California
Vehicle Code
2026

California Vehicle Code 2026

Snape Legal Publishing

California Vehicle Code 2026

ISBN # 978-1-948593-16-8

California Vehicle Code 2026

California Vehicle Code 2026

This compilation does not incorporate any amendments, repeals, additions, or other legislative actions occurring after January 1, 2026. Users should consult the official state publications or the legislature's current online resources to verify whether a section has been modified, superseded, or repealed subsequent to that date. If the applicability or legal force of any provision is uncertain, the official statutory text should be consulted before relying on this volume in any legal or professional context.

General Provisions

(General Provisions enacted by Stats. 1959, Ch. 3.)

1. This act shall be known as the Vehicle Code.

(Enacted by Stats. 1959, Ch. 3.)

2. The provisions of this code, insofar as they are substantially the same as existing provisions relating to the same subject matter, shall be construed as restatements and continuations thereof and not as new enactments.

(Enacted by Stats. 1959, Ch. 3.)

3. All persons who, at the time this code goes into effect, hold office under the code repealed by this code, which offices are continued by this code, continue to hold them according to their former tenure.

(Enacted by Stats. 1959, Ch. 3.)

4. No action or proceeding commenced before this code takes effect, and no right accrued, is affected by the provisions of this code, but all procedure thereafter taken therein shall conform to the provisions of this code so far as possible.

(Enacted by Stats. 1959, Ch. 3.)

5. If any portion of this code is held unconstitutional, such decision shall not affect the validity of any other portion of this code.

(Enacted by Stats. 1959, Ch. 3.)

6. Unless the provision or the context otherwise requires, these general provisions and rules of construction shall govern the construction of this code.

(Enacted by Stats. 1959, Ch. 3.)

7. Division, chapter, and article headings do not in any manner affect the scope, meaning, or intent of the provisions of this code.

(Amended by Stats. 1959, Ch. 1996.)

8. Whenever, by the provisions of this code, a power is granted to a public officer or a duty imposed upon such an officer, the power may be exercised or the duty performed by a deputy of the officer or by a person authorized pursuant to law by the officer.

(Enacted by Stats. 1959, Ch. 3.)

9. Whenever any notice, report, statement, or record is required by this code, it shall be made in writing in the English language.

(Enacted by Stats. 1959, Ch. 3.)

10. Whenever any reference is made to any portion of this code or of any other law, such reference shall apply to all amendments and additions heretofore or hereafter made.

(Enacted by Stats. 1959, Ch. 3.)

11. "Section" means a section of this code unless some other statute is specifically mentioned and "subdivision" means a subdivision of the section in which that term occurs unless some other section is expressly mentioned.

(Enacted by Stats. 1959, Ch. 3.)

12. The present tense includes the past and future tenses; and the future, the present.

(Enacted by Stats. 1959, Ch. 3.)

12.2. "Spouse" includes "registered domestic partner," as required by Section 297.5 of the Family Code.

(Added by Stats. 2016, Ch. 50, Sec. 117. (SB 1005) Effective January 1, 2017.)

13. The masculine gender includes the feminine and neuter.

(Enacted by Stats. 1959, Ch. 3.)

14. The singular number includes the plural, and the plural the singular.

(Enacted by Stats. 1959, Ch. 3.)

15. "Shall" is mandatory and "may" is permissive.

(Enacted by Stats. 1959, Ch. 3.)

16. "Oath" includes affirmation.

(Enacted by Stats. 1959, Ch. 3.)

17. "Signature" or "subscription" includes mark when the signer or subscriber cannot write, such signer's or subscriber's name being written near the mark by a witness who writes his own name near the signer's or subscriber's name; but a signature or subscription by mark can be acknowledged or can serve as a signature or subscription to a sworn statement only when two witnesses so sign their own names thereto.

(Enacted by Stats. 1959, Ch. 3.)

18. Officers and employees of the Department of Motor Vehicles and the Department of the California Highway Patrol are, for the purposes of this code, authorized to administer oaths and acknowledge signatures, for which no fee shall be charged.

(Enacted by Stats. 1959, Ch. 3.)

19. Whenever the acknowledgement of any document is required by this code or any regulation of either department, the signature of the applicant attested to in his presence by the signature of a subscribing witness is sufficient.

(Enacted by Stats. 1959, Ch. 3.)

20. It is unlawful to use a false or fictitious name, or to knowingly make any false statement or knowingly conceal any material fact in any document filed with the Department of Motor Vehicles or the Department of the California Highway Patrol.

(Enacted by Stats. 1959, Ch. 3.)

21. (a) Except as otherwise expressly provided, the provisions of this code are applicable and uniform throughout the state and in all counties and municipalities therein, and a local authority shall not enact or enforce any ordinance or resolution on the matters covered by this code, including ordinances or resolutions that establish regulations or procedures for, or assess a fine, penalty, assessment, or fee for a violation of, matters covered by this code, unless expressly authorized by this code.

(b) To the extent permitted by current state law, this section does not impair the current lawful authority of the Mountains Recreation and Conservation Authority, a joint powers authority, or any member agency constituted therein as of July 1, 2010, to enforce an ordinance or resolution relating to the management of public lands within its jurisdiction.

(Amended by Stats. 2010, Ch. 616, Sec. 1. (SB 949) Effective January 1, 2011. Operative July 1, 2011, by Sec. 6 of Ch. 616.)

22. Whenever notice is required to be given under this code by a department or any division, officer, employee, or agent, the notice shall be given either by personal delivery to the person to be notified, by certified mail, return receipt requested, by mailing the notice, postage prepaid, addressed to the person at their address as shown by the records of the department, or by electronic notification, as authorized pursuant to Section 1801.2.

(Amended by Stats. 2023, Ch. 131, Sec. 214. (AB 1754) Effective January 1, 2024.)

23. The giving of notice by personal delivery is complete upon delivery of a copy of the notice to the person to be notified. The giving of notice by mail is complete upon the expiration of four days after deposit of the notice in the mail, except that in the case of a notice informing a person of an offense against them under Section 40001, the notice is complete 10 days after mailing. The giving of notice by electronic notification, as authorized pursuant to Section 1801.2, is complete upon sending the electronic notification.

(Amended by Stats. 2022, Ch. 838, Sec. 2. (SB 1193) Effective January 1, 2023.)

24. Proof of the giving of notice may be made by the certificate of any officer, employee, or agent of the Department of Motor Vehicles and the Department of the California Highway Patrol or of any peace officer, or by an affidavit of any person over 18 years of age, naming the person to whom the notice was given and specifying the time, place, and manner of the giving of the notice.

(Amended by Stats. 1996, Ch. 1154, Sec. 55. Effective September 30, 1996.)

24.5. All civil process in actions brought against the director and the Department of Motor Vehicles and all subpoenas for the production of department records shall be served upon the director or his appointed representatives at the department's headquarters.

(Added by Stats. 1971, Ch. 699.)

25. (a) It is unlawful for a person to display or cause or permit to be displayed any sign, mark, or advertisement indicating an official connection with either the Department of Motor Vehicles or the Department of the California Highway Patrol unless the person has lawful authority, permission, or right to make that display.

(b) It is unlawful for the holder of an occupational license issued pursuant to Division 5 (commencing with Section 11100) to use the initials "DMV," the Department of Motor Vehicles logogram, or the words "Department of Motor Vehicles" in any business name, telephone number, or internet domain name, as defined in Section 17527 of the Business and Professions Code. An occupational licensee shall not use the initials, logogram, or words in any advertisement in a way that indicates, or could be construed to indicate, an official connection with the Department of Motor Vehicles other than as a licensee.

(Amended by Stats. 2025, Ch. 68, Sec. 1. (AB 1272) Effective January 1, 2026.)

25.5. It is unlawful for any person to falsely represent himself or herself in any manner as an employee of the Department of Motor Vehicles for the purpose of obtaining records or information to which he or she is not entitled.

(Amended by Stats. 1982, Ch. 466, Sec. 105.)

27. Any person who without authority impersonates, or wears the badge of, a member of the California Highway Patrol with intention to deceive anyone is guilty of a misdemeanor.

(Enacted by Stats. 1959, Ch. 3.)

28. (a) Whenever possession is taken of any vehicle by or on behalf of its legal owner under the terms of a security agreement or lease agreement, the person taking possession shall contact, for the purpose of providing the information required pursuant to subdivision (d), within one hour after taking possession of the vehicle, by the most expeditious means available, the city police department where the taking of possession occurred, if within an incorporated city, or the sheriff's department of the county where the taking of possession occurred, if outside an incorporated city, or the police department of a campus of the University of California or the California State University, if the taking of possession occurred on that campus. If, after an attempt to notify, law enforcement is unable to receive and record the notification required pursuant to subdivision (d), the person taking possession of the vehicle shall continue to attempt notification until the information required pursuant to subdivision (d) is provided.

(b) If possession is taken of more than one vehicle, the possession of each vehicle shall be considered and reported as a separate event.

(c) Any person failing to notify the city police department, sheriff's department, or campus police department as required by this section is guilty of an infraction, and shall be fined a minimum of three hundred dollars ($300), and up to five hundred dollars ($500). The district attorney, city attorney, or city prosecutor shall promptly notify the Bureau of Security and Investigative Services of any conviction resulting from a violation of this section.

(d) For the notification required by this section, the person shall report only the following information and in the following order:

(1) The approximate location of the repossession.

(2) The date and approximate time of the repossession.

(3) The vehicle year, make, and model.

(4) The last six digits of the vehicle identification number.

(5) The registered owner as provided on the repossession assignment.

(6) The legal owner requesting the repossession as provided on the repossession assignment.

(7) The name of the repossession agency.

(8) The telephone number of the repossession agency.

(Amended by Stats. 2015, Ch. 740, Sec. 13. (AB 281) Effective January 1, 2016.)

29. Wherever a notice or other communication is required by this code to be mailed by registered mail by or to a person or corporation, the mailing of that notice or other communication by certified mail, or by electronic notification, as authorized pursuant to Section 1801.2, shall be deemed to be a sufficient compliance with the requirements of law.

(Amended by Stats. 2022, Ch. 838, Sec. 3. (SB 1193) Effective January 1, 2023.)

30. It is declared as a matter of legislative policy that red lights and sirens on vehicles should be restricted to authorized emergency vehicles engaged in police, fire and lifesaving services; and that other types of vehicles which are engaged in activities which create special hazards upon the highways should be equipped with flashing amber warning lamps.

(Added by Stats. 1961, Ch. 653.)

31. No person shall give, either orally or in writing, information to a peace officer while in the performance of his duties under the provisions of this code when such person knows that the information is false.

(Added by Stats. 1965, Ch. 1264.)

32. Whenever local authorities are given the power to take action by ordinance pursuant to Division 11 (commencing with Section 21000) and Division 15 (commencing with Section 35000), they shall also have the power to take such action by resolution.

(Added by Stats. 1972, Ch. 1095.)

Division 1. Words and Phrases Defined

(Division 1 enacted by Stats. 1959, Ch. 3.)

100. Unless the provision or context otherwise requires, these definitions shall govern the construction of this code.

(Enacted by Stats. 1959, Ch. 3.)

102. "Ability to respond in damages" means financial responsibility.

(Added by renumbering Section 95 by Stats. 1992, Ch. 974, Sec. 2. Effective September 28, 1992.)

105. An "agricultural water-well boring rig" is a motor vehicle which is used exclusively in the boring of water-wells on agricultural property.

(Enacted by Stats. 1959, Ch. 3.)

108. "Airbrakes" means a brake system using compressed air either for actuating the service brakes at the wheels of the vehicle or as a source of power for controlling or applying service brakes which are actuated through hydraulic or other intermediate means.

(Added by Stats. 1963, Ch. 207.)

109. "Alcoholic beverage" includes any liquid or solid material intended to be ingested by a person which contains ethanol, also known as ethyl alcohol, drinking alcohol, or alcohol, including, but not limited to, alcoholic beverages as defined in Section 23004 of the Business and Professions Code, intoxicating liquor, malt beverage, beer, wine, spirits, liqueur, whiskey, rum, vodka, cordials, gin, and brandy, and any mixture containing one or more alcoholic beverages. Alcoholic beverage includes a mixture of one or more alcoholic beverages whether found or ingested separately or as a mixture.

For purposes of the Driver License Compact, "intoxicating liquor" as used in Section 15023 has the same meaning as "alcoholic beverage" as used in this code.

(Added by renumbering Section 23151 by Stats. 1982, Ch. 53, Sec. 25. Effective February 18, 1982.)

110. "Alley" is any highway having a roadway not exceeding 25 feet in width which is primarily used for access to the rear or side entrances of abutting property; provided, that the City and County of San Francisco may designate by ordinance or resolution as an "alley" any highway having a roadway not exceeding 25 feet in width.

(Amended by Stats. 1965, Ch. 833.)

111. (a) "All-terrain vehicle" means a motor vehicle subject to subdivision (a) of Section 38010 that is all of the following:

(1) Designed for operation off of the highway by an operator with no more than one passenger.

(2) Fifty inches or less in width.

(3) Nine hundred pounds or less unladen weight.

(4) Suspended on three or more low-pressure tires.

(5) Has a single seat designed to be straddled by the operator, or a single seat designed to be straddled by the operator and a seat for no more than one passenger.

(6) Has handlebars for steering control.

(b) Notwithstanding subdivision (a), for purposes of Chapter 6 (commencing with Section 3000) of Division 2 and Chapter 4 (commencing with Section 11700) of Division 5, "all-terrain vehicle" also means a recreational off-highway vehicle as defined in Section 500 and a utility-terrain vehicle as defined in Section 531.

(Amended by Stats. 2014, Ch. 279, Sec. 1. (AB 988) Effective January 1, 2015.)

111.3. An "all-terrain vehicle safety instructor" is a person who is sponsored by an all-terrain vehicle safety training organization, who has completed a course in all-terrain vehicle safety instruction administered by an approved all-terrain vehicle safety training organization, and who has been licensed by the department pursuant to Section 11105.1.

(Added by Stats. 1987, Ch. 881, Sec. 2.)

111.5. An "all-terrain vehicle safety training organization" is any organization which is approved to offer a program of instruction in all-terrain vehicle safety, including all-terrain vehicle safety instruction training, by the Off-Highway Vehicle Safety Education Committee and which has been issued a license by the department pursuant to Section 11105.6.

(Added by Stats. 1987, Ch. 881, Sec. 3.)

112. "Amber" has the same meaning as "yellow," and is within the chromaticity coordinate boundaries for yellow specified in regulations adopted by the Department of the California Highway Patrol.

(Added by Stats. 1977, Ch. 287.)

115. An "armored car" is a vehicle that is equipped with materials on either the front, sides, or rear for the protection of persons therein from missiles discharged from firearms.

(Enacted by Stats. 1959, Ch. 3.)

165. An authorized emergency vehicle is:

(a) Any publicly owned and operated ambulance, lifeguard, or lifesaving equipment or any privately owned or operated ambulance licensed by the Commissioner of the California Highway Patrol to operate in response to emergency calls.

(b) Any publicly owned vehicle operated by the following persons, agencies, or organizations:

(1) Any federal, state, or local agency, department, or district employing peace officers as that term is defined in Chapter 4.5 (commencing with Section 830) of Part 2 of Title 3 of the Penal Code, for use by those officers in the performance of their duties.

(2) Any forestry or fire department of any public agency or fire department organized as provided in the Health and Safety Code.

(c) Any vehicle owned by the state, or any bridge and highway district, and equipped and used either for fighting fires, or towing or servicing other vehicles, caring for injured persons, or repairing damaged lighting or electrical equipment.

(d) Any state-owned vehicle used in responding to emergency fire, rescue, or communications calls and operated either by the Office of Emergency Services or by any public agency or industrial fire department to which the Office of Emergency Services has assigned the vehicle.

(e) (1) Any vehicle owned or operated by a federally recognized Indian tribe used in responding to emergency, fire, ambulance, or lifesaving calls. For the purposes of this section and the provisions of Sections 2501 and 2510, a vehicle used in responding to emergency, fire, ambulance, or lifesaving calls owned or operated by a federally recognized Indian tribe is considered an authorized emergency vehicle.

(2) Any vehicle owned or operated by any department or agency of the United States government when the vehicle is used in responding to emergency fire, ambulance, or lifesaving calls or is actively engaged in law enforcement work.

(f) Any vehicle for which an authorized emergency vehicle permit has been issued by the Commissioner of the California Highway Patrol.

(Amended by Stats. 2021, Ch. 282, Sec. 1. (AB 798) Effective January 1, 2022.)

165.5. No act or omission of any rescue team operating in conjunction with an authorized emergency vehicle as defined in Section 165, while attempting to resuscitate any person who is in immediate danger of loss of life, shall impose any liability upon the rescue team or the owners or operators of any authorized emergency vehicle, if good faith is exercised.

For the purposes of this section, "rescue team" means a special group of physicians and surgeons, nurses, volunteers, or employees of the owners or operators of the authorized emergency vehicle who have been trained in cardiopulmonary resuscitation and have been designated by the owners or operators of the emergency vehicle to attempt to resuscitate persons who are in immediate danger of loss of life in cases of emergency.

This section shall not relieve the owners or operators of any other duty imposed upon them by law for the designation and training of members of a rescue team or for any provisions regarding maintenance of equipment to be used by the rescue team.

Members of a rescue team shall receive the training in a program approved by, or conforming to, standards prescribed by an emergency medical care committee established pursuant to Article 3 (commencing with Section 1797.270) of Chapter 4 of Division 2.5 of the Health and Safety Code, or a voluntary area health planning agency established

pursuant to Section 127155 of the Health and Safety Code.
(Amended by Stats. 1996, Ch. 1023, Sec. 421. Effective September 29, 1996.)

166. An "autobroker" or "auto buying service" is a dealer, as defined in Section 285, who engages in the business of brokering, as defined in Section 232.5.
(Added by Stats. 1994, Ch. 1253, Sec. 3. Effective January 1, 1995.)

175. An "autoette" is a motor vehicle, located on a natural island with an area in excess of 20,000 acres and that is within a county having a population in excess of 4,000,000, that meets all of the following requirements:

(a) Has three or more wheels in contact with the ground.

(b) Has an unladed weight of no greater than 1,800 pounds.

(c) Has an overall length of no more than 130 inches, including the front and rear bumpers.

(d) Has a width of no more than 55 inches, as measured from its widest part.
(Amended by Stats. 2023, Ch. 91, Sec. 1. (AB 705) Effective January 1, 2024.)

210. An "automated enforcement system" is any system operated by a governmental agency, in cooperation with a law enforcement agency, that photographically records a driver's responses to a rail or rail transit signal or crossing gate, or both, or to an official traffic control signal described in Section 21450, and is designed to obtain a clear photograph of a vehicle's license plate and the driver of the vehicle.
(Amended (as amended by Stats. 1995, Ch. 922, Sec. 1) by Stats. 1998, Ch. 54, Sec. 1. Effective January 1, 1999.)

220. (a) An "automobile dismantler" is a person not otherwise expressly excluded by Section 221 who is engaged in the business of buying, selling, or dealing in vehicles of a type required to be registered under this code, including nonrepairable vehicles, for the purpose of dismantling the vehicles, who buys or sells the integral parts and component materials thereof, in whole or in part, or deals in used motor vehicle parts. This section does not apply to the occasional and incidental dismantling of vehicles by dealers who have secured dealer plates from the department for the current year whose principal business is buying and selling new and used vehicles, or by owners who desire to dismantle not more than three personal vehicles within any 12-month period.

(b) Notwithstanding subdivision (a), "automobile dismantler" includes a person not otherwise expressly excluded by Section 221 who keeps or maintains on real property owned by the person, or under their possession or control, either of the following vehicles or catalytic converters, whether for the purpose of resale of used parts, for the purpose of reclaiming for use some or all of the materials, whether metal, glass, fabric, or otherwise, or to dispose of them, or for any other purpose:

(1) Two or more unregistered motor vehicles no longer intended for, or in condition for, legal use on the highways.

(2) Nine or more used catalytic converters that have been cut from a motor vehicle using a sharp implement.

(c) (1) Notwithstanding paragraph (2) of subdivision (b), a "junk dealer," as defined in Section 21601 of the Business and Professions Code, a "recycler," as defined in Section 21605 of the Business and Professions Code, or a "commercial enterprise" or "core recycler," as defined in Section 21610 of the Business and Professions Code, is not an automobile dismantler even if it possesses nine or more used catalytic converters that have been cut from a motor vehicle using a sharp implement.

(2) This subdivision does not apply to a "commercial enterprise" described in subparagraph (A) of paragraph (2) of subdivision (a) of Section 21610 of the Business and Professions Code.
(Amended by Stats. 2023, Ch. 537, Sec. 1. (AB 641) Effective January 1, 2024.)

221. (a) The term "automobile dismantler" does not include any of the following:

(1) The owner or operator of any premises on which two or more unregistered and inoperable vehicles are held or stored, or a person who possesses nine or more catalytic converters, if the vehicles or catalytic converters are used for restoration or replacement parts or otherwise in conjunction with any of the following:

(A) Any business of a licensed dealer, manufacturer, or transporter.

(B) The operation and maintenance of any fleet of motor vehicles used for the transportation of persons or property.

(C) Any agricultural, farming, mining, or ranching business that does not sell parts of the vehicles, except for either of the following purposes:

(i) For use in repairs performed by that business.

(ii) For use by a licensed dismantler or an entity described in paragraph (3).

(D) Any motor vehicle repair business registered with the Bureau of Automotive Repair, or those exempt from registration under the Business and Professions Code or applicable regulations, that does not sell parts of the vehicles, except for either of the following purposes:

(i) For use in repairs performed by that business.

(ii) For use by a licensed dismantler or an entity described in paragraph (3).

(2) A person engaged in the restoration of vehicles of the type described in Section 5004 or in the restoration of other vehicles having historic or classic significance.

(3) The owner of a steel mill, scrap metal processing facility, or similar establishment purchasing vehicles of a type subject to registration, not for the purpose of selling the vehicles, in whole or in part, but exclusively for the purpose of reducing the vehicles to their component materials, if either the facility obtains, on a form approved or provided by the department, a certification by the person from whom the vehicles are obtained that each of the vehicles has been cleared for dismantling pursuant to Section 5500 or 11520, or the facility complies with Section 9564.

(4) Any person who acquires used parts or components for resale from vehicles which have been previously cleared for dismantling pursuant to Section 5500 or 11520.

Nothing in this paragraph permits a dismantler to acquire or sell used parts or components during the time the dismantler license is under suspension.

(b) Any vehicle acquired for the purpose specified in paragraph (3) of subdivision (a) from other than a licensed dismantler, or from other than an independent hauler who obtained the vehicle, or parts thereof from a licensed dismantler, shall be accompanied by either a receipt issued by the department evidencing proof of clearance for dismantling under Section 5500, or a copy of the ordinance or order issued by a local authority for the abatement of the vehicle pursuant to Section 22660. The steel mill, scrap metal processing facility, or similar establishment acquiring the vehicle shall attach the form evidencing clearance or abatement to the certification required pursuant to this section.

All forms specified in paragraph (3) of subdivision (a) and in this subdivision shall be available for inspection by a peace officer during business hours.
(Amended by Stats. 2023, Ch. 537, Sec. 2. (AB 641) Effective January 1, 2024.)

223. Any reference in this code to "automobile driver training" shall be deemed to refer to the laboratory phase of driver education described by Section 51852 of the Education Code.
(Amended by Stats. 1980, Ch. 676, Sec. 305.)

225. An "auxiliary dolly" is a vehicle, not designed for carrying persons or property on its own structure, which is so constructed and used in conjunction with a semitrailer as to support a portion of the weight of the semitrailer and any load thereon, but not permanently attached to the semitrailer, although a part of the weight of such dolly may rest on another vehicle.
(Enacted by Stats. 1959, Ch. 3.)

230. An "axle" is a structure or portion of a structure consisting of one or more shafts, spindles, or bearings in the same vertical transverse plane by means of which, in conjunction with wheels mounted on said shafts, spindles, or bearings, a portion of the weight of a vehicle and its load, if any, is continuously transmitted to the roadway when the vehicle is in motion.

(Enacted by Stats. 1959, Ch. 3.)

230.5. A "B-train assembly" is a rigid frame extension attached to the rear frame of a semitrailer which allows for a fifth wheel connection point for a second semitrailer.

(Added by Stats. 1991, Ch. 13, Sec. 13. Effective February 13, 1991.)

231. A bicycle is a device upon which a person may ride, propelled exclusively by human power, except as provided in Section 312.5, through a belt, chain, or gears, and having one or more wheels. A person riding a bicycle is subject to the provisions of this code specified in Sections 21200 and 21200.5. An electric bicycle is a bicycle.

(Amended by Stats. 2021, Ch. 311, Sec. 1. (SB 814) Effective January 1, 2022.)

231.5. A "bicycle path" or "bike path" is a Class I bikeway, as defined in subdivision (a) of Section 890.4 of the Streets and Highways Code.

(Added by Stats. 2009, Ch. 200, Sec. 5. (SB 734) Effective January 1, 2010.)

231.6. (a) A "bicycle path crossing" is either of the following:

(1) That portion of a roadway included within the prolongation or connection of the boundary lines of a bike path at intersections where the intersecting roadways meet at approximately right angles.

(2) Any portion of a roadway distinctly indicated for bicycle crossing by lines or other markings on the surface.

(b) Notwithstanding subdivision (a), there shall not be a bicycle path crossing where local authorities have placed signs indicating no crossing.

(Added by Stats. 2009, Ch. 200, Sec. 6. (SB 734) Effective January 1, 2010.)

232. The "board" is the New Motor Vehicle Board.

(Added by Stats. 1973, Ch. 996.)

232.5. "Brokering" is an arrangement under which a dealer, for a fee or other consideration, regardless of the form or time of payment, provides or offers to provide the service of arranging, negotiating, assisting, or effectuating the purchase of a new or used motor vehicle, not owned by the dealer, for another or others.

(Added by Stats. 1994, Ch. 1253, Sec. 4. Effective January 1, 1995.)

233. (a) Except as provided in subdivision (b), a "bus" is any vehicle, including a trailer bus, designed, used, or maintained for carrying more than 15 persons including the driver.

(b) A vehicle designed, used, or maintained for carrying more than 10 persons, including the driver, which is used to transport persons for compensation or profit, or is used by any nonprofit organization or group, is also a bus.

(c) This section does not alter the definition of a schoolbus, school pupil activity bus, general public paratransit vehicle, farm labor vehicle, or youth bus.

(d) A vanpool vehicle is not a bus.

(Amended by Stats. 1994, Ch. 675, Sec. 1. Effective January 1, 1995.)

234. A "business" includes a proprietorship, partnership, corporation, and any other form of commercial enterprise.

(Added by Stats. 1990, Ch. 1563, Sec. 1.)

235. A "business district" is that portion of a highway and the property contiguous thereto (a) upon one side of which highway, for a distance of 600 feet, 50 percent or more of the contiguous property fronting thereon is occupied by buildings in use for business, or (b) upon both sides of which highway, collectively, for a distance of 300 feet, 50 percent or more of the contiguous property fronting thereon is so occupied. A business district may be longer than the distances specified in this section if the above ratio of buildings in use for business to the length of the highway exists.

(Enacted by Stats. 1959, Ch. 3.)

236. A "business representative" means a proprietor, a limited or general partner, a managerial employee, a stockholder, a director, or an officer who is active in the management, direction, and control of that part of a business which is a licensed activity.

(Added by Stats. 1990, Ch. 1563, Sec. 2.)

240. In determining whether a highway is within a business or residence district, the following limitations shall apply and shall qualify the definitions in Sections 235 and 515:

(a) No building shall be regarded unless its entrance faces the highway and the front of the building is within 75 feet of the roadway.

(b) Where a highway is physically divided into two or more roadways only those buildings facing each roadway separately shall be regarded for the purpose of determining whether the roadway is within a district.

(c) All churches, apartments, hotels, multiple dwelling houses, clubs, and public buildings, other than schools, shall be deemed to be business structures.

(d) A highway or portion of a highway shall not be deemed to be within a district regardless of the number of buildings upon the contiguous property if there is no right of access to the highway by vehicles from the contiguous property.

(Enacted by Stats. 1959, Ch. 3.)

241. A "buy-here-pay-here" dealer is a dealer, as defined in Section 285, who is not otherwise expressly excluded by Section 241.1, and who does all of the following:

(a) Enters into conditional sale contracts, within the meaning of subdivision (a) of Section 2981 of the Civil Code, and subject to the provisions of Chapter 2b (commencing with Section 2981) of Title 14 of Part 4 of Division 3 of the Civil Code, or lease contracts, within the meaning of Section 2985.7 of the Civil Code, and subject to the provisions of Chapter 2d (commencing with Section 2985.7) of Title 14 of Part 4 of Division 3 of the Civil Code.

(b) Assigns less than 90 percent of all unrescinded conditional sale contracts and lease contracts to unaffiliated third-party finance or leasing sources within 45 days of the consummation of those contracts.

(c) For purposes of this section, a conditional sale contract does not include a contract for the sale of a motor vehicle if all amounts owed under the contract are paid in full within 30 days.

(d) The department may promulgate regulations as necessary to implement this section.

(Added by Stats. 2012, Ch. 741, Sec. 2. (AB 1534) Effective January 1, 2013.)

241.1. The term "buy-here-pay-here" dealer does not include any of the following:

(a) A lessor who primarily leases vehicles that are two model years old or newer.

(b) A dealer that does both of the following:

(1) Certifies 100 percent of used vehicle inventory offered for sale at retail price pursuant to Section 11713.18.

(2) Maintains an onsite service and repair facility that is licensed by the Bureau of Automotive Repair and employs a minimum of five master automobile technicians that are certified by the National Institute for Automotive Service Excellence.

(Added by Stats. 2012, Ch. 741, Sec. 3. (AB 1534) Effective January 1, 2013.)

242. A "camp trailer" is a vehicle designed to be used on a highway, capable of human habitation for camping or recreational purposes, that does not exceed 16 feet in overall length from the foremost point of the trailer hitch to the rear extremity of the trailer body and does not exceed 96 inches in width and includes any tent trailer. Where a trailer telescopes for travel, the size shall apply to the trailer as fully extended. Notwithstanding any other provision of law, a camp trailer shall not be deemed to be a trailer coach.

(Added by Stats. 1971, Ch. 1536.)

243. A "camper" is a structure designed to be mounted upon a motor vehicle and to provide facilities for human habitation or camping purposes. A camper having one axle shall not be considered a vehicle.

(Amended by Stats. 1968, Ch. 228.)

245. A "carry-all" is that type of earth-moving equipment which is not self-propelled but which is designed for use behind tractors or other motive power and which is self-loading by means of a cutting blade which is lowered at an angle to dig into the ground. The term includes, but is not limited to, such types of vehicles as carry the trade names of

LaPlant-Choate, LeTourneau, and Be Ge.
(Enacted by Stats. 1959, Ch. 3.)

246. A "certificate of compliance" for the purposes of this code is an electronic or printed document issued by a state agency, board, or commission, or authorized person, setting forth that the requirements of a particular law, rule or regulation, within its jurisdiction to regulate or administer has been satisfied.
(Amended by Stats. 1999, Ch. 1007, Sec. 15. Effective January 1, 2000.)

250. A "chop shop" is any building, lot, or other premises where any person has been engaged in altering, destroying, disassembling, dismantling, reassembling, or storing any motor vehicle or motor vehicle part known to be illegally obtained by theft, fraud, or conspiracy to defraud, in order to do either of the following:

(a) Alter, counterfeit, deface, destroy, disguise, falsify, forge, obliterate, or remove the identity, including the vehicle identification number, of a motor vehicle or motor vehicle part, in order to misrepresent the identity of the motor vehicle or motor vehicle part, or to prevent the identification of the motor vehicle or motor vehicle part.

(b) Sell or dispose of the motor vehicle or motor vehicle part.
(Added by Stats. 1993, Ch. 386, Sec. 1. Effective September 8, 1993.)

255. "City" includes every city and city and county within this State.
(Enacted by Stats. 1959, Ch. 3.)

257. A "clean fuel vehicle" means any passenger or commercial vehicle or pickup truck that is fueled by alternative fuels, as defined in Section 301 of the Energy Policy Act of 1992 (P.L. 102-486), and produces emissions which do not exceed whichever of the following standards, as defined by regulations of the State Air Resources Board in effect on January 1, 1994, is applicable to the model year of the vehicle:

(a) For a vehicle of the 1994 to 1996, inclusive, model year, the emission standard applicable to a transitional low-emission vehicle.

(b) For a vehicle of the 1997 model year, the emission standard applicable to a low-emission vehicle.

(c) For a vehicle of the 1998 to 2000, inclusive, model year, the emission standard applicable to an ultra low-emission vehicle.
(Added by Stats. 1993, Ch. 1159, Sec. 4. Effective January 1, 1994.)

259. "Collector motor vehicle" means a motor vehicle owned by a collector, as defined in subdivision (a) of Section 5051, and the motor vehicle is used primarily in shows, parades, charitable functions, and historical exhibitions for display, maintenance, and preservation, and is not used primarily for transportation.
(Added by Stats. 2004, Ch. 107, Sec. 1. Effective January 1, 2005.)

260. (a) A "commercial vehicle" is a motor vehicle of a type required to be registered under this code used or maintained for the transportation of persons for hire, compensation, or profit or designed, used, or maintained primarily for the transportation of property.

(b) Passenger vehicles and house cars that are not used for the transportation of persons for hire, compensation, or profit are not commercial vehicles. This subdivision shall not apply to Chapter 4 (commencing with Section 6700) of Division 3.

(c) Any vanpool vehicle is not a commercial vehicle.

(d) The definition of a commercial vehicle in this section does not apply to Chapter 7 (commencing with Section 15200) of Division 6.
(Amended by Stats. 2003, Ch. 222, Sec. 1. Effective January 1, 2004.)

265. The "commissioner" is the Commissioner of the California Highway Patrol.
(Enacted by Stats. 1959, Ch. 3.)

266. A "consignment" is an arrangement under which a dealer agrees to accept possession of a vehicle of a type required to be registered under this code from an owner for the purpose of selling the vehicle and to pay the owner or the owner's designee from the proceeds of the sale.
(Amended by Stats. 1991, Ch. 815, Sec. 1.)

267. A "converter" is a person, other than a vehicle manufacturer, who, prior to the retail sale of a new vehicle, does any of the following to the vehicle:

(a) Assembles, installs, or affixes a body, cab, or special equipment to the vehicle chassis.

(b) Substantially adds to, subtracts from, or modifies the vehicle, if it is a previously assembled or manufactured new vehicle.
(Added by Stats. 1995, Ch. 211, Sec. 1. Effective January 1, 1996.)

270. "County" includes every county and city and county within this State.
(Enacted by Stats. 1959, Ch. 3.)

273. A "crib sheet" or "cribbing device" is any paper or device designed for cheating by supplying examination answers without questions to an applicant for the purpose of fraudulently qualifying the applicant for any class of driver's license, permit, or certificate.
(Added by Stats. 1986, Ch. 960, Sec. 1.)

275. "Crosswalk" is either:

(a) That portion of a roadway included within the prolongation or connection of the boundary lines of sidewalks at intersections where the intersecting roadways meet at approximately right angles, except the prolongation of such lines from an alley across a street.

(b) Any portion of a roadway distinctly indicated for pedestrian crossing by lines or other markings on the surface.

Notwithstanding the foregoing provisions of this section, there shall not be a crosswalk where local authorities have placed signs indicating no crossing.
(Enacted by Stats. 1959, Ch. 3.)

280. "Darkness" is any time from one-half hour after sunset to one-half hour before sunrise and any other time when visibility is not sufficient to render clearly discernible any person or vehicle on the highway at a distance of 1,000 feet.
(Amended by Stats. 1974, Ch. 635.)

285. "Dealer" is a person not otherwise expressly excluded by Section 286 who:

(a) For commission, money, or other thing of value, sells, exchanges, buys, or offers for sale, negotiates or attempts to negotiate, a sale or exchange of an interest in, a vehicle subject to registration, a motorcycle, snowmobile, or all-terrain vehicle subject to identification under this code, or a trailer subject to identification pursuant to Section 5014.1, or induces or attempts to induce any person to buy or exchange an interest in a vehicle and, who receives or expects to receive a commission, money, brokerage fees, profit, or any other thing of value, from either the seller or purchaser of the vehicle.

(b) Is engaged wholly or in part in the business of selling vehicles or buying or taking in trade, vehicles for the purpose of resale, selling, or offering for sale, or consigned to be sold, or otherwise dealing in vehicles, whether or not the vehicles are owned by the person.
(Amended by Stats. 2005, Ch. 270, Sec. 8. Effective January 1, 2006.)

286. The term "dealer" does not include any of the following:

(a) Insurance companies, banks, finance companies, public officials, or any other person coming into possession of vehicles in the regular course of business, who sells vehicles under a contractual right or obligation, in performance of an official duty, or in authority of any court of law, if the sale is for the purpose of saving the seller from loss or pursuant to the authority of a court.

(b) Persons who sell or distribute vehicles of a type subject to registration or trailers subject to identification pursuant to Section 5014.1 for a manufacturer to vehicle dealers licensed under this code, or who are employed by manufacturers or distributors to promote the sale of vehicles dealt in by those manufacturers or distributors. However, any of those persons who also sell vehicles at retail are vehicle dealers and are subject to this code.

(c) Persons regularly employed as salespersons by vehicle dealers licensed under this code while acting within the scope of that employment.

(d) Persons engaged exclusively in the bona fide business of exporting vehicles or of soliciting orders for the sale and delivery of vehicles outside the territorial limits of the United States, if no federal excise tax is legally payable or refundable on any of the transactions. Persons not engaged exclusively in the bona fide business of exporting vehicles, but who are engaged in the business of soliciting orders for the sale and delivery of vehicles, outside the territorial limits of the United States are exempt from licensure as dealers only if their sales of vehicles produce less than 10 percent of their total gross revenue from all business transacted.

(e) Persons not engaged in the purchase or sale of vehicles as a business, who dispose of any vehicle acquired and used in good faith, for their own personal use, or for use in their business, and not for the purpose of avoiding the provisions of this code.

(f) Persons who are engaged in the purchase, sale, or exchange of vehicles, other than motorcycles, all-terrain vehicles, or trailers subject to identification under this code, that are not intended for use on the highways.

(g) Persons temporarily retained as auctioneers solely for the purpose of disposing of vehicle stock inventories by means of public auction on behalf of the owners at the owners' place of business, or as otherwise approved by the department, if intermediate physical possession or control of, or an ownership interest in, the inventory is not conveyed to the persons so retained.

(h) Persons who are engaged exclusively in the business of purchasing, selling, servicing, or exchanging racing vehicles, parts for racing vehicles, and trailers designed and intended by the manufacturer to be used exclusively for carrying racing vehicles. For purposes of this subdivision, "racing vehicle" means a motor vehicle of a type used exclusively in a contest of speed or in a competitive trial of speed which is not intended for use on the highways.

(i) A person who is a lessor.

(j) A person who is a renter.

(k) A salvage pool.

(l) A yacht broker who is subject to the Yacht and Ship Brokers Act (Article 2 (commencing with Section 700) of Chapter 5 of Division 3 of the Harbors and Navigation Code) and who sells used boat trailers in conjunction with the sale of a vessel.

(m) A licensed automobile dismantler who sells vehicles that have been reported for dismantling as provided in Section 11520.

(n) The Director of Corrections when selling vehicles pursuant to Section 2813.5 of the Penal Code.

(o) (1) Any public or private nonprofit charitable, religious, or educational institution or organization that sells vehicles if all of the following conditions are met:

(A) The institution or organization qualifies for state tax-exempt status under Section 23701d of the Revenue and Taxation Code, and tax-exempt status under Section 501(c)(3) of the federal Internal Revenue Code.

(B) The vehicles sold were donated to the nonprofit charitable, religious, or educational institution or organization.

(C) The vehicles subject to retail sale meet all of the applicable equipment requirements of Division 12 (commencing with Section 24000) and are in compliance with emission control requirements as evidenced by the issuance of a certificate pursuant to subdivision (b) of Section 44015 of the Health and Safety Code. Under no circumstances may any institution or organization transfer the responsibility of obtaining a smog inspection certificate to the buyer of the vehicle.

(D) The proceeds of the sale of the vehicles are retained by that institution or organization for its charitable, religious, or educational purposes.

(2) An institution or organization described in paragraph (1) may sell vehicles on behalf of another institution or organization under the following conditions:

(A) The nonselling institution or organization meets the requirements of paragraph (1).

(B) The selling and nonselling institutions or organizations enter into a signed, written agreement pursuant to subparagraph (A) of paragraph (3) of subdivision (a) of Section 1660.

(C) The selling institution or organization transfers the proceeds from the sale of each vehicle to the nonselling institution or organization within 45 days of the sale. All net proceeds transferred to the nonselling institution or organization shall clearly be identifiable to the sale of a specific vehicle. The selling institution or organization may retain a percentage of the proceeds from the sale of a particular vehicle. However, any retained proceeds shall be used by the selling institution or organization for its charitable, religious, or educational purposes.

(D) At the time of transferring the proceeds, the selling institution or organization shall provide to the nonselling institution or organization, an itemized listing of the vehicles sold and the amount for which each vehicle was sold.

(E) In the event the selling institution or organization cannot complete a retail sale of a particular vehicle, or if the vehicle cannot be transferred as a wholesale transaction to a dealer licensed under this code, the vehicle shall be returned to the nonselling institution or organization and the written agreement revised to reflect that return. Under no circumstances may a selling institution or organization transfer or donate the vehicle to a third party that is excluded from the definition of a dealer under this section.

(3) An institution or organization described in this subdivision shall retain all records required to be retained pursuant to Section 1660.

(p) A motor club, as defined in Section 12142 of the Insurance Code, that does not arrange or negotiate individual motor vehicle purchase transactions on behalf of its members but refers members to a new motor vehicle dealer for the purchase of a new motor vehicle and does not receive a fee from the dealer contingent upon the sale of the vehicle.

(Amended by Stats. 2004, Ch. 836, Sec. 2. Effective January 1, 2005.)

288. "Declared combined gross weight" equals the total unladen weight of the combination of vehicles plus the heaviest load that will be transported by that combination of vehicles.

(Added by Stats. 2000, Ch. 861, Sec. 12. Effective September 29, 2000. Operative December 31, 2001, pursuant to Sec. 67 of Ch. 861.)

289. "Declared gross vehicle weight" means weight that equals the total unladen weight of the vehicle plus the heaviest load that will be transported on the vehicle.

(Added by Stats. 2000, Ch. 861, Sec. 13. Effective September 29, 2000. Operative December 31, 2001, pursuant to Sec. 67 of Ch. 861.)

290. "Department" means the Department of Motor Vehicles except, when used in Chapter 2 (commencing with Section 2100) of Division 2 and in Divisions 11 (commencing with Section 21000), 12 (commencing with Section 24000), 13 (commencing with Section 29000), 14 (commencing with Section 31600), 14.1 (commencing with Section 32000), 14.3 (commencing with Section 32100), 14.5 (commencing with Section 33000), 14.7 (commencing with Section 34000), and 14.8 (commencing with Section 34500), it shall mean the Department of the California Highway Patrol.

(Amended by Stats. 1988, Ch. 1384, Sec. 1.)

291. Any reference in this code to the Department of Public Works shall be deemed to refer to the Department of Transportation, which is part of the Business, Transportation and Housing Agency as provided by Section 13975 of the Government Code.

(Amended by Stats. 1982, Ch. 454, Sec. 178.)

295. The "director" is the Director of Motor Vehicles.

(Enacted by Stats. 1959, Ch. 3.)

295.5. A "disabled person" is any of the following:

(a) Any person who has lost, or has lost the use of, one or more lower extremities or both hands, or who has significant limitation in the use of lower extremities, or who has a diagnosed disease or disorder which substantially impairs or interferes with mobility, or who is so severely disabled as to be unable to move without the aid of an assistant device.

(b) Any person who is blind to the extent that the person's central visual acuity does not exceed 20/200 in the better eye, with corrective lenses, as measured by the Snellen test, or visual acuity that is greater than 20/200, but with a limitation in the field of vision such that the widest diameter of the visual field subtends an angle not greater than 20 degrees.

(c) Any person who suffers from lung disease to the extent of any of the following:

(1) The person's forced (respiratory) expiratory volume for one second when measured by spirometry is less than one liter.

(2) The person's arterial oxygen tension (pO2) is less than 60 mm/Hg on room air while the person is at rest.

(d) Any person who is impaired by cardiovascular disease to the extent that the person's functional limitations are classified in severity as class III or class IV based upon standards accepted by the American Heart Association.

(Added by Stats. 1989, Ch. 554, Sec. 1.)

295.7. A "disabled veteran" is any person who, as a result of injury or disease suffered while on active service with the armed forces of the United States, suffers any of the following:

(a) Has a disability which has been rated at 100 percent by the Department of Veterans Affairs or the military service from which the veteran was discharged, due to a diagnosed disease or disorder which substantially impairs or interferes with mobility.

(b) Is so severely disabled as to be unable to move without the aid of an assistant device.

(c) Has lost, or has lost use of, one or more limbs.

(d) Has suffered permanent blindness, as defined in Section 19153 of the Welfare and Institutions Code.

(Added by Stats. 1989, Ch. 554, Sec. 2.)

296. A "distributor" is any person other than a manufacturer who sells or distributes new vehicles subject to registration under this code, new trailers subject to identification pursuant to Section 5014.1, or new off-highway motorcycles or all-terrain vehicles subject to identification under this code, to dealers in this state and maintains representatives for the purpose of contacting dealers or prospective dealers in this state.

(Amended by Stats. 2004, Ch. 836, Sec. 3. Effective January 1, 2005.)

297. A "distributor branch" is an office maintained by a distributor for the sale of new vehicles or new trailers subject to identification pursuant to Section 5014.1 to dealers or for directing or supervising, in whole or in part, the distributor's representatives.

(Amended by Stats. 2001, Ch. 539, Sec. 4. Effective January 1, 2002.)

300. A "drawbar" is a rigid structure forming a connection between a trailer and a towing vehicle, securely attached to both vehicles by nonrigid means and carrying no part of the load of either vehicle.

(Enacted by Stats. 1959, Ch. 3.)

303. A "driveaway-towaway operation" is any operation in which any motor vehicle or combination of motor vehicles coupled together constitutes the commodity being transported, when one or more sets of wheels of any such motor vehicle or motor vehicles are on the roadway, and when one or more of such vehicles are being operated under a manufacturer's, dealer's, or transporter's special plates.

(Added by Stats. 1961, Ch. 1989.)

305. A "driver" is a person who drives or is in actual physical control of a vehicle. The term "driver" does not include the tillerman or other person who, in an auxiliary capacity, assists the driver in the steering or operation of any articulated firefighting apparatus.

(Amended by Stats. 1971, Ch. 213.)

310. A "driver's license" is a valid license to drive the type of motor vehicle or combination of vehicles for which a person is licensed under this code or by a foreign jurisdiction.

(Amended by Stats. 1971, Ch. 213.)

310.4. A "driving instructor" is, except as provided in Section 11105.5, an employee of a driving school licensed by the department to instruct others in the operation of motor vehicles.

(Added by Stats. 1975, Ch. 703.)

310.6. A "driving school" is a business which, for compensation, conducts or offers to conduct instruction in the operation of motor vehicles. As used in this section, "instruction" includes classroom driver education, in-vehicle driver training, and correspondence study.

(Added by Stats. 1975, Ch. 703.)

310.8. A "driving school operator" is either a driving school owner who operates his own driving school or an employee of a driving school who is designated by the driving school owner of such school to personally direct and manage the school for the owner.

(Added by renumbering Section 311.5 by Stats. 1975, Ch. 703.)

311. A "driving school owner" is any person licensed by the department to engage in the business of giving instruction for compensation in the driving of motor vehicles or in the preparation of an applicant for examination for a driver's license issued by the department.

(Amended by Stats. 1975, Ch. 703.)

312. The term "drug" means any substance or combination of substances, other than alcohol, which could so affect the nervous system, brain, or muscles of a person as to impair, to an appreciable degree, his ability to drive a vehicle in the manner that an ordinarily prudent and cautious man, in full possession of his faculties, using reasonable care, would drive a similar vehicle under like conditions.

(Added by Stats. 1971, Ch. 1530.)

312.5. (a) An "electric bicycle" is a bicycle equipped with fully operable pedals and an electric motor that does not exceed 750 watts of power.

(1) A "class 1 electric bicycle," or "low-speed pedal-assisted electric bicycle," is a bicycle equipped with a motor that provides assistance only when the rider is pedaling, that is not capable of exclusively propelling the bicycle, except as provided in paragraph (4), that ceases to provide assistance when the bicycle reaches the speed of 20 miles per hour, and that is not capable of providing assistance to reach speeds greater than 20 miles per hour.

(2) A "class 2 electric bicycle," or "low-speed throttle-assisted electric bicycle," is a bicycle equipped with a motor that may be used exclusively to propel the bicycle, and that is not capable of providing assistance when the bicycle reaches the speed of 20 miles per hour.

(3) A "class 3 electric bicycle," or "speed pedal-assisted electric bicycle," is a bicycle equipped with a motor that provides assistance only when the rider is pedaling, that is not capable of exclusively propelling the bicycle, except as provided in paragraph (4), and that ceases to provide assistance when the bicycle reaches the speed of 28 miles per hour, and equipped with a speedometer.

(4) A class 1 or class 3 electric bicycle may have start assistance or a walk mode that propels the electric bicycle on motor power alone, up to a maximum speed of 3.7 miles per hour.

(b) A person riding an electric bicycle, as defined in this section, is subject to Article 4 (commencing with Section 21200) of Chapter 1 of Division 11.

(c) On and after January 1, 2017, manufacturers and distributors of electric bicycles shall apply a label that is permanently affixed, in a prominent location, to each electric bicycle. The label shall contain the classification number, top assisted speed, and motor wattage of the electric bicycle, and shall be printed in Arial font in at least 9-point type.

(d) The following vehicles are not electric bicycles under this code and shall not be advertised, sold, offered for sale, or labeled as electric bicycles:

(1) A vehicle with two or three wheels powered by an electric motor that is intended by the manufacturer to be modifiable to attain a speed greater than 20 miles per hour on motor power alone or to attain more than 750 watts of power.

(2) A vehicle that is modified to attain a speed greater than 20 miles per hour on motor power alone or to have motor power of more than 750 watts.

(3) A vehicle that is modified to have its operable pedals removed.

(Amended by Stats. 2024, Ch. 791, Sec. 2 (SB 1271) Effective January 1, 2025.)

313. The term "electric personal assistive mobility device" or "EPAMD" means a self-balancing, nontandem two-wheeled device, that is not greater than 20 inches deep and 25 inches wide and can turn in place, designed to transport only one person, with an electric propulsion system averaging less than 750 watts (1 horsepower), the maximum speed of which, when powered solely by a propulsion system on a paved level surface, is no more than 12.5 miles per hour.

(Amended by Stats. 2007, Ch. 106, Sec. 1. Effective January 1, 2008.)

313.5. An "electrically motorized board" is any wheeled device that has a floorboard designed to be stood upon when riding that is not greater than 60 inches deep and 18 inches wide, is designed to transport only one person, and has an electric propulsion system averaging less than 1,000 watts, the maximum speed of which, when powered solely by a propulsion system on a paved level surface, is no more than 20 miles per hour. The device may be designed to also be powered by human propulsion.

(Added by Stats. 2015, Ch. 777, Sec. 1. (AB 604) Effective January 1, 2016.)

314. An "expressway" is a portion of highway that is part of either of the following:

(a) An expressway system established by a county under Section 941.4 of the Streets and Highways Code.

(b) An expressway system established by a county before January 1, 1989, as described in subdivision (g) of Section 941.4 of the Streets and Highways Code.

(Added by Stats. 2004, Ch. 615, Sec. 17. Effective January 1, 2005.)

315. "Essential parts" are all integral and body parts of a vehicle of a type required to be registered under this code, the removal, alteration, or substitution of which would tend to conceal the identity of the vehicle or substantially alter its appearance.

(Enacted by Stats. 1959, Ch. 3.)

320. "Established place of business" is a place actually occupied either continuously or at regular periods by any of the following:

(a) A dealer, remanufacturer, remanufacturer branch, manufacturer, manufacturer branch, distributor, distributor branch, automobile driving school, or traffic violator school where the books and records pertinent to the type of business being conducted are kept.

(b) An automobile dismantler where the books and records pertinent to the type of business being conducted are kept. A place of business of an automobile dismantler which qualified as an "established place of business" before September 17, 1970, is an "established place of business" as defined in this section.

(c) A registration service where the books and records pertinent to the type of business being conducted are kept.

(Amended by Stats. 1992, Ch. 1243, Sec. 54. Effective September 30, 1992.)

320.5. An "extralegal load" is a single unit or an assembled item which, due to its design, cannot be reasonably reduced or dismantled in size or weight so that it can be legally transported as a load without a permit as required by Section 35780. This section does not apply to loads on passenger cars.

(Added by Stats. 1983, Ch. 145, Sec. 1. Effective June 28, 1983.)

321. "Factory-built housing" is a structure as defined in Section 19971 of the Health and Safety Code. As used in this code, factory-built housing is a trailer coach which is in excess of eight feet in width or in excess of 40 feet in length.

(Added by Stats. 1980, Ch. 1150, Sec. 7.)

322. (a) A "farm labor vehicle" is any motor vehicle designed, used, or maintained for the transportation of nine or more farmworkers, in addition to the driver, to or from a place of employment or employment-related activities.

(b) For the purpose of this section, a farmworker is any person engaged in rendering personal services for hire and compensation in connection with the production or harvesting of any farm products.

(c) "Farm labor vehicle" does not include:

(1) Any vehicle carrying only members of the immediate family of the owner or driver thereof.

(2) Any vehicle while being operated under specific authority granted by the Public Utilities Commission or under specific authority granted to a transit system by an authorized city or county agency.

(Amended by Stats. 2000, Ch. 308, Sec. 1. Effective January 1, 2001.)

324. A "fifth-wheel travel trailer" is a vehicle designed for recreational purposes to carry persons or property on its own structure and so constructed as to be drawn by a motor vehicle by means of a kingpin connecting device.

(Added by Stats. 1990, Ch. 1358, Sec. 1.)

324.5. A "former prisoner of war" is any person who, while serving as a member of the United States Armed Forces, as a member of the Philippine Commonwealth Armed Forces, as a part of a United States Expeditionary Force, or as a United States civilian, was held as a prisoner of war by forces hostile to the United States during any armed conflict and is currently a resident of California.

(Added by Stats. 1991, Ch. 893, Sec. 1.)

325. A "foreign jurisdiction" is any other state, the District of Columbia, territories or possessions of the United States, and foreign states, provinces, or countries.

(Enacted by Stats. 1959, Ch. 3.)

330. A "foreign vehicle" is a vehicle of a type required to be registered under this code brought into this State from a foreign jurisdiction other than in the ordinary course of business, by or through a manufacturer or dealer and not registered in this State.

(Enacted by Stats. 1959, Ch. 3.)

331. (a) A "franchise" is a written agreement between two or more persons having all of the following conditions:

(1) A commercial relationship of definite duration or continuing indefinite duration.

(2) The franchisee is granted the right to offer for sale or lease, or to sell or lease at retail new motor vehicles or new trailers subject to identification pursuant to Section 5014.1 manufactured or distributed by the franchisor or the right to perform authorized warranty repairs and service, or the right to perform any combination of these activities.

(3) The franchisee constitutes a component of the franchisor's distribution system.

(4) The operation of the franchisee's business is substantially associated with the franchisor's trademark, trade name, advertising, or other commercial symbol designating the franchisor.

(5) The operation of a portion of the franchisee's business is substantially reliant on the franchisor for a continued supply of new vehicles, parts, or accessories.

(b) The term "franchise" does not include an agreement entered into by a manufacturer or distributor and a person where all the following apply:

(1) The person is authorized to perform warranty repairs and service on vehicles manufactured or distributed by the manufacturer or distributor.

(2) The person is not a new motor vehicle dealer franchisee of the manufacturer or distributor.

(3) The person's repair and service facility is not located within the relevant market area of a new motor vehicle dealer franchisee of the manufacturer or distributor.

(Amended by Stats. 2001, Ch. 539, Sec. 5. Effective January 1, 2002.)

331.1. A "franchisee" is any person who, pursuant to a franchise, receives new motor vehicles subject to registration under this code, new off-highway motorcycles, as defined in Section 436, new all-terrain vehicles, as defined in Section 111, or new trailers subject to identification pursuant to Section 5014.1 from the franchisor and who offers for sale or lease, or sells or leases the vehicles at retail or is granted the right to perform authorized warranty repairs and service, or the right to perform any combination of these activities.

(Amended by Stats. 2004, Ch. 836, Sec. 4. Effective January 1, 2005.)

331.2. A "franchisor" is any person who manufactures, assembles, or distributes new motor vehicles subject to registration under this

code, new off-highway motorcycles, as defined in Section 436, new all-terrain vehicles, as defined in Section 111, or new trailers subject to identification pursuant to Section 5014.1 and who grants a franchise.
(Amended by Stats. 2004, Ch. 836, Sec. 5. Effective January 1, 2005.)

331.3. A "recreational vehicle franchise" is a written agreement between two or more persons having both of the following conditions:

(a) A commercial relationship of definite duration or continuing indefinite duration.

(b) The franchisee is granted the right to offer for sale or lease, or to sell or lease at retail, new recreational vehicles, as defined in subdivision (a) of Section 18010 of the Health and Safety Code, that are manufactured or distributed by the franchisor, or the right to perform authorized warranty repairs and service, or the right to perform any combination of these activities.
(Added by Stats. 2008, Ch. 743, Sec. 1. Effective January 1, 2009.)

332. "Freeway" is a highway in respect to which the owners of abutting lands have no right or easement of access to or from their abutting lands or in respect to which such owners have only limited or restricted right or easement of access.
(Enacted by Stats. 1959, Ch. 3.)

335. A "gantry truck" is a motor vehicle so designed and constructed that it straddles the load to be transported and by means of appropriate mechanism picks up the load and supports it during transportation.
(Enacted by Stats. 1959, Ch. 3.)

336. "General public paratransit vehicle" means any motor vehicle designed for carrying no more than 24 persons and the driver, that provides local transportation to the general public, including transportation of pupils at or below the 12th-grade level to or from a public or private school or school activity, under the exclusive jurisdiction of a publicly owned and operated transit system through one of the following modes: dial-a-ride, subscription service, or route-deviated bus service. Vehicles used in the exclusive transportation of disabled persons as defined in Section 99206.5 of the Public Utilities Code, or of persons 55 years of age or older, including any persons necessary to provide assistance to these passengers, are not general public paratransit vehicles.

However, transportation of attendants, companions, or both traveling together with those individuals with disabilities who are determined to be eligible for complementary paratransit services in accordance with Title II of the Americans with Disabilities Act of 1990 (Public Law 101-336) and federal regulations adopted pursuant thereto, shall not be sufficient to qualify a vehicle as a general public paratransit vehicle.

A vehicle that provides local transportation for the general public through one of the following modes: dial-a-ride, subscription service, or route-deviated bus service, but does not provide transportation of pupils at or below the 12th-grade level to or from a public or private school or school activity, is a transit bus, as defined by Section 642, and is not a general public paratransit vehicle.
(Amended by Stats. 1993, Ch. 844, Sec. 1. Effective January 1, 1994.)

340. A "garage" is a building or other place wherein the business of storing or safekeeping vehicles of a type required to be registered under this code and which belong to members of the general public is conducted for compensation.
(Enacted by Stats. 1959, Ch. 3.)

345. A "golf cart" is a motor vehicle having not less than three wheels in contact with the ground, having an unladen weight less than 1,300 pounds, which is designed to be and is operated at not more than 15 miles per hour and designed to carry golf equipment and not more than two persons, including the driver.
(Added by Stats. 1968, Ch. 1303.)

350. (a) "Gross vehicle weight rating" (GVWR) means the weight specified by the manufacturer as the loaded weight of a single vehicle.

(b) Gross combination weight rating (GCWR) means the weight specified by the manufacturer as the loaded weight of a combination or articulated vehicle. In the absence of a weight specified by the manufacturer, GCWR shall be determined by adding the GVWR of the power unit and the total unladen weight of the towed units and any load thereon.
(Added by renumbering Section 390 by Stats. 2000, Ch. 861, Sec. 14. Effective September 29, 2000. Operative December 31, 2001, pursuant to Sec. 67 of Ch. 861.)

353. "Hazardous material" is any substance, material, or device posing an unreasonable risk to health, safety, or property during transportation, as defined by regulations adopted pursuant to Section 2402.7. "Hazardous material" includes explosives and hazardous wastes or substances as defined by regulations adopted pursuant to Section 25141 of the Health and Safety Code and medical wastes, as defined in Section 117690 of the Health and Safety Code.
(Amended by Stats. 1996, Ch. 1023, Sec. 422. Effective September 29, 1996.)

360. "Highway" is a way or place of whatever nature, publicly maintained and open to the use of the public for purposes of vehicular travel. Highway includes street.
(Enacted by Stats. 1959, Ch. 3.)

362. A "house car" is a motor vehicle originally designed, or permanently altered, and equipped for human habitation, or to which a camper has been permanently attached. A motor vehicle to which a camper has been temporarily attached is not a house car except that, for the purposes of Division 11 (commencing with Section 21000) and Division 12 (commencing with Section 24000), a motor vehicle equipped with a camper having an axle that is designed to support a portion of the weight of the camper unit shall be considered a three-axle house car regardless of the method of attachment or manner of registration. A house car shall not be deemed to be a motortruck.
(Amended by Stats. 1968, Ch. 875.)

365. An "intersection" is the area embraced within the prolongation of the lateral curb lines, or, if none, then the lateral boundary lines of the roadways, of two highways which join one another at approximately right angles or the area within which vehicles traveling upon different highways joining at any other angle may come in conflict.
(Enacted by Stats. 1959, Ch. 3.)

370. A "legal owner" is a person holding a security interest in a vehicle which is subject to the provisions of the Uniform Commercial Code, or the lessor of a vehicle to the State or to any county, city, district, or political subdivision of the State, or to the United States, under a lease, lease-sale, or rental-purchase agreement which grants possession of the vehicle to the lessee for a period of 30 consecutive days or more.
(Amended by Stats. 1963, Ch. 1867.)

371. Lessee includes "bailee" and is a person who leases, offers to lease, or is offered the lease of a motor vehicle for a term exceeding four months.
(Added by Stats. 1976, Ch. 1284.)

372. A "lessor" is a person who, for a term exceeding four months, leases or offers for lease, negotiates or attempts to negotiate a lease, or induce any person to lease a motor vehicle; and who receives or expects to receive a commission, money, brokerage fees, profit or any other thing of value from the lessee of said vehicle. "Lessor" includes "bailor" and "lease" includes "bailment."
(Added by Stats. 1976, Ch. 1284.)

373. A "lessor-retailer" is a lessor or renter who, except under the circumstances described in subdivision (a) of Section 286, makes a retail sale or sales of a previously leased or rented vehicle or vehicles to other than any of the following:

(a) The lessee of the vehicle, or the person who, for a period of at least one year, has been designated by the lessee as the driver of the vehicle covered by a written lease agreement.

(b) A buyer for agricultural, business, or commercial purposes.

(c) A government or governmental agency or instrumentality.
(Amended by Stats. 1979, Ch. 561.)

375. "Lighting equipment" is any of the following lamps or devices:

(a) A headlamp, auxiliary driving, passing, or fog lamp, fog taillamp,

taillamp, stoplamp, supplemental stoplamp, license plate lamp, clearance lamp, side marker lamp, signal lamp or device, supplemental signal lamp, deceleration signal device, cornering lamp, running lamp, red, blue, amber, or white warning lamp, flashing red schoolbus lamp, side-mounted turn signal lamp, and schoolbus side lamp.

(b) An operating unit or canceling mechanism for turn signal lamps or for the simultaneous flashing of turn signal lamps as vehicular hazard signals, and an advance stoplamp switch.

(c) A flasher mechanism for turn signals, red schoolbus lamps, warning lamps, the simultaneous flashing of turn signal lamps as vehicular hazard signals, and the headlamp flashing systems for emergency vehicles.

(d) Any equipment regulating the light emitted from a lamp or device or the light sources therein.

(e) A reflector, including reflectors for use on bicycles, and reflectors used for required warning devices.

(f) An illuminating device that emits radiation predominantly in the infrared or ultraviolet regions of the spectrum, whether or not these emissions are visible to the unaided eye.

(g) An illuminated sign installed on a bus that utilizes an electronic display to convey the route designation, route number, run number, public service announcement, or any combination of this information, or an illuminated sign utilized pursuant to Section 25353.1.

(Amended by Stats. 2011, Ch. 529, Sec. 2. (AB 607) Effective January 1, 2012.)

377. A "limit line" is a solid white line not less than 12 nor more than 24 inches wide, extending across a roadway or any portion thereof to indicate the point at which traffic is required to stop in compliance with legal requirements.

(Enacted by Stats. 1959, Ch. 3.)

378. (a) "Limousine" means any sedan or sport utility vehicle, of either standard or extended length, with a seating capacity of not more than 10 passengers including the driver, used in the transportation of passengers for hire on a prearranged basis within this state.

(b) "Modified limousine" means any vehicle that has been modified, altered, or extended in a manner that increases the overall wheelbase of the vehicle, exceeding the original equipment manufacturer's published wheelbase dimension for the base model and year of the vehicle, in any amount sufficient to accommodate additional passengers with a seating capacity of not more than 10 passengers including the driver, and is used in the transportation of passengers for hire. For purposes of this subdivision, "wheelbase" means the longitudinal distance between the vertical centerlines of the front and rear wheels.

(Added by Stats. 2014, Ch. 860, Sec. 10. (SB 611) Effective September 30, 2014.)

380. "Liquefied petroleum gas" means normal butane, isobutane, propane, or butylene (including isomers) or mixtures composed predominantly thereof in liquid or gaseous state having a vapor pressure in excess of 40 pounds per square inch absolute at a temperature of 100 degrees Fahrenheit.

(Amended by Stats. 1977, Ch. 825.)

385. "Local authorities" means the legislative body of every county or municipality having authority to adopt local police regulations.

(Enacted by Stats. 1959, Ch. 3.)

385.2. A "logging dolly" is a vehicle designed for carrying logs, having one or more axles that, if there are more than one, are not more than 54 inches apart, and used in connection with a motor truck solely for the purpose of transporting logs and securely connected with the towing vehicle both by a reach and by the load.

(Added by Stats. 2013, Ch. 523, Sec. 20. (SB 788) Effective January 1, 2014.)

385.3. A "logging vehicle" is a vehicle used exclusively in the conduct of logging operations and not designed for the transportation of persons or property on a highway.

(Added by Stats. 2013, Ch. 523, Sec. 21. (SB 788) Effective January 1, 2014.)

385.5. (a) A "low-speed vehicle" is a motor vehicle that meets all of the following requirements:

(1) Has four wheels.

(2) Can attain a speed, in one mile, of more than 20 miles per hour and not more than 25 miles per hour, on a paved level surface.

(3) Has a gross vehicle weight rating of less than 3,000 pounds.

(b) (1) For the purposes of this section, a "low-speed vehicle" is not a golf cart, except when operated pursuant to Section 21115 or 21115.1.

(2) A "low-speed vehicle" is also known as a "neighborhood electric vehicle."

(Amended by Stats. 2006, Ch. 66, Sec. 1. Effective July 12, 2006.)

386. A "managerial employee" is a person who exercises control over a business licensed under this code, whether compensated by salary or commission, including, but not limited to, any person who is employed as a general manager, business manager, assistant general manager, finance and insurance manager, advertising manager, or sales manager.

(Added by Stats. 1982, Ch. 791, Sec. 1.)

387. "Manufactured home" is a manufactured home, as defined in Section 18007 of the Health and Safety Code, a commercial coach, as defined in Section 18001. 8 of the Health and Safety Code, a mobilehome, as defined in Section 18008 of the Health and Safety Code, factory-built housing, as defined in Section 18971 of the Health and Safety Code, and a trailer coach which is in excess of 102 inches in width, or in excess of 40 feet in overall length measured from the foremost point of the trailer hitch to the rear extremity of the trailer. Manufactured home does not include a recreational vehicle, as defined in Section 18010 of the Health and Safety Code.

(Amended by Stats. 1986, Ch. 1185, Sec. 1.)

389. A "manufacturer branch" is an office maintained by a manufacturer for the sale of new vehicles to dealers or for directing or supervising in whole or in part the manufacturer's representatives.

(Amended by Stats. 1978, Ch. 797.)

395. A "metal tire" is a tire the surface of which in contact with the highway is wholly or partly of metal or other hard nonresilient material.

(Enacted by Stats. 1959, Ch. 3.)

395.5. A "mobile billboard advertising display" means an advertising display that is attached to a mobile, nonmotorized vehicle, device, or bicycle, that carries, pulls, or transports a sign or billboard, and is for the primary purpose of advertising.

(Amended by Stats. 2011, Ch. 538, Sec. 1. (AB 1298) Effective January 1, 2012.)

396. "Mobilehome" is a structure as defined in Section 18008 of the Health and Safety Code. For the purposes of enforcement of highway safety laws and regulations, a mobilehome is a trailer coach which is in excess of 102 inches in width, or in excess of 40 feet in overall length measured from the foremost point of the trailer hitch to the rear extremity of the trailer.

(Amended by Stats. 1986, Ch. 1185, Sec. 2.)

400. (a) A "motorcycle" is a motor vehicle having a seat or saddle for the use of the rider, designed to travel on not more than three wheels in contact with the ground.

(b) A motor vehicle that has four wheels in contact with the ground, two of which are a functional part of a sidecar, is a motorcycle if the vehicle otherwise comes within the definition of subdivision (a).

(c) A farm tractor is not a motorcycle.

(d) A three-wheeled motor vehicle that otherwise meets the requirements of subdivision (a), has a partially or completely enclosed seating area for the driver and passenger, is used by local public agencies for the enforcement of parking control provisions, and is operated at slow speeds on public streets, is not a motorcycle. However, a motor vehicle described in this subdivision shall comply with the applicable sections of this code imposing equipment installation requirements on motorcycles.

(Amended by Stats. 2008, Ch. 672, Sec. 1. Effective January 1, 2009.)

405. A "motor-driven cycle" is any motorcycle with a motor that displaces less than 150 cubic centimeters. A motor-driven cycle does not include a motorized bicycle, as defined in Section 406.

(Amended by Stats. 1995, Ch. 342, Sec. 1. Effective January 1, 1996.)

406. (a) A "motorized bicycle" or "moped" is a two-wheeled or three-wheeled device having fully operative pedals for propulsion by human power, or having no pedals if powered solely by electrical energy, and an automatic transmission and a motor that produces less than 4 gross brake horsepower and is capable of propelling the device at a maximum speed of not more than 30 miles per hour on level ground.

(b) Every manufacturer of a motorized bicycle or moped, as defined in this section, shall provide a disclosure to buyers that advises buyers that their existing insurance policies may not provide coverage for these bicycles and that they should contact their insurance company or insurance agent to determine if coverage is provided. The disclosure shall meet both of the following requirements:

(1) The disclosure shall be printed in not less than 14-point boldface type on a single sheet of paper that contains no information other than the disclosure.

(2) The disclosure shall include the following language in capital letters:

"YOUR INSURANCE POLICIES MAY NOT PROVIDE COVERAGE FOR ACCIDENTS INVOLVING THE USE OF THIS BICYCLE. TO DETERMINE IF COVERAGE IS PROVIDED YOU SHOULD CONTACT YOUR INSURANCE COMPANY OR AGENT."

(Amended by Stats. 2015, Ch. 568, Sec. 2. (AB 1096) Effective January 1, 2016.)

407. A "motorized quadricycle" is a four-wheeled device, and a "motorized tricycle" is a three-wheeled device, designed to carry not more than two persons, including the driver, and having either an electric motor or a motor with an automatic transmission developing less than two gross brake horsepower and capable of propelling the device at a maximum speed of not more than 30 miles per hour on level ground. The device shall be utilized only by a person who by reason of physical disability is otherwise unable to move about as a pedestrian or by a senior citizen as defined in Section 13000.

(Amended by Stats. 1993, Ch. 1292, Sec. 3. Effective January 1, 1994.)

407.5. (a) A "motorized scooter" is any two-wheeled device that has handlebars, has either a floorboard that is designed to be stood upon when riding or a seat and footrests in place of the floorboard, and is powered by an electric motor. This device may also be designed to be powered by human propulsion. For purposes of this section, a motorcycle, as defined in Section 400, a motor-driven cycle, as defined in Section 405, or a motorized bicycle or moped, as defined in Section 406, is not a motorized scooter.

(b) A device meeting the definition in subdivision (a) that is powered by a source other than electrical power is also a motorized scooter.

(c) (1) A manufacturer of motorized scooters shall provide a disclosure to buyers that advises buyers that the buyers' existing insurance policies may not provide coverage for these scooters and that the buyers should contact their insurance company or insurance agent to determine if coverage is provided.

(2) The disclosure required under paragraph (1) shall meet both of the following requirements:

(A) The disclosure shall be printed in not less than 14-point boldface type on a single sheet of paper that contains no information other than the disclosure.

(B) The disclosure shall include the following language in capital letters:

"YOUR INSURANCE POLICIES MAY NOT PROVIDE COVERAGE FOR ACCIDENTS INVOLVING THE USE OF THIS SCOOTER. TO DETERMINE IF COVERAGE IS PROVIDED, YOU SHOULD CONTACT YOUR INSURANCE COMPANY OR AGENT."

(d) (1) A manufacturer of motorized scooters shall provide a disclosure to a buyer that advises the buyer that the buyer may not modify or alter the exhaust system to cause that system to amplify or create an excessive noise, or to fail to meet applicable emission requirements.

(2) The disclosure required under paragraph (1) shall meet both of the following requirements:

(A) The disclosure shall be printed in not less than 14-point boldface type on a single sheet of paper that contains no information other than the disclosure.

(B) The disclosure shall include the following language in capital letters:

"YOU MAY NOT MODIFY OR ALTER THE EXHAUST SYSTEM OF THIS SCOOTER TO CAUSE IT TO AMPLIFY OR CREATE EXCESSIVE NOISE PER VEHICLE CODE SECTION 21226, OR TO FAIL TO MEET APPLICABLE EMISSION REQUIREMENTS PER VEHICLE CODE 27156."

(Amended by Stats. 2021, Ch. 311, Sec. 2. (SB 814) Effective January 1, 2022.)

408. "Motor carrier" is the registered owner, lessee, licensee, or bailee of any vehicle set forth in Section 34500, who operates or directs the operation of any such vehicle on either a for-hire or not-for-hire basis. "Motor carrier" also includes a motor carrier's agents, officers, and representatives, as well as employees responsible for the hiring, supervising, training, assigning, or dispatching of drivers and employees concerned with the installation, inspection, and maintenance of motor vehicle equipment or accessories.

(Amended by Stats. 2016, Ch. 208, Sec. 7. (AB 2906) Effective January 1, 2017.)

410. A "motor truck" or "motortruck" is a motor vehicle designed, used, or maintained primarily for the transportation of property.

(Amended by Stats. 1993, Ch. 272, Sec. 11. Effective August 2, 1993.)

415. (a) A "motor vehicle" is a vehicle that is self-propelled.

(b) "Motor vehicle" does not include a self-propelled wheelchair, motorized tricycle, or motorized quadricycle, if operated by a person who, by reason of physical disability, is otherwise unable to move about as a pedestrian.

(c) For purposes of Chapter 6 (commencing with Section 3000) of Division 2, "motor vehicle" includes a recreational vehicle as that term is defined in subdivision (a) of Section 18010 of the Health and Safety Code, but does not include a truck camper.

(Amended by Stats. 2004, Ch. 404, Sec. 1. Effective January 1, 2005.)

425. A "muffler" is a device consisting of a series of chambers or baffle plates, or other mechanical design, for the purpose of receiving exhaust gas from an internal combustion engine, and effective in reducing noise.

(Enacted by Stats. 1959, Ch. 3.)

426. "New motor vehicle dealer" is a dealer, as defined in Section 285, who, in addition to the requirements of that section, either acquires for resale new and unregistered motor vehicles from manufacturers or distributors of those motor vehicles or acquires for resale new off-highway motorcycles, or all-terrain vehicles from manufacturers or distributors of the vehicles. A distinction shall not be made, nor any different construction be given to the definition of "new motor vehicle dealer" and "dealer" except for the application of the provisions of Chapter 6 (commencing with Section 3000) of Division 2 and Sections 4456, 4750.6, and 11704.5. Sections 3001 and 3003 do not, however, apply to a dealer who deals exclusively in motorcycles, all-terrain vehicles, or recreational vehicles, as defined in subdivision (a) of Section 18010 of the Health and Safety Code.

(Amended by Stats. 2020, Ch. 8, Sec. 20. (AB 85) Effective June 29, 2020.)

430. A "new vehicle" is a vehicle constructed entirely from new parts that has never been the subject of a retail sale, or registered with the department, or registered with the appropriate agency or authority of any other state, District of Columbia, territory or possession of the United States, or foreign state, province, or country.

(Amended by Stats. 1994, Ch. 1253, Sec. 6. Effective January 1, 1995.)

431. A "nonrepairable vehicle" is a vehicle of a type otherwise subject to registration that meets the criteria specified in subdivision (a), (b), or (c). The vehicle shall be issued a nonrepairable vehicle certificate and the vehicle, the vehicle frame, or unitized frame and body, as applicable, and as defined in Section 670.5, shall not be titled or registered.

(a) A nonrepairable vehicle is a vehicle that has no resale value except as a source of parts or scrap metal, and which the owner irreversibly designates solely as a source of parts or scrap metal.

(b) A nonrepairable vehicle is a completely stripped vehicle (a surgical strip) recovered from theft, missing all of the bolt on sheet metal body panels, all of the doors and hatches, substantially all of the interior components, and substantially all of the grill and light assemblies, or that the owner designates has little or no resale value other than its worth as a source of scrap metal, or as a source of a vehicle identification number that could be used illegally.

(c) A nonrepairable vehicle is a completely burned vehicle (burned hulk) that has been burned to the extent that there are no more usable or repairable body or interior components, tires and wheels, or drive train components, and which the owner irreversibly designates as having little or no resale value other than its worth as scrap metal or as a source of a vehicle identification number that could be used illegally.

(Amended by Stats. 2002, Ch. 670, Sec. 1. Effective January 1, 2003.)

432. A "nonrepairable vehicle certificate" is a vehicle ownership document issued to the owner of a nonrepairable vehicle. Ownership of the vehicle may only be transferred two times on a nonrepairable vehicle certificate. A vehicle for which a nonrepairable vehicle certificate has been issued may not be titled or registered for use on the roads or highways of California. A nonrepairable vehicle certificate shall be conspicuously labeled with the word "nonrepairable" across the front.

(Added by Stats. 1994, Ch. 1008, Sec. 6.5. Effective January 1, 1995. Operative July 1, 1995, by Sec. 19 of Ch. 1008.)

435. "Nonresident" is a person who is not a resident of this State.

(Enacted by Stats. 1959, Ch. 3.)

435.5. "Nonresident daily commuter" means a person who is not a resident of this state, but who enters and leaves this state on a daily basis for the purpose of employment and whose vehicle is principally garaged out of this state.

(Added by Stats. 1985, Ch. 1090, Sec. 1. Effective September 27, 1985.)

436. An "off-highway motorcycle" means a motorcycle or motor-driven cycle which is subject to identification under this code.

(Added by Stats. 1982, Ch. 1584, Sec. 5.)

436.1. An "off-highway electric motorcycle," commonly referred to as an eMoto, is an off-highway motorcycle subject to identification under this code that meets all of the following requirements:

(a) Is designed by the manufacturer for operation primarily off the highway.

(b) Is powered by an electric motor for which a motor number is not required.

(c) Has handlebars for steering control.

(d) Has a straddle seat provided by the manufacturer.

(e) Has two wheels.

(f) Is not equipped with pedals from the manufacturer.

(Added by Stats. 2025, Ch. 588, Sec. 1. (SB 586) Effective January 1, 2026.)

440. An "official traffic control device" is any sign, signal, marking, or device, consistent with Section 21400, placed or erected by authority of a public body or official having jurisdiction, for the purpose of regulating, warning, or guiding traffic, but does not include islands, curbs, traffic barriers, speed humps, speed bumps, or other roadway design features.

(Amended by Stats. 1994, Ch. 1220, Sec. 51. Effective September 30, 1994.)

445. An "official traffic control signal" is any device, whether manually, electrically or mechanically operated, by which traffic is alternately directed to stop and proceed and which is erected by authority of a public body or official having jurisdiction.

(Enacted by Stats. 1959, Ch. 3.)

450. An "oil well production service unit" is any vehicle specifically designed for and used exclusively in servicing oil wells which is only incidentally operated or moved on a highway.

(Added by Stats. 1969, Ch. 133.)

455. "Original driver's license" means the first driver's license issued a person under this code.

(Enacted by Stats. 1959, Ch. 3.)

460. An "owner" is a person having all the incidents of ownership, including the legal title of a vehicle whether or not such person lends, rents, or creates a security interest in the vehicle; the person entitled to the possession of a vehicle as the purchaser under a security agreement; or the State, or any county, city, district, or political subdivision of the State, or the United States, when entitled to the possession and use of a vehicle under a lease, lease-sale, or rental-purchase agreement for a period of 30 consecutive days or more.

(Amended by Stats. 1963, Ch. 1867.)

461. The Senate, Assembly, or any committees thereof, or the Governor's office in possession and using vehicles under a lease, lease-sale, or rental-purchase agreement for a period of 30 consecutive days or more, unless otherwise provided in the lease or rental agreement, shall be exempt from the provisions of Section 460, upon the giving of written notice to the department of the desire to be so exempt.

(Added by Stats. 1967, Ch. 162.)

462. A "paratransit vehicle" is a passenger vehicle, other than a bus, schoolbus, school pupil activity bus, youth bus, general public paratransit vehicle, or taxicab that is both of the following:

(a) (1) Operated for hire by a business, nonprofit organization, or the state, or a political subdivision of the state utilizing drivers who receive compensation for their services and who spend a majority of their workweek operating a passenger vehicle.

(2) For the purposes of this subdivision, compensation does not include reimbursement to volunteer drivers of the cost of providing transportation services at a rate not greater than that approved by the United States Internal Revenue Service for volunteers.

(3) For the purposes of this subdivision, "for hire" means that the entity providing transportation services is compensated for the transportation under contract or agreement.

(b) Regularly used to provide transportation services to any of the following:

(1) Disabled persons who meet the definition of handicapped persons, as defined in Section 99206.5 of the Public Utilities Code.

(2) Persons with a developmental disability, as defined in subdivision (a) of Section 4512 of the Welfare and Institutions Code.

(3) Individuals with disabilities who are determined to be eligible for complementary paratransit services under Title II of the Americans with Disabilities Act of 1990 (P.L.101-336).

(4) Persons who are 55 years of age or older.

(Amended by Stats. 2004, Ch. 404, Sec. 2. Effective January 1, 2005.)

463. "Park or parking" shall mean the standing of a vehicle, whether occupied or not, otherwise than temporarily for the purpose of and while actually engaged in loading or unloading merchandise or passengers.

(Added by Stats. 1961, Ch. 1608.)

464. A "passenger transportation vehicle" is any vehicle, including a trailer bus, designed, used, or maintained for carrying more than 10 persons including the driver, which requires the person to have in his or her immediate possession a valid driver's license for the appropriate class of vehicle to be driven endorsed for passenger transportation.

(Added by Stats. 1990, Ch. 1360, Sec. 1.5.)

465. A "passenger vehicle" is any motor vehicle, other than a motortruck, truck tractor, or a bus, as defined in Section 233, and used or maintained for the transportation of persons. The term "passenger vehicle" shall include a housecar.

(Amended by Stats. 1999, Ch. 1008, Sec. 1. Effective January 1, 2000.)

467. (a) A "pedestrian" is a person who is afoot or who is using any of the following:

(1) A means of conveyance propelled by human power other than a bicycle.

(2) An electric personal assistive mobility device.

(b) "Pedestrian" includes a person who is operating a self-propelled wheelchair, motorized tricycle, or motorized quadricycle and, by reason of physical disability, is otherwise unable to move about as a pedestrian, as specified in subdivision (a).

(Amended (as amended by Stats. 2004, Ch. 404, Sec. 3) by Stats. 2007, Ch. 106, Sec. 2. Effective January 1, 2008.)

467.5. "Pedicab" means any of the following:

(a) A bicycle, including an electric bicycle, that has three or more wheels, that transports, or is capable of transporting, passengers on seats attached to the bicycle, that is operated by a person, and that is being used for transporting passengers for hire.

(b) A bicycle, including an electric bicycle, that pulls a trailer, sidecar, or similar device, that transports, or is capable of transporting, passengers on seats attached to the trailer, sidecar, or similar device, that is operated by a person, and that is being used for transporting passengers for hire.

(c) A four-wheeled device that is primarily or exclusively pedal-powered, has a seating capacity for eight or more passengers, cannot travel in excess of 15 miles per hour, and is being used for transporting passengers for hire. A pedicab defined under this subdivision is subject to the requirements of Article 4.5 (commencing with Section 21215) of Chapter 1 of Division 11.

(Amended by Stats. 2021, Ch. 311, Sec. 3. (SB 814) Effective January 1, 2022.)

468. The department shall commence the "permanent trailer identification plate program," on or after December 31, 2001, and may designate the method, consistent with this code, to be used by trailers, as defined in Section 5014.1, to receive an assigned permanent trailer identification plate for all trailers, except for trailer coaches and park trailers as described in subdivision (b) of Section 18010 of the Health and Safety Code, for identification purposes. An auxiliary dolly or tow dolly may be assigned a permanent trailer identification plate. The plate shall be in a size and design as determined by the department.

(Added by Stats. 2000, Ch. 861, Sec. 15. Effective September 29, 2000. Operative December 31, 2001, pursuant to Sec. 67 of Ch. 861.)

470. "Person" includes a natural person, firm, copartnership, association, limited liability company, or corporation.

(Amended by Stats. 1994, Ch. 1010, Sec. 225. Effective January 1, 1995.)

471. A "pickup truck" is a motor truck with a manufacturer's gross vehicle weight rating of less than 11,500 pounds, an unladen weight of less than 8,001 pounds, and which is equipped with an open box-type bed not exceeding 9 feet in length. "Pickup truck" does not include a motor vehicle otherwise meeting the above definition, that is equipped with a bed-mounted storage compartment unit commonly called a "utility body."

(Amended by Stats. 1997, Ch. 652, Sec. 8. Effective January 1, 1998.)

472. A "pilot car" is a motor vehicle, except a motorcycle, motorized bicycle, or motorized quadricycle, which is used to escort one or more other vehicles, when required, due to the vehicles' size or character of load, in accordance with conditions set forth in a permit issued by the appropriate state agency or by a local authority.

(Added by Stats. 1982, Ch. 568, Sec. 1.)

473. (a) A "pocket bike" is a two-wheeled motorized device that has a seat or saddle for the use of the rider, and that is not designed or manufactured for highway use. "Pocket bike" does not include an off-highway motorcycle, as defined in Section 436.

(b) For purposes of this section, a vehicle is designed for highway use if it meets the applicable Federal Motor Vehicle Safety Standards, as contained in Title 49 of the Code of Federal Regulations, and is equipped in accordance with the requirements of this code.

(Added by Stats. 2005, Ch. 323, Sec. 1. Effective January 1, 2006.)

475. A "pole or pipe dolly" is a vehicle, other than a motor vehicle, having one or more axles which axles, if there be more than one, are not more than 54 inches apart, and two or more wheels, used in connection with a motor vehicle solely for the purpose of transporting poles, timbers, pipes, or integral structural materials and connected with the towing vehicle both by chain, rope, cable, or drawbar, and by the load, without any part of the weight of the dolly resting upon the towing vehicle.

(Enacted by Stats. 1959, Ch. 3.)

480. A "power brake" is any breaking gear or mechanism that aids in applying the brakes of a vehicle and which utilizes vacuum, compressed air, electricity, or hydraulic pressure developed by the motive power of that vehicle for that purpose.

(Amended by Stats. 1977, Ch. 102.)

485. A "pneumatic tire" is a tire inflated or capable of inflation with compressed air.

(Enacted by Stats. 1959, Ch. 3.)

490. "Private road or driveway" is a way or place in private ownership and used for vehicular travel by the owner and those having express or implied permission from the owner but not by other members of the public.

(Enacted by Stats. 1959, Ch. 3.)

492. A "private school" is any school, whether conducted for profit or not, giving a course of training similar to that given in a public school at or below the twelfth grade, including but not limited to schools owned or operated by any church.

(Amended by Stats. 1977, Ch. 406.)

500. "Recreational off-highway vehicle" means a motor vehicle meeting all of the following criteria:

(a) Designed by the manufacturer for operation primarily off of the highway.

(b) Has a steering wheel for steering control.

(c) Has nonstraddle seating provided by the manufacturer for the operator and all passengers.

(d) (1) Has a maximum speed capability of greater than 30 miles per hour.

(2) A vehicle designed by the manufacturer with a maximum speed capability of 30 miles per hour or less but is modified so that it has a maximum speed capability of greater than 30 miles per hour satisfies the criteria set forth in this subdivision.

(e) Has an engine displacement equal to or less than 1,000cc (61 ci).

(Added by Stats. 2012, Ch. 165, Sec. 1. (AB 1595) Effective January 1, 2013.)

505. A "registered owner" is a person registered by the department as the owner of a vehicle.

(Enacted by Stats. 1959, Ch. 3.)

505.2. (a) A "registration service" is a person engaged in the business of soliciting or receiving an application for the registration, renewal of registration, or transfer of registration or ownership, of a vehicle of a type subject to registration under this code, or of soliciting or receiving an application for a motor carrier permit under Division 14.85 (commencing with Section 34600), or of transmitting or presenting those documents to the department, when any compensation is solicited or received for the service. "Registration service" includes, but is not limited to, a person who, for compensation, processes registration documents, conducts lien sales, or processes vehicle dismantling documents.

(b) "Registration service" does not include the following:

(1) A person performing registration services on a vehicle acquired by that person for his or her own personal use or for use in the regular course of that person's business.

(2) A person who solicits applications for or sells, for compensation, nonresident permits for the operation of vehicles within this state.

(3) An employee of one or more dealers or dismantlers, or a combination thereof, who performs either of the following:

(A) Registration services for vehicles acquired by, consigned to, or sold by one or more of the employing dealers or dismantlers.

(B) Vehicle transactions on behalf of one or more of the employing dealers or dismantlers, if the transaction is for an employing dealer or dismantler who is a qualified business partner in compliance with the Business Partner Automation Program established by the department pursuant to Section 1685.

(4) A motor club, as defined in Section 12142 of the Insurance Code.

(5) A common carrier acting in the regular course of its business in transmitting applications.

(Amended by Stats. 2006, Ch. 419, Sec. 2. Effective January 1, 2007.)

506. "Registration year" is the period of time beginning with the date the vehicle is first required to be registered in this state and ending on the date designated by the director for expiration of the registration or the period of time designated for subsequent renewal thereof.
(Added by Stats. 1973, Ch. 889.)

507. The "relevant market area" is any area within a radius of 10 miles from the site of a potential new dealership.
(Added by Stats. 1973, Ch. 996.)

507.5. A "remanufactured vehicle" is a vehicle that has been constructed by a licensed remanufacturer and consists of any used or reconditioned integral parts, including, but not limited to, frame, engine, transmission, axles, brakes, or suspension. Remanufactured vehicles may be sold under a distinctive trade name. An existing vehicle which is incidently repaired, restored, or modified by replacing or adding parts or accessories is not a remanufactured vehicle.
(Added by Stats. 1983, Ch. 1286, Sec. 11.)

507.8. A "remanufacturer" is any person who for commission, money, or other thing of value, produces a vehicle that consists of any used or reconditioned integral parts, including, but not limited to, frame, engine, transmission, axles, brakes, or suspension which is subject to registration under this code. A remanufacturer is not a person who incidently repairs, restores, or modifies an existing vehicle by replacing or adding parts or accessories.
(Added by Stats. 1983, Ch. 1286, Sec. 12.)

508. A "renter" is a person who is engaged in the business of renting, leasing or bailing vehicles for a term not exceeding four months and for a fixed rate or price.
(Added by Stats. 1976, Ch. 1284.)

510. A "repair shop" is a place where vehicles subject to registration under this code are repaired, rebuilt, reconditioned, repainted, or in any way maintained for the public at a charge.
(Enacted by Stats. 1959, Ch. 3.)

512. A "representative" is any person regularly employed by a manufacturer or distributor for the purpose of negotiating or promoting the sale of the manufacturer's or distributer's vehicles to their franchisees or for regularly supervising or contacting franchisees or prospective franchisees in this state for any purpose.
(Added by Stats. 1973, Ch. 996.)

515. A "residence district" is that portion of a highway and the property contiguous thereto, other than a business district, (a) upon one side of which highway, within a distance of a quarter of a mile, the contiguous property fronting thereon is occupied by 13 or more separate dwelling houses or business structures, or (b) upon both sides of which highway, collectively, within a distance of a quarter of a mile, the contiguous property fronting thereon is occupied by 16 or more separate dwelling houses or business structures. A residence district may be longer than one-quarter of a mile if the above ratio of separate dwelling houses or business structures to the length of the highway exists.
(Enacted by Stats. 1959, Ch. 3.)

516. "Resident" means any person who manifests an intent to live or be located in this state on more than a temporary or transient basis. Presence in the state for six months or more in any 12-month period gives rise to a rebuttable presumption of residency.

The following are evidence of residency for purposes of vehicle registration:

(a) Address where registered to vote.

(b) Location of employment or place of business.

(c) Payment of resident tuition at a public institution of higher education.

(d) Attendance of dependents at a primary or secondary school.

(e) Filing a homeowner's property tax exemption.

(f) Renting or leasing a home for use as a residence.

(g) Declaration of residency to obtain a license or any other privilege or benefit not ordinarily extended to a nonresident.

(h) Possession of a California driver's license.

(i) Other acts, occurrences, or events that indicate presence in the state is more than temporary or transient.
(Amended by Stats. 1991, Ch. 13, Sec. 17. Effective February 13, 1991.)

520. A "retail sale" is a sale of goods to a person for the purpose of consumption and use, and not for resale to others, including, but not limited to, an arrangement where a motor vehicle is consigned to a dealer for sale.
(Added by Stats. 1976, Ch. 1284.)

521. A "retarder" is a device, other than a brake, which, when activated by the driver, applies a retarding force to the wheels of a vehicle without the use of friction. A retarder may be installed in or on the engine, exhaust system, drive train, or wheels of a motor vehicle, or an axle or wheels of a towed vehicle. A retarder may operate by altering the valve timing of the engine, by controlling the flow of a circulating fluid, by applying an electromagnetic force, by controlling the release of gases from the exhaust system, or by other means. A retarder may or may not be capable of stopping the vehicle upon which it is installed.
(Added by Stats. 1991, Ch. 648, Sec. 1.)

521.5. "Revived salvage vehicle" means a total loss salvage vehicle as defined in Section 544, or a vehicle reported for dismantling pursuant to Section 5500 or 11520, that has been rebuilt or restored to legal operating condition with new or used component parts.
(Added by Stats. 2002, Ch. 670, Sec. 2. Effective January 1, 2003.)

522. "Ridesharing" means two or more persons traveling by any mode, including, but not limited to, carpooling, vanpooling, buspooling, taxipooling, jitney, and public transit.
(Added by Stats. 1982, Ch. 185, Sec. 5.)

525. "Right-of-way" is the privilege of the immediate use of the highway.
(Enacted by Stats. 1959, Ch. 3.)

527. (a) "Road" means any existing vehicle route established before January 1, 1979, with significant evidence of prior regular travel by vehicles subject to registration pursuant to Article 1 (commencing with Section 4000) of Chapter 1 of Division 3; provided, that "road" does not mean any route traversed exclusively by bicycles as defined in Section 39001, motorcycles as defined in Section 400, motor-driven cycles as defined in Section 405, or off-highway motor vehicles as defined in Section 38012.

(b) Even though nature may alter or eliminate portions of an existing vehicle route, the route shall still be considered a road where there is evidence of periodic use.

(c) A vehicle route need not necessarily be a publicly or privately maintained surface to be a road, as defined, for purposes of this section. Nothing contained herein shall pertain to any property in an incorporated area or properties held in private ownership.

(d) This section is definitional only and nothing contained herein shall be deemed to affect, alter, create, or destroy any right, title, or interest in real property, including, but not limited to, any permit, license, or easement; nor shall this chapter be deemed to affect the liability, or lack thereof, of any owner of an interest of real property based upon the use, possession, or ownership of such interest in real property or the entry upon such property by any person.

(e) This section shall only apply in a county where the board of supervisors has adopted a resolution or enacted an ordinance providing for such application.
(Added by Stats. 1980, Ch. 361, Sec. 1.)

530. A "roadway" is that portion of a highway improved, designed, or ordinarily used for vehicular travel.
(Enacted by Stats. 1959, Ch. 3.)

531. "Utility-terrain vehicle" means a motor vehicle subject to subdivision (a) of Section 38010 that is all of the following:

(a) Designed for operation off of the highway.

(b) Suspended on four tires.

(c) Has a steering wheel for steering control.

(d) Has one seat to accommodate a driver and one passenger sitting side by side.

(Added by Stats. 2012, Ch. 168, Sec. 1. (AB 2111) Effective January 1, 2013.)

535. Safety glazing material is any glazing material so constructed, treated, or combined with other materials as to reduce, in comparison with ordinary sheet, plate, or floatglass, the likelihood of injury to persons by glazing material whether it may be broken or unbroken.

(Amended by Stats. 1979, Ch. 723.)

540. A "safety zone" is the area or space lawfully set apart within a roadway for the exclusive use of pedestrians and which is protected, or which is marked or indicated by vertical signs, raised markers or raised buttons, in order to make such area or space plainly visible at all times while the same is set apart as a safety zone.

(Enacted by Stats. 1959, Ch. 3.)

543. "Salvage pool" means a person engaged exclusively in the business of disposing of total loss salvage vehicles, nonrepairable vehicles, or recovered stolen vehicles sent to it by, or on behalf of, insurance companies, authorized adjusters, leasing companies, self-insured persons, or financial institutions.

(Amended by Stats. 1994, Ch. 1008, Sec. 7. Effective January 1, 1995. Operative July 1, 1995, by Sec. 19 of Ch. 1008.)

543.5. "Salvage vehicle rebuilder" means any person who rebuilds a total loss salvage vehicle, as defined in Section 544, or a vehicle reported for dismantling pursuant to Section 11520, for subsequent resale. A person who, for personal use, rebuilds a total loss salvage vehicle, or a vehicle reported for dismantling, and registers that vehicle in his or her name, is not a salvage vehicle rebuilder. Nothing in this section exempts a salvage vehicle rebuilder from any applicable licensing requirements under this code.

(Added by Stats. 2002, Ch. 670, Sec. 3. Effective January 1, 2003.)

544. "Total loss salvage vehicle" means either of the following:

(a) A vehicle, other than a nonrepairable vehicle, of a type subject to registration that has been wrecked, destroyed, or damaged, to the extent that the owner, leasing company, financial institution, or the insurance company that insured or is responsible for repair of the vehicle, considers it uneconomical to repair the vehicle and because of this, the vehicle is not repaired by or for the person who owned the vehicle at the time of the event resulting in damage.

(b) A vehicle that was determined to be uneconomical to repair, for which a total loss payment has been made by an insurer, whether or not the vehicle is subsequently repaired, if prior to or upon making the payment to the claimant, the insurer obtains the agreement of the claimant to the amount of the total loss settlement, and informs the client that, pursuant to subdivision (a) or (b) of Section 11515, the total loss settlement must be reported to the Department of Motor Vehicles, which will issue a salvage certificate for the vehicle.

(Amended by Stats. 2003, Ch. 451, Sec. 4. Effective January 1, 2004.)

545. (a) A "schoolbus" is a motor vehicle designed, used, or maintained for the transportation of any school pupil at or below the 12th grade level to or from a public or private school or to or from public or private school activities, except the following:

(1) A motor vehicle of any type carrying only members of the household of the owner of the vehicle.

(2) A motortruck transporting pupils who are seated only in the passenger compartment, or a passenger vehicle designed for and carrying not more than 10 persons, including the driver, unless the vehicle or truck is transporting two or more disabled pupils confined to wheelchairs.

(3) A motor vehicle operated by a common carrier, or by and under the exclusive jurisdiction of a publicly owned or operated transit system, only during the time it is on a scheduled run and is available to the general public, or on a run scheduled in response to a request from a disabled pupil confined to a wheelchair, or from a parent of the disabled pupil, for transportation to or from nonschool activities, and the motor vehicle is designed for and actually carries not more than 16 persons including the driver, is available to eligible persons of the general public, and the school does not provide the requested transportation service.

(4) A school pupil activity bus.

(5) A motor vehicle operated by a carrier licensed by the federal Surface Transportation Board that is transporting pupils on a school activity entering or returning to the state from another state or country.

(6) A youth bus.

(7) Notwithstanding any other provisions of this section, the governing board of a district maintaining a community college may, by resolution, designate any motor vehicle operated by or for the district, a schoolbus within the meaning of this section, if it is primarily used for the transportation of community college students to or from a public community college or to or from public community college activities. The designation shall not be effective until written notification thereof has been filed with the Department of the California Highway Patrol.

(8) A state-owned motor vehicle being operated by a state employee upon the driveways, paths, parking facilities, or grounds specified in Section 21113 that are under the control of a state hospital under the jurisdiction of the State Department of Developmental Services if the posted speed limit is not more than 20 miles per hour. The motor vehicle may also be operated for a distance of not more than one-quarter mile upon a public street or highway that runs through the grounds of a state hospital under the jurisdiction of the State Department of Developmental Services, if the posted speed limit on the public street or highway is not more than 25 miles per hour and if all traffic is regulated by posted stop signs or official traffic control signals at the points of entry and exit by the motor vehicle.

(9) A general public paratransit vehicle, if the general public paratransit vehicle does not duplicate existing schoolbus service, does not transport a public school pupil at or below the 12th grade level to a destination outside of that pupil's school district, and is not used to transport public school pupils in areas where schoolbus services were available during the 1986–87 school year. In areas where expanded school services require expanded transportation of public school pupils, as determined by the governing board of a school district, general public paratransit vehicles shall not be used to transport those pupils for a period of three years from the date that a need for expansion is identified. For purposes of this section, a pupil is defined as a student at or below the 12th grade level who is being transported to a mandated school activity.

(10) A schoolbus with the flashing red light signal system, the amber warning system, and the schoolbus signs covered, while being used for transportation of persons other than pupils, to or from school or school-related activities.

(11) A motor vehicle, other than a motor vehicle described in paragraph (2), that is designed to carry not more than 25 persons including the driver, while being used for the transportation of pupils to or from school-related activities if the vehicle is operated by a passenger charter-party carrier certified and licensed by the Public Utilities Commission pursuant to Chapter 8 (commencing with Section 5351) of Division 2 of the Public Utilities Code that is not under a contractual agreement with a school or school district, and the transportation does not duplicate schoolbus service or any other transportation services for pupils contracted, arranged, or otherwise provided by the school or school district.

(b) This section shall not be construed to prohibit the use of a schoolbus for any activity authorized by any other law, including Section 39837.5 of the Education Code.

(Amended by Stats. 2018, Ch. 92, Sec. 208. (SB 1289) Effective January 1, 2019.)

545.1. (a) Notwithstanding Section 545, a motor vehicle is not a schoolbus if it is operated for the purpose of transporting any pupil to or from a community college or to or from activities at that college, irrespective of the age of the pupil or the grade level of the pupil, if the pupil is a current enrollee in classes of the college providing the transportation.

(b) A driver of a motor vehicle that meets the criteria established by subdivision (a) shall escort pupils as required by subdivision (d) of Section 22112 and shall meet the requirements of Section 12517.

(c) This section shall apply to a community college district that includes within its boundaries one or more counties, each of which has a population of 250,000 or less.

(Amended by Stats. 2001, Ch. 739, Sec. 2. Effective January 1, 2002.)

545.5. (a) Notwithstanding Section 545, a bus of the type commonly known as a coach bus is not a schoolbus when it is operated by the Trona Unified School District to transport pupils to route-deviated school activities.

(b) A coach bus operated pursuant to subdivision (a) shall be inspected annually by the Department of the California Highway Patrol, shall meet the equipment safety standards established by the federal government for schoolbuses, and shall be used to transport pupils only if the driver has obtained a certificate to operate a schoolbus pursuant to Section 12517.

(Added by Stats. 1995, Ch. 400, Sec. 1. Effective January 1, 1996.)

546. A "school pupil activity bus" is any motor vehicle, other than a schoolbus, operated by a common carrier, or by and under the exclusive jurisdiction of a publicly owned or operated transit system, or by a passenger charter-party carrier, used under a contractual agreement between a school and carrier to transport school pupils at or below the 12th-grade level to or from a public or private school activity, or used to transport pupils to or from residential schools, when the pupils are received and discharged at off-highway locations where a parent or adult designated by the parent is present to accept the pupil or place the pupil on the bus. As used in this section, common carrier, publicly owned or operated transit system, and passenger charter-party carrier refer to carriers in business for the principal purpose of transporting members of the public on a commercial basis. This section shall not apply to a motor vehicle operated by a carrier licensed by the Interstate Commerce Commission that is transporting pupils on a school activity trip entering or returning to the state from another state or country.

The driver of a school pupil activity bus shall be subject to the regulations adopted by the California Highway Patrol governing schoolbus drivers, except that the regulations shall not require drivers to duplicate training or schooling that they have otherwise received which is equivalent to that required pursuant to the regulations, and the regulations shall not require drivers to take training in first aid. However, a valid certificate to drive a school pupil activity bus shall not entitle the bearer to drive a schoolbus.

(Added by Stats. 1981, Ch. 813, Sec. 6.)

550. A "semitrailer" is a vehicle designed for carrying persons or property, used in conjunction with a motor vehicle, and so constructed that some part of its weight and that of its load rests upon, or is carried by, another vehicle.

(Enacted by Stats. 1959, Ch. 3.)

553. "Shade trailer" means a device designed and utilized to provide shade pursuant to Section 3395 of Title 8 of the California Code of Regulations.

(Added by Stats. 2012, Ch. 168, Sec. 2. (AB 2111) Effective January 1, 2013.)

554. "Shared mobility device" means an electrically motorized board, as defined in Section 313.5, motorized scooter, as defined in Section 407.5, electric bicycle, as defined in Section 312.5, bicycle, as defined in Section 231, or other similar personal transportation device, except as provided in subdivision (b) of Section 415, that is made available to the public by a shared mobility device service provider for shared use and transportation in exchange for financial compensation via a digital application or other electronic or digital platform.

(Added by Stats. 2022, Ch. 206, Sec. 1. (AB 2174) Effective January 1, 2023.)

555. "Sidewalk" is that portion of a highway, other than the roadway, set apart by curbs, barriers, markings or other delineation for pedestrian travel.

(Amended by Stats. 1959, Ch. 979.)

557. A "snowmobile" is a motor vehicle designed to travel over ice or snow in whole or in part on skis, belts, or cleats, which is commonly referred to as an Over Snow Vehicle (OSV).

(Amended by Stats. 1989, Ch. 533, Sec. 2.)

558. A "snow-tread tire" is a tire which has a relatively deep and aggressive tread pattern compared with conventional passenger tread pattern.

(Added by Stats. 1961, Ch. 26.)

560. A "solid tire" is a tire of rubber or other resilient material which does not depend upon compressed air for the support of the load. A nonpneumatic tire, as defined in Section 571.129 of Title 49 of the Code of Federal Regulations, is not a "solid tire" for purposes of complying with Division 12.

(Amended by Stats. 2023, Ch. 219, Sec. 4. (SB 891) Effective January 1, 2024.)

565. "Special construction equipment" is:

(a) Any vehicle used primarily off the highways for construction purposes and which moves only occasionally over the highways and which because of the length, height, width, or unladen weight may not move over the public highways unladen without the permit specified in Section 35780.

(b) Any vehicle which is designed and used primarily either for grading of highways, paving of highways, earth moving, and other construction work on highways, or for construction or maintenance work on railroad rights-of-way, and which is not designed or used primarily for the transportation of persons or property and which is only incidentally operated or moved over the highway. It includes, but is not limited to, road and railroad construction and maintenance machinery so designed and used such as portable air compressors, air drills, asphalt spreaders, bituminous mixers, bucket loaders, tracktype tractors, crawler tractors, ditchers, leveling graders, finishing machines, motor graders, paving mixers, road rollers, scarifiers, earth moving scrapers and carryalls, lighting plants, welders, pumps, water wagons, power shovels and draglines, speed swings, skip loaders, weed mowers, self-propelled and tractor-drawn earth moving equipment and machinery, including dump trucks and tractor-dump trailer combinations which either (1) are in excess of 96 inches in width or (2) which, because of their length, height or unladen weight, may not be moved on a public highway without the permit specified in Section 35780 of this code and which are not operated laden except within the boundaries of the job construction site, and other similar types of construction equipment.

(Amended by Stats. 1969, Ch. 90.)

570. "Special construction equipment" does not include any of the following:

(a) A vehicle originally designed for the transportation of persons or property to which machinery has been attached unless specifically designated as such in Section 565.

(b) Dump trucks originally designed to comply with the size and weight provisions of this code notwithstanding any subsequent modification which would require a permit, as specified in Section 35780 of this code, to operate such vehicles on a highway, truck-mounted transit mixers, cranes and shovels.

(Amended by Stats. 1961, Ch. 1659.)

575. "Special mobile equipment" is a vehicle, not self-propelled, not designed or used primarily for the transportation of persons or property, and only incidentally operated or moved over a highway, excepting implements of husbandry.

(Enacted by Stats. 1959, Ch. 3.)

580. A "specially constructed vehicle" is a vehicle which is built for private use, not for resale, and is not constructed by a licensed manufacturer or remanufacturer. A specially constructed vehicle may be built from (1) a kit; (2) new or used, or a combination of new and used, parts; or (3) a vehicle reported for dismantling, as required by Section 5500 or 11520, which, when reconstructed, does not resemble the original make of the vehicle dismantled. A specially constructed

vehicle is not a vehicle which has been repaired or restored to its original design by replacing parts.
(Amended by Stats. 1983, Ch. 1286, Sec. 13.)

585. A "station wagon" is a dual purpose vehicle designed for the transportation of persons and also designed in such a manner that the seats may be removed or folded out of the way for the purpose of increasing the property carrying space within the vehicle. The term includes, but is not limited to, types of vehicles which carry the trade names of station wagon, estate wagon, town and country wagon, and country sedan. A vehicle used primarily for the transportation of cadavers to or from a funeral home, mortuary, or burial site is not a station wagon.
(Amended by Stats. 2013, Ch. 523, Sec. 22. (SB 788) Effective January 1, 2014.)

587. "Stop or stopping" when prohibited shall mean any cessation of movement of a vehicle, whether occupied or not, except when necessary to avoid conflict with other traffic or in compliance with the direction of a police officer or official traffic control device or signal.
(Added by Stats. 1961, Ch. 1917.)

590. "Street" is a way or place of whatever nature, publicly maintained and open to the use of the public for purposes of vehicular travel. Street includes highway.
(Enacted by Stats. 1959, Ch. 3.)

591. A "street" or "highway" shall not include those portions of a way or place in or upon which construction, alteration, or repair work is being performed insofar as the equipment performing such work and its operation are concerned. Where the work consists of a street or highway project, the limits of the project as shown or described in the plans or specifications of the awarding body shall be so excluded with reference to the equipment actually engaged in performing the work. The authority having jurisdiction over such way or place may include any or all of the requirements set forth in Divisions 11, 12, 13, 14 and 15 in any permit issued for work on such way or place and the awarding body on any such street or highway project may include such requirements in the specifications for such project. It is the intention of the Legislature, in enacting this section, that this section shall not be construed to relieve any person from the duty of exercising due care.
(Added by Stats. 1959, Ch. 659.)

592. "Highway", for the purposes of Division 3 (commencing with Section 4000), Division 12 (commencing with Section 24000), Division 13 (commencing with Section 29000), Division 14.8 (commencing with Section 34500), and Division 15 (commencing with Section 35000), does not include a way or place under the jurisdiction of a federal governmental agency, which lies on national forest or private lands, is open to public use, and for which the cost of maintenance of such way or place is borne or contributed to directly by any users thereof.
(Amended by Stats. 1969, Ch. 1213.)

593. "Supplemental restraint system" means an automatic passive restraint system consisting of a bag that is designed to inflate upon collision, commonly referred to as an "airbag."
(Added by Stats. 2002, Ch. 670, Sec. 4. Effective January 1, 2003.)

595. "Terminal" is a place where a vehicle of a type listed in Section 34500 is regularly garaged or maintained, or from which the vehicle is operated or dispatched.
(Added by Stats. 1994, Ch. 832, Sec. 1. Effective January 1, 1995.)

600. A "through highway" is a highway or portion thereof at the entrance to which vehicular traffic from intersecting highways is regulated by stop signs or traffic control signals or is controlled when entering on a separated right-turn roadway by a yield-right-of-way sign.
(Amended by Stats. 1969, Ch. 168.)

605. "Tire traction devices" are devices or mechanisms having a composition and design capable of improving vehicle traction, braking, and cornering ability upon snow or ice-covered surfaces. Tire traction devices shall be constructed and assembled to provide sufficient structural integrity and to prevent accidental detachment from vehicles. Tire traction devices shall, at the time of manufacture or final assembly, bear a permanent impression indicating the name, initials, or trademark of the assembling company or primary manufacturer, and the country in which the devices were manufactured or assembled in final form.
(Added by Stats. 1990, Ch. 71, Sec. 1. Effective May 1, 1990.)

610. "Tire tread" is that portion of the tire, consisting of the ribs and grooves, which comes in contact with the roadway.
(Added by Stats. 1970, Ch. 216.)

611. A "toll highway" or "toll road" is a publicly owned way or place open to the use of the public for purposes of vehicular travel which use requires the payment of a fee.
(Added by Stats. 1992, Ch. 1241, Sec. 6. Effective January 1, 1993.)

612. (a) "Tour bus" means a bus, which is operated by or for a charter-party carrier of passengers, as defined in Section 5360 of the Public Utilities Code, or a passenger stage corporation, as defined in Section 226 of the Public Utilities Code.

(b) "Tour bus" includes a bus described in subdivision (a) that has had its roof substantially structurally modified or removed.
(Amended by Stats. 2017, Ch. 310, Sec. 1. (AB 25) Effective January 1, 2018.)

615. (a) A "tow truck" is a motor vehicle which has been altered or designed and equipped for, and primarily used in the business of, transporting vehicles by means of a crane, hoist, tow bar, tow line, or dolly or is otherwise primarily used to render assistance to other vehicles. A "roll-back carrier" designed to carry up to two vehicles is also a tow truck. A trailer for hire that is being used to transport a vehicle is a tow truck. "Tow truck" does not include an automobile dismantlers' tow vehicle or a repossessor's tow vehicle.

(b) "Repossessor's tow vehicle" means a tow vehicle which is registered to a repossessor licensed or registered pursuant to Chapter 11 (commencing with Section 7500) of Division 3 of the Business and Professions Code that is used exclusively in the course of the repossession business.

(c) "Automobile dismantlers' tow vehicle" means a tow vehicle which is registered by an automobile dismantler licensed pursuant to Chapter 3 (commencing with Section 11500) of Division 5 and which is used exclusively to tow vehicles owned by that automobile dismantler in the course of the automobile dismantling business.
(Amended by Stats. 1999, Ch. 456, Sec. 14. Effective January 1, 2000.)

617. A "tow dolly" is a vehicle towed by a motor vehicle and designed and used exclusively to transport another motor vehicle and upon which the front or rear wheels of the towed motor vehicle are mounted, while the other wheels of the towed motor vehicle remain in contact with the ground. "Tow dolly" does not include a portable or collapsible dolly used as specified in Section 4014.
(Added by Stats. 1983, Ch. 708, Sec. 1.)

620. The term "traffic" includes pedestrians, ridden animals, vehicles, street cars, and other conveyances, either singly or together, while using any highway for purposes of travel.
(Enacted by Stats. 1959, Ch. 3.)

625. A "traffic officer" is any member of the California Highway Patrol, or any peace officer who is on duty for the exclusive or main purpose of enforcing Division 10 (commencing with Section 20000) or 11 (commencing with Section 21000).
(Amended by Stats. 1983, Ch. 142, Sec. 159.)

626. A "traffic violator school" is a business that, for compensation, provides, or offers to provide, instruction in traffic safety, including, but not limited to, classroom traffic violator curricula, for persons referred by a court pursuant to Section 42005 or to other persons who elect to attend.
(Amended by Stats. 2001, Ch. 457, Sec. 1. Effective January 1, 2002.)

626.2. A "traffic violator school branch or classroom location" is any place where a traffic violator school conducts instruction or maintains records.
(Added by Stats. 1985, Ch. 396, Sec. 2. Effective July 30, 1985.)

626.4. A "traffic violator school instructor" is any person who provides

instruction to traffic violators on behalf of a traffic violator school.
(Added by Stats. 1985, Ch. 396, Sec. 3. Effective July 30, 1985.)

626.6. A "traffic violator school operator" is the person who directs and manages the operations of a traffic violator school.

A "traffic violator school operator" may be either the traffic violator school owner or another person designated by the traffic violator school owner to personally direct and manage the traffic violator school for the traffic violator school owner.
(Added by Stats. 1985, Ch. 396, Sec. 4. Effective July 30, 1985.)

626.8. A "traffic violator school owner" is any natural person, association, or corporation that owns a traffic violator school.
(Added by Stats. 1985, Ch. 396, Sec. 5. Effective July 30, 1985.)

627. (a) "Engineering and traffic survey," as used in this code, means a survey of highway and traffic conditions in accordance with methods determined by the Department of Transportation for use by state and local authorities.

(b) An engineering and traffic survey shall include, among other requirements deemed necessary by the department, consideration of all of the following:

(1) Prevailing speeds as determined by traffic engineering measurements.

(2) Accident records.

(3) Highway, traffic, and roadside conditions not readily apparent to the driver.

(c) When conducting an engineering and traffic survey, local authorities, in addition to the factors set forth in paragraphs (1) to (3), inclusive, of subdivision (b) may consider all of the following:

(1) Residential density, if any of the following conditions exist on the particular portion of highway and the property contiguous thereto, other than a business district:

(A) Upon one side of the highway, within a distance of a quarter of a mile, the contiguous property fronting thereon is occupied by 13 or more separate dwelling houses or business structures.

(B) Upon both sides of the highway, collectively, within a distance of a quarter of a mile, the contiguous property fronting thereon is occupied by 16 or more separate dwelling houses or business structures.

(C) The portion of highway is longer than one-quarter of a mile but has the ratio of separate dwelling houses or business structures to the length of the highway described in either subparagraph (A) or (B).

(2) Safety of bicyclists and pedestrians, with increased consideration for vulnerable pedestrian groups including children, seniors, persons with disabilities, users of personal assistive mobility devices, and the unhoused.
(Amended by Stats. 2021, Ch. 690, Sec. 1. (AB 43) Effective January 1, 2022.)

630. A "trailer" is a vehicle designed for carrying persons or property on its own structure and for being drawn by a motor vehicle and so constructed that no part of its weight rests upon any other vehicle. As used in Division 15 (commencing with Section 35000), "trailer" includes a semitrailer when used in conjunction with an auxiliary dolly, if the auxiliary dolly is of a type constructed to replace the function of the drawbar and the front axle or axles of a trailer.
(Amended by Stats. 1984, Ch. 542, Sec. 1.)

635. A "trailer coach" is a vehicle, other than a motor vehicle, designed for human habitation or human occupancy for industrial, professional, or commercial purposes, for carrying property on its own structure, and for being drawn by a motor vehicle. A "park trailer," as described in Section 18009.3 of the Health and Safety Code, is a trailer coach.
(Amended by Stats. 2000, Ch. 566, Sec. 3. Effective January 1, 2001.)

636. A "trailer bus" is a trailer or semitrailer designed, used, or maintained for the transportation of more than 15 persons, including the driver, and includes a connected towing motor vehicle that is a motor truck, truck tractor, or bus.
(Amended by Stats. 1994, Ch. 58, Sec. 1. Effective April 26, 1994.)

640. A "transferee" is a person who has acquired the sole ownership of or an equity in a vehicle of a type required to be registered under this code.
(Enacted by Stats. 1959, Ch. 3.)

642. A "transit bus" is any bus owned or operated by a publicly owned or operated transit system, or operated under contract with a publicly owned or operated transit system, and used to provide to the general public, regularly scheduled transportation for which a fare is charged. A general public paratransit vehicle is not a transit bus.
(Added by Stats. 1989, Ch. 1136, Sec. 2. Operative July 1, 1990, by Sec. 9 of Ch. 1136.)

645. (a) A "transporter" is a person engaged in the business of moving any owned or lawfully possessed vehicle by lawful methods over the highways for the purpose of delivery of such vehicles to dealers, sales agents of a manufacturer, purchasers, or to a new location as requested by the owner.

(b) The term "transporter" does not include a person engaged in the business of operating a tow car.
(Amended by Stats. 1963, Ch. 444.)

650. A "trolley coach" is a vehicle which is propelled by electric power obtained from overhead trolley wires, but not operated upon rails.
(Enacted by Stats. 1959, Ch. 3.)

655. (a) A "truck tractor" is a motor vehicle designed and used primarily for drawing other vehicles and not so constructed as to carry a load, other than a part of the weight of the vehicle and the load so drawn. As used in this section, "load" does not include items carried on the truck tractor in conjunction with the operation of the vehicle if the load carrying space for these items does not exceed 34 square feet.

(b) Notwithstanding subdivision (a), a truck tractor, operated by a motor carrier whose owner is licensed by the Department of the California Highway Patrol to transport explosives pursuant to Division 14 (commencing with Section 31600), may be equipped with a cargo container used exclusively for the transportation of explosives or munitions-related security material, as specified by the United States Department of Defense.
(Amended by Stats. 1994, Ch. 88, Sec. 1. Effective January 1, 1995.)

657. A "truss" is an assemblage of beams, bars, or rods typically arranged in a triangle or combination of triangles to form a rigid framework and used as a structural support in buildings.
(Added by Stats. 1979, Ch. 299.)

660. The "unladen weight" of a vehicle is the weight equipped and ready for operation on the road including the body, fenders, oil in motor, radiator full of water, with five gallons of gasoline or equivalent weight of other motor fuel; also equipment required by law, and unless exempted under Section 661, any special cabinets, boxes or body parts permanently attached to the vehicle, and any machinery, equipment or attachment which is attendant to the efficient operation of the body or vehicle. Unladen weight shall not include any load or any machinery or mechanical apparatus, such as, but not limited to, wood saws, well-drilling machines, spray apparatus, tow truck cranes, and grinding equipment. The unladen weight of a vehicle shall have no application in determining any fee under this code or the Revenue and Taxation Code other than Section 9400.
(Amended by Stats. 1988, Ch. 924, Sec. 2.)

661. Unladen weight shall not include the following machinery, equipment or attachment which is attendant to the efficient operation of the body or vehicle:

(a) Equipment used for loading, compacting, or unloading of refuse.

(b) Transitmix cement equipment.

(c) Temporary equipment used to contain or support the load which does not change the body classification.

(d) Any camper unit that is temporarily attached to a vehicle.

(e) Refrigeration equipment.
(Added by Stats. 1963, Ch. 2108.)

665. A "used vehicle" is a vehicle that has been sold, or has been registered with the department, or has been sold and operated upon the highways, or has been registered with the appropriate agency of authority, of any other state, District of Columbia, territory or possession of the United States or foreign state, province or country, or unregistered vehicles regularly used or operated as demonstrators in the sales work of a dealer or unregistered vehicles regularly used or operated by a manufacturer in the sales or distribution work of such manufacturer. The word "sold" does not include or extend to: (1) any sale made by a manufacturer or a distributor to a dealer, (2) any sale by a new motor vehicle dealer franchised to sell a particular line-make to another new motor vehicle dealer franchised to sell the same line-make, or (3) any sale by a dealer to another dealer licensed under this code involving a mobilehome, as defined in Section 396, a recreational vehicle, as defined in Section 18010.5 of the Health and Safety Code, a commercial coach, as defined in Section 18012 of the Health and Safety Code, an off-highway motor vehicle subject to identification, as defined in Section 38012, or a commercial vehicle, as defined in Section 260.

(Amended by Stats. 1988, Ch. 1583, Sec. 2.)

665.5. A "U-turn" is the turning of a vehicle upon a highway so as to proceed in the opposite direction whether accomplished by one continuous movement or not.

(Added by Stats. 1970, Ch. 620.)

667. (a) A "utility trailer" is a trailer or semitrailer used solely for the transportation of the user's personal property, not in commerce, which does not exceed a gross weight of 10,000 pounds or a manufacturer's gross vehicle weight rating of 10,000 pounds.

(b) Notwithstanding subdivision (a), a "utility trailer" includes a trailer or semitrailer designed and used for the transportation of livestock, not in commerce, which does not exceed a gross weight of 10,000 pounds or a manufacturer's gross vehicle weight rating of 10,000 pounds.

(Added by Stats. 2010, Ch. 491, Sec. 35. (SB 1318) Effective January 1, 2011.)

668. A "vanpool vehicle" is any motor vehicle, other than a motortruck or truck tractor, designed for carrying more than 10 but not more than 15 persons including the driver, which is maintained and used primarily for the nonprofit work-related transportation of adults for the purposes of ridesharing.

(Added by Stats. 1982, Ch. 46, Sec. 8.)

670. A "vehicle" is a device by which any person or property may be propelled, moved, or drawn upon a highway, excepting a device moved exclusively by human power or used exclusively upon stationary rails or tracks.

(Amended by Stats. 1975, Ch. 987.)

670.5. A "vehicle frame" is defined as the main longitudinal structural members of the chassis of the vehicle, or for vehicles with unitized body construction, the lowest main longitudinal structural members of the body of the vehicle, used as the major support in the construction of the motor vehicle.

(Added by Stats. 2002, Ch. 670, Sec. 5. Effective January 1, 2003.)

671. (a) A "vehicle identification number" is the motor number, serial number, or other distinguishing number, letter, mark, character, or datum, or any combination thereof, required or employed by the manufacturer or the department for the purpose of uniquely identifying a motor vehicle or motor vehicle part or for the purpose of registration.

(b) Whenever a vehicle is constructed of component parts identified with one or more different vehicle identification numbers, the vehicle identification number stamped or affixed by the manufacturer or authorized governmental entity on the frame or unitized frame and body, as applicable, and as defined in Section 670.5, shall determine the identity of the vehicle for registration purposes.

(Amended by Stats. 2002, Ch. 670, Sec. 6. Effective January 1, 2003.)

672. (a) "Vehicle manufacturer" is any person who produces from raw materials or new basic components a vehicle of a type subject to registration under this code, off-highway motorcycles or all-terrain vehicles subject to identification under this code, or trailers subject to identification pursuant to Section 5014.1, or who permanently alters, for purposes of retail sales, new commercial vehicles by converting the vehicles into house cars that display the insignia of approval required by Section 18056 of the Health and Safety Code and any regulations issued pursuant thereto by the Department of Housing and Community Development. As used in this section, "permanently alters" does not include the permanent attachment of a camper to a vehicle.

(b) A vehicle manufacturer that produces a vehicle of a type subject to registration that consists of used or reconditioned parts, for the purposes of the code, is a remanufacturer, as defined in Section 507.8.

(c) Unless a vehicle manufacturer either grants franchises to franchisees in this state, or issues vehicle warranties directly to franchisees in this state or consumers in this state, the manufacturer shall have an established place of business or a representative in this state.

(d) The scope and application of this section are limited to Division 2 (commencing with Section 1500) and Division 5 (commencing with Section 11100).

(Amended by Stats. 2004, Ch. 836, Sec. 7. Effective January 1, 2005.)

675. (a) "Vehicle salesperson" is a person not otherwise expressly excluded by this section, who does one or a combination of the following:

(1) Is employed as a salesperson by a dealer, as defined in Section 285, or who, under any form of contract, agreement, or arrangement with a dealer, for commission, money, profit, or other thing of value, sells, exchanges, buys, or offers for sale, negotiates, or attempts to negotiate, a sale, or exchange of an interest in a vehicle required to be registered under this code.

(2) Induces or attempts to induce any person to buy or exchange an interest in a vehicle required to be registered, and who receives or expects to receive a commission, money, brokerage fees, profit, or any other thing of value, from either the seller or purchaser of the vehicle.

(3) Exercises managerial control over the business of a licensed vehicle dealer or who supervises vehicle salespersons employed by a licensed dealer, whether compensated by salary or commission, including, but not limited to, any person who is employed by the dealer as a general manager, assistant general manager, or sales manager, or any employee of a licensed vehicle dealer who negotiates with or induces a customer to enter into a security agreement or purchase agreement or purchase order for the sale of a vehicle on behalf of the licensed vehicle dealer.

(b) The term "vehicle salesperson" does not include any of the following:

(1) Representatives of insurance companies, finance companies, or public officials, who in the regular course of business, are required to dispose of or sell vehicles under a contractual right or obligation of the employer, or in the performance of an official duty, or under the authority of any court of law, if the sale is for the purpose of saving the seller from any loss or pursuant to the authority of a court of competent jurisdiction.

(2) Persons who are licensed as a manufacturer, remanufacturer, transporter, distributor, or representative.

(3) Persons exclusively employed in a bona fide business of exporting vehicles, or of soliciting orders for the sale and delivery of vehicles outside the territorial limits of the United States.

(4) Persons not engaged in the purchase or sale of vehicles as a business, disposing of vehicles acquired for their own use, or for use in their business when the vehicles have been so acquired and used in good faith, and not for the purpose of avoiding the provisions of this code.

(5) Persons regularly employed as salespersons by persons who are engaged in a business involving the purchase, sale, or exchange of boat trailers.

(6) Persons regularly employed as salespersons by persons who are engaged in a business activity which does not involve the purchase, sale, or exchange of vehicles, except incidentally in connection with the purchase, sale, or exchange of vehicles of a type not subject to registration under this code, boat trailers, or midget autos or racers advertised as being built exclusively for use by children.

(7) Persons licensed as a vehicle dealer under this code doing business

as a sole ownership or member of a partnership or a stockholder and director of a corporation or a member and manager of a limited liability company licensed as a vehicle dealer under this code. However, those persons shall engage in the activities of a salesperson, as defined in this section, exclusively on behalf of the sole ownership or partnership or corporation or limited liability company in which they own an interest or stock, and those persons owning stock shall be directors of the corporation; otherwise, they are vehicle salespersons and subject to Article 2 (commencing with Section 11800) of Chapter 4 of Division 5.

(8) Persons regularly employed as salespersons by a vehicle dealer authorized to do business in California under Section 11700.1 of the Vehicle Code.

(Amended by Stats. 1994, Ch. 1200, Sec. 92. Effective September 30, 1994.)

675.5. A "vehicle verifier" is a person not expressly excluded by Section 675.6 who inspects, records, documents, and submits to the department, or its authorized representative, such proof of vehicle identification as may be required by the department for the purpose of registering or transferring the ownership of vehicles.

(Added by Stats. 1975, Ch. 700.)

675.6. (a) "Vehicle verifier" does not include any of the following:

(1) A peace officer.

(2) An authorized employee of the department.

(3) An agent of the National Insurance Crime Bureau.

(4) An employee of an organization certified under the provisions of Part 5 (commencing with Section 12140) of Division 2 of the Insurance Code whose duties require or authorize the verification of vehicles.

(b) Any person specified in subdivision (a) may perform the duties of a vehicle verifier without obtaining the special permit required in Section 11300.

(Amended by Stats. 2018, Ch. 198, Sec. 17. (AB 3246) Effective January 1, 2019.)

676. "Year-round registration" is a system whereby the director designates a date for the expiration of registration of a vehicle and renewal thereof in order to equalize the volume of such renewals throughout the year.

(Added by Stats. 1973, Ch. 889.)

676.5. A "water tender vehicle" is a vehicle designed to carry not less than 1,500 gallons of water and used primarily for transporting and delivering water to be applied by other vehicles or pumping equipment at fire emergency scenes.

(Amended by Stats. 1995, Ch. 91, Sec. 169. Effective January 1, 1996.)

680. (a) A "youth bus" is any bus, other than a schoolbus, designed for and when actually carrying not more than 16 persons and the driver, used to transport children at or below the 12th-grade level directly from a public or private school to an organized nonschool-related youth activity within 25 miles of the school or directly from a location which provides the organized nonschool-related youth activity to a public or private school within 25 miles of that location.

(b) In addition to the destinations specified in subdivision (a), a youth bus may also be used to transport children at or below the 12th-grade level to or from their place of residence if the driver has met the requirements of Section 12523 and received additional instruction and training approved by the Department of the California Highway Patrol.

(Amended by Stats. 1996, Ch. 774, Sec. 1. Effective January 1, 1997.)

681. (a) "Real ID driver's license or identification card" means a driver's license or identification card that has been issued by a state that has been certified by the Department of Homeland Security to be in compliance with the requirements of the Real ID Act of 2005 (Public Law 109-13) and the regulations adopted pursuant to the act.

(b) This section shall become operative on January 1, 2018.

(Added by Stats. 2016, Ch. 339, Sec. 3. (SB 838) Effective September 13, 2016. Section operative January 1, 2018, by its own provisions.)

Division 2. Administration

(Division 2 enacted by Stats. 1959, Ch. 3.)

Chapter 1. The Department of Motor Vehicles

(Chapter 1 enacted by Stats. 1959, Ch. 3.)

Article 1. Organization of Department

(Article 1 enacted by Stats. 1959, Ch. 3.)

1500. (a) There is in the Transportation Agency the Department of Motor Vehicles.

(b) Whenever the term "Business, Transportation and Housing Agency" appears within the Vehicle Code, it shall refer to the Transportation Agency, and whenever the term "Secretary of Business, Transportation and Housing" appears within the Vehicle Code, it shall refer to the Secretary of Transportation.

(Amended by Stats. 2013, Ch. 352, Sec. 517. (AB 1317) Effective September 26, 2013. Operative July 1, 2013, by Sec. 543 of Ch. 352.)

1501. The department is the successor to and is hereby vested with all of the powers, duties, purposes, responsibilities, and jurisdiction now or hereafter vested by law in the Department of Motor Vehicles, the Motor Vehicle Department, the Motor Vehicle Department of California, the Division of Motor Vehicles of the Department of Finance, the Division of Motor Vehicles of the Department of Public Works, and all other state agencies of similar designation, or in the several heads, members, officers, and employees of each thereof.

(Enacted by Stats. 1959, Ch. 3.)

1502. The department has possession and control of all records, books, papers, offices, equipment, moneys, funds, appropriations, and all other property, real or personal, now or hereafter held for the benefit or use of any state agency mentioned in Section 1501.

(Enacted by Stats. 1959, Ch. 3.)

1503. Except as in this division otherwise provided, the provisions of Chapter 2 (commencing at Section 11150) of Part 1 of Division 3 of Title 2 of the Government Code shall govern and apply to the conduct of the department in every respect the same as if the provisions were set forth in this code, and wherever in that chapter the term "head of the department" or similar designation occurs, for the purposes of this division, it shall mean the director.

(Amended by Stats. 1959, Ch. 1996.)

1504. The department is under the control of a civil executive officer known as the Director of Motor Vehicles. The director shall be appointed by, and hold office at the pleasure of, the Governor.

(Amended by Stats. 1984, Ch. 268, Sec. 32.2. Effective June 29, 1984.)

1505. The director, with the approval of the Governor and the Secretary of Transportation, shall organize the department in a manner that he or she may deem necessary to conduct the work of the department.

(Amended by Stats. 2013, Ch. 352, Sec. 518. (AB 1317) Effective September 26, 2013. Operative July 1, 2013, by Sec. 543 of Ch. 352.)

1507. The director may appoint and, in accordance with law fix the salaries of:

(a) A deputy director.

(b) Such other officers, deputies, technical experts, and employees as may be necessary for the proper discharge of the duties of the department.

(Enacted by Stats. 1959, Ch. 3.)

Article 2. Powers and Duties

(Article 2 enacted by Stats. 1959, Ch. 3.)

1650. The director shall administer and enforce the provisions of this code relating to the department.

(Enacted by Stats. 1959, Ch. 3.)

1651. (a) The director may adopt and enforce rules and regulations as may be necessary to carry out the provisions of this code relating to the department.

(b) Rules and regulations shall be adopted, amended, or repealed

in accordance with the Administrative Procedure Act (Chapter 3.5 (commencing with Section 11340) of Part 1 of Division 3 of Title 2 of the Government Code).
(Amended by Stats. 2003, Ch. 594, Sec. 13. Effective January 1, 2004.)

1651.2. Whenever in the judgment of the department, any person has engaged, or is about to engage, in any acts or practices that constitute, or will constitute, an offense against Division 5 (commencing with Section 11100) by engaging in any act subject to license requirements without having obtained a license, the department may apply to the appropriate court for an order enjoining the acts or practices, and, upon showing by the department that the person has engaged, or is about to engage, in any of those acts or practices, an injunction, restraining order, or other order that may be appropriate shall be granted by the court, including the costs incurred by the department in obtaining the order.
(Added by Stats. 1994, Ch. 584, Sec. 1. Effective January 1, 1995.)

1651.3. It is the policy of this state to recognize the training and experience that individuals gain while serving in the Armed Forces of the United States. In furtherance of this policy, the department, in conjunction with the military services of the United States, shall develop policies to assist persons who are leaving active duty to obtain commercial driver's licenses. These policies shall not waive any requisites or examinations required by law for a commercial driver's license. Except as otherwise authorized, these policies shall specify how this training and experience may be used to obtain these licenses. The department shall consult with the Department of Veterans Affairs before adopting these policies. The department shall perform the duties required by this section within existing budgetary resources of the agency within which the department operates.
(Amended by Stats. 2020, Ch. 47, Sec. 1. (AB 2141) Effective January 1, 2021.)

1651.5. (a) The director may assign or reassign dates for the expiration of registration for a vehicle registered pursuant to this code. The director may establish a registration year for any vehicle consisting of any period from seven months to 18 months, inclusive, with subsequent renewals being required at yearly intervals thereafter. The director shall assign an expiration date of the last day of the calendar month to all trailers and to all motor vehicles subject to additional fees under the provisions of Section 9400. Any vehicle being registered on a quarterly basis shall be assigned or reassigned an expiration date of December 31 for the registration year. The director shall have the authority to exclude from year-round registration any type of vehicle that the director deems appropriate for exclusion.

(b) In order to implement a year-round registration for vehicles registered pursuant to the International Registration Plan as described in Article 4 (commencing with Section 8050) of Chapter 4 of Division 3, the director, on or before January 1, 2009, shall assign or reassign a date for the expiration of registration of those vehicles described in this subdivision and may utilize the applicable practices and procedures set forth under subdivision (a) in order to implement this subdivision.
(Amended by Stats. 2006, Ch. 169, Sec. 1. Effective January 1, 2007.)

1652. (a) The department shall prescribe and provide suitable forms of applications, certificates of ownership, registration cards, drivers' licenses, and all other forms requisite or deemed necessary for the purposes of this code and shall prepay all transportation charges thereon.

(b) The department may require that any application or document filed with the department be signed and submitted under penalty of perjury.
(Amended by Stats. 1982, Ch. 830, Sec. 1.)

1653. The department shall examine and determine the genuineness and regularity of every application or document filed with it under this code and may require additional information or reject any such application or document if not satisfied of the genuineness and regularity thereof or the truth of any statement contained therein.
(Amended by Stats. 1961, Ch. 58.)

1653.5. (a) Each form prescribed by the department for use by an applicant for the issuance or renewal by the department of a driver's license or identification card pursuant to Division 6 (commencing with Section 12500) shall contain a section for the applicant's social security account number.

(b) Each form prescribed by the department for use by an applicant for the issuance, renewal, or transfer of the registration or certificate of title to a vehicle shall contain a section for the applicant's driver's license or identification card number.

(c) Except as provided in Section 12801, a person who submits to the department a form that, pursuant to subdivision (a), contains a section for the applicant's social security account number, or pursuant to subdivision (b), the applicant's driver's license or identification card number, if any, shall furnish the appropriate number in the space provided.

(d) Except as provided in Section 12801, the department shall not complete an application that does not include the applicant's social security account number or driver's license or identification card number as required under subdivision (c).

(e) An applicant's social security account number shall not be included by the department on a driver's license, identification card, registration, certificate of title, or any other document issued by the department.

(f) Notwithstanding any other law, information regarding an applicant's social security account number, or ineligibility for a social security number, obtained by the department pursuant to this section, is not a public record and shall not be disclosed by the department except for any of the following purposes:

(1) Responding to a request for information from an agency operating pursuant to, and carrying out the provisions of, Part A (Block Grants to States for Temporary Assistance for Needy Families), or Part D (Child Support and Establishment of Paternity), of Subchapter IV of Chapter 7 of Title 42 of the United States Code.

(2) Implementation of Section 12419.10 of the Government Code.

(3) Responding to information requests from the Franchise Tax Board for the purpose of tax administration.

(4) Responding to information requests from the Employment Development Department for purposes relating to tax administration and ensuring compliance with family temporary disability insurance, unemployment compensation disability, and unemployment compensation benefit requirements.

(g) This section shall become inoperative on the effective date of a final judicial determination made by any court of appellate jurisdiction that any provision of the act that added this section, or its application, either in whole or in part, is enjoined, found unconstitutional, or held invalid for any reason. The department shall post this information on its internet website.
(Amended (as amended by Stats. 2014, Ch. 452, Sec. 2) by Stats. 2020, Ch. 14, Sec. 11. (AB 82) Effective June 29, 2020. Conditionally inoperative as provided in subd. (h). See later operative version, as amended by Sec. 168 of Stats. 2014, Ch. 71.)

1653.5. (a) Each form prescribed by the department for use by an applicant for the issuance or renewal by the department of a driver's license or identification card pursuant to Division 6 (commencing with Section 12500) shall contain a section for the applicant's social security account number.

(b) Each form prescribed by the department for use by an applicant for the issuance, renewal, or transfer of the registration or certificate of title to a vehicle shall contain a section for the applicant's driver's license or identification card number.

(c) A person who submits to the department a form that, pursuant to subdivision (a), contains a section for the applicant's social security account number, or pursuant to subdivision (b), the applicant's driver's license or identification card number, if any, shall furnish the appropriate number in the space provided.

(d) The department shall not complete an application that does not include the applicant's social security account number or driver's license or identification card number as required under subdivision (c).

(e) An applicant's social security account number shall not be included by the department on a driver's license, identification card, registration, certificate of title, or any other document issued by the department.

(f) Notwithstanding any other law, information regarding an applicant's social security account number, obtained by the department pursuant to this section, is not a public record and shall not be disclosed by the department except for any of the following purposes:

(1) Responding to a request for information from an agency operating pursuant to, and carrying out the provisions of, Part A (Block Grants to States for Temporary Assistance for Needy Families), or Part D (Child Support and Establishment of Paternity), of Subchapter IV of Chapter 7 of Title 42 of the United States Code.

(2) Implementation of Section 12419.10 of the Government Code.

(3) Responding to information requests from the Franchise Tax Board for the purpose of tax administration.

(g) This section shall become operative on the effective date of a final judicial determination made by any court of appellate jurisdiction that any provision of the act that added this section, or its application, either in whole or in part, is enjoined, found unconstitutional, or held invalid for any reason. The department shall post this information on its Internet Web site.

(Amended (as added by Stats. 2013, Ch. 524, Sec. 5) by Stats. 2014, Ch. 71, Sec. 168. (SB 1304) Effective January 1, 2015. Section conditionally operative as prescribed by its own provisions.)

1654. The director may purchase or lease such real estate and erect such buildings as the department or any of its divisions require, subject to the approval of the Department of General Services.

(Amended by Stats. 1965, Ch. 371.)

1655. (a) The director and deputy director of the department, the Deputy Director, Investigations Division, the Chief, Field Investigations Branch, and the investigators of the department, including rank-and-file, supervisory, and management personnel, shall have the powers of peace officers for the purpose of enforcing those provisions of law committed to the administration of the department or enforcing the law on premises occupied by the department.

(b) Any person designated in subdivision (a) may inspect any vehicle of a type required to be registered under this code, or any component part thereof, in any garage, repair shop, parking lot, used car lot, automobile dismantler's lot, steel mill, scrap metal processing facility, or other establishment engaged in the business of selling, repairing, or dismantling vehicles, or reducing vehicles or the integral parts thereof to their component materials for the purpose of investigating the title and registration of the vehicle, inspecting wrecked or dismantled vehicles, or locating stolen vehicles.

(Amended by Stats. 2004, Ch. 615, Sec. 18. Effective January 1, 2005.)

1656. The department shall publish a synopsis or summary of the laws regulating the operation of vehicles and the use of the highways and may deliver a copy of the synopsis or summary without charge with each original vehicle registration and each original driver's license. The department shall publish as many copies of the synopsis or summary in Spanish as the director determines are needed to meet the demand for those copies. The department shall furnish both English and Spanish copies to its field offices and to law enforcement agencies for general distribution and, when it does so, shall furnish the copies without charge.

(Amended by Stats. 2021, Ch. 254, Sec. 1. (AB 174) Effective September 23, 2021.)

1656.1. The Department of Justice shall, in conjunction with the department and the Commission on Peace Officer Standards and Training, develop and create a video demonstrating the proper conduct by a peace officer and an individual during a traffic stop. The department shall post this video on its internet website.

(Added by Stats. 2022, Ch. 332, Sec. 2. (AB 2537) Effective January 1, 2023.)

1656.2. (a) The department shall prepare and publish a printed summary describing the penalties for noncompliance with Sections 16000 and 16028, which shall be included with each motor vehicle registration, registration renewal, and transfer of registration and with each driver's license and license renewal. The printed summary may contain, but is not limited to, the following wording:

"IMPORTANT FACTS ABOUT ENFORCEMENT OF CALIFORNIA'S COMPULSORY FINANCIAL RESPONSIBILITY LAW

California law requires every driver to carry written evidence of valid automobile liability insurance, a $35,000 bond, a $35,000 cash deposit, or a certificate of self-insurance that has been issued by the Department of Motor Vehicles.

You must provide evidence of financial responsibility when you renew the registration of a motor vehicle, and after you are cited by a peace officer for a traffic violation or are involved in any traffic accident. The law requires that you provide the officer with the name and address of your insurer and the policy identification number. Your insurer will provide written evidence of this number. Failure to provide evidence of your financial responsibility can result in fines of up to $500 and loss of your driver's license. Falsification of evidence can result in fines of up to $750 or 30 days in jail, or both, in addition to a one-year suspension of driving privileges.

Under existing California law, if you are involved in an accident that results in damages of over $1,000 to the property of any person or in any injury or fatality, you must file a report of the accident with the Department of Motor Vehicles within 10 days of the accident. If you fail to file a report or fail to provide evidence of financial responsibility on the report, your driving privilege will be suspended for up to four years. Your suspension notice will notify you of the department's action and of your right to a hearing. Your suspension notice will also inform you that if you request a hearing, it must be conducted within 30 days of your written request, and that a decision is to be rendered within 15 days of the conclusion of the hearing."

(b) This section shall become operative on January 1, 2017.

(Repealed (in Sec. 19) and added by Stats. 2015, Ch. 451, Sec. 20. (SB 491) Effective January 1, 2016. Section operative January 1, 2017, by its own provisions.)

1656.3. (a) The department shall include within the California Driver's Handbook, as specified in Section 1656, information regarding each of the following:

(1) Rail transit safety.

(2) Abandonment or dumping of any animal on a highway.

(3) The importance of respecting the right-of-way of others, particularly pedestrians, bicycle riders, and motorcycle riders.

(4) A person's civil rights during a traffic stop. The information shall address the extent and limitations of a peace officer's authority during a traffic stop and the legal rights of drivers and passengers, including, but not limited to, the right to file complaints against a peace officer. The information to be included in the handbook shall be developed by the civil rights section of the Department of Justice in consultation with the Department of Motor Vehicles, the Department of the California Highway Patrol, the Commission on Peace Officer Standards and Training, and civil rights organizations, including community-based organizations.

(5) The requirement that a peace officer disclose the reason for a traffic or pedestrian stop before engaging in questioning related to a criminal investigation or traffic violation, unless the officer reasonably believes that withholding the reason for the stop is necessary to protect life or property from imminent threat, and the requirement for the officer to document the reason for the stop on any citation or police report resulting from the stop.

(b) In order to minimize costs, the information referred to in paragraphs (4) and (5) of subdivision (a) shall be initially included at the earliest opportunity when the handbook is otherwise revised or reprinted.

(c) This section shall become operative on January 1, 2024.

(Repealed (in Sec. 3) and added by Stats. 2022, Ch. 805, Sec. 4. (AB 2773) Effective January 1, 2023. Operative January 1, 2024, by its own provisions.)

1656.4. (a) The department, in consultation with the Department of Consumer Affairs, shall make available on its Internet web site, on or before July 1, 1997, information to assist consumers who plan to purchase a vehicle or who have purchased a vehicle. The information shall, at a minimum, contain the names, addresses, electronic addresses, and telephone numbers of all of the following:

(1) State and federal government agencies that deal with consumer affairs and vehicles.

(2) Vehicle arbitration services.

(3) Consumer organizations that provide information and direct assistance to consumers with vehicle concerns.

(b) Money deposited in the Consumer Fraud Protection Program Fund shall be available, upon appropriation by the Legislature, for the consumer protection activities of the department, including, but not limited to, expenditures by the department to comply with the requirements specified in subdivision (a).

(Added by Stats. 1996, Ch. 722, Sec. 1. Effective January 1, 1997.)

1656.5. (a) The Legislature finds that the department, by virtue of its interaction with millions of California drivers and vehicle owners each year, represents a valuable resource for the disbursement of important public safety and consumer information.

(b) The department may enter into a contract with a private vendor for the purpose of acquiring and utilizing message display systems. These systems may be used on the department's mailings or other property owned, leased, or controlled by the department. The information displayed shall be of appropriate benefit to the motoring public and the state's consumers, as determined by the department.

(c) A vendor under contract with the department may utilize a portion of the available time and space on the display systems that it provides for the purpose of advertising products or services. The advertising on a message display system shall not exceed 15 minutes in a 60-minute period. The extent of the access shall be established under the terms of the contract.

(d) The department shall determine whether a vendor's advertised product or service is consistent with and appropriate to the best interests of the motoring public. The department shall not enter into a contract with a vendor whose advertised product or service the department determines is not consistent with or appropriate to the best interests of the motoring public.

(Added by Stats. 2007, Ch. 407, Sec. 1. Effective January 1, 2008.)

1657. The director may assign qualified employees of the department to advise with the State Board of Education and with the governing boards of districts maintaining secondary schools in the preparation, establishment, and conduct of courses in automobile driver education and automobile driver training in secondary schools under the provisions of the Education Code.

(Amended by Stats. 1971, Ch. 438.)

1658. The department may pay membership fees, join, and participate in affairs of associations having for their purpose the interchange of information relating to the registration of vehicles and the issuance of operators' licenses, financial responsibility, and subjects relating to highway safety and to the powers and duties of the department.

(Enacted by Stats. 1959, Ch. 3.)

1659. The department may develop criteria, establish standards for, and coordinate a program of motor vehicle driver education and motor vehicle driver training for drivers whose licenses have been suspended or revoked.

The purpose of the program shall be to promote safe driving. To carry out this purpose the department may seek the advice or cooperation of the schools, courts, and other interested persons.

(Added by Stats. 1965, Ch. 447.)

1660. (a) Any institution or organization described in subdivision (o) of Section 286 shall keep the following records for not less than three years:

(1) The name and address of each vehicle donor and the year, make, vehicle identification number, and, if available, the license plate number of the donated vehicle.

(2) An itemized listing by vehicle identification number of the date each vehicle was donated, the date sold, and the amount for which it was sold.

(3) If the donated vehicle is being sold by an institution or organization on behalf of another institution or organization pursuant to paragraph (2) of subdivision (o) of Section 286, the following documentation shall be retained in the following manner:

(A) A signed, written agreement shall remain on the premises that identifies the percentage of the proceeds that may be retained by the selling institution or organization, a statement that each vehicle meets, or, unless sold at wholesale, by the time of sale will meet, the equipment requirements of Division 12 (commencing with Section 24000), and a statement that each vehicle is in compliance, or, unless sold at wholesale, at the time of sale will be in compliance, with emission control certification requirements pursuant to subdivision (b) of Section 44015 of the Health and Safety Code.

(B) A separate listing that identifies each vehicle by year, make, and vehicle identification number.

(C) All itemized listings pursuant to subparagraph (D) of paragraph (2) of subdivision (o) of Section 286.

(D) The selling institution or organization shall retain all documentation pertaining to the sale of vehicles on behalf of another institution or organization in the same manner as is required for the sale of vehicles donated to the selling institution or organization.

(b) The department may inspect the records of any nonprofit institution or organization that obtains donated vehicles in order to ascertain whether it meets the conditions specified in subdivision (o) of Section 286.

(Amended by Stats. 2001, Ch. 460, Sec. 2. Effective January 1, 2002.)

1661. (a) Except for vehicles registered pursuant to Article 5 (commencing with Section 9700) of Chapter 6 of Division 3, the department shall notify the registered owner of each vehicle of the date that the registration renewal fees for the vehicle are due, at least 60 days prior to that due date. The department shall indicate the fact that the required notice was mailed by a notation in the department's records.

(b) The department shall include in any final notice of delinquent registration provided to the registered owner of a vehicle whose registration has not been properly renewed as required under this code, information relating to the potential removal and impoundment of that vehicle under subdivision (o) of Section 22651.

(c) Commencing on May 1, 2011, subdivision (a) shall not apply to vehicles with registration expiring on or after July 1, 2011. This subdivision shall become inoperative on January 1, 2012.

(Amended by Stats. 2011, Ch. 21, Sec. 2. (SB 94) Effective May 4, 2011.)

1663. (a) The department shall, in the synopsis or summary of laws regulating the operation of vehicles and the use of the highways published under Section 1656, provide a warning which states that, in certain accidents, the lack of a shoulder harness may cause, or aggravate, serious and fatal injuries, especially to the head, spinal column, and abdominal organs.

(b) This section does not limit or impair the rights or remedies that are otherwise available to any person under existing law.

(Amended by Stats. 2021, Ch. 254, Sec. 2. (AB 174) Effective September 23, 2021.)

1664. The department shall publicize the Safe Streets Act of 1994 when mailing vehicle registrations, driver's licenses, and driver's license suspension and revocation notices, and in other educational materials made available by the department.

(Added by Stats. 1994, Ch. 1133, Sec. 2. Effective January 1, 1995.)

1665. Notwithstanding any other provision of law, the department by rule or regulation may provide for the issuance and renewal on a two-year basis of licenses or other indicia of authority issued pursuant to this code by the department or any agency in the department.

The department may, by rule or regulation, set the fee for such two-year license, certificate of registration, or other indicia, not to exceed twice the annual fee for issuance or renewal set by statute.

This section shall not apply to any driver's license or vehicle or vessel license or certificate of registration issued pursuant to this code.
(Added by Stats. 1975, Ch. 57.)

1666. The department shall do all of the following:

(a) Include at least one question in each test of an applicant's knowledge and understanding of the provisions of this code, as administered pursuant to Section 12804.9 or 12814, to verify that the applicant has read and understands the table of blood alcohol concentration published in the Driver's Handbook made available pursuant to Section 1656. In order to minimize costs, the question or questions shall be initially included at the earliest opportunity when the test is otherwise revised or reprinted.

(b) Include with each driver's license or certificate of renewal and each vehicle registration renewal mailed by the department, information that shows with reasonable certainty the amount of alcohol consumption necessary for a person to reach a 0.08 percent blood alcohol concentration by weight.

(c) Include at least one question in each test of an applicant's knowledge and understanding of the provisions of this code as administered pursuant to Section 12804.9 or 12814, to verify that the applicant has read and understands the rights of pedestrians. In order to minimize costs, the question or questions shall be initially included at the earliest opportunity when the test is otherwise revised or reprinted.
(Amended by Stats. 2021, Ch. 254, Sec. 3. (AB 174) Effective September 23, 2021.)

1666.1. Upon updating the California Driver's Handbook, the department shall include at least one question in any of the noncommercial driver's license examinations, as administered under Section 12804.9, of an applicant's knowledge and understanding of this code, to verify that the applicant has an understanding of the risks and punishments associated with eluding a pursuing officer's motor vehicle.
(Added by Stats. 2005, Ch. 485, Sec. 5. Effective January 1, 2006.)

1666.5. The department shall include, on a rotating basis, at least one question in at least 20 percent of the tests of an applicant's knowledge and understanding of the provisions of this code, as administered pursuant to Section 12803 or 12814, to verify that the applicant has read and understands that the abandonment or dumping of any animal is a criminal offense that can create a severe traffic safety hazard.
(Added by Stats. 2001, Ch. 300, Sec. 2. Effective January 1, 2002.)

1666.7. The department shall include, on a rotating basis, at least one question in at least 20 percent of the tests of an applicant's knowledge and understanding of the provisions of this code, as administered pursuant to Section 12803 or 12814, to verify that the applicant has read and understands that driving with an unsafe, unsecured load, such as driving with ladders, buckets, and loose items in the back of a pickup truck, is a violation of law, including, but not limited to, Sections 23114, 23115, and 24002, and may create a severe traffic safety hazard for other motorists.
(Added by Stats. 2018, Ch. 124, Sec. 1. (AB 1925) Effective January 1, 2019.)

1667. (a) As part of its motor vehicle registration and registration renewal process, other than upon the initial registration of a new motor vehicle, the department shall inform motor vehicle owners of the vehicle smog indexing program. That notice shall be in the form developed by the State Air Resources Board in consultation with the department pursuant to subdivision (c) of Section 44254 of the Health and Safety Code.

(b) This section shall become inoperative five years from the date determined pursuant to Section 32 of the act adding this section, and on the January 1 following that date is repealed.
(Added by Stats. 1994, Ch. 1192, Sec. 31.1. Effective January 1, 1995. Operative on date prescribed by Sec. 32 of Ch. 1192. Inoperative five years after operative date. Repealed on January 1 after inoperative date, by its own provisions.)

1668. (a) The department may provide fingerprint service to the general public. When that service is provided, the department shall charge a fee of not less than five dollars ($5) for each person fingerprinted.

(b) Whenever the department submits the fingerprints of an applicant for a license or certificate to the Department of Justice, and is required to pay a fee pursuant to subdivision (e) of Section 11105 of the Penal Code, the department, without the necessity of adopting regulations, shall charge the applicant a fee sufficient to reimburse the department for that fee.
(Amended by Stats. 1990, Ch. 1360, Sec. 1.5.)

1669. It is the intent of the Legislature that the department implement procedures to ensure, to the fullest extent permitted by the resources made available to it, that any person who is requesting services relating to registration of vessels or vehicles, or who is applying for an original or renewal of a driver's license or identification card, will not be required under normal circumstances to wait in any one line for service longer than one-half hour during the department's published or posted hours of operation. Every office of the department shall have posted, at or near the entrance thereto, its hours of operation.
(Added by Stats. 1983, Ch. 786, Sec. 1.)

1670. A licensee issued an occupational license by the department and conducting more than one type of business from an established place of business shall provide a clear physical division between the types of business involving vehicles or their component parts. The established place of business shall be open to inspection of the premises, pertinent records, and vehicles by any peace officer during business hours.
(Added by Stats. 1985, Ch. 106, Sec. 164.)

1671. (a) The established place of business of a dealer, remanufacturer, remanufacturer branch, manufacturer, manufacturer branch, distributor, distributor branch, automobile driving school, or traffic violator school shall have an office and a dealer, manufacturer, or remanufacturer shall also have a display or manufacturing area situated on the same property where the business peculiar to the type of license issued by the department is or may be transacted. When a room or rooms in a hotel, roominghouse, apartment house building, or a part of any single- or multiple-unit dwelling house is used as an office or offices of an established place of business, the room or rooms shall be devoted exclusively to and occupied for the office or offices of the dealer, manufacturer, manufacturer branch, remanufacturer, remanufacturer branch, distributor, distributor branch, automobile driving school, or traffic violator school, shall be located on the ground floor, and shall be so constructed as to provide a direct entrance into the room or rooms from the exterior of the building. A dealer who does not offer new or used vehicles for sale at retail, a dealer who has been issued an autobroker's endorsement to his or her dealer's license and who does not also sell motor vehicles at retail, or a dealer who is a wholesaler involved for profit only in the sale of vehicles between licensed dealers, shall have an office, but a display area is not required.

(b) The established place of business of an automobile dismantler shall have an office and a dismantling area located in a zone properly zoned for that purpose by the city or county.
(Amended by Stats. 2006, Ch. 538, Sec. 653. Effective January 1, 2007.)

1672. (a) The department shall make available, in the public area of each office of the department where applications for driver's licenses or identification cards are received, space for a sign or notice briefly describing the Uniform Anatomical Gift Act (Chapter 3.5 (commencing with Section 7150) of Part 1 of Division 7 of the Health and Safety Code) and information about the California Organ and Tissue Donor Registry and about how private donations may be made.

(b) The department shall make available to the public in its offices a pamphlet or brochure providing more detailed information on the California Organ and Tissue Donor Registry and information about how private donations may be made.

(c) The signs, notices, pamphlets, and brochures specified in subdivisions (a) and (b) shall be provided without cost to the department by responsible private parties associated with the anatomical gift program.
(Amended by Stats. 2003, Ch. 405, Sec. 5. Effective January 1, 2004.)

1672.3. (a) The director shall determine the date when the department's inventory of driver's license and identification card forms, as that inventory exists in accordance with the law in effect on December 31, 1998, has been depleted.

(b) The director shall make written notification of the date determined under subdivision (a) to the following persons:

(1) The Secretary of State.

(2) The Chair of the Senate Committee on Transportation.

(3) The Chair of the Assembly Committee on Transportation.

(c) The written notice required under subdivision (b) shall state that it is being submitted in accordance with this section.

(Added by Stats. 1998, Ch. 887, Sec. 4. Effective January 1, 1999.)

1672.5. For purposes of providing a means of identifying persons who have elected to make an anatomical gift under the Uniform Anatomical Gift Act (Chapter 3.5 (commencing with Section 7150) of Part 1 of Division 7 of the Health and Safety Code), the department shall design the driver's licenses and identification cards in order that a sticker may be affixed to the licenses and cards. The sticker shall indicate a person's willingness to make an anatomical gift, and shall be affixed with a substance that is resistant to any unintentional removal.

(Added by Stats. 1998, Ch. 887, Sec. 5. Effective January 1, 1999.)

1673. For the purposes of refunding the smog impact fee, as prescribed in Sections 1673.2 and 1673.4, "registered owner or lessee" means the person or persons to whom the registration or title was issued when the transaction that included the imposition of the smog impact fee under Chapter 3.3 (commencing with Section 6261) of Part 1 of Division 2 of the Revenue and Taxation Code was completed.

(Added by Stats. 2000, Ch. 31, Sec. 3. Effective June 8, 2000.)

1673.2. (a) The department, in coordination with the Department of Finance, shall do all of the following:

(1) Search its records to identify the registered owner or lessee. Except as required under Section 1673.4, the department shall mail to the registered owner or lessee a refund notification form notifying the registered owner or lessee that he or she is eligible for a refund of the smog impact fee. This form shall identify the vehicle make and year, and include a refund claim that shall be signed, under penalty of perjury, and returned to the department.

(2) Shall acknowledge by mail claims for refund from registered owners or lessees received prior to the effective date of this section.

(3) Except as provided in Section 1673.4, shall verify whether the information provided in any claim is true and correct and shall refund the three hundred dollar ($300) smog impact fee, plus the amount of any penalty collected for late payment of the smog impact fee, and any interest earned on those charges, to the person shown to be the registered owner or lessee.

(b) Notwithstanding any other provision of law, interest shall be paid on all claims at a single annual rate, calculated by the Department of Finance, that averages the annualized interest rates earned by the Pooled Money Investment Account for the period beginning October 1990 and ending on the effective date of this section. Interest on each refund shall be calculated from the date the smog impact fee and vehicle registration transaction was completed to the date the refund is issued. Accrual of interest shall terminate one year after the effective date of this section.

(c) (1) Notwithstanding any other provision of law, those who paid the smog impact fee between October 15, 1990, and October 19, 1999, may file a claim for refund.

(2) Claims for refund by a registered owner or lessee shall be filed with the Department of Motor Vehicles within three years of the effective date of this section.

(Amended by Stats. 2010, Ch. 719, Sec. 64. (SB 856) Effective October 19, 2010.)

1673.4. (a) Any claim submitted by a person other than a registered owner or lessee shall be filed within 30 days from the effective date of this section.

(b) If a claimant other than the registered owner or lessee files a claim, or has filed a claim prior to the effective date of this section, for refund in a manner and form verified by the department, the department shall mail a notification to the registered owner or lessee informing that person that he or she is eligible for a refund of the smog impact fee and that a competing claim for that fee has been filed. The registered owner or lessee shall have three years from the effective date of this section to inform the department that the registered owner or lessee opposes payment of the smog impact fee refund to the competing claimant. In that case, the refund shall be made to the registered owner or lessee and notice of that action shall be sent to the competing claimant. If the registered owner or lessee does not notify the department within the three-year period that he or she opposes the payment, the department shall pay the refund to the competing claimant.

(c) If any refund paid by the department under this section is disputed, any party that filed a claim may commence an action in small claims court. The small claims court action may not be filed if three years or more have elapsed from the date the department mailed the refund to either party.

(d) The State of California, its departments and agencies, and their officers or employees shall not be a party to a lawsuit between competing claimants relating to smog impact fee refunds.

(Added by Stats. 2000, Ch. 31, Sec. 5. Effective June 8, 2000.)

1673.5. The department shall attempt to recover any refund of the smog impact fee, or part thereof, that is erroneously made. Collection shall be initiated if the recipient fails to respond to the Department of Motor Vehicles' notice to pay the erroneous refund within 90 days in accordance with existing collection procedures utilized by the department.

(Added by Stats. 2000, Ch. 31, Sec. 6. Effective June 8, 2000.)

1673.6. It is unlawful to use a false or fictitious name, to knowingly make any false statement, or conceal any material fact on a refund claim for the smog impact fee that is filed with the department. A violation of this provision is punishable under Section 72 of the Penal Code. Any signed claim form submitted to the department for a refund of the smog impact fee shall be signed under penalty of perjury.

(Added by Stats. 2000, Ch. 31, Sec. 7. Effective June 8, 2000.)

1673.7. (a) The department shall include the following notice with each check issued as a refund of the smog impact fee:

"The enclosed check is a refund of the $300 Smog Impact Fee you paid to the Department of Motor Vehicles when you initially registered an out-of-state vehicle in California. In the case of Jordan v. Department of Motor Vehicles (1999) 75 Cal.App.4th 449, the court ruled the smog impact fee unconstitutional. The enclosed check includes an interest payment which has been calculated from the date the fee was paid to the date the refund is issued.

"If you have any questions about the enclosed refund, please contact your local office of the Department of Motor Vehicles."

(b) No notice other than the one required under subdivision (a) may be included with a smog impact fee refund check.

(Added by Stats. 2000, Ch. 31, Sec. 8. Effective June 8, 2000.)

1674. The department shall develop a program to foster a positive atmosphere that is conducive to encouraging drivers to succeed in passing any visual tests or written or behind-the-wheel driving tests administered by the department.

(Added by Stats. 2000, Ch. 985, Sec. 3. Effective January 1, 2001.)

1674.4. In order to address any conscious or unconscious bias against a driver by persons administering the department's visual tests or written or behind-the-wheel driving tests, the department shall implement a component in its training and development program for test administrators that encourages sensitivity to the issues of youth and aging.

(Added by Stats. 2000, Ch. 985, Sec. 5. Effective January 1, 2001.)

1674.6. (a) The Legislature finds and declares that persons should be provided with transportation alternatives when their privilege to drive is lost because of failure to pass visual tests or written or behind-the-wheel driving tests. While a partial obligation for addressing this issue rests with families, communities, social service agencies, and local governments, the Legislature recognizes an obligation to promote, facilitate, and share in the funding of alternative modes of transportation for persons who have lost their driving privilege.

(b) Accordingly, it is the intent of the Legislature, not later than January 1, 2003, to provide an affordable and equitable mode of transportation to fulfill the reasonable transportation needs of persons who have lost their driver's licenses due to a failure to pass a visual test or a written or behind-the-wheel driving test.

(c) In furtherance of the intent set forth in subdivision (b), the Business, Transportation and Housing Agency shall establish a task force to analyze potential sources of funding and modes of transportation for persons who have lost their driver's licenses due to a failure to pass a visual test or a written or behind-the-wheel driving test. The Business, Transportation and Housing Agency shall prepare and submit a report on the findings of the task force to the Legislature not later than July 1, 2001.

(Added by Stats. 2000, Ch. 985, Sec. 6. Effective January 1, 2001.)

1675. (a) The director shall establish standards and develop criteria for the approval of initial and renewal driver improvement courses specifically designed for the safe driving needs of drivers who are 55 years of age or older, which shall be known as mature driver improvement courses.

(b) The curricula for the courses provided for in subdivision (a) shall include, but is not limited to, all of the following components:

(1) How impairment of visual and audio perception affects driving performance and how to compensate for that impairment.

(2) The effects of fatigue, medications, and alcohol on driving performance, when experienced alone or in combination, and precautionary measures to prevent or offset ill effects.

(3) Updates on rules of the road and equipment, including, but not limited to, safety belts and safe and efficient driving techniques under present day road and traffic conditions.

(4) How to plan travel time and select routes for safety and efficiency.

(5) How to make crucial decisions in dangerous, hazardous, and unforeseen situations.

(c) The initial mature driver improvement course shall include not less than 400 minutes of instruction, and shall not exceed 25 students per single day of instruction or 30 students per two days of instruction.

(d) Upon satisfactory completion of an initial mature driver improvement course, participants shall receive and retain a certificate provided by the department, awarded and distributed by the course provider, which shall be suitable evidence of satisfactory course completion, and eligibility for three years, from the date of completion, for the mature driver vehicle liability insurance premium reduction pursuant to Section 11628.3 of the Insurance Code.

(e) (1) The certificate may be renewed by successfully completing a subsequent renewal mature driver improvement course within one year of the expiration of the certificate, or if more than one year has elapsed since the expiration, a mature driver improvement course in accordance with the standards established in subdivision (c).

(2) The renewal mature driver improvement course shall include not less than 240 minutes of instruction.

(f) For the purposes of this section, and Sections 1676 and 1677, "course provider" means any person offering a mature driver improvement course approved by the department pursuant to subdivision (a).

(Amended by Stats. 2006, Ch. 129, Sec. 1. Effective January 1, 2007.)

1676. (a) A course provider conducting a mature driver improvement course pursuant to Section 1675 may charge a tuition not to exceed thirty dollars ($30).

(b) A course provider shall issue a receipt for the tuition it collects from an individual who registers for or attends a mature driver improvement course.

(c) The department shall charge a fee not to exceed three dollars ($3) for each completion certificate issued to a mature driver improvement course provider, pursuant to subdivision (d) of Section 1675. The amount of the fee shall be determined by the department and shall be sufficient to defray the actual costs incurred by the department for administering the mature driver improvement program, for evaluating the program, and for any other activities deemed necessary by the department to assure high quality education for participants of the program. A course provider shall not charge a fee in excess of the fee charged by the department pursuant to this subdivision for furnishing a certificate of completion or duplicate thereof. The department shall transmit all fees it receives for deposit in the Motor Vehicle Account in the State Transportation Fund pursuant to Section 42270.

(Amended by Stats. 2006, Ch. 129, Sec. 2. Effective January 1, 2007.)

1677. (a) The department may collect a fee, to be determined by the department, from each course provider who shall be responsible for the development and operation of a mature driver improvement course, for the approval of the course, but not to exceed the actual cost of approval of the course. The department shall transmit all fees it receives for deposit in the Motor Vehicle Account in the State Transportation Fund pursuant to Section 42270.

(b) Each course provider, who has received course approval from the department, is responsible for the delivery, instruction, and content of his or her mature driver improvement course.

(c) The department shall investigate claims of impropriety on the part of a course provider. The department may withdraw the approval of courses in violation of Section 1675 or 1676, as determined by the department, for just cause, including, but not limited to any of the following:

(1) Furnishing course completion certificates to course enrollees prior to, or in the absence of, completion of the curriculum specified in subdivisions (b) and (c) of Section 1675.

(2) Charging fees in excess of the amounts specified in subdivisions (a) and (c) of Section 1676.

(d) Mature driver improvement courses approved by the department shall continue to be approved until either of the following occurs:

(1) The course provider does not meet the conditions of approval.

(2) The department finds just cause to terminate the approval pursuant to subdivision (c).

(Amended by Stats. 2001, Ch. 739, Sec. 4. Effective January 1, 2002.)

1678. (a) Between January 1, 2004, and December 31, 2004, inclusive, the fee amounts set forth in Section 488.385 of the Code of Civil Procedure, Section 10902 of the Revenue and Taxation Code, and Sections 4604, 5014, 5036, 6700.25, 9102.5, 9250.8, 9250.13, 9252, 9254, 9258, 9261, 9265, 9702, 11515, 11515.2, 14900, 14900.1, 14901, 14902, 15255.1, 15255.2, 38121, 38225.4, 38225.5, 38232, 38255, 38260, and 38265, and subdivision (b) of Section 9250, of this code, shall be the base fee amounts charged by the department.

(b) On January 1, 2005, and every January 1 thereafter, the department shall adjust the fees imposed under the sections listed in subdivision (a) by increasing each fee in an amount equal to the increase in the California Consumer Price Index for the prior year, as calculated by the Department of Finance, with amounts equal to or greater than fifty cents ($0.50) rounded to the next highest whole dollar.

(c) Any increases to the fees imposed under the sections listed in subdivision (a) that are enacted by legislation subsequent to January 1, 2005, shall be deemed to be changes to the base fee for purposes of the calculation performed pursuant to subdivision (b).

(Amended by Stats. 2016, Ch. 339, Sec. 4. (SB 838) Effective September 13, 2016.)

1679. On and after July 1, 2006, in any document mailed by the department that offers a person the opportunity to register to vote pursuant to the National Voter Registration Act of 1993 (42 U.S.C. Sec. 1973gg), the department shall include a notice informing prospective voters that if they have not received voter registration information within 30 days of requesting it, they should contact their local elections office or the office of the Secretary of State.

(Added by Stats. 2005, Ch. 660, Sec. 2. Effective January 1, 2006.)

1680. (a) It shall be unlawful for any person to sell, or offer for sale, an appointment with the department.

(b) For purposes of this section, "appointment" means an arrangement to receive a government service at a specified time.

(Added by Stats. 2019, Ch. 608, Sec. 1. (AB 317) Effective January 1, 2020.)

1685. (a) In order to continue improving the quality of products and services it provides to its customers, the department, in conformance with Article 4 (commencing with Section 19130) of Chapter 5 of Part 2 of Division 5 of Title 2 of the Government Code, may establish contracts for electronic programs that allow qualified private industry partners to join the department in providing services that include processing and payment programs for vehicle registration and titling transactions, and services related to reporting vehicle sales and producing temporary license plates pursuant to Sections 4456 and 4456.2.

(b) (1) The department may enter into contractual agreements with qualified private industry partners. There are the following three types of private industry partnerships authorized under this section:

(A) First-line business partner is an industry partner that receives data directly from the department and uses it to complete registration and titling activities for that partner's own business purposes.

(B) First-line service provider is an industry partner that receives information from the department and then transmits it to another authorized industry partner.

(C) Second-line business partner is a partner that receives information from a first-line service provider.

(2) The private industry partner contractual agreements shall include the following minimum requirements:

(A) Filing of an application and payment of an application fee, as established by the department.

(B) Submission of information, including, but not limited to, fingerprints and personal history statements, focusing on and concerning the applicant's character, honesty, integrity, and reputation as the department may consider necessary.

(C) Posting a bond in an amount consistent with Section 1815.

(3) The department shall, through regulations, establish any additional requirements for the purpose of safeguarding privacy and protecting the information authorized for release under this section.

(c) (1) The director may establish, through the adoption of regulations, the maximum amount that a qualified private industry partner may charge its customers in providing the services authorized under subdivision (a).

(2) On or before September 1, 2022, and each January 1 thereafter, the department shall adjust the amount determined pursuant to paragraph (1) in accordance with the most recent available data on growth in the California Consumer Price Index for All Urban Consumers, except the initial adjustment made on or before September 1, 2022, shall be based on growth in the California Consumer Price Index for All Urban Consumers in the period since the end of the 2021 calendar year. The amount of the fee shall be rounded to the nearest whole dollar, with amounts equal to, or greater than, fifty cents ($0.50) rounded to the next highest whole dollar.

(d) The department shall charge a three-dollar ($3) transaction fee for the information and services provided pursuant to subdivision (a). The private industry partner may pass on the transaction fee to the customer, but the total charge to a customer may not exceed the amount established by the director under subdivision (c). The department may establish, through the adoption of regulations, exemptions from the transaction fee for transactions other than an original registration or transfer of ownership.

(e) All fees collected by the department pursuant to subdivision (d) shall be deposited in the Motor Vehicle Account. On January 1 of each year, the department shall adjust the fee in accordance with the California Consumer Price Index. The amount of the fee shall be rounded to the nearest whole dollar, with amounts equal to, or greater than, fifty cents ($0.50) rounded to the next highest whole dollar.

(f) The department shall adopt regulations and procedures that ensure adequate oversight and monitoring of qualified private industry partners to protect vehicle owners from the improper use of vehicle records. These regulations and procedures shall include provisions for qualified private industry partners to periodically submit records to the department, and the department shall review those records as necessary. The regulations shall also include provisions for the dedication of department resources to program monitoring and oversight; the protection of confidential records in the department's files and databases; and the duration and nature of the contracts with qualified private industry partners.

(g) The department shall, annually, by October 1, provide a report to the Legislature that shall include all of the following information gathered during the fiscal year immediately preceding the report date:

(1) Listing of all qualified private industry partners, including names and business addresses.

(2) Volume of transactions, by type, completed by business partners.

(3) Total amount of funds, by transaction type, collected by business partners.

(4) Total amount of funds received by the department.

(5) Description of any fraudulent activities identified by the department.

(6) Evaluation of the benefits of the program.

(7) Recommendations for any administrative or statutory changes that may be needed to improve the program.

(h) Nothing in this section impairs or limits the authority provided in Section 4610 or Section 12155 of the Insurance Code.

(i) (1) Commencing July 1, 2025, in addition to, and in accordance with, the transaction fee described in subdivision (d), the department shall charge private industry partners a one-dollar ($1) transaction fee for the implementation of the private industry partners' proportionate share of departmentwide system improvements. All fees collected by the department pursuant to this subdivision shall be deposited in the Motor Vehicle Account.

(2) (A) The fee required by this subdivision shall be discontinued when the director determines that sufficient funds have been received to pay for the system improvements as described in paragraph (1), or on December 31, 2028, whichever occurs first. If sufficient funds are received first, the director shall execute a declaration making that determination, which shall be posted on the department's internet website and retained by the director.

(B) This subdivision shall become inoperative when the declaration described in subparagraph (A) has been executed and posted, or on December 31, 2028, whichever occurs first.

(Amended by Stats. 2025, Ch. 16, Sec. 2. (SB 128) Effective June 27, 2025.)

1685.1. (a) In order to provide electronic vehicle registration services, the department may enter into an interstate carrier partnership, established under this section, with an interstate carrier partner, if the partner meets all of the following requirements:

(1) Agrees to provide electronic vehicle registration services capable of accepting, completing, and transmitting registration transaction data to the department using a departmental registration system or system approved by the department.

(2) Maintains, protects, and issues apportioned vehicle registration documents, and indicia as applicable on behalf of the department to its customers.

(3) Demonstrates International Registration Plan knowledge proficiency, as determined by the department and established pursuant to subdivision (d).

(4) Meets qualification standards, as established by the department pursuant to subdivision (d).

(b) (1) The department may enter into contractual agreements with interstate carrier partners that utilize the departmental apportioned registration system or a system approved by the department. The following three types of partnerships are authorized under this section:

(A) A registration service, as defined in Section 505.2.

(B) A vehicle leasing company or vehicle rental company.

(C) A motor carrier association.

(2) For purposes of this section, the following definitions shall apply:

(A) "Vehicle leasing company" or "vehicle rental company" means a transportation provider that rents commercial vehicles to the public.

(B) "Motor carrier association" means an association that represents interstate motor carriers for the purpose of providing apportioned registration services for its members.

(c) An interstate carrier partner applicant shall submit an application to the department on the form adopted by the department pursuant to subdivision (d). The applicant shall also include with the application any other information the department may require.

(d) The department may adopt regulations to carry out the purposes of this section, including, but not limited to:

(1) Program administration structure.

(2) Fees.

(3) Financial responsibility.

(4) Compliance requirements.

(5) Adequate oversight and monitoring.

(6) Safeguards for privacy and protecting information authorized for release under this section.

(7) Minimum transaction requirements.

(8) Performance standards to ensure accuracy and efficiency.

(e) The director may establish, through the adoption of regulations pursuant to subdivision (d), the maximum amount that an interstate carrier partner may charge its customers in providing the services authorized under subdivision (a).

(Added by Stats. 2016, Ch. 456, Sec. 1. (AB 2107) Effective January 1, 2017.)

Article 3. Records of Department

(Article 3 enacted by Stats. 1959, Ch. 3.)

1800. (a) The department shall file each application received for the registration of a vehicle and shall keep a record of each as follows:

(1) Under a distinctive registration number assigned to the vehicle.

(2) Alphabetically, under the name of the owner.

(3) Under the motor or a permanent identifying number of the vehicle as may be determined by the department.

(4) In the discretion of the department, in any other manner it may deem desirable.

(b) The department shall file every application for a license to operate a motor vehicle received by it and maintain all of the following:

(1) A suitable index containing, in alphabetical order, all applications denied. On the applications shall be noted the reasons for the denial.

(2) A suitable index containing, in alphabetical order, all applications granted.

(3) A suitable index containing, in alphabetical order, the name of every licensee whose license has been suspended or revoked by the department or by a court and after each name notes the reasons for the action and the period of revocation or suspension.

(Amended by Stats. 2003, Ch. 594, Sec. 14. Effective January 1, 2004.)

1801. (a) Whenever any notice, report, statement, court abstract, or record is required to be submitted to the department by this code, the document may be submitted to the department by electronic transmission or other means approved by the department.

(b) All records maintained by the department may be stored in any feasible manner, including, but not limited to, any electronic media or any other form of data compilation.

(c) Notwithstanding any other provision of law, the records shall be deemed original documents and shall be admissible in evidence in all administrative, quasi-judicial, and judicial proceedings.

(Amended by Stats. 1996, Ch. 10, Sec. 9. Effective February 9, 1996.)

1801.1. (a) Notwithstanding any other law, the department may allow a person to submit a document required to be submitted to the department by using electronic media deemed feasible by the department instead of requiring the actual submittal of the original document.

(b) If a signature on a document is required by law in order to complete a transaction, and the document is submitted electronically, that signature requirement may be met by an electronically submitted signature.

(c) The department may establish minimum transaction volume levels, audit and security standards, and technological requirements, or terms and conditions, including methods of authentication for electronically submitted signatures, it deems necessary for the approval of this process.

(d) An electronically submitted document, once accepted by the department, is deemed the same as an original document, and is admissible in all administrative, quasi-judicial, and judicial proceedings.

(Amended by Stats. 2018, Ch. 400, Sec. 2. (AB 3163) Effective September 14, 2018.)

1801.2. (a) For a provision of this code or of Title 13 of the California Code of Regulations that requires the department to mail, notify, deliver via certified or first class mail, provide information in written form, or otherwise references the use of paper, a writing, or the mail to convey information to a person, including to notify a person of any departmental actions related to a permit, license, identification card, endorsement, certificate, or vehicle registration, that requirement may be satisfied by electronic notification, including, but not limited to, email, if the all of the following are established by the department:

(1) The department identified the person prior to accepting their consent to receive the type of document or information that is electronically delivered.

(2) The person consented to the electronic receipt of the type of document or information delivered.

(3) The department permits a person to withdraw their consent to electronically receive the type of document or information.

(4) The department records do not indicate the person withdrew their consent to electronically receive this type of document or information as of the date the document or information was electronically sent.

(b) For a provision of this code that refers to an address for any kind of notice or mailing, and mailing is effected pursuant to this section, an email or electronic delivery address provided to the department by the recipient may be used.

(c) A person who provides an electronic delivery address to the department shall notify the department of any change to that address.

(d) The consent to accept electronic notification may be made electronically.

(e) The department may adopt regulations to implement this section.

(Added by Stats. 2022, Ch. 838, Sec. 4. (SB 1193) Effective January 1, 2023.)

1802. Every judge of a court not of record shall keep a full record of every case in which a person is charged with any violation of this code.

(Enacted by Stats. 1959, Ch. 3.)

1803. (a) (1) The clerk of a court in which a person was convicted of a violation of this code, was convicted of a violation of subdivision (a), (b), (c), (d), (e), or (f) of Section 655 of the Harbors and Navigation Code pertaining to a mechanically propelled vessel but not to manipulating any water skis, an aquaplane, or similar device, was convicted of a violation of Section 655.2, 655.6, 658, or 658.5 of the Harbors and Navigation Code, a violation of subdivision (a) of Section 192.5 of the Penal Code, or a violation of subdivision (b) of Section 5387 of the Public Utilities Code, was convicted of an offense involving use or possession of controlled substances under Division 10 (commencing with Section 11000) of the Health and Safety Code, was convicted of a felony offense when a commercial motor vehicle, as defined in subdivision (b) of Section 15210, was involved in or incidental to the commission of the offense, or was convicted of a violation of any other statute relating to the safe operation of vehicles, shall prepare within five days after conviction and immediately forward to the department at its office at Sacramento an abstract of the record of the court covering the case in which the person was so convicted. If sentencing is not pronounced in conjunction with the conviction, the abstract shall be forwarded to the department within five days after sentencing and the abstract shall be certified by the person so required to prepare it to be true and correct.

(2) For the purposes of this section, a forfeiture of bail shall be equivalent to a conviction.

(b) The following violations are not required to be reported under subdivision (a):

(1) Division 3.5 (commencing with Section 9840).

(2) Section 21113, with respect to parking violations.

(3) Chapter 9 (commencing with Section 22500) of Division 11, except Section 22526.

(4) Division 12 (commencing with Section 24000), except Sections 24002, 24004, 24250, 24409, 24604, 24800, 25103, 26707, 27151, 27315, 27360, 27800, and 27801 and Chapter 3 (commencing with Section 26301).

(5) Division 15 (commencing with Section 35000), except Chapter 5 (commencing with Section 35550).

(6) Violations for which a person was cited as a pedestrian or while operating a bicycle or a motorized scooter.

(7) Division 16.5 (commencing with Section 38000), except Sections 38301, 38301.3, 38301.5, 38304.1, and 38504.1.

(8) Subdivision (b) of Section 23221, subdivision (b) of Section 23223, subdivision (b) of Section 23225, and subdivision (b) of Section 23226.

(c) If the court determines that a prior judgment of conviction of a violation of Section 23152 or 23153 is valid or is invalid on constitutional grounds pursuant to Section 41403, the clerk of the court in which the determination is made shall prepare an abstract of that determination and forward it to the department in the same manner as an abstract of record pursuant to subdivision (a).

(d) Within five days of an order terminating or revoking probation under Section 23602, the clerk of the court in which the order terminating or revoking probation was entered shall prepare and immediately forward to the department at its office in Sacramento an abstract of the record of the court order terminating or revoking probation and any other order of the court to the department required by law.

(e) This section shall remain in effect only until January 1, 2027, and as of that date is repealed.

(Amended by Stats. 2024, Ch. 226, Sec. 8. (AB 3278) Effective January 1, 2025. Repealed as of January 1, 2027, by its own provisions. See later operative version added by Sec. 9 of Stats. 2024, Ch. 226.)

1803. (a) (1) (A) The clerk of a court in which a person was convicted of a violation listed in subparagraph (B) shall prepare an abstract of the record of the court covering the case within five days after conviction and immediately forward that abstract to the department at its office at Sacramento.

(B) Pursuant to subparagraph (A), the clerk of the court shall prepare an abstract of the record of the court covering the case for a violation of any of the following:

(i) This code.

(ii) Subdivisions (a) to (f), inclusive, of Section 655 of the Harbors and Navigation Code pertaining to a mechanically propelled vessel but not to manipulating a water ski, an aquaplane, or similar device.

(iii) Section 655.2, 655.6, 658, or 658.5 of the Harbors and Navigation Code.

(iv) Subdivision (a) of Section 192.5 of the Penal Code.

(v) Subdivision (b) of Section 5387 of the Public Utilities Code.

(vi) An offense involving use or possession of controlled substances under Division 10 (commencing with Section 11000) of the Health and Safety Code.

(vii) A felony offense when a commercial motor vehicle, as defined in subdivision (b) of Section 15210, was involved in, or incidental to, the commission of the offense.

(viii) Any other statute relating to the safe operation of vehicles.

(C) If sentencing is not pronounced in conjunction with the conviction, the abstract shall be forwarded to the department within five days after sentencing, and the abstract shall be certified by the person so required to prepare it to be true and correct.

(2) For the purposes of this section, a forfeiture of bail shall be equivalent to a conviction.

(b) The following violations are not required to be reported under subdivision (a):

(1) Division 3.5 (commencing with Section 9840).

(2) Section 21113, with respect to parking violations.

(3) Chapter 9 (commencing with Section 22500) of Division 11, except Section 22526.

(4) Division 12 (commencing with Section 24000), except Sections 24002, 24004, 24250, 24409, 24604, 24800, 25103, 26707, 27151, 27315, 27360, 27800, and 27801 and Chapter 3 (commencing with Section 26301).

(5) Division 15 (commencing with Section 35000), except Chapter 5 (commencing with Section 35550).

(6) A violation for which a person was cited as a pedestrian or while operating a bicycle or a motorized scooter.

(7) Division 16.5 (commencing with Section 38000), except Sections 38301, 38301.3, 38301.5, 38304.1, and 38504.1.

(8) Subdivision (b) of Section 23221, subdivision (b) of Section 23223, subdivision (b) of Section 23225, and subdivision (b) of Section 23226.

(9) Section 40508.

(c) If the court determines that a prior judgment of conviction of a violation of Section 23152 or 23153 is valid or is invalid on constitutional grounds pursuant to Section 41403, the clerk of the court in which the determination is made shall prepare an abstract of that determination and forward it to the department in the same manner as an abstract of record pursuant to subdivision (a).

(d) Within five days of an order terminating or revoking probation under Section 23602, the clerk of the court in which the order terminating or revoking probation was entered shall prepare and immediately forward to the department at its office in Sacramento an abstract of the record of the court order terminating or revoking probation and any other order of the court to the department required by law.

(e) This section shall become operative on January 1, 2027.

(Repealed (in Sec. 8) and added by Stats. 2024, Ch. 226, Sec. 9. (AB 3278) Effective January 1, 2025. Operative January 1, 2027, by its own provisions.)

1803.3. (a) The clerk of any court that reverses a conviction for an offense described in subdivision (a) of Section 1803, which is not exempted under subdivision (b) of that section, shall prepare and forward to the department at its office in Sacramento an abstract of the record of the court covering the case in which the conviction was reversed. In addition, if a court dismisses a charge of a violation of Section 40508 for which a notice was given to the department pursuant to former Section 40509 or former Section 40509.5, the court shall notify the department of the dismissal.

(b) The abstract shall be forwarded within 30 days of the date the judgment of reversal becomes final. The notice of dismissal shall be given to the department not later than 30 days after the dismissal. Within 30 days of receiving the abstract or notice, the department shall remove any record of that conviction, or notice received pursuant to former Section 40509 or former Section 40509.5, from the driver's record.

(c) As used in this section, "reverse" includes any action by which a conviction is nullified or set aside.

(Amended by Stats. 2022, Ch. 800, Sec. 3. (AB 2746) Effective January 1, 2023.)

1803.4. Any record regarding the providing of information pursuant to Section 13106, or record of persons personally given notice by the department or a court, by a peace officer pursuant to Section 13382 or 13388, or otherwise pursuant to this code regarding the suspension or revocation of a person's privilege to operate a motor vehicle shall, upon request, be provided as follows:

(a) Immediately to any peace officer, as defined in Chapter 4.5 (commencing with Section 830) of Title 3 of Part 2 of the Penal Code, acting within the scope of his or her duties.

(b) Clearly stated on the record provided to any court of this state.

(Amended by Stats. 1999, Ch. 22, Sec. 6. Effective May 26, 1999.)

1803.5. (a) In accordance with Section 41501 or 42005, the clerk of a court or hearing officer, when a person who receives a notice to appear at a court or board proceeding for a violation of any statute relating to the safe operation of vehicles is granted a continuance of the proceeding in consideration for completion of a program at a school for traffic violators, that results in a designation of the conviction as confidential in consideration for that completion, shall prepare an abstract of the record of the court or board proceeding that indicates that the person was convicted of the violation and ordered to complete a traffic violator program, certify the abstract to be true and correct, and cause the abstract to be forwarded to the department at its office at Sacramento within five days after receiving proof that the program was completed or the due date to which the proceeding was continued, whichever comes first.

(b) This section shall become operative on July 1, 2011.

(Repealed (in Sec. 1.5) and added by Stats. 2010, Ch. 599, Sec. 1.7. (AB 2499) Effective January 1, 2011. Section operative July 1, 2011, by its own provisions.)

1804. (a) The abstract shall be made upon a form furnished or approved by the department and shall contain all necessary information to identify the defendant, including, but not limited to, the person's driver's license number, name, and date of birth, the date and nature of the offense, the vessel number, if any, of the vessel involved in the offense, the license plate number of the vehicle involved in the offense, the date of hearing, and the judgment, except that in the case of infractions where the court has not directed the department to suspend or restrict the defendant's driver's license, only the conviction and not the judgment need be set forth in the abstract. The abstract shall also indicate whether the vehicle involved in the offense is a commercial motor vehicle, as defined in subdivision (b) of Section 15210, whether the vehicle was of a type requiring the driver to have a certificate issued pursuant to Section 2512, 12517, 12519, 12523, or 12523.5 or any endorsement issued pursuant to paragraph (2) or (5) of subdivision (a) of Section 15278, and whether the vehicle was transporting hazardous material at the time of the offense, or whether the vessel involved in the offense was a recreational vessel, as defined in Section 651 of the Harbors and Navigation Code.

(b) As to any abstract for which the original arrest and final conviction was for a violation of subdivision (b), (c), (d), (e), or (f) of Section 655 of the Harbors and Navigation Code or Section 23152 or 23153 of this code, the abstract shall contain a statement indicating the percentage of alcohol, by weight, in the person's blood whenever that percentage was determined by a chemical test. The information regarding the chemical test shall be compiled if it is available to the clerk of the court. All information required to be compiled pursuant to this subdivision shall be kept confidential in the records of the department pursuant to Section 1808.5. The department may use the information for research and statistical purposes and for determining the eligibility of any person to operate a motor vehicle on the highways of this state. The information shall not be released to any other public or private agency, except for research and statistical summary purposes and, for those purposes, the name and address of the person and any other identifying information shall not be disclosed.

(c) The Legislature finds and declares that blood-alcohol percentages have valuable research potential in providing statistical summary information on impaired drivers but that a specific blood-alcohol percentage is only an item of evidence for purposes of criminal and licensing sanctions imposed by law. The Legislature recognizes that the accuracy of the determination of a specific blood-alcohol percentage is not the critical determination in a conviction for driving under the influence of an alcoholic beverage if the blood-alcohol percentage exceeds the statutory amount.

(Amended by Stats. 2024, Ch. 72, Sec. 65. (SB 156) Effective July 2, 2024.)

1805. The failure, refusal, or neglect of any such judicial officer to comply with any of the requirements of Sections 1802, 1803, 1804 and 1816 is misconduct in office and is ground for removal therefrom.

(Amended by Stats. 1959, Ch. 1622.)

1806. (a) The department shall file all accident reports and abstracts of court records of convictions received under this code, and in connection therewith, shall maintain convenient records or make suitable notations in order that an individual record of each license showing the convictions of the licensee and all traffic accidents in which the individual was involved, except those where, in the opinion of a reporting officer, another individual was at fault, are readily ascertainable. At its discretion the department may file and maintain these accident reports and abstracts by electronic recording and storage media and after transcribing electronically all available data from the accident reports and abstracts of conviction may destroy the original documents. Notwithstanding any other provisions of law, the recorded facts from any electronic recording and storage device maintained by the department shall constitute evidence of the facts in any administrative actions instituted by the department.

(b) When the department receives notification pursuant to subdivision (c) of Section 1872.45 of the Insurance Code, the department shall remove from the license record of each victim any record of his or her involvement in the accident which is the subject of the criminal complaint.

(Amended by Stats. 1999, Ch. 885, Sec. 9. Effective January 1, 2000.)

1806.1. If a person has entered into a stipulated vehicle release agreement pursuant to paragraph (2) of subdivision (d) of Section 14607.6, the department shall maintain a record of that fact for seven years from the date the person signed the agreement.

(Added by Stats. 1994, Ch. 1133, Sec. 3. Effective January 1, 1995.)

1806.5. Notwithstanding Section 1808, the department shall not furnish information filed pursuant to Section 1806 to any person if the furnishing of that information would violate the federal Fair Credit Reporting Act (15 U.S.C. Sec. 1681 et seq.).

(Added by Stats. 1986, Ch. 1117, Sec. 1.)

1807. (a) The department is not required to maintain records relating to drivers of motor vehicles after the records are, in the opinion of the director, no longer necessary, except as follows:

(1) Records of convictions shall be maintained so long as they may form the basis of license suspensions or revocations as prior convictions or with other records of conviction constitute a person a "negligent driver."

(2) Records of convictions of violating Section 38301.3 shall be maintained for seven years.

(b) Records that are not required to be maintained may be destroyed with the approval of the Department of General Services.

(Amended by Stats. 2005, Ch. 571, Sec. 2. Effective January 1, 2006.)

1807.5. (a) Notwithstanding Section 1808, any record of the department of a conviction of Section 23103 as specified in Section 23103.5, or of a conviction of Section 23152 or 23153 which occurred before January 1, 1987, is not a public record on and after a date which is five years after the date of conviction of that offense, and the department shall, thereafter, make any information relating to that conviction available only to persons authorized by law to receive the information.

(b) For the purposes of this section, "persons authorized by law to receive the information" means any of the following:

(1) The courts of the state.

(2) Peace officers, as defined in Section 830.1 of the Penal Code; subdivision (a) of Section 830.2 of the Penal Code; subdivisions (a), (b), and (j) of Section 830.3 of the Penal Code; and subdivisions (a), (b), and (c) of Section 830.5 of the Penal Code.

(3) The Attorney General.

(4) District attorneys of any county within the state.

(5) Prosecuting city attorneys or city prosecutors of any city within the state.

(6) Probation officers of any city or county of the state.

(7) Parole officers of any city or county of the state.

(Amended by Stats. 2017, Ch. 299, Sec. 4. (AB 1418) Effective January 1, 2018.)

1808. (a) Except where a specific provision of law prohibits the disclosure of records or information or provides for confidentiality, all records of the department relating to the registration of vehicles, other information contained on an application for a driver's license, abstracts of convictions, and abstracts of accident reports required to be sent to the department in Sacramento, except for abstracts of accidents where, in the opinion of a reporting officer, another individual was at fault, shall be open to public inspection during office hours. All abstracts of accident reports shall be available to law enforcement agencies and courts of competent jurisdiction.

(b) The department shall make available or disclose abstracts of convictions and abstracts of accident reports required to be sent to the department in Sacramento, as described in subdivision (a), if the date of the occurrence is not later than the following:

(1) Ten years for a violation pursuant to Section 23140, 23152, or 23153.

(2) Seven years for a violation designated as two points pursuant to Section 12810, except as provided in paragraph (1) of this subdivision.

(3) Three years for accidents and all other violations.

(c) The department shall make available or disclose suspensions and revocations of the driving privilege while the suspension or revocation is in effect and for three years following termination of the action or reinstatement of the privilege, except that driver's license suspension actions taken pursuant to former Sections 13202.6 and 13202.7, Section 17520 of the Family Code, or Section 256 or former Section 11350.6 of the Welfare and Institutions Code shall be disclosed only during the actual time period in which the suspension is in effect.

(d) The department shall not make available or disclose a suspension or revocation that has been judicially set aside or stayed.

(e) The department shall not make available or disclose personal information about a person unless the disclosure is in compliance with the Driver's Privacy Protection Act of 1994 (18 U.S.C. Sec. 2721 et seq.). However, a disclosure is subject to the prohibition in paragraph (2) of subdivision (a) of Section 12800.5.

(f) The department shall make available or disclose to the courts and law enforcement agencies a conviction of Section 23103, as specified in Section 23103.5, or a conviction of Section 23140, 23152, or 23153, or Section 655 of the Harbors and Navigation Code, or paragraph (1) of subdivision (c) of Section 192 of the Penal Code for a period of 10 years from the date of the offense for the purpose of imposing penalties mandated by this code, or by other applicable provisions of California law.

(g) The department shall make available or disclose to the courts and law enforcement agencies a conviction of Section 191.5, or subdivision (a) of Section 192.5 of the Penal Code, punished as a felony, for the purpose of imposing penalties mandated by Section 23550.5, or by other applicable provisions of California law.

(Amended by Stats. 2019, Ch. 505, Sec. 8. (SB 485) Effective January 1, 2020.)

1808.1. (a) The prospective employer of a driver who drives a vehicle specified in subdivision (k) shall obtain a report showing the driver's current public record as recorded by the department. For purposes of this subdivision, a report is current if it was issued less than 30 days before the date the employer employs the driver. The report shall be reviewed, signed, and dated by the employer and maintained at the employer's place of business until receipt of the pull-notice system report pursuant to subdivisions (b) and (c). These reports shall be presented upon request to an authorized representative of the Department of the California Highway Patrol during regular business hours.

(b) The employer of a driver who drives a vehicle specified in subdivision (k) shall participate in a pull-notice system, which is a process for the purpose of providing the employer with a report showing the driver's current public record as recorded by the department, and any subsequent convictions, failures to appear, accidents, driver's license suspensions, driver's license revocations, or any other actions taken against the driving privilege or certificate, added to the driver's record while the employer's notification request remains valid and uncanceled. As used in this section, participation in the pull-notice system means obtaining a requester code and enrolling all employed drivers who drive a vehicle specified in subdivision (k) under that requester code.

(c) The employer of a driver of a vehicle specified in subdivision (k) shall, additionally, obtain a periodic report from the department at least every 12 months. The employer shall verify that each employee's driver's license has not been suspended or revoked, the employee's traffic violation point count, and whether the employee has been convicted of a violation of Section 23152 or 23153. The report shall be signed and dated by the employer and maintained at the employer's principal place of business. The report shall be presented upon demand to an authorized representative of the Department of the California Highway Patrol during regular business hours.

(d) Upon the termination of a driver's employment, the employer shall notify the department to discontinue the driver's enrollment in the pull-notice system.

(e) For the purposes of the pull-notice system and periodic report process required by subdivisions (b) and (c), an owner, other than an owner-operator as defined in Section 34624, and an employer who drives a vehicle described in subdivision (k) shall be enrolled as if he or she were an employee. A family member and a volunteer driver who drives a vehicle described in subdivision (k) shall also be enrolled as if he or she were an employee.

(f) An employer who, after receiving a driving record pursuant to this section, employs or continues to employ as a driver a person against whom a disqualifying action has been taken regarding his or her driving privilege or required driver's certificate, is guilty of a public offense, and upon conviction thereof, shall be punished by confinement in a county jail for not more than six months, by a fine of not more than one thousand dollars ($1,000), or by both that confinement and fine.

(g) As part of its inspection of bus maintenance facilities and terminals required at least once every 13 months pursuant to subdivision (c) of Section 34501, the Department of the California Highway Patrol shall determine whether each transit operator, as defined in Section 99210 of the Public Utilities Code, is then in compliance with this section and Section 12804.6, and shall certify each operator found to be in compliance. Funds shall not be allocated pursuant to Chapter 4 (commencing with Section 99200) of Part 11 of Division 10 of the Public Utilities Code to a transit operator that the Department of the California Highway Patrol has not certified pursuant to this section.

(h) (1) A request to participate in the pull-notice system established by this section shall be accompanied by a fee determined by the department to be sufficient to defray the entire actual cost to the department for the notification service. For the receipt of subsequent reports, the employer shall also be charged a fee established by the department pursuant to Section 1811. An employer who qualifies pursuant to Section 1812 shall be exempt from any fee required pursuant to this section. Failure to pay the fee shall result in automatic cancellation of the employer's participation in the notification services.

(2) A regularly organized fire department, having official recognition of the city, county, city and county, or district in which the department is located, shall participate in the pull-notice program and shall not be subject to the fee established pursuant to this subdivision.

(3) The Board of Pilot Commissioners for the Bays of San Francisco, San Pablo, and Suisun, and its port agent shall participate in the pull-notice system established by this section, subject to Section 1178.5 of the Harbors and Navigation Code, and shall not be subject to the fees established pursuant to this subdivision.

(i) The department, as soon as feasible, may establish an automatic procedure to provide the periodic reports to an employer by mail or via an electronic delivery method, as required by subdivision (c), on a regular basis without the need for individual requests.

(j) (1) The employer of a driver who is employed as a casual driver is not required to enter that driver's name in the pull-notice system, as otherwise required by subdivision (a). However, the employer of a casual driver shall be in possession of a report of the driver's current public record as recorded by the department, before allowing a casual driver to drive a vehicle specified in subdivision (k). A report is current if it was issued less than six months before the date the employer employs the driver.

(2) For the purposes of this subdivision, a driver is employed as a casual driver when the employer has employed the driver less than 30 days during the preceding six months. "Casual driver" does not include a driver who operates a vehicle that requires a passenger transportation endorsement.

(k) This section applies to a vehicle for the operation of which the driver is required to have a class A or class B driver's license, a class C license with any endorsement issued pursuant to Section 15278, a class C license issued pursuant to Section 12814.7, or a certificate issued pursuant to Section 12517, 12519, 12520, 12523, 12523.5, or 12527, a passenger vehicle having a seating capacity of not more than 10 persons, including the driver, operated for compensation by a charter-party carrier of passengers or passenger stage corporation pursuant to a certificate of public convenience and necessity or a permit issued by the Public Utilities Commission, or a permitted taxicab company as described in Section 53075.5 of the Government Code.

(l) This section shall not be construed to change the definition of "employer," "employee," or "independent contractor" for any purpose.

(m) A motor carrier who contracts with a person to drive a vehicle described in subdivision (k) that is owned by, or leased to, that motor carrier, is subject to subdivisions (a), (b), (c), (d), (f), (j), (k), and (l) and the employer obligations in those subdivisions.

(n) Reports issued pursuant to this section, but only those for a driver of a taxicab engaged in transportation service as described in subdivision (a) of Section 53075.5 of the Government Code, shall be presented upon request, during regular business hours, to an authorized representative of the administrative agency responsible for issuing permits to taxicab transportation services pursuant to Section 53075.5 of the Government Code.

(Amended by Stats. 2018, Ch. 92, Sec. 209. (SB 1289) Effective January 1, 2019.)

1808.2. In addition to those specified in Section 1808.4, the home address of any inspector or investigator regularly employed and paid as such in the office of a district attorney or any peace officer employee of the Board of Prison Terms appearing in any record of the department is confidential.

(Added by Stats. 1980, Ch. 616, Sec. 2. Operative July 1, 1981, by Sec. 4 of Ch. 616.)

1808.21. (a) Any residence address in any record of the department is confidential and shall not be disclosed to any person, except a court, law enforcement agency, or other government agency, or as authorized in Section 1808.22 or 1808.23.

(b) Release of any mailing address or part thereof in any record of the department may be restricted to a release for purposes related to the reasons for which the information was collected, including, but not limited to, the assessment of driver risk, or ownership of vehicles or vessels. This restriction does not apply to a release to a court, a law enforcement agency, or other governmental agency, or a person who has been issued a requester code pursuant to Section 1810.2.

(c) Any person providing the department with a mailing address shall declare, under penalty of perjury, that the mailing address is a valid, existing, and accurate mailing address and shall consent to receive service of process pursuant to subdivision (b) of Section 415.20, subdivision (a) of Section 415.30, and Section 416.90 of the Code of Civil Procedure at the mailing address.

(d) (1) Any registration or driver's license record of a person may be suppressed from any other person, except those persons specified in subdivision (a), if the person requesting the suppression submits either of the following:

(A) A certificate or identification card issued to the person as a program participant by the Secretary of State pursuant to Chapter 3.1 (commencing with Section 6205) of Division 7 of Title 1 of the Government Code.

(B) Verification acceptable to the department that he or she has reasonable cause to believe either of the following:

(i) That he or she is the subject of stalking, as specified in Section 1708.7 of the Civil Code or Section 646.9 of the Penal Code.

(ii) That there exists a threat of death or great bodily injury to his or her person, as defined in Section 12022.7 of the Penal Code.

(2) Upon suppression of a record, each request for information about that record shall be authorized by the subject of the record or verified as legitimate by other investigative means by the department before the information is released.

(e) (1) The suppression of a record pursuant to a verification under subparagraph (B) of paragraph (1) of subdivision (d) shall occur for one year after approval by the department. Not less than 60 days prior to the date the suppression of the record would otherwise expire, the department shall notify the subject of the record of its impending expiration. The suppression may be continued for two additional periods of one year each if a letter is submitted to the department stating that the person continues to have a reasonable cause to believe that he or she is the subject of stalking or that there exists a threat of death or great bodily injury as described in subparagraph (B) of paragraph (1) of subdivision (d). The suppression may be additionally continued at the end of the second one-year period by submitting verification acceptable to the department. The notification described in this subdivision shall instruct the person of the method to reapply for record suppression.

(2) The suppression of a record made in accordance with the submission of a certificate or identification card under subparagraph (A) of paragraph (1) of subdivision (d) shall occur for four years following the submission of the certificate or identification card described in this paragraph. The suppression may be continued for an additional four-year period, and for subsequent four-year periods, upon the submission of a current certificate or identification card described in this paragraph.

(f) For the purposes of subdivisions (d) and (e), "verification acceptable to the department" means recent police reports, court documentation, or other documentation from a law enforcement agency.

(Amended by Stats. 2003, Ch. 720, Sec. 1. Effective January 1, 2004.)

1808.22. (a) Section 1808.21 does not apply to a financial institution licensed by the state or federal government to do business in the State of California, if the financial institution states under penalty of perjury that it has obtained a written waiver of Section 1808.21 signed by the individual whose address is requested, or to providing the address of a person who has entered into an agreement held by that institution prior to July 1, 1990, so long as that agreement remains in effect.

(b) (1) Section 1808.21 does not apply to an insurance company licensed to do business in California, or to an authorized contractor acting on behalf of that insurance company, pursuant to a contractual agreement, if the company or contractor, under penalty of perjury, requests the information for the purpose of obtaining the address of another motorist or vehicle owner involved in an accident with the company's insured.

(2) Section 1808.21 does not apply to an insurance company licensed to do business in California if the company, under penalty of perjury, requests the information on an individual who has signed a written waiver of Section 1808.21 or on the individuals insured under a policy if a named insured of that policy has signed a written waiver.

(c) (1) Notwithstanding any other provisions of the Vehicle Code and regulations adopted by the department, all information obtained from the department pursuant to the exemptions in subdivision (b) shall be subject to the existing use or disclosure limitations and data security requirements for the principal under applicable state and federal law.

(2) Use or disclosure limitations and data security requirements imposed on an authorized contractor by this subdivision shall be enforced by the department in compliance with its existing regulations governing the use or disclosure of information obtained from the department

pursuant to subdivision (b).

(3) The use or disclosure of information obtained from the department by an authorized contractor of the insurance company pursuant to paragraph (1) of subdivision (b) shall be permitted only for the purpose of obtaining the address of another motorist or vehicle owner involved in an accident with the company's insured. The information shall not be used or disclosed for any other purpose, other than the reason for which the information was requested, or to any other person.

(4) An insurance company shall be responsible for any misuse of the information by the authorized contractor.

(5) An authorized contractor is subject to all of the following requirements:

(A) All information obtained by the contractor from the department pursuant to paragraph (1) of subdivision (b), and any copies made of that information, shall be destroyed by the contractor pursuant to Section 1798.81 of the Civil Code, once the contractor has used the information for the purpose of obtaining the address of a motorist or vehicle owner involved in an accident with individuals insured with the insurer.

(B) The contractor shall not sell the information obtained from the department or store, combine, or link that information with a database for resale or for any purpose other than obtaining the address of a motorist or vehicle owner involved in an accident with individuals insured with the insurer.

(C) The contractor shall maintain a log to track the receipt, use, and dissemination of the information. The log shall be immediately available to the department upon request and maintained for four years from the date of the request.

(D) The contractor shall maintain a surety bond in the amount of fifty thousand dollars ($50,000), consistent with subdivision (c) of Section 1810.2 and Section 350.24 of Title 13 of the California Code of Regulations.

(E) A contractor that violates this section shall be liable to the department for civil penalties up to the amount of one hundred thousand dollars ($100,000), and, if the contractor is a commercial requester pursuant to Section 1810.2, the contractor shall also have his or her requester code suspended for a period of five years, or revoked, pursuant to Section 1808.46.

(d) Section 1808.21 does not apply to an attorney if the attorney states, under penalty of perjury, that the motor vehicle or vessel registered owner or driver residential address information is necessary in order to represent his or her client in a criminal or civil action that directly involves the use of the motor vehicle or vessel that is pending, is to be filed, or is being investigated. Information requested pursuant to this subdivision is subject to all of the following:

(1) The attorney shall state that the criminal or civil action that is pending, is to be filed, or is being investigated relates directly to the use of that motor vehicle or vessel.

(2) The case number, if any, or the names of expected parties to the extent they are known to the attorney requesting the information, shall be listed on the request.

(3) A residence address obtained from the department shall not be used for any purpose other than in furtherance of the case cited or action to be filed or that is being investigated.

(4) If an action is not filed within a reasonable time, the residence address information shall be destroyed.

(5) An attorney shall not request residential address information pursuant to this subdivision in order to sell the information to a person.

(6) Within 10 days of receipt of a request, the department shall notify every individual whose residence address has been requested pursuant to this subdivision.

(e) A knowing violation of paragraph (1), (2), (3), (4), or (5) of subdivision (d) is a misdemeanor. A knowing violation of paragraph (1), (2), (3), (4), or (5) of subdivision (d) in furtherance of another crime is subject to the same penalties as that other crime.

(Amended by Stats. 2010, Ch. 353, Sec. 1. (AB 953) Effective January 1, 2011.)

1808.23. (a) Section 1808.21 does not apply to any of the following:

(1) A vehicle manufacturer licensed to do business in this state if the manufacturer, or its agent, under penalty of perjury, requests and uses the information only for the purpose of safety, warranty, including a warranty issued in compliance with Section 1795.92 of the Civil Code, emission, or product recall if the manufacturer offers to make and makes any changes at no cost to the vehicle owner.

(2) A dealer licensed to do business in this state if the dealer, or its agent, under penalty of perjury, requests and uses the information only for the purpose of completing registration transactions and documents.

(3) A person who, under penalty of perjury, requests and uses the information as permitted under subdivision (h) of Section 1798.24 of the Civil Code, if the request specifies that no persons will be contacted by mail or otherwise at the address included with the information released. The information released by the department under this subdivision shall not be in a form that identifies any person.

(4) An electrical corporation as defined in Section 218 of the Public Utilities Code or a local publicly owned electric utility as defined in Section 224.3 of the Public Utilities Code, if the corporation or utility, or its agent, under penalty of perjury, requests and uses the information only for the purposes of identifying where an electric vehicle is registered. All of the following shall apply to this paragraph:

(A) The department may disclose to the electrical corporation or local publicly owned utility only the type of vehicle and address of the electric vehicle owner. The department shall not disclose the name of the electric vehicle owner.

(B) Within 15 days of receiving residence address information from the department pursuant to this section, an electrical corporation or local publicly owned utility shall provide a clear, express disclosure to the electric vehicle owner that his or her residence address information is permitted by law to be shared with the corporation or utility. The disclosure shall not contain marketing information or a solicitation for the purchase of goods or services.

(C) Confidential home address and type of vehicle information of electric vehicle owners disclosed pursuant to this paragraph shall only be used for the purpose of identifying where an electric vehicle is registered and shall not be used or disclosed for any other purpose, including for purposes of identifying the individual or individuals residing at the address, or to any other person.

(D) The electrical corporation or local publicly owned utility and its agents shall not sell, share, or further disclose, including to any subsidiaries, the residence address or type of vehicle information of electric vehicle owners obtained pursuant to this paragraph, or name information determined by matching residence information against the corporation or utility's customer records.

(b) Residential addresses released shall not be used for direct marketing or solicitation for the purchase of any consumer product or service.

(Amended by Stats. 2011, Ch. 346, Sec. 1. (SB 859) Effective January 1, 2012.)

1808.24. Information regarding any motor vehicle liability insurance policy or surety bond provided to the department pursuant to Section 4000.37 or provided electronically is confidential and shall not be disclosed to any person, except to the following:

(a) A court of competent jurisdiction.

(b) A law enforcement or other governmental agency.

(c) An insurance company or its assigns to verify a record the company or its assigns previously submitted to the department.

(d) A person whose vehicle or property has been involved in an accident reported to the department, or who suffered bodily injury or death in an accident reported to the department, pursuant to Chapter 1 (commencing with Section 16000) of Division 7, or the person's authorized representative, employer, parent, or legal guardian.

(Added by Stats. 1999, Ch. 880, Sec. 2. Effective January 1, 2000.)

1808.25. (a) The department shall implement a program to provide residence address information to an accredited degree-granting nonprofit independent institution of higher education incorporated in the state, that has concluded a memorandum of understanding pursuant to subdivision (b) of Section 830.7 of the Penal Code if, under penalty of perjury, the institution requests and uses the information solely for the purpose of enforcing parking restrictions.

(b) The memorandum of understanding executed by the sheriff or chief of police within whose jurisdiction the independent institution is located shall expressly permit the institution to enforce parking restrictions pursuant to subdivision (b) of Section 830.7 of the Penal Code. For the purposes of this subdivision, a participating institution shall enter into a contractual agreement with the department that, at a minimum, requires the institution to do all of the following:

(1) Establish and maintain procedures, to the satisfaction of the department, for persons to contest parking violation notices issued by the institution.

(2) Remit a fee, as determined by the department, to cover the department's costs of providing each address to the institution.

(3) Agree that access to confidential residence address information from the department's vehicle registration database will be provided only through an approved commercial requester account.

(4) Establish and maintain a system that ensures that confidential address information obtained from the department is used solely for the purpose specified in subdivision (a).

(c) The director may terminate a contract authorized by subdivision (b) at any time the department determines that the independent institution of higher education fails to maintain adequate safeguards to ensure that the operation of the program does not adversely affect those individuals whose records are maintained in the department's files, or that the information is used for any purpose other than that specified in subdivision (a).

(d) Sections 1808.45, 1808.46, and 1808.47 are applicable to persons who obtain department records pursuant to this section and the department may pursue any appropriate civil or criminal action against any individual at an independent institution who violates the provisions of this section.

(e) For purposes of this article only, any confidential information obtained from the department for administration or enforcement of this article shall be held confidential, except to the extent necessary for the enforcement of parking restrictions, and may not be used for any purpose other than the administration or enforcement of parking restrictions.

(Amended by Stats. 2003, Ch. 410, Sec. 1. Effective January 1, 2004.)

1808.4. (a) For all of the following persons, the person's home address that appears in a record of the department is confidential if the person requests the confidentiality of that information:

(1) Attorney General.

(2) State Public Defender.

(3) A Member of the Legislature.

(4) An active or retired judge or court commissioner.

(5) A district attorney.

(6) A public defender.

(7) An attorney employed by the Department of Justice, the office of the State Public Defender, or a county office of the district attorney or public defender.

(8) A city attorney, city prosecutor, or an attorney who submits verification from their public employer that the attorney represents the city in matters that routinely place the attorney in personal contact with persons under investigation for, charged with, or convicted of, committing criminal acts, if that attorney is employed by a city attorney or city prosecutor.

(9) A nonsworn police dispatcher.

(10) A child abuse investigator or social worker, working in child protective services within a social services department.

(11) An active or retired peace officer, as defined in Chapter 4.5 (commencing with Section 830) of Title 3 of Part 2 of the Penal Code.

(12) An employee of the Department of Corrections and Rehabilitation, Division of Juvenile Facilities, or the California Correctional Training and Rehabilitation Authority specified in Sections 20403 and 20405 of the Government Code.

(13) A nonsworn employee of a city police department, a county sheriff's office, the Department of the California Highway Patrol, a federal, state, or local detention facility, or a local juvenile hall, camp, ranch, or home, who submits agency verification that, in the normal course of the employee's employment, the employee controls or supervises inmates or is required to have a prisoner in the employee's care or custody.

(14) A county counsel assigned to child abuse cases.

(15) An investigator employed by the Department of Justice, a county district attorney, or a county public defender.

(16) A member of a city council.

(17) A member of a board of supervisors.

(18) A federal prosecutor, criminal investigator, or National Park Service Ranger working in this state.

(19) An active or retired city enforcement officer engaged in the enforcement of the Vehicle Code or municipal parking ordinances.

(20) An employee of a trial court.

(21) A psychiatric social worker employed by a county.

(22) A police or sheriff department employee designated by the chief of police of the department or the sheriff of the county as being in a sensitive position. A designation pursuant to this paragraph shall, for purposes of this section, remain in effect for three years subject to additional designations that, for purposes of this section, shall remain in effect for additional three-year periods.

(23) A state employee in one of the following classifications:

(A) Licensing-Registration Examiner, Department of Motor Vehicles.

(B) Motor Carrier Specialist I, Department of the California Highway Patrol.

(C) Museum Security Officer and Supervising Museum Security Officer.

(D) Licensing Program Analyst, State Department of Social Services.

(24) (A) The spouse or child of a person listed in paragraphs (1) to (23), inclusive, regardless of the spouse's or child's place of residence.

(B) The surviving spouse or child of a peace officer, as defined in Chapter 4.5 (commencing with Section 830) of Title 3 of Part 2 of the Penal Code, if the peace officer died in the line of duty.

(C) The surviving spouse or child of a judge or court commissioner, if the judge or court commissioner died in the performance of their duties.

(D) (i) Subparagraphs (A), (B), and (C) do not apply if the person listed in those subparagraphs was convicted of a crime and is on active parole or probation.

(ii) For requests made on or after January 1, 2011, the person requesting confidentiality for their spouse or child listed in subparagraph (A), (B), or (C) shall declare, at the time of the request for confidentiality, whether the spouse or child has been convicted of a crime and is on active parole or probation.

(iii) Neither the listed person's employer nor the department shall be required to verify, or be responsible for verifying, that a person listed in subparagraph (A), (B), or (C) was convicted of a crime and is on active parole or probation.

(E) (i) The department shall discontinue holding a home address confidential pursuant to this subdivision for a person specified in subparagraph (A), (B), or (C) who is the child or spouse of a person described in paragraph (4), (9), (11), (13), or (22) if the child or spouse is convicted of a felony in this state or is convicted of an offense in another jurisdiction that, if committed in California, would be a felony.

(ii) The department shall comply with this subparagraph upon receiving notice of a disqualifying conviction from the agency that employs or formerly employed the parent or spouse of the convicted person, or as soon as the department otherwise becomes aware of the disqualifying conviction.

(b) The confidential home address of a person listed in subdivision (a) shall not be disclosed, except to any of the following:

(1) A court.

(2) A law enforcement agency.

(3) The State Board of Equalization.

(4) An attorney in a civil or criminal action that demonstrates to a court the need for the home address, if the disclosure is made pursuant to a subpoena.

(5) A governmental agency to which, under any law, information is required to be furnished from records maintained by the department.

(c) (1) A record of the department containing a confidential home address shall be open to public inspection, as provided in Section 1808, if the address is completely obliterated or otherwise removed from the record.

(2) Following termination of office or employment, a confidential home address shall be withheld from public inspection for three years, unless the termination is the result of conviction of a criminal offense or a request to remove confidentiality protections has been made by an employing agency pursuant to paragraph (6). If the termination or separation is the result of the filing of a criminal complaint, a confidential home address shall be withheld from public inspection during the time in which the terminated individual may file an appeal from termination, while an appeal from termination is ongoing, and until the appeal process is exhausted, after which confidentiality shall be at the discretion of the employing agency if the termination or separation is upheld. Upon reinstatement to an office or employment, the protections of this section are available.

(3) With respect to a retired peace officer, the peace officer's home address shall be withheld from public inspection permanently upon request of confidentiality at the time the information would otherwise be opened. The home address of the surviving spouse or child listed in subparagraph (B) of paragraph (24) of subdivision (a) shall be withheld from public inspection for three years following the death of the peace officer.

(4) The department shall inform a person who requests a confidential home address what agency the individual whose address was requested is employed by or the court at which the judge or court commissioner presides.

(5) With respect to a retired judge or court commissioner, the retired judge or court commissioner's home address shall be withheld from public inspection permanently upon request of confidentiality at the time the information would otherwise be opened. The home address of the surviving spouse or child listed in subparagraph (C) of paragraph (24) of subdivision (a) shall be withheld from public inspection for three years following the death of the judge or court commissioner.

(6) Following a termination of employment, the terminated individual's employing agency may request that the department remove the confidentiality protections of this section for the terminated individual if no appeal to the termination is filed or if the termination or separation is upheld. The employing agency shall certify in its request to the department that no appeal to the termination has been filed or that the termination or separation has been upheld. If the terminated individual files an appeal from termination, the individual's confidential home address shall be withheld from public inspection while the appeal from termination is ongoing and until the appeal process is exhausted. The department shall comply with a request made pursuant to this paragraph within 45 days of receipt. This paragraph shall not apply to terminations of employment resulting from the filing of a criminal complaint.

(d) A violation of subdivision (a) by the disclosure of the confidential home address of a peace officer, as specified in paragraph (11) of subdivision (a), a nonsworn employee of the city police department or county sheriff's office, a judge or court commissioner, as specified in paragraph (4) of subdivision (a), or the spouses or children of these persons, including, but not limited to, the surviving spouse or child listed in subparagraph (B) or (C) of paragraph (24) of subdivision (a), that results in bodily injury to the peace officer, employee of the city police department or county sheriff's office, judge or court commissioner, or the spouses or children of these persons is a felony.

(Amended by Stats. 2025, Ch. 241, Sec. 71. (SB 857) Effective January 1, 2026.)

1808.45. The willful, unauthorized disclosure of information from any department record to any person, or the use of any false representation to obtain information from a department record or any use of information obtained from any department record for a purpose other than the one stated in the request or the sale or other distribution of the information to a person or organization for purposes not disclosed in the request is a misdemeanor, punishable by a fine not exceeding five thousand dollars ($5,000) or by imprisonment in the county jail not exceeding one year, or both fine and imprisonment.

(Added by Stats. 1989, Ch. 1213, Sec. 7.)

1808.46. No person or agent shall directly or indirectly obtain information from the department files using false representations or distribute restricted or confidential information to any person or use the information for a reason not authorized or specified in a requester code application. Any person who violates this section, in addition to any other penalty provided in this code, is liable to the department for civil penalties up to one hundred thousand dollars ($100,000) and shall have its requester code privileges suspended for a period of up to five years, or revoked. The regulatory agencies having jurisdiction over any licensed person receiving information pursuant to this chapter shall implement procedures to review the procedures of any licensee which receives information to ensure compliance with the limitations on the use of information as part of the agency's regular oversight of the licensees. The agency shall report noncompliance to the department.

(Amended by Stats. 1990, Ch. 1635, Sec. 2. Effective September 30, 1990.)

1808.47. Any person who has access to confidential or restricted information from the department shall establish procedures to protect the confidentiality of those records. If any confidential or restricted information is released to any agent of a person authorized to obtain information, the person shall require the agent to take all steps necessary to ensure confidentiality and prevent the release of any information to a third party. No agent shall obtain or use any confidential or restricted records for any purpose other than the reason the information was requested.

(Amended by Stats. 1999, Ch. 880, Sec. 3. Effective January 1, 2000.)

1808.48. Notwithstanding any other law, no government agency or department, law enforcement agency, commercial entity, or other person shall obtain, access, use, or otherwise disclose, noncriminal history information maintained by the department, for the purpose of immigration enforcement, as defined in subdivision (f) of Section 7284.4. of the Government Code.

(Added by Stats. 2022, Ch. 482, Sec. 6. (AB 1766) Effective January 1, 2023.)

1808.5. Except as provided in Section 22511.58, all records of the department relating to the physical or mental condition of any person, and convictions of any offense involving the use or possession of controlled substances under Division 10 (commencing with Section 11000) of the Health and Safety Code not arising from circumstances involving a motor vehicle, are confidential and not open to public inspection.

(Amended by Stats. 1998, Ch. 828, Sec. 11. Effective January 1, 1999.)

1808.51. Notwithstanding Sections 1808.5 and 12800.5, any of the following may obtain copies of fullface engraved pictures or photographs of individuals directly from the department:

(a) The Bureau of Real Estate, as a department, individually, or through its staff, for purposes of enforcing the Real Estate Law (Part 1 (commencing with Section 10000) of Division 4 of the Business and Professions Code) or the Subdivided Lands Law (Chapter 1 (commencing with Section 11000) of Part 2 of Division 4 of the Business and Professions Code).

(b) The city attorney of a city and county and his or her investigators for purposes of performing functions related to city and county operations.

(c) The Bureau of Automotive Repair, as a department, individually, or through its staff, for purposes of enforcing the Automotive Repair Act (Chapter 20.3 (commencing with Section 9880) of Division 3 of the Business and Professions Code) or the Motor Vehicle Inspection Program (Chapter 5 (commencing with Section 44000) of Part 5 of Division 26 of the Health and Safety Code).

(Amended by Stats. 2018, Ch. 503, Sec. 4. (AB 3141) Effective January 1, 2019.)

1808.6. (a) In addition to those specified in Section 1808.4, the home address of any of the following persons, that appears in any record of the department, is confidential, if the person requests the confidentiality of that information:

(1) The chairperson, executive officer, commissioners, and deputy commissioners of the Board of Prison Terms.

(2) The chairperson, members, executive director, and hearing representatives of the Youthful Offender Parole Board.

(3) The spouse or children of persons listed in this section, regardless of the spouse's or child's place of residence.

(b) The confidential home address of any of the persons listed in subdivision (a) shall not be disclosed to any person, except a court, a law enforcement agency, the State Board of Equalization, or any governmental agency to which, under any provision of law, information is required to be furnished from records maintained by the department.

(c) Any record of the department containing a confidential home address shall be open to public inspection, as provided in Section 1808, if the address is completely obliterated or otherwise removed from the record. The home address shall be withheld from public inspection for three years following termination of office or employment, except with respect to retired peace officers, whose home addresses shall be withheld from public inspection permanently upon request of confidentiality at the time the information would otherwise be opened. The department shall inform any person who requests a confidential home address of the name of the agency that employs the individual whose address was requested.

(Amended by Stats. 1996, Ch. 880, Sec. 1. Effective January 1, 1997.)

1808.7. (a) The record of the department relating to the first proceeding and conviction under Section 1803.5 in any 18-month period for completion of a traffic violator school program is confidential, shall not be disclosed to any person, except a court and as provided for in subdivision (b), and shall be used only for statistical purposes by the department. No violation point count shall be assessed pursuant to Section 12810 if the conviction is confidential.

(b) The record of a conviction described in subdivision (a) shall not be confidential if any of the following circumstances applies:

(1) The person convicted holds a commercial driver's license as defined by Section 15210.

(2) The person convicted holds a commercial driver's license in another state, in accordance with Part 383 of Title 49 of the Code of Federal Regulations.

(3) The violation occurred in a commercial motor vehicle, as defined in subdivision (b) of Section 15210.

(4) The conviction would result in a violation point count of more than one point pursuant to Section 12810.

(c) This section shall become operative on July 1, 2011.

(Repealed (in Sec. 2) and added by Stats. 2010, Ch. 599, Sec. 2.5. (AB 2499) Effective January 1, 2011. Section operative July 1, 2011, by its own provisions.)

1808.8. (a) Dismissal of any driver certified pursuant to Section 12517, 12523, or 12523.5, for a cause relating to pupil transportation safety, shall be reported by the carrier to the department within five days of the dismissal date.

(b) Reinstatement of any driver whose dismissal has been reported under subdivision (a) shall be reported by the carrier to the department within five days of the reinstatement date.

(Added by Stats. 1989, Ch. 359, Sec. 2.)

1808.9. (a) Except for retired peace officers whose home address is permanently withheld from public inspection under subdivision (c) of Section 1808.4 or subdivision (c) of Section 1808.6, a person whose home address is confidential in any record of the department under Section 1808.2, 1808.4, or 1808.6 may be required by the department to demonstrate his or her continued eligibility for that confidentiality upon renewal of a driver's license or identification card issued by the department. Not later than 90 days prior to the expiration of a driver's license or identification card, the department shall notify the person whose record is confidential of any requirement to demonstrate the continued eligibility.

(b) A person whose driver's license or identification card is renewed within one year of the first request for address confidentiality under this section shall not be required to demonstrate his or her eligibility for that confidentially again until the subsequent renewal.

(Added by Stats. 1996, Ch. 880, Sec. 2. Effective January 1, 1997.)

1808.10. The record of the department relating to the first proceeding and conviction for a driver licensed with a class A license, class B license, or commercial class C driver's license in any 18-month period who is allowed, for a traffic offense while operating a vehicle requiring only a class C or a class M license, to complete a course of instruction at a traffic violator school, is not confidential and shall be disclosed for purposes of Title 49 of the Code of Federal Regulations and to insurers by the department for insurance underwriting and rating purposes.

(Added by Stats. 2012, Ch. 302, Sec. 1. (AB 1888) Effective January 1, 2013.)

1809. The department may prepare and disseminate information relating to prevention of traffic accidents.

(Enacted by Stats. 1959, Ch. 3.)

1810. (a) Except as provided in Sections 1806.5, 1808.2, 1808.4, 1808.5, 1808.6, 1808.7, 1808.8, and paragraph (2) of subdivision (a) of Section 12800.5, the department may permit inspection of information from its records concerning the registration of a vehicle or information from the files of drivers' licenses at a charge that shall not exceed the actual cost to the department for providing the inspection of the information, including, but not limited to, costs incurred by the department in carrying out subdivision (b), with the charge for the information to be determined by the director. This section does not apply to statistical information of the type previously compiled and distributed by the department.

(b) (1) With respect to the inspection of information concerning the registration of a vehicle or of information from the files of drivers' licenses, the department shall establish, by regulation, administrative procedures under which a person making a request for that information shall be required to identify themselves and state the reason for making the request. The procedures shall provide for the verification of the name and address of the person making a request for the information, and the department may require the person to produce that information as it determines is necessary to ensure that the name and address of the person is the true name and address. The procedures may provide for a 10-day delay in the release of the requested information. The procedures shall also provide for notification to the person to whom the information primarily relates, as to what information was provided and to whom it was provided. The department shall establish, by regulation, a reasonable period of time for which a record of all the foregoing shall be maintained.

(2) The procedures required by paragraph (1) do not apply to a governmental entity, a person or an organization who has applied for and has been issued a requester code by the department, or a court of competent jurisdiction.

(c) With respect to the inspection of information from the files of drivers' licenses, the department may require both the full name of the driver and either the driver's license number or date of birth as identifying points of the record, except that the department may disclose a record without two identifying points if the department determines that the public interest in disclosure outweighs the public interest in personal privacy.

(d) With respect to the inspection of information from the files of

drivers' licenses, certificates of ownership, and registration cards, the department shall not allow, for a fee or otherwise, copying by the public.
(Amended by Stats. 2021, Ch. 90, Sec. 1. (AB 398) Effective January 1, 2022.)

1810.2. (a) The department may establish commercial requester accounts for individuals or organizations and issue requester codes for the purpose of obtaining information from the department's files, except as prohibited by Section 1808.21.

(b) Commercial requester account applications shall include the requester's name, address, type of business, a specific reason for requesting information, and the name of the person responsible for the business or firm.

(c) The department shall establish a commercial requester account when it determines that the applicant has a legitimate business need for the information requested and when the applicant files a bond in the amount of fifty thousand dollars ($50,000) and pays a two hundred fifty dollar ($250) filing fee. If the applicant does not request and is not issued a requester code permitting the applicant access to residence address information, only a filing fee of fifty dollars ($50) shall be required with the original application and each biennial renewal application.

(d) An individual requester code shall be issued for a period not to exceed five years and may be renewed upon application for additional periods not to exceed five years each.

(e) A requester code may be denied to any person unless the proposed use of the information from department records is related to legitimate business or commercial purposes of that person. A requester code may be canceled immediately if the requested information is used for a purpose other than the purpose for which the requester code was issued.
(Amended by Stats. 1991, Ch. 579, Sec. 3.)

1810.3. (a) Using the information made available in the accident reports provided to the department by law enforcement agencies under Section 20012, the department may provide information consisting of the following, for each vehicle that is included in those reports:

(1) The license plate number.

(2) The accident report number.

(b) Notwithstanding Section 16005, 20012, or 20014, or any other provision of law, the department may make the information available to a person who has done both of the following:

(1) Established a commercial requester account under Section 1810.2.

(2) Entered into an agreement described under subdivision (c).

(c) The department shall not provide information under this section unless the person requesting the information has entered into an agreement with the department that includes the following stipulations:

(1) The information provided may not be used for the purpose of identifying or contacting any person or for any other purpose, except as specified in paragraph (2).

(2) The information may be used only to identify a vehicle that has been reported to be in a traffic accident.

(3) The law enforcement agency accident report number and license plate number provided under this section shall be used only for the internal verification purposes of the business that receives the information and may not be disclosed to any party other than the department or the Department of the California Highway Patrol.

(4) The requester agrees to investigate and promptly correct any error that is brought to its attention.

(d) Use of the information provided under this section in violation of paragraph (1), (2), or (3) of subdivision (c) is a violation of Sections 1808.45 and 1808.46.
(Added by Stats. 2004, Ch. 336, Sec. 1. Effective August 30, 2004.)

1810.5. The Attorney General, district attorneys, law enforcement agencies, city attorneys and city prosecutors prosecuting misdemeanor actions under Section 41803.5 or 72193 of the Government Code, public defenders, and public defender investigators shall have access, including, but not limited to, telephone access, to the records of the department. For purposes of obtaining a governmental entity requester code from the department, the office of a city attorney or city prosecutor engaged in the prosecution of criminal actions shall be deemed a law enforcement entity.
(Amended by Stats. 2017, Ch. 299, Sec. 6. (AB 1418) Effective January 1, 2018.)

1810.7. (a) Except as provided in Sections 1806.5, 1808.2, 1808.4, 1808.5, 1808.6, 1808.7, and 1808.21, the department may authorize, by special permit, any person to access the department's electronic database, as provided for in this section, for the purpose of obtaining information for commercial use.

(b) The department may limit the number of permits issued under this section, and may restrict, or establish priority for, access to its files as the department deems necessary to avoid disruption of its normal operations, or as the department deems is in the best interest of the public.

(c) The department may establish minimum volume levels, audit and security standards, and technological requirements, or any terms and conditions it deems necessary for the permits.

(d) As a condition of issuing a permit under this section, the department shall require each direct-access permittee to file a performance bond or other financial security acceptable to the department, in an amount the department deems appropriate.

(e) The department shall charge fees for direct-access service permits, and shall charge fees pursuant to Section 1810 for any information copied from the files.

(f) The department shall ensure that information provided under this section includes only the public portions of records.

(g) On and after January 1, 1992, the director shall report every three years to the Legislature on the implementation of this section. The report shall include the number and location of direct-access permittees, the volume and nature of direct-access inquiries, procedures the department has taken to ensure the security of its files, and the costs and revenues associated with the project.

(h) The department shall establish procedures to ensure confidentiality of any records of residence addresses and mailing addresses as required by Sections 1808.21, 1808.22, 1808.45, 1808.46, and 1810.2.
(Amended by Stats. 2003, Ch. 594, Sec. 16. Effective January 1, 2004.)

1811. The department may sell copies of all or any part of its records at a charge sufficient to pay at least the entire actual cost to the department of the copies, the charge for the records and the conditions under which they may be sold to be determined by the director.
(Amended by Stats. 1961, Ch. 216.)

1812. The department shall not charge for copies of records or for information from its records given to any county, city, any transit operator as defined in Section 99210 of the Public Utilities Code, state department, or the United States government.
(Amended by Stats. 1987, Ch. 726, Sec. 4. Operative July 1, 1988, by Sec. 11 of Ch. 726.)

1813. The director and such officers of the department as he may designate may, upon request, prepare under the seal of the department and deliver without charge a certified copy of any record of the department received or maintained under this code.
(Enacted by Stats. 1959, Ch. 3.)

1814. Any person engaged in the business of examining the records of the department and supplying information relative thereto to the public for compensation shall first obtain a permit from the director. The director shall grant such a permit when he determines that the applicant is qualified and intends in good faith to carry on such business, and when the applicant files with the director a bond in the amount of five thousand dollars ($5,000).
(Enacted by Stats. 1959, Ch. 3.)

1815. The bond shall be to the satisfaction of the director and shall obligate the principal and sureties to compensate the officers of the department and any other person who may suffer loss or damage by reason of any failure or neglect of the principal, the principal's agents, or employees to preserve carefully and surrender any records examined in the department and by reason of any act of the principal, the principal's agents, or employees in respect to the loss, alteration, substitution, or mutilation of any records of the department.

(Amended by Stats. 1982, Ch. 517, Sec. 386.)

1816. Every judge of the juvenile court, juvenile hearing officer, duly constituted referee of a juvenile court, or other person responsible for the disposition of cases involving traffic offenses required to be reported under Section 1803 committed by persons under 18 years of age shall keep a full record of every case in which a person is charged with such a violation, and shall report the offense to the department at its office in Sacramento not more than 30 days after the date on which it was committed, and in no case less than 10 days after adjudication. The report required by this section shall be required for any determination that a minor committed the violation, including any determination that because of the act the minor is a person described in Section 601 or 602 of the Welfare and Institutions Code or that a program of supervision should be instituted for the minor. No report shall be made if it is found that the alleged offense was not committed.

The report required by this section shall be made upon a form furnished by the department and shall contain all necessary information as to the identity of the offender, the arresting agency, the date and nature of the offense, and the date the finding was made.

(Amended by Stats. 2003, Ch. 149, Sec. 80. Effective January 1, 2004.)

1817. Written allegations received by the department from members of the public identifying motor vehicles or other vehicles by license number from which any flaming or glowing substance has been thrown, or discharged, shall be forwarded to the Department of Forestry and Fire Protection together with any information as to the identity of the registered owner of the vehicle as shown by the records of the department.

(Amended by Stats. 1992, Ch. 427, Sec. 165. Effective January 1, 1993.)

1818. Any record of, or information from any record concerning, an abstract of conviction kept by the department shall contain an appropriate notation indicating the commercial or noncommercial nature or the license plate number of the vehicle involved in the offense.

(Added by Stats. 1967, Ch. 683.)

1819. All records of the department containing information as to the actual mileage of motor vehicles submitted as required by subdivision (b) of Section 4456 and Sections 5900 and 5901 shall be open to inspection by the public during the office hours of the department.

(Amended by Stats. 1994, Ch. 180, Sec. 4. Effective July 11, 1994.)

1821. (a) The department shall establish and maintain a data and monitoring system to evaluate the efficacy of intervention programs for persons convicted of violations of Section 23152 or 23153.

(b) The system may include a recidivism tracking system. The recidivism tracking system may include, but not be limited to, jail sentencing, license restriction, license suspension, level I (first offender) and II (multiple offender) alcohol and drug education and treatment program assignment, alcohol and drug education treatment program readmission and dropout rates, adjudicating court, length of jail term, actual jail or alternative sentence served, type of treatment program assigned, actual program compliance status, subsequent crashes related to driving under the influence of alcohol or drugs, and subsequent convictions of violations of Section 23152 or 23153.

(c) The systems described in subdivisions (a) and (b) shall include an evaluation of the efficacy of the increased level of intervention resulting from the act that added this subdivision.

(d) The department shall submit an annual report of its evaluations to the Legislature. The evaluations shall include a ranking of the relative efficacy of criminal penalties, other sanctions, and intervention programs and the various combinations thereof, including, but not limited to, those described in subdivision (c).

(Amended by Stats. 2022, Ch. 81, Sec. 2. (AB 2198) Effective January 1, 2023.)

1822. The Legislature finds that driving under the influence of alcohol or drugs continues to be a primary safety issue on the state's highways, and the major cause of traffic deaths. It is imperative that violators who drive while under the influence of alcohol or drugs be fully prosecuted under the law. The Legislature also finds that too often violators have not had their driving records at the Department of Motor Vehicles appropriately updated. Therefore, it is the intent of the Legislature that the department, working with the courts, establish and maintain a data and monitoring system to track violations of driving under the influence of alcohol or drugs, including, but not limited to, violations of Article 1.3 (commencing with Section 23136), Article 1.5 (commencing with Section 23140), and Article 2 (commencing with Section 23152), of Chapter 12 of Division 11. The system shall match arrests for driving under the influence of alcohol or drug violations with convictions reported to the department.

(Added by Stats. 1996, Ch. 224, Sec. 1. Effective January 1, 1997.)

1825. (a) The department shall conduct a quarterly random audit of applications submitted and processed pursuant to Section 5007 or 22511.55 or subdivision (b) or (c) of Section 22511.59 to verify the authenticity of the certificates and information submitted in support of those applications. The department shall seek the cooperation of the Medical Board of California or the appropriate regulatory boards in conducting the audits.

(b) The audit provisions of subdivision (a) only apply to those applications that were initially submitted to the department after January 1, 2001.

(Amended by Stats. 2017, Ch. 485, Sec. 1. (SB 611) Effective January 1, 2018.)

Chapter 2. Department of the California Highway Patrol

(Chapter 2 enacted by Stats. 1959, Ch. 3.)

Article 1. Administration

(Article 1 enacted by Stats. 1959, Ch. 3.)

2100. There is in the Transportation Agency the Department of the California Highway Patrol.

(Amended by Stats. 2013, Ch. 352, Sec. 520. (AB 1317) Effective September 26, 2013. Operative July 1, 2013, by Sec. 543 of Ch. 352.)

2101. As used in this chapter, "department" means the Department of the California Highway Patrol.

(Amended by Stats. 1959, Ch. 1996.)

2102. Wherever in any statute "California Highway Patrol" is used, it means the Department of the California Highway Patrol.

(Enacted by Stats. 1959, Ch. 3.)

2103. The department is the successor to and is vested with the duties, powers, purposes, responsibilities, and jurisdiction of the former Division of Enforcement of the Department of Motor Vehicles, known as the California Highway Patrol, and of the officers and employees thereof.

(Enacted by Stats. 1959, Ch. 3.)

2104. The department has possession and control of all records, books, papers, offices, or equipment, and all other property, real or personal, now or hereafter held for the benefit or use of the former Division of Enforcement of the Department of Motor Vehicles, known as the California Highway Patrol.

(Enacted by Stats. 1959, Ch. 3.)

2105. Except as in this chapter otherwise provided, the provisions of Chapter 2 (commencing at Section 11150) of Part 1 of Division 3 of Title 2 of the Government Code shall govern and apply to the conduct of the department in every respect the same as if the provisions were set forth in this code, and wherever in that chapter the term "head of the department" or similar designation occurs, for the purposes of this division, it shall mean the commissioner.

(Amended by Stats. 1959, Ch. 1996.)

2106. The department shall maintain its main office within 20 miles of Sacramento.

(Amended by Stats. 2007, Ch. 9, Sec. 1. Effective January 1, 2008.)

2107. The department is under the control of a civil executive officer,

known as the Commissioner of the California Highway Patrol. The commissioner shall be appointed by the Governor with the advice and consent of the Senate to serve at the pleasure of the Governor, and shall have resided within the state continuously for at least five years immediately preceding appointment.
(Amended by Stats. 2021, Ch. 133, Sec. 103. (SB 272) Effective July 23, 2021.)

2108. The commissioner shall perform all duties, exercise all powers and jurisdiction, assume and discharge all responsibilities, and carry out and effect all purposes vested by law in the department.

Notwithstanding any other provision of law, the commissioner may administratively determine the geographic area of residence of any member of the department in order to assure the availability of such member for emergency service and the discharge of departmental responsibilities.
(Amended by Stats. 1963, Ch. 1231.)

2109. The commissioner shall organize the department with the approval of the Governor and the Secretary of Transportation and may arrange and classify the work of the department and may, with the approval of the Governor and the Secretary of Transportation, create or abolish divisions thereof.
(Amended by Stats. 2013, Ch. 352, Sec. 521. (AB 1317) Effective September 26, 2013. Operative July 1, 2013, by Sec. 543 of Ch. 352.)

2110. The Assistant Commissioner of the California Highway Patrol shall be appointed by the commissioner, subject to the approval of the Governor, pursuant to the provisions of Article XXIV of the State Constitution.
(Amended by Stats. 1984, Ch. 268, Sec. 32.4. Effective June 30, 1984.)

2111. The assistant commissioner shall carry out and execute such duties, with respect to traffic law enforcement, as may be specified by the commissioner.
(Enacted by Stats. 1959, Ch. 3.)

2112. The chief administrative officer of the department shall be appointed by the commissioner subject to the approval of the Governor, pursuant to the provisions of Article XXIV of the State Constitution.
(Amended by Stats. 1984, Ch. 268, Sec. 32.5. Effective June 30, 1984.)

2113. The chief administrative officer shall carry out and execute such duties with respect to the administrative affairs of the department as may be specified by the commissioner.
(Enacted by Stats. 1959, Ch. 3.)

2114. The department may pay membership fees, join, and participate in the affairs of associations having for their purpose the interchange of information relating to law enforcement, accident prevention, and subjects related to the powers and duties of the department.
(Enacted by Stats. 1959, Ch. 3.)

Article 2. The California Highway Patrol

(Article 2 enacted by Stats. 1959, Ch. 3.)

2250. The California Highway Patrol in the Department of the California Highway Patrol consists of the following members: the commissioner, the deputy commissioner, assistant commissioners, chiefs, assistant chiefs, captains, lieutenants, sergeants, and officers.
(Amended by Stats. 2005, Ch. 270, Sec. 9. Effective January 1, 2006.)

2250.1. (a) The commissioner shall establish special designations of peace officers within the Department of the California Highway Patrol to assist in the transfer of responsibilities from the California State Police Division to the Department of the California Highway Patrol. The peace officers so designated include all peace officers of the former California State Police Division on July 11, 1995. These specially designated peace officers are peace officers as defined in subdivision (a) of Section 830.2 of the Penal Code.

(b) Peace officers designated in subdivision (a) shall become members of the Department of the California Highway Patrol, as described in Section 2250, by meeting the training requirements and qualifications for those positions as established pursuant to Section 19818.6 of the Government Code or with the approval of the State Personnel Board Executive Officer.

(c) Individuals granted reemployment or reinstatement on or after July 12, 1995, to peace officer positions formerly within the California State Police Division shall be reinstated to the peace officer designations established by the commissioner pursuant to this section.
(Added by Stats. 1996, Ch. 305, Sec. 65. Effective January 1, 1997.)

2251. All promotions to the classes of deputy chief, assistant chief, captain, lieutenant, and sergeant shall be made from promotional eligible lists resulting from promotional examination of persons in the next lower class.
(Amended by Stats. 1977, Ch. 615.)

2252. Such specialized positions as shall be designated by the commissioner with the approval of the Personnel Board shall be filled pursuant to open competitive examinations held pursuant to law.
(Enacted by Stats. 1959, Ch. 3.)

2253. For the purpose of determining the scope of employment of any member of the California Highway Patrol under the workers' compensation laws, any such member shall be deemed to be on duty and acting within the scope of the person's employment when actually exercising any of the powers or performing any of the duties imposed or authorized by law at any time during the 24 hours of the day.
(Amended by Stats. 1974, Ch. 1454.)

2254. In the event any dispute arises between the department and any of its members in an industrial disability case, such member or his attorney, upon demand, shall be entitled to examine any record of the department or of the State Compensation Insurance Fund which has any bearing on said case.
(Enacted by Stats. 1959, Ch. 3.)

2255. No member of the California Highway Patrol, appointed to serve in any county, shall be assigned by the commissioner for service outside the county for a longer period than one week, except:

(a) Pursuant to a request by the employee for a transfer.

(b) As may be necessitated by temporary traffic emergencies requiring an increase in the number of patrol members in one locality or seasonal changes making expedient a decrease in the number of patrol members in one locality, but in such latter events no assignment shall be made for disciplinary purposes.

An assignment under this section shall be made by the commissioner.
(Enacted by Stats. 1959, Ch. 3.)

2256. Notwithstanding Section 18932 of the Government Code, the minimum age limit for appointment to the position of entry level peace officer of the Department of the California Highway Patrol, shall be 21 years, and the maximum age limit for examination shall be 35 years.
(Amended by Stats. 2001, Ch. 162, Sec. 1. Effective January 1, 2002.)

2257. The commissioner shall issue to each member of the California Highway Patrol a badge of authority with the seal of the State of California in the center thereof, the words "California Highway Patrol" encircling the seal and below the designation of the position held by each member to whom issued.
(Enacted by Stats. 1959, Ch. 3.)

2258. Neither the commissioner nor any other person shall issue a badge to any person who is not a duly appointed member of the California Highway Patrol.
(Enacted by Stats. 1959, Ch. 3.)

2259. The Department of the California Highway Patrol shall pay to the member, or his estate, the cost of repairing the uniforms and equipment of the member of the California Highway Patrol which are damaged in the line of duty. If the uniforms or equipment are damaged beyond repair, the department shall pay an amount equal to the actual value thereof at the time the damage occurred, which shall be determined by the commissioner.

The term "equipment," as used in this section, shall include equipment required by the department or personal accoutrements necessary for the patrol member to perform his duty.

(Amended by Stats. 1961, Ch. 1473.)

2259.5. The commissioner shall make certified bulletproof vests available to members of the California Highway Patrol while engaged in enforcement activities. The commissioner may make the equipment available to the remainder of the personnel of the California Highway Patrol. The equipment shall remain the property of the Department of the California Highway Patrol and shall be returned upon request of the commissioner. This section shall not be construed to require that the commissioner provide one certified bulletproof vest for each member of the California Highway Patrol. It is the intent of this section that a sufficient number of vests be available for the use of members of the California Highway Patrol while engaged in enforcement activities. The vests may be passed from one shift to another in the interests of economy.

(Amended by Stats. 2021, Ch. 133, Sec. 104. (SB 272) Effective July 23, 2021.)

2260. The commissioner may advance the cost of, or obtain and furnish, one complete uniform, including such items of clothing and equipment as may be required by the commissioner, to each new member of the California Highway Patrol hereafter employed. The cost to the commissioner shall be deducted from the salary of such member in installments within the first year after he has completed the training school.

(Enacted by Stats. 1959, Ch. 3.)

2261. A uniform substantially similar to the official uniform of members of the California Highway Patrol shall not be worn by any other law enforcement officer or by any other person except duly appointed members of the California Highway Patrol and persons authorized by the commissioner to wear such uniform in connection with a program of entertainment. A uniform shall be deemed substantially similar to the uniform of the California Highway Patrol if it so resembles such official uniform as to cause an ordinary reasonable person to believe that the person wearing the uniform is a member of the California Highway Patrol.

(Amended by Stats. 1968, Ch. 1192.)

2262. The commissioner shall establish a school for the training and education of the members of the California Highway Patrol, and for other employees of the department deemed necessary, in traffic regulation, in the performance of their duties, and in the proper enforcement of this code and laws respecting use of the highways. The commissioner may contract with any county, city, district, or other subdivision of the state for the use of school facilities in the training of enforcement officers.

(Amended by Stats. 2021, Ch. 133, Sec. 105. (SB 272) Effective July 23, 2021.)

2263. Shooting practice and instruction in the use of firearms shall constitute part of the training to be given to members of the California Highway Patrol. Firearm training may be given in connection with the school or otherwise and may include participation by patrol members in shooting competition.

(Enacted by Stats. 1959, Ch. 3.)

2264. The commissioner may procure and issue appropriate badges to patrol members for excellence in marksmanship.

(Enacted by Stats. 1959, Ch. 3.)

2265. The Department of the California Highway Patrol shall not assess against any member of the department the cost of replacing any article of uniform clothing or accessories which employees are required to wear when the replacement is necessary as a result of a change in uniform regulations by the department after the effective date of this section.

(Added by Stats. 1959, Ch. 1704.)

2266. (a) The Legislature finds and declares all of the following:

(1) The public safety dispatchers and public safety operators of the Department of the California Highway Patrol are among the lowest paid when compared to operators employed by other law enforcement agencies in the state. The department's communication centers suffer from significant staff shortages and high turnover rates. Increasing the wages paid to these public safety dispatchers and public safety operators will increase their professionalism while reducing their rate of turnover.

(2) The recruitment and retention problem is especially evident in the classifications of Public Safety Dispatcher and Public Safety Operator.

(3) In order for the state to recruit and retain the highest qualified and capable public safety dispatchers and public safety operators, those employees should be compensated in an amount equal to the estimated average total compensation for the classifications corresponding to Public Safety Dispatcher and Public Safety Operator within the police departments in the Cities of Los Angeles, Oakland, San Diego, and San Jose and the City and County of San Francisco.

(4) This section is not in violation of the Ralph C. Dills Act (Chapter 10.3 (commencing with Section 3512) of Division 4 of Title 1 of the Government Code), which requires that changes for salaries and benefits be collectively bargained between representatives of the state and the employee's union. This section does not circumvent that process. This section simply authorizes the Department of Human Resources, when determining compensation for public safety dispatchers and public safety operators in the Department of the California Highway Patrol, to consider the total compensation for public safety dispatchers and public safety operators in other jurisdictions.

(b) When determining compensation for public safety dispatchers and public safety operators in the Department of the California Highway Patrol, the Department of Human Resources may consider the total compensation for public safety dispatchers and public safety operators in comparable positions in the police departments specified in paragraph (3) of subdivision (a).

(Amended by Stats. 2014, Ch. 66, Sec. 1. (SB 1025) Effective January 1, 2015.)

2268. (a) Any member of the Department of the California Highway Patrol, as specified in Sections 2250 and 2250.1, shall be capable of fulfilling the complete range of official duties administered by the commissioner pursuant to Section 2400 and other critical duties that may be necessary for the preservation of life and property. Members of the California Highway Patrol shall not be assigned to permanent limited duty positions which do not require the ability to perform these duties.

(b) Subdivision (a) does not apply to any member of the California Highway Patrol who, after sustaining serious job-related physical injuries, returned to duty with the California Highway Patrol and who received a written commitment from the appointing power allowing his or her continued employment as a member of the California Highway Patrol. This subdivision applies only to commitments made prior to January 1, 1984.

(c) Nothing in subdivision (a) entitles a member of the California Highway Patrol to, or precludes a member from receiving, an industrial disability retirement.

(Amended by Stats. 1996, Ch. 305, Sec. 66. Effective January 1, 1997.)

2269. (a) The commissioner shall provide, as safety equipment, boots to each member of the California Highway Patrol who is assigned to ride motorcycles. This safety equipment shall remain the property of the state. Items lost or damaged because of the negligence of the officer shall be replaced by the officer at his or her expense.

(b) The commissioner shall pay the cost of aviation boots to each member of the California Highway Patrol who is assigned to aircraft operations and shall make aviation boots directly available for purchase by those members.

(Added by renumbering Section 2267 (as added by Stats. 1982, Ch. 23) by Stats. 1987, Ch. 56, Sec. 168.)

Article 3. Powers and Duties

(Article 3 enacted by Stats. 1959, Ch. 3.)

2400. (a) The commissioner shall administer Chapter 4 (commencing with Section 10850) of Division 4, Article 3 (commencing with Section 17300) of Chapter 1 of Division 9, Division 10 (commencing with Section 20000), Division 11 (commencing with Section 21000) except Chapter 11 (commencing with Section 22950), Division 12 (commencing with Section 24000), Division 13 (commencing with Section 29000), Division 14 (commencing with Section 31600), Division 14.1 (commencing with Section 32000), Division 14.5 (commencing with Section 33000), Division 14.7 (commencing with Section 34000), Division 14.8 (commencing with Section 34500), Division 15 (commencing with Section 35000), Division 16 (commencing with Section 36000) except Chapter 2 (commencing with Section 36100) and Chapter 3 (commencing with Section 36300), and Division 16.5 (commencing with Section 38000) except Chapter 2 (commencing with Section 38010).

(b) The commissioner shall enforce all laws regulating the operation of vehicles and the use of the highways except that, on ways or places to which Section 592 makes reference, the commissioner shall not be required to provide patrol or enforce any provisions of this code other than those provisions applicable to private property.

(c) The commissioner shall not be required to provide patrol for or enforce Division 16.5 (commencing with Section 38000).

(d) The commissioner shall have full responsibility and primary jurisdiction for the administration and enforcement of the laws, and for the investigation of traffic accidents, on all toll highways and state highways constructed as freeways, including transit-related facilities located on or along the rights-of-way of those toll highways or freeways, except facilities of the San Francisco Bay Area Rapid Transit District. However, city police officers while engaged primarily in general law enforcement duties may incidentally enforce state and local traffic laws and ordinances on toll highways and state freeways within incorporated areas of the state. In any city having either a population in excess of 2,000,000 or an area of more than 300 square miles, city police officers shall have full responsibility and primary jurisdiction for the administration and enforcement of those laws and ordinances, unless the city council of the city by resolution requests administration and enforcement of those laws by the commissioner.

(e) The commissioner shall have full responsibility and primary jurisdiction for the administration and enforcement of the laws, and for the investigation of traffic accidents, on all highways within a city and county with a population of less than 25,000, if, at the time the city and county government is established, the county contains no municipal corporations.

(f) The commissioner may enter into any interagency agreement with the State Board of Equalization for the purpose of enforcement of statutes requiring commercial vehicles from foreign jurisdictions to have a diesel fuel tax permit and to make payments to the board as required.

(g) The commissioner shall assume those duties and responsibilities of providing protection to state property and employees actually being performed by the California State Police Division on and before July 11, 1995.

(h) The commissioner may provide for the physical security of any current or former constitutional officer of the state and current or former legislator of the state.

(i) Upon request of the Chief Justice of the California Supreme Court, the commissioner may provide appropriate protective services to any current or former member of the State Court of Appeal or the California Supreme Court.

(j) The commissioner shall have full responsibility as the certifying official of the Annual State of California Size and Weight Certification for the enforcement of all state size and weight laws on the federal-aid interstate, primary urban, and secondary systems in accordance with Sections 657.13 and 657.15 of Title 23 of the Code of Federal Regulations.
(Amended by Stats. 2022, Ch. 295, Sec. 2. (AB 2956) Effective January 1, 2023.)

2400.6. The commissioner shall enforce all laws regulating the operation of vehicles on, and the use of any portion of, State Highway Route 1 in the City of Malibu, if requested by the city, and if a contract is entered into between the state and the city. The contract shall require that an amount be paid to the commissioner that is equal to the costs incurred by the department for services provided under the contract.
(Added by Stats. 1992, Ch. 394, Sec. 1. Effective January 1, 1993.)

2400.7. (a) The commissioner may enforce all laws regulating the operation of vehicles and on, and the use of, any portion of any expressway in the County of Santa Clara, if requested by a city or the county with respect to the portion of the highway within that city or county and if a contract is entered into between the state and that city or the county or any combination thereof.

(b) The contract shall require affected cities or the County of Santa Clara, or both, as the case may be, to pay to the commissioner, for deposit in the Motor Vehicle Account in the State Transportation Fund, an amount that is equal to the costs incurred by the department for services provided under the contract.
(Added by Stats. 1997, Ch. 467, Sec. 2. Effective September 25, 1997.)

2401. The commissioner shall make adequate provision for patrol of the highways at all times of the day and night.
(Enacted by Stats. 1959, Ch. 3.)

2401.1. The commissioner may enforce those provisions relating to the transportation of hazardous waste found in Article 6 (commencing with Section 25160), Article 6.5 (commencing with Section 25167.1), and Article 8 (commencing with Section 25180), of Chapter 6.5 of Division 20 of the Health and Safety Code, pursuant to subdivision (d) of Section 25180 of the Health and Safety Code and the provisions relating to the transportation of medical waste found in Chapter 6 (commencing with Section 118000) of, and Chapter 10 (commencing with Section 118325) of, Part 14 of Division 104 of the Health and Safety Code.
(Amended by Stats. 1996, Ch. 1023, Sec. 423. Effective September 29, 1996.)

2402. The commissioner may make and enforce such rules and regulations as may be necessary to carry out the duties of the department. Rules and regulations shall be adopted, amended, or repealed in accordance with the Administrative Procedure Act, commencing with Section 11370 of the Government Code.
(Amended by Stats. 1965, Ch. 1500.)

2402.6. (a) The commissioner may adopt and enforce regulations and standards with respect to fuel containers and fuel systems on vehicles using compressed or liquefied natural gas and liquefied petroleum gas used in conjunction with a propulsion system certified by the State Air Resources Board as producing as few or fewer emissions as a State Air Resources Board approved system using compressed or liquefied natural gas or liquefied petroleum gas and with respect to the operation of vehicles using any of those fuels to ensure the safety of the equipment and vehicles and of persons and property using the highways.

(b) The commissioner may also adopt and enforce regulations and standards with respect to fuel containers and fuel systems on vehicles using compressed or liquefied hydrogen gas or liquid fuels that generate hydrogen gas.

(c) All motor vehicles with compressed natural gas fuel systems used for propulsion shall comply either with the regulations adopted pursuant to subdivision (a) or with National Fire Protection Administration Standard NFPA 52, "Compressed Natural Gas (CNG) Vehicular Fuel Systems" in effect at the time of manufacture, until standards for those fuel systems have been incorporated into the Federal Motor Vehicle Safety Standards by the United States Department of Transportation. Whenever those Federal Motor Vehicle Safety Standards include requirements for gaseous fuel systems, all motor vehicles with gaseous fuel systems which are manufactured after the effective date of those requirements shall comply with those requirements.

(d) It is an infraction for any person to operate any motor vehicle in violation of any provision of a regulation adopted pursuant to this section.

(e) The operator of every facility for filling portable liquefied natural gas or liquefied petroleum gas containers having a capacity of four pounds or more but not more than 200 pounds of gas shall post in a conspicuous place the regulations applicable to that filling procedure.
(Amended by Stats. 2002, Ch. 610, Sec. 2. Effective January 1, 2003.)

2402.7. The commissioner shall adopt the definitions designated by the United States Department of Transportation under Title 49 (commencing with Section 1801) of the United States Code and Title

49 (commencing with Section 107) of the Code of Federal Regulations relating to hazardous materials, substances, or wastes, including, but not limited to, definitions relating to any radioactive material, poison, flammable gas, nonflammable gas, flammable liquid, oxidizer, flammable solid, corrosive material (liquid or solid), irritating materials, combustible liquids, explosives, blasting agents, etiologic agents, organic peroxides, hazardous wastes, and other regulated materials of classes A, B, C, D and E.

(Amended by Stats. 1981, Ch. 860, Sec. 3.)

2403. The commissioner may create highway patrol districts for the efficient administration and enforcement of this code and the laws respecting the use of highways. The commissioner may establish branch offices where necessary.

(Amended by Stats. 2021, Ch. 133, Sec. 106. (SB 272) Effective July 23, 2021.)

2403.5. The commissioner, or a designated representative, may enter into reciprocal operational agreements with authorized representatives of the Oregon State Police, the Nevada Department of Motor Vehicles and Public Safety, and the Arizona Department of Public Safety to promote expeditious and effective law enforcement service to the public, and assistance between the members of the California Highway Patrol and those agencies, in areas adjacent to the borders of this state and each of the adjoining states pursuant to Section 830.39 of the Penal Code. The reciprocal operational agreement shall be in writing and may cover the reciprocal exchange of law enforcement services, resources, facilities, and any other necessary and proper matters between the Department of the California Highway Patrol and the respective agency. Any agreement shall specify the involved departments, divisions, or units of the agencies, the duration and purpose of the agreement, the responsibility for damages, the method of financing any joint or cooperative undertaking, and the methods to be employed to terminate an agreement. The commissioner may establish operational procedures in implementation of any reciprocal operational agreement that are necessary to achieve the purposes of the agreement.

(Amended by Stats. 2014, Ch. 345, Sec. 11. (AB 2752) Effective January 1, 2015.)

2404. The commissioner shall establish, in counties having charters, except in counties of the first or second class, headquarters or substations for the efficient performance of the duties of the department, and may establish, in other localities deemed most suitable, headquarters or substations.

(Amended by Stats. 2021, Ch. 133, Sec. 107. (SB 272) Effective July 23, 2021.)

2404.5. The department shall obtain a vehicle suitable for registration and commercial safety inspections at border crossings into Mexico.

(Amended by Stats. 2016, Ch. 86, Sec. 299. (SB 1171) Effective January 1, 2017.)

2405. The commissioner may purchase or lease such real estate and erect such buildings as the department or any of its divisions require, subject to the approval of the Department of General Services.

(Amended by Stats. 1965, Ch. 371.)

2406. The commissioner may provide that any highway patrol vehicle shall be equipped with a stretcher and emergency first aid equipment for use in transporting injured persons.

(Enacted by Stats. 1959, Ch. 3.)

2407. The department shall prepare and on request supply to police departments, coroners, sheriffs, and other suitable agencies or individuals, forms for accident reports required under this code, which reports shall call for sufficiently detailed information to disclose with reference to a traffic accident the cause, conditions then existing, and the persons and vehicles involved.

(Enacted by Stats. 1959, Ch. 3.)

2408. The department shall tabulate and may analyze all accident reports and publish annually or at more frequent intervals statistical information based thereon as to the number and location of traffic accidents, as well as other information relating to traffic accident prevention. Based upon its findings after such analysis, the department may conduct further necessary detailed research to more fully determine the cause and control of highway accidents. It may further conduct experimental field tests within areas of the State to prove the practicability of various ideas advanced in traffic control and accident prevention.

(Enacted by Stats. 1959, Ch. 3.)

2409. All members of the California Highway Patrol have the powers of a peace officer as provided in Section 830.2 of the Penal Code.

(Amended by Stats. 1971, Ch. 938.)

2410. Members of the California Highway Patrol are authorized to direct traffic according to law, and, in the event of a fire or other emergency, or to expedite traffic or insure safety, may direct traffic as conditions may require notwithstanding the provisions of this code.

(Enacted by Stats. 1959, Ch. 3.)

2410.5. (a) The department may contract with a person or governmental entity that is conducting a special event which will impose extraordinary traffic control requirements at and near the site of the special event to provide supplemental patrol services to coordinate and direct traffic at and near the special event site. A contract entered into pursuant to this section shall include provisions for reimbursement to the department, and may include a requirement for the posting of a bond, for the cost of providing the supplemental patrol services, as determined by the commissioner.

(b) The patrol services, if any, provided under this section shall be rendered by officers of the department.

(c) Contract patrol services authorized under this section shall not reduce the normal and regular services of the department.

(d) Any contract fees received by the department pursuant to a contract under this section shall be deposited in the Motor Vehicle Account in the State Transportation Fund.

(Added by Stats. 1983, Ch. 54, Sec. 1. Effective May 27, 1983.)

2411. Members of the California Highway Patrol are authorized to serve all warrants relating to the enforcement of this code.

(Enacted by Stats. 1959, Ch. 3.)

2412. All members of the California Highway Patrol may investigate accidents resulting in personal injuries or death and gather evidence for the purpose of prosecuting the person or persons guilty of any violation of the law contributing to the happening of such accident.

(Enacted by Stats. 1959, Ch. 3.)

2413. (a) The Commissioner of the California Highway Patrol is designated as the Statewide Vehicle Theft Investigation and Apprehension Coordinator. The commissioner may establish vehicle theft prevention, investigation, and apprehension programs. The commissioner may assist local, state, and federal law enforcement agencies by coordinating multijurisdictional vehicle theft investigations and may establish programs to improve the ability of law enforcement to combat vehicle theft.

(b) The Department of the California Highway Patrol may retain license plate data captured by a license plate reader (LPR) for no more than 60 days, except in circumstances when the data is being used as evidence or for all felonies being investigated, including, but not limited to, auto theft, homicides, kidnaping, burglaries, elder and juvenile abductions, Amber Alerts, and Blue Alerts.

(c) The Department of the California Highway Patrol shall not sell LPR data for any purpose and shall not make the data available to an agency that is not a law enforcement agency or an individual who is not a law enforcement officer. The data may be used by a law enforcement agency only for purposes of locating vehicles or persons when either are reasonably suspected of being involved in the commission of a public offense.

(d) The Department of the California Highway Patrol shall monitor internal use of the LPR data to prevent unauthorized use.

(e) The Department of the California Highway Patrol shall, as a part of the annual automobile theft report submitted to the Legislature pursuant to subdivision (b) of Section 10901, report the LPR practices and usage, including the number of LPR data disclosures, a record of the agencies to which data was disclosed and for what purpose, and any changes in policy that affect privacy concerns.

(Amended by Stats. 2011, Ch. 38, Sec. 6. (AB 115) Effective June 30, 2011.)

2414. When lost, stolen, abandoned or otherwise unclaimed property, except vehicles subject to registration under this code, comes into possession of the department, the department may hold or store the same with some responsible person until it is claimed and all just and reasonable charges for saving and storage thereof have been paid.

(Enacted by Stats. 1959, Ch. 3.)

2415. (a) If the owner or other person entitled to the possession thereof fails to claim the property within six months and pay the charges, the department may sell it to the highest bidder at public auction at the place where the same may be held or stored, having first caused notice of sale to be given at least five days before the time fixed therefor, by publication once in a newspaper of general circulation published in the county where the sale is to be held.

(b) Any excess in the proceeds of the sale after paying such charges and expenses of sale including but not limited to the costs of advertising and a fee of not exceeding ten dollars ($10) to be charged by the department for making the sale shall be deposited in the State Treasury in the special deposit fund as money remaining unclaimed in the hands of the department.

(c) On payment of the price bid for the property sold, the delivery of the property with the commissioner's bill of sale vests title in the purchaser.

(d) In any case where there is no bid offered for the property, or if the highest bid offered does not exceed the charges for saving, holding, and storage and the expenses of sale, the same shall become the property of the department as compensation for expenses incurred.

(Enacted by Stats. 1959, Ch. 3.)

2416. (a) The Commissioner of the California Highway Patrol may issue authorized emergency vehicle permits only for the following vehicles, and then only upon a finding in each case that the vehicle is used in responding to emergency calls for fire or law enforcement, the immediate preservation of life or property, or the apprehension of law violators:

(1) Any vehicle maintained in whole or in part by the state, a city, a county, or a city and county, and privately owned and operated by a marshal, deputy marshal, or person who is a member of, receives salary from, and is regularly employed by, a police department or sheriff's department, if the state, a city, a county, or a city and county does not furnish to that person a publicly owned authorized emergency vehicle.

(2) Any vehicle owned and operated by a public utility, used primarily to accomplish emergency repairs to utility facilities or used primarily by railroad police officers, who are commissioned by the Governor, in the performance of their duties.

(3) Firefighting or rescue equipment designed and operated exclusively as such.

(4) Any vehicle operated by the chief, assistant chief, or one other uniformed person designated by the chief of a fire department organized as provided in the Health and Safety Code or the Government Code or a special act of the Legislature.

(5) Any vehicle of an air pollution control district used to enforce law relating to air pollution from motor vehicles.

(6) Any vehicle operated by the chief of a fire department established on any base of the Armed Forces of the United States.

(7) Any vehicle owned and operated by a fire company organized pursuant to Part 4 (commencing with Section 14825) of Division 12 of the Health and Safety Code.

(8) A privately owned ambulance licensed pursuant to Chapter 2.5 (commencing with Section 2500).

(9) Any vehicle other than a privately owned ambulance used by privately owned ambulance operators exclusively to transport medical supplies, lifesaving equipment, or personnel to the scene of an emergency when a request for medical supplies, lifesaving equipment, or personnel has been made by any person or public agency responsible for providing emergency medical transportation. The vehicle shall display a sign or lettering not less than two and one-half inches in height, in a color providing a sharp contrast to its background, on each side showing the name of the ambulance operator.

(10) Any vehicle owned and operated by an office or department of a city, county, city and county, or district that is designated by an ordinance adopted by the governing body of that local agency as a hazardous materials response team vehicle for response to hazardous materials emergencies.

(11) Any vehicle owned by a county, city, or city and county office of emergency services only while that vehicle is being used by a public employee who is employed by the office in responding to any disaster, including, but not limited to, a fire, flood, earthquake, tsunami, or hazardous materials spill.

(b) The commissioner may adopt and enforce regulations to implement this section.

(c) Violation of any regulation adopted by the commissioner pursuant to this section is a misdemeanor.

(Amended by Stats. 2025, Ch. 152, Sec. 1. (AB 438) Effective January 1, 2026.)

2417. (a) The commissioner may suspend or revoke any permit issued for an authorized emergency vehicle under the following conditions:

(1) The vehicle is operated in violation of any of the provisions of this code.

(2) The vehicle is operated in violation of the rules and regulations relating to authorized emergency vehicles as promulgated by the commissioner.

(3) The vehicle is not equipped as required by this code.

(b) The permittee of any authorized emergency vehicle whose permit has been suspended or revoked shall be entitled, upon request, to a hearing in accordance with Chapter 5 (commencing with Section 11500) of Part 1 of Division 3 of Title 2 of the Government Code.

(c) When any authorized emergency vehicle permit has been suspended or revoked under provisions of this section, any additional authorized emergency vehicle permit issued in the name of the permittee may be likewise suspended or revoked.

(Amended by Stats. 1978, Ch. 272.)

2418. The department shall adopt reasonable rules and regulations to ensure that all foreign commercial vehicles entering into, and operating within, this state meet those standards already in effect for other commercial vehicles and shall address, but not be limited to, the following concerns:

(a) Vehicle maintenance.

(b) Maximum hours of service for drivers.

(c) Insurance.

(d) Enforcement of criminal, civil, and administrative actions, including, but not limited to, impoundment of vehicles for second or subsequent violations of rules and regulations adopted under this section.

(Added by Stats. 1998, Ch. 727, Sec. 3. Effective January 1, 1999. Pursuant to Sec. 5 of Ch. 727, this addition became operative only if funding was provided in the 1998 Budget Act.)

2418.1. For purposes of enforcing the provisions of Section 2418, the department and the State Air Resources Board shall, to the maximum extent possible, conduct vehicle safety and emissions inspections at the California-Mexican border crossings. Inspections shall be conducted at the Otay Mesa and Calexico commercial vehicle inspection facilities operated by the department and at other random roadside locations as determined by the department, in consultation with the board. Inspections for safety and emissions shall be consistent with the inspection procedures specified in Title 13 (commencing with Section 2175) of the California Code of Regulations as they pertain to vehicle inspections.

(Added by Stats. 1998, Ch. 727, Sec. 4. Effective January 1, 1999. Pursuant to Sec. 5 of Ch. 727, this addition became operative only if funding was provided in the 1998 Budget Act.)

2418.5. (a) Notwithstanding any other provision of law, every emergency ambulance that is operated within this state by any public or private agency, including, but not limited to, any emergency ambulance that is operated by the State of California, any charter or general law city or county, or any district, shall be equipped at all times with a resuscitator.

(b) For purposes of this section "emergency ambulance" means a vehicle that is designed or intended to be used in providing emergency transportation of wounded, injured, sick, disabled, or incapacitated human beings.

(c) For the purposes of this section, a "resuscitator" means a device that adequately, effectively and safely restores breathing, including, but not limited to, a portable hand-operated, self-refilling bag-valve mask unit for inflation of the lungs with either air or oxygen. The resuscitator shall not have any straps that could be used to attach the resuscitator to the human head.

(Amended by Stats. 2004, Ch. 404, Sec. 6. Effective January 1, 2005.)

2419. (a) Any member of the California Highway Patrol may give flares to any person as replacement for flares used by such person to warn traffic of an accident or other hazardous condition on a highway, provided such person was not required by law to give such warning, or was not involved in the accident or the creation of the hazardous condition. The officer shall not replace such flares unless he is reasonably satisfied that such person in fact placed the flares for which replacement is requested.

(b) Notwithstanding any other provision of law, the person requesting replacement of flares shall not be required to file any claim for such flares.

(Amended by Stats. 1969, Ch. 167.)

2420. Upon request of the California Highway Patrol, manufacturers of motorcycles shall furnish a certification of gross brake horsepower to the department. If any manufacturer of motorcycles fails to comply with such request within 30 days from the date such request has been deposited in the mail, then and in that event no dealer shall sell or offer for sale the particular make and model of motocycle for which the certification was requested.

(Added by Stats. 1963, Ch. 422.)

2420.5. (a) The department may enter into a contract to conduct an inspection of vehicles that are subject to Section 500.100 of Title 29 of the Code of Federal Regulations and issue the vehicle inspection sticker authorized under subdivision (b) of that section to qualified vehicles.

(b) Any contract entered into under subdivision (a) shall provide that the amount to be paid to the department shall be equal to the costs incurred by the department for services provided under the contract.

(Added by Stats. 1998, Ch. 877, Sec. 36. Effective January 1, 1999.)

2421. Notwithstanding Section 11032 of the Government Code, the commissioner may approve the out-of-state travel within the United States of members of the California Highway Patrol, in numbers the commissioner deems appropriate, to attend out-of-state funerals of law enforcement officers or to attend out-of-state events related to the funerals of law enforcement officers, including the National Peace Officers Memorial. Reimbursement for actual and necessary traveling expenses shall be allowed for members of the California Highway Patrol approved to travel out of state pursuant to this section up to a maximum aggregate amount of forty thousand dollars ($40,000) in any fiscal year.

(Added by Stats. 1998, Ch. 220, Sec. 1. Effective January 1, 1999.)

2421.5. (a) When any Service Authority for Freeway Emergencies has imposed additional fees on vehicles pursuant to Section 2555 of the Streets and Highways Code, the authority may contract with the department or a private or public entity to handle calls originating from the authority's motorist aid call box system.

(b) (1) If the contract is with the department, its terms shall comply with the requirements specified in paragraph (2) for the system on the portions of the California Freeway and Expressway System and on county roads in rural, unincorporated areas of the county and on state highway routes that connect segments of these systems, if they are located within the county in which the authority is established and the Department of the California Highway Patrol has law enforcement responsibility over them.

(2) The contract shall contain guidelines, as jointly agreed to between the authority and the department, following consultation with the authority, for services to be provided, including, but not limited to, reporting requirements, immediate transfer of emergency calls and traffic management information to the department, computer interface capability with the department, performance standards, and coordination with the eligible tow service providers.

(c) If the contract is with a private or public entity, the authority shall ensure that the specifications in the "CHP/Cal Trans Call Box and Motorist Aid Guidelines" are met and coordinate with the department to determine which calls will be transferred to it for response. The authority shall reimburse the department for all costs incurred under this subdivision in accordance with the "CHP/Cal Trans Call Box and Motorist Aid Guidelines." If an authority has a contract with a private or public entity having a commencement date of July 1, 2003, or prior, the performance standards of those contracts shall remain in effect until modifications are made to the applicable sections of the statewide guidelines.

(d) The authority may contract with the Department of the California Highway Patrol to perform duties as mutually agreed by the parties.

(Amended by Stats. 2003, Ch. 374, Sec. 4. Effective January 1, 2004.)

2422. The department shall determine and implement the basic level of emergency medical dispatcher training for dispatchers employed by the department based on guidelines developed by the Emergency Medical Services Authority with the concurrence of the department. The commissioner may adopt a higher level of training for department dispatchers where appropriate.

(Amended by Stats. 2020, Ch. 70, Sec. 3. (AB 2038) Effective January 1, 2021.)

2423. In approving the additional instruction and training required under subdivision (b) of Section 680, the department shall consider the requirements of Chapter 3 (commencing with Section 40080) of Part 23.5 of the Education Code, as those provisions relate to instruction and training requirements for schoolbus drivers and school pupil activity bus drivers.

(Amended by Stats. 2006, Ch. 538, Sec. 654. Effective January 1, 2007.)

2424. (a) The Commissioner of the California Highway Patrol may enter into agreements with providers of towing, emergency road, and storage services for the purpose of determining which providers shall be summoned by the department when those services are necessary for public assistance or to carry out the duties and responsibilities of the department. Chapter 3.5 (commencing with Section 11340) of Part 1 of Division 3 of Title 2 of the Government Code shall not apply to the agreements. The department shall confer with the towing industry, as necessary, to reach agreements mutually beneficial to the public, the towing industry, and the department.

(b) This section does not prohibit a member of the public from selecting any vehicle towing, emergency road service, or storage provider, except when towing or storage is ordered by a member of the department under the provisions of law.

(c) These agreements shall be implemented in cooperation with representatives of the towing industry, and shall include, but not be limited to, the following subjects: liability insurance requirements, towing, emergency road service, and storage fees, inspection of business and storage facilities and equipment, recordkeeping, minimum equipment requirements, and the establishment of tow districts.

(d) Failure of a towing, emergency road service, or storage provider to comply with the provisions of the agreement may result in the suspension or termination of the agreement. In the event of suspension or termination of the agreement, and at the request of the towing, emergency road service, or storage provider, the department shall provide a hearing and appeal process to the provider.

(e) Chapter 5 (commencing with Section 11500) of Part 1 of Division 3 of Title 2 of the Government Code does not apply to the hearing and appeal process specified in subdivision (d).

(Amended by Stats. 1991, Ch. 488, Sec. 2.)

2426. The department shall prepare a one-page information sheet describing its Designated Driver Program. The sheet shall include information concerning the person or entity an alcoholic beverage licensee may contact for assistance in establishing a Designated Driver Program.
(Added by Stats. 1990, Ch. 1337, Sec. 3.)

2427. Whenever the department submits the fingerprints of an applicant for a license or certificate to the Department of Justice, and is required to pay a fee pursuant to subdivision (e) of Section 11105 of the Penal Code, the department, without the necessity of adopting regulations, shall charge the applicant a fee sufficient to reimburse the department for that fee.
(Added by Stats. 1990, Ch. 1360, Sec. 4.)

2428. (a) The Department of the California Highway Patrol may fix the cost or pro rata share, or, in its discretion, an amount it considers equivalent to the cost or pro rata share, and collect from each state agency in advance or upon any other basis that it may determine the cost of providing protective services for state employees and property.

(b) Payments for services provided shall be made by direct transfer as described in Section 11255 of the Government Code. All money received by the department pursuant to this section shall be deposited in the Protective Services Fund, which is hereby created. When appropriated by the Legislature, funds in the Protective Services Fund shall be used by the department to fulfill those responsibilities set forth in subdivisions (g), (h), and (i) of Section 2400.

(c) If a state agency refuses to pay the charges fixed by the Department of the California Highway Patrol for security services rendered, the department may file a claim for those charges against any appropriations made for the support or maintenance of all or any part of the work and affairs of the state agency. The Controller shall draw his or her warrant in accordance with law upon the claim in favor of the Department of the California Highway Patrol.
(Added by Stats. 1996, Ch. 305, Sec. 68. Effective January 1, 1997.)

2429. The department shall develop an "800" telephone number system to facilitate public reporting of violations of Article 2 (commencing with Section 31400) of Chapter 5 of Division 13. The department shall include in the department's "El Protector Program" public outreach activities that publicize the "800" telephone number system.
(Added by Stats. 1999, Ch. 557, Sec. 1. Effective September 29, 1999.)

2429.3. (a) The commissioner shall appoint a committee of 12 members to develop a public awareness and outreach campaign to educate manufacturers, sellers, and owners of house cars, as described in subdivision (b) of Section 12804.10, regarding locations where those vehicles may be legally operated within the state. The committee shall consist of the commissioner, two members representing owners or operators of house cars, and one representative from each of the following:

(1) The Department of Transportation.

(2) The Department of Motor Vehicles.

(3) The Recreational Vehicle Industry Association.

(4) The California Recreational Vehicle Dealers Association.

(5) The National Recreational Vehicle Dealers Association.

(6) The Family Motor Coach Association.

(7) The Good Sam Club.

(8) The recreational vehicle manufacturing industry.

(9) The California Travel Parks Association.

(b) The committee shall develop a driver education safety video for operators of house cars. The video, as well as a map of the approved highways on which those vehicles may operate, shall be made available to dealers of house cars. The committee shall encourage dealers to make copies of the video and map available to purchasers of those vehicles. The video shall be produced at no cost to the state.

(c) Committee members shall serve at the pleasure of the commissioner and without compensation.
(Added by Stats. 2001, Ch. 658, Sec. 1. Effective October 10, 2001.)

2429.5. The department, in cooperation with county and local farm bureaus, shall provide a program to educate growers and farmers and farm labor vehicle owners and drivers regarding farm labor vehicle certification requirements, including, but not limited to, certification requirements for farm labor vehicle drivers.
(Added by Stats. 1999, Ch. 556, Sec. 2. Effective September 29, 1999.)

2429.7. (a) The commissioner shall appoint an impaired driving task force to develop recommendations for best practices, protocols, proposed legislation, and other policies that will address the issue of impaired driving, including driving under the influence of cannabis and controlled substances. The task force shall also examine the use of technology, including field testing technologies and validated field sobriety tests, to identify drivers under the influence of prescription drugs, cannabis, and controlled substances. The task force shall include, but is not limited to, the commissioner, who shall serve as chairperson, and at least one member from each of the following:

(1) The Office of Traffic Safety.

(2) The National Highway Traffic Safety Administration.

(3) Local law enforcement.

(4) District attorneys.

(5) Public defenders.

(6) California Association of Crime Laboratory Directors.

(7) California Attorneys for Criminal Justice.

(8) The California Cannabis Research Program, known as the Center for Medicinal Cannabis Research, authorized pursuant to Section 11362.9 of the Health and Safety Code.

(9) An organization that represents medicinal cannabis patients.

(10) Licensed physicians with expertise in substance abuse disorder treatment.

(11) Researchers with expertise in identifying impairment caused by prescription medications and controlled substances.

(12) Nongovernmental organizations committed to social justice issues.

(13) A nongovernmental organization that focuses on improving roadway safety.

(b) The members of the task force shall serve at the pleasure of the commissioner and without compensation.

(c) The task force members shall be free of economic relationships with any company that profits from the sale of technologies or equipment that is intended to identify impairment. Members and their organizations shall not receive pay from, grants from, or any form of financial support from companies or entities that sell such technologies or equipment.

(d) The task force shall make recommendations regarding prevention of impaired driving, means of identifying impaired driving, and responses to impaired driving that reduce reoccurrence, including, but not limited to, evidence-based approaches that do not rely on incarceration.

(e) The task force shall make recommendations regarding how to best capture data to evaluate the impact that cannabis legalization is having on roadway safety.

(f) By January 1, 2021, the task force shall report to the Legislature its policy recommendations and the steps state agencies are taking regarding impaired driving. The report shall be submitted in compliance with Section 9795 of the Government Code.
(Added by Stats. 2017, Ch. 27, Sec. 173. (SB 94) Effective June 27, 2017.)

2429.9. (a) On or before January 1, 2027, the Department of the California Highway Patrol shall make the following available to city and county law enforcement agencies subject to this section:

(1) At no charge, training on enforcement of laws related to commercial vehicles, as defined in Section 260 of the California Vehicle Code, including, but not limited to, truck route enforcement.

(2) Course completion certificates for city and county law enforcement personnel who have completed the training described in paragraph (1).

(b) All jurisdictions that are required to update a circulation element or to adopt an ordinance pursuant to Section 65098.1 of the Government Code shall have at least one enforcement officer that has received a completion certificate pursuant to paragraph (2) of subdivision (a) by the date upon which that circulation element is updated or ordinance is adopted.

(c) Nothing in this section shall be construed to require the department to provide training for which it has not received funding or to require a jurisdiction to have an enforcement officer that has received a course completion certificate if the department has not made the training described in subdivision (a) available to law enforcement personnel at no charge.

(Added by Stats. 2025, Ch. 316, Sec. 16. (SB 415) Effective January 1, 2026.)

Article 3.3. Tow Truck Drivers

(Article 3.3 added by Stats. 1991, Ch. 488, Sec. 3.)

2430.1. As used in this article, each of the following terms has the following meaning:

(a) "Tow truck driver" means a person who operates a tow truck, who renders towing service or emergency road service to motorists while involved in freeway service patrol operations, pursuant to an agreement with a regional or local entity, and who has or will have direct and personal contact with the individuals being transported or assisted. As used in this subdivision, "towing service" has the same meaning as defined in Section 2436.

(b) "Employer" means a person or organization that employs those persons defined in subdivision (a), or who is an owner-operator who performs the activity specified in subdivision (a), and who is involved in freeway service patrol operations pursuant to an agreement or contract with a regional or local entity.

(c) "Regional or local entity" means a public organization established as a public transportation planning entity pursuant to Title 7.1 (commencing with Section 66500) of the Government Code or authorized to impose a transaction and use tax for transportation purposes by the Public Utilities Code or the service authority for freeway emergencies described in Section 2551 of the Streets and Highways Code.

(d) "Emergency road service" has the same meaning as defined in Section 2436.

(e) "Freeway service patrol" has the same meaning as defined in Section 2561 of the Streets and Highways Code.

(Amended by Stats. 2008, Ch. 179, Sec. 214. Effective January 1, 2009.)

2430.2. "Regional or local entity," as defined by subdivision (c) of Section 2430.1, also includes the transportation planning entity established pursuant to Section 130050.1 of the Public Utilities Code or the service authority for freeway emergencies described in Section 2551 of the Streets and Highways Code.

(Amended by Stats. 2003, Ch. 374, Sec. 6. Effective January 1, 2004.)

2430.3. (a) Every freeway service patrol tow truck driver and any California Highway Patrol rotation tow truck operator shall notify each of his or her employers and prospective employers and the Department of the California Highway Patrol of an arrest or conviction of any crime specified in paragraph (1), (2), (3), or (4) of subdivision (a) of Section 13377 prior to beginning the next workshift for that employer.

(b) For the purpose of conducting criminal history and driver history checks of any California Highway Patrol rotation tow truck operator, the commissioner may utilize the California Law Enforcement Telecommunications System (CLETS).

(Amended by Stats. 2001, Ch. 127, Sec. 5. Effective July 30, 2001.)

2430.5. (a) Every employer intending to hire a tow truck driver on or after July 1, 1992, shall require the applicant for employment to submit a temporary tow truck driver certificate issued by the department or a permanent tow truck driver certificate issued by the Department of Motor Vehicles. The employer shall review the certificate and obtain a copy to be maintained as required by subdivision (c). The employer shall not hire any tow truck driver in any freeway service patrol operations who does not provide a temporary tow truck driver certificate issued by the department or a permanent tow truck driver certificate issued by the Department of Motor Vehicles. The employer shall not allow a tow truck driver who is not certified to participate in any freeway service patrol operations. If the issuance date on the certificate is more than 90 days from the proposed date of hire, the employer shall contact the department to reverify eligibility.

(b) On or after July 1, 1992, every employer, whose currently employed tow truck drivers are required to obtain a tow truck driver certificate pursuant to Section 12520, shall require the employees to submit to the employer a temporary tow truck driver certificate issued by the department or a permanent tow truck driver certificate issued by the Department of Motor Vehicles. The employer shall review the certificate and obtain a copy to be maintained as required by subdivision (c).

(c) Every employer shall maintain a tow truck driver certificate file for all tow truck drivers hired on or after July 1, 1992, or all currently employed tow truck drivers who are required to obtain a tow truck driver certificate pursuant to Section 12520. The employer shall retain employee rosters and copies of tow truck driver certificates for all tow truck drivers. The roster shall be comprised of the following two lists:

(1) Drivers who have valid tow truck driver certificates.

(2) Drivers who would be prohibited, pursuant to subdivision (a) of Section 13377, from involvement in any freeway service patrol operation.

Every employer shall make available for inspection by the department at the employer's primary place of business in this state. In addition, the employer shall maintain a personnel roster, also available for inspection, of all current tow truck drivers and their date of hire by the employer.

(d) Upon notification that a tow truck driver has been arrested for, or convicted of, any crime specified in paragraph (1), (2), (3), or (4) of subdivision (a) of Section 13377, the employer shall remove that tow truck driver from any position involving freeway service patrol operations.

(e) A violation of this section by an employer is a misdemeanor.

(Amended by Stats. 1992, Ch. 1241, Sec. 8. Effective January 1, 1993.)

2431. (a) For the purposes of conducting criminal history and driver history screening of tow truck drivers and employers, the commissioner shall do all of the following:

(1) Obtain fingerprints from tow truck drivers and employers. The fingerprint cards will be submitted to the Department of Justice for criminal history checks.

(2) Obtain a second set of fingerprints from applicants who have not continuously resided in the state for the previous seven years, and submit that card to the Federal Bureau of Investigation for out-of-state criminal history checks. The department may charge a fee sufficient to cover the additional expense of processing the fingerprint cards through the Federal Bureau of Investigation.

(3) Verify that the tow truck driver or employer, or both, have a valid California driver's license, through the use of the automated records system.

(b) On and after July 1, 1992, all tow truck drivers shall submit an application for the issuance of a tow truck driver certificate with the department and pay an application fee equal to the actual costs of a criminal history check and issuance of the tow truck driver's certificate, but not more than fifty dollars ($50). Applicants for the renewal of an expired tow truck driver certificate or applicants for a duplicate tow truck driver certificate shall submit an application for issuance of a new tow truck driver certificate to the Department of Motor Vehicles and pay an application fee of twelve dollars ($12).

All fees collected pursuant to this section shall be deposited in the Motor Vehicle Account in the State Transportation Fund. An amount equal to the fees paid shall be made available, upon appropriation, to the Department of Motor Vehicles for its administrative costs, for the cost of criminal history checks to be conducted by the Department of Justice, and to the department for its administrative costs. In no case shall the fees collected exceed the costs of administering this section.

(c) Applicants for an original tow truck driver certificate shall be fingerprinted by the department, on a form issued by the department, for submission to the Department of Justice for the purpose of determining whether the applicant has been convicted for a violation of a crime specified in paragraph (1), (2), (3), or (4) of subdivision (a) of Section 13377.

(d) Information released to the department or the Department of Motor Vehicles shall be related to their inquiry and shall remain confidential.

(e) The department shall issue a temporary tow truck driver certificate, provided by the Department of Motor Vehicles, to applicants who have cleared the specified criminal history check pursuant to paragraph (1) of subdivision (a) and the driver history check through the automated records system, and who meet all other applicable provisions of this code. The term of the temporary tow truck driver's certificate shall be for a period of 90 days from the date of issuance.

(Amended by Stats. 2010, Ch. 280, Sec. 2. (SB 938) Effective January 1, 2011.)

2432. (a) It is unlawful for a freeway service patrol tow truck driver to knowingly provide false information on the application prepared and submitted to the department pursuant to subdivision (b) of Section 2431.

(b) It is unlawful for a California Highway Patrol rotation tow truck operator, including, but not limited to, a freeway service patrol tow truck driver, to fail to comply with the notification requirements in Section 2430.3.

(c) A violation of this section is punishable as a misdemeanor.

(Amended by Stats. 2001, Ch. 127, Sec. 6. Effective July 30, 2001.)

2432.1. (a) If the commissioner determines that an employer has failed to comply with the requirements of this article or Article 3.5 (commencing with Section 2435), the commissioner may, after a hearing, suspend the highway safety carrier's identification number issued pursuant to Section 2436.3 for a period not to exceed two years.

(b) If the commissioner determines that an employer has failed to comply with the requirements of this article or Article 3.5 (commencing with Section 2435) twice within a period of 24 consecutive months, the commissioner may, after a hearing, prohibit the employer from participating in any freeway service patrol operation for two years.

(c) Chapter 5 (commencing with Section 11500) of Part 1 of Division 3 of Title 2 of the Government Code does not apply to the hearing specified in subdivision (a) or (b).

(Added by Stats. 1991, Ch. 488, Sec. 3.)

2432.3. (a) This article does not preempt the authority of any city, city and county, or county to regulate, pursuant to subdivision (g) of Section 21100, any of the matters covered by this article.

(b) (1) For the purposes of verifying the criminal history of individuals involved in the operation of tow truck services, law enforcement agencies of any city, city and county, or county may conduct criminal history checks for all of the following:

(A) Applicants for employment to drive tow trucks.

(B) Those who drive tow trucks.

(C) Tow truck owners-operators.

(2) The law enforcement agency may obtain the fingerprints of the individuals on a form approved by the Department of Justice and provided by the agency. The fingerprint samples shall be submitted to the Department of Justice for the purpose of determining whether the individual has been convicted of any violation, including, but not limited to, Section 220, subdivision (1), (2), (3), or (4) of Section 261, or Section 264.1, 267, 288, or 289 of the Penal Code, or any felony or three misdemeanors as set forth in subparagraph (B) of paragraph (2) of subdivision (a) of Section 5164 of the Public Resources Code.

(3) For purposes of conducting criminal history screening of tow truck driver applicants, employees, and employers who have not resided continuously in the state for the previous seven years, the law enforcement agency of any city, city and county, or county, may obtain a second set of fingerprints, when necessary, and may submit that card to the Federal Bureau of Investigation for out-of-state criminal history checks.

(c) The law enforcement agency of any city, city and county, or county may charge a fee sufficient to cover the cost of obtaining and processing the fingerprint cards through the Department of Justice.

(d) For the purposes of conducting driver history screening of applicants to drive tow trucks, employees, and owners-operators, the law enforcement agency of any city, city and county, or county may verify that the applicant or owner-operator, as the case may be, has a valid California driver's license of the proper class, through the use of the automated records system.

(e) The Department of Justice shall develop a procedure whereby it will notify the requesting law enforcement agency if the person fingerprinted has been convicted of any of the specified crimes or is convicted of a specified crime subsequent to employment or beginning operation of a tow service. The Department of Justice shall release the requested information to the requesting agency.

(f) Information released to the requesting agency may be utilized for licensing and regulating procedures established pursuant to subdivision (g) of Section 21100.

(g) Information released to the requesting agency shall be related to its inquiry, shall remain confidential, and shall not be made public.

(Amended by Stats. 2004, Ch. 184, Sec. 5. Effective July 23, 2004.)

Article 3.5. Emergency Roadside Assistance

(Article 3.5 added by Stats. 1991, Ch. 488, Sec. 4.)

2435. (a) The Legislature finds and declares that the emergency roadside assistance provided by highway service organizations is a valuable service that benefits millions of California motorists. The Legislature further finds and declares that emergency roadside assistance is provided statewide, in cooperation with, and shares resources with, public safety agencies. The Legislature also finds that the Department of the California Highway Patrol, in cooperation with the Department of Transportation, is responsible for the rapid removal of impediments to traffic on highways within the state and that the Department of the California Highway Patrol may enter into agreements with employers for freeway service patrol operations under an agreement or contract with a regional or local entity. The Legislature declares that it is important to the public safety that drivers who provide emergency roadside service not have criminal records that include violent crimes against persons.

(b) The Legislature also declares that the Department of the California Highway Patrol, in cooperation with the Department of Transportation, shall be responsible for establishing the minimum training standards for highway service organization employees and employers who participate in freeway service patrol operations pursuant to an agreement or contract with a regional or local entity.

(Amended by Stats. 2003, Ch. 374, Sec. 7. Effective January 1, 2004.)

2436. For the purposes of this article, each of the following terms has the meaning given in this section:

(a) "Emergency road service" is the adjustment, repair, or replacement by a highway service organization of the equipment, tires, or mechanical parts of a motor vehicle so as to permit it to be operated under its own power. "Towing service" is the drafting or moving by a highway service organization of a motor vehicle from one place to another under power other than its own.

(b) "Emergency roadside assistance" means towing service or emergency road service.

(c) "Employer" has the same meaning as defined in Section 2430.1.

(d) "Freeway service patrol" has the same meaning as defined in Section 2561 of the Streets and Highways Code.

(e) "Highway service organization" means a motor club, as defined by Section 12142 of the Insurance Code and, in addition, includes any person or organization that operates or directs the operation of highway service vehicles to provide emergency roadside assistance to motorists, or any person or organization that is reimbursed or reimburses others for the cost of providing emergency roadside assistance, and any employer and includes any person or organization that directly or indirectly, with or without compensation, provides emergency roadside assistance.

(f) "Regional or local entity" has the same meaning as defined in Section 2430.1.

(g) "Tow truck driver" has the same meaning as defined in Section 2430.1.

(Amended by Stats. 2003, Ch. 374, Sec. 8. Effective January 1, 2004.)

2436.3. (a) On and after July 1, 1992, every employer shall obtain from the department a carrier identification number. Application for a carrier identification number shall be on forms furnished by the department. The number shall be displayed on both sides of each tow truck utilized in any freeway service patrol operation, in accordance with Section 27907.

(b) No employer shall operate a tow truck in any freeway service patrol operation if the carrier identification number issued pursuant to subdivision (a) has been suspended by the commissioner pursuant to Section 2432.1.

(c) The carrier identification number shall be removed before sale, transfer, or other disposal of the vehicle, or upon termination of an agreement or contract for freeway service patrol operations.

(d) A violation of this section is a misdemeanor.

(Added by Stats. 1991, Ch. 488, Sec. 4.)

2436.5. (a) The department, in cooperation with the Department of Transportation, shall provide training, pursuant to a reimbursable agreement or contract with a regional or local entity, for all employers and tow truck drivers who are involved in freeway service patrol operations pursuant to an agreement or contract with the regional or local entity. Dispatchers for freeway service patrol operations shall be employees of the department or the Department of Transportation.

(b) The training shall include, but not be limited to, all of the following:

(1) Tow truck driver and motorist safety.

(2) Patrol responsibility.

(3) Vehicle operation.

(4) Traffic control and scene management.

(5) Communication procedures.

(6) Demeanor and courtesy.

(Added by Stats. 1991, Ch. 488, Sec. 4.)

2436.7. (a) Every tow truck driver and employer, involved in a freeway service patrol operation under an agreement or contract with a regional or local entity, shall attend the training specified in subdivision (b) of Section 2436.5.

(b) Upon successful completion of the training, each trainee shall be issued a certificate of completion. The certificate shall state the name of the training organization, the name and signature of the trainer, the name of the trainee, and the date of completion of the training.

(c) The trainee shall provide a copy of the certificate of training to the employer. The employer shall maintain this information in the tow truck driver files established pursuant to subdivision (c) of Section 2430.5.

(d) Every employer shall make the file available for inspection by the department at the employer's primary place of business in this state.

(Added by Stats. 1991, Ch. 488, Sec. 4.)

Article 4. Highway Spill Containment and Abatement of Hazardous Substances

(Article 4 added by Stats. 1980, Ch. 922, Sec. 1.)

2450. This article shall be known and may be cited as the Hazardous Substances Highway Spill Containment and Abatement Act.

(Added by Stats. 1980, Ch. 922, Sec. 1.)

2451. The Legislature finds and declares that a statewide program for the management of hazardous substances highway spills, under the jurisdiction of the California Highway Patrol, is necessary to protect the public health and environment.

(Added by Stats. 1980, Ch. 922, Sec. 1.)

2452. "Hazardous substance" means any hazardous material defined in Section 353 and any toxic substance defined pursuant to Section 108145 of the Health and Safety Code.

(Amended by Stats. 1996, Ch. 1023, Sec. 424. Effective September 29, 1996.)

2453. The California Highway Patrol shall serve as statewide information, assistance, and notification coordinator for all hazardous substances spill incidents occurring on highways within the State of California. The California Highway Patrol shall establish a single notification mechanism to serve as a central focus point for a hazardous substances spill response system. To assure timely notification of emergency personnel, the notification mechanism established pursuant to this section shall complement and not conflict with the system established pursuant to subdivision (b) of Section 8574.17 of the Government Code.

(Amended by Stats. 1994, Ch. 1214, Sec. 7. Effective January 1, 1995.)

2454. (a) The authority for incident command at the scene of an on-highway hazardous substance incident is vested in the appropriate law enforcement agency having primary traffic investigative authority on the highway where the incident occurs. Responsibility for incident command at the scene of an on-highway hazardous substance incident shall continue until all emergency operations at the scene have been completed and order has been restored.

(b) Notwithstanding subdivision (a), the local governing body of a city, whether general law or chartered, which has jurisdiction over the location where an on-highway hazardous substance incident occurs may assign the authority for incident command at the scene of an on-highway hazardous substance incident on local streets and roads, other than freeways, to either the local law enforcement agency or the local fire protection agency. However, the department is responsible for incident command at the scene of an on-highway hazardous substance incident on all highways where the department has primary traffic investigative authority. Any law enforcement agency having primary traffic investigative authority may enter into written agreements with other public agencies to facilitate incident command at the scene of an on-highway hazardous substance incident on local streets and roads other than freeways.

(c) For purposes of this section, "incident command at the scene of an on-highway hazardous substance incident" means coordination of operations which occur at the location of a hazardous substance incident. This coordinating function does not include how the specialized functions provided by the various other responding agencies are to be performed. The incident commander at the scene of an on-highway hazardous substance incident shall consult with other response agencies at the scene to ensure that all appropriate resources are properly utilized, and shall perform his or her coordinating function in a manner designed to minimize the risk of death or injury to other persons.

(Amended by Stats. 1992, Ch. 1241, Sec. 10. Effective January 1, 1993.)

Article 5. Renderers and Transporters of Inedible Kitchen Grease

(Article 5 added by Stats. 1998, Ch. 394, Sec. 3.)

2460. (a) The definitions set forth in Article 1 (commencing with Section 19200) of Chapter 5 of Part 3 of Division 9 of the Food and Agricultural Code apply for purposes of interpreting this article. The definitions set forth elsewhere in this section also apply for purposes of interpreting this article.

(b) A "licensed renderer" is a renderer licensed under Article 6 (commencing with Section 19300) of Chapter 5 of Part 3 of Division 9 of the Food and Agricultural Code.

(c) A "registered transporter" is a transporter of inedible kitchen grease registered under Article 6.5 (commencing with Section 19310) of Chapter 5 of Part 3 of Division 9 of the Food and Agricultural Code.

(d) A "peace officer" is any peace officer defined in Chapter 4.5 (commencing with Section 830) of Title 3 of Part 2 of the Penal Code.

(e) A "container" is a receptacle, including, but not limited to, a box, barrel, tank, or jar, for holding meat or meat products, poultry meat or poultry meat products, animal carcasses or parts, inedible kitchen grease, packinghouse waste, or other such items.

(f) A "manifest" is a written or electronic record that contains information required by Section 1180.24 of Article 42 of Subchapter 2 of Chapter 4 of Division 2 of Title 3 of the California Code of Regulations.

(g) "Transportation" means the movement of inedible kitchen grease and the loading, unloading, or storage incidental to that movement.

(h) "Inedible kitchen grease" means any fat or used cooking grease or oils from any source.

(i) "Rendering" means all recycling, processing, and conversion of animal and fish materials and carcasses and inedible kitchen grease into fats, oils, proteins, and other products that are used in the animal, poultry, and pet food industries and other industries.

(j) "Collection center" means a receiving area for the temporary storage of animal carcasses, packinghouse waste, or other products before transportation to a licensed rendering plant or pet food processor.

(k) "Licensed collection center" means a collection center licensed pursuant to Section 19300.5 of the Food and Agricultural Code.

(Amended by Stats. 2014, Ch. 595, Sec. 10. (AB 1566) Effective January 1, 2015.)

2462. (a) In addition to any other records required to be maintained and retained pursuant to Chapter 5 (commencing with Section 19200) of Part 3 of Division 9 of the Food and Agricultural Code, each licensed renderer and collection center shall record and maintain for two years, in connection with the receipt of kitchen grease that is not intended for human food, all of the information required by Section 1180.24 of Article 42 of Subchapter 2 of Chapter 4 of Division 2 of Title 3 of the California Code of Regulations, including, but not limited to, the following:

(1) The name of each registered transporter of inedible kitchen grease who has delivered that material to the licensed renderer or collection center.

(2) The total amount of inedible kitchen grease purchased in each transaction.

(3) The date of delivery for each transaction.

(b) Each registered transporter shall record and maintain for two years a manifest that includes, but is not limited to, all of the following:

(1) The name and address of each location from which the registered transporter obtained the inedible kitchen grease.

(2) The quantity of inedible kitchen grease received from each location.

(3) The date on which the inedible kitchen grease was obtained from each location.

(Amended by Stats. 2014, Ch. 595, Sec. 11. (AB 1566) Effective January 1, 2015.)

2464. All records required to be retained pursuant to this article shall be maintained and retained at the regular place of business of each licensed renderer, collection center, and registered transporter for two years. Those records shall be exhibited on demand to any peace officer or authorized employee of the Department of the California Highway Patrol or the Department of Food and Agriculture.

(Amended by Stats. 2014, Ch. 595, Sec. 12. (AB 1566) Effective January 1, 2015.)

2466. A peace officer or an authorized employee of the Department of the California Highway Patrol or the Department of Food and Agriculture may, during normal business hours, inspect any premises maintained by a licensed renderer, collection center, or registered transporter, and any inedible kitchen grease located on the premises, for the purpose of determining whether that renderer, collection center, or transporter is complying with the record maintenance requirements of this article.

(Amended by Stats. 2014, Ch. 595, Sec. 13. (AB 1566) Effective January 1, 2015.)

2468. (a) A licensed renderer, collection center, or registered transporter who fails in any respect to keep the records required by this article, or to set out in that record any matter required by this article to be set out in the record, is guilty of a misdemeanor.

(b) Each licensed renderer or collection center, or registered transporter, who refuses, upon demand of any peace officer or authorized employee of the Department of the California Highway Patrol or the Department of Food and Agriculture, to exhibit any record required by this article, or who destroys that record within two years after making the final entry of any information required by this article, is guilty of a misdemeanor.

(c) A violation of subdivision (a) or (b) is punishable as follows:

(1) For a first offense, by a fine of not less than one thousand dollars ($1,000), or by imprisonment in the county jail for not more than 30 days, or by both that fine and imprisonment.

(2) For a second offense within a period of one year, by a fine of not less than five thousand dollars ($5,000), or by imprisonment in the county jail for not more than 30 days, or by both that fine and imprisonment. In addition to any other punishment imposed pursuant to this paragraph, the court may enjoin the defendant from engaging in the business as a transporter, collection center, or renderer for a period not to exceed 30 days.

(3) For a third or any subsequent offense within a period of two years, by a fine of not less than ten thousand dollars ($10,000), or by imprisonment in the county jail for not more than six months, or by both that fine and imprisonment. In addition to any other sentence imposed pursuant to this paragraph, the court shall enjoin the defendant from engaging in the business as a transporter, collection center, or renderer for a period of 30 days.

(Amended by Stats. 2014, Ch. 595, Sec. 14. (AB 1566) Effective January 1, 2015.)

2470. It is unlawful for a person to engage in the transportation of inedible kitchen grease without being registered with the Department of Food and Agriculture and without being in possession of a valid registration certificate issued by that department, or a copy of the certificate, and a manifest for the inedible kitchen grease being transported.

(Amended by Stats. 2014, Ch. 595, Sec. 15. (AB 1566) Effective January 1, 2015.)

2472. (a) It is unlawful for any person who is not a licensed renderer or collection center or registered transporter of inedible kitchen grease to transport that product from any place within this state to any place outside the borders of this state.

(b) It is unlawful for any person who is not a licensed renderer or collection center or registered transporter of inedible kitchen grease to transport that product from any place outside this state to any place inside the borders of this state.

(Amended by Stats. 2014, Ch. 595, Sec. 16. (AB 1566) Effective January 1, 2015.)

2474. It is unlawful for any person to steal, misappropriate, contaminate, or damage inedible kitchen grease, or containers thereof.

(Added by Stats. 1998, Ch. 394, Sec. 3. Effective January 1, 1999.)

2476. A licensed renderer or collection center, registered transporter, or any other person shall not take possession of inedible kitchen grease from an unregistered transporter, unlicensed renderer or collection center, or any other person, or knowingly take possession of stolen inedible kitchen grease.

(Amended by Stats. 2014, Ch. 595, Sec. 17. (AB 1566) Effective January 1, 2015.)

2478. (a) Any person who is found guilty of violating Section 2470, 2472, 2474, or 2476, or the rules and regulations promulgated under those provisions, is subject to imprisonment in a county jail for not more than one year, or a fine of not more than five thousand dollars ($5,000), or both that imprisonment and fine.

(b) If the conviction is a second or subsequent conviction of a violation described in subdivision (a), or the violation is committed with intent to defraud or mislead, the person is subject to imprisonment pursuant to subdivision (h) of Section 1170 of the Penal Code, or a fine of not more than fifteen thousand dollars ($15,000), or both that imprisonment and fine.

(Amended by Stats. 2012, Ch. 303, Sec. 6. (AB 2378) Effective January 1, 2013.)

2480. (a) A peace officer may remove a vehicle, within the territorial limits in which the officer may act, if the vehicle is involved in the theft or movement of stolen inedible kitchen grease. If a peace officer removes a vehicle pursuant to this subdivision, the officer may, after citing or arresting the responsible person, seize the vehicle, which may be impounded for up to 15 days.

(b) The registered and legal owner of a vehicle removed and seized pursuant to subdivision (a) or their agents shall be provided the opportunity for a storage hearing to determine the validity of the storage in accordance with Section 22852.

(c) (1) Notwithstanding Chapter 10 (commencing with Section 22650) of Division 11 or any other law, an impounding agency shall release a motor vehicle to the registered owner or his or her agent prior to the conclusion of the impoundment period described in subdivision (a) under any of the following circumstances:

(A) If the vehicle is a stolen vehicle and reported as stolen in accordance with then existing state and local law.

(B) If the legal owner or registered owner of the vehicle is a rental car agency.

(C) If, prior to the conclusion of the impoundment period, a citation or notice is dismissed under Section 40500, criminal charges are not filed by the district attorney because of a lack of evidence, or the charges are otherwise dismissed by the court.

(2) A vehicle shall be released pursuant to this subdivision only if the registered owner or his or her agent presents a currently valid driver's license to operate the vehicle and proof of current vehicle registration, or if ordered by a court.

(d) A vehicle seized and removed pursuant to subdivision (a) shall be released to the legal owner of the vehicle, or the legal owner's agent, on or before the 15th day of impoundment if all of the following conditions are met:

(1) The legal owner is a motor vehicle dealer, bank, credit union, acceptance corporation, or other licensed financial institution legally operating in this state, or is another person, not the registered owner, holding a security interest in the vehicle.

(2) The legal owner or the legal owner's agent pays all towing and storage fees related to the impoundment of the vehicle. No lien sale processing fees shall be charged to a legal owner who redeems the vehicle on or before the seventh day of impoundment.

(3) The legal owner or the legal owner's agent presents foreclosure documents or an affidavit of repossession for the vehicle.

(e) (1) The registered owner or his or her agent is responsible for all towing and storage charges related to the impoundment, and any administrative charges authorized under Section 22850.5.

(2) If the vehicle is a rental vehicle, the rental car agency may require the person to whom the vehicle was rented to pay all towing and storage charges related to the impoundment and any administrative charges authorized under Section 22850.5 incurred by the rental car agency in connection with obtaining possession of the vehicle.

(3) The owner is not liable for any towing and storage charges related to the impoundment if acquittal or dismissal occurs.

(4) The vehicle shall not be sold prior to the defendant's conviction.

(Amended by Stats. 2015, Ch. 303, Sec. 532. (AB 731) Effective January 1, 2016.)

2482. (a) To assist law enforcement personnel in enforcing this article, each vehicle transporting inedible kitchen grease shall have a current registration decal issued by the Department of Food and Agriculture permanently affixed and prominently displayed on the upper right corner of the vehicle windshield or in a conspicuous location on the right side of the trailer being towed.

(b) Each vehicle used in the transportation of inedible kitchen grease shall conspicuously display the following information on both front doors of the vehicle in letters not less than two inches high:

(1) The name of the business or person registered as a transporter with the Department of Food and Agriculture.

(2) The address of the company or owner, or the carrier identification number issued by the California Highway Patrol.

(c) Removable signs shall also display the information specified in subdivision (b).

(d) A violation of this section shall be a correctable offense pursuant to Section 40303.5.

(Added by Stats. 2014, Ch. 595, Sec. 19. (AB 1566) Effective January 1, 2015.)

Chapter 2.5. Licenses Issued by California Highway Patrol

(Chapter 2.5 added by Stats. 1968, Ch. 1309.)

Article 1. General Provisions

(Article 1 added by Stats. 1968, Ch. 1309.)

2500. The provisions of this chapter shall apply to all licenses issued by the Department of the California Highway Patrol unless the particular provisions applicable to each license otherwise provide.

(Added by Stats. 1968, Ch. 1309.)

2501. (a) The Commissioner of the California Highway Patrol may issue licenses for the operation of privately owned or operated ambulances used to respond to emergency calls, armored cars, fleet owner inspection and maintenance stations, and for the transportation of hazardous material, including the transportation of explosives. Licenses issued under this section shall be issued in accordance with this chapter and regulations adopted by the commissioner pursuant thereto. Licenses issued by the commissioner shall expire one year from the date of issue, and may be renewed upon application and payment of the renewal fees if the application for renewal is made within the 30-day period before the date of expiration. A person whose license has expired shall immediately cease the activity requiring a license, but the commissioner shall accept applications for renewal during the 30-day period following the date of expiration if they are accompanied by the new license fee. A license shall not be renewed when the application is received more than 30 days after the date of expiration.

(b) Notwithstanding subdivision (a) and this chapter, licenses shall not be required under this chapter for ambulances owned or operated by a fire department of a federally recognized tribe or operators of those ambulances.

(Amended by Stats. 2021, Ch. 282, Sec. 2. (AB 798) Effective January 1, 2022.)

2502. (a) Except as otherwise provided in this section, each application for a new or renewal license shall be accompanied by a fee of ten dollars ($10) for a new license or five dollars ($5) for a renewal license. This subdivision does not apply to licenses for transportation of hazardous material or operation of ambulances.

(b) Each application for a new or renewal license for the operation of ambulances shall be accompanied by a fee not to exceed two hundred dollars ($200) for a new license or one hundred fifty dollars ($150) for a renewal license.

(c) Each application for a new or renewal license to transport hazardous material shall be accompanied by a fee of not to exceed one hundred dollars ($100) for a new license and not to exceed seventy-five dollars ($75) for a renewal license.

(d) Each application shall be made upon a form furnished by the commissioner. It shall contain information concerning the applicant's background and experience which the commissioner may prescribe, in addition to other information required by law.

(Amended by Stats. 1996, Ch. 539, Sec. 26. Effective January 1, 1997.)

2503. (a) Licenses issued by the commissioner shall not be transferable. A change in ownership or control of the licensed activity shall render the existing license null and void and a new license shall be required. A change in ownership or control includes, but is not limited to, a change in corporate status, or a stock transfer of shares possessing more than 50 percent of the voting power of the corporation. A change in ownership or control does not include the addition or deletion of partners, officers, directors, or board members comprising 50 percent or less ownership or control of the licensed activity if both of the following are complied with:

(1) The new partners, officers, directors, or board members have not committed any acts described in Section 2541.

(2) An amended license application form indicating the changes and

any other information required pursuant to subdivision (d) of Section 2502 is submitted to the commissioner within 10 days of the change.

(b) In the event of a change of name, not involving a change of ownership or control, the license shall be returned to the commissioner for cancellation, and a new license application form shall be submitted. The commissioner shall cancel the returned license and issue a new license for the unexpired term without a fee.

(c) In the event of loss, destruction, or mutilation of a license issued by the commissioner, the person to whom it was issued may obtain a duplicate upon paying a fee of five dollars ($5). Any person who loses a license issued by the commissioner and who, after obtaining a duplicate, finds the original license, shall immediately surrender the original license to the commissioner.

(d) Any change of address or relocation of a licensed service shall be reported to the commissioner within 10 days.

(Amended by Stats. 1999, Ch. 1008, Sec. 3. Effective January 1, 2000.)

2504. It is unlawful to violate any regulation adopted by the commissioner pursuant to this chapter.

(Amended by Stats. 1970, Ch. 1067.)

2505. Notwithstanding Sections 2501 and 2502, for the purpose of staggering license renewals subject to this chapter, the commissioner may, during any 12-month period, issue licenses that expire 6 to 18 months from the date of issue. Subsequent renewal of these licenses shall be for a period of 12 months. Fees with respect to these licenses for more or less than one year shall be prorated accordingly.

This section applies only to licenses for the transportation of hazardous materials established on or after January 1, 1982.

(Added by Stats. 1984, Ch. 1230, Sec. 8.)

Article 2. Privately Owned and Operated Ambulances and Armored Cars

(Article 2 added by Stats. 1968, Ch. 1309.)

2510. (a) (1) A person applying for a license to operate ambulances or armored cars shall provide separate identification data and reports of inspection for each vehicle as prescribed by the commissioner.

(2) A person who operates ambulances owned or operated by a fire department of a federally recognized Indian tribe shall be exempt from the requirements set forth under paragraph (1) and this chapter.

(b) (1) A person shall not operate a privately owned emergency ambulance or armored car until the California Highway Patrol has determined that the vehicle is in compliance with this code and regulations adopted by the commissioner. Ambulances licensed by the department shall be inspected by the department not less often than once annually.

(2) Notwithstanding paragraph (1), the department shall not inspect ambulances owned or operated by a fire department of a federally recognized Indian tribe.

(Amended by Stats. 2021, Ch. 282, Sec. 3. (AB 798) Effective January 1, 2022.)

2511. Licenses for the operation of ambulances may be issued only to those persons or entities which operate ambulances designed and operated exclusively as such and which are used to respond to emergency calls.

(Added by Stats. 1968, Ch. 1309.)

2512. (a) The commissioner, after consultation with, and pursuant to the recommendations of, the Emergency Medical Service Authority and the department, shall adopt and enforce reasonable regulations as the commissioner determines are necessary for the public health and safety regarding the operation, equipment, and certification of drivers of all ambulances used for emergency services. The regulations shall not conflict with standards established by the Emergency Medical Service Authority pursuant to Section 1797.170 of the Health and Safety Code. The commissioner shall exempt, upon request of the county board of supervisors that an exemption is necessary for public health and safety, noncommercial ambulances operated within the county from the regulations adopted under this section as are specified in the board of supervisors' request. The Emergency Medical Service Authority shall be notified by the county boards of supervisors of any exemptions.

(b) The department, in cooperation with the Department of the California Highway Patrol and the Emergency Medical Service Authority, may adopt and administer regulations relating to the issuance, suspension, or revocation of ambulance driver's certificates. In addition to the fee authorized in Section 2427, the department shall charge a fee of twenty-five dollars ($25) for the issuance of an original certificate and twelve dollars ($12) for the renewal of that certificate, and, in the administration thereof, to exercise the powers granted to the commissioner by this section.

(c) This section shall not preclude the adoption of more restrictive regulations by local authorities, except that inspection of ambulances pursuant to subdivision (b) of Section 2510 shall not be duplicated by local authorities. It is the intent of the Legislature that regulations adopted by the commissioner pursuant to this section shall be the minimum necessary to protect public health and safety, and shall not be so restrictive as to preclude compliance by ambulances operated in sparsely populated areas. This subdivision does not relieve the owner or driver of any ambulance from compliance with Section 21055.

(d) The Department of the California Highway Patrol after consultation with the department and the Emergency Medical Service Authority shall prepare, and make available for purchase, an ambulance driver's handbook.

(Amended by Stats. 1996, Ch. 440, Sec. 5. Effective January 1, 1997.)

Article 3.5. Inspection and Maintenance Stations

(Heading of Article 3.5 amended by Stats. 1975, Ch. 502.)

2525. For purposes of this article:

(a) "Fleet owner" means an owner of a fleet of three or more vehicles that are any one or more of the types specified in Section 34500 who is engaged in the transportation of persons or property and whose vehicles are registered in California.

(b) "Inspection and maintenance station" means a facility operated by a fleet owner to inspect and maintain his own vehicles and licensed by the commissioner pursuant to this chapter.

(Amended by Stats. 1975, Ch. 502.)

2525.2. The commissioner may adopt such regulations as are necessary to administer the provisions of this article. A fleet owner licensed by the commissioner as an inspection and maintenance station pursuant to this chapter shall comply with such regulations.

(Amended by Stats. 1975, Ch. 502.)

2525.4. (a) Fleet owners licensed as inspection and maintenance stations shall do all of the following:

(1) Conduct all installations, adjustments, inspections, and maintenance under the supervision of, and subject to the regulations of, the department, and subject to Division 12 (commencing with Section 24000).

(2) If engaged in interstate transportation, also conduct inspections and maintenance in accordance with the requirements of the United States Department of Transportation.

(3) If operating or maintaining vehicles described in subdivisions (a), (b), (d), (e), (f), or (g), of Section 34500, enroll each licensed inspection and maintenance station for inspection by the Department of the California Highway Patrol pursuant to subdivision (d) of Section 34501.12 and pay the fees required by subdivision (e) of that section.

(b) Fleet owners may not certify vehicle safety systems, as described in Section 9888.5 of the Business and Professions Code, or the installation, inspection, repair, or servicing of motor vehicle pollution control devices or systems, except for vehicles in the owner's fleet.

(Amended by Stats. 2023, Ch. 681, Sec. 23. (AB 1263) Effective January 1, 2024.)

2525.6. Each fleet owner licensed as an inspection and maintenance station may place upon a vehicle which it has inspected and maintained, or upon which it has installed or adjusted required equipment, a sticker, in a form approved by the commissioner, certifying the compliance of such vehicle with all pertinent requirements imposed upon such vehicle by this code or regulations adopted thereunder and, if applicable, by the United States Department of Transportation. Such stickers shall remain valid for a period of one year and shall not be placed on any vehicle which is not part of the fleet.

(Amended by Stats. 1975, Ch. 502.)

2525.8. The commissioner shall make and enforce regulations with respect to the issuance of stickers to be displayed upon vehicles owned or operated by a fleet owner which has complied with Section 2525.6.

(Added by Stats. 1970, Ch. 1067.)

2525.10. It is unlawful and constitutes a separate offense for any person to knowingly place or knowingly permit to be placed any sticker authorized by this article on any vehicle which does not comply with all the equipment requirements of this code or regulations adopted thereunder.

(Added by Stats. 1970, Ch. 1067.)

2525.12. The commissioner may charge a fee for the stickers furnished to fleet owner inspection and maintenance stations. The fee charged shall be established by regulation and shall not produce a total estimated revenue which, together with license fees charged pursuant to Sections 2502 and 2503, is in excess of the estimated total cost to the department of the administration of the statutes relating to fleet owner inspection and maintenance stations.

(Amended by Stats. 1975, Ch. 502.)

Article 4. Transportation of Hazardous Material

(Article 4 repealed and added by Stats. 1981, Ch. 860, Sec. 11.)

2531. In addition to taking action pursuant to Article 5 (commencing with Section 2540), the commissioner may deny, suspend, or revoke a license to transport hazardous material when it is evident that the applicant or licensee or his or her employees have repeatedly violated any provision of law to such an extent as to demonstrate that it would be unsafe and not in the public interest to permit the applicant or licensee to operate or permit the operation of any vehicle owned or controlled by him or her for the transportation of hazardous material upon the public highways.

(Amended by Stats. 1989, Ch. 161, Sec. 2.)

2532. The commissioner may adopt such regulations as are necessary to administer the provisions of this article.

(Repealed and added by Stats. 1981, Ch. 860, Sec. 11.)

Article 5. Denial, Suspension and Revocation

(Article 5 added by Stats. 1968, Ch. 1309.)

2540. Any license issued may be suspended or revoked by the commissioner. The commissioner may refuse to issue a license to any applicant for the reasons set forth in Section 2531 or 2541. The proceedings under this article shall be conducted in accordance with Chapter 5 (commencing with Section 11500) of Part 1 of Division 3 of Title 2 of the Government Code, and the commissioner shall have all the powers granted therein.

(Amended by Stats. 1981, Ch. 860, Sec. 12.)

2541. (a) The commissioner may deny a license if the applicant or any partner, officer, or director thereof:

(1) Fails to meet the qualifications established by the department pursuant to this chapter for the issuance of the license applied for.

(2) Was previously the holder of a license issued under this chapter which license has been revoked and never reissued or which license was suspended and the terms of the suspension have not been fulfilled.

(3) Has committed any act which, if committed by any licensee, would be grounds for the suspension or revocation of a license issued pursuant to this chapter.

(4) Has committed any act involving dishonesty, fraud, or deceit whereby another is injured or whereby the applicant has benefited.

(5) Has acted in the capacity of a licensed person or firm under this chapter without having a license therefor.

(6) Has entered a plea of guilty or nolo contendere to, or been found guilty of, or been convicted of, a felony, or a crime involving moral turpitude, and the time for appeal has elapsed or the judgment of conviction has been affirmed on appeal, irrespective of an order granting probation following such conviction, suspending the imposition of sentence, or of a subsequent order under the provisions of Section 1203.4 of the Penal Code allowing such person to withdraw his plea of guilty and to enter a plea of not guilty, or setting aside the plea or verdict of guilty, or dismissing the accusation or information.

(b) The commissioner may also deny a license if a corporation is the applicant and the policy or activities of the corporation are or will be directed, controlled, or managed by individuals or shareholders who are ineligible for a license, and the licensing of that corporation would likely defeat the purpose of this section.

(Amended by Stats. 1982, Ch. 16, Sec. 5.)

2542. The commissioner may suspend, revoke, or take other disciplinary action against a license as provided in this article if the licensee or any partner, officer, director, controlling shareholder, or manager thereof:

(a) Violates any section of this code which relates to his or her licensed activities.

(b) Is convicted of any felony.

(c) Is convicted of any misdemeanor involving moral turpitude.

(d) Violates any of the regulations promulgated by the commissioner pursuant to this chapter.

(e) Commits any act involving dishonesty, fraud, or deceit whereby another is injured or any act involving moral turpitude.

(f) Has misrepresented a material fact in obtaining a license.

(g) Aids or abets an unlicensed person to evade this chapter.

(h) Fails to make and keep records showing his or her transactions as a licensee, or fails to have these records available for inspection by the commissioner or his or her duly authorized representative for a period of not less than three years after completion of any transaction to which the records refer, or refuses to comply with a written request of the commissioner to make such record available for inspection.

(i) Violates or attempts to violate this chapter relating to the particular activity for which he or she is licensed.

(j) Fails to equip or maintain his or her vehicles, as required by this code or by the regulations adopted pursuant to this code.

(Amended by Stats. 1989, Ch. 161, Sec. 3.)

2543. A plea or verdict of guilty or a conviction following a plea of nolo contendere is deemed to be a conviction within the meaning of this article. The commissioner may order the license suspended or revoked, or may decline to issue a license, when the time for appeal has elapsed, or the judgment of conviction has been affirmed on appeal, or when an order granting probation is made suspending the imposition of sentence, irrespective of a subsequent order under the provisions of Section 1203.4 of the Penal Code allowing such person to withdraw his plea of guilty and to enter a plea of not guilty, or setting aside the verdict of guilty, or dismissing the accusation, information or indictment.

(Added by Stats. 1968, Ch. 1309.)

2544. The commissioner may take disciplinary action against any licensee after a hearing as provided in this chapter by any of the following:

(a) Imposing probation upon terms and conditions to be set forth by the commissioner.

(b) Suspending the license.

(c) Revoking the license.

(Added by Stats. 1968, Ch. 1309.)

2545. Upon the effective date of any order of suspension or revocation of any license governed by this chapter, the licensee shall surrender the license to the commissioner.

(Added by Stats. 1968, Ch. 1309.)

2546. The expiration or suspension of a license by operation of

law or by order or decision of the commissioner or a court of law, or the voluntary surrender of a license by a licensee shall not deprive the commissioner of jurisdiction to proceed with any investigation of or action or disciplinary proceedings against such licensee, or to render a decision suspending or revoking such license.
(Added by Stats. 1968, Ch. 1309.)

2547. All accusations against licensees shall be filed within three years after the act or omission alleged as the ground for disciplinary action, except that with respect to an accusation alleging a violation of subdivision (f) of Section 2542, the accusation may be filed within two years after the discovery by the California Highway Patrol of the alleged facts constituting the fraud or misrepresentation prohibited by said section.
(Added by Stats. 1968, Ch. 1309.)

2548. When any license has been revoked or suspended following a hearing under the provisions of this chapter, any additional license issued under this chapter in the name of the licensee may be likewise revoked or suspended by the commissioner.
(Added by Stats. 1968, Ch. 1309.)

2549. After suspension of the license upon any of the grounds set forth in this article, the commissioner may reinstate the license upon proof of compliance by the applicant with all provisions of the decision as to reinstatement. After revocation of a license upon any of the grounds set forth in this article, the license shall not be reinstated or reissued within a period of one year after the effective date of revocation.
(Added by Stats. 1968, Ch. 1309.)

Article 7. Transportation of School Pupils

(Article 7 added by Stats. 1990, Ch. 1563, Sec. 3.6.)

2570. It is the intent of the Legislature, in enacting this chapter, that the public be provided additional protection through the licensing of private schoolbus contractors transporting school pupils under contracts with school districts, and that the Department of the California Highway Patrol be authorized to inspect and license the contractors described in subdivision (a), giving special attention directed to negligent operators or repeat violators.
(Added by Stats. 1990, Ch. 1563, Sec. 3.6.)

2571. Every private schoolbus contractor who contracts with a school district for the transportation of school pupils shall be licensed in accordance with regulations adopted by the commissioner. The license fee shall be one hundred dollars ($100) for an initial license and seventy-five dollars ($75) for each annual renewal.
(Added by Stats. 1990, Ch. 1563, Sec. 3.6.)

2572. (a) The commissioner may adopt whatever regulations are necessary to administer this chapter. The regulations shall be consistent with regulations regarding schoolbuses and schoolbus drivers adopted by the commissioner pursuant to other provisions of law.

(b) In addition to any other requirements, it is unlawful for the private schoolbus contractor or the person who directs the driver to operate a vehicle transporting school pupils, when that transportation requires a license, to knowingly cause the operation of the vehicle unless the private schoolbus contractor holds a valid license for the transportation of school pupils. A violation of this subdivision shall be punished by a fine of not more than two thousand dollars ($2,000).
(Added by Stats. 1990, Ch. 1563, Sec. 3.6.)

2573. (a) The commissioner may temporarily suspend a license to transport school pupils under contract with a school district, subject to a hearing conducted pursuant to Chapter 5 (commencing with Section 11500) of Part 1 of Division 3 of Title 2 of the Government Code, when, in the commissioner's opinion, the action is necessary to prevent an imminent and substantial danger to the public health.

(b) The commissioner may, following a hearing, suspend a license to transport school pupils under contract with a school district, for a period of at least 30 days but not more than 90 days, if the holder of the license knowingly permits the transportation of school pupils by a person who does not possess the appropriate driver's license and driver's certificate.

(c) The suspensions authorized pursuant to subdivisions (a) and (b) may, at the discretion of the commissioner, be enforced for all operations of a schoolbus contractor, or for the operations of the contractor in the school district in which the alleged violations occurred, or for the operations of the contractor in the contractor's terminal in which the alleged violations occurred.

(d) The commissioner shall provide notification of a suspension hearing to those school districts whose terminals would be affected by the suspension.
(Added by Stats. 1990, Ch. 1563, Sec. 3.6.)

2574. (a) All fees collected by the Department of the California Highway Patrol pursuant to the issuance or renewal of a license for the transportation of school pupils under contract with a school district shall be deposited in the Motor Vehicle Account of the State Transportation Fund.

(b) All moneys collected from these fees shall be used for the support of the licensing program of the department upon appropriation therefor by the Legislature.
(Added by Stats. 1990, Ch. 1563, Sec. 3.6.)

Chapter 4. Administration and Enforcement

(Chapter 4 enacted by Stats. 1959, Ch. 3.)

Article 1. Lawful Orders and Inspections

(Article 1 enacted by Stats. 1959, Ch. 3.)

2800. (a) It is unlawful to willfully fail or refuse to comply with a lawful order, signal, or direction of a peace officer, as defined in Chapter 4.5 (commencing with Section 830) of Title 3 of Part 2 of the Penal Code, when that peace officer is in uniform and is performing duties pursuant to any of the provisions of this code, or to refuse to submit to a lawful inspection pursuant to this code.

(b) (1) Except as authorized pursuant to Section 24004, it is unlawful to fail or refuse to comply with a lawful out-of-service order issued by an authorized employee of the Department of the California Highway Patrol or by an authorized enforcement officer as described in subdivision (d).

(2) It is unlawful for a driver transporting hazardous materials in a commercial motor vehicle that is required to display a placard pursuant to Section 27903 to violate paragraph (1).

(3) It is unlawful for a driver of a vehicle designed to transport 16 or more passengers, including the driver, to violate paragraph (1).

(c) It is unlawful to fail or refuse to comply with a lawful out-of-service order issued by the United States Secretary of the Department of Transportation.

(d) "Out-of-Service order" means a declaration by an authorized enforcement officer of a federal, state, Canadian, Mexican, or local jurisdiction that a driver, a commercial motor vehicle, or a motor carrier operation is out-of-service pursuant to Section 386.72, 392.5, 392.9a, 395.13, or 396.9 of Title 49 of the Code of Federal Regulations, state law, or the North American Standard Out-of-Service Criteria.

(e) It is unlawful for a driver of a commercial vehicle subject to inspection under this code to fail to comply with any vehicle inspection testing and associated procedures as required by an authorized member of the California Highway Patrol.
(Amended by Stats. 2022, Ch. 295, Sec. 3. (AB 2956) Effective January 1, 2023.)

2800.1. (a) Any person who, while operating a motor vehicle and with the intent to evade, willfully flees or otherwise attempts to elude a pursuing peace officer's motor vehicle, is guilty of a misdemeanor punishable by imprisonment in a county jail for not more than one year if all of the following conditions exist:

(1) The peace officer's motor vehicle is exhibiting at least one lighted red lamp visible from the front and the person either sees or reasonably should have seen the lamp.

(2) The peace officer's motor vehicle is sounding a siren as may be reasonably necessary.

(3) The peace officer's motor vehicle is distinctively marked.

(4) The peace officer's motor vehicle is operated by a peace officer, as defined in Chapter 4.5 (commencing with Section 830) of Title 3 of Part 2 of the Penal Code, and that peace officer is wearing a distinctive uniform.

(b) Any person who, while operating a motor vehicle and with the intent to evade, willfully flees or otherwise attempts to elude a pursuing peace officer's bicycle, is guilty of a misdemeanor punishable by imprisonment in a county jail for not more than one year if the following conditions exist:

(1) The peace officer's bicycle is distinctively marked.

(2) The peace officer's bicycle is operated by a peace officer, as defined in paragraph (4) of subdivision (a), and that peace officer is wearing a distinctive uniform.

(3) The peace officer gives a verbal command to stop.

(4) The peace officer sounds a horn that produces a sound of at least 115 decibels.

(5) The peace officer gives a hand signal commanding the person to stop.

(6) The person is aware or reasonably should have been aware of the verbal command, horn, and hand signal, but refuses to comply with the command to stop.

(Amended by Stats. 2005, Ch. 485, Sec. 6. Effective January 1, 2006.)

2800.2. (a) If a person flees or attempts to elude a pursuing peace officer in violation of Section 2800.1 and the pursued vehicle is driven in a willful or wanton disregard for the safety of persons or property, the person driving the vehicle, upon conviction, shall be punished by imprisonment in the state prison, or by confinement in the county jail for not less than six months nor more than one year. The court may also impose a fine of not less than one thousand dollars ($1,000) nor more than ten thousand dollars ($10,000), or may impose both that imprisonment or confinement and fine.

(b) For purposes of this section, a willful or wanton disregard for the safety of persons or property includes, but is not limited to, driving while fleeing or attempting to elude a pursuing peace officer during which time either three or more violations that are assigned a traffic violation point count under Section 12810 occur, or damage to property occurs.

(Amended by Stats. 1998, Ch. 472, Sec. 1. Effective January 1, 1999.)

2800.3. (a) Whenever willful flight or attempt to elude a pursuing peace officer in violation of Section 2800.1 proximately causes serious bodily injury to any person, the person driving the pursued vehicle, upon conviction, shall be punished by imprisonment in the state prison for three, five, or seven years, by imprisonment in a county jail for not more than one year, or by a fine of not less than two thousand dollars ($2,000) nor more than ten thousand dollars ($10,000), or by both that fine and imprisonment.

(b) Whenever willful flight or attempt to elude a pursuing peace officer in violation of Section 2800.1 proximately causes death to a person, the person driving the pursued vehicle, upon conviction, shall be punished by imprisonment in the state prison for a term of 4, 6, or 10 years.

(c) Nothing in this section shall preclude the imposition of a greater sentence pursuant to Section 190 of the Penal Code or any other provisions of law applicable to punishment for an unlawful death.

(d) For the purposes of this section, "serious bodily injury" has the same meaning as defined in paragraph (4) of subdivision (f) of Section 243 of the Penal Code.

(Amended by Stats. 2005, Ch. 485, Sec. 7. Effective January 1, 2006.)

2800.4. Whenever a person willfully flees or attempts to elude a pursuing peace officer in violation of Section 2800.1, and the person operating the pursued vehicle willfully drives that vehicle on a highway in a direction opposite to that in which the traffic lawfully moves upon that highway, the person upon conviction is punishable by imprisonment for not less than six months nor more than one year in a county jail or by imprisonment in the state prison, or by a fine of not less than one thousand dollars ($1,000) nor more than ten thousand dollars ($10,000), or by both that fine and imprisonment.

(Amended by Stats. 2012, Ch. 43, Sec. 111. (SB 1023) Effective June 27, 2012.)

2801. It is unlawful to wilfully fail or refuse to comply with any lawful order, signal, or direction of any member of any fire department, paid, volunteer, or company operated, when wearing the badge or insignia of a fireman and when in the course of his duties he is protecting the personnel and fire department equipment.

(Enacted by Stats. 1959, Ch. 3.)

2802. (a) Any traffic officer having reason to believe that a vehicle is not safely loaded or that the height, width, length, or weight of a vehicle and load is unlawful may require the driver to stop and submit to an inspection, measurement, or weighing of the vehicle. The weighing may be done either by means of portable or stationary scales and the officer may require that the vehicle be driven to the nearest scale facility, in the event the scales are within five road miles.

(b) Selected inspection facilities and platform scales operated by the Department of the California Highway Patrol may, at the discretion of the commissioner, be open for extended hours, up to and including 24 hours every day. The primary purpose of the extended hours is to assist in the detection of overweight vehicles. These inspection facilities and platform scales shall be located near primary border route points of entry into the state and key routes within the state.

(c) An amount not to exceed one million dollars ($1,000,000) shall be available annually from the Motor Vehicle Account in the State Transportation Fund, upon appropriation by the Legislature, for the expanded operation of the scale facilities, as specified in subdivision (b). It is the intent of the Legislature that the funds made available pursuant to this subdivision shall be the only funds available for purposes of this section.

(Amended by Stats. 1993, Ch. 19, Sec. 1. Effective January 1, 1994.)

2803. (a) If the traffic officer determines that the vehicle is not safely loaded or that the height, width, length, or weight is unlawful, he may require the driver to stop in a suitable place and reload or remove such portion of the load as may be necessary to render the load safe or to reduce it to the limits permitted under this code. A suitable place is an area which allows the least obstruction to the highway and which requires the least travel on the highway by the vehicle. Determination of the suitability of an area shall be made by the traffic officer who requires the adjustment. All material so unloaded shall be cared for by the owner or operator of the vehicle at the risk of the owner or operator.

(b) If a certified weight certificate or bill of lading accompanies a vehicle which has been determined to be overweight due to the load on the vehicle, the driver shall submit the certified weight certificate or bill of lading, whichever is appropriate, to the traffic officer when the overweight load is removed in the presence of the officer. The officer may note on the certified weight certificate or bill of lading submitted by the driver the fact that a portion of the load has been removed to bring the vehicle and load within the allowable weight limit specified in this code, and the officer shall return the certificate or bill of lading to the driver.

(c) If the height, width, or length of the vehicle is unlawful, irrespective of any load thereon, or if an unladen vehicle is overweight, the traffic officer may prohibit further movement of the vehicle until a permit is obtained as provided in Section 35780.

(Amended by Stats. 1977, Ch. 506.)

2804. A member of the California Highway Patrol upon reasonable belief that any vehicle is being operated in violation of any provisions of this code or is in such unsafe condition as to endanger any person, may require the driver of the vehicle to stop and submit to an inspection of the vehicle, and its equipment, license plates, and registration card.

(Enacted by Stats. 1959, Ch. 3.)

2805. (a) For the purpose of locating stolen vehicles, (1) any member of the California Highway Patrol, or (2) a member of a city police department, a member of a county sheriff's office, or a district attorney investigator, whose primary responsibility is to conduct vehicle theft investigations, may inspect any vehicle of a type required to be registered under this code, or any identifiable vehicle component thereof, on a highway or in any public garage, repair shop, terminal, parking lot, new or used car lot, automobile dismantler's lot, vehicle shredding facility, vehicle leasing or rental lot, vehicle equipment rental yard, vehicle salvage pool, or other similar establishment, or any agricultural or construction work location where work is being actively performed, and may inspect the title or registration of vehicles, in order to establish the rightful ownership or possession of the vehicle or identifiable vehicle component.

As used in this subdivision, "identifiable vehicle component" means any component which can be distinguished from other similar components by a serial number or other unique distinguishing number, sign, or symbol.

(b) A member of the California Highway Patrol, a member of a city police department or county sheriff's office, or a district attorney investigator whose primary responsibility is to conduct vehicle theft investigations, may also inspect, for the purposes specified in subdivision (a), implements of husbandry, special construction equipment, forklifts, and special mobile equipment in the places described in subdivision (a) or when that vehicle is incidentally operated or transported upon a highway.

(c) Whenever possible, inspections conducted pursuant to subdivision (a) or (b) shall be conducted at a time and in a manner so as to minimize any interference with, or delay of, business operations.

(Amended by Stats. 2000, Ch. 688, Sec. 21. Effective January 1, 2001.)

2806. Any regularly employed and salaried police officer or deputy sheriff, or any reserve police officer or reserve deputy sheriff listed in Section 830.6 of the Penal Code, having reasonable cause to believe that any vehicle or combination of vehicles is not equipped as required by this code or is in any unsafe condition as to endanger any person, may require the driver to stop and submit the vehicle or combination of vehicles to an inspection and those tests as may be appropriate to determine the safety to persons and compliance with the code.

(Amended by Stats. 2003, Ch. 292, Sec. 5. Effective January 1, 2004.)

2806.5. (a) A peace officer making a traffic or pedestrian stop, before engaging in questioning related to a criminal investigation or traffic violation, shall state the reason for the stop. The officer shall document the reason for the stop on any citation or police report resulting from the stop.

(b) Subdivision (a) does not apply when the officer reasonably believes that withholding the reason for the stop is necessary to protect life or property from imminent threat, including, but not limited to, cases of terrorism or kidnaping.

(c) This section shall become operative on January 1, 2024.

(Added by Stats. 2022, Ch. 805, Sec. 5. (AB 2773) Effective January 1, 2023. Operative January 1, 2024, by its own provisions.)

2807. (a) The California Highway Patrol shall inspect every schoolbus at least once each school year to ascertain whether its construction, design, equipment, and color comply with all provisions of law.

(b) No person shall drive any schoolbus unless there is displayed therein a certificate issued by the California Highway Patrol stating that on a certain date, which shall be within 13 months of the date of operation, an authorized employee of the California Highway Patrol inspected the bus and found that on the date of inspection the bus complied with the applicable provisions of state law relating to construction, design, equipment, and color. The Commissioner of the California Highway Patrol shall provide by rule or regulation for the issuance and display of distinctive inspection certificates.

(Amended by Stats. 1969, Ch. 580.)

2807.1. (a) The Department of the California Highway Patrol shall inspect and certify every school pupil activity bus specified in Section 546 at least once each year to ascertain whether its condition complies with all provisions of the law.

(b) No person shall drive any motor vehicle specified in subdivision (a) unless there is displayed therein a certificate issued by the Department of the California Highway Patrol stating that on a certain date, which shall be within 13 months of the date of operation, an authorized employee of the Department of the California Highway Patrol inspected such motor vehicle and found that on the date of inspection such motor vehicle complied with the applicable provisions of the state law. The Commissioner of the California Highway Patrol shall provide by rule or regulation for the issuance and display of distinctive inspection certificates.

(Amended by Stats. 1981, Ch. 813, Sec. 7.)

2807.2. The Department of the California Highway Patrol shall, by regulation, provide for a preventive maintenance inspection guide for use by operators of tour buses, motor vehicles specified in Sections 2807 and 2807.1, and vehicles described in subdivisions (a), (b), (d), (e), (f), and (g) of Section 34500. The regulations shall provide that the record of inspection shall be signed by the person making the inspection, and the record of the inspections shall be retained on file by the operator for review and inspection by the Department of the California Highway Patrol.

(Amended by Stats. 1988, Ch. 1586, Sec. 4. Operative July 1, 1989, by Sec. 14 of Ch. 1586.)

2807.3. (a) The Department of the California Highway Patrol shall inspect and certify every youth bus at least once each school year to ascertain whether its condition complies with all provisions of law.

(b) No person shall drive any youth bus unless there is displayed therein a certificate issued by the Department of the California Highway Patrol stating that on a certain date, which shall be within 13 months of the date of operation, an authorized employee of the Department of the California Highway Patrol inspected the youth bus and found that on the date of inspection the youth bus complied with the applicable provisions of state law. The Commissioner of the California Highway Patrol shall provide, by rule or regulation, for the issuance and display of distinctive inspection certificates.

(c) The Commissioner of the California Highway Patrol may determine the fee and method of collection for the annual inspection of youth buses. The fee, established by regulation, shall be sufficient to cover the cost to the department for youth bus inspections and testing of drivers pursuant to Section 12523. All fees received shall be deposited in the Motor Vehicle Account in the State Transportation Fund.

(Amended by Stats. 1982, Ch. 1273, Sec. 4.)

2808. (a) Except as provided in subdivision (b), all schoolbuses transporting pupils to or from any private school or private school activity shall be subject to the same statutes, rules, and regulations relating to construction, design, operation, equipment, and color as are now or hereafter applicable to schoolbuses transporting pupils to or from any public school or public school activity.

(b) Schoolbuses shall be exempt from such statutes, rules, and regulations relating to construction, design, safe operation, and equipment as the Commissioner of the California Highway Patrol shall determine necessary to permit such schoolbuses to continue in operation or when it appears that the results intended to be attained by such rules and regulations are being accomplished by the use of other methods. Such exemption shall be specified by rule or regulation of the commissioner. No such exemption shall be made which in the opinion of the commissioner would jeopardize the safety of the pupils so transported.

(Amended by Stats. 1977, Ch. 406.)

2809. All scales and weighing instruments used by any member of the California Highway Patrol to enforce the provisions of this code with respect to weight limitations shall be inspected and certified as to accuracy at least once in each calendar year by the Bureau of Weights and Measures of the Department of Food and Agriculture or by a county sealer of weights and measures.

(Amended by Stats. 1974, Ch. 545.)

2810. (a) A member of the California Highway Patrol may stop any vehicle transporting any timber products, livestock, poultry, farm produce, crude oil, petroleum products, or inedible kitchen grease, and inspect the bills of lading, shipping or delivery papers, or other evidence to determine whether the driver is in legal possession of the load, and, upon reasonable belief that the driver of the vehicle is not in legal possession, shall take custody of the vehicle and load and turn them over to the custody of the sheriff of the county in which the timber products, livestock, poultry, farm produce, crude oil, petroleum products, or inedible kitchen grease, or any part thereof, is apprehended.

(b) The sheriff shall receive and provide for the care and safekeeping of the apprehended timber products, livestock, poultry, farm produce, crude oil, petroleum products, or inedible kitchen grease, or any part thereof, and immediately, in cooperation with the department, proceed with an investigation and its legal disposition.

(c) Any expense incurred by the sheriff in the performance of his or her duties under this section shall be a legal charge against the county.

(Amended by Stats. 1999, Ch. 83, Sec. 187. Effective January 1, 2000.)

2810.1. (a) Any traffic officer may stop any commercial vehicle, as defined in Section 260, that is a rental vehicle and inspect the bills of lading, shipping, delivery papers, or other evidence to determine whether the driver is transporting household goods in violation of the Household Movers Act (Chapter 3.1 (commencing with Section 19225)) of Division 8 of the Business and Professions Code. The officer may only stop and inspect where the officer has probable cause to believe that the vehicle is being operated in violation of that act.

(b) It is a public offense, for which an officer may issue a citation, for a driver to unlawfully transport household goods in violation of the Household Movers Act. That public offense is punishable as prescribed in Article 8 (commencing with Section 19277) of Chapter 3.1 of Division 3 of the Business and Professions Code. It is an infraction to refuse to submit to an inspection as authorized by subdivision (a).

(c) A copy of the citation for any offense described in subdivision (b) shall be sent by the department that employs the traffic officer to the Chief of the Bureau of Household Goods and Services. A copy of a citation shall be removed from any record of the bureau upon a showing that the person was not convicted of the offense or that bail was not forfeited for that offense. A person for whom a copy of a citation has been sent to the bureau and is on file with the bureau may request the bureau for an administrative hearing on that matter.

(Amended by Stats. 2022, Ch. 295, Sec. 4. (AB 2956) Effective January 1, 2023.)

2810.2. (a) (1) A peace officer, as described in Chapter 4.5 (commencing with Section 830) of Title 3 of Part 2 of the Penal Code, may stop a vehicle transporting agricultural irrigation supplies that are in plain view to inspect the bills of lading, shipping, or delivery papers, or other evidence to determine whether the driver is in legal possession of the load, if the vehicle is on a rock road or unpaved road that is located in a county that has elected to implement this section and the road is located as follows:

(A) Located under the management of the Department of Parks and Recreation, the Department of Fish and Wildlife, the Department of Forestry and Fire Protection, the State Lands Commission, a regional park district, the United States Forest Service, or the federal Bureau of Land Management.

(B) Located within the respective ownership of a timberland production zone, as defined in Chapter 6.7 (commencing with Section 51100) of Part 1 of Division 1 of Title 5 of the Government Code, either that is larger than 50,000 acres or for which the owner of more than 2,500 acres has given express written permission for a vehicle to be stopped within that zone pursuant to this section.

(2) Upon reasonable belief that the driver of the vehicle is not in legal possession, the law enforcement officer specified in paragraph (1) shall take custody of the vehicle and load and turn them over to the custody of the sheriff of the county that has elected to implement this section where the agricultural irrigation supplies are apprehended.

(b) The sheriff shall receive and provide for the care and safekeeping of the apprehended agricultural irrigation supplies that were in plain view within the boundaries of public lands under the management of the entities listed in subparagraph (A) of paragraph (1) of subdivision (a) or on a timberland production zone as specified in subparagraph (B) of paragraph (1) of subdivision (a), and immediately, in cooperation with the department, proceed with an investigation and its legal disposition.

(c) An expense incurred by the sheriff in the performance of his or her duties under this section shall be a legal charge against the county.

(d) Except as provided in subdivision (e), a peace officer shall not cause the impoundment of a vehicle at a traffic stop made pursuant to subdivision (a) if the driver's only offense is a violation of Section 12500.

(e) During the conduct of pulling a driver over in accordance with subdivision (a), if the peace officer encounters a driver who is in violation of Section 12500, the peace officer shall make a reasonable attempt to identify the registered owner of the vehicle. If the registered owner is present, or the peace officer is able to identify the registered owner and obtain the registered owner's authorization to release the motor vehicle to a licensed driver during the vehicle stop, the vehicle shall be released to either the registered owner of the vehicle if he or she is a licensed driver or to the licensed driver authorized by the registered owner of the vehicle. If a notice to appear is issued, the name and the driver's license number of the licensed driver to whom the vehicle was released pursuant to this subdivision shall be listed on the officer's copy of the notice to appear issued to the unlicensed driver. If a vehicle cannot be released, the vehicle shall be removed pursuant to subdivision (p) of Section 22651, whether a notice to appear has been issued or not.

(f) For purposes of this section, "agricultural irrigation supplies" include agricultural irrigation water bladder and one-half inch diameter or greater irrigation line.

(g) This section shall be implemented only in a county where the board of supervisors adopts a resolution authorizing the enforcement of this section.

(Amended by Stats. 2014, Ch. 71, Sec. 169. (SB 1304) Effective January 1, 2015.)

2811. Any traffic officer who observes a fence along any highway, which has been damaged as a result of a traffic accident, shall promptly report same to the owner, lessee, occupant, or person in charge of the property enclosed by the fence, or to the local headquarters of the department.

(Enacted by Stats. 1959, Ch. 3.)

2812. Whenever poisonous gas, explosives, dust, smoke, or other similar substances, or fire exist upon or so near a public highway as to create a menace to public health or safety, members of the California Highway Patrol, police departments, or sheriff's office may close any highway to traffic when necessary to protect the public from such dangers. Whenever a highway is closed, the governmental agency having control over the highway shall be immediately notified of the reason of the closing and the location.

(Enacted by Stats. 1959, Ch. 3.)

2812.5. Whenever visibility limitations pose a significant safety hazard, as determined by a member of the California Highway Patrol, that member may restrict or prohibit the use of any highway by any vehicle subject to regulation by the Department of the California Highway Patrol pursuant to Section 34500.

(Added by Stats. 1992, Ch. 119, Sec. 1. Effective January 1, 1993.)

2813. Every driver of a commercial vehicle shall stop and submit the vehicle to an inspection of the vehicle's size, weight, equipment, loading, and smoke emissions, as well as the driver's license, medical qualifications, and hours-of-service compliance of a driver of the vehicle at any location where members of the California Highway Patrol are conducting tests and inspections of commercial vehicles and when signs are displayed requiring the stop. Every driver who fails or refuses to stop and submit the vehicle to an inspection when signs are displayed

requiring that stop is guilty of a misdemeanor.
(Amended by Stats. 2022, Ch. 295, Sec. 5. (AB 2956) Effective January 1, 2023.)

2813.5. (a) The commissioner shall have exclusive authority in the issuance of stickers as evidence that commercial vehicles have been inspected pursuant to Section 2813 and have been found to be in compliance with minimum safety standards established by the department. The commissioner may make and enforce regulations with respect to the issuance and display of the stickers upon commercial vehicles.

(b) It is unlawful for any unauthorized person, company, corporation, or public or private entity to possess, issue, or display upon a vehicle an unauthorized commercial vehicle safety inspection sticker or a sticker that is either a facsimile of, or is substantially similar to, that issued by the commissioner.

(c) Any violation of subdivision (b) is a misdemeanor.
(Amended by Stats. 2004, Ch. 183, Sec. 345. Effective January 1, 2005.)

2814. Every driver of a passenger vehicle shall stop and submit the vehicle to an inspection of the mechanical condition and equipment of the vehicle at any location where members of the California Highway Patrol are conducting tests and inspections of passenger vehicles and when signs are displayed requiring such stop.

The Commissioner of the California Highway Patrol may make and enforce regulations with respect to the issuance of stickers or other devices to be displayed upon passenger vehicles as evidence that the vehicles have been inspected and have been found to be in safe mechanical condition and equipped as required by this code and equipped with certified motor vehicle pollution control devices as required by Part 5 (commencing with Section 43000) of Division 26 of the Health and Safety Code which are correctly installed and in operating condition. Any sticker so issued shall be placed on the windshield within a seven-inch square as provided in Section 26708.

If, upon such inspection of a passenger vehicle, it is found to be in unsafe mechanical condition or not equipped as required by this code and the provisions of Part 5 (commencing with Section 43000) of Division 26 of the Health and Safety Code, the provisions of Article 2 (commencing with Section 40150) of Chapter 1 of Division 17 of this code shall apply.

The provisions of this section relating to motor vehicle pollution control devices apply to vehicles of the United States or its agencies, to the extent authorized by federal law.
(Amended by Stats. 1975, Ch. 957.)

2814.1. (a) A board of supervisors of a county may, by ordinance, establish, on highways under its jurisdiction, a vehicle inspection checkpoint program to check for violations of Sections 27153 and 27153.5. The program shall be conducted by the local agency or department with the primary responsibility for traffic law enforcement.

(b) A driver of a motor vehicle shall stop and submit to an inspection conducted under subdivision (a) when signs and displays are posted requiring that stop.

(c) A county that elects to conduct the program described under subdivision (a) may fund that program through fine proceeds deposited with the county under Section 1463.15 of the Penal Code.

(d) State and local law enforcement agencies shall not conduct motorcycle only checkpoints.
(Amended by Stats. 2012, Ch. 89, Sec. 2. (AB 1047) Effective January 1, 2013.)

2814.2. (a) A driver of a motor vehicle shall stop and submit to a sobriety checkpoint inspection conducted by a law enforcement agency when signs and displays are posted requiring that stop.

(b) Notwithstanding Section 14602.6 or 14607.6, a peace officer or any other authorized person shall not cause the impoundment of a vehicle at a sobriety checkpoint if the driver's only offense is a violation of Section 12500.

(c) During the conduct of a sobriety checkpoint, if the law enforcement officer encounters a driver who is in violation of Section 12500, the law enforcement officer shall make a reasonable attempt to identify the registered owner of the vehicle. If the registered owner is present, or the officer is able to identify the registered owner and obtain the registered owner's authorization to release the motor vehicle to a licensed driver by the end of the checkpoint, the vehicle shall be released to either the registered owner of the vehicle if he or she is a licensed driver or to the licensed driver authorized by the registered owner of the vehicle. If a notice to appear is issued, the name and driver's license number of the licensed driver to whom the vehicle was released pursuant to this subdivision shall be listed on the officer's copy of the notice to appear issued to the unlicensed driver. When a vehicle cannot be released, the vehicle shall be removed pursuant to subdivision (p) of Section 22651, whether a notice to appear has been issued or not.
(Added by Stats. 2011, Ch. 653, Sec. 2. (AB 353) Effective January 1, 2012.)

2815. Any person who shall disregard any traffic signal or direction given by a nonstudent school crossing guard, appointed pursuant to Section 21100, or authorized by any city police department, any board of supervisors of a county, or the Department of the California Highway Patrol, when the guard is wearing the official insignia of such a school crossing guard, and when in the course of the guard's duties the guard is protecting any person in crossing a street or highway in the vicinity of a school or while returning thereafter to a place of safety, shall be guilty of an infraction and subject to the penalties provided in Section 42001.1.
(Amended by Stats. 1984, Ch. 69, Sec. 1. Effective April 5, 1984.)

2816. It is unlawful to load or discharge children onto or from a youth bus upon a highway at any location where the children must cross the highway upon which the youth bus is stopped, unless traffic is controlled by a traffic officer or an official traffic control signal.
(Added by Stats. 1982, Ch. 383, Sec. 4. Effective July 4, 1982. Operative on date (not sooner than October 1, 1982, or later than January 1, 1983) prescribed by Sec. 13 of Ch. 383.)

2817. Any person who disregards any traffic signal or direction given by a peace officer authorized pursuant to subdivision (d) of Section 70 of the Penal Code to escort funeral processions, if the peace officer is in a peace officer's uniform, and is in the process of escorting a funeral procession, shall be guilty of an infraction and subject to the penalties provided in subdivision (a) of Section 42001.
(Added by Stats. 1984, Ch. 1108, Sec. 1.)

2818. It is unlawful to traverse an electronic beacon pattern, a flare pattern, cone pattern, or combination of electronic beacon, flare, or cone patterns, provided for the regulation of traffic, or provided in a situation where public safety personnel are engaged in traffic control or emergency scene management.
(Amended by Stats. 2008, Ch. 120, Sec. 1. Effective January 1, 2009.)

Chapter 5. California Traffic Safety Program

(Chapter 5 added by Stats. 1967, Ch. 1492.)

Article 1. Traffic Safety

(Heading of Article 1 added by Stats. 1985, Ch. 547, Sec. 1.)

2900. There is in this state, the California Traffic Safety Program, which consists of a comprehensive plan in conformity with the laws of this state to reduce traffic accidents and deaths, injuries, and property damage resulting from accidents. The program shall include, but not be limited to, provisions to improve driver performance, including, but not limited to, driver education, driver testing to determine proficiency to operate motor vehicles, and driver examinations and driver licensing, and provisions to improve bicyclist and pedestrian education and performance. In addition, the program shall include, but not be limited to, provisions for an effective record system of accidents, including injuries and deaths resulting from accidents; accident investigations to determine the probable causes of accidents, injuries, and deaths; vehicle registration, operation, and inspection; highway design and maintenance including lighting, markings, and surface treatment; traffic control; vehicle codes and laws; surveillance of traffic for detection and correction of high or potentially high accident locations; and emergency services.

(Amended by Stats. 2000, Ch. 181, Sec. 1. Effective January 1, 2001.)

2901. The Governor may appoint a highway safety representative who shall serve in the Transportation Agency and who shall, in consultation with the Governor and Secretary of Transportation, prepare the California Traffic Safety Program. The Governor is responsible for the administration of the program, and has final approval of all phases of the program, and may take all action necessary to secure the full benefits available to the program under the Federal Highway Safety Act of 1966, and any amendments thereto. The highway safety representative serves at the pleasure of the secretary.

(Amended by Stats. 2013, Ch. 352, Sec. 522. (AB 1317) Effective September 26, 2013. Operative July 1, 2013, by Sec. 543 of Ch. 352.)

2902. To the maximum extent permitted by federal law and regulations and the laws of this state, the Governor may delegate to the Secretary of Transportation and the highway safety representative the authority necessary to administer the program, and the secretary and the representative may exercise this authority once delegated.

(Amended by Stats. 2013, Ch. 352, Sec. 523. (AB 1317) Effective September 26, 2013. Operative July 1, 2013, by Sec. 543 of Ch. 352.)

2903. The Governor may establish an Advisory Committee on the California Traffic Safety Program which shall consist of various officials of state and local government and other persons who are interested in the establishment of a comprehensive program of traffic safety in this state including, but not limited to, representatives of agriculture, railroads, the Institute of Transportation and Traffic Engineering of the University of California, the motor vehicle manufacturing industry, the automobile aftermarket equipment servicing and manufacturing industry, automobile dealers, the trucking industry, labor, motor vehicle user organizations, and traffic safety organizations.

(Added by Stats. 1967, Ch. 1492.)

2904. The California Traffic Safety Program shall include a local traffic safety program designed to encourage the political subdivisions of this state to establish traffic safety programs consistent with the objectives of the California Traffic Safety Program.

(Added by Stats. 1967, Ch. 1492.)

2905. On or before the fifth legislative day of the 1968 legislative session and each year thereafter, the Governor shall submit a report to the Legislature through such interim committee or committees as may be designated by legislative resolution. Such report shall include a detailed presentation of the California Traffic Safety Program, a statement concerning the progress made in implementing the program and recommendations concerning possible legislative action deemed necessary or desirable to implement the program.

(Added by Stats. 1967, Ch. 1492.)

2906. The California Traffic Safety Program Fund is hereby created in the State Treasury to consist of the funds referred to in Section 2907.

(Added by Stats. 1967, Ch. 1492.)

2907. Any funds which are appropriated by Congress for the purposes of carrying out Section 402 of Title 23, United States Code (P.L. 89-564; 80 Stats. 731) and which are apportioned to this state by the Secretary of Commerce pursuant to Section 402 of Title 23, United States Code (P.L. 89-564; 80 Stats. 731) are continuously appropriated for the purposes and uses of the California Traffic Safety Program.

(Added by Stats. 1967, Ch. 1492.)

2908. The Governor shall apportion any funds contained in the California Traffic Safety Program Fund among the various state agencies and local political subdivisions as shall effectuate the purposes of the program, and, in accordance with any federal formula for apportionment or other federal requirements as contained in federal enactments, regulations, or standards promulgated by the Secretary of Commerce.

(Added by Stats. 1967, Ch. 1492.)

2909. Any local political subdivision of this state, including, but not limited to, a city, a county, a city and county, a district, or a special district, is authorized to participate in a local traffic safety program within its jurisdiction if such local program is approved by the Governor; provided, however, that any local political subdivision may participate in a traffic safety program other than that promulgated pursuant to the federal Highway Safety Act of 1966.

(Added by Stats. 1967, Ch. 1492.)

2910. Such local political subdivision may use, in implementing its local traffic safety program, any funds which are apportioned to it from the California Traffic Safety Program Fund by the Governor pursuant to Section 2908.

(Added by Stats. 1967, Ch. 1492.)

2911. All traffic safety programs that receive state funds and that include public awareness campaigns involving emergency vehicle operations shall include in the public awareness campaign, information on the risks to public safety of peace officer motor vehicle pursuits, and the penalties that may result from evading a peace officer.

(Added by Stats. 2005, Ch. 485, Sec. 8. Effective January 1, 2006.)

Article 2. Motorcycle Safety

(Article 2 added by Stats. 1985, Ch. 547, Sec. 2.)

2930. (a) "Commissioner" means the Commissioner of the California Highway Patrol.

(b) "Fund" means the California Motorcyclist Safety Fund.

(c) "Program" means the motorcyclist safety program established in this article.

(Added by Stats. 1985, Ch. 547, Sec. 2.)

2931. A motorcyclist safety program is hereby established in the Department of the California Highway Patrol, to be administered by the commissioner.

(Added by Stats. 1985, Ch. 547, Sec. 2.)

2932. The commissioner may, through contracts with other public agencies or with private entities, do all of the following:

(a) Provide financial or other support to projects aimed at enhancing motorcycle operation and safety, including, but not limited to, motorcyclist safety training programs. The motorcyclist safety training programs shall comply with criteria which the commissioner, in consultation with other state agencies and national motorcycle safety organizations, may adopt to provide validated motorcyclist safety training programs in the state.

(b) Sponsor and coordinate efforts aimed at increasing motorists' awareness of motorcyclists.

(c) Sponsor research into effective communication techniques to reach all highway users on matters of motorcyclist safety.

(d) Establish an advisory committee of persons from other state and local agencies with an interest in motorcycle safety; persons from the motorcycle industry; motorcycle safety organizations; motorcycle enthusiast organizations; and others with an interest in motorcycle safety, to assist in the establishment of a comprehensive program of motorcycle safety.

(e) Adopt standards for course content, contact hours, curriculum, instructor training and testing, and instructional quality control, and setting forth a maximum amount for course fees for the novice rider training course specified in subdivisions (g) and (i) of Section 12804.9.

(f) (1) Adopt standards for course content, contact hours, curriculum, instructor training and testing, and instructional quality control, for a premier motorcyclist safety training program. Motorcycle safety training courses offered under a premier motorcyclist safety training program shall meet all of the following requirements:

(A) Provide a core curriculum approved for the novice rider training course specified in subdivision (e).

(B) Additional course requirements established by the commissioner.

(2) On and after January 1, 2008, the commissioner shall not impose a maximum amount for course fees for courses provided under the premier motorcyclist safety training program.

(3) All administrative costs of a premier motorcyclist safety training

program shall be paid for by the provider, and none of the costs shall be paid for by the state.

(Amended by Stats. 2006, Ch. 711, Sec. 2. Effective January 1, 2007.)

2933. The commissioner shall not directly manage or provide program services. Any program service financed under this article shall be provided under contractual arrangements or grant funding. All public agencies assisting or providing program services under this article shall be fully reimbursed for their costs by the commissioner. The commissioner shall monitor and evaluate any contracts or grants executed pursuant to this article to ensure that the provisions of the contracts or grants are adhered to by the recipients.

(Added by Stats. 1985, Ch. 547, Sec. 2.)

2934. (a) The California Motorcyclist Safety Fund is hereby created in the State Treasury. The money in the fund is available, when appropriated by the Legislature, to fund programs established pursuant to this article and to defray related costs incurred. Moneys in the fund are and shall be held as trust funds for the exclusive trust purposes specified in this article.

(b) The commissioner shall not in any way encumber moneys in the fund beyond that amount which is actually available in the fund at the time of encumbrance, and shall not in any manner pledge or encumber future revenues to accrue to the fund from any source.

(Added by Stats. 1985, Ch. 547, Sec. 2.)

2935. The Department of Motor Vehicles shall, in addition to other fees, collect a fee of two dollars ($2) upon initial registration and renewal of registration of every motorcycle subject to registration fees. These additional fees shall be deposited in the fund.

(Added by Stats. 1985, Ch. 547, Sec. 2.)

Chapter 6. New Motor Vehicle Board

(Heading of Chapter 6 amended by Stats. 1974, Ch. 545.)

Article 1. Organization of Board

(Article 1 added by Stats. 1967, Ch. 1397.)

3000. There is in the Department of Motor Vehicles a New Motor Vehicle Board, which consists of nine members.

(Amended by Stats. 1973, Ch. 996.)

3001. (a) Four of the appointive members of the board shall be new motor vehicle dealers as defined in Section 426 who have engaged for a period of not less than five years preceding their appointment in activities regulated by Article 1 (commencing with Section 11700) of Chapter 4 of Division 5. These members shall be appointed by the Governor.

(b) Each of the five remaining appointive members shall be a public member who is not a licentiate under Article 1 (commencing with Section 11700) or 2 (commencing with Section 11800) of Chapter 4 of Division 5 or an employee of such licentiate at the time of appointment and one of these five appointive members shall have been admitted to practice law in the state for at least 10 years immediately preceding his or her appointment. One public member shall be appointed by the Senate Committee on Rules, one by the Speaker of the Assembly, and three by the Governor.

(c) Each member shall be of good moral character.

(d) This section does not apply to a dealer who deals exclusively in motorcycles, all-terrain vehicles, as defined in Section 111, or recreational vehicles, as defined in subdivision (a) of Section 18010 of the Health and Safety Code.

(Amended by Stats. 2014, Ch. 279, Sec. 2. (AB 988) Effective January 1, 2015.)

3002. The appointments of the appointive members shall be made effective as of the effective date of this article.

(Added by Stats. 1967, Ch. 1397.)

3003. (a) Each appointive member of the board shall be appointed for a term of four years and shall hold office until the appointment and qualification of his or her successor or until one year has elapsed since the expiration of the time for which he or she was appointed, whichever occurs first.

(b) The terms of the members of the board first appointed shall expire as follows: one public member and one new motor vehicle dealer member, January 15, 1969; two public members and one new motor vehicle dealer member, January 15, 1970; two public members and two new motor vehicle dealer members, January 15, 1971. The terms shall thereupon expire in the same relative order.

(c) Vacancies occurring shall be filled by appointment for the unexpired term.

This section does not apply to a dealer who deals exclusively in motorcycles, all-terrain vehicles, as defined in Section 111, or recreational vehicles, as defined in subdivision (a) of Section 18010 of the Health and Safety Code.

(Amended by Stats. 2014, Ch. 279, Sec. 3. (AB 988) Effective January 1, 2015.)

3004. Members of the board shall take an oath of office as provided in the Constitution and the Government Code.

(Added by Stats. 1967, Ch. 1397.)

3005. The appointing authority has the power to remove from office at any time, any member of the board appointed by such appointing authority for continued neglect of duties required by law, or for incompetence, or unprofessional or dishonorable conduct. Nothing in this section shall be construed as a limitation or restriction on the power of the appointing authority, conferred by any other provision of law, to remove any member of the board.

(Added by Stats. 1967, Ch. 1397.)

3006. The board shall organize and elect a president from among its members for a term of one year at the first meeting of each year. The newly elected president shall assume his or her duties at the conclusion of the meeting at which he or she was elected. Reelection to office during membership is unrestricted.

(Amended by Stats. 2013, Ch. 512, Sec. 2. (SB 155) Effective January 1, 2014.)

3007. The board shall meet at least twice during each calendar year.

Special meetings may be called at any time by the president or by any five members of the board upon notice for such time and in such manner as the board may provide.

(Added by Stats. 1967, Ch. 1397.)

3008. All meetings of the board shall be open and public, and all persons shall be permitted to attend any meeting of the board, except that the board may hold executive sessions to deliberate on the decision to be reached upon the evidence introduced in a proceeding conducted in accordance with Chapter 5 (commencing with Section 11500) of Part 1 of Division 3 of Title 2 of the Government Code.

(Amended by Stats. 2022, Ch. 295, Sec. 6. (AB 2956) Effective January 1, 2023.)

3010. Five members of the board shall constitute a quorum for the transaction of business, for the performance of any duty or the exercise of any power or authority of the board, except that three members of the board, who are not new motor vehicle dealers, shall constitute a quorum for the purposes of Article 4 (commencing with Section 3060) and the consideration of a petition pursuant to subdivision (b) of Section 3050 that involves a dispute between a franchisee and franchisor.

(Amended by Stats. 2019, Ch. 796, Sec. 2. (AB 179) Effective January 1, 2020.)

3011. A vacancy on the board shall not impair the power of the remaining members to perform all duties and exercise all powers of the board, providing the members remaining constitute a quorum.

(Added by Stats. 1967, Ch. 1397.)

3012. Each member of the board shall receive a per diem of one hundred dollars ($100) for each day actually spent in the discharge of official duties, and he or she shall be reimbursed for traveling and other expenses necessarily incurred in the performance of his or her duties. The per diem and reimbursement shall be wholly defrayed from funds that shall be provided in the annual budget of the department.

(Amended by Stats. 2013, Ch. 512, Sec. 4. (SB 155) Effective January 1, 2014.)

3013. The board shall adopt a seal and such other device as the members may desire thereon, by which they shall authenticate all papers and documents under their control.

Copies of all records and papers in the board's office shall be received in evidence in all cases when certified under the hand and seal of the board, equally and with like effect as the originals.
(Added by Stats. 1967, Ch. 1397.)

3014. The board may appoint an executive director, who shall be exempt from civil service requirements, and who shall devote as much time as may be necessary to discharge the functions of the board as herein provided. The department shall provide the board with the necessary personnel, office space, equipment, supplies, and services that, in the opinion of the board, may be necessary to administer this chapter. However, the board may contract with the department or another state agency for office space, equipment, supplies, and services, as determined by the board to be appropriate, for the administration of this chapter.
(Amended by Stats. 2003, Ch. 451, Sec. 5. Effective January 1, 2004.)

3015. In addition to the office of the executive director in Sacramento, the department shall, as the need therefor occurs, secure adequate rooms for the meetings of the board in Los Angeles, San Francisco, Sacramento, or other locations in the state as may be required in the discretion of the board, to administer this chapter.
(Amended by Stats. 2003, Ch. 451, Sec. 6. Effective January 1, 2004.)

3016. (a) New motor vehicle dealers and other licensees under the jurisdiction of the board shall be charged fees sufficient to fully fund the activities of the board other than those conducted pursuant to Section 472.5 of the Business and Professions Code. The board may recover the direct cost of the activities required by Section 472.5 of the Business and Professions Code by charging the Department of Consumer Affairs a fee which shall be paid by the Department of Consumer Affairs with funds appropriated from the Certification Account in the Consumer Affairs Fund. All fees shall be deposited, and held separate from other moneys, in the Motor Vehicle Account in the State Transportation Fund, and shall not be transferred to the State Highway Account pursuant to Section 42273.

(b) The fees shall be available, when appropriated, exclusively to fund the activities of the board. If, at the conclusion of any fiscal year, the amount of fees collected exceeds the amount of expenditures for this purpose during the fiscal year, the surplus shall be carried over into the succeeding fiscal year.
(Amended by Stats. 1997, Ch. 17, Sec. 143. Effective January 1, 1998.)

Article 2. Powers and Duties of Board

(Article 2 added by Stats. 1967, Ch. 1397.)

3050. The board shall do all of the following:

(a) Adopt rules and regulations in accordance with Chapter 3.5 (commencing with Section 11340) of Part 1 of Division 3 of Title 2 of the Government Code governing those matters that are specifically committed to its jurisdiction.

(b) Consider any matter concerning the activities or practices of any person applying for or holding a license as a new motor vehicle dealer, manufacturer, manufacturer branch, distributor, distributor branch, or representative pursuant to Chapter 4 (commencing with Section 11700) of Division 5 submitted by any person. A member of the board who is a new motor vehicle dealer may not participate in, hear, comment, advise other members upon, or decide any matter considered by the board pursuant to this subdivision that involves a dispute between a franchisee and franchisor. After that consideration, the board may do any one or any combination of the following:

(1) Direct the department to conduct investigation of matters that the board deems reasonable, and make a written report on the results of the investigation to the board within the time specified by the board.

(2) (A) Undertake to mediate, arbitrate, or otherwise resolve any honest difference of opinion or viewpoint existing between any member of the public and any new motor vehicle dealer, manufacturer, manufacturer branch, distributor, distributor branch, or representative.

(B) The board does not have jurisdiction over a dispute pursuant to this paragraph involving any member of the public, including a consumer or other person who is not applying for or holding a license as a new motor vehicle dealer, manufacturer, manufacturer branch, distributor, distributor branch, or representative pursuant to Chapter 4 (commencing with Section 11700) of Division 5, unless that person has filed the dispute with the board or consents to jurisdiction by the board.

(3) Order the department to exercise any and all authority or power that the department may have with respect to the issuance, renewal, refusal to renew, suspension, or revocation of the license of any new motor vehicle dealer, manufacturer, manufacturer branch, distributor, distributor branch, or representative as that license is required under Chapter 4 (commencing with Section 11700) of Division 5.

(c) Hear and decide, within the limitations and in accordance with the procedure provided, a protest presented by a franchisee pursuant to Section 3060, 3062, 3064, 3065, 3065.1, 3065.3, 3065.4, 3070, 3072, 3074, 3075, or 3076. A member of the board who is a new motor vehicle dealer may not participate in, hear, comment, advise other members upon, or decide, any matter involving a protest filed pursuant to Article 4 (commencing with Section 3060), unless all parties to the protest stipulate otherwise.

(d) Hear and decide, within the limitations and in accordance with the procedure provided, a protest presented by an association challenging a policy of a manufacturer, manufacturer branch, distributor, or distributor branch pursuant to Section 3085. A member of the board who is a new motor vehicle dealer may not participate in, hear, comment, advise other members upon, or decide, any matter involving a protest filed pursuant to Article 6 (commencing with Section 3085), unless all participants to the protest stipulate otherwise.

(e) Notwithstanding subdivisions (b), (c), and (d), the courts have jurisdiction over all common law and statutory claims originally cognizable in the courts. For those claims, a party may initiate an action directly in any court of competent jurisdiction.

(f) This section shall remain in effect only until January 1, 2030, and as of that date is repealed.
(Amended by Stats. 2019, Ch. 796, Sec. 3. (AB 179) Effective January 1, 2020. Repealed as of January 1, 2030, by its own provisions. See later operative version added by Sec. 4 of Stats. 2019, Ch. 796.)

3050. The board shall do all of the following:

(a) Adopt rules and regulations in accordance with Chapter 3.5 (commencing with Section 11340) of Part 1 of Division 3 of Title 2 of the Government Code governing those matters that are specifically committed to its jurisdiction.

(b) Consider any matter concerning the activities or practices of any person applying for or holding a license as a new motor vehicle dealer, manufacturer, manufacturer branch, distributor, distributor branch, or representative pursuant to Chapter 4 (commencing with Section 11700) of Division 5 submitted by any person. A member of the board who is a new motor vehicle dealer may not participate in, hear, comment, advise other members upon, or decide, any matter considered by the board pursuant to this subdivision that involves a dispute between a franchisee and franchisor. After that consideration, the board may do any one or any combination of the following:

(1) Direct the department to conduct investigation of matters that the board deems reasonable, and make a written report on the results of the investigation to the board within the time specified by the board.

(2) (A) Undertake to mediate, arbitrate, or otherwise resolve any honest difference of opinion or viewpoint existing between any member of the public and any new motor vehicle dealer, manufacturer, manufacturer branch, distributor, distributor branch, or representative.

(B) The board does not have jurisdiction over a dispute pursuant to this paragraph involving any member of the public, including a consumer, or other person that is not applying for or holding a license as a new motor vehicle dealer, manufacturer, manufacturer branch, distributor, distributor branch, or representative pursuant to Chapter 4 (commencing with Section 11700) of Division 5, unless that person has filed the dispute with the board or consents to jurisdiction by the board.

(3) Order the department to exercise any and all authority or power that the department may have with respect to the issuance, renewal, refusal to renew, suspension, or revocation of the license of any new motor vehicle dealer, manufacturer, manufacturer branch, distributor, distributor branch, or representative as that license is required under Chapter 4 (commencing with Section 11700) of Division 5.

(c) Hear and decide, within the limitations and in accordance with the procedure provided, a protest presented by a franchisee pursuant to Section 3060, 3062, 3064, 3065, 3065.1, 3065.3, 3065.4, 3070, 3072, 3074, 3075, or 3076. A member of the board who is a new motor vehicle dealer may not participate in, hear, comment, advise other members upon, or decide, any matter involving a protest filed pursuant to Article 4 (commencing with Section 3060), unless all parties to the protest stipulate otherwise.

(d) Notwithstanding subdivisions (b) and (c), the courts have jurisdiction over all common law and statutory claims originally cognizable in the courts. For those claims, a party may initiate an action directly in any court of competent jurisdiction.

(e) This section shall become operative on January 1, 2030.

(Repealed (in Sec. 3) and added by Stats. 2019, Ch. 796, Sec. 4. (AB 179) Effective January 1, 2020. Section operative January 1, 2030, by its own provisions.)

3050.1. (a) In a proceeding, hearing, or in the discharge of duties imposed under this chapter, the board, its executive director, or an administrative law judge designated by the board may administer oaths, take depositions, certify to official acts, and issue subpoenas to compel attendance of witnesses and the production of books, records, papers, and other documents in any part of the state.

(b) For purposes of discovery, the board or its executive director may, if deemed appropriate and proper under the circumstances, authorize the parties to engage in the civil action discovery procedures in Title 4 (commencing with Section 2016.010) of Part 4 of the Code of Civil Procedure, excepting the provisions of Chapter 13 (commencing with Section 2030.010) of that title. Discovery shall be completed no later than 15 days prior to the commencement of the proceeding or hearing before the board. This subdivision shall apply only to those proceedings or hearings involving a petition filed pursuant to subdivision (b) of Section 3050 or protest filed pursuant to subdivision (c) or (d) of Section 3050. The board, its executive director, or an administrative law judge designated by the board may issue subpoenas to compel attendance at depositions of persons having knowledge of the acts, omissions, or events that are the basis for the proceedings, as well as the production of books, records, papers, and other documents.

(c) This section shall remain in effect only until January 1, 2030, and as of that date is repealed.

(Amended by Stats. 2019, Ch. 796, Sec. 5. (AB 179) Effective January 1, 2020. Repealed as of January 1, 2030, by its own provisions. See later operative version added by Sec. 6 of Stats. 2019, Ch. 796.)

3050.1. (a) In a proceeding, hearing, or in the discharge of duties imposed under this chapter, the board, its executive director, or an administrative law judge designated by the board may administer oaths, take depositions, certify to official acts, and issue subpoenas to compel attendance of witnesses and the production of books, records, papers, and other documents in any part of the state.

(b) For purposes of discovery, the board or its executive director may, if deemed appropriate and proper under the circumstances, authorize the parties to engage in the civil action discovery procedures in Title 4 (commencing with Section 2016.010) of Part 4 of the Code of Civil Procedure, excepting the provisions of Chapter 13 (commencing with Section 2030.010) of that title. Discovery shall be completed no later than 15 days prior to the commencement of the proceeding or hearing before the board. This subdivision shall apply only to those proceedings or hearings involving a petition filed pursuant to subdivision (b) of Section 3050 or protest filed pursuant to subdivision (c) of Section 3050. The board, its executive director, or an administrative law judge designated by the board may issue subpoenas to compel attendance at depositions of persons having knowledge of the acts, omissions, or events that are the basis for the proceedings, as well as the production of books, records, papers, and other documents.

(c) This section shall become operative on January 1, 2030.

(Repealed (in Sec. 5) and added by Stats. 2019, Ch. 796, Sec. 6. (AB 179) Effective January 1, 2020. Section operative January 1, 2030, by its own provisions.)

3050.2. (a) Obedience to subpoenas issued to compel attendance of witnesses, or the production of books, records, papers, and other documents at the proceeding or hearing, may be enforced by application to the superior court as set forth in Article 2 (commencing with Section 11180) of Chapter 2 of Part 1 of Division 3 of Title 2 of the Government Code.

(b) Compliance with discovery procedures authorized pursuant to subdivision (b) of Section 3050.1 may be enforced by application to the executive director of the board. The executive director may, at the direction of the board, upon a showing of failure to comply with authorized discovery without substantial justification for that failure, dismiss the protest or petition or suspend the proceedings pending compliance. The executive director may, at the direction of the board, upon a failure to comply with authorized discovery without substantial justification for that failure, require payment of costs incurred by the board, as well as attorney's fees and costs of the party who successfully makes or opposes a motion to compel enforcement of discovery. Nothing in this section precludes the executive director from making application to the superior court to enforce obedience to subpoenas or compliance with other discovery procedures authorized pursuant to subdivision (b) of Section 3050.1.

(Amended by Stats. 2003, Ch. 451, Sec. 8. Effective January 1, 2004.)

3050.3. A witness, other than an officer or employee of the state or of a political subdivision of the state, who appears by order of the board or its executive director, shall receive for his or her attendance the same fees and the same mileage allowed by law to witnesses in civil cases. The amount shall be paid by the party at whose request the witness is subpoenaed. The mileage and fees, if any, of a witness subpoenaed by the board or its executive director, but not at the request of a party, shall be paid from the funds provided for the use of the board in the same manner that other expenses of the board are paid.

(Amended by Stats. 2003, Ch. 451, Sec. 9. Effective January 1, 2004.)

3050.4. In a protest or petition before the board, the board, its executive director, or an administrative law judge designated by the board or its executive director, may order a mandatory settlement conference. The failure of a party to appear, to be prepared, or to have authority to settle the matter may result in one or more of the following:

(a) The board, its executive director, or an administrative law judge designated by the board or its executive director, may suspend all proceedings before the board in the matter until compliance.

(b) The board, its executive director, or an administrative law judge designated by the board or its executive director, may dismiss the proceedings or any part thereof before the board with or without prejudice.

(c) The board, its executive director, or an administrative law judge designated by the board or its executive director, may require all the board's costs to be paid by the party at fault.

(d) The board, its executive director, or an administrative law judge designated by the board or its executive director, may deem that the party at fault has abandoned the matter.

(Amended by Stats. 2003, Ch. 451, Sec. 10. Effective January 1, 2004.)

3050.5. Pursuant to Section 3016, the board shall establish a fee for the initial filing by any party in regard to any protest or petition filed pursuant to this chapter.

(Amended by Stats. 2019, Ch. 796, Sec. 7. (AB 179) Effective January 1, 2020.)

3050.6. The board or its executive director may, in the event of a granting of a continuance of a scheduled matter, assess costs of the board upon the party receiving the continuance.

(Amended by Stats. 2003, Ch. 451, Sec. 11. Effective January 1, 2004.)

3050.7. (a) The board may adopt stipulated decisions and orders, without a hearing pursuant to Section 3066, 3080, or 3085.2, to resolve one or more issues raised by a protest or petition filed with the board. Whenever the parties to a protest or petition submit a proposed stipulated decision and order of the board, a copy of the proposed stipulated decision and order shall be transmitted by the executive director of the board to each member of the board. The proposed stipulated decision and order shall be deemed to be adopted by the board unless a member of the board notifies the executive director of the board of an objection thereto within 10 days after that board member has received a copy of the proposed stipulated decision and order.

(b) If the board adopts a stipulated decision and order to resolve a protest filed pursuant to Section 3060 or 3070 in which the parties stipulate that good cause exists for the termination of the franchise of the protestant, and the order provides for a conditional or unconditional termination of the franchise of the protestant, paragraph (2) of subdivision (a) of Section 3060 and paragraph (2) of subdivision (a) of Section 3070, which require a hearing to determine whether good cause exists for termination of the franchise, is inapplicable to the proceedings. If the stipulated decision and order provides for an unconditional termination of the franchise, the franchise may be terminated without further proceedings by the board. If the stipulated decision and order provides for the termination of the franchise, conditioned upon the failure of a party to comply with specified conditions, the franchise may be terminated upon a determination, according to the terms of the stipulated decision and order, that the conditions have not been met. If the stipulated decision and order provides for the termination of the franchise conditioned upon the occurrence of specified conditions, the franchise may be terminated upon a determination, according to the terms of the stipulated decision and order, that the stipulated conditions have occurred.

(c) This section shall remain in effect only until January 1, 2030, and as of that date is repealed.

(Amended by Stats. 2019, Ch. 796, Sec. 8. (AB 179) Effective January 1, 2020. Repealed as of January 1, 2030, by its own provisions. See later operative version added by Sec. 9 of Stats. 2019, Ch. 796.)

3050.7. (a) The board may adopt stipulated decisions and orders, without a hearing pursuant to Section 3066 or 3080, to resolve one or more issues raised by a protest or petition filed with the board. Whenever the parties to a protest or petition submit a proposed stipulated decision and order of the board, a copy of the proposed stipulated decision and order shall be transmitted by the executive director of the board to each member of the board. The proposed stipulated decision and order shall be deemed to be adopted by the board unless a member of the board notifies the executive director of the board of an objection thereto within 10 days after that board member has received a copy of the proposed stipulated decision and order.

(b) If the board adopts a stipulated decision and order to resolve a protest filed pursuant to Section 3060 or 3070 in which the parties stipulate that good cause exists for the termination of the franchise of the protestant, and the order provides for a conditional or unconditional termination of the franchise of the protestant, paragraph (2) of subdivision (a) of Section 3060 and paragraph (2) of subdivision (a) of Section 3070, which require a hearing to determine whether good cause exists for termination of the franchise, is inapplicable to the proceedings. If the stipulated decision and order provides for an unconditional termination of the franchise, the franchise may be terminated without further proceedings by the board. If the stipulated decision and order provides for the termination of the franchise, conditioned upon the failure of a party to comply with specified conditions, the franchise may be terminated upon a determination, according to the terms of the stipulated decision and order, that the conditions have not been met. If the stipulated decision and order provides for the termination of the franchise conditioned upon the occurrence of specified conditions, the franchise may be terminated upon a determination, according to the terms of the stipulated decision and order, that the stipulated conditions have occurred.

(c) This section shall become operative on January 1, 2030.

(Repealed (in Sec. 8) and added by Stats. 2019, Ch. 796, Sec. 9. (AB 179) Effective January 1, 2020. Section operative January 1, 2030, by its own provisions.)

3051. This chapter does not apply to any person licensed as a transporter under Article 1 (commencing with Section 11700) or as a salesperson under Article 2 (commencing with Section 11800) of Chapter 4 of Division 5, or to any licensee who is not a new motor vehicle dealer, motor vehicle manufacturer, manufacturer branch, new motor vehicle distributor, distributor branch, or representative. This chapter does not apply to transactions involving "mobilehomes," as defined in Section 18008 of the Health and Safety Code, "recreational vehicles," as defined in subdivision (b) of Section 18010 of the Health and Safety Code, truck campers, "commercial coaches," as defined in Section 18001.8 of the Health and Safety Code, or off-highway motor vehicles subject to identification, as defined in Section 38012, except off-highway motorcycles, as defined in Section 436, and all-terrain vehicles, as defined in Section 111. Except as otherwise provided in this chapter, this chapter applies to a new motor vehicle dealer, a dealer of new recreational vehicles, as defined in subdivision (a) of Section 18010 of the Health and Safety Code, except a dealer who deals exclusively in truck campers, a vehicle manufacturer as defined in Section 672, a manufacturer branch as defined in Section 389, a distributor as defined in Section 296, a distributor branch as defined in Section 297, a representative as defined in Section 512, or an applicant therefor.

(Amended by Stats. 2003, Ch. 703, Sec. 5. Effective January 1, 2004.)

Article 4. Hearings on Franchise Modification, Replacement, Termination, Refusal to Continue, Delivery and Preparation Obligations, and Warranty Reimbursement

(Heading of Article 4 amended by Stats. 1974, Ch. 384.)

3060. (a) Notwithstanding Section 20999.1 of the Business and Professions Code or the terms of any franchise, no franchisor shall terminate or refuse to continue any existing franchise unless all of the following conditions are met:

(1) The franchisee and the board have received written notice from the franchisor as follows:

(A) Sixty days before the effective date thereof setting forth the specific grounds for termination or refusal to continue.

(B) Fifteen days before the effective date thereof setting forth the specific grounds with respect to any of the following:

(i) Transfer of any ownership or interest in the franchise without the consent of the franchisor, which consent shall not be unreasonably withheld.

(ii) Misrepresentation by the franchisee in applying for the franchise.

(iii) Insolvency of the franchisee, or filing of any petition by or against the franchisee under any bankruptcy or receivership law.

(iv) Any unfair business practice after written warning thereof.

(v) Failure of the motor vehicle dealer to conduct its customary sales and service operations during its customary hours of business for seven consecutive business days, giving rise to a good faith belief on the part of the franchisor that the motor vehicle dealer is in fact going out of business, except for circumstances beyond the direct control of the motor vehicle dealer or by order of the department.

(C) The written notice shall contain, on the first page thereof in at least 12-point bold type and circumscribed by a line to segregate it from the rest of the text, one of the following statements, whichever is applicable:

[To be inserted when a 60-day notice of termination is given.]

"NOTICE TO DEALER: You have the right to file a protest with the

NEW MOTOR VEHICLE BOARD in Sacramento and have a hearing in which you may protest the termination of your franchise under provisions of the California Vehicle Code. You must file your protest with the board within 30 calendar days after receiving this notice or within 30 days after the end of any appeal procedure provided by the franchisor or your protest right will be waived."

[To be inserted when a 15-day notice of termination is given.]

"NOTICE TO DEALER: You have the right to file a protest with the NEW MOTOR VEHICLE BOARD in Sacramento and have a hearing in which you may protest the termination of your franchise under provisions of the California Vehicle Code. You must file your protest with the board within 10 calendar days after receiving this notice or within 10 days after the end of any appeal procedure provided by the franchisor or your protest right will be waived."

(2) Except as provided in Section 3050.7, the board finds that there is good cause for termination or refusal to continue, following a hearing called pursuant to Section 3066. The franchisee may file a protest with the board within 30 days after receiving a 60-day notice, satisfying the requirements of this section, or within 30 days after the end of any appeal procedure provided by the franchisor, or within 10 days after receiving a 15-day notice, satisfying the requirements of this section, or within 10 days after the end of any appeal procedure provided by the franchisor. When a protest is filed, the board shall advise the franchisor that a timely protest has been filed, that a hearing is required pursuant to Section 3066, and that the franchisor may not terminate or refuse to continue until the board makes its findings.

(3) The franchisor has received the written consent of the franchisee, or the appropriate period for filing a protest has elapsed.

(b) (1) Notwithstanding Section 20999.1 of the Business and Professions Code or the terms of any franchise, no franchisor shall modify or replace a franchise with a succeeding franchise if the modification or replacement would substantially affect the franchisee's sales or service obligations or investment, unless the franchisor has first given the board and each affected franchisee written notice thereof at least 60 days in advance of the modification or replacement. Within 30 days of receipt of the notice, satisfying the requirement of this section, or within 30 days after the end of any appeal procedure provided by the franchisor, a franchisee may file a protest with the board and the modification or replacement does not become effective until there is a finding by the board that there is good cause for the modification or replacement. If, however, a replacement franchise is the successor franchise to an expiring or expired term franchise, the prior franchise shall continue in effect until resolution of the protest by the board. In the event of multiple protests, hearings shall be consolidated to expedite the disposition of the issue.

(2) The written notice shall contain, on the first page thereof in at least 12-point bold type and circumscribed by a line to segregate it from the rest of the text, the following statement:

"NOTICE TO DEALER: Your franchise agreement is being modified or replaced. If the modification or replacement will substantially affect your sales or service obligations or investment, you have the right to file a protest with the NEW MOTOR VEHICLE BOARD in Sacramento and have a hearing in which you may protest the proposed modification or replacement of your franchise under provisions of the California Vehicle Code. You must file your protest with the board within 30 calendar days of your receipt of this notice or within 30 days after the end of any appeal procedure provided by the franchisor or your protest rights will be waived."

(Amended by Stats. 1998, Ch. 662, Sec. 3. Effective January 1, 1999.)

3061. In determining whether good cause has been established for modifying, replacing, terminating, or refusing to continue a franchise, the board shall take into consideration the existing circumstances, including, but not limited to, all of the following:

(a) Amount of business transacted by the franchisee, as compared to the business available to the franchisee.

(b) Investment necessarily made and obligations incurred by the franchisee to perform its part of the franchise.

(c) Permanency of the investment.

(d) Whether it is injurious or beneficial to the public welfare for the franchise to be modified or replaced or the business of the franchisee disrupted.

(e) Whether the franchisee has adequate motor vehicle sales and service facilities, equipment, vehicle parts, and qualified service personnel to reasonably provide for the needs of the consumers for the motor vehicles handled by the franchisee and has been and is rendering adequate services to the public.

(f) Whether the franchisee fails to fulfill the warranty obligations of the franchisor to be performed by the franchisee.

(g) Extent of franchisee's failure to comply with the terms of the franchise.

(Amended by Stats. 1983, Ch. 142, Sec. 160.)

3062. (a) (1) Except as otherwise provided in subdivision (b), if a franchisor seeks to enter into a franchise establishing an additional motor vehicle dealership, or seeks to relocate an existing motor vehicle dealership, that has a relevant market area within which the same line-make is represented, the franchisor shall, in writing, first notify the board and each franchisee in that line-make in the relevant market area of the franchisor's intention to establish an additional dealership or to relocate an existing dealership. Within 20 days of receiving the notice, satisfying the requirements of this section, or within 20 days after the end of an appeal procedure provided by the franchisor, a franchisee required to be given the notice may file with the board a protest to the proposed dealership establishment or relocation described in the franchisor's notice. If, within this time, a franchisee files with the board a request for additional time to file a protest, the board or its executive director, upon a showing of good cause, may grant an additional 10 days to file the protest. When a protest is filed, the board shall inform the franchisor that a timely protest has been filed, that a hearing is required pursuant to Section 3066, and that the franchisor may not establish the proposed dealership or relocate the existing dealership until the board has held a hearing as provided in Section 3066, nor thereafter, if the board has determined that there is good cause for not permitting the establishment of the proposed dealership or relocation of the existing dealership. In the event of multiple protests, hearings may be consolidated to expedite the disposition of the issue.

(2) If a franchisor seeks to enter into a franchise that authorizes a satellite warranty facility to be established at, or relocated to, a proposed location that is within two miles of a dealership of the same line-make, the franchisor shall first give notice in writing of the franchisor's intention to establish or relocate a satellite warranty facility at the proposed location to the board and each franchisee operating a dealership of the same line-make within two miles of the proposed location. Within 20 days of receiving the notice satisfying the requirements of this section, or within 20 days after the end of an appeal procedure provided by the franchisor, a franchisee required to be given the notice may file with the board a protest to the establishing or relocating of the satellite warranty facility. If, within this time, a franchisee files with the board a request for additional time to file a protest, the board or its executive director, upon a showing of good cause, may grant an additional 10 days to file the protest. When a protest is filed, the board shall inform the franchisor that a timely protest has been filed, that a hearing is required pursuant to Section 3066, and that the franchisor may not establish or relocate the proposed satellite warranty facility until the board has held a hearing as provided in Section 3066, nor thereafter, if the board has determined that there is good cause for not permitting the satellite warranty facility. In the event of multiple protests, hearings may be consolidated to expedite the disposition of the issue.

(3) The written notice shall contain, on the first page thereof in at least 12-point bold type and circumscribed by a line to segregate it from the

rest of the text, the following statement:

"NOTICE TO DEALER: You have the right to file a protest with the NEW MOTOR VEHICLE BOARD in Sacramento and have a hearing on your protest under the terms of the California Vehicle Code if you oppose this action. You must file your protest with the board within 20 days of your receipt of this notice, or within 20 days after the end of any appeal procedure that is provided by us to you. If within this time you file with the board a request for additional time to file a protest, the board or its executive director, upon a showing of good cause, may grant you an additional 10 days to file the protest."

(b) Subdivision (a) does not apply to either of the following:

(1) The relocation of an existing dealership to a location that is both within the same city as, and within one mile from, the existing dealership location.

(2) The establishment at a location that is both within the same city as, and within one-quarter mile from, the location of a dealership of the same line-make that has been out of operation for less than 90 days.

(c) Subdivision (a) does not apply to a display of vehicles at a fair, exposition, or similar exhibit if actual sales are not made at the event and the display does not exceed 30 days. This subdivision may not be construed to prohibit a new vehicle dealer from establishing a branch office for the purpose of selling vehicles at the fair, exposition, or similar exhibit, even though the event is sponsored by a financial institution, as defined in Section 31041 of the Financial Code or by a financial institution and a licensed dealer. The establishment of these branch offices, however, shall be in accordance with subdivision (a) where applicable.

(d) For the purposes of this section, the reopening of a dealership that has not been in operation for one year or more shall be deemed the establishment of an additional motor vehicle dealership.

(e) As used in this section, the following definitions apply:

(1) "Motor vehicle dealership" or "dealership" means an authorized facility at which a franchisee offers for sale or lease, displays for sale or lease, or sells or leases new motor vehicles.

(2) "Satellite warranty facility" means a facility operated by a franchisee where authorized warranty repairs and service are performed and the offer for sale or lease, the display for sale or lease, or the sale or lease of new motor vehicles is not authorized to take place.

(Amended by Stats. 2013, Ch. 512, Sec. 10. (SB 155) Effective January 1, 2014.)

3063. In determining whether good cause has been established for not entering into a franchise or relocating an existing dealership of the same line-make, the board shall take into consideration the existing circumstances, including, but not limited to, all of the following:

(a) Permanency of the investment.

(b) Effect on the retail motor vehicle business and the consuming public in the relevant market area.

(c) Whether it is injurious to the public welfare for an additional franchise to be established or an existing dealership to be relocated.

(d) Whether the franchisees of the same line-make in the relevant market area are providing adequate competition and convenient consumer care for the motor vehicles of the line-make in the market area, which shall include the adequacy of motor vehicle sales and service facilities, equipment, supply of vehicle parts, and qualified service personnel.

(e) Whether the establishment of an additional franchise would increase competition and therefore be in the public interest.

(f) For purposes of this section, the terms "motor vehicle dealership" and "dealership" shall have the same meaning as defined in Section 3062.

(Amended by Stats. 2013, Ch. 512, Sec. 11. (SB 155) Effective January 1, 2014.)

3064. (a) Every franchisor shall specify to its franchisees the delivery and preparation obligations of the franchisees prior to delivery of new motor vehicles to retail buyers. A copy of the delivery and preparation obligations, which shall constitute the franchisee's only responsibility for product liability between the franchisee and the franchisor but shall not in any way affect the franchisee's responsibility for product liability between the purchaser and either the franchisee or the franchisor, and a schedule of compensation to be paid to franchisees for the work and services they shall be required to perform in connection with those delivery and preparation obligations shall be filed with the board by franchisors, and shall constitute the compensation as set forth on the schedule. The schedule of compensation shall be reasonable, with the reasonableness thereof being subject to the approval of the board, if a franchisee files a notice of protest with the board. In determining the reasonableness of the schedules, the board shall consider all relevant circumstances, including, but not limited to, the time required to perform each function that the dealer is obligated to perform and the appropriate labor rate.

(b) Upon delivery of the vehicle, the franchisee shall give a copy of the delivery and preparation obligations to the purchaser and a written certification that the franchisee has fulfilled these obligations.

(Amended by Stats. 2013, Ch. 512, Sec. 12. (SB 155) Effective January 1, 2014.)

3065. (a) Every franchisor shall properly fulfill every warranty agreement made by it and adequately and fairly compensate each of its franchisees for labor and parts used to satisfy the warranty obligations of the franchisor, including, but not limited to, diagnostics, repair, and servicing and shall file a copy of its warranty reimbursement schedule with the board. The warranty reimbursement schedule shall be reasonable with respect to the time and compensation allowed to the franchisee for the warranty diagnostics, repair, servicing, and all other conditions of the obligation, including costs directly associated with the disposal of hazardous materials that are associated with a warranty repair.

(1) The franchisor shall use time allowances for the diagnosis and performance of work and service that are reasonable and adequate for a qualified technician to perform the work or services. A franchisor shall not unreasonably deny a written request submitted by a franchisee for modification of a franchisor's uniform time allowance for a specific warranty repair, or a request submitted by a franchisee for an additional time allowance for either diagnostic or repair work on a specific vehicle covered under warranty, provided the request includes any information and documentation reasonably required by the franchisor to assess the merits of the franchisee's request.

(2) A franchisor shall not replace, modify, or supplement the warranty reimbursement schedule to impose a fixed percentage or other reduction in the time or compensation allowed to the franchisee for warranty repairs not attributable to a specific repair. A franchisor may reduce the allowed time or compensation applicable to a specific warranty repair only upon 15 days' prior written notice to the franchisee.

(3) Any protest challenging a reduction in time or compensation applicable to specific parts or labor operations shall be filed within six months following the franchisee's receipt of notice of the reduction, and the franchisor shall have the burden of establishing the reasonableness of the reduction and adequacy and fairness of the resulting reduction in time or compensation.

(b) In determining what constitutes a reasonable warranty reimbursement schedule under this section, a franchisor shall compensate each of its franchisees for parts and labor at rates equal to the franchisee's retail labor rate and retail parts rate, as established pursuant to Section 3065.2. Nothing in this subdivision prohibits a franchisee and a franchisor from entering into a voluntary written agreement signed by both parties that compensates for labor and parts used to satisfy the warranty obligations of the franchisor at rates other than the franchisee's retail rates, provided that the warranty reimbursement schedule adequately and fairly compensates the franchisee.

(c) If any franchisor disallows a franchisee's claim for a defective part, alleging that the part, in fact, is not defective, the franchisor shall return the part alleged not to be defective to the franchisee at the expense of the franchisor, or the franchisee shall be reimbursed for the franchisee's cost of the part, at the franchisor's option.

(d) (1) All claims made by franchisees pursuant to this section shall be either approved or disapproved within 30 days after their receipt by the franchisor. Any claim not specifically disapproved in writing within 30 days from receipt by the franchisor shall be deemed approved on the 30th day. All claims made by franchisees under this section and Section 3064 for labor and parts shall be paid within 30 days after approval.

(2) A franchisor shall not disapprove a claim unless the claim is false or fraudulent, repairs were not properly made, repairs were inappropriate to correct a nonconformity with the written warranty due to an improper act or omission of the franchisee, or for material noncompliance with reasonable and nondiscriminatory documentation and administrative claims submission requirements.

(3) When any claim is disapproved, the franchisee who submits it shall be notified in writing of its disapproval within the required period, and each notice shall state the specific grounds upon which the disapproval is based. The franchisor shall provide for a reasonable appeal process allowing the franchisee at least 30 days after receipt of the written disapproval notice to provide additional supporting documentation or information rebutting the disapproval. If disapproval is based upon noncompliance with documentation or administrative claims submission requirements, the franchisor shall allow the franchisee at least 30 days from the date of receipt of the notice to cure any material noncompliance. If the disapproval is rebutted, and material noncompliance is cured before the applicable deadline, the franchisor shall approve the claim.

(4) If the franchisee provides additional supporting documentation or information purporting to rebut the disapproval, attempts to cure noncompliance relating to the claim, or otherwise appeals denial of the claim and the franchisor continues to deny the claim, the franchisor shall provide the franchisee with a written notification of the final denial within 30 days of completion of the appeal process, which shall conspicuously state "Final Denial" on the first page.

(5) Failure to approve or pay within the above specified time limits, in individual instances for reasons beyond the reasonable control of the franchisor, shall not constitute a violation of this article.

(6) Within six months after either receipt of the written notice described in paragraph (3) or (4), whichever is later, a franchisee may file a protest with the board for determination of whether the franchisor complied with the requirements of this subdivision. In any protest pursuant to this subdivision, the franchisor shall have the burden of proof.

(e) (1) Audits of franchisee warranty records may be conducted by the franchisor on a reasonable basis for a period of nine months after a claim is paid or credit issued. A franchisor shall not select a franchisee for an audit, or perform an audit, in a punitive, retaliatory, or unfairly discriminatory manner. A franchisor may conduct no more than one random audit of a franchisee in a nine-month period. The franchisor's notification to the franchisee of any additional audit within a nine-month period shall be accompanied by written disclosure of the basis for that additional audit.

(2) Previously approved claims shall not be disapproved or charged back to the franchisee unless the claim is false or fraudulent, repairs were not properly made, repairs were inappropriate to correct a nonconformity with the written warranty due to an improper act or omission of the franchisee, or for material noncompliance with reasonable and nondiscriminatory documentation and administrative claims submission requirements. A franchisor shall not disapprove or chargeback a claim based upon an extrapolation from a sample of claims, unless the sample of claims is selected randomly and the extrapolation is performed in a reasonable and statistically valid manner.

(3) If the franchisor disapproves of a previously approved claim following an audit, the franchisor shall provide to the franchisee, within 30 days after the audit, a written disapproval notice stating the specific grounds upon which the claim is disapproved. The franchisor shall provide a reasonable appeal process allowing the franchisee a reasonable period of not less than 30 days after receipt of the written disapproval notice to respond to any disapproval with additional supporting documentation or information rebutting the disapproval and to cure noncompliance, with the period to be commensurate with the volume of claims under consideration. If the franchisee rebuts any disapproval and cures any material noncompliance relating to a claim before the applicable deadline, the franchisor shall not chargeback the franchisee for that claim.

(4) If the franchisee provides additional supporting documentation or information purporting to rebut the disapproval, attempts to cure noncompliance relating to the claim, or otherwise appeals denial of the claim and the franchisor continues to deny the claim, the franchisor shall provide the franchisee with a written notification of the final denial within 30 days of completion of the appeal process, which shall conspicuously state "Final Denial" on the first page.

(5) The franchisor shall not chargeback the franchisee until 45 days after receipt of the written notice described in paragraph (3) or paragraph (4), whichever is later. Any chargeback to a franchisee for warranty parts or service compensation shall be made within 90 days of receipt of that written notice. If the franchisee files a protest pursuant to this subdivision prior to the franchisor's chargeback for denied claims, the franchisor shall not offset or otherwise undertake to collect the chargeback until the board issues a final order on the protest. If the board sustains the chargeback or the protest is dismissed, the franchisor shall have 90 days following issuance of the final order or the dismissal to make the chargeback, unless otherwise provided in a settlement agreement.

(6) Within six months after either receipt of the written disapproval notice or completion of the franchisor's appeal process, whichever is later, a franchisee may file a protest with the board for determination of whether the franchisor complied with this subdivision. In any protest pursuant to this subdivision, the franchisor shall have the burden of proof.

(f) If a false claim was submitted by a franchisee with the intent to defraud the franchisor, a longer period for audit and any resulting chargeback may be permitted if the franchisor obtains an order from the board.

(Amended by Stats. 2019, Ch. 796, Sec. 11. (AB 179) Effective January 1, 2020.)

3065.1. (a) All claims made by a franchisee for payment under the terms of a franchisor incentive program shall be either approved or disapproved within 30 days after receipt by the franchisor. When any claim is disapproved, the franchisee who submits it shall be notified in writing of its disapproval within the required period, and each notice shall state the specific grounds upon which the disapproval is based. Any claim not specifically disapproved in writing within 30 days from receipt shall be deemed approved on the 30th day.

(b) Franchisee claims for incentive program compensation shall not be disapproved unless the claim is false or fraudulent, the claim is ineligible under the terms of the incentive program as previously communicated to the franchisee, or for material noncompliance with reasonable and nondiscriminatory documentation and administrative claims submission requirements.

(c) The franchisor shall provide for a reasonable appeal process allowing the franchisee at least 30 days after receipt of the written disapproval notice to respond to any disapproval with additional supporting documentation or information rebutting the disapproval. If disapproval is based upon noncompliance with documentation or administrative claims submission requirements, the franchisor shall allow the franchisee at least 30 days from the date of receipt of the written disapproval notice to cure any material noncompliance. If the disapproval is rebutted, and material noncompliance is cured before the applicable deadline, the franchisor shall approve the claim.

(d) If the franchisee provides additional supporting documentation or information purporting to rebut the disapproval, attempts to cure noncompliance relating to the claim, or otherwise appeals denial of the claim, and the franchisor continues to deny the claim, the franchisor shall provide the franchisee with a written notification of the final denial within 30 days of completion of the appeal process, which shall conspicuously state "Final Denial" on the first page.

(e) Following the disapproval of a claim, a franchisee shall have six months from receipt of the written notice described in either subdivision (a) or (d), whichever is later, to file a protest with the board for determination of whether the franchisor complied with subdivisions (a), (b), (c), and (d). In any hearing pursuant to this subdivision or subdivision (a), (b), (c), or (d), the franchisor shall have the burden of proof.

(f) All claims made by franchisees under this section shall be paid within 30 days following approval. Failure to approve or pay within the above specified time limits, in individual instances for reasons beyond the reasonable control of the franchisor, do not constitute a violation of this article.

(g) (1) Audits of franchisee incentive records may be conducted by the franchisor on a reasonable basis, and for a period of nine months after a claim is paid or credit issued. A franchisor shall not select a franchisee for an audit, or perform an audit, in a punitive, retaliatory, or unfairly discriminatory manner. A franchisor may conduct no more than one random audit of a franchisee in a nine-month period. The franchisor's notification to the franchisee of any additional audit within a nine-month period shall be accompanied by written disclosure of the basis for that additional audit.

(2) Previously approved claims shall not be disapproved and charged back unless the claim is false or fraudulent, the claim is ineligible under the terms of the incentive program as previously communicated to the franchisee, or for material noncompliance with reasonable and nondiscriminatory documentation and administrative claims submission requirements. A franchisor shall not disapprove a claim or chargeback a claim based upon an extrapolation from a sample of claims, unless the sample of claims is selected randomly and the extrapolation is performed in a reasonable and statistically valid manner.

(3) If the franchisor disapproves of a previously approved claim following an audit, the franchisor shall provide to the franchisee, within 30 days after the audit, a written disapproval notice stating the specific grounds upon which the claim is disapproved. The franchisor shall provide a reasonable appeal process allowing the franchisee a reasonable period of not less than 30 days after receipt of the written disapproval notice to respond to any disapproval with additional supporting documentation or information rebutting the disapproval and to cure any material noncompliance, with the period to be commensurate with the volume of claims under consideration. If the franchisee rebuts any disapproval and cures any material noncompliance relating to a claim before the applicable deadline, the franchisor shall not chargeback the franchisee for that claim.

(4) If the franchisee provides additional supporting documentation or information purporting to rebut the disapproval, attempts to cure noncompliance relating to the claim, or otherwise appeals denial of the claim, and the franchisor continues to deny the claim, the franchisor shall provide the franchisee with a written notification of the final denial within 30 days of completion of the appeal process, which shall conspicuously state "Final Denial" on the first page.

(5) The franchisor shall not chargeback the franchisee until 45 days after the franchisee receives the written notice described in paragraph (3) or (4), whichever is later. If the franchisee cures any material noncompliance relating to a claim, the franchisor shall not chargeback the dealer for that claim. Any chargeback to a franchisee for incentive program compensation shall be made within 90 days after the franchisee receives that written notice. If the board sustains the chargeback or the protest is dismissed, the franchisor shall have 90 days following issuance of the final order or the dismissal to make the chargeback, unless otherwise provided in a settlement agreement.

(6) Within six months after either receipt of the written notice described in paragraph (3) or (4), a franchisee may file a protest with the board for determination of whether the franchisor complied with this subdivision. If the franchisee files a protest pursuant to this subdivision prior to the franchisor's chargeback for denied claims, the franchisor shall not offset or otherwise undertake to collect the chargeback until the board issues a final order on the protest. In any protest pursuant to this subdivision, the franchisor shall have the burden of proof.

(h) If a false claim was submitted by a franchisee with the intent to defraud the franchisor, a longer period for audit and any resulting chargeback may be permitted if the franchisor obtains an order from the board.

(Amended by Stats. 2013, Ch. 512, Sec. 14. (SB 155) Effective January 1, 2014.)

3065.2. (a) A franchisee seeking to establish or modify its retail labor rate, retail parts rate, or both, to determine a reasonable warranty reimbursement schedule shall, no more frequently than once per calendar year, complete the following requirements:

(1) The franchisee shall submit in writing to the franchisor whichever of the following is fewer in number:

(A) Any 100 consecutive qualified repair orders completed, including any nonqualified repair orders completed in the same period.

(B) All repair orders completed in any 90-consecutive-day period.

(2) The franchisee shall calculate its retail labor rate by determining the total charges for labor from the qualified repair orders submitted and dividing that amount by the total number of hours that generated those charges.

(3) The franchisee shall calculate its retail parts rate by determining the total charges for parts from the qualified repair orders submitted, dividing that amount by the franchisee's total cost of the purchase of those parts, subtracting one, and multiplying by 100 to produce a percentage.

(4) The franchisee shall provide notice to the franchisor of its retail labor rate and retail parts rate calculated in accordance with this subdivision.

(b) For purposes of subdivision (a), qualified repair orders submitted under this subdivision shall be from a period occurring not more than 180 days before the submission. Repair orders submitted pursuant to this section may be transmitted electronically. A franchisee may submit either of the following:

(1) A single set of qualified repair orders for purposes of calculating both its retail labor rate and its retail parts rate.

(2) A set of qualified repair orders for purposes of calculating only its retail labor rate or only its retail parts rate.

(c) Charges included in a repair order arising from any of the following shall be omitted in calculating the retail labor rate and retail parts rate under this section:

(1) Manufacturer, manufacturer branch, distributor, or distributor branch special events, specials, or promotional discounts for retail customer repairs.

(2) Parts sold, or repairs performed, at wholesale.

(3) Routine maintenance, including, but not limited to, the replacement of bulbs, fluids, filters, batteries, and belts that are not provided in the course of, and related to, a repair.

(4) Items that do not have individual part numbers including, but not limited to, nuts, bolts, and fasteners.

(5) Vehicle reconditioning.

(6) Accessories.

(7) Repairs of conditions caused by a collision, a road hazard, the force of the elements, vandalism, theft, or owner, operational, or third-party negligence or deliberate act.

(8) Parts sold or repairs performed for insurance carriers.

(9) Vehicle emission inspections required by law.

(10) Manufacturer-approved goodwill or policy repairs or replacements.

(11) Repairs for government agencies or service contract providers.

(12) Repairs with aftermarket parts, when calculating the retail parts rate, but not the retail labor rate.

(13) Repairs on aftermarket parts.

(14) Replacement of or work on tires, including front-end alignments and wheel or tire rotations.

(15) Repairs of motor vehicles owned by the franchisee or an employee thereof at the time of the repair.

(d) (1) A franchisor may contest to the franchisee the material accuracy of the retail labor rate or retail parts rate that was calculated by the franchisee under this section within 30 days after receiving notice from the franchisee or, if the franchisor requests supplemental repair orders pursuant to paragraph (4), within 30 days after receiving the supplemental repair orders. If the franchisor seeks to contest the retail labor rate, retail parts rate, or both, the franchisor shall submit no more than one notification to the franchisee. The notification shall be limited to an assertion that the rate is materially inaccurate or fraudulent, and shall provide a full explanation of any and all reasons for the allegation, evidence substantiating the franchisor's position, a copy of all calculations used by the franchisor in determining the franchisor's position, and a proposed adjusted retail labor rate or retail parts rate, as applicable, on the basis of the repair orders submitted by the franchisee or, if applicable, on the basis provided in paragraph (5). After submitting the notification, the franchisor shall not add to, expand, supplement, or otherwise modify any element of that notification, including, but not limited to, its grounds for contesting the retail labor rate, retail parts rate, or both, without justification. A franchisor shall not deny the franchisee's submission for the retail labor rate, retail parts rate, or both, under subdivision (a).

(2) If the franchisee agrees with the conclusions of the franchisor and any corresponding adjustment to the retail labor rate or retail parts rate, no further action shall be required. The new adjusted rate shall be deemed effective as of the 30th calendar day after the franchisor's receipt of the notice submitted pursuant to subdivision (a).

(3) In the event the franchisor provides all of the information required by paragraph (1) to the franchisee, and the franchisee does not agree with the adjusted rate proposed by the franchisor, the franchisor shall pay the franchisee at the franchisor's proposed adjusted retail labor rate or retail parts rate until a decision is rendered upon any board protest filed pursuant to Section 3065.4 or until any mutual resolution between the franchisor and the franchisee. The franchisor's proposed adjusted rate shall be deemed to be effective as of the 30th day after the franchisor's receipt of the notice submitted pursuant to subdivision (a).

(4) If the franchisor determines from the franchisee's set of repair orders submitted pursuant to subdivisions (a) and (b) that the franchisee's submission for a retail labor rate or retail parts rate is substantially higher than the franchisee's current warranty rate, the franchisor may request, in writing, within 30 days after the franchisor's receipt of the notice submitted pursuant to subdivision (a), all repair orders closed within the period of 30 days immediately preceding, or 30 days immediately following, the set of repair orders submitted by the franchisee. If the franchisee fails to provide the supplemental repair orders, all time periods under this section shall be suspended until the supplemental repair orders are provided.

(5) If the franchisor requests supplemental repair orders pursuant to paragraphs (1) and (4), the franchisor may calculate a proposed adjusted retail labor rate or retail parts rate, as applicable, based upon any set of the qualified repair orders submitted by the franchisee, if the franchisor complies with all of the following requirements:

(A) The franchisor uses the same requirements applicable to the franchisee's submission pursuant to paragraph (1) of subdivision (a).

(B) The franchisor uses the formula to calculate retail labor rate or retail parts as provided in subdivision (a).

(C) The franchisor omits all charges in the repair orders as provided in subdivision (c).

(e) If the franchisor does not contest the retail labor rate or retail parts rate that was calculated by the franchisee, or if the franchisor fails to contest the rate pursuant to subdivision (d), within 30 days after receiving the notice submitted by the franchisee pursuant to subdivision (a), the uncontested retail labor rate or retail parts rate shall take effect on the 30th day after the franchisor's receipt of the notice and the franchisor shall use the new retail labor rate or retail parts rate, or both, if applicable, to determine compensation to fulfill warranty obligations to the franchisee pursuant to this section.

(f) When calculating the retail parts rate and retail labor rate, all of the following shall apply:

(1) Promotional reward program cash-equivalent pay methods shall not be considered discounts.

(2) (A) The franchisor is prohibited from establishing or implementing a special part or component number for parts used in warranty work, if the result of the special part or component lowers compensation to the franchisee below that amount calculated pursuant to this section.

(B) This paragraph does not apply to parts or components that are subject to a recall and are issued a new special part or component number. This paragraph does not prohibit a franchisor from changing prices of parts in the ordinary course of business.

(g) When the franchisor is compensating the franchisee for the retail parts rate, all of the following shall apply:

(1) If the franchisor furnishes a part to a franchisee at no cost for use in performing warranty obligations, the franchisor shall compensate the franchisee the amount resulting from multiplying the wholesale value of the part by the franchisee's retail parts rate determined pursuant to this section.

(2) If the franchisor furnishes a part to a franchisee at a reduced cost for use in performing warranty obligations, the franchisor shall compensate the franchisee the amount resulting from multiplying the wholesale value of the part by the franchisee's retail parts rate determined pursuant to this section, plus the franchisee's cost of the part.

(3) The wholesale value of the part, for purposes of this subdivision, shall be the greater of:

(A) The amount the franchisee paid for the part or a substantially identical part if already owned by the franchisee.

(B) The cost of the part shown in a current franchisor's established price schedule.

(C) The cost of a substantially identical part shown in a current franchisor's established price schedule.

(h) When a franchisee submits for the establishment or modification of a retail labor rate, retail parts rate, or both, pursuant to this section, a franchisee's retail labor rate or retail parts rate shall be calculated only using the method prescribed in this section. When a franchisee submits for the establishment or modification of a retail labor rate, retail parts rate, or both, pursuant to this section, a franchisor shall not use, or require a franchisee to use, any other method, including, but not limited to, any of the following:

(1) Substituting any other purported repair sample for that submitted by a franchisee.

(2) Imposing any method related to the establishment of a retail labor rate or retail parts rate that is unreasonable or time consuming, or require the use of information that is unreasonable or time consuming to obtain, including part-by-part or transaction-by-transaction calculations or utilization of the franchisee's financial statement.

(3) Unilaterally calculating a retail labor rate or retail parts rate for a franchisee, except as provided in subdivision (d).

(4) Using a franchisee's sample, submitted for establishing or increasing its retail parts rate, to establish or reduce the franchisee's retail labor rate or using a franchisee's sample, submitted for establishing or increasing its retail labor rate, to establish or reduce the franchisee's retail parts rate.

(i) A franchisor shall not do any of the following:

(1) Attempt to influence a franchisee to implement or change the prices for which the franchisee sells parts or labor in retail repairs because the franchisee is seeking compensation or exercising any right pursuant to this section.

(2) Directly or indirectly, take or threaten to take any adverse action against a franchisee for seeking compensation or exercising any right pursuant to this section, by any action including, but not limited to, the following:

(A) Assessing penalties, surcharges, or similar costs to a franchisee.

(B) Transferring or shifting any costs to a franchisee.

(C) Limiting allocation of vehicles or parts to a franchisee.

(D) Failing to act other than in good faith.

(E) Hindering, delaying, or rejecting the proper and timely payment of compensation due under this section to a franchisee.

(F) Establishing, implementing, enforcing, or applying any discriminatory policy, standard, rule, program, or incentive regarding compensation due under this section.

(G) Conducting or threatening to conduct nonroutine or nonrandom warranty, nonwarranty repair, or other service-related audits in response to a franchisee seeking compensation or exercising any right pursuant to this section.

(3) This subdivision does not prohibit a franchisor from increasing prices of vehicles or parts in the ordinary course of business.

(j) As used in this section, a "qualified repair order" is a repair order, closed at the time of submission, for work that was performed outside of the period of the manufacturer's warranty and paid for by the customer, but that would have been covered by a manufacturer's warranty if the work had been required and performed during the period of warranty.

(Amended by Stats. 2020, Ch. 370, Sec. 265. (SB 1371) Effective January 1, 2021.)

3065.25. As used in Sections 3065, 3065.2, and 3065.4, the following terms shall have the following meanings:

(a) "Parts" includes, but is not limited to, engine, transmission, and other part assemblies.

(b) "Warranty" includes a new vehicle warranty, a certified preowned warranty, a repair pursuant to a technical service bulletin on a vehicle covered under the period of warranty, a repair pursuant to a customer service campaign on a vehicle covered under the period of warranty, and a recall conducted pursuant to Sections 30118 to 30120, inclusive, of Title 49 of the United States Code.

(Added by Stats. 2019, Ch. 796, Sec. 13. (AB 179) Effective January 1, 2020.)

3065.3. (a) No franchisor shall establish or maintain a performance standard, sales objective, or program for measuring a dealer's sales, service, or customer service performance that is inconsistent with the standards set forth in subdivision (g) of Section 11713.13.

(b) No franchisor shall allocate vehicles or parts in a manner inconsistent with the standards set forth in subdivision (a) of Section 11713.3.

(c) No franchisor shall impose a facility or equipment policy inconsistent with the standards set forth in subdivision (a), (b), (c), or (k) of Section 11713.13.

(d) No franchisor shall compete with a dealer in violation of subdivision (o) of Section 11713.3.

(e) A franchisee may file a protest with the board for determination of whether a franchisor has complied with this section and in that proceeding the franchisor shall have the burden of proof.

(Amended by Stats. 2023, Ch. 332, Sec. 2. (AB 473) Effective January 1, 2024.)

3065.4. (a) If a franchisor fails to comply with Section 3065.2, or if a franchisee disputes the franchisor's proposed adjusted retail labor rate or retail parts rate, the franchisee may file a protest with the board for a declaration of the franchisee's retail labor rate or retail parts rate. In any protest under this section, the franchisor shall have the burden of proof that it complied with Section 3065.2 and that the franchisee's determination of the retail labor rate or retail parts rate is materially inaccurate or fraudulent.

(b) Upon a decision by the board pursuant to subdivision (a), the board may determine the difference between the amount the franchisee has actually received from the franchisor for fulfilled warranty obligations and the amount that the franchisee would have received if the franchisor had compensated the franchisee at the retail labor rate and retail parts rate as determined in accordance with Section 3065.2 for a period beginning 30 days after receipt of the franchisee's initial submission under subdivision (a) of Section 3065.2. The franchisee may submit a request to the franchisor to calculate the unpaid warranty reimbursement compensation and the franchisor shall provide this calculation to the franchisee within 30 days after receipt of the request. The request for the calculation will also be deemed a request for payment of the unpaid warranty reimbursement compensation.

(c) If the franchisor fails to make full payment within 30 days after the franchisee submits a request for payment, the franchisee may file an action in superior court for injunctive and other appropriate relief to enforce the determination or order of the board. The franchisee may also recover in superior court its actual reasonable expenses in bringing and maintaining an enforcement action in superior court.

(d) Either the franchisor or the franchisee may seek judicial review of the board's determination pursuant to Section 3068.

(Added by Stats. 2019, Ch. 796, Sec. 15. (AB 179) Effective January 1, 2020.)

3066. (a) Upon receiving a protest pursuant to Section 3060, 3062, 3064, 3065, 3065.1, 3065.3, or 3065.4, the board shall fix a time within 60 days of the order, and place of hearing, and shall send by certified mail a copy of the order to the franchisor, the protesting franchisee, and all individuals and groups that have requested notification by the board of protests and decisions of the board. Except in a case involving a franchisee who deals exclusively in motorcycles, the board or its executive director may, upon a showing of good cause, accelerate or postpone the date initially established for a hearing, but the hearing shall not be rescheduled more than 90 days after the board's initial order. For the purpose of accelerating or postponing a hearing date, "good cause" includes, but is not limited to, the effects upon, and any irreparable harm to, the parties or interested persons or groups if the request for a change in hearing date is not granted. The board or an administrative law judge designated by the board shall hear and consider the oral and documented evidence introduced by the parties and other interested individuals and groups, and the board shall make its decision solely on the record so made. Chapter 4.5 (commencing with Section 11400) of Part 1 of Division 3 of Title 2 of the Government Code and Sections 11507.3, 11507.6, 11507.7, 11511, 11511.5, 11513, 11514, 11515, and 11517 of the Government Code apply to these proceedings.

(b) In a hearing on a protest filed pursuant to Section 3060 or 3062, the franchisor shall have the burden of proof to establish that there is good cause to modify, replace, terminate, or refuse to continue a franchise. The franchisee shall have the burden of proof to establish that there is good cause not to enter into a franchise establishing an additional motor vehicle dealership or relocating an existing motor vehicle dealership.

(c) Except as otherwise provided in this chapter, in a hearing on a protest alleging a violation of, or filed pursuant to, Section 3064, 3065, or 3065.1, the franchisee shall have the burden of proof, but the franchisor has the burden of proof to establish that a franchisee acted with intent to defraud the franchisor when that issue is material to a protest filed pursuant to Section 3065 or 3065.1.

(d) In a hearing on a protest filed pursuant to Section 3065.3, the franchisor shall have the burden of proof to establish that the franchisor complied with subdivision (g) of Section 11713.13.

(e) In a hearing on a protest filed pursuant to Section 3065.4, the franchisor shall have the burden of proof to establish that the franchisor complied with Section 3065.2 and that the franchisee's determination of the retail labor rate or retail parts rate is materially inaccurate or fraudulent.

(f) A member of the board who is a new motor vehicle dealer may not participate in, hear, comment, or advise other members upon, or decide, a matter involving a protest filed pursuant to this article unless all parties to the protest stipulate otherwise.

(Amended by Stats. 2019, Ch. 796, Sec. 16. (AB 179) Effective January 1, 2020.)

3067. (a) The decision of the board shall be in writing and shall contain findings of fact and a determination of the issues presented. The decision shall sustain, conditionally sustain, overrule, or conditionally overrule the protest. Conditions imposed by the board shall be for the purpose of assuring performance of binding contractual agreements between franchisees and franchisors or otherwise serving the purposes of this article. If the board fails to act within 30 days after the hearing, within 30 days after the board receives a proposed decision when the case is heard before an administrative law judge alone, or within a period necessitated by Section 11517 of the Government Code, or as may be mutually agreed upon by the parties, then the proposed action shall be deemed to be approved. Copies of the board's decision shall be delivered to the parties personally or sent to them by certified mail, as well as to all individuals and groups that have requested notification by the board of protests and decisions by the board. The board's decision shall be final upon its delivery or mailing and a reconsideration or rehearing is not permitted.

(b) Notwithstanding subdivision (c) of Section 11517 of the Government Code, if a protest is heard by an administrative law judge alone, 10 days after receipt by the board of the administrative law judge's proposed decision, a copy of the proposed decision shall be filed by the board as a public record and a copy shall be served by the board on each party and his or her attorney.

(Amended by Stats. 2015, Ch. 407, Sec. 4. (AB 759) Effective January 1, 2016.)

3068. Either party may seek judicial review of final decisions of the board. Time for filing for the review shall not be more than 45 days from the date on which the final order of the board is made public and is delivered to the parties personally or is sent to them by certified mail.

(Amended by Stats. 2015, Ch. 407, Sec. 5. (AB 759) Effective January 1, 2016.)

3069. The provisions of this article shall be applicable to all franchises existing between dealers and manufacturers, manufacturer branches, distributors and distributor branches at the time of its enactment and to all such future franchises.

(Added by Stats. 1973, Ch. 996.)

3069.1. Sections 3060 to 3065.4, inclusive, do not apply to a franchise authorizing a dealership, as defined in subdivision (d) of Section 3072.

(Amended by Stats. 2022, Ch. 295, Sec. 7. (AB 2956) Effective January 1, 2023.)

Article 5. Hearings on Recreational Vehicle Franchise Modification, Replacement, Termination, Refusal to Continue, Establishment, and Relocation, and Consumer Complaints

(Article 5 added by Stats. 2003, Ch. 703, Sec. 11.)

3070. (a) Notwithstanding Section 20999.1 of the Business and Professions Code or the terms of any franchise, a franchisor of a dealer of new recreational vehicles, as defined in subdivision (a) of Section 18010 of the Health and Safety Code, except a dealer who deals exclusively in truck campers, may not terminate or refuse to continue a franchise unless all of the following conditions are met:

(1) The franchisee and the board have received written notice from the franchisor as follows:

(A) Sixty days before the effective date thereof setting forth the specific grounds for termination or refusal to continue.

(B) Fifteen days before the effective date thereof setting forth the specific grounds with respect to any of the following:

(i) Transfer of any ownership or interest in the franchise without the consent of the franchisor, which consent may not be unreasonably withheld.

(ii) Misrepresentation by the franchisee in applying for the franchise.

(iii) Insolvency of the franchisee, or filing of any petition by or against the franchisee under any bankruptcy or receivership law.

(iv) Any unfair business practice after written warning thereof.

(v) Failure of the dealer to conduct its customary sales and service operations during its customary hours of business for seven consecutive business days, giving rise to a good faith belief on the part of the franchisor that the recreational vehicle dealer is in fact going out of business, except for circumstances beyond the direct control of the recreational vehicle dealer or by order of the department.

(C) The written notice shall contain, on the first page thereof in at least 12-point bold type and circumscribed by a line to segregate it from the rest of the text, one of the following statements, whichever is applicable:

(i) To be inserted when a 60-day notice of termination is given:

"NOTICE TO DEALER: You have the right to file a protest with the NEW MOTOR VEHICLE BOARD in Sacramento and have a hearing in which you may protest the termination of your franchise under provisions of the California Vehicle Code. You must file your protest with the board within 30 calendar days after receiving this notice or within 30 days after the end of any appeal procedure provided by the franchisor or your protest right will be waived."

(ii) To be inserted when a 15-day notice of termination is given:

"NOTICE TO DEALER: You have the right to file a protest with the NEW MOTOR VEHICLE BOARD in Sacramento and have a hearing in which you may protest the termination of your franchise under provisions of the California Vehicle Code. You must file your protest with the board within 10 calendar days after receiving this notice or within 10 days after the end of any appeal procedure provided by the franchisor or your protest right will be waived."

(2) Except as provided in Section 3050.7, the board finds that there is good cause for termination or refusal to continue, following a hearing called pursuant to Section 3080. The franchisee may file a protest with the board within 30 days after receiving a 60-day notice, satisfying the requirements of this section, or within 30 days after the end of any appeal procedure provided by the franchisor, or within 10 days after receiving a 15-day notice, satisfying the requirements of this section, or within 10 days after the end of any appeal procedure provided by the franchisor. When a protest is filed, the board shall advise the franchisor that a timely protest has been filed, that a hearing is required pursuant to Section 3080, and that the franchisor may not terminate or refuse to continue until the board makes its findings.

(3) The franchisor has received the written consent of the franchisee, or the appropriate period for filing a protest has elapsed.

(b) (1) Notwithstanding Section 20999.1 of the Business and Professions Code or the terms of any franchise, a franchisor of a dealer of recreational vehicles may not modify or replace a franchise with a succeeding franchise if the modification or replacement would substantially affect the franchisee's sales or service obligations or investment, unless the franchisor has first given the board and each affected franchisee written notice thereof at least 60 days in advance of the modification or replacement. Within 30 days of receipt of a notice satisfying the requirements of this section, or within 30 days after the end of any appeal procedure provided by the franchisor, a franchisee may file a protest with the board and the modification or replacement does not become effective until there is a finding by the board that there is good cause for the modification or replacement. If, however, a replacement franchise is the successor franchise to an expiring or expired term franchise, the prior franchise shall continue in effect until resolution of the protest by the board. In the event of multiple protests, hearings shall be consolidated to expedite the disposition of the issue.

(2) The written notice shall contain, on the first page thereof in at least 12-point bold type and circumscribed by a line to segregate it from the rest of the text, the following statement:

"NOTICE TO DEALER: Your franchise agreement is being modified or replaced. If the modification or replacement will substantially affect your sales or service obligations or investment, you have the right to file a protest with the NEW MOTOR VEHICLE BOARD in Sacramento and have a hearing in which you may protest the proposed modification or replacement of your franchise under provisions of the California Vehicle Code. You must file your protest with the board within 30 calendar days of your receipt of this notice or within 30 days after the end of any appeal procedure provided by the franchisor or your protest rights will be waived."

(Amended by Stats. 2015, Ch. 407, Sec. 6. (AB 759) Effective January 1, 2016.)

3071. In determining whether good cause has been established for modifying, replacing, terminating, or refusing to continue a franchise of a dealer of new recreational vehicles, the board shall take into consideration the existing circumstances, including, but not limited to, all of the following:

(a) The amount of business transacted by the franchisee, as compared to the business available to the franchisee.

(b) The investment necessarily made and obligations incurred by the franchisee to perform its part of the franchise.

(c) The permanency of the investment.

(d) Whether it is injurious or beneficial to the public welfare for the franchise to be modified or replaced or the business of the franchisee disrupted.

(e) Whether the franchisee has adequate new recreational vehicle sales and, if required by the franchise, service facilities, equipment, vehicle parts, and qualified service personnel, to reasonably provide for the needs of the consumers of the recreational vehicles handled by the franchisee and has been and is rendering adequate services to the public.

(f) Whether the franchisee fails to fulfill the warranty obligations agreed to be performed by the franchisee in the franchise.

(g) The extent of franchisee's failure to comply with the terms of the franchise.

(Added by Stats. 2003, Ch. 703, Sec. 11. Effective January 1, 2004.)

3072. (a) (1) Except as otherwise provided in subdivision (b), if a franchisor seeks to enter into a franchise establishing an additional recreational vehicle dealership, or seeks to relocate an existing recreational vehicle dealership, that has a relevant market area in which the same recreational vehicle line-make is represented, the franchisor shall, in writing, first notify the board and each franchisee in that recreational vehicle line-make in the relevant market area of the franchisor's intention to establish an additional dealership or to relocate an existing dealership. Within 20 days of receiving the notice, satisfying the requirements of this section, or within 20 days after the end of any appeal procedure provided by the franchisor, any franchisee required to be given the notice may file with the board a protest to the proposed dealership establishment or relocation described in the franchisor's notice. If, within this time, a franchisee files with the board a request for additional time to file a protest, the board or its executive director, upon a showing of good cause, may grant an additional 10 days to file the protest. When a protest is filed, the board shall inform the franchisor that a timely protest has been filed, that a hearing is required pursuant to Section 3080, and that the franchisor shall not establish the proposed dealership or relocate the existing dealership until the board has held a hearing as provided in Section 3080, nor thereafter, if the board has determined that there is good cause for not permitting the establishment of the proposed recreational vehicle dealership or relocation of the existing recreational vehicle dealership. In the event of multiple protests, hearings may be consolidated to expedite the disposition of the issue.

(2) The written notice shall contain, on the first page thereof in at least 12-point bold type and circumscribed by a line to segregate it from the rest of the text, the following statement:

"NOTICE TO DEALER: You have the right to file a protest with the NEW MOTOR VEHICLE BOARD in Sacramento and have a hearing on your protest under the terms of the California Vehicle Code if you oppose this action. You must file your protest with the board within 20 days of your receipt of this notice, or within 20 days after the end of any appeal procedure that is provided by us to you. If, within this time, you file with the board a request for additional time to file a protest, the board or its executive director, upon a showing of good cause, may grant you an additional 10 days to file the protest."

(b) Subdivision (a) does not apply to any of the following:

(1) The relocation of an existing dealership to any location that is both within the same city as, and within one mile of, the existing dealership location.

(2) The establishment at any location that is both within the same city as, and within one-quarter mile of, the location of a dealership of the same recreational vehicle line-make that has been out of operation for less than 90 days.

(3) A display of vehicles at a fair, exposition, or similar exhibit if no actual sales are made at the event and the display does not exceed 30 days. This paragraph may not be construed to prohibit a new vehicle dealer from establishing a branch office for the purpose of selling vehicles at the fair, exposition, or similar exhibit, even though that event is sponsored by a financial institution, as defined in Section 31041 of the Financial Code, or by a financial institution and a licensed dealer. The establishment of these branch offices, however, shall be in accordance with subdivision (a) where applicable.

(4) An annual show sponsored by a national trade association of recreational vehicle manufacturers that complies with all of the requirements of subdivision (d) of Section 11713.15.

(c) For the purposes of this section, the reopening of a dealership that has not been in operation for one year or more shall be deemed the establishment of an additional recreational vehicle dealership.

(d) For the purposes of this section and Section 3073, a "recreational vehicle dealership" or "dealership" is any authorized facility at which a franchisee offers for sale or lease, displays for sale or lease, or sells or leases new recreational vehicles, as defined in subdivision (a) of Section 18010 of the Health and Safety Code. A "recreational vehicle dealership" or "dealership" does not include a dealer who deals exclusively in truck campers.

(Amended by Stats. 2015, Ch. 407, Sec. 7. (AB 759) Effective January 1, 2016.)

3072.5. For the purposes of this article, a "recreational vehicle line-make" is a group or groups of recreational vehicles defined by the terms of a written agreement that complies with Section 331.3.

(Amended by Stats. 2015, Ch. 407, Sec. 8. (AB 759) Effective January 1, 2016.)

3073. In determining whether good cause has been established for not entering into a recreational vehicle franchise or relocating an existing dealership of the same recreational vehicle line-make, the board shall take into consideration the existing circumstances, including, but not limited to, all of the following:

(a) The permanency of the investment.

(b) The effect on the retail recreational vehicle business and the consuming public in the relevant market area.

(c) Whether it is injurious to the public welfare for an additional recreational vehicle franchise to be established or an existing dealership be relocated.

(d) Whether the franchisees of the same recreational vehicle line-make in the relevant market area are providing adequate competition and convenient consumer care for the motor vehicles of the recreational vehicle line-make in the market area. In making this determination, the board shall consider the adequacy of recreational vehicle sales and, if required by the franchise, service facilities, equipment, supply of vehicle parts, and qualified service personnel.

(e) Whether the establishment of an additional franchise would increase competition and therefore be in the public interest.

(Amended by Stats. 2015, Ch. 407, Sec. 9. (AB 759) Effective January 1, 2016.)

3074. (a) A franchisor shall specify to its franchisees the delivery and preparation obligations of the franchisees prior to delivery of new recreational vehicles to retail buyers. A copy of the delivery and preparation obligations, which shall constitute the franchisee's only responsibility for product liability between the franchisee and the franchisor but which shall not in any way affect the franchisee's responsibility for product liability between the purchaser and either the franchisee or the franchisor, and a schedule of compensation to be paid franchisees for the work and services they shall be required to perform in connection with the delivery and preparation obligations shall be filed with the board by franchisors, and shall constitute the compensation as set forth on the schedule. The schedule of compensation shall be reasonable, with the reasonableness thereof being subject to the approval of the board, if a franchisee files a notice of protest with the board. In determining the reasonableness of the schedules, the board shall consider all relevant circumstances, including, but not limited to, the time required to perform each function that the dealer is obligated to perform and the appropriate labor rate.

(b) Upon delivery of the vehicle, the franchisee shall give a copy of the delivery and preparation obligations to the purchaser and a written certification that the franchisee has fulfilled these obligations.

(Amended by Stats. 2015, Ch. 407, Sec. 10. (AB 759) Effective January 1, 2016.)

3075. (a) A franchisor shall properly fulfill every warranty agreement made by it and adequately and fairly compensate each of its franchisees for labor and parts used to fulfill that warranty when the franchisee has fulfilled warranty obligations of repair and servicing and shall file a copy of its warranty reimbursement schedule or formula with the board. The warranty reimbursement schedule or formula shall be reasonable with respect to the time and compensation allowed the franchisee for the warranty work and all other conditions of the obligation. The reasonableness of the warranty reimbursement schedule or formula shall be determined by the board if a franchisee files a notice of protest with the board.

(b) In determining the adequacy and fairness of the compensation, the franchisee's effective labor rate charged to its various retail customers may be considered together with other relevant criteria.

(c) If a franchisor disallows a franchisee's claim for a defective part, alleging that the part, in fact, is not defective, the franchisor shall return the part alleged not to be defective to the franchisee at the expense of the franchisor, or the franchisee shall be reimbursed for the franchisee's cost of the part, at the franchisor's option.

(d) All claims made by franchisees pursuant to this section shall be either approved or disapproved within 30 days after their receipt by the franchisor. A claim not specifically disapproved in writing within 30 days from receipt by the franchisor shall be deemed approved on the 30th day. When a claim is disapproved, the franchisee who submits it shall be notified in writing of its disapproval within the required period, and the notice shall state the specific grounds upon which the disapproval is based. All claims made by franchisees under this section and Section 3074 for labor and parts shall be paid within 30 days following approval. Failure to approve or pay within the above specified time limits, in individual instances for reasons beyond the reasonable control of the franchisor, do not constitute a violation of this article.

(e) Audits of franchisee warranty records may be conducted by the franchisor on a reasonable basis, and for a period of 12 months after a claim is paid or credit issued. Franchisee claims for warranty compensation shall not be disapproved except for good cause, including, but not limited to, performance of nonwarranty repairs, lack of material documentation, or fraud. Any chargeback to a franchisee for warranty parts or service compensation shall be made within 90 days of the completion of the audit. If a false claim was submitted by a franchisee with intent to defraud the franchisor, a longer period for audit and any resulting chargeback may be permitted if the franchisor obtains an order from the board.

(Added by Stats. 2003, Ch. 703, Sec. 11. Effective January 1, 2004.)

3076. (a) All claims made by a franchisee for payment under the terms of a franchisor incentive program shall be either approved or disapproved within 30 days after receipt by the franchisor. When a claim is disapproved, the franchisee who submits it shall be notified in writing of its disapproval within the required period, and each notice shall state the specific grounds upon which the disapproval is based. A claim not specifically disapproved in writing within 30 days from receipt shall be deemed approved on the 30th day. Following the disapproval of a claim, a franchisee shall have one year from receipt of the notice of disapproval in which to appeal the disapproval to the franchisor and file a protest with the board. All claims made by franchisees under this section shall be paid within 30 days following approval. Failure to approve or pay within the above specified time limits, in individual instances for reasons beyond the reasonable control of the franchisor, do not constitute a violation of this article.

(b) Audits of franchisee incentive records may be conducted by the franchisor on a reasonable basis, and for a period of 18 months after a claim is paid or credit issued. Franchisee claims for incentive program compensation shall not be disapproved except for good cause, such as ineligibility under the terms of the incentive program, lack of material documentation, or fraud. Any chargeback to a franchisee for incentive program compensation shall be made within 90 days of the completion of the audit. If a false claim was submitted by a franchisee with the intent to defraud the franchisor, a longer period for audit and any resulting chargeback may be permitted if the franchisor obtains an order from the board.

(Added by Stats. 2003, Ch. 703, Sec. 11. Effective January 1, 2004.)

3077. (a) In addition to fees imposed under Sections 3016 and 11723, the department shall impose a one-time additional fee on those dealers subject to this article for the issuance or renewal of a license, in an amount determined by the department to be sufficient to cover the costs incurred by the department and the board in the implementation of this article for the first year, or in an amount sufficient to cover costs of not more than three hundred fifty thousand dollars ($350,000), whichever amount is less.

(b) The fee authorized under subdivision (a) may not be imposed on and after January 1, 2005.

(c) All funds derived from the imposition of the fee required under subdivision (a) shall be deposited in the Motor Vehicle Account in the State Transportation Fund and shall be available, upon appropriation, for expenditure to cover the costs incurred by the department and the board in the initial implementation of this article.

(Added by Stats. 2003, Ch. 703, Sec. 11. Effective January 1, 2004.)

3078. (a) If the board receives a complaint from a member of the public seeking a refund involving the sale or lease of, or a replacement of, a recreational vehicle, as defined in subdivision (a) of Section 18010 of the Health and Safety Code, from a recreational vehicle dealership, as defined in subdivision (d) of Section 3072, the board shall recommend that the complainant consult with the Department of Consumer Affairs.

(b) This chapter does not affect a person's rights regarding a transaction involving a recreational vehicle as defined in subdivision (a), to maintain an action under any other statute, including, but not limited to, applicable provisions of Title 1.7 (commencing with Section 1790) of Part 4 of Division 3 of the Civil Code.

(Amended by Stats. 2015, Ch. 407, Sec. 11. (AB 759) Effective January 1, 2016.)

3079. This article applies only to a recreational vehicle franchise entered into or renewed on or after January 1, 2004.

(Amended by Stats. 2015, Ch. 407, Sec. 12. (AB 759) Effective January 1, 2016.)

3080. (a) Upon receiving a protest pursuant to Section 3070, 3072, 3074, 3075, or 3076, the board shall fix a time and place of hearing within 60 days of the order, and shall send by certified mail a copy of the order to the franchisor, the protesting franchisee, and all individuals and groups that have requested notification by the board of protests and decisions of the board. The board or its executive director may, upon a showing of good cause, accelerate or postpone the date initially established for a hearing, but the hearing shall not be rescheduled more than 90 days after the board's initial order. For the purpose of accelerating or postponing a hearing date, "good cause" includes, but is not limited to, the effects upon, and any irreparable harm to, the parties or interested persons or groups if the request for a change in hearing date is not granted. The board or an administrative law judge designated by the board shall hear and consider the oral and documented evidence introduced by the parties and other interested individuals and groups, and the board shall make its decision solely on the record so made. Chapter 4.5 (commencing with Section 11400) of Part 1 of Division 3 of Title 2 of the Government Code and Sections 11507.3, 11507.6, 11507.7, 11511, 11511.5, 11513, 11514, 11515, and 11517 of the Government Code apply to these proceedings.

(b) In a hearing on a protest filed pursuant to Section 3070 or 3072, the franchisor shall have the burden of proof to establish that there is good cause to modify, replace, terminate, or refuse to continue a franchise. The franchisee shall have the burden of proof to establish that there is good cause not to enter into a franchise establishing an additional recreational vehicle dealership or relocating an existing recreational vehicle dealership.

(c) Except as otherwise provided in this chapter, in a hearing on a protest alleging a violation of, or filed pursuant to, Section 3074, 3075, or 3076, the franchisee shall have the burden of proof, but the franchisor has the burden of proof to establish that a franchisee acted with intent to defraud the franchisor when that issue is material to a protest filed pursuant to Section 3075 or 3076.

(Added by Stats. 2015, Ch. 407, Sec. 13. (AB 759) Effective January 1, 2016.)

3081. (a) The decision of the board shall be in writing and shall contain findings of fact and a determination of the issues presented. The decision shall sustain, conditionally sustain, overrule, or conditionally overrule the protest. Conditions imposed by the board shall be for the purpose of assuring performance of binding contractual agreements between franchisees and franchisors or otherwise serving the purposes of this article. If the board fails to act within 30 days after the hearing, within 30 days after the board receives a proposed decision when the case is heard before an administrative law judge alone, or within a period necessitated by Section 11517 of the Government Code, or as may be mutually agreed upon by the parties, then the proposed action shall be deemed to be approved. Copies of the board's decision shall be delivered to the parties personally or sent to them by certified mail, as well as to all individuals and groups that have requested notification by the board of protests and decisions by the board. The board's decision shall be final upon its delivery or mailing and a reconsideration or rehearing is not permitted.

(b) Notwithstanding subdivision (c) of Section 11517 of the Government Code, if a protest is heard by an administrative law judge alone, 10 days after receipt by the board of the administrative law judge's proposed decision, a copy of the proposed decision shall be filed by the board as a public record and a copy shall be served by the board on each party and his or her attorney.

(Added by Stats. 2015, Ch. 407, Sec. 14. (AB 759) Effective January 1, 2016.)

3082. Either party may seek judicial review of final decisions of the board. Time for filing for the review shall not be more than 45 days from the date on which the final order of the board is made public and is delivered to the parties personally or is sent to them by certified mail.

(Added by Stats. 2015, Ch. 407, Sec. 15. (AB 759) Effective January 1, 2016.)

Article 6. Export and Sale-for-Resale Prohibition Hearings

(Article 6 added by Stats. 2019, Ch. 796, Sec. 17.)

3085. (a) An association may bring a protest challenging the legality of an export or sale-for-resale prohibition policy of a manufacturer, manufacturer branch, distributor, or distributor branch at any time on behalf of two or more dealers subject to the challenged policy pursuant to subdivision (y) of Section 11713.3.

(b) For the purpose of this article, an association is an organization primarily owned by, or comprised of, new motor vehicle dealers and that primarily represents the interests of dealers.

(c) Relief for a protest pursuant to this section is limited to a declaration that an export or sale-for-resale prohibition policy of a manufacturer, manufacturer branch, distributor, or distributor branch violates the prohibitions of subdivision (y) of Section 11713.3. No monetary relief may be sought on behalf of the association or any dealers represented by the association.

(d) In a protest pursuant to this section, the association shall have the burden of proof to show that the challenged export or sale-for-resale prohibition policy violates subdivision (y) of Section 11713.3.

(Added by Stats. 2019, Ch. 796, Sec. 17. (AB 179) Effective January 1, 2020. Repealed as of January 1, 2030, pursuant to Section 3085.10.)

3085.2. (a) Upon receiving a protest pursuant to Section 3085, the board shall fix a time and place of hearing within 60 days, and shall send by certified mail a copy of the order to the manufacturer, manufacturer branch, distributor, distributor branch, the protesting association, and all individuals and groups that have requested notification by the board of protests and decisions of the board. The board or an administrative law judge designated by the board shall hear and consider the oral and documented evidence introduced by the parties and other interested individuals and groups, and the board shall make its decision solely on the record so made. Chapter 4.5 (commencing with Section 11400) of Part 1 of Division 3 of Title 2 of the Government Code and Sections 11507.3, 11507.6, 11507.7, 11511, 11511.5, 11513, 11514, 11515, and 11517 of the Government Code apply to these proceedings.

(b) In a hearing on a protest filed pursuant to Section 3085, the association shall have the burden of proof to establish a violation of the applicable section by the subject manufacturer, manufacturer branch, distributor, or distributor branch.

(c) A member of the board who is a new motor vehicle dealer may not participate in, hear, comment, or advise other members upon, or decide, a matter involving a protest filed pursuant to this article unless all parties to the protest stipulate otherwise.

(Added by Stats. 2019, Ch. 796, Sec. 17. (AB 179) Effective January 1, 2020. Repealed as of January 1, 2030, pursuant to Section 3085.10.)

3085.4. (a) The decision of the board shall be in writing and shall contain findings of fact and a determination of the issues presented. The decision shall sustain, conditionally sustain, overrule, or conditionally overrule the protest. Conditions imposed by the board shall be for the purpose of assuring performance of binding contractual agreements between franchisees and franchisors or otherwise serving the purposes of this article. The board shall act within 30 days after the hearing, within 30 days after the board receives a proposed decision when the case is heard before an administrative law judge alone, or within a period necessitated by Section 11517 of the Government Code, or as may be mutually agreed upon by the parties. Copies of the board's decision shall be delivered to the parties personally or sent to them by certified mail, as well as to all individuals and groups that have requested notification by the board of protests and decisions by the board. The board's decision shall be final upon its delivery or mailing and a reconsideration or rehearing is not permitted.

(b) Notwithstanding subdivision (c) of Section 11517 of the Government Code, if a protest is heard by an administrative law judge alone, 10 days after receipt by the board of the administrative law judge's proposed decision, a copy of the proposed decision shall be filed by the board as a public record and a copy shall be served by the board on each party and the party's attorney.

(Added by Stats. 2019, Ch. 796, Sec. 17. (AB 179) Effective January 1, 2020. Repealed as of January 1, 2030, pursuant to Section 3085.10.)

3085.6. Either party may seek judicial review of final decisions of the board. An appeal shall be filed within 45 days from the date on which the final order of the board is made public and is delivered to the parties personally or is sent to them by certified mail.

(Added by Stats. 2019, Ch. 796, Sec. 17. (AB 179) Effective January 1, 2020. Repealed as of January 1, 2030, pursuant to Section 3085.10.)

3085.8. The provisions of this article shall be applicable to any association which is primarily owned by or comprised of new motor vehicle dealers and acts on behalf of its new motor vehicle franchisees.

(Added by Stats. 2019, Ch. 796, Sec. 17. (AB 179) Effective January 1, 2020. Repealed as of

January 1, 2030, pursuant to Section 3085.10.)

3085.10. This article shall remain in effect only until January 1, 2030, and as of that date is repealed, unless a later enacted statute, that is enacted before January 1, 2030, deletes or extends that date.

(Added by Stats. 2019, Ch. 796, Sec. 17. (AB 179) Effective January 1, 2020. Repealed as of January 1, 2030, by its own provisions. Note: Repeal affects Article 6, commencing with Section 3085.)

Chapter 7. Road Usage Charge Pilot Program

(Chapter 7 added by Stats. 2014, Ch. 835, Sec. 2.)

3090. (a) The Chair of the California Transportation Commission shall create, in consultation with the Secretary of the Transportation Agency, a Road Usage Charge (RUC) Technical Advisory Committee.

(b) (1) The purpose of the technical advisory committee is to guide the development and evaluation of a pilot program to assess the potential for mileage-based revenue collection for California's roads and highways as an alternative to the gas tax system.

(2) Commencing January 1, 2019, the technical advisory committee shall continue to assess the potential for mechanisms, including, but not limited to, a mileage-based revenue collection system, to use as alternative methods to the existing gas tax system for generating the revenue necessary to maintain and operate the state's transportation system.

(c) The technical advisory committee shall consist of 15 members. In selecting the members of the technical advisory committee, the chair shall consider individuals who are representative of the telecommunications industry, highway user groups, the data security and privacy industry, privacy rights advocacy organizations, regional transportation agencies, national research and policymaking bodies, including, but not limited to, the Transportation Research Board and the American Association of State Highway and Transportation Officials, Members of the Legislature, and other relevant stakeholders as determined by the chair.

(d) Pursuant to Section 14512 of the Government Code, the technical advisory committee may request the Department of Transportation to perform such work as the technical advisory committee deems necessary to carry out its duties and responsibilities.

(e) The technical advisory committee shall study RUC alternatives to the gas tax. The technical advisory committee shall gather public comment related to the activities described in subdivision (b) and shall make recommendations to the Secretary of the Transportation Agency on the design of a pilot program to test alternative RUC approaches. The technical advisory committee may also make recommendations on the criteria to be used to evaluate the pilot program.

(f) In studying alternatives to the current gas tax system and developing recommendations on the design of a pilot program to test alternative RUC approaches pursuant to subdivision (e), the technical advisory committee shall take all of the following into consideration:

(1) The availability, adaptability, reliability, and security of methods that might be used in recording and reporting highway use.

(2) The necessity of protecting all personally identifiable information used in reporting highway use.

(3) The ease and cost of recording and reporting highway use.

(4) The ease and cost of administering the collection of taxes and fees as an alternative to the current system of taxing highway use through motor vehicle fuel taxes.

(5) Effective methods of maintaining compliance.

(6) The ease of reidentifying location data, even when personally identifiable information has been removed from the data.

(7) Increased privacy concerns when location data is used in conjunction with other technologies.

(8) Public and private agency access, including law enforcement, to data collected and stored for purposes of the RUC to ensure individual privacy rights are protected pursuant to Section 1 of Article I of the California Constitution.

(g) The technical advisory committee shall consult with highway users and transportation stakeholders, including representatives of vehicle users, vehicle manufacturers, and fuel distributors as part of its duties pursuant to subdivision (f).

(Amended by Stats. 2018, Ch. 698, Sec. 1. (SB 1328) Effective January 1, 2019. Repealed as of January 1, 2027, pursuant to Section 3093.)

3091. (a) Based on the recommendations of the RUC Technical Advisory Committee, the Transportation Agency shall implement a pilot program to identify and evaluate issues related to the potential implementation of an RUC program in California by January 1, 2017.

(b) At a minimum, the pilot program shall accomplish all of the following:

(1) Analyze alternative means of collecting road usage data, including at least one alternative that does not rely on electronic vehicle location data.

(2) Collect a minimum amount of personal information including location tracking information, necessary to implement the RUC program.

(3) Ensure that processes for collecting, managing, storing, transmitting, and destroying data are in place to protect the integrity of the data and safeguard the privacy of drivers.

(c) The agency shall not disclose, distribute, make available, sell, access, or otherwise provide for another purpose, personal information or data collected through the RUC program to any private entity or individual unless authorized by a court order, as part of a civil case, by a subpoena issued on behalf of a defendant in a criminal case, by a search warrant, or in aggregate form with all personal information removed for the purposes of academic research.

(Added by Stats. 2014, Ch. 835, Sec. 2. (SB 1077) Effective January 1, 2015. Repealed as of January 1, 2027, pursuant to Section 3093.)

3092. (a) The Transportation Agency shall prepare and submit a report of its findings based on the results of the pilot program to the RUC Technical Advisory Committee, the California Transportation Commission, and the appropriate policy and fiscal committees of the Legislature by no later than June 30, 2018. The report shall include, but not be limited to, a discussion of all of the following issues:

(1) Cost.

(2) Privacy, including recommendations regarding public and private access, including law enforcement, to data collected and stored for purposes of the RUC to ensure individual privacy rights are protected pursuant to Section 1 of Article I of the California Constitution.

(3) Jurisdictional issues.

(4) Feasibility.

(5) Complexity.

(6) Acceptance.

(7) Use of revenues.

(8) Security and compliance, including a discussion of processes and security measures necessary to minimize fraud and tax evasion rates.

(9) Data collection technology, including a discussion of the advantages and disadvantages of various types of data collection equipment and the privacy implications and considerations of the equipment.

(10) Potential for additional driver services.

(11) Implementation issues.

(b) The California Transportation Commission shall include its recommendations regarding the pilot program in its annual report to the Legislature as specified in Sections 14535 and 14536 of the Government Code.

(Added by Stats. 2014, Ch. 835, Sec. 2. (SB 1077) Effective January 1, 2015. Repealed as of January 1, 2027, pursuant to Section 3093.)

3092.5. (a) Commencing on or after January 1, 2023, the Transportation Agency, in consultation with the California Transportation Commission, shall implement a pilot program to identify and evaluate issues related to the collection of revenue for a road charge program.

(b) The Road Usage Charge Technical Advisory Committee shall, by no later than July 1, 2023, make recommendations to the Transportation Agency on the design of the pilot program to test revenue collection, including the group of vehicles to participate in the pilot.

(1) In deciding which group of vehicles to recommend for the pilot, the committee shall consider input from industry experts and relevant stakeholders.

(2) If a vehicle group other than state-owned vehicles is selected, participation in the pilot shall be voluntary.

(3) The committee may make recommendations on the criteria to be used to evaluate the pilot program.

(c) The Transportation Agency shall consult with appropriate state agencies, which may include, but are not limited to, the Department of Transportation, the Department of Motor Vehicles, the California Department of Tax and Fee Administration, and the Controller to design a process for collecting road charge revenue from vehicles. The road charge may be collected by the Transportation Agency or by any entities or persons designated by the agency.

(d) Participants in the pilot program shall be charged a mileage-based fee as specified in subdivision (e), and receive a credit or a refund for the estimated state fuel taxes and electric vehicle fees paid to operate a vehicle during the pilot. The credit or refund for electric vehicle fees described in Section 9250.6, which are paid annually, shall be prorated.

(e) For purposes of calculating the mileage-based fee, participating vehicles shall be equally subdivided and randomly assigned to one of two study groups. One group will be subject to a fee per mile traveled, determined by the committee no later than July 1, 2023, that will be the same for all vehicles in that group. The other group will be subject to an individually calculated fee per mile traveled, that is equal to the state per-gallon fuel tax divided by the United States Environmental Protection Agency's estimated fuel economy rating for that vehicle based on the manufacturer, model, and year of the vehicle.

(f) The pilot program shall not affect funding levels for each program or purpose supported by state fuel tax and electric vehicle fee revenues.

(g) Paragraphs (2) and (3) of subdivision (b) and subdivision (c) of Section 3091 shall apply to the pilot program.

(h) The Transportation Agency, in consultation with the California Transportation Commission and the committee, shall, by no later than July 1, 2024, prepare and submit an interim report on the status of the pilot program, and by no later than December 31, 2026, the Transportation Agency, in consultation with the California Transportation Commission and the committee, shall prepare and submit a final report of its findings based on the results of the pilot program, to the appropriate policy and fiscal committees of the Legislature. The final report shall include, but not be limited to, a discussion of costs and implementation issues, and an evaluation and comparison of the two fee-calculation methodologies described in subdivision (e), including the effectiveness of those methodologies in ensuring sustainable funding for transportation and their alignment with the state's climate, air quality, zero-emissions vehicle, and equity goals. The reports required by this subdivision shall be submitted in compliance with Section 9795 of the Government Code.

(Added by Stats. 2021, Ch. 308, Sec. 2. (SB 339) Effective January 1, 2022. Repealed as of January 1, 2027, pursuant to Section 3093.)

3093. This chapter shall remain in effect only until January 1, 2027, and as of that date is repealed, unless a later enacted statute, that is enacted before January 1, 2027, deletes or extends that date.

(Amended by Stats. 2021, Ch. 308, Sec. 3. (SB 339) Effective January 1, 2022. Repealed as of January 1, 2027, by its own provisions. Note: Repeal affects Chapter 7, commencing with Section 3090.)

Division 3. Registration of Vehicles and Certificates of Title

(Division 3 enacted by Stats. 1959, Ch. 3.)

Chapter 1. Original and Renewal of Registration; Issuance of Certificates of Title

(Chapter 1 enacted by Stats. 1959, Ch. 3.)

Article 1. Vehicles Subject to Registration

(Article 1 enacted by Stats. 1959, Ch. 3.)

4000. (a) (1) A person shall not drive, move, or leave standing upon a highway, or in an offstreet public parking facility, any motor vehicle, trailer, semitrailer, pole or pipe dolly, or logging dolly, unless it is registered and the appropriate fees have been paid under this code or registered under the permanent trailer identification program, except that an off-highway motor vehicle which displays an identification plate or device issued by the department pursuant to Section 38010 may be driven, moved, or left standing in an offstreet public parking facility without being registered or paying registration fees.

(2) For purposes of this subdivision, "offstreet public parking facility" means either of the following:

(A) Any publicly owned parking facility.

(B) Any privately owned parking facility for which no fee for the privilege to park is charged and which is held open for the common public use of retail customers.

(3) This subdivision does not apply to any motor vehicle stored in a privately owned offstreet parking facility by, or with the express permission of, the owner of the privately owned offstreet parking facility.

(4) (A) (i) A violation of this subdivision shall not be the sole basis for any enforcement action before the second month after the month of expiration of the vehicle's registration.

(ii) Notwithstanding clause (i), if a vehicle is stopped for any other violation of this code, enforcement action for a violation of this subdivision may be taken before the second month following the month of expiration.

(B) This paragraph shall be operative from July 1, 2024, to January 1, 2030, inclusive.

(b) A person shall not drive, move, or leave standing upon a highway any motor vehicle, as defined in Chapter 2 (commencing with Section 39010) of Part 1 of Division 26 of the Health and Safety Code, that has been registered in violation of Part 5 (commencing with Section 43000) of Division 26 of the Health and Safety Code.

(c) Subdivisions (a) and (b) do not apply to off-highway motor vehicles operated pursuant to Sections 38025 and 38026.5.

(d) This section does not apply, following payment of fees due for registration, during the time that registration and transfer is being withheld by the department pending the investigation of any use tax due under the Revenue and Taxation Code.

(e) Subdivision (a) does not apply to a vehicle that is towed by a tow truck on the order of a sheriff, marshal, or other official acting pursuant to a court order or on the order of a peace officer acting pursuant to this code.

(f) Subdivision (a) applies to a vehicle that is towed from a highway or offstreet parking facility under the direction of a highway service organization when that organization is providing emergency roadside assistance to that vehicle. However, the operator of a tow truck providing that assistance to that vehicle is not responsible for the violation of subdivision (a) with respect to that vehicle. The owner of an unregistered vehicle that is disabled and located on private property, shall obtain a permit from the department pursuant to Section 4003 prior to having the vehicle towed on the highway.

(g) (1) Pursuant to Section 4022 and to subparagraph (B) of paragraph (3) of subdivision (o) of Section 22651, a vehicle obtained by a licensed repossessor as a release of collateral is exempt from registration pursuant to this section for purposes of the repossessor removing the vehicle to their storage facility or the facility of the legal owner. A law enforcement agency, impounding authority, tow yard, storage facility, or any other person in possession of the collateral shall release the vehicle without requiring current registration and pursuant to subdivision (f) of Section 14602.6.

(2) The legal owner of collateral shall, by operation of law and without requiring further action, indemnify and hold harmless a law enforcement agency, city, county, city and county, the state, a tow yard, storage facility, or an impounding yard from a claim arising out of the release of the collateral to a licensee, and from any damage to the collateral after its release, including reasonable attorney's fees and costs associated with defending a claim, if the collateral was released in compliance with this subdivision.

(h) For purposes of this section, possession of a California driver's license by the registered owner of a vehicle shall give rise to a rebuttable presumption that the owner is a resident of California.

(Amended by Stats. 2023, Ch. 297, Sec. 1. (AB 256) Effective January 1, 2024.)

4000.1. (a) Except as otherwise provided in subdivision (b), (c), or (d) of this section, or subdivision (b) of Section 43654 of the Health and Safety Code, the department shall require upon initial registration, and upon transfer of ownership and registration, of any motor vehicle subject to Part 5 (commencing with Section 43000) of Division 26 of the Health and Safety Code, a valid certificate of compliance or a certificate of noncompliance, as appropriate, issued in accordance with Section 44015 of the Health and Safety Code.

(b) With respect to new motor vehicles certified pursuant to Chapter 2 (commencing with Section 43100) of Part 5 of Division 26 of the Health and Safety Code, the department shall accept a statement completed pursuant to subdivision (b) of Section 24007 in lieu of the certificate of compliance.

(c) For purposes of determining the validity of a certificate of compliance or noncompliance submitted in compliance with the requirements of this section, the definitions of new and used motor vehicle contained in Chapter 2 (commencing with Section 39010) of Part 1 of Division 26 of the Health and Safety Code shall control.

(d) Subdivision (a) does not apply to a transfer of ownership and registration under any of the following circumstances:

(1) The initial application for transfer is submitted within the 90-day validity period of a smog certificate as specified in Section 44015 of the Health and Safety Code.

(2) The transferor is the parent, grandparent, sibling, child, grandchild, or spouse of the transferee.

(3) A motor vehicle registered to a sole proprietorship is transferred to the proprietor as owner.

(4) The transfer is between companies the principal business of which is leasing motor vehicles, if there is no change in the lessee or operator of the motor vehicle or between the lessor and the person who has been, for at least one year, the lessee's operator of the motor vehicle.

(5) The transfer is between the lessor and lessee of the motor vehicle, if there is no change in the lessee or operator of the motor vehicle.

(6) The motor vehicle was manufactured prior to the 1976 model-year.

(7) Except for diesel-powered vehicles, the transfer is for a motor vehicle that is four or less model-years old. The department shall impose a fee of eight dollars ($8) on the transferee of a motor vehicle that is four or less model-years old. Revenues generated from the imposition of that fee shall be deposited into the Vehicle Inspection and Repair Fund.

(e) The State Air Resources Board, under Part 5 (commencing with Section 43000) of Division 26 of the Health and Safety Code, may exempt designated classifications of motor vehicles from subdivision (a) as it deems necessary, and shall notify the department of that action.

(f) Subdivision (a) does not apply to a motor vehicle when an additional individual is added as a registered owner of the motor vehicle.

(g) For purposes of subdivision (a), any collector motor vehicle, as defined in Section 259, is exempt from those portions of the test required by subdivision (f) of Section 44012 of the Health and Safety Code, if the collector motor vehicle meets all of the following criteria:

(1) Submission of proof that the motor vehicle is insured as a collector motor vehicle, as shall be required by regulation of the bureau.

(2) The motor vehicle is at least 35 model-years old.

(3) The motor vehicle complies with the exhaust emissions standards for that motor vehicle's class and model year as prescribed by the department, and the motor vehicle passes a functional inspection of the fuel cap and a visual inspection for liquid fuel leaks.

(Amended by Stats. 2009, Ch. 200, Sec. 7. (SB 734) Effective January 1, 2010.)

4000.15. (a) Effective January 1, 2020, the department shall confirm, prior to the initial registration or the transfer of ownership and registration of a diesel-fueled vehicle with a gross vehicle weight rating of more than 14,000 pounds, that the vehicle is compliant with, or exempt from, applicable air pollution control technology requirements pursuant to Division 26 (commencing with Section 39000) of the Health and Safety Code and regulations of the State Air Resources Board adopted pursuant to that division.

(b) Except as otherwise provided in subdivision (c), for diesel-fueled vehicles subject to Section 43018 of the Health and Safety Code, as applied to the reduction of emissions of diesel particulate matter, oxides of nitrogen, and other criteria pollutants from in-use diesel-fueled vehicles, and Section 2025 of Title 13 of the California Code of Regulations as it read January 1, 2017, or as subsequently amended:

(1) The department shall refuse registration, or renewal or transfer of registration, for a diesel-fueled vehicle with a gross vehicle weight rating of 14,001 pounds to 26,000 pounds for the following vehicle model years:

(A) Effective January 1, 2020, vehicle model years 2004 and older.

(B) Effective January 1, 2021, vehicle model years 2007 and older.

(C) Effective January 1, 2023, vehicle model years 2010 and older.

(2) The department shall refuse registration, or renewal or transfer of registration, for a diesel-fueled vehicle with a gross vehicle weight rating of more than 26,000 pounds for the following vehicle model years:

(A) Effective January 1, 2020, vehicle model years 2000 and older.

(B) Effective January 1, 2021, vehicle model years 2005 and older.

(C) Effective January 1, 2022, vehicle model years 2007 and older.

(D) Effective January 1, 2023, vehicle model years 2010 and older.

(c) (1) As determined by the State Air Resources Board, notwithstanding effective dates and vehicle model years identified in subdivision (b), the department may allow registration, or renewal or transfer of registration, for a diesel-fueled vehicle that has been reported to the State Air Resources Board, and is using an approved exemption, or is compliant with applicable air pollution control technology requirements pursuant to Division 26 (commencing with Section 39000) of the Health and Safety Code and regulations of the State Air Resources Board adopted pursuant to that division, including vehicles equipped with the required model year emissions equivalent engine or otherwise using an approved compliance option.

(2) The State Air Resources Board shall notify the department of the vehicles allowed to be registered pursuant to this subdivision.

(Added by Stats. 2017, Ch. 5, Sec. 45. (SB 1) Effective April 28, 2017.)

4000.17. (a) For purposes of this section, "heavy-duty vehicle" means a nongasoline heavy-duty onroad motor vehicle with a gross vehicle weight rating of more than 14,000 pounds, as defined by the State Air Resources Board pursuant to Section 44152 of the Health and Safety Code.

(b) No later than one year after the effective date of a regulation implementing the Heavy-Duty Vehicle Inspection and Maintenance Program (Chapter 5.5 (commencing with Section 44150) of Part 5 of Division 26 of the Health and Safety Code), the department shall confirm prior to the initial registration, the transfer of ownership, or the renewal of registration that a heavy-duty vehicle is compliant with, or exempt from, the Heavy-Duty Vehicle Inspection and Maintenance Program.

(c) Subdivision (b) does not apply to a transfer of ownership and registration under any of the following circumstances:

(1) A motor vehicle registered to a sole proprietorship is transferred to the proprietor as owner.

(2) The transfer is between companies the principal business of which is leasing motor vehicles, if there is no change in the lessee or operator of the motor vehicle or between the lessor and the person who has been, for at least one year, the lessee's operator of the motor vehicle.

(3) The transfer is between the lessor and lessee of the motor vehicle, if there is no change in the lessee or operator of the motor vehicle.

(4) An additional individual is added as a registered owner of the motor vehicle.

(d) The State Air Resources Board shall notify the department of the motor vehicles allowed to be registered pursuant to this section.

(Added by Stats. 2019, Ch. 298, Sec. 3. (SB 210) Effective January 1, 2020.)

4000.2. (a) Except as otherwise provided in subdivision (b) of Section 43654 of the Health and Safety Code, and, commencing on April 1, 2005, except for model-years exempted from biennial inspection pursuant to Section 44011 of the Health and Safety Code, the department shall require upon registration of a motor vehicle subject to Part 5 (commencing with Section 43000) of Division 26 of the Health and Safety Code, previously registered outside this state, a valid certificate of compliance or a certificate of noncompliance, as appropriate, issued in accordance with Section 44015 of the Health and Safety Code.

(b) For the purposes of determining the validity of a certificate of compliance or noncompliance submitted in compliance with the requirements of this section, the definitions of new and used motor vehicle contained in Chapter 2 (commencing with Section 39010) of Part 1 of Division 26 of the Health and Safety Code shall control.

(Amended by Stats. 2004, Ch. 704, Sec. 4. Effective January 1, 2005. Operative April 1, 2005, by Sec. 7 of Ch. 704.)

4000.3. (a) Except as otherwise provided in Section 44011 of the Health and Safety Code, the department shall require biennially, upon renewal of registration of any motor vehicle subject to Part 5 (commencing with Section 43000) of Division 26 of the Health and Safety Code, a valid certificate of compliance issued in accordance with Section 44015 of the Health and Safety Code. The department, in consultation with the Department of Consumer Affairs, shall develop a schedule under which vehicles shall be required biennially to obtain certificates of compliance.

(b) The Department of Consumer Affairs shall provide the department with information on vehicle classes that are subject to the motor vehicle inspection and maintenance program.

(c) The department shall include any information pamphlet provided by the Department of Consumer Affairs with notification of the inspection requirement and with its renewal notices. The information pamphlet in the renewal notice shall also notify the owner of the motor vehicle of the right to have the vehicle pretested pursuant to Section 44011.3 of the Health and Safety Code.

(Amended by Stats. 1998, Ch. 938, Sec. 2. Effective January 1, 1999.)

4000.37. (a) Upon application for renewal of registration of a motor vehicle, the department shall require that the applicant submit either a form approved by the department, but issued by the insurer, as specified in paragraph (1), (2), or (3), or any of the items specified in paragraph (4), as evidence that the applicant is in compliance with the financial responsibility laws of this state.

(1) For vehicles covered by private passenger automobile liability policies and having coverage as described in subdivisions (a) and (b) of Section 660 of the Insurance Code, or policies and coverages for private passenger automobile policies as described in subdivisions (a) and (b) of that section and issued by an automobile assigned risk plan, the form shall include all of the following:

(A) The primary name of the insured covered by the policy or the vehicle owner, or both.

(B) The year, make, and vehicle identification number of the vehicle.

(C) The name, the National Association of Insurance Commissioners (NAIC) number, and the address of the insurance company or surety company providing a policy or bond for the vehicle.

(D) The policy or bond number, and the effective date and expiration date of that policy or bond.

(E) A statement from the insurance company or surety company that the policy or bond meets the requirements of Section 16056 or 16500.5. For the purposes of this section, policies described in Section 11629.71 of the Insurance Code are deemed to meet the requirements of Section 16056.

(2) For vehicles covered by commercial or fleet policies, and not private passenger automobile liability policies, as described in paragraph (1), the form shall include all of the following:

(A) The name and address of the vehicle owner or fleet operator.

(B) The name, the NAIC number, and the address of the insurance company or surety company providing a policy or bond for the vehicle.

(C) The policy or bond number, and the effective date and expiration date of the policy or bond.

(D) A statement from the insurance company or surety company that the policy or bond meets the requirements of Section 16056 or 16500.5 and is a commercial or fleet policy. For vehicles registered pursuant to Article 9.5 (commencing with Section 5301) or Article 4 (commencing with Section 8050) of Chapter 4, one form may be submitted per fleet as specified by the department.

(3) (A) The director may authorize an insurer to issue a form that does not conform to paragraph (1) or (2) if the director does all of the following:

(i) Determines that the entity issuing the alternate form is or will begin reporting the insurance information required under paragraph (1) or (2) to the department through electronic transmission.

(ii) Determines that use of the alternate form furthers the interests of the state by enhancing the enforcement of the state's financial responsibility laws.

(iii) Approves the contents of the alternate form as providing an adequate means for persons to prove compliance with the financial responsibility laws.

(B) The director may authorize the use of the alternate form in lieu of the forms otherwise required under paragraph (1) or (2) for a period of four years or less and may renew that authority for additional periods of four years or less.

(4) In lieu of evidence of insurance as described in paragraphs (1), (2), and (3), one of the following documents as evidence of coverage under an alternative form of financial responsibility may be provided by the applicant:

(A) An evidence form, as specified by the department, that indicates either a certificate of self-insurance or an assignment of deposit letter has been issued by the department pursuant to Sections 16053 or 16054.2.

(B) An insurance covering note or binder pursuant to Section 382 or 382.5 of the Insurance Code.

(C) An evidence form that indicates coverage is provided by a charitable risk pool operating under Section 5005.1 of the Corporations Code, if the registered owner of the vehicle is a nonprofit organization that is exempt from taxation under paragraph (3) of subsection (c) of Section 501 of the United States Internal Revenue Code. The evidence form shall include:

(i) The name and address of the vehicle owner or fleet operator.

(ii) The name and address of the charitable risk pool providing the policy for the vehicle.

(iii) The policy number, and the effective date and expiration date of the policy.

(iv) A statement from the charitable risk pool that the policy meets the requirements of subdivision (b) of Section 16054.2.

(b) This section does not apply to any of the following:

(1) A vehicle for which a certification has been filed pursuant to Section

4604, until the vehicle is registered for operation upon the highway.

(2) A vehicle that is owned or leased by, or under the direction of, the United States or any public entity that is included in Section 811.2 of the Government Code.

(3) A vehicle registration renewal application where there is a change of registered owner.

(4) A vehicle for which evidence of liability insurance information has been electronically filed with the department.

(Amended by Stats. 2005, Ch. 435, Sec. 18. Effective January 1, 2006.)

4000.38. (a) The department shall suspend, cancel, or revoke the registration of a vehicle when it determines that any of the following circumstances has occurred:

(1) The registration was obtained by providing false evidence of financial responsibility to the department.

(2) Upon notification by an insurance company that the required coverage has been canceled and a sufficient period of time has elapsed since the cancellation notification, as determined by the department, for replacement coverage to be processed and received by the department.

(3) Evidence of financial responsibility has not been submitted to the department within 30 days of the issuance of a registration certificate for the original registration or transfer of registration of a vehicle.

(b) (1) Prior to suspending, canceling, or revoking the registration of a vehicle, the department shall notify the vehicle owner of its intent to suspend, cancel, or revoke the registration, and shall provide the vehicle owner a reasonable time, not less than 45 days in cases under paragraph (2) of subdivision (a), to provide evidence of financial responsibility or to establish that the vehicle is not being operated.

(2) For the low-cost automobile insurance program established under Section 11629.7 of the Insurance Code, the department shall provide residents with information on the notification document, in plain, boldface type not less than 12 point in size, and in both English and Spanish, stating the following:

"California Low-Cost Auto Insurance: A program offering affordable automobile insurance is available. Visit (insert Internet Web site address provided by the Department of Insurance) or call toll free (insert toll-free telephone number for the California Automobile Assigned Risk Plan or its successor as provided by the Department of Insurance). Qualified applicants must be 19 years of age or older, have a driver's license for the past three years, and meet income eligibility requirements (insert income example provided by Department of Insurance)."

(c) (1) Notwithstanding any other provision of this code, before a registration is reinstated after suspension, cancellation, or revocation, there shall be paid to the department, in addition to any other fees required by this code, a fee sufficient to pay the cost of the reissuance as determined by the department.

(2) Commencing on January 1, 2011, the reissuance fee imposed by paragraph (1) shall not apply to a member of the California National Guard or the United States Armed Forces who was on active duty, serving outside of this state in a military conflict during a time of war, as defined in Section 18 of the Military and Veterans Code, at the time of the suspension, cancellation, or revocation of his or her vehicle registration. The person shall submit a copy of his or her official military orders upon requesting the registration reinstatement.

(Amended by Stats. 2011, Ch. 401, Sec. 4. (AB 1024) Effective January 1, 2012.)

4000.4. (a) Except as provided in Sections 6700, 6702, and 6703, any vehicle which is registered to a nonresident owner, and which is based in California or primarily used on California highways, shall be registered in California.

(b) For purposes of this section, a vehicle is deemed to be primarily or regularly used on the highways of this state if the vehicle is located or operated in this state for a greater amount of time than it is located or operated in any other individual state during the registration period in question.

(Amended by Stats. 1988, Ch. 1008, Sec. 2.)

4000.5. (a) The department shall register an autoette, as defined in Section 175, as a motor vehicle.

(b) The owner of an autoette shall remove the license plates from the vehicle and return them to the department when the autoette is removed from a natural island, as described in Section 175.

(Added by Stats. 2006, Ch. 322, Sec. 2. Effective January 1, 2007.)

4000.6. A commercial motor vehicle, singly or in combination, that operates with a declared gross or combined gross vehicle weight that exceeds 10,000 pounds shall be registered pursuant to Section 9400.1.

(a) A person submitting an application for registration of a commercial motor vehicle operated in combination with a semitrailer, trailer, or any combination thereof, shall include the declared combined gross weight of all units when applying for registration with the department, except as exempted under subdivision (a) of Section 9400.1.

(b) This section does not apply to pickups nor to any commercial motor vehicle or combination that does not exceed 10,000 pounds gross vehicle weight.

(c) A peace officer, as defined in Chapter 4.5 (commencing with Section 830) of Title 3 of Part 2 of the Penal Code, having reason to believe that a commercial motor vehicle is being operated, either singly or in combination, in excess of its registered declared gross or combined gross vehicle weight, may require the driver to stop and submit to an inspection or weighing of the vehicle or vehicles and an inspection of registration documents.

(d) A person shall not operate a commercial motor vehicle, either singly or in combination, in excess of its registered declared gross or combined gross vehicle weight.

(e) A violation of this section is an infraction punishable by a fine in an amount equal to the amount specified in Section 42030.1.

(Amended by Stats. 2004, Ch. 615, Sec. 21. Effective January 1, 2005.)

4001. All vehicles exempt from the payment of registration fees shall be registered as otherwise required by this code by the person having custody thereof, and he shall display upon the vehicle a license plate bearing distinguishing marks or symbols, which shall be furnished by the department free of charge.

(Enacted by Stats. 1959, Ch. 3.)

4002. When moved or operated under a permit issued by the department, registration is not required of:

(a) A vehicle not previously registered while being moved or operated from a dealer's, distributor's, or manufacturer's place of business to a place where essential parts of the vehicle are to be altered or supplied.

(b) A vehicle while being moved from a place of storage to another place of storage.

(c) A vehicle while being moved to or from a garage or repair shop for the purpose of repairs or alteration.

(d) A vehicle while being moved or operated for the purpose of dismantling or wrecking the same and permanently removing it from the highways.

(e) A vehicle, while being moved from one place to another for the purpose of inspection by the department, assignment of a vehicle identification number, inspection of pollution control devices, or weighing the vehicle.

(f) A vehicle, the construction of which has not been completed, until such time as the construction thereof is completed and final weights and costs can be determined for registration purposes.

(Amended by Stats. 1977, Ch. 326.)

4003. A permit, as described in Section 9258, may be issued by the department for operating any of the following vehicles, except a crane:

(a) A vehicle while being moved or operated unladen for one continuous trip from a place within this state to another place either within or without this state or from a place without this state to a place within this state.

(b) A vehicle while being moved or operated for one round trip to be completed within 60 days from one place to another for the purpose of participating as a vehicular float or display in a lawful parade or exhibition, provided that the total round trip does not exceed 100 miles.

The department may issue a quantity of permits under this subsection in booklet form upon payment of the proper fee for each permit contained in such booklet. Each permit shall be valid for only one vehicle and for only one continuous trip. Such permit shall be posted upon the windshield or other prominent place upon a vehicle and shall identify the vehicle to which it is affixed. When so affixed, such permit shall serve in lieu of California registration.

(Amended by Stats. 1977, Ch. 326.)

4003.5. (a) Upon payment of the fee specified in Section 9258.5, the department shall issue to a manufacturer or dealer a one-trip permit authorizing a new trailer, semitrailer, or auxiliary dolly that has never been registered in any state, or a used trailer, semitrailer, or auxiliary dolly that is not currently registered, to be moved or operated laden within, entering, or leaving this state for not more than 10 days as part of one continuous trip from the place of manufacture for a new vehicle, or from the place of dispatch or entry into this state for a used vehicle, to a place where the vehicle will be offered for sale.

(b) Any permit issued pursuant to this section authorizes the operation of a single trailer, semitrailer, or auxiliary dolly, and the permit shall identify the trailer, semitrailer, or auxiliary dolly authorized by make, model, and vehicle identification number. The permit shall include the name and license number of the manufacturer from whom the new vehicle is sent, or the name and license number of the dealer from whom the used vehicle is sent, the name and address of the person or business receiving the load, a description of the load being carried, and the name and license number of the dealer who will be offering the trailer, semitrailer, or auxiliary dolly for sale. Each permit shall be completed prior to operation of the trailer or semitrailer or auxiliary dolly on a highway. The permit shall be carried on the trailer, semitrailer, or auxiliary dolly to which it applies in an appropriate receptacle inaccessible from the inside of the cab and shall be readily available for inspection by a peace officer. Each permit is valid at the time of inspection by a peace officer only if it has been completed as required by the department and has been placed in the appropriate receptacle as required by this section. The manufacturer or dealer issued the permit may allow a third party to move or operate the vehicle.

(c) The privilege of securing and displaying a permit authorized pursuant to this section shall not be extended to a manufacturer, carrier, or dealer located in a jurisdiction with which the state does not have vehicle licensing reciprocity.

(d) The privilege of securing and displaying a permit authorized pursuant to this section shall not be granted more than once without the sale and registration of the trailer, semitrailer, or auxiliary dolly.

(Amended by Stats. 2014, Ch. 301, Sec. 1. (AB 27) Effective January 1, 2015.)

4004. (a) (1) Commercial motor vehicles meeting the registration requirements of a foreign jurisdiction, and subject to registration but not entitled to exemption from registration or licensing under any of the provisions of this code or any agreements, arrangements, or declarations made under Article 3 (commencing with Section 8000) of Chapter 4, may, as an alternate to registration, secure a temporary registration to operate in this state for a period of not to exceed 90 days, or a trip permit to operate in this state for a period of four consecutive days.

(2) Each trip permit shall authorize the operation of a single commercial motor vehicle for a period of not more than four consecutive days, commencing with the day of first use and three consecutive days thereafter. Every permit shall identify, as the department may require, the commercial motor vehicle for which it is issued. Each trip permit shall be completed prior to operation of the commercial motor vehicle on any highway in this state and shall be carried in the commercial motor vehicle to which it applies and shall be readily available for inspection by a peace officer. Each permit shall be valid at the time of inspection by a peace officer only if it has been completed as required by the department and has been placed in the appropriate receptacle as required by this section. It is unlawful for any person to fail to comply with the provisions of this section.

(b) The privilege of securing and using a trip permit or a temporary registration not to exceed 90 days shall not extend to a vehicle that is based within this state and is operated by a person having an established place of business within this state. For purposes of this paragraph, a commercial motor vehicle shall be considered to be based in this state if it is primarily operated or dispatched from or principally garaged or serviced or maintained at a site with an address within this state.

(c) Any trailer or semitrailer identified in paragraph (1) of subdivision (a) of Section 5014.1 that enters the state without a currently valid license plate issued by California or another jurisdiction shall be immediately subject to full identification fees as specified in subdivision (e) of Section 5014.1.

(Amended by Stats. 2011, Ch. 315, Sec. 8. (AB 28) Effective January 1, 2012.)

4004.5. The owner of any motor vehicle subject to the registration provisions of this chapter, or exempted therefrom, may file with the department, at the time he registers or renews the registration of such motor vehicle, a signed statement that he resides in more than one county for a period of more than 30 days, or uses such vehicle in a county other than the county of his legal residence for business purposes. Such statement shall specify the address at which the owner resides in any county for more than 30 days, if any, or the length of time during which such owner uses the motor vehicle for business purposes in any county.

The department shall provide forms for the filing of such statements and shall take into consideration the length of time during which owners reside or use motor vehicles in counties, in accordance with the statements filed with the department, to determine the total number of vehicles registered or exempted from registration in any particular county.

(Added by Stats. 1967, Ch. 1485.)

4004.7. (a) If the apportioned registration issued under Article 4 (commencing with Section 8050) of Chapter 4 for a commercial vehicle or vehicle combination that was last registered by a California resident has expired or has been terminated, the department, upon receipt of a completed application, a fee of thirty dollars ($30), and proof of financial responsibility for the vehicle, may issue an unladen operation permit to authorize the unladen operation of that vehicle or vehicle combination for a period of not more than 15 continuous days.

(b) This section does not apply to any vehicle or vehicle combination for which any vehicle registration fees, other than those for the current year, vehicle license fees, or penalties, or any combination of those are due.

(c) Operation of a laden vehicle or vehicle combination under an unladen operation permit issued pursuant to this section is an infraction.

(Added by Stats. 2001, Ch. 539, Sec. 9. Effective January 1, 2002.)

4005. Any vehicle subject to registration may be operated within a disaster area or region for the purpose of assisting in disaster relief work, under a special permit to be issued by the department for such purpose, without the registration of such vehicle.

Said permit shall be issued only if the Department of Transportation or the responsible local authority has determined that the vehicle is necessary for such purpose, and shall be valid only during a period of a state of emergency as proclaimed by the Governor under the provisions of the California Emergency Services Act.

(Amended by Stats. 1974, Ch. 545.)

4006. A vehicle which is driven or moved upon a highway only for the purpose of crossing the highway from one property to another in accordance with a permit issued by the Department of Transportation is exempt from registration.

(Amended by Stats. 1974, Ch. 545.)

4007. The department, the Public Utilities Commission, and the State Board of Equalization shall enter into an interagency agreement to establish a coordinated system for the issuance of temporary operating authority to carriers of passengers for compensation by motor vehicles

which are operating under the laws of another state or country. The agreement shall designate a lead agency from among the parties to the agreement to which the carrier may make a single application for the temporary operating authority required under the laws of this state. The lead agency shall coordinate and expedite all matters relating to issuance of the temporary operating authority and the collection and distribution of fees therefor with every other state agency having jurisdiction, so as to promptly prepare and issue the required operating authority.
(Added by Stats. 1986, Ch. 510, Sec. 3.)

4009. A vehicle transported upon a highway, no part of which is in contact with the highway, is exempt from registration.
(Enacted by Stats. 1959, Ch. 3.)

4010. Special construction equipment and special mobile equipment are exempt from registration.
(Amended by Stats. 1961, Ch. 1659.)

4012. Any vehicle, implement, or equipment specifically designed or altered for and used exclusively in the maintenance or operation of cemetery grounds, which is only incidentally operated or moved on a highway is exempt from registration.
(Amended by Stats. 1968, Ch. 999.)

4013. Any forklift truck which is designed primarily for loading and unloading and for stacking materials and is operated upon a highway only for the purpose of transporting products or material across a highway in the loading, unloading or stacking process, and is in no event operated along a highway for a greater distance than one-quarter mile is exempt from registration.
(Enacted by Stats. 1959, Ch. 3.)

4014. Any portable or collapsible dolly carried in a tow truck or in a truck used by an automobile dismantler and used upon a highway exclusively for towing disabled vehicles is exempt from registration.
(Amended by Stats. 1988, Ch. 924, Sec. 3.)

4015. Any privately owned vehicle designed or capable of being used for firefighting purposes when operated upon a highway only in responding to, and returning from, emergency fire calls is exempt from registration.
(Amended by Stats. 1965, Ch. 1643.)

4016. Notwithstanding the provisions of Section 4000, unregistered vehicles may be left standing upon a highway adjacent to a vehicle dealer's place of business when done so in connection with the loading and unloading of vehicles to be used in the dealer's business, unless otherwise prohibited by law.
(Added by Stats. 1959, Ch. 1233.)

4017. The provisions of Section 4000 shall not apply to the moving or operating of a vehicle during the period of time in which application may be made for registration of the vehicle without penalty as provided in Section 4152.5.
(Amended by Stats. 1974, Ch. 1330.)

4018. Any logging vehicle is exempt from registration.
(Added by Stats. 1975, Ch. 517.)

4019. A golf cart operated pursuant to Section 21115 is exempt from registration.
(Added by Stats. 1968, Ch. 1303.)

4020. A motorized bicycle operated upon a highway is exempt from registration.
(Added by Stats. 1975, Ch. 987.)

4021. Any vehicle that is designed or altered for, and used exclusively for, the refueling of aircraft at a public airport is exempt from registration, if the vehicle is operated upon a highway under the control of a local authority for a continuous distance not exceeding one-half mile each way to and from a bulk fuel storage facility.
(Amended by Stats. 1996, Ch. 1154, Sec. 57. Effective September 30, 1996.)

4022. A vehicle repossessed pursuant to the terms of a security agreement is exempt from registration solely for the purpose of transporting the vehicle from the point of repossession to the storage facilities of the repossessor, and from the storage facilities to the legal owner or a licensed motor vehicle auction, provided that the repossessor transports with the vehicle the appropriate documents authorizing the repossession and makes them available to a law enforcement officer on request.
(Added by Stats. 1995, Ch. 505, Sec. 38. Effective January 1, 1996.)

4023. A low-speed vehicle operated pursuant to Section 21115 or 21115.1 is exempt from registration.
(Added by Stats. 1999, Ch. 140, Sec. 2. Effective January 1, 2000.)

Article 2. Original Registration

(Article 2 enacted by Stats. 1959, Ch. 3.)

4150. Application for the original or renewal registration of a vehicle of a type required to be registered under this code shall be made by the owner to the department upon the appropriate form furnished by it and shall contain all of the following:

(a) The true, full name, business or residence and mailing address, and driver's license or identification card number, if any, of the owner, and the true, full name and business or residence or mailing address of the legal owner, if any.

(b) The name of the county in which the owner resides.

(c) A description of the vehicle, including the following data insofar as they may exist:

(1) The make, model, and type of body.

(2) The vehicle identification number or any other identifying number as may be required by the department.

(3) The date first sold by a manufacturer, remanufacturer, or dealer to a consumer.

(d) Any other information that is reasonably required by the department to enable it to determine whether the vehicle is lawfully entitled to registration.
(Amended by Stats. 1994, Ch. 1221, Sec. 2. Effective January 1, 1995.)

4150.1. (a) On a form provided by the department, the registered owner of record, lessee, or the owner's designee shall certify and report the declared gross or combined gross vehicle weight of any commercial motor vehicle, singly or in combination, in excess of 10,000 pounds.

(b) A single form may be used or referenced for multiple vehicles.
(Amended by Stats. 2001, Ch. 826, Sec. 10. Effective January 1, 2002.)

4150.2. Application for the original registration or renewal of the registration of a motorcycle shall be made by the owner to the department upon the appropriate form furnished by it, and shall contain all of the following:

(a) The true, full name, business or residence and mailing address, and driver's license or identification card number, if any, of the owner, and the true, full name and business or residence or mailing address of the legal owner, if any.

(b) The name of the county in which the owner resides.

(c) A description of the motorcycle, including the following data insofar as they may exist:

(1) The make and type of body.

(2) The motor and vehicle identification numbers recorded exactly as they appear on the engine and frame, respectively, by the manufacturer, and any other identifying number of the motorcycle as may be required by the department.

(3) The date first sold by a manufacturer, remanufacturer, or dealer to a consumer.

(d) Any other information that is reasonably required by the department to enable it to determine whether the vehicle is lawfully entitled to registration.

(e) The department shall maintain a cross-index file of motor and vehicle identification numbers registered with it.
(Amended by Stats. 1994, Ch. 1221, Sec. 3. Effective January 1, 1995.)

4150.5. Ownership of title to a vehicle subject to registration may be held by two (or more) coowners as provided in Section 682 of the

Civil Code, except that:

(a) A vehicle may be registered in the names of two (or more) persons as coowners in the alternative by the use of the word "or." A vehicle so registered in the alternative shall be deemed to be held in joint tenancy. Each coowner shall be deemed to have granted to the other coowners the absolute right to dispose of the title and interest in the vehicle. Upon the death of a coowner the interest of the decedent shall pass to the survivor as though title or interest in the vehicle was held in joint tenancy unless a contrary intention is set forth in writing upon the application for registration.

(b) A vehicle may be registered in the names of two (or more) persons as coowners in the alternative by the use of the word "or" and if declared in writing upon the application for registration by the applicants to be community property, or tenancy in common, shall grant to each coowner the absolute power to transfer the title or interest of the other coowners only during the lifetime of such coowners.

(c) A vehicle may be registered in the names of two (or more) persons as coowners in the conjunctive by the use of the word "and" and shall thereafter require the signature of each coowner or his personal representative to transfer title to the vehicle, except where title to the vehicle is set forth in joint tenancy, the signature of each coowner or his personal representative shall be required only during the lifetime of the coowners, and upon death of a coowner title shall pass to the surviving coowner.

(d) The department may adopt suitable abbreviations to appear upon the certificate of registration and certificate of ownership to designate the manner in which title to the vehicle is held if set forth by the coowners upon the application for registration.

(Added by Stats. 1965, Ch. 891.)

4150.7. (a) Ownership of title to a vehicle subject to registration may be held in beneficiary form that includes a direction to transfer ownership of the vehicle to a designated beneficiary on the death of the owner if both of the following requirements are satisfied:

(1) Only one owner is designated.

(2) Only one TOD beneficiary is designated.

(b) A certificate of ownership issued in beneficiary form shall include, after the name of the owner, the words "transfer on death to" or the abbreviation "TOD" followed by the name of the beneficiary.

(c) During the lifetime of the owner, the signature or consent of the beneficiary is not required for any transaction relating to the vehicle for which a certificate of ownership in beneficiary form has been issued.

(d) The fee for registering ownership of a vehicle in a beneficiary form is ten dollars ($10).

(Added by Stats. 1991, Ch. 1055, Sec. 58. Operative January 1, 1993, by Sec. 64 of Ch. 1055.)

4151. The department shall not accept an application for the original registration of a vehicle in this State unless the vehicle at the time of application is within this State unless the provisions of Section 4152 are complied with.

(Enacted by Stats. 1959, Ch. 3.)

4152. (a) The department may accept an application for registration of a vehicle which is not within this state, but which is to be registered to a resident of this state, at the time all documents and fees, as determined by the department in accordance with the provisions of this division, are submitted to the department.

(b) Any fees submitted pursuant to subdivision (a) shall not be subject to refund based upon the fact that the vehicle has not been and is not within this state.

(Amended by Stats. 1975, Ch. 1220.)

4152.5. Except as provided for in subdivision (c) of Section 9553, when California registration is required of a vehicle last registered in a foreign jurisdiction, an application for registration shall be made to the department within 20 days following the date registration became due. The application shall be deemed an original application.

(Amended by Stats. 2000, Ch. 1035, Sec. 7. Effective January 1, 2001.)

4153. If the vehicle to be registered is a specially constructed or remanufactured vehicle, the application shall also state that fact and contain additional information as may reasonably be required by the department to enable it properly to register the vehicle.

(Amended by Stats. 1983, Ch. 1286, Sec. 18.)

4154. The department may not issue or renew the registration of a farm labor vehicle unless the owner of the vehicle provides verification to the department that the inspection required by Section 31401 has been performed. For these purposes, the department shall determine what constitutes appropriate verification.

(Added by Stats. 1999, Ch. 557, Sec. 1.5. Effective September 29, 1999.)

4155. Registration under this code shall apply to any vehicle owned by the United States government, the state, or any city, county, or political subdivision of the state, except in the following particulars:

(a) A license plate issued for a vehicle while publicly owned need not display the year number for which it is issued, but shall display a distinguishing symbol or letter.

(b) The registration of the vehicle and the registration card issued therefor shall not be renewed annually but shall remain valid until the certificate of ownership is suspended, revoked, or canceled by the department or upon a transfer of any interest shown in the certificate of ownership. If ownership of the vehicle is transferred to any person, the vehicle shall be reregistered as a privately owned vehicle and the special license plates shall be surrendered to the department.

(c) An identification plate used for special construction, cemetery, or special mobile equipment need not display a distinguishing symbol or letter.

(Amended by Stats. 1969, Ch. 1242.)

4156. (a) Notwithstanding any other provision of this code, and except as provided in subdivision (b), the department in its discretion may issue a temporary permit to operate a vehicle when a payment of fees has been accepted in an amount to be determined by, and paid to the department, by the owner or other person in lawful possession of the vehicle. The permit shall be subject to the terms and conditions, and shall be valid for the period of time, that the department shall deem appropriate under the circumstances.

(b) (1) The department shall not issue a temporary permit pursuant to subdivision (a) to operate a vehicle for which a certificate of compliance is required pursuant to Section 4000.3, and for which that certificate of compliance has not been issued, unless the department is presented with sufficient evidence, as determined by the department, that the vehicle has failed its most recent smog check inspection.

(2) Only one temporary permit may be issued pursuant to this subdivision to a vehicle owner in a two-year period.

(3) A temporary permit issued pursuant to paragraph (1) is valid for either 60 days after the expiration of the registration of the vehicle or 60 days after the date that vehicle is removed from nonoperation, whichever is applicable at the time that the temporary permit is issued.

(4) A temporary permit issued pursuant to paragraph (1) is subject to Section 9257.5.

(c) (1) The department may issue a temporary permit pursuant to subdivision (a) to operate a vehicle for which registration may be refused pursuant to Section 4000.15.

(2) Only one temporary permit may be issued pursuant to this subdivision for any vehicle, unless otherwise approved by the State Air Resources Board.

(3) A temporary permit issued pursuant to paragraph (1) is valid for either 90 days after the expiration of the registration of the vehicle or 90 days after the date that vehicle is removed from nonoperation, whichever is applicable at the time the temporary permit is issued.

(Amended by Stats. 2017, Ch. 20, Sec. 21. (AB 115) Effective June 27, 2017.)

4156.5. (a) Except as provided in subdivision (b), the department in its discretion may issue a temporary permit to operate a vehicle when a payment of fees has been accepted in an amount to be determined by, and paid to, the department by the owner or other person in lawful possession of the vehicle, for a vehicle for which registration may be refused pursuant to Section 4000.17. The permit shall be subject to the terms and conditions that the department shall deem appropriate under the circumstances.

(b) The department shall not issue a temporary permit pursuant to subdivision (a) to operate a vehicle for which a certificate of compliance is required pursuant to Section 4000.17, and for which that certificate of compliance has not been issued, unless the department is presented with sufficient evidence, as determined by the department, that the vehicle has failed its most recent inspection pursuant to the Heavy-Duty Vehicle Inspection and Maintenance Program (Chapter 5.5 (commencing with Section 44150) of Part 5 of Division 26 of the Health and Safety Code).

(c) Only one temporary permit may be issued pursuant to this section for any vehicle, unless otherwise approved by the State Air Resources Board.

(d) A temporary permit issued pursuant to this section is valid for either 60 days after the expiration of the registration of the vehicle or 60 days after the date that vehicle is removed from nonoperation, whichever is applicable at the time the temporary permit is issued.

(e) (1) A fee of fifty dollars ($50) shall be paid for a temporary permit issued pursuant to this section.

(2) The fee authorized pursuant to paragraph (1) shall be adjusted annually based on the California Consumer Price Index as compiled and reported by the Department of Industrial Relations.

(3) After deducting its administrative costs, the department shall deposit fees collected pursuant to paragraph (1) in the Truck Emission Check (TEC) Fund created pursuant to Section 44154 of the Health and Safety Code, to be used for regulatory activities under the Heavy-Duty Vehicle Inspection and Maintenance Program (Chapter 5.5 (commencing with Section 44150) of Part 5 of Division 26 of the Health and Safety Code).

(Added by Stats. 2019, Ch. 298, Sec. 4. (SB 210) Effective January 1, 2020.)

4157. In the absence of the regularly required supporting evidence of ownership upon application for registration or transfer of a vehicle, the department may accept an undertaking or bond which shall be conditioned to protect the department and all officers and employees thereof and any subsequent purchaser of the vehicle, any person acquiring a lien or security interest thereon, or the successor in interest of such purchaser or person against any loss or damage on account of any defect in or undisclosed claim upon the right, title, and interest of the applicant or other person in and to the vehicle.

(Amended by Stats. 1963, Ch. 819.)

4158. In the event the vehicle is no longer registered in this state and the currently valid certificate of ownership is surrendered to the department, the bond or undertaking shall be returned and surrendered at the end of three years or prior thereto.

(Amended by Stats. 1982, Ch. 517, Sec. 387.)

4159. Whenever any person after making application for the registration of a vehicle required to be registered under this code, or after obtaining registration either as owner or legal owner, moves or acquires a new address different from the address shown in the application or upon the certificate of ownership or registration card, such person shall, within 10 days thereafter, notify the department of his old and new address.

(Amended by Stats. 1976, Ch. 552.)

4160. Any registered owner of a vehicle who moves or acquires a new address different from the address shown upon the registration card issued for the vehicle shall within 10 days mark out the former address shown on the face of the card and with pen and ink write or type the new address on the face of the card immediately below the former address with the initials of the registered owner.

(Amended by Stats. 1959, Ch. 964.)

4161. (a) Whenever a motor vehicle engine or motor is installed, except temporarily, in a motor vehicle which is identified on the ownership and registration certificates by motor or engine number or by both the motor and frame numbers and subject to registration under this code, the owner of the motor vehicle shall, within 10 days thereafter, give notice to the department upon a form furnished by it containing a description of the motor vehicle engine or motor installed, including any identifying number thereon and the date of the installation. The owner of the motor vehicle shall also submit to the department with the notice the certificate of ownership and registration card covering the motor vehicle in which the motor vehicle engine or motor is installed and evidence of ownership covering the new or used motor vehicle engine or motor installed and such other documents as may be required by the department.

(b) Upon receipt of motor vehicle engine or motor change notification and other required documents, the department shall assign a distinguishing vehicle identification number to motor vehicles, other than motorcycles or motor-driven cycles registered under a motor number or motor and frame numbers. When the distinguishing vehicle identification number is placed on the vehicle as authorized, the vehicle shall thereafter be identified by the distinguishing identification number assigned.

(c) Notwithstanding any other provision of this section or any other provision of law, whenever an application is made to the department to register a replacement engine case for any motorcycle, the department shall request the Department of the California Highway Patrol to inspect the motorcycle to determine its proper identity. If the replacement engine case bears the same identifying numbers as the engine case being replaced, the original engine case shall be destroyed. A determination verifying proof of destruction shall be made by the Department of the California Highway Patrol.

(Amended by Stats. 2001, Ch. 94, Sec. 1. Effective January 1, 2002.)

4163. The owner of three or more motor vehicles is not required to notify the department or to pay the fee required under Section 9257 when motor vehicle engines or motors owned by him are installed in or transferred between the motor vehicles owned by him until the motor vehicle is sold, transferred, or otherwise disposed of by him.

(Amended by Stats. 1961, Ch. 58.)

4166. The department may assign a distinguishing vehicle identification number to a motor vehicle whenever the motor or other identifying number thereon is removed, destroyed or obliterated, and any motor vehicle to which a distinguishing vehicle identification number is assigned as authorized herein shall be registered under the number so assigned when registration of the motor vehicle is required under this code.

(Amended by Stats. 1970, Ch. 824.)

Article 3. Registration of Foreign Vehicles

(Article 3 enacted by Stats. 1959, Ch. 3.)

4300. Upon application for registration of a vehicle previously registered outside this State, the application shall be certified by the applicant and shall state that the vehicle previously has been registered outside this State, the time and place of the last registration of such vehicle outside this State, the name and address of the governmental officer, agency, or authority making the registration, and such further information relative to its previous registration as may reasonably be required by the department, including the time and place of original registration, if known, and if different from the last foreign registration.

(Enacted by Stats. 1959, Ch. 3.)

4300.5. An application for registration under this chapter of a vehicle previously registered outside of this state shall be accompanied by payment of the amount required to be paid under Part 1 (commencing with Section 6001) of Division 2 of the Revenue and Taxation Code with respect to the use of the vehicle by the applicant.

(Amended by Stats. 1984, Ch. 144, Sec. 205.)

4301. The applicant shall surrender to the department all unexpired

license plates, seals, certificates, or other evidence of foreign registration as may be in his possession or under his control. The department may require a certification from the jurisdiction of last registry when the applicant fails to surrender the last issued unexpired license plates.
(Enacted by Stats. 1959, Ch. 3.)

4302. Upon application made at the time of their surrender to the department and upon payment of a fee of one dollar ($1), the department shall return the unexpired license plates to the official in charge of the registration of motor vehicles in the state of issue of the license plates.
(Enacted by Stats. 1959, Ch. 3.)

4303. If in the course of interstate operation of a vehicle registered in another state it is desirable to retain registration in such state, the applicant need not surrender the evidence of foreign registration, but shall deliver it to the department for purposes of inspection, and the department upon a proper showing shall register the vehicle in this State, but shall not issue a certificate of ownership for the vehicle.
(Enacted by Stats. 1959, Ch. 3.)

4304. Upon application for registration of a vehicle previously registered outside this State, the department shall grant full faith and credit to the currently valid certificate of title describing the vehicle, the ownership thereof, and any liens thereon, issued by the state in which the vehicle was last registered, except that the laws of the state shall provide for the notation upon the certificate of title of any and all liens and encumbrances other than those dependent upon possession.
(Enacted by Stats. 1959, Ch. 3.)

4305. In the absence of knowledge by the department that any certificate of title issued by another state is forged, fraudulent, or void, the acceptance thereof by the department shall be a sufficient determination of the genuineness and regularity of the certificate and of the truth of the recitals therein, and no liability shall be incurred by any officer or employee of the department by reason of so accepting a certificate of title.
(Enacted by Stats. 1959, Ch. 3.)

4306. In the event a certificate of title issued by another state shows any lien or encumbrance upon the vehicle therein described, then the department upon registering the vehicle in this State and upon issuing a certificate of ownership shall include therein the name of the lienholder as legal owner unless documents submitted with the foreign certificate of title establish that the lien or encumbrance has been fully satisfied.
(Enacted by Stats. 1959, Ch. 3.)

4307. In the event application is made in this state for registration of a vehicle and the department is not satisfied as to the ownership of the vehicle or the existence of foreign liens thereon, then the department may register the vehicle and issue a distinctive registration card and appropriate license plates but shall withhold issuance of a California certificate of ownership unless the applicant shall present documents sufficient to reasonably satisfy the department of the applicant's ownership of the vehicle and sufficient to identify any liens thereon or the applicant shall post a bond pursuant to Section 4157.
(Amended by Stats. 1981, Ch. 636, Sec. 2.)

4308. In the event the department refuses to grant an application for registration in this State of a vehicle previously registered in another state, the department shall immediately return to the applicant all documents submitted by the applicant with the application.
(Enacted by Stats. 1959, Ch. 3.)

4309. The department shall forthwith mail a notice of the filing of any application for registration of a vehicle previously registered outside this state upon written request of the governmental officer, agency, or authority which made the last registration of the vehicle outside this state. The notice shall contain like data as required on the application filed with the department. This section shall not apply to applications to register commercial vehicles operating in interstate transportation nor to vehicles last registered in a foreign province or country.
(Amended by Stats. 1967, Ch. 1141.)

Article 4. Evidences of Registration

(Article 4 enacted by Stats. 1959, Ch. 3.)

4450. The department upon registering a vehicle shall issue a certificate of ownership to the legal owner and a registration card to the owner, or both to the owner if there is no legal owner of the vehicle.
(Enacted by Stats. 1959, Ch. 3.)

4450.5. (a) On or before January 1, 2012, the director shall develop an Electronic Lien and Title (ELT) Program, in consultation with lienholders, licensed dealers, and other stakeholders, to require that all lienholders' title information be held in an electronic format, if the department determines that the program is cost effective compared to the current paper title and registration system.

(b) The director may establish an auto loan business volume threshold below which a lienholder is not required to participate in the program developed pursuant to subdivision (a).
(Added by Stats. 2009, Ch. 540, Sec. 1. (AB 1515) Effective January 1, 2010.)

4451. The certificate of ownership shall contain all of the following:

(a) Not less than the information required upon the face of the registration card.

(b) Provision for notice to the department of a transfer of the title or interest of the owner or legal owner.

(c) Provision for application for transfer of registration by the transferee.

(d) Provision for an odometer disclosure statement pursuant to subsection (a) of Section 32705 of Title 49 of the United States Code.
(Amended by Stats. 2000, Ch. 1035, Sec. 8. Effective January 1, 2001.)

4452. The department may issue a certificate of ownership to the legal owner of a vehicle without requiring registration, and may issue a facsimile copy of the certificate to the owner if there is no legal owner, the application is submitted in proper form, and one of the following conditions exist:

(a) The vehicle is registered pursuant to Section 5014.1.

(b) A certification has been filed with the department, pursuant to subdivision (a) of Section 4604, that the vehicle has not been driven, moved, or left standing upon any highway so as to require payment of fees and that the owner will not thereafter permit that operation or movement of the vehicle or leave the vehicle standing on any highway without surrendering, or arranging to surrender, the certificate of ownership to the department and without first making an application for the regular registration of the vehicle and full payment of all fees required to be paid under this code and Part 5 (commencing with Section 10701) of Division 2 of the Revenue and Taxation Code.
(Amended by Stats. 2001, Ch. 826, Sec. 11. Effective January 1, 2002.)

4453. (a) The registration card shall contain upon its face, the date issued, the name and residence or business address or mailing address of the owner and of the legal owner, if any, the registration number assigned to the vehicle, and a description of the vehicle as complete as that required in the application for registration of the vehicle.

(b) The following motor vehicles shall be identified as such on the face of the registration card whenever the department is able to ascertain that fact at the time application is made for initial registration or transfer of ownership of the vehicle:

(1) A motor vehicle rebuilt and restored to operation that was previously declared to be a total loss salvage vehicle because the cost of repairs exceeds the retail value of the vehicle.

(2) A motor vehicle rebuilt and restored to operation that was previously reported to be dismantled pursuant to Section 11520.

(3) A motor vehicle previously registered to a law enforcement agency and operated in law enforcement work.

(4) A motor vehicle formerly operated as a taxicab.

(5) A motor vehicle manufactured outside of the United States and not intended by the manufacturer for sale in the United States.

(6) A park trailer, as described in Section 18009.3 of the Health and Safety Code, that when moved upon the highway is required to be moved

under a permit pursuant to Section 35780.

(7) A motor vehicle that has been reacquired under circumstances described in subdivision (c) of Section 1793.23 of the Civil Code, a vehicle with out-of-state titling documents reflecting a warranty return, or a vehicle that has been identified by an agency of another state as requiring a warranty return title notation, pursuant to the laws of that state. The notation made on the face of the registration and pursuant to this subdivision shall state "Lemon Law Buyback."

(c) The director may modify the form, arrangement, and information appearing on the face of the registration card and may provide for standardization and abbreviation of fictitious or firm names on the registration card whenever the director finds that the efficiency of the department will be promoted by so doing.

(Amended by Stats. 2003, Ch. 451, Sec. 17. Effective January 1, 2004.)

4453.2. In addition to the information required under Section 4453, the registration card of every farm labor vehicle shall contain the words, "Farm Labor Vehicle," in conjunction with the vehicle identification information.

(Added by Stats. 1999, Ch. 557, Sec. 2. Effective September 29, 1999.)

4453.5. (a) In the case of leased vehicles, the lessor and the lessee shall be shown on the registration card as the owner and the lessee of a vehicle, and the department shall designate their relationships upon the card and the ownership certificate by the words "lessor" and "lessee" and, at the election of the lessor, the department may designate thereon either the address of the lessor or the lessee.

(b) Transfers of ownership involving vehicles registered as provided in subdivision (a) shall only be effected upon the signature release of the lessor.

(c) The lessor shall provide the address, or the name and address, of the lessee on a form prescribed by the department in all cases where the information is not on the registration card and ownership certificate. Information received under this subdivision shall be used only for law enforcement and shall be available only to law enforcement officials at their request.

(d) A lessor, upon written request of the lessee or, if designated in writing, the lessee's designee, shall disclose any pertinent information regarding the amount of payment and the documents necessary to exercise any option held by the lessee to purchase the leased vehicle.

(Amended by Stats. 2003, Ch. 151, Sec. 1. Effective January 1, 2004.)

4453.6. On request of any member of the California Highway Patrol, any regularly employed and salaried police officer or deputy sheriff, or any reserve police officer or reserve deputy sheriff listed in Section 830.6 of the Penal Code, or any employee or officer of the department specified in Section 1655, who is conducting an investigation of a public offense, the lessor of a vehicle shall furnish the name and address of the lessee of a vehicle if that information does not appear on the registration card.

(Amended by Stats. 2003, Ch. 292, Sec. 6. Effective January 1, 2004.)

4454. (a) Every owner, upon receipt of a registration card, shall maintain the same or a facsimile copy thereof with the vehicle for which issued.

(b) This section does not apply when a registration card is necessarily removed from the vehicle for the purpose of application for renewal or transfer of registration, or when the vehicle is left unattended.

(c) Any violation of this section shall be cited in accordance with the provisions of Section 40610.

(Amended by Stats. 1999, Ch. 106, Sec. 1. Effective January 1, 2000.)

4455. Any permit issued under Section 4004 shall be carried in the vehicle for which issued at all times while it is being operated in this State.

(Enacted by Stats. 1959, Ch. 3.)

4456. (a) When selling a vehicle, dealers and lessor-retailers shall report the sale using the reporting system described in Section 4456.2. After providing information to the reporting system, the dealer or lessor-retailer shall do all of the following:

(1) The dealer or lessor-retailer shall attach for display a copy of the report-of-sale form provided by the reporting system on the vehicle before the vehicle is delivered to the purchaser.

(2) The dealer or lessor-retailer shall submit to the department an application accompanied by all fees and penalties due for registration or transfer of registration of the vehicle within 30 days from the date of sale, as provided in subdivision (c) of Section 9553, if the vehicle is a used vehicle, and within 20 days if the vehicle is a new vehicle. Penalties due for noncompliance with this paragraph shall be paid by the dealer or lessor-retailer. The dealer or lessor-retailer shall not charge the purchaser for the penalties.

(3) (A) Pursuant to the regulations adopted by the department under subdivision (f) of Section 6295 of the Revenue and Taxation Code, for retail sales of vehicles occurring on and after January 1, 2021, the dealer shall also submit with the application payment of the applicable sales tax required by the Sales and Use Tax Law (Part 1 (commencing with Section 6001) of Division 2 of the Revenue and Taxation Code) and the Bradley-Burns Uniform Local Sales and Use Tax Law (Part 1.5 (commencing with Section 7200) of Division 2 of the Revenue and Taxation Code) and the applicable transactions and use taxes required by the Transactions and Use Tax Law (Part 1.6 (commencing with Section 7251) of Division 2 of the Revenue and Taxation Code) to the department within 30 days from the date of sale.

(B) The amendments to this section made by the act adding this subparagraph do not constitute a change in, but are declaratory of, existing law.

(C) For purposes of this paragraph, "dealer" shall not include a new motor vehicle dealer as defined by Section 426, a manufacturer or remanufacturer holding a license issued pursuant to Chapter 4 (commencing with Section 11700) of Division 5, an automobile dismantler holding a license and certificate issued pursuant to Chapter 3 (commencing with Section 11500) of Division 5, or a lessor-retailer holding a license issued pursuant to Chapter 3.5 (commencing with Section 11600) of Division 5, and subject to the provisions of Section 11615.5.

(4) As part of an application to transfer registration of a used vehicle, the dealer or lessor-retailer shall include all of the following information on the certificate of title, application for a duplicate certificate of title, or form prescribed by the department:

(A) Date of sale and report-of-sale number.

(B) Purchaser's name and address.

(C) Dealer's name, address, number, and signature, or signature of authorized agent.

(D) Salesperson number.

(5) If the department returns an application and the application was first received by the department within 30 days of the date of sale of the vehicle if the vehicle is a used vehicle, and within 20 days if the vehicle is a new vehicle, the dealer or lessor-retailer shall submit a corrected application to the department within 50 days from the date of sale of the vehicle if the vehicle is a used vehicle, and within 40 days if the vehicle is a new vehicle, or within 30 days from the date that the application was first returned by the department if the vehicle is a used vehicle, and within 20 days if the vehicle is a new vehicle, whichever is later.

(6) If the department returns an application and the application was first received by the department more than 30 days from the date of sale of the vehicle if the vehicle is a used vehicle, and more than 20 days if the vehicle is a new vehicle, the dealer or lessor-retailer shall submit a corrected application to the department within 50 days from the date of sale of the vehicle if the vehicle is a used vehicle, and within 40 days if the vehicle is a new vehicle.

(7) An application first received by the department more than 50 days from the date of sale of the vehicle if the vehicle is a used vehicle, and more than 40 days if the vehicle is a new vehicle, is subject to the penalties specified in subdivisions (a) and (b) of Section 4456.1.

(8) The dealer or lessor-retailer shall report the sale pursuant to

Section 5901.

(9) If the vehicle does not display license plates previously issued by the department, the dealer or lessor-retailer shall attach the temporary license plates issued by the reporting system.

(b) (1) A transfer that takes place through a dealer conducting a wholesale vehicle auction shall be reported to the department electronically in a manner approved by the department. The report shall contain, at a minimum, all of the following information:

(A) The name and address of the seller.

(B) The seller's dealer number, if applicable.

(C) The date of delivery to the dealer conducting the auction.

(D) The actual mileage of the vehicle as indicated by the vehicle's odometer at the time of delivery to the dealer conducting the auction.

(E) The name, address, and occupational license number of the dealer conducting the auction.

(F) The name, address, and occupational license number of the buyer.

(G) The signature of the dealer conducting the auction.

(2) Submission of the electronic report specified in paragraph (1) to the department shall fully satisfy the requirements of subdivision (a) and subdivision (a) of Section 5901 with respect to the dealer selling at auction and the dealer conducting the auction.

(3) The electronic report required by this subdivision does not relieve a dealer of any obligation or responsibility that is required by any other law.

(c) A vehicle displaying a report-of-sale form or temporary license plate issued pursuant to paragraph (8) of subdivision (a) may be operated without license plates until either of the following, whichever occurs first:

(1) The license plates and registration card are received by the purchaser.

(2) A 90-day period, commencing with the date of sale of the vehicle, has expired.

(d) Notwithstanding subdivision (c), a vehicle may continue to display a report-of-sale form or temporary license plates after 90 days if the owner provides proof that the owner has submitted an application to the department pursuant to Section 4457 and it has been no more than 14 days since the permanent license plates were issued to the owner. A violation of this paragraph is a correctable offense pursuant to Section 40303.5.

(e) This section shall become operative January 1, 2019.

(Amended by Stats. 2021, Ch. 256, Sec. 26. (AB 176) Effective September 23, 2021.)

4456.1. (a) A dealer or lessor-retailer who violates paragraph (1), (2), or (7) of subdivision (a) of Section 4456 shall pay to the department an administrative service fee of five dollars ($5) for each violation.

(b) A dealer or lessor-retailer who violates paragraph (4), (5), or (6) of subdivision (a) of Section 4456 shall pay to the department an administrative service fee of twenty-five dollars ($25) for each violation.

(c) Subject to subdivision (d), each violation of Section 4456 is, in addition to the obligation to pay an administrative service fee, a separate cause for discipline pursuant to Section 11613 or 11705.

(d) A violation of subdivision (a) of Section 4456 because of a dealer or lessor-retailer's failure to submit to the department an application for registration or transfer of registration is a cause for disciplinary action pursuant to Section 11613 or 11705 only if the initial application is submitted 50 days or more following the date of sale of the vehicle if the vehicle is a used vehicle, and 40 days if the vehicle is a new vehicle.

(Amended by Stats. 1996, Ch. 1155, Sec. 3.1. Effective January 1, 1997.)

4456.2. (a) The department shall develop a system for dealers and lessor-retailers to electronically report the sale of a vehicle before the vehicle is delivered to the purchaser. At minimum, the system shall conform to the following conditions:

(1) The system shall provide a licensed dealer with the forms for use as prescribed in subdivision (a) of Section 4456.

(2) For a vehicle that does not already display license plates, the system shall also produce a temporary license plate to be used and displayed in lieu of license plates, pursuant to subdivision (c) of Section 4456. The temporary license plate shall display the report-of-sale number, expiration date, and any other information deemed necessary by the department.

(3) The dealer reporting system shall assign each transaction a unique report-of-sale number that will be displayed on the report-of-sale forms and any temporary license plate.

(4) The system shall record the vehicle identification number, vehicle year, model and make, name of dealer or lessor-retailer, purchaser name and address, and any other information deemed necessary by the department.

(b) The department shall develop standards for temporary license plates produced pursuant to this section. The standards shall specify content, format, and physical attributes that are cost effective and reasonably necessary to create appropriately durable and legible temporary license plates, including the type and quality of paper, ink, and printer required to create the temporary license plates.

(c) Access to the dealer reporting system shall be restricted to authorized users of the department's vehicle registration and occupational licensing databases.

(d) The department shall make the dealer reporting system operational for use no later than January 1, 2019.

(Added by Stats. 2016, Ch. 90, Sec. 4. (AB 516) Effective January 1, 2017.)

4456.3. (a) The department shall charge a dealer or lessor-retailer a fee, as established by the director pursuant to subdivision (b), for each vehicle sold by a dealer or lessor-retailer and reported on a report-of-sale form issued by the department to a dealer or lessor-retailer, or for every vehicle sold by a dealer or lessor-retailer if that licensee does not use a report-of-sale form issued by the department because the report of the sale is given electronically or otherwise. The department shall collect the fee and the fees shall be paid to the Consumer Motor Vehicle Recovery Corporation as described in Chapter 11 (commencing with Section 12200) of Division 5. The department shall not charge more than a total of two thousand five hundred dollars ($2,500) in fees under this section to a dealer licensee within a calendar year.

(b) The director shall establish the fee at one dollar ($1) and shall collect the fee. The director shall deposit the fees received in the Motor Vehicle Account. Notwithstanding Section 13340 of the Government Code, the revenues from the fees deposited in the Motor Vehicle Account, less an amount that the director determines is equal to the department's costs related to collecting and processing the fees, is hereby continuously appropriated to the department for quarterly payment to the Consumer Motor Vehicle Recovery Corporation until the Consumer Motor Vehicle Recovery Corporation notifies the department that the balance in the recovery fund maintained by the corporation has reached five million dollars ($5,000,000). Within 90 days after being notified by the Consumer Motor Vehicle Recovery Corporation, the director shall cease collecting the fee. Thereafter, if the amount in the recovery fund maintained by the corporation is less than two million dollars ($2,000,000), the Consumer Motor Vehicle Recovery Corporation shall notify the department of the amount necessary to return the recovery fund balance to five million dollars ($5,000,000). Within 90 days of being notified, the director shall collect the fee and pay the fee revenue required by this subdivision until the Consumer Motor Vehicle Recovery Corporation notifies the director that the recovery fund has reached five million dollars ($5,000,000). Within 90 days of being notified, the director shall cease collecting the fee.

(c) (1) The Consumer Motor Vehicle Recovery Corporation shall reimburse the department for all reasonable expenses incurred in implementing this section.

(2) The Consumer Motor Vehicle Recovery Corporation shall reimburse the department for all reasonable startup expenses incurred by the department to comply with this section within 90 days after the department begins collecting the fees and transmitting them to the Corporation as provided in this section.

(d) This section shall become operative on July 1, 2008.

(Added by Stats. 2007, Ch. 437, Sec. 2. Effective January 1, 2008. Section operative July 1, 2008, by its own provisions.)

4456.4. (a) A motor vehicle sold or leased by a new motor vehicle dealer shall be registered by the dealer using electronic programs provided by a qualified private industry partner pursuant to Section 1685 if the department permits the transaction to be processed electronically.

(b) This section does not apply to the sale or lease of a motorcycle or off-highway motor vehicle subject to identification under Section 38010 or a recreational vehicle as defined in Section 18010 of the Health and Safety Code.

(c) This section shall become operative on July 1, 2012.

(Added by Stats. 2011, Ch. 329, Sec. 9. (AB 1215) Effective January 1, 2012. Section operative July 1, 2012, by its own provisions.)

4456.5. (a) A dealer may charge the purchaser or lessee of a vehicle the following charges:

(1) A document processing charge for the preparation and processing of documents, disclosures, and titling, registration, and information security obligations imposed by state and federal law. The dealer document processing charge shall not be represented as a governmental fee.

(A) If a dealer has a contractual agreement with the department to be a private industry partner pursuant to Section 1685, the document processing charge shall not exceed eighty-five dollars ($85).

(B) If a dealer does not have a contractual agreement with the department to be a private industry partner pursuant to Section 1685, the document processing charge shall not exceed seventy dollars ($70).

(2) An electronic filing charge, not to exceed the actual amount the dealer is charged by a first-line service provider for providing license plate processing, postage, and the fees and services authorized pursuant to subdivisions (a) and (d) of Section 1685, including services related to reporting vehicle sales and producing temporary license plates pursuant to Sections 4456 and 4456.2. The electronic filing charge shall not be used to pay for additional fees, goods, or services not directly related to the electronic registration of a motor vehicle, including, but not limited to, the receipt by the dealer of free or discounted goods, services, or financial incentives. The director may establish, through the adoption of regulations, the maximum amount that a first-line service provider may charge a dealer. The electronic filing charge shall not be represented as a governmental fee.

(b) As used in this section, the term "first-line service provider" shall have the same meaning as defined in subdivision (b) of Section 1685.

(c) This section does not prohibit a first-line service provider from entering into contracts with dealers for products and services unrelated to electronic vehicle registration services.

(d) This section shall become operative on January 1, 2019.

(Repealed (in Sec. 5) and added by Stats. 2016, Ch. 90, Sec. 6. (AB 516) Effective January 1, 2017. Section operative January 1, 2019, by its own provisions.)

4457. If any registration card or license plate is stolen, lost, mutilated, or illegible, the owner of the vehicle for which the same was issued, as shown by the records of the department, shall immediately make application for and may, upon the applicant furnishing information satisfactory to the department, obtain a duplicate or a substitute or a new registration under a new registration number, as determined to be most advisable by the department. An application for a duplicate registration card is not required in conjunction with any other application.

(Amended by Stats. 1988, Ch. 1268, Sec. 1.)

4458. If both license plates or a permanent trailer identification plate are lost or stolen, the registered owner shall immediately notify a law enforcement agency, and shall immediately apply to the department for new plates in lieu of the plates stolen or lost. The department shall in every proper case, except in the case of plates which are exempt from fees, cause to be issued applicable license plates of a different number and assign the registration number to the vehicle for which the plates are issued.

(Amended by Stats. 2001, Ch. 826, Sec. 12. Effective January 1, 2002.)

4459. If any certificate of ownership is stolen, lost, mutilated or illegible, the legal owner or, if none, then the owner of the vehicle for which the same was issued as shown by the records of the department shall immediately make application for and may, upon the applicant furnishing information satisfactory to the department, obtain a duplicate.

(Enacted by Stats. 1959, Ch. 3.)

4460. (a) The Department of Motor Vehicles, the Traffic Adjudication Board, and the Department of the California Highway Patrol, any regularly employed and salaried police officer or deputy sheriff or any reserve police officer or reserve deputy sheriff listed in Section 830.6 of the Penal Code may take possession of any certificate, card, placard, permit, license, or license plate issued under this code, upon expiration, revocation, cancellation, or suspension thereof or which is fictitious or which has been unlawfully or erroneously issued. Any license plate which is not attached to the vehicle for which issued, when and in the manner required under this code, may be seized, and attachment to the proper vehicle may be made or required.

(b) Any document, placard, or license plate seized shall be delivered to the Department of Motor Vehicles.

(Amended by Stats. 2003, Ch. 292, Sec. 7. Effective January 1, 2004.)

4461. (a) A person shall not lend a certificate of ownership, registration card, license plate, special plate, validation tab, or permit issued to him or her if the person desiring to borrow it would not be entitled to its use, and a person shall not knowingly permit its use by one not entitled to it.

(b) A person to whom a disabled person placard has been issued shall not lend the placard to another person, and a disabled person shall not knowingly permit the use for parking purposes of the placard or identification license plate issued pursuant to Section 5007 by one not entitled to it. A person to whom a disabled person placard has been issued may permit another person to use the placard only while in the presence or reasonable proximity of the disabled person for the purpose of transporting the disabled person. A violation of this subdivision is subject to the issuance of a notice of parking violation imposing a civil penalty of not less than two hundred fifty dollars ($250) and not more than one thousand dollars ($1,000), for which enforcement shall be governed by the procedures set forth in Article 3 (commencing with Section 40200) of Chapter 1 of Division 17 or is a misdemeanor punishable by a fine of not less than two hundred fifty dollars ($250) and not more than one thousand dollars ($1,000), imprisonment in the county jail for not more than six months, or both that fine and imprisonment.

(c) Except for the purpose of transporting a disabled person as specified in subdivision (b), a person shall not display a disabled person placard that was not issued to him or her or that has been canceled or revoked pursuant to Section 22511.6. A violation of this subdivision is subject to the issuance of a notice of parking violation imposing a civil penalty of not less than two hundred fifty dollars ($250) and not more than one thousand dollars ($1,000), for which enforcement shall be governed by the procedures set forth in Article 3 (commencing with Section 40200) of Chapter 1 of Division 17 or is a misdemeanor punishable by a fine of not less than two hundred fifty dollars ($250) and not more than one thousand dollars ($1,000), imprisonment in the county jail for not more than six months, or both that fine and imprisonment.

(d) Notwithstanding subdivisions (a), (b), and (c), a person using a vehicle displaying a special identification license plate issued to another pursuant to Section 5007 shall not park in those parking stalls or spaces designated for disabled persons pursuant to Section 22511.7 or 22511.8, unless transporting a disabled person. A violation of this subdivision is subject to the issuance of a notice of parking violation imposing a civil penalty of not less than two hundred fifty dollars ($250) and not more than one thousand dollars ($1,000), for which enforcement shall be governed by the procedures set forth in Article 3 (commencing with Section 40200) of Chapter 1 of Division 17 or is a misdemeanor punishable by a fine of not less than two hundred fifty dollars ($250) and not more than one thousand dollars ($1,000), imprisonment in the county jail for not more than six months, or both that fine and imprisonment.

(e)For the purposes of subdivisions (b) and (c), "disabled person placard" means a placard issued pursuant to Section 22511.55 or 22511.59.

(Amended by Stats. 2009, Ch. 415, Sec. 2. (AB 144) Effective January 1, 2010.)

4461.3. In addition to any fine imposed for conviction of a violation of Section 4461 or 22507.8, a city or county may adopt an ordinance or resolution to assess an additional penalty of one hundred dollars ($100). All revenue generated from imposition of the penalty shall be used specifically for the purpose of improving enforcement of the provisions of this code relating to disabled parking spaces and placards within the city or county. Revenue generated from imposition of the penalty may not be used to supplant funds used for other general parking enforcement purposes, but may be used to offset the cost of establishing a new disabled parking enforcement program.

(Added by Stats. 2003, Ch. 555, Sec. 4. Effective January 1, 2004.)

4461.5. In addition to, or instead of, any fine imposed for conviction of a violation of subdivision (c) or (d) of Section 4461, the court may impose a civil penalty of not more than one thousand five hundred dollars ($1,500) for each conviction.

(Added by Stats. 2000, Ch. 215, Sec. 1. Effective January 1, 2001.)

4462. (a) The driver of a motor vehicle shall present the registration or identification card or other evidence of registration of any or all vehicles under his or her immediate control for examination upon demand of any peace officer.

(b) A person shall not display upon a vehicle, nor present to any peace officer, any registration card, identification card, temporary receipt, license plate, temporary license plate, device issued pursuant to Section 4853, or permit not issued for that vehicle or not otherwise lawfully used thereon under this code.

(c) This section shall become operative January 1, 2019.

(Repealed (in Sec. 7) and added by Stats. 2016, Ch. 90, Sec. 8. (AB 516) Effective January 1, 2017. Section operative January 1, 2019, by its own provisions.)

4462.5. Every person who commits a violation of subdivision (b) of Section 4462, with intent to avoid compliance with vehicle registration requirements of Article 1 (commencing with Section 4000) of Chapter 1 or Article 1 (commencing with Section 5600) of Chapter 2, is guilty of a misdemeanor.

(Added by Stats. 1988, Ch. 640, Sec. 2.)

4463. (a) A person who, with intent to prejudice, damage, or defraud, commits any of the following acts is guilty of a felony and upon conviction thereof shall be punished by imprisonment pursuant to subdivision (h) of Section 1170 of the Penal Code for 16 months, or two or three years, or by imprisonment in a county jail for not more than one year:

(1) Alters, forges, counterfeits, or falsifies a certificate of ownership, registration card, certificate, license, license plate, temporary license plate, device issued pursuant to Sections 4853 and 4854, special plate, or permit provided for by this code or a comparable certificate of ownership, registration card, certificate, license, license plate, temporary license plate, device comparable to that issued pursuant to Sections 4853 and 4854, special plate, or permit provided for by a foreign jurisdiction, or alters, forges, counterfeits, or falsifies the document, device, or plate with intent to represent it as issued by the department, or alters, forges, counterfeits, or falsifies with fraudulent intent an endorsement of transfer on a certificate of ownership or other document evidencing ownership, or with fraudulent intent displays or causes or permits to be displayed or have in their possession a blank, incomplete, canceled, suspended, revoked, altered, forged, counterfeit, or false certificate of ownership, registration card, certificate, license, license plate, temporary license plate, device issued pursuant to Sections 4853 and 4854, special plate, or permit.

(2) Utters, publishes, passes, or attempts to pass, as true and genuine, a false, altered, forged, or counterfeited matter listed in paragraph (1) knowing it to be false, altered, forged, or counterfeited.

(b) A person who, with intent to prejudice, damage, or defraud, commits any of the following acts is guilty of a misdemeanor, and upon conviction thereof shall be punished by imprisonment in a county jail for six months, a fine of not less than five hundred dollars ($500) and not more than one thousand dollars ($1,000), or both that fine and imprisonment, which penalty shall not be suspended:

(1) Forges, counterfeits, or falsifies a disabled person placard or a comparable placard relating to parking privileges for disabled persons provided for by a foreign jurisdiction, or forges, counterfeits, or falsifies a disabled person placard with intent to represent it as issued by the department.

(2) Passes, or attempts to pass, as true and genuine, a false, forged, or counterfeit disabled person placard knowing it to be false, forged, or counterfeited.

(3) Acquires, possesses, sells, or offers for sale a genuine or counterfeit disabled person placard.

(c) A person who, with fraudulent intent, displays or causes or permits to be displayed a forged, counterfeit, or false disabled person placard, is subject to the issuance of a notice of parking violation imposing a civil penalty of not less than two hundred fifty dollars ($250) and not more than one thousand dollars ($1,000), for which enforcement shall be governed by the procedures set forth in Article 3 (commencing with Section 40200) of Chapter 1 of Division 17, or is guilty of a misdemeanor punishable by imprisonment in a county jail for six months, a fine of not less than two hundred fifty dollars ($250) and not more than one thousand dollars ($1,000), or both that fine and imprisonment, which penalty shall not be suspended.

(d) For purposes of subdivision (b) or (c), "disabled person placard" means a placard issued pursuant to Section 22511.55 or 22511.59.

(e) A person who, with intent to prejudice, damage, or defraud, commits any of the following acts is guilty of an infraction, and upon conviction thereof shall be punished by a fine of not less than one hundred dollars ($100) and not more than two hundred fifty dollars ($250) for a first offense, not less than two hundred fifty dollars ($250) and not more than five hundred dollars ($500) for a second offense, and not less than five hundred dollars ($500) and not more than one thousand dollars ($1,000) for a third or subsequent offense, which penalty shall not be suspended:

(1) Forges, counterfeits, or falsifies a Clean Air Sticker or a comparable clean air sticker relating to high-occupancy vehicle lane privileges provided for by a foreign jurisdiction, or forges, counterfeits, or falsifies a Clean Air Sticker with intent to represent it as issued by the department.

(2) Passes, or attempts to pass, as true and genuine, a false, forged, or counterfeit Clean Air Sticker knowing it to be false, forged, or counterfeited.

(3) Acquires, possesses, sells, or offers for sale a counterfeit Clean Air Sticker.

(4) Acquires, possesses, sells, or offers for sale a genuine Clean Air Sticker separate from the vehicle for which the department issued that sticker.

(f) As used in this section, "Clean Air Sticker" means a label or decal issued pursuant to Sections 5205.5 and 21655.9.

(Amended by Stats. 2022, Ch. 746, Sec. 1. (AB 984) Effective January 1, 2023.)

4463.3. In addition to, or instead of, any fine imposed for conviction of a violation of subdivision (b) or (c) of Section 4463, the court may impose a civil penalty of not more than two thousand five hundred dollars ($2,500) for each conviction.

(Added by Stats. 2000, Ch. 215, Sec. 2. Effective January 1, 2001.)

4463.5. (a) No person shall manufacture or sell a decorative or facsimile license plate of a size substantially similar to the license plate issued by the department.

(b) Notwithstanding subdivision (a), the director may authorize the manufacture and sale of decorative or facsimile license plates for special events or media productions.

(c) A violation of this section is a misdemeanor punishable by a fine of not less than five hundred dollars ($500).

(Added by Stats. 1986, Ch. 859, Sec. 1.)

4464. A person shall not display upon a vehicle a license plate that is altered from its original markings.

(Amended by Stats. 2012, Ch. 702, Sec. 2. (AB 2489) Effective January 1, 2013.)

4465. (a) A legal owner of record of a vehicle may request, and the department shall furnish, information regarding the current registration status of the vehicle, including the license plate number and address of the registered owner of the vehicle. The department may charge a fee to pay for the cost of furnishing this information.

(b) (1) By January 1, 2010, the department shall be in full compliance with the federal Anti Car Theft Act of 1992 (P.L. 102-519) and the United States Department of Justice (DOJ) rules governing the federal National Motor Vehicle Title Information System (NMVTIS) (49 U.S.C. Sec. 30501 et seq.), to the extent practicable.

(2) Notwithstanding paragraph (1), by January 1, 2010, the department shall eliminate any restrictions to consumer access to titling, branding, and theft information provided by the department to NMVTIS, to ensure that prospective purchasers have instant and reliable access to California's data.

(Amended by Stats. 2010, Ch. 328, Sec. 226. (SB 1330) Effective January 1, 2011.)

4466. (a) The department shall not issue a duplicate or substitute certificate of title or license plate if, after a search of the records of the department, the registered owner's address, as submitted on the application, is different from that which appears in the records of the department, unless the registered owner applies in person and presents all of the following:

(1) Proof of ownership of the vehicle that is acceptable to the department. Proof of ownership may be the certificate of title, registration certificate, or registration renewal notice, or a facsimile or photocopy of any of those documents, if the facsimile or photocopy matches the vehicle record of the department.

(2) A driver's license or identification card containing a picture of the licensee or cardholder issued to the registered owner by the department pursuant to Chapter 1 (commencing with Section 12500) of Division 6. The department shall conduct a search of its records to verify the authenticity of any document submitted under this paragraph.

(A) If the registered owner is a resident of another state or country, the registered owner shall present a driver's license or identification card issued by that state or country. In addition, the registered owner shall provide photo documentation in the form of a valid passport, military identification card, identification card issued by a state or United States government agency, student identification card issued by a college or university, or identification card issued by a California-based employer. If a resident of another state is unable to present the required photo identification, the department shall verify the authenticity of the driver's license or identification card by contacting the state that issued the driver's license or identification card.

(B) If the registered owner is not an individual, the person submitting the application shall submit the photo identification required pursuant to this paragraph, as well as documentation acceptable to the department that demonstrates that the person is employed by an officer of the registered owner.

(3) If the application is for the purpose of replacing a license plate that was stolen, a copy of a police report identifying the plate as stolen.

(4) If the application is for the purpose of replacing a certificate of title or license plate that was mutilated or destroyed, the remnants of the mutilated or destroyed document or plate.

(5) If the department has a record of a prior issuance of a duplicate or substitute certificate of title or license plate for the vehicle within the past 90 days, a copy of a report from the Department of the California Highway Patrol verifying the vehicle identification number of the vehicle.

(b) Subdivision (a) does not apply if any of the following applies:

(1) The registered owner's name, address, and driver's license or identification card number submitted on the application match the name, address, and driver's license or identification card number contained in the department's records.

(2) An application for a duplicate or substitute certificate of title or license plate is submitted by or through one of the following:

(A) A legal owner, if the legal owner is not the same person as the registered owner or as the lessee under Section 4453.5.

(B) A dealer or an agent of the dealer.

(C) A dismantler.

(D) An insurer or an agent of the insurer.

(E) A salvage pool.

(c) At the discretion of the department, subdivision (a) does not apply in any of the following circumstances:

(1) An application for a duplicate or substitute certificate of title or license plate is submitted by a licensed registration service representing any of the following:

(A) A person or entity listed in subparagraphs (A) to (E), inclusive, of paragraph (2) of subdivision (b).

(B) A business entity recognized under the laws of this state or the laws of any foreign or domestic jurisdiction whose laws are in parity with the laws of this state.

(C) A court-appointed bankruptcy referee.

(D) A person who is an individual, is not included in subparagraphs (A) to (C), inclusive, and submits to the licensed registration service an application with a signature that is validated by a notary public. The licensed registration service shall maintain full and complete records of its transactions conducted pursuant to this subparagraph and shall make those records available for inspection by an investigator of the Department of Motor Vehicles, investigator of the Department of the California Highway Patrol, a city police department, a county sheriff's office, or a district attorney's office, if the investigator requests access to the record and the request is for the purpose of a criminal investigation.

(2) The vehicle is registered under the International Registration Plan pursuant to Section 8052 or under the Permanent Fleet Registration program pursuant to Article 9.5 (commencing with Section 5301).

(3) The vehicle is an implement of husbandry, as defined in Section 36000, or a tow dolly, or has been issued an identification plate under Section 5014 or 5014.1.

(d) The department shall issue one or more license plates only to the registered owner or lessee. The department shall issue the certificate of title only to the legal owner, or if none, then to the registered owner, as shown on the department's records.

(Amended by Stats. 2010, Ch. 328, Sec. 227. (SB 1330) Effective January 1, 2011.)

4467. (a) Notwithstanding any other law, the department shall issue new and different license plates immediately upon request to the registered owner of a vehicle who appears in person and submits a completed application, if all of the following are provided:

(1) Proof of ownership of the vehicle that is acceptable to the department.

(2) A driver's license or identification card containing a picture of the licensee or cardholder issued to the registered owner by the department pursuant to Chapter 1 (commencing with Section 12500) of Division 6. The department shall conduct a search of its records to verify the authenticity of any document submitted under this paragraph.

(3) The previously issued license plates from the vehicle.

(4) The payment of required fees under subdivision (c) of Section 4850 and subdivision (b) of Section 9265 for the issuance of duplicate license plates.

(5) One of the following:

(A) A copy of a police report, court documentation, or other law enforcement documentation identifying the registered owner of the vehicle as the victim of an incident of domestic violence, as specified in Section 1708.6 of the Civil Code, the subject of stalking, as specified in Section 1708.7 of the Civil Code or Section 646.9 of the Penal Code, the victim of a rape, as defined in Section 261 or former Section 262 of the Penal Code, or the victim of a sexual battery, as defined in Section

1708.5 of the Civil Code.

(B) A written acknowledgment, dated within 30 days of submission, on the letterhead of a domestic violence agency or a rape crisis center, that the registered owner is actively seeking assistance or has sought assistance from that agency within the past year.

(C) An active protective order as defined in Section 6218 of the Family Code, or issued pursuant to Section 527.6 or 527.8 of the Code of Civil Procedure, that names the registered owner as a protected party.

(b) Subdivision (a) does not apply to special license plates issued under Article 8 (commencing with Section 5000) of Chapter 1 of Division 3, special interest license plates issued under Article 8.4 (commencing with Section 5060) of Chapter 1 of Division 3, or environmental license plates issued under Article 8.5 (commencing with Section 5100) of Chapter 1 of Division 3.

(Amended by Stats. 2021, Ch. 626, Sec. 73. (AB 1171) Effective January 1, 2022.)

Article 5. Renewal of Registration

(Article 5 enacted by Stats. 1959, Ch. 3.)

4600. Certificates of ownership shall not be renewed annually but shall remain valid until suspended, revoked, or canceled by the department for cause or upon a transfer of any interest shown therein.

(Enacted by Stats. 1959, Ch. 3.)

4601. (a) Except as otherwise provided in this code, every vehicle registration and registration card expires at midnight on the expiration date designated by the director pursuant to Section 1651.5, and shall be renewed prior to the expiration of the registration year. The department may, upon payment of the proper fees, renew the registration of vehicles.

(b) Notwithstanding any other provision of law, renewal of registration for any vehicle that is either currently registered or for which a certification pursuant to Section 4604 has been filed may be obtained not more than 75 days prior to the expiration of the current registration or certification.

(c) Notwithstanding subdivision (b) or any other law, commencing upon the effective date of the act that added this subdivision, the renewal of registration for a vehicle that expires on or before June 30, 2011, may be obtained not more than 75 days prior to the expiration of the current registration or certification and the renewal of registration for a vehicle that expires on or after July 1, 2011, or for which a certification, pursuant to Section 4604, has been filed, may not be obtained until the expiration of the current registration or certification or until the department has issued a notice of renewal, whichever occurs first. This subdivision shall become inoperative on January 1, 2012.

(Amended by Stats. 2011, Ch. 21, Sec. 4. (SB 94) Effective May 4, 2011.)

4601.5. Notwithstanding Section 4601, the registration for vehicles registered pursuant to the Partial Year Registration Program as described in Article 5 (commencing with Section 9700) of Chapter 6 of Division 3, expires at midnight of December 31 of the registration year. However, for the purposes of applying any future reductions or increases in the vehicle license fee, the vehicle registrations subject to this section shall be deemed to have a final expiration date in the succeeding calendar year.

(Amended by Stats. 2006, Ch. 169, Sec. 2. Effective January 1, 2007.)

4602. Application for renewal of a vehicle registration shall be made by the owner not later than midnight of the expiration date, and shall be made by presentation of the registration card last issued for the vehicle or by presentation of a potential registration card issued by the department for use at the time of renewal and by payment of the full registration year fee for the vehicle as provided in this code. If the registration card and potential registration card are unavailable, a fee as specified in Section 9265 shall not be paid.

(Amended by Stats. 1988, Ch. 1268, Sec. 2.)

4603. Whenever in his opinion the interests of the State will be promoted thereby, the director with the approval of the Governor may extend for a period not to exceed 10 days the closing of the period during which applications for renewal of registration may be presented without the payment of penalties.

(Enacted by Stats. 1959, Ch. 3.)

4604. (a) Except as otherwise provided in subdivision (d), prior to the expiration of the registration of a vehicle, if that registration is not to be renewed prior to its expiration, the owner of the vehicle shall file, under penalty of perjury, a certification that the vehicle will not be operated, moved, or left standing upon a highway without first making an application for registration of the vehicle, including full payment of all fees. The certification is valid until the vehicle's registration is renewed pursuant to subdivision (c).

(b) Each certification filed pursuant to subdivision (a) shall be accompanied by a filing fee of fifteen dollars ($15).

(c) (1) An application for renewal of registration, except when accompanied by an application for transfer of title to, or an interest in, the vehicle, shall be submitted to the department with payment of the required fees for the current registration year and without penalty for delinquent payment of fees imposed under this code or under Part 5 (commencing with Section 10701) of Division 2 of the Revenue and Taxation Code if the department receives the application prior to or on the date the vehicle is first operated, moved, or left standing upon a highway during the current registration year and the certification required pursuant to subdivision (a) was timely filed with the department.

(2) If an application for renewal of registration is accompanied by an application for transfer of title, that application may be made without incurring a penalty for delinquent payment of fees not later than 20 days after the date the vehicle is first operated, moved, or left standing on a highway if a certification pursuant to subdivision (a) was timely filed with the department.

(d) A certification is not required to be filed pursuant to subdivision (a) for one or more of the following:

(1) A vehicle on which the registration expires while being held as inventory by a dealer or lessor-retailer or while being held pending a lien sale by the keeper of a garage or operator of a towing service.

(2) A vehicle registered pursuant to Article 4 (commencing with Section 8050) of Chapter 4 of Division 3.

(3) A vehicle described in Section 5004, 5004.5, or 5051, as provided in Section 4604.2. However, the registered owner may file a certificate of nonoperation in lieu of the certification specified in subdivision (a).

(4) A vehicle registered pursuant to Article 5 (commencing with Section 9700) of Chapter 6 if the registered owner has complied with subdivision (c) of Section 9706.

(e) Notwithstanding Section 670, for purposes of this section, a "vehicle" is a device by which a person or property may be propelled, moved, or driven upon a highway having intact and assembled its major component parts including, but not limited to, the frame or chassis, cowl, and floor pan or, in the case of a trailer, the frame and wheels or, in the case of a motorcycle, the frame, front fork, and engine. For purposes of this section, "vehicle" does not include a device moved exclusively by human power, a device used exclusively upon stationary rails or tracks, or a motorized wheelchair.

(Amended by Stats. 2006, Ch. 574, Sec. 4. Effective January 1, 2007.)

4604.2. (a) When the registration of a vehicle registered on a partial year basis has expired and the vehicle is not thereafter operated, moved, or left standing upon a highway, and the vehicle is in compliance with subdivision (b) of Section 9706 applying to vehicles registered on a partial year basis, an application for renewal made subsequent to that expiration shall be accompanied by a certificate of nonoperation.

(b) An application for registration or renewal of registration of a vehicle described in Section 5004 or 5004.5 that has not been operated, moved, or left standing upon a highway shall be accompanied by a certificate of nonoperation for the period during which the vehicle was not registered.

(c) A certificate of nonoperation may be accepted for a vehicle registered pursuant to Article 4 (commencing with Section 8050) of Chapter 4 solely for the purpose of waiver of penalties.

(d) The application for registration or renewal of registration of vehicles specified in subdivisions (a) and (b), whether or not accompanied by an application for transfer of title, shall be accepted by the department upon payment of the proper fees for the current registration year without the payment of delinquent fees imposed under this code or Part 5 (commencing with Section 10701) of Division 2 of the Revenue and Taxation Code if the department receives the application and certificate of nonoperation prior to the date the vehicle is first operated, moved, or left standing upon a highway during the current registration year.

(Amended by Stats. 2006, Ch. 574, Sec. 5. Effective January 1, 2007.)

4604.5. (a) (1) If the vehicle has not been operated, moved, or left standing upon any highway subsequent to the expiration of the vehicle's registration, the certification specified in Section 4604 or 4604.2 may be filed after the expiration of the registration of a vehicle, but not later than 90 days after the expiration date, subject to the payment of the filing fee specified in Section 4604 and the penalty specified in paragraph (2).

(2) A penalty shall be collected on any certification specified in Section 4604 or 4604.2 filed later than midnight of the date of expiration of registration. The penalty shall be computed as provided in Sections 9406 and 9559 and after the registration and weight fees have been combined with the license fee specified in Section 10751 of the Revenue and Taxation Code, as follows:

(A) For a delinquency period of 10 days or less, the penalty is 10 percent of the fee.

(B) For a delinquency period of more than 10 days, to and including 30 days, the penalty is 20 percent of the fee.

(C) For a delinquency period of more than 30 days, to and including 90 days, the penalty is 60 percent of the fee.

(3) This subdivision applies to the renewal of registration for vehicles with expiration dates on or before December 31, 2002.

(b) The certification specified in Sections 4604 and 4604.2 may be filed no more than 90 days after the expiration of the registration of a vehicle if the vehicle has not been operated, moved, or left standing upon any highway subsequent to the expiration of the vehicle's registration. A penalty shall be collected on any certification specified in Section 4604 or 4604.2 filed later than midnight of the date of expiration of registration. After 90 days, the vehicle must be registered pursuant to Section 4601. A certification filed pursuant to this subdivision is subject to the payment of the filing fee specified in Section 4604 and the payment of the penalties specified in paragraphs (1), (2), and (3) of this subdivision.

(1) The penalty for late payment of the registration fee provided in Section 9250 is as follows:

(A) For a delinquency period of 10 days or less, the penalty is ten dollars ($10).

(B) For a delinquency period of more than 10 days, to and including 30 days, the penalty is fifteen dollars ($15).

(C) For a delinquency period of more than 30 days, to and including 90 days, the penalty is thirty dollars ($30).

(2) The penalty on the weight fee and the vehicle license fee shall be computed after the weight fee as provided in Section 9400 or 9400.1 plus the vehicle license fee specified in Section 10751 of the Revenue and Taxation Code have been added together as follows:

(A) For a delinquency period of 10 days or less, the penalty is 10 percent of the fee.

(B) For a delinquency period exceeding 10 days, to and including 30 days, the penalty is 20 percent of the fee.

(C) For a delinquency period of more than 30 days, to and including 90 days, the penalty is 60 percent of the fee.

(3) Weight fees not reported and not paid within 20 days, as required by Section 9406, shall be assessed a penalty on the difference in the weight fee, as follows:

(A) For a delinquency period of 10 days or less, the penalty is 10 percent of the fee.

(B) For a delinquency period exceeding 10 days, to and including 30 days, the penalty is 20 percent of the fee.

(C) For a delinquency period of more than 30 days, to and including 90 days, the penalty is 60 percent of the fee.

(c) This section shall apply to registration renewals that expire on or after January 1, 2003.

(Amended by Stats. 2002, Ch. 805, Sec. 12. Effective September 23, 2002.)

4605. Notwithstanding Section 4000 of this code, and notwithstanding Section 38020 of this code, no fees or penalties imposed under this code or under Part 5 (commencing with Section 10701) of Division 2 of the Revenue and Taxation Code shall accrue due to operation of a vehicle in conjunction with the theft or embezzlement of the vehicle if the owner or legal owner submits a certificate in writing setting forth the circumstances of the theft or embezzlement and certifies that the theft or embezzlement of the vehicle has been reported pursuant to the provisions of this code.

(Repealed and added by Stats. 1976, Ch. 935.)

4606. Notwithstanding any provision of subdivision (a) of Section 5204 to the contrary, when an application for the registration of a vehicle has been made as required in Sections 4152.5 and 4602, the vehicle may be operated on the highways until the new indicia of current registration have been received from the department, upon condition that there be displayed on the vehicle the license plates and validating devices, if any, issued to the vehicle for the previous registration year.

(Amended by Stats. 1992, Ch. 258, Sec. 1. Effective January 1, 1993.)

4607. The department, upon renewing a registration, shall issue a new registration card to the owner as upon an original registration.

(Enacted by Stats. 1959, Ch. 3.)

4609. The department may extend the life of the current series of license plates, outstanding during 1957, and may hereafter issue a new series of license plates for an indefinite period of time, but in no event for a period less than five (5) years. During each intervening year of the period for which the plates are issued, the department shall issue a tab, sticker, or other suitable device as herein provided.

Any such series of plates may be canceled by the director with the approval of the Governor at any time after five years from the year of issuance of such series.

(Enacted by Stats. 1959, Ch. 3.)

4610. The department may authorize an endorsement of a receipt or the validation of a registration card or potential registration card as provided in this code by a person or organization holding a certificate of authority issued under the provisions of Part 5 (commencing with Section 12140) of Division 2 of the Insurance Code.

(Amended by Stats. 1982, Ch. 454, Sec. 181.)

Article 6. Refusal of Registration

(Article 6 enacted by Stats. 1959, Ch. 3.)

4750. The department shall refuse registration, or renewal or transfer of registration, upon any of the following grounds:

(a) The application contains any false or fraudulent statement.

(b) The required fee has not been paid.

(c) The registration, or renewal or transfer of registration, is prohibited by the requirements of Part 5 (commencing with Section 43000) of Division 26 of the Health and Safety Code.

(d) The owner of a heavy vehicle, which is subject to the heavy vehicle use tax imposed pursuant to Section 4481 of Title 26 of the United States Code, has not presented sufficient evidence, as determined by the department, that the tax for the vehicle has been paid pursuant to that section.

(e) Evidence of financial responsibility, that is required for a vehicle registration renewal where there is no change in registered owner, has not been provided to the department pursuant to Section 4000.37 or electronically. This subdivision does not apply to any of the following:

(1) A vehicle for which a certification has been filed pursuant to Section 4604, until the vehicle is registered for operation upon the highway.

(2) A vehicle owned or leased by, or under the direction of, the United States or any public entity that is included in Section 811.2 of the Government Code.

(3) A vehicle registration renewal application where there is a change of registered owner.

(Amended by Stats. 1999, Ch. 880, Sec. 7. Effective January 1, 2000.)

4750.1. (a) If the department receives an application for registration of a specially constructed passenger vehicle or pickup truck after it has registered 500 specially constructed vehicles during that calendar year pursuant to Section 44017.4 of the Health and Safety Code, and the vehicle has not been previously registered, the vehicle shall be assigned the same model-year as the calendar year in which the application is submitted, for purposes of determining emissions inspection requirements for the vehicle.

(b) (1) If the department receives an application for registration of a specially constructed passenger vehicle or pickup truck that has been previously registered after it has registered 500 specially constructed vehicles during that calendar year pursuant to Section 44017.4 of the Health and Safety Code, and the application requests a model-year determination different from the model-year assigned in the previous registration, the application for registration shall be denied and the vehicle owner is subject to the emission control and inspection requirements applicable to the model-year assigned in the previous registration.

(2) For a vehicle participating in the amnesty program in effect from July 1, 2011, to June 30, 2012, pursuant to Section 9565, the model-year of the previous registration shall be the calendar year of the year in which the vehicle owner applied for amnesty. However, a denial of an application for registration issued pursuant to this paragraph does not preclude the vehicle owner from applying for a different model-year determination and application for registration under Section 44017.4 of the Health and Safety Code in a subsequent calendar year.

(c) (1) The Bureau of Automotive Repair may charge the vehicle owner who applies to participate in the amnesty program a fee for each referee station inspection conducted pursuant to Section 9565. The fee shall be one hundred sixty dollars ($160) and shall be collected by the referee station performing the inspection.

(2) A contract to perform referee services may authorize direct compensation to the referee contractor from the inspection fees collected pursuant to paragraph (1). The referee contractor shall deposit the inspection fees collected from the vehicle owner into a separate trust account that the referee contractor shall account for and manage in accordance with generally accepted accounting standards and principles. Where the department conducts the inspections pursuant to Section 9565, the inspection fees collected by the department shall be deposited into the Vehicle Inspection and Repair Fund.

(Amended by Stats. 2010, Ch. 388, Sec. 1. (AB 2461) Effective January 1, 2011.)

4750.4. Information provided by an insurer to the department pursuant to Section 11580.10 of the Insurance Code and former Section 4750.2, as added by Chapter 946 of the Statutes of 1991, shall be made available only to law enforcement agencies for law enforcement purposes.

(Amended by Stats. 2004, Ch. 193, Sec. 194. Effective January 1, 2005.)

4750.5. (a) The department shall withhold the registration or the transfer of registration of any vehicle sold at retail to any applicant by any person other than a vehicle manufacturer or dealer holding a license and certificate issued pursuant to Chapter 4 (commencing with Section 11700) of Division 5, or an automobile dismantler holding a license and certificate issued pursuant to Chapter 3 (commencing with Section 11500) of Division 5, or a lessor-retailer holding a license issued pursuant to Chapter 3.5 (commencing with Section 11600) of Division 5, and subject to the provisions of Section 11615.5, until the applicant pays to the department the use tax measured by the sales price of the vehicle as required by the Sales and Use Tax Law (Part 1 (commencing with Section 6001) of Division 2 of the Revenue and Taxation Code), together with penalty, if any, unless the State Board of Equalization finds that no use tax is due. If the applicant so desires, he may pay the use tax and penalty, if any, to the department so as to secure immediate action upon his application for registration or transfer of registration, and thereafter he may apply through the Department of Motor Vehicles to the State Board of Equalization under the provisions of the Sales and Use Tax Law for a refund of the amount so paid.

(b) The department shall transmit to the State Board of Equalization all collections of use tax and penalty made under this section. This transmittal shall be made at least monthly, accompanied by a schedule in such form as the department and board may prescribe.

(c) The State Board of Equalization shall reimburse the department for its costs incurred in carrying out the provisions of this section. Such reimbursement shall be effected under agreement between the agencies, approved by the Department of Finance.

(d) In computing any use tax or penalty thereon under the provisions of this section, dollar fractions shall be disregarded in the manner specified in Section 9559 of this code. Payment of tax and penalty on this basis shall be deemed full compliance with the requirements of the Sales and Use Tax Law insofar as they are applicable to the use of vehicles to which this section relates.

(Amended by Stats. 1976, Ch. 1284.)

4750.6. (a) The department shall transmit to the California Department of Tax and Fee Administration all collections of tax and penalty made under paragraph (3) of subdivision (a) of Section 4456 of this code and Section 6295 of the Revenue and Taxation Code. This transmittal shall be made within 30 days, accompanied by a schedule in such form as the department and California Department of Tax and Fee Administration may prescribe.

(b) The California Department of Tax and Fee Administration shall reimburse the department for its costs incurred in carrying out paragraph (3) of subdivision (a) of Section 4456 of this code and Section 6295 of the Revenue and Taxation Code. The reimbursement shall be effected under agreement between the agencies, approved by the Department of Finance.

(c) In computing any tax or penalty thereon under paragraph (3) of subdivision (a) of Section 4456 of this code and Section 6295 of the Revenue and Taxation Code, dollar fractions shall be disregarded in the manner specified in Section 9559 of this code. Payment of tax and penalty on this basis shall be deemed full compliance with the requirements of the Sales and Use Tax Law insofar as they are applicable to the use of vehicles to which paragraph (3) of subdivision (a) of Section 4456 of this code and Section 6295 of the Revenue and Taxation Code relates.

(d) The amendments to this section made by the act adding this subdivision do not constitute a change in, but are declaratory of, existing law.

(Amended by Stats. 2021, Ch. 256, Sec. 27. (AB 176) Effective September 23, 2021.)

4751. The department may refuse registration or the renewal or transfer of registration of a vehicle in any of the following events:

(a) If the department is not satisfied that the applicant is entitled thereto under this code.

(b) If the applicant has failed to furnish the department with information required in the application or reasonable additional information required by the department.

(c) If the department determines that the applicant has made or permitted unlawful use of any registration certificate, certificate of ownership, or license plates.

(d) If the vehicle is mechanically unfit or unsafe to be operated or moved on the highways.

(e) If the department determines that a manufacturer or dealer has failed during the current or previous year to comply with the provisions of this code relating to the giving of notice to the department of the transfer of a vehicle during the current or previous year.

(f) If the department determines that a lien exists, pursuant to Section 9800, against one or more other vehicles in which the applicant has an ownership interest.

(g) If the applicant has failed to furnish the department with an odometer disclosure statement pursuant to subsection (a) of Section 32705 of Title 49 of the United States Code.

(Amended by Stats. 2000, Ch. 1035, Sec. 9. Effective January 1, 2001.)

4755. The department shall refuse registration, or renewal or transfer of registration for any commercial motor vehicle subject to Section 4000.6, if the owner or operator of the motor vehicle at the time of the application has been cited for a violation, pertaining to that vehicle, of Division 26 (commencing with Section 39000) of the Health and Safety Code or regulations of the State Air Resources Board adopted pursuant to that division, until the violation has been cleared, as determined by the State Air Resources Board.

(Added by Stats. 2007, Ch. 592, Sec. 5. Effective January 1, 2008.)

4760. (a) (1) Except as provided in subdivision (b) or (d), the department shall refuse to renew the registration of a vehicle if the registered owner or lessee has been mailed a notice of delinquent parking violation relating to standing or parking, the processing agency has filed or electronically transmitted to the department an itemization of unpaid parking penalties, including administrative fees pursuant to Section 40220, and the owner or lessee has not paid the parking penalty and administrative fee pursuant to Section 40211, unless he or she pays to the department, at the time of application for renewal, the full amount of all outstanding parking penalties and administrative fees, as shown by records of the department, or the itemization of unpaid parking penalties has been rescinded pursuant to Section 40220.

(2) When the department receives the full amount of all outstanding parking penalties and administrative fees pursuant to paragraph (1), it shall issue a receipt showing each parking penalty and administrative fee that has been paid, the processing agency for that penalty and fee, and a description of the vehicle involved in the parking violations. The receipt shall also state that, to reduce the possibility of impoundment under Section 22651 or immobilization under Section 22651.7 of the vehicle involved in the parking violation, the registered owner or lessee may transmit to that processing agency a copy or other evidence of the receipt.

(b) The department shall not refuse to renew the registration of a vehicle owned by a renter or lessor if the applicant provides the department with the abstract or notice of disposition of parking violation issued pursuant to subdivision (c) for clearing all outstanding parking penalties and administrative fees as shown by the records of the department.

(c) The court or designated processing agency shall issue an abstract or notice of disposition of parking violation to the renter or lessor of a vehicle issued a notice of delinquent parking violation relating to standing or parking if the renter or lessor provides the court or processing agency with the name, address, and driver's license number of the rentee or lessee at the time of occurrence of the parking violation.

(d) The department shall not refuse to renew the registration of a vehicle if the citation was issued prior to the registered owner taking possession of the vehicle.

(e) The department shall allow a registered owner or lessee to file a certification that the vehicle will not be operated, moved, or left standing upon a highway pursuant to Section 4604, if the registered owner or lessee currently owes parking penalties and administrative fees for that vehicle, regardless of whether or not that registered owner or lessee is currently on an active payment plan pursuant to Section 40220.

(Amended by Stats. 2017, Ch. 741, Sec. 2. (AB 503) Effective January 1, 2018.)

4760.1. (a) The department shall, before renewing the registration of any vehicle, check the driver's license record of all registered owners for conviction of traffic violations and traffic accidents.

(b) The department shall, before renewing the registration of any vehicle, check the driver's license record of all registered owners for notices filed with the department pursuant to subdivision (a) of former Section 40509 and notices that the licensee has failed to pay a lawfully imposed fine, penalty, assessment, or bail within the time authorized by the court for any violation that is required to be reported pursuant to Section 1803 and shall refuse to renew the registration of the vehicle if the driver's license record of any registered owner has any such outstanding notices to appear or failures to pay a court-ordered fine, unless the department has received a certificate issued by the magistrate or clerk of the court hearing the case in which the promise was given showing that the case has been adjudicated or unless the registered owner's record is cleared as provided in Chapter 6 (commencing with Section 41500) of Division 17. In lieu of the certificate of adjudication, a notice from the court stating that the original records have been lost or destroyed shall permit the department to renew the registration.

(c) Any notice received by the department pursuant to former Section 40509 that has been on file five years may be removed from the department records and destroyed, in the discretion of the department.

(d) In lieu of the certificate of adjudication or a notice from the court, the department shall with the consent of all registered owners collect the amounts that it has been notified are due pursuant to former Section 40509 and former Section 40509.5, and authorized to be collected pursuant to Article 2 (commencing with Section 14910) of Chapter 5 of Division 6.

(Amended by Stats. 2022, Ch. 800, Sec. 4. (AB 2746) Effective January 1, 2023.)

4761. The department shall include on each potential registration card issued for use at the time of renewal, or on an accompanying document, an itemization of unpaid parking penalties, including administrative fees, showing the amount thereof and the jurisdiction which issued the notice of parking violation relating thereto, which the registered owner or lessee is required to pay pursuant to Section 4760.

(Amended by Stats. 1986, Ch. 939, Sec. 9.)

4762. The department shall remit all parking penalties and administrative fees collected, after deducting the administrative fee authorized by Section 4763, for each notice of delinquent parking violation for which parking penalties and administrative fees have been collected pursuant to Section 4760, to each jurisdiction in the amounts due to each jurisdiction according to its unadjudicated notices of delinquent parking violation. Within 45 days from the time penalties are recorded by the department, the department shall inform each jurisdiction which of its notices of delinquent parking violation have been discharged.

(Amended by Stats. 1986, Ch. 939, Sec. 10.)

4763. (a) The department shall assess a fee for the recording of the notice of delinquent parking violation, which is given to the department by a processing agency pursuant to Section 40220, in an amount, as determined by the department, that is sufficient to provide a total amount equal to its actual costs of administering Sections 4760, 4761, 4762, 4764, and 4765, and administering the system described in Section 4456.2.

(b) This section shall become operative January 1, 2018.

(Repealed (in Sec. 11) and added by Stats. 2016, Ch. 90, Sec. 12. (AB 516) Effective January 1, 2017. Section operative January 1, 2018, by its own provisions.)

4764. (a) If a vehicle is transferred or the registration is not renewed for two renewal periods and the former registered owner or lessee of the vehicle owes a parking penalty for a notice of delinquent parking violation filed with the department pursuant to Section 40220, the department shall notify each jurisdiction of that fact and is not required thereafter to attempt collection of the undeposited parking penalty and administrative fees.

(b) This section does not apply if the transfer of a vehicle is one described in Section 6285 of the Revenue and Taxation Code.

(Amended by Stats. 2013, Ch. 101, Sec. 1. (AB 443) Effective January 1, 2014.)

4765. No exemption from the payment of any fee imposed by this code is an exemption from the obligation of a registered owner or lessee to pay the full amount of parking penalties and administrative fees pursuant to Section 4760.

(Amended by Stats. 1986, Ch. 939, Sec. 13.)

4766. (a) Except as provided in subdivisions (b) and (c), the department shall refuse to renew the registration of a vehicle for which a notice of noncompliance has been transmitted to the department pursuant to subdivision (a) of Section 40002.1 if no certificate of adjudication has been received by the department pursuant to subdivision (b) of that section. The department shall include on each potential registration card issued for use at the time of renewal, or on an accompanying document, an itemization of citations for which notices of noncompliance have been received by the department pursuant to subdivision (a) of Section 40002.1. The itemization shall include the citation number, citation date, and the jurisdiction that issued the underlying notice pursuant to Section 40002 and the administrative service fee for clearing the offense pursuant to subdivision (b) of this section.

(b) Upon application for renewal of vehicle registration for a vehicle subject to subdivision (a), the department shall not refuse registration renewal pursuant to subdivision (a) if the applicant, with respect to each outstanding certificate of noncompliance, has performed both of the following:

(1) Provides the department with a certificate of adjudication for the offense issued pursuant to subdivision (b) of Section 40002.1.

(2) Pays an administrative service fee, which shall be established by the department to, in the aggregate, defray its costs in administering this section.

(c) Whenever registration of a vehicle subject to subdivision (a) is transferred or not renewed for two renewal periods, the department shall notify each court that transmitted a notice of noncompliance affecting the vehicle of the transfer of, or lack of renewal of, the registration and the department shall not thereafter refuse registration renewal pursuant to subdivision (a).

(Amended by Stats. 2008, Ch. 179, Sec. 215. Effective January 1, 2009.)

4767. (a) If delinquent parking or toll violations have been reported to the department for a vehicle for which a transfer of ownership and registration has been requested, the department shall not transfer ownership and registration unless the transferee requesting the transfer pays all of the fines and penalties for those violations to the department, or provides an original abstract or notice of disposition from the court or designated processing agency that the fines and penalties for those violations have been cleared with the parking agency or the court.

(b) This section only applies if the transfer requested is one described in Section 6285 of the Revenue and Taxation Code.

(Added by Stats. 2013, Ch. 101, Sec. 2. (AB 443) Effective January 1, 2014.)

Article 6.5. Refusal of Registration for Nonpayment of Toll Evasion Penalties

(Article 6.5 added by Stats. 1995, Ch. 739, Sec. 5.)

4770. (a) Except as provided in subdivision (c) or (d), the department shall refuse to renew the registration of a vehicle if the registered owner or lessee has been mailed a notice of toll evasion violation, the processing agency has transmitted to the department an itemization of unpaid toll evasion penalties, including administrative fees, pursuant to Section 40267, and the toll evasion penalty and administrative fee have not been paid pursuant to Section 40266, unless the full amount of all outstanding toll evasion penalties and administrative fees, as shown by records of the department are paid to the department at the time of application for renewal.

(b) The designated processing agency shall issue a notice of the disposition of the toll evasion violation or violations to a lessor, if the lessor provides the processing agency with the name, address, and driver's license number of the lessee at the time of the occurrence of the toll evasion violation.

(c) The department shall renew the registration of a vehicle if the applicant provides the department with the notice of the disposition of the toll evasion violation or violations issued pursuant to subdivision (b) for clearing all outstanding toll evasion penalties and administrative fees, as shown by the records of the department, and the applicant has met all other requirements for registration.

(d) The department shall not refuse to renew the registration of a vehicle if the toll evasion violation occurred prior to the date that the registered owner or lessee took possession of the vehicle.

(Amended by Stats. 2008, Ch. 741, Sec. 2. Effective January 1, 2009.)

4771. The department shall include on each vehicle registration renewal notice issued for use at the time of renewal, or on an accompanying document, an itemization of unpaid toll evasion penalties, including administrative fees, showing the amount thereof, the jurisdiction that issued the notice of toll evasion violation, and the date of toll evasion relating thereto, which the registered owner or lessee is required to pay pursuant to Section 4770.

(Added by Stats. 1995, Ch. 739, Sec. 5. Effective January 1, 1996.)

4772. (a) Except as provided in subdivision (b), the department shall remit all toll evasion penalties and administrative fees collected, after deducting the administrative fee authorized by Section 4773, for each notice of delinquent toll evasion violation for which toll evasion penalties and administrative fees have been collected pursuant to Section 4770, to each jurisdiction in the amounts due to each jurisdiction according to its unadjudicated notices of delinquent toll violation. Within 45 days from the time penalties are paid to the department, the department shall inform each jurisdiction which of its notices of delinquent toll evasion violation have been collected.

(b) This subdivision applies to facilities developed pursuant to Section 143 of the Streets and Highways Code. For each notice of delinquent toll evasion violation for which toll evasion penalties and administrative fees have been collected by the department pursuant to Section 4770, each issuing agency is due an amount equal to the sum of the unpaid toll, administrative fees, other costs incurred by the issuing agency that are related to toll evasion, process service fees, and fees and collection costs related to civil debt collection. After deducting the department's administrative fee authorized by Section 4773 and the amounts due each issuing agency for unpaid tolls, administrative fees, other costs incurred by the issuing agency that are related to toll evasion, process service fees, and fees and collection costs related to civil debt collection, the department shall deposit the balance of the toll evasion penalties collected pursuant to Section 4770, if any, in the State Highway Account in the State Transportation Fund.

(Added by Stats. 1995, Ch. 739, Sec. 5. Effective January 1, 1996.)

4773. (a) The department shall assess a fee for the recording of the notice of delinquent toll evasion violation, which is given to the department by a processing agency pursuant to Section 40267, in an amount, as determined by the department, that is sufficient to provide a total amount equal to at least its actual costs of administering Sections 4770, 4771, 4774, and 4775, and administering the system described in Section 4456.2.

(b) This section shall become operative January 1, 2018.

(Repealed (in Sec. 13) and added by Stats. 2016, Ch. 90, Sec. 14. (AB 516) Effective January 1, 2017. Section operative January 1, 2018, by its own provisions.)

4773.5. (a) The department shall require the entire cost of initially implementing this article to be reimbursed by the issuing agencies that are private entities and by the local authorities described in Section 40250, on whose behalf toll processing procedures are carried out pursuant to Article 4 (commencing with Section 40250) of Chapter 1 of Division 17. For purposes of this section, the cost to the department of initially implementing this article includes all of the one-time costs that are incurred by the department in order to implement this article, but does not include ongoing administrative costs associated with this article. The issuing agencies and the local authorities shall each be required to reimburse the department for 50 percent of the reimbursable costs.

(b) (1) The amount collected pursuant to subdivision (a) shall be the actual cost.

(2) The amount of the reimbursement required by subdivision (a) for each issuing agency and local authority shall be determined by

the department in as equitable a manner as possible. In the event of a dispute of the reimbursement required by subdivision (a), an issuing agency may request an audit of applicable costs by a certified public accountant or public accountant. The cost of the audit shall be borne by the issuing agency requesting the audit. The result of the audit shall determine the actual costs.

(c) The processing agency shall access the department's data base via "on-line" techniques or other methods as the department and the processing agency may agree.

(Added by Stats. 1995, Ch. 739, Sec. 5. Effective January 1, 1996.)

4774. (a) If a vehicle is transferred or the registration is not renewed for two renewal periods and the former registered owner or lessee of the vehicle owes a toll evasion penalty for a notice of delinquent toll evasion violation filed with the department pursuant to Section 40267, the department shall notify each jurisdiction of that fact and is not required thereafter to attempt collection of the undeposited toll evasion penalty and administrative fees.

(b) This section does not apply if the transfer of a vehicle is one described in Section 6285 of the Revenue and Taxation Code.

(Amended by Stats. 2013, Ch. 101, Sec. 3. (AB 443) Effective January 1, 2014.)

4775. No exemption from the payment of any fee imposed by this code is an exemption from the obligation of a registered owner or lessee to pay the full amount of toll evasion penalties and administrative fees pursuant to Section 4770.

(Added by Stats. 1995, Ch. 739, Sec. 5. Effective January 1, 1996.)

Article 7. License Plates

(Article 7 enacted by Stats. 1959, Ch. 3.)

4850. (a) The department, upon registering a vehicle, shall issue to the owner two partially or fully reflectorized license plates or devices for a motor vehicle, other than a motorcycle, and one partially or fully reflectorized license plate or device for all other vehicles required to be registered under this code. The plates or devices shall identify the vehicles for which they are issued for the period of their validity.

(b) Notwithstanding any other provision of law, no contract shall be let to any nongovernmental entity for the purchase or securing of reflectorized material for the plates, unless the department has made every reasonable effort to secure qualified bids from as many independent, responsible bidders as possible. No contract shall be let to any nongovernmental entity for the manufacturing of reflectorized safety license plates.

(c) In addition to any other fees specified in this code, a fee of one dollar ($1) for reflectorization shall be paid only by those vehicle owners receiving license plates or devices under this section.

(d) This section does not require vehicle owners with nonreflectorized license plates or devices to replace them with reflectorized plates or devices.

(e) This section shall be known as the Schrade-Belotti Act.

(Amended by Stats. 1985, Ch. 679, Sec. 1. Operative January 1, 1987, by Sec. 4 of Ch. 679.)

4850.5. (a) Notwithstanding subdivision (a) of Section 4850 and Section 5200, the department, upon registering a truck tractor, shall issue to the owner one suitable license plate or other device which identifies the vehicle for which it is issued and for the period of its validity. The license plate or other device shall be attached to the front of the vehicle.

(b) This section shall become operative only when and if the Department of the California Highway Patrol implements a program which requires identifying numbers on the right and left sides of truck tractors.

(Added by Stats. 1985, Ch. 183, Sec. 1. Conditionally operative by its own provisions.)

4851. Every license plate shall have displayed upon it the registration number assigned to the vehicle for which it is issued, together with the word "California" or the abbreviation "Cal." and the year number for which it is issued or a suitable device issued by the department for validation purposes, which device shall contain the year number for which issued.

(Enacted by Stats. 1959, Ch. 3.)

4852. (a) License plates issued for motor vehicles, other than motorcycles, shall be rectangular in shape, 12 inches in length and six inches in width. The number and letter characters on the plates shall have a minimum height of two and three-quarter inches, a minimum width of one and one-quarter inches, and a minimum spacing between characters of five-sixteenths of an inch.

(b) Motorcycle license plates shall measure seven inches in length and four inches in width, and the characters on the plates shall have a minimum height of one and one-half inches and a minimum width of nine-sixteenths inches, and shall have a minimum spacing between characters of three-sixteenths of an inch.

(Amended by Stats. 2000, Ch. 859, Sec. 1. Effective January 1, 2001.)

4853. (a) The department may issue one or more stickers, tabs, or other suitable devices in lieu of the license plates provided for under this code. Except when the physical differences between the stickers, tabs, or devices and license plates by their nature render the provisions of this code inapplicable, all provisions of this code relating to license plates may apply to stickers, tabs, or devices.

(b) The department may establish a pilot program to evaluate the use of alternatives to the stickers, tabs, license plates, and registration cards authorized by this code, subject to all of the following requirements:

(1) The alternative products shall be approved by the Department of the California Highway Patrol.

(2) The pilot program shall be limited to no more than 0.5 percent of registered vehicles for the purpose of road testing and evaluation.

(3) The alternative products to be evaluated shall be provided at no cost to the state.

(4) Any pilot program established by the department pursuant to this subdivision shall be limited to vehicle owners who have voluntarily chosen to participate in the pilot program.

(c) In the conduct of any pilot program pursuant to this section, any data exchanged between the department and any electronic device or the provider of any electronic device shall be limited to those data necessary to display evidence of registration compliance. The department shall not receive or retain any information generated during the pilot program regarding the movement, location, or use of a vehicle participating in the pilot program.

(d) In the conduct of any pilot program pursuant to this section, the department may evaluate the inclusion of participants in the Business Partner Automation Program, pursuant to Section 1685.

(e) Subdivisions (b) to (d), inclusive, shall become inoperative on the effective date of any regulations adopted pursuant to subdivision (b) of Section 4854.

(Amended by Stats. 2022, Ch. 746, Sec. 2. (AB 984) Effective January 1, 2023.)

4854. (a) The department shall establish a program authorizing an entity to issue devices as alternatives to the conventional license plates, stickers, tabs, and registration cards authorized by this code, subject to all of the following requirements:

(1) The alternative device is subject to the approval of the department and the Department of the California Highway Patrol and shall not be used in lieu of a device issued by the Department of Motor Vehicles until that approval has been granted.

(2) (A) Except as specifically authorized in subparagraph (B), an alternative device shall not include vehicle location technology.

(B) (1) (i) Vehicle location technology may be offered for vehicles registered as fleet vehicles, pursuant to Article 9.5 (commencing with Section 5301), commercial vehicles, as defined in Section 260, and those operating under an occupational license, pursuant to Division 5 (commencing with Section 11100).

(ii) Vehicles that began using an alternative device that included vehicle location technology during an authorized pilot program established by Section 4853 may continue to use that alternative device if the vehicle location technology meets the requirements set forth in this section and applicable regulations.

(iii) Beginning on January 1, 2027, and thereafter, any vehicle may be offered an alternative device that includes vehicle location technology.

(2) An alternative device that includes vehicle location technology shall comply with all of the following:

(i) The vehicle location technology shall be capable of being permanently disabled by means of a nonreversible method that ceases all vehicle location functionality and tracking information capabilities.

(ii) The vehicle location technology shall be capable of being manually disabled and enabled by a driver of the vehicle who is inside the vehicle.

(iii) The method of manually disabling and enabling the vehicle location technology shall be prominently located inside the vehicle and easy to use, and shall not require access to a remote or online application, password, or any form of log-in information.

(iv) Once a driver has manually disabled the vehicle location technology from inside the vehicle, the only method of enabling the vehicle location technology shall be to manually enable the technology from inside the vehicle. The registered owner of the license plate, the vehicle manufacturer, the department, or any other entity shall not have the capability of enabling the vehicle location technology through remote means.

(3) If an alternative device is equipped with vehicle location technology, the alternative device shall display a visual indication when the vehicle location technology is in active use.

(4) Data exchanged between the department and the alternative device, or the provider of the alternative device, is limited to that data necessary to display evidence of registration compliance, including the payment of registration fees, plate configurations, and the information or images displayed on the alternative product. If the department receives data from an alternative device or the provider of an alternative device in violation of this paragraph, the department shall immediately delete that data.

(5) Use of an alternative device is optional, and users shall affirmatively opt in to using the alternative device instead of a conventional license plate, sticker, tab, or registration card.

(b) (1) The department shall adopt regulations to carry out this program, including, but not limited to, all of the following:

(A) Determining standards necessary for the safe use of alternative products.

(B) Requirements for product oversight and consumer support.

(C) Requirements for product size, design, display, and functionality.

(D) Introduction of new products through a pilot program.

(E) Transitioning pilot products, and approved enhancements to existing alternative products, to a statewide product offering.

(F) Approval of products for statewide use.

(G) Determining data sharing, privacy, and security protocols pursuant to Section 1 of Article I of the California Constitution's right to privacy and other applicable privacy laws.

(H) Processes for revoking an alternative product's authority for use.

(I) Testing enhancements to approved alternative products.

(J) Determining the types of plates eligible to participate and associated approval processes.

(K) Establishing reasonable fees to reimburse the department for the costs to implement the program.

(L) Reporting requirements.

(M) Requirements to ensure registered users of a device are aware of GPS capability and usage and can deactivate the function.

(N) Requirements to ensure nonregistered vehicle operators are aware of GPS capability and usage. This may include, but is not limited to, live notifications of the GPS function, toll-free communication with the device provider for vehicle location function status and deactivation, or visual indicators of GPS capability or usage.

(2) In developing these regulations, the department may consult with the Department of the California Highway Patrol and shall conduct hearings with the opportunity for public comment on the adoption of any regulation applicable to alternative registration products.

(3) In developing these regulations, the department may specify timeframes for compliance and temporary operating authority for products piloted under Section 4853 that are submitted for approval under this section.

(4) An entity seeking approval to issue an alternative device or electronic vehicle registration card for pilot or statewide use under this section shall submit a business plan for the device to the department for approval that includes, but is not limited to, all of the following:

(A) An administrative oversight plan.

(B) A product support plan, including, but not limited to, methods of providing proof of registration that are not subject to technological failures to be used in the event of the alternative device malfunctioning or failing.

(C) Information technology security, privacy, and cybersecurity evaluations and measures to protect against unauthorized access to information and the device.

(D) Procedures to comply with applicable privacy and security requirements, including, but not limited to, the California Consumer Privacy Act of 2018 (Title 1.81.5 (commencing with Section 1798.100) of Part 4 of Division 3 of the Civil Code). For purposes of this section, a provider of the device shall not share or sell the information obtained to provide the device, or any other information obtained by virtue of contracting with the department to provide the device, including, but not limited to, information collected by the device itself, nor shall it use the information for any purpose other than as strictly necessary to provide the device and show proof of vehicle registration.

(E) Ensuring that the information transmitted between the alternative device or electronic vehicle registration card, the department, and the provider, as well as any mobile application required for the alternative device or electronic vehicle registration card, including storage, is encrypted and protected to the highest reasonable security standards broadly available.

(5) An alternative device intended to serve in lieu of a license plate shall be subject to all of the following requirements:

(A) Have a minimum effective viewable area that meets the size specifications of Section 4852.

(B) Provide legibility and visibility according to standards consistent with those applied to standard metal reflectorized license plates, as set forth in this article.

(C) Be displayed in a manner consistent with Article 9 (commencing with Section 5200).

(D) Display only information and images approved by the department or deemed necessary by the department.

(E) Be readable by automated license plate readers used by the Department of the California Highway Patrol and any other automated enforcement system.

(F) Be readable by the human eye during hours of both daylight and darkness at a distance of no less than 75 feet.

(G) The alphanumeric characters assigned to the vehicle by the department and evidence of valid registration are capable of and shall be displayed on the device whenever a vehicle is in motion, stationary, parked on or off of a road or highway, or unoccupied.

(6) An alternative device intended to serve in lieu of a registration card is subject to both of the following requirements:

(A) Meets the requirements of Section 4453.

(B) May be used to comply with Section 4462.

(7) An alternative device intended to serve in lieu of a license plate or a registration card shall not record or transmit personal identifiable information and shall only record or transmit data limited to what is necessary to display evidence of registration compliance.

(8) The department may establish additional requirements it deems necessary to implement this subdivision.

(9) The department may authorize an alternative device to replicate the appearance of a license plate approved pursuant to any of the following:

(A) Section 5007.

(B) Article 8.4 (commencing with Section 5060).

(C) Article 8.5 (commencing with Section 5100).

(D) Article 8.6 (commencing with Section 5151).

(c) An alternative device failure or malfunction may be deemed a correctable violation if all of the provisions of Section 40610 are met.

(d) The provider of the device, if the device has digital capabilities, shall build into the device a process for frequent notification if the device becomes defective. The provider of the device shall seek to replace defective devices as soon as possible.

(e) Alternative devices issued pursuant to this section may emit diffused nonglaring light only to the extent necessary to meet the visibility requirements of Sections 5201 and 24601.

(f) (1) An employer, or a person acting on behalf of the employer, shall not use an alternative device to monitor employees except during work hours, and only if strictly necessary for the performance of the employee's duties. For purposes of this section, "monitor" includes, but is not limited to, locating, tracking, watching, listening to, or otherwise surveilling the employee.

(2) An employer, or a person acting on behalf of the employer, shall not retaliate against an employee for removing or disabling an alternative device's monitoring capabilities, including vehicle location technology, outside of work hours. An employee who believes they have been subject to a violation of this paragraph may file a complaint with the Labor Commissioner pursuant to Section 98.7 of the Labor Code. In addition to the civil penalties described in this provision, an employee retaliated against in violation of this section shall be entitled to all available penalties, remedies, and compensation, including, but not limited to, reinstatement and reimbursement of lost wages, work benefits, or other compensation caused by the retaliation.

(3) An employer or a person acting on behalf of the employer shall provide an employee with a notice stating that monitoring will occur before conducting any monitoring with an alternative device. The notice shall include, at a minimum, all of the following elements:

(A) A description of the specific activities that will be monitored.

(B) A description of the worker data that will be collected as a part of the monitoring.

(C) A notification of whether the data gathered through monitoring will be used to make or inform any employment-related decisions, including, but not limited to, disciplinary and termination decisions, and, if so, how, including any associated benchmarks.

(D) A description of the vendors or other third parties, if any, to which information collected through monitoring will be disclosed or transferred. The description shall include the name of the vendor or third party and the purpose for the data transfer.

(E) A description of the organizational positions that are authorized to access the data gathered through the alternative device.

(F) A description of the dates, times, and frequency that the monitoring will occur.

(G) A description of where the data will be stored and the length of time it will be retained.

(H) A notification of the employee's right to disable monitoring, including vehicle location technology, outside of work hours.

(4) (A) An employer who violates this subdivision shall be subject to a civil penalty of two hundred fifty dollars ($250) for an initial violation and one thousand dollars ($1,000) per employee for each subsequent violation.

(B) For purposes of determining the penalty described in subparagraph (A), the penalty shall be assessed per employee, per violation, and per day that monitoring without proper notice is conducted.

(C) The Labor Commissioner shall enforce this section using the procedures set forth in Section 1197.1 of the Labor Code, as applicable, including through the issuance of citations against employers who violate this section. The procedures for issuing and contesting citations, and enforcing judgments for civil penalties, that are issued by the Labor Commissioner pursuant to this section shall be the same as those set forth in Section 1197.1 of the Labor Code.

(D) An employer, and any third-party vendor that contracts with an employer to provide GPS tracking of vehicles through an alternative device as described in this section, upon request, shall furnish any report or information that the Labor Commissioner or the Division of Labor Standards Enforcement requires to carry out this section.

(Amended by Stats. 2024, Ch. 756, Sec. 2. (AB 3138) Effective January 1, 2025.)

Article 8. Special Plates

(Article 8 enacted by Stats. 1959, Ch. 3.)

5000. (a) Identification plates issued for trailers, semitrailers, motor-driven cycles, and pole and pipe dollies, and such vehicles as are exempt from the payment of registration fees under this code shall display suitable distinguishing marks or symbols, and the registration numbers assigned to each class of vehicles shall run in a separate numerical series, except that registration numbers assigned to vehicles exempt from the payment of registration fees may run in several separate numerical series.

(b) Vehicles subject to Sections 9400 and 9400.1 shall be issued license plates with suitable distinguishing marks or symbols distinguishing them from other license plates issued.

(c) Vehicles subject to Section 5014.1 shall be issued permanent identification plates with suitable distinguishing marks or symbols that distinguish them from other license plates.

(Amended by Stats. 2000, Ch. 861, Sec. 21. Effective September 29, 2000. Operative December 31, 2001, pursuant to Sec. 67 of Ch. 861.)

5001. The department may issue license plates for vehicles exempt from registration fees in the same series as plates issued for nonexempt vehicles. The plates may be issued for a one-year period and only upon the certification of the department that the issuance of the plates has been requested by the head of a criminal justice or a law enforcement agency of a city, county, or state or federal department, that the vehicle is assigned to persons responsible for investigating actual or suspected violations of the law or the supervision of persons liberated from a state prison or other institution under the jurisdiction of the Department of Corrections by parole or the supervision of persons liberated from an institution under the jurisdiction of the Department of the Youth Authority by parole, and is intended for use in the line of duty.

(Amended by Stats. 1982, Ch. 576, Sec. 1.)

5001.5. The director may enter into agreements or arrangements with motor vehicle departments in other states to provide for a reciprocal exchange of regular series license plates for the purposes of and under the conditions provided in Sections 5001 and 5003.

(Amended by Stats. 1982, Ch. 576, Sec. 2.)

5002. The department may issue regular series plates to the Department of General Services for use on motor vehicles maintained within motor vehicle pools of state-owned vehicles when the vehicles are used for the purposes set forth in Section 5001, except that the Department of General Services shall not assign, dispatch, or otherwise make any of those vehicles available for use by any agency of the state except upon the certification of the department.

(Amended by Stats. 1982, Ch. 576, Sec. 3.)

5002.5. The department shall issue regular series license plates for any motor vehicle owned by, or in the possession and use of, the Senate or Assembly, upon the request of the Rules Committee thereof.

(Added by Stats. 1967, Ch. 162.)

5002.6. (a) The Chancellor or a president of a campus of the California State University, or the president or a chancellor of a campus of the University of California, who is regularly issued a state-owned vehicle may apply to the department for regular series license plates for that vehicle, if a request for that issuance is also made by the Trustees of the

California State University or the Regents of the University of California, as applicable. The request by the president or chancellor and by the trustees or regents shall be in the manner specified by the department.

(b) Regular series license plates issued pursuant to subdivision (a) shall be surrendered to the department by the trustees or regents, as applicable, upon the reassignment of a vehicle, for which those plates have been issued, to a person other than the person who requested those plates.

(Amended by Stats. 1994, Ch. 146, Sec. 219. Effective January 1, 1995.)

5002.7. (a) For a county of over 20,000 square miles in area, a member of the county board of supervisors, or a county assessor, auditor, controller, treasurer, or tax collector, who is regularly issued a county-owned vehicle may apply to the department for regular series license plates for that vehicle, if a request for that issuance is also made by the county board of supervisors. The application and the request shall be in the manner specified by the department.

(b) Regular series license plates issued pursuant to subdivision (a) shall be surrendered to the department by the board member or administrative officer, as applicable, upon the reassignment of a vehicle, for which those plates have been issued, to a person other than the person who requested those plates.

(Amended by Stats. 2007, Ch. 630, Sec. 2. Effective January 1, 2008.)

5002.8. (a) (1) Distinctive license plates issued for a motor vehicle owned by a current or retired Member of the California Legislature, which plates denote that the person is, or was, a Member of the Legislature, and distinctive license plates issued for a vehicle owned by a Member of the Congress of the United States, which plates denote that the person is a Member of Congress, shall be subject to the regular fees for an original registration or renewal of registration.

(2) In addition to the regular fees for an original registration or renewal of registration, the applicant shall be charged the following additional fees:

(b) For an original registration, the applicant shall be charged the fee specified in subdivision (a) of Section 5106.

(c) For a renewal of registration, the applicant shall be charged the fee specified in subdivision (b) of Section 5106.

(d) When a Member or former Member of the California Legislature or a Member of the Congress of the United States who has been issued personalized license plates pursuant to this section applies to the department for transfer of the plates to another passenger vehicle, commercial motor vehicle, trailer, or semitrailer, a transfer fee in the amount specified pursuant to Section 5108 shall be charged in addition to all other appropriate fees.

(e) After deducting the costs incurred by the department to administer this section, the department shall deposit in the California Environmental License Plate Fund, all fees received by the department in payment for the issuance, renewal, or transfer of the special license plates authorized under this section.

(f) This section shall become operative on January 1, 2014.

(Amended by Stats. 2012, Ch. 748, Sec. 2. (AB 2068) Effective January 1, 2013. Amended version operative January 1, 2014, by its own provisions.)

5003. The department shall maintain a record of the registration of exempt vehicles with regular series plates, which record shall not be open to public inspection. The record shall be disclosed in the event of any accident involving a vehicle so registered on demand of the Attorney General or upon an order of court. In the event of an inquiry by a county sheriff, city chief of police, or judge of any court relating to such exempt vehicle in connection with an alleged violation of state or local traffic laws, the department shall notify the supervisor of the person to whom the vehicle was assigned of the inquiry and the alleged violation and shall notify the inquiring official that this has been done without disclosing the name of the person involved.

(Amended by Stats. 1959, Ch. 536.)

5004. (a) Notwithstanding any other provision of this code, any owner of a vehicle described in paragraph (1), (2), or (3) which is operated or moved over the highway primarily for the purpose of historical exhibition or other similar purpose shall, upon application in the manner and at the time prescribed by the department, be issued special identification plates for the vehicle:

(1) A motor vehicle with an engine of 16 or more cylinders manufactured prior to 1965.

(2) A motor vehicle manufactured in the year 1922 or prior thereto.

(3) A vehicle which was manufactured after 1922, is at least 25 years old, and is of historic interest.

(b) The special identification plates assigned to motor vehicles with an engine of 16 or more cylinders manufactured prior to 1965 and to any motor vehicle manufactured in the year 1922 and prior thereto shall run in a separate numerical series, commencing with "Horseless Carriage No. 1".

The special identification plates assigned to vehicles specified in paragraph (3) of subdivision (a) shall run in a separate numerical series, commencing with "Historical Vehicle No. 1".

Each series of plates shall have different and distinguishing colors.

(c) A fee of twenty-five dollars ($25) shall be charged for the initial issuance of the special identification plates. Such plates shall be permanent and shall not be required to be replaced. If such special identification plates become damaged or unserviceable in any manner, replacement for the plates may be obtained from the department upon proper application and upon payment of such fee as is provided for in Section 9265.

(d) All funds received by the department in payment for such identification plates or the replacement thereof shall be deposited in the California Environmental License Plate Fund.

(e) These vehicles shall not be exempt from the equipment provisions of Sections 26709, 27150, and 27600.

(f) As used in this section, a vehicle is of historic interest if it is collected, restored, maintained, and operated by a collector or hobbyist principally for purposes of exhibition and historic vehicle club activities.

(Amended by Stats. 1984, Ch. 918, Sec. 1.)

5004.1. (a) (1) An owner of a vehicle that is a 1980 or older model-year vehicle may, after the requirements for the registration of the vehicle are complied with and with the approval of the department, utilize license plates of this state with the date of year corresponding to the model-year date when the vehicle was manufactured, if the model-year date license plate is legible and serviceable, as determined by the department, in lieu of the license plates otherwise required by this code.

(2) The department may consult with an organization of old car hobbyists in determining whether the date of year of the license plate corresponds to the model-year date when the vehicle was manufactured.

(b) A fee of forty-five dollars ($45) shall be charged for the application for the use of the special plates.

(c) In addition to the regular renewal fee for the vehicle for which the plates are authorized, the applicant for a renewal of the plates shall be charged an additional fee of ten dollars ($10). If payment of a regular vehicle renewal fee is not required by this code, the holder of license plates with a date corresponding to the model-year may retain the plates upon payment of an annual fee of twenty dollars ($20) that shall be due at the expiration of the registration year of the vehicle to which the plates were last assigned under this section.

(d) If a person who is authorized to utilize the special license plates applies to the department for transfer of the plates to another vehicle, a transfer fee of twelve dollars ($12) shall be charged in addition to all other appropriate fees.

(Amended by Stats. 2016, Ch. 157, Sec. 1. (SB 1429) Effective January 1, 2017.)

5004.3. (a) Subject to subdivision (d), the department shall establish the California Legacy License Plate Program and create and issue a series of specialized license plates known as California Legacy License Plates that replicate the look of California license plates from the state's past. The design of the plates shall be identical, to the extent the department determines it to be reasonably feasible under current manufacturing processes, to a regular license plate, except as provided in subdivision (b).

(b) The California Legacy License Plates shall consist of one or more of the following designs:

(1) Yellow background with black lettering per the appearance of California license plates issued by the department from 1956 to 1962, inclusive.

(2) Black background with yellow lettering per the appearance of California license plates issued by the department from 1965 to 1968, inclusive.

(3) Blue background with yellow lettering per the appearance of California license plates issued by the department from 1969 to 1986, inclusive.

(c) An applicant for the specialized license plates described in subdivision (a), who shall be the owner or lessee of the vehicle on which the plates will be displayed, may choose to either accept a license plate character sequence assigned by the department or request a combination of letters or numbers or both, subject to Section 5105.

(d) In addition to the regular fees for an original registration or renewal of registration, the following additional fees shall be paid for the issuance, renewal, retention, or transfer of the specialized license plates:

(1) Fifty dollars ($50) for the original issuance of the plates.

(2) Forty dollars ($40) for a renewal of registration with the plates.

(3) Fifteen dollars ($15) for transfer of the plates to another vehicle.

(4) Thirty-five dollars ($35) for each substitute replacement plate.

(5) Thirty-eight dollars ($38), when the payment of renewal fees is not required as specified in Section 4000 and the holder of the specialized license plates retains the plates. The fee shall be due at the expiration of the registration year of the vehicle to which the specialized license plates were assigned. This paragraph shall not apply when a plate character sequence is assigned by the department pursuant to subdivision (c).

(e) Sections 5106 and 5108 do not apply to the specialized license plates issued pursuant to this section.

(f) The department shall not issue California Legacy License Plates for a vehicle that is exempt from the payment of registration fees pursuant to Section 9101 or 9103.

(g) (1) The department shall not establish the California Legacy License Plate Program until the department has received not less than 7,500 paid applications for plates. The department shall collect and hold applications for the plates. The department shall not issue a specialized license plate until it has received not less than 7,500 paid applications for any one of the particular plates within the time period prescribed in this section.

(2) The department shall have until January 1, 2015, to receive the required number of applications. If, after that date, 7,500 paid applications have not been received for any one of the three plates described in subdivision (b), the department shall immediately refund to all applicants all fees or deposits that have been collected.

(h) (1) Upon a determination by the department that there are sufficient funds for the program, moneys shall be available, upon appropriation by the Legislature, to the department for the necessary administrative costs of establishing the California Legacy License Plate Program.

(2) After deducting its administrative costs under this subdivision, the department shall deposit any additional revenue derived from the issuance, renewal, transfer, retention, and substitution of the specialized license plates into the California Environmental License Plate Fund, for appropriation by the Legislature pursuant to existing law. For purposes of this paragraph, "administrative costs" includes the costs of including the California Legacy License Plates in materials that promote special license plates authorized by this chapter.

(Amended by Stats. 2016, Ch. 208, Sec. 8. (AB 2906) Effective January 1, 2017.)

5004.5. Notwithstanding any other provision of this code, any owner of a motorcycle manufactured in the year 1942 or prior thereto shall, upon application in the manner and at the time prescribed by the department, be issued special license plates for the motorcycle. The special license plates assigned to such motorcycles shall run in a separate numerical series. An additional fee of fifteen dollars ($15) shall be charged for the initial issuance of the special license plates. Such plates shall be permanent and shall not be required to be replaced. If such special license plates become damaged or unserviceable in any manner, replacement for the plates may be obtained from the department upon proper application and upon payment of such fee as is provided for in Section 9265. Except as otherwise provided in this section, such motorcycles shall be subject to the same annual registration fees and provisions of law as are other motorcycles.

All revenues derived from the fees provided for in this section above actual costs of the production and issuance of the special plates for motorcycles, or the replacement thereof, shall be deposited in the California Environmental License Plate Fund by the department.

(Amended by Stats. 1981, Ch. 415, Sec. 3.)

5005. (a) Any person holding an unexpired amateur radio station license issued by the Federal Communications Commission may, after the requirements for the registration of the motor vehicle have been complied with, also apply directly to the department for special license plates, and the department may issue special plates in lieu of the regular license plates. The special license plates shall be affixed to the motor vehicle for which registration is sought and, in lieu of the numbers otherwise prescribed by law, shall display the official amateur radio station call letters of the applicant as assigned by the Federal Communications Commission.

The applicant shall, by satisfactory proof, show that he or she is the holder of an unexpired license.

(b) The department shall not issue more than one set of special plates for any licensed amateur radio station.

(c) In addition to the regular fees for an original registration or renewal of registration, the following special fees shall be paid:

(1) Twenty dollars ($20) for the initial issuance of the special plate.

(2) Twelve dollars ($12) for the transfer of the special plate to another motor vehicle.

(Amended by Stats. 1982, Ch. 1273, Sec. 5.)

5006. (a) The department may issue distinctive license plates for motor vehicles owned or leased by an honorary consular officer or a similar official when the department is otherwise satisfied that the issuance of the license plates is in order. An honorary consular officer or similar official is a citizen of the United States, or a permanent resident of this country, who is appointed by a foreign country for the purpose of facilitating and promoting the interest of that country.

(b) The motor vehicles for which the license plates are issued shall be subject to all regular license and registration fees. In addition to the regular fees for an original registration or renewal of registration, the additional fees specified in Sections 5106 and 5108, as applicable, shall be paid, and shall be deposited in the Motor Vehicle Account in the State Transportation Fund.

(Added by Stats. 1985, Ch. 752, Sec. 1.)

5006.5. (a) The department may issue, for a fee determined by the department to be sufficient to reimburse the department for actual costs incurred pursuant to this section, distinctive license plates for motor vehicles owned or leased by an officer or a designated employee of a foreign organization recognized by the United States pursuant to the Taiwan Relations Act (22 U.S.C. Sec. 3301 et seq.) when the department is otherwise satisfied that the issuance of the license plates is in order.

(b) The distinctive license plates shall be designed by the department and shall contain the words "Foreign Organization."

(c) The department shall establish procedures for both of the following:

(1) To verify the eligibility of an applicant for plates issued pursuant to this section.

(2) To authorize a recognized foreign organization to apply on behalf of its officers for plates issued pursuant to this section.

(Added by Stats. 1994, Ch. 397, Sec. 1. Effective January 1, 1995.)

5007. (a) The department shall, upon application and without additional fees, issue a special license plate or plates pursuant to procedures adopted by the department to all of the following:

(1) A disabled person.

(2) A disabled veteran.

(3) An organization or agency involved in the transportation of disabled persons or disabled veterans if the motor vehicle that will have the special license plate is used solely for the purpose of transporting those persons.

(b) The special license plates issued under subdivision (a) shall run in a regular numerical series that shall include one or more unique two-letter codes reserved for disabled person license plates or disabled veteran license plates. The International Symbol of Access adopted pursuant to Section 3 of Public Law 100-641, commonly known as the "wheelchair symbol" shall be depicted on each plate.

(c) (1) Except as provided in paragraph (3), before issuing a special license plate to a disabled person or disabled veteran, the department shall require the submission of a certificate, in accordance with paragraph (2), signed by the physician and surgeon, or to the extent that it does not cause a reduction in the receipt of federal aid highway funds, by a nurse practitioner, certified nurse-midwife, or physician assistant, substantiating the disability, unless the applicant's disability is readily observable and uncontested. The disability of a person who has lost, or has lost the use of, one or more lower extremities or one hand, for a disabled veteran, or both hands for a disabled person, or who has significant limitation in the use of lower extremities, may also be certified by a licensed chiropractor. The disability of a person related to the foot or ankle may be certified by a licensed podiatrist. The blindness of an applicant shall be certified by a licensed physician and surgeon who specializes in diseases of the eye or a licensed optometrist. The physician and surgeon, nurse practitioner, certified nurse-midwife, physician assistant, chiropractor, or optometrist certifying the qualifying disability shall provide a full description of the illness or disability on the form submitted to the department.

(2) The physician and surgeon, nurse practitioner, certified nurse midwife, physician assistant, chiropractor, podiatrist, or optometrist who signs a certificate submitted under this subdivision shall retain information sufficient to substantiate that certificate and, upon request of the department, shall make that information available for inspection by the Medical Board of California or the appropriate regulatory board.

(3) For a disabled veteran, the department shall accept, in lieu of the certificate described in paragraph (1), a certificate from a county veterans service officer, the Department of Veterans Affairs, or the United States Department of Veterans Affairs that certifies that the applicant is a disabled veteran as described in Section 295.7.

(d) A disabled person or disabled veteran who is issued a license plate or plates under this section shall, upon request, present to a peace officer, or person authorized to enforce parking laws, ordinances, or regulations, a certification form that substantiates the eligibility of the disabled person or veteran to possess the plate or plates. The certification shall be on a form prescribed by the department and contain the name of the disabled person or disabled veteran to whom the plate or plates were issued, and the name, address, and telephone number of the medical professional described in subdivision (c) who certified the eligibility of the person or veteran for the plate or plates.

(e) The certification requirements of subdivisions (c) and (d) do not apply to an organization or agency that is issued a special license plate or plates under paragraph (3) of subdivision (a).

(f) The special license plate shall, upon the death of the disabled person or disabled veteran, be returned to the department within 60 days or upon the expiration of the vehicle registration, whichever occurs first.

(g) When a motor vehicle subject to paragraph (3) of subdivision (a) is sold or transferred, the special license plate or plates issued to an organization or agency under paragraph (3) of subdivision (a) for that motor vehicle shall be immediately returned to the department.

(h) The department shall require a person who applies for a special license plate pursuant to this section to provide proof of the applicant's true full name and date of birth that shall be established by submitting one of the following to the department:

(1) A copy or facsimile of the applicant's state issued driver's license or identification card.

(2) A copy or facsimile of the document required for an applicant for a driver's license or identification card to establish the applicant's true full name.

(3) An applicant unable to establish legal presence in the United States may fulfill the true full name and date of birth requirement by providing the department a copy or facsimile of the documents used to establish identity pursuant to Section 12801.9.

(Amended by Stats. 2020, Ch. 42, Sec. 1. (AB 408) Effective January 1, 2021.)

5007.5. (a) Upon a receipt of request for information by a local law enforcement agency or local or state agency responsible for the administration or enforcement of parking regulations, the department shall make available to the requesting agency any information contained in a physician's certificate submitted to the department to substantiate the disability of a person applying for or who has been issued special license plates pursuant to Section 5007. The department shall not provide the information specified in this subdivision to any private entity or third-party parking citation processing agency.

(b) A local authority may establish a review board or panel, for the purposes of reviewing information contained in applications for special license plates and the certification of qualifying disabilities for persons residing within the jurisdiction of the local authority. The review board shall include a physician or other medical authority. Any findings or determinations by a review board or panel under this section indicating that an application or certification is fraudulent or lacks proper certification shall be transmitted to the department or other appropriate authorities for further review and investigation.

(Added by Stats. 2004, Ch. 404, Sec. 9. Effective January 1, 2005.)

5008. (a) Any person who is regularly employed or engaged as a bona fide newspaper, newsreel, or television photographer or cameraman, may, after the requirements for the registration of the motor vehicle have been complied with, also apply for special license plates, and the department shall issue special license plates in lieu of the regular license plates. The special license plates shall be affixed to the vehicle for which registration is sought and shall display the letters "PP" enclosed by a shield.

The applicant shall, by satisfactory proof, show that he or she is a bona fide newspaper, newsreel, or television photographer or cameraman.

(b) The department shall not issue more than one set of the special plates to any person.

(c) In addition to the regular fees for an original registration or renewal of registration, the following special fees shall be paid:

(1) Twenty dollars ($20) for the initial issuance of the special plate.

(2) Twelve dollars ($12) for the transfer of the special plate to another motor vehicle.

(Amended by Stats. 1982, Ch. 1273, Sec. 5.5.)

5010. Notwithstanding any other provision of this code, when a motor vehicle which is leased to a school district for use as a schoolbus, as defined in Section 545, temporarily reverts to the possession and control of the lessor, and if the motor vehicle thereafter becomes subject to registration, the lessor may, as an alternative to such registration, secure a temporary permit to operate the vehicle in this state for any one or more calendar months. Such permit shall be posted upon the windshield or other prominent place upon the vehicle, and shall identify the vehicle for which it is affixed. When so affixed, such permit shall serve in lieu of registration. If such a lessor operates the motor vehicle under a temporary permit issued pursuant to this section, he shall notwithstanding the provisions of Section 5000 continue to display on the vehicle the exempt license plates issued to the vehicle as a schoolbus. Upon payment of the fees specified in Section 9266, the department may issue a temporary permit under this section.

(Added by Stats. 1968, Ch. 871.)

5011. Every piece of special construction equipment, special mobile equipment, cemetery equipment, trailer, semitrailer, and every logging vehicle shall display an identification plate issued pursuant to Section 5014 or 5014.1.

(Amended by Stats. 2001, Ch. 826, Sec. 13. Effective January 1, 2002.)

5014. An application by a person other than a manufacturer or dealer for an identification plate for special construction equipment, cemetery equipment, special mobile equipment, logging vehicle, cotton trailer, or farm trailer as specified in Section 36109, a vehicle that is farmer-owned and used as provided in subdivision (b) of Section 36101, a motor vehicle that is farmer-owned and operated and used as provided in subdivision (a) of Section 36101, an automatic bale wagon operated as specified in subdivision (a) or (b) of Section 36102, or a farm trailer that is owned, rented, or leased by a farmer and is operated and used as provided in subdivision (b) of Section 36010, shall include the following:

(a) The true, full name and the driver's license or identification card number, if any, of the owner.

(b) A statement by the owner of the use or uses which he or she intends to make of the equipment.

(c) A description of the vehicle, including any distinctive marks or features.

(d) A photograph of the vehicle. Only one photograph of one piece of equipment shall be required to be attached to the application when identification plates are to be obtained for more than one piece of equipment, each of which is of the same identical type.

(e) Other information as may reasonably be required by the department to determine whether the applicant is entitled to be issued an identification plate.

(f) A service fee of fifteen dollars ($15) for each vehicle. The plates shall be renewed between January 1 and February 4 every five calendar years, commencing in 1986. Any part of the year of the first application constitutes a calendar year. An application for renewal of an identification plate shall contain a space for the applicant's driver's license or identification card number, and the applicant shall furnish that number, if any, in the space provided.

(Amended by Stats. 2003, Ch. 719, Sec. 6. Effective January 1, 2004.)

5014.1. (a) Upon the implementation of the permanent trailer identification plate program, the following applies:

(1) All trailers, except in cases where the registrant has elected to apply for trailer identification plates pursuant to Section 5014 or the trailer is exempt from registration pursuant to Section 36100 or 36109, shall receive an identification certificate upon conversion to the permanent trailer identification program. The following trailers, except as provided in Section 5101, may be assigned a trailer identification plate by the department in accordance with this section or an election may be made to keep the current plate on the expiration date of registration:

(A) Logging dolly.

(B) Pole or pipe dolly.

(C) Semitrailer.

(D) Trailer.

(E) Trailer bus.

(2) An auxiliary dolly or tow dolly may be assigned a permanent trailer identification plate.

(3) Trailer coaches and park trailers, as described in subdivision (b) of Section 18010 of the Health and Safety Code, are exempted from the permanent trailer identification plate program.

(b) The permanent trailer identification plate shall be in a size and design as determined by the department.

(c) The permanent trailer identification plate and the permanent trailer identification certificate shall not expire as long as the appropriate fees have been paid.

(d) Upon sale or transfer of the trailer or semitrailer, the assigned permanent trailer identification plate shall remain with the trailer or semitrailer for the life of the vehicle except as provided in Section 5101. Upon transfer of ownership, a new identification certificate shall be issued and the transferee shall pay a fee of seven dollars ($7).

(e) A service fee, sufficient to pay at least the entire actual costs to the department, not to exceed twenty dollars ($20) shall be assessed by the department upon converting to the permanent trailer identification program.

(f) A fee of seven dollars ($7) for substitute permanent trailer identification plates or certificates shall be charged.

(g) All valid trailer and semitrailer license plates and registration indicia that were issued under this code prior to December 31, 2001, upon which is affixed a permanent trailer identification sticker issued by the department, may be displayed in lieu of a permanent trailer identification plate as described in Sections 5011 and 5014.

(h) Every trailer that is submitted for original registration in this state shall be issued a permanent trailer identification plate and identification certificate.

(i) A service fee of ten dollars ($10) shall be charged for each vehicle renewing identification plates pursuant to this section. These plates shall be renewed on the anniversary date of either the trailer plate expiration date or the date of issuance of the original permanent trailer identification plate, every five calendar years commencing December 31, 2006.

(Amended by Stats. 2001, Ch. 826, Sec. 14.5. Effective January 1, 2002.)

5015. (a) The application for an identification plate for special construction equipment, special mobile equipment, cemetery equipment, and any logging vehicle shall be made before that piece of equipment is moved over a highway.

(b) The application for an identification plate for a cotton trailer or a farm trailer as specified in Section 36109, a vehicle that is farmer-owned and used as provided in subdivision (b) of Section 36101, a motor vehicle that is farmer-owned and operated and used as provided in subdivision (a) of Section 36101, or an automatic bale wagon operated as specified in subdivision (a) or (b) of Section 36102 shall be made before any such piece of equipment is moved over a highway.

(c) The application for a permanent trailer identification plate, as described in Section 5014.1, shall be made prior to the equipment or vehicle described in subdivision (a) being moved, towed, or left standing on any highway or in any offstreet public parking facility.

(Amended by Stats. 2000, Ch. 861, Sec. 25. Effective September 29, 2000. Operative December 31, 2001, pursuant to Sec. 67 of Ch. 861.)

5016. Upon proper application and payment of the fees specified in Section 5014.1 or 9261, the department shall issue an identification plate and an identification certificate for the piece of equipment, vehicle, trailer, semitrailer, or implement of husbandry for which application is made.

(Amended by Stats. 2000, Ch. 861, Sec. 26. Effective September 29, 2000. Operative December 31, 2001, pursuant to Sec. 67 of Ch. 861.)

5016.5. (a) The department may issue a special identification plate or other suitable device to a manufacturer or dealer of special construction equipment, special mobile equipment, cemetery equipment, tow dolly, logging vehicle, or implement of husbandry upon payment of the fee specified in subdivision (b) of Section 9261. The identification plate or other suitable device shall be of a size, color, and configuration determined by the department. The form of the application shall also be determined by the department.

(b) A manufacturer or dealer of special construction equipment, special mobile equipment, cemetery equipment, any tow dolly, any logging vehicle, or any implement of husbandry may operate or move such equipment or vehicle upon the highways during the delivery of or during the demonstration for the sale of such piece of equipment or vehicle upon condition that any such equipment or vehicle display thereon an identification plate or other suitable device issued to such manufacturer or dealer; provided, that special permits have been obtained in accordance with the provisions of Article 6 (commencing with Section

35780) of Chapter 5 of Division 15 for the operation or movement of any such equipment or vehicle of a size, weight, or load exceeding the maximum specified in this code.

(Amended by Stats. 1984, Ch. 1077, Sec. 5. Operative July 1, 1985, by Sec. 21 of Ch. 1077.)

5017. (a) Each identification plate issued under Section 5016 shall bear a distinctive number to identify the equipment, logging vehicle, trailer, semitrailer, or implement of husbandry for which it is issued. The owner, upon being issued a plate, shall attach it to the equipment, logging vehicle, trailer, semitrailer, or implement of husbandry for which it is issued and shall carry the identification certificate issued by the department as provided by Section 4454. It shall be unlawful for any person to attach or use the plate upon any other equipment, logging vehicle, trailer, semitrailer, or implement of husbandry. If the equipment, logging vehicle, trailer, semitrailer, or implement of husbandry is destroyed or the ownership thereof transferred to another person, the person to whom the plate was issued shall, within 10 days, notify the department, on a form approved by the department, that the equipment, logging vehicle, trailer, semitrailer, or implement of husbandry has been destroyed or the ownership thereof transferred to another person.

(b) Upon the implementation of the permanent trailer identification plate program, all trailers except those exempted in paragraphs (1) and (3) of subdivision (a) of Section 5014.1 may be assigned a single permanent plate for identification purposes. Upon issuance of the plate, it shall be attached to the vehicle pursuant to Sections 5200 and 5201.

(c) An identification certificate shall be issued for each trailer or semitrailer assigned an identification plate. The identification certificate shall contain upon its face, the date issued, the name and residence or business address of the registered owner or lessee and of the legal owner, if any, the vehicle identification number assigned to the trailer or semitrailer, and a description of the trailer or semitrailer as complete as that required in the application for registration of the trailer or semitrailer. For those trailers registered under Article 4 (commencing with Section 8050) of Chapter 4 on the effective date of the act adding this sentence that are being converted to the permanent trailer identification program, the identification card may contain only the name of the registrant, and the legal owner's name is not required to be shown. Upon transfer of those trailers, the identification card shall contain the name of the owner and legal owner, if any. When an identification certificate has been issued to a trailer or semitrailer, the owner or operator shall make that certificate available for inspection by a peace officer upon request.

(d) The application for transfer of ownership of a vehicle with a trailer plate or permanent trailer identification plate shall be made within 10 days of sale of the vehicle. The permanent trailer identification certificate is not a certificate of ownership as described in Section 38076.

(Amended by Stats. 2002, Ch. 664, Sec. 214. Effective January 1, 2003.)

5018. Whenever the ownership of equipment, a logging vehicle, or an implement of husbandry is transferred, the transferee shall within 10 days thereafter make application to the department for a transfer of ownership and pay the fee specified in subdivision (c) of Section 9261.

(Added by Stats. 1984, Ch. 1077, Sec. 7. Operative July 1, 1985, by Sec. 21 of Ch. 1077.)

5019. The authorizations for the issuance of special license plates referred to in Sections 5005 and 5008 do not apply to trailers.

(Amended by Stats. 1984, Ch. 918, Sec. 3.)

5020. Any person holding an unexpired license for a class D radio station in the Citizens Radio Service issued by the Federal Communications Commission may, at the time he or she makes application for an original or a renewal registration for a motor vehicle, also apply directly to the department for special license plates, to be affixed to the motor vehicle for which registration is sought, on which, in lieu of the numbers otherwise prescribed by law, shall be inscribed the official class D radio station call sign of the applicant as assigned by the Federal Communications Commission.

The applicant shall, by satisfactory proof, show that he or she is the holder of an unexpired license and, in addition to the regular registration fee, may be charged a fee of twenty dollars ($20) for each set of special plates when issued and fifteen dollars ($15) each succeeding year the vehicle is registered. Whenever the vehicle or the ownership of the vehicle for which plates are issued is changed, a fee of twenty dollars ($20) may be charged. When the applicant also pays weight fees, the department shall so indicate on the special license plates.

(Amended by Stats. 1982, Ch. 1273, Sec. 6.)

5021. After the requirements for the registration of the vehicle have been complied with, the department shall issue such plates in lieu of the regular license plates. The department shall not issue more than one set of special plates for any licensed class D radio station in the Citizens Radio Service.

(Added by Stats. 1969, Ch. 1442.)

5022. (a) Until December 31, 1984, a person described in Section 5101 may also apply for a set of commemorative 1984 Olympic reflectorized license plates and the department shall issue those special license plates in lieu of the regular license plates. No commemorative 1984 Olympic reflectorized license plates shall be issued pursuant to an application therefor which is submitted on or after January 1, 1985, but the holder of those plates may thereafter renew or retain them, or transfer them to another vehicle, subject to this section.

(b) The commemorative 1984 Olympic reflectorized license plates shall be of a distinctive design and shall be available in a special series of letters or numbers, or both, as determined by the department after consultation with the Los Angeles Olympic Organizing Committee.

(c) In addition to the regular fees for an original registration or renewal of registration, a special fee of twelve dollars ($12) shall be paid for the transfer of the special plates to another vehicle.

(d) When payment of renewal fees is not required as specified in Section 4000, or when the person determines to retain the plates upon sale, trade, or other release of the vehicle upon which the special plates have been displayed, the person shall notify the department and the person may retain the special plates.

(e) Until December 31, 1989, duplicate, replacement plates shall be identical commemorative 1984 Olympic reflectorized license plates of the same letter, number, and design as originally issued. However, duplicate, replacement plates of the commemorative 1984 Olympic reflectorized license plate series shall not be available on or after January 1, 1990. Thereafter, unless otherwise provided by this code, regular series plates shall be issued for the fee provided in Section 9265 whenever substitute or duplicate plates are requested.

(f) All revenue derived from the additional special fees provided in this section shall be deposited in the California Environmental License Plate Fund pursuant to Section 21191 of the Public Resources Code.

(Amended by Stats. 2013, Ch. 523, Sec. 23. (SB 788) Effective January 1, 2014.)

5023. (a) (1) Until December 31, 2013, a person described in Section 5101 may also apply for a set of commemorative Olympic reflectorized license plates and the department shall issue those special license plates in lieu of regular license plates. The commemorative Olympic reflectorized license plates shall be of a distinctive design and shall be available in a special series of letters or numbers, or both, as determined by the department after consultation with the United States Olympic Committee. The department may issue the commemorative Olympic reflectorized license plates as environmental license plates, as defined in Section 5103, in a combination of numbers or letters, or both, as requested by the owner or lessee of the vehicle.

(2) On or after January 1, 2014, original, substitute, or duplicate Olympic license plates, including those issued as environmental license plates, shall not be available. However, the holder of Olympic license plates may thereafter renew or retain those plates, or transfer them to another vehicle, subject to this section. Unless otherwise provided by this code, regular series plates shall be issued for the fee provided in Section 9265 whenever substitute or duplicate plates are requested.

(3) On or after January 1, 2014, the holder of Olympic license plates issued as environmental license plates, as defined in Section 5103, may apply for other special license plates using the exact combination of numbers or letters, or both, if authorized by this code, whenever the holder requests substitute or duplicate plates.

(b) In addition to the regular fees for an original registration or renewal of registration, the following special fees shall be paid:

(1) Fifteen dollars ($15) for the transfer of the special plates to another vehicle.

(2) Thirty dollars ($30) for the annual renewal of the special plates.

(c) When payment of renewal fees is not required as specified in Section 4000, or when the person determines to retain the plates upon sale, trade, or other release of the vehicle upon which the special plates have been displayed, the person shall notify the department and the person may retain the special plates.

(d) All revenue derived from the additional special fees provided in this section, less costs incurred by the department pursuant to this section, shall be deposited in the General Fund.

(Amended by Stats. 2013, Ch. 523, Sec. 24. (SB 788) Effective January 1, 2014.)

5024. (a) A person described in Section 5101 may also apply for a set of commemorative collegiate reflectorized license plates, and the department shall issue those special license plates in lieu of the regular license plates. The collegiate reflectorized plates shall be of a distinctive design, and shall be available in a special series of letters or numbers, or both, as determined by the department. The collegiate reflectorized plates shall also contain the name of the participating institution as well as the reflectorized logotype, motto, symbol, or other distinctive design, as approved by the department, representing the participating university or college selected by the applicant. The department may issue the commemorative collegiate reflectorized license plates as environmental license plates, as defined in Section 5103, in a combination of numbers or letters, or both, as requested by the owner or lessee of the vehicle.

(b) Any public or private postsecondary educational institution in the state, which is accredited or has been accepted as a recognized candidate for accreditation by the Western Association of Schools and Colleges, may indicate to the department its decision to be included in the commemorative collegiate license plate program and submit its distinctive design for the logotype, motto, symbol, or other design. However, no public or private postsecondary educational institution may be included in the program until not less than 5,000 applications are received for license plates containing that institution's logotype, motto, symbol, or other design. Each participating institution shall collect and hold applications for collegiate license plates until it has received at least 5,000 applications. Once the institution has received at least 5,000 applications, it shall submit the applications, along with the necessary fees, to the department. Upon receiving the first application, the institution shall have one calendar year to receive the remaining required applications. If, after that one calendar year, 5,000 applications have not been received, the institution shall refund to all applicants any fees or deposits which have been collected.

(c) In addition to the regular fees for an original registration, a renewal of registration, or a transfer of registration, the following commemorative collegiate license plate fees shall be paid:

(1) Fifty dollars ($50) for the initial issuance of the plates. These plates shall be permanent and shall not be required to be replaced.

(2) Forty dollars ($40) for each renewal of registration which includes the continued display of the plates.

(3) Fifteen dollars ($15) for transfer of the plates to another vehicle.

(4) Thirty-five dollars ($35) for replacement plates, if the plates become damaged or unserviceable.

(d) When payment of renewal fees is not required as specified in Section 4000, or when the person determines to retain the commemorative collegiate license plates upon sale, trade, or other release of the vehicle upon which the plates have been displayed, the person shall notify the department and the person may retain the plates.

(e) Of the revenue derived from the additional special fees provided in this section, less costs incurred by the department pursuant to this section, one-half shall be deposited in the California Collegiate License Plate Fund, which is hereby created, and one-half shall be deposited in the California Environmental License Plate Fund.

(f) The money in the California Collegiate License Plate Fund is, notwithstanding Section 13340 of the Government Code, continuously appropriated to the Controller for allocation as follows:

(1) To the governing body of participating public institutions in the proportion that funds are collected on behalf of each, to be used for need-based scholarships, distributed according to federal student aid guidelines.

(2) With respect to funds collected on behalf of accredited nonprofit, private, and independent colleges and universities in the state, to the California Student Aid Commission for grants to students at those institutions, in the proportion that funds are collected on behalf of each institution, who demonstrate eligibility and need in accordance with the Cal Grant Program pursuant to Chapter 1.7 (commencing with Section 69430) of Part 42 of the Education Code, but who did not receive an award based on a listing prepared by the California Student Aid Commission.

(g) The scholarships and grants shall be awarded without regard to race, religion, creed, sex, or age.

(h) The Resources License Plate Fund is hereby abolished and all remaining funds shall be transferred to the California Environmental License Plate Fund effective July 1, 2014.

(Amended by Stats. 2014, Ch. 35, Sec. 180. (SB 861) Effective June 20, 2014.)

Article 8.1. Motorized Bicycles

(Article 8.1 added by Stats. 1980, Ch. 1070, Sec. 1.)

5030. A motorized bicycle, as defined in Section 406, is required to display a special license plate issued by the department.

(Added by Stats. 1980, Ch. 1070, Sec. 1.)

5031. An application by a person other than a manufacturer or dealer for a license plate for a motorized bicycle shall include all the following:

(a) The true, full name and the driver's license or identification card number, if any, of the owner.

(b) A description of the motorized bicycle, including any distinctive marks or features.

(c) Other information as may reasonably be required by the department to determine whether a license plate shall be issued for the motorized bicycle.

(Amended by Stats. 1994, Ch. 1221, Sec. 6. Effective January 1, 1995.)

5032. (a) The application for a special license plate for a motorized bicycle shall be made before the motorized bicycle is operated or moved upon a highway, except that, upon the retail sale of a motorized bicycle when there is no license plate, the operator may operate the motorized bicycle for a period of five days from and including the date of sale, at which time application shall be made to the department for a special license plate. If the fifth day should fall on Saturday, Sunday, or a holiday, the application shall be made on the first business day thereafter.

(b) The five-day operating provision set forth in subdivision (a) shall apply only if the operator has in his immediate possession evidence that the motorized bicycle was purchased within the last five days including the date of sale.

(Added by Stats. 1980, Ch. 1070, Sec. 1.)

5033. Upon proper application and payment of the fees specified in Section 5036, the department shall issue a special license plate and an identification card for the motorized bicycle for which application was made. Applications may be submitted by mail unless the department determines that it is not feasible to complete the identification process by such method.

(Added by Stats. 1980, Ch. 1070, Sec. 1.)

5034. (a) The department may issue a special license plate or other suitable device to a manufacturer or dealer of motorized bicycles upon payment of the fee specified in Section 5036. The license plate shall be of a size, color and configuration determined by the department. The form of the application shall also be determined by the department.

(b) A manufacturer or dealer of motorized bicycles may operate or move a motorized bicycle upon the highways during the delivery of, or during the demonstration for the sale of, the motorized bicycle if the motorized bicycle displays thereon a license plate or other suitable device issued to the manufacturer or dealer.

(Added by Stats. 1980, Ch. 1070, Sec. 1.)

5035. Each license plate issued under Section 5033 shall bear a distinctive number to identify the motorized bicycle for which it is issued and shall bear a symbol, letter, or word to distinguish license plates issued under this article from license plates issued for motorcycles and motor-driven cycles. The owner, upon being issued a license plate, shall attach it to the motorized bicycle for which it is issued and shall carry the identification card issued by the department as provided in Section 4454. It shall be unlawful for any person to attach or use the license plate upon any other motorized bicycle or vehicle. If the motorized bicycle is destroyed, the owner shall destroy the license plate and shall within 10 days notify the department on a form approved by the department that the motorized bicycle and license plate have been destroyed.

If the ownership of the motorized bicycle is transferred to another person, that person shall submit, within 10 days, proper application as provided in Section 5031. The license plate shall remain with the motorized bicycle.

(Added by Stats. 1980, Ch. 1070, Sec. 1.)

5036. A service fee of fifteen dollars ($15) shall be paid for the issuance or transfer of a special license plate for motorized bicycles, as defined in Section 406. Publicly-owned motorized bicycles are exempt from the fee.

(Amended by Stats. 2003, Ch. 719, Sec. 7. Effective January 1, 2004.)

5037. (a) No motorized bicycle first sold on or after July 1, 1981, shall be moved or operated upon a highway unless the owner first makes application for a license plate and, when received, attaches it to the motorized bicycle as provided in this article.

(b) Motorized bicycles first sold prior to July 1, 1981, shall not be moved or operated upon a highway after January 1, 1982, unless the owner makes application for a license plate and, when received, attaches it to the motorized bicycle as provided in this article.

(c) Any motorized bicycle currently licensed pursuant to Division 16.7 (commencing with Section 39000) on July 1, 1981, may be operated upon a highway until July 1, 1982.

(Added by Stats. 1980, Ch. 1070, Sec. 1.)

5038. The department shall establish a record system that provides for identification of stolen motorized bicycles.

(Added by Stats. 1980, Ch. 1070, Sec. 1.)

5039. Notwithstanding any other provision of law, no dealer, manufacturer, salesman, or representative of motorized bicycles exclusively is required to be licensed or permitted pursuant to Chapter 4 (commencing with Section 11700) of Division 5.

(Added by Stats. 1980, Ch. 1070, Sec. 1.)

Article 8.3. Historic and Special Interest Vehicles

(Article 8.3 added by Stats. 1975, Ch. 753.)

5050. The Legislature finds and declares that constructive leisure pursuits by California citizens is most important. This article is intended to encourage responsible participation in the hobby of collecting, preserving, restoring, and maintaining motor vehicles of historic and special interest, which hobby contributes to the enjoyment of the citizen and the preservation of California's automotive memorabilia.

(Added by Stats. 1975, Ch. 753.)

5051. As used in this article, unless the context otherwise requires:

(a) "Collector" is the owner of one or more vehicles described in Section 5004 or of one or more special interest vehicles, as defined in this article, who collects, purchases, acquires, trades, or disposes of the vehicle, or parts thereof, for his or her own use, in order to preserve, restore, and maintain the vehicle for hobby or historical purposes.

(b) "Special interest vehicle" is a vehicle of an age that is unaltered from the manufacturer's original specifications and, because of its significance, including, but not limited to, an out-of-production vehicle or a model of less than 2,000 sold in California in a model-year, is collected, preserved, restored, or maintained by a hobbyist as a leisure pursuit.

(c) "Parts car" is a motor vehicle that is owned by a collector to furnish parts for restoration or maintenance of a special interest vehicle or a vehicle described in Section 5004, thus enabling a collector to preserve, restore, and maintain a special interest vehicle or a vehicle described in Section 5004.

(d) "Street rod vehicle" is a motor vehicle, other than a motorcycle, manufactured in, or prior to, 1948 that is individually modified in its body style or design, including through the use of nonoriginal or reproduction components, and may include additional modifications to other components, including, but not limited to, the engine, drivetrain, suspension, and brakes in a manner that does not adversely affect its safe performance as a motor vehicle or render it unlawful for highway use.

(Amended by Stats. 2006, Ch. 574, Sec. 6. Effective January 1, 2007.)

5052. Except as otherwise provided by local ordinance, a collector may maintain one or more vehicles described in Section 5051, whether currently licensed or unlicensed, or whether operable or inoperable, in outdoor storage on private property, if every such vehicle and outdoor storage area is maintained in such manner as not to constitute a health hazard and is located away from public view, or screened from ordinary public view, by means of a suitable fence, trees, shrubbery, opaque covering, or other appropriate means.

(Added by Stats. 1975, Ch. 753.)

Article 8.4. Special Interest License Plates

(Article 8.4 added by Stats. 1992, Ch. 1273, Sec. 2.)

5060. (a) An organization may apply to the department for participation in a special interest license plate program and the department shall issue special license plates for that program if the issuance of those plates is required by this article, the sponsoring organization complies with the requirements of this section, and the organization meets all of the following criteria:

(1) Qualifies for tax-exempt status under Section 501(c)(3) of the Internal Revenue Code and Section 23701d of the Revenue and Taxation Code.

(2) Submits a financial plan describing the purposes for which the revenues described in paragraph (2) of subdivision (e) will be used.

(3) Submits a design of the organization's proposed special interest license plate that, among other things, provides for the placement of the number and letter characters in a manner that allows for law enforcement to readily identify those characters.

(b) Any person described in Section 5101 may apply for special interest license plates, in lieu of the regular license plates.

(c) The design criteria for a special interest license plate are as follows:

(1) The license plate for a passenger vehicle, commercial vehicle, or trailer shall provide a space not larger than 2 inches by 3 inches to the left of the numerical series and a space not larger than five-eighths of an inch in height below the numerical series for a distinctive design, decal, or descriptive message as authorized by this article. The plates shall be issued in sequential numerical order or, pursuant to Section 5103, in a combination of numbers or letters.

(2) Special interest license plates authorized under this article may be issued for use on a motorcycle. That license plate shall contain a five digit configuration issued in sequential numerical order or, pursuant to Section 5103, in a combination of numbers or letters. There shall be a space to the left of the numerical series for a distinctive design or decal

and the characters shall contrast sharply with the uniform background color. No motorcycle plate containing a full plate graphic design is authorized. Those particular special interest license plates that were issued prior to the discontinuation provided by this paragraph may continue to be used and attached to the vehicle for which they were issued and may be renewed, retained, or transferred pursuant to this code.

(d) (1) No organization may be included in the program until not less than 7,500 applications for the particular special interest license plates are received. Each organization shall collect and hold applications for the plates. Once the organization has received at least 7,500 applications, it shall submit the applications, along with the necessary fees, to the department. The department shall not issue any special interest license plate until an organization has received and submitted to the department not less than 7,500 applications for that particular special interest license plate within the time period prescribed in this section. Advanced payment to the department by an organization representing the department's estimated or actual administrative costs associated with the issuance of a particular special interest license plate shall not constitute compliance with this requirement. The organization shall have 12 months, following the effective date of the enactment of the specific legislation enabling the organization to participate in this program, to receive the required number of applications. If, after that 12 months, 7,500 applications have not been received, the organization shall immediately do either of the following:

(A) Refund to all applicants any fees or deposits that have been collected.

(B) Contact the department to indicate the organization's intent to undertake collection of additional applications and fees or deposits for an additional period, not to exceed 12 months, in order to obtain the minimum 7,500 applications. If an organization elects to exercise the option under this paragraph, it shall contact each applicant who has submitted an application with the appropriate fees or deposits to determine if the applicant wishes a refund of fees or deposits or requests the continuance of the holding of the application and fees or deposits until that time that the organization has received 7,500 applications. The organization shall refund the fees or deposits to any applicant so requesting. In no event shall an organization collect and hold applications for a period exceeding 24 months following the date of authorization as described in paragraph (2) of subdivision (a).

(C) Sequential plate fees shall be paid for the original issuance, renewal, retention, replacement, or transfer of the special interest license plate as determined by the organization and authorized by department's regulations. Those plates containing a personalized message are subject to the fees required pursuant to Sections 5106 and 5108 in addition to any fees required by the special interest license plate program.

(2) (A) If the number of currently outstanding and valid special interest license plates in any particular program provided for in this article is less than 7,500, the department shall notify the sponsoring organization of that fact and shall inform the organization that if that number is less than 7,500 one year from the date of that notification, the department will no longer issue or replace those special interest license plates.

(B) Those particular special interest license plates that were issued prior to the discontinuation provided by subparagraph (A) may continue to be used and attached to the vehicle for which they were issued and may be renewed, retained, or transferred pursuant to this code.

(e) (1) The department shall deduct its costs to develop and administer the special interest license plate program from the revenues collected for the plates.

(2) The department shall deposit the remaining revenues from the original issuance, renewal, retention, replacement, or transfer of the special interest license plate in a fund which shall be established by the Controller.

(f) When payment of renewal fees is not required as specified in Section 4000, or when a person determines to retain the special interest license plate upon a sale, trade, or other release of the vehicle upon which the plate has been displayed, the person shall notify the department and the person may retain and use the plate as authorized by department regulations.

(g) An organization that is eligible to participate in a special interest license plate program pursuant to this article and receives funds from the additional fees collected from the sale of special license plates shall not expend annually more than 25 percent of those funds on administrative costs, marketing, or other promotional activities associated with encouraging application for, or renewal of, the special license plates.

(h) (1) Every organization authorized under this article to offer special interest license plates shall prepare and submit an annual accounting report to the department by June 30. The report shall include an accounting of all revenues and expenditures associated with the special interest license plate program.

(2) If an organization submits a report pursuant to paragraph (1) indicating that the organization violated the expenditure restriction set forth in subdivision (g), the department shall immediately cease depositing fees in the fund created by the Controller for that organization under paragraph (2) of subdivision (e) and, instead, shall deposit those fees that would have otherwise been deposited in that fund in a separate fund created by the Controller, which fund is subject to appropriation by the Legislature. The department shall immediately notify the organization of this course of action. The depositing of funds in the account established pursuant to this paragraph shall continue until the organization demonstrates to the satisfaction of the department that the organization is in compliance or will comply with the requirements of subdivision (g). If one year from the date that the organization receives the notice described in this paragraph, the organization is still unable to satisfactorily demonstrate to the department that it is in compliance or will comply with the requirements of subdivision (g), the department shall no longer issue or replace those special interest license plates associated with that organization. Those particular special interest license plates that were issued prior to the discontinuation provided by this paragraph may continue to be used and attached to the vehicle for which they were issued and may be renewed, retained, or transferred pursuant to this code.

(3) Upon receiving the reports required under paragraph (1), the department shall prepare and transmit an annual consolidated report to the Legislature containing the revenue and expenditure data.

(Amended by Stats. 2003, Ch. 185, Sec. 41. Effective January 1, 2004.)

5060.1. Notwithstanding Section 5060 or any other provision of law to the contrary, the department shall not accept an application for participation in a special interest license plate program under Section 5060 and shall not issue, under Section 5060, special interest license plates for a new program.

(Added by Stats. 2006, Ch. 454, Sec. 2. Effective January 1, 2007.)

5061. (a) Notwithstanding any other provision of law, if the department permits the issuance of a special interest license plate for display on a motorcycle, the department shall not approve any design for that plate that incorporates either or both of the following:

(1) Full or partial graphic designs appearing behind the license plate number configuration.

(2) Symbols within the license plate number configuration.

(b) Any special interest license plate issued for display on a motorcycle is subject to the same fees that are collected for the issuance and retention of special interest license plates on other vehicles.

(Added by Stats. 2000, Ch. 859, Sec. 2. Effective January 1, 2001.)

5062. (a) This section shall be known, and may be cited, as the Rosenthal Blue Sky License Plate Program.

(b) The Legislature hereby finds and declares that CALSTART is a California nonprofit consortium dedicated to the development and commercialization of advanced transportation technologies, including clean fuel vehicles, and that CALSTART should be authorized to undertake a special environmental "Blue Sky" license plate program to facilitate the purchase and use of clean fuel vehicles in the state.

(c) CALSTART may, with the approval of the department, participate in this special interest license plate program.

(d) CALSTART may, with the approval of the department, develop a distinctive design, in conformance with Section 5060, for inclusion on a special interest license plate. The license plate shall be known as the Blue Sky license plate and shall signify that the vehicle to which it is assigned is a clean fuel vehicle.

(e) Any person who owns or leases a clean fuel vehicle, as defined in Section 257, and who applies for an original or renewal registration of that vehicle, may apply, through CALSTART, for a set of Blue Sky license plates in lieu of regular license plates.

(f) The Blue Sky license plate is subject to Sections 5106 and 5108. The revenues derived from the sale of the license plates shall be deposited in the California Environmental License Plate Fund, after the department has deducted its costs for developing and administering the program.

(g) Notwithstanding Section 5060, a Blue Sky license plate may, upon application of the holder, be transferred to another clean fuel vehicle. If the vehicle to which transfer is sought is not a clean fuel vehicle, the plates shall be surrendered to the department.

(h) CALSTART, in coordination with the State Air Resources Board, the State Energy Resources Conservation and Development Commission, and the Public Utilities Commission, shall undertake efforts to publicize the availability of Blue Sky license plates.

(i) Notwithstanding Section 5060, CALSTART shall have 12 months, commencing November 1, 1995, to receive the required applications and to notify the department that the requisite number of applications have been received. If, after that 12-month period, 5,000 applications have not been received, CALSTART shall immediately notify the department and refund to all applicants any fees or deposits which have been collected.

(j) If, on November 1, 1996, the department has not received a notice from CALSTART pursuant to subdivision (i) or if, on or before that date CALSTART notifies the department that the requisite number of applications have not been received, the department shall provide that information to the Secretary of State, and this section shall become inoperative upon receipt of that information by the Secretary of State, and shall remain in effect only until January 1, 1997, and as of that date is repealed, unless a later enacted statute, which is enacted before January 1, 1997, deletes or extends that date.

(Added by Stats. 1993, Ch. 1159, Sec. 5. Effective January 1, 1994. Conditionally inoperative as prescribed in subd. (j). If it became inoperative, this section was repealed on January 1, 1997, by its own provisions.)

5064. (a) The department, in consultation with the Yosemite Foundation, shall design and make available for issuance pursuant to this article special environmental design license plates bearing, notwithstanding Section 5060, a full-plate graphic design depicting a significant feature or quality of Yosemite National Park. Any person described in Section 5101, upon payment of the additional fees set forth in subdivision (b), may apply for and be issued a set of special environmental design license plates. Notwithstanding subdivision (a) of Section 5060, the plates may be issued in a combination of numbers or letters, or both, requested by the owner or lessee of the vehicle.

(b) In addition to the regular fees for an original registration or renewal of registration, the following additional fees shall be paid for the issuance, renewal, or transfer of the special environmental design license plates authorized pursuant to this section:

(1) For the original issuance of the plates, fifty dollars ($50).

(2) For a renewal of registration with the plates, forty dollars ($40).

(3) For transfer of the plates to another vehicle, fifteen dollars ($15).

(4) For each substitute replacement plate, thirty-five dollars ($35).

(5) For the conversion of an existing environmental license plate to the special environmental design license plate authorized pursuant to this section, sixty-five dollars ($65).

(c) After deducting its administrative costs under this section, the department shall deposit the additional revenue derived from the issuance, renewal, transfer, and substitution of special environmental design license plates as follows:

(1) One-half in the Yosemite Foundation Account, which is hereby created in the California Environmental License Plate Fund. Upon appropriation by the Legislature, the money in the account shall be allocated by the Controller to the Yosemite Foundation or its successor for expenditure for the exclusive trust purposes of preservation and restoration projects in Yosemite National Park.

(2) One-half in the California Environmental License Plate Fund.

(d) The Yosemite Foundation shall report to the Legislature on or before June 30 of each year on its use and expenditure of the money in the Yosemite Foundation Account, beginning one year after the initial issuance of the special interest license plates authorized by this section.

(Amended by Stats. 1996, Ch. 1154, Sec. 58. Effective September 30, 1996.)

5066. (a) The department, in conjunction with the Department of the California Highway Patrol, shall design and make available for issuance pursuant to this article the California memorial license plate. Notwithstanding Section 5060, the California memorial license plate may be issued in a combination of numbers or letters, or both, as requested by the applicant for the plates. A person described in Section 5101, upon payment of the additional fees set forth in subdivision (b), may apply for and be issued a set of California memorial license plates.

(b) In addition to the regular fees for an original registration or renewal of registration, the following additional fees shall be paid for the issuance, renewal, retention, or transfer of the California memorial license plates authorized pursuant to this section:

(1) For the original issuance of the plates, fifty dollars ($50).

(2) For a renewal of registration of the plates or retention of the plates, if renewal is not required, forty dollars ($40).

(3) For transfer of the plates to another vehicle, fifteen dollars ($15).

(4) For each substitute replacement plate, thirty-five dollars ($35).

(5) In addition, for the issuance of an environmental license plate, as defined in Section 5103, the additional fees required pursuant to Sections 5106 and 5108 shall be deposited proportionately in the funds described in subdivision (c).

(c) The department shall deposit the additional revenue derived from the issuance, renewal, transfer, and substitution of California memorial license plates in the Antiterrorism Fund, which is hereby created in the General Fund.

(1) Upon appropriation by the Legislature, one-half of the money in the fund shall be allocated by the Controller to the Office of Emergency Services to be used solely for antiterrorism activities. The office shall not use more than 5 percent of the money appropriated for local antiterrorism efforts for administrative purposes.

(2) Upon appropriation by the Legislature in the annual Budget Act or in another statute, one-half of the money in the fund shall be used solely for antiterrorism activities.

(d) The department shall deduct its costs to administer, but not to develop, the California memorial license plate program. The department may use an amount of money, not to exceed fifty thousand dollars ($50,000) annually, derived from the issuance, renewal, transfer, and substitution of California memorial license plates for the continued promotion of the California memorial license plate program of this section.

(e) For the purposes of this section, "antiterrorism activities" means activities related to the prevention, detection, and emergency response to terrorism that are undertaken by state and local law enforcement, fire protection, and public health agencies. The funds provided for these activities, to the extent that funds are available, shall be used exclusively for purposes directly related to fighting terrorism. Eligible activities include, but are not limited to, hiring support staff to perform administrative tasks, hiring and training additional law enforcement, fire protection, and public health personnel, response training for existing and additional law enforcement, fire protection, and public health personnel, and hazardous materials and other equipment expenditures.

(f) Beginning January 1, 2007, and each January 1 thereafter, the department shall determine the number of currently outstanding and valid California memorial license plates. If that number is less than 7,500 in any year, then the department shall no longer issue or replace those plates.

(Amended by Stats. 2019, Ch. 32, Sec. 11. (SB 87) Effective June 27, 2019.)

5067. (a) The department, in consultation with the California Coastal Commission, shall design and make available for issuance pursuant to this article special environmental design license plates. Notwithstanding subdivision (a) of Section 5060, the special environmental design license plates shall bear a graphic design depicting a California coastal motif and may be issued in a combination of numbers or letters, or both, as requested by the applicant for the plates. Any person described in Section 5101 may, upon payment of the additional fees set forth in subdivision (b), apply for and be issued a set of special environmental design license plates.

(b) In addition to the regular fees for an original registration or renewal of registration, the following additional fees shall be paid for the issuance, renewal, retention, or transfer of the special environmental design license plates authorized pursuant to this section:

(1) For the original issuance of the plates, fifty dollars ($50).

(2) For a renewal of registration of the plates or retention of the plates, if renewal is not required, forty dollars ($40).

(3) For transfer of the plates to another vehicle, fifteen dollars ($15).

(4) For each substitute replacement plate, thirty-five dollars ($35).

(5) In addition, for the issuance of an environmental license plate, as defined in Section 5103, the additional fees prescribed in Section 5106 and 5108. The additional fees prescribed in Sections 5106 and 5108 shall be deposited in the California Environmental License Plate Fund.

(c) After deducting its administrative costs under this section, the department, except as provided in paragraph (5) of subdivision (b), shall deposit the additional revenue derived from the issuance, renewal, transfer, and substitution of special environmental design license plates as follows:

(1) One-half in the California Beach and Coastal Enhancement Account, which is hereby established in the California Environmental License Plate Fund. Upon appropriation by the Legislature, the money in the account shall be allocated by the Controller as follows:

(A) First to the California Coastal Commission for expenditure for the Adopt-A-Beach program, the Beach Cleanup Day program, coastal public education programs, and grants to local governments and nonprofit organizations for the costs of operating and maintaining public beaches related to these programs.

(B) Second, from funds remaining after the allocation required under subparagraph (A), to the State Coastal Conservancy for coastal natural resource restoration and enhancement projects and for other projects consistent with the provisions of Division 21 (commencing with Section 31000) of the Public Resources Code.

(2) One-half in the California Environmental License Plate Fund.

(Amended by Stats. 2004, Ch. 230, Sec. 19. Effective August 16, 2004.)

5068. (a) (1) (A) A veterans' organization may apply either individually or with other veterans' organizations to meet the application threshold set forth in Section 5060 for special interest plates. An organization that meets the minimum application requirement by applying with other organizations under this subdivision shall be issued a regular license plate bearing a distinctive design or decal approved under subdivision (a) of Section 5060.

(B) The Department of Veterans Affairs may modify the distinctive design or decal described in subparagraph (A), consistent with the design criteria imposed by Section 5060, to honor all veterans, or veterans who served in a particular war or armed conflict as described in subdivision (a) of Section 5068.1. Special interest plates issued under this section and bearing the modified design or decal shall be issued only after all existing plates have been issued.

(2) Any person who is the registered owner or lessee of a passenger vehicle, commercial motor vehicle, motorcycle, trailer, or semitrailer registered or certificated with the department, or any person who applies for an original registration or renewal of registration of that vehicle may apply under this section for a special interest license plate with a decal that honors all veterans or veterans who served in a particular war or armed conflict.

(3) Special interest license plates issued under this section may be issued in a combination of numbers or letters, or both, requested by the owner or lessee of the vehicle, to be displayed in addition to the design or decal authorized under paragraph (1), subject to Section 5105.

(b) In addition to the regular fees for an original registration, a renewal of registration, or a transfer of registration, the following fees shall be paid by individuals applying for a special interest license plate or a decal issued under this section:

(1) Fifty dollars ($50) for the initial issuance of the plates and decals. The plates shall be permanent and shall not be required to be replaced.

(2) Forty dollars ($40) for each renewal of registration that includes the continued display of the plates or decals.

(3) Fifteen dollars ($15) for transfer of the plates to another vehicle.

(4) Thirty-five dollars ($35) for replacement plates, if they become damaged or unserviceable.

(5) Ten dollars ($10) for replacement decals, if they become damaged or unserviceable.

(6) Notwithstanding Section 5106, seventy-eight dollars ($78) for the personalization of the plates, as authorized under paragraph (3) of subdivision (a).

(c) The department shall maintain on its Internet Web site, a link to order online the special interest license plates issued pursuant to this section.

(Amended by Stats. 2013, Ch. 523, Sec. 25. (SB 788) Effective January 1, 2014.)

5068.1. By July 1, 2013, the department shall do all of the following:

(a) Issue a distinctive decal pursuant to subparagraph (B) of paragraph (1) of subdivision (a) of Section 5068 to an applicant for an original or renewal of vehicle registration for veteran plates or plates honoring veterans to allow that applicant the option of recognizing his or her veteran status in, or honoring veterans of, a particular war or armed conflict, including, but not limited to, those who served in the active military, naval, or air service and performed any portion of their service during any of the periods described in Section 980 of the Military and Veterans Code, including active duty in a campaign or expedition for service in which a medal was authorized by the government of the United States.

(b) Make available to an applicant, upon request, a "yellow ribbon/support our troops" decal in lieu of the distinctive decal described in subdivision (a).

(c) Eliminate from inventory any decals for which the department determines that demand is insufficient to maintain that inventory in a cost-effective manner.

(Added by Stats. 2012, Ch. 398, Sec. 2. (AB 1550) Effective January 1, 2013.)

5069. Revenue derived from the additional special fees provided in Section 5068, less costs incurred by the department pursuant to this article, shall be deposited in the Veterans Service Office Fund, created by Section 972.2 of the Military and Veterans Code.

(Amended by Stats. 2010, Ch. 166, Sec. 2. (AB 1908) Effective January 1, 2011.)

5072. (a) Any person described in Section 5101 may also apply for a set of "Have a Heart, Be a Star, Help Our Kids" license plates, and the department shall issue those special license plates in lieu of the regular license plates. The "Have a Heart, Be a Star, Help Our Kids" plates shall be distinct from other existing license plates by the inclusion of a well within the portion of the license plate that has the alpha-numeric sequence. The well may be placed in any position within that portion of the license plate. A heart shape, a five-pointed star, a hand shape, a plus-sign shape, shall be imprinted within the well itself. However, for purposes of processing the alpha-numeric sequence, the symbol within the well shall be read as a blank within the alpha-numeric sequence. The Department of Motor Vehicles shall cooperate with representatives of the California Highway Patrol and the California Correctional Training and Rehabilitation Authority to design the final shape and dimension of the symbols for these license plates.

(b) An applicant for a license plate described in subdivision (a) may choose to either accept a license plate character sequence assigned by the department that includes one of the four symbols or request a specialized license plate character sequence determined by the applicant that includes one of the four symbols, in accordance with instructions which shall be provided by the department.

(c) In addition to the regular fees for an original registration, a renewal of registration, or a transfer of registration, the following "Have a Heart, Be a Star, Help Our Kids" license plate fees shall be paid:

(1) Notwithstanding Section 5106, for those specialized license plates whose character sequence is determined by the license owner or applicant:

(A) Fifty dollars ($50) for the initial issuance of the plates. These plates shall be permanent and shall not be required to be replaced.

(B) Forty dollars ($40) for each renewal of registration which includes the continued display of the plates.

(C) Fifteen dollars ($15) for transfer of the plates to another vehicle.

(D) Thirty-five dollars ($35) for replacement plates, if the plates become damaged or unserviceable.

(2) For those specialized license plates whose character sequence is assigned by the department:

(A) Twenty dollars ($20) for the initial issuance of the plates. These plates shall be permanent and shall not be required to be replaced.

(B) The legally allowed fee for renewal plus fifteen dollars ($15) for each renewal of registration, which includes the continued display of the plates.

(C) Fifteen dollars ($15) for transfer of the plates to another vehicle.

(D) Twenty dollars ($20) for replacement plates, if the plates become damaged or unserviceable.

(d) When payment of renewal fees is not required as specified in Section 4000, or when the person determines to retain the "Have a Heart, Be a Star, Help Our Kids" license plates upon sale, trade, or other release of the vehicle upon which the plates have been displayed, the person shall notify the department and the person may retain the plates.

(e) The revenue derived from the additional special fees provided in this section, less costs incurred by the department, the Department of the California Highway Patrol, and local law enforcement for developing and administering this license plate program pursuant to this section, shall be deposited in the Child Health and Safety Fund, created pursuant to Chapter 4.6 (commencing with Section 18285) of Part 6 of Division 9 of the Welfare and Institutions Code, and, when appropriated by the Legislature shall be available for the purposes specified in that chapter.

(f) It is the intent of the Legislature that the additional special fees specified in subdivision (e) are not used to replace existing appropriation levels in the 1991–92 Budget Act.

(Amended by Stats. 2025, Ch. 241, Sec. 72. (SB 857) Effective January 1, 2026.)

5074. (a) This section shall be known and may be cited as the Polanco-Bates License Plates for the Arts Act of 1993. The California Arts Council shall participate in the special interest license plate program.

(b) In addition to the regular fees for an original registration or renewal of registration, the following additional fees shall be paid for the issuance, transfer, or renewal of license plates bearing, notwithstanding Section 5060, a full-plate graphic design that depicts a significant feature or quality of the State of California, approved by the department in consultation with the California Arts Council:

(1) For the original issuance of the plates, fifty dollars ($50).

(2) For a renewal of registration of the plates, forty dollars ($40).

(3) For the transfer of the special plates to another vehicle, fifteen dollars ($15).

(4) In addition, for the issuance of an environmental license plate, as defined in Section 5103, with a full-plate graphic design, the additional fees prescribed in Sections 5106 and 5108. The additional fees prescribed in Sections 5106 and 5108 shall be deposited in the California Environmental License Plate Fund.

(c) Except as provided in paragraph (4) of subdivision (b), all fees collected under this section, after deduction of the department's costs in administering this section, shall be deposited in the Graphic Design License Plate Account, which is hereby established in the General Fund. The funds in the account shall be used by the California Arts Council, upon appropriation by the Legislature, for arts education and local arts programming.

(d) The California Arts Council shall use the revenue derived from the fee increases authorized by amendment of this section during the 2003–04 Regular Session exclusively for arts education and local arts programming.

(Amended by Stats. 2013, Ch. 221, Sec. 1. (SB 789) Effective January 1, 2014.)

5075. (a) The department, in consultation with the California Tahoe Conservancy, shall design and make available for issuance pursuant to this article special environmental design license plates as described in this section. Notwithstanding subdivision (a) of Section 5060, the special environmental design license plates shall bear a full-plate graphic design depicting a significant feature of Lake Tahoe. Any person described in Section 5101 may, upon payment of the additional fees set forth in subdivision (b), apply for and be issued a set of special environmental design license plates. Notwithstanding subdivision (a) of Section 5060, the special environmental design license plates may be issued as environmental license plates, as defined in Section 5103.

(b) In addition to the regular fees for an original registration or renewal of registration, the following additional fees shall be paid for the issuance, renewal, or transfer of the special environmental design license plates authorized pursuant to this section:

(1) For the original issuance of the plates, fifty dollars ($50).

(2) For a renewal of registration with the plates, forty dollars ($40).

(3) For transfer of the plates to another vehicle, fifteen dollars ($15).

(4) For each substitute replacement plate, thirty-five dollars ($35).

(5) In addition, for the issuance of environmental license plates, as defined in Section 5103, with a full-plate graphic design described in subdivision (a), the additional fees prescribed in Sections 5106 and 5108. The additional fees prescribed in Sections 5106 and 5108 shall be deposited in the Environmental License Plate Fund.

(c) Except as provided in paragraph (5) of subdivision (b), and after deducting its administrative costs under this section, the department shall deposit the additional revenue derived from the issuance, renewal, transfer, and substitution of special environmental design license plates in the Lake Tahoe Conservancy Account, which is hereby created in the California Environmental License Plate Fund. Upon appropriation by the Legislature, the money in the account shall be allocated by the Controller to the California Tahoe Conservancy or its successor for expenditure for the exclusive trust purposes of preservation and restoration projects in the Lake Tahoe area and for the purpose of establishing and improving trails, pathways, and public access for nonmotorized traffic in that area.

(Added by Stats. 1993, Ch. 1303, Sec. 3. Effective October 11, 1993.)

Article 8.5. Environmental License Plates

(Heading of Article 8.5 amended by Stats. 1973, Ch. 265.)

5100. The purpose of this article is to provide revenue for the California Environmental License Plate Fund.

(Amended by Stats. 1979, Ch. 1105.)

5101. Any person who is the registered owner or lessee of a passenger vehicle, commercial motor vehicle, motorcycle, trailer, or semitrailer registered or certificated with the department, or who makes application for an original registration or renewal registration of that vehicle, may, upon payment of the fee prescribed in Section 5106 and those fees required by Sections 5022 to 5024, inclusive, apply to the department for environmental license plates, in the manner prescribed in Section 5105, which plates shall be affixed to the passenger vehicle, commercial motor vehicle, motorcycle, trailer, or semitrailer for which registration is sought in lieu of the regular license plates.

(Amended (as amended by Stats. 2000, Ch. 861, Sec. 28.5) by Stats. 2001, Ch. 826, Sec. 16. Effective January 1, 2002.)

5101.2. (a) A person otherwise eligible under this article who is a firefighter, retired firefighter, or a surviving family member of a firefighter or retired firefighter may apply for special license plates for a vehicle under this article. License plates issued pursuant to this section shall be issued in accordance with Section 5060.

(b) The applicant, by proof satisfactory to the department, shall show that the applicant is a firefighter, retired firefighter, or a surviving family member of a firefighter or retired firefighter, who meets all of the following:

(1) Is presently, was at the time of their death, or has or had retired in good standing as, an officer, an employee, or a member of a fire department or a fire service of the state, a county, a city, a district, or any other political subdivision of the state, whether in a volunteer, partly paid, or fully paid status.

(2) Is or was until retirement or death, regularly employed as a firefighter or regularly enrolled as a volunteer firefighter.

(3) Has, or had before retirement or death, principal duties which fall within the scope of active firefighting and any of the following activities:

(A) Fire prevention service.

(B) Fire training.

(C) Hazardous materials abatement.

(D) Arson investigation.

(E) Emergency medical services.

(c) The special license plates issued under this section shall contain the words "California Firefighter" and shall run in a regular numerical series.

(d) In addition to the regular fees for an original registration, a renewal of registration, or a transfer of registration, the following special license plate fees shall be paid:

(1) A fee of fifty dollars ($50) for the initial issuance of the special license plates. These special license plates shall be permanent and shall not be required to be replaced.

(2) A fee of forty dollars ($40) for each renewal of registration that includes the continued display of the special license plates.

(3) If the special license plates become damaged or unserviceable, a fee of thirty-five dollars ($35) for the replacement of the special license plates, obtained from the department upon proper application therefor.

(4) A fee of fifteen dollars ($15) for the transfer of the special license plates to another vehicle qualifying as a vehicle owned by a firefighter who has met the requirements set forth in subdivision (b).

(5) In addition, for the issuance of environmental license plates, as defined in Section 5103, with the special firefighter personal vehicle license plates and distinctive design or decal, the additional fees prescribed in Sections 5106 and 5108. The additional fees collected pursuant to this paragraph shall be deposited in the California Environmental License Plate Fund.

(e) (1) Upon the death of a person issued special license plates pursuant to this section, their surviving spouse may retain the special license plates. Except as provided in paragraph (2), upon the death of the surviving spouse, the plates shall be returned to the department or destroyed within 60 days after the death of the surviving spouse or upon the expiration of the vehicle registration, whichever occurs first.

(2) (A) In the absence of a surviving spouse or where the surviving spouse dies while in possession of the special license plates, a member of the deceased firefighter's family may retain one of the special license plates as a family heirloom, subject to the conditions set forth in subdivision (f).

(B) As used in this paragraph, "family" means grandparents, stepgrandparents, parents, stepparents, siblings, stepsiblings, stepchildren, natural-born children, or adopted children of the person issued the special license plates under subdivision (a).

(f) The special license plates issued under this section are not valid for use for vehicle registration purposes by a person other than the person issued the special license plates under subdivision (a) and the surviving spouse of that person.

(g) For purposes of this section, the following definitions shall apply:

(1) "Surviving family member" means the spouse and any child, including an adopted child, stepchild, or recognized natural child of a deceased firefighter or deceased retired firefighter. "Surviving family member" does not include a former spouse.

(2) "Spouse" includes a domestic partner in a domestic partnership as described in Section 297 of the Family Code.

(h) Except as provided in paragraph (5) of subdivision (d), the revenues derived from the additional special fees provided in this section, less costs incurred by the department pursuant to this section, shall be deposited in the California Firefighters' Memorial Voluntary Tax Contribution Fund established by Section 18802 of the Revenue and Taxation Code.

(Amended by Stats. 2023, Ch. 602, Sec. 2. (SB 374) Effective January 1, 2024.)

5101.3. (a) Any person otherwise eligible under this article who qualifies under subdivision (b) may apply for special license plates that shall run in a separate numerical series and shall contain the words "Pearl Harbor Survivor." The plates may be issued for any vehicle, except a vehicle used for transportation for hire, compensation, or profit, or a motorcycle, which is owned or coowned by the person.

(b) To qualify for issuance of the special plates, the applicant by satisfactory proof shall show all of the following:

(1) The applicant was a member of the United States Armed Forces on December 7, 1941, and received an honorable discharge from military service.

(2) The applicant was on station at Pearl Harbor, the Island of Oahu, or offshore within a distance of three miles, on December 7, 1941, during the hours of 7:55 a.m. to 9:45 a.m., Hawaii time, as certified by a California chapter of the Pearl Harbor Survivors Association.

(c) Upon the death of a person issued special license plates pursuant to this section, his or her surviving spouse may retain the special license plates subject to the conditions set forth in this section. Upon the death of the spouse, the retained special license plates shall be returned to the department either (1) within 60 days following that death or (2) upon the expiration of the vehicle registration, whichever occurs first.

(d) Sections 5106 and 5108 do not apply to this section.

(Amended by Stats. 1999, Ch. 612, Sec. 1. Effective January 1, 2000.)

5101.4. (a) Any person otherwise eligible under this article who is a recipient of the Army Medal of Honor, Navy Medal of Honor, Air Force Medal of Honor, Army Distinguished Service Cross, Navy Cross, or Air Force Cross may apply for special license plates for the vehicle under this article.

(b) The applicant, by conclusive evidence, shall show that the applicant is a recipient of one of the nation's highest decorations for valor, as specified in subdivision (a).

(c) The special license plates issued under this section shall contain the words "Legion of Valor" and shall run in a regular numerical series. An adhesive sticker denoting which of the nation's highest decorations for valor, as specified in subdivision (a), is held by the applicant shall be affixed in a recess provided for it on the license plates.

(d) Upon the death of a person issued special license plates pursuant to this section, his or her surviving spouse may retain the special license plates subject to the conditions set forth in this section. If there is no surviving spouse, the special license plates shall be returned to the department either (1) within 60 days following that death or (2) upon the expiration of the vehicle registration, whichever occurs first. However, in the absence of a surviving spouse, another surviving member of the deceased medal recipient's family may retain one of the special license plates as a family heirloom, subject to the conditions set forth in subdivision (g).

(e) If a surviving spouse who has elected to retain the special license plates as authorized under subdivision (d) dies while in possession of the special license plates, the special license plates shall be returned to the department either within 60 days following that death, or upon the expiration date of the vehicle registration, whichever date occurs first. However, another surviving member of the deceased medal recipient's family may retain one of the special license plates as a family heirloom, subject to the conditions set forth in subdivision (g).

(f) Sections 5106 and 5108 do not apply to this section.(g) The special license plates issued under this section are not valid for use for vehicle registration purposes or for the purposes of Section 9105, or Section 10783 or 10783.2 of the Revenue and Taxation Code, by a person other than the person issued the special license plates under subdivision (a) and the surviving spouse of that person.

(h) For purposes of this section, "family" means grandparents, stepgrandparents, parents, stepparents, siblings, stepsiblings, children, and stepchildren of the person issued the special license plates under subdivision (a).

(Amended by Stats. 2010, Ch. 181, Sec. 1. (SB 1295) Effective January 1, 2011.)

5101.5. (a) A person otherwise eligible under this article who is a former American prisoner of war may apply for special license plates for the vehicle under this article. The special license plates assigned to the vehicle shall run in a separate numerical series and contain a replica design of the American Prisoner of War Medal followed by the letters "POW" and four numbers. The special license plates issued under this subdivision also shall contain the following words: "Ex-Prisoner of War." The department shall, pursuant to this article, reserve and issue the special license plates provided for by this section only to persons who show by satisfactory proof former prisoner-of-war status. A person otherwise issued license plates within this series pursuant to this article prior to January 1, 1982, may retain them.

(b) Notwithstanding subdivision (a), the department, in consultation with the Department of Veterans Affairs and veterans' service organizations, shall design and make available for issuance pursuant to this article a special environmental design license plate for former American prisoners of war who prefer not to have their former status as a "POW" or "Ex-Prisoner of War" identified by words or other markings or symbols. This section is not intended to prohibit individuals eligible for the special license plate from selecting the existing license plate design specified in subdivision (a). The design criteria for a special interest license plate pursuant to this subdivision are as follows:

(1) The license plate for a passenger vehicle, commercial vehicle, or trailer shall provide a space not larger than two inches by three inches to the left of the numerical series and a space not larger than five-eighths of an inch in height below the numerical series for a distinctive design, decal, or descriptive message as authorized by this subdivision. The license plates shall be issued in sequential numerical order or, pursuant to Section 5103, in a combination of numbers or letters.

(2) The license plate shall not identify "POW" or "Ex-Prisoner of War" by words or other markings or symbols.

(c) Special license plates may be issued pursuant to subdivision (a) only for a vehicle owned or coowned by a former American prisoner of war.

(d) Upon the death of a person issued the special license plates pursuant to this section, his or her surviving spouse may retain the special license plates subject to the conditions set forth in this section. If there is no surviving spouse, the special license plates shall be returned to the department either within 60 days following that death, or upon the expiration date of the vehicle registration, whichever date occurs first. However, in the absence of a surviving spouse, a member of the former prisoner of war's family may retain one of the special license plates as a family heirloom, subject to the conditions set forth in subdivision (i), upon submitting an affidavit to the department agreeing not to attempt to use the special license plates for vehicle registration purposes.

(e) If a surviving spouse who has elected to retain the special license plates as authorized under subdivision (d) dies while in possession of the special license plates, the special license plates shall be returned to the department either within 60 days following that death, or upon the expiration date of the vehicle registration, whichever date occurs first. However, a member of the former prisoner of war's family may retain one of the special license plates as a family heirloom, subject to the conditions set forth in subdivision (i), upon submitting an affidavit to the department agreeing not to attempt to use the special license plates for vehicle registration purposes.

(f) A vehicle exempted from fees by Section 9105 and by Section 10783 of the Revenue and Taxation Code shall lose the exemption upon the death of the former American prisoner of war, except that if a surviving spouse elects to retain the special license plates as authorized under subdivision (d), the exemption pursuant to Section 9105, and Section 10783.2 of the Revenue and Taxation Code, shall extend until the death of that spouse.

(g) Sections 5106 and 5108 do not apply to this section.

(h) The department shall recall all former prisoner-of-war special license plates issued pursuant to this section prior to January 1, 1999, and shall issue to the holder of those special license plates, without charge, the revised special license plates authorized by this section.

(i) The special license plates issued under this section are not valid for use for vehicle registration purposes or for the purposes of Section 9105 or Section 10783 or 10783.2 of the Revenue and Taxation Code by a person other than the person issued the special license plates under subdivision (a) and the surviving spouse of that person.

(j) For purposes of this section, "family" means grandparents, stepgrandparents, parents, stepparents, siblings, stepsiblings, children, and stepchildren of the person issued the special license plates under subdivision (a).

(Amended by Stats. 2010, Ch. 345, Sec. 2. (AB 498) Effective January 1, 2011.)

5101.6. (a) A person otherwise eligible under this article who is a Congressional Medal of Honor recipient may apply for special license plates for the vehicle under this article. The special license plates assigned to the vehicle shall run in a separate numerical series and shall have inscribed on the license plate the words "Congressional Medal of Honor" or "Medal of Honor." The department shall reserve and issue the special license plates to all applicants providing the proof required by subdivision (b).

(b) The applicant shall, by satisfactory proof, show that the applicant is a Congressional Medal of Honor recipient.

(c) Special license plates may be issued pursuant to subdivision (a) only for a vehicle owned or coowned by a Congressional Medal of Honor recipient.

(d) Upon the death of a person issued special license plates pursuant to this section, his or her surviving spouse may retain the special license plates subject to the conditions set forth in this section. If there is no surviving spouse, the special license plates shall be returned to the department either within 60 days following that death, or upon the expiration date of the vehicle registration, whichever date occurs first. However, in the absence of a surviving spouse, a member of the Congressional Medal of Honor recipient's family may retain one of the special license plates as a family heirloom, subject to the conditions set forth in subdivision (h), upon submitting an affidavit to the department agreeing not to attempt to use the special license plates for vehicle registration purposes.

(e) If a surviving spouse who has elected to retain the special license plates as authorized under subdivision (d) dies while in possession of the special license plates, the special license plates shall be returned to the department either within 60 days following that death, or upon the expiration date of the vehicle registration, whichever date occurs first. However, a member of the Congressional Medal of Honor recipient's family may retain one of the special license plates as a family heirloom, subject to the conditions set forth in subdivision (h), upon submitting an affidavit to the department agreeing not to attempt to use the special license plates for vehicle registration purposes.

(f) A vehicle exempted from fees by Section 9105 and by Section 10783 of the Revenue and Taxation Code shall lose the exemption upon the death of the Congressional Medal of Honor recipient, except that if a surviving spouse elects to retain the special license plates as authorized under subdivision (d), the exemption pursuant to Section 9105, and Section 10783.2 of the Revenue and Taxation Code, shall extend until the death of that spouse.

(g) Sections 5106 and 5108 do not apply to this section.

(h) The special license plates issued under this section are not valid for use for vehicle registration purposes or for the purposes of Section 9105 or Section 10783 or 10783.2 of the Revenue and Taxation Code by a person other than the person issued the special license plates under subdivision (a) and the surviving spouse of that person.

(i) For the purposes of this section, "family" means grandparents, stepgrandparents, parents, stepparents, siblings, stepsiblings, children, and stepchildren of the person issued the special license plates under subdivision (a).

(Amended by Stats. 2007, Ch. 357, Sec. 3. Effective January 1, 2008.)

5101.8. (a) Any person otherwise eligible under this article who is a Purple Heart recipient may apply for special license plates for vehicles that are not used for transportation for hire, compensation, or profit, under this article. The special plates assigned to the vehicle shall run in a separate numerical series, shall have inscribed on the plate the Purple Heart insignia, and shall contain the words "Combat Wounded" and "Purple Heart" or at least the letters "PH" as part of the numerical series. The department shall reserve and issue the special plates to all applicants providing the proof required by subdivision (b).

(b) The applicant, by satisfactory proof, shall show that the applicant is a Purple Heart recipient.

(c) Special plates may be issued pursuant to subdivision (a) only for a vehicle owned or coowned by a Purple Heart recipient.

(d) Upon the death of a person issued special license plates pursuant to this section, his or her surviving spouse may retain the special license plates subject to the conditions set forth in this section. If there is no surviving spouse, the special license plates shall be returned to the department either (1) within 60 days following that death or (2) upon the expiration of the vehicle registration, whichever occurs first. However, in the absence of a surviving spouse, another surviving member of the deceased Purple Heart recipient's family may retain one of the special license plates as a family heirloom, subject to the conditions set forth in subdivision (h).

(e) If a surviving spouse who has elected to retain the special license plates as authorized under subdivision (d) dies while in possession of the special license plates, the special license plates shall be returned to the department either within 60 days following that death, or upon the expiration date of the vehicle registration, whichever date occurs first. However, another surviving member of the deceased Purple Heart recipient's family may retain one of the special license plates as a family heirloom, subject to the conditions set forth in subdivision (h).

(f) When an applicant for the Purple Heart license plate qualifies as a disabled veteran, as specified in subdivision (b) of Section 22511.55, the applicant may also apply for a distinguishing placard described in subdivision (a) of Section 22511.55 to be used in conjunction with the Purple Heart license plate for the purpose of allowing special parking privileges pursuant to subdivision (a) of Section 22511.5.

(g) Sections 5106 and 5108 do not apply to this section.(h) The special license plates issued under this section are not valid for use for vehicle registration purposes or for the purposes of Section 9105, or Section 10783 or 10783.2 of the Revenue and Taxation Code, by a person other than the person issued the special license plates under subdivision (a) and the surviving spouse of that person.

(i) For purposes of this section, "family" means grandparents, stepgrandparents, parents, stepparents, siblings, stepsiblings, children, and stepchildren of the person issued the special license plates under subdivision (a).

(Amended by Stats. 2010, Ch. 181, Sec. 2. (SB 1295) Effective January 1, 2011.)

5101.9. (a) Until December 31, 1991, any person described in Section 5101 may apply for a set of commemorative Bicentennial of the Bill of Rights reflectorized license plates and the department shall issue those special license plates in lieu of regular license plates. No commemorative Bicentennial of the Bill of Rights reflectorized license plates shall be issued pursuant to an application submitted on or after January 1, 1992, but the holder of those plates may thereafter renew or retain them, obtain substitute replacements for them, or transfer them to another vehicle, subject to this section. However, substitute replacement plates shall not be available on or after January 1, 1997. Thereafter, unless otherwise provided by law, regular series plates shall be issued for the fee provided in Section 9265 whenever substitute plates are required.

(b) The commemorative Bicentennial of the Bill of Rights reflectorized license plates shall be of a distinctive design and shall be available in a special series of letters or numbers, or both, as determined by the department.

(c) In addition to the regular fees for an original or renewal registration, the applicant shall be charged a fee of thirty-five dollars ($35).

(d) Notwithstanding Section 9265, the applicant for substitute commemorative Bicentennial of the Bill of Rights reflectorized license plates shall be charged a fee of thirty-five dollars ($35).

(e) Whenever any person who has been issued commemorative Bicentennial of the Bill of Rights reflectorized license plates applies to the department for transfer of the plates to another vehicle, a transfer fee of fifteen dollars ($15) shall be charged in addition to all other appropriate fees.

(f) Sections 5106 and 5108 do not apply.

(Added by Stats. 1989, Ch. 312, Sec. 1. Operative July 1, 1990, by Sec. 2 of Ch. 312.)

5102. The environmental license plates shall be the same color and design as regular passenger vehicle, commercial vehicle, motorcycle, or trailer license plates, and shall consist of any combination of numbers or letters, not exceeding seven positions and not less than two positions, if there are no conflicts with existing passenger, commercial, trailer, motorcycle, or special license plates series or with Section 4851.

(Amended by Stats. 1985, Ch. 752, Sec. 2.)

5103. "Environmental license plates," as used in this article, means license plates or permanent trailer identification plates that have displayed upon them the registration number assigned to the passenger vehicle, commercial motor vehicle, motorcycle, trailer, or semitrailer for which a registration number was issued in a combination of letters or numbers, or both, requested by the owner or lessee of the vehicle.

(Amended by Stats. 2000, Ch. 861, Sec. 29.5. Effective September 29, 2000. Operative December 31, 2001, pursuant to Sec. 67 of Ch. 861.)

5104. Environmental license plates shall be issued only to the registered owner or lessee of the vehicle on which they are to be displayed.

(Amended by Stats. 1973, Ch. 265.)

5105. (a) An applicant for issuance of environmental license plates or renewal of such plates in the subsequent year pursuant to this article shall file an application therefor in such form and by such date as the department may require, indicating thereon the combination of letters or numbers, or both, requested as a registration number. There shall be no duplication of registration numbers, and the department may refuse to issue any combination of letters or numbers, or both, that may carry connotations offensive to good taste and decency or which would be misleading or a duplication of license plates provided for in Article 8 (commencing with Section 5000) of Chapter 1 of Division 3.

(b) The department may cancel and order the return of any environmental license plate heretofore or hereafter issued, containing any combination of letters, or numbers, or both, which the department determines carries connotations offensive to good taste and decency or which would be misleading. Whenever the department orders any person to return any such environmental license plate containing any combination of letters or numbers, or both, which the department determines carries connotations offensive to good taste and decency or which would be misleading, the person so ordered may, in writing and within 10 days after receiving the order, demand a hearing, which shall be granted. The provisions of Chapter 5 (commencing with Section 11500), Part 1, Division 3, Title 2 of the Government Code, shall apply to hearings provided for in this subdivision. Any person ordered to return such plates shall either be reimbursed for any additional fees he paid for the plates pursuant to Section 5106 or 5108 for the registration year in which they are recalled, or be given, at no additional cost therefor, replacement environmental license plates, the issuance of which is in compliance with this code.

(c) The department may cancel and order the return of any environmental license plate, without opportunity to be heard, as specified in subdivision (b) of this section, if the license plate issued is a duplication of license plates provided for in Article 8 (commencing with Section 5000) of Chapter 1 of Division 3 or if the fee specified under subdivision (c) of Section 5106 has not been paid.

(Amended by Stats. 1974, Ch. 692.)

5106. (a) In addition to the regular registration fee or a permanent trailer identification fee, the applicant shall be charged a fee of fifty-three dollars ($53) for issuance of environmental license plates.

(b) In addition to the regular renewal fee or a permanent trailer identification fee for the vehicle to which the plates are assigned, the applicant for a renewal of environmental license plates shall be charged an additional fee of forty-three dollars ($43). An applicant with a permanent trailer identification plate shall be charged an annual fee of forty-three dollars ($43) for renewal of environmental license plates. However, applicants for renewal of prisoner-of-war special license plates issued under Section 5101.5 shall not be charged the additional renewal fee under this subdivision.

(c) When payment of renewal fees is not required as specified in Section 4000, the holder of any environmental license plate may retain the plate upon payment of an annual fee of forty-three dollars ($43). The fee shall be due at the expiration of the registration year of the vehicle to which the environmental license plate was last assigned. However, applicants for retention of prisoner-of-war special license plates issued under Section 5101.5 shall not be charged the additional retention fee under this subdivision.

(d) Notwithstanding Section 9265, the applicant for a duplicate environmental license plate shall be charged a fee of forty-three dollars ($43).

(e) This section shall become operative on July 1, 2017.

(Repealed (in Sec. 42) and added by Stats. 2016, Ch. 340, Sec. 42.5. (SB 839) Effective September 13, 2016. Section operative July 1, 2017, by its own provisions.)

5107. (a) All revenue derived from the fees provided for in this article shall be deposited in the California Environmental License Plate Fund.

(b) Not more than fifty cents ($0.50) of the amount collected from each applicant pursuant to Section 5106 on and after January 1, 1999, shall be set aside for use, upon appropriation by the Legislature, by the appropriate agency for the purpose of increasing public awareness of the environmental license plate program.

(Amended by Stats. 1998, Ch. 326, Sec. 6. Effective August 21, 1998.)

5108. (a) Whenever any person who has been issued environmental license plates applies to the department for transfer of the plates to another passenger vehicle, commercial motor vehicle, trailer, or semitrailer, a transfer fee of forty-three dollars ($43) shall be charged in addition to all other appropriate fees.

(b) This section shall become operative on January 1, 2017.

(Repealed (in Sec. 43) and added by Stats. 2016, Ch. 340, Sec. 44. (SB 839) Effective September 13, 2016. Section operative January 1, 2017, by its own provisions.)

5109. When any person who has been issued environmental license plates sells, trades, or otherwise releases ownership of the vehicle upon which the environmental license plates have been displayed, such person shall immediately report the transfer of such plates to an acquired passenger vehicle, commercial vehicle, or trailer pursuant to Section 5108, unless such person determines to retain the plates pursuant to subdivision (c) of Section 5106.

(Amended by Stats. 1976, Ch. 935.)

5110. (a) The director may adopt rules and regulations as necessary to carry out the purposes of this article.

(b) Whenever two or more separate series of special plates are authorized under this article in a period of one year, the director shall coordinate the administrative and technical procedures for preparation and issuance of the plates in order to control costs to the maximum extent.

(Amended by Stats. 1991, Ch. 358, Sec. 2.)

5112. (a) The department shall revise its Internet Web site to provide a direct link on the homepage to information on ordering environmental license plates.

(b) The department may provide links on its Internet Web site to other Internet Web sites that have information regarding the protection and management of ocean and coastal resources and other programs that are supported with funds from the Environmental License Plate Fund.

(c) When existing supplies of forms, publications, and signs have been depleted, or if those forms, publications, and signs are required to be revised in the normal course of operations, the department shall include in the replenishing supplies or the revised forms, publications, and signs, information regarding environmental license plates and the procedures for applying for those plates. This subdivision applies only to forms, publications, and signs, that advertise, facilitate the application for, or are an application for environmental license plates.

(Added by Stats. 2004, Ch. 540, Sec. 6. Effective January 1, 2005.)

Article 8.6. Specialized License Plates

(Article 8.6 added by Stats. 2006, Ch. 454, Sec. 3.)

5151. (a) As used in this article, "state agency" means a state office, officer, department, division, bureau, board, or commission, or any other state body or agency.

(b) It is the intent of the Legislature that this article contain the authority for specialized license plates for state agencies.

(Added by Stats. 2006, Ch. 454, Sec. 3. Effective January 1, 2007.)

5152. A person described in Section 5101 may apply for a specialized license plate under this article, in lieu of regular license plates.

(Added by Stats. 2006, Ch. 454, Sec. 3. Effective January 1, 2007.)

5154. Specialized license plates issued under this article shall have a design or contain a message that publicizes or promotes a state agency, or the official policy, mission, or work of a state agency.

(Added by Stats. 2006, Ch. 454, Sec. 3. Effective January 1, 2007.)

5155. The design criteria for a specialized license plate are as follows:

(a) Except as provided in Section 5161, the license plate for a passenger vehicle, commercial vehicle, or trailer shall provide a space not larger than two inches by three inches to the left of the numerical series and a space not larger than five-eighths of an inch in height below the numerical series for a distinctive design, decal, or descriptive message as authorized by this article. The license plates shall be issued in sequential numerical order or, pursuant to Section 5103, in a combination of numbers or letters.

(b) Specialized license plates authorized under this article may be issued for use on a motorcycle. That license plate shall contain a five-digit configuration issued in sequential numerical order or, pursuant to Section 5103, in a combination of numbers or letters. There shall be a space to the left of the numerical series for a distinctive design or decal and the characters shall contrast sharply with the uniform background color. A motorcycle plate containing a full plate graphic design is not authorized.

(c) Specialized license plates may be issued as environmental license plates, as defined in Section 5103.

(Amended by Stats. 2012, Ch. 39, Sec. 112. (SB 1018) Effective June 27, 2012.)

5156. (a) (1) A state agency may apply to the department to sponsor a specialized license plate program, and the department shall issue specialized license plates for that program, if the agency complies with all of the requirements of this article.

(2) The department shall not issue specialized license plates to a state agency for a vehicle that is exempt from the payment of registration fees pursuant to Section 9101 or 9103.

(b) Except as provided in subdivision (d), the department shall not establish a specialized license plate program for an agency until the department has received not less than 7,500 applications for that agency's specialized license plates. The agency shall collect and hold applications for the plates. Once the agency has received at least 7,500 applications, it shall submit the applications, along with the necessary fees, to the department. The department shall not issue a specialized license plate until the agency has received and submitted to the department not less than 7,500 applications for that particular specialized license plate within the time period prescribed in this section. Advance payment to the department by the agency representing the department's estimated or actual administrative costs associated with the issuance of a particular specialized license plate shall not constitute compliance with this requirement. The agency shall have 12 months, following the date of approval of the agency's initial application to sponsor a specialized license plate program, to receive the required number of applications. If, after that 12 months, 7,500 applications have not been received, the agency shall immediately do either of the following:

(1) Refund to all applicants all fees or deposits that have been collected.

(2) Contact the department to indicate the agency's intent to undertake collection of additional applications and fees or deposits for an additional period, not to exceed 12 months, in order to obtain the minimum 7,500 applications. If the agency elects to exercise the option under this subparagraph, it shall contact each applicant who has submitted an application with the appropriate fees or deposits to determine if the applicant wishes a refund of fees or deposits or requests the continuance of the holding of the application and fees or deposits until that time that the agency has received 7,500 applications. The agency shall refund the fees or deposits to an applicant so requesting. The agency shall not collect and hold applications for a period exceeding 24 months following the date of approval of the agency's initial application to sponsor a specialized license plate program.

(c) (1) If the number of outstanding and valid specialized license plates in a particular program, except as provided in subdivision (d), provided for in this article is less than 7,500, the department shall notify the sponsoring agency of that fact and shall inform the agency that if that number is less than 7,500 one year from the date of that notification, the department will no longer issue or replace those specialized license plates.

(2) Those particular specialized license plates that were issued prior to the discontinuation provided by paragraph (1) may continue to be used and attached to the vehicle for which they were issued and may be renewed, retained, or transferred pursuant to this code.

(d) (1) The Department of Veterans Affairs may sponsor a Gold Star Family specialized license plate program and the department may establish this specialized license plate program in the absence of 7,500 paid applications as provided in subdivision (d) of Section 5157.

(2) The Department of Veterans Affairs shall, upon receiving proof of eligibility from an applicant, authorize the department to issue Gold Star Family specialized license plates for a vehicle owned by an eligible family member of a member of the Armed Forces of the United States who was killed in the line of duty while on active duty during wartime service, or during an international terrorist attack that has been recognized by the United States Secretary of Defense as an attack against the United States or a foreign nation friendly to the United States, or during military operations while serving outside the United States, including commonwealths, territories, and possessions of the United States, or as part of a peacekeeping force, which includes personnel assigned to a force engaged in a peacekeeping operation authorized by the United Nations Security Council. An eligible family member is defined as all of the following:

(A) A person who is otherwise eligible under this article to register a motor vehicle.

(B) A person who shows proof from the United States Department of Veterans Affairs or the Department of Defense that the member who was in the Armed Forces of the United States was killed in the line of duty while on active duty in the military.

(C) A person who bears, and shows proof satisfactory to the Department of Veterans Affairs of, one of the following relationships to the member of the Armed Forces killed in the line of duty while serving on active duty:

(i) Widow.

(ii) Widower.

(iii) Biological parent.

(iv) Adoptive parent.

(v) Stepparent.

(vi) Foster parent in loco parentis.

(vii) Biological child.

(viii) Adoptive child.

(ix) Stepchild.

(x) Sibling.

(xi) Half-sibling.

(xii) Grandparent.

(xiii) Grandchild.

(3) Upon the death of a person issued a Gold Star Family specialized license plate, the license plate shall be transferred to the surviving spouse, if he or she requests, or shall be returned to the department within 60 days after the death of the plateholder or upon the expiration of the vehicle registration, whichever occurs first.

(e) (1) The Department of Veterans Affairs shall apply to the department to sponsor a veterans specialized license plate program, and the department shall issue license plates for that program if the Department of Veterans Affairs meets the requirements prescribed by this section.

(2) The design of the veterans specialized license plate shall be identical to the design of the veterans special interest license plate issued pursuant to Section 5068 on or before January 1, 2010, and the decals for the plate shall be identical to those offered pursuant to Section 5068.

(3) Notwithstanding Section 5157, in addition to the regular fees for an original registration, a renewal of registration, or a transfer of registration, the following fees shall be paid by individuals applying for a special interest license plate or a decal issued under this subdivision:

(A) Fifty dollars ($50) for the initial issuance of the plates and decals. The plates shall be permanent and shall not be required to be replaced.

(B) Forty dollars ($40) for each renewal of registration that includes the continued display of the plates or decals.

(C) Fifteen dollars ($15) for transfer of the plates to another vehicle.

(D) Thirty-five dollars ($35) for replacement plates, if they become damaged or unserviceable.

(E) Ten dollars ($10) for replacement decals, if they become damaged or unserviceable.

(F) Seventy-eight dollars ($78) for the personalization of the plates.

(4) After deducting its administrative costs under this subdivision, the department shall deposit the revenue derived from the additional fees provided in paragraph (3) in the Veterans Service Office Fund created by Section 972.2 of the Military and Veterans Code.

(Amended by Stats. 2013, Ch. 690, Sec. 1. (AB 244) Effective January 1, 2014.)

5156.5. (a) The Office of Emergency Services shall apply to the department to sponsor a domestic violence and sexual assault awareness license plate program pursuant to this article.

(b) The fees specified in Section 5157 shall be imposed for the issuance, renewal, or transfer of specialized license plates authorized by this section. Notwithstanding subdivision (c) of Section 5157, after deducting its administrative costs, the department shall deposit the revenue derived from the additional fees into the California Domestic Violence and Sexual Assault Prevention Fund, which is hereby established in the State Treasury. Upon appropriation by the Legislature, the moneys in that fund shall be allocated to the Office of Emergency Services for purposes of funding the Family Violence Prevention Program described in Section 13823.4 of, and the sexual assault services programs described in Section 13837 of, the Penal Code.

(Amended by Stats. 2015, Ch. 268, Sec. 1. (AB 1338) Effective January 1, 2016.)

5156.7. (a) The State Department of Health Care Services shall apply to the department, pursuant to Section 5156, to sponsor a breast cancer awareness license plate program. The department shall issue specialized license plates for that program if the State Department of Health Care Services complies with the requirements of Section 5156.

(b) The State Department of Health Care Services may accept and use donated artwork from California artists for the license plate.

(c) Notwithstanding subdivision (c) of Section 5157, the additional fees prescribed by Section 5157 for the issuance, renewal, or transfer of the specialized license plates shall be deposited, after the department deducts its administrative costs, in the Breast Cancer Control Account in the Breast Cancer Fund established pursuant to Section 30461.6 of the Revenue and Taxation Code.

(d) It is the intent of the Legislature that the department, in consultation with the State Department of Health Care Services, will design and make available for issuance pursuant to this article special breast cancer awareness license plates. Specifically, it is the intent of the Legislature that the license plates issued pursuant to this section consist of a pink breast cancer awareness ribbon to the left of the numerical series and a breast cancer awareness message, such as, "Early Detection Saves Lives," below the numerical series.

(Amended by Stats. 2015, Ch. 303, Sec. 535. (AB 731) Effective January 1, 2016.)

5157. (a) In addition to the regular fees for an original registration or renewal of registration, the following additional fees shall be paid for the issuance, renewal, or transfer of the specialized license plates:

(1) For the original issuance of the plates, fifty dollars ($50).

(2) For a renewal of registration with the plates, forty dollars ($40).

(3) For transfer of the plates to another vehicle, fifteen dollars ($15).

(4) For each substitute replacement plate, thirty-five dollars ($35).

(5) In addition, for the issuance of environmental license plates, as defined in Section 5103, with a specialized license plate design, the additional fees prescribed in Sections 5106 and 5108. The additional fees prescribed in Sections 5106 and 5108 shall be deposited in the California Environmental License Plate Fund.

(b) The Gold Star Family specialized license plate program as provided in subdivision (d) of Section 5156 shall not be subject to the fees specified in paragraphs (1), (2), and (5) of subdivision (a) and shall only be issued in a sequential series.

(c) Except as provided in paragraph (5) of subdivision (a), and after deducting its administrative costs under this section, the department shall deposit the additional revenue derived from the issuance, renewal, transfer, and substitution of the specialized license plates in the Specialized License Plate Fund, which is hereby established in the State Treasury. Upon appropriation by the Legislature, the moneys in that fund shall be allocated to each sponsoring agency, in proportion to the amount in the fund that is attributable to the agency's specialized license plate program. Except as authorized under Section 5159, the sponsoring agency shall expend all funds received under this section exclusively for projects and programs that promote the state agency's official policy, mission, or work.

(d) (1) The Department of Veterans Affairs may actively request and receive donations for the Gold Star Family License Plate Account which is hereby created in the Specialized License Plate Fund and which may consist of donations from public and private entities. Earnings generated by the Gold Star Family License Plate Account shall be retained by the account.

(2) Upon the determination of the department that there are sufficient funds in the Gold Star Family License Plate Account for this purpose, moneys in the Gold Star Family License Plate Account shall be available, upon appropriation by the Legislature, to the department for the necessary administrative costs of establishing the Gold Star Family specialized license plate program.

(Amended by Stats. 2008, Ch. 309, Sec. 3. Effective January 1, 2009.)

5158. When payment of renewal fees is not required as specified in Section 4000, or when a person determines to retain the specialized license plate upon a sale, trade, or other release of the vehicle upon which the plate has been displayed, the person shall notify the department and the person may retain and use the plate as authorized by departmental regulations.

(Added by Stats. 2006, Ch. 454, Sec. 3. Effective January 1, 2007.)

5159. A state agency that is eligible to participate in a specialized license plate program pursuant to this article and receives funds from the additional fees collected from the sale of specialized plates shall not expend annually more than 25 percent of those funds on administrative costs, marketing, or other promotional activities associated with encouraging application for, or renewal of, the specialized plates.

(Added by Stats. 2006, Ch. 454, Sec. 3. Effective January 1, 2007.)

5160. (a) A state agency authorized under this article to offer specialized license plates shall prepare and submit an annual accounting report to the department by June 30. The report shall include an accounting of all revenues and expenditures associated with the specialized license plate program.

(b) If a state agency submits a report pursuant to subdivision (a) indicating that the agency violated the expenditure restriction set forth in Section 5159, the department shall immediately cease depositing fees for that agency's specialized license plate program in the Specialized License Plate Fund established under Section 5157 and, instead, shall deposit those fees that would have otherwise been deposited in that fund in a separate fund created by the Controller, which fund is subject to appropriation by the Legislature. The department shall immediately notify the agency of this course of action. The depositing of funds in the account established pursuant to this subdivision shall continue until the agency demonstrates to the satisfaction of the department that the agency is in compliance or will comply with the requirements of Section 5159. If one year from the date that the agency receives the notice described in this subdivision, the agency is still unable to satisfactorily demonstrate to the department that it is in compliance or will comply with Section 5159, the department shall no longer issue or replace those specialized license plates associated with that agency. Those particular specialized license plates that were issued prior to the discontinuation provided by this subdivision may continue to be used and attached to the vehicle for which they were issued and may be renewed, retained, or transferred pursuant to this code.

(c) Upon receiving the reports required under subdivision (a), notwithstanding Section 7550.5 of the Government Code, the department shall prepare and transmit an annual consolidated report to the Legislature containing the revenue and expenditure data.

(Amended by Stats. 2007, Ch. 130, Sec. 233. Effective January 1, 2008.)

5161. (a) The department, in consultation with the Department of Parks and Recreation, shall design and make available for issuance pursuant to this article special state parks environmental design license plates as described in this section. Notwithstanding Section 5155, the special state parks environmental design license plates shall bear a full-plate graphic design that the department determines, in consultation with the Department of the California Highway Patrol, does not obscure the readability of the license plate depicting a California redwood tree design as an iconic feature of California's state park system, as approved by the Department of Parks and Recreation. The Department of Parks and Recreation may accept and use donated artwork from California artists for purposes of this requirement. Any person described in Section 5101 may, upon payment of the additional fees set forth in subdivision (b), apply for and be issued a set of special state parks environmental design license plates. The special state parks environmental design license plates may be issued as environmental license plates, as defined in Section 5103.

(b) In addition to the regular fees for an original registration or renewal of registration, the following additional fees shall be paid for the issuance, renewal, or transfer of the special state parks environmental design license plates authorized pursuant to this section:

(1) For the original issuance of the plates, fifty dollars ($50).

(2) For a renewal of registration with the plates, forty dollars ($40).

(3) For transfer of the plates to another vehicle, fifteen dollars ($15).

(4) For each substitute replacement plate, thirty-five dollars ($35).

(5) In addition, for the issuance of environmental license plates, as defined in Section 5103, with a full-plate graphic design described in subdivision (a), the additional fees prescribed in Sections 5106 and 5108. The additional fees prescribed in Sections 5106 and 5108 shall be deposited in the Environmental License Plate Fund.

(c) Except as provided in paragraph (5) of subdivision (b), and after deducting its administrative costs under this section, the department shall deposit the additional revenue derived from the issuance, renewal, transfer, and substitution of special environmental design license plates in the California State Parks Account, which is hereby created in the Specialized License Plate Fund. Upon appropriation by the Legislature, the money in the account shall be allocated by the Controller to the Department of Parks and Recreation for expenditure for the exclusive trust purposes of preservation and restoration of California state parks.

(d) The Department of Parks and Recreation shall collect and hold applications for the special state parks environmental license plates described in this section. The department shall not be required to make the special state parks environmental license plates available for issuance pursuant to this section until the Department of Parks and Recreation has submitted not less than 7,500 applications for the plates to the department.

(Added by Stats. 2012, Ch. 39, Sec. 113. (SB 1018) Effective June 27, 2012.)

5162. The State Department of Public Health shall apply to the department to sponsor a kidney disease awareness license plate program pursuant to this article.

(Added by Stats. 2014, Ch. 359, Sec. 1. (AB 2450) Effective January 1, 2015.)

5163. (a) The Department of Fish and Wildlife shall apply to the department, pursuant to Section 5156, to sponsor a Salton Sea license plate program. The department shall issue specialized license plates for that program if the Department of Fish and Wildlife complies with the requirements of Section 5156.

(b) Notwithstanding subdivision (c) of Section 5157, the additional fees prescribed by Section 5157 for the issuance, renewal, or transfer of the specialized license plates shall be deposited, after the department deducts its administrative costs, in the Salton Sea Restoration Account, which is hereby created in the Specialized License Plate Fund. The funds in the account shall be used, upon appropriation by the Legislature to the Salton Sea Authority, for restoration of the Salton Sea.

(Added by Stats. 2014, Ch. 353, Sec. 1. (AB 1096) Effective January 1, 2015.)

5168. (a) The fees specified in Section 5157 shall be imposed for the issuance, renewal, or transfer of the Pet Lover's specialized license plates. Notwithstanding subdivision (c) of Section 5157, after deducting its administrative costs, the department shall deposit the revenue derived from the additional fees into the Pet Lover's Fund, which is hereby established in the Specialized License Plate Fund.

(b) Upon appropriation by the Legislature, the moneys in the Pet Lover's Fund shall be allocated to the Department of Food and Agriculture. There shall not be an allocation to the Department of Food and Agriculture pursuant to subdivision (c) of Section 5157.

(c) The Department of Food and Agriculture shall allocate those grant funds to eligible veterinary facilities that offer low-cost or no-cost animal sterilization services.

(1) In administering the grants, the Department of Food and Agriculture may prioritize both of the following:

(A) Eligible veterinary facilities located in or serving underserved communities or those that can demonstrate financial need.

(B) Eligible veterinary facilities that have previously provided or currently provide low-cost or no-cost animal sterilization services.

(2) For the purposes of this subdivision, "eligible veterinary facilities" mean those facilities that are all of the following:

(A) Registered and in good standing with the Veterinary Medical Board, pursuant to Section 4853 of the Business and Professions Code.

(B) Overseen by a responsible licensee manager licensed and in good standing with the Veterinary Medical Board, pursuant to Chapter 11 (commencing with Section 4800) of Division 2 of the Business and Professions Code.

(C) (i) Operated by a city, county, city and county, an animal care or control agency, or a nonprofit meeting the requirements of Section 501(c)(3) of the federal Internal Revenue Code that is registered and in good standing with the Secretary of State.

(ii) A city, county, or city and county animal control agency or nonprofit shelter holding a municipal contract that offers spay and neuter services for dogs and cats owned by individual members of the public is required to be current on its yearly rabies reporting requirements to the State Department of Public Health, Veterinary Public Health Section.

(d) Annual administrative costs for the program shall not exceed 25 percent of the funds collected from the issuance of the Pet Lover's license plates, and may include funds for marketing and other promotional activities associated with encouraging application for, or renewal of, Pet Lover's license plates and collaboration expenses. The Department of Food and Agriculture may contract with an eligible nonprofit organization to perform the marketing and promotional activities authorized.

(1) The eligible nonprofit organization selected by the Department of Food and Agriculture pursuant to this subdivision shall not use more than 5 percent of the moneys received pursuant to this section for administrative costs.

(2) For the purposes of this subdivision, "eligible nonprofit organization" means a nonprofit entity that is all of the following:

(A) Qualifies for tax exempt status under Section 501(c)(3) of the Internal Revenue Code and subdivision (b) of Section 23701 of the Revenue and Taxation Code.

(B) Registered and in good standing with the Secretary of State.

(C) Chaptered and headquartered in this state.

(D) Has demonstrated experience in advertising, marketing, and promoting specialized license plates in existence prior to 2016 pursuant to this article.

(e) The Department of Food and Agriculture shall determine eligibility requirements for the grants, establish the grant application process, and develop program specifics. The Department of Food and Agriculture shall collaborate with an eligible nonprofit organization, as defined in paragraph (2) of subdivision (d), to provide advice and consultation for the purposes of developing and implementing the grant program. The Department of Food and Agriculture shall administer and oversee the grant program.

(Amended by Stats. 2020, Ch. 59, Sec. 7. (SB 934) Effective January 1, 2021.)

5169. (a) The California Cultural and Historical Endowment shall apply to the department to sponsor a license plate program pursuant to this article.

(b) The fees specified in Section 5157 shall be imposed for the issuance, renewal, or transfer of specialized license plates authorized by this section. Notwithstanding subdivision (c) of Section 5157, after deducting its administrative costs, the department shall deposit the revenue derived from the additional fees into the California Cultural and Historical Endowment Fund to fund the grant program described in Section 20092 of the Education Code.

(Added by Stats. 2016, Ch. 208, Sec. 9. (AB 2906) Effective January 1, 2017.)

Article 9. Display of Plates, Tabs, and Stickers

(Article 9 enacted by Stats. 1959, Ch. 3.)

5200. (a) When two license plates are issued by the department for use upon a vehicle, they shall be attached to the vehicle for which they were issued, one in the front and the other in the rear.

(b) When only one license plate is issued for use upon a vehicle, it shall be attached to the rear thereof, unless the license plate is issued for use upon a truck tractor, in which case the license plate shall be displayed in accordance with Section 4850.5.

(Amended by Stats. 2003, Ch. 594, Sec. 27. Effective January 1, 2004.)

5201. (a) License plates, including temporary license plates, shall at all times be securely fastened to the vehicle for which they are issued so as to prevent the plates from swinging, shall be mounted in a position so as to be clearly visible, and so that the characters are upright and display from left to right, and shall be maintained in a condition so as to be clearly legible. The rear license plate shall be mounted not less than 12 inches nor more than 60 inches from the ground, and the front license plate shall be mounted not more than 60 inches from the ground, except as follows:

(1) The rear license plate on a tow truck or repossessor's tow vehicle may be mounted on the left-hand side of the mast assembly at the rear of the cab of the vehicle, not less than 12 inches nor more than 90 inches from the ground.

(2) The rear license plate on a tank vehicle hauling hazardous waste, as defined in Section 25117 of the Health and Safety Code, or asphalt material may be mounted not less than 12 inches nor more than 90 inches from the ground.

(3) The rear license plate on a truck tractor may be mounted at the rear of the cab of the vehicle, but not less than 12 inches nor more than 90 inches from the ground.

(4) The rear license plate of a vehicle designed by the manufacturer for the collection and transportation of garbage, rubbish, or refuse that is used regularly for the collection and transportation of that material by a person or governmental entity employed to collect, transport, and dispose of garbage, rubbish, or refuse may be mounted not less than 12 inches nor more than 90 inches from the ground.

(5) The rear license plate on a two-axle livestock trailer may be mounted 12 inches or more, but not more than 90 inches, from the ground.

(6) (A) The rear license plate on a dump bed motortruck equipped with a trailing, load bearing swing axle shall be mounted more than 12 inches, but not more than 107 inches, from the ground.

(B) As used in this section, a trailing, load bearing swing axle is an axle which can be moved from a raised position to a position behind the vehicle that allows for the transfer of a portion of the weight of the vehicle and load to the trailing axle.

(b) Temporary license plates shall be replaced with permanent license plates upon receipt of the permanent license plates, and the temporary license plates shall be destroyed at that time.

(c) A covering shall not be used on license plates except as follows:

(1) The installation of a cover over a lawfully parked vehicle to protect it from the weather and the elements does not constitute a violation of this subdivision. A peace officer or other regularly salaried employee of a public agency designated to enforce laws, including local ordinances, relating to the parking of vehicles may temporarily remove so much of the cover as is necessary to inspect any license plate, tab, or indicia of registration on a vehicle.

(2) The installation of a license plate security cover is not a violation of this subdivision if the device does not obstruct or impair the recognition of the license plate information, including, but not limited to, the issuing state, license plate number, and registration tabs, and the cover is limited to the area directly over the top of the registration tabs. No portion of a license plate security cover shall rest over the license plate number.

(d) A casing, shield, frame, border, shade, tint, product, or other device that obstructs or impairs the reading or recognition of a license plate by an electronic device operated by state or local law enforcement, an electronic device operated in connection with a toll road, high-occupancy toll lane, toll bridge, or other toll facility, or a remote emission sensing device, as specified in Sections 44081 and 44081.6 of the Health and Safety Code, shall not be installed on, or affixed to, a vehicle.

(e) (1) It is the intent of the Legislature that an accommodation be made to persons with disabilities and to those persons who regularly transport persons with disabilities, to allow the removal and relocation of wheelchair lifts and wheelchair carriers without the necessity of removing and reattaching the vehicle's rear license plate. Therefore, it is not a violation of this section if the reading or recognition of a rear license plate is obstructed or impaired by a wheelchair lift or wheelchair carrier and all of the following requirements are met:

(A) The owner of the vehicle has been issued a special identification license plate pursuant to Section 5007, or the person using the wheelchair that is carried on the vehicle has been issued a distinguishing placard under Section 22511.55.

(B) (i) The operator of the vehicle displays a decal, designed and issued by the department, that contains the license plate number assigned to the vehicle transporting the wheelchair.

(ii) The decal is displayed on the rear window of the vehicle, in a location determined by the department, in consultation with the Department of the California Highway Patrol, so as to be clearly visible to law enforcement.

(2) Notwithstanding any other law, if a decal is displayed pursuant to this subdivision, the requirements of this code that require the illumination of the license plate and the license plate number do not apply.

(3) The department shall adopt regulations governing the procedures for accepting and approving applications for decals, and issuing decals, authorized by this subdivision.

(4) This subdivision does not apply to a front license plate.

(f) This section shall become operative January 1, 2019.

(Amended by Stats. 2025, Ch. 179, Sec. 1. (AB 1085) Effective January 1, 2026.)

5201.1. (a) A person shall not sell or manufacture a product or device in this state that obscures, or is intended to obscure, the reading or recognition of a license plate by visual means, or by an electronic device as prohibited by subdivision (c) or (d) of Section 5201.

(b) A person shall not operate a vehicle with a product or device that violates subdivision (a).

(c) A person shall not erase the reflective coating of, paint over the reflective coating of, or alter a license plate to avoid visual or electronic capture of the license plate or its characters.

(d) (1) A conviction for a violation of subdivision (a) is punishable by a fine of one thousand dollars ($1,000) per item sold or manufactured.

(2) A conviction for a violation of subdivision (b) or (c) is punishable by a fine of two hundred fifty dollars ($250) per violation.

(Amended by Stats. 2025, Ch. 179, Sec. 2. (AB 1085) Effective January 1, 2026.)

5202. (a) A license plate issued by this state or any other jurisdiction within or without the United States shall be attached upon receipt and remain attached during the period of its validity to the vehicle for which it is issued while being operated within this state or during the time the vehicle is being held for sale in this state, or until the time that a vehicle with special or identification plates is no longer entitled to those plates; and a person shall not operate, and an owner shall not knowingly permit to be operated, upon any highway, a vehicle unless the license plate is so attached. A special permit or temporary license plate issued in lieu of permanent license plates shall be attached and displayed on the vehicle for which the permit or temporary license plate was issued until the temporary license plate or the special permit expires, or the permanent license plates are received, whichever occurs first.

(b) This section shall become operative January 1, 2019.

(Repealed (in Sec. 17) and added by Stats. 2016, Ch. 90, Sec. 18. (AB 516) Effective January 1, 2017. Section operative January 1, 2019, by its own provisions.)

5203. This chapter does not apply to plates which the department pursuant to law has ordered to be surrendered, transferred to another vehicle, or removed.

(Enacted by Stats. 1959, Ch. 3.)

5204. (a) (1) Except as provided by subdivisions (b) and (c), a tab shall indicate the year of expiration and a tab shall indicate the month of expiration. Current month and year tabs shall be attached to the rear license plate assigned to the vehicle for the last preceding registration year in which license plates were issued, and, when so attached, the license plate with the tabs shall, for the purposes of this code, be deemed to be the license plate, except that truck tractors, and commercial motor vehicles having a declared gross vehicle weight of 10,001 pounds or more, shall display the current month and year tabs upon the front license plate assigned to the truck tractor or commercial motor vehicle. Vehicles that fail to display current month and year tabs or display expired tabs are in violation of this section.

(2) (A) (i) A violation of paragraph (1) shall not be the sole basis for any enforcement action before the second month after the month of expiration of the vehicle's registration.

(ii) Notwithstanding clause (i), if a vehicle is stopped for any other violation of this code, enforcement action for a violation of paragraph (1) may be taken before the second month following the month of expiration.

(B) This paragraph shall be operative from July 1, 2024, to January 1, 2030, inclusive.

(b) The requirement of subdivision (a) that the tabs indicate the year and the month of expiration does not apply to fleet vehicles subject to Article 9.5 (commencing with Section 5301) or vehicles defined in Section 468.

(c) Subdivision (a) does not apply when proper application for registration has been made pursuant to Section 4602 and the new indicia of current registration have not been received from the department.

(d) This section is enforceable against any motor vehicle that is driven, moved, or left standing upon a highway, or in an offstreet public parking facility, in the same manner as provided in subdivision (a) of Section 4000.

(e) Prior to issuing a citation for a violation of this section, a law enforcement officer shall verify, using available department records, that no current registration exists for that vehicle. A citation shall not be issued for failure to comply with this section against any vehicle that has a current registration on file with the department.

(Amended by Stats. 2023, Ch. 297, Sec. 2. (AB 256) Effective January 1, 2024.)

5204.5. The department shall post on its Internet Web site, and any other appropriate online venue used by the department for public outreach, detailed instructions for motorists that describe how to prevent theft of the tabs described in Section 5204.

(Added by Stats. 2016, Ch. 776, Sec. 3. (SB 773) Effective January 1, 2017.)

5205. The department may make appropriate rules and regulations for the use and display of stickers or devices issued in lieu of license plates, and shall publish a summary thereof.

(Enacted by Stats. 1959, Ch. 3.)

5205.5. (a) (1) For purposes of implementing Section 21655.9, the department shall make available for issuance, for a fee determined by the department to be sufficient to reimburse the department for the reasonable costs incurred pursuant to this section, and pursuant to the eligibility provisions in subdivision (b), distinctive decals, labels, and other identifiers that clearly distinguish the following vehicles from other vehicles:

(A) A vehicle that meets the state's super ultra-low emission vehicle (SULEV) standard for exhaust emissions and the federal inherently low-emission vehicle (ILEV) evaporative emission standard, as defined in Part 88 (commencing with Section 88.101-94) of Title 40 of the Code of Federal Regulations.

(B) A vehicle that was produced during the 2004 model year or earlier and meets the state's ultra-low emission vehicle (ULEV) standard for exhaust emissions and the federal ILEV standard. A decal, label, or other identifier issued pursuant to this paragraph is valid until January 1, 2019.

(C) A vehicle that meets the state's enhanced advanced technology partial zero-emission vehicle (enhanced AT PZEV) standard or transitional zero-emission vehicle (TZEV) standard.

(2) (A) A decal, label, or other identifier issued pursuant to subparagraph (A) or (C) of paragraph (1) before January 1, 2017, is valid until January 1, 2019.

(B) (i) A decal, label, or other identifier issued pursuant to subparagraph (A) or (C) of paragraph (1) on or after January 1, 2017, and before March 1, 2018, is valid until January 1, 2019.

(ii) A decal, label, or other identifier issued pursuant to subparagraph (A) or (C) of paragraph (1) between March 1, 2018, and January 1, 2019, is valid until January 1, 2022.

(iii) A decal, label, or other identifier issued pursuant to subparagraph (A) or (C) of paragraph (1) on or after March 1, 2018, for a vehicle that had been issued a decal, label, or other identifier pursuant to subparagraph (A) or (C) of paragraph (1) between January 1, 2017, and March 1, 2018, is valid until January 1, 2022.

(C) Except as provided in clause (iii) of subparagraph (B), a decal, label, or other identifier issued pursuant to subparagraph (A) or (C) of paragraph (1) on or after January 1, 2019, is valid until January 1 of the fourth year after the year of issuance.

(3) (A) Notwithstanding the validity timeframe specified in clause (iii) of subparagraph (B) of paragraph (2), commencing January 1, 2020, and until January 1, 2024, a decal, label, or other identifier may be issued pursuant to subparagraph (A) or (C) of paragraph (1) for a vehicle that had previously been issued a decal, label, or other identifier, and the decal, label, or other identifier shall be valid until January 1, 2024, if the applicant for the decal, label, or other identifier has a household income at or below 80 percent of the state median income, as designated by the Department of Housing and Community Development's list of state income limits adopted pursuant to Section 50093 of the Health and Safety Code. The determination of income eligibility shall be made by a governmental or nonprofit entity selected by the department, in a format prescribed by the department.

(B) A person who obtained a decal, label, or other identifier for a vehicle prior to January 1, 2017, shall not be issued another decal, label, or other identifier pursuant to this paragraph, notwithstanding the person's qualifying income.

(C) The department shall report to the Legislature the number of decals, labels, and other identifiers issued pursuant to this paragraph. The report shall be issued after January 1, 2023, but before June 1, 2023.

(4) Except as provided in clause (iii) of subparagraph (B) of paragraph (2) and paragraph (3), a vehicle shall not be issued a decal, label, or other identifier more than once.

(b) (1) The department shall not issue a decal, label, or other identifier to an applicant who has received a consumer rebate pursuant to the Clean Vehicle Rebate Project, established as part of the Air Quality Improvement Program pursuant to Article 3 (commencing with Section 44274) of Chapter 8.9 of Part 5 of Division 26 of the Health and Safety Code, for a vehicle purchased on or after January 1, 2018, unless the rebate was issued to a buyer whose gross annual income falls below one hundred fifty thousand dollars ($150,000) for a person who files a tax return as a single person, two hundred four thousand dollars ($204,000) for a person who files a tax return as a head of household, and three hundred thousand dollars ($300,000) for a person who files a joint tax return.

(2) The department shall collaborate with the State Air Resources

Board to establish procedures to implement this subdivision, including, but not limited to, all of the following:

(A) The application form for a decal, label, or other identifier issued pursuant to this section and the application for a rebate under the Clean Vehicle Rebate Project shall include a statement indicating that the applicant cannot participate in both programs unless the applicant meets the income restrictions in paragraph (1). Each application shall require the applicant to provide a signature to confirm that the applicant understands this condition.

(B) Notify consumers of the eligibility criteria and conditions using existing education and outreach efforts.

(C) Establish appropriate compliance and enforcement measures.

(D) Establish information sharing between the department and the board to implement the requirements of this subdivision.

(c) The department shall include a summary of the provisions of this section on each motor vehicle registration renewal notice, or on a separate insert, if space is available and the summary can be included without incurring additional printing or postage costs.

(d) The Department of Transportation shall remove individual HOV lanes, or portions of those lanes, during periods of peak congestion from the access provisions provided in subdivision (a), following a finding by the Department of Transportation as follows:

(1) The lane, or portion of the lane, exceeds a level of service C, as discussed in subdivision (b) of Section 65089 of the Government Code.

(2) The operation or projected operation of the vehicles described in subdivision (a) in these lanes, or portions of those lanes, will significantly increase congestion.

(3) The finding shall also demonstrate the infeasibility of alleviating the congestion by other means, including, but not limited to, reducing the use of the lane by noneligible vehicles or further increasing vehicle occupancy.

(e) The State Air Resources Board shall publish and maintain a list of all vehicles eligible for participation in the programs described in this section. The board shall provide that list to the department.

(f) (1) For purposes of subdivision (a), the Department of the California Highway Patrol and the department, in consultation with the Department of Transportation, shall design and specify the placement of the decal, label, or other identifier on the vehicle. Each decal, label, or other identifier issued for a vehicle shall display a unique number, which shall be printed on, or affixed to, the vehicle registration.

(2) Except as provided in clause (iii) of subparagraph (B) of paragraph (2) of subdivision (a), decals, labels, or other identifiers issued pursuant to subparagraph (A) or (C) of paragraph (1) of subdivision (a) before January 1, 2019, shall be distinguishable from the decals, labels, or other identifiers issued on or after January 1, 2019.

(g) If the Metropolitan Transportation Commission, serving as the Bay Area Toll Authority, grants toll-free and reduced-rate passage on toll bridges under its jurisdiction to a vehicle pursuant to Section 30102.5 of the Streets and Highways Code, it shall also grant the same toll-free and reduced-rate passage to a vehicle displaying a valid identifier issued by the department pursuant to subparagraph (A) or (B) of paragraph (1) of subdivision (a).

(h) (1) Notwithstanding Section 21655.9, and except as provided in paragraph (2), a vehicle described in subdivision (a) that displays a valid decal, label, or identifier issued pursuant to this section shall be granted a toll-free or reduced-rate passage in high-occupancy toll lanes as described in Section 149.7 of the Streets and Highways Code unless prohibited by federal law.

(2) (A) Paragraph (1) does not apply to the imposition of a toll imposed for passage on a toll road or toll highway, that is not a high-occupancy toll lane as described in Section 149.7 of the Streets and Highways Code.

(B) Paragraph (1) does not apply to the imposition of a toll charged for crossing a state-owned bridge.

(i) If the Director of Transportation determines that federal law does not authorize the state to allow vehicles that are identified by distinctive decals, labels, or other identifiers on vehicles described in subdivision (a) to use highway lanes or highway access ramps for high-occupancy vehicles regardless of vehicle occupancy, the Director of Transportation shall submit a notice of that determination to the Secretary of State.

(j) This section shall become inoperative on the date the federal authorization pursuant to Section 166 of Title 23 of the United States Code expires, or the date the Secretary of State receives the notice described in subdivision (i), whichever occurs first.

(k) If this section becomes inoperative pursuant to subdivision (j) the driver of a vehicle with an otherwise valid decal, label, or other identifier issued pursuant to this section shall not be cited for a violation of Section 21655.9 within 60 days of the date that this section becomes inoperative.

(l) This section shall remain in effect only until January 1, 2027, and as of that date is repealed.

(Amended by Stats. 2024, Ch. 414, Sec. 2. (AB 2678) Effective January 1, 2025. Inoperative on date prescribed in subd. (j). Repealed as of January 1, 2027, by its own provisions.)

5206. Vehicles for which weight fees are paid on a partial year basis shall display a certificate or insignia issued by the department, which shall state the end of the period for which the vehicle is licensed.

(Amended by Stats. 1981, Ch. 636, Sec. 4.)

Article 9.5. Registration of Fleet Vehicles

(Article 9.5 repealed and added by Stats. 1982, Ch. 695, Sec. 2.)

5301. (a) Notwithstanding any other provision of this code and Part 5 (commencing with Section 10701) of Division 2 of the Revenue and Taxation Code, the registered owner or lessee of a fleet of vehicles consisting of commercial motor vehicles base plated in the state, or passenger automobiles may, upon payment of appropriate fees, apply to the department for license plates, permanent decals, and registration cards.

(b) (1) Fleets shall consist of at least 25 motor vehicles to qualify for this program. However, the department may provide for permanent fleet registration through an association providing a combination of fleets of motor vehicles of 125 or more vehicles with no individual fleet of fewer than 25 motor vehicles.

(2) An association submitting an application of participation in the program shall provide within the overall application a listing identifying the registered owner of each fleet and the motor vehicles within each fleet. Identification of the motor vehicles as provided in this article applies to the ownership of the motor vehicles and not the association submitting the application.

(c) With the concurrence of both the department and the participant, the changes made in this section by the enactment of the Commercial Vehicle Registration Act of 2001 shall not affect those participants who were lawfully participating in the permanent fleet registration program on December 31, 2001. Any fleet that qualifies for permanent fleet registration as of December 31, 2001, will continue to count trailers to qualify as a fleet until January 1, 2007. However, five years following the implementation of the permanent trailer identification program, all participants in the permanent fleet registration program shall meet the requirements of this section in order to continue enrollment in the program described in this section.

(Amended by Stats. 2017, Ch. 441, Sec. 2. (AB 458) Effective January 1, 2018.)

5302. (a) Motor vehicles registered in any state other than California are not permitted to participate in this program.

(b) Section 4604 does not apply to vehicles registered under this article.

(c) The department may conduct an audit of the records of each fleet owner or lessee of the vehicle fleets electing to participate in the program. The department shall be fully reimbursed by the fleet owner or lessee for the costs of conducting the audits.

(Amended by Stats. 2017, Ch. 441, Sec. 3. (AB 458) Effective January 1, 2018.)

5303. (a) The applicant for initial issuance of permanent registration or renewal of registration shall file an application in such form as the department shall require.

(b) Upon initial application, the department shall issue a distinguishing license plate or decal which indicates that the vehicle has been registered under this article.

(c) Display of the distinguishing license plate or decal and registration card shall constitute prima facie evidence that the vehicle is currently registered.

(Repealed and added by Stats. 1982, Ch. 695, Sec. 2.)

5304. Renewal fees shall be paid pursuant to a schedule established by the department. Submission of renewal fees by an association pursuant to subdivision (b) of Section 5301 shall be specific as to each fleet and vehicle thereof covered by the renewal application.

(Amended by Stats. 1983, Ch. 986, Sec. 2.)

5305. In addition to any other fees due for motor vehicles registered pursuant to this article, the department may charge and collect a service fee of one dollar ($1) for each fleet motor vehicle at the time the initial application is submitted to the department and at the time of registration renewal of each fleet vehicle.

(Amended by Stats. 2000, Ch. 861, Sec. 35. Effective September 29, 2000. Operative December 31, 2001, pursuant to Sec. 67 of Ch. 861.)

5306. Upon payment of appropriate fees, the license plate or decal and registration card issued pursuant to this article for the vehicle shall remain valid until the provisions of Section 5307 have been met.

(Repealed and added by Stats. 1982, Ch. 695, Sec. 2.)

5307. (a) A fleet vehicle registered under this article may be deleted from the identified fleet when the fleet operator notifies the department of the proposed deletion on a form approved by the department and the distinguishing license plate or decal and registration card issued for the vehicle are surrendered to the department.

(b) Failure to comply with subdivision (a) will require that the payment of fees due for the registration of the vehicle shall be the responsibility of the fleet owner as though the vehicle remained part of the fleet.

(c) The fees determined to be due and owing under this article shall be a lien upon all vehicles of the applicant of a type subject to registration under this code, and the provisions of Article 6 (commencing with Section 9800) of Chapter 6 shall apply.

(Repealed and added by Stats. 1982, Ch. 695, Sec. 2.)

5308. The director shall adopt procedures for initial application, payment of fees, fleet additions or deletions, and for the cancellation of the distinguishing plates or decals and registration card issued to a vehicle of a fleet owner or lessee who does not comply with this article.

(Repealed and added by Stats. 1982, Ch. 695, Sec. 2.)

5309. The registration of any identified fleet vehicle is required annually.

(Repealed and added by Stats. 1982, Ch. 695, Sec. 2.)

Article 10. Registration of Trailer Coaches

(Article 10 enacted by Stats. 1959, Ch. 3.)

5350. The provisions of this division shall apply to trailer coaches except as otherwise provided in this article.

(Amended by Stats. 1981, Ch. 975, Sec. 35.)

5351. Sections 4452, 4604, 5904, 6052, and 9254, and subdivision (a) of Section 9552 do not apply to the registration or renewal of registration of any trailer coach.

(Enacted by Stats. 1959, Ch. 3.)

5352. Subject to the exemptions stated in Section 5353, registration of any trailer coach in this state is required annually.

(Amended by Stats. 1981, Ch. 975, Sec. 38.)

5353. The registration provisions of this article shall not apply to any of the following:

(a) Any trailer coach which is driven or moved upon a highway in any of the following circumstances:

(1) In conformance with the provisions of this code relating to dealers, manufacturers, transporters, or nonresidents.

(2) Under a temporary permit issued by the department as authorized by Section 4156.

(3) Under a one-trip permit issued by the department as authorized by Section 4003 when such permit is issued to a nonresident.

(b) Any unoccupied trailer coach which is part of an inventory of trailer coaches held for sale by a manufacturer or dealer in the course of his business.

(Amended by Stats. 1981, Ch. 975, Sec. 39.)

5354. The registration of a foreign trailer coach owned by a nonresident shall be subject to and governed by Section 6700.

(Amended by Stats. 1959, Ch. 1021.)

Article 12. Surrender of Registration Documents and License Plates

(Article 12 added by Stats. 1983, Ch. 1286, Sec. 21.)

5500. (a) Any person, other than a licensed dismantler, desiring to disassemble a vehicle of a type required to be registered under this code, either partially or totally, with the intent to use as parts only, to reduce to scrap, or to construct another vehicle shall deliver to the department the certificate of ownership, the registration card, and the license plates last issued to the vehicle before dismantling may begin.

(b) Any person who is convicted of violating subdivision (a) shall be punished upon a first conviction by imprisonment in the county jail for not less than five days or more than six months, or by a fine of not less than fifty dollars ($50) or more than five hundred dollars ($500), or by both that fine and imprisonment; and, upon a second or any subsequent conviction, by imprisonment in the county jail for not less than 30 days or more than one year, or by a fine of not less than two hundred fifty dollars ($250) or more than one thousand dollars ($1,000), or by both that fine and imprisonment.

(Amended by Stats. 1985, Ch. 1022, Sec. 4.)

5501. The provisions of Sections 4457, 4458, and 4459 shall not apply when a vehicle is reported for dismantling. However, any person desiring to dismantle a vehicle shall, in accordance with Section 5500 or 11520, surrender to the department the certificate of ownership, registration card, and license plate or plates last issued for the vehicle. In the event the person so reporting is unable to furnish the certificate of ownership, registration card, and license plate or plates last issued to the vehicle, or any of them, the department may receive the report and application, examine into the circumstances of the case, and may require the filing of suitable affidavits, or other information or documents. No duplicate certificate of ownership, registration card, license plate or plates will be issued when a vehicle is reported for dismantling. No fees shall be required for acceptance of any affidavit provided pursuant to this section or on account of any stolen, lost or damaged certificate, card, plate or plates or duplicates thereof, unless the vehicle is subsequently registered in accordance with Section 11519.

(Added by Stats. 1983, Ch. 1286, Sec. 21.)

5505. (a) This section applies to any vehicle reported to be a total loss salvage vehicle pursuant to Section 11515 and to any vehicle reported for dismantling pursuant to Section 5500 or 11520.

(b) Whenever an application is made to the Department of Motor Vehicles to register a vehicle described in subdivision (a), that department shall inspect the vehicle to determine its proper identity or request that the inspection be performed by the Department of the California Highway Patrol. An inspection by the Department of Motor Vehicles shall not preclude that department from referring the vehicle to the Department of the California Highway Patrol for an additional inspection if deemed necessary.

(c) The Department of the California Highway Patrol shall inspect, on a random basis, those vehicles described in subdivision (a) that have been presented to the Department of Motor Vehicles for registration after completion of the reconstruction process to determine the proper identity of those vehicles. The vehicle being presented for inspection shall be a complete vehicle, in legal operating condition. If the vehicle was originally manufactured with a "supplemental restraint system" as defined in Section 593, the reconstructed vehicle shall also be equipped with a supplemental restraint system in good working order that meets applicable federal motor vehicle safety standards and conforms to the manufacturer's specifications for that vehicle. The inspection conducted pursuant to this subdivision shall be a comprehensive, vehicle identification number inspection.

(d) A salvage vehicle rebuilder, as defined in Section 543.5, or other individual in possession of a vehicle described in subdivision (a), who is submitting the vehicle for registration as described in subdivision (b), shall have available, and shall present upon demand of the Department of the California Highway Patrol, bills of sale, invoices, or other acceptable proof of ownership of component parts, and invoices for minor component parts. Additionally, bills of sale and invoices shall include the year, make, model, and the vehicle identification number of the vehicle from which the parts were removed or sold, the name and signature of the person from whom the parts were acquired, and his or her address, and telephone number. To assist in the identification of the seller of new or used parts, the number of the seller's driver's license, identification card, social security card, or Federal Employer Identification Number shall be provided by the seller to the buyer on the bills of sale and invoice. The seller of a salvage vehicle, or the agent of the seller, shall inform the purchaser of the vehicle that ownership documentation for certain replacement parts used in the repair of the vehicle will be required in the inspection required under this section.

(e) As used in this section, the term "component parts for passenger motor vehicles" includes supplemental restraint systems, the cowl or firewall, front-end assembly, rear clip, including the roof panel, the roof panel when installed separately, and the frame or any portion thereof, or in the case of a unitized body, the supporting structure that serves as the frame, each door, the hood, each fender or quarter panel, deck lid or hatchback, each bumper, both T-tops, replacement transmissions or transaxles, and a replacement motor.

(1) As used in this subdivision, "front-end assembly" includes all of the following: hood, fenders, bumper, and radiator supporting members for these items. For vehicles with a unitized body, the front-end assembly also includes the frame support members.

(2) As used in this subdivision, "rear clip" includes the roof, quarter panels, trunk lid, floor pan, and the support members for each item.

(f) As used in this section, "major component parts for trucks, truck-type or bus-type vehicles" includes the cab, the frame or any portion thereof, and, in the case of a unitized body, the supporting structure which serves as a frame, the cargo compartment floor panel or passenger compartment floor pan, roof panel, and replacement transmissions or transaxles, and replacement motors, each door, hood, each fender or quarter panel, each bumper, and the tailgate. All component parts identified in subdivision (e), common to a truck, truck-type or bus-type vehicle, not listed in this section, shall be considered as included in this section if the part is replaced.

(1) "Major component parts for motorcycles" includes the engine or motor, transmission or transaxle, frame, front fork, and crankcase.

(2) "Minor component parts for motorcycles" includes the fairing and any other body molding.

(g) If the vehicle identification number, year, make, or model required under subdivision (d) cannot be determined, the Department of the California Highway Patrol may accept, in lieu of that information, a certification on a form provided by that department, signed by the person submitting the vehicle for inspection, that the part was not obtained by means of theft or fraud.

(Amended by Stats. 2002, Ch. 670, Sec. 7. Effective January 1, 2003.)

5506. No salvage vehicle rebuilder may resell or transfer ownership of any vehicle that is subject to inspection as provided in Section 5505, unless either a certificate of inspection issued by the Department of the California Highway Patrol, or vehicle verification form completed by an authorized employee of the Department of Motor Vehicles is provided to the buyer upon sale or transfer. Responsibility for compliance with this section shall rest with the salvage vehicle rebuilder selling or transferring the vehicle. This section shall not apply to a salvage vehicle rebuilder who has applied for and received a title in accordance with Section 5505.

(Added by Stats. 2002, Ch. 670, Sec. 8. Effective January 1, 2003.)

Chapter 2. Transfers of Title or Interest

(Chapter 2 enacted by Stats. 1959, Ch. 3.)

Article 1. Procedure to Transfer

(Article 1 enacted by Stats. 1959, Ch. 3.)

5600. (a) No transfer of the title or any interest in or to a vehicle registered under this code shall pass, and any attempted transfer shall not be effective, until the parties thereto have fulfilled either of the following requirements:

(1) The transferor has made proper endorsement and delivery of the certificate of ownership to the transferee as provided in this code and the transferee has delivered to the department or has placed the certificate in the United States mail addressed to the department when and as required under this code with the proper transfer fee, together with the amount required to be paid under Part 1 (commencing with Section 6001), Division 2 of the Revenue and Taxation Code with respect to the use by the transferee of the vehicle, and thereby makes application for a transfer of registration except as otherwise provided in Sections 5905, 5906, 5907, and 5908.

(2) The transferor has delivered to the department or has placed in the United States mail addressed to the department the appropriate documents for the registration or transfer of registration of the vehicle pursuant to the sale or transfer except as provided in Section 5602.

(b) Whenever a person transfers ownership of a vehicle and is required to disclose the mileage of the vehicle, the department may prescribe a secured form to be used for purposes of the odometer mileage disclosure requirements pursuant to subsection (a) of Section 32705 of Title 49 of the United States Code.

(Amended by Stats. 2000, Ch. 1035, Sec. 10. Effective January 1, 2001.)

5600.5. Ownership of title to a vehicle subject to registration may be transferred to two (or more) coowners as transferee to be held provided in Section 682 of the Civil Code, except that:

(a) A vehicle may be registered in the names of two (or more) persons as coowners in the alternative by the use of the word "or." A vehicle so registered in the alternative shall be deemed to be held in joint tenancy. Each coowner shall be deemed to have granted to the other coowners the absolute right to dispose of the title and interest in the vehicle. Upon the death of a coowner the interest of the decedent shall pass to the survivor as though title or interest in the vehicle was held in joint tenancy unless a contrary intention is set forth in writing upon the request for transfer of registration.

(b) A vehicle may be registered in the names of two (or more) persons as coowners in the alternative by the use of the word "or" and if declared in writing upon the application for a transfer of registration by the applicants to be community property, or tenancy in common, shall grant to each coowner the absolute power to transfer the title or interest of the other coowners only during the lifetime of such coowners.

(c) A vehicle may be registered in the names of two (or more) persons as coowners in the conjunctive by the use of the word "and" and shall thereafter require the signature of each coowner or his personal representative to transfer title to the vehicle, except where title to the vehicle is set forth in joint tenancy, the signature of each coowner or his personal representative shall be required only during the lifetime of the coowners, and upon death of a coowner title shall pass to the surviving coowner.

(d) The department may adopt suitable abbreviations to appear upon

the certificate of registration and certificate of ownership to designate the manner in which the interest in or title to the vehicle is held if set forth by the coowners upon the application for transfer of registration.
(Added by Stats. 1965, Ch. 891.)

5601. Section 5600 does not apply to involuntary transfers, as upon the taking of possession by a secured party under a security agreement, or to transfers involving the creation of security interests subject to Chapter 3, commencing at Section 6300.
(Amended by Stats. 1963, Ch. 819.)

5602. An owner who has made a bona fide sale or transfer of a vehicle and has delivered possession of the vehicle to a purchaser is not, by reason of any of the provisions of this code, the owner of the vehicle so as to be subject to civil liability or criminal liability for the parking, abandoning, or operation of the vehicle thereafter by another when the selling or transferring owner, in addition to that delivery and that bona fide sale or transfer, has fulfilled either of the following requirements:

(a) He or she has made proper endorsement and delivery of the certificate of ownership as provided in this code.

(b) He or she has delivered to the department or has placed in the United States mail, addressed to the department, either of the following documents:

(1) The notice as provided in subdivision (b) of Section 4456 or Section 5900 or 5901.

(2) The appropriate documents and fees for registration of the vehicle to the new owner pursuant to the sale or transfer.
(Amended by Stats. 1994, Ch. 180, Sec. 6. Effective July 11, 1994.)

5603. A legal owner may assign his title or interest in or to a vehicle registered under this code to a person other than the owner without the consent of and without affecting the interest of the owner.
(Enacted by Stats. 1959, Ch. 3.)

5604. Every dealer who, upon transferring by sale, lease, or otherwise, any new or used vehicle of a type subject to registration, requires the transferee to insure the vehicle, and every lending agency which, as the holder of any security interest in the vehicle, requires its obligor to insure the vehicle, shall, if the required insurance policy is obtained by the dealer or lending agency and the policy does not insure the transferee or obligor against damages resulting from ownership or operation of the vehicle arising by reason of personal injury or death of any person, or from injury to property, notify the transferee or obligor of that fact in writing on a document other than the insurance policy. The document shall be in duplicate and signed by the transferee or obligor.

If the required insurance policy is obtained by the dealer or lending agency because of the failure or refusal of the transferee or obligor to furnish or renew insurance in accordance with the terms of the contract of sale or the security agreement, and the policy does not insure the transferee or obligor against damages resulting from ownership or operation of the vehicle arising by reason of personal injury or death of any person, or from injury to property, the dealer or lending agency shall notify the transferee or obligor that the policy obtained does not insure the transferee or obligor for liability from any claims. The notice shall be made in writing on a document other than the insurance policy, or the declaration page attached to the policy, and shall be mailed, with postage paid and properly addressed, to the transferee or obligor within 30 days of obtaining the policy.
(Amended by Stats. 1988, Ch. 1407, Sec. 1.)

5604.5. (a) Every dealer who, upon transferring by sale, lease, or otherwise, any new or used vehicle of a type subject to registration, requires the transferee to insure the motor vehicle shall, if the required insurance policy is sold by that dealer at the time of the transfer and the policy does not insure the transferee against damages resulting from ownership or operation of the vehicle arising by reason of personal injury or death of any person, or from damage to property, notify the transferee of that fact in writing on a document other than the insurance policy. The document shall be signed by the transferee and an exact copy shall be furnished to the transferee by the dealer at the time of signature.

(b) The document required under subdivision (a) shall contain a notice in English and Spanish in at least 10-point type that reads as follows:

"INSURANCE WARNING

The motor vehicle physical damage insurance policy you are buying does not allow you to legally drive on the streets of California. Generally, in order to legally drive on the streets of California, you must either purchase a type of insurance called "liability insurance" or deposit a bond with the Department of Motor Vehicles. If you drive this or any other motor vehicle without liability insurance or a bond, a police officer may request evidence of liability insurance or a bond at the time of a traffic stop. If you do not have evidence of liability insurance or a bond during a traffic stop, the fines can be from several hundreds of dollars to an amount that exceeds $1,000. If you get into an accident and do not have liability insurance or a bond, you will lose your driver's license for one year. If you cause the accident and do not have liability insurance or a bond, you may have to pay the injured person yourself and these costs may be substantial.

Liability insurance as well as the insurance needed to obtain a loan for your motor vehicle may be purchased through a licensed insurance agent or broker. The price for both types of insurance may be more or less than the price for the insurance you are being offered by the dealer. The State of California advises you to shop for insurance because prices may vary substantially.

I have read this notice and understand that I am about to buy a type of insurance that is available elsewhere and that does not allow me to drive the motor vehicle legally on the streets of California.

I also understand that if I drive on the streets of California without liability insurance or a bond, then I may be subject to severe financial penalties, including fines and personal payment for any damage to others that I may cause while driving.

(Spanish translation of the above text to be developed by the Department of Motor Vehicles and to be inserted below the above English version text)

Dated: Signed: "

(c) The department shall also make available a translation of the Insurance Warning notice set forth in subdivision (b) in any of the languages used in the most recent statewide voter pamphlet.
(Added by Stats. 2000, Ch. 455, Sec. 2. Effective January 1, 2001.)

Article 2. Endorsement and Delivery of Documents

(Article 2 enacted by Stats. 1959, Ch. 3.)

5750. Upon transfer of the title or any interest of the legal owner or owners in a vehicle registered under this code, the transferor shall write his signature, and the transferee shall write his signature and address, in the appropriate spaces provided on the certificate of ownership issued for the vehicle.
(Amended by Stats. 1967, Ch. 723.)

5751. Upon transfer of the title or interest of the registered owner only in a vehicle registered under this code, the registered owner shall write his signature and address and the transferee shall write his signature and address in the appropriate spaces provided on the certificate of ownership for the vehicle, and the legal owner shall write his signature in the space provided for the new legal owner indicating that he is to retain his legal title and interest.
(Amended by Stats. 1967, Ch. 723.)

5751.5. (a) Upon transfer of the title or interest of the registered owner of a motor vehicle that is subject to Part 5 (commencing with Section 43000) of Division 26 of the Health and Safety Code, if no certificate of compliance or certificate of noncompliance is submitted to the department pursuant to the exemptions described in paragraph (1) of subdivision (d) of Section 4000.1, the transferor of that vehicle shall sign and deliver to the transferee, upon completion of the transaction, the original copy of a statement, under penalty of perjury, that he or she has not modified the emissions system of the vehicle and does not have any personal knowledge of anyone else modifying the system in a manner that causes the emission system to fail to qualify for the issuance of a certificate of compliance pursuant to Section 44015 of the Health and Safety Code. The transferor shall keep a duplicate copy of the statement delivered to the transferee pursuant to this section. The department shall prescribe and make available to transferors the necessary forms to comply with this subdivision.

(b) Any form prescribed by the department pursuant to subdivision (a) shall contain the following statement and a space for the signatures of the transferor and transferee at the end of the statement:

"WARNING TO THE BUYER

"A valid certificate of compliance was submitted to the Department of Motor Vehicles with an application for the renewal of registration of this vehicle. If an application for transfer is submitted to the department within the 90-day validity period of the smog certification, no new smog certification will be required. However, at present, you may be purchasing a vehicle that may not be in compliance with specified emission standards.

"By signing this statement, you acknowledge that the seller is not required to provide you with an additional certificate of compliance prior to the completion of this transaction.

"You may have this vehicle tested at a licensed smog check station prior to completion of this transaction to verify compliance. If the vehicle passes the test, you shall be responsible for the costs of the test. If the vehicle fails the test, the seller is obligated to reimburse you the cost of having the vehicle tested and, without expense to you, must have the vehicle repaired to comply with specified emission standards prior to completion of this transaction.

(Transferor) (Date)

(Transferee) (Date)"

(Amended by Stats. 2004, Ch. 650, Sec. 7. Effective January 1, 2005.)

5752. (a) When the required certificate of ownership is lost, stolen, damaged, or mutilated, the application for transfer may be made upon a form provided by the department for a duplicate certificate of ownership. The transferor shall write his or her signature and address in the appropriate spaces provided upon the application and file the same together with the proper fees for duplicate certificate of ownership and transfer. The application shall also include, if applicable, the notorized signature of the lienholder.

(b) An insurance company or its agent is exempt from the notarized signature requirement of subdivision (a) and may apply, upon a form provided by the department, for a duplicate certificate of ownership and transfer of ownership to the insurance company, if all of the following occur:

(1) The insurance company or its agent obtains from the lienholder a document to verify satisfaction of the lien.

(2) The insurance company has paid a total loss claim for the vehicle.

(3) A lienholder is indicated on the department's records.

(4) The certificate of ownership is lost, stolen, damaged, or mutilated.

(Amended by Stats. 1996, Ch. 451, Sec. 1. Effective January 1, 1997.)

5753. (a) It is unlawful for any person to fail or neglect properly to endorse, date, and deliver the certificate of ownership and, when having possession, to deliver the registration card to a transferee who is lawfully entitled to a transfer of registration.

(b) Except when the certificate of ownership is demanded in writing by a purchaser, a vehicle dealer licensed under this code shall satisfy the delivery requirement of this section by submitting appropriate documents and fees to the department for transfer of registration in accordance with Sections 5906 and 4456 of this code and rules and regulations promulgated thereunder.

(c) (1) Within 15 business days after receiving payment in full for the satisfaction of a security interest and a written instrument signed by the grantor of the security interest designating the transferee and authorizing release of the legal owner's interest, the legal owner shall release its security interest and mail, transmit, or deliver the vehicle's certificate of ownership to the transferee who, due to satisfaction of the security interest, is lawfully entitled to the transfer of legal ownership.

(2) If a lease provides a lessee with the option to purchase the leased vehicle, within 15 business days after receiving payment in full for the purchase, and all documents necessary to effect the transfer, the lessor shall mail, transmit, or deliver the vehicle's certificate of ownership to the transferee, who, due to purchase of the vehicle, is lawfully entitled to the transfer of legal ownership.

(d) The certificate of ownership delivered pursuant to subdivision (c) shall be signed by the legal owner or lessor to reflect release of the legal owner's interest or transfer of the lessor's interest in the vehicle or accompanied by a form provided by the department to accomplish the same result and signed by the legal owner or lessor. If the legal owner or lessor is not in possession or control of the certificate of ownership, the legal owner or lessor shall, within the time provided in subdivision (c) for the mailing, transmittal, or delivery of the certificate of ownership, take any action required by the department to release the legal owner's security interest or transfer the lessor's interest in the vehicle and within that time shall mail, transmit, or deliver written notice of its taking that action to the transferee.

(e) A legal owner or lessor that fails to satisfy the requirements of subdivisions (c) and (d), shall, without offset or reduction, pay the transferee twenty-five dollars ($25) per day for each day that the requirements of subdivisions (c) and (d) remain unsatisfied, not to exceed a maximum payment of two thousand five hundred dollars ($2,500). If the legal owner or lessor fails to pay this amount within 60 days following written demand by the transferee, the amount shall be trebled, not to exceed a maximum payment of seven thousand five hundred dollars ($7,500), and the transferee shall be entitled to costs and reasonable attorneys fees incurred in any court action brought to collect the payment. The right to recover these payments is cumulative with and is not in substitution or derogation of any remedy otherwise available at law or equity.

(f) A legal owner, upon written request of the transferee, shall disclose any pertinent information regarding the amount of payment and the documents necessary to release the obligation secured by the legal owner's interest.

(Amended by Stats. 2003, Ch. 151, Sec. 2. Effective January 1, 2004.)

Article 3. Notice and Application

(Article 3 enacted by Stats. 1959, Ch. 3.)

5900. (a) Whenever the owner of a vehicle registered under this code sells or transfers his or her title or interest in, and delivers the possession of, the vehicle to another, the owner shall, within five calendar days, notify the department of the sale or transfer giving the date thereof, the name and address of the owner and of the transferee, and the description of the vehicle that is required in the appropriate form provided for that purpose by the department.

(b) Except as otherwise provided in subdivision (c), pursuant to subsection (a) of Section 32705 of Title 49 of the United States Code, the owner shall also notify the department of the actual mileage of the vehicle as indicated by the vehicle's odometer at the time of sale or transfer. However, if the vehicle owner has knowledge that the mileage displayed on the odometer is incorrect, the owner shall indicate on the appropriate form the true mileage, if known, of the vehicle at the time of sale or transfer.

Providing false or inaccurate mileage is not a violation of this subdivision unless it is done with the intent to defraud.

(c) If the registered owner is not in possession of the vehicle that is sold or transferred, the person in physical possession of that vehicle shall give the notice required by subdivisions (a) and (b). If the registered owner sells or transfers the vehicle through a dealer conducting a wholesale motor vehicle auction, the owner shall furnish the information required by subdivisions (a) and (b) to that dealer.

(Amended by Stats. 2000, Ch. 1035, Sec. 11. Effective January 1, 2001.)

5901. (a) Every dealer or lessor-retailer, upon transferring by sale, lease, or otherwise any vehicle, whether new or used, of a type subject to registration under this code, shall, not later than the end of the fifth calendar day thereafter not counting the day of sale, give notice of the transfer to the department electronically in a manner approved by the department.

(b) Except as otherwise provided in this subdivision or in subdivision (c), the dealer or lessor-retailer shall enter on the form and pursuant to Section 32705(a) of Title 49 of the United States Code, on the ownership certificate, the actual mileage of the vehicle as indicated by the vehicle's odometer at the time of the transfer. However, if the vehicle dealer or lessor-retailer has knowledge that the mileage displayed on the odometer is incorrect, the licensee shall indicate on the form on which the mileage is entered that the mileage registered by the odometer is incorrect. A vehicle dealer or lessor-retailer need not give the notice when selling or transferring a new unregistered vehicle to a dealer or lessor-retailer.

(c) When the dealer or lessor-retailer is not in possession of the vehicle that is sold or transferred, the person in physical possession of the vehicle shall give the information required by subdivision (b).

(d) A sale is deemed completed and consummated when the purchaser of the vehicle has paid the purchase price, or, in lieu thereof, has signed a purchase contract or security agreement, and has taken physical possession or delivery of the vehicle.

(e) This section shall become operative January 1, 2019.

(Repealed (in Sec. 19) and added by Stats. 2016, Ch. 90, Sec. 20. (AB 516) Effective January 1, 2017. Section operative January 1, 2019, by its own provisions.)

5902. Whenever any person has received as transferee a properly endorsed certificate of ownership, that person shall, within 10 days thereafter, forward the certificate with the proper transfer fee to the department and thereby make application for a transfer of registration. The certificate of ownership shall contain a space for the applicant's driver's license or identification card number, and the applicant shall furnish that number, if any, in the space provided.

(Amended by Stats. 2001, Ch. 826, Sec. 18. Effective January 1, 2002.)

5902.5. (a) If an application for a registration transaction is filed with the department during the 30 days immediately preceding the date of expiration of registration of the vehicle, the application shall be accompanied by the full renewal fees for the ensuing registration year in addition to any other fees that are due and payable.

(b) The requirements of subdivision (a) shall not apply if the expiration of registration occurs on or after July 1, 2011. This subdivision shall become inoperative on January 1, 2012.

(Amended by Stats. 2011, Ch. 21, Sec. 5. (SB 94) Effective May 4, 2011.)

5903. When the department receives a copy of the judgment of abandonment and evidence of sale as specified in Section 798.61 of the Civil Code, the department shall transfer the registration of the trailer coach or recreational vehicle which has been deemed abandoned pursuant to that section, or reregister the trailer coach or vehicle under a new registration number, and issue a new certificate of ownership and registration card to the person or persons presenting the copy of the judgment of abandonment and evidence of sale to the department.

(Added by Stats. 1991, Ch. 564, Sec. 2.)

5904. Whenever the ownership of any vehicle for which a certificate of ownership has been issued without registration under Section 4452 is transferred, an application for transfer shall be made as provided in this chapter.

(Amended by Stats. 1961, Ch. 58.)

5905. When a security interest upon a registered vehicle is satisfied, canceled, or released by the parties thereto duly registered as owner and legal owner respectively and thereafter within a period of 10 days a new security agreement covering the vehicle is executed between the same parties, no application for transfer of registration by reason thereof shall be made and no new certificate of ownership or registration card shall be issued, and all provisions of this code relating to transfers of any title or interest in a vehicle and the registration of the transfers shall be deemed to have been fully complied with, and the new security agreement shall be deemed perfected at the time the new security agreement is executed.

(Amended by Stats. 1963, Ch. 819.)

5906. When the transferee of a vehicle is a dealer who holds the same for resale and operates or moves the same upon the highways under special plates, the dealer is not required to make application for transfer, but upon transferring his title or interest to another person he shall comply with this division.

(Enacted by Stats. 1959, Ch. 3.)

5906.5. (a) Except as otherwise provided in subdivision (b), in the case of any transfer, including, but not limited to, a transfer resulting from a sale, lease, gift, or auction, of a vehicle under 6,001 pounds, manufacturer's maximum gross weight rating, where no application for transfer is required, the person making such transfer, or his authorized representative, shall sign and shall record on the document evidencing the transfer of the vehicle the actual mileage of the vehicle as indicated by the vehicle's odometer at the time of the transfer. However, if the person making the transfer, or his authorized representative, has knowledge that the mileage displayed on the odometer is incorrect, such person shall record on the document the true mileage, if known, of the vehicle at the time of transfer.

(b) Whenever the person making such transfer is not in possession of the vehicle that is transferred, the person in physical possession of such vehicle shall provide the information required by subdivision (a).

(Amended by Stats. 1978, Ch. 797.)

5907. A secured party who holds a security interest in a registered vehicle that constitutes inventory as defined in the Uniform Commercial Code, who has possession of the certificate of ownership issued for that vehicle, if the certificate of ownership has been issued, need not make application for a transfer of registration and the Uniform Commercial Code shall exclusively control the validity and perfection of that security interest. This section does not apply to the extent that subdivisions (a) to (c), inclusive, of Section 9311 of the Uniform Commercial Code apply to a security interest, because the transaction is not described in subdivision (d) of Section 9311 of that code.

(Amended by Stats. 2003, Ch. 235, Sec. 9. Effective January 1, 2004.)

5908. The transferee of a security interest in a registered vehicle need not make application for a transfer of registration when the interest of such transferee arises from a transfer of a security agreement or a lease agreement by the legal owner to the transferee to secure payment or performance of an obligation, and the Uniform Commercial Code shall exclusively control the validity and perfection of such a security interest.

(Amended by Stats. 1963, Ch. 819.)

5909. (a) Whenever the title or interest of any owner or legal owner in or to a vehicle registered under this code passes to another otherwise than by voluntary transfer the new owner or legal owner may obtain a transfer of registration upon application therefor and upon presentation of the last certificate of ownership and registration card issued for the vehicle, if available, and any instruments or documents of authority or certified copies thereof as may be required by the department, or required by law, to evidence or effect a transfer of title or interest in or to chattels in such case.

(b) The department when satisfied of the genuineness and regularity of the transfer shall give notice by mail to the owner and legal owner of the vehicle as shown by the records of the department and five days after the giving of the notice, if still satisfied of the genuineness and regularity of such transfer, shall transfer the registration of the vehicle accordingly. Such notice shall not be required for a transfer described in Section 5601.

(Amended by Stats. 1969, Ch. 384.)

5910. (a) Upon the death of an owner or legal owner of a vehicle registered under this code, without the decedent leaving other property necessitating probate, and irrespective of the value of the vehicle, the following person or persons may secure transfer of registration of the title or interest of the decedent:

(1) The sole person or all of the persons who succeeded to the property of the decedent under Sections 6401 and 6402 of the Probate Code unless the vehicle is, by will, otherwise bequeathed.

(2) The sole beneficiary or all of the beneficiaries who succeeded to the vehicle under the will of the decedent where the vehicle is, by will, so bequeathed.

(b) The person authorized by subdivision (a) may secure a transfer of registration of the title or interest of the decedent upon presenting to the department all of the following:

(1) The appropriate certificate of ownership and registration card, if available.

(2) A certificate of the heir or beneficiary under penalty of perjury containing the following statements:

(A) The date and place of the decedent's death.

(B) The decedent left no other property necessitating probate and no probate proceeding is now being or has been conducted in this state for the decedent's estate.

(C) The declarant is entitled to the vehicle either (i) as the sole person or all of the persons who succeeded to the property of the decedent under Sections 6401 and 6402 of the Probate Code if the decedent left no will or (ii) as the beneficiary or beneficiaries under the decedent's last will if the decedent left a will, and no one has a right to the decedent's vehicle that is superior to that of the declarant.

(D) There are no unsecured creditors of the decedent or, if there are, the unsecured creditors of the decedent have been paid in full or their claims have been otherwise discharged.

(3) If required by the department, a certificate of the death of the decedent.

(4) If required by the department, the names and addresses of any other heirs or beneficiaries.

(c) If the department is presented with the documents specified in paragraphs (1) and (2) of subdivision (b), no liability shall be incurred by the department or any officer or employee of the department by reason of the transfer of registration of the vehicle pursuant to this section. The department or officer or employee of the department may rely in good faith on the statements in the certificate specified in paragraph (2) of subdivision (b) and has no duty to inquire into the truth of any statement in the certificate. The person who secures the transfer of the vehicle pursuant to this section is subject to the provisions of Sections 13109 to 13113, inclusive, of the Probate Code to the same extent as a person to whom transfer of property is made under Chapter 3 (commencing with Section 13100) of Part 1 of Division 8 of the Probate Code.

(d) The department may prescribe a combined form for use under this section and Section 9916.

(Amended by Stats. 1986, Ch. 783, Sec. 26. Operative July 1, 1987, by Sec. 30 of Ch. 783.)

5910.5. (a) On death of the owner of a vehicle owned in beneficiary form, the vehicle belongs to the surviving beneficiary, if any. If there is no surviving beneficiary, the vehicle belongs to the estate of the deceased owner or of the last coowner to die.

(b) A certificate of ownership in beneficiary form may be revoked or the beneficiary changed at any time before the death of the owner by either of the following methods:

(1) By sale of the vehicle with proper assignment and delivery of the certificate of ownership to another person.

(2) By application for a new certificate of ownership without designation of a beneficiary or with the designation of a different beneficiary.

(c) Except as provided in subdivision (b), designation of a beneficiary in a certificate of ownership issued in beneficiary form may not be changed or revoked by will, by any other instrument, by a change of circumstances, or otherwise.

(d) The beneficiary's interest in the vehicle at death of the owner is subject to any contract of sale, assignment, or security interest to which the owner was subject during his or her lifetime.

(e) The surviving beneficiary may secure a transfer of ownership for the vehicle upon presenting to the department all of the following:

(1) The appropriate certificate of ownership.

(2) A certificate under penalty of perjury stating the date and place of the owner's death and that the declarant is entitled to the vehicle as the designated beneficiary.

(3) If required by the department, a certificate of the death of the owner.

(f) After the death of the owner, the surviving beneficiary may transfer his or her interest in the vehicle to another person without securing transfer of ownership into his or her own name by appropriately signing the certificate of ownership for the vehicle and delivering the document to the transferee for forwarding to the department with appropriate fees. The transferee may secure a transfer of ownership upon presenting to the department (1) the certificate of ownership signed by the beneficiary, (2) the certificate described in paragraph (2) of subdivision (e) executed by the beneficiary under penalty of perjury; and (3) if required by the department, a certificate of death of the owner.

(g) A transfer at death pursuant to this section is effective by reason of this section, and shall not be deemed to be a testamentary disposition of property. The right of the designated beneficiary to the vehicle shall not be denied, abridged, or affected on the grounds that the right has not been created by a writing executed in accordance with the laws of this state prescribing the requirements to effect a valid testamentary disposition of property.

(h) A transfer at death pursuant to this section is subject to Section 9653 of the Probate Code.

(i) If there is no surviving beneficiary, the person or persons described in Section 5910 may secure transfer of the vehicle as provided in that section.

(j) The department may prescribe forms for use pursuant to this section.

(Added by Stats. 1991, Ch. 1055, Sec. 59. Operative January 1, 1993, by Sec. 64 of Ch. 1055.)

5910.7. (a) If the department makes a transfer pursuant to Section 5910.5, the department is discharged from all liability, whether or not the transfer is consistent with the beneficial ownership of the vehicle transferred.

(b) The protection provided by subdivision (a) does not extend to a transfer made after the department has been served with a court order restraining the transfer. No other notice or information shown to have been available to the department shall affect its right to the protection afforded by subdivision (a).

(c) The protection provided by this section has no bearing on the rights of parties in disputes between themselves or their successors concerning the beneficial ownership of the vehicle.

(d) The protection provided by this section is in addition to, and not exclusive of, any other protection provided to the department by any other provision of law.

(Added by Stats. 1991, Ch. 1055, Sec. 60. Operative January 1, 1993, by Sec. 64 of Ch. 1055.)

5911. Whenever application is made to the department for a transfer of registration of a vehicle to a new owner or legal owner and the applicant is unable to present the certificate of ownership issued for the vehicle by reason of the same being lost or otherwise not available, the department may receive the application and examine into the circumstances of the case and may require the filing of certifications or other information, and when the department is satisfied that the applicant is entitled to a transfer of registration the department may transfer the registration of the vehicle, or reregister the vehicle under a new registration number, and issue a new certificate of ownership and registration card to the person or persons found to be entitled thereto. The department, however, shall not issue a new certificate of ownership and registration card to the applicant if the department has received notice by registered or certified mail in which it is indicated that the existing ownership certificate is being held for nonpayment of the vehicle. The notice may be forwarded by the registered owner, recorded lienholder, or by a person exempted from recording ownership by Section 5906.

(Amended by Stats. 1988, Ch. 1268, Sec. 6.)

5912. Whenever application is made to the department for a transfer of registration of a vehicle to a new owner or legal owner and the applicant is unable to present the registration card issued for the vehicle by reason of the same being in the possession of the department upon an application for renewal of registration, the department may transfer the registration of such vehicle upon production of the properly endorsed certificate of ownership to the vehicle and a temporary receipt upon a form prescribed by the department and containing such information as the department shall deem necessary, including, but not limited to, the license number assigned to the vehicle for the ensuing registration year, the amount of the fees payable upon renewal of registration, and the vehicle identification number of the vehicle.

(Amended by Stats. 1973, Ch. 889.)

Article 4. Transfer by Department

(Article 4 enacted by Stats. 1959, Ch. 3.)

6050. (a) The department upon receipt of a properly endorsed certificate of ownership and the required fee shall reregister the vehicle under its registration number in the name of the new owner and new legal owner, if any, and shall issue a new registration card and certificate of ownership as provided upon an original registration.

(b) The department shall not issue a new registration card and certificate of ownership pursuant to subdivision (a) on a vehicle that has been issued a nonrepairable vehicle certificate pursuant to Section 11515.2.

(Amended by Stats. 1994, Ch. 1008, Sec. 10. Effective January 1, 1995. Operative July 1, 1995, by Sec. 19 of Ch. 1008.)

6051. If the application for a transfer is made in the manner provided in this code the department shall not be required to withhold the transfer of any right, title, or interest in or to a vehicle if the application on its face appears to be genuine and regular and the department has received neither a request from any law enforcement agency that action on the application be deferred nor an order of a court of the United States or of the State of California restraining the transfer within two years prior thereto.

(Enacted by Stats. 1959, Ch. 3.)

6052. When application is made for transfer of the ownership of a vehicle for which a certificate of ownership has been issued without registration, upon payment of registration, transfer, and other fees required by law, the department shall issue the usual certificate of ownership and registration card unless the vehicle is not to be operated on the highways and the new owner submits an affidavit satisfactory to the department as to those facts required by subdivision (b) of Section 4452, in which case the new certificate of title and facsimile thereof may be issued as provided for in that section.

(Enacted by Stats. 1959, Ch. 3.)

Article 5. Transfers Through Wholesale Auctions

(Article 5 added by Stats. 1992, Ch. 745, Sec. 6.)

6100. (a) A dealer who conducts a wholesale motor vehicle auction and reports the sale of the vehicle in the manner prescribed in subdivision (b) of Section 4456 shall include the phrase "SOLD THROUGH [name of dealer conducting the auction]" and the date of the auction on the certificate of title of every vehicle sold, in a manner prescribed by the department.

(b) This section shall become operative January 1, 2019.

(Repealed (in Sec. 21) and added by Stats. 2016, Ch. 90, Sec. 22. (AB 516) Effective January 1, 2017. Section operative January 1, 2019, by its own provisions.)

6102. For each vehicle sold pursuant to this article, the dealer who conducts the auction shall maintain a copy of the following documents for a period of not less than five years:

(a) The form required by subdivision (b) of Section 4456.

(b) A copy of the auction sales agreement.

(c) A copy of the odometer statement required by Section 5900.

(Amended by Stats. 1994, Ch. 180, Sec. 9. Effective July 11, 1994.)

6104. Notwithstanding any other provision of law, a dealer who purchases a vehicle pursuant to this article has the same rights and remedies against the dealer who conducts the auction sale as if that dealer were an owner and seller of the auctioned vehicle. The purchaser dealer's rights and remedies are in addition to any right or remedy he or she may have against the seller of a vehicle sold at a wholesale motor vehicle auction. The provisions of this section may not be waived or modified by agreement, or by recharacterization of the transaction.

(Added by Stats. 1992, Ch. 745, Sec. 6. Effective January 1, 1993. Section operative July 1, 1993, pursuant to Section 6105.)

6105. This article shall become operative on July 1, 1993.

(Added by Stats. 1992, Ch. 745, Sec. 6. Effective January 1, 1993. Note: This section prescribes a delayed operative date (July 1, 1993) for Article 5, commencing with Section 6100.)

Chapter 2.5. Miscellaneous Title Provisions

(Chapter 2.5 added by Stats. 1994, Ch. 1247, Sec. 6.)

Article 1. Certificate of Title as Evidence

(Article 1 added by Stats. 1994, Ch. 1247, Sec. 6.)

6150. In any criminal proceeding in which ownership, possession, or use of a motor vehicle is an issue, a copy certified by the department as its record of title on file, or with the official custodian of those documents of another state, shall be admissible as evidence of ownership of the motor vehicle. Upon the introduction of evidence that the legal owner of a motor vehicle is not named in the certificate of title or that use or possession was with the consent or authority of the owner, a reasonable continuance shall be granted any party to enable the owner of the vehicle to be brought into court to testify.

(Added by Stats. 1994, Ch. 1247, Sec. 6. Effective January 1, 1995.)

6151. A party to a proceeding described in Section 6150 may provide notice to the opposing party that a showing of need will be made at the arraignment or at any other pretrial hearing, and upon the proof of that notice and the showing of need, the court shall take testimony from the owner or person in control of the motor vehicle which shall be admissible at trial.

(Added by Stats. 1994, Ch. 1247, Sec. 6. Effective January 1, 1995.)

6152. At any hearing, including, but not limited to, a scheduled trial date, involving a proceeding described in Section 6150, upon a showing of need, the court shall order as a condition of granting a continuance that the testimony of a witness then present in court be taken and preserved for subsequent use at a trial or any other stage of the proceeding.

(Added by Stats. 1994, Ch. 1247, Sec. 6. Effective January 1, 1995.)

6153. Where testimony is taken and preserved for use at trial or other stage of the proceeding pursuant to Sections 6151 and 6152, the witness shall be examined in open court by the party on whose behalf he or she is present, and the adverse party shall have the right of cross-examination.

(Added by Stats. 1994, Ch. 1247, Sec. 6. Effective January 1, 1995.)

6154. If any provision of this act or the application thereof to any person or circumstances is held invalid, that invalidity shall not affect other provisions or applications of the act which can be given effect without the invalid provision or application, and to this end the provisions of this act are severable.

(Added by Stats. 1994, Ch. 1247, Sec. 6. Effective January 1, 1995.)

Article 2. Inspection and Cancellation of Titles for Exported Vehicles

(Article 2 added by Stats. 1994, Ch. 1247, Sec. 6.)

6160. The Legislature finds and declares that when vehicles are exported and their title records are not amended to reflect exportation, it is conducive to vehicle theft and insurance fraud. The certificates of title issued by this state are used in insurance frauds in which a claimant falsely states that a vehicle has been stolen or uses that certificate to fraudulently procure insurance when in fact the vehicle has previously been exported from the United States. In the interest of the general welfare of the people of this state, and in order to combat vehicle theft and insurance fraud, it is necessary that the department's record of title reflect the fact that a vehicle is being exported either temporarily or permanently, based upon the true owner's declaration prior to exportation.
(Added by Stats. 1994, Ch. 1247, Sec. 6. Effective January 1, 1995.)

6161. For the purposes of this chapter, the following provisions and definitions apply to the following terms:

(a) "Certified record of permanent exportation" shall include all of the following:

(1) The titled owner's name and address.

(2) A description of the vehicle, including year, make, body type, vehicle identification number, license registration number, and state registration.

(3) The destination of vehicle.

(4) The purpose of export, whether sale, lease, or personal use.

(b) "Declaration that the vehicle will not be permanently located outside the United States" shall include the items specified in paragraphs (1) to (3), inclusive, of subdivision (a), and shall also state the period of time for which it is anticipated that the vehicle will be outside the United States.

(c) "Export" means the shipping or transporting of a vehicle out of the United States by means other than its own power or that of a vehicle drawing or towing it.

(d) "Owner" means the owner of record indicated in a certificate of title issued by this state and includes an agent of that owner acting under a valid power of attorney executed by an owner.

(e) "Title" means the certificate of ownership issued by the department pursuant to Section 4450, but excludes a salvage certificate, as described in Section 11515, a nonrepairable vehicle certificate, as defined in Section 432, and an acquisition bill of sale, as described in Section 11519.

(f) "Vehicle" means every device designed for transportation of persons or property upon land, for which a certificate of title is required.
(Added by Stats. 1994, Ch. 1008, Sec. 11. Effective January 1, 1995. See similar section (except for subd. (e)) added by Stats. 1994, Ch. 1247.)

6161. For the purposes of this act, the term:

(a) "Certified record of permanent exportation" shall include the following:

(1) Titled owner's name and address.

(2) Description of the vehicle, including year, make, body type, vehicle identification number, license registration number, and state registration.

(3) Destination of vehicle.

(4) Purpose of export, whether sale, lease, or personal use.

(b) "Declaration that the vehicle will not be permanently located outside the United States" shall include the items specified in paragraphs (1) to (3), inclusive, of subdivision (a), and shall also state the period of time for which it is anticipated that the vehicle will be outside the United States.

(c) "Export" means the shipping or transporting of a vehicle out of the United States by means other than its own power or that of a vehicle drawing or towing it.

(d) "Owner" means the owner of record indicated in a certificate of title issued by this state and includes an agent of that owner acting under a valid power of attorney executed by an owner.

(e) "Title" means the certificate of ownership issued by the department pursuant to Section 4450, but excludes a salvage certificate as described in Section 11515 and an acquisition bill of sale as described in Section 11519.

(f) "Vehicle" means every device designed for transportation of persons or property upon land, for which a certificate of title is required.
(Added by Stats. 1994, Ch. 1247, Sec. 6. Effective January 1, 1995. See similar section (except for subd. (e)) added by Stats. 1994, Ch. 1008.)

6162. An owner of a vehicle who seeks to export a vehicle titled in this state shall appear at the department with the certificate of title to ascertain whether there are any liens of record outstanding and whether the person exporting the vehicle is the lawful owner. If the certificate of title is found to be in proper order and no unsatisfied lien appears, the department shall enter into its record of title that the vehicle is intended for permanent exportation from the United States. If the owner certifies by filing a declaration with the department that the vehicle will not be permanently located outside the United States, and that he or she intends to return the vehicle to the United States, the department shall enter into its record of title a declaration that the vehicle will not be permanently located outside the United States until notification by the owner that the vehicle has been returned.
(Amended by Stats. 1995, Ch. 91, Sec. 173. Effective January 1, 1996.)

Article 3. Return of Stolen Motor Vehicle Retained as Evidence

(Article 3 added by Stats. 1994, Ch. 1247, Sec. 6.)

6171. When criminal charges have been filed involving a motor vehicle alleged to have been stolen and the vehicle is in the custody of a peace officer for evidentiary purposes, it shall be held in custody or, if a request for its release from custody is made, until the prosecutor has notified the defendant or his or her attorney of that request and both the prosecution and defense have been afforded a reasonable opportunity for an examination of the motor vehicle to determine its true value and to produce or reproduce, by photographs or other identifying techniques, legally sufficient evidence for introduction at trial or other criminal proceedings.
(Added by Stats. 1994, Ch. 1247, Sec. 6. Effective January 1, 1995.)

6172. Upon expiration of a reasonable time for the completion of the examination, which in no event shall exceed 30 days from the date of service of the notice of request or return of the motor vehicle as provided in Section 6171, the property shall be released to the person making that request after satisfactory proof of the person's entitlement to the possession. Notwithstanding the foregoing, upon ex parte application by either party with notice to the other, the court may grant additional time for the examination or order retention of the motor vehicle if it determines that either is necessary to further the interests of justice; however, this provision shall not be construed to require a noticed hearing.
(Added by Stats. 1994, Ch. 1247, Sec. 6. Effective January 1, 1995.)

Chapter 3. Filing Instruments Evidencing Liens or Encumbrances

(Chapter 3 enacted by Stats. 1959, Ch. 3.)

6300. Except as provided in Sections 5905, 5907, and 5908, no security interest in any vehicle registered under this code, irrespective of whether the registration was effected prior or subsequent to the creation of the security interest, is perfected until the secured party or his or her successor or assignee has deposited, either physically or by electronic transmission pursuant to Section 1801.1, with the department, at its office in Sacramento, or at any other office as may be designated by the director, a properly endorsed certificate of ownership to the vehicle subject to the security interest showing the secured party as legal owner if the vehicle is then registered under this code, or, if the vehicle is not so registered, an application in usual form for an original registration, together with an application for registration of the secured party as legal owner, and upon payment of the fees as provided in this code.

(Amended by Stats. 1996, Ch. 440, Sec. 6. Effective January 1, 1997.)

6301. When the secured party, his or her successor, or his or her assignee, has deposited, either physically or by electronic transmission pursuant to Section 1801.1, with the department a properly endorsed certificate of ownership showing the secured party as legal owner or an application in usual form for an original registration, together with an application for registration of the secured party as legal owner, the deposit constitutes perfection of the security interest and the rights of all persons in the vehicle shall be subject to the provisions of the Uniform Commercial Code, but the vehicle subject to the security interest shall be subject to a lien for services and materials as provided in Chapter 6.5 (commencing with Section 3068) of Title 14 of Part 4 of Division 3 of the Civil Code.

(Amended by Stats. 1996, Ch. 440, Sec. 7. Effective January 1, 1997.)

6302. Upon the deposit of an application for registration of a secured party as legal owner and upon the payment of the fees as provided in this code, the department shall register the secured party, his successor or assignee as legal owner in the manner provided for the registration of motor vehicles under the provisions of this chapter.

(Added by Stats. 1963, Ch. 819.)

6303. Except as provided in Sections 5905, 5907 and 5908, the method provided in this chapter for perfecting a security interest on a vehicle registered under this code is exclusive, but the effect of such perfection, and the creation, attachment, priority and validity of such security interest shall be governed by the Uniform Commercial Code.

(Amended by Stats. 1963, Ch. 819.)

Chapter 4. Permits to Nonresident Owners

(Chapter 4 enacted by Stats. 1959, Ch. 3.)

Article 1. Exemption of Nonresidents

(Article 1 repealed and added by Stats. 1984, Ch. 1322, Sec. 7.)

6700. (a) Except as provided in Section 6700.2, the owner of any vehicle of a type otherwise subject to registration under this code, other than a commercial vehicle registered in a foreign jurisdiction, may operate the vehicle in this state until gainful employment is accepted in this state or until residency is established in this state, whichever occurs first, if the vehicle displays valid license plates and has a valid registration issued to the owner, and the owner was a resident of that state at the time of issuance. Application to register the vehicle shall be made within 20 days after gainful employment is accepted in this state or residency is established in this state.

(b) A nonresident owner of a vehicle, otherwise exempt from registration pursuant to this section or Section 6700.2, may operate or permit operation of the vehicle in this state without registering the vehicle in this state if the vehicle is registered in the place of residence of the owner and displays upon it valid license plates issued by that place. This exemption does not apply if the nonresident owner rents, leases, lends, or otherwise furnishes the vehicle to a California resident for regular use on the highways of this state, as defined in subdivision (b) of Section 4000.4.

(c) Any resident who operates upon a highway of this state a vehicle owned by a nonresident who furnished the vehicle to the resident operator for his or her regular use within this state, as defined in subdivision (b) of Section 4000.4, shall cause the vehicle to be registered in California within 20 days after its first operation within this state by the resident.

(Amended by Stats. 2003, Ch. 594, Sec. 30. Effective January 1, 2004.)

6700.1. (a) Notwithstanding any other provision of law, the department may issue an in-transit permit to a resident of a foreign country not more than 30 days before or after the foreign resident purchases a new motor vehicle in California which was manufactured in the United States. The permit authorizes the operation of the vehicle for which it is purchased for up to 30 consecutive days after the first date of operation, and is in lieu of any other registration requirements, including, but not limited to, fees or taxes required by this code or the Revenue and Taxation Code. The seller shall ship or drive the vehicle out of this country before or at the end of 30 consecutive days from the first date of operation, or thereafter shall be subject to, and shall be required to pay, all charges and registration requirements for vehicles subject to registration in this state. In addition, if the vehicle is not so removed from this country, the department shall assess, and the seller shall be required to pay, a penalty of 20 percent of the vehicle registration and license fees and sales tax due upon the vehicle becoming subject to registration.

(b) Subdivision (a) does not apply to commercial vehicles.

(c) Proof of residency in a foreign country for purposes of this section shall be established through the presentation of a valid visa, passport, or other suitable documentation, as determined by the department.

(d) A fee of sixty dollars ($60) shall be paid to the department for each in-transit permit issued.

(e) A permit issued under this section shall be displayed in the manner permitted by paragraph (3) of subdivision (b) of Section 26708.

(f) The permit issued by the department shall clearly and prominently indicate the date of expiration of the authorized in-transit driving privilege.

(g) No California certificate of ownership shall be issued.

(h) A manufacturer's certificate of origin shall prominently indicate that the certificate is valid for transfer of ownership to the purchaser only outside of the United States, the District of Columbia, or the Commonwealth of Puerto Rico.

(i) Notwithstanding Part 1 (commencing with Section 6001) of Division 2 of the Revenue and Taxation Code, the manufacturer of a new motor vehicle sold to a foreign purchaser under the conditions specified in Section 6366.2 of the Revenue and Taxation Code shall reimburse the retailer for an amount equal to the sales tax and all registration charges and fees, and a penalty of 20 percent of those taxes, charges, and fees if the conditions of the in-transit permit are not met, as specified in this section.

(Added by Stats. 1989, Ch. 762, Sec. 3. Effective September 25, 1989. Operative January 1, 1990, by Sec. 6 of Ch. 762.)

6700.2. (a) Notwithstanding Section 4000.4, subdivision (a) of Section 6700, or Section 6702, a nonresident daily commuter may operate a motor vehicle on the highways of this state only if all of the following conditions are met:

(1) The motor vehicle is a passenger vehicle or a commercial vehicle of less than 8,001 pounds unladen weight with not more than two axles of the type commonly referred to as a pickup truck.

(2) The motor vehicle is used regularly to transport passengers on the highways of this state principally between, and to and from, the place of residence in a contiguous state and the place of employment in this state by the owner of the motor vehicle and for no other business purpose.

(3) The motor vehicle is not used in the course of a business within this state, including the transportation of property other than incidental personal property between, and to or from, the place of residence in a contiguous state and the place of employment of the motor vehicle owner in this state.

(4) Nothing in paragraphs (2) and (3) prohibits a nonresident daily commuter operating a motor vehicle that displays currently valid external vehicle identification indicia and who possess a corresponding identification card issued pursuant to Section 6700.25 from using that vehicle for other lawful purposes.

(b) The exception to registration of a motor vehicle under the conditions specified in this section does not supersede any other exception to registration under other conditions provided by law.

(c) This section does not apply to a resident of a foreign country.

(Amended by Stats. 2001, Ch. 825, Sec. 9. Effective January 1, 2002.)

6700.25. (a) The department shall provide a nonresident daily commuter with external vehicle identification indicia and a corresponding identification card, upon application therefor and completion of the form required by Section 6700.3, which indicia and card shall be valid for a period of two years. A vehicle shall be exempt from Sections 4000.4 and 6700 when operated with the requisite indicia and otherwise in accordance with this chapter.

(b) Subdivision (a) applies only to residents and vehicles of residents of a contiguous state which has enacted laws that provide reciprocal privileges to California residents who are employed in the contiguous state. Subdivision (a) does not apply to residents of foreign countries.

(c) Subdivision (a) applies only to the vehicles specified in paragraph (1) of subdivision (a) of Section 6700.2.

(d) Subdivision (a) applies only to vehicles which are licensed in a foreign jurisdiction that are used to commute into California to a destination within a corridor in this state that parallels the border between California and the contiguous state and extends not more than 35 air miles into California from the border at any point. The privilege accorded by subdivision (a) shall be revoked by operation of the vehicle for commuter purposes beyond that 35-mile corridor.

(e) The department shall charge a service fee of fifteen dollars ($15) for each vehicle.

(Amended by Stats. 2003, Ch. 719, Sec. 8. Effective January 1, 2004.)

6700.3. (a) An application by a nonresident daily commuter for indicia and an identification card pursuant to Section 6700.25 shall be filed with the department.

(b) The department shall prescribe a form to be completed by the applicant which shall include all of the following information:

(1) The vehicle license number and the vehicle identification number (VIN) of the vehicle that will display the nonresident daily commuter indicia.

(2) The name of the registered owner of the vehicle that will display the indicia.

(3) A statement that the applicant is a nonresident daily commuter as defined in Section 435.5.

(4) A statement that the indicia will be displayed upon a qualified vehicle as specified in Section 6700.4.

(5) A statement that the place of employment of the nonresident daily commuter is within the 35-mile corridor specified in subdivision (d) of Section 6700.25.

(Added by Stats. 1985, Ch. 1090, Sec. 5. Effective September 27, 1985.)

6700.4. A nonresident daily commuter indicia shall be displayed in a location on the vehicle which is clearly visible and adjacent to the rear license plate. The corresponding nonresident daily commuter identification card shall be carried at all times in the assigned vehicle and shall be presented to any California peace officer upon demand.

(Added by Stats. 1985, Ch. 1090, Sec. 6. Effective September 27, 1985.)

6701. (a) Any nonresident owner of a vehicle registered in a foreign state who is a member or spouse of a member of the armed forces of the United States on active duty within this state, and any resident owner of a vehicle registered in a foreign state who is a member or spouse of a member of the armed forces of the United States returning from active duty in a foreign state, may operate the vehicle in this state without securing California registration after satisfying all of the following requirements:

(1) The license plates displayed on the vehicle are valid plates issued by a foreign jurisdiction.

(2) The vehicle registration and license plates are issued to the military person or spouse of the military person.

(3) The vehicle registration and license plates were issued by the foreign jurisdiction where the military person was last regularly assigned and stationed for duty by military orders or a jurisdiction claimed by the nonresident military person as the permanent state of residence.

(4) If the vehicle is a motor vehicle, the owner or driver has in force one of the forms of financial responsibility specified in Section 16021.

(b) For purposes of paragraph (3) of subdivision (a), military orders do not include military orders for leave, for temporary duty, or for any other assignment of any nature requiring the military person's presence outside the foreign jurisdiction where the owner was regularly assigned and stationed for duty.

(c) This section applies to all vehicles owned by the military person or spouse except any commercial vehicle used in any business manner wherein the military person or spouse receives compensation.

(Amended by Stats. 1999, Ch. 100, Sec. 1. Effective January 1, 2000.)

6702. Every nonresident, including any foreign corporation, having an established place of business within this state, and regularly using a vehicle of a type subject to registration under this code, shall immediately register the vehicle upon entry into this state.

(Repealed and added by Stats. 1984, Ch. 1322, Sec. 7. Operative July 1, 1985, by Sec. 18 of Ch. 1322.)

6703. Any person entering California following discharge from the armed forces of the United States is exempted from registration of passenger vehicles, trailer coaches, and utility trailers only, as provided for and under the conditions prescribed in Section 6700.

(Repealed and added by Stats. 1984, Ch. 1322, Sec. 7. Operative July 1, 1985, by Sec. 18 of Ch. 1322.)

Article 2. Foreign Commercial Vehicles

(Article 2 enacted by Stats. 1959, Ch. 3.)

6850. A nonresident owner of any foreign commercial vehicle shall register the vehicle in this state and pay the fees applicable thereto under this code, except as provided in this article and Article 3 (commencing with Section 8000), and except in the event the vehicle is lawfully registered as a private passenger vehicle in the foreign jurisdiction in which the owner has residence, in which case Section 6700 shall apply.

(Amended by Stats. 1984, Ch. 1322, Sec. 8. Operative July 1, 1985, by Sec. 18 of Ch. 1322.)

6852. The nonresident owner of a foreign vehicle shall be granted such privileges and freedom from registration and payment of fees imposed by this code, or Part 5 of Division 2 of the Revenue and Taxation Code, commencing at Section 10701, as the foreign jurisdiction in which the foreign commercial vehicle is registered or licensed grants to like vehicles registered under this code or as provided in agreements, arrangements, or declarations made under Article 3, commencing at Section 8000.

(Enacted by Stats. 1959, Ch. 3.)

6853. Any vehicle owned by a nonresident owner not registered under this code, which vehicle is leased or rented to a user having an established place of business or residence in this State, for use on the highways of this State shall be subject to registration either by the owner or lessee of the vehicle, unless the vehicle is exempted from registration by the provisions of this division or under any agreement, arrangement, or declaration made pursuant to Article 3, commencing at Section 8000.

(Enacted by Stats. 1959, Ch. 3.)

6854. (a) Any owner or lessor of a commercial vehicle with primary registration and plates issued in a foreign jurisdiction which does not grant reciprocal privileges to California owners of commercial vehicles shall submit to the department proof of financial responsibility issued by an insurance company authorized to do business in California. This section shall apply only to commercial vehicles having an unladen weight of over 7,000 pounds that are used in the transportation of property in the conduct of a business.

(b) As an alternative to the requirements of subdivision (a), proof of financial responsibility may be met by submitting to the department either of the following:

(1) A certificate of registration as a foreign motor carrier or foreign motor private carrier issued by the Interstate Commerce Commission under Part 1171 of Title 49 of the Code of Federal Regulations.

(2) Contractual documents showing to the satisfaction of the department that a trailer or semitrailer subject to registration under Part 1171 of Title 49 of the Code of Federal Regulations will be towed by a truck or truck tractor operated by a motor carrier having highway carrier operating

authority issued by the Public Utilities Commission.
(Amended by Stats. 1992, Ch. 974, Sec. 3. Effective September 28, 1992.)

Article 3. Reciprocity Agreements

(Article 3 repealed and added by Stats. 1989, Ch. 533, Sec. 6.)

8000. The director, or his or her designee, may enter into agreements with foreign jurisdictions that provide for the exemption of fees for commercial vehicles if the foreign jurisdictions provide equivalent exemptions to vehicles registered in this state. The agreements shall be applicable to vehicles that are properly licensed and registered in the foreign jurisdictions. The director, or his or her designee, may also enter into agreements that provide for the exemption of regulatory fees which are, or may be, imposed, by the Public Utilities Code or the department.
(Amended by Stats. 2011, Ch. 315, Sec. 9. (AB 28) Effective January 1, 2012.)

8001. The director, or his or her designee, is authorized to examine the legal requirements of commercial vehicle registration fee statutes of foreign jurisdictions which grant reciprocal privileges to out-of-state vehicles, but which do not authorize negotiations or execution of agreements. After examination of the statutes, the director, or his or her designee, may declare the exemptions, benefits, and privileges that commercial vehicles registered in foreign jurisdictions shall be entitled to in this state.
(Amended by Stats. 2011, Ch. 315, Sec. 10. (AB 28) Effective January 1, 2012.)

Article 4. Apportioned Registration

(Article 4 repealed and added by Stats. 1989, Ch. 533, Sec. 8.)

8050. The Legislature declares that in enacting this article, it adheres to the principle that each state should have the freedom to develop the kind of highway user tax structure that it determines to be most appropriate to itself, that the method of taxation of interstate vehicles should not be a determining factor in developing its user tax structure and that annual taxes or other taxes of the fixed fee type which are not imposed on a basis that reflects the amount of highway use should be apportioned among the states on the basis of vehicle miles traveled within each of the states. If the department determines that apportionment of the taxes on the basis of vehicle miles for a particular fleet of vehicles is impractical, the department may require the taxes on the fleet to be apportioned on an equivalent basis other than miles, as determined by the department.
(Repealed and added by Stats. 1989, Ch. 533, Sec. 8.)

8052. (a) The director, or his or her designee, may, on behalf of the state, enter into, and become, a member of the International Registration Plan Agreement developed by the American Association of Motor Vehicle Administrators. The director, or his or her designee, may adopt rules and regulations necessary to carry out the provisions of the International Registration Plan or other apportioned registration agreements entered into under the authority of this article.

(b) In administering the International Registration Plan, the state may collect all appropriate registration and license fees due other jurisdictions. Foreign jurisdictions that are members of the agreement shall be authorized to collect all appropriate registration and license fees due to the State of California, and remit the fees to this state pursuant to the terms of the agreement.
(Amended by Stats. 2011, Ch. 315, Sec. 13. (AB 28) Effective January 1, 2012.)

8053. Provisions of this code which specify and govern application filing, fee assignment, penalty assessment, and issuance of license plates and registration certificates, shall be applicable to vehicles registered pursuant to this article.
(Added by Stats. 1989, Ch. 533, Sec. 8.)

8054. (a) Upon the application for transfer of ownership of a fleet of vehicles apportionately registered pursuant to this article, the department shall permit registration in the new owners name without reassessing the registration and vehicle license fees, if the application of the new ownership is for the same fleet interstate operation as the previous owner.

(b) The new owner, lessee, or their designee, shall certify the declared gross vehicle weight of the vehicle or vehicles on a single form for all commercial motor vehicles registered in the fleet owner's or lessee's name. The department shall reassess the weight fees if the declared gross vehicle weight is increased. The weight fees will be assessed at a prorated rate.
(Amended by Stats. 2000, Ch. 861, Sec. 40. Effective September 29, 2000. Operative December 31, 2001, pursuant to Sec. 67 of Ch. 861.)

8055. This article does not apply to any owner or lessee of a commercial vehicle with primary registration and license plates issued in a foreign jurisdiction which does not grant reciprocity or apportioned registration to residents of this state owning commercial vehicles while operating within that foreign jurisdiction.
(Added by Stats. 1989, Ch. 533, Sec. 8.)

8056. Any application filed pursuant to this article which contains vehicles powered by diesel fuel shall include information concerning any diesel fuel tax permit issued by the Board of Equalization.
(Added by Stats. 1989, Ch. 533, Sec. 8.)

8057. Any person issued fleet registration pursuant to Article 9.5 (commencing with Section 5301) of Chapter 1 or this article shall:

(a) Maintain fleet records that support the reported mileage, cost, and declared gross or combined gross vehicle weight of all vehicles. Any registrant whose application for apportioned registration has been accepted shall preserve the mileage records on which the application is based, including copies of all permits, for a period of three years after the close of the registration year. Vehicle cost and declared gross or combined gross weight records shall be retained for four years after the close of the registration year in which the vehicle was deleted.

(b) Make fleet records available to the department at its request for audit to verify the accuracy of the records. In the event the records are not made available within 30 days of the request, the department may assess full California fees and penalties and may suspend or cancel apportioned registration privileges. The registrant may be required to reimburse the department auditor per diem and travel expenses under certain conditions as determined by the director.
(Amended by Stats. 2002, Ch. 758, Sec. 4. Effective January 1, 2003.)

8058. (a) The department shall charge interest on any underpaid fees due under this article, at the rate of 1 percent per month of the underpaid portion of the fees, commencing on the date the underpaid portion of the fees were originally due and accruing monthly until paid.

(b) Interest charged under subdivision (a) shall continue to accumulate during any disputation of the underpaid fees or any hearing regarding the underpaid fees. During any disputation or hearing, the registrant may pay the underpaid fees and other charges to avoid additional interest charges and may request a refund of any overpaid fees after final review.

(c) For any underpaid fees, the department may impose a penalty of fifty dollars ($50) or 10 percent of the underpaid fees, whichever is greater, commencing on the date the underpaid fees were determined to be due.

(d) For the purposes of this section, "underpaid fees" include additional vehicle registration, weight, and license fees found to be due to this state.

(e) The director shall have discretion to apply subdivision (b) of Section 9562 instead of subdivision (c) of this section.

(f) The penalty structure set forth in Sections 9554 and 9554.5 shall apply in place of the provisions of this section in those cases where there is a violation of Section 4000, 4000.4, 4002, 4003, 4004, 4004.5, or 4156 for commercial registration that is not apportioned pursuant to Section 8050.
(Amended by Stats. 2002, Ch. 758, Sec. 5. Effective January 1, 2003.)

Article 5. Federal Motor Vehicle Safety Program

(Article 5 added by Stats. 2006, Ch. 169, Sec. 3.)

8100. An application for apportioned registration received on and after January 1, 2008, and filed pursuant to Article 4 (commencing with Section 8050) shall contain the following information:

(a) The United States Department of Transportation Number issued to the person responsible for the safe operation of each vehicle being registered.

(b) The taxpayer identification number corresponding to the United States Department of Transportation number provided in the apportioned registration application. The taxpayer identification number may consist of the federal employer identification number or the social security number, as applicable.

(c) Notwithstanding any other provision of law, the taxpayer identification number provided pursuant to this section is confidential and shall not be disclosed by the department except to law enforcement or a federal agency, or as required by law.

(Added by Stats. 2006, Ch. 169, Sec. 3. Effective January 1, 2007.)

8101. In addition to the reasons specified in Section 4750 or 4751, the department shall refuse an application for apportioned registration for the following grounds:

(a) The applicant has failed to furnish the department with information required in the application under Section 8100.

(b) The person responsible for the safety of the vehicle or fleet is prohibited from operating in interstate commerce by a federal agency.

(Added by Stats. 2006, Ch. 169, Sec. 3. Effective January 1, 2007.)

8102. (a) In addition to the reasons specified in Section 8800, the department may suspend the apportioned registration of a vehicle or a fleet, when the person responsible for the safety of the vehicle or a fleet of vehicles is prohibited from operating in interstate commerce by a federal agency.

(b) Whenever the department suspends the apportioned registration of a vehicle or a fleet pursuant to subdivision (a), the department may refuse the issuance of vehicle registration as authorized pursuant to Section 4751.

(c) Whenever the department suspends the apportioned registration under subdivision (a), the department shall furnish the person responsible for the vehicle or fleet with written notice of the suspension.

(d) When an apportioned registration is suspended pursuant to this section, and that suspension is based wholly or in part on the failure of the person to maintain a vehicle or a fleet in safe operating condition, the person to whom the registration was issued shall not lease, or otherwise allow, another person to operate a vehicle that is subject to the suspension during the period of the suspension.

(e) A person shall not knowingly lease, operate, dispatch, or otherwise utilize a vehicle from another person whose apportioned registration is suspended, when that suspension is based wholly or in part on the failure of the person to maintain a vehicle or a fleet in safe operating condition.

(f) The apportioned registration of a vehicle or a fleet, that was suspended because the vehicle or fleet is prohibited from operating in interstate commerce by a federal agency may be reinstated upon notification from the federal agency that the prohibition has been lifted.

(g) Notwithstanding any other provision of this code, before an apportioned registration may be reissued after a suspension is terminated, there shall, in addition to other fees required by this code, be paid to the department a fee of one hundred fifty dollars ($150). This fee shall be deposited in the Motor Vehicle Account to cover the department's cost of administering this program.

(Added by Stats. 2006, Ch. 169, Sec. 3. Effective January 1, 2007.)

8103. Notwithstanding any other provision of this code, a hearing shall not be provided when the suspension is based solely on notification by a federal agency that interstate operation is prohibited.

(Added by Stats. 2006, Ch. 169, Sec. 3. Effective January 1, 2007.)

8104. Except as provided in subdivision (e), a vehicle or a fleet for which the apportioned registration has been suspended pursuant to this article shall not be operated in interstate or intrastate commerce unless evidence is provided to the department that the vehicle or the fleet is to be operated by a person whose apportioned registration is not subject to a suspension pursuant to this article and who has a valid apportioned registration pursuant to Article 4 (commencing with Section 8050) or Division 14.85.

(Added by Stats. 2006, Ch. 169, Sec. 3. Effective January 1, 2007.)

Article 6. Enforcement of Liens on Apportioned Fleet Vehicles

(Article 6 added by Stats. 1989, Ch. 187, Sec. 2.)

8200. "Registrant," for purposes of this article, means any person issued apportioned fleet registration pursuant to Article 4 (commencing with Section 8050).

(Amended by Stats. 1996, Ch. 124, Sec. 120. Effective January 1, 1997.)

8201. (a) Fees determined to be due, including penalties and service fees, for the operation of a fleet apportionately registered vehicle shall be a lien upon all vehicles operated as part of the fleet and on any other fleet vehicles operated by the registrant. The department may collect the amount of the lien, plus costs, not to exceed two hundred fifty dollars ($250), in an appropriate civil action and by seizure and sale of the vehicle.

(b) Liens arising as the result of an audit expire four years from the date the registration fees first become due unless the lien is perfected pursuant to subdivision (d).

(c) Any lien arising under this section that is not subject to subdivision (b) expires three years from the date the fee or penalty first became due unless the lien is perfected pursuant to subdivision (d).

(d) A lien shall be perfected when a notice is mailed to the registrant at the address shown on the department's records and the lien is recorded on the electronic vehicle registration records of the department. A perfected lien shall expire five years from the date of perfection.

(e) Prior to the expiration of the statute of limitations, the registrant may consent to a waiver which would allow the assessment of fees and penalties past the statute of limitations.

(Amended by Stats. 2002, Ch. 758, Sec. 6. Effective January 1, 2003.)

8202. (a) Within 30 days of the date the notice is mailed pursuant to Section 8201, the registrant may submit documentation not previously available or may request a hearing to contest the existence or the amount of the lien. If no additional documentation is submitted, or if no hearing is requested, the operating privileges of the fleet may be suspended or canceled and a sufficient number of vehicles may be seized and sold to satisfy the lien.

(b) If additional documentation is submitted, the department shall review the documentation and issue its findings to the registrant. Within 30 days of the date the findings are mailed, the registrant may request a hearing.

(c) If a hearing is requested, 10 days' notice shall be given of the time and place of the hearing, which shall be held within the county of residence of the person requesting the hearing or within the county of the established place of business of the registrant. The hearing shall be conducted by a referee who shall submit findings and recommendations to the director or his or her authorized representative, who shall decide the matter. The decision shall be effective on notice thereof to the interested parties. However, the director, or his or her authorized representative, may rescind the decision and reconsider the matter for good cause shown at any time within three years after the date the disputed fee or penalty first became due, or one year from the hearing whichever is later.

(d) Upon final completion of all administrative appeals, the department shall give written notice to the registrant of the right to a review of the decision by a court of competent jurisdiction. Any action brought in court shall be commenced within 90 days from the date notice of the decision is mailed.

(Amended by Stats. 2010, Ch. 478, Sec. 10. (AB 2777) Effective January 1, 2011.)

8203. (a) When a lien is perfected pursuant to Section 8200 and the opportunity to submit additional documentation or to request a hearing has passed, the department may suspend or cancel the operating privileges of the fleet. When the suspension takes effect, the department may seize a sufficient number of vehicles to satisfy the lien without further notice, upon obtaining authorization for the seizure and sale from the director or his or her authorized representative.

(b) Members of the California Highway Patrol, and peace officers employed by local authorities, are agents of the department for the purposes of this section.

(c) In all cases, prior to the sale, a notice of the lien and intent to sell the vehicle shall be given by the department to the registrant, the known legal and registered owners, and to any other person known to be claiming an interest in the vehicle. The department shall also give public notice of the lien by placing an advertisement in a newspaper of general circulation published in the county in which the registrant's place of business is located.

(d) At any time before seizure and sale, any person claiming an interest in the vehicle may pay the department the amount of the lien, plus costs. In that event, the seizure and sale shall not be held, and the vehicle, shall be returned by the department to the person entitled to its possession.

(e) Any property found by the department in any vehicle seized under the provisions of this article shall be handled by the department in the manner provided in Sections 2414 and 2415.

(f) The sale shall be conducted and proceeds distributed pursuant to Section 9802.

(Added by Stats. 1989, Ch. 187, Sec. 2.)

8204. (a) When a transferee or purchaser of an apportionately registered fleet vehicle applies to the department for transfer of ownership and it is determined by the department that there is an outstanding lien against the fleet in which the vehicle was operated, that fees became due prior to the transfer or purchase of the vehicle, and that the transferee or the purchaser was not cognizant of the fact that a lien existed, the department may waive apportioned registration fees and any penalties that are due.

(b) When fees and penalties are waived pursuant to subdivision (a), the apportioned registration fees and penalties shall become the liability of the registrant who failed to pay the fees and penalties when they became due. The fees and penalties may be collected by the department in an appropriate civil action.

(Added by Stats. 1989, Ch. 187, Sec. 2.)

Chapter 5. Offenses Against Registration Laws and Suspension, Revocation, and Cancellation of Registration

(Chapter 5 enacted by Stats. 1959, Ch. 3.)

8800. (a) The department may suspend, cancel, or revoke the registration of a vehicle or a certificate of ownership, registration card, license plate, or permit under any of the following circumstances:

(1) When the department is satisfied that the registration or the certificate, card, plate, or permit was fraudulently obtained or erroneously issued.

(2) When the department determines that a registered vehicle is mechanically unfit or unsafe to be operated or moved upon the highways.

(3) When a registered vehicle has been dismantled or wrecked.

(4) When the department determines that the required fee has not been paid and the same is not paid upon reasonable notice and demand.

(5) When a registration card, license plate, or permit is knowingly displayed upon a vehicle other than the one for which issued.

(6) When the registration could have been refused when last issued or renewed.

(7) When the department determines that the owner or legal owner has committed an offense under Sections 20 (with respect to an application for the registration of a vehicle), 4000, 4159 to 4163, inclusive, 4454, 4456, 4461, 4463, 5202, 10750, and 10751, involving the registration or the certificate, card, plate, or permit to be suspended, canceled, or revoked.

(8) When the department is so authorized pursuant to any other provision of law.

(b) The department may suspend the registration of all vehicles registered in the name of a person, under any of the following circumstances:

(1) When the United States Secretary of the Department of Transportation or his or her designee issues a lawful out-of-service order pursuant to Title 49 of the Code of Federal Regulations.

(2) When the department suspends or revokes a motor carrier of property permit.

(3) When the Public Utilities Commission suspends or revokes operating authority or private registration.

(c) A suspension imposed pursuant to subdivision (b) shall remain in effect and a vehicle for which registration has been suspended shall not be registered in the name of the person until the department verifies that person's federal registration, federal operating authority, California operating authority, California private registration, or motor carrier of property permit is reissued.

(Amended by Stats. 2006, Ch. 288, Sec. 3. Effective January 1, 2007.)

8801. The department may suspend, cancel, revoke, or renew any permanent registration made under Section 4155 when the department determines that it is advisable to reissue the registration.

(Enacted by Stats. 1959, Ch. 3.)

8802. Whenever the department cancels, suspends, or revokes the registration of a vehicle or a certificate of ownership, registration card, or license plates, or any nonresident or other permit, the owner or person in possession shall immediately return the documents, plates, certificates, or other evidence of registration to the department.

(Amended by Stats. 1967, Ch. 482.)

8803. Whenever the department cancels, suspends, or revokes any license issued pursuant to Division 5 (commencing with Section 11100), the licensee or person in possession shall immediately return the license, documents, plates, certificates, and other evidence of the license to the department.

(Amended by Stats. 1990, Ch. 1563, Sec. 5.)

8804. Every person who, while a resident, as defined in Section 516, of this state, with respect to any vehicle owned by him and operated in this state, registers or renews the registration for the vehicle in a foreign jurisdiction, without the payment of appropriate fees and taxes to this state, is guilty of a misdemeanor.

(Added by Stats. 1983, Ch. 409, Sec. 4.)

Chapter 6. Registration and Weight Fees

(Chapter 6 enacted by Stats. 1959, Ch. 3.)

Article 1. Exemptions

(Article 1 enacted by Stats. 1959, Ch. 3.)

9101. No fees specified in this code, except fees not exempted under Section 9103, need be paid for any vehicle operated by the state, or by any county, city, district, or political subdivision of the state, or the United States, as lessee under a lease, lease-sale, or rental-purchase agreement that grants possession of the vehicle to the lessee for a period of 30 consecutive days or more.

(Amended by Stats. 2003, Ch. 594, Sec. 31. Effective January 1, 2004.)

9102. The fees specified in this code except fees for duplicate plates, certificates, or cards need not be paid for any vehicle owned by an educational institution of collegiate grade not conducted for profit and having an enrollment of 5,000 students or more and having an acreage of 5,000 acres or more, if such vehicle is used for fire-fighting purposes within the limits of the acreage of such institution and is operated principally on roads owned by such institution.

(Enacted by Stats. 1959, Ch. 3.)

9102.5. (a) In lieu of all other fees which are specified in this code, except fees for duplicate plates, certificates, or cards, a fee of fifteen dollars ($15) shall be paid for the registration and licensing of any privately owned schoolbus, as defined in Section 545, which is either of the following:

(1) Owned by a private nonprofit educational organization and operated in accordance with the rules and regulations of the Department of Education and the Department of the California Highway Patrol exclusively in transporting school pupils, or school pupils and employees, of the private nonprofit educational organization.

(2) Operated in accordance with the rules and regulations of the Department of Education and the Department of the California Highway Patrol exclusively in transporting school pupils, or school pupils and employees, of any public school or private nonprofit educational organization pursuant to a contract between a public school district or nonprofit educational organization and the owner or operator of the schoolbus.

This section does not apply to any schoolbus which is operated pursuant to any contract which requires the public school district or nonprofit educational organization to pay any amount representing the costs of registration and weight fees unless and until the contract is amended to require only the payment of an amount representing the fee required by this section.

(b) When a schoolbus under contract and registered pursuant to subdivision (a) is to be temporarily operated in such a manner that it becomes subject to full registration fees specified in this code, the owner may, prior to that operation, as an alternative to the full registration, secure a temporary permit to operate the vehicle in this state for any one or more calendar months. The permit shall be posted upon the windshield or other prominent place upon the vehicle, and shall identify the vehicle to which it is affixed. When so affixed, the permit shall serve as indicia of full registration for the period designated on the permit. Upon payment of the fees specified in Section 9266.5, the department may issue a temporary permit under this section.

(c) Notwithstanding any other provision, any schoolbus used exclusively to transport students at or below the 12th-grade level to or from any school, for an education-related purpose, or for an activity sponsored by a nonprofit organization shall be deemed to be a schoolbus for the purposes of this section and shall pay a fee of fifteen dollars ($15) in lieu of all other fees which are specified in this code, except fees for duplicate plates, certificates, or cards.

(d) This section does not apply to a schoolbus, operated to transport persons who are developmentally disabled, as defined by the Lanterman Developmental Disabilities Services Act (Division 4.5 (commencing with Section 4500) of the Welfare and Institutions Code), to or from vocational, prevocational, or work training centers sponsored by the State Department of Developmental Services.

(Amended by Stats. 2003, Ch. 719, Sec. 9. Effective January 1, 2004.)

9103. (a) Fees specified in this code, except fees for duplicate plates, certificates, or cards, are not required to be paid for any vehicle of a type subject to registration under this code owned by the United States or by any state or political subdivision of a state or by any municipality duly organized under the California Constitution or laws of this state.

(b) The registration fees specified in this code, except fees for duplicate plates, certificates, or cards, are not required to be paid for any vehicle owned by a public entity described in subdivision (f) of Section 15975 of the Government Code.

(Amended by Stats. 2009, Ch. 200, Sec. 8. (SB 734) Effective January 1, 2010.)

9104. The fees specified in this code except fees for duplicate plates, certificates, or cards need not be paid for any vehicle of a type subject to registration under this code owned by a public fire department organized as a nonprofit corporation and used exclusively for firefighting or rescue purposes or exclusively as an ambulance, nor for any vehicle owned by a voluntary fire department organized under the laws of this state and used exclusively for firefighting or rescue purposes or exclusively as an ambulance.

(Amended by Stats. 1979, Ch. 517.)

9104.2. The fees specified in this code, except fees for duplicate plates, certificates, or cards need not be paid for a vehicle of a type subject to registration under this code owned by a federally recognized Indian tribe that has entered into a mutual aid agreement with a state, county, city, or other governmental municipality for fire protection and emergency response, and the equipment is used exclusively for firefighting or rescue purposes or exclusively as an ambulance.

(Added by Stats. 2008, Ch. 92, Sec. 1. Effective January 1, 2009.)

9104.5. The fees specified in this code, except fees for registration under Section 9250, need not be paid for any vehicle of a type subject to registration under this code if the vehicle is owned by a federally recognized Indian tribe and the vehicle is used exclusively within the boundaries of lands under the jurisdiction of that Indian tribe, including the incidental use of that vehicle on highways within those boundaries.

(Added by Stats. 1999, Ch. 911, Sec. 2. Effective January 1, 2000.)

9105. (a) Except for fees for duplicate license plates, duplicate certificates, or duplicate cards, the fees specified in this code need not be paid for a vehicle that is of a type subject to registration under this code, and that is not used for transportation for hire, compensation, or profit, when owned by any of the following:

(1) A disabled veteran.

(2) A former American prisoner of war.

(3) The surviving spouse of a former American prisoner of war who has elected to retain the special license plates issued under Section 5101.5.

(4) A Congressional Medal of Honor recipient.

(5) The surviving spouse of a Congressional Medal of Honor recipient who has elected to retain the special license plates issued under Section 5101.6.

(b) The exemption granted by subdivision (a) shall not extend to more than one vehicle owned by a former American prisoner of war, a disabled veteran, or a Congressional Medal of Honor recipient, or a surviving spouse, and is applicable to the same vehicle as described in subdivision (b) of Section 10783, or subdivision (b) of Section 10783.2, of the Revenue and Taxation Code.

(c) (1) The department may require a disabled veteran applying for an exemption under this section to submit a certificate signed by a physician and surgeon, or to the extent that it does not cause a reduction in the receipt of federal aid highway funds, by a nurse practitioner, certified nurse midwife, physician assistant, chiropractor, or optometrist, substantiating the disability.

(2) The department may require a person applying for an exemption under this section for either of the following reasons to do any of the following:

(A) By reason of the person's status as a former prisoner of war, to show, by satisfactory proof, the person's former prisoner-of-war status.

(B) By reason of the person's status of receiving the Congressional Medal of Honor, to show, by satisfactory proof, that the person is a Congressional Medal of Honor recipient.

(d) For the purposes of this section, the term "vehicle" means any of the following:

(1) A passenger motor vehicle.

(2) A motorcycle.

(3) A commercial motor vehicle of less than 8,001 pounds unladen weight.

(e) This section shall remain in effect only until January 1, 2027, and as of that date is repealed.

(Amended by Stats. 2022, Ch. 382, Sec. 1. (AB 2509) Effective January 1, 2023. Repealed as of January 1, 2027, by its own provisions. See later operative version added by Sec. 2 of Stats. 2022, Ch. 382.)

9105. (a) Except for fees for duplicate license plates, duplicate certificates, or duplicate cards, the fees specified in this code need not be paid for a vehicle that is of a type subject to registration under this code, and that is not used for transportation for hire, compensation, or profit, when owned by any of the following:

(1) A disabled veteran.

(2) A former American prisoner of war.

(3) The surviving spouse of a former American prisoner of war who has elected to retain the special license plates issued under Section 5101.5.

(4) A Congressional Medal of Honor recipient.

(5) The surviving spouse of a Congressional Medal of Honor recipient who has elected to retain the special license plates issued under Section 5101.6.

(6) A Purple Heart recipient.

(7) The surviving spouse of a Purple Heart recipient who has elected to retain the special license plates issued under Section 5101.8.

(b) The exemption granted by subdivision (a) does not extend to more than one vehicle owned by a former American prisoner of war, a disabled veteran, a Purple Heart recipient, or a Congressional Medal of Honor recipient, or a surviving spouse, and applies to the same vehicle as described in subdivision (b) of Section 10783, or subdivision (b) of Section 10783.2, of the Revenue and Taxation Code.

(c) (1) The department may require a disabled veteran applying for an exemption under this section to submit a certificate signed by a physician and surgeon, or to the extent that it does not cause a reduction in the receipt of federal aid highway funds, by a nurse practitioner, certified nurse midwife, physician assistant, chiropractor, or optometrist, substantiating the disability.

(2) The department may require a person applying for an exemption under this section for either of the following reasons to do any of the following:

(A) By reason of the person's status as a former prisoner of war, to show, by satisfactory proof, the person's former prisoner-of-war status.

(B) By reason of the person's status of receiving the Congressional Medal of Honor, to show, by satisfactory proof, that the person is a Congressional Medal of Honor recipient.

(C) By reason of the person's status of receiving the Purple Heart, to show, by satisfactory proof, that the person is a Purple Heart recipient.

(d) For the purposes of this section, the term "vehicle" means any of the following:

(1) A passenger motor vehicle.

(2) A motorcycle.

(3) A commercial motor vehicle of less than 8,001 pounds unladen weight.

(e) This section shall become operative on January 1, 2027.

(Repealed (in Sec. 1) and added by Stats. 2022, Ch. 382, Sec. 2. (AB 2509) Effective January 1, 2023. Operative January 1, 2027, by its own provisions.)

9106. The fees specified in this code, except fees for duplicate plates, certificates or cards, need not be paid for any vehicle of a type subject to registration under this code which is operated by the Civil Air Patrol, when the vehicle has been transferred to the Civil Air Patrol by the United States Government, or any agency thereof, if by federal regulation or directive the use of such vehicle is restricted to defined activities of the Civil Air Patrol, and if by federal regulation or directive the vehicle must be returned to the United States Government when no longer required or suited for use by the Civil Air Patrol. Such vehicles shall be registered as otherwise required under this code by the Civil Air Patrol and the Civil Air Patrol shall display a license plate or plates bearing distinguishing marks or symbols as specified in this code, which plate or plates shall be furnished by the department free of charge.

(Enacted by Stats. 1959, Ch. 3.)

9107. The weight fees for commercial vehicles specified in Sections 9400 and 9400.1 do not apply to any of the following:

(a) A vehicle operated by a passenger stage corporation, as defined in Section 226 of the Public Utilities Code, that is subject to the jurisdiction of the Public Utilities Commission, if all of the following conditions are met:

(1) The vehicle is operated exclusively on any line or lines having a one-way route mileage not exceeding 15 miles, and each of those lines is operated in either of the following areas:

(A) In urban or suburban areas or between cities in close proximity.

(B) Between nonadjacent urban or suburban areas or cities, the area between which is substantially residential, commercial, or industrial as distinguished from rural.

(2) The principal business of the passenger stage corporation is the operation of vehicles on a route or routes as defined in paragraph (1).

(b) A vehicle operated exclusively on any line or lines within the limits of a single city by a person engaged as a common carrier of passengers between fixed termini or over a regular route, 98 percent of whose operations, as measured by total route mileage operated, are exclusively within the limits of a single city, and who by reason thereof is not a passenger stage corporation subject to the jurisdiction of the Public Utilities Commission.

(c) Vanpool vehicles.

(d) A vehicle purchased with federal funds under the authority of paragraph (2) of subsection (a) of Section 5310 of Title 49 of the United States Code or Chapter 35 (commencing with Section 3001) of Title 42 of the United States Code for the purpose of providing specialized transportation services to senior citizens and handicapped persons by public and private nonprofit operators of specialized transportation service agencies.

(e) A vehicle operated solely for the purpose of providing specialized transportation services to senior citizens and persons with disabilities, by a nonprofit, public benefit consolidated transportation service agency designated under Section 15975 of the Government Code.

(Amended by Stats. 2003, Ch. 594, Sec. 32. Effective January 1, 2004.)

Article 2. Registration Fees

(Article 2 enacted by Stats. 1959, Ch. 3.)

9250. (a) A registration fee of forty-three dollars ($43) shall be paid to the department for the registration of each vehicle or trailer coach of a type subject to registration under this code, except those vehicles that are expressly exempted under this code from the payment of registration fees. This subdivision applies to all of the following:

(1) The initial or original registration, on or after July 1, 2011, but before April 1, 2017, of any vehicle not previously registered in this state.

(2) The renewal of registration of any vehicle for which the registration period expires on or after July 1, 2011, but before April 1, 2017.

(b) A registration fee of fifty-three dollars ($53) shall be paid to the department for the registration of each vehicle or trailer coach of a type subject to registration under this code, except those vehicles that are expressly exempted under this code from the payment of registration fees. This subdivision applies to all of the following:

(1) The initial or original registration, on or after April 1, 2017, of any vehicle not previously registered in this state.

(2) The renewal or original registration of any vehicle for which the registration period expires on or after April 1, 2017, regardless of whether a renewal application was mailed to the registered owner before April 1, 2017.

(c) The registration fee imposed under this section applies to all vehicles described in Section 5004, whether or not special identification plates are issued to that vehicle.

(d) Trailer coaches are subject to the registration fee provided in subdivision (a) or (b) for each unit of the trailer coach.

(e) The amounts collected pursuant to the increase in the registration fee as specified in subdivision (b) shall be used only for costs incurred in connection with the regulation of vehicles, including administrative costs for vehicle registration.

(Amended by Stats. 2016, Ch. 339, Sec. 6. (SB 838) Effective September 13, 2016.)

9250.1. (a) Beginning July 1, 2008, the fee described in Section 9250 shall be increased by three dollars ($3).

(b) Two dollars ($2) of the increase shall be deposited into the Alternative and Renewable Fuel and Vehicle Technology Fund created by Section 44273 of the Health and Safety Code, and one dollar ($1) shall be deposited into the Enhanced Fleet Modernization Subaccount created by Section 44126 of the Health and Safety Code.

(c) This section shall become inoperative on July 1, 2035, and, as of January 1, 2036, is repealed.

(Amended by Stats. 2023, Ch. 319, Sec. 12. (AB 126) Effective October 7, 2023. Inoperative July 1, 2035, by its own provisions. Repealed as of January 1, 2036, by its own provisions.)

9250.2. (a) The department, if requested by the Sacramento Metropolitan Air Quality Management District pursuant to Section 41081 of the Health and Safety Code, shall impose and collect a surcharge on the registration fees for every motor vehicle registered in that district, not to exceed the amount of six dollars ($6), as specified by the governing body of that district.

(b) This section shall remain in effect only until January 1, 2034, and as of that date is repealed, unless a later enacted statute, that is enacted before January 1, 2034, deletes or extends that date.

(Amended (as amended by Stats. 2013, Ch. 401, Sec. 36) by Stats. 2022, Ch. 355, Sec. 24. (AB 2836) Effective January 1, 2023. Repealed as of January 1, 2034, by its own provisions. See later operative version, as amended by Sec. 25 of Stats. 2022, Ch. 355.)

9250.2. (a) The department, if requested by the Sacramento Metropolitan Air Quality Management District pursuant to Section 41081 of the Health and Safety Code, shall impose and collect a surcharge on the registration fees for every motor vehicle registered in that district, not to exceed four dollars ($4).

(b) This section shall become operative on January 1, 2034.

(Amended (as amended by Stats. 2013, Ch. 401, Sec. 37) by Stats. 2022, Ch. 355, Sec. 25. (AB 2836) Effective January 1, 2023. Operative January 1, 2034, by its own provisions.)

9250.4. (a) The department shall, if requested by a countywide transportation planning agency, collect the fee imposed pursuant to Section 65089.20 of the Government Code upon the registration or renewal of registration of a motor vehicle registered in the county, except those vehicles that are expressly exempted under this code from the payment of registration fees.

(b) The countywide transportation planning agency shall pay for the initial setup and programming costs identified by the department through a direct contract with the department. Any direct contract payment by the board shall be repaid, with no restriction on the funds, to the countywide transportation planning agency as part of the initial revenues available for distribution.

(c) (1) After deducting all costs incurred pursuant to this section, the department shall distribute the net revenues pursuant to subdivision (a) of Section 65089.20 of the Government Code.

(2) The costs deducted under paragraph (1) shall not be counted against the 5-percent administrative cost limit specified in subdivision (d) of Section 65089.20 of the Government Code.

(Added by Stats. 2009, Ch. 554, Sec. 3. (SB 83) Effective January 1, 2010.)

9250.5. (a) The department shall, if requested by the City/County Association of Governments of San Mateo County, collect the fee imposed pursuant to Section 65089.11 of the Government Code upon the registration or renewal of registration of any motor vehicle registered in the county, except those vehicles that are expressly exempted under this code from the payment of registration fees.

(b) The City/County Association of Governments of San Mateo County shall pay for the initial setup and programming costs identified by the Department of Motor Vehicles through a direct contract with the department. Any direct contract payment by the City/County Association of Governments of San Mateo County shall be repaid, with no restriction on the funds, to the City/County Association of Governments of San Mateo County as part of the initial revenues distributed. Regular Department of Motor Vehicles collection costs shall be in accordance with subdivision (c). These costs shall not be counted against the 5-percent administration cost limit specified in subdivision (e) of Section 65089.12.

(c) After deducting all costs incurred pursuant to this section, the department shall distribute the revenues to the City/County Association of Governments of San Mateo County.

(Added by Stats. 2004, Ch. 931, Sec. 2. Effective January 1, 2005.)

9250.6. (a) In addition to any other fees specified in this code, or the Revenue and Taxation Code, commencing July 1, 2020, a road improvement fee of one hundred dollars ($100) shall be paid to the department for registration or renewal of registration of every zero-emission motor vehicle model year 2020 and later subject to registration under this code, except those motor vehicles that are expressly exempted under this code from payment of registration fees.

(b) On January 1, 2021, and every January 1 thereafter, the Department of Motor Vehicles shall adjust the road improvement fee imposed under subdivision (a) by increasing the fee in an amount equal to the increase in the California Consumer Price Index for the prior year, except the first adjustment shall cover the prior six months, as calculated by the Department of Finance, with amounts equal to or greater than fifty cents ($0.50) rounded to the highest whole dollar. The incremental change shall be added to the associated fee rate for that year.

(c) Any changes to the road improvement fee imposed by subdivision (a) that are enacted by legislation subsequent to July 1, 2017, shall be deemed to be changes to the base fee rate for purposes of the California Consumer Price Index calculation and adjustment performed pursuant to subdivision (b).

(d) Revenues from the road improvement fee, after deduction of the department's administrative costs related to this section, shall be deposited in the Road Maintenance and Rehabilitation Account created pursuant to Section 2031 of the Streets and Highways Code.

(e) This section does not apply to a commercial motor vehicle subject to Section 9400.1.

(f) This section does not apply to a vehicle issued apportioned registration pursuant to the International Registration Plan.

(g) The road improvement fee required pursuant to this section does not apply to the initial registration after the purchase of a new zero-emission motor vehicle.

(h) For purposes of this section, "zero-emission motor vehicle" means a motor vehicle as described in subdivision (d) of Section 44258 of the Health and Safety Code.

(Amended by Stats. 2017, Ch. 20, Sec. 22. (AB 115) Effective June 27, 2017.)

9250.7. (a) (1) A service authority established under Section 22710 may impose a service fee of one dollar ($1) on all vehicles, except vehicles described in subdivision (a) of Section 5014.1, registered to an owner with an address in the county that established the service authority. The fee shall be paid to the department at the time of registration, or renewal of registration, or when renewal becomes delinquent, except on vehicles that are expressly exempted under this code from the payment of registration fees.

(2) In addition to the one-dollar ($1) service fee, and upon the implementation of the permanent trailer identification plate program, and as part of the Commercial Vehicle Registration Act of 2001, all commercial motor vehicles subject to Section 9400.1 registered to an owner with an address in the county that established a service authority under this section shall pay an additional service fee of two dollars ($2).

(b) The department, after deducting its administrative costs, shall transmit, at least quarterly, the net amount collected pursuant to subdivision (a) to the Treasurer for deposit in the Abandoned Vehicle Trust Fund, which is hereby created. All money in the fund is continuously appropriated to the Controller for allocation to a service authority that has an approved abandoned vehicle abatement program pursuant to Section 22710, and for payment of the administrative costs of the Controller. After deduction of its administrative costs, the Controller shall allocate the money in the Abandoned Vehicle Trust Fund to each service authority in proportion to the revenues received from the fee imposed by that authority pursuant to subdivision (a). If any funds received by a service authority pursuant to this section are not expended to abate abandoned vehicles pursuant to an approved abandoned vehicle abatement program that has been in existence for at least two full fiscal years within 90 days of the close of the fiscal year in which the funds were received and the amount of those funds exceeds the amount expended by the service authority for the abatement of abandoned vehicles in the previous fiscal year, the fee imposed pursuant to subdivision (a) shall be suspended for one year, commencing on July 1 following the Controller's determination pursuant to subdivision (e).

(c) Every service authority that imposes a fee authorized by subdivision (a) shall issue a fiscal yearend report to the Controller on or before October 31 of each year summarizing all of the following:

(1) The total revenues received by the service authority during the previous fiscal year.

(2) The total expenditures by the service authority during the previous fiscal year.

(3) The total number of vehicles abated during the previous fiscal year.

(4) The average cost per abatement during the previous fiscal year.

(5) Any additional, unexpended fee revenues for the service authority during the previous fiscal year.

(6) The number of notices to abate issued to vehicles during the previous fiscal year.

(7) The number of vehicles disposed of pursuant to an ordinance adopted pursuant to Section 22710 during the previous fiscal year.

(8) The total expenditures by the service authority for towing and storage of abandoned vehicles during the previous fiscal year.

(d) Each service authority that fails to submit the report required pursuant to subdivision (c) by October 31 of each year shall have its fee pursuant to subdivision (a) suspended for one year commencing on July 1 following the Controller's determination pursuant to subdivision (e).

(e) On or before January 1 annually, the Controller shall review the fiscal yearend reports, submitted by each service authority pursuant to subdivision (c) and due no later than October 31, to determine if fee revenues are being utilized in a manner consistent with the service authority's approved program. If the Controller determines that the use of the fee revenues is not consistent with the service authority's program as approved by the Department of the California Highway Patrol, or that an excess of fee revenues exists, as specified in subdivision (b), the authority to collect the fee shall be suspended for one year pursuant to subdivision (b). If the Controller determines that a service authority has not submitted a fiscal yearend report as required in subdivision (c), the authorization to collect the service fee shall be suspended for one year pursuant to subdivisions (b) and (d). The Controller shall inform the Department of Motor Vehicles on or before January 1 annually, that the authority to collect the fee is suspended. A suspension shall only occur if the service authority has been in existence for at least two full fiscal years and the revenue fee surpluses are in excess of those allowed under this section, the use of the fee revenue is not consistent with the service authority's approved program, or the required fiscal yearend report has not been submitted by October 31.

(f) On or before January 1, 2010, and biennially thereafter, the service authority shall have a financial audit of the service authority conducted by a qualified independent third party.

(g) The fee imposed by a service authority shall remain in effect only for a period of 10 years from the date that the actual collection of the fee commenced unless the fee is extended pursuant to this subdivision. The fee may be extended in increments of up to 10 years each if the board of supervisors of the county, by a two-thirds vote, and a majority of the cities having a majority of the incorporated population within the county adopt resolutions providing for the extension of the fee.

(Amended by Stats. 2012, Ch. 728, Sec. 176. (SB 71) Effective January 1, 2013.)

9250.8. (a) In addition to any other fees specified in this code and the Revenue and Taxation Code, a fee of three dollars ($3) shall be paid at the time of registration or renewal of registration of every vehicle, except vehicles described in subdivision (a) of Section 5014.1, subject to registration under this code, except those vehicles that are expressly exempted under this code from the payment of registration fees.

(b) In addition to the fee required under subdivision (a), upon the implementation of the permanent trailer identification plate program, and as part of the Commercial Vehicle Registration Act of 2001, all commercial motor vehicles subject to Section 9400.1 shall pay a fee of six dollars ($6).

(Amended by Stats. 2003, Ch. 719, Sec. 11. Effective January 1, 2004.)

9250.9. All fees received by the department pursuant to Section 9250.8 shall be deposited in the Motor Vehicle Account in the State Transportation Fund. The money deposited in the account pursuant to this section shall be available, upon appropriation by the Legislature, for expenditure to accomplish the following:

(a) To ensure sufficient support for those peace officer members employed on December 31, 1994, and to support an additional 130 peace officer members of the California Highway Patrol.

(b) To offset the costs of maintaining the uniformed field strength of the Department of the California Highway Patrol.

(Amended by Stats. 1994, Ch. 1197, Sec. 2. Effective January 1, 1995.)

9250.10. (a) (1) In addition to any other fees specified in this code and the Revenue and Taxation Code, any additional fees imposed by a service authority for freeway emergencies pursuant to Section 2555 of the Streets and Highways Code shall be paid to the department at the time of registration or renewal of registration of every vehicle, except vehicles described in subdivision (a) of Section 5014.1, subject to registration under this code in the subject counties, except those vehicles that are expressly exempted under this code from the payment of registration fees.

(2) In addition to the additional fees imposed for freeway emergencies, and upon the implementation of the permanent trailer identification plate program, and as part of the Commercial Vehicle Registration Act of 2001, all commercial motor vehicles subject to Section 9400.1 registered to an owner with an address in the county that established a service authority under this section, shall pay an additional service fee of two dollars ($2).

(b) After deducting its administrative costs, the department shall distribute the additional fees collected pursuant to subdivision (a) to the authority in the county in which they were collected.

(Amended by Stats. 2001, Ch. 826, Sec. 21. Effective January 1, 2002.)

9250.11. (a) In addition to any other fees specified in this code and the Revenue and Taxation Code, a fee of one dollar ($1) may be imposed by the South Coast Air Quality Management District and shall be paid to the department, upon renewal of registration of any motor vehicle subject to Part 5 (commencing with Section 43000) of Division 26 of the Health and Safety Code and registered in the south coast district, except any vehicle that is expressly exempted under this code from the payment of registration fees.

(b) Prior to imposing fees pursuant to this section, the south coast district board shall approve the imposition of the fees through the adoption of a resolution by both a majority of the district board and a majority of the district board who are elected officials. After deducting all costs incurred pursuant to this section, the department shall distribute the additional fees collected pursuant to subdivision (a) to the south coast district, which shall use the fees to reduce air pollution from motor vehicles through implementation of Sections 40448.5 and 40448.5.1 of the Health and Safety Code.

(c) Any memorandum of understanding reached between the district and a county prior to the imposition of a one dollar ($1) fee by a county shall remain in effect and govern the allocation of the funds generated in that county by that fee.

(d) The South Coast Air Quality Management District shall adopt accounting procedures to ensure that revenues from motor vehicle registration fees are not commingled with other program revenues.

(Amended by Stats. 2008, Ch. 724, Sec. 2. Effective January 1, 2009.)

9250.12. (a) For purposes of this section, "county" means the City and County of San Francisco.

(b) In addition to any other fees specified in this code and the Revenue and Taxation Code, a fee of four dollars ($4) shall be paid at the time of registration or renewal of registration of every vehicle registered to an address within a county, except those vehicles expressly exempted from payment of registration fees and commercial vehicles weighing more than 4,000 pounds, unladen, if all of the following occur:

(1) The county board of supervisors finds both of the following:

(A) That there is traffic congestion within the county that can be alleviated by the operation of public transit and that the cost of funding public transit exceeds the revenues to be collected from a service fee imposed on vehicles.

(B) That the imposition of the additional registration fee will reduce the need for any public transit fare increases during the period that the fee is in effect.

(2) The county board of supervisors adopts an ordinance or resolution imposing the additional registration fee.

(3) The ordinance or resolution adopted pursuant to paragraph (2) is approved by two-thirds of the voters in the county who voted on the measure.

(c) The fee imposed pursuant to this section shall apply to any original registration occurring on or after the January 1 following the adoption of the ordinance pursuant to paragraph (3) of subdivision (b) and to any renewal of registration with an expiration date on or after that January 1.

(d) After deducting all costs incurred pursuant to this section, the department shall distribute the revenues to the county. The amount of revenues distributed by the department to the county shall be equal to the net amount of revenues received from that county that were derived from the imposition of the additional fees.

(e) Money allocated to the county pursuant to this section shall be expended only to fund programs for the provision of public transit, including capital outlay, security, and maintenance costs, and including, but not limited to, removal of graffiti from public transit vehicles and facilities, and to pay the costs of compliance with paragraph (3) of subdivision (b).

(f) If public transit fees are increased at any time the additional registration fee authorized by the section is in effect, the fee may not continue to be imposed. This section shall become inoperative on the date those fares are increased and shall be repealed on January 1 next following that date. The board of supervisors shall notify the department of any increase in public transit fares occurring while the additional registration fee is in effect.

(Added by Stats. 1993, Ch. 966, Sec. 2. Effective January 1, 1994. Inoperative on date prescribed in subd. (f). Repealed on January 1 after inoperative date, by its own provisions.)

9250.13. (a) (1) In addition to any other fees specified in this code and the Revenue and Taxation Code, a fee of eighteen dollars ($18) shall be paid at the time of registration or renewal of registration of every vehicle, except vehicles described in subdivision (a) of Section 5014.1, subject to registration under this code, except those vehicles that are expressly exempted under this code from the payment of registration fees.

(2) In addition to the fee required under paragraph (1), upon the implementation of the permanent trailer identification plate program, and as part of the Commercial Vehicle Registration Act of 2001 (Chapter 861 of the Statutes of 2000), all commercial motor vehicles subject to Section 9400.1 shall pay a fee of six dollars ($6).

(b) The money realized pursuant to this section shall be available, upon appropriation by the Legislature, for expenditure to offset the costs of increasing the uniformed field strength of the Department of the California Highway Patrol beyond its 1994 staffing level and those costs associated with maintaining this new level of uniformed field strength and carrying out those duties specified in subdivision (a) of Section 830.2 of the Penal Code.

(Amended by Stats. 2008, Ch. 756, Sec. 19. Effective September 30, 2008.)

9250.14. (a) (1) In addition to any other fees specified in this code and the Revenue and Taxation Code, upon the adoption of a resolution by any county board of supervisors, a fee of one dollar ($1) shall be paid at the time of registration or renewal of registration of every vehicle, except vehicles described in subdivision (a) of Section 5014.1, registered to an address within that county except those expressly exempted from payment of registration fees. The fees, after deduction of the administrative costs incurred by the department in carrying out this section, shall be paid quarterly to the Controller.

(2) (A) If a county has adopted a resolution to impose a one-dollar ($1) fee pursuant to paragraph (1), the county may increase the fee specified in paragraph (1) to two dollars ($2) in the same manner as the imposition of the initial fee pursuant to paragraph (1). The two dollars ($2) shall be paid at the time of registration or renewal of registration of a vehicle, and quarterly to the Controller, as provided in paragraph (1).

(B) If a county has not adopted a resolution to impose a one-dollar ($1) fee pursuant to paragraph (1), the county may instead adopt a fee of two dollars ($2) in the manner prescribed in paragraph (1).

(C) A resolution to impose a fee of two dollars ($2) pursuant to subparagraph (A) or (B) shall be submitted to the department at least six months before the operative date of the fee increase.

(3) In addition to the service fee imposed pursuant to paragraph (1), and upon the implementation of the permanent trailer identification plate program, and as part of the Commercial Vehicle Registration Act of 2001 (Chapter 861 of the Statutes of 2000), all commercial motor vehicles subject to Section 9400.1 registered to an owner with an address in the county that established a service authority under this section, shall pay an additional service fee of two dollars ($2).

(4) (A) If a county imposes a service fee of two dollars ($2) by adopting a resolution pursuant to subparagraph (A) or (B) of paragraph (2), the fee specified in paragraph (3) shall be increased to four dollars ($4). The four dollars ($4) shall be paid at the time of registration or renewal of registration of a vehicle, and quarterly to the Controller as provided in paragraph (1).

(B) A resolution to increase the additional service fee from two dollars ($2) to four dollars ($4) pursuant to subparagraph (A) or (B) of paragraph (2) shall be submitted to the department at least six months before the operative date of the fee increase.

(b) Notwithstanding Section 13340 of the Government Code, the moneys paid to the Controller are continuously appropriated, without regard to fiscal years, for the administrative costs of the Controller, and for disbursement by the Controller to each county that has adopted a resolution pursuant to subdivision (a), based upon the number of vehicles registered, or whose registration is renewed, to an address within that county.

(c) (1) Except as otherwise provided in this subdivision, moneys allocated to a county pursuant to subdivision (b) shall be expended exclusively to fund programs that enhance the capacity of local police and prosecutors to deter, investigate, and prosecute vehicle theft crimes. In any county with a population of 250,000 or less, the moneys shall be expended exclusively for those vehicle theft crime programs and for the prosecution of crimes involving driving while under the influence of alcohol or drugs, or both, in violation of Section 23152 or 23153, or vehicular manslaughter in violation of Section 191.5 of the Penal Code or subdivision (c) of Section 192 of the Penal Code, or any combination of those crimes.

(2) For purposes of this subdivision, "vehicle theft crimes" means the theft of a vehicle, unlawful taking of a vehicle, burglary of a vehicle, or theft of vehicle parts or components.

(d) The moneys collected pursuant to this section shall not be expended to offset a reduction in any other source of funds, nor for any purpose not authorized under this section.

(e) Any funds received by a county before January 1, 2000, pursuant to this section, that are not expended to deter, investigate, or prosecute crimes pursuant to subdivision (c) shall be returned to the Controller, for deposit in the Motor Vehicle Account in the State Transportation Fund. Those funds received by a county shall be expended in accordance with this section.

(f) Each county that adopts a resolution under subdivision (a) shall submit, on or before the 13th day following the end of each quarter, a quarterly expenditure and activity report to the designated statewide Vehicle Theft Investigation and Apprehension Coordinator in the Department of the California Highway Patrol.

(g) A county that imposes a fee under subdivision (a) shall issue a fiscal year-end report to the Controller on or before November 30 of each year. The report shall include a detailed accounting of the funds received and expended in the immediately preceding fiscal year, including, at a minimum, all of the following:

(1) The amount of funds received and expended by the county under subdivision (b) for the immediately preceding fiscal year.

(2) The total expenditures by the county under subdivision (c) for the immediately preceding fiscal year.

(3) Details of expenditures made by the county under subdivision (c), including salaries and expenses, purchase of equipment and supplies, and any other expenditures made listed by type with an explanatory comment.

(4) A summary of vehicle theft abatement activities and other vehicle theft programs funded by the fees collected pursuant to this section.

(5) The total number of stolen vehicles recovered and the value of those vehicles during the immediately preceding fiscal year.

(6) The total number of vehicles stolen during the immediately preceding fiscal year as compared to the fiscal year before the immediately preceding fiscal year.

(7) Any additional, unexpended fee revenues received under subdivision (b) for the county for the immediately preceding fiscal year.

(h) A county that imposes a fee under subdivision (a) shall post the report described in subdivision (g) on its internet website.

(i) Each county that fails to submit the report required pursuant to subdivision (g) by November 30 of each year shall have the fee suspended by the Controller for one year, commencing on July 1 following the Controller's determination that a county has failed to submit the report.

(j) (1) On or before January 1 of each year, the Controller shall provide to the Department of the California Highway Patrol copies of the year-end reports submitted by the counties under subdivision (g) and, in consultation with the Department of the California Highway Patrol, shall review the fiscal year-end reports submitted by each county pursuant to subdivision (g) to determine if fee revenues are being utilized in a manner consistent with this section. If the Controller determines that the use of the fee revenues is not consistent with this section, the Controller shall consult with the participating counties' designated regional coordinators. If the Controller determines that use of the fee revenues is still not consistent with this section, the authority to collect the fee by that county shall be suspended for one year.

(2) If the Controller determines that a county has not submitted a fiscal year-end report as required in subdivision (g), the authorization to collect the service fee shall be suspended for one year pursuant to subdivision (i).

(3) If the Controller determines that a fee shall be suspended for a county, the Controller shall inform the Department of Motor Vehicles on or before February 1 of each year that the authority to collect a fee for that county is suspended.

(k) On or before January 1 of each year, the Controller shall prepare and post on the Controller's internet website a revenue and expenditure summary for each participating county that includes all of the following:

(1) The total revenues received by each county.

(2) The total expenditures by each county.

(3) The unexpended revenues for each county.

(l) For the purposes of this section, a county-designated regional coordinator is that agency designated by the participating county's board of supervisors as the agency in control of its countywide vehicle theft apprehension program.

(Amended by Stats. 2025, Ch. 67, Sec. 184. (AB 1170) Effective January 1, 2026.)

9250.15. (a) In addition to any other fees specified in this code, the department shall collect an administrative service fee in the amount authorized under subdivision (b) for each application for registration, renewal of registration, or supplement apportioned registration pursuant to Article 4 (commencing with Section 8050) of Chapter 4.

(b) The administrative service fee required to be collected under subdivision (a) shall be at least the amount determined by the department to be sufficient to pay membership dues to the association acting as the repository for the International Registration Plan under Article 3 (commencing with Section 8000) of Chapter 4, but may not be more than two dollars ($2) for each application.

(c) The money collected by the department under this section, less the department's administrative costs in collecting and transmitting the money, shall be available, upon appropriation, to the department for payment to the association described in subdivision (b).

(d) Funds provided to the association under this section shall be used exclusively for the administration and support of reciprocity activities under the International Registration Plan.

(Amended by Stats. 2001, Ch. 539, Sec. 11. Effective January 1, 2002.)

9250.16. (a) In addition to any other fees specified in this code, the Health and Safety Code, and the Revenue and Taxation Code, a surcharge of one dollar ($1) may be imposed by the San Joaquin Valley Unified Air Pollution Control District and shall be paid to the department as follows:

(1) Upon initial registration of any motor vehicle not previously registered in this state that is registered on or after the date the department begins collecting the fee.

(2) Upon renewal of registration of any motor vehicle for which the registration period expires after the date the department begins collecting the fee.

(3) This subdivision applies to any motor vehicle subject to Part 5 (commencing with Section 43000) of Division 26 of the Health and Safety Code, except any vehicle that is expressly exempted under this code from the payment of registration fees. The department shall begin collecting the fee on January 1 of the fiscal year immediately following the date the department receives the request to do so from the San Joaquin Valley Unified Air Pollution Control District Board.

(b) Prior to the adoption of any surcharge pursuant to this subdivision, the San Joaquin Valley Unified Air Pollution Control District board shall approve the imposition of the surcharge through the adoption of a resolution, as specified in Section 44225 of the Health and Safety Code.

(c) The San Joaquin Valley Unified Air Pollution Control District shall pay for the costs identified by the department to establish the fee collection procedure. After deducting the on-going costs incurred by the department in collecting the fees, the department shall deposit the revenue collected pursuant to this section into the Motor Vehicle Account in the State Transportation Fund for allocation to the district. Subdivision (c) of Section 40605 of the Health and Safety Code does not apply to the costs described in this subdivision.

(Added by Stats. 2003, Ch. 483, Sec. 3. Effective January 1, 2004.)

9250.17. (a) The department shall, if requested by a county air pollution control district, air quality management district, or unified or regional air pollution control district, collect fees established pursuant to Sections 44223 and 44225 of the Health and Safety Code upon the registration or renewal of registration of any motor vehicle registered in the district, except those vehicles which are expressly exempted under this code from the payment of registration fees.

(b) After deducting all costs incurred pursuant to this section, the department shall distribute the revenues to the districts based upon the amount of fees collected from motor vehicles registered within each district.

(c) The department may annually expend for its costs not more than the following percentages of the fees collected pursuant to subdivision (a):

(1) Five percent during the first year after the operative date the fee is imposed or increased.

(2) Three percent during the second year after the operative date the fee is imposed or increased.

(3) One percent during any subsequent year.

(Added by Stats. 1990, Ch. 1705, Sec. 2.)

9250.18. (a) The department shall collect the administrative fee established pursuant to Sections 44081 and 44081.6 of the Health and Safety Code upon the renewal of registration or transfer of ownership of any motor vehicle registered in the state.

(b) On a monthly basis, after deducting its reasonable costs, the department shall transmit all revenues, including accrued interest, received pursuant to this section, for deposit in the Vehicle Inspection and Repair Fund, for use by the Department of Consumer Affairs pursuant to Chapter 5 (commencing with Section 44000) of Part 5 of Division 26 of the Health and Safety Code. Alternatively, the department and the Department of Consumer Affairs may, by interagency agreement, establish a procedure for the Department of Consumer Affairs to reimburse the department for its reasonable costs incurred in collecting the administrative fees.

(Amended by Stats. 1994, Ch. 1220, Sec. 54.2. Effective September 30, 1994.)

9250.19. (a) (1) In addition to any other fees specified in this code and the Revenue and Taxation Code, upon the adoption of a resolution pursuant to this subdivision by any county board of supervisors, a fee of one dollar ($1) shall be paid at the time of registration, renewal, or supplemental application for apportioned registration pursuant to Article 4 (commencing with Section 8050) of Chapter 4 of every vehicle, except vehicles described in subdivision (a) of Section 5014.1, registered to an address within that county except those expressly exempted from payment of registration fees. The fees, after deduction of the administrative costs incurred by the department in carrying out this section, shall be paid quarterly to the Controller.

(2) (A) If a county has adopted a resolution to impose a one-dollar ($1) fee pursuant to paragraph (1), the county may increase the fee specified in paragraph (1) to two dollars ($2) in the same manner as the imposition of the initial fee pursuant to paragraph (1). The two dollars ($2) shall be paid at the time of registration or renewal of registration of a vehicle, and quarterly to the Controller, as provided in paragraph (1).

(B) If a county has not adopted a resolution to impose a one-dollar ($1) fee pursuant to paragraph (1), the county may instead adopt a fee of two dollars ($2) in the manner prescribed in paragraph (1).

(C) A resolution to impose a fee of two dollars ($2) pursuant to subparagraph (A) or (B) shall be submitted to the department at least six months prior to the operative date of the fee increase.

(3) In addition to the one-dollar ($1) service fee, and upon the implementation of the permanent trailer identification plate program, and as part of the Commercial Vehicle Registration Act of 2001, all commercial motor vehicles subject to Section 9400.1 registered to an owner with an address in the county that established a service authority under this section, shall pay an additional service fee of two dollars ($2).

(4) (A) If a county imposes a service fee of two dollars ($2) by adopting a resolution pursuant to subparagraph (A) or (B) of paragraph (2), the fee specified in paragraph (3) shall be increased to four dollars ($4). The four dollars ($4) shall be paid at the time of registration or renewal of registration of a vehicle, and quarterly to the Controller as provided in paragraph (1).

(B) A resolution adopted pursuant to subparagraph (A) or (B) of paragraph (2) shall be submitted to the department at least six months prior to the operative date of the fee.

(5) A resolution adopted pursuant to paragraph (1) or (2) shall include findings as to the purpose of, and the need for, imposing the additional registration fee.

(b) Notwithstanding Section 13340 of the Government Code, the money paid to the Controller pursuant to subdivision (a) is continuously appropriated, without regard to fiscal years, for disbursement by the Controller to each county that has adopted a resolution pursuant to subdivision (a), based upon the number of vehicles registered, or whose registration is renewed, to an address within that county, or supplemental application for apportioned registration, and for the administrative costs of the Controller incurred under this section.

(c) Money allocated to a county pursuant to subdivision (b) shall be expended exclusively to fund programs that enhance the capacity of local law enforcement to provide automated mobile and fixed location fingerprint identification of individuals who may be involved in driving under the influence of alcohol or drugs in violation of Section 23152 or 23153, or vehicular manslaughter in violation of Section 191.5 of the Penal Code or subdivision (c) of Section 192 of the Penal Code, or any combination of those and other vehicle-related crimes, and other crimes committed while operating a motor vehicle.

(d) The data from a program funded pursuant to subdivision (c) shall be made available by the local law enforcement agency to a local public agency that is required by law to obtain a criminal history background of persons as a condition of employment with that local public agency. A local law enforcement agency that provides the data may charge a fee to cover its actual costs in providing that data.

(e) (1) Money collected pursuant to this section shall not be used to offset a reduction in any other source of funds for the purposes authorized under this section.

(2) Funds collected pursuant to this section, upon recommendation of local or regional Remote Access Network Boards to the board of supervisors, shall be used exclusively for the purchase, by competitive bidding procedures, and the operation of equipment that is compatible with the Department of Justice's Cal-ID master plan, as described in Section 11112.2 of the Penal Code, and the equipment shall interface in a manner that is in compliance with the requirement described in the Criminal Justice Information Services, Electronic Fingerprint Transmission Specification, prepared by the Federal Bureau of Investigation and dated August 24, 1995.

(f) Every county that has authorized the collection of the fee pursuant to subdivision (a) shall issue a fiscal yearend report to the Controller on or before November 1 of each year, summarizing all of the following with respect to those fees:

(1) The total revenues received by the county for the fiscal year.

(2) The total expenditures and encumbered funds by the county for the fiscal year. For purposes of this subdivision, "encumbered funds" means funding that is scheduled to be spent pursuant to a determined schedule and for an identified purchase consistent with this section.

(3) Any unexpended or unencumbered fee revenues for the county for the fiscal year.

(4) The estimated annual cost of the purchase, operation, and maintenance of automated mobile and fixed location fingerprint equipment, related infrastructure, law enforcement enhancement programs, and personnel created or utilized in accordance with this section for the fiscal year. The listing shall detail the make and model number of the equipment, and include a succinct description of the related infrastructure items, law enforcement enhancement programs, and the classification or title of any personnel.

(5) How the use of the funds benefits the motoring public.

(g) For each county that fails to submit the report required pursuant to subdivision (f) by November 1 of each year, the Controller shall notify the Department of Motor Vehicles to suspend the fee for that county imposed pursuant to subdivision (a) for one year.

(h) If any funds received by a county pursuant to subdivision (a) are not expended or encumbered in accordance with this section by the close of the fiscal year in which the funds were received, the Controller shall notify the Department of Motor Vehicles to suspend the fee for that county imposed pursuant to subdivision (a) for one year. For purposes of this subdivision, "encumbered funds" means funding that is scheduled to be spent pursuant to a determined schedule and for an identified purchase consistent with this section.

(Amended by Stats. 2014, Ch. 292, Sec. 1. (AB 2393) Effective January 1, 2015.)

9252. (a) In addition to the registration fee specified in Section 9250 and any weight fee, there shall be paid a service fee of fifteen dollars ($15) for the registration within this state of every vehicle purchased new outside this state or previously registered outside this state. If the vehicle has been registered and operated in this state during the same registration year in which application for registration is made, a fee of fifteen dollars ($15) shall be paid.

(b) This section does not apply to vehicles registered as fleet vehicles under Article 4 (commencing with Section 8050) of Chapter 4, except upon application for a certificate of ownership.

(Amended by Stats. 2003, Ch. 719, Sec. 13. Effective January 1, 2004.)

9254. A service fee of fifteen dollars ($15) shall be paid to the department for a certificate of ownership issued without registration of the vehicle.

(Amended by Stats. 2003, Ch. 719, Sec. 14. Effective January 1, 2004.)

9255. Upon application for the transfer of the title or any interest of an owner or legal owner in or to a vehicle registered under this code, or for which a certificate of ownership has been issued without registration under Section 4452, other than upon a transfer to a chattel mortgagee and other than upon a transfer to a transferee not required under this code to obtain the issuance to the owner of a new certificate of ownership and registration card, there shall be paid the following fees:

(1) For a transfer by the owner of an automobile or motorcycle $15

(2) For a transfer by the owner of a trailer coach or commercial vehicle $15

(3) For a transfer by the legal owner $15

(4) When an application is presented showing a transfer by both the owner and legal owner of an automobile or motorcycle $15

(5) When an application is presented showing a transfer by both the owner and legal owner of a trailer coach or commercial vehicle $15

(Amended by Stats. 2002, Ch. 758, Sec. 7. Effective January 1, 2003.)

9255.1. A service fee of two dollars ($2), in addition to other required fees, shall be paid to the department upon the initial issuance of a registration card identifying a motor vehicle of a type included in subdivision (b) of Section 4453. Subsequent transfers of title are exempted from the two-dollar ($2) service fee.

(Added by Stats. 1980, Ch. 856, Sec. 2. Operative October 1, 1981, by Sec. 3 of Ch. 856.)

9255.2. (a) In addition to any other fees specified in this code and the Revenue and Taxation Code, a fee of not more than fifty dollars ($50), as determined by the Department of the California Highway Patrol to cover the costs of implementing and conducting the inspection program required under Section 5505, shall be paid to the Department of Motor Vehicles at the time inspection is made for initial registration or transfer of ownership of a vehicle included in paragraphs (1) and (2) of subdivision (b) of Section 4453.

(b) The fees collected pursuant to subdivision (a) shall be deposited in the Motor Vehicle Account in the State Transportation Fund. The money deposited in the account shall be available, upon appropriation by the Legislature, for distribution as follows:

(1) Not more than three dollars ($3) of each fee collected under subdivision (a) to the Department of Motor Vehicles.

(2) The remainder to the Department of the California Highway Patrol.

(Amended by Stats. 2002, Ch. 670, Sec. 9. Effective January 1, 2003.)

9255.3. Notwithstanding Section 9255, any vehicle transferred pursuant to Section 14607.6 shall be subject to a title transfer fee equal to the department's actual cost of processing that transfer.

(Added by Stats. 1994, Ch. 1133, Sec. 4. Effective January 1, 1995.)

9255.5. Upon application for transfer of registration pursuant to Section 5911, a fee as specified in Section 9265 shall be paid to the department in addition to the regular transfer fee.

(Added by Stats. 1978, Ch. 497.)

9256. Upon filing with the department an application for transfer of registration to the chattel mortgagee as provided herein there shall be paid to the department a fee of three dollars ($3) for each vehicle registered under this code described in and subject to the chattel mortgage.

(Amended by Stats. 1967, Ch. 1717.)

9257. Every notice of the installation in a vehicle of a motor vehicle engine or motor required to be filed under Section 4161 shall be accompanied by a filing fee of two dollars ($2).

(Enacted by Stats. 1959, Ch. 3.)

9257.5. (a) Except as provided in subdivision (c), a fee of fifty dollars ($50) shall be paid for each temporary permit issued pursuant to Section 4156 when a certificate of compliance is required pursuant to Section 4000.3.

(b) After deducting its administrative costs, the department shall deposit fees collected pursuant to subdivision (a) in the High Polluter Repair or Removal Account in the Vehicle Inspection and Repair Fund.

(c) The department shall not charge a fee pursuant to subdivision (a) if the department is presented at the time the temporary permit is issued with sufficient evidence, as determined by the department, that the owner of the vehicle is an income eligible applicant who had his or her vehicle accepted into the Bureau of Automotive Repair Consumer Assistance Program as established pursuant to Chapter 5 (commencing with Section 44000) of Part 5 of Division 26 of the Health and Safety Code.

(Added by Stats. 2008, Ch. 451, Sec. 2. Effective January 1, 2009.)

9258. A fee of fifteen dollars ($15) shall be paid to the department for each one-trip permit issued pursuant to Section 4003.

(Amended by Stats. 2003, Ch. 719, Sec. 15. Effective January 1, 2004.)

9258.5. A fee of thirty-five dollars ($35) shall be paid to the department for each one-trip permit issued pursuant to Section 4003.5.

(Amended by Stats. 1985, Ch. 625, Sec. 2.)

9259. A fee of two dollars ($2) shall be paid for each sticker or device issued under Article 4 (commencing with Section 8050) of Chapter 4 of Division 3 or for each vehicle in a fleet upon transfer of ownership as provided in Section 8054.

(Amended by Stats. 1992, Ch. 1241, Sec. 12. Effective January 1, 1993.)

9259.3. For each application to include an additional operating area or a registration issued under Article 4 (commencing with Section 8050) of Chapter 4 of Division 3, the department shall require a deposit in an amount determined by the department to be sufficient to ensure compliance with that article.

(Added by Stats. 2001, Ch. 539, Sec. 12. Effective January 1, 2002.)

9259.5. For each application for immediate telephone service for a registration issued under Article 4 (commencing with Section 8050) of Chapter 4 of Division 3, the department shall impose a fee in an amount determined by the department to be sufficient to cover its administrative costs under this section.

(Added by Stats. 2001, Ch. 539, Sec. 13. Effective January 1, 2002.)

9260. (a) The fee for a temporary registration issued under Section 4004 is one-quarter of the annual fees in Division 3 (commencing with Section 4000) of this code and Part 5 (commencing with Section 10701) of Division 2 of the Revenue and Taxation Code, for the period that the vehicle is to be operated in this state.

(b) The fee for a trip permit issued under Section 4004 is forty-five dollars ($45) for each commercial motor vehicle.

(Amended by Stats. 2000, Ch. 861, Sec. 47. Effective September 29, 2000. Operative December 31, 2001, pursuant to Sec. 67 of Ch. 861.)

9261. (a) A service fee of fifteen dollars ($15) shall be paid for an identification plate issued pursuant to Section 5014. Publicly owned special construction equipment, cemetery equipment, special mobile equipment, logging vehicles, and implements of husbandry are exempt from the service charge.

(b) A service fee of fifteen dollars ($15) shall be paid for an identification plate issued pursuant to Section 5016.5.

(c) Upon application for the transfer of interest of an owner in a piece of equipment, vehicle, or implement of husbandry identified pursuant to Section 5014, the transferee shall pay a fee of fifteen dollars ($15).

(d) A fee of fifteen dollars ($15) shall be paid upon the renewal of an identification plate issued pursuant to Section 5014 or 5016.5.

(Amended by Stats. 2003, Ch. 719, Sec. 16. Effective January 1, 2004.)

9261.1. (a) Beginning July 1, 2008, the fee described in Section 9261, as adjusted pursuant to Section 1678, shall be increased by five dollars ($5).

(b) Two dollars and fifty cents ($2.50) of the increase shall be deposited into the Alternative and Renewable Fuel and Vehicle Technology Fund created by Section 44273 of the Health and Safety Code, and two dollars and fifty cents ($2.50) shall be deposited into the Air Quality Improvement Fund created by Section 44274.5 of the Health and Safety Code.

(c) This section shall become inoperative on July 1, 2035, and, as of January 1, 2036, is repealed.

(Amended by Stats. 2023, Ch. 319, Sec. 13. (AB 126) Effective October 7, 2023. Inoperative July 1, 2035, by its own provisions. Repealed as of January 1, 2036, by its own provisions.)

9262. (a) The fee for a license issued to dealers and lessor-retailers is as follows:

(1) For the original license, or an ownership change which requires a new application, except as provided by Section 42231, a nonrefundable fee of one hundred seventy-five dollars ($175).

(2) For the annual renewal of a license, a fee of one hundred twenty-five dollars ($125).

(3) If an alteration of an existing license is caused by a firm name change, address change, change in the corporate officer structure, or the addition of a branch location, a fee of seventy dollars ($70).

(b) The fee for a license issued to dismantlers, manufacturers, manufacturer branches, remanufacturers, remanufacturer branches, transporters, distributors, and distributor branches is as follows:

(1) For the original license, or an ownership change which requires a new application, except as provided by Section 42231, a nonrefundable fee of one hundred dollars ($100).

(2) For the annual renewal of a license, a fee of eighty-five dollars ($85).

(3) If an alteration of an existing license is caused by a firm name change, address change, or the addition of a branch location, a fee of fifty dollars ($50).

(4) If an alteration of an existing license is caused by a change in the corporate officer structure, a fee of seventy dollars ($70).

(c) The fee for a license issued to representatives is as follows:

(1) For the original license, or an ownership change which requires a new application, except as provided by Section 42231, a nonrefundable fee of fifty dollars ($50).

(2) For the annual renewal of a license, a fee of eighty-five dollars ($85).

(d) The fee for an autobroker's endorsement to a dealer's license is as follows:

(1) For the original endorsement, a nonrefundable fee of one hundred dollars ($100).

(2) For the annual renewal of the endorsement, a fee of seventy-five dollars ($75).

(e) When the holder of a license for which a fee is provided in this section applies for special plates as provided in subdivision (b) of Section 11505 or subdivision (b) of Section 11714, the fee for the plates and the annual renewal of the plates is the prevailing vehicle registration fee as set forth in Section 9250 for the period for which the special plates are issued or renewed.

(Amended by Stats. 2009, Ch. 556, Sec. 3. (SB 95) Effective January 1, 2010.)

9262.5. It is the intent of the Legislature, in amending Section 9262 in 2009 to increase the fee for the annual renewal of the license of a dealer and of a lessor-retailer to one hundred twenty-five dollars ($125), that forty dollars ($40) of that fee shall, when appropriated, be utilized by the department for the investigation of those dealers and lessor-retailers who demonstrate the greatest potential for causing losses to consumers as shown by repeated consumer complaints, habitual violations of the requirements of their licenses, the issuance of a probationary license by the department, or a violation of other standards and criteria established by the department for these purposes.

(Amended by Stats. 2009, Ch. 556, Sec. 4. (SB 95) Effective January 1, 2010.)

9263. Any automobile dismantler who fails to comply with Section 11520, or any other person who fails to comply with Section 5500 or 11520, shall pay an investigation service fee of fifteen dollars ($15).

(Amended by Stats. 1985, Ch. 1022, Sec. 6.)

9265. Upon application for duplicates or substitutes as permitted under this code, the following fees shall be paid:

(a) For a duplicate certificate of ownership or registration card or equipment identification card............................. $15

(b) For any duplicate license plates, except environmental license plates, or substitute plates, or equipment identification plate for the same vehicle.......................... $15

(Amended by Stats. 2003, Ch. 719, Sec. 17. Effective January 1, 2004.)

9266. The fee for a temporary permit issued under Section 5010 is one-tenth of the annual fees in Division 3 (commencing with Section 4000) of this code and Part 5 (commencing with Section 10701) of Division 2 of the Revenue and Taxation Code, for each calendar month that the vehicle is to be operated in this state. There shall be no proration of fees for any fraction of a calendar month.

(Added by Stats. 1968, Ch. 871.)

9266.5. The fee for a temporary permit issued under subdivision (b) of Section 9102.5 is one-tenth of the annual fees in Division 3 (commencing with Section 4000) of this code and Part 5 (commencing with Section 10701) of Division 2 of the Revenue and Taxation Code, for each calendar month that the vehicle is to be operated in this state. There shall be no proration of fees for any fraction of a calendar month.

(Amended by Stats. 1980, Ch. 147, Sec. 3.)

9268. In addition to any other registration fee and notwithstanding Section 9559, an additional fee of one dollar ($1) shall be collected upon the original registration of a motorcycle pursuant to Section 4150.2.

(Added by Stats. 1970, Ch. 887.)

9269. A licensed automobile dismantler who acquires, for the purpose of dismantling, a vehicle of a type subject to registration under this code, and who complies with Section 11520, is not required to pay fees or penalties that would otherwise be required if that vehicle were to be currently registered.

(Amended by Stats. 1990, Ch. 1352, Sec. 7. Effective September 27, 1990. Applicable from July 1, 1990, pursuant to Sec. 21 of Ch. 1352.)

9270. (a) The department may charge a service fee of not more than fifteen dollars ($15), in addition to other fees payable under this code, for the expedited completion of any of the following services within 72 hours after receipt of a complete and proper application for the service:

(1) Initial registration of a vehicle.

(2) Transfer of registration of a vehicle.

(3) Issuance of a duplicate certificate of ownership.

(b) The services in subdivision (a) shall be available only at the department's headquarters office in Sacramento.

(Amended by Stats. 2004, Ch. 430, Sec. 2. Effective January 1, 2005.)

9271. In addition to any other fees specified in this code, a fee sufficient to cover the department's costs for the inspections performed pursuant to Section 5505 shall be charged to register a vehicle which has been declared a total loss salvage vehicle pursuant to Section 11515 or which has been reported to have been dismantled pursuant to Section 5500 or 11520.

(Amended by Stats. 1989, Ch. 1360, Sec. 155.)

Article 3. Weight Fees

(Article 3 enacted by Stats. 1959, Ch. 3.)

9400. Except as provided in Section 9400.1, and in addition to any other registration fee, there shall be paid the fees set forth in this section for the registration of any commercial motor vehicle that operates with unladen weight. Weight fees for pickup trucks are calculated under this section. Whenever a camper is temporarily attached to a motor vehicle designed to transport property, the motor vehicle shall be subject to the fees imposed by this section. The camper shall be deemed to be a load, and fees imposed by this section upon the motor vehicle shall be based upon the unladen weight of the motor vehicle, exclusive of the camper.

(a) For any electric vehicle designed, used, or maintained as described in this section, fees shall be paid according to the following schedule:

Unladen Weight	Fee
Less than 6,000 lbs.	$ 87
6,000 lbs. or more but less than 10,000 lbs.	266
10,000 lbs. or more	358

(b) For any motor vehicle having not more than two axles and designed, used, or maintained as described in this section, other than an electric vehicle, fees shall be paid according to the following schedule:

Unladen Weight	Fee
Less than 3,000 lbs.	$ 8
3,000 lbs. to and including 4,000 lbs.	24
4,001 lbs. to and including 5,000 lbs.	80
5,001 lbs. to and including 6,000 lbs.	154
6,001 lbs. to and including 7,000 lbs.	204
7,001 lbs. to and including 8,000 lbs.	257
8,001 lbs. to and including 9,000 lbs.	308
9,001 lbs. to and including 10,000 lbs.	360

(c) For any motor vehicle having three or more axles designed, used, or maintained as described in this section, other than an electric vehicle, fees shall be paid according to the following schedule:

Unladen Weight	Fee
2,000 lbs. to and including 3,000 lbs.	$ 43
3,001 lbs. to and including 4,000 lbs.	77
4,001 lbs. to and including 5,000 lbs.	154
5,001 lbs. to and including 6,000 lbs.	231
6,001 lbs. to and including 7,000 lbs.	308
7,001 lbs. to and including 8,000 lbs.	385
8,001 lbs. to and including 9,000 lbs.	462
9,001 lbs. to and including 10,000 lbs.	539

(d) This section is not applicable to any vehicle that is operated or moved over the highway exclusively for the purpose of historical exhibition or other similar noncommercial purpose.

(e) The fee changes effected by this section apply to (1) initial or original registration on or after January 1, 1995, and prior to December 31, 2001, of any commercial vehicle never before registered in this state and (2) to renewal of registration of any commercial vehicle whose registration expires on or after January 1, 1995, and prior to December 31, 2001.

(f) Commercial vehicles, other than those specified in Section 9400.1, with an initial registration or renewal of registration that is due on or after December 31, 2001, are subject to the payment of fees specified in this section.

(Amended (as amended by Stats. 2000, Ch. 973, Sec. 3.5) by Stats. 2001, Ch. 826, Sec. 25. Effective January 1, 2002.)

9400.1. (a) (1) In addition to any other required fee, there shall be paid the fees set forth in this section for the registration of commercial motor vehicles operated either singly or in combination with a declared gross vehicle weight of 10,001 pounds or more. Pickup truck and electric vehicle weight fees are not calculated under this section.

(2) The weight of a vehicle issued an identification plate pursuant to an application under Section 5014, and the weight of an implement of husbandry as defined in Section 36000, shall not be considered when calculating, pursuant to this section, the declared gross vehicle weight of a towing commercial motor vehicle that is owned and operated exclusively by a farmer or an employee of a farmer in the conduct of agricultural operations.

(3) Tow trucks that are utilized to render assistance to the motoring public or to tow or carry impounded vehicles shall pay fees in accordance with this section, except that the fee calculation shall be based only on the gross vehicle weight rating of the towing or carrying vehicle. Upon each initial or transfer application for registration of a tow truck described in this paragraph, the registered owner or lessee or that owner's or lessee's designee, shall certify to the department the gross vehicle weight rating of the tow truck:

Gross Vehicle Weight Range	Fee
10,001–15,000	$ 257
15,001–20,000	353
20,001–26,000	435
26,001–30,000	552
30,001–35,000	648
35,001–40,000	761
40,001–45,000	837
45,001–50,000	948
50,001–54,999	1,039
55,000–60,000	1,173
60,001–65,000	1,282
65,001–70,000	1,398
70,001–75,000	1,650
75,001–80,000	1,700

(b) The fees specified in subdivision (a) apply to both of the following:

(1) An initial or original registration occurring on or after December 31, 2001, to December 30, 2003, inclusive, of a commercial motor vehicle operated either singly or in combination with a declared gross vehicle weight of 10,001 pounds or more.

(2) The renewal of registration of a commercial motor vehicle operated either singly or in combination, with a declared gross vehicle weight of 10,001 pounds or more for which registration expires on or after December 31, 2001, to December 30, 2003, inclusive.

(c) (1) For both an initial or original registration occurring on or after December 31, 2003, of a commercial motor vehicle operated either singly or in combination with a declared gross vehicle weight of 10,001 pounds or more, and the renewal of registration of a commercial motor vehicle operated either singly or in combination, with a declared gross vehicle weight of 10,001 pounds or more for which registration expires on or after December 31, 2003, there shall be paid fees as follows:

Gross Vehicle Weight Range	Weight Code	Fee
10,001–15,000	A	$ 332
15,001–20,000	B	447
20,001–26,000	C	546
26,001–30,000	D	586
30,001–35,000	E	801
35,001–40,000	F	937
40,001–45,000	G	1,028
45,001–50,000	H	1,161
50,001–54,999	I	1,270
55,000–60,000	J	1,431
60,001–65,000	K	1,562
65,001–70,000	L	1,701
70,001–75,000	M	2,004
75,001–80,000	N	2,064

(2) For the purpose of obtaining "revenue neutrality" as described in Sections 1 and 59 of Senate Bill 2084 of the 1999–2000 Regular

Session (Chapter 861 of the Statutes of 2000), the Director of Finance shall review the final 2003–04 Statement of Transactions of the State Highway Account. If that review indicates that the actual truck weight fee revenues deposited in the State Highway Account do not total at least seven hundred eighty-nine million dollars ($789,000,000), the Director of Finance shall instruct the department to adjust the schedule set forth in paragraph (1), but not to exceed the following fee amounts:

Gross Vehicle Weight Range	Weight Code	Fee
10,001–15,000	A	$ 354
15,001–20,000	B	482
20,001–26,000	C	591
26,001–30,000	D	746
30,001–35,000	E	874
35,001–40,000	F	1,024
40,001–45,000	G	1,125
45,001–50,000	H	1,272
50,001–54,999	I	1,393
55,000–60,000	J	1,571
60,001–65,000	K	1,716
65,001–70,000	L	1,870
70,001–75,000	M	2,204
75,001–80,000	N	2,271

(d) (1) In addition to the fees set forth in subdivision (a), a Cargo Theft Interdiction Program fee of three dollars ($3) shall be paid at the time of initial or original registration or renewal of registration of each motor vehicle subject to weight fees under this section.

(2) This subdivision does not apply to vehicles used or maintained for the transportation of persons for hire, compensation or profit, and tow trucks.

(3) For vehicles registered under Article 4 (commencing with Section 8050) of Chapter 4, the fee imposed under this subdivision shall be apportioned as required for registration fees under that article.

(4) Funds collected pursuant to the Cargo Theft Interdiction Program shall not be proportionately reduced for each month and shall be transferred to the Motor Carriers Safety Improvement Fund.

(e) Notwithstanding Section 42270 or any other provision of law, of the moneys collected by the department under this section, one hundred twenty-two dollars ($122) for each initial, original, and renewal registration shall be reported monthly to the Controller, and at the same time, deposited in the State Treasury to the credit of the Motor Vehicle Account in the State Transportation Fund. All other moneys collected by the department under this section shall be deposited to the credit of the State Highway Account in the State Transportation Fund, or directly to the credit of the Transportation Debt Service Fund as provided in paragraph (2) of subdivision (c) of Section 9400.4, as applicable. One hundred twenty-two dollars ($122) of the fee imposed under this section shall not be proportionately reduced for each month. For vehicles registered under Article 4 (commencing with Section 8050) of Chapter 4, the fee shall be apportioned as required for registration under that article.

(f) (1) The department, in consultation with the Department of the California Highway Patrol, shall design and make available a set of distinctive weight decals that reflect the declared gross combined weight or gross operating weight reported to the department at the time of initial registration, registration renewal, or when a weight change is reported to the department pursuant to Section 9406.1. A new decal shall be issued on each renewal or when the weight is changed pursuant to Section 9406.1. The decal for a tow truck that is subject to this section shall reflect the gross vehicle weight rating or weight code.

(2) The department may charge a fee, not to exceed ten dollars ($10), for the department's actual cost of producing and issuing each set of decals issued under paragraph (1).

(3) The weight decal shall be in sharp contrast to the background and shall be of a size, shape, and color that is readily legible during daylight hours from a distance of 50 feet.

(4) Each vehicle subject to this section shall display the weight decal on both the right and left sides of the vehicle.

(5) A person may not display upon a vehicle a decal issued pursuant to this subdivision that does not reflect the declared weight reported to the department.

(6) Notwithstanding subdivision (e) or any other provision of law, the moneys collected by the department under this subdivision shall be deposited in the State Treasury to the credit of the Motor Vehicle Account in the State Transportation Fund.

(7) This subdivision shall apply to vehicles subject to this section at the time of an initial registration, registration renewal, or reported weight change that occurs on or after July 1, 2004.

(8) The following shall apply to vehicles registered under the permanent fleet registration program pursuant to Article 9.5 (commencing with Section 5301) of Chapter 1:

(A) The department, in consultation with the Department of the California Highway Patrol, shall distinguish the weight decals issued to permanent fleet registration vehicles from those issued to other vehicles.

(B) The department shall issue the distinguishable weight decals only to the following:

(i) A permanent fleet registration vehicle that is registered with the department on January 1, 2005.

(ii) On and after January 1, 2005, a vehicle for which the department has an application for initial registration as a permanent fleet registration vehicle.

(iii) On and after January 1, 2005, a permanent fleet registration vehicle that has a weight change pursuant to Section 9406.1.

(C) The weight decal issued under this paragraph shall comply with the applicable provisions of paragraphs (1) to (6), inclusive.

(Amended by Stats. 2013, Ch. 35, Sec. 13. (SB 85) Effective June 27, 2013.)

9400.3. (a) In order to ensure that Chapter 973 of the Statutes of 2000 is implemented as originally intended by the Legislature, the department may not assess the Cargo Theft Interdiction Program fee upon any commercial motor vehicle that has a declared gross vehicle weight of less than 10,001 pounds.

(b) The department shall issue refunds of, or credits for, any Cargo Theft Interdiction Program fee that is assessed upon a vehicle that does not meet the minimum weights described in Section 9400.1 or is a pickup truck or an electric vehicle.

(Amended by Stats. 2004, Ch. 183, Sec. 349. Effective January 1, 2005.)

9400.4. Weight fee revenue deposited into the State Highway Account pursuant to subdivision (e) of Section 9400.1 and subdivision (a) of Section 42205 net of amounts appropriated for other purposes pursuant to subdivision (b) of Section 42205, and weight fee revenues deposited directly into the Transportation Debt Service Fund pursuant to subdivision (e) of Section 9400.1 and subdivision (a) of Section 42205, as applicable, shall be used as follows:

(a) For the 2010–11 fiscal year, seven hundred fifty-six million three hundred ninety-six thousand dollars ($756,396,000) is hereby appropriated from weight fee revenues in the State Highway Account for transfer to the General Fund as transportation bond debt service reimbursement and loans as follows:

(1) The Controller shall transfer all weight fee revenues deposited into the State Highway Account in any month to the Transportation Debt Service Fund for transfer to the General Fund as reimbursement for debt service costs until all of the debt service paid on transportation bonds for projects that the Director of Finance indicates qualify for reimbursement as provided for in Section 16965 of the Government Code have been reimbursed.

(2) After the Director of Finance has notified the Controller that all debt service costs for the 2010–11 fiscal year have been reimbursed, the Controller shall transfer any remaining monthly weight fee revenues in the State Highway Account to the General Fund as a loan until the full amount appropriated in this subdivision has been transferred to the

General Fund. The Director of Finance may repay any remaining portion of the outstanding balance of this loan in any year in which the Director of Finance determines the funds are needed to reimburse the General Fund for current year transportation bond debt service or to redeem or retire those bonds, pursuant to Section 16774 of the Government Code, maturing in a subsequent fiscal year, provided that the loans shall be repaid no later than June 30, 2021. All funds loaned pursuant to this section, upon repayment to the State Highway Account, shall be immediately transferred by the Controller to the Transportation Debt Service Fund for use pursuant to Section 16965 of the Government Code.

(3) By June 15, 2011, the Director of Finance in consultation with the Treasurer shall notify the Controller regarding the final amount of debt service paid from the General Fund during the 2010–11 fiscal year pursuant to Section 16965 of the Government Code and shall direct the Controller to reverse and adjust any transfers made as debt service reimbursements or loans so that a maximum amount of transfers are made for debt service reimbursements and with any loan amounts limited to the difference between this amount and the total amount appropriated in this subdivision. The total amount of weight fee revenues transferred from the State Highway Account for the 2010–11 fiscal year shall not be greater than the total amount of weight fee revenues deposited into the State Highway Account for that year.

(4) With respect to transfers or portions of transfers that cannot be made in any given month if weight fee revenues are insufficient, the first weight fee revenues available in the following month or months shall be used to complete the transfers for the previous month or months before making additional transfers for later months.

(b) For the 2011–12 fiscal year, all revenue generated from weight fees in the State Highway Account, as determined by Sections 9400.1 and 42205, excluding an amount equal to the loan of forty-three million seven hundred thousand dollars ($43,700,000) authorized pursuant to Item 2660-013-0042 of Section 2.00 of the Budget Act of 2011, is hereby appropriated for transfer to the General Fund as debt service reimbursement and loans as follows:

(1) The Controller shall transfer all weight fee revenues deposited into the State Highway Account in any month to the Transportation Debt Service Fund for transfer to the General Fund as reimbursement for debt service costs until all of the debt service paid on transportation bonds for projects that the Director of Finance indicates qualify for reimbursement as provided for in Section 16965 of the Government Code have been reimbursed.

(2) After the Director of Finance has notified the Controller that all debt service costs for the 2011–12 fiscal year have been reimbursed, the Controller shall transfer any remaining weight fee revenues for that fiscal year in the State Highway Account to the General Fund as a loan until all weight fee revenues for that fiscal year appropriated in this subdivision have been transferred to the General Fund, excluding forty-two million dollars ($42,000,000), which shall be transferred to the General Fund as a loan on July 1, 2012. The Director of Finance may repay any portion of the balance of this loan in any year in which the Director of Finance determines the funds are needed to reimburse the General Fund for current year transportation bond debt service or to redeem or retire those bonds, pursuant to Section 16774 of the Government Code, maturing in a subsequent year, provided that the loans shall be repaid no later than June 30, 2021. All funds loaned pursuant to this section, upon repayment to the State Highway Account, shall be immediately transferred by the Controller to the Transportation Debt Service Fund for use pursuant to Section 16965 of the Government Code.

(3) By June 15, 2012, the Director of Finance in consultation with the Treasurer shall notify the Controller regarding the final amount of debt service paid from the General Fund during the 2011–12 fiscal year pursuant to Section 16965 of the Government Code and shall direct the Controller to reverse and adjust any transfers made as debt service reimbursements or loans so that a maximum amount of transfers are made for debt service reimbursements and with any loan amounts limited to the difference between this amount and the total amount appropriated in this subdivision. The total amount of weight fee revenues transferred from the State Highway Account for the 2011–12 fiscal year shall not be greater than the total amount of weight fee revenues deposited into the State Highway Account in that year.

(4) With respect to transfers or portions of transfers that cannot be made in any given month if weight fee revenues are insufficient, the first weight fee revenues available in the following month or months shall be used to complete the transfers for the previous month or months before making additional transfers for later months.

(c) (1) (A) Until the month of first issuance of designated bonds, as defined in subdivision (c) of Section 16773 of the Government Code, and at any time thereafter that a Treasurer's certification pursuant to subparagraph (B) of paragraph (3) of subdivision (a) of Section 16965 of the Government Code applies, all weight fee revenues subject to this section in any month shall be transferred from the State Highway Account to the Transportation Debt Service Fund.

(B) Except as provided in paragraph (3), or when subparagraph (A) applies pursuant to a Treasurer's certification, upon the first issuance of designated bonds, as defined in subdivision (c) of Section 16773 of the Government Code, starting in the month following that first issuance, all weight fee revenues received by the Controller from the first day through the 14th day of every month shall be transferred from the State Highway Account to the Transportation Debt Service Fund.

(C) All funds transferred pursuant to subparagraphs (A) and (B) are hereby appropriated for transfer to the General Fund by the Controller as reimbursement for debt service costs paid with respect to eligible bonds described in paragraph (2) of subdivision (a) of Section 16965 of the Government Code, until all debt service that the Director of Finance indicates qualifies for reimbursement as provided for in subdivision (d), (e), or (f) of Section 16965 of the Government Code has been reimbursed, or to redeem or retire bonds, pursuant to Section 16774 of the Government Code, as referenced in subdivision (d), (e), or (f) of Section 16965 of the Government Code, that are maturing in a subsequent year. After the Director of Finance has notified the Controller that all debt service costs for the fiscal year have been reimbursed, the Controller shall transfer any remaining revenue generated from weight fees subject to this section for that fiscal year in the State Highway Account to the General Fund as a loan. The Director of Finance may repay any portion of the balance of this loan in any year in which the Director of Finance determines that the funds are needed to reimburse the General Fund for current or future year transportation bond debt service or to redeem or retire those bonds pursuant to Section 16774 of the Government Code, maturing in a future fiscal year, provided that the loans shall be repaid no later than June 30, 2021. All funds loaned pursuant to this section, upon repayment to the State Highway Account, shall be immediately transferred by the Controller to the Transportation Debt Service Fund for use pursuant to Section 16965 of the Government Code. By June 15 of each year, the Director of Finance, in consultation with the Treasurer, shall notify the Controller regarding the final amount of debt service paid from the General Fund during that fiscal year pursuant to subdivision (d), (e), or (f) of Section 16965 of the Government Code and shall direct the Controller to reverse or adjust any transfers made as debt service reimbursements or loans so that a maximum amount of transfers are made for debt service reimbursements and with any loan amounts limited to the difference between this amount and the total amount of revenue for that fiscal year generated from weight fees, as determined by Sections 9400.1 and 42205. The total amount of weight fee revenues transferred from the State Highway Account in any fiscal year shall not be greater than the total amount of weight fee revenues deposited into the State Highway Account in that year.

(2) Starting in the month following the first issuance of any designated bonds, unless a Treasurer's certification pursuant to subparagraph (B)

of paragraph (3) of subdivision (a) of Section 16965 of the Government Code applies, all weight fee revenues subject to this section that are received by the Controller from the 15th day of every month, or the first business day thereafter if not a business day, through the last day of the month shall be deposited directly in the Transportation Debt Service Fund and are hereby appropriated for transfer as follows:

(A) First, to the Transportation Bond Direct Payment Account as set forth in subdivision (b) of Section 16965 of the Government Code, to provide for payment of debt service with respect to designated bonds.

(B) Thereafter, as provided in subparagraph (C) of paragraph (1).

(3) Notwithstanding paragraphs (1) and (2), if by the last day of a month the transfer for that month relating to designated bonds required by the Treasurer's certificate described in subdivision (b) of Section 16965 of the Government Code has not been made due to insufficient weight fee revenue, weight fee revenue shall continue to be transferred pursuant to paragraph (2) beginning with the first day of the subsequent month and continuing every day until such time as sufficient revenue for full compliance with the certificate has been transferred.

(4) Except as otherwise provided in paragraph (1), (2), or (3), with respect to any transfers or portions of transfers that cannot be made in any given month if weight fee revenues are insufficient, the first weight fee revenues available in the following month or months shall be used to complete the transfers for the previous month or months before making additional transfers for later months.

(Amended by Stats. 2019, Ch. 32, Sec. 12. (SB 87) Effective June 27, 2019.)

9400.7. (a) Notwithstanding any other provision of law, except for restrictions in existence on June 1, 1989, and except as provided in subdivision (d), so long as any increases in the weight fees required by Section 9400, as enacted by Assembly Bill 471 of the 1989–90 Regular Session, remain in effect, no local agency located within an urbanized area within a county which is required to prepare a congestion management plan pursuant to Section 65089 of the Government Code may restrict the hours of operation on any street or highway which is otherwise open to truck use unless the local agency determines that the restriction is consistent with the adopted congestion management plan and is coordinated with adjacent local agencies so as to not unreasonably interfere with truck operations.

(b) If an inconsistency in access occurs between cities and counties, the inconsistent access provisions of the congestion management plan may be appealed to the California Transportation Commission. The commission shall review the inconsistent access plan and make a finding within 90 days of the appeal being filed. If the commission fails to make a finding within 90 days, the Director of Transportation shall review the issue and make a finding within 30 days.

(c) The access provisions of the congestion management plan shall not go into effect while an appeal is being made. If the commission makes a finding of inconsistency, the access provisions of the congestion management plan shall not become operative.

(d) (1) This section does not apply to Los Angeles County if the City of Los Angeles establishes restrictions on the hours of operation on any street or highway which is otherwise open to truck use.

(2) If the City of Los Angeles establishes restrictions under paragraph (1) and any other city in the County of Los Angeles establishes restrictions on the hours of operation on any street or highway which is otherwise open to truck use, the restrictions in that other city shall conform to the restrictions imposed by the City of Los Angeles, except that the other city may appeal noncomforming restrictions to the commission pursuant to subdivision (b) for a determination as to whether a variance from this paragraph should be granted.

(3) The Legislature finds and declares that, because of unique and special traffic congestion problems in the County of Los Angeles and in the City of Los Angeles, the general provisions of this section cannot be made applicable to that county.

(Added by Stats. 1989, Ch. 1337, Sec. 1.)

9400.8. Notwithstanding any other provision of law, if the voters approve Senate Constitutional Amendment 1 of the 1989–90 Regular Session, no local agency may impose a tax, permit fee, or other charge for the privilege of using its streets or highways, other than a permit fee for extra legal loads, after December 31, 1990, unless the local agency had imposed the fee prior to June 1, 1989.

(Added by Stats. 1989, Ch. 1337, Sec. 2.)

9401. (a) Motor vehicles manufactured in or prior to 1936, are exempted from the payment of the weight fees provided for in Section 9400.

(b) Notwithstanding subdivision (a), any person who owns and operates a commercial vehicle manufactured in or prior to 1936 which is registered to such person, may pay the appropriate weight fees, and the department shall issue license plates of the same type as are issued to vehicles which are required to pay weight fees for such vehicles.

(Added by Stats. 1980, Ch. 622, Sec. 3.)

9404. (a) Station wagons, except those used in the transportation of passengers for hire, are exempted from the payment of weight fees provided for in Section 9400.

Any provision of this code notwithstanding, any person (1) who is bona fide engaged in a business and who owns and operates a station wagon which is registered in the name of such business, or (2) who is bona fide engaged in a business as an employee and who is required by such employment to own and operate a station wagon, which is registered to such person, may pay the appropriate weight fees, and the department shall issue license plates of the same type as are issued to vehicles which are required to pay weight fees.

(b) For purposes of this section, "engaged in a business" means engaged in a bona fide trade, business,, commerce, or in a profession in which the measurement of land, construction quantities, or the dimension of structures, is a function authorized to be performed by the license issued for such profession, but does not include being engaged in any other type of profession.

(Amended by Stats. 1975, Ch. 531.)

9405. Agricultural water-well boring rigs are exempt from the fees provided in Section 9400.

(Enacted by Stats. 1959, Ch. 3.)

9406. Alterations or additions to registered vehicles for which fees have been paid under Section 9400 or 9400.1 placing the vehicles in weight fee classifications under Section 9400 or 9400.1 greater than the weight fees previously paid shall be reported to the department and at the same time the difference between the weight fee previously paid, reduced as provided in Section 9407, and the greater weight fee, reduced as provided in Section 9407, shall be paid to the department upon the operation of the vehicles in the greater weight fee classification under Section 9400 or 9400.1.

(Amended by Stats. 2000, Ch. 861, Sec. 51. Effective September 29, 2000. Operative December 31, 2001, pursuant to Sec. 67 of Ch. 861.)

9406.1. Prior to operation of a vehicle at a declared gross vehicle weight greater than reported to, and registered by, the department, the owner shall make application to the department and pay all appropriate fees.

(Added by Stats. 2000, Ch. 861, Sec. 52. Effective September 29, 2000. Operative December 31, 2001, pursuant to Sec. 67 of Ch. 861.)

9407. The fee required under Section 9400 and 9400.1 shall be reduced proportionately for each month which has elapsed since the expiration of the last issued registration certificate if either of the following applies:

(a) Application for registration is made after the first month of any registration year and a certification was filed pursuant to subdivision (a) of Section 4604.

(b) Application for registration of a vehicle registered on a partial year basis is made after the first month following expiration and a certification was filed pursuant to subdivision (b) of Section 9706.

(Amended by Stats. 2001, Ch. 826, Sec. 28. Effective January 1, 2002.)

9408. (a) Whenever any registered commercial vehicle, including, but not limited to, any commercial vehicle operating in California with apportioned registration, for which fees have been paid under Section 9400 or 9400.1 is withdrawn from service in this state before the expiration of the registration, the owner may surrender the registration card and license plates previously issued for the vehicle to the department and, within 90 days of the time of withdrawal, make application for the registration of another commercial vehicle which is subject to the fees specified in Section 9400 or 9400.1. If the vehicle that is withdrawn from service is operating in this state under Article 4 (commencing with Section 8050 of Chapter 4, credit for any unused fees paid under Section 9400 or 9400.1 may be applied only to a commercial vehicle concurrently added to the same apportioned fleet.

(b) Under the circumstances described in subdivision (a), and upon a proper showing of the facts, the department upon determining the fees payable under this division shall allow as credit thereon the unexpired portion, as of the month of the application, of the fee paid under Section 9400 or 9400.1 for the previous registration, but, in addition to fees otherwise payable under this division less any credit, shall charge and collect an additional fee of two dollars ($2) for issuance of the new registration.

(Amended by Stats. 2001, Ch. 826, Sec. 29. Effective January 1, 2002.)

9409. Any forklift truck which is designed primarily for loading and unloading and for stacking materials and is operated or drawn along a highway unladen is exempt from the provisions of Section 9400.

(Added by Stats. 1963, Ch. 1395.)

9410. (a) One commercial vehicle weighing less than 8,001 pounds unladen, which displays the distinguishing license plate designated in, and is registered to a person who qualifies for the exemption provided by, Section 22511.5, is exempt from the weight fees provided for in Section 9400.

(b) A commercial vehicle displaying a distinguishing placard pursuant to Section 22511.5 is not exempt from weight fees.

(Amended by Stats. 2004, Ch. 404, Sec. 10. Effective January 1, 2005.)

Article 4. Payment of Fees

(Article 4 enacted by Stats. 1959, Ch. 3.)

9550. All fees required to be paid by a vehicle dealer, manufacturer, manufacturer branch, remanufacturer, remanufacturer branch, distributor, distributor branch, representative, or transporter, in accordance with this code, for any license or special plates shall be paid at the time application is made to the department.

(Amended by Stats. 1983, Ch. 1286, Sec. 23.)

9551. All fees required to be paid by an automobile dismantler, in accordance with this code, for any license, or special plates, shall be paid at the time application is made to the department.

(Amended by Stats. 1971, Ch. 1214.)

9551.2. (a) When an application is made for a renewal or initial registration of a vehicle, the department shall apply the amount of any operative offset established by subdivision (a) of Section 10754 of the Revenue and Taxation Code. The department shall alter its billing notice for vehicle license fees to indicate the amount of the vehicle license fee for each vehicle as calculated under Section 10752 or 10752.1 of the Revenue and Taxation Code, or under Section 18115 of the Health and Safety Code, and the amount of the applicable offset as required by subdivision (a) of Section 10754 of the Revenue and Taxation Code. The amount of the offset shall be identified on the billing notice as the "VLF Offset." The Department of Motor Vehicles shall, as required by Section 11000 of the Revenue and Taxation Code, provide information to the Controller with respect to the amount of offsets subject to this subdivision.

(b) This section shall become operative on July 1, 1999, or on that earlier date that is determined by both the director of the department, and the Director of the Department of Housing and Community Development, to be feasible for the implementation of this section.

(Added by Stats. 1998, Ch. 322, Sec. 104. Effective August 20, 1998. Section operative July 1, 1999, or sooner, by its own provisions.)

9552. (a) Whenever any vehicle is operated upon any highway of this state without the fees first having been paid as required by this code, and those fees have not been paid within 20 days of its first operation, those fees are delinquent, except as provided in subdivision (b).

(b) Fees are delinquent whenever application for renewal of registration, or any application for renewal of special license plates, is made after midnight of the expiration date of the registration or special plates, or 60 days after the date the registered owner is notified by the department pursuant to Section 1661, whichever is later.

(c) Whenever any person has received as transferee a properly endorsed certificate of ownership and the transfer fee has not been paid as required by this code within 10 days, the fee is delinquent.

(d) Whenever any person becomes an automobile dismantler, dealer, manufacturer, manufacturer branch, distributor, distributor branch, or transporter without first having paid the license and special plate fees as required by this code, the fees are delinquent.

(Amended by Stats. 2002, Ch. 805, Sec. 13. Effective September 23, 2002.)

9553. (a) A penalty shall be added upon any delinquent application as provided in Section 9552, except as provided in Section 4604 or 9706, or in subdivision (b).

(b) When renewal fee penalties have not accrued with respect to a vehicle and the vehicle is transferred, the transferee has 20 days from the date of the transfer to pay the registration fees which become due without payment of penalties or to file a certification pursuant to subdivision (a) of Section 4604 if the vehicle will not be operated, moved, or left standing upon any highway during the subsequent registration year, except as provided in subdivision (c).

(c) (1) A dealer or lessor-retailer submitting an application for registration or transfer of a used vehicle shall have 30 days from the date of sale to submit the fees, without the penalty that otherwise would be required under subdivision (a).

(2) This subdivision does not apply to penalties due or accrued prior to the date of sale by the dealer or lessor-retailer.

(d) A penalty shall be added if the fees specified in Section 9255 are not paid within 20 days after they become delinquent.

(e) In addition to the imposition of monetary fines or fees as specified in this section, delinquent registration may result in impoundment of the vehicle pursuant to Section 22651.

(Amended by Stats. 2002, Ch. 805, Sec. 14. Effective September 23, 2002.)

9553.5. (a) Whenever fees have not been paid in full for an application for registration of vehicles registered pursuant to Article 4 (commencing with Section 8050) of Chapter 4, the registrant shall have 20 days from the date of notice by the department to pay the balance of the fees due.

(b) Failure to pay the balance of the fees due within 20 days shall subject the application to penalties, as defined in Sections 9554 and 9554.5, on the unpaid portion of the California fees due.

(Amended by Stats. 2008, Ch. 756, Sec. 20. Effective September 30, 2008.)

9553.7. The penalty for delinquency with respect to any transfer is fifteen dollars ($15) and applies only to the last transfer.

(Added by Stats. 2008, Ch. 756, Sec. 21. Effective September 30, 2008.)

9554. (a) (1) A penalty shall be added on any application for renewal of registration made later than midnight of the date of expiration or on or after the date penalties become due. Penalties shall be computed as provided in Section 9559 and shall be collected with the fee.

(2) Notwithstanding paragraph (1), commencing on July 1, 2011, a penalty shall not be added if an application for renewal of registration, or an application for renewal of special license plates, is made within 30 days after midnight of the expiration date of the registration or special plates. This paragraph shall become inoperative on January 1, 2012.

(b) The penalty assessment for the delinquent payment of the registration fee specified in Section 9250 shall be as follows:

(1) Ten dollars ($10) for a delinquency period of 10 days or less.

(2) Fifteen dollars ($15) for a delinquency period of more than 10 days, to and including 30 days.

(3) Thirty dollars ($30) for a delinquency period of more than 30 days, to and including one year.

(4) Fifty dollars ($50) for a delinquency period of more than one year, to and including two years.

(5) One hundred dollars ($100) for a delinquency period of more than two years.

(c) The penalty assessment for the delinquent payment of the weight fee specified in Section 9400 or 9400.1 and the vehicle license fee as specified in Section 10751 of the Revenue and Taxation Code shall be as follows:

(1) Ten percent of the vehicle license fee, or the combined amount of the vehicle license fee and the weight fee if the vehicle is subject to both fees, for a delinquency period of 10 days or less.

(2) Twenty percent of the vehicle license fee, or the combined amount of the vehicle license fee and the weight fee if the vehicle is subject to both fees, for a delinquency period of more than 10 days, to and including 30 days.

(3) Sixty percent of the vehicle license fee, or the combined amount of the vehicle license fee and the weight fee if the vehicle is subject to both fees, for a delinquency period of more than 30 days, to and including one year.

(4) Eighty percent of the vehicle license fee, or the combined amount of the vehicle license fee and the weight fee if the vehicle is subject to both fees, for a delinquency period of more than one year, to and including two years.

(5) One hundred sixty percent of the vehicle license fee, or the combined amount of the vehicle license fee and the weight fee if the vehicle is subject to both fees, for a delinquency period of more than two years.

(d) On or after January 1, 2003, a penalty assessment for weight fees not reported and not paid within 20 days as required by Section 9406 shall be applied to the difference in the weight fee as follows:

(1) Ten percent of the fee for a delinquency period of 10 days or less.

(2) Twenty percent of the fee for a delinquency period more than 10 days, to and including 30 days.

(3) Sixty percent of the fee for a delinquency period more than 30 days, to and including one year.

(4) Eighty percent of the fee for a delinquency period more than one year, to and including two years.

(5) One hundred sixty percent for a delinquency period more than two years.

(e) A single penalty assessment for the delinquent payment of the fees specified in Sections 9250.8 and 9250.13 shall be as follows:

(1) Ten dollars ($10) for a delinquency period of 10 days or less.

(2) Fifteen dollars ($15) for a delinquency period of more than 10 days, to and including 30 days.

(3) Thirty dollars ($30) for a delinquency period of more than 30 days, to and including one year.

(4) Fifty dollars ($50) for a delinquency period of more than one year, to and including two years.

(5) One hundred dollars ($100) for a delinquency period of more than two years.

(6) This subdivision applies to the renewal of registration for vehicles with expiration dates on or after December 1, 2008.

(Amended by Stats. 2011, Ch. 21, Sec. 6. (SB 94) Effective May 4, 2011.)

9554.1. The amount of any penalty calculated pursuant to Section 9554 or subdivision (b) of Section 18116 of the Health and Safety Code shall be reduced by the amount of any offset implemented pursuant to Section 10754 of the Revenue and Taxation Code, or any portion of the amount of that offset.

(Added by Stats. 1998, Ch. 322, Sec. 105. Effective August 20, 1998.)

9554.2. Upon the operation of a commercial motor vehicle at a greater gross vehicle weight than had been reported to and registered by the department, a new registration application shall be made to the department. The greater declared gross vehicle weight fee as required in Section 9400.1 and any penalties defined in this code shall be paid to the department.

(Added by Stats. 2000, Ch. 861, Sec. 54. Effective September 29, 2000. Operative December 31, 2001, pursuant to Sec. 67 of Ch. 861.)

9554.5. (a) On and after January 1, 2003, a penalty shall be added on any application for original registration made later than midnight of the date of expiration or on or after the date penalties become due. Penalties shall be computed as provided in Section 9559 and shall be collected with the fee.

(b) The penalty assessment for the delinquent payment of the registration fee specified in Section 9250 shall be as follows:

(1) Thirty dollars ($30) for a delinquency period of one year or less.

(2) Fifty dollars ($50) for a delinquency period of more than one year, to and including two years.

(3) One hundred dollars ($100) for a delinquency period of more than two years.

(c) The penalty assessment for the delinquent payment of the weight fee specified in Section 9400 or 9400.1 and the vehicle license fee as specified in Section 10751 of the Revenue and Taxation Code shall be as follows:

(1) Forty percent of the vehicle license fee, or the combined amount of the vehicle license fee and the weight fee if the vehicle is subject to both fees, for a delinquency period of one year or less.

(2) Eighty percent of the vehicle license fee, or the combined amount of the vehicle license fee and the weight fee if the vehicle is subject to both fees, for a delinquency period of more than one year, to and including two years.

(3) One hundred sixty percent of the vehicle license fee, or the combined amount of the vehicle license fee and the weight fee if the vehicle is subject to both fees, for a delinquency period of more than two years.

(d) A single penalty assessment for the delinquent payment of the fees specified in Sections 9250.8 and 9250.13 shall be as follows:

(1) Thirty dollars ($30) for a delinquency period of one year or less.

(2) Fifty dollars ($50) for a delinquency period of more than one year, to and including two years.

(3) One hundred dollars ($100) for a delinquency period of more than two years.

(4) This subdivision shall apply to applications for an original registration where the date the fee is due is on or after December 1, 2008.

(e) This section shall become operative January 1, 2009.

(Repealed (in Sec. 24) and added by Stats. 2008, Ch. 756, Sec. 25. Effective September 30, 2008. Section operative January 1, 2009, by its own provisions.)

9555. Whenever any trailer coach is in this State without the registration fee having first been paid as required by this code, the fee is delinquent.

(Enacted by Stats. 1959, Ch. 3.)

9556. Whenever any person or organization authorized by the department under Section 4610 receives an application for renewal of registration accompanied by the proper fee and endorses a receipt or validates a registration card or potential registration card in respect to the application for renewal of registration prior to midnight on the date registration expires in any year, the application and payment of fees shall not be deemed delinquent or subject to penalty, except that the person or organization so receiving the application and fees shall transmit the application and fees to the department as promptly as practicable in the immediate course of business.

This section shall become operative on March 8, 1976, unless a later enacted statute, which is chaptered before March 8, 1976, deletes or extends such date.

(Repealed and added by Stats. 1974, Ch. 1330, Sec. 26.)

9557. (a) No penalty shall be imposed for delinquent payment of any fee required to be paid under this code in the event any instrument for effective payment of such fee is placed in the United States mail or in any postal box maintained by the United States Postal Service with sufficient identification in an envelope with postage thereon prepaid and addressed to the Department of Motor Vehicles at Sacramento, or to one of the regularly established branch offices of the department or to any person or organization authorized by the department under Section 4610, prior to the date or time the fee becomes delinquent.

(b) Any person so mailing an instrument for payment of any fee may file with the department a certificate in writing showing compliance with the provisions of this section. The certificate shall be accepted by the department as prima facie evidence of such mailing.

(Amended by Stats. 1975, Ch. 389.)

9558. If a check in payment of a fee or penalty is not paid by the bank on which it is drawn on its first presentation, the person tendering the check remains liable for the payment of the fee, or fee and penalty, as if he had not tendered the check. The department in its discretion may redeposit a check in payment of the fee, or the fee and penalty, not more than once without assessing additional penalties.

(Amended by Stats. 1969, Ch. 214.)

9559. In computing any registration or weight fee or penalty imposed by this code, whether on a proration or otherwise, a fraction of a dollar is disregarded, unless it equals or exceeds fifty cents ($0.50), in which case it is treated as one full dollar ($1). Computation of any penalty shall be made from the fee after the same has been computed as provided in this section.

Any fee or penalty in an amount of forty-nine cents ($0.49) or less shall be deemed to be one dollar ($1).

(Amended by Stats. 1992, Ch. 1241, Sec. 14. Effective January 1, 1993.)

9559.5. When, by reason of the assignment or reassignment of a renewal registration date by the director, the registration year is less than, or more than, 12 months, the fee due for that renewal shall be decreased or increased by one-twelfth of the annual fee for each month of the period less than, or in excess of, 12 months.

(Added by Stats. 2006, Ch. 169, Sec. 4. Effective January 1, 2007.)

9560. (a) The department shall waive all penalties that may be due for late payment of registration renewal fees on a vehicle for any period during which the registered owner is deployed to a location outside of the state.

(b) (1) For the purposes of this section, "deployed" means being ordered to temporary military duty during a period when a Presidential Executive order specifies that the United States is engaged in combat or homeland defense and the registered owner is one of the following:

(A) A member of the armed forces.

(B) A member of the armed forces reserve or the National Guard who has been called to active duty or active service.

(2) "Deployed" does not include either of the following:

(A) Temporary duty for the sole purpose of training or processing.

(B) A permanent change of station.

(c) This section does not apply to a registered owner who applies for registration renewal more than 60 days after termination of his or her deployment.

(Added by Stats. 2004, Ch. 188, Sec. 1. Effective January 1, 2005.)

9561. (a) When a legal owner or his or her agent repossesses a vehicle on which renewal fees are due, the department shall waive any renewal penalties that are due for late payment if the fees are paid within 60 days of taking possession.

(b) Notwithstanding any other provisions of this code, when a repossessed vehicle is sold through a dealer conducting a wholesale motor vehicle auction as provided in subdivision (b) of Section 4456 and Article 5 (commencing with Section 6100) of Chapter 2 of Division 3, any penalties that may be due are waived, if all renewal fees that are due are paid not later than 60 days after the date of sale at the auction.

(Amended by Stats. 1994, Ch. 180, Sec. 10. Effective July 11, 1994.)

9561.5. The department shall waive any penalties that may be due for late payment of registration renewal fees on a vehicle if all of the following criteria are met:

(a) The vehicle is sold through a dealer conducting a wholesale motor vehicle auction as provided in subdivision (b) of Section 4456 and Article 5 (commencing with Section 6100) of Chapter 2 of Division 3.

(b) Immediately prior to the sale the vehicle was registered as a leased vehicle.

(c) Delivery of the vehicle to the dealer conducting the wholesale motor vehicle auction was not later than 25 days after the termination of the lease.

(d) The date of termination of the lease and the date of delivery to the auction is reported on the application for registration, or application for transfer and registration, in a format that is acceptable to the department.

(Added by Stats. 1997, Ch. 311, Sec. 1. Effective January 1, 1998.)

9562. (a) When a transferee or purchaser of a vehicle applies for transfer of registration, as provided in Section 5902, and it is determined by the department that registration penalties accrued prior to the purchase of the vehicle, and that the transferee or purchaser was not cognizant of the nonpayment of the fees for registration for the current or prior registration years, the department may waive the registration penalties upon payment of the fees for registration due.

(b) Other provisions of this code notwithstanding, the director may, at his or her discretion, investigate into the circumstances of any application for registration to ascertain if penalties had accrued through no fault or intent of the owner. If the director determines that the circumstances justify it, he or she may waive any penalties upon payment of the fees for registration then due.

(c) When a transferee or purchaser of a vehicle applies for transfer of registration of a vehicle, and it is determined by the department that fees for registration of the vehicle for any year are unpaid and due, that the fees became due prior to the transfer or purchase of the vehicle by the transferee or purchaser and that the transferee or purchaser was not cognizant of the fact that the fees were unpaid and due, the department may waive the fees and any penalty thereon if the license plate assigned to the vehicle displays a validating device issued by the department and the validating device contains the year number of the registration year for which the transferee or purchaser is requesting a waiver of fees and penalties.

(d) Upon the transfer of a vehicle for which fees for registration and any penalties thereon are unpaid and due, the fees and penalties are, notwithstanding the provisions of Article 6 (commencing with Section 9800) of this chapter, the personal debt of the transferor of the vehicle who did not pay the fees and penalties when they became due or accrued. The fees and penalties may be collected by the department in an appropriate civil action if the department has waived the fees and penalties pursuant to subdivision (c).

(Amended by Stats. 1993, Ch. 223, Sec. 1. Effective January 1, 1994.)

9563. Notwithstanding any other provisions of this code, when a vehicle is rebuilt and restored to operation after it has been reported to be dismantled pursuant to Section 11520, the application shall be deemed to be an application for original registration of a new vehicle for determination of fees.

(Amended by Stats. 1973, Ch. 889.)

9564. (a) A scrap metal processor, as described in paragraph (3) of subdivision (a) of Section 221, who acquires a vehicle of a type subject to registration under this code, and who complies with all the provisions of this section, is not required to submit a certificate of nonoperation in lieu of fees or to pay fees that would otherwise be required if the vehicle were to be currently registered.

(b) A scrap metal processor who acquires a vehicle as provided in subdivision (a) shall submit either of the following to the department before reducing the vehicle to its component materials:

(1) Documentation that the vehicle was acquired pursuant to Section 22669 and disposed of in compliance with Article 2 (commencing with Section 22850) of Chapter 10 of Division 11.

(2) The properly endorsed certificate of title transferring title to the scrap iron processor and any available license plates or registration documents.

(c) A vehicle delivered to a scrap metal processor under subdivision (a) shall not be reconstructed or made operable, unless it is a vehicle which qualifies for either horseless carriage license plates or historical vehicle license plates pursuant to Section 5004, in which case the vehicle may be reconstructed or made operable.

(Amended by Stats. 1999, Ch. 316, Sec. 2. Effective January 1, 2000.)

Article 5. Partial Year Payment of Weight Fees

(Article 5 repealed and added by Stats. 1981, Ch. 636, Sec. 8.)

9700. With respect to vehicles subject to additional registration fees under Section 9400 or 9400.1, a proportionate share of the additional fees may be paid for any partial period of one month or more, but less than 12 months, in an amount determined to be one-twelfth of the annual registration times the consecutive months, or fraction thereof, of the period of registration.

(Amended by Stats. 2001, Ch. 826, Sec. 30. Effective January 1, 2002.)

9702. An additional fee of fifteen dollars ($15) shall be charged for each application for partial year registration, or renewal thereof, whenever a person pays the fee under Section 9400 or 9400.1, as provided in Section 9700.

(Amended by Stats. 2003, Ch. 719, Sec. 19. Effective January 1, 2004.)

9704. Every partial year vehicle registration and every certificate or insignia issued under this article shall expire at midnight on the last day of the period for which issued. The department may, upon payment of the proper fees, renew the registration of the vehicle for a period of months less than the remainder of the registration year or for the remainder of the registration year.

(Added by Stats. 1981, Ch. 636, Sec. 8.)

9706. (a) Application for partial year registration in conjunction with an application for original California registration shall be made by the owner within 20 days of the date the vehicle first becomes subject to California registration. Any application for partial year registration submitted after that 20-day period shall be denied registration for a partial year, and the vehicle shall be subject to payment of the fees for the entire registration year. In addition to the fee for the registration year, a penalty, as specified in Section 9554, shall be added to the fee for registration.

(b) Any application to renew registration for a part of the remainder of the registration year or for the entire remainder of the registration year shall be made prior to midnight of the expiration date of the last issued registration certificate. Application shall be made upon presentation of the last issued registration card or of a potential registration issued by the department for use at the time of renewal and by payment of the required partial year fees, or, if renewal is for the remainder of the registration year, by payment of the annual fee required by Section 9400 or 9400.1, as reduced pursuant to Section 9407.

(c) Notwithstanding any other provision of law, an owner who registers a vehicle pursuant to this article during a calendar year shall, if the vehicle was not operated, moved, or left standing upon a highway, file a certificate of nonoperation prior to the date of the first operation of the vehicle on the highways in a manner which requires that registration and shall, by December 31 of each calendar year thereafter, file a certification pursuant to subdivisions (a) and (b) of Section 4604 when the vehicle is not registered for operation on the highways for the succeeding calendar year.

(d) Notwithstanding subdivision (c), the owner of any vehicle being moved or operated for the purpose of providing support to firefighting operations while the vehicle or owner is under contract to the United States Forestry Service, the United States Department of the Interior, the Bureau of Land Management, the Department of Forestry and Fire Protection, or the Office of Emergency Services may obtain partial year registration if application is made within 20 days of the date the vehicle is first operated, moved, or left standing on the highway and the owner has obtained a letter of authorization from the department prior to the date that the vehicle is first operated, moved, or left standing on the highway.

(Amended by Stats. 2013, Ch. 352, Sec. 524. (AB 1317) Effective September 26, 2013. Operative July 1, 2013, by Sec. 543 of Ch. 352.)

9706.1. If the registration card or potential registration card is unavailable, payment of the fee prescribed by Section 9265 for the issuance of a duplicate registration shall not be required in addition to the other fees prescribed by subdivision (b) of Section 9706.

(Added by Stats. 1991, Ch. 13, Sec. 22. Effective February 13, 1991.)

9710. When an application for renewal of registration of a vehicle has been made as required by Section 9706, the vehicle may be operated on the highways until the new certificate or insignia of current registration has been received from the department if there is displayed on the vehicle, in addition to the license plates or validating devices issued to the vehicle for the previous year, the certificate or insignia issued to the vehicle for the previous partial year.

(Amended by Stats. 1990, Ch. 1352, Sec. 13. Effective September 27, 1990. Applicable from July 1, 1990, pursuant to Sec. 21 of Ch. 1352.)

9711. This article does not apply to any owner or lessor of a commercial vehicle based in a foreign jurisdiction which does not grant reciprocity or proportionate registration to residents of this state while operating within that jurisdiction.

(Added by Stats. 1988, Ch. 907, Sec. 2.)

Article 6. Enforcement of Liens

(Article 6 repealed and added by Stats. 1982, Ch. 664, Sec. 8.)

9800. (a) Payments for any of the following, and any interest, penalties, or service fees added thereto, required to register or transfer the registration of a vehicle, constitute a lien on the vehicle on which they are due or which was involved in the offense, and on any other vehicle owned by the owner of that vehicle:

(1) Registration fees.

(2) Transfer fees.

(3) License fees.

(4) Use taxes.

(5) Penalties for offenses relating to the standing or parking of a vehicle for which a notice of parking violation has been served on the owner, and any administrative service fee added to the penalty.

(6) Any court-imposed fine or penalty assessment, and any administrative service fee added thereto, which is subject to collection by the department.

(b) Notwithstanding subdivision (a), if a person is cited for a foreign registered auxiliary dolly, semitrailer, or trailer having been operated without current year registration or valid California permits or registration, an amount equal to the minimum registration fees or transfer fees, and any penalty added thereto, from the date they became due, shall, by election of the power unit operator, constitute a lien upon the California registered power unit which was pulling the dolly, semitrailer, or trailer. However, this subdivision is not applicable if the citation is issued at a scale operated by the Department of the California Highway Patrol and registration for the vehicle can be issued there immediately upon payment of the fees due.

(c) Every lien arising under this section expires three years from the date the fee, tax, or parking penalty first became due unless the lien is perfected pursuant to subdivision (d).

(d) A lien is perfected when a notice is mailed to the registered and legal owners at the addresses shown in the department's records and the lien is recorded on the electronic vehicle registration records of the department. A perfected lien shall expire five years from the date of perfection.

(e) Employees and members of the Department of the California Highway Patrol assigned to commercial vehicle scale facilities may possess and sell trip permits approved by the Department of Motor Vehicles.

(Amended by Stats. 1992, Ch. 1199, Sec. 10. Effective September 30, 1992.)

9801. (a) (1) When the payment required for the registration or transfer of a vehicle is delinquent pursuant to subdivision (a) of Section 9800, the department may collect the amount of the lien on the vehicle plus costs, not to exceed two hundred fifty dollars ($250), by the filing of a certificate requesting judgment pursuant to Section 9805, or by appropriate civil action and by the seizure and sale of the vehicle or any other vehicle owned by the owner of the unregistered vehicle.

(2) In the case of a leased vehicle, the authority provided in paragraph (1) to seize and sell the vehicle or any other vehicle owned by the owner of that vehicle shall not apply to a lien for any delinquency for which only the lessee is liable pursuant to paragraph (1) of subdivision (a) of Section 10879 of the Revenue and Taxation Code.

(b) At least 10 days before the seizure, notice of the lien and of the intent to seize and sell the vehicle shall be given by the department to the registered and legal owners, and to any other person known to be claiming an interest in the vehicle, by registered mail addressed to those persons at the last known addresses appearing on the records of the department.

(c) Any person receiving the notice of the lien and the intent to seize and sell the vehicle may request a hearing to contest the existence or amount of the lien. If no hearing is requested, the vehicle shall be seized and sold.

(d) If a hearing is requested, 10 days' notice shall be given of the time and place of the hearing, which shall be held within the county of residence of the person requesting the hearing or of the registered owner. The hearing shall be conducted by a referee who shall submit findings and recommendations to the director or his or her authorized representative, who shall decide the matter. The decision shall be effective on notice thereof to the interested parties. However, the director or his or her authorized representative may rescind the decision and reconsider the matter for good cause shown at any time within three years after the date the disputed fee or tax first became due, or within one year from the hearing, whichever is later.

(e) At any time before seizure or sale, any registered owner, legal owner, or person claiming an interest in the vehicle may pay the department the amount of the lien, plus costs. In that event, the seizure or sale shall not be held and the vehicle, if seized, shall be returned by the department to the person entitled to its possession. This payment shall not constitute a waiver of the right to a hearing.

(f) When the department or an authorized agent has reasonable cause to believe that the lien may be jeopardized within the 10-day notice-of-intent period, the vehicle may be seized without prior notice to the registered or legal owner, upon obtaining authorization for the seizure from the Registrar of Vehicles or authorized representative. In all those cases, a notice of the lien and the intent to sell the vehicle shall be given by the department to the legal and registered owner, and to any other person known to be claiming an interest in the vehicle, within 48 hours after seizure excluding Saturdays, Sundays, and holidays specified in Section 6700 of the Government Code. Any hearing to contest the lien and the seizure shall be requested within 10 days following transmittal of that notice.

(g) When a lien exists against one or more vehicles owned by the same person or persons, the department may seize and sell a sufficient number of the vehicles to pay the lien, plus costs, on one or more of the vehicles in accordance with subdivision (a).

(h) The Department of the California Highway Patrol shall assist with the seizure and impounding of the vehicle. Any municipality or county law enforcement agency may assist with the seizure and impounding of the vehicle.

(i) Any property found by the department in any vehicle seized under the provisions of this article shall be handled by the department in the same manner as is provided in Sections 2414 and 2415.

(Amended by Stats. 1994, Ch. 1211, Sec. 3. Effective September 30, 1994.)

9802. (a) The Registrar of Vehicles or authorized representative shall conduct the sale in the same manner as provided by law for the seizure and sale of personal property by the assessor for the collection of taxes due on personal property.

(b) The department may bid for the vehicle an amount equal to the lien held by the department for registration, transfer, and license fees, use taxes, parking penalties, and any interest, penalties, and costs added thereto. In all cases where the vehicle becomes the property of the department, it shall be reduced to junk and sold.

(c) The proceeds of any sale shall be allocated by the department for the following purposes and in the following order:

(1) Costs incurred by the department.

(2) Registration and transfer fees and any penalty added thereto.

(3) License fees and any penalty added thereto.

(4) Use taxes and any interest or penalty added thereto.

(5) Perfected mechanics' liens.

(6) Perfected security interests.

(7) Penalties for offenses relating to the standing or parking of a vehicle and any administrative service fee added thereto. Any other court-induced liability, and any administrative service fee added thereto, which is subject to collection by the department.

(8) All other fees due the department.

(9) Any remainder to the person whose claim of interest in the vehicle is approved by the department.

(d) Notwithstanding Section 42270, the proceeds of a sale allocated pursuant to paragraphs (4) to (9), inclusive, of subdivision (c) shall not be transmitted to the Treasurer for deposit in the Motor Vehicle Account in the State Transportation Fund.

(e) The department shall transmit to the State Board of Equalization all use taxes, interest, and penalties collected under this article within 60 days after receipt thereof in the form which may be prescribed and approved jointly by the department and the board.

(Amended by Stats. 1992, Ch. 1199, Sec. 11.5. Effective September 30, 1992.)

9803. Nothing in this code prevents a review or other action as may be permitted by the Constitution and laws of this state by a court of competent jurisdiction of any order of the department to seize and sell a vehicle.

(Added by Stats. 1986, Ch. 1212, Sec. 2.)

9804. (a) Any action brought in a court of competent jurisdiction to review any order of the department to seize and sell a vehicle shall be commenced within 90 days from the date notice is given of the order.

(b) Upon final completion of all administrative appeals, the department shall give written notice to the owner of a vehicle ordered for seizure and sale of his or her right to a review of the order by a court pursuant to subdivision (a).

(Added by Stats. 1986, Ch. 1212, Sec. 3.)

9805. (a) The department may file in the office of the Clerk of the Superior Court of Sacramento County, or any other county, a certificate specifying the amount of any fee, tax, penalty, and collection cost due, the name and last known address of the individual, company, or corporation liable for the amount due, and the fact that the department has complied with all the provisions of this division in the computation of the amount due, and a request that judgment be entered against the individual, company, or corporation in the amount of the fee, tax, penalty, and collection cost set forth in the certificate if the fee, tax, penalty, or collection cost constitutes either of the following:

(1) A lien under this division on the vehicle on which it is due is not

paid when due, and there is evidence that the vehicle has been operated in violation of this code or any regulations adopted pursuant to this code.

(2) A lessee liability as provided in Section 10879 of the Revenue and Taxation Code.

(b) Prior to the filing of the certificate, the department shall, by mail, notify the individual, company, or corporation of the amount which is due and of the opportunity for a hearing as provided in this subdivision. At the request of the individual, company, or corporation, the department shall conduct a hearing pursuant to Section 9801, at which it shall be determined whether the claimed fee, tax, penalty, or collection cost in the amount claimed by the department is due and constitutes a lien on the vehicle, and whether the individual, company, or corporation is liable therefor.

(c) If no hearing is requested within 15 days after mailing the notice required by subdivision (b), the certificate required by subdivision (b) may be filed.

(Amended by Stats. 2002, Ch. 784, Sec. 593. Effective January 1, 2003.)

9806. The clerk of the court, immediately upon the filing of the certificate specified in Section 9805, shall enter a judgment for the people of the State of California against the individual, company, or corporation in the amount of any fee, tax, penalty, and collection cost set forth in the certificate. The clerk may file the judgment in a looseleaf book entitled "Department of Motor Vehicles Registration Judgments."

(Amended by Stats. 2002, Ch. 784, Sec. 594. Effective January 1, 2003.)

9808. Execution shall issue upon the judgment specified in Section 9806 upon request of the department in the same manner as execution may issue upon other judgments, and sales shall be held under the execution as prescribed in the Code of Civil Procedure, except that attachment may not issue against any real property.

(Added by Stats. 1990, Ch. 676, Sec. 4.)

Division 3.5. Registration and Transfer of Vessels

(Division 3.5 added by Stats. 1970, Ch. 1428.)

Chapter 1. General Provisions and Definitions

(Chapter 1 added by Stats. 1970, Ch. 1428.)

9840. As used in this division, unless the context clearly requires a different meaning:

(a) "Vessel" includes every description of watercraft used or capable of being used as a means of transportation on water, except the following:

(1) A seaplane on the water.

(2) A watercraft specifically designed to operate on a permanently fixed course, the movement of which is restricted to or guided on such permanently fixed course by means of a mechanical device on a fixed track or arm to which the watercraft is attached or by which the watercraft is controlled, or by means of a mechanical device attached to the watercraft itself.

(3) A floating structure which is designed and built to be used as a stationary waterborne residential dwelling, which (A) does not have and is not designed to have a mode of power of its own, (B) is dependent for utilities upon a continuous utility linkage to a source originating on shore, and (C) has a permanent, continuous hookup to a shoreside sewage system.

(b) "Owner" is a person having all the incidents of ownership, including the legal title, of a vessel whether or not such person lends, rents, or pledges such vessel; the person entitled to the possession of a vessel as the purchaser under a conditional sale contract; or the mortgagor of a vessel. "Owner" does not include a person holding legal title to a vessel under a conditional sales contract, the mortgagee of a vessel, or the renter or lessor of a vessel to the state or to any county, city, district, or political subdivision of the state under a lease, lease-sale, or rental-purchase agreement which grants possession of the vessel to the lessee for a period of 30 consecutive days or more.

(c) "Legal owner" is a person holding the legal title to a vessel under a conditional sale contract, the mortgagee of a vessel, or the renter or lessor of a vessel to the state, or to any county, city, district or political subdivision of the state, under a lease, lease-sale, or rental-purchase agreement which grants possession of the vessel to the lessee for a period of 30 consecutive days or more.

(d) "Registered owner" is the person registered by the department as the owner of the vessel.

(e) "Waters of this state" means any waters within the territorial limits of this state.

(f) "State of principal use" means the state on which waters a vessel is used or intended to be used most during a calendar year.

(g) "Undocumented vessel" means any vessel which is not required to have and does not have a valid marine document issued by the Bureau of Customs of the United States or any federal agency successor thereto.

(h) "Use" means operate, navigate, or employ.

(Amended by Stats. 1984, Ch. 411, Sec. 1.)

9845. The director, deputy director, registrar, deputy registrar, investigators of the department, and peace officers, as defined in Chapter 4.5 (commencing with Section 830) of the Penal Code, may inspect the hull identification number, certificate of number, and certificate of ownership of any vessel, as defined in Section 9840, when transported on a highway, or in any public garage, repair shop, public or private marina, dry storage facility, new or used vessel sales lot or boat yard, or other similar establishment for the purpose of investigating the ownership and registration of vessels, locating stolen vessels, and for inspection of wrecked, dismantled, or abandoned vessels. The authority to inspect pursuant to this section does not extend to any enclosed living area aboard a vessel.

(Added by Stats. 1987, Ch. 298, Sec. 1.)

Chapter 2. Registration

(Chapter 2 added by Stats. 1970, Ch. 1428.)

9850. Every undocumented vessel using the waters or on the waters of this state shall be currently numbered. No person shall operate nor shall any county, city, or political subdivision give permission for the operation of any undocumented vessel on those waters unless the undocumented vessel is numbered in accordance with this chapter, or in accordance with applicable federal law, or in accordance with a federally approved numbering system of another state, and unless (1) the certificate of number issued to such undocumented vessel is in full force and effect, and (2) the identifying number set forth in the certificate of number is displayed on each side of the bow of the undocumented vessel for which the identifying number was issued.

(Amended by Stats. 1987, Ch. 298, Sec. 2.)

9851. The department may adopt rules and regulations for the registration of undocumented vessels belonging to the state, local public agencies, or to the United States without payment of fees specified in this code, except fees for duplicate certificates of ownership, duplicate certificates of number, or substitute current year registration stickers. Any vessel owned by the Department of Boating and Waterways is exempt from any fees specified in this division.

(Amended by Stats. 1990, Ch. 951, Sec. 1. Operative July 1, 1991, by Sec. 5 of Ch. 951.)

9852. The department shall promulgate rules and regulations setting forth requirements relative to establishing proof of ownership to be submitted by the owner at the time of filing initial application for a certificate of number and a certificate of ownership. The issuance of a certificate of ownership or certificate of number under this chapter shall not in any way be construed that the department is warranting or guaranteeing the title of the vessel as it appears on such certificates.

(Amended by Stats. 1973, Ch. 759.)

9852.5. Ownership of an undocumented vessel subject to registration may be held by two or more coowners as follows:

(a) A vessel may be registered in the names of two or more persons as coowners in the alternative by the use of the word "or." A vessel so registered in the alternative shall be deemed to be held in joint tenancy. Each coowner shall be deemed to have granted to the other coowners the absolute right to dispose of the title and interest in the vessel. Upon the death of a coowner the interest of the decedent shall pass to the survivor as though title or interest in the vessel was held in joint tenancy unless a contrary intention is set forth in writing upon the application for registration.

(b) A vessel may be registered in the names of two or more persons as coowners in the alternative by the use of the word "or" and if declared in writing upon the application for registration by the applicants to be community property, or tenancy in common, shall grant to each coowner the absolute power to transfer the title or interest of the other coowners only during the lifetime of such coowners.

(c) A vessel may be registered in the names of two or more persons as coowners in the conjunctive by the use of the word "and" and shall thereafter require the signature of each coowner or his personal representative to transfer title to the vessel, except where title to the vessel is set forth in joint tenancy, the signature of each coowner or his or her personal representative shall be required only during the lifetime of the coowners, and upon death of a coowner title shall pass to the surviving coowner.

(d) The department may adopt suitable abbreviations to appear upon the certificate of ownership and certificate of number to designate the manner in which title to the vessel is held if set forth by the coowners upon the application for registration.

(Added by Stats. 1985, Ch. 982, Sec. 25.)

9852.7. (a) Ownership of an undocumented vessel subject to registration may be held in beneficiary form that includes a direction to transfer ownership of the vessel to a designated beneficiary on death of the owner if both of the following requirements are satisfied:

(1) Only one owner is designated.

(2) Only one TOD beneficiary is designated.

(b) Ownership registration and title issued in beneficiary form shall include, after the name of the owner, the words "transfer on death to" or the abbreviation "TOD" followed by the name of the beneficiary.

(c) During the lifetime of the owner, the signature or consent of the beneficiary is not required for any transaction relating to the vessel for which a certificate of ownership in beneficiary form has been issued.

(d) The fee for registering ownership of a vessel in a beneficiary form is ten dollars ($10).

(Added by Stats. 1991, Ch. 1055, Sec. 61. Operative January 1, 1993, by Sec. 64 of Ch. 1055.)

9852.9. (a) On and after July 1, 2008, the form for an initial application for a number prepared by the department pursuant to Section 9853 shall include both of the following:

(1) Checkoff boxes or line alternatives for the retail seller of an undocumented vessel to certify that a sterndrive or inboard vessel that contains a spark-ignition marine engine below 373 kW (500 hp) rated power output that was manufactured on or after January 1, 2008, and a sterndrive or inboard vessel that contains a spark-ignition marine engine with any rated power output that was manufactured on or after January 1, 2009, has a permanently affixed label indicating that the engine meets or exceeds the 2008 California emissions standards required by Section 2442 of Title 13 of the California Code of Regulations.

(2) A line requiring that an initial application for a vessel described in paragraph (1) be accompanied by the hang tag required by Section 2443.3 of Title 13 of the California Code of Regulations for the engine described in paragraph (1).

(b) As used in this section, "spark-ignition marine engine" has the same meaning as that term is defined in Section 9853.7.

(Added by Stats. 2007, Ch. 609, Sec. 1. Effective January 1, 2008. Operative July 1, 2008, by Sec. 4 of Ch. 609.)

9853. (a) The owner of each vessel requiring numbering by this state shall file an initial application for a number with the department or with an agent authorized by the department on forms approved by the department. The forms shall be prepared in cooperation with the Division of Boating and Waterways. The application shall contain the true name and address of the owner, the true name and address of the legal owner, if any, and the hull identification number of the vessel as may be required by the department. The application shall be signed by the owner of the vessel and shall be accompanied by a fee of nine dollars ($9), in addition to the fees required under subdivision (b).

(b) (1) Whenever the fee for original registration of a vessel becomes due between January 1 and December 31 of any even-numbered year, the application shall be accompanied by a fee of ten dollars ($10), in addition to any other fees that are then due and payable.

(2) Whenever the fee for original registration of a vessel becomes due, or is filed with the department, between January 1 and December 31 of any odd-numbered year, the application shall be accompanied by a fee of twenty dollars ($20) in addition to any other fees that are then due and payable.

(c) (1) The department shall collect, from resident and nonresident vessel owners, separate from the original registration fee, an invasive mussel infestation prevention fee in an amount established by the Division of Boating and Waterways pursuant to Section 675 of the Harbors and Navigation Code.

(2) Upon payment of the fee described in paragraph (1), the department shall issue a vessel an invasive mussel infestation prevention sticker to the vessel owner.

(3) Failure to pay the invasive mussel infestation prevention fee described in paragraph (1) does not prohibit the department from issuing registration of a vessel.

(4) (A) A vessel operator may be issued a citation for operating a recreational vessel in nonmarine waters without a valid state-issued

invasive mussel infestation prevention sticker.

(B) Notwithstanding subparagraph (A), a vessel that is exempt pursuant to Section 5211 of Title 14 of the California Code of Regulations shall not be cited pursuant to subparagraph (A).

(d) The department shall provide documentation of its administrative costs pursuant to this section to the Division of Boating and Waterways.

(Amended by Stats. 2025, Ch. 106, Sec. 17. (AB 149) Effective September 17, 2025.)

9853.1. Upon receipt of the application in approved form, the department shall issue a certificate of ownership to the legal owner and a certificate of number to the owner, or both to the owner if there is no legal owner, stating the number issued to the vessel and the name and address of the owner.

(Added by Stats. 1973, Ch. 759.)

9853.2. The owner shall paint on or attach to each side of the forward half of the vessel the identification number in such manner as may be prescribed by rules and regulations of the department in order that it may be clearly visible. Any such rules and regulations shall be developed in cooperation with the Department of Boating and Waterways. The number shall be maintained in a legible condition. The certificate of number shall be pocket size and shall be available at all times for inspection on the vessel for which issued, whenever the vessel is in use, except as to those vessels subject to Section 9853.3.

(Amended by Stats. 1984, Ch. 144, Sec. 206.)

9853.3. The certificate of number for vessels less than 26 feet in length and leased or rented to another for the latter's noncommercial use of less than 24 hours may be retained on shore by the vessel's owner or his representative at the place from which the vessel departs or returns to the possession of the owner or his representative. A copy of the lease or rental agreement signed by the owner or his authorized representative and by the person leasing or renting the vessel shall be carried aboard the vessel at all times during use.

(Added by Stats. 1973, Ch. 759.)

9853.4. (a) The department may issue one or more stickers, tabs, or other suitable devices to identify vessels as being currently registered. The size, shape, and color of the sticker, tab, or other device and the positioning of the sticker, tab, or other device on the vessel shall be as determined by the department after consultation with the Department of Boating and Waterways, such consultation to consider the responsibilities and duties of the Department of Boating and Waterways as prescribed in the Harbors and Navigation Code.

(b) Whenever the department issues a sticker, tab, or other device pursuant to subdivision (a), the sticker, tab, or device shall only be displayed on the vessel for which it was issued.

(Amended by Stats. 1987, Ch. 298, Sec. 3.)

9853.5. Upon request, the department shall issue for any power-driven pleasure craft which is constructed of wood and which was constructed prior to December 31, 1942, a special plaque which identifies the craft as a vessel of historical interest. The provisions of this section shall apply to documented as well as undocumented vessels. The size, shape, and content of such plaque and its positioning on the vessel shall be determined by the department after consultation with the Department of Boating and Waterways; provided, that such plaque shall be of a durable material and shall be no smaller than six inches in height and six inches in width. A reasonable fee, as determined by the department, sufficient to support the administration of such program, shall be charged for issuance of the plaque. The plaque shall be valid for the life of the vessel.

(Added by Stats. 1980, Ch. 577, Sec. 1.)

9853.7. (a) (1) When the retail seller of an undocumented sterndrive or inboard vessel, that contains a spark-ignition marine engine below 373 kW (500 hp) rated power output that was manufactured on or after January 1, 2008, or contains a spark-ignition marine engine with any rated power output that was manufactured on or after January 1, 2009, files for the purchaser of the vessel the initial application for a number for the vessel, the retail seller shall do both of the following:

(A) Certify on that application, by marking in indelible ink the affirmative checkoff boxes or line alternatives described in subdivision (a) of Section 9852.9, that the spark-ignition marine engine has a permanently affixed label indicating that the engine meets or exceeds the 2008 California emissions standards required by Section 2442 of Title 13 of the California Code of Regulations. The retail seller shall make that certification only after examining the permanently affixed label for the engine and only if the label indicates compliance with Section 2442 of Title 13 of the California Code of Regulations.

(B) Submit with the application, the hang tag required by Section 2443.3 of Title 13 of the California Code of Regulations for the engine, after including on the reserved white space of the hang tag, the engine family name, from the permanently affixed engine label, and the serial number of the engine.

(2) If the retail seller does not file for the purchaser of a vessel described in paragraph (1) the initial application for a number for the vessel, the applicant, upon filing an initial application for a number, shall submit the hang tag required by Section 2443.3 of Title 13 of the California Code of Regulations for the engine. The hang tag shall contain the engine family name, from the permanently affixed engine label, and the serial number of the engine, as inserted by the retail seller of the vessel.

(b) Subdivision (a) does not apply to a vessel originally purchased in another state by a resident of that state who subsequently establishes residence in this state and who provides satisfactory evidence to the department, or the department's agent authorized pursuant to Section 9858, of the previous residence.

(c) The department, and the department's agent authorized pursuant to Section 9858, shall not number a vessel subject to subdivision (a), unless the retail seller certifies on the initial application for a number filed for the purchaser of the vessel that the spark-ignition marine engine has the label described in paragraph (1) of subdivision (a) permanently affixed to the engine, or the applicant submits an application that is accompanied by the hang tag required by subdivision (a).

(d) For the purposes of this section, "spark-ignition marine engine" has the same meaning as that term is defined in paragraph (48) of subdivision (a) of Section 2441 of Title 13 of the California Code of Regulations.

(Added by Stats. 2007, Ch. 609, Sec. 2. Effective January 1, 2008. Operative July 1, 2008, by Sec. 4 of Ch. 609.)

9853.8. (a) This section applies only to a sterndrive or inboard vessel that contains a spark-ignition marine engine below 373 kW (500 hp) rated power output that was manufactured on or after January 1, 2008, or contains a spark-ignition marine engine with any rated power output that was manufactured on or after January 1, 2009.

(b) It is an infraction, punishable by a fine of two hundred fifty dollars ($250), for a person to operate an undocumented vessel, requiring numbering by the state, that is not currently numbered by the state, and that does not comply with the emissions standards required by Section 2442 of Title 13 of the California Code of Regulations.

(c) As used in this section, "spark-ignition marine engine" has the same meaning as that term is defined in Section 9853.7.

(Added by Stats. 2007, Ch. 609, Sec. 3. Effective January 1, 2008. Operative July 1, 2008, by Sec. 4 of Ch. 609.)

9854. The owner of any vessel already covered by a number in full force and effect that has been issued to it pursuant to then operative federal law or a federally approved numbering system of another state shall make application within 30 days after the 60-day reciprocity period provided for in Section 9873. Such application shall be in a manner and pursuant to the procedure required for the issuance of a number under Section 9853.

(Amended by Stats. 2024, Ch. 72, Sec. 66. (SB 156) Effective July 2, 2024.)

9855. If the ownership of an undocumented vessel changes, the existing certificate of ownership and a new application form accompanied by a fee of fifteen dollars ($15) shall be filed with the department and a new certificate of ownership and a new certificate of number shall be issued in the same manner as provided for in the initial issuance of number and the number shall be reassigned to the new owner.

(Amended by Stats. 1990, Ch. 951, Sec. 3. Operative July 1, 1991, by Sec. 5 of Ch. 951.)

9856. (a) It is not required that the department issue, or that an application be made for a new certificate of ownership or a new certificate of number, or that the fee prescribed in Section 9855 be paid on transfer of an undocumented vessel to a dealer in the course of his business as is otherwise provided in this division, if both of the following conditions are satisfied:

(1) The vessel is held and operated by the dealer only for the purpose of resale in the course of his business.

(2) The dealer has been issued a sales permit by the Board of Equalization covering sale of such property.

(b) The certificate of ownership bearing the endorsement of the transferor to the dealer of a vessel registered pursuant to this section and the certificate of number thereof shall be retained by the dealer until a transfer of the vessel by him. During that time the certificates shall be subject to inspection by the department or other authorized agency. Upon transfer of the vessel by the dealer the certificate of ownership shall be endorsed by the dealer and transfer further accomplished as otherwise provided in this division.

(Amended by Stats. 1984, Ch. 411, Sec. 3.)

9857. If an agency of the United States government shall have in force an overall system of identification numbering for undocumented vessels within the United States, the numbering system employed pursuant to this chapter shall be in conformity therewith.

(Added by Stats. 1970, Ch. 1428.)

9858. The department may issue any certificate of ownership and certificate of number or temporary certificate of number directly or the department may authorize any person to act as agent for the issuance of a certificate of number or temporary certificate of number. If a person accepts such authorization, he may be assigned a block of numbers which upon issuance, in conformity with this chapter and with any rules and regulations of the department, shall be valid as if issued directly by the department. Registration of vessels pursuant to the provisions of this code shall be conducted by the department or by any agent authorized by the department to conduct such registration.

(Added by Stats. 1970, Ch. 1428.)

9858.1. Any documentary preparation charge by an authorized agent of the department shall not exceed twenty dollars ($20).

(Added by Stats. 1984, Ch. 1407, Sec. 2.)

9858.5. Any licensed yacht and ship broker acting as an authorized agent of the department may collect use tax on a vessel transfer when applicable, and transmit the use tax and the registration application and applicable fees to the department, or may submit the registration application and applicable fees to the department for collection of any use tax due.

(Added by Stats. 1982, Ch. 665, Sec. 2.)

9859. All money received by an agent from the sale of certificates of number or temporary certificates of number and use tax shall be kept separate and apart from any other funds of the agent, and shall at all times belong to the state.

In case of an assignment for the benefit of creditors, receivership, or bankruptcy, the state shall have a preferred claim against the assignee, receiver, or trustee for all moneys owing the state for the sale of certificates as provided in this code and any use tax, and shall not be estopped from asserting such claim by reason of the commingling of funds or otherwise.

(Amended by Stats. 2009, Ch. 500, Sec. 61. (AB 1059) Effective January 1, 2010.)

9860. (a) Certificates of number shall be renewed before midnight of the expiration date by presentation of the certificate of number last issued for the vessel or by presentation of a potential registration card issued by the department.

(b) The fee for renewal shall be twenty dollars ($20) for each two-year period, and shall accompany the request for renewal.

(c) If the certificate of number and potential registration card are unavailable, the fee specified in Section 9867 shall not be paid.

(d) (1) The department shall collect, from resident and nonresident vessel owners, separate from the fee for renewal, an invasive mussel infestation prevention fee in an amount established by the Department of Boating and Waterways pursuant to Section 675 of the Harbors and Navigation Code.

(2) Failure to pay the fee described in this subdivision does not prohibit the department from issuing renewal registration of the vessel.

(3) (A) A vessel operator may be issued a citation for operating the vessel in nonmarine waters without a valid state-issued invasive mussel infestation prevention sticker.

(B) Notwithstanding subparagraph (A), a vessel that is exempt pursuant to Section 5211 of Title 14 of the California Code of Regulations shall not be cited pursuant to subparagraph (A).

(e) The department shall provide documentation of its administrative costs pursuant to this section to the Department of Boating and Waterways.

(Amended by Stats. 2025, Ch. 106, Sec. 18. (AB 149) Effective September 17, 2025.)

9861. All certificates of number expire on December 31 of every odd-numbered year.

(Amended by Stats. 2005, Ch. 473, Sec. 3. Effective January 1, 2006.)

9862. (a) If the initial application for a number is not received by the department on or before the date set by the department, a penalty of one-half of the fee shall be assessed. If a certificate of number is not renewed on or before midnight of the expiration date, a penalty of one-half of the fee shall be assessed.

(b) If any person has received as the transferee of a vessel a properly endorsed certificate of ownership and certificate of number describing that vessel and the transfer fee has not been paid as required by this code within 30 days, a penalty of one-half of the transfer fee specified in Section 9855 shall be assessed.

(Amended by Stats. 1990, Ch. 1352, Sec. 14. Effective September 27, 1990. Applicable from July 1, 1990, pursuant to Sec. 21 of Ch. 1352.)

9862.5. In computing any penalty imposed under this chapter, a fraction of a dollar shall be disregarded unless it equals or exceeds fifty cents ($0.50), in which case it shall be treated as one dollar ($1).

(Amended by Stats. 2001, Ch. 825, Sec. 12. Effective January 1, 2002.)

9863. (a) Except as required under subdivisions (b) and (c), and except moneys collected under Section 9875, fees received pursuant to this chapter shall be deposited in the Harbors and Watercraft Revolving Fund and, notwithstanding Section 13340 of the Government Code, are continuously appropriated, without regard to fiscal years, for the administration of this chapter by the department. Funds in the Harbors and Watercraft Revolving Fund derived pursuant to this chapter in excess of the amount determined by the Director of Finance, from time to time, to be necessary for expenditure for the administration of this chapter, notwithstanding Section 13340 of the Government Code, are continuously appropriated to the Department of Boating and Waterways, without regard to fiscal years, for expenditure in accordance with Section 663.7 of the Harbors and Navigation Code.

(b) Funds derived from imposition of the biennial registration fee under paragraph (2) of subdivision (b) of Section 9853, or under subdivision (b) of Section 9860, shall be distributed as follows:

(1) One-half shall be continuously appropriated pursuant to subdivision (a).

(2) One-half shall be allocated, upon appropriation, to the Department of Boating and Waterways for expenditure in support of programs under the department's jurisdiction.

(c) Funds derived from the imposition of the invasive mussel prevention fee under subdivision (c) of Section 9853, or under subdivision (d) of Section 9860, shall be distributed as specified in Section 676 of the Harbors and Navigation Code.

(Amended by Stats. 2025, Ch. 106, Sec. 19. (AB 149) Effective September 17, 2025.)

9864. The owner shall furnish the department notice of the wrecking or dismantling, or the destruction or abandonment of an undocumented vessel within 15 days thereof. The wrecking, dismantling, destruction or abandonment shall terminate the certificate of ownership and certificate of number of such undocumented vessel which if in existence shall be surrendered to the department.

The department, upon receiving notice of the abandonment of an undocumented vessel, or upon an official determination that an undocumented vessel has been abandoned, may order the destruction of such vessel at the expiration of 30 days if an investigation by the department has disclosed that no owner, legal owner, or lienholder claims an interest in the vessel, or if those persons have waived their interest. Nothing in this section shall be construed to deny the legal rights, otherwise provided for by law, of any person claiming an interest in an abandoned vessel if that person notifies the department within the time specified therefor.

(Amended by Stats. 1987, Ch. 298, Sec. 4.)

9865. Any holder of a certificate of number shall notify the department within 15 days, if his address no longer conforms to the address appearing on the certificate and shall, as part of such notification, furnish the department with his new address. The department may provide for the surrender of the certificate bearing the former address and its replacement with a certificate bearing the new address or for the alteration of an outstanding certificate to show the new address of the holder.

(Amended by Stats. 1973, Ch. 759.)

9866. No number other than the number issued to an undocumented vessel or granted reciprocity pursuant to this chapter shall be painted, attached, or otherwise displayed on either side of the bow of such undocumented vessel.

(Added by Stats. 1970, Ch. 1428.)

9867. A fee of fifteen dollars ($15) shall be charged for a duplicate of certificate of number, certificate of ownership, or current year registration stickers.

(Amended by Stats. 1990, Ch. 951, Sec. 4. Operative July 1, 1991, by Sec. 5 of Ch. 951.)

9867.5. Upon application for transfer of registration pursuant to Section 9917, a fee as specified in Section 9867 shall be paid to the department in addition to the regular transfer fee.

(Added by Stats. 1978, Ch. 497.)

9868. Fees received pursuant to this chapter are appropriated for payment of refunds of money received or collected in the payment of fees, permits, or services whenever the fee, permit or service cannot lawfully be issued or rendered to the applicant, and in cases where the payment in whole or in part represents overpayment or payment in duplicate.

(Added by Stats. 1970, Ch. 1428.)

9869. The department shall transmit information from each initial application and each transfer application or renewal application to the county assessor in the county of residence of the owner of the vessel and to the county assessor in the county in which the vessel is principally kept if other than the county of residence of the owner, if such other county is known to the department. If an application shows that the owner of the vessel has changed his residence from one county to another county or shows that there has been a change in the county in which the vessel is principally kept, the department shall transmit information of the change to the assessor of the county in which the owner of the vessel formerly resided or to the assessor of the county in which the vessel formerly was principally kept. After the department receives a notice pursuant to Section 9864, the department shall transmit information of the destruction or abandonment to the assessor of the county in which the owner of the vessel resides and to the assessor of the county in which the vessel is or was principally kept, if other than the county of residence of the owner, if such other county was known to the department.

(Added by Stats. 1970, Ch. 1428.)

9870. A nonprofit public benefit corporation governed by the Nonprofit Public Benefit Corporation Law (Part 2 (commencing with Section 5110) of Division 2 of Title 1 of the Corporations Code), which purposes relate to promoting the ability of boys and girls to do things for themselves, to train them in scoutcraft and camping, and to teach them patriotism, courage, self-reliance and kindred virtues, shall not be required to pay the fees provided for in Sections 9853, 9855, and 9860.

(Amended by Stats. 1984, Ch. 411, Sec. 6.)

9871. Upon application for original registration or transfer of registration of an undocumented vessel, the department may assign an appropriate hull identification number to such vessel whenever there is no hull identification number thereon, or when a hull identification number thereon has been destroyed or obliterated; and such hull identification number shall be permanently marked in an integral part of the hull which is accessible for inspection.

(Amended by Stats. 1980, Ch. 617, Sec. 2.)

9871.5. Upon application for renewal of registration of an undocumented vessel, the applicant is required to furnish the hull identification number if the records of the department do not contain such number. If the vessel does not have a hull number, the department may assign an appropriate hull identification number.

(Added by Stats. 1980, Ch. 617, Sec. 3.)

9872. No person shall intentionally deface, destroy, or alter the hull identification number of a vessel required to be numbered under this chapter without written authorization from the department; nor shall any person place or stamp any serial or other number or mark upon an undocumented vessel which might interfere with identification of the hull identification number. This does not prohibit the restoration by an owner of an original number or mark when the restoration is authorized by the department, nor prevent any manufacturer from placing, in the ordinary course of business, numbers or marks upon new vessels or new parts thereof.

(Amended by Stats. 1980, Ch. 617, Sec. 4.)

9872.1. (a) No person shall knowingly buy, sell, offer for sale, receive, or have in his or her possession any vessel, or component part thereof, from which the hull identification number has been removed, defaced, altered, or destroyed, unless the vessel or component part has attached thereto a hull identification number assigned or approved by the department in lieu of the manufacturer's number.

(b) Whenever a vessel, or component part thereof, from which the hull identification number has been removed, defaced, altered, or destroyed, and which does not have attached thereto an assigned or approved number as described in subdivision (a), comes into the custody of a peace officer, the seized vessel or component part is subject, in accordance with the procedures specified in this section, to impoundment and to such disposition as may be provided by order of a court having jurisdiction. This subdivision does not apply with respect to a seized vessel or component part used as evidence in any criminal action or proceeding.

(c) Whenever a vessel or component part described in subdivision (a) comes into the custody of a peace officer, any person from whom the property was seized, and all claimants to the property whose interest or title is on registration records in the department, shall be notified within five days, excluding Saturdays, Sundays, and holidays, after the seizure, of the date, time, and place of the hearing required in subdivision (e). The notice shall contain the information specified in subdivision (d).

(d) Whenever a peace officer seizes a vessel or component part as provided in subdivision (b), any person from whom the property was seized shall be provided a notice of impoundment of the vessel or component part which shall serve as a receipt and contain the following information:

(1) Name and address of person from whom the property was seized.

(2) A statement that the vessel or component part seized has been impounded for investigation of a violation of this section and that the property will be released upon a determination that the hull identification number has not been removed, defaced, altered, or destroyed, or upon the presentation of satisfactory evidence of ownership of the vessel or

component part, provided that no other person claims an interest in the property; otherwise, a hearing regarding the disposition of the vessel or component part shall take place in the proper court.

(3) A statement that any person from whom the property was seized, and all claimants to the property whose interest or title is on registration records in the department, will receive written notification of the date, time, and place of the hearing within five days, excluding Saturdays, Sundays, and holidays, after the seizure.

(4) Name and address of the law enforcement agency where evidence of ownership of the vessel or component part may be presented.

(5) A statement of the contents of this section.

(e) A hearing on the disposition of the property shall be held by the superior court within 60 days after the seizure. The hearing shall be before the court without a jury. A proceeding under this section is a limited civil case.

(1) If the evidence reveals either that the hull identification number has not been removed, altered, or destroyed or that the hull identification number has been removed, altered, or destroyed but satisfactory evidence of ownership has been presented to the seizing agency or court, the property shall be released to the person entitled thereto.

(2) If the evidence reveals that the hull identification number has been removed, altered, or destroyed, and satisfactory evidence of ownership has not been presented, the property shall be destroyed, sold, or otherwise disposed of as provided by court order.

(3) At the hearing, the seizing agency shall have the burden of establishing that the hull identification number has been removed, defaced, altered, or destroyed and that no satisfactory evidence of ownership has been presented.

(f) Nothing in this section precludes the return of a seized vessel or component part to the owner by the seizing agency following presentation of satisfactory evidence of ownership and, if determined necessary, upon the assignment of an identification number to the vessel or component part by the department.

(Amended by Stats. 2002, Ch. 784, Sec. 595. Effective January 1, 2003.)

9872.5. No certificate of ownership shall be issued under this chapter for any "amphibious vehicle" for which a certificate of ownership may be issued by the department under other provisions of this code.

For the purposes of this section, an "amphibious vehicle" is a device by which any person or property may be propelled, moved, or drawn, both upon water and upon a highway on land.

(Added by Stats. 1970, Ch. 1439.)

9873. An undocumented vessel shall not be required to be numbered under this chapter if it is:

(a) Already covered by a number in full force and effect that has been issued to it pursuant to federal law or a federally approved numbering system of another state; provided, that such undocumented vessel shall be subject to the numbering requirements of this chapter if it has changed its state of principal use and has been within this state for a period in excess of 60 consecutive days.

(b) A vessel from a country other than the United States temporarily using the waters of this state.

(c) A public vessel of the United States, another state or subdivision thereof or municipality of such other state.

(d) A ship's lifeboat.

(e) Any vessel belonging to a class of boats that has been exempted from numbering by the department after the department has found that the numbering of vessels of such class will not materially aid in their identification; and, if any agency of the federal government has a numbering system applicable to the class of vessels to which the vessel in question belongs, after the department has further found that the vessel would also be exempt from numbering if it were subject to the federal law. An undocumented vessel propelled solely by oars or paddles and an undocumented vessel eight feet or less propelled solely by sail are exempt from this chapter.

(Amended by Stats. 2024, Ch. 72, Sec. 67. (SB 156) Effective July 2, 2024.)

9874. The department may suspend, cancel, or revoke the registration of a vessel, a certificate of number, sticker, certificate of ownership, or temporary certificate of number in any of the following cases:

(a) When the department is satisfied that the registration or the certificate of number, sticker, certificate of ownership, or temporary certificate of number was fraudulently obtained or erroneously issued.

(b) When the department determines that the required fee has not been paid and the same is not paid upon reasonable notice and demand.

(Added by Stats. 1970, Ch. 1428.)

9875. Except as provided in Section 40000.8, any person who violates any provision of this chapter or any rule or regulation of the department adopted pursuant to this chapter is guilty of an infraction, punishable under Section 42001.

(Amended by Stats. 1991, Ch. 922, Sec. 6.)

9880. (a) The department shall not renew the certificate of number of, or allow a transfer of any title to or interest in, a vessel if the county tax collector has notified the department pursuant to Section 3205 of the Revenue and Taxation Code, that taxes are delinquent upon the vessel, and the department shall not subsequently issue a certificate of number for, or a new certificate of ownership reflecting a transfer of title to or interest in, that vessel until the department receives a certificate of clearance from the county tax collector that the delinquent taxes have been paid on that vessel or until the county tax collector has provided notice to the department that the delinquency has been satisfied.

(b) The department shall record the notice of delinquent taxes on the vessel. If the department is notified by the county tax collector that the delinquency has been satisfied, the department shall, if all other requirements are satisfied, issue a certificate of number for, or a new certificate of ownership reflecting a transfer of title to or interest in, the vessel. The department shall assess a fee upon each county tax collector in an amount that is sufficient to reimburse the department for its actual costs of administering this section.

(c) Whenever a vessel subject to this section is transferred, or not renewed for 26 months, the department shall notify the county tax collector of that fact.

(Amended by Stats. 1997, Ch. 546, Sec. 13. Effective January 1, 1998.)

Chapter 3. Transfer of Title or Interest in Undocumented Vessel

(Chapter 3 added by Stats. 1970, Ch. 1428.)

9900. No transfer of the title or any interest in or to an undocumented vessel numbered under this code shall pass, and any attempted transfer shall not be effective, until the parties thereto have paid any delinquent property taxes with respect to that vessel and fulfilled either of the following requirements:

(a) The transferor has made proper endorsement and delivery of the certificate of ownership to the transferee as provided in this code and the transferee has delivered to the department or has placed the certificates in the United States mail addressed to the department when and as required under this code with the proper transfer fee and thereby makes application for a new certificate of ownership and a new certificate of number.

(b) The transferor has delivered to the department or has placed in the United States mail addressed to the department the appropriate documents for the transfer of ownership of the vessel pursuant to the sale or transfer except as otherwise provided.

(Amended by Stats. 1994, Ch. 940, Sec. 5. Effective January 1, 1995. Operative July 1, 1995, by Sec. 6 of Ch. 940.)

9901. Whenever any person has received as transferee a properly endorsed certificate of ownership, he or she shall, within 10 days thereafter, forward the certificates with the transfer fee specified in Section 9855 to the department, and thereby make application for a certificate of ownership and certificate of number.

(Amended by Stats. 1995, Ch. 766, Sec. 7. Effective January 1, 1996.)

9902. The department, upon receipt of a properly endorsed certificate of ownership and a new application form and the required fee, shall issue a new certificate of ownership and a new certificate of number in the same manner as provided for in the initial issuance of number and the number may be reassigned to the new owner, provided, however, in the case of a transfer of a part interest which does not affect the owner's right to operate such undocumented vessel the transfer shall not terminate the certificate of number.

(Amended by Stats. 1988, Ch. 1268, Sec. 16.)

9903. (a) Prior to the issuance of any certificate of ownership the department shall obtain a statement in writing, signed by the transferee or transferor, showing:

(1) The date of the sale or other transfer of ownership of the vessel.

(2) The name and address of the seller or transferor.

(3) The name and address of the buyer or transferee.

(4) The total consideration (valued in money) given for the sale or other transfer of the vessel, including any motor or other component part of the vessel included in the sale or other transfer.

(b) Upon the transfer of ownership of a vessel the department shall forward to the State Board of Equalization information from its records identifying the vessel together with the data required by subdivision (a). The information shall be transmitted as promptly as feasible and in such form and manner as shall be agreed between the department and the board.

(Added by Stats. 1970, Ch. 1428.)

9905. An owner who has made a bona fide sale or transfer of an undocumented vessel and has delivered possession of the vessel to a purchaser shall not by reason of any of the provisions of this code or the Harbors and Navigation Code be deemed the owner of the vessel so as to be subject to civil liability for the operation of the vessel thereafter by another when the owner, in addition to the foregoing, has fulfilled either of the following requirements:

(a) Made proper endorsement and delivery of the certificate of ownership as provided in this code.

(b) Delivered to the department or placed in the United States mail, addressed to the department, either the notice as provided in Sections 9911 and 9912 or appropriate documents for transfer of the vessel pursuant to the sale or transfer.

(Amended by Stats. 1991, Ch. 13, Sec. 23. Effective February 13, 1991.)

9906. A legal owner may assign his title or interest in or to an undocumented vessel numbered under this code to a person other than the owner without the consent of and without affecting the interest of the owner.

(Added by Stats. 1970, Ch. 1428.)

9907. Upon transfer of the title or any interest of the legal owner or legal owners in an undocumented vessel numbered under this code, the transferor shall write his signature, and the transferee shall write his signature and address, in the appropriate spaces provided upon the reverse side of the certificate of ownership issued for the vessel.

(Added by Stats. 1970, Ch. 1428.)

9908. Upon transfer of the title or interest or any part thereof of the registered owner only in an undocumented vessel numbered under this code, the registered owner shall write his signature and address and the transferee shall write his signature and address in the appropriate spaces provided on the reverse side of the certificate of ownership for the vessel, and the legal owner shall write his signature in the space provided for the new legal owner indicating that he is to retain his legal title and interest.

(Added by Stats. 1970, Ch. 1428.)

9909. When the required certificate of ownership is lost, stolen, damaged, or mutilated, application for transfer may be made upon a form provided by the department for a duplicate certificate of ownership. The transferor shall write his signature and address in the appropriate spaces provided upon the application and file the same together with the proper fees for duplicate certificate of ownership and transfer.

(Added by Stats. 1970, Ch. 1428.)

9910. It is unlawful for any person to fail or neglect to deliver the certificate of number and, when having possession, to properly endorse, date, and deliver the certificate of ownership to a transferee who is lawfully entitled to a transfer of ownership.

(Added by Stats. 1970, Ch. 1428.)

9911. Whenever the owner of an undocumented vessel numbered under this code sells or transfers his or her title or interest in, or any part thereof, and delivers the possession of, the vessel to another, the owner shall, within five calendar days, notify the department of the sale or transfer by giving the date thereof, the name and address of the owner and of the transferee and a description of the vessel as may be required in the appropriate form provided for the purpose by the department.

(Amended by Stats. 1992, Ch. 427, Sec. 166. Effective January 1, 1993.)

9912. Every dealer upon transferring by sale, lease or otherwise any undocumented vessel, whether new or used, required to be numbered under this code, shall, not later than the end of the next business day of the dealer, give written notice of the transfer to the department upon an appropriate form provided by it, but a dealer need not give the notice when selling or transferring a new unnumbered vessel to another dealer.

(Added by Stats. 1970, Ch. 1428.)

9913. When a security interest upon a numbered vessel is satisfied, canceled, or released by the parties thereto who are the registered owner and legal owner respectively of said vessel and thereafter within a period of 10 days a new security interest covering the vessel is executed between the same parties, no application for transfer of ownership by reason thereof shall be made, no new certificate of ownership or certificate of number shall be issued, and all provisions of this code relating to transfers of any title or interest in a vessel shall be deemed to have been fully complied with.

(Added by Stats. 1970, Ch. 1428.)

9914. The transferee of a security interest in the interest of a legal owner of a numbered vessel need not make application for a transfer of ownership when the security interest arises from a pledge of security agreement by the legal owner to the pledgee.

(Added by Stats. 1970, Ch. 1428.)

9915. (a) Whenever the title or interest of any owner or legal owner in or to a vessel numbered under this code passes to another otherwise than by a voluntary transfer, the new owner or legal owner may obtain a transfer of ownership upon application therefor and upon presentation of the last certificate of ownership and certificate of number issued for the vessel, if available, and any instruments or documents of authority or certified copies thereof as may be required by the department, or required by law, to evidence or effect a transfer of title or interest in or to chattels in such case.

(b) The department when satisfied of the genuineness and regularity of the transfer shall give notice by mail to the owner and legal owner of the vessel as shown by the records of the department and five days after the giving of the notice, if still satisfied of the genuineness and regularity of such transfer, shall transfer the ownership of the vessel accordingly and issue a new certificate of ownership and cerificate of number to the person or persons entitled thereto. Such notice shall not be required for an involuntary transfer when repossession involves a secured party.

(Amended by Stats. 1975, Ch. 918.)

9916. (a) If 40 days have elapsed since the death of an owner or legal owner of any vessel numbered under this division without the decedent leaving other property necessitating probate, and irrespective of the value of the vessel, the following person may secure a transfer of ownership of the title or interest of the decedent:

(1) The sole person or all of the persons who succeeded to the property of the decedent under Sections 6401 and 6402 of the Probate Code unless

the vessel is, by will, otherwise bequeathed.

(2) The sole beneficiary or all of the beneficiaries who succeeded to the vessel under the will of the decedent where the vessel is, by will, so bequeathed.

(b) The person authorized by subdivision (a) may secure a transfer of ownership of the title or interest of the decedent upon presenting to the department all of the following:

(1) The appropriate certificate of ownership and certificate of number, if available.

(2) A certificate of the heir or beneficiary under penalty of perjury containing the following statements:

(A) The date and place of the decedent's death.

(B) The decedent left no other property necessitating probate and no probate proceeding is now being or has been conducted in this state for the decedent's estate.

(C) The declarant is entitled to the vessel either (i) as the sole person or all of the persons who succeeded to the property of the decedent under Sections 6401 and 6402 of the Probate Code if the decedent left no will or (ii) as the beneficiary or beneficiaries under the decedent's last will if the decedent left a will, and no one has a right to the decedent's vessel that is superior to that of the declarant.

(D) There are no unsecured creditors of the decedent or, if there are, the unsecured creditors of the decedent have been paid in full or their claims have been otherwise discharged.

(3) If required by the department, a certificate of the death of the decedent.

(4) If required by the department, the names and addresses of any other heirs or beneficiaries.

(c) If the department is presented with the documents specified in paragraphs (1) and (2) of subdivision (b), no liability shall be incurred by the department or any officer or employee of the department by reason of the transfer of registration of the vessel pursuant to this section. The department or officer or employee of the department may rely in good faith on the statements in the certificate specified in paragraph (2) of subdivision (b) and has no duty to inquire into the truth of any statement in the certificate. The person who secures the transfer of the vessel pursuant to this section is subject to the provisions of Section 13109 to 13113, inclusive, of the Probate Code to the same extent as a person to whom transfer of property is made under Chapter 3 (commencing with Section 13100) of Part 1 of Division 8 of the Probate Code.

(Amended by Stats. 1986, Ch. 783, Sec. 27. Operative July 1, 1987, by Sec. 30 of Ch. 783.)

9916.5. (a) On death of the owner of a vessel numbered under this division and owned in beneficiary form, the vessel belongs to the surviving beneficiary, if any. If there is no surviving beneficiary, the vessel belongs to the estate of the deceased owner.

(b) A certificate of ownership in beneficiary form may be revoked or the beneficiary changed at any time before the death of the owner by either of the following methods:

(1) By sale of the vessel with property assignment and delivery of the certificate of ownership to another person.

(2) By application for a new certificate of ownership without designation of a beneficiary or with the designation of a different beneficiary.

(c) Except as provided in subdivision (b), designation of a beneficiary in a certificate of ownership issued in beneficiary form may not be changed or revoked by will, by any other instrument, by a change of circumstances, or otherwise.

(d) The beneficiary's interest in the vessel at death of the owner is subject to any contract of sale, assignment, or security interest to which the owner was subject during his or her lifetime.

(e) The surviving beneficiary may secure a transfer of ownership for the vessel upon presenting to the department all of the following:

(1) The appropriate certificate of ownership.

(2) A certificate under penalty of perjury stating the date and place of the owner's death and that the declarant is entitled to the vessel as the designated beneficiary.

(3) If required by the department, a certificate of the death of the owner.

(f) After the death of the owner, the surviving beneficiary may transfer his or her interest in the vessel to another person without securing transfer of ownership into his or her own name by appropriately signing the certificate of ownership for the vessel and delivering the document to the transferee for forwarding to the department with appropriate fees. The transferee may secure a transfer of ownership upon presenting to the department (1) the certificate of title signed by the beneficiary, (2) the certificate described in paragraph (2) of subdivision (e) executed by the beneficiary under penalty of perjury, and (3) if required by the department, a certificate of death of the owner.

(g) A transfer at death pursuant to this section is effective by reason of this section, and shall not be deemed to be a testamentary disposition of property. The right of the designated beneficiary to the vessel shall not be denied, abridged, or affected on the grounds that the right has not been created by a writing executed in accordance with the laws of this state prescribing the requirements to effect a valid testamentary disposition of property.

(h) A transfer at death pursuant to this section is subject to Section 9653 of the Probate Code.

(i) If there is no surviving beneficiary, the person or persons described in Section 9916 may secure transfer of the vessel as provided in that section.

(j) The department may prescribe forms for use pursuant to this section.

(Added by Stats. 1991, Ch. 1055, Sec. 62. Operative January 1, 1993, by Sec. 64 of Ch. 1055.)

9916.7. (a) If the department makes a transfer pursuant to Section 9916.5, the department is discharged from all liability, whether or not the transfer is consistent with the beneficial ownership of the vessel transferred.

(b) The protection provided by subdivision (a) does not extend to a transfer made after the department has been served with a court order restraining the transfer. No other notice or information shown to have been available to the department shall affect its right to the protection afforded by subdivision (a).

(c) The protection provided by this section has no bearing on the rights of parties in disputes between themselves or their successors concerning the beneficial ownership of the vessel.

(d) The protection provided by this section is in addition to, and not exclusive of, any other protection provided to the department by any other provision of law.

(Added by Stats. 1991, Ch. 1055, Sec. 63. Operative January 1, 1993, by Sec. 64 of Ch. 1055.)

9917. Whenever application is made to the department for a transfer of ownership of a vessel to a new owner or legal owner and the applicant is unable to present the certificate of ownership issued for the vessel by reason of the same being lost or otherwise not available, the department may receive the application and examine into the circumstances of the case and may require the filing of affidavits or other information, and when the department is satisfied that the applicant is entitled to a transfer of ownership, the department may transfer the ownership of the vessel, and issue a new certificate of ownership, and certificate of number to the person or persons found to be entitled thereto.

(Amended by Stats. 1988, Ch. 1268, Sec. 18.)

9918. If the application for a transfer is made in the manner provided in this code, the department shall not be required to withhold the transfer of any right, title or interest in or to a vessel if the application on its face appears to be genuine and regular and the department has received neither a request from any law enforcement agency that action on the application be deferred nor an order of a court of the United States or of the State of California restraining the transfer within two years prior thereto.

(Added by Stats. 1970, Ch. 1428.)

9919. No security interest in any vessel numbered under this code,

irrespective of whether such number was effected prior or subsequent to the creation of such security interest, is perfected, until the secured party, or his successor or assignee, has deposited with the department a properly endorsed certificate of ownership to the vessel, subject to the security interest, showing the secured party as legal owner if the vessel is then numbered under this code; or if the vessel is not so numbered, the owner shall file an initial application for number as provided for in this code, and the certificate of ownership issued under said application shall contain the name and address of the legal owner.
(Added by Stats. 1970, Ch. 1428.)

9920. When the secured party, his successor or assignee, has deposited with the department a properly endorsed certificate of ownership showing the secured party as legal owner, or if the vessel is not numbered when the owner shall file an initial application for number as provided for in this code, and the certificate of ownership issued under said application shows said secured party as the legal owner, and said certificate of ownership is deposited with the department, the deposit constitutes perfection of the security interest.
(Added by Stats. 1970, Ch. 1428.)

9921. Upon the deposit with the department of the certificate of ownership showing the secured party as legal owner as provided in Section 9919 hereof, the department shall on its records show the secured party, his successor or assignee, as legal owner with respect to such vessel.
(Added by Stats. 1970, Ch. 1428.)

9922. The method provided in this chapter for perfecting a security interest in a vessel numbered under this code is exclusive.
(Added by Stats. 1970, Ch. 1428.)

9923. In the absence of the regularly required supporting evidence of ownership upon application for registration or transfer of a vessel, the department may accept an undertaking or bond in the amount of the fair market value of the vessel at the time of the application, as determined by the department, which shall be conditioned to protect the department and all officers and employees thereof and any subsequent purchaser of the vessel, any person acquiring a lien or security interest thereon, or the successor in interest of such purchaser or person, against any loss or damage on account of any defect in or undisclosed claim upon the right, title, and interest of the applicant or other person in and to the vessel.
(Added by Stats. 1970, Ch. 1428.)

9924. In the event the vessel is no longer registered in this state and the currently valid certificate of ownership is surrendered to the department or the vessel has been destroyed or lost, the bond or undertaking shall be returned and surrendered after three years.
(Amended by Stats. 1982, Ch. 517, Sec. 389.)

9928. The department shall withhold the certificate of number or the transfer of registration of any vessel sold at retail to any applicant by any person other than a person holding a seller's permit pursuant to Section 6066 of the Revenue and Taxation Code, and regularly engaged in the business of selling vessels, until the applicant pays to the department the use tax measured by the sales price of the vessel as required by the Sales and Use Tax Law, together with penalty, if any, unless the State Board of Equalization finds that no use tax is due. If the applicant so desires, he may pay the use tax and penalty, if any, to the department so as to secure immediate action upon his application for registration or transfer of registration and thereafter he may apply through the Department of Motor Vehicles to the State Board of Equalization under the provisions of the Sales and Use Tax Law for a refund of the amount so paid.

(b) The department shall transmit to the State Board of Equalization all collections of the use tax and penalty made under this section. This transmittal shall be made at least monthly, accompanied by a schedule in such form as the department and board may prescribe.

(c) The State Board of Equalization shall reimburse the department for its costs incurred in carrying out the provisions of this section.

(d) In computing any use tax or penalty thereon under the provisions of the section, dollar fractions shall be disregarded in the manner specified in Section 9559. Payment of tax and penalty on this basis shall be deemed full compliance with the requirements of the Sales and Use Tax Law insofar as they are applicable to the use of vessels to which this section relates.

(e) The department and the State Board of Equalization shall enter into an agreement for the collection of the use tax pursuant to this section and Section 6294 of the Revenue and Taxation Code. The agreement shall specify the procedures agreed upon by the department and the board for collection of the tax and the reimbursement provided for in subdivision (c). The agreement shall be approved by the Department of Finance.
(Added by Stats. 1982, Ch. 665, Sec. 5.)

Division 3.6. Vehicle Sales

(Division 3.6 added by Stats. 1970, Ch. 1246.)

Chapter 1. Advertising, Brochures, and Manuals

(Chapter 1 added by Stats. 1970, Ch. 1246.)

9950. Any advertisement, brochure, owner's manual, or sales manual relating to any gasoline-powered motor vehicle of a type subject to registration with a manufacturer's gross vehicle weight rating of under 6,000 pounds of 1972 or later year model which contains any reference to the horsepower of the engine of the vehicle shall state only the Society of Automotive Engineers horsepower rating of such engine, as installed (net), as determined by S.A.E. Standard J1349.

(Amended by Stats. 1986, Ch. 1212, Sec. 5.)

9951. (a) A manufacturer of a new motor vehicle sold or leased in this state that is equipped with one or more recording devices commonly referred to as "event data recorders (EDR)" or "sensing and diagnostic modules (SDM)," shall disclose that fact in the owner's manual for the vehicle.

(b) As used in this section, "recording device" means a device that is installed by the manufacturer of the vehicle and does one or more of the following, for the purpose of retrieving data after an accident:

(1) Records how fast and in which direction the motor vehicle is traveling.

(2) Records a history of where the motor vehicle travels.

(3) Records steering performance.

(4) Records brake performance, including, but not limited to, whether brakes were applied before an accident.

(5) Records the driver's seatbelt status.

(6) Has the ability to transmit information concerning an accident in which the motor vehicle has been involved to a central communications system when an accident occurs.

(c) Data described in subdivision (b) that is recorded on a recording device may not be downloaded or otherwise retrieved by a person other than the registered owner of the motor vehicle, except under one of the following circumstances:

(1) The registered owner of the motor vehicle consents to the retrieval of the information.

(2) In response to an order of a court having jurisdiction to issue the order.

(3) For the purpose of improving motor vehicle safety, including for medical research of the human body's reaction to motor vehicle accidents, and the identity of the registered owner or driver is not disclosed in connection with that retrieved data. The disclosure of the vehicle identification number (VIN) for the purpose of improving vehicle safety, including for medical research of the human body's reaction to motor vehicle accidents, does not constitute the disclosure of the identity of the registered owner or driver.

(4) The data is retrieved by a licensed new motor vehicle dealer, or by an automotive technician as defined in Section 9880.1 of the Business and Professions Code, for the purpose of diagnosing, servicing, or repairing the motor vehicle.

(d) A person authorized to download or otherwise retrieve data from a recording device pursuant to paragraph (3) of subdivision (c), may not release that data, except to share the data among the motor vehicle safety and medical research communities to advance motor vehicle safety, and only if the identity of the registered owner or driver is not disclosed.

(e) (1) If a motor vehicle is equipped with a recording device that is capable of recording or transmitting information as described in paragraph (2) or (6) of subdivision (b) and that capability is part of a subscription service, the fact that the information may be recorded or transmitted shall be disclosed in the subscription service agreement.

(2) Subdivision (c) does not apply to subscription services meeting the requirements of paragraph (1).

(f) This section applies to all motor vehicles manufactured on or after July 1, 2004.

(Amended by Stats. 2004, Ch. 183, Sec. 350. Effective January 1, 2005.)

9952. Any person who publishes, or causes to be published, or offers for sale or sells, or gives to another person, any advertisement, brochure, owner's manual, or sales manual which violates Section 9950 is guilty of an infraction.

(Amended by Stats. 1973, Ch. 73.)

9953. Every manufacturer of a new motor vehicle sold in this state which, as equipped, may not be operated with tire chains shall do both of the following:

(a) Indicate that fact in the owner's manual for the vehicle or other written material provided by the manufacturer regarding the vehicle.

(b) Provide each of its franchised new motor vehicle dealers in this state with a list of the affected vehicle models on an annual basis and prior to the manufacturer's introduction of its new model year vehicles. The list shall include sufficient information, including information regarding tire sizes where necessary, to allow the selling dealer to determine when disclosure is required pursuant to Section 11713.6.

(Amended by Stats. 1995, Ch. 452, Sec. 1. Effective January 1, 1996.)

9954. (a) This section applies only to new vehicles sold or leased in this state on or after January 1, 2008, except as provided in subdivision (d) or (e).

(b) A motor vehicle manufacturer of a motor vehicle sold or leased in this state shall provide the means whereby the registered owner of that motor vehicle, through a registered locksmith, can access the information, and only that information, that is necessary to permit the production of a replacement key or other functionally similar device by the registered locksmith that will allow the registered vehicle's owner to enter, start, and operate his or her vehicle. The means to access this information shall be available by telephone or electronically 24 hours a day and seven days a week, as follows:

(1) When a registered locksmith is requested by the motor vehicle's registered owner or the registered owner's family member, to produce a replacement key or other functionally similar device that will allow the vehicle to be entered, started, and operated, and the information is needed from the vehicle manufacturer in order to produce the requested key or other functionally similar device, in addition to the requirement in Section 466.6 of the Penal Code, the registered locksmith shall visually verify the identity of the requesting party through that party's driver's license; shall visually verify that the registration of the vehicle matches the requesting party's identity and address (or last name and address if the requesting party is a family member of the registered owner); and shall visually verify that the vehicle identification number of the vehicle matches with the vehicle identification number on the registration. Upon satisfactory verification of all three requirements, the registered locksmith shall sign an affidavit that he or she has visually verified the information and file the affidavit along with, and for the same time period as, the work order required by Section 466.6 of the Penal Code, and proceed to access the needed information from the vehicle manufacturer.

(2) Upon completing the services, the registered locksmith shall give any key code information obtained from the vehicle manufacturer to the registered owner, or if applicable, the owner's family member, and shall destroy all information accessed from the vehicle manufacturer in his or her possession.

(3) Except in cases of fraud or misappropriation, a registered locksmith who follows these procedures shall incur no liability for theft of the vehicle related to the locksmith's production of a replacement key or functionally similar device that will allow the vehicle to be entered, started, and operated.

(4) When a vehicle manufacturer receives a request from a registered locksmith for information to enable the locksmith to produce a replacement key or other functionally similar device that will allow the vehicle to be entered, started, and operated, and that request is made at the behest of the vehicle's registered owner or the registered owner's family

member, the vehicle manufacturer shall require the registered locksmith to confirm the locksmith's registration with the manufacturer's registry; provide the security password issued by the manufacturer; and comply with any other reasonable authentication procedure. The manufacturer shall also require the registered locksmith to confirm the locksmith's visual identity and vehicle verifications, pursuant to paragraph (1). Upon satisfactory verification of these requirements, and upon presentation of the vehicle identification number and model number, the vehicle manufacturer shall provide to the registered locksmith, for the vehicle identified by the vehicle identification number and model number, the information necessary to enable production of a replacement key or other functionally similar device that allows the vehicle to be entered, started, and operated.

(5) A motor vehicle manufacturer subject to this section shall retain and make the information available in accordance with this section for at least 25 years from the date of manufacture.

(6) A vehicle manufacturer that follows these procedures shall incur no liability for theft of the vehicle related to furnishing the information to a registered locksmith for the production of a replacement key or functionally similar device that will allow the vehicle to be entered, started, and operated.

(c) For purposes of this section the following definitions apply:

(1) "Information" includes, but is not limited to, the vehicle's key code and, if applicable, immobilizer or access code, and its successor technology and terminology.

(2) "Motor vehicle" is a passenger vehicle as defined in Section 465 and pickup truck as defined in Section 471, and does not include a housecar, a motorcycle, or other two-wheeled motor vehicle.

(3) A "registered locksmith" means a locksmith licensed and bonded in California that has registered with a motor vehicle manufacturer, and has been issued a registry number and security password by the manufacturer.

(4) A registered owner, as defined in Section 505, also includes a lessee of the vehicle when the lessee's name appears on the vehicle registration.

(d) (1) This section does not apply to a vehicle line of a motor vehicle manufacturer that on January 1, 2006, does not provide for the production of a replacement key or other functionally similar device that allows the vehicle to be entered, started, and operated, by anyone other than the vehicle manufacturer itself and only itself, provided that the vehicle manufacturer operates a telephone or electronic request line 24 hours a day and seven days a week, and upon a request of the registered owner or family member of the registered owner of the vehicle, a replacement key or other functionally similar device that will allow the vehicle to be entered, started, and operated, is furnished to the registered owner at a reasonable cost within one day of the request or via the next overnight delivery.

(2) If subsequent to January 1, 2008, a vehicle line of the manufacturer exempted by this subdivision provides for the production of a replacement by anyone, other than the vehicle manufacturer itself, of a key or other functionally similar device that will allow the vehicle to be entered, started, and operated, this section shall apply to that vehicle line.

(3) This subdivision shall remain operative until January 1, 2013, and as of that date shall become inoperative, unless a later enacted statute, that is enacted before January 1, 2013, deletes or extends that date.

(e) (1) This section does not apply to a vehicle line of a motor vehicle manufacturer that sold between 2,500 and 5,000 vehicles of that line in the prior calendar year in the state.

(2) This subdivision shall remain operative until January 1, 2013, and as of that date shall become inoperative, unless a later enacted statute, that is enacted before January 1, 2013, deletes or extends that date.

(f) This section shall not apply to a make that sold fewer than 2,500 vehicles in the prior calendar year in the state.

(g) The duties imposed on a manufacturer pursuant to this section may be performed either by the manufacturer or by an agent through a contract.

(h) The provisions of this section are severable. If any provision of this section or its application is held invalid, that invalidity shall not affect other provisions or applications that can be given effect without the invalid provision or application.

(Added by Stats. 2006, Ch. 433, Sec. 2. Effective January 1, 2007.)

9955. (a) A manufacturer of a pocket bike shall affix on the pocket bike a sticker with a disclosure stating that the device is prohibited from being operated on a sidewalk, roadway, or any part of a highway, or on a bikeway, bicycle path or trail, equestrian trail, hiking or recreational trail, or on public lands open to off-highway motor vehicle use.

(b) The disclosure required under subdivision (a) shall meet both of the following requirements:

(1) Be printed in not less than 14-point boldface type on a sticker that contains only the disclosure.

(2) Include the following statement:

(Added by Stats. 2005, Ch. 323, Sec. 2. Effective January 1, 2006.)

Chapter 2. Manufacturer's Responsibility for Safety Defects

(Chapter 2 added by Stats. 1972, Ch. 954.)

9975. Every manufacturer of a motor vehicle who furnishes notification to the registered owner of the motor vehicle of any defect in the motor vehicle or motor vehicle equipment which relates to motor vehicle safety, shall, notwithstanding any limitation in any warranty relating to the motor vehicle, correct such defect without charge to the registered owner of the vehicle or, at the manufacturer's election, reimburse the registered owner for the cost of making such correction.

The manufacturer of such motor vehicle shall not be liable for the cost of such correction if the registered owner of the motor vehicle does not seek to have the correction made within 45 days after receipt of the notification or within the warranty period of the motor vehicle, whichever is longer.

(Added by Stats. 1972, Ch. 954.)

Chapter 3. Engine Manufacturers

(Chapter 3 added by Stats. 1984, Ch. 1264, Sec. 1.)

9980. If the manufacturer of the engine of a new motor vehicle is different from the manufacturer of the vehicle, the vehicle shall be labeled as required by Section 9981.

For purposes of this chapter, the manufacturer of a motor vehicle engine is different from the vehicle manufacturer if a majority of parts, or most of the work of assembly, of the engine is provided by a person other than the vehicle manufacturer or a subsidiary or affiliate of the vehicle manufacturer. For purposes of this chapter, an "affiliate" is an entity that directly, or indirectly through one or more intermediaries, controls or is controlled by, or is under common control with, the manufacturer of the vehicle.

(Amended by Stats. 2000, Ch. 135, Sec. 156. Effective January 1, 2001.)

9981. The manufacturer of any vehicle subject to Section 9980 shall affix a prominent label to the vehicle stating that the engine in the vehicle may have been manufactured by another manufacturer. The label shall be located on or adjacent to the window sticker identifying the manufacturer's suggested retail price for the vehicle or, if none, it shall be located on or adjacent to the window sticker identifying the equipment provided with the vehicle. This label, however, is not required if the manufacturer of the engine contained in the vehicle is disclosed in sales literature or is noted in the sales contract.

(Added by Stats. 1984, Ch. 1264, Sec. 1.)

9982. This chapter applies only to new passenger vehicles and to new motortrucks with an unladen weight under 6,000 pounds, except housecars.

(Added by Stats. 1984, Ch. 1264, Sec. 1.)

Chapter 4. Disclosure of Damage

(Chapter 4 added by Stats. 1990, Ch. 1373, Sec. 1.)

9990. For purposes of this chapter, damage sustained by a motor vehicle is material under any of the following circumstances:

(a) The damage required repairs having a value, including parts and labor calculated at the repairer's cost, exceeding 3 percent of the manufacturer's suggested retail price of the vehicle or five hundred dollars ($500), whichever is greater. The replacement of damaged or stolen components, excluding the cost of repainting or refinishing those components, if replaced by the installation of new original manufacturer's equipment, parts, or accessories that are bolted or otherwise attached as a unit to the vehicle, including, but not limited to, the hood, bumpers, fenders, mechanical parts, instrument panels, moldings, glass, tires, wheels, and electronic instruments, shall be excluded from the damage calculation, except that any damage having a cumulative repair or replacement value which exceeds 10 percent of the manufacturer's suggested retail price of the vehicle shall be deemed material.

(b) The damage was to the frame or drive train of the motor vehicle.

(c) The damage occurred in connection with a theft of the entire vehicle.

(d) The damage was to the suspension of the vehicle requiring repairs other than wheel balancing or alignment.

(Added by Stats. 1990, Ch. 1373, Sec. 1.)

9991. Every dealer shall disclose in writing to the purchaser of a new or previously unregistered motor vehicle, prior to entering into a contract for the vehicle or, if unknown at that time, prior to delivery of the vehicle, any material damage known by the dealer to have been sustained by the vehicle and subsequently repaired.

(Added by Stats. 1990, Ch. 1373, Sec. 1.)

9992. Every dealer shall disclose in writing to the purchaser of a new or previously unregistered motor vehicle, prior to entering into a contract for the vehicle or, if unknown at that time, prior to delivery of the vehicle, any damage, including, but not limited to, material damage, known by the dealer to have been sustained by the vehicle and not repaired.

(Added by Stats. 1990, Ch. 1373, Sec. 1.)

9993. Nothing in this chapter permits any dealer to respond to the inquiry of a purchaser in any untrue or misleading manner.

(Added by Stats. 1990, Ch. 1373, Sec. 1.)

Division 4. Special Antitheft Laws

(Division 4 enacted by Stats. 1959, Ch. 3.)

Chapter 1. Reports of Stolen Vehicles

(Chapter 1 enacted by Stats. 1959, Ch. 3.)

10500. (a) A peace officer, upon receiving a report based on reliable information that a vehicle registered under this code has been stolen, taken, or driven in violation of Section 10851, or that a leased or rented vehicle has not been returned within five days after its owner has made written demand for its return, by certified or registered mail, following the expiration of the lease or rental agreement, or that license plates for a vehicle have been lost or stolen, shall, immediately after receiving that information, report the information to the Department of Justice Stolen Vehicle System. An officer, upon receiving information of the recovery of a vehicle described in this subdivision, or of the recovery of plates which have been previously reported as lost or stolen, shall immediately report the fact of the recovery to the Department of Justice Stolen Vehicle System. At the same time, the recovering officer shall advise the Department of Justice Stolen Vehicle System and the original reporting law enforcement agency of the location and condition of the vehicle or license plates recovered. The original reporting law enforcement agency, upon receipt of the information from the recovering officer, shall immediately attempt to notify the reporting party by telephone, if the telephone number of the reporting party is available or readily accessible, of the location and condition of the recovered vehicle. If the reporting party's telephone number is unknown, or notification attempts were unsuccessful, the original reporting law enforcement agency shall notify the reporting party by placing, in the mail, a notice providing the location and condition of the recovered vehicle. This written notice shall be mailed within 24 hours of the original reporting law enforcement agency's receipt of the information of the recovery of the vehicle, excluding holidays and weekends.

(b) If the recovered vehicle is subject to parking or storage charges, Section 10652.5 applies.

(c) This section shall become operative on January 1, 2024.

(Repealed (in Sec. 1) and added by Stats. 2019, Ch. 609, Sec. 2. (AB 391) Effective January 1, 2020. Section operative January 1, 2024, by its own provisions.)

10501. (a) It is unlawful for any person to make or file a false or fraudulent report of theft of a vehicle required to be registered under this code with any law enforcement agency with intent to deceive.

(b) If a person has been previously convicted of a violation of subdivision (a), he or she is punishable by imprisonment pursuant to subdivision (h) of Section 1170 of the Penal Code for 16 months, or two or three years, or in a county jail for not to exceed one year.

(Amended by Stats. 2011, Ch. 15, Sec. 601. (AB 109) Effective April 4, 2011. Operative October 1, 2011, by Sec. 636 of Ch. 15, as amended by Stats. 2011, Ch. 39, Sec. 68.)

10502. (a) The owner or legal owner of a vehicle registered under this code which has been stolen or embezzled may notify the Department of the California Highway Patrol of the theft or embezzlement, but in the event of an embezzlement other than an embezzlement as specified in Section 10855, may make the report only after having procured the issuance of a warrant for the arrest of the person charged with the embezzlement.

(b) Every owner or legal owner who has given any notice under subdivision (a) shall notify the Department of the California Highway Patrol of a recovery of the vehicle.

(Amended by Stats. 1992, Ch. 290, Sec. 2. Effective January 1, 1993.)

10503. The Department of Justice upon receiving notice under this chapter that a vehicle has been stolen, or taken or driven in violation of Section 10851, or that a vehicle reported stolen, or taken or driven in violation of Section 10851 has been recovered, shall notify the Department of Motor Vehicles of the reported theft, taking or driving, or recovery.

(Amended by Stats. 1972, Ch. 98.)

10504. The department upon receiving a report of a stolen vehicle, or of a vehicle taken or driven in violation of Section 10851, shall place an appropriate notice in the electronic file system which will identify such vehicles during the processing of new certificates of registration, ownership, or registration and ownership. When such vehicles are thus identified, processing shall be discontinued and the Department of Justice shall be notified. New certificates shall not be issued until cleared by the Department of Justice. Notices shall remain in the Department of Motor Vehicles system until a Department of Justice deletion is received.

A report of a stolen vehicle, or of a vehicle taken or driven in violation of Section 10851, is effective for a period of not less than one year from the date first reported or longer as the department may determine.

(Amended by Stats. 1972, Ch. 98.)

10505. Upon the transfer of registration of a vehicle reported as stolen or embezzled, the department shall immediately notify the reporting agency of such fact.

(Enacted by Stats. 1959, Ch. 3.)

Chapter 1.5. Reports of Stolen Vessels

(Chapter 1.5 added by Stats. 1970, Ch. 1428.)

10550. In this chapter, unless the context clearly requires a different meaning, the terms and definitions set forth in Section 9840 shall apply.

(Amended by Stats. 1973, Ch. 759.)

10551. Every peace officer upon receiving a report based on reliable information that any undocumented vessel numbered under this code has been stolen shall immediately after receiving such information report the theft to the Department of Justice, Automated Boat System, and such peace officer upon receiving information of the recovery of any such vessel which he has previously reported as stolen, shall immediately report the fact of the recovery to the Department of Justice, Automated Boat System.

(Amended by Stats. 1980, Ch. 617, Sec. 5.)

10551.5. The Department of Justice upon receiving notice under this chapter that a vessel has been stolen or that a vessel reported stolen has been recovered shall notify the Department of Motor Vehicles of the reported theft or recovery.

(Added by Stats. 1980, Ch. 617, Sec. 6.)

10552. It is unlawful for any person to make or file a false or fraudulent report of the theft of an undocumented vessel required to be numbered under this code with any law enforcement agents with intent to deceive.

(Added by Stats. 1970, Ch. 1428.)

10553. The owner or legal owner of a vessel numbered under this code which has been stolen or embezzled may notify a law enforcement agency of the theft or embezzlement, but in the event of an embezzlement may make the report only after having procured the issuance of a warrant for the arrest of the person charged with such embezzlement. Every owner or legal owner who has given any such notice shall notify the law enforcement agency of a recovery of the vessel.

(Amended by Stats. 1980, Ch. 617, Sec. 7.)

10554. The department upon receiving a report of a stolen or embezzled vessel shall place an appropriate notice in the electronic file system which will identify such vessel during the processing of new certificates of number, ownership, or number and ownership. When such vessels are thus identified, processing shall be discontinued and the agency holding the theft report and the Department of Justice shall be notified. New certificates shall not be issued until cleared by the Department of Justice. Notices shall remain in the Department of Motor Vehicles system until a Department of Justice deletion is received.

A report of a stolen or embezzled vessel is effective for a period of not less than one year from the date first reported, or for such longer period as the department may determine.

(Amended by Stats. 1980, Ch. 617, Sec. 8.)

Chapter 2. Reports of Stored Vehicles

(Chapter 2 enacted by Stats. 1959, Ch. 3.)

10650. (a) Every operator of a towing service and every keeper of a garage or trailer park shall keep a written record of every vehicle of a type subject to registration under this code stored for a period longer than 12 hours.

(b) The record shall contain the name and address of the person storing the vehicle or requesting the towing, the names of the owner and driver of the vehicle, if ascertainable, and a brief description of the vehicle including the name or make, the motor or other number of the vehicle, the nature of any damage to the vehicle, and the license number and registration number shown by the license plates or registration card, if either of the latter is attached to the vehicle in a clearly discernible place.

(c) All records shall be kept for one year from the commencement of storage and shall be open to inspection by any peace officer.

(d) Upon termination of the storage, a statement shall be added to the record as to the disposition of the vehicle, including the name and address of the person to whom the vehicle was released and the date of such release.

(Amended by Stats. 1974, Ch. 271.)

10652. Whenever any vehicle of a type subject to registration under this code has been stored in a garage, repair shop, parking lot, or trailer park for 30 days, the keeper shall report such fact to the Department of Justice by receipted mail, which shall at once notify the legal owner as of record. This section shall not apply to any vehicle stored by a peace officer or employee designated in Section 22651 pursuant to Article 3 (commencing with Section 22850) of Chapter 10 of Division 11.

(Amended by Stats. 2008, Ch. 699, Sec. 24. Effective January 1, 2009.)

10652.5. (a) Whenever the name and address of the legal owner of a motor vehicle is known, or may be ascertained from the registration records in the vehicle or from the records of the Department of Motor Vehicles, no fee or service charge may be imposed upon the legal owner for the parking and storage of the motor vehicle except as follows: (1) The first 15 days of possession and (2) following that 15-day period, the period commencing 3 days after written notice is sent by the person in possession to the legal owner by certified mail, return receipt requested, and continuing for a period not to exceed any applicable time limit set forth in Section 3068 or 3068.1 of the Civil Code.

(b) The costs of notifying the legal owner may be charged as part of the storage fee when the motor vehicle has been stored for an indefinite period of time and notice is given no sooner than the third day of possession. This subdivision also applies if the legal owner refuses to claim possession of the motor vehicle.

(c) In any action brought by, or on behalf of, a legal owner of a motor vehicle to which subdivision (a) applies, to recover a motor vehicle alleged to be withheld by the person in possession of the motor vehicle by demanding storage fees or charges for any number of days in excess of that permitted pursuant to subdivision (a), the prevailing party shall be entitled to reasonable attorney's fees, not to exceed one thousand seven hundred fifty dollars ($1,750). The recovery of those fees is in addition to any other right, remedy, or cause of action of that party.

(d) All storage and towing fees charged to a legal owner of a motor vehicle shall be reasonable. The following rates and fees are presumptively unreasonable:

(1) Administrative or filing fees, except those incurred related to documentation from the Department of Motor Vehicles and those related to the lien sale of a vehicle.

(2) Security fees.

(3) Dolly fees.

(4) Load and unload fees.

(5) Pull-out fees.

(6) Gate fees, except when the owner or insurer of the vehicle requests that the vehicle be released outside of normal business hours.

(7) When gate fees are reasonably assessed, any additional towing

fees that exceed 10 percent of the normal towing rate due to the call originating after normal business hours.

(8) Any storage fees charged for state holidays that exceed the posted standard daily storage rate.

(9) (A) Towing fees when the owner or the operator of a tow truck is directed by a law enforcement officer to remove a vehicle to the nearest shoulder or to level ground adjacent to the roadway for the sole purpose of clearing a roadway to facilitate access by an emergency vehicle at the scene of a state emergency, as defined in Section 8625 of the Government Code, or a local emergency, as defined in Section 8630 of the Government Code.

(B) An owner or operator of a tow truck that removes a vehicle under the circumstances described in subparagraph (A) and acts in good faith shall not be subject to civil liability for any damage to personal property that results from the removal of the vehicle.

(C) The limitation of liability described in subparagraph (B) shall not apply to an act or omission by an owner or operator of a tow truck that constitutes gross negligence or willful or wanton misconduct.

(10) Following a request from the vehicle owner to release their vehicle, and upon payment of all fees then due, storage fees for any day that a storage facility fails to release the vehicle.

(11) Storage fees in excess of 50 percent of the daily storage rate when a vehicle is recovered within the first four hours of storage.

(e) This section is not applicable to any motor vehicle stored by a levying officer acting under the authority of judicial process.

(f) Nothing in subdivision (d) prohibits any fees authorized in a written agreement between a law enforcement agency and a towing or storage company, including, but not limited to, official police garages operating under the jurisdiction of a municipal police commission, if the tow was initiated by the law enforcement agency.

(g) For purposes of this section, "normal business hours" means Monday through Friday from 8:00 a.m. to 5:00 p.m., inclusive, except for state holidays.

(Amended by Stats. 2025, Ch. 345, Sec. 1. (AB 987) Effective January 1, 2026.)

10653. Whenever any vehicle of a type subject to registration under this code which shows evidence of having been struck by a bullet is stored in a garage or repair shop, the keeper thereof shall within 24 hours after receiving the vehicle report such fact to the sheriff's office of the county or police department of the city wherein the garage or repair shop is located, giving the motor or other number of the vehicle, the license number if ascertainable, and the name and address of the person storing the same or the name and address of the owner shown by the registration card, if the same is attached to the vehicle in a clearly discernible place.

(Enacted by Stats. 1959, Ch. 3.)

10654. Every person other than the keeper of a garage renting any private building used as a private garage or space therein for the storage of a vehicle of a type subject to registration under this code, when the agreement to rent includes only the building or space therein, shall within 24 hours after the vehicle is stored therein report such fact together with the name of the tenant, and a description of the vehicle, including the name or make, the motor or other number of the vehicle, and the license number to the sheriff's office of the county or the police department of the city wherein the building is located. "Private garage" as used in this section does not include a public warehouse or public garage.

(Enacted by Stats. 1959, Ch. 3.)

10655. No person required to keep a record or make a report under this chapter shall wilfully fail, refuse, or neglect to comply with this chapter.

(Enacted by Stats. 1959, Ch. 3.)

10656. The director, deputy director, registrar, deputy registrar, investigators of the department, and members of a city police department or county sheriff's office whose primary responsibility is to conduct vehicle theft investigations, may inspect any vehicle of a type required to be registered under this code in any garage, repair shop, parking lot, used car lot, automobile dismantlers lot, or other similar establishment for the purpose of investigating the title and registration of vehicles and inspection of vehicles wrecked or dismantled.

(Amended by Stats. 1979, Ch. 252.)

10658. (a) The provisions of this chapter shall not apply to the storage of any recreational vehicle owned by a mobilehome park resident and stored in a mobilehome park.

(b) As used in this section, "recreational vehicle" shall have the same meaning as defined in Section 18215.5 of the Health and Safety Code, and "mobilehome park" shall have the same meaning as defined in Section 18214 of the Health and Safety Code.

(Added by Stats. 1974, Ch. 646.)

Chapter 3. Alteration or Removal of Numbers

(Chapter 3 enacted by Stats. 1959, Ch. 3.)

10750. (a) No person shall intentionally deface, destroy, or alter the motor number, other distinguishing number, or identification mark of a vehicle required or employed for registration purposes without written authorization from the department, nor shall any person place or stamp any serial, motor, or other number or mark upon a vehicle, except one assigned thereto by the department.

(b) This section does not prohibit the restoration by an owner of the original vehicle identification number when the restoration is authorized by the department, nor prevent any manufacturer from placing in the ordinary course of business numbers or marks upon new motor vehicles or new parts thereof.

(Amended by Stats. 1970. Ch. 824.)

10751. (a) No person shall knowingly buy, sell, offer for sale, receive, or have in his or her possession, any vehicle, or component part thereof, from which any serial or identification number, including, but not limited to, any number used for registration purposes, that is affixed by the manufacturer to the vehicle or component part, in whatever manner deemed proper by the manufacturer, has been removed, defaced, altered, or destroyed, unless the vehicle or component part has attached thereto an identification number assigned or approved by the department in lieu of the manufacturer's number.

(b) Whenever a vehicle described in subdivision (a), including a vehicle assembled with any component part which is in violation of subdivision (a), comes into the custody of a peace officer, it shall be destroyed, sold, or otherwise disposed of under the conditions as provided in an order by the court having jurisdiction. No court order providing for disposition shall be issued unless the person from whom the property was seized, and all claimants to the property whose interest or title is on registration records in the Department of Motor Vehicles, are provided a postseizure hearing by the court having jurisdiction within 90 days after the seizure. This subdivision shall not apply with respect to a seized vehicle or component part used as evidence in any criminal action or proceeding. Nothing in this section shall, however, preclude the return of a seized vehicle or a component part to the owner by the seizing agency following presentation of satisfactory evidence of ownership and, if determined necessary, upon the assignment of an identification number to the vehicle or component part by the department.

(c) Whenever a vehicle described in subdivision (a) comes into the custody of a peace officer, the person from whom the property was seized, and all claimants to the property whose interest or title is on registration records in the Department of Motor Vehicles, shall be notified within five days, excluding Saturdays, Sundays, and holidays, after the seizure, of the date, time, and place of the hearing required in subdivision (b). The notice shall contain the information specified in subdivision (d).

(d) Whenever a peace officer seizes a vehicle described in subdivision (a), the person from whom the property was seized shall be provided a notice of impoundment of the vehicle which shall serve as a receipt and contain the following information:

(1) Name and address of person from whom the property was seized.

(2) A statement that the vehicle seized has been impounded for investigation of a violation of Section 10751 of the California Vehicle Code and that the property will be released upon a determination that the serial or identification number has not been removed, defaced, altered, or destroyed, or upon the presentation of satisfactory evidence of ownership of the vehicle or a component part, if no other person claims an interest in the property; otherwise, a hearing regarding the disposition of the vehicle shall take place in the proper court.

(3) A statement that the person from whom the property was seized, and all claimants to the property whose interest or title is on registration records in the Department of Motor Vehicles, will receive written notification of the date, time, and place of the hearing within five days, excluding Saturdays, Sundays, and holidays, after the seizure.

(4) Name and address of the law enforcement agency where evidence of ownership of the vehicle or component part may be presented.

(5) A statement of the contents of Section 10751 of the Vehicle Code.

(e) A hearing on the disposition of the property shall be held by the superior court within 90 days after the seizure. The hearing shall be before the court without a jury. A proceeding under this section is a limited civil case.

(1) If the evidence reveals either that the serial or identification number has not been removed, defaced, altered, or destroyed or that the number has been removed, defaced, altered, or destroyed but satisfactory evidence of ownership has been presented to the seizing agency or court, the property shall be released to the person entitled thereto. Nothing in this section precludes the return of the vehicle or a component part to a good faith purchaser following presentation of satisfactory evidence of ownership thereof upon the assignment of an identification number to the vehicle or component part by the department.

(2) If the evidence reveals that the identification number has been removed, defaced, altered, or destroyed, and satisfactory evidence of ownership has not been presented, the vehicle shall be destroyed, sold, or otherwise disposed of as provided by court order.

(3) At the hearing, the seizing agency has the burden of establishing that the serial or identification number has been removed, defaced, altered, or destroyed and that no satisfactory evidence of ownership has been presented.

(f) This section does not apply to a scrap metal processor engaged primarily in the acquisition, processing, and shipment of ferrous and nonferrous scrap, and who receives dismantled vehicles from licensed dismantlers, licensed junk collectors, or licensed junk dealers as scrap metal for the purpose of recycling the dismantled vehicles for their metallic content, the end product of which is the production of material for recycling and remelting purposes for steel mills, foundries, smelters, and refiners.

(Amended by Stats. 2002, Ch. 784, Sec. 596. Effective January 1, 2003.)

10752. (a) No person shall, with intent to prejudice, damage, injure, or defraud, acquire, possess, sell, or offer for sale any genuine or counterfeit manufacturer's serial or identification number from or for, or purporting to be from or for, a vehicle or component part thereof.

(b) No person shall, with intent to prejudice, damage, injure, or defraud, acquire, possess, sell, or offer for sale any genuine or counterfeit serial or identification number issued by the department, the Department of the California Highway Patrol, or the vehicle registration and titling agency of any foreign jurisdiction which is from or for, or purports to be from or for, a vehicle or component part thereof.

(c) Every person convicted of a violation of subdivision (a) or (b) shall be punished by imprisonment pursuant to subdivision (h) of Section 1170 of the Penal Code, or in the county jail for not less than 90 days nor more than one year, and by a fine of not less than two hundred fifty dollars ($250) nor more than five thousand dollars ($5,000).

(Amended by Stats. 2011, Ch. 15, Sec. 602. (AB 109) Effective April 4, 2011. Operative October 1, 2011, by Sec. 636 of Ch. 15, as amended by Stats. 2011, Ch. 39, Sec. 68.)

10753. (a) Any person who removes, alters, or obfuscates any vehicle identification number or other unique marking that has been added to a catalytic converter is guilty of a misdemeanor.

(b) Any person who knowingly possesses three or more catalytic converters that have the vehicle identification number or other unique marking removed, altered, or obfuscated is guilty of a misdemeanor.

(c) This subdivision does not apply to either of the following:

(1) Any person who is removing, altering, or obfuscating a vehicle identification number or other unique marking in order to apply a new vehicle identification number or unique marking because the catalytic converter is being lawfully installed on a different vehicle.

(2) Any person that is disassembling, smelting, or otherwise permanently destroying a catalytic converter lawfully in their possession.

(Added by Stats. 2023, Ch. 847, Sec. 1. (AB 1519) Effective January 1, 2024.)

Chapter 3.5. Motor Vehicle Chop Shops

(Chapter 3.5 added by Stats. 1993, Ch. 386, Sec. 3.)

10801. Any person who knowingly and intentionally owns or operates a chop shop is guilty of a public offense and, upon conviction, shall be punished by imprisonment pursuant to subdivision (h) of Section 1170 of the Penal Code for two, three, or four years, or by a fine of not more than fifty thousand dollars ($50,000), or by both the fine and imprisonment, or by up to one year in the county jail, or by a fine of not more than one thousand dollars ($1,000), or by both the fine and imprisonment.

(Amended by Stats. 2011, Ch. 15, Sec. 603. (AB 109) Effective April 4, 2011. Operative October 1, 2011, by Sec. 636 of Ch. 15, as amended by Stats. 2011, Ch. 39, Sec. 68.)

10802. Any person who knowingly alters, counterfeits, defaces, destroys, disguises, falsifies, forges, obliterates, or removes vehicle identification numbers, with the intent to misrepresent the identity or prevent the identification of motor vehicles or motor vehicle parts, for the purpose of sale, transfer, import, or export, is guilty of a public offense and, upon conviction, shall be punished by imprisonment pursuant to subdivision (h) of Section 1170 of the Penal Code for 16 months, or two or three years, or by a fine of not more than twenty-five thousand dollars ($25,000), or by both the fine and imprisonment, or by up to one year in the county jail, or by a fine of not more than one thousand dollars ($1,000), or by both the fine and imprisonment.

(Amended by Stats. 2011, Ch. 15, Sec. 604. (AB 109) Effective April 4, 2011. Operative October 1, 2011, by Sec. 636 of Ch. 15, as amended by Stats. 2011, Ch. 39, Sec. 68.)

10803. (a) Any person who buys with the intent to resell, disposes of, sells, or transfers, more than one motor vehicle or parts from more than one motor vehicle, with the knowledge that the vehicle identification numbers of the motor vehicles or motor vehicle parts have been altered, counterfeited, defaced, destroyed, disguised, falsified, forged, obliterated, or removed for the purpose of misrepresenting the identity or preventing the identification of the motor vehicles or motor vehicle parts, is guilty of a public offense and, upon conviction, shall be punished by imprisonment pursuant to subdivision (h) of Section 1170 of the Penal Code for two, four, or six years, or by a fine of not more than sixty thousand dollars ($60,000), or by both the fine and imprisonment, or by up to one year in the county jail, or by a fine of not more than one thousand dollars ($1,000), or by both the fine and imprisonment.

(b) Any person who possesses, for the purpose of sale, transfer, import, or export, more than one motor vehicle or parts from more than one motor vehicle, with the knowledge that the vehicle identification numbers of the motor vehicles or motor vehicle parts have been altered, counterfeited, defaced, destroyed, disguised, falsified, forged, obliterated, or removed for the purpose of misrepresenting the identity or preventing the identification of the motor vehicles or motor vehicle parts, is guilty of a public offense and, upon conviction, shall be punished by imprisonment pursuant to subdivision (h) of Section 1170 of the Penal Code for 16 months, or two or three years, or by a fine of not more than thirty thousand dollars ($30,000), or by both the fine and imprisonment, or by imprisonment in the county jail not exceeding one year or by a fine of not more than one thousand dollars ($1,000) or by both the fine and imprisonment.

(Amended by Stats. 2011, Ch. 15, Sec. 605. (AB 109) Effective April 4, 2011. Operative October 1, 2011, by Sec. 636 of Ch. 15, as amended by Stats. 2011, Ch. 39, Sec. 68.)

10804. (a) Section 10803 does not apply to a motor vehicle scrap processor who, in the normal legal course of business and in good faith, processes a motor vehicle or motor vehicle part by crushing, compacting, or other similar methods, if any vehicle identification number is not removed from the motor vehicle or motor vehicle part prior to or during the processing.

(b) Section 10803 does not apply to any owner or authorized possessor of a motor vehicle or motor vehicle part which has been recovered by law enforcement authorities after having been stolen or if the condition of the vehicle identification number of the motor vehicle or motor vehicle part is known to, or has been reported to, law enforcement authorities. Law enforcement authorities are presumed to have knowledge of all vehicle identification numbers on a motor vehicle or motor vehicle part which are altered, counterfeited, defaced, disguised, falsified, forged, obliterated, or removed, when law enforcement authorities deliver or return the motor vehicle or motor vehicle part to its owner or an authorized possessor after it has been recovered by law enforcement authorities after having been reported stolen.

(Added by Stats. 1993, Ch. 386, Sec. 3. Effective September 8, 1993.)

Chapter 4. Theft and Injury of Vehicles

(Chapter 4 enacted by Stats. 1959, Ch. 3.)

10850. The provisions of this chapter apply to vehicles upon the highways and elsewhere throughout the State.

(Enacted by Stats. 1959, Ch. 3.)

10851. (a) Any person who drives or takes a vehicle not his or her own, without the consent of the owner thereof, and with intent either to permanently or temporarily deprive the owner thereof of his or her title to or possession of the vehicle, whether with or without intent to steal the vehicle, or any person who is a party or an accessory to or an accomplice in the driving or unauthorized taking or stealing, is guilty of a public offense and, upon conviction thereof, shall be punished by imprisonment in a county jail for not more than one year or pursuant to subdivision (h) of Section 1170 of the Penal Code or by a fine of not more than five thousand dollars ($5,000), or by both the fine and imprisonment.

(b) If the vehicle is (1) an ambulance, as defined in subdivision (a) of Section 165, (2) a distinctively marked vehicle of a law enforcement agency or fire department, taken while the ambulance or vehicle is on an emergency call and this fact is known to the person driving or taking, or any person who is party or an accessory to or an accomplice in the driving or unauthorized taking or stealing, or (3) a vehicle which has been modified for the use of a disabled veteran or any other disabled person and which displays a distinguishing license plate or placard issued pursuant to Section 22511.5 or 22511.9 and this fact is known or should reasonably have been known to the person driving or taking, or any person who is party or an accessory in the driving or unauthorized taking or stealing, the offense is a felony punishable by imprisonment pursuant to subdivision (h) of Section 1170 of the Penal Code for two, three, or four years or by a fine of not more than ten thousand dollars ($10,000), or by both the fine and imprisonment.

(c) In any prosecution for a violation of subdivision (a) or (b), the consent of the owner of a vehicle to its taking or driving shall not in any case be presumed or implied because of the owner's consent on a previous occasion to the taking or driving of the vehicle by the same or a different person.

(d) The existence of any fact which makes subdivision (b) applicable shall be alleged in the accusatory pleading, and either admitted by the defendant in open court, or found to be true by the jury trying the issue of guilt or by the court where guilt is established by plea of guilty or nolo contendere or by trial by the court sitting without a jury.

(e) Any person who has been convicted of one or more previous felony violations of this section, or felony grand theft of a vehicle in violation of subdivision (d) of Section 487 of the Penal Code, former subdivision (3) of Section 487 of the Penal Code, as that section read prior to being amended by Section 4 of Chapter 1125 of the Statutes of 1993, or Section 487h of the Penal Code, is punishable as set forth in Section 666.5 of the Penal Code. The existence of any fact that would bring a person under Section 666.5 of the Penal Code shall be alleged in the information or indictment and either admitted by the defendant in open court, or found to be true by the jury trying the issue of guilt or by the court where guilt is established by plea of guilty or nolo contendere, or by trial by the court sitting without a jury.

(f) This section shall become operative on January 1, 1997.

(Amended by Stats. 2011, Ch. 15, Sec. 606. (AB 109) Effective April 4, 2011. Operative October 1, 2011, by Sec. 636 of Ch. 15, as amended by Stats. 2011, Ch. 39, Sec. 68. Note: The operative date in subd. (f) originated in, and relates to, a prior version.)

10851.5. Any person who takes binder chains, required under regulations adopted pursuant to Section 31510, having a value of nine hundred fifty dollars ($950) or less which chains are not his own, without the consent of the owner thereof, and with intent either permanently or temporarily to deprive the owner thereof of his title to or possession of the binder chains whether with or without intent to steal the same, or any person who is a party or accessory to or an accomplice in the unauthorized taking or stealing is guilty of a misdemeanor, and upon conviction thereof shall be punished by imprisonment in the county jail for not less than six months or by a fine of not less than one thousand dollars ($1,000) or by both such fine and imprisonment. The consent of the owner of the binder chain to its taking shall not in any case be presumed or implied because of such owner's consent on a previous occasion to the taking of the binder chain by the same or a different person.

(Amended by Stats. 2009, 3rd Ex. Sess., Ch. 28, Sec. 54. (SB 18 3x) Effective January 25, 2010.)

10852. No person shall either individually or in association with one or more other persons, wilfully injure or tamper with any vehicle or the contents thereof or break or remove any part of a vehicle without the consent of the owner.

(Enacted by Stats. 1959, Ch. 3.)

10852.5. (a) No person shall purchase a used catalytic converter, including for the purpose of dismantling, recycling, or smelting, except from any of the following:

(1) An automobile dismantler licensed pursuant to Chapter 3 (commencing with Section 11500) of Division 5.

(2) A core recycler, as defined in Section 21610 of the Business and Professions Code, that maintains a fixed place of business and has obtained the catalytic converter pursuant to that section.

(3) A motor vehicle manufacturer, dealer, or lessor-retailer licensed pursuant to Division 5 (commencing with Section 11100).

(4) An automotive repair dealer licensed pursuant to Chapter 20.3 (commencing with Section 9880) of Division 3 of the Business and Professions Code.

(5) Any other licensed business that may reasonably generate, possess, or sell used catalytic converters.

(6) An individual possessing documentation that they are the lawful owner of the used catalytic converter, including, but not limited to, a certificate of title or registration that identifies the individual as the legal or registered owner of the vehicle from which the catalytic converter was detached, and that includes a vehicle identification number that matches the vehicle identification number permanently marked on the catalytic converter.

(b) As used in this section, the following terms have the following meanings:

(1) "Permanently marked" means prominently engraved, etched, welded, metal stamped, acid marked, or otherwise permanently displayed using a similarly reliable method of imparting a lasting mark on the

exterior case of the catalytic converter.

(2) "Used catalytic converter" means a catalytic converter that has been previously installed on a vehicle and has been detached. It does not include a reconditioned or refurbished catalytic converter being sold at retail.

(c) A violation of this section is punishable as an infraction by a fine, as follows:

(1) For a first offense, by a fine of one thousand dollars ($1,000).

(2) For a second offense, by a fine of two thousand dollars ($2,000).

(3) For a third or subsequent offense, by a fine of four thousand dollars ($4,000).

(Added by Stats. 2022, Ch. 514, Sec. 2. (SB 1087) Effective January 1, 2023.)

10853. No person shall with intent to commit any malicious mischief, injury, or other crime, climb into or upon a vehicle whether it is in motion or at rest, nor shall any person attempt to manipulate any of the levers, starting mechanism, brakes, or other mechanism or device of a vehicle while the same is at rest and unattended, nor shall any person set in motion any vehicle while the same is at rest and unattended.

(Enacted by Stats. 1959, Ch. 3.)

10854. Every person having the storage, care, safe-keeping, custody, or possession of any vehicle of a type subject to registration under this code who, without the consent of the owner, takes, hires, runs, drives, or uses the vehicle or who takes or removes any part thereof is guilty of a misdemeanor and upon conviction shall be punished by a fine of not exceeding one thousand dollars ($1,000) or by imprisonment in the county jail for not exceeding one year or by both.

(Enacted by Stats. 1959, Ch. 3.)

10855. (a) If a person who has leased or rented a vehicle willfully and intentionally fails to return the vehicle to its owner within five days after the lease or rental agreement has expired, the person shall be presumed to have embezzled the vehicle.

(b) This section shall become operative on January 1, 2024.

(Repealed (in Sec. 3) and added by Stats. 2019, Ch. 609, Sec. 4. (AB 391) Effective January 1, 2020. Section operative January 1, 2024, by its own provisions.)

10856. (a) A person shall not interfere with the transport of a vehicle to a storage facility, auction, or dealer by an individual who is employed by a repossession agency or who is licensed pursuant to Chapter 11 (commencing with Section 7500) of Division 3 of the Business and Professions Code once repossession is complete as provided in Section 7507.12 of the Business and Professions Code. This subdivision shall not apply to a peace officer while acting in an official capacity.

(b) Any tow yard, impounding agency, or governmental agency, or any person acting on behalf of those entities, shall not refuse to release a vehicle or other collateral to anyone that is legally entitled to that vehicle or other collateral. This subdivision shall not apply to a vehicle being held for evidence by law enforcement or a prosecuting attorney.

(Added by Stats. 2014, Ch. 390, Sec. 11. (AB 2503) Effective September 17, 2014.)

Chapter 5. Motor Vehicle Theft Prevention

(Chapter 5 added by Stats. 1994, Ch. 1248, Sec. 5.)

10900. This chapter shall be known and may be cited as the "Motor Vehicle Theft Prevention Act."

(Added by Stats. 1994, Ch. 1248, Sec. 5. Effective January 1, 1995.)

10901. (a) Pursuant to Section 1872.8 of the Insurance Code, proceeds from the assessment imposed thereunder shall be used to fund prevention and increased investigation of economic automobile theft. Funds received pursuant to Section 1872.8 shall be deposited in the Motor Vehicle Account and appropriated to the Department of the California Highway Patrol for prevention and enhanced investigative efforts to deter economic automobile theft.

(b) Moneys received by the commissioner pursuant to this section shall be used to fund (1) enhanced programs to prevent and investigate economic automobile theft; (2) a program directed at investigating and interdicting the export of stolen motor vehicles and stolen motor vehicle components across an international border; and (3) to operate the CAL H.E.A.T (Californians Help Eliminate Auto Theft) program. Moneys received by a local law enforcement agency pursuant to this section shall be used to fund enhanced programs to prevent and investigate economic automobile theft and shall not be used to supplant or replace funding of existing personnel or equipment.

The commissioner shall submit an annual report to the Legislature, no later than 90 days following the completion of the fiscal year, accounting for all funds received and disbursed pursuant to this section. The report shall detail (A) the uses to which those funds were put, including payment of salaries and expenses, purchase of equipment and supplies, and other expenditures by type; and (B) results achieved as a consequence of expenditures made, including the number of investigations, arrests, complaints filed, convictions, and the number of vehicles recovered and amounts of property losses saved.

(c) As used in this section, "economic automobile theft" means automobile theft perpetrated for financial gain, including, but not limited to, the following:

(1) Theft of a motor vehicle for financial gain.

(2) Reporting that a motor vehicle has been stolen for the purpose of filing a false insurance claim.

(3) Engaging in any act prohibited by Chapter 3.5 (commencing with Section 10801) of Division 4 this code.

(4) Switching of vehicle identification numbers to obtain title to a stolen motor vehicle.

(Added by Stats. 1994, Ch. 1248, Sec. 5. Effective January 1, 1995.)

10902. The Department of the California Highway Patrol shall establish a program entitled "CAL H.E.A.T." (Help Eliminate Auto Theft) for the purpose of reducing the incidence of economic auto theft in California. The program shall be an anti-auto theft program with a toll-free telephone hotline operator funded by the department using funds distributed to it pursuant to Section 10901. The hotline operator shall channel reports from the public regarding auto thefts to state and local law enforcement agencies. In the annual report, the commissioner shall report on the results of this program, including the number of calls from the public reporting a suspected motor vehicle theft, the number of arrests, complaints filed, convictions, and vehicles recovered, and the amount of property losses saved as a result of the program.

If funded by admitted insurers in this state, the program may offer rewards for reports that lead to the arrest and conviction of a person engaged in economic automobile theft. If so funded, the Department of the California Highway Patrol shall establish a claims board, which shall include appointments from state and local law enforcement agencies and the insurance industry, to determine the amount of individual awards.

(Added by Stats. 1994, Ch. 1248, Sec. 5. Effective January 1, 1995.)

10904. The commissioner may develop a public education campaign to deter participation in auto insurance fraud and to encourage reporting of fraudulent claims.

(Added by Stats. 2000, Ch. 867, Sec. 22. Effective January 1, 2001.)

Division 5. Occupational Licensing and Business Regulations

(Division 5 enacted by Stats. 1959, Ch. 3.)

Chapter 1. Driving Schools and Driving Instructors

(Chapter 1 enacted by Stats. 1959, Ch. 3.)

11100. (a) No person shall own or operate a driving school or give driving instruction for compensation, unless a license therefor has been secured from the department.

(b) This section does not apply to the ownership or operation of any school, or the giving of instruction, for the driving of motortrucks of three or more axles which are more than 6,000 pounds unladen weight.

(Amended by Stats. 1988, Ch. 1399, Sec. 2.)

11100.1. No person who instructs others in the operation of all-terrain vehicles shall represent that the instruction given satisfies the requirements of Sections 38503 and 38504, and no certificate shall be issued or awarded for participation in all-terrain vehicle safety instruction unless the instruction is conducted by a licensed all-terrain vehicle safety instructor who is sponsored by an all-terrain vehicle safety training organization.

This section shall become operative on July 1, 1988.

(Added by Stats. 1987, Ch. 881, Sec. 4. Section operative July 1, 1988, by its own provisions.)

11100.5. Whenever it is necessary for a driving school or independent driving instructor to be certified by the Department of Education, or any agency thereof, in order to participate in any state or federal program directed at training or retraining persons in occupational skills, licensing or certification by the Department of Motor Vehicles pursuant to this chapter may operate to fully qualify such school or instructor to participate in the program.

Costs incurred by the department in exercising its functions pursuant to this section shall be borne by the applicant for licensing or certification, and the department may charge the applicant a reasonable fee therefor.

(Added by Stats. 1965, Ch. 1957.)

11101. (a) This chapter does not apply to any of the following:

(1) Public schools or educational institutions in which driving instruction is part of the curriculum.

(2) Nonprofit public service organizations offering instruction without a tuition fee.

(3) Nonprofit organizations engaged exclusively in giving off-the-highway instruction in the operation of motorcycles, if the course of instruction is approved by the National Highway Traffic Safety Administration and is not designed to prepare students for examination by the department for an M1 or M2 drivers license or endorsement.

(4) Commercial schools giving only off-the-highway instruction in the operation of special construction equipment, as defined in this code.

(5) Vehicle dealers or their salesmen giving instruction without charge to purchasers of motor vehicles.

(6) Employers giving instruction to their employees.

(7) Commercial schools engaged exclusively in giving off-the-highway instruction in the operation of racing vehicles or in advanced driving skills to persons holding valid drivers' licenses, except whenever that instruction is given to persons who are being prepared for examination by the department for any class of driver's license.

(b) For purposes of this section, "racing vehicle" means a motor vehicle of a type that is used exclusively in a contest of speed and that is not intended for use on the highways.

(c) (1) Nothing in this chapter shall be construed to direct or restrict courses of instruction in driver education offered by private secondary schools or to require the use of credentialed or certified instructors in driver education courses offered by private secondary schools.

(2) For the purposes of this section, private secondary schools are those subject to Sections 33190 and 48222 of the Education Code.

(Amended by Stats. 2006, Ch. 311, Sec. 6. Effective January 1, 2007.)

11102. (a) A driving school owner, or the principal in an all-terrain vehicle safety training organization, shall meet all of the following requirements:

(1) Maintain an established place of business open to the public. No office or place of business shall be situated within 500 feet of any building used by the department as an office, unless the owner was established at that location on or before January 1, 1976.

(2) Have the proper equipment necessary to give instruction in the operation of the class of vehicles for which the course is designed, which shall include, but not be limited to, training vehicles equipped with all of the following:

(A) An additional functional foot brake affixed to the right side of the front floor.

(B) A rearview mirror placed on the inside of the windshield on the right side, which is additional to the factory-installed mirror in the center of the windshield.

(3) Procure and file with the department a bond of ten thousand dollars ($10,000) executed by an admitted surety insurer and conditioned that the applicant shall not practice any fraud or make any fraudulent representation that will cause a monetary loss to a person taking instruction from the applicant.

(4) Meet the requirements of Section 11105.2 and, if the person is the owner of a driving school, meet the requirements of Section 11102.5. If the owner is not the operator of the driving school, the owner shall designate an operator who shall meet the requirements of Section 11102.5.

(5) (A) File with the department an instrument, in writing, appointing the director as the agent of the applicant upon whom a process may be served in any action commenced against the applicant arising out of any claim for damages suffered by any person by the applicant's violation of any provision of this code or any condition of the bond.

(B) The applicant shall stipulate in the instrument that any process directed to the applicant, when personal service cannot be made in this state after due diligence, may be served upon the director or, if the director is absent from the office, upon any employee in charge of the office of the director, in which case the service is of the same effect as if served upon the applicant personally. The applicant shall further stipulate, in writing, that the agency created by the instrument shall continue during the period covered by the license and so long thereafter as the applicant may be made to answer in damages for a violation of this code or any condition of the bond.

(C) The instrument appointing the director as agent for the applicant for service of process shall be acknowledged by the applicant before a notary public.

(D) If the licensee is served with process by service upon the director, one copy of the summons and complaint shall be left with the director or in the director's office in Sacramento or mailed to the office of the director in Sacramento. A fee of five dollars ($5) shall also be paid to the director at the time of service of the copy of the summons and complaint.

(E) The service on the director is a sufficient service on the licensee if the plaintiff or the plaintiff's attorney also, on the same day, sends notice of the service and a copy of the summons and complaint by registered mail to the licensee. A copy of the summons and complaint shall also be mailed by the plaintiff or his or her attorney to the surety of the applicant's bond at the address of the surety given in the bond, postpaid and registered with request for return receipt.

(F) The director shall keep a record of all process served upon the director under this paragraph showing the day and hour of service, and the director shall retain the summons and complaint served on file.

(G) If the licensee is served with process by service thereof upon the director, the licensee has 30 days after that service within which to answer any complaint or other pleading filed in the cause. For purposes of venue, if the licensee is served with process by service upon the director, the service is deemed to have been made upon the licensee in the county in which the licensee has or last had the licensee's established place of business.

(b) The qualifying requirements referred to in this section shall be met within one year from the date of application for a license, or a new application, examination, and a fee shall be required.

(Amended by Stats. 2000, Ch. 243, Sec. 1. Effective January 1, 2001.)

11102.1. If a deposit is given instead of the bond required by Section 11102:

(a) The director may order the deposit returned at the expiration of three years from the date a driving school licensee has ceased to do business, or three years from the date a licensee has ceased to be licensed, if the director is satisfied that there are no outstanding claims against the deposit. A judge of a superior court may order the return of the deposit prior to the expiration of three years upon evidence satisfactory to the judge that there are no outstanding claims against the deposit.

(b) If either the director, department, or state is a defendant in any action instituted to recover all or any part of the deposit, or any action is instituted by the director, department, or state to determine those entitled to any part of the deposit, the director, department, or state shall be paid reasonable attorney fees and costs from the deposit. Costs shall include those administrative costs incurred in processing claims against the deposit.

(Amended by Stats. 2002, Ch. 784, Sec. 597. Effective January 1, 2003.)

11102.5. (a) A driving school operator shall meet all of the following requirements:

(1) Within three attempts, pass an examination that the department requires on traffic laws, safe driving practices, operation of motor vehicles, teaching methods and techniques, driving school statutes and regulations, and office procedures and recordkeeping.

(2) Pay the department a fee of one hundred dollars ($100), which shall entitle the applicant to three examinations.

(3) Be 21 years of age or older.

(4) Have worked for an established licensed California driving school as a driving instructor for a period of not less than 2,000 hours of actual behind-the-wheel teaching and, on and after July 1, 1973, have satisfactorily completed a course in the teaching of driver education and driver training acceptable to the department, except that the operator, including an owner who is also the operator, of a driving school that exclusively teaches motorcycle driving may, in lieu of the behind-the-wheel teaching requirement, have worked for an established licensed California driving school as a motorcycle driving instructor for not less than 300 hours of actual motorcycle range and street teaching, have taught 300 hours of actual motorcycle range and street instruction under the guidance of the California Motorcyclist Safety Program, or have given comparable training instruction that is acceptable to the department. This paragraph does not apply to any person who is certified by the State Department of Education as fully qualified to teach driver education and driver training and has taught those subjects in the public school system for not less than 1,000 hours.

(b) The qualifying requirements referred to in this section shall be met within one year from the date of application for a license, or a new application, examination, and a fee shall be required.

(Amended by Stats. 2022, Ch. 295, Sec. 8. (AB 2956) Effective January 1, 2023.)

11102.6. (a) Notwithstanding Section 11102.5, a driving school operator who is first licensed to operate a driving school on or after July 1, 2016, and who offers no behind-the-wheel driver training, shall meet all of the following requirements:

(1) Within three attempts, pass an examination that the department requires on traffic laws, safe driving practices, operation of motor vehicles, teaching methods and techniques, driving school statutes and regulations, and office procedures and recordkeeping.

(2) Pay the department a fee for each examination taken, not to exceed the reasonable cost of administering the examination.

(3) Be 21 years of age or older.

(4) Have successfully completed an educational program of not less than 60 hours that is acceptable to the department. The program shall include a minimum of 40 hours of classroom instruction and 20 hours of behind-the-wheel instruction. The program shall include, but not be limited to, driving school operator responsibilities, current vehicle laws, and regulations in Article 4.6 of Chapter 1 of Division 1 of Title 13 of the California Code of Regulations. The instruction may be provided by generally accredited educational institutions, private vocational schools, and education programs and seminars offered by professional societies, organizations, trade associations, and other educational and technical programs that meet the requirements of this section.

(b) The qualifying requirements referred to in this section shall be met within one year from the date of application for a license, or a new application, examination, and a fee for the examination not to exceed the reasonable cost of administering the examination shall be required.

(Amended by Stats. 2016, Ch. 86, Sec. 300. (SB 1171) Effective January 1, 2017.)

11103. A driving school owner and an independent instructor licensed under Section 11105.5 shall maintain bodily injury and property damage liability insurance on motor vehicles while being used in driving instruction, insuring the liability of the driving school, the driving instructor, and any person taking instruction in at least the following amounts: one hundred fifty thousand dollars ($150,000) for bodily injury to or death of one person in any one accident and, subject to the limit for one person, three hundred thousand dollars ($300,000) for bodily injury to or death of two or more persons in any one accident, and the amount of fifty thousand dollars ($50,000) for damage to property of others in any one accident.

The owner or instructor shall file evidence of that insurance coverage in the form of a certificate from the insurance carrier with the department, and the certificate shall stipulate that the insurance shall not be canceled except upon 30 days' prior written notice to the department.

(Amended by Stats. 1986, Ch. 403, Sec. 1.)

11103.1. An all-terrain vehicle safety training organization shall maintain bodily injury and property damage liability insurance on motor vehicles while being used in all-terrain vehicle safety instruction, insuring the liability of the organization, the instructors, and any person taking instruction in at least the following amounts:

(a) One hundred fifty thousand dollars ($150,000) for bodily injury to or death of one person in any one accident.

(b) Subject to the limit specified in paragraph (1) for one person, three hundred thousand dollars ($300,000) for bodily injury to or death of two or more persons in any one accident.

(c) Fifty thousand dollars ($50,000) for damage to property of others in any one accident.

This section shall become operative on July 1, 1988.

(Added by Stats. 1987, Ch. 881, Sec. 7. Section operative July 1, 1988, by its own provisions.)

11103.2. A driving school owner who employs one or more driving instructors or other employees shall sign, under penalty of perjury, a statement in a form determined and retained by the department stating that the owner is in compliance with worker's compensation requirements set forth in Section 3700 of the Labor Code.

(Added by Stats. 1996, Ch. 47, Sec. 1. Effective January 1, 1997.)

11104. (a) Every person, in order to qualify as a driving instructor, as defined in Section 310.4, shall meet all of the following requirements:

(1) On and after July 1, 1973, have a high school education or its equivalent and have satisfactorily completed a course in the teaching of driver education and driver training acceptable to the department.

(2) Within three attempts, pass an examination that the department requires on traffic laws, safe driving practices, operation of motor vehicles, and teaching methods and techniques.

(3) Be physically able to safely operate a motor vehicle and to train others in the operation of motor vehicles.

(4) Hold a valid California driver's license in a class appropriate for the type of vehicle in which instruction will be given.

(5) Not be on probation to the department as a negligent operator.

(6) Have a driving record that does not have an outstanding notice for violating a written promise to appear in court or for willfully failing to pay a lawfully imposed fine, as provided in former Section 40509.

(7) Be 21 years of age or older.

(b) If an applicant cannot meet the requirements of paragraphs (3) and (4) of subdivision (a) because of a physical disability, the department may, at its discretion, issue the applicant a driving school instructor's license restricted to classroom driver education instruction only.

(c) The qualifying requirements referred to in this section shall be met within one year from the date of application for a license, or a new application, examination, and a fee shall be required.

(Amended by Stats. 2022, Ch. 800, Sec. 5. (AB 2746) Effective January 1, 2023.)

11104.3. (a) An all-terrain vehicle safety instructor shall meet all of the following requirements:

(1) Be a person who has not been convicted of a crime involving an act of dishonesty, fraud, or deceit with the intent to benefit themself or another substantially, or to injure another substantially; or has not committed any act that, if done as an all-terrain vehicle safety instructor, would be grounds for the suspension or revocation of the all-terrain vehicle safety instructor's license. A conviction after a plea of nolo contendere shall be deemed to be a conviction within the meaning of this section.

(2) Have a high school education or its equivalent and have satisfactorily completed a course of instruction training in all-terrain vehicle safety as approved by the Off-Highway Vehicle Safety Education Committee.

(3) Within three attempts, pass the examination that the department requires on off-highway vehicle laws, safe driving practices, operation of all-terrain vehicles, and teaching methods and techniques.

(4) Be physically able to safely operate a motor vehicle and to train others in the operation of all-terrain vehicles.

(5) Hold a valid driver's license issued by this state or any contiguous state.

(6) Not be on probation to the department as a negligent operator or the equivalent of that in the state that issued the driver's license.

(7) Have a driver record that does not have an outstanding notice for violating a written promise to appear in court or for willfully failing to pay a lawfully imposed fine, as provided in former Section 40509 or former Section 40509.5 or as provided in equivalent statutes in the state that issued the driver's license.

(8) Be 18 years of age or older.

(9) Be sponsored by an all-terrain vehicle safety training organization.

(b) The qualifying requirements in this section shall be met within one year from the date of application for a license, or a new application, examination, and a fee shall be required.

(Amended by Stats. 2022, Ch. 800, Sec. 6. (AB 2746) Effective January 1, 2023.)

11104.5. Each applicant for a license as a driving school owner, driving school operator, or driving instructor shall submit an application to the department on the forms prescribed by the department. The applicant shall provide the department with any information concerning the applicant's character, honesty, integrity, and reputation which the department may consider necessary.

(Added by Stats. 1987, Ch. 75, Sec. 1.)

11104.6. Each applicant for a license or for renewal of a license under this chapter shall submit an application to the department on the forms prescribed by the department. The applicant shall provide the department any information concerning the applicant's character, honesty, integrity, and reputation which the department considers to be necessary.

This section shall become operative on July 1, 1988.

(Added by Stats. 1987, Ch. 881, Sec. 9. Section operative July 1, 1988, by its own provisions.)

11105. (a) The department shall issue a license certificate to each driving school owner and to each driving school operator when it is satisfied that the owner has met the qualifications required under this chapter. The license shall be for a period of one year from midnight of the last day of the month of issuance unless canceled, suspended, or revoked by the department.

(b) The license shall be renewed annually. The department shall require all of the following for the renewal of the license:

(1) Compliance with the provisions of Sections 11102 and 11105.2 for renewal of a driving school owner's license or Section 11102.5, except paragraph (2) of subdivision (a) of Section 11102.5, for renewal of a driving school operator's license.

(2) Satisfactory completion of an examination as provided in Section 11102.5 at least once during each succeeding three-year period after the initial issuance of a license certificate.

In lieu of any examination for renewal of the license, the department may accept submission by the licensee of evidence of continuing professional education. Professional education, as used in this subdivision, means satisfactory completion of courses related to traffic safety, teaching techniques, or the teaching of driver instruction acceptable to the department or participation in professional seminars approved by the department.

(c) The department may issue a probationary license and certificate subject to conditions to be observed by the licensee in the exercise of the privilege granted. The conditions to be attached to the exercise of the privilege shall not appear on the face of the license or certificate but shall be such as may, in the judgment of the department, be in the public interest and suitable to the qualifications of the applicant as disclosed by the application and investigation by the department of the information contained therein.

(d) Upon notification of death of a driving school licensee the department may issue a certificate of convenience to the executor, executrix, administrator or administratrix of the estate of a deceased holder of a validly outstanding certificate to conduct a driving school, or if no executor, executrix, administrator or administratrix has been appointed, and until a certified copy of an order making such appointment is filed with the department, to the surviving spouse or other heir otherwise entitled to conduct the business of the deceased, permitting such person to conduct the driving school for a period of one year from and after the date of death, and necessary one-year renewals thereafter pending, but not later than, disposal of the business and qualification of the vendee of the business or such surviving spouse or heir for a license certificate to conduct a driving school under the provisions of this division. The department may restrict or condition the certificate and attach to the exercise of the privilege thereunder such terms and conditions as in its judgment the protection of the public requires.

(e) The department shall not issue or renew a license certificate unless it determines that the driving school owner has complied with Section 11103.2.

(Amended by Stats. 1996, Ch. 47, Sec. 2. Effective January 1, 1997.)

11105.1. (a) The department shall issue a license certificate to each driving school instructor and to each all-terrain vehicle safety instructor when it is satisfied that the person has met the qualifications required under this chapter. The original instructor's license and any instructor's license renewed pursuant to subdivisions (b) and (c) is valid for three years from the date issued unless canceled, suspended, or revoked by the department.

(b) A licensee may apply for the renewal of an instructor's license prior to the expiration date of the license. In no event shall an instructor renew the license after the date of expiration.

(c) The department shall require all of the following for the renewal of the instructor's license:

(1) Compliance with Section 11104, except subdivision (c) thereof, for a driving school instructor, or compliance with Section 11104.3, except paragraph (3) of subdivision (a) thereof, for an all-terrain vehicle safety instructor, and, for either, compliance with Section 11105.2.

(2) Satisfactory completion of an examination as provided in Section 11104 or 11104.3, as applicable, at least once during each succeeding three-year period after the initial issuance of an instructor license certificate.

In lieu of any examination for renewal of the license, the department may accept submission by the licensee of evidence of continuing professional education as defined in paragraph (2) of subdivision (b) of Section 11105.

(d) The department may issue a probationary instructor's license and certificate subject to conditions to be observed by the licensee in the exercise of the privilege granted. The conditions to be attached to the exercise of the privilege shall not appear on the face of the license or certificate, but shall be such as may, in the judgment of the department, be in the public interest and suitable to the qualifications of the applicant as disclosed by the application and investigation by the department of the information contained therein.

(e) This section shall become operative on July 1, 1988.

(Repealed (in Sec. 10) and added by Stats. 1987, Ch. 881, Sec. 11. Section operative July 1, 1988, by its own provisions.)

11105.2. (a) The fee for a license issued to a driving school owner or to an all-terrain vehicle safety training organization shall be as follows:

(1) For the original license, or an ownership change which requires a new application, except as provided by Section 42231, a nonrefundable fee of one hundred fifty dollars ($150).

(2) For the annual renewal of a license, a fee of fifty dollars ($50).

(3) If an alteration of an existing license is caused by a firm name change, a change in corporate officer structure, address change, or the addition of a branch location, a fee of seventy dollars ($70).

(4) For replacement of the license when the original license is lost, stolen, or mutilated, a fee of fifteen dollars ($15).

(b) The fee for a license issued to a driving school operator shall be as follows:

(1) For the original license a nonrefundable fee of one hundred dollars ($100).

(2) For the annual renewal of a license, a fee of one hundred dollars ($100).

(3) If an alteration of an existing license is caused by a change in school name or location, or the addition of a branch location, a fee of fifteen dollars ($15).

(4) For replacement of the license when the original license is lost, stolen, or mutilated, a fee of fifteen dollars ($15).

(c) The fee for a license issued to a driving school instructor or to an all-terrain vehicle safety instructor shall be as follows:

(1) For the original license, except as provided by Section 42231, a nonrefundable fee of thirty dollars ($30).

(2) For the triennial renewal of a license, a fee of thirty dollars ($30).

(3) If an alteration of an existing license is caused by a change in the instructor's employing school's name or location, or transfer of the instructor's license to another employing school, a fee of fifteen dollars ($15).

(4) For the replacement of the instructor's license when the original license is lost, stolen, or mutilated, a fee of fifteen dollars ($15).

(d) This section shall become operative on July 1, 1988.

(Repealed (in Sec. 12) and added by Stats. 1987, Ch. 881, Sec. 13. Section operative July 1, 1988, by its own provisions.)

11105.3. Any school owner, operator, or instructor required to be licensed under this chapter who fails to renew the license prior to the expiration of the license in accordance with Sections 11105 and 11105.1 and whose license was not canceled, suspended, or revoked by the department at the time of expiration, may reapply for an original license pursuant to Section 11102, 11102.5, 11104, or 11104.3.

This section shall become operative on July 1, 1988.

(Repealed (in Sec. 14) and added by Stats. 1987, Ch. 881, Sec. 15. Section operative July 1, 1988, by its own provisions.)

11105.5. The department shall issue an independent driving instructor's license to permit instruction in any city with a population of less than 50,000, which does not have within it an established licensed driving school, to any person who meets the requirements of this chapter relating to instructor's and independent instructor's licenses, even though such person is not an employee of, or otherwise associated with or instructing through, a driving school, except that no independent driving instructor's license shall be issued to a person to instruct in counties with a population in excess of 400,000. In addition, an independent instructor must at all times be employed as an accredited teacher of automobile driver education or automobile driver training under the provisions of the Education Code.

(Amended by Stats. 1971, Ch. 438.)

11105.6. (a) The department shall issue a license to an all-terrain vehicle safety training organization when the department is satisfied that the organization has met the qualifications required under this chapter and has been approved and certified by the Off-Highway Vehicle Safety Education Committee. The license shall be valid for a period of one year from midnight of the last day of the month of issuance unless canceled, suspended, or revoked by the department.

(b) The license shall be renewed annually. The department shall require compliance with Sections 11102 and 11105.2 for the renewal of the license.

(c) This section shall become operative on July 1, 1988.

(Added by Stats. 1987, Ch. 881, Sec. 16. Section operative July 1, 1988, by its own provisions.)

11106. (a) Until the department is satisfied that the applicant has met the requirements under this chapter, it may issue a temporary permit to any person applying for a license issued pursuant to this chapter. The temporary permit authorizes the operation of a school or the giving of instruction for a period not to exceed 120 days while the department is completing its investigation and determination of all facts relative to the qualifications of the applicant for the license.

(b) A temporary permit valid for 30 days may be issued to any applicant for an original instructor's license pending satisfactory completion of the course required by subdivision (b) of Section 11104 or paragraph 2 of subdivision (a) of Section 11104.3, as applicable. This subdivision does not extend the period of validity of any temporary permit issued pursuant to subdivision (a).

(c) The department may cancel a temporary permit when it has determined, or has reasonable cause to believe, that the application is incorrect or incomplete or the temporary permit was issued in error. A temporary permit is invalid when canceled or when the applicant's license has been issued or refused.

(d) This section shall become operative on July 1, 1988.

(Repealed (in Sec. 17) and added by Stats. 1987, Ch. 881, Sec. 18. Section operative July 1, 1988, by its own provisions.)

11107. (a) The department may refuse to issue a license certificate under this chapter to any applicant to own or operate a school or to any instructor when it finds and determines any of the following to exist:

(1) The applicant has not met the qualifications required under this chapter.

(2) The applicant was previously the holder of a license under this chapter which was revoked or suspended, which was never reissued by the department after revocation, or which was never reinstated after suspension.

(3) The applicant was previously the holder of an occupational license issued by another state, authorizing the same or similar activities of a license issued under this division; and that license was revoked or suspended for cause and was never reissued, or was suspended for cause, and the terms of suspension have not been fulfilled.

(4) The applicant has done any act or series of acts which would be a cause for suspension or revocation under Section 11110.

(5) If the applicant is a business, a business representative was the

holder of a revoked or suspended license previously issued under this chapter which was never reissued after revocation or which was never reinstated after suspension, or a business representative, though not previously the holder of a license, has done any act or series of acts which would be a cause for revocation or suspension under Section 11110.

(6) By reason of the facts and circumstances relating to the organization, control, and management of the business, it is likely that the policy or operation of the business will be directed, controlled, or managed by a business representative who, by reason of any act, series of acts, or conduct described in paragraph (4) or (5), would be ineligible for a license and that, by licensing the business, the purposes of this division would be defeated.

(7) The applicant has knowingly made a false statement or knowingly concealed a material fact in applying for a license.

(8) The applicant, or one of the business representatives if the applicant is a business, has been convicted of a crime, or has committed any act or engaged in conduct involving moral turpitude, which is substantially related to the qualifications, functions, or duties of the licensed activity. A conviction after a plea of nolo contendere is a conviction within the meaning of this section.

(b) Upon refusal of the department to issue a license, the applicant may demand, in writing, a hearing before the director or the director's representative within 60 days after notice of refusal.

The hearing shall be conducted pursuant to Chapter 5 (commencing with Section 11500) of Part 1 of Division 3 of Title 2 of the Government Code.

(c) A person whose license has been revoked, or whose application for a license has been refused, may reapply for the license after a period of not less than one year has elapsed from the effective date of the decision revoking the license or refusing the application.

(Amended by Stats. 1998, Ch. 877, Sec. 42. Effective January 1, 1999.)

11108. (a) Every person licensed under this chapter shall keep a record showing all of the following:

(1) The name and address and license number of the school.

(2) The name and address of each person given instruction.

(3) Excepting all-terrain vehicle safety training organizations, the instruction permit number or driver's license number of every person given instruction in the driving of a motor vehicle.

(4) Excepting all-terrain vehicle safety training organizations, the date any instruction permit was issued.

(5) The name and instructor's license number of each instructor.

(6) The particular type of instruction given and the date of the instruction.

(7) The amount of time devoted to each type of instruction.

(8) The total number of hours of instruction.

(9) The total cost to the student of the instruction.

(b) The records shall be retained for at least three years and shall be open to the inspection of the department at all reasonable times, but shall be only for the confidential use of the department.

(c) Whenever the licensee suspends or terminates the licensed activity, the licensee shall surrender the records to the department for examination not later than the end of the third day, excluding Saturdays, Sundays, and legal holidays, after the date of suspension or termination. The department may duplicate or make a record of any information contained in the licensee's records. All of the licensee's records shall be returned to the licensee not later than 30 days after the date of surrender.

(d) Every all-terrain vehicle safety training organization shall maintain records for all-terrain vehicle safety instructors who are authorized to offer that organization's courses of instruction.

(e) Each all-terrain vehicle safety instructor shall report the information required under this section to the all-terrain vehicle safety training organization no later than the 15th day of the month following the date instruction was provided. Instructors shall notify the organization, which shall, in turn, notify the department at least 30 days in advance of providing a course of instruction, of the time, date, location, and type of instruction to be given.

(f) This section shall become operative on July 1, 1988.

(Repealed (in Sec. 21) and added by Stats. 1987, Ch. 881, Sec. 22. Section operative July 1, 1988, by its own provisions.)

11108.5. (a) Every school owner licensed pursuant to this chapter shall notify the department within 10 days of any change in the ownership or corporate structure of the licensee.

(b) Every school owner licensed pursuant to this chapter shall immediately notify the department upon changing the site or location of the school's established place of business.

(c) Every school operator and every instructor licensed pursuant to this chapter shall report to the department every change of residence address within five days of the change.

(d) This section shall become operative on July 1, 1988.

(Repealed (in Sec. 23) and added by Stats. 1987, Ch. 881, Sec. 24. Section operative July 1, 1988, by its own provisions.)

11109. Every licensee under this chapter shall maintain all vehicles used in driver training in safe mechanical condition at all times.

(Enacted by Stats. 1959, Ch. 3.)

11110. (a) The department, after notice and hearing, may suspend or revoke a license issued under this chapter if any of the following occurs:

(1) The department finds and determines that the licensee fails to meet the requirements to receive or hold a license under this chapter.

(2) The licensee fails to keep the records required by this chapter.

(3) The licensee (A) permits fraud or engages in fraudulent practices either with reference to an applicant for a driver's license or an all-terrain vehicle safety certificate from the department, or (B) induces or countenances fraud or fraudulent practices on the part of an applicant.

(4) The licensee fails to comply with this chapter or regulation or requirement of the department adopted pursuant thereto.

(5) The licensee represents himself or herself as an agent or employee of the department or uses advertising designed to create the impression, or that would reasonably have the effect of leading persons to believe, that the licensee is in fact an employee or representative of the department; or the licensee makes an advertisement, in any manner or by any means, that is untrue or misleading and that is known, or that by the exercise of reasonable care should be known, to be untrue or misleading.

(6) The licensee, or an employee or agent of the licensee, solicits driver training or instruction or all-terrain vehicle safety instruction in, or within 200 feet of, an office of the department.

(7) The licensee is convicted of violating Section 14606, 20001, 20002, 20003, 20004, 20006, 20008, 23103, 23104, 23105, 23152, or 23153 of this code or subdivision (b) of Section 191.5 or subdivision (c) of Section 192 of the Penal Code. A conviction, after a plea of nolo contendere, is a conviction within the meaning of this paragraph.

(8) The licensee teaches, or permits a student to be taught, the specific tests administered by the department through use of the department's forms or testing facilities.

(9) The licensee conducts training, or permits training by an employee, in an unsafe manner or contrary to safe driving practices.

(10) The licensed school owner or licensed driving school operator teaches, or permits an employee to teach, driving instruction or all-terrain vehicle safety instruction without a valid instructor's license.

(11) The licensed school owner does not have in effect a bond as required by Section 11102.

(12) The licensee permits the use of the license by any other person for the purpose of permitting that person to engage in the ownership or operation of a school or in the giving of driving instruction or all-terrain vehicle safety instruction for compensation.

(13) The licensee holds a secondary teaching credential and explicitly or implicitly recruits or attempts to recruit a pupil who is enrolled in a junior or senior high school to be a customer for a business licensed pursuant to this article that is owned by the licensee or for which the

licensee is an employee.

(b) In the interest of the public's safety, as determined by the department, the department may immediately suspend the license of a licensee for an alleged violation under this chapter and shall conduct a hearing of the alleged violation within 30 days of the suspension.

(Amended by Stats. 2007, Ch. 747, Sec. 14.5. Effective January 1, 2008.)

11110.1. Any of the causes specified in this chapter as a cause for refusal to issue a license under this chapter is cause to suspend or revoke a license under this chapter.

(Added by Stats. 1990, Ch. 1563, Sec. 12.)

11110.2. The license issued to a school owner shall be automatically canceled upon the happening of any of the following:

(a) The abandonment of the established place of business or the change thereof without notice to the department pursuant to Section 11108.5.

(b) The failure to maintain an adequate bond or to procure and file another bond, as required by Section 11102, prior to the effective date of the termination by the surety of any existing bond.

(c) The voluntary or involuntary surrender of the license, except that a surrender or cessation of business by the licensee, or the suspension or revocation of the corporate status of the licensee, does not preclude the department from filing an accusation for revocation or suspension of the surrendered license, as provided in Section 11110, or affect the department's decision to suspend or revoke the license.

(d) Notification to the department that the person designated as licensee has changed.

(e) Suspension or revocation of the corporate status of the licensee.

(Amended by Stats. 1990, Ch. 1563, Sec. 13.)

11110.5. The department may cancel any license issued under this chapter when that license has been issued in error or voluntarily surrendered to the department for cancellation. Whenever a driving school operator's license or an instructor's license is canceled, it shall be without prejudice and shall be surrendered to the department. Any person whose license has been canceled may immediately apply for a license, and the application may be accepted without additional fee or examination under rules and regulations adopted by the department.

This section shall become operative on July 1, 1988.

(Repealed (in Sec. 29) and added by Stats. 1987, Ch. 881, Sec. 30. Section operative July 1, 1988, by its own provisions.)

11110.7. (a) The department, after notice and hearing, on an interim basis, may refuse to issue or may suspend a license issued under this chapter when the applicant or licensee, or a business representative if the applicant or licensee is a business, has been convicted of a crime involving moral turpitude which is substantially related to the qualifications, functions, or duties of the licensed activity, if an appeal of the conviction is pending or the conviction has otherwise not become final. A conviction after a plea of nolo contendere is a conviction within the meaning of this section.

(b) If a conviction, upon which an interim refusal to issue or suspension under subdivision (a) is based, is affirmed on appeal or otherwise becomes final, the refusal to issue or the suspension shall automatically become effective as a denial or revocation, as the case may be, of the license. If the interim refusal to issue or the suspension was stayed under probationary terms and conditions, the subsequent automatic denial or revocation shall also be stayed under the same terms and conditions for a term not to exceed the original term of probation for the interim refusal to issue or suspension.

(c) If a conviction, upon which an interim refusal to issue or suspension under subdivision (a) is based, is reversed on appeal, the department shall set aside immediately that refusal or suspension.

(Added by Stats. 1990, Ch. 1563, Sec. 14.)

11111. (a) Every licensee under this chapter is entitled to notice and hearing prior to cancellation, suspension, or revocation of the license by the department, except that the department shall immediately cancel the license without a hearing for failure of the licensee to meet and maintain the requirements of paragraph (1), (3), or (4) of subdivision (a) of Section 11102, or Section 11103 or 11103.1, or paragraph (4), (5), or (6) of subdivision (a) of Section 11104, or paragraph (4), (5), or (6) of subdivision (a) of Section 11104.3, or Section 11110.2.

(b) The notice and hearings provided for in this chapter shall be pursuant to Chapter 5 (commencing with Section 11500) of Part 1 of Division 3 of Title 2 of the Government Code.

(c) Any action of the department in suspending, canceling, or revoking, or failing to renew a license may be reviewed by any court of competent jurisdiction.

(d) The department may, pending a hearing, temporarily suspend the license or permit of any person licensed under this chapter for not more than 30 days if the director finds that the action is required in the public interest. In that case, a hearing shall be held and a decision issued within 30 days after notice of the temporary suspension.

(e) The suspension, expiration, or cancellation of a license issued under this chapter does not preclude the filing of an accusation for the revocation or suspension of the suspended, expired, or canceled license as provided in Section 11110, and does not invalidate or otherwise preclude a decision by the department to suspend or revoke the license. That determination may be considered in granting or refusing to grant any subsequent license authorized by this chapter to the same licensee, or to any partner, officer, director, or stockholder of the same licensee.

(Amended by Stats. 1990, Ch. 1563, Sec. 15.)

11111.2. Any owner licensed under this chapter who has closed his or her established place of business or any operator or instructor currently or previously licensed under this chapter who no longer resides at the address last filed with the department, may be served with process issued pursuant to Chapter 5 (commencing with Section 11500) of Part 1 of Division 3 of Title 2 of the Government Code by registered mail at that place of business, in the case of an owner, or at that residence, in the case of an operator or instructor, unless the person has notified the department in writing of another address where service may be made.

(Added by Stats. 1988, Ch. 751, Sec. 1.)

11111.5. (a) After the filing of an accusation under this chapter, the director may enter into a stipulated compromise settlement agreement with the consent of the licensee on terms and conditions mutually agreeable to the director, the respondent licensee, and the accuser without further hearing or appeal. The agreement may include, but is not limited to, a period of probation or monetary penalties, or both. The monetary penalty shall not exceed one thousand dollars ($1,000) for driving school owners or for a principal in an all-terrain vehicle safety training organization or five hundred dollars ($500) for driving school operators or for driving instructors or all-terrain vehicle safety instructors for each violation, and the monetary penalty shall be based on the nature of the violation and the effect of the violation on the purposes of this chapter.

(b) A compromise settlement agreement may be entered before, during, or after the hearing, but is valid only if executed and filed pursuant to subdivision (d) before the proposed decision of the hearing officer, if any, is adopted or the case is decided.

(c) The department shall adopt, by regulation, a schedule of maximum and minimum amounts of monetary penalties, the payment of which may be included as a term or condition of a compromise settlement agreement entered under subdivision (a). Any monetary penalty included in a compromise settlement agreement shall be within the range of monetary penalties in that schedule.

(d) Any compromise settlement agreement entered under this section shall be signed by the director, the respondent licensee, and the accuser, or by their authorized representatives. The director shall file, or cause to be filed, the agreement with the Office of Administrative Hearings, together with the department's notice of withdrawal of the accusation or statement of issues upon which the action was initiated.

(e) If the respondent licensee fails to perform all of the terms and conditions of the compromise settlement agreement, the agreement is void and the department may take any action authorized by law notwithstanding the agreement, including, but not limited to, refiling the accusation or imposing license sanctions.

(f) This section shall become operative on July 1, 1988.

(Repealed (in Sec. 33) and added by Stats. 1987, Ch. 881, Sec. 34. Section operative July 1, 1988, by its own provisions.)

11112. Upon refusal of the department to issue a license, the applicant shall be entitled to demand in writing a hearing before the director or his representative within 60 days after notice of refusal.

The hearing shall be conducted pursuant to Chapter 5 (commencing at Section 11500), Part 1, Division 3, Title 2 of the Government Code.

(Added by Stats. 1959, Ch. 1996.)

11113. (a) The director may prescribe rules and regulations for driving schools regarding the conduct of courses of driver education and driver training, including curriculum, facilities, and equipment. The rules and regulations regarding curriculum shall require all the following:

(1) A component relating to the dangers involved in consuming alcohol or drugs in connection with the operation of a motor vehicle.

(2) A component examining driver attitude and motivation that focuses on the reduction of future driving violations, with particular emphasis on aggressive driving behavior and behavior commonly known as "road rage."

(3) Viewing the Department of Justice's video on proper conduct during a traffic stop created pursuant to Section 1656.1.

(b) The director may also prescribe rules and regulations for the conduct of driving instructor training courses required by Sections 11102.5 and 11104, including curriculum, facilities, and equipment. The department shall monitor instruction given by driving schools.

(Amended by Stats. 2022, Ch. 332, Sec. 3. (AB 2537) Effective January 1, 2023.)

11113.3. The rules and regulations adopted pursuant to Section 11113 regarding the curriculum shall include, but are not limited to, the rights and duties of a motorist as they relate to traffic laws and traffic safety.

(Added by Stats. 2000, Ch. 833, Sec. 5. Effective January 1, 2001.)

11113.5. The department shall establish rules and regulations prescribing standards for the licensing and control, as provided in this chapter, of owners, operators, and instructors and the courses of driver education and driver training for driving schools providing training courses for class 1 and class 2 licensed drivers. The standards shall provide for requirements of licensing, training, and control to assure that the owners, operators, and instructors are qualified to provide the type of training needed by drivers for safe operation of large commercial vehicles on the highway.

(Added by Stats. 1985, Ch. 387, Sec. 1.)

11114. The department may require any person licensed under this chapter to submit to a reexamination of his qualifications when there is reasonable cause to believe that the licensee does not have the ability to give driving instruction. If the licensee refuses or fails to submit to such reexamination, the department may peremptorily suspend his license until such time as the licensee shall have submitted to reexamination. The suspension shall be effective upon notice.

(Repealed and added by Stats. 1975, Ch. 703.)

Chapter 1.5. Traffic Violator Schools

(Chapter 1.5 added by Stats. 1984, Ch. 1037, Sec. 4.)

11200. (a) The department shall license schools for traffic violators for purposes of Section 41501 or 42005 and to provide traffic safety instruction to other persons who elect to attend. A person may not own or operate a traffic violator school or, except as provided in Section 11206, give instruction for compensation in a traffic violator school without a currently valid license issued by the department.

(b) (1) Any person who elects to attend a traffic violator school shall receive from the traffic violator school and shall sign a copy of the following consumer disclosure statement prior to the payment of the school fee and attending the school:

"Course content is limited to traffic violator curricula approved by the Department of Motor Vehicles. Students in the classroom include traffic offenders, repeat traffic offenders, adults, and teenagers, and those who have and those who have not been referred by a court. Instructor training, business regulatory standards, and Vehicle Code requirements of traffic violator schools are not equal to the training, standards, and Vehicle Code requirements of licensed driving schools (California Vehicle Code Section 11200(b)(1))."

(2) In the case of a minor who elects to attend a traffic violator school, the minor's parent or guardian shall sign the consumer disclosure statement.

(3) A copy of each signed disclosure statement shall be retained by the traffic violator school for a minimum of 36 months.

(c) New and modified departmental regulations necessitated by this section shall be adopted and effective no later than September 1, 2011.

(d) A licensed traffic violator school shall notify the court by posting on the department's Web-based database established pursuant to subdivision (b) of Section 11205 information regarding successful course completions.

(e) A licensed traffic violator school shall give every person who attends the school for purposes of Sections 41501 or 42005, upon successful completion of the lesson plan and passage of the postlesson knowledge test, a receipt indicating successful completion. The receipt shall include contact information, including the name of the traffic violator school, address of the school's business location, name of the course instructor if classroom-based, telephone number, e-mail address if appropriate, hours of operation, and any other information that may be used to confirm course completion.

(f) This section shall become operative on September 1, 2011.

(Repealed (in Sec. 3) and added by Stats. 2010, Ch. 599, Sec. 3.5. (AB 2499) Effective January 1, 2011. Section operative September 1, 2011, by its own provisions.)

11202. (a) A traffic violator school owner shall meet all of the following criteria before a license may be issued for the traffic violator school:

(1) Maintain an established place of business in this state that is open to the public. An office or place of business of a traffic violator school, including any traffic violator school branch or classroom location, shall not be situated within 500 feet of any court of law or within 50 feet of another licensed traffic violator school. The office or place of business shall be a separate and enclosed space consisting of a minimum of 100 square feet and shall have a lockable entry door.

(2) Be open to the public and maintain regular business hours Monday to Friday, inclusive, excluding state and federal holidays. The business hours shall be posted at the established place of business and on any internet website used or maintained by the traffic violator school.

(3) Have an operator or employee in each office or place of business during regular business hours.

(4) Have a name that does not include a cost, price, or amount of the traffic violator school course, unless that name accurately reflects the cost of the course.

(5) Conform to standards established by regulation of the department. In adopting the standards, the department shall consider those practices and instructional programs that may reasonably foster the knowledge, skills, and judgment necessary for compliance with traffic laws. The department shall establish standards for each instructional modality, which may include requirements specific to each modality. The standards may include, but are not limited to, classroom facilities, school personnel, equipment, curriculum, procedures for the testing and evaluation of students, recordkeeping, and business practices.

(6) Procure and file with the department a bond of fifteen thousand dollars ($15,000) executed by an admitted surety and conditioned upon the applicant not practicing fraud or making a fraudulent representation that will cause a monetary loss to a person taking instruction from the applicant or to the state or any local authority.

(7) Have the proper equipment necessary for giving instruction to traffic violators.

(8) Have a lesson plan approved by the department, and provide not less than the minimum instructional time specified in the approved plan. The approved plan shall include a postlesson knowledge test. The lesson plan for each instructional modality shall require separate approval by the department.

(9) (A) Execute and file with the department an instrument designating the director as agent of the applicant for service of process, as provided in this paragraph, in any action commenced against the applicant arising out of a claim for damages suffered by a person due to the applicant's violation of a provision of this code committed in relation to the specifications of the applicant's traffic violator school or a condition of the bond required by paragraph (6).

(B) The applicant shall stipulate in the instrument that a process directed to the applicant, when personal service cannot be made in this state after due diligence, may be served instead upon the director or, in the director's absence from the department's principal offices, upon an employee in charge of the office of the director, and that this substituted service is of the same effect as personal service on the applicant. The instrument shall further stipulate that the agency created by the designation shall continue during the period covered by the license issued pursuant to this section and so long thereafter as the applicant may be made to answer in damages for a violation of this code for which the surety may be made liable or a condition of the bond.

(C) The instrument designating the director as agent for service of process shall be acknowledged by the applicant before a notary public.

(D) If the director or an employee of the department, in lieu of the director, is served with a summons and complaint on behalf of the licensee, one copy of the summons and complaint shall be left with the director or in the director's office in Sacramento or mailed to the office of the director in Sacramento. A fee of five dollars ($5) shall also be paid to the director or employee at the time of service of the copy of the summons and complaint, or shall be included with a summons and complaint served by mail.

(E) The service on the director or department employee pursuant to this paragraph is sufficient service on the licensee if a notice of the service and a copy of the summons and complaint are, on the same day as the service or mailing of the summons and complaint, sent by registered mail by the plaintiff or the plaintiff's attorney to the licensee. A copy of the summons and complaint shall also be mailed by the plaintiff or plaintiff's attorney to the surety on the licensee's bond at the address of the surety given in the bond, postpaid and registered with request for return receipt.

(F) The director shall keep a record of all processes served pursuant to this paragraph showing the day and hour of service, and shall retain the documents served in the department's files.

(G) If the licensee is served with process by service upon the director or a department employee in lieu of the director, the licensee has 30 days after that service within which to answer any complaint or other pleading filed in the cause. For purposes of venue, if the licensee is served with process by service upon the director or a department employee in lieu of the director, the service is considered to have been made upon the licensee in the county in which the licensee has or last had an established place of business.

(10) (A) Meet the requirements of Section 11202.5, relating to traffic violator school operators, if the owner is also the operator of the traffic violator school. If the owner is not the operator of the traffic violator school, the owner shall designate an employee as operator who shall meet the requirements of Section 11202.5.

(B) A person may be an operator for more than one traffic violator school if (i) the schools have a common owner or owners and (ii) the schools share a single established business address.

(C) A traffic violator school with multiple branch locations may designate a separate licensed operator for each location, but shall designate one of the licensed operators as the primary contact for the department.

(11) Have an instructor who meets the requirements of Section 11206. An owner who is designated as the operator for the school is authorized to act as an instructor without meeting the requirements of Section 11206. The owner license may also include authorization to act as an instructor if the owner is not designated as the operator but meets the requirements of Section 11206. The owner license shall specify if the owner is authorized to offer instruction. If the owner is not approved to act as an instructor, the school must employ an instructor licensed pursuant to Section 11206.

(12) Provide the department with a written assurance that the school will comply with the applicable provisions of Subchapter II or III of the Americans with Disabilities Act of 1990 (42 U.S.C. Sec. 12101 et seq.), and any other federal and state laws prohibiting discrimination against individuals with disabilities. Compliance may include providing sign language interpreters or other accommodations for students with disabilities.

(b) The qualifying requirements specified in subdivision (a) shall be met within one year from the date of application for a license, or a new application and fee are required.

(c) Paragraphs (6) and (9) of subdivision (a) do not apply to public schools or other public agencies, which shall also not be required to post a cash deposit pursuant to Section 11203.

(d) Paragraphs (1), (2), (3), and (10) of subdivision (a) do not apply to public schools or other public educational institutions.

(e) A notice approved by the department shall be posted in every traffic violator school, branch, and classroom location, and prominently displayed on a home study or internet program, stating that any person involved in the offering of, or soliciting for, a completion certificate for attendance at a traffic violator school program in which the person does not attend or does not complete the minimum amount of instruction time may be guilty of violating Section 134 of the Penal Code.

(f) This section shall become operative on July 1, 2020.

(Amended (as added by Stats. 2019, Ch. 307, Sec. 2) by Stats. 2020, Ch. 370, Sec. 266. (SB 1371) Effective January 1, 2021.)

11202.5. (a) The department shall license traffic violator school operators. A person shall not act as a traffic violator school operator without a currently valid license issued by the department, unless the person is an owner/operator and is so designated on the owner's license. Every person, in order to qualify as a traffic violator school operator, shall meet all of the following criteria in order to be issued a traffic violator school operator's license:

(1) Have not committed any act which, if the applicant were licensed as a traffic violator school operator, would be grounds for suspension or revocation of the license.

(2) Within three attempts, pass an examination that the department requires on traffic laws, safe driving practices, operation of motor vehicles, teaching methods and techniques, traffic violator school statutes and regulations, and office procedures and recordkeeping.

(3) Be 21 years of age or older.

(4) Have successfully completed an educational program of not less than four hours. The program shall include, but is not limited to, operator responsibilities, current laws, and the regulations in Article 4 of Title 13 of the California Code of Regulations. The instruction may be provided by generally accredited educational institutions, private vocational schools, and education programs and seminars offered by professional societies, organizations, trade associations, and other educational and technical programs that meet the requirements of this section.

(5) Provide a certification from the owner that the applicant has the knowledge necessary to perform the duties of the operator.

(b) All the qualifying requirements specified in this section shall be met within one year from the date of application for the license or the application shall lapse. However, the applicant may thereafter submit a new application upon payment of the required fee.

(Amended by Stats. 2010, Ch. 599, Sec. 7. (AB 2499) Effective January 1, 2011.)

11203. In lieu of the bond otherwise required by paragraph (3) of subdivision (a) of Section 11202, the applicant may make a deposit pursuant to Article 7 (commencing with Section 995.710) of Chapter 2 of Title 14 of Part 2 of the Code of Civil Procedure. The director may order the deposit returned at the expiration of three years from the date a traffic violator school licensee has ceased to do business, or three years from the date a licensee has ceased to be licensed, if the director is satisfied that there are no outstanding claims against the deposit. A superior court may, upon petition, order the return of the deposit prior to the expiration of three years upon evidence satisfactory to the court that there are no outstanding claims against the deposit. If either the director, department, or state is a defendant in any civil action instituted to recover all or any part of the deposit, or any civil action is instituted by the director, department, or state to determine those entitled to any part of the deposit, the director, department, or state shall be paid reasonable attorney fees and costs from the deposit. Costs shall include those administrative costs incurred in processing claims against the licensee recoverable from the deposit.

(Amended by Stats. 2002, Ch. 784, Sec. 598. Effective January 1, 2003.)

11203.5. If the state or any of its political subdivisions suffers any loss or damage by reason of any fraudulent practice or representation or by reason of any violation of this division by a traffic violator school owner, the department may bring a cause of action against the traffic violator school owner and the surety upon the owner's bond.

(Added by Stats. 1988, Ch. 1221, Sec. 3.)

11204. (a) The department shall issue a license certificate to each traffic violator school owner and each traffic violator school operator licensed pursuant to this chapter. The term of the license shall be for a period of one year from the date of issue unless canceled, suspended, or revoked by the department. The license shall be renewed annually. The department shall require compliance with Section 11202 for renewal of the license of a traffic violator school owner. The department shall require compliance with Section 11202.5 for renewal of the license of a traffic violator school operator.

(b) (1) In lieu of the examination required by Section 11202.5 for renewal of the license of a traffic violator school operator, the department may accept submission of evidence by the licensee of continuing professional education.

(2) "Professional education," as used in paragraph (1), means the satisfactory completion of courses acceptable to the department related to traffic safety, teaching techniques, or the teaching of driver instruction, or the participation in professional seminars approved by the department.

(c) Whenever in its judgment the public interest so requires, the department may issue a probationary license subject to special conditions to be observed by the licensee in the conduct of the traffic violator school. The conditions to be attached to the license shall be any that may, in the judgment of the department, be in the public interest and suitable to the qualifications of the applicant as disclosed by the application and investigation by the department of the information contained therein. The conditions may not appear on the license certificate.

(d) Upon notification of the death of a traffic violator school licensee, the department may issue a temporary license to the executor or administrator of the estate of a deceased holder of a validly outstanding license to conduct a traffic violator school, or if no executor or administrator has been appointed and until a certified copy of an order making an appointment is filed with the department, a temporary license may be issued to the surviving spouse or other heir entitled to conduct the business of the deceased. The temporary license shall permit the holder to conduct the traffic violator school for a period of one year from and after the date of the original licensee's death, and necessary one-year extensions may be granted to permit disposal of the business and qualification for a license of a purchaser of the business or the surviving spouse or heir. The department may restrict or condition a temporary license and attach to the exercise of the privilege thereunder any terms and conditions that in the department's judgment are required for the protection of the public.

(Amended by Stats. 2003, Ch. 594, Sec. 33. Effective January 1, 2004.)

11205. (a) The department shall provide a list of licensed traffic violator schools on its Internet Web site. For each licensed school, the list shall indicate the modalities of instruction offered and specify the cities where classroom instruction is offered. The sequential listing of licensed schools shall be randomized daily.

(b) When a court or traffic assistance program (TAP) provides a hard copy list of licensed traffic violator schools to a traffic violator, the court or TAP shall provide only a current date-stamped list downloaded from the department's Internet Web site. The hard copy list shall be as current as practicable, but in no event shall a list be distributed with a date stamp that is more than 60 days old.

(c) The department shall, by April 1, 2012, develop a Web-based database that will enable the department, the courts, and traffic violator schools to monitor, report, and track participation and course completion. Traffic violator schools shall update course information within three business days of class completion and provide to the courts class completion information on a daily basis.

(d) This section shall become operative on September 1, 2011.

(Repealed (in Sec. 5) and added by Stats. 2010, Ch. 599, Sec. 5.5. (AB 2499) Effective January 1, 2011. Section operative September 1, 2011, by its own provisions.)

11205.1. Until January 1, 2013, the fee authorized in subdivision (d) of Section 11205.2, and after January 1, 2013, the fee authorized in subdivision (c) of Section 11205.2, shall be applicable only in those instances where a traffic violator has agreed to attend or has been ordered to attend a traffic violator school pursuant to Section 41501 or 42005.

(Amended by Stats. 2010, Ch. 599, Sec. 6. (AB 2499) Effective January 1, 2011.)

11205.2. (a) As used in this chapter, a traffic assistance program (TAP) is a public or private nonprofit agency that provides services, under contract with a court to process traffic violators or under contract with the department to assist in oversight activities.

(b) A court may use a TAP to assist the court in performing services related to the processing of traffic violators. As used in this section, "services" means those services relating to the processing of traffic infraction cases at, and for, the court, including printing and providing to the court and traffic violators hard copy county-specific lists printed from the department's Internet Web site, administratively assisting traffic violators, and any other lawful activity relating to the administration of the court's traffic infraction caseload.

(c) The court may charge a traffic violator a fee to defray the costs incurred by a TAP for traffic case administration services provided to the court pursuant to subdivision (b). The court may delegate collection of the fee to the TAP. Fees shall be approved and regulated by the court. The fee shall not exceed the actual costs incurred by the TAP for the activities authorized under subdivision (b).

(d) This section shall become operative on January 1, 2013.

(Repealed (in Sec. 7) and added by Stats. 2010, Ch. 599, Sec. 7.5. (AB 2499) Effective January 1, 2011. Section operative January 1, 2013, by its own provisions.)

11205.4. (a) The department may use a traffic assistance program (TAP), or until January 1, 2013, a CAP established pursuant to Section 11205.2, for monitoring of licensed traffic violator schools, including, but not limited to, audits, inspections, review and examination of business records, class records, business practices, the content of the program of instruction set forth in the lesson plan, or curriculum of a licensee. Inspection includes, but is not limited to, the review of the business office, branch office, and applicable classroom facilities of a licensee. Monitoring includes onsite review of actual presentation of the traffic safety instruction provided in a classroom and any other activity deemed necessary to ensure high-quality education of traffic violators.

(b) This section shall become operative on September 1, 2011.

(Amended (as added by Stats. 2010, Ch. 599) by Stats. 2011, Ch. 296, Sec. 302. (AB 1023) Effective January 1, 2012.)

11206. (a) The department shall license traffic violator school instructors. Except as exempted by this section, no person shall act as a traffic violator school instructor without a currently valid instructor's license issued by the department. Every person, in order to qualify as a traffic violator school instructor, shall meet all of the following requirements before an instructor's license may be issued:

(1) Have a high school education.

(2) Within three attempts, pass an examination, as required by the department, on traffic laws, safe driving practices, operation of motor vehicles, and teaching methods and techniques.

(3) Hold a currently valid California driver's license that is not subject to probation pursuant to Section 14250 due to the applicant being a negligent operator within the meaning of Section 12810 or 12810.5. The applicant's driving record shall not have any outstanding notice for violating a written promise to appear in court or for willfully failing to pay a lawfully imposed fine, as provided in former Section 40509.

(4) Be 18 years of age or older.

(b) All the qualifying requirements specified by this section shall be met within one year from the date of application for a license or the application shall lapse. However, the applicant may thereafter submit a new application upon payment of the requisite fee.

(c) A license issued pursuant to this section is not required to provide instruction to traffic violators in a public school or other public educational institution by a person holding a valid teaching credential with satisfactory training or experience in the subject area, as determined by the department. Persons exempt from licensure under this section are not required to obtain a license certificate pursuant to Section 11207.

(Amended by Stats. 2022, Ch. 800, Sec. 7. (AB 2746) Effective January 1, 2023.)

11206.5. Each applicant for a license as a traffic violator school owner, traffic violator school operator, or traffic violator school instructor shall submit an application to the department on the forms prescribed by the department. The applicant shall provide the department with any information concerning the applicant's character, honesty, integrity, and reputation which the department may consider necessary.

(Added by Stats. 1987, Ch. 75, Sec. 2.)

11207. (a) The department shall issue a license certificate to each traffic violator school instructor when it is satisfied that he or she has met the qualifications required under this chapter. The original instructor license and any license renewed pursuant to subdivisions (b) and (c) shall be valid for a period of three years from the date of issuance unless canceled, suspended, or revoked by the department.

(b) Every application for the renewal of a traffic violator school instructor license may be made by the licensee prior to the expiration date of the license by presenting to the department a completed application on a form provided by the department. In no event shall a traffic violator school instructor renew the license after the date of expiration.

(c) The department shall require all of the following for the renewal of an instructor's license:

(1) Compliance with Section 11206, except subdivision (c) thereof.

(2) Satisfactory completion of an examination as provided in Section 11206 at least once during each succeeding three-year period after the initial issuance of the license. However, in lieu of examination for renewal of the license, the department may accept submission by the licensee of evidence of continuing professional education.

(d) When, in its judgment, the public interest so requires, the department may issue a probationary license subject to special conditions to be observed by the licensee in the exercise of the privilege granted. The conditions to be attached to the license shall be such as may, in the judgment of the department, be in the public interest and suitable to the qualifications of the applicant, as disclosed by the application and investigation by the department of the information contained therein.

(Amended by Stats. 1987, Ch. 111, Sec. 2.)

11208. (a) The department shall charge a fee, to be determined by the department, for the following traffic violator school program activities:

(1) Original issuance of a traffic violator school owner, operator, instructor, and branch or classroom location license.

(2) Renewal of a traffic violator school owner, operator, instructor, and branch or classroom location license.

(3) Issuance of a duplicate or corrected traffic violator school owner, operator, instructor, and branch or classroom location license.

(4) Transfer of an operator or instructor license from one traffic violator school to another.

(5) Approval of curriculum, based on the instructional modality of the curriculum.

(6) Fees for administering the examinations pursuant to Sections 11206 and 11207.

(b) The fees authorized under subdivision (a) shall be sufficient to defray the actual cost to the department to administer the traffic violator school program, except for routine monitoring of instruction.

(c) A single administrative fee shall be assessed against, and collected by the court pursuant to Section 42007.1 from, each driver who is allowed or ordered to attend traffic violator school. Included in this fee shall be an amount determined by the department to be sufficient to defray the cost of routine monitoring of traffic violator school instruction.

(d) This section shall become operative on September 1, 2011.

(Repealed (in Sec. 9) and added by Stats. 2010, Ch. 599, Sec. 10. (AB 2499) Effective January 1, 2011. Section operative September 1, 2011, by its own provisions.)

11209. Any traffic violator school owner, traffic violator school operator, or traffic violator school instructor required to be licensed under this chapter who fails to renew the license before the expiration of the license may not renew that license, but may reapply for an original license pursuant to this chapter. For purposes of this section, a license that has been canceled may not be renewed and a license that is suspended or revoked may not be renewed, until reinstatement or reissuance by the department. If the period of suspension or revocation extends beyond the expiration of a license, it may not be renewed, but the person may apply for a new license thereafter.

(Amended by Stats. 1987, Ch. 111, Sec. 3.)

11210. Pending determination by the department that an applicant for a license fully satisfies the requirements of this chapter, the department may issue a temporary permit to the applicant. A temporary permit may authorize the operation of a traffic violator school or acting as a traffic violator school operator or traffic violator school instructor for a period not to exceed 120 days while the department is completing its investigation and determination of all facts relative to the qualifications of the applicant for the license.

The department may cancel a temporary permit when it has determined or has reasonable cause to believe that the application is incorrect or incomplete or the temporary permit was issued in error. A temporary permit is invalid upon cancellation or once the applicant has been issued or denied the license applied for.

(Amended by Stats. 1985, Ch. 396, Sec. 14. Effective July 30, 1985.)

11211. (a) The department may refuse to issue a license to any applicant under this chapter when it finds and determines that any of the following exist:

(1) The applicant was previously the holder of a license under this chapter which was revoked or suspended.

(2) The applicant was previously the holder of an occupational license issued by another state, authorizing the same or similar activities of a license issued under this division; and that license was revoked or suspended for cause and was never reissued, or was suspended for cause, and the terms of suspension have not been fulfilled.

(3) The applicant has done any act or series of acts which would be a cause for suspension or revocation of licensure under Section 11215,

regardless of whether the applicant was licensed under this chapter at the time of the act or acts.

(4) If the applicant is a business, a business representative was the holder of a previously issued license under this chapter that was suspended or revoked or has done any act or series of acts which would be a cause for suspension or revocation of a license under Section 11215, regardless of whether the business representative was licensed under this chapter at the time of the act or acts.

(5) By reason of the facts and circumstances relating to the organization, control, and management of the business, it is likely that both of the following will occur:

(A) The policy or operation of the business will be directed, controlled, or managed by an individual who, by reason of an act, series of acts, or conduct described in paragraph (3) or (4), would be ineligible for a license.

(B) By licensing the business, the purposes of this division would be defeated.

(6) The applicant has knowingly made a false statement or knowingly concealed a material fact in applying for a license under this chapter.

(7) The applicant, or a business representative if the applicant is a business, has been convicted of a crime, or committed any act or engaged in conduct involving moral turpitude which is substantially related to the qualifications, functions, or duties of the licensed activity. A conviction after a plea of nolo contendere is a conviction within the meaning of this section.

(b) Upon refusal of the department to issue a license under this chapter, the applicant is entitled to a hearing upon demand in writing submitted to the department within 60 days after notice of refusal. The hearing shall be conducted pursuant to Chapter 5 (commencing with Section 11500) of Part 1 of Division 3 of Title 2 of the Government Code.

(c) A person whose license has been revoked or application for a license has been refused may reapply for the license after a period of not less than one year has elapsed from the effective date of the decision revoking the license or refusing the application.

(Amended by Stats. 1998, Ch. 877, Sec. 43. Effective January 1, 1999.)

11212. (a) Every owner licensed under this chapter shall keep a record at the traffic violator school's primary business location showing all of the following for each student:

(1) The name and address and license number of the traffic violator school providing instruction.

(2) The name and address of each person given instruction.

(3) The instruction permit number or driver's license number of every person given instruction.

(4) The name and number of the license issued pursuant to Section 11207 of the traffic violator school instructor.

(5) The particular type of instruction given and the date or dates of the instruction.

(6) A statement as to whether the approved lesson plan was followed.

(7) The total number of hours of instruction.

(8) The total cost to the student of the instruction, which shall not exceed the amount of the fee represented or advertised by the traffic violator school at the time of the student's enrollment.

(9) The court docket number under which the student was referred to a traffic violator school.

(10) The number of the completion certificate issued to the student pursuant to subdivision (e) of Section 11208 and, if different, the number of any copy thereof issued to the student.

(b) The records shall be retained for a minimum of three years and shall be open to the inspection during business hours and at all other reasonable times by the department, the court, a private entity providing monitoring pursuant to Section 11222, the Legislative Analyst, and the State Auditor or authorized employees thereof, but shall be only for confidential use.

(c) Whenever a licensee suspends or terminates the licensed activity, the licensee shall surrender the records specified in subdivision (a) to the department for examination not later than the end of the third day, excluding Saturdays, Sundays, and legal holidays, after the date of suspension or termination. The department may duplicate or make a record of any information contained therein. All these records shall be returned to the licensee not later than 30 days after the date of surrender.

(d) The address of any person kept pursuant to paragraph (2) of subdivision (a) shall only be used by the school for school administrative purposes.

(Amended by Stats. 2001, Ch. 739, Sec. 5. Effective January 1, 2002.)

11213. (a) Every traffic violator school owner licensed pursuant to this chapter shall notify the department within 10 days of any change in the ownership or corporate structure of the licensee.

(b) Every traffic violator school owner shall immediately notify the department of the following activities:

(1) Change of the site or location of the school's established principal place of business.

(2) Addition or deletion of a traffic violator school branch or classroom location.

(c) Every traffic violator school operator and traffic violator school instructor licensed pursuant to this chapter shall report to the department every change of residence address within five days of the change.

(d) The department may require persons licensed pursuant to this chapter to submit additional reports as determined necessary by the department to serve the purposes of this chapter.

(Amended by Stats. 1985, Ch. 396, Sec. 17. Effective July 30, 1985.)

11214. (a) Except as provided in this chapter, the department may audit, inspect, and monitor, all licensed traffic violator schools.

(b) The department may annually audit the records of a licensee. Auditing includes, but is not limited to, the review and examination of business records, class records when applicable, business practices, and the content of the program of instruction set forth in the lesson plan or curriculum of a licensee.

(c) Inspecting includes, but is not limited to, the review of the business office, branch office, and applicable classroom facilities of a licensee.

(d) Monitoring includes the onsite review of the actual presentation of the program of traffic safety instruction provided in a classroom mode of instruction.

(Repealed and added by Stats. 2003, Ch. 518, Sec. 4. Effective January 1, 2004.)

11215. The department, after notice and hearing, may suspend or revoke a license issued under this chapter if any of the following circumstances exist:

(a) The department finds and determines that the licensee ceases to meet any requirement to obtain a license under this chapter.

(b) The holder fails to comply with, or otherwise violates, a provision of this chapter or a regulation or requirement of the department adopted pursuant to this chapter.

(c) The licensee engages in fraudulent practices with respect to its activities licensed under this chapter or induces or fails to promptly report to the department any known fraud or fraudulent practices on the part of an employee of the traffic violator school.

(d) The licensee represents himself or herself as an agent or employee of the department or uses advertising designed to create the impression, or that would reasonably have the effect of leading persons to believe that the licensee was in fact an employee or representative of the department, or whenever the licensee advertises, in any manner or means, a statement that is untrue or misleading and that is known, or that by the exercise of reasonable care should be known, to be untrue or misleading.

(e) The licensee or an employee or agent of the licensee collects fees for or preregisters a person in traffic violator school or solicits traffic violator school instruction in an office of the department or in a court or within 500 feet of a court.

(f) The licensee is convicted of violating Section 20001, 20002, 20003, 20004, 20006, 20008, 23103, 23104, 23105, 23152, or 23153 of this code or subdivision (b) of Section 191.5 or Section 192 of the Penal Code. A conviction after a plea of nolo contendere is a conviction within the meaning of this section.

(g) The traffic violator school owner teaches, or permits an employee to teach, traffic safety instruction without a valid instructor's license.

(h) The traffic violator school owner does not have in effect a bond as provided in paragraph (3) of subdivision (a) of Section 11202 or a deposit in lieu of the bond, as specified in Section 11203.

(Amended by Stats. 2007, Ch. 747, Sec. 15.5. Effective January 1, 2008.)

11215.5. The department, after notice and hearing, may also suspend or revoke any license issued under this chapter when any of the following circumstances exist:

(a) If the main business office of the traffic violator school is located in any county with a population of 400,000 or more in which the traffic violator school conducts its instructional program, and the main business office does not maintain office hours during the time that the day courts in that county are open for business. This subdivision shall not apply to public schools.

(b) If the licensee is found by the department to be selling, or knowingly permitting the sale of, completion certificates.

(c) If the licensee is found by the department to be intentionally cutting instructional time short.

(d) If the licensee is found by the department to be intentionally diverting any student to a traffic school other than the school initially contacted by that student, without disclosure to that student, through the use of the department's list of licensed traffic violator schools.

(Amended by Stats. 1988, Ch. 1196, Sec. 3.)

11215.7. Any of the causes specified in this chapter as a cause for refusal to issue a license under this chapter is cause to suspend or revoke a license under this chapter.

(Added by Stats. 1990, Ch. 1563, Sec. 22.)

11216. Any license issued to a traffic violator school owner under this chapter shall be automatically canceled upon the happening of any of the following:

(a) The abandonment of the established place of business or the change thereof without notice to the department pursuant to Section 11213.

(b) The failure to maintain an adequate bond or to procure and file another bond, as required by Section 11202, prior to the effective date of the termination by the surety of any existing bond.

(c) The voluntary or involuntary surrender of the license, except that a surrender or cessation of business by the licensee, or the suspension or revocation of the corporate status of the licensee, does not preclude the department from filing an accusation for revocation or suspension of the surrendered license, as provided in Section 11215 or 11215.5, or affect the department's decision to suspend or revoke the license.

(d) Notification to the department that the person designated as the licensee has changed.

(e) Suspension or cancellation of the corporate status of the licensee.

(Amended by Stats. 1990, Ch. 1563, Sec. 23.)

11216.2. (a) Any license issued to the owner or operator of a traffic violator school under this chapter shall be automatically suspended for 30 days by the department if the department has been notified that more than one final determination has been made that the traffic violator school has violated a student's rights under the federal Americans with Disabilities Act of 1990 (42 U.S.C. Sec. 12101, et seq.) or any other federal or state law prohibiting discrimination against individuals with disabilities. The final determination shall be made by a federal or state court of competent jurisdiction or an appropriate federal or state administrative agency, including, but not limited to, the Civil Rights Department, or any combination thereof.

For the purpose of this subdivision, "final determination" means that no further appeal of a determination can be taken to any court because the time period for the appeal has expired.

(b) If a traffic violator school subject to suspension under this section is operated by a traffic school operator licensed pursuant to Section 11202.5 who is operating other traffic schools, the licenses of the owners of those traffic schools operated by that traffic school operator also shall be suspended for the 30-day period.

(Amended by Stats. 2022, Ch. 48, Sec. 76. (SB 189) Effective June 30, 2022.)

11216.5. (a) The department, after notice and hearing, on an interim basis, may refuse to issue or may suspend a license issued under this chapter when the applicant or licensee, or a business representative if the applicant or licensee is a business, has been convicted of a crime involving moral turpitude which is substantially related to the qualifications, functions, or duties of the licensed activity, if an appeal of the conviction is pending or the conviction has otherwise not become final. A conviction after a plea of nolo contendere is a conviction within the meaning of this section.

(b) If a conviction, on which an interim refusal to issue or suspension under subdivision (a) is based, is affirmed on appeal or otherwise becomes final, the refusal to issue or the suspension shall automatically take effect as a denial or revocation, as the case may be, of the license. If the interim refusal to issue or suspension was stayed under probationary terms and conditions, the subsequent automatic denial or revocation shall also be stayed under the same terms and conditions for a term not to exceed the original term of probation for the interim refusal to issue or suspension.

(c) If a conviction, upon which an interim refusal to issue or suspension under subdivision (a) is based, is reversed on appeal, the refusal or suspension shall be set aside immediately by the department.

(Added by Stats. 1990, Ch. 1563, Sec. 24.)

11217. (a) Every licensee under this chapter is entitled to notice and hearing prior to suspension or revocation of the license by the department, except that the department shall immediately suspend the license pursuant to subdivision (e) for any act of fraud specified in subdivision (c) or (d) of Section 11215.

(b) Before reinstatement of any license suspended pursuant to subdivision (a) of Section 11215, the licensee shall pay the department a reinstatement fee of five dollars ($5).

(c) The notice and hearings provided for in this division shall be pursuant to Chapter 5 (commencing with Section 11500) of Part 1 of Division 3 of Title 2 of the Government Code.

(d) Any action of the department, in suspending, canceling, revoking, or failing to renew a license issued pursuant to this chapter, may be reviewed by any court of competent jurisdiction.

(e) The department may, pending a hearing, temporarily suspend the license or permit of any traffic violator school owner, operator, or instructor for a period of not more than 30 days if the director finds that the public interest so requires. In that case, a hearing shall be held and a decision issued within 30 days after issuance of the notice of temporary suspension.

(f) The suspension, expiration, or cancellation of a license issued pursuant to this chapter does not preclude the filing of an accusation for the revocation or suspension of the suspended, expired, or canceled license, and does not invalidate or otherwise preclude a decision by the department to suspend or revoke the license, and this determination may be considered by the department in granting or refusing to grant any subsequent license under this chapter to the same licensee or to any business representative of the same licensee.

(Amended by Stats. 1990, Ch. 1563, Sec. 25.)

11217.5. Any owner licensed under this chapter who has closed his or her established place of business or any operator or instructor currently or previously licensed under this chapter who no longer resides at the address last filed with the department, may be served with process issued pursuant to Chapter 5 (commencing with Section 11500) of Part 1 of Division 3 of Title 2 of the Government Code by registered mail at that place of business, in the case of an owner, or at that residence, in the case of an operator or instructor, unless the person has notified the

department in writing of another address where service may be made.
(Added by Stats. 1988, Ch. 751, Sec. 2.)

11218. (a) After the filing of an accusation under this chapter, the director may enter into a stipulated compromise settlement agreement with the consent of the licensee on terms and conditions mutually agreeable to the director, the respondent licensee, and the accuser without further hearing or appeal. The agreement may include, but is not limited to, a period of probation or monetary penalties, or both. The monetary penalty shall not exceed one thousand dollars ($1,000) per violation for a traffic violator school owner or five hundred dollars ($500) per violation for traffic violator school operators or instructors, and shall be based on the nature of the violation and the effect of the violation on the purposes of this chapter.

(b) A compromise settlement agreement may be entered before, during, or after the hearing, but is valid only if executed and filed pursuant to subdivision (d) before the proposed decision of the hearing officer, if any, is adopted or the case is decided.

(c) The department shall adopt, by regulation, a schedule of maximum and minimum amounts of monetary penalties, the payment of which may be included as a term or condition of a compromise settlement agreement entered under subdivision (a). Any monetary penalty included in a compromise settlement agreement shall be within the range of monetary penalties in that schedule.

(d) Any compromise settlement agreement entered under this section shall be signed by the director, the respondent licensee, and the accuser, or by their authorized representatives. The director shall file, or cause to be filed, the agreement with the Office of Administrative Hearings, together with the department's notice of withdrawal of the accusation or statement of issues upon which the action was initiated, unless that accusation or statement has not yet been forwarded to the Office of Administrative Hearings.

(e) If the respondent licensee fails to perform all of the terms and conditions of the compromise settlement agreement, the agreement is void and the department may take any action authorized by law notwithstanding the agreement, including, but not limited to, refiling the accusation or imposing license sanctions.
(Amended by Stats. 1992, Ch. 1243, Sec. 73. Effective September 30, 1992.)

11219. The director may prescribe rules and regulations for traffic violator schools regarding the conduct of courses of education including curriculum, facilities, and equipment. The curriculum shall include, but is not limited to, the rights and duties of a motorist as they pertain to pedestrians and the rights and duties of a pedestrian as they relate to traffic laws and traffic safety. The director may also prescribe rules and regulations for the conduct of instructor training courses.
(Amended by Stats. 2000, Ch. 833, second Sec. 5.5. Effective January 1, 2001.)

11219.3. The curriculum prescribed pursuant to Section 11219 shall include, but is not limited to, the following:

(a) The rights and duties of a motorist as they pertain to pedestrians.

(b) The rights and duties of a pedestrian as they relate to traffic laws and traffic safety.

(c) Information that emphasizes respecting the right-of-way of others, particularly with respect to pedestrians, bicycle riders, and motorcycle riders.
(Amended by Stats. 2006, Ch. 898, Sec. 2. Effective January 1, 2007.)

11219.5. (a) A traffic violator school shall issue a receipt for a fee collected by the traffic violator school from a person who registers for, attends, or completes a program of instruction in traffic safety at the licensed traffic violator school.

(b) In the event of a cancellation of a scheduled class, a licensee under this chapter shall not be required by the department to provide a program of instruction in traffic safety to a person for a fee that is less than the standard fee normally charged by the licensee for its program, if a notice of cancellation of a class is given to a student at least 72 hours prior to the start of the class, or if the class was canceled based upon exigent circumstances beyond the control of the licensee.
(Amended by Stats. 2007, Ch. 396, Sec. 3. Effective January 1, 2008.)

11220. The department may require any person licensed under this chapter to submit to a reexamination of his or her qualifications when there is reasonable cause to believe that the licensee does not have the ability to give instruction. If the licensee refuses or fails to submit to the reexamination, the department may, without a hearing, temporarily suspend his or her license until such time as the licensee submits to the reexamination. The suspension shall be effective upon receipt of notice by the licensee.
(Added by Stats. 1984, Ch. 1037, Sec. 4.)

11222. The department may contract with a nongovernmental entity to administer any part of this chapter, subject to limitations in other laws regarding contracting out for services. No contract shall exceed three years' duration. The contracting entity, and any affiliate or subsidiary thereof monitoring traffic violator schools, shall conform to all of the following requirements:

(a) Engage in no other business activity with traffic violator schools or any of the principals of the traffic violator schools, including the provision of services or supplies.

(b) Provide reports in statistical form to the department and to the Legislature as instructed by the department. These reports shall be issued not less frequently than annually.

(c) Make its records available for inspection by authorized representatives of the department, the Legislative Analyst, and the State Auditor.
(Amended by Stats. 2001, Ch. 739, Sec. 6. Effective January 1, 2002.)

11223. A motorcyclist safety training program established pursuant to Article 2 (commencing with Section 2930) of Chapter 5 of Division 2, that is licensed by the department as a traffic violator school, may administer a motorcyclist training course. In addition to the curriculum prescribed by the department pursuant to Section 11219, the motorcyclist training course may include instruction specific to the safe and lawful operation of motorcycles in accordance with Section 2932.
(Added by Stats. 2016, Ch. 561, Sec. 1. (AB 1932) Effective January 1, 2017.)

Chapter 2. Vehicle Verifiers

(Chapter 2 added by Stats. 1975, Ch. 700.)

11300. It shall be unlawful for any person to act as a vehicle verifier without first having procured a vehicle verifier's permit issued by the department, or when such permit has been canceled, suspended, revoked or invalidated.
(Added by Stats. 1975, Ch. 700.)

11301. Every vehicle verifier shall make application to the department upon the appropriate form, accompanied by a good and sufficient bond, approved as to form by the Attorney General, in the amount of five thousand dollars ($5,000) with corporate surety thereon, duly licensed to do business within the State of California.

(a) The department shall prescribe and provide forms to be used for application for permits to be issued under the terms and provisions of this chapter and require of applicants information including, but not limited to, residence address, fingerprints, and personal history statements touching on and concerning the applicant's character, honesty, integrity, and reputation as it may consider necessary.

(b) Upon receipt of an application in proper form accompanied by the appropriate fee, the department shall within 120 days, make a thorough investigation of the information contained in the application.
(Amended by Stats. 1988, Ch. 751, Sec. 3.)

11301.5. If a deposit is given instead of the bond required by Section 11301:

(a) The Director of Motor Vehicles may order the refund of the deposit three years from the date a vehicle verifier has ceased to be licensed, if the director is satisfied that there are no outstanding claims against the deposit. A judge of a superior court may order the return of the deposit prior to the expiration of three years from the date a vehicle verifier has ceased to be licensed if there is evidence satisfactory to the court that there are no outstanding claims against the deposit.

(b) If the director, department, or state is a defendant in any action instituted to recover all or any part of the deposit, or any action is instituted by the director, department, or state to determine those entitled to any part of the deposit, the director, department, or state shall be paid reasonable attorney fees and costs from the deposit. Costs shall include those administrative costs incurred in processing claims against the deposit.

(Amended by Stats. 2002, Ch. 784, Sec. 599. Effective January 1, 2003.)

11302. (a) The department may issue, or for reasonable cause shown, refuse to issue, a vehicle verifier's permit to any applicant, or may, after notice and hearing, suspend or revoke the permit when satisfied that the applicant or permittee:

(1) Has violated any of the provisions of this division or has committed any acts which are grounds for the refusal to issue, or the suspension or revocation of a permit or license issued under this division.

(2) Was previously the holder of an occupational license issued by another state, authorizing the same or similar activities of a license issued under this division; and that license was revoked or suspended for cause and was never reissued, or was suspended for cause, and the terms of suspension have not been fulfilled.

(3) Has purchased, sold, or otherwise acquired or disposed of, a vehicle which was stolen or embezzled or has performed or submitted to the department, or its authorized representative, documents purporting verification of a vehicle which was stolen or embezzled.

(4) Has, in the course of performing a vehicle verification, acted with negligence or incompetence in the reporting of erroneous information to the department, or its authorized representative, and has thereby caused the department to issue inaccurate certificates of ownership or registration, or any other documents or indices which it would not otherwise have issued.

(b) Every hearing as provided for in this chapter shall be pursuant to the provisions of Chapter 5 (commencing with Section 11500) of Part 1 of Division 3 of Title 2 of the Government Code.

(Amended by Stats. 1998, Ch. 877, Sec. 44. Effective January 1, 1999.)

11302.2. (a) Every person licensed under this chapter shall report to the department every change of residence address within 10 days of the change.

(b) Any person currently or previously licensed under this chapter who no longer resides at the address last filed with the department may be served with process issued pursuant to Chapter 5 (commencing with Section 11500) of Part 1 of Division 3 of Title 2 of the Government Code by registered mail at that residence, unless the person has notified the department in writing of another address where service may be made.

(Added by Stats. 1988, Ch. 751, Sec. 4.)

11302.5. (a) After the filing of an accusation under this chapter, the director may enter into a stipulated compromise settlement agreement with the consent of the licensee on terms and conditions mutually agreeable to the director, the respondent licensee, and the accuser without further hearing or appeal. The agreement may include, but is not limited to, a period of probation or monetary penalties, or both. The monetary penalty shall not exceed five hundred dollars ($500) for each violation, and it shall be based on the nature of the violation and the effect of the violation on the purposes of this chapter.

(b) A compromise settlement agreement may be entered before, during, or after the hearing, but is valid only if executed and filed pursuant to subdivision (d) before the proposed decision of the hearing officer, if any, is adopted or the case is decided.

(c) The department shall adopt, by regulation, a schedule of maximum and minimum amounts of monetary penalties, the payment of which may be included as a term or condition of a compromise settlement agreement entered under subdivision (a). Any monetary penalty included in a compromise settlement agreement shall be within the range of monetary penalties in that schedule.

(d) Any compromise settlement agreement entered under this section shall be signed by the director, the respondent licensee, and the accuser, or by their authorized representatives. The director shall file, or cause to be filed, the agreement with the Office of Administrative Hearings, together with the department's notice of withdrawal of the accusation or statement of issues upon which the action was initiated.

(e) If the respondent licensee fails to perform all of the terms and conditions of the compromise settlement agreement, the agreement is void and the department may take any action authorized by law notwithstanding the agreement, including, but not limited to, refiling the accusation or imposing license sanctions.

(Added by Stats. 1985, Ch. 1022, Sec. 14.)

11305. It shall be unlawful and cause of disciplinary action for the holder of a vehicle verifier's permit:

(a) To submit to the department, or its authorized representative, any document which purports to evidence the verification of any vehicle, without having actually physically inspected such vehicle to determine the existence of proper vehicle identification.

(b) To fail to report to the department, in a manner prescribed by the department, the absence, alteration, or obvious attempt to alter or obliterate any identifying number or number plate, or remove or attempt to remove such plate on any vehicle for which verification is performed.

(c) To fail to physically compare identifying numbers on a vehicle inspected to the information contained in any document of title, registration, or any other form describing such vehicle.

(d) To cause any person to suffer any loss or damage by reason of any fraud or deceit practiced upon such person in the course of the conducting of business under the vehicle verifier's permit.

(e) To violate one or more terms and provisions of Section 20, or of Division 3 (commencing with Section 4000), or of this division of this code, or any rules or regulations adopted pursuant thereto, or of Part 5 (commencing with Section 10701) of Division 2 of the Revenue and Taxation Code.

(Added by Stats. 1975, Ch. 700.)

11306. (a) If the department issues or renews a vehicle verifier's permit requiring conditions of probation, or if the department refuses to issue a vehicle verifier's permit, the applicant shall be entitled to demand, in writing, a hearing as provided in this chapter, before the director, or his representative, within 60 days after notice of refusal or issuance of the probationary permit.

(b) Except where the provisions of this code require the refusal to issue a permit, the department may issue a probationary permit subject to conditions to be observed by the permittee in the exercise of the privilege granted. The conditions to be attached to the exercise of the privilege shall be such as may, in the judgment of the department, be in the public interest and suitable to the qualifications of the applicant as disclosed by the application and investigation by the department of the information contained therein.

(c) The department may, pending a hearing, temporarily suspend the permit issued to a vehicle verifier for a period not to exceed 30 days if the director finds that such action is required in the public interest. In any such case, a hearing shall be held and a decision thereon issued within 30 days after notice of the temporary suspension.

(d) A person whose application for a permit has been denied may reapply for such permit after a period of not less than one year has elapsed from the date of filing of such denial.

(Added by Stats. 1975, Ch. 700.)

11307. (a) A vehicle verifier shall maintain a record of each verification made. The record shall contain all of the following:

(1) The name and address of the person requesting the verification and the fee charged for such verification.

(2) The year model, vehicle identification number, license plate number of the vehicle verified and the state in which the vehicle was

last registered.

(b) All records maintained by a vehicle verifier shall be open to inspection by any peace officer.

(Added by Stats. 1975, Ch. 700.)

11308. The department may adopt rules and regulations concerning the issuance, use, and renewal of a vehicle verifier's permit, and for determining the competence of an applicant therefor.

(Added by Stats. 1975, Ch. 700.)

11309. (a) The following fees for a vehicle verifier's permit shall be paid to the department:

(1) For the application and original permit, except as provided by Section 42231, a nonrefundable fee of fifty dollars ($50).

(2) For an application for renewal, fifteen dollars ($15).

(b) All permits shall be renewed on a biennial basis. All original permits shall be issued for a period of not less than two years, except in the case of a probationary license which, in the discretion of the department, may be issued for a shorter term.

(Amended by Stats. 1982, Ch. 1273, Sec. 13.)

11310. Any person who holds a vehicle verifier's permit issued before the operative date of this chapter shall comply with the provisions of this chapter within three months after its operative date.

(Added by Stats. 1975, Ch. 700.)

11312. The suspension, expiration, or cancellation of a vehicle verifier's permit provided for in this chapter shall not prevent the filing of an accusation for the revocation or suspension of the suspended, expired, or canceled permit as provided in Section 11302 or 11305 or any rules or regulations adopted pursuant to Section 11308, and the department's decision that the permit should be suspended or revoked. That determination may be considered in granting or refusing to grant any subsequent license or permit authorized by this division to that vehicle verifier or to a business representative of that prior vehicle verifier's permit.

(Added by Stats. 1998, Ch. 877, Sec. 45. Effective January 1, 1999.)

Chapter 2.5. Registration Services

(Chapter 2.5 added by Stats. 1990, Ch. 1196, Sec. 3.)

11400. No person shall act as a registration service, engage in the business of soliciting or receiving any application for the registration, renewal of registration, or transfer of registration or ownership of any vehicle of a type subject to registration under this code, or of soliciting or receiving an application for a motor carrier permit under Division 14.85 (commencing with Section 34600), or transmit or present any of those documents to the department, if any compensation is solicited or received for the service, without a license or temporary permit issued by the department pursuant to this chapter, or if that license or temporary permit has expired or been canceled, suspended, or revoked, or the terms and conditions of an agreement entered into pursuant to Section 11408 have not been fulfilled.

(Amended by Stats. 2005, Ch. 148, Sec. 2. Effective January 1, 2006.)

11401. An applicant for a license to be a registration service shall submit an application to the department upon the appropriate form for a license and a distinguishing number. The applicant shall also include with the application any information as to the applicant's character, honesty, integrity, and reputation which the department requires. The application shall include, but not be limited to, all of the following:

(a) The type of ownership, whether an individual, a partnership, or a corporation. If the applicant is a partnership, the names and titles of all partners, except limited partners, shall be furnished. If the applicant is a corporation, the names and titles of all controlling stockholders, directors, and officers who, by reason of the facts and circumstances, could direct, control, or manage the business of the registration service shall be furnished.

(b) The name and address of the business, including street, city, and postal zip code of the principal place of business and any branch location.

(c) A personal history statement and fingerprints from any person required to be identified in subdivision (a), containing the information the department requires.

(d) The name, address, driver's license number, and a brief physical description of all persons employed or otherwise engaged by the registration service to perform registration work.

(e) A bond executed by an admitted surety insurer, approved as to form by the Attorney General, to cover any loss to the public or the State of California arising out of the operation of the registration service.

(f) A nonrefundable application fee, as specified in Section 11409.

(Added by Stats. 1990, Ch. 1196, Sec. 3. Operative July 1, 1991, by Sec. 4 of Ch. 1196.)

11402. (a) The amount of the bond required by subdivision (e) of Section 11401 for the issuance of a registration service license, or for the renewal of such a license is twenty-five thousand dollars ($25,000). Liability under the bond shall remain at that amount.

(b) If the amount of the liability under the bond is decreased, or there is outstanding a final court judgment arising out of a violation of any provision of this code for which the registration service is liable, the license of the registration service shall be automatically suspended. In order to reinstate the license, the registration service shall either file an additional bond or restore the bond on file to the original amount, or shall satisfy the outstanding judgment for which the registration service and surety are liable.

(c) The bond shall remain in effect for three years after cessation of business of the registration service.

(Amended by Stats. 2004, Ch. 430, Sec. 3. Effective January 1, 2005.)

11403. (a) A license to conduct a registration service, or a renewal of that license, shall not be issued to any applicant unless the applicant files with the department an instrument, in writing, in which the applicant appoints the director as the agent of the applicant upon whom all process may be served in any action which may be commenced against the applicant arising out of any claim for damages by any person by reason of the violation by the applicant of any provision of this code in connection with the registration service or any condition of the registration service's bond.

(b) The applicant shall agree in the instrument that any process directed to the applicant, when personal service of process upon the applicant cannot be made in this state after due diligence and, in that case, is served upon the director or, in the event of the director's absence from the office, upon any employee in charge of the office of the director, is of the same force and effect as if served upon the applicant personally.

(c) The applicant shall further agree, in writing, that the agency created by the instrument shall continue during the period covered by any license that may be issued and so long thereafter as the applicant may be required to answer in damages for a violation of this code in connection with the registration service or any condition of the bond.

(d) The instrument appointing the director as the agent for the applicant for service of process shall be acknowledged by the applicant before a notary public.

(e) If the registration service is served with process by service upon the director, one copy of the summons and complaint shall be left with the director or in the director's office in Sacramento or mailed to the office of the director in Sacramento. A fee of five dollars ($5) shall also be paid to the director at the time of service of the copy of the summons and complaint.

(f) Service on the director is a sufficient service on the registration service if a notice of service and a copy of the summons and complaint are immediately sent by registered mail by the plaintiff or the plaintiff's attorney to the registration service. A copy of the summons and complaint shall also be mailed by the plaintiff or the plaintiff's attorney to the surety on the registration service's bond at the address of the surety given in the bond, postpaid and registered with request for return receipt.

(g) The director shall keep a record of all process served on the director pursuant to this section, which shall show the day and hour of service, and shall retain the summons and complaint so served on file.

(h) If the registration service is served with process by service upon the director, the registration service has 30 days from the date of that service within which to answer any complaint or other pleading which may be filed in the cause.

(i) For purposes of venue, if the registration service is served with process by service upon the director, the service is deemed to have been made upon the registration service in the county in which the registration service has, or last had, its principal place of business.

(Added by Stats. 1990, Ch. 1196, Sec. 3. Operative July 1, 1991, by Sec. 4 of Ch. 1196.)

11404. (a) Until the department determines that the applicant meets all of the requirements of this chapter, it may issue a temporary permit to the person applying for a license as a registration service.

(b) The temporary permit shall permit the operation by the registration service or registration agent for not more than 120 days while the department is completing its investigation and determination of all facts relative to the qualifications of the applicant for the license. The department may cancel the temporary permit when it has determined that the application is incorrect or incomplete or that the temporary permit was issued in error.

(c) The temporary permit is invalid when canceled or when the license has been issued or refused.

(Added by Stats. 1990, Ch. 1196, Sec. 3. Operative July 1, 1991, by Sec. 4 of Ch. 1196.)

11405. The department may refuse to issue a license to, or may suspend, revoke, or cancel the license of, a person to act as a registration service for any of the following reasons:

(a) The person has been convicted of a felony or a crime involving moral turpitude which is substantially related to the qualifications, functions, or duties of the licensed activity.

(b) The person is, or has been, the holder, or a managerial employee of the holder, of any occupational license issued by the department which has been suspended or revoked.

(c) The applicant was previously the holder of an occupational license issued by another state, authorizing the same or similar activities of a license issued under this division; and that license was revoked or suspended for cause and was never reissued, or was suspended for cause, and the terms of suspension have not been fulfilled.

(d) The person has used a false or fictitious name, knowingly made any false statement, or knowingly concealed any material fact, in the application for the license.

(e) The person has knowingly made, or acted with negligence or incompetence, or knowingly or negligently accepted or failed to inquire about any false, erroneous, or incorrect statement or information submitted to the registration service or the department in the course of the licensed activity.

(f) The person has knowingly or negligently permitted fraud, or willfully engaged in fraudulent practices, with reference to clients, vehicle registrants, applicants for motor carrier permits under Division 14.85 (commencing with Section 34600), or members of the public, or the department in the course of the licensed activity.

(g) The person has knowingly or negligently committed or was responsible for any violation, cause for license refusal, or cause for discipline under Section 20 or Division 3 (commencing with Section 4000), Division 3.5 (commencing with Section 9840), Division 4 (commencing with Section 10500), or Division 5 (commencing with Section 11100), or Division 14.85 (commencing with Section 34600), or any rules or regulations adopted under those provisions.

(h) The person has failed to obtain and maintain an established place of business in California.

(i) The person has failed to keep the business records required by Section 11406.

(j) The person has violated any term or condition of a restricted license to act as a registration service.

(k) The person has committed or was responsible for any other act, occurrence, or event in California or any foreign jurisdiction which would be cause to refuse to issue a license to, or to suspend, revoke, or cancel the license of, a person to act as a registration service.

(Amended by Stats. 2005, Ch. 148, Sec. 3. Effective January 1, 2006.)

11406. (a) Every registration service shall keep accurate business records containing all of the following information:

(1) The name, address, and license number of the registration service and the name and address of every employee who performs registration work.

(2) The name and address of each client for whom registration work was performed.

(3) The identity of every vehicle by year, make, type, license number, and vehicle identification number on which registration work was performed.

(4) The amount of registration fees or payments collected for each vehicle on which registration work was performed, including the method of payment to the registration service.

(5) The amount of registration fees or payments submitted to the department for each vehicle on which registration work was performed, including the date and method of payment to the department.

(6) The amount of any refunds or additional charges on registration fees or payments collected for each vehicle on which registration work was performed, including the date and method of payment of the refund or additional charge by or to the client, the registration service, or the department.

(7) The name, signature, or initials of each employee performing work on each transaction and the date the work was done.

(8) The cost to each client for the registration work performed on each of the client's vehicles or to obtain a motor carrier permit.

(9) For each motor carrier for which motor carrier permit work was performed, the carrier identification number, business type, business address, carrier type, activities, and number of vehicles.

(10) For each motor carrier for which motor carrier permit work was performed, the amount of fees or payment collected and the method of payment.

(11) For each motor carrier for which motor carrier permit work was performed, the amount of fees or payment submitted to the department, including the date submitted and the method of payment to the department.

(b) As an alternative to maintaining the records required by paragraphs (1) to (11), inclusive, of subdivision (a), a registration service may retain a copy of the listing sheet approved by the department for transmitting registration or motor carrier permit documents to the department.

(c) Every registration service shall provide each customer with a document containing all of the information required by subdivision (a) relative to that customer's transaction, excluding paragraph (7) and excluding the addresses of employees and other customers' names and addresses. This requirement does not apply to transactions for customers of a dealer or dismantler.

(d) Every registration service shall display prominently at its place of business a sign indicating that the service is not a branch of the department and shall inform each customer of that fact.

(e) Every registration service shall provide a disclosure to each customer that the services described in Section 11400 may be provided by the department without an additional fee. If a registration service is providing a service described in Section 11400 in person, the disclosure required pursuant to this subdivision shall be in writing. If a registration service is providing a service described in Section 11400 on an Internet Web site, the disclosure required pursuant to this subdivision shall be in a conspicuous place on the Internet Web site.

(Amended by Stats. 2014, Ch. 128, Sec. 1. (AB 1627) Effective January 1, 2015.)

11406.5. Whenever a customer fails to submit to a registration service any documents, compensation, or fees requested in writing by the registration service, the registration service shall return all documents pertaining to the incomplete transaction, including the department receipt

evidencing any fees paid, within 60 days after the request was sent to the customer, to the last known address of the customer, by registered mail.
(Added by Stats. 1992, Ch. 1243, Sec. 76. Effective September 30, 1992.)

11407. The business records required by Section 11406 shall be maintained for at least four years and shall be open to inspection by the department during normal business hours.

The department may duplicate or make a record of any information contained in any of those records, which shall be for the official use of the department.

All records shall be returned to the licensee not later than 30 days after receipt of the records by the department.
(Added by Stats. 1990, Ch. 1196, Sec. 3. Operative July 1, 1991, by Sec. 4 of Ch. 1196.)

11408. (a) The director may issue an order to grant an unrestricted or a restricted license to act as a registration service, or an order to deny, suspend, revoke, or cancel a license to act as a registration service.

(b) The order shall become final 30 days from issuance, unless the denied or restricted applicant or licensee files with the department a request for a hearing. Hearings shall be held pursuant to Chapter 5 (commencing with Section 11500) of Part 1 of Division 3 of Title 2 of the Government Code.

(c) Any registration service may be served with an accusation issued pursuant to Chapter 5 (commencing with Section 11500) of Part 1 of Division 3 of Title 2 of the Government Code by registered mail to the address of the principal place of business on file with the department, whether or not the business has been closed or terminated, unless the registration service has notified the department in writing of another address where service shall be made.

(d) The department may, pending a hearing, temporarily suspend the license issued to a registration service for not more than 30 days if the director finds that action is required in the public interest. In that case, a hearing shall be held and a decision issued within 30 days after notice of the temporary suspension or cancellation.

(e) The director may, following the filing of a statement of issues or an accusation against an applicant or a registration service, with the consent of the applicant or licensee, enter into a compromise settlement agreement with a stipulated restriction or penalty whereby the applicant or licensee accepts the terms and conditions of the agreement without hearing or appeal by any party thereto.

(1) The compromise settlement agreement may provide for a restricted license, special operating terms and conditions, a higher bond, a monetary penalty, or any other term or condition agreeable to the parties.

(2) The compromise settlement agreement shall be signed by the respondent applicant or licensee, the director, and the accuser, or their authorized representatives, and filed with the Office of Administrative Hearings, together with the department's notice of withdrawal of the statement of issues or the accusation upon which the action was initiated.

(3) A failure of the respondent applicant or licensee to carry out a compromise settlement agreement entered into under this section is a separate cause to refuse to issue, or to suspend, revoke, or cancel, any license authorizing the respondent to act as a registration service.

(f) Any person whose license to act as a registration service was suspended for cause and the terms of the suspension are unfulfilled, or whose license was revoked for cause, may reapply for a license to act as a registration service after not less than one year from the effective date of the suspension or revocation action.

(g) The issuance of a new license to that person is within the sole discretion of the department, and a hearing regarding that issuance shall be held only upon the consent of the director.
(Added by Stats. 1990, Ch. 1196, Sec. 3. Operative July 1, 1991, by Sec. 4 of Ch. 1196.)

11409. The fee for a license issued to a registration service is as follows:

(a) For the original license, or an ownership change which requires a new application, one hundred fifty dollars ($150), which is nonrefundable.

(b) For the annual renewal of a license, fifteen dollars ($15).

(c) For the alteration of an existing license required by a name change, address change, change in corporate officer structure, or the addition of a branch location, seventy dollars ($70).
(Added by Stats. 1990, Ch. 1196, Sec. 3. Operative July 1, 1991, by Sec. 4 of Ch. 1196.)

11410. (a) Every license issued under this chapter is valid for a period of one year from the last day of the month of issuance. Except as provided in subdivision (c), renewal of the license for the ensuing year may be obtained by the person to whom the license was issued upon application to the department and payment of the fee required by Section 11409.

(b) An application for the renewal of a license shall be made by the licensee not more than 90 days prior to the expiration date and shall be made by presenting the completed application form provided by the department and by payment of the renewal fee.

(c) If the application for renewal of the license is not made by midnight of the expiration date, the application may be made within 30 days following expiration of the license by paying the annual renewal fee and a penalty fee equal to the amount of the original application fee for each license held.

(d) A licensee shall not renew the license after the expiration of the 30-day period specified in subdivision (c).
(Amended by Stats. 2008, Ch. 179, Sec. 218. Effective January 1, 2009.)

11411. If a registration service ceases operation for any reason, the owner of the service immediately shall notify the department and, upon demand by the department, shall deliver to the department the registration service license, all records kept pursuant to Section 11406, and all customer transactions then in his or her possession, including any fees or receipts for fees due to the department or to the customer.
(Added by Stats. 1992, Ch. 1243, Sec. 77. Effective September 30, 1992.)

11413. The suspension, expiration, or cancellation of a registration service license provided for in this chapter shall not prevent the filing of an accusation for the revocation or suspension of the suspended, expired, or canceled license as provided in Section 11405 or 11408 or any related rules or regulations, and the department's decision that the license should be suspended or revoked. That determination may be considered in granting or refusing to grant any subsequent license authorized by this division to that licensee or to a business representative of that prior licensee.
(Added by Stats. 1998, Ch. 877, Sec. 47. Effective January 1, 1999.)

Chapter 3. Automobile Dismantlers

(Heading of Chapter 3 amended by Stats. 1963, Ch. 1106.)

11500. (a) (1) It shall be unlawful for any person to act as an automobile dismantler without first having an established place of business that meets the requirements set forth in Section 11514 and without first having procured a license or temporary permit issued by the department, or when such license or temporary permit has been canceled, suspended, revoked, invalidated, expired, or the terms and conditions of an agreement effected pursuant to Section 11509.1 have not been fulfilled. A violation of this subdivision is a misdemeanor, and is subject to the penalties described in paragraph (2).

(2) Notwithstanding Section 42002, a person convicted of a first violation of subdivision (a) for any reason other than described in paragraph (3) shall be punished by a fine of not less than two hundred fifty dollars ($250). A person convicted of a second separate violation of subdivision (a) for this reason shall be punished by a fine of not less than five hundred dollars ($500). A person convicted of a third or subsequent violation of subdivision (a) for this reason shall be punished by a fine of not less than one thousand dollars ($1,000).

(3) A person who violates subdivision (a) due to possessing nine or more catalytic converters that have been cut from a vehicle pursuant to Section 220 is, for a first violation, guilty of an infraction punishable by a fine of not more than one hundred dollars ($100). A person convicted of a second separate violation of subdivision (a) for this reason is guilty

of a misdemeanor punishable by a fine of not less than two hundred fifty dollars ($250). A person convicted of a third separate violation of subdivision (a) for this reason is guilty of a misdemeanor punishable by a fine of not less than five hundred dollars ($500). A person convicted of a fourth or subsequent violation of subdivision (a) for this reason is guilty of a misdemeanor and shall be punished by a fine of not less than one thousand dollars ($1,000).

(b) (1) A building or place used for the purpose of automobile dismantling in violation of subdivision (a) is a public nuisance subject to being enjoined, abated, and prevented, and for which damages may be recovered by any public body or officer.

(2) As used in this section, "public body" means any state agency, county, city, district, or any other political subdivision of the state.

(Amended by Stats. 2024, Ch. 495, Sec. 14. (SB 1518) Effective January 1, 2025.)

11501. Every automobile dismantler shall make application to the department upon the appropriate form for a license containing a general distinguishing number. The applicant shall submit proof of his status as a bona fide automobile dismantler as may reasonably be required by the department.

(Amended by Stats. 1975, Ch. 182.)

11502. The department shall have the power and duty to issue and for reasonable cause shown to refuse to issue a license. The department may refuse to any applicant therefor a license provided for herein, if such applicant does not meet the requirements of the terms and provisions of this code relating to the conduct of an automobile dismantling business.

(Amended by Stats. 1975, Ch. 182.)

11503. The department may refuse to issue a license to an applicant when it determines any of the following:

(a) The applicant was previously the holder, or a managerial employee of the holder, of a license issued under this chapter which was revoked for cause and never reissued by the department, or which was suspended for cause and the terms of suspension have not been fulfilled.

(b) The applicant was previously a business representative whose license issued under this chapter was revoked for cause and never reissued or was suspended for cause and the terms of suspension have not been fulfilled.

(c) If the applicant is a business, a business representative was previously the holder of a license, or was a business representative of a business whose license, issued under this chapter was revoked for cause and never reissued or was suspended for cause and the terms of suspension have not been fulfilled; or, by reason of the facts and circumstances related to the organization, control, and management of the business, the operation of that business will be directed, controlled, or managed by individuals who, by reason of their conviction of violations of this code, would be ineligible for a license and, by licensing that business, the purposes of this chapter would be defeated.

(d) The applicant, or a business representative if the applicant is a business, has been convicted of a crime or has committed any act or engaged in conduct involving moral turpitude which is substantially related to the qualifications, functions, or duties of the licensed activity. A conviction after a plea of nolo contendere is a conviction within the meaning of this section.

(e) The applicant was previously the holder of an occupational license issued by another state, authorizing the same or similar activities of a license issued under this division; and that license was revoked or suspended for cause and was never reissued, or was suspended for cause, and the terms of suspension have not been fulfilled.

(f) The information contained in an application is incorrect.

(g) A decision of the department to cancel, suspend, or revoke a license has been made, and the applicant was a business representative of the business regulated under that license.

(Amended by Stats. 1998, Ch. 877, Sec. 48. Effective January 1, 1999.)

11503.1. Any of the causes specified in this chapter as a cause to suspend or revoke the license issued to an automobile dismantler is cause to refuse to issue a license to an automobile dismantler.

(Amended by Stats. 1990, Ch. 1563, Sec. 28.)

11503.5. (a) The department, after notice and hearing, on an interim basis, may refuse to issue or may suspend a license issued under this chapter when the applicant or licensee, or a business representative if the applicant or licensee is a business, has been convicted of a crime involving moral turpitude which is substantially related to the qualifications, functions, or duties of the licensed activity, if an appeal of the conviction is pending or the conviction has otherwise not become final. A conviction after a plea of nolo contendere is a conviction within the meaning of this section.

(b) When a conviction, upon which an interim refusal to issue or suspension under subdivision (a) is based, is affirmed on appeal or otherwise becomes final, the refusal to issue or suspension shall automatically take effect as a denial or revocation, as the case may be, of the license. If the interim refusal to issue or suspension was stayed under probationary terms and conditions, the subsequent automatic denial or revocation shall also be stayed under the same terms and conditions for a term not to exceed the original term of probation for the interim refusal or suspension.

(c) If a conviction, upon which an interim refusal to issue or suspension under subdivision (a) is based, is reversed on appeal, the refusal or suspension shall be set aside immediately by the department.

(Added by Stats. 1990, Ch. 1563, Sec. 29.)

11504. (a) An applicant who applies for a license pursuant to Section 11501 shall submit an application to the department on the forms prescribed by the department. The applicant shall provide the department with information as to the applicant's character, honesty, integrity, and reputation, as the department may consider necessary. The department, by regulation, shall prescribe what information is required of the applicant for the purposes of this subdivision, and the applicant shall provide that information under penalty of perjury. In addition to any other information required by the department, the department shall require the applicant to furnish all of the following information on any application for a new license or the renewal of a license, if the applicant is required by other provisions of law to have the following permits, numbers, or plan:

(1) Board of Equalization resale permit number.

(2) Identification number issued by the California Environmental Protection Agency.

(3) A statement indicating that the applicant has either filed an application for a stormwater permit or is not required to obtain a stormwater permit.

(4) A statement indicating that the applicant has either filed a hazardous materials business plan or is not required to file that plan.

(5) The tax identification number assigned by the Franchise Tax Board.

(b) Upon receipt of an application for a new license that is accompanied by the appropriate fee, the department shall, not later than 120 days from the receipt of that application, make a thorough investigation of all of the information contained in the application.

(c) (1) Upon receipt of an application for renewal of a license that is accompanied by the appropriate fee, the department shall, not later than 120 days from the receipt of that application, make a thorough investigation of the information contained in the application, except the information specified in paragraphs (1) to (5), inclusive, of subdivision (a).

(2) As of January 1, 2011, upon receipt of an application for the renewal of a license that is accompanied by the appropriate fee, the department shall, not later than 120 days from the receipt of that application, make a thorough investigation of all of the information contained in the application.

(d) A person holding a license issued pursuant to Section 11501 shall notify the department, within 10 days, of any change in the ownership or corporate structure of the licensee.

(Amended by Stats. 2009, Ch. 475, Sec. 1. (AB 805) Effective January 1, 2010.)

11505. (a) The department, upon granting a license shall issue to the applicant a license containing the applicant's name and address and the general distinguishing number assigned to the applicant.

(b) When the department has issued a license pursuant to subdivision (a), the licensee may apply for and the department shall issue special plates which shall have displayed thereon the general distinguishing number assigned to the applicant. Each plate so issued shall also contain a number or symbol identifying the plate from every other plate bearing a like general distinguishing number.

(c) The department shall also furnish books and forms as it may determine necessary, which books and forms are and shall remain the property of the department and may be taken up at any time for inspection.

(Amended by Stats. 1975, Ch. 182.)

11506. Except where the provisions of this code require the refusal to issue a license, the department may issue a license restricted by conditions to be observed in the exercise of the privilege granted. The terms and conditions to be attached to the exercise of the privilege under such restricted license shall be such as may, in the judgment of the department, be in the public interest and suitable to the qualifications of the applicant as disclosed by the application and investigation by the department.

(Amended by Stats. 1975, Ch. 182.)

11507. Pending the satisfaction of the department that the applicant has met the requirements under this code, it may issue a temporary permit to any person applying for an automobile dismantler license. The temporary permit shall permit the operation by the automobile dismantler for a period not to exceed 120 days while the department is completing its investigation and determination of all facts relative to the qualification of the applicant to such license. The department may cancel such temporary permit when it has determined or has reasonable cause to believe that the application is incorrect or incomplete or the temporary permit was issued in error. Such temporary permit shall be invalid when canceled or when the applicant's license has been issued or refused.

(Amended by Stats. 1975, Ch. 182.)

11508. (a) Every occupational license and special plate issued under this chapter shall be valid for a period of one year from midnight of the last day of the month of issuance. Renewal of the occupational license and special plates for the ensuing year may be obtained by the person to whom any plates and license were issued upon application to the department and payment of the fee provided in this code.

(b) Except as provided in subdivision (c), every application for the renewal of an occupational license and special plates which expire pursuant to this section shall be made by the person to whom issued not more than 90 days prior to the expiration date, and shall be made by presenting the completed application form provided by the department and by payment of the full annual renewal fee for the occupational license and special plates.

(c) If the application for renewal of the occupational license and special plates is not made by midnight of the expiration date, the application may be made within 30 days following expiration of the license by paying the annual renewal fee and a penalty fee equal to the amount of the original application fee for each occupational license held. A penalty as specified in Sections 9553 and 9554 shall also be added to each special plate renewed during the 30-day period following expiration of the special plates.

(d) In no event may the licensee renew the occupational license or special plates after the expiration of the 30-day period authorized in subdivision (c).

(Amended by Stats. 1984, Ch. 499, Sec. 10.)

11509. (a) The department, after notice and hearing, may suspend or revoke the license issued to an automobile dismantler upon the determination that the person to whom the license was issued is not lawfully entitled thereto or has done any of the following:

(1) Made or knowingly or negligently permitted any illegal use of the special plates issued to him or her.

(2) Used a false or fictitious name or knowingly made any false statement or concealed any material fact in any application or other document filed with the department.

(3) Failed to provide and maintain a clear physical division between the type of business licensed pursuant to this chapter and any other type of business conducted at the established place of business.

(4) Violated any provision of Division 3 (commencing with Section 4000) or any rule or regulation adopted pursuant thereto.

(5) Violated any provision of Division 4 (commencing with Section 10500) or any rule or regulation adopted pursuant thereto.

(6) Violated any provision of this chapter, except Section 11520, or any rule or regulation adopted pursuant thereto.

(7) Knowingly, repeatedly, or flagrantly violated Section 11520.

(8) Violated any provision of Part 5 (commencing with Section 10701) of Division 2 of the Revenue and Taxation Code or any rule or regulation adopted pursuant thereto.

(9) Purchased, concealed, possessed, or otherwise acquired or disposed of a vehicle, or a part thereof, knowing it to be stolen.

(10) Failed to meet and maintain the requirements for the issuance of an automobile dismantler's license as provided in this code.

(11) Failed to pay, within 30 days after written demand from the department, any fees or penalties due on vehicles acquired for dismantling which are not the subject of dispute. If the dismantler disputes the validity of the fees or penalties, the 30-day period shall not commence until the department, after review, has determined the fee or penalty to be due.

(12) Submitted a check, draft, or money order to the department for any obligation or fees due the state, and it is thereafter dishonored or refused payment upon presentation.

(13) Failed to meet the terms and conditions of a previous agreement entered into pursuant to Section 11509.1.

(b) Any of the causes specified in this chapter as a cause for refusal to issue a license to an automobile dismantler applicant is cause, after notice and hearing, to suspend or revoke a license and special plates issued to an automobile dismantler.

(c) Except as provided in Section 11509.1, every hearing provided for in this chapter shall be held pursuant to Chapter 5 (commencing with Section 11500) of Part 1 of Division 3 of Title 2 of the Government Code.

(Amended by Stats. 1990, Ch. 1563, Sec. 30.)

11509.1. (a) After the filing of an accusation under this chapter, the director may enter into a stipulated compromise settlement agreement with the consent of the licensee on terms and conditions mutually agreeable to the director, the respondent licensee, and the accuser without further hearing or appeal. The agreement may include, but is not limited to, a period of probation or monetary penalties, or both. The monetary penalty shall not exceed one thousand dollars ($1,000) for each violation, and it shall be based on the nature of the violation and the effect of the violation on the purposes of this chapter.

(b) A compromise settlement agreement may be entered before, during, or after the hearing, but is valid only if executed and filed pursuant to subdivision (d) before the proposed decision of the hearing officer, if any, is adopted or the case is decided.

(c) The department shall adopt, by regulation, a schedule of maximum and minimum amounts of monetary penalties, the payment of which may be included as a term or condition of a compromise settlement agreement entered under subdivision (a). Any monetary penalty included in a compromise settlement agreement shall be within the range of monetary penalties in that schedule.

(d) Any compromise settlement agreement entered under this section shall be signed by the director, the respondent licensee, and the accuser, or by their authorized representatives. The director shall file, or cause to be filed, the agreement with the Office of Administrative Hearings, together with the department's notice of withdrawal of the accusation or statement of issues upon which the action was initiated.

(e) If the respondent licensee fails to perform all of the terms and conditions of the compromise settlement agreement, the agreement is void and the department may take any action authorized by law notwithstanding the agreement, including, but not limited to, refiling the accusation or imposing license sanctions.

(Repealed and added by Stats. 1985, Ch. 1022, Sec. 16.)

11509.5. A person whose automobile dismantler's license has been revoked or whose application for a license has been denied may reapply for such license after a period of not less than one year has elapsed from the effective date of the decision revoking the license or denying the application; provided, however, that if such decision was based upon paragraph (3), (9), or (10) of subdivision (a) of Section 11509, or Section 11513, an earlier reapplication may be made accompanied by evidence satisfactory to the department that such grounds no longer exist.

(Amended by Stats. 1979, Ch. 373.)

11510. The department may, pending a hearing, temporarily suspend the license and special plates issued to an automobile dismantler for a period not to exceed 30 days if the director finds that such action is required in the public interest. In any such case a hearing shall be held and a decision thereon issued within 30 days after notice of temporary suspension.

Every hearing as provided for in this section shall be pursuant to the provisions of Chapter 5 (commencing with Section 11500) of Part 1 of Division 3 of Title 2 of the Government Code.

(Amended by Stats. 1971, Ch. 1214.)

11511. In any administrative action to revoke or suspend an automobile dismantler's license:

(a) Proof that a stolen vehicle of a type subject to registration under this code, or a part thereof, was found in the possession of, or upon the premises of, the dismantler shall constitute in evidence a prima facie presumption that the dismantler had knowledge that the vehicle was stolen. This presumption may be rebutted by satisfactory evidence that the dismantler has complied with paragraphs (1), (2), (3), and (5) of subdivision (a) of Section 11520.

(b) Proof that a vehicle of a type subject to registration under this code is found in a partially dismantled condition in the possession of, or upon the premises of, the dismantler shall constitute in evidence a prima facie presumption that the vehicle was partially dismantled by the dismantler. The presumption may be rebutted by a business record of the dismantler reflecting the partially dismantled condition of the vehicle on the date of acquisition.

(Amended by Stats. 1982, Ch. 466, Sec. 109.)

11512. (a) Upon refusal of the department to issue a license to an automobile dismantler the applicant shall be entitled to demand in writing a hearing before the director or his representative within 60 days after notice of refusal.

(b) The hearing shall be conducted pursuant to the provisions of Chapter 5 (commencing with Section 11500) of Part 1 of Division 3 of Title 2 of the Government Code.

(Amended by Stats. 1975, Ch. 182.)

11513. (a) The department shall not issue an automobile dismantler's license to any applicant for that license who has not an established place of business as defined in this code. If the automobile dismantler changes the site or location of his or her established place of business, he or she shall immediately upon making the change notify the department. If the automobile dismantler, for any reason ceases to be in possession of an established place of business from and on which he or she conducts the business for which he or she is licensed, he or she shall immediately notify the department and, upon demand by the department, shall deliver to the department the automobile dismantler's license, and all books and forms provided by the department in his or her possession.

(b) Any person licensed under this chapter who has closed his or her established place of business may be served with process issued pursuant to Chapter 5 (commencing with Section 11500) of Part 1 of Division 3 of Title 2 of the Government Code by registered mail at that place of business, unless the person has notified the department in writing of another address where service may be made.

(Amended by Stats. 1988, Ch. 751, Sec. 5.)

11514. (a) An automobile dismantler's established place of business and such other sites or locations as may be operated and maintained by such automobile dismantler in conjunction with his principal established place of business shall have posted, in a place conspicuous to the public in each and every site or location, the license issued by the department and shall have erected or posted thereon such signs or devices providing information relating to the automobile dismantler's name and the location and address of his established place of business so as to enable any person doing business with such automobile dismantler to identify him properly. Every such sign erected or posted on an established place of business shall have an area of not less than 32 square feet per side displayed and shall contain lettering not less than six inches in height. The sign shall indicate the nature of the dismantler's business by inclusion of "Automobile Dismantler", "Automobile Wrecker", "Motorcycle Dismantler", "Trailer Dismantler", "Vehicle Dismantler", or a combination of such designations on such sign.

(b) Any local authority may provide for a sign and lettering smaller than that specified in subdivision (a); however, no local authority shall require a sign to have an area of less than four square feet per side displayed.

(Amended by Stats. 1977, Ch. 579.)

11515. (a) (1) Whenever an insurance company makes a total loss settlement on a total loss salvage vehicle, the insurance company, an occupational licensee of the department authorized by the insurance company, or a salvage pool authorized by the insurance company, within 10 days from the settlement of the loss, shall forward the properly endorsed certificate of ownership or other evidence of ownership acceptable to the department, the license plates, and a fee in the amount of fifteen dollars ($15), to the department. An occupational licensee of the department may submit a certificate of license plate destruction in lieu of the actual license plate.

(2) If an insurance company, an occupational licensee of the department authorized by the insurance company, or a salvage pool authorized by the insurance company is unable to obtain the properly endorsed certificate of ownership or other evidence of ownership acceptable to the department within 15 days following oral or written acceptance by the owner of an offer of an amount in settlement of a total loss, that insurance company, licensee, or salvage pool, on a form provided by the department and signed under penalty of perjury, may request the department to issue a salvage certificate for the vehicle. The request shall attest that the requester has attempted to obtain the certificate of ownership or other acceptable evidence of title, and shall include the license plates and fee described in paragraph (1). The attempt to obtain the certificate of ownership or other acceptable evidence of title shall be provided concurrently with the payment of the claim or by first-class mail, certificate of mailing, certified mail, other commercially available delivery service showing proof of delivery, or electronic mail.

(3) The department, upon receipt of the certificate of ownership, other evidence of title, or properly executed request described in paragraph (2), the license plates, and the fee, shall issue a salvage certificate for the vehicle.

(b) Whenever the owner of a total loss salvage vehicle retains possession of the vehicle, the insurance company shall notify the department of the retention on a form prescribed by the department. The insurance company shall also notify the insured or owner of the insured's or owner's responsibility to comply with this subdivision. The owner shall, within 10 days from the settlement of the loss, forward the properly endorsed certificate of ownership or other evidence of ownership acceptable to the department, the license plates, and a fee in the amount of fifteen dollars ($15) to the department. The department, upon receipt of the certificate of ownership or other evidence of title, the license plates, and the fee, shall issue a salvage certificate for the vehicle.

(c) Whenever a total loss salvage vehicle is not the subject of an insurance settlement, the owner shall, within 10 days from the loss, forward the properly endorsed certificate of ownership or other evidence of ownership acceptable to the department, the license plates, and a fee in the amount of fifteen dollars ($15) to the department.

(d) Whenever a total loss salvage vehicle is not the subject of an insurance settlement, a self-insurer, as defined in Section 16052, shall, within 10 days from the loss, forward the properly endorsed certificate of ownership or other evidence of ownership acceptable to the department, the license plates, and a fee in the amount of fifteen dollars ($15) to the department.

(e) Prior to the sale or disposal of a total loss salvage vehicle, the owner, owner's agent, or salvage pool, shall obtain a properly endorsed salvage certificate and deliver it to the purchaser within 10 days after payment in full for the salvage vehicle and shall also comply with Section 5900. The department shall accept the endorsed salvage certificate in lieu of the certificate of ownership or other evidence of ownership when accompanied by an application and other documents and fees, including, but not limited to, the fees required by Section 9265, as may be required by the department.

(f) This section does not apply to a vehicle that has been driven or taken without the consent of the owner thereof, until the vehicle has been recovered by the owner and only if the vehicle is a total loss salvage vehicle.

(g) A violation of subdivision (a), (b), (d), or (e) is a misdemeanor, pursuant to Section 40000.11. Notwithstanding Section 40000.11, a violation of subdivision (c) is an infraction, except that, if committed with the intent to defraud, a violation of subdivision (c) is a misdemeanor.

(h) (1) A salvage certificate issued pursuant to this section shall include a statement that the seller and subsequent sellers that transfer ownership of a total loss vehicle pursuant to a properly endorsed salvage certificate are required to disclose to the purchaser at, or prior to, the time of sale that the vehicle has been declared a total loss salvage vehicle.

(2) Effective on and after the department includes in the salvage certificate form the statement described in paragraph (1), a seller who fails to make the disclosure described in paragraph (1) shall be subject to a civil penalty of not more than five hundred dollars ($500).

(3) Nothing in this subdivision affects any other civil remedy provided by law, including, but not limited to, punitive damages.

(Amended by Stats. 2022, Ch. 125, Sec. 1. (AB 2330) Effective January 1, 2023.)

11515.1. A salvage pool shall sell a vehicle only with either of the following:

(a) A salvage certificate, except those vehicles described in subdivision (f) of Section 11515, which may be sold with a certificate of title.

(b) A nonrepairable vehicle certificate, except those vehicles described in subdivision (f) of Section 11515.2, which may be sold with a certificate of title.

(Amended by Stats. 1994, Ch. 1008, Sec. 13. Effective January 1, 1995. Operative July 1, 1995, by Sec. 19 of Ch. 1008.)

11515.2. (a) (1) If an insurance company makes a total loss settlement on a nonrepairable vehicle and takes possession of that vehicle, either itself or through an agent, the insurance company, an occupational licensee of the department authorized by the insurance company, or a salvage pool authorized by the insurance company, shall, within 10 days after receipt of title by the insurer, free and clear of all liens, forward the properly endorsed certificate of ownership or other evidence of ownership acceptable to the department, the license plates, and a fee in the amount of fifteen dollars ($15) to the department. An occupational licensee of the department may submit a certificate of license plate destruction in lieu of the actual license plate. The department, upon receipt of the certificate of ownership or other evidence of title, the license plates, and the fee, shall issue a nonrepairable vehicle certificate for the vehicle.

(2) If an insurance company, an occupational licensee of the department authorized by the insurance company, or a salvage pool authorized by the insurance company is unable to obtain the properly endorsed certificate of ownership or other evidence of ownership acceptable to the department within 15 days following oral or written acceptance by the owner of an offer of an amount in settlement of a total loss, that insurance company, licensee, or salvage pool, on a form provided by the department and signed under penalty of perjury, may request the department to issue a nonrepairable vehicle certificate for the vehicle. The request shall attest that the requester has attempted to obtain the certificate of ownership or other acceptable evidence of title, and shall include the license plates and fee described in paragraph (1). The attempt to obtain the certificate of ownership or other acceptable evidence of title shall be submitted concurrently with the payment of the claim or by first-class mail, certificate of mailing, certified mail, other commercially available delivery service showing proof of delivery, or electronic mail.

(3) The department, upon receipt of the certificate of ownership, other evidence of title, or properly executed request described in paragraph (2), the license plates, and the fee, shall issue a nonrepairable vehicle certificate for the vehicle.

(b) If the owner of a nonrepairable vehicle retains possession of the vehicle, the insurance company shall notify the department of the retention on a form prescribed by the department. The insurance company shall also notify the insured or owner of the insured's or owner's responsibility to comply with this subdivision. The owner shall, within 10 days from the settlement of the loss, forward the properly endorsed certificate of ownership or other evidence of ownership acceptable to the department, the license plates, and a fee in the amount of fifteen dollars ($15) to the department. The department, upon receipt of the certificate of ownership or other evidence of title, the license plates, and the fee, shall issue a nonrepairable vehicle certificate for the vehicle.

(c) If a nonrepairable vehicle is not the subject of an insurance settlement, the owner shall, within 10 days from the loss, forward the properly endorsed certificate of ownership or other evidence of ownership acceptable to the department, the license plates, and a fee in the amount of fifteen dollars ($15) to the department.

(d) If a nonrepairable vehicle is not the subject of an insurance settlement, a self-insurer, as defined in Section 16052, shall, within 10 days of the loss, forward the properly endorsed certificate of ownership or other evidence of ownership acceptable to the department, the license plates, and a fee in the amount of fifteen dollars ($15) to the department.

(e) Prior to sale or disposal of a nonrepairable vehicle, the owner, owner's agent, or salvage pool shall obtain a properly endorsed nonrepairable vehicle certificate and deliver it to the purchaser within 10 days after payment in full for the nonrepairable vehicle and shall also comply with Section 5900. The department shall accept the endorsed nonrepairable vehicle certificate in lieu of the certificate of ownership or other evidence of ownership when accompanied by an application and other documents and fees, including, but not limited to, the fees required by Section 9265, as may be required by the department.

(f) This section does not apply to a vehicle that has been driven or taken without the consent of the owner thereof, until the vehicle has been recovered by the owner and only if the vehicle is a nonrepairable vehicle.

(g) A nonrepairable vehicle certificate shall be conspicuously labeled with the words "NONREPAIRABLE VEHICLE" across the front of the certificate.

(h) A violation of subdivision (a), (b), (d), or (e) is a misdemeanor, pursuant to Section 40000.11. Notwithstanding Section 40000.11, a violation of subdivision (c) is an infraction, except that, if committed with intent to defraud, a violation of subdivision (c) is a misdemeanor.

(Amended by Stats. 2022, Ch. 125, Sec. 2. (AB 2330) Effective January 1, 2023.)

11515.3. (a) If an insurance company requests a salvage pool authorized by the insurance company or an occupational licensee of the department authorized by the insurance company to take possession of a vehicle that is the subject of a total loss claim, and, subsequently, the insurance company does not take ownership of the vehicle, the insurance company may direct the salvage pool or occupational licensee of the department to release the vehicle to the registered and legal owner or lienholder of the vehicle. The insurance company shall provide the salvage pool or occupational licensee of the department with notice authorizing the release of the vehicle to the vehicle's registered and legal owner or lienholder. This notice may be sent by mail, electronic mail, or a proprietary electronic system accessed by both the insurance company and the salvage pool or occupational licensee of the department.

(b) Upon receiving notice from an insurance company pursuant to subdivision (a), the salvage pool or occupational licensee of the department shall send two notices to the registered and legal owner and any lienholder of the vehicle informing the registered and legal owner and lienholder that the vehicle is available to pick up and will be sold or otherwise disposed of if no response is received. The notice shall inform the owner and any lienholder that the registered and legal owner and lienholder has 30 days from the date of mailing of the first notice and 14 days from the date of mailing of the second notice to pick up the vehicle from the salvage pool or occupational licensee of the department before the vehicle is deemed abandoned. The notice shall also inform the registered and legal owner and any lienholder of their right to contact the salvage pool or occupational licensee of the department regarding their intent to pick up the vehicle in order to receive an additional 30 days from the date of contact to pick up the vehicle before the vehicle is deemed abandoned. Notice under this subdivision shall be sent by certified mail or by another commercially available delivery service providing proof of delivery to the address on record with the department and any other known address, or for vehicles last registered in another jurisdiction, to the address on record with that jurisdiction and any other known address.

(c) If the registered and legal owner or any lienholder contacts the salvage pool or occupational licensee of the department regarding their intent to pick up the vehicle within the time periods described in subdivision (b), the salvage pool or occupational licensee shall give the registered and legal owner or any lienholder an additional 30 days from the date of contact to pick up the vehicle before the vehicle is deemed abandoned.

(d) If the registered and legal owner or any lienholder of the vehicle does not pick up the vehicle within 30 days after the date of mailing of the first notice, and within 14 days after the date of mailing of the second notice, as described in subdivision (b), or within 30 days from the date of contact with the salvage pool or occupational licensee of the department, as described in subdivision (c), the vehicle shall be deemed abandoned, the vehicle's certificate of title is deemed to be assigned to the salvage pool or occupational licensee of the department.

(e) The salvage pool or occupational licensee of the department, without surrendering the certificate of title, may request, on a form provided by the department and signed under penalty of perjury, that the department issue a salvage certificate or nonrepairable vehicle certificate that is free and clear of all liens for the vehicle. The request shall be accompanied by an attestation and certification that the insurance company did not take ownership of the vehicle and directed the release of the vehicle to the registered and legal owner or lienholder, an attestation and certification of delivery of the notices required pursuant to subdivision (b) or that the notices were returned undeliverable after the notices were sent to the registered and legal owner and any lienholder, as required pursuant to subdivision (b), the license plates for the vehicle, and the fee required by subdivision (c) of Section 11515 for a salvage vehicle or the fee required by subdivision (c) of Section 11515.2 for a nonrepairable vehicle. Notwithstanding any outstanding liens against the vehicle, the department shall issue a salvage certificate or nonrepairable vehicle certificate that is free and clear of all liens for the vehicle to the salvage pool or occupational licensee of the department in possession of the vehicle. An occupational licensee of the department may submit a certificate of license plate destruction in lieu of the actual license plate.

(f) The salvage pool or occupational licensee of the department shall maintain an accurate record of every vehicle it acquires and disposes of pursuant to this section. The records shall be maintained for two years and be open for inspection by any peace officer during the regular business hours of that salvage pool or occupational licensee of the department. The records shall include, but not be limited to, copies of the notices sent to the registered and legal owner and any lienholder of the vehicle and proof of delivery of the notices as specified in subdivision (b).

(Added by Stats. 2024, Ch. 364, Sec. 1. (AB 1901) Effective January 1, 2025.)

11516. (a) Any automobile dismantler owning or controlling any vehicle of a type otherwise required to be registered under this code, may operate or move the vehicle upon the highways without subjecting the vehicle to registration or transfer, or both, solely for the purpose of moving the vehicle from its location to the established place of business of the automobile dismantler or to a scrap processor, if there are displayed on the vehicle special plates issued to the automobile dismantler as provided in this chapter, in addition to other license plates or permits already assigned and attached to the vehicle in the manner prescribed in Article 9 (commencing with Section 5200) of Chapter 1 of Division 3.

(b) The provisions of this section do not apply to work or service vehicles owned by an automobile dismantler.

(c) Every owner, upon receipt of a registration card issued for special plates, shall maintain the registration card or a facsimile copy of it with the vehicle bearing the special plates.

(Amended by Stats. 1994, Ch. 1220, Sec. 55. Effective September 30, 1994.)

11517. The department may issue a certificate of convenience to the executor, executrix, administrator or administratrix of the estate of a deceased holder of validly outstanding special plates and license issued under this chapter, or if no executor, executrix, administrator or administratrix had been appointed, and until a certified copy of an order making such appointment is filed with the department, to the widow or other heir otherwise entitled to conduct the business of the deceased, permitting such person to exercise the privileges granted by such special plates and license for a period of one year from and after the date of death, pending, but not later than, disposal of the business and qualifications of the vendor of the business or such surviving widow or heir for such special plates and license under the provisions of this chapter. The department may restrict or condition the license and special plates and attach to the exercise of the privileges thereunder such terms and conditions as in its judgment the protection of the public requires.

(Amended by Stats. 1971, Ch. 1214.)

11518. The special plates and license provided for in this chapter shall be automatically canceled if any of the following occurs:

(a) The abandonment of the established place of business of the automobile dismantler or the change thereof without notice to the department pursuant to Section 11513.

(b) The voluntary or involuntary surrender for any cause by the licensee of the special plates and license, except that a surrender of the special plates and license, the cessation of business by the licensee, or the suspension or revocation of the corporate status of the licensee, does not preclude the filing of an accusation for revocation or suspension of the surrendered license as provided in Section 11509, and does not affect the department's decision to suspend or revoke the license. The department's decision to suspend or revoke the license may be considered in issuing or refusing to issue any subsequent license authorized by this division to that licensee or any business representative of that licensee.

(c) When the person designated as the licensee has changed, except that the special plates issued to the original licensee may be transferred upon application as provided in Section 11501 and the newly designated licensee, as transferee, shall succeed to the privileges evidenced by the plates until their expiration.

(d) The suspension or revocation of the corporate status of the licensee.

(e) The suspension or revocation of the seller's permit of the licensee by the State Board of Equalization.

(Amended by Stats. 1990, Ch. 1563, Sec. 31.)

11519. (a) A vehicle that has been reported as a total loss salvage vehicle or dismantled vehicle may not be subsequently registered until there is submitted to the department all of the following:

(1) The prescribed bill of sale.

(2) An appropriate application.

(3) A vehicle safety systems certificate of compliance issued pursuant to Article 6.5 (commencing with Section 9888.5) of Chapter 20.3 of Division 3 of the Business and Professions Code, except that a fleet owner of motor trucks of three or more axles that are more than 6,000 pounds unladen weight, and a fleet owner of truck tractors, may instead submit certification for their own rebuilt vehicle if the fleet owner operates an inspection and maintenance station licensed by the commissioner under subdivision (b) of Section 2525.

(4) With respect to a motor vehicle subject to Part 5 (commencing with Section 43000) of Division 26 of the Health and Safety Code, a valid certificate of compliance from a licensed motor vehicle pollution control device installation and inspection station indicating that the vehicle is properly equipped with a motor vehicle pollution control device that is in proper operating condition and is in compliance with Part 5 (commencing with Section 43000) of Division 26 of the Health and Safety Code.

(5) Any other documents or fees required under law.

(b) The department may not register a vehicle that has been referred to the Department of the California Highway Patrol under subdivision (b) of Section 5505 or that has been selected for inspection by that department under subdivision (c) of that section, until the applicant for registration submits to the department a certification of inspection issued by the Department of the California Highway Patrol and all of the documents required under subdivision (a).

(Amended by Stats. 2023, Ch. 681, Sec. 24. (AB 1263) Effective January 1, 2024.)

11520. (a) A licensed automobile dismantler who acquired, for the purpose of dismantling, actual possession, as a transferee, of a vehicle of a type subject to registration under this code shall do all of the following:

(1) Within five calendar days, not including the day of acquisition, mail a notice of acquisition to the department at its headquarters.

(2) Within five calendar days, not including the day of acquisition, mail a copy of the notice of acquisition to the Department of Justice at its headquarters.

(3) Not begin dismantling until 10 calendar days have elapsed after mailing the notice of acquisition. In the alternative, dismantling may begin any time after the dismantler complies with paragraph (4).

(4) Deliver to the department, within 90 calendar days of the date of acquisition, the documents evidencing ownership and the license plates last issued for the vehicle. Proof that a registered or certified letter of demand for the documents was sent within 90 days of the date of acquisition to the person from whom the vehicle was acquired may be substituted for documents that cannot otherwise be obtained. A certificate of license plate destruction, when authorized by the director, may be delivered in lieu of the license plates.

(5) Maintain a business record of all vehicles acquired for dismantling. The record shall contain the name and address of the person from whom the vehicle was acquired; the date the vehicle was acquired; the license plate number last assigned to the vehicle; and a brief description of the vehicle, including its make, type, and the vehicle identification number used for registration purposes. The record required by this paragraph shall be a business record of the dismantler separate and distinct from the records maintained in those books and forms furnished by the department.

(b) Paragraphs (1) and (2) of subdivision (a) do not apply to vehicles acquired pursuant to Section 11515, 11515.2, 22851.2, or 22851.3 of this code or Section 3071, 3072, or 3073 of the Civil Code.

(c) Paragraphs (1), (2), (3), and (4) of subdivision (a) do not apply to a vehicle acquired from another person if the other person has already notified and cleared the vehicle for dismantling with the department pursuant to this code and a bill of sale has been executed to the dismantler that properly identifies the vehicle and contains evidence of clearance by the department, including, but not limited to, a dismantling report number, temporary receipt number, or other proof of compliance with this section.

(Amended by Stats. 1997, Ch. 945, Sec. 15. Effective January 1, 1998.)

11521. No person required to be licensed as an automobile dismantler under this code shall advertise the services of an automobile dismantler without indicating in the advertisement the occupational license or permit number of the automobile dismantler as issued by the department.

(Added by Stats. 1996, Ch. 265, Sec. 1. Effective January 1, 1997.)

11522. The provisions of this chapter shall not prevent the local authorities of any city, city and county or county by ordinance, within the exercise of the police power of such city, city and county or county, from imposing local regulations with respect to traffic in loose vehicle parts and vehicle accessories.

(Added by Stats. 1961, Ch. 1640.)

11540. (a) A salvage pool shall maintain an accurate record of every vehicle it acquires and every vehicle it disposes of, and shall notify the department of the disposition of any vehicle pursuant to Section 5900.

(b) Whenever a salvage pool acquires a total loss salvage vehicle, a nonrepairable vehicle, or a recovered stolen vehicle and the license plates on the vehicle have not been removed pursuant to subdivision (a) of Section 11515, subdivision (a) of Section 11515.2, subdivision (e) of Section 11515.3, or any other provision of law, the salvage pool shall, prior to disposing of that vehicle, remove and submit the license plates to the department. The salvage pool shall maintain an accurate record of every license plate it acquires and disposes of, which records shall be maintained for two years and be open for inspection by any peace officer during the regular business hours of that salvage pool.

(Amended by Stats. 2024, Ch. 364, Sec. 2. (AB 1901) Effective January 1, 2025.)

11541. The department shall administer and enforce all provisions of this code pertaining to salvage pools.

This section shall become operative on July 1, 1987.

(Added by Stats. 1986, Ch. 952, Sec. 5. Section operative July 1, 1987, by its own provisions.)

Chapter 3.5. Lessor-Retailers

(Chapter 3.5 added by Stats. 1976, Ch. 1284.)

11600. It shall be unlawful for any lessor-retailer to make a retail sale of a vehicle of a type subject to registration without having first procured either a vehicle dealer license or a lessor-retailer license or temporary permit issued by the department or when such license or temporary permit issued by the department has been canceled, suspended, revoked, or invalidated or has expired.

(Added by Stats. 1976, Ch. 1284.)

11601. (a) Every lessor-retailer who sells at retail a vehicle of a type subject to registration shall make application to the department for a license. The applicant shall submit proof of his status as a bona fide lessor-retailer as may reasonably be required by the department.

(b) An application shall be made for the principal place of business, and a separate branch office application shall be made for each branch office location of the licensee as shall be operated and maintained by the applicant in conjunction with the retail sale or sales of vehicles.

(c) "Principal place of business," for the purposes of this chapter, means the place designated by the lessor-retailer as the main business or office location in California whether or not retail sales are made from such location.

(Added by Stats. 1976, Ch. 1284.)

11602. (a) The department shall prescribe and provide forms to be used for application for licenses to be issued under the terms and provisions of this chapter and require of such applicants, where appropriate as a condition precedent to issuance of such license, such information, including but not limited to, fingerprints and personal history statements, touching on and concerning the applicant's character, honesty, integrity and reputation as it may consider necessary; provided, however, that every application for a lessor-retailer license shall contain, in addition to such information that the department may require, a statement of the following facts:

(1) The name and residence address of the applicant and the trade name, if any, under which he intends to conduct his business; and if the applicant be a partnership, the name and residence address of each member thereof, whether a limited or general partner, and the name under which the partnership business is to be conducted; and if the applicant be a corporation, the name of the corporation and the name and address of each of its principal officers and directors.

(2) A complete description, including the city, town or village with the street and number, if any, of its principal place of business in California and such other and additional branch location or locations.

(b) Upon receipt of an application accompanied with the appropriate fee, the department shall make a thorough investigation of the information contained in the application.

(Added by Stats. 1976, Ch. 1284.)

11603. (a) The department may issue, or for reasonable cause shown, refuse to issue, a license to any applicant applying for a lessor-retailer license or branch office location.

(b) The license shall contain the applicant's name, location address and the general distinguishing number assigned to the applicant.

(Added by Stats. 1976, Ch. 1284.)

11604. The department may refuse to issue a lessor-retailer license when it makes any of the following determinations:

(a) The applicant has outstanding an unsatisfied final court judgment rendered in connection with an activity licensed under the authority of this division.

(b) The applicant was previously the holder, or a managerial employee of the holder, of a license issued under this division which was revoked for cause and never reissued by the department, or which was suspended for cause and the terms of suspension have not been fulfilled.

(c) The applicant was previously a business representative whose license issued under this division was revoked for cause and never reissued or was suspended for cause and the terms of suspension have not been fulfilled.

(d) If the applicant is a business, a business representative was previously the holder of a license, or was a business representative of a business whose license, issued under this division, was revoked for cause and never reissued or was suspended for cause and the terms of suspension have not been fulfilled; or, by reason of the facts and circumstances related to the organization, control, and management of the business, the operation of that business will be directed, controlled, or managed by individuals who, by reason of their conviction of violations of this code, would be ineligible for a license and, by licensing that business, the purposes of this chapter would be defeated.

(e) The applicant, or a business representative if the applicant is a business, has been convicted of a crime or committed any act or engaged in conduct involving moral turpitude which is substantially related to the qualifications, functions, or duties of the licensed activity. A conviction after a plea of nolo contendere is a conviction within the meaning of this section.

(f) The applicant was previously the holder of an occupational license issued by another state, authorizing the same or similar activities of a license issued under this division; and that license was revoked or suspended for cause and was never reissued, or was suspended for cause, and the terms of suspension have not been fulfilled.

(g) The information contained in the application is incorrect.

(h) A decision of the department to cancel, suspend, or revoke a license has been made, and the applicant was a business representative of the business regulated under that license.

(i) The applicant does not have a principal place of business in California.

(j) The applicant has failed to pay the full amount of a claim paid by the Consumer Motor Vehicle Recovery Corporation, plus interest at the rate of 10 percent per annum, as described in subdivision (i) of Section 11703.

(Amended by Stats. 2007, Ch. 437, Sec. 3. Effective January 1, 2008.)

11604.1. Any cause specified in this chapter as a cause to suspend or revoke the license issued to a lessor-retailer is a cause to refuse to issue a license to a lessor-retailer.

(Added by Stats. 1990, Ch. 1563, Sec. 33.)

11604.5. (a) The department, after notice and hearing, on an interim basis, may refuse to issue or may suspend a license issued under this chapter when the applicant or licensee, or a business representative if the applicant or licensee is a business, has been convicted of a crime involving moral turpitude which is substantially related to the qualifications, functions, or duties of the licensed activity, if an appeal of the conviction is pending or the conviction has otherwise not become final. A conviction after a plea of nolo contendere is a conviction within the meaning of this section.

(b) When a conviction, upon which an interim refusal to issue or suspension under subdivision (a) is based, is affirmed on appeal or otherwise becomes final, the refusal to issue or suspension shall automatically take effect as a denial or revocation, as the case may be, of the license. If the interim refusal to issue or suspension was stayed under probationary terms and conditions, the subsequent automatic denial or revocation shall also be stayed under the same terms and conditions for a term not to exceed the original term of probation for the interim refusal to issue or suspension.

(c) If a conviction, upon which an interim refusal to issue or suspension under subdivision (a) is based, is reversed on appeal, the refusal or suspension shall be set aside immediately by the department.

(Added by Stats. 1990, Ch. 1563, Sec. 34.)

11605. (a) Upon refusal of the department to issue a license to a lessor-retailer, the applicant shall be entitled to demand in writing a hearing before the director or his representative within 60 days after notice of refusal.

(b) The hearing shall be conducted pursuant to the provisions of Chapter 5 (commencing with Section 11500) of Part 1 of Division 3 of Title 2 of the Government Code.

(Added by Stats. 1976, Ch. 1284.)

11606. Except where the provisions of this code require the refusal to issue a license, the department may issue a probationary license subject to conditions to be observed by the licensee in the exercise of the privilege granted. The conditions to be attached to the exercise of the privilege shall not appear on the face of the license but shall be such as may, in the judgment of the department, be in the public interest and suitable to the qualifications of the applicant as disclosed by the application and investigation by the department of the information contained therein.

(Added by Stats. 1976, Ch. 1284.)

11607. Pending the satisfaction of the department that the applicant has met the requirements under this chapter, it may issue a temporary permit to any person applying for a lessor-retailer license or branch office location. The temporary permit shall permit the operation by the lessor-retailer while the department is completing its investigation and determination of all facts relative to the qualifications of the applicant to such license. The department may cancel such temporary permit when it has determined or has reasonable cause to believe that the application is incorrect or incomplete or the temporary permit was issued in error. Such temporary permit shall be invalid when canceled or when the applicant's license has been issued or refused.

(Amended by Stats. 2018, Ch. 198, Sec. 18. (AB 3246) Effective January 1, 2019.)

11608. The department may issue a certificate of convenience to the executor, executrix, administrator or administratrix of the estate of a deceased holder of a valid license issued under this chapter, or if no executor, executrix, administrator or administratrix has been appointed, and until a certified copy of an order making such appointment is filed with the department, to the widow or other heir otherwise entitled to conduct the business of the deceased, permitting such person to exercise the privileges granted by such license for a period of one year from and after the date of death and necessary one-year renewals thereafter, pending, but not later than, disposal of the business and qualification of the vendee of the business or such surviving widow, heir or other persons for such license under the provisions of this chapter. The department may restrict or condition the license and attach to the exercise of the privileges thereunder such terms and conditions as in its judgment the protection of the public requires.

(Added by Stats. 1976, Ch. 1284.)

11609. Each office location operated and maintained by a lessor-retailer in conjunction with its retail sale of a vehicle or vehicles shall have posted in a place conspicuous to the public the license issued by the department to the lessor, and shall have erected or posted thereon such signs or devices providing information relating to the lessor-retailer's name, the office location and the office address, to enable any person doing business with such lessor to identify him properly.

(Added by Stats. 1976, Ch. 1284.)

11609.5. Every lessor-retailer who displays or offers one or more used vehicles for sale at retail shall post a notice not less than 8 inches high and 10 inches wide, in a place conspicuous to the public, which states the following:

"The prospective purchaser of a vehicle may, at his or her own expense and with the approval of the lessor-retailer, have the vehicle inspected by an independent third party either on or off these premises."

(Added by Stats. 1990, Ch. 1563, Sec. 35.)

11610. (a) If the lessor-retailer changes the location of its principal place of business or any branch office location in California, the lessor-retailer shall immediately upon making the change notify the department.

(b) If a lessor-retailer, for any reason, ceases to be in possession of its principal place of business or any branch office location, the lessor-retailer shall immediately notify the department, and shall deliver to the department the lessor-retailer license issued for the location, and, upon demand, all report of sale books in his or her possession.

(c) Any person licensed under this chapter who has closed his or her principal place of business may be served with process issued pursuant to Chapter 5 (commencing with Section 11500) of Part 1 of Division 3 of Title 2 of the Government Code by registered mail at that place of business, unless the person has notified the department in writing of another address where service may be made.

(Amended by Stats. 1990, Ch. 216, Sec. 114.)

11612. (a) Before any lessor-retailer license shall be issued or renewed by the department to any applicant therefor, the applicant shall procure and file with the department a bond meeting the same requirements as specified for a vehicle dealer's license in Sections 11710 and 11710.2.

(b) Any cause of action or claim specified in Section 11711 against a vehicle dealer's bond shall also be a cause of action or claim against a lessor-retailer's bond.

(Amended by Stats. 1982, Ch. 517, Sec. 395.)

11613. (a) The department, after notice and hearing, may suspend or revoke the license issued to a lessor-retailer upon determining that the person to whom the license was issued is not lawfully entitled thereto, or has done any of the following:

(1) Filed an application for the license using a false or fictitious name not registered with the proper authorities, or knowingly made any false statement or knowingly concealed any material fact, in the application for the license.

(2) Used a false or fictitious name, knowingly made any false statement or knowingly concealed any material fact in any application for the registration of a vehicle, or otherwise committed a fraud in the application.

(3) Knowingly purchased, sold, or otherwise acquired or disposed of a stolen motor vehicle.

(4) Violated any provision of Division 3 (commencing with Section 4000) or rule or regulation adopted pursuant thereto.

(5) Violated any provision of Division 4 (commencing with Section 10500) or rule or regulation adopted pursuant thereto.

(6) Violated any provision of this chapter or rule or regulation adopted pursuant thereto.

(7) Violated any provision of Chapter 2b (commencing with Section 2981) of Title 14 of Part 4 of Division 3 of the Civil Code or rule or regulation adopted pursuant thereto under the authority of Section 1651.

(8) Submitted a check, draft, or money order to the department for any obligation or fee due the state which was thereafter dishonored or refused payment upon presentation.

(9) Caused any person to suffer any loss or damage by reason of any fraud or deceit practiced on, or fraudulent representations made to, that person in the sale of a vehicle or parts or accessories thereof.

For purposes of this subdivision, "fraud" includes any act or omission which is included within the definition of either "actual fraud" or "constructive fraud" as defined in Sections 1572 and 1573 of the Civil Code, and "deceit" has the same meaning as defined in Section 1710 of the Civil Code. In addition, "fraud" and "deceit" include, but are not limited to, a misrepresentation in any manner, whether intentionally false or due to gross negligence, of a material fact; a promise or representation not made honestly and in good faith; an intentional failure to disclose a material fact; and any act within Section 484 of the Penal Code.

For purposes of this subdivision, "person" also includes a governmental entity.

(b) Any of the causes specified in this chapter as a cause for refusal to issue a license to a lessor-retailer applicant is cause to suspend or revoke a license issued to a lessor-retailer.

(c) Every hearing provided for in this section shall be conducted pursuant to Chapter 5 (commencing with Section 11500) of Part 1 of Division 3 of Title 2 of the Government Code.

(Amended by Stats. 1990, Ch. 1563, Sec. 36.)

11613.5. (a) After the filing of an accusation under this chapter, the director may enter into a stipulated compromise settlement agreement with the consent of the licensee on terms and conditions mutually agreeable to the director, the respondent licensee, and the accuser without further hearing or appeal. The agreement may include, but is not limited to, a period of probation or monetary penalties, or both. The monetary penalty shall not exceed one thousand dollars ($1,000) for each violation, and it shall be based on the nature of the violation and the effect of the violation on the purposes of this chapter.

(b) A compromise settlement agreement may be entered before, during, or after the hearing, but is valid only if executed and filed pursuant to subdivision (d) before the proposed decision of the hearing officer, if any, is adopted or the case is decided.

(c) The department shall adopt, by regulation, a schedule of maximum and minimum amounts of monetary penalties, the payment of which may be included as a term or condition of a compromise settlement agreement entered under subdivision (a). Any monetary penalty included in a compromise settlement agreement shall be within the range of monetary penalties in that schedule.

(d) Any compromise settlement agreement entered under this section shall be signed by the director, the respondent licensee, and the accuser, or by their authorized representatives. The director shall file, or cause to be filed, the agreement with the Office of Administrative Hearings, together with the department's notice of withdrawal of the accusation or statement of issues upon which the action was initiated.

(e) If the respondent licensee fails to perform all of the terms and conditions of the compromise settlement agreement, the agreement is void and the department may take any action authorized by law notwithstanding the agreement, including, but not limited to, refiling the accusation or imposing license sanctions.

(Added by Stats. 1985, Ch. 1022, Sec. 18.)

11614. No lessor-retailer licensed under this chapter may do any of the following in connection with any activity for which this license is required:

(a) Make or disseminate, or cause to be made or disseminated, before the public in this state, in any newspaper or other publication, or any advertising device, or by oral representation, or in any other manner or means whatever, any statement that is untrue or misleading and that is known, or which by the exercise of reasonable care should be known, to be untrue or misleading; or make or disseminate, or cause to be made or disseminated, any statement as part of a plan or scheme with the intent not to sell any vehicle, or service so advertised, at the price stated therein, or as so advertised.

(b) Advertise, or offer for sale in any manner, any vehicle not actually for sale at the premises of the lessor-retailer or available within a reasonable time to the lessor-retailer at the time of the advertisement or offer.

(c) Fail within 48 hours to give, in writing, notification to withdraw any advertisement of a vehicle that has been sold or withdrawn from sale.

(d) Advertise any specific vehicle for sale without identifying the vehicle by its model, model year, and either its license number or that portion of the vehicle identification number that distinguishes the vehicle from all other vehicles of the same make, model, and model-year. Model-year is not required to be advertised for current model-year vehicles. Year models are no longer current when ensuing year models are available for purchase at retail in California.

(e) Advertise the total price of a vehicle without including all costs to the purchaser at the time of delivery at the lessor-retailer's premises, except sales tax, vehicle registration fees, finance charges, certificate of compliance or noncompliance fees not exceeding thirty-five dollars ($35) pursuant to any statute, and any dealer documentary preparation charge. The dealer documentary charge shall not exceed thirty-five dollars ($35).

(f) (1) Fail to disclose, in an advertisement of a vehicle for sale, that there will be added to the advertised total price, at the time of sale, charges for sales tax, vehicle registration fees, the fee charged by the state for the issuance of any certificate of compliance or noncompliance pursuant to any statute, finance charges, or any dealer documentary preparation charge.

(2) For purposes of paragraph (1), "advertisement" means any advertisement in a newspaper, magazine, direct mail publication, or handbill that is two or more columns in width or one column in width and more than seven inches in length, or on any Web page of a lessor-retailer's Web site that displays the price of a vehicle offered for sale on the Internet, as that term is defined in paragraph (6) of subdivision (e) of Section 17538 of the Business and Professions Code.

(g) Advertise or otherwise represent, or knowingly allow to be advertised or represented on the lessor-retailer's behalf or at the lessor-retailer's place of business, that no downpayment is required in connection with the sale of a vehicle when a downpayment is in fact required and the buyer is advised or induced to finance the downpayment by a loan in addition to any other loan financing the remainder of the purchase price of the vehicle. The terms "no downpayment," "zero down delivers," or similar terms shall not be advertised unless the vehicle will be sold to any qualified purchaser without a prior payment of any kind or trade-in.

(h) Refuse to sell a vehicle to any person at the advertised total price, exclusive of sales tax, vehicle registration fees, finance charges, certificate of compliance or noncompliance pursuant to any statute, and any dealer documentary preparation charge, which charges shall not exceed thirty-five dollars ($35) for the documentary preparation charge and thirty-five dollars ($35) for the certificate of compliance or noncompliance pursuant to any statute, while the vehicle remains unsold or unleased, unless the advertisement states the advertised total price is good only for a specified time and the time has elapsed.

(i) Engage in the business for which the licensee is licensed without having in force and effect a bond required by Section 11612.

(j) Engage in the business for which the lessor-retailer is licensed without at all times maintaining a principal place of business and any branch office location required by this chapter.

(k) Permit the use of the lessor-retailer license, supplies, or books by any other person for the purpose of permitting that person to engage in the sale of vehicles required to be registered under this code, or to permit the use of the lessor-retailer license, supplies, or books to operate a branch office location to be used by any other person, if, in either situation, the licensee has no financial or equitable interest or investment in the vehicles sold by, or the business of, or branch office location used by, the person, or has no interest or investment other than commissions, compensations, fees, or any other thing of value received for the use of the lessor-retailer license, supplies, or books to engage in the sale of vehicles.

(l) Violate any provision of Article 10 (commencing with Section 28050) of Chapter 5 of Division 12.

(m) Represent the dealer documentary preparation charge, or certificate of compliance or noncompliance fee, as a governmental fee.

(n) Advertise free merchandise, gifts, or services provided by a lessor-retailer contingent on the purchase of a vehicle. "Free" includes merchandise or services offered for sale at a price less than the lessor-retailer's cost of the merchandise or services.

(o) Advertise vehicles and related goods or services with the intent not to supply reasonably expectable demand, unless the advertisement discloses a limitation of quantity.

(p) Use the term "rebate" or similar words such as "cash back" in advertising the sale of a vehicle.

(q) Require a person to pay a higher price for a vehicle and related goods or services for receiving advertised credit terms than the cash price the same person would have to pay to purchase the same vehicle and related goods or services. For the purpose of this subdivision, "cash price" has the meaning as defined in subdivision (e) of Section 2981 of the Civil Code.

(r) Misrepresent the authority of a representative or agent to negotiate the final terms of a transaction.

(s) Violate any law prohibiting bait and switch advertising, including, but not limited to, the guides against bait advertising set forth in Part 238 of Title 16 of the Code of Federal Regulations, as those regulations read on January 1, 1988.

(t) Make any untrue or misleading statement indicating that a vehicle is equipped with all the factory installed optional equipment the manufacturer offers, including, but not limited to, a false statement that a vehicle is "fully factory equipped."

(u) Advertise any underselling claim, such as "we have the lowest prices" or "we will beat any dealer's price," unless the lessor-retailer has conducted a recent survey showing that the lessor-retailer sells its vehicles at lower prices than any other licensee in its trade area and maintains records to adequately substantiate the claim. The substantiating records shall be made available to the department upon request.

(v) To display or offer for sale any used vehicle unless there is affixed to the vehicle the Federal Trade Commission's Buyer's Guide as required by Part 455 of Title 16 of the Code of Federal Regulations.

(w) This section shall become operative on July 1, 2001.

(Amended by Stats. 2002, Ch. 947, Sec. 1. Effective January 1, 2003.)

11614.1. No lessor-retailer licensed under this chapter may do any of the following in connection with any activity for which this license is required:

(a) Use a picture in connection with any advertisement of the price of a specific vehicle or class of vehicles, unless the picture is of the year, make, and model being offered for sale. The picture may not depict a vehicle with optional equipment or a design not actually offered at the advertised price.

(b) Advertise a vehicle for sale that was used by the selling lessor-retailer in its business as a demonstrator, executive vehicle, service vehicle, rental, loaner, or lease vehicle, unless the advertisement clearly and conspicuously discloses the previous use made by that licensee of the vehicle. An advertisement may not describe any of those vehicles as "new."

(c) Advertise any used vehicle of the current or prior model-year without expressly disclosing the vehicle as "used," "previously owned," or a similar term that indicates that the vehicle is used, as defined in this code.

(d) Use the terms "on approved credit" or "on credit approval" in an advertisement for the sale of a vehicle unless those terms are clearly and conspicuously disclosed and unabbreviated.

(e) Advertise an amount described by terms such as "unpaid balance" or "balance can be financed" unless the total sale price is clearly and conspicuously disclosed and is in close proximity to the advertised balance.

(f) Advertise credit terms that fail to comply with the disclosure requirements of Section 226.24 of Title 12 of the Code of Federal Regulations. Advertisements of terms that include escalated payments, balloon payments, or deferred downpayments shall clearly and conspicuously identify those payments as to amounts and time due.

(g) Advertise claims such as "everyone financed," "no credit rejected," or similar claims unless the dealer is willing to extend credit to any person under any and all circumstances.

(h) Advertise the amount of any downpayment unless it represents the total payment required of a purchaser prior to delivery of the vehicle, including any payment for sales tax or license. A statement such as "$____ delivers," is an example of an advertised downpayment.

(i) Fail to clearly and conspicuously disclose in an advertisement for the sale of a vehicle any disclosure required by this code or any qualifying term used in conjunction with advertised credit terms. Unless otherwise provided by statute, the specific size of disclosures or qualifying terms is not prescribed.

(Amended by Stats. 2003, Ch. 62, Sec. 302. Effective January 1, 2004.)

11615. It shall be unlawful and a violation of this code for a lessor-retailer licensed under this chapter when selling at retail a vehicle in a transaction for which this license is required:

(a) To deliver, following sale, a vehicle for operation on California highways, if such vehicle does not meet all of the equipment requirements of Division 12 (commencing with Section 24000) of this code.

(b) To fail to deliver to a transferee lawfully entitled thereto a properly endorsed certificate of ownership.

(c) To violate any of the terms or provisions of Part 5 (commencing with Section 10701) of Division 2 of the Revenue and Taxation Code or rules and regulations adopted pursuant thereto or adopted pursuant to Section 1651 of this code.

(d) To take a vehicle in trade in part or total payment for a vehicle sold by the lessor-retailer.

(e) To sell a vehicle which has not been previously leased, bailed or rented or acquired or contracted for lease or rental by the lessor-retailer.

(f) To display a vehicle for sale at a location other than the principal place of business or branch office authorized by the department for that lessor-retailer.

(Amended by Stats. 1990, Ch. 1563, Sec. 36.7.)

11615.5. It is unlawful and a violation of this code for a person holding a license under this chapter to make a retail sale of a motor vehicle, except to the lessee of such vehicle, required to be registered pursuant to Division 3 (commencing with Section 4000) or subject to identification pursuant to Division 16.5 (commencing with Section 38000) if such person files with the department a report of sale as provided in Section 4456 with respect to such retail sale, without making the return and payment of any sales tax due and required by Section 6451 of the Revenue and Taxation Code.

(Amended by Stats. 1979, Ch. 373.)

11616. If a purchaser of a vehicle pays to the lessor-retailer an amount for the licensing or transfer of title of the vehicle, which amount is in excess of the actual fees due for such licensing or transfer, or which amount is in excess of the amount which has been paid, prior to the sale, by the lessor-retailer to the state in order to avoid penalties that would have accrued because of late payment of such fees, the lessor-retailer shall return such excess amount to the purchaser, whether or not such purchaser requests the return of the excess amount.

(Added by Stats. 1976, Ch. 1284.)

11617. (a) The license provided for in this chapter shall be automatically canceled upon the happening of any of the following:

(1) The abandonment of the principal place of business of the lessor-retailer or the change thereof without notice to the department as provided in Section 11610.

(2) The failure of the licensee to maintain an adequate bond or to procure and file another bond as required by Section 11612 prior to the effective date of the termination by the surety of any existing bond.

(3) The voluntary or involuntary surrender for any cause by the licensee of the license, except that a surrender of the license, or cessation of business by the licensee, or the suspension or revocation of the corporate status of the licensee, does not preclude the filing of an accusation for revocation or suspension of the surrendered license as provided in Section 11613, and does not affect the department's decision to suspend or revoke the license. The department's determination to suspend or revoke the license may be considered in issuing or refusing to issue any subsequent license authorized by this division to that licensee or any business representative of that licensee.

(4) Notification to the department that the person designated as licensee has changed.

(5) The suspension or cancellation of the corporate status of the licensee.

(6) The suspension, revocation, or cancellation of the seller's permit of the licensee by the California Department of Tax and Fee Administration pursuant to Part 1 (commencing with Section 6001) of Division 2 of the Revenue and Taxation Code.

(b) The branch office location license provided for in this chapter shall be automatically canceled upon the abandonment of the branch office location of the lessor-retailer or the change of that branch office without notice to the department as provided in Section 11610.

(Amended by Stats. 2022, Ch. 295, Sec. 9. (AB 2956) Effective January 1, 2023.)

11618. The department may, pending a hearing, temporarily suspend the license issued to a lessor-retailer for a period not to exceed 30 days, if the director finds that such action is required in the public interest. In any such case a hearing shall be held and a decision thereon issued within 30 days after notice of the temporary suspension.

Every hearing as provided for in this section shall be pursuant to the provisions of Chapter 5 (commencing with Section 11500) of Part 1 of Division 3 of Title 2 of the Government Code.

(Added by Stats. 1976, Ch. 1284.)

11620. (a) Every occupational license issued under this chapter shall be valid for a period of one year from midnight of the last day of the month of issuance. Except as provided in subdivision (c), renewal of an occupational license for the ensuing year may be obtained by the person to whom the occupational license was issued upon application to the department and payment of the fee provided in this code.

(b) Every application for the renewal of an occupational license which expires pursuant to this section shall be made by the person to whom issued not more than 90 days prior to the expiration date, and shall be made by presenting the completed application form provided by the department and by payment of the full annual renewal fee for the occupational license.

(c) If the application for renewal of the occupational license is not made by midnight of the expiration date, the application may be made within 30 days following expiration of the license by paying the annual renewal fee and a penalty fee equal to the amount of the original application fee for each occupational license held.

(d) In no event may the licensee renew the occupational license after the expiration of the 30-day period authorized in subdivision (c).

(Amended by Stats. 1984, Ch. 499, Sec. 11.)

Chapter 4. Manufacturers, Transporters, Dealers, and Salesmen

(Chapter 4 enacted by Stats. 1959, Ch. 3.)

Article 1. Issuance of Licenses and Certificates to Manufacturers, Transporters, and Dealers

(Article 1 enacted by Stats. 1959, Ch. 3.)

11700. No person shall act as a dealer, remanufacturer, manufacturer, or transporter, or as a manufacturer branch, remanufacturer branch, distributor, or distributor branch, without having first been issued a license as required in Section 11701 or temporary permit issued by the department, except that, when the license or temporary permit has been canceled, suspended, or revoked or has expired, any vehicle in the dealer's inventory and owned by the dealer when the dealer ceased to be licensed may be sold at wholesale to a licensed dealer. The former licensee shall give the purchasing dealer a statement of facts stating that the seller is not a licensed dealer. Any vehicle on consignment with the dealer when the dealer ceased to be licensed shall be returned to the consignor. Any vehicle in the dealer's possession, but not owned by the dealer and not on consignment when the dealer ceased to be licensed, shall be returned to the owner of the vehicle.

(Amended by Stats. 1990, Ch. 1563, Sec. 38.)

11700.1. A dealer who does not have an established place of business in this state but who is currently authorized to do business as, and who has an established place of business as, a vehicle dealer in another state is not subject to licensure under this article if the business transacted in California is limited to the importation of vehicles for sale to, or the export of vehicles purchased from, persons licensed in California under this chapter.

(Added by Stats. 1979, Ch. 1088.)

11700.2. A dealer who obtains an autobroker's endorsement to his or her dealer's license is subject to all of the licensing, advertising, and other statutory and regulatory requirements and prohibitions applicable to a dealer, regardless of whether that dealer acts as the buyer of a vehicle, the seller of a vehicle, or provides brokering services on behalf of another or others for the purpose of arranging, negotiating, assisting, or effectuating the sale of a vehicle not owned by that dealer.

(Added by Stats. 1995, Ch. 211, Sec. 4. Effective January 1, 1996.)

11700.3. No person may aid and abet a person in the performance of any act in violation of this chapter.

(Added by Stats. 2002, Ch. 407, Sec. 1. Effective January 1, 2003.)

11701. Every manufacturer, manufacturer branch, remanufacturer, remanufacturer branch, distributor, distributor branch, transporter, or dealer of vehicles of a type subject to registration, or snowmobiles, motorcycles, all-terrain vehicles, or trailers of a type subject to identification, shall make application to the department for a license containing a general distinguishing number. The applicant shall submit proof of his or her status as a bona fide manufacturer, manufacturer branch, remanufacturer, remanufacturer branch, distributor, distributor branch, transporter, or dealer as may reasonably be required by the department.

(Amended by Stats. 2004, Ch. 836, Sec. 8. Effective January 1, 2005.)

11702. The department may issue, or for reasonable cause shown, refuse to issue a license to any applicant applying for a manufacturer's, manufacturer's branch, remanufacturer's, remanufacturer's branch, distributor's, distributor's branch, transporter's, or dealer's license.

(Amended by Stats. 1983, Ch. 1286, Sec. 26.)

11703. The department may refuse to issue a license to a manufacturer, manufacturer branch, remanufacturer, remanufacturer branch, distributor, distributor branch, transporter, or dealer, if it determines any of the following:

(a) The applicant was previously the holder, or a managerial employee of the holder, of a license issued under this chapter which was revoked for cause and never reissued by the department, or which was suspended for cause and the terms of suspension have not been fulfilled.

(b) The applicant was previously a business representative of a business whose license issued under this chapter was revoked for cause and never reissued or was suspended for cause and the terms of suspension have not been fulfilled.

(c) If the applicant is a business, a business representative of the business was previously the holder of a license, or was a business representative of a business whose license, issued under this chapter was revoked for cause and never reissued or was suspended for cause and the terms of suspension have not been fulfilled; or, by reason of the facts and circumstances related to the organization, control, and management of the business, the operation of that business will be directed, controlled, or managed by individuals who, by reason of their conviction of violations of the provisions of this code, would be ineligible for a license and, by licensing the business, the purposes of this chapter would be defeated.

(d) The applicant, or a business representative if the applicant is a business, has been convicted of a crime or committed an act or engaged in conduct involving moral turpitude which is substantially related to the qualifications, functions, or duties of the licensed activity. A conviction after a plea of nolo contendere is a conviction within the meaning of this section.

(e) The applicant was previously the holder of an occupational license issued by another state, authorizing the same or similar activities of a license issued under this division; and that license was revoked or suspended for cause and was never reissued, or was suspended for cause, and the terms of suspension have not been fulfilled.

(f) The information contained in the application is incorrect.

(g) Upon investigation, the business history required by Section 11704 contains incomplete or incorrect information, or reflects substantial business irregularities.

(h) A decision of the department to cancel, suspend, or revoke a license has been made and the applicant was a business representative of the business regulated under that license.

(i) The applicant has failed to repay the full amount of a claim paid by the Consumer Motor Vehicle Recovery Corporation, plus interest at the rate of 10 percent per annum. The dealer or lessor-retailer's discharge in bankruptcy shall not relieve the dealer or lessor-retailer from the provisions of this subdivision, except to the extent, if any, mandated by bankruptcy law.

(Amended by Stats. 2007, Ch. 437, Sec. 4. Effective January 1, 2008.)

11703.1. Any of the causes specified in this chapter as a cause to suspend or revoke the license issued to a dealer, manufacturer, manufacturer branch, remanufacturer, remanufacturer branch, distributor, distributor branch, or transporter, is cause to refuse to issue a license to a dealer, manufacturer, manufacturer branch, remanufacturer, remanufacturer branch, distributor, distributor branch, or transporter.

(Amended by Stats. 1990, Ch. 1563, Sec. 40.)

11703.2. The department may refuse to issue a license to a manufacturer, manufacturer branch, remanufacturer, remanufacturer branch, distributor, distributor branch, transporter, or dealer, when the department determines that either of the following apply to the applicant:

(a) An outstanding and unsatisfied final judgment rendered against the applicant exists in connection with the purchase, sale, or lease of any vehicle.

(b) An outstanding and unsatisfied restitution order issued against the applicant under subdivision (a) of Section 11519.1 of the Government Code exists.

(Amended by Stats. 2007, Ch. 93, Sec. 2. Effective January 1, 2008.)

11703.3. A person whose license has been revoked or whose application for a license has been denied may reapply for a license after a period of not less than one year has elapsed from the effective date of the decision revoking the license or denying the application; except that if the decision was entered under the authority of subdivision (a), (b), (c), or (g) of Section 11703, or 11703.2, or paragraph (6) of subdivision (a) of Section 11705, a reapplication accompanied by evidence satisfactory to the department that such grounds no longer exist may be made earlier than such one-year period.

(Amended by Stats. 1976, Ch. 934.)

11703.4. The department may refuse to issue a license to a dealer when it determines that an applicant for a dealer's license has failed to effectively endorse an authorization for disclosure of an account or accounts relating to the operation of the dealership as provided for in Section 7473 of the Government Code.

(Added by Stats. 1976, Ch. 1320.)

11704. (a) Every applicant who applies for a license pursuant to Section 11701 shall submit an application to the department on the forms prescribed by the department. Such applicant shall provide the department with information as to the applicant's character, honesty, integrity, and reputation, as the department may consider necessary. The department, by regulation, shall prescribe what information is required of such an applicant for the purposes of this subdivision.

(b) Upon receipt of an application for a license which is accompanied by the appropriate fee, the department shall, within 120 days, make a thorough investigation of the information contained in the application.

(c) Every person holding a license issued pursuant to Section 11701 shall notify the department, within 10 days, of any change in the ownership or corporate structure of the licensee.

(Repealed and added by Stats. 1977, Ch. 452.)

11704.5. (a) Except as provided in subdivision (e), every person who applies for a dealer's license pursuant to Section 11701 for the purpose of transacting sales of used vehicles on a retail or wholesale basis only shall be required to take and successfully complete a written examination prepared and administered by the department before a license may be issued. The examination shall include, but need not be limited to, all of the following laws and subjects:

(1) Division 12 (commencing with Section 24000), relating to equipment of vehicles.

(2) Advertising.

(3) Odometers.

(4) Vehicle licensing and registration.

(5) Branch locations.

(6) Offsite sales.

(7) Unlawful dealer activities.

(8) Handling, completion, and disposition of departmental forms.

(b) Prior to the first taking of an examination under subdivision (a), every applicant shall successfully complete a preliminary educational program of not less than four hours. The program shall address, but not be limited to, all of the following topics:

(1) Chapter 2B (commencing with Section 2981) of Title 14 of Part 4 of Division 3 of the Civil Code, relating to motor vehicle sales finance.

(2) Motor vehicle financing.

(3) Truth in lending.

(4) Sales and use taxes.

(5) Division 12 (commencing with Section 24000), relating to equipment of vehicles.

(6) Advertising.

(7) Odometers.

(8) Vehicle licensing and registration.

(9) Branch locations.

(10) Offsite sales.

(11) Unlawful dealer activities.

(12) Air pollution control requirements.

(13) Regulations of the Bureau of Automotive Repair.

(14) Handling, completion, and disposition of departmental forms.

(c) (1) Except as provided in paragraph (2) or (3), every dealer who is required to complete a written examination and an educational program pursuant to subdivisions (a) and (b) and who is thereafter issued a dealer's license shall successfully complete, every two years after issuance of that license, an educational program of not less than four hours that offers instruction in the subjects listed under subdivision (a) and the topics listed under subdivision (b), in order to maintain or renew that license.

(2) A dealer is not required to complete the educational program set forth in paragraph (1) if the educational program is completed by a managerial employee employed by the dealer.

(3) Paragraph (1) does not apply to dealers who sell vehicles on a wholesale basis only and who, in a one-year period, deal with less than 50 vehicles that are subject to registration.

(d) Instruction described in subdivisions (b) and (c) may be provided by generally accredited educational institutions, private vocational schools, and educational programs and seminars offered by professional societies, organizations, trade associations, and other educational and technical programs that meet the requirements of this section or by the department.

(e) This section does not apply to any of the following:

(1) An applicant for a new vehicle dealer's license or any employee of that dealer.

(2) A person who holds a valid license as an automobile dismantler, an employee of that dismantler, or an applicant for an automobile dismantler's license.

(3) An applicant for a motorcycle only dealer's license or any employee of that dealer.

(4) An applicant for a trailer only dealer's license or any employee of that dealer.

(5) An applicant for an all-terrain only dealer's license or any employee of that dealer.

(Amended by Stats. 2004, Ch. 836, Sec. 9. Effective January 1, 2005.)

11704.7. Every person who applies to the department to take or retake the examination required under Section 11704.5 shall pay to the department a fee of sixteen dollars ($16).

(Added by Stats. 1996, Ch. 1008, Sec. 4. Effective January 1, 1997.)

11705. (a) The department, after notice and hearing, may suspend or revoke the license issued to a dealer, transporter, manufacturer, manufacturer branch, remanufacturer, remanufacturer branch, distributor, or distributor branch upon determining that the person to whom the license was issued is not lawfully entitled thereto, or has done any of the following:

(1) Filed an application for the license using a false or fictitious name not registered with the proper authorities, or knowingly made a false statement or knowingly concealed a material fact, in the application for the license.

(2) Made, or knowingly or negligently permitted, an illegal use of the special plates issued to the licensee.

(3) Used a false or fictitious name, knowingly made a false statement, or knowingly concealed a material fact, in an application for the registration of a vehicle, or otherwise committed a fraud in the application.

(4) Failed to deliver to a transferee lawfully entitled thereto a properly endorsed certificate of ownership.

(5) Knowingly purchased, sold, or otherwise acquired or disposed of a stolen motor vehicle.

(6) Failed to provide and maintain a clear physical division between the type of business licensed pursuant to this chapter and any other type of business conducted at the established place of business.

(7) Willfully violated Section 3064, 3065, 3074, or 3075 or any rule or regulation adopted pursuant thereto.

(8) Violated any provision of Division 3 (commencing with Section 4000) or any rule or regulation adopted pursuant thereto, or subdivision (a) of Section 38200.

(9) Violated any provision of Division 4 (commencing with Section 10500) or any rule or regulation adopted pursuant thereto.

(10) Violated any provision of Article 1 (commencing with Section 11700) of, or Article 1.1 (commencing with Section 11750) of, Chapter 4 of Division 5 or any rule or regulation adopted pursuant thereto.

(11) Violated any provision of Part 5 (commencing with Section 10701) of Division 2 of the Revenue and Taxation Code or any rule or regulation adopted pursuant thereto.

(12) Violated any provision of Chapter 2b (commencing with Section 2981) of Title 14 of Part 4 of Division 3 of the Civil Code or any rule or regulation adopted pursuant thereto.

(13) Submitted a check, draft, or money order to the department for any obligation or fee due the state which was dishonored or refused payment upon presentation.

(14) (A) Has caused any person to suffer any loss or damage by reason of any fraud or deceit practiced on that person or fraudulent representations made to that person in the course of the licensed activity.

(B) For purposes of this paragraph, "fraud" includes any act or omission which is included within the definition of either "actual fraud" or "constructive fraud" as defined in Sections 1572 and 1573 of the Civil Code, and "deceit" has the same meaning as defined in Section 1710 of the Civil Code. In addition, "fraud" and "deceit" include, but are not limited to, a misrepresentation in any manner, whether intentionally false or due to gross negligence, of a material fact; a promise or representation not made honestly and in good faith; an intentional failure to disclose a material fact; and any act within Section 484 of the Penal Code.

(C) For purposes of this paragraph, "person" also includes a governmental entity.

(15) Failed to meet the terms and conditions of an agreement entered into pursuant to Section 11707.

(16) Violated Section 43151, 43152, or 43153 of, or subdivision (b) of Section 44072.10 of, the Health and Safety Code.

(17) Failed to repay a claim paid by the Consumer Motor Vehicle Recovery Corporation as provided in subdivision (i) of Section 11703.

(18) As a buy-here-pay-here dealer, violated any provision of Chapter 11 (commencing with Section 7500) of Division 3 of the Business and Professions Code or any rule or regulation adopted pursuant to those provisions.

(b) Any of the causes specified in this chapter as a cause for refusal to issue a license to a transporter, manufacturer, manufacturer branch, remanufacturer, remanufacturer branch, distributor, distributor branch, or dealer applicant is cause to suspend or revoke a license issued to a transporter, manufacturer, manufacturer branch, remanufacturer, remanufacturer branch, distributor, distributor branch, or dealer.

(c) Except as provided in Section 11707, every hearing provided for in this section shall be conducted pursuant to Chapter 5 (commencing with Section 11500) of Part 1 of Division 3 of Title 2 of the Government Code.

(Amended by Stats. 2016, Ch. 682, Sec. 3. (AB 287) Effective January 1, 2017.)

11705.4. (a) The department, after notice and hearing, may suspend or revoke the license issued to a dealer, transporter, manufacturer, manufacturer branch, distributor, or distributor branch upon determining that the person to whom the license was issued is not lawfully entitled thereto or has willfully violated the terms and conditions of any warranty responsibilities as set forth in Title 1.7 (commencing with Section 1790) of Part 4 of Division 3 of the Civil Code.

(b) Every hearing as provided for in this section shall be pursuant to the provisions of Chapter 5 (commencing with Section 11500) of Part 1 of Division 3 of Title 2 of the Government Code.

(Amended by Stats. 1977, Ch. 873.)

11706. The department may, pending a hearing, temporarily suspend the license and special plates issued to a manufacturer, manufacturer branch, remanufacturer, remanufacturer branch, distributor, distributor branch, transporter, or dealer, for a period not to exceed 30 days, if the director finds that such action is required in the public interest. In any such case, a hearing shall be held and a decision thereon issued within 30 days after notice of the temporary suspension.

Every hearing, as provided for in this section, shall be conducted pursuant to Chapter 5 (commencing with Section 11500) of Part 1 of Division 3 of Title 2 of the Government Code.

(Amended by Stats. 1983, Ch. 1286, Sec. 32.)

11707. (a) After the filing of an accusation under this article, the director may enter into a stipulated compromise settlement agreement with the consent of the licensee on terms and conditions mutually agreeable to the director, the respondent licensee, and the accuser without further hearing or appeal. The agreement may include, but is not limited to, a period of probation or monetary penalties, or both. Except as provided in Section 11728, the monetary penalty shall not exceed one thousand dollars ($1,000) for each violation, and it shall be based on the nature of the violation and the effect of the violation on the purposes of this article.

(b) A compromise settlement agreement may be entered before, during, or after the hearing, but is valid only if executed and filed pursuant to subdivision (d) before the proposed decision of the hearing officer, if any, is adopted or the case is decided.

(c) The department shall adopt, by regulation, a schedule of maximum and minimum amounts of monetary penalties, the payment of which may be included as a term or condition of a compromise settlement agreement entered under subdivision (a). Any monetary penalty included in a compromise settlement agreement shall be within the range of monetary penalties in that schedule.

(d) Any compromise settlement agreement entered under this section shall be signed by the director, the respondent licensee, and the accuser, or by their authorized representatives. The director shall file, or cause to be filed, the agreement with the Office of Administrative Hearings, together with the department's notice of withdrawal of the accusation or statement of issues upon which the action was initiated.

(e) If the respondent licensee fails to perform all of the terms and conditions of the compromise settlement agreement, the agreement is void and the department may take any action authorized by law, notwithstanding the agreement, including, but not limited to, refiling the accusation or imposing license sanctions.

(Amended by Stats. 1990, Ch. 90, Sec. 3. Effective May 9, 1990.)

11708. (a) Upon refusal of the department to issue a license and special plates to a manufacturer, manufacturer branch, remanufacturer, remanufacturer branch, distributor, distributor branch, transporter, or dealer, the applicant shall be entitled to demand, in writing, a hearing before the director or his or her representative within 60 days after notice of refusal.

(b) The hearing shall be conducted pursuant to Chapter 5 (commencing with Section 11500) of Part 1 of Division 3 of Title 2 of the Government Code.

(Amended by Stats. 1983, Ch. 1286, Sec. 33.)

11709. (a) A dealer's established place of business, and other sites or locations as may be operated and maintained by the dealer in conjunction with his or her established place of business, shall have posted, in a place conspicuous to the public in each and every location, the license, or a true and exact copy of the license, issued by the department to the dealer and to each salesperson employed by the dealer and shall have erected or posted thereon signs or devices providing information relating to the dealer's name and the location and address of the dealer's established place of business to enable any person doing business with the dealer to identify him or her properly. A sign erected or posted pursuant to this subdivision, on an established place of business, shall have an area of not less than two square feet per side displayed and shall contain lettering of sufficient size to enable the sign to be read from a distance of at least

50 feet. This section shall not apply to a dealer who is a wholesaler involved for profit only in the sale of vehicles between licensed dealers.

(b) Notwithstanding Section 11704 and this section, a dealer may display vehicles at a fair, exposition, or similar exhibit without securing a branch license, if no actual sales are made at those events and the display does not exceed 30 days.

(c) A vehicle displayed pursuant to subdivision (b) or (e) shall be identified by a sign or device providing information relating to the dealer's name and the location and address of the dealer's established place of business.

(d) This section shall not be applicable to a dealer who deals only in off-highway vehicles subject to identification, as defined in Section 38012.

(e) Notwithstanding Section 11704 and this section, a vessel dealer may display a trailer and may sell a trailer in conjunction with the sale of a vessel at a fair, exposition, or similar exhibit without securing a branch license if the display does not exceed 30 days.

(Amended by Stats. 2010, Ch. 483, Sec. 1. (SB 1004) Effective January 1, 2011.)

11709.1. Every dealer who displays or offers one or more used vehicles for sale at retail shall post a notice not less than 8 inches high and 10 inches wide, in a place conspicuous to the public, which states the following:

"The prospective purchaser of a vehicle may, at his or her own expense and with the approval of the dealer, have the vehicle inspected by an independent third party either on or off these premises."

(Added by Stats. 1990, Ch. 1563, Sec. 42.)

11709.2. (a) Every dealer shall conspicuously display a notice, not less than 8 inches high and 10 inches wide, in each sales office and sales cubicle of a dealer's established place of business where written terms of specific sale or lease transactions are discussed with prospective purchasers or lessees, and in each room of a dealer's established place of business where sale and lease contracts are regularly executed, which states the following:

"THERE IS NO COOLING-OFF PERIOD UNLESS YOU OBTAIN A CONTRACT CANCELLATION OPTION

California law does not provide for a "cooling-off" or other cancellation period for vehicle lease or purchase contracts. Therefore, you cannot later cancel such a contract simply because you change your mind, decide the vehicle costs too much, or wish you had acquired a different vehicle. After you sign a motor vehicle purchase or lease contract, it may only be canceled with the agreement of the seller or lessor or for legal cause, such as fraud.

However, California law does require a seller to offer a 2-day contract cancellation option on used vehicles with a purchase price of less than $40,000, subject to certain statutory conditions. This contract cancellation option requirement does not apply to the sale of a recreational vehicle, a motorcycle, or an off-highway motor vehicle subject to identification under California law. See the vehicle contract cancellation option agreement for details."

(b) This section shall remain in effect only until October 1, 2026, and as of that date is repealed.

(Amended by Stats. 2025, Ch. 354, Sec. 8. (SB 766) Effective January 1, 2026. Repealed as of October 1, 2026, by its own provisions. See later operative version as added by Sec. 9 of Stats. 2025, Ch. 354.)

11709.2. (a) Every dealer shall conspicuously display a physical notice, in at least 36-point type, in each sales office and sales cubicle of a dealer's established place of business where written terms of specific sale or lease transactions are discussed with prospective purchasers or lessees, and in each room of a dealer's established place of business where sale and lease contracts are regularly executed that states the following:

"CALIFORNIA DOES NOT HAVE A COOLING-OFF PERIOD FOR NEW VEHICLES. BUT IF YOU PURCHASED OR LEASED A USED VEHICLE FOR $50,000 OR LESS, YOU HAVE 3 DAYS TO CANCEL THIS CONTRACT FOR ANY REASON. ADDITIONAL RESTRICTIONS MAY APPLY, INCLUDING A RESTOCKING FEE. ASK THE DEALER FOR MORE INFORMATION ABOUT HOW TO EXERCISE THIS RIGHT."

(b) If the dealer also sells or leases motorcycles or off-highway motor vehicles at the same location as vehicles subject to the right to cancel, the physical notice shall contain the following additional language, in at least 36-point type:

"This cooling-off period also does not apply to the sale of a motorcycle or an off-highway motor vehicle subject to registration under California law. See the vehicle contract for details."

(c) This section shall become operative October 1, 2026.

(Repealed (in Sec. 8) and added by Stats. 2025, Ch. 354, Sec. 9. (SB 766) Effective January 1, 2026. Operative October 1, 2026, by its own provisions.)

11709.3. (a) Every dealer shall clearly and conspicuously display in its showroom at its established place of business, in a place that is easily accessible to prospective purchasers, a clear and conspicuous listing of each vehicle that the dealer has advertised for sale if the vehicle meets all of the following requirements:

(1) The vehicle is advertised for sale in a newspaper or other publication of general circulation, or in any other advertising medium that is disseminated to the public generally, including, but not limited to, radio, television, or the Internet.

(2) The vehicle is advertised at a specific price and is required pursuant to subdivision (a) of Section 11713.1 to be identified in the advertisement by its vehicle identification number or license number.

(3) The vehicle has not been sold or leased during the time that the advertised price is valid.

(4) The vehicle does not clearly and conspicuously have displayed on or in it the advertised price.

(b) The listing required by subdivision (a) may be satisfied by clearly and conspicuously posting in the showroom a complete copy of any print advertisement that includes vehicles currently advertised for sale or by clearly and conspicuously displaying in the showroom a list of currently advertised vehicles described by make, model, model-year, vehicle identification number, or license number, and the advertised price.

(Added by Stats. 2001, Ch. 441, Sec. 1. Effective January 1, 2002.)

11709.4. (a) When a dealer purchases or obtains a vehicle in trade in a retail sale or lease transaction and the vehicle is subject to a prior credit or lease balance, all of the following apply:

(1) If the dealer agreed to pay a specified amount on the prior credit or lease balance owing on the vehicle purchased or obtained in trade, and the agreement to pay the specified amount is contained in a written agreement documenting the transaction, the dealer shall tender the agreed upon amount as provided in the written agreement to the lessor registered in accordance with Section 4453.5, or to the legal owner reflected on the ownership certificate, or to the designee of that lessor or legal owner of the vehicle purchased or obtained in trade within 21 calendar days of purchasing or obtaining the vehicle in trade.

(2) If the dealer did not set forth an agreement regarding payment of a prior credit or lease balance owed on the vehicle purchased or obtained in trade, in a written agreement documenting the transaction, the dealer shall tender to the lessor registered in accordance with Section 4453.5, or to the legal owner reflected on the ownership certificate, or to the designee of that lessor or legal owner of the vehicle purchased or obtained in trade, an amount necessary to discharge the prior credit or lease balance owing on the vehicle purchased or obtained in trade within 21 calendar days of purchasing or obtaining the vehicle in trade.

(3) The time period specified in paragraph (1) or (2) may be shortened if the dealer and consumer agree, in writing, to a shorter time period.

(4) A dealer shall not sell, consign for sale, or transfer any ownership interest in the vehicle purchased or obtained in trade until an amount necessary to discharge the prior credit or lease balance owing on the vehicle has been tendered to the lessor registered in accordance with Section 4453.5, or to the legal owner reflected on the ownership certificate, or to the designee of that lessor or legal owner of the vehicle

purchased or obtained in trade.

(b) A dealer does not violate this section if the dealer reasonably and in good faith gives notice of rescission of the contract promptly, but no later than 21 days after the date on which the vehicle was purchased or obtained in trade, and the contract is thereafter rescinded on any of the grounds in Section 1689 of the Civil Code.

(Amended by Stats. 2010, Ch. 328, Sec. 228. (SB 1330) Effective January 1, 2011.)

11710. (a) Before any dealer's or remanufacturer's license is issued or renewed by the department to any applicant therefor, the applicant shall procure and file with the department a bond executed by an admitted surety insurer, approved as to form by the Attorney General, and conditioned that the applicant shall not practice any fraud or make any fraudulent representation which will cause a monetary loss to a purchaser, seller, financing agency, or governmental agency.

(b) A dealer's bond shall be in the amount of fifty thousand dollars ($50,000), except the bond of a dealer who deals exclusively in motorcycles or all-terrain vehicles shall be in the amount of ten thousand dollars ($10,000). Before the license is renewed by the department, the dealer, other than a dealer who deals exclusively in motorcycles or all-terrain vehicles, shall procure and file a bond in the amount of fifty thousand dollars ($50,000). A remanufacturer bond shall be in the amount of fifty thousand dollars ($50,000).

(c) Liability under the bond is to remain at full value. If the amount of liability under the bond is decreased or there is outstanding a final court judgment for which the dealer or remanufacturer and sureties are liable, the dealer's or remanufacturer's license shall be automatically suspended. In order to reinstate the license and special plates, the licensee shall either file an additional bond or restore the bond on file to the original amount, or shall terminate the outstanding judgment for which the dealer or remanufacturer and sureties are liable.

(d) A dealer's or remanufacturer's license, or renewal of the license, shall not be issued to any applicant therefor, unless and until the applicant files with the department a good and sufficient instrument, in writing, in which the applicant appoints the director as the true and lawful agent of the applicant upon whom all process may be served in any action, or actions, which may thereafter be commenced against the applicant, arising out of any claim for damages suffered by any firm, person, association, or corporation, by reason of the violation of the applicant of any of the terms and provisions of this code or any condition of the dealer's or remanufacturer's bond. The applicant shall stipulate and agree in the appointment that any process directed to the applicant, when personal service of process upon the applicant cannot be made in this state after due diligence and, in that case, is served upon the director or, in the event of the director's absence from the office, upon any employee in charge of the office of the director, shall be of the same legal force and effect as if served upon the applicant personally. The applicant shall further stipulate and agree, in writing, that the agency created by the appointment shall continue for and during the period covered by any license that may be issued and so long thereafter as the applicant may be made to answer in damages for a violation of this code or any condition of the bond. The instrument appointing the director as the agent for the applicant for service of process shall be acknowledged by the applicant before a notary public. In any case where the licensee is served with process by service upon the director, one copy of the summons and complaint shall be left with the director or in the director's office in Sacramento or mailed to the office of the director in Sacramento. A fee of five dollars ($5) shall also be paid to the director at the time of service of the copy of the summons and complaint. Service on the director shall be a sufficient service on the licensee if a notice of service and a copy of the summons and complaint are immediately sent by registered mail by the plaintiff or the plaintiff's attorney to the licensee. A copy of the summons and complaint shall also be mailed by the plaintiff or the plaintiff's attorney to the surety on the applicant's bond at the address of the surety given in the bond, postpaid and registered with request for return receipt. The director shall keep a record of all process so served upon the director, which record shall show the day and hour of service and shall retain the summons and complaint so served on file. Where the licensee is served with process by service upon the director, the licensee shall have and be allowed 30 days from and after the service within which to answer any complaint or other pleading which may be filed in the cause. However, for purposes of venue, where the licensee is served with process by service upon the director, the service is deemed to have been made upon the licensee in the county in which the licensee has or last had an established place of business.

(Amended by Stats. 2004, Ch. 836, Sec. 10. Effective January 1, 2005.)

11710.1. Notwithstanding subdivision (b) of Section 11710, the bond amount of a dealer who sells vehicles on a wholesale basis only, and who sells fewer than 25 vehicles per year, shall be ten thousand dollars ($10,000).

(Added by Stats. 2002, Ch. 1110, Sec. 1. Effective January 1, 2003.)

11710.2. If a deposit is given instead of the bond required by Section 11710 both of the following apply:

(a) (1) The director may order the deposit returned at the expiration of any of the following dates:

(A) Three years from the date an applicant for a dealer's license who has operated a business of selling vehicles under a temporary permit has ceased to do business.

(B) Three years from the date a licensee has ceased to be licensed, if the director is satisfied that there are no outstanding claims against the deposit.

(C) Five years from the date a licensee secured and maintained a dealer bond, pursuant to Section 11710, after posting a deposit, if the director is satisfied that there are no outstanding claims against the deposit.

(2) A judge of a superior court may order the return of the deposit prior to the expiration of the dates provided in paragraph (1) upon evidence satisfactory to the judge that there are no outstanding claims against the deposit.

(b) If either the director, department, or state is a defendant in any action instituted to recover all or any part of the deposit, or any action is instituted by the director, department, or state to determine those entitled to any part of the deposit, the director, department, or state shall be paid reasonable attorney fees and costs from the deposit. Costs shall include those administrative costs incurred in processing claims against the deposit.

(Amended by Stats. 2010, Ch. 483, Sec. 2. (SB 1004) Effective January 1, 2011.)

11711. (a) If any person (1) shall suffer any loss or damage by reason of any fraud practiced on him or fraudulent representation made to him by a licensed dealer or one of such dealer's salesmen acting for the dealer, in his behalf, or within the scope of the employment of such salesman and such person has possession of a written instrument furnished by the licensee, containing stipulated provisions and guarantees which the person believes have been violated by the licensee, or (2) if any person shall suffer any loss or damage by reason of the violation by such dealer or salesman of any of the provisions of Division 3 (commencing with Section 4000) of this code, or (3) if any person is not paid for a vehicle sold to and purchased by a licensee, then any such person shall have a right of action against such dealer, his salesman, and the surety upon the dealer's bond, in an amount not to exceed the value of the vehicle purchased from or sold to the dealer.

(b) If the state or any political subdivision thereof shall suffer any loss or damage by reason of any fraud practiced on the state or fraudulent representation made to the state by a licensed dealer, or one of such dealer's representatives acting for the dealer, in his behalf, or within the scope of employment of such representatives, or shall suffer any loss or damage by reason of the violation of such dealer or representative of any of the provisions of Division 3 (commencing with Section 4000) of this code, or Part 5 (commencing with Section 10701), Division 2 of the Revenue and Taxation Code, the state or any political subdivision thereof, through the department, shall have a right of action against such dealer, his representative, and the surety upon the dealer's bond in an amount not to exceed the value of the vehicles involved.

(c) The failure of a dealer upon demand to pay the fees and penalties determined to be due as provided in Section 4456 hereof is declared to be a violation of Division 3 (commencing with Section 4000) of this code, and Part 5 (commencing with Section 10701), Division 2 of the Revenue and Taxation Code and to constitute loss or damage to the state in the amounts of such fees and penalties determined to be due and not paid.

(d) The claims of the state under subdivision (b) shall be satisfied first and entitled to preference over all claims under subdivision (a).

(e) The claims of any person under subdivision (a) who is not a licensee shall be satisfied first and entitled to preference over all other claims under subdivision (a).

(Amended by Stats. 1972, Ch. 1106.)

11711.3. A person acting as a dealer, who was not licensed as a dealer as required by this article, or a person acting as a lessor-retailer, who was not licensed as a lessor-retailer as required by Chapter 3.5 (commencing with Section 11600), may not enforce any security interest or bring or maintain any action in law or equity to recover any money or property or obtain other relief from the purchaser or lessee of a vehicle in connection with a transaction in which the person was, at the time of the transaction, required to be licensed as a dealer or a lessor-retailer.

(Amended by Stats. 2003, Ch. 62, Sec. 304. Effective January 1, 2004.)

11712. (a) The department shall not issue a dealer's license to any applicant therefor who has not an established place of business as defined in this code. Should the dealer change the site or location of his established place of business, he or she shall, immediately upon making that change, so notify the department. Should a dealer for any reason whatsoever, cease to be in possession of an established place of business from and on which he or she conducts the business for which he or she is licensed, he or she shall immediately notify the department and, upon demand by the department, shall deliver to the department the dealer's license, dealer's special plate or plates, and all report of sale books in his or her possession.

(b) Should the dealer change to, or add another franchise for the sale of new vehicles, or cancel or, for any cause whatever, otherwise lose a franchise for the sale of new vehicles, he or she shall immediately so notify the department.

(c) Any person licensed under this article who has closed his or her established place of business may be served with process issued pursuant to Chapter 5 (commencing with Section 11500) of Part 1 of Division 3 of Title 2 of the Government Code by registered mail at that place of business or at the mailing address of record if different from the established place of business, unless the person has notified the department in writing of another address where service may be made.

(Amended by Stats. 1988, Ch. 751, Sec. 7.)

11712.5. It is unlawful and a violation of this code for a dealer issued a license pursuant to this article to sell, offer for sale, or display any new vehicle, as follows:

(a) A new motorcycle unless there is securely attached thereto a statement as required by Section 24014.

(b) A new light duty truck with a manufacturer's gross vehicle weight rating of 8,500 pounds or less unless there is affixed to the light duty truck the label required by Section 24013.5.

(Amended by Stats. 1987, Ch. 418, Sec. 1.)

11713. A holder of a license issued under this article shall not do any of the following:

(a) Make or disseminate, or cause to be made or disseminated, before the public in this state, in a newspaper or other publication, or an advertising device, or by public outcry or proclamation, or in any other manner or means whatever, a statement that is untrue or misleading and that is known, or that by the exercise of reasonable care should be known, to be untrue or misleading; or to so make or disseminate, or cause to be so disseminated, a statement as part of a plan or scheme with the intent not to sell a vehicle or service so advertised at the price stated therein, or as so advertised.

(b) (1) (A) Advertise or offer for sale or exchange in any manner, a vehicle not actually for sale at the premises of the dealer or available to the dealer directly from the manufacturer or distributor of the vehicle at the time of the advertisement or offer. However, a dealer who has been issued an autobroker's endorsement to the dealer's license may advertise the dealer's service of arranging or negotiating the purchase of a new motor vehicle from a franchised new motor vehicle dealer and may specify the line-makes and models of those new vehicles. Autobrokering service advertisements may not advertise the price or payment terms of a vehicle and shall disclose that the advertiser is an autobroker or auto buying service, and shall clearly and conspicuously state the following: "All new cars arranged for sale are subject to price and availability from the selling franchised new car dealer."

(B) As to printed advertisements, the disclosure statement required by subparagraph (A) shall be printed in not less than 10-point bold type size and shall be textually segregated from the other portions of the printed advertisement.

(2) Notwithstanding subparagraph (A), classified advertisements for autobrokering services that measure two column inches or less are exempt from the disclosure statement in subparagraph (A) pertaining to price and availability.

(3) Radio advertisements of a duration of less than 11 seconds that do not reference specific line-makes or models of motor vehicles are exempt from the disclosure statement required in subparagraph (A).

(c) Fail, within 48 hours, to withdraw in writing an advertisement of a vehicle that has been sold or withdrawn from sale.

(d) Advertise or represent a vehicle as a new vehicle if the vehicle is a used vehicle.

(e) Engage in the business for which the licensee is licensed without having in force and effect a bond as required by this article.

(f) Engage in the business for which the dealer is licensed without at all times maintaining an established place of business as required by this code.

(g) Include, as an added cost to the selling price of a vehicle, an amount for licensing or transfer of title of the vehicle, which is not due to the state unless, prior to the sale, that amount has been paid by a dealer to the state in order to avoid penalties that would have accrued because of late payment of the fees. However, a dealer may collect from the second purchaser of a vehicle a prorated fee based upon the number of months remaining in the registration year for that vehicle, if the vehicle had been previously sold by the dealer and the sale was subsequently rescinded and all the fees that were paid, as required by this code and Chapter 2 (commencing with Section 10751) of Part 5 of Division 2 of the Revenue and Taxation Code, were returned to the first purchaser of the vehicle.

(h) Employ a person as a salesperson who has not been licensed pursuant to Article 2 (commencing with Section 11800), and whose license is not displayed on the premises of the dealer as required by Section 11812, or willfully fail to notify the department by mail within 10 days of the employment or termination of employment of a salesperson.

(i) Deliver, following the sale, a vehicle for operation on California highways, if the vehicle does not meet all of the equipment requirements of Division 12 (commencing with Section 24000). This subdivision does not apply to the sale of a leased vehicle to the lessee if the lessee is in possession of the vehicle immediately prior to the time of the sale and the vehicle is registered in this state.

(j) Use, or permit the use of, the special plates assigned to them for any purpose other than as permitted by Section 11715.

(k) Advertise or otherwise represent, or knowingly allow to be advertised or represented on behalf of, or at the place of business of, the licenseholder that no downpayment is required in connection with the sale of a vehicle when a downpayment is in fact required and the buyer is advised or induced to finance the downpayment by a loan in addition to any other loan financing the remainder of the purchase price of the vehicle. The terms "no downpayment," "zero down delivers," or similar terms shall not be advertised unless the vehicle will be sold to a qualified purchaser without a prior payment of any kind or trade-in.

(l) (1) Participate in the sale of a vehicle required to be reported to the Department of Motor Vehicles under Section 5900 or 5901 without making the return and payment of the full tax due and required by Section 6451 of the Revenue and Taxation Code.

(2) Participate in the sale of a used vehicle required to be reported to the Department of Motor Vehicles under Section 5900 or 5901 without making the payment of the full tax due as required by Section 6295 of the Revenue and Taxation Code.

(3) The amendments to this subdivision made by the act adding this paragraph do not constitute a change in, but are declaratory of, existing law.

(m) Permit the use of the dealer's license, supplies, or books by any other person for the purpose of permitting that person to engage in the purchase or sale of vehicles required to be registered under this code, or permit the use of the dealer's license, supplies, or books to operate a branch location to be used by any other person, whether or not the licensee has any financial or equitable interest or investment in the vehicles purchased or sold by, or the business of, or branch location used by, the other person.

(n) Violate any provision of Article 10 (commencing with Section 28050) of Chapter 5 of Division 12.

(o) Sell a previously unregistered vehicle without disclosing in writing to the purchaser the date on which a manufacturer's or distributor's warranty commenced.

(p) Accept a purchase deposit relative to the sale of a vehicle, unless the vehicle is present at the premises of the dealer or available to the dealer directly from the manufacturer or distributor of the vehicle at the time the dealer accepts the deposit. Purchase deposits accepted by an autobroker when brokering a retail sale shall be governed by Sections 11736 and 11737.

(q) Consign for sale to another dealer a new vehicle.

(r) Display a vehicle for sale at a location other than an established place of business authorized by the department for that dealer or display a new motor vehicle at the business premises of another dealer registered as an autobroker. This subdivision does not apply to the display of a vehicle pursuant to subdivision (b) of Section 11709 or the demonstration of the qualities of a motor vehicle by way of a test drive.

(s) Use a picture in connection with an advertisement of the price of a specific vehicle or class of vehicles, unless the picture is of the year, make, and model being offered for sale. The picture shall not depict a vehicle with optional equipment or a design not actually offered at the advertised price.

(t) Advertise for sale a vehicle that was used by the selling licensee in its business as a demonstrator, executive vehicle, service vehicle, rental, loaner, or lease vehicle, unless the advertisement clearly and conspicuously discloses the previous use made by that licensee of the vehicle. An advertisement shall not describe any of those vehicles as "new."

(u) Advertise the prior use or ownership history of a vehicle in an inaccurate manner.

(v) (1) Offer to a consumer a subscription service for any motor vehicle feature that utilizes components and hardware already installed on the motor vehicle at the time of purchase or lease and would function after activation without ongoing cost to or support by the dealer, manufacturer, distributor, or a third-party service provider.

(2) This subdivision does not apply to navigation system updates, satellite radio, roadside assistance, software-dependent driver assistance or driver automation features, and vehicle-connected services that rely on cellular or other data networks for continued operation.

(3) As used in this subdivision, the following terms have the following meanings:

(A) "Motor vehicle feature" means any convenience or safety function included on the motor vehicle, such as heated seats or driver assistance, that typically is offered to a consumer as an upgrade at the time of purchase or lease of the motor vehicle.

(B) "Subscription service" means a service provided in exchange for a recurring payment, including, but not limited to, a weekly, monthly, or annual payment charged to and made by a consumer, but does not include a consumer's reoccurring payment made pursuant to a conditional sales contract or lease contract, as defined in Chapters 2b (commencing with Section 2981) and 2d (commencing with Section 2985.7) of Title 14 of Part 4 of Division 3 of the Civil Code.

(Amended by Stats. 2023, Ch. 332, Sec. 3. (AB 473) Effective January 1, 2024.)

11713.1. It is a violation of this code for the holder of a dealer's license issued under this article to do any of the following:

(a) Advertise a specific vehicle for sale without identifying the vehicle by its model, model-year, and either its license number or that portion of the vehicle identification number that distinguishes the vehicle from all other vehicles of the same make, model, and model-year. Model-year is not required to be advertised for current model-year vehicles. Year models are no longer current when ensuing year models are available for purchase at retail in California. An advertisement that offers for sale a class of new vehicles in a dealer's inventory, consisting of five or more vehicles, that are all of the same make, model, and model-year is not required to include in the advertisement the vehicle identification numbers or license numbers of those vehicles.

(b) Advertise the total price of a vehicle without including all costs to the purchaser at time of sale, except taxes, vehicle registration fees, the California tire fee, as defined in Section 42885 of the Public Resources Code, emission testing charges not exceeding fifty dollars ($50), actual fees charged for certificates pursuant to Section 44060 of the Health and Safety Code, finance charges, and any dealer document processing charge or charge to electronically register or transfer the vehicle.

(c) (1) Exclude from an advertisement of a vehicle for sale that there will be added to the advertised total price at the time of sale, charges for sales tax, vehicle registration fees, the California tire fee, the fee charged by the state for the issuance of a certificate of compliance or noncompliance pursuant to a statute, finance charges, a charge to electronically register or transfer the vehicle, and a dealer document processing charge.

(2) The obligations imposed by paragraph (1) are satisfied by adding to the advertisement a statement containing no abbreviations and that is worded in substantially the following form: "Plus government fees and taxes, any finance charges, any dealer document processing charge, any electronic filing charge, and any emission testing charge."

(3) For purposes of paragraph (1), "advertisement" means an advertisement in a newspaper, magazine, or direct mail publication that is two or more columns in width or one column in width and more than seven inches in length, or on a Web page of a dealer's Internet Web site that displays the price of a vehicle offered for sale on the Internet, as that term is defined in paragraph (6) of subdivision (f) of Section 17538 of the Business and Professions Code.

(d) Represent the dealer document processing charge, electronic registration or transfer charge, or emission testing charge, as a governmental fee.

(e) Fail to sell a vehicle to a person at the advertised total price, exclusive of taxes, vehicle registration fees, the California tire fee, the fee charged by the state for the issuance of a certificate of compliance or noncompliance pursuant to a statute, finance charges, mobilehome escrow fees, the amount of a city, county, or city and county imposed fee or tax for a mobilehome, a dealer document processing charge, an electronic registration or transfer charge, and a charge for emission testing not to exceed fifty dollars ($50) plus the actual fees charged for certificates pursuant to Section 44060 of the Health and Safety Code, while the vehicle remains unsold, unless the advertisement states the advertised total price is good only for a specified time and the time has elapsed. Advertised vehicles shall be sold at or below the advertised total price, with statutorily permitted exclusions, regardless of whether the purchaser has knowledge of the advertised total price.

(f) (1) Advertise for sale, sell, or purchase for resale a new vehicle of a line-make for which the dealer does not hold a franchise.

(2) This subdivision does not apply to a transaction involving the following:

(A) A mobilehome.

(B) A commercial coach, as defined in Section 18001.8 of the Health and Safety Code.

(C) An off-highway motor vehicle subject to identification as defined in Section 38012.

(D) A manufactured home.

(E) A new vehicle that will be substantially altered or modified by a converter prior to resale.

(F) A commercial vehicle with a gross vehicle weight rating of more than 10,000 pounds.

(G) A vehicle purchased for export and exported outside the territorial limits of the United States without being registered with the department.

(H) A vehicle acquired in the ordinary course of business as a new vehicle by a dealer franchised to sell that vehicle, if all of the following apply:

(i) The manufacturer or distributor of the vehicle files a bankruptcy petition.

(ii) The franchise agreement of the dealer is terminated, canceled, or rejected by the manufacturer or distributor as part of the bankruptcy proceedings and the termination, cancellation, or rejection is not a result of the revocation by the department of the dealer's license or the dealer's conviction of a crime.

(iii) The vehicle is held in the inventory of the dealer on the date the bankruptcy petition is filed.

(iv) The vehicle is sold by the dealer within six months of the date the bankruptcy petition is filed.

(3) Subparagraph (H) of paragraph (2) does not entitle a dealer whose franchise agreement has been terminated, canceled, or rejected to continue to perform warranty service repairs or continue to be eligible to offer or receive consumer or dealer incentives offered by the manufacturer or distributor.

(g) Sell a park trailer, as specified in Section 18009.3 of the Health and Safety Code, without disclosing in writing to the purchaser that a park trailer is required to be moved by a transporter or a licensed manufacturer or dealer under a permit issued by the Department of Transportation or a local authority with respect to highways under their respective jurisdictions.

(h) Advertise free merchandise, gifts, or services provided by a dealer contingent on the purchase of a vehicle. "Free" includes merchandise or services offered for sale at a price less than the seller's cost of the merchandise or services.

(i) (1) Advertise vehicles, and related goods or services, at a specified dealer price, with the intent not to supply reasonably expectable demand, unless the advertisement discloses the number of vehicles in stock at the advertised price. In addition, whether or not there are sufficient vehicles in stock to supply a reasonably expectable demand, when phrases such as "starting at," "from," "beginning as low as," or words of similar import are used in reference to an advertised price, the advertisement shall disclose the number of vehicles available at that advertised price.

(2) For purposes of this subdivision, in a newspaper advertisement for a vehicle that is two model-years old or newer, the actual phrase that states the number of vehicles in stock at the advertised price shall be printed in a type size that is at least equal to one-quarter of the type size, and in the same style and color of type, used for the advertised price. However, in no case shall the phrase be printed in less than 8-point type size, and the phrase shall be disclosed immediately above, below, or beside the advertised price without intervening words, pictures, marks, or symbols.

(3) The disclosure required by this subdivision is in addition to any other disclosure required by this code or any regulation regarding identifying vehicles advertised for sale.

(j) Use "rebate" or similar words, including, but not limited to, "cash back," in advertising the sale of a vehicle unless the rebate is expressed in a specific dollar amount and is in fact a rebate offered by the vehicle manufacturer or distributor, a finance company affiliated with a vehicle manufacturer or distributor, a regulated utility, or a governmental entity directly to the retail purchaser of the vehicle or to the assignee of the retail purchaser.

(k) Require a person to pay a higher price for a vehicle and related goods or services for receiving advertised credit terms than the cash price the same person would have to pay to purchase the same vehicle and related goods or services. For the purpose of this subdivision, "cash price" has the same meaning as defined in subdivision (e) of Section 2981 of the Civil Code.

(l) Advertise a guaranteed trade-in allowance.

(m) Misrepresent the authority of a salesperson, representative, or agent to negotiate the final terms of a transaction.

(n) (1) Use "invoice," "dealer's invoice," "wholesale price," or similar terms that refer to a dealer's cost for a vehicle in an advertisement for the sale of a vehicle or advertise that the selling price of a vehicle is above, below, or at either of the following:

(A) The manufacturer's or distributor's invoice price to a dealer.

(B) A dealer's cost.

(2) This subdivision does not apply to either of the following:

(A) A communication occurring during face-to-face negotiations for the purchase of a specific vehicle if the prospective purchaser initiates a discussion of the vehicle's invoice price or the dealer's cost for that vehicle.

(B) A communication between a dealer and a prospective commercial purchaser that is not disseminated to the general public. For purposes of this subparagraph, a "commercial purchaser" means a dealer, lessor, lessor-retailer, manufacturer, remanufacturer, distributor, financial institution, governmental entity, or person who purchases 10 or more vehicles during a year.

(o) Violate a law prohibiting bait and switch advertising, including, but not limited to, the guides against bait advertising set forth in Part 238 (commencing with Section 238) of Title 16 of the Code of Federal Regulations, as those regulations read on January 1, 1988.

(p) Make an untrue or misleading statement indicating that a vehicle is equipped with all the factory-installed optional equipment the manufacturer offers, including, but not limited to, a false statement that a vehicle is "fully factory equipped."

(q) Except as provided in Section 24014, affix on a new vehicle a supplemental price sticker containing a price that represents the dealer's asking price that exceeds the manufacturer's suggested retail price unless all of the following occur:

(1) The supplemental sticker clearly and conspicuously discloses in the largest print appearing on the sticker, other than the print size used for the dealer's name, that the supplemental sticker price is the dealer's asking price, or words of similar import, and that it is not the manufacturer's suggested retail price.

(2) The supplemental sticker clearly and conspicuously discloses the manufacturer's suggested retail price.

(3) The supplemental sticker lists each item that is not included in the manufacturer's suggested retail price, and discloses the additional price of each item. If the supplemental sticker price is greater than the sum of the manufacturer's suggested retail price and the price of the items added by the dealer, the supplemental sticker price shall set forth

that difference and describe it as "added mark-up."

(r) Advertise an underselling claim, including, but not limited to, "we have the lowest prices" or "we will beat any dealer's price," unless the dealer has conducted a recent survey showing that the dealer sells its vehicles at lower prices than another licensee in its trade area and maintains records to adequately substantiate the claims. The substantiating records shall be made available to the department upon request.

(s) (1) Advertise an incentive offered by the manufacturer or distributor if the dealer is required to contribute to the cost of the incentive as a condition of participating in the incentive program, unless the dealer discloses in a clear and conspicuous manner that dealer participation may affect consumer cost.

(2) For purposes of this subdivision, "incentive" means anything of value offered to induce people to purchase a vehicle, including, but not limited to, discounts, savings claims, rebates, below-market finance rates, and free merchandise or services.

(t) Display or offer for sale a used vehicle unless there is affixed to the vehicle the Federal Trade Commission's Buyer's Guide as required by Part 455 of Title 16 of the Code of Federal Regulations.

(u) Fail to disclose in writing to the franchisor of a new motor vehicle dealer the name of the purchaser, date of sale, and the vehicle identification number of each new motor vehicle sold of the line-make of that franchisor, or intentionally submit to that franchisor a false name for the purchaser or false date for the date of sale.

(v) Enter into a contract for the retail sale of a motor vehicle unless the contract clearly and conspicuously discloses whether the vehicle is being sold as a new vehicle or a used vehicle, as defined in this code.

(w) Use a simulated check, as defined in subdivision (a) of Section 22433 of the Business and Professions Code, in an advertisement for the sale or lease of a vehicle.

(x) Fail to disclose, in a clear and conspicuous manner in at least 10-point boldface type on the face of a contract for the retail sale of a new motor vehicle that this transaction is, or is not, subject to a fee received by an autobroker from the selling new motor vehicle dealer, and the name of the autobroker, if applicable.

(y) Sell or lease a new motor vehicle after October 1, 2012, unless the dealer has a contractual agreement with the department to be a private industry partner pursuant to Section 1685. This subdivision does not apply to the sale or lease of a motorcycle or off-highway motor vehicle subject to identification under Section 38010 or a recreational vehicle as defined in Section 18010 of the Health and Safety Code.

(z) As used in this section, "make" and "model" have the same meaning as is provided in Section 565.12 of Title 49 of the Code of Federal Regulations.

(Amended by Stats. 2018, Ch. 187, Sec. 1. (AB 2227) Effective January 1, 2019.)

11713.2. It shall be unlawful and a violation of this code for any manufacturer, manufacturer branch, distributor, or distributor branch licensed under this code to coerce or attempt to coerce any dealer in this state:

(a) To order or accept delivery of any motor vehicle, part or accessory thereof, appliance, equipment or any other commodity not required by law which shall not have been voluntarily ordered by the dealer.

(b) To order or accept delivery of any motor vehicle with special features, appliances, accessories or equipment not included in the list price of such motor vehicles as publicly advertised by the manufacturer or distributor.

(c) To order for any person any parts, accessories, equipment, machinery, tools, appliances, or any commodity whatsoever.

(d) To participate in an advertising campaign or contest, any promotional campaign, promotional materials, training materials, showroom or other display decorations or materials at the expense of the dealer.

(e) To enter into any agreement with the manufacturer, manufacturer branch, distributor, or distributor branch, or to do any other act prejudicial to the dealer by threatening to cancel a franchise or any contractual agreement existing between the dealer and manufacturer, manufacturer branch, distributor, or distributor branch. Notice in good faith to any dealer of the dealer's violation of any terms or provisions of such franchise or contractual agreement shall not constitute a violation of this article.

(Added by renumbering Section 11713.1 (as added by Stats. 1973, Ch. 996) by Stats. 1979, Ch. 943.)

11713.3. It is unlawful and a violation of this code for a manufacturer, manufacturer branch, distributor, or distributor branch licensed pursuant to this code to do, directly or indirectly through an affiliate, any of the following:

(a) (1) To refuse or fail to deliver in reasonable quantities and within a reasonable time after receipt of an order from a dealer having a franchise for the retail sale of a new vehicle sold or distributed by the manufacturer or distributor, a new vehicle or parts or accessories to new vehicles that are of a model offered by the manufacturer or distributor to other franchisees in this state of the same line-make, if the vehicle, parts, or accessories are publicly advertised as being available for delivery or actually being delivered in this state. This subdivision is not violated, however, if the failure is caused by acts or causes beyond the control of the manufacturer, manufacturer branch, distributor, or distributor branch.

(2) To fail to disclose to any franchisee, upon written request, the basis upon which new motor vehicles of the same line-make are allocated or distributed to franchisees in the state and the basis upon which the current allocation or distribution is being made or will be made to the franchisee.

(b) To prevent or require, or attempt to prevent or require, by contract or otherwise, a change in the capital structure of a dealership or the means by or through which the dealer finances the operation of the dealership, if the dealer at all times meets reasonable capital standards agreed to by the dealer and the manufacturer or distributor, and if a change in capital structure does not cause a change in the principal management or have the effect of a sale of the franchise without the consent of the manufacturer or distributor.

(c) To prevent or require, or attempt to prevent or require, a dealer to change the executive management of a dealership, other than the principal dealership operator or operators, if the franchise was granted to the dealer in reliance upon the personal qualifications of that person.

(d) (1) Except as provided in subdivision (t), to prevent or require, or attempt to prevent or require, by contract or otherwise, a dealer, or an officer, partner, or stockholder of a dealership, the sale or transfer of a part of the interest of any of them to another person. A dealer, officer, partner, or stockholder shall not, however, have the right to sell, transfer, or assign the franchise, or a right thereunder, without the consent of the manufacturer or distributor except that the consent shall not be unreasonably withheld.

(2) (A) For the transferring franchisee to fail, prior to the sale, transfer, or assignment of a franchisee or the sale, assignment, or transfer of all, or substantially all, of the assets of the franchised business or a controlling interest in the franchised business to another person, to notify the manufacturer or distributor of the franchisee's decision to sell, transfer, or assign the franchise. The notice shall be in writing and shall include all of the following:

(i) The proposed transferee's name and address.

(ii) A copy of all of the agreements relating to the sale, assignment, or transfer of the franchised business or its assets.

(iii) The proposed transferee's application for approval to become the successor franchisee. The application shall include forms and related information generally utilized by the manufacturer or distributor in reviewing prospective franchisees, if those forms are readily made available to existing franchisees. As soon as practicable after receipt of the proposed transferee's application, the manufacturer or distributor shall notify the franchisee and the proposed transferee of information needed to make the application complete.

(B) For the manufacturer or distributor, to fail, on or before 60 days after the receipt of all of the information required pursuant to subparagraph (A), or as extended by a written agreement between the manufacturer or distributor and the franchisee, to notify the franchisee of the approval or the disapproval of the sale, transfer, or assignment of the franchise. The notice shall be in writing and shall be personally served or sent by certified mail, return receipt requested, or by guaranteed overnight delivery service that provides verification of delivery and shall be directed to the franchisee. A proposed sale, assignment, or transfer shall be deemed approved, unless disapproved by the franchisor in the manner provided by this subdivision. If the proposed sale, assignment, or transfer is disapproved, the franchisor shall include in the notice of disapproval a statement setting forth the reasons for the disapproval.

(3) In an action in which the manufacturer's or distributor's withholding of consent under this subdivision or subdivision (e) is an issue, whether the withholding of consent was unreasonable is a question of fact requiring consideration of all the existing circumstances.

(e) To prevent, or attempt to prevent, a dealer from receiving fair and reasonable compensation for the value of the franchised business. There shall not be a transfer or assignment of the dealer's franchise without the consent of the manufacturer or distributor. The manufacturer or distributor shall not unreasonably withhold consent or condition consent upon the release, assignment, novation, waiver, estoppel, or modification of a claim or defense by the dealer.

(f) To obtain money, goods, services, or another benefit from a person with whom the dealer does business, on account of, or in relation to, the transaction between the dealer and that other person, other than for compensation for services rendered, unless the benefit is promptly accounted for, and transmitted to, the dealer.

(g) (1) Except as provided in paragraph (3), to obtain from a dealer or enforce against a dealer an agreement, provision, release, assignment, novation, waiver, or estoppel that does any of the following:

(A) Modifies or disclaims a duty or obligation of a manufacturer, manufacturer branch, distributor, distributor branch, or representative, or a right or privilege of a dealer, pursuant to Chapter 4 (commencing with Section 11700) of Division 5 or Chapter 6 (commencing with Section 3000) of Division 2.

(B) Limits or constrains the right of a dealer to file, pursue, or submit evidence in connection with a protest before the board.

(C) Requires a dealer to terminate a franchise.

(D) Requires a controversy between a manufacturer, manufacturer branch, distributor, distributor branch, or representative and a dealer to be referred to a person for a binding determination. However, this subparagraph does not prohibit arbitration before an independent arbitrator, provided that whenever a motor vehicle franchise contract provides for the use of arbitration to resolve a controversy arising out of, or relating to, that contract, arbitration may be used to settle the controversy only if, after the controversy arises, all parties to the controversy consent in writing to use arbitration to settle the controversy. For the purpose of this subparagraph, the terms "motor vehicle" and "motor vehicle franchise contract" shall have the same meanings as defined in Section 1226 of Title 15 of the United States Code. If arbitration is elected to settle a dispute under a motor vehicle franchise contract, the arbitrator shall provide the parties to the arbitration with a written explanation of the factual and legal basis for the award.

(2) An agreement, provision, release, assignment, novation, waiver, or estoppel prohibited by this subdivision shall be unenforceable and void.

(3) This subdivision does not do any of the following:

(A) Limit or restrict the terms upon which parties to a protest before the board, civil action, or other proceeding can settle or resolve, or stipulate to evidentiary or procedural matters during the course of, a protest, civil action, or other proceeding.

(B) Affect the enforceability of any stipulated order or other order entered by the board.

(C) Affect the enforceability of any provision in a contract if the provision is not prohibited under this subdivision or any other law.

(D) Affect the enforceability of a provision in any contract entered into on or before December 31, 2011.

(E) Prohibit a dealer from waiving its right to file a protest pursuant to Section 3065.1 if the waiver agreement is entered into after a franchisor incentive program claim has been disapproved by the franchisor and the waiver is voluntarily given as part of an agreement to settle that claim.

(F) Prohibit a voluntary agreement supported by valuable consideration, other than granting or renewing a franchise, that does both of the following:

(i) Provides that a dealer establish or maintain exclusive facilities, personnel, or display space or provides that a dealer make a material alteration, expansion, or addition to a dealership facility.

(ii) Contains no waiver or other provision prohibited by subparagraph (A), (B), (C), or (D) of paragraph (1).

(G) Prohibit an agreement separate from the franchise agreement that implements a dealer's election to terminate the franchise if the agreement is conditioned only on a specified time for termination or payment of consideration to the dealer.

(H) (i) Prohibit a voluntary waiver agreement, supported by valuable consideration, other than the consideration of renewing a franchise, to waive the right of a dealer to file a protest under Section 3062 for the proposed establishment or relocation of a specific proposed dealership, if the waiver agreement provides all of the following:

(I) The approximate address at which the proposed dealership will be located.

(II) The planning potential used to establish the proposed dealership's facility, personnel, and capital requirements.

(III) An approximation of projected vehicle and parts sales, and number of vehicles to be serviced at the proposed dealership.

(IV) Whether the franchisor or affiliate will hold an ownership interest in the proposed dealership or real property of the proposed dealership, and the approximate percentage of any franchisor or affiliate ownership interest in the proposed dealership.

(V) The line-makes to be operated at the proposed dealership.

(VI) If known at the time the waiver agreement is executed, the identity of the dealer who will operate the proposed dealership.

(VII) The date the waiver agreement is to expire, which may not be more than 30 months after the date of execution of the waiver agreement.

(ii) Notwithstanding the provisions of a waiver agreement entered into pursuant to the provisions of this subparagraph, a dealer may file a protest under Section 3062 if any of the information provided pursuant to clause (i) has become materially inaccurate since the waiver agreement was executed. Any determination of the enforceability of a waiver agreement shall be determined by the board and the franchisor shall have the burden of proof.

(h) To increase prices of motor vehicles that the dealer had ordered for private retail consumers prior to the dealer's receipt of the written official price increase notification. A sales contract signed by a private retail consumer is evidence of the order. In the event of manufacturer price reductions, the amount of the reduction received by a dealer shall be passed on to the private retail consumer by the dealer if the retail price was negotiated on the basis of the previous higher price to the dealer. Price reductions apply to all vehicles in the dealer's inventory that were subject to the price reduction. Price differences applicable to new model or series motor vehicles at the time of the introduction of new models or series shall not be considered a price increase or price decrease. This subdivision does not apply to price changes caused by either of the following:

(1) The addition to a motor vehicle of required or optional equipment pursuant to state or federal law.

(2) Revaluation of the United States dollar in the case of a foreign-make vehicle.

(i) To fail to pay to a dealer, within a reasonable time following receipt of a valid claim by a dealer thereof, a payment agreed to be made by the manufacturer or distributor to the dealer by reason of the fact that a new vehicle of a prior year model is in the dealer's inventory at the time of introduction of new model vehicles.

(j) To deny the widow, widower, or heirs designated by a deceased owner of a dealership the opportunity to participate in the ownership of the dealership or successor dealership under a valid franchise for a reasonable time after the death of the owner.

(k) To offer refunds or other types of inducements to a person for the purchase of new motor vehicles of a certain line-make to be sold to the state or a political subdivision of the state without making the same offer to all other dealers in the same line-make within the relevant market area.

(l) To modify, replace, enter into, relocate, terminate, or refuse to renew a franchise in violation of Article 4 (commencing with Section 3060) or Article 5 (commencing with Section 3070) of Chapter 6 of Division 2.

(m) To employ a person as a representative who has not been licensed pursuant to Article 3 (commencing with Section 11900) of Chapter 4 of Division 5.

(n) To deny a dealer the right of free association with another dealer for a lawful purpose.

(o) (1) To compete with their franchisees in the sale, lease, or warranty service of new motor vehicles.

(2) A manufacturer, branch, or distributor, or an entity that controls or is controlled by a manufacturer, branch, or distributor, shall not, however, be deemed to be competing in the following limited circumstances:

(A) Owning or operating a dealership for a temporary period, not to exceed one year at the location of a former dealership of the same line-make that has been out of operation for less than six months. However, after a showing of good cause by a manufacturer, branch, or distributor that it needs additional time to operate a dealership in preparation for sale to a successor independent franchisee, the board may extend the time period.

(B) Owning an interest in a dealer as part of a bona fide dealer development program that satisfies all of the following requirements:

(i) The sole purpose of the program is to make franchises available to persons lacking capital, training, business experience, or other qualities ordinarily required of prospective franchisees and the dealer development candidate is an individual who is unable to acquire the franchise without assistance of the program.

(ii) The dealer development candidate has made a significant investment subject to loss in the franchised business of the dealer.

(iii) The program requires the dealer development candidate to manage the day-to-day operations and business affairs of the dealer and to acquire, within a reasonable time and on reasonable terms and conditions, beneficial ownership and control of a majority interest in the dealer and disassociation of any direct or indirect ownership or control by the manufacturer, branch, or distributor.

(C) Owning a wholly owned subsidiary corporation of a distributor that sells motor vehicles at retail, if, for at least three years prior to January 1, 1973, the subsidiary corporation has been a wholly owned subsidiary of the distributor and engaged in the sale of vehicles at retail.

(3) (A) A manufacturer, branch, and distributor that owns or operates a dealership in the manner described in subparagraph (A) of paragraph (2) shall give written notice to the board, within 10 days, each time it commences or terminates operation of a dealership and each time it acquires, changes, or divests itself of an ownership interest.

(B) A manufacturer, branch, and distributor that owns an interest in a dealer in the manner described in subparagraph (B) of paragraph (2) shall give written notice to the board, annually, of the name and location of each dealer in which it has an ownership interest, the name of the bona fide dealer development owner or owners, and the ownership interests of each owner expressed as a percentage.

(4) In addition to the exceptions identified in paragraphs (2) and (3), a manufacturer, manufacturer branch, distributor, or distributor branch, or an affiliate thereof, shall not be deemed to be competing with their franchisees in any of the following limited circumstances:

(A) When directly providing an update to or repair of motor vehicle software, if the update or repair is provided over-the-air at no cost.

(B) When creating a new line of motor vehicles and using new or existing franchisees to sell and service those vehicles.

(C) When authorizing a fleet operator or other third party, such as a government entity or a commercial or rental fleet operator, to perform warranty service work on fleet vehicles owned or operated by a fleet owner, operator or other third party, provided that the franchisor does not prohibit or prevent the fleet operator or other third party from obtaining warranty service work from a franchisee of the same line-make.

(D) When owning or operating a dealership for the fleet sale or service of autonomous vehicles, provided that the dealership is of a line-make that does not have franchisees and the dealership does not engage in the sale of consumer goods, as defined by Section 1761 of the Civil Code.

(E) For the purposes of this paragraph, the following definitions shall apply:

(i) "Autonomous vehicles" shall have the same meaning as "autonomous vehicle" in paragraph (2) of subdivision (a) of Section 38750.

(ii) "Fleet vehicles" shall mean five or more vehicles under common ownership or operation.

(iii) "Fleet sale" shall mean a sale to a person that owns, operates, or maintains fleet vehicles.

(5) For the purposes of this subdivision, "warranty" shall have the same meaning as set forth in Section 3065.25.

(p) (1) To unfairly discriminate among its franchisees with respect to warranty reimbursement or authority granted to its franchisees to make warranty adjustments with retail customers.

(2) (A) To require a franchisee to perform service repair or warranty work on any vehicle model that is not currently available to the franchisee for sale or lease as a new vehicle.

(B) This subdivision shall not apply to any vehicle model that is not currently commercially available as a new vehicle. Nothing in this subdivision prohibits a franchisee and a manufacturer, manufacturer branch, distributor, distributor branch, or affiliate from entering into a voluntary written agreement, signed by both parties, to perform service repair or warranty work on any vehicle model provided that the warranty work is reimbursed at the retail labor rate and retail parts rate as established pursuant to Section 3065.2.

(3) As used in this subdivision, "warranty" shall have the same meaning as defined in Section 3065.25.

(q) To sell vehicles to a person not licensed pursuant to this chapter for resale.

(r) To fail to affix an identification number to a park trailer, as described in Section 18009.3 of the Health and Safety Code, that is manufactured on or after January 1, 1987, and that does not clearly identify the unit as a park trailer to the department. The configuration of the identification number shall be approved by the department.

(s) To dishonor a warranty, rebate, or other incentive offered to the public or a dealer in connection with the retail sale of a new motor vehicle, based solely upon the fact that an autobroker arranged or negotiated the sale. This subdivision shall not prohibit the disallowance of that rebate or incentive if the purchaser or dealer is ineligible to receive the rebate or incentive pursuant to any other term or condition of a rebate or incentive program.

(t) To exercise a right of first refusal or other right requiring a franchisee or an owner of the franchise to sell, transfer, or assign to the franchisor, or to a nominee of the franchisor, all or a material part of the franchised business or of the assets of the franchised business unless all of the following requirements are met:

(1) The franchise authorizes the franchisor to exercise a right of first refusal to acquire the franchised business or assets of the franchised business in the event of a proposed sale, transfer, or assignment.

(2) The franchisor gives written notice of its exercise of the right of first refusal no later than 45 days after the franchisor receives all of the information required pursuant to subparagraph (A) of paragraph (2) of subdivision (d).

(3) The sale, transfer, or assignment being proposed relates to not less than all or substantially all of the assets of the franchised business or to a controlling interest in the franchised business.

(4) The proposed transferee is neither a family member of an owner of the franchised business, nor a managerial employee of the franchisee owning 15 percent or more of the franchised business, nor a corporation, partnership, or other legal entity owned by the existing owners of the franchised business. For purposes of this paragraph, a "family member" means the spouse of an owner of the franchised business, the child, grandchild, brother, sister, or parent of an owner, or a spouse of one of those family members. This paragraph does not limit the rights of the franchisor to disapprove a proposed transferee as provided in subdivision (d).

(5) Upon the franchisor's exercise of the right of first refusal, the consideration paid by the franchisor to the franchisee and owners of the franchised business shall equal or exceed all consideration that each of them were to have received under the terms of, or in connection with, the proposed sale, assignment, or transfer, and the franchisor shall comply with all the terms and conditions of the agreement or agreements to sell, transfer, or assign the franchised business.

(6) The franchisor shall reimburse the proposed transferee for expenses paid or incurred by the proposed transferee in evaluating, investigating, and negotiating the proposed transfer to the extent those expenses do not exceed the usual, customary, and reasonable fees charged for similar work done in the area in which the franchised business is located. These expenses include, but are not limited to, legal and accounting expenses, and expenses incurred for title reports and environmental or other investigations of real property on which the franchisee's operations are conducted. The proposed transferee shall provide the franchisor a written itemization of those expenses, and a copy of all nonprivileged reports and studies for which expenses were incurred, if any, within 30 days after the proposed transferee's receipt of a written request from the franchisor for that accounting. The franchisor shall make payment within 30 days after exercising the right of first refusal.

(7) The franchisor does not use, or threaten to use, the exercise of the right of first refusal in bad faith.

(u) (1) To unfairly discriminate in favor of a dealership owned or controlled, in whole or in part, by a manufacturer or distributor or an entity that controls or is controlled by the manufacturer or distributor. Unfair discrimination includes, but is not limited to, the following:

(A) The furnishing to a franchisee or dealer that is owned or controlled, in whole or in part, by a manufacturer, branch, or distributor of any of the following:

(i) A vehicle that is not made available to each franchisee pursuant to a reasonable allocation formula that is applied uniformly, and a part or accessory that is not made available to all franchisees on an equal basis when there is no reasonable allocation formula that is applied uniformly.

(ii) A vehicle, part, or accessory that is not made available to each franchisee on comparable delivery terms, including the time of delivery after the placement of an order. Differences in delivery terms due to geographic distances or other factors beyond the control of the manufacturer, branch, or distributor shall not constitute unfair competition.

(iii) Information obtained from a franchisee by the manufacturer, branch, or distributor concerning the business affairs or operations of a franchisee in which the manufacturer, branch, or distributor does not have an ownership interest. The information includes, but is not limited to, information contained in financial statements and operating reports, the name, address, or other personal information or buying, leasing, or service behavior of a dealer, customer, and other information that, if provided to a franchisee or dealer owned or controlled by a manufacturer or distributor, would give that franchisee or dealer a competitive advantage. This clause does not apply if the information is provided pursuant to a subpoena or court order, or to aggregated information made available to all franchisees.

(iv) Sales or service incentives, discounts, or promotional programs that are not made available to all California franchises of the same line-make on an equal basis.

(B) Referring a prospective purchaser or lessee to a dealer in which a manufacturer, branch, or distributor has an ownership interest, unless the prospective purchaser or lessee resides in the area of responsibility assigned to that dealer or the prospective purchaser or lessee requests to be referred to that dealer.

(2) This subdivision does not prohibit a franchisor from granting a franchise to prospective franchisees or assisting those franchisees during the course of the franchise relationship as part of a program or programs to make franchises available to persons lacking capital, training, business experience, or other qualifications ordinarily required of prospective franchisees.

(v) (1) To access, modify, or extract information from a confidential dealer computer record, as defined in Section 11713.25, without obtaining the prior written consent of the dealer and without maintaining administrative, technical, and physical safeguards to protect the security, confidentiality, and integrity of the information.

(2) Paragraph (1) does not limit a duty that a dealer may have to safeguard the security and privacy of records maintained by the dealer.

(w) (1) To use electronic, contractual, or other means to prevent or interfere with any of the following:

(A) The lawful efforts of a dealer to comply with federal and state data security and privacy laws.

(B) The ability of a dealer to do either of the following:

(i) Ensure that specific data accessed from the dealer's computer system is within the scope of consent specified in subdivision (v).

(ii) Monitor specific data accessed from or written to the dealer's computer system.

(2) Paragraph (1) does not limit a duty that a dealer may have to safeguard the security and privacy of records maintained by the dealer.

(x) (1) To unfairly discriminate against a franchisee selling a service contract, debt cancellation agreement, maintenance agreement, or similar product not approved, endorsed, sponsored, or offered by the manufacturer, manufacturer branch, distributor, or distributor branch or affiliate. For purposes of this subdivision, unfair discrimination includes, but is not limited to, any of the following:

(A) Express or implied statements that the dealer is under an obligation to exclusively sell or offer to sell service contracts, debt cancellation agreements, maintenance agreements, or similar products approved, endorsed, sponsored, or offered by the manufacturer, manufacturer branch, distributor, or distributor branch or affiliate.

(B) Express or implied statements that selling or offering to sell service contracts, debt cancellation agreements, maintenance agreements, or similar products not approved, endorsed, sponsored, or offered by the manufacturer, manufacturer branch, distributor, or distributor branch or affiliate, or the failure to sell or offer to sell service contracts, debt cancellation agreements, maintenance agreements, or similar products approved, endorsed, sponsored, or offered by the manufacturer, manufacturer branch, distributor, or distributor branch or affiliate will have any negative consequences for the dealer.

(C) Measuring a dealer's performance under a franchise agreement based upon the sale of service contracts, debt cancellation agreements, maintenance agreements, or similar products approved, endorsed, sponsored, or offered by the manufacturer, manufacturer branch, distributor, or distributor branch or affiliate.

(D) Requiring a dealer to actively promote the sale of service contracts, debt cancellation agreements, maintenance agreements, or similar products approved, endorsed, sponsored, or offered by the manufacturer, manufacturer branch, distributor, or distributor branch or affiliate.

(E) Conditioning access to vehicles, parts, or vehicle sales or service incentives upon the sale of service contracts, debt cancellation agreements, maintenance agreements, or similar products approved, endorsed, sponsored, or offered by the manufacturer, manufacturer branch, distributor, or distributor branch or affiliate.

(F) Requiring a dealer to provide a disclosure or notice different from the notice set forth in paragraph (4) of this subdivision for the sale of the service contracts.

(2) Unfair discrimination does not include, and nothing shall prohibit a manufacturer from, offering an incentive program to vehicle dealers who voluntarily sell or offer to sell service contracts, debt cancellation agreements, or similar products approved, endorsed, sponsored, or offered by the manufacturer, manufacturer branch, distributor, or distributor branch or affiliate, if the program does not provide vehicle sales or service incentives.

(3) This subdivision does not prohibit a manufacturer, manufacturer branch, distributor, or distributor branch from requiring a franchisee that sells a used vehicle as "certified" under a certified used vehicle program established by the manufacturer, manufacturer branch, distributor, or distributor branch to provide a service contract approved, endorsed, sponsored, or offered by the manufacturer, manufacturer branch, distributor, or distributor branch.

(4) Unfair discrimination does not include, and nothing shall prohibit a franchisor from requiring a franchisee to provide, the following notice prior to the sale of the service contract if the service contract is not provided or backed by the franchisor and the vehicle is of the franchised line-make:"Service Contract DisclosureThe service contract you are purchasing is not provided or backed by the manufacturer of the vehicle you are purchasing. The manufacturer of the vehicle is not responsible for claims or repairs under this service contract.____________________
Signature of Purchaser"

(y) (1) To take or threaten to take any adverse action against a dealer pursuant to an export or sale-for-resale prohibition because the dealer sold or leased a vehicle to a customer who either exported the vehicle to a foreign country or resold the vehicle in violation of the prohibition, unless the export or sale-for-resale prohibition policy was provided to the dealer in writing at least 48 hours before the sale or lease of the vehicle, and the dealer knew or reasonably should have known of the customer's intent to export or resell the vehicle in violation of the prohibition. If the dealer causes the vehicle to be registered in this or any other state, and collects or causes to be collected any applicable sales or use tax due to this state, a rebuttable presumption is established that the dealer did not have reason to know of the customer's intent to export or resell the vehicle. In a proceeding in which a challenge to an adverse action is at issue, the manufacturer, manufacturer branch, distributor, or distributor branch shall have the burden of proof by a preponderance of the evidence to show that the vehicle was exported or resold in violation of an export or sale-for-resale prohibition policy, that the prohibition policy was provided to the dealer in writing at least 48 hours prior to the sale or lease, and that the dealer knew or reasonably should have known of the customer's intent to export the vehicle to a foreign country at the time of the sale or lease.

(2) An export or sale-for-resale prohibition policy shall not include a provision that expressly or implicitly requires a dealer to make further inquiries into a customer's intent, identity, or financial ability to purchase or lease a vehicle based on any of the customer's characteristics listed or defined in Section 51 of the Civil Code. A policy that is in violation of this paragraph is void and unenforceable.

(3) An export or sale-for-resale prohibition policy shall expressly include a provision stating the dealer's rebuttable presumption if the dealer causes the vehicle to be registered in this or any other state and collects or causes to be collected any applicable sales or use tax. A policy that is in violation of this paragraph is void and unenforceable.

(4) For purposes of this subdivision, "adverse action" means any activity that imposes, either expressly or implicitly, a burden, responsibility, or penalty on a dealer, including, but not limited to, nonroutine or nonrandom audits, withholding of incentives, or monetary chargebacks, imposed by the manufacturer, manufacturer branch, distributor, or distributor branch, or through an affiliate.

(z) As used in this section, the following terms have the following meanings:

(1) "Affiliate" means a person who directly or indirectly through one or more intermediaries, controls, is controlled by, or is under the common direction and control with, another person. "Control" means the possession, direct or indirect, of the power to direct or cause the direction of the management and policies of any person.

(2) "Area of responsibility" means a geographic area specified in a franchise that is used by the franchisor for the purpose of evaluating the franchisee's performance of its sales and service obligations.

(Amended by Stats. 2023, Ch. 332, Sec. 4. (AB 473) Effective January 1, 2024.)

11713.4. If a purchaser of a vehicle pays to the dealer an amount for the licensing or transfer of title of the vehicle, which amount is in excess of the actual fees due for such licensing or transfer, or which amount is in excess of the amount which has been paid, prior to the sale, by the dealer to the state in order to avoid penalties that would have accrued because of late payment of such fees, the dealer shall return such excess amount to the purchaser, whether or not such purchaser requests the return of the excess amount.

(Added by renumbering Section 11713.3 by Stats. 1979, Ch. 943.)

11713.5. (a) It is unlawful and a violation of this code for the holder of any license issued under this article to display for sale, offer for sale, or sell, a motor vehicle, representing the motor vehicle to be of a year model different from the year model designated at the time of manufacture or first assembly as a completed vehicle.

(b) It is unlawful and a violation of this code for the holder of any license issued under this article to directly or indirectly authorize or advise another holder of a license issued under this article to change the year model of a motor vehicle in the inventory of the other holder.

(c) It is unlawful and a violation of this code for the holder of any license issued under this article to display for sale, offer for sale, or sell, a housecar which has been manufactured in two or more stages, unless the licensee informs the buyer that the housecar has been so manufactured and the licensee provides the buyer with a form, approved by the department, which sets forth the date of chassis and engine manufacture and the date and model year of the other stages of the vehicle. The licensee shall retain a copy of the form, which shall be signed by the purchaser prior to entering into any sales contract, indicating that the purchaser has received a copy of the form.

(d) This section does not apply to the displaying or offering for sale, or selling, of any new motortruck or truck tractor weighing over 10,000 pounds.

(e) This section does not apply to a vehicle which has been remanufactured by a licensed remanufacturer. The year model of a remanufactured vehicle will be the year the vehicle was remanufactured.

(Amended by Stats. 1983, Ch. 1286, Sec. 36.)

11713.6. (a) It is unlawful and a violation of this code for the holder of any dealer's license issued under this article to fail to disclose in writing to the buyer or lessee of a new motor vehicle, that the vehicle, as equipped, may not be operated on a highway signed for the requirement of tire chains if the owner's manual or other material provided by the manufacturer states that the vehicle, as equipped, may not be operated with tire chains.

(b) The disclosure required under subdivision (a) shall meet both of the following requirements:

(1) The disclosure shall be printed in not less than 14-point boldface type on a single sheet of paper that contains no information other than

the disclosure.

(2) The disclosure shall include the following language in capital letters: "AS EQUIPPED, THIS VEHICLE MAY NOT BE OPERATED WITH TIRE CHAINS BUT MAY ACCOMMODATE SOME OTHER TYPE OF TIRE TRACTION DEVICE. SEE THE OWNER'S MANUAL FOR DETAILS."

(c) Prior to the sale or lease, the dealer shall present the disclosure statement for the buyer's or lessee's signature and then shall provide the buyer or lessee with a copy of the signed disclosure.

(Amended by Stats. 1995, Ch. 452, Sec. 2. Effective January 1, 1996.)

11713.7. Disclosure to a buyer that a vehicle has been remanufactured is required. Disclosure shall be accomplished by all of the following:

(a) Oral notification to the buyer.

(b) The statement "THIS VEHICLE HAS BEEN REMANUFACTURED AND CONTAINS USED OR RECONDITIONED PARTS" shall appear in a type size at least the same as the bulk of the text on the purchase order or conditional sales contract signed by the buyer.

(c) The statement that the vehicle is remanufactured and contains used or reconditioned parts shall appear in any advertisement pertaining to remanufactured vehicles.

(d) Remanufactured vehicles displayed for retail purposes shall be clearly designated as remanufactured. The disclosure statement required in subdivision (b) shall appear on the vehicle or at the location where the vehicles are displayed.

(Added by Stats. 1983, Ch. 1286, Sec. 37.)

11713.8. It is unlawful and a violation of this code for a remanufacturer licensed under this code to fail to do any of the following:

(a) Report to the department an existing vehicle identification number when a used frame is utilized.

(b) Die stamp the vehicle identification number to the frame of the vehicle when a new vehicle identification number is assigned.

(c) Disclose that a vehicle is remanufactured and contains used or reconditioned parts as required by Section 11713.7.

(d) Remove the trade name of the original manufacturer from the vehicle, unless the remanufacturer and the original manufacturer are same.

(e) Maintain for three years bills of sale or invoices for used parts utilized in a remanufactured vehicle.

(f) Maintain for three years proof that the vehicle was reported dismantled, as required by Section 5500 or 11520, when a used frame is utilized in a remanufactured vehicle.

(g) Disclose, on the vehicle identification number plate or label, that the vehicle is remanufactured and includes used parts.

(h) Disclose to the dealer on a document signed by the dealer that the vehicle is remanufactured and contains used parts.

(Added by Stats. 1983, Ch. 1286, Sec. 38.)

11713.9. (a) It is unlawful and a violation of this code for the holder of a dealer's license to knowingly display for sale or offer for sale any new motor vehicle specified in subdivision (b) with an engine manufactured by a manufacturer that is not the same as the vehicle manufacturer, as defined in Section 9980, unless the vehicle is prominently labeled as specified in Section 9981.

(b) This section applies only to new passenger vehicles and to new motortrucks with an unladen weight under 6,000 pounds, except housecars.

(Added by Stats. 1984, Ch. 1264, Sec. 2.)

11713.10. It is unlawful and a violation of this code to sell a low-speed vehicle, as defined in Section 385.5, without disclosing to the buyer the vehicle's maximum speed and the potential risks of driving a low-speed vehicle.

(Added by Stats. 1999, Ch. 140, Sec. 3. Effective January 1, 2000.)

11713.11. No holder of a dealer's license shall do any of the following when conducting an auction of vehicles to the public:

(a) Advertise that a vehicle will be auctioned to the public unless all of the following information is clearly and conspicuously disclosed in the advertisement:

(1) The date or the day of the week of the public auction, or if subdivision (b) applies to the auction, the date of the public auction.

(2) The location of the public auction.

(3) Whether a fee will be charged to attend the auction and the amount of that fee.

(4) The name and dealer number of the auctioning dealer.

(5) Whether a buyer's fee will be charged to a purchaser, in addition to the accepted auction bid price, and, if the fee is a set amount, the dollar amount of that fee. If the buyer's fee is not a set amount, the advertisement shall state the formula or percentage used to calculate the fee.

(b) If vehicles seized by a federal, state, or local public agency or authority are being advertised, advertise that a vehicle will be auctioned to the public unless, in addition to the information required by subdivision (a), the following information is clearly and conspicuously disclosed in the advertisement:

(1) A good faith estimate of the number of vehicles to be auctioned at that date.

(2) A good faith estimate of the number of vehicles seized by a federal, state, or local public agency or authority to be auctioned at that date.

(c) Fail, on the day of auction, to identify each vehicle seized by a federal, state, or local public agency or authority, either in a printed catalog or orally, before bidding begins on the vehicle.

(d) Include in the total price of an auctioned vehicle any costs to the purchaser at the completion of the sale, except the accepted auction bid price, taxes, vehicle registration fees, any charge for emission testing, not to exceed fifty dollars ($50), plus the actual fees charged to a consumer for a certificate pursuant to Section 44060 of the Health and Safety Code, any dealer document preparation charge not exceeding forty-five dollars ($45), and any buyer's fee.

(e) Charge a buyer's fee, unless the dealer conducting the auction delivers to any person permitted to submit bids, and at a time prior to accepting any bids from that person, a disclosure statement required by this subdivision and signed by that person. The disclosure statement, if the buyer's fee is a set amount, shall disclose the amount of the fee, or if the buyer's fee is not a set amount, disclose the formula or percentage used to calculate the fee. The disclosure statement shall be on a separate 81/2 x 11 inch sheet of paper. Except for the information set forth in this subdivision, the disclosure statement shall not contain any other text, except as necessary to identify the dealer conducting the auction sale and to disclose the amount, percentage, or formula used to calculate the buyer's fee, and to provide for the date and the person's acknowledgment of receipt. The heading shall be printed in no smaller than 24-point bold type and the text of the statement shall be printed in no smaller than 12-point type and shall read substantially as follows:

BUYER'S FEE REQUIRED

A buyer's fee is an amount charged by the auctioning dealer for conducting the auction sale. If your bid price is accepted as the winning bid on any vehicle, you will be charged a buyer's fee in addition to the accepted bid price.

The buyer's fee that will be added to your accepted bid price is $ ______________________________.

OR

The buyer's fee that will be added to your accepted bid price will be calculated as follows (insert percentage or other formula for calculating the buyer's fee):

The buyer's fee is part of the purchase price and is subject to sales tax.

Date: ______________

Signature of Bidder ________________________

(f) Fail to comply with or violate this chapter, Title 2.95 (commencing with Section 1812.600) of Part 4 of Division 3 of the Civil Code, Section 2328 of the Commercial Code, or Section 535 of the Penal Code, or any law administered by the State Board of Equalization, relating to the auctioneering business, including, but not limited to, sales and the transfer of title of goods.

(g) For purposes of this section, a "buyer's fee" is any amount that is in addition to the accepted auction bid price, taxes, vehicle registration fees, certificate of compliance or noncompliance fee, or any dealer document preparation charge, which is charged to a purchaser by an auctioning dealer.

(Amended by Stats. 1999, Ch. 672, Sec. 2. Effective January 1, 2000.)

11713.12. (a) The decal required by subdivision (c) of Section 1793.23 of the Civil Code to be affixed by a manufacturer to a motor vehicle, shall be affixed to the left front doorframe of the vehicle, or, if the vehicle does not have a left front doorframe, it shall be affixed in a location designated by the department. The decal shall specify that title to the motor vehicle has been inscribed with the notation "Lemon Law Buyback" and shall be affixed to the vehicle in a manner prescribed by the department.

(b) No person shall knowingly remove or alter any decal affixed to a vehicle pursuant to subdivision (a), whether or not licensed under this code.

(Added by Stats. 1995, Ch. 503, Sec. 6. Effective January 1, 1996.)

11713.13. It is unlawful and a violation of this code for any manufacturer, manufacturer branch, distributor, or distributor branch licensed under this code to do, directly or indirectly through an affiliate, any of the following:

(a) Prevent, or attempt to prevent, by contract or otherwise, a dealer from acquiring, adding, or maintaining a sales or service operation for another line-make of motor vehicles at the same or expanded facility at which the dealer currently operates a dealership if the dealer complies with any reasonable facilities and capital requirements of the manufacturer or distributor.

(b) Require a dealer to establish or maintain exclusive facilities, personnel, or display space if the imposition of the requirement would be unreasonable in light of all existing circumstances, including economic conditions. In any proceeding in which the reasonableness of a facility or capital requirement is an issue, the manufacturer or distributor shall have the burden of proof.

(c) Require, by contract or otherwise, a dealer to make a material alteration, expansion, or addition to any dealership facility, unless the required alteration, expansion, or addition is reasonable in light of all existing circumstances, including economic conditions and advancements in vehicular technology. This subdivision does not limit the obligation of a dealer to comply with any applicable health or safety laws.

(1) A required facility alteration, expansion, or addition shall not be deemed reasonable if it requires that the dealer purchase goods or services from a specific vendor when goods or services of substantially similar kind, quality, and general design concept are available from another vendor. Notwithstanding the prohibitions in this paragraph, a manufacturer, manufacturer branch, distributor, distributor branch, or affiliate may require the dealer to request approval for the use of alternative goods or services in writing. Approval for these requests shall not be unreasonably withheld, and the request shall be deemed approved if not specifically denied in writing within 20 business days of receipt of the dealer's written request. This paragraph does not authorize a dealer to impair or eliminate the intellectual property or trademark rights of the manufacturer, manufacturer branch, distributor, distributor branch, or affiliate, or to permit a dealer to erect or maintain signs that do not conform to the intellectual property usage guidelines of the manufacturer, manufacturer branch, distributor, distributor branch, or affiliate. This paragraph shall not apply to a specific good or service if the manufacturer, manufacturer branch, distributor, distributor branch, or affiliate provides the dealer with a lump-sum payment or series of payments toward a substantial portion of the cost of that good or service, if the payment is intended solely to reimburse the dealer for the purchase of the specified good or service.

(2) In any proceeding in which a required facility alteration, expansion, or addition is an issue, the manufacturer, manufacturer branch, distributor, distributor branch, or affiliate shall have the burden of proof.

(3) (A) A required facility alteration, expansion, or addition shall not be deemed reasonable if the facility has been modified within the last 10 years at a cost of more than two hundred fifty thousand dollars ($250,000), and the modification was required, or was made for the purposes of complying with a franchisor's brand image program, and was approved by the manufacturer, manufacturer branch, distributor, distributor branch, or affiliate.

(B) This paragraph does not apply to a specific facility alteration, expansion, or addition that is necessary to enable the sale or service of zero-emission or near-zero-emission vehicles, as defined in Section 44258 of the Health and Safety Code.

(C) This paragraph does not apply to a specific facility alteration, expansion, or addition involving the exercise of the franchisor's trademark rights that is necessary to erect or maintain signs or to the use of any trademark.

(D) This paragraph does not apply to a specific facility alteration, expansion, or addition that is necessary to comply with any applicable health or safety laws.

(E) This paragraph does not apply to the installation of specialized equipment that is necessary to service a vehicle offered by a franchisor and available for sale by the franchisee.

(F) This paragraph does not apply to voluntary written agreements signed by both parties between a franchisee and a manufacturer, manufacturer branch, distributor, distributor branch, or affiliate.

(d) (1) Fail to pay to a dealer, within 90 days of termination, cancellation, or nonrenewal of a franchise, all of the following:

(A) The dealer cost, plus any charges made by the manufacturer or distributor for vehicle distribution or delivery and the cost of any dealer-installed original equipment accessories, less any amount invoiced to the vehicle and paid by the manufacturer or distributor to the dealer, for all new and undamaged vehicles with less than 500 miles in the dealer's inventory that were acquired by the dealer from the manufacturer, distributor, or another new motor vehicle dealer franchised to sell vehicles of the same line-make, in the ordinary course of business, within 18 months of termination, cancellation, or nonrenewal of the franchise.

(B) The dealer cost for all unused and undamaged supplies, parts, and accessories listed in the manufacturer's current parts catalog and in their original packaging, except that sheet metal may be packaged in a comparable substitute for the original package.

(C) The fair market value of each undamaged sign owned by the motor vehicle dealer and bearing a common name, trade name, or trademark of the manufacturer or distributor if acquisition of the sign was required or made a condition of participation in an incentive program by the manufacturer or distributor.

(D) The fair market value of all special tools, computer systems, and equipment that were required or made a condition of participation in an incentive program by the manufacturer or distributor that are in usable condition, excluding normal wear and tear.

(E) The dealer costs of handling, packing, loading, and transporting any items or inventory for repurchase by the manufacturer or distributor.

(2) This subdivision does not apply to a franchisor of a dealer of new recreational vehicles, as defined in subdivision (a) of Section 18010 of the Health and Safety Code.

(3) This subdivision does not apply to a termination that is implemented as a result of the sale of substantially all of the inventory and fixed assets or stock of a franchised dealership if the dealership continues to operate as a franchisee of the same line-make.

(e) (1) (A) Fail to pay to a dealer of new recreational vehicles, as defined in subdivision (a) of Section 18010 of the Health and Safety Code, within 90 days of termination, cancellation, or nonrenewal of a franchise for a recreational vehicle line-make, as defined in Section 3072.5, the dealer cost, plus any charges made by the manufacturer or distributor for vehicle distribution or delivery and the cost of any dealer-installed original equipment accessories, less any amount invoiced to the vehicle and paid by the manufacturer or distributor to the dealer, for a new recreational vehicle when the termination, cancellation, or nonrenewal is initiated by a recreational vehicle manufacturer. This paragraph only applies to new and unused recreational vehicles that do not currently have or have had in the past, material damage, as defined in Section 9990, and that the dealer acquired from the manufacturer, distributor, or another new motor vehicle dealer franchised to sell recreational vehicles of the same line-make in the ordinary course of business within 12 months of the termination, cancellation, or nonrenewal of the franchise.

(B) For those recreational vehicles with odometers, paragraph (1) shall apply to only those vehicles that have no more than 1,500 miles on the odometer, in addition to the number of miles incurred while delivering the vehicle from the manufacturer's facility that produced the vehicle for delivery to the dealer's retail location.

(C) Damaged recreational vehicles shall be repurchased by the manufacturer provided there is an offset in value for damages, except recreational vehicles that have or had material damage, as defined in Section 9990, may be repurchased at the manufacturer's option provided there is an offset in value for damages.

(2) Fail to pay to a dealer of new recreational vehicles, as defined in subdivision (a) of Section 18010 of the Health and Safety Code, within 90 days of termination, cancellation, or nonrenewal of a franchise, all of the following:

(A) The dealer cost for all unused and undamaged supplies, parts, and accessories listed in the manufacturer's current parts catalog and in their original packaging, except that sheet metal may be packaged in a comparable substitute for the original package.

(B) The fair market value of each undamaged sign owned by the motor vehicle dealer and bearing a common name, trade name, or trademark of the manufacturer or distributor if acquisition of the sign was required or made a condition of participation in an incentive program by the manufacturer or distributor.

(C) The fair market value of all special tools, computer systems, and equipment that were required or made a condition of participation in an incentive program by the manufacturer or distributor that are in usable condition, excluding normal wear and tear.

(D) The dealer costs of handling, packing, loading, and transporting any items or inventory for repurchase by the manufacturer or distributor.

(f) (1) Fail, upon demand, to indemnify any existing or former franchisee and the franchisee's successors and assigns from any and all damages sustained and attorney's fees and other expenses reasonably incurred by the franchisee that result from or relate to any claim made or asserted by a third party against the franchisee to the extent the claim results from any of the following:

(A) The condition, characteristics, manufacture, assembly, or design of any vehicle, parts, accessories, tools, or equipment, or the selection or combination of parts or components manufactured or distributed by the manufacturer or distributor.

(B) Service systems, procedures, or methods the franchisor required or recommended the franchisee to use if the franchisee properly uses the system, procedure, or method.

(C) Improper use or disclosure by a manufacturer or distributor of nonpublic personal information obtained from a franchisee concerning any consumer, customer, or employee of the franchisee.

(D) Any act or omission of the manufacturer or distributor for which the franchisee would have a claim for contribution or indemnity under applicable law or under the franchise, irrespective of and without regard to any prior termination or expiration of the franchise.

(E) Any act or omission of the franchisee that is the result of the franchisee's use of a service provided by a digital vendor preselected by a franchisor and the use of that service violates California law. For purposes of this subdivision, a "service provided by a digital vendor" includes any electronic system that manages consumer data or generates consumer notices or documentation.

(2) Require a franchisee to indemnify its franchisor, or any third party, for the actions of the franchisee that were properly made in compliance with a franchisor's policy, program, or requirement.

(3) This subdivision does not limit, in any way, the existing rights, remedies, or recourses available to any person who purchases or leases vehicles at retail.

(g) (1) Establish or maintain a performance standard, sales objective, or program for measuring a dealer's sales, service, or customer service performance that may materially affect the dealer, including, but not limited to, the dealer's right to payment under any incentive or reimbursement program or establishment of working capital requirements, unless both of the following requirements are satisfied:

(A) The performance standard, sales objective, or program for measuring dealership sales, service, or customer service performance is reasonable in light of all existing circumstances, including, but not limited to, the following:

(i) Demographics in the dealer's area of responsibility.

(ii) Geographical and market characteristics in the dealer's area of responsibility.

(iii) The availability and allocation of vehicles and parts inventory.

(iv) Local and statewide economic circumstances.

(v) Historical sales, service, and customer service performance of the line-make within the dealer's area of responsibility, including vehicle brand preferences of consumers in the dealer's area of responsibility.

(B) Within 30 days after a request by the dealer, the manufacturer, manufacturer branch, distributor, distributor branch, or affiliate provides a written summary of the methodology and data used in establishing the performance standard, sales objective, or program for measuring dealership sales or service performance. The summary shall be in detail sufficient to permit the dealer to determine how the standard was established and applied to the dealer.

(2) In any proceeding in which the reasonableness of a performance standard, sales objective, or program for measuring dealership sales, service, or customer service performance is an issue, the manufacturer, manufacturer branch, distributor, distributor branch, or affiliate shall have the burden of proof.

(3) As used in this subdivision, "area of responsibility" has the same meaning as defined in subdivision (z) of Section 11713.3.

(h) Restrict the ability of a dealer to select a digital service of a dealer's choice that is offered by a vendor of the dealer's choice, provided that the service offered by the vendor is approved by the manufacturer, manufacturer branch, distributor, distributor branch, or affiliate. Approval for services selected by dealers shall not be unreasonably withheld. For purposes of this subdivision, digital service includes, but is not limited to, internet website and data management services, but does not include warranty repair processes for a vehicle.

(i) Restrict, limit, or discourage a franchisee from checking or verifying the applicability of a technical service bulletin or customer service campaign to any vehicle.

(j) Implement or modify a vehicle reservation system for the sale or lease of motor vehicles that does not comply with either of the following requirements:

(1) Any vehicle reservation system designed, implemented, or controlled by a franchisor that allocates vehicles to franchisees shall use customer dealer selection or other objective criteria to allocate the vehicles.

(2) At least 30 days prior to implementing a vehicle reservation system, a franchisor shall make available to its franchisees a description of the reservation program rules and requirements to franchisees through the system, as applicable. Notice of any change to such criteria shall be provided at least 30 days prior to it becoming effective.

(k) (1) Implement a program or policy that coerces or requires the franchisee to install direct current fast charging stations, unless all of the following are satisfied:

(A) If the program or policy requires public access to the direct current fast charging stations, the franchisor shall reimburse the dealer for one-half of all costs to install and maintain the stations, if the dealer pays the franchisor one-half of the net income generated from the ongoing use of the stations. This subparagraph shall not apply to a manufacturer program or policy that encourages the franchisee to install publicly accessible direct current fast charging stations, if the program or policy reimburses the dealer for no less than one-half of the cost of all direct current fast charging stations subject to the program or policy.

(B) The program or policy does not limit the ability of a franchisee to use all available incentives or utility rate plans to minimize total installation cost.

(C) The program or policy does not require installation of more than the number and type of electric vehicle charging stations reasonably necessary to conduct service and sales operations.

(D) The program or policy must be reasonable in light of supply constraints, time constraints, advancements in vehicular technology, and electric grid integration.

(2) For purposes of this subdivision, the term "coerce" shall mean the use of force or threats to persuade, constrain, or compel a franchisee to take a specific action. "Coerce" includes, but is not limited to, threatening to withhold vehicles or parts from a franchisee or charging a franchisee a higher price for vehicles or parts on the basis of the franchisee refusing, declining, or failing to perform a specific behavior.

(l) As used in this section, the following terms have the following meanings:

(1) "Affiliate" means a person who directly or indirectly through one or more intermediaries, controls, is controlled by, or is under the common direction and control with, another person. "Control" means the possession, direct or indirect, of the power to direct or cause the direction of the management and policies of any person.

(2) "Facility" or "facilities" includes, but is not limited to, premises, places, buildings, or structures.

(3) "Vehicle reservation system" means a process that is used to hold open the opportunity for a specified consumer to place an order for the purchase or lease of a new motor vehicle.

(Amended by Stats. 2023, Ch. 332, Sec. 5. (AB 473) Effective January 1, 2024.)

11713.14. (a) Notwithstanding any other provision of law, a person who purchases a vehicle that is sold through a dealer at an auction of vehicles open to the general public shall have the same rights and remedies against the dealer who conducts the auction sale as if that dealer were the owner and seller of the auctioned vehicle. The purchaser's rights and remedies are in addition to any right or remedy he or she may have against an owner of a vehicle sold at a public auto auction.

(b) If any claim or action is filed against a dealer pursuant to subdivision (a) and the vehicle that is the subject of the claim or action was owned by a person other than the dealer at the time of sale by auction, the owner of the vehicle that consigned it to the dealer shall indemnify the dealer for any liability resulting from misrepresentations or other misconduct by the consignor.

(c) A purchaser's rights and remedies under this section may not be waived or modified by an agreement or by a recharacterization of the sales transaction.

(Added by Stats. 1999, Ch. 672, Sec. 3. Effective January 1, 2000.)

11713.15. (a) (1) Prior to being issued a temporary branch license for selling new recreational vehicles, as defined in Section 18010 of the Health and Safety Code, at a show, a dealer shall submit to the department a manufacturer's written authorization for the sale specifying the dates of the show, the location of the show, and the makes of those new recreational vehicles being offered for sale.

(2) If nine or fewer dealers are participating in the show, a temporary branch license may only be issued to a dealer under this subdivision if the location of the show is 50 miles or less from that dealer's established place of business or permanent branch location.

Each dealer described in this paragraph shall certify in his or her application for a temporary branch license that the show location is 50 miles or less from his or her established place of business or permanent branch location.

(3) A temporary branch license may be issued to a dealer for purposes of participating in a show if all of the following conditions exist:

(A) The location of the show is 50 miles or more from the dealer's place of business or that dealer's branch locations, or both.

(B) Ten or more dealers apply for temporary branch licenses for purposes of participating in that show.

(C) Not less than 10 days prior to the conduct of the show, the department receives at least 10 applications for temporary branch licenses together at one of the department's field offices.

(b) (1) Any advertising and promotional materials designed to attract the public to attend a show of recreational vehicles where there are nine or fewer dealers participating shall include the business name of each participating dealer and that dealer's established place of business in a type size that is equivalent to the second largest type used in the advertisement or promotional materials. This information shall be placed at the top of any advertisement or promotional materials.

(2) If the recreational vehicles being offered for sale are used, the word "used" shall immediately precede the identification of the make of the vehicle or be immediately adjacent to the depiction of any used vehicles.

(3) In addition, the promoters of the show shall cause a sign to be conspicuously displayed at the major, public entrance leading directly to the show, printed in 50-point type, containing the information required in paragraph (1).

(c) A recreational vehicle dealer participating in a show for which a temporary branch license is required shall provide each buyer, prior to the sale of any vehicle at the show, a written statement disclosing the identity and the established business location of the dealer that has agreed to render service or warranty work with respect to the vehicle being purchased by the buyer, and if there is no agreement with any dealer to render the service or warranty, to state that fact.

(d) Paragraphs (2) and (3) of subdivision (a) and subdivision (b) do not apply to a dealer participating in an annual show sponsored by a national trade association of recreational vehicle manufacturers, if the show is located in a county with a population of 9,000,000 or more persons, or is at a location within 30 miles from the prior approved location of the show, and at least 10 manufacturers are participating in the show. If the dealer is otherwise eligible to participate in the show, the department shall issue a temporary branch license if all the following occur:

(1) A national trade association of recreational vehicle manufacturers submits a letter to the department that certifies its status as a national trade association of recreational vehicle manufacturers and specifies the dates and location of the show.

(2) Upon receipt of the letter from a national trade association described in paragraph (1) notifying the department of the dates and location of the show, the department provides written acknowledgment to the national trade association submitting the letter.

(3) Each dealer participating in the show attaches a copy of the department letter described in paragraph (2) to the application for a temporary branch license submitted to the department.

(Amended by Stats. 2018, Ch. 537, Sec. 1. (AB 2330) Effective September 19, 2018.)

11713.16. It is a violation of this code for the holder of any dealer's license issued under this article to do any of the following:

(a) Advertise any used vehicle of the current or prior model-year without expressly disclosing the vehicle as "used," "previously owned," or a similar term that indicates that the vehicle is used, as defined in this code.

(b) Use the terms "on approved credit" or "on credit approval" in an advertisement for the sale of a vehicle unless those terms are clearly and conspicuously disclosed and unabbreviated.

(c) Advertise an amount described by terms such as "unpaid balance" or "balance can be financed" unless the total sale price is clearly and conspicuously disclosed and in close proximity to the advertised balance.

(d) Advertise credit terms that fail to comply with the disclosure requirements of Section 226.24 of Title 12 of the Code of Federal Regulations. Advertisements of terms that include escalated payments, balloon payments, or deferred downpayments shall clearly and conspicuously identify those payments as to amounts and time due.

(e) Advertise as the total sales price of a vehicle an amount that includes a deduction for a rebate. However, a dealer may advertise a separate amount that includes a deduction for a rebate provided that the advertisement clearly and conspicuously discloses, in close proximity to the amount advertised, the price of the vehicle before the rebate deduction and the amount of the rebate, each so identified. A dealer may not advertise a rebate deduction that conflicts with another advertised rebate deduction.

(f) Advertise claims such as "everyone financed," "no credit rejected," or similar claims unless the dealer is willing to extend credit to any person under any and all circumstances.

(g) Advertise the amount of any downpayment unless it represents the total payment required of a purchaser prior to delivery of the vehicle, including any payment for sales tax or license. Statements such as "$_____ delivers," "$____ puts you in a new car" are examples of advertised downpayments.

(h) Advertise the price of a new vehicle or class of new vehicles unless the vehicle or vehicles have all of the equipment listed as standard by the manufacturer or distributor or the dealer has replaced the standard equipment with equipment of higher value.

(i) Fail to clearly and conspicuously disclose in an advertisement for the sale of a vehicle any disclosure required by this code or any qualifying term used in conjunction with advertised credit terms. Unless otherwise provided by statute, the specific size of disclosures or qualifying terms is not prescribed.

(Amended by Stats. 2014, Ch. 856, Sec. 3. (AB 1732) Effective January 1, 2015.)

11713.17. (a) Following the retail sale or lease of a motor vehicle for which the department issues two license plates, a dealer may not deliver the motor vehicle unless either of the following occurs:

(1) The motor vehicle is equipped with a bracket or other means of securing a front license plate.

(2) The dealer obtains a signed written acknowledgment from the person taking delivery of the motor vehicle acknowledging both of the following:

(A) The person expressly refused installation of a bracket or other means of securing the front license plate.

(B) The person understands that California law requires a license plate to be displayed from and securely fastened to the front of the motor vehicle and that the hardware necessary to securely fasten the front plate is available from the dealer.

(b) A manufacturer or distributor may not sell or distribute in this state a new motor vehicle for which the department issues two license plates, unless that motor vehicle is equipped or provided with a bracket or other means of securing the license plates.

(Added by Stats. 2004, Ch. 365, Sec. 1. Effective January 1, 2005.)

11713.18. (a) It is a violation of this code for the holder of any dealer's license issued under this article to advertise for sale or sell a used vehicle as "certified" or use any similar descriptive term in the advertisement or the sale of a used vehicle that implies the vehicle has been certified to meet the terms of a used vehicle certification program if any of the following apply:

(1) The dealer knows or should have known that the odometer on the vehicle does not indicate actual mileage, has been rolled back or otherwise altered to show fewer miles, or replaced with an odometer showing fewer miles than actually driven.

(2) The dealer knows or should have known that the vehicle was reacquired by the vehicle's manufacturer or a dealer pursuant to state or federal warranty laws.

(3) The title to the vehicle has been inscribed with the notation "Lemon Law Buyback," "manufacturer repurchase," "salvage," "junk," "nonrepairable," "flood," or similar title designation required by this state or another state.

(4) The vehicle has sustained damage in an impact, fire, or flood, that after repair prior to sale substantially impairs the use or safety of the vehicle.

(5) The dealer knows or should have known that the vehicle has sustained frame damage.

(6) Prior to sale, the dealer fails to provide the buyer with a completed inspection report indicating all the components inspected.

(7) The dealer disclaims any warranties of merchantability on the vehicle.

(8) The vehicle is sold "AS IS."

(9) The term "certified" or any similar descriptive term is used in any manner that is untrue or misleading or that would cause any advertisement to be in violation of subdivision (a) of Section 11713 of this code or Section 17200 or 17500 of the Business and Professions Code.

(b) A violation of this section is actionable under the Consumers Legal Remedies Act (Title 1.5 (commencing with Section 1750) of Part 4 of Division 3 of the Civil Code), the Unfair Competition Law (Chapter 5 (commencing with Section 17200) of Part 2 of Division 7 of the Business and Professions Code), Section 17500 of the Business and Professions Code, or any other applicable state or federal law. The rights and remedies provided by this section are cumulative and shall not be construed as restricting any right or remedy that is otherwise available.

(c) This section does not abrogate or limit any disclosure obligation imposed by any other law.

(d) This section does not apply to the advertisement or sale of a used motorcycle or a used off-highway motor vehicle subject to identification under Section 38010.

(Added by Stats. 2005, Ch. 128, Sec. 8. Effective January 1, 2006. Operative July 1, 2006, by Sec. 12 of Ch. 128.)

11713.19. (a) It is unlawful and a violation of this code for the holder of any dealer's license issued under this article to do any of the following:

(1) Negotiate the terms of a vehicle sale or lease contract and then add charges to the contract for any goods or services without previously disclosing to the consumer the goods and services to be added and obtaining the consumer's consent.

(2) (A) Inflate the amount of an installment payment or down payment or extend the maturity of a sale or lease contract for the purpose of disguising the actual charges for goods or services to be added by the dealer to the contract.

(B) For purposes of subparagraph (A), "goods or services" means any type of good or service, including, but not limited to, insurance and service contracts.

(b) Subdivision (a) does not apply to the sale or lease of a motorcycle or an off-highway motor vehicle subject to identification under Section 38010.

(Added by Stats. 2005, Ch. 128, Sec. 9. Effective January 1, 2006. Operative July 1, 2006, by Sec. 12 of Ch. 128.)

11713.20. (a) A dealer that obtains a consumer credit score, as defined in subdivision (b) of Section 1785.15.1 of the Civil Code, from a consumer credit reporting agency, as defined in subdivision (d) of Section 1785.3 of the Civil Code, for use in connection with an application for credit initiated by a consumer for the purchase or lease of a motor vehicle for personal, family, or household use, shall provide, prior to the sale or lease of the vehicle, the following information to the consumer in at least 10-point type on a document separate from the sale or lease contract:

(1) Each credit score obtained and used by the dealer.

(2) A statement that a consumer report, or a credit report, is a record of the consumer's credit history and includes information about whether the consumer pays his or her obligations on time and how much the consumer owes to creditors.

(3) A statement that a credit score is a number that takes into account information in a consumer report and that a credit score can change over time to reflect changes in the consumer's credit history.

(4) A statement that the consumer's credit score can affect whether the consumer can obtain credit and what the cost of that credit will be.

(5) The range of possible credit scores under the model used to generate that credit score.

(6) The distribution of credit scores among consumers who are scored under the same scoring model that is used to generate the consumer's credit score using the same scale as that of the credit score that is provided to the consumer, presented in the form of a bar graph containing a minimum of six bars that illustrates the percentage of consumers with credit scores within the range of scores reflected in each bar, or by other clear and readily understandable graphical means, or a clear and readily understandable statement informing the consumer how his or her credit score compares to the scores of other consumers. Use of a graph or statement obtained from the person providing the credit score that meets the requirements of this paragraph is deemed to comply with this requirement.

(7) The date the credit score was created.

(8) The name of the consumer reporting agency or other person that provided each credit score obtained and used by the dealer.

(9) A statement that the consumer is encouraged to verify the accuracy of the information contained in the consumer report and has the right to dispute any inaccurate information in the report.

(10) A statement that federal law gives the consumer the right to obtain copies of his or her consumer reports directly from the consumer reporting agencies, including a free report from each of the nationwide consumer reporting agencies once during any 12-month period.

(11) Contact information for the centralized source from which consumers may obtain their free annual consumer reports.

(12) A statement directing consumers to the Internet Web sites of the Federal Reserve Board and Federal Trade Commission to obtain more information about consumer reports.

(b) Appropriate use by a dealer of the model form described in Section 640.5(e)(5) of Title 16 of the Code of Federal Regulations and contained in Title 16 of the Code of Federal Regulations Part B, Appendix B, Model Form B-4, as promulgated on January 15, 2010, is deemed to comply with the requirements of this section. Use of the model form is optional.

(c) This section does not apply to the purchase or lease of a motorcycle or an off-highway motor vehicle subject to identification under Section 38010.

(d) This section does not limit or restrict any rights or remedies otherwise available under existing law.

(Amended by Stats. 2010, Ch. 483, Sec. 3. (SB 1004) Effective January 1, 2011.)

11713.21. (a) (1) A dealer shall not sell a used vehicle, as defined in Section 665 and subject to registration under this code, at retail to an individual for personal, family, or household use without offering the buyer a contract cancellation option agreement that allows the buyer to return the vehicle without cause. This section does not apply to a used vehicle having a purchase price of forty thousand dollars ($40,000) or more, a motorcycle, as defined in Section 400, or a recreational vehicle, as defined in Section 18010 of the Health and Safety Code.

(2) The purchase price for the contract cancellation option shall not exceed the following:

(A) Seventy-five dollars ($75) for a vehicle with a cash price of five thousand dollars ($5,000) or less.

(B) One hundred fifty dollars ($150) for a vehicle with a cash price of more than five thousand dollars ($5,000), but not more than ten thousand dollars ($10,000).

(C) Two hundred fifty dollars ($250) for a vehicle with a cash price of more than ten thousand dollars ($10,000), but not more than thirty thousand dollars ($30,000).

(D) One percent of the purchase price for a vehicle with a cash price of more than thirty thousand dollars ($30,000), but less than forty thousand dollars ($40,000).

The term "cash price" as used in this paragraph has the same meaning as described in subparagraph (A) of paragraph (1) of subdivision (a) of Section 2982 of the Civil Code. "Cash price" also excludes registration, transfer, titling, and license fees, the California tire fee, and any charge to electronically register or transfer the vehicle.

(b) To comply with subdivision (a), and notwithstanding Section 2981.9 of the Civil Code, a contract cancellation option agreement shall be contained in a document separate from the conditional sales contract or other vehicle purchase agreement and shall contain, at a minimum, the following:

(1) The name of the seller and the buyer.

(2) A description and the Vehicle Identification Number of the vehicle purchased.

(3) A statement specifying the time within which the buyer must exercise the right to cancel the purchase under the contract cancellation option and return the vehicle to the dealer. The dealer shall not specify a time that is earlier than the dealer's close of business on the second day following the day on which the vehicle was originally delivered to the buyer by the dealer.

(4) A statement that clearly and conspicuously specifies the dollar amount of any restocking fee the buyer must pay to the dealer to exercise the right to cancel the purchase under the contract cancellation option. The restocking fee shall not exceed one hundred seventy-five dollars ($175) if the vehicle's cash price is five thousand dollars ($5,000) or less, three hundred fifty dollars ($350) if the vehicle's cash price is less than ten thousand dollars ($10,000), and five hundred dollars ($500) if the vehicle cash price is ten thousand dollars ($10,000) or more. The dealer shall apply toward the restocking fee the price paid by the buyer for the contract cancellation option. The price for the purchase of the contract cancellation option is not otherwise subject to setoff or refund.

(5) Notwithstanding paragraph (4), when a buyer, who leased the purchased vehicle immediately preceding the dealer's sale of the vehicle to the buyer, exercises the contract cancellation option, the limit on the amount of a restocking fee required to be paid by the buyer shall be increased. That increased amount shall be the amount the buyer would have been obligated to pay the lessor, at the time of the termination of the lease, for the following charges, as specified in the lease, and as if the buyer had not purchased the contract cancellation option:

(A) Excess mileage.

(B) Unrepaired damage.

(C) Excess wear and tear.

(6) A statement specifying the maximum number of miles that the vehicle may be driven after its original delivery by the dealer to the buyer to remain eligible for cancellation under the contract cancellation option. A dealer shall not specify fewer than 250 miles in the contract cancellation option agreement.

(7) A statement that the contract cancellation option gives the buyer the right to cancel the purchase and obtain a full refund, minus the purchase price for the contract cancellation option agreement; and that the right to cancel will apply only if, within the time specified in the contract cancellation option agreement, the following are personally delivered to the selling dealer by the buyer: a written notice exercising the right to cancel the purchase signed by the buyer; any restocking fee specified in the contract cancellation option agreement minus the purchase price for the contract cancellation option agreement; the original contract cancellation option agreement and vehicle purchase contract and related documents, if the seller gave those original documents to the buyer; all original vehicle titling and registration documents, if the seller gave

those original documents to the buyer; and the vehicle, free of all liens and encumbrances, other than any lien or encumbrance created by or incidental to the conditional sales contract, any loan arranged by the dealer, or any purchase money loan obtained by the buyer from a third party, and in the same condition as when it was delivered by the dealer to the buyer, reasonable wear and tear and any defect or mechanical problem that manifests or becomes evident after delivery that was not caused by the buyer excepted, and which must not have been driven beyond the mileage limit specified in the contract cancellation option agreement. The agreement may also provide that the buyer will execute documents reasonably necessary to effectuate the cancellation and refund and as reasonably required to comply with applicable law.

(8) At the bottom of the contract cancellation option agreement, a statement that may be signed by the buyer to indicate the buyer's election to exercise the right to cancel the purchase under the terms of the contract cancellation option agreement, and the last date and time by which the option to cancel may be exercised, followed by a line for the buyer's signature. A particular form of statement is not required, but the following statement is sufficient: "By signing below, I elect to exercise my right to cancel the purchase of the vehicle described in this agreement." The buyer's delivery of the purchase cancellation agreement to the dealer with the buyer's signature following this statement shall constitute sufficient written notice exercising the right to cancel the purchase pursuant to paragraph (6). The dealer shall provide the buyer with the statement required by this paragraph in duplicate to enable the buyer to return the signed cancellation notice and retain a copy of the cancellation agreement.

(9) If, pursuant to paragraph (5), the limit on the restocking fee is increased by the amount the buyer, who exercises a contract cancellation option would have been obligated to pay the lessor, upon termination of the lease, for charges for excess mileage, unrepaired damage, or excess wear and tear, as specified in the lease, the dealer shall provide the buyer with a notice of the contents of paragraph (5), including a statement regarding the increased restocking fee.

(c) (1) No later than the second day following the day on which the buyer exercises the right to cancel the purchase in compliance with the contract cancellation option agreement, the dealer shall cancel the contract and provide the buyer with a full refund, including that portion of the sales tax attributable to amounts excluded pursuant to Section 6012.3 of the Revenue and Taxation Code.

(2) If the buyer was not charged for the contract cancellation option agreement, the dealer shall return to the buyer, no later than the day following the day on which the buyer exercises the right to cancel the purchase, any motor vehicle the buyer left with the seller as a downpayment or trade-in. If the dealer has sold or otherwise transferred title to the motor vehicle that was left as a downpayment or trade-in, the full refund described in paragraph (1) shall include the fair market value of the motor vehicle left as a downpayment or trade-in, or its value as stated in the contract or purchase order, whichever is greater.

(3) If the buyer was charged for the contract cancellation option agreement, the dealer shall retain any motor vehicle the buyer left with the dealer as a downpayment or trade-in until the buyer exercises the right to cancel or the right to cancel expires. If the buyer exercises the right to cancel the purchase, the dealer shall return to the buyer, no later than the day following the day on which the buyer exercises the right to cancel the purchase, any motor vehicle the buyer left with the seller as a downpayment or trade-in. If the dealer has inadvertently sold or otherwise transferred title to the motor vehicle as the result of a bona fide error, notwithstanding reasonable procedures designed to avoid that error, the inadvertent sale or transfer of title shall not be deemed a violation of this paragraph, and the full refund described in paragraph (1) shall include the retail market value of the motor vehicle left as a downpayment or trade-in, or its value as stated in the contract or purchase order, whichever is greater.

(d) If the dealer received a portion of the purchase price by credit card, or other third-party payer on the buyer's account, the dealer may refund that portion of the purchase price to the credit card issuer or third-party payer for credit to the buyer's account.

(e) Notwithstanding subdivision (a), a dealer is not required to offer a contract cancellation option agreement to an individual who exercised the individual's right to cancel the purchase of a vehicle from the dealer pursuant to a contract cancellation option agreement during the immediately preceding 30 days. A dealer is not required to give notice to a subsequent buyer of the return of a vehicle pursuant to this section. This subdivision does not abrogate or limit any disclosure obligation imposed by any other law.

(f) This section does not affect or alter the legal rights, duties, obligations, or liabilities of the buyer, the dealer, or the dealer's agents or assigns, that would exist in the absence of a contract cancellation option agreement. The buyer is the owner of a vehicle when the buyer takes delivery of a vehicle until the vehicle is returned to the dealer pursuant to a contract cancellation option agreement, and the existence of a contract cancellation option agreement shall not impose permissive user liability on the dealer, or the dealer's agents or assigns, under Section 460 or 17150 or otherwise.

(g) This section does not affect the ability of a buyer to rescind the contract or revoke acceptance under any other law.

(h) This section shall become operative on July 1, 2012.

(i) This section shall remain in effect only until October 1, 2026, and as of that date is repealed.

(Amended by Stats. 2025, Ch. 354, Sec. 10. (SB 766) Effective January 1, 2026. Repealed as of October 1, 2026, by its own provisions.)

11713.22. (a) Upon mutual agreement of the parties to enter into a recreational vehicle franchise, it is unlawful and a violation of this code for a manufacturer, manufacturer branch, distributor, or distributor branch licensed under this code to fail or refuse to provide a recreational vehicle dealer with a written recreational vehicle franchise that complies with the requirements of Section 331.3.

(b) Notwithstanding Section 331.3, a recreational vehicle franchise described in this section shall include, but not be limited to, provisions regarding dealership transfer, dealership termination, sales territory, and reimbursement for costs incurred by the dealer for work related to the manufacturer's warranty for each line-make of recreational vehicle covered by the agreement.

(c) This section applies only to a dealer and manufacturer agreement involving recreational vehicles, as defined in subdivision (a) of Section 18010 of the Health and Safety Code, but does not include an agreement with a dealer who deals exclusively in truck campers.

(Amended by Stats. 2008, Ch. 743, Sec. 2. Effective January 1, 2009.)

11713.23. (a) A recreational vehicle manufacturer, manufacturer branch, distributor, or distributor branch licensed under this code shall not sell a new recreational vehicle in this state to or through a recreational vehicle dealer without having first entered into a written recreational vehicle franchise with that recreational vehicle dealer, that complies with the requirements of Section 331.3 and that has been signed by both parties.

(b) A recreational vehicle dealer shall not sell a new recreational vehicle in this state without having first entered into a written recreational vehicle franchise, that complies with the requirements of Section 331.3, with a recreational vehicle manufacturer, manufacturer branch, distributor, or distributor branch licensed under this code, that has been signed by both parties.

(c) (1) A recreational vehicle manufacturer, manufacturer branch, distributor, or distributor branch shall not ship a new recreational vehicle to a recreational dealer on or after January 1, 2009, without a recreational vehicle franchise that has been signed by both parties.

(2) A recreational vehicle dealer shall not receive a new recreational vehicle from a recreational vehicle manufacturer, manufacturer branch,

distributor, or distributor branch on or after January 1, 2009, without a recreational vehicle franchise that has been signed by both parties.

(d) Any new recreational vehicle inventory that has been purchased by a recreational vehicle dealer, or shipped by a manufacturer, manufacturer branch, distributor, or distributor branch, before January 1, 2009, may be sold at any time without a recreational vehicle franchise.

(e) Following the termination, cancellation, or nonrenewal of a recreational vehicle franchise, any new recreational vehicle inventory that was purchased by the recreational vehicle dealer, or shipped by a manufacturer, manufacturer branch, distributor, or distributor branch, during the period that the written recreational vehicle franchise was in effect, may be sold by that recreational vehicle dealer at any time.

(f) This section applies only to a dealer and manufacturer agreement involving recreational vehicles, as defined in subdivision (a) of Section 18010 of the Health and Safety Code, but does not include an agreement with a dealer who deals exclusively in truck campers.

(Amended by Stats. 2015, Ch. 407, Sec. 19. (AB 759) Effective January 1, 2016.)

11713.25. (a) A computer vendor shall not do any of the following:

(1) Access, modify, or extract information from a confidential dealer computer record or personally identifiable consumer data from a dealer without first obtaining express written consent from the dealer and without maintaining administrative, technical, and physical safeguards to protect the security, confidentiality, and integrity of the information.

(2) (A) Except as provided in subparagraph (B), require a dealer as a condition of doing or continuing to do business, to give express consent to perform the activities specified in paragraph (1).

(B) Express consent may be required as a condition of doing or continuing to do business if the consent is limited to permitting access to personally identifiable consumer data to the extent necessary to do any of the following:

(i) To protect against, or prevent actual or potential fraud, unauthorized transactions, claims, or other liability, or to protect against breaches of confidentiality or security of consumer records.

(ii) To comply with institutional risk control or to resolve consumer disputes or inquiries.

(iii) To comply with federal, state, or local laws, rules, and other applicable legal requirements, including lawful requirements of a law enforcement or governmental agency.

(iv) To comply with lawful requirements of a self-regulatory organization or as necessary to perform an investigation on a matter related to public safety.

(v) To comply with a properly authorized civil, criminal, or regulatory investigation, or subpoena or summons by federal, state, or local authorities.

(vi) To make other use of personally identifiable consumer data with the express written consent of the consumer that has not been revoked by the consumer.

(3) Use electronic, contractual, or other means to prevent or interfere with the lawful efforts of a dealer to comply with federal and state data security and privacy laws and to maintain the security, integrity, and confidentiality of confidential dealer computer records, including, but not limited to, the ability of a dealer to monitor specific data accessed from or written to the dealer computer system. Waiver of this subdivision or purported consents authorizing the activities proscribed by the subdivision is void.

(b) A dealer shall have the right to prospectively revoke an express consent by providing a 10-day written notice to the computer vendor to whom the consent was provided or on any shorter period of notice agreed to by the computer vendor and the dealer. An agreement that requires a dealer to waive its right to prospectively revoke an express consent is void.

(c) For the purposes of this section, the following terms mean as follows:

(1) "Confidential dealer computer record" means a computer record residing on the dealer's computer system that contains, in whole or in part, any personally identifiable consumer data, or the dealer's financial or other proprietary data.

(2) "Computer vendor" means a person, other than a manufacturer, manufacturer branch, distributor, or distributor branch, who in the ordinary course of that person's business configured, sold, leased, licensed, maintained, or otherwise made available to a dealer, a dealer computer system.

(3) "Dealer computer system" means a computer system or computerized application primarily designed for use by and sold to a motor vehicle dealer that, by ownership, lease, license, or otherwise, is used by and in the ordinary course of business of a dealer.

(4) "Express consent" means the unrevoked written consent signed by a dealer that specifically describes the data that may be accessed, the means by which it may be accessed, the purpose for which it may be used, and the person or class of persons to whom it may be disclosed.

(5) "Personally identifiable consumer data" means information that is any of the following:

(A) Information of the type specified in subparagraph (A) of paragraph (6) of subdivision (e) of Section 1798.83 of the Civil Code.

(B) Information that is nonpublic personal information as defined in Section 313.3(n)(1) of Title 16 of the Code of Federal Regulations.

(C) Information that is nonpublic personal information as defined in subdivision (a) of Section 4052 of the Financial Code.

(d) This section does not limit a duty that a dealer may have to safeguard the security and privacy of records maintained by the dealer.

(Added by Stats. 2006, Ch. 353, Sec. 2. Effective January 1, 2007.)

11713.26. (a) A dealer shall not display or offer for sale at retail a used vehicle, as defined in Section 665 and subject to registration under this code, unless the dealer first obtains a NMVTIS vehicle history report from a NMVTIS data provider for the vehicle identification number of the vehicle.

(b) If a NMVTIS vehicle history report for a used vehicle indicates that the vehicle is or has been a junk automobile or a salvage automobile or the vehicle has been reported as a junk automobile or a salvage automobile by a junk yard, salvage yard, or insurance carrier pursuant to Section 30504 of Title 49 of the United States Code, or the certificate of title contains a brand, a dealer shall do both of the following:

(1) Post the following disclosure on the vehicle while it is displayed for sale at retail in at least 14-point bold black type, except for the title "Warning" which shall be in at least 18-point bold black type, on at least a 4 x 5.5 inch red background in close proximity to the Federal Trade Commission's Buyer's Guide:

"WARNING

According to a vehicle history report issued by the National Motor Vehicle Title Information System (NMVTIS), this vehicle has been reported as a total-loss vehicle by an insurance company, has been reported into NMVTIS by a junk or salvage reporting entity, or has a title brand which may materially affect the value, safety, and/or condition of the vehicle. Because of its history as a junk, salvage, or title-branded vehicle, the manufacturer's warranty or service contract on this vehicle may be affected. Ask the dealer to see a copy of the NMVTIS vehicle history report. You may independently obtain the report by checking NMVTIS online at www.vehiclehistory.gov."

(2) Provide the retail purchaser with a copy of the NMVTIS vehicle history report upon request prior to sale.

(c) Subdivisions (a) and (b) do not apply to a used vehicle for which NMVTIS does not have a record if the dealer attempts to obtain a NMVTIS vehicle history report for the vehicle.

(d) As used in this section the following terms have the following meanings:

(1) "NMVTIS" means the National Motor Vehicle Title Information System established pursuant to Section 30501 et seq. of Title 49 of the United States Code.

(2) "NMVTIS vehicle history report" means a report obtained by an NMVTIS data provider that contains:

(A) The date of the report.

(B) Any disclaimer required by the operator of NMVTIS.

(C) If available from NMVTIS, information establishing the following:

(i) Whether the vehicle is titled in a particular state.

(ii) Whether the title to the vehicle was branded by a state.

(iii) The validity and status of a document purporting to be a certificate of title for the vehicle.

(iv) Whether the vehicle is or has been a junk automobile or a salvage automobile.

(v) The odometer mileage disclosure required pursuant to Section 32705 of Title 49 of the United States Code for that vehicle on the date the certificate of title for that vehicle was issued and any later mileage information.

(vi) Whether the vehicle has been reported as a junk automobile or a salvage automobile pursuant to Section 30504 of Title 49 of the United States Code.

(3) "Junk automobile," "operator," and "salvage automobile" shall have the same meanings as defined in Section 25.52 of Title 28 of the Code of Federal Regulations.

(4) "NMVTIS data provider" means a person authorized by the NMVTIS operator as an access portal provider for NMVTIS.

(5) "NMVTIS operator" means the individual or entity authorized or designated as the operator of NMVTIS pursuant to subdivision (b) of Section 30502 of Title 49 of the United States Code, or the office designated by the United States Attorney General, if there is no authorized or designated individual or entity.

(e) Nothing in this section shall prohibit a NMVTIS data provider from including, in a NMVTIS vehicle history report containing the information required by paragraph (2) of subdivision (d), additional vehicle history information obtained from resources other than NMVTIS.

(f) This section shall not create any legal duty upon the dealer related to the accuracy, errors, or omissions contained in a NMVTIS vehicle history report that is obtained from a NMVTIS data provider or any legal duty to provide information added to NMVTIS after the dealer obtained the NMVTIS vehicle history report pursuant to subdivision (a).

(g) (1) In the event that all NMVTIS data providers cease to make NMVTIS vehicle history reports available to the public, this section shall become inoperative.

(2) In the event that all NMVTIS data providers cease to make NMVTIS vehicle history reports available to the public, it is the intent of the Legislature that the United States Department of Justice notify the Legislature and the department.

(h) This section does not apply to the sale of a recreational vehicle, a motorcycle, or an off-highway motor vehicle subject to identification under Section 38010.

(i) This section shall become operative on July 1, 2012.

(Added by Stats. 2011, Ch. 329, Sec. 17. (AB 1215) Effective January 1, 2012. Section operative July 1, 2012, by its own provisions.)

11713.27. (a) A holder of a dealer's license issued under this article is not in violation of paragraph (29) of subdivision (a) of Section 1770 of the Civil Code for excluding from the advertised, displayed, or offered price of a vehicle a fee or charge identified in subdivision (b) of Section 11713.1.

(b) This section shall become operative on July 1, 2024.

(Added by Stats. 2023, Ch. 400, Sec. 10. (SB 478) Effective January 1, 2024. Operative July 1, 2024, by its own provisions.)

11713.28. (a) A motor vehicle manufacturer, or any other person, that advertises a motor vehicle manufacturer's suggested retail price (MSRP) set by an automobile manufacturer, or lease payments based upon an MSRP, does not, by doing so, violate paragraph (29) of subdivision (a) of Section 1770 of the Civil Code.

(b) This section shall become operative on July 1, 2024.

(Added by Stats. 2023, Ch. 400, Sec. 11. (SB 478) Effective January 1, 2024. Operative July 1, 2024, by its own provisions.)

11714. (a) The department, upon granting a license, shall issue to the applicant a license containing the applicant's name and address and the general distinguishing number assigned to the applicant.

(b) A dealer shall not sell any vehicle at retail at a location that is not posted pursuant to Section 11709.

(c) A dealer who is authorized by the department to sell motor vehicles only at wholesale shall not sell any vehicle at retail and shall report every sale to the department as prescribed in subdivision (b) of Section 4456.

(d) When the department has issued a license pursuant to subdivision (a), the licensee may apply for and the department shall issue special plates which shall have displayed thereon the general distinguishing number assigned to the applicant. Each plate so issued shall also contain a number or symbol identifying the plate from every other plate bearing a like general distinguishing number.

(e) The department shall also furnish books and forms as it may determine necessary. Those books and forms are and shall remain the property of the department and may be taken up at any time for inspection.

(f) This section shall become operative January 1, 2019.

(Repealed (in Sec. 23) and added by Stats. 2016, Ch. 90, Sec. 24. (AB 516) Effective January 1, 2017. Section operative January 1, 2019, by its own provisions.)

11715. (a) A manufacturer, remanufacturer, distributor, or dealer owning or lawfully possessing any vehicle of a type otherwise required to be registered under this code may operate or move the vehicle upon the highways without registering the vehicle upon condition that the vehicle displays special plates issued to the owner as provided in this chapter, in addition to other license plates or permits already assigned and attached to the vehicle in the manner prescribed in Sections 5200 to 5203, inclusive. A vehicle for sale or lease by a dealer may also be operated or moved upon the highways without registration for a period not to exceed seven days by a prospective buyer or lessee who is test-driving the vehicle for possible purchase or lease, if the vehicle is in compliance with this condition. The vehicle may also be moved or operated for the purpose of towing or transporting by any lawful method other vehicles.

(b) A transporter may operate or move any owned or lawfully possessed vehicle of like type by any lawful method upon the highways solely for the purpose of delivery, upon condition that there be displayed upon each vehicle in contact with the highway special license plates issued to the transporter as provided in this chapter, in addition to any license plates or permits already assigned and attached to the vehicle in the manner prescribed in Sections 5200 to 5203, inclusive. The vehicles may be used for the purpose of towing or transporting by any lawful method other vehicles when the towing or transporting vehicle is being delivered for sale or to the owner thereof.

(c) This section does not apply to any manufacturer, remanufacturer, transporter, distributor, or dealer operating or moving a vehicle as provided in Section 11716.

(d) This section does not apply to work or service vehicles owned by a manufacturer, remanufacturer, transporter, distributor, or dealer. This section does not apply to vehicles owned and leased by dealers, except those vehicles rented or leased to vehicle salespersons in the course of their employment for purposes of display or demonstration, nor to any unregistered vehicles used to transport more than one load of other vehicles for the purpose of sale.

(e) This section does not apply to vehicles currently registered in this state that are owned and operated by a licensed dealer when the notice of transfer has been forwarded to the department by the former owner of record pursuant to Section 5900 and when a copy of the notice is displayed as follows:

(1) For a motorcycle or motor-driven cycle, the notice is displayed in a conspicuous manner upon the vehicle.

(2) For a vehicle other than a motorcycle or motor-driven cycle, the

notice is displayed in the lower right-hand corner of the windshield of the vehicle, as specified in paragraph (3) of subdivision (b) of Section 26708.

(f) Every owner, upon receipt of a registration card issued for special plates, shall maintain the same or a facsimile copy thereof with the vehicle bearing the special plates.

(Amended by Stats. 2001, Ch. 739, Sec. 6.5. Effective January 1, 2002.)

11716. A manufacturer, remanufacturer, transporter, distributor, or dealer, in the course of business, may operate or move any vehicle of a type otherwise required to be registered under this code without registering the vehicle, and without license or special plates attached thereto, from a vessel, railroad depot, or warehouse over the highways to a warehouse or salesroom upon first having obtained a written permit from the department authorizing that operation.

(Amended by Stats. 1990, Ch. 1563, Sec. 45.)

11717. (a) Every occupational license and special plate issued under this article shall be valid for a period of one year from midnight of the last day of the month of issuance. Except as provided in subdivision (c), renewal of the occupational license and special plates for the ensuing year may be obtained by the person to whom the occupational license and special plates were issued upon application to the department and payment of the fee provided in this code.

(b) Every application for the renewal of an occupational license and special plates which expire pursuant to this section shall be made by the person to whom issued not more than 90 days prior to the expiration date, and shall be made by presenting the completed application form provided by the department and by payment of the full annual renewal fee for the occupational license and special plates.

(c) If the application for renewal of the occupational license and special plates is not made by midnight of the expiration date, the application may be made within 30 days following expiration of the license by paying the annual renewal fee and a penalty fee equal to the amount of the original application fee for each occupational license held. A penalty as specified in Sections 9553 and 9554 shall also be added to each special plate renewed during the 30-day period following expiration of the special plates.

(d) In no event may the licensee renew the occupational license or special plates after the expiration of the 30-day period authorized in subdivision (c).

(Amended by Stats. 1984, Ch. 499, Sec. 12.)

11718. Except where the provisions of this code require the refusal to issue a license, the department may issue a probationary license subject to conditions to be observed by the licensee in the exercise of the privilege granted. The conditions to be attached to the exercise of the privilege shall not appear on the face of the license but shall be such as may, in the judgment of the department, be in the public interest and suitable to the qualifications of the applicant as disclosed by the application and investigation by the department of the information contained therein.

(Amended by Stats. 1971, Ch. 1214.)

11719. Pending the satisfaction of the department that the applicant has met the requirements under this article, it may issue a temporary permit to any person applying for a manufacturer's, manufacturer's branch, remanufacturer's, remanufacturer's branch, distributor's, distributor's branch, transporter's, or dealer's license and special plates. The temporary permit shall permit the operation by the manufacturer, manufacturer branch, remanufacturer, remanufacturer branch, distributor, distributor branch, transporter, or dealer for a period not to exceed 120 days while the department is completing its investigation and determination of all facts relative to the qualifications of the applicant to the license and special plates. The department may cancel the temporary permit when it has determined, or has reasonable cause to believe, that the application is incorrect or incomplete or the temporary permit was issued in error. The temporary permit is invalid when canceled or when the applicant's license has been issued or refused.

(Amended by Stats. 1983, Ch. 1286, Sec. 41.)

11720. The department may issue a certificate of convenience to the executor, executrix, administrator or administratrix of the estate of a deceased holder of validly outstanding special plates and license issued under this article, or if no executor, executrix, administrator or administratrix has been appointed, and until a certified copy of an order making such appointment is filed with the department, to the surviving spouse or other heir otherwise entitled to conduct the business of the deceased, permitting such person to exercise the privileges granted by such special plates and license for a period of one year from and after the date of death and necessary one-year renewals thereafter, pending, but not later than, disposal of the business and qualification of the vendee of the business or such surviving spouse, heir or other persons for such special plates and license under the provisions of this article. The department may restrict or condition the license and attach to the exercise of the privileges thereunder such terms and conditions as in its judgment the protection of the public requires.

(Amended by Stats. 1976, Ch. 1171.)

11721. The special plates and licenses provided for in this article shall be automatically canceled upon the happening of any of the following:

(a) The abandonment of the established place of business of the dealer or the change thereof without notice to the department as provided in Section 11712.

(b) The failure of the licensee to maintain an adequate bond or to procure and file another bond as provided in Section 11710 prior to the effective date of the termination by the surety of any existing bond.

(c) The voluntary or involuntary surrender for any cause by the licensee of the special plates and license, except that the surrender of the special plates and license, the cessation of business by the licensee, or the suspension or revocation of the corporate status of the licensee, does not preclude the filing of an accusation for revocation or suspension of the surrendered license as provided in Section 11705, does not affect the department's decision to suspend or revoke the license. The department's determination to suspend or revoke the license may be considered in issuing or refusing to issue any subsequent license authorized by this division to that licensee or to a business representative of that prior licensee.

(d) Notification to the department that the person designated as licensee has changed, except that the special plates issued to the original licensee may be transferred and the newly designated licensee as transferee shall succeed to the privileges evidenced by the plates until their expiration.

(e) The suspension or revocation of the corporate status of the licensee.

(f) The suspension, revocation, or cancellation of the seller's permit of the licensee by the California Department of Tax and Fee Administration pursuant to Part 1 (commencing with Section 6001) of Division 2 of the Revenue and Taxation Code.

(Amended by Stats. 2022, Ch. 295, Sec. 10. (AB 2956) Effective January 1, 2023.)

11722. Claims, against the surety upon a dealer's bond, of a financing agency that has loaned money to a licensee or assignee thereof shall be allowed only to the extent that the claims of any other person or entity with respect to the bond under Section 11711 shall be satisfied first and entitled to preference over the claims of the financing agency with respect to the bond ; provided, however, that as to any conditional sales contract as defined in Section 2981 of the Civil Code, acquired by way of purchase or pledge, a financing agency shall be entitled to protection under the bond with the same preference set forth under Section 11711 if the financing agency is defrauded by a licensee.

(Amended by Stats. 2002, Ch. 303, Sec. 2. Effective January 1, 2003.)

11723. The board may require that fees shall be paid to the department for the issuance or renewal of a license to do business as a new motor vehicle dealer, dealer branch, manufacturer, manufacturer branch, distributor, distributor branch, or representative. The fees shall be to reimburse the department for costs incurred in licensing those dealers, manufacturers, distributors, branches, and representatives and for related administrative costs incurred on behalf of the board. The board may also require that an additional fee be paid to the department when the licensee has failed to pay the fee authorized by Section 3016 prior to the expiration of its occupational license and special plates and the licensee utilizes the 30-day late renewal period authorized by subdivision (c) of Section 11717.

This section shall not apply to dealers, manufacturers, distributors, or representatives of vehicles not subject to registration under this code, except dealers, manufacturers, manufacturer branches, distributors, distributor branches, or representatives of, off-highway motorcycles, as defined in Section 436, all-terrain vehicles, as defined in Section 111, and trailers subject to identification pursuant to Section 5014.1.

(Amended by Stats. 2004, Ch. 836, Sec. 11. Effective January 1, 2005.)

11724. A dealer, or the agent of a dealer, who has received a notice pursuant to Section 7507.6 of the Business and Professions Code, shall not make a subsequent assignment to skip trace, locate, or repossess a vehicle without simultaneously, and in the same manner by which the assignment is given, advising the assignee of the assignment of the information contained in the notice. As used in this section, "assignment" has the same meaning set forth in Section 7500.1 of the Business and Professions Code.

(Added by Stats. 2007, Ch. 192, Sec. 9. Effective September 7, 2007.)

11725. (a) No person shall transport or drive any motor vehicle from this state outside of the United States with the intent to register or sell such vehicle in a foreign jurisdiction, without first removing the license plates and delivering them to the department. Such person may obtain a permit from the department authorizing the operation of the unlicensed motor vehicle on the public highways of this state in order to reach such foreign jurisdiction. Failure to deliver the license plates as required by this subdivision shall be a misdemeanor.

(b) No holder of any license, or any temporary permit for such license issued under this division, shall deliver any vehicle following sale without first removing all license plates from such vehicle when it is known by the licensee that the vehicle is to be exported to a foreign jurisdiction outside of the United States.

(Amended by Stats. 1976, Ch. 934.)

11726. Any licensee suffering pecuniary loss because of any willful failure by any other licensee to comply with any provision of Article 1 (commencing with Section 11700) or 3 (commencing with Section 11900) of Chapter 4 of Division 5 or with any regulation adopted by the department or any rule adopted or decision rendered by the board under authority vested in them may recover damages and reasonable attorney fees therefor in any court of competent jurisdiction. Any such licensee may also have appropriate injunctive relief in any such court.

(Amended by Stats. 2019, Ch. 796, Sec. 20. (AB 179) Effective January 1, 2020.)

11727. The revocation or suspension of a license of a manufacturer, manufacturer branch, distributor, distributor branch, or representative may be limited to one or more municipalities or counties or any other defined area, or may be revoked or suspended in a defined area only as to certain aspects of its business, or as to a specified dealer or dealers.

(Added by Stats. 1973, Ch. 996.)

11728. As part of a compromise settlement agreement entered into pursuant to Section 11707 or 11808.5, the department may assess a monetary penalty of not more than two thousand five hundred dollars ($2,500) per violation and impose a license suspension of not more than 30 days for any dealer who violates subdivision (r) of Section 11713. The extent of the penalties shall be based on the nature of the violation and effect of the violation on the purposes of this article. Except for the penalty limits provided for in Sections 11707 and 11808.5, all the provisions governing compromise settlement agreements for dealers, salespersons, and wholesalers apply to this section, and Section 11415.60 of the Government Code does not apply.

(Amended by Stats. 1995, Ch. 938, Sec. 90. Effective January 1, 1996. Operative July 1, 1997, by Sec. 98 of Ch. 938.)

11729. (a) Except as provided in subdivision (b), any dealer engaging in a consignment with an owner not licensed as a dealer, manufacturer, manufacturer branch, distributor, or a distributor branch licensed under this code, and the consignment is not otherwise prohibited by this code, shall execute a consignment agreement as prescribed by Section 11730. The failure of a dealer, when required under this section, to complete and comply with the terms of the prescribed consignment agreement for any vehicle which the dealer agrees to accept on consignment, or to pay the agreed amount to the consignor or his or her designee within 20 days after the date of sale of the vehicle, is cause for suspending or revoking the license of the dealer under paragraph (10) of subdivision (a) of Section 11705.

(b) (1) A dealer conducting retail auction sales on behalf of a fleet owner shall execute a consignment agreement applicable to all vehicles consigned for sale during the term of the agreement which contains, at a minimum, substantially all of the terms, phrases, conditions, and disclosures required by Section 11730, except the following are not required:

(A) The description of a specific vehicle by year, make, identification number, license, state, or mileage.

(B) The information contained in paragraph (4) of subdivision (b) of Section 11730.

(2) If mutually agreeable, in lieu of the requirements of paragraph (7) of subdivision (b) of Section 11730, the consignor may provide the documents necessary to transfer the ownership of the vehicle to the consignee prior to the auction being held.

(3) For purposes of this subdivision, "fleet owner" is either of the following:

(A) A person who is the registered or legal owner of 25 or more vehicles registered in this state and is the owner, as recorded in the department's records, of the vehicles consigned for sale to the dealer.

(B) A bankruptcy trustee who owns or has legal control of the vehicles consigned for sale to the dealer, government agency, or financial institution.

(Amended by Stats. 1999, Ch. 672, Sec. 4. Effective January 1, 2000.)

11730. The consignment agreement required by Section 11729 shall contain all the following terms, phrases, conditions, and disclosures:

(a) The date the agreement is executed.

(b) All of the following statements:

(1) "I (We), the undersigned consigner(s), hereby consign and deliver possession of my(our) vehicle, which is a (Year) ____ (Make) ____ (ID#) ____ (License) ____ (State) ____ (Mileage) ____, to (Consignee) ____ (Dealer #) ____ for the sole purpose of selling the vehicle and paying, to the consignor or his or her designee from the proceeds of the sale of the vehicle, the amount agreed upon under terms of this agreement. This agreement is effective and valid only for a period of ____ days from this date."

(2) "At the termination of this agreement, the consignee shall return the vehicle to the consignor, or, at the option of both the consignor and consignee, enter into a new agreement."

(3) "If the vehicle is sold by the consignee during the term of this agreement, the money due the consignor shall be disbursed within 20 days after the date of sale in accordance with the terms of this agreement. As used in this agreement, a "sale" occurs when the consignee either (A) receives the purchase price or its equivalent or executes a conditional sales contract for the vehicle, or (B) when the purchaser takes delivery of the vehicle, whichever occurs first."

(4) "The following information shall be completed prior to the signing of this agreement:

Current market value: $____ Source: ____.

Outstanding liens: $____ Lienholder: ____.

(Any difference between the outstanding amount shown and the actual payoff to the lienholder will be credited to the consignor.)

Repairs to be made: $____ Work Order #____.

Moneys to the consignor: ____ percent of sale price, flat fee of $____

or the following specific formula: ____."

(5) "Within 20 days after sale, the consignee shall make an accounting to the consignor of all of the following: date of sale, repairs authorized by consignor (supported by work records), exact amount of any liens payable to lienholders, evidence of payment of any liens, and the total sales price."

(6) "The consigned vehicle is delivered to the consignee in trust for the exact terms set forth in this agreement. The consignee agrees to receive this vehicle in trust and not to permit its use for any other purpose other than contained in this agreement without the express written consent of the consignor."

(7) "Upon payment of the moneys due the consignor, the consignor agrees to furnish the consignee those documents necessary to transfer the ownership of the vehicle to the purchaser.

Signatures:

_____ Consignor _____ _____ _____ Date _____

_____ Address _____

_____ Consignor _____ _____ _____ Date _____

_____ Address _____ "

(8) "NOTICE TO CONSIGNOR: Failure of the consignee to comply with the terms of this agreement may be a violation of statute which could result in criminal or administrative sanctions, or both. If you feel the consignee has not complied with the terms of this agreement, please contact an investigator of the Department of Motor Vehicles."

(Amended by Stats. 2000, Ch. 1035, Sec. 12. Effective January 1, 2001.)

11735. (a) No dealer shall engage in brokering a retail sales transaction without first paying the fee required by subdivision (d) of Section 9262 and obtaining from the department an autobroker's endorsement to the dealer's license. An autobroker's endorsement shall be automatically cancelled upon the cancellation, suspension, revocation, surrender, or expiration of a dealer's license.

(b) Upon the issuance of an autobroker's endorsement to a dealer's license, the department shall furnish the dealer with an autobroker's log. The autobroker's log shall remain the property of the department and may be taken up at any time for inspection.

(c) The autobroker's log shall contain spaces sufficient for the dealer to record the following information with respect to each retail sale brokered by that dealer:

(1) Vehicle identification number of brokered vehicle.

(2) Date of brokering agreement.

(3) Selling dealer's name, address, and dealer number.

(4) Name of consumer.

(5) Brokering dealer's name and dealer number.

(d) Nothing in this code prohibits a dealer who has been issued an autobroker's endorsement to his or her dealer's license from delivering, with the selling dealer's written approval, motor vehicles that have been sold pursuant to a duly executed motor vehicle purchase agreement or obtaining a consumer's signature on a selling dealer's motor vehicle purchase agreement that has already been executed by the selling dealer.

(e) When brokering a retail sale as an agent of the consumer, selling dealer, or both, the brokering dealer owes a fiduciary duty of utmost care, integrity, honesty, and loyalty in dealings with its principal or principals.

(f) For purposes of this section and Sections 11736, 11737, and 11738, "consumer" means any person who retains a dealer to perform brokering services in connection with a retail sale.

(Amended by Stats. 1995, Ch. 211, Sec. 7. Effective January 1, 1996.)

11736. It is unlawful for any dealer licensed under this article to do any of the following when brokering a retail sale:

(a) Fail to execute a written brokering agreement, as described in Section 11738, and provide a completed copy to both of the following:

(1) Any consumer entering into the brokering agreement. The completed copy shall be provided prior to the consumer's signing of an agreement for the purchase of the vehicle described in the brokering agreement or, prior to accepting one hundred dollars ($100) or more from that consumer, whichever occurs first.

(2) The selling dealer. The completed copy shall be provided prior to the selling dealer's entering into a purchase agreement with the consumer.

(b) Accept a purchase deposit from any consumer that exceeds 2.5 percent of the selling price of the vehicle described in the brokering agreement.

(c) Fail to refund any purchase money, including purchase deposits, upon demand by a consumer at any time prior to the consumer's signing of a vehicle purchase agreement with a selling dealer and taking delivery of the vehicle described in the brokering agreement.

(d) Fail to cancel a brokering agreement and refund, upon demand, any money paid by a consumer, including any brokerage fee, under any of the following circumstances:

(1) When the final price of the brokered vehicle exceeds the purchase price listed in the brokering agreement.

(2) When the vehicle delivered is not as described in the brokering agreement.

(3) When the brokering agreement expires prior to the customer being presented with a purchase agreement from a selling dealer arranged through the brokering dealer that contains a purchase price at or below the price listed in the brokering agreement.

(e) Act as a seller and provide brokering services, both in the same transaction.

(f) Fail to disclose to the consumer and selling dealer, as soon as practicable, whether the autobroker receives or does not receive a fee or other compensation, regardless of the form or time of payment, from the selling dealer and the dollar amount of any fee that the consumer is obligated to pay to the autobroker. This arrangement shall be confirmed in a brokering agreement.

(g) Fail to record in the dealer's autobroker log, for each brokered sale, all of the information specified in subdivision (c) of Section 11735.

(h) Fail to maintain for a minimum of three years a copy of the executed brokering agreement and other notices and documents related to each brokered transaction.

(i) Fail to advise the consumer, prior to accepting any money, that a full refund will be given if the motor vehicle ordered through the autobroker is not obtained for the consumer or if the service orally contracted for is not provided.

(Amended by Stats. 1995, Ch. 211, Sec. 8. Effective January 1, 1996.)

11737. (a) A dealer who brokers a motor vehicle sale shall deposit directly into a trust account any purchase money, including purchase deposits, it receives from a consumer or a consumer's lender. This subdivision does not require a separate trust account for each brokered transaction.

(b) The brokering dealer shall not in any manner encumber the corpus of the trust account except as follows:

(1) In partial or full payment to a selling dealer for a vehicle purchased by the brokering dealer's consumer.

(2) To make refunds.

(c) Subdivision (b) shall not prevent payment of the interest earned on the trust account to the brokering dealer.

(d) The brokering dealer shall serve as trustee of the trust account required by this section. If the brokering dealer is a partnership or a corporation, the managing partner of the partnership or the chief executive officer of the corporation shall be the trustee. The trustee may designate in writing that an officer or employee may manage the trust account if that officer or employee is under the trustee's supervision and control, and the original of that writing is on file with the department.

(e) All trust accounts required by this section shall be maintained at a branch of a bank, savings and loan association, or credit union regulated by the state or the government of the United States.

(f) The brokering dealer has a fiduciary responsibility with respect to all purchase money received from a consumer or consumer's lender relative to a brokered sale transaction.

(g) The following are deemed to be held in trust for consumers who have paid purchase money to a brokering dealer:

(1) All sums received by the brokering dealer whether or not required to be deposited in an actual trust account and regardless of whether any of these sums were required to be deposited or actually were deposited in a trust account.

(2) All property with which any of the sums described in paragraph (1) has been commingled if any of these sums cannot be identified because of the commingling.

(h) Upon any judicially ordered distribution of any money or property required to be held in trust and after all expenses of distribution approved by the court have been paid, every consumer of a brokering dealer has a claim on the trust for purchase money payments made to the brokering dealer. Unless a consumer can identify his or her funds in the trust within the time established by the court, each consumer shall receive a proportional share based on the amount paid.

(Added by Stats. 1994, Ch. 1253, Sec. 14. Effective January 1, 1995.)

11738. The brokering agreement required by Section 11736 shall be printed in no smaller than 10-point type and shall contain not less than the following terms, conditions, requirements, and disclosures:

(a) The name, address, license number, and telephone number of the autobroker.

(b) A complete description, including line-make, model, year model, and color, of the vehicle and the desired options.

(c) The following statement:

"The following information shall be completed prior to the signing of this brokering agreement:Dollar Purchase Price of Vehicle: ______. Date this agreement will expire if a purchase agreement from a selling dealer is not presented for your signature:__________.Fee that you will be obligated to pay us, if any:__________."

(d) One of the following notices, as appropriate, printed in at least 10-point bold type and placed immediately below the statement required by subdivision (c):

(1) "We do not receive a fee from the selling dealer."

(2) "We receive a fee from the selling dealer."

(e) The following notice on the face of the brokering agreement with a heading in at least 14-point bold type and the text in at least 10-point bold type, circumscribed by a line, that reads as follows:

NOTICE

This is an agreement to provide services; it is not an agreement for the purchase of a vehicle. California law gives you the following rights and protection.

Once you have signed this agreement, you have the right to cancel it and receive a full refund of any money paid, including any brokerage fee you may have paid, under any of the following circumstances:

(1) The final price of the vehicle exceeds the purchase price listed above.

(2) The vehicle is not as described above upon delivery.

(3) This agreement expires prior to your being presented with a selling dealer's purchase agreement.

If you have paid a purchase deposit, you have the right to receive a refund of that deposit at any time prior to your signing a vehicle purchase agreement with a selling dealer. Purchase deposits are limited by law to no more than 2.5 percent of the purchase price of a vehicle and must be deposited by an autobroker or auto buying service in a federally insured trust account. If you are unable to resolve a dispute with your autobroker or auto buying service, please contact an investigator of the Department of Motor Vehicles.

(f) The date the agreement is executed.

(g) The signature of the autobroker and consumer.

(Amended by Stats. 2000, Ch. 1035, Sec. 13. Effective January 1, 2001.)

11739. For purposes of title registration, warranties, rebates, and incentives, in a brokered retail new motor vehicle sale, the selling, franchised new car dealer, and not the autobroker, is responsible to apply for title in the name of the purchaser, to secure vehicle registration and the license plates for the purchaser, to secure the manufacturer's warranty in the name of the purchaser, and to make all applications for any manufacturer's rebates and incentives due the purchaser. If there is a manufacturer's recall, the consumer shall be notified directly by the manufacturer.

(Added by Stats. 1994, Ch. 1253, Sec. 16. Effective January 1, 1995.)

11740. The remedies and penalties provided in this code for a violation of this article are cumulative to the remedies and penalties provided by other laws.

(Added by Stats. 2002, Ch. 407, Sec. 3. Effective January 1, 2003.)

Article 1.1. Consumer Automotive Recall Safety Act

(Article 1.1 added by Stats. 2016, Ch. 682, Sec. 4.)

11750. This article shall be known, and may be cited, as the Consumer Automotive Recall Safety Act (CARS Act).

(Added by Stats. 2016, Ch. 682, Sec. 4. (AB 287) Effective January 1, 2017.)

11752. As used in this article, the following definitions apply:

(a) The term "dealer" has the same meaning as in Section 285.

(b) (1) A "manufacturer's recall" is a recall conducted pursuant to Sections 30118 to 30120, inclusive, of Title 49 of the United States Code.

(2) A manufacturer's recall does not include a service campaign or emission recall when the vehicle manufacturer or the National Highway Traffic Safety Administration has not issued a recall notice to owners of affected vehicles, pursuant to Section 30118 of Title 49 of the United States Code.

(c) A "personal vehicle sharing program" has the same meaning as defined in Section 11580.24 of the Insurance Code.

(d) A "recall database" is a database from which an individual may obtain vehicle identification number (VIN) specific manufacturer's recall information relevant to a specific vehicle.

(1) For a vehicle manufacturer that is not subject to the regulations adopted pursuant to Section 31301 of the federal Moving Ahead for Progress in the 21st Century Act (Public Law 112-141), a recall database is one of the following:

(A) The recall data on a vehicle manufacturer's Internet Web site for a specific vehicle's line-make.

(B) The recall data in a vehicle manufacturer's internal system that provides information to its franchisees on vehicles subject to recall.

(C) The recall data in subparagraph (A) or (B) that is contained in a commercially available vehicle history system.

(2) For a vehicle manufacturer that is subject to the regulations adopted pursuant to Section 31301 of the federal Moving Ahead for Progress in the 21st Century Act (Public Law 112-141), a recall database shall include, at a minimum, the recall information required pursuant to Section 573.15 of Title 49 of the Code of Federal Regulations.

(e) A "recall database report" is a report, specific to a vehicle that is identified by its VIN, containing information obtained from a recall database.

(f) A "rental car company" is a person or entity in the business of renting passenger vehicles to the public in California.

(Amended by Stats. 2018, Ch. 591, Sec. 1. (AB 2873) Effective January 1, 2019.)

11754. (a) No later than 48 hours after receiving a notice of a manufacturer's recall, or sooner if practicable, a dealer or rental car company with a motor vehicle fleet of 34 or fewer loaner or rental vehicles shall not loan, rent, or offer for loan or rent a vehicle subject to that recall until the recall repair has been made.

(b) If a recall notification indicates that the remedy for the recall is not immediately available and specifies actions to temporarily repair the vehicle in a manner to eliminate the safety risk that prompted the recall, the dealer or rental car company, after having the repairs completed, may loan or rent the vehicle. Once the remedy for the vehicle becomes available to the dealer or rental car company, the dealer or rental car company shall not loan or rent the vehicle until the vehicle has been repaired.

(c) As soon as practicable but not more than 48 hours after a vehicle is subject to a manufacturer's recall, as defined in subdivision (b) of Section 11752, and a recall notice has been issued by the manufacturer and appears in the recall database provided by the National Highway Traffic Safety Administration pursuant to Section 573.15 of Title 49 of the Code of Federal Regulations, or not more than 48 hours after the personal vehicle sharing program receives notification of a manufacturer's recall by a third party with which the personal vehicle sharing program contracts to provide notification of active recalls, a personal vehicle sharing program shall not facilitate or otherwise arrange for transportation with that vehicle until after any recall notices for that vehicle no longer appear in the recall database provided by the National Highway Traffic Safety Administration.

(d) The changes to this section made by the act adding subdivision (c) shall not apply in any manner to pending litigation.

(e) This section does not affect the determination of whether or not a company is a rental car company or whether or not a company is a personal vehicle sharing company.

(Amended by Stats. 2018, Ch. 591, Sec. 2. (AB 2873) Effective January 1, 2019.)

11755. Notwithstanding Sections 1633.3 of the Civil Code and Section 9975 of this code, a new motor vehicle dealer may receive electronic authorization from consumers consistent with regulations adopted by the Bureau of Automotive Repair for any repair of a manufacturer recall.

(Added by Stats. 2019, Ch. 490, Sec. 2. (AB 596) Effective January 1, 2020.)

11758. The department shall include the following recall disclosure statement on each vehicle registration renewal notice:

"NOTICE: Many vehicles have been recalled recently for needed repairs. Did you know you can check to see if your vehicle has an unrepaired manufacturer's safety recall? For most vehicles, manufacturer safety recalls are repaired for free. You can check for any recalls and how to get the recall repaired at www.safercar.gov."

(Added by Stats. 2016, Ch. 682, Sec. 4. (AB 287) Effective January 1, 2017.)

11760. (a) This article shall not create any legal duty upon the dealer, rental car company, personal vehicle sharing program, or department related to the accuracy, errors, or omissions contained in a recall database report or any legal duty to provide information added to a recall database after the dealer, rental car company, personal vehicle sharing program, or department obtained the recall database report pursuant to Sections 11754 and 11758.

(b) The changes to this section made by the act amending subdivision (a) shall not apply in any manner to pending litigation.

(c) This section does not affect the determination of whether or not a company is a rental car company or whether or not a company is a personal vehicle sharing program.

(Amended by Stats. 2018, Ch. 591, Sec. 3. (AB 2873) Effective January 1, 2019.)

11761. The rights and remedies provided by this article are cumulative and shall not be construed as restricting any right or remedy that is otherwise available.

(Added by Stats. 2016, Ch. 682, Sec. 4. (AB 287) Effective January 1, 2017.)

11762. The provisions of this article are severable. If any provision of this article or its application is held invalid, that invalidity shall not affect other provisions or applications that can be given effect without the invalid provision or application.

(Added by Stats. 2016, Ch. 682, Sec. 4. (AB 287) Effective January 1, 2017.)

Article 2. Vehicle Salespersons

(Heading of Article 2 amended by Stats. 1991, Ch. 13, Sec. 26.)

11800. It shall be unlawful for any person to act as a vehicle salesperson without having first procured a license or temporary permit issued by the department or when that license or temporary permit issued by the department has been canceled, suspended, revoked, or invalidated or has expired.

(Amended by Stats. 1990, Ch. 1563, Sec. 48.)

11802. (a) The department shall prescribe and provide forms to be used for application for licenses to be issued under this article and require of applicants, as a condition of the issuance of a license, information concerning the applicant's character, honesty, integrity, and reputation that it considers necessary. Every application for a vehicle salesperson's license shall contain, in addition to the information that the department requires, a statement of all of the following facts:

(1) The name and address of the applicant.

(2) Whether the applicant has ever had a court judgment rendered for which they have been liable as a result of their activities in conjunction with an occupational license issued under this division, and whether that judgment remains unpaid or unsatisfied.

(3) Whether the applicant ever had a license, issued under this division, revoked, suspended, or subjected to other disciplinary action and whether the applicant was ever a partner in a partnership or an officer, director, or stockholder in a corporation licensed under this division, the license of which was revoked, suspended, or subjected to other disciplinary action.

(b) The department shall issue a license bearing a fullface photograph of the licensee and the following information:

(1) Name and address.

(2) Physical description.

(3) The licensee's usual signature.

(4) Distinguishing vehicle salesperson's license number.

(c) The department may require a new fullface photograph at the time of the renewal of the license.

(Amended by Stats. 2022, Ch. 838, Sec. 5. (SB 1193) Effective January 1, 2023.)

11803. Pending the satisfaction of the department that the applicant has met the requirements of this chapter, it may issue a temporary permit to any person applying for a vehicle salesperson's license. The temporary permit shall permit the operation by the salesperson for a period of not more than 120 days while the department is completing its investigation of the applicant for the license. If the department determines to its satisfaction that the temporary permit was issued upon a fraudulent application or determines or has reasonable cause to believe that the application is incorrect or incomplete or the temporary permit was issued in error, the department may cancel the temporary permit, effective immediately. The temporary permit shall become invalid when canceled or when the applicant's license has been issued or refused.

(Amended by Stats. 2002, Ch. 758, Sec. 10. Effective January 1, 2003.)

11804. The department may issue or, for reasonable cause shown, refuse to issue, a license to any applicant applying for a vehicle salesperson's license.

(Amended by Stats. 1990, Ch. 1563, Sec. 51.)

11806. The department, after notice and hearing, may refuse to issue, or may suspend or revoke, a vehicle salesperson's license when it makes any of the following findings and determinations:

(a) The applicant or licensee has outstanding an unsatisfied final court judgment rendered in connection with an activity licensed under this division.

(b) The applicant or licensee has failed to pay funds or property received in the course of employment to a dealer entitled thereto.

(c) The applicant or licensee has failed to surrender possession of, or failed to return, a vehicle to a dealer lawfully entitled thereto upon termination of employment.

(d) A cause for refusal, suspension, or revocation exists under any provision of Sections 11302 to 11909, inclusive.

(e) The applicant was previously the holder of an occupational license issued by another state authorizing the same or similar activities of a license issued under this division and that license was revoked or suspended for cause and was never reissued, or was suspended for cause, and the terms of suspension have not been fulfilled.

(f) The applicant or licensee has acted as a dealer by purchasing or selling vehicles while employed by a licensed dealer without reporting that fact to the dealer or without utilizing the report of sale documents issued to the dealer.

(g) The applicant or licensee has concurrently acted as a vehicle salesperson and engaged in that activity for, or on behalf of, more than one licensed dealer unless all of the licensed dealers for whom that salesperson works have common controlling ownership. Nothing in this section restricts the number of dealerships of which a person may be an owner, officer, or director, or precludes a vehicle salesperson from working for more than one dealer, provided that all of the licensed dealers for whom that salesperson works have common controlling ownership. For purposes of this subdivision, dealers have common controlling ownership when more than 50 percent of the ownership interests in each dealer are held by the same person or persons, either directly or through one or more wholly owned subsidiary entities.

(h) The applicant or licensee has acted as a vehicle salesperson without having first complied with Section 11812.

(i) The applicant or licensee was a managerial employee of a dealer during the time a person under the direction or control of the managerial employee committed wrongful acts which resulted in the suspension or revocation of the dealer's license.

(j) The applicant or licensee has acted as a dealer by purchasing or selling any vehicle and using the license, report of sale books, purchase drafts, financial institution accounts, or other supplies of a dealer to facilitate that purchase or sale, when the applicant or licensee is not acting on behalf of that dealer.

(Amended by Stats. 2010, Ch. 483, Sec. 4. (SB 1004) Effective January 1, 2011.)

11808. Every hearing provided for in this article shall be conducted pursuant to Chapter 5 (commencing with Section 11500) of Part 1 of Division 3 of Title 2 of the Government Code.

(Amended by Stats. 1990, Ch. 1563, Sec. 53.)

11808.5. (a) After the filing of an accusation under this article, the director may enter into a stipulated compromise settlement agreement with the consent of the licensee on terms and conditions mutually agreeable to the director, the respondent licensee, and the accuser without further hearing or appeal. The agreement may include, but is not limited to, a period of probation or monetary penalties, or both. Except as provided in Section 11728, the monetary penalty shall not exceed five hundred dollars ($500) for each violation, and it shall be based on the nature of the violation and the effect of the violation on the purposes of this article.

(b) A compromise settlement agreement may be entered before, during, or after the hearing, but is valid only if executed and filed pursuant to subdivision (d) before the proposed decision of the hearing officer, if any, is adopted or the case is decided.

(c) The department shall adopt, by regulation, a schedule of maximum and minimum amounts of monetary penalties, the payment of which may be included as a term or condition of a compromise settlement agreement entered under subdivision (a). Any monetary penalty included in a compromise settlement agreement shall be within the range of monetary penalties in that schedule.

(d) Any compromise settlement agreement entered under this section shall be signed by the director, the respondent licensee, and the accuser, or by their authorized representatives. The director shall file, or cause to be filed, the agreement with the Office of Administrative Hearings, together with the department's notice of withdrawal of the accusation or statement of issues upon which the action was initiated.

(e) If the respondent licensee fails to perform all of the terms and conditions of the compromise settlement agreement, the agreement is void and the department may take any action authorized by law, notwithstanding the agreement, including, but not limited to, refiling the accusation or imposing license sanctions.

(Amended by Stats. 1990, Ch. 90, Sec. 5. Effective May 9, 1990.)

11810. (a) The department may, pending a hearing, temporarily suspend the license issued to a vehicle salesperson for a period of not more than 30 days if the director finds that action to be required in the public interest. In that case, a hearing shall be held and a decision thereon issued within 30 days after notice of the temporary suspension.

(b) Except where the provisions of this code require the refusal to issue a license, the department may issue a probationary license subject to conditions to be observed by the licensee in the exercise of the privilege granted. The conditions to be attached to the exercise of the privilege shall be those which may, in the judgment of the department, be in the public interest and suitable to the qualifications of the applicant, as disclosed by the application and investigation by the department of the information contained in the application.

(c) If the department issues or renews a vehicle salesperson's license requiring conditions of probation or if the department refuses to issue a vehicle salesperson's license, the applicant may demand in writing a hearing before the director or the director's representative within 60 days after notice of refusal to issue or issuance of the probationary license.

(d) A person whose license has been revoked or whose application for a license has been denied may reapply for a license after not less than one year has elapsed from the effective date of the decision revoking the license or denying the application, except that if the decision was based upon subdivision (a) of Section 11806, an earlier reapplication may be made accompanied by evidence satisfactory to the department that those grounds for revocation or denial of the license no longer exist.

(Amended by Stats. 1990, Ch. 1563, Sec. 54.)

11812. (a) A vehicle salesperson licensed under this article shall, at the time of employment, deliver his or her salesperson's license to his or her employing dealer for the posting of the salesperson's license or a true and exact copy of the salesperson's license in a place conspicuous to the public at each location where he or she is actually engaged in the selling of vehicles for the employing dealer.

(b) The license, or a true and exact copy of the license, shall be displayed continuously at each location where he or she is actually engaged in the selling of vehicles during the employment. If a vehicle salesperson's employment is terminated, the license shall be returned to the salesperson and all copies of the license used by the dealer for posting or display shall be destroyed by the dealer.

(c) A vehicle salesperson licensed pursuant to this article shall report in writing to the department every change of residence address within five days of the change.

(d) A person currently or previously licensed under this article who no longer resides at the address last filed with the department may be served with process issued pursuant to Chapter 5 (commencing with Section 11500) of Part 1 of Division 3 of Title 2 of the Government Code by registered mail at that residence, unless the person has notified the department in writing of another address where service may be made.

(Amended by Stats. 2010, Ch. 483, Sec. 5. (SB 1004) Effective January 1, 2011.)

11814. (a) Every original vehicle salesperson's license issued, and every vehicle salesperson's license renewed, pursuant to subdivision (b) shall be valid for a period of three years from the date of issuance unless canceled, suspended, or revoked by the department.

(b) Renewal of a vehicle salesperson's license may be made prior to the expiration date. A vehicle salesperson may not renew their license after the date of expiration.

(c) A salesperson shall obtain a duplicate license when the original is either lost or mutilated.

(Amended by Stats. 2022, Ch. 838, Sec. 6. (SB 1193) Effective January 1, 2023.)

11819. It is unlawful for a person:

(a) To lend a salesperson's license to any other person or knowingly permit its use by another.

(b) To display or represent a salesperson's license not issued to the person as being his or her license.

(c) To fail or refuse to surrender to the department, upon its lawful demand, a salesperson's license that has been suspended, revoked, or canceled.

(d) To permit any unlawful use of a salesperson's license issued to him or her.

(e) To photograph, photostat, duplicate, or in any way reproduce a salesperson's license or facsimile thereof in a manner that it could be mistaken for a valid license, or to display or have in possession a photograph, photostat, duplicate, reproduction, or facsimile unless for display by a dealer, or as authorized by this code.

(Amended by Stats. 2010, Ch. 483, Sec. 6. (SB 1004) Effective January 1, 2011.)

11820. The following fees shall be paid to the department:

(a) Except as provided by Section 42231, a nonrefundable fee for the original issuance of a license, fifty dollars ($50).

(b) Fee for license renewal, fifty dollars ($50).

(c) Fee for a duplicate license, fifteen dollars ($15).

(Amended by Stats. 1990, Ch. 90, Sec. 6. Effective May 9, 1990. Operative July 1, 1990, by Sec. 7 of Ch. 90.)

11822. The vehicle salesperson's license or any permit provided in this article shall be automatically canceled upon the failure of a licensee to pay the required fees or to file an application for renewal of the license or permit before the date of expiration of the current license or permit.

(Amended by Stats. 1984, Ch. 499, Sec. 13.)

11824. The suspension, expiration, or cancellation of a vehicle salesperson's license issued under this article does not prevent the filing of an accusation for the revocation or suspension of the suspended, expired, or canceled license as provided in Section 11806, and the department's decision that the license should be suspended or revoked. That determination may be considered in granting or refusing to grant any subsequent license authorized by this division to that licensee.

(Amended by Stats. 1990, Ch. 1563, Sec. 57.)

Article 3. Representatives

(Article 3 added by Stats. 1973, Ch. 996.)

11900. It shall be unlawful for any person to act as a representative on or after July 1, 1974, without having first procured a license or temporary permit issued by the department or when such license or temporary permit has been canceled, suspended, revoked, or invalidated or has expired.

(Amended by Stats. 1974, Ch. 384.)

11901. The department shall prescribe and provide forms to be used for application for licenses to be issued under the terms and provisions of this chapter and require of such applicants, as a condition precedent to issuance of such license, such information touching on and concerning the applicant's character, honesty, integrity and reputation as it may consider necessary. Every application for a representative's license shall contain, in addition to such information as the department may require, a statement of the following facts:

(a) Name and address of the applicant.

(b) Whether the applicant has ever had a court judgment rendered for which he has been liable as a result of his activity in connection with an occupation licensed under this chapter and whether such judgment remains unpaid or unsatisfied.

(c) Whether the applicant ever had a license, issued under the authority of this chapter, revoked, suspended, or subjected to other disciplinary action and whether the applicant was ever a partner in a partnership or an officer, director, or stockholder in a corporation licensed under the authority of this chapter, the license of which was revoked, suspended, or subjected to other disciplinary action.

(d) Name, address, and license number of the manufacturer, manufacturer branch, distributor, or distributor branch employing the applicant.

(Added by Stats. 1973, Ch. 996.)

11902. (a) The department shall issue a representative's license when it finds and determines that the applicant has furnished the required information, and that the applicant intends in good faith to act as a representative and has paid the fees required by Sections 9262 and 11723.

(b) The department may refuse to issue, or may suspend or revoke, a license for any of the following reasons:

(1) The information in the application is incorrect.

(2) The applicant or licensee has been convicted of a crime or committed any act or engaged in any conduct involving moral turpitude which is substantially related to the qualifications, functions, or duties of the licensed activity. A conviction after a plea of nolo contendere is a conviction within the meaning of this section.

(3) The applicant or licensee has outstanding an unpaid final court judgment rendered in connection with an activity licensed under this chapter.

(4) The applicant or licensee was previously the holder of, or was a business representative of a business which was the holder of, a license and certificate issued under this chapter which were revoked for cause and not reissued by the department or which were suspended for cause and the terms of suspension have not been fulfilled.

(5) The applicant was previously the holder of an occupational license issued by another state, authorizing the same or similar activities of a license issued under this division; and that license was revoked or suspended for cause and was never reissued, or was suspended for cause, and the terms of suspension have not been fulfilled.

(6) The applicant or licensee has committed any act prohibited by Section 11713.2 or 11713.3.

(c) Pending the determination of the department that the applicant has met the requirements of this chapter, it may issue a temporary permit to any person applying for a representative's license. The temporary permit shall permit the operation by the representative for a period not to exceed 120 days while the department is completing its investigation and determination of all facts relative to the qualifications of the applicant for a license. The temporary permit is invalid after the applicant's license has been issued or refused.

(d) The department may issue a probationary representative's license based upon the existence of any circumstance set forth in subdivision (b), subject to conditions to be observed in the exercise of the privilege granted, either upon application for the issuance of a license or upon application for the renewal of a license. The conditions to be attached to the exercise of the privilege shall not appear on the face of the license but shall be those which, in the judgment of the department, are in the public interest and suitable to the qualifications of the applicant as disclosed by the application and investigation by the department of the information contained therein.

(Amended by Stats. 1998, Ch. 877, Sec. 52. Effective January 1, 1999.)

11902.5. (a) The department, after notice and hearing, on an interim basis, may refuse to issue or may suspend a license issued under this chapter when the applicant or licensee has been convicted of a crime involving moral turpitude which is substantially related to the qualifications, functions, or duties of the licensed activity, if an appeal of the conviction is pending or the conviction has otherwise not become final. A conviction after a plea of nolo contendere is a conviction within the meaning of this section.

(b) If a conviction, upon which an interim refusal to issue or suspension under subdivision (a) is based, is affirmed on appeal or otherwise becomes final, the refusal to issue or suspension shall automatically take effect as a denial or revocation, as the case may be, of the license. If the interim refusal to issue or suspension was stayed under probationary terms and conditions, the subsequent automatic denial or revocation shall also be stayed under the same terms and conditions for a term not to exceed the original term of probation for the interim refusal or suspension.

(c) If a conviction, upon which an interim refusal to issue or suspension under subdivision (a) is based, is reversed on appeal, the refusal or suspension shall be set aside immediately by the department.

(Added by Stats. 1990, Ch. 1563, Sec. 59.)

11903. (a) If the department suspends or revokes a representative's license, the licensee shall be entitled to an appropriate hearing. Such hearing shall be conducted pursuant to Chapter 5 (commencing with Section 11500) of Part 1 of Division 3 of Title 2 of the Government Code.

(b) If the department issues or renews a representative's license requiring conditions of probation or if the department refuses to issue such license, the applicant shall be entitled to demand in writing a hearing as hereinabove provided before the director or his representative within 60 days after notice of refusal or issuance of the probationary license.

(c) A person whose representative's license has been revoked or whose application for a license has been denied may reapply for such license after a period of not less than one year has elapsed from the effective date of the decision revoking the license or denying the application; provided, however, that if such decision was based upon paragraph (3) or (4) of subdivision (b) of Section 11902, an earlier reapplication may be made accompanied by evidence satisfactory to the department that such grounds no longer exist.

(Amended by Stats. 1976, Ch. 934.)

11903.5. (a) After the filing of an accusation under this article, the director may enter into a stipulated compromise settlement agreement with the consent of the licensee on terms and conditions mutually agreeable to the director, the respondent licensee, and the accuser without further hearing or appeal. The agreement may include, but is not limited to, a period of probation or monetary penalties, or both. The monetary penalty shall not exceed five hundred dollars ($500) for each violation, and it shall be based on the nature of the violation and the effect of the violation on the purposes of this article.

(b) A compromise settlement agreement may be entered before, during, or after the hearing, but is valid only if executed and filed pursuant to subdivision (d) before the proposed decision of the hearing officer, if any, is adopted or the case is decided.

(c) The department shall adopt, by regulation, a schedule of maximum and minimum amounts of monetary penalties, the payment of which may be included as a term or condition of a compromise settlement agreement entered under subdivision (a). Any monetary penalty included in a compromise settlement agreement shall be within the range of monetary penalties in that schedule.

(d) Any compromise settlement agreement entered under this section shall be signed by the director, the respondent licensee, and the accuser, or by their authorized representatives. The director shall file, or cause to be filed, the agreement with the Office of Administrative Hearings, together with the department's notice of withdrawal of the accusation or statement of issues upon which the action was initiated.

(e) If the respondent licensee fails to perform all of the terms and conditions of the compromise settlement agreement, the agreement is void and the department may take any action authorized by law notwithstanding the agreement, including, but not limited to, refiling the accusation or imposing license sanctions.

(Added by Stats. 1985, Ch. 1022, Sec. 22.)

11904. Every representative's license issued hereunder shall expire at midnight on the 30th day of June of each year.

(Added by Stats. 1973, Ch. 996.)

11905. Every application for the renewal of a representative's license which expires on the 30th day of June shall be made by the person to whom issued between June 1st and midnight of June 30th preceding such expiration date and shall be made by presenting the application form provided by the department and by payment of the full annual renewal fee for such license.

(Added by Stats. 1973, Ch. 996.)

11907. The representative's license, or any permit provided for in this chapter, shall be automatically canceled upon the failure of the licensee to file an application for renewal of the license or permit before July 1st following the expiration date of the current license or permit.

(Added by Stats. 1973, Ch. 996.)

11908. The suspension, expiration, or cancellation of the representative's license provided for in this chapter shall not prevent the filing of an accusation for revocation or suspension of the suspended, expired, or canceled license as provided in Section 11903, and the department's decision that such license should be suspended or revoked. Such determination may be considered in granting or refusing to grant any subsequent license authorized by Division 5 (commencing with Section 11100) to such licensee.

(Added by Stats. 1973, Ch. 996.)

11909. Upon issuance by the department to the licensee, the license provided in this article shall be immediately delivered to and posted in a place conspicuous to the public at the place of business of the manufacturer, manufacturer's branch, distributor, distributor's branch from which the representative is directly supervised and shall be continuously exhibited in such place while the representative is employed by such employer.

In the event a representative's employment is terminated, the license shall be forwarded to the department by the manufacturer, manufacturer's branch, distributor, distributor's branch not later than the end of the third business day after termination.

(Added by Stats. 1974, Ch. 384.)

Chapter 5. Sale of Housecars

(Chapter 5 added by Stats. 1980, Ch. 853, Sec. 1.)

11930. As used in this chapter:

(a) "First-stage manufacturer" with reference to a housecar means the manufacturer of the engine, chassis, and drive train of the vehicle.

(b) "Second-stage manufacturer" means the installer of the structure and equipment permanently upon the engine, chassis, and drive train of the vehicle rendering the vehicle complete and suitable for human habitation and ready for delivery to the dealer or the buyer.

(Added by Stats. 1980, Ch. 853, Sec. 1.)

11931. (a) The dealer shall give the purchaser of a new housecar a list of every express warranty, of which he has notice, that has been issued on the housecar, or a part thereof, by the first-stage manufacturer, the second-stage manufacturer, the dealer, or any other party. The dealer shall also give the purchaser a copy of each warranty.

(b) The purchaser shall sign the list as an acknowledgment that he has received each warranty listed. The dealer shall sign to signify that all express warranties applicable to the housecar appear on the list. Both the purchaser and the dealer shall retain a copy of the list.

(c) Violation of this section is an infraction.

(Added by Stats. 1980, Ch. 853, Sec. 1.)

Chapter 6. Sale of Used Vehicles

(Chapter 6 added by Stats. 2012, Ch. 741, Sec. 1.)

11950. (a) A buy-here-pay-here dealer shall affix a label on any used vehicle being offered for retail sale that states the reasonable market value of that vehicle. The label shall meet all of the following conditions:

(1) Be in writing.

(2) Be printed with a heading that reads "REASONABLE MARKET VALUE OF THIS VEHICLE" in at least 16-point bold type and text in at least 12-point type.

(3) Be located adjacent to the window sticker identifying the equipment provided with the vehicle or, if none, it shall be located prominently and conspicuously on the vehicle so that it is readily readable.

(4) Contain the information used to determine the reasonable market value of the vehicle, including, but not limited to, the use of a nationally recognized pricing guide for used vehicles.

(5) Contain the date the reasonable market value was determined.

(6) Indicate that the reasonable market value is being provided only for comparison shopping and is not the retail sale price or the advertised price of the vehicle.

(b) A buy-here-pay-here dealer shall provide to a prospective buyer of the used vehicle a copy of any information obtained from a nationally recognized pricing guide that the buy-here-pay-here dealer used to determine the reasonable market value of the vehicle.

(c) As used in this section:

(1) "Reasonable market value" means the average retail value of a used vehicle based on the condition, mileage, year, make, and model of the vehicle, as determined within the last 60 days by a nationally recognized pricing guide that provides used vehicle retail values or pricing reports to vehicle dealers or the public.

(2) "Nationally recognized pricing guide" includes, but is not limited to, the Kelley Blue Book (KBB), Edmunds, the Black Book, or the National Automobile Dealers' Association (NADA) Guide.

(Added by Stats. 2012, Ch. 741, Sec. 1. (AB 1534) Effective January 1, 2013.)

Chapter 7. Sale of Automobile Parts

(Chapter 7 added by Stats. 1975, Ch. 678.)

12000. The Bureau of Automotive Repair in the Department of Consumer Affairs shall enforce the provisions of this chapter. The Bureau of Automotive Repair shall investigate and inspect retail outlets to insure compliance with this chapter.

(Repealed and added by Stats. 1975, Ch. 678.)

12001. (a) Any person who sells and installs new parts in passenger cars, in the ordinary course of his business, shall provide the customer with an invoice which identifies by brand name, or other comparable designation, the part or parts installed.

(b) Any person who sells and installs used or factory rebuilt parts in passenger cars, in the ordinary course of his business, shall provide the customer with an invoice which specifically designates the used part or parts installed.

(c) This section shall not apply to any fitting or other device necessary to the installation of any new, used or factory rebuilt part subject to the provisions of this section.

(Added by Stats. 1975, Ch. 678.)

12002. No person shall knowingly manufacture, sell, or install in any vehicle, any vehicle part which, under the provisions of Chapter 301 (commencing with Section 30101) of Part A of Subtitle VI of Title 49 of the United States Code, is, or has been, determined to be defective and subject to customer notification or recall.

(Amended by Stats. 2018, Ch. 198, Sec. 20. (AB 3246) Effective January 1, 2019.)

12003. Any violation of this chapter shall be a misdemeanor.

(Added by Stats. 1975, Ch. 678.)

Chapter 8. Private Party Vehicle Markets

(Chapter 8 added by Stats. 1978, Ch. 525.)

12101. Any transaction which is regulated by this chapter shall not be subject to the provisions of Article 4 (commencing with Section 21625) of Chapter 9 of Division 8 of the Business and Professions Code, regulating transactions in identifiable secondhand tangible personal property. No person shall be considered a "secondhand dealer" within the meaning of Section 21661 of the Business and Professions Code because of activities regulated by this chapter.

(Added by Stats. 1978, Ch. 525.)

12102. The following definitions apply with respect to this chapter:

(a) "Private party vehicle market" means any event conducted under any of the following circumstances:

(1) An event at which two or more vehicles are offered or displayed for sale or exchange and a fee is charged for the privilege of offering or displaying the vehicles for sale or exchange.

(2) An event at which a fee is charged to prospective buyers for admission to the area where vehicles are offered or displayed for sale or exchange.

(3) An event, other than one conducted by a person listed in subdivision (a) of Section 286, at which used vehicles are offered or displayed for sale or exchange if such event is held at the same place more than six times in any 12-month period, regardless of the number of persons offering or displaying vehicles or the absence of fees.

(b) "Private party vehicle market operator" means any person who controls, manages, conducts, or otherwise administers a private party vehicle market.

(c) "Vendor" means any person who exchanges, sells, or offers for sale or exchange any vehicle at a private party vehicle market.

(d) Any event arranged or sponsored, or both, by a dealer licensed pursuant to Division 5 (commencing with Section 11100) shall not be considered a private party vehicle market.

(Added by Stats. 1978, Ch. 525.)

12103. (a) Every private party vehicle market operator shall maintain a record, for not less than one year, of all of the following information:

(1) The name of each vendor selling, exchanging, or offering for sale or exchange, any vehicle at a private party vehicle market.

(2) The vendor's driver's license number.

(3) The registration number assigned to the vehicle and the vehicle identification number.

(4) The number of the vehicle's current and valid certificate of compliance.

(5) The make, model, and color of the vehicle.

(b) That information shall be made available, upon request, to any peace officer and to any employee of the department designated by the director.

(Amended by Stats. 1991, Ch. 1054, Sec. 4.)

12104. (a) Every private party vehicle market operator shall supply, to vendors, sufficient forms which are necessary to comply with Section 5900.

(b) Every private party vehicle market operator shall supply, to vendors, all information made available by the department to the general public regarding all existing provisions of law pertaining to requirements for the transfer of vehicle ownership and registration between parties who are not dealers.

(Added by Stats. 1978, Ch. 525.)

Chapter 9. Towing

(Chapter 9 added by Stats. 1983, Ch. 746, Sec. 1.)

12110. (a) Except as provided in subdivision (b), no towing service shall provide and no person or public entity shall accept any direct or indirect commission, gift, or any compensation whatever from a towing service in consideration of arranging or requesting the services of a tow truck. As used in this section, "arranging" does not include the activities of employees or principals of a provider of towing services in responding to a request for towing services.

(b) Subdivision (a) does not preclude a public entity otherwise authorized by law from requiring a fee in connection with the award of a franchise for towing vehicles on behalf of that public entity. However, the fee in those cases may not exceed the amount necessary to reimburse the public entity for its actual and reasonable costs incurred in connection with the towing program.

(c) Any towing service or any employee of a towing service that accepts or agrees to accept any money or anything of value from a repair shop and any repair shop or any employee of a repair shop that pays or agrees to pay any money or anything of value as a commission, referral fee, inducement, or in any manner a consideration, for the delivery or the arranging of a delivery of a vehicle, not owned by the repair shop or towing service, for the purpose of storage or repair, is guilty of a misdemeanor, punishable as set forth in subdivision (d). Nothing in this subdivision prevents a towing service from towing a vehicle to a repair shop owned by the same company that owns the towing service.

(d) Any person convicted of a violation of subdivision (a) or (c) shall be punished as follows:

(1) Upon first conviction, by a fine of not more than five thousand dollars ($5,000) or imprisonment in the county jail for not more than six months, or by both that fine and imprisonment. If the violation of subdivision (a) or (c) is committed by a tow truck driver, the person's privilege to operate a motor vehicle shall be suspended by the department under Section 13351.85. The clerk of the court shall send a certified abstract of the conviction to the department. If the violation of either subdivision (a) or (c) is committed by a tow truck driver, the court may order the impoundment of the tow truck involved for not more than 15 days.

(2) Upon a conviction of a violation of subdivision (a) or (c) that occurred within seven years of one or more separate convictions of violations of subdivision (a) or (c), by a fine of not more than ten thousand dollars ($10,000) or imprisonment in the county jail for not more than one year, or by both that fine and imprisonment. If the violation of subdivision (a) or (c) is committed by a tow truck driver, the person's privilege to operate a motor vehicle shall be suspended by the department under Section 13351.85. The clerk of the court shall send a certified abstract of the conviction to the department. If the violation of either subdivision (a) or (c) is committed by a tow truck owner, the court may order the impoundment of the tow truck involved for not less than 15 days but not more than 30 days.

(Amended by Stats. 2000, Ch. 641, Sec. 1. Effective January 1, 2001.)

12111. (a) Except as provided in subdivision (b), no city or city and county may impose a business license tax for revenue-raising purposes on the operation of a tow truck in its jurisdiction if the vehicle tower maintains no fixed place of business within the boundaries of the city or city and county.

(b) A city or city and county may impose a business license tax upon a vehicle tower doing business within its jurisdiction who has no fixed place of business therein, if the license tax is graduated according to gross receipts attributable to work done within the city or city and county.

(Amended by Stats. 1988, Ch. 924, Sec. 6.)

Chapter 10. Sales of Vehicles by Private Owners

(Chapter 10 added by Stats. 1986, Ch. 668, Sec. 1.)

12120. Only a dealer, a person described in Section 286, or the registered owner of record shall sell or offer for sale a vehicle of a type required to be registered pursuant to Division 3 (commencing with Section 4000) or identified pursuant to Division 16.5 (commencing with Section 38000), except as provided in Section 12121.

(Added by Stats. 1986, Ch. 668, Sec. 1.)

12121. (a) Section 12120 does not apply to a dealer licensed pursuant to Chapter 4 (commencing with Section 11700) when acting under authority of the license, or to his or her authorized agent.

(b) Section 12120 does not prohibit the sale of a vehicle by any of the following persons not engaged in the business of selling vehicles:

(1) Anyone related by blood, adoption, or marriage to the registered owner.

(2) The receiver, administrator, executor, guardian, or other person appointed by, or acting under, a judgment or order of any court.

(3) The trustee of a trust in which the vehicle is registered as an asset.

(4) Any public officer in the performance of his or her official duties.

(5) An attorney on behalf of a client who is the registered owner.

(6) The owner, officer, or designated representative of a business in whose name the vehicle is registered.

(7) The legal owner as shown on the certificate of ownership.

(8) A person who has prior written authorization from the registered owner of the vehicle, and that person does not receive or expect to receive a commission, money, brokerage fees, profit, or any other thing of value from either the seller or purchaser of the vehicle.

(9) An insurer selling the salvage of one of its insured's vehicle or the stolen vehicle of one of its insured which has been recovered.

(Added by Stats. 1986, Ch. 668, Sec. 1.)

Chapter 11. Consumer Recovery Fund

(Chapter 11 added by Stats. 2007, Ch. 437, Sec. 6.)

12200. The following definitions apply to this chapter:

(a) "Application" means an application to the recovery corporation for the payment of an eligible claim from the recovery fund that is filed with the recovery corporation after January 1, 2009.

(b) "Consumer" means a person who either (1) purchased or leased, or became obligated to purchase or lease, a motor vehicle to be used primarily for personal, family, or household purposes from a dealer or lessor-retailer licensed under this code, or (2) consigned for sale a motor vehicle that was used primarily for personal, family, or household purposes to a dealer licensed under this code.

(c) "Eligible claim" means an unsatisfied claim for economic loss, not barred by the statutes of limitation, that accrues after July 1, 2008, as a result of the failure of a dealer licensed under this code, or, if applicable, a lessor-retailer licensed under this code, to do any of the following:

(1) Remit license or registration fees received or contractually obligated to be paid from a consumer to the department.

(2) Pay to the legal owner of a vehicle transferred as a trade-in by a consumer to the dealer or lessor-retailer the amount necessary to discharge the prior credit balance owed to the legal owner.

(3) Pay to the lessor registered in accordance with Section 4453.5 of a vehicle transferred as a trade-in by a consumer to the dealer or lessor-retailer the amount the dealer or lessor-retailer agreed to pay to the lessor.

(4) Pay the amount specified in a consignment agreement to a consumer after the sale of a consigned vehicle.

(5) Provide a consumer who purchased a vehicle from the dealer or lessor-retailer with good title to the vehicle, free from any security interest or other lien, encumbrance, or claim, unless otherwise clearly and conspicuously provided for by the written sale agreement.

(6) Pay to a third party any amount received from, or contractually obligated to be paid by, a consumer for insurance, service contracts, or goods or services purchased through the dealer or lessor-retailer and to be provided by the third party.

(d) "Participant" means a dealer licensed under this code or a lessor-retailer licensed under this code.

(e) "Recovery corporation" means the Consumer Motor Vehicle Recovery Corporation.

(f) "Recovery fund" means the consumer recovery fund established by the recovery corporation pursuant to Section 12203 for the payment of eligible claims.

(Amended by Stats. 2013, Ch. 392, Sec. 3. (AB 501) Effective January 1, 2014.)

12201. (a) Participants shall maintain a corporation under the Nonprofit Mutual Benefit Corporation Law (Part 3 (commencing with Section 7110) of Division 2 of Title 1 of the Corporations Code) that shall operate under the name "Consumer Motor Vehicle Recovery Corporation."

(b) The purpose of the Consumer Motor Vehicle Recovery Corporation is to provide payments to consumers on eligible claims subject to the requirements and limitations set forth in this chapter.

(c) A participant may not charge or collect from a consumer a separate fee or charge to recoup the fee paid by the participant pursuant to Section 4456.3.

(d) The State of California and its officers, agents, or employees shall not be liable for any act or omission of the recovery corporation or its directors, officers, agents, or employees.

(Added by Stats. 2007, Ch. 437, Sec. 6. Effective January 1, 2008.)

12202. (a) The recovery corporation shall have a board of directors composed of six directors, as follows:

(1) One public consumer representative member appointed by the Director of Consumer Affairs who shall serve until the appointment is

revoked, another appointment is made, or until the appointed director resigns. The consumer representative shall be either of the following:

(A) A current or former prosecutor with at least two years of direct experience in the civil or criminal enforcement of consumer protection laws, including laws prohibiting deceptive advertising and unlawful and fraudulent practices.

(B) A current or former employee of a government agency who has at least two years of direct experience in one of the following:

(i) The investigation, mediation, and resolution of consumer complaints.

(ii) Providing counseling, information, education, or referral services to consumers.

(iii) Administering a consumer protection program that provides any of the services described in clause (i) or (ii).

(2) A representative of the Attorney General, who shall serve as an ex officio, nonvoting member.

(3) One member of the general public appointed by the Senate Committee on Rules to a two-year term.

(4) One member of the general public appointed by the Speaker of the Assembly to a two-year term, except that the initial appointment to the board of directors shall be for a one-year term.

(5) Two participants, who shall be appointed by the Governor for two-year terms, except that the initial term of the position of one of the participant directors shall be for a one-year term.

(b) A person is eligible to be nominated and to serve as a participant director if the person satisfies all of the following conditions:

(1) The person's primary occupation, at the time of nomination and continuously during the previous three years, has been as an owner or general manager of a licensed dealer or lessor-retailer.

(2) The person has not been convicted of a crime, including a plea or verdict of guilty or a conviction following a plea of nolo contendere.

(3) The person is not subject to a judgment or administrative order, whether entered after adjudication or stipulation, predicated on that person's commission of an act of dishonesty, fraud, deceit, or violation of this chapter or Chapter 5 (commencing with Section 17200) of Part 2 of Division 7 of the Business and Professions Code.

(4) The person is not a defendant in a pending criminal or civil law enforcement action brought by a public prosecutor.

(5) The person has not served as a participant director of the recovery corporation at any time during the previous 18 months.

(c) A director who does not qualify to be a participant director, whose term has lapsed, or who otherwise becomes unable to serve shall not continue to serve as a director.

(Added by Stats. 2007, Ch. 437, Sec. 6. Effective January 1, 2008.)

12203. (a) The recovery corporation shall establish a consumer recovery fund for the payment of claims as provided in this chapter. The recovery corporation shall receive funds from the department as provided in Section 4456.3 and shall promptly notify the department when the recovery fund balance reaches the amounts specified in subdivision (b) of Section 4456.3.

(b) The recovery corporation shall establish and maintain an operations account within the recovery fund for the payment of costs of operations and administration. The recovery corporation shall prepare, before its fiscal year end, an estimated annual operational budget projecting the costs of operations and administration for the succeeding fiscal year, excluding the amount paid for claims. The recovery corporation shall not expend more than two hundred fifty thousand dollars ($250,000) each fiscal year from the operations account for the administration of this chapter.

(c) The recovery corporation shall invest all funds received from the department pursuant to Section 4456.3, and interest earned on those funds, deposited in the recovery fund, in a federally insured account or in federally insured certificates of deposit at a California state or federally chartered bank or savings bank.

(d) The recovery corporation holds all money in the recovery fund in trust for the purposes provided in this chapter and shall disburse funds only as provided in this chapter.

(e) The recovery corporation shall separately account for disbursements and collections. The accounting shall include a record of each claim paid that indicates the name, address, and phone number of each claimant receiving payment, the amount of the payment, and the name of the participant for which a claim was paid. Quarterly reports shall be provided to the office of the Attorney General, Consumer Protection Section, commencing on or before October 31, 2008, and within 30 days after the end of each quarter thereafter.

(f) The recovery corporation may adopt reasonable written bylaws, rules, and procedures to carry out the purposes of this chapter. The representative of the Attorney General may vote on the adoption of bylaws, rules, and procedures notwithstanding paragraph (2) of subdivision (a) of Section 12202.

(Amended by Stats. 2024, Ch. 853, Sec. 30. (AB 3281) Effective January 1, 2025.)

12204. (a) A consumer may file an application with the recovery corporation for the payment of the consumer's eligible claim if a dealer or lessor-retailer against whom the claim is asserted has ceased selling and leasing motor vehicles to the general public or has become subject to a petition in bankruptcy.

(b) (1) The application shall be verified and shall set forth all of the following information:

(A) The consumer's name, address, and telephone number.

(B) The amount of the eligible claim.

(C) A description of the circumstances demonstrating an eligible claim.

(D) A statement indicating the consumer's belief that the dealer or lessor-retailer has ceased selling and leasing motor vehicles to the general public or has become subject to a petition in bankruptcy and the reasons for this belief.

(E) A statement indicating what action, if any, the applicant has taken to recover the amount of the eligible claim.

(F) A statement indicating that the consumer's application for payment does not include any amount for which the consumer has obtained recovery under the dealer's bond required by Section 11710.

(2) Nothing in this chapter shall be construed to require a consumer to bring a civil action to obtain recovery, file a bankruptcy claim, or file a crime report with a law enforcement agency in order to obtain payment of an eligible claim submitted to the recovery corporation.

(c) The application shall be accompanied by a copy of the agreement between the consumer and the dealer or lessor-retailer, unless the agreement is unnecessary to the recovery corporation's determination of the validity of the claim.

(d) If the eligible claim is based on the failure to remit license or registration fees, the application shall be accompanied by evidence demonstrating that the consumer paid money or other consideration for the fees, or became obligated to pay the fees, and that the fees had not been remitted. The eligible claim shall be limited to the dollar amount of the license or registration fees not remitted and a late charge or penalty.

(e) If the eligible claim is based on the failure to pay the proceeds of a consignment sale, the application shall be accompanied by the consignment agreement, evidence that the consigned vehicle was sold, and by the consumer's verified statement that the consumer did not receive the portion of the proceeds of the sale to which the consumer was entitled. The eligible claim is limited to the dollar amount specified in a written consignment agreement to be paid to the consignor.

(f) If the eligible claim is based on the failure to pay the legal owner of the consumer's trade-in vehicle, the application shall be accompanied by a statement from the legal owner of the amount, if any, that he or she received from the dealer or lessor-retailer. The eligible claim is limited to the dollar amount necessary to discharge the credit balance owing on the trade-in vehicle.

(g) If the eligible claim is based on the failure to pay the lessor of the consumer's trade-in vehicle, the application shall be accompanied by a statement from the lessor of the amount, if any, that the lessor received from the dealer or lessor-retailer. The eligible claim is limited to the dollar amount necessary to pay the lessor the total amount that the dealer or lessor-retailer agreed with the consumer to pay the lessor.

(h) If the eligible claim is based on the failure to provide good title, the application shall be accompanied by a statement from the legal owner or other claimant of the amount, if any, that he or she received from the dealer or lessor-retailer. The eligible claim is limited to the remaining dollar amount necessary to discharge the valid security interest, lien, encumbrance, or other claim clouding title to the vehicle.

(i) If the eligible claim is based on the failure to pay third parties for insurance, service contracts, or goods or services, the application shall be accompanied by a statement from the third party of the amount, if any, that he or she received from the dealer or lessor-retailer. The eligible claim is limited to the difference between the dollar amount the consumer paid or was contractually obligated to pay to the dealer or lessor-retailer for the insurance, service contracts, or goods or services purchased through the dealer or lessor-retailer and to be provided by the third party and the dollar amount actually received by the third party from the dealer or lessor-retailer for the insurance, service contracts, or goods or services.

(j) The recovery corporation may require reasonable additional information designed to facilitate payment of eligible claims.

(k) (1) For claims that have accrued on or after July 1, 2008, and before January 1, 2009, the application shall be filed within 18 months of the date upon which the dealer or lessor-retailer ceased selling or leasing motor vehicles to the general public or became subject to a petition in bankruptcy.

(2) For claims that have accrued on or after January 1, 2009, the application shall be filed within one year of the date upon which the dealer or lessor-retailer ceased selling or leasing motor vehicles to the general public or became subject to a petition in bankruptcy.

(Amended by Stats. 2013, Ch. 392, Sec. 4. (AB 501) Effective January 1, 2014.)

12205. The recovery corporation shall develop a notice fully explaining a consumer's right to make a claim from the fund, an application form, and an explanation of how to complete the application. The notice, application, and explanation shall be in English and Spanish and shall be provided to a person upon request.

(Added by Stats. 2007, Ch. 437, Sec. 6. Effective January 1, 2008.)

12206. (a) Within 30 days of receiving an application, the recovery corporation shall notify the applicant, in writing, that the application is complete or, if the application is incomplete, what additional information is required.

(b) (1) Within 60 days of the recovery corporation providing notice to the applicant of a complete application, the recovery corporation shall either pay the eligible claim from the fund as prescribed in this chapter or deny the claim. A claim shall be deemed granted unless the directors affirmatively vote to deny the claim.

(2) The recovery corporation, for good cause, may extend the 60-day period not more than an additional 90 days to investigate the accuracy of the application or evidence submitted by a dealer or lessor-retailer.

(c) A director shall not be involved in the decision of a claim if the director has a financial interest in the outcome of the decision; has a financial interest in or is employed by the participant that is the subject of the claim; or has a familial or close personal relationship with the claimant or an owner, officer, director, or manager of the participant.

(Added by Stats. 2007, Ch. 437, Sec. 6. Effective January 1, 2008.)

12207. (a) Within 15 days of receiving a complete application, the recovery corporation shall serve a copy of the complete application and the following notice on the dealer or lessor-retailer that is the subject of the claim:

"NOTICE"

"The attached application has been made to the Consumer Motor Vehicle Recovery Corporation for payment of a claim allegedly arising out of your conduct or omission. If you wish to contest payment, you must file a written response to the application that describes any evidence that you have showing that the application is inaccurate or that payment from the fund is not authorized under Section 12200 and following of the Vehicle Code, a copy of which is provided.

"The allegations stated in the attached application may constitute grounds on which disciplinary action may be taken to suspend or revoke your license. In addition, the Department of Motor Vehicles may suspend your license until you have repaid in full the amount paid by the Consumer Motor Vehicle Recovery Corporation on the attached application, plus interest at the rate of 10 percent per annum."

(b) The notice prescribed by subdivision (a), a copy of the application for payment, and a copy of this chapter shall be served on the dealer or lessor-retailer by personal service or certified mail, return receipt requested, at the department's mailing address of record for that licensee.

(Added by Stats. 2007, Ch. 437, Sec. 6. Effective January 1, 2008.)

12208. If the recovery corporation pays the claim, the amount of the payment shall be the total of the amount of the eligible claim, but in no event may the payment exceed thirty-five thousand dollars ($35,000) for a transaction.

(Added by Stats. 2007, Ch. 437, Sec. 6. Effective January 1, 2008.)

12209. If the recovery corporation denies the claim, the recovery corporation shall notify the applicant in writing of the denial, the legal and factual bases for the denial, and the applicant's right to contest the denial in writing within 60 days or any longer period permitted by the recovery corporation. If the applicant does not contest the denial within 60 days or an additional period reasonably requested by the consumer, the decision shall be final. The recovery corporation shall act on the applicant's objection within 30 days. If the claim is denied in whole or in part, the applicant may seek review in the superior court of any of the following counties in which the office of the Attorney General maintains an office: Sacramento, San Francisco, Los Angeles, or San Diego. Review shall be limited to the written record before the recovery corporation and any relevant evidence that could not have been previously presented to the recovery corporation despite the applicant's reasonable diligence. The superior court shall affirm the decision of the recovery corporation if it is supported by substantial evidence.

(Added by Stats. 2007, Ch. 437, Sec. 6. Effective January 1, 2008.)

12210. After the recovery corporation pays or rejects a claim, all of the following apply:

(a) Immediately upon payment, the recovery corporation shall be subrogated to all of the consumer's rights against the dealer or lessor-retailer to the extent of the amount of the payment.

(b) The recovery corporation may bring an action to recover the amount of the payment plus interest at the rate of 10 percent per annum and shall be entitled to recover costs and reasonable attorney's fees.

(c) Within 10 days of paying the claim, the recovery corporation shall inform the department of the payment of the claim, the amount of the payment, and the name and address of the dealer or lessor-retailer that is the subject of the claim. Upon the department's request, the recovery corporation shall provide the department with a copy of the claim application and other documents received by the recovery corporation in connection with the claim.

(d) Within 15 days of paying or rejecting the claim, the recovery corporation shall serve the dealer or lessor-retailer that is the subject of the claim with notice of the recovery corporation's disposition of the claim in the manner provided for service in subdivision (b) of Section 12207.

(e) After the consumer receives payment of the eligible claim from the recovery corporation, the consumer shall not seek to recover the amount received from the recovery corporation for the eligible claim from the dealer's bond required by Section 11710. Nothing in this subdivision affects any other rights the consumer may have as provided in Section 12217.

(Added by Stats. 2007, Ch. 437, Sec. 6. Effective January 1, 2008.)

12211. If the recovery corporation has insufficient funds to pay all eligible claims, the recovery corporation shall pay eligible claims in the order that the claim applications were received and shall hold the remaining claims until funds are available to pay those claims.
(Added by Stats. 2007, Ch. 437, Sec. 6. Effective January 1, 2008.)

12212. (a) Within 30 days after the close of the fiscal year or other reasonable period established by the board of directors, the recovery corporation shall make publicly available a statement of the following information concerning the most recently concluded fiscal year:

(1) The number of claims and approximate dollar amount of the claims received.

(2) The total number of claims and total dollar amount of claims paid.

(3) The approximate number and dollar amount of claims denied or abandoned.

(4) The dollar balance in the recovery fund.

(5) The dollar amount of fees received pursuant to Section 4456.3.

(6) The administrative costs and expenses of the recovery corporation.

(b) The recovery corporation shall make publicly available within 15 days of approval by the board of directors or other reasonable period established by the board of directors, the following information:

(1) The approved minutes of meetings of the board of directors.

(2) The approved estimated annual operational budget projecting the costs of operations and administration for the succeeding fiscal year, excluding the amount to be paid for claims.

(3) The approved bylaws, as amended, of the recovery corporation.

(c) Information may be made publicly available as required by this section by disseminating the information on an Internet Web site or providing the information by electronic mail to a person who has requested the information and provided a valid electronic mail address.
(Added by Stats. 2007, Ch. 437, Sec. 6. Effective January 1, 2008.)

12213. The operation of the recovery corporation shall at all times be subject to the examination and review of the Attorney General and the Attorney General's representatives. The Attorney General and his or her representatives may at any time investigate the affairs and examine the books, accounts, records, and files used by the recovery corporation. The Attorney General and his or her representatives shall have free access to the offices, books, accounts, papers, records, files, safes, and vaults of the recovery corporation and may copy any documents of, or in the possession of, the recovery corporation.
(Added by Stats. 2007, Ch. 437, Sec. 6. Effective January 1, 2008.)

12214. The Attorney General or his or her representative may determine that the recovery corporation has failed or ceased to operate upon a finding that any one of the following has occurred with respect to the recovery corporation:

(a) The recovery corporation was not created.

(b) The recovery corporation is dissolved.

(c) The recovery corporation ceased to operate.

(d) The recovery corporation is insolvent or bankrupt.

(e) The recovery corporation failed to pay its operating costs.

(f) The recovery corporation failed to pay any claim or judgment in a timely manner.

(g) The recovery corporation violated its articles of incorporation or any law of this state.

(h) The recovery corporation invested its funds in violation of this chapter.

(i) The recovery corporation has not diligently made a decision upon a claim made by a person aggrieved.

(j) The recovery corporation violated any section of this chapter.

(k) The recovery corporation neglected or refused to submit its books, papers, and affairs to the inspection of the Attorney General or his or her representatives.
(Added by Stats. 2007, Ch. 437, Sec. 6. Effective January 1, 2008.)

12215. If the recovery corporation is dissolved or ceases to exist, or if the Attorney General or his or her representative makes a determination, pursuant to Section 12214, that the recovery corporation has failed or ceased to operate, all outstanding debts, obligations of the recovery corporation, and amounts due for services rendered shall first be paid from the remaining assets, including the recovery fund. The assets remaining, after settling those liabilities, shall be distributed to the participants, less the costs of that distribution.
(Added by Stats. 2007, Ch. 437, Sec. 6. Effective January 1, 2008.)

12216. All costs and expenses incurred by the Department of Justice in the administration of this chapter shall be paid to the Department of Justice by the recovery corporation. The Department of Justice may institute an action for the recovery of costs and expenses incurred in the administration of this article in any court of competent jurisdiction.
(Added by Stats. 2007, Ch. 437, Sec. 6. Effective January 1, 2008.)

12217. Nothing in this chapter is intended to limit or restrict actions, remedies, penalties, or procedures otherwise available pursuant to any other provision of law.
(Added by Stats. 2007, Ch. 437, Sec. 6. Effective January 1, 2008.)

Division 6. Drivers' Licenses

(Heading of Division 6 amended by Stats. 1961, Ch. 1615.)

Chapter 1. Issuance of Licenses, Expiration, and Renewal

(Chapter 1 enacted by Stats. 1959, Ch. 3.)

Article 1. Persons Required to Be Licensed, Exemptions, and Age Limits

(Article 1 enacted by Stats. 1959, Ch. 3.)

12500. (a) A person may not drive a motor vehicle upon a highway, unless the person then holds a valid driver's license issued under this code, except those persons who are expressly exempted under this code.

(b) A person may not drive a motorcycle, motor-driven cycle, or motorized bicycle upon a highway, unless the person then holds a valid driver's license or endorsement issued under this code for that class, except those persons who are expressly exempted under this code, or those persons specifically authorized to operate motorized bicycles or motorized scooters with a valid driver's license of any class, as specified in subdivision (h) of Section 12804.9.

(c) A person may not drive a motor vehicle in or upon any offstreet parking facility, unless the person then holds a valid driver's license of the appropriate class or certification to operate the vehicle. As used in this subdivision, "offstreet parking facility" means any offstreet facility held open for use by the public for parking vehicles and includes any publicly owned facilities for offstreet parking, and privately owned facilities for offstreet parking where no fee is charged for the privilege to park and which are held open for the common public use of retail customers.

(d) A person may not drive a motor vehicle or combination of vehicles that is not of a type for which the person is licensed.

(e) A motorized scooter operated on public streets shall at all times be equipped with an engine that complies with the applicable State Air Resources Board emission requirements.

(Amended by Stats. 2007, Ch. 630, Sec. 3. Effective January 1, 2008.)

12501. The following persons are not required to obtain a driver's license:

(a) An officer or employee of the United States, while operating a motor vehicle owned or controlled by the United States on the business of the United States, except when the motor vehicle being operated is a commercial motor vehicle, as defined in Section 15210.

(b) Any person while driving or operating implements of husbandry incidentally operated or moved over a highway, except as provided in Section 36300 or 36305.

(c) Any person driving or operating an off-highway motor vehicle subject to identification, as defined in Section 38012, while driving or operating such motor vehicle as provided in Section 38025. Nothing in this subdivision authorizes operation of a motor vehicle by a person without a valid driver's license upon any offstreet parking facility, as defined in subdivision (c) of Section 12500.

(Amended by Stats. 1990, Ch. 1360, Sec. 10.)

12502. (a) The following persons may operate a motor vehicle in this state without obtaining a driver's license under this code:

(1) A nonresident over the age of 18 years having in his or her immediate possession a valid driver's license issued by a foreign jurisdiction of which he or she is a resident, except as provided in Section 12505.

(2)A nonresident, 21 years of age or older, if transporting hazardous material, as defined in Section 353, in a commercial vehicle, having in his or her immediate possession, a valid license with the appropriate endorsement issued by another state or other jurisdiction that is recognized by the department, or a Canadian driver's license and a copy of his or her current training certificate to transport hazardous material that complies with all federal laws and regulations with respect to hazardous materials, both of which shall be in his or her immediate possession.

(3) A nonresident having in his or her immediate possession a valid driver's license, issued by the Diplomatic Motor Vehicle Office of the Office of Foreign Missions of the United States Department of State, for the type of motor vehicle or combination of vehicles that the person is operating.

(b) (1) A driver required to have a commercial driver's license under Part 383 of Title 49 of the Code of Federal Regulations who submits a current medical examiner's certificate to the licensing state in accordance with Section 383.71(h) of Subpart E of Part 383 of Title 49 of the Code of Federal Regulations, documenting that he or she meets the physical qualification requirements of Section 391.41 of Subpart E of Part 391 of Title 49 of the Code of Federal Regulations, is not required to carry on his or her person the medical examiner's certificate or a copy of that certificate.

(2) A driver may use the date-stamped receipt, given to the driver by the licensing state agency, for up to 15 days after the date stamped on the receipt, as proof of medical certification.

(c) A nonresident possessing a medical certificate in accordance with subdivision (b) shall comply with any restriction of the medical certificate issued to that nonresident.

(d) This section shall become operative on January 31, 2014.

(Repealed (in Sec. 2) and added by Stats. 2012, Ch. 670, Sec. 2.5. (AB 2188) Effective January 1, 2013. Section operative January 31, 2014, by its own provisions.)

12503. A nonresident over the age of 18 years whose home state or country does not require the licensing of drivers may operate a foreign vehicle owned by him for not to exceed 30 days without obtaining a license under this code.

(Amended by Stats. 1971, Ch. 1748.)

12504. (a) Sections 12502 and 12503 apply to any nonresident over the age of 16 years but under the age of 18 years. The maximum period during which that nonresident may operate a motor vehicle in this state without obtaining a driver's license is limited to a period of 10 days immediately following the entry of the nonresident into this state except as provided in subdivision (b) of this section.

(b) Any nonresident over the age of 16 years but under the age of 18 years who is a resident of a foreign jurisdiction which requires the licensing of drivers may continue to operate a motor vehicle in this state after 10 days from his or her date of entry into this state if he or she meets both the following:

(1) He or she has a valid driver's license, issued by the foreign jurisdiction, in his or her immediate possession.

(2) He or she has been issued and has in his or her immediate possession a nonresident minor's certificate, which the department issues to a nonresident minor who holds a valid driver's license issued to him or her by his or her home state or country, and who files proof of financial responsibility.

(c) Whenever any of the conditions for the issuance of a nonresident minor's certificate cease to exist, the department shall cancel the certificate and require the minor to surrender it to the department.

(Amended by Stats. 1992, Ch. 974, Sec. 4. Effective September 28, 1992.)

12505. (a) (1) For purposes of this division only and notwithstanding Section 516, residency shall be determined as a person's state of domicile. "State of domicile" means the state where a person has their true, fixed, and permanent home and principal residence and to which the person has manifested the intention of returning whenever they are absent.

Prima facie evidence of residency for driver's licensing purposes includes, but is not limited to, the following:

(A) Address where registered to vote.

(B) Payment of resident tuition at a public institution of higher education.

(C) Filing a homeowner's property tax exemption.

(D) Other acts, occurrences, or events that indicate presence in the state is more than temporary or transient.

(2) California residency is required of a person in order to be issued a commercial driver's license under this code.

(b) The presumption of residency in this state may be rebutted by satisfactory evidence that the licensee's primary residence is in another state.

(c) A person entitled to an exemption under Section 12502, 12503, or 12504 may operate a motor vehicle in this state for not to exceed 10 days from the date the person establishes residence in this state, except that a person shall not operate a motor vehicle for employment in this state after establishing residency without first obtaining a license from the department.

(d) If the State of California is decertified by the federal government and prohibited from issuing an initial, renewal, or upgraded commercial driver's license pursuant to Section 384.405 of Title 49 of the Code of Federal Regulations, the following applies:

(1) An existing commercial driver's license issued pursuant to this code prior to the date that the state is notified of its decertification shall remain valid until its expiration date.

(2) A person who is a resident of this state may obtain a nondomiciled commercial learner's permit or commercial driver's license from any state that elects to issue a nondomiciled commercial learner's permit or commercial driver's license and that complies with the testing and licensing standards contained in subparts F, G, and H of Part 383 of Title 49 of the Code of Federal Regulations.

(3) For the purposes of this subdivision, a nondomiciled commercial learner's permit or commercial driver's license is a commercial learner's permit or commercial driver's license issued by a state to an individual domiciled in a foreign country or in another state.

(e) The department may issue a nondomiciled commercial learner's permit or nondomiciled commercial driver's license to a person who is domiciled in a state or jurisdiction that has been decertified by the federal government or not determined to be in compliance with the testing and licensing standards contained in subparts F, G, and H of Part 383 of Title 49 of the Code of Federal Regulations.

(f) Subject to Section 12504, a person over the age of 16 years who is a resident of a foreign jurisdiction other than a state, territory, or possession of the United States, the District of Columbia, the Commonwealth of Puerto Rico, or Canada, having a valid driver's license issued to the person by any other foreign jurisdiction may operate a motor vehicle in this state without obtaining a license from the department, unless the department determines that the foreign jurisdiction does not meet the licensing standards imposed by this code.

(g) A person who is 18 years of age or older and in possession of a valid commercial learner's permit or commercial driver's license issued by a foreign jurisdiction that meets the licensing standards contained in subparts F, G, and H of Part 383 of Title 49 of the Code of Federal Regulations shall be granted reciprocity to operate vehicles of the appropriate class on the highways of this state.

(h) A person from a foreign jurisdiction that does not meet the licensing standards contained in subparts F, G, and H of Part 383 of Title 49 of the Code of Federal Regulations shall obtain a commercial learner's permit or commercial driver's license from the department before operating on the highways a motor vehicle for which a commercial driver's license is required, as described in Section 12804.9. The medical examination form required for issuance of a commercial driver's license shall be completed by a health care professional, as defined in paragraph (2) of subdivision (a) of Section 12804.9, who is licensed, certified, or registered to perform physical examinations in the United States of America. This subdivision does not apply to (1) drivers of schoolbuses operated in California on a trip for educational purposes or (2) drivers of vehicles used to provide the services of a local public agency.

(i) This section does not authorize the employment of a person in violation of Section 12515.

(Amended by Stats. 2022, Ch. 295, Sec. 11. (AB 2956) Effective January 1, 2023.)

12506. The department may issue a temporary driver's license to any person applying for a driver's license, to any person applying for renewal of a driver's license, or to any licensee whose license is required to be changed, added to, or modified. Notwithstanding paragraph (3) of subdivision (a) of Section 12805, the department may issue a temporary driver's license to an applicant who has previously been licensed in this state or in any other state, territory, or possession of the United States, the District of Columbia, the Commonwealth of Puerto Rico, or the Dominion of Canada, notwithstanding that the applicant has failed the written examination on the person's first attempt.

A temporary license permits the operation of a motor vehicle upon the highways for a period of 60 days, if the licensee has the temporary license in his or her immediate possession, and while the department is completing its investigation and determination of all facts relative to the applicant's right to receive a license. The temporary license is invalid when the applicant's license has been issued or refused.

(Amended by Stats. 2016, Ch. 339, Sec. 7. (SB 838) Effective September 13, 2016.)

12508. When in the opinion of the department it would be in the interest of safety, the department may issue, in individual cases, to any applicant for a driver's license, a license limited in duration to less than the regular term. Upon the expiration of a limited term license the department may extend its duration for an additional period without fee but the duration of the license and extensions shall not exceed the term of a regular license.

(Enacted by Stats. 1959, Ch. 3.)

12509. (a) Except as otherwise provided in subdivision (f) of Section 12514, the department, for good cause, may issue an instruction permit to a physically and mentally qualified person who meets one of the following requirements and who applies to the department for an instruction permit:

(1) Is 15 years and 6 months of age or older, and has successfully completed approved courses in automobile driver education and driver training as provided in paragraph (3) of subdivision (a) of Section 12814.6.

(2) Is 15 years and 6 months of age or older, and has successfully completed an approved course in automobile driver education and is taking driver training as provided in paragraph (3) of subdivision (a) of Section 12814.6.

(3) Is 15 years and 6 months of age and enrolled and participating in an integrated automobile driver education and training program as provided in subparagraph (B) of paragraph (3) of subdivision (a) of Section 12814.6.

(4) Is over 16 years of age and is applying for a restricted driver's license pursuant to Section 12814.7.

(5) Is over 17 years and 6 months of age.

(b) The applicant shall qualify for, and be issued, an instruction permit within 12 months from the date of the application.

(c) An instruction permit issued pursuant to subdivision (a) shall entitle the applicant to operate a vehicle, subject to the limitations imposed by this section and any other provisions of law, upon the highways for a period not exceeding 24 months from the date of the application.

(d) Except as provided in Section 12814.6, a person, while having in their immediate possession a valid permit issued pursuant to paragraphs (1) to (3), inclusive, of, and paragraph (5) of, subdivision (a), may operate a motor vehicle, other than a motorcycle, motorized scooter, or a motorized bicycle, when accompanied by, and under the immediate supervision of, a California-licensed driver with a valid license of the appropriate class who is 18 years of age or over and whose driving privilege is not subject to probation. An accompanying licensed driver at all times shall occupy a position within the driver's compartment that would enable the accompanying licensed driver to assist the person in controlling the vehicle as may be necessary to avoid a collision and to provide immediate guidance in the safe operation of the vehicle.

(e) A person, while having in their immediate possession a valid permit issued pursuant to paragraph (4) of subdivision (a), may only operate a government-owned motor vehicle, other than a motorcycle, motorized scooter, or a motorized bicycle, when taking driver training instruction administered by the California National Guard.

(f) The department may also issue an instruction permit to a person who has been issued a valid driver's license to authorize the person to obtain driver training instruction and to practice that instruction in order to obtain another class of driver's license or an endorsement.

(g) The department may further restrict permits issued under subdivision (a) as it may determine to be appropriate to ensure the safe operation of a motor vehicle by the permittee.

(Amended by Stats. 2022, Ch. 295, Sec. 12. (AB 2956) Effective January 1, 2023.)

12509.5. (a) A person shall obtain an instruction permit issued pursuant to this section before operating, or being issued a class M1 or M2 driver's license to operate, a two-wheel motorcycle, motor-driven cycle, motorized bicycle, moped, or bicycle with an attached motor. The person shall meet the following requirements to obtain an instruction permit for purposes of this section:

(1) If age 15 years and 6 months or older, but under the age of 18 years, the applicant shall meet all of the following requirements:

(A) Have a valid class C license or complete driver education and training pursuant to paragraph (3) of subdivision (a) of Section 12814.6.

(B) Successfully complete a motorcyclist safety program that is operated pursuant to Article 2 (commencing with Section 2930) of Chapter 5 of Division 2.

(C) Pass the motorcycle driver's written exam.

(2) If 18 years of age or older, but under 21 years of age, the applicant shall meet both of the following requirements:

(A) Successfully complete a motorcyclist safety program that is operated pursuant to Article 2 (commencing with Section 2930) of Chapter 5 of Division 2.

(B) Pass the motorcycle driver's written exam.

(3) If 21 years of age or older, pass the motorcycle driver's written exam.

(b) A person described in paragraph (1) or (2) of subdivision (a) shall hold an instruction permit issued pursuant to this section for a minimum of six months before being issued a class M1 or M2 license.

(c) A person issued an instruction permit pursuant to this section shall not operate a two-wheel motorcycle, motor-driven cycle, motorized bicycle, moped, or bicycle with an attached motor during the hours of darkness, shall stay off any freeways that have full control of access and have no crossings at grade, and shall not carry any passenger except an instructor licensed under Chapter 1 (commencing with Section 11100) of Division 5 or a qualified instructor as defined in Section 41907 of the Education Code.

(d) An instruction permit issued pursuant to this section shall be valid for a period not exceeding 24 months from the date of application.

(e) The department may perform, during regularly scheduled computer system maintenance and upgrades, any necessary software updates related to the changes made by the addition, during the 2009–10 Regular Session, of this section.

(Amended by Stats. 2019, Ch. 636, Sec. 6. (AB 1810) Effective January 1, 2020.)

12511. No person shall have in his or her possession or otherwise under his or her control more than one driver's license.

(Amended by Stats. 1988, Ch. 1509, Sec. 4.)

12512. Except as provided in Sections 12513, 12514, and 12814.6, no license to drive shall be issued to a person under the age of 18 years.

(Added by Stats. 2000, Ch. 596, Sec. 6. Effective January 1, 2001.)

12513. (a) Upon application, successful completion of tests and compliance with Sections 17700 to 17705, inclusive, the department may issue a junior permit to any person 14 years of age, but less than 18, who establishes eligibility as required by this section. A person is eligible when, in the opinion of the department, any one or more of the following circumstances exist:

School or other transportation facilities are inadequate for regular attendance at school and at activities authorized by the school. The application for a junior permit shall be accompanied by a signed statement from the school principal verifying such facts. A junior permit issued under this subsection shall be restricted to operating a vehicle from residence to the school and return.

Reasonable transportation facilities are inadequate and operation of a vehicle by a minor is necessary due to illness of a family member. The application shall be accompanied by a signed statement from a physician familiar with the condition, containing a diagnosis and probable date when sufficient recovery will have been made to terminate the emergency.

Transportation facilities are inadequate, and use of a motor vehicle is necessary in the transportation to and from the employment of the applicant and the applicant's income from such employment is essential in the support of the family, or where the applicant's operation of a motor vehicle is essential to an enterprise from which an appreciable portion of the income of the family will be derived. The application shall be accompanied by a signed statement from the parents or the guardian, setting forth the reasons a permit is necessary under this subsection.

(b) The existence of public transportation at reasonable intervals within one mile of the residence of the applicant may be considered adequate grounds for refusal of a junior permit.

(c) The department shall impose restrictions upon junior permits appropriate to the conditions and area under which they are intended to be used.

(Amended by Stats. 1969, Ch. 947, Sec. 1.)

12514. (a) Junior permits issued pursuant to Section 12513 shall not be valid for a period exceeding that established on the original request as the approximate date the minor's operation of a vehicle will no longer be necessary. In any event, no permit shall be valid on or after the 18th birthday of the applicant.

(b) The department may revoke any permit when to do so is necessary for the welfare of the minor or in the interests of safety.

(c) If conditions or location of residence, which required the minor's operation of a vehicle, change prior to expiration of the permit, the department may cancel the permit.

(d) Upon a determination that the permittee has operated a vehicle in violation of restrictions, the department shall revoke the permit.

(e) A junior permit is a form of driver's license that shall include all information required by subdivision (a) of Section 12811 except for an engraved picture or photograph of the permittee, and is subject to all provisions of this code applying to driver's licenses, except as otherwise provided in this section and Section 12513.

(f) An instruction permit valid for a period of not more than six months may be issued after eligibility has been established under Section 12513.

(g) The department shall cancel any permit six months from the date of issuance unless the permittee has complied with one of the conditions prescribed by paragraph (3) of subdivision (a) of Section 12814.6.

(Amended by Stats. 2000, Ch. 1035, Sec. 15. Effective January 1, 2001.)

12515. (a) No person under the age of 18 years shall be employed for compensation by another for the purpose of driving a motor vehicle on the highways.

(b) No person under the age of 21 years shall be employed for compensation by another to drive, and no person under the age of 21 years may drive a motor vehicle, as defined in Section 34500 or subdivision (b) of Section 15210, that is engaged in interstate commerce, or any motor vehicle that is engaged in the interstate or intrastate transportation of hazardous material, as defined in Section 353.

(Amended by Stats. 1988, Ch. 1509, Sec. 5.)

12516. It is unlawful for any person under the age of 18 years to drive a school bus transporting pupils to or from school.

(Enacted by Stats. 1959, Ch. 3.)

12517. (a) (1) A person may not operate a schoolbus while transporting pupils unless that person has in his or her immediate possession a valid driver's license for the appropriate class of vehicle to be driven endorsed for schoolbus and passenger transportation.

(2) When transporting one or more pupils at or below the 12th-grade level to or from a public or private school or to or from public or private school activities, the person described in paragraph (1) shall have in his or her immediate possession a certificate issued by the department to permit the operation of a schoolbus.

(b) A person may not operate a school pupil activity bus unless that person has in his or her immediate possession a valid driver's license for the appropriate class of vehicle to be driven endorsed for passenger transportation. When transporting one or more pupils at or below the 12th-grade level to or from public or private school activities, the person shall also have in his or her immediate possession a certificate issued by the department to permit the operation of school pupil activity buses.

(c) The applicant for a certificate to operate a schoolbus or school pupil activity bus shall meet the eligibility and training requirements specified for schoolbus and school pupil activity busdrivers in this code, the Education Code, and regulations adopted by the Department of the California Highway Patrol, and, in addition to the fee authorized in Section 2427, shall pay a fee of twenty-five dollars ($25) with the application for issuance of an original certificate, and a fee of twelve dollars ($12) for the renewal of that certificate.

(Amended by Stats. 2006, Ch. 574, Sec. 7. Effective January 1, 2007.)

12517.1. (a) A "schoolbus accident" means any of the following:

(1) A motor vehicle accident resulting in property damage in excess of one thousand dollars ($1,000), or personal injury, on public or private property, and involving a schoolbus, youth bus, school pupil activity bus, or general public paratransit vehicle transporting a pupil.

(2) A collision between a vehicle and a pupil or a schoolbus driver while the pupil or driver is crossing the highway when the schoolbus flashing red signal lamps are required to be operated pursuant to Section 22112 or when the schoolbus is stopped for the purpose of loading or unloading pupils.

(3) Injury of a pupil inside a vehicle described in paragraph (1) as a result of acceleration, deceleration, or other movement of the vehicle.

(b) The Department of the California Highway Patrol shall investigate all schoolbus accidents, except that accidents involving only property damage and occurring entirely on private property shall be investigated only if they involve a violation of this code.

(c) This section shall become operative on January 1, 2017.

(Repealed (in Sec. 23) and added by Stats. 2015, Ch. 451, Sec. 24. (SB 491) Effective January 1, 2016. Section operative January 1, 2017, by its own provisions.)

12517.2. (a) Applicants for an original or renewal certificate to drive a schoolbus, school pupil activity bus, youth bus, general public paratransit vehicle, or farm labor vehicle shall submit a report of a medical examination of the applicant given not more than two years prior to the date of the application by a physician licensed to practice medicine, a licensed advanced practice registered nurse qualified to perform a medical examination, a licensed physician assistant, or a licensed doctor of chiropractic listed on the most current National Registry of Certified Medical Examiners, as adopted by the United States Department of Transportation, as published by the notice in the Federal Register, Volume 77, Number 77, Friday, April 20, 2012, on pages 24104 to 24135, inclusive, and pursuant to Section 391.42 of Title 49 of the Code of Federal Regulations. The report shall be on a form approved by the department.

(b) Schoolbus drivers, within the same month of reaching 65 years of age and each 12th month thereafter, shall undergo a medical examination, pursuant to Section 12804.9, and shall submit a report of that medical examination on a form as specified in subdivision (a).

(Amended by Stats. 2013, Ch. 160, Sec. 1. (AB 722) Effective January 1, 2014.)

12517.3. (a) (1) An applicant for an original certificate to drive a schoolbus, school pupil activity bus, youth bus, or general public paratransit vehicle shall be fingerprinted by the Department of the California Highway Patrol, on a form provided or approved by the Department of the California Highway Patrol for submission to the Department of Justice, utilizing the Applicant Expedite Service or an electronic fingerprinting system.

(2) An applicant fingerprint form shall be processed and returned to the office of the Department of the California Highway Patrol from which it originated not later than 15 working days from the date on which the fingerprint form was received by the Department of Justice, unless circumstances, other than the administrative duties of the Department of Justice, warrant further investigation.

(3) Applicant fingerprints that are submitted by utilizing an electronic fingerprinting system shall be processed and returned to the appropriate office of the Department of the California Highway Patrol within three working days.

(4) The commissioner may utilize the California Law Enforcement Telecommunications System to conduct a preliminary criminal and driver history check to determine an applicant's eligibility to hold an original or renewal certificate to drive a schoolbus, school pupil activity bus, youth bus, or general public paratransit vehicle.

(b) (1) Notwithstanding subdivision (a), an applicant for an original certificate to drive a schoolbus, school pupil activity bus, youth bus, or general public paratransit vehicle may be fingerprinted by a public law enforcement agency, a school district, or a county office of education utilizing an electronic fingerprinting system with terminals managed by the Department of Justice.

(2) The Department of Justice shall provide the fingerprint information processed pursuant to this subdivision to the appropriate office of the Department of the California Highway Patrol within three working days of receipt of the information.

(3) An applicant for an original certificate to drive an ambulance shall submit a completed fingerprint card to the department.

(Amended by Stats. 2006, Ch. 311, Sec. 7. Effective January 1, 2007.)

12517.4. This section governs the issuance of a certificate to drive a schoolbus, school pupil activity bus, youth bus, general public paratransit vehicle, or farm labor vehicle.

(a) The driver certificate shall be issued only to applicants meeting all applicable provisions of this code and passing the examinations prescribed by the department and the Department of the California Highway Patrol. The examinations shall be conducted by the Department of the California Highway Patrol, pursuant to Sections 12517, 12519, 12522, 12523, and 12523.5.

(b) A temporary driver certificate shall be issued by the Department of the California Highway Patrol after an applicant has cleared a criminal history background check by the Department of Justice and, if applicable, the Federal Bureau of Investigation, and has passed the examinations and meets all other applicable provisions of this code.

(c) A permanent driver's certificate shall be issued by the department after an applicant has passed all tests and met all applicable provisions of this code. Certificates are valid for a maximum of five years and shall expire on the fifth birthday following the issuance of an original certificate or the expiration of the certificate renewed.

(d) A holder of a certificate may not violate any restriction placed on the certificate. Depending upon the type of vehicle used in the driving test and the abilities and physical condition of the applicant, the Department of the California Highway Patrol and the department may place restrictions on a certificate to assure the safe operation of a motor vehicle and safe transportation of passengers. These restrictions may include, but are not limited to, all of the following:

(1) Automatic transmission only.

(2) Hydraulic brakes only.

(3) Type 2 bus only.

(4) Conventional or type 2 bus only.

(5) Two-axle motor truck or passenger vehicle only.

(e) A holder of a certificate may not drive a motor vehicle equipped with a two-speed rear axle unless the certificate is endorsed: "May drive vehicle with two-speed rear axle."

(f) This section shall become operative on September 20, 2005.

(Amended by Stats. 2004, Ch. 952, Sec. 5. Effective January 1, 2005. Amended version operative September 20, 2005, pursuant to earlier operation of new subdivision (f).)

12517.45. (a) A person shall not operate a motor vehicle described in subdivision (k) of Section 545 while transporting school pupils at or below the 12th-grade level to or from a public or private school or to or from public or private school activities, unless all of the following requirements are met:

(1) The person has in his or her immediate possession all of the following:

(A) A valid driver's license of a class appropriate to the vehicle driven and that is endorsed for passenger transportation.

(B) Either a certificate to drive a schoolbus as described in Section 40082 of the Education Code, or a certificate to drive a school pupil activity bus as described in Section 40083 of the Education Code, issued by the department in accordance with eligibility and training requirements specified by the department, the State Department of Education, and the Department of the California Highway Patrol.

(C) A parental authorization form for each pupil signed by a parent or a legal guardian of the pupil that gives permission for that pupil to be transported to or from the school or school-related activity.

(2) (A) The motor vehicle has passed an annual inspection conducted by the Department of the California Highway Patrol and is in compliance with the charter-party carrier's responsibilities under Section 5374 of the Public Utilities Code.

(B) The Department of the California Highway Patrol may charge a charter-party carrier a reasonable fee sufficient to cover the costs incurred by the Department of the California Highway Patrol in conducting the annual inspection of a motor vehicle.

(b) A driver of a motor vehicle described in subdivision (k) of Section 545 shall comply with the duties specified in subdivision (a) of Section 5384.1 of the Public Utilities Code.

(Added by Stats. 2008, Ch. 649, Sec. 4. Effective January 1, 2009.)

12517.5. A person who is employed as a driver of a paratransit vehicle shall not operate that vehicle unless the person meets both of the following requirements:

(a) Has in his or her immediate possession a valid driver's license of a class appropriate to the vehicle driven.

(b) Successfully completes, during each calendar year, four hours of training administered by, or at the direction of, his or her employer or the employer's agent on the safe operation of paratransit vehicles and four hours of training on the special transportation needs of the persons he or she is employed to transport.

This subdivision may be satisfied if the driver receives transportation training or a certificate, or both, pursuant to Section 40082, 40083, 40085, 40085.5, or 40088 of the Education Code.

The employer shall maintain a record of the current training received by each driver in his or her employ and shall present that record on demand to any authorized representative of the Department of the California Highway Patrol.

(Amended by Stats. 2002, Ch. 664, Sec. 217. Effective January 1, 2003.)

12518. The provisions of Section 12504 shall apply to any nonresident who is under the age of 18 years and who is a member of the armed forces of the United States on active duty within this state, except that the maximum period during which such nonresident may operate a motor vehicle in this state without obtaining a driver's license or a nonresident minor's certificate shall be limited to a period of 60 days immediately following the entry of such nonresident into this state.

(Amended by Stats. 1971, Ch. 1748.)

12519. (a) No person shall operate a farm labor vehicle unless the person has in his or her possession a driver's license for the appropriate class of vehicle to be driven, endorsed for passenger transportation, and, when transporting one or more farmworker passengers, a certificate issued by the department to permit the operation of farm labor vehicles.

(b) The applicants shall present evidence that they have successfully completed the driver training course developed by the Department of Education pursuant to Section 40081 of the Education Code, and approved by the Department of Motor Vehicles and the Department of the California Highway Patrol before a permanent certificate will be issued.

(c) The certificate shall be issued only to applicants qualified by examinations prescribed by the Department of Motor Vehicles and the Department of the California Highway Patrol and upon payment of a fee of twelve dollars ($12) to the Department of the California Highway Patrol.The examinations shall be conducted by the Department of the California Highway Patrol.

(d) A person holding a valid certificate to permit the operation of a farm labor vehicle, issued prior to January 1, 1991, shall not be required to reapply for a certificate to satisfy any additional requirements imposed by the act adding this subdivision until the certificate he or she holds expires or is canceled or revoked.

(Amended by Stats. 1990, Ch. 1360, Sec. 17.)

12520. (a) No person employed as a tow truck driver, as defined in Section 2430.1, shall operate a tow truck unless that person has, in his or her immediate possession, a valid California driver's license of an appropriate class for the vehicle to be driven, and a tow truck driver certificate issued by the department or a temporary tow truck driver certificate issued by the Department of the California Highway Patrol, to permit the operation of the tow truck.

(b) When notified that the applicant has been cleared through the Department of Justice or the Federal Bureau of Investigation, or both, and if the applicant meets all other applicable provisions of this code, the department shall issue a permanent tow truck driver certificate. The permanent tow truck driver certificate shall be valid for a maximum of five years and shall expire on the same date as that of the applicant's driver's license.

(Amended by Stats. 1996, Ch. 1043, Sec. 2. Effective January 1, 1997.)

12521. An operator of a tour bus shall, at all times when operating the tour bus, do all the following:

(a) Use a safety belt.

(b) Report any accidents involving the tour bus to the Department of the California Highway Patrol.

(Repealed and added by Stats. 1990, Ch. 1360, Sec. 22.5.)

12522. (a) Every person who operates a schoolbus or youth bus in the transportation of school pupils shall, in addition to any other requirement for a schoolbus or youth bus driver's certificate, qualify by an examination on first aid practices deemed necessary for schoolbus operators or youth bus operators. Standards for examination shall be determined by the Emergency Medical Services Authority after consultation with the State Department of Education, the Department of Motor Vehicles, and the Department of the California Highway Patrol. The local school authority employing the applicant shall provide a course of instruction concerning necessary first aid practices.

(b) The Department of the California Highway Patrol shall conduct the first aid examination as part of the examination of applicants for a schoolbus or youth bus driver's certificate and shall certify to the Department of Motor Vehicles that the applicant has satisfactorily demonstrated his or her qualifications in first aid practices, knowledge of schoolbus or youth bus laws and regulations, and ability to operate a schoolbus or youth bus. The first aid certifications shall be valid for the term of the schoolbus or youth bus driver's certificate.

(c) The first aid examination may be waived if the applicant possesses either of the following minimum qualifications:

(1) A current first aid certificate issued by the American Red Cross or by an organization whose first aid training program is at least equivalent to the American Red Cross first aid training program, as determined by the Emergency Medical Services Authority. The Emergency Medical Services Authority may charge a fee, sufficient to cover its administrative

costs of approval, to an organization that applies to have its first aid training program approved for purposes of this paragraph.

(2) A current license as a physician and surgeon, osteopathic physician and surgeon, or registered nurse, or a current certificate as a physician's assistant or emergency medical technician. The first aid certificate or license shall be maintained throughout the term of the schoolbus or youth bus driver's certificate and shall be presented upon demand of any traffic officer. The schoolbus or youth bus driver's certificate shall not be valid during any time that the driver fails to maintain and possess that license or certificate after the first aid examination has been waived.

(Amended by Stats. 1993, Ch. 226, Sec. 15. Effective January 1, 1994.)

12523. (a) No person shall operate a youth bus without having in possession a valid driver's license of the appropriate class, endorsed for passenger transportation and a certificate issued by the department to permit the operation of a youth bus.

(b) Applicants for a certificate to drive a youth bus shall present evidence that they have successfully completed a driver training course administered by or at the direction of their employer consisting of a minimum of 10 hours of classroom instruction covering applicable laws and regulations and defensive driving practices and a minimum of 10 hours of behind-the-wheel training in a vehicle to be used as a youth bus. Applicants seeking to renew a certificate to drive a youth bus shall present evidence that they have received two hours of refresher training during each 12 months of driver certificate validity.

(c) The driver certificate shall be issued only to applicants qualified by examinations prescribed by the Department of Motor Vehicles and the Department of the California Highway Patrol, and upon payment of a fee of twenty-five dollars ($25) for an original certificate and twelve dollars ($12) for the renewal of that certificate to the Department of the California Highway Patrol. The examinations shall be conducted by the Department of the California Highway Patrol. The Department of Motor Vehicles may deny, suspend, or revoke a certificate valid for driving a youth bus for the causes specified in this code or in regulations adopted pursuant to this code.

(d) An operator of a youth bus shall, at all times when operating a youth bus, do all of the following:

(1) Use seat belts.

(2) Refrain from smoking tobacco products.

(3) Report any accidents reportable under Section 16000 to the Department of the California Highway Patrol.

(e) A person holding a valid certificate to permit the operation of a youth bus, issued prior to January 1, 1991, shall not be required to reapply for a certificate to satisfy any additional requirements imposed by the act adding this subdivision until the certificate he or she holds expires or is canceled or revoked.

(f) For purposes of this section, "smoking" has the same meaning as in subdivision (c) of Section 22950.5 of the Business and Professions Code.

(g) For purposes of this section, "tobacco product" means a product or device as defined in subdivision (d) of Section 22950.5 of the Business and Professions Code.

(Amended by Stats. 2016, 2nd Ex. Sess., Ch. 7, Sec. 27. (SB 5 2x) Effective June 9, 2016.)

12523.5. (a) No person shall operate a general public paratransit vehicle unless he or she has in his or her possession a valid driver's license of the appropriate class endorsed for passenger transportation when operating a vehicle designed, used, or maintained for carrying more than 10 persons including the driver and either (1) a certificate issued by the department to permit the operation of a general public paratransit vehicle, or (2) a certificate issued by the department to drive a schoolbus or school pupil activity bus pursuant to Section 12517.

(b) Applicants for a certificate to drive a general public paratransit vehicle shall pay a fee to the Department of the California Highway Patrol of twenty-five dollars ($25) for an original certificate and twelve dollars ($12) for a renewal certificate. Applicants for an original certificate shall present evidence that they have successfully completed a driver training course consisting of a minimum of 40 hours of instruction within the previous two years. The instruction shall have covered applicable laws and regulations and defensive driving practices, a minimum of eight hours of certified defensive driving, and a minimum of 20 hours of behind-the-wheel training in a vehicle to be used as a general public paratransit vehicle. Applicants seeking to renew a certificate valid for driving a general public paratransit vehicle shall present evidence that they have received two hours of refresher training during each 12 months of driver certificate validity.

(c) The driver certificate shall be issued only to applicants qualified by examinations prescribed by the Department of Motor Vehicles and the Department of the California Highway Patrol. The examinations shall be conducted by the Department of the California Highway Patrol. The Department of Motor Vehicles may deny, suspend, or revoke a certificate valid for driving a general public paratransit vehicle for the causes specified in this code or the Education Code or in regulations adopted pursuant to this code or the Education Code.

(d) An operator of a general public paratransit vehicle shall do all of the following:

(1) Use seatbelts.

(2) Refrain from smoking.

(3) Report any accident reportable under Section 16000 to the Department of the California Highway Patrol.

(e) A person holding a valid certificate to permit the operation of a general public paratransit vehicle, issued prior to January 1, 1991, shall not be required to reapply for a certificate to satisfy any additional requirements imposed by the act adding this subdivision until the certificate he or she holds expires or is canceled or revoked.

(Amended by Stats. 1990, Ch. 1360, Sec. 24.)

12523.6. (a) (1) On and after March 1, 1998, no person who is employed primarily as a driver of a motor vehicle that is used for the transportation of persons with developmental disabilities, as defined in subdivision (a) of Section 4512 of the Welfare and Institutions Code, shall operate that motor vehicle unless that person has in his or her possession a valid driver's license of the appropriate class and a valid special driver certificate issued by the department.

(2) This subdivision only applies to a person who is employed by a business, a nonprofit organization, or a state or local public agency.

(b) The special driver certificate shall be issued only to an applicant who has cleared a criminal history background check by the Department of Justice and, if applicable, by the Federal Bureau of Investigation.

(1) In order to determine the applicant's suitability as the driver of a vehicle used for the transportation of persons with developmental disabilities, the Department of the California Highway Patrol shall require the applicant to furnish to that department, on a form provided or approved by that department for submission to the Department of Justice, a full set of fingerprints sufficient to enable a criminal background investigation.

(2) Except as provided in paragraph (3), an applicant shall furnish to the Department of the California Highway Patrol evidence of having resided in this state for seven consecutive years immediately prior to the date of application for the certificate.

(3) If an applicant is unable to furnish the evidence required under paragraph (2), the Department of the California Highway Patrol shall require the applicant to furnish an additional full set of fingerprints. That department shall submit those fingerprint cards to the Department of Justice. The Department of Justice shall, in turn, submit the additional full set of fingerprints required under this paragraph to the Federal Bureau of Investigation for a national criminal history record check.

(4) Applicant fingerprint forms shall be processed and returned to the area office of the Department of the California Highway Patrol from which they originated not later than 15 working days from the date on which the fingerprint forms were received by the Department of Justice, unless circumstances, other than the administrative duties of the Department

of Justice, warrant further investigation. Upon implementation of an electronic fingerprinting system with terminals located statewide and managed by the Department of Justice, the Department of Justice shall ascertain the information required pursuant to this subdivision within three working days.

(5) The applicant shall pay, in addition to the fees authorized in Section 2427, a fee of twenty-five dollars ($25) for an original certificate and twelve dollars ($12) for the renewal of that certificate to the Department of the California Highway Patrol.

(c) A certificate issued under this section shall not be deemed a certification to operate a particular vehicle that otherwise requires a driver's license or endorsement for a particular class under this code.

(d) On or after March 1, 1998, no person who operates a business or a nonprofit organization or agency shall employ a person who is employed primarily as a driver of a motor vehicle for hire that is used for the transportation of persons with developmental disabilities unless the employed person operates the motor vehicle in compliance with subdivision (a).

(e) Nothing in this section precludes an employer of persons who are occasionally used as drivers of motor vehicles for the transportation of persons with developmental disabilities from requiring those persons, as a condition of employment, to obtain a special driver certificate pursuant to this section or precludes any volunteer driver from applying for a special driver certificate.

(f) As used in this section, a person is employed primarily as driver if that person performs at least 50 percent of his or her time worked including, but not limited to, time spent assisting persons onto and out of the vehicle, or at least 20 hours a week, whichever is less, as a compensated driver of a motor vehicle for hire for the transportation of persons with developmental disabilities.

(g) This section does not apply to any person who has successfully completed a background investigation prescribed by law, including, but not limited to, health care transport vehicle operators, or to the operator of a taxicab regulated pursuant to Section 21100. This section does not apply to a person who holds a valid certificate, other than a farm labor vehicle driver certificate, issued under Section 12517.4 or 12527. This section does not apply to a driver who provides transportation on a noncommercial basis to persons with developmental disabilities.

(Amended by Stats. 1998, Ch. 877, Sec. 53. Effective January 1, 1999.)

12524. A class A, class B, or class C driver's licenseholder shall not operate a vehicle hauling highway route controlled quantities of radioactive materials, as defined in Section 173.403 of Title 49 of the Code of Federal Regulations, unless the driver possesses a valid license of the appropriate class and a certificate of training as required in Section 397.101(e) of Title 49 of the Code of Federal Regulations.

(Amended by Stats. 2017, Ch. 397, Sec. 2. (SB 810) Effective January 1, 2018.)

12525. Mechanics or other maintenance personnel may operate vehicles requiring a schoolbus endorsement or certificates issued pursuant to Section 2512, 12517, 12519, 12523, or 12523.5 without obtaining a schoolbus endorsement or those certificates if that operation is within the course of their employment and they do not transport pupils or members of the public.

(Amended by Stats. 2006, Ch. 574, Sec. 8. Effective January 1, 2007.)

12527. In addition to satisfying all requirements specified in this code and in regulations adopted pursuant to this code, an applicant for an ambulance driver certificate shall satisfy all of the following requirements:

(a) Except as otherwise provided, every ambulance driver responding to an emergency call or transporting patients shall be at least 18 years of age, hold a driver's license valid in California, possess a valid ambulance driver certificate, and be trained and competent in ambulance operation and the use of safety and emergency care equipment required by the California Code of Regulations governing ambulances.

(b) Except as provided in subdivision (e), a person shall not operate an ambulance unless the person has in their immediate possession a driver's license for the appropriate class of vehicle to be driven and a certificate issued by the department to permit the operation of an ambulance.

(c) An ambulance driver certificate shall only be issued by the department upon the successful completion of an examination conducted by the department and subject to all of the following conditions:

(1) An applicant for an original or renewal driver certificate shall submit a report of medical examination on a form approved by the department, the Federal Motor Carrier Safety Administration, or the Federal Aviation Administration. The report shall be dated within the two years preceding the application date.

(2) An applicant for an original driver certificate shall submit an acceptable fingerprint card.

(3) The certificate to drive an ambulance shall be valid for a period not exceeding five years and six months and shall expire on the same date as the driver's license. The ambulance driver certificate shall only be valid when both of the following conditions exist:

(A) The certificate is accompanied by a medical examination certificate that was issued within the preceding two years and approved by the department, the Federal Motor Carrier Safety Administration, or the Federal Aviation Administration.

(B) A copy of the medical examination report based upon which the certificate was issued is on file with the department.

(4) The ambulance driver certificate is renewable under conditions prescribed by the department. Except as provided in paragraphs (2) and (3) of subdivision (d), an applicant renewing an ambulance driver certificate shall possess certificates or licenses evidencing compliance with the emergency medical training and educational standards for ambulance attendants established by the Emergency Medical Services Authority.

(d) (1) Every ambulance driver shall have been trained to assist the ambulance attendant in the care and handling of the ill and injured.

Except as provided in paragraph (2), the driver of a California-based ambulance shall, within one year of initial issuance of the driver's ambulance driver certificate, possess a certificate or license evidencing compliance with the emergency medical training and educational standards established for ambulance attendants by the Emergency Medical Services Authority. In those emergencies requiring both the regularly assigned driver and attendant to be utilized in providing patient care, the specialized emergency medical training requirement shall not apply to persons temporarily detailed to drive the ambulance.

(2) Paragraph (1) does not apply to an ambulance driver who is a volunteer driver for a volunteer ambulance service if the service is provided in the unincorporated areas of a county with a population of less than 125,000 persons, as determined by the most recent federal decennial census. The operation of an ambulance subject to this paragraph shall only apply if the name of the driver and the volunteer ambulance service and facts substantiating the public health necessity for an exemption are submitted to the department by the county board of supervisors and at least one of the following entities in the county where the driver operates the ambulance:

(A) The county health officer.

(B) The county medical care committee.

(C) The local emergency medical services agency coordinator.

(3) The information required by paragraph (2) shall be submitted to the department at the time of application for an ambulance driver certificate. Upon receipt of that information, the department shall restrict the certificate holder to driving an ambulance for the volunteer ambulance service.

(4) The director may terminate any certificate issued pursuant to paragraph (2) at any time the department determines that the qualifying conditions specified no longer exist.

(5) The exemption granted pursuant to paragraph (2) shall expire on the expiration date of the ambulance driver certificate.

(e) An ambulance certificate is not required for persons operating

ambulances in the line of duty as salaried, regular, full-time police officers, deputy sheriffs, members of a fire department of a public agency, or members of a fire department of a federally recognized tribe. This exemption excludes volunteers and part-time employees or members of a department whose duties are primarily clerical or administrative.
(Amended by Stats. 2021, Ch. 282, Sec. 4. (AB 798) Effective January 1, 2022.)

Article 2. Student Licenses

(Article 2 enacted by Stats. 1959, Ch. 3.)

12650. (a) Any student over 15 years of age taking a course in automobile driver training, maintained pursuant to Article 12 (commencing with Section 41900) of Chapter 5 of Part 24 of Division 3 of Title 2 of the Education Code, in a secondary school or enrolled in a driver training course offered by a private or parochial school of secondary level may apply to the principal of the school for a student license.

(b) The application shall be signed by the applicant before the principal of the school, or a staff member assigned to such duty. The application shall be accompanied by a statement signed by the parents or guardian or person having custody of the minor, consenting to the issuance of a student license to the student and accepting liability for civil damages arising out of the student driving a motor vehicle upon a highway as provided for in Division 9 (commencing with Section 17000) of this code.

(c) Notwithstanding any other provision of this code, if the person or persons required to sign a statement consenting to the issuance of a student license and accepting liability as provided in subdivision (b) are not residents of this state and the student resides at the school, or the student is a foster child with no parents or guardian available to sign this statement, the application may be accepted if the principal of the school or staff member assigned such duties certifies that the school has filed with the department a certificate of insurance carrier or surety company that there is in effect a policy or bond meeting the requirements of Section 16056, and that such policy or bond will cover the liability for civil damages arising out of the student driving a motor vehicle upon a highway.
(Amended by Stats. 1977, Ch. 579.)

12651. The principal or staff member assigned such duty may issue or reissue a student license without cost whenever in his opinion the applicant is qualified to take the course of instruction and has filed a proper application therefor.
(Amended by Stats. 1978, Ch. 162.)

12652. A student license shall limit the operation of a motor vehicle to such times as the licensee is taking driver training in connection with the driver education program and then only at the direction and under the supervision of the instructor and shall be valid only for the period covered by the course and for not more than one year from the date of issuance.
(Enacted by Stats. 1959, Ch. 3.)

12653. A student license may be canceled by the principal of the school or by the department whenever, in the opinion of either, the safety of the licensee or other persons requires the action and shall be canceled upon the written request of the parent or other person who signed the consent to issue the license.
(Amended by Stats. 1978, Ch. 162.)

12660. (a) The department may establish a program authorizing a driving school licensed under Chapter 1 (commencing with Section 11100) of Division 5 to issue a student license to operate a class 3 vehicle to any applicant 15 years of age or older, subject to the conditions specified in subdivision (d).

(b) The department may charge any driving school participating in the program a fee not to exceed two dollars ($2) per applicant to recover the department's cost in establishing and monitoring the program. The fee that a participating school may charge an applicant for a student license may not exceed the fee that the department charges the school for the license.

(c) The department may remove a driving school from the program if the department determines that the school has issued a student license fraudulently, or has otherwise not followed the requirements of the program. This fraudulent conduct may result in cause for suspension or revocation of the driving school license.

(d) (1) Applicants shall meet the qualification standards specified in regulations adopted by the department pursuant to Section 12661. The student license application shall be accompanied by a statement signed by the parents or guardian, or person having custody of the minor, consenting to the issuance of a student license to the applicant.

(2) No licensed driving school may issue a student license to any applicant under the age of 17 years and 6 months unless that applicant shows proof of satisfactory completion of an approved course in driver education, pursuant to standards specified in paragraph (4) of subdivision (a) of Section 12814.6.

(e) A driving school owner or an independent instructor licensed under Section 11105.5 shall maintain liability insurance for bodily injury or property damage caused by the use of a motor vehicle in driving instruction, and for the liability of the driving school, the instructor, and the student, in accordance with Section 11103.

(f) The department shall submit a report to the Legislature on the progress of the program established under subdivision (a) within two years after the program is implemented. The report shall include, but not be limited to, an analysis of the costs and benefits of the program and shall include recommendations by the department.

(g) The director may terminate the program at any time the department determines that continued operation of the program would have an adverse effect on traffic safety. The finding upon which the termination is based shall be reported to the Legislature within 30 days following termination of the program.
(Amended by Stats. 2003, Ch. 768, Sec. 3. Effective January 1, 2004.)

12661. The department, in consultation with the State Department of Education, shall adopt regulations for the issuance of student licenses pursuant to Section 12660. The department and the State Department of Education shall seek advice and input on those regulations from the public, law enforcement, and the driving school industry. The regulations shall include all of the following:

(a) Standards and procedures for the issuance of student licenses pursuant to Section 12660, including the determination of an applicant's qualifications under Section 12805.

(b) Standards and procedures to ensure that all records of a driving school relating to the physical or mental condition of any student are confidential, except to the department.

(c) Standards and procedures for monitoring the issuance of student licenses.

(d) A requirement that each student license issued pursuant to Section 12660 be accompanied by a verbal and written description of the limitations of that license in terms of duration and use.

(e) Any other requirements necessary to carry out Section 12660.
(Added by Stats. 1987, Ch. 1029, Sec. 2.)

Article 3. Issuance and Renewal of Licenses

(Article 3 enacted by Stats. 1959, Ch. 3.)

12800. Each application for an original or a renewal of a driver's license shall contain all of the following information:

(a) (1) The applicant's true full name, age, gender category, mailing address, residence address, and, except as provided in Section 12801, social security account number.

(2) The applicant shall choose their gender category of female, male, or nonbinary.

(3) The department shall not require documentation for an original driver's license applicant's initial choice of a gender category or a licensed applicant's request for an amendment to a gender category other than the following:

(A) The applicant's self-certification of their chosen gender category.

(B) Documentation required by this code and the California Code of Regulations as necessary to establish that an applicant is lawfully entitled to a license.

(b) A brief description of the applicant for the purpose of identification.

(c) A legible print of the thumb or finger of the applicant.

(d) The type of motor vehicle or combination of vehicles the applicant desires to operate.

(e) Whether the applicant has ever previously been licensed as a driver and, if so, when and in what state or country and whether or not the license has been suspended or revoked and, if so, the date of and reason for the suspension or revocation.

(f) Whether the applicant has ever previously been refused a driver's license in this state and, if so, the date of and the reason for the refusal.

(g) Whether the applicant, within the last three years, has experienced, on one or more occasions, either a lapse of consciousness or an episode of marked confusion caused by a condition that may bring about recurrent lapses, or whether the applicant has a disease, disorder, or disability that affects the applicant's ability to exercise reasonable and ordinary control in operating a motor vehicle upon a highway.

(h) Whether the applicant understands traffic signs and signals.

(i) Whether the applicant has ever previously been issued an identification card by the department.

(j) Any other information that is necessary to enable the department to determine whether the applicant is entitled to a license under this code.

(k) (1) Commencing January 1, 2027, a statement informing the person that they may also need to change their address for purposes of their vehicle registration.

(2) The information described in paragraph (1) shall be given to the person orally if the driver's license application or renewal is done in person.

(l) The department shall adopt regulations to provide a process for an amendment to a gender category.

(m) This section shall become operative on January 1, 2019.

(n) This section shall become inoperative on the effective date of a final judicial determination made by any court of appellate jurisdiction that any provision of the act that added this section, or its application, either in whole or in part, is enjoined, found unconstitutional, or held invalid for any reason. The department shall post this information on its internet website.

(Amended (as added by Stats. 2017, Ch. 853, Sec. 16) by Stats. 2022, Ch. 969, Sec. 1. (AB 2594) Effective January 1, 2023. Section operative January 1, 2019, by its own provisions, if a judicial determination as described in subd. (n) has not taken effect. Conditionally inoperative as provided in subd. (n). If a judicial determination as described in subd. (n) takes effect on or after January 1, 2019, see the later operative section amended by Sec. 2 of Stats. 2022, of Ch. 969.)

12800. Each application for an original or a renewal of a driver's license shall contain all of the following information:

(a) (1) The applicant's true full name, age, gender category, mailing address, residence address, and social security account number.

(2) The applicant shall choose their gender category of female, male, or nonbinary.

(3) The department shall not require documentation for an original driver's license applicant's initial choice of a gender category or a licensed applicant's request for an amendment to a gender category other than the following:

(A) The applicant's self-certification of their chosen gender category.

(B) Documentation required by this code and the California Code of Regulations as necessary to establish that an applicant is lawfully entitled to a license.

(b) A brief description of the applicant for the purpose of identification.

(c) A legible print of the thumb or finger of the applicant, which has been confirmed by the department to be on file prior to issuance of a driver's license.

(d) The type of motor vehicle or combination of vehicles the applicant desires to operate.

(e) Whether the applicant has ever previously been licensed as a driver and, if so, when and in what state or country and whether or not the license has been suspended or revoked and, if so, the date of and reason for the suspension or revocation.

(f) Whether the applicant has ever previously been refused a driver's license in this state and, if so, the date of and the reason for the refusal.

(g) Whether the applicant, within the last three years, has experienced, on one or more occasions, either a lapse of consciousness or an episode of marked confusion caused by a condition that may bring about recurrent lapses, or whether the applicant has a disease, disorder, or disability that affects their ability to exercise reasonable and ordinary control in operating a motor vehicle upon a highway.

(h) Whether the applicant understands traffic signs and signals.

(i) Whether the applicant has ever previously been issued an identification card by the department.

(j) Any other information that is necessary to enable the department to determine whether the applicant is entitled to a license under this code.

(k) (1) Commencing January 1, 2027, a statement informing the person that they may also need to change their address for purposes of their vehicle registration.

(2) The information described in paragraph (1) shall be given to the person orally if the driver's license application or renewal is done in person.

(l) The department shall adopt regulations to provide a process for an amendment to a gender category.

(m) This section shall become operative on the effective date of a final judicial determination made by any court of appellate jurisdiction that any provision of the act that added this section, or its application, either in whole or in part, is enjoined, found unconstitutional, or held invalid for any reason. The department shall post this information on its internet website.

(Amended (as amended by Stats. 2021, Ch. 254, Sec. 4) by Stats. 2022, Ch. 969, Sec. 2 (AB 2594) Effective January 1, 2023. This section, pursuant to its own provisions, becomes operative if a judicial determination as described in subd. (m) has taken effect.)

12800.5. (a) (1) A license shall bear a fullface engraved picture or photograph of the licensee.

(2) Notwithstanding any other law, the department shall not, unless requested by the licensee, distribute or sell the licensee's picture or photograph or any information pertaining to the licensee's physical characteristics to any private individual, other than the licensee, or to any firm, copartnership, association, or corporation. This paragraph does not apply to a private business entity that contracts with the department for the production of driver's licenses and identification cards, if the contract prohibits the unauthorized use and disclosure of the information.

(b) (1) A license, including a temporary license issued pursuant to Section 12506, shall bear the following notice: "This license is issued as a license to drive a motor vehicle; it does not establish eligibility for employment, voter registration, or public benefits."

(2) In the next scheduled revision of the driver's license on or after January 1, 2023, the notice specified in paragraph (1) shall be replaced by the following notice requirement:

(A) A Real ID driver's license, as described in Section 681, shall bear a notice including, but not limited to, that the license is issued as a license to drive a motor vehicle, and that it does not establish eligibility for employment, voter registration, or public benefits.

(B) A driver's license that is not a Real ID driver's license, as described in Section 681, shall bear a notice including, but not limited to, that the license is issued as a license to drive a motor vehicle, it does not establish eligibility for employment, firearms purchases, voter registration, or public benefits, and that it is not acceptable for official federal purposes.

(c) The department may demand proof of age prior to the issuance of a license.

(d) This section shall become inoperative on the date the department notifies the Legislature that the driver's license has been revised to include the notices specified in subparagraphs (A) and (B) of paragraph (2) of subdivision (b), and is repealed on January 1 of the following year.
(Amended by Stats. 2022, Ch. 482, Sec. 7. (AB 1766) Effective January 1, 2023. Conditionally inoperative as prescribed by its own provisions. Repealed conditionally by its own provisions. See later operative version added by Sec. 8 of Stats. 2022, Ch. 482.)

12800.5. (a) (1) A license shall bear a fullface engraved picture or photograph of the licensee.

(2) Notwithstanding any other law, the department shall not, unless requested by the licensee, distribute or sell the licensee's picture or photograph or any information pertaining to the licensee's physical characteristics to any private individual, other than the licensee, or to any firm, copartnership, association, or corporation. This paragraph does not apply to a private business entity that contracts with the department for the production of driver's licenses and identification cards, if the contract prohibits the unauthorized use and disclosure of the information.

(b) (1) A Real ID driver's license, as described in Section 681, shall bear a notice including, but not limited to, that the license is issued as a license to drive a motor vehicle, and that it does not establish eligibility for employment, voter registration, or public benefits.

(2) A driver's license that is not a Real ID driver's license, as described in Section 681, shall bear a notice including, but not limited to, that the license is issued as a license to drive a motor vehicle, it does not establish eligibility for employment, firearms purchases, voter registration, or public benefits, and that it is not acceptable for official federal purposes.

(c) The department may demand proof of age prior to the issuance of a license.

(d) This section shall become operative on the date the department notifies the Legislature that the driver's license has been revised to include the notices specified in subdivision (b).
(Repealed (in Sec. 7) and added by Stats. 2022, Ch. 482, Sec. 8. (AB 1766) Effective January 1, 2023. Section conditionally operative by its own provisions.)

12800.6. (a) An application for an original, renewal, or duplicate of a driver's license shall inform the applicant of the Department of Justice's video on proper conduct during a traffic stop created pursuant to Section 1656.1.

(b) The information in subdivision (a) shall be included upon the next scheduled revision of the driver's license application subsequent to the release of the Department of Justice's video on proper conduct during a traffic stop created pursuant to Section 1656.1.
(Added by Stats. 2022, Ch. 332, Sec. 4. (AB 2537) Effective January 1, 2023.)

12800.7. (a) Upon application for an original, renewal, or duplicate of a driver's license the department may require the applicant to produce any identification that it determines is necessary in order to ensure that the name of the applicant stated in the application is their true, full name and that their residence address as set forth in the application is their true residence address.

(b) Notwithstanding any other law, any document provided by the applicant to the department for purposes of proving the applicant's identity, true, full name, California residency, or that the applicant's presence in the United States is authorized under federal law, is not a public record and shall not be disclosed by the department except in response to a subpoena for individual records in a criminal proceeding or a court order, or in response to a law enforcement request to address an urgent health or safety need if the law enforcement agency certifies in writing the specific circumstances that do not permit authorities time to obtain a court order. Immigration enforcement, as defined in Section 7284.4 of the Government Code, does not constitute an urgent health and safety need for purposes of this subdivision.
(Amended by Stats. 2022, Ch. 482, Sec. 9. (AB 1766) Effective January 1, 2023.)

12801. (a) Except as provided in subdivisions (b) and (c) and Section 12801.9, the department shall require an application for a driver's license to contain the applicant's social security account number and any other number or identifier determined to be appropriate by the department.

(b) An applicant who provides satisfactory proof that his or her presence in the United States is authorized under federal law, but who is not eligible for a social security account number, is eligible to receive an original driver's license if he or she meets all other qualifications for licensure.

(c) (1) An applicant applying for a driver's license under Section 12801.9, who has never been issued a social security account number and is not presently eligible for a social security account number, shall satisfy the requirements of this section if he or she indicates in the application described in Section 12800, in the manner prescribed by the department, that he or she has never been issued a social security account number and is not presently eligible for a social security account number.

(2) This subdivision does not apply to applications for a commercial driver's license. The department shall require all applications for a commercial driver's license to include the applicant's social security account number.

(3) This section shall not be used to consider an individual's citizenship or immigration status as a basis for a criminal investigation, arrest, or detention.

(d) The department shall not complete an application for a driver's license unless the applicant is in compliance with the requirements of subdivision (a), (b), or (c).

(e) Notwithstanding any other law, the social security account number collected on a driver's license application shall not be displayed on the driver's license, including, but not limited to, inclusion on a magnetic tape or strip used to store data on the license.

(f) This section shall become operative on January 1, 2015, or on the date that the director executes a declaration pursuant to Section 12801.11, whichever is sooner.

(g) This section shall become inoperative on the effective date of a final judicial determination made by any court of appellate jurisdiction that any provision of the act that added this section, or its application, either in whole or in part, is enjoined, found unconstitutional, or held invalid for any reason. The department shall post this information on its Internet Web site.
(Amended (as amended by Stats. 2014, Ch. 27, Sec. 6) by Stats. 2015, Ch. 303, Sec. 537. (AB 731) Effective January 1, 2016. Conditionally inoperative as provided in subd. (g). See later operative version, as amended by Sec. 171 of Stats. 2014, Ch. 71.)

12801. (a) Notwithstanding any other law, the department shall require an application for a driver's license to contain the applicant's social security account number and any other number or identifier determined to be appropriate by the department.

(b) Notwithstanding subdivision (a), an applicant who provides satisfactory proof that his or her presence in the United States is authorized under federal law, but who is not eligible for a social security account number, is eligible to receive an original driver's license if he or she meets all other qualifications for licensure.

(c) Notwithstanding any other law, the social security account number collected on a driver's license application shall not be displayed on the driver's license, including, but not limited to, inclusion on a magnetic tape or strip used to store data on the license.

(d) This section shall become operative on the effective date of a final judicial determination made by any court of appellate jurisdiction that any provision of the act that added this section, or its application, either in whole or in part, is enjoined, found unconstitutional, or held invalid for any reason. The department shall post this information on its Internet Web site.
(Amended (as added by Stats. 2013, Ch. 524, Sec. 11) by Stats. 2014, Ch. 71, Sec. 171. (SB 1304) Effective January 1, 2015. Section conditionally operative as prescribed by its own provisions.)

12801.2. (a) A person shall not receive financial compensation for the sole purpose of filling out an original driver's license application for another person.

(b) A person in violation of this section is subject to a civil penalty of not more than two thousand five hundred dollars ($2,500) for each offense. Actions for relief pursuant to this section may be commenced in a court of competent jurisdiction by the Attorney General, or by the district attorney, county counsel, or city attorney of the location in which the violation occurred.

(c) Section 40000.1 does not apply to a violation of this section.

(Added by Stats. 2014, Ch. 447, Sec. 1. (AB 852) Effective January 1, 2015.)

12801.5. (a) Except as provided in Section 12801.9, the department shall require an applicant for an original driver's license or identification card to submit satisfactory proof of California residency and that the applicant's presence in the United States is authorized under federal law.

(b) Except as provided in Section 12801.9, the department shall not issue an original driver's license or identification card to a person who does not submit satisfactory proof that the applicant's presence in the United States is authorized under federal law.

(c) The department shall not issue an original driver's license or identification card to a person who does not submit satisfactory proof of California residency.

(d) The department shall adopt regulations to carry out the purposes of this section, including, but not limited to, procedures for (1) verifying that the applicant is a California resident and that his or her presence in the United States is authorized under federal law, (2) issuance of a temporary license pending verification of the applicant's status, and (3) hearings to appeal a denial of a license, temporary license, or identification card.

(e) On January 10 of each year, the department shall submit a supplemental budget report to the Governor and the Legislature detailing the costs of verifying the citizenship or legal residency of applicants for driver's licenses and identification cards, in order for the state to request reimbursement from the federal government.

(f) Notwithstanding Section 40300 or any other law, a peace officer shall not detain or arrest a person solely on the belief that the person is an unlicensed driver, unless the officer has reasonable cause to believe the person driving is under 16 years of age.

(g) The inability of an individual to obtain a driver's license pursuant to this section does not abrogate or diminish in any respect the legal requirement of every driver in this state to obey the motor vehicle laws of this state, including laws with respect to licensing, motor vehicle registration, and financial responsibility.

(h) This section shall become operative on July 1, 2016.

(i) This section shall become inoperative on the effective date of a final judicial determination made by any court of appellate jurisdiction that any provision of the act that added this section, or its application, either in whole or in part, is enjoined, found unconstitutional, or held invalid for any reason. The department shall post this information on its Internet Web site.

(Added by Stats. 2015, Ch. 708, Sec. 2. (AB 1465) Effective January 1, 2016. Pursuant to subd. (h), this version becomes operative on July 1, 2016, only if a judicial determination as described in subd. (i) has not taken effect. Pursuant to subd. (i), this version becomes inoperative on the effective date of a judicial determination as described. On that date, see the later operative version added by Sec. 4 of Ch. 708.)

12801.5. (a) Notwithstanding any other law, the department shall require an applicant for an original driver's license or identification card to submit satisfactory proof of California residency and that the applicant's presence in the United States is authorized under federal law.

(b) The department shall not issue an original driver's license or identification card to a person who does not submit satisfactory proof that the applicant's presence in the United States is authorized under federal law.

(c) The department shall not issue an original driver's license or identification card to a person who does not submit satisfactory proof of California residency.

(d) The department shall adopt regulations to carry out the purposes of this section, including, but not limited to, procedures for (1) verifying that the applicant is a California resident and that his or her presence in the United States is authorized under federal law, (2) issuance of a temporary license pending verification of the applicant's status, and (3) hearings to appeal a denial of a license, temporary license, or identification card.

(e) On January 10 of each year, the department shall submit a supplemental budget report to the Governor and the Legislature detailing the costs of verifying the citizenship or legal residency of applicants for driver's licenses and identification cards, in order for the state to request reimbursement from the federal government.

(f) Notwithstanding Section 40300 or any other law, a peace officer shall not detain or arrest a person solely on the belief that the person is an unlicensed driver, unless the officer has reasonable cause to believe the person driving is under 16 years of age.

(g) The inability of an individual to obtain a driver's license pursuant to this section does not abrogate or diminish in any respect the legal requirement of every driver in this state to obey the motor vehicle laws of this state, including laws with respect to licensing, motor vehicle registration, and financial responsibility.

(h) This section shall become operative on the effective date of a final judicial determination made by any court of appellate jurisdiction that any provision of the act that added this section, or its application, either in whole or in part, is enjoined, found unconstitutional, or held invalid for any reason. The department shall post this information on its Internet Web site.

(Repealed (in Sec. 3) and added by Stats. 2015, Ch. 708, Sec. 4. (AB 1465) Effective January 1, 2016. Pursuant to subd. (h), this version becomes operative on the effective date of a judicial determination as described, but not sooner than July 1, 2016, pursuant to subds. (g) and (h) in the amendment by Sec. 3 of Ch. 708.)

12801.6. (a) Any federal document demonstrating favorable action by the federal government for acceptance of a person into the deferred action for childhood arrivals program shall satisfy the requirements of Section 12801.5.

(b) The department may issue an original driver's license to the person who submits proof of presence in the United States as authorized under federal law pursuant to subdivision (a) and either a social security account number or ineligibility for a social security account number.

(Added by Stats. 2012, Ch. 862, Sec. 3. (AB 2189) Effective January 1, 2013.)

12801.7. (a) The department shall not issue an original driver's license or identification card, or a renewal, duplicate, or replacement driver's license or identification card to any person for whom the department has received notice from the United States Department of Homeland Security that the person has been determined and found by the United States Department of Homeland Security to be a deported person under Section 1252 of Title 8 of the United States Code.

(b) (1) The department shall cancel any driver's license or identification card issued to any person identified as specified in subdivision (a).

(2) The cancellation shall become effective on the 30th day after the date the cancellation notice is mailed to the person, except as authorized under paragraph (3).

(3) The person may request a review of the intended cancellation during the 30-day period specified in paragraph (2) and, if proof is provided to show the person is legally present in the United States as authorized under federal law, the department shall rescind the cancellation.

(4) The cancellation notice shall be mailed to the person's last known address.

(c) The department shall require an applicant for a driver's license whose license was canceled under this section to submit satisfactory proof that the applicant's presence in the United States is authorized under federal law.

(d) This section shall become operative on, and apply only to persons determined and found to be a deported person who is not a citizen or national of the United States after, July 1, 1997.

(Amended by Stats. 2021, Ch. 296, Sec. 61. (AB 1096) Effective January 1, 2022.)

12801.8. (a) In the case of a legal, nonimmigrant driver's license applicant, the department shall issue a temporary driver's license, valid for 90 days, if the applicant has successfully completed the application and the related requirements for the issuance of a driver's license under this code, including paragraph (1) of subdivision (a) of Section 12805. If the United States Department of Homeland Security is unable to verify the applicant's presence before the temporary driver's license expires, the department shall, at least 15 days before the temporary driver's license expires, extend the temporary driver's license for an additional 120 days and notify the applicant by mail that the temporary driver's license is being extended.

(b) If the department adjusts the expiration date of any driver's license issued pursuant to this code so that the date does not exceed the expiration date of a federal document submitted pursuant to subdivision (a) of Section 12801.5, the applicant may, upon receipt of a notice of renewal of the driver's license by the department sent prior to the expiration of the license, request an extension of the term of the driver's license by submitting to the department satisfactory proof that the applicant's presence in the United States has been reauthorized or extended under federal law. After verifying that the applicant's presence in the United States has been reauthorized or extended by federal law, the department shall adjust the expiration date of the driver's license so that it does not exceed the expiration date of the revised federal document submitted pursuant to subdivision (a) of Section 12801.5 and complies with the related requirements of this code.

(c) The department shall establish a procedure for receiving mailed requests for the extension of driver's licenses as described in this section.

(Amended by Stats. 2016, Ch. 339, Sec. 8. (SB 838) Effective September 13, 2016.)

12801.9. (a) (1) Notwithstanding Section 12801.5, the department shall issue an original driver's license to a person who is unable to submit satisfactory proof that the applicant's presence in the United States is authorized under federal law if the person meets all other qualifications for licensure and provides satisfactory proof to the department of the person's identity and California residency.

(2) Notwithstanding Section 12801.5 and commencing no later than July 1, 2027, the department shall issue an identification card to a person who is unable to submit satisfactory proof that the applicant's presence in the United States is authorized under federal law if the person provides satisfactory proof to the department of the person's identity and California residency.

(b) The department shall adopt regulations to carry out the purposes of this section, including, but not limited to, procedures for (1) identifying documents acceptable for the purposes of proving identity and California residency, (2) procedures for verifying the authenticity of the documents, (3) issuance of a temporary license pending verification of any document's authenticity, and (4) hearings to appeal a denial of a license or temporary license, or identification card.

(c) Regulations adopted for purposes of establishing the documents acceptable to prove identity and residency pursuant to subdivision (b) shall be promulgated by the department in consultation with appropriate interested parties, in accordance with the rulemaking provisions of the Administrative Procedure Act (Chapter 3.5 (commencing with Section 11340) of Part 1 of Division 3 of Title 2 of the Government Code), including law enforcement representatives, immigrant rights representatives, labor representatives, and other stakeholders, which may include, but are not limited to, the Department of the California Highway Patrol, the California State Sheriffs' Association, and the California Police Chiefs Association. The department shall accept various types of documentation for this purpose, including, but not limited to, the following documents:

(1) A valid, unexpired consular identification document issued by a consulate from the applicant's country of citizenship, or a valid, unexpired passport from the applicant's country of citizenship.

(2) An original birth certificate, or other proof of age, as designated by the department.

(3) A home utility bill, lease or rental agreement, or other proof of California residence, as designated by the department.

(4) The following documents, which, if in a language other than English, shall be accompanied by a certified translation or an affidavit of translation into English:

(A) A marriage license or divorce certificate.

(B) A foreign federal electoral photo card issued on or after January 1, 1991.

(C) A foreign driver's license.

(5) A United States Department of Homeland Security Form I-589, Application for Asylum and for Withholding of Removal.

(6) An official school or college transcript that includes the applicant's date of birth or a foreign school record that is sealed and includes a photograph of the applicant at the age the record was issued.

(7) A United States Department of Homeland Security Form I-20 or Form DS-2019.

(8) A deed or title to real property.

(9) A property tax bill or statement issued within the previous 12 months.

(10) An income tax return.

(d) (1) (A) A license issued pursuant to this section shall bear the following notice: "This card is not acceptable for official federal purposes. This license is issued only as a license to drive a motor vehicle. It does not establish eligibility for employment, voter registration, or public benefits."

(B) An identification card issued pursuant to this section shall bear the following notice: "This card is not acceptable for official federal purposes. This identification card is issued only as a means of identification. It does not establish eligibility for employment, voter registration, or public benefits."

(2) The notice described in paragraph (1) shall be in lieu of the notice provided in Section 12800.5.

(3) Paragraphs (1) and (2) shall become inoperative upon the department's next scheduled revision of the driver's license or identification card on or after January 1, 2023, at which time, a driver's license and identification card issued pursuant to this section shall bear the notice described in Section 12800.5 or 13005.5, respectively, as added by the act that added this paragraph.

(e) Notwithstanding Section 40300 or any other law, a peace officer shall not detain or arrest a person solely on the belief that the person is an unlicensed driver, unless the officer has reasonable cause to believe the person driving is under 16 years of age.

(f) The inability to obtain a driver's license pursuant to this section does not abrogate or diminish in any respect the legal requirement of every driver in this state to obey the motor vehicle laws of this state, including laws with respect to licensing, motor vehicle registration, and financial responsibility.

(g) It is a violation of law to discriminate against a person because the person holds or presents a license or identification card issued under this section, including, but not limited to, the following:

(1) It is a violation of the Unruh Civil Rights Act (Section 51 of the Civil Code), for a business establishment to discriminate against a person because the person holds or presents a license or identification card issued under this section.

(2) (A) It is a violation of the California Fair Employment and Housing Act (Part 2.8 (commencing with Section 12900) of Division 3 of Title 2 of the Government Code) for an employer or other covered person or entity, pursuant to Section 12940 of the Government Code and subdivision (v) of Section 12926 of the Government Code, to discriminate against a person because the person holds or presents a driver's license or identification card issued pursuant to this section, or for an employer or other covered entity to require a person to present a driver's license, unless possessing a driver's license is required by law or is required by the employer and the employer's requirement is otherwise permitted by

law. This section shall not be construed to limit or expand an employer's authority to require a person to possess a driver's license.

(B) Notwithstanding subparagraph (A), this section shall not be construed to alter an employer's rights or obligations under Section 1324a of Title 8 of the United States Code regarding obtaining documentation evidencing identity and authorization for employment. An action taken by an employer that is required by the federal Immigration and Nationality Act (8 U.S.C. Sec. 1324a) is not a violation of law.

(3) It is a violation of Section 11135 of the Government Code for a state or local governmental authority, agent, or person acting on behalf of a state or local governmental authority, or a program or activity that is funded directly or receives financial assistance from the state, to discriminate against an individual because the individual holds or presents a license or identification card issued pursuant to this section, including by notifying a law enforcement agency of the individual's identity or that the individual carries a license or identification card issued under this section if a notification is not required by law or would not have been provided if the individual held a license issued pursuant to Section 12801 or an identification card issued pursuant to Section 13000.

(h) Driver's license or identification card information obtained by an employer shall be treated as private and confidential, is exempt from disclosure under the California Public Records Act (Division 10 (commencing with Section 7920.000) of Title 1 of the Government Code), and shall not be disclosed to any unauthorized person or used for any purpose other than to establish identity and authorization to drive, as applicable.

(i) Information collected pursuant to this section is not a public record and shall not be disclosed by the department, except as required by law.

(j) Documents provided by applicants to prove identity or residency pursuant to this section are not public records and shall not be disclosed except in response to a subpoena for individual records in a criminal proceeding or a court order, or in response to a law enforcement request to address an urgent health or safety need if the law enforcement agency certifies in writing the specific circumstances that do not permit authorities time to obtain a court order. Immigration enforcement, as defined in Section 7284.4 of the Government Code, does not constitute an urgent health and safety need for purposes of this subdivision.

(k) A license or identification card issued pursuant to this section shall not be used as evidence of an individual's citizenship or immigration status for any purpose.

(l) In addition to the fees required by Section 14902, a person applying for an identification card pursuant to this section may be required to pay an additional fee determined by the department that is sufficient to offset the reasonable administrative costs of implementing the provisions of the act that authorized the issuance of identification cards pursuant to this section. If this additional fee is assessed, it shall only apply until June 30, 2030.

(m) This section shall become inoperative on the effective date of a final judicial determination made by any court of appellate jurisdiction that any provision of the act that added this section, or its application, either in whole or in part, is enjoined, found unconstitutional, or held invalid for any reason. The department shall post this information on its internet website.

(Amended by Stats. 2023, Ch. 311, Sec. 25. (SB 883) Effective January 1, 2024. Conditionally inoperative as provided in subd. (m).)

12801.10. (a) Nothing in Section 1653.5, 12800, 12801, 12801.5, or 12801.9 authorizes an individual to apply for, or be issued, a commercial driver's license without the submission of his or her social security account number upon application.

(b) This section shall become operative on January 1, 2015, or on the date that the director executes a declaration pursuant to Section 12801.11, whichever is sooner.

(c) This section shall become inoperative on the effective date of a final judicial determination made by any court of appellate jurisdiction that any provision of the act that added this section, or its application, either in whole or in part, is enjoined, found unconstitutional, or held invalid for any reason. The department shall post this information on its Internet Web site.

(Added by Stats. 2013, Ch. 524, Sec. 16. (AB 60) Effective January 1, 2014. Section operative January 1, 2015, or sooner, as provided in subd. (m). Conditionally inoperative as provided in subd. (n).)

12801.11. (a) If the director determines that the department is prepared to begin issuing driver's licenses pursuant to Section 12801.9 on a date sooner than January 1, 2015, the director shall execute a declaration stating that determination and date and, within five business days, provide a copy of that declaration to the appropriate fiscal and policy committees of the Legislature and to the Governor, and shall post this information on its Internet Web site.

(b) This section shall become inoperative on the effective date of a final judicial determination made by any court of appellate jurisdiction that any provision of the act that added this section, or its application, either in whole or in part, is enjoined, found unconstitutional, or held invalid for any reason. The department shall post this information on its Internet Web site.

(Added by Stats. 2013, Ch. 524, Sec. 17. (AB 60) Effective January 1, 2014. Conditionally inoperative as prescribed by its own provisions.)

12802. Every original application shall be signed and verified by the applicant under penalty of perjury and the applicant shall submit such evidence of age as the department may require, and, if the applicant is a minor, the application shall also be signed and verified as provided in Chapter 2 (commencing with Section 17700) of Division 9.

(Amended by Stats. 2021, Ch. 254, Sec. 5. (AB 174) Effective September 23, 2021.)

12802.5. Before issuing a driver's license or permit to any person under 21 years of age, both of the following shall occur:

(a) The department shall inform the applicant of the following:

(1) It is unlawful to drive with a blood-alcohol concentration of 0.01 percent or greater, as measured by a preliminary alcohol screening test or other chemical test.

(2) The penalty for so driving is a one-year suspension of the driving privilege.

(3) A refusal to take, or a failure to complete, a preliminary alcohol screening test or other chemical test for the purpose of determining the level of alcohol pursuant to Section 13388 shall result in a one-year suspension of the driving privilege.

(4) The fee for reissuance of a driver's license after suspension for a violation of Section 23136 is one hundred dollars ($100). This fee is in addition to any other fees that may be imposed by the department in connection with reissuance of a driver's license.

(b) The applicant shall sign a statement that acknowledges that he or she has been notified of the information specified in subdivision (a).

(Amended (as amended by Stats. 1998, Ch. 118) by Stats. 1999, Ch. 22, Sec. 7. Effective May 26, 1999. Operative July 1, 1999, by Sec. 46 of Ch. 22.)

12803. Upon application for an original license, except student licenses, the department shall require an examination of the applicant and shall make provision therefor before an officer or employee or authorized representative of the department in the county wherein the applicant resides.

(Enacted by Stats. 1959, Ch. 3.)

12804.2. (a) Notwithstanding Section 15275, a person issued a driver's license by the department is exempt from the endorsement requirements of Section 15275 if all of the following conditions are met:

(1) The person is employed in an agricultural operation and is driving a vehicle, other than a vehicle used in common or contract motor carriage, controlled by a farmer and transporting agricultural products or farm machinery or supplies to or from a farm.

(2) (A) The person has fulfilled the applicable training requirements of Subpart H of Part 172 of Title 49 of the Code of Federal Regulations.

(B) Upon successful completion of the training required by subparagraph

(A), a record of current training, meeting the requirements prescribed by Section 172.704(d) of Title 49 of the Code of Federal Regulations, and a completed application shall be forwarded to the Department of the California Highway Patrol. Upon receipt and validation, the Department of the California Highway Patrol shall issue a verification of training, valid for three years, which shall be carried by the person when operating an implement of husbandry or a motor vehicle required to display placards pursuant to Section 27903. Within 15 days of issuance by the Department of the California Highway Patrol, a copy of the verification shall be forwarded by the person completing the training to the department for inclusion on the permanent driving record of the person, together with a fee of twelve dollars ($12).

(C) The department, in consultation with the Department of the California Highway Patrol, shall develop a suitable form for verification of training.

(3) The person has, within the vehicle, informational material approved by the Department of the California Highway Patrol, in both English and Spanish, outlining basic safety procedures to be followed in the event of an accident. The Department of the California Highway Patrol shall provide the information required by this subdivision and make it available at no cost to the person.

(4) The person is operating a vehicle which is an implement of husbandry or a motor vehicle requiring only a class C driver's license and the distance which the vehicle is being operated between the final point of distribution and the ultimate point of application or from part of a farm to another part thereof, or from one farm to another, is not more than 50 miles.

(5) In lieu of a report of a medical examination required by Section 12804.9, an applicant for a certificate pursuant to paragraph (3) shall, upon application and every two years thereafter, submit medical information on a form approved by the department. A person who obtains a verification of training pursuant to this section, but does not meet the medical requirements for a hazardous materials endorsement established by the department under Section 12804.9, is not qualified to transport hazardous materials.

(6) For purposes of the penalties and sanctions prescribed by Article 7 (commencing with Section 15300) of Chapter 7, the operation of a vehicle pursuant to this subdivision is deemed to be the operation of a commercial motor vehicle.

(b) Implementation dates for this section may be established by the Department of Motor Vehicles by regulation in order to accomplish an orderly certification program.

(Amended by Stats. 2017, Ch. 397, Sec. 3. (SB 810) Effective January 1, 2018.)

12804.5. The class of vehicles permitted to be operated as shown on a driver's license held by a minor shall not be changed, unless the parents, guardians, or person having custody of such minor gives written consent to the department for such a change.

(Added by Stats. 1972, Ch. 97.)

12804.6. (a) A person shall not operate a transit bus transporting passengers unless that person has received from the department a certificate to operate a transit bus or is certified to drive a schoolbus or school pupil activity bus pursuant to Section 12517.

(b) All transit busdrivers shall comply with standards established in Section 40083 of the Education Code. The Department of Motor Vehicles shall establish an implementation program for transit busdrivers to meet these requirements. A transit busdriver who was employed as a busdriver on or before July 1, 1990, shall comply with Section 40085.5 of the Education Code instead of Section 40083 of that code in order to receive his or her original certificate.

(c) Implementation procedures for the issuance of transit busdrivers' certificates may be established by the Department of Motor Vehicles as necessary to implement an orderly transit busdriver training program.

(d) The department shall issue a transit busdriver certificate to a person who provides either of the following:

(1) Proof that he or she has complied with Section 40083 of the Education Code.

(2) Proof that he or she has complied with Section 40085.5 of the Education Code.

(e) The department may charge a fee of ten dollars ($10) to an applicant for an original or a duplicate or renewal certificate under this section.

(f) The department shall issue a certificate to the applicant. The status of the certificate shall also become part of the pull notice and periodic reports issued pursuant to Section 1808.1. The certificate or the pull notice or periodic reports shall become part of, the person's employee records for the purpose of inspection pursuant to Sections 1808.1 and 34501. It shall be unlawful for the employer to permit a person to drive a transit bus who does not have a valid certificate.

(g) The term of a certificate shall be a period not to exceed five years, and shall expire with the driver's license.

(Amended by Stats. 2006, Ch. 574, Sec. 9. Effective January 1, 2007.)

12804.7. Notwithstanding subdivision (b) of Section 12804.9, class C also includes any two-axle motortruck or implement of husbandry weighing 4,000 pounds or more unladen when towing an implement of husbandry as specified in subdivision (n) of Section 36005, except that those vehicles shall not be operated in excess of 25 miles per hour on the highways and for not more than 25 miles on the highway from their point of origin.

(Amended by Stats. 1993, Ch. 272, Sec. 25. Effective August 2, 1993.)

12804.8. (a) Notwithstanding any other provision of law, the department may conduct studies to develop and identify examinations and tests, to more accurately identify persons who, due to physical or mental factors, or both, are not competent or qualified to safely operate a motor vehicle.

(b) In addition to any other tests or examinations required under this code, the department may require any person applying for an original driver's license or renewal of a driver's license, or any person subject to reexamination under Section 13801, to submit to one or more tests or examinations which are part of a study.

(c) The results and information obtained during the study, through the tests and examinations specified in subdivision (a), shall be used only to assess and evaluate the effectiveness of the tests and examinations and to select tests and examinations for use by the department, and for no other purpose. The results of the tests are confidential and shall not be disclosed to any person.

(d) No public entity or employee shall be liable for any loss, detriment, or injury resulting directly or indirectly from the department's acts or failure to act on information received through the studies.

(Added by Stats. 1993, Ch. 546, Sec. 2. Effective January 1, 1994.)

12804.9. (a) (1) The examination shall include all of the following:

(A) A test of the applicant's knowledge and understanding of the provisions of this code governing the operation of vehicles upon the highways.

(B) A test of the applicant's ability to read and understand simple English used in highway traffic and directional signs.

(C) A test of the applicant's understanding of traffic signs and signals, including the bikeway signs, markers, and traffic control devices established by the Department of Transportation.

(D) An actual demonstration of the applicant's ability to exercise ordinary and reasonable control in operating a motor vehicle by driving it under the supervision of an examining officer. The applicant shall submit to an examination appropriate to the type of motor vehicle or combination of vehicles the applicant desires a license to drive, except that the department may waive the driving test part of the examination for any applicant who submits a license issued by another state, territory, or possession of the United States, the District of Columbia, or the Commonwealth of Puerto Rico if the department verifies through any acknowledged national driver record data source that there are no stops, holds, or other impediments to its issuance. The examining officer may request to see evidence of financial responsibility for the vehicle before supervising the demonstration of the applicant's ability to operate the vehicle. The examining officer may refuse to examine an applicant who is unable to provide proof of financial responsibility for the vehicle, unless proof of financial responsibility is not required by this code.

(E) A test of the hearing and eyesight of the applicant, and of other matters that may be necessary to determine the mental and physical fitness of the applicant to operate a motor vehicle upon the highways, and whether any grounds exist for refusal of a license under this code.

(2) (A) Before a class A or class B driver's license, or class C driver's license with a commercial endorsement, may be issued or renewed, the applicant shall have in the applicant's driver record a valid report of a medical examination of the applicant given not more than two years before the date of the application by a health care professional. As used in this paragraph, "health care professional" means a person who is licensed, certified, or registered in accordance with applicable state laws and regulations to practice medicine and perform physical examinations in the United States. Health care professionals are doctors of medicine, doctors of osteopathy, physician assistants, and registered advanced practice nurses, or doctors of chiropractic who are clinically competent to perform the medical examination presently required of motor carrier drivers by the United States Department of Transportation. The report shall be on a form approved by the department. In establishing the requirements, consideration may be given to the standards presently required of motor carrier drivers by the Federal Motor Carrier Safety Administration.

(B) The department may accept a federal waiver of one or more physical qualification standards if the waiver is accompanied by a report of a nonqualifying medical examination for a class A or class B driver's license, or class C driver's license with a commercial endorsement, pursuant to Section 391.41(a)(3)(ii) of Subpart E of Part 391 of Title 49 of the Code of Federal Regulations.

(3) A physical defect of the applicant that, in the opinion of the department, is compensated for to ensure safe driving ability, shall not prevent the issuance of a license to the applicant.

(b) In accordance with the following classifications, an applicant for a driver's license shall be required to submit to an examination appropriate to the type of motor vehicle or combination of vehicles the applicant desires a license to drive:

(1) Class A includes the following:

(A) Except as provided in subparagraph (H) of paragraph (3), a combination of vehicles, if a vehicle being towed has a gross vehicle weight rating or gross vehicle weight of more than 10,000 pounds.

(B) A vehicle towing more than one vehicle.

(C) A trailer bus.

(D) The operation of all vehicles under class B and class C.

(2) Class B includes the following:

(A) Except as provided in subparagraph (H) of paragraph (3), a single vehicle with a gross vehicle weight rating or gross vehicle weight of more than 26,000 pounds.

(B) A single vehicle with three or more axles, except any three-axle vehicle weighing less than 6,000 pounds.

(C) A bus with a gross vehicle weight rating or gross vehicle weight of more than 26,000 pounds, except a trailer bus.

(D) A farm labor vehicle.

(E) A single vehicle with three or more axles or a gross vehicle weight rating or gross vehicle weight of more than 26,000 pounds towing another vehicle with a gross vehicle weight rating or gross vehicle weight of 10,000 pounds or less.

(F) A house car over 40 feet in length, excluding safety devices and safety bumpers.

(G) The operation of all vehicles covered under class C.

(3) Class C includes the following:

(A) A two-axle vehicle with a gross vehicle weight rating or gross vehicle weight of 26,000 pounds or less, including when the vehicle is towing a trailer or semitrailer with a gross vehicle weight rating or gross vehicle weight of 10,000 pounds or less.

(B) Notwithstanding subparagraph (A), a two-axle vehicle weighing 4,000 pounds or more unladen when towing a trailer coach not exceeding 9,000 pounds gross.

(C) A house car of 40 feet in length or less.

(D) A three-axle vehicle weighing 6,000 pounds gross or less.

(E) A house car of 40 feet in length or less or a vehicle towing another vehicle with a gross vehicle weight rating of 10,000 pounds or less, including when a tow dolly is used. A person driving a vehicle may not tow another vehicle in violation of Section 21715.

(F) (i) A two-axle vehicle weighing 4,000 pounds or more unladen when towing either a trailer coach or a fifth-wheel travel trailer not exceeding 10,000 pounds gross vehicle weight rating, when the towing of the trailer is not for compensation.

(ii) A two-axle vehicle weighing 4,000 pounds or more unladen when towing a fifth-wheel travel trailer exceeding 10,000 pounds, but not exceeding 15,000 pounds, gross vehicle weight rating, when the towing of the trailer is not for compensation, and if the person has passed a specialized written examination provided by the department relating to the knowledge of this code and other safety aspects governing the towing of recreational vehicles upon the highway.

(iii) The authority to operate combinations of vehicles under this subparagraph may be granted by endorsement on a class C license upon completion of that written examination.

(G) A vehicle or combination of vehicles with a gross combination weight rating or a gross vehicle weight rating, as those terms are defined in subdivisions (j) and (k), respectively, of Section 15210, of 26,000 pounds or less, if all of the following conditions are met:

(i) Is operated by a farmer, an employee of a farmer, or an instructor credentialed in agriculture as part of an instructional program in agriculture at the high school, community college, or university level.

(ii) Is used exclusively in the conduct of agricultural operations.

(iii) Is not used in the capacity of a for-hire carrier or for compensation.

(H) Firefighting equipment, provided that the equipment is operated by a person who holds a firefighter endorsement pursuant to Section 12804.11.

(I) A motorized scooter.

(J) A bus with a gross vehicle weight rating or gross vehicle weight of 26,000 pounds or less, except a trailer bus.

(K) Class C does not include a two-wheel motorcycle or a two-wheel motor-driven cycle.

(4) Class M1. A two-wheel motorcycle or a motor-driven cycle. Authority to operate a vehicle included in a class M1 license may be granted by endorsement on a class A, B, or C license upon completion of an appropriate examination.

(5) (A) Class M2 includes a motorized bicycle or moped, or a bicycle with an attached motor, except an electric bicycle as described in subdivision (a) of Section 312.5.

(B) Authority to operate vehicles included in class M2 may be granted by endorsement on a class A, B, or C license upon completion of an appropriate examination. Persons holding a class M1 license or endorsement may operate vehicles included in class M2 without further examination.

(c) A driver's license or driver certificate is not valid for operating a commercial motor vehicle, as defined in subdivision (b) of Section 15210, any other motor vehicle listed in paragraph (1) or (2) of subdivision (b), or any other vehicle requiring a driver to hold any driver certificate or any driver's license endorsement under Section 15275, unless a medical certificate approved by the department that has been issued within two years of the date of the operation of that vehicle and a copy of the medical examination report from which the certificate was issued is on file with the department. Otherwise, the license is valid only for operating class

C vehicles that are not commercial vehicles, as defined in subdivision (b) of Section 15210, and for operating class M1 or M2 vehicles, if so endorsed, that are not commercial vehicles, as defined in subdivision (b) of Section 15210.

(d) A license or driver certificate issued before the enactment of Chapter 7 (commencing with Section 15200) is valid to operate the class or type of vehicles specified under the law in existence before that enactment until the license or certificate expires or is otherwise suspended, revoked, or canceled. Upon application for renewal or replacement of a driver's license, endorsement, or certificate required to operate a commercial motor vehicle, a valid medical certificate on a form approved by the department shall be submitted to the department.

(e) The department may accept a certificate of driving skill that is issued by an employer, authorized by the department to issue a certificate under Section 15250, of the applicant, in lieu of a driving test, on class A or B applications, if the applicant has first qualified for a class C license and has met the other examination requirements for the license for which the applicant is applying. The certificate may be submitted as evidence of the applicant's skill in the operation of the types of equipment covered by the license for which the applicant is applying.

(f) The department may accept a certificate of competence in lieu of a driving test on class M1 or M2 applications, when the certificate is issued by a law enforcement agency for its officers who operate class M1 or M2 vehicles in their duties, if the applicant has met the other examination requirements for the license for which the applicant is applying.

(g) The department may accept a certificate of satisfactory completion of a motorcyclist training program approved by the commissioner pursuant to Section 2932 in lieu of a driving test on class M1 or M2 applications, if the applicant has met the other examination requirements for the license for which the applicant is applying. The department shall review and approve the written and driving test used by a program to determine whether the program may issue a certificate of completion.

(h) Notwithstanding subdivision (b), a person holding a valid California driver's license of any class may operate a short-term rental motorized bicycle without taking any special examination for the operation of a motorized bicycle, and without having a class M2 endorsement on that license. As used in this subdivision, "short-term" means 48 hours or less.

(i) A person under 21 years of age shall not be issued a class M1 or M2 license or endorsement unless the person provides evidence satisfactory to the department of completion of a novice motorcycle safety training program that is operated pursuant to Article 2 (commencing with Section 2930) of Chapter 5 of Division 2.

(j) A driver of a vanpool vehicle may operate with a class C license but shall possess evidence of a medical examination required for a class B license when operating vanpool vehicles. In order to be eligible to drive the vanpool vehicle, the driver shall keep in the vanpool vehicle a statement, signed under penalty of perjury, that the driver has not been convicted of reckless driving, drunk driving, or a hit-and-run offense in the last five years.

(k) This section shall remain in effect only until January 1, 2029, and as of that date is repealed.

(Amended (as amended by Stats. 2021, Ch. 610, Sec. 1) by Stats. 2025, Ch. 16, Sec. 3. (SB 128) Effective June 27, 2025. Repealed as of January 1, 2029, by its own provisions. See later operative version amended by Sec. 4 of Stats. 2025, Ch. 16.)

12804.9. (a) (1) The examination shall include all of the following:

(A) A test of the applicant's knowledge and understanding of the provisions of this code governing the operation of vehicles upon the highways.

(B) A test of the applicant's ability to read and understand simple English used in highway traffic and directional signs.

(C) A test of the applicant's understanding of traffic signs and signals, including the bikeway signs, markers, and traffic control devices established by the Department of Transportation.

(D) An actual demonstration of the applicant's ability to exercise ordinary and reasonable control in operating a motor vehicle by driving it under the supervision of an examining officer. The applicant shall submit to an examination appropriate to the type of motor vehicle or combination of vehicles the applicant desires a license to drive, except that the department may waive the driving test part of the examination for any applicant who submits a license issued by another state, territory, or possession of the United States, the District of Columbia, or the Commonwealth of Puerto Rico if the department verifies through any acknowledged national driver record data source that there are no stops, holds, or other impediments to its issuance. The examining officer may request to see evidence of financial responsibility for the vehicle before supervising the demonstration of the applicant's ability to operate the vehicle. The examining officer may refuse to examine an applicant who is unable to provide proof of financial responsibility for the vehicle, unless proof of financial responsibility is not required by this code.

(E) A test of the hearing and eyesight of the applicant, and of other matters that may be necessary to determine the mental and physical fitness of the applicant to operate a motor vehicle upon the highways, and whether any grounds exist for refusal of a license under this code.

(2) (A) Before a class A or class B driver's license, or class C driver's license with a commercial endorsement, may be issued or renewed, the applicant shall have in the applicant's driver record a valid report of a medical examination of the applicant given not more than two years before the date of the application by a health care professional. As used in this paragraph, "health care professional" means a person who is licensed, certified, or registered in accordance with applicable state laws and regulations to practice medicine and perform physical examinations in the United States. Health care professionals are doctors of medicine, doctors of osteopathy, physician assistants, and registered advanced practice nurses, or doctors of chiropractic who are clinically competent to perform the medical examination presently required of motor carrier drivers by the United States Department of Transportation. The report shall be on a form approved by the department. In establishing the requirements, consideration may be given to the standards presently required of motor carrier drivers by the Federal Motor Carrier Safety Administration.

(B) The department may accept a federal waiver of one or more physical qualification standards if the waiver is accompanied by a report of a nonqualifying medical examination for a class A or class B driver's license, or class C driver's license with a commercial endorsement, pursuant to Section 391.41(a)(3)(ii) of Subpart E of Part 391 of Title 49 of the Code of Federal Regulations.

(3) A physical defect of the applicant that, in the opinion of the department, is compensated for to ensure safe driving ability, shall not prevent the issuance of a license to the applicant.

(b) In accordance with the following classifications, an applicant for a driver's license shall be required to submit to an examination appropriate to the type of motor vehicle or combination of vehicles the applicant desires a license to drive:

(1) Class A includes the following:

(A) Except as provided in subparagraph (H) of paragraph (3), a combination of vehicles, if a vehicle being towed has a gross vehicle weight rating or gross vehicle weight of more than 10,000 pounds.

(B) A vehicle towing more than one vehicle.

(C) A trailer bus.

(D) The operation of all vehicles under class B and class C.

(2) Class B includes the following:

(A) Except as provided in subparagraph (H) of paragraph (3), a single vehicle with a gross vehicle weight rating or gross vehicle weight of more than 26,000 pounds.

(B) A single vehicle with three or more axles, except any three-axle vehicle weighing less than 6,000 pounds.

(C) A bus with a gross vehicle weight rating or gross vehicle weight of more than 26,000 pounds, except a trailer bus.

(D) A farm labor vehicle.

(E) A single vehicle with three or more axles or a gross vehicle weight rating or gross vehicle weight of more than 26,000 pounds towing another vehicle with a gross vehicle weight rating or gross vehicle weight of 10,000 pounds or less.

(F) A house car over 40 feet in length, excluding safety devices and safety bumpers.

(G) The operation of all vehicles covered under class C.

(3) Class C includes the following:

(A) A two-axle vehicle with a gross vehicle weight rating or gross vehicle weight of 26,000 pounds or less, including when the vehicle is towing a trailer or semitrailer with a gross vehicle weight rating or gross vehicle weight of 10,000 pounds or less.

(B) Notwithstanding subparagraph (A), a two-axle vehicle weighing 4,000 pounds or more unladen when towing a trailer coach not exceeding 9,000 pounds gross.

(C) A house car of 40 feet in length or less.

(D) A three-axle vehicle weighing 6,000 pounds gross or less.

(E) A house car of 40 feet in length or less or a vehicle towing another vehicle with a gross vehicle weight rating of 10,000 pounds or less, including when a tow dolly is used. A person driving a vehicle may not tow another vehicle in violation of Section 21715.

(F) (i) A two-axle vehicle when towing a trailer exceeding 10,000 pounds, but not exceeding 15,000 pounds gross vehicle weight rating or gross vehicle weight, if all of the following conditions are met:

(I) The towing of the trailer is not for compensation or commercial purposes.

(II) The trailer is coupled to the towing vehicle by a bed-mounted gooseneck hitch or a fifth-wheel and kingpin connection.

(III) The trailer is used exclusively for recreational purposes.

(IV) The trailer is used for the transportation of property or human habitation, or both.

(V) The person has passed a specialized written examination provided by the department relating to the knowledge of this code and other safety aspects governing the towing of recreational vehicles upon the highway.

(ii) A vehicle towing a fifth-wheel travel trailer exceeding 10,000 pounds, but not exceeding 15,000 pounds, gross vehicle weight rating or gross vehicle weight, when the towing of the trailer is not for compensation, and if the person has passed a specialized written examination provided by the department relating to the knowledge of this code and other safety aspects governing the towing of recreational vehicles upon the highway.

(iii) The authority to operate combinations of vehicles under this subparagraph may be granted by endorsement on a class C license upon completion of that written examination.

(G) A vehicle or combination of vehicles with a gross combination weight rating or a gross vehicle weight rating, as those terms are defined in subdivisions (j) and (k), respectively, of Section 15210, of 26,000 pounds or less, if all of the following conditions are met:

(i) Is operated by a farmer, an employee of a farmer, or an instructor credentialed in agriculture as part of an instructional program in agriculture at the high school, community college, or university level.

(ii) Is used exclusively in the conduct of agricultural operations.

(iii) Is not used in the capacity of a for-hire carrier or for compensation.

(H) Firefighting equipment, provided that the equipment is operated by a person who holds a firefighter endorsement pursuant to Section 12804.11.

(I) A motorized scooter.

(J) A bus with a gross vehicle weight rating or gross vehicle weight of 26,000 pounds or less, except a trailer bus.

(K) Class C does not include a two-wheel motorcycle or a two-wheel motor-driven cycle.

(4) Class M1. A two-wheel motorcycle or a motor-driven cycle. Authority to operate a vehicle included in a class M1 license may be granted by endorsement on a class A, B, or C license upon completion of an appropriate examination.

(5) (A) Class M2 includes a motorized bicycle or moped, or a bicycle with an attached motor, except an electric bicycle as described in subdivision (a) of Section 312.5.

(B) Authority to operate vehicles included in class M2 may be granted by endorsement on a class A, B, or C license upon completion of an appropriate examination. Persons holding a class M1 license or endorsement may operate vehicles included in class M2 without further examination.

(c) A driver's license or driver certificate is not valid for operating a commercial motor vehicle, as defined in subdivision (b) of Section 15210, any other motor vehicle listed in paragraph (1) or (2) of subdivision (b), or any other vehicle requiring a driver to hold any driver certificate or any driver's license endorsement under Section 15275, unless a medical certificate approved by the department that has been issued within two years of the date of the operation of that vehicle and a copy of the medical examination report from which the certificate was issued is on file with the department. Otherwise, the license is valid only for operating class C vehicles that are not commercial vehicles, as defined in subdivision (b) of Section 15210, and for operating class M1 or M2 vehicles, if so endorsed, that are not commercial vehicles, as defined in subdivision (b) of Section 15210.

(d) A license or driver certificate issued before the enactment of Chapter 7 (commencing with Section 15200) is valid to operate the class or type of vehicles specified under the law in existence before that enactment until the license or certificate expires or is otherwise suspended, revoked, or canceled. Upon application for renewal or replacement of a driver's license, endorsement, or certificate required to operate a commercial motor vehicle, a valid medical certificate on a form approved by the department shall be submitted to the department.

(e) The department may accept a certificate of driving skill that is issued by an employer, authorized by the department to issue a certificate under Section 15250, of the applicant, in lieu of a driving test, on class A or B applications, if the applicant has first qualified for a class C license and has met the other examination requirements for the license for which the applicant is applying. The certificate may be submitted as evidence of the applicant's skill in the operation of the types of equipment covered by the license for which the applicant is applying.

(f) The department may accept a certificate of competence in lieu of a driving test on class M1 or M2 applications, when the certificate is issued by a law enforcement agency for its officers who operate class M1 or M2 vehicles in their duties, if the applicant has met the other examination requirements for the license for which the applicant is applying.

(g) The department may accept a certificate of satisfactory completion of a motorcyclist training program approved by the commissioner pursuant to Section 2932 in lieu of a driving test on class M1 or M2 applications, if the applicant has met the other examination requirements for the license for which the applicant is applying. The department shall review and approve the written and driving test used by a program to determine whether the program may issue a certificate of completion.

(h) Notwithstanding subdivision (b), a person holding a valid California driver's license of any class may operate a short-term rental motorized bicycle without taking any special examination for the operation of a motorized bicycle, and without having a class M2 endorsement on that license. As used in this subdivision, "short-term" means 48 hours or less.

(i) A person under 21 years of age shall not be issued a class M1 or M2 license or endorsement unless the person provides evidence satisfactory to the department of completion of a novice motorcycle safety training program that is operated pursuant to Article 2 (commencing with Section 2930) of Chapter 5 of Division 2.

(j) A driver of a vanpool vehicle may operate with a class C license but shall possess evidence of a medical examination required for a class B license when operating vanpool vehicles. In order to be eligible to drive the vanpool vehicle, the driver shall keep in the vanpool vehicle a statement, signed under penalty of perjury, that the driver has not been convicted of reckless driving, drunk driving, or a hit-and-run offense in the last five years.

(k) This section shall become operative on January 1, 2029.

(Amended (as added by Stats. 2021, Ch. 610, Sec. 2) by Stats. 2025, Ch. 16, Sec. 4. (SB 128) Effective June 27, 2025. Operative January 1, 2029, by its own provisions.)

12804.10. (a) Notwithstanding any other provision of law, a person issued a class C license under paragraph (3) of subdivision (b) of Section 12804.9 may drive any house car of 40 feet in length or less without obtaining a noncommercial class B driver's license with house car endorsement as described in subdivision (b).

(b) Any person seeking to drive any house car over 40 feet in length, excluding safety devices and safety bumpers, shall obtain a noncommercial class B driver's license with house car endorsement as described in this subdivision. The applicant for that endorsement shall pass a specialized written examination and demonstrate the ability to exercise ordinary and reasonable control in operating that vehicle by driving it under the supervision of an examining officer. Upon satisfactory completion of the examination and demonstration, the applicant shall be issued a noncommercial class B driver's license with house car endorsement by the department. Upon application for an endorsement to operate this vehicle, and every two years thereafter, the applicant shall submit medical information on a form approved by the department.

(Added by Stats. 2001, Ch. 658, Sec. 3. Effective October 10, 2001.)

12804.11. (a) To operate firefighting equipment, a driver, including a tiller operator, is required to do either of the following:

(1) Obtain and maintain a firefighter endorsement issued by the department and obtain and maintain a class C license as described in Section 12804.9, a restricted class A license as described in Section 12804.12, or a noncommercial class B license as described in Section 12804.10.

(2) Obtain and maintain a class A or B license as described in Section 12804.9 and, as appropriate, for the size and configuration of the firefighting equipment operated.

(b) To qualify for a firefighter endorsement the driver shall do all of the following:

(1) (A) Provide to the department proof of current employment as a firefighter or registration as a volunteer firefighter with a fire department and evidence of fire equipment operation training by providing a letter or other indication from the chief of the fire department or his or her designee.

(B) For purposes of this section, evidence of fire equipment operation training means the applicant has successfully completed Fire Apparatus Driver/Operator 1A taught by an instructor registered with the Office of the State Fire Marshal or fire department driver training that meets all of the following requirements:

(i) Meets or exceeds the standards outlined in NFPA 1002, Chapter 4 (2008 version) or the Fire Apparatus Driver/Operator 1A course adopted by the Office of the State Fire Marshal.

(ii) Prepares the applicant to safely operate the department's fire equipment that the applicant will be authorized to operate.

(iii) Includes a classroom (cognitive) portion of at least 16 hours.

(iv) Includes a manipulative portion of at least 14 hours, which includes directly supervised behind-the-wheel driver training.

(C) Driver training shall be conducted by a person who is registered with the Office of the State Fire Marshal to instruct a Fire Apparatus Driver/Operator 1A course or a person who meets all of the following criteria:

(i) Possesses a minimum of five years of fire service experience as an emergency vehicle operator, three of which must be at the rank of engineer or higher.

(ii) Possesses a valid California class A or B license or a class A or B license restricted to the operation of firefighting equipment or a class C license with a firefighter endorsement.

(iii) Is certified as a qualified training instructor or training officer by the State of California, the federal government, or a county training officers' association.

(2) Pass the written firefighter examination developed by the department with the cooperation of the Office of the State Fire Marshal.

(3) Upon application and every two years thereafter, submit medical information on a form approved by the department.

(c) There shall be no additional charge for adding a firefighter endorsement to an original license or when renewing a license. To add a firefighter endorsement to an existing license when not renewing the license, the applicant shall pay the fee for a duplicate license pursuant to Section 14901.

(d) (1) A driver of firefighting equipment is subject to the requirements of subdivision (a) if both of the following conditions exist:

(A) The equipment is operated by a person employed as a firefighter by a federal or state agency, by a regularly organized fire department of a city, county, city and county, or district, or by a tribal fire department or registered as a volunteer member of a regularly organized fire department having official recognition of the city, county, city and county, or district in which the department is located, or of a tribal fire department.

(B) The motor vehicle is used to travel to and from the scene of an emergency situation, or to transport equipment used in the control of an emergency situation, and which is owned, leased, or rented by, or under the exclusive control of, a federal or state agency, a regularly organized fire department of a city, county, city and county, or district, a volunteer fire department having official recognition of the city, county, city and county, or district in which the department is located, or a tribal fire department.

(2) A driver of firefighting equipment is not required to obtain and maintain a firefighter endorsement pursuant to paragraph (1) of subdivision (a) if the driver is operating the firefighting equipment for training purposes, during a nonemergency, while under the direct supervision of a fire department employee who is properly licensed to operate the equipment and is authorized by the fire department to provide training.

(e) For purposes of this section, a tiller operator is the driver of the rear free-axle portion of a ladder truck.

(f) For purposes of this section, "firefighting equipment" means a motor vehicle, that meets the definition of a class A or class B vehicle described in subdivision (b) of Section 12804.9, that is used to travel to and from the scene of an emergency situation, or to transport equipment used in the control of an emergency situation, and that is owned, leased, or rented by, or under the exclusive control of, a federal or state agency, a regularly organized fire department of a city, county, city and county, or district, or a volunteer fire department having official recognition of the city, county, city and county, or district in which the department is located.

(g) Notwithstanding paragraph (1) of subdivision (a), a regularly organized fire department, having official recognition of the city, county, city and county, or district in which the department is located, may require an employee or a volunteer of the fire department who is a driver or operator of firefighting equipment to hold a class A or B license.

(h) This section applies to a person hired by a fire department, or to a person renewing a driver's license, on or after January 1, 2011.

(Amended by Stats. 2014, Ch. 97, Sec. 1. (AB 2438) Effective January 1, 2015.)

12804.12. (a) The department may issue a restricted class A driver's license for the operation of any two-axle vehicle weighing 4,000 pounds or more unladen when towing a trailer coach exceeding 10,000 pounds gross vehicle weight rating, or a fifth-wheel travel trailer exceeding 15,000 pounds gross vehicle weight rating, when the towing of the trailer is not for compensation.

(b) In lieu of a report of a medical examination required by Section 12804.9, an applicant for a restricted license issued pursuant to subdivision (a) shall, upon application and every two years thereafter, submit medical information on a form approved by the department.

(c) This section shall remain in effect only until January 1, 2027, and as of that date is repealed.

(Amended by Stats. 2021, Ch. 610, Sec. 3. (SB 287) Effective January 1, 2022. Repealed as of January 1, 2027, by its own provisions. See later operative version as added by Sec. 4 of Stats. 2021, Ch. 610.)

12804.12. (a) The department may issue a restricted class A driver's license for the operation of a vehicle towing a trailer if all of the following conditions are met:

(1) The towing of the trailer is not for compensation or commercial purposes.

(2) The trailer has a gross vehicle weight rating or gross vehicle weight of more than 10,000 pounds.

(3) The trailer is used exclusively for recreational purposes.

(4) The trailer is used for the transportation of property or human habitation, or both.

(b) In lieu of a report of a medical examination required by Section 12804.9, an applicant for a restricted license issued pursuant to subdivision (a) shall, upon application and every two years thereafter, submit medical information on a form approved by the department.

(c) This section shall become operative on January 1, 2027.

(Repealed (in Sec. 3) and added by Stats. 2021, Ch. 610, Sec. 4. (SB 287) Effective January 1, 2022. Operative January 1, 2027, by its own provisions.)

12804.14. (a) The department may issue a restricted class A driver's license for the operation of any two-axle vehicle weighing 4,000 pounds or more unladen when towing a livestock trailer exceeding 10,000 pounds, but not exceeding 15,000 pounds gross vehicle weight rating or gross vehicle weight, if all of the following conditions are met:

(1) The vehicle is controlled and operated by a farmer.

(2) The vehicle is used to transport livestock to or from a farm.

(3) The vehicle is not used in the operations of a common or contract carrier.

(4) The vehicle is used within 150 miles of the person's farm.

(b) The requirements of subdivision (a) incorporate the guidelines published by the Federal Highway Administration in the Federal Register on September 26, 1988 (53 FR 37313). The department shall follow those guidelines in acting pursuant to this section as those guidelines now exist and as they are hereafter amended.

(c) In lieu of a report of a medical examination required by Sections 12804 and 12804.9, a licensed California driver applying for a restricted license issued pursuant to subdivision (a) shall, upon application and every two years thereafter, submit medical information on a form approved by the department.

(Amended by Stats. 1996, Ch. 10, Sec. 14. Effective February 9, 1996.)

12804.15. (a) Notwithstanding Section 362, for purposes of this section "house car" means a vehicle described in subdivision (b) of Section 12804.10.

(b) (1) Except as provided under paragraph (2), no person may operate a house car unless that person has in his or her possession a valid driver's license of the appropriate class and an endorsement thereto issued by the department to permit operation of the house car.

(2) A nonresident may not operate a house car in this state unless that person is in possession of an out-of-state driver's license authorizing the operation of that vehicle.

(c) An endorsement to drive a house car may be issued only if the applicant meets all of the following conditions:

(1) The applicant successfully completes an examination prescribed by the department to determine qualification for the endorsement.

(2) Upon initial application and every two years thereafter, the applicant submits medical information on a form approved by the department to verify that the person meets the minimum medical requirements established by the department for operation of a house car.

(3) Upon application for issuance of an original driver's license or renewal driver's license pursuant to subdivision (b) of Section 12804.10, there shall be paid to the department a fee of thirty-four dollars ($34) for a license that will expire on the applicant's fifth birthday following the date of the application.

(d) The department may deny, suspend, or revoke an endorsement to drive a house car when the applicant does not meet any requirement for the issuance or retention of the endorsement.

(Added by Stats. 2001, Ch. 658, Sec. 4. Effective October 10, 2001.)

12805. (a) The department shall not issue a driver's license to, or renew a driver's license of, any person:

(1) Who is not of legal age to receive a driver's license.

(2) Whose best corrected visual acuity is 20/200 or worse in that person's better eye, as verified by an optometrist or ophthalmologist. A person shall not use a bioptic telescopic or similar lens to meet the 20/200 visual acuity standards.

(3) Who is unable, as shown by examination, to understand traffic signs or signals or who does not have a reasonable knowledge of the requirements of this code governing the operation of vehicles upon the highways.

(4) When it is determined, by examination or other evidence, that the person is unable to safely operate a motor vehicle upon a highway.

(5) Who is unable to read and understand English used in highway traffic and directional signs.

(6) Who holds a valid driver's license issued by a foreign jurisdiction unless the license has been surrendered to the department, or is lost or destroyed.

(7) Who has ever held, or is the holder of, a license to drive issued by another state, territory, or possession of the United States, the District of Columbia, or the Commonwealth of Puerto Rico, and that license has been suspended by reason, in whole or in part, of a conviction of a traffic violation until the suspension period has terminated, except that the department may issue a license to the applicant if, in the opinion of the department, it will be safe to issue a license to a person whose license to drive was suspended by a state that is not a party to the Driver License Compact provided for in Chapter 6 (commencing with Section 15000) of Division 6.

(8) Who has ever held, or is the holder of, a license to drive issued by another state, territory, or possession of the United States, the District of Columbia or the Commonwealth of Puerto Rico, and that license has been revoked by reason, in whole or in part, of a conviction of a traffic violation, until the revocation has been terminated or after the expiration of one year from the date the license was revoked, whichever occurs first, except that the department may issue a license to the applicant if, in the opinion of the department, it will be safe to issue a license to a person whose license to drive was revoked by a state that is not a party to the Driver License Compact provided for in Chapter 6 (commencing with Section 15000) of Division 6.

(b) The department shall not issue a Real ID driver's license to a person who holds a valid Real ID identification card.

(c) The department may cancel a driver's license in order to enable compliance with subdivision (b).

(d) This section shall become operative on January 1, 2018.

(Repealed (in Sec. 9) and added by Stats. 2016, Ch. 339, Sec. 10. (SB 838) Effective September 13, 2016. Section operative January 1, 2018, by its own provisions.)

12806. The department may refuse to issue to, or renew a driver's license of, any person:

(a) Who is rendered incapable of safely operating a motor vehicle because of alcoholism, excessive and chronic use of alcoholic beverages, or addiction to, or habitual use of, any drug.

(b) Who is addicted to the use of narcotic drugs unless the person is participating in a narcotic treatment program approved pursuant to Article 3 (commencing with Section 11875) of Chapter 1 of Part 3 of Division 10.5 of the Health and Safety Code, in which case the person may be issued a probationary license, subject to reasonable terms and conditions, if that drug usage does not affect the person's ability to exercise reasonable and ordinary control in operating a motor vehicle on the highway.

(c) Who has a disorder characterized by lapses of consciousness or who has experienced, within the last three years, either a lapse of consciousness or an episode of marked confusion caused by any condition which may bring about recurrent lapses, or who has any physical or mental disability, disease, or disorder which could affect the safe operation of a motor vehicle unless the department has medical information which indicates the person may safely operate a motor vehicle. In making its determination, the department may rely on any relevant information available to the department.

(Amended by Stats. 1995, Ch. 455, Ch. 30. Effective September 5, 1995.)

12806.5. The department may adopt regulations specifying, in addition to any cause provided by statute, the circumstances which are grounds for the suspension or revocation of a schoolbus, school pupil activity, youth busdriver, farm labor vehicle, or general public paratransit vehicle certificate.

(Amended by Stats. 1990, Ch. 1360, Sec. 32.)

12807. The department shall not issue or renew a driver's license to any person:

(a) When a license previously issued to the person under this code has been suspended until the expiration of the period of the suspension, unless cause for suspension has been removed.

(b) When a license previously issued to the person under this code has been revoked until the expiration of one year after the date of the revocation, except where a different period of revocation is prescribed by this code, or unless the cause for revocation has been removed.

(c) When the department has received a notice pursuant to former Section 40509 or former Section 40509.5, unless the department has received a certificate as provided in those sections.

(d) This section shall remain in effect only until January 1, 2027, and as of that date is repealed.

(Amended by Stats. 2022, Ch. 800, Sec. 8. (AB 2746) Effective January 1, 2023. Repealed as of January 1, 2027, by its own provisions. See later operative version added by Sec. 9 of Stats. 2022, Ch. 800.)

12807. The department shall not issue or renew a driver's license to any person:

(a) When a license previously issued to the person under this code has been suspended until the expiration of the period of the suspension, unless cause for suspension has been removed.

(b) When a license previously issued to the person under this code has been revoked until the expiration of one year after the date of the revocation, except where a different period of revocation is prescribed by this code, or unless the cause for revocation has been removed.

(c) This section shall become operative on January 1, 2027.

(Repealed (in Sec. 7) and added by Stats. 2022, Ch. 800, Sec. 9. (AB 2746) Effective January 1, 2023. Operative January 1, 2027, by its own provisions.)

12808. (a) The department shall, before issuing or renewing any license, check the record of the applicant for conviction of traffic violations and traffic accidents.

(b) The department shall, before issuing or renewing any license, check the record of the applicant for notices of failure to appear in court filed with it and shall withhold or shall not issue a license to any applicant who has violated their written promise to appear in court unless the department has received a certificate issued by the magistrate or clerk of the court hearing the case in which the promise was given showing that the case has been adjudicated or unless the applicant's record is cleared as provided in Chapter 6 (commencing with Section 41500) of Division 17. In lieu of the certificate of adjudication, a notice from the court stating that the original records have been lost or destroyed shall permit the department to issue a license.

(c) (1) Any notice received by the department pursuant to former Section 40509, Section 40509.1, or former Section 40509.5, except subdivision (c) of former Section 40509.5, that has been on file five years may be removed from the department records and destroyed at the discretion of the department.

(2) Any notice received by the department under subdivision (c) of former Section 40509.5 that has been on file 10 years may be removed from the department records and destroyed at the discretion of the department.

(d) This section shall remain in effect only until January 1, 2027, and as of that date is repealed.

(Amended by Stats. 2022, Ch. 800, Sec. 10. (AB 2746) Effective January 1, 2023. Repealed as of January 1, 2027, by its own provisions. See later operative version added by Sec. 11 of Stats. 2022, Ch. 800.)

12808. (a) The department shall, before issuing or renewing any license, check the record of the applicant for conviction of traffic violations and traffic accidents.

(b) (1) Any notice received by the department pursuant to former Section 40509 or former Section 40509.5, except subdivision (c) of former Section 40509.5, shall be removed from the department records.

(2) Any notice received by the department pursuant to Section 40509.1, that has been on file five years may be removed from the department records and destroyed at the discretion of the department.

(c) This section shall become operative on January 1, 2027.

(Repealed (in Sec. 10) and added by Stats. 2022, Ch. 800, Sec. 11. (AB 2746) Effective January 1, 2023. Operative January 1, 2027, by its own provisions.)

12809. The department may refuse to issue or renew a driver's license to any person:

(a) If the department is satisfied that the applicant is not entitled to the license under this code.

(b) If the applicant has failed to furnish the department the information required in the application or reasonable additional information requested by the department.

(c) If the department determines that the applicant has made or permitted unlawful use of any driver's license.

(d) If the department determines that the person has knowingly used a false or fictitious name in any application for a license or has impersonated another in making application or in taking any test, or has knowingly made a false statement or knowingly concealed a material fact, or otherwise committed any fraud in any application.

(e) If the department determines that the applicant is a negligent or incompetent operator of a motor vehicle.

(f) If the applicant is convicted of any offense involving the transportation for purpose of sale, or the transportation for compensation, of a controlled substance under Division 10 (commencing with Section 11000) of the Health and Safety Code, and the commission of the offense involved the use or operation of a motor vehicle.

If, however, the driving privilege of the applicant is on probation for a cause related to the use or possession of a narcotic controlled substance, the department may refuse to issue or renew a driver's license to the applicant if the applicant is subsequently convicted of any offense involving the use or possession of a narcotic controlled substance, whether or not the commission of the offense involved the use or operation of a motor vehicle.

The maximum period of time for which the department may refuse to issue or renew a driver's license to any person pursuant to this subdivision shall be three years from the date of conviction.

(g) If the applicant fails or refuses to surrender to the department, upon its lawful demand, a nonresident minor's certificate which has been canceled.

(h) If the applicant has failed to appear regarding a citation issued for vehicle abandonment as specified in Section 22523.

(i) This section shall become operative on July 1, 1989.

(Repealed (in Sec. 2) and added by Stats. 1988, Ch. 1267, Sec. 3. Effective September 26, 1988. Section operative July 1, 1989, by its own provisions.)

12810. In determining the violation point count, the following shall apply:

(a) A conviction of failure to stop in the event of an accident in violation of Section 20001 or 20002 shall be given a value of two points.

(b) A conviction of a violation of Section 23152 or 23153 shall be given a value of two points.

(c) A conviction of reckless driving shall be given a value of two points.

(d) (1) A conviction of a violation of subdivision (b) of Section 191.5 or subdivision (c) of Section 192 of the Penal Code, or of Section 2800.2 or 2800.3, subdivision (b) of Section 21651, subdivision (b) of Section 22348, subdivision (a) or (c) of Section 23109, Section 23109.1, or Section 31602 of this code, shall be given a value of two points.

(2) A conviction of a violation of subdivision (a) or (b) of Section 23140 shall be given a value of two points.

(e) A conviction of a violation of Section 14601, 14601.1, 14601.2, 14601.3, or 14601.5 shall be given a value of two points.

(f) Except as provided in subdivision (i), any other traffic conviction involving the safe operation of a motor vehicle upon the highway shall be given a value of one point.

(g) A traffic accident in which the operator is deemed by the department to be responsible shall be given a value of one point.

(h) A conviction of a violation of Section 27360 or 27360.5 shall be given a value of one point.

(i) (1) A violation of paragraph (1), (2), (3), or (5) of subdivision (b) of Section 40001 shall not result in a violation point count being given to the driver if the driver is not the owner of the vehicle.

(2) A conviction of a violation of paragraph (1) or (2) of subdivision (b) of Section 12814.6, subdivision (a) of Section 21116, Section 21207.5, 21708, 21710, 21716, 23120, 24800, or 26707 shall not be given a violation point count.

(3) A violation of subdivision (d) of Section 21712 shall not result in a violation point count.

(4) A violation of Section 23136 shall not result in a violation point count.

(5) A violation of Section 38301, 38301.3, 38301.5, 38304.1, or 38504.1 shall not result in a violation point count.

(j) A conviction for only one violation arising from one occasion of arrest or citation shall be counted in determining the violation point count for the purposes of this section.

(Amended by Stats. 2009, Ch. 414, Sec. 2. (AB 134) Effective January 1, 2010.)

12810.2. (a) Notwithstanding subdivision (f) of Section 12810, a violation point count shall not be given for a conviction of a violation of Section 27315, 27318, or 27319.

(b) The amendments to this section as added by the act that added this subdivision shall be operative on July 1, 2018.

(Amended by Stats. 2017, Ch. 593, Sec. 1.5. (SB 20) Effective January 1, 2018. Amended version operative July 1, 2018, by Stats. 2017, Ch. 593, Sec. 5, and as restated in its own provisions.)

12810.3. Notwithstanding subdivision (f) of Section 12810, a violation point shall be given only for a conviction of a violation of subdivision (a) of Section 23123, subdivision (a) of Section 23123.5, or subdivision (b) of Section 23124, occurring on or after July 1, 2021, that occurs within 36 months of a prior conviction for the same offense.

(Amended by Stats. 2019, Ch. 603, Sec. 1. (AB 47) Effective January 1, 2020.)

12810.4. Notwithstanding any other provision of law, no violation point shall be given for a conviction of a violation of Section 22526.

(Added by Stats. 1993, Ch. 647, Sec. 1. Effective January 1, 1994.)

12810.5. (a) Except as otherwise provided in subdivision (b), a person whose driving record shows a violation point count of four or more points in 12 months, six or more points in 24 months, or eight or more points in 36 months shall be prima facie presumed to be a negligent operator of a motor vehicle. In applying this subdivision to a driver, if the person requests and appears at a hearing conducted by the department, the department shall give due consideration to the amount of use or mileage traveled in the operation of a motor vehicle.

(b) (1) A class A or class B licensed driver, except persons holding certificates pursuant to Section 12517, 12519, 12523, 12523.5, or 12527, or an endorsement issued pursuant to paragraph (2) or (5) of subdivision (a) of Section 15278, who is presumed to be a negligent operator pursuant to subdivision (a), and who requests and appears at a hearing and is found to have a driving record violation point count of six or more points in 12 months, eight or more points in 24 months, or 10 or more points in 36 months is presumed to be a prima facie negligent operator. However, the higher point count does not apply if the department reasonably determines that four or more points in 12 months, six or more points in 24 months, or eight or more points in 36 months are attributable to the driver's operation of a vehicle requiring only a class C license, and not requiring a certificate or endorsement, or a class M license.

(2) For purposes of this subdivision, each point assigned pursuant to Section 12810 shall be valued at one and one-half times the value otherwise required by that section for each violation reasonably determined by the department to be attributable to the driver's operation of a vehicle requiring a class A or class B license, or requiring a certificate or endorsement described in this section.

(c) The department may require a negligent operator whose driving privilege is suspended or revoked pursuant to this section to submit proof of financial responsibility, as defined in Section 16430, on or before the date of reinstatement following the suspension or revocation. The proof of financial responsibility shall be maintained with the department for three years following that date of reinstatement.

(Amended by Stats. 2007, Ch. 630, Sec. 4. Effective January 1, 2008.)

12811. (a) (1) (A) When the department determines that the applicant is lawfully entitled to a license, it shall issue to the person a driver's license as applied for. The license shall state the class of license for which the licensee has qualified and shall contain the distinguishing number assigned to the applicant, the date of expiration, the true full name, age, and mailing address or residence address of the licensee, a brief description and engraved picture or photograph of the licensee for the purpose of identification, and space for the signature of the licensee.

(B) Each license shall also contain a space for the endorsement of a record of each suspension or revocation of the license.

(C) The department shall use whatever process or processes, in the issuance of engraved or colored licenses, that prohibit, as near as possible, the ability to alter or reproduce the license or prohibit the ability to superimpose a picture or photograph on the license without ready detection.

(2) In addition to the requirements of paragraph (1), a license issued to a person under 18 years of age shall display the words "provisional until age 18."

(b) (1) All applications for a driver's license or identification card shall contain a space for an applicant to indicate whether they have served in the Armed Forces of the United States and to give their consent to be contacted regarding eligibility to receive state or federal veterans benefits. The application shall contain the following statement:

"By marking the veteran box on this application, I certify that I am a veteran of the United States Armed Forces and that I want to receive veterans benefits information from the California Department of Veterans Affairs. By marking the veteran box on this application, I also consent to DMV transmitting my name and mailing address to the California Department of Veterans Affairs for this purpose only, and I certify that I have been notified that this transmittal will occur."

(2) The department shall collect the information obtained pursuant to paragraph (1).

(3) As mutually agreed between the department and the Department of Veterans Affairs, the department shall electronically transmit to the Department of Veterans Affairs the following information on each applicant who has identified that they have served in the Armed Forces of the United States since the last data transfer and has consented to be contacted about veterans benefits:

(A) The applicant's true full name.

(B) The applicant's mailing address.

(4) Information obtained by the Department of Veterans Affairs for the purposes of this subdivision shall be used for the purpose of assisting individuals to access veterans benefits and shall not be disseminated except as needed for this purpose.

(5) An application for a driver's license or identification card shall allow an applicant to request the word "VETERAN" be printed on the face of the driver's license or identification card. A verification form shall be developed by the Department of Veterans Affairs in consultation with the Department of Motor Vehicles and the California Association of County Veterans Service Officers to acknowledge verification of veteran status. A county veterans service office shall verify the veteran's status as a veteran, sign the verification form, and return it to the veteran. The Department of Motor Vehicles shall accept the signed verification form as proof of veteran status. The word "VETERAN" shall be printed on the face of a driver's license or identification card, in a location determined by the department, and issued to a person who makes this request and presents the verification form to the department.

(c) A contract shall not be awarded to a nongovernmental entity for the processing of driver's licenses unless the contract conforms to all applicable state contracting laws and all applicable procedures set forth in the State Contracting Manual.

(Amended by Stats. 2023, Ch. 131, Sec. 216. (AB 1754) Effective January 1, 2024.)

12811.1. (a) Upon the applicant's request, the department shall issue an adhesive backed medical information card which contains a format permitting the licensee to specify blood type, allergies, past or present medical problems, any medication being taken, the name of the licensee's doctor, the person to notify in case of an emergency, and whether the licensee is under a doctor's care.

(b) The medical information card, which shall be a different color than the anatomical gift Donor Dot authorized by Section 12811.3, shall be the same size as a driver's license.

(Amended by Stats. 2021, Ch. 211, Sec. 4. (AB 1374) Effective January 1, 2022.)

12811.3. (a) A written or electronic application for an original or renewal driver's license or identification card shall contain a space for the applicant to enroll in the Donate Life California Organ and Tissue Donor Registry. The application shall include check boxes for an applicant to mark either (A) Yes, add my name to the donor registry or (B) I do not wish to register at this time.

(b) (1) The department shall enter into a memorandum of understanding with the Donate Life California Organ and Tissue Donor Registry to mutually agree upon the language accompanying the question of enrollment required in subdivision (a) for the purpose of defining enrollment and providing the corresponding disclosures.

(2) The department shall continue to use existing language accompanying the question of enrollment until a memorandum of understanding, as described in paragraph (1), is in effect.

(3) At any time a memorandum of understanding, as described in paragraph (1), is not in effect, the department shall continue to use the language from the most recent memorandum of understanding until a new one is in effect.

(c) Notwithstanding any other law, a person under 18 years of age may register as a donor. However, the legal guardian of that person shall make the final decision regarding the donation.

(d) The department shall collect donor designation information on all applications for an original or renewal driver's license or identification card.

(e) The department shall print the word "DONOR" or another appropriate designation on the face of a driver's license or identification card to a person who has indicated on the application their intent to enroll in the organ donation program pursuant to this section.

(f) On a weekly basis, the department shall electronically transmit to Donate Life California, a nonprofit organization established and designated as the California Organ and Tissue Donor Registrar pursuant to Section 7150.90 of the Health and Safety Code, all of the following information from every application that indicates the applicant's decision to enroll in the organ donation program:

(1) The applicant's true full name.

(2) The applicant's residence or mailing address.

(3) The applicant's year of birth.

(4) The applicant's California driver's license number or identification card number.

(g) (1) A person who applies for an original or renewal driver's license or identification card may designate a voluntary contribution of two dollars ($2) or more for the purpose of promoting and supporting organ and tissue donation. This contribution shall be collected by the department, and treated as a voluntary contribution to Donate Life California and not as a fee for the issuance of a driver's license or identification card.

(2) The department may use the donations collected pursuant to this section to cover its actual administrative costs incurred pursuant to subdivisions (d) to (f), inclusive. The department shall deposit all revenue derived pursuant to this section and remaining after the department's deduction for administrative costs in the Donate Life California Trust Subaccount that is hereby created in the Motor Vehicle Account in the State Transportation Fund. Notwithstanding Section 13340 of the Government Code, all revenue in this subaccount is continuously appropriated, without regard to fiscal years, to the Controller for allocation to Donate Life California and shall be expended for the purpose of increasing participation in organ donation programs.

(h) The enrollment form shall be posted on the internet websites for the department and the California Health and Human Services Agency.

(i) The enrollment form shall constitute a legal document pursuant to the Uniform Anatomical Gift Act (Chapter 3.5 (commencing with Section 7150) of Part 1 of Division 7 of the Health and Safety Code) and shall remain binding after the donor's death despite any express desires of next of kin opposed to the donation. Except for the provisions relating to a person under 18 years of age, the donation does not require the consent of any other person.

(j) Donate Life California shall ensure that all additions and deletions to the California Organ and Tissue Donor Registry, established pursuant to Section 7150.90 of the Health and Safety Code, shall occur within 30 days of receipt.

(k) Information obtained by Donate Life California for the purposes of this section shall be used for these purposes only and shall not be disseminated further by Donate Life California.

(l) A public entity or employee shall not be liable for loss, detriment, or injury resulting directly or indirectly from false or inaccurate information contained in the enrollment form provided pursuant to this section.

(Added by Stats. 2021, Ch. 211, Sec. 5. (AB 1374) Effective January 1, 2022.)

12811.4. (a) This section shall be known, and may be cited, as Charlie's Law.

(b) An electronic application for an original or renewal driver's license or identification card shall contain a solicitation for the applicant to enroll in the registry operated by the National Marrow Donor Program. The application shall include a question regarding enrollment pursuant to subdivision (c) and check boxes for an applicant to mark either of the following:

(1) Yes, I would like to enroll in the registry to be a potential bone marrow or blood stem cell donor. I consent to my information being shared with the National Marrow Donor Program for the purposes of enrollment. I understand that I am not enrolled at this time and must complete the National Marrow Donor Program enrollment forms and cheek swab to be a registered bone marrow donor. I am aware that after enrollment, if matched, I have the ability to refuse to donate at any point.

(2) No, I do not wish to enroll at this time.

(c) An applicant's election to enroll in the National Marrow Donor

Program's registry shall constitute consent to their information being transmitted to the National Marrow Donor Program for the purposes of completing enrollment in the registry. After submitting their electronic application for an original or renewal driver's license or identification card, the applicant shall receive a followup communication to complete the National Marrow Donor Program application.

(d) The department shall enter into a memorandum of understanding with the National Marrow Donor Program to mutually agree upon all of the following:

(1) The language of the question of enrollment required by subdivision (b). The language may define enrollment and donor requirements, including, but not limited to, limits on the transferring of data to only those eligible for enrollment in the National Marrow Donor Program, and may provide the corresponding disclosures.

(2) The language of the followup communication described in subdivision (c).

(3) The operative date for the provisions specified in subdivisions (b) and (e).

(e) On a weekly basis, the department shall electronically transmit to the National Marrow Donor Program all of the following information from every application that indicates the applicant's intent to enroll as a potential bone marrow or blood stem cell donor:

(1) The applicant's true full name.

(2) The applicant's residence or mailing address.

(3) The applicant's date of birth.

(4) The applicant's telephone number.

(5) The applicant's email address.

(f) The department and the California Health and Human Services Agency shall post the enrollment form on its internet website.

(g) Enrollment in the National Marrow Donor Program registry through the department does not constitute a legal document pursuant to the Uniform Anatomical Gift Act (Chapter 3.5 (commencing with Section 7150) of Part 1 of Division 7 of the Health and Safety Code) and does not require registrants to donate if they are matched.

(h) Information obtained by the National Marrow Donor Program shall be used only for registry operations consistent with the informed consent of the applicant. Information obtained by the National Marrow Donor Program for the purposes of this section shall not be disseminated further by the National Marrow Donor Program.

(i) A public entity or its employee shall not be liable for loss, detriment, or injury resulting directly or indirectly from false or inaccurate information contained in the enrollment form provided pursuant to this section.

(Amended by Stats. 2025, Ch. 16, Sec. 5. (SB 128) Effective June 27, 2025.)

12812. If a driver with a class C or M license, who is not required to have a certificate under any provision of this code, is presumed to be a negligent operator pursuant to Section 12810.5, the department may, as a condition of probation, issue a restricted driver's license to permit driving of a vehicle while in the course of the driver's employment during specified hours of employment or any other restrictions as determined by the department. The restrictions shall be noted on the driver's license.

(Amended by Stats. 1993, Ch. 272, Sec. 31. Effective August 2, 1993.)

12813. (a) The department may, upon issuing a driver's license or after issuance whenever good cause appears, impose restrictions suitable to the licensee's driving ability with respect to the type of, or special mechanical control devices required on, a motor vehicle which the licensee may operate or impose other restrictions applicable to the licensee that the department may determine to be appropriate to assure the safe operation of a motor vehicle by the licensee.

(b) The department may issue either a special restricted license or may set forth the restrictions upon the usual license form.

(c) The authority of the department to issue restricted licenses under this section is subject to Sections 12812, 13352, 13353.3, and 13352.5.

(Amended by Stats. 2011, Ch. 657, Sec. 1. (AB 520) Effective January 1, 2012.)

12814. (a) Application for renewal of a license shall be made at an office of the department by the person to whom the license was issued. The department may in its discretion require an examination of the applicant as upon an original application, or an examination deemed by the department to be appropriate considering the licensee's record of convictions and accidents, or an examination deemed by the department to be appropriate in relation to evidence of a condition that may affect the ability of the applicant to safely operate a motor vehicle. The age of a licensee, by itself, may not constitute evidence of a condition requiring an examination of the driving ability. If the department finds any evidence, the department shall disclose the evidence to the applicant or licensee. If the person is absent from the state at the time the license expires, the director may extend the license for a period of one year from the expiration date of the license.

(b) Renewal of a driver's license shall be under terms and conditions prescribed by the department.

(c) The department may adopt and administer those regulations as shall be deemed necessary for the public safety in the implementation of a program of selective testing of applicants, and, with reference to this section, the department may waive tests for purposes of evaluation of selective testing procedures.

(d) A driver's license renewal notice for a person who is required to pass a knowledge examination in order to renew his or her driver's license shall provide written notice of that requirement.

(Amended by Stats. 2018, Ch. 171, Sec. 1. (AB 2357) Effective January 1, 2019.)

12814.4. (a) The director may establish a program to evaluate the traffic safety and other effects of renewing driver's licenses by virtual or other remote processes, in lieu of submitting an application at an office of the department pursuant to subdivision (a) of Section 12814. Pursuant to that program, the department may renew driver's licenses by virtual or other remote processes.

(b) The director may terminate the renewal by virtual or other remote processes authorized by this section at any time.

(c) On or before January 1, 2034, the department shall provide a report to the Legislature and relevant policy committees detailing the program established under this section.

(1) The report shall include the steps the department took to prevent individuals other than the applicant from taking the knowledge test, the number of individuals on an annual basis that opted to take the knowledge examination virtually or by other remote processes, and the number of individuals that opted to submit a test of their eyesight by virtual or other remote processes, and the process the department took to verify the authenticity of the tests submitted to the department.

(2) The report shall be submitted in compliance with Section 9795 of the Government Code.

(d) A renewal by virtual or other remote processes under this program shall not be granted to a person who is 70 years of age or older without a test of the eyesight of the applicant.

(e) The department shall not renew a driver's license by virtual or other remote processes that has been previously renewed by mail or by virtual or other remote processes two consecutive times for five-year periods, or by an applicant that is 80 years of age or older.

(f) This section shall remain in effect only until January 1, 2035, and as of that date is repealed.

(Added by Stats. 2023, Ch. 373, Sec. 1. (AB 1606) Effective January 1, 2024. Repealed as of January 1, 2035, by its own provisions.)

12814.5. (a) The director may establish a program to evaluate the traffic safety and other effects of renewing driver's licenses by mail. Pursuant to that program, the department may renew by mail driver's licenses for licensees not holding a probationary license, and whose records, for the two years immediately preceding the determination of eligibility for the renewal, show no notification of a violation of subdivision (a) of former Section 40509, a total violation point count not greater than one as determined in accordance with Section 12810, no suspension of the driving privilege pursuant to Section 13353.2, and no refusal to submit to or complete chemical testing pursuant to Section 13353 or 13353.1.

(b) The director may terminate the renewal by mail program authorized by this section at any time the department determines that the program has an adverse impact on traffic safety.

(c) A renewal by mail shall not be granted to any person who is 70 years of age or older.

(d) The department shall notify each licensee granted a renewal by mail pursuant to this section of major changes to the Vehicle Code affecting traffic laws occurring during the prior five-year period.

(e) The department shall not renew a driver's license by mail if the license has been previously renewed by mail two consecutive times for five-year periods.

(Amended (as added by Stats. 2021, Ch. 254, Sec. 7) by Stats. 2022, Ch. 800, Sec. 12. (AB 2746) Effective January 1, 2023.)

12814.6. (a) Except as provided in Section 12814.7, a driver's license issued to a person at least 16 years of age but under 18 years of age shall be issued pursuant to the provisional licensing program contained in this section. The program shall consist of all of the following components:

(1) Upon application for an original license, the applicant shall be issued an instruction permit pursuant to Section 12509. A person who has in their immediate possession a valid permit issued pursuant to Section 12509 may operate a motor vehicle, other than a motorcycle or motorized bicycle, only when the person is either taking the driver training instruction referred to in paragraph (3) or practicing that instruction, provided the person is accompanied by, and is under the immediate supervision of, a California-licensed driver 25 years of age or older whose driving privilege is not on probation. The age requirement of this paragraph does not apply if the licensed driver is the parent, spouse, or guardian of the permitholder or is a licensed or certified driving instructor.

(2) The person shall hold an instruction permit for not less than six months prior to applying for a provisional driver's license.

(3) The person shall have complied with one of the following:

(A) Satisfactory completion of approved courses in automobile driver education and driver training maintained pursuant to provisions of the Education Code in any secondary school of California, or equivalent instruction in a secondary school of another state.

(B) Satisfactory completion of an integrated driver education and training program that is approved by the department and conducted by a driving instructor licensed under Chapter 1 (commencing with Section 11100) of Division 5. The program shall utilize segmented modules, whereby a portion of the educational instruction is provided by, and then reinforced through, specific behind-the-wheel training before moving to the next phase of driver education and training. The program shall contain a minimum of 30 hours of classroom instruction and 6 hours of behind-the-wheel training.

(C) Satisfactory completion of six hours or more of behind-the-wheel instruction by a driving school or an independent driving instructor licensed under Chapter 1 (commencing with Section 11100) of Division 5 and either an accredited course in automobile driver education in any secondary school of California pursuant to provisions of the Education Code or satisfactory completion of equivalent professional instruction acceptable to the department. To be acceptable to the department, the professional instruction shall meet minimum standards to be prescribed by the department, and the standards shall be at least equal to the requirements for driver education and driver training contained in the rules and regulations adopted by the State Board of Education pursuant to the Education Code. A person who has complied with this subdivision shall not be required by the governing board of a school district to comply with subparagraph (A) in order to graduate from high school.

(D) Except as provided under subparagraph (B), a student may not take driver training instruction, unless the student has successfully completed driver education.

(4) The person shall complete 50 hours of supervised driving practice prior to the issuance of a provisional license, which is in addition to any other driver training instruction required by law. Not less than 10 of the required practice hours shall include driving during darkness, as defined in Section 280. Upon application for a provisional license, the person shall submit to the department the certification of a parent, spouse, guardian, or licensed or certified driving instructor that the applicant has completed the required amount of driving practice and is prepared to take the department's driving test. A person without a parent, spouse, guardian, or who is an emancipated minor, may have a licensed driver 25 years of age or older or a licensed or certified driving instructor complete the certification. This requirement does not apply to motorcycle practice.

(5) The person shall successfully complete an examination required by the department. Before retaking a test, the person shall wait for not less than one week after failure of the written test and for not less than two weeks after failure of the driving test.

(b) Except as provided in Section 12814.7, the provisional driver's license shall be subject to all of the following restrictions:

(1) Except as specified in paragraph (2), during the first 12 months after issuance of a provisional license the licensee may not do any of the following unless accompanied and supervised by a licensed driver who is the licensee's parent or guardian, a licensed driver who is 25 years of age or older, or a licensed or certified driving instructor:

(A) Drive between the hours of 11 p.m. and 5 a.m.

(B) Transport passengers who are under 20 years of age.

(2) A licensee may drive between the hours of 11 p.m. and 5 a.m. or transport an immediate family member without being accompanied and supervised by a licensed driver who is the licensee's parent or guardian, a licensed driver who is 25 years of age or older, or a licensed or certified driving instructor, in the following circumstances:

(A) Medical necessity of the licensee when reasonable transportation facilities are inadequate and operation of a vehicle by a minor is necessary. The licensee shall keep in their possession a signed statement from a physician familiar with the condition, containing a diagnosis and probable date when sufficient recovery will have been made to terminate the necessity.

(B) Schooling or school-authorized activities of the licensee when reasonable transportation facilities are inadequate and operation of a vehicle by a minor is necessary. The licensee shall keep in their possession a signed statement from the school principal, dean, or school staff member designated by the principal or dean, containing a probable date that the schooling or school-authorized activity will have been completed.

(C) Employment necessity of the licensee when reasonable transportation facilities are inadequate and operation of a vehicle by a minor is necessary. The licensee shall keep in their possession a signed statement from the employer, verifying employment and containing a probable date that the employment will have been completed.

(D) Necessity of the licensee or the licensee's immediate family member when reasonable transportation facilities are inadequate and operation of a vehicle by a minor is necessary to transport the licensee or the licensee's immediate family member. The licensee shall keep in their possession a signed statement from a parent or legal guardian verifying the reason and containing a probable date that the necessity will have ceased.

(E) The licensee is an emancipated minor.

(c) A law enforcement officer shall not stop a vehicle for the sole purpose of determining whether the driver is in violation of the restrictions imposed under subdivision (b).

(d) A law enforcement officer shall not stop a vehicle for the sole purpose of determining whether a driver who is subject to the license restrictions in subdivision (b) is in violation of Article 2.5 (commencing with Section 118947) of Chapter 4 of Part 15 of Division 104 of the Health and Safety Code.

(e) (1) Upon a finding that any licensee has violated paragraph (1) of subdivision (b), the court shall impose one of the following:

(A) Not less than 8 hours nor more than 16 hours of community service for a first offense and not less than 16 hours nor more than 24 hours of community service for a second or subsequent offense.

(B) A fine of not more than thirty-five dollars ($35) for a first offense and a fine of not more than fifty dollars ($50) for a second or subsequent offense.

(2) If the court orders community service, the court shall retain jurisdiction until the hours of community service have been completed.

(3) If the hours of community service have not been completed within 90 days, the court shall impose a fine of not more than thirty-five dollars ($35) for a first offense and not more than fifty dollars ($50) for a second or subsequent offense.

(f) A conviction of paragraph (1) of subdivision (b), when reported to the department, may not be disclosed as otherwise specified in Section 1808 or constitute a violation point count value pursuant to Section 12810.

(g) Any term of restriction or suspension of the driving privilege imposed on a person pursuant to this subdivision shall remain in effect until the end of the term even though the person becomes 18 years of age before the term ends.

(1) The driving privilege shall be suspended when the record of the person shows one or more notifications issued pursuant to former Section 40509 or former Section 40509.5. The suspension shall continue until any notification issued pursuant to former Section 40509 or former Section 40509.5 has been cleared.

(2) A 30-day restriction shall be imposed when a driver's record shows a violation point count of two or more points in 12 months, as determined in accordance with Section 12810. The restriction shall require the licensee to be accompanied by a licensed parent, spouse, guardian, or other licensed driver 25 years of age or older, except when operating a class M vehicle, or so licensed, with no passengers aboard.

(3) A 6-month suspension of the driving privilege and a one-year term of probation shall be imposed whenever a licensee's record shows a violation point count of three or more points in 12 months, as determined in accordance with Section 12810. The terms and conditions of probation shall include, but not be limited to, both of the following:

(A) The person shall violate no law that, if resulting in conviction, is reportable to the department under Section 1803.

(B) The person shall remain free from accident responsibility.

(h) Whenever action by the department under subdivision (g) arises as a result of a motor vehicle accident, the person may, in writing and within 10 days, demand a hearing to present evidence that they were not responsible for the accident upon which the action is based. Whenever action by the department is based upon a conviction reportable to the department under Section 1803, the person has no right to a hearing pursuant to Article 3 (commencing with Section 14100) of Chapter 3.

(i) The department shall require a person whose driving privilege is suspended or revoked pursuant to subdivision (g) to submit proof of financial responsibility as defined in Section 16430. The proof of financial responsibility shall be filed on or before the date of reinstatement following the suspension or revocation. The proof of financial responsibility shall be maintained with the department for three years following the date of reinstatement.

(j) (1) Notwithstanding any other provision of this code, the department may issue a distinctive driver's license, that displays a distinctive color or a distinctively colored stripe or other distinguishing characteristic, to persons at least 16 years of age and older but under 18 years of age, and to persons 18 years of age and older but under 21 years of age, so that the distinctive license feature is immediately recognizable. The features shall clearly differentiate between driver's licenses issued to persons at least 16 years of age or older but under 18 years of age and to persons 18 years of age or older but under 21 years of age.

(2) If changes in the format or appearance of driver's licenses are adopted pursuant to this subdivision, those changes may be implemented under any new contract for the production of driver's licenses entered into after the adoption of those changes.

(k) The department shall include, on the face of the provisional driver's license, the original issuance date of the provisional driver's license in addition to any other issuance date.

(l) This section shall be known and may be cited as the Brady-Jared Teen Driver Safety Act of 1997.

(Amended by Stats. 2022, Ch. 800, Sec. 13. (AB 2746) Effective January 1, 2023.)

12814.7. (a) Notwithstanding the provisional licensing requirements of subdivisions (a) to (e), inclusive, of Section 12814.6, the department shall issue to a person who is at least 16 years of age, but under 18 years of age, a restricted class C driver's license valid for the operation of United States Army and California National Guard vehicles during the course and scope of their duties with the California National Guard if the following conditions are met:

(1) Upon application, the person provides the department with the executed enlistment contract for the applicant.

(2) The person qualifies for and is issued an instruction permit pursuant to Section 12509.

(3) Prior to the issuance of the class C license, the applicant provides proof satisfactory to the department of successful completion of a driver education and training course administered by the California National Guard.

(b) A driver's license issued pursuant to this section shall be subject to both of the following:

(1) Subdivisions (f) to (k), inclusive, of Section 12814.6.

(2) Pull-notice and periodic reports issued pursuant to Section 1808.1.

(c) The licensee shall comply with all other licensing requirements of this code, including, but not limited to, the requirements of Section 12804.9.

(Added by Stats. 2002, Ch. 418, Sec. 3. Effective January 1, 2003.)

12815. (a) If a driver's license issued under this code is lost, destroyed or mutilated, or a new true, full name is acquired, the person to whom it was issued shall obtain a duplicate upon furnishing to the department (1) satisfactory proof of that loss, destruction, or mutilation and (2) if the licensee is a minor, evidence of permission to obtain a duplicate secured from the parents, guardian, or person having custody of the minor. Any person who loses a driver's license and who, after obtaining a duplicate, finds the original license shall immediately destroy the original license.

(b) A person in possession of a valid driver's license who has been informed either by the department or by a law enforcement agency that the document is mutilated shall surrender the license to the department not later than 10 days after that notification.

(c) A person who submits a change of address pursuant to Section 14600 may apply to the department for a duplicate driver's license. If a person receives a duplicate pursuant to this subdivision, they shall immediately destroy the license with the prior mailing address.

(d) For purposes of this section, a mutilated license is one that has been damaged sufficiently to render any or all of the elements of identity set forth in Sections 12800.5 and 12811 unreadable or unidentifiable through visual, mechanical, or electronic means.

(Amended by Stats. 2025, Ch. 417, Sec. 4. (SB 506) Effective January 1, 2026.)

12816. (a) Every original driver's license expires on the fifth birthday of the applicant following the date of the application for the license.

(b) Renewal of a driver's license shall be made for a term which expires on the fifth birthday of the applicant following the expiration of the license renewed, if application for renewal is made within six months prior to the expiration of the license to be renewed, or within 90 days after expiration of the license. If renewal is not applied for within 90 days after expiration of the license, the application and fee is considered the same as an application for an original license.

(c) The department may accept application for a renewal of a driver's license made more than six months prior to the date of expiration. The renewal shall be made for a term which expires on the fifth birthday of the applicant following the date of the application for the renewal license.

(d) The department may accept an application for a license of a different class made more than six months before the expiration of the license previously issued, if the previously issued license is surrendered for cancellation in accordance with Section 13100. The driver's license issued from that application expires on the fifth birthday of the applicant following the date of the application.

(e) Notwithstanding subdivisions (a), (b), (c), and (d), the department may adjust the expiration date for any driver's license issued pursuant to this code.

(Amended by Stats. 1996, Ch. 1043, Sec. 6. Effective January 1, 1997.)

12817. (a) A California driver's license held by a person who enters or is in the United States Armed Forces shall continue in full force and effect, so long as the service continues and the person remains absent from this state, and for a period not to exceed 30 days following the date the holder of the license is honorably separated from that service or returns to this state, whichever is earlier, unless the license was suspended, canceled, or revoked for cause as provided by law. The license is valid only if it is in the immediate possession of the licensee and the licensee has in their immediate possession discharge or separation papers if the licensee has been discharged or separated from that service.

(b) A California driver's license held by a spouse of a person described in subdivision (a) shall continue in full force and effect, so long as the person described in subdivision (a) continues in the service and remains absent from this state and the spouse remains absent from this state, and for a period not to exceed 30 days following the date the person described in subdivision (a) is honorably separated from that service or the date that the person or the spouse returns to this state, whichever is earlier, unless the spouse's license was suspended, canceled, or revoked for cause as provided by law. The license is valid only if it is in the immediate possession of the licensee and the licensee has in their immediate possession discharge or separation papers of the person described in subdivision (a).

(c) A California driver's license held by a person who enters or is in the United States Foreign Service shall continue in full force and effect, so long as the service continues and the person remains absent from this state, and for a period not to exceed 30 days following the date the holder of the license returns to this state, unless the license was suspended, canceled, or revoked for cause as provided by law. The license is valid only if it is in the immediate possession of the licensee and the licensee has in their immediate possession verification of active service papers.

(d) A California driver's license held by a spouse of a person described in subdivision (c) shall continue in full force and effect, so long as the person described in subdivision (c) continues in the service and remains absent from this state and the spouse remains absent from this state, and for a period not to exceed 30 days following the date the person described in subdivision (c) or the spouse returns to this state, unless the spouse's license was suspended, canceled, or revoked for cause as provided by law. The license is valid only if it is in the immediate possession of the licensee and the licensee has in their immediate possession verification of active service papers of the person described in subdivision (c).

(Amended by Stats. 2019, Ch. 503, Sec. 1. (SB 267) Effective January 1, 2020.)

12818. (a) Upon receipt of a request for reexamination and presentation of a legible copy of a notice of reexamination by a person issued the notice pursuant to Section 21061, the department shall reexamine the person's qualifications to operate a motor vehicle pursuant to Section 13801, notwithstanding the notice requirement of Section 13801.

(b) Based on the department's reexamination of the person's qualifications pursuant to subdivision (a), the department shall determine if either of the following actions should be taken:

(1) Suspend or revoke the driving privilege of that person if the department finds that any of the grounds exist which authorize the refusal to issue a license.

(2) Restrict, make subject to terms and conditions of probation, suspend, or revoke the driving privilege of that person based upon the records of the department as provided in Chapter 3 (commencing with Section 13800).

(c) As an alternative to subdivision (a), the department may suspend or revoke the person's driving privilege as provided under Article 2 (commencing with Section 13950) of Chapter 3.

(d) Upon request, the department shall notify the law enforcement agency which employs the traffic officer who issued the notice of reexamination of the results of the reexamination.

(e) This section shall become operative on January 1, 2011.

(Repealed (in Sec. 13) and added by Stats. 2000, Ch. 985, Sec. 14. Effective January 1, 2001. Section operative January 1, 2011, by its own provisions.)

12819. Unless the person issued the notice of reexamination requests the reexamination pursuant to Section 12818 within five working days after the department receives the notice of reexamination transmitted pursuant to Section 21062, the department shall peremptorily suspend the driving privilege of the person until the person has completed the reexamination and the department has taken the action prescribed in subdivision (b) of Section 12818.

(Added by Stats. 1986, Ch. 304, Sec. 2. Operative July 1, 1987, by Sec. 6 of Ch. 304.)

Article 4. Signature and Display of Licenses

(Article 4 enacted by Stats. 1959, Ch. 3.)

12950. (a) Every person licensed under this code shall write his or her usual signature with pen and ink in the space provided for that purpose on the license issued to him or her, immediately on receipt thereof, and the license is not valid until so signed, except that if the department issues a form of license which bears the facsimile signature of the applicant as shown upon the application, the license is valid even though not so signed.

(b) For purposes of subdivision (a), signature includes a digitized signature.

(Amended by Stats. 2003, Ch. 819, Sec. 3. Effective January 1, 2004.)

12950.5. (a) The department shall require digitized signatures on each driver's license. A digitized signature is an electronic representation of a handwritten signature.

(b) The department shall provide to the Secretary of State the digitized signature of every person who registers to vote on the voter registration card provided by the department.

(c) The department shall provide the Secretary of State with change-of-address information for every voter who indicates that he or she desires to have his or her address changed for voter registration purposes.

(Added by Stats. 2003, Ch. 819, Sec. 4. Effective January 1, 2004.)

12951. (a) The licensee shall have the valid driver's license issued to him or her in his or her immediate possession at all times when driving a motor vehicle upon a highway.

Any charge under this subdivision shall be dismissed when the person charged produces in court a driver's license duly issued to that person and valid at the time of his or her arrest, except that upon a third or subsequent charge the court in its discretion may dismiss the charge. When a temporary, interim, or duplicate driver's license is produced in court, the charge shall not be dismissed unless the court has been furnished proof by the Department of Motor Vehicles that the temporary, interim, or duplicate license was issued prior to the arrest, that the driving privilege and license had not been suspended or revoked, and that the person was eligible for the temporary, interim, or duplicate license.

(b) The driver of a motor vehicle shall present his or her license for examination upon demand of a peace officer enforcing the provisions of this code.

(Amended by Stats. 1993, Ch. 1292, Sec. 8. Effective January 1, 1994.)

12952. A licensee shall display his driver's license upon request of a magistrate or judge before whom he may be brought for violation of any traffic law.

(Enacted by Stats. 1959, Ch. 3.)

12953. In any circumstances involving accidents or violations in which the engineer or any other crewmember of any train is detained by state or local police, the engineer or any other crew member shall not be required to furnish a motor vehicle operator's license, nor shall any citation involving the operation of a train be issued against the motor vehicle operator's license of the engineer or any other crew member of the train.

(Added by Stats. 1980, Ch. 1134, Sec. 11.)

Article 5. Identification Cards

(Article 5 added by Stats. 1968, Ch. 494.)

13000. (a) (1) The department may issue an identification card to any person attesting to the true full name, correct age, and other identifying data as certified by the applicant for the identification card.

(2) The department may not issue a Real ID identification card to a person who holds a Real ID driver's license.

(3) The department may cancel an identification card in order to enable compliance with paragraph (2).

(b) Any person 62 years of age or older may apply for, and the department upon receipt of a proper application therefor shall issue, an identification card bearing the notation "Senior Citizen."

(c) Every application for an identification card shall be signed and verified by the applicant under penalty of perjury and shall be supported by bona fide documentary evidence of the age and identity of the applicant as the department may require.

(d) Prior to the issuance of an identification card, the department shall confirm that a legible print of the thumb or finger of the applicant is on file with the department.

(e) Any person 62 years of age or older, and any other qualified person, may apply for, or possess, an identification card under the provisions of either subdivision (a) or (b), but not under both of those provisions.

(Amended by Stats. 2021, Ch. 254, Sec. 8. (AB 174) Effective September 23, 2021.)

13000.1. (a) The department may refuse to issue or renew an identification card to any person for any of the following reasons:

(1) The department determines that the person has knowingly used a false or fictitious name in any application.

(2) The department determines that the person has impersonated another in making an application.

(3) The department determines that the person has knowingly made a false statement, knowingly concealed a material fact, or otherwise committed any fraud on any application.

(b) The department may declare an identification card invalid upon any of the grounds specified in subdivision (a) as reason to refuse to reissue or renew an identification card. The holder of an identification card that has been declared invalid shall surrender the identification card to the department.

(Added by Stats. 2000, Ch. 787, Sec. 19. Effective January 1, 2001.)

13001. (a) Any federal document demonstrating favorable action by the federal government for acceptance of a person into the federal Deferred Action for Childhood Arrivals program shall satisfy the requirement that the applicant submit satisfactory proof that the applicant's presence in the United States is authorized under federal law.

(b) The department may issue an original identification card to the person who submits proof of presence in the United States as authorized under federal law pursuant to subdivision (a) and either a social security account number or ineligibility for a social security account number.

(Added by Stats. 2013, Ch. 571, Sec. 3. (AB 35) Effective January 1, 2014.)

13001.5. Commencing no later than July 1, 2027, the department shall issue an identification card pursuant to Section 12801.9 to an eligible applicant, other than a person described in Section 13001, who is unable to submit satisfactory proof that the applicant's presence in the United States is authorized under federal law.

(Added by Stats. 2022, Ch. 482, Sec. 11. (AB 1766) Effective January 1, 2023.)

13002. (a) Except as otherwise provided in subdivision (b), every identification card shall expire, unless canceled earlier, on the sixth birthday of the applicant following the date of application for the identification card. Renewal of any identification card, other than a senior citizen identification card, shall be made for a term which shall expire on the sixth birthday of the applicant following expiration of the identification card renewed, unless surrendered earlier. Any application for renewal received after 90 days after expiration of the identification card, including a senior citizen identification card, shall be considered the same as an application for an original identification card. The department shall, at the end of six years and six months after the issuance or renewal of an identification card, other than a senior citizen identification card, destroy any record of the card if it has expired and has not been renewed.

(b) Every senior citizen identification card issued pursuant to subdivision (b) of Section 13000 shall expire, unless canceled earlier, on the eighth birthday of the applicant following the date of application for the identification card. Renewal of any senior citizen identification card shall be made for a term which shall expire on the eighth birthday of the applicant following expiration of the senior citizen identification card renewed, unless surrendered earlier. The department shall, at the end of eight years and six months after the issuance or renewal of a senior citizen identification card, destroy any record of the card if it has expired and has not been renewed.

(c) An identification card may be issued to a person in exchange for the person's driver's license which is surrendered to the department for either of the following reasons:

(1) The person has a physical or mental condition and requests cancellation of the driver's license.

(2) The department has revoked the person's driving privilege based on the person's physical or mental condition.

That card shall be issued without the payment of any additional fee.

(d) Notwithstanding subdivisions (a) and (b), the department may adjust the expiration date of any identification card issued pursuant to this code so that the date does not exceed the expiration date of a document submitted pursuant to subdivision (a) of Section 12801.5.

(e) This section shall become operative on January 1, 2018.

(Repealed (in Sec. 13) and added by Stats. 2016, Ch. 339, Sec. 14. (SB 838) Effective September 13, 2016. Section operative January 1, 2018, by its own provisions.)

13002.1. (a) The director shall establish a program that permits the renewal of identification cards by mail or through the department's Internet Web site.

(b) The initial application for the identification card shall be pursuant to Section 13000. After January 1, 2018, the first renewal for a person 62 years of age or older shall be for an eight-year period with a maximum of one renewal by mail or through the department's Internet Web site. All other renewals shall be for a six-year period with a maximum of two renewals by mail or through the department's Internet Web site.

(c) This section shall become operative on January 1, 2018.

(Repealed (in Sec. 15) and added by Stats. 2016, Ch. 339, Sec. 16. (SB 838) Effective September 13, 2016. Section operative January 1, 2018, by its own provisions.)

13003. (a) If an identification card issued under this code is lost, destroyed, mutilated, or a new true full name is acquired, the person to whom it was issued shall make application for an original identification card as specified in Section 13000. The fee provided in Section 14902 shall be paid to the department upon application for the card. Every identification card issued pursuant to this section shall expire as provided in Section 13002 and shall be deemed an original identification card for that purpose.

(b) A person in possession of a valid identification card who has been informed either by the department or by a law enforcement agency that the document is mutilated shall surrender the identification card to the department not later than 10 days after that notification.

(c) For purposes of this section a mutilated identification card is one that has been damaged sufficiently to render any or all of the elements of identity set forth in Sections 13005 and 13005.5 unreadable or unidentifiable through visual, mechanical, or electronic means.

(Amended by Stats. 1999, Ch. 1008, Sec. 8. Effective January 1, 2000.)

13004. It is unlawful for any person:

(a) To display or cause or permit to be displayed or have in his possession any canceled, fictitious, fraudulently altered, or fraudulently obtained identification card.

(b) To lend his identification card to any other person or knowingly permit the use thereof by another.

(c) To display or represent any identification card not issued to him as being his card.

(d) To permit any unlawful use of an identification card issued to him.

(e) To do any act forbidden or fail to perform any act required by this article.

(f) To photograph, photostat, duplicate, or in any way reproduce any identification card or facsimile thereof in such a manner that it could be mistaken for a valid identification card, or to display or have in his possession any such photograph, photostat, duplicate, reproduction, or facsimile unless authorized by the provisions of this code.

(g) To alter any identification card in any manner not authorized by this code.

(Amended by Stats. 1971, Ch. 1174.)

13004.1. (a) A person shall not manufacture or sell an identification document of a size and form substantially similar to, or that purports to confer the same privileges as, the identification cards issued by the department.

(b) A violation of this section is a misdemeanor punishable as follows:

(1) The court shall impose a fine of not less than two hundred fifty dollars ($250) and not more than one thousand dollars ($1,000), and 24 hours of community service, to be served when the person is not employed or is not attending school. No part of the fine or community service shall be suspended or waived.

(2) In lieu of the penalties imposed under paragraph (1), the court, in its discretion, may impose a jail term of up to one year and a fine of up to one thousand dollars ($1,000). In exercising its discretion the court shall consider the extent of the defendant's commercial motivation for the offense.

(c) Prosecution under this section shall not preclude prosecution under any other applicable provision of law.

(Amended by Stats. 2010, Ch. 684, Sec. 1. (AB 2471) Effective January 1, 2011.)

13005. (a) The identification card shall resemble in appearance, so far as is practicable, a driver's license issued pursuant to this code. It shall adequately describe the applicant, bear the applicant's picture, and be produced in color or engraved by a process or processes that prohibit, as near as possible, the ability to alter or reproduce the identification card, or prohibit the ability to superimpose a picture or photograph on the identification card without ready detection.

(b) Upon issuance of a new identification card, or renewal of an identification card, the department shall provide information on organ and tissue donation, including a standardized written or electronic form to be filled out by an individual who desires to enroll in the California Organ and Tissue Donor Registry with instructions for submitting the completed form to the California Organ and Tissue Donor Registrar established pursuant to subdivision (a) of Section 7150.90 of the Health and Safety Code.

(c) (1) The department shall enter into a memorandum of understanding with the Donate Life California Organ and Tissue Donor Registry to mutually agree upon the written or electronic form for enrollment required by subdivision (b).

(2) (A) At any time a memorandum of understanding, as described in paragraph (1), is not in effect, the department shall, as soon as practicable, produce a written or electronic form that is simple in design, in cooperation with the California Organ and Tissue Donor Registrar, and shall require all of the following information to be supplied by the enrollee:

(i) Date of birth, gender, full name, address, and home telephone number.

(ii) Consent for organs or tissues to be donated for transplant after death.

(iii) Any limitation of the donation to specific organs, tissues, or research.

(B) The form shall also include a description of the process for having a name removed from the registry, and the process for donating money for the benefit of the registry.

(d) The registry enrollment form shall be posted on the internet websites for the department and the California Health and Human Services Agency.

(e) The form shall constitute a legal document under the Uniform Anatomical Gift Act (Chapter 3.5 (commencing with Section 7150) of Part 1 of Division 7 of the Health and Safety Code).

(f) The registrar shall ensure that all additions and deletions to the registry shall occur within 30 days of receipt.

(g) Information obtained by the registrar for the purposes of this subdivision shall be used for these purposes only and shall not further be disseminated by the registrar.

(h) A contract shall not be awarded to a nongovernmental entity for the processing of identification cards unless the contract conforms to all applicable state contracting laws and all applicable procedures set forth in the State Contracting Manual.

(Amended by Stats. 2021, Ch. 211, Sec. 6. (AB 1374) Effective January 1, 2022.)

13005.3. In addition to the requirements of Section 13005, any identification card issued pursuant to subdivision (b) of Section 13000 shall contain the words "Senior Citizen".

(Amended by Stats. 1982, Ch. 1042, Sec. 4.)

13005.5. (a) (1) An identification card issued to any person shall bear a fullface engraved picture or photograph of the person.

(2) Notwithstanding any other law, the department shall not, unless requested by the applicant, distribute or sell the applicant's picture or photograph or any information pertaining to the applicant's physical characteristics to any private individual, other than the applicant, or to any firm, copartnership, association, or corporation. This paragraph does not apply to any private business entity that contracts with the department for the production of driver's licenses and identification cards, if the contract prohibits the unauthorized use and disclosure of the information.

(b) (1) An identification card issued pursuant to Section 13000 shall bear a notice that the identification card is issued only as a means of identification and does not establish eligibility for employment, voter registration, or public benefits.

(2) In the next scheduled revision of the identification card on or after January 1, 2023, the notice requirement specified in paragraph (1) shall be replaced by the following notice requirement:

(A) A Real ID identification card, as described in Section 681, shall bear a notice including, but not limited to, that the identification card is issued only as a means of identification, and that it does not establish eligibility for employment, voter registration, or public benefits.

(B) An identification card that is not a Real ID identification card, as described in Section 681, shall bear a notice including, but not limited to, that the identification card is issued only as a means of identification, it does not establish eligibility for employment, firearms purchases, voter registration, or public benefits, and that it is not acceptable for official federal purposes.

(c) This section shall become inoperative on the date the department notifies the Legislature that the driver's license has been revised to include the notices specified in subparagraphs (A) and (B) of paragraph

(2) of subdivision (b), and is repealed on January 1 of the following year.
(Amended by Stats. 2022, Ch. 482, Sec. 12. (AB 1766) Effective January 1, 2023. Conditionally inoperative as prescribed by its own provisions. Repealed conditionally by its own provisions. See later operative version added by Sec. 13 of Stats. 2022, Ch. 482.)

13005.5. (a) (1) An identification card issued to any person shall bear a fullface engraved picture or photograph of the person.

(2) Notwithstanding any other law, the department shall not, unless requested by the applicant, distribute or sell the applicant's picture or photograph or any information pertaining to the applicant's physical characteristics to any private individual, other than the applicant, or to any firm, copartnership, association, or corporation. This paragraph does not apply to any private business entity that contracts with the department for the production of driver's licenses and identification cards, if the contract prohibits the unauthorized use and disclosure of the information.

(b) (1) A Real ID identification card, as described in Section 681, shall bear a notice including, but not limited to, that the identification card is issued only as a means of identification, and that it does not establish eligibility for employment, voter registration, or public benefits.

(2) An identification card that is not a Real ID identification card, as described in Section 681, shall bear a notice including, but not limited to, that the identification card is issued only as a means of identification, it does not establish eligibility for employment, firearms purchases, voter registration, or public benefits, and that it is not acceptable for official federal purposes.

(c) This section shall become operative on the date the department notifies the Legislature that the identification card has been revised to include the notices specified in subdivision (b).
(Repealed (in Sec. 12) and added by Stats. 2022, Ch. 482, Sec. 13. (AB 1766) Effective January 1, 2023. Section conditionally operative by its own provisions.)

13006. No public entity or employee shall be liable for any loss or injury resulting directly or indirectly from false or inaccurate information contained in identification cards provided for in this article.

No public entity or employee shall be liable for any loss, detriment, or injury resulting directly or indirectly from false or inaccurate information contained in the sticker provided pursuant to subdivision (b) of Section 13005.
(Amended by Stats. 1975, Ch. 325.)

13007. Whenever any person after applying for or receiving an identification card acquires an address different from the address shown on the identification card issued to him, he shall within 10 days thereafter notify the department of his old and new address. The department may thereupon take such action as necessary to insure that the identification card reflects the proper address of the identification card holder.
(Amended by Stats. 1976, Ch. 552.)

13007.5. Notwithstanding anything to the contrary in this code or in the regulations adopted thereunder, including specifically the Driver's License Manual of Procedure, the department may verify the identity of any person born prior to 1916 who applies for an identification card, through United States Census records even though the date and month of birth are not included.

It is unlawful for an applicant to knowingly declare to the department, in writing, that no birth certificate exists for the applicant when, in fact, a birth certificate does exist.
(Amended by Stats. 1992, Ch. 1243, Sec. 86. Effective September 30, 1992.)

13008. When used in reference to an identification card, "cancellation" means that an identification card is terminated without prejudice and must be surrendered. Cancellation of card may be made when a card has been issued through error or when voluntarily surrendered to the department.
(Added by Stats. 1969, Ch. 1340.)

Article 6. Digital Driver's Licenses and Identification Cards

(Article 6 added by Stats. 2021, Ch. 81, Sec. 21.)

13020. (a) The department may establish a pilot program to evaluate the use of optional mobile or digital alternatives to driver's licenses and identification cards, subject to all of the following requirements:

(1) A pilot program established by the department pursuant to this subdivision shall be limited to both of the following:

(A) Persons who have voluntarily chosen to participate in the pilot program.

(B) No more than 15 percent of licensed drivers for the purpose of evaluation.

(2) A participant in a pilot program established by the department pursuant to this subdivision may terminate their participation in the pilot program at any time and may, upon termination, request the deletion of any data associated with their participation in the program. Within 10 days of any such request, the department and all entities contracted with the department for the purpose of effectuating the pilot program shall delete all data collected or maintained pursuant to the participant's participation in the program.

(3) All participants shall receive both a physical and, if requested, an immutable and unique driver's license or identification card.

(b) In developing and implementing the use of digital driver's licenses and identification cards, the department shall ensure the protection of personal information and include security features that protect against unauthorized access to information, including, but not limited to, all of the following:

(1) Ensuring that remote access to the digital driver's license or identification card shall require the express, affirmative, real-time consent of the person whose digital driver's license or identification card is being requested for each piece of information being requested and shall be limited to only the information that is provided on a physical driver's license or identification card.

(2) Ensuring that the digital driver's license or identification card, as well as any mobile application required for the digital driver's license or identification card, shall not contain or collect any information not strictly necessary for the functioning of the digital driver's license, identification card, or mobile application, including, but not limited to, information relating to movement or location.

(3) Ensuring that the information transmitted to the digital driver's license or identification card, as well as any mobile application required for the digital driver's license or identification card, is encrypted and protected to the highest reasonable security standards broadly available, including ISO-18013-5, FIPS 140-3, and NIST 800-53 Moderate, and cannot be intercepted while being transmitted from the department.

(c) (1) In the conduct of a pilot program established pursuant to this section, any data exchanged between the department and an electronic device, between the department and the provider of an electronic device, and between an electronic device and the provider of that electronic device shall be limited to those data necessary to display the information necessary for a driver's license or identification card.

(2) An entity contracted with the department for this purpose shall not use, share, sell, or disclose any information obtained as part of this contract, including, but not limited to, information about the holder of a digital driver's license or identification card, except as is necessary to satisfy the terms of the contract. Upon termination or expiration of a contract entered into for this purpose, the contracting entity shall delete any data collected or generated in the course of activities pursuant to the contract within 30 days.

(d) (1) The holder of a digital driver's license or identification card shall not be required to turn over their electronic device to any person or entity in order to use the digital driver's license or identification card for identity verification.

(2) The holder of a digital driver's license or identification card showing or turning over their electronic device to any person or entity in order to use the digital driver's license or identification card for identity verification shall not constitute consent to a search nor shall it constitute consent for access to any information other than that which is immediately available on the digital driver's license or identification card. Information incidentally obtained in the process of viewing a digital driver's license or identification card in order to verify the identity of the holder shall not be used to establish probable cause for a warrant to search the electronic device.

(3) A request for remote access to their digital driver's license or identification card for identity verification shall require the express consent of the holder of the digital driver's license or identification card shall be limited to the content of the digital driver's license or identification card specified in the request for remote access and shall not exceed the information available on a physical driver's license or identification card.

(4) Consent to remote access to a digital driver's license or identification card by the holder shall not constitute consent to a search nor shall it constitute consent for access to information other than that which is immediately available on the digital driver's license or identification card. Information incidentally obtained in the process of remotely accessing a digital driver's license or identification card shall not be used to establish probable cause for a warrant to search the electronic device.

(e) (1) A participant in a pilot program established by the department pursuant to this section shall not be required to use a digital driver's license or identification card rather than a physical driver's license or identification card for the purpose of identity verification nor shall their participation in the pilot program preclude their use of a physical driver's license or identification card under any circumstances.

(2) A person or entity shall not provide preferential service based on a person's use of a digital driver's license or identification card rather than a physical driver's license or identification card.

(f) The pilot program may include the issuance of mobile or digital Real ID driver's license or identification cards upon authorization of the United States Secretary of Homeland Security.

(g) If the department establishes the pilot program authorized in subdivision (a), the department shall, no later than July 1, 2026, submit a report regarding the pilot program to the Legislature, in compliance with Section 9795 of the Government Code, that includes, but is not limited to, all of the following:

(1) A review of all products evaluated in the pilot program and of the features of those products. The report shall note any security features to protect against unauthorized access to information.

(2) Lessons learned from the pilot program with regards to the utility of a mobile driver's license program or risks and solutions related to the implementation of a mobile driver's license program.

(3) Recommendations for subsequent actions, if any, that should be taken with regard to alternative options for digital driver's licenses or identification cards evaluated in the pilot program.

(4) An estimate of the fiscal impact of the deployment of a mobile driver's license program, including the estimated impact to the Motor Vehicle Account established pursuant to Section 42271.

(h) As part of the 2022–23 budget, the department shall report to the Legislature on the status of the pilot program, including, but not limited to, all of the following:

(1) The scope of the pilot program, including pilot program goals and processes.

(2) The timeline for the pilot program.

(3) The fiscal impact of the pilot program.

(Amended by Stats. 2025, Ch. 109, Sec. 7. (SB 153) Effective September 17, 2025.)

Chapter 2. Suspension or Revocation of Licenses

(Chapter 2 enacted by Stats. 1959, Ch. 3.)

Article 1. General Provisions

(Article 1 enacted by Stats. 1959, Ch. 3.)

13100. When used in reference to a driver's license, "cancellation" means that a driver's license certificate is terminated without prejudice and must be surrendered. Any person whose license has been canceled may immediately apply for a license. Cancellation of license may be made only when specifically authorized in this code, when application is made for a license to operate vehicles of a higher class, or when a license has been issued through error or voluntarily surrendered to the department.

(Amended by Stats. 1974, Ch. 428.)

13101. When used in reference to a driver's license, "revocation" means that the person's privilege to drive a motor vehicle is terminated and a new driver's license may be obtained after the period of revocation.

(Enacted by Stats. 1959, Ch. 3.)

13102. When used in reference to a driver's license, "suspension" means that the person's privilege to drive a motor vehicle is temporarily withdrawn. The department may, before terminating any suspension based upon a physical or mental condition of the licensee, require such examination of the licensee as deemed appropriate in relation to evidence of any condition which may affect the ability of the licensee to safely operate a motor vehicle.

(Amended by Stats. 1999, Ch. 724, Sec. 31. Effective January 1, 2000.)

13103. For purposes of this division, a plea of nolo contendere or a plea of guilty or judgment of guilty, whether probation is granted or not, a forfeiture of bail, or a finding reported under Section 1816, constitutes a conviction of any offense prescribed by this code, other than offenses relating to the unlawful parking of vehicles.

(Amended by Stats. 1972, Ch. 1207.)

13105. For the purposes of this chapter, "convicted" or "conviction" includes a finding by a judge of a juvenile court, a juvenile hearing officer, or referee of a juvenile court that a person has committed an offense, and "court" includes a juvenile court except as otherwise specifically provided.

(Amended by Stats. 2003, Ch. 149, Sec. 81. Effective January 1, 2004.)

13106. (a) When the privilege of a person to operate a motor vehicle is suspended or revoked, the department shall notify the person by first-class mail of the action taken and of the effective date of that suspension or revocation, except for those persons personally given notice by the department, a court, a peace officer pursuant to Section 13388 or 13382, or otherwise pursuant to this code. It shall be a rebuttable presumption, affecting the burden of proof, that a person has knowledge of the suspension or revocation if notice has been sent by first-class mail by the department pursuant to this section to the most recent address reported to the department pursuant to Section 12800 or 14600, or any more recent address on file if reported by the person, a court, or a law enforcement agency, or to the most recent electronic delivery address provided in accordance with Section 1801.2, and the notice has not been returned to the department as undeliverable or unclaimed. It is the responsibility of a holder of a driver's license to report changes of address to the department pursuant to Section 14600.

(b) The department may utilize alternative methods for determining the whereabouts of a driver whose driving privilege has been suspended or revoked pursuant to this code for the purpose of providing the driver with notice of suspension or revocation. Alternative methods may include, but are not limited to, cooperating with other state agencies that maintain more current address information than the department's driver's license files.

(Amended by Stats. 2022, Ch. 838, Sec. 8. (SB 1193) Effective January 1, 2023.)

Article 2. Suspension or Revocation by Court

(Article 2 enacted by Stats. 1959, Ch. 3.)

13200. Whenever any person licensed under this code is convicted of a violation of any provision of this code relating to the speed of vehicles or a violation of Section 23103 the court may, unless this code makes mandatory a revocation by the department, suspend the privilege of the person to operate a motor vehicle for a period of not to exceed 30 days upon a first conviction, for a period of not to exceed 60 days upon a second conviction, and for a period of not to exceed six months upon a third or any subsequent conviction.

(Enacted by Stats. 1959, Ch. 3.)

13200.5. Whenever any person licensed under this code is convicted of a violation of subdivision (b) of Section 22348, the court may, unless this code makes mandatory a revocation by the department, suspend the privilege of the person to operate a motor vehicle for a period of not to exceed 30 days.

(Amended by Stats. 1984, Ch. 276, Sec. 2.)

13201. A court may suspend, for not more than six months, the privilege of a person to operate a motor vehicle upon conviction of any of the following offenses:

(a) Failure of the driver of a vehicle involved in an accident to stop or otherwise comply with Section 20002.

(b) Reckless driving proximately causing bodily injury to a person under Section 23104 or 23105.

(c) Failure of the driver of a vehicle to stop at a railway grade crossing as required by Section 22452.

(d) Evading a peace officer in violation of Section 2800.1 or 2800.2, or in violation of Section 2800.3 if the person's license is not revoked for that violation pursuant to paragraph (3) of subdivision (a) of Section 13351.

(e) (1) Knowingly causing or participating in a vehicular collision, or any other vehicular accident, for the purpose of presenting or causing to be presented any false or fraudulent insurance claim.

(2) In lieu of suspending a person's driving privilege pursuant to paragraph (1), the court may order the privilege to operate a motor vehicle restricted to necessary travel to and from that person's place of employment for not more than six months. If driving a motor vehicle is necessary to perform the duties of the person's employment, the court may restrict the driving privilege to allow driving in that person's scope of employment. Whenever a person's driving privilege is restricted pursuant to this paragraph, the person shall be required to maintain proof of financial responsibility.

(Amended by Stats. 2007, Ch. 682, Sec. 11. Effective January 1, 2008.)

13202.5. (a) (1) For each conviction of a person for an offense specified in subdivision (d), committed while the person was under 21 years of age, but 13 years of age or older, the court shall suspend the person's driving privilege for one year. If the person convicted does not yet have the privilege to drive, the court shall order the department to delay issuing the privilege to drive for one year subsequent to the time the person becomes legally eligible to drive. However, if there is no further conviction for an offense specified in subdivision (d) in a 12-month period after the conviction, the court, upon petition of the person affected, may modify the order imposing the delay of the privilege. For each successive offense, the court shall suspend the person's driving privilege for those possessing a license or delay the eligibility for those not in possession of a license at the time of their conviction for one additional year.

(2) As used in this section, the term "conviction" includes the findings in juvenile proceedings specified in Section 13105.

(b) Whenever the court suspends driving privileges pursuant to subdivision (a), the court in which the conviction is had shall require all driver's licenses held by the person to be surrendered to the court. The court shall within 10 days following the conviction transmit a certified abstract of the conviction, together with any driver's licenses surrendered, to the department.

(c) (1) After a court has issued an order suspending or delaying driving privileges pursuant to subdivision (a), the court, upon petition of the person affected, may review the order and may impose restrictions on the person's privilege to drive based upon a showing of a critical need to drive.

(2) As used in this section, "critical need to drive" means the circumstances that are required to be shown for the issuance of a junior permit pursuant to Section 12513.

(3) The restriction shall remain in effect for the balance of the period of suspension or restriction in this section. The court shall notify the department of any modification within 10 days of the order of modification.

(d) This section applies to violations involving controlled substances or alcohol contained in the following provisions:

(1) Section 191.5 of, and subdivision (a) or (b) of Section 192.5 of, the Penal Code.

(2) Section 23103 when subject to Section 23103.5, Section 23140, and Article 2 (commencing with Section 23152) of Chapter 12 of Division 11 of this code.

(e) Suspension, restriction, or delay of driving privileges pursuant to this section shall be in addition to any penalty imposed upon conviction of a violation specified in subdivision (d).

(Amended by Stats. 2019, Ch. 505, Sec. 12. (SB 485) Effective January 1, 2020.)

13202.8. The restrictions specified in Section 13202.5 for the violations specified in that section may include, but are not limited to, the installation and maintenance of a certified ignition interlock device pursuant to Section 13386. Any restriction is subject to the provisions of Section 13202.5 relating to restrictions.

(Amended by Stats. 1998, Ch. 118, Sec. 1.33. Effective January 1, 1999. Operative July 1, 1999, by Sec. 85 of Ch. 118.)

13203. In no event shall a court suspend the privilege of any person to operate a motor vehicle or as a condition of probation prohibit the operation of a motor vehicle for a period of time longer than that specified in this code. Any such prohibited order of a court, whether imposed as a condition of probation or otherwise, shall be null and void, and the department shall restore or reissue a license to any person entitled thereto irrespective of any such invalid order of a court.

(Amended by Stats. 1974, Ch. 1283.)

13205. The privileges of a nonresident to operate vehicles in this State may be suspended or revoked under the provisions of this chapter in the same manner and to the same extent as the privileges of a resident driver.

(Enacted by Stats. 1959, Ch. 3.)

13206. Whenever a court suspends the privilege of a person to operate a motor vehicle, the court shall require the person's license to be surrendered to it. Unless required by the provisions of Section 13550 to send the license to the department, the court shall retain the license during the period of suspension and return it to the licensee at the end of the period after indorsing thereon a record of the suspension.

(Enacted by Stats. 1959, Ch. 3.)

13207. Whenever a court suspends the privilege of any person to operate a motor vehicle, the suspension shall apply to all driver's licenses held by him, and all licenses shall be surrendered to the court.

(Enacted by Stats. 1959, Ch. 3.)

13208. In any criminal proceeding, without regard to its disposition, wherein the defendant is charged with a violation of Division 11 (commencing with Section 21000), the court may, if it has reason to believe that any of the conditions specified in Section 12805 or 12806 exist, recommend to the department that an investigation be conducted to determine whether the driving privilege of that person should be suspended or revoked. In making the recommendation, the court shall state the basis for the belief that the condition exists and whether the defendant relied upon the condition as a part of his or her defense. The department may provide a form for the court's convenience.

(Amended by Stats. 1987, Ch. 321, Sec. 7.)

13209. Before sentencing a person upon a conviction of a violation of Section 23152 or 23153, the court shall obtain from the department a record of any prior convictions of that person for traffic violations. The department shall furnish that record upon the written request of the court.

Notwithstanding the provisions of Section 1449 of the Penal Code, in any such criminal action the time for pronouncement of judgment shall not commence to run until the time that the court receives the record of prior convictions from the department.

(Amended by Stats. 1981, Ch. 939, Sec. 4.5.)

13210. In addition to the penalties set forth in subdivision (a) of Section 245 of the Penal Code, the court may order the suspension of the driving privilege of any operator of a motor vehicle who commits an assault as described in subdivision (a) of Section 245 of the Penal Code on an operator or passenger of another motor vehicle, an operator of a bicycle, or a pedestrian and the offense occurs on a highway. The suspension period authorized under this section for an assault commonly known as "road rage," shall be six months for a first offense and one year for a second or subsequent offense to commence, at the discretion of the court, either on the date of the person's conviction, or upon the person's release from confinement or imprisonment. The court may, in lieu of or in addition to the suspension of the driving privilege, order a person convicted under this section to complete a court-approved anger management or "road rage" course, subsequent to the date of the current violation.

(Added by Stats. 2000, Ch. 642, Sec. 4. Effective January 1, 2001.)

Article 3. Suspension and Revocation by Department

(Article 3 enacted by Stats. 1959, Ch. 3.)

13350. (a) The department immediately shall revoke the privilege of a person to drive a motor vehicle upon receipt of a duly certified abstract of the record of a court showing that the person has been convicted of any of the following crimes or offenses:

(1) Failure of the driver of a vehicle involved in an accident resulting in injury or death to a person to stop or otherwise comply with Section 20001.

(2) A felony in the commission of which a motor vehicle is used, except as provided in Section 13351, 13352, or 13357.

(3) Reckless driving causing bodily injury.

(b) If a person is convicted of a violation of Section 23152 punishable under Section 23546, 23550, or 23550.5, or a violation of Section 23153 punishable under Section 23550.5 or 23566, including a violation of subdivision (b) of Section 191.5 of the Penal Code as provided in Section 193.7 of that code, the court shall, at the time of surrender of the driver's license or temporary permit, require the defendant to sign an affidavit in a form provided by the department acknowledging his or her understanding of the revocation required by paragraph (5), (6), or (7) of subdivision (a) of Section 13352, and an acknowledgment of his or her designation as a habitual traffic offender. A copy of this affidavit shall be transmitted, with the license or temporary permit, to the department within the prescribed 10 days.

(c) The department shall not reinstate the privilege revoked under subdivision (a) until the expiration of one year after the date of revocation and until the person whose privilege was revoked gives proof of financial responsibility as defined in Section 16430.

(Amended by Stats. 2007, Ch. 747, Sec. 18. Effective January 1, 2008.)

13350.5. Notwithstanding Section 13350, for the purposes of this article, conviction of a violation of subdivision (b) of Section 191.5 of the Penal Code is a conviction of a violation of Section 23153.

(Amended by Stats. 2007, Ch. 747, Sec. 19. Effective January 1, 2008.)

13351. (a) The department immediately shall revoke the privilege of a person to drive a motor vehicle upon receipt of a duly certified abstract of the record of a court showing that the person has been convicted of any of the following crimes or offenses:

(1) Manslaughter resulting from the operation of a motor vehicle, except when convicted under paragraph (2) of subdivision (c) of Section 192 of the Penal Code.

(2) Conviction of three or more violations of Section 20001, 20002, 23103, 23104, or 23105 within a period of 12 months from the time of the first offense to the third or subsequent offense, or a combination of three or more convictions of violations within the same period.

(3) Violation of subdivision (a) of Section 191.5 or subdivision (a) of Section 192.5 of the Penal Code or of Section 2800.3 causing serious bodily injury resulting in a serious impairment of physical condition, including, but not limited to, loss of consciousness, concussion, serious bone fracture, protracted loss or impairment of function of any bodily member or organ, and serious disfigurement.

(b) The department shall not reinstate the privilege revoked under subdivision (a) until the expiration of three years after the date of revocation and until the person whose privilege was revoked gives proof of financial responsibility, as defined in Section 16430.

(Amended by Stats. 2007, Ch. 747, Sec. 20.5. Effective January 1, 2008.)

13351.5. (a) Upon receipt of a duly certified abstract of the record of any court showing that a person has been convicted of a felony for a violation of Section 245 of the Penal Code and that a vehicle was found by the court to constitute the deadly weapon or instrument used to commit that offense, the department immediately shall revoke the privilege of that person to drive a motor vehicle.

(b) The department shall not reinstate a privilege revoked under subdivision (a) under any circumstances.

(c) Notwithstanding subdivision (b), the department shall terminate any revocation order issued under this section on or after January 1, 1995, for a misdemeanor conviction of violating Section 245 of the Penal Code.

(Amended by Stats. 1998, Ch. 606, Sec. 15. Effective January 1, 1999.)

13351.8. Upon receipt of a duly certified abstract of the record of any court showing that the court has ordered the suspension of a driver's license pursuant to Section 13210, on or after January 1, 2001, the department shall suspend the person's driving privilege in accordance with that suspension order commencing either on the date of the person's conviction or upon the person's release from confinement or imprisonment.

(Added by Stats. 2000, Ch. 642, Sec. 5. Effective January 1, 2001.)

13351.85. Upon receipt of a duly certified abstract of any court showing that a person has been convicted of a violation of Section 12110, the department shall suspend that person's driving privilege for four months if the conviction was a first conviction, and for one year, if the conviction was a second or subsequent conviction of a violation of that section that occurred within seven years of the current conviction.

(Added by Stats. 2000, Ch. 641, Sec. 2. Effective January 1, 2001.)

13352. (a) The department shall immediately suspend or revoke the privilege of a person to operate a motor vehicle upon the receipt of an abstract of the record of a court showing that the person has been convicted of a violation of Section 23152 or 23153, subdivision (a) of Section 23109, or Section 23109.1, or upon the receipt of a report of a judge of the juvenile court, a juvenile traffic hearing officer, or a referee of a juvenile court showing that the person has been found to have committed a violation of Section 23152 or 23153, subdivision (a) of Section 23109, or Section 23109.1. If an offense specified in this section occurs in a vehicle defined in Section 15210, the suspension or revocation specified in this subdivision applies also to the noncommercial driving privilege. The commercial driving privilege shall be disqualified as specified in Sections 15300 to 15302, inclusive. For the purposes of this section, suspension or revocation shall be as follows:

(1) (A) Except as provided in this subparagraph, or as required under Section 13352.1 or 13352.4, upon a conviction or finding of a violation of Section 23152 punishable under Section 23536, the privilege shall be suspended for a period of six months. The privilege shall not be reinstated until the person gives proof of financial responsibility and

gives proof satisfactory to the department of successful completion of a driving-under-the-influence program licensed pursuant to Section 11836 of the Health and Safety Code described in subdivision (b) of Section 23538 of this code. If the court, as authorized under paragraph (3) of subdivision (b) of Section 23646, elects to order a person to enroll in, participate in, and complete either program described in subdivision (b) of Section 23542, the department shall require that program in lieu of the program described in subdivision (b) of Section 23538. For the purposes of this paragraph, enrollment in, participation in, and completion of an approved program shall occur subsequent to the date of the current violation. Credit shall not be given to any program activities completed prior to the date of the current violation. Except when the court has ordered installation of a functioning, certified ignition interlock device pursuant to Section 23575.3, the department shall advise the person that they may apply to the department for a restricted driver's license if the person meets all of the following requirements:

(i) The underlying conviction was not only for the use of drugs, as defined in Section 312, at the time of the violation.

(ii) The person satisfactorily provides to the department, subsequent to the violation date of the current underlying conviction, enrollment in, or completion of, a driving-under-the-influence program licensed pursuant to Section 11836 of the Health and Safety Code, as described in subdivision (b) of Section 23538 of this code.

(iii) The person agrees, as a condition of the restriction, to continue satisfactory participation in the program described in clause (ii).

(iv) The person does both of the following:

(I) Submits the "Verification of Installation" form described in paragraph (2) of subdivision (g) of Section 13386.

(II) Agrees to maintain the functioning, certified ignition interlock device as required under subdivision (i).

(v) The person provides proof of financial responsibility, as defined in Section 16430.

(vi) The person pays all reissue fees and any restriction fee required by the department.

(vii) The person pays to the department a fee sufficient to cover the reasonable costs of administering the requirements of this paragraph, as determined by the department.

(B) The restrictions described in this paragraph shall remain in effect for the period required in subdivision (e).

(2) (A) Except as provided in this paragraph, upon a conviction or finding of a violation of Section 23153 punishable under Section 23554, the privilege shall be suspended for a period of one year. The privilege shall not be reinstated until the person gives proof of financial responsibility and gives proof satisfactory to the department of successful completion of a driving-under-the-influence program licensed pursuant to Section 11836 of the Health and Safety Code as described in subdivision (b) of Section 23556 of this code. If the court, as authorized under paragraph (3) of subdivision (b) of Section 23646, elects to order a person to enroll in, participate in, and complete either program described in subdivision (b) of Section 23542, the department shall require that program in lieu of the program described in Section 23556. For the purposes of this paragraph, enrollment in, participation in, and completion of an approved program shall occur subsequent to the date of the current violation. Credit shall not be given to any program activities completed prior to the date of the current violation. The department shall advise the person that they may apply to the department for a restricted driver's license if the person meets all of the following requirements:

(i) The underlying conviction was not only for the use of drugs, as defined in Section 312, at the time of the violation.

(ii) The person satisfactorily provides, subsequent to the violation date of the current underlying conviction, either of the following:

(I) Proof of enrollment in a driving-under-the-influence program licensed pursuant to Section 11836 of the Health and Safety Code, as described in subdivision (b) of Section 23556 of this code.

(II) Proof of enrollment in a program described in subdivision (b) of Section 23542, if the court has ordered the person to enroll in, participate in, and complete either program described in that section, in which case the person shall not be required to provide the proof described in subclause (I).

(iii) The person agrees, as a condition of the restriction, to continue satisfactory participation in the program described in clause (ii).

(iv) The person complies with Section 23575.3.

(v) The person does both of the following:

(I) Submits the "Verification of Installation" form described in paragraph (2) of subdivision (g) of Section 13386.

(II) Agrees to maintain the functioning, certified ignition interlock device as required under subdivision (i).

(vi) The person provides proof of financial responsibility, as defined in Section 16430.

(vii) The person pays all reissue fees and any restriction fee required by the department.

(viii) The person pays to the department a fee sufficient to cover the reasonable costs of administering the requirements of this paragraph, as determined by the department.

(B) The restriction shall remain in effect for the period required in subdivision (e).

(3) (A) Except as provided in this paragraph or in Section 13352.5, upon a conviction or finding of a violation of Section 23152 punishable under Section 23540, the privilege shall be suspended for two years. The privilege shall not be reinstated until the person gives proof of financial responsibility and gives proof satisfactory to the department of successful completion of a driving-under-the-influence program licensed pursuant to Section 11836 of the Health and Safety Code as described in subdivision (b) of Section 23542 of this code. For the purposes of this paragraph, enrollment in, participation in, and completion of an approved program shall occur subsequent to the date of the current violation. Credit shall not be given to any program activities completed prior to the date of the current violation. The department shall advise the person that they may apply to the department for a restricted driver's license if the person meets all of the following requirements:

(i) Completion of 12 months of the suspension period if the underlying conviction was only for the use of drugs, as defined in Section 312, at the time of the violation.

(ii) The person satisfactorily provides, subsequent to the violation date of the current underlying conviction, either of the following:

(I) Proof of enrollment in an 18-month driving-under-the-influence program licensed pursuant to Section 11836 of the Health and Safety Code if a 30-month program is unavailable in the person's county of residence or employment.

(II) Proof of enrollment in a 30-month driving-under-the-influence program licensed pursuant to Section 11836 of the Health and Safety Code, if available in the county of the person's residence or employment.

(iii) The person agrees, as a condition of the restriction, to continue satisfactory participation in the program described in clause (ii).

(iv) The person complies with Section 23575.3, if the underlying conviction involved the use of alcohol.

(v) The person does both of the following:

(I) Submits the "Verification of Installation" form described in paragraph (2) of subdivision (g) of Section 13386.

(II) Agrees to maintain the functioning, certified ignition interlock device as required under subdivision (i).

(vi) The person provides proof of financial responsibility, as defined in Section 16430.

(vii) The person pays all reissue fees and any restriction fee required by the department.

(viii) The person pays to the department a fee sufficient to cover the reasonable costs of administering the requirements of this paragraph, as determined by the department.

(B) The restriction shall remain in effect for the period required in subdivision (e).

(4) (A) Except as provided in this paragraph, upon a conviction or finding of a violation of Section 23153 punishable under Section 23560, the privilege shall be revoked for a period of three years. The privilege may not be reinstated until the person gives proof of financial responsibility, and the person gives proof satisfactory to the department of successful completion of a driving-under-the-influence program licensed pursuant to Section 11836 of the Health and Safety Code, as described in paragraph (4) of subdivision (b) of Section 23562 of this code. For the purposes of this paragraph, enrollment in, participation in, and completion of an approved program shall occur subsequent to the date of the current violation. Credit shall not be given to any program activities completed prior to the date of the current violation. The department shall advise the person that they may apply to the department for a restricted driver's license if the person meets all of the following requirements:

(i) Completion of 12 months of the suspension period if the underlying conviction was only for the use of drugs, as defined in Section 312, at the time of the violation.

(ii) The person satisfactorily provides, subsequent to the violation date of the current underlying conviction, either of the following:

(I) Proof of enrollment in an 18-month driving-under-the-influence program licensed pursuant to Section 11836 of the Health and Safety Code if a 30-month program is unavailable in the person's county of residence or employment.

(II) Proof of enrollment in a 30-month driving-under-the-influence program licensed pursuant to Section 11836 of the Health and Safety Code, if available in the county of the person's residence or employment.

(iii) The person agrees, as a condition of the restriction, to continue satisfactory participation in the program described in clause (ii).

(iv) The person complies with Section 23575.3, if the underlying conviction involved the use of alcohol.

(v) The person does both of the following:

(I) Submits the "Verification of Installation" form described in paragraph (2) of subdivision (g) of Section 13386.

(II) Agrees to maintain the functioning, certified ignition interlock device as required under subdivision (i).

(vi) The person provides proof of financial responsibility, as defined in Section 16430.

(vii) The person pays all applicable reinstatement or reissue fees and any restriction fee required by the department.

(viii) The person pays to the department a fee sufficient to cover the reasonable costs of administering the requirements of this paragraph, as determined by the department.

(B) The restriction shall remain in effect for the period required in subdivision (e).

(5) (A) Except as provided in this paragraph, upon a conviction or finding of a violation of Section 23152 punishable under Section 23546, the privilege shall be revoked for a period of three years. The privilege shall not be reinstated until the person files proof of financial responsibility and gives proof satisfactory to the department of successful completion of an 18-month driving-under-the-influence program licensed pursuant to Section 11836 of the Health and Safety Code, as described in subdivision (b) or (c) of Section 23548 of this code, if a 30-month program is unavailable in the person's county of residence or employment, or, if available in the county of the person's residence or employment, a 30-month driving-under-the-influence program licensed pursuant to Section 11836 of the Health and Safety Code, or a program specified in Section 8001 of the Penal Code. For the purposes of this paragraph, enrollment in, participation in, and completion of an approved program shall occur subsequent to the date of the current violation. Credit shall not be given to any program activities completed prior to the date of the current violation. The department shall advise the person that they may apply to the department for a restricted driver's license if the person meets all of the following requirements:

(i) Completion of 12 months of the suspension period if the underlying conviction was only for the use of drugs, as defined in Section 312, at the time of the violation.

(ii) The person satisfactorily provides, subsequent to the violation date of the current underlying conviction, either of the following:

(I) Proof of enrollment in an 18-month driving-under-the-influence program licensed pursuant to Section 11836 of the Health and Safety Code if a 30-month program is unavailable in the person's county of residence or employment.

(II) Proof of enrollment in a 30-month driving-under-the-influence program licensed pursuant to Section 11836 of the Health and Safety Code, if available in the county of the person's residence or employment.

(iii) The person agrees, as a condition of the restriction, to continue satisfactory participation in the program described in clause (ii).

(iv) The person complies with Section 23575.3, if the underlying conviction involved the use of alcohol.

(v) The person does both of the following:

(I) Submits the "Verification of Installation" form described in paragraph (2) of subdivision (g) of Section 13386.

(II) Agrees to maintain the functioning, certified ignition interlock device as required under Section 23575.3, if applicable.

(vi) The person provides proof of financial responsibility, as defined in Section 16430.

(vii) An individual convicted of a violation of Section 23152 punishable under Section 23546 may also, at any time after sentencing, petition the court for referral to an 18-month driving-under-the-influence program licensed pursuant to Section 11836 of the Health and Safety Code, or, if available in the county of the person's residence or employment, a 30-month driving-under-the-influence program licensed pursuant to Section 11836 of the Health and Safety Code. Unless good cause is shown, the court shall order the referral.

(viii) The person pays all applicable reinstatement or reissue fees and any restriction fee required by the department.

(ix) The person pays to the department a fee sufficient to cover the reasonable costs of administering the requirements of this paragraph, as determined by the department.

(B) The restriction shall remain in effect for the period required in subdivision (e).

(6) (A) Except as provided in this paragraph, upon a conviction or finding of a violation of Section 23153 punishable under Section 23550.5 or 23566, the privilege shall be revoked for a period of five years. The privilege may not be reinstated until the person gives proof of financial responsibility and gives proof satisfactory to the department of successful completion of a driving-under-the-influence program licensed pursuant to Section 11836 of the Health and Safety Code as described in subdivision (b) of Section 23568 of this code, or if available in the county of the person's residence or employment, a 30-month driving-under-the-influence program licensed pursuant to Section 11836 of the Health and Safety Code, or a program specified in Section 8001 of the Penal Code. For the purposes of this paragraph, enrollment in, participation in, and completion of an approved program shall be subsequent to the date of the current violation. Credit shall not be given to any program activities completed prior to the date of the current violation. The department shall advise the person that they may apply to the department for a restricted driver's license if the person meets all of the following requirements:

(i) Completion of 12 months of the suspension period if the underlying conviction was only for the use of drugs, as defined in Section 312, at the time of the violation.

(ii) The person satisfactorily provides, subsequent to the violation date of the current underlying conviction, either of the following:

(I) Proof of enrollment in a 30-month driving-under-the-influence program licensed pursuant to Section 11836 of the Health and Safety Code, if available in the county of the person's residence or employment.

(II) Proof of enrollment in an 18-month driving-under-the-influence program licensed pursuant to Section 11836 of the Health and Safety Code, if a 30-month program is unavailable in the person's county of residence or employment.

(iii) The person agrees, as a condition of the restriction, to continue satisfactory participation in the program described in clause (ii).

(iv) The person complies with Section 23575.3, if the underlying conviction involved alcohol.

(v) The person does both of the following:

(I) Submits the "Verification of Installation" form described in paragraph (2) of subdivision (g) of Section 13386.

(II) Agrees to maintain the functioning, certified ignition interlock device as required under subdivision (i).

(vi) The person provides proof of financial responsibility, as defined in Section 16430.

(vii) An individual convicted of a violation of Section 23153 punishable under Section 23566 may also, at any time after sentencing, petition the court for referral to an 18-month driving-under-the-influence program licensed pursuant to Section 11836 of the Health and Safety Code, or, if available in the county of the person's residence or employment, a 30-month driving-under-the-influence program licensed pursuant to Section 11836 of the Health and Safety Code. Unless good cause is shown, the court shall order the referral.

(viii) The person pays all applicable reinstatement or reissue fees and any restriction fee required by the department.

(ix) The person pays to the department a fee sufficient to cover the reasonable costs of administering the requirements of this paragraph, as determined by the department.

(B) The restriction shall remain in effect for the period required in subdivision (e).

(7) (A) Except as provided in this paragraph, upon a conviction or finding of a violation of Section 23152 punishable under Section 23550 or 23550.5, or of a violation of Section 23153 punishable under Section 23550.5, the privilege shall be revoked for a period of four years. The privilege shall not be reinstated until the person files proof of financial responsibility and gives proof satisfactory to the department of successful completion of an 18-month driving-under-the-influence program licensed pursuant to Section 11836 of the Health and Safety Code, if a 30-month program is unavailable in the person's county of residence or employment, or, if available in the county of the person's residence or employment, a 30-month driving-under-the-influence program licensed pursuant to Section 11836 of the Health and Safety Code, or a program specified in Section 8001 of the Penal Code. For the purposes of this paragraph, enrollment in, participation in, and completion of an approved program shall occur subsequent to the date of the current violation. Credit shall not be given to any program activities completed prior to the date of the current violation. The department shall advise the person that they may apply to the department for a restricted driver's license if the person meets all of the following requirements:

(i) Completion of 12 months of the suspension period if the underlying conviction was only for the use of drugs, as defined in Section 312, at the time of the violation.

(ii) The person satisfactorily provides, subsequent to the violation date of the current underlying conviction, either of the following:

(I) Proof of enrollment in an 18-month driving-under-the-influence program licensed pursuant to Section 11836 of the Health and Safety Code, if a 30-month program is unavailable in the person's county of residence or employment.

(II) Proof of enrollment in a 30-month driving-under-the-influence program licensed pursuant to Section 11836 of the Health and Safety Code, if available in the county of the person's residence or employment.

(iii) The person agrees, as a condition of the restriction, to continue satisfactory participation in the program described in clause (ii).

(iv) The person complies with Section 23575.3, if the underlying conviction involved alcohol.

(v) The person does both of the following:

(I) Submits the "Verification of Installation" form described in paragraph (2) of subdivision (g) of Section 13386.

(II) Agrees to maintain the functioning, certified ignition interlock device as required under subdivision (i).

(vi) The person provides proof of financial responsibility, as defined in Section 16430.

(vii) An individual convicted of a violation of Section 23152 punishable under Section 23550 may also, at any time after sentencing, petition the court for referral to an 18-month driving-under-the-influence program licensed pursuant to Section 11836 of the Health and Safety Code, or, if available in the county of the person's residence or employment, a 30-month driving-under-the-influence program licensed pursuant to Section 11836 of the Health and Safety Code. Unless good cause is shown, the court shall order the referral.

(viii) The person pays all applicable reinstatement or reissue fees and any restriction fee required by the department.

(ix) The person pays to the department a fee sufficient to cover the reasonable costs of administering the requirements of this paragraph, as determined by the department.

(B) The restriction shall remain in effect for the period required in subdivision (e).

(8) (A) Upon a conviction or finding of a violation of subdivision (a) of Section 23109 that is punishable under subdivision (e) of that section or Section 23109.1, the privilege shall be suspended for a period of 90 days to six months, if ordered by the court. The privilege shall not be reinstated until the person gives proof of financial responsibility, as defined in Section 16430.

(B) Commencing January 1, 2029, upon a finding of a violation of subdivision (c) of Section 23109 for engaging in a motor vehicle exhibition of speed, as described in paragraph (2) of subdivision (i) of Section 23109, the privilege shall be suspended for a period of 90 days to six months, if ordered by the court. The privilege shall not be reinstated until the person gives proof of financial responsibility, as defined in Section 16430.

(9) Upon a conviction or finding of a violation of subdivision (a) of Section 23109 that is punishable under subdivision (f) of that section, the privilege shall be suspended for a period of six months, if ordered by the court. The privilege shall not be reinstated until the person gives proof of financial responsibility, as defined in Section 16430.

(b) For the purposes of paragraphs (2) to (9), inclusive, of subdivision (a), the finding of the juvenile court judge, the juvenile hearing officer, or the referee of a juvenile court of a commission of a violation of Section 23152 or 23153, subdivision (a) of Section 23109, or Section 23109.1, as specified in subdivision (a) of this section, is a conviction.

(c) A judge of a juvenile court, juvenile hearing officer, or referee of a juvenile court shall immediately report the findings specified in subdivision (a) to the department.

(d) A conviction of an offense in a state, territory, or possession of the United States, the District of Columbia, the Commonwealth of Puerto Rico, or Canada that, if committed in this state, would be a violation of Section 23152, is a conviction of Section 23152 for the purposes of this section, and a conviction of an offense that, if committed in this state, would be a violation of Section 23153, is a conviction of Section 23153 for the purposes of this section. The department shall suspend or revoke the privilege to operate a motor vehicle pursuant to this section upon receiving notice of that conviction.

(e) (1) The restricted driving privilege shall become effective when the department receives all of the documents and fees required under paragraphs (1) to (7), inclusive, of subdivision (a) and, except as specified in paragraph (2) or (3), shall remain in effect until all reinstatement requirements are satisfied.

(2) For the purposes of the restriction conditions specified in paragraphs

(1) to (7), inclusive, of subdivision (a), the department shall terminate the restriction imposed pursuant to this section and shall suspend or revoke the person's driving privilege upon receipt of notification from the driving-under-the-influence program that the person has failed to comply with the program requirements. The person's driving privilege shall remain suspended or revoked for the remaining period of the original suspension or revocation imposed under this section and until all reinstatement requirements described in this section are met.

(3) The department shall immediately suspend or revoke the privilege to operate a motor vehicle of a person who, with respect to an ignition interlock device installed pursuant to this section attempts to remove, bypass, or tamper with the device, has the device removed prior to the termination date of the restriction, or fails three or more times to comply with any requirement for the maintenance or calibration of the device. The privilege shall remain suspended or revoked for the remaining period of the originating suspension or revocation and until all reinstatement requirements in this section are satisfied, provided, however, that if the person provides proof to the satisfaction of the department that the person is in compliance with the restriction issued pursuant to this section, the department may, in its discretion, restore the privilege to operate a motor vehicle and reimpose the remaining term of the restriction.

(f) Notwithstanding the suspension periods specified in paragraphs (1) to (7), inclusive, of subdivision (a) or Section 13352.1, if the person maintains a functioning, certified ignition interlock device for the mandatory term required under Section 23575.3, inclusive of any term credit earned under Section 13353.6 or 13353.75, the department shall reinstate the person's privilege to operate a motor vehicle at the time the other reinstatement requirements are satisfied.

(g) For the purposes of this section, completion of a program is the following:

(1) Satisfactory completion of all program requirements approved pursuant to program licensure, as evidenced by a certificate of completion issued, under penalty of perjury, by the licensed program.

(2) Certification, under penalty of perjury, by the director of a program specified in Section 8001 of the Penal Code, that the person has completed a program specified in Section 8001 of the Penal Code.

(h) (1) The holder of a commercial driver's license who was operating a motor vehicle other than a commercial vehicle, or a driver who was operating a commercial vehicle, as defined in Section 15210, at the time of the violation that resulted in the suspension of that person's driving privilege pursuant to this section is not eligible for the restricted driver's license authorized under paragraphs (1) to (7), inclusive, of subdivision (a).

(2) Notwithstanding paragraph (1), as authorized under this section, the department shall issue the person a noncommercial driver's license restricted in the same manner and subject to the same conditions and requirements as specified in paragraphs (1) to (7), inclusive, of subdivision (a).

(i) A person whose driving privilege is restricted by the Department of Motor Vehicles pursuant to this section shall arrange for each vehicle with a functioning, certified ignition interlock device to be serviced by the installer at least once every 60 days in order for the installer to recalibrate the device and monitor the operation of the device. The installer shall notify the department if the device is removed or indicates that the person has attempted to remove, bypass, or tamper with the device, or if the person fails three or more times to comply with any requirement for the maintenance or calibration of the ignition interlock device.

(j) The reinstatement of the driving privilege pursuant to this section does not abrogate a person's continuing duty to comply with any restriction imposed pursuant to Section 23575.3.

(k) For purposes of this section, "bypass" means either of the following:

(1) Failure to take any random retest.

(2) Failure to pass a random retest with a breath alcohol concentration not exceeding 0.03 percent, by weight of alcohol, in the person's blood.

(l) For purposes of this section, "random retest" means a breath test performed by the driver upon a certified ignition interlock device at random intervals after the initial engine startup breath test and while the vehicle's motor is running.

(m) The restriction conditions specified in paragraphs (1) to (7), inclusive, of subdivision (a) shall apply only to a person who is convicted for a violation of Section 23152 or 23153 that occurred on or after January 1, 2019.

(n) This section shall become operative on January 1, 2019.

(o) This section shall remain in effect only until January 1, 2033, and as of that date is repealed, unless a later enacted statute that is enacted before January 1, 2033, deletes or extends that date.

(Amended (as amended by Stats. 2025, Ch. 16, Sec. 6) by Stats. 2025, Ch. 689, Sec. 1. (AB 366) Effective January 1, 2026. Repealed as of January 1, 2033, by its own provisions. See later operative version, as amended by Sec. 2 of Stats. 2025, Ch. 689.)

13352. (a) The department shall immediately suspend or revoke the privilege of a person to operate a motor vehicle upon the receipt of an abstract of the record of a court showing that the person has been convicted of a violation of Section 23152 or 23153, subdivision (a) of Section 23109, or Section 23109.1, or upon the receipt of a report of a judge of the juvenile court, a juvenile traffic hearing officer, or a referee of a juvenile court showing that the person has been found to have committed a violation of Section 23152 or 23153, subdivision (a) of Section 23109, or Section 23109.1. If an offense specified in this section occurs in a vehicle defined in Section 15210, the suspension or revocation specified in this subdivision also applies to the noncommercial driving privilege. The commercial driving privilege shall be disqualified as specified in Sections 15300 to 15302, inclusive. For the purposes of this section, suspension or revocation shall be as follows:

(1) Except as required under Section 13352.1 or 13352.4, upon a conviction or finding of a violation of Section 23152 punishable under Section 23536, the privilege shall be suspended for a period of six months. The privilege shall not be reinstated until the person gives proof of financial responsibility and gives proof satisfactory to the department of successful completion of a driving-under-the-influence program licensed pursuant to Section 11836 of the Health and Safety Code described in subdivision (b) of Section 23538 of this code. If the court, as authorized under paragraph (3) of subdivision (b) of Section 23646, elects to order a person to enroll in, participate in, and complete either program described in subdivision (b) of Section 23542, the department shall require that program in lieu of the program described in subdivision (b) of Section 23538. For the purposes of this paragraph, enrollment in, participation in, and completion of an approved program shall occur subsequent to the date of the current violation. Credit shall not be given to any program activities completed prior to the date of the current violation.

(2) Upon a conviction or finding of a violation of Section 23153 punishable under Section 23554, the privilege shall be suspended for a period of one year. The privilege shall not be reinstated until the person gives proof of financial responsibility and gives proof satisfactory to the department of successful completion of a driving-under-the-influence program licensed pursuant to Section 11836 of the Health and Safety Code as described in subdivision (b) of Section 23556 of this code. If the court, as authorized under paragraph (3) of subdivision (b) of Section 23646, elects to order a person to enroll in, participate in, and complete either program described in subdivision (b) of Section 23542, the department shall require that program in lieu of the program described in Section 23556. For the purposes of this paragraph, enrollment, participation, and completion of an approved program shall occur subsequent to the date of the current violation. Credit shall not be given to any program activities completed prior to the date of the current violation.

(3) Except as provided in Section 13352.5, upon a conviction or finding of a violation of Section 23152 punishable under Section 23540, the privilege shall be suspended for two years. The privilege shall not

be reinstated until the person gives proof of financial responsibility and gives proof satisfactory to the department of successful completion of a driving-under-the-influence program licensed pursuant to Section 11836 of the Health and Safety Code as described in subdivision (b) of Section 23542 of this code. For the purposes of this paragraph, enrollment in, participation in, and completion of an approved program shall be subsequent to the date of the current violation. Credit shall not be given to any program activities completed prior to the date of the current violation. The department shall advise the person that they may apply to the department for a restriction of the driving privilege if the person meets all of the following requirements:

(A) Completion of 12 months of the suspension period, or completion of 90 days of the suspension period if the underlying conviction did not include the use of drugs as defined in Section 312 and the person was found to be only under the influence of an alcoholic beverage at the time of the violation.

(B) The person satisfactorily provides, subsequent to the violation date of the current underlying conviction, either of the following:

(i) Proof of enrollment in an 18-month driving-under-the-influence program licensed pursuant to Section 11836 of the Health and Safety Code if a 30-month program is unavailable in the person's county of residence or employment.

(ii) Proof of enrollment in a 30-month driving-under-the-influence program licensed pursuant to Section 11836 of the Health and Safety Code, if available in the county of the person's residence or employment.

(C) The person agrees, as a condition of the restriction, to continue satisfactory participation in the program described in subparagraph (B).

(D) The person submits the "Verification of Installation" form described in paragraph (2) of subdivision (g) of Section 13386.

(E) The person agrees to maintain the ignition interlock device as required under subdivision (g) of Section 23575.

(F) The person provides proof of financial responsibility, as defined in Section 16430.

(G) The person pays all reissue fees and any restriction fee required by the department.

(H) The person pays to the department a fee sufficient to cover the costs of administration of this paragraph, as determined by the department.

(I) The restriction shall remain in effect for the period required in subdivision (f) of Section 23575.

(4) Except as provided in this paragraph, upon a conviction or finding of a violation of Section 23153 punishable under Section 23560, the privilege shall be revoked for a period of three years. The privilege may not be reinstated until the person gives proof of financial responsibility, and the person gives proof satisfactory to the department of successful completion of a driving-under-the-influence program licensed pursuant to Section 11836 of the Health and Safety Code, as described in paragraph (4) of subdivision (b) of Section 23562 of this code. For the purposes of this paragraph, enrollment in, participation in, and completion of an approved program shall occur subsequent to the date of the current violation. Credit shall not be given to any program activities completed prior to the date of the current violation. The department shall advise the person that after the completion of 12 months of the revocation period, which may include credit for a suspension period served under subdivision (c) of Section 13353.3, they may apply to the department for a restricted driver's license if the person meets all of the following requirements:

(A) The person satisfactorily provides, subsequent to the violation date of the current underlying conviction, either of the following:

(i) The initial 12 months of an 18-month driving-under-the-influence program licensed pursuant to Section 11836 of the Health and Safety Code if a 30-month program is unavailable in the person's county of residence or employment.

(ii) The initial 12 months of a 30-month driving-under-the-influence program licensed pursuant to Section 11836 of the Health and Safety Code, if available in the county of the person's residence or employment.

(B) The person agrees, as a condition of the restriction, to continue satisfactory participation in the program described in subparagraph (A).

(C) The person submits the "Verification of Installation" form described in paragraph (2) of subdivision (g) of Section 13386.

(D) The person agrees to maintain the ignition interlock device as required under subdivision (g) of Section 23575.

(E) The person provides proof of financial responsibility, as defined in Section 16430.

(F) The person pays all applicable reinstatement or reissue fees and any restriction fee required by the department.

(G) The restriction shall remain in effect for the period required in subdivision (f) of Section 23575.

(5) Except as provided in this paragraph, upon a conviction or finding of a violation of Section 23152 punishable under Section 23546, the privilege shall be revoked for a period of three years. The privilege shall not be reinstated until the person files proof of financial responsibility and gives proof satisfactory to the department of successful completion of an 18-month driving-under-the-influence program licensed pursuant to Section 11836 of the Health and Safety Code, as described in subdivision (b) or (c) of Section 23548 of this code, if a 30-month program is unavailable in the person's county of residence or employment, or, if available in the county of the person's residence or employment, a 30-month driving-under-the-influence program licensed pursuant to Section 11836 of the Health and Safety Code, or a program specified in Section 8001 of the Penal Code. For the purposes of this paragraph, enrollment in, participation in, and completion of an approved program shall occur subsequent to the date of the current violation. Credit shall not be given to any program activities completed prior to the date of the current violation. The department shall advise the person that they may apply to the department for a restricted driver's license, which may include credit for a suspension period served under subdivision (c) of Section 13353.3, if the person meets all of the following requirements:

(A) Completion of 12 months of the suspension period, or completion of six months of the suspension period if the underlying conviction did not include the use of drugs as defined in Section 312 and the person was found to be only under the influence of an alcoholic beverage at the time of the violation.

(B) The person satisfactorily provides, subsequent to the violation date of the current underlying conviction, either of the following:

(i) Proof of enrollment in an 18-month driving-under-the-influence program licensed pursuant to Section 11836 of the Health and Safety Code if a 30-month program is unavailable in the person's county of residence or employment.

(ii) Proof of enrollment in a 30-month driving-under-the-influence program licensed pursuant to Section 11836 of the Health and Safety Code, if available in the county of the person's residence or employment.

(C) The person agrees, as a condition of the restriction, to continue satisfactory participation in the program described in subparagraph (B).

(D) The person submits the "Verification of Installation" form described in paragraph (2) of subdivision (g) of Section 13386.

(E) The person agrees to maintain the ignition interlock device as required under subdivision (g) of Section 23575.

(F) The person provides proof of financial responsibility, as defined in Section 16430.

(G) An individual convicted of a violation of Section 23152 punishable under Section 23546 may also, at any time after sentencing, petition the court for referral to an 18-month driving-under-the-influence program licensed pursuant to Section 11836 of the Health and Safety Code, or, if available in the county of the person's residence or employment, a 30-month driving-under-the-influence program licensed pursuant to Section 11836 of the Health and Safety Code. Unless good cause is shown, the court shall order the referral.

(H) The person pays all applicable reinstatement or reissue fees and any restriction fee required by the department.

(I) The person pays to the department a fee sufficient to cover the costs of administration of this paragraph, as determined by the department.

(J) The restriction shall remain in effect for the period required in subdivision (f) of Section 23575.

(6) Except as provided in this paragraph, upon a conviction or finding of a violation of Section 23153 punishable under Section 23550.5 or 23566, the privilege shall be revoked for a period of five years. The privilege may not be reinstated until the person gives proof of financial responsibility and gives proof satisfactory to the department of successful completion of a driving-under-the-influence program licensed pursuant to Section 11836 of the Health and Safety Code as described in subdivision (b) of Section 23568 of this code, or if available in the county of the person's residence or employment, a 30-month driving-under-the-influence program licensed pursuant to Section 11836 of the Health and Safety Code, or a program specified in Section 8001 of the Penal Code. For the purposes of this paragraph, enrollment in, participation in, and completion of an approved program shall be subsequent to the date of the current violation. Credit shall not be given to any program activities completed prior to the date of the current violation. The department shall advise the person that after completion of 12 months of the revocation period, which may include credit for a suspension period served under subdivision (c) of Section 13353.3, they may apply to the department for a restricted driver's license if the person meets all of the following requirements:

(A) The person satisfactorily provides, subsequent to the violation date of the current underlying conviction, either of the following:

(i) Completion of the initial 12 months of a 30-month driving-under-the-influence program licensed pursuant to Section 11836 of the Health and Safety Code, if available in the county of the person's residence or employment.

(ii) Completion of the initial 12 months of an 18-month driving-under-the-influence program licensed pursuant to Section 11836 of the Health and Safety Code, if a 30-month program is unavailable in the person's county of residence or employment.

(B) The person agrees, as a condition of the restriction, to continue satisfactory participation in the program described in subparagraph (A).

(C) The person submits the "Verification of Installation" form described in paragraph (2) of subdivision (g) of Section 13386.

(D) The person agrees to maintain the ignition interlock device as required under subdivision (g) of Section 23575.

(E) The person provides proof of financial responsibility, as defined in Section 16430.

(F) An individual convicted of a violation of Section 23153 punishable under Section 23566 may also, at any time after sentencing, petition the court for referral to an 18-month driving-under-the-influence program licensed pursuant to Section 11836 of the Health and Safety Code, or, if available in the county of the person's residence or employment, a 30-month driving-under-the-influence program licensed pursuant to Section 11836 of the Health and Safety Code. Unless good cause is shown, the court shall order the referral.

(G) The person pays all applicable reinstatement or reissue fees and any restriction fee required by the department.

(H) The restriction shall remain in effect for the period required in subdivision (f) of Section 23575.

(7) Except as provided in this paragraph, upon a conviction or finding of a violation of Section 23152 punishable under Section 23550 or 23550.5, or of a violation of Section 23153 punishable under Section 23550.5, the privilege shall be revoked for a period of four years. The privilege shall not be reinstated until the person files proof of financial responsibility and gives proof satisfactory to the department of successful completion of an 18-month driving-under-the-influence program licensed pursuant to Section 11836 of the Health and Safety Code, if a 30-month program is unavailable in the person's county of residence or employment, or, if available in the county of the person's residence or employment, a 30-month driving-under-the-influence program licensed pursuant to Section 11836 of the Health and Safety Code, or a program specified in Section 8001 of the Penal Code. For the purposes of this paragraph, enrollment in, participation in, and completion of an approved program shall occur subsequent to the date of the current violation. Credit shall not be given to any program activities completed prior to the date of the current violation. The department shall advise the person that after completion of 12 months of the revocation period, which may include credit for a suspension period served under subdivision (c) of Section 13353.3, they may apply to the department for a restricted driver's license if the person meets all of the following requirements:

(A) The person satisfactorily provides, subsequent to the violation date of the current underlying conviction, either of the following:

(i) The initial 12 months of an 18-month driving-under-the-influence program licensed pursuant to Section 11836 of the Health and Safety Code, if a 30-month program is unavailable in the person's county of residence or employment.

(ii) The initial 12 months of a 30-month driving-under-the-influence program licensed pursuant to Section 11836 of the Health and Safety Code, if available in the county of the person's residence or employment.

(B) The person agrees, as a condition of the restriction, to continue satisfactory participation in the program described in subparagraph (A).

(C) The person submits the "Verification of Installation" form described in paragraph (2) of subdivision (g) of Section 13386.

(D) The person agrees to maintain the ignition interlock device as required under subdivision (g) of Section 23575.

(E) The person provides proof of financial responsibility, as defined in Section 16430.

(F) An individual convicted of a violation of Section 23152 punishable under Section 23550 may also, at any time after sentencing, petition the court for referral to an 18-month driving-under-the-influence program licensed pursuant to Section 11836 of the Health and Safety Code, or, if available in the county of the person's residence or employment, a 30-month driving-under-the-influence program licensed pursuant to Section 11836 of the Health and Safety Code. Unless good cause is shown, the court shall order the referral.

(G) The person pays all applicable reinstatement or reissue fees and any restriction fee required by the department.

(H) The restriction shall remain in effect for the period required in subdivision (f) of Section 23575.

(8) (A) Upon a conviction or finding of a violation of subdivision (a) of Section 23109 that is punishable under subdivision (e) of that section or Section 23109.1, the privilege shall be suspended for a period of 90 days to six months, if ordered by the court. The privilege shall not be reinstated until the person gives proof of financial responsibility, as defined in Section 16430.

(B) Commencing January 1, 2029, upon a finding of a violation of subdivision (c) of Section 23109 for engaging in a motor vehicle exhibition of speed, as described in paragraph (2) of subdivision (i) of Section 23109, the privilege shall be suspended for a period of 90 days to six months, if ordered by the court. The privilege shall not be reinstated until the person gives proof of financial responsibility, as defined in Section 16430.

(9) Upon a conviction or finding of a violation of subdivision (a) of Section 23109 that is punishable under subdivision (f) of that section, the privilege shall be suspended for a period of six months, if ordered by the court. The privilege shall not be reinstated until the person gives proof of financial responsibility, as defined in Section 16430.

(b) For the purpose of paragraphs (2) to (9), inclusive, of subdivision (a), the finding of the juvenile court judge, the juvenile hearing officer, or the referee of a juvenile court of a commission of a violation of Section 23152 or 23153, subdivision (a) of Section 23109, or Section 23109.1, as specified in subdivision (a) of this section, is a conviction.

(c) A judge of a juvenile court, juvenile hearing officer, or referee of a juvenile court shall immediately report the findings specified in subdivision (a) to the department.

(d) A conviction of an offense in a state, territory, or possession of the United States, the District of Columbia, the Commonwealth of Puerto Rico, or Canada that, if committed in this state, would be a violation of Section 23152, is a conviction of Section 23152 for the purposes of this section, and a conviction of an offense that, if committed in this state, would be a violation of Section 23153, is a conviction of Section 23153 for the purposes of this section. The department shall suspend or revoke the privilege to operate a motor vehicle pursuant to this section upon receiving notice of that conviction.

(e) For the purposes of the restriction conditions specified in paragraphs (3) to (7), inclusive, of subdivision (a), the department shall terminate the restriction imposed pursuant to this section and shall suspend or revoke the person's driving privilege upon receipt of notification from the driving-under-the-influence program that the person has failed to comply with the program requirements. The person's driving privilege shall remain suspended or revoked for the remaining period of the original suspension or revocation imposed under this section and until all reinstatement requirements described in this section are met.

(f) For the purposes of this section, completion of a program is the following:

(1) Satisfactory completion of all program requirements approved pursuant to program licensure, as evidenced by a certificate of completion issued, under penalty of perjury, by the licensed program.

(2) Certification, under penalty of perjury, by the director of a program specified in Section 8001 of the Penal Code, that the person has completed a program specified in Section 8001 of the Penal Code.

(g) The holder of a commercial driver's license who was operating a commercial motor vehicle, as defined in Section 15210, at the time of a violation that resulted in a suspension or revocation of the person's noncommercial driving privilege under this section is not eligible for the restricted driver's license authorized under paragraphs (3) to (7), inclusive, of subdivision (a).

(h) This section shall become operative January 1, 2033.

(Amended (as amended by Stats. 2025, Ch. 16, Sec. 7) by Stats. 2025, Ch. 689, Sec. 2. (AB 366) Effective January 1, 2026. Section operative January 1, 2033, by its own provisions.)

13352.1. (a) Pursuant to subdivision (a) of Section 13352 and except as required under subdivision (c) of this section or Section 13352.4, upon a conviction or finding of a violation of Section 23152 punishable under Section 23536, if the court refers the person to a program pursuant to paragraph (2) of subdivision (b) of Section 23538, the privilege shall be suspended for 10 months.

(b) The privilege may not be reinstated until the person gives proof of financial responsibility and gives proof satisfactory to the department of successful completion of a driving-under-the-influence program licensed pursuant to Section 11836 of the Health and Safety Code described in subdivision (b) of Section 23538 of this code. For the purposes of this subdivision, enrollment, participation, and completion of an approved program shall be subsequent to the date of the current violation. Credit may not be given to any program activities completed prior to the date of the current violation.

(c) (1) Except when the court has ordered installation of a functioning, certified ignition interlock device pursuant to Section 23575.3, the department shall advise the person that the person may apply to the department for a restricted driver's license if the person meets all of the following requirements:

(A) The underlying conviction was not only for the use of drugs, as defined in Section 312, at the time of the violation.

(B) The person satisfactorily provides to the department, subsequent to the violation date of the current underlying conviction, enrollment in, or completion of, a driving-under-the-influence program licensed pursuant to Section 11836 of the Health and Safety Code, as described in paragraph (2) of subdivision (b) of Section 23538 of this code.

(C) The person agrees, as a condition of the restriction, to continue satisfactory participation in the program described in subparagraph (B).

(D) The person does both of the following:

(i) Submits the "Verification of Installation" form described in paragraph (2) of subdivision (g) of Section 13386.

(ii) Agrees to maintain the functioning, certified ignition interlock device as required under subdivision (e).

(E) The person provides proof of financial responsibility, as defined in Section 16430.

(F) The person pays all reissue fees and any restriction fee required by the department.

(G) The person pays to the department a fee sufficient to cover the reasonable costs of administering the requirements of this paragraph, as determined by the department.

(2) The restriction shall remain in effect for the period required in subdivision (d).

(d) (1) The restricted driving privilege shall become effective when the department receives all of the documents and fees required under subdivision (c) and, except as specified in paragraph (2) or (3), shall remain in effect until all reinstatement requirements are satisfied.

(2) For the purposes of the restriction conditions specified in subdivision (c), the department shall terminate the restriction imposed pursuant to this section and shall suspend or revoke the person's driving privilege upon receipt of notification from the driving-under-the-influence program that the person has failed to comply with the program requirements. The person's driving privilege shall remain suspended or revoked for the remaining period of the original suspension or revocation imposed under this section and until all reinstatement requirements described in this section are met.

(3) The department shall immediately suspend or revoke the privilege to operate a motor vehicle of a person who, with respect to an ignition interlock device installed pursuant to Section 23575.3, attempts to remove, bypass, or tamper with the device, has the device removed prior to the termination date of the restriction, or fails three or more times to comply with any requirement for the maintenance or calibration of the device. The privilege shall remain suspended or revoked for the remaining period of the originating suspension or revocation and until all reinstatement requirements in this section are satisfied, provided, however, that if the person provides proof to the satisfaction of the department that the person is in compliance with the restriction issued pursuant to this section, the department may, in its discretion, restore the privilege to operate a motor vehicle and reimpose the remaining term of the restriction.

(e) A person whose driving privilege is restricted by the department pursuant to this section shall arrange for each vehicle with a functioning, certified ignition interlock device to be serviced by the installer at least once every 60 days in order for the installer to recalibrate the device and monitor the operation of the device. The installer shall notify the Department of Motor Vehicles if the device is removed or indicates that the person has attempted to remove, bypass, or tamper with the device, or if the person fails three or more times to comply with any requirement for the maintenance or calibration of the ignition interlock device.

(f) (1) The holder of a commercial driver's license who was operating a motor vehicle other than a commercial vehicle, or a driver who was operating a commercial vehicle, as defined in Section 15210, at the time of the violation that resulted in the suspension of that person's driving privilege under paragraph (1) of subdivision (a) of Section 13352 or this section is not eligible for the restricted driver's license authorized under this section.

(2) Notwithstanding paragraph (1), as authorized under this section, the department shall issue the person a noncommercial driver's license restricted in the same manner and subject to the same conditions and requirements as specified in subdivision (c).

(g) For the purposes of this section, "bypass" means either of the following:

(1) Failure to take any random retest.

(2) Failure to pass a random retest with a breath alcohol concentration not exceeding 0.03 percent, by weight of alcohol, in the person's blood.

(h) For purposes of this section, "random retest" means a breath test performed by the driver upon a certified ignition interlock device at random intervals after the initial engine startup breath test and while the vehicle's motor is running.

(i) The restriction conditions specified in this section shall apply only to a person who is convicted for a violation of Section 23152, as specified in subdivision (a), that occurred on or after January 1, 2019.

(j) This section shall become operative on January 1, 2019.

(k) This section shall remain in effect only until January 1, 2033, and as of that date is repealed.

(Amended (as added by Stats. 2017, Ch. 485, Sec. 5) by Stats. 2025, Ch. 689, Sec. 3. (AB 366) Effective January 1, 2026. Repealed as of January 1, 2033, by its own provisions. See later operative version, as amended by Sec. 4 of Stats. 2025, Ch. 689.)

13352.1. (a) Pursuant to subdivision (a) of Section 13352 and except as required under Section 13352.4, upon a conviction or finding of a violation of Section 23152 punishable under Section 23536, if the court refers the person to a program pursuant to paragraph (2) of subdivision (b) of Section 23538, the privilege shall be suspended for 10 months.

(b) The privilege may not be reinstated until the person gives proof of financial responsibility and gives proof satisfactory to the department of successful completion of a driving-under-the-influence program licensed pursuant to Section 11836 of the Health and Safety Code described in subdivision (b) of Section 23538 of this code. For the purposes of this subdivision, enrollment, participation, and completion of an approved program shall be subsequent to the date of the current violation. Credit may not be given to any program activities completed prior to the date of the current violation.

(c) This section shall become operative on January 1, 2033.

(Amended (as added by Stats. 2017, Ch. 485, Sec. 6) by Stats. 2025, Ch. 689, Sec. 4. (AB 366) Effective January 1, 2026. Section operative January 1, 2033, by its own provisions.)

13352.2. (a) If a person is required under Section 13352 to provide the department with proof of enrollment in a driving-under-the-influence program licensed pursuant to Section 11836 of the Health and Safety Code, or a program specified in Section 8001 of the Penal Code, the department shall deem that requirement satisfied upon receiving at its headquarters proof of enrollment that is satisfactory to the department and has been forwarded to the department by the program provider.

(b) If a person is required under Section 13352 to provide the department with proof of completion of a driving-under-the-influence program licensed pursuant to Section 11836 of the Health and Safety Code, or a program specified in Section 8001 of the Penal Code, the department shall deem that requirement satisfied upon receiving at its headquarters proof of completion that is satisfactory to the department and has been forwarded to the department by the program provider.

(Added by Stats. 2004, Ch. 403, Sec. 1. Effective January 1, 2005.)

13352.3. (a) Notwithstanding any other provision of law, except subdivisions (b), (c), and (d) of Section 13352 and Sections 13367 and 23521, the department immediately shall revoke the privilege of any person to operate a motor vehicle upon receipt of a duly certified abstract of the record of any court showing that the person was convicted of a violation of Section 23152 or 23153 while under 18 years of age, or upon receipt of a report of a judge of the juvenile court, a juvenile hearing officer, or a referee of a juvenile court showing that the person has been found to have committed a violation of Section 23152 or 23153.

(b) The term of the revocation shall be until the person reaches 18 years of age, for one year, or for the period prescribed for restriction, suspension, or revocation specified in subdivision (a) of Section 13352, whichever is longer. The privilege may not be reinstated until the person gives proof of financial responsibility as defined in Section 16430.

(Amended by Stats. 2003, Ch. 149, Sec. 83. Effective January 1, 2004.)

13352.4. (a) Except as provided in subdivision (h), or when the court has ordered installation of a functioning, certified ignition interlock device pursuant to Section 23575.3, the department shall issue a restricted driver's license to a person whose driver's license was suspended under paragraph (1) of subdivision (a) of Section 13352 or Section 13352.1, if the person meets all of the following requirements:

(1) Submits proof satisfactory to the department of either of the following:

(A) Enrollment in a driving-under-the-influence program licensed pursuant to Section 11836 of the Health and Safety Code, as described in subdivision (b) of Section 23538 of this code.

(B) Enrollment in a program described in subdivision (b) of Section 23542, if the court has ordered the person to enroll in, participate in, and complete either program described in that section, in which case the person shall not be required to provide proof of the enrollment described in subparagraph (A).

(2) Submits proof of financial responsibility, as defined in Section 16430.

(3) Pays all applicable reinstatement or reissue fees and any restriction fee required by the department.

(b) The restriction of the driving privilege shall become effective when the department receives all of the documents and fees required under subdivision (a) and shall remain in effect for a period of 12 months and until the date all reinstatement requirements described in Section 13352 or 13352.1 have been met.

(c) The restriction of the driving privilege shall be limited to the hours necessary for driving to and from the person's place of employment, driving during the course of employment, and driving to and from activities required in the driving-under-the-influence program.

(d) Whenever the driving privilege is restricted under this section, proof of financial responsibility, as defined in Section 16430, shall be maintained for three years. If the person does not maintain that proof of financial responsibility at any time during the restriction, the driving privilege shall be suspended until the proof required under Section 16484 is received by the department.

(e) For the purposes of this section, enrollment, participation, and completion of an approved program shall be subsequent to the date of the current violation. Credit may not be given to a program activity completed prior to the date of the current violation.

(f) The department shall terminate the restriction issued under this section and shall suspend the privilege to operate a motor vehicle pursuant to paragraph (1) of subdivision (a) of Section 13352 or Section 13352.1 immediately upon receipt of notification from the driving-under-the-influence program that the person has failed to comply with the program requirements. The privilege shall remain suspended until the final day of the original suspension imposed under paragraph (1) of subdivision (a) of Section 13352 or Section 13352.1, or until the date all reinstatement requirements described in Section 13352 or 13352.1 have been met, whichever date is later.

(g) (1) The holder of a commercial driver's license who was operating a motor vehicle other than a commercial vehicle, or a driver who was operating a commercial vehicle, as defined in Section 15210, at the time of the violation that resulted in the suspension of that person's driving privilege under paragraph (1) of subdivision (a) of Section 13352 or Section 13352.1 is not eligible for the restricted driver's license authorized under this section.

(2) Notwithstanding paragraph (1), as authorized under this section, the department shall issue the person a noncommercial driver's license restricted in the same manner and subject to the same conditions and requirements as specified in subdivision (a).

(h) If, upon conviction, the court has made the determination, as authorized under Section 23536 or paragraph (3) of subdivision (a) of

Section 23538, to disallow the issuance of a restricted driver's license, the department may not issue a restricted driver's license under this section.

(i) This section shall become operative on January 1, 2019.

(j) This section shall remain in effect only until January 1, 2033, and as of that date is repealed, unless a later enacted statute, that is enacted before January 1, 2033, deletes or extends that date.

(Amended (as amended by Stats. 2017, Ch. 485, Sec. 7) by Stats. 2025, Ch. 689, Sec. 5. (AB 366) Effective January 1, 2026. Repealed as of January 1, 2033, by its own provisions. See later operative version, as amended by Sec. 6 of Stats. 2025, Ch. 689.)

13352.4. (a) Except as provided in subdivision (h), the department shall issue a restricted driver's license to a person whose driver's license was suspended under paragraph (1) of subdivision (a) of Section 13352 or Section 13352.1, if the person meets all of the following requirements:

(1) Submits proof satisfactory to the department of either of the following, as applicable:

(A) Enrollment in a driving-under-the-influence program licensed pursuant to Section 11836 of the Health and Safety Code, as described in subdivision (b) of Section 23538 of this code.

(B) Enrollment in a program described in subdivision (b) of Section 23542, if the court has ordered the person to enroll in, participate in, and complete either program described in that section, in which case the person shall not be required to provide proof of the enrollment described in subparagraph (A).

(2) Submits proof of financial responsibility, as defined in Section 16430.

(3) Pays all applicable reinstatement or reissue fees and any restriction fee required by the department.

(b) The restriction of the driving privilege shall become effective when the department receives all of the documents and fees required under subdivision (a) and shall remain in effect until the final day of the original suspension imposed under paragraph (1) of subdivision (a) of Section 13352 or Section 13352.1, or until the date all reinstatement requirements described in Section 13352 or 13352.1 have been met, whichever date is later, and may include credit for any suspension period served under subdivision (c) of Section 13353.3.

(c) The restriction of the driving privilege shall be limited to the hours necessary for driving to and from the person's place of employment, driving during the course of employment, and driving to and from activities required in the driving-under-the-influence program.

(d) Whenever the driving privilege is restricted under this section, proof of financial responsibility, as defined in Section 16430, shall be maintained for three years. If the person does not maintain that proof of financial responsibility at any time during the restriction, the driving privilege shall be suspended until the proof required under Section 16484 is received by the department.

(e) For the purposes of this section, enrollment, participation, and completion of an approved program shall be subsequent to the date of the current violation. Credit may not be given to a program activity completed prior to the date of the current violation.

(f) The department shall terminate the restriction issued under this section and shall suspend the privilege to operate a motor vehicle pursuant to paragraph (1) of subdivision (a) of Section 13352 or Section 13352.1 immediately upon receipt of notification from the driving-under-the-influence program that the person has failed to comply with the program requirements. The privilege shall remain suspended until the final day of the original suspension imposed under paragraph (1) of subdivision (a) of Section 13352 or 13352.1, or until the date all reinstatement requirements described in Section 13352 or Section 13352.1 have been met, whichever date is later.

(g) The holder of a commercial driver's license who was operating a commercial motor vehicle, as defined in Section 15210, at the time of a violation that resulted in a suspension or revocation of the person's noncommercial driving privilege under paragraph (1) of subdivision (a) of Section 13352 or Section 13352.1 is not eligible for the restricted driver's license authorized under this section.

(h) If, upon conviction, the court has made the determination, as authorized under subdivision (d) of Section 23536 or paragraph (3) of subdivision (a) of Section 23538, to disallow the issuance of a restricted driver's license, the department may not issue a restricted driver's license under this section.

(i) This section shall become operative January 1, 2033.

(Amended (as added by Stats. 2016, Ch. 783, Sec. 9) by Stats. 2025, Ch. 689, Sec. 6. (AB 366) Effective January 1, 2026. Section operative January 1, 2033, by its own provisions.)

13352.5. (a) The department shall issue a restricted driver's license to a person whose driver's license was suspended under paragraph (3) of subdivision (a) of Section 13352, if all of the following requirements have been met:

(1) Proof satisfactory to the department of enrollment in, or completion of, a driving-under-the-influence program licensed pursuant to Section 11836 of the Health and Safety Code, as described in subdivision (b) of Section 23542 has been received in the department's headquarters.

(2) The person submits proof of financial responsibility, as described in Section 16430.

(3) The person completes not less than 12 months of the suspension period imposed under paragraph (3) of subdivision (a) of Section 13352. The 12 months may include credit for any suspension period served under subdivision (c) of Section 13353.3.

(4) The person pays all applicable reinstatement or reissue fees and any restriction fee required by the department.

(b) The restriction of the driving privilege shall become effective when the department receives all of the documents and fees required under subdivision (a) and shall remain in effect until the final day of the original suspension imposed under paragraph (3) of subdivision (a) of Section 13352, or until the date all reinstatement requirements described in Section 13352 have been met, whichever date is later.

(c) The restriction of the driving privilege shall be limited to the hours necessary for driving to and from the person's place of employment, driving during the course of employment, and driving to and from activities required in the driving-under-the-influence program.

(d) Whenever the driving privilege is restricted under this section, proof of financial responsibility, as defined in Section 16430, shall be maintained for three years. If the person does not maintain that proof of financial responsibility at any time during the restriction, the driving privilege shall be suspended until the proof required under Section 16484 is received by the department.

(e) For the purposes of this section, enrollment in, participation in, and completion of an approved program shall be subsequent to the date of the current violation. Credit shall not be given to any program activities completed prior to the date of the current violation.

(f) The department shall terminate the restriction imposed pursuant to this section and shall suspend the privilege to drive under paragraph (3) of subdivision (a) of Section 13352 upon receipt of notification from the driving-under-the-influence program that the person has failed to comply with the program requirements.

(g) If, upon conviction, the court has made the determination, as authorized under subdivision (b) of Section 23540 or subdivision (d) of Section 23542, to disallow the issuance of a restricted driver's license, the department shall not issue a restricted driver's license under this section.

(h) A person restricted pursuant to this section may apply to the department for a restricted driver's license, subject to the conditions specified in paragraph (3) of subdivision (a) of Section 13352. Whenever proof of financial responsibility has already been provided and a restriction fee has been paid in compliance with restrictions described in this section, and the offender subsequently receives an ignition interlock device restriction described in paragraph (3) of subdivision (a) of Section 13352, the proof of financial responsibility period shall not be extended beyond the previously established term and no additional restriction fee shall be required.

(i) This section applies to a person who meets all of the following conditions:

(1) Has been convicted of a violation of Section 23152 that occurred on or before July 1, 1999, and is punishable under Section 23540, or former Section 23165.

(2) Was granted probation for the conviction subject to conditions imposed under subdivision (b) of Section 23542, or under subdivision (b) of former Section 23166.

(3) Is no longer subject to the probation described in paragraph (2).

(4) Has not completed the licensed driving-under-the-influence program under paragraph (3) of subdivision (a) of Section 13352 for reinstatement of the driving privilege.

(5) Has no violations in his or her driving record that would preclude issuance of a restricted driver's license.

(Amended (as amended by Stats. 2009, Ch. 193) by Stats. 2010, Ch. 30, Sec. 1. (SB 895) Effective June 22, 2010. Amendments operative July 1, 2010, pursuant to Stats. 2009, Ch. 193, Sec. 9.)

13352.6. (a) The department shall immediately suspend the driving privilege of a person who is 18 years of age or older and is convicted of a violation of Section 23140, upon the receipt of a duly certified abstract of the record of a court showing that conviction. The privilege may not be reinstated until the person provides the department with proof of financial responsibility and until proof satisfactory to the department, of successful completion of a driving-under-the-influence program licensed under Section 11836 of the Health and Safety Code has been received in the department's headquarters. That attendance shall be as follows:

(1) If, within 10 years of the current violation of Section 23140, the person has not been convicted of a separate violation of Section 23140, 23152, or 23153, or of Section 23103, with a plea of guilty under Section 23103.5, or of Section 655 of the Harbors and Navigation Code, or of Section 191.5 of, or subdivision (a) of Section 192.5 of, the Penal Code, the person shall complete, at a minimum, the education component of that licensed driving-under-the-influence program.

(2) If the person does not meet the requirements of paragraph (1), the person shall complete, at a minimum, the program described in paragraph (1) of subdivision (c) of Section 11837 of the Health and Safety Code.

(b) For the purposes of this section, enrollment, participation, and completion of the program shall be subsequent to the date of the current violation. Credit for enrollment, participation, or completion may not be given for any program activities completed prior to the date of the current violation.

(Amended by Stats. 2007, Ch. 747, Sec. 21. Effective January 1, 2008.)

13353. (a) If a person refuses the officer's request to submit to, or fails to complete, a chemical test or tests pursuant to Section 23612, upon receipt of the officer's sworn statement that the officer had reasonable cause to believe the person had been driving a motor vehicle in violation of Section 23140, 23152, or 23153, and that the person had refused to submit to, or did not complete, the test or tests after being requested by the officer, the department shall do one of the following:

(1) Suspend the person's privilege to operate a motor vehicle for a period of one year.

(2) Revoke the person's privilege to operate a motor vehicle for a period of two years if the refusal occurred within 10 years of either (A) a separate violation of Section 23103 as specified in Section 23103.5, or of Section 23140, 23152, or 23153, or of Section 191.5 or subdivision (a) of Section 192.5 of the Penal Code, that resulted in a conviction, or (B) a suspension or revocation of the person's privilege to operate a motor vehicle pursuant to this section or Section 13353.2 for an offense that occurred on a separate occasion.

(3) Revoke the person's privilege to operate a motor vehicle for a period of three years if the refusal occurred within 10 years of any of the following:

(A) Two or more separate violations of Section 23103 as specified in Section 23103.5, or of Section 23140, 23152, or 23153, or of Section 191.5 or subdivision (a) of Section 192.5 of the Penal Code, or any combination thereof, that resulted in convictions.

(B) Two or more suspensions or revocations of the person's privilege to operate a motor vehicle pursuant to this section or Section 13353.2 for offenses that occurred on separate occasions.

(C) Any combination of two or more of those convictions or administrative suspensions or revocations.

The officer's sworn statement shall be submitted pursuant to Section 13380 on a form furnished or approved by the department. The suspension or revocation shall not become effective until 30 days after the giving of written notice thereof, or until the end of a stay of the suspension or revocation, as provided for in Section 13558.

(D) For the purposes of this section, a conviction of an offense in any state, territory, or possession of the United States, the District of Columbia, the Commonwealth of Puerto Rico, or the Dominion of Canada that, if committed in this state, would be a violation of Section 23103, as specified in Section 23103.5, or Section 23140, 23152, or 23153, or Section 191.5 or subdivision (a) of Section 192.5 of the Penal Code, is a conviction of that particular section of the Vehicle Code or Penal Code.

(b) If a person on more than one occasion in separate incidents refuses the officer's request to submit to, or fails to complete, a chemical test or tests pursuant to Section 23612 while driving a motor vehicle, upon the receipt of the officer's sworn statement that the officer had reasonable cause to believe the person had been driving a motor vehicle in violation of Section 23140, 23152, or 23153, the department shall disqualify the person from operating a commercial motor vehicle for the rest of his or her lifetime.

(c) The notice of the order of suspension or revocation under this section shall be served on the person by a peace officer pursuant to Section 23612. The notice of the order of suspension or revocation shall be on a form provided by the department. If the notice of the order of suspension or revocation has not been served by the peace officer pursuant to Section 23612, the department immediately shall notify the person in writing of the action taken. The peace officer who serves the notice, or the department, if applicable, also shall provide, if the officer or department, as the case may be, determines that it is necessary to do so, the person with the appropriate non-English notice developed pursuant to subdivision (d) of Section 14100.

(d) Upon the receipt of the officer's sworn statement, the department shall review the record. For purposes of this section, the scope of the administrative review shall cover all of the following issues:

(1) Whether the peace officer had reasonable cause to believe the person had been driving a motor vehicle in violation of Section 23140, 23152, or 23153.

(2) Whether the person was placed under arrest.

(3) Whether the person refused to submit to, or did not complete, the test or tests after being requested by a peace officer.

(4) Whether, except for a person described in subdivision (a) of Section 23612 who is incapable of refusing, the person had been told that his or her driving privilege would be suspended or revoked if he or she refused to submit to, or did not complete, the test or tests.

(e) The person may request an administrative hearing pursuant to Section 13558. Except as provided in subdivision (e) of Section 13558, the request for an administrative hearing does not stay the order of suspension or revocation.

(f) The suspension or revocation imposed under this section shall run concurrently with any restriction, suspension, or revocation imposed under Section 13352, 13352.4, or 13352.5 that resulted from the same arrest.

(Amended by Stats. 2007, Ch. 747, Sec. 22. Effective January 1, 2008.)

13353.1. (a) If a person refuses an officer's request to submit to, or fails to complete, a preliminary alcohol screening test pursuant to Section 13388 or 13389, upon the receipt of the officer's sworn statement, submitted pursuant to Section 13380, that the officer had reasonable cause to believe the person had been driving a motor vehicle in violation of Section 23136 or 23154, and that the person had refused to submit to, or did not complete, the test after being requested by the officer, the department shall do one of the following:

(1) Suspend the person's privilege to operate a motor vehicle for a period of one year.

(2) Revoke the person's privilege to operate a motor vehicle for a period of two years if the refusal occurred within 10 years of either of the following:

(A) A separate violation of subdivision (a) of Section 23136, that resulted in a finding of a violation, or a separate violation, that resulted in a conviction, of Section 23103, as specified in Section 23103.5, of Section 23140, 23152, or 23153, or of Section 191.5 or subdivision (a) of Section 192.5 of the Penal Code.

(B) A suspension or revocation of the person's privilege to operate a motor vehicle if that action was taken pursuant to this section or Section 13353 or 13353.2 for an offense that occurred on a separate occasion.

(3) Revoke the person's privilege to operate a motor vehicle for a period of three years if the refusal occurred within 10 years of any of the following:

(A) Two or more separate violations of subdivision (a) of Section 23136, that resulted in findings of violations, or two or more separate violations, that resulted in convictions, of Section 23103, as specified in Section 23103.5, of Section 23140, 23152, or 23153, or of Section 191.5 or subdivision (a) of Section 192.5 of the Penal Code, or any combination thereof.

(B) Two or more suspensions or revocations of the person's privilege to operate a motor vehicle if those actions were taken pursuant to this section, or Section 13353 or 13353.2, for offenses that occurred on separate occasions.

(C) Any combination of two or more of the convictions or administrative suspensions or revocations described in subparagraph (A) or (B).

(b) For the purposes of this section, a conviction of an offense in any state, territory, or possession of the United States, the District of Columbia, the Commonwealth of Puerto Rico, or Canada that, if committed in this state, would be a violation of Section 23103, as specified in Section 23103.5, or Section 23140, 23152, or 23153, or Section 191.5 or subdivision (a) of Section 192.5 of the Penal Code, is a conviction of that particular section of the Vehicle or Penal Code.

(c) The notice of the order of suspension or revocation under this section shall be served on the person by the peace officer pursuant to Section 13388 and shall not become effective until 30 days after the person is served with that notice. The notice of the order of suspension or revocation shall be on a form provided by the department. If the notice of the order of suspension or revocation has not been served by the peace officer pursuant to Section 13388, the department immediately shall notify the person in writing of the action taken. The peace officer who serves the notice, or the department, if applicable, also shall provide, if the officer or department, as the case may be, determines that it is necessary to do so, the person with the appropriate non-English notice developed pursuant to subdivision (d) of Section 14100.

(d) Upon the receipt of the officer's sworn statement, the department shall review the record. For the purposes of this section, the scope of the administrative review shall cover all of the following issues:

(1) Whether the peace officer had reasonable cause to believe the person had been driving a motor vehicle in violation of Section 23136.

(2) Whether the person was lawfully detained.

(3) Whether the person refused to submit to, or did not complete, the test after being requested to do so by a peace officer.

(e) The person may request an administrative hearing pursuant to Section 13558. Except as provided in subdivision (e) of Section 13558, the request for an administrative hearing does not stay the order of suspension or revocation.

(Amended by Stats. 2007, Ch. 749, Sec. 1.5. Effective January 1, 2008. Operative January 1, 2009, by Sec. 9 of Ch. 749.)

13353.2. (a) The department shall immediately suspend the privilege of a person to operate a motor vehicle for any one of the following reasons:

(1) The person was driving a motor vehicle when the person had 0.08 percent or more, by weight, of alcohol in his or her blood.

(2) The person was under 21 years of age and had a blood-alcohol concentration of 0.01 percent or greater, as measured by a preliminary alcohol screening test, or other chemical test.

(3) The person was driving a vehicle that requires a commercial driver's license when the person had 0.04 percent or more, by weight, of alcohol in his or her blood.

(4) The person was driving a motor vehicle when both of the following applied:

(A) The person was on probation for a violation of Section 23152 or 23153.

(B) The person had 0.01 percent or more, by weight, of alcohol in his or her blood, as measured by a preliminary alcohol screening test or other chemical test.

(b) The notice of the order of suspension under this section shall be served on the person by a peace officer pursuant to Section 13382 or 13388. The notice of the order of suspension shall be on a form provided by the department. If the notice of the order of suspension has not been served upon the person by the peace officer pursuant to Section 13382 or 13388, upon the receipt of the report of a peace officer submitted pursuant to Section 13380, the department shall mail written notice of the order of the suspension to the person at the last known address shown on the department's records and, if the address of the person provided by the peace officer's report differs from the address of record, to that address.

(c) The notice of the order of suspension shall specify clearly the reason and statutory grounds for the suspension, the effective date of the suspension, the right of the person to request an administrative hearing, the procedure for requesting an administrative hearing, and the date by which a request for an administrative hearing shall be made in order to receive a determination prior to the effective date of the suspension.

(d) The department shall make a determination of the facts in subdivision (a) on the basis of the report of a peace officer submitted pursuant to Section 13380. The determination of the facts, after administrative review pursuant to Section 13557, by the department is final, unless an administrative hearing is held pursuant to Section 13558 and any judicial review of the administrative determination after the hearing pursuant to Section 13559 is final.

(e) The determination of the facts in subdivision (a) is a civil matter that is independent of the determination of the person's guilt or innocence, shall have no collateral estoppel effect on a subsequent criminal prosecution, and shall not preclude the litigation of the same or similar facts in the criminal proceeding. If a person is acquitted of criminal charges relating to a determination of facts under subdivision (a), or if the person's driver's license was suspended pursuant to Section 13388 and the department finds no basis for a suspension pursuant to that section, the department shall immediately reinstate the person's privilege to operate a motor vehicle if the department has suspended it administratively pursuant to subdivision (a), and the department shall return or reissue for the remaining term any driver's license that has been taken from the person pursuant to Section 13382 or otherwise. Notwithstanding subdivision (b) of Section 13558, if criminal charges under Section 23140, 23152, or 23153 are not filed by the district attorney because of a lack of evidence, or if those charges are filed but are subsequently dismissed by the court because of an insufficiency of evidence, the person has a renewed right to request an administrative hearing before the department. The request for a hearing shall be made within one year from the date of arrest.

(f) The department shall furnish a form that requires a detailed explanation specifying which evidence was defective or lacking and detailing why that evidence was defective or lacking. The form shall be made available to the person to provide to the district attorney. The department shall hold an administrative hearing, and the hearing officer shall consider the reasons for the failure to prosecute given by the district attorney on the form provided by the department. If applicable, the hearing officer shall consider the reasons stated on the record by a judge who dismisses the charges. A fee shall not be imposed pursuant to Section 14905 for the return or reissuing of a driver's license pursuant to this subdivision. The disposition of a suspension action under this section does not affect an action to suspend or revoke the person's privilege to operate a motor vehicle under another provision of this code, including, but not limited to, Section 13352 or 13353, or Chapter 3 (commencing with Section 13800).

(Amended (as amended by Stats. 2007, Ch. 749, Sec. 2) by Stats. 2008, Ch. 179, Sec. 219. Effective January 1, 2009.)

13353.3. (a) An order of suspension of a person's privilege to operate a motor vehicle pursuant to Section 13353.2 shall become effective 30 days after the person is served with the notice pursuant to Section 13382 or 13388, or subdivision (b) of Section 13353.2.

(b) The period of suspension of a person's privilege to operate a motor vehicle under Section 13353.2 is as follows:

(1) (A) If the person has not been convicted of a separate violation of Section 23103, as specified in Section 23103.5, or Section 23140, 23152, or 23153, or Section 191.5 or subdivision (a) of Section 192.5 of the Penal Code, the person has not been administratively determined to have refused chemical testing pursuant to Section 13353 or 13353.1 of this code, or the person has not been administratively determined to have been driving with an excessive concentration of alcohol pursuant to Section 13353.2 on a separate occasion, which offense or occurrence occurred within 10 years of the occasion in question, the person's privilege to operate a motor vehicle shall be suspended for four months, except as provided in subparagraph (B).

(B) The four-month suspension pursuant to subparagraph (A) shall terminate if the person has been convicted of a violation arising out of the same occurrence and all of the following conditions are met:

(i) The person is eligible for a restricted driver's license pursuant to Section 13352 or 13352.1.

(ii) The person installs a functioning, certified ignition interlock device as required in Section 13352 or 13352.1 for that restricted driver's license.

(iii) The person complies with all other applicable conditions of Section 13352 or 13352.1 for a restricted driver's license.

(2) (A) If the person has been convicted of one or more separate violations of Section 23103, as specified in Section 23103.5, or Section 23140, 23152, or 23153, or Section 191.5 or subdivision (a) of Section 192.5 of the Penal Code, the person has been administratively determined to have refused chemical testing pursuant to Section 13353 or 13353.1 of this code, or the person has been administratively determined to have been driving with an excessive concentration of alcohol pursuant to Section 13353.2 on a separate occasion, which offense or occasion occurred within 10 years of the occasion in question, the person's privilege to operate a motor vehicle shall be suspended for one year, except as provided in subparagraph (B).

(B) The one-year suspension pursuant to subparagraph (A) shall terminate if the person has been convicted of a violation arising out of the same occurrence and all of the following conditions are met:

(i) The person is eligible for a restricted driver's license pursuant to Section 13352 or 13352.1.

(ii) The person installs a functioning, certified ignition interlock device as required in Section 13352 or 13352.1 for that restricted driver's license.

(iii) The person complies with all other applicable conditions of Section 13352 or 13352.1 for a restricted driver's license.

(3) Notwithstanding any other law, if a person has been administratively determined to have been driving in violation of Section 23136 or to have refused chemical testing pursuant to Section 13353.1, the period of suspension shall not be for less than one year.

(c) If a person's privilege to operate a motor vehicle is suspended pursuant to Section 13353.2 and the person is convicted of a violation of Section 23152 or 23153, including, but not limited to, a violation described in Section 23620, arising out of the same occurrence, both the suspension under Section 13353.2 and the suspension or revocation under Section 13352 shall be imposed, except that the periods of suspension or revocation shall run concurrently, and the total period of suspension or revocation shall not exceed the longer of the two suspension or revocation periods.

(d) For the purposes of this section, a conviction of an offense in any state, territory, or possession of the United States, the District of Columbia, the Commonwealth of Puerto Rico, or Canada that, if committed in this state, would be a violation of Section 23103, as specified in Section 23103.5, or Section 23140, 23152, or 23153, or Section 191.5 or subdivision (a) of Section 192.5 of the Penal Code, is a conviction of that particular section of the Vehicle Code or Penal Code.

(e) This section shall become operative on January 1, 2019.

(f) This section shall remain in effect only until January 1, 2033, and as of that date is repealed, unless a later enacted statute, that is enacted before January 1, 2033, deletes or extends that date.

(Amended (as amended by Stats. 2017, Ch. 485, Sec. 9) by Stats. 2025, Ch. 689, Sec. 7. (AB 366) Effective January 1, 2026. Repealed as of January 1, 2033, by its own provisions. See later operative version, as amended by Sec. 8 of Stats. 2025, Ch. 689.)

13353.3. (a) An order of suspension of a person's privilege to operate a motor vehicle pursuant to Section 13353.2 shall become effective 30 days after the person is served with the notice pursuant to Section 13382 or 13388, or subdivision (b) of Section 13353.2.

(b) The period of suspension of a person's privilege to operate a motor vehicle under Section 13353.2 is as follows:

(1) If the person has not been convicted of a separate violation of Section 23103, as specified in Section 23103.5, or Section 23140, 23152, or 23153, or Section 191.5 or subdivision (a) of Section 192.5 of the Penal Code, the person has not been administratively determined to have refused chemical testing pursuant to Section 13353 or 13353.1 of this code, or the person has not been administratively determined to have been driving with an excessive concentration of alcohol pursuant to Section 13353.2 on a separate occasion, which offense or occurrence occurred within 10 years of the occasion in question, the person's privilege to operate a motor vehicle shall be suspended for four months.

(2) (A) If the person has been convicted of one or more separate violations of Section 23103, as specified in Section 23103.5, or Section 23140, 23152, or 23153, or Section 191.5 or subdivision (a) of Section 192.5 of the Penal Code, the person has been administratively determined to have refused chemical testing pursuant to Section 13353 or 13353.1 of this code, or the person has been administratively determined to have been driving with an excessive concentration of alcohol pursuant to Section 13353.2 on a separate occasion, which offense or occasion occurred within 10 years of the occasion in question, the person's privilege to operate a motor vehicle shall be suspended for one year, except as provided in subparagraphs (B) and (C).

(B) The one-year suspension pursuant to subparagraph (A) shall terminate if the person has been convicted of a violation arising out of the same occurrence and all of the following conditions are met:

(i) The person is eligible for a restricted driver's license pursuant to Section 13352.

(ii) The person installs a functioning, certified ignition interlock device as required in Section 13352 for that restricted driver's license.

(iii) The person complies with all other applicable conditions of Section 13352 for a restricted driver's license.

(C) The one-year suspension pursuant to subparagraph (A) shall terminate after completion of a 90-day suspension period, and the person shall be eligible for a restricted license if the person has been convicted of a violation of Section 23103, as specified in Section 23103.5, arising out of the same occurrence, has no more than two prior alcohol-related convictions within 10 years, as specified pursuant to subparagraph (A), and all of the following conditions are met:

(i) The person satisfactorily provides, subsequent to the underlying violation date, proof satisfactory to the department of enrollment in a nine-month driving-under-the-influence program licensed pursuant to Chapter 9 (commencing with Section 11836) of Part 2 of Division 10.5 of the Health and Safety Code that consists of at least 60 hours of program activities, including education, group counseling, and individual interview sessions.

(ii) The person agrees, as a condition of the restriction, to continue satisfactory participation in the program described in clause (i).

(iii) The person installs a functioning, certified ignition interlock device and submits the "Verification of Installation" form described in paragraph (2) of subdivision (g) of Section 13386.

(iv) The person agrees to maintain the ignition interlock device as required pursuant to subdivision (g) of Section 23575.

(v) The person provides proof of financial responsibility, as defined in Section 16430.

(vi) The person pays all license fees and any restriction fee required by the department.

(vii) The person pays to the department a fee sufficient to cover the costs of administration of this paragraph, as determined by the department.

(D) The department shall advise those persons that are eligible under subparagraph (C) that after completion of 90 days of the suspension period, the person may apply to the department for a restricted driver's license, subject to the conditions set forth in subparagraph (C).

(E) The restricted driving privilege shall become effective when the department receives all of the documents and fees required under subparagraph (C) and remain in effect for at least the remaining period of the original suspension and until the person provides satisfactory proof to the department of successful completion of a driving-under-the-influence program licensed pursuant to Section 11836 of the Health and Safety Code. The restricted driving privilege shall be subject to the following conditions:

(i) If the driving privilege is restricted under this section, proof of financial responsibility, as described in Section 16430, shall be maintained for three years. If the person does not maintain that proof of financial responsibility at any time during the restriction, the driving privilege shall be suspended until the proof required pursuant to Section 16484 is received by the department.

(ii) For the purposes of this section, enrollment, participation, and completion of an approved program shall occur subsequent to the date of the current violation. Credit may not be given to a program activity completed prior to the date of the current violation.

(iii) The department shall terminate the restriction issued pursuant to this section and shall suspend the privilege to operate a motor vehicle pursuant to subparagraph (A) immediately upon receipt of notification from the driving-under-the-influence program that the person has failed to comply with the program requirements. The privilege shall remain suspended until the final day of the original suspension imposed pursuant to subparagraph (A).

(iv) The department shall suspend the privilege to operate a motor vehicle pursuant to subparagraph (A) immediately upon receipt of notification from the installer that a person has attempted to remove, bypass, or tamper with the ignition interlock device, has removed the device prior to the termination date of the restriction, or fails three or more times to comply with any requirement for the maintenance or calibration of the ignition interlock device ordered pursuant to this section. The privilege shall remain suspended for the remaining period of the original suspension imposed pursuant to subparagraph (A), except that if the person provides proof to the satisfaction of the department that the person is in compliance with the restriction issued pursuant to this section, the department may, in its discretion, restore the privilege to operate a motor vehicle and reimpose the remaining term of the restriction.

(3) Notwithstanding any other law, if a person has been administratively determined to have been driving in violation of Section 23136 or to have refused chemical testing pursuant to Section 13353.1, the period of suspension shall not be for less than one year.

(c) If a person's privilege to operate a motor vehicle is suspended pursuant to Section 13353.2 and the person is convicted of a violation of Section 23152 or 23153, including, but not limited to, a violation described in Section 23620, arising out of the same occurrence, both the suspension under Section 13353.2 and the suspension or revocation under Section 13352 shall be imposed, except that the periods of suspension or revocation shall run concurrently, and the total period of suspension or revocation shall not exceed the longer of the two suspension or revocation periods.

(d) For the purposes of this section, a conviction of an offense in any state, territory, or possession of the United States, the District of Columbia, the Commonwealth of Puerto Rico, or Canada that, if committed in this state, would be a violation of Section 23103, as specified in Section 23103.5, or Section 23140, 23152, or 23153, or Section 191.5 or subdivision (a) of Section 192.5 of the Penal Code, is a conviction of that particular section of the Vehicle Code or Penal Code.

(e) The holder of a commercial driver's license who was operating a commercial motor vehicle, as defined in Section 15210, at the time of a violation that resulted in a suspension or revocation of the person's noncommercial driving privilege is not eligible for the restricted driver's license authorized pursuant to this section.

(f) This section shall become operative January 1, 2033.

(Amended (as added by Stats. 2016, Ch. 783, Sec. 12) by Stats. 2025, Ch. 689, Sec. 8. (AB 366) Effective January 1, 2026. Section operative January 1, 2033, by its own provisions.)

13353.4. (a) Except as provided in Section 13353.3, 13353.6, 13353.7, or 13353.8, the driving privilege shall not be restored, and a restricted or hardship permit to operate a motor vehicle shall not be issued, to a person during the suspension or revocation period specified in Section 13353, 13353.1, or 13353.3.

(b) The privilege to operate a motor vehicle shall not be restored after a suspension or revocation pursuant to Section 13352, 13353, 13353.1, or 13353.2 until all applicable fees, including the fees prescribed in Section 14905, have been paid and the person gives proof of financial responsibility, as defined in Section 16430, to the department.

(c) This section shall become operative on January 1, 2019.

(d) This section shall remain in effect only until January 1, 2033, and as of that date is repealed, unless a later enacted statute, that is enacted before January 1, 2033, deletes or extends that date.

(Amended (as added by Stats. 2016, Ch. 783, Sec. 14) by Stats. 2025, Ch. 689, Sec. 9. (AB 366) Effective January 1, 2026. Repealed as of January 1, 2033, by its own provisions. See later operative version, as amended by Sec. 10 of Stats. 2025, Ch. 689.)

13353.4. (a) Except as provided in Section 13353.3, 13353.7, or 13353.8, the driving privilege shall not be restored, and a restricted or hardship permit to operate a motor vehicle shall not be issued, to a person during the suspension or revocation period specified in Section 13353, 13353.1, or 13353.3.

(b) The privilege to operate a motor vehicle shall not be restored after a suspension or revocation pursuant to Section 13352, 13353, 13353.1, or 13353.2 until all applicable fees, including the fees prescribed in Section 14905, have been paid and the person gives proof of financial responsibility, as defined in Section 16430, to the department.

(c) This section shall become operative January 1, 2033.

(Amended (as added by Stats. 2016, Ch. 783, Sec. 15) by Stats. 2025, Ch. 689, Sec. 10. (AB 366) Effective January 1, 2026. Section operative January 1, 2033, by its own provisions.)

13353.45. The department shall, in consultation with the State Department of Health Care Services, with representatives of the county alcohol program administrators, and with representatives of licensed drinking driver program providers, develop a certificate of completion for the purposes of Sections 13352, 13352.4, and 13352.5 and shall develop, implement, and maintain a system for safeguarding the certificates against misuse. The department may charge a reasonable fee for each blank completion certificate distributed to a drinking driver program. The fee shall be sufficient to cover, but shall not exceed, the costs incurred in administering this section, Sections 13352, 13352.4, and 13352.5 or twelve dollars ($12) per person, whichever is less.

(Amended by Stats. 2013, Ch. 22, Sec. 86. (AB 75) Effective June 27, 2013. Operative July 1, 2013, by Sec. 110 of Ch. 22.)

13353.5. (a) If a person whose driving privilege is suspended or revoked under Section 13352, Section 13352.1, former Section 13352.4, Section 13352.4, Section 13352.6, paragraph (1) of subdivision (g) of Section 23247, or paragraph (3) of subdivision (e) of Section 13352 is a resident of another state at the time the mandatory period of suspension or revocation expires, the department may terminate the suspension or revocation, upon written application of the person, for the purpose of allowing the person to apply for a license in the person's state of residence. The application shall include, but need not be limited to, evidence satisfactory to the department that the applicant now resides in another state.

(b) If the person submits an application for a California driver's license within three years after the date of the action to terminate suspension or revocation pursuant to subdivision (a), a license shall not be issued until evidence satisfactory to the department establishes that the person is qualified for reinstatement and no grounds exist including, but not limited to, one or more subsequent convictions for driving under the influence of alcohol or other drugs that would support a refusal to issue a license. The department may waive the three-year requirement if the person provides the department with proof of financial responsibility, as defined in Section 16430, and proof satisfactory to the department of successful completion of a driving-under-the-influence program described in Section 13352, and the driving-under-the-influence program is of the length required under paragraphs (1) to (7), inclusive, of subdivision (a) of Section 13352.

(c) For the purposes of this section, "state" includes a foreign province or country.

(d) This section shall become operative on January 1, 2019.

(e) This section shall remain in effect only until January 1, 2033, and as of that date is repealed, unless a later enacted statute, that is enacted before January 1, 2033, deletes or extends that date.

(Amended (as amended by Stats. 2017, Ch. 485, Sec. 11) by Stats. 2025, Ch. 689, Sec. 11. (AB 366) Effective January 1, 2026. Repealed as of January 1, 2033, by its own provisions. See later operative version, as amended by Sec. 12 of Stats. 2025, Ch. 689.)

13353.5. (a) If a person whose driving privilege is suspended or revoked under Section 13352, Section 13352.1, former Section 13352.4, Section 13352.4, Section 13352.6, paragraph (1) of subdivision (g) of Section 23247, or paragraph (2) of subdivision (f) of Section 23575 is a resident of another state at the time the mandatory period of suspension or revocation expires, the department may terminate the suspension or revocation, upon written application of the person, for the purpose of allowing the person to apply for a license in the person's state of residence. The application shall include, but need not be limited to, evidence satisfactory to the department that the applicant now resides in another state.

(b) If the person submits an application for a California driver's license within three years after the date of the action to terminate suspension or revocation pursuant to subdivision (a), a license shall not be issued until evidence satisfactory to the department establishes that the person is qualified for reinstatement and no grounds exist including, but not limited to, one or more subsequent convictions for driving under the influence of alcohol or other drugs that would support a refusal to issue a license. The department may waive the three-year requirement if the person provides the department with proof of financial responsibility, as defined in Section 16430, and proof satisfactory to the department of successful completion of a driving-under-the-influence program described in Section 13352, and the driving-under-the-influence program is of the length required under paragraphs (1) to (7), inclusive, of subdivision (a) of Section 13352.

(c) For the purposes of this section, "state" includes a foreign province or country.

(d) This section shall become operative January 1, 2033.

(Amended (as amended by Stats. 2017, Ch. 485, Sec. 12) by Stats. 2025, Ch. 689, Sec. 12. (AB 366) Effective January 1, 2026. Section operative January 1, 2033, by its own provisions.)

13353.6. (a) Notwithstanding any other law, a person whose driving privilege has been suspended under Section 13353.2 and who has not been convicted of, or found to have committed, a separate violation of Section 23103, as specified in Section 23103.5, or Section 23140, 23152, or 23153, or Section 191.5 or subdivision (a) of Section 192.5 of the Penal Code, and if the person's privilege to operate a motor vehicle has not been suspended or revoked pursuant to Section 13353 or 13353.2 for an offense that occurred on a separate occasion within 10 years of the occasion in question, may apply to the department for a restricted driver's license on or after the effective date specified in Section 13353.3, if the person meets all of the following requirements:

(1) (A) The person satisfactorily provides proof of enrollment in a driving-under-the-influence program licensed under Section 11836 of the Health and Safety Code, as described in subdivision (b) of Section 23538.

(B) The program shall report any failure to participate in the program to the department and shall certify successful completion of the program to the department.

(C) If a person who has been issued a restricted license under this section fails at any time to participate in the program, the department shall immediately terminate the restriction and reinstate the suspension of the privilege to operate a motor vehicle. The department shall give notice of the suspension under this paragraph in the same manner as prescribed in subdivision (b) of Section 13353.2 for the period specified in Section 13353.3, that is effective upon receipt by the person.

(D) For the purposes of this section, enrollment, participation, and completion of an approved program shall occur subsequent to the date of the current violation. Credit may not be given to a program activity completed prior to the date of the current violation.

(2) The person installs a functioning, certified ignition interlock device on any vehicle that the person operates and submits the "Verification of Installation" form described in paragraph (2) of subdivision (g) of Section 13386.

(3) The person agrees to maintain the functioning, certified ignition interlock device as required under subdivision (f).

(4) (A) The person was 21 years of age or older at the time the offense occurred and gives proof of financial responsibility, as defined in Section 16430.

(B) If the driving privilege is restricted under this section, proof of financial responsibility, as described in Section 16430, shall be maintained for three years. If the person does not maintain that proof of financial responsibility at any time during the restriction, the driving privilege shall be suspended until the proof required pursuant to Section 16484 is received by the department.

(5) The person pays all applicable reinstatement or reissue fees.

(b) The restriction under this section shall remain in effect for the remaining period of the original suspension period under Section 13353.3.

(c) The department shall terminate the restriction issued pursuant to this section and shall immediately reinstate the suspension of the privilege to operate a motor vehicle upon receipt of notification from the ignition interlock device installer that a person has attempted to remove, bypass, or tamper with the ignition interlock device, has removed the device prior to the termination date of the restriction, or fails three or more times to comply with any requirement for the maintenance or calibration of the ignition interlock device. The privilege shall remain suspended for the remaining mandatory suspension period imposed pursuant to Section 13353.3, provided, however, that if the person provides proof to the satisfaction of the department that the person is in compliance with the restriction issued pursuant to this section, the department may, in its discretion, restore the privilege to operate a motor vehicle and reimpose the remaining term of the restriction.

(d) Notwithstanding any other law, a person whose driving privilege has been suspended under Section 13353.2, who is eligible for a restricted driver's license as provided for in this section, and who installs a functioning, certified ignition interlock device pursuant to this section, shall receive credit towards the mandatory term the person is required to install a functioning, certified ignition interlock device pursuant to Section 23575.3 for a conviction of a violation arising out of the same occurrence that led to the person's driving privilege being suspended pursuant to Section 13352 equal to the period of time the person installs a functioning, certified ignition interlock device pursuant to this section or Section 13353.75.

(e) (1) The holder of a commercial driver's license who was operating a motor vehicle other than a commercial vehicle, or a driver who was operating a commercial vehicle, as defined in Section 15210, at the time of the violation that resulted in the suspension of that person's driving privilege pursuant to Section 13353.2 is not eligible for the restricted driver's license authorized under this section.

(2) Notwithstanding paragraph (1), as authorized under this section, the department shall issue the person a noncommercial driver's license restricted in the same manner and subject to the same conditions and requirements as specified in subdivision (a).

(f) A person whose driving privilege is restricted by the department pursuant to this section shall arrange for each vehicle with a functioning, certified ignition interlock device to be serviced by the installer at least once every 60 days in order for the installer to recalibrate the device and monitor the operation of the device. The installer shall notify the department if the device is removed or indicates that the person has attempted to remove, bypass, or tamper with the device, or if the person fails three or more times to comply with any requirement for the maintenance or calibration of the ignition interlock device.

(g) For the purposes of this section, the following definitions apply:

(1) "Bypass" means either of the following:

(A) Failure to take any random retest.

(B) Failure to pass a random retest with a breath alcohol concentration not exceeding 0.03 percent, by weight of alcohol, in the person's blood.

(2) "Operates" includes operating a vehicle that is not owned by the person subject to this section.

(3) "Owned" means solely owned or owned in conjunction with another person or legal entity.

(4) "Random retest" means a breath test performed by the driver upon a certified ignition interlock device at random intervals after the initial engine startup breath test and while the vehicle's motor is running.

(5) "Vehicle" does not include a motorcycle until the state certifies an ignition interlock device that can be installed on a motorcycle. A person subject to an ignition interlock device restriction shall not operate a motorcycle for the duration of the ignition interlock device restriction period.

(h) Notwithstanding subdivisions (a) and (b), and upon a conviction under Section 23152 or 23153 for the current offense, the department shall suspend or revoke the person's privilege to operate a motor vehicle under Section 13352 or 13352.1.

(i) The restriction conditions specified in this section shall apply only to a person who is suspended under Section 13353.2 for a violation that occurred on or after January 1, 2019.

(j) This section shall become operative on January 1, 2019.

(k) This section shall remain in effect only until January 1, 2033, and as of that date is repealed, unless a later enacted statute, that is enacted before January 1, 2033, deletes or extends that date.

(Amended by Stats. 2025, Ch. 689, Sec. 13. (AB 366) Effective January 1, 2026. Repealed as of January 1, 2033, by its own provisions.)

13353.7. (a) Subject to subdivision (c), if the person whose driving privilege has been suspended under Section 13353.2 has not been convicted of, or found to have committed, a separate violation of Section 23103, as specified in Section 23103.5, or Section 23140, 23152, or 23153 of this code, or Section 191.5 or subdivision (a) of Section 192.5 of the Penal Code, and if the person's privilege to operate a motor vehicle has not been suspended or revoked pursuant to Section 13353 or 13353.2 for an offense that occurred on a separate occasion within 10 years of the occasion in question and, if the person subsequently enrolls in a driving-under-the-influence program licensed under Section 11836 of the Health and Safety Code, as described in subdivision (b) of Section 23538, that person, if 21 years of age or older at the time the offense occurred, may apply to the department for a restricted driver's license limited to travel to and from the activities required by the program and to and from and in the course of the person's employment. After receiving proof of enrollment in the program, and if the person has not been arrested subsequent to the offense for which the person's driving privilege has been suspended under Section 13353.2 for a violation of Section 23103, as specified in Section 23103.5, or Section 23140, 23152, or 23153 of this code, or Section 191.5 or subdivision (a) of Section 192.5 of the Penal Code, and if the person's privilege to operate a motor vehicle has not been suspended or revoked pursuant to Section 13353 or 13353.2 for an offense that occurred on a separate occasion, notwithstanding Section 13551, the department shall, after review pursuant to Section 13557, suspend the person's privilege to operate a motor vehicle for 30 days and then issue the person a restricted driver's license under the following conditions:

(1) The program shall report any failure to participate in the program to the department and shall certify successful completion of the program to the department.

(2) The person was 21 years of age or older at the time the offense occurred and gives proof of financial responsibility as defined in Section 16430.

(3) The restriction shall be imposed for a period of five months.

(4) If a person who has been issued a restricted license under this section fails at any time to participate in the program, the department shall suspend the restricted license immediately. The department shall give notice of the suspension under this paragraph in the same manner as prescribed in subdivision (b) of Section 13353.2 for the period specified in Section 13353.3, that is effective upon receipt by the person.

(b) Notwithstanding subdivision (a), and upon a conviction of Section 23152 or 23153, the department shall suspend or revoke the person's privilege to operate a motor vehicle under Section 13352.

(c) If the driver was operating a commercial vehicle, as defined in Section 15210, at the time of the violation that resulted in the suspension of that person's driving privilege under Section 13353.2, the department shall, pursuant to this section, if the person is otherwise eligible, issue the person a class C or class M driver's license restricted in the same manner and subject to the same conditions as specified in subdivision (a), except that the license may not allow travel to and from or in the course of the person's employment.

(d) If the holder of a commercial driver's license was operating a motor vehicle, other than a commercial vehicle as defined in Section 15210, at the time of the violation that resulted in the suspension of that person's driving privilege pursuant to Section 13353.2, the department shall, pursuant to this section, if the person is otherwise eligible, issue the person a class C or class M driver's license restricted in the same manner and subject to the same conditions as specified in subdivision (a).

(e) This section does not apply to a person whose driving privilege has been suspended or revoked pursuant to Section 13353 or 13353.2 for an offense that occurred on a separate occasion, or as a result of a conviction of a separate violation of Section 23103, as specified in Section 23103.5, or Section 23140, 23152, or 23153, when that violation occurred within 10 years of the offense in question. This subdivision shall be operative only so long as a one-year suspension of the driving privilege for a second or subsequent occurrence or offense, with no restricted or hardship licenses permitted, is required by Section 408 or 410 of Title 23 of the United States Code.

(Amended by Stats. 2012, Ch. 670, Sec. 5. (AB 2188) Effective January 1, 2013.)

13353.75. (a) Subject to subdivision (d), a person whose driving privilege has been suspended under Section 13353.2, and who has been previously convicted of, or found to have committed, a separate violation of Section 23103, as specified in Section 23103.5, or Section 23140, 23152, or 23153, or Section 191.5 or subdivision (a) of Section 192.5 of the Penal Code, or whose privilege to operate a motor vehicle has been suspended or revoked pursuant to Section 13353 or 13353.2 for an offense that occurred on a separate occasion within 10 years of the occasion in question may apply to the department for a restricted driver's license on or after the effective date specified in Section 13353.3, if the person meets all of the following requirements:

(1) (A) The person satisfactorily provides proof of enrollment in a driving-under-the-influence program licensed under Section 11836 of the Health and Safety Code, as described in subdivision (b) of Section 23538 of this code.

(B) The program shall report any failure to participate in the program to the department and shall certify successful completion of the program to the department.

(C) If a person who has been issued a restricted license under this section fails at any time to participate in the program, the department shall immediately terminate the restriction and reinstate the suspension of the privilege to operate a motor vehicle. The department shall give notice of the suspension under this paragraph in the same manner as prescribed in subdivision (b) of Section 13353.2 for the period specified in Section 13353.3, that is effective upon receipt by the person.

(D) For the purposes of this section, enrollment, participation, and completion of an approved program shall occur subsequent to the date of the current violation. Credit may not be given to a program activity completed prior to the date of the current violation.

(2) (A) The person was 21 years of age or older at the time the offense occurred and gives proof of financial responsibility, as defined in Section 16430.

(B) If the driving privilege is restricted under this section, proof of financial responsibility, as described in Section 16430, shall be maintained for three years. If the person does not maintain that proof of financial responsibility at any time during the restriction, the driving privilege shall be suspended until the proof required pursuant to Section 16484 is received by the department.

(3) The person installs a functioning, certified ignition interlock device on any vehicle that the person operates and submits the "Verification of Installation" form described in paragraph (2) of subdivision (g) of Section 13386.

(4) The person agrees to maintain the functioning, certified ignition interlock device as required under subdivision (g).

(5) The person pays all applicable reinstatement or reissue fees.

(b) The restriction shall remain in effect for the remaining period of the original suspension period under Section 13353.3.

(c) Notwithstanding subdivisions (a) and (b), and upon a conviction under Section 23152 or 23153 for the current offense, the department shall suspend or revoke the person's privilege to operate a motor vehicle under Section 13352 or 13352.1.

(d) (1) The holder of a commercial driver's license who was operating a motor vehicle other than a commercial vehicle, or a driver who was operating a commercial vehicle, as defined in Section 15210, at the time of the violation that resulted in the suspension of that person's driving privilege pursuant to Section 13353.2 is not eligible for the restricted driver's license authorized under this section.

(2) Notwithstanding paragraph (1), as authorized under this section, the department shall issue the person a noncommercial driver's license restricted in the same manner and subject to the same conditions and requirements as specified in subdivision (a).

(e) The department shall terminate the restriction issued pursuant to this section and shall immediately reinstate the suspension of the privilege to operate a motor vehicle upon receipt of notification from the ignition interlock device installer that a person has attempted to remove, bypass, or tamper with the ignition interlock device, has removed the device prior to the termination date of the restriction, or fails three or more times to comply with any requirement for the maintenance or calibration of the ignition interlock device. The privilege shall remain suspended for the remaining mandatory suspension period imposed pursuant to Section 13353.3. However, if the person provides proof to the satisfaction of the department that the person is in compliance with the restriction issued pursuant to this section, the department may, in its discretion, restore the privilege to operate a motor vehicle and reimpose the remaining term of the restriction.

(f) Notwithstanding any other law, a person whose driving privilege has been suspended under Section 13353.2, who is eligible for a restricted driver's license as provided for in this section, and who installs a functioning, certified ignition interlock device pursuant to this section, shall receive credit toward the mandatory term the person is required to install a functioning, certified ignition interlock device pursuant to Section 23575.3 for a conviction of a violation arising out of the same occurrence that led to the person's driving privilege being suspended pursuant to Section 13352 or 13352.1 equal to the period of time the person installs a functioning, certified ignition interlock device pursuant to this section or Section 13353.75.

(g) A person whose driving privilege is restricted by the department pursuant to this section shall arrange for each vehicle with a functioning, certified ignition interlock device to be serviced by the installer at least once every 60 days in order for the installer to recalibrate the device and monitor the operation of the device. The installer shall notify the department if the device is removed or indicates that the person has attempted to remove, bypass, or tamper with the device, or if the person fails three or more times to comply with any requirement for the maintenance or calibration of the ignition interlock device.

(h) For the purposes of this section, the following definitions apply:

(1) "Bypass" means either of the following:

(A) Failure to take any random retest.

(B) Failure to pass a random retest with a breath alcohol concentration not exceeding 0.03 percent, by weight of alcohol, in the person's blood.

(2) "Operates" includes operating a vehicle that is not owned by the person subject to this section.

(3) "Owned" means solely owned or owned in conjunction with another person or legal entity.

(4) "Random retest" means a breath test performed by the driver upon a certified ignition interlock device at random intervals after the initial engine startup breath test and while the vehicle's motor is running.

(5) "Vehicle" does not include a motorcycle until the state certifies an ignition interlock device that can be installed on a motorcycle. A person subject to an ignition interlock device restriction shall not operate a motorcycle for the duration of the ignition interlock device restriction period.

(i) The restriction conditions specified in this section shall apply only to a person who is suspended under Section 13353.2 for a violation that occurred on or after January 1, 2019.

(j) This section shall become operative January 1, 2019.

(k) This section shall remain in effect only until January 1, 2033, and as of that date is repealed, unless a later enacted statute, that is enacted before January 1, 2033, deletes or extends that date.

(Amended by Stats. 2025, Ch. 689, Sec. 14. (AB 366) Effective January 1, 2026. Repealed

as of January 1, 2033, by its own provisions.)

13353.8. (a) After the department has issued an order suspending or delaying driving privileges as a result of a violation of subdivision (a) of Section 23136, the department, upon the petition of the person affected, may review the order and may impose restrictions on the person's privilege to drive based upon a showing of a critical need to drive, if the department determines that, within 10 years of the current violation of Section 23136, the person has not violated Section 23136 or been convicted of a separate violation of Section 23140, 23152, or 23153, or of Section 23103, with a plea of guilty under Section 23103.5, or of Section 191.5 or subdivision (a) of Section 192.5 of, the Penal Code, and that the person's driving privilege has not been suspended or revoked under Section 13353, 13353.1, or 13353.2 within that 10-year period.

(b) For purposes of this section, a conviction of an offense in a state, territory, or possession of the United States, the District of Columbia, the Commonwealth of Puerto Rico, or the Dominion of Canada that, if committed in this state, would be a violation of Section 23103, as specified in Section 23103.5, or Section 23140, 23152, 23153, or Section 191.5 or subdivision (a) of Section 192.5 of the Penal Code, is a conviction of that particular section of the Vehicle Code or Penal Code.

(c) As used in this section, "critical need to drive" means the circumstances that are required to be shown for the issuance of a junior permit pursuant to Section 12513.

(d) The restriction shall be imposed not earlier than the 31st day after the date the order of suspension became effective and shall remain in effect for the balance of the period of suspension or restriction in this section.

(Amended by Stats. 2007, Ch. 747, Sec. 26. Effective January 1, 2008.)

13355. The department shall immediately suspend the privilege of any person to operate a motor vehicle upon receipt of a duly certified abstract of the record of any court showing that the person has been convicted of a violation of subdivision (b) of Section 22348, or upon a receipt of a report of a judge of a juvenile court, a juvenile hearing officer, or a referee of a juvenile court showing that the person has been found to have committed a violation of subdivision (b) of Section 22348 under the following conditions and for the periods, as follows:

(a) Upon a conviction or finding of an offense under subdivision (b) of Section 22348 that occurred within three years of a prior offense resulting in a conviction of an offense under subdivision (b) of Section 22348, the privilege shall be suspended for a period of six months, or the privilege shall be restricted for six months to necessary travel to and from the person's place of employment and, if driving a motor vehicle is necessary to perform the duties of the person's employment, restricted to driving within the person's scope of employment.

(b) Upon a conviction or finding of an offense under subdivision (b) of Section 22348 that occurred within five years of two or more prior offenses resulting in convictions of offenses under subdivision (b) of Section 22348, the privilege shall be suspended for a period of one year, or the privilege shall be restricted for one year to necessary travel to and from the person's place of employment and, if driving a motor vehicle is necessary to perform the duties of the person's employment, restricted to driving within the person's scope of employment.

(Amended by Stats. 2003, Ch. 149, Sec. 84. Effective January 1, 2004.)

13357. Upon the recommendation of the court the department shall suspend or revoke the privilege to operate a motor vehicle of any person who has been found guilty of a violation of Section 10851.

(Added by Stats. 1967, Ch. 1110.)

13359. The department may suspend or revoke the privilege of any person to operate a motor vehicle upon any of the grounds which authorize the refusal to issue a license.

(Amended by Stats. 1976, Ch. 498.)

13360. Upon receiving satisfactory evidence of any violation of the restrictions of a driver's license, the department may suspend or revoke the same.

(Enacted by Stats. 1959, Ch. 3.)

13361. The department may suspend the privilege of any person to operate a motor vehicle upon receipt of a duly certified abstract of the record of any court showing that the person has been convicted of any of the following crimes or offenses:

(a) Failure to stop in the event of an accident resulting in damage to property only, or otherwise failing to comply with the requirements of Section 20002.

(b) A second or subsequent conviction of reckless driving.

(c) Manslaughter resulting from the operation of a motor vehicle as provided in paragraph (2) of subdivision (c) of Section 192 of the Penal Code.

In any case under this section the department is authorized to require proof of ability to respond in damages as defined in Section 16430.

(Amended by Stats. 1985, Ch. 6, Sec. 3. Effective February 21, 1985.)

13362. The department may require the surrender to it of any driver's license which has been issued erroneously or which contains any erroneous or false statement, or which does not contain any notation required by law or by the department. In the event a licensee does not surrender the license upon proper demand, the department may suspend the licensee's privilege to operate a motor vehicle. The suspension shall continue until the correction of the license by the department or until issuance of another license or temporary license in lieu thereof.

(Enacted by Stats. 1959, Ch. 3.)

13363. (a) The department may, in its discretion, except as provided in Chapter 6 (commencing with Section 15000) of Division 6, of this code, suspend or revoke the privilege of any resident or nonresident to drive a motor vehicle in this State upon receiving notice of the conviction of the person in a state, territory, or possession of the United States, the District of Columbia, the Commonwealth of Puerto Rico, or the Dominion of Canada of an offense therein which, if committed in this State, would be grounds for the suspension or revocation of the privilege to operate a motor vehicle.

(b) Whenever any state, territory, or possession of the United States, the District of Columbia, the Commonwealth of Puerto Rico, or the Dominion of Canada reports the conviction of a violation in such place by a person licensed in this State, the department shall not give effect to such report pursuant to subdivision (a) of this section or Section 15023 unless the department is satisfied that the law of such other place pertaining to the conviction is substantially the same as the law of this State pertaining to such conviction and that the description of the violation from which the conviction arose, is sufficient and that the interpretation and enforcement of such law are substantially the same in such other place as they are in this State.

(Amended by Stats. 1963, Ch. 237.)

13364. (a) Notwithstanding any other provision of this code, a person's privilege to operate a motor vehicle shall be suspended upon notification by a bank or financial institution that a check has been dishonored when that check was presented to the department for either of the following reasons:

(1) In payment of a fine that resulted from an outstanding violation pursuant to Section 40508 or a suspension pursuant to Section 13365.

(2) In payment of a fee or penalty owed by the person, if the fee or penalty is required by this code for the issuance, reissuance, or return of the person's driver's license after suspension, revocation, or restriction of the driving privilege.

(b) The suspension shall remain in effect until payment of all fines, fees, and penalties is made to the department or to the court, as appropriate, and the person's driving record does not contain any notification of a court order issued pursuant to subdivision (a) of Section 42003 or of a violation of subdivision (a) or (b) of Section 40508.

(c) No suspension imposed pursuant to this section shall become effective until 30 days after the mailing of a written notice of the intent to suspend.

(d) The written notice of a suspension imposed pursuant to this section shall be delivered by certified mail.

(e) If any personal check is offered in payment of fines described in paragraph (1) of subdivision (a) and is returned for any reason, the related notice issued pursuant to former Section 40509 or former Section 40509.5 shall be restored to the person's record.

(f) Notwithstanding any other provision of law, any license that has been suspended pursuant to this section shall immediately be reinstated, and the fees and penalties waived, upon the submission of proof acceptable to the department that the check has been erroneously dishonored by the bank or financial institution.

(g) This section shall remain in effect only until January 1, 2027, and as of that date is repealed.

(Amended by Stats. 2022, Ch. 800, Sec. 14. (AB 2746) Effective January 1, 2023. Repealed as of January 1, 2027, by its own provisions. See later operative version added by Sec. 15 of Stats. 2022, Ch. 800.)

13364. (a) Notwithstanding any other provision of this code, a person's privilege to operate a motor vehicle shall be suspended upon notification by a bank or financial institution that a check has been dishonored when that check was presented to the department for either of the following reasons:

(1) In payment of a fine that resulted from an outstanding violation pursuant to Section 40508 or a suspension pursuant to former Section 13365.

(2) In payment of a fee or penalty owed by the person, if the fee or penalty is required by this code for the issuance, reissuance, or return of the person's driver's license after suspension, revocation, or restriction of the driving privilege.

(b) The suspension shall remain in effect until payment of all fines, fees, and penalties is made to the department or to the court, as appropriate, and the person's driving record does not contain any notification of a court order issued pursuant to subdivision (a) of Section 42003 or of a violation of subdivision (a) or (b) of Section 40508.

(c) No suspension imposed pursuant to this section shall become effective until 30 days after the mailing of a written notice of the intent to suspend.

(d) The written notice of a suspension imposed pursuant to this section shall be delivered by certified mail.

(e) If any personal check is offered in payment of fines described in paragraph (1) of subdivision (a) and is returned for any reason, the related notice issued pursuant to former Section 40509 or former Section 40509.5 shall be restored to the person's record.

(f) Notwithstanding any other provision of law, any license that has been suspended pursuant to this section shall immediately be reinstated, and the fees and penalties waived, upon the submission of proof acceptable to the department that the check has been erroneously dishonored by the bank or financial institution.

(g) This section shall become operative on January 1, 2027.

(Repealed (in Sec. 14) and added by Stats. 2022, Ch. 800, Sec. 15. (AB 2746) Effective January 1, 2023. Operative January 1, 2027, by its own provisions.)

13365. (a) Upon receipt of notification of a violation of subdivision (a) of Section 40508, the department shall take the following action:

(1) If the notice is given pursuant to subdivision (a) of former Section 40509, if the driving record of the person who is the subject of the notice contains one or more prior notifications of a violation issued pursuant to former Section 40509 or former Section 40509.5, and if the person's driving privilege is not currently suspended under this section, the department shall suspend the driving privilege of the person.

(2) If the notice is given pursuant to subdivision (a) of Section 40509.5, and if the driving privilege of the person who is the subject of the notice is not currently suspended under this section, the department shall suspend the driving privilege of the person.

(b) (1) A suspension under this section shall not be effective before a date 60 days after the date of receipt, by the department, of the notice given specified in subdivision (a), and the notice of suspension shall not be mailed by the department before a date 30 days after receipt of the notice given specified in subdivision (a).

(2) The suspension shall continue until the suspended person's driving record does not contain any notification of a violation of subdivision (a) of Section 40508.

(c) This section shall remain in effect only until January 1, 2027, and as of that date is repealed.

(Amended by Stats. 2022, Ch. 800, Sec. 16. (AB 2746) Effective January 1, 2023. Repealed as of January 1, 2027, by its own provisions.)

13365.2. (a) Upon receipt of the notice required under subdivision (b) of former Section 40509.5, the department shall suspend the driving privilege of the person upon whom notice was received and shall continue that suspension until receipt of the certificate required under that subdivision.

(b) The suspension required under subdivision (a) shall become effective on the 45th day after the mailing of written notice by the department.

(c) This section shall remain in effect only until January 1, 2027, and as of that date is repealed.

(Amended by Stats. 2022, Ch. 800, Sec. 17. (AB 2746) Effective January 1, 2023. Repealed as of January 1, 2027, by its own provisions.)

13365.5. (a) Upon receipt of a notification issued pursuant to Section 40509.1, the department shall suspend the person's privilege to operate a motor vehicle until compliance with the court order is shown or as prescribed in subdivision (c) of Section 12808. The suspension under this section shall not be effective until 45 days after the giving of written notice by the department.

(b) This section does not apply to a notification of failure to comply with a court order issued for a violation enumerated in paragraph (1), (2), (3), (6), or (7) of subdivision (b) of Section 1803.

(Added by Stats. 1993, Ch. 158, Sec. 21.7. Effective July 21, 1993.)

13366. Whenever in this code the department is required to suspend or revoke the privilege of a person to operate a motor vehicle upon the conviction of such person of violating this code, such suspension or revocation shall begin upon a plea, finding or verdict of guilty.

(Enacted by Stats. 1959, Ch. 3.)

13366.5. (a) Notwithstanding Section 13366, whenever in this code the department is required to disqualify the commercial driving privilege of a person to operate a commercial motor vehicle upon the conviction of that person of a violation of this code, the suspension or revocation shall begin upon receipt by the department of a duly certified abstract of any court record showing that the person has been so convicted.

(b) This section shall become operative on September 20, 2005.

(Added by Stats. 2004, Ch. 952, Sec. 11. Effective January 1, 2005. Section operative September 20, 2005, by its own provisions.)

13367. For purposes of the suspension or revocation of any driver's license issued to a minor, the department shall not provide any lighter penalty than would be given to an adult under similar circumstances.

(Added by Stats. 1959, Ch. 562.)

13368. The department, as a condition to the reinstatement of a suspended license or the issuance of a new license to an individual whose prior license has been revoked, may require the individual to attend the program authorized by the provisions of Section 1659.

(Added by Stats. 1965, Ch. 447.)

13369. (a) This section applies to the following endorsements and certificates:

(1) Passenger transportation vehicle.

(2) Hazardous materials.

(3) Schoolbus.

(4) School pupil activity bus.

(5) Youth bus.

(6) General public paratransit vehicle.

(7) Farm labor vehicle.

(8) Vehicle used for the transportation of developmentally disabled

persons.

(b) The department shall refuse to issue or renew, or shall revoke, the certificate or endorsement of a person who meets the following conditions:

(1) Within three years, has committed any violation that results in a conviction assigned a violation point count of two or more, as defined in Sections 12810 and 12810.5. The department shall not refuse to issue or renew, nor may it revoke, a person's hazardous materials or passenger transportation vehicle endorsement if the violation leading to the conviction occurred in the person's private vehicle and not in a commercial motor vehicle, as defined in Section 15210.

(2) Within three years, has had his or her driving privilege suspended, revoked, or on probation for any reason involving unsafe operation of a motor vehicle. The department shall not refuse to issue or renew, nor may it revoke, a person's passenger transportation vehicle endorsement if the person's driving privilege has, within three years, been placed on probation only for a reason involving unsafe operation of a motor vehicle.

(3) Notwithstanding paragraphs (1) and (2), does not meet the qualifications for issuance of a hazardous materials endorsement set forth in Parts 383, 384, and 1572 of Title 49 of the Code of Federal Regulations.

(c) The department may refuse to issue or renew, or may suspend or revoke, the certificate or endorsement of a person who meets any of the following conditions:

(1) Within 12 months, has been involved as a driver in three accidents in which the driver caused or contributed to the causes of the accidents.

(2) Within 24 months, as a driver, caused or contributed to the cause of an accident resulting in a fatality or serious injury or serious property damage in excess of one thousand dollars ($1,000).

(3) Has violated any provision of this code, or any rule or regulation pertaining to the safe operation of a vehicle for which the certificate or endorsement was issued.

(4) Has violated any restriction of the certificate, endorsement, or commercial driver's license.

(5) Has knowingly made a false statement or failed to disclose a material fact on an application for a certificate or endorsement.

(6) Has been determined by the department to be a negligent or incompetent operator.

(7) Has demonstrated irrational behavior to the extent that a reasonable and prudent person would have reasonable cause to believe that the applicant's ability to perform the duties of a driver may be impaired.

(8) Excessively or habitually uses, or is addicted to, alcoholic beverages, narcotics, or dangerous drugs.

(9) Does not meet the minimum medical standards established or approved by the department.

(d) The department may cancel the certificate or endorsement of any driver who meets any of the following conditions:

(1) Does not have a valid driver's license of the appropriate class.

(2) Has requested cancellation of the certificate or endorsement.

(3) Has failed to meet any of the requirements for issuance or retention of the certificate or endorsement, including, but not limited to, payment of the proper fee, submission of an acceptable medical report and fingerprint cards, and compliance with prescribed training requirements.

(4) Has had his or her driving privilege suspended or revoked for a cause involving other than the safe operation of a motor vehicle.

(e) (1) The department shall refuse to issue or renew, or shall suspend or revoke, the passenger vehicle endorsement of a person who violates subdivision (b) of Section 5387 of the Public Utilities Code.

(2) A person found to be in violation of subdivision (b) of Section 5387 of the Public Utilities Code shall be ineligible for a passenger vehicle endorsement that would permit him or her to drive a bus of any kind, including, but not limited to, a bus, schoolbus, youth bus, school pupil activity bus, trailer bus, or a transit bus, with passengers, for a period of five years.

(f) (1) Reapplication following refusal or revocation under subdivision (b) or (c) may be made after a period of not less than one year from the effective date of denial or revocation, except in cases where a longer period of suspension or revocation is required by law.

(2) Reapplication following cancellation under subdivision (d) may be made at any time without prejudice.

(g) This section shall become operative on January 1, 2017.

(Repealed (in Sec. 25) and added by Stats. 2015, Ch. 451, Sec. 26. (SB 491) Effective January 1, 2016. Section operative January 1, 2017, by its own provisions.)

13370. (a) The department shall refuse to issue or shall revoke a schoolbus, school pupil activity bus, general public paratransit vehicle, or youth bus driver certificate, or a certificate for a vehicle used for the transportation of developmentally disabled persons, if any of the following causes apply to the applicant or certificate holder:

(1) Has been convicted of a sex offense as defined in Section 44010 of the Education Code.

(2) Has been convicted, within two years, of an offense specified in Section 11361.5 of the Health and Safety Code.

(3) Has failed to meet prescribed training requirements for certificate issuance.

(4) Has failed to meet prescribed testing requirements for certificate issuance.

(5) Has been convicted of a violent felony listed in subdivision (c) of Section 667.5 of the Penal Code, or a serious felony listed in subdivision (c) of Section 1192.7 of the Penal Code. This paragraph shall not be applied to revoke a license that was valid on January 1, 2005, unless the certificate holder is convicted for an offense that is committed on or after that date.

(b) The department may refuse to issue or renew, or may suspend or revoke a schoolbus, school pupil activity bus, general public paratransit vehicle, or youth bus driver certificate, or a certificate for a vehicle used for the transportation of developmentally disabled persons, if any of the following causes apply to the applicant or certificate holder:

(1) Has been convicted of a crime specified in Section 44424 of the Education Code within seven years. This paragraph does not apply if denial is mandatory.

(2) Has committed an act involving moral turpitude.

(3) Has been convicted of an offense, not specified in this section and other than a sex offense, that is punishable as a felony, within seven years.

(4) Has been dismissed as a driver for a cause relating to pupil transportation safety.

(5) Has been convicted, within seven years, of an offense relating to the use, sale, possession, or transportation of narcotics, habit-forming drugs, or dangerous drugs, except as provided in paragraph (3) of subdivision (a).

(6) Has been reported to the Department of Motor Vehicles, pursuant to Section 39843 of the Education Code, for leaving a pupil unattended on a schoolbus, school pupil activity bus, or youth bus.

(c) (1) Reapplication following refusal or revocation under paragraph (1), (2), or (3) of subdivision (a) or any paragraph of subdivision (b) may be made after a period of not less than one year after the effective date of refusal or revocation.

(2) Reapplication following refusal or revocation under paragraph (4) of subdivision (a) may be made after a period of not less than 45 days after the date of the applicant's third testing failure.

(3) An applicant or holder of a certificate may reapply for a certificate whenever a felony or misdemeanor conviction is reversed or dismissed. A termination of probation and dismissal of charges pursuant to Section 1203.4 of the Penal Code or a dismissal of charges pursuant to Section 1203.4a of the Penal Code is not a dismissal for purposes of this section.

(4) A former applicant or holder of a certificate whose certificate was revoked pursuant to paragraph (6) of subdivision (b) may reapply for a certificate if the certificate revocation is reversed or dismissed by

the department.

(Amended by Stats. 2016, Ch. 721, Sec. 6. (SB 1072) Effective January 1, 2017.)

13371. This section applies to schoolbus, school pupil activity bus, youth bus, general public paratransit vehicle certificates, and a certificate for a vehicle used for the transportation of developmentally disabled persons.

(a) Any driver or applicant who has received a notice of refusal, suspension, or revocation, may, within 15 days after the mailing date, submit to the department a written request for a hearing. Failure to demand a hearing within 15 days is a waiver of the right to a hearing.

(1) Upon receipt by the department of the hearing request, the department may stay the action until a hearing is conducted and the final decision has been rendered by the Certificate Action Review Board pursuant to paragraph (2) of subdivision (d). The department shall not stay an action when there is reasonable cause to believe the stay would pose a significant risk to the safety of pupils being transported in a schoolbus, school pupil activity bus, youth bus, or persons being transported in a general public paratransit vehicle.

(2) An applicant or driver is not entitled to a hearing whenever the action by the department is made mandatory by this article or any other applicable law or regulation except where the cause for refusal is based on failure to meet medical standards or excessive and habitual use of or addiction to alcoholic beverages, narcotics, or dangerous drugs.

(b) The department shall appoint a hearing officer to conduct the hearing in accordance with Section 14112. After the hearing, the hearing officer shall prepare and submit findings and recommendations to the department.

(c) The department shall mail, as specified in Section 22, a copy of the hearing officer's findings and recommendations to the driver or applicant and to the driver or applicant's hearing representative, either of whom may file a statement of exception to the findings and recommendations within 24 days after the mailing date.

(d) (1) The Certificate Action Review Board consists of the following three members: a chairperson appointed by the director of the department, a member appointed by the Commissioner of the California Highway Patrol, and a member appointed by the Superintendent of Public Instruction.

(2) After a hearing, the board shall review the findings and recommendations of the hearing officer, and any statement of exception, and make a decision concerning disposition of the action taken by the department, which decision shall be final. At this stage, no evidence shall be heard that was not presented at the hearing, unless the person wishing to present the new evidence establishes, to the satisfaction of the board, that it could not have been obtained with due diligence prior to the hearing.

(Amended by Stats. 2005, Ch. 66, Sec. 3. Effective January 1, 2006.)

13372. (a) The department shall refuse to issue or renew, or shall suspend or revoke an ambulance driver certificate if any of the following apply to the applicant or certificate holder:

(1) Is required to register as a sex offender under Section 290 of the Penal Code for any offense involving force, violence, threat, or intimidation.

(2) Habitually or excessively uses or is addicted to narcotics or dangerous drugs.

(3) Is on parole or probation for any felony, theft, or any crime involving force, violence, threat, or intimidation.

(b) The department may refuse to issue or renew, or may suspend or revoke an ambulance driver certificate if any of the following apply to the applicant or certificate holder:

(1) Has been convicted within seven years of any offense punishable as a felony or has been convicted during that period of any theft.

(2) Has committed any act involving moral turpitude, including fraud or intentional dishonesty for personal gain, within seven years.

(3) Habitually and excessively uses intoxicating beverages.

(4) Has been convicted within seven years of any offense relating to the use, sale, possession, or transportation of narcotics or addictive or dangerous drugs, or of any misdemeanor involving force, violence, threat, or intimidation.

(5) Is on probation to the department for a cause involving the unsafe operation of a motor vehicle.

(6) Within three years has had his or her driver's license suspended or revoked by the department for a cause involving the unsafe operation of a motor vehicle, or, within the same period, has been convicted of any of the following:

(A) Failing to stop and render aid in an accident involving injury or death.

(B) Driving-under-the-influence of intoxicating liquor, any drug, or under the combined influence of intoxicating liquor and any drug.

(C) Reckless driving, or reckless driving involving bodily injury.

(7) Has knowingly made a false statement or failed to disclose a material fact in his or her application.

(8) Has been involved as a driver in any motor vehicle accident causing death or bodily injury or in three or more motor vehicle accidents within one year.

(9) Does not meet minimum medical standards specified in this code or in regulations adopted pursuant to this code.

(10) Has demonstrated irrational behavior or incurred a physical disability to the extent that a reasonable and prudent person would have reasonable cause to believe that the ability to perform the duties normally expected of an ambulance driver may be impaired.

(11) Has violated any provision of this code or any rule or regulation adopted by the Commissioner of the California Highway Patrol relating to the operation of emergency ambulances within one year.

(12) Has committed any act that warrants dismissal, as provided in Section 13373.

(c) (1) Reapplication following refusal or revocation under subdivision (a) or (b) may be made after a period of not less than one year after the effective date of the refusal or revocation, except in cases where a longer period of refusal, suspension, or revocation is required by law.

(2) Reapplication following refusal or revocation under subdivision (a) or (b) may be made if a felony or misdemeanor conviction supporting the refusal or revocation is reversed or dismissed. A termination of probation and dismissal of charges under Section 1203.4 of the Penal Code or a dismissal of charges under Section 1203.4a of the Penal Code is not a dismissal for purposes of this section.

(Amended by Stats. 2005, Ch. 66, Sec. 4. Effective January 1, 2006.)

13373. The receipt of satisfactory evidence of any violation of Article 1 (commencing with Section 1100) of Subchapter 5 of Chapter 2 of Title 13 of the California Code of Regulations, the Vehicle Code, or any other applicable law that would provide grounds for refusal, suspension, or revocation of an ambulance driver's certificate or evidence of an act committed involving intentional dishonesty for personal gain or conduct contrary to justice, honesty, modesty, or good morals, may be sufficient cause for the dismissal of any ambulance driver or attendant. Dismissal of a driver or attendant under this section shall be reported by the employer to the Department of Motor Vehicles at Sacramento within 10 days.

(Amended by Stats. 2005, Ch. 66, Sec. 5. Effective January 1, 2006.)

13374. (a) An applicant for, or the holder of, an ambulance driver certificate who has received a notice of refusal, suspension, or revocation may submit, within 15 days after the notice has been mailed by the department, a written request for a hearing. Upon receipt of the request, the department shall appoint a referee who shall conduct an informal hearing in accordance with Section 14104. Failure to request a hearing within 15 days after the notice has been mailed by the department is a waiver of the right to a hearing. A request for a hearing shall not operate to stay the action for which notice is given.

(b) Upon conclusion of an informal hearing, the referee shall prepare and submit findings and recommendations through the department to a committee of three members one each appointed by the Director of the Emergency Medical Service Authority, the director, and the Commissioner of the California Highway Patrol with the appointee of the Commissioner of the California Highway Patrol serving as chairperson. After a review of the findings and recommendations, the committee shall render a final decision on the action taken, and the department shall notify the person involved of the decision.

(Amended by Stats. 2005, Ch. 66, Sec. 6. Effective January 1, 2006.)

13375. For the purposes of this article, any plea or verdict of guilty, plea of nolo contendere, or court finding of guilt in a trial without a jury, or forfeiture of bail, is deemed a conviction, notwithstanding subsequent action under Section 1203.4 or 1203.4a of the Penal Code allowing withdrawal of the plea of guilty and entering a plea of not guilty, setting aside the verdict of guilty, or dismissing the accusation or information.

(Added by Stats. 1990, Ch. 1360, Sec. 41.)

13376. (a) This section applies to the following certificates:

(1) Schoolbus.

(2) School pupil activity bus.

(3) Youth bus.

(4) General public paratransit vehicle.

(5) Vehicle used for the transportation of developmentally disabled persons.

(b) (1) The department shall revoke a certificate listed in subdivision (a) for three years if the certificate holder refuses to submit to a test for, fails to comply with the testing requirements for, or receives a positive test for a controlled substance, as specified in Part 382 (commencing with Section 382.101) of Title 49 of the Code of Federal Regulations and Section 34520. However, the department shall not revoke a certificate under this paragraph if the certificate holder is in compliance with any rehabilitation or return to duty program that is imposed by the employer that meets the controlled substances and alcohol use and testing requirements set forth in Part 382 (commencing with Section 382.101) of Title 49 of the Code of Federal Regulations. The driver shall be allowed to participate in a rehabilitation or return to duty program only once within a three-year period. The employer or program shall report any subsequent positive test result or drop from the program to the department on a form approved by the department.

(2) If an applicant refuses to submit to a test for, fails to comply with the testing requirements for, or receives a positive test for a controlled substance, the department shall refuse the application for a certificate listed in subdivision (a) for three years from the date of the confirmed positive test result.

(3) The carrier that requested the test shall report the refusal, failure to comply, or positive test result to the department not later than five days after receiving notification of the test result on a form approved by the department.

(4) The department shall maintain a record of any action taken for a refusal, failure to comply, or positive test result in the driving record of the applicant or certificate holder for three years from the date of the refusal, failure to comply, or positive test result.

(c) (1) The department may temporarily suspend a schoolbus, school pupil activity bus, youth bus, or general public paratransit driver certificate, or temporarily withhold issuance of a certificate to an applicant, if the holder or applicant is arrested for or charged with any sex offense, as defined in Section 44010 of the Education Code.

(2) Upon receipt of a notice of temporary suspension, or of the department's intent to withhold issuance, of a certificate, the certificate holder or applicant may request a hearing within 10 days of the effective date of the department's action.

(3) The department shall, upon request of the holder of, or applicant for, a certificate, within 10 working days of the receipt of the request, conduct a hearing on whether the public interest requires suspension or withholding of the certificate pursuant to paragraph (1).

(4) If the charge is dismissed or results in a finding of not guilty, the department shall immediately terminate the suspension or resume the application process, and shall expunge the suspension action taken pursuant to this subdivision from the record of the applicant or certificate holder.

(d) An applicant or holder of a certificate may reapply for a certificate whenever a felony or misdemeanor conviction is reversed or dismissed. A termination of probation and dismissal of charges pursuant to Section 1203.4 of the Penal Code or a dismissal of charges pursuant to Section 1203.4a of the Penal Code is not a dismissal for purposes of this section.

(e) The determination of the facts pursuant to this section is a civil matter which is independent of the determination of the person's guilt or innocence, has no collateral estoppel effect on a subsequent criminal prosecution, and does not preclude the litigation of the same or similar facts in a criminal proceeding.

(Amended by Stats. 2005, Ch. 66, Sec. 7. Effective January 1, 2006.)

13377. (a) The department shall not issue or renew, or shall revoke, the tow truck driver certificate of an applicant or holder for any of the following causes:

(1) The tow truck driver certificate applicant or holder has been convicted of a violation of Section 220 of the Penal Code.

(2) The tow truck driver certificate applicant or holder has been convicted of a violation of paragraph (1), (2), (3), or (4) of subdivision (a) of Section 261 of the Penal Code.

(3) The tow truck driver certificate applicant or holder has been convicted of a violation of Section 264.1, 267, 288, or 289 of the Penal Code.

(4) The tow truck driver certificate applicant or holder has been convicted of any felony or three misdemeanors as set forth in subparagraph (B) of paragraph (2) of subdivision (a) of Section 5164 of the Public Resources Code.

(5) The tow truck driver certificate applicant's or holder's driving privilege has been suspended or revoked in accordance with any provisions of this code.

(b) For purposes of this section, a conviction means a plea or verdict of guilty or a conviction following a plea of nolo contendere. For purposes of this section, the record of a conviction, or a copy thereof certified by the clerk of the court or by a judge of the court in which the conviction occurred, is conclusive evidence of the conviction.

(c) Whenever the department receives information from the Department of Justice, or the Federal Bureau of Investigation, that a tow truck driver has been convicted of an offense specified in paragraph (1), (2), (3), or (4) of subdivision (a), the department shall immediately notify the employer and the Department of the California Highway Patrol.

(d) An applicant or holder of a tow truck driver certificate, whose certificate was denied or revoked, may reapply for a certificate whenever the applicable felony or misdemeanor conviction is reversed or dismissed. If the cause for the denial or revocation was based on the suspension or revocation of the applicant's or holder's driving privilege, he or she may reapply for a certificate upon restoration of his or her driving privilege. A termination of probation and dismissal of charges pursuant to Section 1203.4 of the Penal Code or a dismissal of charges pursuant to Section 1203.4a of the Penal Code is not a dismissal for purposes of this section.

(Amended by Stats. 2004, Ch. 184, Sec. 6. Effective July 23, 2004.)

13378. (a) Any applicant for, or holder of, a tow truck driver certificate who has received a notice of refusal or revocation, may submit to the department, within 15 days after the mailing of the notice, a written request for a hearing. Failure to request a hearing, in writing, within 15 days is a waiver of the right to a hearing.

(b) Upon receipt by the department of the hearing request, the department may stay the action until a hearing is conducted and the final decision is made by the hearing officer. The department shall not stay the action when there is reasonable cause to believe that the stay would pose a threat to a member of the motoring public who may require the services of the tow truck driver in question.

(c) An applicant for, or a holder of, a tow truck driver certificate, whose certificate has been refused or revoked, is not entitled to a hearing whenever the action by the department is made mandatory by this article or any other applicable law or regulation.

(d) Upon receipt of a request for a hearing, and when the requesting party is entitled to a hearing under this article, the department shall appoint a hearing officer to conduct a hearing in accordance with Section 14112.

(Amended by Stats. 2005, Ch. 66, Sec. 8. Effective January 1, 2006.)

13380. (a) If a peace officer serves a notice of an order of suspension pursuant to Section 13388, or arrests any person for a violation of Section 23140, 23152, or 23153, the peace officer shall immediately forward to the department a sworn report of all information relevant to the enforcement action, including information that adequately identifies the person, a statement of the officer's grounds for belief that the person violated Section 23136, 23140, 23152, or 23153, a report of the results of any chemical tests that were conducted on the person or the circumstances constituting a refusal to submit to or complete the chemical testing pursuant to Section 13388 or 23612, a copy of any notice to appear under which the person was released from custody, and, if immediately available, a copy of the complaint filed with the court. For the purposes of this section and subdivision (g) of Section 23612, "immediately" means on or before the end of the fifth ordinary business day following the arrest, except that with respect to Section 13388 only, "immediately" has the same meaning as that term is defined in paragraph (3) of subdivision (b) of Section 13388.

(b) The peace officer's sworn report shall be made on forms furnished or approved by the department.

(c) For the purposes of this section, a report prepared pursuant to subdivision (a) and received pursuant to subdivision (a) of Section 1801, is a sworn report when it bears an entry identifying the maker of the document or a signature that has been affixed by means of an electronic device approved by the department.

(Added by Stats. 1998, Ch. 118, Sec. 3.24. Effective January 1, 1999. Operative July 1, 1999, by Sec. 85 of Ch. 118.)

13382. (a) If the chemical test results for a person who has been arrested for a violation of Section 23152 or 23153 show that the person has 0.08 percent or more, by weight, of alcohol in the person's blood, or if the chemical test results for a person who has been arrested for a violation of Section 23140 show that the person has 0.05 percent or more, by weight, of alcohol in the person's blood, the peace officer, acting on behalf of the department, shall serve a notice of order of suspension or revocation of the person's privilege to operate a motor vehicle personally on the arrested person.

(b) If the peace officer serves the notice of order of suspension or revocation, the peace officer shall take possession of any driver's license issued by this state which is held by the person. When the officer takes possession of a valid driver's license, the officer shall issue, on behalf of the department, a temporary driver's license. The temporary driver's license shall be an endorsement on the notice of the order of suspension or revocation and shall be valid for 30 days from the date of arrest.

(c) The peace officer shall immediately forward a copy of the completed notice of order of suspension form, and any driver's license taken into possession under subdivision (b), with the report required by Section 13380, to the department. For the purposes of this section, "immediately" means on or before the end of the fifth ordinary business day following the arrest.

(Added by Stats. 1998, Ch. 118, Sec. 4. Effective January 1, 1999. Operative July 1, 1999, by Sec. 85 of Ch. 118.)

13384. (a) The department shall not issue or renew a driver's license to any person unless the person consents in writing to submit to a chemical test or tests of that person's blood, breath, or urine pursuant to Section 23612, or a preliminary alcohol screening test pursuant to Section 23136, when requested to do so by a peace officer.

(b) All application forms for driver's licenses or driver's license renewal notices shall include a requirement that the applicant sign the following declaration as a condition of licensure:

"I agree to submit to a chemical test of my blood, breath, or urine for the purpose of determining the alcohol or drug content of my blood when testing is requested by a peace officer acting in accordance with Section 13388 or 23612 of the Vehicle Code."

(c) The department is not, incident to this section, required to maintain, copy, or store any information other than that to be incorporated into the standard application form.

(Added by Stats. 1998, Ch. 118, Sec. 5. Effective January 1, 1999. Operative July 1, 1999, by Sec. 85 of Ch. 118.)

13385. (a) On or after July 1, 2008, all application forms for driver's licenses or driver's license renewal notices shall include a requirement that the applicant sign the following declaration as a condition of licensure:

"I am hereby advised that being under the influence of alcohol or drugs, or both, impairs the ability to safely operate a motor vehicle. Therefore, it is extremely dangerous to human life to drive while under the influence of alcohol or drugs, or both. If I drive while under the influence of alcohol or drugs, or both, and as a result, a person is killed, I can be charged with murder."

(b) On all application forms for driver's licenses or driver's license renewal notices printed by the department, in English or a language other than English, the department shall include the declaration in the same language as the application or renewal notice.

(c) The department is not, incident to this section, required to maintain, copy, or store any information other than that to be incorporated into the standard application form.

(Added by Stats. 2007, Ch. 748, Sec. 2. Effective January 1, 2008.)

13386. (a) (1) The department shall certify or cause to be certified ignition interlock devices required by Article 5 (commencing with Section 23575) of Chapter 2 of Division 11.5 and publish a list of approved devices.

(2) (A) The department shall ensure that ignition interlock devices that have been certified according to the requirements of this section continue to meet certification requirements. The department may periodically require manufacturers to indicate in writing whether the devices continue to meet certification requirements.

(B) The department may use denial of certification, suspension or revocation of certification, or decertification of an ignition interlock device in another state as an indication that the certification requirements are not met, if either of the following apply:

(i) The denial of certification, suspension or revocation of certification, or decertification in another state constitutes a violation by the manufacturer of Article 2.55 (commencing with Section 125.00) of Chapter 1 of Division 1 of Title 13 of the California Code of Regulations.

(ii) The denial of certification for an ignition interlock device in another state was due to a failure of an ignition interlock device to meet the standards adopted by the regulation set forth in clause (i), specifically Sections 1 and 2 of the model specification for breath alcohol ignition interlock devices, as published by notice in the Federal Register, Vol. 57, No. 67, Tuesday, April 7, 1992, on pages 11774 to 11787, inclusive, or the Model Specifications for Breath Alcohol Ignition Interlock Devices, as published by notice in the Federal Register, Vol. 78, No. 89, Wednesday, May 8, 2013, on pages 25489 to 26867, inclusive.

(C) Failure to continue to meet certification requirements shall result in suspension or revocation of certification of ignition interlock devices.

(b) (1) A manufacturer shall not furnish an installer, service center, technician, or consumer with technology or information that allows a device to be used in a manner that is contrary to the purpose for which it is certified.

(2) Upon a violation of paragraph (1), the department shall suspend or revoke the certification of the ignition interlock device that is the subject of that violation.

(c) An installer, service center, or technician shall not tamper with, change, or alter the functionality of the device from its certified criteria.

(d) The department shall utilize information from an independent, accredited (ISO/IEC 17025) laboratory to certify ignition interlock devices of the manufacturer or manufacturer's agent, in accordance with the guidelines. The cost of certification shall be borne by the manufacturers of ignition interlock devices. If the certification of a device is suspended or revoked, the manufacturer of the device shall be responsible for, and shall bear the cost of, the removal of the device and the replacement of a certified device of the manufacturer or another manufacturer.

(e) A model of ignition interlock device shall not be certified unless it meets the accuracy requirements and specifications provided in the guidelines adopted by the National Highway Traffic Safety Administration.

(f) All manufacturers of ignition interlock devices that meet the requirements of subdivision (e) and are certified in a manner approved by the department, who intend to sell the devices in this state, first shall apply to the department on forms provided by that department. The application shall be accompanied by a fee in an amount not to exceed the amount necessary to cover the costs incurred by the department in carrying out this section.

(g) The department shall ensure that standard forms and procedures are developed for documenting decisions and compliance and communicating results to relevant agencies. These forms shall include all of the following:

(1) An "Option to Install," to be sent by the department to repeat offenders along with the mandatory order of suspension or revocation. This shall include the alternatives available for early license reinstatement with the installation of an ignition interlock device and shall be accompanied by a toll-free telephone number for each manufacturer of a certified ignition interlock device. Information regarding approved installation locations shall be provided to drivers by manufacturers with ignition interlock devices that have been certified in accordance with this section.

(2) A "Verification of Installation" to be returned to the department by the reinstating offender upon application for reinstatement. Copies shall be provided for the manufacturer or the manufacturer's agent.

(3) A "Notice of Noncompliance" and procedures to ensure continued use of the ignition interlock device during the restriction period and to ensure compliance with maintenance requirements. The maintenance period shall be standardized at 60 days to maximize monitoring checks for equipment tampering.

(h) Every manufacturer and manufacturer's agent certified by the department to provide ignition interlock devices shall adopt fee schedules that provide for the payment of the costs of the device by applicants in amounts commensurate with the applicant's ability to pay.

(i) A person who manufactures, installs, services, or repairs, or otherwise deals in ignition interlock devices shall not disclose, sell, or transfer to a third party any individually identifiable information pertaining to individuals who are required by law to install an ignition interlock device on a vehicle that the individual owns or operates, except to the extent necessary to confirm or deny that an individual has complied with ignition interlock device installation and maintenance requirements.

(j) This section shall become operative January 1, 2033.

(Amended (as added by Stats. 2016, Ch. 783, Sec. 22) by Stats. 2025, Ch. 689, Sec. 16. (AB 366) Effective January 1, 2026. Section operative January 1, 2033, by its own provisions.)

13386. (a) (1) The department shall certify or cause to be certified ignition interlock devices required by Article 5 (commencing with Section 23575) of Chapter 2 of Division 11.5 and publish a list of approved devices.

(2) (A) The department shall ensure that ignition interlock devices that have been certified according to the requirements of this section continue to meet certification requirements. The department may periodically require manufacturers to indicate in writing whether the devices continue to meet certification requirements.

(B) The department may use denial of certification, suspension or revocation of certification, or decertification of an ignition interlock device in another state as an indication that the certification requirements are not met, if either of the following apply:

(i) The denial of certification, suspension or revocation of certification, or decertification in another state constitutes a violation by the manufacturer of Article 2.55 (commencing with Section 125.00) of Chapter 1 of Division 1 of Title 13 of the California Code of Regulations.

(ii) The denial of certification for an ignition interlock device in another state was due to a failure of an ignition interlock device to meet the standards adopted by the regulation set forth in clause (i), specifically Sections 1 and 2 of the model specification for breath alcohol ignition interlock devices, as published by notice in the Federal Register, Vol. 57, No. 67, Tuesday, April 7, 1992, on pages 11774 to 11787, inclusive, or the model specifications for breath alcohol ignition interlock devices, as published by notice in the Federal Register, Vol. 78, No. 89, Wednesday, May 8, 2013, on pages 25489 to 26867, inclusive.

(C) Failure to continue to meet certification requirements shall result in suspension or revocation of certification of ignition interlock devices.

(b) (1) A manufacturer shall not furnish an installer, service center, technician, or consumer with technology or information that allows a device to be used in a manner that is contrary to the purpose for which it is certified.

(2) Upon a violation of paragraph (1), the department shall suspend or revoke the certification of the ignition interlock device that is the subject of that violation.

(c) An installer, service center, or technician shall not tamper with, change, or alter the functionality of the device from its certified criteria.

(d) The department shall utilize information from an independent, accredited (ISO/IEC 17025) laboratory to certify ignition interlock devices of the manufacturer or manufacturer's agent, in accordance with the guidelines. The cost of certification shall be borne by the manufacturers of ignition interlock devices. If the certification of a device is suspended or revoked, the manufacturer of the device shall be responsible for, and shall bear the cost of, the removal of the device and the replacement of a certified device of the manufacturer or another manufacturer.

(e) A model of ignition interlock device shall not be certified unless it meets the accuracy requirements and specifications provided in the guidelines adopted by the National Highway Traffic Safety Administration.

(f) All manufacturers of ignition interlock devices that meet the requirements of subdivision (e) and are certified in a manner approved by the department, who intend to market the devices in this state, first shall apply to the department on forms provided by that department. The application shall be accompanied by a fee in an amount not to exceed the amount necessary to cover the reasonable costs incurred by the department in carrying out this section.

(g) The department shall ensure that standard forms and procedures are developed for documenting decisions and compliance and communicating results to relevant agencies. These forms shall include all of the following:

(1) An "Option to Install," to be sent by the department to all offenders along with the mandatory order of suspension or revocation. This shall include the alternatives available for early license reinstatement with the installation of a functioning, certified ignition interlock device and shall be accompanied by a toll-free telephone number for each manufacturer of a certified ignition interlock device. Information regarding approved installation locations shall be provided to drivers by manufacturers with ignition interlock devices that have been certified in accordance with this section.

(2) A "Verification of Installation" to be returned to the department by the offender upon application for reinstatement. Copies shall be provided for the manufacturer or the manufacturer's agent.

(3) A "Notice of Noncompliance" and procedures to ensure continued use of the ignition interlock device during the restriction period and to ensure compliance with maintenance requirements. The maintenance period shall be standardized at 60 days to maximize monitoring checks for equipment tampering.

(h) The department shall develop rules under which every manufacturer and manufacturer's agent certified by the department to provide ignition interlock devices shall provide a fee schedule to the department of the manufacturer's standard ignition interlock device program costs, stating the standard charges for installation, service and maintenance, and removal of the manufacturer's device, and shall develop a form to be signed by an authorized representative of the manufacturer pursuant to which the manufacturer agrees to provide functioning, certified ignition interlock devices to applicants at the costs described in subdivision (k) of Section 23575.3. The form shall contain an acknowledgment that the failure of the manufacturer, its agents, or authorized installers to comply with subdivision (k) of Section 23575.3 shall result in suspension or revocation of the department's approval for the manufacturer to market ignition interlock devices in this state.

(i) A person who manufactures, installs, services, or repairs, or otherwise deals in ignition interlock devices shall not disclose, sell, or transfer to a third party any individually identifiable information pertaining to individuals who are required by law to install a functioning, certified ignition interlock device on a vehicle that the individual operates, except to the extent necessary to confirm or deny that an individual has complied with ignition interlock device installation and maintenance requirements.

(j) This section shall become operative on January 1, 2019.

(k) This section shall remain in effect only until January 1, 2033, and as of that date is repealed.

(Amended (as added by Stats. 2017, Ch. 485, Sec. 16) by Stats. 2025, Ch. 689, Sec. 15. (AB 366) Effective January 1, 2026. Repealed as of January 1, 2033, by its own provisions. See later operative version, as amended by Sec. 16 of Stats. 2025, Ch. 689.)

13388. (a) If a peace officer lawfully detains a person under 21 years of age who is driving a motor vehicle, and the officer has reasonable cause to believe that the person is in violation of Section 23136, the officer shall request that the person take a preliminary alcohol screening test to determine the presence of alcohol in the person, if a preliminary alcohol screening test device is immediately available. If a preliminary alcohol screening test device is not immediately available, the officer may request the person to submit to chemical testing of his or her blood, breath, or urine, conducted pursuant to Section 23612.

(b) If the person refuses to take, or fails to complete, the preliminary alcohol screening test or refuses to take or fails to complete a chemical test if a preliminary alcohol device is not immediately available, or if the person takes the preliminary alcohol screening test and that test reveals a blood-alcohol concentration of 0.01 percent or greater, or if the results of a chemical test reveal a blood-alcohol concentration of 0.01 percent or greater, the officer shall proceed as follows:

(1) The officer, acting on behalf of the department, shall serve the person with a notice of an order of suspension of the person's driving privilege.

(2) The officer shall take possession of any driver's license issued by this state which is held by the person. When the officer takes possession of a valid driver's license, the officer shall issue, on behalf of the department, a temporary driver's license. The temporary driver's license shall be an endorsement on the notice of the order of suspension and shall be valid for 30 days from the date of issuance, or until receipt of the order of suspension from the department, whichever occurs first.

(3) The officer immediately shall forward a copy of the completed notice of order of suspension form, and any driver's license taken into possession under paragraph (2), with the report required by Section 13380, to the department. For the purposes of this paragraph, "immediately" means on or before the end of the fifth ordinary business day after the notice of order of suspension was served.

(c) For the purposes of this section, a preliminary alcohol screening test device is an instrument designed and used to measure the presence of alcohol in a person based on a breath sample.

(Added by Stats. 1998, Ch. 118, Sec. 7. Effective January 1, 1999. Operative July 1, 1999, by Sec. 85 of Ch. 118.)

13389. (a) If a peace officer lawfully detains a person previously convicted of Section 23152 or 23153 who is driving a motor vehicle, while the person is on probation for a violation of Section 23152 or 23153, and the officer has reasonable cause to believe that the person is in violation of Section 23154, the officer shall request that the person take a preliminary alcohol screening test to determine the presence of alcohol in the person, if a preliminary alcohol screening test device is immediately available. If a preliminary alcohol screening test device is not immediately available, the officer may request the person to submit to chemical testing of his or her blood, breath, or urine, conducted pursuant to Section 23612.

(b) If the person refuses to take, or fails to complete, the preliminary alcohol screening test or refuses to take or fails to complete a chemical test if a preliminary alcohol device is not immediately available, or if the person takes the preliminary alcohol screening test and that test reveals a blood-alcohol concentration of 0.01 percent or greater, the officer shall proceed as follows:

(1) The officer, acting on behalf of the department, shall serve the person with a notice of an order of suspension of the person's driving privilege.

(2) (A) The officer shall take possession of any driver's license issued by this state that is held by the person. When the officer takes possession of a valid driver's license, the officer shall issue, on behalf of the department, a temporary driver's license.

(B) The temporary driver's license shall be an endorsement on the notice of the order of suspension and shall be valid for 30 days from the date of issuance, or until receipt of the order of suspension from the department, whichever occurs first.

(3) (A) The officer shall immediately forward a copy of the completed notice of order of suspension form, and any driver's license taken into possession under paragraph (2), with the report required by Section 13380, to the department.

(B) For the purposes of subparagraph (A), "immediately" means on or before the end of the fifth ordinary business day after the notice of order of suspension was served.

(c) For the purposes of this section, a preliminary alcohol screening test device is an instrument designed and used to measure the presence of alcohol in a person based on a breath sample.

(Added by Stats. 2007, Ch. 749, Sec. 3. Effective January 1, 2008. Operative January 1, 2009, by Sec. 9 of Ch. 749.)

13390. (a) A temporary license issued pursuant to Section 13382 or 13389 shall contain a notice that the person may be able to regain driving privileges with the installation of an ignition interlock device, that financial assistance may be available for that purpose, and a contact for obtaining more information regarding the ignition interlock program.

(b) This section shall become operative on January 1, 2019.

(c) This section shall remain in effect only until January 1, 2033, and as of that date is repealed.

(Amended by Stats. 2025, Ch. 689, Sec. 17. (AB 366) Effective January 1, 2026. Repealed as of January 1, 2033, by its own provisions.)

13392. Any person whose license is suspended or delayed issuance pursuant to Section 13388 shall pay to the department, in addition to any other fees required for the reissuance, return, or issuance of a driver's license, one hundred dollars ($100) for the reissuance, return, or issuance of his or her driver's license.

(Added by Stats. 1998, Ch. 118, Sec. 9. Effective January 1, 1999. Operative July 1, 1999, by Sec. 85 of Ch. 118.)

Article 4. Procedure

(Article 4 enacted by Stats. 1959, Ch. 3.)

13550. Whenever any person is convicted of any offense for which this code makes mandatory the revocation or suspension by the department of the privilege of the person to operate a motor vehicle, the privilege of the person to operate a motor vehicle is suspended or revoked until the department takes the action required by this code, and the court in which the conviction is had shall require the surrender to it of the driver's license or temporary permit issued to the person convicted and the court shall within 10 days after the conviction forward the same with the required report of the conviction to the department.

(Amended by Stats. 1990, Ch. 44, Sec. 3.)

13551. (a) Whenever the department revokes or suspends the privilege of any person to operate a motor vehicle, the revocation or suspension shall apply to all driver's licenses held by that person, and, unless previously surrendered to the court, all of those licenses shall be surrendered to the department, or, pursuant to Section 13388, 23612, or 13382, to a peace officer on behalf of the department. Whenever the department cancels a driver's license, the license shall be surrendered to the department. All suspended licenses shall be retained by the department. The department shall return the license to the licensee, or may issue the person a new license upon the expiration of the period of suspension or revocation, if the person is otherwise eligible for a driver's license.

(b) The department shall return the license to the licensee, or may issue the person a new license, whenever the department determines that the grounds for suspension, revocation, or cancellation did not exist at the time the action was taken, if the person is otherwise eligible for a driver's license.

(Amended by Stats. 1998, Ch. 118, Sec. 3.18. Effective January 1, 1999. Operative July 1, 1999, by Sec. 85 of Ch. 118.)

13552. (a) The privileges of a nonresident to operate vehicles in this state may be suspended or revoked under the provisions of this chapter in the same manner and to the same extent as the privileges of a resident driver.

(b) Any nonresident, whether or not licensed to drive in a foreign jurisdiction, who operates a motor vehicle upon a highway after his privilege of operating a motor vehicle in this state has been suspended or revoked is in violation of Section 14601 or 14601.1.

(c) Whenever the department revokes or suspends the privileges of a nonresident to operate vehicles in this state, it shall send a certified copy of the order to the proper authorities in the state wherein the person is a resident.

(Amended by Stats. 1971, Ch. 438.)

13553. Whenever a court or the department suspends or revokes the privilege of any person to operate a motor vehicle and the person does not hold a valid driver's license, or has never applied for or received a driver's license in this State, the person shall be subject to any and all penalties and disabilities provided in this code for a violation of the terms and conditions of a suspension or revocation of the privilege to operate a motor vehicle.

(Enacted by Stats. 1959, Ch. 3.)

13555. A termination of probation and dismissal of charges pursuant to Section 1203.4 of, or a dismissal of charges pursuant to Section 1203.4a of, or relief granted pursuant to Section 1203.425 of, the Penal Code does not affect any revocation or suspension of the privilege of the person convicted to drive a motor vehicle under this chapter. Such person's prior conviction shall be considered a conviction for the purpose of revoking or suspending or otherwise limiting such privilege on the ground of two or more convictions.

(Amended by Stats. 2019, Ch. 578, Sec. 10. (AB 1076) Effective January 1, 2020.)

13556. (a) Unless otherwise specifically provided in this chapter, no suspension of a license by the department shall be for a longer period than six months, except that the department may suspend a license for a maximum period of 12 months in those cases when a discretionary revocation would otherwise be authorized pursuant to this chapter.

(b) Any discretionary suspension, the ending of which is dependent upon an action by the person suspended and which has been in effect for eight years, may be ended at the election of the department.

(c) Notwithstanding any other provisions of this code, a suspension based upon a physical or mental condition shall continue until evidence satisfactory to the department establishes that the cause for which the action was taken has been removed or no longer renders the person incapable of operating a motor vehicle safely.

(Amended by Stats. 1982, Ch. 612, Sec. 1.)

13557. (a) The department shall review the determination made pursuant to Section 13353, 13353.1, or 13353.2 relating to a person who has received a notice of an order of suspension or revocation of the person's privilege to operate a motor vehicle pursuant to Section 13353, 13353.1, 13353.2, 13382, or 23612,. The department shall consider the sworn report submitted by the peace officer pursuant to Section 23612 or 13380 and any other evidence accompanying the report.

(b) (1) If the department determines in the review of a determination made under Section 13353 or 13353.1, by a preponderance of the evidence, all of the following facts, the department shall sustain the order of suspension or revocation:

(A) The peace officer had reasonable cause to believe that the person had been driving a motor vehicle in violation of Section 23136, 23140, 23152, 23153, or 23154.

(B) The person was placed under arrest or, if the alleged violation was of Section 23136, that the person was lawfully detained.

(C) The person refused or failed to complete the chemical test or tests after being requested by a peace officer.

(D) Except for the persons described in Section 23612 who are incapable of refusing, the person had been told that his or her privilege to operate a motor vehicle would be suspended or revoked if he or she refused to submit to, and complete, the required testing.

(2) If the department determines, by a preponderance of the evidence, that any of the facts required under paragraph (1) were not proven, the department shall rescind the order of suspension or revocation and, if the person is otherwise eligible, return or reissue the person's driver's license pursuant to Section 13551. The determination of the department upon administrative review is final unless a hearing is requested pursuant to Section 13558.

(3) If the department determines in the review of a determination made under Section 13353.2, by the preponderance of the evidence, all of the following facts, the department shall sustain the order of suspension or revocation, or if the person is under 21 years of age and does not yet have a driver's license, the department shall delay issuance of that license for one year:

(A) The peace officer had reasonable cause to believe that the person had been driving a motor vehicle in violation of Section 23136, 23140, 23152, 23153, or 23154.

(B) The person was placed under arrest or, if the alleged violation was of Section 23136, the person was lawfully detained.

(C) The person was driving a motor vehicle under any of the following circumstances:

(i) When the person had 0.08 percent or more, by weight, of alcohol in his or her blood.

(ii) When the person was under 21 years of age and had 0.05 percent or more, by weight, of alcohol in his or her blood.

(iii) When the person was under 21 years of age and had a blood-alcohol concentration of 0.01 percent or greater, as measured by a preliminary alcohol screening test, or other chemical test.

(iv) When the person was driving a vehicle that requires a commercial driver's license and the person had 0.04 percent or more, by weight, of alcohol in his or her blood.

(v) When the person was on probation for a violation of Section

23152 or 23153 and had a blood-alcohol concentration of 0.01 percent or greater, as measured by a preliminary alcohol screening test or other chemical test.

(4) If the department determines that any of those facts required under paragraph (3) were not proven by the preponderance of the evidence, the department shall rescind the order of suspension or revocation and, if the person is otherwise eligible, return or reissue the person's driver's license pursuant to Section 13551. For persons under 21 years of age, the determination of the department pursuant to paragraph (3) is final unless a hearing is requested within 10 days of the determination, which hearing shall be conducted according to Section 13558. For persons over 21 years of age, the determination of the department upon administrative review is final unless a hearing is requested pursuant to Section 13558.

(c) The department shall make the determination upon administrative review before the effective date of the order of suspension or revocation.

(d) The administrative review does not stay the suspension or revocation of a person's privilege to operate a motor vehicle. If the department is unable to make a determination on administrative review within the time limit in subdivision (c), the department shall stay the effective date of the order of suspension or revocation pending the determination and, if the person's driver's license has been taken by the peace officer pursuant to Section 13382, 13388, 13389, or 23612, the department shall notify the person before the expiration date of the temporary permit issued pursuant to Section 13382, 13388, 13389, or 23612, or the expiration date of any previous extension issued pursuant to this subdivision, in a form that permits the person to establish to any peace officer that his or her privilege to operate a motor vehicle is not suspended or revoked.

(e) A person may request and be granted a hearing pursuant to Section 13558 without first receiving the results of an administrative review pursuant to this section. After receiving a request for a hearing, the department is not required to conduct an administrative review of the same matter pursuant to this section.

(f) A determination of facts by the department under this section has no collateral estoppel effect on a subsequent criminal prosecution and does not preclude litigation of those same facts in the criminal proceeding.

(Amended by Stats. 2011, Ch. 296, Sec. 307. (AB 1023) Effective January 1, 2012.)

13558. (a) Any person, who has received a notice of an order of suspension or revocation of the person's privilege to operate a motor vehicle pursuant to Section 13353, 13353.1, 13353.2, 13388, 23612, or 13382 or a notice pursuant to Section 13557, may request a hearing on the matter pursuant to Article 3 (commencing with Section 14100) of Chapter 3, except as otherwise provided in this section.

(b) If the person wishes to have a hearing before the effective date of the order of suspension or revocation, the request for a hearing shall be made within 10 days of the receipt of the notice of the order of suspension or revocation. The hearing shall be held at a place designated by the department as close as practicable to the place where the arrest occurred, unless the parties agree to a different location. Any evidence at the hearing shall not be limited to the evidence presented at an administrative review pursuant to Section 13557.

(c) (1) The only issues at the hearing on an order of suspension or revocation pursuant to Section 13353 or 13353.1 shall be those facts listed in paragraph (1) of subdivision (b) of Section 13557. Notwithstanding Section 14106, the period of suspension or revocation specified in Section 13353 or 13353.1 shall not be reduced and, notwithstanding Section 14105.5, the effective date of the order of suspension or revocation shall not be stayed pending review at a hearing pursuant to this section.

(2) The only issues at the hearing on an order of suspension pursuant to Section 13353.2 shall be those facts listed in paragraph (3) of subdivision (b) of Section 13557. Notwithstanding Section 14106, the period of suspension specified in Section 13353.3 shall not be reduced.

(d) The department shall hold the administrative hearing before the effective date of the order of suspension or revocation if the request for the hearing is postmarked or received by the department on or before 10 days after the person's receipt of the service of the notice of the order of suspension or revocation pursuant to Section 13353.2, 13388, 23612, or 13382.

(e) A request for an administrative hearing does not stay the suspension or revocation of a person's privilege to operate a motor vehicle. If the department does not conduct an administrative hearing and make a determination after an administrative hearing within the time limit in subdivision (d), the department shall stay the effective date of the order of suspension or revocation pending the determination and, if the person's driver's license has been taken by the peace officer pursuant to Section 13388, 23612, or 13382, the department shall notify the person before the expiration date of the temporary permit issued pursuant to Section 13388, 23612, or 13382, or the expiration date of any previous extension issued pursuant to this subdivision, provided the person is otherwise eligible, in a form that permits the person to establish to any peace officer that his or her privilege to operate a motor vehicle is not suspended or revoked.

(f) The department shall give written notice of its determination pursuant to Section 14105. If the department determines, upon a hearing of the matter, to suspend or revoke the person's privilege to operate a motor vehicle, notwithstanding the term of any temporary permit issued pursuant to Section 13388, 23612, or 13382, the temporary permit shall be revoked and the suspension or revocation of the person's privilege to operate a motor vehicle shall become effective five days after notice is given. If the department sustains the order of suspension or revocation, the department shall include notice that the person has a right to review by the court pursuant to Section 13559.

(g) A determination of facts by the department upon a hearing pursuant to this section has no collateral estoppel effect on a subsequent criminal prosecution and does not preclude litigation of those same facts in the criminal proceeding.

(Amended by Stats. 2015, Ch. 451, Sec. 27. (SB 491) Effective January 1, 2016.)

13559. (a) Notwithstanding Section 14400 or 14401, within 30 days of the issuance of the notice of determination of the department sustaining an order of suspension or revocation of the person's privilege to operate a motor vehicle after the hearing pursuant to Section 13558, the person may file a petition for review of the order in the court of competent jurisdiction in the person's county of residence. The filing of a petition for judicial review shall not stay the order of suspension or revocation. The review shall be on the record of the hearing and the court shall not consider other evidence. If the court finds that the department exceeded its constitutional or statutory authority, made an erroneous interpretation of the law, acted in an arbitrary and capricious manner, or made a determination which is not supported by the evidence in the record, the court may order the department to rescind the order of suspension or revocation and return, or reissue a new license to, the person.

(b) A finding by the court after a review pursuant to this section shall have no collateral estoppel effect on a subsequent criminal prosecution and does not preclude litigation of those same facts in the criminal proceeding.

(Amended by Stats. 1990, Ch. 431, Sec. 12. Effective July 26, 1990.)

Chapter 3. Investigation and Hearing

(Chapter 3 enacted by Stats. 1959, Ch. 3.)

Article 1. Investigation and Re-examination

(Article 1 enacted by Stats. 1959, Ch. 3.)

13800. The department may conduct an investigation to determine whether the privilege of any person to operate a motor vehicle should be suspended or revoked or whether terms or conditions of probation should be imposed upon receiving information or upon a showing by its records:

(a) That the licensee has been involved as a driver in an accident causing death or personal injury or serious damage to property.

(b) That the licensee has been involved in three or more accidents within a period of 12 consecutive months.

(c) That the person in three consecutive years has committed three or more offenses that have resulted in convictions involving the consumption of an alcoholic beverage or drug, or both, while operating a motor vehicle, including, but not limited to, offenses under Section 23103.5, 23152, 23153, 23222, or 23224; has been involved in three or more crashes in which the crash reports show that the person was driving and had consumed alcoholic beverages or drugs, or both; or had any combination of three or more of those offenses and crashes.

(d) That the licensee is a reckless, negligent, or incompetent driver of a motor vehicle.

(e) That the licensee has permitted an unlawful or fraudulent use of their driver's license.

(f) That any ground exists for which a license might be refused. The receipt by the department of an abstract of the record of conviction of any offense involving the use or possession of narcotic controlled substances under Division 10 (commencing with Section 11000) of the Health and Safety Code shall be a sufficient basis for an investigation by the department to determine whether grounds exist for which a license might be refused.

(Amended by Stats. 2022, Ch. 81, Sec. 3. (AB 2198) Effective January 1, 2023.)

13801. In addition to the investigation, the department may require the re-examination of the licensee, and shall give 10 days' written notice of the time and place thereof. If the licensee refuses or fails to submit to the re-examination, the department may peremptorily suspend the driving privilege of the person until such time as the licensee shall have submitted to re-examination. The suspension shall be effective upon notice.

(Enacted by Stats. 1959, Ch. 3.)

13802. In applying the provisions of Section 13800 the department shall give due consideration to the amount of use or mileage traveled in the operation of a motor vehicle.

(Amended by Stats. 1961, Ch. 1615.)

Article 2. Notice

(Article 2 enacted by Stats. 1959, Ch. 3.)

13950. Whenever the department determines upon investigation or re-examination that any of the grounds for re-examination are true, or that the safety of the person investigated or re-examined or other persons upon the highways requires such action, and it proposes to revoke or suspend the driving privilege of the person or proposes to impose terms of probation on his driving privilege, notice and an opportunity to be heard shall be given before taking the action.

(Enacted by Stats. 1959, Ch. 3.)

13951. Whenever the department proposes to refuse to issue or renew a driver's license, it shall notify the applicant of such fact and give him an opportunity to be heard.

(Enacted by Stats. 1959, Ch. 3.)

13952. The notice shall contain a statement setting forth the proposed action and the grounds therefor, and notify the person of his right to a hearing as provided in this chapter, or the department, at the time it gives notice of its intention to act may set the date of hearing, giving 10 days' notice thereof.

(Amended by Stats. 1961, Ch. 58.)

13953. In the alternative to the procedure under Sections 13950, 13951, and 13952 and in the event the department determines upon investigation or reexamination that the safety of the person subject to investigation or reexamination or other persons upon the highways require such action, the department shall forthwith and without hearing suspend or revoke the privilege of the person to operate a motor vehicle or impose reasonable terms and conditions of probation which shall be relative to the safe operation of a motor vehicle. No order of suspension or revocation or the imposition of terms or conditions of probation shall become effective until 30 days after the giving of written notice thereof to the person affected, except that the department shall have authority to make any such order effective immediately upon the giving of notice when in its opinion because of the mental or physical condition of the person such immediate action is required for the safety of the driver or other persons upon the highways.

(Amended by Stats. 1969, Ch. 1045.)

13954. (a) Notwithstanding any other provision of this code, the department immediately shall suspend or revoke the driving privilege of a person who the department has reasonable cause to believe was in some manner involved in a crash while operating a motor vehicle under the following circumstances at the time of the crash:

(1) The person had 0.08 percent or more, by weight, of alcohol in their blood.

(2) They proximately caused the crash as a result of an act prohibited, or the neglect of any duty imposed, by law.

(3) The crash occurred within five years of the date of a violation of subdivision (b) of Section 191.5 of the Penal Code that resulted in a conviction.

(b) If a crash described in subdivision (a) does not result in a conviction or finding of a violation of Section 23152 or 23153, the department shall suspend the driving privilege under this section for one year from the date of commencement of the original suspension. After the one-year suspension period, the driving privilege may be reinstated if evidence establishes to the satisfaction of the department that no grounds exist that would authorize the refusal to issue a license and that reinstatement of the driving privilege would not jeopardize the safety of the person or other persons upon the highways, and if the person gives proof of financial responsibility, as defined in Section 16430.

(c) If a crash described in subdivision (a) does result in a conviction or finding of a violation of Section 23152 or 23153, the department shall revoke the driving privilege under this section for three years from the date of commencement of the original revocation. After the three-year revocation period, the driving privilege may be reinstated if evidence establishes to the satisfaction of the department that no grounds exist that would authorize the refusal to issue a license and that reinstatement of the driving privilege would not jeopardize the safety of the person or other persons upon the highways, and if the person gives proof of financial responsibility.

(d) Any revocation action under subdivision (c) shall be imposed as follows:

(1) If the crash results in a first conviction of a violation of Section 23152 or 23153, or if the person was convicted of a separate violation of Section 23152 or 23153 that occurred within five years of the crash, the period of revocation under subdivision (c) shall be concurrent with any period of restriction, suspension, or revocation imposed under Section 13352, 13352.4, or 13352.5.

(2) If the person was convicted of two or more separate violations of Section 23152 or 23153, or both, that occurred within five years of the crash, the period of revocation under subdivision (c) shall be cumulative and shall be imposed consecutively with any period of restriction, suspension, or revocation imposed under Section 13352 or 13352.5.

(e) The department immediately shall notify the person in writing of the action taken and, upon the person's request in writing and within 15 days from the date of receipt of that request, shall grant the person an opportunity for a hearing in the same manner and under the same conditions as provided in Article 3 (commencing with Section 14100) of Chapter 3, except as otherwise provided in this section. For purposes of this section, the scope of the hearing shall cover the following issues:

(1) Whether the peace officer had reasonable cause to believe the person had been driving a motor vehicle in violation of Section 23152 or 23153.

(2) Whether the person had been placed under lawful arrest.

(3) Whether a chemical test of the person's blood, breath, or urine

indicated that the blood-alcohol level was 0.08 percent or more, by weight, at the time of testing.

If the department determines, upon a hearing of the matter, that the person had not been placed under lawful arrest, or that a chemical test of the person's blood, breath, or urine did not indicate a blood-alcohol level of 0.08 percent or more, by weight, at the time of testing, the suspension or revocation shall be terminated immediately.

(f) This section applies if the crash occurred on or after January 1, 1990, without regard for the dates of the violations referred to in subdivisions (a) and (d).

(g) Notwithstanding subdivision (f), if a person's privilege to operate a motor vehicle is required to be suspended or revoked pursuant to this section as it read before January 1, 1990, as a result of a crash that occurred before January 1, 1990, the privilege shall be suspended or revoked pursuant to this section as it read before January 1, 1990.

(Amended by Stats. 2022, Ch. 81, Sec. 4. (AB 2198) Effective January 1, 2023.)

Article 3. Hearing

(Article 3 enacted by Stats. 1959, Ch. 3.)

14100. (a) Whenever the department has given notice, or has taken or proposes to take action under Section 12804.15, 13353, 13353.2, 13950, 13951, 13952, or 13953, the person receiving the notice or subject to the action may, within 10 days, demand a hearing which shall be granted, except as provided in Section 14101.

(b) An application for a hearing does not stay the action by the department for which the notice is given.

(c) The fact that a person has the right to request an administrative hearing within 10 days after receipt of the notice of the order of suspension under this section and Section 16070, and that the request is required to be made within 10 days in order to receive a determination prior to the effective date of the suspension shall be made prominent on the notice.

(d) The department shall make available notices, to accompany the notice provided pursuant to this section, that provide the information required pursuant to subdivision (c) in all non-English languages spoken by a substantial number of the public served by the department, and shall distribute the notices as it determines is appropriate.

(e) The department shall implement the provisions of subdivisions (c) and (d) as soon as practicable, but not later than January 1, 1994.

(Amended by Stats. 2001, Ch. 658, Sec. 5. Effective October 10, 2001.)

14100.1. Hearings granted on refusal, suspension, or revocation of a passenger transportation vehicle or hazardous materials endorsement, or farm labor vehicle certificate shall be conducted according to Chapter 3 (commencing with Section 13800) of Division 6.

(Added by Stats. 1990, Ch. 1360, Sec. 42.)

14101. A person is not entitled to a hearing in either of the following cases:

(a) If the action by the department is made mandatory by this code.

(b) If the person has previously been given an opportunity with appropriate notice for a hearing and failed to request a hearing within the time specified by law.

(Amended by Stats. 1991, Ch. 13, Sec. 32. Effective February 13, 1991.)

14103. Failure to respond to a notice given under this chapter within 10 days is a waiver of the right to a hearing, and the department may take action without a hearing or may, upon request of the person whose privilege of driving is in question, or at its own option, reopen the question, take evidence, change, or set aside any order previously made, or grant a hearing.

(Amended by Stats. 1991, Ch. 13, Sec. 34. Effective February 13, 1991.)

14104. If the department grants a hearing as provided in this chapter, it shall fix a time and place for the hearing and shall give 10 days' notice of the hearing to the applicant or licensee. The notice of hearing shall also include a statement of the discovery rights of the applicant or licensee to review the department's records prior to the hearing.

(Amended by Stats. 1991, Ch. 13, Sec. 35. Effective February 13, 1991.)

14104.2. (a) Any hearing shall be conducted by the director or by a hearing officer or hearing board appointed by him or her from officers or employees of the department.

(b) The entire proceedings at any hearing may be recorded by a phonographic recorder or by mechanical, electronic, or other means capable of reproduction or transcription.

(Added by Stats. 1991, Ch. 13, Sec. 36. Effective February 13, 1991.)

14104.5. (a) Before a hearing has commenced, the department, or the hearing officer or hearing board, shall issue subpoenas or subpoenas duces tecum, or both, at the request of any party, for attendance or production of documents at the hearing. After the hearing has commenced, the department, if it is hearing the case, or the hearing officer sitting alone, or the hearing board, may issue subpoenas or subpoenas duces tecum, or both.

(b) Notwithstanding Section 11450.20 of the Government Code, subpoenas and subpoenas duces tecum issued in conjunction with the hearings may be served by first-class mail.

(Amended by Stats. 1999, Ch. 724, Sec. 32. Effective January 1, 2000.)

14104.7. At any hearing, the department shall consider its official records and may receive sworn testimony. At the hearing, or subsequent to the hearing with the consent of the applicant or licensee, any or all of the following may be submitted as evidence concerning any fact relating to the ability of the applicant or licensee to safely operate a motor vehicle:

(a) Reports of attending or examining physicians and surgeons.

(b) Reports of special investigators appointed by the department to investigate and report upon any facts relating to the ability of the person to operate a vehicle safely.

(c) Properly authenticated reports of hospital records, excerpts from expert testimony received by the department or a hearing board upon similar issues of scientific fact in other cases, and the prior decision of the director upon those issues.

(Added by Stats. 1991, Ch. 13, Sec. 38. Effective February 13, 1991.)

14105. (a) Upon the conclusion of a hearing, the hearing officer or hearing board shall make findings and render a decision on behalf of the department and shall notify the person involved. Notice of the decision shall include a statement of the person's right to a review. The decision shall take effect as stated in the notice, but not less than four nor more than 15 days after the notice is mailed.

(b) The decision may be modified at any time after issuance to correct mistakes or clerical errors.

(Amended by Stats. 1999, Ch. 724, Sec. 33. Effective January 1, 2000.)

14105.5. (a) The person subject to a hearing may request a review of the decision taken under Section 14105 within 15 days of the effective date of the decision.

(b) On receipt of a request for review, the department shall stay the action pending a decision on review, unless the hearing followed an action pursuant to Section 13353, 13353.2, or 13953. The review shall include an examination of the hearing report, documentary evidence, and findings. The hearing officer or hearing board conducting the original hearing may not participate in the review process.

(c) Following the review, a written notice of the department's decision shall be mailed to the person involved. If the action has been stayed pending review, the department's decision shall take effect as stated in the notice, but not less than four nor more than 15 days after the notice is mailed.

(d) The decision may be modified at any time after issuance to correct mistakes or clerical errors.

(Amended by Stats. 1999, Ch. 724, Sec. 34. Effective January 1, 2000.)

14106. Following the mailing of the notice of the department's decision pursuant to Section 14105.5, the department, at its own option or upon the request of the person whose privilege of driving is in question, may reopen the question, take further evidence, or change or set aside any order previously made.

(Amended by Stats. 1991, Ch. 13, Sec. 41. Effective February 13, 1991.)

14112. (a) All matters in a hearing not covered by this chapter shall be governed, as far as applicable, by Chapter 5 (commencing with Section 11500) of Part 1 of Division 3 of Title 2 of the Government Code.

(b) Subdivision (a) of Section 11425.30 of the Government Code does not apply to a proceeding for issuance, denial, revocation, or suspension of a driver's license pursuant to this division.

(Amended by Stats. 2004, Ch. 193, Sec. 196. Effective January 1, 2005.)

Article 4. Probation

(Article 4 enacted by Stats. 1959, Ch. 3.)

14250. Whenever by any provision of this code the department has discretionary authority to suspend or revoke the privilege of a person to operate a motor vehicle, the department may in lieu of suspension or revocation place the person on probation, the terms of which may include a suspension as a condition of probation, issuing a probationary license with such reasonable terms and conditions as shall be deemed by the department to be appropriate.

(Amended by Stats. 1963, Ch. 154.)

14250.5. The department, as a condition of probation, may require a person whose privilege to operate a motor vehicle is subject to suspension or revocation to attend, for not to exceed 24 hours, the program authorized by the provisions of Section 1659.

(Added by Stats. 1965, Ch. 447.)

14251. The department shall have authority to terminate or to modify the terms or conditions of any order of probation whenever good cause appears therefor.

(Enacted by Stats. 1959, Ch. 3.)

14252. The department upon receiving satisfactory evidence of a violation of any of the terms or conditions of probation imposed under this code, may withdraw the probationary license and order the suspension or revocation of the privilege to operate a motor vehicle.

(Enacted by Stats. 1959, Ch. 3.)

14253. Unless probation was imposed for a cause which is continuing, the probationer, after not less than one year, may request in writing the termination of the probation and the return of his regular license. Upon a showing that there has been no violation of the terms or conditions of the probation for a period of one year immediately preceding the request, the department shall terminate the probation and either restore to the person his driver's license or require an application for a new license.

(Enacted by Stats. 1959, Ch. 3.)

Article 5. Review of Orders

(Article 5 enacted by Stats. 1959, Ch. 3.)

14400. Nothing in this code shall be deemed to prevent a review or other action as may be permitted by the Constitution and laws of this State by a court of competent jurisdiction of any order of the department refusing, canceling, suspending, or revoking the privilege of a person to operate a motor vehicle.

(Enacted by Stats. 1959, Ch. 3.)

14401. (a) Any action brought in a court of competent jurisdiction to review any order of the department refusing, canceling, placing on probation, suspending, or revoking the privilege of a person to operate a motor vehicle shall be commenced within 90 days from the date the order is noticed.

(b) Upon final completion of all administrative appeals, the person whose driving privilege was refused, canceled, placed on probation, suspended, or revoked shall be given written notice by the department of his or her right to a review by a court pursuant to subdivision (a).

(Amended by Stats. 1985, Ch. 1008, Sec. 3.)

Chapter 4. Violation of License Provisions

(Chapter 4 enacted by Stats. 1959, Ch. 3.)

14600. (a) Whenever any person after applying for or receiving a driver's license moves to a new residence, or acquires a new mailing address different from the address shown in the application or in the license as issued, he or she shall within 10 days thereafter notify the department of both the old and new address. The department may issue a document to accompany the driver's license reflecting the new address of the holder of the license.

(b) When, pursuant to subdivision (b) of Section 12951, a driver presents his or her driver's license to a peace officer, he or she shall, if applicable, also present the document issued pursuant to subdivision (a) if the driver's license does not reflect the driver's current residence or mailing address.

(Amended by Stats. 1992, Ch. 1243, Sec. 86.4. Effective September 30, 1992.)

14601. (a) No person shall drive a motor vehicle at any time when that person's driving privilege is suspended or revoked for reckless driving in violation of Section 23103, 23104, or 23105, any reason listed in subdivision (a) or (c) of Section 12806 authorizing the department to refuse to issue a license, negligent or incompetent operation of a motor vehicle as prescribed in subdivision (e) of Section 12809, or negligent operation as prescribed in Section 12810.5, if the person so driving has knowledge of the suspension or revocation. Knowledge shall be conclusively presumed if mailed notice has been given by the department to the person pursuant to Section 13106. The presumption established by this subdivision is a presumption affecting the burden of proof.

(b) A person convicted under this section shall be punished as follows:

(1) Upon a first conviction, by imprisonment in a county jail for not less than five days or more than six months and by a fine of not less than three hundred dollars ($300) or more than one thousand dollars ($1,000).

(2) If the offense occurred within five years of a prior offense that resulted in a conviction of a violation of this section or Section 14601.1, 14601.2, or 14601.5, by imprisonment in a county jail for not less than 10 days or more than one year and by a fine of not less than five hundred dollars ($500) or more than two thousand dollars ($2,000).

(c) If the offense occurred within five years of a prior offense that resulted in a conviction of a violation of this section or Section 14601.1, 14601.2, or 14601.5, and is granted probation, the court shall impose as a condition of probation that the person be confined in a county jail for at least 10 days.

(d) Nothing in this section prohibits a person from driving a motor vehicle, that is owned or utilized by the person's employer, during the course of employment on private property that is owned or utilized by the employer, except an offstreet parking facility as defined in subdivision (c) of Section 12500.

(e) When the prosecution agrees to a plea of guilty or nolo contendere to a charge of a violation of this section in satisfaction of, or as a substitute for, an original charge of a violation of Section 14601.2, and the court accepts that plea, except, in the interest of justice, when the court finds it would be inappropriate, the court shall, pursuant to Section 23575, require the person convicted, in addition to any other requirements, to install a certified ignition interlock device on any vehicle that the person owns or operates for a period not to exceed three years.

(f) This section also applies to the operation of an off-highway motor vehicle on those lands to which the Chappie-Z'berg Off-Highway Motor Vehicle Law of 1971 (Division 16.5 (commencing with Section 38000)) applies as to off-highway motor vehicles, as described in Section 38001.

(Amended by Stats. 2007, Ch. 682, Sec. 14. Effective January 1, 2008.)

14601.1. (a) No person shall drive a motor vehicle when his or her driving privilege is suspended or revoked for any reason other than those listed in Section 14601, 14601.2, or 14601.5, if the person so driving has knowledge of the suspension or revocation. Knowledge shall be conclusively presumed if mailed notice has been given by the department to the person pursuant to Section 13106. The presumption established by this subdivision is a presumption affecting the burden of proof.

(b) Any person convicted under this section shall be punished as follows:

(1) Upon a first conviction, by imprisonment in the county jail for

not more than six months or by a fine of not less than three hundred dollars ($300) or more than one thousand dollars ($1,000), or by both that fine and imprisonment.

(2) If the offense occurred within five years of a prior offense which resulted in a conviction of a violation of this section or Section 14601, 14601.2, or 14601.5, by imprisonment in the county jail for not less than five days or more than one year and by a fine of not less than five hundred dollars ($500) or more than two thousand dollars ($2,000).

(c) Nothing in this section prohibits a person from driving a motor vehicle, which is owned or utilized by the person's employer, during the course of employment on private property which is owned or utilized by the employer, except an offstreet parking facility as defined in subdivision (d) of Section 12500.

(d) When the prosecution agrees to a plea of guilty or nolo contendere to a charge of a violation of this section in satisfaction of, or as a substitute for, an original charge of a violation of Section 14601.2, and the court accepts that plea, except, in the interest of justice, when the court finds it would be inappropriate, the court shall, pursuant to Section 23575, require the person convicted, in addition to any other requirements, to install a certified ignition interlock device on any vehicle that the person owns or operates for a period not to exceed three years.

(e) This section also applies to the operation of an off-highway motor vehicle on those lands to which the Chappie-Z'berg Off-Highway Motor Vehicle Law of 1971 (Division 16.5 (commencing with Section 38000)) applies as to off-highway motor vehicles, as described in Section 38001.
(Amended by Stats. 2004, Ch. 908, Sec. 15. Effective January 1, 2005.)

14601.2. (a) A person shall not drive a motor vehicle at any time when that person's driving privilege is suspended or revoked for a conviction of a violation of Section 23152 or 23153 if the person so driving has knowledge of the suspension or revocation.

(b) Except in full compliance with the restriction, a person shall not drive a motor vehicle at any time when that person's driving privilege is restricted if the person so driving has knowledge of the restriction.

(c) Knowledge of the suspension or revocation of the driving privilege shall be conclusively presumed if mailed notice has been given by the department to the person pursuant to Section 13106. Knowledge of the restriction of the driving privilege shall be presumed if notice has been given by the court to the person. The presumption established by this subdivision is a presumption affecting the burden of proof.

(d) A person convicted of a violation of this section shall be punished as follows:

(1) Upon a first conviction, by imprisonment in the county jail for not less than 10 days or more than six months and by a fine of not less than three hundred dollars ($300) or more than one thousand dollars ($1,000), unless the person has been designated a habitual traffic offender under subdivision (b) of Section 23546, subdivision (b) of Section 23550, or subdivision (d) of Section 23550.5, in which case the person, in addition, shall be sentenced as provided in paragraph (3) of subdivision (e) of Section 14601.3.

(2) If the offense occurred within five years of a prior offense that resulted in a conviction of a violation of this section or Section 14601, 14601.1, or 14601.5, by imprisonment in the county jail for not less than 30 days or more than one year and by a fine of not less than five hundred dollars ($500) or more than two thousand dollars ($2,000), unless the person has been designated a habitual traffic offender under subdivision (b) of Section 23546, subdivision (b) of Section 23550, or subdivision (d) of Section 23550.5, in which case the person, in addition, shall be sentenced as provided in paragraph (3) of subdivision (e) of Section 14601.3.

(e) If a person is convicted of a first offense under this section and is granted probation, the court shall impose as a condition of probation that the person be confined in the county jail for at least 10 days.

(f) If the offense occurred within five years of a prior offense that resulted in a conviction of a violation of this section or Section 14601, 14601.1, or 14601.5 and is granted probation, the court shall impose as a condition of probation that the person be confined in the county jail for at least 30 days.

(g) If a person is convicted of a second or subsequent offense that results in a conviction of this section within seven years, but over five years, of a prior offense that resulted in a conviction of a violation of this section or Section 14601, 14601.1, or 14601.5 and is granted probation, the court shall impose as a condition of probation that the person be confined in the county jail for at least 10 days.

(h) Pursuant to Section 23575, the court shall require a person convicted of a violation of this section to install a certified ignition interlock device on a vehicle the person owns or operates. Upon receipt of the abstract of a conviction under this section, the department shall not reinstate the privilege to operate a motor vehicle until the department receives proof of either the "Verification of Installation" form as described in paragraph (2) of subdivision (h) of Section 13386 or the Judicial Council Form I.D. 100.

(i) This section does not prohibit a person who is participating in, or has completed, an alcohol or drug rehabilitation program from driving a motor vehicle that is owned or utilized by the person's employer, during the course of employment on private property that is owned or utilized by the employer, except an offstreet parking facility, as defined in subdivision (c) of Section 12500.

(j) This section also applies to the operation of an off-highway motor vehicle on those lands that the Chappie-Z'berg Off-Highway Motor Vehicle Law of 1971 (Division 16.5 (commencing with Section 38000)) applies as to off-highway motor vehicles, as described in Section 38001.

(k) If Section 23573 is applicable, then subdivision (h) is not applicable.
(Amended by Stats. 2014, Ch. 71, Sec. 173. (SB 1304) Effective January 1, 2015.)

14601.3. (a) It is unlawful for a person whose driving privilege has been suspended or revoked to accumulate a driving record history which results from driving during the period of suspension or revocation. A person who violates this subdivision is designated an habitual traffic offender.

For purposes of this section, a driving record history means any of the following, if the driving occurred during any period of suspension or revocation:

(1) Two or more convictions within a 12-month period of an offense given a violation point count of two pursuant to Section 12810.

(2) Three or more convictions within a 12-month period of an offense given a violation point count of one pursuant to Section 12810.

(3) Three or more accidents within a 12-month period that are subject to the reporting requirements of Section 16000.

(4) Any combination of convictions or accidents, as specified in paragraphs (1) to (3), inclusive, which results during any 12-month period in a violation point count of three or more pursuant to Section 12810.

(b) Knowledge of suspension or revocation of the driving privilege shall be conclusively presumed if mailed notice has been given by the department to the person pursuant to Section 13106. The presumption established by this subdivision is a presumption affecting the burden of proof.

(c) The department, within 30 days of receipt of a duly certified abstract of the record of any court or accident report which results in a person being designated an habitual traffic offender, may execute and transmit by mail a notice of that designation to the office of the district attorney having jurisdiction over the location of the person's last known address as contained in the department's records.

(d) (1) The district attorney, within 30 days of receiving the notice required in subdivision (c), shall inform the department of whether or not the person will be prosecuted for being an habitual traffic offender.

(2) Notwithstanding any other provision of this section, any habitual traffic offender designated under subdivision (b) of Section 23546, subdivision (b) of Section 23550, or subdivision (b) of Section 23550.5, who is convicted of violating Section 14601.2 shall be sentenced as

provided in paragraph (3) of subdivision (e).

(e) Any person convicted under this section of being an habitual traffic offender shall be punished as follows:

(1) Upon a first conviction, by imprisonment in the county jail for 30 days and by a fine of one thousand dollars ($1,000).

(2) Upon a second or any subsequent offense within seven years of a prior conviction under this section, by imprisonment in the county jail for 180 days and by a fine of two thousand dollars ($2,000).

(3) Any habitual traffic offender designated under Section 193.7 of the Penal Code or under subdivision (b) of Section 23546, subdivision (b) of Section 23550, subdivision (b) of Section 23550.5, or subdivision (d) of Section 23566 who is convicted of a violation of Section 14601.2 shall be punished by imprisonment in the county jail for 180 days and by a fine of two thousand dollars ($2,000). The penalty in this paragraph shall be consecutive to that imposed for the violation of any other law.

(f) This section also applies to the operation of an off-highway motor vehicle on those lands to which the Chappie-Z'berg Off-Highway Motor Vehicle Law of 1971 (Division 16.5 (commencing with Section 38000)) applies as to off-highway motor vehicles, as described in Section 38001.

(Amended by Stats. 2004, Ch. 908, Sec. 17. Effective January 1, 2005.)

14601.4. (a) It is unlawful for a person, while driving a vehicle with a license suspended or revoked pursuant to Section 14601.2 to do an act forbidden by law or neglect a duty imposed by law in the driving of the vehicle, which act or neglect proximately causes bodily injury to a person other than the driver. In proving the person neglected a duty imposed by law in the driving of the vehicle, it is not necessary to prove that a specific section of this code was violated.

(b) A person convicted under this section shall be imprisoned in the county jail and shall not be released upon work release, community service, or other release program before the minimum period of imprisonment, prescribed in Section 14601.2, is served. If a person is convicted of that offense and is granted probation, the court shall require that the person convicted serve at least the minimum time of imprisonment, as specified in those sections, as a term or condition of probation.

(c) When the prosecution agrees to a plea of guilty or nolo contendere to a charge of a violation of this section in satisfaction of, or as a substitute for, an original charge of a violation of Section 14601.2, and the court accepts that plea, except, in the interest of justice, when the court finds it should be inappropriate, the court shall, pursuant to Section 23575, require the person convicted, in addition to other requirements, to install a certified ignition interlock device on a vehicle that the person owns or operates for a period not to exceed three years.

(d) This section also applies to the operation of an off-highway motor vehicle on those lands that the Chappie-Z'berg Off-Highway Motor Vehicle Law of 1971 (Division 16.5 (commencing with Section 38000)) applies as to off-highway motor vehicles, as described in Section 38001.

(e) Upon receipt of the abstract of a conviction under this section, the department shall not reinstate the privilege to operate a motor vehicle until the department receives proof of either the "Verification of Installation" form as described in paragraph (2) of subdivision (g) of Section 13386 or the Judicial Council Form I.D. 100.

(f) If Section 23573 is applicable, then subdivisions (c) and (e) are not applicable.

(Amended by Stats. 2008, Ch. 404, Sec. 2. Effective January 1, 2009.)

14601.5. (a) A person shall not drive a motor vehicle at any time when that person's driving privilege is suspended or revoked pursuant to Section 13353, 13353.1, or 13353.2 and that person has knowledge of the suspension or revocation.

(b) Except in full compliance with the restriction, a person shall not drive a motor vehicle at any time when that person's driving privilege is restricted pursuant to Section 13353.7 or 13353.8 and that person has knowledge of the restriction.

(c) Knowledge of suspension, revocation, or restriction of the driving privilege shall be conclusively presumed if notice has been given by the department to the person pursuant to Section 13106. The presumption established by this subdivision is a presumption affecting the burden of proof.

(d) A person convicted of a violation of this section is punishable, as follows:

(1) Upon a first conviction, by imprisonment in the county jail for not more than six months or by a fine of not less than three hundred dollars ($300) or more than one thousand dollars ($1,000), or by both that fine and imprisonment.

(2) If the offense occurred within five years of a prior offense that resulted in a conviction for a violation of this section or Section 14601, 14601.1, 14601.2, or 14601.3, by imprisonment in the county jail for not less than 10 days or more than one year, and by a fine of not less than five hundred dollars ($500) or more than two thousand dollars ($2,000).

(e) In imposing the minimum fine required by subdivision (d), the court shall take into consideration the defendant's ability to pay the fine and may, in the interest of justice, and for reasons stated in the record, reduce the amount of that minimum fine to less than the amount otherwise imposed.

(f) This section does not prohibit a person who is participating in, or has completed, an alcohol or drug rehabilitation program from driving a motor vehicle, that is owned or utilized by the person's employer, during the course of employment on private property that is owned or utilized by the employer, except an offstreet parking facility as defined in subdivision (c) of Section 12500.

(g) When the prosecution agrees to a plea of guilty or nolo contendere to a charge of a violation of this section in satisfaction of, or as a substitute for, an original charge of a violation of Section 14601.2, and the court accepts that plea, except, in the interest of justice, when the court finds it would be inappropriate, the court shall, pursuant to Section 23575, require the person convicted, in addition to other requirements, to install a certified ignition interlock device on a vehicle that the person owns or operates for a period not to exceed three years.

(h) This section also applies to the operation of an off-highway motor vehicle on those lands that the Chappie-Z'berg Off-Highway Motor Vehicle Law of 1971 (Division 16.5 (commencing with Section 38000)) applies as to off-highway motor vehicles, as described in Section 38001.

(i) Upon receipt of the abstract of a conviction under this section, the department shall not reinstate the privilege to operate a motor vehicle until the department receives proof of either the "Verification of Installation" form as described in paragraph (2) of subdivision (g) of Section 13386 or the Judicial Council Form I.D. 100.

(j) If Section 23573 is applicable, then subdivisions (g) and (i) are not applicable.

(Amended by Stats. 2008, Ch. 404, Sec. 3. Effective January 1, 2009.)

14601.8. The judge may, in his or her discretion, allow any person convicted of a violation of Section 14601 or 14601.1 to serve his or her sentence on a sufficient number of consecutive weekend days to complete the sentence.

(Added by renumbering Section 14601.5 by Stats. 1992, Ch. 982, Sec. 1. Effective January 1, 1993.)

14602. In accordance with subdivision (p) of Section 22651, a vehicle removed pursuant to subdivision (c) of Section 2814.2 shall be released to the registered owner or his or her agent at any time the facility to which the vehicle has been removed is open upon presentation of the registered owner's or his or her agent's currently valid driver's license to operate the vehicle and proof of current vehicle registration.

(Added by Stats. 2011, Ch. 653, Sec. 3. (AB 353) Effective January 1, 2012.)

14602.1. (a) Every state and local law enforcement agency, including, but not limited to, city police departments and county sheriffs' offices, shall report to the Department of the California Highway Patrol, on a paper or electronic form developed and approved by the Department of the California Highway Patrol, all motor vehicle pursuit data.

(b) Effective January 1, 2006, the form shall require the reporting of all motor vehicle pursuit data, which shall include, but not be limited to, all of the following:

(1) Whether any person involved in a pursuit or a subsequent arrest was injured, specifying the nature of that injury. For all purposes of this section, the form shall differentiate between the suspect driver, a suspect passenger, and the peace officers involved.

(2) The violations that caused the pursuit to be initiated.

(3) The identity of the peace officers involved in the pursuit.

(4) The means or methods used to stop the suspect being pursued.

(5) All charges filed with the court by the district attorney.

(6) The conditions of the pursuit, including, but not limited to, all of the following:

(A) Duration.

(B) Mileage.

(C) Number of peace officers involved.

(D) Maximum number of law enforcement vehicles involved.

(E) Time of day.

(F) Weather conditions.

(G) Maximum speeds.

(7) Whether a pursuit resulted in a collision, and a resulting injury or fatality to an uninvolved third party, and the corresponding number of persons involved.

(8) Whether the pursuit involved multiple law enforcement agencies.

(9) How the pursuit was terminated.

(c) In order to minimize costs, the department, upon updating the form, shall update the corresponding database to include all of the reporting requirements specified in subdivision (b).

(d) All motor vehicle pursuit data obtained pursuant to subdivision (b) shall be submitted to the Department of the California Highway Patrol no later than 30 days following a motor vehicle pursuit.

(e) The Department of the California Highway Patrol shall submit annually to the Legislature a report that includes, but is not limited to, the following information:

(1) The number of motor vehicle pursuits reported to the Department of the California Highway Patrol during that year.

(2) The number of those motor vehicle pursuits that reportedly resulted in a collision in which an injury or fatality to an uninvolved third party occurred.

(3) The total number of uninvolved third parties who were injured or killed as a result of those collisions during that year.

(Amended by Stats. 2005, Ch. 485, Sec. 9. Effective January 1, 2006.)

14602.5. (a) Whenever a person is convicted for driving any class M1 or M2 motor vehicle, while his or her driving privilege has been suspended or revoked, of which vehicle he or she is the owner, or of which the owner permitted the operation, knowing the person's driving privilege was suspended or revoked, the court may, at the time sentence is imposed on the person, order the motor vehicle impounded in any manner as the court may determine, for a period not to exceed six months for a first conviction, and not to exceed 12 months for a second or subsequent conviction. For the purposes of this section, a "second or subsequent conviction" includes a conviction for any offense described in this section. The cost of keeping the vehicle shall be a lien on the vehicle, pursuant to Chapter 6.5 (commencing with Section 3067) of Title 14 of Part 4 of Division 3 of the Civil Code.

(b) Notwithstanding subdivision (a), any motor vehicle impounded pursuant to this section which is subject to a chattel mortgage, conditional sale contract, or lease contract shall, upon the filing of an affidavit by the legal owner that the chattel mortgage, conditional sale contract, or lease contract is in default, be released by the court to the legal owner, and shall be delivered to him or her upon payment of the accrued cost of keeping the motor vehicle.

(Added by Stats. 1990, Ch. 1359, Sec. 5.)

14602.6. (a) (1) Whenever a peace officer determines that a person was driving a vehicle while his or her driving privilege was suspended or revoked, driving a vehicle while his or her driving privilege is restricted pursuant to Section 13352 or 23575 and the vehicle is not equipped with a functioning, certified interlock device, or driving a vehicle without ever having been issued a driver's license, the peace officer may either immediately arrest that person and cause the removal and seizure of that vehicle or, if the vehicle is involved in a traffic collision, cause the removal and seizure of the vehicle without the necessity of arresting the person in accordance with Chapter 10 (commencing with Section 22650) of Division 11. A vehicle so impounded shall be impounded for 30 days.

(2) The impounding agency, within two working days of impoundment, shall send a notice by certified mail, return receipt requested, to the legal owner of the vehicle, at the address obtained from the department, informing the owner that the vehicle has been impounded. Failure to notify the legal owner within two working days shall prohibit the impounding agency from charging for more than 15 days' impoundment when the legal owner redeems the impounded vehicle. The impounding agency shall maintain a published telephone number that provides information 24 hours a day regarding the impoundment of vehicles and the rights of a registered owner to request a hearing. The law enforcement agency shall be open to issue a release to the registered owner or legal owner, or the agent of either, whenever the agency is open to serve the public for nonemergency business.

(b) The registered and legal owner of a vehicle that is removed and seized under subdivision (a) or their agents shall be provided the opportunity for a storage hearing to determine the validity of, or consider any mitigating circumstances attendant to, the storage, in accordance with Section 22852.

(c) Any period in which a vehicle is subjected to storage under this section shall be included as part of the period of impoundment ordered by the court under subdivision (a) of Section 14602.5.

(d) (1) An impounding agency shall release a vehicle to the registered owner or his or her agent prior to the end of 30 days' impoundment under any of the following circumstances:

(A) When the vehicle is a stolen vehicle.

(B) When the vehicle is subject to bailment and is driven by an unlicensed employee of a business establishment, including a parking service or repair garage.

(C) When the license of the driver was suspended or revoked for an offense other than those included in Article 2 (commencing with Section 13200) of Chapter 2 of Division 6 or Article 3 (commencing with Section 13350) of Chapter 2 of Division 6.

(D) When the vehicle was seized under this section for an offense that does not authorize the seizure of the vehicle.

(E) When the driver reinstates his or her driver's license or acquires a driver's license and proper insurance.

(2) No vehicle shall be released pursuant to this subdivision without presentation of the registered owner's or agent's currently valid driver's license to operate the vehicle and proof of current vehicle registration, or upon order of a court.

(e) The registered owner or his or her agent is responsible for all towing and storage charges related to the impoundment, and any administrative charges authorized under Section 22850.5.

(f) A vehicle removed and seized under subdivision (a) shall be released to the legal owner of the vehicle or the legal owner's agent prior to the end of 30 days' impoundment if all of the following conditions are met:

(1) The legal owner is a motor vehicle dealer, bank, credit union, acceptance corporation, or other licensed financial institution legally operating in this state or is another person, not the registered owner, holding a security interest in the vehicle.

(2) (A) The legal owner or the legal owner's agent pays all towing and storage fees related to the seizure of the vehicle. No lien sale processing fees shall be charged to the legal owner who redeems the vehicle prior to the 15th day of impoundment. Neither the impounding authority nor

any person having possession of the vehicle shall collect from the legal owner of the type specified in paragraph (1), or the legal owner's agent any administrative charges imposed pursuant to Section 22850.5 unless the legal owner voluntarily requested a poststorage hearing.

(B) A person operating or in charge of a storage facility where vehicles are stored pursuant to this section shall accept a valid bank credit card or cash for payment of towing, storage, and related fees by a legal or registered owner or the owner's agent claiming the vehicle. A credit card shall be in the name of the person presenting the card. "Credit card" means "credit card" as defined in subdivision (a) of Section 1747.02 of the Civil Code, except, for the purposes of this section, credit card does not include a credit card issued by a retail seller.

(C) A person operating or in charge of a storage facility described in subparagraph (B) who violates subparagraph (B) shall be civilly liable to the owner of the vehicle or to the person who tendered the fees for four times the amount of the towing, storage, and related fees, but not to exceed five hundred dollars ($500).

(D) A person operating or in charge of a storage facility described in subparagraph (B) shall have sufficient funds on the premises of the primary storage facility during normal business hours to accommodate, and make change in, a reasonable monetary transaction.

(E) Credit charges for towing and storage services shall comply with Section 1748.1 of the Civil Code. Law enforcement agencies may include the costs of providing for payment by credit when making agreements with towing companies on rates.

(3) The legal owner or the legal owner's agent presents a copy of the assignment, as defined in subdivision (b) of Section 7500.1 of the Business and Professions Code; a release from the one responsible governmental agency, only if required by the agency; a government-issued photographic identification card; and any one of the following, as determined by the legal owner or the legal owner's agent: a certificate of repossession for the vehicle, a security agreement for the vehicle, or title, whether paper or electronic, showing proof of legal ownership for the vehicle. Any documents presented may be originals, photocopies, or facsimile copies, or may be transmitted electronically. The law enforcement agency, impounding agency, or any other governmental agency, or any person acting on behalf of those agencies, shall not require any documents to be notarized. The law enforcement agency, impounding agency, or any person acting on behalf of those agencies may require the agent of the legal owner to produce a photocopy or facsimile copy of its repossession agency license or registration issued pursuant to Chapter 11 (commencing with Section 7500) of Division 3 of the Business and Professions Code, or to demonstrate, to the satisfaction of the law enforcement agency, impounding agency, or any person acting on behalf of those agencies, that the agent is exempt from licensure pursuant to Section 7500.2 or 7500.3 of the Business and Professions Code.

No administrative costs authorized under subdivision (a) of Section 22850.5 shall be charged to the legal owner of the type specified in paragraph (1), who redeems the vehicle unless the legal owner voluntarily requests a poststorage hearing. No city, county, city and county, or state agency shall require a legal owner or a legal owner's agent to request a poststorage hearing as a requirement for release of the vehicle to the legal owner or the legal owner's agent. The law enforcement agency, impounding agency, or other governmental agency, or any person acting on behalf of those agencies, shall not require any documents other than those specified in this paragraph. The law enforcement agency, impounding agency, or other governmental agency, or any person acting on behalf of those agencies, shall not require any documents to be notarized. The legal owner or the legal owner's agent shall be given a copy of any documents he or she is required to sign, except for a vehicle evidentiary hold logbook. The law enforcement agency, impounding agency, or any person acting on behalf of those agencies, or any person in possession of the vehicle, may photocopy and retain the copies of any documents presented by the legal owner or legal owner's agent.

(4) A failure by a storage facility to comply with any applicable conditions set forth in this subdivision shall not affect the right of the legal owner or the legal owner's agent to retrieve the vehicle, provided all conditions required of the legal owner or legal owner's agent under this subdivision are satisfied.

(g) (1) A legal owner or the legal owner's agent that obtains release of the vehicle pursuant to subdivision (f) shall not release the vehicle to the registered owner of the vehicle, or the person who was listed as the registered owner when the vehicle was impounded, or any agents of the registered owner, unless the registered owner is a rental car agency, until after the termination of the 30-day impoundment period.

(2) The legal owner or the legal owner's agent shall not relinquish the vehicle to the registered owner or the person who was listed as the registered owner when the vehicle was impounded until the registered owner or that owner's agent presents his or her valid driver's license or valid temporary driver's license to the legal owner or the legal owner's agent. The legal owner or the legal owner's agent or the person in possession of the vehicle shall make every reasonable effort to ensure that the license presented is valid and possession of the vehicle will not be given to the driver who was involved in the original impoundment proceeding until the expiration of the impoundment period.

(3) Prior to relinquishing the vehicle, the legal owner may require the registered owner to pay all towing and storage charges related to the impoundment and any administrative charges authorized under Section 22850.5 that were incurred by the legal owner in connection with obtaining custody of the vehicle.

(4) Any legal owner who knowingly releases or causes the release of a vehicle to a registered owner or the person in possession of the vehicle at the time of the impoundment or any agent of the registered owner in violation of this subdivision shall be guilty of a misdemeanor and subject to a fine in the amount of two thousand dollars ($2,000) in addition to any other penalties established by law.

(5) The legal owner, registered owner, or person in possession of the vehicle shall not change or attempt to change the name of the legal owner or the registered owner on the records of the department until the vehicle is released from the impoundment.

(h) (1) A vehicle removed and seized under subdivision (a) shall be released to a rental car agency prior to the end of 30 days' impoundment if the agency is either the legal owner or registered owner of the vehicle and the agency pays all towing and storage fees related to the seizure of the vehicle.

(2) The owner of a rental vehicle that was seized under this section may continue to rent the vehicle upon recovery of the vehicle. However, the rental car agency may not rent another vehicle to the driver of the vehicle that was seized until 30 days after the date that the vehicle was seized.

(3) The rental car agency may require the person to whom the vehicle was rented to pay all towing and storage charges related to the impoundment and any administrative charges authorized under Section 22850.5 that were incurred by the rental car agency in connection with obtaining custody of the vehicle.

(i) Notwithstanding any other provision of this section, the registered owner and not the legal owner shall remain responsible for any towing and storage charges related to the impoundment, any administrative charges authorized under Section 22850.5, and any parking fines, penalties, and administrative fees incurred by the registered owner.

(j) (1) The law enforcement agency and the impounding agency, including any storage facility acting on behalf of the law enforcement agency or impounding agency, shall comply with this section and shall not be liable to the registered owner for the improper release of the vehicle to the legal owner or the legal owner's agent provided the release complies with the provisions of this section. A law enforcement agency shall not refuse to issue a release to a legal owner or the agent of a legal owner on the grounds that it previously issued a release.

(2) (A) The legal owner of collateral shall, by operation of law and without requiring further action, indemnify and hold harmless a law enforcement agency, city, county, city and county, the state, a tow yard, storage facility, or an impounding yard from a claim arising out of the release of the collateral to a licensed repossessor or licensed repossession agency, and from any damage to the collateral after its release, including reasonable attorney's fees and costs associated with defending a claim, if the collateral was released in compliance with this section.

(B) This subdivision shall apply only when collateral is released to a licensed repossessor, licensed repossession agency, or its officers or employees pursuant to Chapter 11 (commencing with Section 7500) of Division 3 of the Business and Professions Code.

(Amended by Stats. 2015, Ch. 740, Sec. 14. (AB 281) Effective January 1, 2016.)

14602.7. (a) (1) A magistrate presented with the affidavit of a peace officer establishing reasonable cause to believe that a vehicle, described by vehicle type and license number or vehicle identification number, was an instrumentality used in the peace officer's presence in violation of Section 2800.1, 2800.2, 2800.3, 23103, or subdivision (a) or (c) of Section 23109, shall issue a warrant or court order authorizing any peace officer to immediately seize and cause the removal of the vehicle. The warrant or court order may be entered into a computerized database. The vehicle may be impounded for a period not to exceed 30 days.

(2) The impounding agency, within two working days of impoundment, excluding weekends and holidays, shall send a notice by certified mail, return receipt requested, or electronic service as provided for under Section 690.5 of the Penal Code, to the legal owner of the vehicle, at the address obtained from the department, informing the owner that the vehicle has been impounded and providing the owner with a copy of the warrant or court order. Failure to notify the legal owner within two working days shall prohibit the impounding agency from charging for more than 15 days impoundment when a legal owner redeems the impounded vehicle. The law enforcement agency shall be open to issue a release to the registered owner or legal owner, or the agent of either, whenever the agency is open to serve the public for regular, nonemergency business.

(b) (1) An impounding agency shall release a vehicle to the registered owner or their agent before the end of the impoundment period and without the permission of the magistrate authorizing the vehicle's seizure under any of the following circumstances:

(A) When the vehicle is a stolen vehicle.

(B) When the vehicle is subject to bailment and is driven by an unlicensed employee of the business establishment, including a parking service or repair garage.

(C) When the registered owner of the vehicle causes a peace officer to reasonably believe, based on the totality of the circumstances, that the registered owner was not the driver who violated Section 2800.1, 2800.2, or 2800.3, the agency shall immediately release the vehicle to the registered owner or their agent.

(2) A vehicle shall not be released pursuant to this subdivision, except upon presentation of the registered owner's or agent's currently valid driver's license to operate the vehicle and proof of current vehicle registration, or upon order of the court.

(c) (1) Whenever a vehicle is impounded under this section, the magistrate ordering the storage shall provide the vehicle's registered and legal owners of record, or their agents, with the opportunity for a poststorage hearing to determine the validity of the storage.

(2) A notice of the storage hearing shall be sent by certified mail, return receipt requested, or by electronic service pursuant to Section 690.5 of the Penal Code, to the registered and legal owner of the vehicle within 48 hours of impoundment, excluding weekends and holidays, by the person or agency executing the warrant or court order, and shall include all of the following information:

(A) The name, address, and telephone number of the agency providing the notice.

(B) The location of the place of storage and a description of the vehicle, which shall include, if available, the name or make, the manufacturer, the license plate number, and the mileage of the vehicle.

(C) A copy of the warrant or court order and the peace officer's affidavit, as described in subdivision (a).

(D) A statement that, in order to receive their poststorage hearing, the owners, or their agents, are required to request the hearing from the magistrate issuing the warrant or court order within 10 days of the date of the notice, and serve notice of the hearing on the person or agency who executed the warrant or court order.

(3) The poststorage hearing shall be conducted within two court days after receipt of the request for the hearing.

(4) At the hearing, the magistrate may order the vehicle released if they find any of the circumstances described in subdivision (b) or (e) that allow release of a vehicle by the impounding agency. The magistrate may also consider releasing the vehicle when the continued impoundment will cause undue hardship to persons dependent upon the vehicle for employment or to a person with a community property interest in the vehicle.

(5) Failure of either the registered or legal owner, or their agent, to request, or to attend, a scheduled hearing satisfies the poststorage hearing requirement.

(6) The agency employing the peace officer who caused the magistrate to issue the warrant or court order shall be responsible for the costs incurred for towing and storage if it is determined in the poststorage hearing that reasonable cause for the impoundment and storage are not established.

(d) The registered owner or their agent is responsible for all towing and storage charges related to the impoundment, and any administrative charges authorized under Section 22850.5.

(e) A vehicle removed and seized under subdivision (a) shall be released to the legal owner of the vehicle or the legal owner's agent before the end of the impoundment period and without the permission of the magistrate authorizing the seizure of the vehicle if all of the following conditions are met:

(1) The legal owner is a motor vehicle dealer, bank, credit union, acceptance corporation, or other licensed financial institution legally operating in this state or is another person, not the registered owner, holding a financial interest in the vehicle.

(2) (A) The legal owner or the legal owner's agent pays all towing and storage fees related to the seizure of the vehicle. A lien sale processing fees shall not be charged to the legal owner who redeems the vehicle before the 15th day of impoundment. Neither the impounding authority nor any person having possession of the vehicle shall collect from the legal owner of the type specified in paragraph (1), or the legal owner's agent any administrative charges imposed pursuant to Section 22850.5 unless the legal owner voluntarily requested a poststorage hearing.

(B) A person operating or in charge of a storage facility where vehicles are stored pursuant to this section shall accept a valid bank credit card or cash for payment of towing, storage, and related fees by a legal or registered owner or the owner's agent claiming the vehicle. A credit card shall be in the name of the person presenting the card. "Credit card" means "credit card" as defined in subdivision (a) of Section 1747.02 of the Civil Code, except, for the purposes of this section, credit card does not include a credit card issued by a retail seller.

(C) A person operating or in charge of a storage facility described in subparagraph (B) who violates subparagraph (B) shall be civilly liable to the owner of the vehicle or to the person who tendered the fees for four times the amount of the towing, storage and related fees, but not to exceed five hundred dollars ($500).

(D) A person operating or in charge of a storage facility described in subparagraph (B) shall have sufficient funds on the premises of the primary storage facility during normal business hours to accommodate, and make change in, a reasonable monetary transaction.

(E) Credit charges for towing and storage services shall comply with Section 1748.1 of the Civil Code. Law enforcement agencies may include the costs of providing for payment by credit when making agreements with towing companies on rates.

(3) (A) The legal owner or the legal owner's agent presents, to the law enforcement agency, impounding agency, person in possession of the vehicle, or any person acting on behalf of those agencies, a copy of the assignment, as defined in subdivision (b) of Section 7500.1 of the Business and Professions Code; a release from the one responsible governmental agency, only if required by the agency; a government-issued photographic identification card; and any one of the following, as determined by the legal owner or the legal owner's agent: a certificate of repossession for the vehicle, a security agreement for the vehicle, or title, whether paper or electronic, showing proof of legal ownership for the vehicle. Any documents presented may be originals, photocopies, or facsimile copies, or may be transmitted electronically. The law enforcement agency, impounding agency, or any other governmental agency, or any person acting on behalf of those agencies, shall not require any documents to be notarized. The law enforcement agency, impounding agency, or any person acting on behalf of those agencies, may require the agent of the legal owner to produce a photocopy or facsimile copy of its repossession agency license or registration issued pursuant to Chapter 11 (commencing with Section 7500) of Division 3 of the Business and Professions Code, or to demonstrate, to the satisfaction of the law enforcement agency, impounding agency, or any person acting on behalf of those agencies that the agent is exempt from licensure pursuant to Section 7500.2 or 7500.3 of the Business and Professions Code.

(B) Administrative costs authorized under subdivision (a) of Section 22850.5 shall not be charged to the legal owner of the type specified in paragraph (1), who redeems the vehicle unless the legal owner voluntarily requests a poststorage hearing. A city, county, city and county, or state agency shall not require a legal owner or a legal owner's agent to request a poststorage hearing as a requirement for release of the vehicle to the legal owner or the legal owner's agent. The law enforcement agency, impounding agency, or other governmental agency, or any person acting on behalf of those agencies, shall not require any documents other than those specified in this paragraph. The law enforcement agency, impounding agency, or other governmental agency, or any person acting on behalf of those agencies, shall not require any documents to be notarized. The legal owner or the legal owner's agent shall be given a copy of any documents they are required to sign, except for a vehicle evidentiary hold logbook. The law enforcement agency, impounding agency, or any person acting on behalf of those agencies, or any person in possession of the vehicle, may photocopy and retain the copies of any documents presented by the legal owner or legal owner's agent.

(4) A failure by a storage facility to comply with any applicable conditions set forth in this subdivision shall not affect the right of the legal owner or the legal owner's agent to retrieve the vehicle, provided all conditions required of the legal owner or legal owner's agent under this subdivision are satisfied.

(f) (1) A legal owner or the legal owner's agent that obtains release of the vehicle pursuant to subdivision (e) shall not release the vehicle to the registered owner or the person who was listed as the registered owner when the vehicle was impounded of the vehicle or any agents of the registered owner, unless a registered owner is a rental car agency, until the termination of the impoundment period.

(2) The legal owner or the legal owner's agent shall not relinquish the vehicle to the registered owner or the person who was listed as the registered owner when the vehicle was impounded until the registered owner or that owner's agent presents their valid driver's license or valid temporary driver's license to the legal owner or the legal owner's agent. The legal owner or the legal owner's agent shall make every reasonable effort to ensure that the license presented is valid and possession of the vehicle will not be given to the driver who was involved in the original impoundment proceeding until the expiration of the impoundment period.

(3) Before relinquishing the vehicle, the legal owner may require the registered owner to pay all towing and storage charges related to the impoundment and the administrative charges authorized under Section 22850.5 that were incurred by the legal owner in connection with obtaining the custody of the vehicle.

(4) Any legal owner who knowingly releases or causes the release of a vehicle to a registered owner or the person in possession of the vehicle at the time of the impoundment or any agent of the registered owner in violation of this subdivision shall be guilty of a misdemeanor and subject to a fine in the amount of two thousand dollars ($2,000) in addition to any other penalties established by law.

(5) The legal owner, registered owner, or person in possession of the vehicle shall not change or attempt to change the name of the legal owner or the registered owner on the records of the department until the vehicle is released from the impoundment.

(g) (1) A vehicle impounded and seized under subdivision (a) shall be released to a rental car agency before the end of the impoundment period if the agency is either the legal owner or registered owner of the vehicle and the agency pays all towing and storage fees related to the seizure of the vehicle.

(2) The owner of a rental vehicle that was seized under this section may continue to rent the vehicle upon recovery of the vehicle. However, the rental car agency shall not rent another vehicle to the driver who used the vehicle that was seized to evade a police officer until 30 days after the date that the vehicle was seized.

(3) The rental car agency may require the person to whom the vehicle was rented and who evaded the peace officer to pay all towing and storage charges related to the impoundment and any administrative charges authorized under Section 22850.5 that were incurred by the rental car agency in connection with obtaining custody of the vehicle.

(h) Notwithstanding any other provision of this section, the registered owner and not the legal owner shall remain responsible for any towing and storage charges related to the impoundment and the administrative charges authorized under Section 22850.5 and any parking fines, penalties, and administrative fees incurred by the registered owner.

(i) (1) This section does not apply to vehicles abated under the Abandoned Vehicle Abatement Program pursuant to Sections 22660 to 22668, inclusive, and Section 22710, or to vehicles impounded for investigation pursuant to Section 22655, or to vehicles removed from private property pursuant to Section 22658.

(2) This section does not apply to abandoned vehicles removed pursuant to Section 22669 that are determined by the public agency to have an estimated value of three hundred dollars ($300) or less.

(j) The law enforcement agency and the impounding agency, including any storage facility acting on behalf of the law enforcement agency or impounding agency, shall comply with this section and shall not be liable to the registered owner for the improper release of the vehicle to the legal owner or the legal owner's agent provided the release complies with the provisions of this section. The legal owner shall indemnify and hold harmless a storage facility from any claims arising out of the release of the vehicle to the legal owner or the legal owner's agent and from any damage to the vehicle after its release, including the reasonable costs associated with defending any such claims. A law enforcement agency shall not refuse to issue a release to a legal owner or the agent of a legal owner on the grounds that it previously issued a release.

(Amended by Stats. 2024, Ch. 504, Sec. 1. (AB 3085) Effective January 1, 2025.)

14602.8. (a) (1) If a peace officer determines that a person has been convicted of a violation of Section 23140, 23152, or 23153, that the violation occurred within the preceding 10 years, and that one or more of the following circumstances applies to that person, the officer may immediately cause the removal and seizure of the vehicle that the person was driving, under either of the following circumstances:

(A) The person was driving a vehicle when the person had 0.10 percent or more, by weight, of alcohol in his or her blood.

(B) The person driving the vehicle refused to submit to or complete a chemical test requested by the peace officer.

(2) A vehicle impounded pursuant to paragraph (1) shall be impounded for the following period of time:

(A) Five days, if the person has been convicted once of violating Section 23140, 23152, or 23153, and the violation occurred within the preceding 10 years.

(B) Fifteen days, if the person has been convicted two or more times of violating Section 23140, 23152, or 23153, or any combination thereof, and the violations occurred within the preceding 10 years.

(3) Within two working days after impoundment, the impounding agency shall send a notice by certified mail, return receipt requested, to the legal owner of the vehicle, at the address obtained from the department, informing the owner that the vehicle has been impounded. Failure to notify the legal owner within two working days shall prohibit the impounding agency from charging for more than five days' impoundment when the legal owner redeems the impounded vehicle. The impounding agency shall maintain a published telephone number that provides information 24 hours a day regarding the impoundment of vehicles and the rights of a registered owner to request a hearing. The law enforcement agency shall be open to issue a release to the registered owner or legal owner, or the agent of either, whenever the agency is open to serve the public for regular, nonemergency business.

(b) The registered and legal owner of a vehicle that is removed and seized under subdivision (a) or his or her agent shall be provided the opportunity for a storage hearing to determine the validity of, or consider any mitigating circumstances attendant to, the storage, in accordance with Section 22852.

(c) Any period during which a vehicle is subjected to storage under this section shall be included as part of the period of impoundment ordered by the court under Section 23594.

(d) (1) The impounding agency shall release the vehicle to the registered owner or his or her agent prior to the end of the impoundment period under any of the following circumstances:

(A) When the vehicle is a stolen vehicle.

(B) When the vehicle is subject to bailment and is driven by an unlicensed employee of a business establishment, including a parking service or repair garage.

(C) When the driver of the vehicle is not the sole registered owner of the vehicle and the vehicle is being released to another registered owner of the vehicle who agrees not to allow the driver to use the vehicle until after the end of the impoundment period.

(2) A vehicle shall not be released pursuant to this subdivision without presentation of the registered owner's or agent's currently valid driver's license to operate the vehicle and proof of current vehicle registration, or upon order of a court.

(e) The registered owner or his or her agent is responsible for all towing and storage charges related to the impoundment, and any administrative charges authorized under Section 22850.5.

(f) A vehicle removed and seized under subdivision (a) shall be released to the legal owner of the vehicle or the legal owner's agent prior to the end of the impoundment period if all of the following conditions are met:

(1) The legal owner is a motor vehicle dealer, bank, credit union, acceptance corporation, or other licensed financial institution legally operating in this state, or is another person who is not the registered owner and holds a security interest in the vehicle.

(2) (A) The legal owner or the legal owner's agent pays all towing and storage fees related to the seizure of the vehicle. A lien sale processing fee shall not be charged to the legal owner who redeems the vehicle prior to the 10th day of impoundment. The impounding authority or any person having possession of the vehicle shall not collect from the legal owner of the type specified in paragraph (1) or the legal owner's agent any administrative charges imposed pursuant to Section 22850.5 unless the legal owner voluntarily requested a poststorage hearing.

(B) A person operating or in charge of a storage facility where vehicles are stored pursuant to this section shall accept a valid bank credit card or cash for payment of towing, storage, and related fees by a legal or registered owner or the owner's agent claiming the vehicle. A credit card shall be in the name of the person presenting the card. "Credit card" means "credit card" as defined in subdivision (a) of Section 1747.02 of the Civil Code, except, for the purposes of this section, credit card does not include a credit card issued by a retail seller.

(C) A person operating or in charge of a storage facility described in subparagraph (B) who violates subparagraph (B) shall be civilly liable to the owner of the vehicle or to the person who tendered the fees for four times the amount of the towing, storage, and other related fees, but not to exceed five hundred dollars ($500).

(D) A person operating or in charge of a storage facility described in subparagraph (B) shall have sufficient funds on the premises of the primary storage facility during normal business hours to accommodate, and make change in, a reasonable monetary transaction.

(E) Credit charges for towing and storage services shall comply with Section 1748.1 of the Civil Code. Law enforcement agencies may include the costs of providing for payment by credit when making agreements with towing companies on rates.

(3) (A) The legal owner or the legal owner's agent presents to the law enforcement agency or impounding agency, or any person acting on behalf of those agencies, a copy of the assignment, as defined in subdivision (b) of Section 7500.1 of the Business and Professions Code; a release from the one responsible governmental agency, only if required by the agency; a government-issued photographic identification card; and any one of the following as determined by the legal owner or the legal owner's agent: a certificate of repossession for the vehicle, a security agreement for the vehicle, or title, whether paper or electronic, showing proof of legal ownership for the vehicle. The law enforcement agency, impounding agency, or any other governmental agency, or any person acting on behalf of those agencies, shall not require the presentation of any other documents.

(B) The legal owner or the legal owner's agent presents to the person in possession of the vehicle, or any person acting on behalf of the person in possession, a copy of the assignment, as defined in subdivision (b) of Section 7500.1 of the Business and Professions Code; a release from the one responsible governmental agency, only if required by the agency; a government-issued photographic identification card; and any one of the following as determined by the legal owner or the legal owner's agent: a certificate of repossession for the vehicle, a security agreement for the vehicle, or title, whether paper or electronic, showing proof of legal ownership for the vehicle. The person in possession of the vehicle, or any person acting on behalf of the person in possession, shall not require the presentation of any other documents.

(C) All presented documents may be originals, photocopies, or facsimile copies, or may be transmitted electronically. The law enforcement agency, impounding agency, or any person acting on behalf of them, shall not require a document to be notarized. The law enforcement agency, impounding agency, or any person in possession of the vehicle, or anyone acting on behalf of those agencies may require the agent of the legal owner to produce a photocopy or facsimile copy of its repossession agency license or registration issued pursuant to Chapter 11 (commencing with Section 7500) of Division 3 of the Business and Professions Code, or to demonstrate, to the satisfaction of the law enforcement agency, the impounding agency, any other governmental agency, or any person in possession of the vehicle, or anyone acting on behalf of them, that the agent is exempt from licensure pursuant to Section 7500.2 or 7500.3 of the Business and Professions Code.

(D) Administrative costs authorized under subdivision (a) of Section 22850.5 shall not be charged to the legal owner of the type specified in paragraph (1) who redeems the vehicle unless the legal owner voluntarily requests a poststorage hearing. A city, county, city and county, or state agency shall not require a legal owner or a legal owner's agent to request a poststorage hearing as a requirement for release of the vehicle to the legal owner or the legal owner's agent. The law enforcement agency, the impounding agency, any governmental agency, or any person acting on behalf of those agencies shall not require any documents other than those specified in this paragraph. The law enforcement agency, impounding agency, or other governmental agency, or any person acting on behalf of those agencies, shall not require any documents to be notarized. The legal owner or the legal owner's agent shall be given a copy of any documents he or she is required to sign, except for a vehicle evidentiary hold logbook. The law enforcement agency, impounding agency, or any person acting on behalf of those agencies, or any person in possession of the vehicle, may photocopy and retain the copies of any documents presented by the legal owner or legal owner's agent.

(4) A failure by a storage facility to comply with any applicable conditions set forth in this subdivision shall not affect the right of the legal owner or the legal owner's agent to retrieve the vehicle, provided all conditions required of the legal owner or legal owner's agent under this subdivision are satisfied.

(g) (1) A legal owner or the legal owner's agent who obtains release of the vehicle pursuant to subdivision (f) shall not release the vehicle to the registered owner of the vehicle or the person who was listed as the registered owner when the vehicle was impounded or any agents of the registered owner unless the registered owner is a rental car agency, until after the termination of the impoundment period.

(2) The legal owner or the legal owner's agent shall not relinquish the vehicle to the registered owner or the person who was listed as the registered owner when the vehicle was impounded until the registered owner or that owner's agent presents his or her valid driver's license or valid temporary driver's license to the legal owner or the legal owner's agent. The legal owner or the legal owner's agent or the person in possession of the vehicle shall make every reasonable effort to ensure that the license presented is valid and possession of the vehicle will not be given to the driver who was involved in the original impoundment proceeding until the expiration of the impoundment period.

(3) Prior to relinquishing the vehicle, the legal owner may require the registered owner to pay all towing and storage charges related to the impoundment and any administrative charges authorized under Section 22850.5 that were incurred by the legal owner in connection with obtaining custody of the vehicle.

(4) A legal owner who knowingly releases or causes the release of a vehicle to a registered owner or the person in possession of the vehicle at the time of the impoundment or an agent of the registered owner in violation of this subdivision is guilty of a misdemeanor and subject to a fine in the amount of two thousand dollars ($2,000) in addition to any other penalties established by law.

(5) The legal owner, registered owner, or person in possession of the vehicle shall not change or attempt to change the name of the legal owner or the registered owner on the records of the department until the vehicle is released from the impoundment.

(h) (1) A vehicle removed and seized under subdivision (a) shall be released to a rental car agency prior to the end of the impoundment period if the agency is either the legal owner or registered owner of the vehicle and the agency pays all towing and storage fees related to the seizure of the vehicle.

(2) The owner of a rental vehicle that was seized under this section may continue to rent the vehicle upon recovery of the vehicle. However, the rental car agency shall not rent another vehicle to the driver of the vehicle that was seized until the impoundment period has expired.

(3) The rental car agency may require the person to whom the vehicle was rented to pay all towing and storage charges related to the impoundment and any administrative charges authorized under Section 22850.5 that were incurred by the rental car agency in connection with obtaining custody of the vehicle.

(i) Notwithstanding any other provision of this section, the registered owner, and not the legal owner, shall remain responsible for any towing and storage charges related to the impoundment, any administrative charges authorized under Section 22850.5, and any parking fines, penalties, and administrative fees incurred by the registered owner.

(j) The law enforcement agency and the impounding agency, including any storage facility acting on behalf of the law enforcement agency or impounding agency, shall comply with this section and shall not be liable to the registered owner for the improper release of the vehicle to the legal owner or the legal owner's agent provided the release complies with the provisions of this section. The legal owner shall indemnify and hold harmless a storage facility from any claims arising out of the release of the vehicle to the legal owner or the legal owner's agent and from any damage to the vehicle after its release, including the reasonable costs associated with defending any such claims. A law enforcement agency shall not refuse to issue a release to a legal owner or the agent of a legal owner on the grounds that it previously issued a release.

(Amended by Stats. 2011, Ch. 341, Sec. 2. (SB 565) Effective January 1, 2012.)

14602.9. (a) For purposes of this section, "peace officer" means a person designated as a peace officer pursuant to Chapter 4.5 (commencing with Section 830) of Title 3 of Part 2 of the Penal Code.

(b) A peace officer may impound a bus or limousine of a charter-party carrier for 30 days if the officer determines that any of the following violations occurred while the driver was operating the bus or limousine of the charter-party carrier:

(1) The driver was operating the bus or limousine of a charter-party carrier when the charter-party carrier did not have a permit or certificate issued by the Public Utilities Commission, pursuant to Section 5375 of the Public Utilities Code.

(2) The driver was operating the bus or limousine of a charter-party carrier when the charter-party carrier was operating with a suspended permit or certificate from the Public Utilities Commission.

(3) The driver was operating the bus or limousine of a charter-party carrier without having a current and valid driver's license of the proper class, a passenger vehicle endorsement, or the required certificate.

(c) A peace officer may impound a bus or limousine belonging to a passenger stage corporation for 30 days if the officer determines any of the following violations occurred while the driver was operating the bus or limousine:

(1) The driver was operating the bus or limousine when the passenger stage corporation did not have a certificate of public convenience and necessity issued by the Public Utilities Commission as required pursuant to Article 2 (commencing with Section 1031) of Chapter 5 of Part 1 of Division 1 of the Public Utilities Code.

(2) The driver was operating the bus or limousine when the operating rights or certificate of public convenience and necessity of a passenger stage corporation was suspended, canceled, or revoked pursuant to Section 1033.5, 1033.7, or 1045 of the Public Utilities Code.

(3) The driver was operating the bus or limousine without having a current and valid driver's license of the proper class.

(d) Within two working days after impoundment, the impounding agency shall send a notice by certified mail, return receipt requested, to the legal owner of the vehicle, at the address obtained from the department, informing the owner that the vehicle has been impounded. Failure to notify the legal owner within two working days shall prohibit the impounding agency from charging for more than 15 day's impoundment when the legal owner redeems the impounded vehicle. The impounding agency shall maintain a published telephone number that provides information 24 hours a day regarding the impoundment of vehicles and the rights of a registered owner to request a hearing.

(e) The registered and legal owner of a vehicle that is removed and seized under subdivision (b) or (c) or his or her agent shall be provided the opportunity for a storage hearing to determine the validity of, or consider any mitigating circumstances attendant to, the storage, in accordance with Section 22852.

(f) (1) The impounding agency shall release the vehicle to the registered owner or his or her agent prior to the end of the impoundment period under any of the following circumstances:

(A) When the vehicle is a stolen vehicle.

(B) When the vehicle is subject to bailment and is driven by an unlicensed employee of a business establishment, including a parking service or repair garage.

(C) When, for a charter-party carrier of passengers, the driver of the vehicle is not the sole registered owner of the vehicle and the vehicle is being released to another registered owner of the vehicle who agrees not to allow the driver to use the vehicle until after the end of the impoundment period and the charter-party carrier has been issued a valid permit from the Public Utilities Commission, pursuant to Section 5375 of the Public Utilities Code.

(D) When, for a passenger stage corporation, the driver of the vehicle is not the sole registered owner of the vehicle and the vehicle is being released to another registered owner of the vehicle who agrees not to allow the driver to use the vehicle until after the end of the impoundment period and the passenger stage corporation has been issued a valid certificate of public convenience and necessity by the Public Utilities Commission, pursuant to Article 2 (commencing with Section 1031) of Chapter 5 of Part 1 of Division 1 of the Public Utilities Code.

(2) A vehicle shall not be released pursuant to this subdivision without presentation of the registered owner's or agent's currently valid driver's license to operate the vehicle and proof of current vehicle registration, or upon order of a court.

(g) The registered owner or his or her agent is responsible for all towing and storage charges related to the impoundment, and any administrative charges authorized under Section 22850.5.

(h) A vehicle removed and seized under subdivision (b) or (c) shall be released to the legal owner of the vehicle or the legal owner's agent prior to the end of the impoundment period if all of the following conditions are met:

(1) The legal owner is a motor vehicle dealer, bank, credit union, acceptance corporation, or other licensed financial institution legally operating in this state, or is another person who is not the registered owner and holds a security interest in the vehicle.

(2) The legal owner or the legal owner's agent pays all towing and storage fees related to the seizure of the vehicle. A lien sale processing fee shall not be charged to the legal owner who redeems the vehicle prior to the 10th day of impoundment. The impounding authority or any person having possession of the vehicle shall not collect from the legal owner of the type specified in paragraph (1), or the legal owner's agent, any administrative charges imposed pursuant to Section 22850.5 unless the legal owner voluntarily requested a poststorage hearing.

(3) (A) The legal owner or the legal owner's agent presents either lawful foreclosure documents or an affidavit of repossession for the vehicle, and a security agreement or title showing proof of legal ownership for the vehicle. All presented documents may be originals, photocopies, or facsimile copies, or may be transmitted electronically. The impounding agency shall not require a document to be notarized. The impounding agency may require the agent of the legal owner to produce a photocopy or facsimile copy of its repossession agency license or registration issued pursuant to Chapter 11 (commencing with Section 7500) of Division 3 of the Business and Professions Code, or to demonstrate, to the satisfaction of the impounding agency, that the agent is exempt from licensure pursuant to Section 7500.2 or 7500.3 of the Business and Professions Code.

(B) Administrative costs authorized under subdivision (a) of Section 22850.5 shall not be charged to the legal owner of the type specified in paragraph (1), who redeems the vehicle unless the legal owner voluntarily requests a poststorage hearing. A city, county, or state agency shall not require a legal owner or a legal owner's agent to request a poststorage hearing as a requirement for release of the vehicle to the legal owner or the legal owner's agent. The impounding agency shall not require any documents other than those specified in this paragraph. The impounding agency shall not require any documents to be notarized.

(C) As used in this paragraph, "foreclosure documents" means an "assignment" as that term is defined in subdivision (b) of Section 7500.1 of the Business and Professions Code.

(i) (1) A legal owner or the legal owner's agent who obtains release of the vehicle pursuant to subdivision (h) may not release the vehicle to the registered owner of the vehicle or any agents of the registered owner, unless the registered owner is a rental car agency, until after the termination of the impoundment period.

(2) The legal owner or the legal owner's agent shall not relinquish the vehicle to the registered owner until the registered owner or that owner's agent presents his or her valid driver's license or valid temporary driver's license to the legal owner or the legal owner's agent. The legal owner or the legal owner's agent shall make every reasonable effort to ensure that the license presented is valid.

(3) Prior to relinquishing the vehicle, the legal owner may require the registered owner to pay all towing and storage charges related to the impoundment and any administrative charges authorized under Section 22850.5 that were incurred by the legal owner in connection with obtaining custody of the vehicle.

(j) (1) A vehicle removed and seized under subdivision (b) or (c) shall be released to a rental agency prior to the end of the impoundment period if the agency is either the legal owner or registered owner of the vehicle and the agency pays all towing and storage fees related to the seizure of the vehicle.

(2) The owner of a rental vehicle that was seized under this section may continue to rent the vehicle upon recovery of the vehicle. However, the rental agency shall not rent another vehicle to the driver of the vehicle that was seized until the impoundment period has expired.

(3) The rental agency may require the person to whom the vehicle was rented to pay all towing and storage charges related to the impoundment and any administrative charges authorized under Section 22850.5 that were incurred by the rental agency in connection with obtaining custody of the vehicle.

(k) Notwithstanding any other provision of this section, the registered owner, and not the legal owner, shall remain responsible for any towing and storage charges related to the impoundment, any administrative charges authorized under Section 22850.5, and any parking fines, penalties, and administrative fees incurred by the registered owner.

(l) The impounding agency is not liable to the registered owner for the improper release of the vehicle to the legal owner or the legal owner's agent provided the release complies with this section.

(m) This section does not authorize the impoundment of privately owned personal vehicles that are not common carriers nor the impoundment of vehicles used in transportation for compensation by charter-party carriers that are not required to carry individual permits.

(n) For the purposes of this section, a "charter-party carrier" means a charter-party carrier of passengers as defined by Section 5360 of the Public Utilities Code.

(o) For purposes of this section, a "passenger stage corporation" means a passenger stage corporation as defined by Section 226 of the Public Utilities Code.

(Amended by Stats. 2015, Ch. 740, Sec. 15.5. (AB 281) Effective January 1, 2016.)

14603. No person shall operate a vehicle in violation of the provisions of a restricted license issued to him.

(Enacted by Stats. 1959, Ch. 3.)

14604. (a) No owner of a motor vehicle may knowingly allow another person to drive the vehicle upon a highway unless the owner determines that the person possesses a valid driver's license that authorizes the person to operate the vehicle. For the purposes of this section, an owner is required only to make a reasonable effort or inquiry to determine whether the prospective driver possesses a valid driver's license before allowing him or her to operate the owner's vehicle. An owner is not required to inquire of the department whether the prospective driver possesses a valid driver's license.

(b) A rental company is deemed to be in compliance with subdivision (a) if the company rents the vehicle in accordance with Sections 14608 and 14609.

(Amended by Stats. 1995, Ch. 922, Sec. 3.5. Effective January 1, 1996.)

14605. (a) No person who owns or is in control of a motor vehicle shall cause or permit another person to operate the vehicle within or upon an offstreet parking facility if the person has knowledge that the driver does not have a driver's license of the appropriate class or certification to operate the vehicle.

(b) No operator of an offstreet parking facility shall hire or retain in his employment an attendant whose duties involve the operating of motor vehicles unless such attendant, at all times during such employment, is licensed as a driver under the provisions of this code.

(c) As used in this section, "offstreet parking facility" means any offstreet facility held open for use by the public for parking vehicles and includes all publicly owned facilities for offstreet parking, and privately owned facilities for offstreet parking where no fee is charged for the privilege to park and which are held open for the common public use of retail customers.

(Amended by Stats. 1984, Ch. 621, Sec. 4.)

14606. (a) A person shall not employ, hire, knowingly permit, or authorize any person to drive a motor vehicle owned by him or her or under his or her control upon the highways unless that person is licensed for the appropriate class of vehicle to be driven.

(b) Whenever a person fails to qualify, on reexamination, to operate a commercial motor vehicle, an employer shall report that failure to the department within 10 days.

(c) An employer shall obtain from a driver required to have a commercial driver's license or commercial endorsement a copy of the driver's medical certification before allowing the driver to operate a commercial motor vehicle. The employer shall retain the certification as part of a driver qualification file.

(d) This section shall become operative on January 30, 2014.

(Amended (as added by Stats. 2012, Ch. 670, Sec. 7) by Stats. 2013, Ch. 523, Sec. 30. (SB 788) Effective January 1, 2014. Section operative January 30, 2014, by its own provisions.)

14607. No person shall cause or knowingly permit his child, ward, or employee under the age of 18 years to drive a motor vehicle upon the highways unless such child, ward, or employee is then licensed under this code.

(Amended by Stats. 1971, Ch. 1748.)

14607.4. The Legislature finds and declares all of the following:

(a) Driving a motor vehicle on the public streets and highways is a privilege, not a right.

(b) Of all drivers involved in fatal accidents, more than 20 percent are not licensed to drive. A driver with a suspended license is four times as likely to be involved in a fatal accident as a properly licensed driver.

(c) At any given time, it is estimated by the Department of Motor Vehicles that of some 20 million driver's licenses issued to Californians, 720,000 are suspended or revoked. Furthermore, 1,000,000 persons are estimated to be driving without ever having been licensed at all.

(d) Over 4,000 persons are killed in traffic accidents in California annually, and another 330,000 persons suffer injuries.

(e) Californians who comply with the law are frequently victims of traffic accidents caused by unlicensed drivers. These innocent victims suffer considerable pain and property loss at the hands of people who flaunt the law. The Department of Motor Vehicles estimates that 75 percent of all drivers whose driving privilege has been withdrawn continue to drive regardless of the law.

(f) It is necessary and appropriate to take additional steps to prevent unlicensed drivers from driving, including the civil forfeiture of vehicles used by unlicensed drivers. The state has a critical interest in enforcing its traffic laws and in keeping unlicensed drivers from illegally driving. Seizing the vehicles used by unlicensed drivers serves a significant governmental and public interest, namely the protection of the health, safety, and welfare of Californians from the harm of unlicensed drivers, who are involved in a disproportionate number of traffic incidents, and the avoidance of the associated destruction and damage to lives and property.

(g) The Safe Streets Act of 1994 is consistent with the due process requirements of the United States Constitution and the holding of the Supreme Court of the United States in Calero-Toledo v. Pearson Yacht Leasing Co., 40 L. Ed. 2d 452.

(Added by Stats. 1994, Ch. 1133, Sec. 11. Effective January 1, 1995.)

14607.6. (a) Notwithstanding any other provision of law, and except as provided in this section, a motor vehicle is subject to forfeiture as a nuisance if it is driven on a highway in this state by a driver with a suspended or revoked license, or by an unlicensed driver, who is a registered owner of the vehicle at the time of impoundment and has a previous misdemeanor conviction for a violation of subdivision (a) of Section 12500 or Section 14601, 14601.1, 14601.2, 14601.3, 14601.4, or 14601.5.

(b) A peace officer shall not stop a vehicle for the sole reason of determining whether the driver is properly licensed.

(c) (1) If a driver is unable to produce a valid driver's license on the demand of a peace officer enforcing the provisions of this code, as required by subdivision (b) of Section 12951, the vehicle shall be impounded regardless of ownership, unless the peace officer is reasonably able, by other means, to verify that the driver is properly licensed. Prior to impounding a vehicle, a peace officer shall attempt to verify the license status of a driver who claims to be properly licensed but is unable to produce the license on demand of the peace officer.

(2) A peace officer shall not impound a vehicle pursuant to this subdivision if the license of the driver expired within the preceding 30 days and the driver would otherwise have been properly licensed.

(3) A peace officer may exercise discretion in a situation where the driver without a valid license is an employee driving a vehicle registered to the employer in the course of employment. A peace officer may also exercise discretion in a situation where the driver without a valid license is the employee of a bona fide business establishment or is a person otherwise controlled by such an establishment and it reasonably appears that an owner of the vehicle, or an agent of the owner, relinquished possession of the vehicle to the business establishment solely for servicing or parking of the vehicle or other reasonably similar situations, and where the vehicle was not to be driven except as directly necessary to accomplish that business purpose. In this event, if the vehicle can be returned to or be retrieved by the business establishment or registered owner, the peace officer may release and not impound the vehicle.

(4) A registered or legal owner of record at the time of impoundment may request a hearing to determine the validity of the impoundment pursuant to subdivision (n).

(5) If the driver of a vehicle impounded pursuant to this subdivision was not a registered owner of the vehicle at the time of impoundment, or if the driver of the vehicle was a registered owner of the vehicle at the time of impoundment but the driver does not have a previous conviction for a violation of subdivision (a) of Section 12500 or Section 14601, 14601.1, 14601.2, 14601.3, 14601.4, or 14601.5, the vehicle shall be released pursuant to this code and is not subject to forfeiture.

(d) (1) This subdivision applies only if the driver of the vehicle is a registered owner of the vehicle at the time of impoundment. Except as provided in paragraph (5) of subdivision (c), if the driver of a vehicle impounded pursuant to subdivision (c) was a registered owner of the vehicle at the time of impoundment, the impounding agency shall authorize release of the vehicle if, within three days of impoundment, the driver of the vehicle at the time of impoundment presents his or her valid driver's license, including a valid temporary California driver's license or permit, to the impounding agency. The vehicle shall then be released to a registered owner of record at the time of impoundment, or an agent of that owner authorized in writing, upon payment of towing and storage charges related to the impoundment, and any administrative charges authorized by Section 22850.5, providing that the person claiming the vehicle is properly licensed and the vehicle is properly registered. A vehicle impounded pursuant to the circumstances described in paragraph (3) of subdivision (c) shall be released to a registered owner whether or not the driver of the vehicle at the time of impoundment presents a valid driver's license.

(2) If there is a community property interest in the vehicle impounded pursuant to subdivision (c), owned at the time of impoundment by a person other than the driver, and the vehicle is the only vehicle available to the driver's immediate family that may be operated with a class C driver's license, the vehicle shall be released to a registered owner or to the community property interest owner upon compliance with all of the following requirements:

(A) The registered owner or the community property interest owner requests release of the vehicle and the owner of the community property interest submits proof of that interest.

(B) The registered owner or the community property interest owner submits proof that he or she, or an authorized driver, is properly licensed and that the impounded vehicle is properly registered pursuant to this code.

(C) All towing and storage charges related to the impoundment and any administrative charges authorized pursuant to Section 22850.5 are paid.

(D) The registered owner or the community property interest owner signs a stipulated vehicle release agreement, as described in paragraph (3), in consideration for the nonforfeiture of the vehicle. This requirement applies only if the driver requests release of the vehicle.

(3) A stipulated vehicle release agreement shall provide for the consent of the signator to the automatic future forfeiture and transfer of title to the state of any vehicle registered to that person, if the vehicle is driven by a driver with a suspended or revoked license, or by an unlicensed driver. The agreement shall be in effect for only as long as it is noted on a driving record maintained by the department pursuant to Section 1806.1.

(4) The stipulated vehicle release agreement described in paragraph (3) shall be reported by the impounding agency to the department not later than 10 days after the day the agreement is signed.

(5) No vehicle shall be released pursuant to paragraph (2) if the driving record of a registered owner indicates that a prior stipulated vehicle release agreement was signed by that person.

(e) (1) The impounding agency, in the case of a vehicle that has not been redeemed pursuant to subdivision (d), or that has not been otherwise released, shall promptly ascertain from the department the names and addresses of all legal and registered owners of the vehicle.

(2) The impounding agency, within two days of impoundment, shall send a notice by certified mail, return receipt requested, to all legal and registered owners of the vehicle, at the addresses obtained from the department, informing them that the vehicle is subject to forfeiture and will be sold or otherwise disposed of pursuant to this section. The notice shall also include instructions for filing a claim with the district attorney, and the time limits for filing a claim. The notice shall also inform any legal owner of its right to conduct the sale pursuant to subdivision (g). If a registered owner was personally served at the time of impoundment with a notice containing all the information required to be provided by this paragraph, no further notice is required to be sent to a registered owner. However, a notice shall still be sent to the legal owners of the vehicle, if any. If notice was not sent to the legal owner within two working days, the impounding agency shall not charge the legal owner for more than 15-days' impoundment when the legal owner redeems the impounded vehicle.

(3) No processing charges shall be imposed on a legal owner who redeems an impounded vehicle within 15 days of the impoundment of that vehicle. If no claims are filed and served within 15 days after the mailing of the notice in paragraph (2), or if no claims are filed and served within five days of personal service of the notice specified in paragraph (2), when no other mailed notice is required pursuant to paragraph (2), the district attorney shall prepare a written declaration of forfeiture of the vehicle to the state. A written declaration of forfeiture signed by the district attorney under this subdivision shall be deemed to provide good and sufficient title to the forfeited vehicle. A copy of the declaration shall be provided on request to any person informed of the pending forfeiture pursuant to paragraph (2). A claim that is filed and is later withdrawn by the claimant shall be deemed not to have been filed.

(4) If a claim is timely filed and served, then the district attorney shall file a petition of forfeiture with the appropriate juvenile or superior court within 10 days of the receipt of the claim. The district attorney shall establish an expedited hearing date in accordance with instructions from the court, and the court shall hear the matter without delay. The court filing fee of one hundred dollars ($100) shall be paid by the claimant, but shall be reimbursed by the impounding agency if the claimant prevails. To the extent practicable, the civil and criminal cases shall be heard at the same time in an expedited, consolidated proceeding. A proceeding in the civil case is a limited civil case.

(5) The burden of proof in the civil case shall be on the prosecuting agency, by a preponderance of the evidence. All questions that may arise shall be decided and all other proceedings shall be conducted as in an ordinary civil action. A judgment of forfeiture does not require as a condition precedent the conviction of a defendant of an offense which made the vehicle subject to forfeiture. The filing of a claim within the time limits specified in paragraph (3) is considered a jurisdictional prerequisite for the availing of the action authorized by that paragraph.

(6) All right, title, and interest in the vehicle shall vest in the state upon commission of the act giving rise to the forfeiture.

(7) The filing fee in paragraph (4) shall be distributed as follows:

(A) To the county law library fund as provided in Section 6320 of the Business and Professions Code, the amount specified in Sections 6321 and 6322.1 of the Business and Professions Code.

(B) To the Trial Court Trust Fund, the remainder of the fee.

(f) Any vehicle impounded that is not redeemed pursuant to subdivision (d) and is subsequently forfeited pursuant to this section shall be sold once an order of forfeiture is issued by the district attorney of the county of the impounding agency or a court, as the case may be, pursuant to subdivision (e).

(g) Any legal owner who is a motor vehicle dealer, bank, credit union, acceptance corporation, or other licensed financial institution legally operating in this state, or the agent of that legal owner, may take possession and conduct the sale of the forfeited vehicle if the legal owner or agent notifies the agency impounding the vehicle of its intent to conduct the sale within 15 days of the mailing of the notice pursuant to subdivision (e). Sale of the vehicle after forfeiture pursuant to this subdivision may be conducted at the time, in the manner, and on the notice usually given for the sale of repossessed or surrendered vehicles. The proceeds of any sale conducted by or on behalf of the legal owner shall be disposed of as provided in subdivision (i). A notice pursuant to this subdivision may be presented in person, by certified mail, by facsimile transmission, or by electronic mail.

(h) If the legal owner or agent of the owner does not notify the agency impounding the vehicle of its intent to conduct the sale as provided in subdivision (g), the agency shall offer the forfeited vehicle for sale at public auction within 60 days of receiving title to the vehicle. Low value vehicles shall be disposed of pursuant to subdivision (k).

(i) The proceeds of a sale of a forfeited vehicle shall be disposed of in the following priority:

(1) To satisfy the towing and storage costs following impoundment,

the costs of providing notice pursuant to subdivision (e), the costs of sale, and the unfunded costs of judicial proceedings, if any.

(2) To the legal owner in an amount to satisfy the indebtedness owed to the legal owner remaining as of the date of sale, including accrued interest or finance charges and delinquency charges, providing that the principal indebtedness was incurred prior to the date of impoundment.

(3) To the holder of any subordinate lien or encumbrance on the vehicle, other than a registered or legal owner, to satisfy any indebtedness so secured if written notification of demand is received before distribution of the proceeds is completed. The holder of a subordinate lien or encumbrance, if requested, shall furnish reasonable proof of its interest and, unless it does so upon request, is not entitled to distribution pursuant to this paragraph.

(4) To any other person, other than a registered or legal owner, who can reasonably establish an interest in the vehicle, including a community property interest, to the extent of his or her provable interest, if written notification is received before distribution of the proceeds is completed.

(5) Of the remaining proceeds, funds shall be made available to pay any local agency and court costs, that are reasonably related to the implementation of this section, that remain unsatisfied.

(6) Of the remaining proceeds, half shall be transferred to the Controller for deposit in the Vehicle Inspection and Repair Fund for the high-polluter repair assistance and removal program created by Article 9 (commencing with Section 44090) of Chapter 5 of Part 5 of Division 26 of the Health and Safety Code, and half shall be transferred to the general fund of the city or county of the impounding agency, or the city or county where the impoundment occurred. A portion of the local funds may be used to establish a reward fund for persons coming forward with information leading to the arrest and conviction of hit-and-run drivers and to publicize the availability of the reward fund.

(j) The person conducting the sale shall disburse the proceeds of the sale as provided in subdivision (i) and shall provide a written accounting regarding the disposition to the impounding agency and, on request, to any person entitled to or claiming a share of the proceeds, within 15 days after the sale is conducted.

(k) If the vehicle to be sold pursuant to this section is not of the type that can readily be sold to the public generally, the vehicle shall be conveyed to a licensed dismantler or donated to an eleemosynary institution. License plates shall be removed from any vehicle conveyed to a dismantler pursuant to this subdivision.

(l) No vehicle shall be sold pursuant to this section if the impounding agency determines the vehicle to have been stolen. In this event, the vehicle may be claimed by the registered owner at any time after impoundment, providing the vehicle registration is current and the registered owner has no outstanding traffic violations or parking penalties on his or her driving record or on the registration record of any vehicle registered to the person. If the identity of the legal and registered owners of the vehicle cannot be reasonably ascertained, the vehicle may be sold.

(m) Any owner of a vehicle who suffers any loss due to the impoundment or forfeiture of any vehicle pursuant to this section may recover the amount of the loss from the unlicensed, suspended, or revoked driver. If possession of a vehicle has been tendered to a business establishment in good faith, and an unlicensed driver employed or otherwise directed by the business establishment is the cause of the impoundment of the vehicle, a registered owner of the impounded vehicle may recover damages for the loss of use of the vehicle from the business establishment.

(n) (1) The impounding agency, if requested to do so not later than 10 days after the date the vehicle was impounded, shall provide the opportunity for a poststorage hearing to determine the validity of the storage to the persons who were the registered and legal owners of the vehicle at the time of impoundment, except that the hearing shall be requested within three days after the date the vehicle was impounded if personal service was provided to a registered owner pursuant to paragraph (2) of subdivision (e) and no mailed notice is required.

(2) The poststorage hearing shall be conducted not later than two days after the date it was requested. The impounding agency may authorize its own officer or employee to conduct the hearing if the hearing officer is not the same person who directed the storage of the vehicle. Failure of either the registered or legal owner to request a hearing as provided in paragraph (1) or to attend a scheduled hearing shall satisfy the poststorage hearing requirement.

(3) The agency employing the person who directed the storage is responsible for the costs incurred for towing and storage if it is determined that the driver at the time of impoundment had a valid driver's license.

(o) As used in this section, "days" means workdays not including weekends and holidays.

(p) Charges for towing and storage for any vehicle impounded pursuant to this section shall not exceed the normal towing and storage rates for other vehicle towing and storage conducted by the impounding agency in the normal course of business.

(q) The Judicial Council and the Department of Justice may prescribe standard forms and procedures for implementation of this section to be used by all jurisdictions throughout the state.

(r) The impounding agency may act as the agent of the state in carrying out this section.

(s) No vehicle shall be impounded pursuant to this section if the driver has a valid license but the license is for a class of vehicle other than the vehicle operated by the driver.

(t) This section does not apply to vehicles subject to Sections 14608 and 14609, if there has been compliance with the procedures in those sections.

(u) As used in this section, "district attorney" includes a city attorney charged with the duty of prosecuting misdemeanor offenses.

(v) The agent of a legal owner acting pursuant to subdivision (g) shall be licensed, or exempt from licensure, pursuant to Chapter 11 (commencing with Section 7500) of Division 3 of the Business and Professions Code.

(Amended by Stats. 2005, Ch. 75, Sec. 151. Effective July 19, 2005. Operative January 1, 2006, by Sec. 156 of Ch. 75.)

14607.8. Upon a first misdemeanor conviction of a violation of subdivision (a) of Section 12500 or Section 14601, 14601.1, 14601.2, 14601.3, 14601.4, or 14601.5, the court shall inform the defendant that, pursuant to Section 14607.6, a motor vehicle is subject to forfeiture as a nuisance if it is driven on a highway in this state by a driver with a suspended or revoked license, or by an unlicensed driver, who is a registered owner of the vehicle and has a previous misdemeanor conviction for a violation of subdivision (a) of Section 12500 or Section 14601, 14601.1, 14601.2, 14601.3, 14601.4, or 14601.5.

(Added by Stats. 1994, Ch. 1133, Sec. 13. Effective January 1, 1995.)

14608. (a) A person shall not rent a motor vehicle to another person unless both of the following requirements have been met:

(1) The person to whom the vehicle is rented is licensed under this code or is a nonresident who is licensed under the laws of the state or country of his or her residence.

(2) The person renting to another person has inspected the driver's license of the person to whom the vehicle is to be rented and compared either the signature thereon with that of the person to whom the vehicle is to be rented or the photograph thereon with the person to whom the vehicle is to be rented.

(b) This section does not prohibit a blind or disabled person who is a nondriver from renting a motor vehicle if both of the following conditions exist at the time of rental:

(1) The blind or disabled person either holds an identification card issued pursuant to this code or is not a resident of this state.

(2) The blind or disabled person has a driver present who is either licensed to drive a vehicle pursuant to this code or is a nonresident licensed to drive a vehicle pursuant to the laws of the state or country

of the driver's residence.

(Amended by Stats. 2012, Ch. 862, Sec. 4. (AB 2189) Effective January 1, 2013.)

14609. (a) Every person renting a motor vehicle to another person shall keep a record of the registration number of the motor vehicle rented, the name and address of the person to whom the vehicle is rented, his or her driver's license number, the jurisdiction that issued the driver's license, and the expiration date of the driver's license.

(b) If the person renting the vehicle is a nondriver pursuant to subdivision (c) of Section 14608, the record maintained pursuant to this section shall include the name and address of the person renting the vehicle and, if applicable, his or her identification card number, the jurisdiction that issued the identification card, and the expiration date of the identification card. The record shall also include the name and address of the licensed driver, his or her driver's license number, and the expiration date of his or her driver's license.

(Amended by Stats. 1993, Ch. 1292, Sec. 12. Effective January 1, 1994.)

14610. (a) It is unlawful for any person:

(1) To display or cause or permit to be displayed or have in his possession any canceled, revoked, suspended, fictitious, fraudulently altered, or fraudulently obtained driver's license.

(2) To lend his driver's license to any other person or knowingly permit the use thereof by another.

(3) To display or represent any driver's license not issued to him as being his license.

(4) To fail or refuse to surrender to the department upon its lawful demand any driver's license which has been suspended, revoked or canceled.

(5) To permit any unlawful use of a driver's license issued to him.

(6) To do any act forbidden or fail to perform any act required by this division.

(7) To photograph, photostat, duplicate, or in any way reproduce any driver's license or facsimile thereof in such a manner that it could be mistaken for a valid license, or to display or have in his possession any such photograph, photostat, duplicate, reproduction, or facsimile unless authorized by the provisions of this code.

(8) To alter any driver's license in any manner not authorized by this code.

(b) For purposes of this section, "driver's license" includes a temporary permit to operate a motor vehicle.

(Amended by Stats. 1990, Ch. 44, Sec. 5.)

14610.1. (a) A person shall not manufacture or sell an identification document of a size and form substantially similar to, or that purports to confer the same privileges as, the drivers' licenses issued by the department.

(b) A violation of this section is a misdemeanor punishable as follows:

(1) The court shall impose a fine of not less than two hundred fifty dollars ($250) and not more than one thousand dollars ($1,000), and 24 hours of community service, to be served when the person is not employed or is not attending school. No part of the fine or community service shall be suspended or waived.

(2) In lieu of the penalties imposed under paragraph (1), the court, in its discretion, may impose a jail term of up to one year and a fine of up to one thousand dollars ($1,000). In exercising its discretion the court shall consider the extent of the defendant's commercial motivation for the offense.

(c) Prosecution under this section shall not preclude prosecution under any other applicable provision of law.

(Amended by Stats. 2010, Ch. 684, Sec. 2. (AB 2471) Effective January 1, 2011.)

14610.5. (a) It is unlawful for any person to do any of the following:

(1) Sell, offer for sale, distribute, or use any crib sheet or cribbing device that contains the answers to any examination administered by the department for any class of driver's license, permit, or certificate.

(2) Impersonate or allow the impersonation of an applicant for any class of driver's license, permit, or certificate for the purpose of fraudulently qualifying the applicant for any class of driver's license, permit, or certificate.

(b) A first conviction under this section is punishable as either an infraction or a misdemeanor ; a second or subsequent conviction is punishable as a misdemeanor.

(Amended by Stats. 1995, Ch. 243, Sec. 1. Effective January 1, 1996.)

14610.7. It is a misdemeanor for any person to knowingly assist in obtaining a driver's license or identification card for any person whose presence in the United States is not authorized under federal law.

(Added by Stats. 1993, Ch. 820, Sec. 3. Effective January 1, 1994.)

14611. (a) A person shall not knowingly direct the operation of a vehicle transporting a highway route controlled quantity of Class 7 radioactive materials, as defined in Section 173.403 of Title 49 of the Code of Federal Regulations, by a person who does not possess a training certificate pursuant to Section 12524 and a valid driver's license of the appropriate class.

(b) A person convicted under this section shall be punished by a fine of not less than five thousand dollars ($5,000) nor more than ten thousand dollars ($10,000).

(Amended by Stats. 2017, Ch. 397, Sec. 5. (SB 810) Effective January 1, 2018.)

Chapter 5. License Fees

(Chapter 5 enacted by Stats. 1959, Ch. 3.)

Article 1. Imposition of Fees

(Heading of Article 1 added by Stats. 1991, Ch. 13, Sec. 48.)

14900. (a) Upon application for an original class C or M driver's license, a fee of twenty-four dollars ($24), and on and after January 1, 2010, a fee of thirty dollars ($30), shall be paid to the department for a license that will expire on the fifth birthday of the applicant following the date of the application. The payment of the fee entitles the person paying the fee to apply for a driver's license and to take three examinations within a period of 12 months from the date of the application or during the period that an instruction permit is valid, as provided in Section 12509.

(b) In addition to the application fee specified in subdivision (a), a person who fails to successfully complete the driving skill test on the first attempt shall be required to pay an additional fee of five dollars ($5) for each additional driving skill test administered under that application.

(Amended by Stats. 2009, 4th Ex. Sess., Ch. 10, Sec. 10. Effective July 28, 2009.)

14900.1. (a) Except as provided in Section 15255.1, upon application for the renewal of a driver's license or for a license to operate a different class of vehicle, a fee of twenty-four dollars ($24), and on and after January 1, 2010, a fee of thirty dollars ($30), shall be paid to the department for a license that will expire on the fifth birthday of the applicant following the date of the application. The payment of the fee entitles the person paying the fee to apply for a driver's license and to take three examinations within a period of 12 months from the date of the application or during the period that an instruction permit is valid, as provided in Section 12509.

(b) In addition to the application fee specified in subdivision (a), a person who fails to successfully complete the driving skill test on the first attempt shall be required to pay an additional fee of five dollars ($5) for each additional driving skill test administered under that application.

(Amended by Stats. 2017, Ch. 397, Sec. 6. (SB 810) Effective January 1, 2018.)

14900.5. Upon application and payment of the fees for a driver's license pursuant to Section 14900, an identification card may be issued to the applicant if it is determined that a driver's license cannot be issued due to the applicant's physical or mental condition. The identification card, unless canceled earlier, shall expire on the applicant's sixth birthday following the date of application.

(Added by Stats. 1990, Ch. 607, Sec. 2.)

14901. Upon an application for a duplicate driver's license or for a change of name on a driver's license, a fee of nineteen dollars ($19), and on and after January 1, 2010, a fee of twenty-four dollars ($24), shall be paid to the department.

(Amended by Stats. 2009, 4th Ex. Sess., Ch. 10, Sec. 12. Effective July 28, 2009.)

14902. (a) Except as otherwise provided in subdivisions (b), (c), (d), (g), and (h) of this section, subdivision (c) of Section 13002, and subdivision (c) of Section 14900, upon an application for an identification card a fee of twenty-six dollars ($26) shall be paid to the department.

(b) An original or replacement senior citizen identification card issued pursuant to subdivision (b) of Section 13000 shall be issued free of charge.

(c) The fee for an original or replacement identification card issued to a person who has been determined to have a current income level that meets the eligibility requirements for assistance programs under Chapter 2 (commencing with Section 11200) or Chapter 3 (commencing with Section 12000) of Part 3 of, or Part 5 (commencing with Section 17000) of, or Article 9 (commencing with Section 18900) of Chapter 10 of Part 6 of, or Chapter 10.1 (commencing with Section 18930) or Chapter 10.3 (commencing with Section 18937) of Part 6 of, Division 9 of the Welfare and Institutions Code shall be six dollars ($6). The determination of eligibility under this subdivision shall be made by a governmental or nonprofit entity, which shall be subject to regulations adopted by the department.

(d) A fee shall not be charged for an original or replacement identification card issued to any person who can verify their status as a homeless person or homeless child or youth. A homeless services provider that has knowledge of the person's housing status may verify the person's status for purposes of this subdivision. A determination of eligibility pursuant to this subdivision shall be subject to regulations adopted by the department. A person applying for an identification card under this subdivision shall not be charged a fee for verification of their eligibility.

(e) All fees received pursuant to this section shall be deposited in the Motor Vehicle Account.

(f) For purposes of this section, the following definitions apply:

(1) A "homeless child or youth" has the same meaning as the definition of "homeless children and youths" as set forth in the federal McKinney-Vento Homeless Assistance Act (42 U.S.C. Sec. 11301 et seq.).

(2) A "homeless person" has the same meaning as the definition set forth in the federal McKinney-Vento Homeless Assistance Act (42 U.S.C. Sec. 11301 et seq.).

(3) A "homeless services provider" includes:

(A) A governmental or nonprofit agency receiving federal, state, or county or municipal funding to provide services to a "homeless person" or "homeless child or youth," or that is otherwise sanctioned to provide those services by a local homeless continuum of care organization.

(B) An attorney licensed to practice law in this state.

(C) A local educational agency liaison for homeless children and youth designated as such pursuant to Section 11432 (g)(1)(J)(ii) of Title 42 of the United States Code, or a school social worker.

(D) A human services provider or public social services provider funded by the State of California to provide homeless children or youth services, health services, mental or behavioral health services, substance use disorder services, or public assistance or employment services.

(E) A law enforcement officer designated as a liaison to the homeless population by a local police department or sheriff's department within the state.

(F) Any other homeless services provider that is qualified to verify an individual's housing status, as determined by the department.

(g) The fee for a replacement identification card issued to an eligible inmate upon release from a federal correctional facility or a county jail facility is eight dollars ($8). For purposes of this subdivision, "eligible inmate" means an inmate who meets all of the following requirements:

(1) The inmate previously held a California driver's license or identification card.

(2) The inmate has a usable photo on file with the department that is not more than 10 years old.

(3) The inmate has no outstanding fees due for a prior California identification card.

(4) The inmate has provided, and the department has verified, their true full name, date of birth, social security number, and legal presence in the United States, or, upon implementation of paragraph (2) of subdivision (a) of Section 12801.9, if the inmate is unable to submit satisfactory proof that their presence in the United States is authorized under federal law, the inmate has provided proof of their identity pursuant to Section 12801.9.

(5) The inmate currently resides in a federal correctional facility or a county jail facility.

(6) The inmate has provided the department, upon application, a verification of their eligibility under this subdivision that meets all of the following requirements:

(A) Be on federal correctional facility letterhead or county sheriff letterhead.

(B) Be typed or computer generated.

(C) Contain the inmate's name.

(D) Contain the inmate's date of birth.

(E) Contain the original signature of an official from the federal correctional facility or county sheriff's office.

(F) Be dated within 90 days of the date of application.

(h) The fee for an original or replacement identification card issued to an eligible inmate upon release from a state correctional facility is eight dollars ($8). For purposes of this subdivision, "eligible inmate" has the same meaning as that term is defined under subdivision (b) of Section 3007.05 of the Penal Code, and meets both of the following requirements:

(1) The inmate currently resides in a facility housing inmates under the control of the Department of Corrections and Rehabilitation.

(2) The inmate has provided the department, upon application, a verification of their eligibility under this subdivision that meets the requirements described under subparagraphs (A) to (D), inclusive, and (F) of paragraph (6) of subdivision (g) and contains the signature of an official from the state facility.

(i) (1) The fee for an original or replacement identification card issued to an eligible patient treated in a facility of the State Department of State Hospitals is eight dollars ($8). For purposes of this subdivision, "eligible patient" means a patient who is currently housed in a facility described in Section 4100 of the Welfare and Institutions Code, is preparing to be discharged unconditionally or through a conditional release program, and who meets either of the following sets of requirements:

(A) The patient has previously held a California driver's license or identification card and all of the following requirements are met:

(i) The patient has a usable photo on file with the department that is not more than 10 years old or has a new usable photo taken.

(ii) The patient has provided, and the department has verified, their true full name, date of birth, social security number, California residence, and legal presence in the United States, or, upon implementation of paragraph (2) of subdivision (a) of Section 12801.9, if the patient is unable to submit satisfactory proof that their presence in the United States is authorized under federal law, the patient has provided proof of their identity pursuant to Section 12801.9.

(iii) The patient has provided the department, upon application, a verification of their eligibility under this subdivision that meets all of the following requirements:

(I) Be on State Department of State Hospitals letterhead.

(II) Be typed or computer generated.

(III) Contain the patient's name.

(IV) Contain the patient's date of birth.

(V) Contain the original signature of an official from the State Department of State Hospitals.

(VI) Be dated within 90 days of the date of application.

(B) The patient has not previously held a California driver's license or identification card and all of the following requirements are met:

(i) The patient has verified and signed under penalty of perjury a completed application for an identification card.

(ii) The patient has a usable photo taken.

(iii) The patient provides a legible print of the thumb or finger.

(iv) The patient has provided acceptable proof of the information described in clause (ii) of subparagraph (A), subject to verification by the department.

(v) The patient has provided verification of eligibility as described in clause (iii) of subparagraph (A).

(2) The State Department of State Hospitals shall reimburse the Department of Motor Vehicles for any actual costs incurred in providing assistance pursuant to this paragraph.

(Amended by Stats. 2024, Ch. 40, Sec. 34. (SB 159) Effective June 29, 2024.)

14903. (a) A fee shall not be charged for an in person original, renewal, or replacement driver's license or identification card issued to any person who was exonerated, and was released from the state prison within the previous six months.

(b) The Department of Corrections and Rehabilitation shall provide a form to any person who was exonerated and released from the state prison within the previous six months. The form, along with a copy of a court order, if provided by the court, shall be taken by the individual to the Department of Motor Vehicles to qualify for the fee exemption in subdivision (a).

(c) For the purposes of this section, "exonerated" shall have the same meaning as in Section 3007.05 of the Penal Code.

(Added by Stats. 2015, Ch. 403, Sec. 3. (AB 672) Effective January 1, 2016.)

14904. (a) Notwithstanding any other provision of this code, before a driver's license may be issued, reissued, or returned to the licensee after a suspension or a revocation of a person's driving privilege ordered by the department has been terminated, there shall, in addition to any other fees required by this code, be paid to the department a fee sufficient to pay the actual costs of the issuance, reissuance, or return as determined by the department.

(b) This section shall not apply to any suspension or revocation that is set aside by the department or a court.

(c) This section shall not apply to any suspension or revocation based upon a physical or mental condition.

(Amended by Stats. 1991, Ch. 1177, Sec. 2. Effective October 14, 1991.)

14905. (a) Notwithstanding any other provision of this code, in lieu of the fees in Section 14904, before a driver's license may be issued, reissued, or returned to a person after suspension or revocation of the person's privilege to operate a motor vehicle pursuant to Section 13353 or 13353.2, there shall be paid to the department a fee in an amount of one hundred twenty-five dollars ($125) to pay the costs of the administration of the administrative suspension and revocation programs for persons who refuse or fail to complete chemical testing, as provided in Section 13353, or who drive with an excessive amount of alcohol in their blood, as provided in Section 13353.2, any costs of the Department of the California Highway Patrol related to the payment of compensation for overtime for attending any administrative hearings pursuant to Article 3 (commencing with Section 14100) of Chapter 3 and Section 13382, and any reimbursement for costs mandated by the state pursuant to subdivisions (f) and (g) of Section 23612.

(b) This section does not apply to a suspension or revocation that is set aside by the department or a court.

(Amended by Stats. 2002, Ch. 805, Sec. 20. Effective September 23, 2002.)

14906. (a) In addition to the fees required by Section 14904, the department may require payment of a fee sufficient to pay the actual costs, as determined by the department, for giving any notices in connection with suspensions or revocations in accordance with Sections 22, 29, and 13106.

(b) This section does not apply to any suspension or revocation that is set aside by the department or a court.

(Amended by Stats. 1994, Ch. 1221, Sec. 15. Effective January 1, 1995.)

14907. In addition to the fees required pursuant to Section 14904, there shall be paid to the department a fee of one hundred twenty dollars ($120) to pay the costs of a departmental review when requested pursuant to Section 14105.5, following a hearing conducted pursuant to Section 13353 or 13353.2. The fee authorized under this section shall be collected in conjunction with any request for a departmental review received on or after January 1, 2003.

(Added by Stats. 2002, Ch. 805, Sec. 21. Effective September 23, 2002.)

Article 2. Collection of Fees

(Article 2 added by Stats. 1991, Ch. 13, Sec. 49.)

14910. (a) The department shall, with the consent of the applicant, collect the amounts that it has been notified are due pursuant to former Section 40509 and former Section 40509.5, and any service fees added to those amounts, at the time it collects from the applicant any fees and penalties required to issue or renew a driver's license or identification card.

(b) Except as provided in subdivision (c), the department shall remit all amounts collected pursuant to subdivision (a), after deducting the administrative fee authorized in subdivision (c), to each jurisdiction in the amounts due to each jurisdiction according to its notices filed with the department. Within 45 days from the time payment is received by the department, the department shall inform each jurisdiction which of its notices of failure to appear or failure to pay have been discharged.

(c) The department shall assess a fee for posting the bail on each notice of failure to appear or failure to pay that is given to the department pursuant to former Section 40509 or former Section 40509.5, in an amount, as determined by the department, that is sufficient to provide a sum equal to its actual costs of administering this section, not to exceed one dollar ($1) per notice. The fees shall be assessed to each jurisdiction on a regular basis by deducting the amount due to the department pursuant to this subdivision from the bails and fines collected pursuant to subdivision (a), prior to remitting the balance to each jurisdiction pursuant to subdivision (b).

(d) Except as provided in subdivision (e) of Section 13364, if bail is collected under this section for the violation of any provisions of this code, the person shall be deemed to be convicted of those sections violated.

(e) Any amounts collected by the department under this section are nonrefundable by the department.

(f) Notwithstanding Section 42003, payment of bail to the department in accordance with this section shall be paid in full and not in installments.

(Amended by Stats. 2022, Ch. 800, Sec. 18. (AB 2746) Effective January 1, 2023.)

14911. (a) When a notice of failure to appear or failure to pay a fine is recorded on the department records pursuant to former Section 40509 and former Section 40509.5, the fine and any penalty assessments shall be a lien upon all vehicles of the defendant of a type subject to registration under this code.

(b) For every lien arising pursuant to subdivision (a) that is due and not paid, the department may collect the amount of the lien plus costs, and Article 6 (commencing with Section 9800) of Chapter 6 of Division 3.5 shall apply.

(Amended by Stats. 2022, Ch. 800, Sec. 19. (AB 2746) Effective January 1, 2023.)

Chapter 6. Driver License Compact

(Chapter 6 added by Stats. 1963, Ch. 237.)

Article 1. Generally

(Article 1 added by Stats. 1963, Ch. 237.)

15000. The Driver License Compact is hereby enacted into law and entered into with all other jurisdictions legally joining therein in the form substantially contained in Article 2 (commencing with Section

15020), of Chapter 6, Division 6 of this code.
(Added by Stats. 1963, Ch. 237.)

15001. As used in the compact, the term "licensing authority" with reference to this State shall mean the Department of Motor Vehicles. That department shall furnish to the appropriate authorities of any other party state any information or documents reasonably necessary to facilitate the administration of Sections 15022, 15023, and 15024 of the compact.
(Added by Stats. 1963, Ch. 237.)

15002. The compact administrator provided for in Section 15026 of this compact shall not be entitled to any additional compensation on account of his service as such administrator, but shall be entitled to expenses incurred in connection with his duties and responsibilities as such administrator, in the same manner as for expenses incurred in connection with any other duties or responsibilities of his office or employment.
(Amended by Stats. 1972, Ch. 618.)

15003. As used in the compact, with reference to this State, the term "executive head" shall mean the Governor.
(Added by Stats. 1963, Ch. 237.)

Article 2. Compact Terms

(Article 2 added by Stats. 1963, Ch. 237.)

15020. (a) The party states find that:

(1) The safety of their streets and highways is materially affected by the degree of compliance with state laws and local ordinances relating to the operation of motor vehicles.

(2) Violation of such a law or ordinance is evidence that the violator engages in conduct which is likely to endanger the safety of persons and property.

(3) The continuance in force of a license to drive is predicated upon compliance with laws and ordinances relating to the operation of motor vehicles, in whichever jurisdiction the vehicle is operated.

(b) It is the policy of the party states to:

(1) Promote compliance with the laws, ordinances and administrative rules and regulations relating to the operation of motor vehicles by their drivers in each of the jurisdictions where such drivers operate motor vehicles.

(2) Make the reciprocal recognition of licenses to drive and eligibility therefor more just and equitable by considering the overall compliance with motor vehicle laws, ordinances and administrative rules and regulations as a condition precedent to the continuance or issuance of any license by reason of which the licensee is authorized or permitted to operate a motor vehicle in any of the party states.
(Added by Stats. 1963, Ch. 237.)

15021. As used in the compact:

(a) "State" means a state, territory or possession of the United States, the District of Columbia, or the Commonwealth of Puerto Rico.

(b) "Home state" means the state which has issued and has the power to suspend or revoke the use of the license or permit to operate a motor vehicle.

(c) "Conviction" means a conviction of any offense related to the use or operation of a motor vehicle which is prohibited by state law, municipal ordinance or administrative rule or regulation, or a forfeiture of bail, bond or other security deposited to secure appearance by a person charged with having committed any such offense, and which conviction or forfeiture is required to be reported to the licensing authority.
(Added by Stats. 1963, Ch. 237.)

15022. The licensing authority of a party state shall report each conviction of a person from another party state occurring within its jurisdiction to the licensing authority of the home state of the licensee. Such report shall clearly identify the person convicted; describe the violation specifying the section of the statute, code, or ordinance violated; identify the court in which action was taken; indicate whether a plea of guilty or not guilty was entered, or the conviction was a result of the forfeiture of bail, bond or other security; and shall include any special findings made in connection therewith.
(Added by Stats. 1963, Ch. 237.)

15023. (a) The licensing authority in the home state, for the purposes of suspending, revoking, or limiting the license to operate a motor vehicle, shall give the same effect to the conduct reported, pursuant to Section 15022 of this compact, as it would if such conduct had occurred in the home state, in the case of a conviction for:

(1) Manslaughter or negligent homicide resulting from the operation of a motor vehicle;

(2) Driving a motor vehicle while under the influence of intoxicating liquor or a narcotic drug, or under the influence of any other drug to a degree which renders the driver incapable of safely driving a motor vehicle;

(3) Any felony in the commission of which a motor vehicle is used;

(4) Failure to stop and render aid in the event of a motor vehicle accident resulting in the death or personal injury of another.

(b) As to any other conviction, reported pursuant to Section 15022, the licensing authority in the home state shall give such effect to the conduct as is provided by the laws of the home state.

(c) If the laws of a party state do not provide for offenses or violations denominated or described in precisely the words employed in subdivision (a) of this section, such party state shall construe the denominations and descriptions appearing in subdivision (a) hereof as being applicable to and identifying those offenses or violations of a substantially similar nature, and the laws of such party state shall contain such provisions as may be necessary to ensure that full force and effect is given to this section.
(Added by Stats. 1963, Ch. 237.)

15024. Upon application for a license to drive, the licensing authority in a party state shall ascertain whether the applicant has ever held, or is the holder of a license to drive issued by any other party state. The licensing authority in the state where application is made shall not issue a license to drive to the applicant if:

(1) The applicant has held such a license, but the license has been suspended by reason, in whole or in part, of a violation, and if such suspension period has not terminated.

(2) The applicant has held such a license, but the license has been revoked by reason, in whole or in part, of a violation, and if such revocation has not terminated; except that after the expiration of one year from the date the license was revoked, such person may make application for a new license if permitted by law. The licensing authority may refuse to issue a license to any such applicant if, after investigation, the licensing authority determines that it will not be safe to grant to such person the privilege of driving a motor vehicle on the public highways.

(3) The applicant is the holder of a license to drive issued by another party state and currently in force, unless the applicant surrenders such license.
(Added by Stats. 1963, Ch. 237.)

15025. Except as expressly required by provisions of this compact, nothing contained herein shall be construed to affect the right of any party state to apply any of its other laws relating to licenses to drive to any person or circumstance, nor to invalidate or prevent any driver license agreement or other co-operative arrangement between a party state and a nonparty state.
(Added by Stats. 1963 Ch. 237.)

15026. (a) The head of the licensing authority of each party state shall be the administrator of this compact for his state. The administrators of all party states, acting jointly, shall have the power to formulate all necessary and proper procedures for the exchange of information under this compact.

(b) The administrator of each party state shall furnish to the administrator of each other party state any information or documents reasonably necessary to facilitate the administration of this compact.
(Added by Stats. 1963, Ch. 237.)

15027. (a) This compact shall become effective as to any state in which this compact becomes effective as the law of that state.

(b) Any party state may withdraw from this compact by enacting a statute repealing this compact as the law of that state, but no such withdrawal shall take effect until six months after the executive head of the withdrawing state has given notice of the withdrawal to the executive heads of all other party states. No withdrawal shall affect the validity or applicability by the licensing authorities of states remaining party to the compact of any report of conviction occurring prior to the withdrawal.
(Added by Stats. 1963, Ch. 237.)

15028. The compact shall be liberally construed so as to effectuate the purposes thereof. The provisions of the compact shall be severable and if any phrase, clause, sentence, or provisions of the compact is declared to be contrary to the constitution of any party state or of the United States or the applicability thereof to any government, agency, person or circumstance is held invalid, the validity of the remainder of the compact and the applicability thereof to any government, agency, person or circumstance shall not be affected thereby. If the compact shall be held contrary to the constitution of any state party thereto, the compact shall remain in full force and effect as to the remaining states and in full force and effect as to the state affected as to all severable matters.
(Added by Stats. 1963, Ch. 237.)

Chapter 7. Commercial Motor Vehicle Safety Program

(Chapter 7 added by Stats. 1988, Ch. 1509, Sec. 9.)

Article 1. Intent

(Article 1 added by Stats. 1988, Ch. 1509, Sec. 9.)

15200. It is the intent of the Legislature, in enacting this chapter, to adopt those standards required of drivers by the Federal Motor Carrier Safety Administration of the United States Department of Transportation, as set forth in the federal Motor Carrier Safety Improvement Act of 1999 (Public Law 106-159) and to reduce or prevent commercial motor vehicle accidents, fatalities, and injuries by permitting drivers to hold only one license, disqualifying drivers for certain criminal offenses and serious traffic violations, and strengthening licensing and testing standards. This act is a remedial law and shall be liberally construed to promote the public health, safety and welfare. To the extent that this chapter conflicts with general driver licensing provisions, this chapter shall prevail. Where this chapter is silent, the general driver licensing provisions shall apply. It is the further intent of the Legislature that this program be fee supported, and that the department fully recoup its costs within four years of the program's enactment.
(Amended by Stats. 2010, Ch. 216, Sec. 3. (AB 2144) Effective January 1, 2011.)

Article 2. Definitions

(Article 2 added by Stats. 1988, Ch. 1509, Sec. 9.)

15210. Notwithstanding any other provision of this code, as used in this chapter, the following terms have the following meanings:

(a) "Commercial driver's license" means a driver's license issued by a state or other jurisdiction, in accordance with the standards contained in Part 383 of Title 49 of the Code of Federal Regulations, which authorizes the licenseholder to operate a class or type of commercial motor vehicle.

(b) (1) "Commercial motor vehicle" means any vehicle or combination of vehicles that requires a class A or class B license, or a class C license with an endorsement issued pursuant to paragraph (2), (3), (4), or (5) of subdivision (a) of Section 15278.

(2) "Commercial motor vehicle" does not include any of the following:

(A) A recreational vehicle, as defined in Section 18010 of the Health and Safety Code.

(B) An implement of husbandry operated by a person who is not required to obtain a driver's license under this code.

(C) Vehicles operated by persons exempted pursuant to Section 25163 of the Health and Safety Code or a vehicle operated in an emergency situation at the direction of a peace officer pursuant to Section 2800.

(c) "Controlled substance" has the same meaning as defined by the federal Controlled Substances Act (21 U.S.C. Sec. 802).

(d) "Conviction" means an unvacated adjudication of guilt, or a determination that a person has violated or failed to comply with the law in a court of original jurisdiction or by an authorized administrative tribunal, an unvacated forfeiture of bail or collateral deposited to secure the person's appearance in court, a plea of guilty or nolo contendere accepted by the court, the payment of a fine or court costs, or violation of a condition of release without bail, regardless of whether or not the penalty is rebated, suspended, or probated.

(e) "Disqualification" means a prohibition against driving a commercial motor vehicle.

(f) "Driving a commercial vehicle under the influence" means committing any one or more of the following unlawful acts in a commercial motor vehicle:

(1) Driving a commercial motor vehicle while the operator's blood-alcohol concentration level is 0.04 percent or more, by weight in violation of subdivision (d) of Section 23152.

(2) Driving under the influence of alcohol, as prescribed in subdivision (a) or (b) of Section 23152.

(3) Refusal to undergo testing as required under this code in the enforcement of Subpart D of Part 383 or Subpart A of Part 392 of Title 49 of the Code of Federal Regulations.

(g) "Employer" means any person, including the United States, a state, or political subdivision of a state, who owns or leases a commercial motor vehicle or assigns drivers to operate that vehicle. A person who employs himself or herself as a commercial vehicle driver is considered to be both an employer and a driver for purposes of this chapter.

(h) "Fatality" means the death of a person as a result of a motor vehicle accident.

(i) "Felony" means an offense under state or federal law that is punishable by death or imprisonment for a term exceeding one year.

(j) "Gross combination weight rating" means the value specified by the manufacturer as the maximum loaded weight of a combination or articulated vehicle. In the absence of a value specified by the manufacturer, gross vehicle weight rating shall be determined by adding the gross vehicle weight rating of the power unit and the total weight of the towed units and any load thereon.

(k) "Gross vehicle weight rating" means the value specified by the manufacturer as the maximum loaded weight of a single vehicle, as defined in Section 350.

(l) "Imminent hazard" means the existence of a condition that presents a substantial likelihood that death, serious illness, severe personal injury, or substantial endangerment to health, property, or the environment may occur before the reasonably foreseeable completion date of a formal proceeding has begun to lessen the risk of death, illness, injury, or endangerment.

(m) "Noncommercial motor vehicle" means a motor vehicle or combination of motor vehicles that is not included within the definition in subdivision (b).

(n) "Nonresident commercial driver's license" means a commercial driver's license issued to an individual by a state under one of the following provisions:

(1) The individual is domiciled in a foreign country.

(2) The individual is domiciled in another state.

(o) "Schoolbus" is a commercial motor vehicle, as defined in Section 545.

(p) "Serious traffic violation" includes any of the following:

(1) Excessive speeding, as defined pursuant to the federal Commercial Motor Vehicle Safety Act (P.L. 99-570) involving any single offense for any speed of 15 miles an hour or more above the posted speed limit.

(2) Reckless driving, as defined pursuant to the federal Commercial

Motor Vehicle Safety Act (P.L. 99-570), and driving in the manner described under Section 2800.1, 2800.2, or 2800.3, including, but not limited to, the offense of driving a commercial motor vehicle in willful or wanton disregard for the safety of persons or property.

(3) A violation of a state or local law involving the safe operation of a motor vehicle, arising in connection with a fatal traffic accident.

(4) A similar violation of a state or local law involving the safe operation of a motor vehicle, as defined pursuant to the Commercial Motor Vehicle Safety Act (Title XII of P.L. 99-570).

(5) Driving a commercial motor vehicle without a commercial driver's license.

(6) Driving a commercial motor vehicle without the driver having in his or her possession a commercial driver's license, unless the driver provides proof at the subsequent court appearance that he or she held a valid commercial driver's license on the date of the violation.

(7) Driving a commercial motor vehicle when the driver has not met the minimum testing standards for that vehicle as to the class or type of cargo the vehicle is carrying.

(8) Driving a commercial motor vehicle while using an electronic wireless communication device to write, send, or read a text-based communication, as defined in Section 23123.5.

In the absence of a federal definition, existing definitions under this code apply.

(q) "State" means a state of the United States or the District of Columbia.

(r) "Tank vehicle" means a commercial motor vehicle that is designed to transport any liquid or gaseous material within a tank or tanks having an individual rated capacity of more than 119 gallons and an aggregate rated capacity of at least 1,000 gallons that is permanently or temporarily attached to the vehicle or the chassis, including, but not limited to, cargo tanks and portable tanks, as defined in Part 171 of Title 49 of the Code of Federal Regulations. A commercial motor vehicle transporting an empty storage container tank not designed for transportation, with a rated capacity of at least 1,000 gallons that is temporarily attached to a flatbed trailer, is not a tank vehicle.

(Amended by Stats. 2015, Ch. 303, Sec. 540. (AB 731) Effective January 1, 2016.)

Article 3. Driver Notification Requirements

(Article 3 added by Stats. 1988, Ch. 1509, Sec. 9.)

15215. (a) The department shall report each conviction of a person who holds a commercial driver's license from another state occurring within this state to the licensing authority of the home state of the licensee. This report shall clearly identify the person convicted; violation date; describe the violation specifying the section of the statute, code, or ordinance violated; identify the court in which action was taken; indicate whether a plea of guilty or not guilty was entered, or the conviction was a result of the forfeiture of bail, bond, or other security; and include special findings made in connection with the conviction.

(b) For purposes of subdivision (a), "conviction" has the same meaning as defined in subdivision (d) of Section 15210.

(Amended by Stats. 2014, Ch. 71, Sec. 175. (SB 1304) Effective January 1, 2015.)

15220. Any driver of a commercial motor vehicle who has a driver's license issued by the department, and who is convicted of any offense involving the safe operation of a motor vehicle in any other state, shall notify the department, in the manner provided by the department, of the conviction within 30 days of the date of conviction.

(Added by Stats. 1988, Ch. 1509, Sec. 9.)

15222. Any driver of a commercial motor vehicle who is convicted of any offense involving the safe operation of a motor vehicle shall notify his or her employer of the conviction within 30 days of the date of conviction.

(Amended by Stats. 2016, Ch. 208, Sec. 12. (AB 2906) Effective January 1, 2017.)

15224. Any driver who has a driver's license or privilege suspended, revoked, or canceled by any state for any period, or who is disqualified from driving a commercial motor vehicle for any period, shall notify his or her employer of the suspension, revocation, cancellation, or disqualification, before the end of the business day following the action.

(Added by Stats. 1988, Ch. 1509, Sec. 9.)

15226. Any driver who is issued an out-of-service order under the federal Motor Carrier Safety Regulations of the United States Department of Transportation (49 C.F.R. 392.5) shall report the issuance to his or her employer within 24 hours.

(Added by Stats. 1988, Ch. 1509, Sec. 9.)

15228. The driver shall also report the issuance of an out-of-service order described in Section 15226 to the department in the manner provided by the department within 30 days unless the driver requests a review of the order by the United States Department of Transportation. If so, the driver shall report the order to the department within 30 days of an affirmation of the order.

(Added by Stats. 1988, Ch. 1509, Sec. 9.)

15230. Each person who applies for employment as a driver of a commercial motor vehicle shall provide the employer, at the time of the application, with the following information for the 10 years preceding the date of application:

(a) A list of the names and addresses of the applicant's previous employers for which the applicant was a driver of a commercial motor vehicle.

(b) The dates the applicant was employed by each employer.

(c) The reason for leaving that employment.

The applicant shall certify that all information furnished is true and complete. An employer may require an applicant to provide additional information.

(Added by Stats. 1988, Ch. 1509, Sec. 9.)

Article 4. Employer Responsibilities

(Article 4 added by Stats. 1988, Ch. 1509, Sec. 9.)

15240. No employer shall knowingly allow, permit, require, or authorize a driver to drive a commercial motor vehicle under any of the following conditions:

(a) The driver has a driver's license or privilege suspended, revoked, or canceled by any state or has been disqualified from operating a commercial motor vehicle.

(b) The driver has more than one driver's license.

(c) The driver or the commercial motor vehicle or motor carrier operation is subject to an out-of-service order as described in subdivision (b) of Section 2800.

(d) In violation of any law or regulation pertaining to a railroad-highway grade crossing.

(Amended by Stats. 2001, Ch. 504, Sec. 2. Effective January 1, 2002.)

15242. (a) A person who is self-employed as a commercial motor vehicle driver shall comply with both the requirements of this chapter pertaining to employers and those pertaining to employees.

(b) Notwithstanding subdivision (a), a motor carrier that engages a person who owns, leases, or otherwise operates not more than one motor vehicle listed in Section 34500 to provide transportation services under the direction and control of that motor carrier is responsible for the compliance of that person with this chapter and for purposes of the regulations adopted by the department pursuant to Section 34501 during the period of that direction and control.

(c) For the purposes of subdivision (b), "direction and control" means either of the following:

(1) The person is operating under the motor carrier's interstate operating authority issued by the United States Department of Transportation.

(2) The person is operating under a subcontract with the motor carrier that requires the person to operate in intrastate commerce and the person has performed transportation services for a minimum of 60 calendar days within the past 90 calendar days for the motor carrier and has been on duty for that carrier for no less than 36 hours within any week in which

transportation services were provided.

(d) Subdivision (b) shall not be construed to change the definition of "employer," "employee," or "independent contractor" for any purpose.
(Amended by Stats. 2006, Ch. 538, Sec. 659. Effective January 1, 2007.)

Article 5. Commercial Driver's License

(Article 5 added by Stats. 1988, Ch. 1509, Sec. 9.)

15250. (a) (1) A person shall not operate a commercial motor vehicle unless that person has in their immediate possession a valid commercial driver's license of the appropriate class.

(2) A person shall not operate a commercial motor vehicle while transporting hazardous materials unless that person has in their possession a valid commercial driver's license with a hazardous materials endorsement. An instruction permit does not authorize the operation of a vehicle transporting hazardous materials.

(b) (1) Before an application for an original or renewal of a commercial driver's license with a hazardous materials endorsement is submitted to the United States Transportation Security Administration for the processing of a security threat assessment, as required under Part 1572 of Title 49 of the Code of Federal Regulations, the department shall complete a check of the applicant's driving record to ensure that the person is not subject to a disqualification under Part 383.51 of Title 49 of the Code of Federal Regulations.

(2) (A) A person shall not be issued a commercial driver's license until passing a knowledge test and driving test for the operation of a commercial motor vehicle that complies with the minimum federal standards established by the federal Commercial Motor Vehicle Safety Act of 1986 (Public Law 99-570) and Part 383 of Title 49 of the Code of Federal Regulations, and has satisfied all other requirements of that act as well as any other requirements imposed by this code.

(B) The knowledge test required by Sections 383.23 and 383.25 of Title 49 of the Code of Federal Regulations for the issuance of a commercial driver's license or commercial learner's permit may be waived for an applicant who is a current or former member of the United States Armed Forces and who meets the conditions and limitations set forth in subdivision (a) of Section 383.77 of Title 49 of the Code of Federal Regulations, as those conditions and limitations relate to the waiver of the knowledge test for current or former military service members with experience operating commercial vehicles.

(C) The driving skills test required by Section 383.23 of Title 49 of the Code of Federal Regulations for the issuance of a commercial driver's license may be waived for an applicant who is a current or former member of the United States Armed Forces and who meets the conditions and limitations set forth in subdivision (b) of Section 383.77 of Title 49 of the Code of Federal Regulations, as those conditions and limitations relate to the waiver of the driving skills test for current or former military service members with experience operating commercial vehicles.

(D) The specialized knowledge test required for the issuance of a hazardous materials endorsement to a commercial driver's license, or a tank vehicle endorsement to a commercial learner's permit or commercial driver's license, and the driving skills test and specialized knowledge test required for a passenger endorsement to a commercial learner's permit or commercial driver's license, by Section 383.93 of Title 49 of the Code of Federal Regulations, may be waived for an applicant who is a current or former member of the United States Armed Forces and who meets the conditions and limitations set forth in subdivision (c) of Section 383.77 of Title 49 of the Code of Federal Regulations, as those conditions and limitations relate to the waiver of required testing for an endorsement for current or former military service members with experience operating commercial vehicles.

(c) The tests shall be prescribed and conducted by or under the direction of the department. The department may allow a third-party tester to administer the driving test part of the examination required under this section and Section 15275 if all of the following conditions are met:

(1) The tests given by the third party are the same as those that would otherwise be given by the department.

(2) The third party has an agreement with the department that includes, but is not limited to, the following provisions:

(A) Authorization for the United States Secretary of Transportation, or their representative, and the department, or its representative, to conduct random examinations, inspections, and audits without prior notice.

(B) Permission for the department, or its representative, to conduct onsite inspections at least annually.

(C) A requirement that all third-party testers meet the same qualification and training standards as the department's examiners, to the extent necessary to conduct the driving skill tests in compliance with the requirements of Part 383 of Title 49 of the Code of Federal Regulations.

(D) The department may cancel, suspend, or revoke the agreement with a third-party tester if the third-party tester fails to comply with the standards for the commercial driver's license testing program, or with any other term of the third-party agreement, upon 15 days' prior written notice of the action to cancel, suspend, or revoke the agreement by the department to the third party. Any action to appeal or review any order of the department canceling, suspending, or revoking a third-party testing agreement shall be brought in a court of competent jurisdiction under Section 1085 of the Code of Civil Procedure, or as otherwise permitted by the laws of this state. The action shall be commenced within 90 days from the effective date of the order.

(E) Any third-party tester whose agreement has been canceled pursuant to subparagraph (D) may immediately apply for a third-party testing agreement.

(F) A suspension of a third-party testing agreement pursuant to subparagraph (D) shall be for a term of less than 12 months as determined by the department. After the period of suspension, the agreement shall be reinstated upon request of the third-party tester.

(G) A revocation of a third-party testing agreement pursuant to subparagraph (D) shall be for a term of not less than one year. A third-party tester may apply for a new third-party testing agreement after the period of revocation and upon submission of proof of correction of the circumstances causing the revocation.

(H) Authorization for the department to charge the third-party tester a fee, as determined by the department, that is sufficient to defray the actual costs incurred by the department for administering and evaluating the third-party testing program, and for carrying out any other activities deemed necessary by the department to ensure sufficient training for the drivers participating in the program.

(3) Except as provided in Section 15250.3, the tests given by the third party shall not be accepted in lieu of tests prescribed and conducted by the department for applicants for a passenger vehicle endorsement specified in paragraph (2) of subdivision (a) of Section 15278, if the applicant operates or will operate a tour bus.

(d) Commercial driver's license applicants who take and pass driving tests administered by a third party shall provide the department with certificates of driving skill satisfactory to the department that the applicant has successfully passed the driving tests administered by the third party.

(e) If a driving test is administered to a commercial driver's license applicant who is to be licensed in another state pursuant to Section 383.79 of Subpart E of Part 383 of Title 49 of the Code of Federal Regulations, the department may impose a fee on the applicant that does not exceed the reasonable cost of conducting the tests and reporting the results to the driver's state of record.

(f) Implementation dates for the issuance of a commercial driver's license pursuant to this chapter may be established by the department as it determines is necessary to accomplish an orderly commercial driver's license program.

(g) Active duty members of the United States Armed Forces, members of the military reserves, members of the National Guard who are on active duty, including personnel on full-time National Guard duty, personnel on part-time National Guard training, and National Guard military technicians (civilians who are required to wear military uniforms), and active duty personnel of the United States Coast Guard are exempt from all commercial driver's license requirements and sanctions, as provided in Section 383.3(c) of Subpart A of Part 383 of Title 49 of the Code of Federal Regulations when operating motor vehicles for military purposes. This exception shall not apply to United States Armed Forces reserve technicians.

(Amended by Stats. 2020, Ch. 47, Sec. 2. (AB 2141) Effective January 1, 2021.)

15250.1. (a) The department shall, no later than June 5, 2020, adopt regulations related to entry-level driver training requirements for drivers of commercial motor vehicles in compliance with the requirements of Parts 380, 383, and 384 of Title 49 of the Code of Federal Regulations.

(b) The department shall require the course of instruction for entry-level drivers to require an applicant for a class A or B commercial driver's license to complete a minimum of 15 hours of behind-the-wheel training, at least 10 hours of which shall be on a public road. For the purpose of meeting this requirement, every 50 minutes of driving time is deemed to be an hour of training.

(Added by Stats. 2018, Ch. 984, Sec. 1. (SB 1236) Effective January 1, 2019.)

15250.3. The department may allow any employee of an organized camp, as defined in Section 18897 of the Health and Safety Code, regulated by the Public Utilities Commission pursuant to Chapter 8 (commencing with Section 5351) of Division 2 of the Public Utilities Code to operate a tour bus pursuant to employment by the operator of that organized camp, if that employee satisfies the requirements for a class B license and a passenger vehicle endorsement by passing a test administered by a third party in accordance with subdivisions (c), (d), and (e) of Section 15250.

(Added by Stats. 1992, Ch. 208, Sec. 2. Effective January 1, 1993.)

15255.1. (a) Except as otherwise specified in subdivisions (b) and (c), upon an application for an original commercial driver's license, a fee of sixty-four dollars ($64), and on and after January 1, 2010, a fee of sixty-six dollars ($66), shall be paid to the department for a license that will expire on the fifth birthday of the applicant following the date of the application. A fee of sixty-four dollars ($64), and on and after January 1, 2010, a fee of sixty-six dollars ($66), shall also be paid to the department upon an application to change a license classification or to remove a restriction if the change or removal requires a driving-skill test and the license will expire on the fifth birthday of the applicant following the date of the application.

(b) Upon application for an original commercial driver's license or for the renewal of commercial driver's license by a currently licensed class A or class B, or class A or class B, driver who meets the driver record requirements and all other requirements established by Section 383.77 of Title 49 of the Code of Federal Regulations, a fee of thirty-four dollars ($34), and on and after January 1, 2010, a fee of thirty-nine dollars ($39), shall be paid to the department for a license that will expire on the fifth birthday of the applicant following the date of the application.

(c) Upon application for an original class C commercial driver's license or for the renewal of a class C commercial driver's license which requires an endorsement as provided in Section 15278, a fee of thirty-four dollars ($34), and on and after January 1, 2010, a fee of thirty-nine dollars ($39), shall be paid to the department for a license that will expire on the fifth birthday of the applicant following the date of the application.

(d) Following failure in taking a driving-skill test, a fee of thirty dollars ($30) shall be paid to the department for each subsequent administration of the driving-skill test required by the application.

(Amended by Stats. 2009, 4th Ex. Sess., Ch. 10, Sec. 16. Effective July 28, 2009.)

15255.2. Upon application for a duplicate commercial driver's license by a currently licensed class A or class B driver, or a class C commercial driver's license which requires an endorsement as provided in Section 15278, from an applicant who meets the driver record requirements and all other requirements established by Section 383.77 of Title 49 of the Code of Federal Regulations, a fee of twenty-seven dollars ($27), on and after January 1, 2010, a fee of twenty-nine dollars ($29), shall be paid to the department.

(Amended by Stats. 2009, 4th Ex. Sess., Ch. 10, Sec. 17. Effective July 28, 2009.)

15260. (a) Any applicant for a commercial driver's license who does not successfully complete the air-brake component of the knowledge test, or who does not successfully complete the driving-skill test in a vehicle or combination of vehicles equipped with air brakes, shall, if otherwise qualified, receive a commercial driver's license that restricts the licenseholder from operating a commercial motor vehicle equipped with air brakes.

(b) To remove the restriction described in subdivision (a) from a commercial driver's license, the driver is required to make a new application for a commercial driver's license, and, in addition to any other requirements specified in this code, to successfully complete the air-brake component of the knowledge test prescribed by the department, and to pass the driver-skill test in a vehicle or combination of vehicles equipped with air brakes.

(c) For the purposes of the driving-skill test and the restriction described in this section, air brakes shall include any braking system operating fully or partially on the air-brake principle.

(Added by Stats. 1988, Ch. 1509, Sec. 9.)

15263. (a) Any applicant for a commercial driver's license who successfully completes the driving-skill test in a vehicle or combination of vehicles equipped with an automatic transmission, shall, if otherwise qualified, receive a commercial driver's license that restricts the licenseholder from operating a commercial motor vehicle or combination of vehicles equipped with a manual transmission.

(b) To remove the restriction described in subdivision (a) from a commercial driver's license, the driver is required to make a new application for a commercial driver's license, and, in addition to any other requirements specified in this code, successfully complete the driving-skill test in a vehicle or combination of vehicles equipped with a manual transmission.

(Added by Stats. 1988, Ch. 1509, Sec. 9.)

Article 6. Endorsements

(Article 6 added by Stats. 1988, Ch. 1509, Sec. 9.)

15275. (a) A person may not operate a commercial motor vehicle described in this chapter unless that person has in his or her possession a valid commercial driver's license for the appropriate class, and an endorsement issued by the department to permit the operation of the vehicle unless exempt from the requirement to obtain an endorsement pursuant to subdivision (b) of Section 15278.

(b) (1) An endorsement to drive vehicles specified in this article shall be issued only to applicants who are qualified by examinations prescribed by the department and who meet the minimum standards established in Part 383 of Title 49 of the Code of Federal Regulations.

(2) A hazardous materials endorsement shall be issued only to applicants who comply with paragraph (1) and the requirements set forth in Part 1572 of Title 49 of the Code of Federal Regulations.

(c) The department may deny, suspend, revoke, or cancel an endorsement to drive vehicles specified in this article when the applicant does not meet the qualifications for the issuance or retention of the endorsement.

(d) If the department denies, suspends, revokes, or cancels a hazardous materials endorsement because the department received notification that the applicant poses a security threat pursuant to Part 1572 of Title 49 of the Code of Federal Regulations, and, upon appeal by the United States Transportation Security Administration, that endorsement is ordered reinstated, the department shall issue or restore the hazardous materials endorsement to the applicant within the period specified under those

federal regulations.
(Amended by Stats. 2005, Ch. 22, Sec. 201. Effective January 1, 2006.)

15275.1. (a) Except as provided in subdivision (b), a schoolbus endorsement is valid only when the operator possesses or qualifies for a valid commercial driver's license with a passenger endorsement and possesses a schoolbus driver's certificate issued pursuant to Section 12517.

(b) A schoolbus endorsement is valid without a schoolbus driver's certificate for an operator who is employed as a mechanic or a schoolbus driver-trainee if the schoolbus endorsement is restricted to operating a schoolbus when there is no pupil being transported.
(Amended by Stats. 2005, Ch. 199, Sec. 4. Effective January 1, 2006.)

15278. (a) A driver is required to obtain an endorsement issued by the department to operate any commercial motor vehicle that is any of the following:

(1) A double trailer.

(2) A passenger transportation vehicle, which includes, but is not limited to, a bus, farm labor vehicle, or general public paratransit vehicle when designed, used, or maintained to carry more than 10 persons including the driver.

(3) A schoolbus.

(4) A tank vehicle.

(5) A vehicle carrying hazardous materials, as defined in Section 353, that is required to display placards pursuant to Section 27903, unless the driver is exempt from the endorsement requirement as provided in subdivision (b). This paragraph does not apply to any person operating an implement of husbandry who is not required to obtain a driver's license under this code.

(b) This section does not apply to any person operating a vehicle in an emergency situation at the direction of a peace officer pursuant to Section 2800.
(Amended by Stats. 2010, Ch. 360, Sec. 7. (AB 1648) Effective January 1, 2011.)

Article 7. Sanctions

(Article 7 added by Stats. 1988, Ch. 1509, Sec. 9.)

15300. (a) A driver shall not operate a commercial motor vehicle for a period of one year if the driver is convicted of a first violation of any of the following:

(1) Subdivision (a), (b), or (c) of Section 23152 while operating a motor vehicle.

(2) Subdivision (d) of Section 23152.

(3) Subdivision (a) or (b) of Section 23153 while operating a motor vehicle.

(4) Subdivision (d) of Section 23153.

(5) Leaving the scene of an accident involving a motor vehicle operated by the driver.

(6) Using a motor vehicle to commit a felony, other than a felony described in Section 15304.

(7) Driving a commercial motor vehicle when the driver's commercial driver's license is revoked, suspended, or canceled based on the driver's operation of a commercial motor vehicle or when the driver is disqualified from operating a commercial motor vehicle based on the driver's operation of a commercial motor vehicle.

(8) Causing a fatality involving conduct defined pursuant to Section 191.5 of the Penal Code or subdivision (c) of Section 192 of the Penal Code.

(9) While operating a motor vehicle, refuses to submit to, or fails to complete, a chemical test or tests in violation of Section 23612.

(10) A violation of Section 2800.1, 2800.2, or 2800.3 that involves a commercial motor vehicle.

(b) If a violation listed in subdivision (a), or a violation listed in paragraph (2) of subdivision (a) of Section 13350 or Section 13352 or 13357, occurred while transporting a hazardous material, the period specified in subdivision (a) shall be three years.
(Amended by Stats. 2010, Ch. 216, Sec. 4. (AB 2144) Effective January 1, 2011.)

15301. The Department of Motor Vehicles, in conjunction with the State Fire Marshal, shall develop regulations and procedures to temporarily suspend the commercial motor vehicle license of a person who is operating a commercial motor vehicle while transporting dangerous fireworks having a gross weight of 10,000 pounds or more. A driver of a commercial motor vehicle shall not operate a commercial motor vehicle for three years if the driver is convicted of transporting dangerous fireworks having a gross weight of 10,000 pounds or more.
(Added by Stats. 2007, Ch. 563, Sec. 13. Effective January 1, 2008.)

15302. A driver shall not operate a commercial motor vehicle for the rest of his or her life if convicted of more than one violation of any of the following:

(a) Subdivision (a), (b), or (c) of Section 23152 while operating a motor vehicle.

(b) Subdivision (d) of Section 23152.

(c) Subdivision (a) or (b) of Section 23153 while operating a motor vehicle.

(d) Subdivision (d) of Section 23153.

(e) Leaving the scene of an accident involving a motor vehicle operated by the driver.

(f) Using a motor vehicle to commit a felony, other than a felony described in Section 15304.

(g) Driving a commercial motor vehicle when the driver's commercial driver's license is revoked, suspended, or canceled based on the driver's operation of a commercial motor vehicle or when the driver is disqualified from operating a commercial motor vehicle based on the driver's operation of a commercial motor vehicle.

(h) Causing a fatality involving conduct defined pursuant to Section 191.5 of the Penal Code or in subdivision (c) of Section 192 of the Penal Code.

(i) While operating a motor vehicle, refuses to submit to, or fails to complete, a chemical test or tests in violation of Section 23612.

(j) A violation of Section 2800.1, 2800.2, or 2800.3 that involves a commercial motor vehicle.

(k) Any combination of the above violations or a violation listed in paragraph (2) of subdivision (a) of Section 13350 or Section 13352 or 13357 that occurred while transporting a hazardous material.
(Amended by Stats. 2010, Ch. 216, Sec. 5. (AB 2144) Effective January 1, 2011.)

15303. (a) A driver shall not operate a commercial motor vehicle for the rest of their life if convicted of using a commercial motor vehicle in the commission of a felony involving an act or practice of severe forms of human trafficking, as described in Section 7102 of Title 22 of the United States Code.

(b) A driver shall not operate a commercial motor vehicle for the rest of their life if convicted of Section 236.1 of the Penal Code while using a commercial motor vehicle.
(Added by Stats. 2024, Ch. 226, Sec. 10. (AB 3278) Effective January 1, 2025.)

15303.3. Pursuant to Subpart E of Part 383 of Title 49 of the Code of Federal Regulations, a driver shall not operate a commercial motor vehicle if the department receives notice from the federal Drug and Alcohol Clearinghouse that the driver is prohibited from operating a commercial motor vehicle. The term for which a driver shall not operate a commercial motor vehicle shall remain in effect for the period specified by Subpart E of Part 383 of Title 49 of the Code of Federal Regulations.
(Added by Stats. 2024, Ch. 226, Sec. 11. (AB 3278) Effective January 1, 2025.)

15303.5. Pursuant to Subpart E of Part 383 of Title 49 of the Code of Federal Regulations, the department shall not issue, renew, or upgrade a commercial learner's permit or commercial driver's license if the department receives notification from the federal Drug and Alcohol Clearinghouse that the driver is prohibited from operating a commercial motor vehicle.
(Added by Stats. 2024, Ch. 226, Sec. 12. (AB 3278) Effective January 1, 2025.)

15304. (a) A driver may not operate a commercial motor vehicle for the rest of his or her life who uses a motor vehicle in the commission of a felony involving manufacturing, distributing, or dispensing a controlled substance, or possession with intent to manufacture, distribute, or dispense a controlled substance.

(b) This section shall become operative on September 20, 2005.

(Amended by Stats. 2004, Ch. 952, Sec. 19. Effective January 1, 2005. Amended version operative September 20, 2005, pursuant to earlier operation of new subdivision (b).)

15306. A driver shall not operate a commercial motor vehicle for a period of 60 days if the person is convicted of a serious traffic violation involving a commercial or a noncommercial motor vehicle and the offense occurred within three years of a separate offense of a serious traffic violation that resulted in a conviction.

(Amended by Stats. 2010, Ch. 216, Sec. 6. (AB 2144) Effective January 1, 2011.)

15308. (a) A driver shall not operate a commercial motor vehicle for a period of 120 days if the person is convicted of a serious traffic violation involving a commercial or noncommercial motor vehicle and the offense occurred within three years of two or more separate offenses of serious traffic violations that resulted in convictions.

(b) Notwithstanding Section 13366.5, the time period under subdivision (a) shall not commence until all existing suspensions or revocations of the commercial driving privilege have ended.

(Amended by Stats. 2010, Ch. 216, Sec. 7. (AB 2144) Effective January 1, 2011.)

15309. In addition to any other action taken under this code, no driver may operate a commercial motor vehicle for a period of 60 days if the department determines, after a hearing, that the person falsified information on his or her application for a driver's license in violation of the standards set forth in subpart J of part 383 or Section 383.71(a) of Title 49 of the Code of Federal Regulations.

(Added by Stats. 1999, Ch. 724, Sec. 35.4. Effective January 1, 2000.)

15309.5. (a) It is unlawful for any person to do any of the following:

(1) Sell, offer for sale, distribute, or use a crib sheet or cribbing device, as defined in Section 273, that contains answers to any examination administered by the department for a commercial driver's license or permit.

(2) Impersonate or allow the impersonation of an applicant for a commercial driver's license or permit for the purpose of fraudulently qualifying the applicant for a commercial driver's license or permit.

(3) Provide, or use, any unauthorized assistance during any examination administered by the department for a commercial driver's license or permit.

(b) A first conviction under this section is punishable as either an infraction or a misdemeanor, and the driver shall not operate a commercial motor vehicle for a period of one year. A second or subsequent conviction is punishable as a misdemeanor, and the driver shall not operate a commercial motor vehicle for a period of one year.

(Added by Stats. 2013, Ch. 649, Sec. 5. (AB 1047) Effective January 1, 2014.)

15311. (a) A driver shall not operate a commercial motor vehicle for a period of 180 days if the person is convicted of a first violation of an out-of-service order under subdivision (b), (c), or (d) of Section 2800.

(b) A driver shall not operate a commercial motor vehicle for a period of two years if the person is convicted of violating an out-of-service order under subdivision (b), (c), or (d) of Section 2800 while transporting hazardous materials required to be placarded or while operating a vehicle designed to transport 16 or more passengers, including the driver.

(c) A driver shall not operate a commercial motor vehicle for a period of two years if the person is convicted of a second violation of an out-of-service order under subdivision (b), (c), or (d) of Section 2800 during any 10-year period, arising from separate incidents.

(d) A driver shall not operate a commercial motor vehicle for a period of three years if the person is convicted of a second violation of an out-of-service order under subdivision (b), (c), or (d) of Section 2800 while transporting hazardous materials that are required to be placarded or while operating a vehicle designed to transport 16 or more passengers, including the driver.

(e) In addition to the disqualification period required in subdivision (a), (b), (c), or (d), a driver who is convicted of violating an out-of-service order under subdivision (b) of Section 2800 is subject to a civil penalty of not less than two thousand five hundred dollars ($2,500) for a first conviction, and a civil penalty of five thousand dollars ($5,000) for a second or subsequent conviction.

(f) A driver shall not operate a commercial motor vehicle for a period of three years if the person is convicted of a third or subsequent violation of an out-of-service order under subdivision (b), (c), or (d) of Section 2800 during any 10-year period, arising from separate incidents.

(Amended by Stats. 2010, Ch. 216, Sec. 8. (AB 2144) Effective January 1, 2011.)

15311.1. An employer that knowingly allows or requires an employee to operate a commercial motor vehicle in violation of an out-of-service order is, upon conviction, subject to a civil penalty of not less than two thousand seven hundred fifty dollars ($2,750) nor more than twenty-five thousand dollars ($25,000).

(Amended by Stats. 2010, Ch. 216, Sec. 9. (AB 2144) Effective January 1, 2011.)

15312. A driver may not operate a commercial motor vehicle for the following periods:

(a) Not less than 60 days if that person is convicted of a violation of subdivision (a) of Section 2800, or Section 21462, 22451, or 22452, or subdivision (c) or (d) of Section 22526, involving a commercial motor vehicle and the violation occurred at a railroad-highway crossing.

(b) Not less than 120 days if that person is convicted of a violation of subdivision (a) of Section 2800, or Section 21462, 22451, or 22452, or subdivision (c) or (d) of Section 22526, involving a commercial motor vehicle, and that violation occurred at a railroad-highway crossing, during any three-year period of a separate, prior offense of a railroad-highway grade crossing violation, that resulted in a conviction.

(c) Not less than one year if that person is convicted of a violation of subdivision (a) of Section 2800, or Section 21462, 22451, or 22452, or subdivision (c) or (d) of Section 22526, involving a commercial motor vehicle, and that violation occurred at a railroad-highway crossing, at a railroad-highway grade crossing, during any three-year period of two or more prior offenses of a railroad-highway grade crossing violation, that resulted in convictions.

(Amended by Stats. 2010, Ch. 216, Sec. 10. (AB 2144) Effective January 1, 2011.)

15312.1. (a) An employer that knowingly allows or requires an employee to operate a commercial motor vehicle in violation of a federal, state, or local law or regulation pertaining to railroad crossings is, upon conviction, subject to a civil penalty of not more than ten thousand dollars ($10,000).

(b) This section shall become operative on September 20, 2005.

(Added by Stats. 2004, Ch. 952, Sec. 25. Effective January 1, 2005. Section operative September 20, 2005, by its own provisions.)

15315. (a) The department shall not issue a commercial driver's license to a person during a period in which the person is prohibited from operating a commercial motor vehicle, or the person's driving privilege is suspended, revoked, or canceled.

(b) No commercial driver's license may be issued to a person who has a commercial driver's license issued by any other state unless the person first surrenders the commercial driver's license issued by the other state, which license shall be returned to the issuing state.

(Added by Stats. 1988, Ch. 1509, Sec. 9.)

15319. The department may execute or make agreements, arrangements, or declarations to carry out this chapter.

(Added by Stats. 1988, Ch. 1509, Sec. 9.)

15320. The department shall suspend, revoke, or cancel, the privilege of any person to operate a commercial motor vehicle for the periods specified in this article upon receipt of a duly certified abstract of the record of any court that the person has been convicted of any of the offenses set forth in this article.

(Added by Stats. 1999, Ch. 724, Sec. 37. Effective January 1, 2000.)

15325. (a) Pursuant to subpart D of Part 383 of Title 49 of the Code of Federal Regulations, a driver whose driving is determined to constitute an imminent hazard is disqualified from operating a commercial motor vehicle for the period specified by the Federal Motor Carrier Safety Administration.

(b) The disqualification action shall be made part of the driver's record.

(c) A driver who is simultaneously disqualified under this section and any other state law or regulation, shall serve those disqualification periods concurrently.

(d) This section shall become operative on September 20, 2005.

(Added by Stats. 2004, Ch. 952, Sec. 26. Effective January 1, 2005. Section operative September 20, 2005, by its own provisions.)

15326. Upon receiving notification of an administrative action or conviction of a commercial licenseholder in a state, territory, or possession of the United States, the District of Columbia, the Commonwealth of Puerto Rico, or the Dominion of Canada, the department shall impose a suspension, revocation, or disqualification action on that person's commercial driving privilege based upon violations that would result in an administrative action or a conviction pursuant to Section 383.51 of Subpart D of Part 383 and Sections 384.206(b)(3), 384.213, and 384.231 of Subpart B of Part 384 of Title 49 of the Federal Code of Regulations. Those violations include, but are not limited to, all of the following:

(a) Violations of Sections 15300, 15302, and 15304.

(b) Serious traffic violations, as defined in subdivision (p) of Section 15210 and subject to the penalties under Section 15306 or 15308.

(c) Providing false information under Section 15309.

(d) Out-of-service order violations under Section 15311.

(e) Railroad-highway crossing violations under Section 15312.

(Added by Stats. 2012, Ch. 670, Sec. 10. (AB 2188) Effective January 1, 2013.)

Division 6.5. Motor Vehicle Transactions with Minors

(Division 6.5 added by Stats. 1968, Ch. 1020.)

Chapter 1. Driver's License Requirements

(Chapter 1 added by Stats. 1968, Ch. 1020.)

15500. It is unlawful for any minor who does not possess a valid driver's license issued under this code to order, purchase or lease, attempt to purchase or lease, contract to purchase or lease, accept, or otherwise obtain, any vehicle of a type subject to registration.

(Added by Stats. 1968, Ch. 1020.)

15501. It is unlawful for any minor to present or offer to any person offering for sale or lease or to give or otherwise furnish thereto any motor vehicle of a type subject to registration, a driver's license which is false, fraudulent, or not actually his own for the purpose of ordering, purchasing or leasing, attempting to purchase or lease, contracting to purchase or lease, accepting, or otherwise obtaining such a vehicle.

(Added by Stats. 1968, Ch. 1020.)

Division 6.7. Unattended Child in Motor Vehicle Safety Act

(Division 6.7 added by Stats. 2001, Ch. 855, Sec. 2.)

Chapter 1. General Provisions

(Chapter 1 added by Stats. 2001, Ch. 855, Sec. 2.)

15600. This division shall be known and may be cited as "Kaitlyn's Law."

(Added by Stats. 2001, Ch. 855, Sec. 2. Effective January 1, 2002.)

15602. This division applies to motor vehicles upon the highways and elsewhere throughout the state unless expressly provided otherwise.

(Added by Stats. 2001, Ch. 855, Sec. 2. Effective January 1, 2002.)

15603. The purpose of this division is to help prevent injuries to, and the death of, young children from the effects of being left alone in a motor vehicle, to help educate parents and caretakers about the dangers of leaving children alone in a motor vehicle, and to authorize a monetary fine to be imposed on a person for leaving a young child alone in a motor vehicle in circumstances that pose a life safety risk.

(Added by Stats. 2001, Ch. 855, Sec. 2. Effective January 1, 2002.)

Chapter 2. Offenses

(Chapter 2 added by Stats. 2001, Ch. 855, Sec. 2.)

15620. (a) A parent, legal guardian, or other person responsible for a child who is 6 years of age or younger may not leave that child inside a motor vehicle without being subject to the supervision of a person who is 12 years of age or older, under either of the following circumstances:

(1) Where there are conditions that present a significant risk to the child's health or safety.

(2) When the vehicle's engine is running or the vehicle's keys are in the ignition, or both.

(b) A violation of subdivision (a) is an infraction punishable by a fine of one hundred dollars ($100), except that the court may reduce or waive the fine if the defendant establishes to the satisfaction of the court that he or she is economically disadvantaged and the court, instead, refers the defendant to a community education program that includes education on the dangers of leaving young children unattended in motor vehicles, and provides certification of completion of that program. Upon completion of that program, the defendant shall provide that certification to the court. The court may, at its discretion, require any defendant described in this section to attend an education program on the dangers of leaving young children unattended in motor vehicles.

(c) Nothing in this section shall preclude prosecution under both this section and Section 192 of the Penal Code, or Section 273a of that code, or any other provision of law.

(d) (1) Subdivision (b) and Section 40000.1 do not apply if an unattended child is injured or medical services are rendered on that child because of a violation described in subdivision (a).

(2) Nothing in this subdivision precludes prosecution under any other provision of law.

(Amended by Stats. 2002, Ch. 664, Sec. 222. Effective January 1, 2003.)

Chapter 3. Educational Provisions

(Chapter 3 added by Stats. 2001, Ch. 855, Sec. 2.)

15630. Notwithstanding any other provision of law, the fines collected for a violation of this division shall be allocated by the county treasurer, as follows:

(a) (1) Seventy percent to the county or city health department where the violation occurred, to be used for the development and implementation of community education programs on the dangers of leaving young children unattended in motor vehicles.

(2) A county or city health department may develop and implement the community education program described in paragraph (1) or may contract for the development and implementation of that program.

(3) As the proceeds from fines collected under this division become available, each county or city health department shall prepare and annually update a listing of community education programs that provide information on the dangers of leaving young children unattended in motor vehicles and ways to avoid that danger. The county or city health department shall forward the listing to the courts and shall make the listing available to the public, and may distribute it to other agencies or organizations.

(b) Fifteen percent to the county or city for the administration of the program, from which will be paid the cost of the county to account for and disburse fine revenues.

(c) Fifteen percent to the city, to be deposited in its general fund except that, if the violation occurred in an unincorporated area, this amount shall be deposited in the county's general fund.

(Added by Stats. 2001, Ch. 855, Sec. 2. Effective January 1, 2002.)

15632. (a) The department shall include information concerning the dangers of leaving children unattended in motor vehicles, including, but not limited to, the effect of solar heat on the temperature of vehicle interiors and the penalties for noncompliance with Chapter 2 (commencing with Section 15620), in the following materials distributed by the department:

(1) The California Driver's Handbook published under Section 1656.

(2) The driver's license examination administered under Section 12804.9, by including, on a rotating basis, at least one question in one version of the driver's license examination that is periodically administered to applicants.

(3) Any driver's education materials certified by the department.

(4) Courses and examinations for traffic violator schools.

(5) Materials provided to secondary and postsecondary schools and educational institutions.

(6) Any materials provided to community education campaigns undertaken by the department and other state agencies, including, but not limited to, the Department of the California Highway Patrol and the Department of Transportation.

(b) The department shall not republish materials before existing supplies are exhausted, but shall arrange for compliance with this section in the next edition or publication of those materials in the normal course of business.

(Amended by Stats. 2021, Ch. 254, Sec. 9. (AB 174) Effective September 23, 2021.)

Division 7. Financial Responsibility Laws

(Division 7 enacted by Stats. 1959, Ch. 3.)

Chapter 1. Compulsory Financial Responsibility

(Chapter 1 repealed and added by Stats. 1974, Ch. 1409.)

Article 1. Accident Reports

(Article 1 added by Stats. 1974, Ch. 1409.)

16000. (a) The driver of a motor vehicle who is in any manner involved in an accident originating from the operation of the motor vehicle on a street or highway, or is involved in a reportable off-highway accident, as defined in Section 16000.1, that has resulted in damage to the property of any one person in excess of one thousand dollars ($1,000), or in bodily injury, or in the death of any person shall report the accident, within 10 days after the accident, either personally or through an insurance agent, broker, or legal representative, on a form approved by the department, to the office of the department at Sacramento, subject to this chapter. The driver shall identify on the form, by name and current residence address, if available, any person involved in the accident complaining of bodily injury.

(b) A report is not required under subdivision (a) if the motor vehicle involved in the accident was owned or leased by, or under the direction of, the United States, this state, another state, or a local agency.

(c) If none of the parties involved in an accident has reported the accident to the department under this section within one year following the date of the accident, the department is not required to file a report on the accident and the driver's license suspension requirements of Section 16004 or 16070 do not apply.

(d) This section shall become operative on January 1, 2017.

(Repealed (in Sec. 28) and added by Stats. 2015, Ch. 451, Sec. 29. (SB 491) Effective January 1, 2016. Section operative January 1, 2017, by its own provisions.)

16000.1. (a) For purposes of this division, a "reportable off-highway accident" means an accident that includes all of the following:

(1) Occurs off the street or highway.

(2) Involves a vehicle that is subject to registration under this code.

(3) Results in damages to the property of any one person in excess of one thousand dollars ($1,000) or in bodily injury or in the death of any person.

(b) A "reportable off-highway accident" does not include any accident that occurs off-highway in which damage occurs only to the property of the driver or owner of the motor vehicle and no bodily injury or death of a person occurs.

(c) This section shall become operative on January 1, 2017.

(Repealed (in Sec. 30) and added by Stats. 2015, Ch. 451, Sec. 31. (SB 491) Effective January 1, 2016. Section operative January 1, 2017, by its own provisions.)

16000.7. As used in this division an "uninsured motor vehicle" is a motor vehicle for which financial responsibility as provided in Section 16021 was not in effect at the time of the accident.

(Added by Stats. 1979, Ch. 549.)

16000.8. (a) Notwithstanding any other provision of this chapter, if the failure of the driver of a motor vehicle involved in an accident to prove the existence of financial responsibility, as required by Section 16020, was due to the fraudulent acts of an insurance agent or broker, the department shall terminate any suspension action taken pursuant to Section 16070, when both of the following conditions are met:

(1) The driver provides documentation from the Department of Insurance that the insurance agent or broker has been found to have committed fraud in the transaction of automobile liability insurance, or provides documentation that criminal charges have been filed against the agent or broker due to fraud or theft related to the sale of automobile liability insurances.

(2) The driver furnishes proof to the department that financial responsibility meeting the requirements of Section 16021 is currently in effect.

(b) It is the intent of the Legislature in enacting this section that individuals who are the victims of insurance fraud not be penalized for violating the financial responsibility laws when that violation was due to the fraudulent acts of others. Persons with documented evidence of fraud involving their insurance coverage, such as where an insurance agent accepted the premium payment for coverage but willfully failed to obtain the coverage and led the customer to believe insurance was in effect, should retain their driving privileges provided they give evidence that valid liability insurance is currently in effect.

(Added by Stats. 1996, Ch. 1155, Sec. 6. Effective January 1, 1997.)

16001. If the vehicle involved was a driverless runaway vehicle and was parked with the express or implied permission of the registered owner, the registered owner of the vehicle shall be construed to have been the driver of the vehicle for the purposes of this chapter.

(Repealed and added by Stats. 1974, Ch. 1409.)

16002. (a) If the driver at the time of the accident was driving a motor vehicle owned, operated, or leased by the employer of the driver and with the permission of the employer, then the driver shall within five days after the accident report the accident to his employer on a form approved by the employer. Within 10 days after receipt of the report the employer shall transmit a report on a form approved by the department to the office of the department at Sacramento, except that an employer need not transmit such report when the vehicle involved in the accident is owned or operated as described in Section 16051 or 16052, or is owned or operated by any person or corporation who has filed with the department a certificate of an insurance carrier or surety company that there is in effect a policy or bond meeting the requirements of Section 16056 and when such policy or bond is in force with respect to the vehicle at the time of the accident.

(b) The driver of a vehicle that is owned or operated by a publicly owned or operated transit system, or that is operated under contract with a publicly owned or operated transit system, and that is used to provide regularly scheduled transportation to the general public or for other official business of the system shall, within 10 days of the occurrence of the accident, report to the transit system any accident of a type otherwise required to be reported pursuant to subdivision (a) of Section 16000. The transit system shall maintain records of any report filed pursuant to this paragraph. Within 10 days after receipt of the report, the transit system shall transmit a report on a form approved by the department to the office of the department in Sacramento, except that a transit system is not required to submit a report when the vehicle involved in the accident is owned or operated as described in subdivision (b) of Section 16000.

(Amended by Stats. 2001, Ch. 84, first Sec. 2. Effective July 19, 2001.)

16003. If any driver is physically incapable of making the report, and is not the owner of the motor vehicle involved in the accident, the owner shall, as soon as he learns of the accident, report the matter in writing to the department.

(Repealed and added by Stats. 1974, Ch. 1409.)

16004. (a) The department shall suspend the driving privilege of any person who fails, refuses, or neglects to make a report of an accident as required in this chapter.

(b) A suspension taken under this section shall remain in effect until terminated by receipt of the report of the accident or upon receipt of evidence that financial responsibility as provided in Section 16021 is in effect.

(c) The driving privilege shall not be suspended under this section, and, if a suspension has been imposed and is in effect under this section, that suspension shall be terminated, if the driving privilege is suspended under Section 16370 or 16381 as the result of a judgment arising out of the same accident for which the report of the accident is required by this section. The department may suspend or reimpose the suspension of the driving privilege of a person under this section if the suspension under Section 16370 or 16381 is later set aside for a reason other than that the person has satisfied the judgment in full or to the extent provided in Chapter 2 (commencing with Section 16250) and has given proof of financial responsibility, as provided in Chapter 3 (commencing with Section 16430).

(Amended by Stats. 1990, Ch. 314, Sec. 3. Effective July 17, 1990.)

16005. (a) All reports and supplemental reports required by this chapter including insurance information forms shall be without prejudice to the individual so reporting and shall be for the confidential use of the department and any other state department requiring such information, except that the department shall upon request disclose from the reports:

(1) The names and addresses of persons involved in the accident.

(2) The registration numbers and descriptions of vehicles involved in the accident.

(3) The date, time, and location of the accident.

(4) Any suspension action taken by the department.

(5) The names and addresses of insurers.

(b) The information specified in subdivision (a) may be given to any person having a proper interest therein, including:

(1) The driver or drivers involved, or the employer, parent, or legal guardian thereof.

(2) The authorized representative of any person involved in the accident.

(3) Any person injured in the accident.

(4) The owners of vehicles or property damaged in the accident.

(5) Any law enforcement agency.

(6) Any court of competent jurisdiction.

(Repealed and added by Stats. 1974, Ch. 1409.)

Article 2. Financial Responsibility

(Article 2 added by Stats. 1974, Ch. 1409.)

16020. (a) All drivers and all owners of a motor vehicle shall at all times be able to establish financial responsibility pursuant to Section 16021, and shall at all times carry in the vehicle evidence of the form of financial responsibility in effect for the vehicle.

(b) "Evidence of financial responsibility" means any of the following:

(1) A form issued by an insurance company or charitable risk pool, as specified by the department pursuant to Section 4000.37.

(2) If the owner is a self-insurer, as provided in Section 16052 or a depositor, as provided in Section 16054.2, the certificate of self-insurance or the assignment of deposit letter issued by the department.

(3) An insurance covering note or binder pursuant to Section 382 or 382.5 of the Insurance Code.

(4) A showing that the vehicle is owned or leased by, or under the direction of, the United States or a public entity, as defined in Section 811.2 of the Government Code.

(c) For purposes of this section, "evidence of financial responsibility" also may be obtained by a law enforcement officer and court personnel from an electronic reporting system when that system becomes available for use by law enforcement officers.

(d) For purposes of this section, "evidence of financial responsibility" also includes any of the following:

(1) The name of the insurance company and the number of an insurance policy or surety bond that was in effect at the time of the accident or at the time that evidence of financial responsibility is required to be provided pursuant to Section 16028, if that information is contained in the vehicle registration records of the department.

(2) The identifying motor carrier of property permit number issued by the Department of the California Highway Patrol to the motor carrier of property as defined in Section 34601, and displayed on the motor vehicle in the manner specified by the Department of the California Highway Patrol.

(3) The identifying number issued to the household mover by the Bureau of Household Goods and Services and displayed on the motor vehicle in the manner specified by the bureau or an identifying number issued to the passenger stage carrier or transportation charter party carrier by the Public Utilities Commission and displayed on the motor vehicle in the manner specified by the commission.

(e) Evidence of financial responsibility does not include an identification number in paragraph (1), (2), or (3) of subdivision (d) if the carrier is currently suspended by the issuing agency for lack or lapse of insurance or other form of financial responsibility.

(Amended by Stats. 2022, Ch. 295, Sec. 13. (AB 2956) Effective January 1, 2023.)

16020.3. Notwithstanding any other provision of law, any employer that owns a vanpool vehicle, as described in paragraph (1) of subdivision (c) of Section 17149 of the Revenue and Taxation Code, shall maintain evidence of financial responsibility with respect to that vehicle in the same form and amount as described in Section 5391.2 of the Public Utilities Code.

(Added by Stats. 1994, Ch. 622, Sec. 4. Effective January 1, 1995.)

16021. Financial responsibility of the driver or owner is established if the driver or owner of the vehicle involved in an accident described in Section 16000 is:

(a) A self-insurer under the provisions of this division.

(b) An insured or obligee under a form of insurance or bond that complies with the requirements of this division and that covers the driver for the vehicle involved in the accident.

(c) The United States of America, this state, any municipality or subdivision thereof, or the lawful agent thereof.

(d) A depositor in compliance with subdivision (a) of Section 16054.2.

(e) An obligee under a policy issued by a charitable risk pool that complies with subdivision (b) of Section 16054.2.

(f) In compliance with the requirements authorized by the department by any other manner which effectuates the purposes of this chapter.

(Amended by Stats. 2003, Ch. 594, Sec. 41. Effective January 1, 2004.)

16025. (a) Every driver involved in the accident shall, unless rendered incapable, exchange with any other driver or property owner involved in the accident and present at the scene, all of the following information:

(1) Driver's name and current residence address, driver's license number, vehicle identification number, and current residence address of registered owner.

(2) Evidence of financial responsibility, as specified in Section 16020. If the financial responsibility of a person is a form of insurance, then that person shall supply the name and address of the insurance company and the number of the insurance policy.

(b) Any person failing to comply with all of the requirements of this section is guilty of an infraction punishable by a fine not to exceed two hundred fifty dollars ($250).

(Amended by Stats. 1999, Ch. 880, Sec. 10. Effective January 1, 2000.)

16027. (a) Whenever proof of financial responsibility has been established under subdivision (a) of Section 16054.2 and a period of four years has elapsed following the effective date of the suspension, the cash deposit, or any balance thereof remaining, shall be refunded to the person entitled thereto, if the director is satisfied that there are no outstanding or pending claims against the deposit.

(b) If the deposit, or any balance thereof, is refundable under this section but remains unclaimed by the depositor or any other person entitled thereto for a period of six years from the effective date of the suspension, the unclaimed deposit shall be transferred to the Motor Vehicle Account in the State Transportation Fund.

(Amended by Stats. 1985, Ch. 619, Sec. 1.)

16028. (a) Upon the demand of a peace officer pursuant to subdivision (b) or upon the demand of a peace officer or traffic collision investigator pursuant to subdivision (c), every person who drives a motor vehicle upon a highway shall provide evidence of financial responsibility for the vehicle that is in effect at the time the demand is made. The evidence of financial responsibility may be provided using a mobile electronic device. However, a peace officer shall not stop a vehicle for the sole purpose of determining whether the vehicle is being driven in violation of this subdivision.

(b) If a notice to appear is issued for any alleged violation of this code, except a violation specified in Chapter 9 (commencing with Section 22500) of Division 11 or any local ordinance adopted pursuant to that chapter, the cited driver shall furnish written evidence of financial responsibility or may provide electronic verification of evidence of financial responsibility using a mobile electronic device upon request of the peace officer issuing the citation. The peace officer shall request and verify the driver's evidence of financial responsibility, as specified in Section 16020. If the driver fails to provide evidence of financial responsibility at the time the notice to appear is issued, the peace officer may issue the driver a notice to appear for violation of subdivision (a). The notice to appear for violation of subdivision (a) shall be written on the same citation form as the original violation.

(c) If a peace officer, or a regularly employed and salaried employee of a city or county who has been trained as a traffic collision investigator, is summoned to the scene of an accident described in Section 16000, the driver of a motor vehicle that is in any manner involved in the accident shall furnish written evidence of financial responsibility or may provide electronic verification of evidence of financial responsibility using a mobile electronic device upon the request of the peace officer or traffic collision investigator. If the driver fails to provide evidence of financial responsibility when requested, the peace officer may issue the driver a notice to appear for violation of subdivision (a). A traffic collision investigator may cause a notice to appear to be issued for a violation of subdivision (a), upon review of that citation by a peace officer.

(d) (1) If, at the time a notice to appear for a violation of subdivision (a) is issued, the person is driving a motor vehicle owned or leased by the driver's employer, and the vehicle is being driven with the permission of the employer, this section shall apply to the employer rather than the driver. In that case, a notice to appear shall be issued to the employer rather than the driver, and the driver may sign the notice on behalf of the employer.

(2) The driver shall notify the employer of the receipt of the notice issued pursuant to paragraph (1) not later than five days after receipt.

(e) A person issued a notice to appear for a violation of subdivision (a) may personally appear before the clerk of the court, as designated in the notice to appear, and provide written evidence of financial responsibility in a form consistent with Section 16020, showing that the driver was in compliance with that section at the time the notice to appear for violating subdivision (a) was issued. In lieu of the personal appearance, the person may submit by mail to the court written evidence of having had financial responsibility at the time the notice to appear was issued. Upon receipt by the clerk of that written evidence of financial responsibility in a form consistent with Section 16020, further proceedings on the notice to appear for the violation of subdivision (a) shall be dismissed.

(f) For the purposes of this section, "mobile electronic device" means a portable computing and communication device that has a display screen with touch input or a miniature keyboard.

(g) For the purposes of this section, when a person provides evidence of financial responsibility using a mobile electronic device to a peace officer, the peace officer shall only view the evidence of financial responsibility and is prohibited from viewing any other content on the mobile electronic device.

(h) If a person presents a mobile electronic device pursuant to this section, that person assumes all liability for any damage to the mobile electronic device.

(Amended by Stats. 2022, Ch. 295, Sec. 14. (AB 2956) Effective January 1, 2023.)

16029. Notwithstanding any other provision of law, a violation of subdivision (a) of Section 16028 is an infraction and shall be punished as follows:

(a) Upon a first conviction, by a fine of not less than one hundred dollars ($100) and not more than two hundred dollars ($200), plus penalty assessments.

(b) Upon a subsequent conviction, occurring within three years of a prior conviction, by a fine of not less than two hundred dollars ($200) and not more than five hundred dollars ($500), plus penalty assessments.

(c) (1) At the discretion of the court, for good cause, and in addition to the penalties specified in subdivisions (a) and (b), the court may order the impoundment of the vehicle for which the owner could not produce evidence of financial responsibility in violation of subdivision (a) of Section 16028.

(2) A vehicle impounded pursuant to paragraph (1) shall be released to the legal owner of the vehicle or the legal owner's agent if all of the following conditions are met:

(A) The legal owner is a motor vehicle dealer, bank, credit union, acceptance corporation, or other licensed financial institution legally operating in this state.

(B) The legal owner or the legal owner's agent pays all towing and storage fees related to the seizure of the vehicle.

(C) The legal owner or the legal owner's agent presents foreclosure documents or an affidavit of repossession for the vehicle.

(3) (A) A legal owner or the legal owner's agent that obtains release of the vehicle pursuant to paragraph (2) shall not release the vehicle to the registered owner of the vehicle or any agents of the registered owner, unless the registered owner is a rental car agency, except upon presentation of evidence of financial responsibility, as defined in Section 16020, for the vehicle. The legal owner or the legal owner's agent shall make every reasonable effort to ensure that the evidence of financial responsibility that is presented is valid.

(B) Prior to relinquishing the vehicle, the legal owner may require the registered owner to pay all towing and storage charges related to impoundment and any administrative charges authorized under Section 22850.5 that were incurred by the legal owner in connection with obtaining custody of the vehicle.

(4) A vehicle impounded under paragraph (1) shall be released to a rental car agency if the agency is either the legal owner or the registered owner of the vehicle and the agency pays all towing and storage fees related to the seizure of the vehicle.

(5) A vehicle impounded under paragraph (1) shall be released to the registered owner of the vehicle only upon presentation of evidence of financial responsibility, as defined in Section 16020, for that vehicle, and evidence that all towing and storage fees related to the seizure of the vehicle are paid.

This paragraph does not apply to a person, entity, or agency who is entitled to release of a vehicle under paragraph (2) or (4) and is either:

(A) The registered and the legal owner and is described in subparagraph (A) of paragraph (2).

(B) The registered owner or legal owner and is described in paragraph (4).

(d) It is the intent of the Legislature that fines collected pursuant to this section be used to reduce the number of uninsured drivers and not be used to generate revenue for general purposes.

(e) (1) Except as provided in this subdivision, the court shall impose a fine that is greater than the minimum fine specified in subdivision (a) or (b), and may not reduce that fine to the minimum specified fine authorized under those provisions, unless the defendant has presented the court with evidence of financial responsibility, as defined in Section 16020, for the vehicle. In no event may the court impose a fine that is less than the minimum specified in subdivision (a) or (b), or impose a fine that exceeds the maximum specified fine authorized under those subdivisions. In addition to the fine authorized under subdivision (a) or (b), the court may issue an order directing the defendant to maintain insurance coverage satisfying the financial responsibility laws for at least one year from the date of the order.

(2) Notwithstanding any other provision of law, the imposition of the fine required under subdivision (a) or (b) is mandatory upon conviction of a violation of subdivision (a) of Section 16028 and may not be waived, suspended, or reduced below the minimum fines, unless the court in its

discretion reduces or waives the fine based on the defendant's ability to pay. The court may direct that the fine and penalty assessments be paid within a limited time or in installments on specified dates. The Legislature hereby declares that it is in the interest of justice that the minimum fines set forth in subdivisions (a) and (b) for these offenses be enforced by the court, as provided in this subdivision.

(Amended by Stats. 1999, Ch. 880, Sec. 12. Effective January 1, 2000.)

16030. (a) Except as provided in subdivision (c), any person who knowingly provides false evidence of financial responsibility (1) when requested by a peace officer pursuant to Section 16028 or (2) to the clerk of the court as permitted by subdivision (e) of Section 16028, including an expired or canceled insurance policy, bond, certificate of self-insurance, or assignment of deposit letter, is guilty of a misdemeanor punishable by a fine not exceeding seven hundred fifty dollars ($750) or imprisonment in the county jail not exceeding 30 days, or by both that fine and imprisonment. Upon receipt of the court's abstract of conviction, the department shall suspend the driving privilege, effective upon the date of conviction, for a period of one year. The court shall impose an interim suspension of the person's driving privileges pursuant to Section 13550, and shall notify the driver of the suspension pursuant to Section 13106, and all driver's licenses in the possession of the driver shall be surrendered to the court pursuant to Section 13550. Any driver's license surrendered to the court pursuant to this section shall be transmitted by the court, together with the required report of the conviction, to the department within 10 days of the conviction. The suspension may not be terminated until one year has elapsed from the date of the suspension and until the person files proof of financial responsibility, as provided in Chapter 3 (commencing with Section 16430) except that the suspension shall be reinstated if the person fails to maintain proof of financial responsibility for three years.

(b) However, in lieu of suspending a person's driving privileges pursuant to subdivision (a), the court shall restrict the person's driving privileges to driving that is required in the person's course of employment, if driving of a motor vehicle is necessary in order to perform the duties of the person's primary employment. The restriction shall remain in effect for the period of suspension otherwise required by subdivision (a). The court shall provide for endorsement of the restriction on the person's driver's license, and violation of the restriction constitutes a violation of Section 14603 and grounds for suspension or revocation of the license under Section 13360.

(c) This section does not apply to a driver who is driving a motor vehicle owned or leased by the employer of the driver and driven in the course of the driver's employment with the permission of the employer.

(Amended by Stats. 1999, Ch. 880, Sec. 13. Effective January 1, 2000.)

16033. No public entity or employee, agent, or any person or organization authorized under Section 4610 to endorse receipts or validate registration cards or potential registration cards, is liable for any loss, detriment, or injury resulting, directly or indirectly, from any of the following:

(a) Failure to request evidence of financial responsibility.

(b) Failure to notify a vehicle owner that an insurance policy has been terminated.

(c) The discretionary failure to cancel, suspend, or revoke a vehicle registration when an insurance policy has been terminated.

(d) Inaccurately recording that evidence under Section 16028 or as a result of the driver producing false or inaccurate financial responsibility information.

(Amended by Stats. 1999, Ch. 880, Sec. 14. Effective January 1, 2000.)

Article 3. Evidence of Financial Responsibility

(Heading of Article 3 amended by Stats. 2001, Ch. 739, Sec. 11.)

16050. In order to establish evidence of financial responsibility, every driver or employer involved in an accident and required to report the accident under Section 16000 shall establish to the satisfaction of the department that the provisions of this article are applicable to his or her responsibilities arising out of the accident.

(Amended by Stats. 2001, Ch. 739, Sec. 12. Effective January 1, 2002.)

16050.5. The owner of a vehicle, who has a liability insurance policy with respect to the vehicle, shall, upon request, furnish insurance information to a person who, while operating the vehicle with the owner's permission, is involved in a reportable accident with the insured vehicle, or to the department whenever the department is required to establish whether the permitted driver meets the financial responsibility requirements of Section 16020.

(Amended by Stats. 1991, Ch. 1177, Sec. 4. Effective October 14, 1991.)

16051. (a) Evidence may be established by filing a report indicating that the motor vehicle involved in the accident was owned, rented, or leased by or under the direction of the United States, this state, or any political subdivision of this state or municipality thereof.

(b) Evidence may be established by filing a report indicating that the motor vehicle involved in the accident was owned and operated by a peace officer, member of the Department of the California Highway Patrol, or firefighter in the performance of his or her duty, and at the request of or under the direction of the United States, this state, or any political subdivision or municipality of this state.

(Amended by Stats. 2012, Ch. 823, Sec. 4. (AB 2298) Effective January 1, 2013.)

16052. Evidence may be established if the owner of the motor vehicle involved in the accident was a self-insurer. Any person in whose name more than 25 motor vehicles are registered may qualify as a self-insurer by obtaining a certificate of self-insurance issued by the department as provided in this article.

(Amended by Stats. 2001, Ch. 739, Sec. 14. Effective January 1, 2002.)

16053. (a) The department may in its discretion, upon application, issue a certificate of self-insurance when it is satisfied that the applicant in whose name more than 25 motor vehicles are registered is possessed and will continue to be possessed of ability to pay judgments obtained against him or her in amounts at least equal to the amounts provided in Section 16056. The certificate may be issued authorizing the applicant to act as a self-insurer for either property damage or bodily injury or both. Any person duly qualified under the laws or ordinances of any city or county to act as self-insurer and then acting as such, may upon filing with the department satisfactory evidence thereof, along with the application as may be required by the department, be entitled to receive a certificate of self-insurance.

(b) Upon not less than five days' notice and a hearing pursuant to the notice, the department may upon reasonable grounds cancel a certificate of self-insurance. Failure to pay any judgment within 30 days after the judgment has become final and has not been stayed or satisfied shall constitute a reasonable ground for the cancellation of a certificate of self-insurance.

(Amended by Stats. 1991, Ch. 1177, Sec. 5. Effective October 14, 1991.)

16054. (a) Evidence may be established by filing with the department satisfactory documentation:

(1) That the owner had an automobile liability policy, a motor vehicle liability policy, or bond in effect at the time of the accident with respect to the driver or the motor vehicle involved in the accident, unless it is established that at the time of the accident the motor vehicle was being operated without the owner's permission, express or implied, or was parked by a driver who had been operating the vehicle without permission.

(2) That the driver of the motor vehicle involved in the accident, if he or she was not the owner of the motor vehicle, had in effect at the time of the accident an automobile liability policy or bond with respect to his or her operation of the motor vehicle not owned by him or her.

(3) That the liability as may arise from the driver's operation of the motor vehicle involved in the accident is, in the judgment of the department, covered by some form of liability insurance or bond.

(4) That the owner or driver, if he or she is involved in an accident while operating a vehicle of less than four wheels, had in effect at the

time of the accident with respect to the driver or vehicle a liability policy or bond that meets the requirements of Section 16056.

(b) Any automobile liability policy or bond referred to in this section shall comply with the requirements of Section 16056 and Sections 11580, 11580.011, 11580.1, and 11580.2 of the Insurance Code, but need not contain provisions other than those required by those sections, and shall not be governed by Chapter 3 (commencing with Section 16430).

(Amended by Stats. 2001, Ch. 739, Sec. 15. Effective January 1, 2002.)

16054.2. Evidence may also be established by any of the following:

(a) By depositing with the department cash in the amount specified in Section 16056.

(b) By providing documentation of a liability policy covering the operation of the vehicle that (A) is issued by a charitable risk pool operating under Section 5005.1 of the Corporations Code, if the registered owner of the vehicle is a nonprofit organization that is exempt from taxation under paragraph (3) of subsection (c) of Section 501 of the United States Internal Revenue Code and (B) the policy is subject, if the accident has resulted in bodily injury or death, to a limit, exclusive of interest and costs, of not less than fifteen thousand dollars ($15,000) because of bodily injury to or death of one person in any one accident and, subject to that limit for one person, to a limit of not less than thirty thousand dollars ($30,000) because of bodily injury to or death of two or more persons in any one accident, and, if the accident has resulted in injury to, or destruction of property, to a limit of not less than five thousand dollars ($5,000) because of injury to or destruction of property of others in any one accident.

(c) By any other manner authorized by the department which effectuates the purposes of this chapter.

(Amended by Stats. 2001, Ch. 739, Sec. 16. Effective January 1, 2002.)

16055. Evidence of insurance or bond shall be submitted by the insurer or surety in conformance with the requirements of Section 16057. In the event of notice to the department by the company that issued one of the above stated policies or bonds that coverage was not in effect, then the policy or bond shall not operate to establish evidence as provided for by Section 16054.

(Amended by Stats. 2001, Ch. 739, Sec. 17. Effective January 1, 2002.)

16056. (a) A policy or bond shall not be effective under Section 16054 unless issued by an insurance company or surety company admitted to do business in this state by the Insurance Commissioner, except as provided in subdivision (b), and unless the policy or bond is subject to either of the following:

(1) If the accident has resulted in bodily injury or death, to a limit, exclusive of interest and costs, of not less than fifteen thousand dollars ($15,000) because of bodily injury to or death of one person in any one accident and, subject to that limit for one person, to a limit of not less than thirty thousand dollars ($30,000) because of bodily injury to or death of two or more persons in any one accident, and, if the accident has resulted in injury to, or destruction of property, to a limit of not less than five thousand dollars ($5,000) because of injury to or destruction of property of others in any one accident.

(2) Notwithstanding paragraph (1), for any policy or bond issued or renewed on or after January 1, 2025, if the accident has resulted in bodily injury or death, to a limit, exclusive of interest and costs, of not less than thirty thousand dollars ($30,000) because of bodily injury to or death of one person in any one accident and, subject to that limit for one person, to a limit of not less than sixty thousand dollars ($60,000) because of bodily injury to or death of two or more persons in any one accident, and, if the accident has resulted in injury to, or destruction of property, to a limit of not less than fifteen thousand dollars ($15,000) because of injury to or destruction of property of others in any one accident.

(b) A policy or bond shall not be effective under Section 16054 with respect to any vehicle that was not registered in this state or was a vehicle that was registered elsewhere than in this state at the effective date of the policy or bond or the most recent renewal thereof, unless the insurance company or surety company issuing the policy or bond is admitted to do business in this state, or if the company is not admitted to do business in this state, unless it executes a power of attorney authorizing the department to accept service on its behalf of notice or process in any action upon the policy or bond arising out of an accident mentioned in subdivision (a).

(c) Any nonresident driver whose driving privilege has been suspended or revoked based upon an action that requires proof of financial responsibility may, in lieu of providing a certificate of insurance from a company admitted to do business in California, provide a written certificate of proof of financial responsibility that is satisfactory to the department, covers the operation of a vehicle in this state, meets the liability requirements of this section, and is from a company that is admitted to do business in that person's state of residence.

(d) For a policy or bond issued or renewed on or after January 1, 2035, the minimum liability coverage shall be increased by twenty thousand dollars ($20,000) for bodily injury or death for one person, by forty thousand dollars ($40,000) for bodily injury or death for all persons, and by ten thousand dollars ($10,000) for property damage.

(e) This section shall become operative on January 1, 2025.

(Amended (as added by Stats. 2022, Ch. 717, Sec. 3) by Stats. 2023, Ch. 204, Sec. 19. (AB 1140) Effective January 1, 2024. Operative January 1, 2025, by its own provisions.)

16056.1. Notwithstanding the coverage limits specified in Section 16056, an automobile insurance policy described in Section 11629.71 of the Insurance Code shall be effective under Section 16054 when issued by an insurance company admitted to do business in this state by the Insurance Commissioner and the policy is subject, if the accident has resulted in bodily injury or death, to a limit, exclusive of interest and costs, of not less than ten thousand dollars ($10,000) because of bodily injury to or death of one person in any one accident and, subject to that limit for one person, to a limit of not less than twenty thousand dollars ($20,000) because of bodily injury to or death of two or more persons in any one accident, and if the accident has resulted in injury to, or destruction of property, to a limit of not less than three thousand dollars ($3,000) because of injury to or destruction of property of others in any one accident.

(Amended by Stats. 2005, Ch. 435, Sec. 22. Effective January 1, 2006.)

16057. Upon receipt of notice of an accident from the department, the insurance company or surety company named in the notice shall notify the department within such time and in such manner as the department may require whenever the policy or bond was not in effect at the time of the accident.

(Repealed and added by Stats. 1974, Ch. 1409.)

16058. (a) (1) An insurer that issues private passenger automobile liability insurance policies and coverages, or private passenger automobile policies and coverages issued by an automobile assigned risk plan, as those policies, coverages, and plans are described in paragraph (1) of subdivision (a) of Section 4000.37 shall electronically report to the department liability insurance information under subdivisions (b), (c), and (d).

(2) On or before January 1, 2023, an insurer that issues commercial and fleet insurance policies shall electronically report to the department liability insurance information under subdivisions (b), (c), and (d).

(b) (1) An insurer shall report all existing motor vehicle liability insurance policies or coverages described in subdivision (a) issued for vehicles registered in this state or to policyholders with a California address, to the department in a manner that preserves existing reporting relationships and that allows for smaller insurers and those with unusual circumstances to be accommodated, consistent with the intent of this section.

(2) Consistent with the intent of this section, a small insurer or those with unusual circumstances may be accommodated by, among other methods, an extension of the mandatory electronic reporting deadline set forth in paragraph (2) of subdivision(a) to no later than July 1, 2023.

(c) An insurer shall electronically report to the department all issued motor vehicle liability policies or coverages, as described in subdivision (a), within 30 days of the effective date of the coverage.

(d) An insurer shall electronically report to the department the termination of a reported policy or any change of information previously reported under subdivision (b) or (c), as specified by the department, within 45 days of the date of termination or change. This report shall include the effective date of the termination, amendment, or cancellation and any other information that does not exceed that required under subdivision (c).

(e) (1) Those persons with alternative forms of financial responsibility pursuant to subdivision (a), (c), (d), or (e) of Section 16021 shall provide satisfactory evidence of that responsibility as determined by the department.

(2) In addition, the department shall establish an alternative procedure for establishment of satisfactory evidence of financial responsibility to permit the timely renewal of vehicle registration when the electronic data has not been updated due to circumstances beyond the vehicle owner's immediate control. Those circumstances may include, but are not limited to, a vehicle identification error in either the department's or the insurer's records or insurance purchased too recently to have been electronically transmitted to the department. Whenever this alternative procedure is used, the department shall, subsequent to the issuance of the registration certificate and indicia, contact the insurer to obtain electronic data pursuant to subdivision (c).

(f) The department shall adopt regulations for reporting insurance information, including, but not limited to, establishing acceptable timeframes and approved methods for reporting information.

(Amended by Stats. 2021, Ch. 254, Sec. 10. (AB 174) Effective September 23, 2021.)

16058.1. The department shall develop a method by which law enforcement officers and court personnel, on and after July 1, 2006, may electronically verify that an insurance policy or bond for a motor vehicle has been issued.

(Amended by Stats. 2005, Ch. 706, Sec. 38. Effective January 1, 2006.)

Article 4. Suspensions

(Article 4 added by Stats. 1974, Ch. 1409.)

16070. (a) Whenever a driver involved in an accident described in Section 16000 fails to provide evidence of financial responsibility, as required by Section 16020, at the time of the accident, the department shall, pursuant to subdivision (b), suspend the privilege of the driver or owner to drive a motor vehicle, including the driving privilege of a nonresident in this state.

(b) Whenever the department receives an accident report pursuant to this article that alleges that any of the drivers involved in the accident was not in compliance with Section 16020 at the time of the accident, the department shall immediately mail to that driver a notice of intent to suspend the driving privilege of that driver. The department shall suspend the driving privilege 30 days after mailing the notice, unless the driver has, prior to that date, established evidence of financial responsibility at the time of the accident, as specified in Section 16021, with the department. The suspension notice shall notify the driver of the action taken and the right to a hearing under Section 16075.

(Amended by Stats. 2001, Ch. 739, Sec. 18. Effective January 1, 2002.)

16071. The department shall suspend the driving privilege of any person upon receiving notice from another state that the person's driving privilege in that state has been suspended for failure to meet the financial responsibility provisions of the law in that state, if the suspension in that state was taken on grounds that would have resulted in a suspension in this state.

(Amended (as amended by Stats. 1996, Ch. 1126, Sec. 12) by Stats. 1999, Ch. 880, Sec. 17. Effective January 1, 2000.)

16072. (a) The suspension of the driving privilege of a person as provided in Section 16070 shall not be terminated until one year has elapsed from the date of actual commencement of the suspension and until the person files proof of financial responsibility as provided in Chapter 3 (commencing with Section 16430), except that the suspension shall be reinstated if the person fails to maintain proof of financial responsibility for three years. However, in lieu of suspending a person's driving privilege pursuant to this section, the department, upon application, if the person files and thereafter maintains proof of financial responsibility as provided in this section and pays a penalty fee to the department of two hundred fifty dollars ($250), may restrict the person's driving privilege to any of the following situations:

(1) Necessary travel to and from that person's place of employment.

(2) Driving that is required in the person's course of employment, when driving a motor vehicle is necessary in order to perform the duties of the person's primary employment.

(3) Necessary travel to transport a minor dependent in that person's immediate family to and from an institute of primary or secondary instruction, if the chief administrative officer or principal of the educational institution certifies in writing to the department that the minor dependent is enrolled in the educational institution and no form of public transportation or schoolbus is available between the applicant's place of residence and the educational institution.

The restriction shall remain in effect for the period of suspension required by this section, so long as proof of financial responsibility is maintained.

(b) If a suspension has been imposed under Section 16070 and one year has elapsed from the date the suspension actually commenced, that suspension shall be terminated if the driving privilege is suspended under Section 16370 or 16381 as the result of a judgment arising out of the accident for which proof of financial responsibility was required to be established. The department may reimpose the suspension of the driving privilege of a person under Section 16070 if the suspension under Section 16370 or 16381 is later set aside for a reason other than that the person has satisfied the judgment in full or to the extent provided in Chapter 2 (commencing with Section 16250) and has given proof of ability to respond in damages as provided in Chapter 3 (commencing with Section 16430).

(c) Notwithstanding Chapter 2 (commencing with Section 42200) of Division 18, all revenues derived from the penalty fees provided in subdivision (a) shall, after deduction by the department of the costs incurred by the department in administering this section, be deposited in the Financial Responsibility Penalty Account in the General Fund. The balance in this fund on each July 1, which is not subject to appropriation as provided in Section 12980 of the Insurance Code, shall revert to the General Fund.

(d) (1) Subdivision (a) does not apply to a commercial driver's license holder.

(2) A commercial driver's license holder whose driving privilege is otherwise suspended under this chapter is not entitled to a restricted license, unless that person surrenders his or her commercial driver's license and is issued a noncommercial class C or M driver's license.

(Amended by Stats. 2006, Ch. 574, Sec. 16. Effective January 1, 2007.)

16073. (a) The privilege of a person employed for the purpose of driving a motor vehicle for compensation whose occupation requires the use of a motor vehicle in the course of his or her employment to drive a motor vehicle not registered in his or her name and in the course of that person's employment may not be suspended under this chapter even though his or her privilege to drive is otherwise suspended under this chapter.

(b) Subdivision (a) does not apply to a commercial driver's licenseholder. A commercial driver's licenseholder whose driving privilege is otherwise suspended under this chapter may not operate a commercial motor vehicle.

(c) This section shall become operative on September 20, 2005.

(Amended by Stats. 2004, Ch. 952, Sec. 27. Effective January 1, 2005. Amended version

operative September 20, 2005, pursuant to earlier operation of new subdivision (c).)

16074. Whenever the department has taken any action or has failed to take any action under this chapter by reason of having received erroneous information, or by reason of having received no information, it shall take appropriate action to carry out the purposes and effect of this chapter upon receiving correct information.

(Added by Stats. 1974, Ch. 1409.)

16075. (a) The suspension provisions of this article shall not apply to a driver or owner until 30 days after the department sends to the driver or owner notice of its intent to suspend his or her driving privilege, pursuant to subdivision (b) of Section 16070, and advises the driver or owner of his or her right to a hearing as provided in this section.

(b) If the driver or owner receiving the notice of intent to suspend wishes to have a hearing, the request for a hearing shall be made in writing to the department within 10 days of the receipt of the notice. Failure to respond to a notice of intent within 10 days of receipt of the notice is a waiver of the person's right to a hearing.

(c) If the driver or owner makes a timely request for a hearing, the department shall hold the hearing before the effective date of the suspension to determine the applicability of this chapter to the driver or owner, including a determination of whether:

(1) The accident has resulted in property damage in excess of one thousand dollars ($1,000), or bodily injury, or death.

(2) The driver or owner has established evidence of financial responsibility, as provided in Article 3 (commencing with Section 16050), that was in effect at the time of the accident.

(d) A request for a hearing does not stay the suspension of a person's driving privilege. However, if the department does not conduct a hearing and make a determination pursuant thereto within the time limit provided in subdivision (b) of Section 16070, the department shall stay the effective date of the order of suspension pending a determination.

(e) The hearing provided for by this section shall be held in the county of residence of the person requesting the hearing. The hearing shall be conducted pursuant to Article 3 (commencing with Section 14100) of Chapter 3 of Division 6.

(f) The department shall render its decision within 15 days after conclusion of the hearing.

(g) This section shall become operative on January 1, 2017.

(Repealed (in Sec. 34) and added by Stats. 2015, Ch. 451, Sec. 35. (SB 491) Effective January 1, 2016. Section operative January 1, 2017, by its own provisions.)

16076. (a) The department shall notify every person whose driving privilege is suspended, pursuant to Section 16070, of that person's right to apply for a restricted driving privilege authorized under Section 16072.

(b) For purposes of subdivision (a), the department shall prepare and publish a printed summary. The printed summary may contain, but is not limited to, the following wording:

"If your driving privilege is suspended due to involvement in an accident while you were uninsured, you may apply for a restricted license at any office of the Department of Motor Vehicles, accompanied with proof of financial responsibility, payment of a penalty fee of two hundred fifty dollars ($250), and, unless already paid, payment of a reissuance fee.

The Mello-McAlister Restricted Employment Driving Privilege Act allows you to apply for a driver's license limiting you to driving to and from work, and during the course of your primary employment, during the one-year mandatory term of suspension. The restricted license will not be issued if any other suspension or revocation action has been taken against your driving privilege."

(c) This section shall be known and may be cited as the Mello-McAlister Restricted Employment Driving Privilege Act.

(Amended by Stats. 2003, Ch. 451, Sec. 19. Effective January 1, 2004.)

16077. (a) The department, upon application and payment of a fifty dollar ($50) fee and a penalty fee of two hundred dollars ($200), may issue a restricted license to an applicant with serious health problems, or to an applicant with an immediate family member with serious health problems, when the applicant's privilege to drive is otherwise suspended under this chapter. The restricted license may be issued to enable the applicant to drive a motor vehicle for the purpose of receiving medical or mental health treatments of a prolonged and repetitive nature for the applicant or the member of the applicant's immediate family with serious health problems, if the applicant files and maintains proof of financial responsibility on file with the department pursuant to Section 16021 and there is no other suitable means of transportation available.

(b) The application shall set forth the nature of the health problem, the nature of the treatments, the duration and location of the treatments, and the schedule for visits. The applicant shall submit documentation signed by the treating physician and surgeon or licensed psychotherapist, as defined in subdivisions (a), (b), (c), and (e) of Section 1010 of the Evidence Code, as necessary to assist the department in its decision to grant or deny the restricted license. Upon reviewing the application, the department may determine that an investigation as to the person's fitness to operate a motor vehicle is warranted. If the department makes this determination, the department may conduct an investigation in a manner provided for in Chapter 3 (commencing with Section 13800) of Division 6.

(c) In reviewing the application, the department shall give due consideration to the circumstances set forth in the application and shall be guided by principles of fairness and humanity.

(d) Notwithstanding Chapter 2 (commencing with Section 42200) of Division 18, all revenues derived from the penalty fees provided in subdivision (a) shall, after deduction by the department of the costs incurred by the department in administering this section, be deposited in the Financial Responsibility Penalty Account in the General Fund.

(e) (1) Subdivision (a) does not apply to a commercial driver's license holder.

(2) A commercial driver's license holder whose driving privilege is otherwise suspended under this chapter is not entitled to a restricted license unless that person surrenders his or her commercial driver's license and is issued a noncommercial class C or M driver's license.

(Amended by Stats. 2006, Ch. 574, Sec. 17. Effective January 1, 2007.)

16078. Any person who has paid the penalty fee prescribed in subdivision (a) of Section 16072, whether or not the person has received the license restriction authorized by that section, may also apply for and receive a restricted license under Section 16077 without paying the fees prescribed in Section 16077. Any person who has paid the fees prescribed in subdivision (a) of Section 16077, whether or not the person has received the restricted license authorized by that section, may also apply for and receive the license restriction prescribed in Section 16072.

(Added by Stats. 1990, Ch. 1407, Sec. 4.)

Chapter 2. Suspensions Following Unsatisfied Judgments

(Chapter 2 enacted by Stats. 1959, Ch. 3.)

Article 1. Definitions

(Article 1 enacted by Stats. 1959, Ch. 3.)

16250. As used in this chapter and Chapter 3 (commencing with Section 16430), "judgment" means a final judgment of any court of competent jurisdiction in this or any other state or of the United States against a person as defendant upon a cause of action.

(Amended by Stats. 1984, Ch. 144, Sec. 207.)

16251. (a) As used in this chapter and Chapter 3 (commencing with Section 16430), "cause of action" means any cause of action for damage to property in excess of one thousand dollars ($1,000) or for damage in any amount on account of bodily injury to or death of any person resulting from the operation by the defendant or any other person of any motor vehicle upon a highway in this state, except a cause of action based upon statutory liability by reason of signing the application of a minor for a driver's license.

(b) This section shall become operative on January 1, 2017.

(Repealed (in Sec. 36) and added by Stats. 2015, Ch. 451, Sec. 37. (SB 491) Effective January 1, 2016. Section operative January 1, 2017, by its own provisions.)

Article 2. Suspension of Driving Privilege

(Heading of Article 2 amended by Stats. 1975, Ch. 354.)

16370. The department shall suspend the privilege of any person to operate a motor vehicle upon receiving a certified copy of a judgment, or a certified copy of the register of actions (or a comparable court record of another jurisdiction) in an action resulting in a judgment for damages, and a certificate of facts relative to the judgment, on a form provided by the department, indicating that the person has failed for a period of 30 days to satisfy a judgment rendered against him or her.

(Amended by Stats. 2001, Ch. 44, Sec. 10. Effective January 1, 2002.)

16370.5. The department shall suspend the privilege of any person to operate a motor vehicle as specified in Section 116.880 of the Code of Civil Procedure. Except as provided in this section, an action brought under Section 116.880 of the Code of Civil Procedure is not governed by Chapter 2 (commencing with Section 16250) of Division 7.

(Amended by Stats. 2003, Ch. 594, Sec. 42. Effective January 1, 2004.)

16370.7. Documents filed with the department pursuant to Section 16370 shall be accompanied by a fee of not to exceed twenty dollars ($20) to pay for processing the documents and issuing the suspension order.

(Added by Stats. 1988, Ch. 395, Sec. 4. Effective August 11, 1988.)

16371. The suspension shall remain in effect, and no license shall be issued to the judgment debtor until the judgment debtor gives proof of financial responsibility as provided in Chapter 3 (commencing with Section 16430), and until either the judgment is satisfied in full or to the extent provided in this chapter, subject to the exemption provided in Section 16375.

(Amended by Stats. 1989, Ch. 1157, Sec. 6.)

16373. (a) The clerk of a court shall, subject to subdivision (b), issue upon the request of a judgment creditor a certified copy of any judgment or a certified copy of the register of actions in an action resulting in a judgment for damages, and a certificate of facts relative to the judgment on a form provided by the department.

(b) The judgment creditor may pay the required fees and request the documents specified in subdivision (a) upon the expiration of 30 days after the judgment has become final, if the judgment has not been stayed or satisfied within the amounts specified in this chapter as shown by the records of the court. The court shall determine the required fees, which shall be commensurate with the cost incurred by the court in carrying out this section.

(Amended by Stats. 2001, Ch. 44, Sec. 11. Effective January 1, 2002.)

16374. Whenever after a judgment is satisfied and proof of financial responsibility is given, another judgment is rendered against the same person for any accident occurring prior to the date of the giving of the proof and the person fails to satisfy the latter judgment within the amounts specified in this chapter within 15 days after the latter judgment became final, then the department shall again suspend the driver's license of the judgment debtor and shall not issue to him or her any driver's license while the latter judgment remains unsatisfied and subsisting within the amounts specified in this chapter.

(Amended by Stats. 1989, Ch. 1157, Sec. 7.)

16375. Any person whose driver's license has been suspended, or is about to be suspended or shall become subject to suspension under this chapter, may relieve himself from the effect of the judgment by filing with the department an affidavit stating that at the time of the accident upon which the judgment has been rendered he was insured, that the insurer is liable to pay such judgment, and the reason, if known, why the insurance company has not paid the judgment. He shall also file the original policy of insurance or a certified copy thereof, if available, and such other documents as the department may require to show that the loss, injury, or damage for which the judgment was rendered, was covered by the policy of insurance.

If the department is satisfied from such papers that the insurer was authorized to issue the policy of insurance in this state at the time of issuing the policy and that such insurer is liable to pay such judgment, at least to the extent and for the amounts provided in this chapter, the department shall not suspend the license, or if already suspended, shall reinstate it.

(Amended by Stats. 1974, Ch. 714.)

16376. (a) If the person against whom judgment is rendered is a nonresident and the person fails within the prescribed time to satisfy the judgment in full or to the extent specified in this chapter, all privileges of operating a motor vehicle in this state given to the person under this code shall be suspended while the judgment remains in effect and unsatisfied and until the nonresident gives proof of his or her financial responsibility in the manner and to the extent provided in Chapter 3 (commencing with Section 16430) for accidents occurring after the date of the giving of proof.

(b) The department shall forward a certified copy of the judgment of a court of record to the appropriate officer in charge of the licensing of drivers in the state of which the person is a resident.

(Amended by Stats. 2001, Ch. 44, Sec. 12. Effective January 1, 2002.)

16377. (a) For the purposes of this chapter, every judgment shall be deemed satisfied if any of the following apply:

(1) Fifteen thousand dollars ($15,000) has been credited, upon any judgment in excess of that amount, or upon all judgments, collectively, which together total in excess of that amount, for personal injury to, or death of, one person as a result of any one accident.

(2) Subject to the limit of fifteen thousand dollars ($15,000) as to one person, the sum of thirty thousand dollars ($30,000) has been credited, upon any judgment in excess of that amount, or upon all judgments, collectively, which together total in excess of that amount, for personal injury to, or death of, more than one person as a result of any one accident.

(3) Five thousand dollars ($5,000) has been credited, upon any judgment in excess of that amount, or upon all judgments, collectively, each of which is in excess of one thousand dollars ($1,000), and which together total in excess of five thousand dollars ($5,000), for damage to property of others as a result of any one accident.

(4) The judgment debtor or a person designated by him or her has deposited with the department a sum equal to the amount of the unsatisfied judgment for which the suspension action was taken and presents proof, satisfactory to the department, of inability to locate the judgment creditor.

(b) This section shall become operative on January 1, 2017.

(Amended (as added by Stats. 2015, Ch. 451, Sec. 39) by Stats. 2016, Ch. 86, Sec. 301. (SB 1171) Effective January 1, 2017.)

16378. (a) Money deposited pursuant to paragraph (4) of subdivision (a) of Section 16377 shall be:

(1) Deposited by the department in the special deposit fund with the Treasurer.

(2) Payable to the judgment creditor upon presentation of a valid claim establishing that he or she is the judgment creditor for which the deposit was made and that the judgment remains unsatisfied.

(3) Refunded to the person making the deposit or to a person designated by himself or herself if the deposit remains unclaimed by the judgment creditor for a period of two years following the date of the deposit.

(4) The Controller shall draw his or her warrant on the Treasurer for any payment ordered pursuant to this section as ordered by the department.

(b) This section shall become operative on January 1, 2017.

(Repealed (in Sec. 40) and added by Stats. 2015, Ch. 451, Sec. 41. (SB 491) Effective January 1, 2016. Section operative January 1, 2017, by its own provisions.)

16379. (a) The department shall not suspend a license and shall restore any suspended license following nonpayment of a final judgment when the judgment debtor gives proof of financial responsibility for future damages and when the trial court in which the judgment was rendered orders the payment of the judgment in installments and while the payment of any installment payment is not in default.

(b) Whenever the trial court orders the payment of a judgment in installments as provided in this section, upon payment of the required fees by the judgment creditor, it shall forward a certified copy of the order to the department, together with a certified copy of the judgment or a certified copy of the register of actions in an action resulting in a judgment for damages and a certificate of facts relative to the judgment on a form provided by the department.

(c) The court shall determine the required fees, which shall be commensurate with the cost incurred by the court in carrying out the provisions of this section.

(Amended by Stats. 2001, Ch. 44, Sec. 13. Effective January 1, 2002.)

16380. The trial court may order the payment of a judgment in installments only when the defendant is not insured or the insurance policy covering the automobile involved in the accident, for the ownership or operation of which the defendant is held liable, is not sufficient to pay the amount of the judgment, and then only as to such portion of the judgment not covered by the insurance policy. The order shall fix the amounts and times of payment of the installments and shall be without prejudice to any other legal remedies available to the judgment creditor.

(Added by renumbering Section 16486 by Stats. 1967, Ch. 211.)

16381. In the event that it is made to appear to the court that the judgment debtor has failed to pay any installment as permitted by the order of the court, upon the payment of required fees by the judgment creditor, the court shall give notice of the default to the department and the department shall forthwith suspend the driving privilege of the judgment debtor until the judgment is satisfied as provided in this chapter. The court shall determine the required fees, which shall be commensurate with the cost incurred by the court in carrying out the provisions of this section.

(Amended by Stats. 1981, Ch. 362, Sec. 3.)

Chapter 3. Proof of Financial Responsibility

(Heading of Chapter 3 amended by Stats. 1989, Ch. 1157, Sec. 8.5.)

Article 1. Proof Requirements

(Article 1 enacted by Stats. 1959, Ch. 3.)

16430. (a) "Proof of financial responsibility," when required by this code, means proof of financial responsibility resulting from the ownership or operation of a motor vehicle and arising by reason of personal injury to, or death of, any one person, of at least thirty thousand dollars ($30,000), and, subject to the limit of thirty thousand dollars ($30,000) for each person injured or killed, of at least sixty thousand dollars ($60,000) for the injury to, or the death of, two or more persons in any one accident, and for damages to property in excess of one thousand dollars ($1,000), of at least fifteen thousand dollars ($15,000) resulting from any one accident. Proof of financial responsibility may be given in any manner authorized in this chapter.

(b) (1) On January 1, 2035, the minimum liability coverage shall be increased by twenty thousand dollars ($20,000) for bodily injury or death for each person, by forty thousand dollars ($40,000) for bodily injury or death for all persons, and by ten thousand dollars ($10,000) for property damage.

(2) The Insurance Commissioner shall, by July 1, 2033, distribute a bulletin soliciting rate applications from insurers to effectuate the January 1, 2035, increase and shall process and approve them consistent with the manner outlined in Section 12960 of the Insurance Code.

(c) This section shall become operative on January 1, 2025.

(Repealed (in Sec. 4) and added by Stats. 2022, Ch. 717, Sec. 5. (SB 1107) Effective January 1, 2023. Operative January 1, 2025, by its own provisions.)

16431. (a) Proof of financial responsibility may be given by the written certificate or certificates of any insurance carrier duly authorized to do business within the state, that it has issued to or for the benefit of the person named therein a motor vehicle liability policy as defined in Section 16450, an automobile liability policy as defined in Section 16054, or any other liability policy issued for vehicles with less than four wheels that meets the requirements of Section 16056, which, at the date of the certificate or certificates, is in full force and effect. Except as provided in subdivision (b), the certificate or certificates issued under any liability policy set forth in this section shall be accepted by the department and satisfy the requirements of proof of financial responsibility of this chapter. Nothing in this chapter requires that an insurance carrier certify that there is coverage broader than that provided by the actual policy issued by the carrier.

(b) The department shall require that a person whose driver's license has been revoked, suspended, or restricted under Section 13350, 13351, 13352, 13353, 13353.2, 13353.3, 13353.7, or 16370, provide, as proof of financial responsibility, a certificate or certificates that covers all motor vehicles registered to the person before reinstatement of his or her driver's license.

(c) Subdivision (b) does not apply to vehicles in storage if the current license plates and registration cards are surrendered to the department in Sacramento.

(d) (1) A resident of another state may provide proof of financial responsibility when required to do so under this code from a company authorized to do business in that person's state of residence, if that proof is satisfactory to the department, covers the operation of a vehicle in this state, and meets the minimum coverage limit requirements specified in Section 16056.

(2) If the person specified in paragraph (1) becomes a resident of this state during the period that the person is required to maintain proof of financial responsibility with the department, the department may not issue or return a driver's license to that person until the person files a written certificate or certificates, as authorized under subdivision (a), that meets the minimum coverage limit requirements specified in Section 16056 and covers the period during which the person is required to maintain proof of financial responsibility.

(e) This section shall become operative on September 20, 2005.

(Amended by Stats. 2004, Ch. 952, Sec. 28. Effective January 1, 2005. Amended version operative September 20, 2005, pursuant to earlier operation of new subdivision (e).)

16433. A certificate or certificates shall certify, if the liability policy therein cited has been canceled, that the department shall be notified in writing within 10 days after the cancellation of insurance becomes final.

Nothing in this section extends coverage beyond the date stated in the notice of cancellation.

(Amended by Stats. 1990, Ch. 314, Sec. 8. Effective July 17, 1990.)

16434. (a) Proof of financial responsibility may be given by a bond. The bond shall be conditioned for the payment of the amount specified in Section 16430, and shall provide for the entry of judgment on motion of the state in favor of any holder of any final judgment on account of damages to property over one thousand dollars ($1,000) in amount, or injury to any person caused by the operation of the person's motor vehicle.

(b) This section shall become operative on January 1, 2017.

(Repealed (in Sec. 44) and added by Stats. 2015, Ch. 451, Sec. 45. (SB 491) Effective January 1, 2016. Section operative January 1, 2017, by its own provisions.)

16435. (a) Proof of financial responsibility may be given by the deposit of seventy-five thousand dollars ($75,000) as provided in Section 16054.2. The department shall not accept a deposit where any judgment theretofore obtained against that person as a result of damages arising from the operation of any motor vehicle shall not have been paid in full.

(b) The deposit requirement in subdivision (a) shall be increased by fifty thousand dollars ($50,000) on January 1, 2035.

(c) This section shall become operative on January 1, 2025.

(Repealed (in Sec. 6) and added by Stats. 2022, Ch. 717, Sec. 7. (SB 1107) Effective January 1, 2023. Operative January 1, 2025, by its own provisions.)

16436. Proof of financial responsibility may be given by the written certificate of a self-insurer holding a certificate of self-insurance for bodily injury and property damage issued by the department.

The certification shall name the employee in whose behalf it is filed and shall bind the self-insurer in a like manner and to the same amounts as provided for in Section 16430 for damages arising from the operation of a motor vehicle by the employee within the scope of his or her employment by the self-insurer. In that case, the department shall restrict any driver's license issued to the employee to the operation of motor vehicles owned by the self-insurer within the scope of his or her employment by the self-insurer.

The certificate shall be canceled upon 10 days' prior written notice to the department by the self-insurer.

(Amended by Stats. 1989, Ch. 1157, Sec. 14.)

Article 2. Insurance Policy

(Article 2 enacted by Stats. 1959, Ch. 3.)

16450. A "motor vehicle liability policy," as used in Chapters 1 (commencing with Section 16000), 2 (commencing with Section 16250), and 4 (commencing with Section 16500), and this chapter, means an owner's policy or an operator's policy, or both, of liability insurance, certified as provided in Section 16431 as proof of financial responsibility, issued by an insurance carrier authorized to transact that business in this state to or for the benefit of the person named therein as assured. Any requirements set forth in Chapters 1 (commencing with Section 16000), 2 (commencing with Section 16250), and 4 (commencing with Section 16500), and this chapter relating to a motor vehicle liability policy shall apply only to those policies which have been certified as proof of financial responsibility as provided in Section 16431.

(Amended by Stats. 1989, Ch. 1157, Sec. 15.)

16451. (a) (1) An owner's policy of motor vehicle liability insurance shall insure the named insured and any other person using any motor vehicle registered to the named insured with the express or implied permission of the named insured against loss from the liability imposed by law for damages arising out of ownership, maintenance, or use of the motor vehicle within the continental limits of the United States to the extent and aggregate amount, exclusive of interest and costs, with respect to each motor vehicle, of fifteen thousand dollars ($15,000) for bodily injury to or death of each person as a result of any one accident, and, subject to the limit as to one person, the amount of thirty thousand dollars ($30,000) for bodily injury to or death of all persons as a result of any one accident and the amount of five thousand dollars ($5,000) for damage to property of others as a result of any one accident.

(2) Notwithstanding paragraph (1), an owner's policy of motor vehicle liability insurance issued or renewed on or after January 1, 2025, shall insure the named insured and any other person using any motor vehicle registered to the named insured with the express or implied permission of the named insured, against loss from the liability imposed by law for damages arising out of ownership, maintenance, or use of the motor vehicle within the continental limits of the United States to the extent and aggregate amount, exclusive of interest and costs, with respect to each motor vehicle, of thirty thousand dollars ($30,000) for bodily injury to or death of each person as a result of any one accident, and, subject to the limit as to one person, the amount of sixty thousand dollars ($60,000) for bodily injury to or death of all persons as a result of any one accident and the amount of fifteen thousand dollars ($15,000) for damage to property of others as a result of any one accident.

(b) For an owner's policy of motor vehicle liability insurance issued or renewed on or after January 1, 2035, the minimum liability coverage shall be increased by twenty thousand dollars ($20,000) for bodily injury or death for one person, by forty thousand dollars ($40,000) for bodily injury or death for all persons, and by ten thousand dollars ($10,000) for property damage.

(c) This section shall become operative on January 1, 2025.

(Amended (as added by Stats. 2022, Ch. 717, Sec. 9) by Stats. 2023, Ch. 204, Sec. 20. (AB 1140) Effective January 1, 2024. Operative January 1, 2025, by its own provisions.)

16452. An operator's policy of motor vehicle liability insurance shall insure the person named as insured therein against loss from the liability imposed on that person by law for damages arising out of use by that person of any motor vehicle not owned by that person, and for any subsequently acquired motor vehicle for a period not to exceed 10 days from date of purchase, within the same territorial limits and subject to the same limits of liability as are provided for in an owner's policy of liability insurance.

(Amended by Stats. 1989, Ch. 1157, Sec. 17.)

16453. Any motor vehicle liability policy may grant any lawful coverage in excess of or in addition to the coverage herein specified or contain any agreements, provisions or stipulations not in conflict with the provisions of this code and not otherwise contrary to law.

(Enacted by Stats. 1959, Ch. 3.)

16454. Any motor vehicle liability policy need not cover any liability for injury to the assured or any liability of the assured assumed by or imposed upon the assured under any workers' compensation law nor any liability for damage to property in charge of the assured or the assured's employees or agents.

(Amended by Stats. 1974, Ch. 1454.)

16455. The provisions of Section 16451 shall not apply to vehicles in storage if the current license plates and registration cards are surrendered to the department in Sacramento.

(Enacted by Stats. 1959, Ch. 3.)

16457. Whenever proof of financial responsibility is required to be filed pursuant to this chapter, no person of whom that proof is required shall drive any motor vehicle not covered by the certificate of proof of financial responsibility filed by him or her with the department, nor shall any applicant for that proof knowingly fail to disclose ownership of a motor vehicle in the application for proof of financial responsibility or to disclose any subsequently acquired motor vehicle.

(Amended (as amended by Stats. 1996, Ch. 1126, Sec. 14) by Stats. 1999, Ch. 880, Sec. 19. Effective January 1, 2000.)

Article 3. Release of Proof

(Article 3 enacted by Stats. 1959, Ch. 3.)

16480. (a) The department shall upon request, or may at its own discretion, cancel any bond or any certificate of insurance, or the department shall direct the return to the person entitled thereto of any money or securities deposited pursuant to this code as proof of financial responsibility, or the department shall waive the requirement of filing proof of financial responsibility in any of the following events:

(1) When the person is no longer required to maintain the proof under the provisions of this code.

(2) At any time after three years from the date the proof was required.

(3) Upon the death of the person on whose behalf the proof was filed.

(4) The permanent incapacity of the person to operate a motor vehicle if the person surrenders for cancellation his or her driver's license to the department.

(b) The department shall not release proof filed by the bond of individual sureties as set forth in Section 16434, or if given in the manner prescribed by Section 16435, if any action for damages upon a liability referred to in this code is then pending or if any judgment upon any the liability is outstanding and unsatisfied. An affidavit of the applicant of the nonexistence of those facts shall be prima facie evidence thereof.

(Amended by Stats. 1989, Ch. 1157, Sec. 19.)

16482. (a) Any person whose privilege to operate a motor vehicle has been suspended because of failure to satisfy a judgment and the judgment has been outstanding for a period of three years or more, may be relieved of the penalties therein provided and the privilege of the person to operate a motor vehicle may be restored in the event the person files with the department and thereafter maintains proof of financial responsibility notwithstanding that the judgment which gave rise to the order of suspension has not been paid or fully satisfied.

(b) Any person who has filed proof of financial responsibility as required for three years, or who has been eligible to file that proof for three years, may be relieved of the requirement of filing proof as provided in paragraph (2) of subdivision (a) of Section 16480.

(Amended by Stats. 1989, Ch. 1157, Sec. 20.)

16483. The department shall cancel any bond or any certificate of insurance or direct the return of any money or securities to the person entitled thereto, upon the substitution and acceptance of other adequate proof of financial responsibility pursuant to this code.

(Amended by Stats. 1989, Ch. 1157, Sec. 21.)

16484. Except when a nonresident minor's certificate or minor's license is canceled as required by Sections 12504 and 17704, respectively, whenever any evidence of proof of financial responsibility filed by any person under the provisions of this code no longer fulfills the purpose for which required, the department shall require other evidence of financial responsibility as required by Article 1 (commencing with Section 16430) and shall suspend the privilege of the person to operate a motor vehicle upon a highway. The suspension shall remain in effect until adequate proof of financial responsibility is filed with the department by the person.

(Amended by Stats. 1989, Ch. 1157, Sec. 22.)

Chapter 4. Commercial Vehicles

(Heading of Chapter 4 amended by Stats. 1980, Ch. 983, Sec. 1.)

16500. (a) (1) Every owner of a vehicle used in the transportation of passengers for hire, including taxicabs, when the operation of the vehicle is not subject to regulation by the Public Utilities Commission, shall maintain, whenever the owner may be engaged in conducting those operations, either of the following:

(A) Proof of financial responsibility resulting from the ownership or operation of the vehicle and arising by reason of personal injury to, or death of, any one person, of at least fifteen thousand dollars ($15,000), and, subject to the limit of fifteen thousand dollars ($15,000) for each person injured or killed, of at least thirty thousand dollars ($30,000) for the injury to, or the death of, two or more persons in any one accident, and for damages to property of at least five thousand dollars ($5,000) resulting from any one accident.

(B) (i) Notwithstanding subparagraph (A), proof of financial responsibility resulting from the ownership or operation of the vehicle and arising by reason of personal injury to, or death of, any one person, of at least thirty thousand dollars ($30,000), and, subject to the limit of thirty thousand dollars ($30,000) for each person injured or killed, of at least sixty thousand dollars ($60,000) for the injury to, or the death of, two or more persons in any one accident, and for damages to property of at least fifteen thousand dollars ($15,000) resulting from any one accident.

(ii) The proof of financial responsibility limits required by clause (i) shall apply to a motor vehicle liability policy, described in subparagraph (A) of paragraph (2), or bond, described in subparagraph (B) of paragraph (2), issued or renewed on or after January 1, 2025.

(2) Proof of financial responsibility may be maintained by any of the following:

(A) Being insured under a motor vehicle liability policy against that liability.

(B) Obtaining a bond of the same kind, and containing the same provisions, as those bonds specified in Section 16434.

(C) By depositing with the department seventy-five thousand dollars ($75,000), which shall be deposited in a special deposit account with the Controller for the purpose of this section.

(D) Qualifying as a self-insurer under Section 16053.

(b) The department shall return the deposit to the person entitled thereto when the person is no longer required to maintain proof of financial responsibility as required by this section or upon the person's death.

(c) On January 1, 2035, each of the following shall occur:

(1) The minimum liability coverage shall be increased by twenty thousand dollars ($20,000) for bodily injury or death for one person, by forty thousand dollars ($40,000) for bodily injury or death for all persons, and by ten thousand dollars ($10,000) for property damage.

(2) The minimum liability coverage required by paragraph (1) shall apply to a motor vehicle liability policy, described in subparagraph (A) of paragraph (2) of subdivision (a), or bond, described in subparagraph (B) of paragraph (2) of subdivision (a), issued or renewed on or after January 1, 2035.

(3) The deposit requirement in subparagraph (C) of paragraph (2) of subdivision (a) shall be increased by fifty thousand dollars ($50,000).

(d) This section shall become operative on January 1, 2025.

(Amended (as added by Stats. 2022, Ch. 717, Sec. 11) by Stats. 2023, Ch. 204, Sec. 21. (AB 1140) Effective January 1, 2024. Operative January 1, 2025, by its own provisions.)

16500.5. (a) Except as specified in subdivision (b), the owner of the following commercial vehicles shall maintain proof of financial responsibility in the amount required by the director:

(1) A vehicle used to carry passengers for hire, except taxicabs as defined in subdivision (c) of Section 27908.

(2) A vehicle having an unladen weight of over 7,000 pounds which is used in the transportation of property in the conduct of a business.

(b) Subdivision (a) does not apply to the following vehicles:

(1) A schoolbus.

(2) A motor vehicle used by a farmer exclusively in the transportation of his or her livestock, implements of husbandry, and agricultural commodities or in the transportation of supplies to his or her farm.

(3) A motor vehicle used by a resident farmer of this state to occasionally transport from the place of production to a warehouse, regular market, place of storage, or place of shipment the farm products of neighboring farmers in exchange for like services, farm products, or other compensation.

(4) A vehicle used in for-hire transportation which is subject to regulation by the Public Utilities Commission.

(5) A rented vehicle used for noncommercial transportation of property.

(c) The director shall establish the amounts which are determined adequate to cover damages resulting from the ownership or operation of a commercial vehicle or vehicles subject to this section arising by reason of personal injury to, or death of, any person or damage to property, or both. The director shall establish the amounts at levels equal to those prescribed by the Public Utilities Commission for owners and operators of for-hire vehicles subject to its jurisdiction and control.

(d) Proof of financial responsibility may be maintained by any of the following:

(1) Being insured under one or more motor vehicle liability policies against that liability.

(2) Obtaining a bond of the same kind, and containing the same provisions, as those bonds specified in Section 16434.

(3) By depositing with the department five hundred thousand dollars ($500,000), which amount shall be deposited in a special deposit account with the Controller for the purpose of this section.

(4) Qualifying as a self-insurer under Section 16053.

(e) The department shall return the deposit made pursuant to paragraph (3) of subdivision (d) to the person entitled thereto when the owner is no longer required to maintain proof of financial responsibility as required by this section or upon the owner's death.

(f) An insurer, agent, or broker who has been incorrectly informed by an owner of a vehicle or his or her representative that the vehicle is 7,000 pounds or less unladen weight, or is incorrectly informed by the owner or his or her representative that the vehicle is exempt from the requirements of subdivisions (a) and (c) pursuant to the exemptions set forth in subdivision (b), may issue a policy of motor vehicle liability insurance in any amount less than that required by the director but not less than the amounts required under Section 16451. The policy of motor vehicle liability insurance when issued shall not be deemed to provide liability coverage amounts greater than that specifically set forth in the policy notwithstanding that the vehicle weighs in excess of 7,000 pounds unladen weight or is subsequently used in a manner which would have required the vehicle to be insured in the amounts established by the director pursuant to subdivision (c).

(Amended by Stats. 1989, Ch. 1157, Sec. 24.)

16501. The provisions of this chapter shall not prevent local authorities, within the reasonable exercise of the police power, from adopting rules and regulations, by ordinance or resolution, licensing and regulating the operation of any vehicle for hire and the drivers of passenger vehicles for hire.

(Amended by Stats. 1965, Ch. 1554.)

16502. (a) An owner shall not use, or with his or her consent permit the use of, a vehicle used in the transportation of persons or property in the conduct of a business, without maintaining proof of financial responsibility as required by this chapter.

(b) A motor vehicle from another country in which there is no evidence of financial responsibility required pursuant to this chapter or Part 387 (commencing with Section 387.1) of Title 49 of the Code of Federal Regulations shall be denied entry into the state.

(Amended by Stats. 2006, Ch. 288, Sec. 5. Effective January 1, 2007.)

16503. The department shall suspend the registration of all vehicles used in the transportation of persons or property in the conduct of a business, except vehicles subject to regulation by the Public Utilities Commission, which are registered in the name of any person convicted of violating Section 16502 immediately upon receipt of a duly certified abstract of the record of the court in which the person was convicted.

The suspension shall remain in effect and no such vehicle shall be registered in the name of the person until he or she gives the department proof of his or her financial responsibility as required by Section 16500.

(Amended by Stats. 1989, Ch. 1157, Sec. 26.)

Chapter 6. Interstate Highway Carriers

(Chapter 6 added by Stats. 1969, Ch. 1279.)

16560. (a) Any person or corporation who operates or causes to be operated on the highways of this state any motor vehicle in the interstate or foreign transportation of property, other than household goods, for compensation without having first complied with the requirements of paragraph (1) of subdivision (g) of Section 7232 of the Revenue and Taxation Code is guilty of a misdemeanor, and is punishable by a fine of not more than one thousand dollars ($1,000), or by imprisonment in the county jail for not more than three months, or by both that fine and imprisonment.

(b) Any person or corporation who operates or causes to be operated on the highways of this state any motor vehicle in the interstate or foreign transportation of household goods for compensation without having first complied with the requirements of Chapter 3.1 (commencing with Section 19225) of Division 8 of the Business and Professions Code or passengers for compensation without having first complied with the requirements of Chapter 1 (commencing with Section 3901) of Division 2 of the Public Utilities Code is guilty of a misdemeanor, and is punishable by a fine of not more than one thousand dollars ($1,000), or by imprisonment in the county jail for not more than three months, or both that fine and imprisonment.

(Amended by Stats. 2022, Ch. 295, Sec. 15. (AB 2956) Effective January 1, 2023.)

Division 9. Civil Liability

(Division 9 enacted by Stats. 1959, Ch. 3.)

Chapter 1. Civil Liability of Owners and Operators of Vehicles

(Chapter 1 enacted by Stats. 1959, Ch. 3.)

Article 1. Public Agencies

(Article 1 enacted by Stats. 1959, Ch. 3.)

17000. As used in this chapter:

(a) "Employee" includes an officer, employee, or servant, whether or not compensated, but does not include an independent contractor.

(b) "Employment" includes office or employment.

(c) "Public entity" includes the state, the Regents of the University of California, a county, city, district, public authority, public agency, and any other political subdivision or public corporation in the state.

(Amended by Stats. 1965, Ch. 1527.)

17001. A public entity is liable for death or injury to person or property proximately caused by a negligent or wrongful act or omission in the operation of any motor vehicle by an employee of the public entity acting within the scope of his employment.

(Amended by Stats. 1965, Ch. 1527.)

17002. Subject to Article 4 (commencing with Section 825) of Chapter 1 of Part 2 of Division 3.6 of Title 1 of the Government Code, a public entity is liable for death or injury to person or property to the same extent as a private person under the provisions of Article 2 (commencing with Section 17150) of this chapter.

(Repealed and added by Stats. 1965, Ch. 1527.)

17004. A public employee is not liable for civil damages on account of personal injury to or death of any person or damage to property resulting from the operation, in the line of duty, of an authorized emergency vehicle while responding to an emergency call or when in the immediate pursuit of an actual or suspected violator of the law, or when responding to but not upon returning from a fire alarm or other emergency call.

(Amended by Stats. 1965, Ch. 1527.)

17004.5. Any private firm or corporation, or employee thereof, which maintains a fire department and has entered into a mutual aid agreement pursuant to Section 13855, 14095, or 14455.5 of the Health and Safety Code shall have the same immunity from liability for civil damages on account of personal injury to or death of any person or damage to property resulting from the operation of an authorized emergency vehicle while responding to, but not upon returning from, a fire alarm or other emergency call as is provided by law for the district and its employees with which the firm or corporation has entered into a mutual aid agreement, except when the act or omission causing the personal injury to or death of any person or damage to property occurs on property under the control of such firm or corporation.

(Added by Stats. 1961, Ch. 1880, Sec. 5.)

17004.7. (a) The immunity provided by this section is in addition to any other immunity provided by law. The adoption of a vehicle pursuit policy by a public agency pursuant to this section is discretionary.

(b) (1) A public agency employing peace officers that adopts and promulgates a written policy on, and provides regular and periodic training on an annual basis for, vehicular pursuits complying with subdivisions (c) and (d) is immune from liability for civil damages for personal injury to or death of any person or damage to property resulting from the collision of a vehicle being operated by an actual or suspected violator of the law who is being, has been, or believes he or she is being or has been, pursued in a motor vehicle by a peace officer employed by the public entity.

(2) Promulgation of the written policy under paragraph (1) shall include, but is not limited to, a requirement that all peace officers of the public agency certify in writing that they have received, read, and understand the policy. The failure of an individual officer to sign a

certification shall not be used to impose liability on an individual officer or a public entity.

(c) A policy for the safe conduct of motor vehicle pursuits by peace officers shall meet all of the following minimum standards:

(1) Determine under what circumstances to initiate a pursuit. The policy shall define a "pursuit," articulate the reasons for which a pursuit is authorized, and identify the issues that should be considered in reaching the decision to pursue. It should also address the importance of protecting the public and balancing the known or reasonably suspected offense, and the apparent need for immediate capture against the risks to peace officers, innocent motorists, and others to protect the public.

(2) Determine the total number of law enforcement vehicles authorized to participate in a pursuit. Establish the authorized number of law enforcement units and supervisors who may be involved in a pursuit, describe the responsibility of each authorized unit and the role of each peace officer and supervisor, and specify if and when additional units are authorized.

(3) Determine the communication procedures to be followed during a pursuit. Specify pursuit coordination and control procedures and determine assignment of communications responsibility by unit and organizational entity.

(4) Determine the role of the supervisor in managing and controlling a pursuit. Supervisory responsibility shall include management and control of a pursuit, assessment of risk factors associated with a pursuit, and when to terminate a pursuit.

(5) Determine driving tactics and the circumstances under which the tactics may be appropriate.

(6) Determine authorized pursuit intervention tactics. Pursuit intervention tactics include, but are not limited to, blocking, ramming, boxing, and roadblock procedures. The policy shall specify under what circumstances and conditions each approved tactic is authorized to be used.

(7) Determine the factors to be considered by a peace officer and supervisor in determining speeds throughout a pursuit. Evaluation shall take into consideration public safety, peace officer safety, and safety of the occupants in a fleeing vehicle.

(8) Determine the role of air support, where available. Air support shall include coordinating the activities of resources on the ground, reporting on the progress of a pursuit, and providing peace officers and supervisors with information to evaluate whether or not to continue the pursuit.

(9) Determine when to terminate or discontinue a pursuit. Factors to be considered include, but are not limited to, all of the following:

(A) Ongoing evaluation of risk to the public or pursuing peace officer.

(B) The protection of the public, given the known or reasonably suspected offense and apparent need for immediate capture against the risks to the public and peace officers.

(C) Vehicular or pedestrian traffic safety and volume.

(D) Weather conditions.

(E) Traffic conditions.

(F) Speeds.

(G) Availability of air support.

(H) Procedures when an offender is identified and may be apprehended at a later time or when the location of the pursuit vehicle is no longer known.

(10) Determine procedures for apprehending an offender following a pursuit. Safety of the public and peace officers during the law enforcement effort to capture an offender shall be an important factor.

(11) Determine effective coordination, management, and control of interjurisdictional pursuits. The policy shall include, but shall not be limited to, all of the following:

(A) Supervisory control and management of a pursuit that enters another jurisdiction.

(B) Communications and notifications among the agencies involved.

(C) Involvement in another jurisdiction's pursuit.

(D) Roles and responsibilities of units and coordination, management, and control at the termination of an interjurisdictional pursuit.

(12) Reporting and postpursuit analysis as required by Section 14602.1. Establish the level and procedures of postpursuit analysis, review, and feedback. Establish procedures for written postpursuit review and followup.

(d) "Regular and periodic training" under this section means annual training that shall include, at a minimum, coverage of each of the subjects and elements set forth in subdivision (c) and that shall comply, at a minimum, with the training guidelines established pursuant to Section 13519.8 of the Penal Code.

(e) The requirements of subdivision (c) represent minimum policy standards and do not limit an agency from adopting additional policy requirements. The requirements in subdivision (c) are consistent with the 1995 California Law Enforcement Vehicle Pursuit Guidelines developed by the Commission on Peace Officer Standards and Training pursuant to Section 13519.8 of the Penal Code that will assist agencies in the development of their pursuit policies. Nothing in this section precludes the adoption of a policy that limits or restricts pursuits.

(f) A determination of whether a public agency has complied with subdivisions (c) and (d) is a question of law for the court.

(g) This section shall become operative on July 1, 2007.

(Repealed (in Sec. 10) and added by Stats. 2005, Ch. 485, Sec. 11. Effective January 1, 2006. Section operative July 1, 2007, by its own provisions.)

Article 2. Private Owners

(Article 2 enacted by Stats. 1959, Ch. 3.)

17150. Every owner of a motor vehicle is liable and responsible for death or injury to person or property resulting from a negligent or wrongful act or omission in the operation of the motor vehicle, in the business of the owner or otherwise, by any person using or operating the same with the permission, express or implied, of the owner.

(Amended by Stats. 1967, Ch. 702.)

17150.5. The presumptions created by Section 803 of the Family Code as to the acquisition of property by a married woman by an instrument in writing shall not apply in an action based on Section 17150 with respect to the acquisition of a motor vehicle by a married woman and her husband.

(Amended by Stats. 1992, Ch. 163, Sec. 134. Effective January 1, 1993. Operative January 1, 1994, by Sec. 161 of Ch. 163.)

17151. (a) The liability of an owner, bailee of an owner, or personal representative of a decedent imposed by this chapter and not arising through the relationship of principal and agent or master and servant is limited to the amount of fifteen thousand dollars ($15,000) for the death of or injury to one person in any one accident and, subject to the limit as to one person, is limited to the amount of thirty thousand dollars ($30,000) for the death of or injury to more than one person in any one accident and is limited to the amount of five thousand dollars ($5,000) for damage to property of others in any one accident.

(b) An owner, bailee of an owner, or personal representative of a decedent is not liable under this chapter for damages imposed for the sake of example and by way of punishing the operator of the vehicle. Nothing in this subdivision makes an owner, bailee, or personal representative immune from liability for damages imposed for the sake of example and by way of punishing him for his own wrongful conduct.

(Amended by Stats. 1967, Ch. 862, Sec. 8.5.)

17152. In any action against an owner, bailee of an owner, or personal representative of a decedent on account of liability imposed by Sections 17150, 17154, or 17159 for the negligent or wrongful act or omission of the operator of a vehicle, the operator shall be made a party defendant if service of process can be made in a manner sufficient to secure personal jurisdiction over the operator. Upon recovery of judgment, recourse shall first be had against the property of the operator so served.

(Amended by Stats. 1967, Ch. 702.)

17153. If there is recovery under this chapter against an owner, bailee of an owner, or personal representative of a decedent, the owner, bailee of an owner, or personal representative of a decedent is subrogated to all the rights of the person injured or whose property has been injured and may recover from the operator the total amount of any judgment and costs recovered against the owner, bailee of an owner, or personal representative of a decedent.

(Amended by Stats. 1967, Ch. 702.)

17154. If the bailee of an owner with the permission, express or implied, of the owner permits another to operate the motor vehicle of the owner, then the bailee and the driver shall both be deemed operators of the vehicle of the owner within the meaning of Sections 17152 and 17153.

Every bailee of a motor vehicle is liable and responsible for death or injury to person or property resulting from a negligent or wrongful act or omission in the operation of the motor vehicle, in the business of the bailee or otherwise, by any person using or operating the same with the permission, express or implied, of the bailee.

(Amended by Stats. 1967, Ch. 702.)

17155. If two or more persons are injured or killed in one accident, the owner, bailee of an owner, or personal representative of a decedent may settle and pay any bona fide claims for damages arising out of personal injuries or death, whether reduced by judgment or not, and the payments shall diminish, to the extent of those payments, the person's total liability on account of the accident. Payments aggregating the full sum of thirty thousand dollars ($30,000) shall extinguish all liability of the owner, bailee of an owner, or personal representative of a decedent for death or personal injury arising out of the accident that exists pursuant to this chapter, and did not arise through the negligent or wrongful act or omission of the owner, bailee of an owner, or personal representative of a decedent nor through the relationship of principal and agent or master and servant.

(Amended by Stats. 2006, Ch. 538, Sec. 660. Effective January 1, 2007.)

17156. If a motor vehicle is sold under a contract of conditional sale whereby the title to such motor vehicle remains in the vendor, such vendor or his assignee shall not be deemed an owner within the provisions of this chapter, but the vendee or his assignee shall be deemed the owner notwithstanding the terms of such contract, until the vendor or his assignee retake possession of the motor vehicle. A chattel mortgagee of a motor vehicle out of possession is not an owner within the provisions of this chapter.

(Amended by Stats. 1967, Ch. 702.)

17157. If a motor vehicle is gratuitously loaned to a school district, the bailee and not the bailor shall be deemed to be the owner within the provisions of this chapter notwithstanding the terms of any contract, until the bailor retakes possession of the motor vehicle.

(Added by Stats. 1969, Ch. 289.)

17158. No person riding in or occupying a vehicle owned by him and driven by another person with his permission has any right of action for civil damages against the driver of the vehicle or against any other person legally liable for the conduct of the driver on account of personal injury to or the death of the owner during the ride, unless the plaintiff in any such action establishes that the injury or death proximately resulted from the intoxication or willful misconduct of the driver.

(Amended by Stats. 1973, Ch. 803.)

17159. Every person who is a personal representative of a decedent who has control or possession of a motor vehicle subject to administration for the purpose of administration of an estate is, during the period of such administration, or until the vehicle has been distributed under order of the court or he has complied with the requirements of subdivision (a) or (b) of Section 5602, liable and responsible for death or injury to person or property resulting from a negligent or wrongful act or omission in the operation of the motor vehicle by any person using or operating the same with the permission, express or implied, of the personal representative.

(Amended by Stats. 1967, Ch. 702.)

Article 2.5. Uninsured Owners

(Article 2.5 added by Stats. 1983, Ch. 1252, Sec. 10.)

17200. Where an uninsured owner or operator has obtained a judgment against or agreed to a settlement with the owner or operator of an insured motor vehicle based on the negligence of the insured owner or operator, the amount of the judgment or settlement payable by the insured or his or her insurer shall be reduced by the amount paid or payable to the insured owner or operator or occupants of the insured motor vehicles or their heirs or legal representatives from coverage provided by an uninsured motorist endorsement where the claim of the insured, the owner, or occupants of the insured motor vehicle and the uninsured motorist arise out of the same accident. If the insured or his or her insurer becomes entitled to a reduction, the reduction shall not exceed the amount of the settlement or judgment awarded the uninsured owner or operator.

(Added by Stats. 1983, Ch. 1252, Sec. 10.)

17201. The payment of any settlement with an uninsured owner or operator or the payment of any final judgment for damages obtained by an uninsured owner or operator in a civil action against an insured owner or operator shall not be made until the claims of the owner, the operator, or the occupants of the insured motor vehicle, if any, or their heirs or legal representatives for benefits under the uninsured motorist endorsement are settled by the insurer and the claimants under the uninsured motorist endorsement or are determined by the arbitrator in arbitration proceedings conducted pursuant to Section 11580.2 of the Insurance Code.

(Added by Stats. 1983, Ch. 1252, Sec. 10.)

17202. This article is not intended to affect the rights granted pursuant to subdivision (g) of Section 11580.2 of the Insurance Code.

(Added by Stats. 1983, Ch. 1252, Sec. 10.)

Article 3. Liability for Damage to Highway

(Article 3 enacted by Stats. 1959, Ch. 3.)

17300. (a) A person who willfully or negligently damages a street or highway, or its appurtenances, including, but not limited to, guardrails, signs, traffic signals, snow poles, and similar facilities, is liable for the reasonable cost of repair or replacement thereof.

(b) A person who willfully damages or destroys a memorial sign placed by the Department of Transportation, including, but not limited to, a sign memorializing a victim under Section 101.10 of the Streets and Highways Code, is liable for that damage or destruction for the highest of the following amounts:

(1) One thousand five hundred dollars ($1,500).

(2) The actual repair cost or replacement cost, whichever is applicable.

(c) A person who willfully or negligently causes or permits the contents of a vehicle to be deposited upon a street or highway, or its appurtenances, is liable for the reasonable costs of removing those contents from the street or highway or its appurtenances.

(d) The liability stated in this section also applies to an owner of a vehicle operated with the owner's permission, as provided in Article 2 (commencing with Section 17150), and includes liability for the reasonable cost of necessary safety precautions, including, but not limited to, warning traffic, the removal of debris resulting from accidents, the removal of any materials, or providing detours.

(e) The Department of Transportation and local authorities, with respect to highways under their respective jurisdictions, may present claims for liability under this section, bring actions for recovery thereon, and settle and compromise, in their discretion, claims arising under this section.

(f) If the Department of Transportation or a local authority provides services on a highway outside its jurisdiction, at the request of the department or the local authority that has jurisdiction over that highway, the department or the local authority may present a claim for liability for rendering this service under this section, bring actions for recovery thereon, and, in its discretion, settle and compromise the claim.

(Amended by Stats. 2006, Ch. 419, Sec. 3. Effective January 1, 2007.)

17301. (a) Any person driving any vehicle, object, or contrivance over a highway or bridge is liable for all damages which the highway or bridge may sustain as a result of any illegal operation, driving or moving of the vehicle, object, or contrivance, or as a result of operating, driving, or moving any vehicle, object, or contrivance weighing in excess of the maximum weight specified in this code which is operated under a special permit issued by the Department of Transportation.

(b) Whenever the driver is not the owner of the vehicle, object, or contrivance but is operating, driving, or moving the same with the express or implied permission of the owner, the owner and driver are jointly and severally liable for the damage.

(Amended by Stats. 1974, Ch. 545.)

17302. The driver, or the owner and driver, jointly, as the case may be, are also liable for all damages that any highway or bridge sustains as the result of any operation, driving, or moving of any vehicle that exceeds any of the limitations imposed by Division 15 (commencing with Section 35000), Chapter 1 (commencing with Section 29000) of Division 13, Section 21461 with respect to a sign erected under Section 35655, and Sections 21712 and 23114 even though the vehicle is exempted from the limitations by Section 35001, 35104, 35105, 35106, 35108, 35250, 35400, 35414, or 36615.

(Amended by Stats. 1996, Ch. 124, Sec. 124. Effective January 1, 1997.)

17303. Damages under Sections 17301 and 17302 may be recovered in a civil action brought by the authorities in control of the highway or bridge.

(Enacted by Stats. 1959, Ch. 3.)

Article 4. Service of Process

(Article 4 enacted by Stats. 1959, Ch. 3.)

17450. As used in this chapter, "nonresident" means a person who is not a resident of this State at the time the accident or collision occurs.

(Enacted by Stats. 1959, Ch. 3.)

17451. The acceptance by a nonresident of the rights and privileges conferred upon him by this code or any operation by himself or agent of a motor vehicle anywhere within this state, or in the event the nonresident is the owner of a motor vehicle then by the operation of the vehicle anywhere within this state by any person with his express or implied permission, is equivalent to an appointment by the nonresident of the director or his successor in office to be his true and lawful attorney upon whom may be served all lawful processes in any action or proceeding against the nonresident operator or nonresident owner growing out of any accident or collision resulting from the operation of any motor vehicle anywhere within this state by himself or agent, which appointment shall also be irrevocable and binding upon his executor or administrator.

(Amended by Stats. 1967, Ch. 720.)

17452. Where the nonresident has died prior to the commencement of an action brought pursuant to this article, service of process shall be made on the executor or administrator of the nonresident in the same manner and on the same notice as is provided in the case of the nonresident. Where an action has been duly commenced under the provisions of this article by service upon a defendant who dies thereafter, the court shall allow the action to be continued against his executor or administrator upon motion with such notice as the court deems proper.

(Enacted by Stats. 1959, Ch. 3.)

17453. The acceptance of rights and privileges under this code or any operation of a motor vehicle anywhere within this state as specified in Section 17451 shall be a signification of the irrevocable agreement of the nonresident, binding as well upon his executor or administrator, that process against him which is served in the manner provided in this article shall be of the same legal force and validity as if served on him personally in this state.

(Amended by Stats. 1967, Ch. 720.)

17454. Service of process shall be made by leaving one copy of the summons and complaint in the hands of the director or in his office at Sacramento or by mailing either by certified or registered mail, addressee only, return receipt requested, the copy of the summons and complaint to the office of the director in Sacramento. Service shall be effective as of the day the return receipt is received from the director's office. A fee of two dollars ($2) for each nonresident to be served shall be paid to the director at the time of service of the copy of the summons and complaint and such service shall be a sufficient service on the nonresident subject to compliance with Section 17455.

(Amended by Stats. 1959, Ch. 1313.)

17455. A notice of service and a copy of the summons and complaint shall be forthwith sent by registered mail by the plaintiff or his attorney to the defendant. Personal service of the notice and a copy of the summons and complaint upon the defendant wherever found outside this State shall be the equivalent of service by mail.

(Enacted by Stats. 1959, Ch. 3.)

17456. Proof of compliance with Section 17455 shall be made in the event of service by mail by affidavit of the plaintiff or his attorney showing said mailing, together with the return receipt of the United States post office bearing the signature of the defendant. The affidavit and receipt shall be appended to the original summons which shall be filed with the court from out of which the summons issued within such time as the court may allow for the return of the summons.

In the event of personal service outside this State, compliance with Section 17455 may be proved by the return of any duly constituted public officer, qualified to serve like process of and in the state or jurisdiction where the defendant is found, showing such service to have been made. The return shall be appended to the original summons which shall be filed as aforesaid.

(Enacted by Stats. 1959, Ch. 3.)

17457. The court in which the action is pending may order such continuances as may be necessary to afford the defendant reasonable opportunity to defend the action.

(Enacted by Stats. 1959, Ch. 3.)

17458. The director shall keep a record of all process served upon him under this article which record shall show the day and hour of service.

(Enacted by Stats. 1959, Ch. 3.)

17459. The acceptance by a resident of this state of a certificate of ownership or a certificate of registration of any motor vehicle or any renewal thereof, issued under the provisions of this code, shall constitute the consent by the person that service of summons may be made upon him within or without this state, whether or not he is then a resident of this state, in any action brought in the courts of this state upon a cause of action arising in this state out of the ownership or operation of the vehicle.

(Amended by Stats. 1971, Ch. 622.)

17460. The acceptance or retention by a resident of this state of a driver's license issued pursuant to the provisions of this code, shall constitute the consent of the person that service of summons may be made upon him within or without this state, whether or not he is then a resident of this state, in any action brought in the courts of this state upon a cause of action arising in this state out of his operation of a motor vehicle anywhere within this state.

(Amended by Stats. 1972, Ch. 618.)

17461. In the event summons is served outside of this state, pursuant to Sections 17459 and 17460, it may be served and proof of service shall be made, in the manner provided by Sections 17454, 17455, and 17456 for service of summons upon a nonresident, or it may be served pursuant to Chapter 4 (commencing with Section 413.10) of Title 5 of Part 2 of the Code of Civil Procedure.

(Amended by Stats. 1971, Ch. 622.)

17462. In the event of service outside the State, the person so served shall have 60 days in which to appear in the action in which the summons is issued.

(Enacted by Stats. 1959, Ch. 3.)

17463. Notwithstanding any provisions of Section 351 of the Code

of Civil Procedure to the contrary, when summons may be personally served upon a person as provided in Sections 17459 and 17460, the time of his absence from this State is part of the time limited for the commencement of the action described in those sections, except when he is out of this State and cannot be located through the exercise of reasonable diligence, except this section in no event shall be applicable in any action or proceeding commenced on or before September 7, 1956.
(Enacted by Stats. 1959, Ch. 3.)

Chapter 2. Civil Liability of Persons Signing License Applications of Minors

(Chapter 2 enacted by Stats. 1959, Ch. 3.)

17700. For the purposes of this chapter, all persons under 18 years of age are minors.
(Amended by Stats. 1971, Ch. 1748.)

17701. No application for a driver's license shall be granted by the department to any minor unless it is signed and verified by the father and mother of such minor, if both father and mother are living and have custody of the minor.

If only one parent is living or has custody, the application shall be signed and verified by that parent.

If neither parent is living or has custody, the application shall be signed and verified by the guardian, or if there is no guardian, by a person having custody of the minor.

If the minor is a dependent or ward of the court, the application may be signed by a grandparent, sibling over the age of 18 years, aunt, uncle, or foster parent with whom the minor resides. The probation officer or child protective services worker acting as an officer of the court, on behalf of a child, may also sign and verify the application of a minor who is a dependent or ward of the court, if the minor files proof of financial responsibility as provided in Article 1 (commencing with Section 16430) of Chapter 3 of Division 7 at the time of application. Prior to signing the application, the probation officer or child protective services worker shall notify the foster parents or other responsible party of his or her intent to sign and verify the application.
(Amended by Stats. 1992, Ch. 865, Sec. 2. Effective January 1, 1993.)

17702. If a minor under the age of 18 years is married, the application may be signed and verified by the adult spouse of the minor or by the parents of either spouse or in lieu of the signature, the minor may file proof of financial responsibility, as defined in Section 16430.
(Amended by Stats. 1992, Ch. 974, Sec. 12. Effective September 28, 1992.)

17703. If the person or persons required to sign and verify the application of a minor are not residents of this state, the application shall be signed and verified by a person residing within this state who has custody of the minor, or the department may accept an application signed and verified by the minor and accompanied by proof of financial responsibility, as defined in Section 16430.
(Amended by Stats. 1992, Ch. 974, Sec. 13. Effective September 28, 1992.)

17704. If, at any time during the minority of the person who has given proof of financial responsibility, as defined in Section 16430, the proof fails, the department shall immediately cancel the license until proof of the licensee's continued financial responsibility has been given or until the minor has otherwise complied with the requirements of this code relative to the issuance of a driver's license.
(Amended by Stats. 1992, Ch. 974, Sec. 14. Effective September 28, 1992.)

17705. If the person who is required to sign and verify the application of a minor gives his or her written consent, or the minor is emancipated other than by marriage, the department may accept an application signed and verified only by the minor and accompanied by proof of financial responsibility, as defined in Section 16430. The person giving the consent to but not signing or verifying the application shall not be subject to the civil liability specified in Sections 17707 and 17708 merely by reason of having given consent.
(Amended by Stats. 1992, Ch. 974, Sec. 15. Effective September 28, 1992.)

17706. (a) If the person who is required by the provisions of this code to sign and verify the application of a minor gives his written consent, the department may accept an application signed and verified by the minor and his employer, but in such case the department shall issue to the minor only a driver's license restricted to the operation of vehicles by the minor within the scope of his employment by the employer, unless the employer in writing authorizes the issuance of an unrestricted driver's license.

(b) The person giving his consent to, but not signing or verifying, the application as provided in this section shall not be subject to the civil liability specified in Sections 17707 and 17708 merely by reason of having given such consent.
(Enacted by Stats. 1959, Ch. 3.)

17707. Any civil liability of a minor arising out of his driving a motor vehicle upon a highway during his minority is hereby imposed upon the person who signed and verified the application of the minor for a license and the person shall be jointly and severally liable with the minor for any damages proximately resulting from the negligent or wrongful act or omission of the minor in driving a motor vehicle, except that an employer signing the application shall be subject to the provisions of this section only if an unrestricted driver's license has been issued to the minor pursuant to the employer's written authorization.

No liability may be imposed under this section or under Section 17708 on the state or county, or on a probation officer or child protective services worker acting as an officer of the court for damages caused solely by the negligence or willful misconduct of a minor driver whose application for a driver's license was signed by the child protective services worker or probation officer while the minor was a dependent or ward of the court.
(Amended by Stats. 1992, Ch. 865, Sec. 3. Effective January 1, 1993.)

17708. Any civil liability of a minor, whether licensed or not under this code, arising out of his driving a motor vehicle upon a highway with the express or implied permission of the parents or the person or guardian having custody of the minor is hereby imposed upon the parents, person, or guardian and the parents, person, or guardian shall be jointly and severally liable with the minor for any damages proximately resulting from the negligent or wrongful act or omission of the minor in driving a motor vehicle.
(Amended by Stats. 1967, Ch. 702.)

17709. (a) No person, or group of persons collectively, shall incur liability for a minor's negligent or wrongful act or omission under Sections 17707 and 17708 in any amount exceeding fifteen thousand dollars ($15,000) for injury to or death of one person as a result of any one accident or, subject to the limit as to one person, exceeding thirty thousand dollars ($30,000) for injury to or death of all persons as a result of any one accident or exceeding five thousand dollars ($5,000) for damage to property of others as a result of any one accident.

(b) No person is liable under Section 17707 or 17708 for damages imposed for the sake of example and by way of punishing the minor. Nothing in this subdivision makes any person immune from liability for damages imposed for the sake of example and by way of punishing him for his own wrongful conduct.
(Amended by Stats. 1967, Ch. 862.)

17710. The person signing a minor's application for a license is not liable under this chapter for a negligent or wrongful act or omission of the minor committed when the minor is acting as the agent or servant of any person.
(Amended by Stats. 1967, Ch. 702.)

17711. Any person who has signed and verified the application of a minor for a driver's license or any employer who has authorized the issuance of a license to a minor and who desires to be relieved from the joint and several liability imposed by reason of having signed and verified such application, may file a verified application with the department requesting that the license of the minor be canceled. The department shall cancel the license, except as provided in subdivision (e) of Section 17712. Thereafter, the person shall be relieved from the liability imposed under this chapter by reason of having signed and verified the original application on account of any subsequent willful misconduct or negligent operation of a motor vehicle by the minor.

(Amended by Stats. 1976, Ch. 645.)

17712. (a) The department, upon receipt of satisfactory evidence of the death of the father and mother or the person or guardian who signed and verified the application of any minor under Section 17701 or any employer who signed and verified the application of any minor under subdivision (a) of Section 17706, shall cancel the license, except as provided in subdivision (e).

(b) The department, upon receipt of the verified application of a person who has given written consent to the issuance of a license to a minor as prescribed in Sections 17705 and 17706, for the cancellation of such minor's license, shall cancel the license, except as provided in subdivision (e).

(c) The department, upon receipt of satisfactory evidence that there has been a change of custody of a minor licensed under Chapter 1 (commencing with Section 12500) of Division 6, and upon written request by the person to whom custody has been transferred, shall cancel the license.

(d) The department, upon receipt of satisfactory evidence showing that any minor to whom was issued a license pursuant to Section 17706, has left the employ of the employer who signed and verified the application for the license, shall cancel the license, except as provided in subdivision (e).

(e) The department, upon written request by the person to whom custody of a minor has been transferred, shall transfer the liability imposed under this chapter to such person upon receipt of such person's written verified application for acceptance of liability. Upon receipt, by the department, of such application for acceptance of liability, the person who had signed and verified the application of the minor for the driver's license presently held by the minor shall be relieved from the liability imposed under this chapter. If such application for acceptance of liability is on file with the department prior to the receipt of a request for cancellation by the person who had signed the application of the minor for a driver's license, the license issued under such application shall not be canceled so long as the license is otherwise valid. If, however, such application for acceptance of liability is not on file with the department prior to the receipt of a request for cancellation by the person who had signed the application of the minor for a driver's license, the license issued under such application shall be canceled.

(Amended by Stats. 1976, Ch. 645.)

17714. In the event, in one or more actions, judgment is rendered against a defendant under this chapter based upon the negligent or wrongful act or omission of a minor in the operation of a vehicle, and also by reason of such act or omission rendered against such defendant under Article 2 (commencing with Section 17150) of Chapter 1 of Division 9, then such judgment or judgments shall not be cumulative but recovery shall be limited to the amount specified in Section 17709.

(Amended by Stats. 1967, Ch. 702.)

Division 10. Accidents and Accident Reports

(Division 10 enacted by Stats. 1959, Ch. 3.)

Chapter 1. Accidents and Accident Reports

(Heading of Chapter 1 added by Stats. 1989, Ch. 281, Sec. 2.)

20000. The provisions of this division apply upon highways and elsewhere throughout the State, unless expressly provided otherwise.

(Enacted by Stats. 1959, Ch. 3.)

20001. (a) The driver of a vehicle involved in an accident resulting in injury to a person, other than himself or herself, or in the death of a person shall immediately stop the vehicle at the scene of the accident and shall fulfill the requirements of Sections 20003 and 20004.

(b) (1) Except as provided in paragraph (2), a person who violates subdivision (a) shall be punished by imprisonment in the state prison, or in a county jail for not more than one year, or by a fine of not less than one thousand dollars ($1,000) nor more than ten thousand dollars ($10,000), or by both that imprisonment and fine.

(2) If the accident described in subdivision (a) results in death or permanent, serious injury, a person who violates subdivision (a) shall be punished by imprisonment in the state prison for two, three, or four years, or in a county jail for not less than 90 days nor more than one year, or by a fine of not less than one thousand dollars ($1,000) nor more than ten thousand dollars ($10,000), or by both that imprisonment and fine. However, the court, in the interests of justice and for reasons stated in the record, may reduce or eliminate the minimum imprisonment required by this paragraph.

(3) In imposing the minimum fine required by this subdivision, the court shall take into consideration the defendant's ability to pay the fine and, in the interests of justice and for reasons stated in the record, may reduce the amount of that minimum fine to less than the amount otherwise required by this subdivision.

(c) A person who flees the scene of the crime after committing a violation of Section 191.5 of, or paragraph (1) of subdivision (c) of Section 192 of the Penal Code, upon conviction of any of those sections, in addition and consecutive to the punishment prescribed, shall be punished by an additional term of imprisonment of five years in the state prison. This additional term shall not be imposed unless the allegation is charged in the accusatory pleading and admitted by the defendant or found to be true by the trier of fact. The court shall not strike a finding that brings a person within the provisions of this subdivision or an allegation made pursuant to this subdivision.

(d) As used in this section, "permanent, serious injury" means the loss or permanent impairment of function of a bodily member or organ.

(Amended by Stats. 2007, Ch. 747, Sec. 30. Effective January 1, 2008.)

20002. (a) The driver of any vehicle involved in an accident resulting only in damage to any property, including vehicles, shall immediately stop the vehicle at the nearest location that will not impede traffic or otherwise jeopardize the safety of other motorists. Moving the vehicle in accordance with this subdivision does not affect the question of fault. The driver shall also immediately do either of the following:

(1) Locate and notify the owner or person in charge of that property of the name and address of the driver and owner of the vehicle involved and, upon locating the driver of any other vehicle involved or the owner or person in charge of any damaged property, upon being requested, present his or her driver's license, and vehicle registration, to the other driver, property owner, or person in charge of that property. The information presented shall include the current residence address of the driver and of the registered owner. If the registered owner of an involved vehicle is present at the scene, he or she shall also, upon request, present his or her driver's license information, if available, or other valid identification to the other involved parties.

(2) Leave in a conspicuous place on the vehicle or other property damaged a written notice giving the name and address of the driver and of the owner of the vehicle involved and a statement of the circumstances

thereof and shall without unnecessary delay notify the police department of the city wherein the collision occurred or, if the collision occurred in unincorporated territory, the local headquarters of the Department of the California Highway Patrol.

(b) Any person who parks a vehicle which, prior to the vehicle again being driven, becomes a runaway vehicle and is involved in an accident resulting in damage to any property, attended or unattended, shall comply with the requirements of this section relating to notification and reporting and shall, upon conviction thereof, be liable to the penalties of this section for failure to comply with the requirements.

(c) Any person failing to comply with all the requirements of this section is guilty of a misdemeanor and, upon conviction thereof, shall be punished by imprisonment in the county jail not exceeding six months, or by a fine not exceeding one thousand dollars ($1,000), or by both that imprisonment and fine.

(Amended by Stats. 2001, Ch. 825, Sec. 16. Effective January 1, 2002.)

20003. (a) The driver of any vehicle involved in an accident resulting in injury to or death of any person shall also give his or her name, current residence address, the names and current residence addresses of any occupant of the driver's vehicle injured in the accident, the registration number of the vehicle he or she is driving, and the name and current residence address of the owner to the person struck or the driver or occupants of any vehicle collided with, and shall give the information to any traffic or police officer at the scene of the accident. The driver also shall render to any person injured in the accident reasonable assistance, including transporting, or making arrangements for transporting, any injured person to a physician, surgeon, or hospital for medical or surgical treatment if it is apparent that treatment is necessary or if that transportation is requested by any injured person.

(b) Any driver or injured occupant of a driver's vehicle subject to the provisions of subdivision (a) shall also, upon being requested, exhibit his or her driver's license, if available, or, in the case of an injured occupant, any other available identification, to the person struck or to the driver or occupants of any vehicle collided with, and to any traffic or police officer at the scene of the accident.

(Amended by Stats. 1994, Ch. 1247, Sec. 9. Effective January 1, 1995.)

20004. In the event of death of any person resulting from an accident, the driver of any vehicle involved after fulfilling the requirements of this division, and if there be no traffic or police officer at the scene of the accident to whom to give the information required by Section 20003, shall, without delay, report the accident to the nearest office of the Department of the California Highway Patrol or office of a duly authorized police authority and submit with the report the information required by Section 20003.

(Enacted by Stats. 1959, Ch. 3.)

20006. If the driver does not have his driver's license in his possession, he shall exhibit other valid evidences of identification to the occupants of a vehicle with which he collided.

(Enacted by Stats. 1959, Ch. 3.)

20008. (a) The driver of a vehicle, other than a common carrier vehicle, involved in any accident resulting in injuries to or death of any person shall within 24 hours after the accident make or cause to be made a written report of the accident to the Department of the California Highway Patrol or, if the accident occurred within a city, to either the Department of the California Highway Patrol or the police department of the city in which the accident occurred. If the agency which receives the report is not responsible for investigating the accident, it shall immediately forward the report to the law enforcement agency which is responsible for investigating the accident.

On or before the fifth day of each month, every police department which received a report during the previous calendar month of an accident which it is responsible for investigating shall forward the report or a copy thereof to the main office of the Department of the California Highway Patrol at Sacramento.

(b) The owner or driver of a common carrier vehicle involved in any such accident shall make a like report to the Department of California Highway Patrol on or before the 10th day of the month following the accident.

(Amended by Stats. 1970, Ch. 224.)

20009. The Department of the California Highway Patrol may require any driver, or the owner of a common carrier vehicle, involved in any accident of which a report must be made as provided in Section 20008 to file supplemental reports and may require witnesses of accidents to render reports to it whenever the original report is insufficient in the opinion of such department.

(Enacted by Stats. 1959, Ch. 3.)

20010. Whenever the driver of a vehicle is physically incapable of making a required accident report, any occupant in the vehicle at the time of the accident shall make the report or cause it to be made.

(Enacted by Stats. 1959, Ch. 3.)

20011. A coroner or medical examiner shall on or before the 10th day of each month report in writing to the Department of the California Highway Patrol the death of any person during the preceding calendar month as the result of an accident involving a motor vehicle and the circumstances of the accident. Chemical test results, including blood alcohol content and blood drug concentrations, shall be reported in writing when available.

(Amended by Stats. 2022, Ch. 223, Sec. 2. (SB 925) Effective January 1, 2023.)

20012. All required accident reports, and supplemental reports, shall be without prejudice to the individual so reporting and shall be for the confidential use of the Department of Motor Vehicles and the Department of the California Highway Patrol, except that the Department of the California Highway Patrol or the law enforcement agency to whom the accident was reported shall disclose the entire contents of the reports, including, but not limited to, the names and addresses of persons involved or injured in, or witnesses to, an accident, the registration numbers and descriptions of vehicles involved, the date, time and location of an accident, all diagrams, statements of the drivers involved or occupants injured in the accident and the statements of all witnesses, to any person who may have a proper interest therein, including, but not limited to, the driver or drivers involved, or the guardian or conservator thereof, the parent of a minor driver, the authorized representative of a driver, or to any named person injured therein, the owners of vehicles or property damaged thereby, persons who may incur civil liability, including liability based upon a breach of warranty arising out of the accident, and any attorney who declares under penalty of perjury that he or she represents any of the above persons.

A request for a copy of an accident report shall be accompanied by payment of a fee, provided such fee shall not exceed the actual cost of providing the copy.

(Amended by Stats. 1994, Ch. 1247, Sec. 10. Effective January 1, 1995.)

20013. No such accident report shall be used as evidence in any trial, civil or criminal, arising out of an accident, except that the department shall furnish upon demand of any person who has, or claims to have, made such a report or upon demand of any court, a certificate showing that a specified accident report has or has not been made to the department solely to prove a compliance or failure to comply with the requirement that such a report be made to the department.

(Amended by Stats. 1959, Ch. 1996.)

20014. All required accident reports and supplemental reports and all reports made to the Department of the California Highway Patrol by any peace officer, member of the Department of the California Highway Patrol, or other employee of the Department of Motor Vehicles and the Department of the California Highway Patrol, shall be immediately available for the confidential use of any division in the department needing the same, for confidential use of the Department of Transportation, and, with respect to accidents occurring on highways other than state highways, for the confidential use of the local authority having jurisdiction

over the highway.
(Amended by Stats. 1974, Ch. 545.)

20015. (a) No traffic or police officer shall include in any counter report of a property-damage accident, as defined in this section, any determination by the peace officer of fault of the reporting person, including, but not limited to, inattentiveness. This section does not apply to a determination which is the result of an examination of the physical evidence of the accident at the site of the accident by the traffic or police officer or the result of an express, knowing admission of the reporting person if the basis for the determination is also included in the report.

(b) As used in this section, "counter report of a property-damage accident" means any report of an accident involving one or more vehicles which meets the following criteria:

(1) The accident reported caused damage to property, but did not cause personal injury to or the death of any person.

(2) The report is prepared at an office of the California Highway Patrol or local law enforcement agency.

(3) The report is written or recorded by, or with the assistance of, a peace officer.
(Added by Stats. 1984, Ch. 861, Sec. 1.)

20016. Any peace officer, any member of an organized fire department or fire protection district, any employee of the Department of Transportation assigned to maintenance operations, or any member of the California Highway Patrol may transport or arrange for the transportation of any person injured in an accident upon any highway to a physician and surgeon or hospital, if the injured person does not object to such transportation. Any officer, member, or employee exercising ordinary care and precaution shall not be liable for any damages due to any further injury or for any medical, ambulance, or hospital bills incurred in behalf of the injured party.
(Amended by Stats. 1974, Ch. 545.)

20017. Any peace officer who knows, or has reasonable cause to believe, that a pesticide has been spilled or otherwise accidentally released, shall report the spill as required in Section 105215 of the Health and Safety Code.
(Amended by Stats. 1996, Ch. 1023, Sec. 425. Effective September 29, 1996.)

20018. Every law enforcement agency having traffic law enforcement responsibility as specified in subdivision (a) of Section 830.1 and in subdivision (a) of Section 830.2 of the Penal Code may develop, adopt, and implement a written policy for its officers to provide assistance to disabled motorists on highways within its primary jurisdiction. A copy of the policy, if adopted, shall be available to the public upon request.
(Amended by Stats. 1993, Ch. 59, Sec. 18. Effective June 30, 1993.)

Division 11. Rules of the Road
(Division 11 enacted by Stats. 1959, Ch. 3.)

Chapter 1. Obedience to and Effect of Traffic Laws
(Chapter 1 enacted by Stats. 1959, Ch. 3.)

Article 1. Definitions
(Article 1 enacted by Stats. 1959, Ch. 3.)

21000. Wherever in this division "department" occurs, it means the Department of the California Highway Patrol.
(Enacted by Stats. 1959, Ch. 3.)

21001. The provisions of this division refer exclusively to the operation of vehicles upon the highways, unless a different place is specifically referred to.
(Enacted by Stats. 1959, Ch. 3.)

Article 2. Effect of Traffic Laws
(Article 2 enacted by Stats. 1959, Ch. 3.)

21050. Every person riding or driving an animal upon a highway has all of the rights and is subject to all of the duties applicable to the driver of a vehicle by this division and Division 10 (commencing with Section 20000), except those provisions which by their very nature can have no application.
(Amended by Stats. 1967, Ch. 586.)

21051. The following sections apply to trolley coaches:

(a) Sections 1800, 4000, 4001, 4002, 4003, 4006, 4009, 4150, 4151, 4152, 4153, 4155, 4156, 4158, 4166, 4300 to 4309, inclusive, 4450 to 4454, inclusive, 4457, 4458, 4459, 4460, 4600 to 4610, inclusive, 4750, 4751, 4850, 4851, 4852, 4853, 5000, 5200 to 5205, inclusive, 5904, 6052, 8801, 9254, and 40001 with respect to 4000, relating to original and renewal of registration.

(b) Sections 9250, 9265, 9400, 9406, 9407, 9408, 9550, 9552, 9553, 9554, 9800 to 9808, inclusive, 14901, 42230 to 42233, inclusive, relating to registration and other fees.

(c) Sections 2800, 10851, 10852, 10853, 20001 to 20009, inclusive, 21052, 21053, 21054, 21450 to 21457, inclusive, 21461, 21650, 21651, 21658, 21659, 21700, 21701, 21702, 21703, 21709, 21712, 21750, 21753, 21754, 21755, 21800, 21801, 21802, 21806, 21950, 21951, 22106, 22107, 22108, 22109, 22350, 22351, 22352, 22400, 22450 to 22453, inclusive, 23103, 23104, 23105, 23110, 23152, 23153, 40831, 42002 with respect to 10852 and 10853, and 42004, relating to traffic laws.

(d) Sections 26706, 26707, and 26708, relating to equipment.

(e) Sections 17301, 17302, 17303, 21461, 35000, 35100, 35101, 35105, 35106, 35111, 35550, 35551, 35750, 35751, 35753, 40000.1 to 40000.25, inclusive, 40001, 40003, and 42031, relating to the size, weight, and loading of vehicles.
(Amended by Stats. 2007, Ch. 682, Sec. 15. Effective January 1, 2008.)

21052. The provisions of this code applicable to the drivers of vehicles upon the highways apply to the drivers of all vehicles while engaged in the course of employment by this State, any political subdivision thereof, any municipal corporation, or any district, including authorized emergency vehicles subject to those exemptions granted such authorized emergency vehicles in this code.
(Enacted by Stats. 1959, Ch. 3.)

21053. This code, except Chapter 1 (commencing with Section 20000) of Division 10, Article 2 (commencing with Section 23152) of Chapter 12 of Division 11, and Sections 25268 and 25269, does not apply to public employees and publicly owned teams, motor vehicles, and other equipment while actually engaged in work upon the surface of a highway, or work of installation, removal, repairing, or maintaining official traffic control devices. This code does apply to those persons and vehicles when traveling to or from their work.
(Amended by Stats. 1998, Ch. 877, Sec. 62. Effective January 1, 1999.)

21054. The provisions of this division do not apply to the duly authorized representatives of any public agency while actually engaged in performing any of the work described in Section 21053 but apply to such persons when traveling to and from such work.
(Enacted by Stats. 1959, Ch. 3.)

21055. The driver of an authorized emergency vehicle is exempt from Chapter 2 (commencing with Section 21350), Chapter 3 (commencing with Section 21650), Chapter 4 (commencing with Section 21800), Chapter 5 (commencing with Section 21950), Chapter 6 (commencing with 22100), Chapter 7 (commencing with Section 22348), Chapter 8 (commencing with Section 22450), Chapter 9 (commencing with Section 22500), and Chapter 10 (commencing with Section 22650) of this division, and Article 3 (commencing with Section 38305) and Article 4 (commencing with Section 38312) of Chapter 5 of Division 16.5, under all of the following conditions:

(a) If the vehicle is being driven in response to an emergency call or while engaged in rescue operations or is being used in the immediate pursuit of an actual or suspected violator of the law or is responding to, but not returning from, a fire alarm, except that fire department vehicles are exempt whether directly responding to an emergency call or operated from one place to another as rendered desirable or necessary by reason of an emergency call and operated to the scene of the emergency or operated from one fire station to another or to some other location by reason of the emergency call.

(b) If the driver of the vehicle sounds a siren as may be reasonably necessary and the vehicle displays a lighted red lamp visible from the front as a warning to other drivers and pedestrians.

A siren shall not be sounded by an authorized emergency vehicle except when required under this section.
(Amended by Stats. 1977, Ch. 1017.)

21056. Section 21055 does not relieve the driver of a vehicle from the duty to drive with due regard for the safety of all persons using the highway, nor protect him from the consequences of an arbitrary exercise of the privileges granted in that section.
(Enacted by Stats. 1959, Ch. 3.)

21057. Every police and traffic officer is hereby expressly prohibited from using a siren or driving at an illegal speed when serving as an escort of any vehicle, except when the escort or conveyance is furnished for the preservation of life or when expediting movements of supplies and personnel for any federal, state, or local governmental agency during a national emergency, or state of war emergency, or state of emergency, or local emergency as defined in Section 8558 of the Government Code.
(Amended by Stats. 1971, Ch. 131.)

21058. A physician traveling in response to an emergency call shall be exempt from the provisions of Sections 22351 and 22352 if the vehicle so used by him displays an insigne approved by the department indicating that the vehicle is owned by a licensed physician. The provisions of this section do not relieve the driver of the vehicle from the duty to drive with due regard for the safety of all persons using the highway, nor protect the driver from the consequences of an arbitrary exercise of the privileges of this section.
(Amended by Stats. 1959, Ch. 1996.)

21059. Sections 21211, 21650, 21660, 22502, 22504, and subdivision (h) of Section 22500 do not apply to the operation of a rubbish or garbage truck while actually engaged in the collection of rubbish or garbage within a business or residence district, if the front turn signal lamps at each side of the vehicle are being flashed simultaneously and the rear turn signal lamps at each side of the vehicle are being flashed simultaneously.

This provision does not apply when the vehicle is being driven to and from work, and it does not relieve the driver of the vehicle from the duty to drive with due regard for the safety of all persons using the highway or protect him or her from the consequences of an arbitrary exercise of the privilege granted.
(Amended by Stats. 1999, Ch. 1007, Sec. 20. Effective January 1, 2000.)

21060. Between the hours of 1 a.m. and 5 a.m., Sections 21650, 21660, 22502, 22504, and subdivision (h) of Section 22500 do not apply to the operation of a streetsweeper vehicle or watering vehicle, operated by a local authority, while the vehicle is actually sweeping streets or watering landscaping or vegetation within a business or residence district. The exemption is not applicable unless the turn signal lamps at each side of the front and rear of the streetsweeper vehicle or watering vehicle are being flashed simultaneously.

This provision shall not apply when the vehicle is being driven to and from such work, nor does it relieve the driver of such a vehicle from the duty to drive with due regard for the safety of all persons using the highway or protect the driver from the consequences of an arbitrary exercise of the privilege granted.
(Added by Stats. 1979, Ch. 469.)

21061. (a) In addition to any action prescribed in Division 17 (commencing with Section 40000.1), a traffic officer may issue a notice of reexamination to any person who violates any provision of this division and who, at the time of the violation, exhibits evidence of incapacity to the traffic officer which leads the traffic officer to reasonably believe that the person is incapable of operating a motor vehicle in a manner so as not to present a clear or potential danger of risk of injury to that person or others if that person is permitted to resume operation of a motor vehicle.

(b) For purposes of this section, "evidence of incapacity" means evidence, other than violations of this division, of serious physical injury or illness or mental impairment or disorientation which is apparent to the traffic officer and which presents a clear or potential danger or risk of injury to the person or others if that person is permitted to resume operation of a motor vehicle.
(Added by Stats. 1986, Ch. 304, Sec. 3. Operative July 1, 1987, by Sec. 6 of Ch. 304.)

21062. The arresting officer shall, before the end of the next working day, transmit, or cause to be transmitted, a legible copy of the notice of reexamination to the Department of Motor Vehicles, and the department shall enter the record of the notice in the driver's license record maintained by electronic recording and storage media by the department within five working days of its receipt.
(Added by Stats. 1986, Ch. 304, Sec. 4. Operative July 1, 1987, by Sec. 6 of Ch. 304.)

21070. Notwithstanding any other provision of law, a driver who violates any provision of this division, that is punishable as an infraction, and as a result of that violation proximately causes bodily injury or great bodily injury, as defined in Section 12022.7 of the Penal Code, to another person is guilty of the public offense of unsafe operation of a motor vehicle with bodily injury or great bodily injury. That violation is punishable as an infraction pursuant to Section 42001.19.
(Added by Stats. 2006, Ch. 898, Sec. 3. Effective January 1, 2007.)

Article 3. Local Regulation

(Article 3 enacted by Stats. 1959, Ch. 3.)

21100. Local authorities may adopt rules and regulations by ordinance or resolution regarding all of the following matters:

(a) Regulating or prohibiting a procession or assemblage on the highways.

(b) Licensing and regulating the operation of vehicles for hire and drivers of passenger vehicles for hire.

(c) Regulating traffic by means of traffic officers.

(d) Regulating traffic by means of official traffic control devices meeting the requirements of Section 21400.

(e) (1) Regulating traffic by means of a person given temporary or permanent appointment for that duty by the local authority when official traffic control devices are disabled or otherwise inoperable, at the scene of an accident or disaster, or at a location that may require traffic direction for orderly traffic flow.

(2) A person shall not be appointed pursuant to this subdivision

unless and until the local authority has submitted to the commissioner or to the chief law enforcement officer exercising jurisdiction in the enforcement of traffic laws within the area in which the person is to perform the duty, for review, a proposed program of instruction for the training of a person for that duty and unless and until the commissioner or other chief law enforcement officer approves the proposed program. The commissioner or other chief law enforcement officer shall approve a proposed program if they reasonably determine that the program will provide sufficient training for persons assigned to perform the duty described in this subdivision.

(f) Regulating traffic at the site of road or street construction or maintenance by a person authorized for that duty by the local authority.

(g) (1) Licensing and regulating the operation of tow truck service or tow truck drivers whose principal place of business or employment is within the jurisdiction of the local authority, excepting the operation and operators of any auto dismantlers' tow vehicle licensed under Section 11505 or any tow truck operated by a repossessing agency licensed under Chapter 11 (commencing with Section 7500) of Division 3 of the Business and Professions Code and its registered employees.

(2) The Legislature finds that the safety and welfare of the general public is promoted by permitting local authorities to regulate tow truck service companies and operators by requiring licensure, insurance, and proper training in the safe operation of towing equipment, thereby ensuring against towing mistakes that may lead to violent confrontation, stranding motorists in dangerous situations, impeding the expedited vehicle recovery, and wasting state and local law enforcement's limited resources.

(3) This subdivision does not limit the authority of a city or city and county pursuant to Section 12111.

(h) Operation of bicycles and, as specified in Section 21114.5, electric carts by physically disabled persons or persons 50 years of age or older, on public sidewalks.

(i) Providing for the appointment of nonstudent school crossing guards for the protection of persons who are crossing a street or highway in the vicinity of a school or while returning thereafter to a place of safety.

(j) Regulating the methods of deposit of garbage and refuse in streets and highways for collection by the local authority or by any person authorized by the local authority.

(k) Regulating or authorizing the removal by peace officers of vehicles unlawfully parked in a fire lane, as described in Section 22500.1, on private property. A removal pursuant to this subdivision shall be consistent, to the extent possible, with the procedures for removal and storage set forth in Chapter 10 (commencing with Section 22650).

(l) Regulating mobile billboard advertising displays, as defined in Section 395.5, including the establishment of penalties, which may include, but are not limited to, removal of the mobile billboard advertising display, civil penalties, and misdemeanor criminal penalties for a violation of the ordinance or resolution. The ordinance or resolution may establish a minimum distance that a mobile billboard advertising display shall be moved after a specified time period.

(m) Licensing and regulating the operation of pedicabs for hire, as defined in Section 467.5, and operators of pedicabs for hire, including requiring one or more of the following documents:

(1) A valid California driver's license.

(2) Proof of successful completion of a bicycle safety training course certified by the League of American Bicyclists or an equivalent organization as determined by the local authority.

(3) A valid California identification card and proof of successful completion of the written portion of the California driver's license examination administered by the department. The department shall administer, without charging a fee, the original driver's license written examination on traffic laws and signs to a person who states that they are, or intend to become, a pedicab operator and who holds a valid California identification card or has successfully completed an application for a California identification card. If the person achieves a passing score on the examination, the department shall issue a certificate of successful completion of the examination bearing the person's name and identification card number. The certificate shall not serve in lieu of successful completion of the required examination administered as part of any subsequent application for a driver's license. The department is not required to enter the results of the examination into the computerized record of the person's identification card or otherwise retain a record of the examination or results.

(n) (1) This section does not authorize a local authority to enact or enforce an ordinance or resolution that establishes a violation if a violation for the same or similar conduct is provided in this code, nor does it authorize a local authority to enact or enforce an ordinance or resolution that assesses a fine, penalty, assessment, or fee for a violation if a fine, penalty, assessment, or fee for a violation involving the same or similar conduct is provided in this code.

(2) This section does not preclude a local authority from enacting parking ordinances pursuant to existing authority in Chapter 9 (commencing with Section 22500) of Division 11.

(o) (1) Regulating advertising signs on motor vehicles parked or left standing upon a public street. The ordinance or resolution may establish a minimum distance that the advertising sign shall be moved after a specified time period.

(2) Paragraph (1) does not apply to any of the following:

(A) Advertising signs that are permanently affixed to the body of, an integral part of, or a fixture of a motor vehicle for permanent decoration, identification, or display and that do not extend beyond the overall length, width, or height of the vehicle.

(B) If the license plate frame is installed in compliance with Section 5201, paper advertisements issued by a dealer contained within that license plate frame or any advertisements on that license plate frame.

(3) As used in paragraph (2), "permanently affixed" means any of the following:

(A) Painted directly on the body of a motor vehicle.

(B) Applied as a decal on the body of a motor vehicle.

(C) Placed in a location on the body of a motor vehicle that was specifically designed by a vehicle manufacturer, as defined in Section 672, and licensed pursuant to Section 11701, in compliance with both state and federal law or guidelines, for the express purpose of containing an advertising sign.

(Amended by Stats. 2023, Ch. 803, Sec. 1. (AB 436) Effective January 1, 2024.)

21100.1. Whenever any city or county, by ordinance or resolution, permits, restricts, or prohibits the use of public or private highways pursuant to this article, any traffic control device erected by it on or after January 1, 1981, shall conform to the uniform standards and specifications adopted by the Department of Transportation pursuant to Section 21400.

(Added by Stats. 1980, Ch. 671, Sec. 3.)

21100.3. It is unlawful for any person to disobey the traffic directions of a person appointed or authorized by a local authority to regulate traffic pursuant to subdivision (e) of Section 21100 when such appointee is wearing an official insignia issued by the local authority and is acting in the course of his appointed duties.

(Amended by Stats. 1976, Ch. 15.)

21100.4. (a) (1) A magistrate presented with the affidavit of a peace officer or a designated local transportation officer establishing reasonable cause to believe that a vehicle, described by vehicle type and license number, is being operated as a taxicab or other passenger vehicle for hire in violation of licensing requirements adopted by a local authority under subdivision (b) of Section 21100 shall issue a warrant or order authorizing the peace officer or designated local transportation officer to immediately seize and cause the removal of the vehicle. As used in this section, "designated local transportation officer" means any local public officer employed by a local authority to investigate and enforce local taxicab and vehicle for hire laws and regulations.

(2) The warrant or court order may be entered into a computerized database.

(3) A vehicle so impounded may be impounded for a period not to exceed 30 days.

(4) The impounding agency, within two working days of impoundment, shall send a notice by certified mail, return receipt requested, to the legal owner of the vehicle, at an address obtained from the department, informing the owner that the vehicle has been impounded and providing the owner with a copy of the warrant or court order. Failure to notify the legal owner within two working days shall prohibit the impounding agency from charging for more than 15 days' impoundment when a legal owner redeems the impounded vehicle. The law enforcement agency shall be open to issue a release to the registered owner or legal owner, or the agent of either, whenever the agency is open to serve the public for regular, nonemergency business.

(b) (1) An impounding agency shall release a vehicle to the registered owner or his or her agent prior to the end of the impoundment period and without the permission of the magistrate authorizing the vehicle's seizure under any of the following circumstances:

(A) When the vehicle is a stolen vehicle.

(B) When the vehicle was seized under this section for an offense that does not authorize the seizure of the vehicle.

(C) When the vehicle is a rental car.

(2) A vehicle may not be released under this subdivision, except upon presentation of the registered owner's or agent's currently valid license to operate the vehicle under the licensing requirements adopted by the local authority under subdivision (b) of Section 21100, and proof of current vehicle registration, or upon order of the court.

(c) (1) Whenever a vehicle is impounded under this section, the magistrate ordering the storage shall provide the vehicle's registered and legal owners of record, or their agents, with the opportunity for a poststorage hearing to determine the validity of the storage.

(2) A notice of the storage shall be mailed or personally delivered to the registered and legal owners within 48 hours after issuance of the warrant or court order, excluding weekends and holidays, by the person or agency executing the warrant or court order, and shall include all of the following information:

(A) The name, address, and telephone number of the agency providing the notice.

(B) The location of the place of storage and a description of the vehicle, which shall include, if available, the name or make, the manufacturer, the license plate number, and the mileage of the vehicle.

(C) A copy of the warrant or court order and the peace officer's affidavit, as described in subdivision (a).

(D) A statement that, in order to receive their poststorage hearing, the owners, or their agents, are required to request the hearing from the magistrate issuing the warrant or court order in person, in writing, or by telephone, within 10 days of the date of the notice.

(3) The poststorage hearing shall be conducted within two court days after receipt of the request for the hearing.

(4) At the hearing, the magistrate may order the vehicle released if he or she finds any of the circumstances described in subdivision (b) or (e) that allow release of a vehicle by the impounding agency.

(5) Failure of either the registered or legal owner, or his or her agent, to request, or to attend, a scheduled hearing satisfies the poststorage hearing requirement.

(6) The agency employing the peace officer or designated local transportation officer who caused the magistrate to issue the warrant or court order shall be responsible for the costs incurred for towing and storage if it is determined in the poststorage hearing that reasonable grounds for the storage are not established.

(d) The registered owner or his or her agent is responsible for all towing and storage charges related to the impoundment, and any administrative charges authorized under Section 22850.5.

(e) A vehicle removed and seized under subdivision (a) shall be released to the legal owner of the vehicle or the legal owner's agent prior to the end of the impoundment period and without the permission of the magistrate authorizing the seizure of the vehicle if all of the following conditions are met:

(1) The legal owner is a motor vehicle dealer, bank, credit union, acceptance corporation, or other licensed financial institution legally operating in this state or is another person, not the registered owner, holding a security interest in the vehicle.

(2) (A) The legal owner or the legal owner's agent pays all towing and storage fees related to the seizure of the vehicle. A lien sale processing fee shall not be charged to the legal owner who redeems the vehicle prior to the 15th day of impoundment. Neither the impounding authority nor any person having possession of the vehicle shall collect from the legal owner of the type specified in paragraph (1), or the legal owner's agent, any administrative charges imposed pursuant to Section 22850.5 unless the legal owner voluntarily requested a poststorage hearing.

(B) A person operating or in charge of a storage facility where vehicles are stored pursuant to this section shall accept a valid bank credit card or cash for payment of towing, storage, and related fees by a legal or registered owner or the owner's agent claiming the vehicle. A credit card shall be in the name of the person presenting the card. "Credit card" means "credit card" as defined in subdivision (a) of Section 1747.02 of the Civil Code, except, for the purposes of this section, credit card does not include a credit card issued by a retail seller.

(C) A person operating or in charge of a storage facility described in subparagraph (B) who violates subparagraph (B) shall be civilly liable to the owner of the vehicle or to the person who tendered the fees for four times the amount of the towing, storage, and related fees, but not to exceed five hundred dollars ($500).

(D) A person operating or in charge of a storage facility described in subparagraph (B) shall have sufficient funds on the premises of the primary storage facility during normal business hours to accommodate, and make change in, a reasonable monetary transaction.

(E) Credit charges for towing and storage services shall comply with Section 1748.1 of the Civil Code. Law enforcement agencies may include the costs of providing for payment by credit when making agreements with towing companies on rates.

(3) (A) The legal owner or the legal owner's agent presents to the law enforcement agency or impounding agency, or any person acting on behalf of those agencies, a copy of the assignment, as defined in subdivision (b) of Section 7500.1 of the Business and Professions Code; a release from the one responsible governmental agency, only if required by the agency; a government-issued photographic identification card; and any one of the following as determined by the legal owner or the legal owner's agent: a certificate of repossession for the vehicle, a security agreement for the vehicle, or title, whether paper or electronic, showing proof of legal ownership for the vehicle. The law enforcement agency, impounding agency, or any other governmental agency, or any person acting on behalf of those agencies, shall not require the presentation of any other documents.

(B) The legal owner or the legal owner's agent presents to the person in possession of the vehicle, or any person acting on behalf of the person in possession, a copy of the assignment, as defined in subdivision (b) of Section 7500.1 of the Business and Professions Code; a release from the one responsible governmental agency, only if required by the agency; a government-issued photographic identification card; and any one of the following as determined by the legal owner or the legal owner's agent: a certificate of repossession for the vehicle, a security agreement for the vehicle, or title, whether paper or electronic, showing proof of legal ownership for the vehicle. The person in possession of the vehicle, or any person acting on behalf of the person in possession, shall not require the presentation of any other documents.

(C) All presented documents may be originals, photocopies,

or facsimile copies, or may be transmitted electronically. The law enforcement agency, impounding agency, or any person in possession of the vehicle, or anyone acting on behalf of them, shall not require any documents to be notarized. The law enforcement agency, impounding agency, or any person acting on behalf of those agencies, may require the agent of the legal owner to produce a photocopy or facsimile copy of its repossession agency license or registration issued pursuant to Chapter 11 (commencing with Section 7500) of Division 3 of the Business and Professions Code, or to demonstrate, to the satisfaction of the law enforcement agency, impounding agency, or any person in possession of the vehicle, or anyone acting on behalf of them, that the agent is exempt from licensure pursuant to Section 7500.2 or 7500.3 of the Business and Professions Code.

(D) An administrative cost authorized under subdivision (a) of Section 22850.5 shall not be charged to the legal owner of the type specified in paragraph (1) who redeems the vehicle unless the legal owner voluntarily requests a poststorage hearing. A city, county, city and county, or state agency shall not require a legal owner or a legal owner's agent to request a poststorage hearing as a requirement for release of the vehicle to the legal owner or the legal owner's agent. The law enforcement agency, impounding agency, or any other governmental agency, or any person acting on behalf of those agencies, shall not require any documents other than those specified in this paragraph. The law enforcement agency, impounding agency, or other governmental agency, or any person acting on behalf of those agencies, may not require any documents to be notarized. The legal owner or the legal owner's agent shall be given a copy of any documents he or she is required to sign, except for a vehicle evidentiary hold logbook. The law enforcement agency, impounding agency, or any person acting on behalf of those agencies, or any person in possession of the vehicle, may photocopy and retain the copies of any documents presented by the legal owner or legal owner's agent.

(4) A failure by a storage facility to comply with any applicable conditions set forth in this subdivision shall not affect the right of the legal owner or the legal owner's agent to retrieve the vehicle, provided all conditions required of the legal owner or legal owner's agent under this subdivision are satisfied.

(f) (1) A legal owner or the legal owner's agent that obtains release of the vehicle pursuant to subdivision (e) shall not release the vehicle to the registered owner of the vehicle or the person who was listed as the registered owner when the vehicle was impounded or any agents of the registered owner until the termination of the impoundment period.

(2) The legal owner or the legal owner's agent shall not relinquish the vehicle to the registered owner or the person who was listed as the registered owner when the vehicle was impounded until the registered owner or that owner's agent presents his or her valid driver's license or valid temporary driver's license, and an operator's license that is in compliance with the licensing requirements adopted by the local authority under subdivision (b) of Section 21100, to the legal owner or the legal owner's agent. The legal owner or the legal owner's agent or the person in possession of the vehicle shall make every reasonable effort to ensure that the licenses presented are valid and possession of the vehicle will not be given to the driver who was involved in the original impoundment proceeding until the expiration of the impoundment period.

(3) Prior to relinquishing the vehicle, the legal owner may require the registered owner to pay all towing and storage charges related to the impoundment and the administrative charges authorized under Section 22850.5 that were incurred by the legal owner in connection with obtaining the custody of the vehicle.

(4) Any legal owner who knowingly releases or causes the release of a vehicle to a registered owner or the person in possession of the vehicle at the time of the impoundment or any agent of the registered owner in violation of this subdivision shall be guilty of a misdemeanor and subject to a civil penalty in the amount of two thousand dollars ($2,000).

(5) The legal owner, registered owner, or person in possession of the vehicle shall not change or attempt to change the name of the legal owner or the registered owner on the records of the department until the vehicle is released from the impoundment.

(g) Notwithstanding any other provision of this section, the registered owner and not the legal owner shall remain responsible for any towing and storage charges related to the impoundment and the administrative charges authorized under Section 22850.5 and any parking fines, penalties, and administrative fees incurred by the registered owner.

(h) The law enforcement agency and the impounding agency, including any storage facility acting on behalf of the law enforcement agency or impounding agency, shall comply with this section and shall not be liable to the registered owner for the improper release of the vehicle to the legal owner or the legal owner's agent if the release complies with this section. The legal owner shall indemnify and hold harmless a storage facility from any claims arising out of the release of the vehicle to the legal owner or the legal owner's agent and from any damage to the vehicle after its release, including the reasonable costs associated with defending any such claims. A law enforcement agency shall not refuse to issue a release to a legal owner or the agent of a legal owner on the grounds that it previously issued a release.

(Amended by Stats. 2011, Ch. 536, Sec. 14. (AB 957) Effective January 1, 2012.)

21100.5. Notwithstanding any other provisions of law, local authorities of any city which is on a natural island with an area in excess of 20,000 acres and which is within a county having a population in excess of 4,000,000, may, if they determine such rules and regulations to be necessary in view of the special problem existing thereon with respect to the size and nature of the streets of the city and with respect to the characteristics and nature of the city itself, adopt rules and regulations by ordinance or resolution on the following matters:

(a) Regulating the size of vehicles used on streets under their jurisdiction.

(b) Regulating the number of vehicles permitted on streets under their jurisdiction.

(c) Prohibiting the operation, on streets under their jurisdiction, of designated classes of vehicles.

(d) Establishing noise limits, which are different from those prescribed by this code, for vehicles operated on streets under their jurisdiction and prohibiting the operation of vehicles which exceed such limits.

(e) Establishing a maximum speed limit lower than that which the local authority otherwise permitted by this code to establish.

This section shall not apply to vehicles of utilities which are under the jurisdiction of the Public Utilities Commission while engaged in maintenance and construction type service work.

(Amended by Stats. 1974, Ch. 286.)

21100.6. (a) The Counties of Alameda, Contra Costa, and Solano may create a three-year pilot program to regulate the transport of solid waste by commercial nonfranchise solid waste haulers on public roads in unincorporated areas of the county and may adopt an ordinance, as described in subdivision (b), as part of the pilot program.

(b) An ordinance adopted pursuant to this section may include, but is not limited to, provisions requiring commercial nonfranchise solid waste haulers to do any or all of the following:

(1) Obtain a permit to transport solid waste on public roads in unincorporated areas.

(2) Display evidence of the permit described in paragraph (1) when transporting solid waste.

(3) Notwithstanding Section 9400.8, pay a fee to cover the county's reasonable regulatory cost of enforcing the ordinance.

(c) This section does not grant a county any new authority over solid waste hauling operations pursuant to a franchise agreement and does not affect, limit, or abrogate in any manner any franchise granted to a solid waste enterprise for the handling of solid waste.

(d) For purposes of this section, the following definitions apply:"

(1) "Commercial nonfranchise solid waste hauler" means an entity

that charges a fee to haul and dispose of solid waste that is not part of any exclusive or nonexclusive franchise contract or agreement.

(2) "Solid waste" has the same meaning as defined in Section 40191 of the Public Resources Code.

(e) This section shall remain in effect only until January 1, 2028, and as of that date is repealed.

(Added by Stats. 2023, Ch. 202, Sec. 1. (AB 592) Effective January 1, 2024. Repealed as of January 1, 2028, by its own provisions.)

21101. Local authorities, for those highways under their jurisdiction, may adopt rules and regulations by ordinance or resolution, except as provided in subdivision (f), on the following matters:

(a) Closing any highway to vehicular traffic when, in the opinion of the legislative body having jurisdiction, the highway is either of the following:

(1) No longer needed for vehicular traffic.

(2) The closure is in the interests of public safety and all of the following conditions and requirements are met:

(A) The street proposed for closure is located in a county with a population of 6,000,000 or more.

(B) The street has an unsafe volume of traffic and a significant incidence of crime.

(C) The affected local authority conducts a public hearing on the proposed street closure.

(D) Notice of the hearing is provided to residents and owners of property adjacent to the street proposed for closure.

(E) The local authority makes a finding that closure of the street likely would result in a reduced rate of crime.

(b) Designating any highway as a through highway and requiring that all vehicles observe official traffic control devices before entering or crossing the highway or designating any intersection as a stop intersection and requiring all vehicles to stop at one or more entrances to the intersection.

(c) Prohibiting the use of particular highways by certain vehicles, except as otherwise provided by the Public Utilities Commission pursuant to Article 2 (commencing with Section 1031) of Chapter 5 of Part 1 of Division 1 of the Public Utilities Code.

(d) Closing particular streets during regular school hours for the purpose of conducting automobile driver training programs in the secondary schools and colleges of this state.

(e) Temporarily closing a portion of any street for celebrations, parades, local special events, and other purposes when, in the opinion of local authorities having jurisdiction or a public officer or employee that the local authority designates by resolution, the closing is necessary for the safety and protection of persons who are to use that portion of the street during the temporary closing.

(f) Implementing a slow streets program. For purposes of this section, a "slow streets program" may include closures to vehicular traffic or through vehicular traffic of neighborhood local streets with connections to citywide bicycle networks, destinations, such as a business district, that are within walking distance, or green space. A local authority may implement a slow streets program by adopting an ordinance that provides for the closing of streets to vehicular traffic or limiting access and speed on a street using roadway design features, including, but not limited to, islands, curbs, or traffic barriers. A local authority may implement a slow streets program if it meets all of the following requirements:

(1) Conducts an outreach and engagement process that includes notification to residents and owners of property abutting any street being considered for inclusion in the slow streets program.

(2) Determines that the closure or traffic restriction leaves a sufficient portion of the streets in the surrounding area for other public uses, including vehicular, pedestrian, and bicycle traffic.

(3) Provides advance notice of the closure or traffic restriction to residents and owners of property abutting the street.

(4) Clearly designates the street closure or traffic restriction with signage in compliance with the California Manual on Uniform Traffic Control Devices.

(5) Determines that the closure or traffic restriction is necessary for the safety and protection of persons who are to use that portion of the street during the closure or traffic restriction.

(6) Maintains a publically available internet website with information about its slow streets program, a list of streets that are included in the program or are being evaluated for inclusion in the program, and instructions for participating in the public engagement process.

(g) Prohibiting entry to, or exit from, or both, from any street by means of islands, curbs, traffic barriers, or other roadway design features to implement the circulation element of a general plan adopted pursuant to Article 6 (commencing with Section 65350) of Chapter 3 of Division 1 of Title 7 of the Government Code. The rules and regulations authorized by this subdivision shall be consistent with the responsibility of local government to provide for the health and safety of its citizens.

(Amended by Stats. 2022, Ch. 28, Sec. 154. (SB 1380) Effective January 1, 2023.)

21101.2. Local authorities may adopt rules and regulations by ordinance or resolution to provide that if a peace officer, as defined in Chapter 4.5 (commencing with Section 830) of Title 3 of Part 2 of the Penal Code, determines that the traffic load on a particular street or highway, or a portion thereof, is such that little or no vehicular flow is occurring and, additionally, if the peace officer finds that a significant number of vehicles are not promptly moving when an opportunity arises to do so, then the peace officer may divert vehicles, excepting public safety or emergency vehicles, from that street or highway, or portion thereof, subject to traffic congestion until such time as reasonably flowing traffic is restored.

(Added by Stats. 1982, Ch. 710, Sec. 3. Effective September 8, 1982.)

21101.4. (a) A local authority may, by ordinance or resolution, adopt rules and regulations for temporarily closing to through traffic a highway under its jurisdiction when all of the following conditions are, after a public hearing, found to exist:

(1) The local authority finds and determines that, based upon the recommendation of the police department or, in the case of a highway in an unincorporated area, on the joint recommendation of the sheriff's department and the Department of the California Highway Patrol, one of the following concerns exists along the portion of highway recommended for closure:

(A) Serious and continual criminal activity.

(B) Serious and continual illegal dumping.

(2) The highway is not designated as a through highway or arterial street, or, if the highway is so designated, the local authority, in conjunction with law enforcement and traffic engineers, has determined that a temporary closure may be accomplished without significant impact on the normal flow of traffic.

(3) Vehicular or pedestrian traffic on the highway contributes to the concern described in paragraph (1).

(4) The closure will not substantially adversely affect traffic flow, safety on the adjacent streets or in the surrounding neighborhoods, the operation of emergency vehicles, the performance of municipal or public utility services, or the delivery of freight by commercial vehicles in the area of the highway proposed to be temporarily closed.

(b) A highway may be temporarily closed pursuant to subdivision (a) for not more than 18 months, except that this period may be extended for not more than eight additional consecutive periods of not more than 18 months each if, prior to each of those extensions, the local authority holds a public hearing and finds, by ordinance or resolution, that all of the following conditions exist:

(1) Continuation of the temporary closure will assist in preventing the occurrence or reoccurrence of the concern described in paragraph (1), found to exist when the immediately preceding temporary closure was authorized. This finding and determination shall be based upon the recommendation of the police department or, in the case of a highway

in an unincorporated area, on the joint recommendation of the sheriff's department and the Department of the California Highway Patrol.

(2) The highway is not designated as a through highway or arterial street, or, if the highway is so designated, the local authority, in conjunction with law enforcement and traffic engineers, has determined that the immediately preceding temporary closure has been accomplished without significant impact on the normal flow of traffic.

(3) Vehicular or pedestrian traffic on the highway contributes to the concern described in paragraph (1).

(4) The immediately preceding closure has not substantially adversely affected traffic flow, safety on the adjacent streets or in the surrounding neighborhoods, the operation of emergency vehicles, the performance of municipal or public utility services, or the delivery of freight by commercial vehicles in the area of the highway that was temporarily closed.

(c) The local authority shall mail written notice of the public hearing required under subdivision (a) or (b) to all residents and owners, as shown on the last equalized assessment roll, of property adjacent to the portion of highway where a temporary closure or extension of temporary closure is proposed.

(Amended by Stats. 2017, Ch. 34, Sec. 1. (AB 332) Effective January 1, 2018.)

21101.6. Notwithstanding Section 21101, local authorities may not place gates or other selective devices on any street which deny or restrict the access of certain members of the public to the street, while permitting others unrestricted access to the street.

This section is not intended to make a change in the existing law, but is intended to codify the decision of the Court of Appeal in City of Lafayette v. County of Contra Costa (91 Cal. App. 3d 749).

This section shall become operative on January 1, 1990.

(Repealed (in Sec. 2) and added by Stats. 1987, Ch. 689, Sec. 3. Section operative January 1, 1990, by its own provisions.)

21102. Local authorities may adopt rules and regulations by ordinance or resolution closing to vehicular traffic that portion of any street or highway crossing or dividing any school ground or grounds when in the opinion of the legislative body having jurisdiction such closing is necessary for the protection of persons attending such school or school grounds. The closing to vehicular traffic may be limited to such hours and days as the legislative body may specify. No such ordinance or resolution shall be effective until appropriate signs giving notice thereof are posted along the street or highway affected, nor in the case of state highways, until such ordinance or resolution is approved by the Department of Transportation.

(Amended by Stats. 1974, Ch. 545.)

21102.1. Notwithstanding any other provision of law, local authorities may, by ordinance or resolution, adopt rules and regulations restricting vehicular or pedestrian traffic through any alley by means of gates, barriers, or other control devices, when, in the opinion of the local authority having jurisdiction over the alley, the restriction is necessary for the protection or preservation of the public peace, safety, health, or welfare, subject to the following conditions:

(a) No ordinance or resolution adopted pursuant to this section shall be enforceable until appropriate signs giving notice of the restriction are posted at every entrance to the alley.

(b) In the coastal zone, as defined in subdivision (a) of Section 30103 of the Public Resources Code, where the alley provides direct access to any public beach or state waters, the local authority shall comply with Division 20 (commencing with Section 30000) of the Public Resources Code.

(c) In the area administered by the San Francisco Bay Conservation and Development Commission, where the alley provides direct access to any public beach, state waters, or wetlands, the local authority shall first obtain the concurrence by, or on behalf of, the San Francisco Bay Conservation and Development Commission. The concurrence or objection shall be based on the permits issued by the San Francisco Bay Conservation and Development Commission and in conformance with the policies contained in Title 7.2 (commencing with Section 66600) of the Government Code and Division 19 (commencing with Section 29000) of the Public Resources Code.

(d) The local authority shall provide access to utility vehicular or pedestrian traffic in order that the utility may maintain, operate, replace, remove, or renew existing and functioning utility facilities.

(e) No ordinance or resolution adopted pursuant to this section shall prohibit the delivery of freight by commercial vehicles.

(f) No ordinance or resolution adopted pursuant to this section shall be implemented in a manner that adversely affects the operation of emergency vehicles or the performance of municipal services.

(g) No ordinance or resolution adopted pursuant to this section shall restrict the access of certain members of the public to the alley, while permitting others unrestricted access to the alley.

(Added by Stats. 1995, Ch. 215, Sec. 1. Effective January 1, 1996.)

21103. No ordinance or resolution enacted under Section 21101 shall be effective until signs giving notice of the local traffic laws are posted at all entrances to the highway or part thereof affected.

(Amended by Stats. 1980, Ch. 671, Sec. 4.)

21104. No ordinance or resolution proposed to be enacted under Section 21101 or subdivision (d) of Section 21100 is effective as to any highway not under the exclusive jurisdiction of the local authority enacting the same, except that an ordinance or resolution which is submitted to the Department of Transportation by a local legislative body in complete draft form for approval prior to the enactment thereof is effective as to any state highway or part thereof specified in the written approval of the department.

This section does not preclude the application of an ordinance or resolution adopted under Section 21101 or subdivision (d) of Section 21100 to streets maintained by a community services district organized pursuant to Division 3 (commencing with Section 61000) of Title 6 of the Government Code. An ordinance or resolution enacted by a local authority pursuant to subdivision (c) of Section 21101 may impose a fine or penalty of up to one hundred dollars ($100) for a violation of this code.

(Amended by Stats. 2002, Ch. 177, Sec. 1. Effective January 1, 2003.)

21105. No rule or regulation adopted under Sections 21100 or 21101 shall be effective as to boundary line streets where portions thereof are within different jurisdictions unless all authorities having jurisdiction of such portions of the street concerned have approved the same.

(Enacted by Stats. 1959, Ch. 3.)

21106. (a) Local authorities, by ordinance or resolution, may establish crosswalks between intersections.

(b) Local authorities may install signs at or adjacent to an intersection directing that pedestrians shall not cross in a crosswalk indicated at the intersection. It is unlawful for any pedestrian to cross at the crosswalk prohibited by a sign.

(Amended by Stats. 1959, Ch. 417.)

21107. The provisions of this code shall not prevent any city from adopting rules and regulations by ordinance or resolution, regulating vehicular traffic on privately owned and maintained roads located within the boundary of such city, except that no such ordinance or resolution shall be effective until signs giving notice thereof are posted on the roads affected. The provisions of this section shall not apply to any city in which there are publicly maintained city streets.

(Enacted by Stats. 1959, Ch. 3.)

21107.5. (a) Any city or county may, by ordinance or resolution, find and declare that there are privately owned and maintained roads as described in the ordinance or resolution within the city or county that are generally held open for use by the public for vehicular travel and which so connect with highways that the public cannot determine that the roads are not highways. Upon enactment by a city or county of the ordinance or resolution, this code shall apply to the privately owned and maintained road, except as provided in subdivision (b).

(b) No ordinance or resolution enacted under subdivision (a) shall apply to any road on which the owner has erected a notice of a size, shape, and color as to be readily legible during daylight hours from a distance of 100 feet to the effect that the road is privately owned and maintained and that it is not subject to public traffic regulations or control.

(c) No ordinance or resolution shall be enacted under subdivision (a) without a public hearing after 10 days' written notice to the owner of the privately owned and maintained road involved.

(d) The department is not required to provide patrol or enforce any provision of this code on any privately owned and maintained road, except those provisions applicable to private property, other than pursuant to this section.

(Amended by Stats. 1989, Ch. 160, Sec. 1.)

21107.6. (a) Any city or county may, by ordinance, find and declare that there are privately owned and maintained roads as described in such ordinance within the city or county which are generally held open to the public for purposes of vehicular travel to serve commercial establishments. Upon enactment by a city or county of such an ordinance, the provisions of this code shall apply to any such privately owned and maintained road. No ordinance shall be enacted under this section without a public hearing thereon and 10 days' prior notice to the owner of the privately owned and maintained road involved.

(b) Notwithstanding the provisions of subdivision (a) no ordinance enacted thereunder shall apply to any road described therein on which the owner has caused to be erected a notice of such size, shape and color as to be readily legible during daylight hours from a distance of 100 feet, to the effect that the road is privately owned and maintained and that it is not subject to public traffic regulations or control.

(c) The department shall not be required to provide patrol or enforce any provisions of this code on any privately owned and maintained road subjected to the provisions of this code under this section, except those provisions applicable to private property other than by action under this section.

(Added by Stats. 1968, Ch. 514.)

21107.7. (a) Any city or county may, by ordinance or resolution, find and declare that there are privately owned and maintained roads as described in the ordinance or resolution within the city or county that are not generally held open for use of the public for purposes of vehicular travel but, by reason of their proximity to or connection with highways, the interests of any residents residing along the roads and the motoring public will best be served by application of the provisions of this code to those roads. No ordinance or resolution shall be enacted unless there is first filed with the city or county a petition requesting it by a majority of the owners of any privately owned and maintained road, or by at least a majority of the board of directors of a common interest development, as defined by Section 4100 or 6534 of the Civil Code, that is responsible for maintaining the road, and without a public hearing thereon and 10 days' prior written notice to all owners of the road or all of the owners in the development. Upon enactment of the ordinance or resolution, the provisions of this code shall apply to the privately owned and maintained road if appropriate signs are erected at the entrance to the road of the size, shape, and color as to be readily legible during daylight hours from a distance of 100 feet, to the effect that the road is subject to the provisions of this code. The city or county may impose reasonable conditions and may authorize the owners, or board of directors of the common interest development, to erect traffic signs, signals, markings, and devices which conform to the uniform standards and specifications adopted by the Department of Transportation.

(b) The department shall not be required to provide patrol or enforce any provisions of this code on any privately owned and maintained road subjected to the provisions of this code under this section, except those provisions applicable to private property other than by action under this section.

(c) As used in this section, "privately owned and maintained roads" includes roads owned and maintained by a city, county, or district that are not dedicated to use by the public or are not generally held open for use of the public for purposes of vehicular travel.

(Amended (as amended by Stats. 2012, Ch. 181, Sec. 80) by Stats. 2013, Ch. 605, Sec. 49. (SB 752) Effective January 1, 2014.)

21107.8. (a) (1) A city, county, or city and county may, by ordinance or resolution, find and declare that there are privately owned and maintained offstreet parking facilities as described in the ordinance or resolution within the city, county, or city and county that are generally held open for use of the public for purposes of vehicular parking. Upon enactment by a city, county, or city and county of the ordinance or resolution, Sections 22350, 23103, and 23109 and the provisions of Division 16.5 (commencing with Section 38000) shall apply to privately owned and maintained offstreet parking facilities, except as provided in subdivision (b).

(2) (A) If a city, county, or city and county enacts an ordinance or resolution authorized by paragraph (1), the city, county, or city and county may include in that ordinance or resolution authorization for the operator of a privately owned and maintained offstreet parking facility to regulate unauthorized parking in that facility.

(B) (i) If a city, county, or city and county has exercised its authority pursuant to subparagraph (A) and unauthorized parking is regulated in a privately owned and maintained offstreet parking facility, the owner or operator of that facility shall include in a parking fee invoice instructions that describe the manner in which to contest the parking fee invoice.

(ii) If a city, county, or city and county has exercised its authority pursuant to subparagraph (A) and unauthorized parking is regulated in a privately owned and maintained offstreet parking facility, the owner or operator of that facility shall not file with, or transmit to, the Department of Motor Vehicles a parking fee invoice for the purpose of having the Department of Motor Vehicles attempt to collect unpaid parking fees by refusing to renew the registration of a vehicle pursuant to Section 4760.

(b) (1) Notwithstanding subdivision (a), an ordinance or resolution enacted pursuant to that subdivision does not apply to an offstreet parking facility unless the owner or operator has caused to be posted in a conspicuous place at each entrance to that offstreet parking facility a notice not less than 17 by 22 inches in size with lettering not less than one inch in height, to the effect that the offstreet parking facility is subject to public moving vehicle laws and violators may be subject to a parking invoice fee.

(2) If applicable, a parking receipt distributed to drivers shall include language explicitly stating that violators may be subject to a parking invoice fee.

(c) An ordinance or resolution shall not be enacted pursuant to subdivision (a) without a public hearing on the matter and 10 days prior written notice to the owner and operator of the privately owned and maintained offstreet parking facility involved.

(d) Section 22507.8 may be enforced without enactment of an ordinance or resolution as required pursuant to subdivision (a) or the posting of a notice at each entrance to the offstreet parking facility as required by paragraph (1) of subdivision (b).

(e) The department shall not be required to provide patrol or to enforce any provision of this code in a privately owned and maintained offstreet parking facility subject to this section except those provisions applicable to private property actions not described in this section.

(f) A city, county, or city and county that authorizes private parking regulation pursuant to this section shall, in its ordinance or resolution, include provisions that include all of the following:

(1) Procedures for dispute resolution in accordance with Section 40215, including all of the following:

(A) A written and publicly available dispute resolution policy that includes specified time periods for notifications, review, and appeal.

(B) An administrative hearing process that includes all of the following:

(i) Options for a hearing in person or by mail.

(ii) Administrative review.

(iii) A hearing by a third-party examiner who has been adequately trained and who provides an independent, objective, fair, and impartial review.

(iv) Personal delivery or delivery by first-class mail of the examiner's decision.

(v) Authority for the examiner to allow payment of the parking invoice fee in installments for persons showing evidence of inability to pay the parking invoice fee in full.

(2) A prohibition against incentives based on the number of invoices issued or the number or percentage of disputed invoices adjudicated that uphold parking invoice fees.

(3) A cap on a parking invoice fee that is commensurate with the most nearly equivalent municipal parking fine.

(4) Measures to prevent a private parking regulator from representing itself as a government enforcement agency, including a prohibition against the use of terminology in ordinances, resolutions, and parking fee invoices that is restricted to governmental law enforcement and a requirement that a conspicuous statement be included on parking fee invoices to the effect that "This parking invoice fee notice is not issued by the [local government]."

(Amended by Stats. 2017, Ch. 741, Sec. 4. (AB 503) Effective January 1, 2018.)

21107.9. (a) Any city or county, or city and county, may, by ordinance or resolution, find and declare that there are privately owned and maintained roads within a mobilehome park, as defined in Section 18214 of the Health and Safety Code, or within a manufactured housing community, as defined in Section 18801 of the Health and Safety Code, within the city or county, or city and county, that are generally not held open for use by the public for vehicular travel. Upon enactment of the ordinance or resolution, the provisions of this code shall apply to the privately owned and maintained roads within a mobilehome park or manufactured housing community if appropriate signs are erected at the entrance or entrances to the mobilehome park or manufactured housing community of the size, shape, and color as to be readily legible during daylight hours from a distance of 100 feet, to the effect that the roads within the park or community are subject to the provisions of this code. The city or county, or city and county, may impose reasonable conditions and may authorize the owners of the mobilehome park or manufactured housing community to erect traffic signs, markings, or devices which conform to the uniform standards and specifications adopted by the Department of Transportation.

(b) No ordinance or resolution shall be enacted unless there is first filed with the city or county a petition requested by the owner or owners of any privately owned and maintained roads within a mobilehome park or manufactured housing community, who are responsible for maintaining the roads.

(c) No ordinance or resolution shall be enacted without a public hearing thereon and 10 days' prior written notice to all owners of the roads within a mobilehome park or manufactured housing community proposed to be subject to the ordinance or resolution. At least seven days prior to the public hearing, the owner or manager of the mobilehome park or manufactured housing community shall post a written notice about the hearing in a conspicuous area in the park or community clubhouse, or if no clubhouse exists, in a conspicuous public place in the park or community.

(d) For purposes of this section, the prima facie speed limit on any road within a mobilehome park or manufactured housing community shall be 15 miles per hour. This section does not preclude a mobilehome park or manufactured housing community from requesting a higher or lower speed limit if an engineering and traffic survey has been conducted within the community supporting that request.

(e) The department is not required to provide patrol or enforce any provision of this code on any privately owned and maintained road within a mobilehome park or manufactured housing community, except those provisions applicable to private property other than by action under this section.

(Added by Stats. 2002, Ch. 284, Sec. 1. Effective January 1, 2003.)

21108. Local authorities may adopt rules and regulations by ordinance or resolution regulating vehicular traffic on privately owned and maintained roads or ways within the boundaries of a privately owned airport, when the roads or ways are expressly open to the general public for purposes of vehicular traffic.

The rules or regulations shall not be effective until appropriate signs giving notice thereof are posted along the roads or ways affected.

(Enacted by Stats. 1959, Ch. 3.)

21109. (a) Local authorities may adopt rules and regulations by ordinance or resolution regulating vehicular and pedestrian traffic in subways, tubes, and tunnels or upon bridges or viaducts.

(b) The proposed ordinance or resolution shall not be effective as to any state highway until approved in writing by the Department of Transportation. The Department of Transportation, in considering any proposed ordinance or resolution to prohibit or restrict the use by cargo tank vehicles displaying flammable liquids placards in tunnels of a length of 300 feet or greater, shall consult with the Department of the California Highway Patrol and hold a public hearing as provided in Section 21109.5 of the Vehicle Code. In evaluating the feasibility of prohibiting or restricting the use of the structure by cargo tank vehicles displaying flammable liquids placards, the Department of Transportation shall conduct a traffic and engineering survey which includes an analysis of the relative risks to public safety in determining the feasibility of reasonable alternative routes.

(c) The rules or regulations shall not be effective until appropriate signs have been posted giving notice thereof to drivers and pedestrians approaching the highway structures.

(Amended by Stats. 1982, Ch. 1255, Sec. 4.)

21109.5. (a) No restriction or prohibition shall be effective pursuant to subdivision (b) of Section 21109 or Section 34020.5 except upon notice and hearing in the manner prescribed in this section.

(b) Notice of hearing shall be published pursuant to Section 6064 of the Government Code. The notice shall advise all interested parties that they may submit written or oral objections to the proposed action and shall designate a time and place for presentation of the objections. The time for submission of objections shall not expire, and the hearings shall not be held, less than 60 days after the first publication of notice. The hearing shall be conducted by the Department of Transportation and interested parties shall be accorded an adequate opportunity to be heard with respect to their objections.

(Added by Stats. 1982, Ch. 1255, Sec. 5.)

21110. Local authorities may adopt rules and regulations by ordinance or resolution to require that all vehicles stop before entering or crossing the tracks at any highway railroad grade crossing when signs are in place giving notice thereof, but no such ordinance shall be effective unless approved by an order of the Public Utilities Commission.

(Enacted by Stats. 1959, Ch. 3.)

21111. Local authorities may adopt rules and regulations by ordinance or resolution regulating vehicular traffic on privately owned and maintained roads or ways within the boundaries of any housing project or within the site of any housing owned or operated by a housing authority created under and by virtue of the Housing Authorities Law, commencing at Section 34200 of the Health and Safety Code, on privately owned and maintained roads or ways within areas which would be a residence district if the road or way were a public highway, or, with the consent of the owner, on publicly owned and maintained roads and ways within areas which are not owned by such local authorities. The rules or regulations shall not be effective until appropriate signs giving notice thereof are posted along the roads or ways affected.

(Enacted by Stats. 1959, Ch. 3.)

21112. Local authorities may by ordinance license and regulate the

location of stands on streets and highways for use by taxicabs and other public carriers for hire in their respective jurisdictions. No such ordinance shall be effective as to any state highway until approved in writing by the Department of Transportation. Where maintenance of any state highway is delegated by such department to a city, such approval is not required.
(Amended by Stats. 1974, Ch. 545.)

21113. (a) (1) Except as provided in paragraph (2), a person shall not drive a vehicle or animal, or stop, park, or leave standing a vehicle or animal, whether attended or unattended, upon the driveways, paths, parking facilities, or the grounds of any of the following:

(A) A public school, state university, state college, or an educational institution exempted, in whole or in part, from taxation.

(B) A unit of the state park system.

(C) A county park.

(D) A municipal airport.

(E) A rapid transit district, transit development board, transit district, public transportation agency, county transportation commission created pursuant to Section 130050 of the Public Utilities Code, or a joint powers agency operating or managing a commuter rail system.

(F) Any property under the direct control of the legislative body of a municipality.

(G) A state, county, or hospital district institution or building.

(H) Any harbor improvement district or harbor district formed pursuant to Part 2 (commencing with Section 5800) or Part 3 (commencing with Section 6000) of Division 8 of the Harbors and Navigation Code.

(I) A district organized pursuant to Part 3 (commencing with Section 27000) of Division 16 of the Streets and Highways Code.

(J) State grounds served by the Department of the California Highway Patrol.

(K) Any property under the possession or control of a housing authority formed pursuant to Article 2 (commencing with Section 34240) of Chapter 1 of Part 2 of Division 24 of the Health and Safety Code.

(2) The activities described in paragraph (1) may be performed with the permission of, and upon and subject to any condition or regulation that may be imposed by, the legislative body of the municipality, or the governing board or officer of the public school, state university, state college, county park, municipal airport, rapid transit district, transit development board, transit district, public transportation agency, county transportation commission, joint powers agency operating or managing a commuter rail system, or state, county, or hospital district institution or building, or educational institution, or harbor district, or a district organized pursuant to Part 3 (commencing with Section 27000) of Division 16 of the Streets and Highways Code, or housing authority, or the Director of Parks and Recreation regarding units of the state park system or the state agency with jurisdiction over the grounds served by the Department of the California Highway Patrol.

(b) A governing board, legislative body, or officer shall erect or place appropriate signs giving notice of any special conditions or regulations that are imposed under this section and the governing board, legislative body, or officer shall also prepare and keep available at the principal administrative office of the governing board, legislative body, or officer, for examination by all interested persons, a written statement of all those special conditions and regulations adopted pursuant to this section.

(c) When a governing board, legislative body, or officer permits public traffic upon the driveways, paths, parking facilities, or grounds under their control then, except for those conditions imposed or regulations enacted by the governing board, legislative body, or officer applicable to the traffic, all the provisions of this code relating to traffic upon the highways shall be applicable to the traffic upon the driveways, paths, parking facilities, or grounds.

(d) A public transportation agency that imposes any condition or regulation upon a person who parks or leaves standing a vehicle, pursuant to subdivision (a), is authorized to do either of the following:

(1) Enforce that condition or regulation in the manner provided in Article 3 (commencing with Section 40200) of Chapter 1 of Division 17 of this code. The public transportation agency shall be considered the issuing agency for that purpose.

(2) Designate regularly employed and salaried employees, who are engaged in directing traffic or enforcing parking laws and regulations, for the purpose of removing any vehicle in the same manner as a city, county, or jurisdiction of a state agency pursuant to Chapter 10 (commencing with Section 22650) of Division 11 of this code.

(e) With respect to the permitted use of vehicles or animals on property under the direct control of the legislative body of a municipality, no change in the use of vehicles or animals on the property, that had been permitted on January 1, 1976, shall be effective unless and until the legislative body, at a meeting open to the general public, determines that the use of vehicles or animals on the property should be prohibited or regulated.

(f) A transit development board may adopt ordinances, rules, or regulations to restrict, or specify the conditions for, the use of bicycles, motorized bicycles, electric bicycles, skateboards, electrically motorized boards, and roller skates on property under the control of, or any portion of property used by, the board.

(g) A public agency, including, but not limited to, the Regents of the University of California and the Trustees of the California State University, may adopt rules or regulations to restrict, or specify the conditions for, the use of bicycles, motorized bicycles, electric bicycles, skateboards, electrically motorized boards, and roller skates on public property under the jurisdiction of that agency.

(h) "Housing authority," for the purposes of this section, means a housing authority located within a county with a population of over 6,000,000 people, and any other housing authority that complies with the requirements of this section.

(i) "Public transportation agency," for purposes of this section, means a public agency that provides public transportation as defined in paragraph (1) of subdivision (f) of Section 1 of Article XIXA of the California Constitution or a county transportation commission created pursuant to Section 130050 of the Public Utilities Code.
(Amended by Stats. 2016, Ch. 512, Sec. 2. (AB 1943) Effective January 1, 2017.)

21114. If a local authority finds that a city street or county road under its jurisdiction adjacent to an airport has been specifically designed and constructed, with the prior approval of the local authority, so as to safely permit the use thereof by regular vehicular traffic and also the taxiing of aircraft thereon between the airport and the place where such aircraft are hangared or tied down, the local authority may by resolution or ordinance designate such street or road or portion thereof for such combined use and prescribe rules and regulations therefor which shall have the force of law. No such street or road shall be so designated for a distance of more than one-half mile from the airport, provided, the finding of the local authority in this respect shall be conclusive. Upon such designation becoming effective, it shall be the sole responsibility of the local authority to enforce the provisions of the Vehicle Code and all rules and regulations adopted by it upon such street or road. Upon such designation becoming effective it shall be lawful to taxi aircraft upon such street or road in accordance with the rules and regulations prescribed as aforesaid and said aircraft need not be licensed under this code or comply with other provisions thereof.
(Added by Stats. 1963, Ch. 537.)

21114.5. Notwithstanding Section 21663 or any other provision of this code, local authorities may, by ordinance, authorize the operation of electric carts by physically disabled persons, by persons 50 years of age or older, or, while in the course of their employment, by employees of the United States Postal Service, state and local governmental agencies, or utility companies, on public sidewalks. Any ordinance shall, however, contain provisions requiring any disabled person or person 50 years of age or older who owns or leases an electric cart to apply to the local authority for a permit and an identification sticker to so operate the cart, and requiring the person to affix the sticker to the cart in order to operate it on the sidewalk. The permit and sticker shall become invalid if the person ceases to operate, own, or lease the cart.

This section does not apply to devices described in subdivision (b) of Section 415.

(Amended by Stats. 1996, Ch. 124, Sec. 125. Effective January 1, 1997.)

21115. (a) If a local authority finds that a highway under its jurisdiction is located adjacent to, or provides access to, a golf course and between the golf course and the place where golf carts are parked or stored or is within or bounded by a real estate development offering golf facilities and is designed and constructed, so as to safely permit the use of regular vehicular traffic and also the driving of golf carts on the highway, the local authority may, by resolution or ordinance, designate the highway or portion of the highway for combined use and prescribe rules and regulations that shall have the force of law. No highway shall be so designated for a distance of more than one mile from the golf course if the highway is not located within a development or beyond the area of a development, provided, the finding of the local authority in this respect shall be conclusive. Upon the designation becoming effective it shall be lawful to drive golf carts upon the highway in accordance with the prescribed rules and regulations. The rules and regulations may establish crossing zones and speed limits and other operating standards but shall not require that the golf carts conform to any requirements of this code with respect to registration, licensing, or equipment, except that if operated during darkness the golf cart shall be subject to the provisions of Section 24001.5 regarding equipment.

The rules and regulations shall not be effective until appropriate signs giving notice thereof are posted along the highway affected.

A "real estate development offering golf facilities," for purposes of this section, means an area of single-family or multiple-family residences, the owners or occupants of which are eligible for membership in, or the use of, one or more golf courses within the development by virtue of their ownership or occupancy of a residential dwelling unit in the development.

(b) For purposes of this section, a "golf cart" includes a low-speed vehicle.

(Amended by Stats. 1999, Ch. 140, Sec. 4. Effective January 1, 2000.)

21115.1. (a) Notwithstanding Section 21115, a local authority may, by ordinance or resolution, establish crossing zones, for use by golf carts at any time other than during darkness, on any street, other than a state highway, that has a posted speed limit of 45 miles per hour or less and that is immediately adjacent to a golf course. The crossing zones shall be at an angle of approximately 90 degrees to the direction of the roadway. The ordinance or resolution shall not become effective until submitted to the law enforcement agency having primary jurisdiction over the street, the law enforcement agency finds and determines that the conditions pertaining to that street, with the addition of proper signs, markers, or lighting, or any combination of those, will permit the establishment of a golf cart crossing with reasonable safety, and the signs, markers, or lighting specified by the law enforcement agency are in place.

(b) Subdivision (a) does not constitute precedent for the operation of golf carts on any street or highway other than in a crossing zone established pursuant to subdivision (a).

(c) For purposes of this section, a "golf cart" includes a low-speed vehicle.

(Amended by Stats. 1999, Ch. 140, Sec. 5. Effective January 1, 2000.)

21116. (a) No person shall drive any motor vehicle upon a roadway located on a levee, canal bank, natural watercourse bank, or pipeline right-of-way if the responsibility for maintenance of the levee, canal bank, natural watercourse bank, or pipeline right-of-way is vested in the state or in a reclamation, levee, drainage, water or irrigation district, or other local agency, unless such person has received permission to drive upon such roadway from the agency responsible for such maintenance, or unless such roadway has been dedicated as a public right-of-way.

(b) For this section to be applicable to a particular levee, canal bank, natural watercourse bank, or pipeline right-of-way, the state or other agency having responsibility for maintenance of the levee, canal bank, natural watercourse bank, or pipeline right-of-way shall erect or place appropriate signs giving notice that permission is required to be obtained to drive a motor vehicle thereon and giving notice of any special conditions or regulations that are imposed pursuant to this section and shall prepare and keep available at the principal office of the state agency or other agency affected or of the board of such agency, for examination by all interested persons, a written statement, in conformity with the existing rights of such agency to control access to the roadway, describing the nature of the vehicles, if any, to which such permission might be granted and the conditions, regulations, and procedure for the acquisition of such permission adopted pursuant to this section.

(c) Nothing in this section prohibits the establishment of bicycle paths or routes (as prescribed by Article 6.5 (commencing with Section 5078) of Chapter 1 of Division 5 of the Public Resources Code) on levees, canal banks, natural watercourse banks, or pipeline rights-of-way.

(Amended by Stats. 1971, Ch. 1361.)

21117. (a) Local authorities may, notwithstanding Section 21101 or 21101.6, by written agreement approved by their legislative bodies, transfer among themselves the responsibility for maintaining, operating, or controlling public access to any highway under their respective jurisdictions located in or adjacent to an ecological reserve or an environmentally sensitive area within their respective jurisdictions.

(b) An agreement entered into pursuant to subdivision (a) may authorize the local authority having responsibility for the highway under the agreement to do all of the following:

(1) Limit access by motor vehicles to the highway during certain hours of the day or certain days of the week.

(2) Prohibit access by motor vehicles during certain hours of the day or certain days of the week.

(3) Provide for the construction or erection of barricades or other devices designed or intended to separate pedestrians from vehicles or motor vehicles.

(4) Establish and operate a program by which vehicular access is permitted only in conjunction with specified educational programs or for disabled persons, or both.

(5) Issue temporary permits for special events valid for less than one day.

(c) As used in this section, the term "ecological reserve" has the same meaning as defined in Section 1584 of the Fish and Game Code, and "environmentally sensitive area" has the same meaning as defined in Section 30107.5 of the Public Resources Code.

(Added by Stats. 1991, Ch. 541, Sec. 1.)

21118. (a) A local authority may adopt rules and regulations by ordinance or resolution to restrict the routes or streets upon which a tour bus described in subdivision (b) of Section 612 may be operated, if the local authority determines that it is unsafe to operate those vehicles on those routes or streets.

(b) A local authority may adopt rules and regulations by ordinance or resolution to prohibit the use of loudspeakers or public address systems by a tour bus described in subdivision (b) of Section 612, and instead require the use of headphones or similar devices by passengers for any information or presentation provided for the passengers.

(Added by Stats. 2017, Ch. 310, Sec. 2. (AB 25) Effective January 1, 2018.)

Article 4. Operation of Bicycles

(Article 4 added by Stats. 1963, Ch. 479.)

21200. (a) (1) A person riding a bicycle or operating a pedicab upon a highway has all the rights and is subject to all the provisions applicable to the driver of a vehicle by this division, including, but not limited to, provisions concerning driving under the influence of alcoholic beverages or drugs, and by Division 10 (commencing with Section 20000), Section

27400, Division 16.7 (commencing with Section 39000), Division 17 (commencing with Section 40000.1), and Division 18 (commencing with Section 42000), except those provisions which by their very nature can have no application.

(2) A person operating a bicycle on a Class I bikeway, as defined in subdivision (a) of Section 890.4 of the Streets and Highways Code, has all the rights and is subject to all the provisions applicable to the driver of a vehicle pursuant to Section 20001, except those provisions which by their very nature can have no application.

(b) (1) A peace officer, as defined in Chapter 4.5 (commencing with Section 830) of Title 3 of Part 2 of the Penal Code, operating a bicycle during the course of his or her duties is exempt from the requirements of subdivision (a), except as those requirements relate to driving under the influence of alcoholic beverages or drugs, if the bicycle is being operated under any of the following circumstances:

(A) In response to an emergency call.

(B) While engaged in rescue operations.

(C) In the immediate pursuit of an actual or suspected violator of the law.

(2) This subdivision does not relieve a peace officer from the duty to operate a bicycle with due regard for the safety of all persons using the highway.

(Amended by Stats. 2018, Ch. 139, Sec. 1. (AB 1755) Effective January 1, 2019.)

21200.5. Notwithstanding Section 21200, it is unlawful for any person to ride a bicycle upon a highway while under the influence of an alcoholic beverage or any drug, or under the combined influence of an alcoholic beverage and any drug. Any person arrested for a violation of this section may request to have a chemical test made of the person's blood, breath, or urine for the purpose of determining the alcoholic or drug content of that person's blood pursuant to Section 23612, and, if so requested, the arresting officer shall have the test performed. A conviction of a violation of this section shall be punished by a fine of not more than two hundred fifty dollars ($250). Violations of this section are subject to Section 13202.5.

(Amended by Stats. 1999, Ch. 22, Sec. 17. Effective May 26, 1999.)

21201. (a) A person shall not operate a bicycle on a roadway unless it is equipped with a brake that will enable the operator to make one braked wheel skid on dry, level, clean pavement.

(b) A person shall not operate on the highway a bicycle equipped with handlebars so raised that the operator must elevate their hands above the level of their shoulders in order to grasp the normal steering grip area.

(c) A person shall not operate upon a highway a bicycle that is of a size that prevents the operator from safely stopping the bicycle, supporting it in an upright position with at least one foot on the ground, and restarting it in a safe manner.

(d) A bicycle operated during darkness on a highway, a sidewalk where bicycle operation is not prohibited by the local jurisdiction, or a bikeway, as defined in Section 890.4 of the Streets and Highways Code, shall be equipped with all of the following:

(1) A lamp emitting a white light that, while the bicycle is in motion, illuminates the highway, sidewalk, or bikeway in front of the bicyclist and is visible from a distance of 300 feet in front and from the sides of the bicycle.

(2) A red reflector or a solid or flashing red light with a built-in reflector on the rear that shall be visible from a distance of 500 feet to the rear when directly in front of lawful upper beams of headlamps on a motor vehicle.

(3) A white or yellow reflector on each pedal, shoe, or ankle visible from the front and rear of the bicycle from a distance of 200 feet.

(4) A white or yellow reflector on each side forward of the center of the bicycle, and a white or red reflector on each side to the rear of the center of the bicycle, except that bicycles that are equipped with reflectorized tires on the front and the rear need not be equipped with these side reflectors.

The reflectors and reflectorized tires shall be of a type meeting requirements established by the department.

(e) A lamp or lamp combination, emitting a white light, attached to the operator and visible from a distance of 300 feet in front and from the sides of the bicycle, may be used in lieu of the lamp required by paragraph (1) of subdivision (d).

(f) An electric bicycle shall comply with paragraph (2) of subdivision (d) during all hours.

(Amended by Stats. 2025, Ch. 36, Sec. 1. (AB 544) Effective January 1, 2026.)

21201.3. (a) A bicycle or motorized bicycle used by a peace officer, as defined in Section 830.1 of, subdivision (a), (b), (c), (d), (e), (f), (g), or (i) of Section 830.2 of, subdivision (b) or (d) of Section 830.31 of, subdivision (a) or (b) of Section 830.32 of, Section 830.33 of, subdivision (a) of Section 830.36 of, subdivision (a) of Section 830.4 of, or Section 830.6 of, the Penal Code, in the performance of the peace officer's duties, may display a steady or flashing blue warning light that is visible from the front, sides, or rear of the bicycle or motorized bicycle.

(b) No person shall display a steady or flashing blue warning light on a bicycle or motorized bicycle except as authorized under subdivision (a).

(Added by Stats. 1998, Ch. 877, Sec. 65. Effective January 1, 1999.)

21201.5. (a) No person shall sell, or offer for sale, a reflex reflector or reflectorized tire of a type required on a bicycle unless it meets requirements established by the department. If there exists a federal Consumer Product Safety Commission regulation applicable to bicycle reflectors, the provisions of that regulation shall prevail over provisions of this code or requirements established by the department pursuant to this code relative to bicycle reflectors.

(b) No person shall sell, or offer for sale, a new bicycle that is not equipped with a red reflector on the rear, a white or yellow reflector on each pedal visible from the front and rear of the bicycle, a white or yellow reflector on each side forward of the center of the bicycle, and a white or red reflector on each side to the rear of the center of the bicycle, except that bicycles which are equipped with reflectorized tires on the front and rear need not be equipped with these side reflectors.

(c) Area reflectorizing material meeting the requirements of Section 25500 may be used on a bicycle.

(Amended by Stats. 1980, Ch. 399, Sec. 2. Effective July 11, 1980.)

21202. (a) Any person operating a bicycle upon a roadway at a speed less than the normal speed of traffic moving in the same direction at that time shall ride as close as practicable to the right-hand curb or edge of the roadway except under any of the following situations:

(1) When overtaking and passing another bicycle or vehicle proceeding in the same direction.

(2) When preparing for a left turn at an intersection or into a private road or driveway.

(3) When reasonably necessary to avoid conditions (including, but not limited to, fixed or moving objects, vehicles, bicycles, pedestrians, animals, surface hazards, or substandard width lanes) that make it unsafe to continue along the right-hand curb or edge, subject to the provisions of Section 21656. For purposes of this section, a "substandard width lane" is a lane that is too narrow for a bicycle and a vehicle to travel safely side by side within the lane.

(4) When approaching a place where a right turn is authorized.

(b) Any person operating a bicycle upon a roadway of a highway, which highway carries traffic in one direction only and has two or more marked traffic lanes, may ride as near the left-hand curb or edge of that roadway as practicable.

(Amended by Stats. 1996, Ch. 674, Sec. 4. Effective January 1, 1997.)

21203. No person riding upon any motorcycle, motorized bicycle, bicycle, coaster, roller skates, sled, or toy vehicle shall attach the same or himself to any streetcar or vehicle on the roadway.

(Amended by Stats. 1981, Ch. 813, Sec. 11.)

21204. (a) A person operating a bicycle upon a highway shall not ride other than upon or astride a permanent and regular seat attached thereto, unless the bicycle was designed by the manufacturer to be ridden without a seat.

(b) An operator shall not allow a person riding as a passenger, and a person shall not ride as a passenger, on a bicycle upon a highway other than upon or astride a separate seat attached thereto. If the passenger is four years of age or younger, or weighs 40 pounds or less, the seat shall have adequate provision for retaining the passenger in place and for protecting the passenger from the moving parts of the bicycle.

(Amended by Stats. 2009, Ch. 594, Sec. 1. (SB 527) Effective January 1, 2010.)

21205. No person operating a bicycle shall carry any package, bundle or article which prevents the operator from keeping at least one hand upon the handlebars.

(Added by Stats. 1963, Ch. 479.)

21206. This chapter does not prevent local authorities, by ordinance, from regulating the registration of bicycles and the parking and operation of bicycles on pedestrian or bicycle facilities, provided such regulation is not in conflict with the provisions of this code.

(Amended by Stats. 1976, Ch. 751.)

21207. (a) This chapter does not prohibit local authorities from establishing, by ordinance or resolution, bicycle lanes separated from any vehicular lanes upon highways, other than state highways as defined in Section 24 of the Streets and Highways Code and county highways established pursuant to Article 5 (commencing with Section 1720) of Chapter 9 of Division 2 of the Streets and Highways Code.

(b) Bicycle lanes established pursuant to this section shall be constructed in compliance with Section 891 of the Streets and Highways Code.

(Amended by Stats. 1993, Ch. 517, Sec. 4. Effective January 1, 1994.)

21207.5. (a) Notwithstanding Sections 21207 and 23127 of this code, or any other law, a motorized bicycle shall not be operated on a bicycle path or trail, bikeway, bicycle lane established pursuant to Section 21207, equestrian trail, or hiking or recreational trail, unless it is within or adjacent to a roadway or unless the local authority or the governing body of a public agency having jurisdiction over the path or trail permits, by ordinance, that operation.

(b) The local authority or governing body of a public agency having jurisdiction over an equestrian trail, or hiking or recreational trail, may prohibit, by ordinance, the operation of an electric bicycle or any class of electric bicycle on that trail.

(c) The Department of Parks and Recreation may prohibit the operation of an electric bicycle or any class of electric bicycle on any bicycle path or trail within the department's jurisdiction.

(Amended by Stats. 2022, Ch. 343, Sec. 1. (AB 1909) Effective January 1, 2023.)

21208. (a) Whenever a bicycle lane has been established on a roadway pursuant to Section 21207, any person operating a bicycle upon the roadway at a speed less than the normal speed of traffic moving in the same direction at that time shall ride within the bicycle lane, except that the person may move out of the lane under any of the following situations:

(1) When overtaking and passing another bicycle, vehicle, or pedestrian within the lane or about to enter the lane if the overtaking and passing cannot be done safely within the lane.

(2) When preparing for a left turn at an intersection or into a private road or driveway.

(3) When reasonably necessary to leave the bicycle lane to avoid debris or other hazardous conditions.

(4) When approaching a place where a right turn is authorized.

(b) No person operating a bicycle shall leave a bicycle lane until the movement can be made with reasonable safety and then only after giving an appropriate signal in the manner provided in Chapter 6 (commencing with Section 22100) in the event that any vehicle may be affected by the movement.

(Amended by Stats. 1996, Ch. 674, Sec. 5. Effective January 1, 1997.)

21209. (a) No person shall drive a motor vehicle in a bicycle lane established on a roadway pursuant to Section 21207 except as follows:

(1) To park where parking is permitted.

(2) To enter or leave the roadway.

(3) To prepare for a turn within a distance of 200 feet from the intersection.

(b) This section does not prohibit the use of a motorized bicycle in a bicycle lane, pursuant to Section 21207.5, at a speed no greater than is reasonable or prudent, having due regard for visibility, traffic conditions, and the condition of the roadway surface of the bicycle lane, and in a manner which does not endanger the safety of bicyclists.

(Amended by Stats. 1988, Ch. 262, Sec. 1.)

21210. No person shall leave a bicycle lying on its side on any sidewalk, or shall park a bicycle on a sidewalk in any other position, so that there is not an adequate path for pedestrian traffic. Local authorities may, by ordinance or resolution, prohibit bicycle parking in designated areas of the public highway, provided that appropriate signs are erected.

(Added by Stats. 1976, Ch. 751.)

21211. (a) No person may stop, stand, sit, or loiter upon any class I bikeway, as defined in subdivision (a) of Section 890.4 of the Streets and Highways Code, or any other public or private bicycle path or trail, if the stopping, standing, sitting, or loitering impedes or blocks the normal and reasonable movement of any bicyclist.

(b) No person may place or park any bicycle, vehicle, or any other object upon any bikeway or bicycle path or trail, as specified in subdivision (a), which impedes or blocks the normal and reasonable movement of any bicyclist unless the placement or parking is necessary for safe operation or is otherwise in compliance with the law.

(c) This section does not apply to drivers or owners of utility or public utility vehicles, as provided in Section 22512.

(d) This section does not apply to owners or drivers of vehicles who make brief stops while engaged in the delivery of newspapers to customers along the person's route.

(e) This section does not apply to the driver or owner of a rubbish or garbage truck while actually engaged in the collection of rubbish or garbage within a business or residence district if the front turn signal lamps at each side of the vehicle are being flashed simultaneously and the rear turn signal lamps at each side of the vehicle are being flashed simultaneously.

(f) This section does not apply to the driver or owner of a tow vehicle while actually engaged in the towing of a vehicle if the front turn signal lamps at each side of the vehicle are being flashed simultaneously and the rear turn signal lamps at each side of the vehicle are being flashed simultaneously.

(Amended by Stats. 2001, Ch. 127, Sec. 7. Effective July 30, 2001.)

21212. (a) A person under 18 years of age shall not operate a bicycle, a nonmotorized scooter, or a skateboard, wear in-line or roller skates, or ride upon a bicycle, nonmotorized scooter, or skateboard as a passenger upon a street, bikeway, as defined in Section 890.4 of the Streets and Highways Code, or any other public bicycle path or trail unless they are wearing a properly fitted and fastened bicycle helmet that meets the standards of either the American Society for Testing and Materials (ASTM) or the United States Consumer Product Safety Commission (CPSC), or a standard subsequently established by those entities. This requirement also applies to a person who rides upon a bicycle while in a restraining seat that is attached to the bicycle or in a trailer towed by the bicycle.

(b) A helmet sold or offered for sale for use by an operator or passenger of a bicycle, nonmotorized scooter, skateboard, or in-line or roller skates shall be conspicuously labeled in accordance with the standard described in subdivision (a), which shall constitute the manufacturer's certification that the helmet conforms to the applicable safety standard.

(c) A person shall not sell or offer for sale, for use by an operator or passenger of a bicycle, nonmotorized scooter, skateboard, or in-line or roller skates, a helmet that is not of a type meeting requirements established by this section.

(d) A charge under this section shall be dismissed if the person charged alleges in court, under oath, that the charge against the person is the first charge against that person under this section, unless it is otherwise established in court that the charge is not the first charge against the person.

(e) (1) Except as provided in subdivision (d), a violation of this section is an infraction punishable by a fine of not more than twenty-five dollars ($25).

(2) The parent or legal guardian having control or custody of an unemancipated minor whose conduct violates this section shall be jointly and severally liable with the minor for the amount of the fine imposed pursuant to this subdivision.

(f) A record of the action shall not be transmitted to the court and a fee shall not be imposed pursuant to Section 40611 for a citation for not wearing a properly fitted and fastened bicycle helmet pursuant to subdivision (a) if the parent or legal guardian of the person described in subdivision (a) delivers proof to the issuing agency within 120 days after the citation was issued that the person has a helmet meeting the requirements specified in subdivision (a) and the person has completed a local bicycle safety course or, if the violation involved an electric bicycle, a specialized electric bicycle safety course, which may include, but is not limited to, the electric bicycle safety and training program developed by the Department of the California Highway Patrol pursuant to Section 894 of the Streets and Highways Code, or a related safety course, if one is available, as prescribed by authorities in the local jurisdiction.

(g) Notwithstanding Section 1463 of the Penal Code or any other law, the fines collected for a violation of this section shall be allocated as follows:

(1) Seventy-two and one-half percent of the amount collected shall be deposited in a special account of the county health department, to be used for bicycle, nonmotorized scooter, skateboard, and in-line and roller skate safety education and for assisting low-income families in obtaining approved bicycle helmets for persons under 18 years of age, either on a loan or purchase basis. The county may contract for the implementation of this program, which, to the extent practicable, shall be operated in conjunction with the child passenger restraint program pursuant to Section 27360.

(2) Two and one-half percent of the amount collected shall be deposited in the county treasury to be used by the county to administer the program described in paragraph (1).

(3) If the violation occurred within a city, 25 percent of the amount collected shall be transferred to, and deposited in, the treasury of that city. If the violation occurred in an unincorporated area, this 25 percent shall be deposited and used pursuant to paragraph (1).

(Amended by Stats. 2025, Ch. 36, Sec. 2. (AB 544) Effective January 1, 2026.)

21212.5. (a) A person shall not sell a class 3 electric bicycle to a person under 16 years of age.

(b) A violation of this section is an infraction and shall be punishable by a fine not to exceed two hundred and fifty dollars ($250).

(Added by Stats. 2025, Ch. 65, Sec. 1. (AB 965) Effective January 1, 2026.)

21213. (a) A person under 16 years of age shall not operate a class 3 electric bicycle.

(b) A person shall not operate a class 3 electric bicycle, or ride upon a class 3 electric bicycle as a passenger, upon a street, bikeway, as defined in Section 890.4 of the Streets and Highways Code, or any other public bicycle path or trail, unless that person is wearing a properly fitted and fastened bicycle helmet that meets the standards of either the American Society for Testing and Materials (ASTM) or the United States Consumer Product Safety Commission (CPSC), or standards subsequently established by those entities. This helmet requirement also applies to a person who rides upon a class 3 electric bicycle while in a restraining seat that is attached to the bicycle or in a trailer towed by the bicycle.

(Added by Stats. 2015, Ch. 568, Sec. 6. (AB 1096) Effective January 1, 2016.)

21214. (a) On or before January 1, 2026, the Mineta Transportation Institute at San Jose State University, in consultation with relevant stakeholders, shall conduct a study on electric bicycles to inform efforts to improve the safety of all users of the transportation system, and submit a report of the findings from the study to the Legislature. The study shall examine, identify, and analyze available information, including, but not be limited to, all of the following topics:

(1) Data on injuries, crashes, emergency room visits, and deaths related to bicycles and electric bicycles.

(2) Factors and circumstances that are correlated with the crashes of bicycles and electric bicycles.

(3) Best practices for policy to promote safe use of electric bicycles.

(4) Laws in other state vehicle codes pertaining to electric bicycles.

(5) Data on the safety impacts from electric bicycle components and accessories including, but not limited to, headlights, speedometers, brakes, tires, bells, and reflectors.

(6) Data on the safety performance of electric bicycle batteries.

(7) Data on the manufacturing of electric bicycles, including, but not limited to, the market of electric bicycles, manufacturer information, sales patterns, and the number of electric bicycles on California roads, including the usage by city and the reasons behind the usage.

(8) Review of policies that other countries with high electric bicycle ridership use to promote the safe use of electric bicycles, including, but not limited to, cyclist and driver training, street infrastructure policy, and insurance or licensing requirements.

(9) Recommendations for state policy to support expanded use of electric bicycles that protects the safety of riders and other road users, including, but not limited to, recommendations on whether there are needed revisions to the Vehicle Code, and improved data collection on electric bicycles.

(b) (1) A report to be submitted pursuant to subdivision (a) shall be submitted in compliance with Section 9795 of the Government Code.

(2) Pursuant to Section 10231.5 of the Government Code, this section is repealed on January 1, 2030.

(Added by Stats. 2023, Ch. 869, Sec. 2. (SB 381) Effective January 1, 2024. Repealed as of January 1, 2030 by its own provisions.)

21214.5. (a) This section shall be known, and may be cited, as the Marin Electric Bicycle Safety Pilot Program.

(b) A local authority within the County of Marin, or the County of Marin in unincorporated areas, may, by ordinance or resolution, prohibit a person under 16 years of age from operating a class 2 electric bicycle.

(c) A local authority within the County of Marin, or the County of Marin in unincorporated areas, may, by ordinance or resolution, require a person operating a class 2 electric bicycle to wear a bicycle helmet, as described in subdivision (b) of Section 21213.

(d) (1) An ordinance or resolution adopted pursuant to this section shall make a violation punishable by warning notices for the first 60 days after the prohibition comes into effect.

(2) An ordinance or resolution prohibiting a person under 16 years of age from operating a class 2 electric bicycle shall make, after the first 60 days the prohibition has been in effect, a violation an infraction punishable by a fine of twenty-five dollars ($25). A record of the action shall not be transmitted to the court and a fee shall not be imposed upon a citation of this infraction if the parent or legal guardian of the person who violated the prohibition delivers proof to the issuing agency within 120 days after the citation was issued that the person has completed an electric bicycle safety and training course pursuant to Section 894 of the Streets and Highways Code.

(3) An ordinance or resolution requiring a person operating a class 2 electric bicycle to wear a bicycle helmet shall make, after the first 60 days the prohibition has been in effect, a violation an infraction punishable by a fine of twenty-five dollars ($25). A record of the action shall not be transmitted to the court and a fee shall not be imposed upon a citation of this infraction if the person who violated the requirement, or if that person is an unemancipated minor, their parent or guardian,

delivers proof to the issuing agency within 120 days after the citation was issued that the person has a helmet meeting the requirements specified in subdivision (a) of Section 21212 and the person has completed a local bicycle safety course or a related safety course, if one is available, as prescribed by authorities in the local jurisdiction.

(4) If the person who violates an ordinance or resolution adopted pursuant to this section is an unemancipated minor, the parent or legal guardian having control or custody of the minor shall be jointly and severally liable with the minor for the amount of any fine imposed pursuant to this subdivision.

(e) (1) If an ordinance or resolution is adopted pursuant to this section, the county shall, by January 1, 2028, submit a report to the Legislature that includes all of the following:

(A) The total number of traffic stops initiated for violations.

(B) The results of the traffic stops, including whether a warning or citation was issued, property was seized, or an arrest was made.

(C) The number of times a person was stopped for allegedly operating a class 2 electric bicycle while under 16 years of age but was found to be over the age limit.

(D) If a warning or citation was issued, a description of the warning or the violation cited.

(E) If an arrest or traffic stop was made, the offense cited by the officer for the arrest or traffic stop and the perceived race or ethnicity, gender, and approximate age of the person stopped, provided that the identification of these characteristics is solely based on the observation and perception of the peace officer who initiated the traffic stop.

(F) The actions taken by a peace officer during the traffic stops, including, but not limited to, all of the following:

(i) Whether the peace officer asked for consent to search the person, and, if so, whether consent was provided.

(ii) Whether the peace officer searched the person or any property, and, if so, the basis for the search and the type of contraband or evidence discovered.

(iii) Whether the peace officer seized any property and, if so, the type of property that was seized and the basis for seizing the property.

(G) The number of times that a person under 16 years of age was operating an electric bicycle and was involved in a crash that resulted in a permanent, serious injury, as defined in Section 20001, or a fatality in the six months prior to the adoption of the ordinance or resolution, the cause of the crash, and the class of the electric bicycle that was being operated at the time of the crash.

(H) The number of times that a person under 16 years of age was operating an electric bicycle and was involved in a crash that resulted in a permanent, serious injury, as defined in Section 20001, or a fatality after the adoption of the ordinance or resolution, the cause of the crash, and the class of the electric bicycle that was being operated at the time of the crash.

(2) A report submitted pursuant to this section shall be submitted in compliance with Section 9795 of the Government Code.

(f) A local authority or the County of Marin shall administer a public information campaign for at least 30 calendar days prior to the enactment of an ordinance or resolution pursuant to this section, including public announcements in major media outlets and press releases.

(g) This section shall become inoperative on January 1, 2029, and as of that date is repealed.

(Added by Stats. 2024, Ch. 1005, Sec. 1. (AB 1778) Effective January 1, 2025. Repealed as of January 1, 2029, by its own provisions.)

21214.7. (a) This section shall be known, and may be cited, as the San Diego Electric Bicycle Safety Pilot Program.

(b) A local authority within the County of San Diego, or the County of San Diego in unincorporated areas, may, by ordinance or resolution, prohibit a person under 12 years of age from operating a class 1 or 2 electric bicycle.

(c) (1) A violation of an ordinance or resolution adopted pursuant to this section shall be punishable as follows:

(A) For the first 60 days after the prohibition comes into effect, a warning notice.

(B) After the first 60 days, a violation of the ordinance or resolution shall be an infraction punishable by a fine of twenty-five dollars ($25).

(2) A record of the action shall not be transmitted to the court and a fee shall not be imposed upon a citation for this infraction if the parent or legal guardian of the person who violated the prohibition delivers proof to the issuing agency within 120 days after the citation was issued that the person has completed an electric bicycle safety and training program pursuant to Section 894 of the Streets and Highways Code.

(3) If an unemancipated minor violates an ordinance or resolution adopted pursuant to this section, a parent or legal guardian with control or custody of the minor shall be jointly and severally liable with the minor for the amount of a fine imposed pursuant to this subdivision.

(d) (1) If an ordinance or resolution is adopted pursuant to this section, the county shall, by January 1, 2028, submit a report to the Legislature that includes all of the following:

(A) The total number of traffic stops initiated for a violation of the ordinance or resolution adopted pursuant to this section.

(B) The results of those traffic stops, including whether a warning or citation was issued, property was seized, or an arrest was made.

(C) The number of times a person was stopped for allegedly operating a class 1 or class 2 electric bicycle while under 12 years of age but was found to be over the age limit.

(D) If a warning or citation was issued, a description of the warning or the violation cited.

(E) If an arrest or traffic stop was made, the offense cited by the officer for the arrest or traffic stop and the perceived race or ethnicity, gender, and approximate age of the person stopped, provided that the identification of these characteristics is solely based on the observation and perception of the peace officer who initiated the traffic stop.

(F) The actions taken by a peace officer during a traffic stop, including, but not limited to, all of the following:

(i) Whether the peace officer asked for consent to search the person and, if so, whether consent was provided.

(ii) Whether the peace officer searched the person or property and, if so, the basis for the search and the type of contraband or evidence discovered.

(iii) Whether the peace officer seized property and, if so, the type of property that was seized and the basis for seizing the property.

(G) The number of times a person opted to complete, and did complete, the training course in lieu of paying the fine.

(H) The number of times that a person under 12 years of age was operating an electric bicycle and was involved in a crash that resulted in a permanent, serious injury, as defined in Section 20001, or a fatality in the six months prior to the adoption of the ordinance or resolution, the cause of the crash, and the class of the electric bicycle that was being operated at the time of the crash.

(I) The number of times that a person under 12 years of age was operating an electric bicycle and was involved in a crash that resulted in a permanent, serious injury, as defined in Section 20001, or a fatality after the adoption of the ordinance or resolution, the cause of the crash, and the class of the electric bicycle that was being operated at the time of the crash.

(2) A report submitted pursuant to this section shall be submitted in compliance with Section 9795 of the Government Code.

(e) A local authority shall administer a public information campaign for at least 30 calendar days prior to the enactment of an ordinance or resolution adopted pursuant to this section, which shall include public announcements in major media outlets and press releases.

(f) This section shall remain in effect only until January 1, 2029, and as of that date is repealed.

(Amended by Stats. 2025, Ch. 67, Sec. 185. (AB 1170) Effective January 1, 2026. Repealed

as of January 1, 2029, by its own provisions.)

Article 4.5. Operation of Pedicabs

(Article 4.5 added by Stats. 2015, Ch. 496, Sec. 2.)

21215. (a) A pedicab defined in subdivision (c) of Section 467.5 shall operate subject to all of the following requirements:

(1) The pedicab shall have a seating capacity for not more than 15 passengers.

(2) The pedicab shall be authorized by local ordinance or resolution to operate within the applicable local jurisdiction.

(3) The operator of the pedicab shall be at least 21 years of age, with a valid California driver's license.

(4) The pedicab shall be equipped with seatbelts for all passengers, seat backs, brakes, reflectors, headlights, and grab rails. The pedicab shall be inspected annually for compliance with the requirements of this paragraph by an entity designated by the local jurisdiction that authorized the pedicab to operate. The entity may charge a reasonable fee to cover the costs of the inspection. A pedicab that does not meet these requirements shall meet these requirements by January 1, 2017, in order to continue operation.

(5) The operator of the pedicab shall at all times be able to establish financial responsibility in a minimum amount of one million dollars ($1,000,000) general liability insurance coverage and an additional five hundred thousand dollars ($500,000) general umbrella insurance that covers the pedicab. The local jurisdiction that authorized the pedicab to operate may require additional proof of financial responsibility.

(6) A pedicab shall not operate on any highway under the jurisdiction of the local authority unless authorized by resolution or ordinance. A pedicab shall not operate on any freeway and shall not operate on any highway with a posted speed limit in excess of 30 miles per hour, except to cross the highway at an intersection.

(7) The operator of the pedicab shall annually report to the Department of the California Highway Patrol, commencing on January 1, 2016, any accidents caused or experienced by the pedicabs.

(8) The pedicab shall not load or unload passengers on roadways or in the middle of highways.

(9) Pedicabs shall be operated as close as practicable to the right-hand curb or edge of the roadway, except when necessary to overtake another vehicle, to avoid a stationary object, or when preparing to make a left turn.

(b) This article only applies to pedicabs defined by subdivision (c) of Section 467.5, and does not apply to pedicabs defined in subdivision (a) or (b) of Section 467.5.

(Added by Stats. 2015, Ch. 496, Sec. 2. (SB 530) Effective January 1, 2016.)

21215.2. (a) If alcoholic beverages are consumed on board the pedicab, a pedicab defined in subdivision (c) of Section 467.5 shall additionally operate subject to all of the following requirements:

(1) The consumption of alcoholic beverages onboard the pedicab shall be authorized by local ordinance or resolution.

(2) An onboard safety monitor who is 21 years of age or older shall be present whenever alcohol is being consumed by passengers during the operation of the pedicab. The onboard safety monitor shall not be under the influence of any alcoholic beverage and shall be considered as driving the pedicab for purposes of Article 2 (commencing with Section 23152) of Chapter 12 of Division 11 during the operation of the pedicab.

(3) Both the operator and safety monitor shall have completed either the Licensee Education on Alcohol and Drugs (LEAD) program implemented by the Department of Alcoholic Beverage Control or a training course utilizing the curriculum components recommended by the Responsible Beverage Service Advisory Board established by the Director of Alcoholic Beverage Control.

(4) Alcoholic beverages shall not be provided by the operator or onboard safety monitor or any employee or agent of the operator or onboard safety monitor of the pedicab. Alcoholic beverages may only be supplied by the passengers of the pedicab. All alcoholic beverages supplied by passengers of the pedicab shall be in enclosed, sealed, and unopened containers that have been labeled pursuant to Chapter 13 (commencing with Section 25170) of Division 9 of the Business and Professions Code prior to their consumption on board the pedicab.

(5) Alcoholic beverages may be consumed by a passenger of the pedicab only while the passenger is physically on board and within the pedicab.

(6) All passengers shall be 21 years of age or older if alcohol is consumed during the operation of the pedicab.

(7) For purposes of this subdivision, passengers who are pedaling the device are not operators.

(b) A license or permit from the Department of Alcoholic Beverage Control shall not be required of the operator or onboard safety monitor, so long as neither they, nor their employees or agents sell, serve, or furnish any alcoholic beverage to any passenger.

(c) For purposes of this section, "alcoholic beverage" has the same meaning as defined in Section 23004 of the Business and Professions Code.

(Amended by Stats. 2019, Ch. 280, Sec. 1. (SB 543) Effective January 1, 2020.)

21215.5. This article does not preclude a local authority from imposing more stringent operating or equipment requirements on a pedicab subject to this article.

(Added by Stats. 2015, Ch. 496, Sec. 2. (SB 530) Effective January 1, 2016.)

Article 5. Operation of Motorized Scooters

(Article 5 added by Stats. 1999, Ch. 722, Sec. 5.)

21220. (a) The Legislature finds and declares both of the following:

(1) This state has severe traffic congestion and air pollution problems, particularly in its cities, and finding ways to reduce these problems is of paramount importance.

(2) Motorized scooters that meet the definition of Section 407.5 produce no emissions and, therefore, do not contribute to increased air pollution or increase traffic congestion.

(b) It is the intent of the Legislature in adding this article to promote the use of alternative low-emission or no-emission transportation.

(Added by Stats. 1999, Ch. 722, Sec. 5. Effective January 1, 2000.)

21220.5. For the purposes of this article, a motorized scooter is defined in Section 407.5.

(Added by Stats. 1999, Ch. 722, Sec. 5. Effective January 1, 2000.)

21221. Every person operating a motorized scooter upon a highway has all the rights and is subject to all the provisions applicable to the driver of a vehicle by this division, including, but not limited to, provisions concerning driving under the influence of alcoholic beverages or drugs, and by Division 10 (commencing with Section 20000), Division 17 (commencing with Section 40000.1), and Division 18 (commencing with Section 42000), except those provisions which, by their very nature, can have no application.

(Added by Stats. 1999, Ch. 722, Sec. 5. Effective January 1, 2000.)

21221.5. Notwithstanding Section 21221, it is unlawful for any person to operate a motorized scooter upon a highway while under the influence of an alcoholic beverage or any drug, or under the combined influence of an alcoholic beverage and any drug. Any person arrested for a violation of this section may request to have a chemical test made of the person's blood or breath for the purpose of determining the alcoholic or drug content of that person's blood pursuant to subdivision (d) of Section 23612, and, if so requested, the arresting officer shall have the test performed. A conviction of a violation of this section shall be punished by a fine of not more than two hundred fifty dollars ($250).

(Amended by Stats. 2000, Ch. 287, Sec. 25. Effective January 1, 2001.)

21223. (a) Every motorized scooter operated upon any highway during darkness shall be equipped with the following:

(1) Except as provided in subdivision (b), a lamp emitting a white light which, while the motorized scooter is in motion, illuminates the highway in front of the operator and is visible from a distance of 300 feet in front and from the sides of the motorized scooter.

(2) Except as provided in subdivision (c), a red reflector on the rear that is visible from a distance of 500 feet to the rear when directly in front of lawful upper beams of headlamps on a motor vehicle.

(3) A white or yellow reflector on each side visible from the front and rear of the motorized scooter from a distance of 200 feet.

(b) A lamp or lamp combination, emitting a white light, attached to the operator and visible from a distance of 300 feet in front and from the sides of the motorized scooter, may be used in lieu of the lamp required by paragraph (1) of subdivision (a).

(c) A red reflector, or reflectorized material meeting the requirements of Section 25500, attached to the operator and visible from a distance of 500 feet to the rear when directly in front of lawful upper beams of headlamps on a motor vehicle, may be used in lieu of the reflector required by paragraph (2) of subdivision (a).

(Added by Stats. 1999, Ch. 722, Sec. 5. Effective January 1, 2000.)

21224. (a) A person operating a motorized scooter is not subject to the provisions of this code relating to financial responsibility, registration, and license plate requirements, and, for those purposes, a motorized scooter is not a motor vehicle.

(b) A motorized scooter is exempt from the equipment requirements in Division 12 (commencing with Section 24000), except for Sections 24003 and 27400, Article 4 (commencing with Section 27450) of Chapter 5 of Division 12, and Section 27602.

(c) Notwithstanding subdivision (b), any motorized scooter may be equipped with equipment authorized by Division 12 (commencing with Section 24000).

(d) Any motorized scooter equipped with lighting equipment that is authorized by Division 12 (commencing with Section 24000) shall meet the lighting requirements in Article 1 (commencing with Section 24250) of Chapter 2 of Division 12 for that equipment.

(Added by Stats. 1999, Ch. 722, Sec. 5. Effective January 1, 2000.)

21225. This article does not prevent a local authority, by ordinance, from regulating the registration of motorized scooters and the parking and operation of motorized scooters on pedestrian or bicycle facilities and local streets and highways, if that regulation is not in conflict with this code.

(Amended by Stats. 2004, Ch. 755, Sec. 6. Effective January 1, 2005.)

21226. (a) A person shall not sell or offer for sale a motorized scooter that produces a maximum noise level exceeding 80 dbA at a distance of 50 feet from the centerline of travel when tested in accordance with Society of Automotive Engineers (SAE) Recommended Practice J331 JAN00.

(b) A motorized scooter, as defined in subdivision (b) of Section 407.5, shall at all times be equipped with a muffler meeting the requirements of this section, in constant operation and properly maintained to prevent any excessive or unusual noise, and a muffler or exhaust system shall not be equipped with a cutout, bypass, or similar device.

(c) A motorized scooter, as defined in subdivision (b) of Section 407.5, operated off the highways shall at all times be equipped with a muffler meeting the requirements of this section, in constant operation and properly maintained to prevent any excessive or unusual noise, and a muffler or exhaust system shall not be equipped with a cutout, bypass, or similar device.

(d) A person shall not modify the exhaust system of a motorized scooter in a manner that will amplify or increase the noise level emitted by the motor of the scooter so that it is not in compliance with this section or exceeds the noise level limit established by subdivision (a). A person shall not operate a motorized scooter with an exhaust system so modified.

(Added by Stats. 2004, Ch. 755, Sec. 7. Effective January 1, 2005.)

21227. (a) A motorized scooter shall comply with one of the following:

(1) Operate in a manner so that the electric motor is disengaged or ceases to function when the brakes are applied.

(2) Operate in a manner so that the motor is engaged through a switch or mechanism that, when released, will cause the electric motor to disengage or cease to function.

(b) It is unlawful for a person to operate a motorized scooter that does not meet one of the requirements of subdivision (a).

(Added by Stats. 1999, Ch. 722, Sec. 5. Effective January 1, 2000.)

21228. Any person operating a motorized scooter upon a highway at a speed less than the normal speed of traffic moving in the same direction at that time shall ride as close as practicable to the right-hand curb or right edge of the roadway, except under the following situations:

(a) When overtaking and passing another vehicle proceeding in the same direction.

(b) When preparing for a left turn, the operator shall stop and dismount as close as practicable to the right-hand curb or right edge of the roadway and complete the turn by crossing the roadway on foot, subject to the restrictions placed on pedestrians in Chapter 5 (commencing with Section 21950).

(c) (1) When reasonably necessary to avoid conditions, including, but not limited to, fixed or moving objects, vehicles, bicycles, pedestrians, animals, surface hazards, or substandard width lanes, which make it unsafe to continue along the right-hand curb or right edge of the roadway, subject to Section 21656.

(2) For the purposes of paragraph (1), a "substandard width lane" is a lane that is too narrow for a motorized scooter and another vehicle to travel safely side by side within the lane.

(d) Any person operating a motorized scooter upon a highway that carries traffic in one direction only and has two or more marked traffic lanes may operate the motorized scooter as near the left-hand curb or left edge of that roadway as practicable.

However, when preparing for a right turn, the operator shall stop and dismount as close as practicable to the left-hand curb or left edge of the highway and complete the turn by crossing the roadway on foot, subject to the restrictions placed on pedestrians in Chapter 5 (commencing with Section 21950).

(Amended by Stats. 2003, Ch. 62, Sec. 306. Effective January 1, 2004.)

21229. (a) Whenever a class II bicycle lane has been established on a roadway, any person operating a motorized scooter upon the roadway shall ride within the bicycle lane, except that the person may move out of the lane under any of the following situations:

(1) When overtaking and passing another vehicle or pedestrian within the lane or when about to enter the lane if the overtaking and passing cannot be done safely within the lane.

(2) When preparing for a left turn, the operator shall stop and dismount as close as practicable to the right-hand curb or right edge of the roadway and complete the turn by crossing the roadway on foot, subject to the restrictions placed on pedestrians in Chapter 5 (commencing with Section 21950).

(3) When reasonably necessary to leave the bicycle lane to avoid debris or other hazardous conditions.

(4) When approaching a place where a right turn is authorized.

(b) No person operating a motorized scooter shall leave a bicycle lane until the movement can be made with reasonable safety and then only after giving an appropriate signal in the manner provided in Chapter 6 (commencing with Section 22100) in the event that any vehicle may be affected by the movement.

(Added by Stats. 1999, Ch. 722, Sec. 5. Effective January 1, 2000.)

21230. Notwithstanding any other provision of law, a motorized scooter may be operated on a bicycle path or trail or bikeway, unless the local authority or the governing body of a local agency having jurisdiction over that path, trail, or bikeway prohibits that operation by ordinance.

(Added by Stats. 1999, Ch. 722, Sec. 5. Effective January 1, 2000.)

21235. The operator of a motorized scooter shall not do any of the following:

(a) Operate a motorized scooter unless it is equipped with a brake that will enable the operator to make a braked wheel skid on dry, level, clean pavement.

(b) Operate a motorized scooter on a highway with a speed limit in excess of 25 miles per hour unless the motorized scooter is operated within a Class II or Class IV bikeway, except that a local authority may, by ordinance or resolution, authorize the operation of a motorized scooter outside of a Class II or Class IV bikeway on a highway with a speed limit of up to 35 miles per hour. The 15 mile per hour maximum speed limit for the operation of a motorized scooter specified in Section 22411 applies to the operation of a motorized scooter on all highways, including bikeways, regardless of a higher speed limit applicable to the highway.

(c) Operate a motorized scooter without wearing a properly fitted and fastened bicycle helmet that meets the standards described in Section 21212, if the operator is under 18 years of age.

(d) Operate a motorized scooter without a valid driver's license or instruction permit.

(e) Operate a motorized scooter with any passengers in addition to the operator.

(f) Operate a motorized scooter carrying any package, bundle, or article that prevents the operator from keeping at least one hand upon the handlebars.

(g) Operate a motorized scooter upon a sidewalk, except as may be necessary to enter or leave adjacent property.

(h) Operate a motorized scooter on the highway with the handlebars raised so that the operator must elevate his or her hands above the level of his or her shoulders in order to grasp the normal steering grip area.

(i) Leave a motorized scooter lying on its side on any sidewalk, or park a motorized scooter on a sidewalk in any other position, so that there is not an adequate path for pedestrian traffic.

(j) Attach the motorized scooter or himself or herself while on the roadway, by any means, to any other vehicle on the roadway.

(Amended by Stats. 2018, Ch. 552, Sec. 1. (AB 2989) Effective January 1, 2019.)

Article 5.5. Operation of Low-Speed Vehicles

(Heading of Article 5.5 renumbered from Article 5 (as added by Stats. 1999, Ch. 140, Sec. 6) by Stats. 2014, Ch. 71, Sec. 179.)

21250. For the purposes of this article, a low-speed vehicle means a vehicle as defined in Section 385.5. A "low-speed vehicle" is also known as a "neighborhood electric vehicle."

(Amended by Stats. 2004, Ch. 422, Sec. 3. Effective January 1, 2005.)

21251. Except as provided in Chapter 8 (commencing with Section 1965) of Division 2.5 of the Streets and Highways Code, and Sections 4023, 21115, and 21115.1, a low-speed vehicle is subject to all the provisions applicable to a motor vehicle, and the driver of a low-speed vehicle is subject to all the provisions applicable to the driver of a motor vehicle or other vehicle, when applicable, by this code or another code, with the exception of those provisions that, by their very nature, can have no application.

(Amended by Stats. 2018, Ch. 564, Sec. 5. (SB 1151) Effective January 1, 2019.)

21252. A vehicle dealer, selling a low-speed vehicle, shall provide to the buyer a disclosure statement regarding the operation of the vehicle that is in compliance with existing provisions of the California Code of Regulations.

(Added by Stats. 1999, Ch. 140, Sec. 6. Effective January 1, 2000.)

21253. A low-speed vehicle operated or parked on the roadway shall at all times meet federal Motor Vehicle Safety Standards established for low-speed vehicles in Section 571.500 of Title 49 of the Code of Federal Regulations.

(Added by Stats. 1999, Ch. 140, Sec. 6. Effective January 1, 2000.)

21254. A motor vehicle that was originally designated as a low-speed vehicle and that has been modified or altered to exceed 25 miles per hour shall not qualify for the relaxed federal Motor Vehicle Safety Standards established for low-speed vehicles and instead shall meet all federal Motor Vehicle Safety Standards for a passenger vehicle.

(Added by Stats. 1999, Ch. 140, Sec. 6. Effective January 1, 2000.)

21260. (a) Except as provided in paragraph (1) of subdivision (b), or in an area where a neighborhood electric vehicle transportation plan has been adopted pursuant to Chapter 8 (commencing with Section 1965) of Division 2.5 of the Streets and Highways Code, the operator of a low-speed vehicle shall not operate the vehicle on any roadway with a speed limit in excess of 35 miles per hour.

(b) (1) The operator of a low-speed vehicle may cross a roadway with a speed limit in excess of 35 miles per hour if the crossing begins and ends on a roadway with a speed limit of 35 miles per hour or less and occurs at an intersection of approximately 90 degrees.

(2) Notwithstanding paragraph (1), the operator of a low-speed vehicle shall not traverse an uncontrolled intersection with any state highway unless that intersection has been approved and authorized by the agency having primary traffic enforcement responsibilities for that crossing by a low-speed vehicle.

(Amended by Stats. 2018, Ch. 564, Sec. 6. (SB 1151) Effective January 1, 2019.)

21266. (a) Notwithstanding Section 21260, local authorities, by ordinance or resolution, may restrict or prohibit the use of low-speed vehicles.

(b) Notwithstanding Section 21260, a local law enforcement agency with primary traffic enforcement responsibilities or the Department of the California Highway Patrol may prohibit the operation of a low-speed vehicle on any roadway under that agency's or department's jurisdiction when the agency or the department deems the prohibition to be in the best interest of public safety. Any such prohibition shall become effective when appropriate signs giving notice thereof are erected upon the roadway.

(Added by Stats. 1999, Ch. 140, Sec. 6. Effective January 1, 2000.)

Article 6. Electric Personal Assistive Mobility Devices

(Article 6 added by Stats. 2002, Ch. 979, Sec. 6.)

21280. (a) The Legislature finds and declares all of the following:

(1) This state has severe traffic congestion and air pollution problems, particularly in its cities, and finding ways to reduce these problems is of paramount importance.

(2) Reducing the millions of single passenger automobile trips of five miles or less that Californians take each year will significantly reduce the pollution caused by fuel emissions and aggravated by automobile congestion.

(3) Electric personal assistive mobility devices that meet the definition in Section 313 operate solely on electricity and employ advances in technology to safely integrate the user in pedestrian transportation.

(4) Electric personal assistive mobility devices enable California businesses, public officials, and individuals to travel farther and carry more without the use of traditional vehicles, thereby promoting gains in productivity, minimizing environmental impacts, and facilitating better use of public ways.

(b) The Legislature is adding this article as part of its program to promote the use of no-emission transportation.

(Amended by Stats. 2007, Ch. 106, Sec. 4. Effective January 1, 2008.)

21280.5. For purposes of this article, an electric personal assistive mobility device is defined in Section 313.

(Added by Stats. 2002, Ch. 979, Sec. 6. Effective January 1, 2003. Section operative March 1, 2003, pursuant to Section 21283 (later repealed).)

21281. Every electric personal assistive mobility device, or EPAMD, shall be equipped with the following safety mechanisms:

(a) Front, rear, and side reflectors.

(b) A system that enables the operator to bring the device to a controlled stop.

(c) If the EPAMD is operated between one-half hour after sunset and one-half hour before sunrise, a lamp emitting a white light that, while the EPAMD is in motion, illuminates the area in front of the operator and is visible from a distance of 300 feet in front of the EPAMD.

(d) A sound emitting device that can be activated from time to time by the operator, as appropriate, to alert nearby persons.

(Added by Stats. 2002, Ch. 979, Sec. 6. Effective January 1, 2003. Section operative March 1, 2003, pursuant to Section 21283 (later repealed).)

21281.5. (a) A person shall not operate an EPAMD on a sidewalk, bike path, pathway, trail, bike lane, street, road, or highway at a speed greater than is reasonable and prudent having due regard for weather, visibility, pedestrians, and other conveyance traffic on, and the surface, width, and condition of, the sidewalk, bike path, pathway, trail, bike lane, street, road, or highway.

(b) A person shall not operate an EPAMD at a speed that endangers the safety of persons or property.

(c) A person shall not operate an EPAMD on a sidewalk, bike path, pathway, trail, bike lane, street, road, or highway with willful or wanton disregard for the safety of persons or property.

(d) A person operating an EPAMD on a sidewalk, bike path, pathway, trail, bike lane, street, road, or highway shall yield the right-of-way to all pedestrians on foot, including persons with disabilities using assistive devices and service animals that are close enough to constitute a hazard.

(Added by Stats. 2007, Ch. 106, Sec. 5. Effective January 1, 2008.)

21282. Notwithstanding Section 21966, for the purpose of assuring the safety of pedestrians, including seniors, persons with disabilities, and others using sidewalks, bike paths, pathways, trails, bike lanes, streets, roads, and highways, a city, county, or city and county may, by ordinance, regulate the time, place, and manner of the operation of electric personal assistive mobility devices as defined in Section 313, and their use as a pedestrian pursuant to paragraph (2) of subdivision (a) of Section 467, including limiting, prohibiting entirely in the local jurisdiction, or prohibiting use in specified areas as determined to be appropriate by local entities. State agencies may limit or prohibit the time, place, and manner of use on state property.

(Added by Stats. 2002, Ch. 979, Sec. 6. Effective January 1, 2003. Section operative March 1, 2003, pursuant to Section 21283 (later repealed).)

Article 7. Operation of Electrically Motorized Boards

(Article 7 added by Stats. 2015, Ch. 777, Sec. 3.)

21290. (a) For purposes of this article, "bikeway" is defined in Section 890.4 of the Streets and Highways Code.

(b) For purposes of this article, an "electrically motorized board" is defined in Section 313.5.

(Added by Stats. 2015, Ch. 777, Sec. 3. (AB 604) Effective January 1, 2016.)

21291. An electrically motorized board shall be operated only by a person who is 16 years of age or older.

(Added by Stats. 2015, Ch. 777, Sec. 3. (AB 604) Effective January 1, 2016.)

21292. A person shall not operate an electrically motorized board upon a highway, bikeway, or any other public bicycle path, sidewalk, or trail, unless that person is wearing a properly fitted and fastened bicycle helmet that meets the standards described in Section 21212.

(Added by Stats. 2015, Ch. 777, Sec. 3. (AB 604) Effective January 1, 2016.)

21293. (a) Every electrically motorized board operated upon a highway during darkness shall be equipped with all of the following:

(1) Except as provided in subdivision (b), a lamp emitting a white light that, while the electrically motorized board is in motion, illuminates the highway in front of the operator and is visible from a distance of 300 feet in front of the electrically motorized board.

(2) Except as provided in subdivision (c), a red reflector on the rear that is visible from a distance of 500 feet to the rear when directly in front of lawful upper beams of headlamps on a motor vehicle.

(3) Except as provided in subdivision (d), a white or yellow reflector on each side that is visible from a distance of 200 feet from the sides of the electrically motorized board.

(b) A lamp or lamp combination, emitting a white light, attached to the operator and visible from a distance of 300 feet in front of the electrically motorized board, may be used in lieu of the lamp required by paragraph (1) of subdivision (a).

(c) A red reflector, or reflectorizing material meeting the requirements of Section 25500, attached to the operator and visible from a distance of 500 feet to the rear when directly in front of lawful upper beams of headlamps on a motor vehicle, may be used in lieu of the reflector required by paragraph (2) of subdivision (a).

(d) A white or yellow reflector, or reflectorizing material meeting the requirements of Section 25500, attached to the operator and visible from a distance of 200 feet from the sides of the electrically motorized board, may be used in lieu of the reflector required by paragraph (3) of subdivision (a).

(Added by Stats. 2015, Ch. 777, Sec. 3. (AB 604) Effective January 1, 2016.)

21294. (a) An electrically motorized board shall only operate upon a highway designated with a speed limit of 35 miles per hour or less, unless the electrically motorized board is operated entirely within a designated Class II or Class IV bikeway.

(b) A person shall not operate an electrically motorized board upon a highway, bikeway, or any other public bicycle path, sidewalk, or trail, at a speed in excess of 15 miles per hour.

(c) Notwithstanding subdivision (b), a person shall not operate an electrically motorized board at a speed greater than is reasonable or prudent having due regard for weather, visibility, pedestrian and vehicular traffic, and the surface and width of the highway, bikeway, public bicycle path, sidewalk, or trail, and in no event at a speed that endangers the safety of any person or property.

(Amended by Stats. 2016, Ch. 86, Sec. 302. (SB 1171) Effective January 1, 2017.)

21296. (a) It is unlawful for a person to operate an electrically motorized board upon a highway while under the influence of an alcoholic beverage or any drug, or under the combined influence of an alcoholic beverage and any drug.

(b) A person arrested for a violation of this section may request to have a chemical test made of his or her blood or breath for the purpose of determining the alcoholic or drug content of that person's blood pursuant to subdivision (d) of Section 23612, and, if so requested, the arresting officer shall have the test performed.

(c) A conviction for a violation of this section shall be punished by a fine of not more than two hundred fifty dollars ($250).

(Added by Stats. 2015, Ch. 777, Sec. 3. (AB 604) Effective January 1, 2016.)

Article 8. Horseback Riding

(Article 8 added by Stats. 2021, Ch. 175, Sec. 1.)

21300. (a) A person under 18 years of age shall not ride an equestrian animal upon a paved highway unless that person is wearing a properly fitted and fastened helmet that meets the standards of either the American Society for Testing and Materials or the United States Consumer Product Safety Commission, or standards subsequently established by those entities.

(b) A person riding an equestrian animal upon a paved highway during hours of darkness, as defined in Section 280, shall do one of the following:

(1) Wear reflective gear or have reflective gear on the equestrian animal that shall be visible from a distance of 500 feet on the rear and the sides when directly in front of the lawful upper beams of headlamps on a motor vehicle.

(2) Have a lamp emitting a white light attached to either the person or the equestrian animal that is visible from a distance of 300 feet in front of and from the sides of the equestrian animal.

(c) Notwithstanding subdivisions (a) and (b), a person is not required to wear a helmet or reflective gear while riding an equestrian animal when participating in a parade or festival, or while crossing a paved highway from an unpaved highway.

(d) In a civil action, a violation of subdivision (a) or (b) does not establish negligence as a matter of law or negligence per se for comparative fault purposes, but negligence may be proven as a fact without regard to the violation.

(e) A charge under this section shall be dismissed when the person charged alleges in court, under oath, that the charge against the person is the first charge against that person under this section, unless it is otherwise established in court that the charge is not the first charge against the person.

(f) (1) Except as provided in subdivision (e), a violation of this section is an infraction punishable by a fine of not more than twenty-five dollars ($25).

(2) The parent or legal guardian having control or custody of an unemancipated minor whose conduct violates this section shall be jointly and severally liable with the minor for the amount of the fine imposed pursuant to this subdivision.

(Added by Stats. 2021, Ch. 175, Sec. 1. (AB 974) Effective January 1, 2022.)

Chapter 2. Traffic Signs, Signals, and Markings

(Chapter 2 enacted by Stats. 1959, Ch. 3.)

Article 1. Erection and Maintenance

(Article 1 enacted by Stats. 1959, Ch. 3.)

21350. The Department of Transportation shall place and maintain, or cause to be placed and maintained, with respect to highways under its jurisdiction, appropriate signs, signals, and other traffic control devices as required hereunder, and may place and maintain, or cause to be placed and maintained, such appropriate signs, signals, or other traffic control devices as may be authorized hereunder, or as may be necessary properly to indicate and to carry out the provisions of this code, or to warn or guide traffic upon the highways. The Department of Transportation may, with the consent of the local authorities, also place and maintain, or cause to be placed and maintained, in or along city streets and county roads, appropriate signs, signals, and other traffic control devices, or may perform, or cause to be performed, such other work on city streets and county roads, as may be necessary or desirable to control, or direct traffic, or to facilitate traffic flow, to or from or on state highways.

(Amended by Stats. 1974, Ch. 648.)

21351. Local authorities in their respective jurisdictions shall place and maintain or cause to be placed and maintained such traffic signs, signals and other traffic control devices upon streets and highways as required hereunder, and may place and maintain or cause to be placed and maintained, such appropriate signs, signals or other traffic control devices as may be authorized hereunder or as may be necessary properly to indicate and to carry out the provisions of this code or local traffic ordinances or to warn or guide traffic.

(Enacted by Stats. 1959, Ch. 3.)

21351.3. Local authorities in their respective jurisdictions may place and maintain, or cause to be placed and maintained, speed limit, speed advisory, and mileage signs, or suitable plates affixed to or near existing signs, which indicate speeds and distances both in common standards of measures, as specified in Section 12302 of the Business and Professions Code, and in measures of the metric system authorized by Congress.

(Added by Stats. 1974, Ch. 462.)

21351.5. The Department of Transportation or local authorities, with respect to highways under their respective jurisdictions, may erect stop signs to require the traffic on a highway to stop before crossing any railroad grade crossing designated by the agency having jurisdiction of the highway as a major crossing with a demonstrated need for stop signs, except a railroad grade crossing which is controlled by automatic signals, gates, or other train-actuated control devices.

(Added by Stats. 1974, Ch. 58.)

21351.7. Local authorities in their respective jurisdictions may place and maintain, or cause to be placed and maintained, appropriate signs along city streets or county roads which indicate that a deaf child is near.

(Added by Stats. 1983, Ch. 719, Sec. 1.)

21352. The Department of Transportation may erect stop signs at any entrance to any state highway and whenever the department determines that it is necessary for the public safety and the orderly and efficient use of the highways by the public, the department may erect and maintain, or cause to be erected and maintained, on any state highway any traffic control signal or any official traffic control device regulating or prohibiting the turning of vehicles upon the highway, allocating or restricting the use of specified lanes or portions of the highway by moving vehicular traffic, establishing crosswalks at or between intersections, or restricting use of the right-of-way by the public for other than highway purposes.

(Amended by Stats. 1981, Ch. 413, Sec. 1.)

21353. No local authority, except by permission of the Department of Transportation, shall erect or maintain any stop sign or traffic control signal in such manner as to require the traffic on any state highway to stop before entering or crossing any intersecting highway or any railroad grade crossing.

(Amended by Stats. 1981, Ch. 413, Sec. 2.)

21354. Subject to the provisions of Section 21353, a local authority may designate any highway under its jurisdiction as a through highway and may erect stop signs at entrances thereto or may designate any intersection under its exclusive jurisdiction as a stop intersection and erect stop signs at one or more entrances thereto.

(Enacted by Stats. 1959, Ch. 3.)

21355. (a) Stop signs erected under Section 21350, 21351, 21352, or 21354 may be erected either at or near the entrance to an intersection.

The Department of Transportation and local authorities in their respective jurisdictions may erect stop signs at any location so as to control traffic within an intersection.

When a required stop is to apply at the entrance to an intersection from a one-way street with a roadway of 30 feet or more in width, stop signs shall be erected both on the left and the right sides of the one-way street at or near the entrance to the intersection.

Notwithstanding any other provision of this code, stop signs shall not be erected at any entrance to an intersection controlled by official traffic control signals, nor at any railroad grade crossing which is controlled by automatic signals, gates, or other train-actuated control devices except where a stop sign may be necessary to control traffic on intersecting highways adjacent to the grade crossing or when a local authority determines, with the approval of the Public Utilities Commission pursuant to Section 21110, that a railroad grade crossing under its jurisdiction presents a danger warranting a stop sign in addition to a train-activated control device.

(b) Notwithstanding subdivision (a), local authorities, with respect to streets under their jurisdiction, are not required to conform lawfully established intersection configurations existing on January 1, 1985, to meet the requirements of subdivision (a) until January 1, 1990.

(Amended by Stats. 1984, Ch. 700, Sec. 1.)

21356. The Department of Transportation or local authorities, with respect to highways under their respective jurisdictions, may erect yield right-of-way signs at the entrances to intersections or highways. Such yield right-of-way signs shall not be erected upon the approaches to more than one of the intersecting streets.

Yield right-of-way signs shall be located at or near the entrance to the intersection or highway where motorists are required to yield the right-of-way.

(Amended by Stats. 1978, Ch. 287.)

21356.5. Local authorities may place signs, mirrors, or other visual or audible devices at exits from alleys that are under their jurisdiction to warn drivers to watch for pedestrians and bicyclists on the sidewalk prior to exiting the alley.

(Added by Stats. 1997, Ch. 150, Sec. 2. Effective January 1, 1998.)

21357. Speed restriction signs may, but need not, be erected upon any highway other than a state highway at the entrance thereof into a business or residence district unless required in this chapter.

(Amended by Stats. 1959, Ch. 11.)

21358. Where one or more business and residence districts are contiguous, or where, as authorized by this code, speed is to be restricted between two districts, either business or residence, or at the end of either thereof, speed restriction signs affecting traffic on other than state highways as required by Sections 21357 and 21359 need be erected and maintained only at the boundaries of the outside limits of the area in which speed is to be restricted.
(Amended by Stats. 1959, Ch. 11.)

21359. Whenever the Department of Transportation or a local authority as authorized by this code determines and declares a speed limit different from the limit otherwise applicable under Sections 22349 and 22352, appropriate speed restriction signs shall be erected and maintained at the outside entrance of the highway or portion thereof upon which the special speed limit is applicable. The special speed limit is not effective until appropriate signs have been erected.
(Amended by Stats. 1974, Ch. 545.)

21360. Local authorities in their respective jurisdictions may, within the reasonable exercise of their police power and subject to Section 21353, place and maintain official traffic control devices to regulate traffic at the intersection of a highway and a private road or driveway. Official traffic control devices may be erected at or near such intersection, except no such device shall be erected upon a private road or driveway without consent of the owner thereof. When official traffic control devices are installed and in operation, the private road or driveway shall be deemed a highway only for the purpose of determining the existence and location of an intersection.
(Enacted by Stats. 1959, Ch. 3.)

21361. (a) When the outermost boundaries of two or more intersections are confined within a distance of 200 feet, the Department of Transportation in respect to state highways, and a local authority with respect to highways under its jurisdiction, shall have the power to designate a single intersection by the installation and operation of traffic signals which may be supplemented by signs or markings. When so designated, the single intersection shall be the legal intersection for the purposes of traffic movement and regulation.

(b) Whenever a single intersection has been designated by the Department of Transportation or by local authorities as set forth in subdivision (a), the department or such authorities may designate marked crosswalks at certain locations within the intersection or contiguous thereto, and when the marked crosswalks are established, they shall constitute the only crosswalks at the intersection. The department or the local authorities shall erect signs prohibiting pedestrian crossing at locations which, except for the provisions of this section, would constitute unmarked crosswalks.
(Amended by Stats. 1974, Ch. 545.)

21362. Railroad warning approach signs shall be erected by local authorities upon the right-hand side of each approach of every highway under their jurisdiction to a grade crossing of a railroad or electric interurban railway at a reasonable distance from the crossing.
(Amended by Stats. 1959, Ch. 450.)

21362.5. (a) (1) Railroad and rail transit grade crossings may be equipped with an automated rail crossing enforcement system if the system is identified by signs clearly indicating the system's presence and visible to traffic approaching from each direction.

(2) Only a governmental agency, in cooperation with a law enforcement agency, may operate an automated rail crossing enforcement system.

(b) Notwithstanding Article 1 (commencing with Section 7922.500) and Article 2 (commencing with Section 7922.525) of Chapter 1 of Part 3 of Division 10 of Title 1 of the Government Code, or any other provision of law, photographic records made by an automated rail crossing enforcement system shall be confidential, and shall be made available only to governmental agencies and law enforcement agencies for the purposes of this section.
(Amended by Stats. 2021, Ch. 615, Sec. 425. (AB 474) Effective January 1, 2022. Operative January 1, 2023, pursuant to Section 463 of Stats. 2021, Ch. 615.)

21363. Detour signs shall be erected at the nearest points of detour from that portion of a highway, or from any bridge, which is closed to traffic while under construction or repair.
(Enacted by Stats. 1959, Ch. 3.)

21364. The Department of Transportation may authorize an owner of land adjacent to a state highway to erect and maintain signs to indicate the existence of those places where livestock regularly and frequently cross a state highway, and any sign so erected and maintained shall be an official sign. The department shall prescribe the size, shape and character of the signs, which shall be uniform.
(Amended by Stats. 1974, Ch. 545.)

21365. The Department of Transportation, with respect to state highways in open range country, and the board of supervisors of each county, with respect to county highways under its jurisdiction, may place and maintain appropriate signs indicating that the territory traversed is open livestock range and warning against the danger of livestock on the highway.
(Amended by Stats. 1974, Ch. 545.)

21366. At each signal-controlled intersection on streets and highways, there shall be a street name sign clearly visible to traffic approaching from all directions. The cost of erecting and maintaining the street name signs may be paid out of funds derived from the Highway Users Tax Fund or the Motor Vehicle License Fee Fund.
(Amended by Stats. 1963, Ch. 1574.)

21367. (a) As provided in Section 125 of the Streets and Highways Code and in Section 21100 of this code, respectively, the duly authorized representative of the Department of Transportation or local authorities, with respect to highways under their respective jurisdictions, including, but not limited to, persons contracting to perform construction, maintenance, or repair of a highway, may, with the approval of the department or local authority, as the case may be, and while engaged in the performance of that work, restrict the use of, and regulate the movement of traffic through or around, the affected area whenever the traffic would endanger the safety of workers or the work would interfere with or endanger the movement of traffic through the area. Traffic may be regulated by warning signs, lights, appropriate control devices, or by a person or persons controlling and directing the flow of traffic.

(b) It is unlawful to disobey the instructions of a person controlling and directing traffic pursuant to subdivision (a).

(c) It is unlawful to fail to comply with the directions of warning signs, lights, or other control devices provided for the regulation of traffic pursuant to subdivision (a).
(Added by Stats. 1986, Ch. 748, Sec. 2.)

21368. Whenever a marked pedestrian crosswalk has been established in a roadway contiguous to a school building or the grounds thereof, it shall be painted or marked in yellow as shall be all the marked pedestrian crosswalks at an intersection in case any one of the crosswalks is required to be marked in yellow. Other established marked pedestrian crosswalks may be painted or marked in yellow if either (a) the nearest point of the crosswalk is not more than 600 feet from a school building or the grounds thereof, or (b) the nearest point of the crosswalk is not more than 2,800 feet from a school building or the grounds thereof, there are no intervening crosswalks other than those contiguous to the school grounds, and it appears that the facts and circumstances require special painting or marking of the crosswalks for the protection and safety of persons attending the school. There shall be painted or marked in yellow on each side of the street in the lane or lanes leading to all yellow marked crosswalks the following words, "SLOW—SCHOOL XING," except that such words shall not be painted or marked in any lane leading to a crosswalk at an intersection controlled by stop signs, traffic signals, or yield right-of-way signs. A crosswalk shall not be painted or marked yellow at any location other than as required or permitted in this section.
(Amended by Stats. 1976, Ch. 232.)

21369. All speed restriction signs in place on January 1, 1960, are hereby ratified and confirmed and shall establish the applicable prima facie speed limit unless and until changed pursuant to engineering and traffic surveys provided for by this code.
(Added by Stats. 1959, Ch. 1317.)

21370. The Department of Transportation, or its duly authorized representatives with the approval of the department, while engaged in the construction of a state highway upon new alignment may restrict the use of and regulate the movement of traffic upon any highway intersecting the project at or near the place of intersection whenever such work interferes with or endangers the safe movement of traffic through the work.
(Amended by Stats. 1974, Ch. 545.)

21372. The Department of Transportation and local authorities shall, with respect to highways under their respective jurisdictions, establish and promulgate warrants to be used as guidelines for the placement of traffic control devices near schools for the purpose of protecting students going to and from school. Such devices may include flashing signals. Such warrants shall be based upon, but need not be limited to, the following items: pedestrian volumes, vehicle volumes, width of the roadway, physical terrain, speed of vehicle traffic, horizontal and vertical alignment of the roadway, the distance to existing traffic control devices, proximity to the school, and the degree of urban or rural environment of the area.
(Amended by Stats. 1974, Ch. 545.)

21373. The governing board of any school district may request the appropriate city, county, city and county or state agency to install traffic control devices in accordance with the warrants established pursuant to Section 21372. Within 90 days thereafter, the city, county, city and county or state agency involved shall undertake an engineering and traffic survey to determine whether the requested crossing protection meets the warrants established pursuant to Section 21372. The city, county, city and county, or state agency involved may require the requesting school district to pay an amount not to exceed 50 percent of the cost of the survey. If it is determined that such requested protection is warranted, it shall be installed by the city, county, city and county or state agency involved.
(Amended by Stats. 1969, Ch. 1061.)

21374. A local authority may mark or paint the surface of any street or highway under its jurisdiction, or of any state highway, with the approval of the Department of Transportation, with lines, arrows, or other suitable symbols for the purpose of directing visitors and tourists to local points of interest. No such marking shall be of a color or configuration which, as determined by the Department of Transportation, would cause it to be confused with an official traffic control device.
(Added by Stats. 1976, Ch. 472.)

21375. (a) The Department of Transportation shall place and maintain, or cause to be placed and maintained, directional signs on freeways indicating the location of the freeway off ramp which may be used to reach a public or private postsecondary education institution having an enrollment of either 1,000 or more full-time students or the equivalent in part-time students, at the request of the institution. No signs shall be erected pursuant to this subdivision until the department has received donations from private sources covering the costs of erecting the signs.

(b) The Department of Transportation shall place and maintain, or cause to be placed and maintained, freeway directional signs for any institution described in subdivision (a) for which freeway directional signs had previously been erected and which has, on or after January 1, 1980, moved to another location, if that move was done to contribute to the improvement of the institution, as determined by the department. Freeway directional signs erected pursuant to this subdivision shall be at no cost to the institution.

(c) Subdivision (a) applies to a public or private postsecondary institution which is located within two miles of the freeway in a major metropolitan area, within four miles of the freeway in an urban area, or within five miles of the freeway in a rural area. Subdivision (b) applies to a public or private postsecondary education institution which has moved to a location which is within the distances specified in this subdivision.
(Added by Stats. 1990, Ch. 635, Sec. 1.)

21376. The Department of Transportation shall place and maintain on each major state highway entering the state within 500 feet after the state line, a sign that states that the abandonment or dumping of any animal is a crime punishable by a fine of up to one thousand dollars ($1,000) or confinement in a county jail of up to six months, or both.
(Added by Stats. 2001, Ch. 300, Sec. 3. Effective January 1, 2002.)

Article 2. Official Traffic Control Devices

(Article 2 repealed and added by Stats. 1969, Ch. 1033.)

21400. (a) The Department of Transportation shall, after consultation with local agencies and public hearings, adopt rules and regulations prescribing uniform standards and specifications for all official traffic control devices placed pursuant to this code, including, but not limited to, stop signs, yield right-of-way signs, speed restriction signs, railroad warning approach signs, street name signs, lines and markings on the roadway, and stock crossing signs placed pursuant to Section 21364.

(b) The Department of Transportation shall, after notice and public hearing, determine and publicize the specifications for uniform types of warning signs, lights, and devices to be placed upon a highway by a person engaged in performing work that interferes with or endangers the safe movement of traffic upon that highway.

(c) Only those signs, lights, and devices as are provided for in this section shall be placed upon a highway to warn traffic of work that is being performed on the highway.

(d) Control devices or markings installed upon traffic barriers on or after January 1, 1984, shall conform to the uniform standards and specifications required by this section.
(Amended by Stats. 2021, Ch. 690, Sec. 2. (AB 43) Effective January 1, 2022.)

21401. (a) Except as provided in Section 21374, only those official traffic control devices that conform to the uniform standards and specifications promulgated by the Department of Transportation shall be placed upon a street or highway.

(b) Any traffic signal controller that is newly installed or upgraded by the Department of Transportation shall be of a standard traffic signal communication protocol capable of two-way communications. A local authority may follow this requirement.

(c) In recognition of the state and local interests served by the action made optional for a local authority in subdivision (b), the Legislature encourages local agencies to continue taking the action formerly mandated by this section. However nothing in this subdivision may be construed to impose any liability on a local agency that does not continue to take the formerly mandated action.
(Amended by Stats. 2004, Ch. 889, Sec. 6. Effective September 29, 2004.)

Article 3. Offenses Relating to Traffic Devices

(Article 3 enacted by Stats. 1959, Ch. 3.)

21450. Whenever traffic is controlled by official traffic control signals showing different colored lights, color-lighted arrows, or color-lighted bicycle symbols, successively, one at a time, or in combination, only the colors green, yellow, and red shall be used, except for pedestrian control signals, and those lights shall indicate and apply to drivers of vehicles, operators of bicycles, and pedestrians as provided in this chapter.
(Amended (as amended by Stats. 1999, Ch. 277, Sec. 1) by Stats. 2005, Ch. 126, Sec. 1. Effective July 25, 2005. Note: This amended version was effectively added on July 25, 2005, because the prior version, as amended by Stats. 1999, Ch. 277, Sec. 1, had been repealed on January 1, 2005, by its own provisions.)

21450.5. (a) As used in this section, the following terms have the following definitions:

(1) "Accessible pedestrian signal" or "APS" means an integrated

device that communicates information about the "WALK" and "DON'T WALK" intervals at signalized intersections in nonvisual formats, including audible tones, speech messages, and vibrotactile surfaces, to pedestrians who are blind or have low vision.

(2) "Leading pedestrian interval" or "LPI" means an official traffic control signal that advances the "WALK" signal for three to seven seconds while the red signal halting traffic continues to be displayed on parallel through or turning traffic.

(3) "Pedestrian hybrid beacon" means a special type of hybrid beacon used to warn and control traffic at an unsignalized location to assist pedestrians in crossing a street or highway at a marked crosswalk. Following an actuation by a pedestrian, a pedestrian hybrid beacon face shall display to motorists and bicyclists a flashing CIRCULAR YELLOW signal indication, followed by a steady CIRCULAR YELLOW signal indication, followed by both steady CIRCULAR RED signal indications during the pedestrian walk interval and followed by alternating flashing CIRCULAR RED signal indications during the pedestrian change interval. Upon termination of the pedestrian change interval, the pedestrian hybrid beacon faces shall revert to a dark, not illuminated, condition. When a pedestrian makes an actuation, they shall wait for a "WALK" signal to appear on the pedestrian head in order to proceed. After the countdown, a "DON'T WALK" signal appears, and the pedestrian hybrid beacon has to be activated again to initiate a "WALK" signal.

(4) "Replaced" or "replacement" means the relocation or exchange in place of all existing signal poles at an intersection with new signal poles.

(5) A "traffic-actuated signal" is an official traffic control signal, as specified in Section 445, that displays one or more of its indications in response to the presence of traffic detected by mechanical, visual, electrical, or other means.

(6) "Caltrans" means the Department of Transportation.

(b) Upon the first placement of a traffic-actuated signal or replacement of the loop detector of a traffic-actuated signal, the traffic-actuated signal shall, to the extent feasible and in conformance with professional traffic engineering practice, be installed and maintained to detect lawful bicycle or motorcycle traffic on the roadway.

(c) Cities, counties, and cities and counties shall not be required to comply with the provisions contained in subdivision (b) until the Department of Transportation, in consultation with these entities, has established uniform standards, specifications, and guidelines for the detection of bicycles and motorcycles by traffic-actuated signals and related signal timing.

(d) (1) At crosswalks with state-owned or -operated traffic-actuated signals and pedestrian hybrid beacons with pedestrian signal heads, the walk indication and other visual signals, including, but not limited to, LPIs and countdown pedestrian signals, shall comply with the California Manual on Uniform Traffic Control Devices (CA MUTCD), 4E.11. These pedestrian signal heads shall have an APS pushbutton or touch-free APS that activates "WALK" and "DON'T WALK" intervals and other visual signals at signalized intersections in nonvisual formats, including, but not limited to, audible tones, speech messages, and vibrotactile surfaces. These features shall be activated, maintained, and available at all times of the day.

(2) (A) Touch-free APS shall be installed at new signalized pedestrian crossings on capital projects on the state highway system, defined in Section 300 of the Streets and Highways Code, encroachment permit projects, and highway maintenance-funded projects according to the following schedule:

(i) Capital outlay support projects that have a ready to list date.

(ii) Capital outlay support projects that are in construction before October 18, 2021.

(iii) Encroachment permit projects that have been approved on or after October 18, 2021.

(iv) Highway maintenance-funded projects that have a ready to list date on or after October 18, 2021.

(B) (i) When a touch-free APS is installed at an existing signalized pedestrian crossing, or in response to a federal Americans with Disability Act (ADA) access request, on capital projects on the state highway system, all APS at that location shall be upgraded to touch-free APS.

(ii) The installation of touch-free APS shall not require the upgrading of other ADA components, including, but not limited to, curb ramps or sidewalks, unless those components are disturbed.

(3) When performing maintenance and repair activities on capital projects on the state highway system, as defined in Section 300 of the Streets and Highways Code, encroachment permit projects, and highway maintenance-funded projects, the maintenance and repair shall consider using touch-free APS.

(4) Unsignalized pedestrian crossings at signalized intersections, including, but not limited to, intersections with free-right turns, may remain unsignalized.

(e) (1) Upon the first placement or replacement of a state-owned or -operated traffic-actuated signal, the traffic-actuated signal shall be installed and maintained to have an LPI and a touch-free APS, in compliance with the California Manual on Uniform Traffic Control Devices (CA MUTCD). The touch-free APS shall be activated.

(2) Caltrans shall implement LPIs on existing state-owned or -operated traffic-actuated signals capable of being implemented with remote installation or in-person programming when maintenance work is done on the intersection in which the traffic-actuated signal is located, if the traffic-actuated signal is in any of the following areas, unless prohibited by the CA MUTCD:

(A) A residential district, as determined by Section 22507.5.

(B) A business district, as defined in Sections 235 and 240.

(C) A business activity district, as defined in Section 22358.9.

(D) A safety corridor, as defined in Section 2B.13 of the CA MUTCD.

(E) A school zone, as defined in Section 1A.13.185 of the CA MUTCD.

(F) Areas with a high concentration of pedestrians and cyclists, as defined in Section 2B.13 and Table 2B.106(CA) of the CA MUTCD.

(3) (A) As soon as practicable, all existing state-owned or -operated traffic signals located in the areas described in subparagraphs (A) to (F), inclusive, of paragraph (2) shall be identified and recorded in the Caltrans Management System (TMS) inventory database to assist future annual operational review requirements and coordination with local agencies for delegated signals. LPIs shall be implemented at these existing state-owned or -operated traffic signal locations at the next opportunity for regularly scheduled operational reviews. Traffic signals that have been implemented with LPIs shall be recorded in the TMS inventory database.

(B) As soon as practicable, Caltrans' district signal operations units shall formally notify, in writing, local agencies operating state-owned traffic-actuated signals in areas described in subparagraphs (A) to (F), inclusive, of paragraph (2), about the opportunity to implement LPI on the signals. Additionally, these local agencies shall report their implementation of LPIs at these locations to Caltrans so the locations can be included in the TMS inventory database.

(C) For existing traffic signals not in areas described in subparagraphs (A) to (F), inclusive, of paragraph (2), Caltrans shall follow the same criteria for implementing LPIs in paragraph (2).

(4) Depending on the physical location and traffic conditions, locations where LPIs have been implemented pursuant to this subdivision may restrict turns on red using illuminated blank out signs and enhanced signing. LPIs are to be implemented at existing signals with touch-free APS and pedestrian countdown signals.

(Amended by Stats. 2025, Ch. 326, Sec. 1. (SB 671) Effective January 1, 2026.)

21451. (a) A driver facing a circular green signal shall proceed straight through or turn right or left or make a U-turn unless a sign prohibits a U-turn. Any driver, including one turning, shall yield the right-of-way to other traffic and to pedestrians lawfully within the intersection or an adjacent crosswalk.

(b) A driver facing a green arrow signal, shown alone or in combination with another indication, shall enter the intersection only to make the movement indicated by that green arrow or any other movement that is permitted by other indications shown at the same time. A driver facing a left green arrow may also make a U-turn unless prohibited by a sign. A driver shall yield the right-of-way to other traffic and to a pedestrian lawfully within the intersection or an adjacent crosswalk.

(c) A pedestrian facing a circular green signal, unless prohibited by sign or otherwise directed by a pedestrian control signal as provided in Section 21456, may proceed across the roadway within any marked or unmarked crosswalk, but shall yield the right-of-way to vehicles lawfully within the intersection at the time that signal is first shown.

(d) A pedestrian facing a green arrow turn signal, unless otherwise directed by a pedestrian control signal as provided in Section 21456, shall not enter the roadway.

(e) (1) A peace officer, as defined in Chapter 4.5 (commencing with Section 830) of Title 3 of Part 2 of the Penal Code, shall not stop a pedestrian for a violation of subdivision (c) or (d) unless a reasonably careful person would realize there is an immediate danger of a collision with a moving vehicle or other device moving exclusively by human power.

(2) This subdivision does not relieve a pedestrian from the duty of using due care for their safety.

(3) This subdivision does not relieve a driver of a vehicle from the duty of exercising due care for the safety of any pedestrian within the roadway.

(Amended by Stats. 2022, Ch. 957, Sec. 1. (AB 2147) Effective January 1, 2023.)

21452. (a) A driver facing a steady circular yellow or yellow arrow signal is, by that signal, warned that the related green movement is ending or that a red indication will be shown immediately thereafter.

(b) A pedestrian facing a steady circular yellow or a yellow arrow signal, unless otherwise directed by a pedestrian control signal as provided in Section 21456, is, by that signal, warned that there is insufficient time to cross the roadway and shall not enter the roadway.

(c) (1) A peace officer, as defined in Chapter 4.5 (commencing with Section 830) of Title 3 of Part 2 of the Penal Code, shall not stop a pedestrian for a violation of subdivision (b) unless a reasonably careful person would realize there is an immediate danger of a collision with a moving vehicle or other device moving exclusively by human power.

(2) This subdivision does not relieve a pedestrian from the duty of using due care for their safety.

(3) This subdivision does not relieve a driver of a vehicle from the duty of exercising due care for the safety of any pedestrian within the roadway.

(Amended by Stats. 2022, Ch. 957, Sec. 2. (AB 2147) Effective January 1, 2023.)

21453. (a) A driver facing a steady circular red signal alone shall stop at a marked limit line, but if none, before entering the crosswalk on the near side of the intersection or, if none, then before entering the intersection, and shall remain stopped until an indication to proceed is shown, except as provided in subdivision (b).

(b) Except when a sign is in place prohibiting a turn, a driver, after stopping as required by subdivision (a), facing a steady circular red signal, may turn right, or turn left from a one-way street onto a one-way street. A driver making that turn shall yield the right-of-way to pedestrians lawfully within an adjacent crosswalk and to any vehicle that has approached or is approaching so closely as to constitute an immediate hazard to the driver, and shall continue to yield the right-of-way to that vehicle until the driver can proceed with reasonable safety.

(c) A driver facing a steady red arrow signal shall not enter the intersection to make the movement indicated by the arrow and, unless entering the intersection to make a movement permitted by another signal, shall stop at a clearly marked limit line, but if none, before entering the crosswalk on the near side of the intersection, or if none, then before entering the intersection, and shall remain stopped until an indication permitting movement is shown.

(d) Unless otherwise directed by a pedestrian control signal as provided in Section 21456, a pedestrian facing a steady circular red or red arrow signal shall not enter the roadway.

(e) (1) A peace officer, as defined in Chapter 4.5 (commencing with Section 830) of Title 3 of Part 2 of the Penal Code, shall not stop a pedestrian for a violation of subdivision (d) unless a reasonably careful person would realize there is an immediate danger of a collision with a moving vehicle or other device moving exclusively by human power.

(2) This subdivision does not relieve a pedestrian from the duty of using due care for their safety.

(3) This subdivision does not relieve a driver of a vehicle from the duty of exercising due care for the safety of any pedestrian within the roadway.

(Amended by Stats. 2022, Ch. 957, Sec. 3. (AB 2147) Effective January 1, 2023.)

21454. When lane use control signals are placed over individual lanes, those signals shall indicate and apply to drivers of vehicles as follows:

(a) Green indication: A driver may travel in any lane over which a green signal is shown.

(b) Steady yellow indication: A driver is thereby warned that a lane control change is being made.

(c) Steady red indication: A driver shall not enter or travel in any lane over which a red signal is shown.

(d) Flashing yellow indication: A driver may use the lane only for the purpose of making a left turn to or from the highway.

(Amended by Stats. 1981, Ch. 413, Sec. 7.)

21455. If an official traffic control signal is erected and maintained at a place other than an intersection, including a freeway or highway on ramp, this article applies, except those provisions that by their nature can have no application. A stop required shall be made at a sign, crosswalk, or limit line indicating where the stop shall be made, but, in the absence of that sign or marking, the stop shall be made at the signal.

(Amended by Stats. 2017, Ch. 555, Sec. 1. (AB 1094) Effective January 1, 2018.)

21455.5. (a) The limit line, the intersection, or a place designated in Section 21455, where a driver is required to stop, may be equipped with an automated traffic enforcement system if the governmental agency utilizing the system meets both of the following requirements:

(1) Identifies the system by signs posted within 200 feet of an intersection where a system is operating that clearly indicate the system's presence and are visible to traffic approaching from all directions in which the automated traffic enforcement system is being utilized to issue citations. A governmental agency utilizing this type of system does not need to post signs visible to traffic approaching the intersection from directions not subject to the automated traffic enforcement system.

(2) Locates the system at an intersection and ensures that the system meets the criteria specified in Section 21455.7.

(b) Before issuing citations under this section, a local jurisdiction utilizing an automated traffic enforcement system shall commence a program to issue only warning notices for 30 days. The local jurisdiction shall also make a public announcement of the automated traffic enforcement system at least 30 days before commencing the enforcement program.

(c) Only a governmental agency, in cooperation with a law enforcement agency, may operate an automated traffic enforcement system. A governmental agency that operates an automated traffic enforcement system shall do both of the following:

(1) Develop uniform guidelines for screening and issuing violations, including a violation for a prohibited right turn at a steady circular red signal, which shall take into account the relative risk to traffic and pedestrian safety posed by right turns on red compared to proceeding through the intersection against a red signal, and for the processing and storage of confidential information, and establish procedures to ensure compliance with those guidelines.

(2) Perform administrative functions and day-to-day functions, including, but not limited to, all of the following:

(A) Establishing guidelines for the selection of a location. Before installing an automated traffic enforcement system, the governmental agency shall make and adopt a finding of fact establishing that the system is needed at a specific location for reasons related to safety.

(B) Ensuring that the equipment is regularly inspected.

(C) Certifying that the equipment is properly installed and calibrated, and is operating properly.

(D) Regularly inspecting and maintaining warning signs placed under paragraph (1) of subdivision (a).

(E) Overseeing the establishment or change of signal phases and the timing thereof.

(F) Maintaining controls necessary to ensure that only those citations that have been reviewed and approved by law enforcement are delivered to violators.

(d) The activities listed in subdivision (c) that relate to the operation of the system may be contracted out by the governmental agency, if it maintains overall control and supervision of the system. However, the activities listed in paragraph (1) of, and subparagraphs (A), (D), (E), and (F) of paragraph (2) of, subdivision (c) shall not be contracted out to the manufacturer or supplier of the automated traffic enforcement system.

(e) The printed representation of computer-generated information, video, or photographic images stored by an automated traffic enforcement system does not constitute an out-of-court hearsay statement by a declarant under Division 10 (commencing with Section 1200) of the Evidence Code.

(f) (1) Notwithstanding Article 1 (commencing with Section 7922.500) and Article 2 (commencing with Section 7922.525) of Chapter 1 of Part 3 of Division 10 of Title 1 of the Government Code, or any other law, photographic records made by an automated traffic enforcement system shall be confidential, and shall be made available only to governmental agencies and law enforcement agencies and only for the purposes of this article.

(2) Confidential information obtained from the Department of Motor Vehicles for the administration or enforcement of this article shall be held confidential, and shall not be used for any other purpose.

(3) Except for court records described in Section 68152 of the Government Code, the confidential records and information described in paragraphs (1) and (2) may be retained for up to six months from the date the information was first obtained, or until final disposition of the citation, whichever date is later, after which time the information shall be destroyed in a manner that shall preserve the confidentiality of a person included in the record or information.

(g) Notwithstanding subdivision (f), the registered owner or an individual identified by the registered owner as the driver of the vehicle at the time of the alleged violation shall be permitted to review the photographic evidence of the alleged violation.

(h) (1) A contract between a governmental agency and a manufacturer or supplier of automated traffic enforcement equipment shall not include provision for the payment or compensation to the manufacturer or supplier based on the number of citations generated, or as a percentage of the revenue generated, as a result of the use of the equipment authorized under this section.

(2) Paragraph (1) does not apply to a contract that was entered into by a governmental agency and a manufacturer or supplier of automated traffic enforcement equipment before January 1, 2004, unless that contract is renewed, extended, or amended on or after January 1, 2004.

(3) A governmental agency that proposes to install or operate an automated traffic enforcement system shall not consider revenue generation, beyond recovering its actual costs of operating the system, as a factor when considering whether or not to install or operate a system within its local jurisdiction.

(i) A manufacturer or supplier that operates an automated traffic enforcement system pursuant to this section shall, in cooperation with the governmental agency, submit an annual report to the Judicial Council that includes all of the following information if this information is in the possession of, or readily available to, the manufacturer or supplier:

(1) The number of alleged violations captured by the systems they operate.

(2) The number of citations issued by a law enforcement agency based on information collected from the automated traffic enforcement system.

(3) For citations identified in paragraph (2), the number of violations that involved traveling straight through the intersection, turning right, and turning left.

(4) The number and percentage of citations that are dismissed by the court.

(5) The number of traffic collisions at each intersection that occurred before and after the installation of the automated traffic enforcement system.

(j) This section does not affect a local jurisdiction that utilizes an automated traffic enforcement system pursuant to Section 21455.9. A local jurisdiction may utilize an automated traffic enforcement system pursuant to this section or Section 21455.9.

(Amended by Stats. 2025, Ch. 782, Sec. 4. (SB 720) Effective January 1, 2026.)

21455.6. (a) A city council or county board of supervisors shall conduct a public hearing on the proposed use of an automated enforcement system authorized under Section 21455.5 prior to authorizing the city or county to enter into a contract for the use of the system.

(b) (1) The activities listed in subdivision (c) of Section 21455.5 that relate to the operation of an automated enforcement system may be contracted out by the city or county, except that the activities listed in paragraph (1) of, and subparagraphs (A), (D), (E), or (F) of paragraph (2) of, subdivision (c) of Section 21455.5 may not be contracted out to the manufacturer or supplier of the automated enforcement system.

(2) Paragraph (1) does not apply to a contract that was entered into by a city or county and a manufacturer or supplier of automated enforcement equipment before January 1, 2004, unless that contract is renewed, extended, or amended on or after January 1, 2004.

(c) The authorization in Section 21455.5 to use automated enforcement systems does not authorize the use of photo radar for speed enforcement purposes by any jurisdiction.

(Amended by Stats. 2003, Ch. 511, Sec. 2. Effective January 1, 2004.)

21455.7. (a) At an intersection at which there is an automated traffic enforcement system in operation pursuant to Section 21455.5 or 21455.9, the minimum yellow light change interval shall be established in accordance with the California Manual on Uniform Traffic Control Devices.

(b) For purposes of subdivision (a), the minimum yellow light change intervals relating to designated approach speeds provided in the California Manual on Uniform Traffic Control Devices are mandatory minimum yellow light intervals.

(c) A yellow light change interval may exceed the minimum interval established pursuant to subdivision (a).

(Amended by Stats. 2025, Ch. 782, Sec. 5. (SB 720) Effective January 1, 2026.)

21455.9. (a) As used in this section, the following definitions apply:

(1) “Automated traffic enforcement system” or “system” means a fixed system that utilizes automated equipment to detect a violation of a traffic control signal and obtains a clear photograph of the detected vehicle’s license and video recording of the violation.

(2) “Automated traffic enforcement violation” means a violation of a traffic control signal detected by an automated traffic enforcement system operated pursuant to this section.

(3) “Designated jurisdiction” means any city, county, or city and county in the state.

(4) A person is “indigent” if either of the following conditions is met:

(A) The person meets the income criteria set forth in subdivision (b) of Section 68632 of the Government Code.

(B) The person receives public benefits from a program listed in subdivision (a) of Section 68632 of the Government Code.

(5) "Local department of transportation" means a designated jurisdiction's department of transportation or, if a designated jurisdiction does not have a department of transportation, their administrative division, including, but not limited to, a public works department that administers transportation and traffic matters under this code.

(6) "Traffic control signal" means an official traffic control signal, as defined in Section 445.

(b) (1) A designated jurisdiction may establish a program for traffic control signal enforcement that utilizes an automated traffic enforcement system, to be operated by a local department of transportation, at the limit line, the intersection, where a driver is required to stop, if the program meets all of the following requirements:

(A) (i) Identifies the system by signs that clearly indicate the system's presence, are visible to traffic approaching from all directions in which the automated traffic enforcement system is being utilized to issue citations, and are posted within the following distances:

(I) On roads with speed limits of 45 miles per hour or less, one sign within 200 to 300 feet, inclusive, of an intersection where a system is operating.

(II) On roads with speed limits over 45 miles per hour, two signs within 200 to 500 feet, inclusive, of an intersection where a system is operating, with at least 100 feet between the signs.

(ii) A program does not need to post signs visible to traffic approaching the intersection from directions not subject to the automated traffic enforcement system.

(B) Locates the system at an intersection and ensures that the system meets the criteria specified in Section 21455.7. A designated jurisdiction shall not reduce the yellow light interval durations after placement of the system.

(2) An automated traffic enforcement system program developed pursuant to paragraph (1) shall place the systems in locations that are geographically and socioeconomically diverse. The designated jurisdiction shall describe how it has complied with this provision in the automated traffic enforcement system impact report described in subdivision (c).

(3) A designated jurisdiction shall consider traffic data or other evidence supporting the installation and operation of each automated traffic enforcement system and determine that the intersection where an automated traffic enforcement system is to be placed or installed constitutes a heightened safety risk that warrants additional enforcement measures. A designated jurisdiction shall consider placing an automated traffic enforcement system on a street that has had a high number of incidents for motor vehicle contests or motor vehicle exhibitions of speed. For the purposes of this provision, a high number of incidents shall be calls for law enforcement to respond to the area for at least four separate incidences of a motor vehicle contest or motor vehicle exhibition of speed within the last two years before the placement of the automated traffic enforcement system.

(c) (1) For programs implemented after January 1, 2026, the governing body of the designated jurisdiction shall approve an automated traffic enforcement system impact report. The automated traffic enforcement system impact report shall include all of the following information:

(A) Assessment of potential impact of the automated traffic enforcement system on civil liberties and civil rights and any plans to safeguard those public rights.

(B) Description of the automated traffic enforcement system and how it works.

(C) Fiscal costs for the automated traffic enforcement system, including program establishment costs, ongoing costs, and program funding.

(D) If potential deployment locations of systems are predominantly in low-income neighborhoods, a determination of why these locations experience high fatality and injury collisions due to traffic control signal violations at intersections.

(E) Locations where the system may be deployed and traffic data for these locations, including the intersection where the cameras will be located.

(F) Proposed purpose of the automated traffic enforcement system.

(2) The automated traffic enforcement system impact report shall be made available for public review at least 30 calendar days prior to adoption by the governing body at a public hearing.

(3) The governing body of the designated jurisdiction shall consult and work collaboratively with relevant local stakeholder organizations, including racial equity, privacy protection, and economic justice groups, in developing the automated traffic enforcement system impact report.

(d) (1) A designated jurisdiction that operates an automated traffic enforcement system shall do both of the following:

(A) Develop uniform guidelines, consistent with the provisions of this section, for both of the following:

(i) The screening and issuing of notices of violation.

(ii) The processing and storage of confidential information and procedures to ensure compliance with confidentiality requirements.

(B) Perform administrative functions and day-to-day functions, including, but not limited to, all of the following:

(i) Establishing guidelines for the selection of a location. Prior to installing an automated traffic enforcement system after January 1, 2026, the designated jurisdiction shall make and adopt a finding of fact establishing that the system is needed at a specific location for reasons related to safety.

(ii) Ensuring that the equipment is regularly inspected, but at least annually.

(iii) Calibrating the equipment in accordance with the manufacturer's instructions upon installation.

(iv) Regularly inspecting and maintaining warning signs placed under paragraph (1) of subdivision (b).

(v) Overseeing the establishment or change of signal phases and the timing thereof.

(vi) Maintaining controls necessary to ensure that only those citations that have been reviewed and approved by the issuing agency are delivered to violators.

(2) The activities listed in paragraph (1) that relate to the operation of the system may be contracted out by a designated jurisdiction, if it maintains overall control and supervision of the system. However, the activities listed in subparagraph (A) of, and clauses (iv), (v), and (vi) of subparagraph (B) of, paragraph (1) shall not be contracted out to the manufacturer or supplier of the automated traffic enforcement system.

(e) (1) A contract between a designated jurisdiction and a manufacturer or supplier of automated traffic enforcement equipment or a company providing maintenance and processing services shall not include provision for the payment or compensation to the manufacturer, supplier, or company based on the number of citations generated, or as a percentage of the revenue generated, as a result of the use of the equipment authorized under this section.

(2) A designated jurisdiction that proposes to install or operate an automated traffic enforcement system shall not consider revenue generation, beyond recovering its actual costs of operating the system, as a factor when considering whether or not to install or operate a system within its local jurisdiction

(f) A designated jurisdiction that operates an automated traffic enforcement system pursuant to this section shall, in cooperation with the manufacturer or supplier, publish a report that includes, but is not limited to, all of the following information:

(1) The number of alleged violations captured by the systems they operate.

(2) The number of citations issued by the issuing agency based on information collected from the automated traffic enforcement system.

(3) For citations identified in paragraph (2), the number of violations that involved traveling straight through the intersection, turning right, and turning left.

(4) The number and percentage of citations that are dismissed.

(5) The funds generated from the automated traffic enforcement systems.

(g) (1) Prior to issuing citations under this section, a designated jurisdiction utilizing an automated traffic enforcement system shall commence a program to issue only warning notices for 60 days. The designated jurisdiction shall also make a public announcement of the automated traffic enforcement system at least 30 days prior to the commencement of the enforcement program.

(2) A notice of violation issued pursuant to this section shall include a clear photograph of the license plate and rear of the vehicle only, and identify the specific section of the Vehicle Code violated, the camera location, and the date and time when the violation occurred. A notice of violation shall, when practical, exclude images inside of the rear window area of the vehicle. A notice of violation issued from an automated traffic enforcement system that was installed prior to January 1, 2026, may continue to include pictures of the driver at the discretion of the designated jurisdiction.

(3) The photographic and video evidence stored by an automated traffic enforcement system does not constitute an out-of-court hearsay statement by a declarant under Division 10 (commencing with Section 1200) of the Evidence Code.

(4) (A) Notwithstanding any provision of the California Public Records Act, or any other law, photographic, video, and administrative records made by a system shall be confidential. Public agencies shall use and allow access to these records only for the purposes authorized by this section or to assess the impacts of the system. Data about the number of violations issued is not considered an administrative record required to be disclosed by this section.

(B) Confidential information obtained from the Department of Motor Vehicles for the administration of automated traffic enforcement systems and enforcement of this article shall be held confidential and shall not be used for any other purpose. Designated jurisdictions agents shall establish procedures to protect the confidentiality of these records consistent with Section 1808.47.

(C) Except for court records described in Section 68152 of the Government Code, or as provided in subparagraph (D), the confidential records and evidence described in subparagraphs (A) and (B) may be retained for up to 60 days after final disposition of the notice of violation. The designated jurisdiction may retain information that a vehicle has been cited and fined for a violation for up to three years. The designated jurisdiction may adopt a retention period of less than 60 days. Administrative records described in subparagraph (A) may be retained for up to 120 days after final disposition of the notice of violation. Notwithstanding any other law, the confidential records and evidence shall be destroyed in a manner that maintains the confidentiality of any person included in the record or evidence.

(D) Photographic and video evidence that is obtained from an automated traffic enforcement system that does not result in the issuance of a notice of violation shall be destroyed within five business days after the decision to not issue a citation has been made. The use of facial recognition technology in conjunction with an automated traffic enforcement system shall be prohibited.

(E) Information collected and maintained by a designated jurisdiction to administer a program shall only be used to administer the program, and shall not be disclosed to any other persons, including, but not limited to, any other state or federal government agency or official for any other purpose, except as required by state or federal law, court order, or in response to a subpoena in an individual case or proceeding.

(5) Notwithstanding paragraph (4), the registered owner or an individual identified by the registered owner as the driver of the vehicle at the time of the alleged violation shall be permitted to review and obtain a copy of the photographic or video evidence of the alleged violation.

(h) (1) Notwithstanding any other law, a violation of a traffic control signal law pursuant to this chapter that is recorded by an automated traffic enforcement system authorized pursuant to this section shall be subject only to a civil penalty, as provided in paragraph (3), and shall not result in the department suspending or revoking the privilege of a violator to drive a motor vehicle or in a violation point being assessed against the violator.

(2) The automated traffic enforcement system shall capture images of the rear license plate of vehicles that are violating the traffic control signal, and a notice of violation shall only be issued to registered owners of those vehicles based on that evidence.

(3) (A) A civil penalty shall be assessed as follows:

(i) For a violation where no fine has been assessed within the previous three years, by a fine of one hundred dollars ($100).

(ii) For a violation that occurred within three years after a separate previous violation, by a fine of two hundred dollars ($200).

(iii) For a violation that occurred within three years after two separate previous violations, by a fine of three hundred fifty dollars ($350).

(iv) For a violation that occurred within three years after three or more separate previous violations, by a fine of five hundred dollars ($500).

(B) No additional processing fees, other than electronic payment processing fees, may be included.

(C) Late fees for unpaid penalties shall not exceed fifty dollars ($50) for the first late fee and one hundred dollars ($100) for any subsequent late fees for the same violation.

(4) A civil penalty shall not be assessed against an authorized emergency vehicle.

(5) A person shall not be assessed a civil penalty if they are subject to criminal penalties for the same act.

(6) The notice of violation shall be in writing and issued to the registered owner of the vehicle within 15 calendar days of the date of the violation. The notice of violation shall include all of the following information:

(A) The violation, including reference to the traffic control signal law that was violated.

(B) The date, approximate time, and location where the violation occurred.

(C) The vehicle license number and the name and address of the registered owner of the vehicle.

(D) A clear photograph of the traffic control signal and an internet address where they can access the video recording of the violation based on a unique citation number.

(E) A statement that payment is required to be made no later than 30 calendar days from the date of mailing of the notice of violation, or that the violation may be contested pursuant to subdivision (j).

(F) The amount of the civil penalty due for that violation and the procedures for the payment of the civil penalty or for contesting the notice of violation.

(G) An affidavit of nonliability, and information of what constitutes nonliability, information as to the effect of executing the affidavit, and instructions for returning the affidavit to the processor. If the affidavit of nonliability is returned to the processing agency within 30 calendar days of the mailing of the notice of violation, together with proof of a written lease or rental agreement between a bona fide rental company, as defined in Section 1939.01 of the Civil Code, or a personal vehicle sharing program, as defined in Section 11580.24 of the Insurance Code, that identifies the renter or lessee, the processing agency shall serve or mail a notice of violation to the renter or lessee identified in the affidavit of nonliability. If the affidavit of nonliability is returned to the processing agency within 30 calendar days of the mailing of the notice of violation, together with proof of a copy of a police report indicating the vehicle had been stolen at the time of the violation, the processing agency shall not subject the registered owner to a civil penalty and may issue the notice of violation to the identified renter or lessee.

(H) The processing agency shall mail to the registered owner of a vehicle committing a violation of the traffic control signal law a notice of violation by depositing the notice in the United States mail no later than 15 days after the date of the alleged violation. The processing agency shall maintain proof of mailing demonstrating that the notice of violation was mailed to that address. If the registered owner or coowner of the vehicle, or the person designated as having care, custody, or control of the motor vehicle at the time of the violation pursuant to subparagraph (G), initiates a proceeding to challenge the violation pursuant to subdivision (j), such person waives any challenge or dispute as to the delivery of the notice of violation.

(I) An affidavit from a designated jurisdiction that the yellow light change interval was established in accordance with the California Manual on Uniform Traffic Control Devices, as required by Section 21455.7.

(i) (1) Revenues derived from any program utilizing an automated traffic enforcement system shall first be used to recover program costs. Program costs include, but are not limited to, the construction of traffic-calming measures, the installation of automated traffic enforcement systems, the adjudication of violations, and reporting requirements, as specified in this section.

(2) Designated jurisdictions shall maintain their existing commitment of local funds for traffic-calming measures, and shall annually expend not less than the annual average of expenditures for traffic-calming measures during the 2020–21, 2021–22, and 2022–23 fiscal years. For purposes of this subdivision, in calculating average expenditures on traffic-calming measures, restricted funds that may not be available on an ongoing basis, including those from voter-approved bond issuances or tax measures, shall not be included. Any excess revenue shall be used for traffic-calming measures within three years of the end of the fiscal year in which the excess revenue was received. If traffic-calming measures are not planned or constructed after the third year, excess revenue shall revert to the Active Transportation Program established pursuant to Chapter 8 (commencing with Section 2380) of the Streets and Highways Code, to be allocated by the California Transportation Commission pursuant to Section 2381 of the Streets and Highways Code.

(3) "Traffic-calming measures" include, but are not limited to, all of the following:

(A) Bicycle lanes.

(B) Chicanes.

(C) Chokers.

(D) Curb extensions.

(E) Median islands.

(F) Raised crosswalks.

(G) Road diets.

(H) Roundabouts.

(I) Speed humps or speed tables.

(J) Traffic circles.

(j) (1) No later than 30 calendar days from the date of mailing of a notice of violation, the recipient may request an initial review of the notice by the issuing agency. The request may be made by telephone, in writing, electronically, or in person. There shall be no charge for this review. If, following the initial review, the issuing agency is satisfied that the violation did not occur, or that extenuating circumstances make cancellation of the notice of violation appropriate in the interest of justice, the issuing agency shall cancel the notice of violation. The issuing agency shall advise the processing agency, if any, of the cancellation. The issuing agency or the processing agency shall mail the results of the initial review to the person contesting the notice within 60 days of receipt of the recipient's request for an initial review, and, if cancellation of the notice does not occur following that review, include a reason for that denial, notification of the ability to request an administrative hearing, and notice of the procedures adopted by the designated jurisdiction for the administrative hearing, including for waiving prepayment of the civil penalty based upon an inability to pay pursuant to subparagraph (B) of paragraph (2).

(2) (A) If the person contesting the notice of violation is dissatisfied with the results of the initial review, the person may, no later than 21 calendar days following the mailing of the results of the issuing agency's initial review, request an administrative hearing of the violation. The request may be made by telephone, in writing, electronically, or in person.

(B) The person requesting an administrative hearing shall pay the amount of the civil penalty to the processing agency. The issuing agency shall adopt a written procedure to allow a person to request an administrative hearing without payment of the civil penalty upon satisfactory proof of an inability to pay the amount due.

(C) The administrative hearing shall be held within 90 calendar days following the receipt of a request for an administrative hearing. The person requesting the hearing may request one continuance, not to exceed 21 calendar days.

(3) The administrative hearing process shall include all of the following:

(A) The person requesting a hearing shall have the choice of a hearing upon written declaration, video conference, or in person. An in-person hearing shall be conducted within the jurisdiction of the issuing agency.

(B) If the person requesting a hearing is an unemancipated minor, that person shall be permitted to appear at a hearing or admit responsibility for the automated traffic enforcement violation without the appointment of a guardian. The processing agency may proceed against the minor in the same manner as against an adult.

(C) The administrative hearing shall be conducted in accordance with written procedures established by the issuing agency and approved by the governing body or chief executive officer of the issuing agency. The hearing shall provide an independent, objective, fair, and impartial review of contested automated traffic enforcement violations.

(D) (i) The issuing agency's governing body or chief executive officer of the designated jurisdiction shall appoint or contract with qualified independent examiners or administrative hearing providers that employ qualified independent examiners to conduct the administrative hearings. Examiners shall demonstrate the qualifications, training, and objectivity necessary to conduct a fair and impartial review, and shall meet the minimum requirements specified in clause (ii). The examiner shall be separate and independent from the notice of violation issuing and processing functions. An examiner's continued employment, performance evaluation, compensation, and benefits shall not, directly or indirectly, be linked to the amount of civil penalties upheld by the examiner or the number or percentage of violations upheld by the examiner.

(ii) (I) Examiners shall have a minimum of 20 hours of training. The examiner, unless an employee of the designated jurisdiction, is responsible for the costs of the training. The issuing agency may reimburse the examiner for those costs. Training may be provided through any of the following:

(ia) An accredited college or university.

(ib) A program conducted by the Commission on Peace Officer Standards and Training.

(ic) A program conducted by the American Arbitration Association or a similar organization.

(id) Any program approved by the governing body or chief executive officer of the issuing agency, including a program developed and provided by, or for, the agency.

(II) Training programs shall include topics relevant to the administrative hearing, including, but not limited to, applicable laws and regulations, enforcement procedures, due process, evaluation of evidence, hearing procedures, and effective oral and written communication. Upon the approval of the governing body or chief executive officer of the issuing agency, up to 12 hours of relevant experience may be substituted for up to 12 hours of training. Up to eight hours of the training requirements described in this clause may be credited to an individual, at the discretion of the governing body or chief executive officer of the issuing agency, based upon training programs or courses described in this subparagraph that the individual attended within the last five years.

(E) The employee of the designated jurisdiction who issues a notice of violation shall not be required to participate in an administrative hearing. To establish a violation, the issuing agency shall not be required to produce any evidence other than, in proper form, the notice of violation or copy thereof, including the photograph of the vehicle's license plate, a video recording of the violation, and information received from the Department of Motor Vehicles identifying the registered owner of the vehicle. The documentation in proper form shall be prima facie evidence of the violation. If the designated jurisdiction meets its initial burden, the recipient of the notice of violation may present any evidence and argument in defense.

(F) The examiner's final decision following the administrative hearing may be personally delivered to the person by the examiner or sent by first-class mail within 60 days of the date of the conclusion of the administrative hearing.

(G) Following a determination by the examiner that a person has committed the violation, the examiner may, consistent with the written guidelines established by the issuing agency, allow payment of the civil penalty in installments, or an issuing agency may allow for deferred payment or payments in installments, if the person provides evidence satisfactory to the examiner or the issuing agency, as the case may be, of an inability to pay the civil penalty in full. If authorized by the governing body of the issuing agency, the examiner may permit the performance of community service in lieu of payment of the civil penalty.

(H) If a notice of violation is dismissed following an administrative hearing, any civil penalty, if paid, shall be refunded by the issuing agency within 30 days.

(k) (1) Within 30 days after personal delivery or mailing of the final decision described in paragraph (3) of subdivision (j), the contestant may seek review by filing an appeal to the small claims division of the superior court or the traffic division of the superior court, where the case shall be heard de novo, except that the contents of the processing agency's file in the case on appeal shall be lodged by the designated agency at the designated agency's expense and be received into evidence. Notwithstanding any other law, a copy of the notice of violation shall be presumptively admissible as evidence of the facts stated in the notice. A copy of the notice of appeal shall be served in person or by certified first-class mail with return receipt upon the processing agency by the appellant. For purposes of computing the 30-day period, Section 1013 of the Code of Civil Procedure shall be applicable. A proceeding under this paragraph is a limited civil case.

(2) The fee for filing the notice of appeal shall be as provided in Section 70615 of the Government Code. Upon receipt of the notice of appeal, the designated jurisdiction shall lodge its administrative record for the case with the court within 15 calendar days. The court shall notify the appellant of the appearance date by mail or personal delivery. The court shall retain the fee under Section 70615 of the Government Code regardless of the outcome of the appeal. If the appellant prevails, this fee and any payment of the civil penalty shall be promptly refunded by the issuing agency in accordance with the judgment of the court.

(3) The conduct of the hearing on appeal under this section is a subordinate judicial duty that may be performed by a commissioner or other subordinate judicial officer at the direction of the presiding judge of the court.

(4) If a notice of appeal of the examiner's decision is not filed within the period set forth in paragraph (1), the decision shall be deemed final.

(5) If the civil penalty has not been paid and the final decision is adverse to the appellant, the processing agency may, promptly after the decision becomes final, proceed to collect the civil penalty under subdivision (h).

(l) (1) A designated jurisdiction shall offer a diversion program for indigent automated traffic enforcement violation recipients, to perform community service in lieu of paying the penalty for an automated traffic enforcement violation.

(2) A designated jurisdiction shall offer the ability for indigent automated traffic enforcement system violation recipients to pay applicable fines and penalties over a period of time under a payment plan with monthly installments of no more than twenty-five dollars ($25) and shall limit the processing fee to participate in a payment plan to five dollars ($5) or less.

(3) Notwithstanding paragraphs (1) and (2), a designated jurisdiction shall reduce the applicable fines and penalties by 80 percent for indigent persons, and by 50 percent for individuals up to 250 percent above the federal poverty level.

(4) The person may demonstrate that they are indigent or make up to 250 percent above the poverty level or less by providing either of the following information, as applicable:

(A) Proof of income from a pay stub or another form of proof of earnings, such as a bank statement, that shows that the person meets the income criteria set forth in subdivision (b) of Section 68632 of the Government Code, subject to review and approval by the processing agency or its designee. The processing agency or its designee shall not unreasonably withhold its approval.

(B) Proof of receipt of benefits under the programs described in subdivision (a) of Section 68632 of the Government Code, including, but not limited to, an electronic benefits transfer card or another card, subject to review and approval by the processing agency. The processing agency or its designee shall not unreasonably withhold its approval.

(m) This section does not affect a designated jurisdiction that utilizes an automated traffic enforcement system pursuant to Section 21455.5. A designated jurisdiction may utilize an automated traffic enforcement system pursuant to this section or Section 21455.5.

(n) The automated traffic enforcement system, to the extent feasible, shall be angled and focused so as to only capture photographs of the rear license plate and evidence that the vehicle violated the traffic control system and shall not capture identifying images of other drivers or vehicles.

(o) A person shall not be accessed a civil penalty if they are subject to criminal penalties for the same act.

(Added by Stats. 2025, Ch. 782, Sec. 6. (SB 720) Effective January 1, 2026.)

21456. (a) If a pedestrian control signal showing the words "WALK" or "WAIT" or "DON'T WALK" or other approved symbol is in place, the signal shall indicate as follows:

(1) A "WALK" or approved "Walking Person" symbol means a pedestrian facing the signal may proceed across the roadway in the direction of the signal, but shall yield the right-of-way to vehicles lawfully within the intersection at the time that signal is first shown. Except as otherwise directed by a bicycle control signal described in Section 21456.3, the operator of a bicycle facing a pedestrian control signal displaying a "WALK" or approved "Walking Person" symbol may proceed across the roadway in the direction of the signal, but shall yield the right-of-way to any vehicles or pedestrians lawfully within the intersection.

(2) A flashing "DON'T WALK" or "WAIT" or approved "Upraised Hand" symbol with a "countdown" signal indicating the time remaining for a pedestrian to cross the roadway means a pedestrian facing the signal may start to cross the roadway in the direction of the signal, but must complete the crossing prior to the display of the steady "DON'T WALK" or "WAIT" or approved "Upraised Hand" symbol when the "countdown" ends.

(3) A steady "DON'T WALK" or "WAIT" or approved "Upraised Hand" symbol or a flashing "DON'T WALK" or "WAIT" or approved "Upraised Hand" without a "countdown" signal indicating the time remaining for a pedestrian to cross the roadway means a pedestrian facing the signal shall not start to cross the roadway in the direction of the signal, but any pedestrian who started the crossing during the display of the "WALK" or approved "Walking Person" symbol and who has partially completed crossing shall proceed to a sidewalk or safety zone or otherwise leave the roadway while the steady "WAIT" or "DON'T

WALK" or approved "Upraised Hand" symbol is showing.

(b) (1) A peace officer, as defined in Chapter 4.5 (commencing with Section 830) of Title 3 of Part 2 of the Penal Code, shall not stop a pedestrian for a violation of this section unless a reasonably careful person would realize there is an immediate danger of a collision with a moving vehicle or other device moving exclusively by human power.

(2) This subdivision does not relieve a pedestrian from the duty of using due care for their safety.

(3) This subdivision does not relieve a driver of a vehicle from the duty of exercising due care for the safety of any pedestrian within the roadway.

(c) This section shall become operative on January 1, 2024.

(Repealed (in Sec. 4.5) and added by Stats. 2022, Ch. 957, Sec. 4.6. (AB 2147) Effective January 1, 2023. Operative January 1, 2024, by its own provisions.)

21456.1. Whenever an official traffic control signal exhibiting an approved "Walking Person" symbol, an approved "Upraised Hand" symbol, or the words "WALK" or "WAIT" or "DON'T WALK" is shown concurrently with official traffic control signals exhibiting the words "GO" or "CAUTION" or "STOP" or exhibiting different colored lights successively, one at a time or with arrows, a pedestrian facing those traffic control signals shall obey the "Walking Person," "Upraised Hand," "WALK" or "WAIT" or "DON'T WALK" control signal as provided in Section 21456.

(Amended by Stats. 1993, Ch. 272, Sec. 39. Effective August 2, 1993.)

21456.2. (a) Unless otherwise directed by a bicycle signal as provided in Section 21456.3, or as otherwise provided in subdivision (a) of Section 21456, an operator of a bicycle shall obey the provisions of this article applicable to the driver of a vehicle.

(b) Whenever an official traffic control signal exhibiting different colored bicycle symbols is shown concurrently with official traffic control signals or pedestrian control signals exhibiting different colored lights or arrows, an operator of a bicycle facing those traffic control signals shall obey the bicycle signals as provided in Section 21456.3.

(c) This section shall become operative on January 1, 2024.

(Repealed (in Sec. 4) and added by Stats. 2022, Ch. 343, Sec. 5. (AB 1909) Effective January 1, 2023. Operative January 1, 2024, by its own provisions.)

21456.3. (a) An operator of a bicycle facing a green bicycle signal shall proceed straight through or turn right or left or make a U-turn unless a sign prohibits a U-turn. An operator of a bicycle, including one turning, shall yield the right-of-way to other traffic and to pedestrians lawfully within the intersection or an adjacent crosswalk.

(b) An operator of a bicycle facing a steady yellow bicycle signal is, by that signal, warned that the related green movement is ending or that a red indication will be shown immediately thereafter.

(c) Except as provided in subdivision (d), an operator of a bicycle facing a steady red bicycle signal shall stop at a marked limit line, but if none, before entering the crosswalk on the near side of the intersection, or, if none, then before entering the intersection, and shall remain stopped until an indication to proceed is shown.

(d) Except when a sign is in place prohibiting a turn, an operator of a bicycle, after stopping as required by subdivision (c), facing a steady red bicycle signal, may turn right, or turn left from a one-way street onto a one-way street. An operator of a bicycle making a turn shall yield the right-of-way to pedestrians lawfully within an adjacent crosswalk and to traffic lawfully using the intersection.

(e) A bicycle signal may be used only at those locations that meet geometric standards or traffic volume standards, or both, as adopted by the Department of Transportation.

(Amended by Stats. 2005, Ch. 126, Sec. 4. Effective July 25, 2005. Note: This amended version was effectively added on July 25, 2005, because the prior version, as added by Stats. 1999, Ch. 277, had been repealed on January 1, 2005, by its own provisions.)

21457. Whenever an illuminated flashing red or yellow light is used in a traffic signal or with a traffic sign, it shall require obedience by drivers as follows:

(a) Flashing red (stop signal): When a red lens is illuminated with rapid intermittent flashes, a driver shall stop at a clearly marked limit line, but if none, before entering the crosswalk on the near side of the intersection, or if none, then at the point nearest the intersecting roadway where the driver has a view of approaching traffic on the intersecting roadway before entering it, and the driver may proceed subject to the rules applicable after making a stop at a stop sign.

(b) Flashing yellow (caution signal): When a yellow lens is illuminated with rapid intermittent flashes, a driver may proceed through the intersection or past the signal only with caution.

(Amended by Stats. 1981, Ch. 413, Sec. 10.)

21458. (a) Whenever local authorities enact local parking regulations and indicate them by the use of paint upon curbs, the following colors only shall be used, and the colors indicate as follows:

(1) Red indicates no stopping, standing, or parking, whether the vehicle is attended or unattended, except that a bus may stop in a red zone marked or signposted as a bus loading zone.

(2) Yellow indicates stopping only for the purpose of loading or unloading passengers or freight for the time as may be specified by local ordinance.

(3) White indicates stopping for either of the following purposes:

(A) Loading or unloading of passengers for the time as may be specified by local ordinance.

(B) Depositing mail in an adjacent mailbox.

(4) Green indicates time limit parking specified by local ordinance.

(5) Blue indicates parking limited exclusively to the vehicles of disabled persons and disabled veterans.

(b) Regulations adopted pursuant to subdivision (a) shall be effective on days and during hours or times as prescribed by local ordinances.

(Amended by Stats. 1992, Ch. 1243, Sec. 88. Effective September 30, 1992.)

21459. (a) The Department of Transportation in respect to state highways and a local authority with respect to highways under its jurisdiction, is authorized to place and maintain upon highways distinctive roadway markings as described and with the effect set forth in Section 21460.

(b) The distinctive roadway markings shall be employed to designate any portion of a highway where the volume of traffic or the vertical or other curvature of the roadway renders it hazardous to drive on the left side of the marking or to indicate no driving to the left as provided in Section 21460, and shall not be employed for any other purpose.

(c) Any pavement marking other than as described in this section placed by the Department of Transportation or any local authority shall not be effective to indicate no driving over or to the left of the marking.

(Amended by Stats. 1974, Ch. 545.)

21460. (a) If double parallel solid yellow lines are in place, a person driving a vehicle shall not drive to the left of the lines, except as permitted in this section.

(b) If double parallel solid white lines are in place, a person driving a vehicle shall not cross any part of those double solid white lines, except as permitted in this section or Section 21655.8.

(c) If the double parallel lines, one of which is broken, are in place, a person driving a vehicle shall not drive to the left of the lines, except as follows:

(1) If the driver is on the side of the roadway in which the broken line is in place, the driver may cross over the double lines or drive to the left of the double lines when overtaking or passing other vehicles.

(2) As provided in Section 21460.5.

(d) The markings as specified in subdivision (a), (b), or (c) do not prohibit a driver from crossing the marking if (1) turning to the left at an intersection or into or out of a driveway or private road, or (2) making a U-turn under the rules governing that turn, and the markings shall be disregarded when authorized signs have been erected designating offcenter traffic lanes as permitted pursuant to Section 21657.

(e) Raised pavement markers may be used to simulate painted lines

described in this section if the markers are placed in accordance with standards established by the Department of Transportation.
(Amended by Stats. 2011, Ch. 114, Sec. 2. (AB 1105) Effective January 1, 2012.)

21460.5. (a) The Department of Transportation and local authorities in their respective jurisdictions may designate a two-way left-turn lane on a highway. A two-way left-turn lane is a lane near the center of the highway set aside for use by vehicles making left turns in both directions from or into the highway.

(b) Two-way left-turn lanes shall be designated by distinctive roadway markings consisting of parallel double yellow lines, interior line dashed and exterior line solid, on each side of the lane. The Department of Transportation may determine and prescribe standards and specifications governing length, width, and positioning of the distinctive pavement markings. All pavement markings designating a two-way left-turn lane shall conform to the Department of Transportation's standards and specifications.

(c) A vehicle shall not be driven in a designated two-way left-turn lane except when preparing for or making a left turn from or into a highway or when preparing for or making a U-turn when otherwise permitted by law, and shall not be driven in that lane for more than 200 feet while preparing for and making the turn or while preparing to merge into the adjacent lanes of travel. A left turn or U-turn shall not be made from any other lane where a two-way left-turn lane has been designated.

(d) This section does not prohibit driving across a two-way left-turn lane.

(e) Raised pavement markers may be used to simulate the painted lines described in this section when those markers are placed in accordance with standards established by the Department of Transportation.
(Amended by Stats. 1990, Ch. 232, Sec. 1.)

21461. (a) It is unlawful for a driver of a vehicle to fail to obey a sign or signal defined as regulatory in the federal Manual on Uniform Traffic Control Devices, or a Department of Transportation approved supplement to that manual of a regulatory nature erected or maintained to enhance traffic safety and operations or to indicate and carry out the provisions of this code or a local traffic ordinance or resolution adopted pursuant to a local traffic ordinance, or to fail to obey a device erected or maintained by lawful authority of a public body or official.

(b) Subdivision (a) does not apply to acts constituting violations under Chapter 9 (commencing with Section 22500) of this division or to acts constituting violations of a local traffic ordinance adopted pursuant to Chapter 9 (commencing with Section 22500).
(Amended by Stats. 2004, Ch. 203, Sec. 1. Effective January 1, 2005.)

21461.5. (a) It shall be unlawful for any pedestrian to fail to obey any sign or signal erected or maintained to indicate or carry out the provisions of this code or any local traffic ordinance or resolution adopted pursuant to a local traffic ordinance, or to fail to obey any device erected or maintained pursuant to Section 21352.

(b) (1) A peace officer, as defined in Chapter 4.5 (commencing with Section 830) of Title 3 of Part 2 of the Penal Code, shall not stop a pedestrian for a violation of subdivision (a) unless a reasonably careful person would realize there is an immediate danger of a collision with a moving vehicle or other device moving exclusively by human power.

(2) This subdivision does not relieve a pedestrian from the duty of using due care for their safety.

(3) This subdivision does not relieve a driver of a vehicle from the duty of exercising due care for the safety of any pedestrian within the roadway.
(Amended by Stats. 2022, Ch. 957, Sec. 5. (AB 2147) Effective January 1, 2023.)

21462. (a) The driver of a vehicle, the person in charge of an animal, a pedestrian, and the motorist of a streetcar shall obey the instructions of an official traffic signal applicable to them and placed as provided by law, unless otherwise directed by a police or traffic officer or when it is necessary for the purpose of avoiding a collision or in case of other emergency, subject to the exemptions granted by Section 21055.

(b) (1) A peace officer, as defined in Chapter 4.5 (commencing with Section 830) of Title 3 of Part 2 of the Penal Code, shall not stop a pedestrian for a violation of subdivision (a) unless a reasonably careful person would realize there is an immediate danger of a collision with a moving vehicle or other device moving exclusively by human power.

(2) This subdivision does not relieve a pedestrian from the duty of using due care for their safety.

(3) This subdivision does not relieve a driver of a vehicle from the duty of exercising due care for the safety of any pedestrian within the roadway.
(Amended by Stats. 2022, Ch. 957, Sec. 6. (AB 2147) Effective January 1, 2023.)

21463. No person shall operate a manually or traffic actuated signal other than for the purpose of permitting a pedestrian or vehicle to cross a roadway.
(Enacted by Stats. 1959, Ch. 3.)

21464. (a) A person, without lawful authority, may not deface, injure, attach any material or substance to, knock down, or remove, nor may a person shoot at, any official traffic control device, traffic guidepost, traffic signpost, motorist callbox, or historical marker placed or erected as authorized or required by law, nor may a person without lawful authority deface, injure, attach any material or substance to, or remove, nor may a person shoot at, any inscription, shield, or insignia on any device, guide, or marker.

(b) A person may not use, and a vehicle, other than an authorized emergency vehicle or a public transit passenger vehicle, may not be equipped with, any device, including, but not limited to, a mobile infrared transmitter, that is capable of sending a signal that interrupts or changes the sequence patterns of an official traffic control signal unless that device or use is authorized by the Department of Transportation pursuant to Section 21350 or by local authorities pursuant to Section 21351.

(c) A person may not buy, possess, manufacture, install, sell, offer for sale, or otherwise distribute a device described in subdivision (b), including, but not limited to, a mobile infrared transmitter (MIRT), unless the purchase, possession, manufacture, installation, sale, offer for sale, or distribution is for the use of the device by a peace officer or other person authorized to operate an authorized emergency vehicle or a public transit passenger vehicle, in the scope of his or her duties.

(d) Any willful violation of subdivision (a), (b), or (c) that results in injury to, or the death of, a person is punishable by imprisonment pursuant to subdivision (h) of Section 1170 of the Penal Code, or by imprisonment in a county jail for a period of not more than six months, and by a fine of not less than five thousand dollars ($5,000) nor more than ten thousand dollars ($10,000).

(e) Any willful violation of subdivision (a), (b), or (c) that does not result in injury to, or the death of, a person is punishable by a fine of not more than five thousand dollars ($5,000).

(f) The court shall allow the offender to perform community service designated by the court in lieu of all or part of any fine imposed under this section.
(Amended by Stats. 2011, Ch. 15, Sec. 607. (AB 109) Effective April 4, 2011. Operative October 1, 2011, by Sec. 636 of Ch. 15, as amended by Stats. 2011, Ch. 39, Sec. 68.)

21465. No person shall place, maintain, or display upon, or in view of, any highway any unofficial sign, signal, device, or marking, or any sign, signal, device, or marking which purports to be or is an imitation of, or resembles, an official traffic control device or which attempts to direct the movement of traffic or which hides from view any official traffic control device.
(Amended by Stats. 1967, Ch. 486.)

21466. No person shall place or maintain or display upon or in view of any highway any light in such position as to prevent the driver of a vehicle from readily recognizing any official traffic control device.
(Amended by Stats. 1970, Ch. 968.)

21466.5. No person shall place or maintain or display, upon or in view of any highway, any light of any color of such brilliance as to impair the vision of drivers upon the highway. A light source shall be considered vision impairing when its brilliance exceeds the values listed below.

The brightness reading of an objectionable light source shall be measured with a 11/2-degree photoelectric brightness meter placed at the driver's point of view. The maximum measured brightness of the light source within 10 degrees from the driver's normal line of sight shall not be more than 1,000 times the minimum measured brightness in the driver's field of view, except that when the minimum measured brightness in the field of view is 10 foot-lamberts or less, the measured brightness of the light source in foot-lambert shall not exceed 500 plus 100 times the angle, in degrees, between the driver's line of sight and the light source.

The provisions of this section shall not apply to railroads as defined in Section 229 of the Public Utilities Code.

(Added by Stats. 1970, Ch. 968.)

21467. Every prohibited sign, signal, device, or light is a public nuisance, and the Department of Transportation, members of the California Highway Patrol, and local authorities are hereby authorized and empowered without notice to remove the same, or cause the same to be removed, or the Director of Transportation, the commissioner, or local authorities may bring an action as provided by law to abate such nuisance.

(Amended by Stats. 1974, Ch. 545.)

21468. This division does not modify or limit the authority of the Public Utilities Commission to erect or maintain, or cause to be erected and maintained, signs, signals or other traffic control devices as authorized by law.

(Enacted by Stats. 1959, Ch. 3.)

Chapter 3. Driving, Overtaking, and Passing

(Chapter 3 enacted by Stats. 1959, Ch. 3.)

Article 1. Driving on Right Side

(Article 1 enacted by Stats. 1959, Ch. 3.)

21650. Upon all highways, a vehicle shall be driven upon the right half of the roadway, except as follows:

(a) When overtaking and passing another vehicle proceeding in the same direction under the rules governing that movement.

(b) When placing a vehicle in a lawful position for, and when the vehicle is lawfully making, a left turn.

(c) When the right half of a roadway is closed to traffic under construction or repair.

(d) Upon a roadway restricted to one-way traffic.

(e) When the roadway is not of sufficient width.

(f) When the vehicle is necessarily traveling so slowly as to impede the normal movement of traffic, that portion of the highway adjacent to the right edge of the roadway may be utilized temporarily when in a condition permitting safe operation.

(g) This section does not prohibit the operation of bicycles on any shoulder of a highway, on any sidewalk, on any bicycle path within a highway, or along any crosswalk or bicycle path crossing, where the operation is not otherwise prohibited by this code or local ordinance.

(h) This section does not prohibit the operation of a transit bus on the shoulder of a state highway in conjunction with the implementation of a program authorized pursuant to Section 148.1 of the Streets and Highways Code on state highways within the areas served by the transit services of the Monterey-Salinas Transit District or the Santa Cruz Metropolitan Transit District.

(Amended by Stats. 2013, Ch. 426, Sec. 2. (AB 946) Effective January 1, 2014.)

21650.1. A bicycle operated on a roadway, or the shoulder of a highway, shall be operated in the same direction as vehicles are required to be driven upon the roadway.

(Added by Stats. 1988, Ch. 58, Sec. 2.)

21651. (a) Whenever a highway has been divided into two or more roadways by means of intermittent barriers or by means of a dividing section of not less than two feet in width, either unpaved or delineated by curbs, double-parallel lines, or other markings on the roadway, it is unlawful to do either of the following:

(1) To drive any vehicle over, upon, or across the dividing section.

(2) To make any left, semicircular, or U-turn with the vehicle on the divided highway, except through an opening in the barrier designated and intended by public authorities for the use of vehicles or through a plainly marked opening in the dividing section.

(b) It is unlawful to drive any vehicle upon a highway, except to the right of an intermittent barrier or a dividing section which separates two or more opposing lanes of traffic. Except as otherwise provided in subdivision (c), a violation of this subdivision is a misdemeanor.

(c) Any willful violation of subdivision (b) which results in injury to, or death of, a person shall be punished by imprisonment pursuant to subdivision (h) of Section 1170 of the Penal Code, or imprisonment in a county jail for a period of not more than six months.

(Amended by Stats. 2011, Ch. 15, Sec. 608. (AB 109) Effective April 4, 2011. Operative October 1, 2011, by Sec. 636 of Ch. 15, as amended by Stats. 2011, Ch. 39, Sec. 68.)

21652. When any service road has been constructed on or along any public highway and the main thoroughfare of the highway has been separated from the service road, it is unlawful for any person to drive any vehicle into the main thoroughfare from the service road or from the main thoroughfare into the service road except through an opening in the dividing curb, section, separation, or line.

(Amended by Stats. 1963, Ch. 335.)

21654. (a) Notwithstanding the prima facie speed limits, any vehicle proceeding upon a highway at a speed less than the normal speed of traffic moving in the same direction at such time shall be driven in the right-hand lane for traffic or as close as practicable to the right-hand edge or curb, except when overtaking and passing another vehicle proceeding in the same direction or when preparing for a left turn at an intersection or into a private road or driveway.

(b) If a vehicle is being driven at a speed less than the normal speed of traffic moving in the same direction at such time, and is not being driven in the right-hand lane for traffic or as close as practicable to the right-hand edge or curb, it shall constitute prima facie evidence that the driver is operating the vehicle in violation of subdivision (a) of this section.

(c) The Department of Transportation, with respect to state highways, and local authorities, with respect to highways under their jurisdiction, may place and maintain upon highways official signs directing slow-moving traffic to use the right-hand traffic lane except when overtaking and passing another vehicle or preparing for a left turn.

(Amended by Stats. 1974, Ch. 545.)

21655. (a) Whenever the Department of Transportation or local authorities with respect to highways under their respective jurisdictions determines upon the basis of an engineering and traffic investigation that the designation of a specific lane or lanes for the travel of vehicles required to travel at reduced speeds would facilitate the safe and orderly movement of traffic, the department or local authority may designate a specific lane or lanes for the travel of vehicles which are subject to the provisions of Section 22406 and shall erect signs at reasonable intervals giving notice thereof.

(b) Any trailer bus, except as provided in Section 21655.5, and any vehicle subject to the provisions of Section 22406 shall be driven in the lane or lanes designated pursuant to subdivision (a) whenever signs have been erected giving notice of that designation. Except as otherwise provided in this subdivision, when a specific lane or lanes have not been so designated, any of those vehicles shall be driven in the right-hand lane for traffic or as close as practicable to the right edge or curb. If, however, a specific lane or lanes have not been designated on a divided highway having four or more clearly marked lanes for traffic in one direction, any of those vehicles may also be driven in the lane to the immediate left of that right-hand lane, unless otherwise prohibited under this code.

When overtaking and passing another vehicle proceeding in the same direction, the driver shall use either the designated lane, the lane to the immediate left of the right-hand lane, or the right-hand lane for traffic as permitted under this code.

This subdivision does not apply to a driver who is preparing for a left- or right-hand turn or who is entering into or exiting from a highway or to a driver who must necessarily drive in a lane other than the right-hand lane to continue on his or her intended route.

(Amended by Stats. 1988, Ch. 843, Sec. 4.)

21655.1. (a) A person shall not operate a motor vehicle on a portion of a highway that has been designated as a transit-only traffic lane except in compliance with the directions of a peace officer or official traffic control device.

(b) This section does not apply to a driver who is required to enter a lane designated as a transit-only traffic lane in order to make a right turn or a left turn in a location where there is no left-turn lane for motorists, or who is entering into or exiting from a highway, unless there are signs prohibiting turns across the lane or the lane is delineated by a physical separation, including, but not limited to, a curb, fence, landscaping, or other barrier.

(c) (1) The agency with jurisdiction over the highway or a public transit agency shall place and maintain, or cause to be placed and maintained, signs and other official traffic control devices, as necessary, indicating that a portion of a highway has been designated as a transit-only traffic lane for the exclusive use of public transit buses and other vehicles designated by a local authority or the Department of Transportation and to advise motorists of the hours of operation of the lane as a transit-only traffic lane.

(2) A public transit agency placing and maintaining signs and other official traffic control devices pursuant to paragraph (1) shall do so with the agreement of the agency with jurisdiction over the highway.

(d) For purposes of this section, "transit-only traffic lane" shall have the same meaning as that term is defined in Section 40240.

(Amended by Stats. 2023, Ch. 672, Sec. 1. (AB 971) Effective January 1, 2024.)

21655.5. (a) The Department of Transportation and local authorities, with respect to highways under their respective jurisdictions, may authorize or permit exclusive or preferential use of highway lanes for high-occupancy vehicles. Prior to establishing the lanes, competent engineering estimates shall be made of the effect of the lanes on safety, congestion, and highway capacity.

(b) The Department of Transportation and local authorities, with respect to highways under their respective jurisdictions, shall place and maintain, or cause to be placed and maintained, signs and other official traffic control devices to designate the exclusive or preferential lanes, to advise motorists of the applicable vehicle occupancy levels, and, except where ramp metering and bypass lanes are regulated with the activation of traffic signals, to advise motorists of the hours of high-occupancy vehicle usage. A person shall not drive a vehicle upon those lanes except in conformity with the instructions imparted by the official traffic control devices. A motorcycle, a mass transit vehicle, a blood transport vehicle that is clearly and identifiably marked as such on all sides of the vehicle, or a paratransit vehicle that is clearly and identifiably marked on all sides of the vehicle with the name of the paratransit provider may be operated upon those exclusive or preferential use lanes unless specifically prohibited by a traffic control device.

(c) When responding to an existing emergency or breakdown in which a mass transit vehicle is blocking an exclusive or preferential use lane, a clearly marked mass transit vehicle, mass transit supervisor's vehicle, or mass transit maintenance vehicle that is responding to the emergency or breakdown may be operated in the segment of the exclusive or preferential use lane being blocked by the mass transit vehicle, regardless of the number of persons in the vehicle responding to the emergency or breakdown, if both vehicles are owned or operated by the same agency, and that agency provides public mass transit services.

(d) For purposes of this section, the following definitions apply:

(1) "Blood transport vehicle" means a vehicle owned and operated by the American Red Cross or a blood bank that is transporting blood between collection points and hospitals or storage centers.

(2) "Mass transit vehicle" means a transit bus regularly used to transport paying passengers in mass transit service.

(3) "Paratransit vehicle" as defined in Section 462.

(e) It is the intent of the Legislature, in amending this section, to stimulate and encourage the development of ways and means of relieving traffic congestion on California highways and, at the same time, to encourage individual citizens to pool their vehicular resources and thereby conserve fuel and lessen emission of air pollutants.

(f) The provisions of this section regarding mass transit vehicles and paratransit vehicles shall only apply if the Director of Transportation determines that the application will not subject the state to a reduction in the amount of federal aid for highways.

(g) The authority for a blood transport vehicle to use exclusive or preferential lanes in accordance with subdivision (b) shall only be operative under either of the following circumstances:

(1) The Director of Transportation determines that the use of those lanes by those vehicles will not cause a reduction of federal aid funds for highways or otherwise be inconsistent with federal law or regulations, or with any agreement between the state and a federal agency or department, and the director posts that determination on the Department of Transportation's Internet Web site.

(2) The Federal Highway Administration of the United States Department of Transportation, upon the request of the director, makes that determination and the director posts the determination on the Department of Transportation's Internet Web site.

(Amended by Stats. 2017, Ch. 392, Sec. 2 (SB 406) Effective January 1, 2018.)

21655.6. (a) Whenever the Department of Transportation authorizes or permits exclusive or preferential use of highway lanes for high-occupancy vehicles on any highway located within the territory of a transportation planning agency, as defined in Section 99214 of the Public Utilities Code, or a county transportation commission, the department shall obtain the approval of the transportation planning agency or county transportation commission prior to establishing the exclusive or preferential use of the highway lanes.

(b) If the department authorizes or permits additional exclusive or preferential use of highway lanes for high-occupancy vehicles on that portion of State Highway Route 101 located within the boundaries of the City of Los Angeles, the department shall obtain the approval of the Los Angeles County Transportation Commission by at least a two-thirds majority vote of the entire membership eligible to vote prior to establishing the additional exclusion or preferential use of the highway lanes.

(c) If the department restricts or requires the restriction of the use of any lane on any federal-aid highway in the unincorporated areas of Alameda County to high-occupancy vehicles, the Metropolitan Transportation Commission shall review the use patterns of those lanes and shall determine if congestion relief is being efficiently achieved by the creation of the high-occupancy vehicle lanes. The commission shall report its findings and recommendations in its HOV Master Plan Update for the San Francisco Bay area no later than two years after those high-occupancy vehicle lanes become operational.

(Amended by Stats. 1998, Ch. 653, Sec. 1. Effective January 1, 1999.)

21655.7. A local authority, with respect to any highway under its jurisdiction, may authorize or permit a portion of the highway to be used exclusively for a public mass transit guideway.

(Added by Stats. 1981, Ch. 1055, Sec. 12.)

21655.8. (a) Except as required under subdivision (b), when exclusive or preferential use lanes for high-occupancy vehicles are established pursuant to Section 21655.5 and double parallel solid lines are in place to the right thereof, no person driving a vehicle may cross over these double lines to enter into or exit from the exclusive or preferential use lanes, and entrance or exit may be made only in areas designated for these purposes or where a single broken line is in place to the right of the exclusive or preferential use lanes.

(b) Upon the approach of an authorized emergency vehicle displaying a red light or siren, as specified in Section 21806, a person driving a vehicle in an exclusive or preferential use lane shall exit that lane immediately upon determining that the exit can be accomplished with reasonable safety.

(c) Raised pavement markers may be used to simulate painted lines described in this section.

(Amended by Stats. 1996, Ch. 1154, Sec. 67. Effective September 30, 1996.)

21655.9. (a) (1) Whenever the Department of Transportation or a local authority authorizes or permits exclusive or preferential use of highway lanes or highway access ramps for high-occupancy vehicles pursuant to Section 21655.5, the use of those lanes or ramps shall also be extended to vehicles that are issued distinctive decals, labels, or other identifiers pursuant to Section 5205.5 regardless of vehicle occupancy or ownership.

(2) A local authority during periods of peak congestion shall suspend for a lane the access privileges extended pursuant to paragraph (1) for those vehicles issued distinctive decals, labels, or other identifiers pursuant to Section 5205.5, if a periodic review of lane performance by that local authority discloses both of the following factors regarding the lane:

(A) The lane, or a portion of the lane, exceeds a level of service C, as described in subdivision (b) of Section 65089 of the Government Code.

(B) The operation or projected operation of vehicles in the lane, or a portion of the lane, will significantly increase congestion.

(b) A person shall not drive a vehicle described in subdivision (a) of Section 5205.5 with a single occupant upon a high-occupancy vehicle lane pursuant to this section unless the decal, label, or other identifier issued pursuant to Section 5205.5 is properly displayed on the vehicle, and the vehicle registration described in Section 5205.5 is with the vehicle.

(c) A person shall not operate or own a vehicle displaying a decal, label, or other identifier, as described in Section 5205.5, if that decal, label, or identifier was not issued for that vehicle pursuant to Section 5205.5. A violation of this subdivision is a misdemeanor.

(d) If the provisions in Section 5205.5 authorizing the department to issue decals, labels, or other identifiers to hybrid and alternative fuel vehicles become inoperative, vehicles displaying those decals, labels, or other identifiers shall not access high-occupancy vehicle lanes without meeting the occupancy requirements otherwise applicable to those lanes.

(e) (1) This section shall become inoperative on the date the federal authorization pursuant to Section 166 of Title 23 of the United States Code expires, or the date the Secretary of State receives the notice described in subdivision (i) of Section 5205.5, whichever occurs first.

(2) With respect to a vehicle described in subparagraph (B) of paragraph (1) of subdivision (a) of Section 5205.5, this section shall become inoperative on January 1, 2019.

(f) (1) The Department of Transportation shall prepare and submit a report to the Legislature on or before December 1, 2017, on the degradation status of high-occupancy vehicle lanes on the state highway system.

(2) The requirement that a report be submitted pursuant to paragraph (1) shall be inoperative on December 1, 2021, pursuant to Section 10231.5 of the Government Code.

(3) A report submitted pursuant to paragraph (1) shall be submitted in compliance with Section 9795 of the Government Code.

(g) This section shall remain in effect only until January 1, 2027, and as of that date is repealed.

(Amended by Stats. 2024, Ch. 414, Sec. 3. (AB 2678) Effective January 1, 2025. Conditionally inoperative as provided in subd. (e). Repealed as of January 1, 2027, by its own provisions.)

21655.10. (a) The Department of Transportation and local authorities, with respect to highways under their respective jurisdictions, may authorize or temporarily permit exclusive or preferential use of high-occupancy vehicle lanes, high-occupancy toll lanes, and other lanes, regardless of the number of passengers in the vehicle, for the games route network if the vehicle displays a distinctive decal, label, or other identifier issued by the Olympic and Paralympic Games organizers that clearly distinguishes the vehicle is being operated on the games route network during an Olympic and Paralympic Games period. A person shall not drive a vehicle upon those lanes except in conformity with the instructions imparted by the official traffic control devices. Exclusive or preferential use of those lanes shall not exclude emergency response and public safety vehicles.

(b) The design of the decal, label, or other identifier issued by the Olympic and Paralympic Games organizers shall be approved by the Department of Transportation, in collaboration with the Department of the California Highway Patrol, and shall display a serial number or identification number to verify that the decal, label, or other identifier is being used on the vehicle for which it is issued.

(c) For purposes of this section:

(1) "Games route network" means dedicated traffic lanes for travel used during the Olympic and Paralympic Games Period, as identified by the Department of Transportation or a local authority, in consultation with the Olympic and Paralympic Games organizers.

(2) "Olympic and Paralympic Games period" means the days identified by the Department of Transportation for which the games route network shall be operable.

(d) This section shall remain in effect only until January 1, 2029, and as of that date is repealed.

(Added by Stats. 2025, Ch. 16, Sec. 8. (SB 128) Effective June 27, 2025. Repealed as of January 1, 2029, by its own provisions.)

21656. On a two-lane highway where passing is unsafe because of traffic in the opposite direction or other conditions, any vehicle proceeding upon the highway at a speed less than the normal speed of traffic moving in the same direction at that time, behind which five or more vehicles are formed in line, shall turn off the roadway at the nearest place designated as a turnout by signs erected by the authority having jurisdiction over the highway, or wherever sufficient area for a safe turnout exists, in order to permit the vehicles following it to proceed.

(Amended by Stats. 2015, Ch. 265, Sec. 1. (AB 208) Effective January 1, 2016.)

21657. The authorities in charge of any highway may designate any highway, roadway, part of a roadway, or specific lanes upon which vehicular traffic shall proceed in one direction at all or such times as shall be indicated by official traffic control devices. When a roadway has been so designated, a vehicle shall be driven only in the direction designated at all or such times as shall be indicated by traffic control devices.

(Amended by Stats. 1969, Ch. 136.)

21658. Whenever any roadway has been divided into two or more clearly marked lanes for traffic in one direction, the following rules apply:

(a) A vehicle shall be driven as nearly as practical entirely within a single lane and shall not be moved from the lane until such movement can be made with reasonable safety.

(b) Official signs may be erected directing slow-moving traffic to use a designated lane or allocating specified lanes to traffic moving in the same direction, and drivers of vehicles shall obey the directions of the traffic device.

(Amended by Stats. 1975, Ch. 450.)

21658.1. (a) For the purposes of this section, "lane splitting" means driving a motorcycle, as defined in Section 400, that has two wheels in contact with the ground, between rows of stopped or moving vehicles in the same lane, including on both divided and undivided streets, roads, or highways.

(b) The Department of the California Highway Patrol may develop educational guidelines relating to lane splitting in a manner that would ensure the safety of the motorcyclist and the drivers and passengers of the surrounding vehicles.

(c) In developing guidelines pursuant to this section, the department shall consult with agencies and organizations with an interest in road safety and motorcyclist behavior, including, but not limited to, all of the following:

(1) The Department of Motor Vehicles.

(2) The Department of Transportation.

(3) The Office of Traffic Safety.

(4) A motorcycle organization focused on motorcyclist safety.

(Added by Stats. 2016, Ch. 141, Sec. 1. (AB 51) Effective January 1, 2017.)

21659. Upon a roadway which is divided into three lanes a vehicle shall not be driven in the extreme left lane at any time, nor in the center lane except when overtaking and passing another vehicle where the roadway ahead is clearly visible and the center lane is clear of traffic within a safe distance, or in preparation for a left turn, or where the center lane is at the time allocated exclusively to traffic moving in the direction the vehicle is proceeding and is signposted to give notice of such allocation. This section does not apply upon a one-way roadway.

(Enacted by Stats. 1959, Ch. 3.)

21660. Drivers of vehicles proceeding in opposite directions shall pass each other to the right, and, except when a roadway has been divided into traffic lanes, each driver shall give to the other at least one-half of the main traveled portion of the roadway whenever possible.

(Enacted by Stats. 1959, Ch. 3.)

21661. Whenever upon any grade the width of the roadway is insufficient to permit the passing of vehicles approaching from opposite directions at the point of meeting, the driver of the vehicle descending the grade shall yield the right-of-way to the vehicle ascending the grade and shall, if necessary, back his vehicle to a place in the highway where it is possible for the vehicles to pass.

(Enacted by Stats. 1959, Ch. 3.)

21662. The driver of a motor vehicle traveling through defiles or canyons or upon mountain highways shall hold the motor vehicle under control at all times and shall do the following when applicable:

(a) If the roadway has no marked centerline, the driver shall drive as near the right-hand edge of the roadway as is reasonably possible.

(b) If the roadway has insufficient width to permit a motor vehicle to be driven entirely to the right of the center of the roadway, the driver shall give audible warning with the horn of the motor vehicle upon approaching any curve where the view is obstructed within a distance of 200 feet along the highway.

(Amended by Stats. 1984, Ch. 462, Sec. 2.)

21663. Except as expressly permitted pursuant to this code, including Sections 21100.4 and 21114.5, no person shall operate or move a motor vehicle upon a sidewalk except as may be necessary to enter or leave adjacent property.

(Amended by Stats. 1996, Ch. 124, Sec. 126. Effective January 1, 1997.)

21664. It is unlawful for the driver of any vehicle to enter or exit any freeway which has full control of access and no crossings at grade, except upon a designated on ramp with respect to entering the freeway or a designated off ramp with respect to exiting the freeway.

(Amended by Stats. 1988, Ch. 765, Sec. 2.)

Article 2. Additional Driving Rules

(Article 2 enacted by Stats. 1959, Ch. 3.)

21700. No person shall drive a vehicle when it is so loaded, or when there are in the front seat such number of persons as to obstruct the view of the driver to the front or sides of the vehicle or as to interfere with the driver's control over the driving mechanism of the vehicle.

(Amended by Stats. 1965, Ch. 1500.)

21700.5. No person shall knowingly drive a bus within the City of San Diego which is transporting any public or private school pupil who is enrolled in kindergarten or any of grades 1 to 12, inclusive, to or from a public or private school, unless every such pupil is seated in a seat.

(Added by Stats. 1972, Ch. 1124.)

21701. No person shall wilfully interfere with the driver of a vehicle or with the mechanism thereof in such manner as to affect the driver's control of the vehicle. The provisions of this section shall not apply to a drivers' license examiner or other employee of the Department of Motor Vehicles when conducting the road or driving test of an applicant for a driver's license nor to a person giving instruction as a part of a course in driver training conducted by a public school, educational institution or a driver training school licensed by the Department of Motor Vehicles.

(Enacted by Stats. 1959, Ch. 3.)

21702. (a) No person shall drive upon any highway any vehicle designed or used for transporting persons for compensation for more than 10 consecutive hours nor for more than 10 hours spread over a total of 15 consecutive hours. Thereafter, such person shall not drive any such vehicle until eight consecutive hours have elapsed.

Regardless of aggregate driving time, no driver shall drive for more than 10 hours in any 24-hour period unless eight consecutive hours off duty have elapsed.

(b) No person shall drive upon any highway any vehicle designed or used for transporting merchandise, freight, materials or other property for more than 12 consecutive hours nor for more than 12 hours spread over a total of 15 consecutive hours. Thereafter, such person shall not drive any such vehicle until eight consecutive hours have elapsed.

Regardless of aggregate driving time, no driver shall drive for more than 12 hours in any 24-hour period unless eight consecutive hours off duty have elapsed.

(c) This section does not apply in any case of casualty or unavoidable accident or an act of God.

(d) In computing the number of hours under this section, any time spent by a person in driving such a vehicle outside this state shall, upon the vehicle entering this state, be included.

(e) Any person who violates any provision of this section is guilty of a misdemeanor and is punishable by a fine of not less than one hundred dollars ($100) nor more than one thousand dollars ($1,000) for each offense.

(f) This section shall not apply to the driver of a vehicle which is subject to the provisions of Section 34500.

(Amended by Stats. 1983, Ch. 1092, Sec. 391. Effective September 27, 1983. Operative January 1, 1984, by Sec. 427 of Ch. 1092.)

21703. The driver of a motor vehicle shall not follow another vehicle more closely than is reasonable and prudent, having due regard for the speed of such vehicle and the traffic upon, and the condition of, the roadway.

(Enacted by Stats. 1959, Ch. 3.)

21704. (a) The driver of any motor vehicle subject to the speed restriction of Section 22406 that is operated outside of a business or residence district, shall keep the vehicle he is driving at a distance of not less than 300 feet to the rear of any other motor vehicle subject to such speed restriction which is preceding it.

(b) The provisions of this section shall not prevent overtaking and passing nor shall they apply upon a highway with two or more lanes for traffic in the direction of travel.

(Amended by Stats. 1969, Ch. 226.)

21705. Motor vehicles being driven outside of a business or residence district in a caravan or motorcade, whether or not towing other vehicles, shall be so operated as to allow sufficient space and in no event less than 100 feet between each vehicle or combination of vehicles so as to enable any other vehicle to overtake or pass.

(Enacted by Stats. 1959, Ch. 3.)

21706. No motor vehicle, except an authorized emergency vehicle, shall follow within 300 feet of any authorized emergency vehicle being operated under the provisions of Section 21055.

This section shall not apply to a police or traffic officer when serving

as an escort within the purview of Section 21057.
(Amended by Stats. 1972, Ch. 46.)

21706.5. (a) For purposes of this section, the following terms have the following meanings:

(1) "Emergency incident zone" means an area on a freeway that is within 500 feet of, and in the direction of travel of, a stationary authorized emergency vehicle that has its emergency lights activated. Traffic in the opposite lanes of the freeway is not in an "emergency incident zone."

(2) "Operate a vehicle in an unsafe manner" means operating a motor vehicle in violation of an act made unlawful under this division, except a violation of Section 21809.

(b) A person shall not operate a vehicle in an unsafe manner within an emergency incident zone.
(Added by Stats. 2006, Ch. 375, Sec. 1. Effective January 1, 2007.)

21707. No motor vehicle, except an authorized emergency vehicle or a vehicle of a duly authorized member of a fire or police department, shall be operated within the block wherein an emergency situation responded to by any fire department vehicle exists, except that in the event the nearest intersection to the emergency is more than 300 feet therefrom, this section shall prohibit operation of vehicles only within 300 feet of the emergency, unless directed to do so by a member of the fire department or police department, sheriff, deputy sheriff, or member of the California Highway Patrol. The emergency shall be deemed to have ceased to exist when the official of the fire department in charge at the scene of the emergency shall so indicate. Officials of the fire department or police department or the Department of the California Highway Patrol who are present shall make every effort to prevent the closing off entirely of congested highway traffic passing the scene of any such emergency.
(Enacted by Stats. 1959, Ch. 3.)

21708. No person shall drive or propel any vehicle or conveyance upon, over, or across, or in any manner damage any fire hose or chemical hose used by or under the supervision and control of any organized fire department. However, any vehicle may cross a hose provided suitable jumpers or other appliances are installed to protect the hose.
(Enacted by Stats. 1959, Ch. 3.)

21709. No vehicle shall at any time be driven through or within a safety zone.
(Enacted by Stats. 1959, Ch. 3.)

21710. The driver of a motor vehicle when traveling on down grade upon any highway shall not coast with the gears of such vehicle in neutral.
(Enacted by Stats. 1959, Ch. 3.)

21711. No person shall operate a train of vehicles when any vehicle being towed whips or swerves from side to side or fails to follow substantially in the path of the towing vehicle.
(Amended by Stats. 1959, Ch. 44.)

21712. (a) A person driving a motor vehicle shall not knowingly permit a person to ride on a vehicle or upon a portion of a vehicle that is not designed or intended for the use of passengers.

(b) A person shall not ride on a vehicle or upon a portion of a vehicle that is not designed or intended for the use of passengers.

(c) A person driving a motor vehicle shall not knowingly permit a person to ride in the trunk of that motor vehicle.

(d) A person shall not ride in the trunk of a motor vehicle.

(e) A person violating subdivision (c) or (d) shall be punished as follows:

(1) By a fine of one hundred dollars ($100).

(2) For a second violation occurring within one year of a prior violation that resulted in a conviction, a fine of two hundred dollars ($200).

(3) For a third or a subsequent violation occurring within one year of two or more prior violations that resulted in convictions, a fine of two hundred fifty dollars ($250).

(f) Subdivisions (a) and (b) do not apply to an employee engaged in the necessary discharge of his or her duty or in the case of persons riding completely within or upon vehicle bodies in the space intended for a load on the vehicle.

(g) A person shall not drive a motor vehicle that is towing a trailer coach, camp trailer, or trailer carrying a vessel, containing a passenger, except when a trailer carrying or designed to carry a vessel is engaged in the launching or recovery of the vessel.

(h) A person shall not knowingly drive a motor vehicle that is towing a person riding upon a motorcycle, motorized bicycle, bicycle, coaster, roller skates, sled, skis, or toy vehicle.

(i) Subdivision (g) does not apply to a trailer coach that is towed with a fifth-wheel device if the trailer coach is equipped with safety glazing materials wherever glazing materials are used in windows or doors, with an audible or visual signaling device that a passenger inside the trailer coach can use to gain the attention of the motor vehicle driver, and with at least one unobstructed exit capable of being opened from both the interior and exterior of the trailer coach.
(Amended by Stats. 2006, Ch. 900, Sec. 2. Effective January 1, 2007.)

21713. No person shall operate on any highway any privately owned armored car unless a license to operate such car has first been obtained from the commissioner in accordance with Chapter 2.5 (commencing with Section 2500) of Division 2.

Violation of this section is a misdemeanor and upon conviction is punishable by a fine not exceeding one thousand dollars ($1,000) or by imprisonment in the county jail for not to exceed six months or by both such fine and imprisonment.
(Amended by Stats. 1983, Ch. 1092, Sec. 392. Effective September 27, 1983. Operative January 1, 1984, by Sec. 427 of Ch. 1092.)

21714. The driver of a vehicle described in subdivision (f) of Section 27803 shall not operate the vehicle in either of the following areas:

(a) On, or immediately adjacent to, the striping or other markers designating adjacent traffic lanes.

(b) Between two or more vehicles that are traveling in adjacent traffic lanes.
(Amended by Stats. 2008, Ch. 672, Sec. 2. Effective January 1, 2009.)

21715. (a) No passenger vehicle regardless of weight, or any other motor vehicle under 4,000 pounds unladen, shall draw or tow more than one vehicle in combination, except that an auxiliary dolly or tow dolly may be used with the towed vehicle.

(b) No motor vehicle under 4,000 pounds unladen shall tow any vehicle weighing 6,000 pounds or more gross.
(Amended by Stats. 1983, Ch. 708, Sec. 8.)

21716. Except as provided in Section 21115.1 and Chapter 6 (commencing with Section 1950) of Division 2.5 of the Streets and Highways Code, no person shall operate a golf cart on any highway except in a speed zone of 25 miles per hour or less.
(Amended (as amended by Stats. 1997, Ch. 536, Sec. 3) by Stats. 2000, Ch. 155, Sec. 2. Effective January 1, 2001.)

21717. Whenever it is necessary for the driver of a motor vehicle to cross a bicycle lane that is adjacent to his lane of travel to make a turn, the driver shall drive the motor vehicle into the bicycle lane prior to making the turn and shall make the turn pursuant to Section 22100.
(Added by Stats. 1976, Ch. 751.)

21718. (a) No person shall stop, park, or leave standing any vehicle upon a freeway which has full control of access and no crossings at grade except:

(1) When necessary to avoid injury or damage to persons or property.

(2) When required by law or in obedience to a peace officer or official traffic control device.

(3) When any person is actually engaged in maintenance or construction on freeway property or any employee of a public agency is actually engaged in the performance of official duties.

(4) When any vehicle is so disabled that it is impossible to avoid temporarily stopping and another vehicle has been summoned to render assistance to the disabled vehicle or driver of the disabled vehicle. This

paragraph applies when the vehicle summoned to render assistance is a vehicle owned by the donor of free emergency assistance that has been summoned by display upon or within a disabled vehicle of a placard or sign given to the driver of the disabled vehicle by the donor for the specific purpose of summoning assistance, other than towing service, from the donor.

(5) Where stopping, standing, or parking is specifically permitted. However, buses may not stop on freeways unless sidewalks are provided with shoulders of sufficient width to permit stopping without interfering with the normal movement of traffic and without the possibility of crossing over fast lanes to reach the bus stop.

(6) Where necessary for any person to report a traffic accident or other situation or incident to a peace officer or any person specified in paragraph (3), either directly or by means of an emergency telephone or similar device.

(7) When necessary for the purpose of rapid removal of impediments to traffic by the owner or operator of a tow truck operating under an agreement with the Department of the California Highway Patrol.

(b) A conviction of a violation of this section is a conviction involving the safe operation of a motor vehicle upon the highway if a notice to appear for the violation was issued by a peace officer described in Section 830.1 or 830.2 of the Penal Code.

(Added by Stats. 1997, Ch. 945, Sec. 17. Effective January 1, 1998.)

21719. (a) Notwithstanding any other law, in the event of an emergency occurring on a roadway that requires the rapid removal of impediments to traffic or the rendering of assistance to a disabled vehicle obstructing a roadway, a tow truck driver who is operating under an agreement with the law enforcement agency responsible for investigating traffic collisions on the roadway, summoned by the owner or operator of a vehicle involved in a collision or that is otherwise disabled on the roadway, or operating pursuant to subdivision (a) of Section 2430.1 may utilize the center median or right shoulder of a roadway if all of the following conditions are met:

(1) A peace officer employed by the investigating law enforcement agency is at the scene of the roadway obstruction and has determined that the obstruction has caused an unnecessary delay to motorists using the roadway.

(2) A peace officer employed by the investigating law enforcement agency has determined that a tow truck can provide emergency roadside assistance by removing the disabled vehicle and gives explicit permission to the tow truck driver allowing the utilization of the center median or right shoulder of the roadway.

(3) The tow truck is not operated on the center median or right shoulder at a speed greater than what is reasonable or prudent having due regard for weather, visibility, the traffic on, and the surface and width of, the roadway, and in no event at a speed that endangers the safety of persons or property.

(4) The tow truck displays flashing amber warning lamps to the front, rear, and both sides while driving in the center median or right shoulder of a roadway pursuant to this section.

(b) For purposes of this section, "utilize the center median" includes making a U-turn across the center median.

(Amended by Stats. 2016, Ch. 208, Sec. 14. (AB 2906) Effective January 1, 2017.)

21720. A pocket bike shall not be operated on a sidewalk, roadway, or any other part of a highway, or on a bikeway, bicycle path or trail, equestrian trail, hiking or recreational trail, or on public lands open to off-highway motor vehicle use.

(Added by Stats. 2005, Ch. 323, Sec. 3. Effective January 1, 2006.)

21721. (a) A peace officer, as defined in Chapter 4.5 (commencing with Section 830) of Title 3 of Part 2 of the Penal Code, may cause the removal and seizure of a pocket bike, upon the notice to appear for a violation of Section 21720. A pocket bike so seized shall be held for a minimum of 48 hours.

(b) A violator of this section shall be responsible for all costs associated with the removal, seizure, and storage of the pocket bike.

(c) A city, county, or city and county may adopt a regulation, ordinance, or resolution imposing charges equal to its administrative costs relating to the removal, seizure, and storage costs of a pocket bike. The charges shall not exceed the actual costs incurred for the expenses directly related to removing, seizing, and storing a pocket bike.

(d) An agency shall release a seized pocket bike to the owner, violator, or the violator's agent after 48 hours, if all of the following conditions are met:

(1) The violator or authorized agent's request is made during normal business hours.

(2) The applicable removal, seizure, and storage costs have been paid by the owner, or any other responsible party.

(Added by Stats. 2005, Ch. 323, Sec. 4. Effective January 1, 2006.)

Article 3. Overtaking and Passing

(Article 3 enacted by Stats. 1959, Ch. 3.)

21750. (a) The driver of a vehicle overtaking another vehicle proceeding in the same direction shall pass to the left at a safe distance without interfering with the safe operation of the overtaken vehicle, subject to the limitations and exceptions set forth in this article.

(b) This section shall become operative on September 16, 2014.

(Repealed (in Sec. 1) and added by Stats. 2013, Ch. 331, Sec. 2. (AB 1371) Effective January 1, 2014. Section operative September 16, 2014, by its own provisions.)

21751. On a two-lane highway, no vehicle shall be driven to the left side of the center of the roadway in overtaking and passing another vehicle proceeding in the same direction unless the left side is clearly visible and free of oncoming traffic for a sufficient distance ahead to permit such overtaking and passing to be completely made without interfering with the safe operation of any vehicle approaching from the opposite direction.

(Amended by Stats. 1973, Ch. 50.)

21752. No vehicle shall be driven to the left side of the roadway under the following conditions:

(a) When approaching or upon the crest of a grade or a curve in the highway where the driver's view is obstructed within such distance as to create a hazard in the event another vehicle might approach from the opposite direction.

(b) When the view is obstructed upon approaching within 100 feet of any bridge, viaduct, or tunnel.

(c) When approaching within 100 feet of or when traversing any railroad grade crossing.

(d) When approaching within 100 feet of or when traversing any intersection.

This section shall not apply upon a one-way roadway.

(Amended by Stats. 2000, Ch. 596, Sec. 7. Effective January 1, 2001.)

21753. Except when passing on the right is permitted, the driver of an overtaken vehicle shall safely move to the right-hand side of the highway in favor of the overtaking vehicle after an audible signal or a momentary flash of headlights by the overtaking vehicle, and shall not increase the speed of his or her vehicle until completely passed by the overtaking vehicle. This section does not require the driver of an overtaken vehicle to drive on the shoulder of the highway in order to allow the overtaking vehicle to pass.

(Amended by Stats. 1999, Ch. 724, Sec. 40. Effective January 1, 2000.)

21754. The driver of a vehicle may overtake and pass to the right of another vehicle only under the following conditions:

(a) When the vehicle overtaken is making or about to make a left turn.

(b) Upon a highway within a business or residence district with unobstructed pavement of sufficient width for two or more lines of moving vehicles in the direction of travel.

(c) Upon any highway outside of a business or residence district with unobstructed pavement of sufficient width and clearly marked for two or more lines of moving traffic in the direction of travel.

(d) Upon a one-way street.

(e) Upon a highway divided into two roadways where traffic is restricted to one direction upon each of such roadways.

The provisions of this section shall not relieve the driver of a slow moving vehicle from the duty to drive as closely as practicable to the right hand edge of the roadway.

(Amended by Stats. 2010, Ch. 491, Sec. 39. (SB 1318) Effective January 1, 2011.)

21755. (a) The driver of a vehicle may overtake and pass another vehicle upon the right only under conditions permitting that movement in safety. In no event shall that movement be made by driving off the paved or main-traveled portion of the roadway.

(b) This section does not prohibit the use of a bicycle in a bicycle lane or on a shoulder.

(Amended by Stats. 2010, Ch. 491, Sec. 40. (SB 1318) Effective January 1, 2011.)

21756. (a) The driver of a vehicle overtaking any interurban electric or streetcar stopped or about to stop for the purpose of receiving or discharging any passenger shall stop the vehicle to the rear of the nearest running board or door of such car and thereupon remain standing until all passengers have boarded the car or upon alighting have reached a place of safety, except as provided in subdivision (b) hereof.

(b) Where a safety zone has been established or at an intersection where traffic is controlled by an officer or a traffic control signal device, a vehicle need not be brought to a stop before passing any interurban electric or streetcar but may proceed past such car at a speed not greater than 10 miles per hour and with due caution for the safety of pedestrians.

(c) Whenever any trolley coach or bus has stopped at a safety zone to receive or discharge passengers, a vehicle may proceed past such trolley coach or bus at a speed not greater than 10 miles per hour.

(Amended by Stats. 1959, Ch. 969.)

21757. The driver of a vehicle shall not overtake and pass upon the left, nor shall any driver of a vehicle drive upon the left side of, any interurban electric or street car proceeding in the same direction whether the street car is actually in motion or temporarily at rest, except:

(a) When so directed by a police or traffic officer.

(b) When upon a one-way street.

(c) When upon a street where the tracks are so located as to prevent compliance with this section.

(Enacted by Stats. 1959, Ch. 3.)

21758. In the event any vehicle is being operated on any grade outside of a business or residence district at a speed of less than 20 miles per hour, no person operating any other motor vehicle shall attempt to overtake and pass such slow moving vehicle unless the overtaking vehicle is operated at a speed of at least 10 miles per hour in excess of the speed of the overtaken vehicle, nor unless the passing movement is completed within a total distance not greater than one-quarter of a mile.

(Enacted by Stats. 1959, Ch. 3.)

21759. The driver of any vehicle approaching any horse drawn vehicle, any ridden animal, or any livestock shall exercise proper control of his vehicle and shall reduce speed or stop as may appear necessary or as may be signalled or otherwise requested by any person driving, riding or in charge of the animal or livestock in order to avoid frightening and to safeguard the animal or livestock and to insure the safety of any person driving or riding the animal or in charge of the livestock.

(Enacted by Stats. 1959, Ch. 3.)

21760. (a) This section shall be known and may be cited as the Three Feet for Safety Act.

(b) The driver of a motor vehicle overtaking and passing a bicycle that is proceeding in the same direction on a highway shall pass in compliance with the requirements of this article applicable to overtaking and passing a vehicle, and shall do so at a safe distance that does not interfere with the safe operation of the overtaken bicycle, having due regard for the size and speed of the motor vehicle and the bicycle, traffic conditions, weather, visibility, and the surface and width of the highway.

(c) A driver of a motor vehicle shall not overtake or pass a bicycle proceeding in the same direction on a highway at a distance of less than three feet between any part of the motor vehicle and any part of the bicycle or its operator. The driver of a motor vehicle overtaking or passing a bicycle that is proceeding in the same direction and in the same lane of travel shall, if another lane of traffic proceeding in the same direction is available, make a lane change into another available lane with due regard for safety and traffic conditions, if practicable and not prohibited by law, before overtaking or passing the bicycle.

(d) If the driver of a motor vehicle is unable to comply with subdivision (c), due to traffic or roadway conditions, the driver shall slow to a speed that is reasonable and prudent, and may pass only when doing so would not endanger the safety of the operator of the bicycle, taking into account the size and speed of the motor vehicle and bicycle, traffic conditions, weather, visibility, and surface and width of the highway.

(e) (1) A violation of subdivision (b), (c), or (d) is an infraction punishable by a fine of thirty-five dollars ($35).

(2) If a collision occurs between a motor vehicle and a bicycle causing bodily injury to the operator of the bicycle, and the driver of the motor vehicle is found to be in violation of subdivision (b), (c), or (d), a two-hundred-twenty-dollar ($220) fine shall be imposed on that driver.

(Amended by Stats. 2022, Ch. 343, Sec. 6. (AB 1909) Effective January 1, 2023.)

21761. (a) The driver of a vehicle on a public street or highway approaching and overtaking a stopped waste service vehicle shall make a lane change into an available lane adjacent to the waste service vehicle and shall pass at a safe distance without interfering with the safe operation of the waste service vehicle, with due regard for safety and traffic conditions, if practicable and not prohibited by law.

(b) If the maneuver described in subdivision (a) would be unsafe or impractical, a driver approaching and overtaking a stopped waste service vehicle shall slow to a reasonable and prudent speed that is safe for existing weather, road, and vehicular or pedestrian traffic conditions.

(c) For purposes of this section, "waste service vehicle" means a refuse collection vehicle, including a vehicle collecting recyclables or yard waste that is used for curbside collection, and sewer and catch basin maintenance vehicles.

(d) The requirements in subdivisions (a) and (b) apply when both of the following circumstances exist:

(1) The waste service vehicle is readily identifiable as a waste service vehicle based on the vehicle configuration or markings on the vehicle.

(2) The waste service vehicle displays flashing amber lights.

(e) Subdivisions (a) and (b) do not apply to a waste service vehicle that is located on a private driveway or highway, when the waste service vehicle is not adjacent to the street or highway, or is separated from the street or highway by a protective physical barrier.

(f) This section shall be operative on and after January 1, 2020.

(Added by Stats. 2018, Ch. 710, Sec. 1. (AB 2115) Effective January 1, 2019. Section operative January 1, 2020, by its own provisions.)

Chapter 4. Right-of-Way

(Chapter 4 enacted by Stats. 1959, Ch. 3.)

21800. (a) The driver of a vehicle approaching an intersection shall yield the right-of-way to any vehicle which has entered the intersection from a different highway.

(b) (1) When two vehicles enter an intersection from different highways at the same time, the driver of the vehicle on the left shall yield the right-of-way to the vehicle on his or her immediate right, except that the driver of any vehicle on a terminating highway shall yield the right-of-way to any vehicle on the intersecting continuing highway.

(2) For the purposes of this section, "terminating highway" means a highway which intersects, but does not continue beyond the intersection, with another highway which does continue beyond the intersection.

(c) When two vehicles enter an intersection from different highways at the same time and the intersection is controlled from all directions by stop signs, the driver of the vehicle on the left shall yield the right-of-way to the vehicle on his or her immediate right.

(d) (1) The driver of any vehicle approaching an intersection which has official traffic control signals that are inoperative shall stop at the intersection, and may proceed with caution when it is safe to do so.

(2) When two vehicles enter an intersection from different highways at the same time, and the official traffic control signals for the intersection are inoperative, the driver of the vehicle on the left shall yield the right-of-way to the vehicle on his or her immediate right, except that the driver of any vehicle on a terminating highway shall yield the right-of-way to any vehicle on the intersecting continuing highway.

(e) This section does not apply to any of the following:

(1) Any intersection controlled by an official traffic control signal or yield right-of-way sign.

(2) Any intersection controlled by stop signs from less than all directions.

(3) When vehicles are approaching each other from opposite directions and the driver of one of the vehicles intends to make, or is making, a left turn.

(Amended by Stats. 2009, Ch. 200, Sec. 11. (SB 734) Effective January 1, 2010.)

21801. (a) The driver of a vehicle intending to turn to the left or to complete a U-turn upon a highway, or to turn left into public or private property, or an alley, shall yield the right-of-way to all vehicles approaching from the opposite direction which are close enough to constitute a hazard at any time during the turning movement, and shall continue to yield the right-of-way to the approaching vehicles until the left turn or U-turn can be made with reasonable safety.

(b) A driver having yielded as prescribed in subdivision (a), and having given a signal when and as required by this code, may turn left or complete a U-turn, and the drivers of vehicles approaching the intersection or the entrance to the property or alley from the opposite direction shall yield the right-of-way to the turning vehicle.

(Amended by Stats. 1993, Ch. 272, Sec. 40. Effective August 2, 1993.)

21802. (a) The driver of any vehicle approaching a stop sign at the entrance to, or within, an intersection shall stop as required by Section 22450. The driver shall then yield the right-of-way to any vehicles which have approached from another highway, or which are approaching so closely as to constitute an immediate hazard, and shall continue to yield the right-of-way to those vehicles until he or she can proceed with reasonable safety.

(b) A driver having yielded as prescribed in subdivision (a) may proceed to enter the intersection, and the drivers of all other approaching vehicles shall yield the right-of-way to the vehicle entering or crossing the intersection.

(c) This section does not apply where stop signs are erected upon all approaches to an intersection.

(Amended by Stats. 1988, Ch. 623, Sec. 3.)

21803. (a) The driver of any vehicle approaching any intersection which is controlled by a yield right-of-way sign shall, upon arriving at the sign, yield the right-of-way to any vehicles which have entered the intersection, or which are approaching on the intersecting highway close enough to constitute an immediate hazard, and shall continue to yield the right-of-way to those vehicles until he or she can proceed with reasonable safety.

(b) A driver having yielded as prescribed in subdivision (a) may proceed to enter the intersection, and the drivers of all other approaching vehicles shall yield the right-of-way to the vehicle entering or crossing the intersection.

(Amended by Stats. 1988, Ch. 623, Sec. 4.)

21804. (a) The driver of any vehicle about to enter or cross a highway from any public or private property, or from an alley, shall yield the right-of-way to all traffic, as defined in Section 620, approaching on the highway close enough to constitute an immediate hazard, and shall continue to yield the right-of-way to that traffic until he or she can proceed with reasonable safety.

(b) A driver having yielded as prescribed in subdivision (a) may proceed to enter or cross the highway, and the drivers of all other vehicles approaching on the highway shall yield the right-of-way to the vehicle entering or crossing the intersection.

(Amended by Stats. 1988, Ch. 623, Sec. 5.)

21805. (a) The Department of Transportation, and local authorities with respect to highways under their jurisdiction, may designate any intersection of a highway as a bridle path or equestrian crossing by erecting appropriate signs. The signs shall be erected on the highway at or near the approach to the intersection, and shall be of a type approved by the Department of Transportation. The signs shall indicate the crossing and any crossmarks, safety devices, or signals the authorities deem necessary to safeguard vehicular and equestrian traffic at the intersection.

(b) The driver of any vehicle shall yield the right-of-way to any horseback rider who is crossing the highway at any designated equestrian crossing which is marked by signs as prescribed in subdivision (a).

(c) Subdivision (b) does not relieve any horseback rider from the duty of using due care for his or her own safety. No horseback rider shall leave a curb or other place of safety and proceed suddenly into the path of a vehicle which is close enough to constitute an immediate hazard.

(Amended by Stats. 1988, Ch. 623, Sec. 6.)

21806. Upon the immediate approach of an authorized emergency vehicle which is sounding a siren and which has at least one lighted lamp exhibiting red light that is visible, under normal atmospheric conditions, from a distance of 1,000 feet to the front of the vehicle, the surrounding traffic shall, except as otherwise directed by a traffic officer, do the following:

(a) (1) Except as required under paragraph (2), the driver of every other vehicle shall yield the right-of-way and shall immediately drive to the right-hand edge or curb of the highway, clear of any intersection, and thereupon shall stop and remain stopped until the authorized emergency vehicle has passed.

(2) A person driving a vehicle in an exclusive or preferential use lane shall exit that lane immediately upon determining that the exit can be accomplished with reasonable safety.

(b) The operator of every street car shall immediately stop the street car, clear of any intersection, and remain stopped until the authorized emergency vehicle has passed.

(c) All pedestrians upon the highway shall proceed to the nearest curb or place of safety and remain there until the authorized emergency vehicle has passed.

(Amended by Stats. 1996, Ch. 1154, Sec. 68. Effective September 30, 1996.)

21807. The provisions of Section 21806 shall not operate to relieve the driver of an authorized emergency vehicle from the duty to drive with due regard for the safety of all persons and property.

(Added by Stats. 1961, Ch. 653.)

21809. (a) A person driving a vehicle on a highway approaching a stationary authorized emergency vehicle that is displaying emergency lights, a stationary tow truck that is displaying flashing amber warning lights, a stationary marked highway maintenance vehicle that is displaying flashing amber warning lights, or any other stationary vehicle displaying flashing hazard lights or another warning device, including, but not limited to, cones, flares, or retroreflective devices, shall approach with due caution and, before passing in a lane immediately adjacent to the authorized emergency vehicle, tow truck, highway maintenance vehicle, or any other vehicle, absent other direction by a peace officer, proceed to do one of the following:

(1) Make a lane change into an available lane not immediately adjacent to the authorized emergency vehicle that is displaying emergency lights, a stationary tow truck that is displaying flashing amber warning lights, a stationary marked highway maintenance vehicle that is displaying flashing amber warning lights, or any other stationary vehicle displaying flashing hazard lights or another warning device, including, but not limited to, cones, flares, or retroreflective devices, with due regard for safety and traffic conditions, if practicable and not prohibited by law.

(2) If the maneuver described in paragraph (1) would be unsafe or impracticable, slow to a reasonable and prudent speed that is safe for existing weather, road, and vehicular or pedestrian traffic conditions.

(b) A violation of subdivision (a) is an infraction, punishable by a fine of not more than fifty dollars ($50).

(c) The requirements of subdivision (a) do not apply if the stationary authorized emergency vehicle that is displaying emergency lights, the stationary tow truck that is displaying flashing amber warning lights, the stationary marked highway maintenance vehicle that is displaying flashing amber warning lights, or any other stationary vehicle displaying flashing hazard lights or another warning device, including, but not limited to, cones, flares, or retroreflective devices, is not adjacent to the highway or is separated from the highway by a protective physical barrier.

(d) For the purposes of this section, "highway maintenance vehicle" means a vehicle used for the maintenance of highways and roadways in this state and is either of the following:

(1) Owned or operated by the Department of Transportation, a county, or a municipality or other political subdivision of this state.

(2) Owned or operated by a contractor under contract with the Department of Transportation, a county, a municipality, or other political subdivision of this state to maintain highways, roadways, or both.

(Amended by Stats. 2025, Ch. 58, Sec. 1. (AB 390) Effective January 1, 2026.)

Chapter 5. Pedestrians' Rights and Duties

(Chapter 5 enacted by Stats. 1959, Ch. 3.)

21949. (a) The Legislature hereby finds and declares that it is the policy of the State of California that safe and convenient pedestrian travel and access, whether by foot, wheelchair, walker, or stroller, be provided to the residents of the state.

(b) In accordance with the policy declared under subdivision (a), it is the intent of the Legislature that all levels of government in the state, particularly the Department of Transportation, work to provide convenient and safe passage for pedestrians on and across all streets and highways, increase levels of walking and pedestrian travel, and reduce pedestrian fatalities and injuries.

(Added by Stats. 2000, Ch. 833, Sec. 6. Effective January 1, 2001.)

21949.5. (a) On or before January 1, 2028, the Commissioner of the California Highway Patrol, in consultation with the Institute of Transportation Studies at the University of California, shall submit a report to the Legislature regarding statewide pedestrian-related traffic crash data and any associated impacts to traffic safety, including an evaluation of whether and how the changes made to this chapter and Article 3 (commencing with Section 21450) of Chapter 2 by the act that added this section have impacted pedestrian safety.

(b) (1) A report to be submitted pursuant to subdivision (a) shall be submitted in compliance with Section 9795 of the Government Code.

(2) Pursuant to Section 10231.5 of the Government Code, this section is repealed on January 1, 2032.

(Added by Stats. 2022, Ch. 957, Sec. 7. (AB 2147) Effective January 1, 2023. Repealed as of January 1, 2032, by its own provisions.)

21950. (a) The driver of a vehicle shall yield the right-of-way to a pedestrian crossing the roadway within any marked crosswalk or within any unmarked crosswalk at an intersection, except as otherwise provided in this chapter.

(b) This section does not relieve a pedestrian from the duty of using due care for their safety. No pedestrian may suddenly leave a curb or other place of safety and walk or run into the path of a vehicle that is so close as to constitute an immediate hazard. No pedestrian may unnecessarily stop or delay traffic while in a marked or unmarked crosswalk.

(c) The driver of a vehicle approaching a pedestrian within any marked or unmarked crosswalk shall exercise all due care and shall reduce the speed of the vehicle or take any other action relating to the operation of the vehicle as necessary to safeguard the safety of the pedestrian.

(d) Subdivision (b) does not relieve a driver of a vehicle from the duty of exercising due care for the safety of any pedestrian within any marked crosswalk or within any unmarked crosswalk at an intersection.

(e) (1) A peace officer, as defined in Chapter 4.5 (commencing with Section 830) of Title 3 of Part 2 of the Penal Code, shall not stop a pedestrian for a violation of this section unless a reasonably careful person would realize there is an immediate danger of a collision with a moving vehicle or other device moving exclusively by human power.

(2) This subdivision does not relieve a pedestrian from the duty of using due care for their safety.

(3) This subdivision does not relieve a driver of a vehicle from the duty of exercising due care for the safety of any pedestrian within the roadway.

(Amended by Stats. 2022, Ch. 957, Sec. 8. (AB 2147) Effective January 1, 2023.)

21950.5. (a) An existing marked crosswalk may not be removed unless notice and opportunity to be heard is provided to the public not less than 30 days prior to the scheduled date of removal. In addition to any other public notice requirements, the notice of proposed removal shall be posted at the crosswalk identified for removal.

(b) The notice required by subdivision (a) shall include, but is not limited to, notification to the public of both of the following:

(1) That the public may provide input relating to the scheduled removal.

(2) The form and method of providing the input authorized by paragraph (1).

(Added by Stats. 2000, Ch. 833, Sec. 9. Effective January 1, 2001.)

21951. Whenever any vehicle has stopped at a marked crosswalk or at any unmarked crosswalk at an intersection to permit a pedestrian to cross the roadway the driver of any other vehicle approaching from the rear shall not overtake and pass the stopped vehicle.

(Enacted by Stats. 1959, Ch. 3.)

21952. The driver of any motor vehicle, prior to driving over or upon any sidewalk, shall yield the right-of-way to any pedestrian approaching thereon.

(Enacted by Stats. 1959, Ch. 3.)

21953. (a) Whenever any pedestrian crosses a roadway other than by means of a pedestrian tunnel or overhead pedestrian crossing, if a pedestrian tunnel or overhead crossing serves the place where the pedestrian is crossing the roadway, such pedestrian shall yield the right-of-way to all vehicles on the highway so near as to constitute an immediate hazard.

(b) This section shall not be construed to mean that a marked crosswalk, with or without a signal device, cannot be installed where a pedestrian tunnel or overhead crossing exists.

(c) (1) A peace officer, as defined in Chapter 4.5 (commencing with Section 830) of Title 3 of Part 2 of the Penal Code, shall not stop a pedestrian for a violation of subdivision (a) unless a reasonably careful person would realize there is an immediate danger of a collision with a moving vehicle or other device moving exclusively by human power.

(2) This subdivision does not relieve a pedestrian from the duty of using due care for their safety.

(3) This subdivision does not relieve a driver of a vehicle from the duty of exercising due care for the safety of any pedestrian within the roadway.

(Amended by Stats. 2022, Ch. 957, Sec. 9. (AB 2147) Effective January 1, 2023.)

21954. (a) Every pedestrian upon a roadway at any point other than within a marked crosswalk or within an unmarked crosswalk at an intersection shall yield the right-of-way to all vehicles upon the roadway so near as to constitute an immediate hazard.

(b) The provisions of this section shall not relieve the driver of a vehicle from the duty to exercise due care for the safety of any pedestrian upon a roadway.

(c) (1) A peace officer, as defined in Chapter 4.5 (commencing with Section 830) of Title 3 of Part 2 of the Penal Code, shall not stop a pedestrian for a violation of subdivision (a) unless a reasonably careful person would realize there is an immediate danger of a collision with a moving vehicle or other device moving exclusively by human power.

(2) This subdivision does not relieve a pedestrian from the duty of using due care for their safety.

(3) This subdivision does not relieve a driver of a vehicle from the duty of exercising due care for the safety of any pedestrian within the roadway.

(Amended by Stats. 2022, Ch. 957, Sec. 10. (AB 2147) Effective January 1, 2023.)

21955. (a) Between adjacent intersections controlled by traffic control signal devices or by police officers, pedestrians shall not cross the roadway at any place except in a crosswalk.

(b) (1) A peace officer, as defined in Chapter 4.5 (commencing with Section 830) of Title 3 of Part 2 of the Penal Code, shall not stop a pedestrian for a violation of subdivision (a) unless a reasonably careful person would realize there is an immediate danger of a collision with a moving vehicle or other device moving exclusively by human power.

(2) This subdivision does not relieve a pedestrian from the duty of using due care for their safety.

(3) This subdivision does not relieve a driver of a vehicle from the duty of exercising due care for the safety of any pedestrian within the roadway.

(Amended by Stats. 2022, Ch. 957, Sec. 11. (AB 2147) Effective January 1, 2023.)

21956. (a) A pedestrian shall not walk upon a roadway outside of a business or residence district otherwise than close to the pedestrian's left-hand edge of the roadway.

(b) A pedestrian may walk close to their right-hand edge of the roadway if a crosswalk or other means of safely crossing the roadway is not available or if existing traffic or other conditions would compromise the safety of a pedestrian attempting to cross the road.

(c) (1) A peace officer, as defined in Chapter 4.5 (commencing with Section 830) of Title 3 of Part 2 of the Penal Code, shall not stop a pedestrian for a violation of this section unless a reasonably careful person would realize there is an immediate danger of a collision with a moving vehicle or other device moving exclusively by human power.

(2) This subdivision does not relieve a pedestrian from the duty of using due care for their safety.

(3) This subdivision does not relieve a driver of a vehicle from the duty of exercising due care for the safety of any pedestrian within the roadway.

(Amended by Stats. 2022, Ch. 957, Sec. 12. (AB 2147) Effective January 1, 2023.)

21957. No person shall stand in a roadway for the purpose of soliciting a ride from the driver of any vehicle.

(Enacted by Stats. 1959, Ch. 3.)

21959. It is unlawful for any person to ski or toboggan on or across any roadway in such a manner as to interfere with the movement of vehicles thereon. A person on skis proceeding on or across a highway at a pace no greater than a walk is not within the prohibition of this section and shall be considered to be a pedestrian with all the rights and duties thereof as prescribed in this code.

(Amended by Stats. 1972, Ch. 46.)

21960. (a) The Department of Transportation and local authorities, by order, ordinance, or resolution, with respect to freeways, expressways, or designated portions thereof under their respective jurisdictions, to which vehicle access is completely or partially controlled, may prohibit or restrict the use of the freeways, expressways, or any portion thereof by pedestrians, bicycles or other nonmotorized traffic or by any person operating a motor-driven cycle, motorized bicycle, motorized scooter, or electrically motorized board. A prohibition or restriction pertaining to bicycles, motor-driven cycles, motorized scooters, or electrically motorized boards shall be deemed to include motorized bicycles. A person shall not operate a motorized bicycle wherever that prohibition or restriction is in force. Notwithstanding any order, ordinance, or resolution to the contrary, the driver or passengers of a disabled vehicle stopped on a freeway or expressway may walk to the nearest exit, in either direction, on that side of the freeway or expressway upon which the vehicle is disabled, from which telephone or motor vehicle repair services are available.

(b) The prohibitory regulation authorized by subdivision (a) shall be effective when appropriate signs giving notice thereof are erected upon any freeway or expressway and the approaches thereto. If any portion of a county freeway or expressway is contained within the limits of a city within the county, the county may erect signs on that portion as required under this subdivision if the ordinance has been approved by the city pursuant to subdivision (b) of Section 1730 of the Streets and Highways Code.

(c) No ordinance or resolution of local authorities shall apply to any state highway until the proposed ordinance or resolution has been presented to, and approved in writing by, the Department of Transportation.

(d) An ordinance or resolution adopted under this section on or after January 1, 2005, to prohibit pedestrian access to a county freeway or expressway shall not be effective unless it is supported by a finding by the local authority that the freeway or expressway does not have pedestrian facilities and pedestrian use would pose a safety risk to the pedestrian.

(Amended by Stats. 2015, Ch. 777, Sec. 4. (AB 604) Effective January 1, 2016.)

21961. (a) This chapter does not prevent local authorities from adopting ordinances prohibiting pedestrians from crossing roadways at other than crosswalks.

(b) (1) A peace officer, as defined in Chapter 4.5 (commencing with Section 830) of Title 3 of Part 2 of the Penal Code, shall not stop a pedestrian for a violation of an ordinance adopted by a local authority pursuant to this section, unless a reasonably careful person would realize there is an immediate danger of a collision with a moving vehicle or other device moving exclusively by human power.

(2) This subdivision does not relieve a pedestrian from the duty of using due care for their safety.

(3) This subdivision does not relieve a driver of a vehicle from the duty of exercising due care for the safety of any pedestrian within the roadway.

(Amended by Stats. 2022, Ch. 957, Sec. 13. (AB 2147) Effective January 1, 2023.)

21962. Any peace officer having reasonable cause to believe that any pedestrian is stopped or standing on any bridge or overpass for the purpose of violating Section 23110, may lawfully order such person from the bridge or overpass.

(Added by Stats. 1965, Ch. 1673.)

21963. A totally or partially blind pedestrian who is carrying a predominantly white cane (with or without a red tip), or using a guide dog, shall have the right-of-way, and the driver of any vehicle approaching this pedestrian, who fails to yield the right-of-way, or to take all reasonably necessary precautions to avoid injury to this blind pedestrian, is guilty of a misdemeanor, punishable by imprisonment in the county jail not exceeding six months, or by a fine of not less than five hundred dollars ($500) nor more than one thousand dollars ($1,000), or both. This section shall not preclude prosecution under any other applicable provision of law.

(Amended by Stats. 1993, Ch. 1149, Sec. 7. Effective January 1, 1994.)

21964. No person, other than those totally or partially blind, shall carry or use on any highway or in any public building, public facility, or other public place, a predominantly white cane (with or without a red tip).

(Added by Stats. 1968, Ch. 461.)

21965. As used in Sections 21963 and 21964, "blind," "totally blind," and "partially blind," mean having central visual acuity not to exceed 20/200 in the better eye, with corrected lenses, as measured by the Snellen test, or visual acuity greater than 20/200, but with a limitation in the field of vision such that the widest diameter of the visual field subtends an angle not greater than 20 degrees.

(Added by Stats. 1968, Ch. 461.)

21966. (a) A pedestrian shall not proceed along a bicycle path or lane where there is an adjacent adequate pedestrian facility.

(b) (1) A peace officer, as defined in Chapter 4.5 (commencing with

Section 830) of Title 3 of Part 2 of the Penal Code, shall not stop a pedestrian for a violation of subdivision (a) unless a reasonably careful person would realize there is an immediate danger of a collision with a moving vehicle or other device moving exclusively by human power.

(2) This subdivision does not relieve a pedestrian from the duty of using due care for their safety.

(3) This subdivision does not relieve a bicyclist from the duty of exercising due care for the safety of any pedestrian within the roadway.

(Amended by Stats. 2022, Ch. 957, Sec. 14. (AB 2147) Effective January 1, 2023.)

21967. Except as provided in Section 21968, a local authority may adopt rules and regulations by ordinance or resolution prohibiting or restricting persons from riding or propelling skateboards, or electrically motorized boards, on highways, sidewalks, or roadways.

(Amended by Stats. 2015, Ch. 777, Sec. 5. (AB 604) Effective January 1, 2016.)

21968. (a) A motorized skateboard shall not be propelled on any sidewalk, roadway, or any other part of a highway or on any bikeway, bicycle path or trail, equestrian trail, or hiking or recreational trail.

(b) For purposes of this section, an electrically motorized board, as defined in Section 313.5, is not a motorized skateboard.

(Amended by Stats. 2015, Ch. 777, Sec. 6. (AB 604) Effective January 1, 2016.)

21969. A local authority may adopt rules and regulations by ordinance regulating persons engaged in roller skating on a highway, sidewalk, or roadway.

(Added by Stats. 1981, Ch. 145, Sec. 1.)

21970. (a) No person may stop a vehicle unnecessarily in a manner that causes the vehicle to block a marked or unmarked crosswalk or sidewalk.

(b) Subdivision (a) does not preclude the driver of a vehicle facing a steady circular red light from turning right or turning left from a one-way street onto a one-way street pursuant to subdivision (b) of Section 21453.

(Added by Stats. 2000, Ch. 833, Sec. 11. Effective January 1, 2001.)

21971. Notwithstanding any other provision of law, any person who violates subdivision (a) or (b) of Section 21451, subdivision (b) of Section 21453, subdivision (a) of Section 21950, or Section 21952, and causes the bodily injury of anyone other than the driver is guilty of an infraction punishable under Section 42001.18.

(Added by Stats. 2000, Ch. 833, Sec. 12. Effective January 1, 2001.)

Chapter 6. Turning and Stopping and Turning Signals

(Chapter 6 enacted by Stats. 1959, Ch. 3.)

22100. Except as provided in Section 22100.5 or 22101, the driver of any vehicle intending to turn upon a highway shall do so as follows:

(a) Right Turns. Both the approach for a right-hand turn and a right-hand turn shall be made as close as practicable to the right-hand curb or edge of the roadway except:

(1) Upon a highway having three marked lanes for traffic moving in one direction that terminates at an intersecting highway accommodating traffic in both directions, the driver of a vehicle in the middle lane may turn right into any lane lawfully available to traffic moving in that direction upon the roadway being entered.

(2) If a right-hand turn is made from a one-way highway at an intersection, a driver shall approach the turn as provided in this subdivision and shall complete the turn in any lane lawfully available to traffic moving in that direction upon the roadway being entered.

(3) Upon a highway having an additional lane or lanes marked for a right turn by appropriate signs or markings, the driver of a vehicle may turn right from any lane designated and marked for that turning movement.

(b) Left Turns. The approach for a left turn shall be made as close as practicable to the left-hand edge of the extreme left-hand lane or portion of the roadway lawfully available to traffic moving in the direction of travel of the vehicle and, when turning at an intersection, the left turn shall not be made before entering the intersection. After entering the intersection, the left turn shall be made so as to leave the intersection in a lane lawfully available to traffic moving in that direction upon the roadway being entered, except that upon a highway having three marked lanes for traffic moving in one direction that terminates at an intersecting highway accommodating traffic in both directions, the driver of a vehicle in the middle lane may turn left into any lane lawfully available to traffic moving in that direction upon the roadway being entered.

(Amended by Stats. 2004, Ch. 183, Sec. 353. Effective January 1, 2005.)

22100.5. No driver shall make a U-turn at an intersection controlled by official traffic signals except as provided in Section 21451, and then only from the far lefthand lane that is lawfully available to traffic moving in the direction of travel from which the turn is commenced. No driver shall make a U-turn at an intersection controlled by official traffic control devices except from the far lefthand lane that is lawfully available to traffic moving in the direction of travel from which the turn is commenced.

(Amended by Stats. 1984, Ch. 700, Sec. 2.)

22101. (a) The Department of Transportation or local authorities, in respect to highways under their respective jurisdictions, may cause official traffic control devices to be placed or erected within or adjacent to intersections to regulate or prohibit turning movements at such intersections.

(b) When turning movements are required at an intersection, notice of that requirement shall be given by erection of a sign, unless an additional clearly marked traffic lane is provided for the approach to the turning movement, in which event notice as applicable to that additional traffic lane shall be given by an official traffic control device.

(c) When right- or left-hand turns are prohibited at an intersection, notice of that prohibition shall be given by erection of a sign.

(d) When an official traffic control device is placed as required in subdivisions (b) or (c), it is unlawful for a driver of a vehicle to disobey the directions of the official traffic control device.

(e) (1) A person operating a bicycle may travel straight through a right- or left-hand turn only lane when an official traffic control device indicates that the movement is permitted.

(2) The Department of Transportation shall develop standards for lane striping, pavement markings, and appropriate regulatory signs to implement this subdivision.

(Amended by Stats. 2019, Ch. 221, Sec. 1. (AB 1266) Effective January 1, 2020.)

22102. No person in a business district shall make a U-turn, except at an intersection, or on a divided highway where an opening has been provided in accordance with Section 21651. This turning movement shall be made as close as practicable to the extreme left-hand edge of the lanes moving in the driver's direction of travel immediately prior to the initiation of the turning movement, when more than one lane in the direction of travel is present.

(Amended by Stats. 1985, Ch. 47, Sec. 1.)

22103. No person in a residence district shall make a U-turn when any other vehicle is approaching from either direction within 200 feet, except at an intersection when the approaching vehicle is controlled by an official traffic control device.

(Amended by Stats. 1970, Ch. 620.)

22104. No person shall make a U-turn in front of the driveway entrance or approaches to a fire station. No person shall use the driveway entrance or approaches to a fire station for the purpose of turning a vehicle so as to proceed in the opposite direction.

(Amended by Stats. 1970, Ch. 620.)

22105. No person shall make a U-turn upon any highway where the driver of such vehicle does not have an unobstructed view for 200 feet in both directions along the highway and of any traffic thereon.

(Amended by Stats. 1972, Ch. 64.)

22106. No person shall start a vehicle stopped, standing, or parked on a highway, nor shall any person back a vehicle on a highway until

such movement can be made with reasonable safety.
(Enacted by Stats. 1959, Ch. 3.)

22107. No person shall turn a vehicle from a direct course or move right or left upon a roadway until such movement can be made with reasonable safety and then only after the giving of an appropriate signal in the manner provided in this chapter in the event any other vehicle may be affected by the movement.
(Amended by Stats. 1959, Ch. 1996.)

22108. Any signal of intention to turn right or left shall be given continuously during the last 100 feet traveled by the vehicle before turning.
(Enacted by Stats. 1959, Ch. 3.)

22109. No person shall stop or suddenly decrease the speed of a vehicle on a highway without first giving an appropriate signal in the manner provided in this chapter to the driver of any vehicle immediately to the rear when there is opportunity to give the signal.
(Enacted by Stats. 1959, Ch. 3.)

22110. (a) The signals required by this chapter shall be given by signal lamp, unless a vehicle is not required to be and is not equipped with turn signals. Drivers of vehicles not required to be and not equipped with turn signals shall give a hand and arm signal when required by this chapter.

(b) In the event the signal lamps become inoperable while driving, hand and arm signals shall be used in the manner required in this chapter.
(Amended by Stats. 1999, Ch. 1008, Sec. 12. Effective January 1, 2000.)

22111. All required signals given by hand and arm shall be given from the left side of a vehicle in the following manner:

(a) Left turn—hand and arm extended horizontally beyond the side of the vehicle.

(b) Right turn—hand and arm extended upward beyond the side of the vehicle, except that a bicyclist may extend the right hand and arm horizontally to the right side of the bicycle.

(c) Stop or sudden decrease of speed signal—hand and arm extended downward beyond the side of the vehicle.
(Amended by Stats. 1976, Ch. 751.)

22112. (a) On approach to a schoolbus stop where pupils are loading or unloading from a schoolbus, the schoolbus driver shall activate an approved amber warning light system, if the schoolbus is so equipped, beginning 200 feet before the schoolbus stop. The schoolbus driver shall deactivate the amber warning light system after reaching the schoolbus stop. The schoolbus driver shall operate the flashing red light signal system and stop signal arm, as required on the schoolbus, at all times when the schoolbus is stopped for the purpose of loading or unloading pupils. The flashing red light signal system, amber warning lights system, and stop signal arm shall not be operated at any place where traffic is controlled by a traffic officer or at any location identified in subdivision (e) of this section. The schoolbus flashing red light signal system, amber warning lights system, and stop signal arm shall not be operated at any other time.

(b) The schoolbus driver shall stop to load or unload pupils only at a schoolbus stop designated for pupils by the school district superintendent or the head or principal of a private school, or authorized by any of those individuals for school activity trips.

(c) When a schoolbus is stopped on a highway or private road for the purpose of loading or unloading pupils, at a location where traffic is not controlled by a traffic officer, the driver shall, before opening the door, ensure that the flashing red light signal system and stop signal arm are activated, and that it is safe to enter or exit the schoolbus.

(d) When a schoolbus is stopped on a highway or private road for the purpose of loading or unloading pupils, at a location where traffic is not controlled by a traffic officer or official traffic control signal, the schoolbus driver shall do all of the following:

(1) Escort all pupils in prekindergarten, kindergarten, or any of grades 1 to 8, inclusive, who need to cross the highway or private road upon which the schoolbus is stopped. The driver shall use an approved hand-held "STOP" sign while escorting all pupils.

(2) Require all pupils who need to cross the highway or private road upon which the schoolbus is stopped to walk in front of the bus as they cross.

(3) Ensure that all pupils who need to cross the highway or private road upon which the schoolbus is stopped have crossed safely, and that all other pupils and pedestrians are a safe distance from the schoolbus before setting the schoolbus in motion.

(e) Except at a location where pupils are loading or unloading from a schoolbus and must cross a highway or private road upon which the schoolbus is stopped, the schoolbus driver may not activate the amber warning light system, the flashing red light signal system and stop signal arm at any of the following locations:

(1) Schoolbus loading zones on or adjacent to school grounds or during an activity trip, if the schoolbus is lawfully stopped or parked.

(2) Where the schoolbus is disabled due to mechanical breakdown. The driver of a relief bus that arrives at the scene to transport pupils from the disabled schoolbus shall not activate the amber warning light system, the flashing red light system, and stop signal arm.

(3) Where a pupil requires physical assistance from the driver or authorized attendant to board or leave the schoolbus and providing the assistance extends the length of time the schoolbus is stopped beyond the time required to load or unload a pupil that does not require physical assistance.

(4) Where the roadway surface on which the bus is stopped is partially or completely covered by snow or ice and requiring traffic to stop would pose a safety hazard as determined by the schoolbus motor carrier.

(5) On a state highway with a posted speed limit of 55 miles per hour or higher where the schoolbus is completely off the main traveled portion of the highway.

(6) Any location determined by a school district or a private school, with the approval of the Department of the California Highway Patrol, to present a traffic or safety hazard.

(f) Notwithstanding subdivisions (a) to (d), inclusive, the Department of the California Highway Patrol may require the activation of an approved flashing amber warning light system, if the schoolbus is so equipped, or the flashing red light signal system and stop signal arm, as required on the schoolbus, at any location where the department determines that the activation is necessary for the safety of school pupils loading or unloading from a schoolbus.
(Amended by Stats. 2012, Ch. 769, Sec. 35. (AB 2679) Effective January 1, 2013.)

22113. This chapter does not prevent local authorities, by ordinance, from prohibiting the making of any turning movement by any vehicle at any intersection or between any designated intersections.
(Enacted by Stats. 1959, Ch. 3.)

Chapter 7. Speed Laws

(Chapter 7 enacted by Stats. 1959, Ch. 3.)

Article 1. Generally

(Heading of Article 1 amended by Stats. 1959, Ch. 11.)

22348. (a) Notwithstanding subdivision (b) of Section 22351, a person shall not drive a vehicle upon a highway with a speed limit established pursuant to Section 22349 or 22356 at a speed greater than that speed limit.

(b) A person who drives a vehicle upon a highway at a speed greater than 100 miles per hour is guilty of an infraction punishable, as follows:

(1) Upon a first conviction of a violation of this subdivision, by a fine of not to exceed five hundred dollars ($500). The court may also suspend the privilege of the person to operate a motor vehicle for a period not to exceed 30 days pursuant to Section 13200.5.

(2) Upon a conviction under this subdivision of an offense that occurred within three years of a prior offense resulting in a conviction of an offense under this subdivision, by a fine of not to exceed seven

hundred fifty dollars ($750). The person's privilege to operate a motor vehicle shall be suspended by the Department of Motor Vehicles pursuant to subdivision (a) of Section 13355.

(3) Upon a conviction under this subdivision of an offense that occurred within five years of two or more prior offenses resulting in convictions of offenses under this subdivision, by a fine of not to exceed one thousand dollars ($1,000). The person's privilege to operate a motor vehicle shall be suspended by the Department of Motor Vehicles pursuant to subdivision (b) of Section 13355.

(c) A vehicle subject to Section 22406 shall be driven in a lane designated pursuant to Section 21655, or if a lane has not been so designated, in the right-hand lane for traffic or as close as practicable to the right-hand edge or curb. When overtaking and passing another vehicle proceeding in the same direction, the driver shall use either the designated lane, the lane to the immediate left of the right-hand lane, or the right-hand lane for traffic as permitted under this code. If, however, specific lane or lanes have not been designated on a divided highway having four or more clearly marked lanes for traffic in one direction, a vehicle may also be driven in the lane to the immediate left of the right-hand lane, unless otherwise prohibited under this code. This subdivision does not apply to a driver who is preparing for a left- or right-hand turn or who is in the process of entering into or exiting from a highway or to a driver who is required necessarily to drive in a lane other than the right-hand lane to continue on his or her intended route.

(Amended by Stats. 2004, Ch. 300, Sec. 1. Effective January 1, 2005.)

22349. (a) Except as provided in Section 22356, no person may drive a vehicle upon a highway at a speed greater than 65 miles per hour.

(b) Notwithstanding any other provision of law, no person may drive a vehicle upon a two-lane, undivided highway at a speed greater than 55 miles per hour unless that highway, or portion thereof, has been posted for a higher speed by the Department of Transportation or appropriate local agency upon the basis of an engineering and traffic survey. For purposes of this subdivision, the following apply:

(1) A two-lane, undivided highway is a highway with not more than one through lane of travel in each direction.

(2) Passing lanes may not be considered when determining the number of through lanes.

(c) It is the intent of the Legislature that there be reasonable signing on affected two-lane, undivided highways described in subdivision (b) in continuing the 55 miles-per-hour speed limit, including placing signs at county boundaries to the extent possible, and at other appropriate locations.

(Amended by Stats. 1999, Ch. 724, Sec. 41. Effective January 1, 2000.)

22350. No person shall drive a vehicle upon a highway at a speed greater than is reasonable or prudent having due regard for weather, visibility, the traffic on, and the surface and width of, the highway, and in no event at a speed which endangers the safety of persons or property.

(Amended by Stats. 1963, Ch. 252.)

22351. (a) The speed of any vehicle upon a highway not in excess of the limits specified in Section 22352 or established as authorized in this code is lawful unless clearly proved to be in violation of the basic speed law.

(b) The speed of any vehicle upon a highway in excess of the prima facie speed limits in Section 22352 or established as authorized in this code is prima facie unlawful unless the defendant establishes by competent evidence that the speed in excess of said limits did not constitute a violation of the basic speed law at the time, place and under the conditions then existing.

(Enacted by Stats. 1959, Ch. 3.)

22352. The prima facie limits are as follows and shall be applicable unless changed as authorized in this code and, if so changed, only when signs have been erected giving notice thereof:

(a) Fifteen miles per hour:

(1) When traversing a railway grade crossing, if, during the last 100 feet of the approach to the crossing, the driver does not have a clear and unobstructed view of the crossing and of any traffic on the railway for a distance of 400 feet in both directions along the railway. This paragraph does not apply in the case of any railway grade crossing where a human flagperson is on duty or a clearly visible electrical or mechanical railway crossing signal device is installed but does not then indicate the immediate approach of a railway train or car.

(2) When traversing any intersection of highways, if, during the last 100 feet of the driver's approach to the intersection, the driver does not have a clear and unobstructed view of the intersection and of any traffic upon all of the highways entering the intersection for a distance of 100 feet along all those highways, except at an intersection protected by stop signs or yield right-of-way signs or controlled by official traffic control signals.

(3) On any alley.

(b) Twenty-five miles per hour:

(1) On any highway in any business or residence district unless a different speed is determined by local authority or the Department of Transportation under procedures set forth in this code.

(2) When approaching or passing a school building or the grounds thereof, contiguous to a highway and posted with a standard "SCHOOL" warning sign, while children are going to or leaving the school either during school hours or during the noon recess period. The prima facie limit shall also apply when approaching or passing any school grounds which are not separated from the highway by a fence, gate, or other physical barrier while the grounds are in use by children and the highway is posted with a standard "SCHOOL" warning sign. For purposes of this subparagraph, standard "SCHOOL" warning signs may be placed at any distance up to 500 feet away from school grounds.

(3) When passing a senior center or other facility primarily used by senior citizens, contiguous to a street other than a state highway and posted with a standard "SENIOR" warning sign. A local authority may erect a sign pursuant to this paragraph when the local agency makes a determination that the proposed signing should be implemented. A local authority may request grant funding from the Active Transportation Program pursuant to Chapter 8 (commencing with Section 2380) of Division 3 of the Streets and Highways Code, or any other grant funding available to it, and use that grant funding to pay for the erection of those signs, or may utilize any other funds available to it to pay for the erection of those signs, including, but not limited to, donations from private sources.

(c) This section shall remain in effect until January 1, 2031, and as of that date is repealed.

(Amended by Stats. 2025, Ch. 555, Sec. 1. (AB 382) Effective January 1, 2026. Repealed as of January 1, 2031, by its own provisions. See later operative version as added by Sec. 2 of Stats. 2025, Ch. 555.)

22352. The prima facie limits are as follows and shall be applicable unless changed as authorized in this code and, if so changed, only when signs have been erected giving notice thereof:

(a) Fifteen miles per hour:

(1) When traversing a railway grade crossing, if, during the last 100 feet of the approach to the crossing, the driver does not have a clear and unobstructed view of the crossing and of any traffic on the railway for a distance of 400 feet in both directions along the railway. This paragraph does not apply in the case of any railway grade crossing where a human flagperson is on duty or a clearly visible electrical or mechanical railway crossing signal device is installed but does not then indicate the immediate approach of a railway train or car.

(2) When traversing any intersection of highways, if, during the last 100 feet of the driver's approach to the intersection, the driver does not have a clear and unobstructed view of the intersection and of any traffic upon all of the highways entering the intersection for a distance of 100 feet along all those highways, except at an intersection protected by stop signs or yield right-of-way signs or controlled by official traffic

control signals.

(3) On any alley.

(b) Twenty miles per hour in a school zone when any of the following apply:

(1) A school speed limit sign with attached beacons states "speed limit 20 when flashing" and the beacons are flashing.

(2) A school speed limit sign states "children are present" and children are present.

(3) A school speed limit sign with specific hours, which shall be determined by the local jurisdiction.

(c) Twenty-five miles per hour:

(1) On any highway in any business or residence district unless a different speed is determined by local authority or the Department of Transportation under procedures set forth in this code.

(2) When passing a senior center or other facility primarily used by senior citizens, contiguous to a street other than a state highway and posted with a standard "SENIOR" warning sign. A local authority may erect a sign pursuant to this paragraph when the local agency makes a determination that the proposed signing should be implemented. A local authority may request grant funding from the Active Transportation Program pursuant to Chapter 8 (commencing with Section 2380) of Division 3 of the Streets and Highways Code, or any other grant funding available to it, and use that grant funding to pay for the erection of those signs, or may utilize any other funds available to it to pay for the erection of those signs, including, but not limited to, donations from private sources.

(d) For purposes of this section, the following definitions shall apply:

(1) "School zone" means an area of a highway within 500 feet of school grounds in any direction, unless otherwise posted, marked with appropriate signs giving notice of the area.

(2) (A) "Children are present" means whenever either of the following occurs:

(i) Children are going to or leaving the school.

(ii) School grounds are in use by children and the highway is posted with a standard "SCHOOL" warning sign.

(B) "Children are present" does not include children who are separated from the highway by a fence, gate, or other physical barrier.

(e) This section shall become operative on January 1, 2031.

(Repealed (in Sec. 1) and added by Stats. 2025, Ch. 555, Sec. 2. (AB 382) Effective January 1, 2026. Operative January 1, 2031, by its own provisions.)

22352.5. (a) Notwithstanding Section 22352, a local authority may, by ordinance or resolution, determine and declare a prima facie speed limit of 20 miles per hour in a school zone.

(b) For purposes of this section, "school zone" has the same meaning as defined in Section 22352.

(c) This section shall remain in effect until January 1, 2031, and as of that date is repealed.

(Added by Stats. 2025, Ch. 555, Sec. 3. (AB 382) Effective January 1, 2026. Repealed as of January 1, 2031, by its own provisions.)

22353. When conducting an engineering and traffic survey, the City of Norco, in addition to the factors set forth in Section 627, may also consider equestrian safety.

(Added by Stats. 2002, Ch. 186, Sec. 1. Effective January 1, 2003.)

22353.2. The City of Burbank may also consider equestrian safety when conducting an engineering and traffic survey of the public streets within the boundaries of the Rancho Master Plan Area in the City of Burbank, as described in the City of Burbank's General Plan adopted on February 19, 2013, in addition to the factors set forth in Section 627.

(Added by Stats. 2018, Ch. 398, Sec. 1. (AB 2955) Effective January 1, 2019.)

22353.3. The City of Glendale may also consider equestrian safety when conducting an engineering and traffic survey of the public streets within the boundaries of the Horse Overlay Zone, commonly known as the Riverside Rancho Area, in the City of Glendale, as described in Chapter 30.21 of the Glendale Municipal Code, in addition to the factors set forth in Section 627.

(Added by Stats. 2018, Ch. 398, Sec. 2. (AB 2955) Effective January 1, 2019.)

22353.4. The City of Los Angeles may also consider equestrian safety when conducting an engineering and traffic survey of the public streets within the boundaries of the Sylmar Community Plan Area and the Sunland-Tujunga-Lake View Terrace-Shadow Hills-East La Tuna Canyon Community Plan Area in the City of Los Angeles, as described in the Sylmar Community Plan adopted on June 10, 2015, and the Sunland-Tujunga-Lake View Terrace-Shadow Hills-East La Tuna Canyon Community Plan Update adopted on November 18, 1997, respectively, in addition to the factors set forth in Section 627.

(Added by Stats. 2018, Ch. 398, Sec. 3. (AB 2955) Effective January 1, 2019.)

22353.5. When conducting an engineering and traffic survey of the public streets within the boundaries of the common interest development known as Orange Park Acres, in addition to the factors set forth in Section 627, the County of Orange may also consider equestrian safety.

(Added by Stats. 2014, Ch. 282, Sec. 1. (AB 1669) Effective January 1, 2015.)

22354. (a) Whenever the Department of Transportation determines upon the basis of an engineering and traffic survey that the limit of 65 miles per hour is more than is reasonable or safe upon any portion of a state highway where the limit of 65 miles is applicable, the department may determine and declare a prima facie speed limit of 60, 55, 50, 45, 40, 35, 30, 25, 20, or 15 miles per hour, whichever is found most appropriate to facilitate the orderly movement of traffic and is reasonable and safe, which declared prima facie speed limit shall be effective when appropriate signs giving notice thereof are erected upon the highway.

(b) This section shall become operative on the date specified in subdivision (c) of Section 22366.

(Amended by Stats. 2021, Ch. 690, Sec. 4. (AB 43) Effective January 1, 2022.)

22354.5. (a) Whenever the Department of Transportation determines, upon the basis of an engineering and traffic survey, to increase or decrease the existing speed limit on a particular portion of a state highway pursuant to Section 22354, it shall, prior to increasing or decreasing that speed limit, consult with, and take into consideration the recommendations of, the Department of the California Highway Patrol.

(b) The city council or board of supervisors of a city or county through which any portion of a state highway subject to subdivision (a) extends may conduct a public hearing on the proposed increase or decrease at a convenient location as near as possible to that portion of state highway. The Department of Transportation shall take into consideration the results of the public hearing in determining whether to increase or decrease the speed limit.

(Added by Stats. 1991, Ch. 219, Sec. 1.)

22355. Whenever the Department of Transportation determines upon the basis of an engineering and traffic survey that the safe and orderly movement of traffic upon any state highway which is a freeway will be facilitated by the establishment of variable speed limits, the department may erect, regulate, and control signs upon the state highway which is a freeway, or any portion thereof, which signs shall be so designed as to permit display of different speed limits at various times of the day or night. Such signs need not conform to the standards and specifications established by regulations of the Department of Transportation pursuant to Section 21400, but shall be of sufficient size and clarity to give adequate notice of the applicable speed limit. The speed limit upon the freeway at a particular time and place shall be that which is then and there displayed upon such sign.

(Amended by Stats. 1973, Ch. 78.)

22356. (a) Whenever the Department of Transportation, after consultation with the Department of the California Highway Patrol, determines upon the basis of an engineering and traffic survey on existing highway segments, or upon the basis of appropriate design standards and projected traffic volumes in the case of newly constructed highway segments, that a speed greater than 65 miles per hour would facilitate the orderly movement of vehicular traffic and would be reasonable and safe upon any state highway, or portion thereof, that is otherwise subject to a maximum speed limit of 65 miles per hour, the Department of Transportation, with the approval of the Department of the California Highway Patrol, may declare a higher maximum speed of 70 miles per hour for vehicles not subject to Section 22406, and shall cause appropriate signs to be erected giving notice thereof. The Department of Transportation shall only make a determination under this section that is fully consistent with, and in full compliance with, federal law.

(b) No person shall drive a vehicle upon that highway at a speed greater than 70 miles per hour, as posted.

(c) This section shall become operative on the date specified in subdivision (c) of Section 22366.

(Repealed (in Sec. 26) and added by Stats. 1995, Ch. 766, Sec. 27. Effective January 1, 1996. This section became operative, by its own provisions, on the date described in Section 22366.)

22357. (a) Whenever a local authority determines upon the basis of an engineering and traffic survey that a speed greater than 25 miles per hour would facilitate the orderly movement of vehicular traffic and would be reasonable and safe upon any street other than a state highway otherwise subject to a prima facie limit of 25 miles per hour, the local authority may by ordinance determine and declare a prima facie speed limit of 30, 35, 40, 45, 50, 55, or 60 miles per hour or a maximum speed limit of 65 miles per hour, whichever is found most appropriate to facilitate the orderly movement of traffic and is reasonable and safe. The declared prima facie or maximum speed limit shall be effective when appropriate signs giving notice thereof are erected upon the street and shall not thereafter be revised except upon the basis of an engineering and traffic survey. This section does not apply to any 25-mile-per-hour prima facie limit which is applicable when passing a school building or the grounds thereof or when passing a senior center or other facility primarily used by senior citizens.

(b) This section shall become operative on the date specified in subdivision (c) of Section 22366.

(Repealed (in Sec. 28) and added by Stats. 1995, Ch. 766, Sec. 29. Effective January 1, 1996. This section became operative, by its own provisions, on the date described in Section 22366.)

22357.1. Notwithstanding Section 22357, a local authority may, by ordinance or resolution, set a prima facie speed limit of 25 miles per hour on any street, other than a state highway, adjacent to any children's playground in a public park but only during particular hours or days when children are expected to use the facilities. The 25 mile per hour speed limit shall be effective when signs giving notice of the speed limit are posted.

(Added by Stats. 1989, Ch. 508, Sec. 1.)

22358. (a) Whenever a local authority determines upon the basis of an engineering and traffic survey that the limit of 65 miles per hour is more than is reasonable or safe upon any portion of any street other than a state highway where the limit of 65 miles per hour is applicable, the local authority may by ordinance determine and declare a prima facie speed limit of 60, 55, 50, 45, 40, 35, 30, 25, 20, or 15 miles per hour, whichever is found most appropriate to facilitate the orderly movement of traffic and is reasonable and safe, which declared prima facie limit shall be effective when appropriate signs giving notice thereof are erected upon the street.

(b) This section shall become operative on the date specified in subdivision (c) of Section 22366.

(Amended by Stats. 2021, Ch. 690, Sec. 5. (AB 43) Effective January 1, 2022.)

22358.3. Whenever a local authority determines upon the basis of an engineering and traffic survey that the prima facie speed limit of 25 miles per hour in a business or residence district or in a public park on any street having a roadway not exceeding 25 feet in width, other than a state highway, is more than is reasonable or safe, the local authority may, by ordinance or resolution, determine and declare a prima facie speed limit of 20 or 15 miles per hour, whichever is found most appropriate and is reasonable and safe. The declared prima facie limit shall be effective when appropriate signs giving notice thereof are erected upon the street.

(Amended by Stats. 1972, Ch. 1095.)

22358.4. (a) (1) Whenever a local authority determines upon the basis of an engineering and traffic survey that the prima facie speed limit established by subdivision (b) of Section 22352 is more than is reasonable or safe, the local authority may, by ordinance or resolution, determine and declare a prima facie speed limit of 15 miles per hour if justified as the appropriate speed limit by that survey.

(2) An ordinance or resolution adopted under paragraph (1) shall not be effective until appropriate signs giving notice of the speed limit are erected upon the highway and, in the case of a state highway, until the ordinance is approved by the Department of Transportation and the appropriate signs are erected upon the highway.

(b) (1) Notwithstanding subdivision (a) or any other provision of law, a local authority may, by ordinance or resolution, determine and declare prima facie speed limits as follows:

(A) A 15 miles per hour prima facie limit in a residence district, on a highway with a posted speed limit of 30 miles per hour or slower, in a school zone.

(B) A 25 miles per hour prima facie limit on a highway when approaching, at a distance of 500 to 1,000 feet from, a school zone.

(2) The prima facie limit established under subparagraph (A) of paragraph (1) applies only to highways that meet all of the following conditions:

(A) A maximum of two traffic lanes.

(B) A maximum posted 30 miles per hour prima facie speed limit immediately prior to and after the school zone.

(3) The prima facie limits established under paragraph (1) apply to all lanes of an affected highway, in both directions of travel.

(4) When determining the need to lower the prima facie speed limit, the local authority shall take the provisions of Section 627 into consideration.

(5) (A) An ordinance or resolution adopted under paragraph (1) shall not be effective until appropriate signs giving notice of the speed limit are erected upon the highway and, in the case of a state highway, until the ordinance is approved by the Department of Transportation and the appropriate signs are erected upon the highway.

(B) For purposes of subparagraph (A) of paragraph (1), school warning signs indicating a speed limit of 15 miles per hour may be placed at a distance up to 500 feet away from school grounds.

(C) For purposes of subparagraph (B) of paragraph (1), school warning signs indicating a speed limit of 25 miles per hour may be placed at any distance between 500 and 1,000 feet away from the school grounds.

(D) A local authority shall reimburse the Department of Transportation for all costs incurred by the department under this subdivision.

(c) For purposes of this section, "school zone" has the same meaning as defined in Section 22352.

(Amended by Stats. 2025, Ch. 555, Sec. 4. (AB 382) Effective January 1, 2026.)

22358.5. It is the intent of the Legislature that physical conditions such as width, curvature, grade and surface conditions, or any other condition readily apparent to a driver, in the absence of other factors, would not require special downward speed zoning, as the basic rule of section 22350 is sufficient regulation as to such conditions.

(Added by Stats. 1959, Ch. 11.)

22358.6. (a) The Department of Transportation shall, in the next scheduled revision, revise and thereafter maintain the California Manual on Uniform Traffic Control Devices to require the Department of Transportation or a local authority to round speed limits to the nearest five miles per hour of the 85th percentile of the free-flowing traffic.

(b) In cases in which the speed limit needs to be rounded down to the nearest five miles per hour increment of the 85th-percentile speed, the Department of Transportation or a local authority may lower the speed limit by five miles per hour from the nearest five-mile-per-hour increment of the 85th-percentile speed, in compliance with Sections

627 and 22358.5 and the California Manual on Uniform Traffic Control Devices, as it read on March 30, 2021, if the reasons for the lower speed limit are documented in an engineering and traffic survey. The Department of Transportation or a local authority may also take into consideration Sections 22353, 22353.2, 22353.3, 22353.4, and 22353.5, if applicable.

(c) In cases in which the speed limit needs to be rounded up to the nearest five-mile-per-hour increment of the 85th-percentile speed, the Department of Transportation or a local authority may decide to instead round down the speed limit to the lower five-mile-per-hour increment. If the speed limit is rounded down pursuant to this subdivision, the speed limit shall not be reduced any further pursuant to subdivision (b).

(d) In addition to subdivisions (b) and (c), the Department of Transportation or a local authority may additionally lower the speed limit as provided in Section 22358.7.

(e) The total reduction in the speed limit pursuant to subdivisions (a) to (d), inclusive, shall not exceed 12.4 miles per hour from the 85th-percentile speed.

(f) Notwithstanding subdivisions (a) to (e), inclusive, the Department of Transportation or a local authority may retain the currently adopted speed limit as provided in Section 22358.8 without further reduction, or restore the immediately prior adopted speed limit as provided in Section 22358.8 without further reduction.

(Amended by Stats. 2025, Ch. 287, Sec. 2. (AB 1014) Effective January 1, 2026.)

22358.7. (a) If the Department of Transportation or a local authority, after completing an engineering and traffic survey, finds that the speed limit is still more than is reasonable or safe, the Department of Transportation may or the local authority may, by ordinance, determine and declare a prima facie speed limit that has been reduced an additional five miles per hour for either or both of the following reasons:

(1) The portion of highway has been designated as a safety corridor. The Department of Transportation or a local authority shall not deem more than one-fifth of their streets as safety corridors.

(2) The portion of highway is adjacent to any land or facility that generates high concentrations of bicyclists or pedestrians, especially those from vulnerable groups such as children, seniors, persons with disabilities, and the unhoused.

(b) (1) As used in this section, "safety corridor" shall be defined by the Department of Transportation in the next revision of the California Manual on Uniform Traffic Control Devices. In making this determination, the Department of Transportation shall consider highways that have the highest number of serious injuries and fatalities based on collision data that may be derived from, but not limited to, the Statewide Integrated Traffic Records System.

(2) The Department of Transportation shall, in the next revision of the California Manual on Uniform Traffic Control Devices, determine what constitutes land or facilities that generate high concentrations of bicyclists and pedestrians, as used in paragraph (2) of subdivision (a). In making this determination, the Department of Transportation shall consider density, road use type, and bicycle and pedestrian infrastructure present on a section of highway.

(c) A peace officer shall issue only warning citations for violations of exceeding the speed limit by 10 miles per hour or less for the first 30 days that a lower speed limit is in effect as authorized by this section.

(Amended by Stats. 2025, Ch. 287, Sec. 3. (AB 1014) Effective January 1, 2026.)

22358.8. (a) If the Department of Transportation or a local authority, after completing an engineering and traffic survey, finds that the speed limit is still more than is reasonable or safe, the Department of Transportation may or the local authority may, by ordinance, retain the currently adopted speed limit or restore the immediately prior adopted speed limit on a highway that is not a freeway if that speed limit was established with an engineering and traffic survey and if a registered engineer has evaluated the section of highway and determined that no additional general purpose lanes have been added to the roadway since completion of the traffic survey that established that speed limit.

(b) This section does not authorize a speed limit to be reduced by any more than five miles per hour from the currently adopted speed limit nor below the immediately prior speed limit.

(c) A peace officer shall issue only warning citations for violations of exceeding the speed limit by 10 miles per hour or less for the first 30 days that a lower speed limit is in effect as authorized by this section.

(Amended by Stats. 2025, Ch. 287, Sec. 4. (AB 1014) Effective January 1, 2026.)

22358.9. (a) (1) Notwithstanding any other law, the Department of Transportation may or a local authority may, by ordinance, determine and declare a 25- or 20-mile-per-hour prima facie speed limit on a highway that is not a freeway and that is contiguous to a business activity district when posted with a sign that indicates a speed limit of 25 or 20 miles per hour.

(2) The prima facie limits established under paragraph (1) apply only to highways that meet all of the following conditions:

(A) A maximum of four traffic lanes.

(B) A maximum posted 30-mile-per-hour prima facie speed limit immediately prior to and after the business activity district, if establishing a 25-mile-per-hour speed limit.

(C) A maximum posted 25-mile-per-hour prima facie speed limit immediately prior to and after the business activity district, if establishing a 20-mile-per-hour speed limit.

(b) As used in this section, a "business activity district" is that portion of a highway and the property contiguous thereto that includes central or neighborhood downtowns, urban villages, or zoning designations that prioritize commercial land uses at the downtown or neighborhood scale and meets at least three of the following requirements in paragraphs (1) to (4), inclusive:

(1) No less than 50 percent of the contiguous property fronting the highway consists of retail or dining commercial uses, including outdoor dining, that open directly onto sidewalks adjacent to the highway.

(2) Parking, including parallel, diagonal, or perpendicular spaces located alongside the highway.

(3) Traffic control signals or stop signs regulating traffic flow on the highway, located at intervals of no more than 600 feet.

(4) Marked crosswalks not controlled by a traffic control device.

(c) The Department of Transportation or a local authority shall not declare a prima facie speed limit under this section on a portion of a highway where the Department of Transportation or the local authority has already lowered the speed limit as permitted under Section 22358.7, has retained the currently adopted speed limit under Section 22358.8, or has restored the immediately prior adopted speed limit under Section 22358.8.

(d) A peace officer shall issue only warning citations for violations of exceeding the speed limit by 10 miles per hour or less for the first 30 days that a lower speed limit is in effect as authorized by this section.

(Amended by Stats. 2025, Ch. 287, Sec. 5. (AB 1014) Effective January 1, 2026.)

22359. With respect to boundary line streets and highways where portions thereof are within different jurisdictions, no ordinance adopted under Sections 22357 and 22358 shall be effective as to any such portion until all authorities having jurisdiction of the portions of the street concerned have approved the same. This section shall not apply in the case of boundary line streets consisting of separate roadways within different jurisdictions.

(Amended by Stats. 1963, Ch. 209.)

22360. (a) Whenever a local authority determines upon the basis of an engineering and traffic survey that the limit of 65 miles per hour is more than is reasonable or safe upon any portion of a highway other than a state highway for a distance of not exceeding 2,000 feet in length between districts, either business or residence, the local authority may determine and declare a reasonable and safe prima facie limit thereon lower than 65 miles per hour, but not less than 25 miles per hour, which declared prima facie speed limit shall be effective when appropriate signs giving notice thereof are erected upon the street or highway.

(b) This section shall become operative on the date specified in subdivision (c) of Section 22366.

(Repealed (in Sec. 32) and added by Stats. 1995, Ch. 766, Sec. 33. Effective January 1, 1996. This section became operative, by its own provisions, on the date described in Section 22366.)

22361. On multiple-lane highways with two or more separate roadways different prima facie speed limits may be established for different roadways under any of the procedures specified in Sections 22354 to 22359, inclusive.

(Amended by Stats. 1963, Ch. 209.)

22362. It is prima facie a violation of the basic speed law for any person to operate a vehicle in excess of the posted speed limit upon any portion of a highway where officers or employees of the agency having jurisdiction of the same, or any contractor of the agency or his employees, are at work on the roadway or within the right-of-way so close thereto as to be endangered by passing traffic. This section applies only when appropriate signs, indicating the limits of the restricted zone, and the speed limit applicable therein, are placed by such agency within 400 feet of each end of such zone. The signs shall display the figures indicating the applicable limit, which shall not be less than 25 miles per hour, and shall indicate the purpose of the speed restriction. Nothing in this section shall be deemed to relieve any operator of a vehicle from complying with the basic speed law.

(Amended by Stats. 1970, Ch. 515.)

22363. Notwithstanding any speed limit that may be in effect upon the highway, the Department of Transportation in respect to state highways, or a local authority with respect to highways under its jurisdiction, may determine and declare a prima facie speed limit of 40, 35, 30, or 25 miles per hour, whichever is found most appropriate and is reasonable and safe based on the prevailing snow or ice conditions upon such highway or any portion thereof. Signs may be placed and removed as snow or ice conditions vary.

(Amended by Stats. 1974, Ch. 545.)

22364. Whenever the Department of Transportation determines, upon the basis of an engineering and traffic survey, that the safe and orderly movement of traffic upon any state highway will be facilitated by the establishment of different speed limits for the various lanes of traffic, the department may place signs upon the state highway, or any portion thereof. The signs shall designate the speed limits for each of the lanes of traffic.

(Amended by Stats. 1982, Ch. 681, Sec. 84.)

22365. Notwithstanding any other provision of law, any county or city, which is contained, in whole or in part, within the South Coast Air Quality Management District, may, if the county or city determines that it is necessary to achieve or maintain state or federal ambient air quality standards for particulate matter, determine and declare by ordinance a prima facie speed limit that is lower than that which the county or city is otherwise permitted by this code to establish, for any unpaved road under the jurisdiction of the county or city and within the district. That declared prima facie speed limit shall be effective when appropriate signs giving notice thereof are erected along the road.

(Added by Stats. 1997, Ch. 16, Sec. 1. Effective May 30, 1997.)

22366. (a) Whenever the Director of Transportation determines the date upon which the state may establish a maximum speed limit of 65 miles per hour on highways without subjecting the state to a reduction in the amount of federal aid for highways, the director shall notify the Secretary of State of that determination.

(b) The notice required under subdivision (a) shall state that it is being made pursuant to this section.

(c) The notice shall specify a date which is either the date determined pursuant to subdivision (a), or a later date designated by the director.

(Added by Stats. 1995, Ch. 766, Sec. 34. Effective January 1, 1996.)

Article 2. Other Speed Laws

(Article 2 enacted by Stats. 1959, Ch. 3.)

22400. (a) No person shall drive upon a highway at such a slow speed as to impede or block the normal and reasonable movement of traffic unless the reduced speed is necessary for safe operation, because of a grade, or in compliance with law.

No person shall bring a vehicle to a complete stop upon a highway so as to impede or block the normal and reasonable movement of traffic unless the stop is necessary for safe operation or in compliance with law.

(b) Whenever the Department of Transportation determines on the basis of an engineering and traffic survey that slow speeds on any part of a state highway consistently impede the normal and reasonable movement of traffic, the department may determine and declare a minimum speed limit below which no person shall drive a vehicle, except when necessary for safe operation or in compliance with law, when appropriate signs giving notice thereof are erected along the part of the highway for which a minimum speed limit is established.

Subdivision (b) of this section shall apply only to vehicles subject to registration.

(Amended by Stats. 1979, Ch. 364.)

22401. Local authorities in timing traffic signals may so regulate the timing thereof as to permit the movement of traffic in an orderly and safe manner at speeds slightly at variance from the speed otherwise applicable under this code.

(Enacted by Stats. 1959, Ch. 3.)

22402. The Department of Transportation may, in the manner provided in Section 22404 determine the maximum speed, not less than five miles per hour, which can be maintained with safety to any bridge, elevated structure, tube, or tunnel on a state highway. Said department may also make a determination with reference to any other highway upon receiving a request therefor from the board of supervisors or road commissioner of the county, the governing body of the local authority having jurisdiction over the bridge, elevated structure, tube, or tunnel.

(Amended by Stats. 1974, Ch. 545.)

22403. Any local authority may, in the manner provided in Section 22404, determine the maximum speed, not less than five miles per hour, which can be maintained with safety to any bridge, elevated structure, tube, or tunnel under its jurisdiction, or may request the Department of Transportation to make such determination.

(Amended by Stats. 1974, Ch. 545.)

22404. The Department of Transportation or local authority making a determination of the maximum safe speed upon a bridge, elevated structure, tube, or tunnel shall first make an engineering investigation and shall hold a public hearing.

Notice of the time and place of the public hearing shall be posted upon the bridge, elevated structure, tube, or tunnel at least five days before the date fixed for the hearing. Upon the basis of the investigation and all evidence presented at the hearing, the department or local authority shall determine by order in writing the maximum speed which can be maintained with safety to the bridge, elevated structure, tube or tunnel. Thereupon, the authority having jurisdiction over the bridge, elevated structure, tube, or tunnel shall erect and maintain suitable signs specifying the maximum speed so determined at a distance of not more than 500 feet from each end of the bridge, elevated structure, tube, tunnel, or any approach thereto.

(Amended by Stats. 1974, Ch. 545.)

22405. (a) No person shall drive a vehicle on any bridge, elevated structure, tube, or tunnel constituting a part of a highway, at a speed which is greater than the maximum speed which can be maintained with safety to such structure.

(b) Upon the trial of any person charged with a violation of this section with respect to a sign erected under Section 22404, proof of the determination of the maximum speed by the Department of Transportation or local authority and the erection and maintenance of the speed signs

shall constitute prima facie evidence of the maximum speed which can be maintained with safety to the bridge, elevated structure, tube, or tunnel.
(Amended by Stats. 1974, Ch. 545.)

22406. No person may drive any of the following vehicles on a highway at a speed in excess of 55 miles per hour:

(a) A motortruck or truck tractor having three or more axles or any motortruck or truck tractor drawing any other vehicle.

(b) A passenger vehicle or bus drawing any other vehicle.

(c) A schoolbus transporting any school pupil.

(d) A farm labor vehicle when transporting passengers.

(e) A vehicle transporting explosives.

(f) A trailer bus, as defined in Section 636.
(Amended by Stats. 2000, Ch. 787, Sec. 22. Effective January 1, 2001.)

22406.1. (a) A person who operates a commercial motor vehicle, as defined in subdivision (b) of Section 15210, upon a highway at a speed exceeding a posted speed limit established under this code by 15 miles per hour or more, is guilty of a misdemeanor.

(b) A person who holds a commercial driver's license, as defined in subdivision (a) of Section 15210, and operates a noncommerical motor vehicle upon a highway at a speed exceeding a posted speed limit established under this code by 15 miles per hour or more, is guilty of an infraction.

(c) A violation of either subdivision (a) or (b) is a "serious traffic violation," as defined in subdivision (p) of Section 15210, and is subject to the sanctions provided under Section 15306 or 15308, in addition to any other penalty provided by law.

(d) This section shall become operative on September 20, 2005.
(Amended by Stats. 2004, Ch. 952, Sec. 29. Effective January 1, 2005. Amended version operative September 20, 2005, pursuant to earlier operation of new subdivision (d).)

22406.5. Any person who drives a tank vehicle subject to Division 14.7 (commencing with Section 34000) while transporting more than 500 gallons of flammable liquid at a speed greater than the applicable speed limit or in willful or wanton disregard for the safety of persons or property is, in addition to any other applicable penalty, subject to a fine of not less than five hundred dollars ($500) for a first offense and, for a second or subsequent offense within two years of a prior offense, to a fine of not less than two thousand dollars ($2,000) and a suspension of up to six months of a hazardous materials or cargo tank endorsement, or both.
(Added by Stats. 1991, Ch. 1043, Sec. 1.)

22407. Whenever the Department of Transportation or local authority determines upon the basis of engineering studies and a traffic survey that the speed of 55 miles per hour is more than is reasonable or safe for vehicles mentioned in subdivision (a) of Section 22406, which have a manufacturer's gross vehicle weight rating of 10,000 pounds or more, in descending a grade upon any portion of a highway, the department or local authority, with respect to highways under their respective jurisdiction, may determine and declare a speed limit of 50, 45, 40, 35, 30, 25, or 20 miles per hour, whichever is found most appropriate to facilitate the orderly movement of traffic and is reasonable and safe, which declared speed limit shall be effective for such vehicles when appropriate signs giving notice thereof are erected upon the highway.
(Amended by Stats. 1973, Ch. 82, Sec. 1.)

22409. No person shall operate any vehicle equipped with any solid tire when such vehicle has a gross weight as set forth in the following table at any speed in excess of the speed set forth opposite such gross weight:

When gross weight of vehicle and load is:	Maximum speed in miles per hour:
10,000 lbs. or more but less than 16,000 lbs.	25
16,000 lbs. or more but less than 22,000 lbs.	15
22,000 lbs. or more	12

(Enacted by Stats. 1959, Ch. 3.)

22410. No person shall operate any vehicle equipped with any metal tire in contact with the surface of the highway at a speed in excess of six miles per hour.
(Enacted by Stats. 1959, Ch. 3.)

22411. No person shall operate a motorized scooter at a speed in excess of 15 miles per hour.
(Added by Stats. 1999, Ch. 722, Sec. 7. Effective January 1, 2000.)

22413. Whenever a local authority determines upon the basis of an engineering and traffic survey that the prima facie limit of 25 miles per hour is more than is reasonable and safe on any portion of a street having a grade in excess of 10 percent, the local authority may by ordinance determine and declare a maximum limit of 20 or 15 miles per hour, whichever is found most appropriate and is reasonable and safe. The declared maximum speed shall be effective when appropriate signs giving notice thereof are erected upon the street.
(Added by Stats. 1959, Ch. 318.)

Article 3. Speed Safety System Pilot Program

(Article 3 added by Stats. 2023, Ch. 808, Sec. 4.)

22425. (a) As used in this article, the following definitions apply:

(1) "Automated speed violation" means a violation of a speed law detected by a speed safety system operated pursuant to this article.

(2) "Designated jurisdiction" means any of the Cities of Los Angeles, San Jose, Oakland, Glendale, or Long Beach, or the City and County of San Francisco.

(3) A person is "indigent" if either of the following conditions is met:

(A) The person meets the income criteria set forth in subdivision (b) of Section 68632 of the Government Code.

(B) The person receives public benefits from a program listed in subdivision (a) of Section 68632 of the Government Code.

(4) "Local department of transportation" means a designated jurisdiction's department of transportation or, if a designated jurisdiction does not have a department of transportation, their administrative division, including, but not limited to, a public works department that administers transportation and traffic matters under this code.

(5) "School zone" means an area described by subdivision (b) of Section 40802.

(6) "Speed safety system" or "system" means a fixed or mobile radar or laser system or any other electronic device that utilizes automated equipment to detect a violation of speed laws and obtains a clear photograph of a speeding vehicle's license plate.

(b) (1) A designated jurisdiction may establish a program for speed enforcement that utilizes a speed safety system, to be operated by a local department of transportation, in the following areas:

(A) On a street meeting the standards of a safety corridor under Section 22358.7.

(B) On a street a local authority has determined to have had a high number of incidents for motor vehicle speed contests or motor vehicle exhibitions of speed. For the purposes of this provision, a high number of incidents shall be calls for law enforcement to respond to the area for at least four separate incidences of a motor vehicle speed contest or motor vehicle exhibition of speed within the last two years before the placement of the speed safety system.

(C) School zones, subject to subdivision (c).

(2) The number of speed safety systems operated by a designated jurisdiction at any time shall be limited as follows:

(A) For a jurisdiction with a population over 3,000,000, as determined by the United States Census Bureau in the 2020 Census, no more than 125 systems.

(B) For a jurisdiction with a population between 800,000 and 3,000,000, inclusive, as determined by the United States Census Bureau in the 2020 Census, no more than 33 systems.

(C) For a jurisdiction with a population of 300,000 up to 800,000, as determined by the United States Census Bureau in the 2020 Census, no more than 18 systems.

(D) For a jurisdiction with a population of less than 300,000, as determined by the United States Census Bureau in the 2020 Census, no more than 9 systems.

(3) A speed enforcement program developed pursuant to paragraph (1) shall place the speed safety systems in locations that are geographically and socioeconomically diverse. The designated jurisdiction shall describe how it has complied with this provision in the Speed Safety System Impact Report described in subdivision (h).

(c) If a speed safety system is deployed in a school zone and the school zone has a higher posted speed limit when children are not present, a designated jurisdiction may only enforce the school zone speed limit up to one hour before the regular school session begins, 10 minutes after school begins, one hour during lunch period, and up to one hour after regular school session concludes. For these school zones, flashing beacons activated by a time clock, other automatic device, or manual activation shall be installed on a school zone sign and be active to indicate the times during which the school zone speed limit is enforced with a speed safety system.

(d) A speed safety system may be utilized pursuant to subdivision (b) if the program meets all of the following requirements:

(1) Clearly identifies the presence of the speed safety system by signs stating "Photo Enforced," along with the posted speed limit no more than 500 feet before the placement of the system. The signs shall be visible to traffic traveling on the street from the direction of travel for which the system is utilized, and shall be posted at all locations as may be determined necessary by the Department of Transportation after consultation with the California Traffic Control Devices Committee.

(2) Identifies the streets or portions of streets that have been approved for enforcement using a speed safety system and the hours of enforcement on the municipality's internet website, which shall be updated whenever the municipality changes locations of enforcement.

(3) Ensures that the speed safety system is regularly inspected, but no less than once every 60 days, and certifies that the system is installed and operating properly. Each camera unit shall be calibrated in accordance with the manufacturer's instructions, and at least once per year by an independent calibration laboratory. Documentation of the regular inspection, operation, and calibration of the system shall be retained at least 180 days after the date on which the system has been permanently removed from use.

(4) Utilizes fixed or mobile speed safety systems that provide real-time notification to the driver when violations are detected.

(e) A speed safety system shall not be operated on any California state route, as defined in Section 231 of the Streets and Highways Code, including all freeways and expressways, United States highways, interstate highways, or any public road in unincorporated areas of any county where the Commissioner of the California Highway Patrol has full responsibility and primary jurisdiction for the administration and enforcement of the laws, and for the investigation of traffic accidents, pursuant to Section 2400.

(f) Prior to enforcing speed laws utilizing speed safety systems, the designated jurisdiction shall do both of the following:

(1) Administer a public information campaign for at least 30 calendar days prior to the commencement of the program, which shall include public announcements in major media outlets and press releases. The public information campaign shall include the draft Speed Safety System Use Policy pursuant to subdivision (g), the Speed Safety System Impact Report pursuant to subdivision (h), information on when systems will begin detecting violations, the streets, or portions of streets, where systems will be utilized, and the designated jurisdiction's internet website, where additional information about the program can be obtained. Notwithstanding the above, no further public announcement by the municipality shall be required for additional systems that may be added to the program.

(2) (A) Issue warning notices rather than notices of violation for violations detected by the speed safety systems during the first 60 calendar days of enforcement under the program. If additional systems are utilized on additional streets after the initial program implementation, the designated jurisdiction shall issue warning notices rather than notices of violation for violations detected by the new speed safety systems during the first 60 calendar days of enforcement for the additional streets added to the program.

(B) A vehicle's first violation within a designated jurisdiction for traveling 11 to 15 miles per hour over the posted speed limit shall be a warning notice.

(g) The governing body of a designated jurisdiction shall adopt a Speed Safety System Use Policy before entering into an agreement regarding a speed safety system, purchasing or leasing equipment for a program, or implementing a program. The Speed Safety System Use Policy shall set forth the specific purpose for the system, the uses that are authorized, the rules and processes required to be followed by employees and contractors of the designated jurisdiction administering the system prior to its use, and the uses of the equipment and data collected that are prohibited. The policy shall identify the data or information that can be collected by the speed safety system and the individuals who can access or use the collected information, and the rules and processes related to the access, transfer, and use or use of the information. The policy shall also include provisions for protecting data from unauthorized access, data retention, public access, third-party data sharing, training, auditing, and oversight to ensure compliance with the Speed Safety System Use Policy. The Speed Safety System Use Policy shall be made available for public review, including, but not limited to, by posting it on the designated jurisdiction's internet website at least 30 calendar days prior to adoption by the governing body of the designated jurisdiction.

(h) (1) The governing body of the designated jurisdiction also shall approve a Speed Safety System Impact Report prior to implementing a program. The Speed Safety System Impact Report shall include all of the following information:

(A) Assessment of potential impact of the speed safety system on civil liberties and civil rights and any plans to safeguard those public rights.

(B) Description of the speed safety system and how it works.

(C) Fiscal costs for the speed safety system, including program establishment costs, ongoing costs, and program funding.

(D) If potential deployment locations of systems are predominantly in low-income neighborhoods, a determination of why these locations experience high fatality and injury collisions due to unsafe speed.

(E) Locations where the system may be deployed and traffic data for these locations, including the address of where the cameras will be located.

(F) Proposed purpose of the speed safety system.

(2) The Speed Safety System Impact Report shall be made available for public review at least 30 calendar days prior to adoption by the governing body at a public hearing.

(3) The governing body of the designated jurisdiction shall consult and work collaboratively with relevant local stakeholder organizations, including racial equity, privacy protection, and economic justice groups, in developing the Speed Safety System Use Policy and Speed Safety System Impact Report.

(i) The designated jurisdiction shall develop uniform guidelines, consistent with the provisions of this section, for both of the following:

(1) The screening and issuing of notices of violation.

(2) The processing and storage of confidential information and procedures to ensure compliance with confidentiality requirements.

(j) Notices of violation issued pursuant to this section shall include a clear photograph of the license plate and rear of the vehicle only, identify the specific section of the Vehicle Code violated, the camera location, and the date and time when the violation occurred. Notices of violation shall exclude images of the rear window area of the vehicle.

(k) The photographic evidence stored by a speed safety system does not constitute an out-of-court hearsay statement by a declarant under

Division 10 (commencing with Section 1200) of the Evidence Code.

(l) (1) Notwithstanding any provision of the California Public Records Act, or any other law, photographic or administrative records made by a system shall be confidential. Public agencies shall use and allow access to these records only for the purposes authorized by this article or to assess the impacts of the system. Data about the number of violations issued and the speeds at which they were issued is not considered an administrative record required not to be disclosed by this section.

(2) Confidential information obtained from the Department of Motor Vehicles for the administration of speed safety systems and enforcement of this article shall be held confidential, and shall not be used for any other purpose. Designated jurisdictions agents shall establish procedures to protect the confidentiality of these records consistent with Section 1808.47.

(3) Except for court records described in Section 68152 of the Government Code, or as provided in paragraph (4), the confidential records and evidence described in paragraphs (1) and (2) may be retained for up to 60 days after final disposition of the notice of violation. The designated jurisdiction may retain information that a vehicle has been cited and fined for a violation for up to three years. The municipality may adopt a retention period of less than 60 days in the Speed Safety System Use Policy. Administrative records described in paragraph (1) may be retained for up to 120 days after final disposition of the notice of violation. Notwithstanding any other law, the confidential records and evidence shall be destroyed in a manner that maintains the confidentiality of any person included in the record or evidence.

(4) Photographic evidence that is obtained from a speed safety system that does not result in the issuance of a notice of violation shall be destroyed within five business days after the photograph was first made. The use of facial recognition technology in conjunction with a speed safety system shall be prohibited.

(5) Information collected and maintained by a designated jurisdiction to administer a program shall only be used to administer the program, and shall not be disclosed to any other persons, including, but not limited to, any other state or federal government agency or official for any other purpose, except as required by state or federal law, court order, or in response to a subpoena in an individual case or proceeding.

(m) Notwithstanding subdivision (l), the registered owner or an individual identified by the registered owner as the driver of the vehicle at the time of the alleged violation shall be permitted to review and obtain a copy of the photographic evidence of the alleged violation.

(n) A contract between the designated jurisdiction and a manufacturer or supplier of speed safety systems shall allow the local authority to purchase materials, lease equipment, and contract for processing services from the manufacturer or supplier based on the services rendered on a monthly schedule or another schedule agreed upon by the municipality and contractor. The contract shall not allow for payment or compensation based on the number of notices of violation issued, or as a percentage of revenue generated, from the use of the system. The contract shall include a provision that all data collected from the speed safety systems is confidential, and shall prohibit the manufacturer or supplier of the contracted speed safety system from sharing, repurposing, or monetizing collected data, except as specifically authorized in this article. The designated jurisdiction shall oversee, maintain control, and have the final decision over all enforcement activities, including the determination of when a notice of violation should be issued.

(o) Notwithstanding subdivision (n), a designated jurisdiction may contract with a vendor for the processing of notices of violation after an employee of a designated jurisdiction has issued a notice of violation. The vendor shall be a separate legal and corporate entity from, and not related to or affiliated in any manner with, the manufacturer or supplier of speed safety systems used by the designated jurisdiction. Any contract between the designated jurisdiction and a vendor to provide processing services may include a provision for the payment of compensation based on the number of notices of violation processed by the vendor.

(p) (1) A speed safety system at a specific location shall be operated for no more than 18 months after installation of a system, unless one of the following thresholds has been met:

(A) A reduction in the 85th percentile speed of vehicles compared to data collected before the system was in operation.

(B) A 20-percent reduction in vehicles that exceed the posted speed limit by 10 miles per hour or more compared to data collected before the system was in operation.

(C) A 20-percent reduction in the number of violators who received two or more violations at the location since the system became operational.

(2) (A) Paragraph (1) does not apply if a designated jurisdiction adds traffic-calming measures to the street. "Traffic-calming measures" include, but are not limited to, all of the following:

(i) Bicycle lanes.

(ii) Chicanes.

(iii) Chokers.

(iv) Curb extensions.

(v) Median islands.

(vi) Raised crosswalks.

(vii) Road diets.

(viii) Roundabouts.

(ix) Speed humps or speed tables.

(x) Traffic circles.

(xi) Flashing beacons for school zone speed limits.

(B) A designated jurisdiction may continue to operate a speed safety system with a fixed or mobile vehicle speed feedback sign while traffic-calming measures are being planned or constructed, but shall halt their use if construction has not begun within two years.

(3) If the percentage of violations has not decreased by the metrics identified pursuant to paragraph (1) within one year after traffic-calming measures have completed construction, a designated jurisdiction shall either construct additional traffic-calming measures or cease operation of the system on that street.

(q) The speed safety system, to the extent feasible, shall be angled and focused so as to only capture photographs of speeding violations and shall not capture identifying images of other drivers, vehicles, or pedestrians.

(r) Notwithstanding subdivision (c) of Section 21455.6, the designated jurisdictions listed herein may use automated enforcement systems and photo radar for speed enforcement consistent with this article.

(Added by Stats. 2023, Ch. 808, Sec. 4. (AB 645) Effective January 1, 2024. Repealed as of January 1, 2032, pursuant to Section 22431.)

22426. (a) Notwithstanding any other law, a violation of any speed law pursuant to this chapter that is recorded by a speed safety system authorized pursuant to Section 22425 shall be subject only to a civil penalty, as provided in subdivision (c), and shall not result in the department suspending or revoking the privilege of a violator to drive a motor vehicle or in a violation point being assessed against the violator.

(b) The speed safety system shall capture images of the rear license plate of vehicles that are traveling 11 miles per hour or more over the posted speed limit and notices of violation shall only be issued to registered owners of those vehicles based on that evidence.

(c) A civil penalty shall be assessed as follows:

(1) Fifty dollars ($50) for driving at a speed of 11 to 15 miles per hour over the posted speed limit.

(2) One hundred dollars ($100) for driving at a speed of 16 to 25 miles per hour over the posted speed limit.

(3) Two hundred dollars ($200) for driving at a speed of 26 miles per hour or more over the posted speed limit, unless paragraph (4) applies.

(4) Five hundred dollars ($500) for driving at a speed of 100 miles per hour or more.

(d) A civil penalty shall not be assessed against an authorized emergency vehicle.

(e) The notice of violation shall be in writing and issued to the registered owner of the vehicle within 15 calendar days of the date of the violation. The notice of violation shall include all of the following information:

(1) The violation, including reference to the speed law that was violated, the speed of the vehicle, the speed limit for the road on which the violation occurred, and verification of the most recent calibration of the system in accordance with paragraph (3) of subdivision (d) of Section 22425.

(2) The date, approximate time, and location where the violation occurred.

(3) The vehicle license number and the name and address of the registered owner of the vehicle.

(4) A statement that payment is required to be made no later than 30 calendar days from the date of mailing of the notice of violation, or that the violation may be contested pursuant to Section 22427.

(5) The amount of the civil penalty due for that violation and the procedures for the payment of the civil penalty or for contesting the notice of violation.

(6) An affidavit of nonliability, and information of what constitutes nonliability, information as to the effect of executing the affidavit, and instructions for returning the affidavit to the processor. If the affidavit of nonliability is returned to the processing agency within 30 calendar days of the mailing of the notice of violation, together with proof of a written lease or rental agreement between a bona fide rental company, as defined in Section 1939.01 of the Civil Code, or a personal vehicle sharing program, as defined in Section 11580.24 of the Insurance Code, and its customer that identifies the renter or lessee, the processing agency shall serve or mail a notice of violation to the renter or lessee identified in the affidavit of nonliability. If the affidavit of nonliability is returned to the processing agency within 30 calendar days of the mailing of the notice of violation, together with proof of a copy of a police report indicating the vehicle had been stolen at the time of the violation, the processing agency shall not subject the registered owner to a civil violation.

(7) A proof of service consistent with Section 1013a of the Code of Civil Procedure.

(f) Mobile radar or laser systems shall not be used until at least two years after the installation of the first fixed radar or laser system unless the mobile radar or laser system is kept at a fixed location.

(g) (1) Revenues derived from any program utilizing a speed safety system for speed limit enforcement shall first be used to recover program costs. Program costs include, but are not limited to, the construction of traffic-calming measures for the purposes of complying with subdivision (p) of Section 22425, the installation of speed safety systems, the adjudication of violations, and reporting requirements as specified in this section.

(2) Jurisdictions shall maintain their existing commitment of local funds for traffic-calming measures in order to remain authorized to participate in the pilot program, and shall annually expend not less than the annual average of expenditures for traffic-calming measures during the 2016–17, 2017–18, and 2018–19 fiscal years. For purposes of this subdivision, in calculating average expenditures on traffic-calming measures, restricted funds that may not be available on an ongoing basis, including those from voter-approved bond issuances or tax measures, shall not be included. Any excess revenue shall be used for traffic-calming measures within three years of the end of the fiscal year in which the excess revenue was received. If traffic-calming measures are not planned or constructed after the third year, excess revenue shall revert to the Active Transportation Program established pursuant to Chapter 8 (commencing with Section 2380) of the Streets and Highways Code, to be allocated by the California Transportation Commission pursuant to Section 2381 of the Streets and Highways Code.

(h) A person shall not be accessed a civil penalty if they are subject to criminal penalties for the same act.

(i) A speed safety system may only be in operation for five years, or until January 1, 2032, whichever date is sooner.

(Added by Stats. 2023, Ch. 808, Sec. 4. (AB 645) Effective January 1, 2024. Repealed as of January 1, 2032, pursuant to Section 22431.)

22427. (a) No later than 30 calendar days from the date of mailing of a notice of violation, the recipient may request an initial review of the notice by the issuing agency. The request may be made by telephone, in writing, electronically, or in person. There shall be no charge for this review. If, following the initial review, the issuing agency is satisfied that the violation did not occur, or that extenuating circumstances make cancellation of the notice of violation appropriate in the interest of justice, the issuing agency shall cancel the notice of violation. The issuing agency shall advise the processing agency, if any, of the cancellation. The issuing agency or the processing agency shall mail the results of the initial review to the person contesting the notice within 60 days of receipt of the recipient's request for an initial review, and, if cancellation of the notice does not occur following that review, include a reason for that denial, notification of the ability to request an administrative hearing, and notice of the procedures adopted by the designated jurisdiction for the administrative hearing, including for waiving prepayment of the civil penalty based upon an inability to pay pursuant to paragraph (2) of subdivision (b).

(b) (1) If the person contesting the notice of violation is dissatisfied with the results of the initial review, the person may, no later than 21 calendar days following the mailing of the results of the issuing agency's initial review, request an administrative hearing of the violation. The request may be made by telephone, in writing, electronically, or in person.

(2) The person requesting an administrative hearing shall pay the amount of the civil penalty to the processing agency. The issuing agency shall adopt a written procedure to allow a person to request an administrative hearing without payment of the civil penalty upon satisfactory proof of an inability to pay the amount due.

(3) The administrative hearing shall be held within 90 calendar days following the receipt of a request for an administrative hearing. The person requesting the hearing may request one continuance, not to exceed 21 calendar days.

(c) The administrative hearing process shall include all of the following:

(1) The person requesting a hearing shall have the choice of a hearing upon written declaration, video conference, or in person. An in-person hearing shall be conducted within the jurisdiction of the issuing agency.

(2) If the person requesting a hearing is an unemancipated minor, that person shall be permitted to appear at a hearing or admit responsibility for the automated speed violation without the appointment of a guardian. The processing agency may proceed against the minor in the same manner as against an adult.

(3) The administrative hearing shall be conducted in accordance with written procedures established by the issuing agency and approved by the governing body or chief executive officer of the issuing agency. The hearing shall provide an independent, objective, fair, and impartial review of contested automated speed violations.

(4) (A) The issuing agency's governing body or chief executive officer of the designated jurisdiction shall appoint or contract with qualified independent examiners or administrative hearing providers that employ qualified independent examiners to conduct the administrative hearings. Examiners shall demonstrate the qualifications, training, and objectivity necessary to conduct a fair and impartial review, and shall meet the minimum requirements specified in subparagraph (B). The examiner shall be separate and independent from the notice of violation issuing and processing functions. An examiner's continued employment, performance evaluation, compensation, and benefits shall not, directly or indirectly, be linked to the amount of civil penalties upheld by the examiner or the number or percentage of violations upheld by the examiner.

(B) (i) Examiners shall have a minimum of 20 hours of training. The examiner, unless an employee of the designated jurisdiction, is responsible for the costs of the training. The issuing agency may reimburse the examiner for those costs. Training may be provided through any of the following:

(I) An accredited college or university.

(II) A program conducted by the Commission on Peace Officer Standards and Training.

(III) A program conducted by the American Arbitration Association or a similar organization.

(IV) Any program approved by the governing body or chief executive officer of the issuing agency, including a program developed and provided by, or for, the agency.

(ii) Training programs shall include topics relevant to the administrative hearing, including, but not limited to, applicable laws and regulations, enforcement procedures, due process, evaluation of evidence, hearing procedures, and effective oral and written communication. Upon the approval of the governing body or chief executive officer of the issuing agency, up to 12 hours of relevant experience may be substituted for up to 12 hours of training. Up to eight hours of the training requirements described in this subparagraph may be credited to an individual, at the discretion of the governing body or chief executive officer of the issuing agency, based upon training programs or courses described in this subparagraph that the individual attended within the last five years.

(5) The employee of the designated jurisdiction who issues a notice of violation shall not be required to participate in an administrative hearing. To establish a violation, the issuing agency shall not be required to produce any evidence other than, in proper form, the notice of violation or copy thereof, including the photograph of the vehicle's license plate, and information received from the Department of Motor Vehicles identifying the registered owner of the vehicle. The documentation in proper form shall be prima facie evidence of the violation. If the designated jurisdiction meets its initial burden the recipient of the notice of violation may present any evidence and argument in defense.

(6) The examiner's final decision following the administrative hearing may be personally delivered to the person by the examiner or sent by first-class mail within 60 days of the date of the conclusion of the administrative hearing.

(7) Following a determination by the examiner that a person has committed the violation, the examiner may, consistent with the written guidelines established by the issuing agency, allow payment of the civil penalty in installments, or an issuing agency may allow for deferred payment or payments in installments, if the person provides evidence satisfactory to the examiner or the issuing agency, as the case may be, of an inability to pay the civil penalty in full. If authorized by the governing body of the issuing agency, the examiner may permit the performance of community service in lieu of payment of the civil penalty.

(8) If a notice of violation is dismissed following an administrative hearing, any civil penalty, if paid, shall be refunded by the issuing agency within 30 days.

(Added by Stats. 2023, Ch. 808, Sec. 4. (AB 645) Effective January 1, 2024. Repealed as of January 1, 2032, pursuant to Section 22431.)

22428. (a) Within 30 days after personal delivery or mailing of the final decision described in subdivision (c) of Section 22427, the contestant may seek review by filing an appeal to the superior court, where the case shall be heard de novo, except that the contents of the processing agency's file in the case on appeal shall be lodged by the designated agency at the designated agency's expense and be received into evidence. A copy of the notice of violation shall be admitted into evidence as prima facie evidence of the facts stated in the notice. A copy of the notice of appeal shall be served in person or by certified first-class mail with return receipt upon the processing agency by the appellant. For purposes of computing the 30-day period, Section 1013 of the Code of Civil Procedure shall be applicable. A proceeding under this subdivision is a limited civil case.

(b) The fee for filing the notice of appeal shall be as provided in Section 70615 of the Government Code. Upon receipt of the notice of appeal, the designated jurisdiction shall lodge its administrative record for the case with the court within 15 calendar days. The court shall notify the appellant of the appearance date by mail or personal delivery. The court shall retain the fee under Section 70615 of the Government Code regardless of the outcome of the appeal. If the appellant prevails, this fee and any payment of the civil penalty shall be promptly refunded by the issuing agency in accordance with the judgment of the court.

(c) The conduct of the hearing on appeal under this section is a subordinate judicial duty that may be performed by a commissioner or other subordinate judicial officer at the direction of the presiding judge of the court.

(d) If a notice of appeal of the examiner's decision is not filed within the period set forth in subdivision (a), the decision shall be deemed final.

(e) If the civil penalty has not been paid and the final decision is adverse to the appellant, the processing agency may, promptly after the decision becomes final, proceed to collect the civil penalty under Section 22426.

(Added by Stats. 2023, Ch. 808, Sec. 4. (AB 645) Effective January 1, 2024. Repealed as of January 1, 2032, pursuant to Section 22431.)

22429. (a) A designated jurisdiction shall offer a diversion program for indigent speed safety system violation recipients, to perform community service in lieu of paying the penalty for a speed system violation.

(b) A designated jurisdiction shall offer the ability for indigent speed safety system violation recipients to pay applicable fines and penalties over a period of time under a payment plan with monthly installments of no more than twenty-five dollars ($25) and shall limit the processing fee to participate in a payment plan to five dollars ($5) or less.

(c) Notwithstanding subdivisions (a) and (b), a designated jurisdiction shall reduce the applicable fines and penalties by 80 percent for indigent persons, and by 50 percent for individuals up to 250 percent above the federal poverty level.

(d) The person may demonstrate that they are indigent or make up to 250 percent above the poverty level or less by providing either of the following information, as applicable:

(1) Proof of income from a pay stub or another form of proof of earnings, such as a bank statement, that shows that the person meets the income criteria set forth in subdivision (b) of Section 68632 of the Government Code, subject to review and approval by the processing agency or its designee. The processing agency or its designee shall not unreasonably withhold its approval.

(2) Proof of receipt of benefits under the programs described in subdivision (a) of Section 68632 of the Government Code, including, but not limited to, an electronic benefits transfer card or another card, subject to review and approval by the processing agency. The processing agency or its designee shall not unreasonably withhold its approval.

(Added by Stats. 2023, Ch. 808, Sec. 4. (AB 645) Effective January 1, 2024. Repealed as of January 1, 2032, pursuant to Section 22431.)

22430. Any designated jurisdiction that used speed safety systems shall, on or before March 1 of the fifth year in which the system has been implemented, submit to its governing body and the transportation committees of the Legislature, consistent with Section 9795 of the Government Code, an evaluation of the speed safety system in their respective jurisdictions to determine the system's impact on street safety and the system's economic impact on the communities where the system is utilized. The report shall be made available on the internet websites of the respective jurisdictions and shall include all of the following information:

(a) Data, at least three months before and at least six months after implementation of each system, on the number and proportion of vehicles speeding from 11 to 15 miles per hour over the legal speed limit, inclusive, from 16 to 25 miles per hour over the legal speed limit, inclusive, 26 miles per hour over the legal speed limit, and for every violator traveling at a speed of 100 miles per hour or greater. Data shall also be collected on the average speed of vehicles and 85th percentile speed of vehicles.

To the extent feasible, the data should be collected at the same time of day, day of week, and location.

(b) The number of notices of violation issued under the program by month and year, the corridors or locations where violations occurred, and the number of vehicles with two or more violations in a monthly period and a yearly period.

(c) Data, before and after implementation of the system, on the number of traffic collisions that occurred where speed safety systems are used, relative to citywide data, and the transportation mode of the parties involved. The data on traffic collisions shall be categorized by collision type and injury severity, such as property damage only, complaint of pain, other visible injury, or severe or fatal injury.

(d) The number of violations paid, the number of delinquent violations, and the number of violations for which an initial review is requested. For the violations in which an initial review was requested, the report shall indicate the number of violations that went to initial review, administrative hearing, and de novo hearing, the number of notices that were dismissed at each level of review, and the number of notices that were not dismissed after each level of review.

(e) The costs associated with implementation and operation of the speed safety systems, and revenues collected by each jurisdiction.

(f) A racial and economic equity impact analysis, developed in collaboration with local racial justice and economic equity stakeholder groups. The analysis shall include the number of notices of violations issued to indigent individuals, the number of notices of violations issued to individuals of up to 250 percent above the poverty line, and the number of violations issued to each ZIP Code.

(Added by Stats. 2023, Ch. 808, Sec. 4. (AB 645) Effective January 1, 2024. Repealed as of January 1, 2032, pursuant to Section 22431.)

22431. This article shall remain in effect only until January 1, 2032, and as of that date is repealed.

(Added by Stats. 2023, Ch. 808, Sec. 4. (AB 645) Effective January 1, 2024. Repealed as of January 1, 2032, by its own provisions. Repeal affects Article 3, commencing with Section 22425.)

Article 4. The City of Malibu's Speed Safety Pilot Program

(Article 4 added by Stats. 2024, Ch. 631, Sec. 3.)

22435. (a) As used in this article, the following definitions apply:

(1) "Automated speed violation" means a violation of a speed law detected by a speed safety system operated pursuant to this article.

(2) "Designated jurisdiction" means the City of Malibu.

(3) A person is "indigent" if either of the following conditions is met:

(A) The person meets the income criteria set forth in subdivision (b) of Section 68632 of the Government Code.

(B) The person receives public benefits from a program listed in subdivision (a) of Section 68632 of the Government Code.

(4) "Local department of transportation" means the City of Malibu's department that administers transportation and traffic matters under this code.

(5) "Speed safety system" or "system" means a fixed or mobile radar or laser system or any other electronic device that utilizes automated equipment to detect a violation of speed laws and obtains a clear photograph of a speeding vehicle's license plate.

(b) The designated jurisdiction may establish a program for speed enforcement that utilizes up to five speed safety systems, to be operated by the local department of transportation, on the Pacific Coast Highway.

(c) The speed safety system may be utilized pursuant to subdivision (b) if the program meets all of the following requirements:

(1) The designated jurisdiction continues funding the additional traffic enforcement on the Pacific Coast Highway provided by the Department of the California Highway Patrol.

(2) Clearly identifies the presence of the speed safety system by signs stating "Photo Enforced," along with the speed limit signs with flashing beacons and speed feedback signs, no more than 500 feet before the placement of the system. The signs shall be visible to traffic traveling on the street from the direction of travel for which the system is utilized, and shall be posted at locations as may be determined necessary by the Department of Transportation after consultation with the California Traffic Control Devices Committee.

(3) Identifies the street or portions of the street approved for enforcement using a speed safety system and the hours of enforcement on the municipality's internet website, which shall be updated whenever the municipality changes locations of enforcement.

(4) Ensures that the speed safety system is regularly inspected no less than once every 60 days, and certifies that the system is installed and operating properly. Each camera unit shall be calibrated in accordance with the manufacturer's instructions, and at least once per year by an independent calibration laboratory. Documentation of the regular inspection, operation, and calibration of the system shall be retained for at least 180 days after the date on which the system has been permanently removed from use.

(5) Utilizes fixed or mobile speed safety systems that provide real-time notification to the driver when violations are detected.

(d) Prior to enforcing speed laws utilizing speed safety systems, the designated jurisdiction shall do both of the following:

(1) Administer a public information campaign for at least 30 calendar days prior to the commencement of the program, which shall include public announcements in major media outlets and press releases. The public information campaign shall include the draft Speed Safety System Use Policy pursuant to subdivision (e), the Speed Safety System Impact Report pursuant to subdivision (f), information on when systems will begin detecting violations, the street, or portions of the street, where systems will be utilized, and the designated jurisdiction's internet website, where additional information about the program can be obtained. Notwithstanding the above, no further public announcement by the municipality shall be required for additional systems that may be added to the program.

(2) (A) Issue warning notices rather than notices of violation for violations detected by the speed safety system during the first 60 calendar days of enforcement under the program.

(B) A vehicle's first violation for traveling 11 to 15 miles per hour over the posted speed limit shall be a warning notice.

(e) The governing body of the designated jurisdiction shall adopt a Speed Safety System Use Policy before entering into an agreement regarding a speed safety system, purchasing or leasing equipment for a program, or implementing a program. The Speed Safety System Use Policy shall set forth the specific purpose for the system, the uses that are authorized, the rules and processes required to be followed by employees and contractors of the designated jurisdiction administering the system prior to its use, and the uses of the equipment and data collected that are prohibited. The policy shall identify the data or information that can be collected by the speed safety system and the individuals who can access or use the collected information, and the rules and processes related to the access, transfer, and use or use of the information. The policy shall also include provisions for protecting data from unauthorized access, data retention, public access, third-party data sharing, training, auditing, and oversight to ensure compliance with the Speed Safety System Use Policy. The Speed Safety System Use Policy shall be made available for public review, including, but not limited to, by posting it on the designated jurisdiction's internet website at least 30 calendar days prior to adoption by the governing body of the designated jurisdiction.

(f) (1) The governing body of the designated jurisdiction shall approve a Speed Safety System Impact Report prior to implementing a program. The Speed Safety System Impact Report shall include all of the following information:

(A) Assessment of the potential impact of the speed safety system on civil liberties and civil rights and any plans to safeguard those public rights.

(B) Description of the speed safety system and how it works.

(C) Fiscal costs for the speed safety system, including program establishment costs, ongoing costs, and program funding.

(D) If potential deployment locations of systems are predominantly in low-income neighborhoods, a determination of why these locations experience high fatality and injury collisions due to unsafe speed.

(E) Locations where the system may be deployed and traffic data for these locations, including the address where the cameras will be located.

(F) Proposed purpose of the speed safety system.

(2) The Speed Safety System Impact Report shall be made available for public review at least 30 calendar days prior to adoption by the governing body at a public hearing.

(3) The governing body of the designated jurisdiction shall consult and work collaboratively with relevant local stakeholder organizations, including racial equity, privacy protection, and economic justice groups, in developing the Speed Safety System Use Policy and Speed Safety System Impact Report.

(g) The designated jurisdiction shall develop uniform guidelines, consistent with the provisions of this section, for both of the following:

(1) The screening and issuing of notices of violation.

(2) The processing and storage of confidential information and procedures to ensure compliance with confidentiality requirements.

(h) Notices of violation issued pursuant to this section shall include a clear photograph of the license plate and rear of the vehicle only, identify the specific section of the Vehicle Code violated, the camera location, and the date and time when the violation occurred. Notices of violation shall exclude images of the rear window area of the vehicle.

(i) The photographic evidence stored by a speed safety system does not constitute an out-of-court hearsay statement by a declarant under Division 10 (commencing with Section 1200) of the Evidence Code.

(j) (1) Notwithstanding any provision of the California Public Records Act, or any other law, photographic or administrative records made by a system shall be confidential. Public agencies shall use and allow access to these records only for the purposes authorized by this article or to assess the impacts of the system. Data about the number of violations issued and the speeds at which they were issued is not considered an administrative record required not to be disclosed by this section.

(2) Confidential information obtained from the Department of Motor Vehicles for the administration of speed safety systems and enforcement of this article shall be held confidential, and shall not be used for any other purpose. Designated jurisdictions' agents shall establish procedures to protect the confidentiality of these records consistent with Section 1808.47.

(3) Except for court records described in Section 68152 of the Government Code, or as provided in paragraph (4), the confidential records and evidence described in paragraphs (1) and (2) may be retained for up to 60 days after final disposition of the notice of violation. The designated jurisdiction may retain information that a vehicle has been cited and fined for a violation for up to three years. The municipality may adopt a retention period of less than 60 days in the Speed Safety System Use Policy. Administrative records described in paragraph (1) may be retained for up to 120 days after final disposition of the notice of violation. Notwithstanding any other law, the confidential records and evidence shall be destroyed in a manner that maintains the confidentiality of any person included in the record or evidence.

(4) Photographic evidence that is obtained from a speed safety system that does not result in the issuance of a notice of violation shall be destroyed within five business days after the photograph was first made. The use of facial recognition technology in conjunction with a speed safety system shall be prohibited.

(5) Information collected and maintained by a designated jurisdiction to administer a program shall only be used to administer the program, and shall not be disclosed to any other persons, including, but not limited to, any other state or federal governmental agency or official for any other purpose, except as required by state or federal law, court order, or in response to a subpoena in an individual case or proceeding.

(k) Notwithstanding subdivision (j), the registered owner or an individual identified by the registered owner as the driver of the vehicle at the time of the alleged violation shall be permitted to review and obtain a copy of the photographic evidence of the alleged violation.

(l) A contract between the designated jurisdiction and a manufacturer or supplier of speed safety systems shall allow the local authority to purchase materials, lease equipment, and contract for processing services from the manufacturer or supplier based on the services rendered on a monthly schedule or another schedule agreed upon by the municipality and contractor. The contract shall not allow for payment or compensation based on the number of notices of violation issued, or as a percentage of revenue generated, from the use of the system. The contract shall include a provision that all data collected from the speed safety system is confidential, and shall prohibit the manufacturer or supplier of the contracted speed safety system from sharing, repurposing, or monetizing collected data, except as specifically authorized in this article. The designated jurisdiction shall oversee, maintain control, and have the final decision over all enforcement activities, including the determination of when a notice of violation should be issued.

(m) Notwithstanding subdivision (l), a designated jurisdiction may contract with a vendor for the processing of notices of violation after an employee of a designated jurisdiction has issued a notice of violation. The vendor shall be a separate legal and corporate entity from, and not related to or affiliated in any manner with, the manufacturer or supplier of speed safety systems used by the designated jurisdiction. Any contract between the designated jurisdiction and a vendor to provide processing services may include a provision for the payment of compensation based on the number of notices of violation processed by the vendor.

(n) The speed safety system, to the extent feasible, shall be angled and focused so as to only capture photographs of speeding violations and shall not capture identifying images of other drivers, vehicles, or pedestrians.

(o) Notwithstanding subdivision (c) of Section 21455.6, the designated jurisdiction listed herein may use automated enforcement systems and photographic radar for speed enforcement consistent with this article.

(Added by Stats. 2024, Ch. 631, Sec. 3. (SB 1297) Effective January 1, 2025. Repealed as of January 1, 2032, pursuant to Sec. 22441.)

22436. (a) Notwithstanding any other law, a violation of any speed law pursuant to this chapter that is recorded by a speed safety system authorized pursuant to Section 22435 shall be subject only to a civil penalty, as provided in subdivision (c), and shall not result in the department suspending or revoking the privilege of a violator to drive a motor vehicle or in a violation point being assessed against the violator.

(b) The speed safety system shall capture images of the rear license plate of vehicles that are traveling 11 miles per hour or more over the posted speed limit and notices of violation shall only be issued to registered owners of those vehicles based on that evidence.

(c) A civil penalty shall be assessed as follows:

(1) Fifty dollars ($50) for driving at a speed of 11 to 15 miles per hour over the posted speed limit.

(2) One hundred dollars ($100) for driving at a speed of 16 to 25 miles per hour over the posted speed limit.

(3) Two hundred dollars ($200) for driving at a speed of 26 miles per hour or more over the posted speed limit, unless paragraph (4) applies.

(4) Five hundred dollars ($500) for driving at a speed of 100 miles per hour or more.

(d) A civil penalty shall not be assessed against an authorized emergency vehicle.

(e) The notice of violation shall be in writing and issued to the registered owner of the vehicle within 15 calendar days of the date of the violation. The notice of violation shall include all of the following information:

(1) The violation, including reference to the speed law that was violated, the speed of the vehicle, the speed limit for the road on which the violation occurred, and verification of the most recent calibration of the system in accordance with paragraph (4) of subdivision (c) of Section 22435.

(2) The date, approximate time, and location where the violation occurred.

(3) The vehicle license number and the name and address of the registered owner of the vehicle.

(4) A statement that payment is required to be made no later than 30 calendar days from the date of mailing of the notice of violation, or that the violation may be contested pursuant to Section 22437.

(5) The amount of the civil penalty due for that violation and the procedures for the payment of the civil penalty or for contesting the notice of violation.

(6) An affidavit of nonliability, and information of what constitutes nonliability, information as to the effect of executing the affidavit, and instructions for returning the affidavit to the processor. If the affidavit of nonliability is returned to the processing agency within 30 calendar days of the mailing of the notice of violation, together with proof of a written lease or rental agreement between a bona fide rental company, as defined in Section 1939.01 of the Civil Code, or a personal vehicle sharing program, as defined in Section 11580.24 of the Insurance Code, and its customer that identifies the renter or lessee, the processing agency shall serve or mail a notice of violation to the renter or lessee identified in the affidavit of nonliability. If the affidavit of nonliability is returned to the processing agency within 30 calendar days of the mailing of the notice of violation, together with proof of a copy of a police report indicating the vehicle had been stolen at the time of the violation, the processing agency shall not subject the registered owner to a civil violation.

(7) A proof of service consistent with Section 1013a of the Code of Civil Procedure.

(f) Mobile radar or laser systems shall not be used until at least two years after the installation of the first fixed radar or laser system unless the mobile radar or laser system is kept at a fixed location.

(g) (1) Revenues derived from any program utilizing a speed safety system for speed limit enforcement shall first be used to recover program costs. Program costs include, but are not limited to, the installation of speed safety systems, the adjudication of violations, and reporting requirements as specified in this section.

(2) The designated jurisdiction shall maintain their existing commitment of local funds for traffic-calming measures in order to remain authorized to participate in the pilot program, and shall annually expend not less than the annual average of expenditures for traffic-calming measures during the 2016–17, 2017–18, and 2018–19 fiscal years. For purposes of this subdivision, in calculating average expenditures on traffic-calming measures, restricted funds that may not be available on an ongoing basis, including those from voter-approved bond issuances or tax measures, shall not be included. The designated jurisdiction shall enter into an agreement with the Department of Transportation for the use of any excess revenue for traffic calming-measures on the Pacific Coast Highway, in the City of Malibu. Excess revenue shall be used for traffic-calming measures within three years of the end of the fiscal year in which the excess revenue was received. If traffic-calming measures are not planned or constructed after the third year, excess revenue shall revert to the Active Transportation Program established pursuant to Chapter 8 (commencing with Section 2380) of the Streets and Highways Code, to be allocated by the California Transportation Commission pursuant to Section 2381 of the Streets and Highways Code.

(h) A person shall not be assessed a civil penalty if they are subject to criminal penalties for the same act.

(i) A speed safety system may only be in operation for five years, or until January 1, 2032, whichever date is sooner.

(Added by Stats. 2024, Ch. 631, Sec. 3. (SB 1297) Effective January 1, 2025. Repealed as of January 1, 2032, pursuant to Sec. 22441.)

22437. (a) No later than 30 calendar days from the date of mailing of a notice of violation, the recipient may request an initial review of the notice by the issuing agency. The request may be made by telephone, in writing, electronically, or in person. There shall be no charge for this review. If, following the initial review, the issuing agency is satisfied that the violation did not occur, or that extenuating circumstances make cancellation of the notice of violation appropriate in the interest of justice, the issuing agency shall cancel the notice of violation. The issuing agency shall advise the processing agency, if any, of the cancellation. The issuing agency or the processing agency shall mail the results of the initial review to the person contesting the notice within 60 days of receipt of the recipient's request for an initial review, and, if cancellation of the notice does not occur following that review, include a reason for that denial, notification of the ability to request an administrative hearing, and notice of the procedures adopted by the designated jurisdiction for the administrative hearing, including for waiving prepayment of the civil penalty based upon an inability to pay pursuant to paragraph (2) of subdivision (b).

(b) (1) If the person contesting the notice of violation is dissatisfied with the results of the initial review, the person may, no later than 21 calendar days following the mailing of the results of the issuing agency's initial review, request an administrative hearing of the violation. The request may be made by telephone, in writing, electronically, or in person.

(2) The person requesting an administrative hearing shall pay the amount of the civil penalty to the processing agency. The issuing agency shall adopt a written procedure to allow a person to request an administrative hearing without payment of the civil penalty upon satisfactory proof of an inability to pay the amount due.

(3) The administrative hearing shall be held within 90 calendar days following the receipt of a request for an administrative hearing. The person requesting the hearing may request one continuance, not to exceed 21 calendar days.

(c) The administrative hearing process shall include all of the following:

(1) The person requesting a hearing shall have the choice of a hearing upon written declaration, video conference, or in person. An in-person hearing shall be conducted within the jurisdiction of the issuing agency.

(2) If the person requesting a hearing is an unemancipated minor, that person shall be permitted to appear at a hearing or admit responsibility for the automated speed violation without the appointment of a guardian. The processing agency may proceed against the minor in the same manner as against an adult.

(3) The administrative hearing shall be conducted in accordance with written procedures established by the issuing agency and approved by the governing body or chief executive officer of the issuing agency. The hearing shall provide an independent, objective, fair, and impartial review of contested automated speed violations.

(4) (A) The issuing agency's governing body or chief executive officer of the designated jurisdiction shall appoint or contract with qualified independent examiners or administrative hearing providers that employ qualified independent examiners to conduct the administrative hearings. Examiners shall demonstrate the qualifications, training, and objectivity necessary to conduct a fair and impartial review, and shall meet the minimum requirements specified in subparagraph (B). The examiner shall be separate and independent from the notice of violation issuing and processing functions. An examiner's continued employment, performance evaluation, compensation, and benefits shall not, directly or indirectly, be linked to the amount of civil penalties upheld by the examiner or the number or percentage of violations upheld by the examiner.

(B) (i) Examiners shall have a minimum of 20 hours of training. The examiner, unless an employee of the designated jurisdiction, is responsible for the costs of the training. The issuing agency may reimburse the examiner for those costs. Training may be provided through any of the following:

(I) An accredited college or university.

(II) A program conducted by the Commission on Peace Officer Standards and Training.

(III) A program conducted by the American Arbitration Association or a similar organization.

(IV) Any program approved by the governing body or chief executive officer of the issuing agency, including a program developed and provided by, or for, the agency.

(ii) Training programs shall include topics relevant to the administrative hearing, including, but not limited to, applicable laws and regulations, enforcement procedures, due process, evaluation of evidence, hearing procedures, and effective oral and written communication. Upon the approval of the governing body or chief executive officer of the issuing agency, up to 12 hours of relevant experience may be substituted for up to 12 hours of training. Up to eight hours of the training requirements described in this subparagraph may be credited to an individual, at the discretion of the governing body or chief executive officer of the issuing agency, based upon training programs or courses described in this subparagraph that the individual attended within the last five years.

(5) The employee of the designated jurisdiction who issues a notice of violation shall not be required to participate in an administrative hearing. To establish a violation, the issuing agency shall not be required to produce any evidence other than, in proper form, the notice of violation or copy thereof, including the photograph of the vehicle's license plate, and information received from the Department of Motor Vehicles identifying the registered owner of the vehicle. The documentation in proper form shall be prima facie evidence of the violation. If the designated jurisdiction meets its initial burden, the recipient of the notice of violation may present any evidence and argument in defense.

(6) The examiner's final decision following the administrative hearing may be personally delivered to the person by the examiner or sent by first-class mail within 60 days of the date of the conclusion of the administrative hearing.

(7) Following a determination by the examiner that a person has committed the violation, the examiner may, consistent with the written guidelines established by the issuing agency, allow payment of the civil penalty in installments, or an issuing agency may allow for deferred payment or payments in installments, if the person provides evidence satisfactory to the examiner or the issuing agency, as the case may be, of an inability to pay the civil penalty in full. If authorized by the governing body of the issuing agency, the examiner may permit the performance of community service in lieu of payment of the civil penalty.

(8) If a notice of violation is dismissed following an administrative hearing, any civil penalty, if paid, shall be refunded by the issuing agency within 30 days.

(Added by Stats. 2024, Ch. 631, Sec. 3. (SB 1297) Effective January 1, 2025. Repealed as of January 1, 2032, pursuant to Sec. 22441.)

22438. (a) Within 30 days after personal delivery or mailing of the final decision described in subdivision (c) of Section 22437, the contestant may seek review by filing an appeal to the superior court, where the case shall be heard de novo, except that the contents of the processing agency's file in the case on appeal shall be lodged by the designated agency at the designated agency's expense and be received into evidence. A copy of the notice of violation shall be admitted into evidence as prima facie evidence of the facts stated in the notice. A copy of the notice of appeal shall be served in person or by certified first-class mail with return receipt upon the processing agency by the appellant. For purposes of computing the 30-day period, Section 1013 of the Code of Civil Procedure shall be applicable. A proceeding under this subdivision is a limited civil case.

(b) The fee for filing the notice of appeal shall be as provided in Section 70615 of the Government Code. Upon receipt of the notice of appeal, the designated jurisdiction shall lodge its administrative record for the case with the court within 15 calendar days. The court shall notify the appellant of the appearance date by mail or personal delivery. The court shall retain the fee under Section 70615 of the Government Code regardless of the outcome of the appeal. If the appellant prevails, this fee and any payment of the civil penalty shall be promptly refunded by the issuing agency in accordance with the judgment of the court.

(c) The conduct of the hearing on appeal under this section is a subordinate judicial duty that may be performed by a commissioner or other subordinate judicial officer at the direction of the presiding judge of the court.

(d) If a notice of appeal of the examiner's decision is not filed within the period set forth in subdivision (a), the decision shall be deemed final.

(e) If the civil penalty has not been paid and the final decision is adverse to the appellant, the processing agency may, promptly after the decision becomes final, proceed to collect the civil penalty under Section 22436.

(Added by Stats. 2024, Ch. 631, Sec. 3. (SB 1297) Effective January 1, 2025. Repealed as of January 1, 2032, pursuant to Sec. 22441.)

22439. (a) A designated jurisdiction shall offer a diversion program for indigent speed safety system violation recipients, to perform community service in lieu of paying the penalty for a speed system violation.

(b) A designated jurisdiction shall offer the ability for indigent speed safety system violation recipients to pay applicable fines and penalties over a period of time under a payment plan with monthly installments of no more than twenty-five dollars ($25) and shall limit the processing fee to participate in a payment plan to five dollars ($5) or less.

(c) Notwithstanding subdivisions (a) and (b), a designated jurisdiction shall reduce the applicable fines and penalties by 80 percent for indigent persons, and by 50 percent for individuals up to 250 percent above the federal poverty level.

(d) The person may demonstrate that they are indigent or make up to 250 percent above the poverty level or less by providing either of the following information, as applicable:

(1) Proof of income from a pay stub or another form of proof of earnings, such as a bank statement, that shows that the person meets the income criteria set forth in subdivision (b) of Section 68632 of the Government Code, subject to review and approval by the processing agency or its designee. The processing agency or its designee shall not unreasonably withhold its approval.

(2) Proof of receipt of benefits under the programs described in subdivision (a) of Section 68632 of the Government Code, including, but not limited to, an electronic benefits transfer card or another card, subject to review and approval by the processing agency. The processing agency or its designee shall not unreasonably withhold its approval.

(Added by Stats. 2024, Ch. 631, Sec. 3. (SB 1297) Effective January 1, 2025. Repealed as of January 1, 2032, pursuant to Sec. 22441.)

22440. The designated jurisdiction that used a speed safety system shall, on or before March 1 of the fifth year in which the system has been implemented, submit to its governing body and the transportation committees of the Legislature, consistent with Section 9795 of the Government Code, an evaluation of the speed safety system in their respective jurisdictions to determine the system's impact on street safety and the system's economic impact on the communities where the system is utilized. The report shall be made available on the internet website of the jurisdiction and shall include all of the following information:

(a) Data, at least three months before and at least six months after implementation of each system, on the number and proportion of vehicles speeding from 11 to 15 miles per hour over the legal speed limit, inclusive, from 16 to 25 miles per hour over the legal speed limit, inclusive, 26 miles per hour over the legal speed limit, and for every violator traveling at a speed of 100 miles per hour or greater. Data shall also be collected on the average speed of vehicles and 85th percentile speed of vehicles. To the extent feasible, the data should be collected at the same time of day, day of week, and location.

(b) The number of notices of violation issued under the program by month and year, the corridors or locations where violations occurred, and the number of vehicles with two or more violations in a monthly period and a yearly period.

(c) Data, before and after implementation of the system, on the number of traffic collisions that occurred where speed safety systems are used, relative to citywide data, and the transportation mode of the parties involved. The data on traffic collisions shall be categorized by collision type and injury severity, such as property damage only, complaint of pain, other visible injury, or severe or fatal injury.

(d) The number of violations paid, the number of delinquent violations, and the number of violations for which an initial review is requested. For the violations in which an initial review was requested, the report shall indicate the number of violations that went to initial review, administrative hearing, and de novo hearing, the number of notices that were dismissed at each level of review, and the number of notices that were not dismissed after each level of review.

(e) The costs associated with implementation and operation of the speed safety system and revenues collected by the jurisdiction.

(f) A racial and economic equity impact analysis, developed in collaboration with local racial justice and economic equity stakeholder groups. The analysis shall include the number of notices of violations issued to indigent individuals, the number of notices of violations issued to individuals of up to 250 percent above the poverty line, and the number of violations issued to each ZIP Code.

(Added by Stats. 2024, Ch. 631, Sec. 3. (SB 1297) Effective January 1, 2025. Repealed as of January 1, 2032, pursuant to Sec. 22441.)

22441. This article shall remain in effect only until January 1, 2032, and as of that date is repealed.

(Added by Stats. 2024, Ch. 631, Sec. 3. (SB 1297) Effective January 1, 2025. Repealed as of January 1, 2032, by its own provisions. Note: Repeal affects Article 4, commencing with Sec. 22435.)

Article 5. State Highway Work Zone Speed Safety Program

(Article 5 added by Stats. 2025, Ch. 684, Sec. 3.)

22445. (a) As used in this article, the following definitions apply:

(1) "Automated speed violation" means a violation of a speed law detected by a speed safety system operated pursuant to this article.

(2) "Construction Zone Enhanced Enforcement Program" refers to a program whereby the Department of Transportation contracts with the Department of the California Highway Patrol to reimburse the actual and incurred costs for supplemental California Highway Patrol units to assist in the management of traffic passing through state highway construction zones.

(3) "Department" means the Department of Transportation.

(4) A person is "indigent" if either of the following conditions is met:

(A) The person meets the income criteria set forth in subdivision (b) of Section 68632 of the Government Code.

(B) The person receives public benefits from a program listed in subdivision (a) of Section 68632 of the Government Code.

(5) "Maintenance Zone Enhanced Enforcement Program" refers to a program whereby the Department of Transportation contracts with the Department of the California Highway Patrol to reimburse the actual and incurred costs for supplemental California Highway Patrol units to assist in the management of traffic passing through state highway maintenance project zones.

(6) "Speed safety system" means a fixed or mobile radar or laser system or any other electronic device that utilizes automated equipment to detect a violation of speeding laws and is designed to obtain a clear photographic image of a rear vehicle license plate. "Speed safety system" is also known as an automated speed enforcement system.

(7) "State highway work zone" means a state highway construction or maintenance area, during any time when traffic is regulated or restricted through or around that area pursuant to Section 21367.

(b) The department may establish a program for automated speed enforcement that utilizes up to 35 speed safety systems, to be operated by the department in state highway work zones.

(c) The speed safety system may be utilized pursuant to subdivision (b) if the program meets all of the following requirements:

(1) Clearly identifies the presence of the speed safety system by signs stating "Photo Enforced," along with the speed limit signs with flashing beacons and speed feedback signs, between 500 feet and one mile, inclusive, before the placement of the system, as determined by the department. The signs shall be visible to traffic traveling on the highway from the direction of travel for which the system is utilized, and shall be posted at locations as may be determined necessary by the department after consultation with the California Traffic Control Devices Committee.

(2) Identifies the state highway work zones approved for enforcement using a speed safety system and the hours of enforcement on the department's internet website, which shall be updated whenever the department changes locations of enforcement.

(3) Ensures that the speed safety system is regularly inspected no less than once every 60 days, and certifies that the system is installed and operating properly. Each camera unit shall be calibrated in accordance with the manufacturer's instructions, and at least once per year by an independent calibration laboratory. Documentation of the regular inspection, operation, and calibration of the system shall be retained for at least 180 days after the date on which the system has been permanently removed from use.

(4) Utilizes fixed or mobile speed safety systems that provide real-time notification to the driver when violations are detected.

(5) A speed safety system records speed violations and actively issues citations only when workers from the Department of Transportation, including persons contracted to perform construction, maintenance, or repair of a highway, are present in the state highway work zone.

(d) Prior to enforcing speed laws utilizing speed safety systems, the department shall do both of the following:

(1) Administer a public information campaign for at least 30 calendar days prior to the commencement of the program, which shall include public announcements in major media outlets and press releases. The public information campaign shall include the information on when systems will begin detecting violations in state highway work zones, and the department's internet website, where additional information about the program can be obtained. Notwithstanding the above, no further public announcement by the department shall be required for additional systems that may be added to the program.

(2) (A) Issue warning notices rather than notices of violation for violations detected by the speed safety system during the first 60 calendar days of enforcement under the program.

(B) A vehicle's first violation for traveling 11 to 15 miles per hour over the posted speed limit shall be a warning notice.

(e) The department shall adopt written guidelines for the use of speed safety systems prior to entering into an agreement regarding a speed safety system, purchasing or leasing equipment for a program, or implementing a program. In developing the guidelines, the department shall consult with the relevant state agencies and relevant stakeholder organizations, including, but not limited to, racial equity, privacy protection, and economic justice groups. The written guidelines shall be made available for public review at least 30 calendar days prior to adoption. Upon adoption of the guidelines, the department shall post the final adopted guidelines on its internet website. The written guidelines shall include all of the following:

(1) A statement of the specific purpose for the speed safety system, the uses that are authorized and uses that are prohibited, and the procedures required prior to that use.

(2) An identification of the data or information that can be collected by the speed safety system and the individuals who can access or use the

collected information, and the processes related to the access, transfer, or use of the information.

(3) The allowable uses for information collected and maintained is limited to the administration of the state highway work zone speed safety program only.

(4) Procedures for the retention and disposal of data collected by the speed safety system.

(5) Procedures for the screening and issuing of notices of violation.

(6) Procedures for the storage of confidential information to ensure compliance with confidentiality requirements.

(f) The development and adoption of guidelines pursuant to this article are exempt from the Administrative Procedure Act (Chapter 3.5 (commencing with Section 11340) of Part 1 of Division 3 of Title 2 of the Government Code).

(g) Notices of violation issued pursuant to this section shall include a clear image of the license plate and rear of the vehicle only, identify the specific section of the Vehicle Code violated, the camera location, and the date and time when the violation occurred. Notices of violation shall exclude images of the rear window area of the vehicle.

(h) The photographic evidence stored by a speed safety system does not constitute an out-of-court hearsay statement by a declarant under Division 10 (commencing with Section 1200) of the Evidence Code.

(i) (1) Notwithstanding any provision of the California Public Records Act, or any other law, any photographic image or administrative records made by a system shall be confidential. The department shall use and allow access to these records only for the purposes authorized by this article or to assess the impacts of the system. Data about the number of violations issued and the speeds at which they were issued is not considered an administrative record required not to be disclosed by this section.

(2) Confidential information obtained from the Department of Motor Vehicles for the administration of speed safety systems and enforcement of this article shall be held confidential, and shall not be used for any other purpose. The department and its contractors and agents shall establish procedures to protect the confidentiality of these records consistent with Section 1808.47.

(3) Except for court records described in Section 68152 of the Government Code, or as provided in paragraph (4), the confidential records and evidence described in paragraphs (1) and (2) may be retained for up to 60 days after final disposition of the notice of violation. The department may retain information that a vehicle has been cited and fined for a violation for up to three years. The department may adopt a retention period of less than 60 days. Administrative records described in paragraph (1) may be retained for up to 120 days after final disposition of the notice of violation. Notwithstanding any other law, the confidential records and evidence shall be destroyed in a manner that maintains the confidentiality of any person included in the record or evidence.

(4) The photographic evidence that is obtained from a speed safety system that does not result in the issuance of a notice of violation shall be destroyed within five business days after it was first made. The use of facial recognition technology in conjunction with a speed safety system shall be prohibited.

(5) Information collected and maintained by the department to administer the program shall only be used to administer the program, and shall not be disclosed to any other persons, including, but not limited to, any other state or federal governmental agency or official for any other purpose, except as required by a court order, or in response to a subpoena in an individual case or proceeding.

(j) Notwithstanding subdivision (i), the registered owner or an individual identified by the registered owner as the driver of the vehicle at the time of the alleged violation shall be permitted to review and obtain a copy of the photograph of the alleged violation.

(k) A contract between the department and a manufacturer or supplier of speed safety systems shall allow the department to purchase materials, lease equipment, and contract for processing services from the manufacturer or supplier based on the services rendered on a monthly schedule or another schedule agreed upon by the department and contractor. The contract shall not allow for payment or compensation based on the number of notices of violation issued, or as a percentage of revenue generated, from the use of the system. The contract shall include a provision that all data collected from the speed safety system is confidential, and shall prohibit the manufacturer or supplier of the contracted speed safety system from sharing, repurposing, or monetizing collected data, except as specifically authorized in this article. The department shall oversee, maintain control, and have the final decision over all enforcement activities, including the determination of when a notice of violation should be issued.

(l) Notwithstanding subdivision (k), the department may contract with a vendor for the processing of notices of violation after an employee of the department has issued a notice of violation. The vendor shall be a separate legal and corporate entity from, and not related to or affiliated in any manner with, the manufacturer or supplier of speed safety systems used by the department. Any contract between the department and a vendor to provide processing services may include a provision for the payment of compensation based on the number of notices of violation processed by the vendor.

(m) The speed safety system, to the extent feasible, shall be angled and focused so as to only capture rear license plate photographs of speeding violations and shall not capture identifying images of other drivers or vehicles.

(n) Notwithstanding subdivision (c) of Section 21455.6, the department may use automated enforcement systems and photo radar for speed enforcement consistent with this article.

(Added by Stats. 2025, Ch. 684, Sec. 3. (AB 289) Effective January 1, 2026. Repealed as of January 1, 2032, pursuant to Section 22445.6.)

22445.1. (a) Notwithstanding any other law, a violation of any speed law pursuant to this chapter that is recorded by a speed safety system authorized pursuant to Section 22445 shall be subject only to a civil penalty, as provided in subdivision (c), and shall not result in the Department of Motor Vehicles suspending or revoking the privilege of a violator to drive a motor vehicle or in a violation point being assessed against the violator.

(b) The speed safety system shall capture images of the rear license plate of vehicles that are traveling 11 miles per hour or more over the posted speed limit and notices of violation shall only be issued to registered owners of those vehicles based on that evidence.

(c) A civil penalty shall be assessed as follows:

(1) Fifty dollars ($50) for driving at a speed of 11 to 15 miles per hour over the posted speed limit.

(2) One hundred dollars ($100) for driving at a speed of 16 to 25 miles per hour over the posted speed limit.

(3) Two hundred dollars ($200) for driving at a speed of 26 miles per hour or more over the posted speed limit, unless paragraph (4) applies.

(4) Five hundred dollars ($500) for driving at a speed of 100 miles per hour or more.

(d) A civil penalty shall not be assessed against an authorized emergency vehicle.

(e) The notice of violation shall be in writing and issued to the registered owner of the vehicle within 15 calendar days of the date of the violation. The notice of violation shall include all of the following information:

(1) The violation, including reference to the speed law that was violated, the speed of the vehicle, the speed limit for the road on which the violation occurred, and verification of the most recent calibration of the system in accordance with paragraph (3) of subdivision (c) of Section 22445.

(2) The date, approximate time, and location where the violation occurred.

(3) The vehicle license number and the name and address of the registered owner of the vehicle.

(4) A statement that payment is required to be made no later than 30 calendar days from the date of mailing of the notice of violation, or that the violation may be contested pursuant to Section 22445.2.

(5) The amount of the civil penalty due for that violation and the procedures for the payment of the civil penalty or for contesting the notice of violation.

(6) An affidavit of nonliability, and information of what constitutes nonliability, information as to the effect of executing the affidavit, and instructions for returning the affidavit to the processor. If the affidavit of nonliability is returned to the department within 30 calendar days of the mailing of the notice of violation, together with proof of a written lease or rental agreement between a bona fide rental company, as defined in Section 1939.01 of the Civil Code, or a personal vehicle sharing program, as defined in Section 11580.24 of the Insurance Code, and its customer that identifies the renter or lessee, the department shall serve or mail a notice of violation to the renter or lessee identified in the affidavit of nonliability. If the affidavit of nonliability is returned to the department within 30 calendar days of the mailing of the notice of violation, together with proof of a copy of a police report indicating the vehicle had been stolen at the time of the violation, the department shall not subject the registered owner to a civil violation.

(7) A phone number that the recipient may use to request additional information about the State Highway Work Zone Speed Safety Program.

(8) A proof of service consistent with Section 1013a of the Code of Civil Procedure.

(f) (1) Moneys generated from the issuance of citations pursuant to the state highway work zone speed safety program shall be deposited in the Safe Highway Work Zone Account, which is hereby created in the State Transportation Fund. Moneys in the account shall be continuously appropriated to the department for the administration of this program. Any remaining funds shall be used by the department for the Construction Zone Enhanced Enforcement Program and the Maintenance Zone Enhanced Enforcement Program.

(2) It is the intent of the Legislature that speed safety systems complement traffic enforcement by the Department of the California Highway Patrol, and that the program authorized by Section 22445 shall supplement, and not supplant, existing traffic enforcement efforts in highway construction and maintenance zones, including the Construction Zone Enhanced Enforcement Program and the Maintenance Zone Enhanced Enforcement Program.

(3) It is the intent of the Legislature that the department expend for purposes of enhanced traffic enforcement in construction and maintenance zones an amount not less than its expenditures for the Construction Zone Enhanced Enforcement Program and the Maintenance Zone Enhanced Enforcement Program in the 2023–24 fiscal year.

(g) A person shall not be assessed a civil penalty if they are subject to criminal penalties for the same act.

(h) A speed safety system may only be in operation for five years, or until January 1, 2032, whichever date is sooner.

(Added by Stats. 2025, Ch. 684, Sec. 3. (AB 289) Effective January 1, 2026. Repealed as of January 1, 2032, pursuant to Section 22445.6.)

22445.2. (a) No later than 30 calendar days from the date of mailing of a notice of violation, the recipient may request an initial review of the notice by the department. The request may be made by telephone, in writing, electronically, or in person. There shall be no charge for this review. If, following the initial review, the department is satisfied that the violation did not occur, or that extenuating circumstances make cancellation of the notice of violation appropriate in the interest of justice, the department shall cancel the notice of violation. The department shall mail the results of the initial review to the person contesting the notice within 60 days of receipt of the recipient's request for an initial review, and, if cancellation of the notice does not occur following that review, include a reason for that denial, notification of the ability to request an administrative hearing, and notice of the procedures adopted by the department for the administrative hearing, including for waiving prepayment of the civil penalty based upon an inability to pay pursuant to paragraph (2) of subdivision (b).

(b) (1) If the person contesting the notice of violation is dissatisfied with the results of the initial review, the person may, no later than 21 calendar days following the mailing of the results of the department's initial review, request an administrative hearing of the violation. The request may be made by telephone, in writing, electronically, or in person.

(2) The person requesting an administrative hearing shall pay the amount of the civil penalty to the department. There shall be no additional charge for this hearing. The department shall adopt a written procedure to allow a person to request an administrative hearing without payment of the civil penalty upon satisfactory proof of an inability to pay the amount due.

(3) The administrative hearing shall be held within 90 calendar days following the receipt of a request for an administrative hearing. The person requesting the hearing may request one continuance, not to exceed 21 calendar days.

(c) The administrative hearing process shall include all of the following:

(1) The person requesting a hearing shall have the choice of a hearing upon written declaration, video conference, or in person. An in-person hearing shall be conducted within the department district where the violation was issued.

(2) If the person requesting a hearing is an unemancipated minor, that person shall be permitted to appear at a hearing or admit responsibility for the automated speed violation without the appointment of a guardian. The department may proceed against the minor in the same manner as against an adult.

(3) The administrative hearing shall be conducted in accordance with written procedures established by the department. The hearing shall provide an independent, objective, fair, and impartial review of contested automated speed violations.

(4) (A) The department shall appoint or contract with qualified independent examiners or administrative hearing providers that employ qualified independent examiners to conduct the administrative hearings. Examiners shall demonstrate the qualifications, training, and objectivity necessary to conduct a fair and impartial review, and shall meet the minimum requirements specified in subparagraph (B). The examiner shall be separate and independent from the notice of violation issuing and processing functions. An examiner's continued employment, performance evaluation, compensation, and benefits shall not, directly or indirectly, be linked to the amount of civil penalties upheld by the examiner or the number or percentage of violations upheld by the examiner.

(B) (i) Examiners shall have a minimum of 20 hours of training. The examiner, unless an employee of the department, is responsible for the costs of the training. The department may reimburse the examiner for those costs. Training may be provided through any of the following:

(I) An accredited college or university.

(II) A program conducted by the Commission on Peace Officer Standards and Training.

(III) A program conducted by the American Arbitration Association or a similar organization.

(IV) Any program approved by the department, including a program developed and provided by, or for, the department.

(ii) Training programs shall include topics relevant to the administrative hearing, including, but not limited to, applicable laws and regulations, enforcement procedures, due process, evaluation of evidence, hearing procedures, and effective oral and written communication. Upon the approval of the department, up to 12 hours of relevant experience may be substituted for up to 12 hours of training. Up to eight hours of the training requirements described in this subparagraph may be credited to an individual, at the discretion of the department, based upon training programs or courses described in this subparagraph that the individual attended within the last five years.

(5) The employee of the department who issues a notice of violation shall not be required to participate in an administrative hearing. To establish a violation, the department shall not be required to produce any evidence other than, in proper form, the notice of violation or copy thereof, including the photograph of the vehicle's license plate, and information received from the Department of Motor Vehicles identifying the registered owner of the vehicle. The documentation in proper form shall be prima facie evidence of the violation. If the department meets its initial burden, the recipient of the notice of violation may present any evidence and argument in defense.

(6) The examiner's final decision following the administrative hearing may be personally delivered to the person by the examiner or sent by first-class mail within 60 days of the date of the conclusion of the administrative hearing.

(7) Following a determination by the examiner that a person has committed the violation, the examiner or the department shall offer violation recipients who are indigent or who otherwise provide evidence satisfactory to the examiner or the department of an inability to pay the civil penalty in full, the option to pay applicable fines and penalties over a period of time under a payment plan with monthly installments not to exceed twenty-five dollars ($25). Any processing fee to participate in a payment plan shall not exceed five dollars ($5).

(8) If a notice of violation is dismissed following an administrative hearing, any civil penalty, if paid, shall be refunded by the department within 30 days.

(Added by Stats. 2025, Ch. 684, Sec. 3. (AB 289) Effective January 1, 2026. Repealed as of January 1, 2032, pursuant to Section 22445.6.)

22445.3. (a) Within 30 days after personal delivery or mailing of the final decision described in subdivision (c) of Section 22445.2, the contestant may seek review by filing an appeal to the superior court, where the case shall be heard de novo, except that the contents of the department's file in the case on appeal shall be lodged by the department at its expense and be received into evidence. A copy of the notice of violation shall be admitted into evidence as prima facie evidence of the facts stated in the notice. A copy of the notice of appeal shall be served in person or by certified first-class mail with return receipt upon the department by the appellant. For purposes of computing the 30-day period, Section 1013 of the Code of Civil Procedure shall be applicable. A proceeding under this subdivision is a limited civil case.

(b) The fee for filing the notice of appeal shall be as provided in Section 70615 of the Government Code. Upon receipt of the notice of appeal, the department shall lodge its administrative record for the case with the court within 15 calendar days. The court shall notify the appellant of the appearance date by mail or personal delivery. The court shall retain the fee under Section 70615 of the Government Code regardless of the outcome of the appeal. If the appellant prevails, this fee and any payment of the civil penalty shall be promptly refunded by the department in accordance with the judgment of the court.

(c) The conduct of the hearing on appeal under this section is a subordinate judicial duty that may be performed by a commissioner or other subordinate judicial officer at the direction of the presiding judge of the court.

(d) If a notice of appeal of the examiner's decision is not filed within the period set forth in subdivision (a), the decision shall be deemed final.

(e) If the civil penalty has not been paid and the final decision is adverse to the appellant, the department may, promptly after the decision becomes final, proceed to collect the civil penalty under Section 22445.1.

(Added by Stats. 2025, Ch. 684, Sec. 3. (AB 289) Effective January 1, 2026. Repealed as of January 1, 2032, pursuant to Section 22445.6.)

22445.4. (a) The department shall offer the ability for indigent speed safety system violation recipients to pay applicable fines and penalties over a period of time under a payment plan with monthly installments of no more than twenty-five dollars ($25) and shall limit the processing fee to participate in a payment plan to five dollars ($5) or less.

(b) Notwithstanding subdivision (a), the department shall reduce the applicable fines and penalties by 80 percent for indigent persons, and by 50 percent for individuals up to 250 percent above the federal poverty level.

(c) The person may demonstrate that they are indigent or make up to 250 percent above the poverty level or less by providing either of the following information, as applicable:

(1) Proof of income from a pay stub or another form of proof of earnings, such as a bank statement, that shows that the person meets the income criteria set forth in subdivision (b) of Section 68632 of the Government Code, subject to review and approval by the department or its designee. The department or its designee shall not unreasonably withhold its approval.

(2) Proof of receipt of benefits under the programs described in subdivision (a) of Section 68632 of the Government Code, including, but not limited to, an electronic benefits transfer card or another card, subject to review and approval by the department. The department or its designee shall not unreasonably withhold its approval.

(Added by Stats. 2025, Ch. 684, Sec. 3. (AB 289) Effective January 1, 2026. Repealed as of January 1, 2032, pursuant to Section 22445.6.)

22445.5. (a) No later than two years after the commencement of the state highway work zone speed safety program, and annually thereafter, the department shall prepare and submit a report to the Legislature evaluating the state highway work zone speed safety program and its impact on state highway work zone safety. The report shall be made available on the department's internet website and shall include all of the following information:

(1) Data on the number and proportion of vehicles speeding in state highway work zones where speed safety systems were deployed from 11 to 15 miles per hour over the legal speed limit, inclusive, from 16 to 25 miles per hour over the legal speed limit, inclusive, from 26 miles per hour over the legal speed limit, and for every violator traveling at a speed of 100 miles per hour or greater. Data shall also be collected on the average speed of vehicles and 85th percentile speed of vehicles in state highway work zones where speed safety systems were deployed.

(2) The number of notices of violation issued under the program by month and year, the state highway work zones where violations occurred, and the number of vehicles with two or more violations in the same location over a monthly period and a yearly period.

(3) Data on the number of traffic collisions that occurred in state highway work zones where speed safety systems were used, relative to data in all state highway work zones. The data on traffic collisions shall be categorized by collision type and injury severity, such as property damage only, complaint of pain, other visible injury, or severe or fatal injury.

(4) The number of violations paid, the number of delinquent violations, and the number of violations for which an initial review is requested. For the violations in which an initial review was requested, the report shall indicate the number of violations that went to initial review, administrative hearing, and de novo hearing, the number of notices that were dismissed at each level of review, and the number of notices that were not dismissed after each level of review.

(5) The costs associated with implementation and operation of the speed safety systems, and revenues collected.

(6) The number of notices of violations issued to indigent individuals, the number of notices of violations issued to individuals of up to 250 percent above the poverty line, and the number of violations issued to vehicles registered in each California ZIP Code.

(b) The report required by this section shall be submitted in compliance with Section 9795 of the Government Code.

(Added by Stats. 2025, Ch. 684, Sec. 3. (AB 289) Effective January 1, 2026. Repealed as of January 1, 2032, pursuant to Section 22445.6.)

22445.6. This article shall remain in effect only until January 1,

2032, and as of that date is repealed.

(Added by Stats. 2025, Ch. 684, Sec. 3. (AB 289) Effective January 1, 2026. Repealed as of January 1, 2032, by its own provisions. Note: Repeal affects Article 5, commencing with Section 22445.)

Chapter 8. Special Stops Required

(Chapter 8 enacted by Stats. 1959, Ch. 3.)

22450. (a) The driver of any vehicle approaching a stop sign at the entrance to, or within, an intersection shall stop at a limit line, if marked, otherwise before entering the crosswalk on the near side of the intersection.

If there is no limit line or crosswalk, the driver shall stop at the entrance to the intersecting roadway.

(b) The driver of a vehicle approaching a stop sign at a railroad grade crossing shall stop at a limit line, if marked, otherwise before crossing the first track or entrance to the railroad grade crossing.

(c) Notwithstanding any other provision of law, a local authority may adopt rules and regulations by ordinance or resolution providing for the placement of a stop sign at any location on a highway under its jurisdiction where the stop sign would enhance traffic safety.

(Amended by Stats. 2007, Ch. 630, Sec. 8. Effective January 1, 2008.)

22451. (a) The driver of any vehicle or pedestrian approaching a railroad or rail transit grade crossing shall stop not less than 15 feet from the nearest rail and shall not proceed until he or she can do so safely, whenever the following conditions exist:

(1) A clearly visible electric or mechanical signal device or a flagman gives warning of the approach or passage of a train, car, or on-track equipment.

(2) An approaching train, car, or on-track equipment is plainly visible or is emitting an audible signal and, by reason of its speed or nearness, is an immediate hazard.

(b) No driver or pedestrian shall proceed through, around, or under any railroad or rail transit crossing gate while the gate is closed.

(c) Whenever a railroad or rail transit crossing is equipped with an automated enforcement system, a notice of a violation of this section is subject to the procedures provided in Section 40518.

(d) For purposes of this section, "on-track equipment" means any locomotive or any other car, rolling stock, equipment, or other device that, alone or coupled to others, is operated on stationary rails.

(Amended by Stats. 2017, Ch. 110, Sec. 1. (AB 695) Effective January 1, 2018.)

22452. (a) Subdivisions (b) and (d) apply to the operation of the following vehicles:

(1) A bus or farm labor vehicle carrying passengers.

(2) A motortruck transporting employees in addition to those riding in the cab.

(3) A schoolbus and a school pupil activity bus transporting school pupils, except as otherwise provided in paragraph (4) of subdivision (d).

(4) A commercial motor vehicle transporting any quantity of a Division 2.3 chlorine, as classified by Title 49 of the Code of Federal Regulations.

(5) A commercial motor vehicle that is required to be marked or placarded in accordance with the regulations of Title 49 of the Code of Federal Regulations with one of the following federal classifications:

(A) Division 1.1.

(B) Division 1.2, or Division 1.3.

(C) Division 2.3 Poison gas.

(D) Division 4.3.

(E) Class 7.

(F) Class 3 Flammable.

(G) Division 5.1.

(H) Division 2.2.

(I) Division 2.3 Chlorine.

(J) Division 6.1 Poison.

(K) Division 2.2 Oxygen.

(L) Division 2.1.

(M) Class 3 Combustible liquid.

(N) Division 4.1.

(O) Division 5.1.

(P) Division 5.2.

(Q) Class 8.

(R) Class Division 1.4.

(S) A cargo tank motor vehicle, whether loaded or empty, used for the transportation of a hazardous material, as defined in Parts 107 to 180, inclusive, of Title 49 of the Code of Federal Regulations.

(6) A cargo tank motor vehicle transporting a commodity that at the time of loading has a temperature above its flashpoint, as determined under Section 173.120 of Title 49 of the Code of Federal Regulations.

(7) A cargo tank motor vehicle, whether loaded or empty, transporting a commodity under exemption in accordance with Subpart B of Part 107 of Title 49 of the Code of Federal Regulations.

(b) Before traversing a railroad grade crossing, the driver of a vehicle described in subdivision (a) shall stop that vehicle not less than 15 nor more than 50 feet from the nearest rail of the track and while so stopped shall listen, and look in both directions along the track, for an approaching train or on-track equipment and for signals indicating the approach of a train or on-track equipment, and shall not proceed until he or she can do so safely. Upon proceeding, the gears shall not be shifted manually while crossing the tracks.

(c) The driver of a commercial motor vehicle, other than those listed in subdivision (a), upon approaching a railroad grade crossing, shall be driven at a rate of speed that allows the commercial vehicle to stop before reaching the nearest rail of that crossing, and shall not be driven upon, or over, the crossing until due caution is taken to ascertain that the course is clear.

(d) A stop need not be made at a crossing in the following circumstances:

(1) Of railroad tracks running along and upon the roadway within a business or residence district.

(2) Where a traffic officer or an official traffic control signal directs traffic to proceed.

(3) Where an exempt sign was authorized by the Public Utilities Commission prior to January 1, 1978.

(4) Where an official railroad crossing stop exempt sign in compliance with Section 21400 has been placed by the Department of Transportation or a local authority pursuant to Section 22452.5. This paragraph does not apply with respect to a schoolbus or to a school pupil activity bus transporting school pupils.

(e) For purposes of this section, "on-track equipment" means any locomotive or any other car, rolling stock, equipment, or other device that, alone or coupled to others, is operated on stationary rails.

(Amended by Stats. 2017, Ch. 110, Sec. 2. (AB 695) Effective January 1, 2018.)

22452.5. The Department of Transportation and local authorities, with respect to highways under their respective jurisdictions, may place signs at railroad grade crossings permitting any vehicle described in subdivision (a) of Section 22452 to traverse such crossings without stopping. Such signs shall be placed in accordance with criteria adopted by the Public Utilities Commission. Prior to placing such signs, the Department of Transportation or local authority shall consult with the Department of the California Highway Patrol, railroad corporations involved, and the operators involved and shall secure the permission of the Public Utilities Commission if a railroad corporation under the jurisdiction of the Public Utilities Commission is affected. Prior to permitting the placement of such signs, the Public Utilities Commission shall seek the concurrence of the Department of the California Highway Patrol.

(Amended by Stats. 1979, Ch. 373.)

22453. Failure of the driver of a motor vehicle carrying any passenger for hire to stop as required in Section 22452 shall not be imputed to any bona fide passenger for hire in such vehicle.

(Enacted by Stats. 1959, Ch. 3.)

22454. (a) The driver of any vehicle, upon meeting or overtaking, from either direction, any schoolbus equipped with signs as required in this code, that is stopped for the purpose of loading or unloading any schoolchildren and displays a flashing red light signal and stop signal arm, as defined in paragraph (4) of subdivision (b) of Section 25257, if equipped with a stop signal arm, visible from front or rear, shall bring the vehicle to a stop immediately before passing the schoolbus and shall not proceed past the schoolbus until the flashing red light signal and stop signal arm, if equipped with a stop signal arm, cease operation.

(b) (1) The driver of a vehicle upon a divided highway or multiple-lane highway need not stop upon meeting or passing a schoolbus that is upon the other roadway.

(2) For the purposes of this subdivision, a multiple-lane highway is any highway that has two or more lanes of travel in each direction.

(c) (1) If a vehicle was observed overtaking a schoolbus in violation of subdivision (a), and the driver of the schoolbus witnessed the violation, the driver may, within 24 hours, report the violation and furnish the vehicle license plate number and description and the time and place of the violation to the local law enforcement agency having jurisdiction of the offense. That law enforcement agency shall issue a letter of warning prepared in accordance with paragraph (2) with respect to the alleged violation to the registered owner of the vehicle. The issuance of a warning letter under this paragraph shall not be entered on the driving record of the person to whom it is issued, but does not preclude the imposition of any other applicable penalty.

(2) The Attorney General shall prepare and furnish to every law enforcement agency in the state a form letter for purposes of paragraph (1), and the law enforcement agency may issue those letters in the exact form prepared by the Attorney General. The Attorney General may charge a fee to any law enforcement agency that requests a copy of the form letter to recover the costs of preparing and providing that copy.

(d) This section also applies to a roadway upon private property.

(Amended by Stats. 1999, Ch. 647, Sec. 3. Effective October 10, 1999.)

22454.5. Notwithstanding Section 42001, a person convicted of a first violation of Section 22454 shall be punished by a fine of not less than one hundred fifty dollars ($150) or more than two hundred fifty dollars ($250). A person convicted of a second separate violation of Section 22454 shall be punished by a fine of not less than five hundred dollars ($500) or more than one thousand dollars ($1,000). If a person is convicted of a third or subsequent violation of Section 22454 and the offense occurred within three years of two or more separate violations of Section 22454, the Department of Motor Vehicles shall suspend the person's privilege to operate a motor vehicle for one year.

(Amended by Stats. 1990, Ch. 1296, Sec. 2.)

22455. (a) The driver of any commercial vehicle engaged in vending upon a street may vend products on a street in a residence district only after bringing the vehicle to a complete stop and lawfully parking adjacent to the curb, consistent with the requirements of Chapter 9 (commencing with Section 22500) and local ordinances adopted pursuant thereto.

(b) Notwithstanding subdivision (a) of Section 114315 of the Health and Safety Code or any other provision of law, a local authority may, by ordinance or resolution, adopt additional requirements for the public safety regulating the type of vending and the time, place, and manner of vending from vehicles upon any street.

(Amended by Stats. 2008, Ch. 139, Sec. 3. Effective January 1, 2009.)

22456. (a) This section shall be known and may be cited as the Destiny Nicole Stout Memorial Act.

(b) The Legislature finds and declares that motor vehicles engaged in vending ice cream and similar food items in residential neighborhoods can increase the danger to children, and it is necessary that these vehicles are clearly seen and noticed by motorists and pedestrians to protect public safety.

(c) As used in this section, the term "ice cream truck" means a motor vehicle engaged in the curbside vending or sale of frozen or refrigerated desserts, confections, or novelties commonly known as ice cream, or prepackaged candies, prepackaged snack foods, or soft drinks, primarily intended for the sale to children under 12 years of age.

(d) Any ice cream truck shall be equipped at all times, while engaged in vending in a residential area, with signs mounted on both the front and the rear and clearly legible from a distance of 100 feet under daylight conditions, incorporating the words "WARNING" and "CHILDREN CROSSING." Each sign shall be at least 12 inches high by 48 inches wide, with letters of a dark color and at least four inches in height, a one-inch wide solid border, and a sharply contrasting background.

(e) A person may not vend from an ice cream truck that is stopped, parked, or standing on any public street, alley, or highway under any of the following conditions:

(1) On a street, alley, or highway with a posted speed limit greater than 25 miles per hour.

(2) If the street, alley, or highway is within 100 feet of an intersection with an opposing highway that has a posted speed limit greater than 25 miles per hour.

(3) If the vendor does not have an unobstructed view for 200 feet in both directions along the highway and of any traffic on the highway.

(Added by Stats. 2000, Ch. 344, Sec. 1. Effective January 1, 2001.)

Chapter 9. Stopping, Standing, and Parking

(Chapter 9 enacted by Stats. 1959, Ch. 3.)

22500. A person shall not stop, park, or leave standing any vehicle whether attended or unattended, except when necessary to avoid conflict with other traffic or in compliance with the directions of a peace officer or official traffic control device, in any of the following places:

(a) Within an intersection, except adjacent to curbs as may be permitted by local ordinance.

(b) On a crosswalk, except that a bus engaged as a common carrier or a taxicab may stop in an unmarked crosswalk to load or unload passengers when authorized by the legislative body of a city pursuant to an ordinance.

(c) Between a safety zone and the adjacent right-hand curb or within the area between the zone and the curb as may be indicated by a sign or red paint on the curb, which sign or paint was erected or placed by local authorities pursuant to an ordinance.

(d) Within 15 feet of the driveway entrance to a fire station. This subdivision does not apply to any vehicle owned or operated by a fire department and clearly marked as a fire department vehicle.

(e) (1) In front of a public or private driveway, except that a bus engaged as a common carrier, schoolbus, or a taxicab may stop to load or unload passengers when authorized by local authorities pursuant to an ordinance.

(2) In unincorporated territory, where the entrance of a private road or driveway is not delineated by an opening in a curb or by other curb construction, so much of the surface of the ground as is paved, surfaced, or otherwise plainly marked by vehicle use as a private road or driveway entrance, shall constitute a driveway.

(f) On a portion of a sidewalk, or with the body of the vehicle extending over a portion of a sidewalk, except electric carts when authorized by local ordinance, as specified in Section 21114.5. Lights, mirrors, or devices that are required to be mounted upon a vehicle under this code may extend from the body of the vehicle over the sidewalk to a distance of not more than 10 inches.

(g) Alongside or opposite a street or highway excavation or obstruction when stopping, standing, or parking would obstruct traffic.

(h) On the roadway side of a vehicle stopped, parked, or standing at the curb or edge of a highway, except for a schoolbus when stopped to load or unload pupils in a business or residence district where the speed limit is 25 miles per hour or less.

(i) Except as provided under Section 22500.5, alongside curb space authorized for the loading and unloading of passengers of a bus engaged as a common carrier in local transportation when indicated by a sign or red paint on the curb erected or painted by local authorities pursuant to an ordinance.

(j) In a tube or tunnel, except vehicles of the authorities in charge, being used in the repair, maintenance, or inspection of the facility.

(k) Upon a bridge, except vehicles of the authorities in charge, being used in the repair, maintenance, or inspection of the facility, and except that buses engaged as a common carrier in local transportation may stop to load or unload passengers upon a bridge where sidewalks are provided, when authorized by local authorities pursuant to an ordinance, and except that local authorities pursuant to an ordinance or the Department of Transportation pursuant to an order, within their respective jurisdictions, may permit parking on bridges having sidewalks and shoulders of sufficient width to permit parking without interfering with the normal movement of traffic on the roadway. Local authorities, by ordinance or resolution, may permit parking on these bridges on state highways in their respective jurisdictions if the ordinance or resolution is first approved in writing by the Department of Transportation. Parking shall not be permitted unless there are signs in place, as may be necessary, to indicate the provisions of local ordinances or the order of the Department of Transportation.

(l) In front of or upon that portion of a curb that has been cut down, lowered, or constructed to provide wheelchair accessibility to the sidewalk.

(m) In a portion of a highway that has been designated for the exclusive use of public transit buses.

(n) (1) (A) Within 20 feet of the vehicle approach side of any marked or unmarked crosswalk or within 15 feet of any crosswalk where a curb extension is present.

(B) Notwithstanding subparagraph (A), a local authority may establish a different distance if both of the following requirements are met:

(i) A local authority establishes the different distance by ordinance that includes a finding that the different distance is justified by established traffic safety standards.

(ii) A local authority has marked the different distance at the intersection using paint or a sign.

(2) Notwithstanding paragraph (1), a local authority may permit commercial vehicle loading or unloading within 20 feet of the vehicle approach side of any marked or unmarked crosswalk or within 15 feet of any crosswalk where a curb extension is present if both of the following requirements are met:

(A) A local authority authorizes the commercial vehicle loading and unloading by ordinance and identifies the crosswalk or crosswalks in the ordinance.

(B) A local authority has marked the commercial loading and unloading areas with paint or signage.

(3) Notwithstanding paragraph (1), a local authority may permit parking for bicycles or motorized scooters within 20 feet of a crosswalk.

(4) Prior to January 1, 2025, jurisdictions may only issue a warning, and shall not issue a citation, for a violation unless the violation occurs in an area marked using paint or a sign.

(Amended by Stats. 2023, Ch. 652, Sec. 1. (AB 413) Effective January 1, 2024.)

22500.1. In addition to Section 22500, no person shall stop, park, or leave standing any vehicle, whether attended or unattended, except when necessary to avoid conflict with other traffic or in compliance with the directions of a peace officer or official traffic control device along the edge of any highway, at any curb, or in any location in a publicly or privately owned or operated off-street parking facility, designated as a fire lane by the fire department or fire district with jurisdiction over the area in which the place is located.

The designation shall be indicated (1) by a sign posted immediately adjacent to, and visible from, the designated place clearly stating in letters not less than one inch in height that the place is a fire lane, (2) by outlining or painting the place in red and, in contrasting color, marking the place with the words "FIRE LANE", which are clearly visible from a vehicle, or (3) by a red curb or red paint on the edge of the roadway upon which is clearly marked the words "FIRE LANE".

(Amended by Stats. 1984, Ch. 129, Sec. 1. Effective May 21, 1984.)

22500.2. (a) A local authority may, by ordinance, prohibit a person from stopping, parking, or leaving standing a vehicle, whether attended or unattended, except if necessary to avoid conflict with other traffic or in compliance with the directions of a peace officer or official traffic control device, within 15 feet of a driveway that is used by an emergency vehicle owned or operated by a police department, ambulance service care provider, or general acute care hospital, to enter or exit a police station, ambulance service provider facility, or general acute care hospital. This section does not apply to any vehicle owned or operated by a fire department, police department, ambulance service provider, or general acute care hospital, if the vehicle is clearly marked as a fire department vehicle, police department vehicle, ambulance, or general acute care hospital vehicle.

(b) A local authority that enacts an ordinance pursuant to subdivision (a) shall provide appropriate curb markings or "KEEP CLEAR" pavement markings and post signs that delineate the area specified in subdivision (a).

(Added by Stats. 2016, Ch. 358, Sec. 1. (AB 2491) Effective January 1, 2017.)

22500.5. Upon agreement between a transit system operating buses engaged as common carriers in local transportation and a public school district or private school, local authorities may, by ordinance, permit schoolbuses owned by, or operated under contract for, that public school district or private school to stop for the loading or unloading of passengers alongside any or all curb spaces designated for the loading or unloading of passengers of the transit system buses.

(Amended by Stats. 2012, Ch. 769, Sec. 36. (AB 2679) Effective January 1, 2013.)

22501. No ordinance enacted by local authorities pursuant to subdivisions (e) and (k) of Section 22500 or Section 22507.2 shall become effective as to any state highway without prior submission to and approval by the Department of Transportation in the same manner as required by Section 21104. Nothing contained in this section and Section 22500 shall be construed as authorizing local authorities to enact legislation which is contrary to the provisions of Sections 22512 and 25301.

(Amended by Stats. 1980, Ch. 158, Sec. 1. Effective June 11, 1980.)

22502. (a) Except as otherwise provided in this chapter, a vehicle stopped or parked upon a roadway with adjacent curbs or class IV bikeways, as defined in Section 890.4 of the Streets and Highways Code, shall be stopped or parked with the right-hand wheels of the vehicle parallel to, and within 18 inches of, the right-hand curb or the right-hand edge of the class IV bikeway, except that a motorcycle shall be parked with at least one wheel or fender touching the right-hand curb or edge. If no curbs, barriers, or class IV bikeways bound a two-way roadway, right-hand parallel parking is required unless otherwise indicated.

(b) (1) The provisions of subdivision (a) or (e) do not apply to a commercial vehicle if a variation from the requirements of subdivision (a) or (e) is reasonably necessary to accomplish the loading or unloading of merchandise or passengers on, or from, a vehicle and while anything connected with the loading, or unloading, is being executed.

(2) This subdivision does not permit a vehicle to stop or park upon a roadway in a direction opposite to that in which traffic normally moves.

(c) Notwithstanding subdivision (b), a local authority may, by ordinance, prohibit a commercial vehicle from stopping, parking, or standing on one side of a roadway in a business district with the wheels of the vehicle more than 18 inches from the curb or the edge of a class IV bikeway. The ordinance shall be effective only if signs are placed clearly indicating the prohibition in the areas to which it applies.

(d) This section does not apply to vehicles of a public utility when the vehicles are being used in connection with the operation, maintenance, or repair of facilities of the public utility or are being used in connection with providing public utility service.

(e) (1) Upon a one-way roadway, a vehicle may be stopped or parked as provided in subdivision (a) or with the left-hand wheels parallel to, and within 18 inches of, the left-hand curb or left-hand edge of a class IV bikeway, except that a motorcycle, if parked on the left-hand side, shall have either one wheel or one fender touching the curb or edge. If no curb, barriers, or class IV bikeway bound a one-way roadway, parallel parking on either side is required unless otherwise indicated.

(2) This subdivision does not apply upon a roadway of a divided highway.

(f) (1) The City of Long Beach may, by ordinance or resolution, implement a pilot program to authorize vehicles to park on the left-hand side of the roadway parallel to and within 18 inches of the left-hand curb on two-way local residential streets that dead-end with no cul-de-sac or other designated area in which to turn around, if the City of Long Beach has first made a finding, supported by a professional engineering study, that the ordinance or resolution is justified by the need to facilitate the safe and orderly movement of vehicles on the roadways affected by the resolution or ordinance. The area covered by the ordinance or resolution shall be limited to the streets perpendicular to Ocean Boulevard beginning at Balboa Place and ending at 72nd Place, but shall not cover 62nd Place. The ordinance or resolution permitting that parking shall not apply until signs or markings giving adequate notice have been placed near the designated roadways. The city shall submit to the Legislature, two years from the date of the enactment of the ordinance or resolution that establishes the pilot program, a report that outlines the advantages and disadvantages of the pilot program. The report submitted pursuant to this subdivision shall be submitted in compliance with Section 9795 of the Government Code.

(2) The pilot program authorized under this subdivision shall terminate, and this subdivision shall become inoperative, three years from the date of enactment of the ordinance or resolution that establishes the pilot program.

(Amended by Stats. 2016, Ch. 208, Sec. 16. (AB 2906) Effective January 1, 2017.)

22503. Local authorities may by ordinance permit angle parking on any roadway, or left-hand parking upon one-way roadways of divided highways, except that no ordinance is effective with respect to any state highway until the proposed ordinance has been submitted to and approved in writing by the Department of Transportation.

(Amended by Stats. 1974, Ch. 545.)

22503.5. Notwithstanding any other provision of this code, any local authority may, by ordinance or resolution, establish special parking regulations for two-wheeled or three-wheeled motor vehicles.

(Amended by Stats. 1972, Ch. 1095.)

22504. (a) Upon any highway in unincorporated areas, a person shall not stop, park, or leave standing any vehicle, whether attended or unattended, upon the roadway when it is practicable to stop, park, or leave the vehicle off such portion of the highway, but in every event an unobstructed width of the highway opposite a standing vehicle shall be left for the free passage of other vehicles and a clear view of the stopped vehicle shall be available from a distance of 200 feet in each direction upon the highway. This section shall not apply upon a highway where the roadway is bounded by adjacent curbs.

(b) This section does not apply to the driver of any vehicle which is disabled in such a manner and to such extent that it is impossible to avoid stopping and temporarily leaving the disabled vehicle on the roadway.

(c) (1) A schoolbus stop shall not be designated where there is not a clear view of a proposed or existing schoolbus stop from a distance of 200 feet in each direction along a highway, or upon the main traveled portion of a highway where there is not a clear view of the stop from 500 feet in each direction along the highway and the speed limit is more than 25 miles per hour, unless approved by the Department of the California Highway Patrol upon the request of the school district superintendent or the head or principal of a private school. If the schoolbus stop is approved by the Department of the California Highway Patrol, the Department of Transportation, in respect to state highways, and local authorities, in respect to highways under their jurisdiction, shall place sufficient signs along the highway to give adequate notice to motorists that they are approaching such bus stops.

(2) A school bus stop shall not be designated on any divided or multiple-lane highway where pupils must cross the highway to board or after exiting the bus, unless traffic is controlled by a traffic officer or official traffic control signal. For purposes of this section, a multiple-lane highway is defined as any highway having two or more lanes of travel in each direction.

(Amended by Stats. 2012, Ch. 769, Sec. 37. (AB 2679) Effective January 1, 2013.)

22505. (a) The Department of Transportation with respect to highways under its jurisdiction may place signs or markings prohibiting or restricting the stopping, standing, or parking of vehicles, including, but not limited to, vehicles which are six feet or more in height (including any load thereon), in any of the following areas and under the following conditions:

(1) In areas where, in its opinion, stopping, standing, or parking is dangerous to those using the highway or where the stopping, standing, or parking of vehicles would unduly interfere with the free movement of traffic thereon.

(2) In areas within one-half mile of the boundary of any unit of the state park system which the Director of Conservation has determined are unusually high fire hazard areas, upon notification of the Department of Transportation of such determination by the Director of Conservation.

(3) In areas within one-half mile of the boundary of any unit of the state park system which the county health officer has determined are areas where a substantial public health hazard would result if camping were allowed, upon notification of the Department of Transportation of such determination by the county health officer.

(b) No person shall stop, park, or leave standing any vehicle in violation of the restrictions stated on the signs or markings.

(c) This section does not apply to any of the following:

(1) Public utility vehicles while performing a work operation.

(2) The driver of any vehicle which is disabled in such a manner and to such an extent that it is impossible to avoid stopping, parking, or leaving the disabled vehicle standing on the roadway.

(Amended by Stats. 1987, Ch. 455, Sec. 2.)

22506. Local authorities may by ordinance or resolution prohibit or restrict the stopping, standing, or parking of vehicles on a state highway, in their respective jurisdictions, if the ordinance or resolution is first submitted to and approved in writing by the Department of Transportation, except that where maintenance of any state highway is delegated by the Department of Transportation to a city, the department may also delegate to the city the powers conferred on the department.

(Amended by Stats. 1987, Ch. 455, Sec. 3.)

22507. (a) Local authorities may, by ordinance or resolution, prohibit or restrict the stopping, parking, or standing of vehicles, including, but not limited to, vehicles that are six feet or more in height (including any load thereon) within 100 feet of any intersection, on certain streets or highways, or portions thereof, during all or certain hours of the day. The ordinance or resolution may include a designation of certain streets upon which preferential parking privileges are given to residents and merchants adjacent to the streets for their use and the use of their guests, under which the residents and merchants may be issued a permit or permits that exempt them from the prohibition or restriction of the ordinance or resolution. With the exception of alleys, the ordinance or resolution shall not apply until signs or markings giving adequate notice thereof have been placed. A local ordinance or resolution adopted pursuant to this section may contain provisions that are reasonable and necessary to ensure the effectiveness of a preferential parking program.

(b) An ordinance or resolution adopted under this section may also authorize preferential parking permits for members of organizations, professions, or other designated groups, including, but not limited to, school personnel, to park on specified streets if the local authority determines that the use of the permits will not adversely affect parking conditions for residents and merchants in the area.

(Amended by Stats. 2001, Ch. 223, Sec. 1. Effective January 1, 2002.)

22507.1. (a) A local authority may, by ordinance or resolution, designate certain streets or portions of streets for the exclusive or nonexclusive parking privilege of motor vehicles participating in a car share vehicle program or ridesharing program. The ordinance or resolution shall establish the criteria for a public or private company or organization to participate in the program, and may limit the types of motor vehicles that may be included in the program. Under the car share vehicle program, a car share vehicle or ridesharing vehicle shall be assigned a permit, if necessary, by the local authority that allows that vehicle to park in the exclusive or nonexclusive designated parking areas.

(b) If exclusive parking privilege is authorized, the ordinance or resolution described in subdivision (a) does not apply until signs or markings giving adequate notice thereof have been placed.

(c) A local ordinance or resolution adopted pursuant to subdivision (a) may contain provisions that are reasonable and necessary to ensure the effectiveness of a car share vehicle program or ridesharing program.

(d) For purposes of this section, a "car share vehicle" is a motor vehicle that is operated as part of a regional fleet by a public or private car sharing company or organization and provides hourly or daily service.

(Amended by Stats. 2016, Ch. 86, Sec. 303. (SB 1171) Effective January 1, 2017.)

22507.2. Notwithstanding subdivision (e) of Section 22500, a local authority may, by ordinance, authorize the owner or lessee of property to park a vehicle in front of the owner's or lessee's private driveway when the vehicle displays a permit issued pursuant to the ordinance authorizing such parking.

The local authority may charge a nonrefundable fee to defray the costs of issuing and administering the permits.

A local ordinance adopted pursuant to this section may not authorize parking on a sidewalk in violation of subdivision (f) of Section 22500.

(Amended by Stats. 1985, Ch. 45, Sec. 1.)

22507.5. (a) Notwithstanding Section 22507, local authorities may, by ordinance or resolution, prohibit or restrict the parking or standing of vehicles on certain streets or highways, or portions thereof, between the hours of 2 a.m. and 6 a.m., and may, by ordinance or resolution, prohibit or restrict the parking or standing, on any street, or portion thereof, in a residential district, of commercial vehicles having a manufacturer's gross vehicle weight rating of 10,000 pounds or more. The ordinance or resolution relating to parking between the hours of 2 a.m. and 6 a.m. may provide for a system of permits for the purpose of exempting from the prohibition or restriction of the ordinance or resolution, disabled persons, residents, and guests of residents of residential areas, including, but not limited to, high-density and multiple-family dwelling areas, lacking adequate offstreet parking facilities. The ordinance or resolution relating to the parking or standing of commercial vehicles in a residential district, however, shall not be effective with respect to any commercial vehicle, or trailer component thereof, making pickups or deliveries of goods, wares, and merchandise from or to any building or structure located on the restricted streets or highways or for the purpose of delivering materials to be used in the actual and bona fide repair, alteration, remodeling, or construction of any building or structure upon the restricted streets or highways for which a building permit has previously been obtained.

(b) Subdivision (a) of this section is applicable to vehicles specified in subdivision (a) of Section 31303, except that an ordinance or resolution adopted pursuant to subdivision (a) of this section shall not permit the parking of those vehicles which is otherwise prohibited under this code.

(c) For the purpose of implementing this section, each local authority may, by ordinance, define the term "residential district" in accordance with its zoning ordinance. The ordinance is not effective unless the legislative body of the local authority holds a public hearing on the proposed ordinance prior to its adoption, with notice of the public hearing given in accordance with Section 65090 of the Government Code.

(Amended by Stats. 2004, Ch. 518, Sec. 3. Effective January 1, 2005.)

22507.6. Local authorities may, by ordinance or resolution, prohibit or restrict the parking or standing of vehicles on designated streets or highways, or portions thereof, for the purpose of street sweeping. No ordinance or resolution relating to the parking or standing of commercial vehicles in a residential district shall be effective with respect to any commercial vehicle making pickups or deliveries of goods, wares, or merchandise from or to any building or structure located on the restricted street or highway, or for the purpose of delivering materials to be used in the repair, alteration, remodeling, or reconstruction of any building or structure for which a building permit has previously been obtained. No such ordinance or resolution shall be effective until the street or highway, or portion thereof, has been sign-posted in accordance with the uniform standards and specifications of the Department of Transportation, or local authorities have caused to be posted in a conspicuous place at each entrance to the street a notice not less than 17 inches by 22 inches in size, with lettering not less than one inch in height, setting forth the day or days and hours parking is prohibited. As used in this section, "entrance" means the intersection of any street or streets comprising an area of restricted parking for street-sweeping purposes on the same day or days and hours with another street or highway not subject to such a parking restriction, or subject to parking restrictions on different days and hours.

(Amended by Stats. 1982, Ch. 466, Sec. 115.)

22507.8. (a) It is unlawful for any person to park or leave standing any vehicle in a stall or space designated for disabled persons and disabled veterans pursuant to Section 22511.7 or 22511.8 of this code or Section 14679 of the Government Code, unless the vehicle displays either a special identification license plate issued pursuant to Section 5007 or a distinguishing placard issued pursuant to Section 22511.55 or 22511.59.

(b) It is unlawful for any person to obstruct, block, or otherwise bar access to those parking stalls or spaces except as provided in subdivision (a).

(c) It is unlawful for any person to park or leave standing any vehicle, including a vehicle displaying a special identification license plate issued pursuant to Section 5007 or a distinguishing placard issued pursuant to Section 22511.55 or 22511.59, in either of the following places:

(1) On the lines marking the boundaries of a parking stall or space designated for disabled persons or disabled veterans.

(2) In any area of the pavement adjacent to a parking stall or space designated for disabled persons or disabled veterans that is marked by crosshatched lines and is thereby designated, pursuant to any local ordinance, for the loading and unloading of vehicles parked in the stall or space.

(d) Subdivisions (a), (b), and (c) apply to all offstreet parking facilities owned or operated by the state, and to all offstreet parking facilities owned or operated by a local authority. Subdivisions (a), (b), and (c) also apply to any privately owned and maintained offstreet parking facility.

(Amended by Stats. 2009, Ch. 200, Sec. 12. (SB 734) Effective January 1, 2010.)

22507.9. Local authorities may establish a special enforcement unit for the sole purpose of providing adequate enforcement of Section 22507.8 and local ordinances and resolutions adopted pursuant to Section 22511.7.

Local authorities may establish recruitment and employment guidelines that encourage and enable employment of qualified disabled persons in these special enforcement units.

Members of the special enforcement unit may issue notices of parking violation for violations of Section 22507.8 and local ordinances adopted pursuant to Section 22511.7. Members of the special enforcement unit shall not be peace officers and shall not make arrests in the course of their official duties, but shall wear distinctive uniforms and badges while on duty. A two-way radio unit, which may utilize police frequencies or citizens' band, may be issued by the local authority to each member of the special enforcement unit for use while on duty.

The local authority may pay the cost of uniforms and badges for the special enforcement unit, and may provide daily cleaning of the uniforms.

Additionally, the local authority may provide motorized wheelchairs for use by members of the special unit while on duty, including batteries and necessary recharging thereof. Any motorized wheelchair used by a member of the special enforcement unit while on duty shall be equipped with a single headlamp in the front and a single stoplamp in the rear.

Members of the special enforcement unit may be paid an hourly wage without the compensatory benefits provided other permanent and temporary employees, but shall be entitled to applicable workers' compensation benefits as provided by law. Insurance provided by the local authority for disability or liability of a member of the special enforcement unit shall be the same as for other employees performing similar duties.

Nothing in this section precludes a local authority from using regular full-time employees to enforce this chapter and ordinances adopted pursuant thereto.

This section applies to all counties and cities, including every charter city and city and county.

(Amended by Stats. 1996, Ch. 124, Sec. 127. Effective January 1, 1997.)

22508. (a) A local authority shall not establish parking payment zones or fix the rate of fees for those zones except by ordinance. The rate of fees may be variable, based upon criteria identified by the local authority in the ordinance. An ordinance establishing a parking payment zone shall describe the area that would be included within the zone.

(b) A local authority may, by ordinance, cause streets and highways to be marked with white lines designating parking spaces and require vehicles to park within the parking spaces.

(c) An ordinance adopted by a local authority pursuant to this section with respect to a state highway shall not become effective until the proposed ordinance has been submitted to and approved in writing by the Department of Transportation. The proposed ordinance shall be submitted to the department only by action of the local legislative body and the proposed ordinance shall be submitted in complete draft form.

(d) An ordinance adopted pursuant to this section establishing a parking payment zone or fixing rates of fees for that zone shall be subject to local referendum processes in the same manner as if the ordinance dealt with a matter of purely local concern.

(e) Except as described in Section 22508.2, a local authority may accept but shall not require payment of parking meter fees by a mobile device.

(Amended by Stats. 2024, Ch. 858, Sec. 1. (SB 532) Effective January 1, 2025.)

22508.2. (a) A local authority in the City and County of San Francisco, City of Long Beach, or City of Santa Monica may require payment by a mobile device in a parking payment zone only if it meets both of the following requirements:

(1) Installs signs no more than 100 feet from any space where payment is required that clearly states that payment is required and how payments may be made.

(2) Adopts by ordinance or resolution an accessible and equitable parking cash payment plan that does not utilize parking meters or payment centers in parking payment zones. The plan shall provide reasonably accessible alternative means for payment of parking fees using cash. The plan shall assess the feasibility of potential strategies, including, but not limited to, accepting cash payment for parking from a mailed invoice requested through the mobile payment system. The local authority shall consult and work collaboratively with relevant local stakeholder organizations that may include, but are not limited to, racial equity, privacy protection, and economic justice groups, in developing the accessible and equitable parking cash payment plan. The plan shall be approved by the local authority.

(b) A local authority in the City and County of San Francisco, City of Long Beach, or City of Santa Monica that adopts an accessible and equitable parking cash payment plan and implements at least one mobile device parking payment zone pursuant to this section shall, on or before January 1 of the fourth year in which the first mobile device parking payment zone has been implemented, submit to its governing body and the transportation committees of the Legislature, consistent with Section 9795 of the Government Code, an evaluation report of the impact of all mobile device parking payment zones implemented by the local authority on equity, accessibility, and costs. The report shall evaluate the effectiveness, impact on privacy, impact on equity, impact on traffic outcomes, cost to implement, change in citations issued, and generation of revenue.

(c) A civil fine for parking in a parking payment zone that requires payment by mobile device and lacks a parking meter shall be one-half of the civil fine for failing to pay for parking in a metered zone. This subdivision shall not apply to a person who paid for parking but stayed in the spot beyond the period for which the person paid.

(d) A local authority in the City and County of San Francisco, City of Long Beach, or City of Santa Monica may operate a mobile device parking payment zone authorized by this section for five years following the date of creation for each city and county, or city, of the first mobile device parking payment zone, or until January 1, 2033, whichever is sooner.

(e) This section shall remain in effect only until January 1, 2033, and as of that date is repealed.

(Added by Stats. 2024, Ch. 858, Sec. 2. (SB 532) Effective January 1, 2025. Repealed as of January 1, 2033, by its own provisions.)

22508.5. (a) A vehicle may park, for up to the posted time limit, in any parking space that is regulated by an inoperable parking meter or an inoperable parking payment center.

(b) A vehicle may park without time limit in any parking space that does not have a posted time limit and that is regulated by an inoperable parking meter or inoperable parking payment center, subject to any other applicable regulations regarding parking vehicles.

(c) A local authority may limit parking to four hours for a parking space that does not have a posted time limit and that is regulated by an inoperable parking meter or an inoperable parking payment center, if the local authority posts signs clearly providing notice of the time limitation applicable when that parking meter or parking payment center is inoperable.

(d) If a parking space is regulated by a parking meter or parking payment center that cannot physically accept payment, a local authority shall not issue a citation for nonpayment of parking fees notwithstanding the fact that the parking meter or parking payment center may accept payment by other nonphysical means.

(e) Except as provided in subdivision (c), a local authority shall not, by ordinance or resolution, prohibit or restrict the parking of vehicles in a space that is regulated by an inoperable parking meter or inoperable parking payment center.

(f) For purposes of this section:

(1) "Inoperable parking meter" means a meter located next to and designated for an individual parking space that has become inoperable and cannot accept payment in any form or cannot register that a payment in any form has been made.

(2) "Inoperable parking payment center" means an electronic parking meter or pay station serving one or more parking spaces that is closest to the space where a person has parked and that cannot accept payment in any form, cannot register that a payment in any form has been made, or cannot issue a receipt that is required to be displayed in a conspicuous location on or in the vehicle.

(Amended by Stats. 2018, Ch. 92, Sec. 210. (SB 1289) Effective January 1, 2019.)

22509. Local authorities within the reasonable exercise of their police powers may adopt rules and regulations by ordinance or resolution providing that no person driving, or in control of, or in charge of, a motor vehicle shall permit it to stand on any highway unattended when upon any grade exceeding 3 percent within any business or residence district without blocking the wheels of the vehicle by turning them against the curb or by other means.

(Enacted by Stats. 1959, Ch. 3.)

22510. (a) Local authorities may, by ordinance or resolution, prohibit or restrict the parking or standing of vehicles on designated streets or highways within their jurisdiction, or portions thereof, for the purpose of snow removal. The ordinance or resolution shall not be effective until the street or highway, or portion thereof, has been sign-posted in accordance with the uniform standards and specifications of the Department of Transportation, or until the local authorities have caused to be posted in a conspicuous place at each entrance to the street or highway, a notice not less than 17 inches by 22 inches in size, with lettering not less than one inch in height, setting forth the days parking is prohibited. The signs shall, at a minimum, be placed on each affected street or highway, at the boundary of the local authority, and at the beginning and end of each highway or highway segment included in that area. No person shall stop, park, or leave standing any vehicle, whether attended or unattended, within the area marked by signs, except when necessary to avoid conflict with other traffic or in compliance with the directions of a traffic or peace officer.

(b) No ordinance or resolution authorized by subdivision (a) which affects a state highway shall be effective until it is submitted to, and approved by, the Department of Transportation.

(c) The Department of Transportation, with respect to state highways, may restrict the parking or standing of vehicles for purposes of snow removal. The restrictions shall not be effective until the highway, or portion thereof, has been posted with signs in accordance with the uniform standards and specifications of the department. No person shall stop, park, or leave standing any vehicle, whether attended or unattended, within the area marked by parking restriction signs, except when necessary to avoid conflict with other traffic or in compliance with the directions of a traffic or peace officer.

(Repealed and added by Stats. 1990, Ch. 692, Sec. 3.)

22511. (a) (1) A local authority, by ordinance or resolution, and a person in lawful possession of an offstreet parking facility may designate stalls or spaces in an offstreet parking facility owned or operated by that local authority or person for the exclusive purpose of charging and parking a vehicle that is connected for electric charging purposes.

(2) A local authority, by ordinance or resolution, may designate stalls or spaces on a public street within its jurisdiction for the exclusive purpose of charging and parking a vehicle that is connected for electric charging purposes.

(b) If posted in accordance with subdivision (d) or (e), the owner or person in lawful possession of a privately owned or operated offstreet parking facility, after notifying the police or sheriff's department, may cause the removal of a vehicle from a stall or space designated pursuant to subdivision (a) in the facility to the nearest public garage if the vehicle is not connected for electric charging purposes.

(c) (1) If posted in accordance with paragraph (1) of subdivision (d), the local authority owning or operating an offstreet parking facility, after notifying the police or sheriff's department, may cause the removal of a vehicle from a stall or space designated pursuant to paragraph (1) of subdivision (a) in the facility to the nearest garage, as defined in Section 340, that is owned, leased, or approved for use by a public agency if the vehicle is not connected for electric charging purposes.

(2) If posted in accordance with paragraph (2) of subdivision (d), the local authority, after notifying the police or sheriff's department, may cause the removal of a vehicle from a stall or space designated pursuant to paragraph (2) of subdivision (a) to the nearest garage, as defined in Section 340, that is owned, leased, or approved for use by a public agency if the vehicle is not connected for electric charging purposes.

(d) (1) The posting required for an offstreet parking facility owned or operated either privately or by a local authority shall consist of a sign not less than 17 by 22 inches in size with lettering not less than one inch in height that clearly and conspicuously states the following: "Unauthorized vehicles not connected for electric charging purposes will be towed away at owner's expense. Towed vehicles may be reclaimed at
(Address)
or by telephoning
(Telephone number of local law enforcement agency)."

The sign shall be posted in either of the following locations:

(A) Immediately adjacent to, and visible from, the stall or space.

(B) In a conspicuous place at each entrance to the offstreet parking facility.

(2) The posting required for stalls or spaces on a public street designated pursuant to paragraph (2) of subdivision (a) shall follow the California Manual of Uniform Traffic Control Devices.

(e) If the parking facility is privately owned and public parking is prohibited by the posting of a sign meeting the requirements of paragraph (1) of subdivision (a) of Section 22658, the requirements of subdivision (b) may be met by the posting of a sign immediately adjacent to, and visible from, each stall or space indicating that a vehicle not meeting the requirements of subdivision (a) will be removed at the owner's expense and containing the telephone number of the local traffic law enforcement agency.

(f) This section does not interfere with existing law governing the ability of local authorities to adopt ordinances related to parking programs within their jurisdiction, such as programs that provide free parking in metered areas or municipal garages for electric vehicles.

(Amended by Stats. 2017, Ch. 635, Sec. 1. (AB 1452) Effective January 1, 2018.)

22511.1. (a) A person shall not park or leave standing a vehicle in a stall or space designated pursuant to Section 22511 unless the vehicle is connected for electric charging purposes.

(b) A person shall not obstruct, block, or otherwise bar access to parking stalls or spaces described in subdivision (a) except as provided in subdivision (a).

(Amended by Stats. 2011, Ch. 274, Sec. 2. (AB 475) Effective January 1, 2012.)

22511.2. (a) A parking space served by electric vehicle supply equipment or a parking space designated as a future electric vehicle charging space shall count as at least one standard automobile parking space for the purpose of complying with any applicable minimum parking space requirements established by a local jurisdiction.

(b) An accessible parking space with an access aisle served by electric vehicle supply equipment or an accessible parking space with an aisle designated as a future electric vehicle charging space shall count as at least two standard automobile parking spaces for the purpose of complying with any applicable minimum parking space requirements established by a local jurisdiction.

(c) This section does not modify the approval requirements for an electric vehicle charging station pursuant to Section 65850.7 of the Government Code.

(d) The following definitions apply for purposes of this section:

(1) "Electric vehicle supply equipment" has the same definition as that term is used in the latest published version of the California Electrical Code, that is in effect, and applies to any level or capacity of supply equipment installed specifically for the purpose of transferring energy between the premises wiring and the electric vehicle.

(2) "Electric vehicle charging space" means a space designated by a local jurisdiction for charging electric vehicles.

(3) "Local jurisdiction" means a city, including a charter city, county, or city and county.

(Added by Stats. 2019, Ch. 819, Sec. 2. (AB 1100) Effective January 1, 2020.)

22511.3. (a) A veteran displaying special license plates issued under Section 5101.3, 5101.4, 5101.5, 5101.6, or 5101.8 may park his or her motor vehicle, weighing not more than 6,000 pounds gross weight, without charge, in a metered parking space.

(b) Nothing in this section restricts the rights of a person displaying either a special identification license plate issued pursuant to Section 5007 or a distinguishing placard issued pursuant to Section 22511.55 or 22511.59.

(c) (1) This section does not exempt a vehicle displaying special license plates issued under Section 5101.3, 5101.4, 5101.5, 5101.6, or 5101.8 from compliance with any other state law or ordinance, including, but not limited to, vehicle height restrictions, zones that prohibit stopping, parking, or standing of all vehicles, parking time limitations, street sweeping, restrictions of the parking space to a particular type of vehicle, or the parking of a vehicle that is involved in the operation of a street vending business.

(2) This section does not authorize a vehicle displaying special license plates issued under Section 5101.3, 5101.4, 5101.5, 5101.6, or 5101.8 to park in a state parking facility that is designated only for state employees.

(3) This section does not authorize a vehicle displaying special license plates issued under Section 5101.3, 5101.4, 5101.5, 5101.6, or 5101.8 to park during time periods other than the normal business hours of, or the maximum time allotted by, a state or local authority parking facility.

(4) This section does not require the state or a local authority to designate specific parking spaces for vehicles displaying special license plates issued under Section 5101.3, 5101.4, 5101.5, 5101.6, or 5101.8.

(d) A local authority's compliance with subdivision (a) is solely contingent upon the approval of its governing body.

(Added by Stats. 2008, Ch. 588, Sec. 1. Effective January 1, 2009.)

22511.5. (a) (1) A disabled person or disabled veteran displaying special license plates issued under Section 5007 or a distinguishing placard issued under Section 22511.55 or 22511.59 is allowed to park for unlimited periods in any of the following zones:

(A) In any restricted zone described in paragraph (5) of subdivision (a) of Section 21458 or on streets upon which preferential parking privileges and height limits have been given pursuant to Section 22507.

(B) In any parking zone that is restricted as to the length of time parking is permitted as indicated by a sign erected pursuant to a local ordinance.

(2) A disabled person or disabled veteran is allowed to park in any metered parking space without being required to pay parking meter fees.

(3) This subdivision does not apply to a zone for which state law or ordinance absolutely prohibits stopping, parking, or standing of all vehicles, or which the law or ordinance reserves for special types of vehicles, or to the parking of a vehicle that is involved in the operation of a street vending business.

(b) A disabled person or disabled veteran is allowed to park a motor vehicle displaying a special disabled person license plate or placard issued by a foreign jurisdiction with the same parking privileges authorized in this code for any motor vehicle displaying a special license plate or a distinguishing placard issued by the Department of Motor Vehicles.

(Amended by Stats. 2010, Ch. 478, Sec. 11. (AB 2777) Effective January 1, 2011.)

22511.55. (a) (1) A disabled person or disabled veteran may apply to the department for the issuance of a distinguishing placard. The placard may be used in lieu of the special license plate or plates issued under Section 5007 for parking purposes described in Section 22511.5 when (A) suspended from the rearview mirror, (B) if there is no rearview mirror, when displayed on the dashboard of a vehicle, or (C) inserted in a clip designated for a distinguishing placard and installed by the manufacturer on the driver's side of the front window. It is the intent of the Legislature to encourage the use of distinguishing placards because they provide law enforcement officers with a more readily recognizable symbol for distinguishing vehicles qualified for the parking privilege. The placard shall be the size, shape, and color determined by the department and shall bear the International Symbol of Access adopted pursuant to Section 3 of Public Law 100-641, commonly known as the "wheelchair symbol." The department shall incorporate instructions for the lawful use of a placard, and a summary of the penalties for the unlawful use of a placard, into the identification card issued to the placard owner.

(2) (A) The department may establish procedures for the issuance and renewal of the placards. The procedures shall include, but are not limited to, advising an applicant in writing on the application for a placard of the procedure to apply for a special license plate or plates, as described in Section 5007, and the fee exemptions established pursuant to Section 9105 and in subdivision (a) of Section 10783 of the Revenue and Taxation Code. The placards shall have a fixed expiration date of June 30 every two years. A portion of the placard shall be printed in a contrasting color that shall be changed every two years. The size and color of this contrasting portion of the placard shall be large and distinctive enough to be readily identifiable by a law enforcement officer in a passing vehicle.

(B) As used in this section, "year" means the period between the inclusive dates of July 1 through June 30.

(C) Prior to the end of each year, the department shall, for the most current three years available, compare its record of disability placards issued against the records of the Office of Vital Records of the State Department of Public Health, or its successor, and a nationwide vital statistics clearinghouse, and withhold any renewal notices or placards that otherwise would have been sent for a placardholder identified as deceased.

(D) The department shall, six years after the first issuance of a placard and every six years thereafter, send the placardholder a renewal form at least 90 days prior to the June 30 expiration date of the current placard. Certification of medical disability and proof of true full name is not required for the renewal. A placardholder who wishes to renew a placard shall fill out the form and submit it to the department prior to expiration of the current placard.

(3) Except as provided in paragraph (4), a person shall not be eligible for more than one placard at a time.

(4) Organizations and agencies involved in the transportation of disabled persons or disabled veterans may apply for a placard for each vehicle used for the purpose of transporting disabled persons or disabled veterans.

(5) The department shall require a person who applies for a placard pursuant to this section to provide proof of the person's true full name and date of birth that shall be established by submitting one of the following to the department:

(A) A copy or facsimile of the applicant's state issued driver's license or identification card.

(B) A copy or facsimile of the document required for an applicant for a driver's license or identification card to establish the applicant's true full name.

(C) An applicant unable to establish legal presence in the United States may fulfill the true full name and date of birth requirement by providing the department a copy or facsimile of the documents used to establish identity pursuant to Section 12801.9.

(b) (1) Except as provided in paragraph (4), prior to issuing an original distinguishing placard to a disabled person or disabled veteran, the department shall require the submission of a certificate, in accordance with paragraph (2), signed by the physician and surgeon, or to the extent that it does not cause a reduction in the receipt of federal aid highway funds, by a nurse practitioner, certified nurse-midwife, or physician assistant, substantiating the disability, unless the applicant's disability is readily observable and uncontested. The disability of a person who has lost, or has lost use of, one or more lower extremities or one hand, for a disabled veteran, or both hands, for a disabled person, or who has significant limitation in the use of lower extremities, may also be certified by a licensed chiropractor. The disability of a person related to the foot or ankle may be certified by a licensed podiatrist. The blindness of an applicant shall be certified by a licensed physician and surgeon who specializes in diseases of the eye or a licensed optometrist. The physician and surgeon, nurse practitioner, certified nurse-midwife, physician assistant, chiropractor, or optometrist certifying the qualifying disability shall provide a full description of the illness or disability on the form submitted to the department.

(2) The physician and surgeon, nurse practitioner, certified nurse midwife, physician assistant, chiropractor, podiatrist, or optometrist who signs a certificate submitted under this subdivision shall retain

information sufficient to substantiate that certificate and, upon request of the department, shall make that information available for inspection by the Medical Board of California or the appropriate regulatory board.

(3) The department shall maintain in its records all information on an applicant's certification of permanent disability and shall make that information available to eligible law enforcement or parking control agencies upon a request pursuant to Section 22511.58.

(4) For a disabled veteran, the department shall accept, in lieu of the certificate described in paragraph (1), a certificate from a county veterans service officer, the Department of Veterans Affairs, or the United States Department of Veterans Affairs that certifies that the applicant is a disabled veteran as described in Section 295.7.

(c) A person who is issued a distinguishing placard pursuant to subdivision (a) may apply to the department for a substitute placard without recertification of eligibility, if that placard is lost or stolen. The department shall not issue a substitute placard to a person more than four times in a two-year renewal period. A person who requires a substitute placard in excess of the four replacements authorized pursuant to this subdivision shall reapply to the department for a new placard and submit a new certificate of disability as described in subdivision (b).

(d) The distinguishing placard shall be returned to the department not later than 60 days after the death of the disabled person or disabled veteran to whom the placard was issued.

(e) The department shall print on any distinguishing placard issued on or after January 1, 2005, the maximum penalty that may be imposed for a violation of Section 4461. For purposes of this subdivision, the "maximum penalty" is the amount derived from adding all of the following:

(1) The maximum fine that may be imposed under Section 4461.

(2) The penalty required to be imposed under Section 70372 of the Government Code.

(3) The penalty required to be levied under Section 76000 of the Government Code.

(4) The penalty required to be levied under Section 1464 of the Penal Code.

(5) The surcharge required to be levied under Section 1465.7 of the Penal Code.

(6) The penalty authorized to be imposed under Section 4461.3.

(Amended by Stats. 2022, Ch. 71, Sec. 14. (SB 198) Effective June 30, 2022.)

22511.56. (a) A person using a distinguishing placard issued under Section 22511.55 or 22511.59, or a special license plate issued under Section 5007, for parking as permitted by Section 22511.5 shall, upon request of a peace officer or person authorized to enforce parking laws, ordinances, or regulations, present identification and evidence of the issuance of that placard or plate to that person, or that vehicle if the plate was issued pursuant to paragraph (3) of subdivision (a) of Section 5007.

(b) Failure to present the requested identification and evidence of the issuance of that placard or plate shall be a rebuttable presumption that the placard or plate is being misused and that the associated vehicle has been parked in violation of Section 22507.8, or has exercised a disabled person's parking privilege pursuant to Section 22511.5.

(c) In addition to any other applicable penalty for the misuse of a placard, the officer or parking enforcement person may confiscate a placard being used for parking purposes that benefit a person other than the person to whom the placard was issued by the Department of Motor Vehicles. A placard lawfully used by a person transporting a disabled person pursuant to subdivision (b) of Section 4461 may not be confiscated.

(d) In addition to any other applicable penalty for the misuse of a special license plate issued under Section 5007, a peace officer may confiscate the plate being used for parking purposes that benefit a person other than the person to whom the plate was issued by the Department of Motor Vehicles.

(e) After verification with the Department of Motor Vehicles that the user of the placard or plate is not the registered owner of the placard or plate, the appropriate agency that confiscated the placard or plate shall notify the department of the placard or plate number and the department shall cancel the placard or plate. A placard or plate canceled by the department pursuant to this subdivision may be destroyed by the agency that confiscated the placard or plate.

(Amended by Stats. 2006, Ch. 203, Sec. 2. Effective January 1, 2007.)

22511.57. A local authority may, by ordinance or resolution, prohibit or restrict the parking or standing of a vehicle on streets or highways or in a parking stall or space in a privately or publicly owned or operated offstreet parking facility within its jurisdiction when the vehicle displays, in order to obtain special parking privileges, a distinguishing placard or special license plate, issued pursuant to Section 5007, 22511.55, or 22511.59, and any of the following conditions are met:

(a) The records of the Department of Motor Vehicles for the identification number assigned to the placard or license plate indicate that the placard or license plate has been reported as lost, stolen, surrendered, canceled, revoked, or expired, or was issued to a person who has been reported as deceased for a period exceeding 60 days.

(b) The placard or license plate is displayed on a vehicle that is not being used to transport, and is not in the reasonable proximity of, the person to whom the license plate or placard was issued or a person who is authorized to be transported in the vehicle displaying that placard or license plate.

(c) The placard or license plate is counterfeit, forged, altered, or mutilated.

(Amended by Stats. 2011, Ch. 341, Sec. 3. (SB 565) Effective January 1, 2012.)

22511.58. (a) Upon a request to the department by a local public law enforcement agency or local agency responsible for the administration or enforcement of parking regulations, the department shall make available to the requesting agency any information contained in a physician's certificate submitted to the department as part of the application for a disabled person's parking privileges, substantiating the disability of a person applying for or who has been issued a parking placard pursuant to Section 22511.55. The department shall not provide the information specified in this subdivision to any private or other third-party parking citation processing agency.

(b) Local authorities may establish a review board or panel, which shall include a qualified physician or medical authority, for purposes of reviewing information contained in the applications for special parking privileges and the certification of qualifying disabilities for persons residing within the jurisdiction of the local authority. Any findings or determinations by a review board or panel under this section indicating that an application or certification is fraudulent or lacks proper certification may be transmitted to the department or other appropriate authorities for further review and investigation.

(Added by Stats. 1996, Ch. 1033, Sec. 2. Effective January 1, 1997.)

22511.59. (a) Upon the receipt of the applications and documents required by subdivision (b), (c), or (d), the department shall issue a temporary distinguishing placard bearing the International Symbol of Access adopted pursuant to Section 3 of Public Law 100-641, commonly known as the "wheelchair symbol." During the period for which it is valid, the temporary distinguishing placard may be used for the parking purposes described in Section 22511.5 in the same manner as a distinguishing placard issued pursuant to Section 22511.55.

(b) (1) A person who is temporarily disabled for a period of not more than six months may apply to the department for the issuance of the temporary distinguishing placard described in subdivision (a).

(2) Prior to issuing a placard pursuant to this subdivision, the department shall require the submission of a certificate signed by a physician and surgeon, or to the extent that it does not cause a reduction in the receipt of federal aid highway funds, by a nurse practitioner, certified nurse midwife, physician assistant, chiropractor, podiatrist, or optometrist, as described in subdivision (b) of Section 22511.55, substantiating the temporary disability and stating the date upon which

the disability is expected to terminate.

(3) The physician and surgeon, nurse practitioner, certified nurse midwife, physician assistant, chiropractor, podiatrist, or optometrist who signs a certificate submitted under this subdivision shall maintain information sufficient to substantiate that certificate and, upon request of the department, shall make that information available for inspection by the Medical Board of California or the appropriate regulatory board.

(4) A placard issued pursuant to this subdivision shall expire not later than 180 days from the date of issuance or upon the expected termination date of the disability, as stated on the certificate required by paragraph (2), whichever is less.

(5) The fee for a temporary placard issued pursuant to this subdivision shall be six dollars ($6).

(6) A placard issued pursuant to this subdivision shall be renewed a maximum of six times consecutively.

(c) (1) A permanently disabled person or disabled veteran who is not a resident of this state and plans to travel within the state may apply to the department for the issuance of the temporary distinguishing placard described in subdivision (a).

(2) Prior to issuing a placard pursuant to this subdivision, the department shall require certification of the disability, as described in subdivision (b) of Section 22511.55.

(3) The physician and surgeon, nurse practitioner, certified nurse midwife, physician assistant, chiropractor, podiatrist, or optometrist who signs a certificate submitted under this subdivision shall maintain information sufficient to substantiate that certificate and, upon request of the department, shall make that information available for inspection by the Medical Board of California or the appropriate regulatory board.

(4) A placard issued pursuant to this subdivision shall expire not later than 90 days from the date of issuance.

(5) The department shall not charge a fee for issuance of a placard under this subdivision.

(6) A placard issued pursuant to this subdivision shall be renewed a maximum of six times consecutively.

(d) (1) A permanently disabled person or disabled veteran who has been issued either a distinguishing placard pursuant to Section 22511.55 or special license plates pursuant to Section 5007, but not both, may apply to the department for the issuance of the temporary distinguishing placard described in subdivision (a) for the purpose of travel.

(2) Prior to issuing a placard pursuant to this subdivision, the department shall require the applicant to submit either the number identifying the distinguishing placard issued pursuant to Section 22511.55 or the number on the special license plates.

(3) A placard issued pursuant to this subdivision shall expire not later than 30 days from the date of issuance.

(4) The department shall not charge a fee for issuance of a placard under this subdivision.

(5) A placard issued pursuant to this subdivision shall be renewed a maximum of six times consecutively.

(e) The department shall print on a temporary distinguishing placard, the maximum penalty that may be imposed for a violation of Section 4461. For the purposes of this subdivision, the "maximum penalty" is the amount derived from adding all of the following:

(1) The maximum fine that may be imposed under Section 4461.

(2) The penalty required to be imposed under Section 70372 of the Government Code.

(3) The penalty required to be levied under Section 76000 of the Government Code.

(4) The penalty required to be levied under Section 1464 of the Penal Code.

(5) The surcharge required to be levied under Section 1465.7 of the Penal Code.

(6) The penalty authorized to be imposed under Section 4461.3.

(f) The department shall require a person who applies for a temporary placard pursuant to this section to provide proof of his or her true full name and date of birth that shall be established by submitting one of the following to the department:

(1) A copy or facsimile of the applicant's state issued driver's license or identification card.

(2) A copy or facsimile of the document required for an applicant for a driver's license or identification card to establish the applicant's true full name.

(3) An applicant unable to establish legal presence in the United States may fulfill the true full name and date of birth requirement by providing the department a copy or facsimile of the documents used to establish identity pursuant to Section 12801.9.

(Amended by Stats. 2017, Ch. 485, Sec. 20. (SB 611) Effective January 1, 2018.)

22511.6. (a) The Department of Motor Vehicles may cancel or revoke a distinguishing placard issued pursuant to Section 22511.55 or 22511.59 in any of the following events:

(1) When the department is satisfied that the placard was fraudulently obtained or erroneously issued.

(2) When the department determines that the required fee has not been paid and the fee is not paid upon reasonable notice and demand.

(3) When the placard could have been refused when last issued or renewed.

(4) When the department determines that the owner of the placard has committed any offense described in Section 4461 or 4463, involving the placard to be canceled or revoked.

(5) When the department determines that the owner of the placard is deceased.

(b) Whenever the Department of Motor Vehicles cancels or revokes a distinguishing placard, the owner or person in possession of the placard shall immediately return the placard to the department.

(Amended by Stats. 1994, Ch. 1149, Sec. 9. Effective January 1, 1995.)

22511.7. (a) In addition to Section 22511.8 for offstreet parking, a local authority may, by ordinance or resolution, designate onstreet parking spaces for the exclusive use of a vehicle that displays either a special identification license plate issued pursuant to Section 5007 or a distinguishing placard issued pursuant to Section 22511.55 or 22511.59.

(b) (1) Whenever a local authority so designates a parking space, it shall be indicated by blue paint on the curb or edge of the paved portion of the street adjacent to the space. In addition, the local authority shall post immediately adjacent to and visible from the space a sign consisting of a profile view of a wheelchair with occupant in white on a blue background.

(2) The sign required pursuant to paragraph (1) shall clearly and conspicuously state the following: "Minimum Fine $250." This paragraph applies only to signs for parking spaces constructed on or after July 1, 2008, and signs that are replaced on or after July 1, 2008.

(3) If the loading and unloading area of the pavement adjacent to a parking stall or space designated for disabled persons or disabled veterans is to be marked by a border and hatched lines, the border shall be painted blue and the hatched lines shall be painted a suitable contrasting color to the parking space. Blue or white paint is preferred. In addition, within the border the words "No Parking" shall be painted in white letters no less than 12 inches high. This paragraph applies only to parking spaces constructed on or after July 1, 2008, and painting that is done on or after July 1, 2008.

(c) This section does not restrict the privilege granted to disabled persons and disabled veterans by Section 22511.5.

(Amended by Stats. 2009, Ch. 200, Sec. 13. (SB 734) Effective January 1, 2010.)

22511.8. (a) A local authority, by ordinance or resolution, and a person in lawful possession of an offstreet parking facility may designate stalls or spaces in an offstreet parking facility owned or operated by the local authority or person for the exclusive use of a vehicle that displays either a special license plate issued pursuant to Section 5007 or a distinguishing placard issued pursuant to Section 22511.55 or 22511.59. The designation shall be made by posting a sign as described in paragraph (1), and by either of the markings described in paragraph (2) or (3):

(1) (A) By posting immediately adjacent to, and visible from, each stall or space, a sign consisting of a profile view of a wheelchair with occupant in white on a blue background.

(B) The sign shall also clearly and conspicuously state the following: "Minimum Fine $250." This subparagraph applies only to signs for parking spaces constructed on or after July 1, 2008, and signs that are replaced on or after July 1, 2008, or as the State Architect deems necessary when renovations, structural repair, alterations, and additions occur to existing buildings and facilities on or after July 1, 2008.

(2) (A) By outlining or painting the stall or space in blue and outlining on the ground in the stall or space in white or suitable contrasting color a profile view depicting a wheelchair with occupant.

(B) The loading and unloading area of the pavement adjacent to a parking stall or space designated for disabled persons or disabled veterans shall be marked by a border and hatched lines. The border shall be painted blue and the hatched lines shall be painted a suitable contrasting color to the parking space. Blue or white paint is preferred. In addition, within the border the words "No Parking" shall be painted in white letters no less than 12 inches high. This subparagraph applies only to parking spaces constructed on or after July 1, 2008, and painting that is done on or after July 1, 2008, or as the State Architect deems necessary when renovations, structural repair, alterations, and additions occur to existing buildings and facilities on or after July 1, 2008.

(3) By outlining a profile view of a wheelchair with occupant in white on a blue background, of the same dimensions as in paragraph (2). The profile view shall be located so that it is visible to a traffic enforcement officer when a vehicle is properly parked in the space.

(b) The Department of General Services under the Division of the State Architect shall develop pursuant to Section 4450 of the Government Code, as appropriate, conforming regulations to ensure compliance with subparagraph (B) of paragraph (1) of subdivision (a) and subparagraph (B) of paragraph (2) of subdivision (a). Initial regulations to implement these provisions shall be adopted as emergency regulations. The adoption of these regulations shall be considered by the Department of General Services to be an emergency necessary for the immediate preservation of the public peace, health and safety, or general welfare.

(c) If posted in accordance with subdivision (e) or (f), the owner or person in lawful possession of a privately owned or operated offstreet parking facility, after notifying the police or sheriff's department, may cause the removal of a vehicle from a stall or space designated pursuant to subdivision (a) in the facility to the nearest public garage unless a special license plate issued pursuant to Section 5007 or distinguishing placard issued pursuant to Section 22511.55 or 22511.59 is displayed on the vehicle.

(d) If posted in accordance with subdivision (e), the local authority owning or operating an offstreet parking facility, after notifying the police or sheriff's department, may cause the removal of a vehicle from a stall or space designated pursuant to subdivision (a) in the facility to the nearest public garage unless a special license plate issued pursuant to Section 5007 or a distinguishing placard issued pursuant to Section 22511.55 or 22511.59 is displayed on the vehicle.

(e) Except as provided in Section 22511.9, the posting required for an offstreet parking facility owned or operated either privately or by a local authority shall consist of a sign not less than 17 by 22 inches in size with lettering not less than one inch in height which clearly and conspicuously states the following: "Unauthorized vehicles parked in designated accessible spaces not displaying distinguishing placards or special license plates issued for persons with disabilities will be towed away at the owner's expense. Towed vehicles may be reclaimed at:

(Address)

or by telephoning

(Telephone number of local law enforcement agency)."

The sign shall be posted in either of the following locations:

(1) Immediately adjacent to, and visible from, the stall or space.

(2) In a conspicuous place at each entrance to the offstreet parking facility.

(f) If the parking facility is privately owned and public parking is prohibited by the posting of a sign meeting the requirements of paragraph (1) of subdivision (a) of Section 22658, the requirements of subdivision (c) may be met by the posting of a sign immediately adjacent to, and visible from, each stall or space indicating that a vehicle not meeting the requirements of subdivision (a) will be removed at the owner's expense and containing the telephone number of the local traffic law enforcement agency.

(g) This section does not restrict the privilege granted to disabled persons and disabled veterans by Section 22511.5.

(Amended by Stats. 2009, Ch. 200, Sec. 14. (SB 734) Effective January 1, 2010.)

22511.85. A vehicle, identified with a special license plate issued pursuant to Section 5007 or a distinguishing placard issued pursuant to Section 22511.55 or 22511.59, which is equipped with a lift, ramp, or assistive equipment that is used for the loading and unloading of a person with a disability may park in not more than two adjacent stalls or spaces on a street or highway or in a public or private off-street parking facility if the equipment has been or will be used for loading or unloading a person with a disability, and if there is no single parking space immediately available on the street or highway or within the facility that is suitable for that purpose, including, but not limited to, when there is not sufficient space to operate a vehicle lift, ramp, or assistive equipment, or there is not sufficient room for a person with a disability to exit the vehicle or maneuver once outside the vehicle.

(Amended by Stats. 2008, Ch. 179, Sec. 221. Effective January 1, 2009.)

22511.9. Every new or replacement sign installed on or after January 1, 1992, relating to parking privileges for disabled persons shall refer to "disabled persons" rather than "physically handicapped persons" or any other similar term, whenever such a reference is required on a sign.

(Added by Stats. 1991, Ch. 928, Sec. 28. Effective October 14, 1991.)

22511.95. All new or replacement signs installed on or after July 1, 2008, relating to parking privileges for disabled persons shall refer to "persons with disabilities" rather than "disabled persons" or any other similar term, whenever the reference is required on the sign.

(Added by Stats. 2007, Ch. 413, Sec. 5. Effective January 1, 2008.)

22511.10. The Legislature hereby finds and declares all of the following:

(a) Two and one-half million Californians suffer from some form of chronic obstructive pulmonary disease. Those persons who are not in wheelchairs have difficulty walking long distances.

(b) Encouraging those with physical disabilities to engage in activities outside of the home promotes better health and self-esteem, thereby lowering health costs.

(c) Placing disabled person parking spaces closest to the main entrances of buildings does not cost taxpayers, but provides accessibility to the physically disabled.

(d) It is the intent of the Legislature, in enacting Section 22511.11, to direct the Office of the State Architect to propose regulations that require disabled person parking spaces to be located on the shortest accessible route of travel to an accessible entrance or exit of a building or parking facility.

(Added by Stats. 1992, Ch. 1187, Sec. 1. Effective January 1, 1993.)

22511.11. (a) The Office of the State Architect shall propose regulations specifying the location of disabled person parking stalls or spaces designated pursuant to Section 22511.8, for parking facilities constructed or reconstructed pursuant to a building permit issued on or after October 1, 1993. In specifying the placement of those stalls or spaces near buildings or facilities and within parking structures, consideration shall be given to the special access needs of disabled persons.

(b) The Office of the State Architect shall submit the regulations proposed pursuant to subdivision (a) to the State Building Standards Commission on or before July 1, 1993, for approval, adoption, and publication in Title 24 of the California Code of Regulations.

(Added by Stats. 1992, Ch. 1187, Sec. 2. Effective January 1, 1993.)

22512. Except as otherwise indicated in subdivision (b), none of the following provisions shall apply to the driver or owner of any service vehicle owned or operated by or for or operated under contract with a utility or public utility, whether privately, municipally, or publicly owned, used in the construction, operation, removal, or repair of utility or public utility property or facilities, if warning devices are displayed and when the vehicle is stopped, standing, or parked at the site of work involving the construction, operation, removal, or repair of the utility or public utility property or facilities upon, in, over, under, or adjacent to a highway, bicycle lane, bikeway, or bicycle path or trail, or of a vehicle, whether privately, municipally, or publicly owned, if warning devices are displayed and when the vehicle is engaged in authorized work on the highway, bicycle lane, bikeway, or bicycle path or trail:

(a) Sections 21112, 21211, 21707, 21708, 22507.6, 24605, 25253, 25300, 27700, and 27907.

(b) This chapter, except Sections 22507, 22509, 22515, and 22517.

(c) Chapter 10 (commencing with Section 22650).

(Amended by Stats. 1996, Ch. 124, Sec. 128. Effective January 1, 1997.)

22513. (a) (1) It is a misdemeanor for a towing company or the owner or operator of a tow truck to stop or cause a person to stop at the scene of an accident or near a disabled vehicle for the purpose of soliciting an engagement for towing services, either directly or indirectly, to furnish towing services, to move a vehicle from a highway, street, or public property when the vehicle has been left unattended or when there is an injury as the result of an accident, or to accrue charges for services furnished under those circumstances, unless requested to perform that service by a law enforcement officer or public agency pursuant to that agency's procedures, or unless summoned to the scene or requested to stop by the owner or operator of a disabled vehicle.

(2) (A) A towing company or the owner or operator of a tow truck summoned, or alleging it was summoned, to the scene by the owner or operator of a disabled vehicle shall possess all of the following information in writing prior to arriving at the scene:

(i) The first and last name and working telephone number of the person who summoned it to the scene.

(ii) The make, model, year, and license plate number of the disabled vehicle.

(iii) The date and time it was summoned to the scene.

(iv) The name of the person who obtained the information in clauses (i), (ii), and (iii).

(B) A towing company or the owner or operator of a tow truck summoned, or alleging it was summoned, to the scene by a motor club, as defined by Section 12142 of the Insurance Code, pursuant to the request of the owner or operator of a disabled vehicle is exempt from the requirements of subparagraph (A), provided it possesses all of the following information in writing prior to arriving at the scene:

(i) The business name of the motor club.

(ii) The identification number the motor club assigns to the referral.

(iii) The date and time it was summoned to the scene by the motor club.

(3) A towing company or the owner or operator of a tow truck requested, or alleging it was requested, to stop at the scene by the owner or operator of a disabled vehicle shall possess all of the following information in writing upon arriving at the scene:

(A) The first and last name and working telephone number of the person who requested the stop.

(B) The make, model, and license plate number, if one is displayed, of the disabled vehicle.

(C) The date and time it was requested to stop.

(D) The name of the person who obtained the information in subparagraphs (A), (B), and (C).

(4) A towing company or the owner or operator of a tow truck summoned or requested, or alleging it was summoned or requested, by a law enforcement officer or public agency pursuant to that agency's procedures to stop at the scene of an accident or near a disabled vehicle for the purpose of soliciting an engagement for towing services, either directly or indirectly, to furnish towing services, or that is expressly authorized to move a vehicle from a highway, street, or public property when the vehicle has been left unattended or when there is an injury as the result of an accident, shall possess all of the following in writing before leaving the scene:

(A) The identity of the law enforcement agency or public agency.

(B) The log number, call number, incident number, or dispatch number assigned to the incident by law enforcement or the public agency, or the surname and badge number of the law enforcement officer, or the surname and employee identification number of the public agency employee.

(C) The date and time of the summons, request, or express authorization.

(5) For purposes of this section, "writing" includes electronic records.

(b) The towing company or the owner or operator of a tow truck shall make the written information described in subdivision (a) available to law enforcement, upon request, from the time it appears at the scene until the time the vehicle is towed and released to a third party, and shall maintain that information for three years. The towing company or owner or operator of a tow truck shall make that information available for inspection and copying within 48 hours of a written request from any officer or agent of a police department, sheriff's department, the Department of the California Highway Patrol, the Attorney General's office, a district attorney's office, or a city attorney's office.

(c) (1) Prior to attaching a vehicle to the tow truck, if the vehicle owner or operator is present at the time and location of the anticipated tow, the towing company or the owner or operator of the tow truck shall furnish the vehicle's owner or operator with a written itemized estimate of all charges and services to be performed. The estimate shall include all of the following:

(A) The name, address, telephone number, and motor carrier permit number of the towing company.

(B) The license plate number of the tow truck performing the tow.

(C) The first and last name of the towing operator, and if different than the towing operator, the first and last name of the person from the towing company furnishing the estimate.

(D) A description and cost for all services, including, but not limited to, charges for labor, special equipment, mileage from dispatch to return, and storage fees, expressed as a 24-hour rate.

(2) The tow truck operator shall obtain the vehicle owner or operator's signature on the itemized estimate and shall furnish a copy to the person who signed the estimate.

(3) The requirements in paragraph (1) may be completed after the vehicle is attached and removed to the nearest safe shoulder or street if done at the request of law enforcement or a public agency, provided the estimate is furnished prior to the removal of the vehicle from the nearest safe shoulder or street.

(4) The towing company or the owner or operator of a tow truck shall maintain the written documents described in this subdivision for three years, and shall make them available for inspection and copying within 48 hours of a written request from any officer or agent of a police department, sheriff's department, the Department of the California Highway Patrol, the Attorney General's office, a district attorney's office, or a city attorney's office.

(5) This subdivision does not apply to a towing company or the owner or operator of a tow truck summoned to the scene by a motor club, as defined by Section 12142 of the Insurance Code, pursuant to the request of the owner or operator of a disabled vehicle.

(6) This subdivision does not apply to a towing company or the owner or operator of a tow truck summoned to the scene by law enforcement

or a public agency pursuant to that agency's procedures, and operating at the scene pursuant to a contract with that law enforcement agency or public agency.

(d) (1) Except as provided in paragraph (2), a towing company or the owner or operator of a tow truck shall not charge a fee for towing or storage, or both, of a vehicle in excess of the greater of the following:

(A) The fee that would have been charged for that towing or storage, or both, made at the request of a law enforcement agency under an agreement between a towing company and the law enforcement agency that exercises primary jurisdiction in the city in which the vehicle was, or was attempted to be, removed, or if not located within a city, the law enforcement agency that exercises primary jurisdiction in the county in which the vehicle was, or was attempted to be, removed.

(B) The fee that would have been charged for that towing or storage, or both, under the rate approved for that towing operator by the Department of the California Highway Patrol for the jurisdiction from which the vehicle was, or was attempted to be, removed.

(2) Paragraph (1) does not apply to the towing or transportation of a vehicle or temporary storage of a vehicle in transit, if the towing or transportation is performed with the prior consent of the owner or operator of the vehicle.

(3) No charge shall be made in excess of the estimated price without the prior consent of the vehicle owner or operator.

(4) All services rendered by a tow company or tow truck operator, including any warranty or zero cost services, shall be recorded on an invoice, as described in subdivision (e) of Section 22651.07. The towing company or the owner or operator of a tow truck shall maintain the written documents described in this subdivision for three years, and shall make the documents available for inspection and copying within 48 hours of a written request from any officer or agent of a police department, sheriff's department, the Department of the California Highway Patrol, the Attorney General's office, a district attorney's office, or a city attorney's office.

(e) A person who willfully violates subdivision (b), (c), or (d) is guilty of a misdemeanor, punishable by a fine of not more than two thousand five hundred dollars ($2,500), or by imprisonment in a county jail for not more than three months, or by both that fine and imprisonment.

(f) This section shall not apply to the following:

(1) A vehicle owned or operated by, or under contract to, a motor club, as defined by Section 12142 of the Insurance Code, which stops to provide services for which compensation is neither requested nor received, provided that those services may not include towing other than that which may be necessary to remove the vehicle to the nearest safe shoulder. The owner or operator of that vehicle may contact a law enforcement agency or other public agency on behalf of a motorist, but may not refer a motorist to a tow truck owner or operator, unless the motorist is a member of the motor club, the motorist is referred to a tow truck owner or operator under contract to the motor club, and, if there is a dispatch facility that services the area and is owned or operated by the motor club, the referral is made through that dispatch facility.

(2) A tow truck operator employed by a law enforcement agency or other public agency.

(3) A tow truck owner or operator acting under contract with a law enforcement or other public agency to abate abandoned vehicles, or to provide towing service or emergency road service to motorists while involved in freeway service patrol operations, to the extent authorized by law.

(Amended by Stats. 2016, Ch. 518, Sec. 1. (AB 2167) Effective January 1, 2017.)

22513.1. (a) (1) A business taking possession of a vehicle from a tow truck during hours the business is open to the public shall document all of the following:

(A) The name, address, and telephone number of the towing company.

(B) The name and driver's license number, driver's identification number issued by a motor club, as defined in Section 12142 of the Insurance Code, or other government authorized unique identifier of the tow truck operator.

(C) The make, model, and license plate or vehicle identification number.

(D) The date and time that possession was taken of the vehicle.

(2) For purposes of subparagraph (B) of paragraph (1), if a tow truck operator refuses to provide information described in subparagraph (B) of paragraph (1) to a new motor vehicle dealer, as defined in Section 426, a new motor vehicle dealer is in compliance with this section if the new motor vehicle dealer documents the reasonable efforts made to obtain this information from the tow truck operator.

(b) A business taking possession of a vehicle from a tow truck when the business is closed to the public shall document all of the following:

(1) The make, model, and license plate or vehicle identification number.

(2) The date and time that the business first observed the vehicle on its property.

(3) The reasonable effort made by the business to contact the towing company, if identifying information was left with the vehicle, and the vehicle's owner or operator to obtain and document both of the following:

(A) The name, address, and telephone number of the towing company.

(B) The name and driver's license number, driver's identification number issued by a motor club, as defined in Section 12142 of the Insurance Code, or other government authorized unique identifier of the tow truck operator.

(c) The information required in this section shall be maintained for three years and shall be available for inspection and copying within 48 hours of a written request by any officer or agent of a police department, a sheriff's department, the Department of the California Highway Patrol, the Attorney General's office, the Bureau of Automotive Repair, a district attorney's office, or a city attorney's office.

(d) For purposes of this section, a new motor vehicle dealer, as defined in Section 426, is not open to the public during hours its repair shop is closed to the public.

(e) A person who willfully violates this section is guilty of a misdemeanor, and that violation is punishable by a fine of not more than two thousand five hundred dollars ($2,500), or by imprisonment in a county jail for not more than three months, or by both that fine and imprisonment.

(Amended by Stats. 2017, Ch. 561, Sec. 254. (AB 1516) Effective January 1, 2018.)

22514. No person shall stop, park, or leave standing any vehicle within 15 feet of a fire hydrant except as follows:

(a) If the vehicle is attended by a licensed driver who is seated in the front seat and who can immediately move such vehicle in case of necessity.

(b) If the local authority adopts an ordinance or resolution reducing that distance. If the distance is less than 10 feet total length when measured along the curb or edge of the street, the distance shall be indicated by signs or markings.

(c) If the vehicle is owned or operated by a fire department and is clearly marked as a fire department vehicle.

(Amended by Stats. 1987, Ch. 488, Sec. 1.)

22515. (a) No person driving, or in control of, or in charge of, a motor vehicle shall permit it to stand on any highway unattended without first effectively setting the brakes thereon and stopping the motor thereof.

(b) No person in control of, or in charge of, any vehicle, other than a motor vehicle, shall permit it to stand on any highway without first effectively setting the brakes thereon, or blocking the wheels thereof, to effectively prevent the movement of the vehicle.

(Amended by Stats. 1986, Ch. 362, Sec. 3.)

22516. No person shall leave standing a locked vehicle in which there is any person who cannot readily escape therefrom.

(Enacted by Stats. 1959, Ch. 3.)

22517. No person shall open the door of a vehicle on the side available to moving traffic unless it is reasonably safe to do so and can be done

without interfering with the movement of such traffic, nor shall any person leave a door open on the side of a vehicle available to moving traffic for a period of time longer than necessary to load or unload passengers.
(Amended by Stats. 1963, Ch. 162.)

22518. (a) Fringe and transportation corridor parking facilities constructed, maintained, or operated by the Department of Transportation pursuant to Section 146.5 of the Streets and Highways Code shall be used only by persons using a bicycle or public transit, or engaged in ridesharing, including, but not limited to, carpools or vanpools. A person shall not park a vehicle 30 feet or more in length, engage in loitering or camping, or engage in vending or any other commercial activity on any fringe or transportation corridor parking facility.

(b) This section does not apply to alternatively fueled infrastructure programs in park-and-ride lots owned and operated by the Department of Transportation.
(Amended by Stats. 2012, Ch. 676, Sec. 3. (AB 2583) Effective January 1, 2013.)

22519. Local authorities may by ordinance or resolution prohibit, restrict or regulate the parking, stopping or standing of vehicles on any offstreet parking facility which it owns or operates. No such ordinance or resolution shall apply until signs giving notice thereof have been erected.
(Added by Stats. 1959, Ch. 1486.)

22520.5. (a) No person shall solicit, display, sell, offer for sale, or otherwise vend or attempt to vend any merchandise or service while being wholly or partly within any of the following:

(1) The right-of-way of any freeway, including any on ramp, off ramp, or roadway shoulder which lies within the right-of-way of the freeway.

(2) Any roadway or adjacent shoulder within 500 feet of a freeway off ramp or on ramp.

(3) Any sidewalk within 500 feet of a freeway off ramp or on ramp, when vending or attempting to vend to vehicular traffic.

(b) Subdivision (a) does not apply to a roadside rest area or vista point located within a freeway right-of-way which is subject to Section 22520.6, to a tow truck or service vehicle rendering assistance to a disabled vehicle, or to a person issued a permit to vend upon the freeway pursuant to Section 670 of the Streets and Highways Code.

(c) A violation of this section is an infraction. A second or subsequent conviction of a violation of this section is a misdemeanor.
(Amended by Stats. 1988, Ch. 924, Sec. 10.)

22520.6. (a) No person shall engage in any activity within a highway roadside rest area or vista point prohibited by rules and regulations adopted pursuant to Section 225 of the Streets and Highways Code.

(b) A violation of this section is an infraction. A second or subsequent conviction of a violation of this section is a misdemeanor.
(Added by Stats. 1983, Ch. 275, Sec. 3. Effective July 15, 1983.)

22521. No person shall park a vehicle upon any railroad track or within 71/2 feet of the nearest rail.
(Added by Stats. 1968, Ch. 625.)

22522. No person shall park a vehicle within three feet of any sidewalk access ramp constructed at, or adjacent to, a crosswalk or at any other location on a sidewalk so as to be accessible to and usable by the physically disabled, if the area adjoining the ramp is designated by either a sign or red paint.
(Amended by Stats. 1999, Ch. 1007, Sec. 22. Effective January 1, 2000.)

22523. (a) No person shall abandon a vehicle upon any highway.

(b) No person shall abandon a vehicle upon public or private property without the express or implied consent of the owner or person in lawful possession or control of the property.

(c) Any person convicted of a violation of this section shall be punished by a fine of not less than one hundred dollars ($100) and shall provide proof that the costs of removal and disposition of the vehicle have been paid. No part of any fine imposed shall be suspended. The fine may be paid in installments if the court determines that the defendant is unable to pay the entire amount in one payment.

(d) Proof that the costs of removal and disposition of the vehicle have been paid shall not be required if proof is provided to the court that the vehicle was stolen prior to abandonment. That proof may consist of a police report or other evidence acceptable to the court.

(e) The costs required to be paid for the removal and disposition of any vehicle determined to be abandoned pursuant to Section 22669 shall not exceed those for towing and seven days of storage. This subdivision does not apply if the registered owner or legal owner has completed and returned to the lienholder a "Declaration of Opposition" form within the time specified in Section 22851.8.

(f) (1) If a vehicle is abandoned in violation of subdivision (b) and is not redeemed after impound, the last registered owner is guilty of an infraction. In addition to any other penalty, the registered owner shall be liable for any deficiency remaining after disposal of the vehicle under Section 3071 or 3072 of the Civil Code or Section 22851.10 of this code.

(2) The filing of a report of sale or transfer of the vehicle pursuant to Section 5602, the filing of a vehicle theft report with a law enforcement agency, or the filing of a form or notice with the department pursuant to subdivision (b) of Section 4456 or Section 5900 or 5901 relieves the registered owner of liability under this subdivision.
(Amended by Stats. 1996, Ch. 676, Sec. 2. Effective January 1, 1997.)

22524. (a) The abandonment of any vehicle in a manner as provided in Section 22523 shall constitute a prima facie presumption that the last registered owner of record is responsible for the abandonment and is thereby liable for the cost of removal and disposition of the vehicle.

(b) An owner who has made a bona fide sale or transfer of a vehicle and has delivered possession of the vehicle to a purchaser may overcome the presumption prescribed in subdivision (a) by demonstrating that he or she has complied with Section 5900 or providing other proof satisfactory to the court.

(c) This section shall become operative on July 1, 1989.
(Repealed (in Sec. 6) and added by Stats. 1988, Ch. 1267, Sec. 7. Effective September 26, 1988. Section operative July 1, 1989, by its own provisions.)

22524.5. (a) Any insurer that is responsible for coverage for ordinary and reasonable towing and storage charges under an automobile insurance policy to an insured or on behalf of an insured to a valid claimant, is liable for those charges to the person performing those services when a vehicle is towed and stored as a result of an accident or stolen recovery. The insurer may discharge the obligation by making payment to the person performing the towing and storage services or to the insured or on behalf of the insured to the claimant.

(b) Any insured or claimant who has received payment, which includes towing and storage charges, from an insurer for a loss relating to a vehicle is liable for those charges to the person performing those services.

(c) (1) All towing and storage fees charged when those services are performed as a result of an accident or recovery of a stolen vehicle shall be reasonable.

(2) (A) For purposes of this section, a towing and storage charge shall be deemed reasonable if it does not exceed those fees and rates charged for similar services provided in response to requests initiated by a public agency, including, but not limited to, the Department of the California Highway Patrol or local police department.

(B) A storage rate and fee shall also be deemed reasonable if it is comparable to storage-related rates and fees charged by other facilities in the same locale. This does not preclude a rate or fee that is higher or lower if it is otherwise reasonable.

(3) The following rates and fees are presumptively unreasonable:

(A) Administrative or filing fees, except those incurred related to documentation from the Department of Motor Vehicles and those related to the lien sale of a vehicle.

(B) Security fees.

(C) Dolly fees.

(D) Load and unload fees.

(E) Pull-out fees.

(F) Gate fees, except when the owner or insurer of the vehicle requests that the vehicle be released outside of normal business hours.

(G) When gate fees are reasonably assessed, any additional towing fees that exceed 10 percent of the normal towing rate due to the call originating after normal business hours.

(H) Any storage fees charged for state holidays that exceed the posted standard daily storage rate.

(I) (i) Towing fees when the owner or the operator of a tow truck is directed by a law enforcement officer to remove a vehicle to the nearest shoulder or to level ground adjacent to the roadway for the sole purpose of clearing a roadway to facilitate access by an emergency vehicle at the scene of a state emergency, as defined in Section 8625 of the Government Code, or a local emergency, as defined in Section 8630 of the Government Code.

(ii) An owner or operator of a tow truck that removes a vehicle under the circumstances described in clause (i) and acts in good faith shall not be subject to civil liability for any damage to personal property that results from the removal of the vehicle.

(iii) The limitation of liability described in clause (ii) shall not apply to an act or omission by an owner or operator of a tow truck that constitutes gross negligence or willful or wanton misconduct.

(J) Following a request from the vehicle owner to release their vehicle, and upon payment of all fees then due, storage fees for any day that a storage facility fails to release the vehicle.

(K) Storage fees in excess of 50 percent of the daily storage rate when a vehicle is recovered within the first four hours of storage.

(d) Notwithstanding this section, an insurer shall comply with all of its obligations under Section 2695.8 of Chapter 5 of Title 10 of the California Code of Regulations.

(e) Nothing in paragraph (3) of subdivision (c) prohibits any fees authorized in a written agreement between a law enforcement agency and a towing or storage company, including, but not limited to, official police garages operating under the jurisdiction of a municipal police commission, if the tow was initiated by the law enforcement agency.

(f) For purposes of this section, "normal business hours" means Monday through Friday from 8:00 a.m. to 5:00 p.m., inclusive, except for state holidays.

(Amended by Stats. 2025, Ch. 345, Sec. 2. (AB 987) Effective January 1, 2026.)

22525. Local authorities may by ordinance or resolution authorize vanpool vehicles to utilize designated state highway bus stops.

The ordinance or resolution shall be submitted to the Department of Transportation for approval. No ordinance or resolution shall become effective until approved by the department. The department shall review the ordinance or resolution within 45 days after receipt.

(Added by Stats. 1987, Ch. 262, Sec. 1.)

22526. (a) Notwithstanding any official traffic control signal indication to proceed, a driver of a vehicle shall not enter an intersection or marked crosswalk unless there is sufficient space on the other side of the intersection or marked crosswalk to accommodate the vehicle driven without obstructing the through passage of vehicles from either side.

(b) A driver of a vehicle which is making a turn at an intersection who is facing a steady circular yellow or yellow arrow signal shall not enter the intersection or marked crosswalk unless there is sufficient space on the other side of the intersection or marked crosswalk to accommodate the vehicle driven without obstructing the through passage of vehicles from either side.

(c) A driver of a vehicle shall not enter a railroad or rail transit crossing, notwithstanding any official traffic control device or signal indication to proceed, unless there is sufficient undercarriage clearance to cross the intersection without obstructing the through passage of a railway vehicle, including, but not limited to, a train, trolley, or city transit vehicle.

(d) A driver of a vehicle shall not enter a railroad or rail transit crossing, notwithstanding any official traffic control device or signal indication to proceed, unless there is sufficient space on the other side of the railroad or rail transit crossing to accommodate the vehicle driven and any railway vehicle, including, but not limited to, a train, trolley, or city transit vehicle.

(e) A local authority may post appropriate signs at the entrance to intersections indicating the prohibition in subdivisions (a), (b), and (c).

(f) A violation of this section is not a violation of a law relating to the safe operation of vehicles and is the following:

(1) A stopping violation when a notice to appear has been issued by a peace officer described in Section 830.1, 830.2, or 830.33 of the Penal Code.

(2) A parking violation when a notice of parking violation is issued by a person, other than a peace officer described in paragraph (1), who is authorized to enforce parking statutes and regulations.

(g) This section shall be known and may be cited as the Anti-Gridlock Act of 1987.

(Amended by Stats. 2010, Ch. 216, Sec. 11. (AB 2144) Effective January 1, 2011.)

Chapter 10. Removal of Parked and Abandoned Vehicles

(Chapter 10 enacted by Stats. 1959, Ch. 3.)

Article 1. Authority to Remove Vehicles

(Article 1 enacted by Stats. 1959, Ch. 3.)

22650. (a) It is unlawful for a peace officer or an unauthorized person to remove an unattended vehicle from a highway to a garage or to any other place, except as provided in this code.

(b) Any removal of a vehicle is a seizure under the Fourth Amendment of the Constitution of the United States and Section 13 of Article I of the California Constitution, and shall be reasonable and subject to the limits set forth in Fourth Amendment jurisprudence. A removal pursuant to an authority, including, but not limited to, as provided in Section 22651, that is based on community caretaking, is only reasonable if the removal is necessary to achieve the community caretaking need, such as ensuring the safe flow of traffic or protecting property from theft or vandalism.

(c) Those law enforcement and other agencies identified in this chapter as having the authority to remove vehicles shall also have the authority to provide hearings in compliance with the provisions of Section 22852. During these hearings the storing agency shall have the burden of establishing the authority for, and the validity of, the removal.

(d) This section does not prevent a review or other action as may be permitted by the laws of this state by a court of competent jurisdiction.

(Amended by Stats. 2018, Ch. 592, Sec. 1. (AB 2876) Effective January 1, 2019.)

22651. A peace officer, as defined in Chapter 4.5 (commencing with Section 830) of Title 3 of Part 2 of the Penal Code, or a regularly employed and salaried employee who is engaged in directing traffic or enforcing parking laws and regulations of a city, county, or jurisdiction of a state agency in which a vehicle is located may remove a vehicle located within the territorial limits in which the officer or employee may act, under the following circumstances:

(a) If a vehicle is left unattended upon a bridge, viaduct, or causeway or in a tube or tunnel where the vehicle constitutes an obstruction to traffic.

(b) If a vehicle is parked or left standing upon a highway in a position so as to obstruct the normal movement of traffic or in a condition so as to create a hazard to other traffic upon the highway.

(c) If a vehicle is found upon a highway or public land and a report has previously been made that the vehicle is stolen or a complaint has been filed and a warrant thereon is issued charging that the vehicle was embezzled.

(d) If a vehicle is illegally parked so as to block the entrance to a private driveway, and it is impractical to move the vehicle from in front of the driveway to another point on the highway.

(e) If a vehicle is illegally parked so as to prevent access by firefighting equipment to a fire hydrant, and it is impracticable to move the vehicle from in front of the fire hydrant to another point on the highway.

(f) If a vehicle, except highway maintenance or construction equipment, is stopped, parked, or left standing for more than four hours upon the right-of-way of a freeway that has full control of access and no crossings at grade, and the driver, if present, cannot move the vehicle under its own power.

(g) If the person in charge of a vehicle upon a highway or public land is, by reason of physical injuries or illness, incapacitated to an extent so as to be unable to provide for its custody or removal.

(h) (1) If an officer arrests a person driving or in control of a vehicle for an alleged offense, and the officer is, by this code or other law, required or permitted to take, and, except as provided in Section 23109.3, does take, the person into custody.

(2) If an officer serves a notice of an order of suspension or revocation pursuant to Section 13388 or 13389.

(i) (1) If a vehicle, other than a rented vehicle, is found upon a highway or public land, or is removed pursuant to this code, and it is known that the vehicle has been issued five or more notices of parking violations to which the owner or person in control of the vehicle has not responded within 21 calendar days of notice of citation issuance or citation issuance or 14 calendar days of the mailing of a notice of delinquent parking violation to the agency responsible for processing notices of parking violations, or the registered owner of the vehicle is known to have been issued five or more notices for failure to pay or failure to appear in court for traffic violations for which a certificate has not been issued by the magistrate or clerk of the court hearing the case showing that the case has been adjudicated or concerning which the registered owner's record has not been cleared pursuant to Chapter 6 (commencing with Section 41500) of Division 17, the vehicle may be impounded until that person furnishes to the impounding law enforcement agency all of the following:

(A) Evidence of their identity.

(B) An address within this state where they can be located.

(C) Satisfactory evidence that all parking penalties due for the vehicle and all other vehicles registered to the registered owner of the impounded vehicle and all traffic violations of the registered owner have been cleared.

(2) The requirements in subparagraph (C) of paragraph (1) shall be fully enforced by the impounding law enforcement agency on and after the time that the Department of Motor Vehicles is able to provide access to the necessary records.

(3) A notice of parking violation issued for an unlawfully parked vehicle shall be accompanied by a warning that repeated violations may result in the impounding of the vehicle. In lieu of furnishing satisfactory evidence that the full amount of parking penalties or bail has been deposited, that person may demand to be taken without unnecessary delay before a magistrate, for traffic offenses, or a hearing examiner, for parking offenses, within the county where the offenses charged are alleged to have been committed and who has jurisdiction of the offenses and is nearest or most accessible with reference to the place where the vehicle is impounded. Evidence of current registration shall be produced after a vehicle has been impounded, or, at the discretion of the impounding law enforcement agency, a notice to appear for violation of subdivision (a) of Section 4000 shall be issued to that person.

(4) A vehicle shall be released to the legal owner, as defined in Section 370, if the legal owner does all of the following:

(A) Pays the cost of towing and storing the vehicle.

(B) Submits evidence of payment of fees as provided in Section 9561.

(C) Completes an affidavit in a form acceptable to the impounding law enforcement agency stating that the vehicle was not in possession of the legal owner at the time of occurrence of the offenses relating to standing or parking. A vehicle released to a legal owner under this subdivision is a repossessed vehicle for purposes of disposition or sale. The impounding agency shall have a lien on any surplus that remains upon sale of the vehicle, to which the registered owner is or may be entitled, as security for the full amount of the parking penalties for all notices of parking violations issued for the vehicle and for all local administrative charges imposed pursuant to Section 22850.5. The legal owner shall promptly remit to, and deposit with, the agency responsible for processing notices of parking violations from that surplus, on receipt of that surplus, the full amount of the parking penalties for all notices of parking violations issued for the vehicle and for all local administrative charges imposed pursuant to Section 22850.5.

(5) The impounding agency that has a lien on the surplus that remains upon the sale of a vehicle to which a registered owner is entitled pursuant to paragraph (4) has a deficiency claim against the registered owner for the full amount of the parking penalties for all notices of parking violations issued for the vehicle and for all local administrative charges imposed pursuant to Section 22850.5, less the amount received from the sale of the vehicle.

(j) If a vehicle is found illegally parked and there are no license plates or other evidence of registration displayed, the vehicle may be impounded until the owner or person in control of the vehicle furnishes the impounding law enforcement agency evidence of their identity and an address within this state where they can be located.

(k) If a vehicle is parked or left standing upon a highway for 72 or more consecutive hours in violation of a local ordinance authorizing removal.

(l) If a vehicle is illegally parked on a highway in violation of a local ordinance forbidding standing or parking and the use of a highway, or a portion thereof, is necessary for the cleaning, repair, or construction of the highway, or for the installation of underground utilities, and signs giving notice that the vehicle may be removed are erected or placed at least 24 hours prior to the removal by a local authority pursuant to the ordinance.

(m) If the use of the highway, or a portion of the highway, is authorized by a local authority for a purpose other than the normal flow of traffic or for the movement of equipment, articles, or structures of unusual size, and the parking of a vehicle would prohibit or interfere with that use or movement, and signs giving notice that the vehicle may be removed are erected or placed at least 24 hours prior to the removal by a local authority pursuant to the ordinance.

(n) Whenever a vehicle is parked or left standing where local authorities, by resolution or ordinance, have prohibited parking and have authorized the removal of vehicles. Except as provided in subdivisions (v) and (w), a vehicle shall not be removed unless signs are posted giving notice of the removal.

(o) (1) If a vehicle is found or operated upon a highway, public land, or an offstreet parking facility under any of the following circumstances:

(A) (i) With a registration expiration date in excess of six months before the date it is found or operated on the highway, public lands, or the offstreet parking facility.

(ii) Prior to removing a vehicle pursuant to this subparagraph, the officer or employee shall verify, using available Department of Motor Vehicles records, that no current registration exists for the vehicle. A vehicle shall not be removed pursuant to this subparagraph if it has a current registration on file with the Department of Motor Vehicles, regardless of whether the vehicle is in compliance with subdivision (a) of Section 5204. If the officer or employee does not have immediate access to those records, a vehicle shall not be removed pursuant to this subparagraph.

(B) Displaying in, or upon, the vehicle, a registration card, identification card, temporary receipt, license plate, special plate, registration sticker, device issued pursuant to Section 4853, or permit that was not issued for that vehicle or is not otherwise lawfully used on that vehicle under this code.

(C) Displaying in, or upon, the vehicle, an altered, forged, counterfeit, or falsified registration card, identification card, temporary receipt, license plate, special plate, registration sticker, device issued pursuant to Section 4853, or permit.

(D) (i) The vehicle is operating using autonomous technology, without the registered owner or manufacturer of the vehicle having first applied for and obtained a valid permit that is required to operate the vehicle on public roads pursuant to Section 38750, Article 3.7 (commencing with Section 227.00) of Title 13 of the California Code of Regulations, and Article 3.8 (commencing with Section 228.00) of Title 13 of the California Code of Regulations.

(ii) The vehicle is operating using autonomous technology after the registered owner or person in control of the vehicle received notice that the vehicle's permit required for the operation of the vehicle pursuant to Section 38750, Article 3.7 (commencing with Section 227.00) of Title 13 of the California Code of Regulations, and Article 3.8 (commencing with Section 228.00) of Title 13 of the California Code of Regulations is suspended, terminated, or revoked.

(iii) For purposes of this subdivision, the terms "autonomous technology" and "autonomous vehicle" have the same meanings as in Section 38750.

(iv) This subparagraph does not provide the authority for a peace officer to stop an autonomous vehicle solely for the purpose of determining whether the vehicle is operating using autonomous technology without a valid permit required to operate the autonomous vehicle on public roads pursuant to Section 38750, Article 3.7 (commencing with Section 227.00) of Title 13 of the California Code of Regulations, and Article 3.8 (commencing with Section 228.00) of Title 13 of the California Code of Regulations.

(2) If a vehicle described in paragraph (1) is occupied, only a peace officer, as defined in Chapter 4.5 (commencing with Section 830) of Title 3 of Part 2 of the Penal Code, may remove the vehicle.

(3) For the purposes of this subdivision, the vehicle shall be released under any of the following circumstances:

(A) If the vehicle has been removed pursuant to subparagraph (A), (B), or (C) of paragraph (1), to the registered owner of, or person in control of, the vehicle only after the owner or person furnishes the storing law enforcement agency with proof of current registration and a valid driver's license to operate the vehicle.

(B) If the vehicle has been removed pursuant to subparagraph (D) of paragraph (1), to the registered owner of, or person in control of, the autonomous vehicle, after the registered owner or person furnishes the storing law enforcement agency with proof of current registration and a valid driver's license, if required to operate the autonomous vehicle, and either of the following:

(i) Proof of a valid permit required to operate the autonomous vehicle using autonomous technology on public roads pursuant to Section 38750, Article 3.7 (commencing with Section 227.00) of Title 13 of the California Code of Regulations, and Article 3.8 (commencing with Section 228.00) of Title 13 of the California Code of Regulations.

(ii) A declaration or sworn statement to the Department of Motor Vehicles that states that the autonomous vehicle will not be operated using autonomous technology upon public roads without first obtaining a valid permit to operate the vehicle pursuant to Section 38750, Article 3.7 (commencing with Section 227.00) of Title 13 of the California Code of Regulations, and Article 3.8 (commencing with Section 228.00) of Title 13 of the California Code of Regulations.

(C) To the legal owner or the legal owner's agency, without payment of any fees, fines, or penalties for parking tickets or registration and without proof of current registration, if the vehicle will only be transported pursuant to the exemption specified in Section 4022 and if the legal owner does all of the following:

(i) Pays the cost of towing and storing the vehicle.

(ii) Completes an affidavit in a form acceptable to the impounding law enforcement agency stating that the vehicle was not in possession of the legal owner at the time of occurrence of an offense relating to standing or parking. A vehicle released to a legal owner under this subdivision is a repossessed vehicle for purposes of disposition or sale. The impounding agency has a lien on any surplus that remains upon sale of the vehicle to which the registered owner is or may be entitled, as security for the full amount of parking penalties for any notices of parking violations issued for the vehicle and for all local administrative charges imposed pursuant to Section 22850.5. Upon receipt of any surplus, the legal owner shall promptly remit to, and deposit with, the agency responsible for processing notices of parking violations from that surplus, the full amount of the parking penalties for all notices of parking violations issued for the vehicle and for all local administrative charges imposed pursuant to Section 22850.5.

(4) The impounding agency that has a lien on the surplus that remains upon the sale of a vehicle to which a registered owner is entitled has a deficiency claim against the registered owner for the full amount of parking penalties for any notices of parking violations issued for the vehicle and for all local administrative charges imposed pursuant to Section 22850.5, less the amount received from the sale of the vehicle.

(5) As used in this subdivision, "offstreet parking facility" means an offstreet facility held open for use by the public for parking vehicles and includes a publicly owned facility for offstreet parking and a privately owned facility for offstreet parking if a fee is not charged for the privilege to park and it is held open for the common public use of retail customers.

(p) If the peace officer issues the driver of a vehicle a notice to appear for a violation of Section 12500, 14601, 14601.1, 14601.2, 14601.3, 14601.4, 14601.5, or 14604, and the vehicle is not impounded pursuant to Section 22655.5. A vehicle so removed from the highway or public land, or from private property after having been on a highway or public land, shall not be released to the registered owner or their agent, except upon presentation of the registered owner's or their agent's currently valid driver's license to operate the vehicle and proof of current vehicle registration to the impounding law enforcement agency or upon order of a court.

(q) If a vehicle is parked for more than 24 hours on a portion of highway that is located within the boundaries of a common interest development, as defined in Section 4100 or 6534 of the Civil Code, and signs, as required by paragraph (1) of subdivision (a) of Section 22658 of this code, have been posted on that portion of highway providing notice to drivers that vehicles parked thereon for more than 24 hours will be removed at the owner's expense pursuant to a resolution or ordinance adopted by the local authority.

(r) If a vehicle is illegally parked and blocks the movement of a legally parked vehicle.

(s) (1) If a vehicle, except highway maintenance or construction equipment, an authorized emergency vehicle, or a vehicle that is properly permitted or otherwise authorized by the Department of Transportation, is stopped, parked, or left standing for more than eight hours within a roadside rest area or viewpoint.

(2) Notwithstanding paragraph (1), if a commercial motor vehicle, as defined in paragraph (1) of subdivision (b) of Section 15210, is stopped, parked, or left standing for more than 10 hours within a roadside rest area or viewpoint.

(3) For purposes of this subdivision, a roadside rest area or viewpoint is a publicly maintained vehicle parking area, adjacent to a highway, utilized for the convenient, safe stopping of a vehicle to enable motorists to rest or to view the scenery. If two or more roadside rest areas are located on opposite sides of the highway, or upon the center divider, within seven miles of each other, then that combination of rest areas is considered to be the same rest area.

(t) If a peace officer issues a notice to appear for a violation of Section 25279.

(u) If a peace officer issues a citation for a violation of Section 11700, and the vehicle is being offered for sale.

(v) (1) If a vehicle is a mobile billboard advertising display, as defined in Section 395.5, and is parked or left standing in violation of a local resolution or ordinance adopted pursuant to subdivision (m) of Section 21100, if the registered owner of the vehicle was previously issued a warning citation for the same offense pursuant to paragraph (2).

(2) Notwithstanding subdivision (a) of Section 22507, a city or

county, in lieu of posting signs noticing a local ordinance prohibiting mobile billboard advertising displays adopted pursuant to subdivision (m) of Section 21100 may provide notice by issuing a warning citation advising the registered owner of the vehicle that they may be subject to penalties upon a subsequent violation of the ordinance that may include the removal of the vehicle as provided in paragraph (1). A city or county is not required to provide further notice for a subsequent violation prior to the enforcement of penalties for a violation of the ordinance.

(w) (1) If a vehicle is parked or left standing in violation of a local ordinance or resolution adopted pursuant to subdivision (p) of Section 21100, if the registered owner of the vehicle was previously issued a warning citation for the same offense pursuant to paragraph (2).

(2) Notwithstanding subdivision (a) of Section 22507, a city or county, in lieu of posting signs noticing a local ordinance regulating advertising signs adopted pursuant to subdivision (p) of Section 21100 may provide notice by issuing a warning citation advising the registered owner of the vehicle that they may be subject to penalties upon a subsequent violation of the ordinance that may include the removal of the vehicle as provided in paragraph (1). A city or county is not required to provide further notice for a subsequent violation before the enforcement of penalties for a violation of the ordinance.

(Amended by Stats. 2024, Ch. 501, Sec. 1. (AB 1978) Effective January 1, 2025.)

22651.05. (a) A trained volunteer of a state or local law enforcement agency, who is engaged in directing traffic or enforcing parking laws and regulations, of a city, county, or jurisdiction of a state agency in which a vehicle is located, may remove or authorize the removal of a vehicle located within the territorial limits in which an officer or employee of that agency may act, under any of the following circumstances:

(1) When a vehicle is parked or left standing upon a highway for 72 or more consecutive hours in violation of a local ordinance authorizing the removal.

(2) When a vehicle is illegally parked or left standing on a highway in violation of a local ordinance forbidding standing or parking and the use of a highway, or a portion thereof, is necessary for the cleaning, repair, or construction of the highway, or for the installation of underground utilities, and signs giving notice that the vehicle may be removed are erected or placed at least 24 hours prior to the removal by local authorities pursuant to the ordinance.

(3) Wherever the use of the highway, or a portion thereof, is authorized by local authorities for a purpose other than the normal flow of traffic or for the movement of equipment, articles, or structures of unusual size, and the parking of a vehicle would prohibit or interfere with that use or movement, and signs giving notice that the vehicle may be removed are erected or placed at least 24 hours prior to the removal by local authorities pursuant to the ordinance.

(4) Whenever a vehicle is parked or left standing where local authorities, by resolution or ordinance, have prohibited parking and have authorized the removal of vehicles. A vehicle may not be removed unless signs are posted giving notice of the removal.

(5) Whenever a vehicle is parked for more than 24 hours on a portion of highway that is located within the boundaries of a common interest development, as defined in Section 4100 or 6534 of the Civil Code, and signs, as required by Section 22658.2, have been posted on that portion of highway providing notice to drivers that vehicles parked thereon for more than 24 hours will be removed at the owner's expense, pursuant to a resolution or ordinance adopted by the local authority.

(b) The provisions of this chapter that apply to a vehicle removed pursuant to Section 22651 apply to a vehicle removed pursuant to subdivision (a).

(c) For purposes of subdivision (a), a "trained volunteer" is a person who, of his or her own free will, provides services, without any financial gain, to a local or state law enforcement agency, and who is duly trained and certified to remove a vehicle by a local or state law enforcement agency.

(Amended (as amended by Stats. 2012, Ch. 181, Sec. 82) by Stats. 2013, Ch. 605, Sec. 51. (SB 752) Effective January 1, 2014.)

22651.07. (a) A person, including a law enforcement agency, city, county, city and county, the state, a tow yard, storage facility, or an impounding yard, that charges for towing or storage, or both, shall do all of the following:

(1) (A) Except as provided in subparagraph (B), post in the office area of the storage facility, in plain view of the public, the Towing and Storage Fees and Access Notice and have copies readily available to the public.

(B) An automotive repair dealer, registered pursuant to Article 3 (commencing with Section 9884) of Chapter 20.3 of Division 3 of the Business and Professions Code, that does not provide towing services is exempt from the requirements to post the Towing and Storage Fees and Access Notice in the office area.

(2) Provide, upon request, a copy of the Towing and Storage Fees and Access Notice to any owner or operator of a towed or stored vehicle.

(3) Provide a distinct notice on an itemized invoice for any towing or storage, or both, charges stating: "Upon request, you are entitled to receive a copy of the Towing and Storage Fees and Access Notice." This notice shall be contained within a bordered text box, printed in no less than 10-point type.

(b) Prior to receiving payment for any towing, recovery, or storage-related fees, a facility that charges for towing or storage, or both, shall provide an itemized invoice of actual charges to the vehicle owner or his or her agent. If an automotive repair dealer, registered pursuant to Article 3 (commencing with Section 9884) of Chapter 20.3 of Division 3 of the Business and Professions Code, did not provide the tow, and passes along, from the tower to the consumer, any of the information required on the itemized invoice, pursuant to subdivision (g) the automotive repair dealer shall not be responsible for the accuracy of those items of information that remain unaltered.

(c) Prior to paying any towing, recovery, or storage-related fees, a vehicle owner or his or her agent or a licensed repossessor shall, at any facility where the vehicle is being stored, have the right to all of the following:

(1) Receive his or her personal property, at no charge, during normal business hours. Normal business hours for releasing collateral and personal property are Monday through Friday from 8:00 a.m. to 5:00 p.m., inclusive, except state holidays.

(2) Retrieve his or her vehicle during the first 72 hours of storage and not pay a lien fee.

(3) (A) Inspect the vehicle without paying a fee.

(B) Have his or her insurer inspect the vehicle at the storage facility, at no charge, during normal business hours. However, the storage facility may limit the inspection to increments of 45 consecutive minutes in order to provide service to any other waiting customer, after which the insurer may resume the inspection for additional increments of 45 consecutive minutes, as necessary.

(4) Request a copy of the Towing and Storage Fees and Access Notice.

(5) Be permitted to pay by cash, insurer's check, or a valid bank credit card. Credit charges for towing and storage services shall comply with Section 1748.1 of the Civil Code. Law enforcement agencies may include the costs of providing for payment by credit when agreeing with a towing or storage provider on rates.

(d) A storage facility shall be open and accessible during normal business hours, as defined in subdivision (c). Outside of normal business hours, the facility shall provide a telephone number that permits the caller to leave a message. Calls to this number shall be returned no later than six business hours after a message has been left.

(e) The Towing and Storage Fees and Access Notice shall be a standardized document plainly printed in no less that 10-point type. A person may distribute the form using its own letterhead, but the language of the Towing and Storage Fees and Access Notice shall read as follows:

Towing and Storage Fees and Access Notice

Note: The following information is intended to serve as a general summary of some of the laws that provide vehicle owners certain rights when their vehicle is towed. It is not intended to summarize all of the laws that may be applicable nor is it intended to fully and completely state the entire law in any area listed. Please review the applicable California code for a definitive statement of the law in your particular situation.

How much can a towing company charge?

Rates for public tows and storage are generally established by an agreement between the law enforcement agency requesting the tow and the towing company (to confirm the approved rates, you may contact the law enforcement agency that initiated the tow; additionally, these rates are required to be posted at the storage facility).

Rates for private property tows and storage cannot exceed the approved rates for the law enforcement agency that has primary jurisdiction for the property from which the vehicle was removed or the towing company's approved CHP rate.

Rates for owner's request tows and storage are generally established by mutual agreement between the requestor and the towing company, but may be dictated by agreements established between the requestor's motor club and motor club service provider.

Where can you complain about a towing company?

For public tows: Contact the law enforcement agency initiating the tow.

Your rights if your vehicle is towed:

Generally, prior to paying any towing and storage-related fees you have the right to:

- Receive an itemized invoice of actual charges.
- Receive your personal property, at no charge, during normal business hours.
- Retrieve your vehicle during the first 72 hours of storage and not pay a lien fee.
- Request a copy of the Towing and Storage Fees and Access Notice.
- Pay by cash, valid bank credit card, or a check issued by your insurer.
- Inspect your vehicle.
- Have your insurer inspect your vehicle at the storage facility, at no charge, during normal business hours. However, the storage facility may limit the inspection to increments of 45 consecutive minutes in order to provide service to any other waiting customer, after which the insurer may resume the inspection for additional increments of 45 consecutive minutes, as necessary.

You and your insurance company or the insurance company representative have the right to have the vehicle released immediately upon (1) payment of all towing and storage-related fees, (2) presentation of a valid photo identification, (3) presentation of reliable documentation showing that you are the owner, insured, or insurer of the vehicle or that the owner has authorized you to take possession of the vehicle, and (4), if applicable, in the case of a fatality or crime, presentation of any required police or law enforcement release documents.

Prior to your vehicle being repaired:

- You have the right to choose the repair facility and to have no repairs made to your vehicle unless you authorize them in writing.
- Any authorization you sign for towing and any authorization you sign for repair must be on separate forms.

What if I do not pay the towing and storage-related fees or abandon my vehicle at the towing company?

Pursuant to Sections 3068.1 to 3074, inclusive, of the Civil Code, a towing company may sell your vehicle and any moneys received will be applied to towing and storage-related fees that have accumulated against your vehicle.

You are responsible for paying the towing company any outstanding balance due on any of these fees once the sale is complete.

Who is liable if my vehicle was damaged during towing or storage?

Generally the owner of a vehicle may recover for any damage to the vehicle resulting from any intentional or negligent act of a person causing the removal of, or removing, the vehicle.

What happens if a towing company violates the law?

If a tow company does not satisfactorily meet certain requirements detailed in this notice, you may bring a lawsuit in court, generally in small claims court. The tower may be civilly liable for damages up to two times the amount charged, not to exceed $500, and possibly more for certain violations.

(f) "Insurer," as used in this section, means either a first-party insurer or third-party insurer.

(g) "Itemized invoice," as used in this section, means a written document that contains the following information. Any document that substantially complies with this subdivision shall be deemed an "itemized invoice" for purposes of this section:

(1) The name, address, telephone number, and carrier identification number as required by subdivision (a) of Section 34507.5 of the person that is charging for towing and storage.

(2) If ascertainable, the registered owner or operator's name, address, and telephone number.

(3) The date service was initiated.

(4) The location of the vehicle at the time service was initiated, including either the address or nearest intersecting roadways.

(5) A vehicle description that includes, if ascertainable, the vehicle year, make, model, odometer reading, license plate number, or if a license plate number is unavailable, the vehicle identification number (VIN).

(6) The service dispatch time, the service arrival time of the tow truck, and the service completion time.

(7) A clear, itemized, and detailed explanation of any additional services that caused the total towing-related service time to exceed one hour between service dispatch time and service completion time.

(8) The hourly rate or per item rate used to calculate the total towing and recovery-related fees. These fees shall be listed as separate line items.

(9) If subject to storage fees, the daily storage rate and the total number of days stored. The storage fees shall be listed as a separate line item. Storage rates shall comply with the requirements of subdivision (c) of Section 22524.5.

(10) If subject to a gate fee, the date and time the vehicle was released after normal business hours. Normal business hours are Monday through Friday from 8:00 a.m. to 5:00 p.m., inclusive, except state holidays. A gate fee shall be listed as a separate line item. A gate fee shall comply with the requirements in subdivision (c) of Section 22524.5.

(11) A description of the method of towing.

(12) If the tow was not requested by the vehicle's owner or driver, the identity of the person or governmental agency that directed the tow. This paragraph shall not apply to information otherwise required to be redacted under Section 22658.

(13) A clear, itemized, and detailed explanation of any additional services or fees.

(h) "Person," as used in this section, includes those entities described in subdivision (a) and has the same meaning as described in Section 470.

(i) An insurer, insurer's agent, or tow hauler, shall be permitted to pay for towing and storage charges by a valid bank credit card, insurer's check, or bank draft.

(j) Except as otherwise exempted in this section, the requirements of this section apply to any facility that charges for the storage of a vehicle, including, but not limited to, a vehicle repair garage or service station, but not including a new motor vehicle dealer.

(k) A person who violates this section is civilly liable to a registered or legal owner of the vehicle, or a registered owner's insurer, for up to two times the amount charged. Liability in any action brought under this section shall not exceed five hundred dollars ($500) per vehicle.

(l) A suspected violation of this section may be reported by any person, including, without limitation, the legal or registered owner of a vehicle or his or her insurer.

(m) This section shall not apply to the towing or storage of a repossessed vehicle by any person subject to, or exempt from, the Collateral Recovery Act (Chapter 11 (commencing with Section 7500) of Division 3 of the Business and Professions Code).

(n) This section does not relieve a person from the obligation to comply with any other law.

(o) Notwithstanding this section, an insurer shall comply with all of its obligations under Section 2695.8 of Chapter 5 of Title 10 of the California Code of Regulations.

(Amended by Stats. 2018, Ch. 434, Sec. 3. (AB 2392) Effective January 1, 2019.)

22651.08. (a) A peace officer, as defined in Chapter 4.5 (commencing with Section 830) of Title 3 of Part 2 of the Penal Code, may remove a vehicle located within the territorial limits in which the officer may act, under either of the following circumstances:

(1) A person is operating a vehicle with fewer than four wheels that does not meet the definition of an electric bicycle set forth in Section 312.5 and is both of the following:

(A) Powered by an electric motor capable of exclusively propelling the vehicle in excess of 20 miles per hour on a highway.

(B) Being operated by an operator who is not licensed to operate the vehicle.

(2) A person is operating a vehicle that is a class 3 electric bicycle in violation of subdivision (a) of Section 21213.

(b) (1) A city, county, or city and county may adopt at a public meeting a regulation, ordinance, or resolution imposing charges equal to its administrative costs relating to the removal, seizure, and storage costs. The charges shall not exceed the actual costs incurred for the expenses directly related to removing, seizing, and storing the vehicle.

(2) A local jurisdiction that has adopted a regulation, ordinance, or resolution pursuant to paragraph (1) shall publicly and conspicuously post the schedule of charges on their internet website.

(c) An agency shall release a seized vehicle to the owner, violator, or their agent after a minimum of 48 hours, if both of the following conditions are met:

(1) The owner, violator, or authorized agent's request is made during normal business hours.

(2) The applicable removal, seizure, and storage costs have been paid.

(d) If a peace officer removes a vehicle pursuant to paragraph (2) of subdivision (a), an agency may, as a condition of release, require the owner, violator, or the parent or legal guardian of the owner or violator to deliver proof that the violator has completed an electric bicycle safety and training program, as described in Section 894 of the Streets and Highways Code, or a related local bicycle safety course, if one is available, as prescribed by authorities in the local jurisdiction.

(Added by Stats. 2025, Ch. 168, Sec. 1. (AB 875) Effective January 1, 2026.)

22651.1. Persons operating or in charge of any storage facility where vehicles are stored pursuant to Section 22651 shall accept a valid bank credit card or cash for payment of towing and storage by the registered owner, legal owner, or the owner's agent claiming the vehicle. A credit card shall be in the name of the person presenting the card. "Credit card" means "credit card" as defined in subdivision (a) of Section 1747.02 of the Civil Code, except, for the purposes of this section, credit card does not include a credit card issued by a retail seller. A person operating or in charge of any storage facility who refuses to accept a valid bank credit card shall be liable to the owner of the vehicle or to the person who tendered the fees for four times the amount of the towing and storage charges, but not to exceed five hundred dollars ($500). In addition, persons operating or in charge of the storage facility shall have sufficient funds on the premises to accommodate and make change in a reasonable monetary transaction.

Credit charges for towing and storage services shall comply with Section 1748.1 of the Civil Code. Law enforcement agencies may include the costs of providing for payment by credit when agreeing with a towing or storage provider on rates.

(Amended by Stats. 2009, Ch. 322, Sec. 9. (AB 515) Effective January 1, 2010.)

22651.2. (a) Any peace officer, as defined in Chapter 4.5 (commencing with Section 830) of Title 3 of Part 2 of the Penal Code, or any regularly employed and salaried employee, who is engaged in directing traffic or enforcing parking laws and regulations of a city, county, or jurisdiction of a state agency in which a vehicle is located, may remove a vehicle located within the territorial limits in which the officer or employee may act when the vehicle is found upon a highway or any public lands, and if all of the following requirements are satisfied:

(1) Because of the size and placement of signs or placards on the vehicle, it appears that the primary purpose of parking the vehicle at that location is to advertise to the public an event or function on private property or on public property hired for a private event or function to which the public is invited.

(2) The vehicle is known to have been previously issued a notice of parking violation that was accompanied by a notice warning that an additional parking violation may result in the impoundment of the vehicle.

(3) The registered owner of the vehicle has been mailed a notice advising of the existence of the parking violation and that an additional violation may result in the impoundment of the vehicle.

(b) Subdivision (a) does not apply to a vehicle bearing any sign or placard advertising any business or enterprise carried on by or through the use of that vehicle.

(c) Section 22852 applies to the removal of any vehicle pursuant to this section.

(Amended by Stats. 1997, Ch. 17, Sec. 144. Effective January 1, 1998.)

22651.3. (a) Any peace officer, as that term is defined in Chapter 4.5 (commencing with Section 830) of Title 3 of Part 2 of the Penal Code, or any regularly employed and salaried employee, who is engaged in directing traffic or enforcing parking laws and regulations, of a city, county, or jurisdiction of a state agency in which any vehicle, other than a rented vehicle, is located may remove the vehicle from an offstreet public parking facility located within the territorial limits in which the officer or employee may act when the vehicle is known to have been issued five or more notices of parking violation over a period of five or more days, to which the owner or person in control of the vehicle has not responded or when any vehicle is illegally parked so as to prevent the movement of a legally parked vehicle.

A notice of parking violation issued to a vehicle which is registered in a foreign jurisdiction or is without current California registration and is known to have been issued five or more notices of parking violation over a period of five or more days shall be accompanied by a warning that repeated violations may result in the impounding of the vehicle.

(b) The vehicle may be impounded until the owner or person in control of the vehicle furnishes to the impounding law enforcement agency evidence of his or her identity and an address within this state at which he or she can be located and furnishes satisfactory evidence that bail has been deposited for all notices of parking violation issued for the vehicle. In lieu of requiring satisfactory evidence that the bail has been deposited, the impounding law enforcement agency may, in its discretion, issue a notice to appear for the offenses charged, as provided in Article 2 (commencing with Section 40500) of Chapter 2 of Division 17. In lieu of either furnishing satisfactory evidence that the bail has been deposited or accepting the notice to appear, the owner or person in control of the vehicle may demand to be taken without unnecessary delay before a magistrate within the county in which the offenses charged are alleged to have been committed and who has jurisdiction of the offenses and is nearest or most accessible with reference to the place where the vehicle is impounded.

(c) Evidence of current registration shall be produced after a vehicle has been impounded. At the discretion of the impounding law enforcement agency, a notice to appear for violation of subdivision (a) of Section 4000 may be issued to the owner or person in control of the vehicle, if the two days immediately following the day of impoundment are weekend days or holidays.

(Amended by Stats. 1996, Ch. 1142, Sec. 10. Effective September 30, 1996.)

22651.4. (a) A peace officer, as defined in Chapter 4.5 (commencing with Section 830) of Title 3 of Part 2 of the Penal Code, may impound a vehicle and its cargo pursuant to Section 34517.

(b) A member of the department may impound a vehicle and its cargo pursuant to Section 34518.

(c) A member of the department may store or impound a vehicle upon determination that the registrant of the vehicle or the driver of the vehicle has failed to pay registration, regulatory, fuel permit, or other fees, or has an outstanding warrant in a county in the state. The impoundment charges are the responsibility of the owner of the vehicle. The stored or impounded vehicle shall be released upon payment of those fees or fines or the posting of bail. The driver or owner of the vehicle may request a hearing to determine the validity of the seizure.

(Amended by Stats. 2006, Ch. 288, Sec. 6. Effective January 1, 2007.)

22651.5. (a) Any peace officer, as defined in Chapter 4.5 (commencing with Section 830) of Title 3 of Part 2 of the Penal Code, or any regularly employed and salaried employee who is engaged in directing traffic or enforcing parking laws or regulations, may, upon the complaint of any person, remove a vehicle parked within 500 feet of any occupied building of a school, community college, or university during normal hours of operation, or a vehicle parked within a residence or business district, from a highway or from public or private property, if an alarm device or horn has been activated within the vehicle, whether continuously activated or intermittently and repeatedly activated, the peace officer or designated employee is unable to locate the owner of the vehicle within 20 minutes from the time of arrival at the vehicle's location, and the alarm device or horn has not been completely silenced prior to removal.

(b) Upon removal of a vehicle from a highway or from public or private property pursuant to this section, the peace officer or designated employee ordering the removal shall immediately report the removal and the location to which the vehicle is removed to the Stolen Vehicle System of the Department of Justice.

(Amended by Stats. 1997, Ch. 945, Sec. 20. Effective January 1, 1998.)

22651.6. A peace officer or employee specified in Section 22651 may remove a vehicle located within the territorial limits in which the officer or employee may act when the vehicle was used by a person who was engaged in a motor vehicle speed contest, as described in subdivision (a) of Section 23109, and the person was arrested and taken into custody for that offense by a peace officer.

(Added by Stats. 1996, Ch. 884, Sec. 1. Effective January 1, 1997.)

22651.7. (a) In addition to, or as an alternative to, removal, a peace officer, as defined in Chapter 4.5 (commencing with Section 830) of Title 3 of Part 2 of the Penal Code, or a regularly employed and salaried employee who is engaged in directing traffic or enforcing parking laws and regulations, of a jurisdiction in which a vehicle is located may immobilize the vehicle with a device designed and manufactured for the immobilization of vehicles, on a highway or any public lands located within the territorial limits in which the officer or employee may act if the vehicle is found upon a highway or public lands and it is known to have been issued five or more notices of parking violations that are delinquent because the owner or person in control of the vehicle has not responded to the agency responsible for processing notices of parking violation within 21 calendar days of notice of citation issuance or citation issuance or 14 calendar days of the mailing of a notice of delinquent parking violation, or the registered owner of the vehicle is known to have been issued five or more notices for failure to pay or failure to appear in court for traffic violations for which no certificate has been issued by the magistrate or clerk of the court hearing the case showing that the case has been adjudicated or concerning which the registered owner's record has not been cleared pursuant to Chapter 6 (commencing with Section 41500) of Division 17. The vehicle may be immobilized until that person furnishes to the immobilizing law enforcement agency all of the following:

(1) Evidence of his or her identity.

(2) An address within this state at which he or she can be located.

(3) Satisfactory evidence that the full amount of parking penalties has been deposited for all notices of parking violation issued for the vehicle and any other vehicle registered to the registered owner of the immobilized vehicle and that bail has been deposited for all traffic violations of the registered owner that have not been cleared. The requirements in this paragraph shall be fully enforced by the immobilizing law enforcement agency on and after the time that the Department of Motor Vehicles is able to provide access to the necessary records. A notice of parking violation issued to the vehicle shall be accompanied by a warning that repeated violations may result in the impounding or immobilization of the vehicle. In lieu of furnishing satisfactory evidence that the full amount of parking penalties or bail, or both, have been deposited that person may demand to be taken without unnecessary delay before a magistrate, for traffic offenses, or a hearing examiner, for parking offenses, within the county in which the offenses charged are alleged to have been committed and who has jurisdiction of the offenses and is nearest or most accessible with reference to the place where the vehicle is immobilized. Evidence of current registration shall be produced after a vehicle has been immobilized or, at the discretion of the immobilizing law enforcement agency, a notice to appear for violation of subdivision (a) of Section 4000 shall be issued to that person.

(b) A person, other than a person authorized under subdivision (a), shall not immobilize a vehicle.

(Amended by Stats. 2006, Ch. 609, Sec. 2. Effective January 1, 2007.)

22651.8. For purposes of paragraph (1) of subdivision (i) of Section 22651 and Section 22651.7, "satisfactory evidence" includes, but is not limited to, a copy of a receipt issued by the department pursuant to subdivision (a) of Section 4760 for the payment of notices of parking violations appearing on the department's records at the time of payment. The processing agency shall, within 72 hours of receiving that satisfactory evidence, update its records to reflect the payments made to the department. If the processing agency does not receive the amount of the parking penalties and administrative fees from the department within four months of the date of issuance of that satisfactory evidence, the processing agency may revise its records to reflect that no payments were received for the notices of parking violation.

(Added by Stats. 1991, Ch. 587, Sec. 2. Operative July 1, 1992, by Sec. 4 of Ch. 587.)

22651.9. (a) Any peace officer, as defined in Chapter 4.5 (commencing with Section 830) of Title 3 of Part 2 of the Penal Code, or any regularly employed and salaried employee, who is engaged in directing traffic or enforcing parking laws and regulations, of a city, county, or city and county in which a vehicle is located, may remove a vehicle located within the territorial limits in which the officer or employee may act when the vehicle is found upon a street or any public lands, if all of the following requirements are satisfied:

(1) Because of a sign or placard on the vehicle, it appears that the primary purpose of parking the vehicle at that location is to advertise to the public the private sale of that vehicle.

(2) Within the past 30 days, the vehicle is known to have been previously issued a notice of parking violation, under local ordinance, which was accompanied by a notice containing all of the following:

(A) A warning that an additional parking violation may result in the impoundment of the vehicle.

(B) A warning that the vehicle may be impounded pursuant to this section, even if moved to another street, so long as the signs or placards offering the vehicle for sale remain on the vehicle.

(C) A listing of the streets or public lands subject to the resolution or ordinance adopted pursuant to paragraph (4), or if all streets are covered, a statement to that effect.

(3) The notice of parking violation was issued at least 24 hours prior to the removal of the vehicle.

(4) The local authority of the city, county, or city and county has, by resolution or ordinance, authorized the removal of vehicles pursuant to this section from the street or public lands on which the vehicle is located.

(b) Section 22852 applies to the removal of any vehicle pursuant to this section.

(Added by Stats. 1993, Ch. 481, Sec. 1. Effective September 27, 1993.)

22652. (a) A peace officer, as defined in Chapter 4.5 (commencing with Section 830) of Title 3 of Part 2 of the Penal Code, or any regularly employed and salaried employee engaged in directing traffic or enforcing parking laws and regulations of a city, county, or jurisdiction of a state agency may remove any vehicle from a stall or space designated for physically disabled persons pursuant to Section 22511.7 or 22511.8, located within the jurisdictional limits in which the officer or employee is authorized to act, if the vehicle is parked in violation of Section 22507.8 and if the police or sheriff's department or the Department of the California Highway Patrol is notified.

(b) In a privately or publicly owned or operated offstreet parking facility, this section applies only to those stalls and spaces if the posting requirements under subdivisions (a) and (d) of Section 22511.8 have been complied with and if the stalls or spaces are clearly signed or marked.

(Amended by Stats. 2004, Ch. 404, Sec. 17. Effective January 1, 2005.)

22652.5. The owner or person in lawful possession of an offstreet parking facility, or any local authority owning or operating an offstreet parking facility, who causes a vehicle to be removed from the parking facility pursuant to Section 22511.8, or any state, city, or county employee, is not civilly liable for the removal if the police or sheriff's department in whose jurisdiction the offstreet parking facility or the stall or space is located or the Department of the California Highway Patrol has been notified prior to the removal.

(Added by Stats. 1983, Ch. 232, Sec. 1. Effective July 14, 1983.)

22652.6. Any peace officer, as defined in Chapter 4.5 (commencing with Section 830) of Title 3 of Part 2 of the Penal Code, or any regularly employed and salaried employee engaged in directing traffic or enforcing parking laws and regulations of a city or county, may remove any vehicle parked or standing on the streets or highways or from a stall or space of a privately or publicly owned or operated offstreet parking facility within the jurisdiction of the city or county when the vehicle is in violation of a local ordinance or resolution adopted pursuant to Section 22511.57.

(Added by Stats. 1994, Ch. 221, Sec. 3. Effective January 1, 1995. Operative July 1, 1995, by Sec. 5 of Ch. 221.)

22653. (a) Any peace officer, as that term is defined in Chapter 4.5 (commencing with Section 830) of Title 3 of Part 2 of the Penal Code, other than an employee directing traffic or enforcing parking laws and regulations, may remove a vehicle from private property located within the territorial limits in which the officer is empowered to act, when a report has previously been made that the vehicle has been stolen or a complaint has been filed and a warrant thereon issued charging that the vehicle has been embezzled.

(b) Any peace officer, as that term is defined in Chapter 4.5 (commencing with Section 830) of Title 3 of Part 2 of the Penal Code, may, after a reasonable period of time, remove a vehicle from private property located within the territorial limits in which the officer is empowered to act, if the vehicle has been involved in, and left at the scene of, a traffic accident and no owner is available to grant permission to remove the vehicle. This subdivision does not authorize the removal of a vehicle where the owner has been contacted and has refused to grant permission to remove the vehicle.

(c) Any peace officer, as that term is defined in Chapter 4.5 (commencing with Section 830) of Title 3 of Part 2 of the Penal Code, may, at the request of the property owner or person in lawful possession of any private property, remove a vehicle from private property located within the territorial limits in which the officer is empowered to act when an officer arrests any person driving or in control of a vehicle for an alleged offense and the officer is, by this code or other law, required or authorized to take, and does take the person arrested before a magistrate without unnecessary delay.

(Amended by Stats. 1985, Ch. 912, Sec. 3.)

22654. (a) Whenever any peace officer, as that term is defined in Chapter 4.5 (commencing with Section 830) of Title 3 of Part 2 of the Penal Code, or other employee directing traffic or enforcing parking laws and regulations, finds a vehicle standing upon a highway, located within the territorial limits in which the officer or employee is empowered to act, in violation of Sections 22500 and 22504, the officer or employee may move the vehicle or require the driver or other person in charge of the vehicle to move it to the nearest available position off the roadway or to the nearest parking location, or may remove and store the vehicle if moving it off the roadway to a parking location is impracticable.

(b) Whenever the officer or employee finds a vehicle standing upon a street, located within the territorial limits in which the officer or employee is empowered to act, in violation of a traffic ordinance enacted by local authorities to prevent flooding of adjacent property, he or she may move the vehicle or require the driver or person in charge of the vehicle to move it to the nearest available location in the vicinity where parking is permitted.

(c) Any state, county, or city authority charged with the maintenance of any highway may move any vehicle which is disabled or abandoned or which constitutes an obstruction to traffic from the place where it is located on a highway to the nearest available position on the same highway as may be necessary to keep the highway open or safe for public travel. In addition, employees of the Department of Transportation may remove any disabled vehicle which constitutes an obstruction to traffic on a freeway from the place where it is located to the nearest available location where parking is permitted; and, if the vehicle is unoccupied, the department shall comply with the notice requirements of subdivision (d).

(d) Any state, county, or city authority charged with the maintenance or operation of any highway, highway facility, or public works facility, in cases necessitating the prompt performance of any work on or service to the highway, highway facility, or public works facility, may move to the nearest available location where parking is permitted, any unattended vehicle which obstructs or interferes with the performance of the work or service or may remove and store the vehicle if moving it off the roadway to a location where parking is permitted would be impracticable. If the vehicle is moved to another location where it is not readily visible from its former parked location or it is stored, the person causing the movement or storage of the vehicle shall immediately, by the most expeditious means, notify the owner of the vehicle of its location. If for any reason the vehicle owner cannot be so notified, the person causing the vehicle to be moved or stored shall immediately, by the most expeditious means, notify the police department of the city in which the vehicle was parked, or, if the vehicle had been parked in an unincorporated area of a county, notify the sheriff's department and nearest office of the California Highway Patrol in that county. No vehicle may be removed and stored pursuant to this subdivision unless signs indicating that no person shall stop, park, or leave standing any vehicle within the areas marked by the signs because the work or service would be done, were placed at least 24 hours prior to the movement or removal and storage.

(e) Whenever any peace officer finds a vehicle parked or standing upon a highway in a manner so as to obstruct necessary emergency services, or the routing of traffic at the scene of a disaster, the officer may move the vehicle or require the driver or other person in charge of the vehicle to move it to the nearest available parking location. If the vehicle is unoccupied, and moving the vehicle to a parking location is impractical, the officer may store the vehicle pursuant to Sections 22850 and 22852 and subdivision (a) or (b) of Section 22853. If the vehicle so moved or stored was otherwise lawfully parked, no moving or storage

charges shall be assessed against or collected from the driver or owner.
(Amended by Stats. 1983, Ch. 913, Sec. 2.)

22655. (a) When any peace officer, as that term is defined in Chapter 4.5 (commencing with Section 830) of Title 3 of Part 2 of the Penal Code or any regularly employed and salaried employee who is engaged in directing traffic or enforcing parking statutes and regulations, has reasonable cause to believe that a motor vehicle on a highway or on private property open to the general public onto which the public is explicitly or implicitly invited, located within the territorial limits in which the officer is empowered to act, has been involved in a hit-and-run accident, and the operator of the vehicle has failed to stop and comply with Sections 20002 to 20006, inclusive, the officer may remove the vehicle from the highway or from public or private property for the purpose of inspection.

(b) Unless sooner released, the vehicle shall be released upon the expiration of 48 hours after the removal from the highway or private property upon demand of the owner. When determining the 48-hour period, weekends, and holidays shall not be included.

(c) Notwithstanding subdivision (b), when a motor vehicle to be inspected pursuant to subdivision (a) is a commercial vehicle, any cargo within the vehicle may be removed or transferred to another vehicle.

This section shall not be construed to authorize the removal of any vehicle from an enclosed structure on private property that is not open to the general public.
(Amended by Stats. 1997, Ch. 945, Sec. 21. Effective January 1, 1998.)

22655.3. Any peace officer, as defined in Chapter 4.5 (commencing with Section 830) of Title 3 of Part 2 of the Penal Code, pursuing a fleeing or evading person in a motor vehicle may remove and store, or cause to be removed and stored, any vehicle used in violation of Section 2800.1 or 2800.2 from property other than that of the registered owner of the vehicle for the purposes of investigation, identification, or apprehension of the driver if the driver of the vehicle abandons the vehicle and leaves it unattended. All towing and storage fees for a vehicle removed under this section shall be paid by the owner, unless the vehicle was stolen or taken without permission.

No vehicle shall be impounded under this section if the driver is arrested before arrival of the towing equipment or if the registered owner is in the vehicle.

As used in this section, "remove and store a vehicle" means that the peace officer may cause the removal of a vehicle to, and storage of a vehicle in, a private lot where the vehicle may be secured by the owner of the facility or by the owner's representative.

This section is not intended to change current statute and case law governing searches and seizures.
(Added by renumbering Section 22651.7 (as added by Stats. 1987, Ch. 279) by Stats. 1988, Ch. 160, Sec. 181.)

22655.5. A peace officer, as defined in Chapter 4.5 (commencing with Section 830) of Title 3 of Part 2 of the Penal Code, may remove a motor vehicle from the highway or from public or private property within the territorial limits in which the officer may act under the following circumstances:

(a) When any vehicle is found upon a highway or public or private property and a peace officer has probable cause to believe that the vehicle was used as the means of committing a public offense.

(b) When any vehicle is found upon a highway or public or private property and a peace officer has probable cause to believe that the vehicle is itself evidence which tends to show that a crime has been committed or that the vehicle contains evidence, which cannot readily be removed, which tends to show that a crime has been committed.

(c) Notwithstanding Section 3068 of the Civil Code or Section 22851 of this code, no lien shall attach to a vehicle removed under this section unless the vehicle was used by the alleged perpetrator of the crime with the express or implied permission of the owner of the vehicle.

(d) In any prosecution of the crime for which a vehicle was impounded pursuant to this section, the prosecutor may request, and the court may order, the perpetrator of the crime, if convicted, to pay the costs of towing and storage of the vehicle, and any administrative charges imposed pursuant to Section 22850.5.

(e) This section shall become operative on January 1, 1993.
(Amended by Stats. 1996, Ch. 1142, Sec. 12. Effective September 30, 1996.)

22656. Any peace officer, as that term is defined in Chapter 4.5 (commencing with Section 830) of Title 3 of Part 2 of the Penal Code, may remove a vehicle from the right-of-way of a railroad, street railway, or light rail line located within the territorial limits in which the officer is empowered to act if the vehicle is parked or abandoned upon any track or within 71/2 feet of the nearest rail. The officer may also remove a vehicle that is parked beyond 71/2 feet of the nearest rail but within the right-of-way of a railroad, street railway, or light rail if signs are posted giving notice that vehicles may be removed.
(Amended by Stats. 2002, Ch. 438, Sec. 29. Effective January 1, 2003.)

22658. (a) The owner or person in lawful possession of private property, including an association of a common interest development, as defined in Sections 4080 and 4100 or Sections 6528 and 6534 of the Civil Code, may cause the removal of a vehicle parked on the property to a storage facility that meets the requirements of subdivision (n) under any of the following circumstances:

(1) There is displayed, in plain view at all entrances to the property, a sign not less than 17 inches by 22 inches in size, with lettering not less than one inch in height, prohibiting public parking and indicating that vehicles will be removed at the owner's expense, and containing the telephone number of the local traffic law enforcement agency and the name and telephone number of each towing company that is a party to a written general towing authorization agreement with the owner or person in lawful possession of the property. The sign may also indicate that a citation may also be issued for the violation.

(2) The vehicle has been issued a notice of parking violation, and 96 hours have elapsed since the issuance of that notice.

(3) The vehicle is on private property and lacks an engine, transmission, wheels, tires, doors, windshield, or any other major part or equipment necessary to operate safely on the highways, the owner or person in lawful possession of the private property has notified the local traffic law enforcement agency, and 24 hours have elapsed since that notification.

(4) The lot or parcel upon which the vehicle is parked is improved with a single-family dwelling.

(b) The tow truck operator removing the vehicle, if the operator knows or is able to ascertain from the property owner, person in lawful possession of the property, or the registration records of the Department of Motor Vehicles the name and address of the registered and legal owner of the vehicle, shall immediately give, or cause to be given, notice in writing to the registered and legal owner of the fact of the removal, the grounds for the removal, and indicate the place to which the vehicle has been removed. If the vehicle is stored in a storage facility, a copy of the notice shall be given to the proprietor of the storage facility. The notice provided for in this section shall include the amount of mileage on the vehicle at the time of removal, if the vehicle has a visible odometer, and the time of the removal from the property. If the tow truck operator does not know and is not able to ascertain the name of the owner or for any other reason is unable to give the notice to the owner as provided in this section, the tow truck operator shall comply with the requirements of subdivision (c) of Section 22853 relating to notice in the same manner as applicable to an officer removing a vehicle from private property.

(c) This section does not limit or affect any right or remedy that the owner or person in lawful possession of private property may have by virtue of other provisions of law authorizing the removal of a vehicle parked upon private property.

(d) The owner of a vehicle removed from private property pursuant to subdivision (a) may recover for any damage to the vehicle resulting from any intentional or negligent act of a person causing the removal of, or removing, the vehicle.

(e) (1) An owner or person in lawful possession of private property, or an association of a common interest development, causing the removal of a vehicle parked on that property is liable for double the storage or towing charges whenever there has been a failure to comply with paragraph (1), (2), or (3) of subdivision (a) or to state the grounds for the removal of the vehicle if requested by the legal or registered owner of the vehicle as required by subdivision (f).

(2) A property owner or owner's agent or lessee who causes the removal of a vehicle parked on that property pursuant to the exemption set forth in subparagraph (A) of paragraph (1) of subdivision (l) and fails to comply with that subdivision is guilty of an infraction, punishable by a fine of one thousand dollars ($1,000).

(f) An owner or person in lawful possession of private property, or an association of a common interest development, causing the removal of a vehicle parked on that property shall notify by telephone or, if impractical, by the most expeditious means available, the local traffic law enforcement agency within one hour after authorizing the tow. An owner or person in lawful possession of private property, an association of a common interest development, causing the removal of a vehicle parked on that property, or the tow truck operator who removes the vehicle, shall state the grounds for the removal of the vehicle if requested by the legal or registered owner of that vehicle. A towing company that removes a vehicle from private property in compliance with subdivision (l) is not responsible in a situation relating to the validity of the removal. A towing company that removes the vehicle under this section shall be responsible for the following:

(1) Damage to the vehicle in the transit and subsequent storage of the vehicle.

(2) The removal of a vehicle other than the vehicle specified by the owner or other person in lawful possession of the private property.

(g) (1) (A) Possession of a vehicle under this section shall be deemed to arise when a vehicle is removed from private property and is in transit.

(B) Upon the request of the owner of the vehicle or that owner's agent, the towing company or its driver shall immediately and unconditionally release a vehicle that is not yet removed from the private property and in transit.

(C) A person failing to comply with subparagraph (B) is guilty of a misdemeanor.

(2) If a vehicle is released to a person in compliance with subparagraph (B) of paragraph (1), the vehicle owner or authorized agent shall immediately move that vehicle to a lawful location.

(h) A towing company may impose a charge of not more than one-half of the regular towing charge for the towing of a vehicle at the request of the owner, the owner's agent, or the person in lawful possession of the private property pursuant to this section if the owner of the vehicle or the vehicle owner's agent returns to the vehicle after the vehicle is coupled to the tow truck by means of a regular hitch, coupling device, drawbar, portable dolly, or is lifted off the ground by means of a conventional trailer, and before it is removed from the private property. The regular towing charge may only be imposed after the vehicle has been removed from the property and is in transit.

(i) (1) (A) A charge for towing or storage, or both, of a vehicle under this section is excessive if the charge exceeds the greater of the following:

(i) That which would have been charged for that towing or storage, or both, made at the request of a law enforcement agency under an agreement between a towing company and the law enforcement agency that exercises primary jurisdiction in the city in which is located the private property from which the vehicle was, or was attempted to be, removed, or if the private property is not located within a city, then the law enforcement agency that exercises primary jurisdiction in the county in which the private property is located.

(ii) That which would have been charged for that towing or storage, or both, under the rate approved for that towing operator by the Department of the California Highway Patrol for the jurisdiction in which the private property is located and from which the vehicle was, or was attempted to be, removed.

(B) A towing operator shall make available for inspection and copying their rate approved by the Department of the California Highway Patrol, if any, within 24 hours of a request without a warrant to law enforcement, the Attorney General, district attorney, or city attorney.

(2) If a vehicle is released within 24 hours from the time the vehicle is brought into the storage facility, regardless of the calendar date, the storage charge shall be for only one day. Not more than one day's storage charge may be required for a vehicle released the same day that it is stored.

(3) If a request to release a vehicle is made and the appropriate fees are tendered and documentation establishing that the person requesting release is entitled to possession of the vehicle, or is the owner's insurance representative, is presented within the initial 24 hours of storage, and the storage facility fails to comply with the request to release the vehicle or is not open for business during normal business hours, then only one day's storage charge may be required to be paid until after the first business day. A business day is any day in which the lienholder is open for business to the public for at least eight hours. If a request is made more than 24 hours after the vehicle is placed in storage, charges may be imposed on a full calendar day basis for each day, or part thereof, that the vehicle is in storage.

(j) (1) A person who charges a vehicle owner a towing, service, or storage charge at an excessive rate, as described in subdivision (h) or (i), is civilly liable to the vehicle owner for four times the amount charged.

(2) A person who knowingly charges a vehicle owner a towing, service, or storage charge at an excessive rate, as described in subdivision (h) or (i), or who fails to make available their rate as required in subparagraph (B) of paragraph (1) of subdivision (i), is guilty of a misdemeanor, punishable by a fine of not more than two thousand five hundred dollars ($2,500), or by imprisonment in a county jail for not more than three months, or by both that fine and imprisonment.

(k) (1) A person operating or in charge of a storage facility where vehicles are stored pursuant to this section shall accept a valid bank credit card or cash for payment of towing and storage by a registered owner, the legal owner, or the owner's agent claiming the vehicle. A credit card shall be in the name of the person presenting the card. "Credit card" means "credit card" as defined in subdivision (a) of Section 1747.02 of the Civil Code, except, for the purposes of this section, credit card does not include a credit card issued by a retail seller.

(2) A person described in paragraph (1) shall conspicuously display, in that portion of the storage facility office where business is conducted with the public, a notice advising that all valid credit cards and cash are acceptable means of payment.

(3) A person operating or in charge of a storage facility who refuses to accept a valid credit card or who fails to post the required notice under paragraph (2) is guilty of a misdemeanor, punishable by a fine of not more than two thousand five hundred dollars ($2,500), or by imprisonment in a county jail for not more than three months, or by both that fine and imprisonment.

(4) A person described in paragraph (1) who violates paragraph (1) or (2) is civilly liable to the registered owner of the vehicle or the person who tendered the fees for four times the amount of the towing and storage charges.

(5) A person operating or in charge of the storage facility shall have sufficient moneys on the premises of the primary storage facility during normal business hours to accommodate, and make change in, a reasonable monetary transaction.

(6) Credit charges for towing and storage services shall comply with Section 1748.1 of the Civil Code. Law enforcement agencies may include the costs of providing for payment by credit when making agreements with towing companies as described in subdivision (i).

(l) (1) (A) A towing company shall not remove or commence the removal of a vehicle from private property without first obtaining the written authorization from the property owner or lessee, including an association of a common interest development, or an employee or agent thereof, who shall be present at the time of removal and verify the alleged violation, except that presence and verification is not required if the person authorizing the tow is the property owner, or the owner's agent who is not a tow operator, of a residential rental property of 15 or fewer units that does not have an onsite owner, owner's agent or employee, and the tenant has verified the violation, requested the tow from that tenant's assigned parking space, and provided a signed request or email, or has called and provides a signed request or email within 24 hours, to the property owner or owner's agent, which the owner or agent shall provide to the towing company within 48 hours of authorizing the tow. The signed request or email shall contain the name and address of the tenant, and the date and time the tenant requested the tow. A towing company shall obtain, within 48 hours of receiving the written authorization to tow, a copy of a tenant request required pursuant to this subparagraph. For the purpose of this subparagraph, a person providing the written authorization who is required to be present on the private property at the time of the tow does not have to be physically present at the specified location of where the vehicle to be removed is located on the private property.

(B) The written authorization under subparagraph (A) shall include all of the following:

(i) The make, model, vehicle identification number, and license plate number of the removed vehicle. If the vehicle is a shared mobility device or does not have an identifiable make, model, vehicle identification number, or license plate number, the authorization shall include any identification numbers on the vehicle, including, but not limited to, a quick response (QR) code or serial number.

(ii) The name, signature, job title, residential or business address, and working telephone number of the person, described in subparagraph (A), authorizing the removal of the vehicle.

(iii) The grounds for the removal of the vehicle.

(iv) The time when the vehicle was first observed parked at the private property.

(v) The time that authorization to tow the vehicle was given.

(C) (i) When the vehicle owner or their agent claims the vehicle, the towing company prior to payment of a towing or storage charge shall provide a photocopy of the written authorization to the vehicle owner or the agent.

(ii) If the vehicle was towed from a residential property, the towing company shall redact the information specified in clause (ii) of subparagraph (B) in the photocopy of the written authorization provided to the vehicle owner or the agent pursuant to clause (i).

(iii) The towing company shall also provide to the vehicle owner or the agent a separate notice that provides the telephone number of the appropriate local law enforcement or prosecuting agency by stating "If you believe that you have been wrongfully towed, please contact the local law enforcement or prosecuting agency at [insert appropriate telephone number]." The notice shall be in English and in the most populous language, other than English, that is spoken in the jurisdiction.

(D) A towing company shall not remove or commence the removal of a vehicle from private property described in subdivision (a) of Section 22953 unless the towing company has made a good faith inquiry to determine that the owner or the property owner's agent complied with Section 22953.

(E) (i) General authorization to remove or commence removal of a vehicle at the towing company's discretion shall not be delegated to a towing company or its affiliates except in the case of a vehicle unlawfully parked within 15 feet of a fire hydrant or in a fire lane, or in a manner which interferes with an entrance to, or exit from, the private property.

(ii) In those cases in which general authorization is granted to a towing company or its affiliate to undertake the removal or commence the removal of a vehicle that is unlawfully parked within 15 feet of a fire hydrant or in a fire lane, or that interferes with an entrance to, or exit from, private property, the towing company and the property owner, or owner's agent, or person in lawful possession of the private property shall have a written agreement granting that general authorization.

(2) If a towing company removes a vehicle under a general authorization described in subparagraph (E) of paragraph (1) and that vehicle is unlawfully parked within 15 feet of a fire hydrant or in a fire lane, or in a manner that interferes with an entrance to, or exit from, the private property, the towing company shall take, prior to the removal of that vehicle, a photograph of the vehicle that clearly indicates that parking violation. Prior to accepting payment, the towing company shall keep one copy of the photograph taken pursuant to this paragraph, and shall present that photograph and provide, without charge, a photocopy to the owner or an agent of the owner, when that person claims the vehicle.

(3) A towing company shall maintain the original written authorization, or the general authorization described in subparagraph (E) of paragraph (1) and the photograph of the violation, required pursuant to this section, and any written requests from a tenant to the property owner or owner's agent required by subparagraph (A) of paragraph (1), for a period of three years and shall make them available for inspection and copying within 24 hours of a request without a warrant to law enforcement, the Attorney General, district attorney, or city attorney.

(4) A person who violates this subdivision is guilty of a misdemeanor, punishable by a fine of not more than two thousand five hundred dollars ($2,500), or by imprisonment in a county jail for not more than three months, or by both that fine and imprisonment.

(5) A person who violates this subdivision is civilly liable to the owner of the vehicle or their agent for four times the amount of the towing and storage charges.

(m) (1) A towing company that removes a vehicle from private property under this section shall notify the local law enforcement agency of that tow after the vehicle is removed from the private property and is in transit.

(2) A towing company is guilty of a misdemeanor if the towing company fails to provide the notification required under paragraph (1) within 60 minutes after the vehicle is removed from the private property and is in transit or 15 minutes after arriving at the storage facility, whichever time is less.

(3) A towing company that does not provide the notification under paragraph (1) within 30 minutes after the vehicle is removed from the private property and is in transit is civilly liable to the registered owner of the vehicle, or the person who tenders the fees, for three times the amount of the towing and storage charges.

(4) If notification is impracticable, the times for notification, as required pursuant to paragraphs (2) and (3), shall be tolled for the time period that notification is impracticable. This paragraph is an affirmative defense.

(n) A vehicle removed from private property pursuant to this section shall be stored in a facility that meets all of the following requirements:

(1) (A) Is located within a 10-mile radius of the property from where the vehicle was removed.

(B) The 10-mile radius requirement of subparagraph (A) does not apply if a towing company has prior general written approval from the law enforcement agency that exercises primary jurisdiction in the city in which is located the private property from which the vehicle was removed, or if the private property is not located within a city, then the law enforcement agency that exercises primary jurisdiction in the county in which is located the private property.

(2) (A) Remains open during normal business hours and releases vehicles after normal business hours.

(B) A gate fee may be charged for releasing a vehicle after normal business hours, weekends, and state holidays. However, the maximum hourly charge for releasing a vehicle after normal business hours shall be one-half of the hourly tow rate charged for initially towing the vehicle, or less.

(C) Notwithstanding any other provision of law and for purposes of this paragraph, "normal business hours" are Monday to Friday, inclusive, from 8 a.m. to 5 p.m., inclusive, except state holidays.

(3) Has a public pay telephone in the office area that is open and accessible to the public.

(o) (1) It is the intent of the Legislature in the adoption of subdivision (k) to assist vehicle owners or their agents by, among other things, allowing payment by credit cards for towing and storage services, thereby expediting the recovery of towed vehicles and concurrently promoting the safety and welfare of the public.

(2) It is the intent of the Legislature in the adoption of subdivision (l) to further the safety of the general public by ensuring that a private property owner or lessee has provided authorization for the removal of a vehicle from their property, thereby promoting the safety of those persons involved in ordering the removal of the vehicle as well as those persons removing, towing, and storing the vehicle.

(3) It is the intent of the Legislature in the adoption of subdivision (g) to promote the safety of the general public by requiring towing companies to unconditionally release a vehicle that is not lawfully in their possession, thereby avoiding the likelihood of dangerous and violent confrontation and physical injury to vehicle owners and towing operators, the stranding of vehicle owners and their passengers at a dangerous time and location, and impeding expedited vehicle recovery, without wasting law enforcement's limited resources.

(p) The remedies, sanctions, restrictions, and procedures provided in this section are not exclusive and are in addition to other remedies, sanctions, restrictions, or procedures that may be provided in other provisions of law, including, but not limited to, those that are provided in Sections 12110 and 34660.

(q) A vehicle removed and stored pursuant to this section shall be released by the law enforcement agency, impounding agency, or person in possession of the vehicle, or any person acting on behalf of them, to the legal owner or the legal owner's agent upon presentation of the assignment, as defined in subdivision (b) of Section 7500.1 of the Business and Professions Code; a release from the one responsible governmental agency, only if required by the agency; a government-issued photographic identification card; and any one of the following as determined by the legal owner or the legal owner's agent: a certificate of repossession for the vehicle, a security agreement for the vehicle, or title, whether paper or electronic, showing proof of legal ownership for the vehicle. Any documents presented may be originals, photocopies, or facsimile copies, or may be transmitted electronically. The storage facility shall not require any documents to be notarized. The storage facility may require the agent of the legal owner to produce a photocopy or facsimile copy of its repossession agency license or registration issued pursuant to Chapter 11 (commencing with Section 7500) of Division 3 of the Business and Professions Code, or to demonstrate, to the satisfaction of the storage facility, that the agent is exempt from licensure pursuant to Section 7500.2 or 7500.3 of the Business and Professions Code.

(Amended by Stats. 2022, Ch. 206, Sec. 2. (AB 2174) Effective January 1, 2023.)

22658.1. (a) Any towing company that, in removing a vehicle, cuts, removes, otherwise damages, or leaves open a fence without the prior approval of the property owner or the person in charge of the property shall then and there do either of the following:

(1) Locate and notify the owner or person in charge of the property of the damage or open condition of the fence, the name and address of the towing company, and the license, registration, or identification number of the vehicle being removed.

(2) Leave in a conspicuous place on the property the name and address of the towing company, and the license, registration, or identification number of the vehicle being removed, and shall without unnecessary delay, notify the police department of the city in which the property is located, or if the property is located in unincorporated territory, either the sheriff or the local headquarters of the Department of the California Highway Patrol, of that information and the location of the damaged or opened fence.

(b) Any person failing to comply with all the requirements of this section is guilty of an infraction.

(Amended by Stats. 2001, Ch. 854, Sec. 68. Effective January 1, 2002.)

22659. Any peace officer of the Department of the California Highway Patrol or any person duly authorized by the state agency in possession of property owned by the state, or rented or leased from others by the state and any peace officer of the Department of the California Highway Patrol providing policing services to property of a district agricultural association may, subsequent to giving notice to the city police or county sheriff, whichever is appropriate, cause the removal of a vehicle from the property to the nearest public garage, under any of the following circumstances:

(a) When the vehicle is illegally parked in locations where signs are posted giving notice of violation and removal.

(b) When an officer arrests any person driving or in control of a vehicle for an alleged offense and the officer is by this code or other law required to take the person arrested before a magistrate without unnecessary delay.

(c) When any vehicle is found upon the property and report has previously been made that the vehicle has been stolen or complaint has been filed and a warrant thereon issued charging that the vehicle has been embezzled.

(d) When the person or persons in charge of a vehicle upon the property are by reason of physical injuries or illness incapacitated to that extent as to be unable to provide for its custody or removal.

The person causing removal of the vehicle shall comply with the requirements of Sections 22852 and 22853 relating to notice.

(Amended by Stats. 1996, Ch. 305, Sec. 70. Effective January 1, 1997.)

22659.5. Notwithstanding any other provision of law, a city or a county may adopt an ordinance declaring a motor vehicle to be a public nuisance subject to seizure and an impoundment period of up to 30 days when the motor vehicle is used in the commission or attempted commission of an act that violates Section 266h or 266i of, subdivision (h) of Section 374.3 of, or subdivision (b) of Section 647 of, the Penal Code, if the owner or operator of the vehicle has had a prior conviction for the same offense within the past three years. An ordinance adopted pursuant to this section may incorporate any combination or all of these offenses. The vehicle may only be impounded pursuant to a valid arrest of the driver for a violation of one of these provisions. An ordinance adopted pursuant to this section shall, at a minimum, contain all of the following provisions:

(a) Within two working days after impoundment, the impounding agency shall send a notice by certified mail, return receipt requested, to the legal owner of the vehicle, at the address obtained from the department, informing the owner that the vehicle has been impounded. The notice shall also include notice of the opportunity for a poststorage hearing to determine the validity of the storage or to determine mitigating circumstances establishing that the vehicle should be released. The impounding agency shall be prohibited from charging for more than five days' storage if it fails to notify the legal owner within two working days after the impoundment when the legal owner redeems the impounded vehicle. The impounding agency shall maintain a published telephone number that provides information 24 hours a day regarding the impoundment of vehicles and the rights of a legal owner and a registered owner to request a hearing. The notice shall include all of the following information:

(1) The name, address, and telephone number of the agency providing the notice.

(2) The location of the place of storage and description of the vehicle, that shall include, if available, the model or make, the manufacturer, the license plate number, and the mileage.

(3) The authority and purpose for the removal of the vehicle.

(4) A statement that, in order to receive a poststorage hearing, the owners, or their agents, shall request the hearing in person, writing, or by telephone within 10 days of the date appearing on the notice.

(b) The poststorage hearing shall be conducted within 48 hours of the request, excluding weekends and holidays. The public agency may authorize one of its own officers or employees to conduct the hearing if that hearing officer is not the same person who directed the seizure of the vehicle.

(c) Failure of the legal and the registered owners, or their agents, to request or to attend a scheduled hearing shall satisfy the poststorage hearing requirement.

(d) The agency employing the person who directed the storage shall be responsible for the costs incurred for towing and storage if it is determined in the poststorage hearing that reasonable grounds for the storage are not established.

(e) Any period during which a vehicle is subjected to storage under an ordinance adopted pursuant to this section shall be included as part of the period of impoundment.

(f) The impounding agency shall release the vehicle to the registered owner or his or her agent prior to the end of the impoundment period under any of the following circumstances:

(1) The driver of the impounded vehicle was arrested without probable cause.

(2) The vehicle is a stolen vehicle.

(3) The vehicle is subject to bailment and was driven by an unlicensed employee of a business establishment, including a parking service or repair garage.

(4) The driver of the vehicle is not the sole registered owner of the vehicle and the vehicle is being released to another registered owner of the vehicle who agrees not to allow the driver to use the vehicle until after the end of the impoundment period.

(5) The registered owner of the vehicle was neither the driver nor a passenger of the vehicle at the time of the alleged violation, or was unaware that the driver was using the vehicle to engage in activities subject to Section 266h or 266i of, or subdivision (b) of Section 647 of, the Penal Code.

(6) A spouse, registered domestic partner, or other affected third party objects to the impoundment of the vehicle on the grounds that it would create a hardship if the subject vehicle is the sole vehicle in a household. The hearing officer shall release the vehicle where the hardship to a spouse, registered domestic partner, or other affected third party created by the impoundment of the subject vehicle, or the length of the impoundment, outweigh the seriousness and the severity of the act in which the vehicle was used.

(g) Notwithstanding any provision of law, if a motor vehicle is released prior to the conclusion of the impoundment period because the driver was arrested without probable cause, neither the arrested person nor the registered owner of the motor vehicle shall be responsible for the towing and storage charges.

(h) Except as provided in subdivision (g), the registered owner or his or her agent shall be responsible for all towing and storage charges related to the impoundment.

(i) A vehicle removed and seized under an ordinance adopted pursuant to this section shall be released to the legal owner of the vehicle or the legal owner's agent prior to the end of the impoundment period if both of the following conditions are met:

(1) The legal owner is a motor vehicle dealer, bank, credit union, acceptance corporation, or other licensed financial institution legally operating in this state, or is another person who is not the registered owner and holds a security interest in the vehicle.

(2) The legal owner or the legal owner's agent pays all towing and storage fees related to the seizure and impoundment of the vehicle.

(j) (1) No lien sale processing fees shall be charged to the legal owner who redeems the vehicle prior to the 15th day of the impoundment period. Neither the impounding authority nor any person having possession of the vehicle shall collect from the legal owner as described in paragraph (1) of subdivision (i), or the legal owner's agent, any administrative charges imposed pursuant to Section 22850.5, unless the legal owner voluntarily requested a poststorage hearing.

(2) A person operating or in charge of a storage facility where vehicles are stored pursuant to this section shall accept a valid bank credit card or cash for payment of towing, storage, and related fees by a legal or registered owner or the owner's agent claiming the vehicle. A credit card or debit card shall be in the name of the person presenting the card. For purposes of this section, "credit card" is as defined in subdivision (a) of Section 1747.02 of the Civil Code. Credit card does not include a credit card issued by a retail seller.

(3) A person operating or in charge of a storage facility described in paragraph (2) who violates paragraph (2) shall be civilly liable to the owner of the vehicle or the person who tendered the fees for four times the amount of the towing, storage, and related fees not to exceed five hundred dollars ($500).

(4) A person operating or in charge of the storage facility described in paragraph (2) shall have sufficient funds on the premises of the primary storage facility during normal business hours to accommodate, and make change for, a reasonable monetary transaction.

(5) Credit charges for towing and storage services shall comply with Section 1748.1 of the Civil Code. Law enforcement agencies may include the costs of providing for payment by credit when making agreements with towing companies on rates.

(6) A failure by a storage facility to comply with any applicable conditions set forth in this subdivision shall not affect the right of the legal owner or the legal owner's agent to retrieve the vehicle if all conditions required of the legal owner or legal owner's agent under this subdivision are satisfied.

(k) (1) The legal owner or the legal owner's agent shall present to the law enforcement agency, impounding agency, person in possession of the vehicle, or any person acting on behalf of those agencies, a copy of the assignment, as defined in subdivision (b) of Section 7500.1 of the Business and Professions Code, a release from the one responsible governmental agency, only if required by the agency, a government-issued photographic identification card, and any one of the following as determined by the legal owner or the legal owner's agent: a certificate of repossession for the vehicle, a security agreement for the vehicle, or title, whether or not paperless or electronic, showing proof of legal ownership for the vehicle. Any documents presented may be originals, photocopies, or facsimile copies, or may be transmitted electronically. The law enforcement agency, impounding agency, or other governmental agency, or any person acting on behalf of those agencies, shall not require any documents to be notarized. The law enforcement agency, impounding agency, or any person acting on behalf of those agencies may require the agent of the legal owner to produce a photocopy or facsimile copy of its repossession agency license or registration issued pursuant to Chapter 11 (commencing with Section 7500) of Division 3 of the Business and Professions Code, or to demonstrate, to the satisfaction of the law enforcement agency, impounding agency, or any person acting on behalf of those agencies that the agent is exempt from licensure pursuant to Section 7500.2 or 7500.3 of the Business and Professions Code.

(2) Administrative costs authorized under subdivision (a) of Section 22850.5 shall not be charged to the legal owner of the type specified in paragraph (1) of subdivision (i) who redeems the vehicle unless the legal owner voluntarily requests a poststorage hearing. A city, county, city and county, or state agency shall not require a legal owner or a legal owner's agent to request a poststorage hearing as a requirement for release of the vehicle to the legal owner or the legal owner's agent. The law enforcement agency, impounding agency, or other governmental agency, or any person acting on behalf of those agencies, shall not require any

documents other than those specified in this paragraph. The legal owner or the legal owner's agent shall be given a copy of any documents he or she is required to sign, except for a vehicle evidentiary hold log book. The law enforcement agency, impounding agency, or any person acting on behalf of those agencies, or any person in possession of the vehicle, may photocopy and retain the copies of any documents presented by the legal owner or legal owner's agent. The legal owner shall indemnify and hold harmless a storage facility from any claims arising out of the release of the vehicle to the legal owner or the legal owner's agent and from any damage to the vehicle after its release, including the reasonable costs associated with defending any such claims.

(l) A legal owner, who meets the requirements for release of a vehicle pursuant to subdivision (i), or the legal owner's agent, shall not be required to request a poststorage hearing as a requirement for release of the vehicle to the legal owner or the legal owner's agent.

(m) (1) A legal owner, who meets the requirements for release of a vehicle pursuant to subdivision (i), or the legal owner's agent, shall not release the vehicle to the registered owner of the vehicle or an agent of the registered owner, unless the registered owner is a rental car agency, until after the termination of the impoundment period.

(2) Prior to relinquishing the vehicle, the legal owner may require the registered owner to pay all towing and storage charges related to the seizure and impoundment.

(n) (1) A vehicle removed and seized pursuant to an ordinance adopted pursuant to this section shall be released to a rental car agency prior to the end of the impoundment period if the agency is either the legal owner or registered owner of the vehicle and the agency pays all towing and storage fees related to the seizure and impoundment of the vehicle.

(2) The owner of a rental vehicle that was seized under an ordinance adopted pursuant to this section may continue to rent the vehicle upon recovery of the vehicle. However, the rental car agency shall not rent another vehicle to the driver of the vehicle that was seized until the impoundment period has expired.

(3) The rental car agency may require the person to whom the vehicle was rented to pay all towing and storage charges related to the seizure and impoundment.

(Repealed and added by Stats. 2009, Ch. 210, Sec. 2. (AB 14) Effective January 1, 2010.)

22660. Notwithstanding any other provision of law, a city, county, or city and county may adopt an ordinance establishing procedures for the abatement and removal, as public nuisances, of abandoned, wrecked, dismantled, or inoperative vehicles or parts thereof from private or public property, and for the recovery, pursuant to Section 25845 or 38773.5 of the Government Code, or assumption by the local authority, of costs of administration and the removal.

(Amended by Stats. 1988, Ch. 126, Sec. 1.)

22661. Any ordinance establishing procedures for the removal of abandoned vehicles shall contain all of the following provisions:

(a) The requirement that notice be given to the Department of Motor Vehicles within five days after the date of removal, identifying the vehicle or part thereof and any evidence of registration available, including, but not limited to, the registration card, certificates of ownership, or license plates.

(b) Making the ordinance inapplicable to (1) a vehicle or part thereof that is completely enclosed within a building in a lawful manner where it is not visible from the street or other public or private property or (2) a vehicle or part thereof that is stored or parked in a lawful manner on private property in connection with the business of a licensed dismantler, licensed vehicle dealer, or a junkyard. This exception shall not, however, authorize the maintenance of a public or private nuisance as defined under provisions of law other than this chapter.

(c) The requirement that not less than a 10-day notice of intention to abate and remove the vehicle or part thereof as a public nuisance be issued, unless the property owner and the owner of the vehicle have signed releases authorizing removal and waiving further interest in the vehicle or part thereof. However, the notice of intention is not required for removal of a vehicle or part thereof that is inoperable due to the absence of a motor, transmission, or wheels and incapable of being towed, is valued at less than two hundred dollars ($200) by a person specified in Section 22855, and is determined by the local agency to be a public nuisance presenting an immediate threat to public health or safety, provided that the property owner has signed a release authorizing removal and waiving further interest in the vehicle or part thereof. Prior to final disposition under Section 22662 of such a low-valued vehicle or part for which evidence of registration was recovered pursuant to subdivision (a), the local agency shall provide notice to the registered and legal owners of intent to dispose of the vehicle or part, and if the vehicle or part is not claimed and removed within 12 days after the notice is mailed, from a location specified in Section 22662, final disposition may proceed. No local agency or contractor thereof shall be liable for damage caused to a vehicle or part thereof by removal pursuant to this section.

This subdivision applies only to inoperable vehicles located upon a parcel that is (1) zoned for agricultural use or (2) not improved with a residential structure containing one or more dwelling units.

(d) The 10-day notice of intention to abate and remove a vehicle or part thereof, when required by this section, shall contain a statement of the hearing rights of the owner of the property on which the vehicle is located and of the owner of the vehicle. The statement shall include notice to the property owner that he or she may appear in person at a hearing or may submit a sworn written statement denying responsibility for the presence of the vehicle on the land, with his or her reasons for such denial, in lieu of appearing. The notice of intention to abate shall be mailed, by registered or certified mail, to the owner of the land as shown on the last equalized assessment roll and to the last registered and legal owners of record unless the vehicle is in such condition that identification numbers are not available to determine ownership.

(e) The requirement that a public hearing be held before the governing body of the city, county, or city and county, or any other board, commissioner, or official of the city, county, or city and county as designated by the governing body, upon request for such a hearing by the owner of the vehicle or the owner of the land on which the vehicle is located. This request shall be made to the appropriate public body, agency, or officer within 10 days after the mailing of notice of intention to abate and remove the vehicle or at the time of signing a release pursuant to subdivision (c). If the owner of the land on which the vehicle is located submits a sworn written statement denying responsibility for the presence of the vehicle on his or her land within that time period, this statement shall be construed as a request for hearing that does not require the presence of the owner submitting the request. If the request is not received within that period, the appropriate public body, agency, or officer shall have the authority to remove the vehicle.

(f) The requirement that after a vehicle has been removed, it shall not be reconstructed or made operable, unless it is a vehicle that qualifies for either horseless carriage license plates or historical vehicle license plates, pursuant to Section 5004, in which case the vehicle may be reconstructed or made operable.

(g) A provision authorizing the owner of the land on which the vehicle is located to appear in person at the hearing or present a sworn written statement denying responsibility for the presence of the vehicle on the land, with his or her reasons for the denial. If it is determined at the hearing that the vehicle was placed on the land without the consent of the landowner and that he or she has not subsequently acquiesced to its presence, then the local authority shall not assess costs of administration or removal of the vehicle against the property upon which the vehicle is located or otherwise attempt to collect those costs from the owner.

(Amended by Stats. 1993, Ch. 589, Sec. 187. Effective January 1, 1994.)

22662. Vehicles or parts thereof may be disposed of by removal to a scrapyard, automobile dismantler's yard, or any suitable site operated by a local authority for processing as scrap, or other final disposition consistent with subdivision (e) of Section 22661. A local authority may operate such a disposal site when its governing body determines that commercial channels of disposition are not available or are inadequate, and it may make final disposition of such vehicles or parts, or the local agency may transfer such vehicle or parts to another, provided such disposal shall be only as scrap.

(Added by Stats. 1976, Ch. 29.)

22663. Any ordinance adopted pursuant to Section 22660 shall provide for administration of the ordinance by regularly salaried full-time employees of the city, county, or city and county, except that the removal of vehicles or parts thereof from property may be by any other duly authorized person. Any such authorized person may enter upon private property for the purposes specified in the ordinance to examine a vehicle or parts thereof, obtain information as to the identity of a vehicle, and remove or cause the removal of a vehicle or part thereof declared to be a nuisance pursuant to the ordinance.

(Added by Stats. 1976, Ch. 29.)

22664. Any licensed dismantler or commercial enterprise acquiring vehicles removed pursuant to such ordinance shall be excused from the reporting requirements of Section 11520; and any fees and penalties which would otherwise be due the Department of Motor Vehicles are hereby waived, provided that a copy of the resolution or order authorizing disposition of the vehicle is retained in the dismantler's or commercial enterprise's business records.

(Added by Stats. 1976, Ch. 29.)

22665. Notwithstanding Section 22710 or any other provision of law, the department may, at the request of a local authority, other than a service authority, administer on behalf of the authority its abandoned vehicle abatement and removal program established pursuant to Section 22660.

(Amended by Stats. 1990, Ch. 1684, Sec. 4.)

22666. Whenever the department is administering a program pursuant to Section 22665, it shall by regulation establish procedures for the abatement and removal of vehicles that are identical to the requirements specified in Section 22661, except that the department shall provide by agreement with the requesting local authority for the conduct of a public hearing pursuant to subdivision (d) of Section 22661 by the local authority and for the reimbursement of the department for its costs of administration and removal which the local authority is authorized to recover from the property owner pursuant to Section 22660. Such regulations shall also provide for the administration of the regulations by regularly salaried, full-time personnel of the department, except that the removal of vehicles or parts thereof from property may be done by any other duly authorized person. Any such person may enter upon private property for the purposes specified in the regulations to examine a vehicle or parts thereof, obtain information as to the identity of a vehicle, and remove or cause the removal of a vehicle or part thereof declared to be a nuisance pursuant to the regulations.

The provisions of Sections 22662 and 22664 shall also apply to any vehicle removed by the department.

(Added by Stats. 1976, Ch. 29.)

22667. In establishing procedures for the abatement and removal of abandoned vehicles, the department shall give priority to the removal of abandoned vehicles from corridors of the state highway system, from public lands and parks, and from river and wildlife areas.

(Added by Stats. 1976, Ch. 29.)

22668. No local authority whose abandoned vehicle abatement and removal program is administered pursuant to Section 22665 shall be eligible for any disbursement from the Abandoned Vehicle Trust Fund pursuant to Section 22710.

(Added by Stats. 1976, Ch. 29.)

22669. (a) Any peace officer, as that term is defined in Chapter 4.5 (commencing with Section 830) of Title 3 of Part 2 of the Penal Code, or any other employee of the state, county, or city designated by an agency or department of the state or the board of supervisors or city council to perform this function, in the territorial limits in which the officer or employee is authorized to act, who has reasonable grounds to believe that the vehicle has been abandoned, as determined pursuant to Section 22523, may remove the vehicle from a highway or from public or private property.

(b) Any person performing a franchise or contract awarded pursuant to subdivision (a) of Section 22710, may remove a vehicle from a highway or place to which it has been removed pursuant to subdivision (c) of Section 22654 or from public or private property, after a determination by a peace officer, as that term is defined in Chapter 4.5 (commencing with Section 830) of Title 3 of Part 2 of the Penal Code, or other designated employee of the state, county, or city in which the vehicle is located that the vehicle is abandoned, as determined pursuant to Section 22523.

(c) A state, county, or city employee, other than a peace officer or employee of a sheriff's department or a city police department, designated to remove vehicles pursuant to this section may do so only after he or she has mailed or personally delivered a written report identifying the vehicle and its location to the office of the Department of the California Highway Patrol located nearest to the vehicle.

(d) Motor vehicles which are parked, resting, or otherwise immobilized on any highway or public right-of-way and which lack an engine, transmission, wheels, tires, doors, windshield, or any other part or equipment necessary to operate safely on the highways of this state, are hereby declared a hazard to public health, safety, and welfare and may be removed immediately upon discovery by a peace officer or other designated employee of the state, county, or city.

(Amended by Stats. 1987, Ch. 1133, Sec. 4.)

22670. (a) For lien sale purposes, the public agency causing the removal of the vehicle shall determine if the estimated value of the vehicle that has been ordered removed, towed, or stored is five hundred dollars ($500) or less, over five hundred dollars ($500) but four thousand dollars ($4,000) or less, or over four thousand dollars ($4,000).

(b) If the public agency fails or refuses to put a value on, or to estimate the value of, the vehicle within three days after the date of removal of the vehicle, the garage keeper specified in Section 22851 or the garage keeper's agent shall determine, under penalty of perjury, if the estimated value of the vehicle that has been ordered removed, towed, or stored, is five hundred dollars ($500) or less, over five hundred dollars ($500) but four thousand dollars ($4,000) or less, or over four thousand dollars ($4,000).

(Amended by Stats. 2004, Ch. 650, Sec. 10. Effective January 1, 2005.)

22671. A local authority may either issue a franchise or execute a contract for the removal of abandoned vehicles in accordance with the provisions of this chapter.

(Added by renumbering Section 22706 by Stats. 1980, Ch. 1111, Sec. 26.)

22710. (a) A service authority for the abatement of abandoned vehicles may be established, and a one dollar ($1) vehicle registration fee imposed, in a county if the board of supervisors of the county, by a two-thirds vote, and a majority of the cities having a majority of the incorporated population within the county have adopted resolutions providing for the establishment of the authority and imposition of the fee. The membership of the authority shall be determined by concurrence of the board of supervisors and a majority vote of the majority of the cities within the county having a majority of the incorporated population.

(b) The authority may contract and may undertake any act convenient or necessary to carry out a law relating to the authority. The authority shall be staffed by existing personnel of the city, county, or county transportation commission.

(c) (1) Notwithstanding any other provision of law, a service authority may adopt an ordinance establishing procedures for the abatement, removal, and disposal, as a public nuisance, of an abandoned, wrecked, dismantled, or inoperative vehicle or part of the vehicle from private or public property; and for the recovery, pursuant to Section 25845 or 38773.5 of the Government Code, or assumption by the service authority, of costs associated with the enforcement of the ordinance. Cost recovery shall only be undertaken by an entity that may be a county or city or the department, pursuant to contract with the service authority as provided in this section.

(2) (A) The money received by an authority pursuant to Section 9250.7 and this section shall be used only for the abatement, removal, or the disposal as a public nuisance of any abandoned, wrecked, dismantled, or inoperative vehicle or part of the vehicle from private or public property. The money received shall not be used to offset the costs of vehicles towed under authorities other than an ordinance adopted pursuant to paragraph (1) or when costs are recovered under Section 22850.5.

(B) The money received by a service authority pursuant to Section 9250.7 and this section that are unexpended in a fiscal year may be carried forward by the service authority for the abandoned vehicle abatement program in the following fiscal year as agreed upon by the service authority and its member agencies.

(d) (1) An abandoned vehicle abatement program and plan of a service authority shall be implemented only with the approval of the county and a majority of the cities having a majority of the incorporated population.

(2) (A) The department shall provide guidelines for an abandoned vehicle abatement program. An authority's abandoned vehicle abatement plan and program shall be consistent with those guidelines, and shall provide for, but not be limited to, an estimate of the number of abandoned vehicles, a disposal and enforcement strategy including contractual agreements, and appropriate fiscal controls.

(B) The department's guidelines provided pursuant to this paragraph shall include, but not be limited to, requiring each service authority receiving funds from the Abandoned Vehicle Trust Fund to report to the Controller on an annual basis pursuant to subdivision (c) of Section 9250.7, in a manner prescribed by the department, and pursuant to an approved abandoned vehicle abatement program.

(C) A service authority may carry out an abandoned vehicle abatement from a public property after providing a notice as specified by the local ordinance adopted pursuant to Section 22660 of the jurisdiction in which the abandoned vehicle is located and that notice has expired.

(3) After a plan has been approved pursuant to paragraph (1), the service authority shall, not later than August 1 of the year in which the plan was approved, submit it to the department for review, and the department shall, not later than October 1 of that same year, either approve the plan as submitted or make recommendations for revision. After the plan has received the department's approval as being consistent with the department's guidelines, the service authority shall submit it to the Controller.

(4) Except as provided in subdivision (e), the Controller shall not make an allocation for a fiscal year, commencing on July 1 following the Controller's determination to suspend a service authority when a service authority has failed to comply with the provisions set forth in Section 9250.7.

(5) A governmental agency shall not receive funds from a service authority for the abatement of abandoned vehicles pursuant to an approved abandoned vehicle abatement program unless the governmental agency has submitted an annual report to the service authority stating the manner in which the funds were expended, and the number of vehicles abated. The governmental agency shall receive that percentage of the total funds collected by the service authority that is equal to its share of the formula calculated pursuant to paragraph (6).

(6) Each service authority shall calculate a formula for apportioning funds to each governmental agency that receives funds from the service authority and submit that formula to the Controller with the annual report required pursuant to paragraph (2). The formula shall apportion 50 percent of the funds received by the service authority to a governmental agency based on the percentage of vehicles abated by that governmental agency of the total number of abandoned vehicles abated by all member agencies, and 50 percent based on population and geographic area, as determined by the service authority. When the formula is first submitted to the Controller, and each time the formula is revised thereafter, the service authority shall include a detailed explanation of how the service authority determined the apportionment between per capita abatements and service area.

(7) Notwithstanding any other provision of this subdivision, the Controller may allocate to the service authority in the County of Humboldt the net amount of the abandoned vehicle abatement funds received from the fee imposed by that authority, as described in subdivision (b) of Section 9250.7, for calendar years 2000 and 2001.

(e) A plan that has been submitted to the Controller pursuant to subdivision (d) may be revised pursuant to the procedure prescribed in that subdivision, including compliance with any dates described therein for submission to the department and the Controller, respectively, in the year in which the revisions are proposed by the service authority. Compliance with that procedure shall only be required if the revisions are substantial.

(f) For purposes of this section, "abandoned vehicle abatement" means the removal of a vehicle from public or private property by towing or any other means after the vehicle has been marked as abandoned by an official of a governmental agency that is a member of the service authority.

(g) A service authority shall cease to exist on the date that all revenues received by the authority pursuant to this section and Section 9250.7 have been expended.

(h) In the event of a conflict with other provisions of law, this section shall govern the disbursement of money collected pursuant to this section and from the Abandoned Vehicle Trust Fund for the implementation of the abandoned vehicle abatement program.

(Amended by Stats. 2007, Ch. 389, Sec. 2. Effective January 1, 2008.)

22711. Notwithstanding any other provision of law, the California Highway Patrol, any city, county, or city and county which has an abandoned vehicle abatement program, and any service authority established under Section 22710, upon satisfying all applicable reporting requirements provided in this chapter, may, with the consent of the Director of Corrections, transport any abandoned vehicle to, and dispose of any abandoned vehicle at, any institution under the jurisdiction of the director which has a program established pursuant to Section 2813.5 of the Penal Code.

(Added by Stats. 1991, Ch. 1157, Sec. 2.)

Article 2. Vehicle Disposition

(Heading of Article 2 renumbered from Article 3 by Stats. 1980, Ch. 1111, Sec. 28.)

22850. Whenever an officer or employee removes a vehicle from a highway, or from public or private property, unless otherwise provided, he shall take the vehicle to the nearest garage or other place of safety or to a garage designated or maintained by the governmental agency of which the officer or employee is a member, where the vehicle shall be placed in storage.

At the time of such removal, the officer or employee shall determine the amount of mileage on the vehicle.

(Amended by Stats. 1975, Ch. 239.)

22850.3. (a) A vehicle placed in storage pursuant to Section 22850 shall be released to the owner or person in control of the vehicle only if the owner or person furnishes, to the law enforcement agency or employee who placed the vehicle in storage, satisfactory proof of current vehicle registration. The agency which caused the vehicle to be stored may, in its discretion, issue a notice to appear for the registration violation, if the two days immediately following the day of impoundment are weekend days or holidays.

(b) At every storage facility there shall be posted in a conspicuous place a notice to the effect that a vehicle placed in storage pursuant to Section 22850 may be released only on proof of current registration or, at the discretion of the impounding agency, upon the issuance of a notice to appear for the registration violation by the local agency which caused the vehicle to be stored, specifying the name and telephone number of that local agency.

(Amended by Stats. 1994, Ch. 1220, Sec. 64. Effective September 30, 1994.)

22850.5. (a) A city, county, or city and county, or a state agency may adopt a regulation, ordinance, or resolution establishing procedures for the release of properly impounded vehicles to the registered owner or the agent of the registered owner and for the imposition of a charge equal to its administrative costs relating to the removal, impound, storage, or release of the vehicles to the registered owner or to the agent of the registered owner. Those administrative costs may be waived by the local or state authority upon verifiable proof that the vehicle was reported stolen at the time the vehicle was removed.

(b) The following apply to any charges imposed for administrative costs pursuant to subdivision (a):

(1) The charges shall only be imposed on the registered owner or the agents of that owner and shall not include any vehicle towed under an abatement program or sold at a lien sale pursuant to Sections 3068.1 to 3074, inclusive, of, and Section 22851 of, the Civil Code unless the sale is sufficient in amount to pay the lienholder's total charges and proper administrative costs.

(2) Any charges shall be collected by the local or state authority only from the registered owner or an agent of the registered owner.

(3) The charges shall be in addition to any other charges authorized or imposed pursuant to this code.

(4) No charge may be imposed for any hearing or appeal relating to the removal, impound, storage, or release of a vehicle unless that hearing or appeal was requested in writing by the registered or legal owner of the vehicle or an agent of that registered or legal owner. In addition, the charge may be imposed only upon the person requesting that hearing or appeal.

No administrative costs authorized under subdivision (a) shall be charged to the legal owner who redeems the vehicle unless the legal owner voluntarily requests a poststorage hearing. No city, county, city and county, or state agency shall require a legal owner or a legal owner's agent to request a poststorage hearing as a requirement for release of the vehicle to the legal owner or the legal owner's agent. The impounding agency, or any person acting on behalf of the agency, shall not require the legal owner or the legal owner's agent to produce any documents other than those specified in paragraph (3) of subdivision (f) of Section 14602.6 or paragraph (3) of subdivision (e) of Section 14602.7. The impounding agency, or any person acting on behalf of the agency, shall not require any documents to be notarized.

(Amended by Stats. 2015, Ch. 740, Sec. 17. (AB 281) Effective January 1, 2016.)

22851. (a) (1) Whenever a vehicle has been removed to a garage under this chapter and the keeper of the garage has received the notice or notices as provided herein, the keeper shall have a lien dependent upon possession for his or her compensation for towage and for caring for and keeping safe the vehicle for a period not exceeding 60 days or, if an application for an authorization to conduct a lien sale has been filed pursuant to Section 3068.1 of the Civil Code within 30 days after the removal of the vehicle to the garage, 120 days and, if the vehicle is not recovered by the owner within that period or the owner is unknown, the keeper of the garage may satisfy his or her lien in the manner prescribed in this article. The lien shall not be assigned. Possession of the vehicle is deemed to arise when a vehicle is removed and is in transit, or when vehicle recovery operations or load salvage operations that have been requested by a law enforcement agency have begun at the scene.

(2) Whenever a vehicle owner returns to a vehicle that is in possession of a towing company prior to the removal of the vehicle, the owner may regain possession of the vehicle from the towing company if the owner pays the towing company the towing charges.

(b) No lien shall attach to any personal property in or on the vehicle. The personal property in or on the vehicle shall be given to the current registered owner or the owner's authorized agent upon demand and without charge during normal business hours. Notwithstanding any other provision of law, normal business hours are Monday to Friday, inclusive, from 8 a.m. to 5 p.m., inclusive, except state holidays. A gate fee may be charged for returning property after normal business hours, weekends, and state holidays. The maximum hourly charge for nonbusiness hours releases shall be one-half the hourly tow rate charged for initially towing the vehicle, or less. The lienholder is not responsible for property after any vehicle has been disposed of pursuant to this chapter.

(Amended by Stats. 2001, Ch. 127, Sec. 8. Effective July 30, 2001.)

22851.1. (a) If the vehicle is impounded pursuant to subdivision (i) of Section 22651 and not released as provided in that subdivision, the vehicle may be sold pursuant to this chapter to satisfy the liens specified in Section 22851 and in subdivision (b) of this section.

(b) A local authority impounding a vehicle pursuant to subdivision (i) of Section 22651 shall have a lien dependent upon possession by the keeper of the garage for satisfaction of bail for all outstanding notices of parking violation issued by the local authority for the vehicle, when the conditions specified in subdivision (c) have been met. This lien shall be subordinate in priority to the lien established by Section 22851, and the proceeds of any sale shall be applied accordingly. Consistent with this order of priority, the term "lien," as used in this article and in Chapter 6.5 (commencing with Section 3067) of Title 14 of Part 4 of Division 3 of the Civil Code, includes a lien imposed by this subdivision. In any action brought to perfect the lien, where required by subdivision (d) of Section 22851.8 of this code, or by subdivision (d) of Section 3071 or subdivision (d) of Section 3072 of the Civil Code, it shall be a defense to the recovery of bail that the owner of the vehicle at the time of impoundment was not the owner of the vehicle at the time of the parking offense.

(c) A lien shall exist for bail with respect to parking violations for which no person has answered the charge in the notice of parking violation given, or filed an affidavit of nonownership pursuant to and within the time specified in subdivision (b) of Section 41103.

(Amended by Stats. 1996, Ch. 124, Sec. 129. Effective January 1, 1997.)

22851.2. (a) Excepting a vehicle removed pursuant to Section 22669, if the vehicle is determined to have a value not exceeding five hundred dollars ($500) pursuant to Section 22670, the public agency that removed the vehicle shall do all of the following:

(1) Within 48 hours after removal of the vehicle, notify the Stolen Vehicle System of the Department of Justice in Sacramento of the removal.

(2) Prepare and give to the lienholder a report that includes all of the following:

(A) The value of the vehicle estimated pursuant to Section 22670.

(B) The identification of the estimator.

(C) The location of the vehicle.

(D) A description of the vehicle, including the make, year model, identification number, license number, state of registration, and, if a motorcycle, an engine number.

(E) The statutory authority for storage.

(b) If the vehicle is in a condition that there is no means of determining ownership, the public agency that removed the vehicle may give authorization to dispose of the vehicle. If authorization for disposal is not issued, a vehicle identification number shall be assigned prior to commencing the lien sale proceedings.

(Amended by Stats. 2004, Ch. 650, Sec. 12. Effective January 1, 2005.)

22851.3. Whenever a peace officer, as defined in Chapter 4.5 (commencing with Section 830) of Title 3 of Part 2 of the Penal Code, or any other employee of a public agency authorized pursuant to Section 22669, removes, or causes the removal of, a vehicle pursuant to Section 22669 and the public agency or, at the request of the public agency, the lienholder determines the estimated value of the vehicle is five hundred dollars ($500) or less, the public agency that removed, or caused the removal of, the vehicle shall cause the disposal of the vehicle under this section, subject to all of the following requirements:

(a) Not less than 72 hours before the vehicle is removed, the peace officer or the authorized public employee has securely attached to the vehicle a distinctive notice which states that the vehicle will be removed by the public agency. This subdivision does not apply to abandoned vehicles removed pursuant to subdivision (d) of Section 22669 which are determined by the public agency to have an estimated value of three hundred dollars ($300) or less.

(b) Immediately after removal of the vehicle, the public agency which removed, or caused the removal of, the vehicle shall notify the Stolen Vehicle System of the Department of Justice in Sacramento of the removal.

(c) The public agency that removed, or caused the removal of, the vehicle or, at the request of the public agency, the lienholder shall obtain a copy of the names and addresses of all persons having an interest in the vehicle, if any, from the Department of Motor Vehicles either directly or by use of the California Law Enforcement Telecommunications System. This subdivision does not require the public agency or lienholder to obtain a copy of the actual record on file at the Department of Motor Vehicles.

(d) Within 48 hours of the removal, excluding weekends and holidays, the public agency that removed, or caused the removal of, the vehicle or, at the request of the public agency, the lienholder shall send a notice to the registered and legal owners at their addresses of record with the Department of Motor Vehicles, and to any other person known to have an interest in the vehicle. A notice sent by the public agency shall be sent by certified or first-class mail, and a notice sent by the lienholder shall be sent by certified mail. The notice shall include all of the following information:

(1) The name, address, and telephone number of the public agency providing the notice.

(2) The location of the place of storage and description of the vehicle which shall include, if available, the vehicle make, license plate number, vehicle identification number, and mileage.

(3) The authority and purpose for the removal of the vehicle.

(4) A statement that the vehicle may be disposed of 15 days from the date of the notice.

(5) A statement that the owners and interested persons, or their agents, have the opportunity for a poststorage hearing before the public agency that removed, or caused the removal of, the vehicle to determine the validity of the storage if a request for a hearing is made in person, in writing, or by telephone within 10 days from the date of notice; that, if the owner or interested person, or his or her agent, disagrees with the decision of the public agency, the decision may be reviewed pursuant to Section 11523 of the Government Code; and that during the time of the initial hearing, or during the time the decision is being reviewed pursuant to Section 11523 of the Government Code, the vehicle in question may not be disposed of.

(e) (1) A requested hearing shall be conducted within 48 hours of the request, excluding weekends and holidays. The public agency that removed the vehicle may authorize its own officers to conduct the hearing if the hearing officer is not the same person who directed the storage of the vehicle.

(2) Failure of either the registered or legal owner or interested person, or his or her agent, to request or to attend a scheduled hearing shall satisfy the poststorage validity hearing requirement of this section.

(f) The public agency employing the person, or utilizing the services of a contractor or franchiser pursuant to subdivision (b) of Section 22669, that removed, or caused the removal of, the vehicle and that directed any towing or storage, is responsible for the costs incurred for towing and storage if it is determined in the hearing that reasonable grounds to believe that the vehicle was abandoned are not established.

(g) An authorization for disposal may not be issued by the public agency that removed, or caused the removal of, the vehicle to a lienholder who is storing the vehicle prior to the conclusion of a requested poststorage hearing or any judicial review of that hearing.

(h) If, after 15 days from the notification date, the vehicle remains unclaimed and the towing and storage fees have not been paid, and if no request for a poststorage hearing was requested or a poststorage hearing was not attended, the public agency that removed, or caused the removal of, the vehicle shall provide to the lienholder who is storing the vehicle, on a form approved by the Department of Motor Vehicles, authorization to dispose of the vehicle. The lienholder may request the public agency to provide the authorization to dispose of the vehicle.

(i) If the vehicle is claimed by the owner or his or her agent within 15 days of the notice date, the lienholder who is storing the vehicle may collect reasonable fees for services rendered, but may not collect lien sale fees as provided in Section 22851.12.

(j) Disposal of the vehicle by the lienholder who is storing the vehicle may only be to a licensed dismantler or scrap iron processor. A copy of the public agency's authorization for disposal shall be forwarded to the licensed dismantler within five days of disposal to a licensed dismantler. A copy of the public agency's authorization for disposal shall be retained by the lienholder who stored the vehicle for a period of 90 days if the vehicle is disposed of to a scrap iron processor.

(k) If the names and addresses of the registered and legal owners of the vehicle are not available from the records of the Department of Motor Vehicles, either directly or by use of the California Law Enforcement Telecommunications System, the public agency may issue to the lienholder who stored the vehicle an authorization for disposal at any time after the removal.

The lienholder may request the public agency to issue an authorization for disposal after the lienholder ascertains that the names and addresses of the registered and legal owners of the vehicle are not available from the records of the Department of Motor Vehicles either directly or by use of the California Law Enforcement Telecommunications System.

(l) A vehicle disposed of pursuant to this section may not be reconstructed or made operable, unless it is a vehicle that qualifies for either horseless carriage license plates or historical vehicle license plates, pursuant to Section 5004, in which case the vehicle may be reconstructed or made operable.

(Amended by Stats. 2003, Ch. 67, Sec. 1. Effective January 1, 2004.)

22851.4. If the vehicle is determined to have a value exceeding five hundred dollars ($500) pursuant to Section 22670, the lien shall be satisfied pursuant to Sections 3067 to 3074, inclusive, of the Civil Code.

(Amended by Stats. 2004, Ch. 650, Sec. 13. Effective January 1, 2005.)

22851.5. (a) The Counties of Alameda and Los Angeles may implement a program to dispose of recreational vehicles subject to the requirements described in subdivision (b).

(b) Whenever a peace officer, as defined in Chapter 4.5 (commencing with Section 830) of Title 3 of Part 2 of the Penal Code, or any other employee of a public agency authorized pursuant to Section 22669, removes, or causes the removal of, a recreational vehicle pursuant to Section 22669, and the public agency or, at the request of the public agency, the lienholder determines the estimated value of the recreational vehicle is four thousand dollars ($4,000) or less, the public agency that removed, or caused the removal of, the recreational vehicle shall cause the disposal of the recreational vehicle subject to all of the following requirements:

(1) Not less than 72 hours before the recreational vehicle is removed, the peace officer or the authorized public employee has securely attached to the recreational vehicle a distinctive notice which states that the recreational vehicle will be removed by the public agency and that if the recreational vehicle is towed, it can be recovered for at least 30 days after the public agency notifies the registered owner of the recreational vehicle pursuant to paragraph (4). The notice shall also include contact information for an individual to learn where their recreational vehicle and other possessions may be recovered. This subdivision does not apply to abandoned recreational vehicles removed pursuant to subdivision (d)

of Section 22669 which are determined by the public agency to have an estimated value of three hundred dollars ($300) or less.

(2) Immediately after removal of the recreational vehicle, the public agency which removed, or caused the removal of, the vehicle shall notify the Stolen Vehicle System of the Department of Justice in Sacramento of the removal.

(3) The public agency that removed, or caused the removal of, the recreational vehicle or, at the request of the public agency, the lienholder shall obtain a copy of the names and addresses of all persons having an interest in the recreational vehicle, if any, from the Department of Motor Vehicles either directly or by use of the California Law Enforcement Telecommunications System. This paragraph does not require the public agency or lienholder to obtain a copy of the actual record on file at the Department of Motor Vehicles.

(4) Within 48 hours of the removal, excluding weekends and holidays, the public agency that removed, or caused the removal of, the recreational vehicle or, at the request of the public agency, the lienholder shall send a notice to the registered and legal owners at their addresses of record with the Department of Motor Vehicles, and to any other person known to have an interest in the recreational vehicle. A notice sent by the public agency shall be sent by certified or first-class mail, and a notice sent by the lienholder shall be sent by certified mail. The notice shall include all of the following information:

(A) The name, address, and telephone number of the public agency providing the notice.

(B) The location of the place of storage and description of the recreational vehicle, which shall include, if available, the vehicle make, license plate number, vehicle identification number, and mileage.

(C) The authority and purpose for the removal of the recreational vehicle.

(D) A statement that the registered owner has up to 30 days from the date of notice to claim the recreational vehicle.

(E) A statement that the owners and interested persons, or their agents, have the opportunity for a poststorage hearing before the public agency that removed, or caused the removal of, the recreational vehicle to determine the validity of the storage if a request for a hearing is made in person, in writing, or by telephone within 10 days from the date of notice; that, if the owner or interested person, or their agent, disagrees with the decision of the public agency, the decision may be reviewed pursuant to Section 11523 of the Government Code; and that during the time of the initial hearing, or during the time the decision is being reviewed pursuant to Section 11523 of the Government Code, the recreational vehicle in question may not be disposed of.

(5) If the agency performing the removal is unable to collect the information necessary to identify the registered and legal owner of the recreational vehicle, including, but not limited to, the vehicle identification number, and is consequently unable to send the notice described in paragraph (4), the agency shall instead place and affix at least two copies of the notice within close geographic proximity to the removal location within 48 hours of the removal.

(6) (A) A requested hearing shall be conducted within 48 hours of the request, excluding weekends and holidays. The public agency that removed the recreational vehicle may authorize its own officers to conduct the hearing if the hearing officer is not the same person who directed the storage of the recreational vehicle.

(B) Failure of either the registered or legal owner or interested person, or their agent, to request or to attend a scheduled hearing shall satisfy the poststorage validity hearing requirement of this section.

(7) The public agency employing the person, or utilizing the services of a contractor or franchiser pursuant to subdivision (b) of Section 22669, that removed, or caused the removal of, the recreational vehicle and that directed any towing or storage, is responsible for the costs incurred for towing and storage if it is determined in the hearing that reasonable grounds to believe that the recreational vehicle was abandoned are not established.

(8) The public agency that removed, or caused the removal of, the recreational vehicle and that directed any towing and storage pursuant to subdivision (d) of Section 22669, is responsible for the costs incurred for towing and storage if it is determined in the hearing that the recreational vehicle was not inoperable or was not a hazard to public health, safety, and welfare.

(9) An authorization for disposal may not be issued by the public agency that removed, or caused the removal of, the recreational vehicle to a lienholder who is storing the recreational vehicle prior to the conclusion of a requested poststorage hearing or any judicial review of that hearing.

(10) (A) If, after 30 days from the notification date, the recreational vehicle remains unclaimed and the towing and storage fees have not been paid, and if no poststorage hearing was requested or a poststorage hearing was not attended, the public agency that removed, or caused the removal of, the recreational vehicle shall provide to the lienholder who is storing the recreational vehicle, on a form approved by the Department of Motor Vehicles, authorization to dispose of the recreational vehicle. Except as provided in subparagraph (B), the authorization to dispose of the recreational vehicle shall include a verification that the recreational vehicle is inoperable. The lienholder may request the public agency to provide the authorization to dispose of the recreational vehicle.

(B) If the recreational vehicle is operable, the public agency may authorize the disposal of the recreational vehicle only if it was towed due to it posing an environmental or public safety hazard.

(11) If the recreational vehicle is claimed by the owner or their agent within 30 days of the notice date, the lienholder who is storing the vehicle may collect reasonable fees for services rendered, but may not collect lien sale fees as provided in Section 22851.12.

(12) Disposal of the recreational vehicle by the lienholder who is storing the vehicle may only be to a licensed dismantler or scrap iron processor. A copy of the public agency's authorization for disposal shall be forwarded to the licensed dismantler within five days of disposal to a licensed dismantler. A copy of the public agency's authorization for disposal shall be retained by the lienholder who stored the recreational vehicle for a period of 90 days if the recreational vehicle is disposed of to a scrap iron processor.

(13) (A) If the names and addresses of the registered and legal owners of the recreational vehicle are not available from the records of the Department of Motor Vehicles, either directly or by use of the California Law Enforcement Telecommunications System, the public agency may issue to the lienholder who stored the recreational vehicle an authorization for disposal at any time after the removal.

(B) The lienholder may request the public agency to issue an authorization for disposal after the lienholder ascertains that the names and addresses of the registered and legal owners of the recreational vehicle are not available from the records of the Department of Motor Vehicles either directly or by use of the California Law Enforcement Telecommunications System.

(14) A recreational vehicle disposed of pursuant to this section may not be reconstructed or made operable, unless it is a vehicle that qualifies for either horseless carriage license plates or historical vehicle license plates, pursuant to Section 5004, in which case the vehicle may be reconstructed or made operable.

(15) Local public agencies authorized and designated to remove recreational vehicles pursuant to this section shall annually report to their governing body the following information regarding recreational vehicles removed pursuant to this section for the preceding year:

(A) The number of recreational vehicles removed.

(B) The number of people found in recreational vehicles prior to removal.

(C) The number of recreational vehicles that were operable.

(D) The number of recreational vehicles that were inoperable.

(c) For the purposes of this section, the following definitions apply:

(1) A "recreational vehicle" has the same meaning as defined in Section 18010 of the Health and Safety Code.

(2) A recreational vehicle is "inoperable" if it can only be moved by a tow truck.

(d) This section shall remain in effect only until January 1, 2030, and as of that date is repealed.

(Added by Stats. 2025, Ch. 699, Sec. 1. (AB 630) Effective January 1, 2026. Repealed as of January 1, 2030, by its own provisions.)

22851.6. (a) Lienholders who acquire a vehicle subject to Section 22851.2 shall satisfy their lien pursuant to Sections 22851.8 and 22851.10 if the vehicle has a value not exceeding five hundred dollars ($500), as determined pursuant to Section 22670.

(b) All forms required by Sections 22851.8 and 22851.10 shall be prescribed by the Department of Motor Vehicles. The language used in the notices and declarations shall be simple and nontechnical.

(Amended by Stats. 2004, Ch. 650, Sec. 14. Effective January 1, 2005.)

22851.8. (a) The lienholder shall, within 15 working days following the date of possession of the vehicle, make a request to the Department of Motor Vehicles for the names and addresses of all persons having an interest in the vehicle. A storage charge may not accrue beyond the 15-day period unless the lienholder has made a request to the Department of Motor Vehicles as provided for in this section.

(b) By certified mail with return receipt requested or by United States Postal Service Certificate of Mailing, the lienholder shall immediately, upon receipt of this information, send the following prescribed forms and enclosures to the registered owner and legal owner at their addresses of record with the Department of Motor Vehicles, and to any other person known to have an interest in the vehicle:

(1) A completed form entitled "Notice of Intent to Dispose of a Vehicle Valued at $500 or Less."

(2) A blank form entitled "Declaration of Opposition."

(3) A return envelope preaddressed to the lienholder.

(c) All notices to persons having an interest in the vehicle shall be signed under penalty of perjury and shall include all of the following:

(1) A description of the vehicle, including make, year, model, identification number, license number, and state of registration. For motorcycles, the engine number shall also be included.

(2) The names and addresses of the registered and legal owners of the vehicle and any other person known to have an interest in the vehicle.

(3) The following statements and information:

(A) The amount of the lien.

(B) The facts concerning the claim that gives rise to the lien.

(C) The person has a right to a hearing in court.

(D) If a hearing in court is desired, a Declaration of Opposition form shall be signed under penalty of perjury and returned to the lienholder within 10 days of the date the notice form specified in paragraph (1) of subdivision (b) was mailed.

(E) If the Declaration of Opposition form is signed and mailed, the lienholder shall be allowed to dispose of the vehicle only if the lienholder obtains a court judgment or a subsequent release from the declarant or if the declarant cannot be served as described in subdivision (e).

(F) If a court action is filed, the declarant shall be notified of the lawsuit at the address shown on the Declaration of Opposition form, and the declarant may appear to contest the claim.

(G) The declarant may be liable for court costs if a judgment is entered in favor of the lienholder.

(4) A statement that the lienholder may dispose of the vehicle to a licensed dismantler or scrap iron processor if it is not redeemed or if a Declaration of Opposition form is not signed and mailed to the lienholder within 10 days of the date the notice form specified in paragraph (1) of subdivision (b) was mailed.

(d) If the lienholder receives a completed Declaration of Opposition form within the time prescribed, the vehicle shall not be disposed of unless the lienholder files an action in court within 20 days of the date the notice form specified in paragraph (1) of subdivision (b) was mailed and a judgment is subsequently entered in favor of the lienholder or unless the declarant subsequently releases his or her interest in the vehicle. If a money judgment is entered in favor of the lienholder and the judgment is not paid within five days after becoming final, then the lienholder may dispose of the vehicle through a dismantler or scrap iron processor.

(e) (1) Service on the declarant in person or by certified mail, return receipt requested, signed by the addressee at the address shown on the Declaration of Opposition form, shall be effective for the serving of process.

(2) If the lienholder has served the declarant by certified mail, return receipt requested, at the address shown on the Declaration of Opposition form and the mail has been returned unclaimed, or if the lienholder has attempted to effect service on the declarant in person with a marshal, sheriff, or licensed process server and the marshal, sheriff, or licensed process server has been unable to effect service on the declarant, the lienholder may proceed with the judicial proceeding or proceed with the lien sale without a judicial proceeding. The lienholder shall notify the Department of Motor Vehicles of the inability to effect service on the declarant and shall provide the Department of Motor Vehicles with a copy of the documents with which service on the declarant was attempted. Upon receipt of the notification of unsuccessful service, the Department of Motor Vehicles shall send authorization of the sale to the lienholder and send notification of the authorization to the declarant. If service is effected on the declarant, the proof of service shall be submitted to the Department of Motor Vehicles with the documents specified in Section 22851.10.

(Amended by Stats. 2004, Ch. 650, Sec. 15. Effective January 1, 2005.)

22851.10. (a) A vehicle determined to have a value not exceeding five hundred dollars ($500) pursuant to Section 22670 that was stored pursuant to this chapter, and that remains unclaimed, or for which reasonable towing and storage charges remain unpaid, shall be disposed of only to a licensed dismantler or scrap iron processor not earlier than 15 days after the date the Notice of Intent to Dispose of a Vehicle Valued at $500 or Less form required pursuant to subdivision (b) of Section 22851.8 was mailed, unless a Declaration of Opposition form has been signed and returned to the lienholder.

(b) If the vehicle has been disposed of to a licensed dismantler or scrap iron processor, the lienholder shall forward the following forms and information to the licensed dismantler or scrap iron processor within five days:

(1) A statement, signed under penalty of perjury, that a properly executed Declaration of Opposition form was not received.

(2) A copy of the notice sent to all interested parties.

(3) A certification from the public agency that made the determination of value pursuant to Section 22670.

(4) The proof of service pursuant to subdivision (e) of Section 22851.8 or a copy of the court judgment, if any in favor of the lienholder entered pursuant to subdivision (d) of Section 22851.8.

(5) The name, address, and telephone number of the licensed dismantler or scrap iron processor who received the vehicle.

(6) The amount the lienholder received for the vehicle.

(c) A vehicle disposed of pursuant to this section shall not be reconstructed or made operable, unless it is a vehicle that qualifies for either horseless carriage license plates or historical vehicle license plates, pursuant to Section 5004, in which case the vehicle may be reconstructed or made operable.

(Amended by Stats. 2004, Ch. 650, Sec. 16. Effective January 1, 2005.)

22851.12. The lienholder may charge a fee for lien-sale preparations not to exceed seventy dollars ($70) in the case of a vehicle having a value determined to be four thousand dollars ($4,000) or less and not to exceed one hundred dollars ($100) in the case of a vehicle having a value determined to be greater than four thousand dollars ($4,000), from any person who redeems the vehicle prior to disposal or is sold through a lien sale pursuant to this chapter. These charges may commence and become part of the possessory lien when the lienholder requests the names and addresses of all persons having an interest in the vehicle from the department. Not more than 50 percent of the allowable fee may be charged until the lien sale notifications are mailed to all interested parties and the lienholder or the registration service agent has possession of the required lien processing documents. This charge shall not be made in the case of any vehicle redeemed prior to 72 hours from the initial storage.

(Amended by Stats. 1998, Ch. 203, Sec. 7. Effective January 1, 1999.)

22852. (a) Whenever an authorized member of a public agency directs the storage of a vehicle, as permitted by this chapter, or upon the storage of a vehicle as permitted under this section (except as provided in subdivision (f) or (g)), the agency or person directing the storage shall provide the vehicle's registered and legal owners of record, or their agents, with the opportunity for a poststorage hearing to determine the validity of the storage.

(b) A notice of the storage shall be mailed or personally delivered to the registered and legal owners within 48 hours, excluding weekends and holidays, and shall include all of the following information:

(1) The name, address, and telephone number of the agency providing the notice.

(2) The location of the place of storage and description of the vehicle, which shall include, if available, the name or make, the manufacturer, the license plate number, and the mileage.

(3) The authority and purpose for the removal of the vehicle.

(4) A statement that, in order to receive their poststorage hearing, the owners, or their agents, shall request the hearing in person, writing, or by telephone within 10 days of the date appearing on the notice.

(c) The poststorage hearing shall be conducted within 48 hours of the request, excluding weekends and holidays. The public agency may authorize its own officer or employee to conduct the hearing if the hearing officer is not the same person who directed the storage of the vehicle.

(d) Failure of either the registered or legal owner, or his or her agent, to request or to attend a scheduled hearing shall satisfy the poststorage hearing requirement.

(e) The agency employing the person who directed the storage shall be responsible for the costs incurred for towing and storage if it is determined in the poststorage hearing that reasonable grounds for the storage are not established.

(f) This section does not apply to vehicles abated under the Abandoned Vehicle Abatement Program pursuant to Sections 22660 to 22668, inclusive, and Section 22710, or to vehicles impounded for investigation pursuant to Section 22655, or to vehicles removed from private property pursuant to Section 22658.

(g) This section does not apply to abandoned vehicles removed pursuant to Section 22669 that are determined by the public agency to have an estimated value of five hundred dollars ($500) or less.

(Amended by Stats. 2004, Ch. 650, Sec. 17. Effective January 1, 2005.)

22852.5. (a) Whenever the possessory lien upon any vehicle is lost through trick, fraud, or device, the repossession of the vehicle by the lienholder revives the possessory lien, but any lien so revived is subordinate to any right, title, or interest of any person under any sale, transfer, encumbrance, lien, or other interest acquired or secured in good faith and for value between the time of the loss of possession and the time of repossession.

(b) It is a misdemeanor for any person to obtain possession of any vehicle or any part thereof subject to a lien pursuant to the provisions of this chapter by trick, fraud, or device.

(c) It is a misdemeanor for any person claiming a lien on a vehicle to knowingly violate any provision of this chapter.

(Added by Stats. 1980, Ch. 1111, Sec. 36.)

22853. (a) Whenever an officer or an employee removing a California registered vehicle from a highway or from public property for storage under this chapter does not know and is not able to ascertain the name of the owner or for any other reason is unable to give notice to the owner as required by Section 22852, the officer or employee shall immediately notify, or cause to be notified, the Department of Justice, Stolen Vehicle System, of its removal. The officer or employee shall file a notice with the proprietor of any public garage in which the vehicle may be stored. The notice shall include a complete description of the vehicle, the date, time, and place from which removed, the amount of mileage on the vehicle at the time of removal, and the name of the garage or place where the vehicle is stored.

(b) Whenever an officer or an employee removing a vehicle not registered in California from a highway or from public property for storage under this chapter does not know and is not able to ascertain the owner or for any other reason is unable to give the notice to the owner as required by Section 22852, the officer or employee shall immediately notify, or cause to be notified, the Department of Justice, Stolen Vehicle System. If the vehicle is not returned to the owner within 120 hours, the officer or employee shall immediately send, or cause to be sent, a written report of the removal by mail to the Department of Justice at Sacramento and shall file a copy of the notice with the proprietor of any public garage in which the vehicle may be stored. The report shall be made on a form furnished by that department and shall include a complete description of the vehicle, the date, time, and place from which the vehicle was removed, the amount of mileage on the vehicle at the time of removal, the grounds for removal, and the name of the garage or place where the vehicle is stored.

(c) Whenever an officer or employee or private party removing a vehicle from private property for storage under this chapter does not know and is not able to ascertain the name of the owner or for any other reason is unable to give the notice to the owner as required by Section 22852 and if the vehicle is not returned to the owner within a period of 120 hours, the officer or employee or private party shall immediately send, or cause to be sent, a written report of the removal by mail to the Department of Justice at Sacramento and shall file a copy of the notice with the proprietor of any public garage in which the vehicle may be stored. The report shall be made on a form furnished by that department and shall include a complete description of the vehicle, the date, time, and place from which the vehicle was removed, the amount of mileage on the vehicle at the time of removal, the grounds for removal, and the name of the garage or place where the vehicle is stored.

(Repealed and added by Stats. 1983, Ch. 913, Sec. 6.)

22854. The Department of Justice upon receiving notice under Section 22853 of the removal of a vehicle from a highway, or from public or private property, shall notify the registered and legal owner in writing at the addresses of such persons as shown by the records of the Department of Motor Vehicles, if the vehicle is registered in this state, of the removal of such vehicle, and give the name of the officer reporting such removal, the grounds upon which the removal was authorized and the location of the vehicle. If the vehicle is not registered in this state, the department shall make reasonable effort to notify the legal or registered owner of the removal and location of the vehicle. The notice to the registered or legal owner shall list the amount of mileage on the vehicle at the time of removal.

(Amended by Stats. 1975, Ch. 239.)

22854.5. Whenever an officer or employee of a public agency directs the storage of a vehicle under this chapter, the officer, employee, or agency directing that storage may notify the National Law Enforcement Telecommunication System by transmitting by any means available, including, but not limited to, electronic means, the vehicle identification number, the information listed in paragraphs (1), (2), and (3) of subdivision (b) of Section 22852, and the information described under Section 22853.

(Added by Stats. 2003, Ch. 622, Sec. 1. Effective January 1, 2004.)

22855. The following persons shall have the authority to make appraisals of the value of vehicles for purposes of this chapter, subject to the conditions stated in this chapter:

(a) Any peace officer of the Department of the California Highway Patrol designated by the commissioner.

(b) Any regularly employed and salaried deputy sheriff, any reserve deputy sheriff listed under Section 830.6 of the Penal Code, or any other employee designated by the sheriff of any county.

(c) Any regularly employed and salaried police officer, any reserve police officer listed under Section 830.6 of the Penal Code, or any other employee designated by the chief of police of any city.

(d) Any officer or employee of the Department of Motor Vehicles designated by the director of that department.

(e) Any regularly employed and salaried police officer, or reserve police officer, or other employee of the University of California Police Department designated by the chief of the department.

(f) Any regularly salaried employee of a city, county, or city and county designated by a board of supervisors or a city council pursuant to subdivision (a) of Section 22669.

(g) Any regularly employed and salaried police officer, or reserve police officer, or other employee of the police department of a California State University designated by the chief thereof.

(h) Any regularly employed and salaried security officer or other employee of a transit district security force designated by the chief thereof.

(i) Any regularly employed and salaried peace officer, or reserve peace officer, or other employee of the Department of Parks and Recreation designated by the director of that department.

(Amended by Stats. 2003, Ch. 292, Sec. 8. Effective January 1, 2004.)

22856. Notwithstanding any other provision of law, no cause of action for despoliation of evidence shall arise against any towing company that sells any vehicle at, or disposes of any vehicle after, a lien sale, unless the company knew, or should have known, that the vehicle will be needed as evidence in a legal action.

(Added by Stats. 1989, Ch. 457, Sec. 3.)

Chapter 11. Parking Lots

(Chapter 11 enacted by Stats. 1959, Ch. 3.)

22950. Any city having a population of over 2,000,000 inhabitants shall regulate offstreet parking facilities within its jurisdiction in a manner not inconsistent with any provisions of this chapter.

(Repealed and added by Stats. 1976, Ch. 802.)

22951. No operator of any offstreet parking facility shall park the vehicle of a patron of the facility in any street or alley.

(Added by renumbering Section 22518 by Stats. 1965, Ch. 1041.)

22952. Every person engaged in the operation of off-street parking facilities is guilty of a violation, who:

(a) Tows or removes or authorizes the towing and removal of any vehicle within 24 hours of the expiration of the period for which a particular fee is charged. This subdivision shall not affect or limit any parking lot operator from charging parking fees in accordance with his posted schedule for the additional time such vehicle is parked.

(b) Tows or removes or authorizes the towing and removal of any vehicle when such parking facilities are held open for public use and there was no attendant on duty or other facilities permitting the patron to pay or remit the parking charges at the time such vehicle was first parked. This subdivision shall not affect or limit any parking lot operator from charging parking fees in accordance with his posted schedule for the time such vehicle is parked.

(Amended by Stats. 1968, Ch. 1192.)

22953. (a) An owner or person in lawful possession of private property that is held open to the public, or a discernible portion thereof, for parking of vehicles at no fee, or an employee or agent thereof, shall not tow or remove, or cause the towing or removal, of a vehicle within one hour of the vehicle being parked.

(b) Notwithstanding subdivision (a), a vehicle may be removed immediately after being illegally parked within 15 feet of a fire hydrant, in a fire lane, in a manner that interferes with an entrance to, or an exit from, the private property, or in a parking space or stall legally designated for disabled persons.

(c) Subdivision (a) does not apply to property designated for parking at residential property, or to property designated for parking at a hotel or motel where the parking stalls or spaces are clearly marked for a specific room.

(d) It is the intent of the Legislature in the adoption of subdivision (a) to avoid causing the unnecessary stranding of motorists and placing them in dangerous situations, when traffic citations and other civil remedies are available, thereby promoting the safety of the general public.

(e) A person who violates subdivision (a) is civilly liable to the owner of the vehicle or his or her agent for two times the amount of the towing and storage charges.

(Amended by Stats. 2006, Ch. 609, Sec. 5. Effective January 1, 2007.)

Chapter 12. Public Offenses

(Chapter 12 enacted by Stats. 1959, Ch. 3.)

Article 1. Driving Offenses

(Heading of Article 1 added by Stats. 1981, Ch. 940, Sec. 9.)

23100. The provisions of this chapter apply to vehicles upon the highways and elsewhere throughout the State unless expressly provided otherwise.

(Enacted by Stats. 1959, Ch. 3.)

23103. (a) A person who drives a vehicle upon a highway in willful or wanton disregard for the safety of persons or property is guilty of reckless driving.

(b) A person who drives a vehicle in an offstreet parking facility, as defined in subdivision (c) of Section 12500, in willful or wanton disregard for the safety of persons or property is guilty of reckless driving.

(c) Except as otherwise provided in Section 40008, persons convicted of the offense of reckless driving shall be punished by imprisonment in a county jail for not less than five days nor more than 90 days or by a fine of not less than one hundred forty-five dollars ($145) nor more than one thousand dollars ($1,000), or by both that fine and imprisonment, except as provided in Section 23104 or 23105.

(Amended by Stats. 2010, Ch. 685, Sec. 2. (AB 2479) Effective January 1, 2011.)

23103.5. (a) If the prosecution agrees to a plea of guilty or nolo contendere to a charge of a violation of Section 23103 in satisfaction of, or as a substitute for, an original charge of a violation of Section 23152, the prosecution shall state for the record a factual basis for the satisfaction or substitution, including whether or not there had been consumption of an alcoholic beverage or ingestion or administration of a drug, or both, by the defendant in connection with the offense. The statement shall set forth the facts that show whether or not there was a consumption of an alcoholic beverage or the ingestion or administration of a drug by the defendant in connection with the offense.

(b) The court shall advise the defendant, prior to the acceptance of the plea offered pursuant to a factual statement pursuant to subdivision (a), of the consequences of a conviction of a violation of Section 23103 as set forth in subdivision (c).

(c) If the court accepts the defendant's plea of guilty or nolo contendere to a charge of a violation of Section 23103 and the prosecutor's statement under subdivision (a) states that there was consumption of an alcoholic beverage or the ingestion or administration of a drug by the defendant in connection with the offense, the resulting conviction shall be a prior offense for the purposes of Section 23540, 23546, 23550, 23560, 23566, or 23622, as specified in those sections.

(d) The court shall notify the Department of Motor Vehicles of each conviction of Section 23103 that is required under this section to be a prior offense for purposes of Section 23540, 23546, 23550, 23560, 23566, or 23622.

(e) Except as provided in paragraph (1) of subdivision (f), if the court places the defendant on probation for a conviction of Section 23103 that is required under this section to be a prior offense for purposes of Section 23540, 23546, 23550, 23560, 23566, or 23622, the court shall order the defendant to enroll in an alcohol and drug education program licensed under Chapter 9 (commencing with Section 11836) of Part 2 of Division 10.5 of the Health and Safety Code and complete, at a minimum, the educational component of that program, as a condition of probation. If compelling circumstances exist that mitigate against including the education component in the order, the court may make an affirmative finding to that effect. The court shall state the compelling circumstances and the affirmative finding on the record, and may, in these cases, exclude the educational component from the order.

(f) (1) If the court places on probation a defendant convicted of a violation of Section 23103 that is required under this section to be a prior offense for purposes of Section 23540, 23546, 23550, 23560, 23566, or 23622, and that offense occurred within 10 years of a separate conviction of a violation of Section 23103, as specified in this section, or within 10 years of a conviction of a violation of Section 23152 or 23153, the court shall order the defendant to participate for nine months or longer, as ordered by the court, in a program licensed under Chapter 9 (commencing with Section 11836) of Part 2 of Division 10.5 of the Health and Safety Code that consists of at least 60 hours of program activities, including education, group counseling, and individual interview sessions.

(2) The court shall revoke the person's probation, except for good cause shown, for the failure to enroll in, participate in, or complete a program specified in paragraph (1).

(g) Commencing January 1, 2019, the court may require a person convicted on or after January 1, 2019, of a violation of Section 23103, as described in this section, to install a functioning, certified ignition interlock device on any vehicle that the person operates and prohibit that person from operating a motor vehicle unless that vehicle is equipped with a functioning, certified ignition interlock device. If the court orders the ignition interlock device restriction, the term shall be determined by the court for a period of at least three months, but no longer than the term specified in Section 23575.3 that would have applied to the defendant had the defendant instead been convicted of a violation of Section 23152, from the date of conviction. The court shall notify the Department of Motor Vehicles, as specified in subdivision (a) of Section 1803, of the terms of the restrictions in accordance with subdivision (a) of Section 1804. The Department of Motor Vehicles shall place the restriction in the person's records in the Department of Motor Vehicles. A person who is required to install a functioning, certified ignition interlock device pursuant to this subdivision shall submit the "Verification of Installation" form described in paragraph (2) of subdivision (g) of Section 13386 and maintain the ignition interlock device as required under subdivision (f) of Section 23575.3. The department shall monitor the installation and maintenance of the ignition interlock device installed pursuant to this subdivision.

(h) The Department of Motor Vehicles shall include in its annual report to the Legislature under Section 1821 an evaluation of the effectiveness of the programs described in subdivisions (e) and (g) as to treating persons convicted of violating Section 23103.

(i) This section shall remain in effect only until January 1, 2033, and as of that date is repealed, unless a later enacted statute, that is enacted before January 1, 2033, deletes or extends that date.

(Amended (as amended by Stats. 2016, Ch. 783, Sec. 24) by Stats. 2025, Ch. 689, Sec. 18. (AB 366) Effective January 1, 2026. Repealed as of January 1, 2033, by its own provisions. See later operative version, as amended by Sec. 19 of Stats. 2025, Ch. 689.)

23103.5. (a) If the prosecution agrees to a plea of guilty or nolo contendere to a charge of a violation of Section 23103 in satisfaction of, or as a substitute for, an original charge of a violation of Section 23152, the prosecution shall state for the record a factual basis for the satisfaction or substitution, including whether or not there had been consumption of an alcoholic beverage or ingestion or administration of a drug, or both, by the defendant in connection with the offense. The statement shall set forth the facts that show whether or not there was a consumption of an alcoholic beverage or the ingestion or administration of a drug by the defendant in connection with the offense.

(b) The court shall advise the defendant, prior to the acceptance of the plea offered pursuant to a factual statement pursuant to subdivision (a), of the consequences of a conviction of a violation of Section 23103 as set forth in subdivision (c).

(c) If the court accepts the defendant's plea of guilty or nolo contendere to a charge of a violation of Section 23103 and the prosecutor's statement under subdivision (a) states that there was consumption of an alcoholic beverage or the ingestion or administration of a drug by the defendant in connection with the offense, the resulting conviction shall be a prior offense for the purposes of Section 23540, 23546, 23550, 23560, 23566, or 23622, as specified in those sections.

(d) The court shall notify the Department of Motor Vehicles of each conviction of Section 23103 that is required under this section to be a prior offense for purposes of Section 23540, 23546, 23550, 23560, 23566, or 23622.

(e) Except as provided in paragraph (1) of subdivision (f), if the court places the defendant on probation for a conviction of Section 23103 that is required under this section to be a prior offense for purposes of Section 23540, 23546, 23550, 23560, 23566, or 23622, the court shall order the defendant to enroll in an alcohol and drug education program licensed under Chapter 9 (commencing with Section 11836) of Part 2 of Division 10.5 of the Health and Safety Code and complete, at a minimum, the educational component of that program, as a condition of probation. If compelling circumstances exist that mitigate against including the education component in the order, the court may make an affirmative finding to that effect. The court shall state the compelling circumstances and the affirmative finding on the record, and may, in these cases, exclude the educational component from the order.

(f) (1) If the court places on probation a defendant convicted of a violation of Section 23103 that is required under this section to be a prior offense for purposes of Section 23540, 23546, 23550, 23560, 23566, or 23622, and that offense occurred within 10 years of a separate conviction of a violation of Section 23103, as specified in this section, or within 10 years of a conviction of a violation of Section 23152 or 23153, the court shall order the defendant to participate for nine months or longer, as ordered by the court, in a program licensed under Chapter 9 (commencing with Section 11836) of Part 2 of Division 10.5 of the Health and Safety Code that consists of at least 60 hours of program activities, including education, group counseling, and individual interview sessions.

(2) The court shall revoke the person's probation, except for good cause shown, for the failure to enroll in, participate in, or complete a program specified in paragraph (1).

(g) The Department of Motor Vehicles shall include in its annual report to the Legislature under Section 1821 an evaluation of the effectiveness of the programs described in subdivisions (e) and (f) as to treating persons convicted of violating Section 23103.

(h) This section shall become operative January 1, 2033.

(Amended (as added by Stats. 2016, Ch. 783, Sec. 25) by Stats. 2025, Ch. 689, Sec. 19. (AB 366) Effective January 1, 2026. Section operative January 1, 2033, by its own provisions.)

23104. (a) Except as provided in subdivision (b), whenever reckless driving of a vehicle proximately causes bodily injury to a person other than the driver, the person driving the vehicle shall, upon conviction thereof, be punished by imprisonment in the county jail for not less than 30 days nor more than six months or by a fine of not less than two hundred twenty dollars ($220) nor more than one thousand dollars ($1,000), or by both the fine and imprisonment.

(b) A person convicted of reckless driving that proximately causes great bodily injury, as defined in Section 12022.7 of the Penal Code, to a person other than the driver, who previously has been convicted of a violation of Section 23103, 23104, 23105, 23109, 23109.1, 23152, or 23153, shall be punished by imprisonment pursuant to subdivision (h) of Section 1170 of the Penal Code, by imprisonment in the county jail for not less than 30 days nor more than six months or by a fine of not less than two hundred twenty dollars ($220) nor more than one thousand dollars ($1,000) or by both the fine and imprisonment.

(Amended by Stats. 2011, Ch. 15, Sec. 609. (AB 109) Effective April 4, 2011. Operative October 1, 2011, by Sec. 636 of Ch. 15, as amended by Stats. 2011, Ch. 39, Sec. 68.)

23105. (a) A person convicted of reckless driving in violation of Section 23103 that proximately causes one or more of the injuries specified in subdivision (b) to a person other than the driver, shall be punished by imprisonment pursuant to subdivision (h) of Section 1170 of the Penal Code, or by imprisonment in a county jail for not less than 30 days nor more than six months, or by a fine of not less than two hundred twenty dollars ($220) nor more than one thousand dollars ($1,000), or by both that fine and imprisonment.

(b) This section applies to all of the following injuries:

(1) A loss of consciousness.

(2) A concussion.

(3) A bone fracture.

(4) A protracted loss or impairment of function of a bodily member or organ.

(5) A wound requiring extensive suturing.

(6) A serious disfigurement.

(7) Brain injury.

(8) Paralysis.

(c) This section does not preclude or prohibit prosecution under any other provision of law.

(Amended by Stats. 2011, Ch. 15, Sec. 610. (AB 109) Effective April 4, 2011. Operative October 1, 2011, by Sec. 636 of Ch. 15, as amended by Stats. 2011, Ch. 39, Sec. 68.)

23109. (a) A person shall not engage in a motor vehicle speed contest on a highway or in an offstreet parking facility. As used in this section, a motor vehicle speed contest includes a motor vehicle race against another vehicle, a clock, or other timing device. For purposes of this section, an event in which the time to cover a prescribed route of more than 20 miles is measured, but in which the vehicle does not exceed the speed limit, is not a speed contest.

(b) A person shall not aid or abet in a motor vehicle speed contest on a highway or in an offstreet parking facility.

(c) A person shall not engage in a motor vehicle exhibition of speed on a highway or in an offstreet parking facility, and a person shall not aid or abet in a motor vehicle exhibition of speed on a highway or in an offstreet parking facility.

(d) A person shall not, for the purpose of facilitating or aiding or as an incident to a motor vehicle speed contest or exhibition upon a highway or in an offstreet parking facility, in any manner obstruct or place a barricade or obstruction or assist or participate in placing a barricade or obstruction upon a highway or in an offstreet parking facility.

(e) (1) A person convicted of a violation of subdivision (a) shall be punished by imprisonment in a county jail for not less than 24 hours nor more than 90 days or by a fine of not less than three hundred fifty-five dollars ($355) nor more than one thousand dollars ($1,000), or by both that fine and imprisonment. That person shall also be required to perform 40 hours of community service. The court may order the privilege to operate a motor vehicle suspended for 90 days to six months, as provided in paragraph (8) of subdivision (a) of Section 13352. The person's privilege to operate a motor vehicle may be restricted for 90 days to six months to necessary travel to and from that person's place of employment and, if driving a motor vehicle is necessary to perform the duties of the person's employment, restricted to driving in that person's scope of employment. This subdivision does not interfere with the court's power to grant probation in a suitable case.

(2) If a person is convicted of a violation of subdivision (a) and that violation proximately causes bodily injury to a person other than the driver, the person convicted shall be punished by imprisonment in a county jail for not less than 30 days nor more than six months or by a fine of not less than five hundred dollars ($500) nor more than one thousand dollars ($1,000), or by both that fine and imprisonment.

(f) (1) If a person is convicted of a violation of subdivision (a) for an offense that occurred within five years of the date of a prior offense that resulted in a conviction of a violation of subdivision (a), that person shall be punished by imprisonment in a county jail for not less than four days nor more than six months and by a fine of not less than five hundred dollars ($500) nor more than one thousand dollars ($1,000).

(2) If the perpetration of the most recent offense within the five-year period described in paragraph (1) proximately causes bodily injury to a person other than the driver, a person convicted of that second violation shall be imprisoned in a county jail for not less than 30 days nor more than six months and by a fine of not less than five hundred dollars ($500) nor more than one thousand dollars ($1,000).

(3) If the perpetration of the most recent offense within the five-year period described in paragraph (1) proximately causes serious bodily injury, as defined in paragraph (4) of subdivision (f) of Section 243 of the Penal Code, to a person other than the driver, a person convicted of that second violation shall be imprisoned in the state prison, or in a county jail for not less than 30 days nor more than one year, and by a fine of not less than five hundred dollars ($500) nor more than one thousand dollars ($1,000).

(4) The court shall order the privilege to operate a motor vehicle of a person convicted under paragraph (1), (2), or (3) suspended for a period of six months, as provided in paragraph (9) of subdivision (a) of Section 13352. In lieu of the suspension, the person's privilege to operate a motor vehicle may be restricted for six months to necessary travel to and from that person's place of employment and, if driving a motor vehicle is necessary to perform the duties of the person's employment, restricted to driving in that person's scope of employment.

(5) This subdivision does not interfere with the court's power to grant probation in a suitable case.

(g) If the court grants probation to a person subject to punishment under subdivision (f), in addition to subdivision (f) and any other terms and conditions imposed by the court, which may include a fine, the court shall impose as a condition of probation that the person be confined in a county jail for not less than 48 hours nor more than six months. The court shall order the person's privilege to operate a motor vehicle to be suspended for a period of six months, as provided in paragraph (9) of subdivision (a) of Section 13352 or restricted pursuant to subdivision (f).

(h) If a person is convicted of a violation of subdivision (a) and the vehicle used in the violation is registered to that person, the vehicle may be impounded at the registered owner's expense for not less than 1 day nor more than 30 days.

(i) (1) A person who violates subdivision (b), (c), or (d) shall upon conviction of that violation be punished by imprisonment in a county jail for not more than 90 days, by a fine of not more than five hundred dollars ($500), or by both that fine and imprisonment.

(2) (A) (i) Commencing January 1, 2029, the court may order the privilege to operate a motor vehicle suspended for 90 days to six months for a person who violates subdivision (c), as provided in subparagraph (B) of paragraph (8) of subdivision (a) of Section 13352, only if the violation occurred as part of a sideshow.

(ii) For purposes of this section, "sideshow" is defined as an event in which two or more persons block or impede traffic on a highway or in an offstreet parking facility for the purpose of performing motor vehicle stunts, motor vehicle speed contests, motor vehicle exhibitions of speed, or reckless driving, for spectators. A sideshow is also known as a street takeover.

(B) A person's privilege to operate a motor vehicle may be restricted for 90 days to six months to necessary travel to and from that person's place of employment and, if driving a motor vehicle is necessary to perform the duties of the person's employment, restricted to driving in that person's scope of employment.

(C) If the court is considering suspending or restricting the privilege to operate a motor vehicle pursuant to this paragraph, the court shall also consider whether a medical, personal, or family hardship exists that requires a person to have a driver's license for such limited purpose as the court deems necessary to address the hardship. This subdivision does not interfere with the court's power to grant probation in a suitable case.

(j) If a person's privilege to operate a motor vehicle is restricted by a court pursuant to this section, the court shall clearly mark the restriction and the dates of the restriction on that person's driver's license and promptly notify the Department of Motor Vehicles of the terms of the restriction in a manner prescribed by the department. The Department of Motor Vehicles shall place that restriction in the person's records in the Department of Motor Vehicles and enter the restriction on a license subsequently issued by the Department of Motor Vehicles to that person during the period of the restriction.

(k) The court may order that a person convicted under this section, who is to be punished by imprisonment in a county jail, be imprisoned on days other than days of regular employment of the person, as determined by the court.

(l) For purposes of this section, "offstreet parking facility" has the same meaning as in subdivision (c) of Section 12500.

(m) This section shall be known and may be cited as the Louis Friend Memorial Act.

(Amended by Stats. 2025, Ch. 16, Sec. 9. (SB 128) Effective June 27, 2025.)

23109.1. (a) A person convicted of engaging in a motor vehicle speed contest in violation of subdivision (a) of Section 23109 that proximately causes one or more of the injuries specified in subdivision (b) to a person other than the driver, shall be punished by imprisonment pursuant to subdivision (h) of Section 1170 of the Penal Code, or by imprisonment in a county jail for not less than 30 days nor more than six months, or by a fine of not less than five hundred dollars ($500) nor more than one thousand dollars ($1,000), or by both that fine and imprisonment.

(b) This section applies to all of the following injuries:

(1) A loss of consciousness.

(2) A concussion.

(3) A bone fracture.

(4) A protracted loss or impairment of function of a bodily member or organ.

(5) A wound requiring extensive suturing.

(6) A serious disfigurement.

(7) Brain injury.

(8) Paralysis.

(c) This section does not preclude or prohibit prosecution under any other provision of law.

(Amended by Stats. 2011, Ch. 15, Sec. 612. (AB 109) Effective April 4, 2011. Operative October 1, 2011, by Sec. 636 of Ch. 15, as amended by Stats. 2011, Ch. 39, Sec. 68.)

23109.2. (a) (1) Whenever a peace officer determines that a person was engaged in an activity set forth in paragraph (2), the peace officer may immediately arrest and take into custody that person and may cause the removal and seizure of the motor vehicle used in that offense pursuant to Chapter 10 (commencing with Section 22650). A motor vehicle that is seized may be impounded for not more than 30 days.

(2) (A) A motor vehicle speed contest, as described in subdivision (a) of Section 23109.

(B) Reckless driving on a highway, as described in subdivision (a) of Section 23103.

(C) Reckless driving in an offstreet parking facility, as described in subdivision (b) of Section 23103.

(D) (i) Exhibition of speed on a highway or in an offstreet parking facility, as described in subdivision (c) of Section 23109.

(ii) This subparagraph does not apply to aiding or abetting an exhibition of speed on any highway or in an offstreet parking facility.

(b) The registered and legal owner of a vehicle removed and seized under subdivision (a) or their agents shall be provided the opportunity for a storage hearing to determine the validity of the storage in accordance with Section 22852.

(c) (1) Notwithstanding Chapter 10 (commencing with Section 22650) or any other law, an impounding agency shall release a motor vehicle to the registered owner or their agent prior to the conclusion of the impoundment period described in subdivision (a) under any of the following circumstances:

(A) If the vehicle is a stolen vehicle.

(B) If the person alleged to have been engaged in the motor vehicle speed contest, as described in subdivision (a), was not authorized by the registered owner of the motor vehicle to operate the motor vehicle at the time of the commission of the offense.

(C) If the registered owner of the vehicle was neither the driver nor a passenger of the vehicle at the time of the alleged violation pursuant to subdivision (a), or was unaware that the driver was using the vehicle to engage in an activity described in subdivision (a).

(D) If the legal owner or registered owner of the vehicle is a rental car agency.

(E) If, prior to the conclusion of the impoundment period, a citation or notice is dismissed under Section 40500, criminal charges are not filed by the district attorney because of a lack of evidence, or the charges are otherwise dismissed by the court.

(2) A vehicle shall be released pursuant to this subdivision only if the registered owner or their agent presents a currently valid driver's license to operate the vehicle and proof of current vehicle registration, or if ordered by a court.

(3) If, pursuant to subparagraph (E) of paragraph (1), a motor vehicle is released prior to the conclusion of the impoundment period, neither the person charged with a violation of subdivision (a) of Section 23109 nor the registered owner of the motor vehicle is responsible for towing and storage charges nor shall the motor vehicle be sold to satisfy those charges.

(d) A vehicle seized and removed under subdivision (a) shall be released to the legal owner of the vehicle, or the legal owner's agent, on or before the 30th day of impoundment if all of the following conditions are met:

(1) The legal owner is a motor vehicle dealer, bank, credit union, acceptance corporation, or other licensed financial institution legally operating in this state, or is another person, not the registered owner, holding a security interest in the vehicle.

(2) The legal owner or the legal owner's agent pays all towing and storage fees related to the impoundment of the vehicle. Lien sale processing fees shall not be charged to a legal owner who redeems the vehicle on or before the 15th day of impoundment.

(3) The legal owner or the legal owner's agent presents foreclosure documents or an affidavit of repossession for the vehicle.

(e) (1) The registered owner or the registered owner's agent is responsible for all towing and storage charges related to the impoundment, and any administrative charges authorized under Section 22850.5.

(2) Notwithstanding paragraph (1), if the person convicted of engaging in the activities set forth in paragraph (2) of subdivision (a) was not authorized by the registered owner of the motor vehicle to operate the motor vehicle at the time of the commission of the offense, the court shall order the convicted person to reimburse the registered owner for any towing and storage charges related to the impoundment, and any administrative charges authorized under Section 22850.5 incurred by the registered owner to obtain possession of the vehicle, unless the court finds that the person convicted does not have the ability to pay all or part of those charges.

(3) If the vehicle is a rental vehicle, the rental car agency may require the person to whom the vehicle was rented to pay all towing and storage charges related to the impoundment and any administrative charges

authorized under Section 22850.5 incurred by the rental car agency in connection with obtaining possession of the vehicle.

(4) The owner is not liable for any towing and storage charges related to the impoundment if acquittal or dismissal occurs.

(5) The vehicle may not be sold prior to the defendant's conviction.

(6) The impounding agency is responsible for the actual costs incurred by the towing agency as a result of the impoundment should the registered owner be absolved of liability for those charges pursuant to paragraph (3) of subdivision (c). Notwithstanding this provision, an impounding agency is not prohibited from making prior payment arrangements to satisfy this requirement.

(f) A period when a vehicle is subjected to storage under this section shall be included as part of the period of impoundment ordered by the court under subdivision (h) of Section 23109.

(Amended by Stats. 2024, Ch. 502, Sec. 1. (AB 2186) Effective January 1, 2025.)

23109.3. If a peace officer arrests a person for a violation of subdivision (d) of Section 23109 and causes the removal and seizure of the vehicle used to commit the violation pursuant to paragraph (1) of subdivision (h) of Section 22651, the peace officer shall not be required to take the person into custody.

(Added by Stats. 2024, Ch. 501, Sec. 2. (AB 1978) Effective January 1, 2025.)

23109.5. (a) In any case charging a violation of subdivision (a) of Section 23109 and where the offense occurs within five years of one or more prior offenses which resulted in conviction of violation of subdivision (a) of Section 23109, the court shall not strike any prior conviction of those offenses for purposes of sentencing in order to avoid imposing, as part of the sentence or term of probation, the minimum time of imprisonment, as provided in subdivision (f) of Section 23109, or for purposes of avoiding revocation, suspension, or restriction of the privilege to operate a motor vehicle, as provided in Section 13352 or 23109.

(b) In any case charging a violation of subdivision (a) of Section 23109, the court shall obtain a copy of the driving record of the person charged from the Department of Motor Vehicles and may obtain any records from the Department of Justice or any other source to determine if one or more prior convictions of the person for violation of subdivision (a) of Section 23109 have occurred within five years of the charged offense.

(Added by Stats. 1983, Ch. 953, Sec. 3.)

23110. (a) Any person who throws any substance at a vehicle or any occupant thereof on a highway is guilty of a misdemeanor.

(b) Any person who with intent to do great bodily injury maliciously and willfully throws or projects any rock, brick, bottle, metal or other missile, or projects any other substance capable of doing serious bodily harm at such vehicle or occupant thereof is guilty of a felony and upon conviction shall be punished by imprisonment in the state prison.

(Amended (as amended by Stats. 2011, Ch. 15, Sec. 613) by Stats. 2011, Ch. 39, Sec. 65. (AB 117) Effective June 30, 2011. Operative October 1, 2011, pursuant to Secs. 68 and 69 of Ch. 39.)

23111. No person in any vehicle and no pedestrian shall throw or discharge from or upon any road or highway or adjoining area, public or private, any lighted or nonlighted cigarette, cigar, match, or any flaming or glowing substance. This section shall be known as the Paul Buzzo Act.

(Amended by Stats. 1970, Ch. 1548.)

23112. (a) No person shall throw or deposit, nor shall the registered owner or the driver, if such owner is not then present in the vehicle, aid or abet in the throwing or depositing upon any highway any bottle, can, garbage, glass, nail, offal, paper, wire, any substance likely to injure or damage traffic using the highway, or any noisome, nauseous, or offensive matter of any kind.

(b) No person shall place, deposit, or dump, or cause to be placed, deposited, or dumped, any rocks, refuse, garbage, or dirt in or upon any highway, including any portion of the right-of-way thereof, without the consent of the state or local agency having jurisdiction over the highway.

(Amended by Stats. 1980, Ch. 74, Sec. 4.)

23112.5. (a) Any person who dumps, spills, or causes the release of hazardous material, as defined by Section 353, or hazardous waste, as defined by Section 25117 of the Health and Safety Code, upon any highway shall notify the Department of the California Highway Patrol or the agency having traffic jurisdiction for that highway of the dump, spill, or release, as soon as the person has knowledge of the dump, spill, or release and notification is possible. Upon receiving notification pursuant to this section, the Department of the California Highway Patrol shall, as soon as possible, notify the Office of Emergency Services of the dump, spill, or release, except for petroleum spills of less than 42 gallons from vehicular fuel tanks.

(b) Any person who is convicted of a violation of this section shall be punished by a mandatory fine of not less than two thousand dollars ($2,000).

(Amended by Stats. 2013, Ch. 352, Sec. 525. (AB 1317) Effective September 26, 2013. Operative July 1, 2013, by Sec. 543 of Ch. 352.)

23112.7. (a) (1) A motor vehicle used for illegal dumping of waste matter on public or private property is subject to impoundment pursuant to subdivision (c).

(2) A motor vehicle used for illegal dumping of harmful waste matter on public or private property is subject to impoundment and civil forfeiture pursuant to subdivision (d).

(b) For the purposes of this section, the following terms have the following meanings:

(1) "Illegal dumping" means the willful or intentional depositing, dropping, dumping, placing, or throwing of any waste matter onto public or private property that is not expressly designated for the purpose of disposal of waste matter. "Illegal dumping" does not include the discarding of small quantities of waste matter related to consumer goods and that are reasonably understood to be ordinarily carried on or about the body of a living person, including, but not limited to, beverage containers and closures, packaging, wrappers, wastepaper, newspaper, magazines, or other similar waste matter that escapes or is allowed to escape from a container, receptacle, or package.

(2) "Waste matter" means any form of tangible matter described by any of the following:

(A) All forms of garbage, refuse, rubbish, recyclable materials, and solid waste.

(B) Dirt, soil, rock, decomposed rock, gravel, sand, or other aggregate material dumped or deposited as refuse.

(C) Abandoned or discarded furniture; or commercial, industrial, or agricultural machinery, apparatus, structure, or other container; or a piece, portion, or part of these items.

(D) All forms of liquid waste not otherwise defined in or deemed to fall within the purview of Section 25117 of the Health and Safety Code, including, but not limited to, water-based or oil-based paints, chemical solutions, water contaminated with any substance rendering it unusable for irrigation or construction, oils, fuels, and other petroleum distillates or byproducts.

(E) Any form of biological waste not otherwise designated by law as hazardous waste, including, but not limited to, body parts, carcasses, and any associated container, enclosure, or wrapping material used to dispose these matters.

(F) A physical substance used as an ingredient in any process, now known or hereafter developed or devised, to manufacture a controlled substance specified in Section 11054, 11055, 11056, 11057, or 11058 of the Health and Safety Code, or that is a byproduct or result of the manufacturing process of the controlled substance.

(3) "Harmful waste matter" is a hazardous substance as defined in Section 374.8 of the Penal Code; a hazardous waste as defined in Section 25117 of the Health and Safety Code; waste that, pursuant to Division 30 (commencing with Section 40000) of the Public Resources Code, cannot be disposed in a municipal solid waste landfill without special handling, processing, or treatment; or waste matter in excess of one cubic yard.

(c) (1) Whenever a person, who has one or more prior convictions of Section 374.3 or 374.8 of the Penal Code that are not infractions, is convicted of a misdemeanor violation of Section 374.3 of the Penal Code, or of a violation of Section 374.8 of the Penal Code, for illegally dumping waste matter or harmful waste matter that is committed while driving a motor vehicle of which he or she is the registered owner of the vehicle, or is the registered owner's agent or employee, the court at the time of sentencing may order the motor vehicle impounded for a period of not more than six months.

(2) In determining the impoundment period imposed pursuant to paragraph (1), the court shall consider both of the following factors:

(A) The size and nature of the waste matter dumped.

(B) Whether the dumping occurred for a business purpose.

(3) The cost of keeping the vehicle is a lien on the vehicle pursuant to Chapter 6.5 (commencing with Section 3067) of Title 14 of Part 4 of Division 3 of the Civil Code.

(4) Notwithstanding paragraph (1), a vehicle impounded pursuant to this subdivision shall be released to the legal owner or his or her agent pursuant to subdivision (b) of Section 23592.

(5) The impounding agency shall not be liable to the registered owner for the release of the vehicle to the legal owner or his or her agent when made in compliance with paragraph (4).

(6) This subdivision does not apply if there is a community property interest in the vehicle that is owned by a person other than the defendant and the vehicle is the only vehicle available to the defendant's immediate family that may be operated on the highway with a class A, class B, or class C driver's license.

(d) (1) Notwithstanding Section 86 of the Code of Civil Procedure and any other provision of law otherwise prescribing the jurisdiction of the court based upon the value of the property involved, whenever a person, who has two or more prior convictions of Section 374.3 or 374.8 of the Penal Code that are not infractions, is charged with a misdemeanor violation of Section 374.3 of the Penal Code, or of a violation of Section 374.8 of the Penal Code, for illegally dumping harmful waste matter, the court with jurisdiction over the offense may, upon a motion of the prosecutor or the county counsel in a criminal action, declare a motor vehicle if used by the defendant in the commission of the violation, to be a nuisance, and upon conviction order the vehicle sold pursuant to Section 23596, if the person is the registered owner of the vehicle or the registered owner's employee or agent.

(2) The proceeds of the sale of the vehicle pursuant to this subdivision shall be distributed and used in decreasing order of priority, as follows:

(A) To satisfy all costs of the sale, including costs incurred with respect to the taking and keeping of the vehicle pending sale.

(B) To the legal owner in an amount to satisfy the indebtedness owed to the legal owner remaining as of the date of the sale, including accrued interest or finance charges and delinquency charges.

(C) To recover the costs made, incurred, or associated with the enforcement of this section, the abatement of waste matter, and the deterrence of illegal dumping.

(3) A vehicle shall not be sold pursuant to this subdivision in either of the following circumstances:

(A) The vehicle is owned by the employer or principal of the defendant and the use of the vehicle was made without the employer's or principal's knowledge and consent, and did not provide a direct benefit to the employer's or principal's business.

(B) There is a community property interest in the vehicle that is owned by a person other than the defendant and the vehicle is the only vehicle available to the defendant's immediate family that may be operated on the highway with a class A, class B, or class C driver's license.

(Added by Stats. 2006, Ch. 765, Sec. 1. Effective January 1, 2007.)

23113. (a) Any person who drops, dumps, deposits, places, or throws, or causes or permits to be dropped, dumped, deposited, placed, or thrown, upon any highway or street any material described in Section 23112 or in subdivision (d) of Section 23114 shall immediately remove the material or cause the material to be removed.

(b) If the person fails to comply with subdivision (a), the governmental agency responsible for the maintenance of the street or highway on which the material has been deposited may remove the material and collect, by civil action, if necessary, the actual cost of the removal operation in addition to any other damages authorized by law from the person made responsible under subdivision (a).

(c) A member of the Department of the California Highway Patrol may direct a responsible party to remove the aggregate material described in subdivision (d) of Section 23114 from a highway when that material has escaped or been released from a vehicle.

(d) Notwithstanding any other provision of law, a government agency described in subdivision (b), the Department of the California Highway Patrol, or the employees or officers of those agencies, may not be held liable for any damage to material, to cargo, or to personal property caused by a negligent act or omission of the employee or officer when the employee or officer is acting within the scope and purpose of subdivision (b) or (c). Nothing in this subdivision affects liability for purposes of establishing gross negligence or willful misconduct. This subdivision applies to the negligent performance of a ministerial act, and does not affect liability under any provision of law, including liability, if any, derived from the failure to preserve evidence in a civil or criminal action.

(Amended by Stats. 1999, Ch. 421, Sec. 2. Effective January 1, 2000.)

23114. (a) Except as provided in Subpart I (commencing with Section 393.100) of Title 49 of the Code of Federal Regulations related to hay and straw, a vehicle shall not be driven or moved on any highway unless the vehicle is so constructed, covered, or loaded as to prevent any of its contents or load other than clear water or feathers from live birds from dropping, sifting, leaking, blowing, spilling, or otherwise escaping from the vehicle.

(b) (1) Aggregate material shall only be carried in the cargo area of a vehicle. The cargo area shall not contain any holes, cracks, or openings through which that material may escape, regardless of the degree to which the vehicle is loaded, except as provided in paragraph (2).

(2) Every vehicle used to transport aggregate materials, regardless of the degree to which the vehicle is loaded, shall be equipped with all of the following:

(A) Properly functioning seals on any openings used to empty the load, including, but not limited to, bottom dump release gates and tailgates.

(B) Splash flaps behind every tire, or set of tires, regardless of the position on the truck, truck tractor, or trailer.

(C) Center flaps at a location to the rear of each bottom dump release gate as to trucks or trailers equipped with bottom dump release gates. The center flap may be positioned directly behind the bottom dump release gate and in front of the rear axle of the vehicle, or it may be positioned to the rear of the rear axle in line with the splash flaps required behind the tires. The width of the center flap may extend not more than one inch from one sidewall to the opposite sidewall of the inside tires and shall extend to within five inches of the pavement surface, and may be not less than 24 inches from the bottom edge to the top edge of that center flap.

(D) Fenders starting at the splash flap with the leading edge of the fenders extending forward at least six inches beyond the center of the axle that cover the tops of tires not already covered by the truck, truck tractor, or trailer body.

(E) Complete enclosures on all vertical sides of the cargo area, including, but not limited to, tailgates.

(F) Shed boards designed to prevent aggregate materials from being deposited on the vehicle body during top loading.

(c) Vehicles comprised of full rigid enclosures are exempt only from subparagraphs (C) and (F) of paragraph (2) of subdivision (b).

(d) For purposes of this section, "aggregate material" means rock fragments, pebbles, sand, dirt, gravel, cobbles, crushed base, asphalt, and other similar materials.

(e) (1) In addition to subdivisions (a) and (b), a vehicle may not transport any aggregate material upon a highway unless the material is covered.

(2) Vehicles transporting loads composed entirely of asphalt material are exempt only from the provisions of this section requiring that loads be covered.

(3) Vehicles transporting loads composed entirely of petroleum coke material are not required to cover their loads if they are loaded using safety procedures, specialized equipment, and a chemical surfactant designed to prevent materials from blowing, spilling, or otherwise escaping from the vehicle.

(4) Vehicles transporting loads of aggregate materials are not required to cover their loads if the load, where it contacts the sides, front, and back of the cargo container area, remains six inches from the upper edge of the container area, and if the load does not extend, at its peak, above any part of the upper edge of the cargo container area.

(f) A person who provides a location for vehicles to be loaded with an aggregate material or other material shall provide a location for vehicle operators to comply with this section before entering a highway.

(1) A person is exempt from the requirements of this subdivision if the location that he or she provides for vehicles to be loaded with the materials described in this subdivision has 100 yards or less between the scale houses where the trucks carrying aggregate material are weighed and the point of egress to a public road.

(2) A driver of a vehicle loaded with aggregate material leaving locations exempted from the requirements of this subdivision is authorized to operate on public roads only until that driver is able to safely cover the load at a site near the location's point of egress to the public road. Except as provided under paragraph (4) of subdivision (e), an uncovered vehicle described in this paragraph may not operate more than 200 yards from the point of egress to the public road.

(Amended by Stats. 2008, Ch. 250, Sec. 1. Effective January 1, 2009.)

23115. (a) No vehicle transporting garbage, swill, used cans or bottles, wastepapers, waste cardboard, ashes, refuse, trash, or rubbish, or any noisome, nauseous, or offensive matter, or anything being transported for disposal or recycling shall be driven or moved upon any highway unless the load is totally covered in a manner that will prevent the load or any part of the load from spilling or falling from the vehicle.

(b) Subdivision (a) does not prohibit a rubbish vehicle from being without cover while in the process of acquiring its load if no law, administrative regulation, or local ordinance requires that it be covered in those circumstances.

(c) Vehicles transporting wastepaper, waste cardboard, or used cans or bottles, are in compliance with subdivision (a) if appropriate binders including, but not limited to, bands, wires, straps, or netting are used to prevent the load, or any part of the load, from spilling or falling from the vehicle.

(d) This section does not apply to any vehicle engaged in transporting wet waste fruit or vegetable matter, or waste products to or from a food processing establishment.

(Amended by Stats. 2001, Ch. 279, Sec. 1. Effective January 1, 2002.)

23116. (a) No person driving a pickup truck or a flatbed motortruck on a highway shall transport any person in or on the back of the truck.

(b) No person shall ride in or on the back of a truck or flatbed motortruck being driven on a highway.

(c) Subdivisions (a) and (b) do not apply if the person in the back of the truck is secured with a restraint system. The restraint system shall meet or exceed the federal motor vehicle safety standards published in Sections 571.207, 571.209, and 571.210 of Title 49 of the Code of Federal Regulations.

(d) Subdivisions (a), (b), and (c) do not apply to any person transporting one or more persons in the back of a truck or flatbed motortruck owned by a farmer or rancher, if that vehicle is used exclusively within the boundaries of lands owned or managed by that farmer or rancher, including the incidental use of that vehicle on not more than one mile of highway between one part of the farm or ranch to another part of that farm or ranch.

(e) Subdivisions (a), (b), and (c) do not apply if the person in the back of the truck or the flatbed is being transported in an emergency response situation by a public agency or pursuant to the direction or authority of a public agency.

As used in this subdivision, "emergency response situation" means instances in which necessary measures are needed in order to prevent injury or death to persons or to prevent, confine, or mitigate damage or destruction to property.

(f) Subdivisions (a) and (b) do not apply if the person in the back of the truck or flatbed motortruck is being transported in a parade that is supervised by a law enforcement agency and the speed of the truck while in the parade does not exceed eight miles per hour.

(Amended by Stats. 2000, Ch. 308, Sec. 2. Effective January 1, 2001.)

23117. (a) No person driving a motor vehicle shall transport any animal in the back of the vehicle in a space intended for any load on the vehicle on a highway unless the space is enclosed or has side and tail racks to a height of at least 46 inches extending vertically from the floor, the vehicle has installed means of preventing the animal from being discharged, or the animal is cross tethered to the vehicle, or is protected by a secured container or cage, in a manner which will prevent the animal from being thrown, falling, or jumping from the vehicle.

(b) This section does not apply to any of the following:

(1) The transportation of livestock.

(2) The transportation of a dog whose owner either owns or is employed by a ranching or farming operation who is traveling on a road in a rural area or who is traveling to and from a livestock auction.

(3) The transportation of a dog for purposes associated with ranching or farming.

(Added by Stats. 1987, Ch. 224, Sec. 1.)

23118. (a) (1) A magistrate presented with the affidavit of a peace officer establishing reasonable cause to believe that a vehicle, described by vehicle type and license number, is being used or operated in violation of Section 7502.1 of the Business and Professions Code shall issue a warrant or order authorizing any peace officer to immediately seize and cause the removal of the vehicle.

(2) The warrant or court order may be entered into a computerized database.

(3) Any vehicle so impounded may be impounded until such time as the owner of the property, or the person in possession of the property at the time of the impoundment, produces proof of licensure pursuant to Chapter 11 (commencing with Section 7500) of Division 3 of the Business and Professions Code, or proof of an exemption from licensure pursuant to Section 7500.2 or 7500.3 of the Business and Professions Code.

(4) The impounding agency, within two working days of impoundment, shall send a notice by certified mail, return receipt requested, to the legal owner of the vehicle, at an address obtained from the department, informing the owner that the vehicle has been impounded and providing the owner with a copy of the warrant or court order. Failure to notify the legal owner within two working days shall prohibit the impounding agency from charging for more than 15 days impoundment when a legal owner redeems the impounded vehicle. The law enforcement agency shall be open to issue a release to the registered owner or legal owner, or the agent of either, whenever the agency is open to serve the public for regular, nonemergency business.

(b) (1) An impounding agency shall release a vehicle to the registered owner or his or her agent prior to the end of the impoundment period and without the permission of the magistrate authorizing the vehicle's seizure under any of the following circumstances:

(A) When the vehicle is a stolen vehicle.

(B) When the vehicle was seized under this section for an offense that does not authorize the seizure of the vehicle.

(2) No vehicle may be released under this subdivision, except upon presentation of the registered owner's or agent's currently valid license to operate the vehicle, and proof of current vehicle registration, or upon order of the court.

(c) (1) Whenever a vehicle is impounded under this section, the magistrate ordering the storage shall provide the vehicle's registered and legal owners of record, or their agents, with the opportunity for a poststorage hearing to determine the validity of the storage.

(2) A notice of the storage shall be mailed or personally delivered to the registered and legal owners within 48 hours after issuance of the warrant or court order, excluding weekends and holidays, by the person or agency executing the warrant or court order, and shall include all of the following information:

(A) The name, address, and telephone number of the agency providing the notice.

(B) The location of the place of storage and a description of the vehicle, which shall include, if available, the name or make, the manufacturer, the license plate number, and the mileage of the vehicle.

(C) A copy of the warrant or court order and the peace officer's affidavit, as described in subdivision (a).

(D) A statement that, in order to receive their poststorage hearing, the owners, or their agents, are required to request the hearing from the magistrate issuing the warrant or court order in person, in writing, or by telephone, within 10 days of the date of the notice.

(3) The poststorage hearing shall be conducted within two court days after receipt of the request for the hearing.

(4) At the hearing, the magistrate may order the vehicle released if he or she finds any of the circumstances described in subdivision (b) or (e) that allow release of a vehicle by the impounding agency.

(5) Failure of either the registered or legal owner, or his or her agent, to request, or to attend, a scheduled hearing satisfies the poststorage hearing requirement.

(6) The agency employing the peace officer who caused the magistrate to issue the warrant or court order shall be responsible for the costs incurred for towing and storage if it is determined in the poststorage hearing that reasonable grounds for the storage are not established.

(d) The registered owner or his or her agent is responsible for all towing and storage charges related to the impoundment, and any administrative charges authorized under Section 22850.5.

(e) A vehicle removed and seized under subdivision (a) shall be released to the legal owner of the vehicle or the legal owner's agent prior to the end of the impoundment period and without the permission of the magistrate authorizing the seizure of the vehicle if all of the following conditions are met:

(1) The legal owner is a motor vehicle dealer, bank, credit union, acceptance corporation, or other licensed financial institution legally operating in this state or is another person, not the registered owner, holding a security interest in the vehicle.

(2) (A) The legal owner or the legal owner's agent pays all towing and storage fees related to the seizure of the vehicle. Except as specifically authorized by this subdivision, no other fees shall be charged to the legal owner or the agent of the legal owner. No lien sale processing fees shall be charged to the legal owner who redeems the vehicle prior to the 15th day of impoundment. Neither the impounding authority nor any person having possession of the vehicle shall collect from the legal owner of the type specified in paragraph (1), or the legal owner's agent any administrative charges imposed pursuant to Section 22850.5 unless the legal owner voluntarily requested a poststorage hearing.

(B) A person operating or in charge of a storage facility where vehicles are stored pursuant to this section shall accept a valid bank credit card or cash for payment of towing, storage, and related fees by a legal or registered owner or the owner's agent claiming the vehicle. A credit card shall be in the name of the person presenting the card. "Credit card" means "credit card" as defined in subdivision (a) of Section 1747.02 of the Civil Code, except, for the purposes of this section, credit card does not include a credit card issued by a retail seller.

(C) A person operating or in charge of a storage facility described in subparagraph (B) who violates subparagraph (B) shall be civilly liable to the owner of the vehicle or to the person who tendered the fees for four times the amount of the towing, storage, and related fees, but not to exceed five hundred dollars ($500).

(D) A person operating or in charge of the storage facility shall have sufficient funds on the premises of the primary storage facility during normal business hours to accommodate, and make change in, a reasonable monetary transaction.

(E) Credit charges for towing and storage services shall comply with Section 1748.1 of the Civil Code. Law enforcement agencies may include the costs of providing for payment by credit when making agreements with towing companies on rates.

(3) (A) The legal owner or the legal owner's agent presents to the law enforcement agency or impounding agency, or any person acting on behalf of those agencies, a copy of the assignment, as defined in subdivision (b) of Section 7500.1 of the Business and Professions Code; a release from the one responsible governmental agency, only if required by the agency; a government-issued photographic identification card; and any one of the following as determined by the legal owner or the legal owner's agent: a certificate of repossession for the vehicle, a security agreement for the vehicle, or title, whether paper or electronic, showing proof of legal ownership for the vehicle. The law enforcement agency, impounding agency, or any other governmental agency, or any person acting on behalf of those agencies, shall not require the presentation of any other documents.

(B) The legal owner or the legal owner's agent presents to the person in possession of the vehicle, or any person acting on behalf of the person in possession, a copy of the assignment, as defined in subdivision (b) of Section 7500.1 of the Business and Professions Code; a release from the one responsible governmental agency, only if required by the agency; a government-issued photographic identification card; and any one of the following as determined by the legal owner or the legal owner's agent: a certificate of repossession for the vehicle, a security agreement for the vehicle, or title, whether paper or electronic, showing proof of legal ownership for the vehicle. The person in possession of the vehicle, or any person acting on behalf of the person in possession, shall not require the presentation of any other documents.

(C) All presented documents may be originals, photocopies, or facsimile copies, or may be transmitted electronically. The law enforcement agency, impounding agency, or any person in possession of the vehicle, or anyone acting on behalf of them, shall not require a document to be notarized. The law enforcement agency, impounding agency, or any person acting on behalf of those agencies, may require the agent of the legal owner to produce a photocopy or facsimile copy of its repossession agency license or registration issued pursuant to Chapter 11 (commencing with Section 7500) of Division 3 of the Business and Professions Code, or to demonstrate, to the satisfaction of the law enforcement agency, impounding agency, or any person in possession of the vehicle, or anyone acting on behalf of them, that the agent is exempt from licensure pursuant to Section 7500.2 or 7500.3 of the Business and Professions Code.

(D) No administrative costs authorized under subdivision (a) of Section 22850.5 shall be charged to the legal owner of the type specified in paragraph (1), who redeems the vehicle unless the legal owner voluntarily requests a poststorage hearing. No city, county, city and county, or state agency shall require a legal owner or a legal owner's agent to request a poststorage hearing as a requirement for release of the vehicle to the legal owner or the legal owner's agent. The law enforcement agency, impounding agency, or any other governmental agency, or any person acting on behalf of those agencies, shall not require any documents other than those specified in this paragraph. The law enforcement agency, impounding agency, or other governmental agency, or any person acting on behalf of those agencies, may not require any documents to be notarized. The legal owner or the legal owner's agent shall be given a copy of any documents he or she is required to sign, except for a vehicle evidentiary hold logbook. The law enforcement agency, impounding agency, or any person acting on behalf of those agencies, or any person in possession of the vehicle, may photocopy and retain the copies of any documents presented by the legal owner or legal owner's agent.

(4) A failure by a storage facility to comply with any applicable conditions set forth in this subdivision shall not affect the right of the legal owner or the legal owner's agent to retrieve the vehicle, provided all conditions required of the legal owner or legal owner's agent under this subdivision are satisfied.

(f) (1) A legal owner or the legal owner's agent that obtains release of the vehicle pursuant to subdivision (e) shall not release the vehicle to the registered owner of the vehicle or the person who was listed as the registered owner when the vehicle was impounded or the person in possession of the vehicle at the time of the impound or any agents of the registered owner until the termination of the impoundment period.

(2) The legal owner or the legal owner's agent shall not relinquish the vehicle to the registered owner or the person who was listed as the registered owner when the vehicle was impounded until the registered owner or that owner's agent presents his or her valid driver's license or valid temporary driver's license to the legal owner or the legal owner's agent. The legal owner or the legal owner's agent or the person in possession of the vehicle shall make every reasonable effort to ensure that the licenses presented are valid and possession of the vehicle will not be given to the driver who was involved in the original impound proceeding until the expiration of the impoundment period.

(3) Prior to relinquishing the vehicle, the legal owner may require the registered owner to pay all towing and storage charges related to the impoundment and the administrative charges authorized under Section 22850.5 that were incurred by the legal owner in connection with obtaining the custody of the vehicle.

(4) Any legal owner who knowingly releases or causes the release of a vehicle to a registered owner or the person in possession of the vehicle at the time of the impound or any agent of the registered owner in violation of this subdivision shall be guilty of a misdemeanor and subject to a fine in the amount of two thousand dollars ($2,000) in addition to any other penalties established by law.

(5) The legal owner, registered owner, or person in possession of the vehicle shall not change or attempt to change the name of the legal owner or the registered owner on the records of the department until the vehicle is released from the impound.

(g) Notwithstanding any other provision of this section, the registered owner and not the legal owner shall remain responsible for any towing and storage charges related to the impoundment and the administrative charges authorized under Section 22850.5 and any parking fines, penalties, and administrative fees incurred by the registered owner.

(h) The law enforcement agency and the impounding agency, including any storage facility acting on behalf of the law enforcement agency or impounding agency, shall comply with this section and shall not be liable to the registered owner for the improper release of the vehicle to the legal owner or the legal owner's agent provided the release complies with the provisions of this section. The legal owner shall indemnify and hold harmless a storage facility from any claims arising out of the release of the vehicle to the legal owner or the legal owner's agent and from any damage to the vehicle after its release, including the reasonable costs associated with defending any such claims. A law enforcement agency shall not refuse to issue a release to a legal owner or the agent of a legal owner on the grounds that it previously issued a release.

(Added by Stats. 2009, Ch. 322, Sec. 11. (AB 515) Effective January 1, 2010.)

23120. No person shall operate a motor vehicle while wearing glasses having a temple width of one-half inch or more if any part of such temple extends below the horizontal center of the lens so as to interfere with lateral vision.

(Added by Stats. 1959, Ch. 531.)

23123. (a) A person shall not drive a motor vehicle while using a wireless telephone unless that telephone is specifically designed and configured to allow hands-free listening and talking, and is used in that manner while driving.

(b) A violation of this section is an infraction punishable by a base fine of twenty dollars ($20) for a first offense and fifty dollars ($50) for each subsequent offense.

(c) This section does not apply to a person using a wireless telephone for emergency purposes, including, but not limited to, an emergency call to a law enforcement agency, health care provider, fire department, or other emergency services agency or entity.

(d) This section does not apply to an emergency services professional using a wireless telephone while operating an authorized emergency vehicle, as defined in Section 165, in the course and scope of his or her duties.

(e) This section does not apply to a person driving a schoolbus or transit vehicle that is subject to Section 23125.

(f) This section does not apply to a person while driving a motor vehicle on private property.

(g) This section shall become operative on July 1, 2011.

(Amended (as added by Stats. 2006, Ch. 290, Sec. 5) by Stats. 2007, Ch. 214, Sec. 3. Effective January 1, 2008. Section operative July 1, 2011, by its own provisions.)

23123.5. (a) A person shall not drive a motor vehicle while holding and operating a handheld wireless telephone or an electronic wireless communications device unless the wireless telephone or electronic wireless communications device is specifically designed and configured to allow voice-operated and hands-free operation, and it is used in that manner while driving.

(b) This section shall not apply to manufacturer-installed systems that are embedded in the vehicle.

(c) A handheld wireless telephone or electronic wireless communications device may be operated in a manner requiring the use of the driver's hand while the driver is operating the vehicle only if both of the following conditions are satisfied:

(1) The handheld wireless telephone or electronic wireless communications device is mounted on a vehicle's windshield in the same manner a portable Global Positioning System (GPS) is mounted pursuant to paragraph (12) of subdivision (b) of Section 26708 or is mounted on or affixed to a vehicle's dashboard or center console in a manner that does not hinder the driver's view of the road.

(2) The driver's hand is used to activate or deactivate a feature or function of the handheld wireless telephone or wireless communications device with the motion of a single swipe or tap of the driver's finger.

(d) A violation of this section is an infraction punishable by a base fine of twenty dollars ($20) for a first offense and fifty dollars ($50) for each subsequent offense.

(e) This section does not apply to an emergency services professional using an electronic wireless communications device while operating an authorized emergency vehicle, as defined in Section 165, in the course and scope of his or her duties.

(f) For the purposes of this section, "electronic wireless communications device" includes, but is not limited to, a broadband personal communication device, a handheld device or laptop computer with mobile data access, or a pager.

(Amended by Stats. 2017, Ch. 297, Sec. 1. (AB 1222) Effective January 1, 2018.)

23124. (a) This section applies to a person under the age of 18 years.

(b) Notwithstanding Sections 23123 and 23123.5, a person described in subdivision (a) shall not drive a motor vehicle while using a wireless telephone or an electronic wireless communications device, even if equipped with a hands-free device.

(c) A violation of this section is an infraction punishable by a base fine of twenty dollars ($20) for a first offense and fifty dollars ($50) for each subsequent offense.

(d) A law enforcement officer shall not stop a vehicle for the sole purpose of determining whether the driver is violating subdivision (b).

(e) Subdivision (d) does not prohibit a law enforcement officer from stopping a vehicle for a violation of Section 23123 or 23123.5.

(f) This section does not apply to a person using a wireless telephone or a mobile service device for emergency purposes, including, but not limited to, an emergency call to a law enforcement agency, health care provider, fire department, or other emergency services agency or entity.

(g) For the purposes of this section, "electronic wireless communications device" includes, but is not limited to, a broadband personal communication device, specialized mobile radio device, handheld device or laptop computer with mobile data access, pager, and two-way messaging device.

(Amended by Stats. 2013, Ch. 754, Sec. 1. (SB 194) Effective January 1, 2014.)

23125. (a) A person may not drive a schoolbus or transit vehicle, as defined in subdivision (g) of Section 99247 of the Public Utilities Code, while using a wireless telephone.

(b) This section does not apply to a driver using a wireless telephone for work-related purposes, or for emergency purposes, including, but not limited to, an emergency call to a law enforcement agency, health care provider, fire department, or other emergency service agency or entity.

(c) Notwithstanding any other provision of law, a violation of subdivision (a) does not constitute a serious traffic violation within the meaning of subdivision (i) of Section 15210.

(Added by Stats. 2004, Ch. 505, Sec. 1. Effective January 1, 2005.)

23127. No person shall operate an unauthorized motor vehicle on any state, county, city, private, or district hiking or horseback riding trail or bicycle path that is clearly marked by an authorized agent or owner with signs at all entrances and exits and at intervals of not more than one mile indicating no unauthorized motor vehicles are permitted on the hiking or horseback riding trail or bicycle path, except bicycle paths which are contiguous or adjacent to a roadway dedicated solely to motor vehicle use.

For the purpose of this section "unauthorized motor vehicle" means any motor vehicle that is driven upon a hiking or horseback riding trail or bicycle path without the written permission of an agent or the owner of the trail or path.

This section does not apply to the operation of an authorized emergency or maintenance vehicle on a hiking or horseback riding trail or bicycle path whenever necessary in furtherance of the purpose for which the vehicle has been classed as an authorized emergency vehicle. Any person who violates this section is guilty of a misdemeanor.

(Amended by Stats. 1973, Ch. 951.)

23128. It is unlawful for any person to operate a snowmobile in the following manner:

(a) On a highway except as provided in Section 38025.

(b) In a careless or negligent manner so as to endanger a person or property.

(c) For the purpose of pursuing deer or other game mammal with intent to harass such animals.

(d) For the purpose of violating Section 602 of the Penal Code.

(Amended by Stats. 1972, Ch. 973.)

23129. No person shall drive a motor vehicle upon which is mounted a camper containing any passengers unless there is at least one unobstructed exit capable of being opened from both the interior and exterior of such camper.

(Added by Stats. 1972, Ch. 432.)

23135. It is unlawful for any person to operate upon a highway any vehicle which was originally manufactured as a motorized bicycle, as defined in Section 406, and which has been modified in such a manner that it no longer conforms to the definition of a motorized bicycle.

(Added by Stats. 1978, Ch. 421.)

Article 1.3. Offenses by Persons Under 21 Years of Age Involving Alcohol

(Article 1.3 added by Stats. 1993, Ch. 899, Sec. 11.)

23136. (a) Notwithstanding Sections 23152 and 23153, it is unlawful for a person under the age of 21 years who has a blood-alcohol concentration of 0.01 percent or greater, as measured by a preliminary alcohol screening test or other chemical test, to drive a vehicle. However, this section shall not be a bar to prosecution under Section 23152 or 23153 or any other provision of law.

(b) A person shall be found to be in violation of subdivision (a) if the person was, at the time of driving, under the age of 21 years, and the trier of fact finds that the person had consumed an alcoholic beverage and was driving a vehicle with a blood-alcohol concentration of 0.01 percent or greater, as measured by a preliminary alcohol screening test or other chemical test.

(c) (1) Any person under the age of 21 years who drives a motor vehicle is deemed to have given his or her consent to a preliminary alcohol screening test or other chemical test for the purpose of determining the presence of alcohol in the person, if lawfully detained for an alleged violation of subdivision (a).

(2) The testing shall be incidental to a lawful detention and administered at the direction of a peace officer having reasonable cause to believe the person was driving a motor vehicle in violation of subdivision (a).

(3) The person shall be told that his or her failure to submit to, or the failure to complete, a preliminary alcohol screening test or other chemical test as requested will result in the suspension or revocation of the person's privilege to operate a motor vehicle for a period of one year to three years, as provided in Section 13353.1.

(Amended by Stats. 1996, Ch. 10, Sec. 18. Effective February 9, 1996.)

Article 1.5. Juvenile Offenses Involving Alcohol

(Article 1.5 added by Stats. 1986, Ch. 1105, Sec. 1.)

23140. (a) It is unlawful for a person under the age of 21 years who has 0.05 percent or more, by weight, of alcohol in his or her blood to drive a vehicle.

(b) A person may be found to be in violation of subdivision (a) if the person was, at the time of driving, under the age of 21 years and under the influence of, or affected by, an alcoholic beverage regardless of whether a chemical test was made to determine that person's blood-alcohol concentration and if the trier of fact finds that the person had consumed an alcoholic beverage and was driving a vehicle while having a concentration of 0.05 percent or more, by weight, of alcohol in his or her blood.

(c) Notwithstanding any provision of law to the contrary, upon a finding that a person has violated this section, the clerk of the court shall prepare within 10 days after the finding and immediately forward to the department an abstract of the record of the court in which the finding is made. That abstract shall be a public record and available for public inspection in the same manner as other records reported under Section 1803.

(Amended by Stats. 2007, Ch. 263, Sec. 32. Effective January 1, 2008.)

Article 2. Offenses Involving Alcohol and Drugs

(Article 2 added by Stats. 1981, Ch. 940, Sec. 32.)

23152. (a) It is unlawful for a person who is under the influence of any alcoholic beverage to drive a vehicle.

(b) It is unlawful for a person who has 0.08 percent or more, by weight, of alcohol in his or her blood to drive a vehicle.

For purposes of this article and Section 34501.16, percent, by weight, of alcohol in a person's blood is based upon grams of alcohol per 100 milliliters of blood or grams of alcohol per 210 liters of breath.

In any prosecution under this subdivision, it is a rebuttable presumption that the person had 0.08 percent or more, by weight, of alcohol in his or her blood at the time of driving the vehicle if the person had 0.08 percent or more, by weight, of alcohol in his or her blood at the time of the performance of a chemical test within three hours after the driving.

(c) It is unlawful for a person who is addicted to the use of any drug to drive a vehicle. This subdivision shall not apply to a person who is participating in a narcotic treatment program approved pursuant to Article 3 (commencing with Section 11875) of Chapter 1 of Part 3 of Division 10.5 of the Health and Safety Code.

(d) It is unlawful for a person who has 0.04 percent or more, by weight, of alcohol in his or her blood to drive a commercial motor vehicle, as defined in Section 15210. In a prosecution under this subdivision, it is a rebuttable presumption that the person had 0.04 percent or more, by weight, of alcohol in his or her blood at the time of driving the vehicle if the person had 0.04 percent or more, by weight, of alcohol in his or her blood at the time of the performance of a chemical test within three hours after the driving.

(e) Commencing July 1, 2018, it shall be unlawful for a person who has 0.04 percent or more, by weight, of alcohol in his or her blood to drive a motor vehicle when a passenger for hire is a passenger in the vehicle at the time of the offense. For purposes of this subdivision, "passenger for hire" means a passenger for whom consideration is contributed or expected as a condition of carriage in the vehicle, whether directly or indirectly flowing to the owner, operator, agent, or any other person having an interest in the vehicle. In a prosecution under this subdivision, it is a rebuttable presumption that the person had 0.04 percent or more, by weight, of alcohol in his or her blood at the time of driving the vehicle if the person had 0.04 percent or more, by weight, of alcohol in his or her blood at the time of the performance of a chemical test within three hours after the driving.

(f) It is unlawful for a person who is under the influence of any drug to drive a vehicle.

(g) It is unlawful for a person who is under the combined influence of any alcoholic beverage and drug to drive a vehicle.

(Amended by Stats. 2016, Ch. 765, Sec. 1. (AB 2687) Effective January 1, 2017.)

23152.5. Notwithstanding Section 23152, a person who is under the influence of a drug or the combined influence of an alcoholic beverage and drug who is under the supervision of, and on the property of, the Department of the California Highway Patrol may drive a vehicle for purposes of conducting research on impaired driving.

(Added by Stats. 2019, Ch. 68, Sec. 1. (AB 127) Effective July 10, 2019.)

23153. (a) It is unlawful for a person, while under the influence of any alcoholic beverage, to drive a vehicle and concurrently do any act forbidden by law, or neglect any duty imposed by law in driving the vehicle, which act or neglect proximately causes bodily injury to any person other than the driver.

(b) It is unlawful for a person, while having 0.08 percent or more, by weight, of alcohol in his or her blood to drive a vehicle and concurrently do any act forbidden by law, or neglect any duty imposed by law in driving the vehicle, which act or neglect proximately causes bodily injury to any person other than the driver.

In any prosecution under this subdivision, it is a rebuttable presumption that the person had 0.08 percent or more, by weight, of alcohol in his or her blood at the time of driving the vehicle if the person had 0.08 percent or more, by weight, of alcohol in his or her blood at the time of the performance of a chemical test within three hours after driving.

(c) In proving the person neglected any duty imposed by law in driving the vehicle, it is not necessary to prove that any specific section of this code was violated.

(d) It is unlawful for a person, while having 0.04 percent or more, by weight, of alcohol in his or her blood to drive a commercial motor vehicle, as defined in Section 15210 and concurrently to do any act forbidden by law or neglect any duty imposed by law in driving the vehicle, which act or neglect proximately causes bodily injury to any person other than the driver. In a prosecution under this subdivision, it is a rebuttable presumption that the person had 0.04 percent or more, by weight, of alcohol in his or her blood at the time of driving the vehicle if the person had 0.04 percent or more, by weight, of alcohol in his or her blood at the time of performance of a chemical test within three hours after driving.

(e) Commencing July 1, 2018, it shall be unlawful for a person, while having 0.04 percent or more, by weight, of alcohol in his or her blood to drive a motor vehicle when a passenger for hire is a passenger in the vehicle at the time of the offense, and concurrently to do any act forbidden by law or neglect any duty imposed by law in driving the vehicle, which act or neglect proximately causes bodily injury to any person other than the driver. For purposes of this subdivision, "passenger for hire" means a passenger for whom consideration is contributed or expected as a condition of carriage in the vehicle, whether directly or indirectly flowing to the owner, operator, agent, or any other person having an interest in the vehicle. In a prosecution under this subdivision, it is a rebuttable presumption that the person had 0.04 percent or more, by weight, of alcohol in his or her blood at the time of driving the vehicle if the person had 0.04 percent or more, by weight, of alcohol in his or her blood at the time of performance of a chemical test within three hours after driving.

(f) It is unlawful for a person, while under the influence of any drug, to drive a vehicle and concurrently do any act forbidden by law, or neglect any duty imposed by law in driving the vehicle, which act or neglect proximately causes bodily injury to any person other than the driver.

(g) It is unlawful for a person, while under the combined influence of any alcoholic beverage and drug, to drive a vehicle and concurrently do any act forbidden by law, or neglect any duty imposed by law in driving the vehicle, which act or neglect proximately causes bodily injury to any person other than the driver.

(Amended by Stats. 2016, Ch. 765, Sec. 2. (AB 2687) Effective January 1, 2017.)

23154. (a) It is unlawful for a person who is on probation for a violation of Section 23152 or 23153 to operate a motor vehicle at any time with a blood-alcohol concentration of 0.01 percent or greater, as measured by a preliminary alcohol screening test or other chemical test.

(b) A person may be found to be in violation of subdivision (a) if the person was, at the time of driving, on probation for a violation of Section 23152 or 23153, and the trier of fact finds that the person had consumed an alcoholic beverage and was driving a vehicle with a blood-alcohol concentration of 0.01 percent or greater, as measured by a preliminary alcohol screening test or other chemical test.

(c) (1) A person who is on probation for a violation of Section 23152 or 23153 who drives a motor vehicle is deemed to have given his or her consent to a preliminary alcohol screening test or other chemical test for the purpose of determining the presence of alcohol in the person, if lawfully detained for an alleged violation of subdivision (a).

(2) The testing shall be incidental to a lawful detention and administered at the direction of a peace officer having reasonable cause to believe the person is driving a motor vehicle in violation of subdivision (a).

(3) The person shall be told that his or her failure to submit to, or the failure to complete, a preliminary alcohol screening test or other chemical test as requested will result in the suspension or revocation of the person's privilege to operate a motor vehicle for a period of one year to three years, as provided in Section 13353.1.

(Added by Stats. 2007, Ch. 749, Sec. 5. Effective January 1, 2008. Operative January 1, 2009, by Sec. 9 of Ch. 749.)

23155. Beginning January 1, 2022, when a disposition described in Section 13151 of the Penal Code is a conviction for a violation of subdivision (f) of Section 23152 or subdivision (f) of Section 23153 for which cannabis was the sole drug, the disposition report shall state that the convicted offense was due to cannabis.

(Added by Stats. 2019, Ch. 610, Sec. 1. (AB 397) Effective January 1, 2020.)

23158. (a) Notwithstanding any other provision of law, only a licensed physician and surgeon, registered nurse, licensed vocational nurse, duly licensed clinical laboratory scientist or clinical laboratory bioanalyst, a person who has been issued a "certified phlebotomy technician" certificate pursuant to Section 1246 of the Business and Professions Code, unlicensed laboratory personnel regulated pursuant to Sections 1242, 1242.5, and 1246 of the Business and Professions Code, or certified paramedic acting at the request of a peace officer may withdraw blood for the purpose of determining the alcoholic content therein. This limitation does not apply to the taking of breath specimens. An emergency call for paramedic services takes precedence over a peace officer's request for a paramedic to withdraw blood for determining its alcoholic content. A certified paramedic shall not withdraw blood for this purpose unless authorized by his or her employer to do so.

(b) The person tested may, at his or her own expense, have a licensed physician and surgeon, registered nurse, licensed vocational nurse, duly licensed clinical laboratory scientist or clinical laboratory bioanalyst, person who has been issued a "certified phlebotomy technician" certificate pursuant to Section 1246 of the Business and Professions Code, unlicensed laboratory personnel regulated pursuant to Sections 1242, 1242.5, and 1246 of the Business and Professions Code, or any other person of his or her own choosing administer a test in addition to any test administered at the direction of a peace officer for the purpose of determining the amount of alcohol in the person's blood at the time alleged as shown by chemical analysis of his or her blood, breath, or urine. The failure or inability to obtain an additional test by a person does not preclude the admissibility in evidence of the test taken at the direction of a peace officer.

(c) Upon the request of the person tested, full information concerning the test taken at the direction of the peace officer shall be made available to the person or the person's attorney.

(d) Notwithstanding any other provision of law, no licensed physician and surgeon, registered nurse, licensed vocational nurse, duly licensed clinical laboratory scientist or clinical laboratory bioanalyst, person who has been issued a "certified phlebotomy technician" certificate pursuant to Section 1246 of the Business and Professions Code, unlicensed laboratory personnel regulated pursuant to Sections 1242, 1242.5, and 1246 of the Business and Professions Code, or certified paramedic, or hospital, laboratory, or clinic employing or utilizing the services of the licensed physician and surgeon, registered nurse, licensed vocational nurse, duly licensed clinical laboratory scientist or clinical laboratory bioanalyst, person who has been issued a "certified phlebotomy technician" certificate pursuant to Section 1246 of the Business and Professions Code, unlicensed laboratory personnel regulated pursuant to Sections 1242, 1242.5, and 1246 of the Business and Professions Code, or certified paramedic, owning or leasing the premises on which tests are performed, shall incur any civil or criminal liability as a result of the administering of a blood test in a reasonable manner in a hospital, clinical laboratory, medical clinic environment, jail, or law enforcement facility, according to accepted venipuncture practices, without violence by the person administering the test, and when requested in writing by a peace officer to administer the test.

(e) Notwithstanding any other provision of law, a person who has been issued a "certified phlebotomy technician" certificate pursuant to Section 1246 of the Business and Professions Code and who is authorized by this section to draw blood at the request and in the presence of a peace officer for purposes of determining its alcoholic content, may do so in a jail, law enforcement facility, or medical facility, with general supervision. The "certified phlebotomy technician" shall draw blood following the policies and procedures approved by a physician and surgeon licensed under Chapter 5 (commencing with Section 2000) of Division 2 of the Business and Professions Code, appropriate to the location where the blood is being drawn and in accordance with state regulations.

(f) The Certified Phlebotomy Technician I or II shall carry a current, valid identification card issued by the State Department of Health Services, attesting to the technician's name, certificate type, and effective dates of certification, when performing blood withdrawals.

(g) As used in this section, "general supervision" means that the supervisor of the technician is licensed under the Business and Professions Code as a physician and surgeon, physician assistant, clinical laboratory bioanalyst, registered nurse, or clinical laboratory scientist, and reviews the competency of the technician before the technician may perform blood withdrawals without direct supervision, and on an annual basis thereafter. The supervisor is also required to review the work of the technician at least once a month to ensure compliance with venipuncture policies, procedures, and regulations. The supervisor, or another person licensed as a physician and surgeon, physician assistant, clinical laboratory bioanalyst, registered nurse, or clinical laboratory scientist, shall be accessible to the location where the technician is working to provide onsite, telephone, or electronic consultation, within 30 minutes when needed.

(h) Nothing in this section shall be construed as requiring the certified phlebotomy technician who is authorized to withdraw blood by this section at the request and in the presence of a peace officer for purposes of determining alcoholic content to be associated with a clinical laboratory or to be directly supervised after competency has been established.

(i) If the test given under Section 23612 is a chemical test of urine, the person tested shall be given such privacy in the taking of the urine specimen as will ensure the accuracy of the specimen and, at the same time, maintain the dignity of the individual involved.

(j) The department, in cooperation with the State Department of Health Services or any other appropriate agency, shall adopt uniform standards for the withdrawal, handling, and preservation of blood samples prior to analysis.

(k) As used in this section, "certified paramedic" does not include any employee of a fire department.

(l) Consent, waiver of liability, or the offering to, acceptance by, or refusal of consent or waiver of liability by the person on whom a test is administered, is not an issue or relevant to the immunity from liability for medical or law enforcement personnel or other facilities designated under subdivision (d).

(Amended by Stats. 2004, Ch. 14, Sec. 2. Effective February 11, 2004.)

23213. No patient or other person residing in a social rehabilitation facility licensed pursuant to Chapter 3 (commencing with Section 1500) of Division 2 of the Health and Safety Code for the rehabilitation of persons who have abused alcohol or drugs, shall have a motor vehicle registered in the name of that patient or person on or near the premises of that facility unless the patient or person has an operator's license issued pursuant to this code which is not suspended or revoked.

(Added by Stats. 1982, Ch. 1339, Sec. 30. Effective September 24, 1982.)

23215. The department may, but shall not be required to, provide patrol or enforce the provisions of Section 23152 for offenses which occur other than upon a highway.

(Added by Stats. 1981, Ch. 940, Sec. 32.)

23216. (a) The provisions of Sections 2, 6, 7, and 10 expressly apply to the provisions of this article, and, further, for any recidivist or enhancement purpose, reference to an offense by section number is a reference to the provisions contained in that section, insofar as they were renumbered by Chapter 940 of the Statutes of 1981 without substantive change, and those provisions shall be construed as restatements and continuations thereof and not as new enactments.

(b) Any reference in the provisions of this code to a separate violation of Section 23152 shall include a separate offense under Section 23102 or 23105, as those sections read prior to January 1, 1982.

(c) Any reference in the provisions of the Vehicle Code to a separate violation of Section 23153 shall include a separate offense under Section 23101 or 23106 as those sections read prior to January 1, 1982.

(d) The provisions of this section are to be given retroactive effect.

(Added by Stats. 1984, Ch. 1205, Sec. 13.)

23217. The Legislature finds and declares that some repeat offenders of the prohibition against driving under the influence of alcohol or drugs, when they are addicted or when they have too much alcohol in their systems, may be escaping the intent of the Legislature to punish the offender with progressively greater severity if the offense is repeated one or more times within a 10-year period. This situation may occur when a conviction for a subsequent offense occurs before a conviction is obtained on an earlier offense.

The Legislature further finds and declares that the timing of court proceedings should not permit a person to avoid aggravated mandatory minimum penalties for multiple separate offenses occurring within a 10-year period. It is the intent of the Legislature to provide that a person be subject to enhanced mandatory minimum penalties for multiple offenses within a period of 10 years, regardless of whether the convictions are obtained in the same sequence as the offenses had been committed.

Nothing in this section requires consideration of judgment of conviction in a separate proceeding that is entered after the judgment in the present proceeding, except as it relates to violation of probation.

Nothing in this section or the amendments to Section 23540, 23546, 23550, 23560, 23566, 23622, or 23640 made by Chapter 1205 of the Statutes of 1984 affects the penalty for a violation of Section 23152 or 23153 occurring prior to January 1, 1985.

(Amended by Stats. 2004, Ch. 550, Sec. 11. Effective January 1, 2005.)

23220. (a) A person shall not drink any alcoholic beverage or smoke or ingest marijuana or any marijuana product while driving a motor vehicle on any lands described in subdivision (c).

(b) A person shall not drink any alcoholic beverage or smoke or ingest marijuana or any marijuana product while riding as a passenger in any motor vehicle being driven on any lands described in subdivision (c).

(c) As used in this section, "lands" means those lands to which the Chappie-Z'berg Off-Highway Motor Vehicle Law of 1971 (Division 16.5 (commencing with Section 38000)) applies as to off-highway motor vehicles, as described in Section 38001.

(d) A violation of subdivision (a) or (b) shall be punished as an infraction.

(Amended by Stats. 2017, Ch. 232, Sec. 1. (SB 65) Effective January 1, 2018.)

23221. (a) A driver shall not drink any alcoholic beverage or smoke or ingest marijuana or any marijuana product while driving a motor vehicle upon a highway.

(b) A passenger shall not drink any alcoholic beverage or smoke or ingest marijuana or any marijuana product while in a motor vehicle being driven upon a highway.

(c) A violation of this section shall be punished as an infraction.

(Amended by Stats. 2017, Ch. 232, Sec. 2. (SB 65) Effective January 1, 2018.)

23222. (a) A person shall not have in their possession on their person, while driving a motor vehicle upon a highway or on lands, as described in subdivision (c) of Section 23220, a bottle, can, or other receptacle, containing an alcoholic beverage which has been opened, or a seal broken, or the contents of which have been partially removed.

(b) (1) Except as authorized by law, a person who has in their possession on their person, while driving a motor vehicle upon a highway or on lands, as described in subdivision (c) of Section 23220, a receptacle containing cannabis or cannabis products, as defined by Section 11018.1 of the Health and Safety Code, which has been opened or has a seal broken, or loose cannabis flower not in a container, is guilty of an infraction punishable by a fine of not more than one hundred dollars ($100).

(2) Paragraph (1) does not apply to a person who has a receptacle containing cannabis or cannabis products that has been opened, has a seal broken, or the contents of which have been partially removed, or to a person who has a loose cannabis flower not in a container, if the receptacle or loose cannabis flower not in a container is in the trunk of the vehicle.

(c) Subdivision (b) does not apply to a qualified patient or person with an identification card, as defined in Section 11362.7 of the Health and Safety Code, if both of the following apply:

(1) The person is carrying a current identification card or a physician's recommendation.

(2) The cannabis or cannabis product is contained in a container or receptacle that is either sealed, resealed, or closed.

(Amended by Stats. 2019, Ch. 610, Sec. 2. (AB 397) Effective January 1, 2020.)

23223. (a) A driver shall not have in the driver's possession, while in a motor vehicle upon a highway or on lands, as described in subdivision (c) of Section 23220, any bottle, can, or other receptacle, containing any alcoholic beverage that has been opened, or a seal broken, or the contents of which have been partially removed.

(b) A passenger shall not have in the passenger's possession, while in a motor vehicle upon a highway or on lands, as described in subdivision (c) of Section 23220, any bottle, can, or other receptacle containing any alcoholic beverage that has been opened or a seal broken, or the contents of which have been partially removed.

(Amended by Stats. 2019, Ch. 497, Sec. 275. (AB 991) Effective January 1, 2020.)

23224. (a) No person under 21 years of age shall knowingly drive any motor vehicle carrying any alcoholic beverage, unless the person is accompanied by a parent, responsible adult relative, any other adult designated by the parent, or legal guardian for the purpose of transportation of an alcoholic beverage, or is employed by a licensee under the Alcoholic Beverage Control Act (Division 9 (commencing with Section 23000) of the Business and Professions Code), and is driving the motor vehicle during regular hours and in the course of the person's employment. If the driver was unaccompanied, they shall have a complete defense if they were following, in a timely manner, the reasonable instructions of a parent, legal guardian, responsible adult relative, or adult designee relating to disposition of the alcoholic beverage.

(b) No passenger in any motor vehicle who is under 21 years of age shall knowingly possess or have under that person's control any alcoholic beverage, unless the passenger is accompanied by a parent, legal guardian, responsible adult relative, any other adult designated by the parent, or legal guardian for the purpose of transportation of an alcoholic beverage, or is employed by a licensee under the Alcoholic Beverage Control Act (Division 9 (commencing with Section 23000) of the Business and Professions Code), and possession or control is during regular hours and in the course of the passenger's employment. If the passenger was unaccompanied, they shall have a complete defense if they were following, in a timely manner, the reasonable instructions of a parent, legal guardian, responsible adult relative or adult designee relating to disposition of the alcoholic beverage.

(c) If the vehicle used in any violation of subdivision (a) or (b) is registered to an offender who is under 21 years of age, the vehicle may be impounded at the owner's expense for not less than one day nor more than 30 days for each violation.

(d) Any person convicted for a violation of subdivision (a) or (b) is guilty of a misdemeanor and shall be punished upon conviction by a fine of not more than one thousand dollars ($1,000) or by imprisonment in the county jail for not more than six months, or by both that fine and imprisonment.

(Amended by Stats. 2019, Ch. 505, Sec. 14. (SB 485) Effective January 1, 2020.)

23225. (a) (1) It is unlawful for the registered owner of any motor vehicle to keep in a motor vehicle, when the vehicle is upon any highway or on lands, as described in subdivision (c) of Section 23220, any bottle, can, or other receptacle containing any alcoholic beverage that has been opened, or a seal broken, or the contents of which have been partially removed, unless the container is kept in the trunk of the vehicle.

(2) If the vehicle is not equipped with a trunk and is not an off-highway motor vehicle subject to identification, as defined in Section 38012, the bottle, can, or other receptacle described in paragraph (1) shall be kept in some other area of the vehicle that is not normally occupied by the driver or passengers. For the purposes of this paragraph, a utility compartment or glove compartment shall be deemed to be within the area occupied by the driver and passengers.

(3) If the vehicle is not equipped with a trunk and is an off-highway motor vehicle subject to identification, as defined in subdivision (a) of Section 38012, the bottle, can, or other receptacle described in paragraph (1) shall be kept in a locked container. As used in this paragraph, "locked container" means a secure container that is fully enclosed and locked by a padlock, key lock, combination lock, or similar locking device.

(b) Subdivision (a) is also applicable to a driver of a motor vehicle if the registered owner is not present in the vehicle.

(c) This section shall not apply to the living quarters of a housecar or camper.

(Amended by Stats. 2019, Ch. 497, Sec. 276. (AB 991) Effective January 1, 2020.)

23226. (a) It is unlawful for any driver to keep in the passenger compartment of a motor vehicle, when the vehicle is upon any highway or on lands, as described in subdivision (c) of Section 23220, any bottle, can, or other receptacle containing any alcoholic beverage that has been opened, or a seal broken, or the contents of which have been partially removed.

(b) It is unlawful for any passenger to keep in the passenger compartment of a motor vehicle, when the vehicle is upon any highway or on lands, as described in subdivision (c) of Section 23220, any bottle, can, or other receptacle containing any alcoholic beverage that has been opened or a seal broken, or the contents of which have been partially removed.

(c) This section does not apply to the living quarters of a housecar or camper.

(Amended by Stats. 2019, Ch. 497, Sec. 277. (AB 991) Effective January 1, 2020.)

23229. (a) Except as provided in Section 23229.1, Section 23221, as it applies to an alcoholic beverage, and Section 23223 do not apply to passengers in any bus, taxicab, or limousine for hire licensed to transport passengers pursuant to the Public Utilities Code or proper local authority, the living quarters of a housecar or camper, or of a pedicab operated pursuant to Article 4.5 (commencing with Section 21215) of Chapter 1.

(b) Except as provided in Section 23229.1, Section 23225 does not apply to the driver or owner of a bus, taxicab, or limousine for hire licensed to transport passengers pursuant to the Public Utilities Code or proper local authority, or of a pedicab operated pursuant to Article 4.5 (commencing with Section 21215) of Chapter 1.

(Amended by Stats. 2019, Ch. 636, Sec. 8. (AB 1810) Effective January 1, 2020.)

23229.1. (a) Subject to subdivision (b), Sections 23223 and 23225 apply to any driver providing transportation services on a prearranged basis as a charter-party carrier of passengers, as defined in Section 5360 of the Public Utilities Code, when the driver of the vehicle transports any passenger under 21 years of age and fails to comply with the requirements of Section 5384.1 of the Public Utilities Code.

(b) For purposes of subdivision (a), it is not a violation of Section 23225 for any driver providing transportation services on a prearranged basis as a charter-party carrier of passengers that is licensed pursuant to the Public Utilities Code to keep any bottle, can, or other receptacle containing any alcoholic beverage in a locked utility compartment within the area occupied by the driver and passengers.

(c) In addition to the requirements of Section 1803, every clerk of a court in which any driver in subdivision (a) was convicted of a violation of Section 23225 shall prepare within 10 days after conviction, and immediately forward to the Public Utilities Commission at its office in San Francisco, an abstract of the record of the court covering the case in which the person was convicted. If sentencing is not pronounced in conjunction with the conviction, the abstract shall be forwarded to the commission within 10 days after sentencing, and the abstract shall be certified, by the person required to prepare it, to be true and correct. For the purposes of this subdivision, a forfeiture of bail is equivalent to a conviction.

(Amended by Stats. 2012, Ch. 461, Sec. 6. (AB 45) Effective January 1, 2013.)

Article 4. Ignition Interlock Device

(Article 4 repealed and added by Stats. 1994, Ch. 1237, Sec. 3.)

23247. (a) It is unlawful for a person to knowingly rent, lease, or lend a motor vehicle to another person known to have had their driving privilege restricted as provided in Section 13352, 13352.1, 13353.6, 13353.75, 23575, 23575.3, or 23700, unless the vehicle is equipped with a functioning, certified ignition interlock device. A person, whose driving privilege is restricted pursuant to Section 13352, 13352.1, 13353.6, 13353.75, 23575, 23575.3, or 23700, shall notify any other person who rents, leases, or loans a motor vehicle to them of the driving restriction imposed under that section.

(b) It is unlawful for any person whose driving privilege is restricted pursuant to Section 13352, 13352.1, 13353.6, 13353.75, 23575, 23575.3, or 23700 to request or solicit any other person to blow into an ignition interlock device or to start a motor vehicle equipped with the device for the purpose of providing the person so restricted with an operable motor vehicle.

(c) It is unlawful to blow into an ignition interlock device or to start a motor vehicle equipped with the device for the purpose of providing an operable motor vehicle to a person whose driving privilege is restricted pursuant to Section 13352, 13352.1, 13353.6, 13353.75, 23575, 23575.3, or 23700.

(d) It is unlawful to remove, bypass, or tamper with, an ignition interlock device.

(e) It is unlawful for any person whose driving privilege is restricted pursuant to Section 13352, 13352.1, 13353.6, 13353.75, 23575, 23575.3, or 23700 to operate any vehicle not equipped with a functioning ignition interlock device.

(f) Any person convicted of a violation of this section shall be punished by imprisonment in a county jail for not more than six months or by a fine of not more than five thousand dollars ($5,000), or by both that fine and imprisonment.

(g) (1) If any person whose driving privilege is restricted pursuant to Section 13352, 13352.1, 13353.6, or 13353.75 is convicted of a violation of subdivision (e), the court shall notify the Department of Motor Vehicles, which shall immediately terminate the restriction and shall suspend or revoke the person's driving privilege for the remaining period of the originating suspension or revocation and until all reinstatement requirements in Section 13352 or 13353.3 are met.

(2) If any person who is restricted pursuant to Section 23575.3, subdivision (a) or (i) of Section 23575, or Section 23700 is convicted of a violation of subdivision (e), the department shall suspend the person's driving privilege for one year from the date of the conviction.

(h) Notwithstanding any other law, if a vehicle in which a functioning, certified ignition interlock device has been installed is impounded, the manufacturer or installer of the device shall have the right to remove the device from the vehicle during normal business hours. No charge shall be imposed for the removal of the device nor shall the manufacturer or installer be liable for any removal, towing, impoundment, storage, release, or administrative costs or penalties associated with the impoundment. Upon request, the person seeking to remove the device shall present documentation to justify removal of the device from the vehicle. Any damage to the vehicle resulting from the removal of the device is the responsibility of the person removing it.

(i) This section shall become operative on January 1, 2019.

(j) This section shall remain in effect only until January 1, 2033, and as of that date is repealed, unless a later enacted statute, that is enacted before January 1, 2033, deletes or extends that date.

(Amended (as amended by Stats. 2017, Ch. 485, Sec. 21) by Stats. 2025, Ch. 689, Sec. 20. (AB 366) Effective January 1, 2026. Repealed as of January 1, 2033, by its own provisions. See later operative version, as amended by Sec. 21 of Stats. 2025, Ch. 689.)

23247. (a) It is unlawful for a person to knowingly rent, lease, or lend a motor vehicle to another person known to have had their driving privilege restricted as provided in Section 13352, 23575, or 23700, unless the vehicle is equipped with a functioning, certified ignition interlock device. A person, whose driving privilege is restricted pursuant to Section 13352, 23575, or 23700, shall notify any other person who rents, leases, or loans a motor vehicle to them of the driving restriction imposed under that section.

(b) It is unlawful for any person whose driving privilege is restricted pursuant to Section 13352, 23575, or 23700 to request or solicit any other person to blow into an ignition interlock device or to start a motor vehicle equipped with the device for the purpose of providing the person so restricted with an operable motor vehicle.

(c) It is unlawful to blow into an ignition interlock device or to start a motor vehicle equipped with the device for the purpose of providing an operable motor vehicle to a person whose driving privilege is restricted pursuant to Section 13352, 23575, or 23700.

(d) It is unlawful to remove, bypass, or tamper with, an ignition interlock device.

(e) It is unlawful for any person whose driving privilege is restricted pursuant to Section 13352, 23575, or 23700 to operate any vehicle not equipped with a functioning, certified ignition interlock device.

(f) Any person convicted of a violation of this section shall be punished by imprisonment in a county jail for not more than six months or by a fine of not more than five thousand dollars ($5,000), or by both that fine and imprisonment.

(g) (1) If any person whose driving privilege is restricted pursuant to Section 13352 is convicted of a violation of subdivision (e), the court shall notify the Department of Motor Vehicles, which shall immediately terminate the restriction and shall suspend or revoke the person's driving privilege for the remaining period of the originating suspension or revocation and until all reinstatement requirements in Section 13352 are met.

(2) If any person who is restricted pursuant to subdivision (a) or (l) of Section 23575 or Section 23700 is convicted of a violation of subdivision (e), the department shall suspend the person's driving privilege for one year from the date of the conviction.

(h) Notwithstanding any other law, if a vehicle in which a functioning, certified ignition interlock device has been installed is impounded, the manufacturer or installer of the device shall have the right to remove the device from the vehicle during normal business hours. No charge shall be imposed for the removal of the device nor shall the manufacturer or installer be liable for any removal, towing, impoundment, storage, release, or administrative costs or penalties associated with the impoundment. Upon request, the person seeking to remove the device shall present documentation to justify removal of the device from the vehicle. Any damage to the vehicle resulting from the removal of the device is the responsibility of the person removing it.

(i) This section shall become operative January 1, 2033.

(Amended (as added by Stats. 2016, Ch. 783, Sec. 28) by Stats. 2025, Ch. 689, Sec. 21. (AB 366) Effective January 1, 2026. Section operative January 1, 2033, by its own provisions.)

Article 5. Alcohol and Drug Problem Assessment Program

(Article 5 repealed (as Article 4, comm. with Section 23240) and added by Stats. 1988, Ch. 160, Sec. 183.)

23249.50. (a) The Legislature finds and declares all of the following:

(1) Driving under the influence of an alcoholic beverage or a drug is a serious problem, constituting the largest group of misdemeanor violations in many counties.

(2) Studies of first offenders have found that more than half of first offenders are alcoholics or problem drinkers. There are higher percentages of problem drinkers among second offenders than among first offenders.

(3) As the link between the health and legal aspects of the problem has become recognized, the courts have sought more information on a presentence basis in determining the appropriate sentence.

(4) Laws relating to driving under the influence of an alcoholic beverage or a drug allow the courts to order a presentence investigation to determine whether a person can benefit from an education, training, or treatment program. The Legislature thus finds that, to adequately assess whether an individual arrested for driving under the influence of an alcoholic beverage or a drug is chemically dependent, it is important to develop and implement screening programs in order to continue to address the problem of driving under the influence of alcoholic beverages or drugs in the state.

(b) It is therefore the intent of the Legislature to establish an additional procedure to assist the courts in the use of presentence investigations of individuals convicted of driving under the influence of an alcoholic beverage or a drug and to enable the courts to make appropriate dispositions in these cases. As part of this process, the courts should obtain and consider a presentence investigation report detailing the defendant's driving and criminal record, and, where possible, an alcohol or drug problem assessment report. In all cases, an alcohol or drug problem assessment report should be completed by qualified personnel prior to the determination of an education or treatment plan and subsequent sentencing by the courts.

(Added by Stats. 1988, Ch. 160, Sec. 183.)

Chapter 13. Vehicular Crossings and Toll Highways

(Heading of Chapter 13 amended by Stats. 1992, Ch. 1241, Sec. 22.)

Article 1. General Provisions

(Article 1 enacted by Stats. 1959, Ch. 3.)

23250. All of the provisions of this code not inconsistent with the provisions of this chapter shall be applicable to vehicular crossings and toll highways. This chapter shall control over any provision of this code inconsistent with this chapter.

(Amended by Stats. 1996, Ch. 1154, Sec. 72. Effective September 30, 1996.)

23251. (a) The Department of the California Highway Patrol shall provide for proper and adequate policing of all toll highways and all vehicular crossings to ensure the enforcement thereon of this code and of any other law relating to the use and operation of vehicles upon toll highways, highways or vehicular crossings, and of the rules and regulations of the Department of Transportation in respect thereto, and to cooperate with the Department of Transportation to the end that vehicular crossings be operated at all times in a manner as to carry traffic efficiently. The authority of the Department of the California Highway Patrol is exclusive except as to the authority conferred by law upon the Department of Transportation in respect to vehicular crossings.

(b) Notwithstanding subdivision (a), a private operator of a toll highway may make temporary arrangements, not to exceed 30 days, for traffic law enforcement services with an agency that employs peace officers as described in Section 830.1 of the Penal Code, if the Department of the California Highway Patrol cannot fulfill its responsibilities as described in this section, as determined by the Secretary of the Business, Transportation and Housing Agency.

(c) The services provided by the Department of the California Highway Patrol for all toll highways that are operated by a private entity shall be reimbursed pursuant to Section 30809.1 of the Streets and Highways Code. If the private operator of a toll highway and the Department of the California Highway Patrol reach an impasse in negotiating an agreement for reimbursement, the Secretary of the Business, Transportation and Housing Agency shall assist in resolving the impasse.

(Amended by Stats. 1992, Ch. 1241, Sec. 23. Effective January 1, 1993.)

23252. The chief of toll services, captains, lieutenants, and sergeants employed by the Department of Transportation shall have the powers and authority of peace officers as listed in Section 830.4 of the Penal Code while so employed on any vehicular crossing or as may be necessary to the performance of their duties while not upon such vehicular crossing. Captains, lieutenants, and sergeants so employed shall wear, while on duty, a uniform which shall be distinctly different from that of the California Highway Patrol, to be specified by the Director of Transportation.

(Amended by Stats. 1974, Ch. 545.)

23253. All persons in, or upon, any toll highway or vehicular crossing shall at all times comply with any lawful order, signal, or direction by voice or hand of any member of the California Highway Patrol or an employee of the Department of Transportation who is a peace officer.

(Amended by Stats. 1992, Ch. 1241, Sec. 24. Effective January 1, 1993.)

23254. A "vehicular crossing" is any toll bridge or toll highway crossing and the approaches thereto, constructed or acquired by the Department of Transportation under the provisions of the California Toll Bridge Authority Act.

(Amended by Stats. 1974, Ch. 545.)

23255. An "approach" is that portion of a state highway leading to or from a toll bridge or toll highway crossing which lies between one end of the bridge or crossing and the nearest intersection of a highway with the state highway. A ramp or other structure designed exclusively for use in connection with a toll bridge or toll highway crossing shall not be deemed an intersecting highway but is a part of the approach.

(Enacted by Stats. 1959, Ch. 3.)

Article 2. Towing on Vehicular Crossings

(Article 2 enacted by Stats. 1959, Ch. 3.)

23270. (a) No person shall commence to tow any vehicle or other object on any vehicular crossing unless authorized to do so by the Department of Transportation and unless the towing is done by means of a tow truck as defined in Section 615. No person, other than a member of the California Highway Patrol or an employee of the Department of Transportation, shall, by means of pushing with another vehicle, propel any vehicle or object on a vehicular crossing. No person, other than an employee of the Department of Transportation, shall, on any vehicular crossing, tow any vehicle or other object except a vehicle or object constructed and designed to be towed by a vehicle of a type similar to that being used for this purpose.

(b) The California Transportation Commission shall, by regulation, establish the maximum towing fee which may be charged by any person authorized to tow a vehicle pursuant to subdivision (a). No authorized person shall charge a fee for towing a vehicle which is in excess of the maximum fee established by the California Transportation Commission.

(c) The Director of Transportation may grant a special permit to any person to tow any vehicle or object over and completely across any vehicular crossing when in his or her judgment the towing vehicle is so constructed and equipped that the vehicle or object can be towed across the vehicular crossing without endangering persons or property and without interrupting the orderly traffic across the vehicular crossing.

(d) The prohibitions of this section shall apply only on those vehicular crossings upon which a towing service is maintained by the Department of Transportation.

(Amended by Stats. 1990, Ch. 216, Sec. 119.)

23271. A towing service may be maintained on each vehicular crossing by the Department of Transportation, and the department may furnish such service as is necessary to permit the orderly flow of traffic upon such crossing. The Department of Transportation may prescribe and collect reasonable rates for towing services furnished.

(Amended by Stats. 1974, Ch. 1053.)

23272. When any vehicle or object on any vehicular crossing, upon which towing service is maintained, is stopped for any reason and is obstructing or may obstruct traffic, the vehicle or object shall be towed by the towing service either to the nearest property of the Department of Transportation designated for the parking or storing of vehicles, or to a suitable parking location on a public street or highway and thereupon left in the custody of the owner or operator of the vehicle or object, or his agent, or, if no owner, operator, or agent is present, or if an owner, operator, or agent so requests, to a public garage or off-street parking facility. The department may prescribe the limits within which the towing service shall be operated.

Notwithstanding the foregoing provisions, the department may furnish and deliver fuel to vehicles, the supply of which is exhausted, or change tires, and may charge a reasonable sum for the services and materials furnished or, if the department deems it safe and advisable, and the owner or operator of the vehicle or object so requests, it may be towed from the vehicular crossing.

(Amended by Stats. 1982, Ch. 681, Sec. 85.)

23273. Sections 24605, 25253, 27700, and 27907 do not apply to vehicles operated by the Department of Transportation pursuant to this article.

(Amended by Stats. 1974, Ch. 545.)

Article 3. Tolls and Other Charges

(Article 3 enacted by Stats. 1959, Ch. 3.)

23300. The Department of Transportation shall erect appropriate signs at each entrance to a vehicular crossing to notify traffic that it is entering upon a vehicular crossing.

(Amended by Stats. 1974, Ch. 545.)

23301. Except as provided in Sections 23301.3 and 23301.5, a vehicle that enters into or upon a vehicular crossing is liable for those tolls and other charges prescribed by the California Transportation Commission.

(Amended by Stats. 2022, Ch. 871, Sec. 1. (AB 2949) Effective January 1, 2023.)

23301.3. (a) A vehicle described in subdivision (b) is exempt from a toll or other charge on a toll road, toll bridge, toll highway, vehicular crossing, or other toll facility.

(b) The exemption described in subdivision (a) applies only to a vehicle that meets all of the following criteria:

(1) The vehicle is registered to a veteran.

(2) The vehicle is displaying one of the following license plates:

(A) A license plate issued to a disabled veteran, pursuant to Section 5007.

(B) A license plate issued to a Pearl Harbor survivor, pursuant to Section 5101.3.

(C) A license plate issued to a recipient of the Army Medal of Honor, Navy Medal of Honor, Air Force Medal of Honor, Army Distinguished Service Cross, Navy Cross, or Air Force Cross, pursuant to Section 5101.4.

(D) A license plate issued to a former American prisoner of war, pursuant to Section 5101.5.

(E) A license plate issued to a recipient of the Congressional Medal of Honor, pursuant to Section 5101.6.

(F) A license plate issued to a recipient of the Purple Heart, pursuant to Section 5101.8.

(3) The vehicle is registered to a transponder or other electronic toll payment device account with an issuing agency as defined in Section 40250.

(c) This section does not exempt a vehicle described in subdivision (b) from a toll on a high-occupancy toll (HOT) lane.

(d) Sections 23302 and 23302.5 do not apply to a vehicle exempt pursuant to this section.

(Added by Stats. 2022, Ch. 871, Sec. 2. (AB 2949) Effective January 1, 2023.)

23301.5. (a) An authorized emergency vehicle is exempt from any requirement to pay a toll or other charge on a vehicular crossing, toll highway, or high-occupancy toll (HOT) lane, including the requirements of Section 23301, if all of the following conditions are satisfied:

(1) The authorized emergency vehicle is properly displaying an exempt California license plate, and is properly identified or marked as an authorized emergency vehicle, including, but not limited to, displaying an external surface-mounted red warning light, blue warning light, or both, and displaying either of the following:

(A) Public agency identification, including, but not limited to, "Fire Department," "Sheriff," or "Police."

(B) "Ambulance."

(2) (A) The vehicle is being driven while responding to or returning from an urgent or emergency call, engaged in an urgent or emergency response, or engaging in a fire station coverage assignment directly related to an emergency response.

(B) For purposes of this paragraph, an "urgent" response or call means an incident or circumstance that requires an immediate response to a public safety-related incident, but does not warrant the use of emergency warning lights. "Urgent" does not include any personal use, commuting, training, or administrative uses.

(C) Notwithstanding subparagraph (A), an authorized emergency vehicle, when returning from an urgent or emergency call, or from being engaged in an urgent or emergency response, or from engaging in a fire station coverage assignment directly related to an emergency response, shall not be exempt from any requirement to pay a toll or other charge imposed while traveling on a HOT lane.

(3) The driver of the vehicle determines that the use of the toll facility shall likely improve the availability or response and arrival time of the authorized emergency vehicle and its delivery of essential public safety services.

(b) If the operator of a toll facility elects to send a bill or invoice to the public agency for the use of the toll facility by an authorized emergency vehicle, exempt pursuant to subdivision (a), the fire chief, police chief, county sheriff, head of the public agency, ambulance corporation chief executive, or their designee, is authorized to certify in writing that the authorized emergency vehicle was responding to or returning from an emergency call or response and is exempt from the payment of the toll or other charge in accordance with this section. The letter shall be accepted by the toll operator in lieu of payment and is a public document.

(c) An authorized emergency vehicle that does not comply with this section is not exempt from the requirement to pay a toll or other charge on a toll highway, vehicular crossing, or HOT lane. Upon information and belief of the toll operator that an authorized emergency vehicle is not in compliance with this section, the fire chief, police chief, county sheriff, head of the public agency, ambulance corporation chief executive, or their designee, upon the written request of the owner or operator of the toll facility, shall provide or otherwise make accessible to the toll operator the dispatch records or log books relevant to the time period when the vehicle was in use on the toll highway, vehicular crossing, or HOT lane.

(d) Upon the request of a private or public local emergency service provider, an owner or operator of a toll facility shall enter into an agreement to establish mutually agreed upon terms for the use of the toll facility by the emergency service provider, including, but not limited to, being exempt from toll payment. This section shall not prohibit the owner or operator of a toll facility from having a policy that meets or exceeds this section. If at any time an emergency service provider or the owner or operator of a toll facility opts to terminate an agreement regarding the payment and processing of tolls or other charges, this section shall apply to the emergency service provider and the toll facility. An agreement between an emergency service provider and the owner or operator of a toll facility does not exempt other emergency service providers not named in the original agreement and the toll facility from the requirements of this section when those other emergency service providers use a toll facility in the jurisdiction of the owner or operator of the toll facility.

(e) Sections 23302 and 23302.5 do not apply to authorized emergency vehicles exempt pursuant to this section.

(f) As used in this section, "toll facility" includes a toll road, HOT lane, toll bridge, toll highway, a vehicular crossing for which payment of a toll or charge is required, or any other toll facility.

(Amended by Stats. 2025, Ch. 87, Sec. 1. (AB 1114) Effective January 1, 2026.)

23301.8. Where an issuing agency permits pay-by-plate toll payment as described in subdivision (e) of Section 23302, it shall communicate, as practicable, the pay-by-plate toll amount in the same manner as it communicates other toll payment methods. The issuing agency shall provide publicly available information on how pay-by-plate toll payment works, including the toll amount, process for payment, and period of time a vehicle has to resolve the payment before an issuing agency may process the trip as a violation under Section 40255. Communication of this information may include the Department of Transportation's approved signage, posting of information on the issuing agency's Internet Web site, media advertising, public meeting or disclosure as required by the issuing agency's policies, or other methods of communication. Except where the issuing agency has an agreement with a vehicle owner that specifies in advance any administrative fees that will be imposed on the owner for pay-by-plate toll payment, administrative costs shall be incorporated into the pay-by-plate toll amount, and no additional administrative costs shall be added above the posted pay-by-plate toll amount.

(Added by Stats. 2009, Ch. 459, Sec. 1. (AB 628) Effective January 1, 2010.)

23302. (a) (1) It is unlawful for a driver to fail to pay tolls or other charges on any vehicular crossing or toll highway. Except as otherwise provided in subdivision (b), (c), or (d), it is prima facie evidence of a violation of this section for a person to drive a vehicle onto any vehicular crossing or toll highway without either lawful money of the United States in the driver's immediate possession in an amount sufficient to pay the prescribed tolls or other charges due from that driver or a transponder or other electronic toll payment device associated with a valid Automatic Vehicle Identification account with a balance sufficient to pay those tolls.

(2) Except as specified in paragraph (3), if a transponder or other electronic toll payment device is used to pay tolls or other charges due, the device shall be located in or on the vehicle in a location so as to be visible for the purpose of enforcement at all times when the vehicle is located on the vehicular crossing or toll highway. If required by the operator of a vehicular crossing or toll highway, this requirement applies even if the operator offers free travel or nontoll accounts to certain classes of users.

(3) If a motorcyclist uses a transponder or other electronic toll payment device to lawfully enter a vehicle crossing or toll highway, the motorcyclist shall use any one of the following methods as long as the transponder or device is able to be read by the toll operator's detection equipment:

(A) Place the transponder or other electronic toll payment device in the motorcyclist's pocket.

(B) Place the transponder or other electronic toll payment device inside a cycle net that drapes over the gas tank of the motorcycle.

(C) Mount the transponder or other electronic toll payment device on license plate devices provided by the toll operator, if the toll operator provides those devices.

(D) Keep the transponder or other electronic toll payment device in the glove or storage compartment of the motorcycle.

(E) Mount the transponder or other electronic toll payment device on the windshield of the motorcycle.

(b) For vehicular crossings and toll highways that use electronic toll collection as the only method of paying tolls or other charges, it is prima facie evidence of a violation of this section for a driver to drive a vehicle onto the vehicular crossing or toll highway without a transponder or other electronic toll payment device associated with a valid Automatic Vehicle Identification account with a balance sufficient to pay those tolls.

(c) For vehicular crossings and toll highways where the issuing agency, as defined in Section 40250, permits pay-by-plate payment of tolls and other charges, in accordance with policies adopted by the issuing agency, it is prima facie evidence of a violation of this section for a driver to drive a vehicle onto the vehicular crossing or toll highway without at least one of the following:

(1) Lawful money of the United States in the driver's immediate possession in an amount sufficient to pay the prescribed tolls or other charges due from that person.

(2) A transponder or other electronic toll payment device associated with a valid Automatic Vehicle Identification account with a balance sufficient to pay those tolls.

(3) Valid vehicle license plates, registered to a vehicle with an up-to-date vehicle registration address pursuant to Section 4159, properly attached pursuant to Section 4850.5 or 5200 to the vehicle in which that driver enters onto the vehicular crossing or toll highway.

(d) For vehicular crossings and toll highways where the issuing agency, as defined in Section 40250, permits pay-by-plate payment of tolls and other charges in accordance with policies adopted by the issuing agency, and where electronic toll collection is the only other method of paying tolls or other charges, it is prima facie evidence of a violation of this section for a driver to drive a vehicle onto the vehicular crossing or toll highway without either a transponder or other electronic toll payment device associated with a valid Automatic Vehicle Identification account with a balance sufficient to pay those tolls or valid vehicle license plates, registered to a vehicle with an up-to-date vehicle registration address pursuant to Section 4159, properly attached to the vehicle pursuant to Section 4850.5 or 5200 in which that driver enters onto the vehicular crossing or toll highway.

(e) As used in this article, "pay-by-plate toll payment" means an issuing agency's use of on-road vehicle license plate identification recognition technology to accept payment of tolls in accordance with policies adopted by the issuing agency.

(f) This section does not require an issuing agency to offer pay-by-plate toll processing as a method for paying tolls.

(Amended by Stats. 2022, Ch. 969, Sec. 3. (AB 2594) Effective January 1, 2023.)

23302.5. (a) No person shall evade or attempt to evade the payment of tolls or other charges on any vehicular crossing or toll highway.

(b) A violation of subdivision (a) is subject to civil penalties and is neither an infraction nor a public offense, as defined in Section 15 of the Penal Code. The enforcement of those civil penalties shall be governed by the civil administrative procedures set forth in Article 4 (commencing with Section 40250) of Chapter 1 of Division 17.

(Added by Stats. 1995, Ch. 739, Sec. 7. Effective January 1, 1996.)

23303. The Department of Transportation shall have a lien and may enforce such lien, as provided in Chapter 6.5 (commencing with Section 3067) of Title 14 of Part 4 of Division 3 of the Civil Code, for all tolls and charges provided by this chapter.

(Amended by Stats. 1974, Ch. 545.)

23304. (a) With respect to a toll bridge, an issuing agency that permits pay-by-plate toll payment as described in subdivision (e) of Section 23302 or that permits payment by a transponder or other electronic toll payment device shall send an invoice by mail for any unpaid toll to the registered vehicle owner. The invoice shall include a notice to the registered owner that, unless the registered owner pays the toll by the due date shown on the invoice, a toll evasion penalty will be assessed. The invoice due date shall not be less than 30 days from the invoice date.

(b) If a toll invoice is not paid by the due date shown on the invoice, the nonpayment shall be deemed an evasion of tolls and the issuing agency, or processing agency as the case may be, shall mail a notice of toll evasion violation to the registered owner pursuant to subdivision (a) of Section 40254.

(c) This section shall become operative on July 1, 2024.

(Added by Stats. 2022, Ch. 969, Sec. 4. (AB 2594) Effective January 1, 2023. Operative July 1, 2024, by its own provisions.)

23305. (a) An issuing agency shall allow a driver of a rental vehicle to register the rental vehicle to a transponder or other electronic toll payment device account with the issuing agency prior to traveling on the issuing agency's toll facility for the purpose of paying all tolls with a credit or debit card. The issuing agency may require the use of a transponder for this purpose.

(b) The public entities operating or planning to implement a toll facility in this state shall cooperate to publish an internet website at which the public and rental car agencies can view and download, or that provides direct links to, information about how to open an account or acquire a transponder or other electronic toll payment device, for use of each issuing agency's toll facility. The rental car agency shall provide the customer with a written or electronic notice, including the electronic link for the internet website. The notice shall be separate from the rental contract and, if an electronic notice, emailed to the rental customer.

(c) This section shall become operative on July 1, 2024.

(Added by Stats. 2022, Ch. 969, Sec. 5. (AB 2594) Effective January 1, 2023. Operative July 1, 2024, by its own provisions.)

23306. (a) (1) An issuing agency that operates an electronic toll collection system that permits payment by a transponder or other electronic toll payment device shall, directly or through a third-party vendor, make the transponder or other electronic toll payment device available for acquisition online, by mail, and in person at a retail outlet, the office of an issuing agency or processing agency, as defined in Section 40253, or customer service center.

(2) At least one retail outlet, kiosk, or customer service center that offers the transponder or other electronic toll payment device associated with the issuing agency shall be located within the jurisdiction of the issuing agency.

(3) The issuing agency shall post on an internet website related to its electronic toll collection system locations where tolls may be paid with cash, and locations at which a transponder or other electronic toll payment device may be acquired.

(b) The price of the transponder or other electronic toll payment device shall not exceed the reasonable cost to the issuing agency based on the estimated cost to procure and distribute the device.

(c) As used in this article, "retail outlet" includes a store managed by the issuing agency, a cash payment location, or other locations not managed by the issuing agency.

(d) This section shall become operative on July 1, 2024.

(Added by Stats. 2022, Ch. 969, Sec. 6. (AB 2594) Effective January 1, 2023. Operative July 1, 2024, by its own provisions.)

23307. (a) If an issuing agency offers a transponder or other electronic toll payment device, a person shall be allowed to acquire a transponder or other electronic toll payment device with cash, or with a credit or debit card, and shall be allowed to load a minimum of one hundred dollars ($100) onto the associated account with cash or with a credit or debit card.

(b) Except as otherwise provided in subdivision (b) of Section 23306, there shall be no additional transaction fee charged to acquire the transponder or other electronic toll payment device.

(c) An issuing agency shall not assess any additional transaction fee to the amount a person is charged by a cash payment network company to load funds to an account using cash through a cash payment network.

(d) This section shall become operative on July 1, 2024.

(Added by Stats. 2022, Ch. 969, Sec. 7. (AB 2594) Effective January 1, 2023. Operative July 1, 2024, by its own provisions.)

23308. (a) Subject to extenuating circumstances and holidays, the hours during which one of the issuing or processing agency's offices or customer service centers are open to the public to provide customer service related to electronic toll collection shall include at least five hours per week between the hours of 6 a.m. to 8 a.m. or 5 p.m. to 7 p.m., or on a Saturday.

(b) A person shall be able to conduct all of the following transactions at either the issuing agency's office or customer service center:

(1) Acquire the issuing agency's transponder or other electronic toll payment device.

(2) Load money onto an account with the issuing agency.

(3) Pay a toll notice, including fines and penalties.

(4) Register or remove a license plate to or from a transponder or other electronic toll payment device account with the issuing agency for payment of tolls.

(c) Except as otherwise provided in subdivision (b) of Section 23306, the issuing agency shall not charge persons paying cash an additional transaction fee for any transaction listed in paragraphs (1) to (3), inclusive, of subdivision (b) that are conducted at the issuing or processing agency's office, or customer service center. There shall be at least one issuing or processing agency's office or customer service center within the issuing agency's jurisdiction.

(d) The issuing agency shall have two or more physical locations within each county in which a toll facility operated by the issuing agency is located for purposes of conducting the transactions set forth in paragraphs (2) and (3) of subdivision (b).

(e) This section shall become operative on July 1, 2024.

(Added by Stats. 2022, Ch. 969, Sec. 8. (AB 2594) Effective January 1, 2023. Operative July 1, 2024, by its own provisions.)

23309. (a) Subject to extenuating circumstances and holidays, the issuing agency, directly or through a third-party vendor, shall maintain a customer service telephone line that shall be operated by a live person for at least 35 hours per week between the hours of 8 a.m. to 5 p.m. and an additional 5 hours per week between the hours of 6 a.m. to 8 a.m., from 5 p.m. to 7 p.m., or on a Saturday. The customer service telephone line shall be available to address questions related to acquiring a transponder or other electronic toll payment device, paying toll notices, disputing tolls and penalties, setting up payment plans, and registering the license plate of a vehicle to a transponder or other electronic toll payment device account.

(b) The customer service telephone line shall provide language interpreter services and assistance for deaf or hard-of-hearing individuals.

(c) This section shall become operative on July 1, 2024.

(Added by Stats. 2022, Ch. 969, Sec. 9. (AB 2594) Effective January 1, 2023. Operative July 1, 2024, by its own provisions.)

Article 4. Special Traffic Regulations

(Article 4 enacted by Stats. 1959, Ch. 3.)

23330. Except where a special permit has been obtained from the Department of Transportation under the provisions of Article 6 (commencing with Section 35780) of Chapter 5 of Division 15, none of the following shall be permitted on any vehicular crossing:

(a) Animals while being led or driven, even though tethered or harnessed.

(b) Bicycles, motorized bicycles, or motorized scooters, unless the department by signs indicates that bicycles, motorized bicycles, or motorized scooters, or any combination thereof, are permitted upon all or any portion of the vehicular crossing.

(c) Vehicles having a total width of vehicle or load exceeding 102 inches.

(d) Vehicles carrying items prohibited by regulations promulgated by the Department of Transportation.

(Amended by Stats. 1999, Ch. 722, Sec. 8. Effective January 1, 2000.)

23331. Pedestrians shall not be permitted upon any vehicular crossing, unless unobstructed sidewalks of more than three feet in width are constructed and maintained and signs indicating that pedestrians are permitted are in place.

(Enacted by Stats. 1959, Ch. 3.)

23332. It is unlawful for any person to be upon any portion of a vehicular crossing which is not intended for public use without the permission of the Department of Transportation. This section does not apply to a person engaged in the operation, maintenance, or repair of a vehicular crossing or any facility thereon nor to any person attempting to effect a rescue.

(Amended by Stats. 1974, Ch. 545.)

23333. No vehicle shall stop, stand, or be parked in or upon any vehicular crossing except:

(a) When necessary to avoid injury or damage to persons or property.

(b) When necessary for the repair, maintenance or operation of a publicly owned toll bridge.

(c) In compliance with the direction of a member of the California Highway Patrol or an employee of the Department of Transportation who is a peace officer or with the direction of a sign or signal.

(d) In such places as may be designated by the Director of Transportation.

(Amended by Stats. 1974, Ch. 545.)

23334. The Department of Transportation may adopt rules and regulations not inconsistent with this chapter for the control of traffic on any vehicular crossing to aid and insure the safe and orderly flow of traffic, and shall, so far as practicable, notify the public of the rules and regulations by signs on the vehicular crossing.

(Amended by Stats. 1974, Ch. 545.)

23335. The Department of Transportation shall cause to be published and made available to the public at the tollgates of each vehicular crossing copies of those traffic laws and rules and regulations particularly applicable thereto.

(Amended by Stats. 1974, Ch. 545.)

23336. It is unlawful to violate any rules or regulations adopted under Section 23334, notice of which has been given either by a sign on a vehicular crossing or by publication as provided in Section 23335.

(Enacted by Stats. 1959, Ch. 3.)

Division 11.5. Sentencing for Driving While Under the Influence

(Division 11.5 added by Stats. 1998, Ch. 118, Sec. 84.)

Chapter 1. Court-Imposed Penalties: Persons Less Than 21 Years Of Age

(Chapter 1 added by Stats. 1998, Ch. 118, Sec. 84.)

Article 1. General Provisions

(Article 1 added by Stats. 1998, Ch. 118, Sec. 84.)

23500. This chapter applies to the imposition of penalties and sanctions by the courts on persons who were less than 21 years of age at the time of the commission of the driving while under the influence offenses described in Chapter 12 (commencing with Section 23100) of Division 11.

(Added by Stats. 1998, Ch. 118, Sec. 84. Effective January 1, 1999. Section operative July 1, 1999, pursuant to Section 23675.)

Article 2. Penalties for a Violation of Section 23140

(Article 2 repealed and added by Stats. 2000, Ch. 1063, Sec. 4.)

23502. (a) Notwithstanding any other provision of law, if a person who is at least 18 years of age is convicted of a first violation of Section 23140, in addition to any penalties, the court shall order the person to attend a program licensed under Section 11836 of the Health and Safety Code, subject to a fee schedule developed under paragraph (2) of subdivision (b) of Section 11837.4 of the Health and Safety Code.

(b) The attendance in a licensed driving-under-the-influence program required under subdivision (a) shall be as follows:

(1) If, within 10 years of the current violation of Section 23140, the person has not been convicted of a separate violation of Section 23140, 23152, or 23153, or of Section 23103, with a plea of guilty under Section 23103.5, or of Section 655 of the Harbors and Navigation Code, or of Section 191.5 of, or subdivision (a) of Section 192.5 of, the Penal Code, the person shall complete, at a minimum, the education component of that licensed driving-under-the-influence program.

(2) If the person does not meet the requirements of paragraph (1), the person shall complete, at a minimum, the program described in paragraph (1) of subdivision (c) of Section 11837 of the Health and Safety Code.

(c) The person's privilege to operate a motor vehicle shall be suspended by the department as required under Section 13352.6, and the court shall require the person to surrender his or her driver's license to the court in accordance with Section 13550.

(d) The court shall advise the person at the time of sentencing that the driving privilege will not be restored until the person has provided the department with proof satisfactory to the department that the person has successfully completed the driving-under-the-influence program required under this section.

(Amended by Stats. 2007, Ch. 747, Sec. 32. Effective January 1, 2008.)

Article 3. Youthful Drunk Driver Visitation Program

(Article 3 added by Stats. 1998, Ch. 118, Sec. 84.)

23509. This article shall be known and may be cited as the "Youthful Drunk Driver Visitation Program Act."

(Added by Stats. 1998, Ch. 118, Sec. 84. Effective January 1, 1999. Section operative July 1, 1999, pursuant to Section 23675.)

23510. The Legislature finds and declares all of the following:

(a) Young drivers often do not realize the consequences of drinking alcohol or ingesting any other drugs, whether legal or not, and driving a motor vehicle while their physical capabilities to drive safely are impaired by those substances.

(b) Young drivers who use alcohol or other drugs are likely to become dependent on those substances and prompt intervention is needed to protect other persons, as well as the young driver, from death or serious injury.

(c) The conviction of a young driver for driving under the influence of an alcoholic beverage, a drug, or both, identifies that person as a risk to the health and safety of others, as well as that young driver, because of the young driver's inability to control his or her conduct.

(d) It has been demonstrated that close observation of the effects on others of alcohol and other drugs, both chronic and acute, by a young driver convicted of driving under the influence has a marked effect on recidivism and should therefore be encouraged by the courts, prehospital emergency medical care personnel, and other officials charged with cleaning up the carnage and wreckage caused by drunk drivers.

(e) The program prescribed in this article provides guidelines for the operation of an intensive program to discourage recidivism by convicted young drunk drivers.

(Added by Stats. 1998, Ch. 118, Sec. 84. Effective January 1, 1999. Section operative July 1, 1999, pursuant to Section 23675.)

23512. For the purposes of this article, "program" means the Youthful Drunk Driver Visitation Program prescribed in this article.

(Added by Stats. 1998, Ch. 118, Sec. 84. Effective January 1, 1999. Section operative July 1, 1999, pursuant to Section 23675.)

23514. (a) If a person is found to be in violation of Section 23140, is convicted of, or is adjudged a ward of the juvenile court for, a violation of Section 21200.5, 23140, or 23152 punishable under Section 23536, or Section 23220, 23221, or 23222, subdivision (a) or (b) of Section 23224, or Section 23225 or 23226, and is granted probation, the court may order, with the consent of the defendant or ward, as a term and condition of probation in addition to any other term and condition required or authorized by law, that the defendant or ward participate in the program.

(b) The court shall give preference for participation in the program to defendants or wards who were less than 21 years of age at the time of the offense if the facilities of the program in the jurisdiction are limited to fewer than the number of defendants or wards eligible and consenting to participate.

(c) The court shall require that the defendant or ward not drink any alcoholic beverage at all before reaching the age of 21 years and not use illegal drugs.

(Added by Stats. 1998, Ch. 118, Sec. 84. Effective January 1, 1999. Section operative July 1, 1999, pursuant to Section 23675.)

23516. The court shall investigate and consult with the defendant or ward, defendant's or ward's counsel, if any, and any proposed supervisor of a visitation under the program, and the court may consult with any other person whom the court finds may be of value, including, but not limited to, the defendant's or ward's parents or other family members, in order to ascertain that the defendant or ward is suitable for the program, that the visitation will be educational and meaningful to the defendant or ward, and that there are no physical, emotional, or mental reasons to believe the program would not be appropriate or would cause any injury to the defendant or ward.

(Added by Stats. 1998, Ch. 118, Sec. 84. Effective January 1, 1999. Section operative July 1, 1999, pursuant to Section 23675.)

23517. (a) To the extent that personnel and facilities are made available to the court, the court may include a requirement for supervised visitation by the defendant or ward to all, or any, of the following:

(1) A trauma facility, as defined in Section 1798.160 of the Health and Safety Code, a base hospital designated pursuant to Section 1798.100 or 1798.101 of the Health and Safety Code, or a general acute care hospital having a basic emergency medical services special permit issued pursuant to subdivision (c) of Section 1277 of the Health and Safety Code that regularly receives victims of vehicle crashes, between the hours of 10 p.m. and 2 a.m. on a Friday or Saturday night to observe appropriate victims of vehicle crashes involving drinking drivers, under

the supervision of any of the following:

(A) A registered nurse trained in providing emergency trauma care or prehospital advanced life support.

(B) An emergency room physician.

(C) An emergency medical technician-paramedic or an emergency medical technician II.

(2) If approved by the county coroner, the county coroner's office or the county morgue to observe appropriate victims of vehicle crashes involving drinking drivers, under the supervision of the coroner or a deputy coroner.

(b) As used in this section, "appropriate victims" means victims whose condition is determined by the visitation supervisor to demonstrate the results of crashes involving drinking drivers without being excessively gruesome or traumatic to the probationer.

(c) If persons trained in counseling or substance abuse are made available to the court, the court may coordinate the visitation program or the visitations at any facility designated in subdivision (a) through those persons.

(d) Any visitation shall include, before any observation of victims or disabled persons by the probationer, a comprehensive counseling session with the visitation supervisor at which the supervisor shall explain and discuss the experiences that may be encountered during the visitation in order to ascertain whether the visitation is appropriate for the probationer.

(e) If at any time, whether before or during a visitation, the supervisor of the probationer determines that the visitation may be or is traumatic or otherwise inappropriate for the probationer, or is uncertain whether the visitation may be traumatic or inappropriate, the visitation shall be terminated without prejudice to the probationer.

(f) Prior to the court including a requirement for supervised visitation, pursuant to subdivision (a), the court shall consider the speed of the vehicle, the severity of any injuries sustained as a result of the violation, and whether the defendant or ward was engaged in a speed competition, as defined in Section 23109.

(Amended by Stats. 2022, Ch. 81, Sec. 5. (AB 2198) Effective January 1, 2023.)

23518. (a) The program may include a personal conference after the visitations described in Section 23517 between the sentencing judge or judicial officer or the person responsible for coordinating the program for the judicial district and the probationer, his or her counsel, and, if available, the probationer's parents to discuss the experiences of the visitation and how those experiences may impact the probationer's future conduct.

(b) If a personal conference described in subdivision (a) is not practicable, because of the probationer's absence from the jurisdiction, conflicting time schedules, or other reasons, the program should provide for a written report or letter by the probationer to the court discussing the experiences and their impact on the probationer.

(Added by Stats. 1998, Ch. 118, Sec. 84. Effective January 1, 1999. Section operative July 1, 1999, pursuant to Section 23675.)

23518.5. The county, a court, any facility visited pursuant to the program, the agents, employees, or independent contractors of the court, county, or facility visited pursuant to the program, and any person supervising a probationer during the visitation, is not liable for any civil damages resulting from injury to the probationer, or civil damages caused by the probationer, during, or from any activities relating to, the visitation, except for willful or grossly negligent acts intended to, or reasonably expected to result in, that injury or damage and except for workers' compensation for the probationer as prescribed by law if the probationer performs community service at the facility as an additional term or condition of probation.

(Added by Stats. 1998, Ch. 118, Sec. 84. Effective January 1, 1999. Section operative July 1, 1999, pursuant to Section 23675.)

Article 4. Penalties for a Violation of Section 23152 or 23153

(Article 4 added by Stats. 1998, Ch. 118, Sec. 84.)

23520. (a) Whenever, in any county specified in subdivision (b), a judge of a juvenile court, a juvenile hearing officer, or referee of a juvenile court finds that a person has committed a first violation of Section 23152 or 23153, the person shall be required to participate in and successfully complete an alcohol or drug education program, or both of those programs, as designated by the court. The expense of the person's attendance in the program shall be paid by the person's parents or guardian so long as the person is under the age of 18 years, and shall be paid by the person thereafter. However, in approving the program, each county shall require the program to provide for the payment of the fee for the program in installments by any person who cannot afford to pay the full fee at the commencement of the program and shall require the program to provide for the waiver of the fee for any person who is indigent, as determined by criteria for indigency established by the board of supervisors. Whenever it can be done without substantial additional cost, each county shall require that the program be provided for juveniles at a separate location from, or at a different time of day than, alcohol and drug education programs for adults.

(b) This section applies only in those counties that have one or more alcohol or drug education programs certified by the county alcohol program administrator and approved by the board of supervisors.

(Amended by Stats. 2003, Ch. 149, Sec. 85. Effective January 1, 2004.)

23521. (a) Any finding of a juvenile court judge, juvenile hearing officer, or referee of a juvenile court of a commission of an offense in any state, territory, possession of the United States, the District of Columbia, the Commonwealth of Puerto Rico, or the Dominion of Canada that, if committed in this state, would be a violation of Section 23152, is a conviction of a violation of Section 23152 for the purposes of Sections 13352, 13352.3, 13352.4, and 13352.5, and the finding of a juvenile court judge, juvenile hearing officer, or referee of a juvenile court of a commission of an offense that, if committed in this state, would be a violation of Section 23153 is a conviction of a violation of Section 23153 for the purposes of Sections 13352 and 13352.3.

(b) This section shall become operative on September 20, 2005.

(Amended by Stats. 2004, Ch. 551, Sec. 14. Effective January 1, 2005. Amended version operative September 20, 2005, pursuant to earlier operation of new subdivision (b).)

Chapter 2. Court Penalties

(Chapter 2 added by Stats. 1998, Ch. 118, Sec. 84.)

Article 1. General Provisions

(Article 1 added by Stats. 1998, Ch. 118, Sec. 84.)

23530. This chapter applies to the imposition of penalties, sanctions, and probation upon persons convicted of violating driving while under the influence offenses that are set forth in Chapter 12 (commencing with Section 23100) of Division 11.

(Added by Stats. 1998, Ch. 118, Sec. 84. Effective January 1, 1999. Section operative July 1, 1999, pursuant to Section 23675.)

Article 2. Penalties for a Violation of Section 23152

(Article 2 added by Stats. 1998, Ch. 118, Sec. 84.)

23536. (a) If a person is convicted of a first violation of Section 23152, that person shall be punished by imprisonment in the county jail for not less than 96 hours, at least 48 hours of which shall be continuous, nor more than six months, and by a fine of not less than three hundred ninety dollars ($390), nor more than one thousand dollars ($1,000).

(b) The court shall order that a person punished under subdivision (a), who is to be punished by imprisonment in the county jail, be imprisoned on days other than days of regular employment of the person, as determined by the court. If the court determines that 48 hours of continuous imprisonment would interfere with the person's work schedule, the court shall allow the person to serve the imprisonment whenever the person is normally scheduled for time off from work. The court may make this determination based upon a representation from the defendant's attorney or upon an affidavit or testimony from the defendant.

(c) The person's privilege to operate a motor vehicle shall be suspended by the department under paragraph (1) of subdivision (a) of Section 13352 or Section 13352.1. The court shall require the person to surrender the driver's license to the court in accordance with Section 13550.

(d) Whenever, when considering the circumstances taken as a whole, the court determines that the person punished under this section would present a traffic safety or public safety risk if authorized to operate a motor vehicle during the period of suspension imposed under paragraph (1) of subdivision (a) of Section 13352 or Section 13352.1, the court may disallow the issuance of a restricted driver's license required under Section 13352.4.

(Amended by Stats. 2006, Ch. 692, Sec. 5. Effective January 1, 2007.)

23538. (a) (1) If the court grants probation to person punished under Section 23536, in addition to the provisions of Section 23600 and any other terms and conditions imposed by the court, the court shall impose as a condition of probation that the person pay a fine of at least three hundred ninety dollars ($390), but not more than one thousand dollars ($1,000). The court may also impose, as a condition of probation, that the person be confined in a county jail for at least 48 hours, but not more than six months.

(2) The person's privilege to operate a motor vehicle shall be suspended by the department under paragraph (1) of subdivision (a) of Section 13352 or Section 13352.1. The court shall require the person to surrender the driver's license to the court in accordance with Section 13550.

(3) Whenever, when considering the circumstances taken as a whole, the court determines that the person punished under this section would present a traffic safety or public safety risk if authorized to operate a motor vehicle during the period of suspension imposed under paragraph (1) of subdivision (a) of Section 13352 or Section 13352.1, the court may disallow the issuance of a restricted driver's license required under Section 13352.4.

(b) In any county where the board of supervisors has approved, and the State Department of Health Care Services has licensed, a program or programs described in Section 11837.3 of the Health and Safety Code, the court shall also impose as a condition of probation that the driver shall enroll and participate in, and successfully complete a driving-under-the-influence program, licensed pursuant to Section 11836 of the Health and Safety Code, in the driver's county of residence or employment, as designated by the court. For the purposes of this subdivision, enrollment in, participation in, and completion of an approved program shall be subsequent to the date of the current violation. Credit may not be given for any program activities completed prior to the date of the current violation.

(1) The court shall refer a first offender whose blood-alcohol concentration was less than 0.20 percent, by weight, to participate for at least three months or longer, as ordered by the court, in a licensed program that consists of at least 30 hours of program activities, including those education, group counseling, and individual interview sessions described in Chapter 9 (commencing with Section 11836) of Part 2 of Division 10.5 of the Health and Safety Code.

(2) The court shall refer a first offender whose blood-alcohol concentration was 0.20 percent or more, by weight, or who refused to take a chemical test, to participate for at least nine months or longer, as ordered by the court, in a licensed program that consists of at least 60 hours of program activities, including those education, group counseling, and individual interview sessions described in Chapter 9 (commencing with Section 11836) of Part 2 of Division 10.5 of the Health and Safety Code.

(3) The court shall advise the person at the time of sentencing that the driving privilege shall not be restored until proof satisfactory to the department of successful completion of a driving-under-the-influence program of the length required under this code that is licensed pursuant to Section 11836 of the Health and Safety Code has been received in the department's headquarters.

(c) (1) The court shall revoke the person's probation pursuant to Section 23602, except for good cause shown, for the failure to enroll in, participate in, or complete a program specified in subdivision (b).

(2) The court, in establishing reporting requirements, shall consult with the county alcohol program administrator. The county alcohol program administrator shall coordinate the reporting requirements with the department and with the State Department of Health Care Services. That reporting shall ensure that all persons who, after being ordered to attend and complete a program, may be identified for either (A) failure to enroll in, or failure to successfully complete, the program, or (B) successful completion of the program as ordered.

(Amended by Stats. 2013, Ch. 22, Sec. 87. (AB 75) Effective June 27, 2013. Operative July 1, 2013, by Sec. 110 of Ch. 22.)

23540. (a) If a person is convicted of a violation of Section 23152 and the offense occurred within 10 years of a separate violation of Section 23103, as specified in Section 23103.5, 23152, or 23153, that resulted in a conviction, that person shall be punished by imprisonment in the county jail for not less than 90 days nor more than one year and by a fine of not less than three hundred ninety dollars ($390) nor more than one thousand dollars ($1,000). The person's privilege to operate a motor vehicle shall be suspended by the department pursuant to paragraph (3) of subdivision (a) of Section 13352. The court shall require the person to surrender the driver's license to the court in accordance with Section 13550.

(b) Whenever, when considering the circumstances taken as a whole, the court determines that the person punished under this section would present a traffic safety or public safety risk if authorized to operate a motor vehicle during the period of suspension imposed under paragraph (3) of subdivision (a) of Section 13352, the court may disallow the issuance of a restricted driver's license required under Section 13352.5.

(c) This section shall become operative on September 20, 2005.

(Repealed (in Sec. 17.3) and added by Stats. 2004, Ch. 551, Sec. 17.5. Effective January 1, 2005. Section operative September 20, 2005, by its own provisions.)

23542. (a) (1) If the court grants probation to a person punished under Section 23540, in addition to the provisions of Section 23600 and any other terms and conditions imposed by the court, the court shall impose as conditions of probation that the person be confined in county jail and fined under either of the following:

(A) For at least 10 days, but not more than one year, and pay a fine of at least three hundred ninety dollars ($390), but not more than one thousand dollars ($1,000).

(B) For at least 96 hours, but not more than one year, and pay a fine of at least three hundred ninety dollars ($390), but not more than one thousand dollars ($1,000). A sentence of 96 hours of confinement shall be served in two increments consisting of a continuous 48 hours each. The two 48-hour increments may be served nonconsecutively.

(2) The person's privilege to operate a motor vehicle shall be suspended by the department under paragraph (3) of subdivision (a) of Section 13352. The court shall require the person to surrender the driver's license to the court in accordance with Section 13550.

(b) In addition to the conditions specified in subdivision (a), the court shall require the person to do either of the following:

(1) Enroll and participate, for at least 18 months subsequent to the date of the underlying violation and in a manner satisfactory to the court, in a driving-under-the-influence program licensed pursuant to Section 11836 of the Health and Safety Code, as designated by the court. The person shall complete the entire program subsequent to, and shall not be given any credit for any program activities completed prior to, the date of the current violation. The program shall provide for persons who

cannot afford the program fee pursuant to paragraph (2) of subdivision (b) of Section 11837.4 of the Health and Safety Code in order to enable those persons to participate.

(2) Enroll and participate, for at least 30 months subsequent to the date of the underlying violation and in a manner satisfactory to the court, in a driving-under-the-influence program licensed pursuant to Section 11836 of the Health and Safety Code. The person shall complete the entire program subsequent to, and shall not be given any credit for any program activities completed prior to, the date of the current violation.

(c) The court shall advise the person at the time of sentencing that the driving privilege shall not be restored until proof satisfactory to the Department of Motor Vehicles of successful completion of a driving-under-the-influence program of the length required under this code licensed pursuant to Section 11836 of the Health and Safety Code has been received in the department's headquarters.

(d) Whenever, when considering the circumstances taken as a whole, the court determines that the person punished under this section would present a traffic safety or public safety risk if authorized to operate a motor vehicle during the period of suspension imposed under paragraph (3) of subdivision (a) of Section 13352, the court may disallow the issuance of a restricted driver's license required under Section 13352.5.

(e) This section shall become operative on September 20, 2005.

(Repealed (in Sec. 18.3) and added by Stats. 2004, Ch. 551, Sec. 18.5. Effective January 1, 2005. Section operative September 20, 2005, by its own provisions.)

23546. (a) If a person is convicted of a violation of Section 23152 and the offense occurred within 10 years of two separate violations of Section 23103, as specified in Section 23103.5, 23152, or 23153, or any combination thereof, that resulted in convictions, that person shall be punished by imprisonment in the county jail for not less than 120 days nor more than one year and by a fine of not less than three hundred ninety dollars ($390) nor more than one thousand dollars ($1,000). The person's privilege to operate a motor vehicle shall be revoked by the Department of Motor Vehicles as required in paragraph (5) of subdivision (a) of Section 13352. The court shall require the person to surrender his or her driver's license to the court in accordance with Section 13550.

(b) A person convicted of a violation of Section 23152 punishable under this section shall be designated as a habitual traffic offender for a period of three years, subsequent to the conviction. The person shall be advised of this designation pursuant to subdivision (b) of Section 13350.

(Amended by Stats. 2004, Ch. 550, Sec. 14. Effective January 1, 2005.)

23548. (a) (1) If the court grants probation to any person punished under Section 23546, in addition to the provisions of Section 23600 and any other terms and conditions imposed by the court, the court shall impose as conditions of probation that the person be confined in the county jail for at least 120 days but not more than one year and pay a fine of at least three hundred ninety dollars ($390) but not more than one thousand dollars ($1,000).

(2) The person's privilege to operate a motor vehicle shall be revoked by the department under paragraph (5) of subdivision (a) of Section 13352. The court shall require the person to surrender the driver's license to the court in accordance with Section 13550.

(b) In addition to subdivision (a), if the court grants probation to any person punished under Section 23546, the court may order as a condition of probation that the person participate, for at least 30 months subsequent to the underlying conviction and in a manner satisfactory to the court, in a driving-under-the-influence program licensed pursuant to Section 11836 of the Health and Safety Code. In lieu of the minimum term of imprisonment specified in subdivision (a), the court shall impose as a condition of probation under this subdivision that the person be confined in the county jail for at least 30 days but not more than one year. The court shall not order the treatment prescribed by this subdivision unless the person makes a specific request and shows good cause for the order, whether or not the person has previously completed a treatment program pursuant to paragraph (4) of subdivision (b) of Section 23542 or paragraph (4) of subdivision (b) of Section 23562. In order to enable all required persons to participate, each person shall pay the program costs commensurate with the person's ability to pay as determined pursuant to Section 11837.4 of the Health and Safety Code. No condition of probation required pursuant to this subdivision is a basis for reducing any other probation requirement in this section or Section 23600 or for avoiding the mandatory license revocation provisions of paragraph (5) of subdivision (a) of Section 13352.

(c) In addition to the provisions of Section 23600 and subdivision (a), if the court grants probation to any person punished under Section 23546 who has not previously completed a treatment program pursuant to paragraph (4) of subdivision (b) of Section 23542 or paragraph (4) of subdivision (b) of Section 23562, and unless the person is ordered to participate in and complete a driving-under-the-influence program under subdivision (b), the court shall impose as a condition of probation that the person, subsequent to the date of the current violation, enroll and participate, for at least 18 months and in a manner satisfactory to the court, in a driving-under-the-influence program licensed pursuant to Section 11836 of the Health and Safety Code, as designated by the court. The person shall complete the entire program subsequent to, and shall not be given any credit for program activities completed prior to, the date of the current violation. Any person who has previously completed a 12-month or 18-month program licensed pursuant to Section 11836 of the Health and Safety Code shall not be eligible for referral pursuant to this subdivision unless a 30-month licensed driving-under-the-influence program is not available for referral in the county of the person's residence or employment. The program shall provide for persons who cannot afford the program fee pursuant to paragraph (2) of subdivision (b) of Section 11837.4 of the Health and Safety Code in order to enable those persons to participate. No condition of probation required pursuant to this subdivision is a basis for reducing any other probation requirement in this section or Section 23600 or for avoiding the mandatory license revocation provisions of paragraph (5) of subdivision (a) of Section 13352.

(d) The court shall advise the person at the time of sentencing that the driving privilege may not be restored until the person provides proof satisfactory to the department of successful completion of a driving-under-the-influence program of the length required under this code that is licensed pursuant to Section 11836 of the Health and Safety Code.

(e) This section shall become operative on September 20, 2005.

(Amended by Stats. 2004, Ch. 551, Sec. 19. Effective January 1, 2005. Amended version operative September 20, 2005, pursuant to earlier operation of new subdivision (e).)

23550. (a) If a person is convicted of a violation of Section 23152 and the offense occurred within 10 years of three or more separate violations of Section 23103, as specified in Section 23103.5, or Section 23152 or 23153, or any combination thereof, that resulted in convictions, that person shall be punished by imprisonment pursuant to subdivision (h) of Section 1170 of the Penal Code, or in a county jail for not less than 180 days nor more than one year, and by a fine of not less than three hundred ninety dollars ($390) nor more than one thousand dollars ($1,000). The person's privilege to operate a motor vehicle shall be revoked by the Department of Motor Vehicles pursuant to paragraph (7) of subdivision (a) of Section 13352. The court shall require the person to surrender the driver's license to the court in accordance with Section 13550.

(b) A person convicted of a violation of Section 23152 punishable under this section shall be designated as a habitual traffic offender for a period of three years, subsequent to the conviction. The person shall be advised of this designation pursuant to subdivision (b) of Section 13350.

(Amended by Stats. 2011, Ch. 15, Sec. 614. (AB 109) Effective April 4, 2011. Operative October 1, 2011, by Sec. 636 of Ch. 15, as amended by Stats. 2011, Ch. 39, Sec. 68.)

23550.5. (a) A person is guilty of a public offense, punishable by imprisonment in the state prison or confinement in a county jail for not more than one year and by a fine of not less than three hundred ninety dollars ($390) nor more than one thousand dollars ($1,000) if that person is convicted of a violation of Section 23152 or 23153, and the offense occurred within 10 years of any of the following:

(1) A separate violation of Section 23152 that was punished as a felony under Section 23550 or this section, or both, or under former Section 23175 or former Section 23175.5, or both.

(2) A separate violation of Section 23153 that was punished as a felony.

(3) A separate violation of paragraph (1) of subdivision (c) of Section 192 of the Penal Code that was punished as a felony.

(b) Each person who, having previously been convicted of a violation of subdivision (a) of Section 191.5 of the Penal Code, a felony violation of subdivision (b) of Section 191.5, or a violation of subdivision (a) of Section 192.5 of the Penal Code, is subsequently convicted of a violation of Section 23152 or 23153 is guilty of a public offense punishable by imprisonment in the state prison or confinement in a county jail for not more than one year and by a fine of not less than three hundred ninety dollars ($390) nor more than one thousand dollars ($1,000).

(c) The privilege to operate a motor vehicle of a person convicted of a violation that is punishable under subdivision (a) or (b) shall be revoked by the department pursuant to paragraph (7) of subdivision (a) of Section 13352, unless paragraph (6) of subdivision (a) of Section 13352 is also applicable, in which case the privilege shall be revoked under that provision. The court shall require the person to surrender the driver's license to the court in accordance with Section 13550.

(d) A person convicted of a violation of Section 23152 or 23153 that is punishable under this section shall be designated as a habitual traffic offender for a period of three years, subsequent to the conviction. The person shall be advised of this designation under subdivision (b) of Section 13350.

(Amended by Stats. 2014, Ch. 509, Sec. 1. (AB 2690) Effective January 1, 2015.)

23552. (a) (1) If the court grants probation to a person punished under Section 23550, in addition to the provisions of Section 23600 and any other terms and conditions imposed by the court, the court shall impose as conditions of probation that the person be confined in a county jail for at least 180 days but not more than one year and pay a fine of at least three hundred ninety dollars ($390) but not more than one thousand dollars ($1,000).

(2) The person's privilege to operate a motor vehicle shall be revoked by the department under paragraph (7) of subdivision (a) of Section 13352. The court shall require the person to surrender the driver's license to the court in accordance with Section 13550.

(b) In addition to subdivision (a), if the court grants probation to any person punished under Section 23550, the court may order as a condition of probation that the person participate, for at least 30 months subsequent to the underlying conviction and in a manner satisfactory to the court, in a driving-under-the-influence program licensed pursuant to Section 11836 of the Health and Safety Code. In lieu of the minimum term of imprisonment in subdivision (a), the court shall impose as a condition of probation under this subdivision that the person be confined in the county jail for at least 30 days but not more than one year. The court shall not order the treatment prescribed by this subdivision unless the person makes a specific request and shows good cause for the order, whether or not the person has previously completed a treatment program pursuant to subdivision (b) of Section 23542 or paragraph (4) of subdivision (b) of Section 23562. In order to enable all required persons to participate, each person shall pay the program costs commensurate with the person's ability to pay as determined pursuant to Section 11837.4 of the Health and Safety Code. No condition of probation required pursuant to this subdivision is a basis for reducing any other probation requirement in this section or Section 23600 or for avoiding the mandatory license revocation provisions of paragraph (7) of subdivision (a) of Section 13352.

(c) In addition to Section 23600 and subdivision (a), if the court grants probation to any person punished under Section 23550 who has not previously completed a treatment program pursuant to subdivision (b) of Section 23542 or paragraph (4) of subdivision (b) of Section 23562, and unless the person is ordered to participate in, and complete, a program under subdivision (b), the court shall impose as a condition of probation that the person, subsequent to the date of the current violation, enroll in and participate, for at least 18 months and in a manner satisfactory to the court, in a driving-under-the-influence program licensed pursuant to Section 11836 of the Health and Safety Code, as designated by the court. The person shall complete the entire program subsequent to, and shall not be given any credit for program activities completed prior to, the date of the current violation. A person who has previously completed a 12-month or 18-month driving-under-the-influence program licensed pursuant to Section 11836 of the Health and Safety Code shall not be eligible for referral pursuant to this subdivision unless a 30-month driving-under-the-influence program licensed pursuant to Section 11836 of the Health and Safety Code is not available for referral in the county of the person's residence or employment. A condition of probation required pursuant to this subdivision is not a basis for reducing any other probation requirement in this section or Section 23600 or for avoiding the mandatory license revocation provisions of paragraph (7) of subdivision (a) of Section 13352.

(d) The court shall advise the person at the time of sentencing that the driving privilege may not be restored until the person provides proof satisfactory to the department of successful completion of a driving-under-the-influence program of the length required under this code that is licensed pursuant to Section 11836 of the Health and Safety Code.

(Amended by Stats. 2010, Ch. 301, Sec. 5. (AB 1601) Effective January 1, 2011.)

Article 3. Penalties for a Violation of Section 23153

(Article 3 added by Stats. 1998, Ch. 118, Sec. 84.)

23554. If any person is convicted of a first violation of Section 23153, that person shall be punished by imprisonment in the state prison, or in a county jail for not less than 90 days nor more than one year, and by a fine of not less than three hundred ninety dollars ($390) nor more than one thousand dollars ($1,000). The person's privilege to operate a motor vehicle shall be suspended by the Department of Motor Vehicles pursuant to paragraph (2) of subdivision (a) of Section 13352. The court shall require the person to surrender the driver's license to the court in accordance with Section 13550.

(Amended by Stats. 2002, Ch. 545, Sec. 28. Effective January 1, 2003.)

23556. (a) (1) If the court grants probation to any person punished under Section 23554, in addition to the provisions of Section 23600 and any other terms and conditions imposed by the court, the court shall impose as a condition of probation that the person be confined in the county jail for at least five days but not more than one year and pay a fine of at least three hundred ninety dollars ($390) but not more than one thousand dollars ($1,000).

(2) The person's privilege to operate a motor vehicle shall be suspended by the department under paragraph (2) of subdivision (a) of Section 13352. The court shall require the person to surrender the driver's license to the court in accordance with Section 13550.

(b) (1) In a county where the county alcohol program administrator has certified, and the board of supervisors has approved, a program or programs, the court shall also impose as a condition of probation that the driver shall participate in, and successfully complete, an alcohol and other drug education and counseling program, established pursuant to Section 11837.3 of the Health and Safety Code, as designated by the court.

(2) In any county where the board of supervisors has approved and the State Department of Health Care Services has licensed an alcohol and other drug education and counseling program, the court shall also impose as a condition of probation that the driver enroll in, participate in, and successfully complete, a driving-under-the-influence program licensed pursuant to Section 11836 of the Health and Safety Code, in the driver's county of residence or employment, as designated by the

court. For the purposes of this paragraph, enrollment in, participation in, and completion of, an approved program shall be subsequent to the date of the current violation. Credit may not be given to any program activities completed prior to the date of the current violation.

(3) The court shall refer a first offender whose blood-alcohol concentration was less than 0.20 percent, by weight, to participate for three months or longer, as ordered by the court, in a licensed program that consists of at least 30 hours of program activities, including those education, group counseling, and individual interview sessions described in Chapter 9 (commencing with Section 11836) of Part 2 of Division 10.5 of the Health and Safety Code.

(4) The court shall refer a first offender whose blood-alcohol concentration was 0.20 percent or more, by weight, or who refused to take a chemical test, to participate for nine months or longer, as ordered by the court, in a licensed program that consists of at least 60 hours of program activities, including those education, group counseling, and individual interview sessions described in Chapter 9 (commencing with Section 11836) of Part 2 of Division 10.5 of the Health and Safety Code.

(c) (1) The court shall revoke the person's probation pursuant to Section 23602, except for good cause shown, for the failure to enroll in, participate in, or complete a program specified in subdivision (b).

(2) The court, in establishing reporting requirements, shall consult with the county alcohol program administrator. The county alcohol program administrator shall coordinate the reporting requirements with the department and with the State Department of Health Care Services. That reporting shall ensure that all persons who, after being ordered to attend and complete a program, may be identified for either (A) failure to enroll in, or failure to successfully complete, the program, or (B) successful completion of the program as ordered.

(d) The court shall advise the person at the time of sentencing that the driving privilege shall not be restored until the person has provided proof satisfactory to the department of successful completion of a driving-under-the-influence program of the length required under this code that is licensed pursuant to Section 11836 of the Health and Safety Code.

(e) This section shall become operative on September 20, 2005.

(Amended by Stats. 2013, Ch. 22, Sec. 88. (AB 75) Effective June 27, 2013. Operative July 1, 2013, by Sec. 110 of Ch. 22.)

23558. A person who proximately causes bodily injury or death to more than one victim in any one instance of driving in violation of Section 23153 of this code or in violation of Section 191.5 of, or subdivision (a) of Section 192.5 of, the Penal Code, shall, upon a felony conviction, and notwithstanding subdivision (g) of Section 1170.1 of the Penal Code, receive an enhancement of one year in the state prison for each additional injured victim. The enhanced sentence provided for in this section shall not be imposed unless the fact of the bodily injury to each additional victim is charged in the accusatory pleading and admitted or found to be true by the trier of fact. The maximum number of one year enhancements that may be imposed pursuant to this section is three.

Notwithstanding any other provision of law, the court may strike the enhancements provided in this section if it determines that there are circumstances in mitigation of the additional punishment and states on the record its reasons for striking the additional punishment.

(Amended by Stats. 2007, Ch. 747, Sec. 34. Effective January 1, 2008.)

23560. If a person is convicted of a violation of Section 23153 and the offense occurred within 10 years of a separate violation of Section 23103, as specified in Section 23103.5, 23152, or 23153 that resulted in a conviction, that person shall be punished by imprisonment in the state prison, or in a county jail for not less than 120 days nor more than one year, and by a fine of not less than three hundred ninety dollars ($390) nor more than five thousand dollars ($5,000). The person's privilege to operate a motor vehicle shall be revoked by the Department of Motor Vehicles pursuant to paragraph (4) of subdivision (a) of Section 13352. The court shall require the person to surrender the driver's license to the court in accordance with Section 13550.

(Amended by Stats. 2004, Ch. 550, Sec. 16. Effective January 1, 2005.)

23562. If the court grants probation to a person punished under Section 23560, in addition to the provisions of Section 23600 and any other terms and conditions imposed by the court, the court shall impose as conditions of probation that the person be subject to either subdivision (a) or (b), as follows:

(a) Be confined in the county jail for at least 120 days and pay a fine of at least three hundred ninety dollars ($390), but not more than five thousand dollars ($5,000). The person's privilege to operate a motor vehicle shall be revoked by the department under paragraph (4) of subdivision (a) of Section 13352. The court shall require the person to surrender the driver's license to the court in accordance with Section 13550.

(b) All of the following apply:

(1) Be confined in the county jail for at least 30 days, but not more than one year.

(2) Pay a fine of at least three hundred ninety dollars ($390), but not more than one thousand dollars ($1,000).

(3) The privilege to operate a motor vehicle shall be revoked by the department under paragraph (4) of subdivision (a) of Section 13352. The court shall require the person to surrender the driver's license to the court in accordance with Section 13550.

(4) Either of the following:

(A) Enroll and participate, for at least 18 months subsequent to the date of the underlying violation and in a manner satisfactory to the court, in a driving-under-the-influence program licensed pursuant to Section 11836 of the Health and Safety Code, if available in the county of the person's residence or employment, as designated by the court. The person shall complete the entire program subsequent to, and shall not be given any credit for program activities completed prior to, the date of the current violation. The program shall provide for persons who cannot afford the program fee pursuant to paragraph (2) of subdivision (b) of Section 11837.4 of the Health and Safety Code in order to enable those persons to participate.

(B) Enroll and participate, for at least 30 months subsequent to the date of the underlying violation and in a manner satisfactory to the court, in a driving-under-the-influence program licensed pursuant to Section 11836 of the Health and Safety Code, if available in the county of the person's residence or employment. The person shall complete the entire program subsequent to, and shall not be given any credit for program activities completed prior to, the date of the current violation.

(c) The court shall advise the person at the time of sentencing that the driving privilege shall not be restored until the person has provided proof satisfactory to the department of successful completion of a driving-under-the-influence program of the length required under this code that is licensed pursuant to Section 11836 of the Health and Safety Code.

(d) This section shall become operative on September 20, 2005.

(Amended by Stats. 2004, Ch. 551, Sec. 22. Effective January 1, 2005. Amended version operative September 20, 2005, pursuant to earlier operation of new subdivision (d).)

23566. (a) If a person is convicted of a violation of Section 23153 and the offense occurred within 10 years of two or more separate violations of Section 23103, as specified in Section 23103.5, or Section 23152 or 23153, or any combination of these violations, that resulted in convictions, that person shall be punished by imprisonment in the state prison for a term of two, three, or four years and by a fine of not less than one thousand fifteen dollars ($1,015) nor more than five thousand dollars ($5,000). The person's privilege to operate a motor vehicle shall be revoked by the Department of Motor Vehicles pursuant to paragraph (6) of subdivision (a) of Section 13352. The court shall require the person to surrender the driver's license to the court in accordance with Section 13550.

(b) If a person is convicted of a violation of Section 23153, and the act or neglect proximately causes great bodily injury, as defined in

Section 12022.7 of the Penal Code, to any person other than the driver, and the offense occurred within 10 years of two or more separate violations of Section 23103, as specified in Section 23103.5, or Section 23152 or 23153, or any combination of these violations, that resulted in convictions, that person shall be punished by imprisonment in the state prison for a term of two, three, or four years and by a fine of not less than one thousand fifteen dollars ($1,015) nor more than five thousand dollars ($5,000). The person's privilege to operate a motor vehicle shall be revoked by the Department of Motor Vehicles pursuant to paragraph (6) of subdivision (a) of Section 13352. The court shall require the person to surrender the driver's license to the court in accordance with Section 13550.

(c) If a person is convicted under subdivision (b), and the offense for which the person is convicted occurred within 10 years of four or more separate violations of Section 23103, as specified in Section 23103.5, or Section 23152 or 23153, or any combination of these violations, that resulted in convictions, that person shall, in addition and consecutive to the sentences imposed under subdivision (b), be punished by an additional term of imprisonment in the state prison for three years.

The enhancement allegation provided in this subdivision shall be pleaded and proved as provided by law.

(d) A person convicted of Section 23153 punishable under this section shall be designated as a habitual traffic offender for a period of three years, subsequent to the conviction. The person shall be advised of this designation pursuant to subdivision (b) of Section 13350.

(e) A person confined in state prison under this section shall be ordered by the court to participate in an alcohol or drug program, or both, that is available at the prison during the person's confinement. Completion of an alcohol or drug program under this section does not meet the program completion requirement of paragraph (6) of subdivision (a) of Section 13352, unless the drug or alcohol program is licensed under Section 11836 of the Health and Safety Code, or is a program specified in Section 8001 of the Penal Code.

(Amended by Stats. 2010, Ch. 301, Sec. 6. (AB 1601) Effective January 1, 2011.)

23568. (a) If the court grants probation to a person punished under Section 23566, in addition to the provisions of Section 23600 and any other terms and conditions imposed by the court, the court shall impose as conditions of probation that the person be confined in the county jail for at least one year, that the person pay a fine of at least three hundred ninety dollars ($390) but not more than five thousand dollars ($5,000), and that the person make restitution or reparation pursuant to Section 1203.1 of the Penal Code. The person's privilege to operate a motor vehicle shall be revoked by the department under paragraph (6) of subdivision (a) of Section 13352. The court shall require the person to surrender the driver's license to the court in accordance with Section 13550.

(b) In addition to Section 23600 and subdivision (a), if the court grants probation to a person punished under Section 23566, the court shall impose as a condition of probation that the person enroll in and complete, subsequent to the date of the underlying violation and in a manner satisfactory to the court, an 18-month driving-under-the-influence program licensed pursuant to Section 11836 of the Health and Safety Code or, if available in the county of the person's residence or employment, a 30-month driving-under-the-influence program licensed pursuant to Section 11836 of the Health and Safety Code, as designated by the court. The person shall complete the entire program subsequent to, and shall not be given any credit for program activities completed prior to, the date of the current violation. In lieu of the minimum term of imprisonment in subdivision (a), the court shall impose as a minimum condition of probation under this subdivision that the person be confined in the county jail for at least 30 days but not more than one year. Except as provided in this subdivision, if the court grants probation under this section, the court shall order the treatment prescribed by this subdivision, whether or not the person has previously completed a treatment program pursuant to subdivision (b) of Section 23542 or paragraph (4) of subdivision (b) of Section 23562. In order to enable all required persons to participate, each person shall pay the program costs commensurate with the person's ability to pay as determined pursuant to Section 11837.4 of the Health and Safety Code. No condition of probation required pursuant to this subdivision is a basis for reducing any other probation requirement in this section or Section 23600 or for avoiding the mandatory license revocation provisions of paragraph (6) of subdivision (a) of Section 13352.

(c) The court shall advise the person at the time of sentencing that the driving privilege may not be restored until the person provides proof satisfactory to the department of successful completion of a driving-under-the-influence program of the length required under this code that is licensed pursuant to Section 11836 of the Health and Safety Code.

(Amended by Stats. 2010, Ch. 301, Sec. 7. (AB 1601) Effective January 1, 2011.)

Article 4. Additional Punishments

(Article 4 added by Stats. 1998, Ch. 118, Sec. 84.)

23572. (a) If any person is convicted of a violation of Section 23152 and a minor under 14 years of age was a passenger in the vehicle at the time of the offense, the court shall impose the following penalties in addition to any other penalty prescribed:

(1) If the person is convicted of a violation of Section 23152 punishable under Section 23536, the punishment shall be enhanced by an imprisonment of 48 continuous hours in the county jail, whether or not probation is granted, no part of which shall be stayed.

(2) If a person is convicted of a violation of Section 23152 punishable under Section 23540, the punishment shall be enhanced by an imprisonment of 10 days in the county jail, whether or not probation is granted, no part of which may be stayed.

(3) If a person is convicted of a violation of Section 23152 punishable under Section 23546, the punishment shall be enhanced by an imprisonment of 30 days in the county jail, whether or not probation is granted, no part of which may be stayed.

(4) If a person is convicted of a violation of Section 23152 which is punished as a misdemeanor under Section 23550, the punishment shall be enhanced by an imprisonment of 90 days in the county jail, whether or not probation is granted, no part of which may be stayed.

(b) The driving of a vehicle in which a minor under 14 years of age was a passenger shall be pled and proven.

(c) No punishment enhancement shall be imposed pursuant to this section if the person is also convicted of a violation of Section 273a of the Penal Code arising out of the same facts and incident.

(Amended by Stats. 1999, Ch. 22, Sec. 38. Effective May 26, 1999. Operative July 1, 1999, by Sec. 46 of Ch. 22.)

Article 5. Additional Penalties and Sanctions

(Article 5 added by Stats. 1998, Ch. 118, Sec. 84.)

23573. (a) The Department of Motor Vehicles, upon receipt of the court's abstract of conviction for a violation listed in subdivision (j), shall inform the convicted person of the requirements of this section and the term for which the person is required to have a functioning, certified ignition interlock device installed. The records of the department shall reflect the mandatory use of the device for the term required and the time when the device is required to be installed pursuant to this code.

(b) The department shall advise the person that installation of a functioning, certified ignition interlock device on a vehicle does not allow the person to drive without a valid driver's license.

(c) A person who is notified by the department pursuant to subdivision (a) shall, within 30 days of notification, complete all of the following:

(1) Arrange for each vehicle operated by the person to be fitted with a functioning, certified ignition interlock device by a certified ignition interlock device provider under Section 13386.

(2) Notify the department and provide to the department proof of installation by submitting the "Verification of Installation" form described in paragraph (2) of subdivision (g) of Section 13386.

(3) Pay to the department a fee sufficient to cover the costs of administration of this section, including startup costs, as determined by the department.

(d) The department shall place a restriction on the driver's license record of the convicted person that states the driver is restricted to driving only vehicles equipped with a functioning, certified ignition interlock device.

(e) (1) A person who is notified by the department pursuant to subdivision (a) shall arrange for each vehicle with an ignition interlock device to be serviced by the installer at least once every 60 days in order for the installer to recalibrate and monitor the operation of the device.

(2) The installer shall notify the department if the device is removed or indicates that the person has attempted to remove, bypass, or tamper with the device, or if the person fails three or more times to comply with any requirement for the maintenance or calibration of the ignition interlock device.

(f) The department shall monitor the installation and maintenance of the functioning, certified ignition interlock device installed pursuant to subdivision (a).

(g) (1) A person who is notified by the department, pursuant to subdivision (a), is exempt from the requirements of subdivision (c) if all of the following circumstances occur:

(A) Within 30 days of the notification, the person certifies to the department all of the following:

(i) The person does not own a vehicle.

(ii) The person does not have access to a vehicle at their residence.

(iii) The person no longer has access to the vehicle being driven by the person when the person was arrested for a violation that subsequently resulted in a conviction for a violation listed in subdivision (j).

(iv) The person acknowledges that they are only allowed to drive a vehicle that is fitted with a functioning, certified ignition interlock device and that they are required to have a valid driver's license before they can drive.

(v) The person is subject to the requirements of this section when the person purchases or has access to a vehicle.

(B) The person's driver's license record has been restricted pursuant to subdivision (d).

(C) The person complies with this section immediately upon commencing operation of a vehicle subject to the required installation of a functioning, certified ignition interlock device.

(2) A person who has been granted an exemption pursuant to this subdivision and who subsequently drives a vehicle in violation of the exemption is subject to the penalties of subdivision (i) in addition to any other applicable penalties in law.

(h) This section does not permit a person to drive without a valid driver's license.

(i) A person who is required under subdivision (c) to install a functioning, certified ignition interlock device who willfully fails to install the ignition interlock device within the time period required under subdivision (c) is guilty of a misdemeanor and shall be punished by imprisonment in a county jail for not more than six months or by a fine of not more than five thousand dollars ($5,000), or by both that fine and imprisonment.

(j) In addition to all other requirements of this code, a person convicted of any of the following violations shall be punished as follows:

(1) Upon a conviction of a violation of Section 14601.2, 14601.4, or 14601.5 subsequent to one prior conviction of a violation of Section 23103.5, 23152, or 23153, within a 10-year period, the person shall immediately install a functioning, certified ignition interlock device, pursuant to this section, in all vehicles operated by that person for a term of one year.

(2) Upon a conviction of a violation of Section 14601.2, 14601.4, or 14601.5 subsequent to two prior convictions of a violation of Section 23103.5, 23152, or 23153, within a 10-year period, or one prior conviction of Section 14601.2, 14601.4, or 14601.5, within a 10-year period, the person shall immediately install a functioning, certified ignition interlock device, pursuant to this section, in all vehicles operated by that person for a term of two years.

(3) Upon a conviction of a violation of Section 14601.2, 14601.4, or 14601.5 subsequent to three or more prior convictions of a violation of Section 23103.5, 23152, or 23153, within a 10-year period, or two or more prior convictions of Section 14601.2, 14601.4, or 14601.5, within a 10-year period, the person shall immediately install a functioning, certified ignition interlock device, pursuant to this section, in all vehicles operated by that person for a term of three years.

(k) The department shall notify the court if a person subject to this section has failed to show proof of installation within 30 days of the department informing the person that the person is required to install a functioning, certified ignition interlock device.

(l) Subdivisions (g), (h), (j), (k), and (l) of Section 23575 apply to this section.

(m) The requirements of this section are in addition to any other requirements of law.

(n) This section shall become operative on January 1, 2019.

(o) This section shall remain in effect only until January 1, 2033, and as of that date is repealed, unless a later enacted statute, that is enacted before January 1, 2033, deletes or extends that date.

(Amended (as amended by Stats. 2017, Ch. 485, Sec. 23) by Stats. 2025, Ch. 689, Sec. 22. (AB 366) Effective January 1, 2026. Repealed as of January 1, 2033, by its own provisions. See later operative version, as amended by Sec. 23 of Stats. 2025, Ch. 689.)

23573. (a) The Department of Motor Vehicles, upon receipt of the court's abstract of conviction for a violation listed in subdivision (j), shall inform the convicted person of the requirements of this section and the term for which the person is required to have a functioning, certified ignition interlock device installed. The records of the department shall reflect the mandatory use of the device for the term required and the time when the device is required to be installed pursuant to this code.

(b) The department shall advise the person that installation of a functioning, certified ignition interlock device on a vehicle does not allow the person to drive without a valid driver's license.

(c) A person who is notified by the department pursuant to subdivision (a) shall, within 30 days of notification, complete all of the following:

(1) Arrange for each vehicle operated by the person to be fitted with a functioning, certified ignition interlock device by a certified ignition interlock device provider under Section 13386.

(2) Notify the department and provide to the department proof of installation by submitting the "Verification of Installation" form described in paragraph (2) of subdivision (g) of Section 13386.

(3) Pay to the department a fee sufficient to cover the costs of administration of this section, including startup costs, as determined by the department.

(d) The department shall place a restriction on the driver's license record of the convicted person that states the driver is restricted to driving only vehicles equipped with a functioning, certified ignition interlock device.

(e) (1) A person who is notified by the department pursuant to subdivision (a) shall arrange for each vehicle with an ignition interlock device to be serviced by the installer at least once every 60 days in order for the installer to recalibrate and monitor the operation of the device.

(2) The installer shall notify the department if the device is removed or indicates that the person has attempted to remove, bypass, or tamper with the device, or if the person fails three or more times to comply with any requirement for the maintenance or calibration of the ignition interlock device.

(f) The department shall monitor the installation and maintenance of the ignition interlock device installed pursuant to subdivision (a).

(g) (1) A person who is notified by the department, pursuant to subdivision (a), is exempt from the requirements of subdivision (c) if all of the following circumstances occur:

(A) Within 30 days of the notification, the person certifies to the department all of the following:

(i) The person does not own a vehicle.

(ii) The person does not have access to a vehicle at their residence.

(iii) The person no longer has access to the vehicle being driven by the person when the person was arrested for a violation that subsequently resulted in a conviction for a violation listed in subdivision (j).

(iv) The person acknowledges that they are only allowed to drive a vehicle that is fitted with a functioning, certified ignition interlock device and that they are required to have a valid driver's license before they can drive.

(v) The person is subject to the requirements of this section when the person purchases or has access to a vehicle.

(B) The person's driver's license record has been restricted pursuant to subdivision (d).

(C) The person complies with this section immediately upon commencing operation of a vehicle subject to the required installation of a functioning, certified ignition interlock device.

(2) A person who has been granted an exemption pursuant to this subdivision and who subsequently drives a vehicle in violation of the exemption is subject to the penalties of subdivision (i) in addition to any other applicable penalties in law.

(h) This section does not permit a person to drive without a valid driver's license.

(i) A person who is required under subdivision (c) to install a functioning, certified ignition interlock device who willfully fails to install the ignition interlock device within the time period required under subdivision (c) is guilty of a misdemeanor and shall be punished by imprisonment in a county jail for not more than six months or by a fine of not more than five thousand dollars ($5,000), or by both that fine and imprisonment.

(j) In addition to all other requirements of this code, a person convicted of any of the following violations shall be punished as follows:

(1) Upon a conviction of a violation of Section 14601.2, 14601.4, or 14601.5 subsequent to one prior conviction of a violation of Section 23103.5, 23152, or 23153, within a 10-year period, the person shall immediately install a functioning, certified ignition interlock device, pursuant to this section, in all vehicles operated by that person for a term of one year.

(2) Upon a conviction of a violation of Section 14601.2, 14601.4, or 14601.5 subsequent to two prior convictions of a violation of Section 23103.5, 23152, or 23153, within a 10-year period, or one prior conviction of Section 14601.2, 14601.4, or 14601.5, within a 10-year period, the person shall immediately install a functioning, certified ignition interlock device, pursuant to this section, in all vehicles operated by that person for a term of two years.

(3) Upon a conviction of a violation of Section 14601.2, 14601.4, or 14601.5 subsequent to three or more prior convictions of a violation of Section 23103.5, 23152, or 23153, within a 10-year period, or two or more prior convictions of Section 14601.2, 14601.4, or 14601.5, within a 10-year period, the person shall immediately install a functioning, certified ignition interlock device, pursuant to this section, in all vehicles operated by that person for a term of three years.

(k) The department shall notify the court if a person subject to this section has failed to show proof of installation within 30 days of the department informing the person that the person is required to install a functioning, certified ignition interlock device.

(l) Subdivisions (j), (k), (m), (n), and (o) of Section 23575 apply to this section.

(m) The requirements of this section are in addition to any other requirements of law.

(n) This section shall become operative January 1, 2033.

(Amended (as amended by Stats. 2017, Ch. 485, Sec. 24) by Stats. 2025, Ch. 689, Sec. 23. (AB 366) Effective January 1, 2026. Section operative January 1, 2033, by its own provisions.)

23575. (a) The court shall require a person convicted of a violation of Section 14601.2 to install a functioning, certified ignition interlock device on any vehicle that the person operates and prohibit the person from operating a motor vehicle unless the vehicle is equipped with a functioning, certified ignition interlock device. The term of the restriction shall be determined by the court for a period not to exceed three years from the date of conviction. The court shall notify the Department of Motor Vehicles, as specified in subdivision (a) of Section 1803, of the terms of the restrictions in accordance with subdivision (a) of Section 1804. The Department of Motor Vehicles shall place the restriction in the person's records in the Department of Motor Vehicles.

(b) The court shall include on the abstract of conviction or violation submitted to the Department of Motor Vehicles under Section 1803 or 1816 the requirement and term for the use of a functioning, certified ignition interlock device. The records of the department shall reflect mandatory use of the device for the term ordered by the court.

(c) The court shall advise the person that installation of an ignition interlock device on a vehicle does not allow the person to drive without a valid driver's license.

(d) A person whose driving privilege is restricted by the court pursuant to this section shall arrange for each vehicle with a functioning, certified ignition interlock device to be serviced by the installer at least once every 60 days in order for the installer to recalibrate and monitor the operation of the device. The installer shall notify the court if the device is removed or indicates that the person has attempted to remove, bypass, or tamper with the device, or if the person fails three or more times to comply with any requirement for the maintenance or calibration of the ignition interlock device. There is no obligation for the installer to notify the court if the person has complied with all of the requirements of this article.

(e) The court shall monitor the installation and maintenance of a functioning, certified ignition interlock device restriction ordered pursuant to subdivision (a) or (i). If a person fails to comply with the court order, the court shall give notice of the fact to the department pursuant to Section 40509.1.

(f) Nothing in this section permits a person to drive without a valid driver's license.

(g) Pursuant to this section, an out-of-state resident who otherwise would qualify for an ignition interlock device restricted license in California shall be prohibited from operating a motor vehicle in California unless that vehicle is equipped with a functioning, certified ignition interlock device. An ignition interlock device is not required to be installed on any vehicle owned by the defendant that is not driven in California.

(h) If a medical problem does not permit a person to breathe with sufficient strength to activate the device, that person shall only have the suspension option.

(i) This section does not restrict a court from requiring installation of a functioning, certified ignition interlock device and prohibiting operation of a motor vehicle unless that vehicle is equipped with a functioning, certified ignition interlock device for a person to whom subdivision (a) does not apply. The term of the restriction shall be determined by the court for a period not to exceed three years from the date of conviction. The court shall notify the Department of Motor Vehicles, as specified in subdivision (a) of Section 1803, of the terms of the restrictions in accordance with subdivision (a) of Section 1804. The Department of Motor Vehicles shall place the restriction in the person's records in the Department of Motor Vehicles.

(j) For the purposes of this section, "vehicle" does not include a motorcycle until the state certifies an ignition interlock device that can be installed on a motorcycle. Any person subject to an ignition interlock device restriction shall not operate a motorcycle for the duration of the ignition interlock device restriction period.

(k) (1) For the purposes of this section, "owned" means solely owned or owned in conjunction with another person or legal entity.

(2) For purposes of this section, "operates" includes operating a vehicle that is not owned by the person subject to this section.

(l) For the purposes of this section, "bypass" means either of the following:

(1) Failure to take any random retest.

(2) Failure to pass any random retest with a breath alcohol concentration not exceeding 0.03 percent breath alcohol concentration.

(m) The department shall adopt regulations specifying the intervals between random retests.

(n) For purposes of this section, "random retest" means a breath test performed by the driver upon a certified ignition interlock device at random intervals after the initial engine startup breath test and while the vehicle's motor is running.

(o) This section shall become operative on January 1, 2019.

(p) This section shall remain in effect only until January 1, 2033, and as of that date is repealed, unless a later enacted statute, that is enacted before January 1, 2033, deletes or extends that date.

(Amended (as amended by Stats. 2017, Ch. 485, Sec. 26) by Stats. 2025, Ch. 689, Sec. 24. (AB 366) Effective January 1, 2026. Repealed as of January 1, 2033, by its own provisions. See later operative version, as amended by Sec. 25 of Stats. 2025, Ch. 689.)

23575. (a) (1) In addition to any other law, the court may require that a person convicted of a first offense violation of Section 23152 or 23153 install a functioning, certified ignition interlock device on any vehicle that the person operates and prohibit that person from operating a motor vehicle unless that vehicle is equipped with a functioning, certified ignition interlock device. The court shall give heightened consideration to applying this sanction to a first offense violator with 0.15 percent or more, by weight, of alcohol in their blood at arrest, or with two or more prior moving traffic violations, or to persons who refused the chemical tests at arrest. If the court orders the ignition interlock device restriction, the term shall be determined by the court for a period not to exceed three years from the date of conviction. The court shall notify the Department of Motor Vehicles, as specified in subdivision (a) of Section 1803, of the terms of the restrictions in accordance with subdivision (a) of Section 1804. The Department of Motor Vehicles shall place the restriction in the person's records in the Department of Motor Vehicles.

(2) The court shall require a person convicted of a violation of Section 14601.2 to install a functioning, certified ignition interlock device on any vehicle that the person operates and prohibit the person from operating a motor vehicle unless the vehicle is equipped with a functioning, certified ignition interlock device. The term of the restriction shall be determined by the court for a period not to exceed three years from the date of conviction. The court shall notify the Department of Motor Vehicles, as specified in subdivision (a) of Section 1803, of the terms of the restrictions in accordance with subdivision (a) of Section 1804. The Department of Motor Vehicles shall place the restriction in the person's records in the Department of Motor Vehicles.

(b) The court shall include on the abstract of conviction or violation submitted to the Department of Motor Vehicles under Section 1803 or 1816 the requirement and term for the use of a functioning, certified ignition interlock device. The records of the department shall reflect mandatory use of the device for the term ordered by the court.

(c) The court shall advise the person that installation of a functioning, certified ignition interlock device on a vehicle does not allow the person to drive without a valid driver's license.

(d) A person whose driving privilege is restricted by the court pursuant to this section shall arrange for each vehicle with a functioning, certified ignition interlock device to be serviced by the installer at least once every 60 days in order for the installer to recalibrate and monitor the operation of the device. The installer shall notify the court if the device is removed or indicates that the person has attempted to remove, bypass, or tamper with the device, or if the person fails three or more times to comply with any requirement for the maintenance or calibration of the ignition interlock device. There is no obligation for the installer to notify the court if the person has complied with all of the requirements of this article.

(e) The court shall monitor the installation and maintenance of a functioning, certified ignition interlock device restriction ordered pursuant to subdivision (a) or (l). If a person fails to comply with the court order, the court shall give notice of the fact to the department pursuant to Section 40509.1.

(f) (1) If a person is convicted of a violation of Section 23152 or 23153 and the offense occurred within 10 years of one or more separate violations of Section 23152 or 23153 that resulted in a conviction, or if a person is convicted of a violation of Section 23103, as specified in Section 23103.5, and is suspended for one year under Section 13353.3, the person may apply to the Department of Motor Vehicles for a restricted driver's license pursuant to Section 13352 or 13353.3 that prohibits the person from operating a motor vehicle unless that vehicle is equipped with a functioning, certified ignition interlock device, certified pursuant to Section 13386. The restriction shall remain in effect for at least the remaining period of the original suspension or revocation and until all reinstatement requirements in Section 13352 or 13353.4 are met.

(2) Pursuant to subdivision (g), the Department of Motor Vehicles shall immediately terminate the restriction issued pursuant to Section 13352 or 13353.3 and shall immediately suspend or revoke the privilege to operate a motor vehicle of a person who attempts to remove, bypass, or tamper with the device, who has the device removed prior to the termination date of the restriction, or who fails three or more times to comply with any requirement for the maintenance or calibration of the ignition interlock device ordered pursuant to Section 13352 or 13353.3. The privilege shall remain suspended or revoked for the remaining period of the originating suspension or revocation and until all reinstatement requirements in Section 13352 or 13353.4 are met, except that if the person provides proof to the satisfaction of the department that the person is in compliance with the restriction issued pursuant to this section, the department may, in its discretion, restore the privilege to operate a motor vehicle and reimpose the remaining term of the restriction.

(g) A person whose driving privilege is restricted by the Department of Motor Vehicles pursuant to Section 13352 or 13353.3 shall arrange for each vehicle with a functioning, certified ignition interlock device to be serviced by the installer at least once every 60 days in order for the installer to recalibrate the device and monitor the operation of the device. The installer shall notify the Department of Motor Vehicles if the device is removed or indicates that the person has attempted to remove, bypass, or tamper with the device, or if the person fails three or more times to comply with any requirement for the maintenance or calibration of the ignition interlock device. There is no obligation on the part of the installer to notify the department or the court if the person has complied with all of the requirements of this section.

(h) This section does not permit a person to drive without a valid driver's license.

(i) The Department of Motor Vehicles shall include information along with the order of suspension or revocation for repeat offenders informing them that after a specified period of suspension or revocation has been completed, the person may either install a functioning, certified ignition interlock device on any vehicle that the person operates or remain with a suspended or revoked driver's license.

(j) Pursuant to this section, an out-of-state resident who otherwise would qualify for a functioning, certified ignition interlock device restricted license in California shall be prohibited from operating a motor vehicle in California unless that vehicle is equipped with a functioning, certified ignition interlock device. An ignition interlock device is not required to be installed on any vehicle owned by the defendant that is not driven in California.

(k) If a medical problem does not permit a person to breathe with sufficient strength to activate the device, that person shall only have the suspension option.

(l) This section does not restrict a court from requiring installation of a functioning, certified ignition interlock device and prohibiting operation of a motor vehicle unless that vehicle is equipped with a functioning, certified ignition interlock device for a person to whom subdivision (a) or (b) does not apply. The term of the restriction shall be determined by the court for a period not to exceed three years from the date of conviction. The court shall notify the Department of Motor Vehicles, as specified in subdivision (a) of Section 1803, of the terms of the restrictions in accordance with subdivision (a) of Section 1804. The Department of Motor Vehicles shall place the restriction in the person's records in the Department of Motor Vehicles.

(m) For the purposes of this section, "vehicle" does not include a motorcycle until the state certifies an ignition interlock device that can be installed on a motorcycle. Any person subject to an ignition interlock device restriction shall not operate a motorcycle for the duration of the ignition interlock device restriction period.

(n) (1) For the purposes of this section, "owned" means solely owned or owned in conjunction with another person or legal entity.

(2) For purposes of this section, "operates" includes operating a vehicle that is not owned by the person subject to this section.

(o) For the purposes of this section, "bypass" means either of the following:

(1) Failure to take any random retest.

(2) Failure to pass a random retest with a breath alcohol concentration not exceeding 0.03 percent breath alcohol concentration.

(p) For purposes of this section, "random retest" means a breath test performed by the driver upon a certified ignition interlock device at random intervals after the initial engine startup breath test and while the vehicle's motor is running.

(q) This section shall become operative January 1, 2033.

(Amended (as amended by Stats. 2017, Ch. 485, Sec. 27) by Stats. 2025, Ch. 689, Sec. 25. (AB 366) Effective January 1, 2026. Section operative January 1, 2033, by its own provisions.)

23575.1. The department may undertake a study and report its findings of that study to the Legislature on or before January 1, 2013, regarding the overall effectiveness of the use of ignition interlock devices (IID) to reduce the recidivism rate of first-time violators of Section 23152 or 23153. If the department exercises this authority, the study shall focus on those drivers who actually have an IID installed in their vehicles rather than on those who are subject to a judicial order to have an IID installed.

(Added by Stats. 2008, Ch. 392, Sec. 2. Effective January 1, 2009.)

23575.3. (a) In addition to any other requirement imposed by law, a court shall notify a person convicted of a violation listed in subdivision (h) that the person is required to install a functioning, certified ignition interlock device on any vehicle that the person operates and that the person is prohibited from operating a motor vehicle unless that vehicle is equipped with a functioning, certified ignition interlock device in accordance with this section.

(b) The Department of Motor Vehicles, upon receipt of the court's abstract of conviction for a violation listed in subdivision (h), shall inform the convicted person of the requirements of this section, including the term for which the person is required to have a certified ignition interlock device installed. The records of the department shall reflect the mandatory use of the device for the term required and the time when the device is required to be installed by this code.

(c) The department shall advise the person that installation of a functioning, certified ignition interlock device on a vehicle does not allow the person to drive without a valid driver's license.

(d) (1) A person who is notified by the department pursuant to subdivision (b) shall do all of the following:

(A) Arrange for each vehicle operated by the person to be equipped with a functioning, certified ignition interlock device by a certified ignition interlock device provider under Section 13386.

(B) Provide to the department proof of installation by submitting the "Verification of Installation" form described in paragraph (2) of subdivision (g) of Section 13386.

(C) Pay a fee, determined by the department, that is sufficient to cover the costs of administration of this section.

(2) A person who is notified by the department pursuant to subdivision (b), is exempt from the requirements of this subdivision until the time the person purchases or has access to a vehicle if, within 30 days of the notification, the person certifies to the department all of the following:

(A) The person does not own a vehicle.

(B) The person does not have access to a vehicle at their residence.

(C) The person no longer has access to the vehicle they were driving at the time they were arrested for a violation that subsequently resulted in a conviction for a violation listed in subdivision (h).

(D) The person acknowledges that they are only allowed to drive a vehicle that is equipped with a functioning, certified ignition interlock device.

(E) The person acknowledges that they are required to have a valid driver's license before they can drive.

(F) The person acknowledges that they are subject to the requirements of this section when the person purchases or has access to a vehicle.

(e) In addition to any other restrictions the department places on the driver's license record of the convicted person when the person is issued a restricted driver's license pursuant to Section 13352 or 13352.4, the department shall place a restriction on the driver's license record of the person that states the driver is restricted to driving only vehicles equipped with a functioning, certified ignition interlock device for the applicable term.

(f) (1) A person who is notified by the department pursuant to subdivision (b) shall arrange for each vehicle with a functioning, certified ignition interlock device to be serviced by the installer at least once every 60 days in order for the installer to recalibrate and monitor the operation of the device.

(2) The installer shall notify the department if the device is removed or indicates that the person has attempted to remove, bypass, or tamper with the device, or if the person fails three or more times to comply with any requirement for the maintenance or calibration of the ignition interlock device.

(g) The department shall monitor the installation and maintenance of the ignition interlock device installed pursuant to subdivision (d).

(h) A person is required to install a functioning, certified ignition interlock device pursuant to this section for the applicable term, as follows:

(1) A person convicted of a violation of subdivision (a), (b), (d), (e), or (g) of Section 23152 shall be required to do the following, as applicable:

(A) Upon a conviction with no priors, punishable under Section 23536, only one of the following may occur:

(i) The court may order installation of a functioning, certified ignition interlock device on any vehicle that the person operates and prohibit that person from operating a motor vehicle unless that vehicle is equipped with a functioning, certified ignition interlock device. If the court orders the ignition interlock device restriction, the term shall be determined by the court for a period not to exceed six months from the date of conviction. The court shall notify the department of the conviction as specified in subdivision (a) of Section 1803 or Section 1816, and shall specify the terms of the ignition interlock device restriction in accordance with subdivision (a) of Section 1804. The department shall place the restriction on the driver's license record of the person that states the driver is restricted to driving only vehicles equipped with a functioning, certified ignition interlock device for the applicable term.

(ii) The person may apply to the department for a restriction of the driving privilege under Section 13352.4.

(iii) The person may apply to the department for a restriction of the driving privilege under paragraph (1) of subdivision (a) of Section 13352 or subdivision (c) of Section 13352.1.

(B) Upon a conviction with one prior, punishable under Section 23540, the person shall install a functioning, certified ignition interlock device in the vehicle, as ordered by the court, that is operated by that person for a mandatory term of 12 months.

(C) Upon a conviction with two priors, punishable under Section 23546, the person shall install a functioning, certified ignition interlock device in the vehicle, as ordered by the court, that is operated by that person for a mandatory term of 24 months.

(D) Upon a conviction with three or more priors punishable under Section 23550, or a conviction punishable under Section 23550.5, the person shall install a functioning, certified ignition interlock device in the vehicle, as ordered by the court, that is operated by that person for a mandatory term of 36 months.

(2) A person convicted of a violation of subdivision (a), (b), (d), (e), or (g) of Section 23153 shall install a functioning, certified ignition interlock device, as follows:

(A) Upon a conviction with no priors, punishable under Section 23554, the person shall install a functioning, certified ignition interlock device in the vehicle, as ordered by the court, that is operated by that person for a mandatory term of 12 months.

(B) Upon a conviction with one prior, punishable under Section 23560, the person shall install a functioning, certified ignition interlock device in the vehicle, as ordered by the court, that is operated by that person for a mandatory term of 24 months.

(C) Upon a conviction with two priors, punishable under Section 23550 or 23566, the person shall install a functioning, certified ignition interlock device in the vehicle, as ordered by the court, that is operated by that person for a mandatory term of 36 months.

(D) Upon a conviction with one prior punishable under Section 23550.5, the person shall install a functioning, certified ignition interlock device in the vehicle, as ordered by the court, that is operated by that person for a mandatory term of 48 months.

(3) For the purposes of paragraphs (1) and (2), "prior" means a conviction for a separate violation of Section 23103, as specified in Section 23103.5, or Section 23152 or 23153, subdivision (a) or (b) of Section 191.5 of, or subdivision (a) of Section 192.5 of, the Penal Code, or subdivision (b), (c), (d), (e), or (f) of Section 655 of the Harbors and Navigation Code, that occurred within 10 years of the current violation.

(4) The terms prescribed in this subdivision shall begin once a person has complied with subparagraph (B) of paragraph (1) of subdivision (d) and either upon the reinstatement of the privilege to drive pursuant to Section 13352 or the issuance of a restricted driver's license pursuant to Section 13352. A person shall receive credit for any period in which they had a restricted driver's license issued pursuant to Section 13353.6 or 13353.75.

(i) Subdivisions (g), (h), (j), and (k) of Section 23575 apply to this section.

(j) If a person fails to comply with any of the requirements regarding ignition interlock devices, the period in which the person was not in compliance shall not be credited towards the mandatory term for which the ignition interlock device is required to be installed.

(k) (1) Every manufacturer and manufacturer's agent certified by the department to provide ignition interlock devices, under Section 13386, shall adopt the following fee schedule that provides for the payment of the costs of the certified ignition interlock device by offenders subject to this chapter in amounts commensurate with that person's income relative to the federal poverty level, as defined in Section 127400 of the Health and Safety Code:

(A) A person with an income at 100 percent of the federal poverty level or below and who provides income verification pursuant to paragraph (2) is responsible for 10 percent of the cost of the manufacturer's standard ignition interlock device program costs, and any additional costs accrued by the person for noncompliance with program requirements.

(B) A person with an income at 101 to 200 percent of the federal poverty level and who provides income verification pursuant to paragraph (2) is responsible for 25 percent of the cost of the manufacturer's standard ignition interlock device program costs, and any additional costs accrued by the person for noncompliance with program requirements.

(C) A person with an income at 201 to 300 percent of the federal poverty level and who provides income verification pursuant to paragraph (2) is responsible for 50 percent of the cost of the manufacturer's standard ignition interlock device program costs, and any additional costs accrued by the person for noncompliance with program requirements.

(D) A person who is receiving CalFresh benefits and who provides proof of those benefits to the manufacturer or manufacturer's agent or authorized installer is responsible for 50 percent of the cost of the manufacturer's standard ignition interlock device program costs, and any additional costs accrued by the person for noncompliance with program requirements.

(E) A person with an income at 301 to 400 percent of the federal poverty level and who provides income verification pursuant to paragraph (2) is responsible for 90 percent of the cost of the manufacturer's standard ignition interlock device program costs, and any additional costs accrued by the person for noncompliance with program requirements.

(F) All other offenders are responsible for 100 percent of the cost of the ignition interlock device.

(G) The manufacturer is responsible for the percentage of costs that the offender is not responsible for pursuant to subparagraphs (A) to (E), inclusive.

(2) The ignition interlock device provider shall verify the offender's income to determine the cost of the ignition interlock device pursuant to this subdivision by verifying one of the following documents from the offender:

(A) The previous year's federal income tax return.

(B) The previous three months of weekly or monthly income statements.

(C) Employment Development Department verification of unemployment benefits.

(l) The Department of Consumer Affairs may impose a civil assessment not to exceed one thousand dollars ($1,000) upon a manufacturer or manufacturer's agent certified to provide ignition interlock devices who fails to inform an offender subject to this chapter of the provisions of subdivision (k), or who fails to comply with the provisions of subdivision (k).

(m) This section does not permit a person to drive without a valid driver's license.

(n) The requirements of this section are in addition to any other requirements of law.

(o) For the purposes of this section, the following definitions apply:

(1) "Bypass" means either of the following:

(A) Failure to take any random retest.

(B) Failure to pass a random retest with a breath alcohol concentration not exceeding 0.03 percent, by weight of alcohol, in the person's blood.

(2) "Operates" includes operating a vehicle that is not owned by the person subject to this section.

(3) "Owned" means solely owned or owned in conjunction with another person or legal entity.

(4) "Random retest" means a breath test performed by the driver upon a certified ignition interlock device at random intervals after the initial engine startup breath test and while the vehicle's motor is running.

(5) "Vehicle" does not include a motorcycle until the state certifies an ignition interlock device that can be installed on a motorcycle. A person subject to an ignition interlock device restriction shall not operate a motorcycle for the duration of the ignition interlock device restriction period.

(p) The requirements of this section shall apply only to a person who is convicted for a violation of Section 23152 or 23153 that occurred on or after January 1, 2019.

(q) This section shall become operative on January 1, 2019.

(r) This section shall remain in effect only until January 1, 2033, and as of that date is repealed, unless a later enacted statute, that is enacted before January 1, 2033, deletes or extends that date.

(Amended by Stats. 2025, Ch. 689, Sec. 26. (AB 366) Effective January 1, 2026. Repealed as of January 1, 2033, by its own provisions.)

23575.5. (a) On or before March 1, 2024, the Department of Motor Vehicles shall report data to the Transportation Agency regarding the implementation and efficacy of the program enacted by the act that added this section.

(b) The data described in subdivision (a) shall, at a minimum, include all of the following:

(1) The number of individuals who were required to have a functioning, certified ignition interlock device installed as a result of the program who killed or injured anyone in a crash while they were operating a vehicle under the influence of alcohol.

(2) The number of individuals who were required to have a functioning, certified ignition interlock device installed as a result of the program who were convicted of an alcohol-related violation of Section 23103, as specified in Section 23103.5, or Section 23140, 23152, or 23153, or Section 191.5 or subdivision (a) of Section 192.5 of the Penal Code during the term in which the person was required to have the ignition interlock device installed.

(3) The number of injuries and deaths resulting from alcohol-related motor vehicle crashes between January 1, 2019, and January 1, 2024, inclusive, and during periods of similar duration prior to the implementation of the program.

(4) The number of individuals who have been convicted more than one time for driving under the influence of alcohol between January 1, 2019, and January 1, 2024, inclusive, and periods of similar duration prior to the implementation of the program.

(5) Any other information requested by the Transportation Agency to assess the effectiveness of the statewide ignition interlock device requirement in reducing recidivism for driving-under-the-influence violations.

(c) The Transportation Agency may contract with educational institutions to obtain and analyze the data required by this section.

(d) The Transportation Agency shall assess the program based on the data provided pursuant to subdivision (b) and shall report to the Legislature on the outcomes of the program no later than January 1, 2025.

(e) The report described in subdivision (a) shall be submitted in compliance with Section 9795 of the Government Code.

(f) (1) This section shall become operative on January 1, 2019.

(2) This section is repealed as of January 1, 2029, unless a later enacted statute, that becomes operative on or before January 1, 2029, deletes or extends the dates on which it becomes inoperative and is repealed.

(Amended by Stats. 2022, Ch. 81, Sec. 6. (AB 2198) Effective January 1, 2023. Repealed as of January 1, 2029, by its own provisions.)

23576. (a) Notwithstanding Sections 13352, 13352.1, 13353.6, 13353.75, 23573, 23575, 23575.3, and 23700, if a person is required to operate a motor vehicle in the course and scope of their employment and if the vehicle is owned by the employer, the person may operate that vehicle without installation of a functioning, certified approved ignition interlock device if the employer has been notified by the person that the person's driving privilege has been restricted pursuant to Section 13352, 13352.1, 13353.6, 13353.75, 23573, 23575, 23575.3, or 23700 and if the person has proof of that notification in their possession, or if the notice, or a facsimile copy thereof, is with the vehicle.

(b) A motor vehicle owned by a business entity that is all or partly owned or controlled by a person otherwise subject to Section 13352, 13352.1, 13353.6, 13353.75, 23573, 23575, 23575.3, or 23700, is not a motor vehicle owned by the employer subject to the exemption in subdivision (a).

(c) This section shall become operative on January 1, 2019.

(d) This section shall remain in effect only until January 1, 2033, and as of that date is repealed, unless a later enacted statute, that is enacted before January 1, 2033, deletes or extends that date.

(Amended (as amended by Stats. 2017, Ch. 485, Sec. 29) by Stats. 2025, Ch. 689, Sec. 27. (AB 366) Effective January 1, 2026. Repealed as of January 1, 2033, by its own provisions. See later operative version, as amended by Sec. 28 of Stats. 2025, Ch. 689.)

23576. (a) Notwithstanding Sections 23575 and 23700, if a person is required to operate a motor vehicle in the course and scope of their employment and if the vehicle is owned by the employer, the person may operate that vehicle without installation of a functioning, certified ignition interlock device if the employer has been notified by the person that the person's driving privilege has been restricted pursuant to Section 23575 or 23700 and if the person has proof of that notification in their possession, or if the notice, or a facsimile copy thereof, is with the vehicle.

(b) A motor vehicle owned by a business entity that is all or partly owned or controlled by a person otherwise subject to Section 23575 or 23700 is not a motor vehicle owned by the employer subject to the exemption in subdivision (a).

(c) This section shall become operative January 1, 2033.

(Amended (as added by Stats. 2016, Ch. 783, Sec. 39) by Stats. 2025, Ch. 689, Sec. 28. (AB 366) Effective January 1, 2026. Section operative January 1, 2033, by its own provisions.)

23577. (a) If a person is convicted of a violation of Section 23152 or 23153, and at the time of the arrest leading to that conviction that person willfully refused a peace officer's request to submit to, or willfully failed to complete, the breath or urine tests pursuant to Section 23612, the court shall impose the following penalties:

(1) If the person is convicted of a first violation of Section 23152, notwithstanding any other provision of subdivision (a) of Section 23538, the terms and conditions of probation shall include the conditions in paragraph (1) of subdivision (a) of Section 23538.

(2) If the person is convicted of a first violation of Section 23153, the punishment shall be enhanced by an imprisonment of 48 continuous hours in the county jail, whether or not probation is granted and no part of which may be stayed, unless the person is sentenced to, and incarcerated in, the state prison and the execution of that sentence is not stayed.

(3) If the person is convicted of a second violation of Section 23152, punishable under Section 23540, or a second violation of Section 23153, punishable under Section 23560, the punishment shall be enhanced by an imprisonment of 96 hours in the county jail, whether or not probation is granted and no part of which may be stayed, unless the person is sentenced to, and incarcerated in, the state prison and execution of that sentence is not stayed.

(4) If the person is convicted of a third violation of Section 23152, punishable under Section 23546, the punishment shall be enhanced by an imprisonment of 10 days in the county jail, whether or not probation is granted and no part of which may be stayed.

(5) If the person is convicted of a fourth or subsequent violation of Section 23152, punishable under Section 23550 or 23550.5, the punishment shall be enhanced by imprisonment of 18 days in the county jail, whether or not probation is granted and no part of which may be stayed.

(b) The willful refusal or failure to complete the breath or urine test required pursuant to Section 23612 shall be pled and proven.

(c) The penalties in this section do not apply to a person who refused to submit to or complete a blood test pursuant to Section 23612. This section does not prohibit imposition of administrative actions involving driving privileges.

(Amended by Stats. 2018, Ch. 177, Sec. 1. (AB 2717) Effective January 1, 2019.)

23578. In addition to any other provision of this code, if a person is convicted of a violation of Section 23152 or 23153, the court shall consider a concentration of alcohol in the person's blood of 0.15 percent or more, by weight, or the refusal of the person to take a breath or urine test, as a special factor that may justify enhancing the penalties in sentencing,

in determining whether to grant probation, and, if probation is granted, in determining additional or enhanced terms and conditions of probation.
(Amended by Stats. 2018, Ch. 177, Sec. 2 (AB 2717) Effective January 1, 2019.)

23580. (a) If any person is convicted of a violation of Section 23152 or 23153 and the offense was a second or subsequent offense punishable under Section 23540, 23546, 23550, 23550.5, 23560, or 23566, the court shall require that any term of imprisonment that is imposed include at least one period of not less than 48 consecutive hours of imprisonment or, in the alternative and notwithstanding Section 4024.2 of the Penal Code, that the person serve not less than 10 days of community service.

(b) Notwithstanding any other provision of law, except Section 2900.5 of the Penal Code, unless the court expressly finds in the circumstances that the punishment inflicted would be cruel or unusual punishment prohibited by Section 17 of Article I of the California Constitution, no court or person to whom a person is remanded for execution of sentence shall release, or permit the release of, a person from the requirements of subdivision (a), including, but not limited to, any work-release program, weekend service of sentence program, diversion or treatment program, or otherwise.

(c) For the purposes of this section, "imprisonment" means confinement in a jail, in a minimum security facility, or in an inpatient rehabilitation facility, as provided in Part 1309 (commencing with Section 1309.1) of Title 23 of the Code of Federal Regulations.
(Amended by Stats. 2002, Ch. 664, Sec. 223. Effective January 1, 2003.)

23582. (a) Any person who drives a vehicle 30 or more miles per hour over the maximum, prima facie, or posted speed limit on a freeway, or 20 or more miles per hour over the maximum, prima facie, or posted speed limit on any other street or highway, and in a manner prohibited by Section 23103 during the commission of a violation of Section 23152 or 23153 shall, in addition to the punishment prescribed for that person upon conviction of a violation of Section 23152 or 23153, be punished by an additional and consecutive term of 60 days in the county jail.

(b) If the court grants probation or suspends the execution of sentence, it shall require as a condition of probation or suspension that the defendant serve 60 days in the county jail, in addition and consecutive to any other sentence prescribed by this chapter.

(c) On a first conviction under this section, the court shall order the driver to participate in, and successfully complete, an alcohol or drug education and counseling program, or both an alcohol and a drug education and counseling program. Except in unusual cases where the interests of justice would be served, a finding making this section applicable to a defendant shall not be stricken pursuant to Section 1385 of the Penal Code or any other provision of law. If the court decides not to impose the additional and consecutive term, it shall specify on the court record the reasons for that order.

(d) The additional term provided in this section shall not be imposed unless the facts of driving in a manner prohibited by Section 23103 and driving the vehicle 30 or more miles per hour over the maximum, prima facie, or posted speed limit on a freeway, or 20 or more miles per hour over the maximum, prima facie, or posted speed limit on any other street or highway, are charged in the accusatory pleading and admitted or found to be true by the trier of fact. A finding of driving in that manner shall be based on facts in addition to the fact that the defendant was driving while under the influence of alcohol, any drug, or both, or with a specified percentage of alcohol in the blood.
(Added by Stats. 1998, Ch. 118, Sec. 84. Effective January 1, 1999. Section operative July 1, 1999, pursuant to Section 23675.)

Article 6. Additional Court-Imposed Orders and Directions

(Article 6 added by Stats. 1998, Ch. 118, Sec. 84.)

23592. (a) (1) Whenever a person is convicted of any of the following offenses committed while driving a motor vehicle of which he or she is the owner, the court, at the time sentence is imposed on the person, may order the motor vehicle impounded for a period of not more than six months for a first conviction, and not more than 12 months for a second or subsequent conviction:

(A) Driving with a suspended or revoked driver's license.

(B) A violation of Section 2800.2 resulting in an accident or Section 2800.3, if either violation occurred within seven years of one or more separate convictions for a violation of any of the following:

(i) Section 23103, if the vehicle involved in the violation was driven at a speed of 100 or more miles per hour.

(ii) Section 23152.

(iii) Section 23153.

(iv) Subdivisions (a) and (b) of Section 191.5 of the Penal Code.

(v) Subdivision (c) of Section 192 of the Penal Code.

(vi) Subdivision (a) of Section 192.5 of the Penal Code.

(2) The cost of keeping the vehicle is a lien on the vehicle pursuant to Chapter 6.5 (commencing with Section 3067) of Title 14 of Part 4 of Division 3 of the Civil Code.

(b) Notwithstanding subdivision (a), a motor vehicle impounded pursuant to this section that is subject to a chattel mortgage, conditional sale contract, or lease contract shall be released by the court to the legal owner upon the filing of an affidavit by the legal owner that the chattel mortgage, conditional sale contract, or lease contract is in default and shall be delivered to the legal owner upon payment of the accrued cost of keeping the vehicle.
(Amended by Stats. 2007, Ch. 747, Sec. 35. Effective January 1, 2008.)

23593. (a) The court shall advise a person convicted of a violation of Section 23103, as specified in Section 23103.5, or a violation of Section 23152 or 23153, as follows:

"You are hereby advised that being under the influence of alcohol or drugs, or both, impairs your ability to safely operate a motor vehicle. Therefore, it is extremely dangerous to human life to drive while under the influence of alcohol or drugs, or both. If you continue to drive while under the influence of alcohol or drugs, or both, and, as a result of that driving, someone is killed, you can be charged with murder."

(b) The advisory statement may be included in a plea form, if used, or the fact that the advice was given may be specified on the record.

(c) The court shall include on the abstract of the conviction or violation submitted to the department under Section 1803 or 1816, the fact that the person has been advised as required under subdivision (a).
(Amended by Stats. 2005, Ch. 279, Sec. 24. Effective January 1, 2006.)

23594. (a) Except as provided in subdivision (b), the interest of any registered owner of a motor vehicle that has been used in the commission of a violation of Section 23152 or 23153 for which the owner was convicted, is subject to impoundment as provided in this section. Upon conviction, the court may order the vehicle impounded at the registered owner's expense for not less than one nor more than 30 days.

If the offense occurred within five years of a prior offense which resulted in conviction of a violation of Section 23152 or 23153, the prior conviction shall also be charged in the accusatory pleading and if admitted or found to be true by the jury upon a jury trial or by the court upon a court trial, the court shall, except in an unusual case where the interests of justice would best be served by not ordering impoundment, order the vehicle impounded at the registered owner's expense for not less than one nor more than 30 days.

If the offense occurred within five years of two or more prior offenses which resulted in convictions of violations of Section 23152 or 23153, the prior convictions shall also be charged in the accusatory pleading and if admitted or found to be true by the jury upon a jury trial or by the court upon a court trial, the court shall, except in an unusual case where the interests of justice would best be served by not ordering impoundment, order the vehicle impounded at the registered owner's expense for not less than one nor more than 90 days.

For the purposes of this section, the court may consider in the interests of justice factors such as whether impoundment of the vehicle would result in a loss of employment of the offender or the offender's family, impair the ability of the offender or the offender's family to attend school or obtain medical care, result in the loss of the vehicle because of inability to pay impoundment fees, or unfairly infringe upon community property rights or any other facts the court finds relevant. When no impoundment is ordered in an unusual case pursuant to this section, the court shall specify on the record and shall enter in the minutes the circumstances indicating that the interests of justice would best be served by that disposition.

(b) No vehicle which may be lawfully driven on the highway with a class C or class M driver's license, as specified in Section 12804.9, is subject to impoundment under this section if there is a community property interest in the vehicle owned by a person other than the defendant and the vehicle is the sole vehicle available to the defendant's immediate family which may be operated on the highway with a class C or class M driver's license.

(Added by Stats. 1998, Ch. 118, Sec. 84. Effective January 1, 1999. Section operative July 1, 1999, pursuant to Section 23675.)

23596. (a) (1) Upon its own motion or upon motion of the prosecutor in a criminal action for a violation of any of the following offenses, the court with jurisdiction over the offense, notwithstanding Section 86 of the Code of Civil Procedure and any other provision of law otherwise prescribing the jurisdiction of the court based upon the value of the property involved, may declare the motor vehicle driven by the defendant to be a nuisance if the defendant is the registered owner of the vehicle:

(A) A violation of Section 191.5 of, or subdivision (a) of Section 192.5 of, the Penal Code.

(B) A violation of Section 23152 that occurred within seven years of two or more separate offenses of Section 191.5 of, or subdivision (a) of Section 192.5 of, the Penal Code, or Section 23152 or 23153, or any combination thereof, that resulted in convictions.

(C) A violation of Section 23153 that occurred within seven years of one or more separate offenses of Section 191.5 of, or subdivision (a) of Section 192.5 of, the Penal Code, or Section 23152 or 23153, that resulted in convictions.

(2) The court or the prosecutor shall give notice of the motion to the defendant, and the court shall hold a hearing before a motor vehicle may be declared a nuisance under this section.

(b) Except as provided in subdivision (g), upon the conviction of the defendant and at the time of pronouncement of sentence, the court with jurisdiction over the offense shall order a vehicle declared to be a nuisance pursuant to subdivision (a) to be sold. A vehicle ordered to be sold pursuant to this subdivision shall be surrendered to the sheriff of the county or the chief of police of the city in which the violation occurred. The officer to whom the vehicle is surrendered shall promptly ascertain from the department the names and addresses of all legal and registered owners of the vehicle and, within five days of receiving that information, shall send by certified mail a notice to all legal and registered owners of the vehicle other than the defendant, at the addresses obtained from the department, informing them that the vehicle has been declared a nuisance and will be sold or otherwise disposed of pursuant to this section and of the approximate date and location of the sale or other disposition. The notice shall also inform a legal owner of its right to conduct the sale pursuant to subdivision (c).

(c) The legal owner who is a motor vehicle dealer, bank, credit union, acceptance corporation, or other licensed finance institution legally operating in this state, or the agent of that legal owner, may take possession and conduct the sale of the vehicle declared to be a nuisance if it notifies the officer to whom the vehicle is surrendered of its intent to conduct the sale within 15 days of the mailing of the notice pursuant to subdivision (b). Sale of the vehicle pursuant to this subdivision may be conducted at the time, in the manner, and on the notice usually given for the sale of repossessed or surrendered vehicles. The proceeds of a sale conducted by the legal owner shall be disposed of as provided in subdivision (e). A notice pursuant to this subdivision may be presented in person, by certified mail, by facsimile transmission, or by electronic mail. The agent of a legal owner acting pursuant to this subdivision shall be licensed, or exempt from licensure, pursuant to Chapter 11 (commencing with Section 7500) of Division 3 of the Business and Professions Code.

(d) If the legal owner or the agent of the legal owner does not notify the officer to whom the vehicle is surrendered of its intent to conduct the sale as provided in subdivision (c), the officer shall offer the vehicle for sale at public auction within 60 days of receiving the vehicle. At least 10 days but not more than 20 days prior to the sale, not counting the day of the sale, the officer shall give notice of the sale by advertising once in a newspaper of general circulation published in the city or county, as the case may be, in which the vehicle is located, that notice shall contain a description of the make, year, model, identification number, and license number of the vehicle and the date, time, and location of the sale. For motorcycles, the engine number shall also be included. If there is no newspaper of general circulation published in the county, notice shall be given by posting a notice of sale containing the information required by this subdivision in three of the most public places in the city or county in which the vehicle is located, and at the place where the vehicle is to be sold, for 10 consecutive days prior to and including the day of the sale.

(e) The proceeds of a sale conducted pursuant to this section shall be disposed of in the following priority:

(1) To satisfy the costs of the sale, including costs incurred with respect to the taking and keeping of the vehicle pending sale.

(2) To the legal owner in an amount to satisfy the indebtedness owed to the legal owner remaining as of the date of the sale, including accrued interest or finance charges and delinquency charges.

(3) To the holder of a subordinate lien or encumbrance on the vehicle to satisfy any indebtedness so secured if written notification of demand is received before distribution of the proceeds is completed. The holder of a subordinate lien or encumbrance, if requested, shall reasonably furnish reasonable proof of its interest and, unless it does so on request, is not entitled to distribution pursuant to this paragraph.

(4) To any other person who can establish an interest in the vehicle, including a community property interest, to the extent of his or her provable interest.

(5) If the vehicle was forfeited as a result of a felony violation of subdivision (a) of Section 191.5 of, or subdivision (a) of Section 192.5 of, the Penal Code, or of Section 23153 that resulted in serious bodily injury to a person other than the defendant, the balance, if any, to the city or county in which the violation occurred, to be deposited in its general fund.

(6) Except as provided in paragraph (5), the balance, if any, to the city or county in which the violation occurred, to be expended for community-based adolescent substance abuse treatment services.

The person conducting the sale shall disburse the proceeds of the sale as provided in this subdivision, and provide a written accounting regarding the disposition to all persons entitled to or claiming a share of the proceeds, within 15 days after the sale is conducted.

(f) If the vehicle to be sold under this section is not of the type that can readily be sold to the public generally, the vehicle shall be destroyed or donated to an eleemosynary institution.

(g) No vehicle shall be sold pursuant to this section in either of the following circumstances:

(1) The vehicle is stolen, unless the identity of the legal and registered owners of the vehicle cannot be reasonably ascertained.

(2) The vehicle is owned by another, or there is a community property interest in the vehicle owned by a person other than the defendant and the vehicle is the only vehicle available to the defendant's immediate family that may be operated on the highway with a class 3 or class 4 driver's license.

(h) The Legislature finds and declares it to be the public policy of this state that no policy of insurance shall afford benefits that would alleviate the financial detriment suffered by a person as a direct or indirect result of a confiscation of a vehicle pursuant to this section.

(Amended by Stats. 2007, Ch. 747, Sec. 36. Effective January 1, 2008.)

23597. (a) Notwithstanding Sections 13202.5, 13203, and 13352, a court may order a 10-year revocation of the driver's license of a person who has been convicted of three or more separate violations of Section 23152 or 23153, the last of which is punishable under Section 23546, 23550, 23550.5, or 23566. When making this order, the court shall consider all of the following:

(1) The person's level of remorse for the acts.

(2) The period of time that has elapsed since the person's previous convictions.

(3) The person's blood-alcohol level at the time of the violation.

(4) The person's participation in an alcohol treatment program.

(5) The person's risk to traffic or public safety.

(6) The person's ability to install a functioning, certified ignition interlock device in each motor vehicle that the person operates.

(b) Upon receipt of a duly certified abstract of the record of the court showing the court has ordered a 10-year revocation of a driver's license pursuant to this section, the department shall revoke the person's driver's license for 10 years, except as provided in subdivision (c).

(c) (1) Five years from the date of the last conviction of a violation of Section 23152 or 23153, a person whose license was revoked pursuant to subdivision (a) may apply to the department to have their privilege to operate a motor vehicle reinstated, subject to the condition that the person submits the "Verification of Installation" form described in paragraph (2) of subdivision (g) of Section 13386 and agrees to maintain a functioning, certified ignition interlock device as required under subdivision (f) of Section 23575.3. Notwithstanding Chapter 5 (commencing with Section 23700) or Section 23575.3, the ignition interlock device shall remain on the person's motor vehicle for two years following the reinstatement of the person's driving privilege pursuant to this section.

(2) The department shall reinstate the person's license pursuant to paragraph (1), if the person satisfies all of the following conditions:

(A) The person was not convicted of any drug- or alcohol-related offenses, under state law, during the driver's license revocation period.

(B) The person successfully completed a driving-under-the-influence program, licensed pursuant to Section 11836 of the Health and Safety Code, following the date of the last conviction of a violation of Section 23152 or 23153 of this code.

(C) The person was not convicted of violating Section 14601, 14601.1, 14601.2, 14601.4, or 14601.5 during the driver's license revocation period.

(3) The department shall immediately revoke the privilege to operate a motor vehicle of a person who attempts to remove, bypass, or tamper with the device, who has the device removed prior to the termination date of the restriction, or who fails three or more times to comply with any requirement for the maintenance or calibration of the ignition interlock device. The privilege shall remain revoked for the remaining period of the original revocation and until all reinstatement requirements are met, provided, however, that if the person provides proof to the satisfaction of the department that the person is in compliance with the restriction issued pursuant to this section, the department may, in its discretion, restore the privilege to operate a motor vehicle and reimpose the remaining term of the restriction.

(d) This section shall become operative on January 1, 2019.

(e) This section shall remain in effect only until January 1, 2033, and as of that date is repealed, unless a later enacted statute, that is enacted before January 1, 2033, deletes or extends that date.

(Amended (as amended by Stats. 2017, Ch. 485, Sec. 30) by Stats. 2025, Ch. 689, Sec. 29. (AB 366) Effective January 1, 2026. Repealed as of January 1, 2033, by its own provisions. See later operative version, as amended by Sec. 30 of Stats. 2025, Ch. 689.)

23597. (a) Notwithstanding Sections 13202.5, 13203, and 13352, a court may order a 10-year revocation of the driver's license of a person who has been convicted of three or more separate violations of Section 23152 or 23153, the last of which is punishable under Section 23546, 23550, 23550.5, or 23566. When making this order, the court shall consider all of the following:

(1) The person's level of remorse for the acts.

(2) The period of time that has elapsed since the person's previous convictions.

(3) The person's blood-alcohol level at the time of the violation.

(4) The person's participation in an alcohol treatment program.

(5) The person's risk to traffic or public safety.

(6) The person's ability to install a certified ignition interlock device in each motor vehicle that the person owns or operates.

(b) Upon receipt of a duly certified abstract of the record of the court showing the court has ordered a 10-year revocation of a driver's license pursuant to this section, the department shall revoke the person's driver's license for 10 years, except as provided in subdivision (c).

(c) (1) Five years from the date of the last conviction of a violation of Section 23152 or 23153, a person whose license was revoked pursuant to subdivision (a) may apply to the department to have their privilege to operate a motor vehicle reinstated, subject to the condition that the person submits the "Verification of Installation" form described in paragraph (2) of subdivision (g) of Section 13386 and agrees to maintain the ignition interlock device as required under subdivision (g) of Section 23575. Notwithstanding Chapter 5 (commencing with Section 23700) or subdivision (f) of Section 23575, the ignition interlock device shall remain on the person's motor vehicle for two years following the reinstatement of the person's driving privilege pursuant to this section.

(2) The department shall reinstate the person's license pursuant to paragraph (1), if the person satisfies all of the following conditions:

(A) The person was not convicted of any drug- or alcohol-related offenses, under state law, during the driver's license revocation period.

(B) The person successfully completed a driving-under-the-influence program, licensed pursuant to Section 11836 of the Health and Safety Code, following the date of the last conviction of a violation of Section 23152 or 23153.

(C) The person was not convicted of violating Section 14601, 14601.1, 14601.2, 14601.4, or 14601.5 during the driver's license revocation period.

(3) The department shall immediately terminate the restriction issued pursuant to this section and shall immediately revoke the privilege to operate a motor vehicle of a person who attempts to remove, bypass, or tamper with the device, who has the device removed prior to the termination date of the restriction, or who fails three or more times to comply with any requirement for the maintenance or calibration of the ignition interlock device. The privilege shall remain revoked for the remaining period of the original revocation and until all reinstatement requirements are met.

(d) This section shall become operative January 1, 2033.

(Amended (as added by Stats. 2016, Ch. 783, Sec. 42) by Stats. 2025, Ch. 689, Sec. 30. (AB 366) Effective January 1, 2026. Section operative January 1, 2033, by its own provisions.)

Article 7. Alternative to Alcohol or Drug Education Program

(Article 7 added by Stats. 1998, Ch. 118, Sec. 84.)

23598. In lieu of the alcohol or drug education program prescribed by Section 23538, 23542, 23548, 23552, 23556, 23562, or 23568, a court may impose, as a condition of probation, that the person complete, subsequent to the underlying conviction, a program specified in Section 8001 of the Penal Code, if the person consents and has been accepted into that program. Acceptance into that program shall be verified by a certification, under penalty of perjury, by the director of the program.

(Added by Stats. 1998, Ch. 118, Sec. 84. Effective January 1, 1999. Section operative July 1, 1999, pursuant to Section 23675.)

Chapter 3. Probation

(Chapter 3 added by Stats. 1998, Ch. 118, Sec. 84.)

23600. (a) If any person is convicted of a violation of Section 23152 or 23153, the court shall not stay or suspend pronouncement of sentencing, and shall pronounce sentence in conjunction with the conviction in a reasonable time, including time for receipt of any presentence investigation report ordered pursuant to Section 23655.

(b) If any person is convicted of a violation of Section 23152 or 23153 and is granted probation, the terms and conditions of probation shall include, but not be limited to, the following:

(1) Notwithstanding Section 1203a of the Penal Code, a period of probation not less than three nor more than five years; provided, however, that if the maximum sentence provided for the offense may exceed five years in the state prison, the period during which the sentence may be suspended and terms of probation enforced may be for a longer period than three years but may not exceed the maximum time for which sentence of imprisonment may be pronounced.

(2) A requirement that the person shall not drive a vehicle with any measurable amount of alcohol in his or her blood.

(3) A requirement that the person, if arrested for a violation of Section 23152 or 23153, shall not refuse to submit to a chemical test of his or her blood, breath, or urine, pursuant to Section 23612, for the purpose of determining the alcoholic content of his or her blood.

(4) A requirement that the person shall not commit any criminal offense.

(c) The court shall not absolve a person who is convicted of a violation of Section 23152 or 23153 from the obligation of spending the minimum time in confinement, if any, or of paying the minimum fine imposed by law.

(d) In addition to any other provision of law, if any person violates paragraph (2) or (3) of subdivision (b) and the person had a blood alcohol concentration of over 0.04 percent as determined by a chemical test, the court shall revoke or terminate the person's probation as provided by Section 23602, regardless of any other proceeding, and shall only grant a new term of probation of not more than five years on the added condition that the person be confined in the county jail for not less than 48 hours for each of these violations of probation, except in unusual cases where the interests of justice would best be served if this additional condition were not imposed.

(Amended by Stats. 1999, Ch. 22, Sec. 40.6. Effective May 26, 1999. Operative July 1, 1999, by Sec. 46 of Ch. 22.)

23601. (a) Except as provided in subdivision (c), an order to pay any fine, restitution, or assessment, imposed as a condition of the grant of probation or as part of a judgment of conditional sentence for a violation of Section 23152 or 23153, may be enforced in the same manner provided for the enforcement of money judgments.

(b) A willful failure to pay any fine, restitution, or assessment during the term of probation is a violation of the terms and conditions of probation.

(c) If an order to pay a fine as a condition of probation is stayed, a writ of execution shall not be issued, and any failure to pay the fine is not willful, until the stay is removed.

(Added by Stats. 1998, Ch. 118, Sec. 84. Effective January 1, 1999. Section operative July 1, 1999, pursuant to Section 23675.)

23602. Except as otherwise expressly provided in this code, if a person has been convicted of a violation of Section 23152 or 23153 and the court has suspended execution of the sentence for that conviction and has granted probation, and during the time of that probation, the person is found by the court to have violated a required term or condition of that probation, the court shall revoke the suspension of sentence, revoke or terminate probation, and shall proceed in the manner provided in subdivision (c) of Section 1203.2 of the Penal Code.

(Amended by Stats. 1999, Ch. 22, Sec. 41. Effective May 26, 1999. Operative July 1, 1999, by Sec. 46 of Ch. 22.)

Chapter 4. Procedures

(Chapter 4 added by Stats. 1998, Ch. 118, Sec. 84.)

Article 1. General Provisions

(Article 1 added by Stats. 1998, Ch. 118, Sec. 84.)

23610. (a) Upon the trial of any criminal action, or preliminary proceeding in a criminal action, arising out of acts alleged to have been committed by any person while driving a vehicle while under the influence of an alcoholic beverage in violation of subdivision (a) of Section 23152 or subdivision (a) of Section 23153, the amount of alcohol in the person's blood at the time of the test as shown by chemical analysis of that person's blood, breath, or urine shall give rise to the following presumptions affecting the burden of proof:

(1) If there was at that time less than 0.05 percent, by weight, of alcohol in the person's blood, it shall be presumed that the person was not under the influence of an alcoholic beverage at the time of the alleged offense.

(2) If there was at that time 0.05 percent or more but less than 0.08 percent, by weight, of alcohol in the person's blood, that fact shall not give rise to any presumption that the person was or was not under the influence of an alcoholic beverage, but the fact may be considered with other competent evidence in determining whether the person was under the influence of an alcoholic beverage at the time of the alleged offense.

(3) If there was at that time 0.08 percent or more, by weight, of alcohol in the person's blood, it shall be presumed that the person was under the influence of an alcoholic beverage at the time of the alleged offense.

(b) Percent, by weight, of alcohol in the person's blood shall be based upon grams of alcohol per 100 milliliters of blood or grams of alcohol per 210 liters of breath.

(c) This section shall not be construed as limiting the introduction of any other competent evidence bearing upon the question of whether the person ingested any alcoholic beverage or was under the influence of an alcoholic beverage at the time of the alleged offense.

(Added by Stats. 1998, Ch. 118, Sec. 84. Effective January 1, 1999. Section operative July 1, 1999, pursuant to Section 23675.)

23612. (a) (1) (A) A person who drives a motor vehicle is deemed to have given his or her consent to chemical testing of his or her blood or breath for the purpose of determining the alcoholic content of his or her blood, if lawfully arrested for an offense allegedly committed in violation of Section 23140, 23152, or 23153. If a blood or breath test, or both, are unavailable, then paragraph (2) of subdivision (d) applies.

(B) A person who drives a motor vehicle is deemed to have given his or her consent to chemical testing of his or her blood for the purpose of determining the drug content of his or her blood, if lawfully arrested for an offense allegedly committed in violation of Section 23140, 23152, or 23153. If a blood test is unavailable, the person shall be deemed to have given his or her consent to chemical testing of his or her urine and shall submit to a urine test.

(C) The testing shall be incidental to a lawful arrest and administered at the direction of a peace officer having reasonable cause to believe the person was driving a motor vehicle in violation of Section 23140, 23152, or 23153.

(D) The person shall be told that his or her failure to submit to, or the failure to complete, the required breath or urine testing will result in a fine and mandatory imprisonment if the person is convicted of a violation of Section 23152 or 23153. The person shall also be told that his or her failure to submit to, or the failure to complete, the required breath, blood, or urine tests will result in (i) the administrative suspension by the department of the person's privilege to operate a motor vehicle for a period of one year, (ii) the administrative revocation by the department of the person's privilege to operate a motor vehicle for a period of two years if the refusal occurs within 10 years of a separate violation of Section 23103 as specified in Section 23103.5, or of Section 23140, 23152, or 23153 of this code, or of Section 191.5 or subdivision (a) of Section 192.5 of the Penal Code that resulted in a conviction, or if the person's privilege to operate a motor vehicle has been suspended or revoked pursuant to Section 13353, 13353.1, or 13353.2 for an offense that occurred on a separate occasion, or (iii) the administrative revocation by the department of the person's privilege to operate a motor vehicle for a period of three years if the refusal occurs within 10 years of two or more separate violations of Section 23103 as specified in Section 23103.5, or of Section 23140, 23152, or 23153 of this code, or of Section 191.5 or subdivision (a) of Section 192.5 of the Penal Code, or any combination thereof, that resulted in convictions, or if the person's privilege to operate a motor vehicle has been suspended or revoked two or more times pursuant to Section 13353, 13353.1, or 13353.2 for offenses that occurred on separate occasions, or if there is any combination of those convictions, administrative suspensions, or revocations.

(2) (A) If the person is lawfully arrested for driving under the influence of an alcoholic beverage, the person has the choice of whether the test shall be of his or her blood or breath and the officer shall advise the person that he or she has that choice. If the person arrested either is incapable, or states that he or she is incapable, of completing the chosen test, the person shall submit to the remaining test. If a blood or breath test, or both, are unavailable, then paragraph (2) of subdivision (d) applies.

(B) If the person is lawfully arrested for driving under the influence of any drug or the combined influence of an alcoholic beverage and any drug, the person has the choice of whether the test shall be of his or her blood or breath, and the officer shall advise the person that he or she has that choice.

(C) A person who chooses to submit to a breath test may also be requested to submit to a blood test if the officer has reasonable cause to believe that the person was driving under the influence of a drug or the combined influence of an alcoholic beverage and a drug and if the officer has reasonable cause to believe that a blood test will reveal evidence of the person being under the influence. The officer shall state in his or her report the facts upon which those beliefs are based. The officer shall advise the person that he or she is required to submit to an additional test. The person shall submit to and complete a blood test. If the person arrested is incapable of completing the blood test, the person shall submit to and complete a urine test.

(3) If the person is lawfully arrested for an offense allegedly committed in violation of Section 23140, 23152, or 23153, and, because of the need for medical treatment, the person is first transported to a medical facility where it is not feasible to administer a particular test of, or to obtain a particular sample of, the person's blood or breath, the person has the choice of those tests, including a urine test, that are available at the facility to which that person has been transported. In that case, the officer shall advise the person of those tests that are available at the medical facility and that the person's choice is limited to those tests that are available.

(4) The officer shall also advise the person that he or she does not have the right to have an attorney present before stating whether he or she will submit to a test or tests, before deciding which test or tests to take, or during administration of the test or tests chosen, and that, in the event of refusal to submit to a test or tests, the refusal may be used against him or her in a court of law.

(5) A person who is unconscious or otherwise in a condition rendering him or her incapable of refusal is deemed not to have withdrawn his or her consent and a test or tests may be administered whether or not the person is told that his or her failure to submit to, or the noncompletion of, the test or tests will result in the suspension or revocation of his or her privilege to operate a motor vehicle. A person who is dead is deemed not to have withdrawn his or her consent and a test or tests may be administered at the direction of a peace officer.

(b) A person who is afflicted with hemophilia is exempt from the blood test required by this section, but shall submit to, and complete, a urine test.

(c) A person who is afflicted with a heart condition and is using an anticoagulant under the direction of a licensed physician and surgeon is exempt from the blood test required by this section, but shall submit to, and complete, a urine test.

(d) (1) A person lawfully arrested for an offense allegedly committed while the person was driving a motor vehicle in violation of Section 23140, 23152, or 23153 may request the arresting officer to have a chemical test made of the arrested person's blood or breath for the purpose of determining the alcoholic content of that person's blood, and, if so requested, the arresting officer shall have the test performed.

(2) If a blood or breath test is not available under subparagraph (A) of paragraph (1) of subdivision (a), or under subparagraph (A) of paragraph (2) of subdivision (a), or under paragraph (1) of this subdivision, the person shall submit to the remaining test in order to determine the percent, by weight, of alcohol in the person's blood. If both the blood and breath tests are unavailable, the person shall be deemed to have given his or her consent to chemical testing of his or her urine and shall submit to a urine test.

(e) If the person, who has been arrested for a violation of Section 23140, 23152, or 23153, refuses or fails to complete a chemical test or tests, or requests that a blood or urine test be taken, the peace officer, acting on behalf of the department, shall serve the notice of the order of suspension or revocation of the person's privilege to operate a motor vehicle personally on the arrested person. The notice shall be on a form provided by the department.

(f) If the peace officer serves the notice of the order of suspension or revocation of the person's privilege to operate a motor vehicle, the peace officer shall take possession of all driver's licenses issued by this state that are held by the person. The temporary driver's license shall be an endorsement on the notice of the order of suspension and shall be valid for 30 days from the date of arrest.

(g) (1) The peace officer shall immediately forward a copy of the completed notice of suspension or revocation form and any driver's license taken into possession under subdivision (f), with the report required by Section 13380, to the department. If the person submitted to a blood or urine test, the peace officer shall forward the results immediately to the appropriate forensic laboratory. The forensic laboratory shall forward the results of the chemical tests to the department within 15 calendar days of the date of the arrest.

(2) (A) Notwithstanding any other law, a document containing data prepared and maintained in the governmental forensic laboratory computerized database system that is electronically transmitted or retrieved through public or private computer networks to or by the department is the best available evidence of the chemical test results in all administrative proceedings conducted by the department. In addition, any other official record that is maintained in the governmental forensic laboratory, relates to a chemical test analysis prepared and maintained in the governmental forensic laboratory computerized database system, and is electronically transmitted and retrieved through a public or private computer network to or by the department is admissible as evidence in the department's administrative proceedings. In order to be admissible as evidence in administrative proceedings, a document described in this subparagraph shall bear a certification by the employee of the department who retrieved the document certifying that the information was received or retrieved directly from the computerized database system of a governmental forensic laboratory and that the document accurately reflects the data received or retrieved.

(B) Notwithstanding any other law, the failure of an employee of the department to certify under subparagraph (A) is not a public offense.

(h) A preliminary alcohol screening test that indicates the presence or concentration of alcohol based on a breath sample in order to establish reasonable cause to believe the person was driving a vehicle in violation of Section 23140, 23152, or 23153 is a field sobriety test and may be used by an officer as a further investigative tool.

(i) If the officer decides to use a preliminary alcohol screening test, the officer shall advise the person that he or she is requesting that person to take a preliminary alcohol screening test to assist the officer in determining if that person is under the influence of alcohol or drugs, or a combination of alcohol and drugs. The person's obligation to submit to a blood, breath, or urine test, as required by this section, for the purpose of determining the alcohol or drug content of that person's blood, is not satisfied by the person submitting to a preliminary alcohol screening test. The officer shall advise the person of that fact and of the person's right to refuse to take the preliminary alcohol screening test.

(Amended by Stats. 2018, Ch. 177, Sec. 3. (AB 2717) Effective January 1, 2019.)

23614. (a) In addition to the requirements of Section 23612, a person who chooses to submit to a breath test shall be advised before or after the test that the breath-testing equipment does not retain any sample of the breath and that no breath sample will be available after the test which could be analyzed later by that person or any other person.

(b) The person shall also be advised that, because no breath sample is retained, the person will be given an opportunity to provide a blood or urine sample that will be retained at no cost to the person so that there will be something retained that may be subsequently analyzed for the alcoholic content of the person's blood. If the person completes a breath test and wishes to provide a blood or urine sample to be retained, the sample shall be collected and retained in the same manner as if the person had chosen a blood or urine test initially.

(c) The person shall also be advised that the blood or urine sample may be tested by either party in any criminal prosecution. The failure of either party to perform this test shall place neither a duty upon the opposing party to perform the test nor affect the admissibility of any other evidence of the alcoholic content of the blood of the person arrested.

(d) No failure or omission to advise pursuant to this section shall affect the admissibility of any evidence of the alcoholic content of the blood of the person arrested.

(Added by Stats. 1998, Ch. 118, Sec. 84. Effective January 1, 1999. Section operative July 1, 1999, pursuant to Section 23675.)

Article 2. Prior and Separate Offenses

(Article 2 added by Stats. 1998, Ch. 118, Sec. 84.)

23620. (a) For the purposes of this division, Section 13352, and Chapter 12 (commencing with Section 23100) of Division 11, a separate offense that resulted in a conviction of a violation of subdivision (f) of Section 655 of the Harbors and Navigation Code or of Section 191.5 of, or subdivision (a) of Section 192.5 of, the Penal Code is a separate offense of a violation of Section 23153.

(b) For the purposes of this division and Chapter 12 (commencing with Section 23100) of Division 11, and Section 13352, a separate offense that resulted in a conviction of a violation of subdivision (b), (c), (d), or (e) of Section 655 of the Harbors and Navigation Code is a separate violation of Section 23152.

(Amended by Stats. 2007, Ch. 747, Sec. 38. Effective January 1, 2008.)

23622. (a) In any case charging a violation of Section 23152 or 23153 and the offense occurred within 10 years of one or more separate violations of Section 23103, as specified in Section 23103.5, that occurred on or after January 1, 1982, 23152, or 23153, or any combination thereof, that resulted in convictions, the court shall not strike any separate conviction of those offenses for purposes of sentencing in order to avoid imposing, as part of the sentence or term of probation, the minimum time of imprisonment and the minimum fine, as provided in this chapter, or for purposes of avoiding revocation, suspension, or restriction of the privilege to operate a motor vehicle, as provided in this code.

(b) In any case charging a violation of Section 23152 or 23153, the court shall obtain a copy of the driving record of the person charged from the Department of Motor Vehicles and may obtain any records from the Department of Justice or any other source to determine if one or more separate violations of Section 23103, as specified in Section 23103.5, that occurred on or after January 1, 1982, 23152, or 23153, or any combination thereof, that resulted in convictions, have occurred within 10 years of the charged offense. The court may obtain, and accept as rebuttable evidence, a printout from the Department of Motor Vehicles of the driving record of the person charged, maintained by electronic and storage media pursuant to Section 1801 for the purpose of proving those separate violations.

(c) If any separate convictions of violations of Section 23152 or 23153 are reported to have occurred within 10 years of the charged offense, the court shall notify each court where any of the separate convictions occurred for the purpose of enforcing terms and conditions of probation pursuant to Section 23602.

(Amended by Stats. 2004, Ch. 550, Sec. 20. Effective January 1, 2005.)

23624. Only one challenge shall be permitted to the constitutionality of a separate conviction of a violation of Section 14601, 14601.2, 23152, or 23153, which was entered in a separate proceeding. When a proceeding to declare a separate judgment of conviction constitutionally invalid has been held, a determination by the court that the separate conviction is constitutional precludes any subsequent attack on constitutional grounds in a subsequent prosecution in which the same separate conviction is charged. In addition, any determination that a separate conviction is unconstitutional precludes any allegation or use of that separate conviction in any judicial or administrative proceeding, and the department shall strike that separate conviction from its records. Pursuant to Section 1803, the court shall report to the Department of Motor Vehicles any determination upholding a conviction on constitutional grounds and any determination that a conviction is unconstitutional.

This section shall not preclude a subsequent challenge to a conviction if, at a later time, a subsequent statute or appellate court decision having retroactive application affords any new basis to challenge the constitutionality of the conviction.

(Added by Stats. 1998, Ch. 118, Sec. 84. Effective January 1, 1999. Section operative July 1, 1999, pursuant to Section 23675.)

23626. A conviction of an offense in any state, territory, or possession of the United States, the District of Columbia, the Commonwealth of Puerto Rico, or the Dominion of Canada that, if committed in this state, would be a violation of Section 23152 or 23153 of this code, or Section 191.5 of, or subdivision (a) of Section 192.5 of, the Penal Code, is a conviction of Section 23152 or 23153 of this code, or Section 191.5 of, or subdivision (a) of Section 192.5 of, the Penal Code for the purposes of this code.

(Amended by Stats. 2007, Ch. 747, Sec. 39. Effective January 1, 2008.)

Article 3. Defenses

(Article 3 added by Stats. 1998, Ch. 118, Sec. 84.)

23630. The fact that any person charged with driving under the influence of any drug or the combined influence of alcoholic beverages and any drug in violation of Section 23152 or 23153 is, or has been entitled to use, the drug under the laws of this state shall not constitute a defense against any violation of the sections.

(Added by Stats. 1998, Ch. 118, Sec. 84. Effective January 1, 1999. Section operative July 1, 1999, pursuant to Section 23675.)

Article 4. Dismissal on the Record

(Article 4 added by Stats. 1998, Ch. 118, Sec. 84.)

23635. When an allegation of a violation of Section 23152 is dismissed by the court, an allegation of a different or lesser offense is substituted for an allegation of a violation of Section 23152, or an allegation of a separate conviction is dismissed or stricken, the court shall specify on the record its reason or reasons for the order. The court shall also specify on the record whether the dismissal, substitution, or striking was requested by the prosecution and whether the prosecution concurred in or opposed the dismissal, substitution, or striking.

When the prosecution makes a motion for a dismissal or substitution, or for the striking of a separate conviction, the prosecution shall submit a written statement which shall become part of the court record and which gives the reasons for the motion. The reasons shall include, but need not be limited to, problems of proof, the interests of justice, why another offense is more properly charged, if applicable, and any other pertinent reasons. If the reasons include the "interests of justice," the written statement shall specify all of the factors which contributed to this conclusion.

(Added by Stats. 1998, Ch. 118, Sec. 84. Effective January 1, 1999. Section operative July 1, 1999, pursuant to Section 23675.)

Article 5. Court Restrictions

(Article 5 added by Stats. 1998, Ch. 118, Sec. 84.)

23640. (a) In any case in which a person is charged with a violation of Section 23152 or 23153, prior to acquittal or conviction, the court shall neither suspend nor stay the proceedings for the purpose of allowing the accused person to attend or participate, nor shall the court consider dismissal of or entertain a motion to dismiss the proceedings because the accused person attends or participates during that suspension, in any one or more education, training, or treatment programs, including, but not limited to, a driver improvement program, a treatment program for persons who are habitual users of alcohol or other alcoholism program, a program designed to offer alcohol services to problem drinkers, an alcohol or drug education program, or a treatment program for persons who are habitual users of drugs or other drug-related program.

(b) This section shall not apply to any attendance or participation in any education, training, or treatment programs after conviction and sentencing, including attendance or participation in any of those programs as a condition of probation granted after conviction when permitted.

(Amended by Stats. 1999, Ch. 22, Sec. 42. Effective May 26, 1999. Operative July 1, 1999, by Sec. 46 of Ch. 22.)

Article 6. Alcohol Assessment

(Article 6 added by Stats. 1998, Ch. 118, Sec. 84.)

23645. (a) Except as otherwise provided in subdivision (c), any person convicted of a violation of Section 23152 or 23153 shall, in addition to any other fine, assessment, or imprisonment imposed pursuant to law, pay an alcohol abuse education and prevention penalty assessment in an amount not to exceed fifty dollars ($50) for deposit and distribution pursuant to Section 1463.25 of the Penal Code.

(b) The payment of the penalty assessment under this section shall be ordered upon conviction of a person of a violation of Section 23152 or 23153 irrespective of any other proceeding and, if probation is granted, the payment of the penalty assessment shall also be ordered as a condition of probation, except in unusual cases that are subject to subdivision (d) of Section 1464 of the Penal Code.

(c) The court shall determine if the defendant has the ability to pay a penalty assessment. If the court determines that the defendant has the ability to pay a penalty assessment, the court may set the amount to be paid and order the defendant to pay that sum to the county in the manner in which the court believes reasonable and compatible with the defendant's financial ability. In making a determination of whether a defendant has the ability to pay, the court shall take into account the amount of any fine imposed upon the defendant and any amount the defendant has been ordered to pay in restitution. If the court determines that the defendant does not have the ability to pay a penalty assessment, the defendant shall not be required to pay a penalty assessment.

(d) Five percent of the funds allocated to primary prevention programs to the school and the communities pursuant to subdivision (a) of Section 11802 of the Health and Safety Code shall be used to conduct an annual evaluation. The annual evaluation shall be conducted by the office of the county superintendent of schools in counties where the program is operating in a single county or in the office of the county superintendent of schools in the county designated as the lead county in counties where the program is operating as a consortium of counties. The evaluation shall contain the following:

(1) A needs assessment evaluation that provides specific data regarding the problem to be resolved.

(2) A written report of the planning process outlining the deliberations, considerations, and conclusions following a review of the needs assessment.

(3) An end of fiscal year accountability evaluation that will indicate the program's continuing ability to reach appropriate program beneficiaries, deliver the appropriate benefits, and use funds appropriately.

(4) An impact evaluation charged with the task of assessing the effectiveness of the program. Guidelines for the evaluation report format and the timeliness for the submission of the report shall be developed by the State Department of Education. Each county shall submit an evaluation report annually to the State Department of Education and the State Department of Education shall write and submit a report to the Legislature and Governor.

(Added by Stats. 1998, Ch. 118, Sec. 84. Effective January 1, 1999. Section operative July 1, 1999, pursuant to Section 23675.)

23646. (a) Each county alcohol program administrator or the administrator's designee shall develop, implement, operate, and administer an alcohol and drug problem assessment program pursuant to this article for each person described in subdivision (b). The alcohol and drug problem assessment program may include a referral and client tracking component.

(b) (1) The court shall order a person to participate in an alcohol and drug problem assessment program pursuant to this section and Sections 23647 to 23649, inclusive, and the related regulations of the State Department of Health Care Services, if the person was convicted of a violation of Section 23152 or 23153 that occurred within 10 years of a separate violation of Section 23152 or 23153 that resulted in a conviction.

(2) A court may order a person convicted of a violation of Section 23152 or 23153 to attend an alcohol and drug problem assessment program pursuant to this article.

(3) The court shall order a person convicted of a violation of Section 23152 or 23153 who has previously been convicted of a violation of Section 23152 or 23153 that occurred more than 10 years ago, or has been previously convicted of a violation of subdivision (f) of Section 647 of the Penal Code, to attend and complete an alcohol and drug problem assessment program under this article. In order to determine whether a previous conviction for a violation occurring more than 10 years ago exists, the court shall rely on state summary criminal history information, local summary history information, or records made available to the judge through the district attorney.

(c) The State Department of Health Care Services shall establish minimum specifications for alcohol and other drug problem assessments and reports.

(Amended by Stats. 2017, Ch. 485, Sec. 31. (SB 611) Effective January 1, 2018.)

23647. (a) Any person convicted of a violation of Section 23152 or 23153 who is required to participate in a county alcohol and drug problem assessment program shall participate in that program.

(b) Any person convicted of a violation of Section 23103, as specified in Section 23103.5, in a judicial district that participates in a county alcohol and drug problem assessment program pursuant to this article, may be ordered to participate in the program.

(Added by renumbering Section 23249.53 by Stats. 1999, Ch. 22, Sec. 30. Effective May 26, 1999. Operative July 1, 1999, by Sec. 46 of Ch. 22.)

23648. (a) Each county shall prepare, or contract to be prepared, an alcohol and drug problem assessment report on each person described in subdivision (b) of Section 23646.

(b) The assessment report shall include, if applicable, a recommendation for any additional treatment and the duration of the treatment. The treatment shall be in addition to the education and counseling program required under Section 11837 of the Health and Safety Code. The assessment report shall be submitted to the court not more than 14 days after the date the assessment was conducted.

(c) Within 30 days of the receipt of the report, the court shall order the person to complete the recommendations set forth in the report in satisfaction of, and consistent with, the terms and conditions of probation.

If the court elects not to order the completion of the recommended plan, the court shall specify on the record its reason for not adopting these recommendations.

(d) This section shall become operative on January 1, 2000.

(Added by renumbering Section 23249.54 (as added by Stats. 1998, Ch. 656, Sec. 7) by Stats. 1999, Ch. 22, Sec. 32. Effective May 26, 1999. Renumbering action operative July 1, 1999, by Sec. 46 of Ch. 22. Section operative January 1, 2000, by its own provisions.)

23649. (a) Notwithstanding any other provision of law, in addition to any other fine or penalty assessment, there shall be levied an assessment of not more than one hundred dollars ($100) upon every fine, penalty, or forfeiture imposed and collected by the courts for a violation of Section 23152 or 23153 in any judicial district that participates in a county alcohol and drug problem assessment program. An assessment of not more than one hundred dollars ($100) shall be imposed and collected by the courts from each person convicted of a violation of Section 23103, as specified in Section 23103.5, who is ordered to participate in a county alcohol and drug problem assessment program pursuant to Section 23647.

(b) The court shall determine if the defendant has the ability to pay the assessment. If the court determines that the defendant has the ability to pay the assessment then the court may set the amount to be reimbursed and order the defendant to pay that sum to the county in the manner that the court determines is reasonable and compatible with the defendant's financial ability. In making a determination of whether a defendant has the ability to pay, the court shall take into account the amount of any fine imposed upon the defendant and any amount the defendant has been ordered to pay in restitution.

(c) Notwithstanding Section 1463 or 1464 of the Penal Code or any other provision of law, all moneys collected pursuant to this section shall be deposited in a special account in the county treasury and shall be used exclusively by the county alcohol program administrator or the administrator's designee to pay for the costs of developing, implementing, operating, maintaining, and evaluating alcohol and drug problem assessment programs.

(d) On January 15 of each year, the treasurer of each county that administers an alcohol and drug problem assessment program shall determine those moneys in the special account that were not expended during the preceding fiscal year, and shall transfer those moneys to the general fund of the county.

(e) Any moneys remaining in the special account, if and when the alcohol and drug problem assessment program is terminated, shall be transferred to the general fund of the county.

(f) The county treasurer shall annually transfer an amount of money equal to the county's administrative cost incurred pursuant to this section, as he or she shall determine, from the special account to the general fund of the county.

(Amended by Stats. 2000, Ch. 1064, Sec. 13. Effective September 30, 2000.)

23650. The Office of Traffic Safety shall adopt rules and guidelines to implement Sections 23646 to 23649, inclusive.

(Amended by Stats. 1999, Ch. 22, Sec. 43. Effective May 26, 1999. Operative July 1, 1999, by Sec. 46 of Ch. 22.)

Article 7. Presentence Investigation

(Article 7 added by Stats. 1998, Ch. 118, Sec. 84.)

23655. (a) Upon any conviction of a violation of Section 23152 or 23153, any judge of the court may order a presentence investigation to determine whether a person convicted of the violation would benefit from one or more education, training, or treatment programs, and the court may order suitable education, training, or treatment for the person, in addition to imposing any penalties required by this code.

(b) In determining whether to require, as a condition of probation, the participation in a program pursuant to subdivision (b) of Section 23538, subdivision (b) of Section 23542, subdivision (b) of Section 23548, subdivision (b) of Section 23552, subdivision (b) of Section 23556, subdivision (b) of Section 23562, or subdivision (b) of Section 23568, the court may consider any relevant information about the person made available pursuant to a presentence investigation, which is permitted but not required by subdivision (a), or other screening procedure. That information shall not be furnished to the court by any person who also provides services in a privately operated, approved program or who has any direct interest in a privately operated, approved program. In addition, the court shall obtain from the Department of Motor Vehicles a copy of the person's driving record to determine whether the person is eligible to participate in an approved program.

(c) The Judicial Council shall adopt a standard form for use by all courts, defendants, and alcohol or drug education programs in certifying to the court that the person has achieved both of the following:

(1) Enrolled within the specified time period.

(2) Successfully completed any program required by Section 23538 or 23556.

(Amended by Stats. 1999, Ch. 22, Sec. 44. Effective May 26, 1999. Operative July 1, 1999, by Sec. 46 of Ch. 22.)

Article 8. Surrender and Notification of License Restriction

(Article 8 added by Stats. 1998, Ch. 118, Sec. 84.)

23660. (a) If a person's privilege to operate a motor vehicle is required to be suspended or revoked by the department under other provisions of this code upon the conviction of an offense described in Article 2 (commencing with Section 23152) of Chapter 12 of Division 11, that person shall surrender each and every operator's license of that person to the court upon conviction. The court shall transmit the license or licenses required to be suspended or revoked to the department under Section 13550, and the court shall notify the department.

(b) This section does not apply to an administrative proceeding by the department to suspend or revoke the driving privilege of any person pursuant to other provisions of law.

(c) This section shall become operative on September 20, 2005.

(Amended by Stats. 2004, Ch. 551, Sec. 24. Effective January 1, 2005. Amended version operative September 20, 2005, pursuant to earlier operation of new subdivision (c).)

23662. If a person is placed on probation, the court shall promptly notify the Department of Motor Vehicles of the probation and probationary term and conditions in a manner prescribed by the department. The department shall place the fact of probation and the probationary term and conditions on the person's records in the department.

(Added by renumbering Section 23203 (as amended by Stats. 1998, Ch. 756) by Stats. 1999, Ch. 22, Sec. 23. Effective May 26, 1999. Operative July 1, 1999, by Sec. 46 of Ch. 22.)

Article 9. Delayed Suspensions and Revocations

(Article 9 added by Stats. 1998, Ch. 118, Sec. 84.)

23665. (a) If a person is convicted of a violation of Section 20001, or of Section 23152 or 23153 and is sentenced to one year in a county jail or more than one year in the state prison under Section 23540, 23542, 23546, 23548, 23550, 23550.5, 23552, 23554, 23556, 23558, 23560, 23562, 23566, or 23568, the court may postpone the revocation or suspension of the person's driving privilege until the term of imprisonment is served.

(b) This section shall become operative on September 20, 2005.

(Amended by Stats. 2004, Ch. 551, Sec. 25. Effective January 1, 2005. Amended version operative September 20, 2005, pursuant to earlier operation of new subdivision (b).)

Article 10. Conflict of Interest

(Article 10 added by Stats. 1998, Ch. 118, Sec. 84.)

23670. A court shall not order or refer any person to any program, including an alcohol and other drug education program or a program licensed pursuant to Chapter 9 (commencing with Section 11836) of Part 2 of Division 10.5 of the Health and Safety Code, or to a provider of a program, in which any employee of the court has a direct or indirect economic interest.

(Added by Stats. 1998, Ch. 118, Sec. 84. Effective January 1, 1999. Section operative July 1, 1999, pursuant to Section 23675. Operative July 1, 1999, by Section 23675.)

Article 11. Operative Date

(Article 11 added by Stats. 1998, Ch. 118, Sec. 84.)

23675. This division shall become operative on July 1, 1999.

(Added by Stats. 1998, Ch. 118, Sec. 84. Effective January 1, 1999. Note: This section prescribes a delayed operative date (July 1, 1999) for Division 11.5, commencing with Section 23500.)

Division 12. Equipment of Vehicles

(Division 12 enacted by Stats. 1959, Ch. 3.)

Chapter 1. General Provisions

(Chapter 1 enacted by Stats. 1959, Ch. 3.)

24000. Wherever in this division the word "department" occurs, it means the Department of the California Highway Patrol.

(Enacted by Stats. 1959, Ch. 3.)

24001. This division and Division 13 (commencing at Section 29000), unless otherwise provided, applies to all vehicles whether publicly or privately owned when upon the highways, including all authorized emergency vehicles.

(Amended by Stats. 1959, Ch. 1996.)

24001.5. A golf cart as defined in Section 345 shall only be subject to the provisions of this division which are applicable to a motorcycle.

(Amended by Stats. 1972, Ch. 973.)

24002. (a) It is unlawful to operate any vehicle or combination of vehicles which is in an unsafe condition, or which is not safely loaded, and which presents an immediate safety hazard.

(b) It is unlawful to operate any vehicle or combination of vehicles which is not equipped as provided in this code.

(c) A motor carrier shall not require a person to drive a commercial motor vehicle unless the driver can, by reason of experience, training, or both, determine whether the cargo being transported, including baggage in a passenger-carrying commercial vehicle, has been properly located, distributed, and secured in or on the commercial motor vehicle operated by the driver.

(d) A driver shall not operate a commercial motor vehicle unless the driver can, by reason of experience, training, or both, demonstrate familiarity with the methods and procedures for securing cargo in or on the commercial motor vehicle operated by the driver.

(e) Drivers and motor carriers of commercial motor vehicles shall comply with Section 392.9 of Title 49 of the Code of Federal Regulations.

(f) For purposes of this section, "commercial motor vehicle" has the same meaning as defined in subdivision (b) of Section 15210, and also includes any vehicle listed in Section 34500.

(Amended by Stats. 2015, Ch. 451, Sec. 47. (SB 491) Effective January 1, 2016.)

24002.5. (a) No person may operate a farm labor vehicle that is in a condition that presents an immediate safety hazard or in violation of Section 24004 or 31402.

(b) A violation of this section is a misdemeanor punishable by a fine of not less than one thousand dollars ($1,000) and not more than five thousand dollars ($5,000), or both that fine and a sentence of confinement for not more than six months in the county jail. No part of any fine imposed under this section may be suspended.

(c) As used in this section, an "immediate safety hazard" is any equipment violation described in subdivision (a) of Section 31401 or Section 31405, including any violation of a regulation adopted pursuant to those provisions.

(d) Any member of the Department of the California Highway Patrol may impound a farm labor vehicle operated in violation of this section pursuant to Section 34506.4.

(Added by Stats. 2000, Ch. 873, Sec. 2. Effective January 1, 2001.)

24003. No vehicle shall be equipped with any lamp or illuminating device not required or permitted in this code, nor shall any lamp or illuminating device be mounted inside a vehicle unless specifically permitted by this code. This section does not apply to:

(a) Interior lamps such as door, brake and instrument lamps, and map, dash, and dome lamps designed and used for the purpose of illuminating the interior of the vehicle.

(b) Lamps needed in the operation or utilization of those vehicles mentioned in Section 25801, or vehicles used by public utilities in the repair or maintenance of their service, or used only for the illumination of cargo space of a vehicle while loading or unloading.

(c) Warning lamps mounted inside an authorized emergency vehicle and meeting requirements established by the department.
(Amended by Stats. 1979, Ch. 723.)

24004. No person shall operate any vehicle or combination of vehicles after notice by a peace officer, as defined in Section 830.1 or subdivision (a) of Section 830.2 of the Penal Code, that the vehicle is in an unsafe condition or is not equipped as required by this code, except as may be necessary to return the vehicle or combination of vehicles to the residence or place of business of the owner or driver or to a garage, until the vehicle and its equipment have been made to conform with the requirements of this code.

The provisions of this section shall not apply to an employee who does not know that such notice has been issued, and in such event the provisions of Section 40001 shall be applicable.
(Amended by Stats. 1979, Ch. 171.)

24005. It is unlawful for any person to sell, offer for sale, lease, install, or replace, either for himself or as the agent or employee of another, or through such agent or employee, any glass, lighting equipment, signal devices, brakes, vacuum or pressure hose, muffler, exhaust, or any kind of equipment whatsoever for use, or with knowledge that any such equipment is intended for eventual use, in any vehicle, that is not in conformity with this code or regulations made thereunder.
(Amended by Stats. 1971, Ch. 734.)

24005.5. It is unlawful for any person to sell or offer for sale for use on loads regulated by the department any type of synthetic fiber rope or webbing strap material unless it meets requirements established by the department.
(Amended by Stats. 1979, Ch. 723.)

24006. No person shall sell or offer for sale either separately or as a part of the equipment of a new motor vehicle any equipment or device subject to requirements established by the department unless the equipment or device bears thereon the trademark or name and type or model designation under requirements established by the department and is accompanied by any printed instructions which may be required by the department as to the light source to be used with lamps, any particular methods of mounting or adjustment of lamps or other devices, and any other instructions as determined by the department necessary for compliance with this code.
(Amended by Stats. 1979, Ch. 723.)

24007. (a) (1) No dealer or person holding a retail seller's permit shall sell a new or used vehicle that is not in compliance with this code and departmental regulations adopted pursuant to this code, unless the vehicle is sold to another dealer, sold for the purpose of being legally wrecked or dismantled, or sold exclusively for off-highway use.

(2) Paragraph (1) does not apply to any vehicle sold by either (A) a dismantler after being reported for dismantling pursuant to Section 11520 or (B) a salvage pool after obtaining a salvage certificate pursuant to Section 11515 or a nonrepairable vehicle certificate issued pursuant to Section 11515.2.

(3) Notwithstanding paragraph (1), the equipment requirements of this division do not apply to the sale of a leased vehicle by a dealer to a lessee if the lessee is in possession of the vehicle immediately prior to the time of the sale and the vehicle is registered in this state.

(b) (1) Except as provided in Section 24007.5, no person shall sell, or offer or deliver for sale, to the ultimate purchaser, or to any subsequent purchaser a new or used motor vehicle, as those terms are defined in Chapter 2 (commencing with Section 39010) of Part 1 of Division 26 of the Health and Safety Code, subject to Part 5 (commencing with Section 43000) of that Division 26 which is not in compliance with that part and the rules and regulations of the State Air Resources Board, unless the vehicle is sold to a dealer or sold for the purpose of being legally wrecked or dismantled.

(2) Prior to or at the time of delivery for sale, the seller shall provide the purchaser a valid certificate of compliance or certificate of noncompliance, as appropriate, issued in accordance with Section 44015 of the Health and Safety Code.

(3) Paragraph (2) does not apply to any vehicle whose transfer of ownership and registration is described in subdivision (d) of Section 4000.1.

(4) Paragraphs (1) and (2) do not apply to any vehicle sold by either (A) a dismantler after being reported for dismantling pursuant to Section 11520 or (B) a salvage pool after obtaining a salvage certificate pursuant to Section 11515 or a nonrepairable vehicle certificate issued pursuant to Section 11515.2.

(c) (1) With each application for initial registration of a new motor vehicle or transfer of registration of a motor vehicle subject to Part 5 (commencing with Section 43000) of Division 26 of the Health and Safety Code, a dealer, the purchaser, or their authorized representative, shall transmit to the Department of Motor Vehicles a valid certificate of compliance or noncompliance, as appropriate, issued in accordance with Section 44015 of the Health and Safety Code.

(2) Notwithstanding paragraph (1) of this subdivision, with respect to new vehicles certified pursuant to Chapter 2 (commencing with Section 43100) of Part 5 of Division 26 of the Health and Safety Code, a dealer may transmit, in lieu of a certificate of compliance, a statement, in a form and containing information deemed necessary and appropriate by the Director of Motor Vehicles and the Executive Officer of the State Air Resources Board, to attest to the vehicle's compliance with that chapter. The statement shall be certified under penalty of perjury, and shall be signed by the dealer or the dealer's authorized representative.

(3) Paragraph (1) does not apply to a transfer of ownership and registration under any of the circumstances described in subdivision (d) of Section 4000.1.

(d) A salvage vehicle rebuilder, when selling a total loss salvage vehicle, including a revived salvage loss vehicle, shall provide the purchaser with a valid vehicle safety systems certificate of compliance issued pursuant to Article 6.5 (commencing with Section 9888.5) of Chapter 20.3 of Division 3 of the Business and Professions Code prior to, or at the time of, delivery for sale, unless the vehicle is sold to a dealer or sold for the purpose of being legally wrecked or dismantled.
(Amended by Stats. 2023, Ch. 681, Sec. 25. (AB 1263) Effective January 1, 2024.)

24007.1. (a) The manufacturer of equipment used in the assembly of an authorized emergency vehicle, as defined in Section 165, used by a local public fire service agency shall, upon request of the fire department, reimburse the agency for the cost of repairs to the vehicle if (1) the repair was made to correct a manufacturer's defect, and (2) the vehicle is placed on a safety-related recall to correct that defect.

(b) A final stage equipment manufacturer is deemed to be an original equipment manufacturer in the event of a warranty dispute with a local public fire service agency regarding the failure of component parts used in the assembly of the agency's authorized emergency vehicle. As used in this section, "final stage equipment manufacturer" means the manufacturer who assembles the authorized emergency vehicle from one or more components supplied by other manufacturers.

(c) The Legislature finds and declares that local public fire service agencies of this state are entitled to safe and efficient use of their equipment, and that defects in emergency equipment, especially emergency vehicles, endanger the firefighters of California and the public they serve. It is the intent of the Legislature to ensure that these defects are repaired as expeditiously as possible and with no expense to the local public fire service agencies.
(Added by Stats. 1994, Ch. 1220, Sec. 65. Effective September 30, 1994.)

24007.2. If a dealer, or a person holding a retail seller's permit, sells to an elderly low-income person, as defined in Section 39026.5 of the Health and Safety Code, a 1966 through 1970 model year motor vehicle which is not equipped, as required pursuant to Sections 43654 and 43656 of that code, with a certified device to control its exhaust emission of oxides of nitrogen, the dealer or such person, as the case may be, shall install the required certified device on the motor vehicle without cost to the elderly low-income person.

(Added by Stats. 1976, Ch. 231.)

24007.5. (a) (1) No auctioneer or public agency shall sell, at public auction, any vehicle specified in subdivision (a) of Section 24007, which is not in compliance with this code.

(2) Paragraph (1) does not apply to a vehicle that is sold under the conditions specified in subdivision (c), (d), (e), or (g) or is sold to a dealer or for the purpose of being wrecked or dismantled or is sold exclusively for off-highway use.

(b) Except with respect to the sale of a vehicle specified in paragraph (2) of subdivision (a), the consignor of any vehicle, specified in subdivision (b) of Section 24007, sold at public auction, shall provide the purchaser a valid certificate of compliance or certificate of noncompliance, as appropriate, issued in accordance with Section 44015 of the Health and Safety Code.

(c) Notwithstanding any other provision of this code, if, in the opinion of a public utility or public agency, the cost of repairs to a vehicle exceeds the value of the vehicle to the public utility or public agency, the public utility or public agency shall, as transferee or owner, surrender the certificates of registration, documents satisfactory to the Department of Motor Vehicles showing proof of ownership, and the license plates issued for the vehicle to the Department of Motor Vehicles. As used in this section, "public utility" means a public utility as described in Sections 218, 222, and 234 of the Public Utilities Code.

(d) The public utility or public agency having complied with subdivision (c) shall, upon sale of the vehicle, give to the purchaser a bill of sale which includes, in addition to any other required information, the last issued license plate number.

(e) (1) Subdivisions (a) and (b) do not apply to any judicial sale, including, but not limited to, a bankruptcy sale, conducted pursuant to a writ of execution or order of court.

(2) Subdivision (b) does not apply to any lien sale if the lienholder does both of the following:

(A) Gives the notice required by subdivisions (a) and (b) of Section 5900.

(B) Notifies the buyer that California law requires that the buyer obtain a certificate of compliance or noncompliance and register the vehicle with the department, and that failure to comply will result in a lien against any vehicle owned by the buyer pursuant to Section 10876 of the Revenue and Taxation Code, enforceable pursuant to Section 10877 of the Revenue and Taxation Code and Article 6 (commencing with Section 9800) of Chapter 6 of Division 3. Receipt of the notice required by this subparagraph shall be evidenced by the signature of the buyer.

(f) The exceptions in this section do not apply to any requirements for registration of a vehicle pursuant to Section 4000.1, 4000.2, or 4000.3.

(g) Except as otherwise provided in subdivision (e), any public agency or auctioneer which sells, at public auction, any vehicle specified in subdivision (b) of Section 24007, which is registered to a public agency or a public utility, shall provide each bidder with a notice in writing that certificates of compliance are required to be obtained, certifying that the vehicle complies with Part 5 (commencing with Section 43000) of Division 26 of the Health and Safety Code and Article 6.5 (commencing with Section 9888.5) of Chapter 20.3 of Division 3 of the Business and Professions Code, before the vehicle may be registered in this state, unless the vehicle is sold to a dealer or for the purpose of being wrecked or dismantled or is sold exclusively for off-highway use. Prior to the sale of the vehicle, a public agency or public utility shall remove the license plates from the vehicle and surrender them to the department. The purchaser of the vehicle shall be given a bill of sale which includes, in addition to any other required information, the vehicle's last issued license plate number.

(Amended by Stats. 2023, Ch. 681, Sec. 26. (AB 1263) Effective January 1, 2024.)

24007.6. Except for vehicles sold to a dealer or for the purpose of being wrecked or dismantled or sold exclusively for off-highway use, a salvage pool shall do both of the following:

(a) Give the notice required by subdivisions (a) and (b) of Section 5900.

(b) Notify the buyer that California law requires that the buyer obtain a certificate of compliance or noncompliance and to register the vehicle with the department, and that failure to comply will result in a lien against any vehicle owned by the buyer pursuant to Section 10876 of the Revenue and Taxation Code, enforceable pursuant to Section 10877 of the Revenue and Taxation Code and Article 6 (commencing with Section 9800) of Chapter 6 of Division 3. Receipt of the notice required by this paragraph shall be evidenced by the signature of the buyer.

(Added by Stats. 1991, Ch. 996, Sec. 4.)

24008.5. (a) No person shall operate any motor vehicle with a frame height or body floor height greater than specified in subdivisions (b) and (c).

(b) The maximum frame height is as follows:

Vehicle Type	Frame Height
(1) Passenger vehicles, except housecars	23 inches
(2) All other motor vehicles, including housecars, as follows:	
Up to 4,500 pounds GVWR	27 inches
4,501 to 7,500 pounds GVWR	30 inches
7,501 to 10,000 pounds GVWR	31 inches

(c) The lowest portion of the body floor shall not be more than five inches above the top of the frame.

(d) The following definitions govern the construction of this section:

(1) "Frame" means the main longitudinal structural members of the chassis of the vehicle or, for vehicles with unitized body construction, the lowest main longitudinal structural members of the body of the vehicle.

(2) "Frame height" means the vertical distance between the ground and the lowest point on the frame, measured when the vehicle is unladen on a level surface at the lowest point on the frame midway between the front axle and the second axle on the vehicle.

(3) "GVWR" means the manufacturer's gross vehicle weight rating, as defined in Section 390, whether or not the vehicle is modified by use of parts not originally installed by the manufacturer.

(Amended by Stats. 1987, Ch. 718, Sec. 1.)

24009. No person shall sell or offer for sale a new motor truck, truck tractor, or bus that is not equipped with an identification plate or marking bearing the manufacturer's name and the manufacturer's gross vehicle weight rating of such vehicle.

(Added by Stats. 1967, Ch. 1287.)

24010. (a) No person engaged in the rental of any vehicle, for periods of 30 days or less, shall rent, lease or otherwise allow the operation of such vehicle unless all of the following requirements are met:

(1) All necessary equipment required by this code and regulations adopted pursuant to this code for the operation of the vehicle upon a highway has been provided or offered to the lessee for his or her use.

(2) The vehicle conforms to all applicable federal motor vehicle safety standards established pursuant to Chapter 301 (commencing with Section 30101) of Part A of Subtitle VI of Title 49 of the United States Code, and the regulations adopted pursuant to those provisions.

(3) The vehicle is mechanically sound and safe to operate within the meaning of Section 24002.

(b) In order to ensure compliance with this section, the department may conduct periodic inspections, without prior notice, of the business premises of persons engaged in the rental of vehicles for periods of 30 days or less and of the vehicles themselves, for the purpose of ascertaining that the vehicles are in compliance with this section. Any vehicle which is found not in compliance shall not be rented or leased until proof of full compliance with this section is made to the satisfaction of the department.

(c) The contract or rental agreement shall include the name of the person from whom the vehicle is rented, leased or obtained, the address of that person's place of business in this state where the vehicle is rented, leased, or delivered, and a statement of any required equipment refused by the person to whom the vehicle is rented, leased, or delivered.

(Amended by Stats. 2018, Ch. 198, Sec. 23. (AB 3246) Effective January 1, 2019.)

24011. Whenever a federal motor vehicle safety standard is established under federal law (49 U.S.C. Sec. 30101 et seq.), no dealer shall sell or offer for sale a vehicle to which the standard is applicable, and no person shall sell or offer for sale for use upon a vehicle an item of equipment to which the standard is applicable, unless:

(a) The vehicle or equipment conforms to the applicable federal standard.

(b) The vehicle or equipment bears thereon a certification by the manufacturer or distributor that it complies with the applicable federal standards. The certification may be in the form of a symbol prescribed in the federal standards or, if there is no federal symbol, by a symbol acceptable to the department.

(Amended by Stats. 2004, Ch. 615, Sec. 29. Effective January 1, 2005.)

24011.3. (a) Every manufacturer or importer of new passenger vehicles for sale or lease in this state, shall affix to a window or the windshield of the vehicle a notice with either of the following statements, whichever is appropriate:

(1) "This vehicle is equipped with bumpers that can withstand an impact of 2.5 miles per hour with no damage to the vehicle's body and safety systems, although the bumper and related components may sustain damage. The bumper system on this vehicle conforms to the current federal bumper standard of 2.5 miles per hour."

(2) "This vehicle is equipped with a front bumper of a type that has been tested at an impact speed of (here specify the appropriate number) miles per hour, and a rear bumper of a type that has been tested at an impact speed of (here specify the appropriate number) miles per hour, resulting in no damage to the vehicle's body and safety systems and minimal damage to the bumper and attachment hardware. Minimal damage to the bumper means minor cosmetic damage that can be repaired with the use of common repair materials and without replacing any parts. The stronger the bumper, the less likely the vehicle will require repair after a low-speed collision. This vehicle exceeds the current federal bumper standard of 2.5 miles per hour."

(b) The impact speed required to be specified in the notice pursuant to paragraph (2) of subdivision (a) is the maximum speed of impact upon the bumper of the vehicle at which the vehicle sustains no damage to the body and safety systems and only minimal damage to the bumper when subjected to the fixed barrier and pendulum impact tests, and when subjected to the corner impact test at not less than 60 percent of that maximum speed, conducted pursuant to Part 581 of Title 49 of the Code of Federal Regulations.

(c) (1) A manufacturer who willfully fails to affix the notice required by subdivision (a), or willfully misstates any information in the notice, is guilty of a misdemeanor, which shall be punishable by a fine of not more than five hundred dollars ($500). Each failure or misstatement is a separate offense.

(2) A person who willfully defaces, alters, or removes the notice required by subdivision (a) prior to the delivery of the vehicle, to which the notice is required to be affixed, to the registered owner or lessee is guilty of a misdemeanor, which shall be punishable by a fine of not more than five hundred dollars ($500). Each willful defacement, alteration, or removal is a separate offense.

(d) For purposes of this section, the following terms have the following meanings:

(1) "Manufacturer" is any person engaged in the manufacture or assembly of new passenger vehicles for distribution or sale, and includes an importer of new passenger vehicles for distribution or sale and any person who acts for, or is under the control of, a manufacturer in connection with the distribution or sale of new passenger vehicles.

(2) "Passenger vehicle" means, notwithstanding Section 465, a motor vehicle subject to impact testing conducted pursuant to Part 581 of Title 49 of the Code of Federal Regulations.

(3) "No damage" means that, when a passenger vehicle is subjected to impact testing, conducted pursuant to the conditions and test procedures of Sections 581.6 and 581.7 of Part 581 of Title 49 of the Code of Federal Regulations, the vehicle sustains no damage to the body and safety systems.

(4) For purposes of paragraph (2) of subdivision (a) and subdivision (b), "minimal damage to the bumper and attachment hardware" means damage that can be repaired with the use of common repair materials and without replacing any parts. In addition, not later than 30 minutes after completion of each pendulum or barrier impact test, the bumper face bar shall have no permanent deviation greater than three-quarters of one inch from its original contour and position relative to the vehicle frame and no permanent deviation greater than three-eighths of one inch from its original contour on areas of contact with the barrier face or impact ridge of the pendulum test device, measured from a straight line connecting the bumper contours adjoining the contact area.

(e) The notice required by this section may be included in any notice or label required by federal law to be affixed to a window or windshield of the vehicle.

(f) The notice required by this section shall, in an autonomous vehicle, as defined in Section 38750, that is not capable of operation by a human driver seated in the vehicle and not equipped with a windshield or windows, be affixed in the doorjamb, provided that this modification is consistent with, or authorized by, any applicable federal law, regulation, or exemption thereto.

(Amended by Stats. 2021, Ch. 428, Sec. 1. (SB 570) Effective January 1, 2022.)

24011.5. (a) A dealer or manufacturer shall not sell any new passenger vehicle that is equipped with any partial driving automation feature, or provide any software update or other vehicle upgrade that adds any partial driving automation feature, without, at the time of delivering or upgrading the vehicle, providing the buyer or owner with a distinct notice that provides the name of the feature and clearly describes the functions and limitations of the feature.

(b) A manufacturer or dealer shall not name any partial driving automation feature, or describe any partial driving automation feature in marketing materials, using language that implies or would otherwise lead a reasonable person to believe, that the feature allows the vehicle to function as an autonomous vehicle, as defined in Section 38750, or otherwise has functionality not actually included in the feature. A violation of this subdivision shall be considered a misleading advertisement for the purposes of Section 11713.

(c) As used in this section, "partial driving automation feature" has the same meaning as "Level 2 partial driving automation" in the Society of Automotive Engineers (SAE) Standard J3016 (April 2021).

(d) Compliance with this section shall not alter any existing duty of care or limit the civil liability of a manufacturer or dealer, including, but not limited to, claims for negligence or product defect.

(e) Before delivering a passenger vehicle equipped with a partial driving automation feature to a dealer, a manufacturer shall provide information to enable the dealer to comply with subdivision (a). This information shall include specific language recommended for the notice required in that subdivision. A dealer may reasonably rely on the information provided by the manufacturer and a dealer shall not be held in violation of subdivision (a) if the manufacturer fails to provide this information to the dealer or if the information provided is deemed to be not in compliance with this section.

(f) A manufacturer shall not be held in violation of subdivision (a) if the manufacturer provides a dealer with the information required under subdivision (e) and the dealer fails to provide the required notice to the buyer or owner.

(Added by Stats. 2022, Ch. 308, Sec. 1. (SB 1398) Effective January 1, 2023.)

24011.7. (a) Nothing in Chapter 20.4 (commencing with Section 9889.50) of Division 3 of the Business and Professions Code, shall be construed as having any effect on the existing inspection program conducted by the department. Rather, it is the intent of the Legislature that such program continue and that a cooperative relationship between the department and the Department of Consumer Affairs be established, under which the department can inform the Department of Consumer Affairs of the results and experiences of the department in order to provide data on exhaust and noise emission control device tampering and performance deterioration following mandatory inspections.

(Added by Stats. 1973, Ch. 1154.)

24012. All lighting equipment or devices subject to requirements established by the department shall comply with the engineering requirements and specifications, including mounting and aiming instructions, determined and publicized by the department.

(Amended by Stats. 1979, Ch. 723.)

24013. No new motor vehicle shall be sold unless the seller provides the buyer with a statement of the minimum octane number of the gasoline for such vehicle.

As used in this section "octane number" means the octane number of the gasoline adopted by the Federal Trade Commission, and if the Federal Trade Commission does not adopt an octane number, then the American Society for Testing Materials research octane number of the gasoline as defined by Section 20710 of the Business and Professions Code.

(Added by Stats. 1971, Ch. 711.)

24013.5. (a) No dealer shall sell, offer for sale, or display for sale any new light duty truck with a manufacturer's gross vehicle weight rating of 8,500 pounds or less unless there is securely affixed to the windshield or side window of the light duty truck a label on which the manufacturer has endorsed clearly, distinctly, and legibly, true and correct entries disclosing the following information concerning the light duty truck:

(1) The make, model, and serial or identification number or numbers.

(2) The retail price of the light duty truck as suggested by the manufacturer.

(3) The retail delivered price, as suggested by the manufacturer, for each accessory or item of optional equipment which is physically attached to the light duty truck at the time of its delivery to the dealer and which is not included within the price of the light duty truck as stated pursuant to paragraph (2).

(4) The amount charged, if any, to the dealer for the transportation of the light duty truck to the location at which it is delivered to the dealer.

(5) The total of the amounts specified pursuant to paragraphs (2), (3), and (4).

(b) Subdivision (a) applies to every light duty truck sold, offered for sale, or displayed in California which is manufactured on or after September 1, 1988.

(Added by Stats. 1987, Ch. 418, Sec. 2.)

24014. (a) A dealer shall not sell, offer for sale, or display, any new, assembled motorcycle on its premises, unless there is securely attached to its handlebar a label, in the form of a hang tag, approved by the Department of Motor Vehicles, furnished by the manufacturer, on which the manufacturer shall clearly indicate the following for that specific motorcycle:

(1) The recommended retail price of the motorcycle.

(2) The recommended price for each accessory or item of optional equipment physically attached to the motorcycle at the time of its delivery to the dealer.

(3) The manufacturer's suggested retail price for the motorcycle, which is the sum of the prices in paragraphs (1) and (2).

(4) The vehicle identification number.

(b) A dealer shall not affix to a new motorcycle a supplemental price label containing a price that represents the dealer's asking price that exceeds the manufacturer's suggested retail price unless the label is in compliance with all of the following:

(1) The supplemental price label, in lieu of the supplemental sticker provided for in subdivision (q) of Section 11713.1, is securely attached to the handlebar of the motorcycle in a way that does not prevent access to the manufacturer's hang tag and clearly and conspicuously discloses in the largest print appearing on the label, other than the print size used for the dealer's name, that the supplemental label price is the dealer's asking price, or words of similar import, and that it is not the manufacturer's suggested retail price.

(2) The supplemental label clearly and conspicuously discloses the manufacturer's suggested retail price.

(3) The supplemental label lists each item for which the dealer imposes a charge that is not included in the manufacturer's suggested retail price, and discloses the additional price of each item, including, but not limited to, the amount charged by the dealer for assembly, preparation, or both, and the amount charged by the dealer for transportation to the dealership. Charges disclosed shall be net of reimbursement received by the dealer from the manufacturer.

(4) If the supplemental label price is greater than the sum of the manufacturer's suggested retail price and the price of the items disclosed pursuant to paragraph (3), the supplemental label shall set forth that difference and describe it as "added mark-up."

(Amended by Stats. 2018, Ch. 187, Sec. 2. (AB 2227) Effective January 1, 2019.)

24015. (a) Motorized bicycles shall comply with those federal motor vehicle safety standards established pursuant to Chapter 301 (commencing with Section 30101) of Part A of Subtitle VI of Title 49 of the United States Code that apply to a motor-driven cycle, as that term is defined in regulations adopted pursuant to those provisions. These standards include, but are not limited to, provisions requiring a headlamp, taillamp, stoplamp, side and rear reflex reflectors, and adequate brakes.

(b) In addition to equipment required in subdivision (a), all motorized bicycles operated upon a highway shall be equipped with a mirror as required in subdivision (a) of Section 26709, a horn as required in Section 27000, and an adequate muffler as required in subdivision (a) of Section 27150.

(c) Except as provided in subdivisions (a) and (b), none of the provisions of this chapter relating to motorcycles and motor-driven cycles, as defined in this code, shall apply to a motorized bicycle.

(Amended by Stats. 2018, Ch. 198, Sec. 24. (AB 3246) Effective January 1, 2019.)

24016. (a) An electric bicycle described in subdivision (a) of Section 312.5 shall meet the following criteria:

(1) Comply with the equipment and manufacturing requirements for bicycles adopted by the United States Consumer Product Safety Commission (16 C.F.R. 1512.1, et seq.).

(2) Operate in a manner so that the electric motor is disengaged or ceases to function when the brakes are applied, or operate in a manner such that the motor is engaged through a switch or mechanism that, if released or activated, will cause the electric motor to disengage or cease to function.

(b) A person operating an electric bicycle is not subject to the provisions of this code relating to financial responsibility, driver's licenses, registration, and license plate requirements, and an electric bicycle is not a motor vehicle.

(c) Every manufacturer of an electric bicycle shall certify that it complies with the equipment and manufacturing requirements for bicycles adopted by the United States Consumer Product Safety Commission (16 C.F.R. 1512.1, et seq.).

(d) A person shall not tamper with or modify an electric bicycle described in subdivision (a) of Section 312.5 so as to change the speed capability of the bicycle, unless the bicycle continues to meet the definition of an electric bicycle under subdivision (a) of Section 312.5 and the person appropriately replaces the label indicating the classification required in subdivision (c) of Section 312.5.

(e) A person shall not sell a product, device, or application that can modify the speed capability of an electric bicycle such that it no longer meets the definition of an electric bicycle under subdivision (a) of Section 312.5.

(Amended by Stats. 2025, Ch. 37, Sec. 1. (AB 545) Effective January 1, 2026.)

24017. (a) A commercial motor vehicle, as defined in Section 260, operated by a motor carrier, whether the motor carrier is a private company or a public agency shall be equipped with a speedometer that shall be maintained in good working order. The speedometer shall indicate the vehicle's speed in miles per hour or kilometers (km) per hour and shall be accurate to within plus or minus 5 miles per hour (8 km/hour) at a speed of 50 miles per hour (80 km/hour).

(b) This section does not apply to an autonomous vehicle, as defined in Section 38750, that is not capable of operation by a human driver seated in the vehicle, provided that this exemption is consistent with, or authorized by, any applicable federal law, regulation, or exemption thereto.

(Amended by Stats. 2021, Ch. 428, Sec. 2. (SB 570) Effective January 1, 2022.)

24018. (a) Every transit bus operated by a motor carrier, whether that motor carrier is a private company or a public agency, that provides public transportation services shall be equipped with a two-way communication device that enables the driver to contact the motor carrier in the event of an emergency. The two-way communication devices shall be maintained in good working order.

(b) For the purposes of this section, "two-way communication device" is a radio, cellular telephone, or other similar device permitting communication between the transit bus driver and personnel responsible for the safety of operations of the motor carrier, including, but not limited to, the motor carrier's dispatcher.

(c) This section does not apply to buses operated by a school district or on behalf of a school district.

(d) The commissioner shall upon request grant a nonrenewable one year extension to any motor carrier to comply with the requirements of this section.

(e) Nothing in this section shall require a motor carrier to replace an existing two-way communication device that currently meets the requirements of this section.

(Added by Stats. 2002, Ch. 937, Sec. 3. Effective January 1, 2003.)

24019. (a) A nongasoline heavy-duty onroad motor vehicle with a gross vehicle weight rating of more than 14,000 pounds shall not be operated on a public road in this state if that vehicle has an illuminated malfunction indicator light (MIL) displaying the International Standards Organization (ISO) 2575 engine symbol F01, consistent with subdivision (d) of Section 1971.1 of Title 13 of the California Code of Regulations.

(b) A violation of this section shall be considered a mechanical violation under Section 40610. A peace officer shall not stop a vehicle solely on suspicion of a violation of this section.

(c) (1) A violation of this section is a correctable violation pursuant to Article 4 (commencing with Section 40610) of Chapter 2 of Division 17. Except as provided in subdivision (d), an owner or operator of a vehicle found to be in violation of this section shall have 45 days to correct the violation and the vehicle shall not be prohibited from being used during this time.

(2) Except as provided in subdivision (d), an owner or operator of a vehicle that is used exclusively in the conduct of agricultural operations and that is found to be in violation of this section shall have a time period determined by the State Air Resources Board that is not less than 75 days from the date of the citation to correct the violation and the vehicle shall not be prohibited from being used during that time.

(d) Notwithstanding subdivision (c), a vehicle found to have willfully tampered emission controls, including the vehicle's onboard diagnostics system, shall not be operated.

(Added by Stats. 2019, Ch. 298, Sec. 5. (SB 210) Effective January 1, 2020.)

24020. (a) No dealer or person holding a retail seller's permit shall sell a new or used vehicle equipped with a catalytic converter unless the catalytic converter has been permanently marked with the vehicle identification number (VIN) of the vehicle to which it is attached.

(b) This section does not apply to any of the following:

(1) A collector motor vehicle.

(2) A vehicle sold in any of the of the following circumstances:

(A) By a licensed automobile dismantler after being reported for dismantling pursuant to Section 11520.

(B) By or through a salvage pool after obtaining a salvage certificate pursuant to Section 11515, a nonrepairable vehicle certificate pursuant to Section 11515.2, a certificate of title for a vehicle described in subdivision (f) of Section 11515 or subdivision (f) of Section 11515.2, or a similar ownership document issued by another state.

(C) By or through a salvage disposal auction. For purposes of this section, "salvage disposal auction" means an auction where a person or entity, engaged primarily in the business of selling total loss salvage vehicles on behalf of insurance companies and that has more than eight business locations in California, sells total loss salvage vehicles.

(D) By or through a wholesale motor vehicle auction. For purposes of this section, "wholesale motor vehicle auction" means an auction where the dealer conducting the auction does not take ownership of the vehicle and the vehicle is sold to a nonretail buyer for resale.

(3) A vehicle where the buyer declines the seller's offer to permanently mark the catalytic converter pursuant to subdivision (a) and the dealer discloses the catalytic converter permanent marking as a body part marking product in accordance with Sections 2981 and 2982.2 of the Civil Code.

(4) A motorcycle, as defined in Section 400.

(c) As used in this section, "permanently marked" means prominently engraved, etched, welded, metal stamped, acid marked, or otherwise permanently imprinted using a similarly reliable method of imparting a lasting mark on the exterior case of the catalytic converter.

(d) A dealer or person holding a retail seller's permit who violates this section shall be guilty of an infraction punishable pursuant to Section 42001.

(e) This section shall become operative on January 1, 2025.

(Repealed (in Sec. 2) and added by Stats. 2023, Ch. 858, Sec. 3. (SB 55) Effective January 1, 2024. Operative January 1, 2025, by its own provisions.)

Chapter 2. Lighting Equipment

(Chapter 2 enacted by Stats. 1959, Ch. 3.)

Article 1. General Provisions

(Article 1 enacted by Stats. 1959, Ch. 3.)

24250. During darkness, a vehicle shall be equipped with lighted lighting equipment as required for the vehicle by this chapter.

(Enacted by Stats. 1959, Ch. 3.)

24251. Any requirement in this chapter as to the distance from which any lighting equipment shall render a person or vehicle visible or within which any lighting equipment shall be visible shall apply during darkness, directly ahead upon a straight, level unlighted highway, and under normal atmospheric conditions, unless a different time, direction, or condition is expressly stated.

(Enacted by Stats. 1959, Ch. 3.)

24252. (a) (1) All lighting equipment of a required type installed on a vehicle shall at all times be maintained in good working order. Lamps shall be equipped with bulbs of the correct voltage rating corresponding to the nominal voltage at the lamp socket.

(2) For purposes of this section, "lighting equipment of a required type" includes lighting equipment specifically required by this code and lighting equipment required pursuant to Part 393 or Part 571 of Title 49 of the Code of Federal Regulations.

(b) The voltage at a tail, stop, license plate, side marker or clearance lamp socket on a vehicle shall not be less than 85 percent of the design voltage of the bulb. Voltage tests shall be conducted with the engine operating.

(c) Two or more lamp or reflector functions may be combined, provided each function subject to requirements established by the department meets those requirements.

(1) A turn signal lamp may not be combined optically with a stoplamp

unless the stoplamp is extinguished when the turn signal is flashing.

(2) A clearance lamp may not be combined optically with a taillamp or identification lamp.

(Amended by Stats. 2021, Ch. 311, Sec. 5. (SB 814) Effective January 1, 2022.)

24253. (a) All motor vehicles manufactured and first registered after January 1, 1970, shall be equipped so all taillamps are capable of remaining lighted for a period of at least one-quarter hour with the engine inoperative. This requirement shall be complied with by an energy storing system which is recharged by energy produced by the vehicle.

(b) All motorcycles manufactured and first registered after January 1, 1971, shall be equipped so all taillamps, when turned on, will remain lighted automatically for a period of at least one-quarter hour if the engine stops.

(Amended by Stats. 1970, Ch. 217.)

24254. Whenever a requirement is declared as to the mounted height of lamps or reflectors, the height shall be measured from the center of the lamp or reflector to the level surface upon which the vehicle stands when it is without a load.

(Added by renumbering Section 25952 by Stats. 1969, Ch. 341.)

24255. (a) A vehicle may be equipped with a system to supplement the driver's visibility of the roadway to the front or rear of the vehicle during darkness. This system may incorporate an illuminating device that emits radiation predominantly in the infrared region of the electromagnetic spectrum and a display monitor to provide an image visible to the driver of the vehicle. The system, or any portion of it, shall not obstruct the vision of the driver, and shall not emit any glaring light visible in any direction or to any person. The illuminating device may be mounted inside the vehicle, if it is constructed and mounted so as to prevent any direct or reflected light, other than a monitorial indicator emitted from the device, from being visible to the driver.

(b) The system shall be operated only with the headlamps lighted. An illuminating device for the system shall be interlocked with the headlamp switch so that it is operable only when the headlamps are lighted.

(c) (1) No part of the illuminating device may be physically or optically combined with any other required or permitted lighting device.

(2) The illuminating device may be installed within a housing containing other required or permitted lighting devices, if the function of the other devices is not impaired thereby.

(Added by Stats. 2004, Ch. 198, Sec. 2. Effective January 1, 2005.)

Article 2. Headlamps and Auxiliary Lamps

(Article 2 enacted by Stats. 1959, Ch. 3.)

24400. (a) A motor vehicle, other than a motorcycle, shall be equipped with at least two headlamps, with at least one on each side of the front of the vehicle, and, except as to vehicles registered prior to January 1, 1930, they shall be located directly above or in advance of the front axle of the vehicle. The headlamps and every light source in any headlamp unit shall be located at a height of not more than 54 inches nor less than 22 inches.

(b) A motor vehicle, other than a motorcycle, shall be operated during darkness, or inclement weather, or both, with at least two lighted headlamps that comply with subdivision (a).

(c) As used in subdivision (b), "inclement weather" is a weather condition that is either of the following:

(1) A condition that prevents a driver of a motor vehicle from clearly discerning a person or another motor vehicle on the highway from a distance of 1,000 feet.

(2) A condition requiring the windshield wipers to be in continuous use due to rain, mist, snow, fog, or other precipitation or atmospheric moisture.

(Amended by Stats. 2010, Ch. 491, Sec. 43. (SB 1318) Effective January 1, 2011.)

24401. Whenever any motor vehicle is parked or standing upon a highway any headlamp that is lighted shall be dimmed or on the lower beam.

(Enacted by Stats. 1959, Ch. 3.)

24402. (a) Any motor vehicle may be equipped with not to exceed two auxiliary driving lamps mounted on the front at a height of not less than 16 inches nor more than 42 inches. Driving lamps are lamps designed for supplementing the upper beam from headlamps and may not be lighted with the lower beam.

(b) Any motor vehicle may be equipped with not to exceed two auxiliary passing lamps mounted on the front at a height of not less than 24 inches nor more than 42 inches. Passing lamps are lamps designed for supplementing the lower beam from headlamps and may also be lighted with the upper beam.

(Enacted by Stats. 1959, Ch. 3.)

24403. (a) A motor vehicle may be equipped with not more than two foglamps that may be used with, but may not be used in substitution of, headlamps.

(b) On a motor vehicle other than a motorcycle, the foglamps authorized under this section shall be mounted on the front at a height of not less than 12 inches nor more than 30 inches and aimed so that when the vehicle is not loaded none of the high-intensity portion of the light to the left of the center of the vehicle projects higher than a level of four inches below the level of the center of the lamp from which it comes, for a distance of 25 feet in front of the vehicle.

(c) On a motorcycle, the foglamps authorized under this section shall be mounted on the front at a height of not less than 12 inches nor more than 40 inches and aimed so that when the vehicle is not loaded none of the high-intensity portion of the light to the left of the center of the vehicle projects higher than a level of four inches below the level of the center of the lamp from which it comes, for a distance of 25 feet in front of the vehicle.

(Amended by Stats. 2003, Ch. 451, Sec. 20. Effective January 1, 2004.)

24404. (a) A motor vehicle may be equipped with not to exceed two white spotlamps, which shall not be used in substitution of headlamps.

(b) No spotlamp shall be equipped with any lamp source exceeding 32 standard candlepower or 30 watts nor project any glaring light into the eyes of an approaching driver.

(c) Every spotlamp shall be so directed when in use: That no portion of the main substantially parallel beam of light will strike the roadway to the left of the prolongation of the left side line of the vehicle.

That the top of the beam will not strike the roadway at a distance in excess of 300 feet from the vehicle.

(d) This section does not apply to spotlamps on authorized emergency vehicles.

(e) No spotlamp when in use shall be directed so as to illuminate any other moving vehicle.

(Amended by Stats. 1967, Ch. 544.)

24405. (a) Not more than four lamps of the following types showing to the front of a vehicle may be lighted at any one time:

(1) Headlamps.

(2) Auxiliary driving or passing lamps.

(3) Fog lamps.

(4) Warning lamps.

(5) Spot lamps.

(6) Gaseous discharge lamps specified in Section 25258.

(b) For the purpose of this section each pair of a dual headlamp system shall be considered as one lamp.

(c) Subdivision (a) does not apply to any authorized emergency vehicle.

(Amended by Stats. 1976, Ch. 234.)

24406. Except as otherwise provided, the headlamps, or other auxiliary driving lamps, or a combination thereof, on a motor vehicle during darkness shall be so arranged that the driver may select at will between distributions of light projected to different elevations, and the lamps may, in addition, be so arranged that the selection can be made automatically.

(Enacted by Stats. 1959, Ch. 3.)

24407. Multiple-beam road lighting equipment shall be designed and aimed as follows:

(a) There shall be an uppermost distribution of light, or composite beam, so aimed and of such intensity as to reveal persons and vehicles at a distance of at least 350 feet ahead for all conditions of loading.

(b) There shall be a lowermost distribution of light, or composite beam so aimed and of sufficient intensity to reveal a person or vehicle at a distance of at least 100 feet ahead. On a straight level road under any condition of loading none of the high intensity portion of the beam shall be directed to strike the eyes of an approaching driver.

(Amended by Stats. 1963, Ch. 547.)

24408. (a) Every new motor vehicle registered in this state after January 1, 1940, which has multiple-beam road lighting equipment shall be equipped with a beam indicator, which shall be lighted whenever the uppermost distribution of light from the headlamps is in use, and shall not otherwise be lighted.

(b) The indicator shall be so designed and located that when lighted it will be readily visible without glare to the driver of the vehicle so equipped. Any such lamp on the exterior of the vehicle shall have a light source not exceeding two candlepower, and the light shall not show to the front or sides of the vehicle.

(c) This section does not apply to an autonomous vehicle, as defined in Section 38750, that is not capable of operation by a human driver seated in the vehicle, provided that this exemption is consistent with, or authorized by, any applicable federal law, regulation, or exemption thereto.

(Amended by Stats. 2021, Ch. 428, Sec. 3. (SB 570) Effective January 1, 2022.)

24409. Whenever a motor vehicle is being operated during darkness, the driver shall use a distribution of light, or composite beam, directed high enough and of sufficient intensity to reveal persons and vehicles at a safe distance in advance of the vehicle, subject to the following requirements and limitations:

(a) Whenever the driver of a vehicle approaches an oncoming vehicle within 500 feet, he shall use a distribution of light or composite beam so aimed that the glaring rays are not projected into the eyes of the oncoming driver.

The lowermost distribution of light specified in this article shall be deemed to avoid glare at all times regardless of road contour.

(b) Whenever the driver of a vehicle follows another vehicle within 300 feet to the rear, he shall use the lowermost distribution of light specified in this article.

(Amended by Stats. 1965, Ch. 37.)

24410. Headlamps arranged to provide a single distribution of light not supplemented by auxiliary driving lamps are permitted on motor vehicles manufactured and sold prior to September 19, 1940, in lieu of multiple-beam road lighting equipment if the single distribution of light complies with the following requirements and limitations:

(a) The headlamps shall be so aimed that when the vehicle is not loaded none of the high-intensity portion of the light shall at a distance of 25 feet ahead project higher than a level of five inches below the level of the center of the lamp from which it comes, and in no case higher than 42 inches above the level on which the vehicle stands at a distance of 75 feet ahead.

(b) The intensity shall be sufficient to reveal persons and vehicles at a distance of at least 200 feet.

(Enacted by Stats. 1959, Ch. 3.)

24411. Notwithstanding any other provision of law, a vehicle may be equipped with not more than eight lamps for use as headlamps while the vehicle is operated or driven off the highway. The lamps shall be mounted at a height of not less than 16 inches from the ground, or more than 12 inches above the top of the passenger compartment, at any place between the front of the vehicle and a line lying on a point 40 inches to the rear of the seat occupied by the driver, shall be wired independently of all other lighting circuits, and, whenever the vehicle is operated or driven upon a highway, shall be covered or hooded with an opaque hood or cover, and turned off.

(Amended by Stats. 1986, Ch. 149, Sec. 1.)

Article 3. Rear Lighting Equipment

(Article 3 enacted by Stats. 1959, Ch. 3.)

24600. During darkness every motor vehicle which is not in combination with any other vehicle and every vehicle at the end of a combination of vehicles shall be equipped with lighted taillamps mounted on the rear as follows:

(a) Every vehicle shall be equipped with one or more taillamps.

(b) Every vehicle, other than a motorcycle, manufactured and first registered on or after January 1, 1958, shall be equipped with not less than two taillamps, except that trailers and semitrailers manufactured after July 23, 1973, which are less than 30 inches wide, may be equipped with one taillamp which shall be mounted at or near the vertical centerline of the vehicles. If a vehicle is equipped with two taillamps, they shall be mounted as specified in subdivision (d).

(c) Every vehicle or vehicle at the end of a combination of vehicles, subject to subdivision (a) of Section 22406 shall be equipped with not less than two taillamps.

(d) When two taillamps are required, at least one shall be mounted at the left and one at the right side respectively at the same level.

(e) Taillamps shall be red in color and shall be plainly visible from all distances within 500 feet to the rear except that taillamps on vehicles manufactured after January 1, 1969, shall be plainly visible from all distances within 1,000 feet to the rear.

(f) Taillamps on vehicles manufactured on or after January 1, 1969, shall be mounted not lower than 15 inches nor higher than 72 inches, except that a tow truck, in addition to being equipped with the required taillamps, may also be equipped with two taillamps which may be mounted not lower than 15 inches nor higher than the maximum allowable vehicle height and as far forward as the rearmost portion of the driver's seat in the rearmost position. The additional taillamps on a tow truck shall be lighted whenever the headlamps are lighted.

(Amended by Stats. 1988, Ch. 924, Sec. 11.)

24601. Either the taillamp or a separate lamp shall be so constructed and placed as to illuminate with a white light the rear license plate during darkness and render it clearly legible from a distance of 50 feet to the rear. When the rear license plate is illuminated by a lamp other than a required taillamp, the two lamps shall be turned on or off only by the same control switch at all times.

(Amended by Stats. 1965, Ch. 1313.)

24602. (a) A vehicle may be equipped with not more than two red fog taillamps mounted on the rear which may be lighted, in addition to the required taillamps, only when atmospheric conditions, such as fog, rain, snow, smoke, or dust, reduce the daytime or nighttime visibility of other vehicles to less than 500 feet.

(b) The lamps authorized under subdivision (a) shall be installed as follows:

(1) When two lamps are installed, one shall be mounted at the left side and one at the right side at the same level and as close as practical to the sides. When one lamp is installed, it shall be mounted as close as practical to the left side or on the center of the vehicle.

(2) The lamps shall be mounted not lower than 12 inches nor higher than 60 inches.

(3) The edge of the lens of the lamp shall be no closer than four inches from the edge of the lens of any stoplamp.

(4) The lamps shall be wired so they can be turned on only when the headlamps are on and shall have a switch that allows them to be turned off when the headlamps are on.

(5) A nonflashing amber pilot light that is lighted when the lamps are turned on shall be mounted in a location readily visible to the driver.

(Amended by Stats. 2005, Ch. 270, Sec. 11. Effective January 1, 2006.)

24603. Every motor vehicle that is not in combination with any other vehicle and every vehicle at the end of a combination of vehicles shall at all times be equipped with stoplamps mounted on the rear as follows:

(a) Each vehicle shall be equipped with one or more stoplamps.

(b) Each vehicle, other than a motorcycle, manufactured and first registered on or after January 1, 1958, shall be equipped with two stoplamps, except that trailers and semitrailers manufactured after July 23, 1973, which are less than 30 inches wide, may be equipped with one stoplamp which shall be mounted at or near the vertical centerline of the trailer. If such vehicle is equipped with two stoplamps, they shall be mounted as specified in subdivision (d).

(c) Except as provided in subdivision (h), stoplamps on vehicles manufactured on or after January 1, 1969, shall be mounted not lower than 15 inches nor higher than 72 inches, except that a tow truck or a repossessor's tow vehicle, in addition to being equipped with the required stoplamps, may also be equipped with two stoplamps which may be mounted not lower than 15 inches nor higher than the maximum allowable vehicle height and as far forward as the rearmost portion of the driver's seat in the rearmost position.

(d) When two stoplamps are required, at least one shall be mounted at the left and one at the right side, respectively, at the same level.

(e) (1) Stoplamps on vehicles manufactured on or after January 1, 1979, shall emit a red light. Stoplamps on vehicles manufactured before January 1, 1979, shall emit a red or yellow light.

(2) Paragraph (1) does not apply to commercial motor vehicles, as defined in Section 15210 or 34500. Stoplamps on a commercial motor vehicle shall emit red light. A commercial motor vehicle shall not be equipped with an amber stoplamp, amber taillamp, or other amber lamp that is optically combined with a stoplamp or taillamp.

(f) All stoplamps shall be plainly visible and understandable from a distance of 300 feet from the rear of the vehicle both during normal sunlight and at nighttime, except that stoplamps on a vehicle of a size required to be equipped with clearance lamps shall be visible from a distance of 500 feet from the rear of the vehicle during those times.

(g) (1) Stoplamps shall be activated upon application of the service (foot) brake and the hand control head for air, vacuum, or electric brakes. In addition, all stoplamps may be activated by a mechanical device designed to function only upon sudden release of the accelerator while the vehicle is in motion. Stoplamps on vehicles equipped with a manual transmission may be manually activated by a mechanical device when the vehicle is downshifted if the device is automatically rendered inoperative while the vehicle is accelerating.

(2) For an autonomous vehicle, as defined in Section 38750, that is not capable of operation by a human driver seated in the vehicle, stoplamps shall be activated upon the remote or autonomous activation of the braking system, provided that this modification is consistent with, or authorized by, any applicable federal law, regulation, or exemption thereto.

(h) (1) Any vehicle may be equipped with supplemental stoplamps mounted to the rear of the rearmost portion of the driver's seat in its rearmost position in addition to the lamps required to be mounted on the rear of the vehicle. Supplemental stoplamps installed after January 1, 1979, shall be red in color and mounted not lower than 15 inches above the roadway. The supplemental stoplamp on that side of a vehicle toward which a turn will be made may flash as part of the supplemental turn signal lamp.

(2) A supplemental stoplamp may be mounted inside the rear window of a vehicle, if it is mounted at the centerline of the vehicle and is constructed and mounted so as to prevent any light, other than a monitorial indicator emitted from the device, either direct or reflected, from being visible to the driver.

(i) Any supplemental stoplamp installed after January 1, 1987, shall comply with Federal Motor Vehicle Safety Standard No. 108 (49 C.F.R. 571.108). Any vehicle equipped with a stoplamp that complies with the federal motor vehicle safety standards applicable to that make and model vehicle shall conform to that applicable safety standard unless modified to comply with the federal motor vehicle safety standard designated in this subdivision.

(Amended by Stats. 2021, Ch. 428, Sec. 4. (SB 570) Effective January 1, 2022.)

24604. (a) Whenever the load upon any vehicle extends, or whenever any integral part of any vehicle projects, to the rear four feet or more beyond the rear of the vehicle, as measured from the taillamps, there shall be displayed at the extreme end of the load or projecting part of the vehicle during darkness, in addition to the required taillamp, two red lights with a bulb rated not in excess of six candlepower plainly visible from a distance of at least 500 feet to the sides and rear. At any other time there shall be displayed at the extreme end of the load or projecting part of the vehicle a solid red or fluorescent orange flag or cloth not less than 18 inches square.

(b) There shall be a single flag or cloth at the extreme rear if the projecting load is two feet wide or less. Two warning flags or cloths are required if the projecting load is wider than two feet. Flags or cloths shall be located to indicate maximum width of loads that extend beyond the sides or rear of the vehicle.

(Amended by Stats. 2015, Ch. 451, Sec. 49. (SB 491) Effective January 1, 2016.)

24605. (a) A tow truck or an automobile dismantler's tow vehicle used to tow a vehicle shall be equipped with and carry a taillamp, a stoplamp, and turn signal lamps for use on the rear of a towed vehicle.

(b) Whenever a tow truck or an automobile dismantler's tow vehicle is towing a vehicle and a stoplamp and turn signal lamps cannot be lighted and displayed on the rear of the towed vehicle, the operator of the tow truck or the automobile dismantler's tow vehicle shall display to the rear a stoplamp and turn signal lamps mounted on the towed vehicle, except as provided in subdivision (c). During darkness, if a taillamp on the towed vehicle cannot be lighted, the operator of the tow truck or the automobile dismantler's tow vehicle shall display to the rear a taillamp mounted on the towed vehicle. No other lighting equipment need be displayed on the towed vehicle.

(c) Whenever any motor vehicle is towing another motor vehicle, stoplamps and turn signal lamps are not required on the towed motor vehicle, but only if a stoplamp and a turn signal lamp on each side of the rear of the towing vehicle is plainly visible to the rear of the towed vehicle. This subdivision does not apply to driveaway-towaway operations.

(Amended by Stats. 2009, Ch. 322, Sec. 12. (AB 515) Effective January 1, 2010.)

24606. (a) Every motor vehicle, other than a motorcycle, of a type subject to registration and manufactured on and after January 1, 1969, shall be equipped with one or more backup lamps either separately or in combination with another lamp. Any vehicle may be equipped with backup lamps.

(b) Backup lamps shall be so directed as to project a white light illuminating the highway to the rear of the vehicle for a distance not to exceed 75 feet. A backup lamp may project incidental red, amber, or white light through reflectors or lenses that are adjacent or close to, or a part of, the lamp assembly.

(c) Backup lamps shall not be lighted except when the vehicle is about to be or is backing or except in conjunction with a lighting system which activates the lights for a temporary period after the ignition system is turned off.

(d) Any motor vehicle may be equipped with a lamp emitting white light on each side near or on the rear of the vehicle which is designed to provide supplemental illumination in an area to the side and rear not lighted by the backup lamps. These lamps shall be lighted only with the backup lamps.

(Amended by Stats. 1981, Ch. 813, Sec. 17.)

24607. Every vehicle subject to registration under this code shall at all times be equipped with red reflectors mounted on the rear as follows:

(a) Every vehicle shall be equipped with at least one reflector so maintained as to be plainly visible at night from all distances within 350 to 100 feet from the vehicle when directly in front of the lawful upper headlamp beams.

(b) Every vehicle, other than a motorcycle or a low-speed vehicle, manufactured and first registered on or after January 1, 1965, shall be equipped with at least two reflectors meeting the visibility requirements of subdivision (a), except that trailers and semitrailers manufactured after July 23, 1973, that are less than 30 inches wide, may be equipped with one reflector which shall be mounted at or near the vertical centerline of the trailer. If the vehicle is equipped with two reflectors, they shall be mounted as specified in subdivision (d).

(c) Every motortruck having an unladen weight of more than 5,000 pounds, every trailer coach, every camp trailer, every vehicle, or vehicle at the end of a combination of vehicles, subject to subdivision (a) of Section 22406, and every vehicle 80 or more inches in width manufactured on or after January 1, 1969, shall be equipped with at least two reflectors maintained so as to be plainly visible at night from all distances within 600 feet to 100 feet from the vehicle when directly in front of lawful upper headlamp beams.

(d) When more than one reflector is required, at least one shall be mounted at the left side and one at the right side, respectively, at the same level. Required reflectors shall be mounted not lower than 15 inches nor higher than 60 inches, except that a tow truck, in addition to being equipped with the required reflectors, may also be equipped with two reflectors which may be mounted not lower than 15 inches nor higher than the maximum allowable vehicle height and as far forward as the rearmost portion of the driver's seat in the rearmost position. Additional reflectors of a type meeting requirements established by the department may be mounted at any height.

(e) Reflectors on truck tractors may be mounted on the rear of the cab. Any reflector installed on a vehicle as part of its original equipment prior to January 1, 1941, need not meet the requirements of the department provided it meets the visibility requirements of subdivision (a).

(f) Area reflectorizing material may be used in lieu of the reflectors required or permitted in subdivisions (a), (b), (c), (d), and (e), provided each installation is of sufficient size to meet the photometric requirement for those reflectors.

(Amended by Stats. 1999, Ch. 140, Sec. 7. Effective January 1, 2000.)

24608. (a) Motortrucks, trailers, semitrailers, and buses 80 or more inches in width manufactured on or after January 1, 1968, shall be equipped with an amber reflector on each side at the front and a red reflector on each side at the rear. Any vehicle may be so equipped.

(b) Motortrucks, trailers, semitrailers, housecars, and buses 80 or more inches in width and 30 or more feet in length manufactured on or after January 1, 1968, shall be equipped with an amber reflector mounted on each side at the approximate midpoint of the vehicle. Any such vehicle manufactured prior to January 1, 1968, may be so equipped.

(c) Required reflectors on the sides of vehicles shall be mounted not lower than 15 inches nor higher than 60 inches. Additional reflectors of a type meeting requirements established by the department may be mounted at any height.

(d) Reflectors required or permitted in subdivisions (a) and (b) shall be so maintained as to be plainly visible at night from all distances within 600 feet to 100 feet from the vehicle when directly in front of lawful upper headlamp beams.

(e) Area reflectorizing material may be used in lieu of the reflectors required or permitted in subdivisions (a) and (b), provided each installation is of sufficient size to meet the photometric requirement for such reflectors.

(Amended by Stats. 1979, Ch. 723.)

24609. (a) A vehicle may be equipped with white or amber reflectors that are mounted on the front of the vehicle at a height of 15 inches or more, but not more than 60 inches from the ground.

(b) A schoolbus may be equipped with a set of two devices, with each device in the set consisting of an amber reflector integrated into the lens of an amber light that is otherwise permitted under this code, if the set is mounted with one device on the left side and one on the right side of the vehicle, and with each device at the same level.

(Amended by Stats. 2003, Ch. 594, Sec. 44. Effective January 1, 2004.)

24610. A reflector placed on vehicles under Section 24609 which is of the button or other multiple-unit type shall contain not less than seven units with a total of not less than three square inches of reflecting surface. The red reflectors required may be separate units or a part of the red taillamps, but in either event the reflector and taillamps shall comply with all of the requirements of Sections 24600, 24602, and 24609, and any reflector constituting an integral part of a taillamp shall comply with all photometric requirements applicable to a separate reflector.

(Amended by Stats. 1965, Ch. 1313.)

24611. Trailers that are equipped with red and white reflective sheeting or reflectors on both the sides and rear and displayed in accordance with federal Motor Vehicle Safety Standard regulations (49 C.F.R. 571.108) for trailers with a width of 80 inches or more and having a gross vehicle weight rating of over 10,000 pounds need not be equipped with the reflectors required by Section 24607 or 24608.

(Added by Stats. 1995, Ch. 766, Sec. 37. Effective January 1, 1996.)

24612. (a) All trailers and semitrailers having an overall width of 80 inches or more and a gross vehicle weight rating of more than 10,000 pounds, and manufactured on or after December 1, 1993, except those designed exclusively for living or office use, and all truck tractors manufactured on or after July 1, 1997, shall be equipped with the conspicuity system specified in federal Motor Vehicle Safety Standard No. 108 (49 C.F.R. 571.108). The conspicuity system shall consist of either retroreflective sheeting or reflex reflectors, or a combination of retroreflective sheeting and reflex reflectors, as specified in the federal standard applicable on the date of manufacture of the vehicle.

(b) Any motor truck having an overall width of 80 inches or more and manufactured prior to December 1, 1993, and any truck tractor manufactured prior to July 1, 1997, may be equipped with the conspicuity system described in subdivision (a).

(c) All trailers and semitrailers having an overall width of 80 inches or more and a gross vehicle weight rating of more than 10,000 pounds, and manufactured before December 1, 1993, shall comply with Section 393.13 of Title 49 of the Code of Federal Regulations.

(Amended by Stats. 2016, Ch. 208, Sec. 18. (AB 2906) Effective January 1, 2017.)

24615. It is unlawful to operate upon a public highway any vehicle or combination of vehicles, which is designed to be and is operated at a speed of 25 miles per hour or less, unless the rearmost vehicle displays a "slow-moving vehicle emblem," except upon vehicles used by a utility, whether publicly or privately owned, for the construction, maintenance, or repair of its own facilities or upon vehicles used by highway authorities or bridge or highway districts in highway maintenance, inspection, survey, or construction work, while such vehicle is engaged in work at the jobsite upon a highway. Any other vehicle or combination of vehicles, when operated at a speed of 25 miles per hour or less, may display such emblem. The emblem shall be mounted on the rear of the vehicle, base down, and at a height of not less than three nor more than five feet from ground to base. Such emblem shall consist of a truncated equilateral triangle having a minimum height of 14 inches with a red reflective border not less than 13/4 inches in width and a fluorescent orange center.

This emblem shall not be displayed except as permitted or required by this section.

(Amended by Stats. 1971, Ch. 287.)

24616. (a) A motor vehicle may be equipped with one or two rear-facing auxiliary lamps. For the purposes of this section, a rear-facing auxiliary lamp is a lamp that is mounted on the vehicle facing rearward. That lamp shall meet the photometric and performance requirements of the Society of Automotive Engineers Standard J1424 for cargo lamps.

(b) A rear-facing auxiliary lamp may project only a white light, with the main cone of light projecting both rearward and downward. The main cone of light shall illuminate the road surface or ground immediately rearward of a line parallel to the rear of the vehicle for a distance not greater than 50 feet. The main cone of light may not project to the front or sides of the vehicle.

(c) A rear-facing auxiliary lamp may be activated only when the vehicle is stopped. A vehicle equipped with a rear-facing auxiliary lamp shall also be equipped with a system that allows activation of the lamp only when the vehicle is in the "park" setting, if the vehicle is equipped with an automatic transmission, or in the "neutral" setting with the parking brake engaged, if the vehicle is equipped with a manual transmission.

(d) A vehicle equipped with a rear-facing auxiliary lamp may have an activation switch accessible to the operator from the rear of the vehicle.

(Added by Stats. 2001, Ch. 739, Sec. 20. Effective January 1, 2002.)

24617. (a) A transit bus may be authorized to be equipped with a yield right-of-way sign on the left rear of the bus. The yield right-of-way sign may flash simultaneously with the rear turn signal lamps, but is not required to do so. The sign may also be a static decal that is affixed to the left rear of the bus. If the sign is a flashing light-emitting diode (LED) sign, it shall be both of the following:

(1) Designed to warn a person operating a motor vehicle approaching the rear of the bus that the bus is entering traffic.

(2) Illuminated by a red flashing light when the bus is signaling in preparation for entering a traffic lane after having stopped to receive or discharge passengers.

(b) This section does not require a transit agency to install the yield right-of-way sign described in subdivision (a).

(c) This section does not relieve the driver of a transit bus from the duty to drive the bus with due regard for the safety of all persons and property. This section does not exempt the driver of a transit bus from Section 21804.

(d) This section applies only if the governing board of the transit agency approves a resolution, after a public hearing on the issue, requesting that this section be made applicable to it.

(e) A participating transit agency shall undertake a public education program to encourage motorists to yield to a transit bus when the sign specified in subdivision (a) is activated.

(Amended by Stats. 2024, Ch. 555, Sec. 1. (AB 1904) Effective January 1, 2025.)

Article 4. Parking Lamps

(Article 4 enacted by Stats. 1959, Ch. 3.)

24800. No vehicle shall be driven at any time with the parking lamps lighted except when the lamps are being used as turn signal lamps or when the headlamps are also lighted.

(Amended by Stats. 1961, Ch. 58.)

24801. Parking lamps are those lamps permitted by Section 25106, or any lamps mounted on the front of a vehicle, designed to be displayed primarily when the vehicle is parked.

(Enacted by Stats. 1959, Ch. 3.)

24802. No lights need be displayed upon a vehicle which is:

(a) Parked off the roadway and not in a hazardous position on the highway; or

(b) Parked with a wheel within 18 inches of a curb; or

(c) Parked within a business or residence district with a wheel within 18 inches of a curb or edge of the roadway.

(Amended by Stats. 1977, Ch. 620.)

Article 5. Signal Lamps and Devices

(Article 5 enacted by Stats. 1959, Ch. 3.)

24950. Whenever any motor vehicle is towing a trailer coach or a camp trailer the combination of vehicles shall be equipped with a lamp-type turn signal system.

(Amended by Stats. 1971, Ch. 1536.)

24951. (a) Any vehicle may be equipped with a lamp-type turn signal system capable of clearly indicating any intention to turn either to the right or to the left.

(b) The following vehicles shall be equipped with a lamp-type turn signal system meeting the requirements of this chapter.

(1) Motortrucks, truck tractors, buses and passenger vehicles, other than motorcycles, manufactured and first registered on or after January 1, 1958.

(2) Trailers and semitrailers manufactured and first registered between December 31, 1957, and January 1, 1969, having a gross weight of 6,000 pounds or more.

(3) Trailers and semitrailers 80 or more inches in width manufactured on or after January 1, 1969.

(4) Motorcycles manufactured and first registered on or after January 1, 1973, except motor-driven cycles whose speed attainable in one mile is 30 miles per hour or less.

The requirements of this subdivision shall not apply to special mobile equipment, or auxiliary dollies.

(c) Turn signal lamps on vehicles manufactured on or after January 1, 1969, shall be mounted not lower than 15 inches.

(Amended by Stats. 1975, Ch. 475.)

24952. A lamp-type turn signal shall be plainly visible and understandable in normal sunlight and at nighttime from a distance of at least 300 feet to the front and rear of the vehicle, except that turn signal lamps on vehicles of a size required to be equipped with clearance lamps shall be visible from a distance of 500 feet during such times.

(Amended by Stats. 1965, Ch. 1012.)

24953. (a) Any turn signal system used to give a signal of intention to turn right or left shall project a flashing white or amber light visible to the front and a flashing red or amber light visible to the rear.

(b) Side-mounted turn signal lamps projecting a flashing amber light to either side may be used to supplement the front and rear turn signals. Side-mounted turn signal lamps mounted to the rear of the center of the vehicle may project a flashing red light no part of which shall be visible from the front.

(c) In addition to any required turn signal lamps, any vehicle may be equipped with supplemental rear turn signal lamps mounted to the rear of the rearmost portion of the driver's seat in its rearmost position.

(d) In addition to any required or authorized turn signal lamps, any vehicle may be equipped with supplemental rear turn signal lamps that are mounted on, or are an integral portion of, the outside rearview mirrors, so long as the lamps flash simultaneously with the rear turn signal lamps, the light emitted from the lamps is projected only to the rear of the vehicle and is not visible to the driver under normal operating conditions, except for a visual indicator designed to allow monitoring of lamp operation, and the lamps do not project a glaring light.

(Amended by Stats. 1997, Ch. 945, Sec. 22. Effective January 1, 1998.)

Article 6. Side and Fender Lighting Equipment

(Article 6 enacted by Stats. 1959, Ch. 3.)

25100. (a) Except as provided in subdivisions (b) and (d), every vehicle 80 inches or more in overall width shall be equipped during darkness as follows:

(1) At least one amber clearance lamp on each side mounted on a forward-facing portion of the vehicle and visible from the front and at least one red clearance lamp on each side mounted on a rearward-facing portion of the vehicle and visible from the rear.

(2) At least one amber side-marker lamp on each side near the front and at least one red side-marker lamp on each side near the rear.

(3) At least one amber side-marker lamp on each side at or near the center on trailers and semitrailers 30 feet or more in length and which are manufactured and first registered after January 1, 1962. Any such vehicle manufactured and first registered prior to January 1, 1962, may be so equipped.

(4) At least one amber side-marker lamp mounted at approximate midpoint of housecars, motortrucks, and buses 30 or more feet in length and manufactured on or after January 1, 1969. Any such vehicle

manufactured prior to January 1, 1969, may be so equipped.

(5) Combination clearance and side-marker lamps mounted as side-marker lamps and meeting the visibility requirements for both types of lamps may be used in lieu of required individual clearance or side-marker lamps.

(b) The following vehicles when 80 inches or more in overall width and not equipped as provided in subdivision (a) shall be equipped during darkness as follows:

(1) Truck tractors shall be equipped with at least one amber clearance lamp on each side on the front of the cab or sleeper and may be equipped with amber side-marker lamps on each side.

(2) Truck tractors manufactured on or after January 1, 1969, shall be equipped with one amber side-marker lamp on each side near the front.

(3) Pole or pipe dollies, or logging dollies, shall be equipped with at least one combination clearance and side-marker lamp on each side showing red to the front, side, and rear.

(4) Vehicles, except truck tractors, which are 80 inches or more in width over a distance not exceeding three feet from front to rear shall be equipped with at least one amber combination clearance lamp and side-marker lamp on each side visible from the front, side, and rear if the projection is near the front of the vehicle and at least one red lamp if the projection is near the rear of the vehicle.

(5) Towing motor vehicles engaged in driveaway-towaway operations shall be equipped with at least one amber clearance lamp at each side on the front and at least one amber side-marker lamp on each side near the front.

(6) Towed motor vehicles engaged in driveaway-towaway operations shall be equipped with at least one amber side-marker lamp on each side of intermediate vehicles, and the rearmost vehicle shall be equipped with at least one red side-marker lamp on each side and at least one red clearance lamp on each side on the rear.

(7) Trailers and semitrailers designed for transporting single boats in a cradle-type mounting and for launching the boat from the rear of the trailer need not be equipped with front and rear clearance lamps provided amber clearance lamps showing to the front and red clearance lamps showing to the rear are located on each side at or near the midpoint between the front and rear of the trailer to indicate the extreme width of the trailer.

(c) Loads extending beyond the side of a vehicle where the overall width of the vehicle and load is 80 inches or more shall be equipped with an amber combination clearance and side-marker lamp on the side at the front and a red combination clearance and side-marker lamp on the side at the rear. In lieu of the foregoing requirement, projecting loads not exceeding three feet from front to rear at the extreme width shall be equipped with at least one amber combination clearance and side-marker lamp on the side visible from the front, side, and rear if the projection is near the front of the vehicle and at least one red lamp if the projection is near the rear of the vehicle.

(d) Clearance and side-marker lamps are not required on auxiliary dollies or on passenger vehicles other than a housecar.

(e) Clearance lamps shall be visible from all distances between 500 feet and 50 feet to the front or rear of the vehicle, and side-marker lamps shall be visible from all distances between 500 feet and 50 feet to the side of the vehicle.

(f) Clearance lamps shall, so far as is practicable, be mounted to indicate the extreme width of the vehicle. Side-marker lamps shall be mounted not lower than 15 inches on vehicles manufactured on and after January 1, 1968. Combination clearance and side-marker lamps required on loads shall be mounted so the lenses project to the outer extremity of the vehicle or load.

(Amended by Stats. 1981, Ch. 714, Sec. 446.)

25100.1. Notwithstanding any other provisions of this code, an ambulance may be equipped with clearance and side-marker lamps.

(Added by Stats. 1975, Ch. 616.)

25102. In addition to the lamps otherwise permitted by this chapter, any motor vehicle may be equipped with lamps on the sides thereof, visible from the side of the vehicle but not from the front or rear thereof, which lamps, together with mountings or receptacles, shall be set into depressions or recesses in the body of the vehicle and shall not protrude beyond or outside the body of the vehicle. The light source in each of the lamps shall not exceed two candlepower and shall emit diffused light of any color, except that the color red is permitted only on authorized emergency vehicles.

(Enacted by Stats. 1959, Ch. 3.)

25102.5. (a) A schoolbus may be equipped with lamps mounted so as to be visible from the sides of the bus which may be lighted, in addition to other required lights, when, and only when, atmospheric conditions such as fog, rain, snow, smoke, or dust, reduce the visibility of other vehicles to less than 500 feet.

(b) The type and mounting requirements of such lamps shall be established by regulations adopted by the department. The regulations shall be adopted by January 1, 1980.

(Amended by Stats. 1979, Ch. 723.)

25103. Whenever the load upon any vehicle extends from the left side of the vehicle one foot or more, there shall be displayed at the extreme left side of the load during darkness:

(a) An amber lamp plainly visible for 300 feet to the front and rear of the vehicle.

(b) An amber lamp at the front visible for 300 feet to the front and a red lamp at the rear plainly visible for 300 feet to the rear of the vehicle if the projecting load exceeds 120 inches in length.

The lamp shall not contain a bulb rated in excess of six candlepower.

(Amended by Stats. 1981, Ch. 774, Sec. 1.)

25104. (a) Any vehicle or equipment that requires a permit issued pursuant to Article 6 (commencing with Section 35780) of Chapter 5 of Division 15 because it is wider than permitted under Chapter 2 (commencing with Section 35100) of Division 15 shall display a solid red or fluorescent orange flag or cloth not less than 18 inches square at the extremities of the vehicle or equipment, if the vehicle or equipment is being operated other than during darkness.

(b) Any vehicle defined in Section 34500 transporting a load that extends beyond the sides of the vehicle by more than four inches shall also comply with subdivision (a).

(Amended by Stats. 2015, Ch. 451, Sec. 50. (SB 491) Effective January 1, 2016.)

25105. (a) Any motor vehicle may be equipped with running board or door-mounted courtesy lamps. The bulbs in the lamps shall not exceed six standard candlepower and shall emit either a green or white light without glare. The beams of the lamps shall not be visible to the front or rear of the vehicle.

(b) Any motor vehicle may be equipped with inside door-mounted red lamps or red reflectorizing devices or material visible to the rear of the vehicle when the doors are open. The bulbs in the lamps shall not exceed six standard candlepower.

(c) Any motor vehicle may be equipped with exterior lamps for the purpose of lighting the entrances and exits of the vehicles, which lamps may be lighted only when the vehicles are not in motion. The lamp source of the exterior lamps shall not exceed 32 standard candlepower, or 30 watts, nor project any glaring light into the eyes of an approaching driver.

(Amended by Stats. 1995, Ch. 348, Sec. 1. Effective January 1, 1996.)

25106. (a) Any motor vehicle may be equipped with lighted white or amber cowl or fender lamps on the front. Any vehicle may be equipped with not more than one amber side lamp on each side near the front, nor more than one red side lamp on each side near the rear. The light source of each such lamp shall not exceed four standard candlepower.

(b) Lamps meeting requirements established by the department for side-marker or combination clearance and side-marker lamps may be installed on the sides of vehicles at any location, but any lamp installed within 24 inches of the rear of the vehicle shall be red, and any lamp installed at any other location shall be amber.

(Amended by Stats. 1979, Ch. 723.)

25107. Any motor vehicle may be equipped with not more than two cornering lamps designed and of sufficient intensity for the purpose of revealing objects only in the direction of turn while the vehicle is turning or while the turn signal lamps are operating to signal an intention to turn. The lamps shall be designed so that no glaring light is projected into the eyes of an approaching driver.

(Amended by Stats. 1965, Ch. 1313.)

25108. (a) Any motor vehicle may be equipped with not more than two amber turn-signal pilot indicators mounted on the exterior. The light output from any indicator shall not exceed five candlepower unless a provision is made for operating the indicator at reduced intensity during darkness in which event the light output shall not exceed five candlepower during darkness or 15 candlepower at any other time. The center of the beam shall be projected toward the driver.

(b) Any vehicle may be equipped with pilot indicators visible from the front to monitor the functioning or condition of parts essential to the operation of the vehicle or of equipment attached to the vehicle that is necessary for protection of the cargo or load. The pilot indicators shall be steady-burning, having a projected lighted lens area of not more than three-quarters of a square inch and have a light output of not more than five candlepower. The pilot indicator may be of any color except red.

(c) Other exterior pilot indicators of any color may be used for monitoring exterior lighting devices, provided that the area of each indicator is less than 0.20 square inches, the intensity of each indicator does not exceed 0.10 candlepower, and the color red is not visible to the front.

(d) Any towed vehicle may be equipped with an exterior-mounted indicator lamp used only to indicate the functional status of an antilock braking system providing that either of the following conditions are met:

(1) The indicator lamp complies with the applicable requirements of the federal motor vehicle safety standards.

(2) The indicator lamp is designed and located so that it will be readily visible, with the assistance of a rearview mirror if necessary, to the driver of the towing motor vehicle and the indicator lamp has a light source not exceeding five candlepower. The light shall not show to the sides or rear of the vehicle and the indicator lamp may emit any color except red.

(e) (1) Notwithstanding any other provision of law, any motor vehicle may be equipped with not more than two exterior-lighted data monitors that transmit information to the driver of the vehicle regarding the efficient or safe operation, or both the efficient and safe operation, of the vehicle.

(2) Data monitors shall comply with all of the following conditions:

(A) Be mounted to the vehicle in a manner so that they are readily visible to the driver of the vehicle when the driver is seated in the normal driving position. Data monitors shall not be designed to convey information to any person other than the driver of the vehicle.

(B) Be limited in size to not more than two square inches of lighted area each.

(C) Not emit a light brighter than reasonably necessary to convey the intended information.

(D) Not project a glaring light to the driver or, to other motorists, or to any other person.

(3) Data monitors may incorporate flashing or changing elements only as necessary to convey the intended information. Data monitors shall not resemble any official traffic-control device or required lighting device or be combined with any required lighting device.

(4) Data monitors may display any color, except that the color red shall not be visible to the front of the vehicle.

(Amended by Stats. 2001, Ch. 739, Sec. 21. Effective January 1, 2002.)

25109. Any motor vehicle may be equipped with two white or amber running lamps mounted on the front, one at each side, which shall not be lighted during darkness except while the motor vehicle is parked.

(Added by Stats. 1965, Ch. 858.)

25110. (a) The following vehicles may be equipped with utility flood or loading lamps mounted on the rear, and sides, that project a white light illuminating an area to the side or rear of the vehicle for a distance not to exceed 75 feet at the level of the roadway:

(1) Tow trucks that are used to tow disabled vehicles may display utility floodlights, but only during the period of preparation for towing at the location from which a disabled vehicle is to be towed.

(2) Ambulances used to respond to emergency calls may display utility flood and loading lights, but only at the scene of an emergency or while loading or unloading patients.

(3) Firefighting equipment designed and operated exclusively as such may display utility floodlamps only at the scene of an emergency.

(4) Vehicles used by law enforcement agencies or organizations engaged in the detoxification of alcoholics may display utility flood or loading lights when loading or unloading persons under the influence of intoxicants for transportation to detoxification centers or places of incarceration.

(5) Vehicles used by law enforcement agencies for mobile blood alcohol testing, drug evaluation, or field sobriety testing .

(6) Vehicles used by publicly or privately owned public utilities may display utility flood or loading lights when engaged in emergency roadside repair of electric, gas, telephone, telegraph, water, or sewer facilities.

(b) Lamps permitted under subdivision (a) shall not be lighted during darkness, except while the vehicle is parked, nor project any glaring light into the eyes of an approaching driver.

(Amended by Stats. 1996, Ch. 124, Sec. 132. Effective January 1, 1997.)

Article 7. Flashing and Colored Lights

(Article 7 enacted by Stats. 1959, Ch. 3.)

25250. Flashing lights are prohibited on vehicles except as otherwise permitted.

(Amended by Stats. 1963, Ch. 223.)

25251. (a) Flashing lights are permitted on vehicles as follows:

(1) To indicate an intention to turn or move to the right or left upon a roadway, turn signal lamps and turn signal exterior pilot indicator lamps and side lamps permitted under Section 25106 may be flashed on the side of a vehicle toward which the turn or movement is to be made.

(2) When disabled or parked off the roadway but within 10 feet of the roadway, or when approaching, stopped at, or departing from, a railroad grade crossing, turn signal lamps may be flashed as warning lights if the front turn signal lamps at each side are being flashed simultaneously and the rear turn signal lamps at each side are being flashed simultaneously.

(3) To warn other motorists of accidents or hazards on a roadway, turn signal lamps may be flashed as warning lights while the vehicle is approaching, overtaking, or passing the accident or hazard on the roadway if the front turn signal lamps at each side are being flashed simultaneously and the rear turn signal lamps at each side are being flashed simultaneously.

(4) For use on authorized emergency vehicles.

(5) To warn other motorists of a funeral procession, turn signal lamps may be flashed as warning lights on all vehicles actually engaged in a funeral procession, if the front turn signal lamps at each side are being flashed simultaneously and the rear turn signal lamps at each side are being flashed simultaneously.

(b) Turn signal lamps shall be flashed as warning lights whenever a vehicle is disabled upon the roadway and the vehicle is equipped with a device to automatically activate the front turn signal lamps at each side to flash simultaneously and the rear turn signal lamps at each side to flash simultaneously, if the device and the turn signal lamps were not rendered inoperative by the event which caused the vehicle to be disabled.

(c) Side lamps permitted under Section 25106 and used in conjunction with turn signal lamps may be flashed with the turn signal lamps as part of the warning light system, as provided in paragraphs (2) and (3) of subdivision (a).

(d) Required or permitted lamps on a trailer or semitrailer may flash when the trailer or semitrailer has broken away from the towing vehicle and the connection between the vehicles is broken.

(e) Hazard warning lights, as permitted by paragraphs (2) and (3) of subdivision (a) may be flashed in a repeating series of short and long flashes when the driver is in need of help.

(Amended by Stats. 1997, Ch. 945, Sec. 23. Effective January 1, 1998.)

25251.1. Any implement of husbandry displaying a slow moving vehicle emblem, as defined in Section 24615, and being operated at a speed of 25 miles per hour or less, may be equipped with double-faced amber turn signals which may be flashed simultaneously as warning lights.

(Added by Stats. 1978, Ch. 252.)

25251.2. Any motorcycle may be equipped with a means of modulating the upper beam of the headlamp between a high and a lower brightness at a rate of 200 to 280 flashes per minute. Such headlamps shall not be so modulated during darkness.

(Added by Stats. 1980, Ch. 35, Sec. 1. Effective March 7, 1980.)

25251.3. No civil liability shall attach to any person for the use or nonuse of turn signal lamps in the manner permitted by paragraph (3) or (5) of subdivision (a) of Section 25251, except for such civil liability as would attach for the use or nonuse of any other device required by this article or Article 8 (commencing with Section 25300).

(Amended by Stats. 1983, Ch. 410, Sec. 2.)

25251.4. Any motor vehicle may also be equipped with a theft alarm system which flashes any of the lights required or permitted on the motor vehicle and which operates as specified in Article 13 (commencing with Section 28085) of Chapter 5 of this division.

(Added by Stats. 1977, Ch. 993.)

25251.5. (a) Any motor vehicle may also be equipped with a system in which an amber light is center mounted on the rear of a vehicle to communicate a component of deceleration of the vehicle, and which light pulses in a controlled fashion at a rate which varies exponentially with a component of deceleration.

(b) Any motor vehicle may be equipped with two amber lamps on the rear of the vehicle which operate simultaneously with not more than four flashes within four seconds after the accelerator pedal is in the deceleration position and which are not lighted at any other time. The lamps shall be mounted at the same height, with one lamp located on each side of the vertical centerline of the vehicle, not higher than the bottom of the rear window, or if the vehicle has no rear window, not higher than 60 inches. The light output from each of the lamps shall not exceed 200 candlepower at any angle horizontal or above. The amber lamps may be used either separately or in combination with another lamp.

(c) Any stoplamp or supplemental stoplamp required or permitted by Section 24603 may be equipped so as to flash not more than four times within the first four seconds after actuation by application of the brakes.

(Amended by Stats. 1983, Ch. 410, Sec. 3.)

25252. Every authorized emergency vehicle shall be equipped with at least one steady burning red warning lamp visible from at least 1,000 feet to the front of the vehicle to be used as provided in this code.

In addition, authorized emergency vehicles may display revolving, flashing, or steady red warning lights to the front, sides or rear of the vehicles.

(Amended by Stats. 1974, Ch. 635.)

25252.5. (a) Every authorized emergency vehicle may be equipped with a system which flashes the upper-beam headlamps of the vehicle with the flashes occurring alternately from the front headlamp on one side of the vehicle to the front headlamp on the other side of the vehicle. The flashing of the headlamps shall consist only of upper-beam flashing, and not the flashing of any other light beam.

(b) "Upper-beam headlamp," as used in this section, means a headlamp or that part of a headlamp which projects a distribution of light, or composite beam, so aimed and of such intensity as to reveal persons and vehicles at a distance of at least 350 feet ahead for all conditions of loading.

(c) The system provided for in subdivision (a) shall only be used when an authorized emergency vehicle is being operated pursuant to Section 21055.

(Amended by Stats. 1983, Ch. 1017, Sec. 4.)

25253. (a) Tow trucks used to tow disabled vehicles shall be equipped with flashing amber warning lamps. This subdivision does not apply to a tractor-trailer combination.

(b) Tow trucks may display flashing amber warning lamps while providing service to a disabled vehicle. A flashing amber warning lamp upon a tow truck may be displayed to the rear when the tow truck is towing a vehicle and moving at a speed slower than the normal flow of traffic.

(c) A tow truck shall not display flashing amber warning lamps on a freeway except when an unusual traffic hazard or extreme hazard exists.

(Amended (as amended by Stats. 2006, Ch. 375, Sec. 3) by Stats. 2009, Ch. 33, Sec. 2. (SB 159) Effective January 1, 2010.)

25253.1. An automobile dismantler's tow vehicle used to tow a disabled vehicle may be equipped with flashing amber warning lamps.

A flashing amber warning lamp upon an automobile dismantler's tow vehicle may be displayed to the rear when the automobile dismantler's tow vehicle is towing a vehicle and moving at a speed slower than the normal flow of traffic.

(Added by Stats. 1985, Ch. 710, Sec. 4.)

25256. Vehicles used by highway authorities or bridge and highway districts, and vehicles of duly authorized representatives thereof, used in highway maintenance, inspection, survey or construction work may display flashing amber warning lights to the front, sides or rear when such vehicles are parked or working on the highway.

(Amended by Stats. 1967, Ch. 544.)

25257. (a) Every schoolbus, when operated for the transportation of schoolchildren, shall be equipped with a flashing red light signal system.

(b) (1) Every schoolbus manufactured on or after September 1, 1992, shall also be equipped with a stop signal arm. Any schoolbus manufactured before September 1, 1992, may be equipped with a stop signal arm.

(2) Any schoolbus manufactured on or after July 1, 1993, shall also be equipped with an amber warning light system, in addition to the flashing red light signal system. Any schoolbus manufactured before July 1, 1993, may be equipped with an amber warning light system.

(3) On or before September 1, 1992, the department shall adopt regulations governing the specifications, installation, and use of stop signal arms, to comply with federal standards.

(4) A "stop signal arm" is a device that can be extended outward from the side of a schoolbus to provide a signal to other motorists not to pass the bus because it has stopped to load or unload passengers, that is manufactured pursuant to the specifications of Federal Motor Vehicle Safety Standard No. 131, issued on April 25, 1991.

(Amended by Stats. 1992, Ch. 624, Sec. 7. Effective September 14, 1992.)

25257.2. If a schoolbus is used for the transportation of persons of any age who are developmentally disabled, as defined by the Lanterman Developmental Disabilities Services Act (Division 4.5 (commencing with Section 4500) of the Welfare and Institutions Code), the amber light signal system, flashing red light signal system, and stop signal arm shall not be used other than as required by Sections 22112 and 22454.

(Amended by Stats. 1992, Ch. 624, Sec. 8. Effective September 14, 1992.)

25257.5. To warn other motorists or pedestrians on a roadway during a backing maneuver, the operator of a schoolbus may flash turn signal lamps if the front turn signal lamps at each side are flashed simultaneously and the rear signal lamps at each side are flashed simultaneously.

(Added by Stats. 1984, Ch. 127, Sec. 1.)

25257.7. (a) A schoolbus may be equipped with a white strobe light mounted so as to be visible from the front, sides, or rear of the bus. The strobe light may only be lighted when visibility is reduced to 500 feet or less due to atmospheric conditions including, but not limited to, fog, rain, snow, smoke, or dust. Reduced visibility due to atmospheric conditions does not include the time of darkness from one-half hour after sunset to one-half hour before sunrise.

(b) The type and mounting requirements of strobe lights authorized by subdivision (a) shall be established by regulations adopted by the department by April 1, 1991. No schoolbus shall be equipped with a strobe light until the regulations are adopted.

(Added by Stats. 1990, Ch. 169, Sec. 1. Effective June 22, 1990.)

25258. (a) An authorized emergency vehicle operating under the conditions specified in Section 21055 may display a flashing white light from a gaseous discharge lamp designed and used for the purpose of controlling official traffic control signals.

(b) (1) An authorized emergency vehicle used by a peace officer, as defined in Section 830.1 of, subdivision (a), (b), (c), (d), (e), (f), (g), or (i) of Section 830.2 of, subdivision (n) of Section 830.3 of, subdivision (b) of Section 830.31 of, subdivision (a) or (b) of Section 830.32 of, Section 830.33 of, subdivision (a) of Section 830.36 of, subdivision (a) of Section 830.4 of, or Section 830.6 of, or a probation officer, as defined in Section 830.5 of, the Penal Code, in the performance of the peace officer's duties, may, in addition, display a steady or flashing blue warning light visible from the front, sides, or rear of the vehicle.

(2) Before a probation officer operates an emergency vehicle with a blue warning light, the officer shall complete a four-hour classroom training course regarding the operation of emergency vehicles that is certified by the Standards and Training for Corrections Division of the Board of State and Community Corrections.

(3) This subdivision does not expand any existing authority of a probation officer to conduct a high-speed vehicle pursuit, nor does it change any existing training requirements for high-speed vehicle pursuits.

(c) Except as provided in subdivision (a), a vehicle shall not be equipped with a device that emits any illumination or radiation that is designed or used for the purpose of controlling official traffic control signals.

(Amended by Stats. 2018, Ch. 92, Sec. 211. (SB 1289) Effective January 1, 2019.)

25259. (a) Any authorized emergency vehicle may display flashing amber warning lights to the front, sides, or rear.

(b) A vehicle operated by a police or traffic officer while in the actual performance of his or her duties may display steady burning or flashing white lights to either side mounted above the roofline of the vehicle.

(c) Any authorized emergency vehicle may display not more than two flashing white warning lights to the front mounted above the roofline of the vehicle and not more than two flashing white warning lights to the front mounted below the roofline of the vehicle. These lamps may be in addition to the flashing headlamps permitted under Section 25252.5.

(Amended by Stats. 1997, Ch. 945, Sec. 25. Effective January 1, 1998.)

25259.1. (a) Any vehicle operated by a disaster service worker who has received training in accordance with subdivision (b) and used by that worker in the performance of emergency or disaster services ordered by lawful authority during a state of war emergency, a state of emergency, or a local emergency, as those terms are defined in Section 8558 of the Government Code, may display flashing amber warning lights to the front, sides, or rear while at the scene of the emergency or disaster.

(b)Any disaster service worker operating a vehicle that displays flashing amber warning lights shall receive a training course from the public agency, disaster council, or emergency organization described in Section 3101 of the Government Code concerning the safe operation of the use of flashing amber warning lights prior to operating a vehicle that displays flashing amber warning lights.

(c) A person operating a vehicle that is authorized to display flashing amber warning lights under this section shall either completely cover or remove those lights when the lights are not in use.

(Added by Stats. 1997, Ch. 144, Sec. 1. Effective January 1, 1998.)

25259.5. An emergency response or disaster service vehicle owned or leased and operated by the American National Red Cross, or any chapter or branch thereof, and equipped and clearly marked as a Red Cross emergency service or disaster service vehicle, may display flashing amber warning lights to the front, sides, or rear of the vehicle while at the scene of an emergency or disaster operation. Vehicles not used on emergency response shall not be included.

(Amended by Stats. 1997, Ch. 144, Sec. 2. Effective January 1, 1998.)

25260. (a) Public utility vehicles, and vehicles of duly authorized representatives of a public utility, actually engaged in the construction, removal, maintenance, or inspection of public utility facilities, including the cutting or trimming of trees immediately adjacent thereto, may display flashing amber warning lights to the front, sides, or rear when necessarily parked on a highway or when moving at a speed slower than the normal flow of traffic.

(b) Vehicles owned by public transit operators which provide assistance to a disabled district bus may display flashing amber warning lights to the front, sides, or rear when necessarily parked on a highway.

(Amended by Stats. 1980, Ch. 399, Sec. 5. Effective July 11, 1980.)

25260.1. Vehicles actually engaged in the construction, removal, maintenance, or inspection of any oil or gas pipeline may display flashing amber warning lights to the front, sides, or rear when necessarily parked on a highway or when necessarily moving at a speed slower than the normal flow of traffic and only in accordance with Section 25268.

(Added by Stats. 1978, Ch. 120.)

25260.3. Any vehicle having personnel aerial lift equipment, actually engaged in the construction, removal, maintenance or inspection of any building, structure, or appurtenances thereto, including the cutting or trimming of trees immediately adjacent thereto, may display flashing amber warning lights to the front, sides, or rear when necessarily parked on a highway or when moving at a speed slower than the normal flow of the traffic.

(Added by Stats. 1976, Ch. 334.)

25260.4. Any hazardous substance spill response vehicle, under contract to the Department of Transportation for the cleanup of hazardous substance spills, may display flashing amber warning lights to the front, sides, or rear of the vehicle while it is engaged in the actual cleanup of the spill. The warning lights shall be removed or covered with opaque material whenever the vehicle is not actually engaged in the cleanup of a hazardous substance at the scene of the spill.

(Added by Stats. 1984, Ch. 887, Sec. 1. Effective September 5, 1984.)

25261. Vehicles used by a county or county department of agriculture and vehicles of duly authorized representatives thereof, actually engaged in weed control or pest detection, may display flashing amber warning lights to the front, sides, or rear when necessarily parked on a highway or when moving at a speed slower than the normal flow of traffic.

(Added by Stats. 1969, Ch. 218.)

25262. An armored car may be equipped with red lights which may be used while resisting armed robbery. At all other times the red lights shall not be lighted. The authority to use red lights granted by this section does not constitute an armored car an authorized emergency vehicle, and all other provisions of this code applicable to drivers of vehicles apply to drivers of armored cars.

(Amended by Stats. 1969, Ch. 9.)

25263. Trucks actually engaged in the towing of houses or buildings upon any highway may display flashing amber warning lights to the front, sides or rear on the vehicle or load.

(Amended by Stats. 1961, Ch. 653.)

25264. Any motor vehicle operated by a coroner, or by a deputy coroner, and which is at the scene of any violent highway death, may display flashing amber warning lights to the front or rear.

(Repealed and added by Stats. 1961, Ch. 653.)

25265. Repair vehicles of sanitary districts or county sanitation districts necessarily parked other than adjacent to the curb in a highway for purposes of repairing district facilities, may display flashing amber warning lights to the front, sides or rear, but these lights shall not be lighted when the vehicle is in motion.

(Amended by Stats. 1961, Ch. 653.)

25266. Vehicles owned by the state and operated by officers or employees of the state who are actually engaged in aqueduct or levee construction, maintenance, patrol, or inspection, or in stream measurement work, may display flashing amber warning lights to the front, sides and rear when parked on the traveled roadway so as to partially obstruct the free flow of traffic, or when moving at a speed slower than the normal flow of traffic.

(Amended by Stats. 1973, Ch. 763.)

25267. Vehicles used by mosquito abatement districts or pest abatement districts when dispersing insecticides may display flashing amber warning lights to the front or rear while the vehicles are parked or working on the highway.

(Added by Stats. 1961, Ch. 653.)

25268. No person shall display a flashing amber warning light on a vehicle as permitted by this code except when an unusual traffic hazard exists.

(Added by Stats. 1961, Ch. 653.)

25269. No person shall display a flashing or steady burning red warning light on a vehicle except as permitted by Section 21055 or when an extreme hazard exists.

(Added by Stats. 1961, Ch. 653.)

25270. Any pilot car required by the permit referred to in Section 35780 or 35790, or any vehicle or combination of vehicles subject to the permit if specified in the permit, shall be equipped with flashing amber warning lights to the front, sides or rear. The pilot car and any vehicles required by the permit to have flashing amber warning lights, shall display the flashing amber warning lights while actually engaged in the movement described in the permit. The warning lamps shall be removed or covered with opaque material whenever the pilot car is not escorting the movement described in the permit.

(Amended by Stats. 1988, Ch. 460, Sec. 1.)

25270.5. Any motor vehicle engaged in, or aiding in, the herding of livestock along or across a public roadway may display flashing amber warning lights to the front, sides, or rear of the vehicle while it is stopped in the roadway near the livestock or is proceeding with the livestock along the roadway.

(Amended by Stats. 1977, Ch. 287.)

25271. Any publicly owned vehicle or any vehicle operated by a corporation incorporated under Part 4 (commencing with Section 10400) of Division 2 of Title 1 of the Corporations Code for the purpose of the prevention of cruelty to animals, when used for removing dead animals, injured animals, or loose livestock, may, display flashing amber warning lights to the front or rear when necessarily parked on the roadway or when moving at a speed slower than the normal flow of traffic.

(Added by Stats. 1961, Ch. 653.)

25271.5. Any publicly owned vehicle used for the enforcement of animal control laws contained in a statute, local ordinance, or regulation may display flashing or revolving amber warning lights to the front, sides, or rear of the vehicle when actually engaged in the enforcement of those laws and when necessarily parked on a roadway or moving at a speed slower than the normal flow of traffic.

(Added by Stats. 1985, Ch. 131, Sec. 1.)

25272. A motor vehicle used by a rural mail carrier may display flashing amber warning lights to the front and rear of the vehicle while the vehicle is necessarily stopped or stopping upon a roadway for the delivery of United States mail.

(Added by Stats. 1961, Ch. 653.)

25273. Any motor vehicle owned and operated by a school district with an average daily attendance in excess of 400,000 while being used to measure the distance from school to a school pupil's residence may display a flashing amber warning light to the rear of the vehicle when moving at a speed substantially slower than the normal flow of traffic.

(Added by Stats. 1963, Ch. 404.)

25274. Any vehicle owned by a cable television company and operated by employees, or duly authorized representatives, of a cable television company, when actually engaged in the construction, removal, maintenance or inspection of cable television facilities, including but not limited to, the cutting or trimming of trees immediately adjacent thereto, may display flashing amber warning lights to the front, sides, or rear when necessarily parked on a highway or when moving at a speed slower than the normal flow of traffic.

For the purposes of this section, "cable television company" means any person engaged in the business of transmitting television programs by cable to subscribers for a fee.

(Added by Stats. 1972, Ch. 406.)

25275. Any truck or truck tractor which is primarily used in the transportation of loads specified in subdivision (a) of Section 35414, may be equipped with a flashing amber warning lamp. Such lamp may be displayed to the front, sides, or rear of the combination only when its length exceeds 75 feet and when an unusual traffic hazard exists.

(Added by Stats. 1973, Ch. 64.)

25275.5. Any bus operated either by a public agency or under the authority of a certificate of public convenience and necessity issued by the Public Utilities Commission may be equipped with a system of crime alarm lights. The system of crime alarm lights shall consist of the installation of additional lamp sources, not exceeding 32 standard candlepower or 30 watts, in the front and rear clearance lamps required or permitted by Section 25100. Such lamps shall be operated by a flasher unit or units that are not audible inside the bus. When actuated, both rear crime alarm lights shall flash simultaneously and both front crime alarm lights shall flash simultaneously. Crime alarm lights shall be actuated only when a crime is in progress on board the bus or has recently been committed on board the bus.

(Amended by Stats. 1979, Ch. 723.)

25276. (a) A motor vehicle designed for carrying more than eight persons, including the driver, owned by a private, nonprofit organization that provides training or other activities for persons who have intellectual or physical disabilities, or both, and that is certified by the Department of Rehabilitation or licensed by the State Department of Developmental Services, with respect to the providing of this training or other activities, may be equipped with a flashing amber light signal system.

(b) A motor vehicle, described in subdivision (a), may, while actually engaged in the transportation of persons described in subdivision (a) to or from a training or activity center operated by the organization, display the flashing amber lights of the system when necessarily parked upon a highway and in the process of loading or unloading persons.

(c) Subdivisions (a) and (b) apply to a motor vehicle that is rented, leased, or chartered by the organization.

(Amended by Stats. 2012, Ch. 457, Sec. 45. (SB 1381) Effective January 1, 2013.)

25277. Any vehicle used by any police department, sheriff's office, or other governmental agency for the purpose of enforcing parking laws contained in the Vehicle Code or in a local ordinance or regulation may display flashing or revolving amber warning lights to the front, sides, or rear of the vehicle when actually engaged in the enforcement of such laws and when either necessarily stopped on a street, or when moving at a speed slower than the normal flow of traffic.

(Added by Stats. 1976, Ch. 234.)

25278. Any vehicle owned or operated by a land surveyor or civil engineer licensed to practice in this state may display flashing amber warning lights to the front, sides, or rear, if the vehicle is engaged in any phase of a project that requires surveying or surveying related activities to be performed on a highway, or in the vicinity of a highway, and the vehicle is parked on the highway or moving at a speed lower than the normal flow of traffic. The use of, or absence of, amber warning lights as authorized in this section shall not serve as the basis for any civil action, a defense to a civil action, or establish negligence as a matter of law or negligence per se for comparative fault purposes.

(Amended by Stats. 1995, Ch. 91, Sec. 181. Effective January 1, 1996.)

25279. (a) Vehicles owned and operated by private security agencies and utilized exclusively on privately owned and maintained roads to which this code is made applicable by local ordinance or resolution, may display flashing amber warning lights to the front, sides, or rear, while being operated in response to emergency calls for the immediate preservation of life or property.

(b) (1) Vehicles owned by a private security agency and operated by personnel who are registered with the Department of Consumer Affairs under Article 3 (commencing with Section 7582) of Chapter 11.5 of Division 3 of the Business and Professions Code may be equipped with a flashing amber warning light system while the vehicle is operated on a highway, if the vehicle is in compliance with Section 27605 and is distinctively marked with the words "PRIVATE SECURITY" or "SECURITY PATROL" on the rear and both sides of the vehicle in a size that is legible from a distance of not less than 50 feet.

(2) The flashing amber warning light system authorized under paragraph (1) shall not be activated while the vehicle is on the highway, unless otherwise directed by a peace officer, as defined in Chapter 4.5 (commencing with Section 830) of Title 3 of Part 2 of the Penal Code.

(c) A peace officer may order that the flashing amber warning light system of a vehicle that is found to be in violation of this section be immediately removed at the place of business of the vehicle's owner or a garage.

(d) A flashing amber warning light system shall not be installed on a vehicle that has been found to be in violation of this section, unless written authorization is obtained from the Commissioner of the California Highway Patrol.

(Amended by Stats. 1996, Ch. 1154, Sec. 76. Effective September 30, 1996.)

25280. Vehicles operated by a local public entity, or pursuant to a permit, license, contract, or franchise with a local public entity, and used to collect and transport garbage, rubbish, or refuse may display flashing amber warning lights to the front, sides, or rear while stopped upon a street and actually engaged in the collection of garbage, rubbish, or refuse, or while moving between stops at a speed not greater than 10 miles per hour.

(Added by Stats. 1981, Ch. 280, Sec. 1.)

25281. A privately owned or operated water tender vehicle, when used exclusively for contract emergency services provided to any public agency, may display flashing amber warning lights to the front, sides, or rear of the vehicle when necessarily parked on a highway or other public road, blocking or partially blocking a highway or other public road, traveling at a speed slower than the normal flow of traffic, or crossing or entering a highway or other public road. The flashing amber lights shall not be displayed when the water tender vehicle is traveling to or from an emergency at the normal speed and flow of traffic, except when the vehicle is traveling in escort with a fire engine or other authorized emergency vehicle. The lights shall be covered with an opaque material when not being displayed.

(Added by Stats. 1994, Ch. 207, Sec. 4. Effective July 18, 1994.)

25282. Any vehicle owned or operated by a contractor or a construction company licensed to operate in this state pursuant to the Business and Professions Code may display flashing amber warning lights to the front, sides, or rear, if the vehicle is engaged in any phase of a construction project performed on a highway, or in the vicinity of a highway, and the vehicle is parked on the highway or moving at a speed lower than the normal flow of traffic. The use of, or absence of, amber warning lights as authorized in this section shall not serve as the basis for any civil action, a defense to civil action, or establish negligence as a matter of law or negligence per se for comparative fault purposes.

(Added by Stats. 1996, Ch. 10, Sec. 21. Effective February 9, 1996.)

Article 8. Warning Lights and Devices

(Article 8 enacted by Stats. 1959, Ch. 3.)

25300. (a) Every vehicle which, if operated during darkness, would be subject to the requirements of Section 25100, and every truck tractor, irrespective of width, shall at all times be equipped with at least three red emergency reflectors. The reflectors need be carried by only one vehicle in a combination.

All reflectors shall be maintained in good working condition.

(b) When the vehicle is disabled on the roadway during darkness, reflectors of the type specified in subdivision (a) shall be immediately placed as follows:

(1) One at the traffic side of the disabled vehicle, not more than 10 feet to the front or rear of the vehicle.

(2) One at a distance of approximately 100 feet to the rear of the disabled vehicle in the center of the traffic lane occupied by the vehicle.

(3) One at a distance of approximately 100 feet to the front of the disabled vehicle in the center of the traffic lane occupied by such vehicle.

(4) If disablement of the vehicle occurs within 500 feet of a curve, crest of a hill, or other obstruction to view, the driver shall so place the reflectors in that direction as to afford ample warning to other users of the highway, but in no case less than 100 nor more than 500 feet from the disabled vehicle.

(5) If disablement of the vehicle occurs upon any roadway of a divided or one-way highway, the driver shall place one reflector at a distance of approximately 200 feet and one reflector at a distance of approximately 100 feet to the rear of the vehicle in the center of the lane occupied by the stopped vehicle, and one reflector at the traffic side of the vehicle not more than 10 feet to the rear of the vehicle.

(c) When the vehicle is disabled or parked off the roadway but within 10 feet thereof during darkness, warning reflectors of the type specified in subdivision (a) shall be immediately placed by the driver as follows: one at a distance of approximately 200 feet and one at a distance of approximately 100 feet to the rear of the vehicle, and one at the traffic side of the vehicle not more than 10 feet to the rear of the vehicle. The reflectors shall, if possible, be placed between the edge of the roadway and the vehicle, but in no event less than two feet to the left of the widest portion of the vehicle or load thereon.

(d) (1) Until the reflectors required by this section can be placed properly, the requirements of this section may be complied with temporarily either by placing lighted red fusees or liquid-burning flares in the required locations or by using turn signal lamps, but only if front turn signal lamps at each side are being flashed simultaneously and rear turn signal lamps at each side are being flashed simultaneously.

(2) The driver of a commercial motor vehicle equipped with fusees or liquid-burning flares shall place a lighted fusee or liquid-burning flare at each of the locations specified in subdivision (b). There shall be at least one lighted fusee or liquid-burning flare at each of the prescribed locations for as long as the commercial motor vehicle is stopped. Before the stopped commercial vehicle is moved, the driver shall properly extinguish and remove each fusee or liquid-burning flare.

(3) If gasoline or any other flammable or combustible liquid or gas seeps or leaks from a fuel container or commercial motor vehicle stopped upon a highway, an emergency warning signal producing a flame shall not be lighted or placed except at a distance from the liquid or gas as will assure the prevention of a fire or explosion.

(4) (A) A driver shall not use or permit the use of any flame-producing emergency signal for protecting any of the following:

(i) A commercial vehicle transporting Division 1.1, Division 1.2, or Division 1.3 explosives, as classified by the United States Department of Transportation.

(ii) A cargo tank motor vehicle, whether loaded or empty, used for the transportation of any Class 3 flammable liquid or Division 2.1 flammable gas, as classified by the United States Department of Transportation.

(iii) A commercial motor vehicle using compressed gas as a motor fuel.

(B) In lieu of a flame-producing emergency signal, emergency reflective triangles, red electric lanterns, or red emergency reflectors shall be used, the placement of which shall be in the same manner as prescribed in Section 392.22(b) of Title 49 of the Code of Federal Regulations.

(e) The reflectors shall be displayed continuously during darkness while the vehicle remains disabled upon the roadway or parked or disabled within 10 feet thereof.

(f) Subdivisions (b), (c), (d), and (e) do not apply to a vehicle under either of the following circumstances:

(1) Parked in a legal position within the corporate limits of any city.

(2) Parked in a legal position upon a roadway bounded by adjacent curbs.

(g) In addition to the reflectors specified in subdivision (a), an emergency warning sign or banner may be attached to a vehicle which is disabled upon the roadway or which is parked or disabled within 10 feet of a roadway.

(Amended by Stats. 2016, Ch. 208, Sec. 19. (AB 2906) Effective January 1, 2017.)

25301. When utility or public utility vehicles are parked, stopped or standing at the site of work as described in Section 22512, warning devices shall be displayed as follows:

(a) During daylight warning devices shall consist of either:

A warning flag or barricade striping on the front and rear of the vehicle.

A warning flag, sign, or barrier on the highway not more than 50 feet in advance of the vehicle and not more than 50 feet to the rear thereof, except that in zones where the speed limit is in excess of 25 miles per hour the 50-foot distance may be increased up to 500 feet from the vehicle as circumstances may warrant.

(b) During darkness the warning devices shall consist of either:

One or more flashing amber warning lights on the vehicle giving warning to approaching traffic from each direction.

A warning light, flare, fusee, or reflector on the highway not more than 50 feet in advance of the vehicle and not more than 50 feet to the rear thereof, except that in zones where the speed limit is in excess of 25 miles per hour the 50-foot distance may be increased up to 500 feet from the vehicle where circumstances may warrant.

(c) The provisions of subdivision (a) or (b) do not prevent the display of both types of the warning devices during daylight or darkness.

(d) During either daylight or darkness, no warning device is necessary if the vehicle is equipped with the flashing warning lights visible to approaching traffic from each direction as provided in subdivision (b).

(Amended by Stats. 1961, Ch. 653.)

25305. (a) No person shall place, deposit, or display upon or adjacent to any highway any lighted fusee, except as a warning to approaching vehicular traffic or railroad trains, or both, of an existing hazard upon or adjacent to the highway or highway-railroad crossing.

(b) It is unlawful to use any fusee which produces other than a red light. The provisions of this subdivision shall not apply to any railroad, as defined in Section 229 of the Public Utilities Code.

(c) No person shall attach or permit any person to attach a lighted fusee to any part of a vehicle.

(Amended by Stats. 2015, Ch. 451, Sec. 51. (SB 491) Effective January 1, 2016.)

Article 9. Commercial and Common Carrier Vehicles

(Article 9 enacted by Stats. 1959, Ch. 3.)

25350. Any passenger common carrier motor vehicle manufactured prior to January 1, 1968, may be equipped with green identification lamps. Any bus may be equipped with an illuminated termini sign, an illuminated identification sign, or any combination thereof, which shall not project any glaring light. Internally illuminated termini signs, identification signs, or any combination thereof, meeting the requirements of Section 25400 may be mounted inside a bus. Any commercial vehicle, other than a passenger common carrier motor vehicle, may be equipped with an illuminated identification sign upon the front thereof which shall not exceed 24 inches in length or 8 inches in width and which emits diffused white light without glare.

(Amended by Stats. 1981, Ch. 813, Sec. 18.)

25351. (a) A commercial vehicle and any other vehicle 80 or more inches in width may be equipped with identification lamps mounted on the front or rear.

(b) Identification lamps on vehicles described in subdivision (a) manufactured prior to January 1, 1968, may exhibit either amber, green, or white light to the front and red light to the rear.

(c) Identification lamps on vehicles described in subdivision (a) manufactured on or after January 1, 1968, may exhibit only amber light to the front and red light to the rear.

(Amended by Stats. 2021, Ch. 311, Sec. 6. (SB 814) Effective January 1, 2022.)

25352. Any bus operated by a publicly owned transit system on regularly scheduled service may be equipped with a device capable of sending a signal that interrupts or changes the sequence patterns of an official traffic control signal, under the following conditions:

(a) If such a device is a flashing gaseous discharge lamp, such lamp shall not emit a visible light exceeding an average of 0.0003 candela per flash of any color measured at a distance of 10 feet.

(b) Such device shall not be installed or used unless and until authorized on specific routes by either the Department of Transportation pursuant to Section 21350 or local authorities pursuant to Section 21351.

(c) Any bus or system operating under the conditions specified herein shall allow emergency vehicles operating pursuant to Section 25258 or 21055 to have priority in changing the sequence patterns of an official traffic control signal.

(Amended by Stats. 1980, Ch. 399, Sec. 6. Effective July 11, 1980.)

25353. (a) Notwithstanding Sections 25400 and 25950, a bus operated by a publicly owned transit system on regularly scheduled service may be equipped with illuminated signs that include destination signs, route-number signs, run-number signs, public service announcement signs, or a combination thereof, visible from any direction of the vehicle, that emit any light color, other than the color red emitted from forward-facing signs, pursuant to the following conditions:

(1) Each illuminated sign shall emit diffused nonglaring light.

(2) Each illuminated sign shall be limited in size to a display area of not greater than 720 square inches.

(3) Each illuminated sign shall not resemble nor be installed in a position that interferes with the visibility or effectiveness of a required lamp, reflector, or other device upon the vehicle.

(4) Each illuminated sign shall display information directly related to public transit service, including, but not limited to, route number, destination description, run number, and public service announcements.

(5) The mixing of individually colored light emitting diode elements, including red, is allowed as long as the emitted color formed by the combination of light emitting diode elements is not red.

(b) (1) An illuminated sign may be operated as a dynamic message sign in a paging or streaming mode.

(2) The following definitions shall govern the construction of paragraph (1):

(A) "Paging," meaning character elements or other information presented for a period of time and then disappearing all at once before the same or new elements are presented, is permitted if the display time of each message is between 2.7 and 10 seconds. Blanking times between each message shall be between 0.5 and 25 seconds.

(B) "Streaming," meaning character elements or other information moving smoothly and continuously across the display, is permitted if the character movement time, from one end of the display to the other, is at least 2.7 seconds, and the movement time of the entire message does not exceed 10 seconds.

(c) A regulation adopted pursuant to this section shall comply with

applicable federal law, including, but not limited to, the federal Americans with Disabilities Act of 1990 (42 U.S.C. Sec. 12101 et seq.).
(Added by Stats. 2006, Ch. 881, Sec. 2. Effective January 1, 2007.)

Article 10. Diffused Lights

(Article 10 enacted Stats. 1959, Ch. 3.)

25400. (a) Any vehicle may be equipped with a lamp or device on the exterior of the vehicle that emits a diffused nonglaring light of not more than 0.05 candela per square inch of area.

(b) Any diffused nonglaring light shall not display red to the front, but may display other colors. A diffused nonglaring light shall not resemble nor be installed within 12 inches or in such position as to interfere with the visibility or effectiveness of any required lamp, reflector, or other device upon the vehicle.

(c) A diffused nonglaring lamp or device, other than a display sign authorized by subdivision (d), shall be limited in size to an area of 720 square inches and where any lease, rental, or donation is involved the installation of the lamp or device shall be limited to those vehicles operated either primarily within business or residential districts or municipalities, or between business districts, residential districts, and municipalities in close proximity.

(d) An internally illuminated sign emitting not more than 0.25 candela per square inch and possessing copy which does not contain a white background may be displayed on each side, but not on the front or rear, of a trolley coach or of a bus being operated in urban or suburban service as described in Section 35107 of this code.
(Amended by Stats. 1968, Ch. 582.)

25401. No diffused nonglaring light on a vehicle shall resemble any official traffic control device.
(Enacted by Stats. 1959, Ch. 3.)

Article 11. Acetylene Lamps

(Article 11 enacted by Stats. 1959, Ch. 3.)

25450. Any motor vehicle, other than a motorcycle, equipped with lighted acetylene headlamps complies with the provisions of this code concerning lighted headlamps when it has two lighted acetylene headlamps of approximately equal candlepower mounted upon the front of the motor vehicle and fitted with clear plane glass fronts and bright six-inch spherical mirrors and standard acetylene five-eighths or three-quarters foot burners, not more and not less, projecting sufficient light ahead to reveal any vehicle, person or substantial object upon the roadway within 200 feet.
(Enacted by Stats. 1959, Ch. 3.)

25451. Any motorcycle equipped with one lighted acetylene headlamp complies with the provisions of this code concerning lighted headlamps on motorcycles when the acetylene headlamp is fitted with a clear plane glass front and a bright six-inch spherical mirror and a standard acetylene one-half or five-eighths foot burner, projecting sufficient light ahead to reveal any vehicle, person, or substantial object upon the roadway within a distance of 115 feet.
(Enacted by Stats. 1959, Ch. 3.)

25452. No acetylene lamp shall emit any glaring light.
(Enacted by Stats. 1959, Ch. 3.)

Article 12. Reflectorizing Material

(Article 12 enacted by Stats. 1959, Ch. 3.)

25500. (a) Area reflectorizing material may be displayed on any vehicle, provided: the color red is not displayed on the front; designs do not tend to distort the length or width of the vehicle; and designs do not resemble official traffic control devices, except that alternate striping resembling a barricade pattern may be used.

No vehicle shall be equipped with area reflectorizing material contrary to these provisions.

(b) The provisions of this section shall not apply to license plate stickers or tabs affixed to license plates as authorized by the Department of Motor Vehicles.
(Amended by Stats. 1971, Ch. 1536.)

Article 13. Headlamps on Motorcycles and Motor-Driven Cycles

(Heading of Article 13 amended by Stats. 1970, Ch. 923.)

25650. Every motorcycle during darkness shall be equipped with at least one and not more than two lighted headlamps which shall conform to the requirements and limitations of this division.
(Enacted by Stats. 1959, Ch. 3.)

25650.5. Every motorcycle manufactured and first registered on and after January 1, 1978, shall be equipped with at least one and not more than two headlamps which automatically turn on when the engine of the motorcycle is started and which remain lighted as long as the engine is running. This section does not preclude equipping motorcycles used as authorized emergency vehicles with a switch to be used to turn off the headlamp during emergency situations or when the light would interfere with law enforcement, if the switch is removed prior to resale of the motorcycle.
(Amended by Stats. 1984, Ch. 247, Sec. 3.)

25651. The headlamp upon a motor-driven cycle may be of the single-beam or multiple-beam type, but in either event, when the vehicle is operated during darkness, the headlamp shall comply with the requirements and limitations as follows:

(a) The headlamp shall be of sufficient intensity to reveal a person or a vehicle at a distance of not less than 100 feet when the motor-driven cycle is operated at any speed less than 25 miles per hour and at a distance of not less than 200 feet when operated at a speed of 25 to not exceeding 35 miles per hour, and at a distance of 300 feet when operated at a speed greater than 35 miles per hour.

(b) In the event the motor-driven cycle is equipped with a multiple-beam headlamp, the upper beam shall meet the minimum requirements set forth above and the lowermost beam shall meet the requirements applicable to a lowermost distribution of light as set forth in subdivision (b) of Section 24407.

(c) In the event the motor-driven cycle is equipped with a single-beam lamp, it shall be so aimed that when the vehicle is loaded none of the high intensity portion of light, at a distance of 25 feet ahead, shall project higher than the level of the center of the lamp from which it comes.
(Amended by Stats. 1959, Ch. 1996.)

Article 14. Vehicles Exempted

(Article 14 enacted by Stats. 1959, Ch. 3.)

25800. The provisions of Sections 24012, 24250, 24251, 24400 to 24404, inclusive, and Articles 3 (commencing with Section 24600), 4 (commencing with Section 24800), 5 (commencing with Section 24950), 6 (commencing with Section 25100), 9 (commencing with Section 25350), 11 (commencing with Section 25450), and 13 (commencing with Section 25650), shall not apply to special mobile equipment. Such equipment shall be subject to the provisions of Sections 24254, 25803, and 25950, and Article 12 (commencing with Section 25500) .
(Amended by Stats. 1972, Ch. 618.)

25801. The provisions of Sections 24012, 24250, 24251, 24254, 24400 to 24404, inclusive, 24600 to 24604, inclusive, 24606 to 24610, inclusive, Section 25950, and Articles 4 (commencing with Section 24800), 5 (commencing with Section 24950), 6 (commencing with Section 25100), 9 (commencing with Section 25350), 11 (commencing with Section 25450), 12 (commencing with Section 25500), and 13 (commencing with Section 25650) and shall not apply to special construction or maintenance equipment, nor to motortrucks equipped with snow removal or sanding devices, but shall apply to motortrucks and automobiles used independently of such equipment.

The provisions of Section 25803 shall be applicable to such equipment.
(Amended by Stats. 1972, Ch. 618.)

25802. Sections 24002, 24005, 24012, 24250, 24251, 24400 to 24404, inclusive, 24600 to 24604, inclusive, 24606 to 24610, inclusive, Article 4 (commencing with Section 24800), Article 5 (commencing with Section 24950), Article 6 (commencing with Section 25100), Article 9 (commencing with Section 25350), Article 11 (commencing with Section 25450), and Article 13 (commencing with Section 25650) of Chapter 2 of this division, Chapter 3 (commencing with Section 26301), Chapter 4 (commencing with Section 26700), and Chapter 5 (commencing with Section 27000) of this division, and Chapter 5 (commencing with Section 31301) of Division 13 do not apply to logging vehicles or any vehicle of a type subject to registration under this code that is not designed, used, or maintained for the transportation of persons or property and that is operated or moved over a highway only incidentally; but any such vehicle shall be subject to Sections 2800, 2806, 24004, 25260, 25803, 25950, 25952, 26457, 27454, 27602, 31500, and 40150, and to Article 12 (commencing with Section 25500) of Chapter 2 of this division.
(Amended by Stats. 2016, Ch. 208, Sec. 20. (AB 2906) Effective January 1, 2017.)

25803. (a) All vehicles not otherwise required to be equipped with headlamps, rear lights, or reflectors by this chapter shall, if operated on a highway during darkness, be equipped with a lamp exhibiting a red light visible from a distance of 500 feet to the rear of the vehicle. In addition, all of these vehicles operated alone or as the first vehicle in a combination of vehicles, shall be equipped with at least one lighted lamp exhibiting a white light visible from a distance of 500 feet to the front of the vehicle.

(b) A vehicle shall also be equipped with an amber reflector on the front near the left side and a red reflector on the rear near the left side. The reflectors shall be mounted on the vehicle not lower than 16 inches nor higher than 60 inches above the ground and so designed and maintained as to be visible during darkness from all distances within 500 feet from the vehicle when directly in front of a motor vehicle displaying lawful lighted headlamps undimmed.

(c) In addition, if a vehicle described in subdivision (a) or the load thereon has a total outside width in excess of 100 inches there shall be displayed during darkness at the left outer extremity at least one amber light visible under normal atmospheric conditions from a distance of 500 feet to the front, sides, and rear. At all other times there shall be displayed at the left outer extremity a solid red or fluorescent orange flag or cloth not less than 18 inches square.
(Amended by Stats. 2015, Ch. 451, Sec. 52. (SB 491) Effective January 1, 2016.)

25804. Notwithstanding any other provision of this code, original lighting equipment installed on a vehicle manufactured prior to January 1, 1946, need not meet the requirements established by the department when the vehicle is used primarily for the purpose of historical exhibition.
(Amended by Stats. 1979, Ch. 723.)

25805. Notwithstanding any other provision of this article, a forklift truck which is towed upon the highway at the end of a combination of vehicles shall at all times be equipped with at least one stop lamp mounted upon the rear of the vehicle and shall be equipped with lamp-type turn signals. Such vehicle shall, during the hours of darkness, be equipped with at least one taillamp and one red reflector mounted upon the rear of the vehicle and shall be equipped with clearance lamps if the vehicle is 80 or more inches in width.
(Added by Stats. 1969, Ch. 132.)

25806. Sections 24003 and 27002 shall not apply to the installation of warning lamps and sirens on ambulances or firetrucks which are used solely for demonstration purposes in the sales work of a licensed dealer, distributor, or vehicle manufacturer and shall not apply to ambulances or firetrucks being operated on a highway solely for the purpose of delivery from the licensee to a purchaser. Warning lamps shall be removed or covered with opaque material and the siren controls disabled whenever the vehicle is upon a highway.
(Added by Stats. 1982, Ch. 217, Sec. 1.)

Article 15. Light Restrictions and Mounting

(Article 15 enacted by Stats. 1959, Ch. 3.)

25950. This section applies to the color of lamps and to any reflector exhibiting or reflecting perceptible light of 0.05 candela or more per foot-candle of incident illumination. Unless provided otherwise, the color of lamps and reflectors upon a vehicle shall be as follows:

(a) The emitted light from all lamps and the reflected light from all reflectors, visible from in front of a vehicle, shall be white or yellow, except as follows:

(1) Rear side marker lamps required by Section 25100 may show red to the front.

(2) The color of foglamps described in Section 24403 may be in the color spectrum from white to yellow.

(3) An illuminating device, as permitted under Section 24255, shall emit radiation predominantly in the infrared region of the electromagnetic spectrum. Any incidental visible light projecting to the front of the vehicle shall be predominantly yellow to white. Any incidental visible light projecting to the rear of the vehicle shall be predominantly red. Any incidental visible light from an illuminating device, as permitted under Section 24255, shall not resemble any other required or permitted lighting device or official traffic control device.

(4) ADS marker lamps, as described in subdivision (i) of Section 38750, on an autonomous vehicle.

(b) The emitted light from all lamps and the reflected light from all reflectors, visible from the rear of a vehicle, shall be red except as follows:

(1) Stoplamps on vehicles manufactured before January 1, 1979, may show yellow to the rear.

(2) Turn signal lamps may show yellow to the rear.

(3) Front side marker lamps required by Section 25100 may show yellow to the rear.

(4) Backup lamps shall show white to the rear.

(5) The rearward facing portion of a front-mounted double-faced turn signal lamp may show amber to the rear while the headlamps or parking lamps are lighted, if the intensity of the light emitted is not greater than the parking lamps and the turn signal function is not impaired.

(6) A reflector meeting the requirements of, and installed in accordance with, Section 24611 shall be red or white, or both.

(7) ADS marker lamps, as described in subdivision (i) of Section 38750, on an autonomous vehicle.

(c) All lamps and reflectors visible from the front, sides, or rear of a vehicle, except headlamps, may have any unlighted color, provided the emitted light from all lamps or reflected light from all reflectors complies with the required color. Except for backup lamps, the entire effective projected luminous area of lamps visible from the rear or mounted on the sides near the rear of a vehicle shall be covered by an inner lens of the required color when the unlighted color differs from the required emitted light color. Taillamps, stoplamps, and turn signal lamps that are visible to the rear may be white when unlighted on vehicles manufactured before January 1, 1974.
(Amended by Stats. 2025, Ch. 415, Sec. 1. (SB 480) Effective January 1, 2026.)

25951. Any lighted lamp or device upon a motor vehicle other than headlamps, spotlamps, signal lamps, or auxiliary driving lamps, warning lamps which projects a beam of light of an intensity greater than 300 candlepower shall be so directed that no part of the beam will strike the level of the roadway at a distance of more than 75 feet from the vehicle.
(Amended by Stats. 1965, Ch. 1313.)

25952. (a) Lamps, reflectors, and area reflectorizing material of a type required or permitted on a vehicle may be mounted on a load carried by the vehicle in lieu of, or in addition to, such equipment on the vehicle. Such equipment shall be mounted on the load in a manner that would comply with the requirements of this code and regulations adopted pursuant to this code if the load were an integral part of the vehicle.

(b) Lamps on vehicles carried as a load shall not be lighted unless such lamps are mounted in accordance with subdivision (a).

(Added by Stats. 1969, Ch. 341.)

Article 16. Equipment Testing

(Article 16 repealed and added by Stats. 1979, Ch. 723.)

26100. (a) A person shall not sell or offer for sale for use upon or as part of the equipment of a vehicle any lighting equipment, safety glazing material, or other device that does not meet the provisions of Section 26104.

(b) A person shall not use upon a vehicle, and a person shall not drive a vehicle upon a highway that is equipped with, any lighting equipment, safety glazing material, or other device that is not in compliance with Section 26104.

(c) This section does not apply to a taillamp or stop lamp in use on or prior to December 1, 1935.

(Amended by Stats. 2010, Ch. 491, Sec. 44. (SB 1318) Effective January 1, 2011.)

26101. (a) A person shall not sell or offer for sale for use upon or as part of the equipment of a vehicle any device that is intended to modify the original design or performance of any lighting equipment, safety glazing material, or other device, unless the modifying device meets the provisions of Section 26104.

(b) A person shall not use upon a vehicle, and a person shall not drive a vehicle upon a highway that has installed a device that is intended to modify the original design or performance of a lighting, safety glazing material, or other device, unless the modifying device complies with Section 26104.

(c) This section does not apply to a taillamp or stop lamp in use on or prior to December 1, 1935, or to lamps installed on authorized emergency vehicles.

(Amended by Stats. 2010, Ch. 491, Sec. 45. (SB 1318) Effective January 1, 2011.)

26102. In the event any equipment in actual use meets the requirements of this code or a department regulation adopted pursuant to this code, a subsequent regulation shall not require the replacement of the equipment and shall be applicable only to equipment installed after the effective date of the regulation.

(Repealed and added by Stats. 1979, Ch. 723.)

26103. (a) The department may adopt and enforce regulations establishing standards and specifications for safety belts, safety glazing material, safety helmets, sirens, tire traction devices, bunk stakes, and synthetic binders. The standards and specifications may include installation and aiming requirements.

(b) Notwithstanding rulemaking provisions of the Administrative Procedure Act (Chapter 3.5 (commencing with Section 11340) of Part 1 of Division 3 of Title 2 of the Government Code), the department shall adopt regulations for lighting devices permitted by this code and incorporate by reference the applicable standards published by SAE International for these devices and a corresponding publication date. Notwithstanding the specified publication date, a person may sell or use upon a vehicle a device meeting the requirements of a revised standard.

(c) A federal motor vehicle safety standard adopted pursuant to Chapter 301 (commencing with Section 30101) of Part A of Subtitle VI of Title 49 of the United States Code that covers the same aspect of performance of a device shall prevail over provisions of this code or regulations adopted pursuant to this code. Lamps, devices, and equipment certified by the manufacturer to meet applicable federal motor vehicle safety standards as original equipment on new vehicles and the identical replacements for those items need not be certified to the department.

(Amended by Stats. 2021, Ch. 311, Sec. 7. (SB 814) Effective January 1, 2022.)

26104. (a) Every manufacturer who sells, offers for sale, or manufactures for use upon a vehicle devices subject to requirements established by the department shall, before the device is offered for sale, have laboratory test data showing compliance with such requirements. Tests may be conducted by the manufacturer.

(b) The department may at any time request from the manufacturer a copy of the test data showing proof of compliance of any device with the requirements established by the department and additional evidence that due care was exercised in maintaining compliance during production. If the manufacturer fails to provide such proof of compliance within 30 days of notice from the department, the department may prohibit the sale of the device in this state until acceptable proof of compliance is received by the department.

(Amended by Stats. 1980, Ch. 399, Sec. 8. Effective July 11, 1980.)

26105. The department may purchase any equipment sold for use on vehicles and test or retest the same as to conformance with the requirements of this code and department regulations adopted pursuant to this code and any expense incurred in such purchase and test shall be a legal charge against the Motor Vehicle Fund.

(Repealed and added by Stats. 1979, Ch. 723.)

26106. The department may issue a permit for the use of equipment for experimental purposes. The use of such equipment under the permit is not a violation of this code.

(Repealed and added by Stats. 1979, Ch. 723.)

Chapter 3. Brakes

(Chapter 3 enacted by Stats. 1959, Ch. 3.)

Article 1. Brake Requirements

(Article 1 enacted by Stats. 1959, Ch. 3.)

26301. Any motor vehicle first registered in this state after January 1, 1940, shall be equipped with power brakes if its gross weight exceeds 14,000 pounds, except that any such vehicle having a gross weight of less than 18,000 pounds may, in lieu of power brakes, be equipped with two-stage hydraulic actuators of a type designed to increase braking effect of its brakes.

(Amended by Stats. 1982, Ch. 789, Sec. 1.)

26301.5. Every passenger vehicle manufactured and first registered after January 1, 1973, except motorcycles, shall be equipped with an emergency brake system so constructed that rupture or leakage-type failure of any single pressure component of the service brake system, except structural failures of the brake master cylinder body or effectiveness indicator body, shall not result in complete loss of function of the vehicle's brakes when force on the brake pedal is continued.

(Added by Stats. 1971, Ch. 1110.)

26302. (a) Every trailer or semitrailer, manufactured and first registered after January 1, 1940, and having a gross weight of 6,000 pounds or more and which is operated at a speed of 20 miles per hour or over shall be equipped with brakes.

(b) Every trailer or semitrailer manufactured and first registered after January 1, 1966, and having a gross weight of 3,000 pounds or more shall be equipped with brakes on at least two wheels.

(c) Every trailer or semitrailer manufactured after January 1, 1982, and equipped with air brakes shall be equipped with brakes on all wheels.

(d) Brakes required on trailers or semitrailers shall be adequate, supplemental to the brakes on the towing vehicle, to enable the combination of vehicles to comply with the stopping distance requirements of Section 26454.

(e) The provisions of this section shall not apply to any vehicle being used to support the boom or mast attached to a mobile crane or shovel.

(Amended by Stats. 1981, Ch. 774, Sec. 6.)

26303. Every trailer coach and every camp trailer having a gross weight of 1,500 pounds or more, but exclusive of passengers, shall be equipped with brakes on at least two wheels which are adequate, supplemental to the brakes on the towing vehicle, to enable the combination of vehicles to comply with the stopping distance requirements of Section 26454.

(Amended by Stats. 1971, Ch. 1536.)

26304. (a) Power brakes on any trailer or semitrailer manufactured after December 31, 1955, operated over public highways and required to be equipped with brakes shall be designed to be automatically applied upon breakaway from the towing vehicle and shall be capable of stopping and holding such vehicle stationary for not less than 15 minutes.

(b) Every new truck or truck tractor manufactured after December 31, 1955, operated over public highways and used in towing a vehicle shall be equipped with service brakes capable of stopping the truck or truck tractor in the event of breakaway of the towed vehicle.

(Amended by Stats. 1972, Ch. 733.)

26305. Any auxiliary dolly or tow dolly may be equipped with brakes.

(Amended by Stats. 1983, Ch. 708, Sec. 9.)

26307. No forklift truck manufactured after January 1, 1970, shall be towed behind another vehicle unless it is equipped with brakes on the wheels of the rearmost axle when the forklift truck is in the towing position, which brakes shall be adequate, supplemental to the brakes on the towing vehicle, to enable the combination of vehicles to comply with the stopping distance requirements of Section 26454.

(Added by Stats. 1969, Ch. 132.)

26311. (a) Every motor vehicle shall be equipped with service brakes on all wheels in contact with the roadway, except as follows:

(1) Trucks and truck tractors manufactured before July 25, 1980, having three or more axles need not have brakes on the front wheels, except when such vehicles are equipped with at least two steerable axles, the wheels of one such axle need not be equipped with brakes.

(2) The final towed vehicle in a triple saddle-mount driveaway-towaway operation.

(3) Any vehicle manufactured prior to 1930.

(4) Any two-axle truck tractor manufactured prior to 1964.

(5) Any sidecar attached to a motorcycle.

(6) Any motorcycle manufactured prior to 1966. Such motorcycle shall be equipped with brakes on at least one wheel.

(b) Any bus, truck, or truck tractor may be equipped with a manual or automatic means for reducing the braking effort on the front wheels. The manual means shall be used only when operating under adverse road conditions, such as wet, snowy, or icy roads.

(c) Vehicles and combinations of vehicles exempted in subdivisions (a) and (b) from the requirements of brakes on all wheels shall comply with the stopping distance requirements of Section 26454.

(Amended by Stats. 2015, Ch. 451, Sec. 53. (SB 491) Effective January 1, 2016.)

Article 2. Operation of Brakes

(Article 2 enacted by Stats. 1959, Ch. 3.)

26450. Every motor vehicle shall be equipped with a service brake system and every motor vehicle, other than a motorcycle, shall be equipped with a parking brake system. Both the service brake and parking brake shall be separately applied.

If the two systems are connected in any way, they shall be so constructed that failure of any one part, except failure in the drums, brakeshoes, or other mechanical parts of the wheel brake assemblies, shall not leave the motor vehicle without operative brakes.

(Amended by Stats. 1967, Ch. 369.)

26451. The parking brake system of every motor vehicle shall comply with the following requirements:

(a) The parking brake shall be adequate to hold the vehicle or combination of vehicles stationary on any grade on which it is operated under all conditions of loading on a surface free from snow, ice or loose material. In any event the parking brake shall be capable of locking the braked wheels to the limit of traction.

(b) The parking brake shall be applied either by the driver's muscular efforts, by spring action, or by other energy which is isolated and used exclusively for the operation of the parking brake or the combination parking brake and emergency stopping system.

(c) The parking brake shall be held in the applied position solely by mechanical means.

(Amended by Stats. 1981, Ch. 774, Sec. 8.)

26452. All motor vehicles shall be so equipped as to permit application of the brakes at least once for the purpose of bringing the vehicle to a stop within the legal stopping distance after the engine has become inoperative.

(Enacted by Stats. 1959, Ch. 3.)

26453. All brakes and component parts thereof shall be maintained in good condition and in good working order. The brakes shall be so adjusted as to operate as equally as practicable with respect to the wheels on opposite sides of the vehicle.

(Amended by Stats. 1959, Ch. 2183.)

26454. (a) The service brakes of every motor vehicle or combination of vehicles shall be adequate to control the movement of and to stop and hold the vehicle or combination of vehicles under all conditions of loading.

(b) Every motor vehicle or combination of vehicles, at any time and under all conditions of loading, shall, upon application of the service brake, be capable of stopping from an initial speed of 20 miles per hour according to the following requirements:

Maximum Stopping Distance (feet)

(1) Passenger-carrying vehicles with a seating capacity of 10 or fewer persons, including the driver, and built on a passenger car chassis 20

(2) Passenger-carrying vehicles with a seating capacity of more than 10 persons, including the driver, and built on a passenger car chassis; vehicles built on a truck or bus chassis and having a GVWR of 10,000 pounds or less..... 25

(3) All other passenger-carrying vehicles 35

(4) Single-unit property-carrying vehicles having a GVWR of 10,000 pounds or less 25

(5) Single-unit property-carrying vehicles having a GVWR of more than 10,000 pounds, except truck tractors; combinations of a 2-axle towing vehicle and trailer having a GVWR of 3,000 pounds or less; all combinations of 2 or fewer vehicles in driveaway or towaway operation 35

(6) All other property-carrying vehicles and combinations of property-carrying vehicles 40

(c) Every motor vehicle or combination of vehicles, at any time and under all conditions of loading, shall, upon application of the service brake, be capable of developing a braking force at least equal to the percentage of its gross weight according to the following requirements:

Braking force as a percentage of gross vehicle or combination weight

(1) Passenger-carrying vehicles with a seating capacity of 10 or fewer persons, including the driver, and built on a passenger car chassis 65.2

(2) Passenger-carrying vehicles with a seating capacity of more than 10 persons, including driver, and built on a passenger car chassis; vehicles built on a truck or bus chassis and having a GVWR of 10,000 pounds or less.. 52.8

(3) All other passenger-carrying vehicles 43.5

(4) Single-unit property-carrying vehicles having a GVWR of 10,000 pounds or less 52.8

(5) Single-unit property-carrying vehicles having a GVWR of more than 10,000 pounds, except truck tractors; combinations of a 2-axle towing vehicle and trailer having a GVWR of 3,000 pounds or less; all combinations of 2 or fewer vehicles in driveaway or towaway operation 43.5

(6) All other property-carrying vehicles and combinations of property-carrying vehicles 43.5

(d) Every motor vehicle or combination of vehicles, at any time and under all conditions off loading, shall, upon application of the service brake, be capable of decelerating to a stop from 20 miles per hour at not less than the rate specified in the following requirements:

Deceleration in feet per second

(1) Passenger-carrying vehicles with a seating capacity of 10 or fewer persons, including the driver, and built on a passenger car chassis 21

(2) Passenger-carrying vehicles with a seating capacity of more than 10 persons, including the driver, and built on a passenger car chassis; vehicles built on a truck or bus chassis and having a GVWR of 10,000 pounds or less..... 17

(3) All other passenger-carrying vehicles 14

(4) Single-unit property-carrying vehicles having a GVWR of 10,000 pounds or less 17

(5) Single-unit property-carrying vehicles having a GVWR of more than 10,000 pounds, except truck tractors; combinations of a 2-axle towing vehicle and trailer having a GVWR of 3,000 pounds or less; all combinations of 2 or fewer vehicles in driveaway or towaway operation 14

(6) All other property-carrying vehicles and combinations of property-carrying vehicles 14

(e) Upon application of its service brakes, a motor vehicle or combination of motor vehicles shall, under any condition of loading in which it is found on a public highway, be capable of stopping within the distance specified in subdivision (b) and developing only the braking force specified in subdivision (c), if braking force is measured by a performance-based brake tester that meets the requirements of functional specifications for performance-based brake testers for commercial motor vehicles and braking force is the sum of the braking force at each wheel of the vehicle or vehicle combination as a percentage of gross vehicle or combination weight.

(f) Upon application of its emergency brake system and with no other brake system applied, a motor vehicle or combination of motor vehicles shall, under any condition of loading in which it is found on a public highway, be capable of stopping from 20 miles per hour in a distance, measured from the point at which movement of the emergency brake control begins, that is not greater than the distance specified in the following:

Maximum Stopping Distance (feet)

(1) Passenger-carrying vehicles with a seating capacity of 10 or fewer persons, including the driver, and built on a passenger car chassis 54

(2) Passenger-carrying vehicles with a seating capacity of more than 10 persons, including the driver, and built on a passenger car chassis; vehicles built on a truck or bus chassis and having a GVWR of 10,000 pounds or less..... 66

(3) All other passenger-carrying vehicles 85

(4) Single-unit property-carrying vehicles having a GVWR of 10,000 pounds or less 66

(5) Single-unit property-carrying vehicles having a GVWR of more than 10,000 pounds, except truck tractors; combinations of a 2-axle towing vehicle and trailer having a GVWR of 3,000 pounds or less; all combinations of 2 or fewer vehicles in driveaway or towaway operation 85

(6) All other property-carrying vehicles and combinations of property-carrying vehicles 90

(g) Conformity to the stopping-distance requirements of this section shall be determined under the following conditions:

(1) Any test shall be made with the vehicle on a hard surface that is substantially level, dry, smooth, and free of loose material.

(2) The vehicle shall be in the center of a 12-foot-wide lane when the test begins and shall not deviate from that lane during the test.

(h) For purposes of this section, "GVWR" means the manufacturer's gross vehicle weight rating, as defined in Section 350.

(Amended by Stats. 2016, Ch. 208, Sec. 21. (AB 2906) Effective January 1, 2017.)

26455. In respect to any motor vehicle designed, used or maintained primarily for the transportation of property which is not equipped with a plate or marker showing the manufacturer's gross vehicle weight rating, for purposes of stopping distance requirements, the weight of a vehicle shall be determined as follows:

(a) Any motor vehicle having less than six wheels is the equivalent of a vehicle having a manufacturer's gross vehicle weight rating of less than 10,000 pounds.

(b) Any motor vehicle having six wheels or more is the equivalent of a vehicle having a manufacturer's gross vehicle weight rating of 10,000 pounds or more.

(Enacted by Stats. 1959, Ch. 3.)

26456. Stopping distance requirement tests shall be conducted on a substantially level, dry, smooth, hard-surfaced road that is free from loose material and where the grade does not exceed plus or minus 1 percent. Stopping distance shall be measured from the instant brake controls are moved and from an initial speed of approximately 20 miles per hour. No test of brake performance shall be made upon a highway at a speed in excess of 25 miles per hour.

(Enacted by Stats. 1959, Ch. 3.)

26457. Special mobile equipment, logging vehicles, equipment operated under special permit, and any chassis without body or load are not subject to stopping distance requirements, but if any such vehicle or equipment cannot be stopped within 32 feet from an initial speed of 15 miles per hour, it shall not be operated at a speed in excess of that permitting a stop in 32 feet.

(Amended by Stats. 1975, Ch. 517.)

26458. (a) The braking system on every motor vehicle used to tow another vehicle shall be so arranged that one control on the towing vehicle shall, when applied, operate all the service brakes on the power unit and combination of vehicles when either or both of the following conditions exist:

(1) The towing vehicle is required to be equipped with power brakes.

(2) The towed vehicle is required to be equipped with brakes and is equipped with power brakes.

(b) Subdivision (a) shall not be construed to prohibit motor vehicles from being equipped with an additional control to be used to operate the brakes on the trailer or trailers.

(c) Subdivision (a) does not apply to any of the following combinations of vehicles, if the combination of vehicles meets the stopping distance requirements of Section 26454:

(1) Vehicles engaged in driveaway-towaway operations.

(2) Disabled vehicles, while being towed.

(3) Towed motor vehicles.

(4) Trailers equipped with inertially controlled brakes which are designed to be applied automatically upon breakaway from the towing vehicle and which are capable of stopping and holding the trailer stationary for not less than 15 minutes.

(Amended by Stats. 1991, Ch. 121, Sec. 1.)

26458.5. Pursuant to Section 26458, whenever a motor vehicle is equipped with an additional control to operate the brakes on a trailer, that control shall not be used in lieu of the service brake control, except in the case of failure of the service brake system.

(Added by Stats. 1989, Ch. 316, Sec. 1.)

Article 3. Airbrakes

(Article 3 added by Stats. 1959, Ch. 420.)

26502. (a) Airbrakes of every motor vehicle and combination of vehicles shall be so adjusted and maintained as to be capable of providing full service brake application at all times except as provided in subdivision (b) of Section 26311. A full service brake application shall deliver to all brake chambers not less than 90 percent of the air reservoir pressure remaining with the brakes applied.

(b) The department may by regulation authorize the use of special devices or systems to automatically reduce the maximum air pressure delivered to the brake chambers in order to compensate for load variation and to obtain balanced braking. Permitted systems shall be of the fail safe type and shall not increase the vehicle stopping distance.

(Repealed and added by Stats. 1965, Ch. 1789.)

26503. Every motor vehicle equipped with airbrakes or equipped to operate airbrakes on towed vehicles shall be equipped with a standard type safety valve which shall be installed so as to have an uninterrupted connection with the air reservoir or tank. It shall be adjusted and maintained so that it will open and discharge the air system under any condition at a pressure of not to exceed 150 pounds per square inch and close and reseat itself at a point above the maximum air governor setting. The department may by regulation prescribe a higher maximum opening pressure for air pressure systems designed for, and capable of safely operating with, pressure safety valves with a higher opening pressure.

(Amended by Stats. 1967, Ch. 1578.)

26504. The air governor cut-in and cut-out pressures of every motor vehicle equipped with airbrakes or equipped to operate airbrakes on towed vehicles shall be adjusted so that the maximum pressure in the air system and the minimum cut-in pressure shall be within limits prescribed by the department. In adopting regulations specifying such pressures the department shall consider the safe operating capacities of the various airbrake systems which are now or may be used on motor vehicles and shall be guided by the designed capabilities of those systems.

(Amended by Stats. 1967, Ch. 1578.)

26505. A motor vehicle equipped with airbrakes or equipped to operate airbrakes on towed vehicles shall be equipped with a pressure gauge of reliable and satisfactory construction and maintained in an efficient working condition, accurate within 10 percent of the actual air reservoir pressure, and visible and legible to a person when seated in the driving position.

(Amended by Stats. 2010, Ch. 491, Sec. 46. (SB 1318) Effective January 1, 2011.)

26506. (a) Every motor vehicle airbrake system used to operate the brakes on a motor vehicle or on a towed vehicle shall be equipped with a low air pressure warning device that complies with either the requirements set forth in the Federal Motor Vehicle Safety Standards in effect at the time of manufacture or the requirements of subdivision (b).

(b) The device shall be readily visible or audible to the driver and shall give a satisfactory continuous warning when the air supply pressure drops below a fixed pressure, which shall be not more than 75 pounds per square inch nor less than 55 pounds per square inch with the engine running. A gauge indicating pressure shall not satisfy this requirement.

(Amended by Stats. 1992, Ch. 1241, Sec. 25. Effective January 1, 1993.)

26507. A check valve shall be installed and properly maintained in the air supply piping of every motor vehicle equipped with airbrakes, either between the air compressor and the first reservoir or tank immediately adjacent to the air intake of said reservoir, or between No. 1 reservoir (wet tank) and No. 2 reservoir (dry tank) immediately adjacent to the air intake of the No. 2 reservoir; provided, that the air supply for the brakes is not drawn from the No. 1 reservoir and that the No. 1 and No. 2 reservoirs are connected by only one pipeline.

(Added by Stats. 1959, Ch. 510.)

26508. Every vehicle or combination of vehicles using compressed air at the wheels for applying the service brakes shall be equipped with an emergency stopping system meeting the requirements of this section and capable of stopping the vehicle or combination of vehicles in the event of failure in the service brake air system as follows:

(a) Every motor vehicle operated either singly or in a combination of vehicles and every towed vehicle shall be equipped with an emergency stopping system.

(b) Motor vehicles used to tow vehicles that use compressed air at the wheels for applying the service brakes shall be equipped with a device or devices with both a manual and automatic means of actuating the emergency stopping system on the towed vehicle as follows:

(1) The automatic device shall operate automatically in the event of reduction of the service brake air supply of the towing vehicle to a fixed pressure which shall be not lower than 20 pounds per square inch nor higher than 45 pounds per square inch.

(2) The manual device shall be readily operable by a person seated in the driver's seat, with its emergency position or method of operation clearly indicated. In no instance may the manual means be so arranged as to permit its use to prevent operation of the automatic means.

(c) Motor vehicles manufactured prior to 1964 shall be deemed to be in compliance with subdivisions (e) and (f) when equipped with axle-by-axle protected airbrakes using a separate air tank system for each of at least two axles, provided that each system independently meets all other requirements of this section. Each system shall be capable of being manually applied, released, and reapplied from the driver's seat but shall not be capable of being released from the driver's seat after any reapplication unless there is available a means which can be applied from the driver's seat to stop and hold the vehicle or combination of vehicles.

(d) Towed vehicles shall be deemed to be in compliance with this section when:

(1) The towed vehicle is equipped with a no-bleed-back relay-emergency valve or equivalent device, so designed that the supply reservoir used to provide air for the brakes is safeguarded against backflow of air from the reservoir through the supply line,

(2) The brakes are applied automatically and promptly upon breakaway from the towing vehicle and maintain application for at least 15 minutes, and

(3) The combination of vehicles is capable of stopping within the distance and under the conditions specified in Section 26454.

(e) If the service brake system and the emergency stopping system are connected in any way, they shall be so constructed that a failure or malfunction in any one part of either system, including brake chamber diaphragm failure but not including failure in the drums, brake shoes, or other mechanical parts of the wheel brake assemblies, shall not leave the vehicle without one operative stopping system capable of complying with the performance requirements in Section 26454.

(f) Every emergency stopping system shall be designed so that it is capable of being manually applied, released, and reapplied by a person seated in the driver's seat. The system shall be designed so that it cannot be released from the driver's seat after any reapplication unless immediate further application can be made from the driver's seat to stop and hold the vehicle or combination of vehicles. The emergency stopping system may also be applied automatically.

(g) A vehicle or combination of vehicles upon failure of the service brake air system shall not be driven on a highway under its own power except to the extent necessary to move the vehicles off the roadway to the nearest place of safety.

(h) A vehicle or combination of vehicles shall not be equipped with an emergency stopping system that creates a hazard on the highway, or increases the service brake stopping distance of a vehicle or combination of vehicles, or interferes in any way with the application of the service brakes on any vehicle or combination of vehicles.

(i) Any energy-storing device which is a part of the emergency stopping system shall be designed so that it is recharged or reset from the course of compressed air or other energy produced by the vehicle, except that energy to release the emergency stopping system may be produced by the driver's muscular effort from the driver's seat. A device shall not be used that can be set to prevent automatic delivery of air to protected air supply reservoirs of motor vehicle emergency stopping systems when air is available in the service brake air supply system.

(j) Any vehicle manufactured on or after January 1, 1964, which uses axle-by-axle protected airbrakes as the emergency stopping system shall use a separate air tank system for each axle, except that motor vehicles equipped with a dual or tandem treadle valve system need have no more than two protected air tanks in such system, one for each valve.

(k) This section does not apply to any of the following:

(1) Auxiliary dollies, special mobile equipment, or special construction equipment.

(2) Motor vehicles which are operated in a driveaway-towaway operation and not registered in this state.

(3) Disabled vehicles when being towed.

(4) Vehicles which are operated under a one-trip permit as provided in Section 4003.

(5) Vehicles which because of unladen width, length, height or weight may not be moved upon the highway without the permit specified in Section 35780.

(l) Every owner or lessee shall instruct and require that the driver be thoroughly familiar with the requirements of this section. The driver of a vehicle or combination of vehicles required to comply with the requirements of this section shall be able to demonstrate the application and release of the emergency system on the vehicle and each vehicle in the combination.

(Amended by Stats. 2016, Ch. 208, Sec. 22. (AB 2906) Effective January 1, 2017.)

Article 4. Vacuum Brakes

(Article 4 added by Stats. 1963, Ch. 386.)

26520. Motor vehicles required to be equipped with power brakes and which are equipped with vacuum or vacuum-assisted brakes shall be equipped with a properly maintained vacuum gauge of reliable and satisfactory construction, accurate within 10 percent of the actual vacuum in the supply reservoir, and visible and legible to the driver at all times.

This section shall not apply to a two-axle motor truck operated singly.

(Added by Stats. 1963, Ch. 386.)

26521. Motor vehicles required to be equipped with power brakes and equipped with vacuum or vacuum-assisted brakes and motor vehicles used to tow vehicles equipped with vacuum brakes or vacuum-assisted brakes shall be equipped with either an audible or visible warning signal to indicate readily to the driver when the vacuum drops to eight inches of mercury and less. A vacuum gauge shall not be deemed to meet this requirement.

This section shall not apply to a two-axle motor truck operated singly nor to any motor vehicle manufactured prior to 1964.

(Added by Stats. 1963, Ch. 386.)

26522. Vehicles required to be equipped with power brakes and equipped with vacuum or vacuum-assisted brakes shall have a check valve installed and properly maintained in the vacuum system between the source of vacuum and the vacuum reserve.

(Added by Stats. 1963, Ch. 386.)

Chapter 4. Windshields and Mirrors

(Chapter 4 enacted by Stats. 1959, Ch. 3.)

26700. (a) Except as provided in subdivision (b) or (c), a passenger vehicle, other than a motorcycle, and every bus, motortruck or truck tractor, and every firetruck, fire engine or other fire apparatus, whether publicly or privately owned, shall be equipped with an adequate windshield.

(b) Subdivision (a) does not apply to any vehicle issued identification plates pursuant to Section 5004 which was not required to be equipped with a windshield at the time it was first sold or registered under the laws of this state, another state, or foreign jurisdiction.

(c) This section does not apply to an autonomous vehicle, as defined in Section 38750, that is not capable of operation with a human occupant in the vehicle, provided that this exemption is consistent with, or authorized by, any applicable federal law, regulation, or exemption thereto.

(Amended by Stats. 2021, Ch. 428, Sec. 5. (SB 570) Effective January 1, 2022.)

26701. (a) No person shall sell, offer for sale, or operate any motor vehicle, except a motorcycle, manufactured after January 1, 1936, unless it is equipped with safety glazing material wherever glazing materials are used in interior partitions, doors, windows, windshields, auxiliary wind deflectors or openings in the roof.

(b) No person shall sell or offer for sale any camper manufactured after January 1, 1968, nor shall any person operate a motor vehicle registered in this state which is equipped with that camper, unless the camper is equipped with safety glazing materials wherever glazing materials are used in outside windows and doors, interior partitions, and openings in the roof.

(c) No person shall operate a motorcycle manufactured after January 1, 1969, equipped with a windshield containing glazing material unless it is safety glazing material.

(d) No person shall sell, offer for sale, or operate any motor vehicle equipped with red, blue, or amber translucent aftermarket material in any partitions, windows, windshields, or wind deflectors.

(e) No person shall sell, offer for sale, or operate any trailer coach manufactured after January 1, 1977, that is capable of being towed with a fifth-wheel device unless the trailer coach is equipped with safety glazing materials wherever glazing materials are used in windows or doors, interior partitions, and openings in the roof.

(Amended by Stats. 1993, Ch. 540, Sec. 2. Effective January 1, 1994.)

26703. (a) No person shall replace any glazing materials used in interior partitions, doors, windows, or openings in the roof in any motor vehicle, in the outside windows, doors, interior partitions, or openings in the roof of any camper, or in windows, doors, interior partitions, or openings in the roof of a trailer coach capable of being towed with a fifth-wheel device, with any glazing material other than safety glazing material.

(b) No person shall replace any glazing material used in the windshield, rear window, auxiliary wind deflectors, or windows to the left and right of the driver with any material other than safety glazing material.

(Amended by Stats. 1976, Ch. 900.)

26704. Wherever the term "safety glazing material" is used in this article, it means safety glazing material of a type meeting requirements established by the department.

(Repealed and added by Stats. 1979, Ch. 723.)

26705. On or after January 1, 1969, no person shall sell or offer for sale for use upon or as part of the equipment of a motorcycle any motorcycle windshield unless the glazing material used therein is safety glazing material.

(Repealed and added by Stats. 1968, Ch. 1469.)

26706. (a) Every motor vehicle, except motorcycles, equipped with a windshield shall also be equipped with a self-operating windshield wiper.

(b) Every new motor vehicle first registered after December 31, 1949, except motorcycles, shall be equipped with two windshield wipers, one mounted on the right half and one on the left half of the windshield, except that any motor vehicle may be equipped with a single wiper so long as it meets the wiped area requirements in Federal Motor Vehicle Safety Standards Governing Windshield Wiping and Washing Systems.

(c) This section does not apply to snow removal equipment equipped with adequate manually operated windshield wipers.

(d) This section does not apply to an autonomous vehicle, as defined in Section 38750, that is not capable of operation by a human driver seated in the vehicle, provided that this exemption is consistent with, or authorized by, any applicable federal law, regulation, or exemption thereto.

(Amended by Stats. 2021, Ch. 428, Sec. 6. (SB 570) Effective January 1, 2022.)

26707. Windshield wipers required by this code shall be maintained in good operating condition and shall provide clear vision through the windshield for the driver. Wipers shall be operated under conditions of fog, snow, or rain and shall be capable of effectively clearing the windshield under all ordinary storm or load conditions while the vehicle is in operation.

(Enacted by Stats. 1959, Ch. 3.)

26708. (a) (1) A person shall not drive any motor vehicle with any object or material placed, displayed, installed, affixed, or applied upon the windshield or side or rear windows.

(2) A person shall not drive any motor vehicle with any object or material placed, displayed, installed, affixed, or applied in or upon the vehicle that obstructs or reduces the driver's clear view through the windshield or side windows.

(3) This subdivision applies to a person driving a motor vehicle with the driver's clear vision through the windshield, or side or rear windows, obstructed by snow or ice.

(b) This section does not apply to any of the following:

(1) Rearview mirrors.

(2) Adjustable nontransparent sunvisors that are mounted forward of the side windows and are not attached to the glass.

(3) Signs, stickers, or other materials that are displayed in a seven-inch square in the lower corner of the windshield farthest removed from the driver, signs, stickers, or other materials that are displayed in a seven-inch square in the lower corner of the rear window farthest removed from the driver, or signs, stickers, or other materials that are displayed in a five-inch square in the lower corner of the windshield nearest the driver.

(4) Side windows that are to the rear of the driver.

(5) Direction, destination, or terminus signs upon a passenger common carrier motor vehicle or a schoolbus, if those signs do not interfere with the driver's clear view of approaching traffic.

(6) Rear window wiper motor.

(7) Rear trunk lid handle or hinges.

(8) The rear window or windows, if the motor vehicle is equipped with outside mirrors on both the left- and right-hand sides of the vehicle that are so located as to reflect to the driver a view of the highway through each mirror for a distance of at least 200 feet to the rear of the vehicle.

(9) A clear, transparent lens affixed to the side window opposite the driver on a vehicle greater than 80 inches in width and that occupies an area not exceeding 50 square inches of the lowest corner toward the rear of that window and that provides the driver with a wide-angle view through the lens.

(10) Sun screening devices meeting the requirements of Section 26708.2 installed on the side windows on either side of the vehicle's front seat, if the driver or a passenger in the front seat has in their possession a letter or other document signed by a licensed physician and surgeon certifying that the person must be shaded from the sun due to a medical condition, or has in their possession a letter or other document signed by a licensed optometrist certifying that the person must be shaded from the sun due to a visual condition. The devices authorized by this paragraph shall not be used during darkness.

(11) An electronic communication device affixed to the center uppermost portion of the interior of a windshield within an area that is not greater than five inches square, if the device provides either of the following:

(A) The capability for enforcement facilities of the Department of the California Highway Patrol to communicate with a vehicle equipped with the device.

(B) The capability for electronic toll and traffic management on public or private roads or facilities.

(12) A portable Global Positioning System (GPS), which may be mounted in a seven-inch square in the lower corner of the windshield farthest removed from the driver or in a five-inch square in the lower corner of the windshield nearest to the driver and outside of an airbag deployment zone, if the system is used only for door-to-door navigation while the motor vehicle is being operated.

(13) (A) A video event recorder with the capability of monitoring driver performance to improve driver safety, which may be mounted in a seven-inch square in the lower corner of the windshield farthest removed from the driver, in a five-inch square in the lower corner of the windshield nearest to the driver and outside of an airbag deployment zone, or in a five-inch square mounted to the center uppermost portion of the interior of the windshield. As used in this section, "video event recorder" means a video recorder that continuously records in a digital loop, recording audio, video, and G-force levels, but saves video only when triggered by an unusual motion or crash or when operated by the driver to monitor driver performance.

(B) A vehicle equipped with a video event recorder shall have a notice posted in a visible location which states that a passenger's conversation may be recorded.

(C) Video event recorders shall store no more than 30 seconds before and after a triggering event.

(D) The registered owner or lessee of the vehicle may disable the device.

(E) The data recorded to the device is the property of the registered owner or lessee of the vehicle.

(F) When a person is driving for hire as an employee in a vehicle with a video event recorder, the person's employer shall provide unedited copies of the recordings upon the request of the employee or the employee's representative. These copies shall be provided free of charge to the employee and within five days of the request.

(14) Vehicle safety technology, as defined in Section 393.5 of Title 49 of the Code of Federal Regulations, installed on any vehicle listed in Section 34500 and subject to Section 34500.7 that is otherwise in compliance with Section 393.60 of Title 49 of the Code of Federal Regulations.

(c) Notwithstanding subdivision (a), transparent material may be installed, affixed, or applied to the topmost portion of the windshield if the following conditions apply:

(1) The bottom edge of the material is at least 29 inches above the undepressed driver's seat when measured from a point five inches in front of the bottom of the backrest with the driver's seat in its rearmost and lowermost position with the vehicle on a level surface.

(2) The material is not red or amber in color.

(3) There is no opaque lettering on the material and any other lettering does not affect primary colors or distort vision through the windshield.

(4) The material does not reflect sunlight or headlight glare into the eyes of occupants of oncoming or following vehicles to any greater extent than the windshield without the material.

(d) Notwithstanding subdivision (a), clear, colorless, and transparent material may be installed, affixed, or applied to the front side windows, located to the immediate left and right of the front seat if the following conditions are met:

(1) The material has a minimum visible light transmittance of 88 percent.

(2) The window glazing with the material applied meets all requirements of Federal Motor Vehicle Safety Standard No. 205 (49 C.F.R. 571.205), including the specified minimum light transmittance of 70 percent and the abrasion resistance of AS–14 glazing, as specified in that federal standard.

(3) The material is designed and manufactured to enhance the ability of the existing window glass to block the sun's harmful ultraviolet A rays.

(4) The driver has in their possession, or within the vehicle, a certificate signed by the installing company certifying that the windows with the material installed meet the requirements of this subdivision and the certificate identifies the installing company and the material's manufacturer by full name and street address, or, if the material was installed by the vehicle owner, a certificate signed by the material's manufacturer certifying that the windows with the material installed according to manufacturer's instructions meet the requirements of this subdivision and the certificate identifies the material's manufacturer by full name and street address.

(5) If the material described in this subdivision tears or bubbles, or is

otherwise worn to prohibit clear vision, it shall be removed or replaced.

(e) Notwithstanding subdivision (a), clear, colorless, and transparent material may be installed, affixed, or applied to the windshield, side, or rear windows of a motor vehicle if the following conditions are met:

(1) The material has a minimum visible light transmittance of 88 percent.

(2) The window glazing with the material applied meets all requirements of Federal Motor Vehicle Safety Standard No. 205 (49 C.F.R. 571.205), including the specified minimum light transmittance of 70 percent and the abrasion resistance of AS–14 glazing, as specified in that federal standard.

(3) The material is designed and manufactured to enhance the ability of the existing window glass to block the sun's harmful ultraviolet A rays.

(4) The driver has in their possession, or within the vehicle, a certificate signed by a licensed dermatologist certifying that the person should not be exposed to ultraviolet rays because of a medical condition that necessitates clear, colorless, and transparent film material to be installed on the windshield, side, or rear windows.

(5) If the material described in this subdivision tears or bubbles, or is otherwise worn to prohibit clear vision, it shall be removed or replaced.

(Amended by Stats. 2025, Ch. 417, Sec. 5. (SB 506) Effective January 1, 2026.)

26708.2. Sun screening devices permitted by paragraph (10) of subdivision (b) of Section 26708 shall meet the following requirements:

(a) The devices shall be held in place by means allowing ready removal from the window area, such as a frame, a rigid material with temporary fasteners, or a flexible roller shade.

(b) Devices utilizing transparent material shall be green, gray, or a neutral smoke in color and shall have a luminous transmittance of not less than 35 percent.

(c) Devices utilizing nontransparent louvers or other alternating patterns of opaque and open sections shall have an essentially uniform pattern over the entire surface, except for framing and supports. At least 35 percent of the device area shall be open and no individual louver or opaque section shall have a projected vertical dimension exceeding 3/16 inch.

(d) The devices shall not have a reflective quality exceeding 35 percent on either the inner or outer surface.

(Added by Stats. 1984, Ch. 74, Sec. 2.)

26708.5. (a) No person shall place, install, affix, or apply any transparent material upon the windshield, or side or rear windows, of any motor vehicle if the material alters the color or reduces the light transmittance of the windshield or side or rear windows, except as provided in subdivision (b), (c), or (d) of Section 26708.

(b) Tinted safety glass may be installed in a vehicle if (1) the glass complies with motor vehicle safety standards of the United States Department of Transportation for safety glazing materials, and (2) the glass is installed in a location permitted by those standards for the particular type of glass used.

(Amended by Stats. 1998, Ch. 476, Sec. 2. Effective January 1, 1999.)

26708.7. Notwithstanding any other law, a vehicle operated and owned or leased by a federal, state, or local agency, department, or district, that employs peace officers, as defined by Chapter 4.5 (commencing with Section 830) of Title 3 of Part 2 of the Penal Code, for use by those peace officers in the performance of their duties, is exempt from California law, and regulations adopted pursuant thereto, prohibiting or limiting material that may be placed, displayed, installed, affixed, or applied to the side or rear windows, commonly referred to as window tinting or glazing.

(Added by Stats. 2012, Ch. 171, Sec. 1. (AB 2660) Effective January 1, 2013.)

26709. (a) (1) Every motor vehicle registered in a foreign jurisdiction and every motorcycle subject to registration in this state shall be equipped with a mirror so located as to reflect to the driver a view of the highway for a distance of at least 200 feet to the rear of such vehicle.

(2) Every motor vehicle subject to registration in this state, except a motorcycle, shall be equipped with not less than two mirrors, including one affixed to the left-hand side.

(b) The following described types of motor vehicles, of a type subject to registration, shall be equipped with mirrors on both the left- and right-hand sides of the vehicle so located as to reflect to the driver a view of the highway through each mirror for a distance of at least 200 feet to the rear of such vehicle:

(1) A motor vehicle so constructed or loaded as to obstruct the driver's view to the rear.

(2) A motor vehicle towing a vehicle and the towed vehicle or load thereon obstructs the driver's view to the rear.

(3) A bus or trolley coach.

(c) The provisions of subdivision (b) shall not apply to a passenger vehicle when the load obstructing the driver's view consists of passengers.

(d) This section does not apply to an autonomous vehicle, as defined in Section 38750, that is not capable of operation by a human driver seated in the vehicle, provided that this exemption is consistent with, or authorized by, any applicable federal law, regulation, or exemption thereto.

(Amended by Stats. 2021, Ch. 428, Sec. 7. (SB 570) Effective January 1, 2022.)

26710. (a) It is unlawful to operate any motor vehicle upon a highway when the windshield or rear window is in such a defective condition as to impair the driver's vision either to the front or rear.

(b) Notwithstanding subdivision (a), it is unlawful to operate any motor vehicle described in Section 34500 upon a highway when the condition of the windshield is other than described in Section 393.60(c) of Title 49 of the Code of Federal Regulations.

(c) In the event any windshield or rear window fails to comply with this code the officer making the inspection shall direct the driver to make the windshield and rear window conform to the requirements of this code within 48 hours. The officer may also arrest the driver and give them notice to appear and further require the driver or the owner of the vehicle to produce in court satisfactory evidence that the windshield or rear window has been made to conform to the requirements of this code.

(Amended by Stats. 2022, Ch. 295, Sec. 16. (AB 2956) Effective January 1, 2023.)

26711. Every bus or trolley coach, except those first registered prior to January 1, 1960, and engaged in urban and suburban service as defined in Section 35107, shall be equipped with movable eyeshades of sufficient size to shade the eyes of the operator of a bus or trolley coach while it is being driven facing the sun.

(Amended by Stats. 1963, Ch. 661.)

26712. (a) Every passenger vehicle used or maintained for the transportation of persons for hire, compensation, or profit shall be equipped with a defrosting device that is adequate to remove snow, ice, frost, fog, or internal moisture from the windshield.

(b) This section does not apply to an autonomous vehicle, as defined in Section 38750, that is not capable of operation by a human driver seated in the vehicle, provided that this exemption is consistent with, or authorized by, any applicable federal law, regulation, or exemption thereto.

(Amended by Stats. 2021, Ch. 428, Sec. 8. (SB 570) Effective January 1, 2022.)

Chapter 5. Other Equipment

(Chapter 5 enacted by Stats. 1959, Ch. 3.)

Article 1. Horns, Sirens and Amplification Devices

(Heading of Article 1 amended by Stats. 1978, Ch. 1306.)

27000. (a) A motor vehicle, when operated upon a highway, shall be equipped with a horn in good working order and capable of emitting sound audible under normal conditions from a distance of not less than 200 feet, but no horn shall emit an unreasonably loud or harsh sound. An authorized emergency vehicle may be equipped with, and use in conjunction with the siren on that vehicle, an air horn that emits sounds that do not comply with the requirements of this section.

(b) A refuse or garbage truck shall be equipped with an automatic backup audible alarm that sounds on backing and is capable of emitting sound audible under normal conditions from a distance of not less than 100 feet or shall be equipped with an automatic backup device that is in good working order, located at the rear of the vehicle and that immediately applies the service brake of the vehicle on contact by the vehicle with any obstruction to the rear. The backup device or alarm shall also be capable of operating automatically when the vehicle is in neutral or a forward gear but rolls backward.

(c) A refuse or garbage truck, except a vehicle, known as a rolloff vehicle, that is used for the express purpose of transporting waste containers such as open boxes or compactors, purchased after January 1, 2010, shall also be equipped with a functioning camera providing a video display for the driver that enhances or supplements the driver's view behind the truck for the purpose of safely maneuvering the truck.

(d) (1) A construction vehicle with a gross vehicle weight rating (GVWR) in excess of 14,000 pounds that operates at, or transports construction or industrial materials to and from, a mine or construction site, or both, shall be equipped with an automatic backup audible alarm that sounds on backing and is capable of emitting sound audible under normal conditions from a distance of not less than 200 feet.

(2) As used in this subdivision, "construction vehicle" includes, but is not limited to, all of the following:

(A) A vehicle designed to transport concrete, cement, clay, limestone, aggregate material as defined in subdivision (d) of Section 23114, or other similar construction or industrial material, including a transfer truck or a tractor trailer combination used exclusively to pull bottom dump, end dump, or side dump trailers.

(B) A vehicle that is a concrete mixer truck, a truck with a concrete placing boom, a water tank truck, a single engine crane with a load rating of 35 tons or more, or a tractor that exclusively pulls a low-boy trailer.

(Amended by Stats. 2011, Ch. 235, Sec. 1. (SB 341) Effective January 1, 2012.)

27001. (a) The driver of a motor vehicle when reasonably necessary to insure safe operation shall give audible warning with his horn.

(b) The horn shall not otherwise be used, except as a theft alarm system which operates as specified in Article 13 (commencing with Section 28085) of this chapter.

(Amended by Stats. 1977, Ch. 993.)

27002. (a) No vehicle, except an authorized emergency vehicle, shall be equipped with, nor shall any person use upon a vehicle any siren except that an authorized emergency vehicle shall be equipped with a siren meeting requirements established by the department.

(b) An authorized emergency vehicle may also be equipped with a Hi-Lo audible warning sound meeting requirements established by the department.

(c) A Hi-Lo warning sound may only be used to notify the public of an immediate evacuation in case of an emergency and is not a siren. For the purposes of Section 21055, a Hi-Lo shall not be used in lieu of a siren if the sounding of a siren is reasonably necessary pursuant to that section.

(Amended by Stats. 2020, Ch. 262, Sec. 1. (SB 909) Effective September 29, 2020.)

27003. An armored car may be equipped with a siren which may be used while resisting armed robbery. At all other times, the siren shall not be sounded. The authority to use a siren granted by this section does not constitute an armored car an authorized emergency vehicle, and all other provisions of this code applicable to drivers of vehicles apply to drivers of armored cars.

(Enacted by Stats. 1959, Ch. 3.)

27007. No driver of a vehicle shall operate, or permit the operation of, any sound amplification system which can be heard outside the vehicle from 50 or more feet when the vehicle is being operated upon a highway, unless that system is being operated to request assistance or warn of a hazardous situation.

This section does not apply to authorized emergency vehicles or vehicles operated by gas, electric, communications, or water utilities. This section does not apply to the sound systems of vehicles used for advertising, or in parades, political or other special events, except that the use of sound systems on those vehicles may be prohibited by a local authority by ordinance or resolution.

(Amended by Stats. 1989, Ch. 538, Sec. 1.)

Article 2. Exhaust Systems

(Article 2 enacted by Stats. 1959, Ch. 3.)

27150. (a) Every motor vehicle equipped with an internal combustion engine and subject to registration shall at all times be equipped with an adequate muffler in constant operation and properly maintained to prevent any excessive or unusual noise, and no muffler or exhaust system shall be equipped with a cutout, bypass, or similar device.

(b) Except as provided in Division 16.5 (commencing with Section 38000) with respect to off-highway motor vehicles subject to identification, every passenger vehicle operated off the highways shall at all times be equipped with an adequate muffler in constant operation and properly maintained so as to meet the requirements of Article 2.5 (commencing with Section 27200), and no muffler or exhaust system shall be equipped with a cutout, bypass, or similar device.

(c) The provisions of subdivision (b) shall not be applicable to passenger vehicles being operated off the highways in an organized racing or competitive event conducted under the auspices of a recognized sanctioning body or by permit issued by the local governmental authority having jurisdiction, or to vehicles not equipped with an internal combustion engine.

(Amended by Stats. 2021, Ch. 428, Sec. 9. (SB 570) Effective January 1, 2022.)

27150.1. No person engaged in a business that involves the selling of motor vehicle exhaust systems, or parts thereof, including, but not limited to, mufflers, shall offer for sale, sell, or install, a motor vehicle exhaust system, or part thereof, including, but not limited to, a muffler, unless it meets the regulations and standards applicable pursuant to this article. Motor vehicle exhaust systems or parts thereof include, but are not limited to, nonoriginal exhaust equipment.

A violation of this section is a misdemeanor.

(Amended by Stats. 2002, Ch. 569, Sec. 2. Effective January 1, 2003.)

27150.2. (a) Stations providing referee functions pursuant to Section 44036 of the Health and Safety Code shall provide for the testing of vehicular exhaust systems and the issuance of certificates of compliance only for those vehicles that have received a citation for a violation of Section 27150 or 27151.

(b) A certificate of compliance for a vehicular exhaust system shall be issued pursuant to subdivision (a) if the vehicle complies with Sections 27150 and 27151. Exhaust systems installed on motor vehicles, other than motorcycles, with a manufacturer's gross vehicle weight rating of less than 6,000 pounds comply with Sections 27150 and 27151 if they emit no more than 95 dbA when tested in accordance with the most current SAE International standard.

(c) An exhaust system certificate of compliance issued pursuant to subdivision (a) shall identify, to the extent possible, the make, model, year, license number, and vehicle identification number of the vehicle tested, and the make and model of the exhaust system installed on the vehicle.

(d) The station shall charge a fee for the exhaust system certificate of compliance issued pursuant to subdivision (a). The fee charged shall be calculated to recover the costs incurred by the Department of Consumer Affairs to implement this section. The fees charged by the station shall be deposited in the Vehicle Inspection and Repair Fund established by Section 44062 of the Health and Safety Code.

(e) Vehicular exhaust systems are exempt from the requirements of Sections 27150 and 27151 if compliance with those sections, or the regulations adopted pursuant thereto, would cause an unreasonable hardship without resulting in a sufficient corresponding benefit with respect to noise level control.

(f) This section shall remain in effect only until January 1, 2027, and as of that date is repealed.

(Amended by Stats. 2022, Ch. 595, Sec. 1. (AB 2496) Effective January 1, 2023. Repealed as of January 1, 2027, by its own provisions. See later operative version added by Sec. 2 of Stats. 2022, Ch. 595.)

27150.2. (a) Stations providing referee functions pursuant to Section 44036 of the Health and Safety Code shall provide for the testing of exhaust systems of motor vehicles, including motorcycles, and the issuance of certificates of compliance in accordance with Section 27151.1 only for those vehicles that have received a citation for a violation of Section 27150, 27150.3, or 27151.

(b) (1) A certificate of compliance for an exhaust system of a motor vehicle, including motorcycles, with a manufacturer's gross vehicle weight rating up to 14,000 pounds shall be issued pursuant to subdivision (a) if the vehicle complies with Sections 27150, 27150.3, and 27151.

(2) Exhaust systems installed on motor vehicles with a manufacturer's gross vehicle weight rating less than 6,000 pounds comply with this subdivision if they emit no more than 95 dbA when tested in accordance with the most current SAE International standard.

(3) Exhaust systems installed on motor vehicles with a manufacturer's gross vehicle weight rating between 6,000 and 14,000 pounds comply with this subdivision if they emit no more than the decibel limits set in Section 27204 when tested in accordance with the most current SAE International standard.

(c) An exhaust system certificate of compliance issued pursuant to subdivision (a) shall identify, to the extent possible, the make, model, year, license number, and vehicle identification number of the vehicle tested, and the make and model of the exhaust system installed on the vehicle.

(d) The station shall charge a fee for the exhaust system certificate of compliance issued pursuant to subdivision (a). The fee charged shall be calculated to recover the costs incurred by the Department of Consumer Affairs to implement this section. The fees charged by the station shall be deposited in the Vehicle Inspection and Repair Fund established by Section 44062 of the Health and Safety Code.

(e) Vehicular exhaust systems are exempt from the requirements of Sections 27150 and 27151 if compliance with those sections, or the regulations adopted pursuant thereto, would cause an unreasonable hardship without resulting in a sufficient corresponding benefit with respect to noise level control.

(f) This section shall become operative on January 1, 2027.

(Repealed (in Sec. 1) and added by Stats. 2022, Ch. 595, Sec. 2. (AB 2496) Effective January 1, 2023. Operative January 1, 2027, by its own provisions.)

27150.3. (a) A person may not modify the exhaust system of a motor vehicle with a whistle-tip.

(b) A person may not operate a motor vehicle if that vehicle's exhaust system is modified in violation of subdivision (a).

(c) A person may not engage in the business of installing a whistle-tip onto a motor vehicle's exhaust system.

(d) For purposes of subdivisions (a) and (c), a "whistle-tip" is a device that is applied to, or is a modification of, a motor vehicle's exhaust pipe for the sole purpose of creating a high-pitched or shrieking noise when the motor vehicle is operated.

(Added by Stats. 2003, Ch. 432, Sec. 1. Effective January 1, 2004.)

27150.4. (a) The Department of the California Highway Patrol shall evaluate the efficacy of sound-activated enforcement devices by evaluating devices from at least three different companies.

(b) (1) On or before January 1, 2025, the department shall prepare and submit its findings and recommendations from the evaluation in a report to the Legislature, which shall include all of the following information:

(A) How effective the devices are at determining that a vehicle was not equipped with an adequate muffler in constant operation and properly maintained in accordance with the requirements of Article 2.5 (commencing with Section 27200).

(B) How often the device identified a potential violation that was not related to a violation of Section 27150, and the types of sounds other than a loud muffler that triggered the device.

(C) What percentage of time an officer was unable to determine the source of the sound that activated the device.

(D) How often the device was required to be serviced.

(E) What, if any, technology does the sound-activated enforcement system use to determine the direction or source of the sound that violated the sound limits provided for in Article 2.5 (commencing with Section 27200).

(F) Where the devices were located, and whether the location had any consequences to the effectiveness of the device.

(G) The number of devices the department tested and from which companies were the devices that were tested.

(H) Recommendations on all of the following:

(i) Which, if any, device or devices would the department recommend be used for the purposes of enforcing Sections 27150 and 27151, and the reasons for that determination. If the department determines that it does not recommend any of the devices tested, the report shall include the standards and parameters that shall be met by future technology.

(ii) What, if any, restrictions should be placed on the use of sound-activated enforcement devices in enforcing Sections 27150 and 27151, including, but not limited to, the decibel level setting for triggering a potential violation for the purposes of enforcement.

(iii) Where the devices should be optimally located in order to reduce the chances of a false violation.

(iv) Descriptions and explanation of any necessary and associated training that an individual reviewing these violations would need to go through in order to operate the device, including recommendations for what is necessary for a robust human review process.

(v) Any other recommendations the department believes would be necessary for authorizing the use of sound-activated enforcement devices.

(I) A video demonstrating the device. The video shall be edited to remove any personally identifying information, including the blurring of persons recorded in the video, street addresses, and license plates.

(2) The report required by this subdivision shall be submitted in compliance with Section 9795 of the Government Code.

(c) The department shall delete all videos recorded on a highway by a device within five days of the video being recorded. However, the department shall keep 15 videos from the devices of each company evaluated for the purposes of preparing the report required by this section and documenting the issues related to each device that helped the department make its recommendations. The department shall not keep any recording that picked up audio of a person speaking, if recorded on a highway.

(d) Notwithstanding Division 10 (commencing with Section 7920.000) of Title 1 of the Government Code, or any other law, information collected and maintained by the department using a sound-activated enforcement device that could be used to identify the identity or location of any individual shall be confidential and only be used for purposes of this section, and shall not be disclosed to any other persons, including, but not limited to, any other state or federal government agency or official for any other purpose, except as required by the reporting requirements in this section, state or federal law, court order, or in response to a subpoena in an individual case or proceeding.

(e) For purposes of this section, "sound-activated enforcement device" or "device" means an electronic device that utilizes automated equipment that activates when the noise levels have exceeded the legal sound limit established in Section 27151 and is designed to obtain clear video of a vehicle and its license plate. A sound-activated enforcement device shall do all of the following:

(1) Record audio, precision accuracy noise levels, and high definition video in two directions.

(2) Utilize an automated system that triggers when excessive vehicle noise over the limit is detected and save the data for review.

(3) Automatically delete any evidence not related to a violation.

(4) Permit the department to manually review evidence to ensure a violation has occurred.

(5) Conform to the class 1 accuracy standards in the International Electrotechnical Commission's (IEC) standard IEC 61672:2013, or any other accuracy standard determined to be appropriate by the department.

(Added by Stats. 2022, Ch. 449, Sec. 1. (SB 1079) Effective January 1, 2023.)

27150.5. Any person holding a retail seller's permit who sells or installs an exhaust system, or part thereof, including, but not limited to, a muffler, in violation of Section 27150.1 or 27150.2 or the regulations adopted pursuant thereto, shall thereafter be required to install an exhaust system, or part thereof, including, but not limited to, a muffler, which is in compliance with such regulations upon demand of the purchaser or registered owner of the vehicle concerned, or to reimburse the purchaser or registered owner for the expense of replacement and installation of an exhaust system, or part thereof, including, but not limited to, a muffler, which is in compliance, at the election of such purchaser or registered owner.

(Added by Stats. 1971, Ch. 1769.)

27150.7. A court may dismiss any action in which a person is prosecuted for operating a vehicle in violation of Section 27150 or 27151 if a certificate of compliance has been issued by a station pursuant to Section 27150.2, or if the defendant had reasonable grounds to believe that the exhaust system was in good working order and had reasonable grounds to believe that the vehicle was not operated in violation of Section 27150 or 27151.

(Amended by Stats. 2002, Ch. 569, Sec. 4. Effective January 1, 2003.)

27151. (a) A person shall not modify the exhaust system of a motor vehicle in a manner which will amplify or increase the noise emitted by the motor of the vehicle so that the vehicle is not in compliance with the provisions of Section 27150 or exceeds the noise limits established for the type of vehicle in Article 2.5 (commencing with Section 27200). A person shall not operate a motor vehicle with an exhaust system so modified.

(b) For the purposes of exhaust systems installed on motor vehicles with a manufacturer's gross vehicle weight rating of less than 6,000 pounds, other than motorcycles, a sound level of 95 dbA or less, when tested in accordance with the most current SAE International standard, complies with this section. Motor vehicle exhaust systems or parts thereof include, but are not limited to, nonoriginal exhaust equipment.

(Amended by Stats. 2022, Ch. 295, Sec. 18. (AB 2956) Effective January 1, 2023.)

27151.1. (a) For a violation of Section 27150.3 or 27151 of a vehicle under 14,000 pounds gross vehicle weight rating, a court shall require a certificate of compliance for a vehicular exhaust system in compliance with subdivision (b) of Section 27150.2. A court shall utilize the notification procedures set forth in Section 40002. If a certificate of compliance is not provided to the court within three months of the violation date, the court shall treat this failure as noncompliance pursuant to subdivision (c) of Section 40002 and follow the provisions of Section 40002.1 to inform the Department of Motor Vehicles.

(b) The department shall, before renewing the registration of any vehicle, check to see whether the court has issued a hold on the vehicle registration for a violation of Section 27150.3 or 27151, and shall refuse to renew the registration until it has received a notification from the court that a certificate of compliance has been issued.

(c) This section shall become operative on January 1, 2027.

(Added by Stats. 2022, Ch. 595, Sec. 3. (AB 2496) Effective January 1, 2023. Operative January 1, 2027, by its own provisions.)

27152. The exhaust gases from a motor vehicle shall not be directed to the side of the vehicle between 2 feet and 11 feet above the ground.

(Enacted by Stats. 1959, Ch. 3.)

27153. (a) A motor vehicle shall not be operated in a manner resulting in the escape of excessive smoke, flame, gas, oil, or fuel residue.

(b) A nongasoline heavy-duty onroad motor vehicle with a gross vehicle weight rating of more than 14,000 pounds shall not be operated in a manner resulting in the escape of visible smoke, except during active regeneration.

(c) (1) A violation of this section is a correctable violation pursuant to Article 4 (commencing with Section 40610) of Chapter 2 of Division 17. Except as provided in paragraph (2) and subdivision (d), an owner or operator of a vehicle found to be in violation of this section shall have 45 days to correct the violation and the vehicle shall not be prohibited from being used during this time.

(2) Except as provided in subdivision (d), an owner or operator of a vehicle that is used exclusively in the conduct of agricultural operations and that is found to be in violation of this section shall have a time period determined by the State Air Resources Board that is not less than 75 days from the date of the citation to correct the violation and the vehicle shall not be prohibited from being used during that time.

(d) Notwithstanding subdivision (c), a vehicle found to have willfully tampered emission controls, including the vehicle's onboard diagnostics system, shall not be operated.

(e) This section applies to motor vehicles of the United States or its agencies, to the extent authorized by federal law.

(Amended by Stats. 2019, Ch. 298, Sec. 6. (SB 210) Effective January 1, 2020.)

27153.5. (a) No motor vehicle first sold or registered as a new motor vehicle on or after January 1, 1971, shall discharge into the atmosphere at elevation of less than 4,000 feet any air contaminant for a period of more than 10 seconds which is:

(1) As dark or darker in shade as that designated as No. 1 on the Ringelmann Chart, as published by the United States Bureau of Mines, or

(2) Of such opacity as to obscure an observer's view to a degree equal to or greater than does smoke described in paragraph (1) of this subdivision.

(b) No motor vehicle first sold or registered prior to January 1, 1971, shall discharge into the atmosphere at elevation of less than 4,000 feet any air contaminant for a period of more than 10 seconds which is:

(1) As dark or darker in shade than that designated as No. 2 on the Ringelmann Chart, as published by the United States Bureau of Mines, or

(2) Of such opacity as to obscure an observer's view to a degree equal to or greater than does smoke described in paragraph (1) of this subdivision.

(c) The provisions of this section apply to motor vehicles of the United States or its agencies, to the extent authorized by federal law.

(Amended by Stats. 1973, Ch. 216.)

27154. The cab of any motor vehicle shall be reasonably tight against the penetration of gases and fumes from the engine or exhaust system. The exhaust system, including the manifold, muffler, and exhaust pipes shall be so constructed as to be capable of being maintained and shall be maintained in a reasonably gastight condition.

(Enacted by Stats. 1959, Ch. 3.)

27154.1. (a) The flooring in all motor vehicles shall be substantially constructed, free of unnecessary holes and openings and shall be maintained so as to minimize the entrance of fumes, exhaust gases, or fire.

(b) Floors shall not be permeated with oil or other substances likely to cause injury to persons using the floor as a traction surface.

(Added by Stats. 2015, Ch. 451, Sec. 54. (SB 491) Effective January 1, 2016.)

27155. No motor vehicle shall be operated or parked upon any highway unless the filling spout for the fuel tank is closed by a cap or cover of noncombustible material.

(Amended by Stats. 1965, Ch. 453.)

27156. (a) No person shall operate or leave standing upon a highway a motor vehicle that is a gross polluter, as defined in Section 39032.5 of the Health and Safety Code.

(b) No person shall operate or leave standing upon a highway a motor vehicle that is required to be equipped with a motor vehicle pollution control device under Part 5 (commencing with Section 43000) of Division 26 of the Health and Safety Code or any other certified motor vehicle pollution control device required by any other state law or any rule or regulation adopted pursuant to that law, or required to be equipped with a motor vehicle pollution control device pursuant to the National Emission Standards Act (42 U.S.C. Secs. 7521 to 7550, inclusive) and the standards and regulations adopted pursuant to that federal act, unless the motor vehicle is equipped with the required motor vehicle pollution control device that is correctly installed and in operating condition. No person shall disconnect, modify, or alter any such required device.

(c) No person shall install, sell, offer for sale, or advertise any device, apparatus, or mechanism intended for use with, or as a part of, a required motor vehicle pollution control device or system that alters or modifies the original design or performance of the motor vehicle pollution control device or system.

(d) If the court finds that a person has willfully violated this section, the court shall impose the maximum fine that may be imposed in the case, and no part of the fine may be suspended.

(e) "Willfully," as used in this section, has the same meaning as the meaning of that word prescribed in Section 7 of the Penal Code.

(f) No person shall operate a vehicle after notice by a traffic officer that the vehicle is not equipped with the required certified motor vehicle pollution control device correctly installed in operating condition, except as may be necessary to return the vehicle to the residence or place of business of the owner or driver or to a garage, until the vehicle has been properly equipped with such a device.

(g) The notice to appear issued or complaint filed for a violation of this section shall require that the person to whom the notice to appear is issued, or against whom the complaint is filed, produce proof of correction pursuant to Section 40150 or proof of exemption pursuant to Section 4000.1 or 4000.2.

(h) This section shall not apply to an alteration, modification, or modifying device, apparatus, or mechanism found by resolution of the State Air Resources Board to do either of the following:

(1) Not to reduce the effectiveness of a required motor vehicle pollution control device.

(2) To result in emissions from the modified or altered vehicle that are at levels that comply with existing state or federal standards for that model-year of the vehicle being modified or converted.

(i) Aftermarket and performance parts with valid State Air Resources Board Executive Orders may be sold and installed concurrent with a motorcycle's transfer to an ultimate purchaser.

(j) This section applies to motor vehicles of the United States or its agencies, to the extent authorized by federal law.

(Amended by Stats. 2007, Ch. 325, Sec. 1. Effective January 1, 2008.)

27156.1. The installation, prior to January 1, 1974, of an auxiliary gasoline fuel tank for use on a 1973 or earlier model year motor vehicle, which vehicle is required, pursuant to Part 5 (commencing with Section 43000) of Division 26 of the Health and Safety Code or the National Emission Standards Act (42 U.S.C., Secs. 1857f-1 to 1857f-7, inclusive), to be equipped with a fuel system evaporative loss control device, shall not be deemed a violation of Section 27156 of this code. As used in this section, the term "auxiliary gasoline fuel tank," has the same meaning as defined in subdivision (b) of Section 43834 of the Health and Safety Code.

(Amended by Stats. 1975, Ch. 957.)

27156.2. Notwithstanding any other provision of law, any publicly owned authorized emergency vehicle operated by a peace officer, as defined in Section 830 of the Penal Code, any authorized emergency vehicle, as defined in Section 165 and used for fighting fires or responding to emergency fire calls pursuant to paragraph (2) of subdivision (b) or pursuant to subdivision (c) or (d) of that section, and any publicly owned authorized emergency vehicle used by an emergency medical technician-paramedic, as defined in Section 1797.84 of the Health and Safety Code, is exempt from requirements imposed pursuant to California law and the regulations adopted pursuant thereto for motor vehicle pollution control devices.

(Added by Stats. 1981, Ch. 595, Sec. 1.)

27156.3. Notwithstanding any other provision of law, any motor vehicle of mosquito abatement, vector control, or pest abatement districts or agencies, any authorized emergency vehicle as defined in Section 165, except subdivision (f) thereof, and any ambulance used by a private entity under contract with a public agency, is exempt from requirements imposed pursuant to California law and the regulations adopted pursuant thereto for motor vehicle pollution control devices.

(Added by renumbering Section 27156.2 (as added by Stats. 1981, Ch. 669) by Stats. 1982, Ch. 466, Sec. 116.)

27157. The State Air Resources Board, after consultation with, and pursuant to the recommendations of, the commissioner, shall adopt such reasonable regulations as it determines are necessary for the public health and safety regarding the maximum allowable emissions of pollutants from vehicles upon a highway. Such regulations shall apply only to vehicles required by Part 5 (commencing with Section 43000) of Division 26 of the Health and Safety Code or any federal law or regulation to be equipped with devices or systems to control emission of pollutants from the exhaust and shall not be stricter than the emission standards required of that model year motor vehicle when first manufactured.

(Amended by Stats. 1979, Ch. 373.)

27157.5. The State Air Resources Board, after consultation with, and pursuant to the recommendations of, the commissioner, shall adopt such reasonable standards as it determines are necessary for the public health and safety for the emission of air pollutants from the exhaust of motor vehicles of 1955 through 1965 model years. These standards shall be based on the normal emissions of such cars when the timing and carburetor are in proper adjustment and the spark plugs are in proper operating condition.

(Added by Stats. 1971, Ch. 1095.)

27158. After notice by a traffic officer that a vehicle does not comply with any regulation adopted pursuant to Section 27157, no person shall operate, and no owner shall permit the operation of, such vehicle for more than 30 days thereafter unless a certificate of compliance has been issued for such vehicle in accordance with the provisions of Section 9889.18 of the Business and Professions Code or unless the department has checked the vehicle and determined that the vehicle has been made to comply with such regulation adopted pursuant to Section 27157. A certificate of compliance issued for such vehicle shall, for a period of one year from date of issue, constitute proof of compliance with any regulations adopted pursuant to Section 27157 provided that no required pollution control device has been disconnected, modified, or altered or has been adjusted by other than a licensed installer in a licensed motor vehicle pollution control device installation and inspection station subsequent to the issuance of the certificate of compliance. The provisions of this section shall apply to the United States and its agencies to the extent authorized by federal law.

(Amended by Stats. 1974, Ch. 769.)

27158.1. (a) Commencing one year after the effective date of a regulation implementing the Heavy-Duty Vehicle Inspection and Maintenance Program (Chapter 5.5 (commencing with Section 44150) of Part 5 of Division 26 of the Health and Safety Code), a legal owner or registered owner of a nongasoline heavy-duty onroad motor vehicle with a gross vehicle weight rating of more than 14,000 pounds shall maintain a Heavy-Duty Vehicle Inspection and Maintenance Compliance Certificate, as described in Section 44152 of the Health and Safety Code, or a facsimile or electronic copy of that certificate of compliance, with the vehicle for which the certificate is issued.

(b) Subdivision (a) does not apply when a Heavy-Duty Vehicle Inspection and Maintenance Compliance Certificate is necessarily removed from the vehicle for the purpose of renewal or when the vehicle is left unattended.

(c) A violation of this section shall be cited in accordance with Section 40610.

(Added by Stats. 2019, Ch. 298, Sec. 7. (SB 210) Effective January 1, 2020.)

27158.2. (a) The driver of a nongasoline heavy-duty onroad motor vehicle with a gross vehicle weight rating of more than 14,000 pounds shall present a Heavy-Duty Vehicle Inspection and Maintenance Compliance Certificate, as described in Section 44152 of the Health and Safety Code, or other evidence of that certificate of compliance, of the vehicle under the driver's immediate control for examination upon demand by any peace officer.

(b) The driver of the vehicle described in subdivision (a) shall not present to any peace officer a Heavy-Duty Vehicle Inspection and Maintenance Compliance Certificate not issued for that vehicle.

(Added by Stats. 2019, Ch. 298, Sec. 8. (SB 210) Effective January 1, 2020.)

27158.5. After notice by a traffic officer that a motor vehicle does not comply with any standard adopted pursuant to Section 27157.5, no person shall operate, and no owner shall permit the operation of, such motor vehicle for more than 30 days thereafter unless a certificate of compliance has been issued for such vehicle in accordance with the provisions of Section 9889.18 of the Business and Professions Code or unless the department has checked the vehicle and determined that the vehicle has been made to comply with such standard adopted pursuant to Section 27157.5. A certificate of compliance issued for such vehicle shall, for a period of one year from date of issue, constitute proof of compliance with the standards determined pursuant to Section 27157.5.

(Amended by Stats. 1974, Ch. 769.)

27159. Any uniformed member of the California Highway Patrol may order a vehicle stored when it is located within the territorial limits in which the member may act if requested by a representative of the State Air Resources Board to remove the vehicle from service pursuant to subdivision (f) of Section 44011.6 of the Health and Safety Code. All towing and storage fees for a vehicle removed under this section shall be paid by the owner.

(Added by Stats. 1990, Ch. 1433, Sec. 24.)

Article 2.5. Noise Limits

(Article 2.5 added by Stats. 1975, Ch. 83.)

27200. (a) The Department of Motor Vehicles shall not register on a dealer's report of sale a new motor vehicle, except an off-highway motor vehicle subject to identification as provided in Division 16.5 (commencing with Section 38000), which produces a maximum noise exceeding the applicable noise limit at a distance of 50 feet from the centerline of travel under test procedures established by the Department of the California Highway Patrol.

(b) The Department of Motor Vehicles may accept a dealer's certificate as proof of compliance with this article.

(c) Test procedures for compliance with this article shall be established by the Department of the California Highway Patrol, taking into consideration the test procedures of the Society of Automotive Engineers.

(d) No person shall sell or offer for sale a new motor vehicle, except an off-highway motor vehicle subject to identification as provided in Division 16.5 (commencing with Section 38000), which produces a maximum noise exceeding the applicable noise limit specified in this article, and for which noise emission standards or regulations have not been adopted by the Administrator of the Environmental Protection Agency pursuant to the Noise Control Act of 1972 (P.L. 92-574).

(e) No person shall sell or offer for sale a new motor vehicle, except an off-highway motor vehicle subject to identification as provided in Division 16.5 (commencing with Section 38000), which produces noise that exceeds or in any way violates the noise emission standards or regulations adopted for such a motor vehicle by the Administrator of the Environmental Protection Agency pursuant to the Noise Control Act of 1972 (P.L. 92-574).

(f) As used in this section, the term "register" is equivalent to the term "licensing" as used in Section 6(e)(2) of the Noise Control Act of 1972 (P.L. 92-574; Title 42, United States Code, Section 4905(e)(2)).

(Amended by Stats. 1977, Ch. 558.)

27201. For the purposes of Section 27200, the noise limit of 92 dbA shall apply to any motorcycle manufactured before 1970.

(Added by Stats. 1975, Ch. 83.)

27202. For the purposes of Section 27200, the following noise limits shall apply to any motorcycle, other than a motor-driven cycle, manufactured:

(1) After 1969, and before 1973 .... 88 dbA
(2) After 1972, and before 1975 .... 86 dbA
(3) After 1974, and before 1986 .... 83 dbA
(4) After 1985 .... 80 dbA

(Amended by Stats. 1982, Ch. 356, Sec. 1.)

27202.1. (a) Notwithstanding any other law, a person shall not park, use, or operate a motorcycle, registered in the State of California, that does not bear the required applicable federal Environmental Protection Agency exhaust system label pursuant to Subparts D (commencing with Section 205.150) and E (commencing with Section 205.164) of Part 205 of Title 40 of the Code of Federal Regulations. A violation of this section shall be considered a mechanical violation and a peace officer shall not stop a motorcycle solely on a suspicion of a violation of this section. A peace officer shall cite a violation of this section as a secondary infraction.

(b) A violation of this section is punishable as follows:

(1) For a first conviction, by a fine of not less than fifty dollars ($50), nor more than one hundred dollars ($100).

(2) For a second or subsequent conviction, by a fine of not less than one hundred dollars ($100), nor more than two hundred fifty dollars ($250).

(c) (1) The notice to appear issued or complaint filed for a violation of this section shall require that the person to whom the notice to appear is issued, or against whom the complaint is filed, produce proof of correction pursuant to Section 40150.

(2) Upon producing proof of correction to the satisfaction of the court, the court may dismiss the penalty imposed pursuant to subdivision (b) for a first violation of this section.

(d) (1) This section is applicable to a person operating a motorcycle that is manufactured on or after January 1, 2013, or a motorcycle with aftermarket exhaust system equipment that is manufactured on or after January 1, 2013.

(2) Penalties imposed pursuant to this section are in addition to penalties imposed pursuant to any other applicable laws or regulations.

(3) This section does not supersede, negate, or otherwise alter any other applicable laws or regulations.

(Added by Stats. 2010, Ch. 407, Sec. 1. (SB 435) Effective January 1, 2011.)

27203. For the purposes of Section 27200, the noise limit of 82 dbA shall apply to any snowmobile manufactured after 1972.

(Added by Stats. 1975, Ch. 83.)

27204. For the purposes of Section 27200, the following noise limits shall apply to any motor vehicle within the specified manufacturer's gross vehicle weight rating and date of manufacture:

GVWR—Pounds	Date of Manufacture	Noise Limit (dbA)
Over 6,000	after 1967 and before 1973	88
Over 6,000	after 1972 and before 1975	86
Over 6,000	after 1974 and before 1978	83
Over 8,500	after 1977 and before 1982	83
Over 6,000 but not over 8,500	after 1977	80
Over 8,500 but not over 10,000	after 1981	80
Over 10,000	after 1981 and before 1988	83

GVWR—Pounds	Date of Manufacture	Noise Limit (dbA)
Over 10,000	after 1987	80

(Amended by Stats. 1985, Ch. 274, Sec. 1.)

27206. For the purposes of Section 27200, the following noise limits shall apply to any other motor vehicle, not specified in this article, manufactured:

(1) After 1967, and before 1973 ....86 dbA
(2) After 1972, and before 1975 ....84 dbA
(3) After 1974 ....80 dbA

(Added by renumbering Section 27205 by Stats. 1977, Ch. 558.)

27207. No motor vehicle with a gross vehicle weight rating of more than 10,000 pounds and equipped with an engine speed governor shall produce a sound level exceeding 88 dbA, measured on an open site at a distance of 50 feet from the longitudinal centerline of the vehicle, when its engine is accelerated from idle with wide open throttle to governed speed with the vehicle stationary, transmission in neutral, and clutch, if any, engaged. Test procedures for compliance with this section shall be established by the department, taking into consideration the procedures of the United States Department of Transportation. The procedures may provide for measuring at other distances, in which case the measurement shall be corrected so as to provide for measurements equivalent to the noise limit established by this section measured at 50 feet.

(Amended by Stats. 1996, Ch. 124, Sec. 134. Effective January 1, 1997.)

Article 3. Safety Belts and Inflatable Restraint Systems

(Heading of Article 3 amended by Stats. 1999, Ch. 449, Sec. 1.)

27302. No person shall sell or offer for sale any seatbelt or attachments thereto for use in a vehicle unless it complies with requirements established by the department.

(Amended by Stats. 1979, Ch. 723.)

27304. All vehicles owned and utilized in driver training by a driver training school licensed under the provisions of Chapter 1 (commencing with Section 11100) of Division 5 or in a course in automobile driver training in any secondary school maintained under the Education Code shall be equipped with a seatbelt for the driver and each passenger. Such seatbelt shall comply with requirements established by the department.

It shall be unlawful for any driver or passenger to operate or ride in such a vehicle while it is being operated for the purposes of driver training, unless such person is utilizing an installed seatbelt in the proper manner.

(Amended by Stats. 1979, Ch. 723.)

27305. All publicly owned firefighting vehicles designed for and used in responding to emergency fire calls and in combating fires shall be equipped with seatbelts for each seat utilized by personnel when such vehicles are being operated. Such seatbelts shall comply with requirements established by the department.

(Amended by Stats. 1979, Ch. 723.)

27314. (a) No dealer shall sell or offer for sale any used passenger vehicle that was manufactured on or after January 1, 1962, other than a motorcycle, unless it is equipped with at least two seatbelts which are installed for the use of persons in the front seat of the vehicle.

(b) No dealer shall sell or offer for sale any used passenger vehicle manufactured on or after January 1, 1968, other than a motorcycle, unless it is equipped with seatbelts for each seating position.

(c) Seatbelts required in subdivisions (a) and (b) shall comply with regulations established by the department.

(d) The requirements of this section shall not apply to sales to dealers, automobile dismantlers, or junk dealers.

(Amended by Stats. 1979, Ch. 723.)

27314.5. (a) (1) Subject to paragraph (3), no dealer shall sell or offer for sale any used passenger vehicle of a model year of 1972 to 1990, inclusive, unless there is affixed to the window of the left front door or, if there is no window, to another suitable location so that it may be seen and read by a person standing outside the vehicle at that location, a notice, printed in 14-point type, which reads as follows:

"WARNING: While use of all seat belts reduces the chance of ejection, failure to install and use shoulder harnesses with lap belts can result in serious or fatal injuries in some crashes. Lap-only belts increase the chance of head and neck injury by allowing the upper torso to move unrestrained in a crash and increase the chance of spinal column and abdominal injuries by concentrating excessive force on the lower torso. Because children carry a disproportionate amount of body weight above the waist, they are more likely to sustain those injuries. Shoulder harnesses may be available that can be retrofitted in this vehicle. For more information call the Auto Safety Hotline at 1-800-424-9393."

(2) The notice shall remain affixed to the vehicle pursuant to paragraph (1) at all times that the vehicle is for sale.

(3) The notice is not required to be affixed to any vehicle equipped with both a lap belt and a shoulder harness for the driver and one passenger in the front seat of the vehicle and for at least two passengers in the rear seat of the vehicle.

(b) (1) In addition to the requirements of subdivision (a), and subject to paragraph (3) and subdivision (c), the dealer shall affix, to one rear seat lap belt buckle of every used passenger vehicle of a model year of 1972 to 1990, inclusive, that has a rear seat, a notice, printed in 10-point type, that reads as follows:

"WARNING: While use of all seat belts reduces the chance of ejection, failure to install and use shoulder harnesses with lap belts can result in serious or fatal injuries in some crashes. Shoulder harnesses may be available that can be retrofitted in this vehicle. For more information, call the Auto Safety Hotline at 1-800-424-9393."

(2) The notice shall remain affixed to the vehicle pursuant to paragraph (1) at all times that the vehicle is for sale.

(3) The message is not required to be affixed to any vehicle either equipped with both a lap belt and a shoulder harness for at least two passengers in the rear seat or having no rear seat lap belts.

(c) A dealer is not in violation of subdivision (b) unless a private nonprofit entity has furnished a supply of the appropriate notices suitable for affixing as required free of charge or, having requested a resupply of notices, has not received the resupply.

(d) The department shall furnish, to a nonprofit private entity for purposes of this section, for a fee not to exceed its costs in so furnishing, at least once every six months, a list of all licensed dealers who sell used passenger vehicles.

(Amended by Stats. 1997, Ch. 619, Sec. 11. Effective January 1, 1998.)

27315. (a) The Legislature finds that a mandatory seatbelt law will contribute to reducing highway deaths and injuries by encouraging greater usage of existing manual seatbelts, that automatic crash protection systems that require no action by vehicle occupants offer the best hope of reducing deaths and injuries, and that encouraging the use of manual safety belts is only a partial remedy for addressing this major cause of death and injury. The Legislature declares that the enactment of this section is intended to be compatible with support for federal motor vehicle safety standards requiring automatic crash protection systems and should not be used in any manner to rescind federal requirements for installation of automatic restraints in new cars.

(b) This section shall be known and may be cited as the Motor Vehicle Safety Act.

(c) (1) As used in this section, "motor vehicle" means a passenger vehicle, a motortruck, or a truck tractor, but does not include a motorcycle.

(2) For purposes of this section, a "motor vehicle" also means a farm labor vehicle, regardless of the date of certification under Section 31401.

(d) (1) A person shall not operate a motor vehicle on a highway unless that person and all passengers 16 years of age or over are properly restrained by a safety belt. This paragraph does not apply to the operator of a taxicab, as defined in Section 27908, when the taxicab is driven on a city street and is engaged in the transportation of a fare-paying passenger. The safety belt requirement established by this paragraph is the minimum safety standard applicable to employees being transported in a motor vehicle. This paragraph does not preempt more stringent or restrictive standards imposed by the Labor Code or another state or federal regulation regarding the transportation of employees in a motor vehicle.

(2) For purposes of this section the phrase, "properly restrained by a safety belt" means that the lower (lap) portion of the belt crosses the hips or upper thighs of the occupant and the upper (shoulder) portion of the belt, if present, crosses the chest in front of the occupant.

(3) The operator of a limousine for hire or the operator of an authorized emergency vehicle, as defined in subdivision (a) of Section 165, shall not operate the limousine for hire or authorized emergency vehicle unless the operator and any passengers eight years of age or over in the front seat, are properly restrained by a safety belt.

(4) The operator of a taxicab shall not operate the taxicab unless any passengers eight years of age or over in the front seat, are properly restrained by a safety belt.

(e) A person 16 years of age or over shall not be a passenger in a motor vehicle on a highway unless that person is properly restrained by a safety belt. This subdivision does not apply to a passenger in a sleeper berth, as defined in subdivision (x) of Section 1201 of Title 13 of the California Code of Regulations.

(f) An owner of a motor vehicle, including an owner or operator of a taxicab, as defined in Section 27908, or a limousine for hire, operated on a highway shall maintain safety belts in good working order for the use of the occupants of the vehicle. The safety belts shall conform to motor vehicle safety standards established by the United States Department of Transportation. This subdivision, however, does not require installation or maintenance of safety belts if it is not required by the laws of the United States applicable to the vehicle at the time of its initial sale.

(g) This section does not apply to a passenger or operator with a physically disabling condition or medical condition that would prevent appropriate restraint in a safety belt, if the condition is duly certified by a licensed physician and surgeon or by a licensed chiropractor who shall state the nature of the condition, as well as the reason the restraint is inappropriate. This section also does not apply to a public employee, if the public employee is in an authorized emergency vehicle as defined in paragraph (1) of subdivision (b) of Section 165, or to a passenger in a seat behind the front seat of an authorized emergency vehicle as defined in paragraph (1) of subdivision (b) of Section 165 operated by the public employee, unless required by the agency employing the public employee.

(h) Notwithstanding subdivision (a) of Section 42001, a violation of subdivision (d), (e), or (f) is an infraction punishable by a fine of not more than twenty dollars ($20) for a first offense, and a fine of not more than fifty dollars ($50) for each subsequent offense. In lieu of the fine and any penalty assessment or court costs, the court, pursuant to Section 42005, may order that a person convicted of a first offense attend a school for traffic violators or another court-approved program in which the proper use of safety belts is demonstrated.

(i) In a civil action, a violation of subdivision (d), (e), or (f), or information of a violation of subdivision (h), does not establish negligence as a matter of law or negligence per se for comparative fault purposes, but negligence may be proven as a fact without regard to the violation.

(j) If the United States Secretary of Transportation fails to adopt safety standards for manual safety belt systems by September 1, 1989, a motor vehicle manufactured after that date for sale or sold in this state shall not be registered unless it contains a manual safety belt system that meets the performance standards applicable to automatic crash protection devices adopted by the United States Secretary of Transportation pursuant to Federal Motor Vehicle Safety Standard No. 208 (49 C.F.R. 571.208) as in effect on January 1, 1985.

(k) A motor vehicle offered for original sale in this state that has been manufactured on or after September 1, 1989, shall comply with the automatic restraint requirements of Section S4.1.2.1 of Federal Motor Vehicle Safety Standard No. 208 (49 C.F.R. 571.208), as published in Volume 49 of the Federal Register, No. 138, page 29009. An automobile manufacturer that sells or delivers a motor vehicle subject to this subdivision, and fails to comply with this subdivision, shall be punished by a fine of not more than five hundred dollars ($500) for each sale or delivery of a noncomplying motor vehicle.

(l) Compliance with subdivision (j) or (k) by a manufacturer shall be made by self-certification in the same manner as self-certification is accomplished under federal law.

(m) This section does not apply to a person actually engaged in delivery of newspapers to customers along the person's route if the person is properly restrained by a safety belt prior to commencing and subsequent to completing delivery on the route.

(n) This section does not apply to a person actually engaged in collection and delivery activities as a rural delivery carrier for the United States Postal Service if the person is properly restrained by a safety belt prior to stopping at the first box and subsequent to stopping at the last box on the route.

(o) This section does not apply to a driver actually engaged in the collection of solid waste or recyclable materials along that driver's collection route if the driver is properly restrained by a safety belt prior to commencing and subsequent to completing the collection route.

(p) Subdivisions (d), (e), (f), (g), and (h) shall become inoperative immediately upon the date that the United States Secretary of Transportation, or their delegate, determines to rescind the portion of the Federal Motor Vehicle Safety Standard No. 208 (49 C.F.R. 571.208) that requires the installation of automatic restraints in new motor vehicles, except that those subdivisions shall not become inoperative if the secretary's decision to rescind that Standard No. 208 is not based, in any respect, on the enactment or continued operation of those subdivisions.

(q) This section shall remain in effect only until January 1, 2027, and as of that date is repealed.

(Amended by Stats. 2025, Ch. 434, Sec. 1. (AB 435) Effective January 1, 2026. Repealed as of January 1, 2027, by its own provisions. See later operative version as added by Sec. 2 of Stats. 2025, Ch. 434.)

27315. (a) The Legislature finds that a mandatory seatbelt law will contribute to reducing highway deaths and injuries by encouraging greater usage of existing manual seatbelts, that automatic crash protection systems that require no action by vehicle occupants offer the best hope of reducing deaths and injuries, and that encouraging the use of manual safety belts is only a partial remedy for addressing this major cause of death and injury. The Legislature declares that the enactment of this section is intended to be compatible with support for federal motor vehicle safety standards requiring automatic crash protection systems and should not be used in any manner to rescind federal requirements for installation of automatic restraints in new cars.

(b) This section shall be known and may be cited as the Motor Vehicle Safety Act.

(c) For purposes of this section, the following terms and phrases have the following meanings:

(1) (A) "Motor vehicle" means a passenger vehicle, a motortruck, or a truck tractor, but does not include a motorcycle.

(B) "Motor vehicle" also means a farm labor vehicle, regardless of the date of certification under Section 31401.

(2) "Properly restrained by a safety belt" means the person meets all of the following requirements of the 5-Step test:

(A) The person is sitting all the way back against the auto seat.

(B) The knees of the person bend over the edge of the auto seat.

(C) The shoulder belt snugly crosses the center of the person's chest and shoulder, not the person's neck.

(D) The lap belt is as low as possible and is touching the person's thighs.

(E) The person can stay seated like this for the whole trip.

(d) (1) A person shall not operate a motor vehicle on a highway unless that person and all passengers 16 years of age or over are properly restrained by a safety belt. This paragraph does not apply to the operator of a taxicab, as defined in Section 27908, when the taxicab is driven on a city street and is engaged in the transportation of a fare-paying passenger. The safety belt requirement established by this paragraph is the minimum safety standard applicable to employees being transported in a motor vehicle. This paragraph does not preempt more stringent or restrictive standards imposed by the Labor Code or another state or federal regulation regarding the transportation of employees in a motor vehicle.

(2) The operator of a limousine for hire or the operator of an authorized emergency vehicle, as defined in subdivision (a) of Section 165, shall not operate the limousine for hire or authorized emergency vehicle unless the operator and any passengers eight years of age or over in the front seat, are properly restrained by a safety belt.

(3) The operator of a taxicab shall not operate the taxicab unless any passengers eight years of age or over in the front seat, are properly restrained by a safety belt.

(e) A person 16 years of age or over shall not be a passenger in a motor vehicle on a highway unless that person is properly restrained by a safety belt. This subdivision does not apply to a passenger in a sleeper berth, as defined in subdivision (x) of Section 1201 of Title 13 of the California Code of Regulations.

(f) An owner of a motor vehicle, including an owner or operator of a taxicab, as defined in Section 27908, or a limousine for hire, operated on a highway shall maintain safety belts in good working order for the use of the occupants of the vehicle. The safety belts shall conform to motor vehicle safety standards established by the United States Department of Transportation. This subdivision, however, does not require installation or maintenance of safety belts if it is not required by the laws of the United States applicable to the vehicle at the time of its initial sale.

(g) This section does not apply to a passenger or operator with a physically disabling condition or medical condition that would prevent appropriate restraint in a safety belt, if the condition is duly certified by a licensed physician and surgeon or by a licensed chiropractor who shall state the nature of the condition, as well as the reason the restraint is inappropriate. This section also does not apply to a public employee, if the public employee is in an authorized emergency vehicle as defined in paragraph (1) of subdivision (b) of Section 165, or to a passenger in a seat behind the front seat of an authorized emergency vehicle as defined in paragraph (1) of subdivision (b) of Section 165 operated by the public employee, unless required by the agency employing the public employee.

(h) Notwithstanding subdivision (a) of Section 42001, a violation of subdivision (d), (e), or (f) is an infraction punishable by a fine of not more than twenty dollars ($20) for a first offense, and a fine of not more than fifty dollars ($50) for each subsequent offense. In lieu of the fine and any penalty assessment or court costs, the court, pursuant to Section 42005, may order that a person convicted of a first offense attend a school for traffic violators or another court-approved program in which the proper use of safety belts is demonstrated.

(i) In a civil action, a violation of subdivision (d), (e), or (f), or information of a violation of subdivision (h), does not establish negligence as a matter of law or negligence per se for comparative fault purposes, but negligence may be proven as a fact without regard to the violation.

(j) If the United States Secretary of Transportation fails to adopt safety standards for manual safety belt systems by September 1, 1989, a motor vehicle manufactured after that date for sale or sold in this state shall not be registered unless it contains a manual safety belt system that meets the performance standards applicable to automatic crash protection devices adopted by the United States Secretary of Transportation pursuant to Federal Motor Vehicle Safety Standard No. 208 (49 C.F.R. 571.208) as in effect on January 1, 1985.

(k) A motor vehicle offered for original sale in this state that has been manufactured on or after September 1, 1989, shall comply with the automatic restraint requirements of Section S4.1.2.1 of Federal Motor Vehicle Safety Standard No. 208 (49 C.F.R. 571.208), as published in Volume 49 of the Federal Register, No. 138, page 29009. An automobile manufacturer that sells or delivers a motor vehicle subject to this subdivision, and fails to comply with this subdivision, shall be punished by a fine of not more than five hundred dollars ($500) for each sale or delivery of a noncomplying motor vehicle.

(l) Compliance with subdivision (j) or (k) by a manufacturer shall be made by self-certification in the same manner as self-certification is accomplished under federal law.

(m) This section does not apply to a person actually engaged in delivery of newspapers to customers along the person's route if the person is properly restrained by a safety belt prior to commencing and subsequent to completing delivery on the route.

(n) This section does not apply to a person actually engaged in collection and delivery activities as a rural delivery carrier for the United States Postal Service if the person is properly restrained by a safety belt prior to stopping at the first box and subsequent to stopping at the last box on the route.

(o) This section does not apply to a driver actually engaged in the collection of solid waste or recyclable materials along that driver's collection route if the driver is properly restrained by a safety belt prior to commencing and subsequent to completing the collection route.

(p) Subdivisions (d), (e), (f), (g), and (h) shall become inoperative immediately upon the date that the United States Secretary of Transportation, or their delegate, determines to rescind the portion of the Federal Motor Vehicle Safety Standard No. 208 (49 C.F.R. 571.208) that requires the installation of automatic restraints in new motor vehicles, except that those subdivisions shall not become inoperative if the secretary's decision to rescind that Standard No. 208 is not based, in any respect, on the enactment or continued operation of those subdivisions.

(q) This section shall become operative on January 1, 2027.

(Repealed (in Sec. 1) and added by Stats. 2025, Ch. 434, Sec. 2. (AB 435) Effective January 1, 2026. Operative January 1, 2027, by its own provisions.)

27315.1. Section 27315 applies to any person in a fully enclosed three-wheeled motor vehicle that is not less than seven feet in length and not less than four feet in width, and has an unladen weight of 900 pounds or more.

(Added by Stats. 1997, Ch. 710, Sec. 2. Effective January 1, 1998.)

27315.3. (a) As used in this section, "passenger motor vehicle" means a passenger vehicle as defined in Section 465 and a motortruck as defined in Section 410 of less than 6,001 pounds unladen weight, but does not include a motorcycle as defined in Section 400.

(b) Every sheriff's department and city police department and the Department of the California Highway Patrol shall maintain safety belts in good working order for the use of occupants of a vehicle that it operates on a highway for the purpose of patrol. The safety belts shall conform to motor vehicle safety standards established by the United States Department of Transportation. This subdivision does not, however, require installation or maintenance of safety belts where not required by the laws of the United States applicable to the vehicle at the time of its initial sale.

(c) Notwithstanding subdivision (a) of Section 42001, a violation of subdivision (b) is an infraction punishable by a fine, including all penalty assessments and court costs imposed on the convicted department, of not more than twenty dollars ($20) for a first offense, and a fine, including all penalty assessments and court costs imposed on the convicted department, of not more than fifty dollars ($50) for each subsequent offense.

(d) (1) For a violation of subdivision (b), in addition to the fines provided for pursuant to subdivision (c) and the penalty assessments provided for pursuant to Section 1464 of the Penal Code, an additional penalty assessment of two dollars ($2) shall be levied for a first offense, and an additional penalty assessment of five dollars ($5) shall be levied for any subsequent offense.

(2) All money collected pursuant to this subdivision shall be utilized in accordance with Section 1464 of the Penal Code.

(e) In a civil action, a violation of subdivision (b) or information of a violation of subdivision (c) shall not establish negligence as a matter of law or negligence per se for comparative fault purposes, but negligence may be proven as a fact without regard to the violation.

(f) Subdivisions (b) and (c) shall become inoperative immediately upon the date that the Secretary of the United States Department of Transportation, or his or her delegate, determines to rescind the portion of the Federal Motor Vehicle Safety Standard No. 208 (49 C.F.R. 571.208) that requires the installation of automatic restraints in new passenger motor vehicles, except that those subdivisions shall not become inoperative if the secretary's decision to rescind Standard No. 208 is not based, in any respect, on the enactment or continued operation of those subdivisions or subdivisions (d) to (h), inclusive, of Section 27315.

(Amended by Stats. 2011, Ch. 474, Sec. 2. (SB 929) Effective January 1, 2012.)

27315.5. All law enforcement agencies shall, not later than January 1, 1991, establish a policy and issue an order, in writing, which states whether or not their officers are required to wear seat belts. When a law enforcement agency is developing a safety belt policy, the agency shall consider the officer's safety, comfort, and convenience.

(Added by Stats. 1990, Ch. 33, Sec. 3. Effective March 26, 1990.)

27316. (a) Unless specifically prohibited by the National Highway Traffic Safety Administration, all schoolbuses purchased or leased for use in California shall be equipped at all designated seating positions with a combination pelvic and upper torso passenger restraint system, if the schoolbus is either of the following:

(1) Type 1, as defined in paragraph (1) of subdivision (b) of Section 1201 of Title 13 of the California Code of Regulations, and is manufactured on or after July 1, 2005.

(2) Type 2, as defined in paragraph (2) of subdivision (b) of Section 1201 of Title 13 of the California Code of Regulations, and is manufactured on or after July 1, 2004.

(b) For purposes of this section, a "passenger restraint system" means any of the following:

(1) A restraint system that is in compliance with Federal Motor Vehicle Safety Standard 209, for a type 2 seatbelt assembly, and with Federal Motor Vehicle Safety Standard 210, as those standards were in effect on the date the schoolbus was manufactured.

(2) A restraint system certified by the schoolbus manufacturer that is in compliance with Federal Motor Vehicle Safety Standard 222 and incorporates a type 2 lap/shoulder restraint system.

(c) A person, school district, or organization, with respect to a schoolbus equipped with passenger restraint systems pursuant to this section, shall not be charged for a violation of this code or any regulation adopted thereunder requiring a passenger to use a passenger restraint system, if a passenger on the schoolbus fails to use or improperly uses the passenger restraint system.

(d) It is the intent of the Legislature, in implementing this section, that school pupil transportation providers work to prioritize the allocation of schoolbuses purchased, leased, or contracted for on or after July 1, 2004, for type 2 schoolbuses, or on or after July 1, 2005, for type 1 schoolbuses, to ensure that elementary level schoolbus passengers receive first priority for new schoolbuses whenever feasible.

(e) On or before July 1, 2035, all schoolbuses in use in California shall be equipped with a passenger restraint system.

(Amended by Stats. 2018, Ch. 206, Sec. 1. (AB 1798) Effective January 1, 2019.)

27316.5. (a) Unless specifically prohibited by the National Highway Traffic Safety Administration, all type 2 school pupil activity buses, manufactured on or after July 1, 2004, purchased or leased for use in California shall be equipped at all designated seating positions with a combination pelvic and upper torso passenger restraint system.

(b) For purposes of this section, a "passenger restraint system" is either of the following:

(1) A restraint system that is in compliance with Federal Motor Vehicle Safety Standard 209, for a type 2 seatbelt assembly, and with Federal Motor Vehicle Safety Standard 210, as those standards were in effect on the date that the school pupil activity bus was manufactured.

(2) A restraint system certified by the school pupil activity bus manufacturer that is in compliance with Federal Motor Vehicle Safety Standard 222 and incorporates a type 2 lap-shoulder restraint system.

(c) No person, school district, or organization, with respect to a type 2 school pupil activity bus equipped with passenger restraint systems pursuant to this section, may be charged for a violation of this code or any regulation adopted thereunder requiring a passenger to use a passenger restraint system, if a passenger on the school pupil activity bus fails to use or improperly uses the passenger restraint system.

(Amended by Stats. 2017, Ch. 397, Sec. 8. (SB 810) Effective January 1, 2018.)

27317. (a) A person shall not knowingly and intentionally manufacture, import, install, reinstall, distribute, sell, or offer for sale any device intended to replace a supplemental restraint system component in any motor vehicle if the device is a counterfeit supplemental restraint system component or a nonfunctional airbag, or does not meet federal safety requirements as provided in Section 571.208 of Title 49 of the Code of Federal Regulations.

(b) A person shall not knowingly and intentionally sell, install, or reinstall in a vehicle, any device that causes the vehicle's diagnostic systems to fail to warn when the vehicle is equipped with a counterfeit supplemental restraint system component or nonfunctional airbag, or when no airbag is installed.

(c) A violation of subdivision (a) or (b) is a misdemeanor punishable by a fine of up to five thousand dollars ($5,000) or by imprisonment in a county jail for up to one year, or by both the fine and imprisonment.

(d) An installation or reinstallation shall not have occurred for purposes of this section until the work is complete.

(e) The following definitions shall apply for purposes of this section:

(1) "Airbag" means a motor vehicle inflatable occupant restraint system device that is part of a supplemental restraint system.

(2) "Counterfeit supplemental restraint system component" means a replacement supplemental restraint system component, including, but not limited to, an airbag that displays a mark identical or substantially similar to the genuine mark of a motor vehicle manufacturer or a supplier of parts to the manufacturer of a motor vehicle without authorization from that manufacturer or supplier, respectively.

(3) "Nonfunctional airbag" means a replacement airbag that meets any of the following criteria:

(A) The airbag was previously deployed or damaged.

(B) The airbag has an electric fault that is detected by the vehicle's airbag diagnostic systems when the installation procedure is completed and the vehicle is returned to the customer who requested the work to be performed or when ownership is intended to be transferred.

(C) The airbag includes a part or object, including, but not limited to, a supplemental restraint system component installed in a motor vehicle to mislead the owner or operator of the motor vehicle into believing that a functional airbag has been installed.

(D) The airbag is subject to the prohibitions of subsection (j) of Section 30120 of Title 49 of the United States Code.

(4) "Supplemental restraint system," commonly referred to as an "SRS," means a passive inflatable motor vehicle occupant crash protection system designed for use in conjunction with active restraint systems, as defined in Section 571.208 of Title 49 of the Code of Federal Regulations. A supplemental restraint system includes one or more airbags and all components required to ensure that an airbag works as designed by the vehicle manufacturer, including both of the following:

(A) The airbag operates in the event of a crash.

(B) The airbag is designed in accordance with federal motor vehicle safety standards for the specific make, model, and year of the motor vehicle in which it is or will be installed.

(f) This section does not affect any duties, rights, or remedies otherwise available at law.

(g) This section does not preclude prosecution under any other law.

(Repealed and added by Stats. 2016, Ch. 694, Sec. 2. (AB 2387) Effective January 1, 2017.)

27318. (a) A passenger who is 16 years of age or older in a bus shall be properly restrained by a safety belt.

(b) A parent, legal guardian, or chartering party shall not transport on a bus, or permit to be transported on a bus, a child, ward, or passenger who is eight years of age or older, but under 16 years of age, unless they are properly restrained by a safety belt.

(c) Except as provided in subdivision (d), a parent, legal guardian, or chartering party shall not transport on a bus, or permit to be transported on a bus, a child, ward, or passenger who is under eight years of age and under four feet nine inches in height, unless they are acceptably restrained by a safety belt.

(d) If it is not possible to ensure a child, ward, or passenger who is under eight years of age and under four feet nine inches in height is acceptably restrained by a safety belt because of their size, a parent, legal guardian, or chartering party shall either secure them in an appropriate child passenger restraint system that meets applicable federal motor vehicle safety standards, or if the child, ward, or passenger is under two years of age, may authorize a parent, legal guardian, or chartering party to hold them.

(e) (1) For purposes of this section, "acceptably restrained by a safety belt" means all of the following:

(A) The latch plate is securely fastened in the buckle.

(B) The lap belt shall be adjusted to fit low and tight across the hips or upper thighs, not the stomach area.

(C) The shoulder belt shall be adjusted snugly across the chest and the middle of the shoulder, away from the neck.

(D) The shoulder belt shall not be placed behind the back or under the arm.

(2) For purposes of this section, "properly restrained by a safety belt" means that the lap belt crosses the hips or upper thighs of the occupant and the shoulder belt, if present, crosses the chest in front of the occupant.

(3) For purposes of this section, "bus" means a bus that is equipped with safety belts, including a bus that is required to be equipped with a seatbelt assembly pursuant to Federal Motor Vehicle Safety Standard No. 208 (49 C.F.R. 571.208).

(f) Subdivisions (a), (b), (c), and (d) do not apply to a passenger that is leaving, has left, or is returning from their seat to use an onboard bathroom.

(g) If the bus is equipped with safety belts, the motor carrier shall maintain safety belts in good working order for the use of passengers of the vehicle.

(h) A motor carrier operating a bus equipped with safety belts shall do one of the following:

(1) Require the bus driver, before departure of a bus carrying passengers, to inform passengers of the requirement to wear the seatbelt under California law and inform passengers that not wearing a seatbelt is punishable by a fine.

(2) Post, or allow to be posted, signs or placards that inform passengers of the requirement to wear a seatbelt under California law and that not wearing a seatbelt is punishable by a fine. The signs or placards shall be in a font type and font size that is reasonably easy to read and shall be affixed to a bus in multiple, conspicuous locations.

(i) Notwithstanding subdivision (a) of Section 42001, a violation of subdivision (a), (b), (c), or (d) is an infraction punishable by a fine of not more than twenty dollars ($20) for a first offense, and a fine of not more than fifty dollars ($50) for each subsequent offense.

(j) This section does not apply to a schoolbus described in Section 27316 or a school pupil activity bus described in Section 27316.5.

(k) This section shall remain in effect only until January 1, 2027, and as of that date is repealed.

(Amended by Stats. 2025, Ch. 434, Sec. 3. (AB 435) Effective January 1, 2026. Repealed as of January 1, 2027, by its own provisions. See later operative version as added by Sec. 4 of Stats. 2025, Ch. 434.)

27318. (a) A passenger who is 16 years of age or older in a bus shall be properly restrained by a safety belt.

(b) Except as provided in subdivision (c), a parent, legal guardian, or chartering party shall not transport on a bus, or permit to be transported on a bus, a child, ward, or passenger who is under 16 years of age unless they are properly restrained by a safety belt.

(c) If it is not possible to ensure a child, ward, or passenger who is under eight years of age and under four feet nine inches in height is properly restrained by a safety belt because of their size, a parent, legal guardian, or chartering party shall either secure them in an appropriate child passenger restraint system that meets applicable federal motor vehicle safety standards, or if the child, ward, or passenger is under two years of age, may authorize a parent, legal guardian, or chartering party to hold them.

(d) (1) For purposes of this section, the following terms and phrases have the following meanings:

(2) "Bus" means a bus that is equipped with safety belts, including a bus that is required to be equipped with a seatbelt assembly pursuant to Federal Motor Vehicle Safety Standard No. 208 (49 C.F.R. 571.208).

(3) "Properly restrained by a safety belt" means the child, ward, or passenger meets all of the following requirements of the 5-Step test:

(A) The child, ward, or passenger is sitting all the way back against the auto seat.

(B) The knees of the child, ward, or passenger bend over the edge of the auto seat.

(C) The shoulder belt snugly crosses the center of the child, ward, or passenger's chest and shoulder, not the child, ward, or passenger's neck.

(D) The lap belt is as low as possible and is touching the child, ward, or passenger's thighs.

(E) The child, ward, or passenger can stay seated like this for the whole trip.

(e) Subdivisions (a), (b), and (c) do not apply to a passenger that is leaving, has left, or is returning from their seat to use an onboard bathroom.

(f) If the bus is equipped with safety belts, the motor carrier shall maintain safety belts in good working order for the use of passengers of the vehicle.

(g) A motor carrier operating a bus equipped with safety belts shall do one of the following:

(1) Require the bus driver, before departure of a bus carrying passengers, to inform passengers of the requirement to wear the seatbelt under California law and inform passengers that not wearing a seatbelt is punishable by a fine.

(2) Post, or allow to be posted, signs or placards that inform passengers of the requirement to wear a seatbelt under California law and that not wearing a seatbelt is punishable by a fine. The signs or placards shall be in a font type and font size that is reasonably easy to read and shall be affixed to a bus in multiple, conspicuous locations.

(h) Notwithstanding subdivision (a) of Section 42001, a violation of subdivision (a), (b), or (c) is an infraction punishable by a fine of not more than twenty dollars ($20) for a first offense, and a fine of not more than fifty dollars ($50) for each subsequent offense.

(i) This section does not apply to a schoolbus described in Section 27316 or a school pupil activity bus described in Section 27316.5.

(j) This section shall become operative on January 1, 2027.

(Repealed (in Sec. 3) and added by Stats. 2025, Ch. 434, Sec. 2. (AB 435) Effective January 1, 2026. Operative January 1, 2027, by its own provisions.)

27319. (a) If a bus is equipped with a driver safety belt, the driver of the bus shall not operate the vehicle unless he or she is properly restrained by the safety belt.

(b) If a bus is equipped with a driver safety belt, the motor carrier shall maintain the safety belt in good working order for the use of the driver.

(c) Notwithstanding subdivision (a) of Section 42001, a violation of this section is an infraction punishable by a fine of not more than twenty dollars ($20) for a first offense and a fine of not more than fifty dollars ($50) for each subsequent offense.

(d) The requirements of this section are intended to satisfy the requirements of Section 392.16 of Title 49 of the Code of Federal Regulations, or any similar federal law or regulation, but shall remain in effect in the absence of those laws.

(e) This section shall be operative July 1, 2018.

(Added by Stats. 2017, Ch. 593, Sec. 3. (SB 20) Effective January 1, 2018. Section operative July 1, 2018, by its own provisions.)

Article 3.3. Child Safety Belt and Passenger Restraint Requirements

(Heading of Article 3.3 amended by Stats. 1994, Ch. 1101, Sec. 3.)

27360. (a) Except as provided in Section 27363, a parent, legal guardian, or driver who transports a child under eight years of age on a highway in a motor vehicle, as defined in paragraph (1) of subdivision (c) of Section 27315, shall properly secure that child in a rear seat in an appropriate child passenger restraint system meeting applicable federal motor vehicle safety standards.

(b) Except as provided in Section 27363, a parent, legal guardian, or driver who transports a child under two years of age on a highway in a motor vehicle, as defined in paragraph (1) of subdivision (c) of Section 27315, shall properly secure the child in a rear-facing child passenger restraint system that meets applicable federal motor vehicle safety standards, unless the child weighs 40 or more pounds or is 40 or more inches tall. The child shall be secured in a manner that complies with the height and weight limits specified by the manufacturer of the child passenger restraint system.

(c) This section does not apply to a driver if the parent or legal guardian of the child is a passenger in the motor vehicle.

(d) This section shall become operative January 1, 2017.

(Repealed (in Sec. 1) and added by Stats. 2015, Ch. 292, Sec. 2. (AB 53) Effective January 1, 2016. Section operative January 1, 2017, by its own provisions.)

27360.5. (a) A parent, legal guardian, or driver shall not transport on a highway in a motor vehicle, as defined in paragraph (1) of subdivision (c) of Section 27315, a child or ward who is eight years of age or older, but less than 16 years of age, without properly securing that child or ward in an appropriate child passenger restraint system or safety belt meeting applicable federal motor vehicle safety standards.

(b) Subdivision (a) does not apply to a driver if the parent or legal guardian of the child is also present in the motor vehicle and is not the driver.

(c) This section shall remain in effect only until January 1, 2027, and as of that date is repealed.

(Amended by Stats. 2025, Ch. 434, Sec. 5. (AB 435) Effective January 1, 2026. Repealed as of January 1, 2027, by its own provisions. See later operative version as added by Sec. 6 of Stats. 2025, Ch. 434.)

27360.5. (a) A parent, legal guardian, or driver shall not transport on a highway in a motor vehicle, as defined in paragraph (1) of subdivision (c) of Section 27315, a child or ward who is eight years of age or older, but less than 16 years of age, without properly securing that child or ward in an appropriate child passenger restraint system meeting applicable federal motor vehicle safety standards or unless the child or ward is properly restrained by a safety belt.

(b) Subdivision (a) does not apply to a driver if the parent or legal guardian of the child is also present in the motor vehicle and is not the driver.

(c) For purposes of this section, "properly restrained by a safety belt" means the child or ward meets all of the following requirements of the 5-Step test:

(1) The child or ward is sitting all the way back against the auto seat.

(2) The knees of the child or ward bend over the edge of the auto seat.

(3) The shoulder belt snugly crosses the center of the child's chest and shoulder, not the child's neck.

(4) The lap belt is as low as possible and is touching the child or ward's thighs.

(5) The child or ward can stay seated like this for the whole trip.

(d) This section shall become operative on January 1, 2027.

(Repealed (in Sec. 5) and added by Stats. 2025, Ch. 434, Sec. 2. (AB 435) Effective January 1, 2026. Operative January 1, 2027, by its own provisions.)

27360.6. (a) (1) For a conviction under Section 27360 or 27360.5, a first offense is punishable by a fine of one hundred dollars ($100), except that the court may reduce or waive the fine if the defendant establishes to the satisfaction of the court that he or she is economically disadvantaged, and the court, instead, refers the defendant to a community education program that includes, but is not limited to, education on the proper installation and use of a child passenger restraint system for children of all ages, and provides certification to the court of completion of that program. Upon completion of the program, the defendant shall provide proof of participation in the program. If an education program on the proper installation and use of a child passenger restraint system is not available within 50 miles of the residence of the defendant, the requirement to participate in that program shall be waived. If the fine is paid, waived, or reduced, the court shall report the conviction to the department pursuant to Section 1803.

(2) The court may require a defendant described under paragraph (1) to attend an education program that includes demonstration of proper installation and use of a child passenger restraint system and provides certification to the court that the defendant has presented for inspection a child passenger restraint system that meets applicable federal safety standards.

(b) (1) A second or subsequent conviction under Section 27360 or 27360.5 is punishable by a fine of two hundred fifty dollars ($250), no part of which may be waived by the court, except that the court may reduce or waive the fine if the defendant establishes to the satisfaction of the court that he or she is economically disadvantaged, and the court, instead refers the defendant to a community education program that includes, but is not limited to, education on the proper installation and use of child passenger restraint systems for children of all ages, and provides certification to the court of completion of that program. Upon completion of the program, the defendant shall provide proof of participation in the program. If an education program on the proper installation and use of a child passenger restraint system is not available within 50 miles of the residence of the defendant, the requirement to participate in that program shall be waived. If the fine is paid, waived, or reduced, the court shall report the conviction to the department pursuant to Section 1803.

(2) The court may require a defendant described under paragraph (1) to attend an education program that includes demonstration of proper installation and use of a child passenger restraint system and provides certification to the court that the defendant has presented for inspection a child passenger restraint system that meets applicable federal safety standards.

(c) Notwithstanding any other law, the fines collected under this section shall be allocated as follows:

(1) (A) Sixty percent to health departments of local jurisdictions where the violation occurred, to be used for a community education and assistance program that includes, but is not limited to, demonstration of the proper installation and use of child passenger restraint systems for children of all ages and assistance to economically disadvantaged families in obtaining a restraint system through a low-cost purchase or loan. The county or city health department shall designate a coordinator to facilitate the creation of a special account and to develop a relationship

with the court system to facilitate the transfer of funds to the program. The county or city may contract for the implementation of the program. Prior to obtaining possession of a child passenger restraint system pursuant to this subdivision, a person shall attend an education program that includes demonstration of proper installation and use of a child passenger restraint system.

(B) As the proceeds from fines become available, county or city health departments shall prepare and maintain a listing of all child passenger restraint low-cost purchase or loaner programs in their counties, including a semiannual verification that all programs listed are in existence. Each county or city shall forward the listing to the Office of Traffic Safety in the Business, Transportation and Housing Agency and the courts, birthing centers, community child health and disability prevention programs, county clinics, prenatal clinics, women, infants, and children programs, and county hospitals in that county, who shall make the listing available to the public. The Office of Traffic Safety shall maintain a listing of all of the programs in the state.

(2) Twenty-five percent to the county or city for the administration of the community education program.

(3) Fifteen percent to the city, to be deposited in its general fund except that, if the violation occurred in an unincorporated area, this amount shall be allocated to the county for purposes of paragraph (1).

(Added by Stats. 2011, Ch. 474, Sec. 7. (SB 929) Effective January 1, 2012.)

27361. A law enforcement officer reasonably suspecting a violation of Section 27360 or 27360.5, or both of those sections, may stop a vehicle transporting a child appearing to the officer to be within the age specified in Section 27360 or 27360.5. The officer may issue a notice to appear for a violation of Section 27360 or 27360.5.

(Amended by Stats. 2011, Ch. 474, Sec. 8. (SB 929) Effective January 1, 2012.)

27362. (a) A manufacturer, wholesaler, or retailer shall not sell, offer for sale, or install in a motor vehicle, a child passenger restraint system that does not conform to all applicable federal motor vehicle safety standards on the date of manufacture. Responsibility for compliance with this section shall rest with the individual selling the system, offering the system for sale, or installing the system. A person who violates this section is guilty of a misdemeanor and shall be punished as follows:

(1) Upon a first conviction, by a fine not exceeding four hundred dollars ($400), or by imprisonment in a county jail for a period of not more than 90 days, or both.

(2) Upon a second or subsequent conviction, by a fine not exceeding one thousand dollars ($1,000), or by imprisonment in a county jail for a period of not more than 180 days, or both.

(b) The fines collected for a violation of this section shall be allocated as follows:

(1) (A) Sixty percent to the county or city health department where the violation occurred, to be used for a child passenger restraint low-cost purchase or loaner program which shall include, but not be limited to, education on the proper installation and use of a child passenger restraint system. The county health department shall designate a coordinator to facilitate the creation of a special account and to develop a relationship with the superior court to facilitate the transfer of funds to the program. The county may contract for the implementation of the program. Prior to obtaining possession of a child passenger restraint system pursuant to this section, a person shall receive information relating to the importance of utilizing that system.

(B) As the proceeds from fines become available, county health departments shall prepare and maintain a listing of all child passenger restraint low-cost purchase or loaner programs in their counties, including a semiannual verification that all programs listed are in existence. Each county shall forward the listing to the Office of Traffic Safety in the Business, Transportation and Housing Agency and the courts, birthing centers, community child health and disability prevention programs, and county hospitals in that county, who shall make the listing available to the public. The Office of Traffic Safety shall maintain a listing of all of the programs in the state.

(2) Twenty-five percent to the county for the administration of the program.

(3) Fifteen percent to the city, to be deposited in its general fund except that, if the violation occurred in an unincorporated area, this amount shall be allocated to the county for purposes of paragraph (1).

(Amended by Stats. 2005, Ch. 22, Sec. 204. Effective January 1, 2006.)

27362.1. (a) No individual may sell or offer for sale a child passenger restraint system that was in use by a child during an accident involving a motor vehicle.

(b) A violation of this section shall be punished by a fine of one hundred dollars ($100).

(Added by Stats. 2002, Ch. 703, Sec. 2. Effective January 1, 2003.)

27363. (a) The court may exempt from the requirements of this article any class of child by age, weight, or size if it is determined that the use of a child passenger restraint system would be impractical by reason of physical unfitness, medical condition, or size. The court may require satisfactory proof of the child's physical unfitness, medical condition, or size and that an appropriate special needs child passenger restraint system is not available.

(b) In case of a life-threatening emergency, or when a child is being transported in an authorized emergency vehicle, if there is no child passenger restraint system available, a child may be transported without the use of that system, but the child shall be secured by a seatbelt.

(c) A child weighing more than 40 pounds may be transported in the backseat of a vehicle while wearing only a lap safety belt when the backseat of the vehicle is not equipped with a combination lap and shoulder safety belt.

(d) Notwithstanding Section 27360, a child or ward under eight years of age who is four feet nine inches in height or taller may be properly restrained by a safety belt, as defined in paragraph (2) of subdivision (d) of Section 27315, rather than by a child passenger restraint system.

(e) Notwithstanding Section 27360, a child or ward under eight years of age may ride properly secured in an appropriate child passenger restraint system meeting applicable federal motor vehicle safety standards in the front seat of a motor vehicle under any of the following circumstances:

(1) There is no rear seat.

(2) The rear seats are side-facing jump seats.

(3) The rear seats are rear-facing seats.

(4) The child passenger restraint system cannot be installed properly in the rear seat.

(5) All rear seats are already occupied by children seven years of age or under.

(6) Medical reasons necessitate that the child or ward not ride in the rear seat. The court may require satisfactory proof of the child's medical condition.

(f) Notwithstanding subdivision (e), a child shall not be transported in a rear-facing child passenger restraint system in the front seat of a motor vehicle that is equipped with an active frontal passenger airbag.

(g) This section shall remain in effect only until January 1, 2027, and as of that date is repealed.

(Amended by Stats. 2025, Ch. 434, Sec. 7. (AB 435) Effective January 1, 2026. Repealed as of January 1, 2027, by its own provisions. See later operative version as added by Sec. 8 of Stats. 2025, Ch. 434.)

27363. (a) The court may exempt from the requirements of this article any class of child by age, weight, or size if it is determined that the use of a child passenger restraint system would be impractical by reason of physical unfitness, medical condition, or size. The court may require satisfactory proof of the child's physical unfitness, medical condition, or size and that an appropriate special needs child passenger restraint system is not available.

(b) In case of a life-threatening emergency, or when a child is being transported in an authorized emergency vehicle, if there is no child passenger restraint system available, a child may be transported without the use of that system, but the child shall be secured by a seatbelt.

(c) A child weighing more than 40 pounds may be transported in the backseat of a vehicle while wearing only a lap safety belt when the backseat of the vehicle is not equipped with a combination lap and shoulder safety belt.

(d) Notwithstanding Section 27360, a child or ward under eight years of age who is four feet nine inches in height or taller may be properly restrained by a safety belt rather than by a child passenger restraint system.

(e) Notwithstanding Section 27360, a child or ward under eight years of age may ride properly secured in an appropriate child passenger restraint system meeting applicable federal motor vehicle safety standards in the front seat of a motor vehicle under any of the following circumstances:

(1) There is no rear seat.

(2) The rear seats are side-facing jump seats.

(3) The rear seats are rear-facing seats.

(4) The child passenger restraint system cannot be installed properly in the rear seat.

(5) All rear seats are already occupied by children seven years of age or under.

(6) Medical reasons necessitate that the child or ward not ride in the rear seat. The court may require satisfactory proof of the child's medical condition.

(f) Notwithstanding subdivision (e), a child shall not be transported in a rear-facing child passenger restraint system in the front seat of a motor vehicle that is equipped with an active frontal passenger airbag.

(g) For purposes of this section, "properly restrained by a safety belt" means the child or ward meets all of the following requirements of the 5-Step test:

(1) The child or ward is sitting all the way back against the auto seat.

(2) The knees of the child or ward bend over the edge of the auto seat.

(3) The shoulder belt snugly crosses the center of the child's chest and shoulder, not the child's neck.

(4) The lap belt is as low as possible and is touching the child or ward's thighs.

(5) The child or ward can stay seated like this for the whole trip.

(h) This section shall become operative on January 1, 2027.

(Repealed (in Sec. 7) and added by Stats. 2025, Ch. 434, Sec. 2. (AB 435) Effective January 1, 2026. Operative January 1, 2027, by its own provisions.)

27363.5. (a) A public or private hospital, clinic, or birthing center shall, at the time of the discharge of a child, provide to and discuss with the parents or the person to whom the child is released, if the child is under eight years of age, information on the current law requiring child passenger restraint systems, safety belts, and the transportation of children in rear seats.

(b) A public or private hospital, clinic, or birthing center shall also provide to and discuss with the parent or person to whom the child is released, if the child is under eight years of age, contact information to direct the person to an Internet Web site or other contact that could provide, at no cost or low cost, information and assistance relating to child passenger restraint system requirements, installation, and inspection. Pursuant to this subdivision, the hospital, clinic, or birthing center does not have any additional obligation to provide patients with any assistance relating to child passenger restraint systems, other than providing the contact information as set forth in this subdivision. This contact information may include the following:

(1) Call 1-866-SEAT-CHECK or visit www.seatcheck.org to find a nearby location.

(2) The telephone number of the local office of the Department of the California Highway Patrol.

(3) The Internet Web site for the National Highway Traffic Safety Administration's Child Safety Seat Inspection Station Locator.

(4) The Internet Web site for the State Department of Public Health's child passenger restraint system safety inspection locator.

(c) A public or private hospital, clinic, or birthing center shall not be responsible for the failure of the parent or person to whom the child is released to properly transport the child.

(Amended by Stats. 2012, Ch. 185, Sec. 2. (AB 1452) Effective January 1, 2013.)

27364. (a) It is the intent of the Legislature, in enacting this article, to insure that children, who are, because of their tender years, helpless dependent passengers, are provided with the safest transportation possible.

(b) It is the further intent of the Legislature to stress and communicate to all drivers in this state the importance of using child passenger restraint systems.

(c) Nothing in this article shall be construed to extend application of these provisions to a class of children other than the class of children herein specified.

(Amended by Stats. 1995, Ch. 512, Sec. 9. Effective January 1, 1996.)

27365. (a) (1) A car rental agency in California shall inform each of its customers of Section 27360 by posting, in a place conspicuous to the public in each established place of business of the agency, a notice not smaller than 15 by 20 inches which states the following:

"CALIFORNIA LAW REQUIRES ALL CHILDREN UNDER 8 YEARS OF AGE TO BE TRANSPORTED IN THE REAR SEAT OF THE VEHICLE IN A CHILD RESTRAINT SYSTEM. THIS AGENCY IS REQUIRED TO PROVIDE FOR RENTAL OF A CHILD RESTRAINT SYSTEM IF YOU DO NOT HAVE A CHILD RESTRAINT SYSTEM YOURSELF."

(2) The posted notice specified in paragraph (1) is not required if the car rental agency's place of business is located in a hotel that has a business policy prohibiting the posting of signs or notices in any area of the hotel. In that case, a car rental agency shall furnish a written notice to each customer that contains the same information as required for the posted notice.

(b) Every car rental agency in California shall have available for, and shall, upon request, provide for rental to, adults traveling with children under eight years of age, child passenger restraint systems that are certified by the manufacturer to meet applicable federal motor vehicle safety standards for use by children, are in good and safe condition, with no missing original parts, and are not older than five years.

(c) A violation of this section is an infraction punishable by a fine of one hundred dollars ($100).

(Amended by Stats. 2011, Ch. 474, Sec. 11. (SB 929) Effective January 1, 2012.)

27366. (a) The department shall do the following:

(1) Prepare and disseminate materials for the purpose of educating the public about the importance of using passenger restraints for infants and children under 15 years of age. These materials shall include, but are not limited to, audiovisual aids and written materials that explain the effects of motor vehicle accidents on infants and children and the reduction in risk of injury or death as a result of the utilization of passenger restraints for infants and children.

(2) As funding is available, produce and administer a billboard campaign stressing the importance of utilizing child passenger restraint systems and instructing the public on where to obtain those systems.

(b) The department, the Office of Traffic Safety, and the State Department of Health Services shall meet annually to coordinate, share information about, and outline the programs that each organization is pursuing in the area of child passenger restraint systems.

(Added by Stats. 1995, Ch. 512, Sec. 10. Effective January 1, 1996.)

27368. This article applies to child passengers in a fully enclosed three-wheeled motor vehicle that is not less than seven feet in length and not less than four feet in width, and has an unladen weight of 900 pounds or more.

(Added by Stats. 1997, Ch. 710, Sec. 3. Effective January 1, 1998.)

Article 3.4. Emergency Exits for Charter-Party Carriers of Passengers

(Article 3.4 added by Stats. 2013, Ch. 752, Sec. 2.)

27375. (a) Any person who operates a modified limousine shall ensure that the vehicle has at least two rear side doors, as specified in paragraph (2), and one or two rear windows, as specified in paragraph (1), that the rear seat passengers or all passengers of the vehicle may open from the inside of the vehicle in case of any fire or other emergency that may require the immediate exit of the passengers of the vehicle. A limousine subject to this subdivision shall be equipped with both of the following:

(1) (A) Except as provided in subparagraph (B), at least two rear push-out windows that are accessible to all passengers. At least one push-out window shall be located on each side of the vehicle, unless the design of the limousine precludes the installation of a push-out window on one side of the vehicle, in which case the second push-out window shall instead be located in the roof of the vehicle.

(B) If the design of the limousine precludes the installation of even one push-out window on a side of the vehicle, one push-out window shall instead be located in the roof of the vehicle.

(C) The Department of the California Highway Patrol shall establish, by regulation, standards to ensure that window exits are operable and sufficient in emergency situations for limousine passengers. The department shall ensure that these regulations comply with any applicable federal motor vehicle safety standards.

(D) For modified limousines modified prior to July 1, 2015, the requirements of this paragraph shall apply on and after January 1, 2018.

(2) (A) At least two rear side doors that are accessible to all passengers and that may be opened manually by any passenger. At least one rear side door shall be located on each side of the vehicle.

(B) For modified limousines modified on or after July 1, 2015, at least one of these side doors shall be located near the driver's compartment and another near the back of the vehicle.

(C) The rear side doors shall comply with any applicable federal motor vehicle safety standards as deemed necessary by the Department of the California Highway Patrol.

(b) In the case of a fire or other emergency that requires the immediate exit of the passengers from the limousine, the driver of the limousine shall unlock the doors so that the rear side doors can be opened by the passengers from the inside of the vehicle.

(c) An owner or operator of a limousine shall do all of the following:

(1) Instruct all passengers on the safety features of the vehicle prior to the beginning of any trip, including, but not limited to, instructions for lowering the partition between the driver and passenger compartments and for communicating with the driver by the use of an intercom or other onboard or wireless device.

(2) Disclose to the contracting party and the passengers whether the limousine meets the safety requirements described in this section.

(3) If paragraph (1) of subdivision (d) applies, the owner or operator of a limousine shall further disclose to the contracting party and the passengers that the limousine does not meet the safety requirements required in subdivision (a) regarding vehicle escape options because of its exempt status, and therefore may pose a greater risk to passengers should emergency escape be necessary.

(d) (1) Except as provided in paragraph (2), subdivision (a) shall not apply to any limousine manufactured before 1970 that has an active transportation charter-party carrier (TCP) number that was issued by the commission as of August 15, 2013.

(2) Subdivision (a) shall apply to any limousine manufactured before 1970 if it was modified after August 15, 2013.

(Amended by Stats. 2016, Ch. 711, Sec. 1. (SB 812) Effective January 1, 2017.)

Article 3.5. Headsets and Earplugs

(Article 3.5 added by Stats. 1973, Ch. 87.)

27400. A person operating a motor vehicle or bicycle may not wear a headset covering, earplugs in, or earphones covering, resting on, or inserted in, both ears. This prohibition does not apply to any of the following:

(a) A person operating authorized emergency vehicles, as defined in Section 165.

(b) A person engaged in the operation of either special construction equipment or equipment for use in the maintenance of any highway.

(c) A person engaged in the operation of refuse collection equipment who is wearing a safety headset or safety earplugs.

(d) A person wearing personal hearing protectors in the form of earplugs or molds that are specifically designed to attenuate injurious noise levels. The plugs or molds shall be designed in a manner so as to not inhibit the wearer's ability to hear a siren or horn from an emergency vehicle or a horn from another motor vehicle.

(e) A person using a prosthetic device that aids the hard of hearing.

(Amended by Stats. 2015, Ch. 451, Sec. 55. (SB 491) Effective January 1, 2016.)

Article 3.6. Charter-Party Carrier Safety Equipment

(Article 3.6 added by Stats. 2016, Ch. 705, Sec. 2.)

27425. (a) A vehicle described in paragraph (1) of subdivision (b) of Section 5363 of the Public Utilities Code that is designed to carry 39 or more passengers and that is manufactured on or after July 1, 2020, shall be equipped with emergency lighting fixtures that will turn on in the event of an impact or collision.

(b) A vehicle as specified in subdivision (a) shall at all times meet applicable federal motor vehicle safety standards (FMVSS) issued by the United States Department of Transportation. This section shall not be construed to conflict with those standards.

(Added by Stats. 2016, Ch. 705, Sec. 2. (SB 247) Effective January 1, 2017.)

27426. No later than July 1, 2018, the department shall adopt standards and criteria for the implementation of the safety equipment requirements specified in Section 27425.

(Added by Stats. 2016, Ch. 705, Sec. 2. (SB 247) Effective January 1, 2017.)

27427. This article does not alter or affect the requirements of the Passenger Charter-party Carriers' Act (Chapter 8 (commencing with Section 5351) of Division 2 of the Public Utilities Code).

(Amended by Stats. 2017, Ch. 561, Sec. 256. (AB 1516) Effective January 1, 2018.)

Article 4. Tires

(Article 4 enacted by Stats. 1959, Ch. 3.)

27450. When any vehicle is equipped with any solid tire, the solid tire shall have a minimum thickness of resilient rubber as follows:

(a) If the width of the tire is three inches but less than six inches, one inch thick.

(b) If the width of the tire is six inches but not more than nine inches, 11/4 inches thick.

(c) If the width of the tire is more than nine inches, 11/2 inches thick.

(Enacted by Stats. 1959, Ch. 3.)

27451. The rubber of a solid tire shall be measured between the surface of the roadway and the nearest metal part of the base flange to which the tire is attached at the point where the concentrated weight of the vehicle bears upon the surface of the roadway.

(Enacted by Stats. 1959, Ch. 3.)

27452. The required thickness of rubber shall extend evenly around the entire periphery of the tire. The entire solid tire shall be securely attached to the channel base and shall be without flat spots or bumpy rubber.

(Enacted by Stats. 1959, Ch. 3.)

27453. There shall not be an average difference greater than 1/8 inch between the outside diameters of each single tire composing a dual solid rubber tire.

(Enacted by Stats. 1959, Ch. 3.)

27454. A tire on a vehicle upon a highway shall not have on its periphery any block, stud, flange, cleat, ridge, bead, or any other protuberance of metal or wood that projects beyond the tread of the traction surface of the tire.

This section does not apply to any of the following:

(a) Tire traction devices of reasonable size used to prevent skidding when upon wet surfaces or when upon snow or ice.

(b) Pneumatic tires that have embedded therein wire not to exceed 0.075 of an inch in diameter and that are constructed so that under no conditions will the percentage of metal in contact with the roadway exceed 5 percent of the total tire area in contact with the roadway, except that during the first 1,000 miles of use or operation of the tire, the metal in contact with the roadway may exceed 5 percent of the tire area in contact with the roadway, but shall in no event exceed 20 percent of the area.

(c) Vehicles operated upon unimproved roadways when necessary in the construction or repair of highways.

(d) Traction engines or tractors when operated under the conditions of a permit first obtained from the Department of Transportation.

(e) (1) Pneumatic tires containing metal-type studs of tungsten carbide or other suitable material that are inserted or constructed so that under no condition will the number of studs or the percentage of metal in contact with the roadway exceed 3 percent of the total tire area in contact with the roadway, between November 1 and April 30 of each year. A vehicle may be equipped year-round with tires that have studs that retract pneumatically or mechanically when not in use, if the studs are retracted between May 1 and October 31 of each year. A tire on a vehicle shall not be worn to a point at which the studs protrude beyond the tire tread when retracted.

(2) The commissioner, after consultation with the Department of Transportation, may extend the period during which the studded pneumatic tires may be used with studs deployed or inserted in areas of the state for the protection of the public because of adverse weather conditions.

(f) Pneumatic tires used on an authorized emergency vehicle, as defined in Section 165, containing metal-type studs of tungsten carbide or other suitable material, if the studs are inserted or constructed so that under no conditions will the number of studs or the percentage of metal in contact with the roadway exceed 3 percent of the total tire area in contact with the roadway. Notwithstanding subdivision (e), authorized emergency vehicles are permitted the unrestricted use of studded pneumatic tires throughout the year.

(Amended by Stats. 2008, Ch. 220, Sec. 1. Effective January 1, 2009.)

27455. (a) On and after January 1, 1975, no person shall sell or offer for sale an inner tube for use in a radial tire unless, at the time of manufacture, the tube valve stem is colored red or is distinctly marked in accordance with rules and regulations adopted by the department, taking into consideration the recommendations of manufacturers of inner tubes.

(b) No person shall install an inner tube in a radial tire unless the inner tube is designed for use in a radial tire.

(Added by Stats. 1973, Ch. 741.)

27459. No person shall operate any motor vehicle, trailer or semitrailer upon any portion of a highway without tire traction devices when that portion of the highway is signed for the requirement of tire traction devices. In any case where a passenger vehicle or motortruck having an unladen weight of 6,000 pounds or less may be required by the Department of Transportation or local authorities to be equipped with tire traction devices, the devices shall be placed on at least two drive wheels, or the department or local authorities may provide, in the alternative, that the vehicle may be equipped with snow-tread tires on at least two drive wheels when the weather and surface conditions at the time are such that the stopping, tractive, and cornering abilities of the snow-tread tires are adequate. The snow-tread tires shall be of a type and design manufactured for use on snow as a replacement for tire chains or tire traction devices, shall be in good condition, and shall bear the marking of M-S, M/S, or other marking indicating that the tire was manufactured for use on snow, or, in the case of tires purchased before January 1, 1987, shall either bear the markings or, in the opinion of the inspecting officer, comply with the tread pattern requirements of Section 558.

(Amended by Stats. 1990, Ch. 71, Sec. 4. Effective May 1, 1990.)

27459.5. (a) No person shall sell, offer for sale, lease, install, or replace on a vehicle for use on a highway, any tire traction devices which are not in compliance with requirements specified in Section 605.

(b) Every manufacturer who sells, offers for sale, or manufactures for use upon a vehicle, tire traction devices subject to the requirements of Section 605 shall, before the device is offered for sale, have laboratory test data showing compliance with those requirements. Tests may be conducted by the manufacturer.

(Added by Stats. 1990, Ch. 71, Sec. 5. Effective May 1, 1990.)

27460. Any passenger vehicle or motortruck having an unladen weight of 6,500 pounds or less and operated and equipped with four-wheel drive and with snow-tread tires on all four drive wheels may be operated upon any portion of a highway without tire traction devices, notwithstanding the fact that the highway is signed for the requirement of those devices and provided that tire traction devices for at least one set of drive wheels are carried in or upon the vehicle. The snow-tread tires shall meet the requirements specified in Section 27459, and the vehicle shall not, when so operated, tow another vehicle except as may be necessary to move a disabled vehicle from the roadway.

No person shall use those tires on four-wheel drive vehicles in place of tire traction devices whenever weather and roadway conditions at the time are such that the stopping, tractive, and cornering abilities of the tires are not adequate or whenever the Department of Transportation or local authorities, in their respective jurisdictions, place signs prohibiting their operation unless equipped with tire traction devices.

(Amended by Stats. 1990, Ch. 71, Sec. 7. Effective May 1, 1990.)

27460.5. No person shall knowingly sell or offer or expose for sale any motor vehicle tire except a commercial vehicle tire, or any motor vehicle equipped with any tire except a commercial vehicle tire, which has been recut or regrooved. For purposes of this section a recut or regrooved tire is an unretreaded or unrecapped tire into which new grooves have been cut or burned.

(Added by Stats. 1965, Ch. 1518.)

27461. No person shall cause or permit the operation of and no driver shall knowingly operate any motor vehicle except a commercial vehicle, on any street or highway, which is equipped with one or more recut or regrooved tires. For purposes of this section a recut or regrooved tire is an unretreaded or unrecapped tire into which new grooves have been cut or burned.

(Added by Stats. 1965, Ch. 1518.)

27465. (a) No dealer or person holding a retail seller's permit shall sell, offer for sale, expose for sale, or install on a vehicle axle for use on a highway, a pneumatic tire when the tire has less than the tread depth specified in subdivision (b). This subdivision does not apply to any person who installs on a vehicle, as part of an emergency service rendered to a disabled vehicle upon a highway, a spare tire with which the disabled vehicle was equipped.

(b) No person shall use on a highway a pneumatic tire on a vehicle axle when the tire has less than the following tread depth, except when temporarily installed on a disabled vehicle as specified in subdivision (a):

(1) One thirty-second (1/32) of an inch tread depth in any two adjacent grooves at any location of the tire, except as provided in paragraphs (2) and (3).

(2) Four thirty-second (4/32) of an inch tread depth at all points in all major grooves on a tire on the steering axle of any motor vehicle specified in Section 34500, and two thirty-second (2/32) of an inch tread depth at all points in all major grooves on all other tires on the axles of these vehicles.

(3) Six thirty-second (6/32) of an inch tread depth at all points in all major grooves on snow tires used in lieu of tire traction devices in posted tire traction device control areas.

(c) The measurement of tread depth shall not be made where tie bars, humps, or fillets are located.

(d) The requirements of this section shall not apply to implements of husbandry.

(e) The department, if it determines that such action is appropriate and in keeping with reasonable safety requirements, may adopt regulations establishing more stringent tread depth requirements than those specified in this section for those vehicles defined in Sections 322 and 545, and may adopt regulations establishing tread depth requirements different from those specified in this section for those vehicles listed in Section 34500.

(Amended by Stats. 1990, Ch. 71, Sec. 8. Effective May 1, 1990.)

27470. (a) A nonpneumatic tire shall comply with the standards contained in Part 571 of Title 49 of the Code of Federal Regulations.

(b) A nonpneumatic tire shall be considered a pneumatic tire for purposes of Sections 27454, 27459, 27459.5, 27460, 27460.5, 27461, 27465, and 27502.

(c) The department may adopt regulations relating to standards for nonpneumatic tires for a vehicle type as it determines necessary to provide for public safety.

(1) A person shall not install or use on a highway a nonpneumatic tire that is not in conformance with the regulations adopted pursuant to this subdivision.

(2) In adopting regulations, the department shall consider Part 571 of Title 49 of the Code of Federal Regulations and guidance issued by the National Highway Traffic Safety Administration.

(d) For purposes of this section, "nonpneumatic tire" has the same meaning as defined in Section 571.129 of Title 49 of the Code of Federal Regulations.

(Added by Stats. 2023, Ch. 219, Sec. 5. (SB 891) Effective January 1, 2024.)

27500. (a) The department may adopt regulations relating to standards for pneumatic tires of a vehicle type as it determines necessary to provide for public safety.

(b) In adopting these regulations, the department shall consider as evidence of generally accepted standards, the rules and regulations which have been adopted by the Federal Highway Administration and Rubber Manufacturers Assocation.

(Amended by Stats. 1970, Ch. 216.)

27501. (a) No dealer or person holding a retail seller's permit shall sell, offer for sale, expose for sale, or install on a vehicle for use on a highway, a pneumatic tire which is not in compliance with regulations adopted pursuant to Section 27500. This subdivision shall not apply to any person who installs on a vehicle, as part of an emergency service rendered to a vehicle upon a highway, a spare tire with which such disabled vehicle was equipped.

(b) No person shall use on a highway a pneumatic tire which is not in conformance with such regulations.

(Amended by Stats. 1976, Ch. 70.)

27502. No dealer or person holding a retail seller's permit shall sell, offer for sale, expose for sale, or install on a vehicle for use on a highway, a tire which is not in compliance with regulations adopted pursuant to Section 27503.

(Added by Stats. 1971, Ch. 1197. Operative, by Sec. 3 of Ch. 1197, on operative date of regulations adopted pursuant to Section 27503.)

27503. (a) The commissioner, after public hearings, shall adopt regulations setting noise standards for pneumatic tires. Such standards shall be the lowest level of noise consistent with economic and technological feasibility and with public safety as stated in the regulations adopted pursuant to Section 27500. Such standards may be adopted for each tire-vehicle type combination. The regulations may require the manufacturer to prove to the commissioner that the tire meets the standards, subject to such inspection as the commissioner prescribes. The regulations shall be filed with the Legislature eight months after the federal study on tire noise is available, and shall become operative one year after such filing.

(b) It is the intent of the Legislature in enacting this section that the commissioner shall consider recommendations of the United States Department of Transportation before developing independent standards for tire noise.

(Added by Stats. 1971, Ch. 1197.)

Article 5. Fenders, Ornaments, and Television

(Article 5 enacted by Stats. 1959, Ch. 3.)

27600. No person shall operate any motor vehicle having three or more wheels, any trailer, or semitrailer unless equipped with fenders, covers, or devices, including flaps or splash aprons, or unless the body of the vehicle or attachments thereto afford adequate protection to effectively minimize the spray or splash of water or mud to the rear of the vehicle and all such equipment or such body or attachments thereto shall be at least as wide as the tire tread. This section does not apply to those vehicles exempt from registration, trailers and semitrailers having an unladen weight of under 1,500 pounds, or any vehicles manufactured and first registered prior to January 1, 1971, having an unladen weight of under 1,500 pounds.

(Amended by Stats. 1970, Ch. 215.)

27602. (a) A person shall not drive a motor vehicle if a television receiver, a video monitor, or a television or video screen, or any other similar means of visually displaying a television broadcast or video signal that produces entertainment or business applications, is operating and is located in the motor vehicle at a point forward of the back of the driver's seat, or is operating and the monitor, screen, or display is visible to the driver while driving the motor vehicle.

(b) Subdivision (a) does not apply to the following equipment when installed in a vehicle:

(1) A vehicle information display.

(2) A global positioning display.

(3) A mapping display.

(4) A visual display used to enhance or supplement the driver's view forward, behind, or to the sides of a motor vehicle for the purpose of maneuvering the vehicle.

(5) A television receiver, video monitor, television or video screen, or any other similar means of visually displaying a television broadcast or video signal, if that equipment satisfies one of the following requirements:

(A) The equipment has an interlock device that, when the motor vehicle is driven, disables the equipment for all uses except as a visual display as described in paragraphs (1) to (4), inclusive.

(B) The equipment is designed, operated, and configured in a manner that prevents the driver of the motor vehicle from viewing the television broadcast or video signal while operating the vehicle in a safe and reasonable manner.

(6) A mobile digital terminal that is fitted with an opaque covering that does not allow the driver to view any part of the display while driving, even though the terminal may be operating, installed in a vehicle that is owned or operated by any of the following:

(A) An electrical corporation, as defined in Section 218 of the Public Utilities Code.

(B) A gas corporation, as defined in Section 222 of the Public Utilities Code.

(C) A sewer system corporation, as defined in Section 230.6 of the Public Utilities Code.

(D) A telephone corporation, as defined in Section 234 of the Public Utilities Code.

(E) A water corporation, as defined in Section 241 of the Public Utilities Code.

(F) A local publicly owned electric utility, as defined in Section 224.3 of the Public Utilities Code.

(G) A city, joint powers agency, or special district, if that local entity uses the vehicle solely in the provision of sewer service, gas service, water service, or wastewater service.

(c) Subdivision (a) does not apply to a mobile digital terminal installed in an authorized emergency vehicle or to a motor vehicle providing emergency road service or roadside assistance.

(d) Subdivision (a) does not apply to a mobile digital terminal installed in a vehicle when the vehicle is deployed in an emergency to respond to an interruption or impending interruption of electrical, natural gas, telephone, sewer, water, or wastewater service, and the vehicle is owned or operated by any of the following:

(1) An electrical corporation, as defined in Section 218 of the Public Utilities Code.

(2) A gas corporation, as defined in Section 222 of the Public Utilities Code.

(3) A sewer system corporation, as defined in Section 230.6 of the Public Utilities Code.

(4) A telephone corporation, as defined in Section 234 of the Public Utilities Code.

(5) A water corporation, as defined in Section 241 of the Public Utilities Code.

(6) A local publicly owned electric utility, as defined in Section 224.3 of the Public Utilities Code.

(7) A city, joint powers agency, or special district, if that local entity uses the vehicle solely in the provision of sewer service, gas service, water service, or wastewater service.

(Amended by Stats. 2010, Ch. 328, Sec. 231. (SB 1330) Effective January 1, 2011.)

27603. When a motor vehicle formerly used as a schoolbus is sold to any person and is used exclusively for purposes other than the transportation of pupils pursuant to Article 3 (commencing with Section 39830) of Chapter 5 of Part 23 of the Education Code, it shall be painted by the purchaser a color different than that prescribed by the Department of the California Highway Patrol for schoolbuses before it is operated on any street or highway other than to have the vehicle painted or moved to a place of storage.

The provisions of this section shall not apply where the ownership of a schoolbus is transferred to a nonprofit organization under a contractual arrangement under which the ownership is required to be retransferred to the original owner within 90 days of the date of the original transfer.

(Amended by Stats. 1980, Ch. 676, Sec. 314.)

27604. (a) When a motor vehicle, painted, as required by Section 40800, and formerly used in the enforcement of the provisions of Division 10 (commencing with Section 20000) or 11 (commencing with Section 21000), is sold to any person and is used for purposes other than law enforcement, the vehicle shall be painted or partially painted by the seller or agency formerly using such vehicle so that it will no longer resemble a vehicle complying with Section 40800 and any insignia or other marking of the vehicle identifying it as a traffic law enforcement vehicle shall be removed by the seller or agency formerly using such vehicle before it shall be operated on any street or highway, other than to have the vehicle moved to be painted or to a place of storage.

(b) This section shall not apply to former law enforcement vehicles, without insignia, which are painted one solid color, or which are used exclusively for movie or television production and display signs stating "movie car" prominently on the doors, or which are motorcycles, as defined in Section 400, without insignia.

(c) This section shall not apply to a vehicle, if all of the following conditions are satisfied:

(1) The vehicle is possessed by a federal, state, or local historical society or museum that is open to the public.

(2) The vehicle is secured from unauthorized operation.

(3) The vehicle is not operated on any public road or highway, unless one of the following applies:

(A) The vehicle is being operated within a temporary street closure for the purposes of celebrations, parades, local special events, and other purposes when the operation is approved by local authorities having jurisdiction over the street closure.

(B) The vehicle is of a model year of at least twenty-five years prior to the year of operation.

(Amended by Stats. 2019, Ch. 260, Sec. 1. (AB 309) Effective January 1, 2020.)

27605. (a) No person shall own or operate a motor vehicle painted in the manner described in Section 40800 to resemble a motor vehicle used by a peace officer or traffic officer on duty for the primary purpose of enforcing the provisions of Division 10 (commencing with Section 20000) or Division 11 (commencing with Section 21000) pursuant to Section 40800.

(b) This section shall not apply to vehicles which are painted one solid color or to vehicles first registered on or before January 1, 1979. These provisions shall not apply to vehicles that are any of the following:

(1) Owned by vehicle manufacturers or dealers.

(2) Used by law enforcement agencies in the enforcement of the provisions of Division 10 (commencing with Section 20000) or Division 11 (commencing with Section 21000).

(3) Owned by persons or companies who use the vehicles exclusively for movie or television production and display signs stating "movie car" prominently on the doors.

(4) Owned by persons or companies who use the vehicles exclusively for funeral escort purposes.

(5) Motorcycles, as defined in Section 400, without insignia.

(c) This section shall not apply to a vehicle, if all of the following conditions are satisfied:

(1) The vehicle is possessed by a federal, state, or local historical society or museum that is open to the public.

(2) The vehicle is secured from unauthorized operation.

(3) The vehicle is not operated on any public road or highway, unless one of the following applies:

(A) The vehicle is being operated within a temporary street closure for the purposes of celebrations, parades, local special events, and other purposes when the operation is approved by local authorities having jurisdiction over the street closure.

(B) The vehicle is of a model year of at least twenty-five years prior to the year of operation.

(Amended by Stats. 2019, Ch. 260, Sec. 2. (AB 309) Effective January 1, 2020.)

27606. (a) No person shall own or operate a motor vehicle which is equipped with a light bar, or facsimile thereof, to resemble a motor vehicle used by a peace officer or traffic officer while on duty within that jurisdiction for the primary purpose of enforcing Division 10 (commencing with Section 20000) or Division 11 (commencing with Section 21000) pursuant to Section 40800.

(b) For purposes of this section the following definitions apply:

(1) A "light bar" means any light or device affixed to or mounted upon the roof of a vehicle and extending the width of the roof, or a substantial portion thereof, which emits amber, red, or blue, or any combination of those lights.

(2) A "facsimile of a light bar" is any device designed or contrived to resemble a light bar regardless of the degree of light emission or lack thereof.

(c) This section shall not apply to a vehicle, if all of the following conditions are satisfied:

(1) The vehicle is possessed by a federal, state, or local historical society or museum that is open to the public.

(2) The vehicle is secured from unauthorized operation.

(3) The vehicle is not operated on any public road or highway, unless one of the following applies:

(A) The vehicle is being operated within a temporary street closure for the purposes of celebrations, parades, local special events, and other purposes when the operation is approved by local authorities having jurisdiction over the street closure.

(B) The vehicle is of a model year of at least twenty-five years prior to the year of operation.

(Amended by Stats. 2019, Ch. 260, Sec. 3. (AB 309) Effective January 1, 2020.)

27607. (a) Section 27606 does not apply to vehicles owned or used by persons licensed pursuant to Article 3.1 (commencing with Section 7540) or Article 3.2 (commencing with Section 7544) of Chapter 11.5 of, or Chapter 11.6 (commencing with Section 7590) of, Division 3 of the Business and Professions Code in the performance of their duties under those provisions.

(b) This section does not authorize those persons described in subdivision (a) to equip a vehicle with a light bar if prohibited by other provisions of existing law or regulation.

(Added by Stats. 1986, Ch. 759, Sec. 2.)

Article 6. Tow Trucks

(Heading of Article 6 amended by Stats. 1989, Ch. 1360, Sec. 160.)

27700. (a) Tow trucks shall be equipped with and carry all of the following:

(1) One or more brooms, and the driver of the tow truck engaged to remove a disabled vehicle from the scene of an accident shall remove all glass and debris deposited upon the roadway by the disabled vehicle which is to be towed.

(2) One or more shovels, and whenever practical the tow truck driver engaged to remove any disabled vehicle shall spread dirt upon that portion of the roadway where oil or grease has been deposited by the disabled vehicle.

(3) One or more fire extinguishers of the dry chemical or carbon dioxide type with an aggregate rating of at least 4-B, C units and bearing the approval of a laboratory nationally recognized as properly equipped to make the approval.

(b) A person licensed as a repossession agency pursuant to Chapter 11 (commencing with Section 7500) of Division 3 of the Business and Professions Code is exempt from this section.

(Amended by Stats. 1988, Ch. 924, Sec. 17.)

Article 7. Motorcycles

(Article 7 enacted by Stats. 1959, Ch. 3.)

27800. It is unlawful for a driver of a motorcycle or a motorized bicycle to carry any other person thereon, except on a seat securely fastened to the machine at the rear of the driver and provided with footrests, or in a sidecar attached to a motorcycle and designed for the purpose of carrying a passenger. Every passenger on a motorcycle or a motorized bicycle shall keep his feet on the footrests while such vehicle is in motion.

(Amended by Stats. 1978, Ch. 421.)

27801. A person shall not drive a two-wheel motorcycle that is equipped with either of the following:

(a) A seat so positioned that the driver, when sitting astride the seat, cannot reach the ground with his or her feet.

(b) Handlebars so positioned that the hands of the driver, when upon the grips, are more than six inches above his or her shoulder height when sitting astride the seat.

(Amended by Stats. 2004, Ch. 280, Sec. 1. Effective January 1, 2005.)

27802. (a) The department may adopt reasonable regulations establishing specifications and standards for safety helmets offered for sale, or sold, for use by drivers and passengers of motorcycles and motorized bicycles as it determines are necessary for the safety of those drivers and passengers. The regulations shall include, but are not limited to, the requirements imposed by Federal Motor Vehicle Safety Standard No. 218 (49 C.F.R. Sec. 571.218) and may include compliance with that federal standard by incorporation of its requirements by reference. Each helmet sold or offered for sale for use by drivers and passengers of motorcycles and motorized bicycles shall be conspicuously labeled in accordance with the federal standard which shall constitute the manufacturer's certification that the helmet conforms to the applicable federal motor vehicle safety standards.

(b) No person shall sell, or offer for sale, for use by a driver or passenger of a motorcycle or motorized bicycle any safety helmet which is not of a type meeting requirements established by the department.

(Amended by Stats. 1985, Ch. 163, Sec. 1.)

27803. (a) A driver and any passenger shall wear a safety helmet meeting requirements established pursuant to Section 27802 when riding on a motorcycle, motor-driven cycle, or motorized bicycle.

(b) It is unlawful to operate a motorcycle, motor-driven cycle, or motorized bicycle if the driver or any passenger is not wearing a safety helmet as required by subdivision (a).

(c) It is unlawful to ride as a passenger on a motorcycle, motor-driven cycles, or motorized bicycle if the driver or any passenger is not wearing a safety helmet as required by subdivision (a).

(d) This section applies to persons who are riding on motorcycles, motor-driven cycles, or motorized bicycles operated on the highways.

(e) For the purposes of this section, "wear a safety helmet" or "wearing a safety helmet" means having a safety helmet meeting the requirements of Section 27802 on the person's head that is fastened with the helmet straps and that is of a size that fits the wearing person's head securely without excessive lateral or vertical movement.

(f) This section does not apply to a person operating, or riding as a passenger in, a fully enclosed three-wheeled motor vehicle that is not less than seven feet in length and not less than four feet in width, and has an unladen weight of 900 pounds or more, if the vehicle meets or exceeds all of the requirements of this code, the Federal Motor Vehicle Safety Standards, and the rules and regulations adopted by the United States Department of Transportation and the National Highway Traffic Safety Administration.

(g) In enacting this section, it is the intent of the Legislature to ensure that all persons are provided with an additional safety benefit while operating or riding a motorcycle, motor-driven cycle, or motorized bicycle.

(Amended by Stats. 1997, Ch. 710, Sec. 4. Effective January 1, 1998.)

Article 8. Signs

(Article 8 enacted by Stats. 1959, Ch. 3.)

27900. (a) A motor vehicle or combination of vehicles used to carry the property of others for hire or used to carry passengers for hire, a truck or truck tractor with three or more axles or a truck tractor with a semitrailer, and all commercial motor vehicles, as defined in subdivision (c) of Section 34601, shall have displayed on both sides of each vehicle or on both sides of one of the vehicles in each combination of vehicles the name or trademark of the person under whose authority the vehicle or combination of vehicles is being operated.

(b) The name or trademark of the motor carrier operating a vehicle or combination of vehicles listed in subdivision (a) under a rental agreement with a term of not more than 30 calendar days is not required to be displayed if all of the following requirements are met:

(1) The name or trademark of the lessor is displayed on both sides of each vehicle or on both sides of one of the vehicles in each combination of vehicles.

(2) Any of the following numbers issued to the lessor are displayed on both sides of each vehicle or on both sides of one of the vehicles in each combination of vehicles:

(A) The carrier identification number issued by the United States Department of Transportation.

(B) A valid operating authority number.

(C) A valid motor carrier of property number.

(3) (A) A copy of the rental agreement entered into by the lessor and the vehicle operator is in the vehicle or combination of vehicles.

(B) The rental agreement shall be available for inspection immediately upon the request of an authorized employee of the department, any regularly employed and salaried police officer or deputy sheriff, or any reserve police officer or reserve deputy sheriff listed in Section 830.6 of the Penal Code.

(C) If the rented vehicle or combination of vehicles is operated in conjunction with a commercial enterprise, the rental agreement shall include the operator's carrier identification number or motor carrier of property permit number.

(c) A vehicle or combination of vehicles that is in compliance with Section 390.21 of Title 49 of the Code of Federal Regulations shall be deemed to be in compliance with subdivision (b).

(d) All names, trademarks, and other identifiers for companies no longer in business, no longer operating with the same name, or no longer operating under the same operating authority, shall be removed from or covered over on every motor vehicle or combination of vehicles listed in subdivision (a), within 60 days from the change of company ownership or operation. Those vehicles or combinations of vehicles shall be remarked pursuant to subdivision (a) before they may be operated on the highways.

(Amended by Stats. 2021, Ch. 311, Sec. 8. (SB 814) Effective January 1, 2022.)

27901. The display of the name or trademark shall be in letters in sharp contrast to the background and shall be of such size, shape, and color as to be readily legible during daylight hours from a distance of 50 feet.

This section does not prohibit additional displays not inconsistent with this article.

(Enacted by Stats. 1959, Ch. 3.)

27902. Section 27900 does not apply to any motor vehicle having an unladen weight of 6,000 pounds or less or to any vehicle towed by such motor vehicles, or to any motor vehicle operating under manufacturers, dealers, or transporters special plates, or to any motor vehicle operated by a passenger stage corporation subject to the jurisdiction of the Public Utilities Commission.

(Amended by Stats. 1963, Ch. 1021.)

27903. (a) A vehicle transporting an explosive, blasting agent, flammable liquid, flammable solid, oxidizing material, corrosive, compressed gas, poison, radioactive material, or other hazardous materials, of the type and in quantities that require the display of placards or markings on the vehicle exterior by the United States Department of Transportation pursuant to Parts 172, 173, and 177 of Title 49 of the Code of Federal Regulations shall display those placards and markings in the manner and under conditions prescribed by those regulations.

(b) Notwithstanding subdivision (a), a vehicle shall not display hazardous materials placards or markings unless permitted or required by Subparts D and F of Part 172 of Title 49 of the Code of Federal Regulations.

(c) This section does not apply to any of the following:

(1) A vehicle transporting not more than 20 pounds of smokeless powder or not more than five pounds of black sporting powder or any combination thereof.

(2) The operation of a vehicle excepted by subdivision (b) of Section 34501.

(Amended by Stats. 2023, Ch. 219, Sec. 6. (SB 891) Effective January 1, 2024.)

27904. There shall be displayed in a conspicuous place on both the right and left sides of a pilot car a sign showing the name of the company which owns or operates the pilot car. The name shall contrast with the background and shall be of a size, shape, and color as to be readily legible during daylight hours from a distance of 50 feet. Additional markings which do not interfere with the legibility of the name may also be displayed.

(Amended by Stats. 1988, Ch. 460, Sec. 2.)

27904.5. Subject to Section 35783.5, a pilot car shall display neat, clean, and legible signs containing the word "OVERSIZE." The words "OVERSIZE LOAD," "WIDE LOAD," or "LONG LOAD" may be substituted as applicable. The sign shall be a minimum of 48 inches above the ground and shall be legible at 45 degrees from either side when read from the front or rear. The sign shall have a bright yellow background with a minimum projected area of 440 square inches. The lettering shall be black with a 1-inch minimum brush stroke width and a 6-inch minimum letter height.

(Added by Stats. 1988, Ch. 460, Sec. 3.)

27905. It is unlawful to display on a vehicle any sign with the words "fire" or "fire department" thereon, except on vehicles owned and operated by a regularly organized fire department, fire district, forestry service, or the State Fire Marshal's Office, and on the privately owned vehicles of any regular member of any such fire departments.

(Enacted by Stats. 1959, Ch. 3.)

27906. (a) Every schoolbus, while being used for the transportation of school pupils at or below the 12th-grade level shall bear upon the front and rear of the bus a plainly visible sign containing the word "schoolbus" in letters not less than eight inches in height. The letters on schoolbus signs shall be of proportionate width.

Except as provided in subdivision (b), no other vehicle shall display a sign containing the word "schoolbus."

(b) Notwithstanding subdivision (a), a schoolbus which is also used to transport persons of any age who are developmentally disabled, as defined by the Lanterman Developmental Disabilities Services Act (Division 4.5 (commencing with Section 4500) of the Welfare and Institutions Code), may display a sign containing the word "schoolbus" while transporting those persons to or from vocational, prevocational, or work training centers sponsored by the State Department of Developmental Services.

(c) Every schoolbus, when operated for the transportation of school pupils at or below the 12th-grade level, shall bear upon the rear of the bus, below the rear windows, a plainly visible sign containing the words "Stop When Red Lights Flash" in letters not less than six inches in height. The letters on schoolbus signs shall be of proportionate width.

(Amended by Stats. 1986, Ch. 678, Sec. 3.)

27906.5. Every youth bus, when operated for the transportation of school pupils, shall bear, upon the front and rear of the youth bus, a plainly visible sign containing the words "YOUTH BUS" in letters not less than eight inches in height. The letters on youth bus signs shall be of proportionate width and the letters shall be in sharp contrast to the background.

(Added by Stats. 1982, Ch. 383, Sec. 6. Effective July 4, 1982. Operative on date (not sooner than October 1, 1982, or later than January 1, 1983) prescribed by Sec. 13 of Ch. 383.)

27906.7. (a) A school district, county office of education, or charter school using a zero-emission schoolbus to transport pupils at or below the 12th-grade level may place signage on the rear of the zero-emission schoolbus that identifies the schoolbus as a clean air zero-emission bus. The signage may specify the fuel type of the zero-emission schoolbus.

(b) The Department of the California Highway Patrol may issue guidelines governing the size and placement of the signage described in subdivision (a).

(Added by Stats. 2023, Ch. 413, Sec. 1. (SB 775) Effective January 1, 2024.)

27907. There shall be displayed in a conspicuous place on both the right and left side of a tow truck, a repossessor's tow vehicle, or an automobile dismantler's tow vehicle used to tow or carry vehicles a sign showing the name of the company or the owner or operator of the tow truck or tow vehicle. The sign shall also contain the business address and telephone number of the owner or driver. The letters and numbers of the sign shall not be less than 2 inches in height and shall be in contrast to the color of the background upon which they are placed.

A person licensed as a repossession agency pursuant to Chapter 11 (commencing with Section 7500) of Division 3 of the Business and Professions Code, or a registrant of the agency, may use the license number issued to the agency by the Department of Consumer Affairs in lieu of a name, business address, and telephone number.

(Amended by Stats. 1999, Ch. 456, Sec. 16. Effective January 1, 2000.)

27908. (a) In every taxicab operated in this state there shall be a sign of heavy material, not smaller than 6 inches by 4 inches, or such other size as the agency regulating the operation of the taxicab provides for other notices or signs required to be in every taxicab, securely attached and clearly displayed in view of the passenger at all times, providing in letters as large as the size of the sign will reasonably allow, all of the following information:

(1) The name, address, and telephone number of the agency regulating the operation of the taxicab.

(2) The name, address, and telephone number of the firm licensed or controlled by the agency regulating the operation of the taxicab.

(b) In the event more than one local regulatory agency has jurisdiction over the operation of the taxicab, the notice required by paragraph (1) of subdivision (a) shall provide the name, address, and telephone number of the agency having jurisdiction in the area where the taxicab operator conducts its greatest volume of business; or, if this cannot readily be ascertained, the agency having jurisdiction in the area where the taxicab operator maintains its offices or primary place of business, provided that the operator conducts a substantial volume of business in such area; or, if neither of the foregoing provisions apply, any agency having jurisdiction of an area where the taxicab operator conducts a substantial volume of business.

(c) As used in this section, "taxicab" means a passenger vehicle designed for carrying not more than eight persons, excluding the driver, and used to carry passengers for hire. "Taxicab" shall not include a charter-party carrier of passengers within the meaning of the Passenger Charter-party Carriers' Act, Chapter 8 (commencing with Section 5351) of Division 2 of the Public Utilities Code.

(Added by Stats. 1973, Ch. 1158.)

27909. Any vehicle which carries liquefied petroleum gas fuel or natural gas, in a tank attached to a vehicle, in any concealed area, including trunks, compartments, or under the vehicle, shall display on the exterior of the vehicle the letters "CNG," "LNG," or "LPG," whichever type fuel is utilized, in block letters at least one inch high. The letters shall be of contrasting color and shall be placed as near as possible to the area of the location of the tank. Any vehicle fueled by liquefied petroleum gas fuel or by natural gas may also comply with this section by displaying on each side of the vehicle words or letters at least 0.25 inch high indicating that the vehicle is fueled by liquefied petroleum gas or natural gas. It is unlawful to dispense liquefied petroleum gas fuel or natural gas into any tank in a concealed area of any vehicle registered in California, unless the vehicle complies with the requirements of this section.

(Amended by Stats. 1983, Ch. 142, Sec. 171.)

27910. The Department of the California Highway Patrol shall initiate a 12-month study to determine an effective means to enforce the provisions of the Commercial Vehicle Registration Act of 2001. The Department of the California Highway Patrol, after consultation with representatives from the Department of Transportation, the Board of Equalization, the Department of Motor Vehicles, and the commercial vehicle industry, shall provide, on or before July 1, 2003, recommendations to the Legislature for actions to be taken to ensure compliance with that act.

(Added by Stats. 2000, Ch. 861, Sec. 55. Effective September 29, 2000. Operative December 31, 2001, pursuant to Sec. 67 of Ch. 861.)

Article 9. Refrigeration Equipment

(Article 9 added by Stats. 1961, Ch. 1335.)

28000. Every refrigerator van equipped with one or more doors designed to lock automatically upon closure shall have at least one door which can be opened from inside the van as an emergency means of exit.

For the purposes of this article, "refrigerator van" means any motor truck, semitrailer, or trailer, with a fully enclosed cargo body having an enclosed volume of 15 cubic feet or more, which utilizes a mechanical refrigeration system to reduce the temperature within the enclosed portion of the vehicle to 32 degrees Fahrenheit or less, or which provides refrigeration by the use of dry ice.

(Added by Stats. 1961, Ch. 1335.)

Article 10. Odometers

(Article 10 added by Stats. 1967, Ch. 1109.)

28050. It is unlawful for any person to advertise for sale, to sell, to use, or to install on any part of a motor vehicle or on an odometer in a motor vehicle any device which causes the odometer to register any mileage other than the true mileage driven. For the purposes of this section the true mileage driven is that mileage driven by the car as registered by the odometer within the manufacturer's designed tolerance.

(Added by Stats. 1967, Ch. 1109.)

28050.5. It is unlawful for any person with the intent to defraud to operate a motor vehicle on any street or highway knowing that the odometer of such vehicle is disconnected or nonfunctional.

(Added by Stats. 1967, Ch. 1210.)

28051. It is unlawful for any person to disconnect, turn back, advance, or reset the odometer of any motor vehicle with the intent to alter the number of miles indicated on the odometer gauge.

(Amended by Stats. 1973, Ch. 774.)

28051.5. It is unlawful for any person to advertise for sale, to sell, or to use, any device designed primarily for the purpose of turning back or resetting the odometer of any motor vehicle to reduce the number of miles indicated on the odometer gauge.

(Added by Stats. 1970, Ch. 841.)

28052. If a manufacturer, distributor, or dealer of a new motor vehicle makes any warranty to the purchaser of, and with respect to, a new motor vehicle which is based on the amount of miles that the motor vehicle is driven, only those miles which the motor vehicle has been driven on and after the date that the motor vehicle has first been sold as new to the purchaser shall be considered for purposes of the warranty.

The mileage indicated upon the odometer of the motor vehicle on the date that the motor vehicle is first sold as new to the purchaser shall, for purposes of the warranty, be the mileage upon which the warranty shall commence.

Nothing in this section shall be construed to relieve any person of any criminal punishment to which he would otherwise be subject under Section 28051.

The provisions of this section shall apply only to motor vehicles which are sold on or after the effective date of this section.

(Added by Stats. 1969, Ch. 111.)

28053. (a) Nothing in this article prevents the service, repair, or replacement of an odometer, if the mileage indicated thereon remains the same as before the service, repair, or replacement. If the odometer is incapable of registering the same mileage as before the service, repair, or replacement, the odometer shall be adjusted to read zero and a notice in writing shall be attached to the left doorframe of the vehicle by the person performing the service, repair, or replacement specifying the mileage prior to the service, repair or replacement of the odometer and the date on which it was serviced, repaired, or replaced.

(b) No person shall fail to adjust an odometer or affix a notice regarding the adjustment as required by subdivision (a).

(c) No person shall, with intent to defraud, remove or alter any notice affixed to a vehicle pursuant to subdivision (a).

(Repealed and added by Stats. 1987, Ch. 130, Sec. 2.)

Article 11. Fire Extinguishers

(Article 11 added by Stats. 1972, Ch. 392.)

28060. (a) No person shall sell or offer for sale a new recreational vehicle or new camper which is equipped with cooking equipment or heating equipment, and no dealer or person holding a retail seller's permit shall sell or offer for sale a used recreational vehicle or a used camper which is equipped with cooking or heating equipment, unless such new or used vehicle or new or used camper is equipped with at least one fire extinguisher, filled and ready for use, of the dry chemical or carbon dioxide type with an aggregate rating of at least 4-B:C units, which meets the requirements specified in Section 13162 of the Health and Safety Code.

(b) The operator of a recreational vehicle, or a vehicle to which a camper is attached, which recreational vehicle or camper is equipped with a fire extinguisher as required by subdivision (a), shall carry such fire extinguisher in such recreational vehicle or camper and shall maintain the fire extinguisher in an efficient operating condition.

(c) As used in this section:

(1) "Cooking equipment" means a device designed for cooking which utilizes combustible material, including, but not limited to, materials such as charcoal or any flammable gas or liquid, and "heating equipment" means a device designed for heating which utilizes combustible material, including, but not limited to, materials such as charcoal or any flammable gas or liquid.

(2) "Recreational vehicle" has the same meaning as defined in Section 18010.5 of the Health and Safety Code.

(Added by Stats. 1972, Ch. 392.)

28062. (a) A modified limousine shall be equipped with two readily accessible and fully charged fire extinguishers having at least a 2A10BC 5 pound rating and maintained in efficient operating condition. One fire extinguisher shall be securely mounted in the driver's compartment and at least one shall be accessible to the passengers.

(b) The driver or operator of a modified limousine shall notify the passengers of the location of each fire extinguisher prior to the commencement of any trip.

(Added by Stats. 2014, Ch. 860, Sec. 15. (SB 611) Effective September 30, 2014.)

Article 11.5. Bumpers

(Heading of Article 11.5 renumbered from Article 11 by Stats. 1976, Ch. 1079.)

28070. As used in this article, "passenger vehicle" means "passenger vehicle" as defined in Section 34710.

(Added by Stats. 1972, Ch. 272.)

28071. Every passenger vehicle registered in this state shall be equipped with a front bumper and with a rear bumper. As used in this section, "bumper" means any device designed and intended by a manufacturer to prevent the front or rear of the body of the vehicle from coming into contact with any other motor vehicle. This section shall not apply to any passenger vehicle that is required to be equipped with an energy absorption system pursuant to either state or federal law, or to any passenger vehicle which was not equipped with a front or rear bumper, or both, at the time that it was first sold and registered under the laws of this or any other state or foreign jurisdiction.

(Amended by Stats. 1973, Ch. 451.)

Article 12. Camper Signaling Devices

(Article 12 added by Stats. 1973, Ch. 292.)

28080. (a) Every motor vehicle upon which a camper is mounted shall be equipped with an audible or visual signaling device which can be activated from inside the camper and which is constructed so as to allow any person inside the camper to gain the attention of the driver of the motor vehicle. In no event shall a horn, as required by Section 27000, be used to comply with this subdivision.

(b) No person shall drive a motor vehicle upon which is mounted a camper containing any passenger unless the motor vehicle is equipped as required by subdivision (a).

(Added by Stats. 1973, Ch. 292.)

28081. The provisions of Section 28080 shall not apply to either of the following:

(a) Any motor vehicle upon which a camper is mounted if a person is able to move between the cab portion of the motor vehicle and the camper.

(b) Any motor vehicle upon which a camper is mounted, which motor vehicle is equipped with a sliding or removable rear window which can be opened or removed by a person inside such camper.

(Added by Stats. 1973, Ch. 292.)

Article 13. Theft Alarm System

(Article 13 added by Stats. 1977, Ch. 993.)

28085. Any motor vehicle may be equipped with a theft alarm system which flashes the lights of the vehicle, or sounds an audible signal, or both, and which operates as follows:

(a) The system may flash any of the lights required or permitted on the vehicle.

(b) The system may sound an audible signal.

(c) No vehicle shall be equipped with a theft alarm system which emits the sound of a siren.

(Amended by Stats. 1994, Ch. 516, Sec. 1. Effective January 1, 1995.)

Article 14. Cellular Telephones

(Article 14 added by Stats. 1987, Ch. 1306, Sec. 1.)

28090. Every renter of a motor vehicle with cellular radio telephone equipment shall provide the person who rents the motor vehicle with written operating instructions concerning the safe use of the equipment. The equipment shall also be clearly labeled with operating instructions concerning the safe use of the equipment.

(Added by Stats. 1987, Ch. 1306, Sec. 1.)

Article 15. Pilot Cars

(Article 15 added by Stats. 1988, Ch. 460, Sec. 4.)

28100. A pilot car shall display at least one red warning flag on each side of the vehicle. The flags shall be a minimum of 16 inches square, and shall be mounted so as to be visible from both the front and rear of the vehicle. The flags shall be removed or covered when the vehicle is not operating as a pilot car.

(Added by Stats. 1988, Ch. 460, Sec. 4.)

28101. In addition to the lighting, sign, and flag requirements in Sections 25270, 27904, 27904.5, and 28100, a pilot car shall meet all of the following requirements:

(a) Be a vehicle not less than 60 inches in width.

(b) Be equipped with all of the following:

(1) One STOP/SLOW paddle.

(2) One orange vest, shirt, or jacket.

(3) One red hand flag (24 inches square).

(4) One two-way radio communication device.

(Added by Stats. 1988, Ch. 460, Sec. 4.)

28102. Pilot cars equipped with vertical clearance measuring devices shall comply with Section 35252.

(Added by Stats. 1988, Ch. 460, Sec. 4.)

28103. It is unlawful and an infraction for any person to violate any provision of this article or to fail to have any required equipment in good working order.

(Added by Stats. 1988, Ch. 460, Sec. 4.)

Article 16. Methanol or Ethanol Fueled Vehicles

(Article 16 added by Stats. 1989, Ch. 1301, Sec. 1.)

28110. As used in this article, "antisiphoning device" means a device which prevents the removal by suction of fuel from a motor vehicle.

(Added by Stats. 1989, Ch. 1301, Sec. 1.)

28111. Except as otherwise provided in Section 28112, any 1993 and later model-year vehicle which is capable of operating on methanol or ethanol and is imported into the state, or sold, purchased, leased, rented, or acquired in the state, shall be equipped with an antisiphoning device.

(Added by Stats. 1989, Ch. 1301, Sec. 1.)

28112. Notwithstanding subdivision (a) of Section 28111, the State Air Resources Board may adopt regulations providing for exemptions from antisiphoning device requirements for categories of vehicles of 1993 and later model-years which it determines not susceptible to siphoning.

(Added by Stats. 1989, Ch. 1301, Sec. 1.)

28113. (a) Every light-duty and medium-duty motor vehicle operated for compensation to transport persons in an air quality management district or air pollution control district, which does not meet all applicable state ambient air quality standards, shall be a low-emission vehicle, as defined by regulation of the State Air Resources Board. If the vehicle is capable of operating on more than one fuel, it shall be operated within any nonattainment area to the maximum extent practicable either on the designated clean fuel on which the low-emission vehicle was certified or on any other fuel designated by the State Air Resources Board as a substitute fuel for the designated clean fuel. Any air quality management district or air pollution control district may adopt regulations for the enforcement of this section which are consistent with regulations of the State Air Resources Board.

(b) As used in this section, "motor vehicle operated for compensation to transport persons" includes a taxi cab, bus, airport shuttle vehicle, transit authority or transit district vehicle, or a vehicle owned by a private entity providing transit service under contract with a transit district or transportation authority.

(c) As used in this section, "light-duty" has the same meaning as defined in Section 39035 of the Health and Safety Code.

(d) As used in this section, "medium-duty" has the same meaning as defined in Section 39037.5 of the Health and Safety Code.

(e) This section applies to all new light-duty motor vehicles purchased on or after January 1, 1997, and to all new medium-duty vehicles purchased on or after January 1, 1998.

(Added by Stats. 1991, Ch. 496, Sec. 3.)

28114. (a) Every heavy-duty vehicle operated by a transit authority or transit district, or owned by a private entity providing transit service under contract with a transit district or transportation authority, and used to transport persons for compensation shall meet the emission standards adopted by the State Air Resources Board pursuant to Section 43806 of the Health and Safety Code.

(b) As used in this section, "heavy-duty" has the same meaning as defined in Section 39033 of the Health and Safety Code.

(c) This section applies to all new heavy-duty motor vehicles purchased on or after January 1, 1996, and all new or replacement engines purchased on or after January 1, 1996, for use in heavy-duty vehicles.

(Added by Stats. 1991, Ch. 496, Sec. 4.)

Article 17. Jamming Devices

(Article 17 added by Stats. 1998, Ch. 493, Sec. 1.)

28150. (a) No vehicle shall be equipped with any device that is designed for, or is capable of, jamming, scrambling, neutralizing, disabling, or otherwise interfering with radar, laser, or any other electronic device used by a law enforcement agency to measure the speed of moving objects.

(b) No person shall use, buy, possess, manufacture, sell, or otherwise distribute any device that is designed for jamming, scrambling, neutralizing, disabling, or otherwise interfering with radar, laser, or any other electronic device used by a law enforcement agency to measure the speed of moving objects.

(c) Except as provided in subdivision (d), a violation of subdivision (a) or (b) is an infraction.

(d) When a person possesses four or more devices in violation of subdivision (b), the person is guilty of a misdemeanor.

(e) Notwithstanding any other provision of law, a person who has a valid federal license for operating the devices described in this section may transport one or more of those devices if the license is carried in the vehicle transporting the device at all times when the device is being transported.

(Added by Stats. 1998, Ch. 493, Sec. 1. Effective January 1, 1999.)

Article 17.5. Driver Monitoring Defeat Devices

(Article 17.5 added by Stats. 2024, Ch. 604, Sec. 1.)

28155. (a) A vehicle shall not be equipped with a device that is specifically designed for, marketed for, or being used for, neutralizing, disabling, or otherwise interfering with a driver monitoring system that is engaged when drivers are utilizing advanced driver assistance system features or autonomous technology, as defined in Section 38750.

(b) A person shall not use, buy, possess, manufacture, sell, advertise for sale, or otherwise distribute a device that is specifically designed for neutralizing, disabling, or otherwise interfering with a driver monitoring system that is engaged when drivers are utilizing advanced driver assistance system features or autonomous technology, as defined in Section 38750.

(c) A violation of subdivision (a) or (b) is an infraction.

(d) All of the following are exempt from subdivision (a) or (b):

(1) A manufacturer while operating under a testing permit issued pursuant to Section 38750.

(2) A person or entity conducting motor vehicle diagnostic services, repairs, or enhancements consistent with the original equipment manufacturer's safety standards, whether physically or remotely.

(3) In connection with an update or enhancement of the driver monitoring system by the original equipment manufacturer.

(4) In connection with a repair of a vehicle malfunction corrected by the manufacturer or manufacturer-approved third-party vendor.

(5) To remedy a defect corrected by the manufacturer or manufacturer-approved third-party vendor.

(6) For modifications or compliance pursuant to applicable provisions of the federal Americans with Disabilities Act of 1990 (42 U.S.C. Sec. 12101 et seq.).

(e) For purposes of this section, "advanced driver assistance system" means Level 2 of SAE International's Taxonomy and Definitions for Terms Related to Driving Automation Systems for On-Road Motor Vehicles, standard J3016 (APR 2021).

(f) For purposes of this section, a "direct driver monitoring system" includes exterior camera systems, interior camera systems, or other detection devices designed specifically to monitor the alertness of the driver while advanced driver assistance system technology or autonomous technology that meets the definition of a Level 3, 4 or 5 SAE International's Taxonomy and Definitions for Terms Related to Driving Automation Systems for On-Road Motor Vehicles, standard J3016 (APR2021) is engaged, systems that require a driver to maintain their hands on the steering wheel, pressure sensors, safety sensors, distracted driver sensors, systems that help the driver to continue to pay attention to the traffic situation, systems that warn the driver when the driver is distracted, and any other system that has been shown to be effective in monitoring drivers while they are utilizing advanced driver assistance system or autonomous technology.

(g) This section shall not be construed to do either of the following:

(1) Restrict or prohibit access to a motor vehicle's onboard computer systems to conduct diagnostics, repairs, or enhancements consistent with the original equipment manufacturer's safety standards, whether physically or remotely.

(2) Prevent a person from taking immediate steps to protect the life or physical safety of the driver or other people in the vehicle.

(Added by Stats. 2024, Ch. 604, Sec. 1. (SB 1313) Effective January 1, 2025.)

Article 18. Child Safety Alert System

(Article 18 added by Stats. 2016, Ch. 721, Sec. 7.)

28160. (a) On or before January 1, 2018, the department shall adopt regulations governing the specifications, installation, and use of child safety alert systems.

(b) (1) (A) Except as provided in subparagraphs (B) and (C), on or before March 1, 2019, each schoolbus, school pupil activity bus, except school pupil activity buses described in paragraph (2), youth bus, and child care motor vehicle shall be equipped with an operational child safety alert system.

(B) If a school district, county office of education, or charter school with an average daily attendance of 4,000 pupils or fewer, or a private school with 4,000 pupils or fewer in attendance, cannot meet the requirements of this section on or before March 1, 2019, the school district, county office of education, charter school, or private school shall submit to the department, on or before March 1, 2019, documentation that demonstrates that it has, before March 1, 2019, ordered or purchased the child safety alert system or child safety alert systems, and includes an estimate of repairs or installation, the total number of vehicles described in subparagraph (A) in the fleet and the number of vehicles described in subparagraph (A) that do not have an installed child safety alert system, the proposed date of installation, and the name of the vendor or individual who will install the child safety alert system or child safety alert systems. Upon providing this documentation, the school district, county office of education, charter school, or private school shall have an additional six months, not to extend beyond September 1, 2019, to meet the requirements of this section.

(C) Any entity other than a school district, county office of education, charter school, or private school that operates a schoolbus, school pupil activity bus, except school pupil activity buses described in paragraph (2), youth bus, or child care motor vehicle that is subject to the requirements of this section may submit documentation as specified in subparagraph (B) to the department. Upon providing this documentation, the entity shall have an additional six months, not to extend beyond September 1, 2019, to meet the requirements of this section.

(D) This section shall apply to all school districts, county offices of education, charter schools, and private schools, including those that began the 2018–19 school year before September 1, 2018.

(2) A school pupil activity bus is not required to be equipped with an operational child safety alert system if all of the following apply:

(A) The school pupil activity bus is not used exclusively to transport pupils.

(B) When the school pupil activity bus is used to transport pupils, the pupils are accompanied by at least one adult chaperone selected by a school official. If an adult chaperone is not a school employee, the chaperone shall meet the requirements for a school volunteer established by the policies of the school district, county office of education, charter school, or private school.

(C) One adult chaperone has a list of every pupil and adult chaperone, including a school employee, who is on the school pupil activity bus at the time of departure.

(D) The driver has reviewed all safety and emergency procedures before the initial departure and the driver and adult chaperone have signed a form with the time and date acknowledging that the safety plan and procedures were reviewed.

(E) Immediately before departure from any location, the adult chaperone shall account for each pupil on the list of pupils, verify the number of pupils to the driver, and sign a form indicating that all pupils are present or accounted for.

(F) After pupils have exited a school pupil activity bus, and before driving away, the driver shall check all areas of the bus, including, but not limited to, overhead compartments and bathrooms, to ensure that the bus is vacant.

(G) The driver shall sign a form with the time and date verifying that all required procedures have been followed.

(H) The information required to be recorded pursuant to subparagraphs (D), (E), and (G) may be recorded on a single form. These forms shall be retained by the school district, county office of education, charter school, or private school for a minimum of two years.

(c) The department shall consult with the State Department of Education to develop frequently asked questions related to the implementation of this section and of Section 1294 of Title 13 of the California Code of Regulations. The department shall also consult with, at a minimum, the California Association of School Transportation Officials when developing the frequently asked questions. The department and the State Department of Education shall each post the frequently asked questions on their respective Internet Web sites.

(d) A "child safety alert system" is a device located at the interior rear of a vehicle that requires the driver to either manually contact or scan the device before exiting the vehicle, thereby prompting the driver to inspect the entirety of the interior of the vehicle before exiting.

(e) For purposes of this section, the following definitions apply:

(1) "Child care motor vehicle" means a vehicle designed, used, or maintained for more than eight persons, including the driver, that is used by a child care provider to transport children.

(2) "Child care provider" has the same meaning as provided for "day care center" in Section 1596.76 of the Health and Safety Code.

(Amended by Stats. 2018, Ch. 426, Sec. 34. (AB 1840) Effective September 17, 2018.)

Chapter 6. Connected Vehicle Service

(Chapter 6 added by Stats. 2024, Ch. 655, Sec. 2.)

Article 1. General Provisions

(Article 1 added by Stats. 2024, Ch. 655, Sec. 2.)

28200. Unless the context requires otherwise, for purposes of this chapter, the following terms have the following meanings:

(a) "Account holder" means a person who is a party to or a user of services provided under a contract for connected vehicle service with a covered provider, and includes, but is not limited to, a subscriber, customer, or registered user.

(b) "Connected vehicle location access" is a type of connected vehicle service that allows a person who is outside of a vehicle, excluding a covered provider or vehicle cellular data provider, to view or track the location of the vehicle, including, but not limited to, a location determined by a Global Positioning System (GPS), whether through the internet, an app-based technology, or any other remote wireless connectivity technology.

(c) "Connected vehicle service" means any capability provided by or on behalf of a vehicle manufacturer that enables a person, excluding a covered provider or vehicle cellular data provider, to remotely obtain data from, or send commands to, a vehicle, which may be accomplished through a software application that is designed to be operated on a mobile device.

(d) "Connected vehicle service account" means an account or other means by which a person enrolls in or obtains access to a connected vehicle service.

(e) "Connected vehicle service request" means a request by a driver to terminate a person's access to connected vehicle service.

(f) "Covered provider" means a vehicle manufacturer or an entity acting on behalf of the vehicle manufacturer that provides connected vehicle service.

(Added by Stats. 2024, Ch. 655, Sec. 2. (SB 1394) Effective January 1, 2025. Operative July 1, 2025, pursuant to Sec. 28206.)

28202. (a) A vehicle with connected vehicle service shall clearly indicate to a person who is inside the vehicle when a person who is outside the vehicle has accessed either of the following:

(1) Connected vehicle service.

(2) Connected vehicle location access.

(b) This section shall become operative on January 1, 2028.

(Added by Stats. 2024, Ch. 655, Sec. 2. (SB 1394) Effective January 1, 2025. Operative January 1, 2028, by its own provisions.)

28204. The provisions of this chapter are severable. If any provision of this chapter or its application is held invalid, that invalidity shall not affect other provisions or applications that can be given effect without the invalid provision or application.

(Added by Stats. 2024, Ch. 655, Sec. 2. (SB 1394) Effective January 1, 2025. Operative July 1, 2025, pursuant to Sec. 28206.)

28206. (a) This article, except Section 28202, and Article 2 (commencing with Section 28220) shall become operative on July 1, 2025, and apply to vehicles that have connected vehicle service.

(b) Article 3 (commencing with Section 28240) shall become operative as follows:

(1) On January 1, 2028, for vehicles manufactured on or after January 1, 2028, that have connected vehicle location access.

(2) On July 1, 2026, for vehicles manufactured prior to January 1, 2028, that have connected vehicle location access, and have the capability to receive software updates that provide for the functionality required by Article 3 (commencing with Section 28240).

(c) This chapter does not apply to vehicles owned or operated by a rental company, as defined in Section 1939.01 of the Civil Code.

(Added by Stats. 2024, Ch. 655, Sec. 2. (SB 1394) Effective January 1, 2025.)

28210. A covered provider or any officer, director, employee, vendor, or agent of a covered provider shall not be subject to liability for any claims deriving from an action taken in compliance with this chapter.

(Added by Stats. 2024, Ch. 655, Sec. 2. (SB 1394) Effective January 1, 2025. Operative July 1, 2025, pursuant to Sec. 28206.)

Article 2. Access to Connected Vehicle Service

(Article 2 added by Stats. 2024, Ch. 655, Sec. 2.)

28220. (a) A covered provider shall provide a process that includes a prominent and clearly visible link entitled "HOW TO DISCONNECT REMOTE VEHICLE ACCESS" on its internet website to complete both of the following transactions:

(1) Submit a connected vehicle service request.

(2) Obtain a new connected vehicle service account.

(b) A covered provider shall ensure that all communications provided pursuant to this article are clear, concise, and written in accessible language. It is imperative that drivers, particularly those who are abuse survivors, receive support and clear guidance throughout the process for submitting a connected vehicle service request or obtaining a new connected vehicle service account.

(Added by Stats. 2024, Ch. 655, Sec. 2. (SB 1394) Effective January 1, 2025. Operative July 1, 2025, pursuant to Sec. 28206.)

28222. To enhance transparency and communication, the process to submit a connected vehicle service request or obtain a new connected vehicle service account shall be efficient, secure, user-friendly, and include all of the following features:

(a) Upon submission of a connected vehicle service request or request to obtain a new connected vehicle service account, the covered provider shall automatically send a confirmation email to the driver, acknowledging the receipt of the request. This email shall contain a reference number for the request and an outline of the subsequent steps in the process.

(b) Upon completing the review of the request, the covered provider shall inform the driver of the action taken, including, as applicable, whether a person's access to connected vehicle service has been terminated, or if additional information or proof of legal possession of the vehicle is needed. This alert shall clearly state any relevant details or further actions required from the driver to complete a successful connected vehicle service request.

(c) If a connected vehicle service request is approved, the covered provider shall provide the driver with a clear explanation and guidance on how to create their own connected vehicle service account, if applicable, to ensure that the driver can maintain control over the connected vehicle service once another person's access to connected vehicle service has been terminated.

(Added by Stats. 2024, Ch. 655, Sec. 2. (SB 1394) Effective January 1, 2025. Operative July 1, 2025, pursuant to Sec. 28206.)

28224. (a) A driver shall demonstrate to a covered provider the authority to terminate a person's access to connected vehicle service by providing both of the following:

(1) The vehicle identification number.

(2) Proof of legal possession of the vehicle, which may be a legal title to the vehicle, or a dissolution decree, temporary court order, or domestic violence restraining order that awards possession or exclusive use of the vehicle to the driver. A court order awarding sole possession or exclusive use of a vehicle shall take priority over a vehicle title showing joint ownership for purposes of this article.

(b) A covered provider shall not require a driver to provide any proof of legal possession other than what is required in subdivision (a) to establish the authority to terminate a person's access to connected vehicle service.

(c) A covered provider shall not require a driver to take any action to terminate a person's access to connected vehicle service other than what is set forth in this section, including, but not limited to, requiring any of the following:

(1) Payment of a fee, penalty, or other charge to complete a connected vehicle service request.

(2) Maintaining or extending the term of a connected vehicle service account.

(3) Approval by any account holder, including, but not limited to, the named account holder, of the change in access.

(4) An increase in the rate charged for the connected vehicle service.

(d) A covered provider shall terminate a person's access to connected vehicle service within two business days after the date of receiving a completed request from a driver who meets the requirements of this section.

(Added by Stats. 2024, Ch. 655, Sec. 2. (SB 1394) Effective January 1, 2025. Operative July 1, 2025, pursuant to Sec. 28206.)

28226. (a) If a covered provider terminated a person's access to connected vehicle service in response to a connected vehicle service request, the covered provider shall not provide to the person any data or information regarding the driver, the vehicle, or any new connected vehicle service account that was generated after that person's access to the connected vehicle service was terminated.

(b) A covered provider shall ensure that all personal information provided during the process to terminate a person's access to connected vehicle service is handled with appropriate security and privacy, adhering to relevant data protection laws and regulations.

(c) A covered provider and any officer, director, employee, vendor, or agent thereof shall treat any information submitted by a driver pursuant to this article as confidential and shall comply with applicable privacy laws.

(d) A covered provider shall not share information submitted by a driver pursuant to this article with any third party without the affirmative consent of the driver, unless sharing that information is required to effectuate a connected vehicle service request.

(e) Nothing in this section shall preclude a covered provider from responding to a court order or warrant.

(Added by Stats. 2024, Ch. 655, Sec. 2. (SB 1394) Effective January 1, 2025. Operative July 1, 2025, pursuant to Sec. 28206.)

28228. The termination of connected vehicle service pursuant to this article shall not be deemed to impact legal ownership of a vehicle.

(Added by Stats. 2024, Ch. 655, Sec. 2. (SB 1394) Effective January 1, 2025. Operative July 1, 2025, pursuant to Sec. 28206.)

Article 3. Disabling Connected Vehicle Location Access

(Article 3 added by Stats. 2024, Ch. 655, Sec. 2.)

28240. If a vehicle includes connected vehicle location access, a covered provider shall provide a mechanism that can be used by a driver who is inside a vehicle to immediately disable connected vehicle location access.

(Added by Stats. 2024, Ch. 655, Sec. 2. (SB 1394) Effective January 1, 2025. Conditionally operative pursuant to Sec. 28206.)

28242. A mechanism for disabling connected vehicle location access shall meet all of the following requirements:

(a) Be prominently located and easy to use.

(b) Not require access to, or use of, a remote or online application.

(c) (1) Not require account creation, a password, or login information.

(2) A vehicle manufacturer may require a driver to input a mobile number associated with the connected vehicle service account. If a

vehicle manufacturer requires a driver to input a mobile number in order to disable the connected vehicle location access connection, it shall not require any further information in order to allow the driver to disable the connection, including, but not limited to, using that number as part of a two-factor authentication process that results in sending a code to the mobile number.

(d) Allow connected vehicle location access that has been disabled from inside the vehicle to be enabled only by a driver who is located inside the vehicle.

(Added by Stats. 2024, Ch. 655, Sec. 2. (SB 1394) Effective January 1, 2025. Conditionally operative pursuant to Sec. 28206.)

28244. Disabling the connected vehicle location access from inside the vehicle shall not result in an account holder of the connected vehicle service, vehicle manufacturer, or a third-party service provider receiving any notification related to the connected vehicle location access being disabled, including, but not limited to, an alert, email, text, or telephone call.

(Added by Stats. 2024, Ch. 655, Sec. 2. (SB 1394) Effective January 1, 2025. Conditionally operative pursuant to Sec. 28206.)

Division 12.5. Zero-Emission Vehicles

(Division 12.5 heading added by Stats. 2023, Ch. 585, Sec. 2.)

Chapter 1. Public Agency Utility Medium- and Heavy-Duty Vehicles

(Chapter 1 added by Stats. 2023, Ch. 585, Sec. 3.)

28500. (a) "Public agency utility" means a local publicly owned electric utility, as defined in Section 224.3 of the Public Utilities Code, a community water system, as defined in Section 116275 of the Health and Safety Code, a water district, as defined in Section 20200 of the Water Code, and a wastewater treatment provider, as defined in Section 116773.2 of the Health and Safety Code.

(b) Any state regulation that seeks to require, or otherwise compel, the procurement of medium- and heavy-duty zero-emission vehicles shall authorize public agency utilities to purchase replacements for traditional utility-specialized vehicles that are at the end of life, as determined by the State Air Resources Board in consultation with public agency utilities, when needed to maintain reliable service and respond to major foreseeable events, including, but not limited to, severe weather, wildfires, natural disasters, and physical attacks, without regard to the model year of the vehicle being replaced. For the purposes of determining the daily usage of a medium- or heavy-duty vehicle, a public agency utility may provide comprehensive usage data for a class of vehicles that does not exclusively rely on the lowest mileage reading and does not exclude the highest usage days.

(Added by Stats. 2023, Ch. 585, Sec. 3. (AB 1594) Effective January 1, 2024.)

Division 13. Towing and Loading Equipment

(Division 13 enacted by Stats. 1959, Ch. 3.)

Chapter 1. Towing Equipment

(Chapter 1 enacted by Stats. 1959, Ch. 3.)

29000. Unless specified, this chapter does not apply to tow trucks or to the drawbar or other connection between a motor vehicle and a pole or pipe dolly or logging dolly or to any lawful trailer used as a pole or pipe dolly.

(Amended by Stats. 1988, Ch. 924, Sec. 19.)

29001. The upper and lower halves of every fifth wheel connecting device on any semitrailer and truck-tractor or auxiliary dolly shall be securely affixed to the vehicles to prevent shifting of the device on the vehicle to which it is attached.

(Added by renumbering Section 29000 by Stats. 1969, Ch. 338.)

29002. Every fifth wheel mechanism, including adapters, shall be equipped with a locking device which will not permit the upper and lower halves to be separated without the operation of a positive manual release. The manual release shall be designed, installed, and maintained so that it cannot be accidentally operated. Automatic locking devices on fifth wheels designed and constructed to be readily separable are required on any vehicle first required to be registered in this state after January 1, 1954.

(Added by renumbering Section 29001 by Stats. 1969, Ch. 338.)

29003. (a) Every hitch or coupling device used as a means of attaching the towed and towing vehicles shall be properly and securely mounted and be structurally adequate for the weight drawn. The mounting of the hitch or coupling device on the towing and towed vehicle shall include sufficient reinforcement or bracing of the frame to provide sufficient strength and rigidity to prevent undue distortion of the frame.

(b) The drawbar, tongue, or other connection between the towing and towed vehicles shall be securely attached and structurally adequate for the weight drawn.

(c) The raised end of any motor vehicle being transported by another motor vehicle using a tow dolly shall be secured to the tow dolly by two separate chains, cables, or equivalent devices adequate to prevent shifting or separation of the towed vehicle and the tow dolly.

(Amended by Stats. 1983, Ch. 708, Sec. 10.)

29004. (a) (1) Except as required under paragraph (2), a towed vehicle shall be coupled to the towing vehicle by means of a safety chain, cable, or equivalent device in addition to the regular drawbar, tongue, or other connection.

(2) A vehicle towed by a tow truck shall be coupled to the tow truck by means of at least two safety chains in addition to the primary restraining system. The safety chains shall be securely affixed to the truck frame, bed, or towing equipment, independent of the towing sling, wheel lift, or under-reach towing equipment.

(3) A vehicle transported as a load on a trailer, using vehicles other than those described in Section 34500, shall be secured by at least four tiedown chains, straps, or an equivalent device, independent of the winch or loading cable.

(b) All safety connections and attachments shall be of sufficient strength to control the towed vehicle in the event of failure of the regular hitch, coupling device, drawbar, tongue, or other connection. All safety connections and attachments also shall have a positive means of ensuring that the safety connection or attachment does not become dislodged while in transit.

(c) No more slack may be left in a safety chain, cable, or equivalent device than is necessary to permit proper turning. When a drawbar is used as the towing connection, the safety chain, cable, or equivalent device shall be connected to the towed and towing vehicle and to the drawbar so as to prevent the drawbar from dropping to the ground if the drawbar fails.

(d) Subdivision (a) does not apply to a semitrailer having a connecting device composed of a fifth wheel and kingpin assembly, and does not apply to a towed motor vehicle when steered by a person who holds a license for the type of vehicle being towed.

(e) For purposes of this section, a "tow truck" includes both of the following:

(1) A repossessor's tow vehicle, as defined in subdivision (b) of Section 615.

(2) An automobile dismantler's tow vehicle, as defined in subdivision (c) of Section 615.

(f) A vehicle towed by a repossessor's tow vehicle, as defined in subdivision (b) of Section 615, is exempt from the multisafety chain requirement of paragraph (2) of subdivision (a) so long as the vehicle is not towed more than one mile on a public highway and is secured by one safety chain.

(Amended by Stats. 2021, Ch. 311, Sec. 9. (SB 814) Effective January 1, 2022.)

29004.5. No recreational vehicle, as described in Section 18010.5 of the Health and Safety Code, designed to be towed, shall be manufactured for sale in this state, sold, offered for sale, leased, or rented unless it is equipped with a safety connection in compliance with Section 29004 with breaking strength which equals or exceeds the gross weight of the towed vehicle. The retail seller, renter, or lessor shall supply instructions to the purchaser, renter, or lessee of such recreational vehicle on proper methods of making the connection between the towed and towing vehicles. Nothing in this section shall, however, require a lessor of a recreational vehicle to supply to the lessee of such vehicle the required instructions if such vehicle is sold to the lessor by a third party and such third party or the agent of the third party delivers possession of the vehicle to the lessee. In such case, such third party shall supply to the lessee the required instructions.

(Added by Stats. 1978, Ch. 932.)

29005. When one vehicle is towing another, the drawbar or other connection shall not exceed 15 feet.

(Added by Stats. 1961, Ch. 58.)

29006. (a) No person shall operate a vehicle towing another motor vehicle upon a freeway unless the towing vehicle is coupled to the towed vehicle by a rigid structure attached securely to both vehicles by nonrigid means.

(b) The requirements of subdivision (a) are not applicable to a vehicle towing a motor vehicle which has been disabled and is being towed from the point of disablement to the nearest and most accessible exit from the freeway.

(Added by Stats. 1970, Ch. 334.)

29007. The requirements of Section 29004 shall not apply to vehicles engaged in driveaway-towaway operations if all the following conditions are met:

(a) The towed vehicle has one end supported by the towing vehicle.

(b) The towed vehicle is secured to the towing vehicle by a device designed and constructed as to be readily demountable and to perform the functions of a fifth-wheel-type connection.

(c) The fifth-wheel-type connection device is securely affixed to the vehicles to prevent shifting of the device on the vehicles to which it is attached.

(d) The fifth-wheel-type connection device provides a means of variation of inclination between the towing and towed vehicle due to vertical curvatures of the highway. Such means shall not depend upon either the looseness or deformation of the connection or the vehicles to provide for such variation.

(e) No more than three saddle-mounts may be used in any combination.

(f) No more than one tow-bar or ball-and-socket type coupling device may be used in any combination.

(g) Driveaway-towaway combinations shall comply with all provisions specified in Section 393.71 of Title 49 of the Code of Federal Regulations.

(Amended by Stats. 2015, Ch. 451, Sec. 56. (SB 491) Effective January 1, 2016.)

29008. Sections 29004 and 29005 shall not apply to trailers or dollies used to support booms attached to truck cranes if the following conditions are met:

(a) The trailer or dolly is connected to the boom by a pin, coupling device, or fifth wheel assembly.

(b) The trailer is secured to the boom with a chain, cable, or equivalent device of sufficient strength to control the trailer or dolly in case of failure of the connection consisting of a pin, coupling device, or fifth wheel assembly.

(Amended by Stats. 2006, Ch. 538, Sec. 664. Effective January 1, 2007.)

29009. The requirements of Section 29004 do not apply to a dolly used to support a portion of special construction equipment, as defined in Section 565, which, due to its size or weight is being operated under the authority of a permit issued by the Department of Transportation, if the dolly is secured to the construction equipment, and the construction equipment is secured to the towing vehicle, by chain, cable, or equivalent devices of sufficient strength to control the construction equipment and dolly.

(Added by Stats. 1988, Ch. 907, Sec. 3.)

Chapter 5. Transporting Other Loads

(Chapter 5 enacted by Stats. 1959, Ch. 3.)

Article 1. Hazardous Materials

(Heading of Article 1 amended by Stats. 1984, Ch. 1683, Sec. 1.)

31301. (a) No person shall transport any explosive substance, flammable liquid, liquefied petroleum gas or poisonous gas in a tank truck, trailer, or semitrailer through the Caldecott Tunnel located on State Highway, Route 24, near the Alameda-Contra Costa County boundary, connecting Oakland with Contra Costa County in the East Bay area at any time other than between the hours of 3 a.m. to 5 a.m.

(b) The Department of Transportation may, in compliance with the requirements of Article 1 (commencing with Section 22400) of Division 11, determine and declare a reduced speed limit, lower than the maximum speed of 55 miles per hour, found most appropriate for traffic safety between the hours of 3 a.m. and 5 a.m.

(c) Nothing in this section shall be construed as a limitation or restriction on the power of the Department of Transportation, conferred by any other provision of law, to adopt regulations with regard to the movement of vehicles, including, but not limited to, tank truck vehicles transporting any cargo specified under subdivision (a) through the Caldecott Tunnel.

If, pursuant to any such other law, the Department of Transportation adopts or amends regulations after the effective date of this section, which adopted or amended regulations govern the movement of vehicles subject to subdivision (a), then on the operative date of those regulations, this section shall no longer be operative.

(Added by Stats. 1982, Ch. 1140, Sec. 1. Effective September 20, 1982. Conditionally inoperative as provided in subd. (c).)

31303. (a) The provisions of this section apply to the highway transportation of hazardous materials and hazardous waste for which the display of placards or markings is required pursuant to Section 27903. This section does not apply to hazardous materials being transported on specified routes pursuant to Section 31616 or 33000.

(b) Unless restricted or prohibited pursuant to Section 31304, the transportation shall be on state or interstate highways which offer the least overall transit time whenever practicable.

(c) The transporter shall avoid, whenever practicable, congested thoroughfares, places where crowds are assembled, and residence districts as defined in Section 515.

(d) Vehicles used for the transportation shall not be left unattended or parked overnight in a residence district as defined in Section 515.

(e) When transporting hazardous waste pursuant to Section 25169.3 of the Health and Safety Code, all provisions of the waste hauler transportation safety plan, as approved by the State Department of Health Services, shall be complied with.

(f) Transportation which deviates from the routes required by this section shall not be excused on the basis of operating convenience.

(g) Notwithstanding subdivisions (b) and (c), vehicles engaged in the transportation may also use any of the following highways:

(1) Highways which provide necessary access to local pickup or delivery points consistent with safe vehicle operation.

(2) Highways which provide reasonable access to fuel, repairs, rest, or food facilities that are designed and intended to accommodate commercial vehicle parking, when that access is consistent with safe vehicle operation and when the facility is within one-half road mile of points of entry or exit from the state or interstate highway being used.

(3) Highways restricted or prohibited pursuant to this section when no other lawful alternative exists.

(h) This section shall become operative on January 1, 1987.

(Repealed (in Sec. 1) and added by Stats. 1985, Ch. 814, Sec. 2. Section operative January 1, 1987, by its own provisions. Note: See this section as modified on July 17, 1991, in Governor's Reorganization Plan No. 1 of 1991.)

31304. (a) The transportation of hazardous materials and hazardous waste for which the display of placards or markings is required pursuant to Section 27903 may be restricted or prohibited, by the Department of the California Highway Patrol, after consultation with the Department of Transportation, with regard to state or interstate highways, or by a city or county by ordinance or resolution, after formal notice to the Department of the California Highway Patrol and with the concurrence of their appropriate transportation planning agency defined in Section 29532 of the Government Code, with regard to specified highways under their control, if all of the following requirements are met:

(1) The respective highway is appreciably less safe than a reasonable alternate highway as determined by using either of the following criteria:

(A) The "Guidelines for Applying Criteria to Designate Routes for Transporting Hazardous Materials" prepared by the Federal Highway Administration (FHWA A-IP-80-15).

(B) The Department of the California Highway Patrol or the city or county, whichever has jurisdiction pursuant to subdivision (a), determines that the respective highway is located within the watershed of a drinking water reservoir which meets all of the following requirements:

(i) The reservoir is owned or operated by a public water system, as defined in Section 116275 of the Health and Safety Code.

(ii) The reservoir has a capacity of at least 10,000 acre feet.

(iii) The reservoir directly serves a water treatment plant, as defined in Section 116275 of the Health and Safety Code.

(iv) The reservoir is impounded by a dam, as defined in Section 6002 of the Water Code.

(v) The reservoir's shoreline is located within 500 feet of the highway.

(2) The restriction or prohibition on the use of the highway pursuant to this section is not precluded or preempted by federal law.

(3) The restriction or prohibition does not eliminate necessary access to local pickup or delivery points consistent with safe vehicle operation; does not eliminate reasonable access to fuel, repairs, rest, or food facilities that are designed and intended to accommodate commercial vehicle parking, when that access is consistent with safe vehicle operation and when the facility is within one-half road mile of points of entry or exit from the state or interstate highway being used; or does not restrict or prohibit the use of highways when no other lawful alternative exists.

(4) Written concurrence has been obtained from affected surrounding jurisdictions, including, but not limited to, state agencies, counties, cities, special districts, or other political subdivisions of the state, that the proposed restriction or prohibition is not incompatible with through transportation. If written concurrence is not granted by one of the affected surrounding jurisdictions, that action may be appealed to the appropriate transportation planning agency for final resolution.

(5) The highway is posted by the agency responsible for highway signs on that highway in conformity with standards of the Department

of Transportation.

(6) A list of the routes restricted or prohibited is submitted to the Department of the California Highway Patrol.

(7) The highway is included in a list of highways restricted or prohibited pursuant to this section which is published by the Department of the California Highway Patrol and is available to interested parties for not less than 14 days.

(b) Notwithstanding any prohibition or restriction adopted pursuant to subdivision (a), deviation from restricted or prohibited routes is authorized in an emergency or other special circumstances with the concurrence of a member of the agency having traffic law enforcement authority for the highway.

(Amended by Stats. 2002, Ch. 104, Sec. 1. Effective January 1, 2003.)

31305. (a) Upon receipt of a written petition from a local jurisdiction or motor carrier adversely affected by a restriction or prohibition adopted pursuant to Section 31304, the Department of the California Highway Patrol may preempt any local restriction or prohibition that, in its opinion, is not compatible with reasonable and necessary access or the use of highways when no other lawful alternative exists as provided for in paragraph (3) of subdivision (a) of that section, or through transportation as provided for in paragraph (4) of subdivision (a) of that section.

(b) Upon receipt of a written petition from a local jurisdiction or motor carrier adversely affected by a preemption issued pursuant to subdivision (a), the Department of the California Highway Patrol, after holding a public hearing, shall render a decision upholding or denying the petition.

(c) This section shall become operative on January 1, 1987.

(Added by Stats. 1985, Ch. 814, Sec. 4. Section operative January 1, 1987, by its own provisions.)

31306. (a) A list of highways restricted or prohibited pursuant to subdivision (a) of Section 31304 shall be published or updated by the Department of the California Highway Patrol semiannually.

(b) This section shall become operative on January 1, 1987.

(Added by Stats. 1985, Ch. 814, Sec. 5. Section operative January 1, 1987, by its own provisions.)

31307. (a) It is unlawful for the owner of any vehicle or the authorized agent of the owner to drive, or to direct or knowingly permit the driving of, the vehicle in violation of Section 31303 or 31304. Violation of any of these sections is a misdemeanor punishable as follows:

(1) For a first violation, a fine not exceeding five hundred dollars ($500), imprisonment in the county jail not exceeding 60 days, or both the fine and imprisonment.

(2) For a second violation within a 12-month period, a fine not exceeding one thousand dollars ($1,000), imprisonment in the county jail not exceeding 60 days, or both the fine and imprisonment.

(3) For a third or subsequent violation within a 12-month period, a fine not exceeding two thousand five hundred dollars ($2,500), imprisonment in the county jail not exceeding 120 days, or both the fine and imprisonment.

(b) Additionally, upon recommendation of the Department of the California Highway Patrol, three or more violations of these sections constitute grounds for suspension or revocation of registration, or denial of an application for registration under Section 25163 of the Health and Safety Code by the State Department of Health Services. Proceedings in these cases shall be subject to Chapter 5 (commencing with Section 11500) of Part 1 of Division 3 of Title 2 of the Government Code.

(c) This section shall become operative on January 1, 1987.

(Added by Stats. 1985, Ch. 814, Sec. 6. Section operative January 1, 1987, by its own provisions. Note: See this section as modified on July 17, 1991, in Governor's Reorganization Plan No. 1 of 1991.)

31308. (a) Nothing contained in Section 31303 or 31304 shall be deemed to exempt any person subject to these sections from other provisions of this code.

(b) This section shall become operative on January 1, 1987.

(Added by Stats. 1985, Ch. 814, Sec. 7. Section operative January 1, 1987, by its own provisions.)

31309. Notwithstanding Section 34500 and subdivision (a) of Section 34501, the transportation of hazardous materials in a manner requiring that placards be displayed on the transporting vehicle pursuant to Section 27903, shall comply with regulations adopted by the California Highway Patrol pursuant to subdivision (b) of Section 34501.

(Added by Stats. 1990, Ch. 429, Sec. 3.)

Article 2. Vehicles Transporting Workmen

(Article 2 repealed and added by Stats. 1968, Ch. 1019.)

31400. Trucks used primarily or regularly for the transportation of workmen shall be:

(a) Equipped with seats securely fastened to the vehicle.

(b) Equipped, if a motortruck, with a railing or other suitable enclosure on the sides and end of the vehicle not less than 46 inches above the floor of the vehicle.

(c) Equipped with steps, stirrups, or other equivalent devices so placed and arranged that the vehicle may be safely mounted and dismounted.

(Added by Stats. 1968, Ch. 1019.)

31401. (a) The department shall adopt regulations designed to promote the safe operation of farm labor vehicles described in Section 322, including, but not limited to, vehicular design, equipment, passenger safety, and seating.

(b) The department shall inspect every farm labor vehicle described in Section 322 at least once annually to ascertain whether its construction, design, and equipment comply with all provisions of law. No person shall drive any farm labor vehicle described in Section 322 unless there is displayed therein a certificate issued by the department stating that on a stated day, which shall be within 13 months of the date of operation, an authorized employee of the department inspected the vehicle and found on the date of inspection the vehicle complied with applicable regulations relating to construction, design, and equipment. The commissioner shall provide by rule or regulation for the issuance and display of distinctive inspection certificates.

(c) The department may inspect any vehicle subject to these regulations in maintenance facilities, terminals, labor camps, or other private property of the vehicle owner or the farm labor contractor to insure compliance with the provisions of this code and regulations adopted pursuant to this section.

(d) The owner of any farm labor vehicle or any farm labor contractor, as defined in Section 1682 of the Labor Code, who rents a farm labor vehicle or who otherwise uses a farm labor vehicle to transport individuals is responsible for the inspection required under subdivision (b).

(e) An owner of any farm labor vehicle or any farm labor contractor who operates a farm labor vehicle under the circumstances described in subdivision (d) may not operate that vehicle unless the vehicle has a current certificate described in subdivision (b).

(f) It is unlawful to violate any provision of these regulations or this section.

(Amended by Stats. 1999, Ch. 556, Sec. 3. Effective September 29, 1999.)

31401.5. (a) The department shall develop, by regulation, specifications for a display sticker that shall be clearly displayed on every farm labor vehicle. This display sticker shall list the inspection certification date pursuant to this section and the "800" telephone reporting system required by Section 2429.

(b) The regulations of the department shall require every owner or operator of a farm labor vehicle to request the scheduling of the inspection required under subdivision (b) of Section 31401 as follows:

(1) The owner or operator of a farm labor vehicle that has a current inspection certificate pursuant to Section 31401 shall make the request for inspection not later than four weeks prior to the expiration date of the certificate.

(2) The owner or operator of a farm labor vehicle required to have its initial inspection shall make the request for inspection not later than

three business days prior to the requested date.

(c) In no event shall the owner or operator of a farm labor vehicle allow the operation of a farm labor vehicle without the proper certification requirements specified under Section 31401.

(Added by Stats. 1999, Ch. 557, Sec. 4. Effective September 29, 1999.)

31402. (a) No person may operate any farm labor vehicle except as may be necessary to return the unladen vehicle or combination of vehicles to the residence or place of business of the owner or driver, or to a garage, after notice by the department to the owner that the vehicle is in an unsafe condition or is not equipped as required by this code, or any regulations adopted thereunder, until the vehicle and its equipment have been made to conform with the requirements of this code, or any regulations adopted thereunder, and approved by the department.

(b) (1) A person who operates a farm labor vehicle in violation of this section while the vehicle is in a condition that presents an immediate safety hazard is guilty of a misdemeanor punishable by a fine of not less than one thousand dollars ($1,000) and not more than five thousand dollars ($5,000), or both that fine and a sentence of confinement for not more than six months in the county jail. No part of any fine imposed under this subdivision may be suspended.

(2) As used in this subdivision, an "immediate safety hazard" is any equipment violation described in subdivision (a) of Section 31401 or Section 31405, including any violation of a regulation adopted pursuant to that provision or those provisions.

(c) Any member of the Department of the California Highway Patrol may impound a farm labor vehicle operated in violation of this section pursuant to Section 34506.4. A farm labor vehicle shall not be impounded unless a member of that department determines that a person has failed to comply with subdivision (a) or a person fails to comply with a lawful out-of-service order, as described in subdivision (b) of Section 2800.

(Amended by Stats. 2000, Ch. 873, Sec. 3. Effective January 1, 2001.)

31403. A farm labor vehicle known to an owner, farm labor contractor, or driver, to be unsafe, or not equipped as required by this code, or any regulations adopted thereunder, shall not be used for transporting any passengers until it is examined and repaired or equipped as required by this code, or any regulations adopted thereunder, and certified by a competent mechanic to be safe and lawfully equipped.

(Added by Stats. 1974, Ch. 1447.)

31404. Any person who operates, or any owner or farm labor contractor who knowingly allows the operation of, a farm labor vehicle in violation of subdivision (b) or (d) of Section 31401 or Section 31402 or 31403 is guilty of a misdemeanor. When a person has been convicted of willfully violating those provisions, the person shall, in addition, be fined not less than one thousand dollars ($1,000) for each violation, and no part of the fine may be suspended. If passengers are in the vehicle at the time of the violation, the person shall, in addition, be fined five hundred dollars ($500) for each passenger, not to exceed a total of five thousand dollars ($5,000) for each violation, and no part of this fine may be suspended. As used in this section, the terms "knowingly" and "willfully" have the same meaning as prescribed in Section 7 of the Penal Code.

(Amended by Stats. 1999, Ch. 556, Sec. 4. Effective September 29, 1999.)

31405. (a) Except as authorized under paragraph (1) of subdivision (e), every farm labor vehicle issued an inspection certificate under Section 31401 shall be equipped at each passenger position with a Type 1 or Type 2 seatbelt assembly, conforming to the specifications set forth in Section 571.209 of Title 49 of the Code of Federal Regulations, that is anchored to the vehicle in a manner that conforms to the specifications of Section 571.210 of Title 49 of the Code of Federal Regulations.

(b) Except as authorized under paragraph (1) of subdivision (e), the department may not issue an initial inspection certificate under Section 31401 to any farm labor vehicle that is not equipped with a seatbelt assembly at each passenger position, as described in subdivision (a).

(c) The owner of a farm labor vehicle shall maintain all seatbelt assemblies and seatbelt assembly anchorages required under this section in good working order for the use of passengers.

(d) Except as authorized under paragraph (1) of subdivision (e) or subdivision (d) of Section 23116, no person may operate a farm labor vehicle on a highway unless that person and all passengers are properly restrained by a seatbelt assembly that conforms to this section.

(e) (1) Until January 1, 2007, this section does not apply to a farm labor vehicle that meets the definition in subdivision (a) of Section 233, meets all state and federal standards for safety and construction, and is not currently required to have seatbelts.

(2) On or after January 1, 2007, any farm labor vehicle that meets the conditions set forth in paragraph (1) shall be equipped at each passenger position with a seatbelt assembly as described in subdivision (a), unless exempted from this requirement under the regulations promulgated under Section 31401.

(f) The department shall adopt regulations to implement this section.

(Amended by Stats. 2000, Ch. 308, Sec. 3. Effective January 1, 2001.)

31406. (a) No person may be transported in a farm labor vehicle that does not have all passenger seating positions in compliance with Section 571.207 of Title 49 of the Code of Federal Regulations, as that provision exists now or may hereafter be amended.

(b) No person may install a seat or seating system in a farm labor vehicle unless that seat or seating system is in compliance with Section 571.207 of Title 49 of the Code of Federal Regulations, as that provision exists now or may hereafter be amended.

(c) This section shall become operative on March 31, 2002.

(Added by Stats. 2000, Ch. 308, Sec. 4. Effective January 1, 2001. Section operative March 31, 2002, by its own provisions.)

31407. All cutting tools or tools with sharp edges carried in the passenger compartment of a farm labor vehicle shall be placed in securely latched containers that are firmly attached to the vehicle. All other tools, equipment, or materials carried in the passenger compartment shall be secured to the body of the vehicle to prevent their movement while the vehicle is in motion. Under no circumstances shall those tools, equipment, or materials obstruct an aisle or an emergency exit.

(Added by Stats. 2000, Ch. 308, Sec. 5. Effective January 1, 2001.)

31408. No person may operate a farm labor vehicle on a highway unless both headlamps required under Section 24400 are lighted, regardless of the time of day.

(Added by Stats. 1999, Ch. 556, Sec. 5. Effective September 29, 1999.)

31409. Notwithstanding paragraph (2) of subdivision (c) of Section 322, any vehicle owned or operated by or for a public transit system that is purchased with funds appropriated pursuant to Item 2660-103-0046 of Section 2.00 of the Budget Act of 2000 (Chapter 52 of the Statutes of 2000) or pursuant to Section 5309 of Title 49 of the United States Code and is used to transport farmworkers for any farmworker transportation program shall comply with the farm labor vehicle provisions contained in, and the regulations promulgated under, this chapter, relating to the following:

(a) (1) Annual farm labor vehicle inspection and certification.

(2) Following initial certification, the inspection and certification of buses designed, used, or maintained for carrying more than 15 persons, including the driver, shall be conducted during the inspection required by subdivision (c) of Section 34501.

(b) Seatbelt installation.

(c) Illumination of headlamps.

(d) Storage and securing of tools in passenger compartments.

(Added by Stats. 2000, Ch. 308, Sec. 6. Effective January 1, 2001.)

Article 7. Tank Containers

(Article 7 added by Stats. 1963, Ch. 1580.)

31540. (a) The department shall adopt and enforce such regulations as it determines are necessary for public safety regarding the transportation of:

(1) Freight van or tank containers which can be removed from the running gear or chassis of a truck or trailer, and

(2) Collapsible containers used to transport liquids on flatbed vehicles.

(b) It is unlawful to fail to comply with any provision of the regulations adopted by the department.

(Amended by Stats. 1968, Ch. 1192.)

Article 8. Waste Tires

(Article 8 added by Stats. 1996, Ch. 304, Sec. 5.)

31560. (a) A person operating a vehicle, or combination of vehicles, in the transportation of 10 or more used tires or waste tires, or a combination of used tires and waste tires totaling 10 or more, as defined in Section 42950 of the Public Resources Code, shall be registered with the California Integrated Waste Management Board, unless specifically exempted, as provided in Chapter 19 (commencing with Section 42950) of Part 3 of Division 30 of the Public Resources Code and in regulations adopted by the board to implement that chapter.

(b) It is unlawful and constitutes an infraction for a person engaged in the transportation of 10 or more used tires or waste tires, or a combination of used tires and waste tires totaling 10 or more, to violate a provision of this article or Section 42951 of the Public Resources Code.

(Amended by Stats. 2008, Ch. 696, Sec. 31. Effective September 30, 2008.)

Division 14. Transportation of Explosives

(Division 14 enacted by Stats. 1959, Ch. 3.)

31600. For the purposes of this division "explosive" or "explosives" means any substance, or combination of substances, the primary or common purpose of which is detonation or rapid combustion and which is capable of a relatively instantaneous or rapid release of gas and heat. "Explosive" or "explosives" includes, but is not necessarily limited to, explosives as defined in Section 12000 of the Health and Safety Code, and any of the following:

(a) Dynamite, nitroglycerine, picric acid, lead azide, fulminate of mercury, black powder, smokeless powder, propellant explosives, detonating primers, blasting caps, commercial boosters, ammonium nitrate-fuel oil mixture (blasting agent), or any explosives as defined in Section 841 of Title 18 of the United States Code and published pursuant to Section 555.23 of Title 27 of the Code of Federal Regulations, when transported in a combined load with any explosive, as defined in this section.

(b) Substances determined to be division 1.1, 1.2, 1.3, or 1.6 explosives as classified by the United States Department of Transportation.

(c) "Explosive" or "explosives" does not include small arms ammunition or any other division 1.4 explosive.

(d) This division shall not apply to special fireworks classified by the United States Department of Transportation as division 1.2 or 1.3 explosives when those special fireworks are regulated by and in conformance with Part 2 (commencing with Section 12500) of Division 11 of the Health and Safety Code.

(e) Nothing in this chapter supersedes any regulations for the transportation of hazardous materials as defined in Section 2402.7 or as regulated in Division 14.1 (commencing with Section 32000).

(Amended by Stats. 2004, Ch. 247, Sec. 17. Effective August 23, 2004.)

31601. (a) This division shall apply to the operation of any motor vehicle on any highway, and to the operation and parking of any vehicle on any property designated pursuant to this division as a safe stopping place for the purpose of transporting any explosive in any amount when the transportation is rendered as a delivery service or for hire, or in any other event for the purpose of transporting any explosive or a combined load of any explosive and ammonium nitrate-fuel oil mixture (blasting agent) in an amount in excess of 1,000 pounds. The transportation of quantities of explosives of 1,000 pounds or less, or other than on a public highway, is governed by Division 11 (commencing at Section 12000) of the Health and Safety Code. Notwithstanding other provisions of this section, a license required by Section 31602 may be used to transport quantities of less than 1,000 pounds of explosives if all other requirements of this division are met.

(b) It is the legislative intention in enacting this division and with particular reference to requiring licenses for transportation of explosives as set forth herein that such provisions shall apply uniformly throughout the State of California and that such license to be obtained from the Department of the California Highway Patrol, as provided in Chapter 2.5 (commencing with Section 2500) of Division 2, shall be in lieu of any requirement for any license to be obtained by any such owner from any local authority within the state.

(Amended by Stats. 1981, Ch. 912, Sec. 6. Effective September 28, 1981.)

31602. (a) It is a misdemeanor for any owner of a vehicle to drive or permit the driving of the vehicle on any public highway for the purpose of transporting any explosive as defined herein and within the scope of Section 31601 unless the owner then holds a valid license for the transportation of explosives as provided in this division, except such persons as are expressly exempted in this division.

(b) It is a misdemeanor for the owner, or authorized agent of the owner, of any vehicle transporting explosives to drive, or to permit the driving of the vehicle, or for the driver to drive such vehicle, upon any public highway, not designated in regulations adopted by the Department of the California Highway Patrol as a route for the transportation of explosives, unless the use of the highway is required to permit delivery of, or the loading of, explosives at a point not on a highway designated as a route for the transportation of explosives, or unless the use of the highway is required to permit the vehicle to proceed to, and return from, a point designated as an inspection stop pursuant to this division.

(c) It is a misdemeanor for the driver of any vehicle transporting explosives to stop at any place not designated as a safe stopping place unless the vehicle is disabled or except when necessary to avoid conflict with other traffic or to comply with the orders of a peace officer or an official traffic control device. A safe stopping place is any location designated by the Department of the California Highway Patrol where the driver may stop for food, fuel or other necessary reasons and any location designated by the Department of the California Highway Patrol as a safe parking place, a safe stopping place, or as an inspection stop for purposes of this division.

(d) In the event the owner of a vehicle leases the same to be used in the transportation of explosives for which a license is required, the lessee shall be deemed the owner for the purposes of this division.

(Amended by Stats. 1970, Ch. 1315.)

31607. (a) Any person operating or permitting the operation of a vehicle or combination of vehicles used in the transportation of explosives and subject to this division shall make or cause to be made an inspection of every said vehicle or combination of vehicles as hereinafter set forth.

(b) Such inspection as called for in Section 31608 shall be made immediately preceding the actual transportation of explosives by the vehicle and whenever there is an interchange of any vehicle operating in combination with any other vehicle in the transportation of explosives.

(c) Inspection of tires and brakes shall also be made en route at suitable intervals, off the roadway, at inspection stops established by the Department of the California Highway Patrol, at regular stops, terminal points, or driver-change points.

(Amended by Stats. 1961, Ch. 228.)

31608. The inspection of a vehicle required under subdivision (b) of Section 31607 shall include inspection of the following:

(a) Brakes and the brake system.

(b) The ignition and lighting systems.

(c) All tires on the equipment.

(d) All supplemental equipment as required by Section 31610.

(Amended by Stats. 1959, Ch. 1996.)

31609. Every person operating a vehicle or combination of vehicles in the transportation of explosives subject to this division shall complete a record of every inspection which is required under Sections 31607 and 31608 in such form as approved by the Department of the California Highway Patrol showing the time and place of every inspection. The person making the inspection shall certify the fact in the record. The forms may be based upon the type used by the United States Department of Transportation. The record of every inspection shall be made at the time such inspection is conducted.

The driver of the vehicle shall display the record upon demand of any member of the California Highway Patrol or any police officer of a city who is on duty for the exclusive or main purpose of enforcing the provisions of this code.

(Amended by Stats. 1970, Ch. 1315.)

31610. Every vehicle or combination of vehicles used in the transportation of explosives and subject to this division, in addition to any other equipment required by law, shall be equipped and maintained as required by this section.

(a) Brakes and the brake system shall be maintained in good and safe operating condition.

(b) The ignition and lighting systems shall be maintained in good operating condition.

(c) All tires shall be in good condition, properly matched and inflated. Except as may be necessary to cause immediate replacement, no vehicle shall be driven unless all tires in actual use on the vehicle are properly inflated.

(d) Fire extinguishers and other safety equipment prescribed by regulations adopted by the department pursuant to subdivision (f) of Section 34500 and Section 34501 shall be carried in each vehicle or combination of vehicles.

(e) No flare, fusee, oil lantern, or any signal device producing a flame shall be carried upon any vehicle or combination of vehicles.

(Amended by Stats. 1971, Ch. 754.)

31611. Every owner of a vehicle used in the transportation of explosives and subject to this division shall make available in each vehicle the latest map showing the routes which are to be used for the transportation of explosives which has been furnished for the vehicle by the Department of the California Highway Patrol and a list of the safe stopping places prescribed by the regulations of the Department of the California Highway Patrol for vehicles transporting explosives. The owner shall require that the driver be thoroughly familiar with the provisions of this division before operating any vehicle in the transportation of explosives.

(Amended by Stats. 1971, Ch. 754.)

31612. Persons operating vehicles, or combinations of vehicles, in the transportation of explosives and subject to this division, shall not accept any explosives for transportation unless the shipment is accompanied by a bill of lading or other shipping paper supplied by the shipper, showing the kind of explosives and bearing a statement that they have been packaged, labeled and marked in accordance with regulations of the United States Department of Transportation, and the bill of lading or other shipping paper shall be carried in the vehicle while en route and shall be displayed upon demand of any member of the California Highway Patrol or any police officer of a city who is on duty for the exclusive or main purpose of enforcing the provisions of this code.

(Amended by Stats. 1970, Ch. 1315.)

31613. There shall not be included in any cargo of explosives any flammable liquids, acids, or corrosive liquids, oxidizers, or combustible materials, other than the explosives themselves, which may have such characteristics. Blasting caps or detonators shall not be transported upon the same vehicle with other explosives, nor shall electric blasting caps be transported upon any vehicle equipped with a radio transmitter. The foregoing provisions of this section shall be subject to such exceptions as are permitted by the United States Department of Transportation loading chart for cargoes of explosives.

(Amended by Stats. 1970, Ch. 1315.)

31614. The following provisions shall apply to any vehicle transporting explosives subject to this division:

(a) When transporting explosives through or into a city or any other congested area for which a route has not been designated by the Department of the California Highway Patrol, drivers shall follow such routes as may be prescribed or established by local authorities.

(b) Where routes are not prescribed by local authority, every driver of a vehicle transporting explosives shall avoid, so far as practicable, and, where feasible, by prearrangement of routes, driving into or through congested thoroughfares, places where crowds are assembled, streetcar tracks, tunnels, viaducts, and dangerous crossings.

(c) No driver or other person in charge of any vehicle on any public or private property shall permit any explosive to be loaded into, or on, or to be unloaded from any motor vehicle with the engine running, and, whenever any loading operation is in progress, the parking brake on the motor vehicle shall be securely set and all reasonable precautions taken to prevent movement of the motor vehicle during loading or unloading.

(d) No driver or other person in charge of such vehicle shall operate or permit the operation of any vehicle transporting explosives unless all of that portion of the lading which consists of explosives is contained entirely within the body of the motor vehicle or within the horizontal outline thereof, without overhang or projection of any part of the load, and if such motor vehicle has a tailboard or tailgate it shall be closed and secured in place during such transportation.

(e) Every motor vehicle transporting explosives shall have either a closed body or have the explosive cargo covered with a fire- and water-resistant tarpaulin, and in either event, care shall be taken to protect the load from moisture and sparks. Subject to other exceptions as are permitted by the United States Department of Transportation regulations, explosives may be transported on flat-bed vehicles if the explosive portion of the load on each vehicle is packed in fire- and water-resistant containers or covered with a fire- and water-resistant tarpaulin.

(f) No person shall operate any vehicle transporting explosives past any fire of any kind burning on or near the highway until the driver ascertains that such passing can be made with safety.

(g) No motor vehicle transporting explosives shall be left unattended upon any street or highway except in extreme emergency. The vehicle shall be deemed attended whenever a driver or person in charge thereof is in or upon the vehicle or is in a position to observe the vehicle at all times. The driver or person in charge of a vehicle transporting explosives may, however, leave the vehicle unattended at any place designated as a safe parking place on the list of safe stopping places prepared by the Department of the California Highway Patrol unless conditions exist, which are known to the driver, which make it unreasonable to do so.

(h) No driver or other person shall smoke or light any match or otherwise have or produce any fire or flame while in, upon, or near any vehicle transporting explosives.

(i) No person shall transport any explosives in a passenger vehicle, or bus, which is subject to this division.

(Amended by Stats. 1971, Ch. 754.)

31615. Nothing contained in this division shall be deemed to exempt any vehicle transporting explosives and subject to this division, or the owner or any other person, from other provisions of this code, but all such other provisions relating to the driving and movement of vehicles, the size, weight, and equipment thereof, shall be deemed to apply as applicable to each and every vehicle engaged in transporting explosives subject to this division.

(Enacted by Stats. 1959, Ch. 3.)

31616. The Department of the California Highway Patrol, after consultation with the officials having the responsibility for the prevention and suppression of fire in communities through which routes for the transporting of explosives pass, representatives of transportation companies concerned, explosives manufacturers, and the State Fire Marshal shall, by regulation, designate the routes in this state which are to be used for the transportation of explosives. The Department of the California Highway Patrol shall prepare for distribution to persons engaged in the transportation of explosives, maps which clearly indicate the routes, as established in regulations, which are to be used for the transportation of explosives. The Department of the California Highway Patrol shall prepare for distribution to persons engaged in the transportation of explosives a list of locations of required inspection stops, safe parking places, and safe stopping places and shall revise the list to keep it current. Notwithstanding any other provision of law, regulations adopted pursuant to this section shall be adopted in accordance with Chapter 3.5 (commencing with Section 11340) of Part 1 of Division 3 of Title 2 of the Government Code, except that, for the purposes of subdivision (a) of Section 11346.4 of the Government Code, the public comment period shall be 30 days, and the regulations shall become effective upon filing with the Secretary of State.

(Amended by Stats. 1988, Ch. 63, Sec. 1. Effective March 30, 1988.)

31616.5. Notwithstanding Section 11349.3 of the Government Code, the review by the Office of Administrative Law of regulations adopted pursuant to Section 31616 shall be completed within 15 days after the regulations have been submitted to the Office of Administrative Law for review.

(Added by Stats. 1988, Ch. 63, Sec. 2. Effective March 30, 1988.)

31617. In the event of an emergency, the Department of the California Highway Patrol is authorized to suspend or change any designated route for the transportation of explosives or to temporarily designate new or additional routes for such transportation. The Department of the California Highway Patrol shall, unless the nature of the emergency makes it impracticable to do so, consult with local fire officials in the area or areas affected before making any such changes or new designations. If the changes or new designations are made before they can be discussed with those officials, the Department of the California Highway Patrol shall immediately notify the appropriate officials of his action.

The change in or new designation of routes shall not be effective for more than 90 days from the date of such action, unless the Department of the California Highway Patrol determines that the change or new designation should become permanent, in which case the Department of the California Highway Patrol shall, within the 90-day period, initiate action to make the change or new designation permanent in accordance with the provisions of Section 31616 and in which case the emergency change or designation shall remain in effect until superseded by a regulation of the Department of the California Highway Patrol.

(Amended by Stats. 1970, Ch. 1315.)

31618. Where not specifically provided otherwise, it is a misdemeanor for any person to violate any provision of this division. Every person convicted of a misdemeanor for a violation of any of the provisions of this division shall be punished as follows:

(a) For a first violation, by a fine of not less than one thousand dollars ($1,000), or by imprisonment for not more than six months, or by both fine and imprisonment.

(b) For a second or subsequent violation, by a fine of not less than two thousand dollars ($2,000) or by imprisonment for not more than six months, or by both fine and imprisonment.

(Amended by Stats. 1988, Ch. 1384, Sec. 3.)

31619. When not in conflict with any local ordinance pertaining to the transportation of explosives, it shall be lawful to transport smokeless powder in an amount not exceeding 100 pounds if packed in containers prescribed by the United States Department of Transportation upon a highway not designated by the Department of the California Highway Patrol as a route for the transportation of explosives.

(Amended by Stats. 1970, Ch. 1315.)

31620. The Department of the California Highway Patrol, upon application of any interested party, with the concurrence of the fire chief or chiefs in the area or areas affected, and if he determines that such action may be taken without jeopardizing the public safety, may suspend, or waive compliance with, the whole or any part of the requirements of this division insofar as they apply to the delivery or transportation of explosives in sparsely populated, unincorporated areas or in any area where there may be practical difficulties or unnecessary or unreasonable hardship in carrying out the provisions of this division. No person shall be charged with any crime for any violation of the provisions of this division when such a suspension or waiver by the Department of the California Highway Patrol is in effect in the area in which the alleged violation occurs.

(Amended by Stats. 1970, Ch. 1315.)

Division 14.1. Transportation of Hazardous Material

(Division 14.1 added by Stats. 1981, Ch. 860, Sec. 13.)

Chapter 1. Licensing

(Heading of Chapter 1 added by Stats. 1988, Ch. 1222, Sec. 1.)

32000. It is the intent of the Legislature, by enacting this division, that the public be provided additional protection through the licensing of motor carriers transporting hazardous material. The Department of the California Highway Patrol shall be authorized to inspect and license the motor carriers with special attention directed to the negligent operators or repeat violators.

(Added by Stats. 1981, Ch. 860, Sec. 13.)

32000.5. (a) A motor carrier who directs the transportation of an explosive and a motor carrier who directs the transportation of a hazardous material, who is required to display placards pursuant to Section 27903, and a motor carrier who transports for a fee in excess of 500 pounds of hazardous materials of the type requiring placards pursuant to Section 27903, shall be licensed in accordance with this code, unless specifically exempted by this code or regulations adopted pursuant to this code. This license shall be available for examination and shall be displayed in accordance with the regulations adopted by the commissioner.

(b) (1) Except as provided in Section 32001, this division shall not apply to a person hauling only hazardous waste, as defined in Section 25115 or 25117 of the Health and Safety Code, and who is registered pursuant to subdivision (a) of Section 25163 of the Health and Safety Code or who is exempt from that registration pursuant to subdivision (b) of that section.

(2) A motor carrier that is transporting a hazardous waste and is required to display placards pursuant to Section 27903 shall comply with all provisions of Section 32001 except paragraph (3) of subdivision (c) of that section.

(c) This division does not apply to implements of husbandry, as defined in Section 36000.

(d) This division does not apply to the hauling of division 1.3 explosives classified as special fireworks or to division 1.4 explosives classified as common fireworks by the United States Department of Transportation if those fireworks are transported by a motor carrier under the authority of, and in conformance with, a license issued to the motor carrier by the State Fire Marshal pursuant to Part 2 (commencing with Section 12500) of Division 11 of the Health and Safety Code. In that case, a copy of the license shall be carried in the vehicle and presented to a peace officer upon request.

(e) (1) The department shall not issue a license to transport hazardous materials to a motor carrier unless each terminal from which hazardous materials carrying vehicles are operated is in compliance with Section 34501.12 and is currently rated satisfactory.

(2) The department shall adopt rules and regulations that provide for a temporary license to transport hazardous materials for a carrier who, within the previous three years, has not been issued an unsatisfactory rating as a result of an inspection conducted pursuant to Section 34501, 34501.12, or 34520.

(3) It is the intent of the Legislature that a carrier's license to transport hazardous materials should not be unreasonably hindered as a result of the department's verification and issuance process.

(f) This section does not prevent the department from issuing a new or initial license to transport hazardous materials to a motor carrier that applies for a license to transport hazardous materials and that, within the previous three years, has been issued an unsatisfactory rating as a result of an inspection conducted pursuant to Section 34501, 34501.12, or 34520, if the motor carrier has corrected the unsatisfactory rating before applying for the license to transport hazardous materials.

(Amended by Stats. 2009, Ch. 111, Sec. 1. (AB 463) Effective January 1, 2010.)

32001. (a) (1) Any authorized employee of the department may inspect any sealed or unsealed vehicle, container, or shipment subject to this division in maintenance facilities, terminals, or other public or private property to ascertain the quantity and kind of hazardous material and to ensure compliance with the provisions of this code and regulations adopted pursuant to this code.

(2) If a seal is opened for inspection, the department shall reseal any vehicle, container, or shipment prior to further transportation.

(b) Unless specifically stated, nothing contained in this division shall be deemed to exempt any vehicle transporting a hazardous material subject to this division or the operator or any other person from other provisions of this code.

(c) No motor carrier shall direct the transportation of any shipment of a hazardous material in any vehicle unless all of the following are complied with:

(1) The vehicle is equipped as required by this code and applicable regulations adopted pursuant to law.

(2) The shipment complies with laws and regulations pertaining to the shipment or transportation of hazardous material.

(3) The motor carrier holds a valid license for the transportation of hazardous materials.

(4) (A) A vehicle or combination of vehicles required to display placards pursuant to Section 27903 is equipped with a two-way communication device, maintained in good working order, that enables the driver to contact the personnel responsible for the safety operations of the motor carrier in the event of an emergency.

(B) For the purposes of this section, "two-way communication device" means a radio, cellular telephone, or other similar device that permits communication between the driver and personnel responsible for the safety operations of the motor carrier.

(5) (A) The enclosed cargo body, when the display of placards is required pursuant to Section 27903, shall be locked and remain locked during transit of the hazardous materials so as to prevent any unauthorized entry and shall be opened only during loading, unloading, or at the direction of a peace officer, an authorized employee of the department, or a person authorized pursuant to Section 25185 of the Health and Safety Code.

(B) A driver transporting hazardous material in a locked cargo body shall verify that all locks are in place if the vehicle has been left unattended for any length of time. Each driver shall make a notation in his or her log book of the time and date that the verification occurred.

(C) For the purposes of this section, "cargo body" means a fully enclosed area that is an integral part of the vehicle and designed to encapsulate the entire load, such as a van body or an intermodal freight container, and does not mean a tank or flatbed type of vehicle.

(d) The commissioner may issue exemptions from the provisions of this section.

(e) Nothing in this section shall limit the ability of other state or local agencies to carry out their regulatory, enforcement, or emergency response duties under other provisions of law.

(Amended by Stats. 2002, Ch. 610, Sec. 4. Effective January 1, 2003.)

32002. (a) The commissioner may adopt any regulations that are necessary to administer this division. It is a misdemeanor for any motor carrier to violate this division or regulations adopted pursuant to this division.

(b) Notwithstanding subdivision (a), it is unlawful for the motor carrier or the person who directs the driver to operate a vehicle transporting hazardous material, when that transportation requires a license pursuant to this division, to cause the operation of the vehicle unless the motor carrier holds a valid license for the transportation of hazardous materials. A violation of this subdivision shall be punished as follows:

(1) For a first violation, by a fine of not less than two thousand dollars ($2,000).

(2) For a second or subsequent violation, by a fine of not less than

four thousand dollars ($4,000).

(Amended by Stats. 1988, Ch. 1384, Sec. 4.)

32002.5. (a) The commissioner may temporarily suspend a license to haul hazardous material prior to any hearing, when, in the commissioner's opinion, the action is necessary to prevent an imminent and substantial danger to the public health. The commissioner shall notify the holder of the license of the temporary suspension and the effective date thereof and, at the same time, shall serve the person with an accusation. Upon receipt of a notice of defense to the accusation, the commissioner shall set the matter for a hearing which shall be held as soon as possible, but not later than 10 days after receipt of the notice of defense. The temporary suspension shall remain in effect until the hearing is completed and the commissioner has made a final determination on the merits, which, in any event, shall be made within 10 days after the completion of the hearing. If the determination is not transmitted within 10 days after the hearing is completed, the temporary suspension is of no further effect.

(b) The commissioner shall suspend a license to transport hazardous material of a person or motorcarrier, for a period of at least 90 days but not more than 180 days, if the holder of the license permits the transportation of fissile class III shipments or highway route controlled quantity radioactive materials, as defined in Subpart I (commencing with Section 173.401) of Part 173 of Title 49 of the Code of Federal Regulations, by a person who does not possess a license of the appropriate class and an attached radioactive materials driver's certificate or an endorsement issued under Article 6 (commencing with Section 15275) of Chapter 7 of Division 6.

(Amended by Stats. 1992, Ch. 1243, Sec. 92. Effective September 30, 1992.)

32003. (a) All fees collected by the department pursuant to the issuance or renewal of a license for the transportation of hazardous material shall be deposited in the Motor Vehicle Account of the State Transportation Fund.

(b) All moneys collected from these fees shall be used for the support of the hazardous materials inspection and licensing program of the department upon appropriation therefor by the Legislature.

(Added by Stats. 1981, Ch. 860, Sec. 13.)

32004. Any violation of any provision of this division may be enjoined in a civil action brought by the Attorney General in the name of the people of the State of California, upon request of the department, except that it shall not be necessary to show lack of adequate remedy at law or to show irreparable damage or loss.

(Added by Stats. 1981, Ch. 860, Sec. 13.)

Chapter 2. Notification of Routes

(Chapter 2 added by Stats. 1988, Ch. 1222, Sec. 2.)

32050. (a) Prior to the transport of anhydrous hydrazine, methylhydrazine, dimethylhydrazine, Aerozine 50, fuming nitric acid, liquid fluorine, or nitrogen tetroxide in bulk packaging, except when that packaging contains only residue, outside the confines of a facility where that material was used or stored, or prior to the delivery of that bulk material to a carrier for transport, each carrier shall provide advance notification, in writing, of the shipment, to the department, which, in turn, shall notify the sheriff of each county and police chief of each city in which is located the proposed route. Notification shall be made through the Department of Justice's California Law Enforcement Telecommunications System. The sheriffs and police chiefs shall, in turn, make timely notification to the fire chiefs within their respective jurisdictions through a mutually agreed upon communications system.

(b) Subdivision (a) applies only to the extent that it does not conflict with federal law.

(c) For the purposes of this section, the following definitions apply:

(1) "Bulk packaging" has the same meaning as defined in Section 171.8 of Title 49 of the Code of Federal Regulations.

(2) "Fire chief" means the fire chief of each county and city fire department and the fire chief of each fire protection district serving a population greater than 15,000 in which is located the proposed route. This paragraph does not apply to any fire chief of a fire department or fire protection district that is composed of 50 percent or more volunteer firefighters.

(3) "Residue" has the same meaning as defined in Section 171.8 of Title 49 of the Code of Federal Regulations.

(Amended by Stats. 1996, Ch. 124, Sec. 135. Effective January 1, 1997.)

32051. (a) Each advance notification required by Section 32050 shall contain all of the following information:

(1) The name, address, and emergency telephone number of the manufacturer, shipper, carrier, and receiver of the shipment.

(2) A current copy of a material data safety sheet, as designated by the department, regarding the material.

(3) If the shipment is originating within California, the point of origin of the shipment and the 48-hour period during which departure of the shipment is estimated to occur, the destination of the shipment within California, and the 48-hour period during which the shipment is estimated to arrive.

(4) If the shipment is originating outside of California, the point of origin of the shipment and the 48-hour period during which the shipment is estimated to arrive at the state boundary, the destination of the shipment within California, and the 48-hour period during which the shipment is estimated to arrive.

(5) A telephone number and address for current shipment information.

(b) The department shall design a standard notification form to include all of the information specified in subdivision (a) and shall make these forms available by April 1, 1989.

(Added by Stats. 1988, Ch. 1222, Sec. 2.)

32052. (a) The notification required by Section 32050 shall reach the department at least 72 hours before the beginning of the 48-hour period during which departure of the shipment of any material designated in Section 32050 is estimated to occur, and the department shall notify the sheriffs and the police chiefs as specified in subdivision (a) of Section 32050 at least 36 hours before the beginning of the 48-hour departure period specified in subdivision (a) of Section 32051, who shall notify the fire chiefs, as provided in Section 32050. A copy of the notification shall be retained by the department for three years.

(b) The carrier shall also notify, by telephone or telegram, the department if there are any changes in the scheduling of a shipment, in the routes to be used for shipment, or any cancellation of a shipment. The department shall, in turn, notify the sheriffs and the police chiefs specified in subdivision (a) of Section 32050 that would be affected by these changes in the scheduling of a shipment, in the routes to be used for a shipment, or the cancellation of a shipment, who shall notify the fire chiefs, as provided in Section 32050. The department shall maintain for three years a record of each telegram and telephonic notification.

(Added by Stats. 1988, Ch. 1222, Sec. 2.)

32053. (a) Any carrier who violates Section 32050, 32051, or 32052, in addition to any other penalty provided by law, is subject to a civil penalty of not less than five hundred dollars ($500) or more than one thousand dollars ($1,000) for each violation. For purposes of this section, each day of a continuing violation is a separate violation.

(b) When establishing the amount of the civil penalty, the court shall consider, in addition to other relevant circumstances, all of the following:

(1) The extent of the harm caused by the violation.

(2) The persistence of the violation.

(3) The number of prior violations by the same violator.

(4) The deterrent value of the penalty based on the financial resources of the violator.

(Added by Stats. 1988, Ch. 1222, Sec. 2.)

Division 14.3. Transportation of Inhalation Hazards

(Division 14.3 added by Stats. 1988, Ch. 1384, Sec. 5.)

32100. It is the intent of the Legislature, in enacting this division, to create a special category of inhalation hazards and poison gases and to establish special safeguards for their transportation.

These materials are highly toxic, spread rapidly, and require rapid and widespread evacuation if there is loss of containment or a fire. For these reasons, the Legislature intends to more rigorously restrict and otherwise control the transportation of these materials.

(Added by Stats. 1988, Ch. 1384, Sec. 5.)

32100.5. This division applies to the transportation of inhalation hazards in bulk packaging, except when that packaging contains only residue.

(Added by Stats. 1988, Ch. 1384, Sec. 5.)

32101. As used in this division:

(a) "Inhalation hazard" means any material defined as "Poison A" pursuant to Section 173.326 of Title 49 of the Code of Federal Regulations or for which a "Poison-Inhalation Hazard" or "Inhalation Hazard" shipping paper description is required pursuant to Section 172.203 of Title 49 of the Code of Federal Regulations.

(b) "Bulk packaging" means the same as defined in Section 171.8 of Title 49 of the Code of Federal Regulations.

(c) "Residue" means the same as defined in Section 171.8 of Title 49 of the Code of Federal Regulations.

(d) "Inspection stop" means any location designated as such in regulations adopted pursuant to this division or any safe stopping place.

(e) "Safe parking place" means any loading or unloading facility or motor carrier terminal where the driver may safely and lawfully park and leave the vehicle unattended when authorized by the owner or person in charge of the facility or terminal.

(f) "Safe stopping place" means any place designated by the department pursuant to this division where a driver may stop for food, fuel, or any other necessary reason, provided the vehicle is attended at all times. A vehicle is "attended" when the driver or person in charge of it is awake and occupies any part of it except the sleeper berth, or is within 100 feet of the vehicle and has an unobstructed view of it.

(Added by Stats. 1988, Ch. 1384, Sec. 5.)

32102. (a) The department may adopt any regulations that are necessary to administer this division. It is a misdemeanor for any person to violate this division or regulations adopted pursuant to this division.

(b) The department shall, by regulation, designate through routes in this state which are to be used for the transportation of inhalation hazards. The department may also designate separate through routes for the transportation of inhalation hazards composed of any chemical rocket propellant specified in Section 32050. The Department of Transportation shall assist the department in developing the recommended routes. The department shall hold public hearings in each field operation division of the department in which are located proposed routes. In recommending the through routes, the department shall do both of the following:

(1) Perform a risk assessment which shall include, but not be limited to, consideration of the population density, capabilities of the emergency response personnel near the proposed routes, and the safety of the roadways.

(2) Consult with officials having the responsibility for the prevention and suppression of fire in communities in which are located the proposed routes, the representatives of persons engaged in the transportation of inhalation hazards, manufacturers of inhalation hazards, and the State Fire Marshal.

(c) The department shall prepare for distribution to persons engaged in the transportation of inhalation hazards maps which clearly indicate the routes which are to be used for the transportation of inhalation hazards.

(d) The department shall prepare for distribution to persons engaged in the transportation of inhalation hazards a list of locations of required inspection stops and safe stopping places and shall revise the list to keep it current.

(e) Until other routes are designated by the department for the transportation of chemical rocket propellants pursuant to subdivision (b), the designated through routes for the transportation of chemical rocket propellants to Vandenberg Air Force Base shall be those routes designated in the letter of agreement between the department and the United States Department of the Air Force executed in 1992.

(Amended by Stats. 1992, Ch. 516, Sec. 1. Effective January 1, 1993.)

32103. (a) Every motor carrier shall make available in each vehicle used in the transportation of inhalation hazards the latest map showing the routes to be used for the transportation of inhalation hazards and a list of the safe stopping places and inspection stops for vehicles transporting inhalation hazards as prescribed by regulations of the department. The carrier shall require that the driver be thoroughly familiar with this division before operating any vehicle in the transportation of inhalation hazards.

(b) This section shall become operative on January 1, 1992.

(Added by Stats. 1988, Ch. 1384, Sec. 5. Section operative January 1, 1992, by its own provisions.)

32104. (a) It is unlawful for the motor carrier or its authorized agent to drive or to permit the driving of any vehicle transporting inhalation hazards, or for the driver to drive the vehicle, upon any public highway not designated in regulations adopted by the department as a route for the transportation of inhalation hazards. This subdivision shall not apply when the use of the highway is required (1) to permit delivery of, or the loading of, inhalation hazards at a point not on a highway designated as a route for the transportation of inhalation hazards, or (2) to permit the vehicle to proceed to, and return from, an inspection stop, safe stopping place, or safe parking place.

(b) It is unlawful for the driver of any vehicle transporting inhalation hazards to stop at any place other than a safe stopping place, safe parking place, or an inspection stop unless the vehicle is disabled or except when necessary to avoid conflict with other traffic or to comply with the orders of a peace officer or an official traffic control device.

(c) This section shall become operative on January 1, 1992.

(Added by Stats. 1988, Ch. 1384, Sec. 5. Section operative January 1, 1992, by its own provisions.)

32105. (a) Unless there is no practicable alternative, every driver of a vehicle transporting inhalation hazards shall avoid, by prearrangement of routes, driving into or through heavily populated areas, congested thoroughfares, or places where crowds are assembled. Operating convenience is not a basis for determining whether it is practicable to operate a vehicle in accordance with this subdivision.

(b) No vehicle transporting inhalation hazards shall be left unattended upon any street or highway.

(c) Inspection of the following items of equipment shall be made immediately preceding the actual transportation of an inhalation hazard:

(1) Brakes and the brake system.

(2) Steering, connection devices, and lighting systems.

(3) All tires.

(4) All supplemental equipment as required by Section 32106.

(d) En route inspection of tires and brakes on vehicles transporting inhalation hazards shall be performed at the following locations:

(1) At an inspection stop at least every four hours or 150 miles traveled, whichever occurs first, or as close thereto as is practicable, depending upon the proximity of those inspection stops.

(2) Regardless of elapsed time or miles traveled, at the top of and prior to descending any grade upon which the Department of Transportation has declared a speed limit for trucks of less than 55 miles per hour as provided by Section 22407. The inspection shall be made off the roadway.

(3) Regardless of elapsed time or miles traveled, at any location designated in regulations of the department as a required inspection stop.

(e) (1) Every person operating a vehicle transporting an inhalation hazard shall complete a record of every inspection which is required pursuant to this section in the form approved by the department showing the time and place of every inspection.

(2) The record of every inspection shall be made at the time the inspection is conducted.

(3) The person making the inspection shall certify the fact in the record.

(f) This section shall become operative on January 1, 1992.

(Added by Stats. 1988, Ch. 1384, Sec. 5. Section operative January 1, 1992, by its own provisions.)

32106. Every vehicle used in the transportation of an inhalation hazard, in addition to any other equipment required by law, shall be equipped and maintained as required by this section.

(a) Brakes and the brake system shall be maintained in good and safe operating condition.

(b) Steering, connection devices, and lighting systems shall be maintained in good operating condition.

(c) All tires shall be in good condition, properly matched and inflated. Except as may be necessary to cause immediate replacement, no vehicle shall be driven unless all tires in actual use on the vehicle are properly inflated.

(d) Fire extinguishers and other safety equipment prescribed by regulations adopted by the department pursuant to Section 34501 shall be carried in each vehicle or combination of vehicles.

(Added by Stats. 1988, Ch. 1384, Sec. 5.)

32107. Every vehicle, or combination of vehicles, transporting an inhalation hazard shall contain a self-contained breathing apparatus and equipment capable of immediate communication with emergency personnel.

(Added by Stats. 1988, Ch. 1384, Sec. 5.)

32109. Nothing in this division exempts any vehicle transporting inhalation hazards and subject to this division, or the owner or any other person, from other provisions of this code. All those other provisions relating to the driving and movement of vehicles, and the size, weight and equipment thereof, shall apply as applicable to each and every vehicle engaged in transporting inhalation hazards subject to this division.

(Added by Stats. 1988, Ch. 1384, Sec. 5.)

Division 14.5. Transportation of Radioactive Materials

(Division 14.5 added by Stats. 1959, Ch. 1810.)

33000. Subject to the provisions of Section 114765 of the Health and Safety Code, the Department of the California Highway Patrol, after consulting with the State Department of Health Services, shall adopt regulations specifying the time that shipments may occur and the routes that are to be used in the transportation of cargoes of hazardous radioactive materials, as are defined in regulations of the State Department of Health Services.

(Amended by Stats. 1996, Ch. 1023, Sec. 427. Effective September 29, 1996.)

33002. (a) Prior to the transport of any hazardous radioactive materials containing cargoes of commercially produced, spent radioactive fuel outside the confines of a facility where that material was used or stored, or prior to the delivery of these materials to a carrier for transport, each carrier shall provide advance notification, in writing, of the shipment to the Department of the California Highway Patrol, which, in turn, shall notify all of the following persons:

(1) The fire chiefs of each city and county fire department and the fire chiefs of each fire protection district serving a population greater than 15,000, which city, county, or fire protection district is located along the proposed route. The Department of the California Highway Patrol, however, shall notify only those fire chiefs who have requested, in writing, to be so notified. A fire chief may revoke this request, in writing, at any time.

This paragraph does not apply to any fire chief of a fire department or fire protection district that is composed of 50 percent or more volunteer firefighters.

(2) The police chiefs of each city where surface transportation would occur along the proposed route.

(b) Subdivision (a) applies only to the extent that it does not conflict with federal law.

(c) Each advance notification shall contain the following information:

(1) The name, address, and telephone number of the shipper, carrier, and receiver of the shipment.

(2) If the shipment originates within California, the point of origin of the shipment and the 48-hour period during which departure of the shipment is estimated to occur, the destination of the shipment within California, and the 48-hour period during which the shipment is estimated to arrive.

(3) If the shipment originates outside of California, the point of origin of the shipment and the 48-hour period during which the shipment is estimated to arrive at state boundaries, the destination of the shipment within California, and the 48-hour period during which the shipment is estimated to arrive.

(4) A telephone number and address for current shipment information.

(d) The Department of the California Highway Patrol shall design a standard notification form to include all of the information specified in subdivision (c) and shall make these forms available by April 1, 1984.

(e) The notification is required to reach the Department of the California Highway Patrol at least 72 hours before the beginning of the 48-hour period during which departure of the shipment is estimated to occur, and the Department of the California Highway Patrol shall notify the fire chiefs who have requested notification and the police chiefs specified in subdivision (a) at least 36 hours before the beginning of this 48-hour period. A copy of the notification shall be retained by the Department of the California Highway Patrol for three years.

(f) The carrier shall also notify, by telephone or telegram, the Department of the California Highway Patrol if there are any changes in the scheduling of a shipment, in the routes to be used for a shipment, or any cancellation of a shipment. The Department of the California Highway Patrol shall, in turn, notify the fire chiefs who have requested notification and the police chiefs specified in subdivision (a) who would be affected by these changes in the scheduling of a shipment, in the routes to be used for a shipment, or the cancellation of a shipment. The Department of the California Highway Patrol shall maintain for three years a record of each telegram and telephonic notification.

(g) Any person or agency that receives any information pursuant to this section shall not disseminate or reveal this information to any other person, state agency, city, county, or local agency unless the person or agency determines that disseminating or revealing this information is necessary to protect the public health and safety or the environment.

(h) The Governor shall appoint the fire chiefs eligible to request notification, as specified in paragraph (1) of subdivision (a), as the designated representatives of the Governor pursuant to paragraph (1) of subsection (c) of Section 73.21 of Title 10 of the Code of Federal Regulations for the purpose of receiving information classified as safeguards information pursuant to Part 73 of Title 10 of the Code of Federal Regulations.

(i) Any carrier who violates this section, in addition to any penalty provided by law, is subject to a civil penalty of not more than five hundred dollars ($500) for each violation. For purposes of this section, each day of a continuing violation is a separate and distinct violation.

When establishing the amount of civil liability pursuant to this subdivision, the court shall consider, in addition to other relevant circumstances, the following:

(1) The extent of the harm caused by the violation.

(2) The persistence of the violation.

(3) The number of prior violations by the same violator.

(4) The deterrent value of the penalty based on the financial resources of the violator.

(Amended by Stats. 1996, Ch. 124, Sec. 136. Effective January 1, 1997.)

Division 14.7. Flammable and Combustible Liquids

(Heading of Division 14.7 amended by Stats. 1977, Ch. 825.)

Article 1. Administration

(Article 1 added by Stats. 1967, Ch. 1106.)

34000. It is the intent of the Legislature to provide additional protection to the public and reduce the risk of possible hazards in the highway transportation of hazardous waste and of flammable and combustible liquids in tank vehicles. It is further the intent of the Legislature that the Department of the California Highway Patrol shall place as a high priority the random inspection of cargo tanks and hazardous waste transport vehicles and containers for compliance with this code.

(Amended by Stats. 1996, Ch. 539, Sec. 28. Effective January 1, 1997.)

34001. The provisions of this division refer to vehicles having a cargo tank and to hazardous waste transport vehicles and containers, as defined in Section 25167.4 of the Health and Safety Code, that are operating on highways within this state.

(Amended by Stats. 1997, Ch. 945, Sec. 28. Effective January 1, 1998.)

34002. (a) It is the legislative intention that the regulations adopted by the commissioner pursuant to this division shall apply uniformly throughout the State of California, and no state agency, city, city and county, county, or other political subdivision of this state, including, but not limited to, a chartered city, city and county, or county, shall adopt or enforce any ordinance or regulation which is inconsistent with this division.

(b) No other state agency, city, city and county, county, or other public agency of this state, including, but not limited to, a chartered city, city and county, or county, shall enforce any provisions regarding the design and construction of any cargo tank subject to this division, regardless of the location of the cargo tank, or the area of operation of the cargo tank, within this state.

(Amended by Stats. 1983, Ch. 661, Sec. 3.)

34003. For purposes of this division:

(a) "Cargo tank" has the same meaning as defined in Section 171.8 of Title 49 of the Code of Federal Regulations.

(b) "Cargo tank vehicle" means a truck, trailer, or semitrailer with one or more permanently attached cargo tanks to or forming an integral part of the vehicle.

(c) "Flammable liquids" and "combustible liquids" have the same meanings as defined in Section 173.120 of Title 49 of the Code of Federal Regulations.

(Repealed and added by Stats. 2023, Ch. 219, Sec. 8. (SB 891) Effective January 1, 2024.)

34004. The provisions of this division shall apply equally to new as well as existing cargo tanks.

(Repealed and added by Stats. 1967, Ch. 1106.)

34006. The provisions of this division shall not apply to "wine," as defined by Section 23007 of the Business and Professions Code, or any other aqueous solution, having an alcoholic content less than, or equal to, 24 percent by volume. This exemption applies only if the nonalcohol portion of the aqueous solution does not fall within the definition of flammable or combustible liquid.

(Added by Stats. 1978, Ch. 868.)

Article 2. Regulations

(Article 2 added by Stats. 1967, Ch. 1106.)

34019. (a) The commissioner shall adopt reasonable regulations with respect to the following:

(1) The design, construction, and structural safety of cargo tanks and fire auxiliary equipment.

(2) To the extent permitted by federal law, the stability of tank vehicles.

(b) For intrastate shipments in this state, the commissioner shall, as soon as feasible, incorporate any new United States Department of

Transportation standards concerning interstate shipments.

(Amended by Stats. 1991, Ch. 1043, Sec. 2.)

34020.5. (a) The Department of Transportation, after consultation with the Department of the California Highway Patrol, the State Fire Marshal, and affected local agencies, and following a public hearing subject to Section 21109.5, may regulate the time when tank vehicles may travel through a tunnel on state highways.

(b) In evaluating the use of a tunnel on a state highway, the Department of Transportation shall conduct a traffic and engineering survey which includes an analysis of the relative risks to public safety in determining the feasibility of reasonable alternative routes.

(c) For the purposes of this section, a tunnel is a horizontal passage enclosed on the sides and top containing a roadway of a length of not less than 300 feet.

(d) No prohibition or restriction adopted pursuant to this section shall be effective until appropriate signs have been posted giving notice thereof to drivers approaching the tunnel.

(Added by Stats. 1982, Ch. 1255, Sec. 12.)

34021. The regulations adopted by the commissioner shall make reasonable allowances for cargo tanks in existence when the regulations become effective. No allowance shall, however, be made for any cargo tank which because of its design or construction constitutes a distinct hazard to life or property.

(Amended by Stats. 1983, Ch. 661, Sec. 5.)

34022. In adopting the regulations, the commissioner shall consider, as evidence of generally accepted safety standards, the publications of the National Fire Protection Association and the United States Department of Transportation.

(Amended by Stats. 1983, Ch. 661, Sec. 6.)

34024. The regulations adopted by the commissioner pursuant to this division shall be adopted, amended, and repealed in accordance with Chapter 3.5 (commencing with Section 11340) of Part 1 of Division 3 of Title 2 of the Government Code.

(Amended by Stats. 1985, Ch. 106, Sec. 166.)

Article 4. Enforcement

(Article 4 added by Stats. 1967, Ch. 1106.)

34060. The commissioner shall provide for the establishment, operation, and enforcement of random on- and off-highway inspections of cargo tanks and hazardous waste transport vehicles and containers. The commissioner shall also provide training in the inspection of cargo tanks and hazardous waste transport vehicles and containers to employees of the department whose primary duties include the enforcement of laws and regulations relating to commercial vehicles and who, thereafter, are required to perform random inspections of cargo tanks and hazardous waste transport vehicles and containers to determine whether or not the cargo tanks and hazardous waste transport vehicles and containers are designed, constructed, and maintained in accordance with the regulations adopted by the commissioner pursuant to this code and Chapter 6.5 (commencing with Section 25100) of Division 20 of the Health and Safety Code.

(Amended by Stats. 1997, Ch. 945, Sec. 29. Effective January 1, 1998.)

34060.5. Any required pressure, vacuum, or hydrostatic testing of a cargo tank shall be performed, or be caused to be performed, by the carrier, operator, or consultant who shall certify in writing that the cargo tank meets the requirements of the United States Department of Transportation, the State Air Resources Board, and the commissioner. An authorized representative of the department may observe or require these tests. Records of these certifications shall be maintained at the carrier's place of business.

(Amended by Stats. 1983, Ch. 661, Sec. 11.)

34061. The department shall compile data and annually publish a report relating to the level of cargo tank and hazardous waste transport vehicle and container inspections conducted during the previous year. The data included in the report shall include, but need not be limited to, all of the following:

(a) The number of inspections conducted.

(b) The number of violations recorded.

(c) The number of on-highway incidents involving cargo tanks and hazardous waste transport vehicles and containers that were reported to the Office of Emergency Services under Section 8574.17 of the Government Code.

(Amended by Stats. 2013, Ch. 352, Sec. 526. (AB 1317) Effective September 26, 2013. Operative July 1, 2013, by Sec. 543 of Ch. 352.)

34064. Any duly authorized employee of the department may inspect cargo tanks and hazardous waste transport vehicles and containers, or the appurtenances and equipment thereof, in terminals, yards, or similar places, as often as may be necessary for the purpose of ascertaining and causing to be corrected any conditions likely to cause damage to any personal or real property or injury or death to any person or animal or any violation of the provisions or intent of this division. Any duly authorized employee of the department may enter upon private property to conduct those inspections. The owner, lessee, bailee, manager, or operator of that property shall permit any duly authorized employee of the department to enter the property and inspect cargo tanks and hazardous waste transport vehicles and containers for the purpose stated in this division.

(Amended by Stats. 1996, Ch. 539, Sec. 36. Effective January 1, 1997.)

Article 5. Violations

(Article 5 added by Stats. 1967, Ch. 1106.)

34100. A violation of this division or of any regulation adopted by the commissioner pursuant to this division is a misdemeanor. No person shall operate a tank vehicle upon a highway in violation of this division or of any regulation adopted by the commissioner pursuant to this division.

(Added by renumbering Section 34102 by Stats. 1996, Ch. 539, Sec. 40. Effective January 1, 1997.)

Division 14.8. Safety Regulations

(Division 14.8 added by Stats. 1963, Ch. 2148.)

34500. The department shall regulate the safe operation of the following vehicles:

(a) Motortrucks of three or more axles that are more than 10,000 pounds gross vehicle weight rating.

(b) Truck tractors.

(c) Buses, schoolbuses, school pupil activity buses, youth buses, farm labor vehicles, modified limousines, and general public paratransit vehicles.

(d) Trailers and semitrailers designed or used for the transportation of more than 10 persons, and the towing motor vehicle.

(e) Trailers and semitrailers, pole or pipe dollies, auxiliary dollies, and logging dollies used in combination with vehicles listed in subdivision (a), (b), (c), (d), or (j). This subdivision does not include camp trailers, trailer coaches, and utility trailers.

(f) A combination of a motortruck and a vehicle or vehicles set forth in subdivision (e) that exceeds 40 feet in length when coupled together.

(g) A vehicle, or a combination of vehicles, transporting hazardous materials.

(h) Manufactured homes that, when moved upon the highway, are required to be moved pursuant to a permit, as specified in Section 35780 or 35790.

(i) A park trailer, as described in Section 18009.3 of the Health and Safety Code, that, when moved upon a highway, is required to be moved pursuant to a permit pursuant to Section 35780.

(j) Any other motortruck regulated by the Department of Motor Vehicles, the Department of Consumer Affairs, or the United States Secretary of Transportation.

(k) A commercial motor vehicle with a gross vehicle weight rating of 26,001 or more pounds or a commercial motor vehicle of any gross vehicle weight rating towing a vehicle described in subdivision (e) with a gross vehicle weight rating of more than 10,000 pounds, except combinations including camp trailers, trailer coaches, or utility trailers. For purposes of this subdivision, the term "commercial motor vehicle" has the same meaning as defined in subdivision (b) of Section 15210.

(Amended by Stats. 2024, Ch. 226, Sec. 13. (AB 3278) Effective January 1, 2025.)

34500.1. In addition to the duties imposed by Section 34500, the department shall regulate the safe operation of tour buses.

(Added by Stats. 1986, Ch. 1306, Sec. 13.)

34500.2. No additional inspection shall be required under this division on any vehicle which is owned and operated by a public agency and is used for responding to and returning from an emergency, as defined in subdivision (c) of Section 35002, during the duration of the emergency, as determined by the public agency, if an inspection pursuant to Section 1215 of Title 13 of the California Code of Regulations has been completed on the vehicle within the past 24 hours. Any vehicle used in responding to an emergency shall be inspected immediately upon the termination of the emergency.

(Added by Stats. 1990, Ch. 899, Sec. 1. Effective September 14, 1990.)

34500.3. (a) The department shall adopt rules and regulations that are designed to promote the safe operation of vehicles, regarding cargo securement standards. The regulations adopted pursuant to this section shall be consistent with the securement regulations adopted by the United States Department of Transportation in Part 393 (commencing with Section 393.1) of Title 49 of the Code of Federal Regulations, as those regulations now exist or are amended in the future.

(b) Regulations adopted pursuant to subdivision (a) do not apply to a farmer transporting his or her own hay or straw, incidental to his or her farming operation, if that transportation requires that the farmer use a highway, except that this subdivision does not relieve the farmer from loading and securing the hay or straw in a safe manner.

(Amended by Stats. 2015, Ch. 451, Sec. 57. (SB 491) Effective January 1, 2016.)

34500.4. (a) Not later than July 1, 2017, the Department of the California Highway Patrol shall implement a program to conduct safety inspections of modified limousine terminals that are operated by passenger stage corporations pursuant to Article 2 (commencing with Section 1031) of Chapter 5 of Part 1 of Division 1 of the Public Utilities Code or by charter-party carriers of passengers pursuant to the Passenger Charter-party Carriers' Act (Chapter 8 (commencing with Section 5351) of Division 2 of the Public Utilities Code).

(b) (1) The inspection program shall include, but is not limited to, the safe operation of the vehicle, the installation of safety equipment, the retention of maintenance logs, accident reports, and records of driver discipline, compliance with federal and state motor vehicle safety standards, the examination of a preventative maintenance program, and, if ownership of the modified limousine has been transferred, the transmission of relevant safety and maintenance information of the limousine.

(2) Pursuant to the safety inspection program, the department shall conduct an inspection of each terminal of a charter-party carrier of passengers and passenger stage corporation that operates modified limousines at least once every 13 months.

(3) The department shall adopt emergency regulations for purposes of this subdivision. The adoption by the department of regulations implementing this section shall be deemed to be an emergency and necessary to avoid serious harm to the public peace, health, safety, or general welfare for purposes of Sections 11346.1 and 11349.6 of the Government Code, and the department is hereby exempted from the requirement that it describe facts showing the need for immediate action to the Office of Administrative Law. The emergency regulations shall remain in effect for no more than one year, by which time final regulations shall be adopted.

(4) (A) The department shall adopt regulations to establish an inspection fee to be collected every 13 months, based on the number of modified limousines operated by a single charter-party carrier or passenger stage corporation. The fee shall be in an amount sufficient to offset the costs to administer the inspection program and shall not be used to supplant or support any other inspection program conducted by the department. The fee shall be in addition to any other required fee. When developing the regulations, the department shall consider measures that increase efficiencies to limit the financial impact to charter-party carriers of passengers and passenger stage corporations subject to the fee. The department shall promulgate the regulations in consultation with appropriate interested parties.

(B) The fee structure established pursuant to this subdivision shall apply to modified limousines that are required to undergo a safety inspection pursuant to this section.

(C) The fee established pursuant to this subdivision shall be collected by the Public Utilities Commission and deposited into the Motor Vehicle Account in the State Transportation Fund to cover the costs of the inspections conducted by the department.

(5) The department shall transmit to the Public Utilities Commission inspection data of modified limousine terminals inspected pursuant to this program, as specified in the program regulations.

(c) Regulations adopted pursuant to this section shall be consistent with the established inspection program administered by the department for buses pursuant to this division.

(Amended by Stats. 2015, Ch. 480, Sec. 2. (AB 863) Effective January 1, 2016.)

34500.5. For purposes of this division, the term "commercial motor vehicle" has the same meaning as defined in subdivision (b) of Section 15210, or any vehicle listed in Section 34500.

(Amended by Stats. 2015, Ch. 451, Sec. 58. (SB 491) Effective January 1, 2016.)

34500.6. (a) For purposes of this division, an agricultural vehicle is a vehicle or combination of vehicles with a gross combination weight rating or a gross vehicle weight rating of 26,000 pounds or less if all of the following conditions are met:

(1) Is operated by a farmer, an employee of a farmer, or an instructor

credentialed in agriculture as part of an instructional program in agriculture at the high school, community college, or university level.

(2) Is used exclusively in the conduct of agricultural operations when operating in commerce.

(3) Is not used in the capacity of a for-hire carrier or for compensation.

(4) The towing vehicle has a gross weight rating of 16,000 pounds or less.

(5) Is used solely in intrastate commerce.

(b) This section shall remain in effect only until January 1, 2031, and as of that date is repealed, unless a later enacted statute, that is enacted before January 1, 2031, deletes or extends that date.

(Amended by Stats. 2025, Ch. 61, Sec. 1. (AB 525) Effective January 1, 2026. Repealed as of January 1, 2031, by its own provisions.)

34500.7. (a) Subject to Section 34500, motor carriers, drivers, and vehicles shall comply with the Federal Motor Carrier Safety Regulations in Parts 385, 392, 393, 396, and 397 of Title 49 of the Code of Federal Regulations.

(b) Notwithstanding subdivision (a), Daily Vehicle Inspection Reports are required for intrastate drivers and motor carriers pursuant to Section 1215 of Title 13 of the California Code of Regulations.

(Added by Stats. 2023, Ch. 219, Sec. 10. (SB 891) Effective January 1, 2024.)

34501. (a) (1) The department shall adopt reasonable rules and regulations that, in the judgment of the department, are designed to promote the safe operation of vehicles described in Section 34500, regarding, but not limited to, controlled substances and alcohol testing of drivers by motor carriers, hours of service of drivers, equipment, fuel containers, fueling operations, inspection, maintenance, recordkeeping, accident reports, and drawbridges. The rules and regulations shall not, however, be applicable to schoolbuses, which shall be subject to rules and regulations adopted pursuant to Section 34501.5.

The rules and regulations shall exempt local law enforcement agencies, within a single county, engaged in the transportation of inmates or prisoners when those agencies maintain other motor vehicle operations records which furnish hours of service information on drivers which are in substantial compliance with the rules and regulations. This exemption does not apply to any local law enforcement agency engaged in the transportation of inmates or prisoners outside the county in which the agency is located, if that agency would otherwise be required, by existing law, to maintain driving logs.

(2) The department may adopt rules and regulations relating to commercial vehicle safety inspection and out-of-service criteria. In adopting the rules and regulations, the commissioner may consider the commercial vehicle safety inspection and out-of-service criteria adopted by organizations such as the Commercial Vehicle Safety Alliance, other intergovernmental safety group, or the United States Department of Transportation. The commissioner may provide departmental representatives to that alliance or other organization for the purpose of promoting the continued improvement and refinement of compatible nationwide commercial vehicle safety inspection and out-of-service criteria.

(3) The commissioner shall appoint a committee of 15 members, consisting of representatives of industry subject to the regulations to be adopted pursuant to this section, to act in an advisory capacity to the department, and the department shall cooperate and confer with the advisory committee so appointed. The commissioner shall appoint a separate committee to advise the department on rules and regulations concerning wheelchair lifts for installation and use on buses, consisting of persons who use the wheelchair lifts, representatives of transit districts, representatives of designers or manufacturers of wheelchairs and wheelchair lifts, and representatives of the Department of Transportation.

(4) The department may inspect any vehicles in maintenance facilities or terminals, as well as any records relating to the dispatch of vehicles or drivers, and the pay of drivers, to ensure compliance with this code and regulations adopted pursuant to this section.

(b) (1) The department, using the definitions adopted pursuant to Section 2402.7, shall adopt regulations for the transportation of hazardous materials in this state, except the transportation of materials that are subject to other provisions of this code, that the department determines are reasonably necessary to ensure the safety of persons and property using the highways. The regulations may include provisions governing the filling, marking, packing, labeling, and assembly of, and containers that may be used for, hazardous materials shipments, and the manner by which the shipper attests that the shipments are correctly identified and in proper condition for transport.

(2) (A) The regulations adopted under this section for vehicles engaged in interstate or intrastate commerce shall establish hazardous materials requirements that are consistent with the hazardous materials regulations adopted by the United States Department of Transportation in Chapter I of, and Part 397 of Subchapter B of Chapter III of, Subtitle B of Title 49 of the Code of Federal Regulations.

(B) If a carrier not subject to federal jurisdiction finds a regulation adopted pursuant to this section to be unnecessarily burdensome or impracticable, the carrier may apply to the department, at no cost, for an alternate method of compliance.

(3) Regulations adopted pursuant to this subdivision do not apply to the following:

(A) The transportation of explosives in an authorized emergency vehicle, as defined in paragraph (1) of subdivision (b) of Section 165, when operated by a peace officer, as defined in Sections 830.1 and 830.2 of the Penal Code, under the following conditions:

(i) The transportation is necessary for tactical operations or explosives detection or removal duties.

(ii) Storage and security is in compliance with the applicable provisions of "ATV Federal Explosives Laws and Regulations," published by the Bureau of Alcohol, Tobacco, Firearms, and Explosives.

(B) The transportation of seized fireworks by a public agency as authorized by Part 2 (commencing with Section 12500) of Division 11 of the Health and Safety Code.

(c) (1) At least once every 13 months, the department shall inspect every maintenance facility or terminal of any person who at any time operates any bus. If the bus operation includes more than 100 buses, the inspection shall be without prior notice.

(2) This subdivision does not preclude the department from conducting inspections of tour bus operations with fewer than 100 buses without prior notice. To the extent possible, the department shall conduct inspections without prior notice of any tour bus operation, including tour bus operations that have a history of noncompliance with safety laws or regulations, that have received unsatisfactory ratings, or that have had buses ordered out of service for safety violations.

(3) If a tour bus operator receives an unsatisfactory rating, the department shall conduct a followup inspection between 30 and 90 days after the initial inspection during which the unsatisfactory rating was received.

(d) The commissioner shall adopt and enforce regulations which will make the public or private users of any bus aware of the operator's last safety rating.

(e) It is unlawful and constitutes a misdemeanor for any person to operate any bus without the inspections specified in subdivision (c) having been conducted.

(f) The department may adopt regulations restricting or prohibiting the movement of any vehicle from a maintenance facility or terminal if the vehicle is found in violation of this code or regulations adopted pursuant to this section.

(Amended by Stats. 2022, Ch. 295, Sec. 20. (AB 2956) Effective January 1, 2023.)

34501.1. A manufacturer or distributor of wheelchair lifts for buses, schoolbuses, youth buses, and general public transit vehicles, regardless of capacity, shall, prior to the distribution of the wheelchair lift model in California, provide to the Department of the California Highway

Patrol proof of certification from an independent laboratory or registered mechanical engineer of this state that the wheelchair lift model complies with the California and any federal law and the regulations adopted pursuant thereto.

(Added by Stats. 1989, Ch. 428, Sec. 1.)

34501.2. (a) The regulations adopted under Section 34501 for vehicles engaged in interstate or intrastate commerce shall establish hours-of-service regulations for drivers of those vehicles that are consistent with the hours-of-service regulations adopted by the United States Department of Transportation in Title 49 of the Code of Federal Regulations, as those regulations now exist or are hereafter amended.

(b) The regulations adopted under Section 34501 for vehicles engaged in intrastate commerce that are not transporting hazardous substances or hazardous waste, as those terms are defined by regulations in Section 171.8 of Title 49 of the Code of Federal Regulations, as those regulations now exist or are hereafter amended, shall have the following exceptions:

(1) (A) The maximum driving time within a work period shall be 12 hours for a driver of a truck or truck tractor, except for a driver of a tank vehicle with a capacity of more than 500 gallons transporting flammable liquid, who shall not drive for more than 10 hours within a work period.

(B) Notwithstanding subparagraph (A), the regulations may authorize a driver to exceed the maximum driving time prescribed in subparagraph (A) and on-duty time prescribed in paragraph (2) during a state of emergency declared by the Governor when operating within the state to transport fuel, pursuant to a contract with this state or the United States, used for the purpose of refueling aircraft used in emergency-related activities, including fire suppression.

(2) Except as provided in subparagraph (B) of paragraph (1), a motor carrier shall not permit or require a driver to drive, nor shall a driver drive, for any period after having been on duty for 80 hours in any consecutive eight days.

(3) (A) A driver employed by an electrical corporation, as defined in Section 218 of the Public Utilities Code, a local publicly owned electric utility, as defined in Section 224.3 of that code, a gas corporation, as defined in Section 222 of that code, a telephone corporation, as defined in Section 234 of that code, a water corporation, as defined in Section 241 of that code, or a public water district as defined in Section 20200 of the Water Code, is exempt from all hours-of-service regulations while operating a public utility or public water district vehicle.

(B) A driver hired directly as a contractor by an electrical corporation, a local publicly owned electric utility, a gas corporation, a telephone corporation, a water corporation, or a public water district, as those entities are defined in subparagraph (A), or as a subcontractor hired directly by the original contractor, is exempt from all hours-of-service regulations while operating a vehicle for the purpose of restoring utility service during an emergency on behalf of the entity that hired the original contractor. The driver shall maintain a driver's record of duty status and shall keep a duplicate copy in their possession when driving a vehicle subject to this chapter. These records shall be presented immediately upon request by any authorized employee of the department, or any police officer or deputy sheriff.

(C) For purposes of subparagraph (B), "emergency" means a sudden, unexpected occurrence involving a clear and imminent danger, demanding immediate action to prevent or mitigate loss of, or damage to, life, health, property, or essential public services. "Unexpected occurrence" includes, but is not limited to, fires, floods, earthquakes or other soil or geologic movements, riots, accidents, inclement weather, natural disaster, sabotage, or other occurrence, whether natural or man-made, that interrupts the delivery of essential services, such as electricity, medical care, sewer, water, telecommunications, and telecommunication transmissions, or otherwise immediately threatens human life or public welfare.

(4) Any other exceptions applicable to drivers assigned to governmental fire suppression and prevention, as determined by the department.

(5) A driver employed by a law enforcement agency, as defined in Section 390.3(f)(2) of Title 49 of the Code of Federal Regulations, as that section now exists or is hereafter amended, during an emergency or to restore the public peace.

(c) The regulations adopted under Section 34501 for vehicles engaged in the transportation of farm products in intrastate commerce shall include all of the following provisions:

(1) A driver employed by an agricultural carrier, including a carrier holding a seasonal permit, or by a private carrier, when transporting farm products from the field to the first point of processing or packing, shall not drive for any period after having been on duty 16 hours or more following 8 consecutive hours off duty and shall not drive for any period after having been on duty for 112 hours in any consecutive eight-day period, except that a driver transporting special situation farm products from the field to the first point of processing or packing, or transporting livestock from pasture to pasture, may be permitted, during one period of not more than 28 consecutive days or a combination of two periods totaling not more than 28 days in a calendar year, to drive for not more than 12 hours during any workday of not more than 16 hours. A driver who thereby exceeds the driving time limits specified in paragraph (2) of subdivision (b) shall maintain a driver's record of duty status, and shall keep a duplicate copy in their possession when driving a vehicle subject to this chapter. These records shall be presented immediately upon request by any authorized employee of the department, or any police officer or deputy sheriff.

(2) Upon the request of the Secretary of Food and Agriculture, the commissioner may, for good cause, temporarily waive the maximum on-duty time limits applicable to any eight-day period when an emergency exists due to inclement weather, natural disaster, or an adverse economic condition that threatens to disrupt the orderly movement of farm products during harvest for the duration of the emergency. For purposes of this paragraph, an emergency does not include a strike or labor dispute.

(3) For purposes of this subdivision, the following terms have the following meanings:

(A) "Farm products" means every agricultural, horticultural, viticultural, or vegetable product of the soil, honey and beeswax, oilseeds, poultry, livestock, milk, or timber.

(B) "First point of processing or packing" means a location where farm products are dried, canned, extracted, fermented, distilled, frozen, ginned, eviscerated, pasteurized, packed, packaged, bottled, conditioned, or otherwise manufactured, processed, or preserved for distribution in wholesale or retail markets.

(C) "Special situation farm products" means fruit, tomatoes, sugar beets, grains, wine grapes, grape concentrate, cotton, or nuts.

(Amended by Stats. 2025, Ch. 417, Sec. 6. (SB 506) Effective January 1, 2026.)

34501.3. (a) No motor carrier shall schedule a run or permit or require the operation of any motor vehicle subject to this division between points within a period of time which would do either of the following:

(1) Necessitate the vehicle being operated at speeds greater than those prescribed by this code.

(2) Require the driver of the vehicle to exceed the applicable maximum hours of service.

(b) A logbook of a driver, which reflects a trip or trips between points within a period of time which would have necessitated excessive speed to complete, shall give rise to a rebuttable presumption that the driver exceeded the lawful speed limit.

(c) For a violation of paragraph (2) of subdivision (a), a first offense is punishable by a fine of not more than one thousand dollars ($1,000), a second offense by a fine of not more than two thousand five hundred dollars ($2,500), and a third or subsequent offense by a fine of not more than five thousand dollars ($5,000).

(Amended by Stats. 1991, Ch. 392, Sec. 1.)

34501.4. Any driver subject to the hours of service limitations and logbook requirements of this division, who is unable to produce upon request of a representative of the department any driver's logbook or is only able to produce an incomplete driver's log book for the prior 24-hour period, is rebuttably presumed to be in violation of the hours of service limitations in Sections 34501 and 34501.2.

(Added by Stats. 1986, Ch. 1306, Sec. 15.)

34501.5. (a) The Department of the California Highway Patrol shall adopt reasonable rules and regulations that, in the judgment of the department, are designed to promote the safe operation of vehicles described in Sections 39830 and 82321 of the Education Code and Sections 545 and 34500 of this code. The Commissioner of the California Highway Patrol shall appoint a committee of 11 members to act in an advisory capacity when developing and adopting regulations affecting school pupil transportation buses and school pupil transportation operations. The advisory committee shall consist of 11 members appointed as follows:

(1) One member of the State Department of Education.

(2) One member of the Department of Motor Vehicles.

(3) One member of the Department of the California Highway Patrol.

(4) One member who is employed as a schoolbus driver.

(5) One member of the California Office of Traffic Safety in the Transportation Agency.

(6) Two members who are schoolbus contractors, one of whom shall be from an urban area of the state and one of whom shall be from a rural area of the state, as determined by the department.

(7) Two members who are representatives of school districts, one of whom shall be from an urban area of the state and one of whom shall be from a rural area of the state, as determined by the department.

(8) One professionally licensed member of the American Academy of Pediatrics.

(9) One member representing school pupil transportation operations other than schoolbus operations.

(b) The department shall cooperate and confer with the advisory committee appointed pursuant to this section prior to adopting rules or regulations affecting school pupil transportation buses and school pupil transportation operations.

(Amended by Stats. 2025, Ch. 417, Sec. 7. (SB 506) Effective January 1, 2026.)

34501.6. The governing board of a local educational agency that provides for the transportation of pupils shall adopt procedures that limit the operation of schoolbuses when atmospheric conditions reduce visibility on the roadway to 200 feet or less during regular home-to-school transportation service. Operational policies for school activity trips shall give schoolbus drivers discretionary authority to discontinue schoolbus operation if the driver determines that it is unsafe to continue operation because of reduced visibility.

(Added by Stats. 1992, Ch. 624, Sec. 9. Effective September 14, 1992.)

34501.7. (a) Any rules or regulations adopted pursuant to Section 34501 for the construction, testing, or certification of wheelchair lifts for installation and use on buses shall take into consideration the costs of implementing the regulations and shall be reviewed and brought up to date by the department annually.

(b) This section shall become operative on July 1, 1987.

(Added by Stats. 1986, Ch. 969, Sec. 4. Section operative July 1, 1987, by its own provisions.)

34501.8. (a) The Department of the California Highway Patrol shall inspect every general public paratransit vehicle, as defined in Section 336, at least once each year to certify that its condition complies with all provisions of law, including being equipped with a fire extinguisher, first-aid kit, and three-point tie downs for transporting wheelchair passengers.

(b) On or after July 1, 1989, no person shall drive any general public paratransit vehicle unless there is displayed therein a certificate issued by the Department of the California Highway Patrol stating that on a certain date, which shall be within 13 months of the date of operation, an authorized employee of the Department of the California Highway Patrol inspected the general public paratransit vehicle and found that on the date of inspection the general public paratransit vehicle complied with the applicable provisions of state law. The Commissioner of the California Highway Patrol shall provide, by rule or regulation, for the issuance and display of distinctive inspection certificates.

(c) The Commissioner of the California Highway Patrol shall determine a fee and method of collection for the annual inspection of general public paratransit vehicles. The fee, established by regulation, shall be sufficient to cover the cost to the department for general public paratransit vehicle inspections. All fees received shall be deposited in the Motor Vehicle Account in the State Transportation Fund.

This section shall become operative January 1, 1989.

(Amended by Stats. 1988, Ch. 683, Sec. 5. Effective August 29, 1988. Section is inoperative from August 29, 1988, until January 1, 1989, by its own provisions from this amendment.)

34501.9. (a) Nothing in this division or the regulations adopted under this division is intended to, or shall, affect the rate of payment of wages, including, but not limited to, regular, premium, or overtime rates, paid to any person whether for on-duty hours or driving hours or otherwise.

(b) Nothing in this division or the regulations adopted under this division is intended to, or shall, affect the regulations adopted pursuant to other provisions of law concerning the rate or rates of payment of wages by any other public agency, including, but not limited to, the Industrial Welfare Commission or the Division of Labor Standards Enforcement of the Department of Industrial Relations.

(Amended by Stats. 1987, Ch. 747, Sec. 2.5.)

34501.10. The employer of any person required to keep log books, records of physical examination, and other driver records as may be required by the Department of the California Highway Patrol, the Department of Motor Vehicles, or the State Department of Health Services, shall register with the Department of the California Highway Patrol the address where the log books and other records are available for inspection.

(Added by Stats. 1988, Ch. 1452, Sec. 3. Effective September 28, 1988. Note: See this section as modified on July 17, 1991, in Governor's Reorganization Plan No. 1 of 1991.)

34501.12. (a) Vehicles and the operation thereof, subject to this section, are those described in subdivision (a), (b), (e), (f), (g), or (k) of Section 34500, except an agricultural vehicle as defined in Section 34500.6.

(b) It is unlawful for a motor carrier to operate any vehicle of a type described in subdivision (a) without identifying to the department all terminals, as defined in Section 34515, in this state where vehicles may be inspected by the department pursuant to paragraph (4) of subdivision (a) of Section 34501 and where vehicle inspection and maintenance records and driver records will be made available for inspection. Motor carriers shall make vehicles and records available for inspection upon request by an authorized representative of the department. If a motor carrier fails to provide vehicles and records, an unsatisfactory terminal rating shall be issued by the department.

(1) The number of vehicles that will be selected for inspection by the department at a terminal shall be based on terminal fleet size and applied separately to a terminal fleet of power units and trailers, according to the following schedule:

Fleet Size	Representative Sample
1 or 2	All
3 to 8	3
9 to 15	4
16 to 25	6
26 to 50	9
51 to 90	14
91 or more	20

(2) The lessor of any vehicle described in subdivision (a) shall make vehicles available for inspection upon request of an authorized representative of the department in the course of inspecting the terminal of the lessee. This section does not affect whether the lessor or driver provided by the lessor is an employee of the authorized carrier lessee, and

compliance with this section and its attendant administrative requirements does not imply an employee-employer relationship.

(c) (1) The department may inspect any terminal, as defined in Section 34515, of a motor carrier who, at any time, operates any vehicle described in subdivision (a).

(2) The department shall establish a performance-based truck terminal inspection selection priority system. In adopting the system's rules, the department shall incorporate methodologies consistent with those used by the Federal Motor Carrier Safety Administration, including those related to the quantitative analysis of safety-related motor carrier performance data, collected during the course of inspection or enforcement contact by authorized representatives of the department or any authorized federal, state, or local safety official, in categories, including, but not limited to, driver fatigue, driver fitness, vehicle maintenance, and controlled substances and alcohol use. The department shall also incorporate other safety-related motor carrier performance data in this system, including citations and accident information. The department shall create a database to include all performance-based data specified in this section that shall be updated in a manner to provide real-time information to the department on motor carrier performance. The department shall prioritize for selection those motor carrier terminals never previously inspected by the department, those identified by the inspection priority selection system, and those terminals operating vehicles listed in subdivision (g) of Section 34500. The department is not required to inspect a terminal pursuant to this section after a terminal receives a satisfactory compliance rating as the result of a terminal inspection conducted by the department pursuant to this section or Section 34501, or if the department has not received notification by the system of a motor carrier operating while exceeding the threshold of the inspection selection priority system. Any motor carrier that is inspected and receives less than a satisfactory compliance rating, or that falls below the threshold of the selection priority system, shall be subject to periodic inquiries and inspections as outlined in subdivision (f), and these inquiries and inspections shall be based on the severity of the violations.

(3) As used in this section and Section 34505.6, subdivision (f) of Section 34500 includes only those combinations in which the gross vehicle weight rating of the towing vehicle exceeds 10,000 pounds, but does not include a pickup truck or any combination never operated in commercial use, and subdivision (g) of Section 34500 includes only those vehicles transporting hazardous material for which the display of placards is required pursuant to Section 27903, a license is required pursuant to Section 32000.5, or for which hazardous waste transporter registration is required pursuant to Section 25163 of the Health and Safety Code. Notwithstanding Section 5014.1, vehicles that display special identification plates in accordance with Section 5011, historical vehicles, as described in Section 5004, implements of husbandry and farm vehicles, as defined in Chapter 1 (commencing with Section 36000) of Division 16, and vehicles owned or operated by an agency of the federal government are not subject to this section or Section 34505.6.

(d) It is unlawful for a motor carrier to operate, or cause to be operated, any vehicle that is subject to this section, Section 34520, or Division 14.85 (commencing with Section 34600), unless the motor carrier is knowledgeable of, and in compliance with, all applicable statutes and regulations.

(e) It is unlawful for a motor carrier to contract or subcontract with, or otherwise engage the services of, another motor carrier, subject to this section, unless the contracted motor carrier has complied with subdivision (d). A motor carrier shall not contract or subcontract with, or otherwise engage the services of, another motor carrier until the contracted motor carrier provides certification of compliance with subdivision (d). This certification shall be completed in writing by the contracted motor carrier in a manner prescribed by the department. The certification, or a copy of the certification, shall be maintained by each involved party for the duration of the contract or the period of service plus two years, and shall be presented for inspection immediately upon the request of an authorized employee of the department. The certifications required by this subdivision and subdivision (b) of Section 34620 may be combined.

(f) (1) An inspected terminal that receives an unsatisfactory compliance rating shall be reinspected by the department within 120 days after the issuance of the unsatisfactory compliance rating.

(2) If a motor carrier's Motor Carrier of Property Permit or Public Utilities Commission operating authority is suspended as a result of an unsatisfactory compliance rating, the department shall not conduct a reinspection for permit or authority reinstatement until requested to do so by the Department of Motor Vehicles or the Public Utilities Commission, as appropriate.

(g) A motor carrier issued an unsatisfactory terminal rating may request a review of the rating within five business days of receipt of the notification of the rating. The department shall conduct and evaluate the review within 10 business days of the request.

(h) The department shall publish performance-based inspection completion data and make the data available for public review.

(i) This section shall be known, and may be cited, as the Basic Inspection of Terminals program or BIT program.

(j) This section shall remain in effect only until January 1, 2031, and as of that date is repealed, unless a later enacted statute, that is enacted before January 1, 2031, deletes or extends that date.

(Amended (as amended by Stats. 2024, Ch. 226, Sec. 14) by Stats. 2025, Ch. 61, Sec. 2. (AB 525) Effective January 1, 2026. Repealed as of January 1, 2031, by its own provisions. See later operative version, as amended by Sec. 3 of Stats. 2025, Ch. 61.)

34501.12. (a) Vehicles and the operation thereof, subject to this section, are those described in subdivision (a), (b), (e), (f), (g), or (k) of Section 34500.

(b) It is unlawful for a motor carrier to operate any vehicle of a type described in subdivision (a) without identifying to the department all terminals, as defined in Section 34515, in this state where vehicles may be inspected by the department pursuant to paragraph (4) of subdivision (a) of Section 34501 and where vehicle inspection and maintenance records and driver records will be made available for inspection. Motor carriers shall make vehicles and records available for inspection upon request by an authorized representative of the department. If a motor carrier fails to provide vehicles and records, an unsatisfactory terminal rating shall be issued by the department.

(1) The number of vehicles that will be selected for inspection by the department at a terminal shall be based on terminal fleet size and applied separately to a terminal fleet of power units and trailers, according to the following schedule:

Fleet Size	Representative Sample
1 or 2	All
3 to 8	3
9 to 15	4
16 to 25	6
26 to 50	9
51 to 90	14
91 or more	20

(2) The lessor of any vehicle described in subdivision (a) shall make vehicles available for inspection upon request of an authorized representative of the department in the course of inspecting the terminal of the lessee. This section does not affect whether the lessor or driver provided by the lessor is an employee of the authorized carrier lessee, and compliance with this section and its attendant administrative requirements does not imply an employee-employer relationship.

(c) (1) The department may inspect any terminal, as defined in Section 34515, of a motor carrier who, at any time, operates any vehicle described in subdivision (a).

(2) The department shall establish a performance-based truck terminal inspection selection priority system. In adopting the system's rules, the department shall incorporate methodologies consistent with those used by

the Federal Motor Carrier Safety Administration, including those related to the quantitative analysis of safety-related motor carrier performance data, collected during the course of inspection or enforcement contact by authorized representatives of the department or any authorized federal, state, or local safety official, in categories, including, but not limited to, driver fatigue, driver fitness, vehicle maintenance, and controlled substances and alcohol use. The department shall also incorporate other safety-related motor carrier performance data in this system, including citations and accident information. The department shall create a database to include all performance-based data specified in this section that shall be updated in a manner to provide real-time information to the department on motor carrier performance. The department shall prioritize for selection those motor carrier terminals never previously inspected by the department, those identified by the inspection priority selection system, and those terminals operating vehicles listed in subdivision (g) of Section 34500. The department is not required to inspect a terminal pursuant to this section after a terminal receives a satisfactory compliance rating as the result of a terminal inspection conducted by the department pursuant to this section or Section 34501, or if the department has not received notification by the system of a motor carrier operating while exceeding the threshold of the inspection selection priority system. Any motor carrier that is inspected and receives less than a satisfactory compliance rating, or that falls below the threshold of the selection priority system, shall be subject to periodic inquiries and inspections as outlined in subdivision (f), and these inquiries and inspections shall be based on the severity of the violations.

(3) As used in this section and Section 34505.6, subdivision (f) of Section 34500 includes only those combinations in which the gross vehicle weight rating of the towing vehicle exceeds 10,000 pounds, but does not include a pickup truck or any combination never operated in commercial use, and subdivision (g) of Section 34500 includes only those vehicles transporting hazardous material for which the display of placards is required pursuant to Section 27903, a license is required pursuant to Section 32000.5, or for which hazardous waste transporter registration is required pursuant to Section 25163 of the Health and Safety Code. Notwithstanding Section 5014.1, vehicles that display special identification plates in accordance with Section 5011, historical vehicles, as described in Section 5004, implements of husbandry and farm vehicles, as defined in Chapter 1 (commencing with Section 36000) of Division 16 and vehicles owned or operated by an agency of the federal government are not subject to this section or Section 34505.6.

(d) It is unlawful for a motor carrier to operate, or cause to be operated, any vehicle that is subject to this section, Section 34520, or Division 14.85 (commencing with Section 34600), unless the motor carrier is knowledgeable of, and in compliance with, all applicable statutes and regulations.

(e) It is unlawful for a motor carrier to contract or subcontract with, or otherwise engage the services of, another motor carrier, subject to this section, unless the contracted motor carrier has complied with subdivision (d). A motor carrier shall not contract or subcontract with, or otherwise engage the services of, another motor carrier until the contracted motor carrier provides certification of compliance with subdivision (d). This certification shall be completed in writing by the contracted motor carrier in a manner prescribed by the department. The certification, or a copy of the certification, shall be maintained by each involved party for the duration of the contract or the period of service plus two years, and shall be presented for inspection immediately upon the request of an authorized employee of the department. The certifications required by this subdivision and subdivision (b) of Section 34620 may be combined.

(f) (1) An inspected terminal that receives an unsatisfactory compliance rating shall be reinspected by the department within 120 days after the issuance of the unsatisfactory compliance rating.

(2) If a motor carrier's Motor Carrier of Property Permit or Public Utilities Commission operating authority is suspended as a result of an unsatisfactory compliance rating, the department shall not conduct a reinspection for permit or authority reinstatement until requested to do so by the Department of Motor Vehicles or the Public Utilities Commission, as appropriate.

(g) A motor carrier issued an unsatisfactory terminal rating may request a review of the rating within five business days of receipt of the notification of the rating. The department shall conduct and evaluate the review within 10 business days of the request.

(h) The department shall publish performance-based inspection completion data and make the data available for public review.

(i) This section shall be known, and may be cited, as the Basic Inspection of Terminals program or BIT program.

(j) This section shall become operative on January 1, 2031.

(Amended (as amended by Stats. 2024, Ch. 226, Sec. 15) by Stats. 2025, Ch. 61, Sec. 3. (AB 525) Effective January 1, 2026. Operative January 1, 2031, by its own provisions.)

34501.13. If the inspection of a carrier facility, maintenance facility, or terminal of any person who operates a schoolbus results in an unsatisfactory terminal rating by the department, the department shall notify the school board of the district that is responsible for the terminal.

(Amended by Stats. 1999, Ch. 1007, Sec. 24.5. Effective January 1, 2000.)

34501.14. (a) Notwithstanding Section 34501.12, for purposes of this division, safety inspections of grape gondolas are governed by this section.

(b) Every registered owner of a grape gondola shall submit an application and the fee specified in subdivision (g) to the department for the initial inspection required by this section. The initial application shall be submitted on or before July 1, 1993. The inspection term for a grape gondola shall expire 25 months from the date the department conducts the inspection, and issues a certificate indicating the gondola has passed the inspection, and every 25 months thereafter. Applications and fees for subsequent inspections and certificates shall be submitted not later than seven months before the expiration of the then current inspection term. If the registered owner has submitted the inspection application and the required accompanying fees, but the department is unable to complete the inspection within the 25-month inspection period, then no additional fee shall be required for the inspection requested in the original application.

(c) On and after July 1, 1993, no person may operate any grape gondola without having submitted an inspection application and the required fees to the department as required by this section.

(d) On and after January 1, 1995, no person may operate any grape gondola, without the inspection described in subdivision (e) having been performed and a certificate having been issued to the owner.

(e) The safety inspection undertaken pursuant to this section shall be limited to an inspection of the brake system, steering, lights, connections, wheels and tires, frame, and suspension.

(f) For purposes of undertaking the inspection of grape gondolas under this section, the department shall schedule all inspections at one central location during a continuous eight-week period every odd-numbered year with at least two days of each week during that eight-week period devoted to the actual inspection. If the gondola does not pass its first inspection, it may be reinspected during the eight-week period at no additional cost.

(g) Fees shall be established by the department in an amount equal to the actual costs incurred by the department in carrying out this section, but not to exceed twenty-five dollars ($25) for each inspection or reinspection.

(h) As used in this section, "grape gondola" means a motor vehicle which has been permanently altered and is attached to a grape tank by two means. The first mean is by use of a kingpin on the trunk which is centered through a turntable assembly on the tank. The second means of attachment is through the use of a pair of horizontal crossarms between the drive axle and the rear tank axle. The tank is designed to pivot off of the chassis on two support arms during dumping, and is further designed to be specifically compatible with dumping facilities of the wineries.

(i) This section only applies to a grape gondola that is used under all of the following conditions:

(1) For 60 days or less during any calendar year.

(2) For not more than 500 miles in any calendar year.

(3) Only for the transportation of grapes.

(Added by Stats. 1992, Ch. 724, Sec. 1. Effective January 1, 1993.)

34501.15. (a) The regulations adopted pursuant to Section 34501 shall require that any driver of a commercial motor vehicle, as defined in Section 15210, be ordered out of service for 24 hours if the driver is found to have 0.01 percent or more, by weight, of alcohol in his or her blood.

(b) This section shall become operative on January 1, 1992, and shall remain operative until the director determines that federal regulations adopted pursuant to the Commercial Motor Vehicle Safety Act of 1986 (49 U.S.C. Sec. 2701 et seq.) contained in that act and Section 391.15 of Title 49 of the Code of Federal Regulations do not require the state to order the operator of a commercial vehicle out of service for 24 hours when the operator has a measurable concentration of alcohol in his or her blood.

(c) The director shall submit a notice of the determination under subdivision (b) to the Secretary of State, and this section shall be repealed upon the receipt of that notice.

(Added by Stats. 1989, Ch. 1114, Sec. 40. Section operative January 1, 1992, by its own provisions. Inoperative upon determination described in subd. (b). Repealed upon notification prescribed in subd. (c).)

34501.16. (a) Every employer of a commercial driver shall provide information to that employee at the time of hiring and to all employed commercial drivers annually, concerning all of the following:

(1) The prohibition against driving a commercial motor vehicle with over 0.04 percent or more, by weight, alcohol in his or her blood on and after January 1, 1992.

(2) The requirement to be placed out of service for 24 hours if the person's blood-alcohol concentration is tested to be 0.01 percent or more, by weight, on and after January 1, 1992.

(b) The Department of Motor Vehicles shall include the information prescribed in subdivision (a), together with information concerning the alcohol concentration in a person's blood resulting from consumption of alcoholic beverages, in each publication of the commercial driver's handbook published after January 1, 1990.

(c) This section shall remain operative until the director determines that federal regulations adopted pursuant to the Commercial Motor Vehicle Safety Act of 1986 (49 U.S.C. Sec. 2701 et seq.) do not require the state to implement the prohibitions and requirements in paragraphs (1) and (2) of subdivision (a).

(d) The director shall submit a notice of the determination under subdivision (c) to the Secretary of State, and this section shall be repealed upon the receipt of that notice.

(Added by Stats. 1989, Ch. 1114, Sec. 41. Inoperative upon determination described in subd. (c). Repealed upon notification prescribed in subd. (d).)

34501.17. (a) All paratransit vehicles shall be regularly and systematically inspected, maintained, and lubricated by the owner or operator in accordance with the manufacturer's recommendations, or more often if necessary to ensure the safe operating condition of the vehicle. The maintenance shall include, at a minimum, in-depth inspection of the vehicle's brake system, steering components, lighting system, and wheels and tires, to be performed at intervals in accordance with the manufacturer's recommendations.

(b) All owners or operators of paratransit vehicles shall document each systematic inspection, maintenance, and lubrication and repair performed for each vehicle subject to this section. Required records shall include service performed, the name of the person performing the service, the date that the service was performed, and the odometer reading of the vehicle at the time of the service. The records shall be maintained for the period that the vehicle is in service at the place of business in this state of the owner or operator of the vehicle, and shall be presented upon demand to any authorized representative of the department. The odometer of a paratransit vehicle shall be maintained in proper working order.

(Added by Stats. 1998, Ch. 241, Sec. 3. Effective January 1, 1999.)

34501.18. (a) Every motor carrier regularly employing more than 20 full-time drivers shall report to the department whenever it replaces more than half of its drivers within a 30-day period. Within 21 days of receipt of that report, the department shall inspect the motor carrier to ensure that the motor carrier is complying with all safety of operations requirements, including, but not limited to, controlled substances testing and hours-of-service regulations. The reporting requirement of this subdivision does not apply to a motor carrier who, through normal seasonal fluctuations in the business operations of the carrier, or through termination of a contract for transportation services, other than a collective bargaining agreement, replaces drivers in one geographical location with drivers in another geographical location.

(b) For the purposes of subdivision (a), "employing" means having an employer-employee relationship with a driver or contracting with an owner-operator, as described in Section 34624, to provide transportation services for more than 30 days within the previous year.

(c) For the purposes of subdivision (a), "full-time" means that the driver is on-duty with the motor carrier for an average of 30 hours or more per week during the course of his or her employment or contract with the motor carrier.

(Added by Stats. 2001, Ch. 789, Sec. 1. Effective January 1, 2002.)

34501.19. A vehicle described in Section 34500 shall comply with the equipment requirements specified in Part 393 of Title 49 of the Code of Federal Regulations, relating to automatic brake adjusters and brake adjustment indicators, antilock brake systems, frames, cab and body components, wheels, suspension systems, and steering wheel systems. In the application of this section to a vehicle, "commercial motor vehicle" and "motor vehicle" have the same meanings as those terms are defined in Section 390.5 of Title 49 of the Code of Federal Regulations.

(Added by Stats. 2022, Ch. 295, Sec. 21. (AB 2956) Effective January 1, 2023.)

34502. In adopting rules and regulations, the Department of the California Highway Patrol shall consider as evidence of generally accepted safety standards the rules and regulations which have been adopted by the Public Utilities Commission.

(Added by Stats. 1963, Ch. 2148.)

34503. It is the legislative intention in enacting this division that the rules and regulations adopted by the Department of the California Highway Patrol pursuant to this division shall apply uniformly throughout the State of California, and no state agency, city, city and county, county, or other political subdivision of this State, including, but not limited to, a chartered city, city and county, or county, shall adopt or enforce any ordinance or regulation which is inconsistent with the rules and regulations adopted by the department pursuant to this division.

(Added by Stats. 1963, Ch. 2148.)

34504. The Department of the California Highway Patrol shall enforce the rules and regulations adopted pursuant to Section 34501. Rules and regulations adopted pursuant to Section 34501 shall become effective on March 1, 1965.

(Added by Stats. 1963, Ch. 2148.)

34505. (a) Tour bus operators shall, in addition to the systematic inspection, maintenance, and lubrication services required of all motor carriers, require each tour bus to be inspected at least every 45 days, or more often if necessary to ensure safe operation. This inspection shall include, but not be limited to, all of the following:

(1) Brake adjustment.

(2) Brake system components and leaks.

(3) Steering and suspension systems.

(4) Tires and wheels.

(b) A tour bus shall not be used to transport passengers until all defects listed during the inspection conducted pursuant to subdivision (a) have been corrected and attested to by the signature of the operator's authorized representative.

(c) Records of inspections conducted pursuant to subdivision (a) shall be kept at the operator's maintenance facility or terminal where the tour bus is regularly garaged. The records shall be retained by the operator for one year, and shall be made available for inspection upon request by any authorized employee of the department. Each record shall include, but not be limited to, all of the following:

(1) Identification of the vehicle, including make, model, license number, or other means of positive identification.

(2) Date and nature of each inspection and any repair performed.

(3) Signature of operator's authorized representative attesting to the inspection and to the completion of all required repairs.

(4) Company vehicle number.

(Added by Stats. 1986, Ch. 1306, Sec. 16.)

34505.1. (a) Upon determining that a tour bus carrier or modified limousine carrier has either failed to comply with the requirements specified in paragraph (1) or (2), or has been issued an out-of-service order for either an imminent hazard or an unsatisfactory or unfit rating by the United States Secretary of Transportation, the department shall recommend to the Public Utilities Commission that the carrier's operating authority be suspended, denied, or revoked, or to the United States Department of Transportation that appropriate administrative action be taken against the carrier's interstate operating authority, whichever is appropriate:

(1) The tour bus carrier or modified limousine carrier has failed to maintain any vehicle of the carrier in a safe operating condition or to comply with the Vehicle Code or with regulations contained in Title 13 of the California Code of Regulations relative to motor carrier safety, and, in the department's opinion, the failure presents an imminent danger to public safety or constitutes such a consistent failure as to justify a recommendation to the Public Utilities Commission or the United States Department of Transportation.

(2) The tour bus carrier or modified limousine carrier has failed to enroll all drivers in the pull-notice system as required by Section 1808.1.

(b) For purposes of this section, two consecutive unsatisfactory compliance ratings for an inspected terminal assigned because the tour bus carrier or modified limousine carrier failed to comply with the periodic report requirements of Section 1808.1 or the cancellation of the carrier's enrollment by the Department of Motor Vehicles for nonpayment of required fees may be determined by the department to be a consistent failure. However, when recommending denial of an application for new or renewal authority, the department need not conclude that the carrier's failure presents an imminent danger to public safety or that it constitutes a consistent failure. The department need only conclude that the carrier's compliance with the safety-related matters described in paragraph (1) of subdivision (a) is sufficiently unsatisfactory to justify a recommendation for denial. The department shall retain a record, by carrier, of every recommendation made pursuant to this section.

(c) Before transmitting a recommendation pursuant to subdivision (a), the department shall notify the carrier in writing of all of the following:

(1) That the department has determined that the carrier's safety record is unsatisfactory, furnishing a copy of any documentation or summary of any other evidence supporting the determination.

(2) That the determination may result in a suspension, revocation, or denial of the carrier's operating authority by the Public Utilities Commission or the United States Department of Transportation, as appropriate.

(3) That the carrier may request a review of the determination by the department within five days of its receipt of the notice required under this subdivision. If a review is requested by the carrier, the department shall conduct and evaluate that review prior to transmitting a notification pursuant to subdivision (a).

(d) Notwithstanding subdivision (a) or (c), upon determining during a terminal inspection or at any other time that the condition of a tour bus shows multiple safety violations of a nature that operation of the tour bus could constitute an imminent danger to public safety, the department shall immediately order the tour bus out of service. The tour bus shall not be subsequently operated with passengers until all of the safety violations have been corrected and the department has verified the correction of the safety violations upon a subsequent inspection by the department of the tour bus, which shall occur within five business days of the submission of a reinspection request from the tour bus carrier to the department.

(Amended by Stats. 2021, Ch. 311, Sec. 10. (SB 814) Effective January 1, 2022.)

34505.2. (a) In furtherance of the requirements specified in subdivision (c) of Section 34501, upon the request of, and in consultation with, representatives of a local government in a jurisdiction where tour buses operate, the Department of the California Highway Patrol shall develop protocols for entering into memoranda of understanding with local governments to allow the department to increase the number of the locally operating tour buses that are being inspected by the department.

(b) A memorandum of understanding entered into with a local government pursuant to subdivision (a) shall include a provision that the local government will reimburse the department for all actual costs associated with conducting additional inspections.

(c) Any inspection conducted pursuant to subdivision (a) shall not be duplicative of an inspection conducted by the department to meet the requirements specified in subdivision (c) of Section 34501.

(Added by Stats. 2016, Ch. 685, Sec. 1. (AB 1677) Effective January 1, 2017.)

34505.5. (a) Motor carriers operating any vehicle described in subdivision (a), (b), (e), (f), (g), or (k) of Section 34500, except those vehicles exempted under Section 34501.12, shall, as a part of the systematic inspection, maintenance, and lubrication services required of all motor carriers, require the vehicle or vehicles for which it is responsible pursuant to Section 34501.12 to be inspected at least every 90 days, or more often if necessary to ensure safe operation. Vehicles that are out of service for periods greater than 90 calendar days are not required to be inspected at 90-day intervals if they are inspected before operation on the highway. This inspection shall include, but not be limited to, all of the following:

(1) Brake adjustment.

(2) Brake system components and leaks.

(3) Steering and suspension systems.

(4) Tires and wheels.

(5) Vehicle connecting devices.

(b) No vehicle subject to this section shall be operated on the highway other than to a place of repair until all defects listed during the inspection conducted pursuant to subdivision (a) have been corrected and attested to by the signature of the motor carrier's authorized representative.

(c) Records of inspections conducted pursuant to subdivision (a) shall be kept at the motor carrier's terminals, as designated in accordance with Section 34501.12. The records shall be retained by the motor carrier for two years, and shall be made available for inspection upon request by any authorized employee of the department. Each record shall include, but not be limited to, all of the following:

(1) Identification of the vehicle, including make, model, license number, company vehicle number, or other means of positive identification.

(2) Date and nature of each inspection and any repair performed.

(3) Signature of the motor carrier's authorized representative attesting to the inspection and to the completion of all required repairs.

(d) Printouts of inspection and maintenance records maintained in computer systems shall be accepted in lieu of signed inspection or repair records if the printouts include the information required in paragraphs (1) and (2) of subdivision (c).

(e) Notwithstanding subdivisions (a) to (d), inclusive, records of 90-day inspections need not be retained in California for interstate vehicles that are not physically based in California. However, when these vehicles are

present in California, they are subject to inspection by the department. If the inspection results indicate maintenance program deficiencies, the department may require the motor carrier to produce the maintenance records or copies of those records for inspection within 10 working days.
(Amended by Stats. 2024, Ch. 226, Sec. 16. (AB 3278) Effective January 1, 2025.)

34505.6. (a) Upon determining that a motor carrier of property, as defined in Section 34601, either is subject to paragraph (1) or (2), or has been issued an out-of-service order for either an imminent hazard or an unsatisfactory or unfit rating by the United States Secretary of Transportation, the department shall recommend that the Department of Motor Vehicles suspend or revoke the carrier's motor carrier permit, or, for interstate operators, the department shall recommend to the Federal Motor Carrier Safety Administration that appropriate administrative action be taken against the carrier.

(1) The motor carrier of property has failed to maintain any vehicle of a type described above in a safe operating condition or to comply with the Vehicle Code or with regulations contained in Title 13 of the California Code of Regulations relative to motor carrier safety, and, in the department's opinion, that failure presents an imminent danger to public safety or constitutes a consistent failure so as to justify a recommendation to the Department of Motor Vehicles.

(2) The motor carrier of property has failed to enroll all drivers in the pull-notice system as required by Section 1808.1.

(b) Upon determining that a household mover, or a household mover transporting used office, store, or institution furniture and fixtures under its household mover permit issued under Section 19241 of the Business and Professions Code, either is subject to paragraph (1) or (2), or has been issued an out-of-service order for either an imminent hazard or an unsatisfactory or unfit rating by the United States Secretary of Transportation, the department shall recommend that the Department of Consumer Affairs deny, suspend, or revoke the carrier's household mover permit, or, for interstate operators, the department shall recommend to the Federal Motor Carrier Safety Administration that appropriate administrative action be taken against the household mover.

(1) The motor carrier of property has failed to maintain any vehicle of the carrier in a safe operating condition or to comply with the Vehicle Code or with regulations contained in Title 13 of the California Code of Regulations relative to motor carrier safety, and, in the department's opinion, that failure presents an imminent danger to public safety or constitutes a consistent failure so as to justify a recommendation to the Department of Consumer Affairs.

(2) The motor carrier of property has failed to enroll all drivers in the pull-notice system as required by Section 1808.1.

(c) For purposes of this section, two consecutive unsatisfactory compliance ratings for an inspected terminal assigned because the motor carrier failed to comply with the periodic report requirements of Section 1808.1 or the cancellation of the carrier's enrollment by the Department of Motor Vehicles for the nonpayment of required fees is a consistent failure. The department shall retain a record, by operator, of every recommendation made pursuant to this section.

(d) Before transmitting a recommendation pursuant to subdivision (a), the department shall notify the carrier in writing of all of the following:

(1) That the department has determined that the carrier's safety record or compliance with Section 1808.1 is unsatisfactory, furnishing a copy of any documentation or summary of any other evidence supporting the determination.

(2) That the determination may result in a suspension, revocation, or denial of the carrier's motor carrier permit by the Department of Motor Vehicles, suspension, revocation, or denial of the carrier's household mover permit suspended, revoked, or denied, by the Department of Consumer Affairs, or administrative action by the Federal Motor Carrier Safety Administration.

(3) That the carrier may request a review of the determination by the department within five days of its receipt of the notice required under this subdivision. If a review pursuant to this paragraph is requested by the carrier, the department shall conduct and evaluate that review prior to transmitting any notification pursuant to subdivision (a) or (b).

(e) Upon receipt of a written recommendation from the department that a motor carrier permit or household mover permit be suspended, revoked, or denied, the Department of Motor Vehicles or Department of Consumer Affairs, as appropriate, shall, pending a hearing in the matter pursuant to Section 34623 or appropriate Department of Consumer Affairs authority, suspend the motor carrier permit or household mover permit. The written recommendation shall specifically indicate compliance with subdivision (d).
(Amended by Stats. 2022, Ch. 295, Sec. 22. (AB 2956) Effective January 1, 2023.)

34505.7. (a) Upon determining that a private carrier of passengers, as defined in Section 34681 of the Vehicle Code, has either failed to comply with the requirements specified in paragraph (1) or (2), or has been issued an out-of-service order for either an imminent hazard or an unsatisfactory rating by the United States Secretary of Transportation, the department shall make a written recommendation to the Department of Motor Vehicles that the carrier's registration be suspended:

(1) The private carrier of passengers has failed to maintain any vehicle of the carrier in a safe operating condition or to comply with the Vehicle Code or with regulations contained in Title 13 of the California Code of Regulations relative to motor carrier safety, and, in the department's opinion, the failure presents an imminent danger to public safety or constitutes such a consistent failure as to justify a recommendation to the Department of Motor Vehicles.

(2) The private carrier of passengers has failed to enroll all drivers in the pull-notice system as required by Section 1808.1.

(b) For purposes of this section, two consecutive unsatisfactory terminal ratings assigned for failure to comply with the periodic report requirements in Section 1808.1, or cancellation of an employer's enrollment by the Department of Motor Vehicles for nonpayment of fees, constitutes a consistent failure. The department shall retain a record, by operator, of every recommendation made pursuant to this section.

(c) Before transmitting a recommendation pursuant to subdivision (a), the department shall give written notice to the carrier of all of the following:

(1) That the department has determined that the carrier's safety record is unsatisfactory, furnishing a copy of any documentation or summary of any other evidence supporting the determination.

(2) That the determination may result in a suspension or revocation of the carrier's registration by the Department of Motor Vehicles.

(3) That the carrier may request a review of the determination by the department within five days of its receipt of the notice required by this subdivision. If a review pursuant to this paragraph is requested by the carrier, the department shall conduct and evaluate that review prior to transmitting a notification pursuant to subdivision (a).

(d) Commercial vehicle inspection facilities along the border of Mexico, including those in Calexico and Otay Mesa, shall be staffed at all times by a Department of the California Highway Patrol inspector whenever those facilities are open to the public. The Department of the California Highway Patrol shall also assign, as staffing permits, a commercial inspector to control truck traffic entering the United States at the Tecate border crossing.
(Amended by Stats. 2021, Ch. 311, Sec. 11. (SB 814) Effective January 1, 2022.)

34505.8. (a) A charter-party carrier of passengers engaged in charter bus transportation shall ensure that the driver of a vehicle as described in paragraph (1) of subdivision (b) of Section 5363 of the Public Utilities Code that is designed to carry 39 or more passengers shall instruct or play a video for all passengers on the safety equipment and emergency exits on the vehicle prior to the beginning of any trip and provide each passenger with written or video instructions that include, at a minimum, a demonstration of the location and operation of all exits, including emergency exits, the requirement to wear a seatbelt, if available, and that not wearing a seatbelt is punishable by a fine.

(b) Notwithstanding any other law, no later than July 1, 2018, the department shall adopt standards and criteria for the implementation of the safety requirements specified in this section.

(c) This section does not alter or affect the requirements of the Passenger Charter-party Carriers' Act (Chapter 8 (commencing with Section 5351) of Division 2 of the Public Utilities Code).

(d) The amendments to this section as added by the act that added this subdivision shall be operative on July 1, 2018.

(Amended by Stats. 2017, Ch. 593, Sec. 4. (SB 20) Effective January 1, 2018. Amended version operative July 1, 2018, pursuant to earlier operation of new subdivision (d).)

34505.9. (a) An ocean marine terminal that receives and dispatches intermodal chassis may conduct the intermodal roadability inspection program, as described in this section, in lieu of the inspection required by Section 34505.5, if the terminal meets all of the following conditions:

(1) More than 1,000 chassis are based at the ocean marine terminal.

(2) The ocean marine terminal, following the two most recent consecutive inspections required by Section 34501.12, has received satisfactory compliance ratings, and the terminal has received no unsatisfactory compliance ratings as a result of any inspection conducted in the interim between the consecutive inspections conducted under Section 34501.12.

(3) Each intermodal chassis exiting the ocean marine terminal shall have a current decal and supporting documentation in accordance with Section 396.17 of Title 49 of the Code of Federal Regulations.

(4) The ocean marine terminal's intermodal roadability inspection program shall consist of all of the following:

(A) Each time an intermodal chassis is released from the ocean marine terminal, the chassis shall be inspected. The inspection shall include, but not be limited to, brake adjustment, brake system components and leaks, suspension systems, tires and wheels, vehicle connecting devices, and lights and electrical system, and shall include a visual inspection of the chassis to determine that it has not been tampered with.

(B) Each inspection shall be recorded on a daily roadability inspection report that shall include, but not be limited to, all of the following:

(i) Positive identification of the intermodal chassis, including company identification number and vehicle license plate number.

(ii) Date and nature of each inspection.

(iii) Signature, under penalty of perjury, of the ocean marine terminal operator or an authorized representative that the inspection has been performed.

(iv) The inspector shall affix a green tag to a chassis that has passed inspection and a red tag to a chassis that has failed inspection. The tag shall contain the name of the inspector and the date and time that the inspection was completed and shall be placed in a conspicuous location so that it may be viewed from the rear of the vehicle. The tag shall be provided by the marine terminal operator and shall meet specifications determined by the Department of the California Highway Patrol. The provisions of this subparagraph shall also be applicable to an intermodal chassis inspected by a marine terminal operator pursuant to Section 34505.5.

(C) Records of each inspection conducted pursuant to subparagraph (A) shall be retained for 90 days at the ocean marine terminal at which each chassis is based and shall be made available upon request by any authorized employee of the department.

(D) Defects noted on any intermodal chassis shall be repaired, and the repairs shall be recorded on the intermodal chassis maintenance file, before the intermodal chassis is released from the control of the ocean marine terminal. No vehicle subject to this section shall be released to a motor carrier or operated on the highway other than to a place of repair until all defects listed during the inspection conducted pursuant to subparagraph (A) have been corrected and attested to by the signature of the operator's authorized representative.

(E) Records of maintenance or repairs performed pursuant to the inspection in subparagraph (A) shall be maintained at the ocean marine terminal for two years and shall be made available upon request of the department. Repair records may be retained in a computer system if printouts of those records are provided to the department upon request.

(F) Individuals performing ocean marine terminal roadability inspections pursuant to this section shall be qualified, at a minimum, as set forth in Section 396.19 of Title 49 of the Code of Federal Regulations. Evidence of each inspector's qualification shall be retained by the ocean marine terminal operator for the period during which the inspector is performing intermodal roadability inspections.

(b) The records maintained pursuant to paragraphs (C) and (E) of subdivision (a) and Section 34505.5 shall be made available during normal business hours to any motor carrier or driver or the authorized representative thereof who has been engaged to transport an intermodal container on a chassis inspected pursuant to this section or Section 34505.5 from the ocean marine terminal.

(c) Any citation issued for the violation of any state or federal law related to the defective condition of an intermodal chassis subject to inspection pursuant to this section or Section 34505.5, that is not owned by that motor carrier or commercial driver, shall be issued to the entity responsible for the inspection and maintenance of the intermodal chassis, unless the officer determines that the defective condition of the intermodal chassis was caused by the failure of the driver to operate a commercial motor vehicle in a safe manner.

(d) Any provision contained in a contract between the registered owner or lessee of an intermodal chassis subject to inspection pursuant to this section, or any other entity responsible for the inspection and maintenance of the intermodal chassis, and any motor carrier or any contract between a motor carrier and another motor carrier engaged to transport an intermodal container on a chassis subject to inspection pursuant to this section that contains a hold harmless or indemnity clause concerning defects in the physical condition of that chassis shall be void as against public policy. This subdivision shall not apply to damage to the intermodal chassis caused by the negligent or willful failure of the motor carrier to operate a commercial motor vehicle in a safe manner.

(e) Following a terminal inspection in which the department determines that an operator of an ocean marine terminal has failed to comply with the requirements of this section, the department shall conduct a reinspection within 120 days as specified in subdivision (h) of Section 34501.12. If the terminal fails the reinspection, the department shall direct the operator to comply with the requirements of Section 34505.5 until eligibility to utilize the inspection program described in this section is reestablished pursuant to subdivision (a). If any inspection results in an unsatisfactory rating due to conditions presenting an imminent danger to the public safety or due to the operator's repeated failure to inspect and repair intermodal chassis pursuant to this section, the department shall immediately forward a recommendation to the Department of Motor Vehicles to suspend the operator's motor carrier property permit, and forward a recommendation to the Federal Motor Carrier Safety Administration for administrative or other action deemed necessary against the carrier's interstate operating authority, pursuant to Section 34505.6 or 34505.7.

(f) Any driver who believes that an intermodal chassis is in an unsafe operating condition may request that the chassis be reinspected by the entity responsible for the inspection and maintenance of the chassis pursuant to this section or Section 34505.5. The request for reinspection, any corrective action taken, or the reason why corrective action was not taken shall be recorded in the intermodal chassis maintenance file.

(g) No commercial driver shall be threatened, coerced, or otherwise retaliated against by any ocean marine terminal operator for contacting a law enforcement agency with regard to the physical condition of an intermodal chassis or for requesting that the intermodal chassis be reinspected or repaired.

(h) For the purposes of this section, the following definitions shall apply:

(1) "Intermodal chassis" means a trailer designed to carry intermodal freight containers.

(2) "Ocean marine terminal" means a terminal, as defined in Section 34515, located at a port facility that engages in the loading and unloading of the cargo of oceangoing vessels.

(i) Nothing in this section shall relieve a commercial driver or commercial motor carrier of any duty imposed by state or federal law related to the safe operation of a commercial motor vehicle.

(j) Nothing in this section shall affect the rights, duties, and obligations set forth in Section 2802 of the Labor Code.

(Amended by Stats. 2002, Ch. 897, Sec. 1. Effective January 1, 2003.)

34505.10. Motor carriers who contract or subcontract transportation service for other motor carriers shall retain all required records relating to the dispatch of vehicles and drivers and the pay of drivers that are not required to be retained by the carrier for whom the contracted or subcontracted service is performed.

(Added by Stats. 1997, Ch. 652, Sec. 12. Effective January 1, 1998.)

34506. It is a misdemeanor to fail to comply with any rule or regulation adopted by the Department of the California Highway Patrol pursuant to Section 34501, 34501.5, 34508, or 34513 regarding any of the following:

(a) Hours of service of drivers.

(b) Hazardous material transportation.

(c) Schoolbus construction, design, color, equipment, maintenance, or operation.

(d) Youth bus equipment, maintenance, or operation.

(e) Tour bus equipment, maintenance, or operation.

(f) Equipment, maintenance, or operation of any vehicle described in subdivision (a), (b), (c), (d), (e), (f), or (g) of Section 34500.

(g) Equipment, maintenance, or operation of any school pupil activity bus.

(Amended by Stats. 1991, Ch. 928, Sec. 36. Effective October 14, 1991.)

34506.3. Except as otherwise provided in this division, it is an infraction to fail to comply with any rule or regulation adopted by the department pursuant to this division.

(Amended by Stats. 1991, Ch. 298, Sec. 2.)

34506.4. (a) Any member of the Department of the California Highway Patrol may remove from the highway and have placed in a storage facility, any vehicle described in subdivision (a) of Section 22406, subdivision (g) of Section 34500, and any motortruck with a gross vehicle weight rating of more than 10,000 pounds, which is in an unsafe condition.

(b) Any member of the Department of the California Highway Patrol may impound any farm labor vehicle operated in violation of subdivision (b) of Section 2800, subdivision (a) of Section 24002.5, or subdivision (a) of Section 31402, subject to the following requirements:

(1) A farm labor vehicle impounded for a first violation of subdivision (b) of Section 2800, subdivision (a) of Section 24002.5, or subdivision (a) of Section 31402 may be released within 24 hours upon delivery to the impounding authority of satisfactory proof that the vehicle will be legally moved or transported to a place of repair.

(2) A farm labor vehicle shall be impounded for not less than 10 days for a second violation of subdivision (b) of Section 2800, subdivision (a) of Section 24002.5, or subdivision (a) of Section 31402, or any combination of two of those provisions, if the original equipment or maintenance violation has not been repaired to comply with existing law. The farm labor vehicle shall be released after 10 days upon delivery to the impounding authority of satisfactory proof that the vehicle has been repaired to comply with existing law, or upon delivery to the impounding agency of satisfactory proof that the vehicle will be lawfully moved or transported to a place of repair.

(3) A farm labor vehicle shall be impounded for not less than 30 days for a third or subsequent violation of subdivision (b) of Section 2800, subdivision (a) of Section 24002.5, or subdivision (a) of Section 31402, or any combination of three or more of those provisions, if the original equipment or maintenance violation has not been repaired to comply with existing law. The farm labor vehicle shall be released after 30 days upon delivery to the impounding authority of satisfactory proof that the vehicle has been repaired to comply with existing law, or upon delivery to the impounding agency of satisfactory proof that the vehicle will be lawfully moved or transported to a place of repair.

(c) All towing and storage fees for a vehicle removed under this section shall be paid by the owner.

(Amended by Stats. 2000, Ch. 873, Sec. 4. Effective January 1, 2001.)

34506.5. (a) A farm labor vehicle is subject to forfeiture as a nuisance if it is driven on a highway in violation of subdivision (b) of Section 2800, subdivision (a) of Section 24002.5, or subdivision (a) of Section 31402 and has been impounded for a second or subsequent time pursuant to paragraph (3) of subdivision (b) of Section 34506.4.

(b) (1) A registered or legal owner of record at the time of impoundment may request a hearing to determine the validity of the impoundment pursuant to paragraph (1) or (2) of subdivision (n) of Section 14607.6.

(2) If it is determined that the necessary repairs had been completed and the farm labor vehicle complied with existing laws at the time of impoundment, the agency employing the person who directed the impoundment shall be responsible for the costs incurred for towing and storage.

(c) Procedures established in subdivisions (e), (f), (g), (h), (i), (j), (k), (l), (o), (p), (q), (r), (t), (u), and (v) of Section 14607.6 shall be utilized for the forfeiture of an impounded farm labor vehicle.

(Added by Stats. 2000, Ch. 873, Sec. 5. Effective January 1, 2001.)

34507. To assist the department in enforcing this division, a vehicle that is subject to this division and to the jurisdiction, control, and regulation of the Department of Motor Vehicles, the Public Utilities Commission, or the United States Secretary of the Department of Transportation shall have displayed prominently a distinctive identifying symbol as required by Section 34507.5.

(Amended by Stats. 2006, Ch. 288, Sec. 16. Effective January 1, 2007.)

34507.5. (a) A motor carrier, as defined in Section 408, whose principal place of business is in this state, who operates from a terminal in this state, or who is required to be licensed pursuant to Section 32000.5, a motor carrier of property, and a for-hire motor carrier of property, as defined in Section 34601, shall obtain a carrier identification number from the department. Application for a carrier identification number shall be on a form furnished by the department. The department may furnish the form online and require the form to be completed and submitted electronically via the department's internet website. Information provided in connection with an application for a carrier identification number shall be true and accurate. Information relating to a carrier identification number shall be updated by a motor carrier upon request from the department and within 15 days of a change of information, or the cessation or resumption of regulated activity at any of the motor carrier's terminals.

(1) A motor carrier required to obtain a carrier identification number shall first obtain a United States Department of Transportation number from the Federal Motor Carrier Safety Administration and provide that number on the application for a carrier identification number. The department shall not assign a carrier identification number unless the application includes the United States Department of Transportation number assigned to, and properly identifying, the motor carrier.

(2) A motor carrier shall ensure information associated with the United States Department of Transportation number assigned to the motor carrier is true and accurate. The information shall be updated as required by Section 390.19T of Title 49 of the Code of Federal Regulations, before the motor carrier operates a commercial motor vehicle, at least once every two calendar years, and within 15 days of any change of information, or cessation or resumption of regulated activity.

(b) The carrier identification number assigned to the motor carrier under whose operating authority or motor carrier permit the vehicle or combination of vehicles is being operated shall be displayed on both sides of each vehicle, or on both sides of at least one motor vehicle in each combination of the following vehicles:

(1) Each vehicle set forth in Section 34500.

(2) A motortruck of two or more axles that is more than 10,000 pounds gross vehicle weight rating.

(3) Any other motortruck or motor vehicle used to transport property for compensation.

(c) The carrier identification number of a motor carrier operating a vehicle or combination of vehicles listed in subdivision (b) under a rental agreement with a term of not more than 30 calendar days need not be displayed if all of the following requirements are met:

(1) The name or trademark of the lessor are displayed on both sides of each vehicle or on both sides of one of the vehicles in each combination of vehicles.

(2) Any of the following numbers issued to the lessor are displayed on both sides of each vehicle or on both sides of one of the vehicles in each combination of vehicles:

(A) The carrier identification number issued by the United States Department of Transportation.

(B) A valid operating authority number.

(C) A valid motor carrier of property number.

(3) (A) A copy of the rental agreement entered into by the lessor and the vehicle operator is in the vehicle or combination of vehicles.

(B) The rental agreement shall be available for inspection immediately upon the request of an authorized employee of the department, a regularly employed and salaried police officer or deputy sheriff, or a reserve police officer or reserve deputy sheriff listed pursuant to Section 830.6 of the Penal Code.

(C) If the rented vehicle or combination of vehicles is operated in conjunction with a commercial enterprise, the rental agreement shall include the operator's carrier identification number or motor carrier of property permit number.

(d) A vehicle or combination of vehicles that is in compliance with Section 390.21T of Title 49 of the Code of Federal Regulations shall be deemed to be in compliance with subdivision (c).

(e) This section does not apply to any of the following vehicles:

(1) A vehicle described in subdivision (f) of Section 34500, that is operated by a private carrier as defined in subdivision (d) of Section 34601, if the gross vehicle weight rating of the towing vehicle is 10,000 pounds or less, or the towing vehicle is a pickup truck, as defined in Section 471. This exception does not apply to a vehicle combination described in subdivision (k) of Section 34500.

(2) A vehicle described in subdivision (g) of Section 34500, that is operated by a private carrier as defined in subdivision (d) of Section 34601, if the hazardous material transportation does not require the display of placards pursuant to Section 27903, a license pursuant to Section 32000.5, or hazardous waste hauler registration pursuant to Section 25163 of the Health and Safety Code.

(3) A historical vehicle, as described in Section 5004, and a vehicle that displays special identification plates in accordance with Section 5011.

(4) An implement of husbandry as defined in Chapter 1 (commencing with Section 36000) of Division 16.

(5) A vehicle owned or operated by an agency of the federal government.

(6) A pickup truck, as defined in Section 471, and a two-axle daily rental truck with a gross vehicle weight rating of less than 26,001 pounds, when operated in noncommercial use.

(f) Subdivision (b) does not apply to the following:

(1) A vehicle that displays a valid identification number assigned by the United States Secretary of the Department of Transportation.

(2) A vehicle that is regulated by, and that displays a valid operating authority number issued by, the Bureau of Household Goods and Services, including a household mover as defined in Section 19225.5 of the Business and Professions Code.

(3) A for-hire motor carrier of passengers.

(g) The display of the carrier identification number shall be in sharp contrast to the background, and shall be of a size, shape, and color that it is readily legible during daylight hours from a distance of 50 feet.

(h) The carrier identification number for a company no longer in business, no longer operating with the same name, or no longer operating under the same operating authority, identification number, or motor carrier permit shall be removed before sale, transfer, or other disposal of a vehicle marked pursuant to this section.

(Amended by Stats. 2022, Ch. 295, Sec. 23. (AB 2956) Effective January 1, 2023.)

34507.6. (a) Every operator of transportation service which is exempt from regulation as a charter-party carrier of passengers pursuant to subdivision (k) or (l) of Section 5353 of the Public Utilities Code, and which furnishes that transportation service in a bus, shall obtain a carrier identification number from the Department of the California Highway Patrol. Application for a carrier identification number shall be on a form furnished by the Department of the California Highway Patrol.

(b) (1) The carrier identification number so obtained by the operator shall be displayed on both sides of each bus used in that transportation service.

(2) The display of the carrier identification number shall be in sharp contrast to the background, and shall be of a size, shape, and color as to be readily legible during daylight hours from a distance of at least 50 feet.

(3) The carrier identification number shall be removed before the sale, transfer, or other disposal of the bus.

(Added by Stats. 1988, Ch. 1039, Sec. 2.)

34508. The Department of the California Highway Patrol shall adopt and enforce rules and regulations relating to the equipment, maintenance, construction, design, color, and operation of schoolbuses.

(Amended by Stats. 1981, Ch. 774, Sec. 11.)

34509. Vanpool vehicles, as defined in Section 668, and vanpool vehicles when used for purposes other than traveling to and from a work location and transporting not more than 10 persons including the driver, shall be exempt from the regulations adopted pursuant to Section 34501, except that the following shall apply:

(a) The vanpool vehicle shall be equipped with an operable fire extinguisher which is of the dry chemical or carbon dioxide type with an aggregate rating of at least 4-B:C and which is securely mounted and readily accessible.

(b) The vanpool vehicle shall be equipped with a first aid kit, conforming to the minimum requirements for schoolbuses. First aid kits shall be readily visible, accessible, and plainly marked "First Aid Kit."

(c) The vanpool vehicle shall be regularly and systematically inspected, maintained, and lubricated in accordance with the manufacturer's recommendations, or more often if necessary to ensure the safe operating condition of the vehicle. The maintenance shall include, as a minimum, an in-depth inspection of the vehicle's brake system, steering components, lighting system, and wheels and tires, to be performed at intervals of not more than every six months or 6,000 miles, whichever occurs first.

(d) Operators of vanpool vehicles shall document each systematic inspection, maintenance, and lubrication and repair performed for each vehicle under their control. Required records shall include services performed, the person performing the service, the date, and the mileage on the vehicle at the time of the repair. The records shall be maintained with the vehicle for one year, and shall be presented upon demand to any authorized representative of the California Highway Patrol.

(e) Vanpool vehicles being operated pursuant to the exemptions specified in this section shall display, upon the rear and sides of the vehicle, a sign or placard, clearly visible and discernable for a distance of not less than 50 feet, indicating that the vehicle is being used as a vanpool vehicle.

(Added by Stats. 1982, Ch. 46, Sec. 11.)

34510. Persons operating vehicles, or combinations of vehicles, in the transportation of hazardous material and subject to this division, shall carry in the vehicle while en route any shipping papers required to accompany the vehicle in accordance with regulations adopted pursuant to Section 2402. The bill of lading or other shipping paper shall be displayed upon demand of any member of the California Highway Patrol or any police officer of a city who is on duty for the exclusive or main purpose of enforcing the provisions of this code.

(Amended by Stats. 2001, Ch. 504, Sec. 8. Effective January 1, 2002.)

34510.5. (a) (1) A broker of construction trucking services, as defined in Section 3322 of the Civil Code, shall not furnish construction transportation services to any construction project unless it has secured a surety bond of not less than fifteen thousand dollars ($15,000) executed by an admitted surety insurer. The surety bond shall ensure the payment of the claims of a contracted motor carrier of property in dump truck equipment if the broker fails to pay the contracted motor carrier within the time period specified in paragraph (1) of subdivision (a) of Section 3322 of the Civil Code.

(2) (A) A broker of construction trucking services annually shall provide written evidence of the broker's valid surety bond to a third-party nonprofit organization that is related to the industry and regularly maintains a published database of bonded brokers or post a current copy of the surety bond on the broker's Internet Web site.

(B) When a copy of a surety bond is provided to a third-party nonprofit organization, the broker shall notify the third-party nonprofit organization if at any time the surety bond is cancelled or expired. When a copy of the surety bond is posted on the broker's Internet Web site, the broker shall remove the copy of the surety bond from his or her Internet Web site if at any time the surety bond is cancelled or expired.

(C) A third-party nonprofit organization shall not charge a broker for posting evidence of a valid surety bond or limit the posting of the bond only to the organization's members.

(D) A third-party nonprofit organization shall not be liable for any damages caused by the publication of any information provided pursuant to this paragraph that is erroneous or outdated.

(b) A broker of construction trucking services shall not hire, or otherwise engage the services of, a motor carrier of property to furnish construction transportation services unless the broker provides, prior to the commencement of work each calendar year, written evidence of the broker's valid surety bond to any person that hires, or otherwise engages the services of, the broker to furnish construction transportation services and also to the hired motor carrier of property.

(c) A broker of construction trucking services who furnishes construction transportation services in violation of this section is guilty of a misdemeanor and subject to a fine of up to five thousand dollars ($5,000).

(d) In any civil action brought against a broker of construction trucking services by a motor carrier of property in dump truck equipment with whom the broker contracted during any period of time in which the broker did not have a surety bond in violation of this section, the failure to have the bond shall create a rebuttable presumption that the broker failed to pay to the motor carrier the amount due and owing.

(e) For purposes of this section, "a broker of construction trucking services" does not include a facility that meets all the following requirements:

(1) Arranges for transportation services of its product.

(2) Primarily handles raw materials to produce a new product.

(3) Is a rock product operation (such as an "aggregate" operation), a hot mixing asphalt plant, or a concrete, concrete product, or Portland cement product manufacturing facility.

(4) Does not accept a fee for the arrangement.

(f) For the purposes of this section, "written evidence of the broker's valid surety bond" includes a copy of the surety bond, a certificate of insurance, a continuation certificate, or other similar documentation originally issued from the surety that includes the surety's and broker's name, the bond number, and the effective and expiration dates of the bond.

(Amended by Stats. 2013, Ch. 76, Sec. 197. (AB 383) Effective January 1, 2014.)

34511. Any violation of any provision of this division or regulation adopted pursuant thereto may be enjoined in a civil action brought by the Attorney General in the name of the people of the State of California, upon request of the department, except that it shall not be necessary to show lack of adequate remedy at law or to show irreparable damage or loss.

The department may not submit a request for civil action and the Attorney General may not bring action pursuant to this section unless the person charged with a violation of this division or regulation adopted pursuant thereto fails to take corrective action after being notified of the violation by the department, in writing, on at least two occasions over a 60-day period. Prior to the submission of the department's request for civil action, the person charged shall receive, at his or her request, a departmental hearing on the matter and the department's request for civil action shall be forwarded by the department to, and approved by, the Commissioner of the California Highway Patrol.

(Added by Stats. 1982, Ch. 789, Sec. 3.)

34513. The department shall adopt rules and regulations relating to the equipment and maintenance of tour buses.

(Added by Stats. 1986, Ch. 1306, Sec. 19.)

34514. (a) Beginning with the 1990–91 fiscal year, the department shall, upon appropriation of the requisite funds by the Legislature, annually conduct additional roadside vehicle safety inspections of vehicles described in Section 34501.12. These roadside inspections shall be in addition to the maintenance facility and terminal inspections required by that section, and over and above the number of roadside vehicle safety inspections conducted during the 1987–88 fiscal year.

(b) It is the intent of the Legislature that, beginning with the 1990–91 fiscal year, funds are to be appropriated to the department annually, for the purposes of subdivision (a), from the Motor Vehicle Account in the State Transportation Fund, to the extent that sufficient funds are collected pursuant to Section 34501.12.

(Amended by Stats. 1992, Ch. 1243, Sec. 100. Effective September 30, 1992.)

34515. (a) As used in this division and in regulations adopted pursuant to this division, "maintenance facility or terminal" means any place or places where a vehicle of a type listed in Section 34500 is regularly garaged or maintained, or from which it is operated or dispatched. "Maintenance facility or terminal" includes a private business or residence.

(b) For the purpose of the inspections conducted pursuant to Section 34501.12, "terminal" means the location or locations in this state that are designated by a motor carrier, where subject vehicles may be inspected by the department and where vehicle maintenance and inspection records and drivers' records will be made available for inspection.

(c) This section shall become operative on January 1, 2016.

(Repealed (in Sec. 11) and added by Stats. 2013, Ch. 500, Sec. 12. (AB 529) Effective January 1, 2014. Section operative January 1, 2016, by its own provisions.)

34516. (a) No person shall use or arrange for the use of a refrigerated motor vehicle, tank truck, dry van, or other motor vehicle, to provide transportation of food products for human consumption if the vehicle has been used to transport solid waste destined for landfills, or if precluded from use in accordance with subdivision (c).

(b) A violation of this section is a misdemeanor.

(c) If, pursuant to a federal statute having the same purposes as the act which added this section to the Public Utilities Code during the 1990 portion of the 1989–90 Regular Session, the United States Secretary of Transportation publishes a list of categories of solid waste or hazardous substances which he or she determines make food unsafe as a result of having been transported in a refrigerated motor vehicle, tank truck, dry van, or other motor vehicle also used to transport food products for human consumption, subdivisions (a) and (b) apply to those substances.

(d) A person or corporation charged with a violation of this section may avoid liability upon a showing by clear and convincing evidence that the transportation alleged to violate this section did not in fact endanger the public health, due to the specific protective or remedial actions taken by the person or corporation charged.

(Added by Stats. 1990, Ch. 1685, Sec. 12.)

34517. (a) With respect to a commercial motor vehicle from another country, a person shall not operate the vehicle outside the boundaries of a designated commercial zone unless the required operating authority from the United States Secretary of the Department of Transportation has first been obtained.

(b) A violation of subdivision (a) is an infraction punishable by a fine of one thousand dollars ($1,000).

(c) Notwithstanding subdivision (b), a peace officer, as defined in Chapter 4.5 (commencing with Section 830) of Title 3 of Part 2 of the Penal Code, shall issue a citation for a violation of subdivision (a) to the driver of the vehicle and order the driver of the vehicle to return the vehicle to its country of origin. The peace officer may impound a vehicle cited pursuant to this section and its cargo until the citation and all charges related to the impoundment are cleared. The impoundment charges are the responsibility of the vehicle's owner.

(d) As used in this section, "designated commercial zone" means a commercial zone, as defined in Part 372 (commencing with Section 372.101) of Title 49 of the Code of Federal Regulations.

(Amended by Stats. 2006, Ch. 288, Sec. 18. Effective January 1, 2007.)

34518. (a) A foreign motor carrier or foreign private motor carrier required to have a certificate of registration issued by the United States Secretary of the Department of Transportation pursuant to Part 368 (commencing with Section 368.1), or required to be registered pursuant to Part 365 (commencing with Section 365.101), of Title 49 of the Code of Federal Regulations shall not do any of the following:

(1) Operate in this state without the required certificate in the vehicle.

(2) Operate beyond the limitations or restrictions specified in the certificate as issued.

(3) Refuse to show the certificate upon request of a peace officer.

(4) Provide point-to-point transportation services, including express delivery services, within the United States for goods other than international cargo.

(b) A motor carrier required to be registered with the United States Secretary of the Department of Transportation pursuant to Section 13902 of Title 49 of the United States Code, Part 365 (commencing with Section 365.101), Part 390 (commencing with Section 390.1), or Section 392.9a of Title 49 of the Code of Federal Regulations shall not do any of the following:

(1) Operate in this state without the required registration.

(2) Operate beyond the limitations or restrictions specified in its registration.

(3) Operate in this state without the required operating authority.

(c) A violation of subdivision (a) or (b) is an infraction punishable by a fine of one thousand dollars ($1,000).

(d) A member of the Department of the California Highway Patrol may impound a vehicle operated in violation of subdivision (a) or (b) and its cargo, until the citation and all charges related to the impoundment are cleared. The impoundment charges are the responsibility of the vehicle's owner.

(e) (1) A motor carrier granted permanent operating authority pursuant to subdivision (a) shall not operate a vehicle on a highway, unless the vehicle is inspected by a Commercial Vehicle Safety Alliance-certified inspector every three months and displays a current safety inspection decal attesting to the successful completion of those inspections for at least three years after receiving permanent operating authority.

(2) Paragraph (1) does not apply to a motor carrier granted authority to operate solely in a commercial zone on the United States-Mexico International Border.

(f) As used in this section "limitations" or "restrictions" include definitions of "commercial zones," "municipality," "contiguous municipalities," "unincorporated area," and "terminal areas," in Part 372 (commencing with Section 372.101) of Title 49 of the Code of Federal Regulations.

(Amended by Stats. 2010, Ch. 491, Sec. 48. (SB 1318) Effective January 1, 2011.)

34520. (a) Motor carriers and drivers shall comply with the controlled substances and alcohol use, transportation, and testing requirements of the United States Secretary of Transportation as set forth in Part 382 (commencing with Section 382.101) of, and Sections 392.4 and 392.5 of, Title 49 of the Code of Federal Regulations.

(b) (1) A motor carrier shall make available for inspection, upon the request of an authorized employee of the department, copies of all results and other records pertaining to controlled substances and alcohol use and testing conducted pursuant to federal law, as specified in subdivision (a), including those records contained in individual driver qualification files.

(2) For the purposes of complying with the return-to-duty alcohol or controlled substances test requirements, or both, of Section 382.309 of Title 49 of the Code of Federal Regulations and the followup alcohol or controlled substances test requirements, or both, of Section 382.311 of that title, the department may use those test results to monitor drivers who are motor carriers.

(3) Evidence derived from a positive test result in the possession of a motor carrier shall not be admissible in a criminal prosecution concerning unlawful possession, sale, or distribution of controlled substances.

(c) A drug or alcohol testing consortium, as defined in Section 382.107 of Title 49 of the Code of Federal Regulations, shall mail a copy of all drug and alcohol positive test result summaries to the department within three days of the test. This requirement applies only to drug and alcohol positive tests of those drivers employed by motor carriers who operate terminals within this state.

(d) A transit agency receiving federal financial assistance under Section 3, 9, or 18 of the Federal Transit Act, or under Section 103(e)(4) of Title 23 of the United States Code, shall comply with the controlled substances and alcohol use and testing requirements of the United States Secretary of Transportation as set forth in Part 655 (commencing with Section 655.1) of Title 49 of the Code of Federal Regulations.

(e) The owner-operator shall notify all other motor carriers with whom he or she is under contract when the owner-operator has met the requirements of subdivision (c) of Section 15242. Notwithstanding subdivision (i), a violation of this subdivision is an infraction.

(f) Except as provided in Section 382.301 of Title 49 of the Code of Federal Regulations, an applicant for employment as a commercial driver or an owner-operator seeking to provide transportation services and meeting the requirements of subdivision (b) of Section 34624, may not be placed on duty by a motor carrier until a preemployment test for controlled substances and alcohol use meeting the requirements of the federal regulations referenced in subdivision (a) have been completed and a negative test result has been reported.

(g) An applicant for employment as a commercial driver or an owner-operator, seeking to provide transportation services and meeting the requirements of subdivision (b) of Section 34624, may not be placed on duty by a motor carrier until the motor carrier has completed a full investigation of the driver's employment history meeting the requirements of the federal regulations cited under subdivision (a). Every motor carrier, whether making or receiving inquiries concerning a driver's history, shall document all activities it has taken to comply with this subdivision.

(h) A motor carrier that utilizes a preemployment screening service to review applications is in compliance with the employer duties under subdivisions (e) and (f) if the preemployment screening services that are provided satisfy the requirements of state and federal law and the motor carrier abides by any findings that would, under federal law, disqualify an applicant from operating a commercial vehicle.

(i) It is a misdemeanor punishable by imprisonment in the county jail for six months and a fine not to exceed five thousand dollars ($5,000), or by both the imprisonment and fine, for a person to willfully violate this section. As used in this subdivision, "willfully" has the same meaning as defined in Section 7 of the Penal Code.

(j) This section does not apply to a peace officer, as defined in Section 830.1 or 830.2 of the Penal Code, who is authorized to drive vehicles described in Section 34500, or to a firefighter, as defined in subdivision (f) of Section 15250.6, who is authorized to operate firefighting equipment as defined in subdivision (g) of Section 15250.6, if that peace officer or firefighter is participating in a substance abuse detection program within the scope of his or her employment.

(Amended by Stats. 2015, Ch. 451, Sec. 59. (SB 491) Effective January 1, 2016.)

34520.3. (a) For the purposes of this section, a "school transportation vehicle" is a vehicle that is not a schoolbus, school pupil activity bus, or youth bus, and is used by a school district or county office of education for the primary purpose of transporting children.

(b) A school district or county office of education that employs drivers to drive a school transportation vehicle, and the driver of those vehicles, who are not otherwise required to participate in a testing program of the United States Secretary of Transportation, shall participate in a program that is consistent with the controlled substances and alcohol use and testing requirements of the United States Secretary of Transportation that apply to schoolbus drivers and are set forth in Part 382 (commencing with Section 382.101) of, and Sections 392.5(a)(1) and (3) of, Title 49 of the Code of Federal Regulations.

(c) It is the intent of the Legislature that this section be implemented in a manner that does not require a school district or county office of education to administer a program for drivers of school transportation vehicles that imposes controlled substance and alcohol use and testing requirements greater than those applicable to school bus drivers under existing law.

(Added by Stats. 2005, Ch. 324, Sec. 1. Effective January 1, 2006.)

34520.5. (a) All employers of drivers who operate paratransit vehicles, and the drivers of those vehicles, who are not otherwise required to participate in a testing program of the United States Secretary of Transportation, shall participate in a program consistent with the controlled substances and alcohol use and testing requirements of the United States Secretary of Transportation as set forth in Part 382 (commencing with Section 382.101), Part 653 (commencing with Section 653.1), or Part 654 (commencing with Section 654.1) of Title 49 of the Code of Federal Regulations.

(b) Section 34520 is applicable to any controlled substances or alcohol testing program undertaken under this section.

(c) The employer of a paratransit vehicle driver shall participate in the pull notice system defined in Section 1808.1.

(Amended by Stats. 1999, Ch. 1007, Sec. 25. Effective January 1, 2000.)

Division 14.85. Motor Carriers of Property Permit Act

(Division 14.85 added by Stats. 1996, Ch. 1042, Sec. 53.)

Chapter 1. General Provisions and Definitions

(Chapter 1 added by Stats. 1996, Ch. 1042, Sec. 53.)

34600. This division shall be known and may be cited as the Motor Carriers of Property Permit Act.

(Added by Stats. 1996, Ch. 1042, Sec. 53. Effective September 29, 1996.)

34601. (a) As used in this division, "motor carrier of property" means any person who operates any commercial motor vehicle as defined in subdivision (c). "Motor carrier of property" does not include a household mover, as defined in Section 19225.5 of the Business and Professions Code, a household mover transporting used office, store, and institution furniture and fixtures under its household mover permit pursuant to Section 19237 of the Business and Professions Code, persons providing only transportation of passengers, or a passenger stage corporation transporting baggage and express upon a passenger vehicle incidental to the transportation of passengers.

(b) As used in this division, "for-hire motor carrier of property" means a motor carrier of property as defined in subdivision (a) who transports property for compensation.

(c) (1) As used in this division, except as provided in paragraph (2), a "commercial motor vehicle" means any self-propelled vehicle listed in subdivisions (a), (b), (f), (g), and (k) of Section 34500, any motortruck of two or more axles that is more than 10,000 pounds gross vehicle weight rating, and any other motor vehicle used to transport property for compensation.

(2) As used in this division, "commercial motor vehicle" does not include any of the following:

(A) Vehicles identified in subdivision (f) of Section 34500, if the gross vehicle weight rating of the towing vehicle is 10,000 pounds or less.

(B) Vehicles identified in subdivision (g) of Section 34500, if the hazardous material transportation does not require the display of placards under Section 27903, a license under Section 32000.5, or a hazardous waste transporter registration under Section 25163 of the Health and Safety Code, and the vehicle is not operated in commercial use.

(C) Vehicles operated by a household mover, as defined in Section 19225.5 of the Business and Professions Code, under the household mover permit pursuant to Section 19237 of that code.

(D) Vehicles operated by a household mover to transport used office, store, and institution furniture and fixtures under its household mover permit pursuant to Section 19237 of the Business and Professions Code.

(E) Pickup trucks as defined in Section 471, if the conditions in subparagraphs (A) and (B) are also met.

(F) Two-axle daily rental trucks with a gross vehicle weight rating of less than 26,001 pounds, when operated in noncommercial use.

(G) Vehicles never operated in commercial use, including motortrucks or two-axle truck tractors, with a gross vehicle weight rating of less than 26,001 pounds, when operated singly, or, when used to tow a camp trailer, trailer coach, fifth-wheel travel trailer, trailer designed to transport watercraft, or a utility trailer, never operated in commercial use. Vehicle combinations described in this subparagraph are not subject to Section 27900, 34501.12, or 34507.5.

(d) For purposes of this chapter, "private carrier" means a motor carrier of property, who transports only their own property, including, but not limited to, the delivery of goods sold by that carrier.

(e) This section shall become operative on January 1, 2016.

(Amended by Stats. 2022, Ch. 295, Sec. 24. (AB 2956) Effective January 1, 2023.)

34602. As used in this division, "fund" means the Motor Vehicle Account in the State Transportation Fund.

(Amended by Stats. 2002, Ch. 805, Sec. 22. Effective September 23, 2002. Operative July 1, 2003, by Sec. 26 of Ch. 805.)

34603. The Department of the California Highway Patrol, the Public

Utilities Commission, the Bureau of Household Goods and Services, and the State Board of Equalization shall furnish, upon request, whatever information from their records may be required to assist the department in the effective development and enforcement of this division.

(Amended by Stats. 2022, Ch. 295, Sec. 25. (AB 2956) Effective January 1, 2023.)

34604. The department may adopt reasonable rules and regulations necessary to administer this division. The department may also adopt rules and regulations necessary to administer civil sanction proceedings and impose fines for failure to comply with Division 14.8 (commencing with Section 34500), or this division, or regulations adopted pursuant to this code.

(Added by Stats. 1996, Ch. 1042, Sec. 53. Effective September 29, 1996.)

34605. (a) The department may contract with the Office of Administrative Hearings to administer proceedings and impose fines for failure to comply with Division 14.8 (commencing with Section 34500), or this division, or regulations adopted pursuant to this code.

(b) The department and the California Highway Patrol may also contract with the Public Utilities Commission to administer this division in a manner described by the contract, or if permitted by the Department of Motor Vehicles, in a manner as existed on January 1, 1996. This temporary authority shall be terminated on December 31, 1997.

(c) All fees collected under this contract shall be deposited in the Motor Vehicle Account in the State Transportation Fund.

(Amended by Stats. 2002, Ch. 805, Sec. 23. Effective September 23, 2002. Operative July 1, 2003, by Sec. 26 of Ch. 805.)

Chapter 2. Motor Carrier Permits

(Chapter 2 added by Stats. 1996, Ch. 1042, Sec. 53.)

34620. (a) Except as provided in subdivision (b) and Section 34622, a motor carrier of property shall not operate a commercial motor vehicle on any public highway in this state, unless it has complied with Section 34507.5 and has registered with the department its carrier identification number authorized or assigned thereunder, and holds a valid motor carrier permit issued to that motor carrier by the department. The department shall issue a motor carrier permit upon the carrier's written request, compliance with Sections 34507.5, 34630, and 34640, and subdivisions (e) and (h) of Section 34501.12 for motor carriers listed in that section, and the payment of the fee required by this chapter.

(b) A person shall not contract with, or otherwise engage the services of, a motor carrier of property, unless that motor carrier holds a valid motor carrier of property permit issued by the department. A motor carrier of property or broker of construction trucking services, as defined in Section 3322 of the Civil Code, shall not contract or subcontract with, or otherwise engage the services of, a motor carrier of property, until the contracted motor carrier of property provides certification in the manner prescribed by this section, of compliance with subdivision (a). This certification shall be completed by the contracted motor carrier of property and shall include a provision requiring the contracted motor carrier of property to immediately notify the person to whom they are contracted if the contracted motor carrier of property's permit is suspended or revoked. A copy of the contracted motor carrier of property's permit shall accompany the required certificate. The Department of the California Highway Patrol shall, by regulation, prescribe the format for the certificate and may make available an optional specific form for that purpose. The certificate, or a copy thereof, shall be maintained by each involved party for the duration of the contract or period of service plus two years, and shall be presented for inspection at the location designated by each carrier under Section 34501.10, immediately upon the request of an authorized employee of the Department of the California Highway Patrol.

(c) (1) A motor carrier of property shall not retrieve a vehicle through the use of a tow truck, as defined in subdivision (a) of Section 615, from the premises of another motor carrier of property until the retrieving motor carrier provides a copy of its motor carrier permit to the releasing motor carrier.

(2) A motor carrier of property shall not release a vehicle to another motor carrier of property utilizing a tow truck, as defined in subdivision (a) of Section 615, until the releasing motor carrier obtains a copy of the motor carrier permit from the retrieving motor carrier. The motor carrier releasing the vehicle shall maintain a copy of the motor carrier permit for a period of two years after the transaction, and, upon the request of an authorized employee of the Department of the California Highway Patrol, shall immediately present the permit for inspection at the location designated by the releasing motor carrier under Section 34501.10.

(3) This subdivision does not apply to a person licensed pursuant to the Collateral Recovery Act (Chapter 11 (commencing with Section 7500) of Division 3 of the Business and Professions Code).

(Amended by Stats. 2013, Ch. 96, Sec. 1. (AB 306) Effective January 1, 2014.)

34621. (a) The fee required by Section 7232 of the Revenue and Taxation Code shall be paid to the department upon initial application for a motor carrier permit and for annual renewal.

(b) An application for an original or a renewal motor carrier permit shall contain all of the following information:

(1) The full name of the motor carrier; any fictitious name under which it is doing business; address, both physical and mailing; and business telephone number.

(2) Status as individual, partnership, owner-operator, or corporation, and officers of corporation and all partners.

(3) Name, address, and driver's license number of owner-operator.

(4) California carrier number, number of commercial motor vehicles in fleet, interstate or intrastate operations, State Board of Equalization, federal Department of Transportation or the Federal Motor Carrier Safety Administration number, as applicable.

(5) Transporter or not a transporter of hazardous materials or petroleum.

(6) Evidence of financial responsibility.

(7) Evidence of workman's compensation coverage, if applicable.

(8) Carrier certification of enrollment in the biennial inspection of terminals (BIT) program under subdivisions (e) and (h) of Section 34501.12, unless otherwise exempted.

(9) Carrier certification of enrollment in a controlled substance and alcohol use and testing (CSAT) program required under Section 34520, unless otherwise exempted.

(10) Any other information necessary to enable the department to determine whether the applicant is entitled to a permit.

(c) Notwithstanding any provision of this chapter, a motor carrier of property may continue to operate for 30 days past the expiration date of the motor carrier permit, if the motor carrier of property meets all of the following conditions:

(1) Applied to the department for a renewal of a motor carrier permit, as required by this section, before the expiration of the motor carrier permit.

(2) Holds a valid motor carrier permit for the previous year.

(3) Maintains compliance with Section 34507.5 for the 30 days past the expiration date.

(4) Not rated unsatisfactory for any of the motor carriers' terminals inspected by the Department of the California Highway Patrol pursuant to either Section 34501.12 or Section 34520, for the 30 days past the expiration date.

(Amended by Stats. 2019, Ch. 636, Sec. 9. (AB 1810) Effective January 1, 2020.)

34622. This chapter does not apply to any of the following:

(a) Vehicles described in Section 5004 or 5011, and those that are exempt from vehicle registration fees.

(b) A household mover transporting used office, store, and institution furniture and fixtures under its household mover permit pursuant to Section 19241 of the Business and Professions Code.

(Amended by Stats. 2022, Ch. 295, Sec. 26. (AB 2956) Effective January 1, 2023.)

34623. (a) The Department of the California Highway Patrol has exclusive jurisdiction for the regulation of safety of operation of motor carriers of property.

(b) The motor carrier permit of a motor carrier of property may be suspended for failure to do either of the following:

(1) Maintain any vehicle of the carrier in a safe operating condition or to comply with this code or with applicable regulations contained in Title 13 of the California Code of Regulations, if that failure is either a consistent failure or presents an imminent danger to public safety.

(2) Enroll all drivers in the pull-notice system as required by Section 1808.1.

(c) The motor carrier permit of a motor carrier of property shall be suspended for failure to either (1) comply with the requirements of federal law described in subdivision (a) of Section 34520 of the Vehicle Code, or (2) make copies of results and other records available as required by subdivision (b) of that section. The suspension shall be as follows:

(1) For a serious violation, which is a willful failure to perform substance abuse testing in accordance with state or federal law:

(A) For a first offense, a mandatory five-day suspension.

(B) For a second offense within three years of a first offense, a mandatory three-month suspension.

(C) For a third offense within three years of a first offense, a mandatory one-year suspension.

(2) For a nonserious violation, the time recommended to the department by the Department of the California Highway Patrol.

(3) For the purposes of this subdivision, "willful failure" means any of the following:

(A) An intentional and uncorrected failure to have a controlled substances and alcohol testing program in place.

(B) An intentional and uncorrected failure to enroll an employed driver into the controlled substances and alcohol testing program.

(C) A knowing use of a medically disqualified driver, including the failure to remove the driver from safety-sensitive duties upon notification of the medical disqualification.

(D) An attempt to conceal legal deficiencies in the motor carrier's controlled substances and alcohol testing program.

(d) The department, pending a hearing in the matter pursuant to subdivision (f), may suspend a carrier's permit.

(e) (1) A motor carrier whose motor carrier permit is suspended pursuant to subdivision (b) may obtain a reinspection of its terminal and vehicles by the Department of the California Highway Patrol by submitting a written request for reinstatement to the department and paying a reinstatement fee as required by Section 34623.5.

(2) The department shall deposit all reinstatement fees collected from motor carriers of property pursuant to this section in the fund. Upon receipt of the fee, the department shall forward a request to the Department of the California Highway Patrol, which shall perform a reinspection within a reasonable time, or shall verify receipt of the application or fee or both the application and fee. Following the term of a suspension imposed under Section 34670, the department shall reinstate a carrier's motor carrier permit suspended under subdivision (b) upon notification by the Department of the California Highway Patrol that the carrier's safety compliance has improved to the satisfaction of the Department of the California Highway Patrol, unless the permit is suspended for another reason or has been revoked.

(f) Whenever the department suspends the permit of any carrier pursuant to subdivision (b), (c), or paragraph (3) of subdivision (i), the department shall furnish the carrier with written notice of the suspension and shall provide for a hearing within a reasonable time, not to exceed 21 days, after a written request is filed with the department. At the hearing, the carrier shall show cause why the suspension should not be continued. Following the hearing, the department may terminate the suspension, continue the suspension in effect, or revoke the permit. The department may revoke the permit of any carrier suspended pursuant to subdivision (b) at any time that is 90 days or more after its suspension if the carrier has not filed a written request for a hearing with the department or has failed to submit a request for reinstatement pursuant to subdivision (e).

(g) Notwithstanding any other provision of this code, a hearing shall not be provided if the suspension of the motor carrier permit is based solely upon the failure of the motor carrier to maintain satisfactory proof of financial responsibility as required by this code.

(h) A motor carrier of property may not operate a commercial motor vehicle on any public highway in this state during any period its motor carrier of property permit is suspended pursuant to this division.

(i) (1) A motor carrier of property whose motor carrier permit is suspended pursuant to this section or Section 34505.6, which suspension is based wholly or in part on the failure of the motor carrier to maintain any vehicle in safe operating condition, may not lease, or otherwise allow, another motor carrier to operate the vehicles of the carrier subject to the suspension, during the period of the suspension.

(2) A motor carrier of property may not knowingly lease, operate, dispatch, or otherwise utilize any vehicle from a motor carrier of property whose motor carrier permit is suspended, which suspension is based wholly or in part on the failure of the motor carrier to maintain any vehicle in safe operating condition.

(3) The department may immediately suspend the motor carrier permit of any motor carrier that the department determines to be in violation of paragraph (2).

(j) This section shall become operative on January 1, 2016.

(Repealed (in Sec. 17) and added by Stats. 2013, Ch. 500, Sec. 18. (AB 529) Effective January 1, 2014. Section operative January 1, 2016, by its own provisions.)

34623.1. The motor carrier permit of a licensee may be suspended pursuant to Section 494.5 of the Business and Professions Code if a licensee's name is included on a certified list of tax delinquencies provided by the State Board of Equalization or the Franchise Tax Board pursuant to Section 7063 or Section 19195, respectively of the Revenue and Taxation Code.

(Added by Stats. 2011, Ch. 455, Sec. 17. (AB 1424) Effective January 1, 2012.)

34623.5. Except as provided under subdivision (c) of Section 34630 and subdivision (d) of Section 34640, before a permit may be reissued after a suspension is terminated, there shall, in addition to any other fees required by this code, be paid to the department a fee of one hundred fifty dollars ($150).

(Amended by Stats. 2007, Ch. 58, Sec. 1. Effective January 1, 2008.)

34624. (a) The department shall establish a classification of motor carrier of property known as owner-operators.

(b) As used in this section and in Sections 1808.1 and 34501.12, an owner-operator is a person who meets all of the following requirements:

(1) Holds a class A or class B driver's license or a class C license with a hazardous materials endorsement.

(2) Owns, leases, or otherwise operates not more than one power unit and not more than three towed vehicles.

(3) Is required to obtain a permit as a motor carrier of property by the department under this division.

(c) (1) As used in this section, "power unit" is a motor vehicle described in subdivision (a), (b), (g), (f), or (k) of Section 34500, or a motortruck of two or more axles that is more than 10,000 pounds gross vehicle weight rating, but does not include those vehicles operated by household goods carriers, as defined in Section 5109 of the Public Utilities Code or persons providing transportation of passengers. A "towed vehicle" is a nonmotorized vehicle described in subdivision (d), (e), (f), (g), or (k) of that section.

(2) As used in this section, subdivision (f) of Section 34500 includes only those combinations where the gross vehicle weight rating of the towing vehicle exceeds 11,500 pounds, and subdivision (g) of Section 34500 includes only those vehicles transporting hazardous materials for which the display of placards is required pursuant to Section 27903, a license is required pursuant to Section 32000.5, or for which a hazardous waste transporter registration is required pursuant to Section 25163 of the Health and Safety Code.

(d) The department, upon suspending or revoking the driving privilege of an owner-operator shall also suspend the owner-operator's motor carrier permit, unless the owner-operator, within 15 days, shows good cause why the permit should not be suspended.

(e) Every motor carrier who is within the classification established by this section is responsible for notifying all other motor carriers with whom he or she is under contract when the status of the motor carrier changes so that he or she is no longer within the classification established by this section.

(f) This section shall not be construed to change the definition of "employer," "employee," or "independent contractor" for any other purpose.

(Amended by Stats. 2002, Ch. 774, Sec. 6. Effective September 21, 2002.)

Chapter 3. Insurance

(Chapter 3 added by Stats. 1996, Ch. 1042, Sec. 53.)

34630. (a) A motor carrier permit shall not be granted to any motor carrier of property until there is filed with the department proof of financial responsibility in the form of a currently effective certificate of insurance, issued by a company licensed to write that insurance in this state or by a nonadmitted insurer subject to Section 1763 of the Insurance Code, if the policy represented by the certificate meets the minimum insurance requirements contained in Section 34631.5. The certificate of insurance or surety bond shall provide coverage with respect to the operation, maintenance, or use of any vehicle for which a permit is required, although the vehicle may not be specifically described in the policy, or a bond of surety issued by a company licensed to write surety bonds in this state, or written evidence of self-insurance by providing the self-insured number granted by the department on a form approved by the department.

(b) Proof of financial responsibility shall be continued in effect during the active life of the motor carrier permit. The certificate of insurance shall not be cancelable on less than 30 days' written notice from the insurer to the department except in the event of cessation of operations as a permitted motor carrier of property.

(c) Whenever the department determines or is notified that the certificate of insurance or surety bond of a motor carrier of property will lapse or be terminated, the department shall suspend the carrier's permit effective on the date of lapse or termination unless the carrier provides evidence of valid insurance coverage pursuant to subdivision (a).

(1) If the carrier's permit is suspended, the carrier shall pay a reinstatement fee as set forth in Section 34623.5, and prior to conducting on-highway operations, present proof of financial responsibility pursuant to subdivision (a) in order to have the permit reinstated.

(2) If the evidence provided by the carrier of valid insurance coverage pursuant to subdivision (a) demonstrates that a lapse in coverage for the carrier's operation did not occur, the reinstatement fee shall be waived.

(Amended by Stats. 2007, Ch. 58, Sec. 2. Effective January 1, 2008.)

34631. The proof of financial responsibility required under Section 34630 shall be evidenced by the deposit with the department, covering each vehicle used or to be used under the motor carrier permit applied for, of one of the following:

(a) A certificate of insurance, issued by a company licensed to write insurance in this state, or by a nonadmitted insurer subject to Section 1763 of the Insurance Code, if the policies represented by the certificate comply with Section 34630 and the rules promulgated by the department pursuant to Section 34604.

(b) A bond of a surety company licensed to write surety bonds in the state.

(c) Evidence of qualification of the carrier as a self-insurer as provided for in subdivision (a) of Section 34630. However, any certificate of self-insurance granted to a motor carrier of property shall be limited to serve as proof of financial responsibility under paragraphs (1) and (2) of subdivision (a) of Section 34631.5 minimum limits only and shall not be acceptable as proof of financial responsibility for the coverage required pursuant to paragraph (3) or (4) of subdivision (a) of Section 34631.5.

(d) Evidence on a form that indicates that coverage is provided by a charitable risk pool operating under Section 5005.1 of the Corporations Code, if the registered owner of the vehicle is a nonprofit organization that is exempt from taxation under paragraph (3) of subsection (c) of Section 501 of the United States Internal Revenue Code. The form shall include all of the following:

(1) The name and address of the motor carrier.

(2) The name and address of the charitable risk pool providing the policy for the motor carrier.

(3) The policy number, effective date, and liability limits of the policy.

(4) A statement from the charitable risk pool that the policy meets the requirements of Section 34631.5.

(Amended by Stats. 2002, Ch. 758, Sec. 15. Effective January 1, 2003.)

34631.5. (a) (1) Every motor carrier of property as defined in Section 34601, except those subject to paragraph (2), (3), or (4), shall provide and thereafter continue in effect adequate protection against liability imposed by law upon those carriers for the payment of damages in the amount of a combined single limit of not less than seven hundred fifty thousand dollars ($750,000) on account of bodily injuries to, or death of, one or more persons, or damage to or destruction of, property other than property being transported by the carrier for any shipper or consignee whether the property of one or more than one claimant in any one accident.

(2) Every motor carrier of property, as defined in Section 34601, who operates only vehicles under 10,000 pounds GVWR and who does not transport any commodity subject to paragraph (3) or (4), shall provide and thereafter continue in effect adequate protection against liability imposed by law for the payment of damages caused by bodily injuries to or the death of any person; or for damage to or destruction of property of others, other than property being transported by the carrier, in an amount not less than three hundred thousand dollars ($300,000).

(3) Every intrastate motor carrier of property, as defined in Section 34601, who transports petroleum products in bulk, including waste petroleum and waste petroleum products, shall provide and thereafter continue in effect adequate protection against liability imposed by law upon the carrier for the payment of damages for personal bodily injuries (including death resulting therefrom) in the amount of not less than five hundred thousand dollars ($500,000) on account of bodily injuries to, or death of, one person; and protection against a total liability of those carriers on account of bodily injuries to, or death of more than one person as a result of any one accident, but subject to the same limitation for each person in the amount of not less than one million dollars ($1,000,000); and protection in an amount of not less than two hundred thousand dollars ($200,000) for one accident resulting in damage to or destruction to property other than property being transported by the carrier for any shipper or consignee, whether the property of one or more than one claimant; or a combined single limit in the amount of not less than one million two hundred thousand dollars ($1,200,000) on account of bodily injuries to, or death of, one or more persons or damage to or destruction of property, or both, other than property being transported by the carrier for any shipper or consignee whether the property of one or more than one claimant in any one accident.

(4) Except as provided in paragraph (3), every motor carrier of property, as defined in Section 34601, that transports any hazardous material, as defined by Section 353, shall provide and thereafter continue in effect adequate protection against liability imposed by law on those carriers for the payment of damages for personal injury or death, and damage to or destruction of property, in amounts of not less than the minimum levels of financial responsibility specified for carriers of hazardous materials by the United States Department of Transportation in Part 387 (commencing with Section 387.1) of Title 49 of the Code of Federal Regulations. The applicable minimum levels of financial responsibility required are as follows:

Commodity Transported:	Combined Single Limit Coverage
(A) Oil listed in Section 172.101 of Title 49 of the Code of Federal Regulations; or hazardous waste, hazardous materials and hazardous substances defined in Section 171.8 of Title 49 of the Code of Federal Regulations and listed in Section 172.101 of Title 49 of the Code of Federal Regulations, but not mentioned in subparagraph (C) or (D).	$1,000,000
(B) Hazardous waste as defined in Section 25117 of the Health and Safety Code and in Article 1 (commencing with Section 66261.1) of Chapter 11 of Division 4.5 of Title 22 of the California Code of Regulations, but not mentioned in subparagraph (C) or (D).	$1,000,000
(C) Hazardous substances, as defined in Section 171.8 of Title 49 of the Code of Federal Regulations, or liquefied compressed gas or compressed gas, transported in cargo tanks, portable tanks, or hopper-type vehicle with capacities in excess of 3,500 water gallons	$5,000,000
(D) Any quantity of division 1.1, 1.2, or 1.3 explosives; any quantity of poison gas (Poison A); or highway route controlled quantity radioactive materials as defined in Section 173.403 of Title 49 of the Code of Federal Regulations.	$5,000,000

(b) (1) The protection required under subdivision (a) shall be evidenced by the deposit with the department, covering each vehicle used or to be used in conducting the service performed by each motor carrier of property, an authorized certificate of public liability and property damage insurance, issued by a company licensed to write the insurance in the State of California, or by a nonadmitted insurer subject to Section 1763 of the Insurance Code.

(2) The protection required under subdivision (a) by every motor carrier of property engaged in interstate or foreign transportation of property in or through California, shall be evidenced by the filing and acceptance of a department authorized certificate of insurance, or qualification as a self-insurer as may be authorized by law.

(3) A certificate of insurance, evidencing the protection, shall not be cancelable on less than 30 days' written notice to the department, the notice to commence to run from the date notice is actually received at the office of the department in Sacramento.

(4) Every insurance certificate or equivalent protection to the public shall contain a provision that the certificate or equivalent protection shall remain in full force and effect until canceled in the manner provided by paragraph (3).

(5) Upon cancellation of an insurance certificate or the cancellation of equivalent protection authorized by the Department of Motor Vehicles, the motor carrier permit of any motor carrier of property, shall stand suspended immediately upon the effective date of the cancellations.

(6) No carrier shall engage in any operation on any public highway of this state during the suspension of its permit.

(7) No motor carrier of property, whose permit has been suspended under paragraph (5) shall resume operations unless and until the carrier has filed an insurance certificate or equivalent protection in effect at the time and that meets the standards set forth in this section. The operative rights of the complying carriers shall be reinstated from suspension upon the filing of an insurance certificate or equivalent protection.

(8) In order to expedite the processing of insurance filings by the department, each insurance filing made should contain the insured's California carrier number, if known, in the upper right corner of the certificate.

(c) (1) Notwithstanding any other provision of law, the operator of a for-hire tow truck who is in compliance with subdivision (a) may perform emergency moves, irrespective of the load carried aboard the vehicle being moved.

(2) For the purposes of paragraph (1), an "emergency move" is limited to one or more of the following activities:

(A) Removal of a disabled or damaged vehicle or combination of vehicles from a highway.

(B) Removal of a vehicle or combination of vehicles from public or private property following a traffic collision.

(C) Removal of a vehicle or combination of vehicles from public or private property to protect public health, safety, or property.

(D) Removal of a vehicle or combination of vehicles from any location for impound or storage, at the direction of a peace officer.

(3) The authority granted under paragraph (1) applies only to the first one-way carriage of property from the scene of the emergency to the nearest safe location. Any subsequent move of that property shall be subject to subdivision (a), including, but not limited to, a requirement that the for-hire tow truck operator have a level of liability protection that is adequate for the commodity being transported by the towed vehicle or combination of vehicles.

(4) Any transportation of property by an operator of an operator of a for-hire tow truck that is not an emergency move, as authorized under paragraph (1), shall be subject to subdivision (a), including, but not limited to, a requirement that the for-hire tow truck operator have a level of liability protection that is adequate for the commodity being transported by the towed vehicle or combination of vehicles.

(Amended by Stats. 1999, Ch. 724, Sec. 48. Effective January 1, 2000.)

34632. (a) Every motor carrier of property shall furnish the department annually, as specified by the department, a list, prepared under oath, of all vehicles, described in Section 34601, used in transportation during the preceding year.

(b) If the carrier's insurer informs the department that the carrier has failed to obtain insurance coverage for any vehicle reported on the list, the department shall, in addition to any other applicable penalty provided in this division, suspend the carrier's permit.

(Added by Stats. 1996, Ch. 1042, Sec. 53. Effective September 29, 1996.)

34633. Every motor carrier of property with a carrier fleet of 20 or more commercial motor vehicles as defined in Section 34601 shall, under oath, file annually a report with the department indicating the number, classification, and compensation of all employees and owner-operator drivers hired or engaged during the reporting period. The department shall submit a copy of the report to the administrator of the corporation's workers' compensation self-insurance plan if the corporation is self-insured, or to the carrier's workers' compensation insurer if the carrier's workers' compensation protection is provided by a policy or policies of insurance.

(Added by Stats. 1996, Ch. 1042, Sec. 53. Effective September 29, 1996.)

34634. (a) Upon receipt of a stop order issued by the Director of Industrial Relations pursuant to Section 3710.1 of the Labor Code, the department shall determine whether the motor carrier of property has filed a false statement relative to workers' compensation insurance coverage, in violation of statute, or rules or orders of the department. If, after notice and opportunity to be heard, the department determines that there has been a violation of statute, or rules or orders of the department, the department shall, in addition to any other applicable penalty provided in this division, suspend the carrier's permit.

(b) Upon notification from the Director of Industrial Relations that a final judgment has been entered against any motor carrier of property as a result of an award having been made to an employee pursuant to Section 3716.2 of the Labor Code, the department shall, 30 days from the date the carrier is mailed the notice pursuant to subdivision (c), revoke the carrier's permit unless the judgment has been satisfied or has been discharged in accordance with the bankruptcy laws of the United States or the carrier requests a hearing pursuant to subdivision (c).

(c) Within seven days of notification from the Director of Industrial Relations that a final judgment has been entered against any motor carrier of property as a result of an award having been made to an employee pursuant to Section 3716.2 of the Labor Code, the department shall furnish to the carrier named in the final judgment written notice of the right to a hearing regarding the revocation of the permit and the procedure to follow to request a hearing. The notice shall state that the department is required to revoke the carrier's permit pursuant to subdivision (b) after 30 days from the date the notice is mailed unless the carrier provides proof that the judgment is satisfied or has been discharged in accordance with the bankruptcy laws of the United States and the department has been so notified seven days prior to the conclusion of the 30-day waiting period. The carrier may request a hearing within 10 days from the date the notice is sent by the department. The request for the hearing shall stay the revocation. The hearing shall be held within 30 days of the receipt of the request. If the department finds that an unsatisfied judgment exists concerning a debt arising under Section 3717 of the Labor Code, the department shall immediately revoke the carrier's permit.

(Added by Stats. 1996, Ch. 1042, Sec. 53. Effective September 29, 1996.)

Chapter 4. Workers' Compensation

(Chapter 4 added by Stats. 1996, Ch. 1042, Sec. 53.)

34640. (a) A motor carrier permit shall not be granted to any motor carrier of property until one of the following is filed with the department:

(1) A certificate of workers' compensation coverage for its employees issued by an admitted insurer.

(2) A certification of consent to self-insure issued by the Director of Industrial Relations, and the identity of the administrator of the carrier's workers' compensation self-insurance plan.

(3) A statement, under penalty of perjury, stating that, in its operations as a motor carrier of property, it does not employ any person in any manner so as to become subject to the workers' compensation laws of this state.

(b) The workers' compensation certified under paragraph (1) of subdivision (a) shall be effective until canceled. The insurer shall provide to the motor carrier of property and to the department a notice of cancellation not less than 30 days in advance of the effective date.

(c) If, after filing the statement described in paragraph (3) of subdivision (a), the carrier becomes subject to the workers' compensation laws of this state, the carrier shall promptly notify the department that the carrier is withdrawing its statement under paragraph (3) of subdivision (a), and shall simultaneously file the certificate described in either paragraph (1) or (2) of subdivision (a).

(d) Whenever the department determines or is notified that the certificate of workers' compensation insurance or certification to self-insure a motor carrier of property will lapse or be terminated, the department shall suspend the carrier's permit effective on the date of the lapse or termination, unless the motor carrier provides evidence of valid insurance coverage pursuant to subdivision (a).

(1) If the carrier's permit is suspended, the carrier shall pay a reinstatement fee as set forth in Section 34671, and prior to conducting on-highway operations, present proof of valid insurance coverage pursuant to subdivision (a) in order to have the permit reinstated.

(2) If the evidence provided by the carrier of valid insurance coverage pursuant to subdivision (a) demonstrates that a lapse in coverage for the carrier's operation did not occur, the reinstatement fee shall be waived.

(Amended by Stats. 2007, Ch. 58, Sec. 3. Effective January 1, 2008.)

Chapter 6. Fines and Penalties

(Chapter 6 added by Stats. 1996, Ch. 1042, Sec. 53.)

34660. (a) A motor carrier of property, after its motor carrier permit has been suspended by the department, who continues to operate as a motor carrier, either independently or for another motor carrier, is guilty of a misdemeanor, punishable by a fine of not more than two thousand five hundred dollars ($2,500), or by imprisonment in the county jail for not more than three months, or by both that fine and imprisonment.

(b) Each violation of this section is a separate and distinct offense, and, in the case of a continuing violation, each day's continuance of operation as a carrier in violation of this section is a separate and distinct offense.

(c) Upon finding that a motor carrier of property is willfully violating this section after being advised that it is not operating in compliance with the laws of this state, the court may issue an injunction to stop the carrier's continued operation.

(d) A member of the Department of the California Highway Patrol may impound a vehicle or combination of vehicles operated by a motor carrier of property, when the vehicle or combination of vehicles is found upon a highway, any public lands, or an offstreet parking facility and the motor carrier is found to be in violation of this section or of subdivision (a) of Section 34620. For purposes of this subdivision, the vehicle shall be released to the registered owner or authorized agent only after the registered owner or authorized agent furnishes the Department of the California Highway Patrol with proof of current registration, a currently valid driver's license of the appropriate class to operate the vehicle or combination of vehicles, and proof of compliance with this division. The registered owner or authorized agent is responsible for all towing and storage charges related to the impoundment.

(Amended by Stats. 1997, Ch. 652, Sec. 22. Effective January 1, 1998.)

34661. Any person or corporation who violates any provision of this division is guilty of a misdemeanor, punishable by a fine of not more than two thousand five hundred dollars ($2,500), or by imprisonment in the county jail for not more than three months, or by both that fine and imprisonment.

(Added by Stats. 1996, Ch. 1042, Sec. 53. Effective September 29, 1996.)

34670. Any violation of Division 14.8 (commencing with Section 34500) or any violation that results in a suspension or revocation of the motor carrier permit pursuant to Section 34505.6 or 34623, or subdivision (d) of Section 34624, in addition to any other penalties, shall be sanctioned as follows:

(a) If there have been no prior sanctions imposed on the permitholder, the permit shall be suspended for 30 days.

(b) If the permit had been suspended once prior in the previous 36 months, the permit shall be suspended for 60 days.

(c) If the permit had been previously suspended two or more times in the previous 36 months, the permit shall be suspended for 90 days, and a fine of one thousand five hundred dollars ($1,500) shall be imposed.

(Amended by Stats. 1997, Ch. 652, Sec. 23. Effective January 1, 1998.)

34671. Except as provided under subdivision (c) of Section 34630 and subdivision (d) of Section 34640, a motor carrier permit suspended or revoked under the provisions of this code shall not be reinstated until a fee of one hundred fifty dollars ($150) has been paid, and the motor carrier permitholder has met all requirements for the issuance of a permit.

(Amended by Stats. 2007, Ch. 58, Sec. 4. Effective January 1, 2008.)

34672. If a motor carrier permit is paid for by a check that is dishonored by the bank, the permit shall be canceled. The department shall notify the carrier that the check was dishonored and that the permit will be canceled 30 days from the date of notification if the applicant does not make restitution. If the applicant does not make restitution for the dishonored check, and pay the dishonored check fee within 30 days of the notice, the application for a motor carrier permit shall be canceled.

(Amended by Stats. 2001, Ch. 825, Sec. 18. Effective January 1, 2002.)

Division 14.86. Private Carriers of Passengers Registration Act

(Division 14.86 added by Stats. 2017, Ch. 421, Sec. 40.)

34680. This division may be cited as the Private Carriers of Passengers Registration Act.

(Added by Stats. 2017, Ch. 421, Sec. 40. (SB 19) Effective January 1, 2018. Operative July 1, 2018, pursuant to Section 34693.)

34681. (a) For purposes of this division, "private carrier" means a not-for-hire motor carrier, as defined in Section 408, who transports passengers and is required to obtain a carrier identification number pursuant to Section 34507.5, including an organization that provides transportation services incidental to the operation of a youth camp that is either a nonprofit organization that qualifies for tax exemption under Section 501(c)(3) of the Internal Revenue Code or an organization that operates an organized camp, as defined in Section 18897 of the Health and Safety Code, serving youth 18 years of age or younger.

(b) For purposes of this division, "private carrier" does not include either of the following:

(1) The operator of an automobile rental business that uses vehicles owned or leased by that operator, without charge other than as may be included in the automobile rental charges, to carry its customers to or from its office or facility where rental vehicles are furnished or returned after the rental period.

(2) The operator of a hotel, motel, or other place of temporary lodging that provides transportation service in vehicles owned or leased by that operator, without charge other than as may be included in the charges for lodging, between the lodging facility and an air, rail, water, or bus passenger terminal or between the lodging facility and any place of entertainment or commercial attraction, including, but not limited to, facilities providing snow skiing. Nothing in this subdivision authorizes the operator of a hotel, motel, or other place of temporary lodging to provide any round-trip sightseeing service without a permit, as required by subdivision (c) of Section 5384 of the Public Utilities Code.

(Added by Stats. 2017, Ch. 421, Sec. 40. (SB 19) Effective January 1, 2018. Operative July 1, 2018, pursuant to Section 34693.)

34682. The California Department of Tax and Fee Administration shall furnish, upon request, whatever information from its records may be required to assist the department and the Department of the California Highway Patrol in the effective enforcement of this division.

(Added by Stats. 2017, Ch. 421, Sec. 40. (SB 19) Effective January 1, 2018. Operative July 1, 2018, pursuant to Section 34693.)

34683. (a) Except as provided in Section 34686, a private carrier of passengers shall not operate a motor vehicle on any public highway in this state unless its operation is currently registered with the department. The department shall grant registration upon the filing of the application and the payment of the fee as required by this division, subject to the private carrier of passengers' compliance with this division. A private carrier of passengers who is exempt from registration need not file a notice of exemption.

(b) To satisfy the registration requirement described in subdivision (a), a private carrier of passengers shall submit required fees and all of the following information and documents to the department:

(1) The carrier identification number issued to the applicant by the Department of the California Highway Patrol.

(2) Identification information, including business name, form of business, addresses, including mailing address, contact person's name, and phone number.

(3) Whether the registrant provides transportation services incidental to operation of an organized camp, as defined in Section 18897 of the Health and Safety Code, or as a nonprofit that qualifies for a tax exemption under Section 501(c)(3) of the Internal Revenue Code, or neither.

(4) Proof of insurance or financial responsibility as required under Section 34687.

(5) The dated signature of the person completing the form that declares under penalty of perjury that the information provided is true and correct.

(Added by Stats. 2017, Ch. 421, Sec. 40. (SB 19) Effective January 1, 2018. Operative July 1, 2018, pursuant to Section 34693.)

34684. A fee of thirty-five dollars ($35) shall be paid to the department for the filing of the initial registration of private carriers of passengers, and an annual renewal fee of thirty dollars ($30) shall also be paid by private carriers of passengers. The fees required to be paid by private carriers of passengers pursuant to this section shall be deposited in the Motor Vehicle Account in the State Transportation Fund.

(Added by Stats. 2017, Ch. 421, Sec. 40. (SB 19) Effective January 1, 2018. Operative July 1, 2018, pursuant to Section 34693.)

34685. (a) When the Department of the California Highway Patrol issues a carrier identification number pursuant to Section 34507.5 to a private carrier of passengers, it shall inform the carrier of the provisions of this division and the requirement that the carrier register with the department.

(b) The Department of the California Highway Patrol shall periodically, but not less frequently than quarterly, transmit to the department a list of the persons, firms, and corporations identified as private carriers of passengers to which it has issued a carrier identification number. Upon receipt of the list, the department shall notify the private carriers of passengers of the registration requirements and of the penalties for failure to register.

(Added by Stats. 2017, Ch. 421, Sec. 40. (SB 19) Effective January 1, 2018. Operative July 1, 2018, pursuant to Section 34693.)

34686. The State of California and its agencies and political subdivisions are exempt from the registration requirements of this division.

(Added by Stats. 2017, Ch. 421, Sec. 40. (SB 19) Effective January 1, 2018. Operative July 1, 2018, pursuant to Section 34693.)

34687. (a) Registration shall not be granted to a private carrier of passengers until proof of financial responsibility is filed by an insurer or surety with the department. The department may accept only a currently effective certificate of insurance issued by a company licensed to write that insurance in this state or by a nonadmitted insurer subject to Section 1763 of the Insurance Code, and only if the policy represented by the certificate meets the minimum insurance requirements contained in Section 34692, or a surety bond evidencing protection against liability imposed by law for the payment of damages for personal injury to, or death of, a person or property damage, or both. Each certificate shall be valid until canceled, and may only be canceled upon 30 days' written notice submitted to the department by the carrier or surety.

(b) Whenever the department determines that the certificate of insurance or surety bond of a private carrier of passengers has lapsed or been terminated, the department shall suspend the private carrier of passengers' registration. Registration of a private carrier or organization providing transportation services incidental to operation of a youth camp shall stand suspended immediately upon the effective date of the cancellation.

(c) The department shall notify the private carrier of passengers of an action taken under subdivision (b).

(Amended by Stats. 2018, Ch. 92, Sec. 212. (SB 1289) Effective January 1, 2019.)

34688. A private carrier of passengers shall display the carrier identification number, as required by Section 34507.5, on the vehicles operated pursuant to the registration granted under this division.

(Added by Stats. 2017, Ch. 421, Sec. 40. (SB 19) Effective January 1, 2018. Operative July 1, 2018, pursuant to Section 34693.)

34689. The department shall periodically, but not less frequently than quarterly, transmit to the Department of the California Highway Patrol a list of persons, firms, and corporations that have received a carrier identification number from the Department of the California Highway Patrol, but that have not registered with the department. The Department of the California Highway Patrol may use this list in its normal enforcement activities, including terminal inspections and roadside enforcement, as prima facie evidence of a failure to register.

(Added by Stats. 2017, Ch. 421, Sec. 40. (SB 19) Effective January 1, 2018. Operative July 1, 2018, pursuant to Section 34693.)

34690. (a) Any person or corporation that violates any provision of this division is guilty of a misdemeanor, and is punishable by a fine of not more than two thousand five hundred dollars ($2,500), or by imprisonment in the county jail for not more than three months, or both.

(b) A violation of this section is an infraction subject to the procedures described in Sections 19.6 and 19.7 of the Penal Code when the conditions specified in either paragraph (1) or (2) of subdivision (d) of Section 17 of the Penal Code are met.

(Added by Stats. 2017, Ch. 421, Sec. 40. (SB 19) Effective January 1, 2018. Operative July 1, 2018, pursuant to Section 34693.)

34691. (a) Upon receipt of a written recommendation from the Department of the California Highway Patrol that the registration of a private carrier of passengers be suspended for failure to either (1) maintain any vehicle of the carrier in a safe operating condition or to comply with this code or with regulations contained in Title 13 of the California Code of Regulations relative to motor carrier safety, if that failure is either a consistent failure or presents an imminent danger to public safety, or (2) enroll all drivers in the pull-notice system as required by Section 1808.1, the department shall, pending a hearing in the matter pursuant to subdivision (d), suspend the carrier's registration. The Department of the California Highway Patrol's written recommendation shall specifically indicate compliance with subdivision (c).

(b) A private carrier of passengers whose registration is suspended pursuant to subdivision (a) may obtain a reinspection of its terminal and vehicles by the Department of the California Highway Patrol by submitting a written request for reinstatement to the department and paying a reinstatement fee of one hundred twenty-five dollars ($125). The fees required to be paid by carriers of passengers pursuant to this section shall be deposited in the Motor Vehicle Account in the State Transportation Fund. Upon payment of the fee, the department shall forward a request for reinspection to the Department of the California Highway Patrol, which shall perform a reinspection within a reasonable time. The department shall reinstate a carrier's registration suspended under subdivision (a) promptly upon receipt of a written recommendation from the Department of the California Highway Patrol that the carrier's safety compliance has improved to the satisfaction of the Department of the California Highway Patrol, unless the registration is suspended for another reason or has been revoked.

(c) Before transmitting a recommendation pursuant to subdivision (a) to the department, the Department of the California Highway Patrol shall notify the private carrier of passengers in writing of all of the following:

(1) That the Department of the California Highway Patrol has determined that the carrier's safety record is unsatisfactory, furnishing a copy of any documentation or summary of any other evidence supporting the determination.

(2) That the determination may result in a suspension or revocation of the carrier's registration by the department.

(3) That the carrier may request a review of the determination by the Department of the California Highway Patrol within five days of its receipt of the notice required under this subdivision. If a review pursuant to this paragraph is requested by the carrier, the Department of the California Highway Patrol shall conduct and evaluate that review prior to transmitting any notification to the department pursuant to subdivision (a).

(d) Whenever the department suspends the registration of any private carrier of passengers pursuant to subdivision (a), the department shall furnish the carrier written notice of the suspension and shall hold a hearing within a reasonable time, not to exceed 21 days, after a written request therefor is filed with the department, with a copy thereof furnished to the Department of the California Highway Patrol. At the hearing, the carrier shall show cause why the suspension should not be continued. At the conclusion of the hearing, the department may terminate the suspension, continue the suspension in effect, or revoke the registration. The department may revoke the registration of any carrier suspended pursuant to subdivision (a) at any time 90 days or more after its suspension if the department has not received a written recommendation for reinstatement from the Department of the California Highway Patrol and the carrier has not filed a written request for a hearing with the department.

(Added by Stats. 2017, Ch. 421, Sec. 40. (SB 19) Effective January 1, 2018. Operative July 1, 2018, pursuant to Section 34693.)

34692. (a) Except as provided in subdivision (b), a private carrier of passengers, as defined in Section 34681, that is required to register under Section 34683 shall provide and thereafter continue in effect on each vehicle, so long as the carrier may be engaged in conducting those operations, adequate protection against liability imposed by law upon a carrier in accordance with the following:

(1) For the payment of damages for bodily injury to, or death of, one person in any one accident in the amount of at least fifteen thousand dollars ($15,000).

(2) Subject to the limit for one person, in the amount of at least thirty thousand dollars ($30,000) for bodily injury to, or death of, two or more persons in any one accident.

(3) For injury to, or destruction of, property of others in the amount of at least five thousand dollars ($5,000) for any one accident.

(b) Transportation services incidental to operation of a youth camp that are provided by either a nonprofit organization described in Section 501(c)(3) of the Internal Revenue Code (26 U.S.C. Sec. 501 (c)(3)), that is exempt from taxation under Section 501(a) of that code (26 U.S.C. Sec. 501(a)), or an organization that operates an organized camp, as defined in Section 18897 of the Health and Safety Code, serving youth 18 years of age or younger shall provide and thereafter continue in effect, so long as it may be engaged in conducting those operations, the following minimum amounts of general liability insurance coverage for vehicles that are used to transport youth:

(1) A minimum of five hundred thousand dollars ($500,000) of general liability insurance coverage for passenger vehicles designed to carry up to eight passengers. For organized camps, as defined in Section 18897 of the Health and Safety Code, there shall be an additional two hundred fifty thousand dollars ($250,000) of general umbrella policy that covers vehicles.

(2) A minimum of one million dollars ($1,000,000) of general liability insurance coverage for vehicles designed to carry up to 15 passengers. For organized camps, as defined in Section 18897 of the Health and Safety Code, there shall be an additional five hundred thousand dollars ($500,000) of general umbrella policy that covers vehicles.

(3) A minimum of one million five hundred thousand dollars ($1,500,000) of general liability insurance coverage for vehicles designed to carry more than 15 passengers, and an additional three million five hundred thousand dollars ($3,500,000) of general umbrella liability insurance policy that covers vehicles.

(Amended by Stats. 2018, Ch. 92, Sec. 213. (SB 1289) Effective January 1, 2019.)

34693. This division shall become operative on July 1, 2018.

(Added by Stats. 2017, Ch. 421, Sec. 40. (SB 19) Effective January 1, 2018. Note: Operative date applies to Division 14.86, commencing with Section 34680.)

Division 14.9. Motor Vehicle Damage Control

(Division 14.9 added by Stats. 1971, Ch. 598.)

Chapter 1. Short Title

(Chapter 1 added by Stats. 1971, Ch. 598.)

34700. This division may be cited as the Greene-Harmer Motor Vehicle Damage Control Act.

(Added by Stats. 1971, Ch. 598.)

Chapter 2. General Provisions and Definitions

(Chapter 2 added by Stats. 1971, Ch. 598.)

34710. As used in this division, "passenger vehicle" means any motor vehicle defined in Section 465, except any of the following motor vehicles:

(a) Motorcycles.

(b) Housecars.

(c) Specially constructed vehicles.

(d) Motor vehicles equipped with four-wheel drive.

(e) Motor vehicles constructed on a truck chassis.

(f) Motor vehicles operated for hire, compensation, or profit.

(g) Makes of motor vehicles of a model year manufactured or sold in California in quantities of less than 2,000 units for each such model year.

(h) Motor vehicles designed and constructed by the manufacturer of such vehicles, for off-highway use, as determined by the Department of Motor Vehicles.

(Amended by Stats. 1974, Ch. 635.)

34715. No new passenger vehicle, except a passenger vehicle certified by its manufacturer as having been manufactured prior to September 1, 1973, shall be sold or registered on and after September 1, 1973, unless it has a manufacturer's warranty that it is equipped with an appropriate energy-absorption system that meets the requirement for energy absorption systems set by the National Highway Traffic Safety Administration.

(Amended by Stats. 1977, Ch. 880.)

Chapter 3. Departmental Action

(Chapter 3 added by Stats. 1971, Ch. 598.)

34725. Any violation of any provisions of this division may be enjoined in a civil action brought by the Attorney General in the name of the people of the State of California, upon request of the Department of Motor Vehicles, except that it shall not be necessary to show lack of adequate remedy at law or to show irreparable damage or loss.

(Added by Stats. 1971, Ch. 598.)

Division 15. Size, Weight, and Load

(Division 15 enacted by Stats. 1959, Ch. 3.)

Chapter 1. General Provisions

(Chapter 1 enacted by Stats. 1959, Ch. 3.)

35000. The provisions of this division refer exclusively to the size and weight of, and loads upon, vehicles when operated upon the highways.

(Enacted by Stats. 1959, Ch. 3.)

35001. The provisions of this division, except those requiring a permit for overweight loads, do not apply to motor trucks equipped with snow removal devices.

(Enacted by Stats. 1959, Ch. 3.)

35002. (a) (1) This division does not apply to an authorized emergency vehicle owned or operated by a governmental agency while being used in responding to and returning from emergency fire calls, while being moved from place to place in anticipation of emergency fire calls, when used during training in any fire service application or during fire prevention activities, or when vehicles ordinarily used for those purposes are necessarily transported for vehicle maintenance, repair, or service. This subdivision only applies to vehicles purchased prior to January 1, 1994. Vehicles purchased on January 1, 1992, to and including December 31, 1993, shall meet the applicable requirements of Standards 1901 to 1904, inclusive, of the National Fire Protection Association, as those standards were in effect on December 31, 1991.

(2) All vehicles described in paragraph (1) first purchased on or after January 1, 1994, shall comply with the applicable permit requirements adopted by the Department of Transportation.

(3) For purposes of this section, "purchased" means the date that the operating agency enters into a contract to purchase the vehicle.

(b) All vehicles described in subdivision (a) purchased on or after January 1, 1994, shall meet the following requirements:

(1) It shall be the responsibility of the manufacturer to provide a gross axle weight rating (GAWR), gross combined weight rating (GCWR), and gross vehicle weight rating (GVWR), adequate to carry a full water tank with the allowance for personnel and miscellaneous equipment, including hose load, shown in the table below:

	Personnel	Misc. Equipment
Pumpers	1,200 lbs.	2,000 lbs.
Light attack apparatus	600 lbs.	900 lbs.
Water towers	1,200 lbs.	1,500 lbs.
Aerial platforms with ground ladders	1,200 lbs.	2,500 lbs.
Aerial ladders with ground ladders	1,200 lbs.	2,500 lbs.

Fire apparatus shall be weighed and certified by the manufacturer to determine compliance with the table above prior to acceptance by the purchaser. Apparatus and chassis manufacturers shall furnish certification of the gross vehicle weight rating (GVWR), gross combined weight rating (GCWR), and gross axle weight rating (GAWR) on a nameplate affixed to the apparatus.

(2) A fire apparatus exceeding 31,000 pounds gross vehicle weight rating (GVWR) shall be equipped with a retarder.

(3) For purposes of this section, a "fire apparatus" is a vehicle designed, maintained, and used under emergency conditions to transport personnel and equipment, or for the suppression of fires or mitigation of other hazardous situations, consistent with the 2009 edition of Standard 1901 of the National Fire Protection Association.

(4) Notwithstanding the weight exemption provided for in Chapter 7 of Division 2 of Title 21 of the California Code of Regulations, effective on July 2, 2010, nor any other provision of law, a fire apparatus vehicle is prohibited from towing or hauling any other vehicle or equipment while operating under an overweight permit.

(5) This chapter and Chapter 7 of Division 2 of Title 21 of the California Code of Regulations do not limit the discretion of the department or a local government to deny an application for an overweight permit on the basis of good cause.

(c) A vehicle owned, operated, or rented by a public agency that is being used in responding to or returning from an emergency, may be operated as required, if a reasonable effort is first made by the agency to obtain verbal permission from an authorized officer or employee of the agency having jurisdiction of the highways used, and, upon termination of the emergency, when the vehicle is returning from the site of the emergency, the public agency either obtains a permit at the location of the emergency or makes a reasonable effort to obtain verbal permission from an authorized officer or employee of the agency having jurisdiction of the highways used, and obtains a written permit for that use pursuant to Section 35780 not later than three days after the date of the emergency. As used in this subdivision, "emergency" means a condition that poses an imminent threat of loss of property or a hazard to life, as determined by the public agency charged with responsibility to respond thereto.

(d) A governmental agency operating an authorized emergency vehicle or other vehicle subject to this section is liable to the governmental agency having jurisdiction of a state or county highway for the damage to the highway or a highway structure caused by the operation of the vehicle of a size or weight of vehicle or load exceeding that specified in this division. The cost of repair of the damage is a proper charge against the support fund of the governmental agency operating the oversize or overweight vehicle.

(e) Neither the state nor an agency thereof is liable for damage to a highway or highway structure caused by vehicles operated, pursuant to this section, by or on behalf of a local authority or any other local governmental entity.

(Amended by Stats. 2010, Ch. 487, Sec. 1. (SB 1220) Effective September 29, 2010.)

35003. For the purpose of this division, booms, masts, machinery or other equipment which is not attendant to the efficient operation of the body of the vehicle but which may be attached to the body or chassis or connected with the driving mechanism, shall be regarded as a load.

(Added by Stats. 1968, Ch. 12.)

Chapter 2. Width

(Chapter 2 enacted by Stats. 1959, Ch. 3.)

35100. (a) The total outside width of any vehicle or its load shall not exceed 102 inches, except as otherwise provided in this chapter.

(b) Notwithstanding any other provision of law, safety devices which the Secretary of Transportation determines to be necessary for the safe and efficient operation of motor vehicles shall not be included in the calculation of width as specified in subdivision (a).

(c) Any city or county may, by ordinance, prohibit a combination of vehicles of a total width in excess of 96 inches upon highways under its jurisdiction. The ordinance shall not be effective until appropriate signs are erected indicating the streets affected.

(Amended by Stats. 1988, Ch. 1452, Sec. 5. Effective September 28, 1988.)

35100.1. For purposes of subdivision (a) of Section 35100, the following apply:

(a) The metric equivalent of 102 inches, 2.6 meters, meets the requirement of Section 35100.

(b) The width measurement of any vehicle with side walls shall be made from the outside wall of the two opposite sides of the vehicle.

(Added by Stats. 1988, Ch. 1452, Sec. 6. Effective September 28, 1988.)

35100.5. The total outside width of a cotton module mover operated on the highways pursuant to Section 35555 and the load thereon shall not exceed 130 inches in width. However, a county board of supervisors, with respect to any or all county highways within its jurisdiction or any portion thereof, may by resolution prohibit or limit the operation of cotton module movers exceeding the maximum width specified in Section 35100.

(Added by Stats. 1984, Ch. 270, Sec. 3. Effective July 3, 1984.)

35101. When any vehicle is equipped with pneumatic tires, the maximum width from the outside of one wheel and tire to the outside of the opposite outer wheel and tire shall not exceed 108 inches, but the outside width of the body of the vehicle or the load thereon shall not exceed 102 inches.

Vehicles manufactured, reconstructed, or modified after the effective date of amendments to this section enacted during the 1983 portion of the 1983–84 Regular Session of the Legislature, to utilize the 102 inch maximum width dimension, shall be equipped with axles, tires, and wheels of sufficient width to adequately and safely stabilize the vehicle. The Department of the California Highway Patrol shall conduct tests relating to the dynamic stability of vehicles utilizing body widths over 96 inches, up to and including 102 inches, to determine the necessity for establishing performance standards under the authority of Section 34500. Such standards if established shall be consistent with width standards established by or under the authority of the United States Department of Transportation.

(Amended by Stats. 1983, Ch. 145, Sec. 2. Effective June 28, 1983.)

35102. When any vehicle carries a load of loosely piled agricultural products such as hay, straw, or leguminous plants in bulk but not crated, baled, boxed, or sacked, such load of loosely piled material and any loading racks retaining the same shall not exceed 120 inches in width.

(Enacted by Stats. 1959, Ch. 3.)

35103. (a) A vehicle used for recreational purposes may exceed the maximum width established under Section 35100 if the excess width is attributable to an appurtenance, excluding a safety device, that does not exceed six inches beyond either sidewall of the vehicle.

(b) For the purposes of subdivision (a), an appurtenance is an integral part of a vehicle and includes, but is not limited to, awnings, grab handles, lighting equipment, cameras, and vents. An appurtenance may not be used as a load carrying device.

(Added by Stats. 2003, Ch. 222, Sec. 3. Effective January 1, 2004.)

35104. The limitations as to width do not apply to the following vehicles except that these vehicles shall not exceed a width of 120 inches:

(a) Special mobile equipment.

(b) Special construction or highway maintenance equipment.

(c) Motor vehicles designed for, and used exclusively to, haul feed for livestock that are exempted from registration by subdivision (c) of Section 36102, except when operated on a highway during darkness.

(Amended by Stats. 1984, Ch. 1021, Sec. 1.)

35105. Any city organized under a freeholders' charter may by ordinance permit a total outside width of vehicle and load in excess of the limits set forth in Sections 35100, 35101, 35102, 35104, and 35106 when the vehicle is used exclusively within the boundary limits of the city.

(Amended by Stats. 1983, Ch. 145, Sec. 4. Effective June 28, 1983.)

35106. (a) Motor coaches or buses may have a maximum width not exceeding 102 inches.

(b) Notwithstanding subdivision (a), motor coaches or buses operated under the jurisdiction of the Public Utilities Commission in urban or suburban service may have a maximum outside width not exceeding 104 inches, when approved by order of the Public Utilities Commission for use on routes designated by it. Motor coaches or buses operated by common carriers of passengers for hire in urban or suburban service and not under the jurisdiction of the Public Utilities Commission may have a maximum outside width not exceeding 104 inches.

(Amended by Stats. 2006, Ch. 538, Sec. 665. Effective January 1, 2007.)

35107. "Urban and suburban service" means a service performed in urban or suburban areas, or between municipalities in close proximity, except that:

(a) The one-way route mileage of the service shall not be more than 50 miles.

(b) Designated motor coach routes over state highways outside limits of incorporated cities where the one-way route mileage is over 25 miles, but does not exceed 50 miles, shall be approved by the Department of Transportation.

(Amended by Stats. 1974, Ch. 545.)

35109. Lights, mirrors, or devices which are required to be mounted upon a vehicle under this code may extend beyond the permissible width of the vehicle to a distance not exceeding 10 inches on each side of the vehicle.

(Amended by Stats. 1983, Ch. 145, Sec. 7. Effective June 28, 1983.)

35110. (a) Door handles, hinges, cable cinchers, chain binders, aerodynamic devices, holders for the display of placards warning of hazardous materials, and a tarping system and all nonproperty carrying devices or components thereof, may extend three inches on each side of the vehicle.

(b) For purposes of this section, "aerodynamic device" means a device that uses technologies that minimize drag and improve airflow over an entire tractor-trailer vehicle. These include gap fairings that reduce turbulence between the tractor and trailer, side skirts that minimize wind under the trailer, and rear fairings that reduce turbulence and pressure drop at the rear of the trailer, provided that these devices shall not adversely impact the vehicle's swept width and turning characteristics and that the primary purpose of the device is not for advertising.

(c) (1) For purposes of this section, "a tarping system" means a movable device used to enclose the cargo area of flatbed semitrailers or trailers.

(2) Subdivision (a) applies to all component parts of a tarping system, including the following:

(A) The transverse structure at the front of the vehicle to which the sliding walls and roof of the tarp mechanism are attached, provided the structure is not also intended or designed to comply with Section 393.106 of Title 49 of the Code of Federal Regulations. The transverse structure may be up to 108 inches wide if properly centered so that neither side extends more than three inches beyond the structural edge of the vehicle.

(B) The side rails running the length of the vehicle.

(C) The rear doors, provided the only function of the rear doors is to seal the cargo area and anchor the sliding walls and roof.

(D) The "wings" designed to close the gap between a headerboard designed to comply with Section 393.106 of Title 49 of the Code of Federal Regulations and the movable walls and roof of a tarping system, provided they are add-on pieces designed to bear only the load of the tarping system itself and are not integral parts of the load-bearing headerboard structure.

(d) For purposes of this section, a "headerboard designed to comply with Section 393.106 of Title 49 of the Code of Federal Regulations" is load bearing and does not exceed 102 inches in width.

(Amended by Stats. 2014, Ch. 133, Sec. 1. (SB 469) Effective January 1, 2015.)

35111. No passenger vehicle shall be operated on any highway with any load carried thereon extending beyond the line of the fenders on its left side or more than six inches beyond the line of the fenders on its right side.

(Amended by Stats. 1961, Ch. 120.)

Chapter 3. Height

(Chapter 3 enacted by Stats. 1959, Ch. 3.)

35250. No vehicle or load shall exceed a height of 14 feet measured from the surface upon which the vehicle stands, except that a double-deck bus may not exceed a height of 14 feet, 3 inches. Any vehicle or load which exceeds a height of 13 feet, 6 inches, shall only be operated on those highways where deemed to be safe by the owner of the vehicle or the entity operating the bus.

(Amended by Stats. 1984, Ch. 1287, Sec. 1. Effective September 19, 1984. Operative January 1, 1985, by Sec. 5 of Ch. 1287.)

35251. (a) A boom or mast which is designed to be raised and lowered by hydraulic mechanisms and which is a constituent part of or an attachment to a vehicle or machine, shall be securely chained or otherwise restrained to ensure compliance with Section 35250 while the vehicle or machine is being transported as a load or driven upon any highway.

(b) Subdivision (a) does not apply when the configuration and design of the hydraulic boom effectively restrain the movement of the boom during transit.

(Amended by Stats. 1994, Ch. 704, Sec. 21. Effective January 1, 1995.)

35252. (a) A pilot car may operate a vertical clearance measuring device with a height in excess of 14 feet when escorting a permitted overheight load. The pilot car may also operate the vertical clearance measuring device when surveying a route for a permitted overheight load.

(b) Any vertical measuring device used by a pilot car shall be designed and operated so as to avoid any damages to overhead structures. The measuring device shall be securely affixed to the pilot car, and shall be operated in a manner that does not create a hazard to surrounding traffic.

(c) The operator of the pilot car shall not reduce the vehicle's speed more than 20 miles per hour below the posted speed limit on the roadway to measure overhead clearance, nor exit the vehicle to measure the clearance of overhead structures from a vantage point on or above the roadway.

(Added by Stats. 1988, Ch. 460, Sec. 5.)

Chapter 4. Length

(Chapter 4 enacted by Stats. 1959, Ch. 3.)

35400. (a) A vehicle may not exceed a length of 40 feet.

(b) This section does not apply to any of the following:

(1) A vehicle used in a combination of vehicles when the excess length is caused by auxiliary parts, equipment, or machinery not used as space to carry any part of the load, except that the combination of vehicles shall not exceed the length provided for combination vehicles.

(2) A vehicle, when the excess length is caused by any parts necessary to comply with the fender and mudguard regulations of this code.

(3) (A) An articulated bus or articulated trolley coach that does not exceed a length of 60 feet.

(B) An articulated bus or articulated trolley coach described in subparagraph (A) may be equipped with a folding device attached to the front of the bus or trolley if the device is designed and used exclusively for transporting bicycles. The device, including any bicycles transported thereon, shall be mounted in a manner that does not materially affect efficiency or visibility of vehicle safety equipment, and shall not extend more than 36 inches from the front body of the bus or trolley coach when fully deployed. The handlebars of a bicycle that is transported on a device described in this subparagraph shall not extend more than 42 inches from the front of the bus.

(C) (i) An articulated bus or articulated trolley coach described in subparagraph (A) may be equipped with a folding device attached to the front of the bus or trolley if the device is designed and used exclusively for transporting bicycles. The device, including any bicycles transported thereon, shall be mounted in a manner that does not materially affect efficiency or visibility of vehicle safety equipment, and shall not extend more than 40 inches from the front body of the bus or trolley coach when fully deployed. The handlebars of a bicycle that is transported on a device described in this subparagraph shall not extend more than 46 inches from the front of the bus.

(ii) In order for a public agency operating transit services to operate an articulated bus or articulated trolley coach equipped with a front-mounted bicycle rack, as described in and pursuant to clause (i), the public agency shall establish a route review committee comprised of four members as follows:

(I) One member of the public agency who is appointed by the general manager of the public agency.

(II) One member who is a traffic engineer and is employed and appointed by the public agency that has jurisdiction over the largest proportional share of routes among all affected agencies.

(III) One member appointed by the labor organization that is the exclusive representative of the bus drivers of the public agency.

(IV) One member of the law enforcement agency that has jurisdiction over the largest proportional share of routes among all affected agencies.

(iii) The committee members shall be appointed not more than 30 days after receipt of a public agency proposal to equip a 60-foot articulated bus or articulated trolley coach with a front-mounted bicycle rack, as described in clause (i).

(iv) The purpose of the committee is to ensure the safe operation of a 60-foot articulated bus or articulated trolley coach that is equipped with a front-mounted bicycle rack, as described in clause (i). The committee, by a majority vote, shall make a determination of which routes are suitable for the safe operation of a 60-foot articulated bus or articulated trolley coach that is equipped with a front-mounted bicycle rack, as described in clause (i). The committee may include a field review of the proposed routes.

(4) A semitrailer while being towed by a motortruck or truck tractor, if the distance from the kingpin to the rearmost axle of the semitrailer does not exceed 40 feet for semitrailers having two or more axles, or 38 feet for semitrailers having one axle if the semitrailer does not, exclusive of attachments, extend forward of the rear of the cab of the motortruck or truck tractor.

(5) A bus or house car when the excess length is caused by the projection of a front safety bumper or a rear safety bumper, or both. The safety bumper shall not cause the length of the vehicle to exceed the maximum legal limit by more than one foot in the front and one foot in the rear. For the purposes of this chapter, "safety bumper" means any device that is fitted on an existing bumper or which replaces the bumper and is constructed, treated, or manufactured to absorb energy upon impact.

(6) A schoolbus, when the excess length is caused by the projection of a crossing control arm. For the purposes of this chapter, "crossing control arm" means an extendable and retractable device fitted to the front of a schoolbus that is designed to impede movement of pupils exiting the schoolbus directly in front of the schoolbus so that pupils are visible to the driver while they are moving in front of the schoolbus. An operator of a schoolbus shall not extend a crossing control arm while the schoolbus is in motion. Except when activated, a crossing control arm shall not cause the maximum length of the schoolbus to be extended by more than 10 inches, inclusive of any front safety bumper. Use of a crossing control arm by the operator of a schoolbus does not, in and of itself, fulfill his or her responsibility to ensure the safety of students crossing a highway or private road pursuant to Section 22112.

(7) A bus, when the excess length is caused by a device, located in front of the front axle, for lifting wheelchairs into the bus. That device shall not cause the length of the bus to be extended by more than 18 inches, inclusive of any front safety bumper.

(8) A bus, when the excess length is caused by a device attached to the rear of the bus designed and used exclusively for the transporting of bicycles. This device may be up to 10 feet in length, if the device, along with any other device permitted pursuant to this section, does not cause the total length of the bus, including any device or load, to exceed 50 feet.

(9) A bus operated by a public agency or a passenger stage corporation, as defined in Section 226 of the Public Utilities Code, used in transit system service, other than a schoolbus, when the excess length is caused by a folding device attached to the front of the bus which is designed and used exclusively for transporting bicycles. The device, including any bicycles transported thereon, shall be mounted in a manner that does not materially affect efficiency or visibility of vehicle safety equipment, and shall not extend more than 40 inches from the front body of the bus when fully deployed. The handlebars of a bicycle that is transported on a device described in this paragraph shall not extend more than 46 inches from the front of the bus. A device described in this paragraph may not be used on a bus that, exclusive of the device, exceeds 40 feet in length, or 60 feet in length pursuant to paragraph (3), or on a bus having a device attached to the rear of the bus pursuant to paragraph (8).

(10) (A) A bus of a length of up to 45 feet when operating on those highways specified in subdivision (a) of Section 35401.5. The Department of Transportation or local authorities, with respect to highways under their respective jurisdictions, may not deny reasonable access to a bus of a length of up to 45 feet between the highways specified in subdivision (a) of Section 35401.5 and points of loading and unloading for motor carriers of passengers as required by the federal Intermodal Surface Transportation Efficiency Act of 1991 (Public Law 102-240).

(B) (i) A bus operated by a public agency and on those highways specified in subparagraph (A) may be equipped with a folding device attached to the front of the bus that is designed and used exclusively for transporting bicycles. The device, including all bicycles transported thereon, may be mounted in a manner that does not materially affect efficiency or visibility of vehicle safety equipment, and may not extend more than 36 inches from the front body of the bus when fully deployed. The handlebars of a bicycle that is transported on a device described in this subparagraph may not extend more than 42 inches from the front of the bus. The total length of the bus, including the folding device or load, may not exceed 48.5 feet.

(ii) A route review committee, established under this subparagraph, shall review the routes where a public agency proposes to operate a 45-foot bus equipped with a front-mounted bicycle rack. The committee shall be comprised of three members as follows:

(I) One member from the public agency appointed by the general manager of the public agency.

(II) One member who is a traffic engineer and is employed and selected by the public agency that has jurisdiction over the largest proportional share of routes among all affected agencies.

(III) One member appointed by the labor organization that is the exclusive representative of the bus drivers of the public agency. If there is no exclusive representative of the bus drivers, a bus driver member shall be chosen by a majority vote of the bus drivers employed by the agency.

(iii) The members of the committee shall be selected not more than 30 days after receipt of a public agency proposal to equip a 45-foot bus with a front-mounted bicycle rack.

(iv) The review shall include a field review of the proposed routes. The purpose of the committee is to ensure the safe operation of a 45-foot bus that is equipped with a front-mounted bicycle rack. The committee by a unanimous vote, shall make a determination of which routes are suitable for the safe operation of a 45-foot bus that is equipped with a front-mounted bicycle rack. These determinations shall be consistent with the operating requirements specified in subparagraph (A). It is the intent of the Legislature that the field review required under this subparagraph include consultation with traffic engineers from affected public agencies that have jurisdiction over segments of the route or routes under review, to ensure coordination with all affected state and local public road agencies that may potentially be impacted due to the operation of a 45-foot bus with a front-mounted bicycle rack.

(11) (A) A house car of a length of up to 45 feet when operating on the National System of Interstate and Defense Highways or when using those portions of federal aid primary system highways that have been qualified by the United States Secretary of Transportation for that use, or when using routes appropriately identified by the Department of Transportation or local authorities, with respect to highways under their respective jurisdictions.

(B) A house car described in subparagraph (A) may be operated on a highway that provides reasonable access to facilities for purposes limited to fuel, food, and lodging when that access is consistent with the safe operation of the vehicle and when the facility is within one road mile of identified points of ingress and egress to or from highways specified in subparagraph (A) for use by that vehicle.

(C) As used in this paragraph and paragraph (10), "reasonable access" means access substantially similar to that authorized for combinations of vehicles pursuant to subdivision (c) of Section 35401.5.

(D) Any access route established by a local authority pursuant to subdivision (d) of Section 35401.5 is open for access by a house car of a length of up to 45 feet. In addition, local authorities may establish a process whereby access to services by house cars of a length of up to 45 feet may be applied for upon a route not previously established as an access route. The denial of a request for access to services shall be only on the basis of safety and an engineering analysis of the proposed access route. In lieu of processing an access application, local authorities, with respect to highways under their jurisdiction, may provide signing, mapping, or a listing of highways, as necessary, to indicate the use of these specific routes by a house car of a length of up to 45 feet.

(c) The Legislature, by increasing the maximum permissible kingpin to rearmost axle distance to 40 feet effective January 1, 1987, as provided in paragraph (4) of subdivision (b), does not intend this action to be considered a precedent for any future increases in truck size and length limitations.

(d) Any transit bus equipped with a folding device installed on or after January 1, 1999, that is permitted under subparagraph (B) of paragraph (3) of subdivision (b) or under paragraph (9) of subdivision (b) shall be additionally equipped with any of the following:

(1) An indicator light that is visible to the driver and is activated whenever the folding device is in an extended position.

(2) Any other device or mechanism that provides notice to the driver that the folding device is in an extended position.

(3) A mechanism that causes the folding device to retract automatically from an extended position.

(e) (1) A person may not improperly or unsafely mount a bicycle on a device described in subparagraph (B) of paragraph (3) of subdivision (b), or in paragraph (9) or (10) of subdivision (b).

(2) Notwithstanding subdivision (a) of Section 23114, or subdivision (a) of Section 24002, or any other law, when a bicycle is improperly or unsafely loaded by a passenger onto a transit bus, the passenger, and not the driver, is liable for any violation of this code that is attributable to the improper or unlawful loading of the bicycle.

(Amended by Stats. 2018, Ch. 22, Sec. 1. (AB 3124) Effective January 1, 2019.)

35400.5. Subdivision (a) of Section 35400 does not apply to a motortruck used solely as a cotton module mover and which does not exceed 48 feet in length.

(Amended by Stats. 1984, Ch. 270, Sec. 4. Effective July 3, 1984.)

35400.6. (a) Subdivision (a) of Section 35400 does not apply to a fifth-wheel travel trailer that does not exceed the following lengths:

(1) Forty-eight feet in length from the foremost point of the trailer to the rear extremity of the trailer.

(2) (A) For a fifth-wheel travel trailer with a single axle, 38 feet in length from the kingpin to the rearmost axle.

(B) For a fifth-wheel travel trailer with two or more axles, 40 feet in length from the kingpin to the rearmost axle.

(b) A manufacturer of a fifth-wheel travel trailer described by subdivision (a) shall include in the delivery documents the information necessary to register that fifth-wheel travel trailer, including its overall length pursuant to paragraph (1) of subdivision (a) and a declaration that its length is in compliance with subparagraph (A) or subparagraph (B) of paragraph (2) of subdivision (a). The dealer may reject acceptance of the fifth-wheel travel trailer if this documentation is not provided.

(Added by Stats. 2013, Ch. 548, Sec. 1. (AB 64) Effective January 1, 2014.)

35400.7. (a) Notwithstanding Section 35400, the Alameda-Contra Costa Transit District created pursuant to Part 1 (commencing with Section 24501) of Division 10 of the Public Utilities Code may install a folding device attached to the front of a bus that is designed and used exclusively for transporting bicycles if the following conditions are met:

(1) The device does not extend more than 40 inches from the front body of the bus when fully deployed.

(2) The device, including all bicycles transported thereon, is mounted in a manner that does not materially affect efficiency or visibility of vehicle safety equipment.

(3) The handlebars of a bicycle that is transported on a device described in this subdivision does not extend more than 46 inches from the front of the bus.

(b) (1) The Alameda-Contra Costa Transit District shall establish a route review committee prior to the installation of the initial folding device, pursuant to subdivision (a), on a bus that is 45 feet in length. The purpose of the committee is to ensure the safe operation of a 45-foot bus that is equipped with a front-mounted bicycle rack.

(2) The committee established pursuant to this subdivision shall perform an initial review of the routes on which the district proposes to operate a 45-foot bus equipped with a front-mounted bicycle rack. The review shall include a field review of the proposed routes.It is the intent of the Legislature that the field review required under this paragraph include consultation with traffic engineers from affected public agencies that have jurisdiction over segments of the route or routes under review, to ensure coordination with all affected state and local public road agencies that may potentially be impacted due to the operation of a 45-foot bus with a front-mounted bicycle rack.

(3) By unanimous vote of all voting members, the committee shall make a determination of the routes that are suitable for the safe operation of a 45-foot bus that is equipped with a front-mounted bicycle rack.

(4) Upon any proposal to make substantive changes or additions to approved routes, those changes shall be subject to review and certification pursuant to paragraph (2) prior to being approved by the committee.

(5) The members of the committee shall be selected not more than 30 days after receipt of the district proposal to equip a 45-foot bus with a front-mounted bicycle rack and shall be comprised of the following members:

(A) One member from the district who shall be appointed by the district's general manager and who shall be a voting member of the committee.

(B) One member who is a traffic engineer selected by the district and who shall be a voting member of the committee.

(C) One member appointed by the labor organization that is the exclusive representative of the busdrivers of the district. If there is no exclusive representative of the busdrivers, a busdriver member shall be chosen by a majority vote of the busdrivers employed by the district. This member shall be a voting member of the committee.

(D) One member appointed by the governing board who shall be a representative of the bicycling community and who shall reside in the district. This member shall be a nonvoting member of the committee.

(c) If a folding device is installed pursuant to subdivision (a), the Alameda-Contra Costa Transit District shall submit a report to the Assembly Committee on Transportation and the Senate Committee on Transportation and Housing on or before December 31, 2014. The report shall include a summary of any incidents where the size of the folding devices was a factor, and a summary of the mobility improvements these folding devices provide.

(Added by Stats. 2009, Ch. 369, Sec. 1. (AB 652) Effective January 1, 2010.)

35400.75. (a) Notwithstanding Section 35400, the Los Angeles County Metropolitan Transportation Authority created pursuant to Chapter 2 (commencing with Section 130050) of Division 12 of the Public Utilities Code may operate articulated buses that do not exceed a length of 82 feet on the route designated as the Orange Line in the County of Los Angeles, and between that route, terminals, and maintenance facilities.

(b) (1) The authority shall establish a route review committee prior to the operation of any bus, pursuant to subdivision (a), that is greater than 60 feet in length.

(2) The committee shall perform a review of the Orange Line route and any necessary routes from the Orange Line to maintenance and storage yards upon which the authority proposes to operate a bus greater than 60 feet in length, pursuant to subdivision (a), prior to the operation of those

buses. The reviews shall include field reviews of the Orange Line and proposed routes. The field reviews shall include both of the following:

(A) Consultation with traffic engineers from public agencies that have jurisdiction over the routes where the buses are proposed to be operated pursuant to subdivision (a), to ensure coordination with the affected state and local public agencies for purposes of public safety.

(B) Consultation with pavement engineers from public agencies that have jurisdiction over the routes where the buses are proposed to be operated pursuant to subdivision (a), to ensure that any impacts of the weight of the vehicles upon any streets and roads that are used to access the right-of-way or are crossed by the right-of-way are considered.

(3) The route review committee shall be comprised of four members, as follows:

(A) A member representing the authority who shall be appointed by the authority's general manager.

(B) A member who is a traffic engineer who shall be appointed by the authority's general manager.

(C) A member appointed by the labor organization that is the exclusive representative of the bus drivers of the authority.

(D) A member representing law enforcement appointed by the law enforcement agency having authority over the proposed routes.

(4) The route review committee shall determine, by majority vote, whether the Orange Line is suitable for the safe operation of a bus exceeding 60 feet in length, but not exceeding 82 feet in length, and shall determine, by majority vote, routes that are suitable for the safe operation of those buses between the Orange Line, maintenance facilities, and storage yards.

(c) Implementation of this section is subject to all of the following:

(1) The collective bargaining requirements under Article 10 (commencing with Section 30750) of Chapter 5 of Part 3 of Division 10 of the Public Utilities Code and the Los Angeles County Metropolitan Transportation Authority Transit Employer-Employee Relations Act (Chapter 7 (commencing with Section 99560) of Part 11 of Division 10 of the Public Utilities Code).

(2) Determination by a majority vote of the route review committee that the Orange Line and the routes between the Orange Line, maintenance facilities, and storage yards are suitable for the safe operation of buses pursuant to subdivision (a).

(3) If portions of the proposed routes are on highways under the jurisdiction of the Department of Transportation, a determination by the Department of the California Highway Patrol and a determination by the Department of Transportation that those portions of the routes are suitable for the operation of buses pursuant to subdivision (a).

(Added by Stats. 2015, Ch. 479, Sec. 1. (AB 726) Effective January 1, 2016.)

35400.8. (a) Notwithstanding Section 35400, the Sacramento Regional Transit District, created pursuant to Article 1 (commencing with Section 6500) of Chapter 5 of Division 7 of Title 1 of the Government Code as a joint powers agency, may install a folding device attached to the front of a bus that is designed and used exclusively for transporting bicycles if the following conditions are met:

(1) The device does not extend more than 40 inches from the front body of the bus when fully deployed.

(2) The device, including all bicycles transported on the device, is mounted in a manner that does not materially affect efficiency or visibility of vehicle safety equipment.

(3) The handlebars of a bicycle that is transported on a device described in this subdivision do not extend more than 46 inches from the front of the bus.

(b) For purposes of this section, "district" means the Sacramento Regional Transit District.

(c) (1) The district shall establish a route review committee prior to the installation of the initial folding device, pursuant to subdivision (a), on a bus that is 45 feet in length. The purpose of the committee is to ensure the safe operation of a 45-foot bus that is equipped with a front-mounted bicycle rack.

(2) The committee established pursuant to this subdivision shall perform an initial review of the routes on which the district proposes to operate a 45-foot bus equipped with a front-mounted bicycle rack. The review shall include a field review of the proposed routes, including consultation with licensed traffic engineers from affected public agencies that have jurisdiction over segments of the route or routes under review in order to ensure coordination with all affected state and local public road agencies that may potentially be impacted due to the operation of a 45-foot bus with a front-mounted bicycle rack.

(3) (A) By unanimous vote of all members, the committee shall make a determination of the routes that are suitable for the safe operation of a 45-foot bus that is equipped with a front-mounted bicycle rack.

(B) Before conducting a vote pursuant to subparagraph (A), the committee shall obtain certification approved by a licensed traffic engineer that all proposed routes are safe for travel by 45-foot buses equipped with the bicycle racks specified in subdivision (a).

(4) Upon any proposal to make substantive changes to additions to approved routes, those changes shall be subject to review and certification pursuant to paragraph (2) prior to being approved by the committee.

(5) The members of the committee shall be selected not more than 30 days after receipt of the district's proposal to equip a 45-foot bus with a front-mounted bicycle rack and shall be comprised of the following members:

(A) One member from the district who shall be appointed by the district's general manager and who shall be a voting member of the committee.

(B) One member who is a licensed traffic engineer selected by the governing board of the district and who shall be a voting member of the committee.

(C) One member appointed by the labor organization that is the exclusive representative of the busdrivers of the district. This member shall be a voting member of the committee.

(D) One member appointed by the governing board of the district who shall be a representative of the bicycling community and who shall reside within the area of the district jurisdiction. This member shall be a nonvoting member of the committee.

(d) If a folding device is installed pursuant to subdivision (a), the district shall submit a report in compliance with Section 9795 of the Government Code to the Assembly Committee on Transportation and the Senate Committee on Transportation and Housing on or before December 31, 2018. The report shall include a summary of any vehicular or traffic incidents where the size of the folding device was a factor, and a summary of the mobility improvements that these folding devices provide.

(Added by Stats. 2013, Ch. 95, Sec. 1. (AB 206) Effective January 1, 2014.)

35400.9. (a) Notwithstanding Section 35400, Gold Coast Transit (GCT), created pursuant to Article 1 (commencing with Section 6500) of Chapter 5 of Division 7 of Title 1 of the Government Code as a joint powers agency, may install a folding device attached to the front of a bus that is designed and used exclusively for transporting bicycles if all of the following conditions are met:

(1) The device does not extend more than 40 inches from the front body of the bus when fully deployed.

(2) The device, including all bicycles transported on the device, is mounted in a manner that does not materially affect efficiency or visibility of vehicle safety equipment.

(3) The handlebars of a bicycle that is transported on a device described in this subdivision do not extend more than 46 inches from the front of the bus.

(b) (1) GCT shall establish a route review committee prior to the installation of the initial folding device, pursuant to subdivision (a), on a bus that is 45 feet in length. The purpose of the committee is to ensure the safe operation of a 45-foot bus that is equipped with a front-mounted bicycle rack.

(2) The committee established pursuant to this subdivision shall perform an initial review of the routes on which GCT proposes to operate a 45-foot bus equipped with a front-mounted bicycle rack. The review shall include a field review of the proposed routes. It is the intent of the Legislature that the field review required under this paragraph include consultation with licensed traffic engineers from affected public agencies that have jurisdiction over segments of the route or routes under review, to ensure coordination with all affected state and local public road agencies that may potentially be impacted due to the operation of a 45-foot bus with a front-mounted bicycle rack.

(3) (A) By unanimous vote of all voting members, the committee shall make a determination of the routes that are suitable for the safe operation of a 45-foot bus that is equipped with a front-mounted bicycle rack.

(B) Before conducting a vote pursuant to subparagraph (A), the committee shall obtain certification approved by a licensed traffic engineer that all proposed routes are safe for travel by 45 foot buses equipped with the bicycle racks specified in subdivision (a).

(4) Upon any proposal to make substantive changes or additions to approved routes, those changes shall be subject to review and certification pursuant to paragraph (2) prior to being approved by the committee.

(5) The members of the committee shall be selected not more than 30 days after receipt of the GCT proposal to equip a 45-foot bus with a front-mounted bicycle rack and shall be comprised of the following members:

(A) One member from GCT who shall be appointed by GCT's general manager and who shall be a voting member of the committee.

(B) One member who is a licensed traffic engineer selected by the governing board of GCT and who shall be a voting member of the committee.

(C) One member appointed by the labor organization that is the exclusive representative of the busdrivers of GCT. If there is no exclusive representative of the busdrivers, a busdriver member shall be chosen by a majority vote of the busdrivers employed by GCT. This member shall be a voting member of the committee.

(D) One member appointed by the governing board of GCT who shall be a representative of the bicycling community and who shall reside within the area of GCT's jurisdiction. This member shall be a nonvoting member of the committee.

(c) If a folding device is installed pursuant to subdivision (a), GCT shall submit a report in compliance with Section 9795 of the Government Code to the Assembly Committee on Transportation and the Senate Committee on Transportation and Housing on or before December 31, 2017. The report shall include a summary of any vehicular or traffic incidents where the size of the folding devices was a factor, and a summary of the mobility improvements that these folding devices provide.

(Added by Stats. 2012, Ch. 376, Sec. 1. (AB 2488) Effective January 1, 2013.)

35401. (a) Except as provided in subdivisions (b), (c), and (d), a combination of vehicles coupled together, including attachments, may not exceed a total length of 65 feet.

(b) (1) A combination of vehicles coupled together, including attachments, that consists of a truck tractor, a semitrailer, and a semitrailer or trailer, may not exceed a total length of 75 feet, if the length of neither the semitrailers nor the trailer in the combination of vehicles exceeds 28 feet 6 inches.

(2) A B-train assembly is excluded from the measurement of semitrailer length when used between the first and second semitrailers of a truck tractor-semitrailer-semitrailer combination of vehicles. However, if there is no second semitrailer mounted to the B-train assembly, it shall be included in the length measurement of the semitrailer to which it is attached.

(c) (1) A tow truck in combination with a single disabled vehicle or a single abandoned vehicle that is authorized to travel on the highways by this chapter is exempt from subdivision (a) when operating under a valid annual transportation permit.

(2) A tow truck, in combination with a disabled or abandoned combination of vehicles that are authorized to travel on the highways by this chapter, is exempt from subdivision (a) when operating under a valid annual transportation permit and within a 100-mile radius of the location specified in the permit.

(3) A tow truck may exceed the 100-mile radius restriction imposed under paragraph (2) if a single trip permit is obtained from the Department of Transportation.

(d) A city or county may, by ordinance, prohibit a combination of vehicles of a total length in excess of 60 feet upon highways under its respective jurisdiction. The ordinance may not be effective until appropriate signs are erected indicating either the streets affected by the ordinance or the streets not affected, as the local authority determines will best serve to give notice of the ordinance.

(e) A city or county, upon a determination that a highway or portion of highway under its jurisdiction cannot, in consideration of public safety, sustain the operation of trailers or semitrailers of the maximum kingpin to rearmost axle distances permitted under Section 35400, may, by ordinance, establish lesser distances consistent with the maximum distances that the highway or highway portion can sustain, except that a city or county may not restrict the kingpin to rearmost axle measurement to less than 38 feet on those highways or highway portions. A city or county considering the adoption of an ordinance shall consider, but not be limited to, consideration of, all of the following:

(1) A comparison of the operating characteristics of the vehicles to be limited as compared to operating characteristics of other vehicles regulated by this code.

(2) Actual traffic volume.

(3) Frequency of accidents.

(4) Any other relevant data.

In addition, the city or county may appoint an advisory committee consisting of local representatives of those interests that are likely to be affected and shall consider the recommendations of the advisory committee in adopting the ordinance. The ordinance may not be effective until appropriate signs are erected indicating the highways or highway portions affected by the ordinance.

This subdivision shall only become operative upon the adoption of an enabling ordinance by a city or county.

(f) Whenever, in the judgment of the Department of Transportation, a state highway cannot, in consideration of public safety, sustain the operation of trailers or semitrailers of the maximum kingpin to rearmost axle distances permitted under Section 35400, the director, in consultation with the Department of the California Highway Patrol, shall compile data on total traffic volume, frequency of use by vehicles covered by this subdivision, accidents involving these vehicles, and other relevant data to assess whether these vehicles are a threat to public safety and should be excluded from the highway or highway segment. The study, containing the conclusions and recommendations of the director, shall be submitted to the Secretary of the Business, Transportation and Housing Agency. Unless otherwise notified by the secretary, the director shall hold public hearings in accordance with the procedures set forth in Article 3 (commencing with Section 35650) of Chapter 5 for the purpose of determining the maximum kingpin to rear axle length, which shall be not less than 38 feet, that the highway or highway segment can sustain without unreasonable threat to the safety of the public. Upon the basis of the findings, the Director of Transportation shall declare in writing the maximum kingpin to rear axle lengths which can be maintained with safety upon the highway. Following the declaration of maximum lengths as provided by this subdivision, the Department of Transportation shall erect suitable signs at each end of the affected portion of the highway and at any other points that the Department of Transportation determines to be necessary to give adequate notice of the length limits.

The Department of Transportation, in consultation with the Department of the California Highway Patrol, shall compile traffic volume, geometric, and other relevant data, to assess the maximum kingpin to rearmost axle distance of vehicle combinations appropriate for those state highways or portion of highways, affected by this section, that cannot safely accommodate trailers or semitrailers of the maximum kingpin to rearmost axle distances permitted under Section 35400. The department shall erect suitable signs appropriately restricting truck travel on those highways, or portions of highways.

(g) This section shall become operative on January 1, 2010.

(Amended (as added by Stats. 2006, Ch. 450, Sec. 2) by Stats. 2008, Ch. 394, Sec. 2. Effective January 1, 2009. Section operative January 1, 2010, by its own provisions.)

35401.1. A combination of vehicles operated pursuant to Section 35400 or 35401 with a kingpin to rearmost axle measurement of greater than 38 feet but not more than 40 feet may be operated on those highways under the jurisdiction of local authorities only where it is deemed to be safe by the owner of the vehicle or the person operating the vehicle and where its operation is not specifically prohibited by local ordinance pursuant to subdivision (d) of Section 35401.

(Added by Stats. 1986, Ch. 1378, Sec. 3.)

35401.3. (a) Notwithstanding subdivisions (a) and (b) of Section 35401, a combination of vehicles designed and used to transport motor vehicles, camper units, or boats, which consists of a motortruck and stinger-steered semitrailer, shall be allowed a length of up to 70 feet if the kingpin is at least 3 feet behind the rear drive axle of the motortruck. This combination shall not be subject to subdivision (a) of Section 35411, but the load upon the rear vehicle of the combination shall not extend more than 6 feet 6 inches beyond the allowable length of the vehicle.

(b) A combination of vehicles designed and used to transport motor vehicles, camper units, or boats, which consists of a motortruck and stinger-steered semitrailer, shall be allowed a length of up to 75 feet if all of the following conditions are maintained:

(1) The distance from the steering axle to the rear drive axle of the motortruck does not exceed 24 feet.

(2) The kingpin is at least 5 feet behind the rear drive axle of the motortruck.

(3) The distance from the kingpin to the rear axle of the semitrailer does not exceed 34 feet except that the distance from the kingpin to the rear axle of a triple axle semitrailer does not exceed 36 feet.

This combination shall not be subject to subdivision (a) of Section 35411, but the load upon the rear vehicle of the combination shall not extend more than 6 feet 6 inches beyond the allowable length of the vehicle.

(Amended by Stats. 2000, Ch. 860, Sec. 11. Effective January 1, 2001.)

35401.5. (a) A combination of vehicles consisting of a truck tractor and semitrailer, or of a truck tractor, semitrailer, and trailer, is not subject to the limitations of Sections 35400 and 35401, when operating on the Dwight D. Eisenhower National System of Interstate and Defense Highways or when using those portions of federal-aid primary system highways that have been qualified by the United States Secretary of Transportation for that use, or when using routes appropriately identified by the Department of Transportation or local authorities as provided in subdivision (c) or (d), if all of the following conditions are met:

(1) The length of the semitrailer in exclusive combination with a truck tractor does not exceed 48 feet. A semitrailer not more than 53 feet in length shall satisfy this requirement when configured with two or more rear axles, the rearmost of which is located 40 feet or less from the kingpin or when configured with a single axle which is located 38 feet or less from the kingpin. For purposes of this paragraph, a motortruck used in combination with a semitrailer, when that combination of vehicles is engaged solely in the transportation of motor vehicles, camper units, or boats, is considered to be a truck tractor.

(2) Neither the length of the semitrailer nor the length of the trailer when simultaneously in combination with a truck tractor exceeds 28 feet 6 inches.

(b) Subdivisions (b), (d), and (e) of Section 35402 do not apply to combinations of vehicles operated subject to the exemptions provided by this section.

(c) Combinations of vehicles operated pursuant to subdivision (a) may also use highways not specified in subdivision (a) that provide reasonable access to terminals and facilities for purposes limited to fuel, food, lodging, and repair when that access is consistent with the safe operation of the combinations of vehicles and when the facility is within one road mile of identified points of ingress and egress to or from highways specified in subdivision (a) for use by those combinations of vehicles.

(d) The Department of Transportation or local authorities may establish a process whereby access to terminals or services may be applied for upon a route not previously established as an access route. The denial of a request for access to terminals and services shall be only on the basis of safety and an engineering analysis of the proposed access route. If a written request for access has been properly submitted and has not been acted upon within 90 days of receipt by the department or the appropriate local agency, the access shall be deemed automatically approved. Thereafter, the route shall be deemed open for access by all other vehicles of the same type regardless of ownership. In lieu of processing an access application, the Department of Transportation or local authorities with respect to highways under their respective jurisdictions may provide signing, mapping, or a listing of highways as necessary to indicate the use of specific routes as terminal access routes. For purposes of this subdivision, "terminal" means either of the following:

(1) A facility where freight originates, terminates, or is handled in the transportation process.

(2) A facility where a motor carrier maintains operating facilities.

(e) Nothing in subdivision (c) or (d) authorizes state or local agencies to require permits of terminal operators or to charge terminal operators fees for the purpose of attaining access for vehicles described in this section.

(f) Notwithstanding subdivision (d), the limitations of access specified in that subdivision do not apply to licensed carriers of household goods when directly en route to or from a point of loading or unloading of household goods, if travel on highways other than those specified in subdivision (a) is necessary and incidental to the shipment of the household goods.

(g) (1) Notwithstanding Sections 35400 and 35401, a combination of vehicles consisting solely of a truck tractor semitrailer combination with a kingpin to rearmost axle measurement limit of not more than 46 feet, a trailer length of not more than 56 feet, and used exclusively or primarily in connection with motorsports, may operate on the routes identified in subdivision (a) as well as on any other routes authorized for that purpose by the Department of Transportation in consultation with the Department of the California Highway Patrol, when issued a permit as set forth in paragraph (3). As used in this subdivision, "motorsports" means an event, and all activities leading up to that event, including, but not limited to, administration, testing, practice, promotion, and merchandising, that is sanctioned under the auspices of the member organizations of the Automobile Competition Committee for the United States.

(2) (A) The Department of Transportation shall conduct field tests of the truck tractor semitrailer combination authorized under paragraph (1) for motorsport trucks with a trailer length of not more than 56 feet to evaluate their performance on transition routes connecting to the Auto Club Speedway in Fontana.

(B) (i) The Legislature finds and declares that the Department of Transportation established the existing transition routes described in subparagraph (A) based on records from the 1990s.

(ii) The Department of Transportation shall update the transition routes to reflect road projects completed since the 1990s and shall update the transition routes every five years thereafter.

(iii) The Department of Transportation shall develop new transition routes, as necessary, for the truck tractor semitrailer combination authorized under paragraph (1) for motorsport trucks with a trailer length of not more than 56 feet.

(C) The Department of Transportation shall, no later than January 1, 2017, submit a report to the Legislature, in compliance with Section 9795 of the Government Code, that includes the results of the field tests for the Auto Club Raceway in Pomona, the Sonoma Raceway, and the Auto Club Speedway in Fontana, an overview of the related roadway improvements identified and made, and, in consultation with the Department of the California Highway Patrol, a recommendation as to whether the maximum 56 foot trailer length should be reauthorized.

(D) Notwithstanding Section 10231.5 of the Government Code, the requirement for submitting a report under this paragraph is inoperative on January 1, 2019.

(3) Permits for a combination of vehicles consisting solely of a truck tractor semitrailer combination with a kingpin to rearmost axle measurement limit of not more than 46 feet, a trailer length of not more than 56 feet, for use exclusively or primarily in connection with motorsports, to operate on the routes identified in subdivision (a) as well as on any other routes authorized for that purpose, as provided in paragraph (1), shall be issued by the Department of Transportation, pursuant to Article 6 (commencing with Section 35780) of Chapter 5. The permit requirement for travel on a specific route to or from the Auto Club Raceway in Pomona, the Sonoma Raceway, or the Auto Club Speedway in Fontana, shall apply only until field tests for each of those raceways by the Department of Transportation determine that no additional projects need to be performed on the specific route, or, if projects are required to be performed on the specific route, until those projects are completed.

(h) The Legislature finds and declares both of the following:

(1) In authorizing the use of 53-foot semitrailers, it is the intent of the Legislature to conform with Section 31111(b)(1)(C) of Title 49 of the United States Code by permitting the continued use of semitrailers of the dimensions as those that were in actual and legal use on December 1, 1982, and does not intend this action to be a precedent for future increases in the parameters of any of those vehicles that would adversely affect the turning maneuverability of vehicle combinations.

(2) In authorizing the department to issue special transportation permits for motorsports, it is the intent of the Legislature to conform with Section 31111(b)(1)(F) of Title 49 of the United States Code. It is also the intent of the Legislature that this action not be a precedent for future increases in the distance from the kingpin to the rearmost axle of semitrailers and trailers that would adversely affect the turning maneuverability of vehicle combinations.

(Amended by Stats. 2014, Ch. 786, Sec. 1. (SB 1175) Effective January 1, 2015.)

35401.7. (a) The limitations of access specified in subdivision (d) of Section 35401.5 do not apply to licensed carriers of livestock when those carriers are directly en route to or from a point of loading or unloading of livestock on those portions of State Highway Route 101 located in the Counties of Del Norte, Humboldt, and Mendocino from its junction with State Highway Route 1 near Leggett north to the Oregon border, if the travel is necessary and incidental to the shipment of the livestock.

(b) The exemption allowed under this section does not apply unless all of the following conditions are met:

(1) The length of the truck tractor, in combination with the semitrailer used to transport the livestock, does not exceed a total of 70 feet.

(2) The distance from the kingpin to the rearmost axle of the semitrailer does not exceed 43 feet.

(3) The length of the semitrailer does not exceed a total of 48 feet.

(c) The exemption allowed under this section does not apply to travel conducted on the day prior to, or on the day of, any federally recognized holiday.

(d) (1) Because route improvements in Richardson Grove that will allow the combination of vehicles described in Section 35401.5 to fully operate on all portions of State Highway Route 101 located in the Counties of Del Norte, Humboldt, and Mendocino are ongoing and not yet completed, this section shall remain in effect only until both of the following conditions are satisfied:

(A) All route improvements in Richardson Grove are completed without restraint, including, but not limited to, judicial or injunctive restraints.

(B) The Director of Transportation determines that the combination of vehicles described in Section 35401.5 is authorized to operate on all portions of State Highway Route 101 located in the Counties of Del Norte, Humboldt, and Mendocino. When the director makes the determination described in this subparagraph, the director shall post a declaration on the Internet Web site of the Department of Transportation.

(2) This section is repealed as of the date that the declaration described in subparagraph (B) of paragraph (1) is posted on the Department of Transportation's Internet Web site.

(3) The declaration described in subparagraph (B) of paragraph (1) shall state that it is being made pursuant to this section.

(e) (1) If, prior to the completion of the route improvements in Richardson Grove as described in paragraph (1) of subdivision (d), the Director of Transportation determines that the only adjustment to State Highway Route 101 possible to accommodate the truck sizes allowed to travel on portions of State Highway Route 101, pursuant to subdivisions (a) and (b), is the removal of any tree that has a diameter of 42 inches or greater, measured outside the bark, at 12 inches above ground on the side adjacent to the highest ground level, the director shall notify the Secretary of State of that determination.

(2) If, prior to the completion of the route improvements in Richardson Grove as described in paragraph (1) of subdivision (d), the Director of Transportation determines that safety improvements to the portion of State Highway Route 101 described in subdivision (a) have resulted in the reclassification of the entire segment as a terminal access route pursuant to subdivision (d) of Section 35401.5, the director shall notify the Secretary of State of that determination.

(3) The notice required under paragraph (1) or (2) shall state that it is being made pursuant to this section.

(4) This section is repealed on the date the Secretary of State receives either of the notices described in this subdivision.

(Amended by Stats. 2015, Ch. 303, Sec. 542. (AB 731) Effective January 1, 2016. Repealed on earlier of dates prescribed in subd. (d) and subd. (e).)

35401.9. Notwithstanding Section 35401, a driveaway-towaway combination, as described in Section 303, shall not exceed 97 feet in length when transporting up to three saddle-mounted vehicles and one full-mounted vehicle.

(Added by Stats. 2016, Ch. 208, Sec. 25. (AB 2906) Effective January 1, 2017.)

35402. (a) Any extension or device, including any adjustable axle added to the front or rear of a vehicle, used to increase the carrying capacity of a vehicle shall be included in measuring the length of a vehicle, except that a drawbar shall not be included in measuring the length of a vehicle but shall be included in measuring the overall length of a combination of vehicles.

(b) Notwithstanding subdivision (a), extensions of not more than 18 inches in length on each end of a vehicle or combination of vehicles used exclusively to transport vehicles shall not be included in measuring the length of a vehicle or combination of vehicles when the vehicles are loaded.

(c) Notwithstanding subdivision (a), an extension of not more than 18 inches in length on the last trailer in a combination of vehicles transporting loads shall not be included in measuring the length of a vehicle or combination of vehicles when the vehicles are loaded. Additionally, an extension of not more than 18 inches in length on the front of the first trailer in a combination of vehicles transporting loads shall not be included in measuring the length of a vehicle or combination of vehicles when the vehicles are loaded and on highways, other than those highways designated by the United States Department of Transportation as national network routes.

(d) Notwithstanding subdivision (a), any extension or device which is not used to carry any load and which does not exceed three feet in length, added to the rear of a vehicle, and is used exclusively for pushing the vehicle or a combination of vehicles, which vehicle or combination of vehicles is designed and used exclusively to transport earth, sand, gravel, and similar materials, shall be included in measuring the length of the vehicle but shall not be included in measuring the overall length of the combination of vehicles.

(e) Notwithstanding subdivision (a), a truck semitrailer combination, but not a truck tractor and semitrailer combination, may use a sliding fifth wheel, or a truck tractor, semitrailer, trailer, and a truck-trailer combination may use a sliding drawbar, to extend the length of the combination by not more than 2 feet 6 inches while traveling 35 miles per hour or less on any highway, except a freeway. These provisions shall apply, however, to freeway onramps and offramps and freeway connectors. The sliding fifth wheel or drawbar when extended shall not be included in measuring the overall length of the combination of vehicles if the pivot point of the semitrailer connection is more than two feet to the rear of the center of the rearmost axle of the motortruck or if the distance from the pivot point to the center of the rearmost axle of the semitrailer does not exceed 34 feet.

Combinations of vehicles permitted by this subdivision shall be in compliance with the weight limits provided in Article 1 (commencing with Section 35550) of Chapter 5 whenever any drawbar or sliding fifth wheel is extended, contracted, or in any intermediate position as provided for by this subdivision.

(Amended by Stats. 2000, Ch. 860, Sec. 13. Effective January 1, 2001.)

35403. Safety devices which are required to be mounted upon a vehicle pursuant to provisions of this code, may extend beyond the permissible length of a vehicle, or a combination of vehicles, to a distance not exceeding 10 inches.

(Added by Stats. 1974, Ch. 1117.)

35404. Any county having a population in excess of 4,000,000 and having within its limits a natural island with an area in excess of 20,000 acres may, by ordinance, prohibit the use of any highway or lane, hereafter established in unincorporated area thereon, (1) by any vehicle exceeding an overall length of 170 inches and an overall width of 65 inches, or (2) by any such vehicle and all vehicles driven by internal combustion engines. Notwithstanding the provisions of Section 906 of the Streets and Highways Code, no such ordinance shall be enacted unless the board of supervisors shall have theretofore adopted, by a four-fifths vote, a resolution determining that the public convenience and necessity require that such highway or lane have a width of 35 feet or less and a roadway width of 22 feet or less.

Any ordinance enacted pursuant to this section shall be subject to Sections 35718 to 35720, inclusive, of this code and shall not apply to authorized emergency vehicles.

(Added by Stats. 1969, Ch. 723.)

35405. (a) An aerodynamic device that extends no more than five feet beyond the rear of a vehicle shall not be included in measuring the length of the vehicle or combination of vehicles, if both of the following conditions are met:

(1) The device does not have the strength, rigidity, or mass to damage a vehicle, or injure a passenger in a vehicle, that strikes the vehicle equipped with the device from the rear.

(2) The device does not obscure tail lamps, turn signals, marker lamps, identification lamps, or any other required safety devices, including, but not limited to, hazardous materials placards or conspicuity markings.

(b) For purposes of this section, "aerodynamic device" has the same meaning as defined in Section 35110.

(Added by Stats. 2014, Ch. 133, Sec. 2. (SB 469) Effective January 1, 2015.)

35406. (a) Except as provided in subdivision (b), the load upon any vehicle operated alone, or the load upon the front vehicle of a combination of vehicles, shall not extend more than three feet beyond the foremost part of the front tires of the vehicle or the front bumper of the vehicle, if it is equipped with a front bumper.

(b) When the load is composed solely of vehicles, the load upon the front vehicle of a combination of vehicles shall not extend more than four feet beyond the foremost part of the front tires of the vehicle or the front bumper of the vehicle, if it is equipped with a front bumper.

(Amended by Stats. 1972, Ch. 434.)

35407. Section 35406 does not apply to the booms or masts of shovels, cranes or water well drilling and servicing equipment carried upon a motor vehicle if the following conditions are met:

(a) The booms or masts shall not extend more than two-thirds of the wheelbase beyond the front tires of such vehicle.

(b) The projecting structure or attachments thereto shall be securely held in place to prevent dropping or swaying.

(c) No part of the structure which extends beyond the front tires shall be less than seven feet from the roadway.

(d) The driver's vision shall not be impaired by the projecting or supporting structure.

(Amended by Stats. 1959, Ch. 816.)

35407.5. Section 35406 and subdivisions (a) and (d) of Section 35407 do not apply to the booms or masts of a self-propelled heel-boom log loader first sold in this state prior to January 1, 1988, if all of the following conditions are met:

(a) A system of mirrors or other view enhancements permits the driver to see in any area blocked from view.

(b) The log loader is operated together with a four wheeled lead vehicle which remains a reasonable distance ahead to guide the movement of the log loader.

(c) Two-way radio communication equipment is maintained in good working condition on the log loader and the pilot car, and is used between those vehicles during movement upon any highway.

(Added by Stats. 1988, Ch. 550, Sec. 1.)

35408. In no event shall a front bumper on a motor vehicle be constructed or installed so as to project more than two feet forward of the foremost part of either the fenders or cab structure or radiator, whichever extends farthest toward the front of such vehicle.

(Enacted by Stats. 1959, Ch. 3.)

35409. (a) Any motor vehicle used for the purpose of taking photographs, motion pictures, or television pictures or for teaching safe driving may be equipped with a dismountable platform or other device extending forward of either the fenders or cab structure or radiator, whichever extends farthest toward the front of such vehicle, for a distance not exceeding five feet while such vehicle is in use for such purpose.

(b) Any device used for the sole purpose of teaching safe driving, as provided in subdivision (a), shall be of a type authorized by the Department of the California Highway Patrol and the Department of Motor Vehicles.

(Amended by Stats. 1979, Ch. 723.)

35410. The load upon any motor vehicle alone or an independent load only upon a trailer or semitrailer shall not extend to the rear beyond the last point of support for a greater distance than that equal to two-thirds of the length of the wheelbase of the vehicle carrying such load, except that the wheelbase of a semitrailer shall be considered as the distance between the rearmost axle of the towing vehicle and the rearmost axle of the semitrailer.

(Enacted by Stats. 1959, Ch. 3.)

35411. (a) Except as provided in subdivision (b), the load upon any combination of vehicles shall not exceed 75 feet measured from the front extremity of the front vehicle or load to the rear extremity of the last vehicle or load.

(b) The load upon any combination of vehicles operating pursuant to Section 35401 or 35401.5, when the overall length of the combination of vehicles exceeds 75 feet, shall be confined within the exterior dimensions of the vehicles.

(Amended by Stats. 1983, Ch. 145, Sec. 17. Effective June 28, 1983.)

35414. (a) Except where a load can be transported consistent with the limitations on vehicle and load length specified in other sections of this chapter, the limitations of this chapter as to length of vehicles do not apply when only poles, timbers, pipes, integral structural materials, or single unit component parts, including, but not limited to, missile components, aircraft assemblies, drilling equipment, and tanks not exceeding 80 feet in length are being transported upon any of the following:

(1) Upon a pole or pipe dolly or otherwise lawful trailer used as a pole or pipe dolly in connection with a motor vehicle.

(2) Upon a semitrailer, except for the limitations provided in Section 35410.

(3) Upon a semitrailer and a pole or pipe dolly used in connection with a truck tractor to haul flexible integral structural material.

(b) Poles and the tools and materials incidental to the work to be performed may be transported on a pole or pipe dolly or otherwise lawful semitrailer used as a pole or pipe dolly, transporting not more than three poles not exceeding 80 feet in length and when used by public utility companies or local public agencies engaged in the business of supplying electricity or telephone service, by the Department of Transportation, or by a licensed contractor in the performance of work for a utility, the department, or a local public agency, when such transportation is between a storage yard and job location where such tools and materials are to be used, in which event the limitations of this chapter as to length of vehicles and loads shall not apply.

(Amended by Stats. 1998, Ch. 135, Sec. 1. Effective July 13, 1998.)

Chapter 5. Weight

(Chapter 5 enacted by Stats. 1959, Ch. 3.)

Article 1. Axle Limits

(Article 1 enacted by Stats. 1959, Ch. 3.)

35550. (a) The gross weight imposed upon the highway by the wheels on any one axle of a vehicle shall not exceed 20,000 pounds and the gross weight upon any one wheel, or wheels, supporting one end of an axle, and resting upon the roadway, shall not exceed 10,500 pounds.

(b) The gross weight limit provided for weight bearing upon any one wheel, or wheels, supporting one end of an axle shall not apply to vehicles the loads of which consist of livestock.

(c) The maximum wheel load is the lesser of the following:

(1) The load limit established by the tire manufacturer, as molded on at least one sidewall of the tire.

(2) A load of 620 pounds per lateral inch of tire width, as determined by the manufacturer's rated tire width as molded on at least one sidewall of the tire for all axles except the steering axle, in which case paragraph (1) applies.

(Amended by Stats. 1996, Ch. 1154, Sec. 82. Effective September 30, 1996.)

35551. (a) Except as otherwise provided in this section or Section 35551.5, the total gross weight in pounds imposed on the highway by any group of two or more consecutive axles shall not exceed that given for the respective distance in the following table:

Distance in feet between the extremes of any group of 2 or more consecutive					
axles	2 axles	3 axles	4 axles	5 axles	6 axles
4	34,000	34,000	34,000	34,000	34,000
5	34,000	34,000	34,000	34,000	34,000
6	34,000	34,000	34,000	34,000	34,000
7	34,000	34,000	34,000	34,000	34,000
8	34,000	34,000	34,000	34,000	34,000
9	39,000	42,500	42,500	42,500	42,500
10	40,000	43,500	43,500	43,500	43,500
11	40,000	44,000	44,000	44,000	44,000
12	40,000	45,000	50,000	50,000	50,000
13	40,000	45,500	50,500	50,500	50,500
14	40,000	46,500	51,500	51,500	51,500
15	40,000	47,000	52,000	52,000	52,000
16	40,000	48,000	52,500	52,500	52,500
17	40,000	48,500	53,500	53,500	53,500
18	40,000	49,500	54,000	54,000	54,000
19	40,000	50,000	54,500	54,500	54,500
20	40,000	51,000	55,500	55,500	55,500
21	40,000	51,500	56,000	56,000	56,000
22	40,000	52,500	56,500	56,500	56,500
23	40,000	53,000	57,500	57,500	57,500
24	40,000	54,000	58,000	58,000	58,000
25	40,000	54,500	58,500	58,500	58,500
26	40,000	55,500	59,500	59,500	59,500
27	40,000	56,000	60,000	60,000	60,000
28	40,000	57,000	60,500	60,500	60,500
29	40,000	57,500	61,500	61,500	61,500
30	40,000	58,500	62,000	62,000	62,000
31	40,000	59,000	62,500	62,500	62,500
32	40,000	60,000	63,500	63,500	63,500
33	40,000	60,000	64,000	64,000	64,000
34	40,000	60,000	64,500	64,500	64,500
35	40,000	60,000	65,500	65,500	65,500
36	40,000	60,000	66,000	66,000	66,000
37	40,000	60,000	66,500	66,500	66,500
38	40,000	60,000	67,500	67,500	67,500
39	40,000	60,000	68,000	68,000	68,000
40	40,000	60,000	68,500	70,000	70,000
41	40,000	60,000	69,500	72,000	72,000
42	40,000	60,000	70,000	73,280	73,280
43	40,000	60,000	70,500	73,280	73,280
44	40,000	60,000	71,500	73,280	73,280
45	40,000	60,000	72,000	76,000	80,000
46	40,000	60,000	72,500	76,500	80,000
47	40,000	60,000	73,500	77,500	80,000
48	40,000	60,000	74,000	78,000	80,000
49	40,000	60,000	74,500	78,500	80,000
50	40,000	60,000	75,500	79,000	80,000
51	40,000	60,000	76,000	80,000	80,000
52	40,000	60,000	76,500	80,000	80,000
53	40,000	60,000	77,500	80,000	80,000
54	40,000	60,000	78,000	80,000	80,000
55	40,000	60,000	78,500	80,000	80,000

Distance in feet between the extremes of any group of 2 or more consecutive					
axles	2 axles	3 axles	4 axles	5 axles	6 axles
56	40,000	60,000	79,500	80,000	80,000
57	40,000	60,000	80,000	80,000	80,000
58	40,000	60,000	80,000	80,000	80,000
59	40,000	60,000	80,000	80,000	80,000
60	40,000	60,000	80,000	80,000	80,000

(b) In addition to the weights specified in subdivision (a), two consecutive sets of tandem axles may carry a gross weight of 34,000 pounds each if the overall distance between the first and last axles of the consecutive sets of tandem axles is 36 feet or more. The gross weight of each set of tandem axles shall not exceed 34,000 pounds and the gross weight of the two consecutive sets of tandem axles shall not exceed 68,000 pounds.

(c) The distance between axles shall be measured to the nearest whole foot. When a fraction is exactly six inches, the next larger whole foot shall be used.

(d) This section does not affect the right to prohibit the use of any highway or any bridge or other structure thereon in the manner and to the extent specified in Article 4 (commencing with Section 35700) and Article 5 (commencing with Section 35750) of this chapter.

(e) The gross weight limits expressed by this section and Section 35550 shall include all enforcement tolerances.

(Amended by Stats. 2024, Ch. 219, Sec. 1. (AB 1953) Effective January 1, 2025.)

35551.5. (a) The provisions of this section shall apply only to combinations of vehicles which contain a trailer or semitrailer. Each vehicle in such combination of vehicles, and every such combination of vehicles, shall comply with either Section 35551 or with subdivisions (b), (c), and (d) of this section.

(b) The gross weight imposed upon the highway by the wheels on any one axle of a vehicle shall not exceed 18,000 pounds and the gross weight upon any one wheel, or wheels, supporting one end of an axle and resting upon the roadway, shall not exceed 9,500 pounds, except that the gross weight imposed upon the highway by the wheels on any front steering axle of a motor vehicle shall not exceed 12,500 pounds. The gross weight limit provided for weight bearing upon any one wheel, or wheels, supporting one end of an axle shall not apply to vehicles the loads of which consist of livestock. The following vehicles are exempt from the front axle weight limits specified in this subdivision:

(1) Trucks transporting vehicles.
(2) Trucks transporting livestock.
(3) Dump trucks.
(4) Cranes.
(5) Buses.
(6) Transit mix concrete or cement trucks, and trucks that mix concrete or cement at, or adjacent to, a jobsite.
(7) Motor vehicles that are not commercial vehicles.
(8) Vehicles operated by any public utility furnishing electricity, gas, water, or telephone service.
(9) Trucks or truck tractors with a front axle at least four feet to the rear of the foremost part of the truck or truck tractor, not including the front bumper.
(10) Trucks transporting garbage, rubbish, or refuse.
(11) Trucks equipped with a fifth wheel when towing a semitrailer.
(12) Tank trucks which have a cargo capacity of at least 1,500 gallons.
(13) Trucks transporting bulk grains or bulk livestock feed.

(c) The total gross weight with load imposed on the highway by any group of two or more consecutive axles of a vehicle in such combination of vehicles or of such combination of vehicles where the distance between the first and last axles of the two or more consecutive axles is 18 feet or less shall not exceed that given for the respective distance in the following table:

Distance in feet between first and **last axles of group**	**Allowed load in pounds on group of axles**
4	32,000
5	32,000
6	32,200
7	32,900
8	33,600
9	34,300
10	35,000
11	35,700
12	36,400
13	37,100
14	43,200
15	44,000
16	44,800
17	45,600
18	46,400

(d) The total gross weight with load imposed on the highway by any vehicle in such combination of vehicles or of such combination of vehicles where the distance between the first and last axles is more than 18 feet shall not exceed that given for the respective distances in the following table:

Distance **in feet**	**Allowed load in pounds**
19	47,200
20	48,000
21	48,800
22	49,600
23	50,400
24	51,200
25	55,250
26	56,100
27	56,950
28	57,800
29	58,650
30	59,500
31	60,350
32	61,200
33	62,050
34	62,900
35	63,750
36	64,600
37	65,450
38	66,300
39	68,000
40	70,000
41	72,000
42	73,280
43	73,280
44	73,280

Distance in feet	Allowed load in pounds
45	73,280
46	73,280
47	73,280
48	73,280
49	73,280
50	73,280
51	73,280
52	73,600
53	74,400
54	75,200
55	76,000
56 or over	76,800

(e) The distance between axles shall be measured to the nearest whole foot. When a fraction is exactly six inches, the next larger whole foot shall be used.

(f) The gross weight limits expressed by this section shall include all enforcement tolerances.

(g) Nothing in this section shall affect the right to prohibit the use of any highway or any bridge or other structure thereon in the manner and to the extent specified in Article 4 (commencing with Section 35700) and Article 5 (commencing with Section 35750) of Chapter 5 of Division 15.

(h) The Legislature, in enacting this section, does not intend to increase, and this section shall not be construed to allow, statutory weights any greater than existed prior to January 1, 1976.

(Added by Stats. 1980, Ch. 784, Sec. 4.)

35552. (a) This section applies only to trucks and vehicle combinations while transporting loads composed solely of logs.

(b) One set of tandem axles of such a truck or vehicle combination shall be deemed to be in compliance with Section 35551 if the total gross weight of 34,000 pounds on such a set that is permitted by Section 35551 is not exceeded by more than 1,500 pounds. In addition, such a truck and vehicle combination that has two consecutive sets of tandem axles shall be deemed to be in compliance with Section 35551 if such consecutive sets of tandem axles do not carry a combined total gross weight of more than 69,000 pounds, if the total gross weight on any one such set does not exceed 35,500 pounds, and if the overall distance between the first and last axle of such consecutive sets of tandem axles is 34 feet or more. All such truck and vehicle combinations shall be subject to all other provisions of Section 35551 or any other provision made applicable to the total gross weight of such a truck or vehicle combination in lieu of Section 35551.

(c) The gross weight limits expressed in this section shall include all enforcement tolerances.

(d) If any total gross weight permitted by this section is exceeded, the allowed weight in pounds set forth in subdivision (a) of Section 35551 shall be the maximum permitted weight for purposes of determining the amount of fine for such violation as specified in the table in Section 42030; except that, whenever the violation is for exceeding the total gross weight for two consecutive sets of tandem axles, and if the overall distance between the first and last axle of such sets is 34 feet or more, the allowed weight on the two consecutive sets shall be 68,000 pounds.

(e) This section shall have no application to highways which are a part of the National System of Interstate and Defense Highways (as referred to in subdivision (a) of Section 108 of the Federal-aid Highway Act of 1956).

This section may be cited as the Christensen-Belotti Act.

(Amended by Stats. 1976, Ch. 249.)

35553. The provisions of this article shall not apply to any vehicle in the immediate vicinity of an unloading or loading area while actually preparing for or in the process of unloading or loading, provided any overload is incidental to and necessitated by such action; and provided that such action does not occur on a bridge or highway structure.

This section shall have no application to highways which are a part of the national system of interstate and defense highways (as referred to in subdivision (a) of Section 108 of the Federal-aid Highway Act of 1956).

(Amended by Stats. 1972, Ch. 733.)

35554. (a) (1) Notwithstanding Section 35550, the maximum gross weight on any one axle of a bus shall not exceed 20,500 pounds.

(2) This subdivision does not apply to a transit bus procured through a solicitation process pursuant to which a solicitation was issued before January 1, 2016. This subdivision does not apply to a bus purchased during an option period in a multiyear contract to purchase transit buses that is entered into before January 1, 2016, by a publicly owned or operated transit system, or an operator of a transit system under contract with a publicly owned or operated transit system, provided, however, that the option period does not exceed five years from the date of the original contract, or extend beyond January 1, 2021, whichever is earlier.

(b) A transit bus is not subject to Section 35550.

(c) Notwithstanding subdivision (a), the following provisions shall apply to a transit bus:

(1) The curb weight on any one axle of a transit bus procured through a solicitation process pursuant to which a solicitation was issued between January 1, 2016, and December 31, 2018, inclusive, shall not exceed 23,000 pounds.

(2) The curb weight on any one axle of a transit bus procured through a solicitation process pursuant to which a solicitation was issued on or after January 1, 2019, shall not exceed 22,000 pounds.

(d) Notwithstanding subdivisions (a) and (c), the following provisions shall apply to an articulated transit bus or zero-emission transit bus:

(1) The curb weight on any one axle of an articulated transit bus or zero-emission transit bus procured through a solicitation process pursuant to which a solicitation was issued between January 1, 2016, and December 31, 2017, inclusive, shall not exceed 25,000 pounds.

(2) The curb weight on any one axle of an articulated transit bus or zero-emission transit bus procured through a solicitation process pursuant to which a solicitation was issued between January 1, 2018, and December 31, 2019, inclusive, shall not exceed 24,000 pounds.

(3) The curb weight on any one axle of an articulated transit bus or zero-emission transit bus procured through a solicitation process pursuant to which a solicitation was issued between January 1, 2020, and December 31, 2021, inclusive, shall not exceed 23,000 pounds.

(4) The curb weight on any one axle of an articulated transit bus or zero-emission transit bus procured through a solicitation process pursuant to which a solicitation was issued on or after January 1, 2022, shall not exceed 22,000 pounds.

(e) Nothing in this article shall be construed to authorize a vehicle described in paragraph (2) of subdivision (a) or described in subdivision (c) or (d) to be operated in violation of Section 35753.

(f) A transit operator operating an articulated transit bus shall, by July 1, 2016, provide notice to all cities and counties in whose jurisdiction the bus will operate in the upcoming calendar year, identifying the approximate routes upon which the bus is expected to be scheduled for service, including the names of streets and roads upon which that service is likely to take place. Thereafter, a transit operator operating an articulated transit bus shall annually provide notice by July 1, to all cities and counties in whose jurisdiction the bus will operate in the upcoming calendar year, identifying any changes to the service on those routes and any new routes upon which the bus is expected to be scheduled for the upcoming year. The notice shall include data from information provided by the bus manufacturer to the transit operator, identifying the weight of the articulated bus.

(g) For purposes of this section, the term "curb weight" means the total weight of a fully loaded transit bus, including maximum fuel, oil, and coolant, and all equipment used in the normal operation of the bus, except without passengers or a driver.

(h) Notwithstanding subdivisions (a) to (g), inclusive, a transit bus shall not operate on the Dwight D. Eisenhower System of Interstate and Defense Highways in excess of the weight limitation for transit buses specified in federal law.

(i) If the gross weight imposed upon the highway by the wheels on any one axle of a transit bus exceeds 20,000 pounds, the axle shall be supported by four wheels bearing load upon the highway.

(Amended (as amended by Stats. 2014, Ch. 263, Sec. 2) by Stats. 2015, Ch. 484, Sec. 1. (AB 1250) Effective January 1, 2016.)

35555. (a) During the period commencing September 15 of each year and ending March 15 of the following year, the weight limitations of Section 35551 do not apply to any cotton module mover or any truck tractor pulling a semitrailer that is a cotton module mover, when operated as follows:

(1) Laterally across a state highway at grade of the state highway.

(2) Upon any county highway within the Counties of Butte, Colusa, Fresno, Glenn, Imperial, Kern, Kings, Madera, Merced, Riverside, Sacramento, San Benito, San Bernardino, San Joaquin, Stanislaus, Sutter, Tehama, Tulare, Yolo, and Yuba, except as prohibited or limited on county highways or portions thereof by resolution of the county board of supervisors having jurisdiction.

(b) A cotton module mover may be operated upon a state highway within the counties and during the period set forth in subdivision (a) if all of the following are met:

(1) The operator is in possession of a driver's license of the class required for operation of the mover.

(2) The mover is operated in compliance with Sections 24002 and 24012; Article 1 (commencing with Section 24250) of, Article 3 (commencing with Section 24600) of, Article 4 (commencing with Section 24800) of, Article 5 (commencing with Section 24950) of, Article 6 (commencing with 25100) of, Article 9 (commencing with 25350) of, Article 11 (commencing with 25450) of, Chapter 2 of Division 12; and Article 2 (commencing with 26450) and Article 3 (commencing with 26502) of Chapter 3 of Division 12.

(3) The mover does not exceed the maximum allowable gross axle weight for tandem axles set forth in Section 35551 by more than 6,000 pounds.

(4) The operator of a mover that exceeds the maximum allowable gross axle weight for tandem axle vehicles as set forth in Section 35551 shall possess a commercial driver's license as defined in subdivision (a) of Section 15210.

(c) This section does not apply to those highways designated by the United States Department of Transportation as national network routes.

(Amended by Stats. 2001, Ch. 497, Sec. 1. Effective October 4, 2001.)

35557. (a) Only upon request to, and approval by, and in accordance with regulations adopted by, the Director of Food and Agriculture, all of the following are available for inspection by district attorneys and are subject to legal process for admission in any criminal or civil proceeding arising out of a violation of this chapter:

(1) Vehicle weight certificates issued on or after January 1, 1984, pursuant to Chapter 7 (commencing with Section 12700), Chapter 7.3 (commencing with Section 12740), and Chapter 7.7 (commencing with Section 12770) of Division 5 of the Business and Professions Code.

(2) Other records of vehicle weight relating to those certificates.

(3) Copies of those certificates and records.

(b) All certificates, records, and copies thereof, issued before January 1, 1984, shall not be available for inspection and are not admissible in any criminal or civil proceedings arising out of a violation of this chapter.

(Added by Stats. 1983, Ch. 1319, Sec. 1.)

35558. Any person or business which has an axle weight scale at its loading facilities shall, upon the request of the driver, weigh any load being transported for that person or business before the vehicle leaves the loading facility. In a port facility, this requirement only applies if the scale is located in outbound lanes. The request to weigh shall be based upon a reasonable assumption that the load is overweight.

(Added by Stats. 1990, Ch. 217, Sec. 1.)

35559. (a) (1) Notwithstanding any provision of this article, the power unit of a near-zero emission or zero-emission vehicle may exceed the allowable gross weight limits by up to a maximum of 2,000 pounds.

(2) The maximum allowance may apply to a single power unit or be distributed between more than one power unit, but shall not exceed a total of 2,000 pounds across a single vehicle or combination of vehicles.

(3) The maximum gross vehicle weight shall not exceed 82,000 pounds.

(b) This section shall not be construed to exempt any near-zero-emission or zero-emission vehicle from the weight limits prescribed in Article 2 (commencing with Section 35600), Article 3 (commencing with Section 35650), Article 4 (commencing with Section 35700), or Article 5 (commencing with Section 35750) of this chapter.

(c) This section shall not be construed to exempt any near-zero-emission or zero-emission vehicle from tire weight limits imposed by this code or in regulations adopted by the Department of the California Highway Patrol.

(d) For purposes of this section, "power unit" means a single unit or a combination of units in a near-zero emission or zero-emission vehicle that provide motive power to a drive system independent of any other power source.

(e) The terms "near-zero-emission vehicle" and "zero-emission vehicle" have the same meanings as defined in subdivisions (c) and (d) of Section 44258 of the Health and Safety Code.

(f) This section applies only to the extent expressly authorized by federal law.

(Added by Stats. 2024, Ch. 219, Sec. 2. (AB 1953) Effective January 1, 2025.)

Article 1.5. Intermodal Weight Determination Program

(Article 1.5 added by Stats. 1988, Ch. 865, Sec. 1.)

35580. (a) The Legislature finds and declares that a substantial number of container trailers using California highways exceed weight limitations authorized for California highways. Intermodal container trailers are containers which have been unloaded from ships or trains and placed on truck chassis, or are piggyback trailers unloaded from trains, for subsequent transport upon the highways. Container trailers are usually loaded by shippers in other states or foreign countries where gross and axle weight restrictions imposed by this code are of no concern to the loader. These loading practices often result in overweight vehicles traveling on California highways, which contributes to highway deterioration.

(b) The Legislature further finds and declares that the continued growth of intermodal transportation within the United States and the Pacific Rim makes it important for California to initiate a program to allow intermodal freight to be weighed at major terminal locations prior to operation on the highways, to ensure that these vehicles are within the established weight limits. The Legislature finds that the imposition of heavy fines and assessments is one means of reducing the number of overweight vehicles on the highways. A more effective, and preferable, alternative is to assure that intermodal container trailers are properly loaded at the outset by the party responsible for loading goods into the container trailer, so that vehicles meet weight requirements prior to their operation on the highways.

(Added by Stats. 1988, Ch. 865, Sec. 1.)

35581. (a) The Department of Transportation, in cooperation with the Department of the California Highway Patrol, shall develop a plan for implementing or identifying new or existing scale facilities at major intermodal terminals which may serve as intermodal weighing facilities for weighing commercial vehicles which transport intermodal freight, prior to their entry onto any highway which is not specifically exempted from weight limitations by a local authority. The plan shall include consideration of options for financing the construction of required intermodal weighing facilities. The plan shall be submitted to the Legislature not later than August 1, 1989.

(b) The Department of Transportation may enter into agreements with local authorities or private entities to provide for exemption from weight restrictions for short distance movement to an intermodal weighing facility.

(Amended by Stats. 2001, Ch. 745, Sec. 229. Effective October 12, 2001.)

Article 2. Tire Limits

(Article 2 enacted by Stats. 1959, Ch. 3.)

35600. The gross weight upon a solid tire upon a vehicle shall not exceed 600 pounds upon any inch of the channel base width of such tire.

(Enacted by Stats. 1959, Ch. 3.)

35601. The gross weight of any vehicle and load resting upon any metal tire in contact with the roadway shall not exceed 500 pounds upon any inch of the width of such tire but this limitation shall not apply to traction engines or tractors, the propulsive power of which is not exerted through wheels resting upon the roadway but by means of a flexible band or chain, known as a movable track, when the portions of the movable tracks in contact with the surface of the roadway present plane surfaces.

(Enacted by Stats. 1959, Ch. 3.)

Article 3. Limit Changes on State Highways

(Article 3 enacted by Stats. 1959, Ch. 3.)

35650. The Department of Transportation, whenever it determines after an engineering investigation that any highway under its jurisdiction will with safety to itself sustain vehicles and loads weighing more than the maximum weight limits set forth in this code, shall have authority to declare and to fix a weight limit for the highway greater than the maximum weight limit set forth in this code. Thereafter it shall be lawful to operate or move vehicles and loads of a gross weight upon the highways designated, equal to but not in excess of the maximum weight limit fixed by the department.

(Amended by Stats. 1974, Ch. 545.)

35651. Whenever in the judgment of the Department of Transportation any state highway will not with safety to itself sustain the maximum weights permitted under this code for the highway, the department shall determine, after a public hearing, the maximum weight which the highway will sustain.

(Amended by Stats. 1974, Ch. 545.)

35652. The Department of Transportation shall give notice of the time and place of the hearing by posting a notice in the county seat of each county in which any affected portion of the highway is located and shall also post copies of the notice at intervals of not more than one mile along said highway and a notice at each end of the affected portion thereof. Notice of the hearing shall be given for not less than 10 days and the hearing shall be had at the county seat of the county in which the affected highway is situated or at some other place convenient to the portion of the highway affected.

(Amended by Stats. 1974, Ch. 545.)

35653. The hearing shall be conducted by one or more engineers appointed by the Director of Transportation. The engineers shall hear all evidence presented at the time and place mentioned in the notice and shall report findings made in writing to the Director of Transportation. Upon the basis of the findings, the Director of Transportation shall declare in writing the maximum weight which can be maintained with safety upon the state highway. In no event shall the weight be less than 16,000 pounds.

(Amended by Stats. 1974, Ch. 545.)

35654. Following the declaration of maximum weight as provided in this article, the Department of Transportation shall erect suitable signs at each end of the affected portion of the highway and at such other points as the department deems necessary to give adequate notice of the weight limits.

(Amended by Stats. 1974, Ch. 545.)

35655. (a) No person shall drive a vehicle on any state highway when the weight of the vehicle and load is greater than the maximum weight which the highway will sustain. Violations of this subdivision shall be punished in accordance with the schedule of fines set forth in Section 42030.

(b) Upon the trial of any person charged with a violation with respect to signs erected under Section 35654, proof of the determination and the maximum weight by the Department of Transportation and the existence of the signs constitutes prima facie evidence of the maximum weight which the state highway will sustain.

(Amended by Stats. 1984, Ch. 542, Sec. 5.)

35655.5. (a) Notwithstanding this article or any other provision of law, no vehicle, as described in Sections 410 and 655, with a gross weight of 9,000 pounds or more, shall be operated on the segment of Interstate Route 580 (I-580) that is located between Grand Avenue in the City of Oakland and the city limits of the City of San Leandro. This subdivision does not apply to passenger buses or paratransit vehicles.

(b) The Department of Transportation shall erect suitable signs at each end of the portion of highway described in subdivision (a) and at any other points that the department deems necessary to give adequate notice of the weight limit imposed under this section.

(Added by Stats. 2000, Ch. 212, Sec. 1. Effective January 1, 2001.)

35655.6. (a) Except as provided in subdivision (b), a person shall not drive a commercial vehicle with three or more axles, or a gross vehicle weight or a combined gross weight of 9,000 pounds or more, on the segment of State Route 2 (SR-2) that is located between Interstate Route 210 (I-210) in the City of La Canada Flintridge and County Route N4 (Big Pine Highway) in the County of Los Angeles.

(b) Subdivision (a) does not apply to any of the following vehicles:

(1) An authorized emergency vehicle.

(2) A vehicle operated by a publicly or privately owned public utility.

(3) A vehicle operated by a government agency.

(4) A transit bus servicing facilities accessible only from that portion of State Route 2 specified in subdivision (a).

(5) A tow truck providing assistance to a vehicle that is accessible only from that portion of State Route 2 specified in subdivision (a).

(6) A commercial vehicle making deliveries to or from, or servicing, property that is either of the following:

(A) Located within the city limits of the City of La Canada Flintridge.

(B) Is accessible only from the portion of State Route 2 specified in subdivision (a).

(7) A commercial vehicle involved in a motion picture, commercial, or television production conducting motion picture, commercial, or television production activities in areas that are accessible only from that portion of State Route 2 specified in subdivision (a).

(c) A person who violates this section shall, upon conviction, be punished by a fine pursuant to subdivision (a) of Section 42030 or one thousand dollars ($1,000), whichever is greater.

(d) The Department of Transportation shall erect suitable signs at each end of the portion of State Route 2 specified in subdivision (a) and any other points that the department deems necessary to give adequate notice of the prohibition pursuant to this section.

(Added by Stats. 2009, Ch. 147, Sec. 1. Effective August 6, 2009.)

Article 4. Local Authorities

(Article 4 enacted by Stats. 1959, Ch. 3.)

35700. (a) The legislative body of any county or city may by ordinance permit the operation and moving of vehicles and loads upon highways under their respective jurisdictions of a maximum gross weight in excess of the maximum gross weight of vehicles and loads specified in this code.

(b) This section does not apply to state highways.

(Enacted by Stats. 1959, Ch. 3.)

35700.5. (a) The Department of Transportation, upon adoption of an ordinance or resolution that is in conformance with the provisions of this section by the City of Carson, the City of Long Beach, and the City of Los Angeles, covering designated routes, may issue a special permit to the operator of a vehicle, combination of vehicles, or mobile equipment, permitting the operation and movement of the vehicle, combination, or equipment, and its load, on the 3.66-mile portion of State Route 47 and State Route 103 known as the Terminal Island Freeway, between Willow Street in the City of Long Beach and Terminal Island in the City of Long Beach and the City of Los Angeles, and on the 2.4-mile portion of State Highway Route 1, that is between Sanford Avenue in the City of Los Angeles and Harbor Avenue in the City of Long Beach, if the vehicle, combination, or equipment meets all of the following criteria:

(1) The vehicle, combination of vehicles, or mobile equipment is used to transport intermodal cargo containers that are moving in international commerce.

(2) The vehicle, combination of vehicles, or mobile equipment, in combination with its load, has a maximum gross weight in excess of the maximum gross weight limit of vehicles and loads specified in this chapter, but does not exceed 95,000 pounds gross vehicle weight.

(3) (A) The vehicle, combination of vehicles, or mobile equipment conforms to the axle weight limits specified in Section 35550.

(B) The vehicle, combination of vehicles, or mobile equipment conforms to the axle weight limits in Section 35551, except as specified in subparagraph (C).

(C) Vehicles, combinations of vehicles, or mobile equipment that impose more than 80,000 pounds total gross weight on the highway by any group of two or more consecutive axles, exceed 60 feet in length between the extremes of any group of two or more consecutive axles, or have more than six axles shall conform to weight limits that shall be determined by the Department of Transportation.

(b) The permit issued by the Department of Transportation shall be required to authorize the operation or movement of a vehicle, combination of vehicles, or mobile equipment described in subdivision (a). The permit shall not authorize the movement of hazardous materials or hazardous wastes, as those terms are defined by local, state, and federal law. The following criteria shall be included in the application for the permit:

(1) A description of the loads and vehicles to be operated under the permit.

(2) An agreement wherein each applicant agrees to be responsible for all injuries to persons and for all damage to real or personal property of the state and others directly caused by or resulting from the operation of the applicant's vehicles or combination of vehicles under the conditions of the permit. The applicant shall agree to hold harmless and indemnify the state and all its agents for all costs or claims arising out of or caused by the movement of vehicles or combination of vehicles under the conditions of the permit.

(3) The applicant shall provide proof of financial responsibility that covers the movement of the shipment as described in subdivision (a). The insurance shall meet the minimum requirements established by law.

(4) An agreement to carry a copy of the permit in the vehicle at all times and furnish the copy upon request of an employee of the Department of the California Highway Patrol or the Department of Transportation.

(5) An agreement to place an indicia, developed by the Department of Transportation, in consultation with the Department of the California Highway Patrol, upon the vehicle identifying it as a vehicle possibly operating under this section. The indicia shall be displayed in the lower right area of the front windshield of the power unit. The Department of Transportation may charge a fee to cover the cost of producing and issuing this indicia.

(c) The permit issued pursuant to subdivision (a) shall be valid for one year. The permit may be canceled by the Department of Transportation for any of the following reasons:

(1) The failure of the applicant to maintain any of the conditions required pursuant to subdivision (b).

(2) The failure of the applicant to maintain a satisfactory rating, as required by Section 34501.12.

(3) A determination by the Department of Transportation that there is sufficient cause to cancel the permit because the continued movement of the applicant's vehicles under the permit would jeopardize the safety of the motorists on the roadway or result in undue damage to the highways listed in this section.

(d) This section does not authorize an applicant or holder of a special permit under subdivision (a) to operate a vehicle or combination of vehicles in excess of the maximum gross weight limit of vehicles and loads specified in this chapter outside of the designated corridors identified in subdivision (a). A violation of this subdivision shall result in the revocation of the permit.

(e) The Department of Transportation may charge a fee to cover the cost of issuing a permit pursuant to subdivision (a).

(Amended by Stats. 2011, Ch. 298, Sec. 2. (AB 1128) Effective January 1, 2012.)

35700.6. (a) The Department of Transportation, upon adoption of an ordinance or resolution that is in conformance with the provisions of this section by the City of Oakland, covering the designated route, may issue a special permit to the operator of a vehicle, combination of vehicles, or mobile equipment, permitting the operation and movement of the vehicle, combination, or equipment, and its load, on the 1.7-mile portion of State Route 185 that is between High Street and Hegenberger Road known as International Boulevard in the City of Oakland, if the vehicle, combination, or equipment meets all of the following criteria:

(1) The vehicle, combination of vehicles, or mobile equipment is used to transport intermodal cargo containers that are moving in international commerce.

(2) The vehicle, combination of vehicles, or mobile equipment, in combination with its load, has a maximum gross weight in excess of the maximum gross weight limit of vehicles and loads specified in this chapter, but does not exceed 95,000 pounds gross vehicle weight.

(3) (A) The vehicle, combination of vehicles, or mobile equipment conforms to the axle weight limits specified in Section 35550.

(B) The vehicle, combination of vehicles, or mobile equipment conforms to the axle weight limits in Section 35551, except as specified in subparagraph (C).

(C) Vehicles, combinations of vehicles, or mobile equipment that impose more than 80,000 pounds total gross weight on the highway by any group of two or more consecutive axles, exceed 60 feet in length between the extremes of any group of two or more consecutive axles, or have more than six axles shall conform to weight limits that shall be determined by the Department of Transportation.

(4) The vehicle, combination of vehicles, or mobile equipment only operate during the hours determined to be appropriate by the Department of Transportation, in concurrence with the City of Oakland.

(b) The permit issued by the Department of Transportation shall be required to authorize the operation or movement of a vehicle, combination of vehicles, or mobile equipment described in subdivision (a). The permit shall not authorize the movement of hazardous materials or hazardous wastes, as those terms are defined by local, state, and federal law. The following criteria shall be included in the application for the permit:

(1) A description of the loads and vehicles to be operated under the permit.

(2) An agreement wherein each applicant agrees to be responsible for all injuries to persons and for all damage to real or personal property of the state and others directly caused by or resulting from the operation of the applicant's vehicles or combination of vehicles under the conditions of the permit. The applicant shall agree to hold harmless and indemnify the state and all its agents for all costs or claims arising out of or caused by the movement of vehicles or combination of vehicles under the

conditions of the permit.

(3) The applicant shall provide proof of financial responsibility that covers the movement of the shipment as described in subdivision (a). The insurance shall meet the minimum requirements established by law.

(4) An agreement to carry a copy of the permit in the vehicle at all times and furnish the copy upon request of an employee of the Department of the California Highway Patrol or the Department of Transportation.

(5) An agreement to place an indicia, developed by the Department of Transportation, in consultation with the Department of the California Highway Patrol, upon the vehicle identifying it as a vehicle possibly operating under this section. The indicia shall be displayed in the lower right area of the front windshield of the power unit. The Department of Transportation may charge a fee to cover the cost of producing and issuing this indicia.

(c) The permit issued pursuant to subdivision (a) shall be valid for one year. The permit may be canceled by the Department of Transportation for any of the following reasons:

(1) The failure of the applicant to maintain any of the conditions required pursuant to subdivision (b).

(2) The failure of the applicant to maintain a satisfactory rating, as required by Section 34501.12.

(3) A determination by the Department of Transportation that there is sufficient cause to cancel the permit because the continued movement of the applicant's vehicles under the permit would jeopardize the safety of the motorists on the roadway or result in undue damage to the highways listed in this section.

(d) This section does not authorize an applicant or holder of a special permit under subdivision (a) to operate a vehicle or combination of vehicles in excess of the maximum gross weight limit of vehicles and loads specified in this chapter outside of the designated corridors identified in subdivision (a). A violation of this subdivision shall result in the revocation of the permit.

(e) The Department of Transportation may charge a fee to cover the cost of issuing a permit pursuant to subdivision (a).

(f) On or before January 1, 2031, the City of Oakland shall submit to the Legislature and the Department of Transportation, in conformance with Section 9795 of the Government Code, a report on all of the following:

(1) The cost of road repairs caused by the vehicle, combination of vehicles, or mobile equipment on International Boulevard.

(2) Community impacts, including safety impacts, of the vehicle, combination of vehicles, or mobile equipment on International Boulevard.

(3) Status of evaluating and implementing an alternate truck route providing freight movement direct access to San Leandro Street instead of International Boulevard.

(g) This section shall remain in effect only until an alternate truck route to San Leandro Street becomes available pursuant to a notice by the Department of Transportation, or until December 31, 2031, whichever occurs first, and as of that date is repealed.

(Added by Stats. 2025, Ch. 109, Sec. 8. (SB 153) Effective September 17, 2025. Conditionally repealed on or before December 31, 2031, as prescribed by its own provisions.)

35701. (a) Any city, or county for a residence district, may, by ordinance, prohibit the use of a street by any commercial vehicle or by any vehicle exceeding a maximum gross weight limit, except with respect to any vehicle which is subject to Sections 1031 to 1036, inclusive, of the Public Utilities Code, and except with respect to vehicles used for the collection and transportation of garbage, rubbish, or refuse using traditionally used routes in San Diego County when the solid waste management plan prepared under Section 66780.1 of the Government Code is amended to designate each traditionally used route used for the purpose of transporting garbage, rubbish, or refuse which intersects with a local or regional arterial circulation route contained within a city or county's traffic circulation element and which provides access to a solid waste disposal site.

(b) The ordinance shall not be effective until appropriate signs are erected indicating either the streets affected by the ordinance or the streets not affected, as the local authority determines will best serve to give notice of the ordinance.

(c) No ordinance adopted pursuant to this section after November 10, 1969, shall apply to any state highway which is included in the National System of Interstate and Defense Highways, except an ordinance which has been approved by a two-thirds vote of the California Transportation Commission.

(d) The solid waste management plan prepared under Section 66780.1 of the Government Code by San Diego County may designate the traditionally used routes.

(e) "Traditionally used route," for purposes of this section, means any street used for a period of one year or more as access to or from a solid waste disposal site.

(Amended by Stats. 1987, Ch. 616, Sec. 1.)

35702. No ordinance proposed under Section 35701 is effective with respect to any highway which is not under the exclusive jurisdiction of the local authority enacting the ordinance, or, in the case of any state highway, until the ordinance has been submitted by the governing body of the local authority to, and approved in writing by, the Department of Transportation. In submitting a proposed ordinance to the department for approval, the governing body of the local authority shall designate therein, an alternate route for the use of vehicles, which route shall remain unrestricted by any local regulation as to weight limits or types of vehicles so long as the ordinance proposed shall remain in effect. The approval of the proposed ordinance by the Department of Transportation shall constitute an approval by it of the alternate route so designated.

(Amended by Stats. 1998, Ch. 877, Sec. 71. Effective January 1, 1999.)

35703. No ordinance adopted pursuant to Section 35701 shall prohibit any commercial vehicles coming from an unrestricted street having ingress and egress by direct route to and from a restricted street when necessary for the purpose of making pickups or deliveries of goods, wares, and merchandise from or to any building or structure located on the restricted street or for the purpose of delivering materials to be used in the actual and bona fide repair, alteration, remodeling, or construction of any building or structure upon the restricted street for which a building permit has previously been obtained.

(Enacted by Stats. 1959, Ch. 3.)

35704. No ordinance adopted pursuant to Section 35701 to decrease weight limits shall apply to any vehicle owned by a public utility or a licensed contractor while necessarily in use in the construction, installation, or repair of any public utility.

(Amended by Stats. 1987, Ch. 371, Sec. 1.)

35705. Section 35701 shall not be applicable to any city street on which money from the State Highway Account in the State Transportation Fund has been or is used for construction or maintenance except in such cases as the legislative body of the city, after notice and hearing, determines to reduce weight limits on such streets. Notice of the hearing shall be published as provided in Section 6064 of the Government Code. The notice shall advise all interested parties that they may submit written and oral objections to the proposed action and shall designate a time and place for presentation of such objections. The time for submission of objections shall not expire, and the hearing may not be held, less than 60 days after the first publication of notice. The hearing shall be held before the legislative body of the city. All objections shall be considered and interested parties shall be afforded an adequate opportunity to be heard in respect to their objections.

(Amended by Stats. 1974, Ch. 545.)

35706. Boards of supervisors in their respective counties may by ordinance reduce the permissible weight of vehicles and loads upon unimproved county highways or upon county bridges.

(Enacted by Stats. 1959, Ch. 3.)

35707. Boards of supervisors in their respective counties may by ordinance reduce the permissible weights upon improved highways only which by reason of deterioration will be destroyed unless the weight limits are reduced, but no such reduction shall extend for a period of more than 90 days unless actual repair of the highway is begun within that time and thereafter continuously carried on to completion.

For the purposes of this section, an improved county highway means a highway paved with cement concrete or asphaltic concrete, or a highway with a roadway of hard surface not less than four inches thick made up of a mixture of rock, sand, or gravel bound together by an artificial binder other than natural soil.

(Enacted by Stats. 1959, Ch. 3.)

35708. In the event any person protests in writing to the clerk of the board of supervisors within 15 days after the adoption of an ordinance reducing the permissible gross weight upon an improved highway, the reduction in weight shall not become final until the Department of Transportation after a hearing approves the action of the board of supervisors in making such reduction.

(Amended by Stats. 1974, Ch. 545.)

35709. The hearing shall be held in the county in which the highway is located within 25 days after a request therefor, and shall be conducted by one or more engineers of the Department of Transportation to be designated by the Director of Transportation. The engineers shall hear all evidence presented and report their findings in writing to the director. Such director shall, upon the basis of the findings, declare in writing the approval or disapproval of the reduction.

(Amended by Stats. 1974, Ch. 545.)

35710. Whenever any weight limit different from those specified in this code is fixed in accordance with Section 35706 or 35707, the board of supervisors shall cause signs indicating the weight so fixed to be erected at all entrances to the highway upon which the permissible gross weight is altered.

(Enacted by Stats. 1959, Ch. 3.)

35711. No ordinance adopted pursuant to Section 35706 or 35707 or 35712 shall prohibit any commercial vehicle from using any county highway by direct route to or from a state highway for the purpose of delivering or loading for transportation goods, wares, or merchandise.

(Amended by Stats. 1969, Ch. 1598.)

35712. (a) Any county may, by ordinance, prohibit the use of any highway located in an unincorporated residential or subdivision area by any commercial vehicle exceeding a gross weight of 14,000 pounds.

(b) Any county of the third class, as defined by Section 28024 of the Government Code, or of the ninth class, as defined by Section 28030 of the Government Code, may, by ordinance, prohibit the use of any highway located in an unincorporated residential or subdivision area by any commercial vehicle exceeding a gross weight of 5,000 pounds.

(c) This section does not apply to a vehicle operated by, or on behalf of, a public utility in connection with the installation, operation, maintenance, or repair of its facilities.

(Amended by Stats. 1998, Ch. 877, Sec. 72. Effective January 1, 1999.)

35713. No ordinance closing a highway under Section 35712 or 35715 is effective until appropriate signs are erected indicating either the highways affected by the ordinance or the highways not affected as the county may determine will best serve to give notice of the ordinance, nor shall any ordinance be effective with respect to any county highway unless the board of supervisors designates in the ordinance an alternate route for the use of the vehicles which shall remain unrestricted by any local regulation as to commercial vehicles so long as the ordinance proposed shall remain in effect.

(Amended by Stats. 1975, Ch. 660.)

35714. No ordinance adopted pursuant to Section 35712 shall be effective with respect to:

(a) Any vehicle which is subject to the provisions of Article 2 (commencing with Section 1031) of Chapter 5 of Part 1 of Division 1 of the Public Utilities Code.

(b) Any highway, any portion of which is also under the jurisdiction of a city, unless the consent of the governing body of the city is first obtained.

(c) Any commercial vehicle coming from an unrestricted highway having ingress and egress by direct route to and from the restricted highway when necessary for the purpose of making pickups or deliveries of goods, wares, and merchandise from or to any building or structure located on the restricted highway or for the purpose of delivering materials to be used in the actual and bona fide repair, alteration, remodeling, or construction of any building or structure upon the restricted highway for which a building permit has previously been obtained.

(d) The operation of ambulances or hearses.

(e) Any vehicle owned, operated, controlled, or used by a public utility in connection with the construction, installation, operation, maintenance, or repair of any public utility facilities.

(f) Any state highway, until the proposed ordinance has been submitted by the board of supervisors of the county to and approved in writing by the Department of Transportation. In submitting a proposed ordinance to the department for approval, the board of supervisors shall designate therein, an alternate route for the use of the vehicles which shall remain unrestricted by any local regulation as to commercial vehicles so long as the ordinance proposed shall remain in effect. The approval of the proposed ordinance by the Department of Transportation shall constitute an approval by the department of the alternate route so designated.

(g) Vehicles operated as an incident to any industrial, commercial or agricultural enterprise conducted within the boundaries of the unincorporated residential subdivision area.

(Amended by Stats. 1998, Ch. 877, Sec. 73. Effective January 1, 1999.)

35715. (a) The County of Nevada may by ordinance prohibit the use of Northwoods Boulevard in such county by any commercial vehicle exceeding a gross weight specified in the ordinance.

(b) No ordinance adopted pursuant to this section shall be effective with respect to:

(1) Any commercial vehicle coming from an unrestricted highway having ingress and egress by direct route to and from the restricted highway when necessary for the purpose of making pickups or deliveries of goods, wares, and merchandise from or to any building or structure located on the restricted highway or for the purpose of delivering materials to be used in the actual and bona fide repair, alteration, remodeling, or construction of any building or structure upon the restricted highway for which a building permit has previously been obtained.

(2) The operation of ambulances or hearses.

(3) Any vehicle owned, operated, controlled, or used by a public utility in connection with the construction, installation, operation, maintenance, or repair of any public utility facilities.

(Added by Stats. 1975, Ch. 660.)

35715.1. (a) The County of Tuolumne may by ordinance prohibit the use of Old Priest Grade in that county by a vehicle or combination of vehicles that exceeds a weight limit of 7,500 pounds or more. The weight limit shall be determined by the County Board of Supervisors and specified in the ordinance.

(b) An ordinance adopted pursuant to this section is not effective with respect to the following:

(1) A vehicle or combination of vehicles coming from an unrestricted highway having ingress and egress by direct route to and from the restricted highway when necessary for the purpose of making pickups or deliveries of goods, wares, and merchandise from or to any building or structure located on the restricted highway or for the purpose of delivering materials to be used in the actual and bona fide repair, alteration, remodeling, or construction of a building or structure upon the restricted highway for which a building permit has previously been obtained.

(2) The operation of ambulances, hearses, or vehicles providing emergency roadside services or roadside assistance.

(3) A vehicle or combination of vehicles owned, operated, controlled, or used by a public utility in connection with the construction, installation, operation, maintenance, or repair of a public utility facility.

(Added by Stats. 2003, Ch. 15, Sec. 1. Effective January 1, 2004.)

35716. No ordinance adopted by a city to decrease weight limits shall apply to any vehicle owned, leased, operated or controlled by any licensed contractor while necessarily in use in the construction, maintenance, or repair of a public works project, or by any highway carrier regulated by the Public Utilities Commission while transporting any materials to or from a public works project, when the bids were opened prior to the adoption of the ordinance unless an alternate direct route is provided substantially within and by the city enacting the ordinance.

(Amended by Stats. 1969, Ch. 393.)

35717. Notwithstanding any provision to the contrary, any county may by ordinance prohibit the use of any street, road or highway by any commercial vehicle exceeding a maximum gross weight of 14,000 pounds if, by accepted engineering standards, the street, road or highway cannot support such vehicle.

(Added by Stats. 1959, Ch. 1732.)

35718. No ordinance adopted pursuant to Section 35717 shall be effective until appropriate signs are erected indicating either the streets, roads or highways affected by the ordinance or the streets, roads or highways not affected, as the board of supervisors may determine will best serve to give notice of the ordinance.

(Added by Stats. 1959, Ch. 1732.)

35719. No ordinance adopted pursuant to Section 35717 shall be effective with respect to any street, road or highway which connects with, or is a continuation of, any street, road or highway of an adjoining county unless the board of supervisors of each county in which the street, road or highway is a through highway, by concurrent action and like limitation, prohibit the use of such street, road or highway pursuant to this section.

(Added by Stats. 1959, Ch. 1732.)

35720. No ordinance adopted pursuant to Section 35717 shall be effective with respect to:

(a) Any vehicle which is subject to the provisions of Article 2 (commencing with Section 1031) of Chapter 5 of Part 1 of Division 1 of the Public Utilities Code or any farm labor vehicle.

(b) Any street, road or highway which is not under the exclusive jurisdiction of the board of supervisors enacting such ordinance, except as otherwise provided in Section 35719, or, in the case of any state highway, until such proposed ordinance has been submitted by the board of supervisors to and approved in writing by the Department of Transportation. In submitting such a proposed ordinance to the department for approval, the board of supervisors shall designate therein, an alternate route or routes for the use of such vehicles which shall remain unrestricted by any local regulation as to weight limits or types of vehicles so long as the ordinance proposed shall remain in effect. The approval of such proposed ordinances by the Department of Transportation shall constitute an approval by the department of such alternate route or routes so designated.

(c) Any commercial vehicle coming from an unrestricted street, road or highway having ingress and egress by direct route to and from such restricted streets, roads, and highways when necessary for the purpose of making pickups or deliveries of goods, wares and merchandise from or to any building or structure located on such restricted streets, roads or highways or for the purpose of delivering materials to be used in the actual and bona fide repair, alteration, remodeling or construction of any building or structure upon such restricted street, road or highway for which a building permit, if required, has previously been obtained therefor, or vehicles, machinery, or construction equipment used in connection with, the construction, repair or maintenance of such restricted street or public work projects located thereon.

(d) Any vehicle operated as an incident to any industrial, commercial, or agricultural enterprise conducted upon any such street, road, or highway.

(e) Any vehicle owned, operated, controlled, or used by a public utility or licensed contractor in connection with the construction, installation, operation, maintenance, or repair of any public utility facilities or public works projects.

(f) The operation of ambulances or hearses.

(Amended by Stats. 1980, Ch. 676, Sec. 317.)

35721. No ordinance shall be adopted pursuant to Section 35717 except upon notice and hearing in the manner prescribed in this section.

Notice of hearing shall be published as prescribed in Section 6064 of the Government Code. The notice shall advise all interested parties that they may submit written or oral objections to the proposed action and shall designate a time and place for presentation of such objections. The time for submission of objections shall not expire, and the hearing may not be held, less than 60 days after the first publication of notice. The hearing shall be held before the board of supervisors and interested parties shall be afforded an adequate opportunity to be heard with respect to their objections.

(Added by Stats. 1959, Ch. 1732.)

35722. Prior to the execution of freeway agreements for State Highway Route 85 in Santa Clara County, with the concurrence of each city within the highway corridor, the Board of Supervisors of the County of Santa Clara may, after a public hearing, adopt a proposed ordinance imposing a maximum gross truck weight limit of 9,000 pounds on Route 85 from State Highway Route 280 in Cupertino south and east to State Highway Route 101 in San Jose, and submit the proposed ordinance to the Department of Transportation for approval.

Upon approval of the proposed ordinance by the department, this weight limit shall be stipulated in the applicable freeway agreements with the local entities in the Route 85 corridor.

If the proposed ordinance is approved by the department, the weight limit shall become effective upon opening of any portion of the new Route 85 freeway corridor as defined in this section, and the department shall post appropriate signs, similar to the signs on State Highway Route 580 in Oakland. Except as otherwise provided in this section, this article shall be applicable to an ordinance adopted pursuant to this section.

(Added by Stats. 1987, Ch. 1250, Sec. 1.)

Article 5. Bridges and Other Structures

(Article 5 enacted by Stats. 1959, Ch. 3.)

35750. (a) The Department of Transportation may, in the manner provided in Section 35751, determine the maximum weight of vehicle and load, lower than the maximum weight otherwise permitted under this code which a bridge or other structure with safety to itself will sustain.

(b) The city council or the board of supervisors of a city or county with a population of 1,100,000 or more, as determined by the 1970 federal decennial census, may, in the manner provided in Section 35751, determine the maximum weight of vehicle and load, lower than the maximum weight otherwise permitted under this code which a bridge or other structure under its jurisdiction with safety to itself will sustain.

(Amended by Stats. 1974, Ch. 545.)

35751. (a) The Department of Transportation or the city council or board of supervisors of a city or county with a population of 1,100,000 or more, as determined by the 1970 federal decennial census, as the case may be, shall make an engineering investigation and hold a public hearing whenever such a determination appears necessary.

(b) Notice of the time and place of the hearing shall be posted upon the bridge or other structure at least five days before the date fixed for the hearing. Upon the basis of the investigation and all evidence presented at the hearing, the department or the city council or board of supervisors, as the case may be, shall determine by order in writing the maximum weight of vehicle and load which the bridge or other structure with safety to itself will sustain.

(c) With respect to any bridge or other structure not under its jurisdiction, the department shall not proceed under subdivisions (a) and (b) unless it first receives a request to do so from the city council or the board of supervisors having jurisdiction over the bridge or other structure.

(Amended by Stats. 1974, Ch. 545.)

35752. Thereupon, the authority having jurisdiction over the bridge or other structure shall erect and maintain suitable signs specifying the maximum weight so determined, at a distance of not more than 500 feet from each end of the bridge or other structure or any approach thereto.

The standards and specifications for such signs shall be established in accordance with Section 21400 of this code.

(Amended by Stats. 1969, Ch. 1033.)

35753. (a) No person shall drive a vehicle over any bridge, causeway, viaduct, trestle, or dam constituting a part of a highway when the weight of the vehicle and load thereon is greater than the maximum weight which the bridge or other structure with safety to itself will sustain. Violations of this subdivision shall be punished in accordance with the schedule of fines set forth in Section 42030.

(b) Upon the trial of any person charged with a violation with respect to a weight restriction sign erected pursuant to Section 35752, proof of the determination of the maximum weight by the Department of Transportation and the existence of the weight restriction signs constitute prima facie evidence of the maximum weight which the bridge or other structure with safety to itself will sustain.

(Amended by Stats. 1984, Ch. 542, Sec. 6.)

35754. Whenever, in the opinion of a local authority, a bridge under its jurisdiction is in a dangerous or weak condition, it may temporarily erect suitable signs at all entrances to such bridge specifying the maximum weight which it believes the bridge with safety to itself will sustain. The maximum weight limit so fixed and posted shall remain in effect for not more than 90 days.

(Amended by Stats. 1972, Ch. 597.)

35755. Whenever a state highway bridge is in a dangerous or weak condition, the Department of Transportation may temporarily erect suitable signs at all entrances to such bridge specifying the maximum weight which the bridge may safely sustain. Under no circumstances shall the maximum weight limit so fixed and posted pursuant to this section remain in effect for more than 90 days.

(Amended by Stats. 1974, Ch. 545.)

Article 6. Permits and Agreements

(Article 6 enacted by Stats. 1959, Ch. 3.)

35780. (a) The Department of Transportation or local authorities, with respect to highways under their respective jurisdictions, may, at their discretion upon application and if good cause appears, issue a special permit authorizing the applicant:

(1) To operate or move a vehicle or combination of vehicles or special mobile equipment of a size or weight of vehicle or load exceeding the maximum specified in this code.

(2) To use corrugations on the periphery of the movable tracks on a traction engine or tractor, the propulsive power of which is not exerted through wheels resting upon the roadway but by means of a flexible band or chain.

(3) Under emergency conditions, to operate or move a type of vehicle otherwise prohibited hereunder, upon any highway under the jurisdiction of the party granting the permit and for the maintenance of which the party is responsible.

(4) To operate or move a vehicle or combination of vehicles transporting loads composed of logs only for the purpose of crossing a highway from one private property to another without complying with any or all of the equipment requirements of Division 12 (commencing with Section 24000) and Division 13 (commencing with Section 29000). These crossings shall be as near to a right angle to the roadway as is practical and shall not include any travel parallel to the roadway. The Department of Transportation shall determine standards and conditions upon which permits shall be issued and any permit not in compliance with those standards and conditions shall be invalid, except that a permit may contain more restrictive conditions if the issuing authority deems it appropriate.

(b) Under conditions prescribed by the Department of Transportation or the local authority, the Department of Transportation or local authority may accept applications made by, and issue permits directly to, an applicant or permit service by any of the following processes:

(1) In writing.

(2) By an authorized facsimile process.

(3) Through an authorized computer and modem connection.

(Amended by Stats. 1992, Ch. 391, Sec. 3. Effective January 1, 1993.)

35780.3. A permit issued under Section 35780 for the movement of a park trailer, as described in Section 18009.3 of the Health and Safety Code, shall not be issued except to transporters, or licensed manufacturers and dealers.

(Amended by Stats. 2000, Ch. 566, Sec. 8. Effective January 1, 2001.)

35780.5. (a) Notwithstanding Section 320.5, the Department of Transportation or a local authority, with respect to highways under their respective jurisdictions, may, upon application, issue a special permit authorizing the applicant to operate or move a vehicle carrying a load, lying in the horizontal position, of stacked trusses or wall panels that are used as single width components in the manufacture of a finished product, that exceeds the maximum width specified by this code, if the load does not exceed 12 feet in width and the permittee complies with the regulations of the Department of Transportation or a local authority, as the case may be, governing the transportation of these loads.

(b) Under conditions prescribed by the Department of Transportation or the local authority, the Department of Transportation or local authority may accept applications and issue permits directly to an applicant or permit service, by any of the following processes:

(1) In writing.

(2) By an authorized facsimile process.

(3) Through an authorized computer and modem connection.

(c) The special permit allowed pursuant to this section shall, under conditions prescribed by the Department of Transportation or a local authority, be granted on either a per trip or annual basis.

(d) As used in this section, "truss" means a designed and manufactured assemblage of structural elements typically arranged in a triangle or combination of triangles to form a rigid framework and used as a structural support in buildings.

(e) As used in this section, "wall panel" means a designed and manufactured assemblage of structural elements constructed in the same manner as site-built walls to form a rigid framework and used as a structural support in buildings, which may have attached various types of sheathing products including wood structural panels, foam panels, and gypsum board that do not exceed more than one foot beyond the main structural elements.

(Added by Stats. 2007, Ch. 514, Sec. 3. Effective January 1, 2008.)

35781. The Department of Transportation shall develop a standard application form and a standard permit form for the application for, and the issuance of, a permit. The standard permit form may be used as the standard application form. The application for a permit shall specifically describe the vehicle and load to be operated or moved and the particular highways over which permit to operate is requested, and whether the permit is requested for a single trip or for continuous operation. Local authorities shall use the standard application form and the standard permit form developed by the Department of Transportation. The standard application form and the standard permit form shall be developed in cooperation with representatives of local government and the commercial trucking industry.

(Amended by Stats. 1996, Ch. 464, Sec. 1. Effective January 1, 1997.)

35782. (a) The Department of Transportation or a local authority may issue or withhold the permit at its discretion, or, if the permit is issued, do any of the following when necessary to protect against injury to the road, foundations, surfaces, or structures:

(1) Limit the number of trips.

(2) Establish seasonal or other time limitations within which the vehicle or vehicles described may be operated on the highways indicated.

(3) Otherwise limit or prescribe conditions of operation of the vehicle.

(b) The Department of Transportation or a local authority may not require the posting of a bond as a condition of the issuance of a permit, except that a requirement of extra insurance or other financial security may be imposed as a condition for a permit for unusually large or heavy loads that pose a substantial risk to public facilities.

(c) Except as provided in subdivision (b), the Department of Transportation or a local authority may not require proof of financial responsibility in an amount greater than that required for compliance with Section 16500.5 as a condition of the permit, and shall accept evidence of financial responsibility that complies with Section 16020.

(Amended by Stats. 1996, Ch. 124, Sec. 137. Effective January 1, 1997.)

35783. Every permit shall be carried in the vehicle or combination of vehicles to which it refers and shall be open to inspection of any peace officer, traffic officer, authorized agent of the Department of Transportation, or any other officer or employee charged with the care or protection of such highways.

(Amended by Stats. 1974, Ch. 545.)

35783.5. Warning signs required by the terms of a permit shall either be removed from the vehicle or covered from the view of other motorists whenever the vehicle is operating without the load that required the permit.

(Added by Stats. 1978, Ch. 287.)

35784. (a) Except as provided in subdivision (b), it is unlawful for any person to violate any of the terms or conditions of any special permit.

(b) In an incorporated city where compliance with the route described in a special permit would result in a violation of local traffic regulations, the permittee may detour from the prescribed route to avoid violating the local traffic regulations if the permittee returns as soon as possible to the prescribed route. A detour under this subdivision shall be made only on nonresidential streets.

(c) If a violation under subdivision (a) consists of an extralegal load not being on the route described in the special permit, and the violation is directly caused by the action of an employee under the supervision of, or by the action of any independent contractor working for, a permittee subject to this section, the employee or independent contractor causing the violation is guilty of a misdemeanor. This subdivision applies only if the employee or independent contractor has been provided written direction on the route to travel and has not been directed to take a different route by a peace officer.

(d) The guilt of an employee or independent contractor under subdivision (c) shall not extend to the permittee employing that person unless the permittee is separately responsible for an action causing the violation.

(e) A violation of equipment requirements contained in Division 12 (commencing with Section 24000), by any person operating a pilot car shall not be considered a violation of any terms or conditions of a special permit under subdivision (a).

(f) (1) Any person convicted of a violation of the terms and conditions of a special permit shall be punished by a fine not exceeding five hundred dollars ($500) or by imprisonment in the county jail for a period not exceeding six months, or by both that fine and imprisonment.

(2) In addition, if the violation involves weight in excess of that authorized by the permit, an additional fine shall be levied as specified in Section 42030 on the amount of weight in excess of the amount authorized by the permit.

(Amended by Stats. 1988, Ch. 460, Sec. 6.)

35784.5. (a) Any person convicted of transporting an extralegal load on a highway, or causing or directing the operation of or driving on a highway any vehicle or combination of vehicles for which a permit is required pursuant to this article, without having obtained a permit issued in accordance with this article, shall be punished by a fine not exceeding five hundred dollars ($500) or by imprisonment in the county jail for a period not exceeding six months, or by both that fine and imprisonment.

(b) If the violation involves excess weight, an additional fine shall be levied as specified in Section 42030 on the amount of weight in excess of that authorized pursuant to this chapter.

(Added by Stats. 1984, Ch. 542, Sec. 8.)

35785. (a) The axle weight limitations imposed in Sections 35550 and 35551 shall not apply to the transportation of a single saw log which does not exceed 8 feet in diameter and 21 feet in length or 6 feet in diameter and 33 feet in length, if such log is hauled on a combination of vehicles consisting of a three-axle truck and a two-axle logging dolly under permit issued by the Department of Transportation or by local authorities with respect to highways under their respective jurisdictions. Such permit may be granted for not more than thirty (30) days and may be revocable upon notice by the department or local authorities, as the case may be. (b) When so transported, the vehicle shall not be operated over any bridge or causeway at a speed of more than 15 miles per hour or on the highway at more than 25 miles per hour, on routes designated in the permit. Diameter measurements of the logs shall be made on the large end.

(Amended by Stats. 1974, Ch. 545.)

35786. Truck booster power units may be used to aid in propelling or moving any motor truck or lawful combination of motor vehicles upon a highway upon an ascending or descending grade, subject to the following conditions:

(a) A permit for such operation must be obtained as provided in this article.

(b) The truck booster power unit shall be operated only on such highways and at such times and according to such conditions and requirements as may be specified in the permit.

(Enacted by Stats. 1959, Ch. 3.)

35787. The Department of Transportation or local authority, as the case may be, shall issue a truck booster power unit permit only if in its opinion the proposed operation would not tend to endanger the traveling public or to damage the highway, bridge or any highway structure.

The Department of Transportation and local authorities, in issuing a permit, may make such conditions and requirements as in their opinion are necessary or desirable for the safety of the traveling public and of the highway, including bridges and other highway structures.

(Amended by Stats. 1974, Ch. 545.)

35788. Upon application to the Director of Transportation for permission to use and operate on highways private or contract vehicles for the purpose of hauling loads which weigh in excess of the maximum load weight limits, the director may enter into an agreement with the applicant, permitting such overloads, specifying protective restrictions and providing for the payment of a financial contribution for the issuance of such permission, except that the overload shall not exceed 25 percent of the maximum load weight limitation, in pounds, set forth in this code. The agreement shall not permit the applicant to transport such excess weight loads on highways for distances exceeding 75 miles. All contributions received by the Department of Transportation shall be used for the construction, improvement, or maintenance of the highway designated in the permission to operate overweight loads. Sections 188 and 188.8 of the Streets and Highways Code does not apply to contributions received pursuant to this section, and any expenditures of the contributions by the department shall not be credited against amounts required to be expended pursuant to Sections 188 and 188.8 of the Streets and Highways Code.

This section does not apply to highways which are a part of the

National System of Interstate and Defense Highways.

(Amended by Stats. 1982, Ch. 827, Sec. 16. Effective September 10, 1982.)

35789. Any housemoving contractor or other person who by contract or otherwise moves or transports a dwelling house or other building across railroad tracks shall furnish to the division or district superintendent of the railroad company operating such tracks written notice of intention to make such movement at least 36 hours prior to doing so. The written notice of intention to make such a movement shall contain the name of the street, highway or road over which such dwelling house or other building will be moved across the railroad tracks, the approximate time of day such movement will be made and such other information as may be necessary to enable the railroad company to take precautionary measures to avoid a collision by a train with such dwelling house or other building.

(Added by renumbering Section 25789 by Stats. 1959, Ch. 1996.)

35789.5. (a) The Legislature finds and declares all of the following:

(1) Current restrictions on the movement on the highways of manufactured homes in excess of 14 feet in width has caused the closure of some manufactured housing manufacturing facilities, that have, in turn, relocated to other states in order to compete with interstate commerce.

(2) Those restrictions on the movement of manufactured homes could cause the closure of at least three more manufacturing facilities within the next 12 months, thereby laying off some 500 employees, while at the same time those manufacturing facilities relocate to other states.

(3) The Department of Transportation has a policy allowing permitted loads in excess of 14 feet in width for the general trucking industry and the boating industry.

(4) The Legislature supports allowing the movement on the highways of manufactured homes in excess of 14 feet in width, with appropriate safeguards, because this policy will result in both of the following:

(A) Enable the manufactured housing industry to produce homes for export to other states, thereby keeping jobs within the state and benefiting the state's economy.

(B) Permit the building of manufactured homes with eaves, which provide structural and aesthetic benefits to the homes.

(b) The Legislature further finds and declares that allowing the movement on the highways of manufactured homes that are 16 feet in width, with appropriate safeguards, will benefit the state's economy and will allow production of more affordable and aesthetic manufactured homes.

(Amended by Stats. 1996, Ch. 278, Sec. 1. Effective January 1, 1997.)

35790. (a) The Department of Transportation or local authorities with respect to highways under their respective jurisdictions may, upon application in writing and if good cause appears, issue a special or annual permit in writing authorizing the applicant to move any manufactured home in excess of the maximum width but not exceeding 14 feet in total width, exclusive of lights and devices provided for in Sections 35109 and 35110, upon any highway under the jurisdiction of the party granting the permit.

(b) A public agency, in the exercise of its discretion in granting permits for the movement of overwidth manufactured homes, and in considering the individual circumstances of each case, may use merchandising or relocation of residence as a basis for movement for good cause.

(c) (1) The application for a special permit shall specifically describe the manufactured home to be moved and the particular highways over which the permit to operate is requested.

(2) The application for an annual permit shall specifically describe the power unit to be used to tow the overwidth manufactured homes and the particular highways over which the permit to operate is requested. The annual permit shall be subject to all of the conditions of this section and any additional conditions imposed by the public agency.

(d) The Department of Transportation or local authority may establish seasonal or other time limitations within which a manufactured home may be moved on the highways indicated, and may require an undertaking or other security as it deems necessary to protect the highways and bridges from injury or to provide indemnity for any injury resulting from the operation.

(e) Permits for the movement of manufactured homes under this section shall not be issued except to transporters or licensed manufacturers and dealers and only under the following conditions:

(1) The manufactured home for which the permit is issued shall comply with Sections 35550 and 35551.

(2) In the case of a permit issued on an individual or repetitive trip basis, the applicant has first received the approval of a city or county if the trip will include movement on streets or highways under the jurisdiction of the city or county. The application for such a permit shall indicate the complete route of the proposed move and shall specify all cities and counties that have approved the move. This paragraph shall not be construed to require the Department of Transportation to verify the information provided by an applicant with respect to movement on streets or highways under local jurisdiction.

(3) It is a violation of any permit, which is issued by the Department of Transportation and authorizes a move only on a state highway, for that move to be extended to a street or highway under the jurisdiction of a city or county unless the move has been approved by the city or county.

(f) The Department of Transportation, in cooperation with the Department of the California Highway Patrol, or the local authority may establish additional reasonable permit regulations as they may deem necessary in the interest of public safety, which regulations shall be consistent with this section.

(g) Every permit, the consent form or forms as required by Section 18099.5 of the Health and Safety Code, and a copy of the tax clearance certificate, certificate of origin, or dealer's notice of transfer, when the certificate or notice is required to be issued, shall be carried in the manufactured home or power unit to which it refers and shall be open to inspection by any peace officer or traffic officer, any authorized agent of the Department of Transportation, or any other officer or employee charged with the care and protection of the highways.

(h) It is unlawful for any person to violate any of the terms or conditions of any permit.

(Amended by Stats. 1996, Ch. 124, Sec. 138. Effective January 1, 1997.)

35790.1. In addition to the requirements and conditions contained in Section 35790 and notwithstanding any other provision of law, all of the following conditions and specifications shall be complied with to move any manufactured home, as defined in Section 18007 of the Health and Safety Code, that is in excess of 14 feet in total width, but not exceeding 16 feet in total width, exclusive of lights and devices provided for in Sections 35109 and 35110, upon any highway under the jurisdiction of the entity granting the permit:

(a) For the purposes of width requirements under this code, the overall width of manufactured housing specified in this section shall be the overall width, including roof overhang, eaves, window shades, porch roofs, or any other part of the manufactured house that cannot be removed for the purposes of transporting upon any highway.

(b) Unless otherwise exempted under this code, all combinations of motor vehicles and manufactured housing shall be equipped with service brakes on all wheels. Service brakes required under this subdivision shall be adequate, supplemental to the brakes on the towing vehicle, to enable the combination of vehicles to comply with the stopping distance requirements of Section 26454.

(c) In addition to the requirements contained in Section 26304, the breakaway brake device on any manufactured housing unit equipped with electric brakes shall be powered by a wet cell rechargeable battery that is of the same voltage rating as the brakes and has sufficient charge to hold the brakes applied for not less than 15 minutes.

(d) Notwithstanding any other provision of this code, the weight imposed upon any tire, wheel, axle, drawbar, hitch, or other suspension component on a manufactured housing unit shall not exceed the manufacturer's maximum weight rating for the item or component.

(e) In addition to the requirements in subdivision (d), the maximum allowable weight upon one manufactured housing unit axle shall not exceed 6,000 pounds, and the maximum allowable weight upon one manufactured housing unit wheel shall not exceed 3,000 pounds.

(f) Manufactured housing unit tires shall be free from defects, have at least2/32 of an inch tread depth, as determined by tire tread wear indicators, and shall comply with specifications and requirements contained in Section 3280.904(b)(8) of Title 24 of the Code of Federal Regulations.

(g) Manufactured housing unit manufacturers shall provide transporters with a certification of compliance document, certifying the manufactured housing unit complies with the specifications and requirements contained in subdivisions (d), (e), and (f). Each certification of compliance document shall identify, by serial or identification number, the specific manufactured housing unit being transported and shall be signed by a representative of the manufacturer. Each transporter of manufactured housing units shall have in his or her immediate possession a copy of the certification of compliance document and shall make the document available upon request by any member of the Department of the California Highway Patrol, any authorized employee of the Department of Transportation, or any regularly employed and salaried municipal police officer or deputy sheriff.

(h) Manufactured housing unit dealers shall provide transporters with a certification of compliance document, specifying that all modifications, equipment additions, or loading changes by the dealer have not exceeded the gross vehicle weight rating of the manufactured housing unit or the axle and wheel requirements contained in subdivisions (d), (e), and (f). Each certification of compliance document shall identify, by serial or identification number, the specific manufactured housing unit being transported and shall be signed by a representative of the dealer. Each transporter of manufactured housing units shall have in his or her immediate possession a copy of the certification of compliance document and shall make the document available upon request by any member of the Department of the California Highway Patrol, any authorized employee of the Department of Transportation, any regularly employed and salaried municipal police officer or deputy sheriff, or any reserve police officer or reserve deputy sheriff listed under Section 830.6 of the Penal Code.

(i) Transporters of manufactured housing units shall not transport any additional load in, or upon, the manufactured housing unit that has not been certified by the manufactured housing unit's manufacturer or dealer.

(j) Every hitch, coupling device, drawbar, or other connections between the towing unit and the towed manufactured housing unit shall be securely attached and shall comply with Subpart J of Part 3280 of Title 24 of the Code of Federal Regulations.

(k) Manufactured housing units shall be equipped with an identification plate, specifying the manufacturer's name, the manufactured housing unit's serial number, the gross vehicle weight rating of the manufactured housing unit, and the gross weight of the cargo that may be transported in or upon the manufactured housing unit without exceeding the gross vehicle weight rating. The identification plate shall be permanently attached to the manufactured housing unit and shall be positioned adjacent to, and meet the same specifications and requirements applicable to, the certification label required by Subpart A of Part 3280 of Title 24 of the Code of Federal Regulations.

(l) Manufactured housing units shall be subject to all lighting requirements contained in Sections 24603, 24607, 24608, and 24951. When transported during darkness, manufactured housing units shall additionally be subject to Sections 24600 and 25100.

(m) Manufactured housing units shall have all open sides covered by plywood, hard board, or other rigid material, or by other suitable plastics or flexible material. Plastic or flexible side coverings shall not billow or flap in excess of six inches in any one place. Units that are opened on both sides may be transported empty with no side coverings.

(n) Transporters of manufactured housing units shall make available all permits, licenses, certificates, forms, and any other relative document required for the transportation of manufactured housing upon request by any member of the Department of the California Highway Patrol, any authorized employee of the Department of Transportation, any regularly employed and salaried municipal police officer or deputy sheriff, or any reserve police officer or reserve deputy sheriff listed under Section 830.6 of the Penal Code.

(o) The Department of Transportation, in cooperation with the Department of the California Highway Patrol, or the local authority, shall require pilot car or special escort services for the movement of any manufactured housing unit pursuant to this section, and may establish additional reasonable permit regulations, including special routing requirements, as necessary in the interest of public safety and consistent with this section.

(p) The Department of Transportation shall not issue a permit to move a manufactured home that is in excess of 14 feet in total width unless that department determines that all of the conditions and specifications set forth in this section have been met.

(Amended by Stats. 2003, Ch. 292, Sec. 11. Effective January 1, 2004.)

35790.4. The Legislature finds and declares that current restrictions on the movement of combinations of manufactured homes have unduly restricted the ability of the California manufactured housing industry to meet the needs of the consumer in this state.

The Legislature further finds and declares that the improved movement of manufactured homes, with appropriate safeguards, will benefit the state's economy and will allow production of more affordable and aesthetic manufactured homes.

(Added by Stats. 1984, Ch. 1312, Sec. 1.)

35790.5. (a) A permit issued pursuant to Section 35790 may authorize an exemption from length limitations otherwise applicable to vehicles and combinations of vehicles for the transportation of more than one unit of a manufactured home if all of the following conditions are met:

(1) The units are parts of a manufactured home that, when completed, connect two or more modular units.

(2) The units are mounted or loaded on a single vehicle or chassis in a manner so that their narrowest dimension represents the loaded width on the highway.

(3) The units are loaded in tandem only with respect to length, and the dimension from the front of the forward unit to the rear of the last unit does not exceed the length of vehicles in combination that would otherwise be permitted under this section.

(b) Applications for permits issued pursuant to this section shall specifically describe the manufactured home units to be moved and shall include a written statement of good cause satisfying the requirements of this section.

(c) Permits, other than annual permits, issued pursuant to this section shall describe the particular highways over which the permit is valid and shall be subject to all of the conditions of this article and any additional conditions imposed by the public agency issuing the permit.

(Added by Stats. 1984, Ch. 1312, Sec. 2.)

35790.6. A permit issued pursuant to Section 35780 or 35790 may authorize an exemption from the height limitations in Section 35250 for manufactured homes, including manufactured homes with a height in excess of 15 feet, measured from the surface upon which the vehicle stands, if the proposed route can accommodate the vehicle.

(Added by Stats. 1986, Ch. 350, Sec. 2. Effective July 15, 1986.)

35791. The Department of Transportation and any local authority may, with respect to such highways as may be agreed upon under their respective jurisdictions which traverse any area within the boundaries of the local authority, contract for the issuance by either authority of a single permit authorizing the operation or movement of a vehicle or a combination of vehicles or special mobile equipment in the same manner

as if each authority had issued separate permits pursuant to Section 35780.
(Amended by Stats. 1974, Ch. 545.)

35795. (a) (1) The Department of Transportation may charge a fee for the issuance of permits pursuant to this article.

(2) The fee established by the Department of Transportation pursuant to this section shall be established by a regulation adopted pursuant to Chapter 4.5 (commencing with Section 11371) of Part 1 of Division 3 of Title 2 of the Government Code, and shall be calculated to produce a total estimated revenue that is not more than the estimated total cost to that department for administering this article.

(3) Special services necessitated by unusually large or heavy loads requiring engineering investigations, or other services, may be billed separately for each permit.

(4) The funds collected by the Department of Transportation pursuant to this subdivision shall be deposited in the State Highway Account in the State Transportation Fund.

(b) (1) Local authorities may charge a fee for the issuance of permits pursuant to this article. However, the fee established by a local authority pursuant to this section shall be established by ordinance or resolution adopted after notice and hearing. The fee shall be calculated to produce a total estimated revenue that is not more than the estimated total cost incurred by the local authority in administering its authority under this article and shall not exceed the fee developed by the Department of Transportation pursuant to subdivision (a). The fee for the issuance of permits shall be developed in consultation with representatives of local government and the commercial trucking industry. Notice of the hearing shall be by publication as provided in Section 6064 of the Government Code. The hearing shall be held before the legislative body of the local authority. All objections shall be considered and interested parties shall be afforded an adequate opportunity to be heard in respect to their objections.

(2) Special services necessitated by unusually large or heavy loads requiring engineering investigations, escorts, tree trimming, or other services, excluding services necessary to provide the notification required under this section and services that are within the scope of the local authority's ordinary duty to provide, shall be billed separately for each permit.

(3) For purposes of determining whether, under paragraph (2), special services are necessitated by an unusually large or heavy load, a local authority shall be governed by the criteria set forth in subdivision (b) of Section 1411.3 of Title 21 of the California Code of Regulations.

(c) Nothing in this section shall limit or restrict the application of Section 35782.
(Amended by Stats. 2006, Ch. 242, Sec. 1. Effective January 1, 2007.)

35796. Any or all of the powers granted to local authorities in this article may, by ordinance or resolution, be delegated by such local authorities to the road commissioner or to such other local official as may be performing functions substantially the same as a road commissioner in the county or municipality enacting such ordinance or resolution.
(Added by Stats. 1971, Ch. 380.)

Division 16. Implements of Husbandry

(Division 16 added by Stats. 1963, Ch. 2149.)

Chapter 1. Definitions

(Chapter 1 added by Stats. 1963, Ch. 2149.)

36000. An "implement of husbandry" is a vehicle which is used exclusively in the conduct of agricultural operations.

An implement of husbandry does not include a vehicle if its existing design is primarily for the transportation of persons or property on a highway, unless specifically designated as such by some other provision of this code.
(Amended by Stats. 1986, Ch. 973, Sec. 4.)

36005. An implement of husbandry includes, but is not limited to, all of the following:

(a) A lift carrier or other vehicle designed and used exclusively for the lifting and carrying of implements of husbandry or tools used exclusively for the production or harvesting of agricultural products, when operated or moved upon a highway.

(b) A trailer of the tip-bed type when used exclusively in the transportation of other implements of husbandry or tools used exclusively for the production or harvesting of agricultural products.

(c) A trailer or semitrailer having no bed, and designed and used solely for transporting a hay loader or swather.

(d) A spray or fertilizer applicator rig used exclusively for spraying or fertilizing in the conduct of agricultural operations. This subdivision does not apply to anhydrous ammonia fertilizer applicator rigs which have a transportation capacity in excess of 500 gallons.

(e) (1) A trailer or semitrailer that has a maximum transportation capacity in excess of 500 gallons, but not more than 1,000 gallons, used exclusively for the transportation and application of anhydrous ammonia, if the vehicle is either equipped with operating brakes or is towed upon a highway by a motortruck that is assigned a manufacturer's gross vehicle weight rating of 3/4 ton or more.

(2) These vehicles are subject to Section 24603 if the stoplamps of the towing vehicle are not clearly visible.

(3) For purposes of this subdivision, a combination of vehicles is limited to two vehicles in tandem.

(f) A nurse rig or equipment auxiliary to the use of and designed or modified for the fueling, repairing, or loading of an applicator rig or an airplane used for the dusting, spraying, fertilizing, or seeding of crops.

(g) A row duster.

(h) A wagon or van used exclusively for carrying products of farming from one part of a farm to another part thereof, or from one farm to another farm, and used solely for agricultural purposes, including any van used in harvesting alfalfa or cotton, which is only incidentally operated or moved on a highway as a trailer.

(i) A wagon or portable house on wheels used solely by shepherds as a permanent residence in connection with sheep raising operations and moved from one part of a ranch to another part thereof or from one ranch to another ranch, which is only incidentally operated or moved on a highway as a trailer.

(j) Notwithstanding subdivision (f) of Section 36101, a trap wagon, as defined in Section 36016, moved from one part of a ranch to another part of the same ranch or from one ranch to another, which is only operated or moved on a highway incidental to agricultural operations. The fuel tank or tanks of the trap wagon shall not exceed 1,000 gallons total capacity.

(k) Any vehicle that is operated upon a highway only for the purpose of transporting agricultural products and is in no event operated along a highway for a total distance greater than one mile from the point of origin of the trip.

(l) A portable honey-extracting trailer or semitrailer.

(m) A fertilizer nurse tank or trailer that is not self-propelled and which is moved unladen on the highway and auxiliary to the use of a spray or fertilizer applicator rig.

(n) Any cotton trailer when used on the highways for the exclusive purpose of transporting cotton from a farm to a cotton gin, and returning the empty trailer to such farm, except that Section 5014 shall apply to such trailers.

(o) A truck tractor or truck tractor and semitrailer combination specified in this subdivision which is owned by a farmer and operated on the highways, (1) only incidental to a farming operation, (2) not for compensation, and (3) for a distance of not more than two miles (on the highway) each way. This subdivision applies only to truck tractors with a manufacturer's gross vehicle weight rating over 10,000 pounds that are equipped with all-wheel drive and off-highway traction tires on all wheels, and only to semitrailers used in combination with such a truck tractor and exclusively in production or harvesting of tomatoes. The vehicles specified in this subdivision shall not be operated in excess of 25 miles per hour on the highways.

(p) An all-terrain or utility-terrain vehicle used exclusively in agricultural operations.

(Amended by Stats. 2012, Ch. 168, Sec. 3. (AB 2111) Effective January 1, 2013.)

36010. A "farm trailer" is either of the following:

(a) A trailer or semitrailer owned and operated by a farmer in the conduct of agricultural operations, and used exclusively to transport agricultural products upon the highway to the point of first handling and return.

(b) A trailer or semitrailer equipped with rollers on the bed, with a frame not taller than 10 inches high, and with a gross vehicle weight rating of 10,000 pounds or less, that is owned, rented, or leased by a farmer and operated by that farmer in the conduct of agricultural operations, used exclusively to transport fruit and vegetables upon the highway to the point of first handling and return, and that was manufactured and in use prior to January 1, 1997. These vehicles may also be operated on the highways without a load for the purposes of delivering a rented or leased vehicle to the renting or leasing farmer's farm, or returning empty to the owner's premises.

(Amended by Stats. 2000, Ch. 861, Sec. 56. Effective September 29, 2000. Operative December 31, 2001, pursuant to Sec. 67 of Ch. 861.)

36011. An "automatic bale wagon" is a motor vehicle capable of transporting property on a highway and equipped with apparatus specifically designed to pick up single bales of hay or straw from a field and to load and unload baled hay or straw.

(Added by Stats. 1977, Ch. 627.)

36012. A "cotton module mover" is a motortruck, semitrailer, or a truck tractor, in combination with a semitrailer, that is equipped with a self-loading bed and is designed and used exclusively to transport field manufactured cotton modules to a cotton gin.

(Amended by Stats. 1997, Ch. 641, Sec. 1. Effective January 1, 1998.)

36015. "Implement of husbandry" includes any farm tractor, otherwise an implement of husbandry used upon a highway to draw a farm trailer carrying farm produce, or to draw any trailer or semitrailer carrying other implements of husbandry, between farms, or from a farm to a processing or handling point and returning with or without the trailer.

(Added by Stats. 1963, Ch. 2149.)

36016. A "trap wagon" is a trailer or semitrailer used exclusively in the conduct of agricultural operations to fuel, service, or repair implements of husbandry. A trap wagon may be equipped with tools, spare parts, lubricating supplies, or fuel tanks.

(Added by Stats. 1986, Ch. 973, Sec. 7.)

36017. For the exclusive purpose of this division, empty bins, pallets, and tiedown straps shall not be considered a load when transported within the parameters of agricultural operations. Any farm trailer or other vehicle transporting these items shall continue to be regulated pursuant to this division. The total outside width of any of the transported items shall not exceed 102 inches.

(Added by Stats. 1986, Ch. 973, Sec. 8.)

Chapter 2. Registration of Implements of Husbandry

(Chapter 2 added by Stats. 1963, Ch. 2149.)

36100. Implements of husbandry which are only incidentally operated or moved over a highway and implements of husbandry listed in Section 36005 or 36015 are exempt from registration.

(Added by Stats. 1963, Ch. 2149.)

36101. The following farm vehicles are exempt from registration, if they have and display an identification plate as specified in Section 5014, and the vehicles shall not be deemed to be implements of husbandry and they shall be subject to all equipment and device requirements as if registered:

(a) A motor vehicle of a size so as to require a permit under Section 35780 owned and operated by a farmer, designed and used exclusively for carrying, or returning empty from carrying, feed and seed products of farming, and used on a highway between one part of a farm to another part of that farm or from one farm to another farm.

(b) A vehicle equipped with a water tank owned by a farmer and used exclusively to service his or her own implements of husbandry.

(c) A water tank truck that is owned by a farmer, not operated for compensation, and used extensively in the conduct of agricultural operations, when used exclusively (1) for sprinkling water on dirt roads providing access to agricultural fields or (2) transportation of water for irrigation of crops or trees.

(d) (1) A cotton module mover, as defined in Section 36012.

(2) In order to maintain the exemption from registration granted under this subdivision for a truck tractor, when combined with a semitrailer, the owner of that truck tractor shall not operate it during the exemption period in any manner other than as a cotton module mover, as defined in Section 36012, and shall do all of the following:

(A) Register the vehicle with the department before operating it as a commercial motor vehicle.

(B) Apply to the department on a yearly basis for any renewal of the exemption from registration.

(3) Exemption from registration under this subdivision does not exempt a truck tractor, when combined with a semitrailer, operating as a cotton module mover pursuant to Section 36012 and this subdivision from the applicable safety requirements of this code or any regulation adopted pursuant to any statute, including, but not limited to, equipment standards, driver licensing requirements, maximum driving and on-duty hours provisions, log book requirements, drug and alcohol testing, maintenance of vehicles, and any driver or vehicle standards specified in Division 14.8 (commencing with Section 34500).

(4) Truck tractors exempt from registration under this subdivision are subject to the fees imposed under Sections 9250, 9250.8, and 9250.13, and to any other vehicle fees that are imposed by statute on or after January 1, 1998, that are deposited in the Motor Vehicle Account.

(e) A trailer that is equipped with a plenum chamber for the drying of agricultural commodities.

(f) Except as provided in subdivision (j) of Section 36005, a trap wagon, as defined in Section 36016, that is equipped with a fuel tank or tanks. The fuel tank or tanks shall not exceed 3,000 gallons total capacity.

(g) A forklift truck, operated by a farmer not for compensation. For purposes of this section, a hay-squeeze shall be deemed a forklift.

(h) A truck tractor or truck tractor and semitrailer combination specified in this subdivision that is owned by a farmer and operated on the highways only incidental to a farming operation and not for compensation. This subdivision applies only to truck tractors with a manufacturer's gross vehicle weight rating over 10,000 pounds that are equipped with all-wheel drive and off-highway traction tires on all wheels, and only to semitrailers used in combination with that truck tractor and exclusively in the production or harvesting of melons. The vehicles specified in this subdivision shall not be operated in excess of 25 miles per hour on the highways.

The Commissioner of the California Highway Patrol may, by regulation, prohibit the vehicles specified in this subdivision from operating on specific routes. These vehicles shall not be operated laden on the highway for more than two miles from the point of origin and shall not be operated for more than 30 miles unladen on the highway from the point of origin. These vehicles shall not be operated for more than 15 miles unladen on the highway from the point of origin, unless accompanied by an escort vehicle to the front, and an escort vehicle to the rear.

(i) A motor vehicle specifically designed for, and used exclusively in, an agricultural operation for purposes of carrying, or returning empty from carrying, silage that is operated by a farmer, an employee of the farmer, or a contracted employee of the farmer between one part of a farm to another part of that farm or from one farm to another farm, on a highway for a distance not to exceed 20 miles from the point of origin of the trip. This subdivision does not include a vehicle that is used for the transportation of silage for retail sales.

For the purposes of this subdivision, "silage" includes field corn, sorghum, grass, legumes, cereals, or cereal mixes, either green or mature, converted into feed for livestock.

(Amended by Stats. 1998, Ch. 877, Sec. 74. Effective January 1, 1999.)

36102. The following vehicles are exempt from registration if they have and display identification plates, as specified in Section 5014; and these vehicles, except when operated pursuant to subdivision (k) of Section 36005, shall not be deemed to be implements of husbandry and they shall be subject to all equipment and device requirements as if registered:

(a) An automatic bale wagon operated unladen on a highway.

(b) An automatic bale wagon when transporting baled hay or straw for a distance of not more than five continuous road miles on a highway from one parcel of property owned, leased, or controlled by a farmer to another parcel of property owned, leased, or controlled by such farmer.

(c) A motor vehicle which is designed for, and used exclusively to, haul feed for livestock and which is owned and operated exclusively by a farmer or an employee of a farmer. A vehicle exempted by this subdivision may be operated only on those highways that are maintained by local authorities, only pursuant to a permit issued as provided in Section 35780 by the local authority having jurisdiction over the highways used, and only for a distance of not more than five continuous road miles from one parcel of property owned, leased, or controlled by the farmer to another parcel of property owned, leased, or controlled by the farmer. This subdivision does not apply to transportation for compensation.

(Amended by Stats. 1984, Ch. 1077, Sec. 12.5. Operative July 1, 1985, by Sec. 21 of Ch. 1077.)

36105. A trailer or semitrailer owned and used exclusively by a farmer to haul his or her own implements of husbandry, portable sanitary facility, shade trailer, or tools used exclusively for the production or harvesting of agricultural products is exempt from registration.

(Amended by Stats. 2012, Ch. 168, Sec. 4. (AB 2111) Effective January 1, 2013.)

36109. "Farm trailers," as defined in Section 36010, having a gross weight of 10,000 pounds or less, are exempt from registration except that Section 5014 shall apply to such trailers.

(Amended by Stats. 2000, Ch. 861, Sec. 57. Effective September 29, 2000. Operative December 31, 2001, pursuant to Sec. 67 of Ch. 861.)

36115. (a) Any person who owns an implement of husbandry which is exempt from registration may obtain an identification plate as provided in Section 5014 for the implement.

(b) The department shall issue an identification plate as applied for to any manufacturer or dealer of an implement of husbandry which is exempt from registration as provided in Section 5016.5. That manufacturer or dealer may obtain more than one plate.

(Amended by Stats. 1984, Ch. 1077, Sec. 14. Operative July 1, 1985, by Sec. 21 of Ch. 1077.)

36130. (a) On and after January 1, 1986, original applications for identification plates on vehicles specified in Division 16 (commencing with Section 36000) shall be submitted pursuant to Section 5014 or Section 5016.5.

(b) Effective January 1, 1986, identification plates that expired on December 31, 1983, shall not be eligible for renewal. Applicants shall apply for identification plates pursuant to Section 5014 or Section 5016.5.

(c) Commencing with 1987 renewals, all expiring identification plates are canceled and owners of vehicles defined in Division 16 (commencing with Section 36000), that are required to display these plates, shall submit applications pursuant to Section 5014 or Section 5016.5.

(Repealed and added by Stats. 1984, Ch. 1077, Sec. 19. Operative July 1, 1985, by Sec. 21 of Ch. 1077.)

Chapter 3. Drivers' Licenses

(Chapter 3 added by Stats. 1963, Ch. 2149.)

36300. Any person, while driving or operating an implement of husbandry incidentally operated or moved over a highway is not required to obtain a driver's license; except that the driver of any farm tractor while being used to draw a farm trailer carrying farm produce between farms or from a farm to a processing or handling point and return, and the driver of an automatic bale wagon which is being operated as specified in Section 36102, but is not being operated as provided in subdivision (k) of Section 36005, shall be in possession of a driver's license of the appropriate class other than a junior permit.

(Amended by Stats. 1977, Ch. 627.)

36305. The driver of any implement of husbandry shall possess a valid class C driver's license when operating a combination of vehicles at a speed in excess of 25 miles per hour or towing any implement of husbandry as specified in subdivision (d), (e), or (j) of Section 36005.

(Amended by Stats. 1993, Ch. 272, Sec. 55. Effective August 2, 1993.)

Chapter 4. Speed Laws

(Chapter 4 added by Stats. 1963, Ch. 2149.)

36400. No person shall move or drive a lift-carrier or other vehicle designed and used exclusively for the lifting and carrying of implements of husbandry or tools used exclusively for the production or harvesting of agricultural products at a speed in excess of 35 miles per hour.

(Amended by Stats. 1971, Ch. 1135.)

Chapter 5. Equipment of Implements of Husbandry

(Chapter 5 added by Stats. 1963, Ch. 2149.)

36500. The provisions of Sections 24012, 24250, 24251, 24400 to 24404, inclusive, and Articles 3 (commencing with Section 24600), 4 (commencing with Section 24800), 5 (commencing with Section 24950), 6 (commencing with Section 25100), 9 (commencing with Section 25350), 11 (commencing with Section 25450), and 13 (commencing with Section 25650) of Chapter 2 of Division 12 shall not apply to implements of husbandry. Such vehicles shall be subject to the provisions of Sections 24254, 24615, 25803, and 25950, and Article 12 (commencing with Section 25500) of Chapter 2 of Division 12.

(Amended by Stats. 1972, Ch. 618.)

36505. Farm tractors as defined in Section 36015, and trailers displaying an identification plate, as provided for in Section 36115 or 36130, when operated during darkness shall not be exempted from the provisions of Sections 24400 and 25100.

(Amended by Stats. 1996, Ch. 124, Sec. 139. Effective January 1, 1997.)

36508. After July 1, 1970, no new implement of husbandry designed or intended by the manufacturer to be operated or moved at a speed not in excess of 25 miles per hour shall be sold in this state unless it is equipped by the manufacturer with a slow-moving vehicle emblem as prescribed by Section 24615, and such an emblem shall thereafter be displayed and maintained on such implement of husbandry while the implement is able to be operated upon a public highway.

(Amended by Stats. 1969, Ch. 949.)

36509. (a) An implement of husbandry, a farm vehicle, or any vehicle escorting or towing an implement of husbandry or farm vehicle, may display flashing amber warning lamps or flashing amber turn signals:

(1) When the vehicle is required to display a "slow moving vehicle" emblem as defined in Section 24615.

(2) When the width, length, height, or speed of the vehicle may cause a hazard to other traffic on the highway.

(b) An implement of husbandry, a farm vehicle, or any vehicle towing an implement of husbandry or farm vehicle, when the load upon the vehicle exceeds 120 inches in width, shall display either:

(1) Flashing amber warning lamps.

(2) Flashing amber turn signals.

(3) During daylight hours, red flags, each of which shall be not less than 16 inches square, mounted at the left and right outer extremities of the vehicle or load whichever has the greater horizontal dimension.

(Added by Stats. 1986, Ch. 973, Sec. 11.)

36510. Implements of husbandry are not subject to stopping distance requirements contained in Section 26454, but if any such vehicle cannot be stopped within 32 feet from an initial speed of 15 miles per hour, it shall not be operated at a speed in excess of that permitting a stop in 32 feet.

(Added by Stats. 1963, Ch. 2149.)

36515. The provisions of Section 26700 relating to windshields shall not apply to implements of husbandry.

(Added by Stats. 1963, Ch. 2149.)

36520. The provisions of Section 26706 relating to windshield wipers shall not apply to implements of husbandry.

(Added by Stats. 1963, Ch. 2149.)

Chapter 6. Size, Weight and Load of Implements of Husbandry

(Chapter 6 added by Stats. 1963, Ch. 2149.)

36600. (a) The limitations as to width as set forth in Chapter 2 (commencing with Section 35100) of Division 15 do not apply to implements of husbandry incidentally operated, transported, towed, or otherwise moved over a highway.

(b) Notwithstanding subdivision (a), when an implement of husbandry is transported or moved over a highway which is a part of the National System of Interstate and Defense Highways (as referred to in Section 108 of the Federal-aid Highway Act of 1956) as a load on another vehicle, if the load exceeds 102 inches in width, the vehicle and load shall not be operated for a distance in excess of 25 miles from the point of origin of the trip. The operator of the transporting vehicle shall be a farmer or a person regularly employed by a farmer or farm corporation, and the operator transporting the load shall have in his or her immediate possession a writing signed by the farmer or farm corporation agent which states the origin and destination of the trip.

(c) Notwithstanding subdivision (a), when an implement of husbandry is transported or moved over any other highway as a load on another vehicle, if the load exceeds 120 inches in width, the vehicle and load shall not be operated for a distance in excess of 25 miles from the point of origin of the trip. The operator of the transporting vehicle shall be a farmer or a person employed by a farmer or farm corporation, and the operator transporting the load shall have in his or her immediate possession a writing signed by the farmer or farm corporation agent which states the origin and destination of the trip.

(Amended by Stats. 1988, Ch. 103, Sec. 1. Effective May 11, 1988.)

36605. The limitations as to width, as set forth in Chapter 2 (commencing with Section 35100) of Division 15, do not apply to any trailer or semitrailer, including lift carriers and tip-bed trailers, used exclusively for the transportation of implements of husbandry or tools used exclusively for the production or harvesting of agricultural products by farmers or implement dealers, except as follows:

(1) With respect to any trailer or semitrailer transporting a grain-harvesting combine, that vehicle shall not exceed a width of 144 inches.

(2) With respect to any other vehicle described in this section, that vehicle, or the load on that vehicle when that load consists of tools, shall not exceed a width of 120 inches.

(3) With respect to any trailer or semitrailer described in subdivision (c) of Section 36005, that vehicle, when towed upon a highway shall not exceed a width of 174 inches and shall be subject to subdivisions (b) and (c) of Section 36600.

(Amended by Stats. 1986, Ch. 973, Sec. 13.)

36606. (a) The limitations as to width, as set forth in Chapter 2 (commencing with Section 35100) of Division 15, do not apply to automatic bale wagons while operated as specified in Section 36102, except that such vehicles or the load thereon may not exceed 120 inches in width.

(b) This section shall have no application to highways which are a part of the National System of Interstate and Defense Highways (as referred to in subdivision (a) of Section 108 of the Federal-Aid Highway Act of 1956).

(Added by Stats. 1977, Ch. 627.)

36610. (a) The limitations as to height of vehicles contained in Chapter 3 (commencing with Section 35250) of Division 15 do not apply to implements of husbandry incidentally operated, transported, towed, or otherwise moved over a highway.

(b) Notwithstanding subdivision (a), when an implement of husbandry is transported or moved over a highway as a load on another vehicle and the load exceeds 14 feet in height, the vehicle and load shall not be operated for a distance in excess of 25 miles from the point of origin of the trip. The operator of the transporting vehicle shall be a farmer or a person regularly employed by a farmer or farm corporation, and the operator transporting the vehicle shall have in his or her immediate possession a writing signed by the farmer or farm corporation agent which states the origin and destination of the trip.

(Amended by Stats. 1982, Ch. 686, Sec. 2.)

36615. The limitations as to length of vehicles contained in Chapter 4 (commencing with Section 35400) do not apply to implements of husbandry operated or moved over a highway incidental to agricultural operations. Notwithstanding Section 36626, when an implement of husbandry is operated in a combination of vehicles that exceeds the length requirements of Section 35401, the combination is limited to two vehicles in tandem.

(Amended by Stats. 1986, Ch. 973, Sec. 14.)

36625. The provisions of Section 21715 do not apply to any vehicle drawing or towing unladen implements of husbandry.

(Added by Stats. 1963, Ch. 2149.)

36626. Notwithstanding the provisions of Section 21715, a motor truck with an unladen weight of not less than 3,500 pounds and a gross weight of not less than 4,200 pounds may tow a combination of two cotton trailers operated on the highways for the exclusive purpose of transporting cotton from a farm to a cotton gin and returning the empty trailers to such farm. Extra weight or ballast may be added to meet the requirements of this section and shall be in the form of 100-pound bags of sand.

(Added by Stats. 1963, Ch. 2004.)

36627. Notwithstanding the provisions of Section 21715, a motortruck with an unladen weight of not less than 3,500 pounds and a gross weight of not less than 4,200 pounds may tow a combination of two almond trailers operated on the highways for the exclusive purpose of transporting almonds from a farm to an almond huller and returning the empty trailers to such farm. Extra weight or ballast may be added to meet the requirements of this section and shall be in the form of 100-pound bags of sand.

(Added by Stats. 1973, Ch. 293.)

Chapter 7. Other Requirements

(Heading of Chapter 7 amended by Stats. 1977, Ch. 627.)

36700. All implements of husbandry, farm trailers or any other vehicles subject to the provisions of this division, and any owner, operator or driver of such vehicles, shall also comply with and be subject to all other provisions of this code which are not in conflict with the specific provisions contained in this division.

(Added by Stats. 1963, Ch. 2149.)

36705. No automatic bale wagon exceeding 96 inches in width or carrying a load in excess of 100 inches in width may be operated on any highway during darkness.

(Added by Stats. 1977, Ch. 627.)

Chapter 8. General Provisions

(Chapter 8 added by Stats. 1963, Ch. 2149.)

36800. The provisions of this division, unless otherwise provided, apply to all vehicles, whether publicly or privately owned, when upon the highways.

(Added by Stats. 1963, Ch. 2149.)

Division 16.5. Off-Highway Vehicles

(Division 16.5 added by Stats. 1971, Ch. 1816.)

Chapter 1. General Provisions

(Chapter 1 added by Stats. 1971, Ch. 1816.)

38000. This division may be cited as the Chappie-Z'berg Off-Highway Motor Vehicle Law of 1971.

(Added by Stats. 1971, Ch. 1816.)

38001. (a) Except as otherwise provided, this division applies to off-highway motor vehicles, as defined in Section 38006, on lands, other than a highway, that are open and accessible to the public, including any land acquired, developed, operated, or maintained, in whole or in part, with money from the Off-Highway Vehicle Trust Fund, except private lands under the immediate control of the owner or his or her agent where permission is required and has been granted to operate a motor vehicle. For purposes of this division, the term "highway" does not include fire trails, logging roads, service roads regardless of surface composition, or other roughly graded trails and roads upon which vehicular travel by the public is permitted.

(b) Privately owned and maintained parking facilities that are generally open to the public are exempt from this division, unless the facilities are specifically declared subject to this division by the procedure specified in Section 21107.8.

(Amended by Stats. 2002, Ch. 563, Sec. 37. Effective January 1, 2003.)

38006. As used in this division, an "off-highway motor vehicle" is any of the following:

(a) A motor vehicle subject to the provisions of subdivision (a) of Section 38010.

(b) A motor vehicle registered under Section 4000, when such motor vehicle is operated on land to which this division has application.

(c) A motor vehicle owned or operated by a nonresident of this state, whether or not such motor vehicle is identified or registered in a foreign jurisdiction, when such motor vehicle is operated on lands to which this division has application.

(Added by Stats. 1976, Ch. 1093.)

38007. The Off-Highway Motor Vehicle Recreation Division of the Department of Parks and Recreation shall adopt courses of instruction in off-highway motor vehicle safety, operation, and principles of environmental preservation by January 1, 2005. For this purpose the division shall consult with the Department of the California Highway Patrol and other public and private agencies or organizations. The division shall make this course of instruction available directly, through contractual agreement, or through volunteers authorized by the division to conduct a course of instruction.

(Amended by Stats. 2002, Ch. 563, Sec. 38. Effective January 1, 2003.)

Chapter 2. Registration of Off-Highway Vehicles; Original and Renewal of Identification; Issuance of Certificates of Ownership

(Chapter 2 added by Stats. 1971, Ch. 1816.)

Article 1. Motor Vehicles Subject to Identification

(Article 1 added by Stats. 1971, Ch. 1816.)

38010. (a) Except as otherwise provided in subdivision (b), a motor vehicle specified in subdivision (b) of Section 38012 that is not registered under this code because it is to be operated or used exclusively off the highways, except as provided in this division, shall display an identification plate or device issued by the department.

(b) Subdivision (a) does not apply to any of the following:

(1) Motor vehicles specifically exempted from registration under this code, including, but not limited to, motor vehicles exempted pursuant to Sections 4006, 4010, 4012, 4013, 4015, 4018, and 4019.

(2) Implements of husbandry.

(3) Motor vehicles owned by the state, or any county, city, district,

or political subdivision of the state, or the United States.

(4) Motor vehicles owned or operated by, or operated under contract with a utility, whether privately or publicly owned, when used as specified in Section 22512.

(5) Special construction equipment described in Section 565, regardless of whether those motor vehicles are used in connection with highway or railroad work.

(6) A motor vehicle with a currently valid special permit issued under Section 38087.5 that is owned or operated by a nonresident of this state and the vehicle is not identified or registered in a foreign jurisdiction. For the purposes of this paragraph, a person who holds a valid driver's license issued by a foreign jurisdiction is presumed to be a nonresident.

(7) Commercial vehicles weighing more than 6,000 pounds unladen.

(8) A motorcycle manufactured in the year 1942 or prior.

(9) Four-wheeled motor vehicles operated solely in organized racing or competitive events upon a closed course when those events are conducted under the auspices of a recognized sanctioning body or by permit issued by the local governmental authority having jurisdiction.

(10) A motor vehicle with a currently valid identification or registration permit issued by another state, if the other state recognizes an identification plate or device issued by the department pursuant to subdivision (a) as valid for use in that state.

(Amended by Stats. 2025, Ch. 588, Sec. 2. (SB 586) Effective January 1, 2026.)

38012. (a) As used in this division, "off-highway motor vehicle subject to identification" means a motor vehicle subject to subdivision (a) of Section 38010.

(b) As used in this division, "off-highway motor vehicle" includes, but is not limited to, the following:

(1) A motorcycle or motor-driven cycle, except for any motorcycle that is eligible for a special transportation identification device issued pursuant to Section 38088.

(2) A snowmobile or other vehicle designed to travel over snow or ice, as defined in Section 557.

(3) A motor vehicle commonly referred to as a sand buggy, dune buggy, or all-terrain vehicle.

(4) A motor vehicle commonly referred to as a jeep.

(5) A recreational off-highway vehicle as defined in Section 500.

(6) An off-highway electric motorcycle as defined in Section 436.1.

(Amended by Stats. 2025, Ch. 588, Sec. 3. (SB 586) Effective January 1, 2026.)

38013. Unless otherwise provided, the terms "identification" and "identification certificate" shall have the same meaning as the terms "registration" and "registration card," respectively, as used in Division 3 (commencing with Section 4000).

(Added by Stats. 1971, Ch. 1816.)

38014. As used in this division, "closed course" includes, but is not limited to, a speedway, racetrack, or a prescribed and defined route of travel on or off a highway that is closed to all motor vehicles other than those of participants. A closed course is one which is not available at any time for vehicular access by the general public.

(Added by Stats. 1975, Ch. 1050.)

38020. Except as otherwise provided in this division, a person shall not operate or leave standing an off-highway motor vehicle subject to identification under this code that is not registered under the provisions of Division 3 (commencing with Section 4000), unless it is identified under the provisions of this chapter. A violation of this section is an infraction. Riding in violation of seasons established by Section 2412(f) and 2415 of Title 13 of the California Code of Regulations constitutes a violation of this section. This section shall not apply to the operation, transportation, or leaving standing of an off-highway vehicle pursuant to a valid special permit.

(Amended by Stats. 2014, Ch. 345, Sec. 18. (AB 2752) Effective January 1, 2015.)

38021. (a) A manufacturer, dealer, or distributor, or his agent, owning or lawfully possessing any off-highway motor vehicle of a type otherwise required to be identified hereunder may operate or use such vehicle without an identification certificate and plate or device upon condition that each such vehicle is accompanied by a special permit issued to the manufacturer, dealer, or distributor as provided in this division.

(b) Persons licensed pursuant to Article 1 (commencing with Section 11700) of Chapter 4 of Division 5 need not obtain such a permit provided the vehicle is operated or used under special plates issued to the licensee.

(Amended by Stats. 1976, Ch. 1093.)

38022. Notwithstanding the provisions of Section 4000, motorcycles issued a special transportation identification device pursuant to Section 38088 may be transported upon a highway to and from a closed course.

(Added by Stats. 1975, Ch. 1050.)

38025. In accordance with subdivision (c) of Section 4000, a motor vehicle issued a plate or device pursuant to Section 38160 may be operated or driven upon a highway but only as follows:

(a) On a two-lane highway, only to cross the highway at an angle of approximately 90 degrees to the direction of the roadway and at a place where a quick and safe crossing may be made, or only when the roadway is not maintained by snow removal equipment and is closed to motor vehicles that are subject to registration pursuant to Division 3 (commencing with Section 4000), or only to cross a highway in the manner specified in subdivision (b).

(b) With respect to the crossing of a highway having more than two lanes, or a highway having limited access, a motor vehicle may cross a highway but only at a place designated by the Department of Transportation or local authorities with respect to a highway under their respective jurisdictions as a place where a motor vehicle, or specified types of motor vehicle, may cross a highway, and a vehicle shall cross the highway only at that designated place and only in a quick and safe manner.

(c) The Department of Transportation and local authorities with respect to a highway under their respective jurisdictions may designate, by the erection of an appropriate sign of a type approved by the Department of Transportation, a place where a motor vehicle, or specified type of motor vehicle, may cross a highway having more than two lanes or having limited access.

(d) A motor vehicle identified pursuant to Section 38010 may be towed upon a highway, but not driven, if the vehicle displays a plate or device issued pursuant to Section 38160.

(e) A motorcycle identified pursuant to Section 38010 may be pushed upon a highway, but not ridden, if the motorcycle has displayed upon it a plate or device issued pursuant to Section 38160.

(f) A peace officer, as defined in Chapter 4.5 (commencing with Section 830) of Title 3 of Part 2 of the Penal Code, may operate or drive an off-highway vehicle identified pursuant to Section 38010 upon a highway in an emergency response situation.

(Amended by Stats. 2003, Ch. 135, Sec. 1. Effective January 1, 2004.)

38026. (a) In addition to Section 38025 and after complying with subdivision (c) of this section, if a local authority, an agency of the federal government, or the Director of Parks and Recreation finds that a highway, or a portion of a highway, under the jurisdiction of the authority, agency, or the director, as the case may be, is located in a manner that provides a connecting link between off-highway motor vehicle trail segments, between an off-highway motor vehicle recreational use area and necessary service facilities, or between lodging facilities and an off-highway motor vehicle recreational facility and if it is found that the highway is designed and constructed so as to safely permit the use of regular vehicular traffic and also the driving of off-highway motor vehicles on that highway, the local authority, by resolution or ordinance, agency of the federal government, or the Director of Parks and Recreation, as the case may be, may designate that highway, or a portion of a highway, for combined use and shall prescribe rules and regulations therefor. A highway, or portion of a highway, shall not be so designated for a distance of more than three miles, except as provided in Sections 38026.1, 38026.2, and 38026.3. A freeway shall not be designated under this section.

(b) The Off-Highway Motor Vehicle Recreation Commission may propose highway segments for consideration by local authorities, an agency of the federal government, or the Director of Parks and Recreation for combined use.

(c) Prior to designating a highway or portion of a highway on the motion of the local authority, an agency of the federal government, or the Director of Parks and Recreation, or as a recommendation of the Off-Highway Motor Vehicle Recreation Commission, a local authority, an agency of the federal government, or the Director of Parks and Recreation shall notify the Commissioner of the California Highway Patrol, and shall not designate any segment pursuant to subdivision (a) which, in the opinion of the commissioner, would create a potential traffic safety hazard.

(d) (1) A designation of a highway, or a portion of a highway, under subdivision (a) shall become effective upon the erection of appropriate signs of a type approved by the Department of Transportation on and along the highway, or portion of the highway.

(2) The cost of the signs shall be reimbursed from the Off-Highway Vehicle Trust Fund, when appropriated by the Legislature, or by expenditure of funds from a grant or cooperative agreement made pursuant to Section 5090.50 of the Public Resources Code.

(Amended by Stats. 2024, Ch. 592, Sec. 1. (SB 632) Effective January 1, 2025.)

38026.2. (a) Except as provided in subdivision (e), the City of Needles may establish a pilot project to designate combined-use highways on roads in the city for no more than 10 miles so that the combined-use highways can be used to link existing off-highway motor vehicle trails and trailheads on federal Bureau of Land Management or United States Forest Service lands, and to link off-highway motor vehicle recreational-use areas with necessary service and lodging facilities, in order to provide a unified system of trails for off-highway motor vehicles, preserve traffic safety, improve natural resource protection, reduce off-highway vehicle trespass on private land, and minimize impacts on city residents.

(b) A pilot project established pursuant to this section shall do all of the following:

(1) Prescribe a procedure for highway, road, or route selection and designation. The procedure shall be approved by a vote of a majority of the city council.

(2) Prescribe a procedure for the city to remove a combined-use designation, including a designation that is removed as a result of the conclusion of the pilot program.

(3) In cooperation with the Department of Transportation, establish uniform specifications and symbols for signs, markers, and traffic control devices to control off-highway motor vehicles, including, but not limited to, all of the following:

(A) Devices to warn of dangerous conditions, obstacles, or hazards.

(B) Designations of the right-of-way for regular vehicular traffic and off-highway motor vehicles.

(C) A description of the nature and destination of the off-highway motor vehicle trail.

(D) Warning signs for pedestrians and motorists of the presence of off-highway motor vehicle traffic.

(4) Require that off-highway motor vehicles subject to the pilot project meet the safety requirements of federal and state law regarding proper drivers' licensing, helmet usage, and the requirements specified in Section 38026.5.

(5) Prohibit off-highway motor vehicles from traveling faster than 35 miles per hour on highways designated under this section.

(6) (A) Prohibit a combined-use highway road segment designated under this section from exceeding 10 miles.

(B) Notwithstanding subparagraph (A), two or more combined-use highway road segments may share a common starting point or ending point and may partially overlap as long as the resulting network of the highway road segments does not include more than three distinct locations of shared starting or ending points, or both.

(7) Include an opportunity for public comment at a public hearing held by the city in order to evaluate the pilot project.

(c) A pilot project established pursuant to this section may include use of a state highway, subject to the approval of the Department of Transportation, or any crossing of a highway designated pursuant to Section 38025.

(d) (1) By selecting and designating a highway for combined use pursuant to this section, the city agrees to defend and indemnify the state against any and all claims, including legal defense and liability arising from a claim, for any safety-related losses or injuries arising or resulting from use by off-highway motor vehicles of a highway designated as a combined-use highway by the city council pursuant to this section.

(2) This subdivision does not alter the requirements of subdivision (e).

(e) The city shall not designate a highway for combined use pursuant to this section unless the Commissioner of the Department of the California Highway Patrol finds that designating the highway for combined use would not create a potential traffic safety hazard.

(f) (1) Not later than January 1, 2027, the City of Needles, in consultation with the Department of the California Highway Patrol, the Department of Transportation, and the Department of Parks and Recreation, shall prepare and submit to the Legislature a report evaluating the pilot project, and containing all of the following:

(A) A description of the road segments designated to allow combined use for over three miles, as approved or adopted by a majority vote of the members of the City of Needles city council.

(B) An evaluation of the overall safety and effectiveness of the pilot project, including its impact on traffic flows, safety, off-highway vehicle usage on existing trails, incursions into areas not designated for off-highway vehicle usage, and nonmotorized recreation.

(C) A description of the public comments received at a public hearing held by the city in regards to an evaluation of the pilot project.

(2) On or before January 1, 2027, the City of Needles, in consultation with the entities listed in paragraph (1), shall prepare and submit a report to the Legislature that includes the information specified in paragraph (1).

(g) On or before January 1, 2027, the City of Needles, in consultation with the Department of Fish and Wildlife and the Mojave Desert Air Quality Management District, shall prepare and submit a report to the Legislature on the operation and impacts of the combined-use highways designated pursuant to this section, and the portions of any adjoining trails in close proximity to those highways, including impacts to neighboring lands affected by the system, if any. The report shall include the latest available information, including, but not limited to, impacts on cultural resources and archaeological sites, streambed modifications and water quality impacts, impacts on protections for wildlife and aquatic habitat, native plants, and wildlife, traffic, particulate pollution, and noise.

(h) (1) The reports submitted pursuant to subdivisions (f) and (g) shall be submitted in compliance with Section 9795 of the Government Code.

(2) This section shall remain in effect only until January 1, 2028, and as of that date is repealed, unless a later enacted statute that is enacted before January 1, 2028, deletes or extends that date.

(Added by Stats. 2022, Ch. 185, Sec. 4. (AB 2152) Effective January 1, 2023. Repealed as of January 1, 2028, by its own provisions.)

38026.3. (a) Except as provided in subdivision (d), the Department of Parks and Recreation may establish a pilot project to designate combined-use highways on roads in Red Rock Canyon State Park for no more than 10 miles so that the combined-use highways can be used to link existing off-highway motor vehicle trails and trailheads on federal Bureau of Land Management or United States Forest Service lands, and to link off-highway motor vehicle recreational-use areas with necessary service and lodging facilities, in order to provide a unified system of trails for off-highway motor vehicles, preserve traffic safety, improve natural resource protection, and reduce off-highway vehicle trespass on private land.

(b) A pilot project established pursuant to this section shall do all of the following:

(1) Prescribe a procedure for highway, road, or route selection and designation. The procedure shall be approved by the director of the department.

(2) Prescribe a procedure for the department to remove a combined-use designation, including a designation that is removed as a result of the conclusion of the pilot project.

(3) In cooperation with the Department of Transportation, establish uniform specifications and symbols for signs, markers, and traffic control devices to control off-highway motor vehicles, including, but not limited to, all of the following:

(A) Devices to warn of dangerous conditions, obstacles, or hazards.

(B) Designations of the right-of-way for regular vehicular traffic and off-highway motor vehicles.

(C) A description of the nature and destination of the off-highway motor vehicle trail.

(D) Warning signs for pedestrians and motorists of the presence of off-highway motor vehicle traffic.

(4) Require that off-highway motor vehicles subject to the pilot project meet the safety requirements of federal and state law regarding proper drivers' licensing, helmet usage, and the requirements specified in Section 38026.5.

(5) Prohibit off-highway motor vehicles from traveling faster than 35 miles per hour on highways designated under this section.

(6) (A) Prohibit a combined-use highway road segment designated under this section from exceeding 10 miles.

(B) Notwithstanding subparagraph (A), two or more combined-use highway road segments may share a common starting point or ending point and may partially overlap as long as the resulting network of the highway road segments does not include more than three distinct locations of shared starting or ending points, or both.

(7) Include an opportunity for public comment at a public hearing held by the department in order to evaluate the pilot project.

(c) A pilot project established pursuant to this section may include use of a state highway, subject to the approval of the Department of Transportation, or any crossing of a highway designated pursuant to Section 38025.

(d) The department shall not designate a highway for combined use pursuant to this section unless the Commissioner of the Department of the California Highway Patrol finds that designating the highway for combined use would not create a potential traffic safety hazard.

(e) (1) Not later than January 1, 2029, the department, in consultation with the Department of the California Highway Patrol and the Department of Transportation, shall prepare and submit to the Legislature a report evaluating the pilot project that contains all of the following:

(A) A description of the road segments designated to allow combined use for over three miles.

(B) An evaluation of the overall safety and effectiveness of the pilot project, including its impact on traffic flows, safety, off-highway vehicle usage on existing trails, incursions into areas not designated for off-highway vehicle usage, and nonmotorized recreation.

(C) A description of the public comments received at a public hearing held by the department in regards to an evaluation of the pilot project.

(2) The report required by this subdivision shall be submitted in compliance with Section 9795 of the Government Code.

(f) This section shall remain in effect only until January 1, 2030, and as of that date is repealed, unless a later enacted statute that is enacted before January 1, 2030, deletes or extends that date.

(Added by Stats. 2024, Ch. 592, Sec. 2. (SB 632) Effective January 1, 2025. Repealed as of January 1, 2030, by its own provisions.)

38026.5. (a) In accordance with subdivision (c) of Section 4000, a motor vehicle issued a plate or device pursuant to Section 38160 may be operated or driven on a local highway, or a portion of the local highway, that is designated pursuant to Section 38026, 38026.1, 38026.2, or 38026.3 if the operation is in conformance with this code and the vehicle complies with off-highway vehicle equipment requirements specified in this division.

(b) Notwithstanding subdivision (a), it is unlawful for a person using an off-highway vehicle on a combined-use highway to do any of the following:

(1) Operate an off-highway motor vehicle on the highway during the hours of darkness.

(2) Operate a vehicle on the highway that does not have an operational stoplight.

(3) Operate a vehicle on the highway that does not have rubber tires.

(4) Operate a vehicle without a valid driver's license of the appropriate class for the vehicle operation in possession.

(5) Operate a vehicle on the highway without complying with Article 2 (commencing with Section 16020) of Chapter 1 of Division 7.

(Amended by Stats. 2024, Ch. 592, Sec. 3. (SB 632) Effective January 1, 2025.)

38027. Motor-driven cycles issued a plate or device pursuant to Section 38160 may be moved, by nonmechanical means only, adjacent to a roadway, in such a manner so as to not interfere with traffic upon the highway, only for the purpose of gaining access to, or returning from, areas designed for the operation of off-highway vehicles, when no other route is available. The Department of Transportation or local authority may designate access routes leading to off-highway parks as suitable for the operation of off-highway vehicles, if such access routes are available to the general public only for pedestrian and off-highway motor vehicle travel.

(Amended by Stats. 1976, Ch. 1093.)

38030. Notwithstanding the provisions of Section 38020, an unidentified off-highway motor vehicle subject to identification may be left standing upon a highway or public or private property adjacent to the place of business of a dealer of such motor vehicles when done so in connection with the loading and unloading or storage of such vehicles to be used in the dealer's business, unless already prohibited by law.

(Amended by Stats. 1973, Ch. 78.)

Article 2. Original Identification

(Article 2 added by Stats. 1971, Ch. 1816.)

38040. Application for the original identification of a motor vehicle, other than a motorcycle, required to be identified pursuant to this division shall be made by the owner to the department upon the appropriate form furnished by it and shall contain all of the following:

(a) The true, full name, business or residence and mailing address, and the driver's license or identification card number, if any, of the owner and the legal owner, if any.

(b) The name of the county in which the owner resides.

(c)A description of the vehicle, including the following, insofar as it may exist:

(1) The make, model, and type of body.

(2) The vehicle identification number or any other number as may be required by the department.

(d) Information as may reasonably be required by the department to enable it to determine whether the vehicle is lawfully entitled to identification.

(Amended by Stats. 1994, Ch. 1221, Sec. 18. Effective January 1, 1995.)

38041. Application for the original identification of a motorcycle shall be made by the owner to the department upon the appropriate form furnished by it, and shall contain:

(a) The true, full name, business or residence and mailing address, and the driver's license or identification card number, if any, of the owner and the legal owner, if any.

(b) The name of the county in which the owner resides.

(c) A description of the motorcycle including the following data insofar as it may exist:

(1) The make and type of body.

(2) The motor and frame numbers recorded exactly as stamped on the engine and frame, respectively, by the manufacturer, and any other identifying number of the motorcycle as may be required by the department.

(3) The date first sold by a manufacturer or dealer to a consumer.

(d) Such information as may reasonably be required by the department to enable it to determine whether the vehicle is lawfully entitled to identification.

(e) The department shall maintain a cross-index file of motor and frame numbers identified with it.

The application shall be accompanied by a tracing, tape lift, or photograph of the motor or frame numbers, or where the facsimile of the motor or frame numbers cannot be obtained, a verification of the numbers shall be required.

(Amended by Stats. 1994, Ch. 1221, Sec. 19. Effective January 1, 1995.)

38045. Ownership of title to an off-highway motor vehicle subject to identification under this division may be held by two (or more) coowners as provided in Section 682 of the Civil Code, except that:

(a) A vehicle may be identified in the names of two (or more) persons as coowners in the alternative by the use of the word "or." A vehicle so identified in the alternative shall be deemed to be held in joint tenancy. Each coowner shall be deemed to have granted to the other coowners the absolute right to dispose of the title and interest in the vehicle. Upon the death of a coowner, the interest of the decedent shall pass to the survivor as though title or interest in the vehicle was held in joint tenancy, unless a contrary intention is set forth in writing upon the application for identification.

(b) A vehicle may be identified in the names of two (or more) persons as coowners in the alternative by the use of the word "or" and if declared in writing upon the application for identification by the applicants to be community property, or tenancy in common, shall grant to each coowner the absolute power to transfer the title or interest of the other coowners only during the lifetime of such coowners.

(c) A vehicle may be identified in the names of two (or more) persons as coowners in the conjunctive by the use of the word "and" and shall thereafter require the signature of each coowner or his personal representative to transfer title to the vehicle, except where title to the vehicle is set forth in joint tenancy, the signature of each coowner or his personal representative shall be required only during the lifetime of the coowners, and upon death of a coowner title shall pass to the surviving coowner.

(d) The department may adopt suitable abbreviations to appear upon the certificate of identification and certificate of ownership to designate the manner in which title to the vehicle is held if set forth by the coowners upon the application for identification.

(Added by Stats. 1971, Ch. 1816.)

38050. In the absence of the regularly required supporting evidence of ownership upon application for identification or transfer of a vehicle, the department may accept an undertaking or bond which shall be conditioned to protect the department and all officers and employees thereof and any subsequent purchaser of the vehicle, any person acquiring a lien or security interest thereon, or the successor in interest of such purchaser or person against any loss or damage on account of any defect in or undisclosed claim upon the right, title, and interest of the applicant or other person in and to the vehicle.

(Added by Stats. 1971, Ch. 1816.)

38055. In the event the vehicle is no longer identified in this state and the currently valid certificate of ownership is surrendered to the department, the bond or undertaking shall be returned and surrendered at the end of three years or prior thereto.

(Amended by Stats. 1982, Ch. 517, Sec. 402.)

38060. (a) Whenever any person, after making application for identification of an off-highway motor vehicle subject to identification, or after the identification either as owner or legal owner, moves or acquires a new address different from the address shown in the application or upon the certificate of ownership or identification certificate, that person shall, within 10 days thereafter, notify the department of his or her old and new addresses.

(b) Any owner having notified the department as required in subdivision (a), shall immediately mark out the former on the face of the certificate and write with pen and ink or type the new on the face of the certificate immediately below the former address and initial the entry.

(Amended by Stats. 1982, Ch. 466, Sec. 118.)

Article 3. Evidences of Identification

(Article 3 added by Stats. 1971, Ch. 1816.)

38070. The department, upon identifying an off-highway motor vehicle subject to identification, shall issue a certificate of ownership to the legal owner and an identification certificate to the owner, or both to the owner if there is no legal owner.

(Amended by Stats. 1976, Ch. 1093.)

38075. (a) The identification certificate shall contain upon the face thereof the date issued, the name and residence or business or mailing address of the owner and of the legal owner, if any, the identification number to the vehicle, and a description of the vehicle as complete as that required in the application for the identification of a vehicle.

(b) The director may modify the form, arrangement, and information appearing on the face of the identification certificate and may provide for standardization and abbreviation of fictitious or firm names thereon whenever he finds that the efficiency of the department will be promoted thereby, except that general delivery or post office box numbers shall not be permitted as the address of the identified owner unless there is no other address.

(Amended by Stats. 1989, Ch. 1213, Sec. 17.)

38076. The certificate of ownership shall contain:

(a) Not less than the information required upon the face of the identification certificate.

(b) Provision for notice to the department of a transfer of the title or interest of the owner or legal owner.

(c) Provision for application for transfer of identification by the transferee.

(Added by Stats. 1971, Ch. 1816.)

38080. (a) The department may authorize, under Section 4456, dealers licensed under Article 1 (commencing with Section 11700) of Chapter 4 of Division 5 to use the process described in Section 4456 and corresponding temporary identification devices upon off-highway motor vehicles subject to identification that they sell.

(b) Off-highway motor vehicles subject to identification that are purchased from dealers not required to be licensed under Article 1 (commencing with Section 11700) of Chapter 4 of Division 5, or that are specially constructed by the owner or owners, may be operated off-highway, as provided by this division, without an identification plate or device or identification certificate, provided a receipt or other suitable device issued by the department is displayed upon the vehicle evidencing an application has been made and appropriate fees paid pursuant to this division, until the identification plate or device and identification certificate are received from the department.

(c) This section shall become operative January 1, 2019.

(Repealed (in Sec. 25) and added by Stats. 2016, Ch. 90, Sec. 26. (AB 516) Effective January 1, 2017. Section operative January 1, 2019, by its own provisions.)

38085. (a) Every owner upon receipt of an identification certificate shall maintain the same or a facsimile copy thereof with the vehicle for which it is issued at all times when the vehicle is operated or transported.

(b) The provisions of this section do not apply when an identification certificate is removed from the vehicle for the purpose of application for renewal or transfer of identification.

(Amended by Stats. 1988, Ch. 1268, Sec. 19.)

38087. (a) Upon payment of the fees specified in Section 38231, the department may issue to manufacturers, dealers, distributors, or their agents, a special permit to operate or use for the purpose of delivery, demonstration, or display, off-highway motor vehicles otherwise required to be identified under this division.

(b) Special permits issued pursuant to this section shall expire at midnight on the 30th day of June in the second calendar year following the year of issuance of such permit.

(Amended by Stats. 1976, Ch. 1093.)

38087.5. (a) Upon payment of the fee specified in Section 38231.5, the Department of Parks and Recreation may issue to a nonresident of this state a special permit to operate an off-highway motor vehicle otherwise required to be identified under this chapter.

(b) Special permits issued under this section shall expire on December 31 in the year of their issuance.

(Added by Stats. 1996, Ch. 572, Sec. 2. Effective January 1, 1997.)

38087.7. (a) Upon payment of the fee specified in Section 38231.7, the Department of Parks and Recreation shall issue an annual special permit, to be known as the "sanctioned event permit," to California residents to operate an off-road motorcycle at a sanctioned event. The sanctioned event permit shall be available for online purchase beginning January 1, 2026.

(b) A sanctioned event permit shall expire on December 31 of the year that the permit is issued.

(c) A sanctioned event permit shall only be available to California residents and for model year 2022 and newer off-road motorcycles that are not eligible for the "Green Sticker" or "Red Sticker" off-highway vehicle identification issued by the department.

(d) A sanctioned event permit shall be displayed on the left side of an off-road motorcycle and shall be visible for inspection at sanctioned events. A sanctioned event permit shall be nonrefundable, nonreplaceable, and void if removed from an off-road motorcycle.

(e) For purposes of this section, "sanctioned event" means an event approved by an agency within its guidelines for off-highway vehicle competition or racing events.

(Added by Stats. 2024, Ch. 446, Sec. 1. (SB 708) Effective January 1, 2025.)

38088. (a) Upon payment of the fee specified in Section 38232, the department shall issue to the owner of a motorcycle, which the owner has certified as being used exclusively in racing events on a closed course, a special transportation identification device for the purpose of identifying the motorcycle while it is being transported upon a highway to and from racing events on a closed course. Such device may be either a plate or a sticker, whichever is determined by the department to be the most appropriate.

(b) Such device is nonrenewable, nontransferrable, and becomes invalid when the vehicle for which it was issued is sold or dismantled.

(c) A certificate of ownership may not be issued in conjunction with a special transportation identification device.

(Added by Stats. 1975, Ch. 1050.)

38090. If any identification certificate or identification plate or device is stolen, lost, mutilated or illegible, the owner of the vehicle for which the same was issued, as shown by the records of the department, shall immediately make application for and may, upon furnishing information satisfactory to the department, obtain a duplicate or substitute or a new identification under a new number, as determined to be most advisable by the department. An application for a duplicate identification certificate is not required in conjunction with any other application.

(Amended by Stats. 1988, Ch. 1268, Sec. 20.)

38095. If any certificate of ownership is stolen, lost, mutilated or illegible, the legal owner or, if none, the owner of the vehicle for which the same was issued as shown by the records of the department shall immediately make application for and may, upon furnishing information satisfactory to the department, obtain a duplicate.

(Added by Stats. 1971, Ch. 1816.)

38100. The provisions of Sections 4458, 4460, 4461, 4462, 4463, and 4464 shall be fully applicable to motor vehicles identified under this division and the terms "identification" and "identification certificate" shall have the same meaning as the terms "registration" and "registration card," respectively, as used in those sections.

(Amended by Stats. 1976, Ch. 1093.)

Article 4. Renewal of Identification

(Article 4 added by Stats. 1971, Ch. 1816.)

38110. Certificates of ownership shall not be renewed but shall remain valid until suspended, revoked, or canceled by the department for cause or upon transfer of any interest shown therein.

(Added by Stats. 1971, Ch. 1816.)

38115. Every motor vehicle identification and identification certificate issued pursuant to this division shall expire at midnight on the 30th day of June in the second calendar year following the year of issuance of such certificate. The department may upon payment of the proper fees renew such identification.

(Amended by Stats. 1976, Ch. 1093.)

38120. (a) Application for renewal of identification of off-highway motor vehicles subject to identification shall be made by the owner not later than midnight of the 30th day of June of the expiration year. The application shall contain the true, full name and driver's license or identification card number, if any, of the owner.

(b) Whenever any application for identification or transfer of ownership of an off-highway motor vehicle subject to identification is filed with the department between June 1 and June 30 of the year of expiration, the application shall be accompanied by the full renewal fees in addition to any other fees then due and payable.

(c) Whenever an application for identification or transfer of ownership of an off-highway motor vehicle subject to identification is filed with the department between January 1 and May 31 of the year of expiration, the application may be accompanied by full renewal fees in addition to any other fees then due and payable, which renewal fees shall be for the two-year period following June 30th of the year in which paid.

(Amended by Stats. 1994, Ch. 1221, Sec. 20. Effective January 1, 1995.)

38121. (a) Prior to the expiration of the identification of an off-highway motor vehicle, if that identification is not to be renewed prior to its expiration, the owner of the vehicle shall file, under penalty of perjury, a certification that the vehicle will not be operated, used, or transported on public property or private property in a manner so as to subject the vehicle to identification during the subsequent identification period without first making an application for identification of the vehicle, including full payment of all fees. The certification of nonoperation is valid until the identification is renewed under subdivision (c).

(b) Each certification of nonoperation filed pursuant to subdivision (a) shall be accompanied by a filing fee of fifteen dollars ($15).

(c) An application for renewal of identification, whether or not accompanied by an application for transfer of title to, or any interest in, the vehicle, shall be submitted to the department with payment of the required fees for the current identification period and without penalty for delinquent payment of fees imposed under this code if the department receives the application on or before the date the vehicle is first operated, used, or transported on public property or private property in a manner so as to subject the vehicle to identification and certification of nonoperation required pursuant to subdivision (a).

(d) A certification of nonoperation is not required to be filed pursuant to subdivision (a) for a vehicle on which the identification expires while being held as inventory by a dealer or lessor-retailer.

(Amended by Stats. 2003, Ch. 719, Sec. 27. Effective January 1, 2004.)

38125. Whenever by reason of the theft or embezzlement of an off-highway motor vehicle subject to identification the owner or legal owner is not in possession of the vehicle at the time penalties accrue for failure to obtain identification, or renewal thereof, the owner or legal owner may secure the identification or renewal of the identification of the vehicle within 20 days after its recovery upon filing an affidavit setting forth the circumstances of the theft or embezzlement if the theft or embezzlement of the vehicle has been reported pursuant to provisions of this code, without penalty for delinquent payment of fees imposed under this division.

(Amended by Stats. 1974, Ch. 947.)

38130. When application for identification of an off-highway motor vehicle subject to identification has been made as required by this division, the vehicle may be operated pursuant to this division until the new indicia of current identification have been received from the department on condition that there be displayed on the vehicle the identification plate or device and validating device, if any, issued to the vehicle for the previous identification term.

(Added by Stats. 1971, Ch. 1816.)

38135. The department may, upon renewing of an identification of off-highway motor vehicles subject to identification, issue a new identification certificate or may endorse or authorize the endorsement of a receipt or validation upon payment of the required fees. The receipt or validation to be stamped upon the identification certificate last issued for the vehicle during the preceding period, or upon a potential identification certificate issued near the close of the preceding period, which identification certificate so endorsed or validated shall constitute the identification certificate for the ensuing two-year period. If the identification certificate and potential identification certificate are unavailable, a fee as specified in Section 38260 shall not be paid.

(Amended by Stats. 1988, Ch. 1268, Sec. 21.)

Article 5. Refusal of Identification

(Article 5 added by Stats. 1971, Ch. 1816.)

38145. The department shall refuse the identification or renewal or transfer of identification of an off-highway motor vehicle subject to identification upon any of the following grounds:

(a) That the application contains any false or fraudulent statement.

(b) That the required fee has not been paid.

(Added by Stats. 1971, Ch. 1816.)

38150. The department may refuse the identification or renewal or transfer of identification of an off-highway motor vehicle subject to identification in any of the following circumstances:

(a) If the department is satisfied that the applicant is not entitled thereto under this code.

(b) If the applicant has failed to furnish the department with information required in the application or reasonable additional information required by the department.

(c) If the department determines that the applicant has made or permitted unlawful use of any identification certificate, certificate of ownership, identification plates, or other identifying indicia.

(Amended by Stats. 1976, Ch. 1093.)

Article 6. Identification Plate or Device

(Article 6 added by Stats. 1971, Ch. 1816.)

38160. The department, upon identifying an off-highway motor vehicle subject to identification, shall issue to the owner a suitable identification plate or device which is capable of being attached to the vehicle in such a manner so as to not endanger the operator or passengers of the vehicle, and which shall identify the vehicle for which it is issued for the period of its validity.

(Added by Stats. 1971, Ch. 1816.)

38165. (a) The department shall determine the size, color, and letters or number of the plate or device issued pursuant to this division and the life of the series of plate or device issued, but in no event less than six years. The design of the plate or device shall have the identification number as the most prominent feature of the device. During the intervening identification periods for which the plate or device is issued, the department shall issue a tab, sticker, or other suitable device to indicate the term for which such plate or device will be valid.

(b) On or before July 1, 2009, the department, in conjunction with the Division of Off-Highway Motor Vehicle Recreation of the Department of Parks and Recreation, shall report to the Assembly Committee on Water, Parks and Wildlife and the Senate Committee on Natural Resources and Water, regarding recommendations to improve the identification of off-highway motor vehicles. At a minimum, the report shall examine the benefits and challenges of all of the following:

(1) Using multiple identification stickers for each vehicle.

(2) Using large-print identifying numbers or letters.

(3) Various identifying devices, such as license plates and stickers.

(4) Requiring license plates or other device alternatives for certain off-highway vehicle types.

(5) Including a unique number for special nonresident permits issued under Section 38087.5.

(c) In preparing the report, the department and the Division of Off-Highway Motor Vehicle Recreation shall work with vehicle manufacturers to evaluate feasibility.

(Amended by Stats. 2007, Ch. 541, Sec. 23. Effective January 1, 2008.)

38170. (a) Every off-highway motor vehicle subject to identification shall have displayed upon it the identification number assigned to the vehicle for which it is issued, together with the word "California" or the abbreviation "CAL" and the year number for which it is issued or a suitable device issued by the department for validation purposes, which device shall contain the year for which it is issued.

(b) The identification plate or device shall at all times be securely fastened to the vehicle for which it is issued and shall be mounted or affixed in a position to be clearly visible, and shall be maintained in a condition so as to be clearly legible. No covering shall be used on the identification plate or device.

(c) All identification plates or devices issued on or after January 1, 1996, shall be displayed as follows:

(1) On the left fork leg of a motorcycle, either horizontal or vertical, and shall be visible from the left side of the motorcycle.

(2) On the left quadrant of the metal frame member of sand rails, rail-type buggies, and dune buggies, visible from the rear of the vehicle.

(3) On the left rear quadrant on permanent plastic or metal frame members of all-terrain vehicles, visible to outside inspections.

(4) On the left tunnel on the back quadrant of snowmobiles.

(Amended by Stats. 1994, Ch. 14, Sec. 1. Effective January 1, 1995.)

Article 7. Dismantling of Off-Highway Motor Vehicles

(Article 7 added by Stats. 1971, Ch. 1816.)

38180. Chapter 3 (commencing with Section 11500) of Division 5 shall be applicable to off-highway motor vehicles subject to identification, except as provided in this article.

(Added by Stats. 1971, Ch. 1816.)

38185. No off-highway motor vehicle subject to identification which has been reported dismantled or sold as salvage may be subsequently identified until it has been inspected by the department.

(Added by Stats. 1971, Ch. 1816.)

Article 8. Transfers of Title or Interest

(Heading of Article 8 renamed from Chapter 3 (and placed in Chapter 2) by Stats. 1976, Ch. 1093.)

38195. The provisions of Chapter 2 (commencing with Section 5600) of Division 3 shall be applicable to off-highway motor vehicles subject to identification, and the terms "registration," "registration card," and "registered" as used therein, shall apply to the terms "identification," "identification certificate," and "identified," respectively, except that

Sections 5901, 5902, 5903, 5904, 5906, and 6052 shall not apply.
(Added by Stats. 1971, Ch. 1816.)

38200. (a) Every licensed dealer upon transferring by sale, lease, or otherwise any off-highway motor vehicle subject to identification, whether new or used, of a type subject to identification under this division, shall, not later than the end of the fifth calendar day thereafter, not counting the day of sale, lease, or other transfer, give written notice of the transfer to the department upon an appropriate form provided by it; but a dealer need not give the notice when selling or transferring a new unidentified off-highway motor vehicle subject to identification to another dealer.

A "sale" shall be deemed completed and consummated when the purchaser of that vehicle has paid the purchase price, or, in lieu thereof, has signed a purchase contract or security agreement, and taken physical possession or delivery of that vehicle.

(b) Every dealer of off-highway motor vehicles subject to identification who is not licensed with the department, and who engages only in the sale of vehicles of a type not properly equipped for operation upon the highway and that are restricted to off-highway operation or use, shall comply with the provisions of Section 5900, or such regulations as the director determines are necessary to carry out the provisions of this division.
(Amended by Stats. 1975, Ch. 440.)

38205. Whenever any person has received as transferee a properly endorsed certificate of ownership, he or she shall, within 10 days thereafter, endorse the ownership certificate as required and forward the ownership certificate with the proper transfer fee and, if required under Section 38120, any other fee due and thereby make application for transfer of identification. The certificate of ownership shall contain a space for the applicant's driver's license or identification card number, and the applicant shall furnish that number, if any, in the space provided.
(Amended by Stats. 1994, Ch. 1221, Sec. 21. Effective January 1, 1995.)

38210. When the transferee of an off-highway motor vehicle subject to identification is a dealer who holds such vehicle for resale, the dealer is not required to make application for transfer, but upon transferring his title or interest to another person he shall comply with this division.
(Added by Stats. 1971, Ch. 1816.)

38211. (a) The department shall withhold identification of or the transfer of ownership of any vehicle subject to identification under this division until the applicant pays to the department the use tax measured by the sales price of the vehicle as required by the Sales and Use Tax Law, together with penalty, if any, unless the purchaser presents evidence on a form prescribed by the State Board of Equalization that sales tax will be paid by the seller or that use tax has been collected by the seller or that the State Board of Equalization finds that no use tax is due. If the applicant so desires, he may pay the use tax and penalty, if any, to the department so as to secure immediate action upon his application for identification or transfer of ownership, and thereafter he may apply through the Department of Motor Vehicles to the State Board of Equalization under the provisions of the Sales and Use Tax Law for a refund of the amount so paid.

(b) The department shall transmit to the State Board of Equalization all collections of use tax and penalty made under this section. This transmittal shall be made at least monthly, accompanied by a schedule in such form as the department and board may prescribe.

(c) The State Board of Equalization shall reimburse the department for its costs incurred in carrying out the provisions of this section. Such reimbursement shall be effected under agreement between the agencies, approved by the Department of Finance.

(d) In computing any use tax or penalty thereon under the provisions of this section dollar fractions shall be disregarded in the manner specified in Section 9559 of this code. Payment of tax and penalty on this basis shall be deemed full compliance with the requirements of the Sales and Use Tax Law insofar as they are applicable to the use of vehicles to which this section relates.
(Added by Stats. 1971, Ch. 1816.)

Article 9. Identification Fees

(Heading of Article 9 renamed from Chapter 4 (and placed in Chapter 2) by Stats. 1976, Ch. 1093.)

38225. (a) A service fee of seven dollars ($7) shall be paid to the department for the issuance or renewal of identification of off-highway motor vehicles subject to identification, except as expressly exempted under this division.

(b) In addition to the service fee required by subdivision (a), a special fee of thirty-three dollars ($33) shall be paid at the time of payment of the service fee for the issuance or renewal of an identification plate or device.

(c) All money transferred pursuant to Section 8352.6 of the Revenue and Taxation Code, all fees received by the department pursuant to subdivision (b), and all day use, overnight use, or annual or biennial use fees for state vehicular recreation areas received by the Department of Parks and Recreation shall be deposited in the Off-Highway Vehicle Trust Fund, which is hereby created. There shall be a separate reporting of special fee revenues by vehicle type, including four-wheeled vehicles, all-terrain vehicles, motorcycles, and snowmobiles. All money shall be deposited in the fund, and, upon appropriation by the Legislature, shall be allocated according to Section 5090.61 of the Public Resources Code.

(d) Any money temporarily transferred by the Legislature from the Off-Highway Vehicle Trust Fund to the General Fund shall be reimbursed, without interest, by the Legislature within two fiscal years of the transfer.
(Amended by Stats. 2017, Ch. 456, Sec. 1. (SB 159) Effective October 3, 2017.)

38225.4. In addition to the service fees specified in subdivision (a) of Section 38225, as amended by Section 6 of Chapter 964 of the Statutes of 1992, a fee of three dollars ($3) shall be paid at the time of issuance or renewal of identification of off-highway motor vehicles subject to identification, except as expressly exempted under this division. The department shall deposit the fee received under this section in the Motor Vehicle Account in the State Transportation Fund. The money deposited in the account pursuant to this section shall be available, upon appropriation by the Legislature, for expenditure to offset the costs of maintaining the uniformed field strength of the Department of the California Highway Patrol.
(Amended (as added by Stats. 1994, Ch. 1197) by Stats. 2003, Ch. 719, Sec. 29. Effective January 1, 2004.)

38225.5. In addition to the service fees specified in Section 38225, a fee of three dollars ($3) shall be paid at the time of issuance or renewal of identification of off-highway vehicles subject to identification, except as expressly exempted under this division. The department shall deposit the fee received under this section in the Motor Vehicle Account in the State Transportation Fund. The money deposited in the account pursuant to this section shall be available, upon appropriation by the Legislature, for expenditure to offset the costs of increasing the uniformed field strength of the Department of the California Highway Patrol beyond its 1994 staffing level and those costs associated with maintaining this new level of uniformed field strength and carrying out those duties specified in subdivision (a) of Section 830.2 of the Penal Code.
(Amended by Stats. 2003, Ch. 719, Sec. 30. Effective January 1, 2004.)

38230. In addition to the fees imposed by Section 38225, there shall be paid a four-dollar ($4) fee for the issuance or renewal of identification for every off-highway motor vehicle subject to identification. The fee imposed by this section is in lieu of all taxes according to value levied for state or local purposes.
(Added by Stats. 1971, Ch. 1816.)

38231. The fees for a special permit issued under Section 38087 shall be the prevailing identification fees as set forth in Sections 38225 and 38230 and shall be deposited and distributed as are identification fees under this chapter.
(Added by Stats. 1972, Ch. 973.)

38231.5. (a) The fee for a special permit issued under Section 38087.5 shall be not less than twenty dollars ($20), as established by the Department of Parks and Recreation. The Department of Parks and Recreation may adjust the special permit fee for a permit issued to a nonresident of this state under Section 38087.5, as necessary, to recover the costs of this program. After deducting its administrative and vendor costs, the Department of Parks and Recreation shall deposit the fees received under this section in the Off-Highway Vehicle Trust Fund. Money in the fund shall be allocated, upon appropriation, as provided in Sections 5090.50 and 5090.64 of the Public Resources Code.

(b) The Department of Parks and Recreation shall print the special permits required by Section 38087.5 and shall supervise the sale of those permits throughout the state.

(c) The Department of Parks and Recreation shall either distribute and sell the special permits directly or contract with vendors according to rules and regulations established by that department. The vendors shall receive a commission in an amount not to exceed 5 percent of the fee imposed pursuant to subdivision (a) for each special permit sold. The Department of Parks and Recreation may solicit the participation of qualified retail commercial enterprises engaged in the sale or rental of off-highway vehicles, equipment, accessories, or supplies to act as authorized vendors of the special permits and may authorize local and federal agencies that provide off-highway vehicle opportunities to act as authorized vendors of the special permits.

(Amended by Stats. 2002, Ch. 563, Sec. 41. Effective January 1, 2003.)

38231.7. The Department of Parks and Recreation shall set, and may adjust, the amount of the fee to recover the operating and administrative costs of a sanctioned event permit issued pursuant to Section 38087.7. The Department of Parks and Recreation shall deposit fees received pursuant to this section in the Off-Highway Vehicle Trust Fund.

(Added by Stats. 2024, Ch. 446, Sec. 2. (SB 708) Effective January 1, 2025.)

38232. A special fee of fifteen dollars ($15) shall be paid to the department for the issuance of a special transportation identification device issued pursuant to Section 38088 and shall be deposited in the Motor Vehicle Account in the Transportation Tax Fund. The fee is in lieu of the fees provided in Section 38225.

(Amended by Stats. 2003, Ch. 719, Sec. 31. Effective January 1, 2004.)

38235. All money collected by the department under Section 38230 shall be reported monthly to the Controller and at the same time be deposited in the State Treasury to the credit of the Off-Highway License Fee Fund, which is hereby created.

(Amended by Stats. 1995, Ch. 970, Sec. 5. Effective January 1, 1996.)

38240. (a) The Controller shall allocate the fees collected under Section 38230 in July and January of each fiscal year to cities and counties based upon the proportional estimated off-highway motor vehicle use and related activity within the respective jurisdictions pursuant to the report described in subdivision (d) of Section 5090.15 of the Public Resources Code.

(b) The funds collected under Section 38230 shall be used for the purposes set forth in Sections 5090.50 and 5090.64 of the Public Resources Code.

(c) In addition to the purposes set forth in subdivision (b), funds received by a city or county pursuant to this section may be expended for facilities located outside the limits of the city or county if both of the following conditions are met:

(1) The funds are expended for the purposes of acquiring, developing, and constructing trails, areas, or other facilities for the use of off-highway motor vehicles.

(2) The funds are expended pursuant to an agreement with the city in which the facility is located or with the county in which the facility is located if the facility is located in an unincorporated territory.

(d) This section shall become operative on January 1, 2006.

(Repealed (in Sec. 21) and added by Stats. 2004, Ch. 908, Sec. 22. Effective January 1, 2005. Section operative January 1, 2006, by its own provisions.)

38245. Whenever an off-highway motor vehicle subject to identification is operated or transported in this state without the fees required by this division having first been paid, the fee is delinquent.

(Amended by Stats. 1973, Ch. 974.)

38246. (a) A penalty shall be added upon any application for renewal of identification made on or after the day following the expiration date, except as provided in Section 4605, 38121, or 38247.

(b) If the fee specified in subdivision (a) or (b) of Section 38255 is not paid within 10 days after the fee becomes delinquent, a penalty shall be assessed.

(c) If renewal fee penalties have not accrued and the ownership of the vehicle is transferred, the transferee has 20 days from the date of transfer to pay the identification fees that become due without payment of any penalties that would otherwise be required under subdivision (a) or to file a certificate of nonoperation pursuant to subdivision (a) of Section 38121, if the vehicle will not be operated, used, or transported on public property or private property in a manner so as to subject the vehicle to identification during the subsequent identification period without first making application for identification of the vehicle, including full payment of all fees.

(d) Except as otherwise provided in this section, if any fee is not paid within 20 days after the fee becomes delinquent, a penalty shall be assessed.

(Amended by Stats. 1999, Ch. 1008, Sec. 17. Effective January 1, 2000.)

38247. (a) When a transferee or purchaser of a vehicle applies for transfer of identification, as provided in Section 38205, and it is determined by the department that penalties accrued prior to the purchase of the vehicle, and that the transferee or purchaser was not cognizant of the nonpayment of the fees for identification for the current or prior identification years, the department may waive the identification penalties upon payment of the fees for identification due.

(b) Other provisions of this code notwithstanding, the director may at his discretion investigate into the circumstances of any application for identification to ascertain if penalties had accrued through no fault or intent of the owner. Provided such circumstances prevail, the director may waive any penalties upon payment of the fees for identification then due.

(c) When a transferee or purchaser of a vehicle applies for transfer of identification of a vehicle, and it is determined by the department that fees for identification of the vehicle for any year are unpaid and due, that such fees became due prior to the purchase of the vehicle by the transferee or purchaser and that the transferee or purchaser was not cognizant of the fact that such fees were unpaid and due, the department may waive such fees and any penalty thereon when the identification fees due for the vehicle for the current year are paid.

(d) Upon the transfer of a vehicle for which fees for identification and any penalties thereon are unpaid and due, such fees and penalties are, notwithstanding the provisions of Article 6 (commencing with Section 9800) of this chapter, the personal debt of the transferor of the vehicle who did not pay such fees and penalties when they became due or accrued. Such fees and penalties may be collected by the department in an appropriate civil action if the department has waived such fees and penalties pursuant to subdivision (c).

(Added by Stats. 1976, Ch. 935.)

38250. Whenever any person has received as transferee a properly endorsed certificate of ownership and the transfer fee has not been paid as required by this division within 10 days, the fee is delinquent.

(Amended by Stats. 1988, Ch. 1268, Sec. 23.)

38255. Upon application for transfer of ownership or any interest of an owner, or legal owner in or to any off-highway motor vehicle identified under this division, there shall be paid the following fees:

(a) For a transfer by the owner $15

(b) For a transfer by the legal owner $15

(c) When application is presented showing a transfer by

both the owner and legal owner... $15

(Amended by Stats. 2003, Ch. 719, Sec. 32. Effective January 1, 2004.)

38260. Upon application for a duplicate ownership certificate or identification certificate, or a duplicate or substitute identification plate or device, or any other tabs, stickers, or devices, there shall be paid a fee in the amount of fifteen dollars ($15).

(Amended by Stats. 2003, Ch. 719, Sec. 33. Effective January 1, 2004.)

38265. (a) The penalty for delinquency in respect to any transfer shall be fifteen dollars ($15), and shall apply only to the last transfer.

(b) The penalty for delinquency in respect to the fees imposed by Sections 38225 and 38230 shall be equal to one-half the fee after it has been computed.

(Amended by Stats. 2003, Ch. 719, Sec. 34. Effective January 1, 2004.)

Chapter 5. Off-Highway Vehicle Operating Rules

(Chapter 5 repealed and added by Stats. 1976, Ch. 1093.)

Article 1. Traffic Signs, Signals, and Markings

(Article 1 added by Stats. 1976, Ch. 1093.)

38280. Federal, state, or local authorities having jurisdiction over public lands may place or cause to be placed and maintained, such appropriate signs, signals and other traffic control devices as may be necessary to properly indicate and carry out any provision of law or any duly adopted regulation of such governmental authority or to warn or guide traffic.

(Repealed and added by Stats. 1976, Ch. 1093.)

38285. Only those signs, signals, markings, or devices that conform to the uniform standards and specifications adopted by the Department of Parks and Recreation, with the approval of the Off-Highway Motor Vehicle Recreation Commission, shall be placed as provided in Section 38280.

Special signs, signals, markings, or devices may be used on a temporary basis for purposes of directing traffic on and at sanctioned events conducted on public lands with permission of the agency having administrative jurisdiction over such lands.

(Amended by Stats. 1984, Ch. 729, Sec. 1.)

38286. The provisions of Article 3 (commencing with Section 38305), Article 4 (commencing with Section 38312), Article 5 (commencing with Section 38316), Section 38319 of this chapter, and subdivision (h) of Section 38370 shall not apply to a motor vehicle being operated in an organized racing event that is conducted under the auspices of a recognized sanctioning body or by permit issued by the governmental authority having jurisdiction.

(Amended by Stats. 2002, Ch. 563, Sec. 44. Effective January 1, 2003.)

38300. It is unlawful for the driver of any vehicle to disobey any sign, signal, or traffic control device placed or maintained pursuant to Section 38280.

(Repealed and added by Stats. 1976, Ch. 1093.)

38301. (a) It is unlawful to operate a vehicle in violation of special regulations which have been promulgated by the governmental agency having jurisdiction over public lands, including, but not limited to, regulations governing access, routes of travel, plants, wildlife, wildlife habitat, water resources, and historical sites.

(b) A person who operates a motor vehicle in an area closed to that vehicle is guilty of a public offense and shall be punished as follows:

(1) Except as provided in paragraphs (2) and (3), the offense is an infraction punishable by a fine not exceeding fifty dollars ($50).

(2) For a second offense committed within seven years after a prior violation for which there was a conviction punishable under paragraph (1), the offense is an infraction punishable by a fine not exceeding seventy-five dollars ($75).

(3) For a third or subsequent offense committed within seven years after two or more prior violations for which there were convictions punishable under this section, the offense is punishable by a fine not exceeding one hundred fifty dollars ($150). In addition to the fine, the court may assess costs sufficient to repair property damage resulting from the violation.

(Amended by Stats. 2007, Ch. 541, Sec. 25. Effective January 1, 2008.)

38301.3. Notwithstanding subdivision (d) of Section 5008 of the Public Resources Code, or any other provision of state law, and to the extent authorized under federal law, a person who violates a state or federal regulation that prohibits entry of a motor vehicle into all or portions of an area designated as a federal or state wilderness area is guilty of a public offense and shall be punished as follows:

(a) Except as provided in subdivisions (b) and (c), the offense is an infraction punishable by a fine not exceeding one hundred fifty dollars ($150).

(b) For a second offense committed within seven years after a prior violation for which there was a conviction punishable under subdivision (a), the offense is an infraction punishable by a fine not exceeding two hundred twenty-five dollars ($225).

(c) (1) For a third or subsequent offense committed within seven years after two or more prior violations for which there were convictions punishable under this section, the offense is a misdemeanor punishable by a fine not exceeding three hundred dollars ($300) or by imprisonment in the county jail not exceeding 90 days, or by both that fine and imprisonment.

(2) In addition to the fine imposed under paragraph (1), the court may order impoundment of the vehicle used in the offense under the following conditions:

(A) The person convicted under this subdivision is the owner of the vehicle.

(B) The vehicle is subject to Section 4000 or 38010.

(3) The period of impoundment imposed pursuant to this subdivision shall be not less than one day nor more than 30 days. The impoundment shall be at the owner's expense.

(Added by Stats. 2005, Ch. 571, Sec. 4. Effective January 1, 2006.)

38301.5. Every person convicted of violating a local ordinance which is adopted by a city with a population over 2,000,000 persons pursuant to Section 38301 and which prohibits entry into all or portions of an area designated by ordinance as a mountain fire district shall be punished as follows:

(a) Except as provided in subdivisions (b) and (c), the offense is an infraction punishable by a fine not exceeding one hundred fifty dollars ($150).

(b) For a second offense committed within one year of a prior violation for which there was a conviction punishable under subdivision (a), the offense is punishable as an infraction by a fine not exceeding two hundred fifty dollars ($250).

(c) (1) For a third or subsequent offense committed within one year of two or more prior violations for which there were convictions punishable under this section, the offense is punishable as a misdemeanor by a fine not exceeding one thousand dollars ($1,000) or by imprisonment in the county jail not exceeding 90 days, or by both that fine and imprisonment. Additionally, the court may order impoundment of the vehicle used in the offense under the following conditions:

(A) The person convicted under this subdivision is the owner of the vehicle.

(B) The vehicle is subject to Section 38010.

(2) The period of impoundment imposed pursuant to this subdivision shall be not less than one day nor more than 30 days. The impoundment shall be at the owner's expense.

(Added by Stats. 1984, Ch. 1015, Sec. 1.)

38302. It is unlawful for any person to place or erect any sign, signal, or traffic control device for off-highway traffic upon public lands unless authorized by law.

(Added by Stats. 1976, Ch. 1093.)

Article 2. Operating Controls

(Article 2 added by Stats. 1976, Ch. 1093.)

38304. The operator of an off-highway motor vehicle shall be able to reach and operate all controls necessary to safely operate the vehicle.
(Added by Stats. 1976, Ch. 1093.)

38304.1. (a) Neither a parent or guardian of a child who is under 14 years of age, nor an adult who is authorized by the parent or guardian to supervise that child, shall grant permission to, or knowingly allow, that child to operate an off-highway motor vehicle in a manner that violates Section 38304.

(b) A person convicted of a violation of subdivision (a) is punishable as follows:

(1) For a first conviction, the court shall impose a fine of thirty-five dollars ($35).

(2) For a second conviction, a fine of not less than thirty-five dollars ($35) nor more than fifty dollars ($50).

(3) For a third or any subsequent conviction, a fine of not less than fifty dollars ($50) nor more than seventy-five dollars ($75).
(Added by Stats. 2009, Ch. 414, Sec. 3. (AB 134) Effective January 1, 2010.)

Article 3. Speed Laws

(Article 3 added by Stats. 1976, Ch. 1093.)

38305. No person shall drive an off-highway motor vehicle at a speed greater than is reasonable or prudent and in no event at a speed which endangers the safety of other persons or property.
(Added by Stats. 1976, Ch. 1093.)

38310. The prima facie speed limit within 50 feet of any campground, campsite, or concentration of people or animals shall be 15 miles per hour unless changed as authorized by this code and, if so changed, only when signs have been erected giving notice thereof.
(Added by Stats. 1976, Ch. 1093.)

Article 4. Turning and Starting

(Article 4 added by Stats. 1976, Ch. 1093.)

38312. No person shall place in motion an off-highway motor vehicle that is stopped, standing, or parked until such movement can be made with reasonable safety.
(Added by Stats. 1976, Ch. 1093.)

38314. No person shall turn an off-highway motor vehicle from a direct course or move right or left until such movement can be made with reasonable safety.
(Added by Stats. 1976, Ch. 1093.)

Article 5. Reckless Driving

(Article 5 added by Stats. 1976, Ch. 1093.)

38316. (a) It is unlawful for any person to drive any off-highway motor vehicle with a willful and wanton disregard for the safety of other persons or property.

(b) Any person who violates this section shall, upon conviction thereof, be punished by imprisonment in the county jail for not less than five days nor more than 90 days or by fine of not less than fifty dollars ($50) nor more than five hundred dollars ($500) or by both such fine and imprisonment, except as provided in Section 38317.
(Amended by Stats. 1983, Ch. 1092, Sec. 397. Effective September 27, 1983. Operative January 1, 1984, by Sec. 427 of Ch. 1092.)

38317. Whenever reckless driving of an off-highway motor vehicle proximately causes bodily injury to any person, the person driving the vehicle shall, upon conviction thereof, be punished by imprisonment in the county jail for not less than 30 days nor more than six months or by fine of not less than one hundred dollars ($100) nor more than one thousand dollars ($1,000) or by both such fine and imprisonment.
(Amended by Stats. 1983, Ch. 1092, Sec. 398. Effective September 27, 1983. Operative January 1, 1984, by Sec. 427 of Ch. 1092.)

38318. (a) Any person who throws any substance at an off-highway motor vehicle or occupant thereof is guilty of a misdemeanor and shall be punished pursuant to Section 42002 by a fine of not more than one thousand dollars ($1,000) or by imprisonment in the county jail for not more than six months, or by both the fine and imprisonment.

(b) Any person who, with intent to do great bodily injury, maliciously and willfully throws or projects any rock, brick, bottle, metal, or other missile, projects any other substance capable of doing serious bodily harm, or discharges a firearm at an off-highway motor vehicle or occupant thereof is guilty of a felony.
(Amended by Stats. 1984, Ch. 729, Sec. 1.5.)

38318.5. (a) Any person who maliciously removes or alters trail, danger, or directional markers or signs provided for the safety or guidance of off-highway motor vehicles is guilty of a misdemeanor and shall be punished pursuant to Section 42002 by a fine of not more than one thousand dollars ($1,000) or by imprisonment in the county jail for not more than six months, or by both the fine and imprisonment.

(b) Any person who, with intent to do great bodily injury (1) proximately causes great bodily injury to any person as a result of acts prohibited by subdivision (a), or (2) erects or places any cable, chain, rope, fishing line, or other similar material which is unmarked or intentionally placed, or both, for malicious purpose is guilty of a felony.

(c) Any person convicted under subdivision (a) or (b) shall, if the violation proximately causes one or more adverse environmental impacts, also be liable in civil damages for the cost of mitigation, restoration, or repair thereof, in addition to any other liability imposed by law.
(Amended by Stats. 1985, Ch. 1322, Sec. 1.)

Article 6. Littering and Environmental Protection

(Article 6 added by Stats. 1976, Ch. 1093.)

38319. No person shall operate, nor shall an owner permit the operation of, an off-highway motor vehicle in a manner likely to cause malicious or unnecessary damage to the land, wildlife, wildlife habitat or vegetative resources.
(Added by Stats. 1976, Ch. 1093.)

38320. (a) No person shall throw or deposit, nor shall the registered owner or the driver, if such owner is not then present in the vehicle, aid or abet in the throwing or depositing, upon any area, public or private, any bottle, can, garbage, glass, nail, offal, paper, wire, any substance likely to injure or kill wild or domestic animal or plant life or damage traffic using such area, or any noisome, nauseous or offensive matter of any kind.

(b) No person shall place, deposit or dump, or cause to be placed, deposited or dumped, any rocks or dirt in or upon any area, public or private, without the consent of the property owner or public agency having jurisdiction over the area.

(c) Any person who violates this section shall, upon conviction thereof, be punished by a fine of not less than fifty dollars ($50). No part of such fine shall be suspended. The court may permit the fine required by this section to be paid in installments if the court determines that the defendant is unable to pay the fine in one lump sum.
(Amended by Stats. 1983, Ch. 1092, Sec. 399. Effective September 27, 1983. Operative January 1, 1984, by Sec. 427 of Ch. 1092.)

38321. (a) Any person who drops, dumps, deposits, places, or throws, or causes or permits to be dropped, dumped, deposited, placed, or thrown, upon any area, any material described in Section 38320, shall immediately remove the material or cause it to be removed.

(b) If such person fails to comply with the provisions of this section, the governmental agency responsible for the maintenance of the area, or the property owner of the land on which the material has been deposited, may remove such material and collect, by civil action, if necessary, the actual cost of the removal operation in addition to any other damages authorized by law from the person who did not comply with the requirements of this section.
(Added by Stats. 1976, Ch. 1093.)

Chapter 6. Equipment of Off-Highway Vehicles

(Chapter 6 repealed and added by Stats. 1976, Ch. 1093.)

Article 1. General Provisions

(Article 1 added by Stats. 1976, Ch. 1093.)

38325. The provisions of this chapter shall apply to all off-highway motor vehicles, as defined in Section 38006, when operated in areas in which this division has application.

(Added by Stats. 1976, Ch. 1093.)

38330. It is unlawful to operate any vehicle or combination of vehicles which is in an unsafe condition, which is not equipped as required by this chapter or the equipment regulations of the governmental agency having jurisdiction over public lands, or which is not safely loaded.

(Added by Stats. 1976, Ch. 1093.)

Article 2. Lighting Equipment

(Article 2 added by Stats. 1976, Ch. 1093.)

38335. When operated from one-half hour after sunset to one-half hour before sunrise, each motor vehicle shall be equipped with at least one lighted white headlamp directed toward the front of the vehicle. Such lamp shall be of an intensity sufficient to reveal persons and vehicles at a distance of at least 200 feet.

(Added by Stats. 1976, Ch. 1093.)

38345. When operated from one-half hour after sunset to one-half hour before sunrise, each motor vehicle which is not in combination with any other vehicle shall be equipped with at least one lighted red taillamp which shall be clearly visible from the rear.

(a) Every such vehicle or vehicles at the end of a combination of vehicles shall be equipped with one lighted red taillamp when operated from one-half hour after sunset to one-half hour before sunrise.

(Added by Stats. 1976, Ch. 1093.)

38346. A person shall not display a flashing or steady burning red or blue warning light on an off-highway motor vehicle except as permitted by Section 21055 or when an extreme hazard exists.

(Added by Stats. 2004, Ch. 908, Sec. 24. Effective January 1, 2005.)

Article 3. Brakes

(Article 3 added by Stats. 1976, Ch. 1093.)

38355. (a) Except as provided in subdivision (b), every motor vehicle shall be equipped with a service brake system which is in good working order and adequate to control the movement of, and to stop and hold to the limit of traction of, such vehicle or combination of vehicles under all conditions of loading and upon any grade on which it is operated.

(b) Any motor vehicle, such as an air-cushioned vehicle, which is unable to comply with the requirements of this section due to the method of operation, is exempt, if the operator is able to exercise safe control over the movement of such vehicle.

(Added by Stats. 1976, Ch. 1093.)

Article 4. Equipment

(Article 4 added by Stats. 1976, Ch. 1093.)

38365. (a) Every off-highway motor vehicle, as defined in Section 38006, shall at all times be equipped with an adequate muffler in constant operation and properly maintained so as to meet the requirements of Section 38370, and no muffler or exhaust system shall be equipped with a cutout, bypass, or similar device.

(b) The provisions of subdivision (a) shall not be applicable to vehicles being operated off the highways in an organized racing or competitive event upon a closed course or in a hill climb or drag race, which is conducted under the auspices of a recognized sanctioning body or by permit issued by the local governmental authority having jurisdiction.

(Added by Stats. 1976, Ch. 1093.)

38366. (a) Notwithstanding Section 4442 of the Public Resources Code, and except for vehicles with mufflers as provided in Article 2 (commencing with Section 27150) of Chapter 5 of Division 12, no person shall use, operate, or allow to be used or operated, any off-highway motor vehicle, as defined in Section 38006, on any forest-covered land, brush-covered land, or grass-covered land unless the vehicle is equipped with a spark arrester maintained in effective working order.

(b) A spark arrester affixed to the exhaust system of a vehicle subject to this section shall not be placed or mounted in such a manner as to allow flames or heat from the exhaust system to ignite any flammable material.

(c) A spark arrester is a device constructed of nonflammable materials specifically for the purpose of removing and retaining carbon and other flammable particles over 0.0232 of an inch in size from the exhaust flow of an internal combustion engine or which is qualified and rated by the United States Forest Service.

(d) Subdivision (a) shall not be applicable to vehicles being operated off the highway in an organized racing or competitive event upon a closed course, which is conducted under the auspices of a recognized sanctioning body and by permit issued by the fire protection authority having jurisdiction.

(Added by Stats. 1987, Ch. 1027, Sec. 28.)

38370. (a) The Department of Motor Vehicles shall not identify any new off-highway motor vehicle, which is subject to identification and which produces a maximum noise level that exceeds the following noise limit, at a distance of 50 feet from the centerline of travel, under test procedures established by the Department of the California Highway Patrol.

(1) Any such vehicle manufactured before January 1, 1973 .... 92 dBA

(2) Any such vehicle manufactured on or after January 1, 1973, and before January 1, 1975 .... 88 dBA

(3) Any such vehicle manufactured on or after January 1, 1975, and before January 1, 1986 .... 86 dBA

(4) Any such vehicle manufactured on or after January 1, 1986 .... 82 dBA

(b) The department may accept a dealer's certificate as proof of compliance with this section.

(c) Test procedures for compliance with this section shall be established by the Department of the California Highway Patrol, taking into consideration the test procedures of the Society of Automotive Engineers.

(d) No person shall sell or offer for sale any new off-highway motor vehicle which is subject to identification and which produces a maximum noise level that exceeds the noise limits in subdivision (a), and for which noise emission standards or regulations have not been adopted by the Administrator of the Environmental Protection Agency pursuant to the Federal Noise Control Act of 1972 (P.L. 92-574).

(e) No person shall sell or offer for sale any new off-highway motor vehicle which is subject to identification and which produces a noise level that exceeds, or in any way violates, the noise emission standards or regulations adopted for such a motor vehicle by the Administrator of the Environmental Protection Agency pursuant to the Federal Noise Control Act of 1972 (P.L. 92-574).

(f) As used in this section, the term "identify" is equivalent to the term "licensing" as used in Section 6(e)(2) of the Federal Noise Control Act of 1972 (P.L. 92-574).

(g) Any off-highway motor vehicle, when operating pursuant to Section 38001, shall at all times be equipped with a silencer, or other device, which limits noise emissions to not more than 101 dBA if manufactured on or after January 1, 1975, or 105 dBA if manufactured before January 1, 1975, when measured from a distance of 20 inches using test procedures established by the Society of Automotive Engineers under Standard J-1287. This subdivision shall only be operative until January 1, 2003.

(h) On and after January 1, 2003, off-highway motor vehicles, when operating pursuant to Section 38001, shall at all times be equipped with a silencer, or other device, which limits noise emissions.

(1) Noise emissions of competition off-highway vehicles manufactured

on or after January 1, 1998, shall be limited to not more than 96 dBA, and if manufactured prior to January 1, 1998, to not more than 101 dBA, when measured from a distance of 20 inches using test procedures established by the Society of Automotive Engineers under Standard J-1287, as applicable. Noise emissions of all other off-highway vehicles shall be limited to not more than 96 dBA if manufactured on or after January 1, 1986, and not more than 101 dBA if manufactured prior to January 1, 1986, when measured from a distance of 20 inches using test procedures established by the Society of Automotive Engineers under Standard J-1287, as applicable.

(2) The Off-Highway Motor Vehicle Recreation Division of the Department of Parks and Recreation shall evaluate and reassess the dates specified in paragraph (1) and include the findings and recommendations in the noise report required in subdivision (o) of Section 5090.32 of the Public Resources Code.

(i) Off-highway vehicle manufacturers or their agents prior to the sale to the general public in California of any new off-highway vehicle model manufactured after January 1, 2003, shall provide to the Off-Highway Motor Vehicle Recreation Division of the California Department of Parks and Recreation rpm data needed to conduct the J-1287 test, where applicable.

(Amended by Stats. 2004, Ch. 908, Sec. 25. Effective January 1, 2005.)

38375. (a) An off-highway motor vehicle, except an authorized emergency vehicle, shall not be equipped with a siren.

(b) A person driving an off-highway motor vehicle, except the driver of an authorized emergency vehicle as permitted by Section 21055, shall not use a siren.

(Added by Stats. 2004, Ch. 908, Sec. 26. Effective January 1, 2005.)

38380. (a) Because of specialized conditions such as fire hazard, public safety or other circumstances, any local authority, or state or federal agencies having control over public lands may require that vehicles being operated off highway be equipped with additional equipment.

(b) When such additional equipment is required in a specific location, the governmental agency having jurisdiction over that location shall insure that such regulations are posted in a manner that operators of off-highway motor vehicles using those locations will be aware of the special requirements.

(Added by Stats. 1976, Ch. 1093.)

Article 5. Emission Control Equipment

(Article 5 added by Stats. 1976, Ch. 1093.)

38390. No person shall operate or maintain in a condition of readiness for operation any off-highway motor vehicle which is required to be equipped with a motor vehicle pollution control device under Part 5 (commencing with Section 43000) of Division 26 of the Health and Safety Code or with any other certified motor vehicle pollution control device required by any other state law or any rule or regulation adopted pursuant to such law, or required to be equipped with a motor vehicle pollution control device pursuant to the Clean Air Act (42 U.S.C. 1857 et seq.) and the standards and regulations promulgated thereunder, unless it is equipped with the required motor vehicle pollution control device which is correctly installed and in operating condition. No person shall disconnect, modify, or alter any such required device. Notwithstanding Section 43107 of the Health and Safety Code, this section shall apply only to off-highway motor vehicles of the 1978 or later model year.

(Added by Stats. 1976, Ch. 1093.)

38391. No person shall install, sell, offer for sale, or advertise any device, apparatus, or mechanism intended for use with, or as a part of, any required off-highway motor vehicle pollution control device or system which alters or modifies the original design or performance of any such motor vehicle pollution control device or system.

(Added by Stats. 1976, Ch. 1093.)

38392. When the court finds that a person has willfully violated any provision of this article, such person shall be fined the maximum amount that may be imposed for such an offense, and no part of the fine may be suspended.

"Willfully", as used in this section, has the same meaning as the meaning of that word prescribed in Section 7 of the Penal Code.

(Added by Stats. 1976, Ch. 1093.)

38393. No person shall operate an off-highway motor vehicle after notice by a traffic officer or other authorized public officer that such vehicle is not equipped with the required certified motor vehicle pollution control device correctly installed in operating condition, except as may be necessary to return the vehicle to the residence or place of business of the owner or driver or to a garage, until the vehicle has been properly equipped with such a device.

(Added by Stats. 1976, Ch. 1093.)

38394. The notice to appear issued or complaint filed for a violation of any provision of this article shall require that the person to whom the notice to appear is issued or against whom the complaint is filed produce proof of correction pursuant to Section 40150.

(Added by Stats. 1976, Ch. 1093.)

38395. This article shall not apply to an alteration, modification, or modifying device, apparatus, or mechanism found by resolution of the State Air Resources Board either:

(a) To not reduce the effectiveness of any required off-highway motor vehicle pollution control device; or

(b) To result in emissions from any such modified or altered off-highway vehicle which are at levels which comply with existing state or federal standards for that model year of the vehicle being modified or converted.

(Added by Stats. 1976, Ch. 1093.)

38396. The provisions of this article apply to off-highway motor vehicles of the United States or its agencies, to the extent authorized by federal law.

(Added by Stats. 1976, Ch. 1093.)

38397. Except as provided in Section 38390, this article shall be applicable to all off-highway motor vehicles, whether or not subject to identification pursuant to this division and without limitation by the exceptions contained in Section 38001, and to all off-highway motor vehicles operated or maintained in a condition of readiness for operation on private or public property.

(Added by Stats. 1976, Ch. 1093.)

Chapter 7. All-Terrain Vehicles

(Heading of Chapter 7 renumbered from Chapter 6 (as added by Stats. 1987, Ch. 881) by Stats. 1988, Ch. 160, Sec. 165.)

38500. The Off-Highway Vehicle Safety Education Committee is hereby established. The committee consists of the Commissioner of the California Highway Patrol, the Deputy Director of Parks and Recreation for Off-Highway Vehicles, the Director of Motor Vehicles, or their designees, and a member of the Off-Highway Motor Vehicle Recreation Commission appointed by the members of the commission. The committee shall receive staff assistance in its operations from the Off-Highway Motor Vehicle Recreation Division in the Department of Parks and Recreation.

(Added by Stats. 1987, Ch. 881, Sec. 37.)

38500.1. The Off-Highway Vehicle Safety Education Committee shall meet periodically to perform all of the following:

(a) Develop minimum criteria for certification as an approved all-terrain vehicle safety training organization. The criteria shall include, but not be limited to, the following:

(1) Curriculum and materials for training instructors to teach all-terrain vehicle operation and safety.

(2) Curriculum and materials for training all-terrain vehicle safety.

(3) Curriculum for teaching responsible use of off-highway vehicles with respect to environmental considerations, private property restrictions, off-highway vehicle operating laws, including noise and spark arrestor

laws, and prohibitions against operating off-highway vehicles under the influence of alcohol or drugs.

(4) Record keeping and insurance requirements to satisfy the requirements of Sections 11103.1 and 11108.

(b) Upon presentation to the committee of a proposed program by an applicant to become an approved all-terrain vehicle safety training organization, the committee shall determine whether the applicant's program meets the minimum criteria and, if approved, shall recommend the organization for licensing pursuant to Section 11105.6.

(Added by Stats. 1987, Ch. 881, Sec. 37.)

38501. (a) An all-terrain vehicle safety training organization, commencing on January 1, 1989, shall issue an all-terrain vehicle safety certificate furnished by the department to any individual who successfully completes a course of instruction in all-terrain vehicle operation and safety as approved and certified by the Off-highway Vehicle Safety Education Committee.

(b) The department shall charge a fee not to exceed three dollars ($3) for each all-terrain vehicle safety certificate issued by an all-terrain vehicle safety training organization to each person completing a course of instruction from an all-terrain vehicle safety instructor using the approved course of instruction of the all-terrain vehicle safety training organization. The amount of the fee shall be determined by the department and shall be sufficient to defray the actual costs incurred by the department for administering and monitoring this program.

(c) An all-terrain vehicle safety training organization shall not charge a fee in excess of the fee charged by the department pursuant to subdivision (b) for furnishing an all-terrain vehicle safety certificate. An organization may charge a fee not to exceed three dollars ($3) in addition to the fee charged by the department for the issuance of a duplicate certificate and shall provide a duplicate certificate if requested by the person who completed the course.

(Added by Stats. 1987, Ch. 881, Sec. 37.)

38502. The department, on and after July 1, 1988, may monitor any all-terrain vehicle safety training organization or any all-terrain vehicle safety instructor without advance notice. The monitoring may include, but is not limited to, the instruction provided, business practices, and records required by Section 11108.

(Added by Stats. 1987, Ch. 881, Sec. 37.)

38503. No person under the age of 18 years, on and after January 1, 1990, shall operate an all-terrain vehicle on public lands of this state unless the person satisfies one of the following conditions:

(a) The person is taking a prescribed safety training course under the direct supervision of a certified all-terrain vehicle safety instructor.

(b) The person is under the direct supervision of an adult who has in their possession an appropriate safety certificate issued by this state, or issued under the authority of another state.

(c) The person has in possession an appropriate safety certificate issued by this state or issued under the authority of another state.

(Added by Stats. 1987, Ch. 881, Sec. 37.)

38504. No person under 14 years of age, on and after January 1, 1990, shall operate an all-terrain vehicle on public lands of this state unless the person satisfies one of the conditions set forth in Section 38503 and, in addition, is accompanied by and under the direct supervision of a parent or guardian or is accompanied by and under the direct supervision of an adult who is authorized by the parent or guardian.

(Added by Stats. 1987, Ch. 881, Sec. 37.)

38504.1. (a) Neither a parent or guardian of a child who is under 14 years of age, nor an adult who is authorized by the parent or guardian to supervise that child shall grant permission to, or knowingly allow, that child to operate an all-terrain vehicle in a manner that violates Section 38504.

(b) A person convicted of a violation of subdivision (a) is punishable as follows:

(1) For a first conviction, the court shall either impose a fine of one hundred twenty-five dollars ($125) or order the person to take or retake and complete an all-terrain vehicle safety training course pursuant to Section 38501. If ordered to take or retake and complete the safety training course, the person shall provide the court a copy of the all-terrain vehicles safety certificate issued as a result of that completion.

(2) For a second conviction, a fine of not less than one hundred twenty-five dollars ($125) nor more than two hundred fifty dollars ($250).

(3) For a third or any subsequent conviction, a fine of not less than two hundred fifty dollars ($250) nor more than five hundred dollars ($500).

(Added by Stats. 2006, Ch. 195, Sec. 1. Effective January 1, 2007.)

38504.2. If a person under 14 years of age was not properly supervised or accompanied in accordance with Section 38504, and the parent or guardian of that child or the adult who was authorized by the parent or guardian to supervise or accompany that child is in violation of Section 38504.1, upon a conviction pursuant to Section 38504, the court may order that child to attend and complete the all-terrain vehicle safety training course accompanied by the person who violated Section 38504.1. If so ordered, the child under 14 years of age shall provide the court a copy of the all-terrain vehicles safety certificate issued as a result of that completion.

(Added by Stats. 2006, Ch. 195, Sec. 2. Effective January 1, 2007.)

38505. A person, on and after January 1, 1989, shall not operate, ride, or be otherwise propelled on an all-terrain vehicle on public lands, as described in Section 38001, unless the person wears a safety helmet meeting requirements established for motorcycles and motorized bicycles, pursuant to Section 27802.

(Amended by Stats. 2019, Ch. 469, Sec. 10. (SB 785) Effective January 1, 2020.)

38506. An operator of an all-terrain vehicle shall not carry a passenger when operating on public lands, as described in Section 38001.

However, the operator of an all-terrain vehicle, that is designed for operation off of the highway by an operator with no more than one passenger, may carry a passenger when operating on public lands, as described in Section 38001.

(Amended by Stats. 2019, Ch. 469, Sec. 11. (SB 785) Effective January 1, 2020.)

Chapter 8. Recreational Off-Highway Vehicles

(Chapter 8 added by Stats. 2012, Ch. 165, Sec. 3.)

38600. A person operating a recreational off-highway vehicle on lands, as described in Section 38001, shall be at least 16 years of age, or be directly supervised in the vehicle by a parent or guardian or by an adult authorized by the parent or guardian.

(Amended by Stats. 2019, Ch. 469, Sec. 12. (SB 785) Effective January 1, 2020.)

38601. A person shall not operate, or allow a passenger in, a recreational off-highway vehicle on public lands, as described in Section 38001, unless the person and the passenger are wearing safety helmets meeting the requirements established for motorcycles and motorized bicycles pursuant to Section 27802.

(Amended by Stats. 2019, Ch. 469, Sec. 13. (SB 785) Effective January 1, 2020.)

38602. A person operating, and any passenger in, a recreational off-highway vehicle on lands, as described in Section 38001, shall wear a seatbelt and shoulder belt or safety harness that is properly fastened when the vehicle is in motion.

(Amended by Stats. 2019, Ch. 469, Sec. 14. (SB 785) Effective January 1, 2020.)

38603. (a) A person operating a recreational off-highway vehicle with a model year of 2014 or later on lands, as described in Section 38001, shall not allow a passenger to occupy a separate seat location not designed and provided by the manufacturer for a passenger.

(b) Seats that are installed in a separate seat location not designed and provided by the manufacturer for a passenger in a vehicle with a model year of 2013 or earlier on lands, as described in Section 38001, may be occupied by a passenger if the occupant of the seat is fully contained inside of the vehicle's rollover protection structure at all times while the vehicle is being operated.

(Amended by Stats. 2019, Ch. 469, Sec. 15. (SB 785) Effective January 1, 2020.)

38604. (a) A person operating a recreational off-highway vehicle on lands, as described in Section 38001, shall not ride with a passenger, unless the passenger, while seated upright with their back against the seatback, can grasp the occupant handhold with the seatbelt and shoulder belt or safety harness properly fastened.

(b) For purposes of this chapter, "occupant handhold" means any factory or aftermarket device grasped by an occupant to provide support and to assist in keeping arms and hands within the recreational off-highway vehicle. The steering wheel shall be considered an occupant handhold for the recreational off-highway vehicle operator.

(c) Occupant handholds shall be designed to allow the recreational off-highway vehicle passenger to exit the vehicle without interference from the handholds.

(Amended by Stats. 2019, Ch. 469, Sec. 16. (SB 785) Effective January 1, 2020.)

Division 16.6. Autonomous Vehicles

(Division 16.6 added by Stats. 2012, Ch. 570, Sec. 2.)

38750. (a) For purposes of this division, the following definitions apply:

(1) "Autonomous technology" means technology that has the capability to drive a vehicle without the active physical control or monitoring by a human operator.

(2) (A) "Autonomous vehicle" means any vehicle equipped with autonomous technology that has been integrated into that vehicle that meets the definition of Level 3, Level 4, or Level 5 of SAE International's "Taxonomy and Definitions for Terms Related to Driving Automation Systems for On-Road Motor Vehicles, standard J3016 (APR2021)," as may be revised.

(B) An autonomous vehicle does not include a vehicle that is equipped with one or more collision avoidance systems, including, but not limited to, electronic blind spot assistance, automated emergency braking systems, park assist, adaptive cruise control, lane keep assist, lane departure warning, traffic jam and queuing assist, or other similar systems that enhance safety or provide driver assistance, but are not capable, collectively or singularly, of driving the vehicle without the active control or monitoring of a human operator.

(3) "Department" means the Department of Motor Vehicles.

(4) An "operator" of an autonomous vehicle is the person who is seated in the driver's seat, or, if there is no person in the driver's seat, causes the autonomous technology to engage.

(5) A "manufacturer" of autonomous technology is the person, as defined in Section 470, that originally manufactures a vehicle and equips autonomous technology on the originally completed vehicle or, in the case of a vehicle not originally equipped with autonomous technology by the vehicle manufacturer, the person that modifies the vehicle by installing autonomous technology to convert it to an autonomous vehicle after the vehicle was originally manufactured.

(b) An autonomous vehicle may be operated on public roads for testing purposes by a driver who possesses the proper class of license for the type of vehicle being operated if all of the following requirements are met:

(1) The autonomous vehicle is being operated on roads in this state solely by employees, contractors, or other persons designated by the manufacturer of the autonomous technology.

(2) The driver shall be seated in the driver's seat, monitoring the safe operation of the autonomous vehicle, and capable of taking over immediate manual control of the autonomous vehicle in the event of an autonomous technology failure or other emergency.

(3) Prior to the start of testing in this state, the manufacturer performing the testing shall obtain an instrument of insurance, surety bond, or proof of self-insurance in the amount of five million dollars ($5,000,000), and shall provide evidence of the insurance, surety bond, or self-insurance to the department in the form and manner required by the department pursuant to the regulations adopted pursuant to subdivision (d).

(c) Except as provided in subdivision (b), an autonomous vehicle shall not be operated on public roads until the manufacturer submits an application to the department, and that application is approved by the department pursuant to the regulations adopted pursuant to subdivision (d). The application shall contain, at a minimum, all of the following certifications:

(1) A certification by the manufacturer that the autonomous technology satisfies all of the following requirements:

(A) The autonomous vehicle has a mechanism to engage and disengage the autonomous technology that is easily accessible to the operator.

(B) The autonomous vehicle has a visual indicator inside the cabin to indicate when the autonomous technology is engaged.

(C) The autonomous vehicle has a system to safely alert the operator if an autonomous technology failure is detected while the autonomous technology is engaged, and when an alert is given, the system shall do either of the following:

(i) Require the operator to take control of the autonomous vehicle.

(ii) If the operator does not or is unable to take control of the autonomous vehicle, the autonomous vehicle shall be capable of coming to a complete stop.

(D) The autonomous vehicle shall allow the operator to take control in multiple manners, including, without limitation, through the use of the brake, the accelerator pedal, or the steering wheel, and it shall alert the operator that the autonomous technology has been disengaged.

(E) The autonomous vehicle's autonomous technology meets Federal Motor Vehicle Safety Standards for the vehicle's model year and all other applicable safety standards and performance requirements set forth in state and federal law and the regulations promulgated pursuant to those laws.

(F) The autonomous technology does not make inoperative any Federal Motor Vehicle Safety Standards for the vehicle's model year and all other applicable safety standards and performance requirements set forth in state and federal law and the regulations promulgated pursuant to those laws.

(G) The autonomous vehicle has a separate mechanism, in addition to, and separate from, any other mechanism required by law, to capture and store the autonomous technology sensor data for at least 30 seconds before a collision occurs between the autonomous vehicle and another vehicle, object, or natural person while the vehicle is operating in autonomous mode. The autonomous technology sensor data shall be captured and stored in a read-only format by the mechanism so that the data is retained until extracted from the mechanism by an external device capable of downloading and storing the data. The data shall be preserved for three years after the date of the collision.

(2) A certification that the manufacturer has tested the autonomous technology on public roads and has complied with the testing standards, if any, established by the department pursuant to subdivision (d).

(3) A certification that the manufacturer will maintain, an instrument of insurance, a surety bond, or proof of self-insurance as specified in regulations adopted by the department pursuant to subdivision (d), in an amount of five million dollars ($5,000,000).

(d) (1) The department shall adopt regulations setting forth requirements for the submission of evidence of insurance, surety bond, or self-insurance required by subdivision (b), the submission and approval of an application to operate an autonomous vehicle pursuant to subdivision (c), and processes related to notices of autonomous vehicle noncompliance pursuant to Section 38752.

(2) The regulations shall include any testing, equipment, and performance standards, in addition to those established for purposes of subdivision (b), that the department concludes are necessary to ensure the safe operation of autonomous vehicles on public roads, with or without the presence of a driver inside the vehicle. In developing these regulations, the department may consult with the Department of the California Highway Patrol, the Institute of Transportation Studies at the University of California, or any other entity identified by the department that has expertise in automotive technology, automotive safety, and autonomous system design.

(3) The department may establish additional requirements by the adoption of regulations, which it determines, in consultation with the Department of the California Highway Patrol, are necessary to ensure the safe operation of autonomous vehicles on public roads, including, but not limited to, regulations regarding the aggregate number of deployments of autonomous vehicles on public roads, special rules for the registration of autonomous vehicles, new license requirements for operators of autonomous vehicles, regulations for notices of autonomous vehicle noncompliance, and rules for revocation, suspension, or denial of any license or any approval issued pursuant to this division.

(4) The department shall hold public hearings on the adoption of any regulation applicable to the operation of an autonomous vehicle without the presence of a driver inside the vehicle.

(e) (1) The department shall approve an application submitted by a manufacturer pursuant to subdivision (c) if it finds that the applicant has submitted all information and completed testing necessary to satisfy the department that the autonomous vehicles are safe to operate on public roads and the applicant has complied with all requirements specified in the regulations adopted by the department pursuant to subdivision (d).

(2) Notwithstanding paragraph (1), if the application seeks approval for autonomous vehicles capable of operating without the presence of a driver inside the vehicle, the department may impose additional requirements it deems necessary to ensure the safe operation of those vehicles, and may require the presence of a driver in the driver's seat of the vehicle if it determines, based on its review pursuant to paragraph (1), that such a requirement is necessary to ensure the safe operation of those vehicles on public roads.

(f) The department shall post a public notice on its internet website when it adopts the regulations required by subdivision (d). The department shall not approve an application submitted pursuant to the regulations until 30 days after the public notice is provided.

(g) Federal regulations promulgated by the National Highway Traffic Safety Administration shall supersede the provisions of this division when found to be in conflict with any other state law or regulation.

(h) The manufacturer of the autonomous technology installed on a vehicle shall provide a written disclosure to the purchaser of an autonomous vehicle that describes what information is collected by the autonomous technology equipped on the vehicle. The department may promulgate regulations to assess a fee upon a manufacturer that submits an application pursuant to subdivision (c) to operate autonomous vehicles on public roads in an amount necessary to recover all costs reasonably incurred by the department.

(i) Commencing January 1, 2026, an autonomous vehicle may be equipped with automated driving system (ADS) marker lamps in accordance with SAE International's "Recommended Practice, Automated Driving System (ADS) Marker Lamp, standard J3134 (MAY2019)," as may be revised, and SAE International's "Chromaticity Requirements for Ground Vehicle Lamps and Lighting Equipment, standard J578 (APR2020)," as may be revised. For purposes of this subdivision, an "ADS marker lamp" means a device that emits a light to indicate when an ADS is engaged in the operation of the vehicle.

(j) (1) Commencing January 1, 2030, to the extent authorized by federal law, any autonomous vehicle with a model year of 2031 or later and a gross vehicle weight rating of less than 8,501 pounds shall only be operated pursuant to a deployment permit pursuant to Article 3.8 (commencing with Section 228.00) of Chapter 1 of Division 1 of Title 13 of the California Code of Regulations if the vehicle is a zero-emission vehicle, as defined in Section 44258 of the Health and Safety Code.

(2) The department shall not commence rulemaking for the adoption of regulations implementing this subdivision before January 1, 2027.

(Amended by Stats. 2025, Ch. 415, Sec. 2. (SB 480) Effective January 1, 2026.)

38751. (a) For purposes of this section, the following definitions apply:

(1) "Emergency geofencing message" means a message delivered using commonly available communication methods to identify a location using a street address, intersection, coordinates, or any other reasonable and customary way of identifying a location, that directs an autonomous vehicle to leave or avoid an area because of an emergency.

(2) "Emergency response official" includes, but is not limited to, emergency dispatchers, peace officers as defined in Chapter 4.5 (commencing with Section 830) of Title 3 of Part 2 of the Penal Code, and first responders.

(3) "Emergency" means a sudden, unexpected occurrence demanding immediate action to prevent or mitigate loss or damage to life, health, property, or essential public services.

(b) A manufacturer shall comply with all of the following requirements:

(1) (A) A manufacturer operating an autonomous vehicle under a testing permit or deployment permit issued by the department shall

maintain a dedicated emergency response telephone line that is available for emergency response officials during all hours when an autonomous vehicle is on a public road. The telephone line shall be available at no cost to public agencies.

(B) The manufacturer shall continuously monitor the status of each autonomous vehicle on a public road and shall equip and staff the telephone line to ensure that calls are picked up within 30 seconds by a remote human operator who has situational awareness of all autonomous vehicles on public roads.

(C) The remote human operator shall have the ability to immobilize the autonomous vehicle, allow an emergency response official to move the autonomous vehicle, or cause the autonomous vehicle to move as directed by an emergency response official.

(2) (A) A manufacturer operating an autonomous vehicle under a testing permit or deployment permit issued by the department shall equip each autonomous vehicle with a two-way voice communication device that enables emergency response officials that are near the vehicle to communicate effectively with a remote human operator who has situational awareness about the autonomous vehicle. The manufacturer shall ensure that an emergency response official is able to reach a remote human operator within 30 seconds after making a request through the device.

(B) The remote human operator shall have the ability to immobilize the autonomous vehicle, allow an emergency response official to move the autonomous vehicle, or cause the autonomous vehicle to move as directed by an emergency response official.

(3) Autonomous vehicles equipped with an override system in the vehicle that allows someone physically present to move the vehicle, pursuant to subparagraphs (A) and (D) of paragraph (1) of subdivision (c) of Section 38750 shall provide access to the override system to law enforcement and firefighters in case of emergency to allow law enforcement and firefighters to completely immobilize the vehicle or cause the vehicle to move as necessary to address the emergency. The manufacturer shall provide training for law enforcement and firefighters on the use of the override system. The training shall be reviewed on a regular basis by the manufacturer and updated as changes are needed.

(c) The department shall not renew, reinstate, or approve an expansion of the operational design domain of a permit unless the manufacturer certifies that it is in full compliance with the requirements under subdivision (b).

(d) (1) An emergency response official may issue an emergency geofencing message to a manufacturer.

(2) Within two minutes of receiving an emergency geofencing message, a manufacturer shall issue direction to its fleet to leave or avoid the area identified.

(3) Within 30 business days of receiving a notice that an emergency response official wishes to begin issuing emergency geofencing messages, a manufacturer shall provide the emergency response official with all information necessary for the emergency response official to begin issuing and for the manufacturer to receive and respond to emergency geofencing messages.

(4) An emergency geofencing message shall include the initial duration for the defined avoidance area based on a reasonable assessment of the emergency. Where necessary, an emergency response official may extend the duration for the avoidance area.

(e) This section shall only apply to manufacturers of autonomous vehicles that operate without a human operator physically present in the vehicle.

(f) Paragraphs (2) and (3) of subdivision (b) and subdivision (c) shall not apply to a commercial motor vehicle with a gross vehicle weight rating or gross vehicle weight of at least 10,001 pounds, whichever is greater. This subdivision does not apply to a passenger transportation vehicle as defined in Section 464. The department may establish requirements by the adoption of regulations, determined in consultation with the Department of the California Highway Patrol, to ensure the safe interaction between autonomous commercial motor vehicles and emergency response officials.

(g) This section shall become operative on July 1, 2026.

(Added by Stats. 2024, Ch. 682, Sec. 2. (AB 1777) Effective January 1, 2025. Operative July 1, 2026, by its own provisions.)

38752. (a) A "notice of autonomous vehicle noncompliance" means a notice issued by a peace officer, as defined in Chapter 4.5 (commencing with Section 830) of Title 3 of Part 2 of the Penal Code, that identifies, at minimum, an alleged violation of this code or an alleged violation of a local traffic ordinance adopted pursuant to this code by an autonomous vehicle while the autonomous technology is engaged, the date, time, and location of the alleged violation, and the license plate number of the vehicle.

(b) A peace officer, as defined in Chapter 4.5 (commencing with Section 830) of Title 3 of Part 2 of the Penal Code, may issue a notice of autonomous vehicle noncompliance upon observing an alleged violation of this code or an alleged violation of a local traffic ordinance adopted pursuant to this code.

(c) A manufacturer of an autonomous vehicle shall provide any issued notice of autonomous vehicle noncompliance to the department within 72 hours of issuance, or within a timeframe otherwise determined by the department. The department shall make available a means by which the manufacturer can provide the notice.

(d) The issuance of a notice of autonomous vehicle noncompliance shall not create a presumption that the autonomous vehicle is unsafe and shall not limit the manufacturer's ability to contest the nature or occurrence of an alleged violation identified in the notice.

(e) This section shall not become operative until the department issues regulations addressing notices of autonomous vehicle noncompliance, as required by Section 38750.

(Added by Stats. 2024, Ch. 682, Sec. 3. (AB 1777) Effective January 1, 2025. Conditionally operative by its own provisions.)

38753. The provisions of this division are severable. If any provision of this division or its application is held invalid, that invalidity shall not affect other provisions or applications that can be given effect without the invalid provision or application.

(Added by Stats. 2024, Ch. 682, Sec. 4. (AB 1777) Effective January 1, 2025.)

38755. (a) Notwithstanding Section 38750, the Contra Costa Transportation Authority is authorized to conduct a pilot project for the testing of autonomous vehicles that do not have a driver seated in the driver's seat and are not equipped with a steering wheel, a brake pedal, or an accelerator provided the following requirements are met:

(1) The testing shall be conducted only at a privately owned business park designated by the authority, inclusive of public roads within the designated business park, and at GoMentum Station located within the boundaries of the former Concord Naval Weapons Station.

(2) The autonomous vehicle shall operate at speeds of less than 35 miles per hour.

(b) A change in ownership of the property comprising the GoMentum Station shall not affect the authorization to conduct testing pursuant to this section.

(c) Prior to the start of the testing of an autonomous vehicle that does not have a driver seated in the driver's seat on or across a public road, the Contra Costa Transportation Authority or a private entity, or a combination of the two, shall do both of the following:

(1) Obtain an instrument of insurance, surety bond, or proof of self-insurance in an amount of five million dollars ($5,000,000), and shall provide evidence of the insurance, surety bond, or proof of self-insurance to the Department of Motor Vehicles in the form and manner required by the department.

(2) Submit a detailed description of the testing program to the department. The detailed description shall include all of the following:

(A) Certification that, prior to testing on public roads, the autonomous vehicle has been tested under controlled conditions that simulate, as closely as practicable, the real world conditions that the autonomous vehicle will be subject to during this pilot project, and that the Contra Costa Transportation Authority or a private entity, or a combination of the two, has made a reasonable determination that it is safe to operate the autonomous vehicle on public roads under these conditions.

(B) Evidence satisfactory to the department that the City of San Ramon and any other local authorities with jurisdiction over the public roads in the designated privately owned business park approve of the geographic area and environmental, traffic, and speed conditions authorized for purposes of this pilot project.

(C) Certification that the autonomous vehicle can only operate in autonomous mode in the geographic area and environmental, traffic, and speed conditions authorized in this specific pilot project.

(D) Certification that this pilot project complies, or will comply, with National Highway Traffic Safety Administration guidance, if any, on the safe testing, deployment, and operation of autonomous vehicles.

(E) Certification that the autonomous vehicle used in the pilot project complies with all applicable federal Motor Vehicle Safety Standards, or written evidence that the National Highway Traffic Safety Administration either considers the absence of a steering wheel, a brake pedal, or an accelerator permissible under federal Motor Vehicle Safety Standards or has granted the autonomous vehicle an exemption from compliance with the relevant federal Motor Vehicle Safety Standards.

(F) Identify to the department the autonomous vehicles that are to be tested on public roads during this pilot project. For each vehicle, the manufacturer shall provide to the department the make, model, and model year of the vehicle, the full vehicle identification number, and the license plate number and the state of issuance.

(G) Certification that the vehicle is equipped with a communication link between the vehicle and a remote operator to provide information on the vehicle's location and status and to allow two-way communication between the remote operator and any passengers if the vehicle experiences any failures that would endanger the safety of the vehicle's passengers or other road users while operating without a driver.

(H) Certification that the autonomous vehicle is designed to detect and respond to roadway conditions in compliance with all provisions of this code and local regulations applicable to the operation of motor vehicles.

(I) A copy of a law enforcement interaction plan, which includes information that the Contra Costa Transportation Authority or a private entity, or a combination of the two, will provide to the law enforcement agencies whose jurisdiction covers the designated privately owned business park to instruct those agencies on how to interact with the vehicle in emergency and traffic enforcement situations.

(d) The operator of the autonomous vehicle technology tested pursuant to this section shall disclose to an individual who participates in the pilot project what personal information, if any, concerning the pilot project participant is collected by an autonomous vehicle.

(e) For the testing of autonomous vehicles within the designated business park, the department may require data collection for evaluating the safety of the vehicles, including, but not limited to, both of the following:

(1) A report to the department of any accident originating from the operation of the autonomous vehicle on a public road that resulted in the damage of property or in bodily injury or death. Accidents shall be reported within 10 days in the form and manner specified by the department pursuant to the regulations adopted by the department under Section 38750.

(2) The submission to the department of an annual report in the form and manner specified by the department pursuant to the regulations adopted under Section 38750 summarizing information on unplanned technology disengagements that occurred while the autonomous vehicle was being tested on public roads. "Disengagement" means a deactivation of the autonomous mode when a failure of the autonomous technology is detected or when the safe operation of the vehicle required disengagement from the autonomous mode.

(f) This section does not limit the authority of the department to promulgate regulations governing the testing and operation of autonomous vehicles on public roads, with or without the presence of a driver inside the vehicle, pursuant to Section 38750.

(g) It is the intent of the Legislature, in enacting the act that added this section, to address the specific circumstances of the pilot project proposed in the County of Contra Costa. Pursuant to Section 38750, the Department of Motor Vehicles is developing regulations for the testing and operation of autonomous vehicles, and it is not the intent of the Legislature to influence the content of those statewide regulations through the adoption of the act that added this section, which is only intended to govern the establishment of one local pilot project.

(h) This section shall remain in effect only until 180 days after the operative date of regulations promulgated by the department to allow testing of autonomous vehicles without a driver in the vehicle, on which date any testing of autonomous vehicles by the Contra Costa Transportation Authority shall conform to those regulations, and as of the January 1 following that date this section is repealed, unless a later enacted statute, that is enacted before that January 1, deletes or extends that date.

(Added by Stats. 2016, Ch. 814, Sec. 1. (AB 1592) Effective January 1, 2017. Inoperative on date prescribed by its own provisions. Repealed, by its own provisions, on January 1 following inoperative date.)

Division 16.7. Registration and Licensing of Bicycles

(Heading of Division 16.7 amended by Stats. 1975, Ch. 1250.)

39000. "Bicycle", for the purposes of this division, means any device upon which a person may ride, which is propelled by human power through a system of belts, chains, or gears having either two or three wheels (one of which is at least 20 inches in diameter) or having a frame size of at least 14 inches, or having four or more wheels.

(Amended by Stats. 1978, Ch. 421.)

39001. (a) The department shall procure and distribute bicycle license indicia and registration forms to all counties and cities which have adopted a bicycle licensing ordinance or resolution. Those counties and cities shall issue the indicia and registration form to the owner of any new bicycle, and may, upon request of the owner, issue an indicia and registration form to the owner of any bicycle which complies with Section 39007.

The department shall charge and collect a fee, not to exceed the cost of procuring and distributing the license indicia and registration form, for each bicycle license indicia and registration form issued. All fees collected pursuant to this section shall be deposited in the Motor Vehicle Account in the State Transportation Fund. Those fees are hereby continuously appropriated from the account for use by the department to defray costs to procure and distribute the bicycle license indicia and registration forms.

(b) The director shall design the bicycle license indicia and registration form described in subdivision (a), and shall establish procedures for the distribution of the indicia and registration form to counties and cities. The indicia shall be adhesive, durable, flexible, and of a size to permit it to be affixed to the front of the seat tube of the bicycle frame. Each indicia shall bear a unique license number and shall be permanently assigned to a bicycle. Each registration form shall comply with Section 39005.

(c) Bicycle licenses shall be renewed uniformly throughout the state on January 1 of the third year following the year of registration. Renewal of a bicycle license shall be indicated by a supplementary adhesive device affixed parallel to, and above or below, the indicia, with the expiration date showing.

(Amended by Stats. 1988, Ch. 1268, Sec. 25. Operative July 1, 1989, by Sec. 27 of Ch. 1268.)

39002. (a) A city or county, which adopts a bicycle licensing ordinance or resolution, shall not prohibit the operation of an unlicensed bicycle.

(b) It is unlawful for any person to tamper with, destroy, mutilate, or alter any license indicia or registration form, or to remove, alter, or mutilate the serial number, or the identifying marks of a licensing agency's identifying symbol, on any bicycle frame licensed under this division.

(Amended by Stats. 2022, Ch. 343, Sec. 7. (AB 1909) Effective January 1, 2023.)

39003. If a city or county has or adopts a bicycle licensing ordinance or resolution, indicia and a copy of the registration form obtained from the department shall be issued to the owner by the city or county or other licensing agency designated by it.

(Amended by Stats. 1975, Ch. 1250.)

39004. Each licensing agency, by ordinance or resolution, may adopt rules and regulations for the collection of license fees. Revenues from license fees shall be retained by the licensing city or county and shall be used for the support of such bicycle ordinance or resolution, and may be used to reimburse retailers for services rendered. In addition, fees collected shall be used to improve bicycle safety programs and establish bicycle facilities, including bicycle paths and lanes, within the limits of the jurisdiction.

The fees required to be paid pursuant to this division are as follows:

(a) For each new bicycle license and registration certificate, the sum shall not exceed four dollars ($4) per year or any portion thereof.

(b) For each transfer of registration certificate, the sum shall not exceed two dollars ($2).

(c) For each replacement of a bicycle license or registration certificate, the sum shall not exceed two dollars ($2).

(d) For each bicycle license renewal, the sum shall not exceed two dollars ($2) per year.

(Amended by Stats. 1999, Ch. 277, Sec. 4. Effective January 1, 2000.)

39005. Cities and counties having a bicycle licensing ordinance or resolution shall maintain records of each bicycle registered. Such records shall include, but not be limited to, the license number, the serial number of the bicycle, the make and type, of the bicycle, and the name and address of the licensee.

Records shall be maintained by the licensing agency during the period of validity of the license or until notification that the bicycle is no longer to be operated.

(Amended by Stats. 1975, Ch. 1250.)

39006. (a) Each bicycle retailer and each bicycle dealer shall supply to each purchaser a preregistration form provided by the licensing agency and shall include, on the sales check or receipt given to the purchaser, a record of the following information: name of retailer, address of retailer, year and make of the bicycle, serial number of the bicycle if delivered to the purchaser in an assembled state, general description of the bicycle, name of purchaser, and address of purchaser. A copy of the preregistration form shall be filled out and forwarded by the purchaser to the appropriate licensing agency within 10 days from the date of sale.

(b) For the purposes of this division, a bicycle dealer is any person who sells, gives away, buys, or takes in trade for the purpose of resale, more than five bicycles in any one calendar year, whether or not such bicycles are owned by such person. "Bicycle dealer" also includes agents or employees of such person.

(Amended by Stats. 1975, Ch. 1250.)

39007. After December 31, 1976, no bicycle retailer shall sell any new bicycle in this state unless such bicycle has legibly and permanently stamped or cast on its frame a serial number, no less than one-eighth inch in size, and unique to the particular bicycle of each manufacturer. The serial number only shall be stamped or cast in the head of the frame, either side of the seat tube, the toeplate, or the bottom sprocket (crank) housing.

(Amended by Stats. 1975, Ch. 1250.)

39008. (a) Whenever any person sells or otherwise disposes of a bicycle, he shall endorse upon the registration certificate previously issued for such bicycle a written transfer of same, setting forth the name, address, telephone number of the transferee, date of transfer, and signature of the transferrer, and shall deliver the registration certificate, so endorsed, to the licensing agency within 10 days.

(b) Any person who purchases or otherwise acquires possession of a bicycle shall, within 10 days of taking possession, apply for the transfer of license to his own name. Cities and counties may establish rules and regulations to govern and enforce the provisions of this section.

(Amended by Stats. 1975, Ch. 1250.)

39009. (a) Whenever the owner of a bicycle licensed pursuant to an ordinance or resolution of a city or county changes his address, he shall within 10 days notify the appropriate licensing agency of the old and new address.

(b) In the event that any bicycle license indicia or registration form issued pursuant to the provisions of this division is lost, stolen, or mutilated, the licensee of such bicycle shall immediately notify the licensing agency, and, within 10 days after such notification, shall apply to the licensing agency for a duplicate license indicia or registration form. Thereupon, the licensing agency shall issue to such licensee a replacement indicia or registration form upon payment to the licensing agency of the appropriate fee.

(Amended by Stats. 1975, Ch. 1250.)

39011. No fine imposed for any violation of an ordinance or resolution, which is adopted pursuant to this division, shall exceed ten dollars ($10).

(Amended by Stats. 1983, Ch. 1092, Sec. 400. Effective September 27, 1983. Operative January 1, 1984, by Sec. 427 of Ch. 1092.)

Division 17. Offenses and Prosecution

(Division 17 enacted by Stats. 1959, Ch. 3.)

Chapter 1. Offenses

(Chapter 1 enacted by Stats. 1959, Ch. 3.)

Article 1. Violation of Code

(Article 1 enacted by Stats. 1959, Ch. 3.)

40000.1. Except as otherwise provided in this article, it is unlawful and constitutes an infraction for any person to violate, or fail to comply with any provision of this code, or any local ordinance adopted pursuant to this code.

(Added by Stats. 1971, Ch. 1178.)

40000.3. A violation expressly declared to be a felony, or a public offense which is punishable, in the discretion of the court, either as a felony or misdemeanor, or a willful violation of a court order which is punishable as contempt pursuant to subdivision (a) of Section 42003, is not an infraction.

(Amended by Stats. 1973, Ch. 1162.)

40000.5. A violation of any of the following provisions shall constitute a misdemeanor, and not an infraction:

Section 20, relating to false statements.

Section 27, relating to impersonating a member of the California Highway Patrol.

Section 31, relating to giving false information.

Paragraph (3) of subdivision (a), or subdivision (b), or both, of Section 221, relating to proper evidence of clearance for dismantling.

(Amended by Stats. 1999, Ch. 316, Sec. 3. Effective January 1, 2000.)

40000.6. A violation of any of the following is a misdemeanor and not an infraction:

(a) Subdivision (b) of Section 1808.1, relating to enrollment in the pull notice system.

(b) Subdivision (f) of Section 1808.1, relating to employment of disqualified drivers.

(Amended by Stats. 1991, Ch. 928, Sec. 37. Effective October 14, 1991.)

40000.61. A violation of Section 1808.45, relating to unauthorized disclosure of department records, is a misdemeanor, and not an infraction.

(Added by Stats. 1989, Ch. 1213, Sec. 18.)

40000.65. A violation of Section 2430.5 or 2432, relating to emergency road service, is a misdemeanor and not an infraction.

(Added by Stats. 1991, Ch. 488, Sec. 9.)

40000.7. (a) A violation of any of the following provisions is a misdemeanor, and not an infraction:

(1) Section 2416, relating to regulations for emergency vehicles.

(2) Section 2800, relating to failure to obey an officer's lawful order or submit to a lawful inspection.

(3) Section 2800.1, relating to fleeing from a peace officer.

(4) Section 2801, relating to failure to obey a firefighter's lawful order.

(5) Section 2803, relating to unlawful vehicle or load.

(6) Section 2813, relating to stopping for inspection.

(7) Subdivisions (b), (c), and (d) of Section 4461 and subdivisions (b) and (c) of Section 4463, relating to disabled person placards and disabled person and disabled veteran license plates.

(8) Section 4462.5, relating to deceptive or false evidence of vehicle registration.

(9) Section 4463.5, relating to deceptive or facsimile license plates.

(10) Section 5500, relating to the surrender of registration documents and license plates before dismantling may begin.

(11) Section 5506, relating to the sale of a total loss salvage vehicle, or of a vehicle reported for dismantling by a salvage vehicle rebuilder.

(12) Section 5753, relating to delivery of certificates of ownership and registration when committed by a dealer or any person while a dealer within the preceding 12 months.

(13) Section 5901, relating to dealers and lessor-retailers giving notice.

(14) Section 5901.1, relating to lessors giving notice and failure to pay fee.

(15) Section 8802, relating to the return of canceled, suspended, or revoked certificates of ownership, registration cards, or license plates, when committed by any person with intent to defraud.

(16) Section 8803, relating to return of canceled, suspended, or revoked documents and license plates of a dealer, manufacturer, remanufacturer, transporter, dismantler, or salesman.

(b) This section shall become operative on January 1, 2001.

(Amended by Stats. 2010, Ch. 709, Sec. 26. (SB 1062) Effective January 1, 2011.)

40000.70. A violation of Section 23112.5, relating to notification of an on-highway hazardous material or hazardous waste spill, is a misdemeanor and not an infraction.

(Added by Stats. 1990, Ch. 429, Sec. 10.)

40000.77. A violation of Article 7 (commencing with Section 2570) of Chapter 2.5 of Division 2, relating to transportation of school pupils, is a misdemeanor, and not an infraction.

(Added by Stats. 1990, Ch. 1563, Sec. 62.)

40000.8. A violation of any of the following provisions is a misdemeanor, and not an infraction:

Section 9872, relating to the registration of vessels.

Section 9872.1, relating to unidentified vessels.

(Amended by Stats. 1991, Ch. 922, Sec. 7.)

40000.9. A violation of any of the following provisions shall constitute a misdemeanor, and not an infraction:

Section 10501, relating to false report of vehicle theft.

Sections 10750 and 10751, relating to altered or defaced vehicle identifying numbers.

Section 10851.5, relating to theft of binder chains.

Sections 10852 and 10853, relating to injuring or tampering with a vehicle.

Section 10854, relating to unlawful use of stored vehicle.

(Added by Stats. 1971, Ch. 1178.)

40000.10. A violation of subdivision (a) of Section 12500 shall be punished as follows:

(a) Except as provided in subdivision (b), as an infraction by a fine of one hundred dollars ($100) for a first or second violation.

(b) As a misdemeanor or an infraction as prescribed by Section 19.8 of the Penal Code if a person has a prior driver's license suspension or revocation for a violation of subdivision (c) of Section 192 of the Penal Code, subdivision (e) of Section 12809, or of Section 13353, 13353.1, 13353.2, 23103, 23104, 23105, 23109, 23152, 23153, or 23154.

(c) As a misdemeanor or an infraction as prescribed by Section 19.8 of the Penal Code for a third or subsequent violation.

(Added by Stats. 2022, Ch. 800, Sec. 20. (AB 2746) Effective January 1, 2023.)

40000.11. A violation of any of the following provisions is a misdemeanor, and not an infraction:

(a) Division 5 (commencing with Section 11100), relating to occupational licensing and business regulations.

(b) Section 12515, subdivision (b), relating to persons under 21 years of age driving, and the employment of those persons to drive, vehicles engaged in interstate commerce or transporting hazardous substances or wastes.

(c) Section 12517, relating to a special driver's certificate to operate a schoolbus or school pupil activity bus.

(d) Section 12517.45, relating to a special driver's certificate and vehicle inspection for the transportation of pupils to or from school-related activities by a passenger charter-party carrier as defined in subdivision (k) of Section 545.

(e) Section 12519, subdivision (a), relating to a special driver's certificate to operate a farm labor vehicle.

(f) Section 12520, relating to a special driver's certificate to operate a tow truck.

(g) Section 12951, subdivision (b), relating to refusal to display license.

(h) Section 13004, relating to unlawful use of an identification card.

(i) Section 13004.1, relating to identification documents.

(j) Sections 14601, 14601.1, 14601.2, and 14601.5, relating to driving with a suspended or revoked driver's license.

(k) Section 14604, relating to unlawful use of a vehicle.

(l) Section 14610, relating to unlawful use of a driver's license.

(m) Section 14610.1, relating to identification documents.

(n) Section 15501, relating to use of false or fraudulent license by a minor.

(Amended by Stats. 2023, Ch. 131, Sec. 218. (AB 1754) Effective January 1, 2024.)

40000.13. A violation of any of the following provisions is a misdemeanor, and not an infraction:

(a) Section 16560, relating to interstate highway carriers.

(b) Sections 20002 and 20003, relating to duties at accidents.

(c) Section 21200.5, relating to riding a bicycle while under the influence of an alcoholic beverage or any drug.

(d) Subdivision (b) of Section 21651, relating to wrong-way driving on divided highways.

(e) Subdivision (c) of Section 21655.9, relating to illegal use of decals, labels, or other identifiers.

(f) Section 22520.5, a second or subsequent conviction of an offense relating to vending on or near freeways.

(g) Section 22520.6, a second or subsequent conviction of an offense relating to roadside rest areas and vista points.

(h) This section shall remain in effect only until the date that the Secretary of State receives the notice from the Director of Transportation as described in Section 5205.5, and as of that date is repealed.

(Amended (as amended by Stats. 2006, Ch. 614, Sec. 5) by Stats. 2010, Ch. 215, Sec. 3. (SB 535) Effective January 1, 2011. Repealed on date prescribed by its own provisions. See later operative version, as amended by Sec. 4 of Ch. 215.)

40000.13. A violation of any of the following provisions is a misdemeanor, and not an infraction:

(a) Section 16560, relating to interstate highway carriers.

(b) Sections 20002 and 20003, relating to duties at accidents.

(c) Section 21200.5, relating to riding a bicycle while under the influence of an alcoholic beverage or any drug.

(d) Subdivision (b) of Section 21651, relating to wrong-way driving on divided highways.

(e) Section 22520.5, a second or subsequent conviction of an offense relating to vending on or near freeways.

(f) Section 22520.6, a second or subsequent conviction of an offense relating to roadside rest areas and vista points.

(g) This section shall become operative on the date that the Secretary of State receives the notice from the Director of Transportation as described in Section 5205.5.

(Amended (as amended by Stats. 2006, Ch. 614, Sec. 6) by Stats. 2010, Ch. 215, Sec. 4. (SB 535) Effective January 1, 2011. Section operative on date prescribed by its own provisions.)

40000.14. A violation of subdivision (b) or (c) of Section 21367 is an infraction, except as follows:

(a) A willful violation is a misdemeanor.

(b) A willful violation committed in a manner exhibiting a wanton disregard for the safety of persons is a misdemeanor punishable by imprisonment in the county jail for not more than one year.

(Added by Stats. 1986, Ch. 748, Sec. 3.)

40000.15. A violation of any of the following provisions shall constitute a misdemeanor, and not an infraction:

Subdivision (g), (j), (k), (l), or (m) of Section 22658, relating to unlawfully towed or stored vehicles.

Sections 23103 and 23104, relating to reckless driving.

Section 23109, relating to speed contests or exhibitions.

Subdivision (a) of Section 23110, relating to throwing at vehicles.

Section 23152, relating to driving under the influence.

Subdivision (b) of Section 23222, relating to possession of marijuana.

Subdivision (a) or (b) of Section 23224, relating to persons under 21 years of age knowingly driving, or being a passenger in, a motor vehicle carrying any alcoholic beverage.

Section 23253, relating to directions on toll highways or vehicular crossings.

Section 23332, relating to trespassing.

Section 24002.5, relating to unlawful operation of a farm vehicle.

Section 24011.3, relating to vehicle bumper strength notices.

Section 27150.1, relating to sale of exhaust systems.

Section 27362, relating to child passenger seat restraints.

Section 28050, relating to true mileage driven.

Section 28050.5, relating to nonfunctional odometers.

Section 28051, relating to resetting odometers.

Section 28051.5, relating to devices to reset odometers.

Subdivision (d) of Section 28150, relating to possessing four or more jamming devices.

(Amended by Stats. 2006, Ch. 609, Sec. 6. Effective January 1, 2007.)

40000.16. A second or subsequent violation of Section 23114, relating to preventing the escape of materials from vehicles, occurring within two years of a prior violation of that section is a misdemeanor, and not an infraction.

(Amended by Stats. 1997, Ch. 945, Sec. 32. Effective January 1, 1998.)

40000.18. A violation of subdivision (b) of Section 31401 or Section 31402 or 31403, relating to farm labor vehicles, is a misdemeanor and not an infraction.

(Added by Stats. 1988, Ch. 613, Sec. 2.)

40000.19. A violation of any of the following provisions is a misdemeanor, and not an infraction:

(a) Section 31303, relating to transportation of hazardous waste.

(b) Division 14 (commencing with Section 31600), relating to transportation of explosives.

(c) Division 14.1 (commencing with Section 32000), relating to the transportation of hazardous material.

(d) Division 14.3 (commencing with Section 32100), relating to transportation of inhalation hazards.

(e) Division 14.5 (commencing with Section 33000), relating to transportation of radioactive materials.

(f) Division 14.7 (commencing with Section 34001), relating to flammable liquids.

(Amended by Stats. 1988, Ch. 1384, Sec. 6.)

40000.20. A third or subsequent violation of Section 23225, relating to the storage of an opened container of an alcoholic beverage, or Section 23223, relating to the possession of an open container of an alcoholic beverage, by a driver of a vehicle used to provide transportation services on a prearranged basis, operating under a valid certificate or permit pursuant to the Passenger Charter-party Carriers' Act (Chapter 8 (commencing with Section 5351) of Division 2 of the Public Utilities Code), is a misdemeanor.

(Amended by Stats. 2013, Ch. 76, Sec. 198. (AB 383) Effective January 1, 2014.)

40000.21. A violation of any of the following provisions is a misdemeanor, and not an infraction:

(a) Subdivision (a) of Section 34506, relating to the hours of service of drivers.

(b) Subdivision (b) of Section 34506, relating to the transportation of hazardous materials.

(c) Subdivision (c) of Section 34506, relating to schoolbuses.

(d) Subdivision (d) of Section 34506, relating to youth buses.

(e) Section 34505 or subdivision (e) of Section 34506, relating to tour buses.

(f) Section 34505.5 or subdivision (f) of Section 34506, relating to vehicles described in subdivisions (a) to (g), inclusive, of Section 34500.

(g) Subdivision (a) of Section 34501.3, relating to unlawful scheduling of runs by motor carriers.

(h) Subdivision (g) of Section 34506, relating to school pupil activity buses.

(i) Subparagraph (D) of paragraph (4) of subdivision (a) of Section 34505.9, relating to intermodal chassis.

(Amended by Stats. 1998, Ch. 340, Sec. 4. Effective August 24, 1998.)

40000.22. (a) A violation of subdivision (e) of Section 34501, subdivision (b) or (d) of Section 34501.12, or subdivision (c) of Section 34501.14, relating to applications for inspections, is a misdemeanor and not an infraction.

(b) A violation of Division 14.85 (commencing with Section 34600), relating to motor carriers of property, is a misdemeanor and not an infraction.

(c) This section shall become operative on January 1, 2016.

(Repealed (in Sec. 19) and added by Stats. 2013, Ch. 500, Sec. 20. (AB 529) Effective January 1, 2014. Section operative January 1, 2016, by its own provisions.)

40000.23. A violation of any of the following provisions is a misdemeanor, and not an infraction:

(a) Paragraph (1) of subdivision (c) of Section 35784, relating to special permit violations.

(b) Subdivision (a) of Section 35784.5 relating to extralegal loads and operation of vehicles without a special permit.

(c) Other provisions of Chapter 5 (commencing with Section 35550) of Division 15, which relate to weight restrictions, except in cases of weight violations where the amount of excess weight is less than 4,501 pounds.

(Amended by Stats. 1984, Ch. 542, Sec. 9.)

40000.24. A violation of any of the following provisions shall constitute a misdemeanor and not an infraction:

(a) Subdivision (c) of Section 38301.5, relating to unauthorized operation of a vehicle within a mountain fire district.

(b) Section 38316, relating to reckless driving.

(c) Section 38317, relating to reckless driving with injury.

(d) Subdivision (a) of Section 38318 or subdivision (a) of Section 38318.5, relating to off-highway vehicles.

(e) Section 38319, relating to protection of the environment.

(f) Section 38320, relating to the depositing of matter.

(Amended by Stats. 1984, Ch. 1015, Sec. 3.)

40000.25. A violation of any of the following provisions shall constitute a misdemeanor, and not an infraction:

Section 40005, relating to owner's responsibility.

Section 40504, relating to false signatures.

Section 40508, relating to failure to appear or to pay fine.

Section 40519, relating to failure to appear.

Section 40614, relating to use of a fictitious name.

Section 40616, relating to a willful violation of a notice to correct.

(Amended by Stats. 2023, Ch. 85, Sec. 1. (AB 466) Effective January 1, 2024.)

40000.26. A violation of subdivision (g) of Section 34501.12 or subdivision (d) of Section 34501.14, relating to inspections, is a misdemeanor and not an infraction.

(Amended by Stats. 1992, Ch. 1243, Sec. 107.1. Effective September 30, 1992. Operative January 1, 1993, by Sec. 117 of Ch. 1243.)

40000.28. Any offense which would otherwise be an infraction is a misdemeanor if a defendant has been convicted of three or more violations of this code or any local ordinance adopted pursuant to this code within the 12-month period immediately preceding the commission of the offense and such prior convictions are admitted by the defendant or alleged in the accusatory pleading. For this purpose, a bail forfeiture shall be deemed to be a conviction of the offense charged.

This section shall have no application to violations by pedestrians.

(Amended by Stats. 1975, Ch. 635.)

40001. (a) It is unlawful for the owner, or any other person, employing or otherwise directing the driver of any vehicle to cause the operation of the vehicle upon a highway in any manner contrary to law.

(b) It is unlawful for an owner to request, cause, or permit the operation of any vehicle that is any of the following:

(1) Not registered or for which any fee has not been paid under this code.

(2) Not equipped as required in this code.

(3) Not in compliance with the size, weight, or load provisions of this code.

(4) Not in compliance with the regulations promulgated pursuant to this code, or with applicable city or county ordinances adopted pursuant to this code.

(5) Not in compliance with the provisions of Part 5 (commencing with Section 43000) of Division 26 of the Health and Safety Code and the rules and regulations of the State Air Resources Board.

(c) Any employer who violates an out-of-service order, that complies with Section 396.9 of Title 49 of the Code of Federal Regulations, or who knowingly requires or permits a driver to violate or fail to comply with that out-of-service order, is guilty of a misdemeanor.

(d) An employer who is convicted of allowing, permitting, requiring, or authorizing a driver to operate a commercial motor vehicle in violation of any statute or regulation pertaining to a railroad-highway grade crossing is subject to a fine of not more than ten thousand dollars ($10,000).

(e) Whenever a violation is chargeable to the owner or lessee of a vehicle pursuant to subdivision (a) or (b), the driver shall not be arrested or cited for the violation unless the vehicle is registered in a state or country other than California, or unless the violation is for an offense that is clearly within the responsibility of the driver.

(f) Whenever the owner, or lessee, or any other person is prosecuted for a violation pursuant to this section, the court may, on the request of the defendant, take appropriate steps to make the driver of the vehicle, or any other person who directs the loading, maintenance, or operation of the vehicle, a codefendant. However, the court may make the driver a codefendant only if the driver is the owner or lessee of the vehicle, or the driver is an employee or a contractor of the defendant who requested the court to make the driver a codefendant. If the codefendant is held solely responsible and found guilty, the court may dismiss the charge against the defendant.

(g) In any prosecution under this section, it is a rebuttable presumption that any person who gives false or erroneous information in a written certification of actual gross cargo weight has directed, requested, caused, or permitted the operation of a vehicle in a manner contrary to law in violation of subdivision (a) or (b), or both.

(Amended by Stats. 2004, Ch. 193, Sec. 200. Effective January 1, 2005.)

40002. (a) (1) If there is a violation of Section 40001, an owner or any other person subject to Section 40001, who was not driving the vehicle involved in the violation, may be mailed a written notice to appear. An exact and legible duplicate copy of that notice when filed with the court, in lieu of a verified complaint, is a complaint to which the defendant may plead "guilty."

(2) If, however, the defendant fails to appear in court or does not deposit lawful bail, or pleads other than "guilty" of the offense charged, a verified complaint shall be filed which shall be deemed to be an original complaint, and thereafter proceedings shall be had as provided by law, except that a defendant may, by an agreement in writing, subscribed by the defendant and filed with the court, waive the filing of a verified complaint and elect that the prosecution may proceed upon a written notice to appear.

(3) A verified complaint pursuant to paragraph (2) shall include a paragraph that informs the person that unless he or she appears in the court designated in the complaint within 21 days after being given the complaint and answers the charge, renewal of registration of the vehicle involved in the offense may be precluded by the department, or a warrant of arrest may be issued against him or her.

(b) (1) If a person mailed a notice to appear pursuant to paragraph (1) of subdivision (a) fails to appear in court or deposit bail, a warrant of arrest shall not be issued based on the notice to appear, even if that notice is verified. An arrest warrant may be issued only after a verified complaint pursuant to paragraph (2) of subdivision (a) is given the person and the person fails to appear in court to answer that complaint.

(2) If a person mailed a notice to appear pursuant to paragraph (1) of subdivision (a) fails to appear in court or deposit bail, the court may give by mail to the person a notice of noncompliance. A notice of noncompliance shall include a paragraph that informs the person that unless he or she appears in the court designated in the notice to appear within 21 days after being given by mail the notice of noncompliance and answers the charge on the notice to appear, or pays the applicable fine and penalties if an appearance is not required, renewal of registration of the vehicle involved in the offense may be precluded by the department.

(c) A verified complaint filed pursuant to this section shall conform to Chapter 2 (commencing with Section 948) of Title 5 of Part 2 of the Penal Code.

(d) (1) The giving by mail of a notice to appear pursuant to paragraph (1) of subdivision (a) or a notice of noncompliance pursuant to paragraph (2) of subdivision (b) shall be done in a manner prescribed by Section 22.

(2) The verified complaint pursuant to paragraph (2) of subdivision (a) shall be given in a manner prescribed by Section 22.

(Amended by Stats. 2010, Ch. 328, Sec. 232. (SB 1330) Effective January 1, 2011.)

40002.1. (a) Whenever a person has failed to appear in the court designated in the notice to appear or a verified complaint specified in Section 40002, following personal service of the notice of noncompliance or deposit in the mail pursuant to Section 22, the magistrate or clerk of the court may give notice of that fact to the department.

(b) Whenever the matter is adjudicated, including a dismissal of the charges upon forfeiture of bail or otherwise, the magistrate or clerk of the court hearing the matter shall immediately do all of the following:

(1) Endorse a certificate to that effect.

(2) Provide the person or the person's attorney with a copy of the certificate.

(3) Transmit a copy of the certificate to the department.

(c) A notice of noncompliance shall not be transmitted to the department pursuant to subdivision (a) if a warrant of arrest has been issued on the same offense pursuant to subdivision (b) of Section 40002. A warrant of arrest shall not be issued pursuant to subdivision (b) of Section 40002 if a notice of noncompliance has been transmitted to the department on the same offense pursuant to this section, except that, when a notice has been received by the court pursuant to subdivision (c) of Section 4766 or recalled by motion of the court, a warrant may then be issued.

(Amended by Stats. 2007, Ch. 452, Sec. 4. Effective January 1, 2008.)

40003. Whenever an employee is prosecuted for a violation of any provision of this code, or regulations promulgated pursuant to this code, relating to the size, weight, registration, equipment, or loading of a vehicle while operating a vehicle he was employed to operate, and which is owned by his employer, the court shall on the request of the employee take appropriate proceedings to make the owner of the vehicle a codefendant. In the event it is found that the employee had reasonable grounds to believe that the vehicle operated by him as an employee did not violate such provisions, and in the event the owner is found guilty under the provisions of Section 40001, the court may dismiss the charges against the employee.

In those cases in which the charges against the employee are dismissed, the abstract of the record of the court required by Section 1803 shall clearly indicate that such charges were dismissed and that the owner of the vehicle was found guilty under Section 40001.

(Amended by Stats. 1967, Ch. 819.)

40004. (a) The period for commencing criminal action against any person having filed or caused to be filed any false, fictitious, altered, forged or counterfeit document with the Department of Motor Vehicles or the Department of the California Highway Patrol shall, if the offense is a misdemeanor, expire one year from time of discovery of such act.

(b) The period for commencing criminal action against any person having filed or caused to be filed any false, fictitious, altered, forged or counterfeit document with the Department of Motor Vehicles or the Department of the California Highway Patrol shall, if the offense is a felony, expire three years from time of discovery of such act.

(c) The time allowed for commencing criminal proceedings as provided in subdivisions (a) and (b) of this section shall not extend beyond five years from the date of commission of the act.

(Repealed and added by Stats. 1968, Ch. 1192.)

40005. Whenever a driver is cited for a violation of any provision of this code, or regulations promulgated pursuant to this code, relating to the size, weight, equipment, registration, fees, or loading of a vehicle, while operating a vehicle he was employed or otherwise directed to operate, and which is not owned by him, and the driver gives the citation to the owner or any other person referred to in Section 40001, if the owner or other person undertakes to answer the charge or otherwise to cause its disposition without any further action by the driver and then fails to act in accordance with the undertaking as a consequence of which a warrant is issued for the arrest of the driver, the owner or other person is guilty of a misdemeanor.

(Added by Stats. 1965, Ch. 294.)

40006. Whenever a disabled vehicle, being taken to a repair shop, garage, or other place of storage, is being towed upon a highway by a tow car and the vehicle is determined to be in violation of subdivision (a) of Section 4000, the violation shall be charged as prescribed in Section 40001.

(Added by Stats. 1979, Ch. 152.)

40007. Division 5 (commencing with Section 11100) does not preclude the application of any other statutory provision which is applicable to any act violating any provision of Division 5.

(Added by Stats. 1985, Ch. 93, Sec. 1.)

40008. (a) Notwithstanding any other provision of law, except as otherwise provided in subdivision (c), any person who violates Section 21701, 21703, or 23103, with the intent to capture any type of visual image, sound recording, or other physical impression of another person for a commercial purpose, is guilty of a misdemeanor and not an infraction and shall be punished by imprisonment in a county jail for not more than six months and by a fine of not more than two thousand five hundred dollars ($2,500).

(b) Notwithstanding any other provision of law, except as otherwise provided in subdivision (c), any person who violates Section 21701, 21703, or 23103, with the intent to capture any type of visual image, sound recording, or other physical impression of another person for a commercial purpose and who causes a minor child or children to be placed in a situation in which the child's person or health is endangered, is guilty of a misdemeanor and not an infraction and shall be punished by imprisonment in a county jail for not more than one year and by a fine of not more than five thousand dollars ($5,000).

(c) Pursuant to Section 654 of the Penal Code, an act or omission described in subdivision (a) or (b) that is punishable in different ways by different provisions of law shall be punished under the provision that provides for the longest potential term of imprisonment, but in no case shall the act or omission be punished under more than one provision. An acquittal or conviction and sentence under any one provision bars a prosecution for the same act or omission under any other provision.

(Added by Stats. 2010, Ch. 685, Sec. 3. (AB 2479) Effective January 1, 2011.)

Article 2. Procedure on Equipment and Registration Violations

(Heading of Article 2 amended by Stats. 1980, Ch. 544, Sec. 3.)

40150. Whenever any vehicle or combination of vehicles is found to be in an unsafe mechanical condition or is not equipped as required by this code, and a notice to appear is issued or a complaint filed for such violation, the notice to appear or the complaint may require that the person to whom the notice to appear is issued or against whom the complaint is filed shall produce in court satisfactory evidence that the vehicle or its equipment has been made to conform with the requirements of this code.

(Amended by Stats. 1961, Ch. 1728.)

40151. (a) Whenever any lighting equipment or device does not meet requirements established by the Department of the California Highway Patrol, the officer making the inspection shall direct the driver to remove the lighting equipment or device within 24 hours.

(b) Whenever any lighting equipment or device meets requirements established by the department but by reason of faulty adjustment or otherwise fails to comply with this code, the officer making the inspection shall direct the driver to make it comply with this code within 48 hours.

(Amended by Stats. 1979, Ch. 723.)

40152. (a) Whenever any vehicle or combination of vehicles is found to be not registered as required by this code, and a notice to appear is issued or a complaint is filed for that violation, the person to whom the notice to appear is issued or against whom the complaint is filed shall produce in court satisfactory evidence that the vehicle or combination of vehicles has been registered or has had the appropriate fees paid, or has been reduced to junk, to conform with the requirements of this code. The court shall not dismiss the offense until that evidence is produced.

(b) A four-day, nonresident commercial trip permit of the type authorized in Section 4004 may not be accepted as evidence of registration compliance as required in subdivision (a) of this section.

(Amended by Stats. 1996, Ch. 1154, Sec. 83. Effective September 30, 1996.)

Article 3. Procedure on Parking Violations

(Article 3 added by Stats. 1986, Ch. 939, Sec. 15.)

40200. (a) Any violation of any regulation that is not a misdemeanor governing the standing or parking of a vehicle under this code, under any federal statute or regulation, or under any ordinance enacted by local authorities is subject to a civil penalty. The enforcement of those civil penalties shall be governed by the civil administrative procedures set forth in this article.

(b) Except as provided in Section 40209, the registered owner and driver, rentee, or lessee of a vehicle cited for any violation of any regulation governing the parking of a vehicle under this code, under any federal statute or regulation, or under any ordinance enacted by a local authority shall be jointly liable for parking penalties imposed under this article, unless the owner can show that the vehicle was used without consent of that person, express or implied. An owner who pays any parking penalty, civil judgment, costs, or administrative fees pursuant to this article shall have the right to recover the same from the driver, rentee, or lessee.

(c) The driver of a vehicle who is not the owner thereof but who uses or operates the vehicle with the express or implied permission of the owner shall be considered the agent of the owner to receive notices of parking violations served in accordance with this article and may contest the notice of violation.

(Amended by Stats. 1993, Ch. 1093, Sec. 3. Effective January 1, 1994.)

40200.1. A person shall not be subject to both a notice of parking violation and a notice to appear for the same violation.

(Added by Stats. 2009, Ch. 415, Sec. 5. (AB 144) Effective January 1, 2010.)

40200.3. (a) All parking penalties collected by the processing agency, which may be the issuing agency, including process service fees and fees and collection costs related to civil debt collection, shall be deposited to the account of the issuing agency, except that those sums attributable to the issuance of a notice of parking violation by a peace officer of the Department of the California Highway Patrol shall be deposited in the account in the jurisdiction where the violation occurred, and except those sums payable to a county pursuant to Chapter 12 (commencing with Section 76000) of Title 8 of the Government Code and that portion of any parking penalty which is attributable to an increase in the parking bail amount effective between September 16, 1988, and July 1, 1992, inclusive, pursuant to Section 1463.28 of the Penal Code. Those funds attributable to this increase in bail shall be transferred to the county treasurer and deposited in the general fund. Any increase in parking penalties effective after July 1, 1992, shall accrue to the benefit of the issuing agency.

(b) The processing agency shall prepare a report at the end of each fiscal year setting forth the number of cases processed, and all sums received and distributed, together with any other information that may be required by the issuing agency or the Controller. This report is a public record and shall be delivered to each issuing agency. Copies shall be made available, upon request, to the county auditor, the Controller, and the grand jury.

(Amended by Stats. 1996, Ch. 305, Sec. 72. Effective January 1, 1997.)

40200.4. (a) The processing agency shall deposit with the county treasurer all sums due the county as the result of processing a parking violation not later than 45 calendar days after the last day of the month in which the parking penalty was received.

(b) Except as provided in subdivisions (c) and (d), if a court within a county has been processing notices of parking violations and notices of delinquent parking violations for a city, a district, or any other issuing agency, the issuing agency and the county shall provide in an agreement for the orderly transfer of the processing activity as soon as possible but not later than January 1, 1994. The agreement shall permit the court to phase out, and the issuing agency to phase in, or transfer, personnel, equipment, and facilities that may have been acquired or need to be acquired in contemplation of a long-term commitment to processing of notices of parking violations and notices of delinquent parking violations for the issuing agency under this article. The court shall transfer the processing function for parking citations issued by the Department of the California Highway Patrol to the processing agency in the city or county where the violation occurred.

(c) If Contra Costa County or San Mateo County, or a court in either county, had a contract in effect on January 1, 1992, to process notices of parking violations and notices of delinquent parking violations for a city, district, or other issuing agency within the particular county or counties, the county may continue to provide those services to the issuing agencies pursuant to the terms of the contract and any amendments thereto, to and including June 30, 1996, after which Section 40200.5 shall govern any contracts entered into for these services.

(d) San Francisco Municipal Court employees engaged in processing notices of parking violations and the positions of those employees shall be transferred to equivalent civil service positions in the City and County of San Francisco.

(e) No court employee shall be terminated or otherwise released from employment as a result of the transfer of processing notices of parking violations and notices of delinquent parking violations from the courts to the issuing agencies.

(f) As used in this article, "parking penalty" includes the fine authorized by law, including assessments authorized by this article, any late payment penalty, and costs of collection as provided by law.

(Amended by Stats. 1996, Ch. 305, Sec. 73. Effective January 1, 1997.)

40200.5. (a) Except as provided in subdivision (c) of Section 40200.4, an issuing agency may elect to contract with the county, with a private vendor, or with any other city or county processing agency, other than the Department of the California Highway Patrol or other state law enforcement agency, within the county, with the consent of that other entity, for the processing of notices of parking violations and notices of delinquent parking violations, prior to filing with the court pursuant to Section 40230.

If an issuing agency contracts with a private vendor for processing services, it shall give special consideration to minority business enterprise participation in providing those services. For purposes of this subdivision, "special consideration" has the same meaning as specified in subdivision (c) of Section 14838 of the Government Code, as it relates to small business preference.

(b) A contract entered pursuant to subdivision (a) shall provide for monthly distribution of amounts collected between the parties, except those amounts payable to a county pursuant to Chapter 12 (commencing with Section 76000) of Title 8 of the Government Code and amounts payable to the Department of Motor Vehicles pursuant to Section 4763 of this code.

(c) If a contract entered into pursuant to subdivision (a) includes the provision of qualified examiners or administrative hearing providers, the contract shall be based on either a fixed monthly rate or on the number of notices processed and shall not include incentives for the processing entity based on the number of notices upheld or denied or the amount of fines collected.

(Amended by Stats. 2008, Ch. 13, Sec. 1. Effective January 1, 2009.)

40200.6. (a) If a contract is entered into pursuant to Section 40200.5, for the purposes of this article, "processing agency" means the contracting party responsible for the processing of the notices of parking violations and notices of delinquent parking violations.

(b) The governing body of the issuing agency shall establish written policies and procedures pursuant to which the contracting party shall provide services.

(c) The issuing agency shall be responsible for all actions taken by contracting parties and shall exercise effective oversight over the parties. "Effective oversight" includes, at a minimum, an annual review of the services of the processing agency and a review of complaints made by motorists using the services of the processing agency. The issuing agency shall establish procedures to investigate and resolve complaints by motorists about any processing agency.

(d) Subdivision (c) does not apply to an issuing agency that is a law enforcement agency if the issuing agency does not also act as the processing agency.

(Amended by Stats. 1995, Ch. 734, Sec. 5. Effective January 1, 1996.)

40200.8. The parking processing agency shall notify the department and recall any hold on the registration of a vehicle that it filed with the department in connection with a parking citation if the processing agency is awarded a civil judgment for the citation pursuant to subdivision (b) or (c) of Section 40220, or if the processing agency has granted a review of the issuance of the citation pursuant to Section 40200.7 or Section 40215.

(Added by Stats. 1995, Ch. 766, Sec. 41. Effective January 1, 1996.)

40202. (a) If a vehicle is unattended during the time of the violation, the peace officer or person authorized to enforce parking laws and regulations shall securely attach to the vehicle a notice of parking violation setting forth the violation, including reference to the section of this code or of the Public Resources Code, the local ordinance, or the federal statute or regulation so violated; the date; the approximate time thereof; the location where the violation occurred; a statement printed on the notice indicating that the date of payment is required to be made not later than 21 calendar days from the date of citation issuance; and the procedure for the registered owner, lessee, or rentee to deposit the parking penalty or, pursuant to Section 40215, contest the citation. The notice of parking violation shall also set forth the vehicle license number and registration expiration date if they are visible, the last four digits of the vehicle identification number, if that number is readable through the windshield, the color of the vehicle, and, if possible, the make of the vehicle. The notice of parking violation, or copy thereof, shall be considered a record kept in the ordinary course of business of the issuing agency and the processing agency and shall be prima facie evidence of the facts contained therein.

(b) The notice of parking violation shall be served by attaching it to the vehicle either under the windshield wiper or in another conspicuous place upon the vehicle so as to be easily observed by the person in charge of the vehicle upon the return of that person.

(c) Once the issuing officer has prepared the notice of parking violation and has attached it to the vehicle as provided in subdivisions (a) and (b), the officer shall file the notice with the processing agency. Any person, including the issuing officer and any member of the officer's department or agency, or any peace officer who alters, conceals, modifies, nullifies, or destroys, or causes to be altered, concealed, modified, nullified, or destroyed the face of the remaining original or any copy of a citation that was retained by the officer, for any reason, before it is filed with the processing agency or with a person authorized to receive the deposit of the parking penalty, is guilty of a misdemeanor.

(d) If, during the issuance of a notice of parking violation, without regard to whether the vehicle was initially attended or unattended, the vehicle is driven away prior to attaching the notice to the vehicle, the issuing officer shall file the notice with the processing agency. The processing agency shall mail, within 15 calendar days of issuance of the notice of parking violation, a copy of the notice of parking violation or transmit an electronic facsimile of the notice to the registered owner.

(e) If, within 21 days after the notice of parking violation is attached to the vehicle, the issuing officer or the issuing agency determines that, in the interest of justice, the notice of parking violation should be canceled, the issuing agency, pursuant to subdivision (a) of Section 40215, shall cancel the notice of parking violation or, if the issuing agency has contracted with a processing agency, shall notify the processing agency to cancel the notice of parking violation pursuant to subdivision (a) of Section 40215. The reason for the cancellation shall be set forth in writing.

If, after a copy of the notice of parking violation is attached to the vehicle, the issuing officer determines that there is incorrect data on the notice, including, but not limited to, the date or time, the issuing officer may indicate in writing, on a form attached to the original notice, the necessary correction to allow for the timely entry of the notice on the processing agency's data system. A copy of the correction shall be mailed to the registered owner of the vehicle.

(f) Under no circumstances shall a personal relationship with any officer, public official, or law enforcement agency be grounds for cancellation.

(Amended by Stats. 1998, Ch. 885, Sec. 3. Effective January 1, 1999.)

40203. The notice of parking violation shall be accompanied by a written notice of the amount of the parking penalty due for that violation, the address of the person authorized to receive a deposit of the parking penalty, a statement in bold print that payments of the parking penalty for the parking violation may be sent through the mail, and instructions on obtaining information on the procedures to contest the notice of parking violation.

(Amended by Stats. 1995, Ch. 734, Sec. 8. Effective January 1, 1996.)

40203.5. (a) The schedule of parking penalties for parking violations and late payment penalties shall be established by the governing body of the jurisdiction where the notice of violation is issued. To the extent possible, issuing agencies within the same county shall standardize parking penalties.

(b) Parking penalties under this article shall be collected as civil penalties.

(c) (1) Notwithstanding subdivision (a) the penalty for a violation of Section 22507.8 or an ordinance or resolution adopted pursuant to Section 22511.57 shall be not less than two hundred fifty dollars ($250) and not more than one thousand dollars ($1,000).

(2) The issuing agency may suspend the imposition of the penalty in paragraph (1), if the violator, at the time of the offense, possesses but failed to display a valid special identification license plate issued pursuant to Section 5007 or a distinguishing placard issued pursuant to Section 22511.55 or 22511.59.

(3) A penalty imposed pursuant to this subdivision may be paid in installments if the issuing agency determines that the violator is unable to pay the entire amount in one payment.

(Amended by Stats. 2009, Ch. 415, Sec. 6. (AB 144) Effective January 1, 2010.)

40203.6. (a) In addition to an assessment levied pursuant to any other law, an additional assessment equal to 10 percent of the penalty established pursuant to Section 40203.5 shall be imposed by the governing body of the jurisdiction where the notice of parking violation is issued for a civil violation of any of the following:

(1) Subdivisions (b), (c), and (d) of Section 4461.

(2) Subdivision (c) of Section 4463.

(3) Section 22507.8.

(4) An ordinance or resolution adopted pursuant to Section 22511.57.

(5) Section 22522.

(b) An assessment imposed pursuant to this section shall be deposited with the city or county where the violation occurred.

(Added by Stats. 2009, Ch. 415, Sec. 7. (AB 144) Effective January 1, 2010.)

40204. (a) If the parking penalty is received by the person authorized to receive the deposit of the parking penalty and there is no contest as to that parking violation, the proceedings under this article shall terminate.

(b) The issuing agency may, consistent with the written guidelines established by the agency, allow payment of the parking penalty in installments if the violator provides evidence satisfactory to the issuing agency of an inability to pay the parking penalty in full.

(Amended by Stats. 2015, Ch. 112, Sec. 1. (AB 1151) Effective January 1, 2016.)

40205. If a person contests the parking violation, the processing agency shall proceed in accordance with Section 40215.

(Amended by Stats. 1992, Ch. 1244, Sec. 18. Effective January 1, 1993. Operative July 1, 1993, by Sec. 39 of Ch. 1244.)

40206. (a) If the payment of the parking penalty is not received by the person authorized to receive a deposit of the parking penalty by the date fixed on the notice of parking violation under Section 40202, the processing agency shall deliver to the registered owner a notice of delinquent parking violation.

(b) Delivery of a notice of delinquent parking violation under this section may be made by personal service or by first-class mail addressed to the registered owner, as shown on records of the Department of Motor Vehicles.

(Amended by Stats. 1992, Ch. 1244, Sec. 19. Effective January 1, 1993. Operative July 1, 1993, by Sec. 39 of Ch. 1244.)

40206.5. (a) Within 15 days of a request, by mail or in person, the processing agency shall mail or otherwise provide to any person who has received a notice of delinquent parking violation, or his or her agent, a photostatic copy of the original notice of parking violation or an electronically produced facsimile of the original notice of parking violation. The issuing agency may charge a fee sufficient to recover the actual cost of providing the copy, not to exceed two dollars ($2). Until the issuing agency complies with a request for a copy of the original notice of parking violation, the processing agency may not proceed pursuant to subdivision (i) of Section 22651, Section 22651.7, or Section 40220.

(b) If the description of the vehicle on the notice of parking violation does not substantially match the corresponding information on the registration card for that vehicle and the processing agency is satisfied that the vehicle has not been incorrectly described due to the intentional switching of license plates, the processing agency shall, on written request of the person cancel the notice of parking violation without the necessity of an appearance by that person.

(c) For purposes of this section, a copy of the notice of parking violation may be a photostatic copy or an electronically produced facsimile.

(Amended by Stats. 1993, Ch. 1093, Sec. 9. Effective January 1, 1994.)

40207. (a) The notice of delinquent parking violation shall contain the information specified in subdivision (a) of Section 40202 or subdivision (a) of Section 40248, as applicable, and Section 40203, and, additionally shall contain a notice to the registered owner that, unless the registered owner pays the parking penalty or contests the citation within 21 calendar days from the date of issuance of the citation or 14 calendar days after the mailing of the notice of delinquent parking violation or completes and files an affidavit of nonliability that complies with Section 40208 or 40209, the renewal of the vehicle registration shall be contingent upon compliance with the notice of delinquent parking violation. If the registered owner, by appearance or by mail, makes payment to the processing agency within 21 calendar days from the date of issuance of the citation or 14 calendar days after the mailing of the notice of delinquent parking violation, the parking penalty shall consist solely of the amount of the original penalty. Additional fees, assessments, or other charges shall not be added.

(b) This section shall become operative on January 1, 2016.

(Amended (as amended by Stats. 2010, Ch. 471, Sec. 2) by Stats. 2011, Ch. 325, Sec. 2. (AB 1041) Effective January 1, 2012. Section operative January 1, 2016, by its own provisions.)

40208. The notice of delinquent parking violation shall contain, or be accompanied with, an affidavit of nonliability and information of what constitutes nonliability, information as to the effect of executing the affidavit, and instructions for returning the affidavit to the issuing agency.

(Added by Stats. 1986, Ch. 939, Sec. 15.)

40209. If the affidavit of nonliability is returned to the processing agency within 30 calendar days of the mailing of the notice of delinquent parking violation together with the proof of a written lease or rental agreement between a bona fide rental or leasing company, and its customer which identifies the rentee or lessee and provides the driver's license number, name, and address of the rentee or lessee, the processing agency shall serve or mail to the rentee or lessee identified in the affidavit of nonliability a notice of delinquent parking violation. If payment is not received within 21 calendar days from the date of issuance of the citation or 14 calendar days after the mailing of the notice of delinquent parking violation, the processing agency may proceed against the rentee or lessee pursuant to Section 40220.

(Amended by Stats. 1996, Ch. 1156, Sec. 8. Effective January 1, 1997.)

40210. (a) If the affidavit of nonliability is returned and indicates that the registered owner served has made a bona fide sale or transfer of the vehicle and has delivered possession of the vehicle to the purchaser prior to the date of the alleged violation, the processing agency shall obtain verification from the department that the registered owner has complied with Section 5602.

(b) If the registered owner has complied with Section 5602, the processing agency shall cancel the notice of delinquent parking violation or violations with respect to the registered owner.

(c) If the registered owner has not complied with Section 5602, the processing agency shall inform the registered owner that the citation shall be paid in full or contested pursuant to Section 40215 unless the registered owner delivers evidence within 15 days of the notice that establishes that the transfer of ownership and possession of the vehicle occurred prior to the date of the alleged violation. If the registered owner does not comply with this notice, the processing agency shall proceed pursuant to Section 40220. If the registered owner delivers the evidence within 15 days of the notice, the processing agency shall cancel the notice of delinquent parking violation or violations with respect to the registered owner.

(d) For purposes of subdivision (c), evidence sufficient to establish that the transfer of ownership and possession occurred prior to the date of the alleged violation or violations shall include, but is not limited to, a copy of the executed agreement showing the date of the transfer of vehicle ownership.

(e) This section does not limit or impair the ability or the right of the processing agency to pursue the collection of delinquent parking penalties from the person having ownership and possession of the vehicle on the date the alleged violation occurred.

(Amended by Stats. 2008, Ch. 741, Sec. 3. Effective January 1, 2009.)

40211. (a) If the registered owner, or an agent of the registered owner, or a rentee or lessee who was served with the notice of delinquent parking violation pursuant to Section 40206 or Section 40209, or any other person who presents the notice of parking violation or notice of delinquent parking violation after the notice of delinquent parking violation has been issued for delivery under Section 40206, deposits the parking penalty with a person authorized to receive it, the processing agency shall do both of the following:

(1) Deliver a copy of one of the following: the notice of delinquent

parking violation issued under Section 40206; a true and correct abstract containing the information set forth in the notice of parking violation if the citation was issued electronically; or an electronically reproduced listing of the citation information presented in a notice of delinquent parking violation to the person and record the name, address, and driver's license number of the person actually given the copy in the records of the issuing agency.

For the purposes of this paragraph, a copy of the notice of delinquent parking violation may be a photostatic copy.

(2) Determine whether the notice of delinquent parking violation has been filed with the department pursuant to subdivision (b) of Section 40220 or a civil judgment has been entered pursuant to Section 40220.

(b) If the notice of delinquent parking violation has not been filed with the department or judgment entered and payment of the parking penalty, including any applicable assessments, is received, the proceedings under this article shall terminate.

(c) If the notice of delinquent parking violation has been filed with the department, has been returned under subdivision (b) or (c) of Section 4760 or Section 4764, and payment of the parking penalty together with the administrative service fee of the processing agency for costs of service and any applicable assessments is received, the proceedings under this article shall terminate.

(d) If the notice of delinquent parking violation has been filed with the department and has not been returned under Section 4760, 4762, and 4764, and payment of the parking penalty for, and any applicable costs of, service in connection with civil debt collection, is received by the processing agency, the processing agency shall do all of the following:

(1) Deliver a certificate of payment to the registered owner, the agent, the lessee, or the rentee or other person making the payment.

(2) Immediately transmit the payment information to the department in the manner prescribed by the department.

(3) Terminate proceedings on the notice of delinquent parking violation.

(4) Transmit for deposit all parking penalties and assessments in accordance with law.

(Amended by Stats. 1995, Ch. 734, Sec. 13. Effective January 1, 1996.)

40215. (a) For a period of 21 calendar days from the issuance of a notice of parking violation or 14 calendar days from the mailing of a notice of delinquent parking violation, exclusive of any days from the day the processing agency receives a request for a copy or facsimile of the original notice of parking violation pursuant to Section 40206.5 and the day the processing agency complies with the request, a person may request an initial review of the notice by the issuing agency. The request may be made by telephone, in writing, or in person. There shall not be a charge for this review. If, following the initial review, the issuing agency is satisfied that the violation did not occur, that the registered owner was not responsible for the violation, or that extenuating circumstances make dismissal of the citation appropriate in the interest of justice, the issuing agency shall cancel the notice of parking violation or notice of delinquent parking violation. The issuing agency shall advise the processing agency, if any, of the cancellation. The issuing agency or the processing agency shall mail the results of the initial review to the person contesting the notice, and, if following that review, cancellation of the notice does not occur, include a reason for that denial, notification of the ability to request an administrative hearing, and notice of the procedure adopted pursuant to subdivision (b) for waiving prepayment of the parking penalty based upon an inability to pay.

(b) If the person is dissatisfied with the results of the initial review, the person may request an administrative hearing of the violation no later than 21 calendar days following the mailing of the results of the issuing agency's initial review. The request may be made by telephone, in writing, or in person. The person requesting an administrative hearing shall deposit the amount of the parking penalty with the processing agency. The issuing agency shall adopt a written procedure to allow a person who is indigent, as defined in Section 40220, to request an administrative hearing without payment of the parking penalty upon satisfactory proof of an inability to pay the amount due. An administrative hearing shall be held within 90 calendar days following the receipt of a request for an administrative hearing, excluding time tolled pursuant to this article. The person requesting the hearing may request one continuance, not to exceed 21 calendar days.

(c) The administrative hearing process shall include all of the following:

(1) The person requesting a hearing shall have the choice of a hearing by mail, in person, or, if offered by the issuing agency, by telephone or electronic means. An in-person hearing shall be conducted within the jurisdiction of the issuing agency. If an issuing agency contracts with an administrative provider, in-person hearings shall be held within the jurisdiction of the issuing agency or within the county of the issuing agency.

(2) If the person requesting a hearing is a minor, that person shall be permitted to appear at a hearing or admit responsibility for the parking violation without the necessity of the appointment of a guardian. The processing agency may proceed against the minor in the same manner as against an adult.

(3) The administrative hearing shall be conducted in accordance with written procedures established by the issuing agency and approved by the governing body or chief executive officer of the issuing agency. The hearing shall provide an independent, objective, fair, and impartial review of contested parking violations.

(4) (A) The issuing agency's governing body or chief executive officer shall appoint or contract with qualified examiners or administrative hearing providers that employ qualified examiners to conduct the administrative hearings. Examiners shall demonstrate those qualifications, training, and objectivity necessary to conduct a fair and impartial review. An examiner shall not be employed, managed, or controlled by a person whose primary duties are parking enforcement or parking citation, processing, collection, or issuance. The examiner shall be separate and independent from the citation, collection, or processing function. An examiner's continued employment, performance evaluation, compensation, and benefits shall not, directly or indirectly, be linked to the amount of fines collected by the examiner.

(B) (i) Examiners shall have a minimum of 20 hours of training. The examiner is responsible for the costs of the training. The issuing agency may reimburse the examiner for those costs.

(ii) Training may be provided through any of the following:

(I) An accredited college or university.

(II) A program conducted by the Commission on Peace Officer Standards and Training.

(III) American Arbitration Association or a similar established organization.

(IV) Through a program approved by the governing board of the issuing agency, including a program developed and provided by, or for, the issuing agency.

(iii) Training programs may include topics relevant to the administrative hearing, including, but not limited to, applicable laws and regulations, parking enforcement procedures, due process, evaluation of evidence, hearing procedures, and effective oral and written communication.

(iv) Upon the approval of the governing board of the issuing agency, up to 12 hours of relevant experience may be substituted for up to 12 hours of training. In addition, up to eight hours of the training requirements described in clause (i) may be credited to an individual, at the discretion of the governing board of the issuing agency, based upon training programs or courses described in clause (ii) that the individual attended within the last five years.

(5) The officer or person who issues a notice of parking violation shall not be required to participate in an administrative hearing. The issuing agency shall not be required to produce any evidence other than the notice of parking violation or copy of the notice and information received from the Department of Motor Vehicles identifying the registered owner

of the vehicle. The documentation in proper form shall be prima facie evidence of the violation.

(6) The examiner's decision following the administrative hearing may be personally delivered to the person by the examiner or sent by first-class mail, and, if the notice is not cancelled, include a written reason for that denial.

(7) The examiner or the issuing agency may, at any time, and consistent with the written guidelines established by the issuing agency, allow payment of the parking penalty in installments, or the issuing agency may allow for deferred payment or allow for a reduction or waiver of the parking penalty if the person provides evidence satisfactory to the examiner or the issuing agency, as the case may be, of either an inability to pay the parking penalty in full, or any other extenuating circumstances relevant to payment of the parking penalty, including, but not limited to, documented homelessness status and financial hardship. If authorized by the governing board of the issuing agency, the examiner may permit the performance of community service in lieu of payment of a parking penalty.

(d) The provisions of this section relating to the administrative appeal process do not apply to an issuing agency that is a law enforcement agency if the issuing agency does not also act as the processing agency.

(Amended by Stats. 2025, Ch. 346, Sec. 1. (AB 1299) Effective January 1, 2026.)

40220. (a) Except as otherwise provided in Sections 40220.5, 40221, and 40222, the processing agency may proceed under one of the following options in order to collect an unpaid parking penalty and related service fees:

(1) (A) File an itemization of unpaid parking penalties and related service fees with the department for collection with the registration of the vehicle pursuant to Section 4760. For unpaid parking penalties issued on and after July 1, 2018, and related service fees, the processing agency shall not file an itemization with the department unless all of the following conditions have been satisfied:

(i) The processing agency provides a payment plan option for indigent persons that, at a minimum, does all of the following:

(I) Allows payment of unpaid parking penalties and related service fees in monthly installments of no more than twenty-five dollars ($25) for total amounts due that are five hundred dollars ($500) or less. The amount of late fees and penalty assessments waived pursuant to subclause (II) shall not be counted in calculating that total amount of five hundred dollars ($500) or less. Unpaid parking penalties and fees shall be paid off within 24 months. There shall be no prepayment penalty for paying off the balance prior to the payment period expiring.

(II) Waives all late fees and penalty assessments, exclusive of any state surcharges described in Sections 70372, 76000, and 76000.3 of the Government Code, if an indigent person enrolls in the payment plan. Waived late fees and penalty assessments may be reinstated if the person falls out of compliance with the payment plan.

(III) Limits the processing fee to participate in a payment plan to five dollars ($5) or less for indigent persons. The processing fee for an indigent person may be added to the payment plan amount, at the discretion of the indigent person. If a processing agency offers a payment plan option to persons who are not indigent, limits the processing fee to participate in the payment plan to twenty-five dollars ($25) or less.

(IV) Allows a person to file a request to participate in a payment plan at any time.

(ii) The processing agency includes the information described in subclauses (I) and (II) in the notice of parking violation, and includes both in the notice of parking violation and on its public internet website, a web page link and telephone number to more information on the payment program. Each processing agency shall ensure that the linked internet web page is readily accessible in a prominent location on the parking citation payment section of the agency's internet website and includes all of the following information:

(I) The availability of an installment payment plan and the timeframe in which to apply.

(II) The person's right to request an indigency determination and the timeframe in which the person must apply.

(III) Clear language about how the person can request an indigency determination and what that determination will entail.

(IV) Documents needed by the processing agency to make an indigency determination.

(iii) The person fails to enroll in the payment plan within the time specified in the notice or is not eligible for the payment plan because the person is not indigent.

(B) The processing agency shall allow a person who falls out of compliance with the payment plan a one-time extension of 45 calendar days from the date the payment plan becomes delinquent to resume payments before the processing agency files an itemization of unpaid parking penalties and related service fees with the department pursuant to subparagraph (A).

(C) The processing agency shall rescind the filing of an itemization of unpaid parking penalties and related service fees with the department for an indigent person, for one time only, if the registered owner or lessee enrolls in a payment plan and pays a late fee of no more than five dollars ($5).

(D) (i) Each California State University and community college district governing board shall adopt a parking citation payment plan for persons with multiple unpaid parking citations. A parking citation payment policy adopted under this subparagraph shall include, but not be limited to, all of the following requirements:

(I) Late fees shall be placed in abeyance while the payment plan is in place and the person adheres to its terms, and shall be waived once the payment plan is completed.

(II) Once the payment plan is in place and the person adheres to its terms, an itemization of unpaid parking penalties and service fees as described in subparagraph (A) shall not be filed with the department.

(III) Each California State University and community college district campus shall post the parking citation payment policy on its internet website for students' awareness and access.

(ii) A California State University or community college district governing board that fails to implement a parking citation payment plan pursuant to clause (i) shall implement the payment plan as provided in subparagraphs (A) to (C), inclusive, and subdivision (c).

(2) (A) If more than four hundred dollars ($400) in unpaid penalties and fees have been accrued by a person or registered owner, proof thereof may be filed with the court and shall have the same effect as a civil judgment. Execution may be levied and other measures may be taken for the collection of the judgment as are authorized for the collection of an unpaid civil judgment entered against a defendant in an action on a debtor. The court may assess costs against a judgment debtor to be paid upon satisfaction of the judgment. The processing agency shall send a notice by first-class mail to the person or registered owner indicating that a judgment shall be entered for the unpaid penalties, fees, and costs and that, after 21 calendar days from the date of the mailing of the notice, the judgment shall have the same effect as an entry of judgment against a judgment debtor. The person or registered owner shall also be notified at that time that execution may be levied against their assets, liens may be placed against their property, their wages may be garnished, and other steps may be taken to satisfy the judgment. If a judgment is rendered for the processing agency, the processing agency may contract with a collection agency to collect the amount of the judgment.

(B) Notwithstanding any other law, the processing agency shall pay the established first paper civil filing fee at the time an entry of civil judgment is requested.

(3) If the registration of the vehicle has not been renewed for 60 days beyond the renewal date, and the citation has not been collected by the department pursuant to Section 4760, file proof of unpaid penalties and fees with the court with the same effect as a civil judgment as provided

in paragraph (2).

(b) This section does not apply to a registered owner of a vehicle if the citation was issued prior to the registered owner taking possession of the vehicle, and the department has notified the processing agency pursuant to Section 4764.

(c) (1) For purposes of paragraph (1) of subdivision (a), a person is "indigent" if any of the following conditions is met:

(A) The person meets the income criteria set forth in subdivision (b) of Section 68632 of the Government Code.

(B) The person receives public benefits from a program listed in subdivision (a) of Section 68632 of the Government Code.

(2) The person may demonstrate that the person is indigent by providing either of the following information, as applicable:

(A) Proof of income from a pay stub or another form of proof of earnings, such as a bank statement, that shows that the person meets the income criteria set forth in subdivision (b) of Section 68632 of the Government Code, subject to review and approval by the processing agency or its designee. The processing agency or its designee shall not unreasonably withhold its approval.

(B) Proof of receipt of benefits under the programs described in subparagraph (B) of paragraph (1), including, but not limited to, an electronic benefits transfer card or another card, subject to review and approval by the processing agency. The processing agency or its designee shall not unreasonably withhold its approval.

(3) If a defendant's indigent status is found to have been willfully fraudulent, the defendant's penalties and fees reduction shall be overturned and the full amount of penalties and fees shall be restored.

(Amended by Stats. 2025, Ch. 346, Sec. 2. (AB 1299) Effective January 1, 2026.)

40220.5. (a) (1) A processing agency may only use the process set forth in Section 4760 to collect unpaid parking penalties that were issued before July 1, 2018, and related service fees, if the processing agency provides indigent persons with the payment plan program described in this section.

(2) A processing agency shall not be required to comply with this section to collect unpaid parking penalties that were issued before July 1, 2018, and related service fees, pursuant to the process set forth in Section 4760 for a person who does not file an application for an indigency determination, a person who falls out of compliance with a payment plan, except as set forth in subdivision (d), or a person who the processing agency has determined is not an indigent person.

(b) A processing agency shall provide notice on its internet website of a person's ability to request an indigency determination to qualify for a payment plan pursuant to this section. The notice shall include all of the following information:

(1) The availability of a payment plan for indigent persons to pay parking penalties that were issued before July 1, 2018, and related service fees.

(2) Clear language about how a person can request an indigency determination and what that determination will entail.

(3) Documents needed by the processing agency to make an indigency determination.

(c) A processing agency shall provide an indigent person an opportunity to pay unpaid parking penalties that were issued before July 1, 2018, and related service fees, pursuant to a payment plan that, at a minimum, does all of the following:

(1) Allows payment of unpaid parking penalties that were issued before July 1, 2018, and related service fees, in monthly installments of no more than twenty-five dollars ($25) for total amounts due that are three hundred dollars ($300) or less. The amount of late fees and penalty assessments waived pursuant to paragraph (2) shall not be counted in calculating that total amount of three hundred dollars ($300) or less. Unpaid parking penalties and related service fees shall be paid off within 18 months. There shall be no prepayment penalty for paying off the balance prior to the payment period expiring.

(2) Waives all late fees and penalty assessments, exclusive of any state surcharges described in Sections 70372, 76000, and 76000.3 of the Government Code. Waived late fees and penalty assessments may be reinstated if the indigent person falls out of compliance with the payment plan.

(3) Limits the processing fee to participate in a payment plan to five dollars ($5) or less. The processing fee may be added to the payment plan amount, at the discretion of the indigent person.

(d) A processing agency shall allow an indigent person who falls out of compliance with the payment plan a one-time extension of 45 calendar days from the date the payment plan became delinquent to resume payment.

(e) A processing agency shall rescind the collection of unpaid parking penalties that were issued before July 1, 2018, and related service fees, with the department pursuant to the process set forth in Section 4760 for an indigent person, if the indigent person enrolls in a payment plan pursuant to this section.

(f) "Indigent" shall have the same meaning as set forth in subdivision (c) of Section 40220.

(g) This section shall remain in effect until January 1, 2027, and as of that date is repealed.

(Amended by Stats. 2019, Ch. 495, Sec. 2. (AB 833) Effective October 3, 2019. Repealed as of January 1, 2027, by its own provisions.)

40221. The processing agency shall not file a civil judgment with the court relating to a parking violation which has been filed with the department unless the processing agency has determined that the registration of the vehicle has not been renewed for 60 days beyond the renewal date and the citation has not been collected by the department pursuant to Section 4760.

(Amended by Stats. 1992, Ch. 1244, Sec. 28. Effective January 1, 1993. Operative July 1, 1993, by Sec. 39 of Ch. 1244.)

40222. The processing agency shall terminate proceedings on a notice of a delinquent parking violation or violations in all of the following cases:

(a) Upon receipt of collected penalties and administrative fees remitted by the department under Section 4762 for that notice of delinquent parking violation or violations. The termination under this subdivision is by satisfaction of the parking penalty or penalties.

(b) If the notice of a delinquent parking violation or violations was returned to the processing agency pursuant to Section 4764 and five years have elapsed since the date of the last violation. The termination under this subdivision is by the running of a statute of limitation of proceedings.

(c) The processing agency receives information, that it shall verify with the department, that the penalty or penalties have been paid to the department pursuant to Section 4762.

(d) (1) If the registered owner of the vehicle provides proof to the processing agency that he or she was not the registered owner on the date of the violation.

(2) This subdivision does not limit or impair the ability or the right of the processing agency to pursue the collection of a delinquent parking violation or violations from the person who was the registered owner or lessee of the vehicle on the date of the violation.

(Amended by Stats. 2008, Ch. 741, Sec. 5. Effective January 1, 2009.)

40224. The time limitation provided by law for commencement of a civil action for a violation specified in Section 40200 shall be tolled from and after the date a notice of delinquent parking violation is filed with the department pursuant to subdivision (b) of Section 40220 until the notice is returned to the processing agency under subdivision (b) of Section 4760 or Section 4762 or 4764 or is recalled by the processing agency pursuant to subdivision (d) of Section 40211.

(Amended by Stats. 1995, Ch. 734, Sec. 17. Effective January 1, 1996.)

40225. (a) An equipment violation entered on the notice of parking violation attached to the vehicle under Section 40203 shall be processed in accordance with this article. All of the violations entered on the notice of parking violation shall be noticed in the notice of delinquent parking violation delivered pursuant to Section 40206, together with the amount of civil penalty.

(b) (1) Whether or not a vehicle is in violation of any regulation governing the standing or parking of a vehicle but is in violation of subdivision (a) of Section 5204, a person authorized to enforce parking laws and regulations shall verify, using available Department of Motor Vehicle records, that no current registration exists for that vehicle. A citation shall not be issued for failure to comply with subdivision (a) of Section 5204 against any vehicle that has a current registration on file with the department. If the person authorized to enforce parking laws and regulations does not have immediate access to those records, a citation shall not be issued for failure to comply with subdivision (a) of Section 5204. A person authorized to enforce parking laws and regulations shall issue a written notice of parking violation for a vehicle that does not have a tab or a verified current registration, setting forth the alleged violation. The violation shall be processed pursuant to this section.

(2) Commencing on July 1, 2024, a violation of paragraph (1) shall not be the basis for any enforcement action before the second month after the month of expiration of the vehicle's registration. This paragraph shall become inoperative on January 1, 2030.

(c) The civil penalty for each equipment violation, including failure to properly display a license plate, is the amount established for the violation in the Uniform Bail and Penalty Schedule, as adopted by the Judicial Council, except that upon proof of the correction to the processing agency, the penalty shall be reduced to ten dollars ($10). The reduction provided for in this subdivision involving failure to properly display license plates shall only apply if, at the time of the violation, valid license plates were issued for that vehicle in accordance with this code. The civil penalty for each violation of Section 5204 is the amount established for the violation in the Uniform Bail and Penalty Schedule, as adopted by the Judicial Council, except that upon proof of the correction to the processing agency, the penalty shall be reduced to ten dollars ($10).

(d) Fifty percent of any penalty collected pursuant to this section for registration or equipment violations by a processing agency shall be paid to the county for remittance to the State Treasurer and the remaining 50 percent shall be retained by the issuing agency and processing agency subject to the terms of the contract described in Section 40200.5.

(e) Subdivisions (a) and (b) do not preclude the recording of a violation of subdivision (a) or (b) of Section 4000 on a notice of parking violation or the adjudication of that violation under the civil process set forth in this article.

(Amended by Stats. 2023, Ch. 297, Sec. 3. (AB 256) Effective January 1, 2024.)

40226. An issuing agency may, in lieu of collecting a fine for a citation for failure to display a disabled placard, charge an administrative fee not to exceed twenty-five dollars ($25) to process cancellation of a citation in any case where the individual who received the citation can show proof that he or she had been issued a valid placard at the time the citation was received.

(Added by Stats. 2002, Ch. 640, Sec. 5. Effective January 1, 2003.)

40230. (a) Within 30 calendar days after the mailing or personal delivery of the final decision described in subdivision (b) of Section 40215, the contestant may seek review by filing an appeal to be heard by the superior court where the same shall be heard de novo, except that the contents of the processing agency's file in the case shall be received in evidence. A copy of the notice of parking violation or, if the citation was issued electronically, a true and correct abstract containing the information set forth in the notice of parking violation shall be admitted into evidence as prima facie evidence of the facts stated therein. A copy of the notice of appeal shall be served in person or by first-class mail upon the processing agency by the contestant. For purposes of computing the 30-calendar-day period, Section 1013 of the Code of Civil Procedure shall be applicable. A proceeding under this subdivision is a limited civil case.

(b) The fee for filing the notice of appeal is as provided in Section 70615 of the Government Code. The court shall request that the processing agency's file on the case be forwarded to the court, to be received within 15 calendar days of the request. The court shall notify the contestant of the appearance date by mail or personal delivery. The court shall retain the fee under Section 70615 of the Government Code regardless of the outcome of the appeal. If the court finds in favor of the contestant, the amount of the fee shall be reimbursed to the contestant by the processing agency. Any deposit of parking penalty shall be refunded by the processing agency in accordance with the judgment of the court.

(c) The conduct of the appeal under this section is a subordinate judicial duty that may be performed by traffic trial commissioners and other subordinate judicial officials at the direction of the presiding judge of the court.

(d) If no notice of appeal of the processing agency's decision is filed within the period set forth in subdivision (a), the decision shall be deemed final.

(e) If the parking penalty has not been deposited and the decision is against the contestant, the processing agency shall, after the decision becomes final, proceed to collect the penalty pursuant to Section 40220.

(Amended by Stats. 2007, Ch. 738, Sec. 43. Effective January 1, 2008.)

Article 3.5. Procedure on Video Imaging of Parking Violations Occurring in Transit-Only Lanes

(Article 3.5 added by Stats. 2007, Ch. 377, Sec. 3.)

40240. (a) A public transit operator, as defined in Section 99210 of the Public Utilities Code, may install automated forward facing parking control devices on city-owned or district-owned public transit vehicles, as defined by Section 99211 of the Public Utilities Code, for the purpose of video imaging of parking violations occurring in transit-only traffic lanes and at transit stops. Citations shall be issued only for violations captured during the posted hours of operation for a transit-only traffic lane or during the scheduled operating hours at transit stops. The devices shall be angled and focused so as to capture video images of parking violations and not unnecessarily capture identifying images of other drivers, vehicles, and pedestrians. The devices shall record the date and time of the violation at the same time as the video images are captured. Transit agencies may share the relevant data, video, and images of parking violations collected by automated forward facing parking control devices with the local parking enforcement entity and local agency in the jurisdiction where the violation occurred. A transit operator, including the City and County of San Francisco and the Alameda-Contra Costa Transit District, may only install forward facing cameras pursuant to this section if the examiner or issuing agency, as described in Section 40215, includes options to reduce or waive the payment of a parking penalty if the examiner or issuing agency determines that the person is an indigent person as defined in Section 40220.

(b) Prior to issuing notices of parking violations pursuant to subdivision (a) of Section 40241, a public transit operator, in partnership with a city, county, city and county, or local enforcement authority, shall commence a program to issue only warning notices for 60 days and shall also make a public announcement of the program and provide the public with information about the enforcement program, existing parking regulations, and the payment options available for low-income persons at least 60 days prior to commencement of issuing notices of parking violations.

(c) A designated employee of a city, county, city and county, or a contracted law enforcement agency for a special transit district, who is qualified by a city, county, city and county, or district to issue parking citations, shall review video image recordings for the purpose of determining whether a parking violation occurred in a transit-only traffic lane or at a transit stop. A violation of a statute, regulation, or ordinance governing vehicle parking under this code, under a federal or state statute or regulation, or under an ordinance enacted by a city, county, city and county, or special transit district occurring in a transit-only traffic lane or at a transit stop observed by the designated employee in the recordings is subject to a civil penalty.

(d) The registered owner shall be permitted to review the video image evidence of the alleged violation during normal business hours at no cost.

(e) (1) Except as it may be included in court records described in Section 68152 of the Government Code, or as provided in paragraph (2), the video image evidence may be retained for up to six months from the date the information was first obtained, or 60 days after final disposition of the citation, whichever date is later, after which time the information shall be destroyed.

(2) Notwithstanding Section 26202.6 of the Government Code, video image evidence from forward facing automated enforcement devices that does not contain evidence of a parking violation occurring in a transit-only traffic lane or at a transit stop shall be destroyed within 15 days after the information was first obtained. Video image data and records collected pursuant to this section shall not be used or processed by an automated license plate recognition system, as defined in Section 1798.90.5 of the Civil Code, unless the public transit operator, city, county, city and county, or local enforcement authority meets the requirements in this paragraph and paragraph (1), the requirements of subdivision (f), and the requirements of subdivision (e) of Section 40241.

(f) Notwithstanding Article 1 (commencing with Section 7922.500) and Article 2 (commencing with Section 7922.525) of Chapter 1 of Part 3 of Division 10 of Title 1 of the Government Code, or any other law, the video image records are confidential. Public agencies shall use and allow access to these records only for the purposes authorized by this article.

(g) The following definitions shall apply for purposes of this article:

(1) "Local agency" means a public transit operator as defined in Section 99210 of the Public Utilities Code or a local city, county, or city and county parking enforcement authority.

(2) "Transit-only traffic lane" means any designated transit-only lane on which use is restricted to mass transit vehicles, or other designated vehicles including taxis and vanpools, during posted times.

(h) This section shall remain in effect only until January 1, 2027, and as of that date is repealed.

(Amended (as amended by Stats. 2021, Ch. 709, Sec. 1) by Stats. 2022, Ch. 28, Sec. 155. (SB 1380) Effective January 1, 2023. Repealed as of January 1, 2027, by its own provisions. See later operative version, as amended by Sec. 156 of Stats. 2022, Ch. 28.)

40240. (a) The City and County of San Francisco may install automated forward facing parking control devices on city-owned or district-owned public transit vehicles, as defined in Section 99211 of the Public Utilities Code, for the purpose of video imaging of parking violations occurring in transit-only traffic lanes and at transit stops. Citations shall be issued only for violations captured during the posted hours of operation for a transit-only traffic lane or during the scheduled operating hours at transit stops. The devices shall be angled and focused so as to capture video images of parking violations and not unnecessarily capture identifying images of other drivers, vehicles, and pedestrians. The devices shall record the date and time of the violation at the same time as the video images are captured. Transit agencies may share the relevant data, video, and images of parking violations collected by automated forward facing parking control devices with the local parking enforcement entity and local agency in the jurisdiction where the violation occurred. The City and County of San Francisco may only install forward facing cameras pursuant to this section if the examiner or issuing agency, as described in Section 40215, includes options to reduce or waive the payment of a parking penalty if the examiner or issuing agency determines that the person is an indigent person as defined in Section 40220.

(b) Prior to issuing notices of parking violations pursuant to subdivision (a) of Section 40241, the City and County of San Francisco shall commence a program to issue only warning notices for 60 days and shall also make a public announcement of the program and provide the public with information about the enforcement program, existing parking regulations, and the payment options available for low-income persons at least 60 days prior to commencement of issuing notices of parking violations.

(c) A designated employee of the City and County of San Francisco who is qualified to issue parking citations shall review video image recordings for the purpose of determining whether a parking violation occurred in a transit-only traffic lane or at a transit stop. A violation of a statute, regulation, or ordinance governing vehicle parking under this code, under a federal or state statute or regulation, or under an ordinance enacted by the City and County of San Francisco occurring in a transit-only traffic lane or at a transit stop observed by the designated employee in the recordings is subject to a civil penalty.

(d) The registered owner shall be permitted to review the video image evidence of the alleged violation during normal business hours at no cost.

(e) (1) Except as it may be included in court records described in Section 68152 of the Government Code, or as provided in paragraph (2), the video image evidence may be retained for up to six months from the date the information was first obtained, or 60 days after final disposition of the citation, whichever date is later, after which time the information shall be destroyed.

(2) Notwithstanding Section 26202.6 of the Government Code, video image evidence from forward facing automated enforcement devices that does not contain evidence of a parking violation occurring in a transit-only traffic lane or at a transit stop shall be destroyed within 15 days after the information was first obtained. Video image data and records collected pursuant to this section shall not be used or processed by an automated license plate recognition system, as defined in Section 1798.90.5 of the Civil Code, unless the public transit operator, city, county, city and county, or local enforcement authority meets the requirements of this paragraph and paragraph (1), the requirements of subdivision (f), and the requirements of subdivision (e) of Section 40241.

(f) Notwithstanding Article 1 (commencing with Section 7922.500) and Article 2 (commencing with Section 7922.525) of Chapter 1 of Part 3 of Division 10 of Title 1 of the Government Code or any other law, the video image records are confidential. Public agencies shall use and allow access to these records only for the purposes authorized by this article.

(g) For purposes of this article, "transit-only traffic lane" means any designated transit-only lane on which use is restricted to mass transit vehicles or other designated vehicles, including taxis and vanpools, during posted times.

(h) This section shall become operative on January 1, 2027.

(Amended (as added by Stats. 2021, Ch. 709, Sec. 2) by Stats. 2022, Ch. 28, Sec. 156. (SB 1380) Effective January 1, 2023. Operative January 1, 2027, by its own provisions.)

40240.5. (a) A public transit operator, including the Alameda-Contra Costa Transit District, that implements an automated enforcement system to enforce parking violations occurring in transit-only traffic lanes and at transit stops pursuant to this article, shall provide to the transportation, privacy, and judiciary committees of the Legislature an evaluation report of the enforcement system's effectiveness, impact on privacy, impact on traffic outcomes, cost to implement, change in citations issued, and generation of revenue, no later than January 1, 2025. This section shall not apply to the City and County of San Francisco.

(b) A report submitted pursuant to this section shall be submitted in compliance with Section 9795 of the Government Code.

(Repealed and added by Stats. 2021, Ch. 709, Sec. 4. (AB 917) Effective January 1, 2022.)

40241. (a) A designated employee of the local agency, including a contracted law enforcement agency, shall issue a notice of parking violation to the registered owner of a vehicle within 15 calendar days of the date of the violation. A designated employee or contracted law enforcement agency may decline to issue a ticket based on the evidence in the video illustrating hardship. The notice of parking violation shall set forth the violation of a statute, regulation, or ordinance governing vehicle parking under this code, under a federal or state statute or regulation, or under an ordinance enacted by the local agency occurring in a transit-only traffic lane or at a transit stop, a statement indicating that payment is required within 21 calendar days from the date of citation issuance, and the procedure for the registered owner, lessee, or rentee to deposit the parking penalty or contest the citation pursuant to Section 40215. The notice of parking violation shall also set forth the date, time, and location of the violation, the vehicle license number, registration expiration date, if visible, the color of the vehicle, and, if possible, the make of the vehicle. The notice of parking violation, or copy of the notice, shall be considered a record kept in the ordinary course of business of the local agency and shall be prima facie evidence of the facts contained in the notice. The local agency shall send information regarding the process for requesting review of the video image evidence along with the notice of parking violation.

(b) The notice of parking violation shall be served by depositing the notice in the United States mail to the registered owner's last known address listed with the Department of Motor Vehicles. Proof of mailing demonstrating that the notice of parking violation was mailed to that address shall be maintained by the local agency. If the registered owner, by appearance or by mail, makes payment to the processing agency or contests the violation within either 21 calendar days from the date of mailing of the citation, or 14 calendar days after the mailing of the notice of delinquent parking violation, the parking penalty shall consist solely of the amount of the original penalty.

(c) If, within 21 days after the notice of parking violation is issued, the local agency determines that, in the interest of justice, the notice of parking violation should be canceled, the local agency shall cancel the notice of parking violation pursuant to subdivision (a) of Section 40215. The reason for the cancellation shall be set forth in writing.

(d) Following an initial review by the local agency, and an administrative hearing, pursuant to Section 40215, a contestant may seek court review by filing an appeal pursuant to Section 40230.

(e) A local agency or a contracted law enforcement agency, may contract with a private vendor for the processing of notices of parking violations and notices of delinquent violations. The local agency shall maintain overall control and supervision of the program.

(f) This section shall remain in effect only until January 1, 2027, and as of that date is repealed.

(Amended by Stats. 2021, Ch. 709, Sec. 5. (AB 917) Effective January 1, 2022. Repealed as of January 1, 2027, by its own provisions. See later operative version as added by Sec. 6 of Stats. 2021, Ch. 709.)

40241. (a) A designated employee of the City and County of San Francisco, including a contracted law enforcement agency, shall issue a notice of parking violation to the registered owner of a vehicle within 15 calendar days of the date of the violation. A designated employee or contracted law enforcement agency may decline to issue a ticket based on the evidence in the video illustrating hardship. The notice of parking violation shall set forth the violation of a statute, regulation, or ordinance governing vehicle parking under this code, under a federal or state statute or regulation, or under an ordinance enacted by the City and County of San Francisco occurring in a transit-only traffic lane or at a transit stop, a statement indicating that payment is required within 21 calendar days from the date of citation issuance, and the procedure for the registered owner, lessee, or rentee to deposit the parking penalty or contest the citation pursuant to Section 40215. The notice of parking violation shall also set forth the date, time, and location of the violation, the vehicle license number, registration expiration date, if visible, the color of the vehicle, and, if possible, the make of the vehicle. The notice of parking violation, or copy of the notice, shall be considered a record kept in the ordinary course of business of the City and County of San Francisco and shall be prima facie evidence of the facts contained in the notice. The City and County of San Francisco shall send information regarding the process for requesting review of the video image evidence along with the notice of parking violation.

(b) The notice of parking violation shall be served by depositing the notice in the United States mail to the registered owner's last known address listed with the Department of Motor Vehicles. Proof of mailing demonstrating that the notice of parking violation was mailed to that address shall be maintained by the City and County of San Francisco. If the registered owner, by appearance or by mail, makes payment to the processing agency or contests the violation within either 21 calendar days from the date of mailing of the citation, or 14 calendar days after the mailing of the notice of delinquent parking violation, the parking penalty shall consist solely of the amount of the original penalty.

(c) If, within 21 days after the notice of parking violation is issued, the City and County of San Francisco determines that, in the interest of justice, the notice of parking violation should be canceled, the City and County of San Francisco shall cancel the notice of parking violation pursuant to subdivision (a) of Section 40215. The reason for the cancellation shall be set forth in writing.

(d) Following an initial review by the City and County of San Francisco and an administrative hearing pursuant to Section 40215, a contestant may seek court review by filing an appeal pursuant to Section 40230.

(e) The City and County of San Francisco or a contracted law enforcement agency may contract with a private vendor for the processing of notices of parking violations and notices of delinquent violations. The City and County of San Francisco shall maintain overall control and supervision of the program.

(f) This section shall become operative on January 1, 2027.

(Repealed (in Sec. 5) and added by Stats. 2021, Ch. 709, Sec. 6. (AB 917) Effective January 1, 2022. Operative January 1, 2027, by its own provisions.)

Article 3.6. Procedure on Photographic Imaging of Parking Violations Occurring in Bicycle Lanes

(Article 3.6 added by Stats. 2023, Ch. 432, Sec. 1.)

40245. (a) A local agency may install automated forward facing parking control devices on city-owned or district-owned parking enforcement vehicles for the purpose of taking photographs of parking violations occurring in bicycle lanes, as described in Section 21207. The devices shall be angled and focused so as to only capture photographs of parking violations and not capture identifying images of other drivers, vehicles, and pedestrians. The devices shall record the date and time of the violation at the same time as the photographs are captured. A local agency may only install forward facing cameras pursuant to this section if the examiner or issuing agency, as described in Section 40215, includes options to reduce or waive the payment of a parking penalty if the examiner or issuing agency determines that the person is an indigent person as defined in Section 40220.

(b) Prior to issuing notices of parking violations pursuant to Section 21211, a local agency shall commence a program to issue only warning notices for 60 days and shall also make a public announcement of the program and provide the public with information about the enforcement program, existing parking regulations, and the payment options available for low-income persons at least 60 days prior to commencement of issuing notices of parking violations.

(c) A designated employee of a city, county, city and county, or a contracted law enforcement agency for a special transit district, who is qualified by a city, county, city and county, or district to issue parking citations, shall review photographs for the purpose of determining whether a parking violation occurred in a bicycle lane. A violation of a statute, regulation, or ordinance governing vehicle parking under this code, under a federal or state statute or regulation, or under an ordinance enacted by a city, county, city and county, or special transit district occurring in a bicycle lane observed by the designated employee in the recordings is subject to a civil penalty.

(d) The registered owner shall be permitted to review the photographic evidence of the alleged violation during normal business hours at no cost.

(e) (1) Except as it may be included in court records described in Section 68152 of the Government Code, or as provided in paragraph (2), the photographic evidence may be retained for up to 30 days after final disposition of the citation. The photographic evidence shall not be retained for more than six months from the date the information was first obtained, after which time the information shall be destroyed.

(2) Notwithstanding Section 26202.6 of the Government Code, photographic evidence from forward facing automated enforcement devices that does not contain evidence of a parking violation occurring in a bicycle lane shall be destroyed within 15 days after the information was first obtained. Photographic data and records collected pursuant to this section shall not be used or processed by an automated license plate recognition system, as defined in Section 1798.90.5 of the Civil Code, unless the local agency meets the requirements of this subdivision, the requirements of subdivision (f), and the requirements of subdivision (e) of Section 40247.

(f) Notwithstanding Article 1 (commencing with Section 7922.500) and Article 2 (commencing with Section 7922.525) of Chapter 1 of Part 3 of Division 10 of Title 1 of the Government Code, or any other law, the photographic records are confidential. Public agencies shall use and allow access to these records only for the purposes authorized by this article.

(g) For purposes of this article, "local agency" means a public transit operator as defined in Section 99210 of the Public Utilities Code or a local city, county, or city and county parking enforcement authority.

(Added by Stats. 2023, Ch. 432, Sec. 1. (AB 361) Effective January 1, 2024. Repealed as of January 1, 2030, pursuant to Section 40248.)

40246. (a) A local agency that implements an automated enforcement system to enforce parking violations occurring in bicycle lanes pursuant to this article shall provide to the transportation, privacy, and judiciary committees of the Legislature an evaluation report of the enforcement system's effectiveness, impact on privacy, impact on traffic outcomes, cost to implement, change in citations issued, and generation of revenue, no later than December 31, 2028.

(b) A report submitted pursuant to this section shall be submitted in compliance with Section 9795 of the Government Code.

(Added by Stats. 2023, Ch. 432, Sec. 1. (AB 361) Effective January 1, 2024. Repealed as of January 1, 2030, pursuant to Section 40248.)

40247. (a) A designated employee of a local agency, including a contracted law enforcement agency, shall issue a notice of parking violation to the registered owner of a vehicle within 15 calendar days of the date of the violation. A designated employee or contracted law enforcement agency may decline to issue a ticket based on the evidence in the photograph illustrating hardship. The notice of parking violation shall set forth the violation of a statute, regulation, or ordinance governing vehicle parking under this code, under a federal or state statute or regulation, or under an ordinance enacted by the local agency in a bicycle lane, a statement indicating that payment is required within 21 calendar days from the date of citation issuance, and the procedure for the registered owner, lessee, or rentee to deposit the parking penalty or contest the citation pursuant to Section 40215. The notice of parking violation shall also set forth the date, time, and location of the violation, the vehicle license number, the registration expiration date, if visible, the color of the vehicle, and a copy of the photographic evidence. The notice of parking violation, or copy of the notice, shall be considered a record kept in the ordinary course of business of the local agency and shall be prima facie evidence of the facts contained in the notice. The local agency shall send information regarding the process for requesting review of the photographic evidence along with the notice of parking violation.

(b) The notice of parking violation shall be served by depositing the notice in the United States mail to the registered owner's last known address listed with the Department of Motor Vehicles. Proof of mailing demonstrating that the notice of parking violation was mailed to that address shall be maintained by the local agency. If the registered owner, by appearance or by mail, makes payment to the processing agency or contests the violation within either 21 calendar days from the date of mailing of the citation, or 14 calendar days after the mailing of the notice of delinquent parking violation, the parking penalty shall consist solely of the amount of the original penalty.

(c) If, within 21 days after the notice of parking violation is issued, the local agency determines that, in the interest of justice, the notice of parking violation should be canceled, the local agency shall cancel the notice of parking violation pursuant to subdivision (a) of Section 40215. The reason for the cancellation shall be set forth in writing.

(d) Following an initial review by the local agency and an administrative hearing pursuant to Section 40215, a contestant may seek court review by filing an appeal pursuant to Section 40230.

(e) A local agency or a contracted law enforcement agency may contract with a private vendor for the processing of notices of parking violations and notices of delinquent violations. The local agency shall maintain overall control and supervision of the program.

(Added by Stats. 2023, Ch. 432, Sec. 1. (AB 361) Effective January 1, 2024. Repealed as of January 1, 2030, pursuant to Section 40248.)

40248. This article shall remain in effect only until January 1, 2030, and as of that date is repealed.

(Added by Stats. 2023, Ch. 432, Sec. 1. (AB 361) Effective January 1, 2024. Repealed as of January 1, 2030, by its own provisions. Repeal affects Article 3.6, commencing with Section 40245.)

Article 4. Procedure on Toll Evasion Violations

(Article 4 added by Stats. 1995, Ch. 739, Sec. 8.)

40250. (a) Except where otherwise specifically provided, a violation of a statute, regulation, or ordinance governing the evasion of tolls on toll facilities under this code, under a federal or state statute or regulation, or under an ordinance enacted by a local authority including a joint powers authority, or a district organized pursuant to Part 3 (commencing with Section 27000) of Division 16 of the Streets and Highways Code is subject to a civil penalty. The enforcement of a civil penalty is governed by the civil administrative procedures set forth in this article.

(b) Except as provided in Section 40264, the registered owner, driver, rentee, or lessee of a vehicle cited for a toll evasion violation of a toll facility, under an applicable statute, regulation, or ordinance shall be jointly and severally liable for the toll evasion penalty imposed under this article, unless the owner can show that the vehicle was used without the express or implied consent of that person. A person who pays a toll evasion penalty, a civil judgment, costs, or administrative fees pursuant to this article has the right to recover the same from the driver, rentee, or lessee.

(c) The driver of a vehicle who is not the vehicle owner but who uses or operates the vehicle with the express or implied permission of the owner is the agent of the owner to receive a notice of a toll evasion violation served in accordance with this article and may contest the notice of violation.

(d) If the driver of the vehicle is in violation of a statute, regulation, or ordinance governing toll evasion violations, and if the driver is arrested pursuant to Article 1 (commencing with Section 40300) of Chapter 2, this article does not apply.

(e) For the purposes of this article, the following definitions apply:

(1) "Issuing agency" is an entity, public or private, authorized to collect tolls.

(2) "Registered owner" is either of the following:

(A) A person described in Section 505.

(B) A person registered as the owner of the vehicle by the appropriate agency or authority of another state, the District of Columbia, or a territory or possession of the United States.

(Amended by Stats. 2007, Ch. 150, Sec. 1. Effective July 27, 2007.)

40251. All toll evasion penalties collected by the processing agency, as defined in Section 40253, including all administrative fees, process service fees, and fees and collection costs related to civil debt collection, shall be deposited to the account of the issuing agency, except that those sums attributable to the issuance of a toll evasion violation by a member of the California Highway Patrol shall be deposited in accordance with Article 1 (commencing with Section 42200) of Chapter 2 of Division 18 in the city or county where the violation occurred. At the end of each fiscal year, the issuing agencies of facilities which have been developed pursuant to Section 143 of the Streets and Highways Code shall deposit in the State Highway Account in the State Transportation Fund any amounts collected under Section 40253 in excess of the sum of the unpaid toll, administrative fees, other costs incurred by the issuing agency that are related to toll evasion, process service fees, and fees and collection costs related to civil debt collection.

(Added by Stats. 1995, Ch. 739, Sec. 8. Effective January 1, 1996.)

40252. (a) An issuing agency may elect to contract with the state, the county, a local authority, or a district organized pursuant to Part 3 (commencing with Section 27000) of Division 16 of the Streets and Highways Code, or with a private vendor, for the processing of notices of toll evasion violations and notices of delinquent toll evasion violations, prior to filing with the court pursuant to Section 40256.

(b) As used in this article, "toll evasion penalty" includes, but is not limited to, any late payment penalty, administrative fee, fine, assessment, and costs of collection as provided by law.

(Added by Stats. 1995, Ch. 739, Sec. 8. Effective January 1, 1996.)

40253. If a contract is entered into pursuant to Section 40252, for the purpose of this article, "processing agency" means the party responsible for the processing of the notices of toll evasions and notices of delinquent toll evasions. Absent such contract, "processing agency" shall be synonymous with "issuing agency."

(Added by Stats. 1995, Ch. 739, Sec. 8. Effective January 1, 1996.)

40254. (a) If a vehicle is found, by automated devices, visual observation, or otherwise, to have evaded tolls on a toll road or toll bridge, and subdivision (d) of Section 40250 does not apply, an issuing agency or a processing agency, as the case may be, shall, within 21 days of the violation, forward to the registered owner a notice of toll evasion violation setting forth the violation, including reference to the section violated, the approximate time thereof, and the location where the violation occurred. If accurate information concerning the identity and address of the registered owner is not available to the processing agency within 21 days of the violation, the processing agency shall have an additional 45 calendar days to obtain such information and forward the notice of toll evasion violation. If the registered owner is a repeat violator, the processing agency shall forward the notice of toll evasion violation within 90 calendar days of the violation. "Repeat violator" means any registered owner for whom more than five violations have been issued pursuant to this section in any calendar month within the preceding 12-month period. The notice of toll evasion violation shall also set forth, if applicable, all of the following:

(1) The vehicle license plate number.

(2) If practicable, the registration expiration date and the make of the vehicle.

(3) If a vehicle is found, by automated devices, to have evaded the toll through failure to meet occupancy requirements in a high-occupancy toll lane, a copy of photographic evidence on which the determination was based.

(4) A clear and concise explanation of the procedures for contesting the violation and appealing an adverse decision pursuant to Sections 40255 and 40256.

(b) After the authorized person has notified the processing agency of a toll evasion violation, the processing agency shall prepare and forward the notice of violation to the registered owner of the vehicle cited for the violation. Any person, including the authorized person and any member of the person's department or agency, or any peace officer who, with intent to prejudice, damage, or defraud, is found guilty of altering, concealing, modifying, nullifying, or destroying, or causing to be altered, concealed, modified, nullified, or destroyed, the face of the original or any copy of a notice that was retained by the authorized person before it is filed with the processing agency or with a person authorized to receive the deposit of the toll evasion violation is guilty of a misdemeanor.

(c) If, after a copy of the notice of toll evasion violation has been sent to the registered owner, the issuing person determines that, due to a failure of proof of apparent violation, the notice of toll evasion violation should be dismissed, the issuing agency may recommend, in writing, that the charges be dismissed. The recommendation shall cite the reasons for the recommendation and shall be filed with the processing agency.

(d) If the processing agency makes a finding that there are grounds for dismissal, the notice of toll evasion violation shall be canceled pursuant to Section 40255.

(e) A personal relationship with any law enforcement officer, public official, law enforcement agency, processing agency, or toll operating agency or entity shall not be grounds for dismissal of the violation.

(f) The processing agency shall use its best efforts to obtain accurate information concerning the identity and address of the registered owner for the purpose of forwarding a notice of toll evasion violation pursuant to subdivision (a).

(Amended by Stats. 2019, Ch. 497, Sec. 278. (AB 991) Effective January 1, 2020.)

40255. (a) Within 21 days from the issuance of the notice of toll evasion violation, or within 30 days from the mailing of the notice of delinquent toll evasion, whichever occurs later, a person may contest a notice of toll evasion violation or a notice of delinquent toll evasion, without having to deposit the outstanding toll or toll evasion penalty. In that case, the processing agency shall do the following:

(1) The processing agency shall either investigate with its own records and staff or request that the issuing agency investigate the circumstances of the notice with respect to the contestant's written explanation of reasons for contesting the toll evasion violation. At a minimum, the processing agency or issuing agency shall review the evidence on which the alleged violation was based, including any photographs of the alleged violation, the department's registered owner information, and confirmation that a full and complete payment was not made. If, based upon the results of that investigation, the processing agency is satisfied that the violation did not occur or that the registered owner was not responsible for the violation, the processing agency shall cancel the notice of toll evasion violation and make an adequate record of the reasons for canceling the notice. The processing agency shall mail the results of the investigation to the person who contested the notice of toll evasion violation or the notice of delinquent toll evasion violation, or may email the results if the person contesting the notice requests email notification in lieu of mail and provides an email address.

(2) If the person contesting a notice of toll evasion violation or notice of delinquent toll evasion violation is not satisfied with the results of the investigation provided for in paragraph (1), the person may, within 15 days of the mailing or emailing of the results of the investigation, deposit the amount of the toll evasion penalty and request an administrative review. If the person meets the income criteria in subdivision (a) of Section 40269.5, as verified by the issuing or processing agency or their designee, the person shall only be required to deposit the amount of the toll, and not the amount of the toll evasion penalty. After January 1, 1996, an administrative hearing shall be held within 90 calendar days following the receipt of a request for an administrative hearing, excluding any time tolled pursuant to this article. The person requesting the hearing may request one continuance, not to exceed 21 calendar days.

(b) The administrative review procedure shall consist of the following:

(1) The person requesting an administrative review shall indicate to the processing agency their election for a review by mail or personal conference.

(2) If the person requesting an administrative review is a minor, that person shall be permitted to appear at an administrative review or

admit responsibility for a toll evasion violation without the necessity of the appointment of a guardian. The processing agency may proceed against that person in the same manner as if that person were an adult.

(3) (A) The administrative review shall be conducted before a reviewer designated to conduct the review by the issuing agency's governing body or chief executive officer. In the case of violations on facilities developed pursuant to Section 143 of the Streets and Highways Code, the processing agency shall contract with a public agency or a private entity that has no financial interest in the facility for the provision of administrative review services pursuant to this subdivision. The costs of those administrative review services shall be included in the administrative fees authorized by this article.

(B) In addition to any other requirements of employment, a reviewer shall demonstrate those qualifications, training, and objectivity prescribed by the issuing agency's governing body or chief executive as are necessary and which are consistent with the duties and responsibilities set forth in this article.

(C) The examiner's continued employment, performance evaluation, compensation, and benefits shall not be directly or indirectly linked to the amount of fines collected by the examiner.

(4) The officer or person authorized to issue a notice of toll evasion violation shall not be required to participate in an administrative review. The issuing agency shall not be required to produce any evidence other than the notice of toll evasion violation or copy thereof, information received from the department identifying the registered owner of the vehicle, and a statement under penalty of perjury from the person reporting the violation. The documentation in proper form shall be considered prima facie evidence of the violation.

(5) For a toll evasion violation that occurs on a vehicular crossing or toll highway where the issuing agency allows pay-by-plate toll payment, as defined in subdivision (e) of Section 23302, the officer or person authorized to issue a notice of toll evasion violation shall not be required to participate in an administrative review. The issuing agency shall not be required to produce any evidence other than the notice of toll evasion violation or copy thereof, information received from the department identifying the registered owner of the vehicle, and a statement from the officer or person authorized to issue a notice of toll evasion that the tolls or other charges and any applicable fee was not paid in accordance with the issuing agency's policies for pay-by-plate toll payment. Any officer or person who knowingly provides false information pursuant to this paragraph shall be subject to a civil penalty for each violation in the minimum amount of two hundred fifty dollars ($250) up to a maximum amount of two thousand five hundred dollars ($2,500). An action for a civil penalty may be brought by any public prosecutor in the name of the people of the State of California. The documentation in proper form shall be considered prima facie evidence of the violation.

(6) The review shall be conducted in accordance with the written procedure established by the processing agency which shall ensure fair and impartial review of contested toll evasion violations. The agency's final decision may be delivered personally or by first-class mail.

(c) This section shall become operative on July 1, 2024.

(Repealed (in Sec. 10) and added by Stats. 2022, Ch. 969, Sec. 11. (AB 2594) Effective January 1, 2023. Operative July 1, 2024, by its own provisions.)

40256. (a) Within 20 days after the mailing of the final decision described in subdivision (b) of Section 40255, the contestant may seek review by filing an appeal to the superior court, where the same shall be heard de novo, except that the contents of the processing agency's file in the case on appeal shall be received in evidence. A copy of the notice of toll evasion violation shall be admitted into evidence as prima facie evidence of the facts stated therein. A copy of the notice of appeal shall be served in person or by first-class mail upon the processing agency by the contestant. For purposes of computing the 20-day period, Section 1013 of the Code of Civil Procedure shall be applicable. A proceeding under this subdivision is a limited civil case.

(b) Notwithstanding Section 72055 of the Government Code, the fee for filing the notice of appeal shall be twenty-five dollars ($25). If the appellant prevails, this fee, together with any deposit of toll evasion penalty, shall be promptly refunded by the processing agency in accordance with the judgment of the court.

(c) The conduct of the hearing on appeal under this section is a subordinate judicial duty which may be performed by commissioners and other subordinate judicial officials at the direction of the presiding judge of the court.

(d) If no notice of appeal of the processing agency's decision is filed within the period set forth in subdivision (a), the decision shall be deemed final.

(e) If the toll evasion penalty has not been deposited and the decision is adverse to the contestant, the processing agency may, promptly after the decision becomes final, proceed to collect the penalty under Section 40267.

(Amended by Stats. 2002, Ch. 784, Sec. 602. Effective January 1, 2003.)

40257. The notice of toll evasion violation shall be accompanied by a written notice of the toll evasion penalty due for that violation and the address of the person authorized to receive a deposit of the toll evasion penalty, to whom payments may be sent, and a statement in bold print that payments of the toll evasion penalty for the toll evasion violation may be sent through the mail.

(Added by Stats. 1995, Ch. 739, Sec. 8. Effective January 1, 1996.)

40258. (a) (1) The schedule of toll evasion penalties for a toll evasion violation on a toll bridge shall not exceed twenty-five dollars ($25) for the notice of toll evasion violation, and shall not exceed fifty dollars ($50) for the notice of delinquent toll evasion violation for a cumulative total of fifty dollars ($50) for each individual toll evasion violation.

(2) Notwithstanding paragraph (1), the schedule of toll evasion penalties may include any administrative fee, fine, or assessment imposed by the state after enactment of this chapter in addition to the cumulative fifty-dollar ($50) limit per each individual toll evasion violation.

(b) If the registered owner, by appearance or by mail, makes payment to the processing agency within 15 days of the mailing of the notice of toll evasion violation issued pursuant to subdivision (a) of Section 40254 for a bridge toll evasion, the amount owed shall consist of the amount of the toll without any additional penalties, administrative fees, or charges.

(c) The maximum penalty for each toll evasion violation included in a notice of toll evasion for either a toll highway, toll road, or express lane shall be sixty dollars ($60). The maximum cumulative toll evasion penalty shall not exceed one hundred dollars ($100) for each individual toll evasion violation.

(d) Toll evasion penalties under this article shall be collected as civil penalties.

(e) The amounts specified in this section may be adjusted periodically by an issuing agency at a rate not to exceed any increase in the California Consumer Price Index as compiled and reported by the Department of Industrial Relations.

(f) An issuing agency shall waive the toll evasion penalty for a first violation with the issuing agency if the person contacts, as applicable, the issuing or processing agency customer service center within 21 days from the mailing of the notice of toll evasion violation, and the person is not currently an accountholder with the issuing agency, signs up for an account, and pays the outstanding toll.

(g) This section shall become operative on July 1, 2024.

(Repealed (in Sec. 12) and added by Stats. 2022, Ch. 969, Sec. 13. (AB 2594) Effective January 1, 2023. Operative July 1, 2024, by its own provisions.)

40259. If the toll evasion penalty is received by the person authorized to receive the deposit of the toll evasion penalty and there is no contest as to that toll evasion violation, the proceedings under this article shall terminate.

(Added by Stats. 1995, Ch. 739, Sec. 8. Effective January 1, 1996.)

40260. (a) If the payment of the toll evasion penalty is not received by the person authorized to receive a deposit of the toll evasion penalty by the time and date fixed for appearance on the notice of toll evasion violation under Section 40254, the processing agency shall serve or mail to the registered owner a notice of delinquent toll evasion violation.

(b) Delivery of a notice of delinquent toll evasion violation under this section may be made by personal service or by first-class mail addressed to the registered owner.

(Added by Stats. 1995, Ch. 739, Sec. 8. Effective January 1, 1996.)

40261. (a) Within 10 days from the mailing of a notice of delinquent toll evasion violation, any person or his or her agent, may request by mail or in person a photostatic copy or an electronically produced facsimile of the original notice of toll evasion violation. The issuing agency may charge a fee sufficient to recover the actual cost of providing the copy, not to exceed two dollars ($2). Within 15 days of the request, the processing agency shall mail or otherwise provide the copy. Until the issuing agency complies with a request for a copy of the original notice of toll evasion violation, the processing agency may not proceed pursuant to subdivision (i) of Section 22651, or Section 22651.7 or 40267.

(b) If the description of the vehicle on the notice of toll evasion violation does not match the department's corresponding vehicle registration record, the processing agency may, on written request of the person, cancel the notice of toll evasion violation without the necessity of an appearance by that person.

(Added by Stats. 1995, Ch. 739, Sec. 8. Effective January 1, 1996.)

40262. (a) (1) The notice of delinquent toll evasion violation shall contain the information specified in Section 40254 and, additionally shall contain a notice to the registered owner that, unless the registered owner pays the toll evasion penalty or contests the notice within 30 days after mailing of the notice of delinquent toll evasion violation or completes and files an affidavit of nonliability that complies with Section 40263 or 40264, the renewal of the vehicle registration shall be contingent upon compliance with the notice of delinquent toll evasion violation.

(2) If the toll evasion penalty is not paid as specified in the notice of delinquent toll evasion violation, the issuing agency may notify the department and the department shall refuse to renew that person's vehicle registration pursuant to Section 4770. If the registered owner pays the toll, toll evasion penalty, and all related fees, or enters into a payment plan pursuant to Section 40269.5 and makes the first payment, the issuing or processing agency shall notify the department electronically, and the department shall not refuse renewal of the person's vehicle registration. If the issuing agency subsequently notifies the department electronically that the registered owner is delinquent under the payment plan for more than 10 business days, the department shall refuse to renew the vehicle registration until the registered owner has fully satisfied the terms of the payment plan and the issuing agency has notified the department electronically.

(3) Notwithstanding paragraph (2), if a registered owner pays the toll, toll evasion penalty, and all related fees, or has entered into a payment plan authorized pursuant to subdivision (e) of Section 40269.5, and meets the agency's requirements for that payment plan, the issuing or processing agency shall notify the department electronically, and the department shall not refuse renewal of the person's vehicle registration. If the registered owner is delinquent under the payment plan for more than 10 business days and the issuing agency or processing agency subsequently notifies the department electronically, the department shall refuse to renew the vehicle registration until the registered owner has fully satisfied the terms of the payment plan and the issuing agency and the issuing agency has notified the department electronically.

(b) If the registered owner, by appearance or by mail, makes payment to the processing agency within 15 days of the mailing of the notice of delinquent toll evasion violation, the toll evasion penalty shall consist of the amount of the original penalty without any additional administrative fees or charges.

(c) This section shall become operative on July 1, 2024.

(Repealed (in Sec. 14) and added by Stats. 2022, Ch. 969, Sec. 15. (AB 2594) Effective January 1, 2023. Operative July 1, 2024, by its own provisions.)

40262.5. If the registered owner fails to pay the toll evasion penalty, as required in Section 40262, or fails to contest the violation, as provided in Section 40255, the registered owner shall be deemed liable for the violation by operation of law, and the toll evasion penalty and any administrative fees or charges shall be considered a debt due and owing the issuing agency by the registered owner.

(Added by Stats. 1995, Ch. 739, Sec. 8. Effective January 1, 1996.)

40263. The notice of delinquent toll evasion violation shall contain, or be accompanied with, an affidavit of nonliability and information of what constitutes nonliability, information as to the effect of executing the affidavit, and instructions for returning the affidavit to the issuing agency.

(Added by Stats. 1995, Ch. 739, Sec. 8. Effective January 1, 1996.)

40264. If the affidavit of nonliability is returned to the agency within 30 days of the mailing of the notice of toll evasion violation together with the proof of a written rental agreement or lease between a bona fide renting or leasing company and its customer which identifies the rentee or lessee and provides the driver's license number, name, and address of the rentee or lessee, the processing agency shall serve or mail to the rentee or lessee identified in the affidavit of nonliability a notice of delinquent toll evasion violation. If payment is not received within 15 days of the mailing of the notice of delinquent toll evasion violation, the processing agency may proceed against the rentee or lessee pursuant to Section 40267.

(Added by Stats. 1995, Ch. 739, Sec. 8. Effective January 1, 1996.)

40265. (a) If the affidavit of nonliability is returned and indicates that the registered owner served has made a bona fide sale or transfer of the vehicle and has delivered possession of the vehicle to the purchaser prior to the date of the alleged violation, the processing agency shall obtain verification from the department that the registered owner has complied with subdivision (b) of Section 5602.

(b) If the registered owner has complied with subdivision (b) of Section 5602, the processing agency shall cancel the notice of toll evasion violation with respect to the registered owner.

(c) If the registered owner has not complied with subdivision (b) of Section 5602, the processing agency shall inform the registered owner that the notice shall be paid in full or contested pursuant to Section 40255 unless the registered owner delivers evidence within 15 days of the notice that establishes that the transfer of ownership and possession of the vehicle occurred prior to the date of the alleged violation. If the registered owner does not comply with this notice, the processing agency shall proceed pursuant to Section 40220. If the registered owner delivers the evidence within 15 days of the notice, the processing agency shall cancel the notice of delinquent toll evasion violation or violations with respect to the registered owner.

(d) For purposes of subdivision (c), evidence sufficient to establish that the transfer of ownership and possession occurred prior to the date of the alleged violation or violations shall include, but is not limited to, a copy of the executed agreement showing the date of the transfer of vehicle ownership.

(e) This section does not limit or impair the ability or the right of the processing agency to pursue the collection of delinquent toll evasion penalties from the person having ownership and possession of the vehicle on the date the alleged violation occurred.

(Amended by Stats. 2008, Ch. 741, Sec. 6. Effective January 1, 2009.)

40266. (a) If the registered owner, or an agent of the registered owner, or a rentee or lessee who was served with the notice of delinquent toll evasion violation pursuant to Section 40260 or 40264, or any other person who presents the notice of toll evasion violation or notice of delinquent toll evasion violation after the notice of delinquent toll evasion violation has been issued for delivery under Section 40260, deposits that toll evasion violation penalty with a person authorized to receive it, the processing agency shall do both of the following:

(1) Deliver a copy of the notice of delinquent toll evasion violation issued under Section 40260, or a listing of the notice information presented in a notice of delinquent toll evasion violation to the person and record the name, address, and driver's license number of the person actually given the copy in the records of the issuing agency.

For the purposes of this paragraph, a copy of the notice of delinquent toll evasion violation may be a photostatic copy.

(2) Determine whether the notice of delinquent toll evasion violation has been filed with the department pursuant to subdivision (b) of Section 40267 or a civil judgment has been entered pursuant to Section 40267.

(b) If the notice of delinquent toll evasion violation has not been filed with the department or judgment entered and payment of the toll evasion penalty and any applicable assessments is received, the proceedings under this article shall terminate.

(c) If the notice of delinquent toll evasion violation has been filed with the department, has been returned to the processing agency pursuant to subdivision (b) or (c) of Section 4770 or pursuant to Section 4774, and payment of the toll evasion penalty together with the administrative service fee of the processing agency for costs of service and any applicable assessment is received, the proceedings under this article shall terminate.

(d) If the notice of delinquent toll evasion violation has been filed with the department and has not been returned to the processing agency pursuant to Section 4770, 4772, or 4774, and payment of the toll evasion penalty together with the administrative fee of the department established under Section 4773, and administrative service fee of the issuing agency for costs of service, and any applicable assessments is received by the processing agency, the processing agency shall do all of the following:

(1) Immediately transmit the payment information to the department in the manner prescribed by the department.

(2) Terminate proceedings on the notice of delinquent toll evasion violation.

(3) Transmit for deposit all toll evasion penalties and assessments in accordance with law.

(Added by Stats. 1995, Ch. 739, Sec. 8. Effective January 1, 1996.)

40267. Except as otherwise provided in Sections 40268 and 40269, the processing agency shall proceed under one or more of the following options to collect an unpaid toll evasion penalty:

(a) The processing agency may file an itemization of unpaid toll evasion penalties and administrative and service fees with the department for collection with the registration of the vehicle pursuant to Section 4770.

(b) (1) If more than four hundred dollars ($400) in unpaid penalties and fees have been accrued by a person or registered owner, the processing agency may file proof of that fact with the court with the same effect as a civil judgment. Execution may be levied and other measures may be taken for the collection of the judgment as are authorized for the collection of an unpaid civil judgment entered against a defendant in an action on a debt. The court may assess costs against a judgment debtor to be paid upon satisfaction of the judgment. The processing agency shall send a notice by first-class mail to the person or registered owner indicating that a judgment shall be entered for the unpaid penalties, fees, and costs and that, after 30 days from the date of the mailing of the notice, the judgment shall have the same effect as an entry of judgment against a judgment debtor. The person or registered owner shall also be notified at that time that execution may be levied against his or her assets, liens may be placed against his or her property, his or her wages may be garnished, and other steps may be taken to satisfy the judgment. The filing fee plus any costs of collection shall be added to the judgment amount.

(2) Notwithstanding any other provision of law, the processing agency shall pay the established first paper civil filing fee, if required by law, at the time an entry of civil judgment is requested.

(c) If the registration of the vehicle has not been renewed for 60 days beyond the renewal date, and the notice has not been collected by the department pursuant to Section 4770, the processing agency may file proof of unpaid penalties and fees with the court with the same effect as a civil judgment as provided in subdivision (b), except that if the amount of the unpaid penalties and fees is not more than four hundred dollars ($400), the filing fee shall be collectible by the court from the debtor.

(d) The issuing agency may contract with a collection agency to collect unpaid toll evasion penalties, fees, and charges.

(e) This section does not apply to the registered owner of a vehicle if the toll evasion violation occurred prior to the registered owner taking possession of the vehicle and the department has notified the processing agency pursuant to Section 4774.

(Amended by Stats. 2008, Ch. 741, Sec. 7. Effective January 1, 2009.)

40268. The processing agency shall not file a civil judgment with the court relating to a toll evasion violation which has been filed with the department unless the processing agency has determined that the registration of the vehicle has not been renewed for 60 days beyond the renewal date and the notice has not been collected by the department pursuant to Section 4770.

(Added by Stats. 1995, Ch. 739, Sec. 8. Effective January 1, 1996.)

40269. (a) The processing agency shall terminate proceedings on the notice of a delinquent toll evasion violation in any of the following cases:

(1) Upon receipt of collected penalties and administrative fees remitted by the department under Section 4772 for that notice of delinquent toll evasion violation. The termination under this subdivision is by satisfaction of the toll evasion penalty.

(2) If the notice of delinquent toll evasion violation was returned to the processing agency pursuant to Section 4774 and five years have elapsed since the date of the violation. The termination under this subdivision is by the running of a statute of limitation of proceedings.

(3) The processing agency receives information, which it shall verify with the department, that the penalty has been paid to the department pursuant to Section 4772.

(4) If the registered owner of the vehicle provides proof to the processing agency that he or she was not the registered owner on the date of the toll evasion violation.

(b) This section does not limit or impair the ability or the right of the processing agency to pursue the collection of delinquent toll evasion penalties from the person who was the registered owner or lessee of the vehicle on the date of the alleged toll evasion violation.

(Amended by Stats. 2008, Ch. 741, Sec. 8. Effective January 1, 2009.)

40269.5. (a) (1) An issuing agency shall make a payment plan option available to a person whose monthly income is 200 percent of the current poverty guidelines, or less, as updated periodically in the Federal Register by the United States Department of Health and Human Services under the authority of paragraph (2) of Section 9902 of Title 42 of the United States Code, as determined by the issuing agency or processing agency or their designee.

(2) For purposes of verifying a person's eligibility an issuing agency or processing agency or their designee shall accept all of the following: (A) unexpired proof of enrollment of participation in the CalFresh program established pursuant to (Chapter 10 (commencing with Section 18900) of Part 6 of Division 9 of the Welfare and Institutions Code), Medi-Cal, or another low-income program with the same or more exacting low-income requirement; or (B) an unexpired county benefit eligibility letter. Other evidence of the persons' income may also be accepted, as determined to be sufficient by the issuing agency or processing agency or their designee.

(b) The payment plan option for qualifying individuals shall do all of the following:

(1) Apply to toll evasion penalties in excess of one hundred dollars ($100).

(2) Require payment of no more than twenty-five dollars ($25) per month for total outstanding toll evasion penalties of six hundred dollars

($600) or less.

(3) Include no prepayment penalty for paying off the balance prior to the payment period expiring.

(4) Include a process for removal of any registration hold placed pursuant to Section 4770.

(c) Information regarding the issuing agency's payment plan policy shall be posted on an internet website related to the issuing agency's electronic toll collection system.

(d) Notwithstanding subdivision (a), the issuing agency shall not be required to offer more than one payment plan to a person at any given time. The issuing agency shall not be required to offer a person more than two payment plans in a six-year period. The issuing agency shall not be required to offer a payment plan if the person has more than two thousand five hundred dollars ($2,500) in outstanding toll evasion penalties.

(e) The requirements of subdivisions (a) and (b) are minimum standards only, and shall not limit the discretion of the issuing agency to establish or provide payment plan options that exceed the minimum requirements in those subdivisions, including, but not limited to, allowing payment plans for a person who owes less than the amount specified in paragraph (1) of subdivision (b), and making a payment plan available to more individuals than those who meet the economic criteria in subdivision (a). For those individuals who exceed the income criteria set forth in subdivision (a), the issuing agency may set payment plan requirements that differ from those established in subdivision (a) or (b), such as requiring higher monthly payments than those specified in paragraph (2) of subdivision (b), or similar requirements.

(f) This section shall become operative on July 1, 2023, for toll bridges. With respect to toll highways, toll roads, and express lanes, this section shall become operative on July 1, 2024.

(Added by Stats. 2022, Ch. 969, Sec. 16. (AB 2594) Effective January 1, 2023.)

40270. If the notice of delinquent toll evasion violation is filed with the department pursuant to subdivision (b) of Section 40267 and the department returns the notice of delinquent toll evasion violation by notice of noncollection pursuant to subdivision (b) of Section 4770 or Section 4774, the processing agency may cancel the notice of delinquent toll evasion violation.

(Added by Stats. 1995, Ch. 739, Sec. 8. Effective January 1, 1996.)

40271. The time limitation provided by law for commencement of a civil action for a violation specified in Section 40250 shall be tolled from and after the date a notice of delinquent toll evasion violation is filed with the department pursuant to subdivision (b) of Section 40267 until the notice is returned to the processing agency under subdivision (b) of Section 4770, or Section 4772 or 4774, or is recalled by the processing agency pursuant to subdivision (b) of Section 40255.

(Added by Stats. 1995, Ch. 739, Sec. 8. Effective January 1, 1996.)

40272. Notwithstanding any other provision of law, an imposition of civil liability for a violation of Section 23302.5 shall not be deemed a conviction of a driver, rentee, lessee, or registered owner and shall not be made part of the driving record of the person upon whom that liability is imposed, nor shall it be used for insurance purposes in connection with the provision of motor vehicle insurance coverage.

(Added by Stats. 1995, Ch. 739, Sec. 8. Effective January 1, 1996.)

40273. Any information obtained pursuant to this article through the use of automated devices shall not be used for any purpose other than to identify, and obtain the mailing address information of, either of the following:

(a) Toll evasion violators, to facilitate the serving of notices of toll evasion violations and notices of delinquent toll evasion violations.

(b) Persons entering a vehicular crossing and toll highway where pay-by-plate toll payment, as defined in Section 23302, is permitted by the toll operator to facilitate the collection of tolls.

(Amended by Stats. 2009, Ch. 459, Sec. 4. (AB 628) Effective January 1, 2010.)

Chapter 2. Procedure on Arrests

(Chapter 2 enacted by Stats. 1959, Ch. 3.)

Article 1. Arrests

(Article 1 enacted by Stats. 1959, Ch. 3.)

40300. The provisions of this chapter shall govern all peace officers in making arrests for violations of this code without a warrant for offenses committed in their presence, but the procedure prescribed herein shall not otherwise be exclusive of any other method prescribed by law for the arrest and prosecution of a person for an offense of like grade.

(Enacted by Stats. 1959, Ch. 3.)

40300.2. Whenever a person is arrested for a violation of this code, or a violation of any other statute required to be reported under Section 1803, the written complaint, notice to appear in court, or other notice of violation, shall indicate whether the vehicle involved in the offense is a commercial motor vehicle, as defined in subdivision (b) of Section 15210.

(Added by Stats. 1988, Ch. 1509, Sec. 10.)

40300.5. In addition to the authority to make an arrest without a warrant pursuant to paragraph (1) of subdivision (a) of Section 836 of the Penal Code, a peace officer may, without a warrant, arrest a person when the officer has reasonable cause to believe that the person had been driving while under the influence of an alcoholic beverage or any drug, or under the combined influence of an alcoholic beverage and any drug when any of the following exists:

(a) The person is involved in a traffic crash.

(b) The person is observed in or about a vehicle that is obstructing a roadway.

(c) The person will not be apprehended unless immediately arrested.

(d) The person may cause injury to themselves or damage property unless immediately arrested.

(e) The person may destroy or conceal evidence of the crime unless immediately arrested.

(Amended by Stats. 2022, Ch. 81, Sec. 7. (AB 2198) Effective January 1, 2023.)

40300.6. Section 40300.5 shall be liberally interpreted to further safe roads and the control of driving while under the influence of an alcoholic beverage or any drug in order to permit arrests to be made pursuant to that section within a reasonable time and distance away from the scene of a traffic crash.

The enactment of this section during the 1985–86 Regular Session of the Legislature does not constitute a change in, but is declaratory of, the existing law.

(Amended by Stats. 2022, Ch. 81, Sec. 8. (AB 2198) Effective January 1, 2023.)

40301. Except as provided in this chapter, whenever a person is arrested for any violation of this code declared to be a felony, he shall be dealt with in like manner as upon arrest for the commission of any other felony.

(Enacted by Stats. 1959, Ch. 3.)

40302. Whenever any person is arrested for any violation of this code, not declared to be a felony, the arrested person shall be taken without unnecessary delay before a magistrate within the county in which the offense charged is alleged to have been committed and who has jurisdiction of the offense and is nearest or most accessible with reference to the place where the arrest is made in any of the following cases:

(a) When the person arrested fails to present both his or her driver's license or other satisfactory evidence of his or her identity and an unobstructed view of his or her full face for examination.

(b) When the person arrested refuses to give his or her written promise to appear in court.

(c) When the person arrested demands an immediate appearance before a magistrate.

(d) When the person arrested is charged with violating Section 23152.

(Amended by Stats. 2015, Ch. 82, Sec. 1. (AB 346) Effective January 1, 2016.)

40302.5. Whenever any person under the age of 18 years is taken into custody in connection with any traffic infraction case, and he is not taken directly before a magistrate, he shall be delivered to the custody of the probation officer. Unless sooner released, the probation officer shall keep the minor in the juvenile hall pending his appearance before a magistrate. When a minor is cited for an offense not involving the driving of a motor vehicle, the minor shall not be taken into custody pursuant to subdivision (a) of Section 40302 solely for failure to present a driver's license.

(Added by Stats. 1980, Ch. 1299, Sec. 2.)

40303. (a) Whenever a person is arrested for any of the offenses listed in subdivision (b) and the arresting officer is not required to take the person without unnecessary delay before a magistrate, the arrested person shall, in the judgment of the arresting officer, either be given a 10 days' notice to appear, or be taken without unnecessary delay before a magistrate within the county in which the offense charged is alleged to have been committed and who has jurisdiction of the offense and is nearest or most accessible with reference to the place where the arrest is made. The officer may require that the arrested person, if he or she does not have satisfactory identification, place a right thumbprint, or a left thumbprint or fingerprint if the person has a missing or disfigured right thumb, on the 10 days' notice to appear when a 10 days' notice is provided. Except for law enforcement purposes relating to the identity of the arrestee, a person or entity shall not sell, give away, allow the distribution of, include in a database, or create a database with, this print.

(b) Subdivision (a) applies to the following offenses:

(1) Section 10852 or 10853, relating to injuring or tampering with a vehicle.

(2) Section 23103 or 23104, relating to reckless driving.

(3) Subdivision (a) of Section 2800, insofar as it relates to a failure or refusal of the driver of a vehicle to stop and submit to an inspection or test of the lights upon the vehicle pursuant to Section 2804, that is punishable as a misdemeanor.

(4) Subdivision (a) of Section 2800, insofar as it relates to a failure or refusal of the driver of a vehicle to stop and submit to a brake test that is punishable as a misdemeanor.

(5) Subdivision (a) of Section 2800, relating to the refusal to submit vehicle and load to an inspection, measurement, or weighing as prescribed in Section 2802 or a refusal to adjust the load or obtain a permit as prescribed in Section 2803.

(6) Subdivision (a) of Section 2800, insofar as it relates to a driver who continues to drive after being lawfully ordered not to drive by a member of the Department of the California Highway Patrol for violating the driver's hours of service or driver's log regulations adopted pursuant to subdivision (a) of Section 34501.

(7) Subdivision (b), (c), or (d) of Section 2800, relating to a failure or refusal to comply with a lawful out-of-service order.

(8) Section 20002 or 20003, relating to duties in the event of an accident.

(9) Section 23109, relating to participating in a speed contest or exhibition of speed.

(10) Section 14601, 14601.1, 14601.2, or 14601.5, relating to driving while the privilege to operate a motor vehicle is suspended or revoked.

(11) When the person arrested has attempted to evade arrest.

(12) Section 23332, relating to persons upon vehicular crossings.

(13) Section 2813, relating to the refusal to stop and submit a vehicle to an inspection of its size, weight, and equipment.

(14) Section 21461.5, insofar as it relates to a pedestrian who, after being cited for a violation of Section 21461.5, is, within 24 hours, again found upon the freeway in violation of Section 21461.5 and thereafter refuses to leave the freeway after being lawfully ordered to do so by a peace officer and after having been informed that his or her failure to leave could result in his or her arrest.

(15) Subdivision (a) of Section 2800, insofar as it relates to a pedestrian who, after having been cited for a violation of subdivision (a) of Section 2800 for failure to obey a lawful order of a peace officer issued pursuant to Section 21962, is within 24 hours again found upon the bridge or overpass and thereafter refuses to leave after being lawfully ordered to do so by a peace officer and after having been informed that his or her failure to leave could result in his or her arrest.

(16) Section 21200.5, relating to riding a bicycle while under the influence of an alcoholic beverage or a drug.

(17) Section 21221.5, relating to operating a motorized scooter while under the influence of an alcoholic beverage or a drug.

(c) (1) A person contesting a charge by claiming under penalty of perjury not to be the person issued the notice to appear may choose to submit a right thumbprint, or a left thumbprint if the person has a missing or disfigured right thumb, to the issuing court through his or her local law enforcement agency for comparison with the one placed on the notice to appear. A local law enforcement agency providing this service may charge the requester no more than the actual costs. The issuing court may refer the thumbprint submitted and the notice to appear to the prosecuting attorney for comparison of the thumbprints. When there is no thumbprint or fingerprint on the notice to appear, or when the comparison of thumbprints is inconclusive, the court shall refer the notice to appear or copy thereof back to the issuing agency for further investigation, unless the court finds that referral is not in the interest of justice.

(2) Upon initiation of the investigation or comparison process by referral of the court, the court shall continue the case and the speedy trial period shall be tolled for 45 days.

(3) Upon receipt of the issuing agency's or prosecuting attorney's response, the court may make a finding of factual innocence pursuant to Section 530.6 of the Penal Code if the court determines that there is insufficient evidence that the person cited is the person charged and shall immediately notify the Department of Motor Vehicles of its determination. If the Department of Motor Vehicles determines the citation or citations in question formed the basis of a suspension or revocation of the person's driving privilege, the department shall immediately set aside the action.

(4) If the prosecuting attorney or issuing agency fails to respond to a court referral within 45 days, the court shall make a finding of factual innocence pursuant to Section 530.6 of the Penal Code, unless the court finds that a finding of factual innocence is not in the interest of justice.

(5) The citation or notice to appear may be held by the prosecuting attorney or issuing agency for future adjudication should the arrestee who received the citation or notice to appear be found.

(Amended by Stats. 2006, Ch. 288, Sec. 19. Effective January 1, 2007.)

40303.5. An arresting officer shall permit a person arrested for any of the following offenses to execute a notice containing a promise to correct the violation in accordance with the provisions of Section 40610 unless the arresting officer finds that any of the disqualifying conditions specified in subdivision (b) of Section 40610 exist:

(a) A registration infraction set forth in Division 3 (commencing with Section 4000).

(b) A driver's license infraction set forth in Division 6 (commencing with Section 12500), and subdivision (a) of Section 12951, relating to possession of a driver's license.

(c) Section 21201, relating to bicycle equipment.

(d) Subdivision (a) of Section 21212.

(e) An infraction involving equipment set forth in Division 12 (commencing with Section 24000), Division 13 (commencing with Section 29000), Division 14.8 (commencing with Section 34500), Division 16 (commencing with Section 36000), Division 16.5 (commencing with Section 38000), and Division 16.7 (commencing with Section 39000).

(f) Section 2482, relating to registration decals for vehicles transporting inedible kitchen grease.

(g) Section 9850, relating to expired vessel registration.

(h) Section 9853.2, relating to the display of vessel identification numbers.

(i) Section 678.11 of the Harbors and Navigation Code, relating to possessing a vessel operator card.

(j) Subparagraph (a) or (c) of Section 190.00 of Title 13 of the California Code of Regulations, relating to the display of vessel identification numbers.

(k) Section 190.01 of Title 13 of the California Code of Regulations, relating to vessel registration stickers.

(l) Section 6565.8 of Title 14 of the California Code of Regulations, relating to personal floatation devices on vessels.

(m) Section 6569 of Title 14 of the California Code of Regulations, relating to serviceable fire extinguishers on vessels.

(n) Section 6572 of Title 14 of the California Code of Regulations, relating to markings on fire extinguishers on vessels.

(Amended by Stats. 2021, Ch. 57, Sec. 1. (AB 591) Effective January 1, 2022.)

40304. Whenever any person is arrested by any member of the California Highway Patrol for any violation of any state law regulating the operation of vehicles or the use of the highways declared to be a misdemeanor but which offense is not specified in this code, he shall, in the judgment of the arresting officer, either be given a 10-day notice to appear in the manner provided in this chapter or be taken without unnecessary delay before a magistrate within the county in which the offense charged is alleged to have been committed and who has jurisdiction of the offense and is nearest or most accessible with reference to the place where the arrest is made, or, upon demand of the person arrested, before a magistrate in the judicial district in which the offense is alleged to have been committed.

(Enacted by Stats. 1959, Ch. 3.)

40304.5. Notwithstanding any other provision of law, whenever any person is taken into custody for bail to be collected on two or fewer outstanding warrants for failure to appear on a citation for a parking offense or a traffic infraction, the person shall be provided the opportunity immediately to post bail, and shall not be booked, photographed, or fingerprinted, nor shall an arrest record be made, when the amount of bail required to be paid on the warrant may be ascertained by reference to the face thereof or to a fixed schedule of bail, unless and until all of the following requirements have been exhausted:

(a) If the person has sufficient cash in his or her possession, that person shall be given the opportunity immediately to post bail with the person in charge of the jail or his or her designee.

(b) If the person does not have sufficient cash in his or her possession, that person shall be informed of his or her rights and given the opportunity to do all of the following:

(1) Make not less than three completed telephone calls to obtain bail. The person shall be permitted the use of the police or sheriff's department telephone to make not less than three completed local or collect long-distance telephone calls to obtain bail.

(2) Have not less than three hours in which to arrange for the deposit of bail.

(Added by Stats. 1984, Ch. 35, Sec. 3. Effective March 8, 1984. Operative March 31, 1984, by Sec. 7 of Ch. 35.)

40305. (a) Whenever a nonresident is arrested for violating any section of this code while driving a motor vehicle and does not furnish satisfactory evidence of identity and an address within this state at which he or she can be located, he or she may, in the discretion of the arresting officer, be taken immediately before a magistrate within the county where the offense charged is alleged to have been committed, and who has jurisdiction over the offense and is nearest or most accessible with reference to the place where the arrest is made. If the magistrate is not available at the time of the arrest and the arrested person is not taken before any other person authorized to receive a deposit of bail, and if the arresting officer does not have the authority or is not required to take the arrested person before a magistrate or other person authorized to receive a deposit of bail by some other provision of law, the officer may require the arrested person, if he or she has no satisfactory identification, to place a right thumbprint, or a left thumbprint or fingerprint if the person has a missing or disfigured right thumb, on the notice to appear as provided in Article 2 (commencing with Section 40500).

Except for law enforcement purposes relating to the identity of the arrestee, no person or entity may sell, give away, allow the distribution of, include in a database, or create a database with, this print.

(b) (1) A person contesting a charge by claiming under penalty of perjury not to be the person issued the notice to appear may choose to submit a right thumbprint, or a left thumbprint if the person has a missing or disfigured right thumb, to the issuing court through his or her local law enforcement agency for comparison with the one placed on the notice to appear. A local law enforcement agency providing this service may charge the requester no more than the actual costs. The issuing court may refer the thumbprint submitted and the notice to appear to the prosecuting attorney for comparison of the thumbprints. When there is no thumbprint or fingerprint on the notice to appear, or when the comparison of thumbprints is inconclusive, the court shall refer the notice to appear or copy thereof back to the issuing agency for further investigation, unless the court finds that referral is not in the interest of justice.

(2) Upon initiation of the investigation or comparison process by referral of the court, the court shall continue the case and the speedy trial period shall be tolled for 45 days.

(3) Upon receipt of the issuing agency's or prosecuting attorney's response, the court may make a finding of factual innocence pursuant to Section 530.6 of the Penal Code if the court determines that there is insufficient evidence that the person cited is the person charged and shall immediately notify the Department of Motor Vehicles of its determination. If the Department of Motor Vehicles determines the citation or citations in question formed the basis of a suspension or revocation of the person's driving privilege, the department shall immediately set aside the action.

(4) If the prosecuting attorney or issuing agency fails to respond to a court referral within 45 days, the court shall make a finding of factual innocence pursuant to Section 530.6 of the Penal Code, unless the court determines that a finding of factual innocence is not in the interest of justice.

(5) The citation or notice to appear may be held by the prosecuting attorney or issuing agency for future adjudication should the arrestee who received the citation or notice to appear be found.

(Amended by Stats. 2003, Ch. 467, Sec. 5. Effective January 1, 2004.)

40305.5. (a) If a nonresident is arrested for violating this code while driving a commercially registered motor vehicle, excluding house cars, with an unladen weight of 7,000 pounds or more, and does not furnish satisfactory evidence of identity and an address within this state at which he or she can be located, the arresting officer may, in lieu of the procedures set forth in Section 40305, accept a guaranteed traffic arrest bail bond certificate, and the nonresident shall be released from custody upon giving a written promise to appear as provided in Article 2 (commencing with Section 40500). The officer may require the arrested person, if he or she has no satisfactory identification, to place a right thumbprint, or a left thumbprint or fingerprint if the person has a missing or disfigured right thumb, on the notice to appear as provided in Article 2 (commencing with Section 45000). Except for law enforcement purposes relating to the identity of the arrestee, a person or entity shall not sell, give away, allow the distribution of, include in a database, or create a database with, this print.

(b) Every guaranteed traffic arrest bail bond certificate shall contain all of the following information:

(1) The name and address of the surety and of the issuer, if other than the surety.

(2) The name, address, driver's license number and signature of the individual covered by the certificate.

(3) The maximum amount guaranteed.

(4) Exclusions from coverage.

(5) A statement that the issuing company guarantees the appearance of a person to whom a guaranteed traffic arrest bail bond certificate is issued and, in the event of the failure of the person to appear in court at the time of trial, the issuing company shall pay any fine or forfeiture imposed on the person, not to exceed the amount stated on the certificate.

(6) The expiration date of the certificate.

(c) A guaranteed traffic arrest bail bond certificate may be issued by a surety admitted in this state. The certificate may also be issued by an association of motor carriers if all of the following conditions are met:

(1) The association is incorporated, or authorized to do business, in this state.

(2) The association is covered by a guaranteed traffic arrest bail bond issued by a surety admitted in this state.

(3) The association agrees to pay fines or bail assessed against the guaranteed traffic arrest bail bond certificate.

(4) The surety guarantees payment of fines or bail assessed against the guaranteed traffic arrest bail bond certificates issued by the association.

(d) The arresting officer shall file the guaranteed traffic arrest bail bond certificate with the notice to appear required to be filed by Section 40506.

(e) A "guaranteed traffic arrest bail bond certificate" is a document that guarantees the payment of fines or bail assessed against an individual for violation of this code, except driving while under the influence of alcohol or drugs, driving without a license or driving with a suspended or revoked license, operating a motor vehicle without the permission of the owner, or any violation punishable as a felony.

(f) A "guaranteed traffic arrest bail bond" is a bond issued by a surety guaranteeing the obligations of the issuer of guaranteed traffic arrest bail bond certificates. The bond shall be in the amount of fifty thousand dollars ($50,000) and shall be filed with the Secretary of State. Any court in this state may assess against the surety the amount of covered fines or bail that the issuer of a guaranteed traffic arrest bail bond certificate fails to pay.

(g) (1) A person contesting a charge by claiming under penalty of perjury not to be the person issued the notice to appear may choose to submit a right thumbprint, or a left thumbprint if the person has a missing or disfigured right thumb, to the issuing court through his or her local law enforcement agency for comparison with the one placed on the notice to appear. A local law enforcement agency providing this service may charge the requester no more than the actual costs. The issuing court may refer the thumbprint submitted and the notice to appear to the prosecuting attorney for comparison of the thumbprints. If there is no thumbprint or fingerprint on the notice to appear or the comparison of thumbprints is inconclusive, the court shall refer the notice to appear or copy of the notice to appear back to the issuing agency for further investigation, unless the court finds that referral is not in the interest of justice.

(2) Upon initiation of the investigation or comparison process by referral of the court, the court shall continue the case and the speedy trial period shall be tolled for 45 days.

(3) Upon receipt of the issuing agency's or prosecuting attorney's response, the court may make a finding of factual innocence pursuant to Section 530.6 of the Penal Code if the court determines that there is insufficient evidence that the person cited is the person charged and shall immediately notify the Department of Motor Vehicles of its determination. If the Department of Motor Vehicles determines the citation or citations in question formed the basis of a suspension or revocation of the person's driving privilege, the department shall immediately set aside the action.

(4) If the prosecuting attorney or issuing agency fails to respond to a court referral within 45 days, the court shall make a finding of factual innocence pursuant to Section 530.6 of the Penal Code, unless the court determines that a finding of factual innocence is not in the interest of justice.

(5) The citation or notice to appear may be held by the prosecuting attorney or issuing agency for future adjudication should the arrestee who received the citation or notice to appear be found.

(Amended by Stats. 2011, Ch. 296, Sec. 310. (AB 1023) Effective January 1, 2012.)

40306. (a) Whenever a person is arrested for a misdemeanor or an infraction and is taken before a magistrate, the arresting officer shall file with the magistrate a complaint stating the offense with which the person is charged.

(b) The person taken before a magistrate shall be entitled to at least five days continuance of his case in which to plead and prepare for trial and the person shall not be required to plead or be tried within the five days unless he waives such time in writing or in open court.

(c) The person taken before a magistrate shall thereupon be released from custody upon his own recognizance or upon such bail as the magistrate may fix.

(Amended by Stats. 1968, Ch. 1192.)

40307. (a) When an arresting officer attempts to take a person arrested for a misdemeanor or infraction of this code before a magistrate and the magistrate or person authorized to act for him or her is not available, the arresting officer shall take the person arrested, without unnecessary delay, before one of the following:

(1) The clerk of the magistrate, who shall admit the person to bail for the full amount set for the offense in a schedule fixed as provided in Section 1269b of the Penal Code.

(2) The officer in charge of the most accessible county or city jail or other place of detention within the county, who shall admit the person to bail for the full amount set for the offense in a schedule fixed as provided in Section 1269b of the Penal Code or may, in lieu of bail, release the person on his or her written promise to appear as provided in subdivisions (a) to (f), inclusive, of Section 853.6 of the Penal Code.

(b) Whenever a person is taken into custody pursuant to subdivision (a) of Section 40302 and is arrested for a misdemeanor or infraction of this code pertaining to the operation of a motor vehicle, the officer in charge of the most accessible county or city jail or other place of detention within the county may detain the person arrested for a reasonable period of time, not to exceed two hours, in order to verify his or her identity.

(Amended by Stats. 2007, Ch. 738, Sec. 44. Effective January 1, 2008.)

40309. Whenever a notice of parking violation is issued in accordance with Sections 40202 and 40203, or a notice of delinquent parking violation is issued pursuant to Section 40206, the amount fixed as a parking penalty for the violation charged may be forwarded by United States mail to the person authorized to receive a deposit of the parking penalty. Payment of a parking penalty forwarded by mail is effective only when actually received, and the presumption that a letter duly directed and mailed was received does not apply. Section 40512 is applicable to a parking penalty posted pursuant to this section.

(Amended by Stats. 1986, Ch. 939, Sec. 16.)

40310. The Judicial Council shall annually adopt a uniform traffic penalty schedule which shall be applicable to all nonparking infractions specified in this code, unless in a particular case before the court the judge or authorized hearing officer specifies a different penalty. No penalty shall be established for any infraction in an amount, exclusive of any additional penalty levied pursuant to Section 1464 of the Penal Code, in excess of the amount of the maximum fine pursuant to Section 42001 or 42001.5, and penalties shall be set without regard to residence. In case a traffic penalty is not paid within 20 days following mailing of a notice that the penalty has been assessed, a late charge shall be due in the amount of 50 percent of total initial penalty.

In establishing a uniform traffic penalty schedule, the Judicial Council shall classify the offenses into four or fewer penalty categories, according to the severity of offenses, so as to permit convenient notice and payment of the scheduled penalty.

(Amended by Stats. 1992, Ch. 696, Sec. 93. Effective September 15, 1992.)

40311. Whenever a person is arrested under authority of a warrant, the court to which such person is taken shall, with his consent, have jurisdiction to arraign him at that time for any other alleged violation of this code or an ordinance relating to traffic offenses for which he has been issued a written notice to appear in court, notwithstanding the fact that the time for appearance specified in such notice has not yet arrived.

(Added by Stats. 1959, Ch. 977.)

40312. A peace officer shall not arrest, on the basis of an outstanding warrant arising from a violation of this code, any person who presents to the peace officer a receipt, from a proper official of the court, indicating that the person has paid the fine for the violation that caused the warrant to be issued. The receipt shall contain sufficient information to identify the name and number of the court issuing the receipt, the date the case was adjudicated or the fine was paid, the case number or docket number, and the violations disposed of.

(Added by Stats. 1982, Ch. 290, Sec. 1.)

40313. If a notice of reexamination was issued pursuant to Section 21061, the record of arrest for the traffic violation, or any notice to appear issued under this article, or both, shall include a notation indicating that the notice of reexamination was issued to the arrested person and the driver's license record maintained by the department shall contain a record of the notice of reexamination. The record of the notice of reexamination shall be considered confidential by the department pursuant to Section 1808.5.

(Added by Stats. 1986, Ch. 304, Sec. 5. Operative July 1, 1987, by Sec. 6 of Ch. 304.)

Article 2. Release Upon Promise to Appear

(Article 2 enacted by Stats. 1959, Ch. 3.)

40500. (a) Whenever a person is arrested for any violation of this code not declared to be a felony, or for a violation of an ordinance of a city or county relating to traffic offenses and he or she is not immediately taken before a magistrate, as provided in this chapter, the arresting officer shall prepare in triplicate a written notice to appear in court or before a person authorized to receive a deposit of bail, containing the name and address of the person, the license number of his or her vehicle, if any, the name and address, when available, of the registered owner or lessee of the vehicle, the offense charged and the time and place when and where he or she shall appear. If the arrestee does not have a driver's license or other satisfactory evidence of identity in his or her possession, the officer may require the arrestee to place a right thumbprint, or a left thumbprint or fingerprint if the person has a missing or disfigured right thumb, on the notice to appear. Except for law enforcement purposes relating to the identity of the arrestee, no person or entity may sell, give away, allow the distribution of, include in a database, or create a database with, this print.

(b) The Judicial Council shall prescribe the form of the notice to appear.

(c) Nothing in this section requires the law enforcement agency or the arresting officer issuing the notice to appear to inform any person arrested pursuant to this section of the amount of bail required to be deposited for the offense charged.

(d) Once the arresting officer has prepared the written notice to appear, and has delivered a copy to the arrested person, the officer shall deliver the remaining original and all copies of the notice to appear as provided by Section 40506.

Any person, including the arresting officer and any member of the officer's department or agency, or any peace officer, who alters, conceals, modifies, nullifies, or destroys, or causes to be altered, concealed, modified, nullified, or destroyed, the face side of the remaining original or any copy of a citation that was retained by the officer, for any reason, before it is filed with the magistrate or with a person authorized by the magistrate or judge to receive a deposit of bail, is guilty of a misdemeanor.

If, after an arrested person has signed and received a copy of a notice to appear, the arresting officer or other officer of the issuing agency, determines that, in the interest of justice, the citation or notice should be dismissed, the arresting agency may recommend, in writing, to the magistrate or judge that the case be dismissed. The recommendation shall cite the reasons for the recommendation and be filed with the court.

If the magistrate or judge makes a finding that there are grounds for dismissal, the finding shall be entered on the record and the infraction or misdemeanor dismissed.

Under no circumstances shall a personal relationship with any officer, public official, or law enforcement agency be grounds for dismissal.

(e) (1) A person contesting a charge by claiming under penalty of perjury not to be the person issued the notice to appear may choose to submit a right thumbprint, or a left thumbprint if the person has a missing or disfigured right thumb, to the issuing court through his or her local law enforcement agency for comparison with the one placed on the notice to appear. A local law enforcement agency providing this service may charge the requester no more than the actual costs. The issuing court may refer the thumbprint submitted and the notice to appear to the prosecuting attorney for comparison of the thumbprints. When there is no thumbprint or fingerprint on the notice to appear, or when the comparison of thumbprints is inconclusive, the court shall refer the notice to appear or copy thereof back to the issuing agency for further investigation, unless the court determines that referral is not in the interest of justice.

(2) Upon initiation of the investigation or comparison process by referral of the court, the court shall continue the case and the speedy trial period shall be tolled for 45 days.

(3) Upon receipt of the issuing agency's or prosecuting attorney's response, the court may make a finding of factual innocence pursuant to Section 530.6 of the Penal Code if the court determines that there is insufficient evidence that the person cited is the person charged and shall immediately notify the Department of Motor Vehicles of its determination. If the Department of Motor Vehicles determines the citation or citations in question formed the basis of a suspension or revocation of the person's driving privilege, the department shall immediately set aside the action.

(4) If the prosecuting attorney or issuing agency fails to respond to a court referral within 45 days, the court shall make a finding of factual innocence pursuant to Section 530.6 of the Penal Code, unless the court determines that a finding of factual innocence is not in the interest of justice.

(5) The citation or notice to appear may be held by the prosecuting attorney or issuing agency for future adjudication should the arrestee who received the citation or notice to appear be found.

(Amended by Stats. 2003, Ch. 467, Sec. 7. Effective January 1, 2004.)

40501. (a) The time specified in the notice to appear shall be a specific date which is at least 21 days after the arrest, except that the court having jurisdiction over the offense charged may authorize the arresting officer to specify on the notice that an appearance may be made before the time specified.

(b) In the case of juveniles, the court having jurisdiction over the offense charged may require the arresting officer to indicate on the notice "to be notified" rather than specifying a specific date pursuant to subdivision (a).

(Amended by Stats. 1986, Ch. 557, Sec. 1. Effective August 22, 1986.)

40502. The place specified in the notice to appear shall be any of the following:

(a) Before a magistrate within the county in which the offense charged is alleged to have been committed and who has jurisdiction of the offense and is nearest or most accessible with reference to the place where the arrest is made.

(b) Upon demand of the person arrested, before a judge or other magistrate having jurisdiction of the offense at the county seat of the county in which the offense is alleged to have been committed. This subdivision applies only if the person arrested resides, or the person's principal place of employment is located, closer to the county seat than to the magistrate nearest or most accessible to the place where the arrest is made.

(c) Before a person authorized to receive a deposit of bail.

The clerk and deputy clerks of the superior court are persons authorized to receive bail in accordance with a schedule of bail approved by the judges of that court.

(d) Before the juvenile court, a juvenile court referee, or a juvenile hearing officer within the county in which the offense charged is alleged to have been committed, if the person arrested appears to be under the age of 18 years. The juvenile court shall by order designate the proper person before whom the appearance is to be made.

In a county that has implemented the provisions of Section 603.5 of the Welfare and Institutions Code, if the offense alleged to have been committed by a minor is classified as an infraction under this code, or is a violation of a local ordinance involving the driving, parking, or operation of a motor vehicle, the citation shall be issued as provided in subdivision (a), (b), or (c); provided, however, that if the citation combines an infraction and a misdemeanor, the place specified shall be as provided in subdivision (d).

If the place specified in the notice to appear is within a county where a department of the superior court is to hold a night session within a period of not more than 10 days after the arrest, the notice to appear shall contain, in addition to the above, a statement notifying the person arrested that the person may appear before a night session of the court.

(Amended by Stats. 2003, Ch. 149, Sec. 87. Effective January 1, 2004.)

40503. Every notice to appear or notice of violation and every complaint or information charging a violation of any provision of this code regulating the speed of vehicles upon a highway shall specify the approximate speed at which the defendant is alleged to have driven and exactly the prima facie or maximum speed limit applicable to the highway at the time and place of the alleged offense and shall state any other speed limit alleged to have been exceeded if applicable to the particular type of vehicle or combination of vehicles operated by the defendant.

(Amended by Stats. 1969, Ch. 1056.)

40504. (a) The officer shall deliver one copy of the notice to appear to the arrested person and the arrested person in order to secure release must give his or her written promise to appear in court or before a person authorized to receive a deposit of bail by signing two copies of the notice which shall be retained by the officer, and the officer may require the arrested person, if this person has no satisfactory identification, to place a right thumbprint, or a left thumbprint or fingerprint if the person has a missing or disfigured right thumb, on the notice to appear. Thereupon, the arresting officer shall forthwith release the person arrested from custody. Except for law enforcement purposes relating to the identity of the arrestee, no person or entity may sell, give away, allow the distribution of, include in a database, or create a database with, this print.

(b) Any person who signs a written promise to appear with a false or fictitious name is guilty of a misdemeanor regardless of the disposition of the charge upon which he or she was originally arrested.

(c) (1) A person contesting a charge by claiming under penalty of perjury not to be the person issued the notice to appear may choose to submit a right thumbprint, or a left thumbprint if the person has a missing or disfigured right thumb, to the issuing court through his or her local law enforcement agency for comparison with the one placed on the notice to appear. A local law enforcement agency providing this service may charge the requester no more than the actual costs. The issuing court may refer the thumbprint submitted and the notice to appear to the prosecuting attorney for comparison of the thumbprints. When there is no thumbprint or fingerprint on the notice to appear, or when the comparison of thumbprints is inconclusive, the court shall refer the notice to appear or copy thereof back to the issuing agency for further investigation, unless the court finds that referral is not in the interest of justice.

(2) Upon initiation of the investigation or comparison process by referral of the court, the court shall continue the case and the speedy trial period shall be tolled for 45 days.

(3) Upon receipt of the issuing agency's or prosecuting attorney's response, the court may make a finding of factual innocence pursuant to Section 530.6 of the Penal Code if the court determines that there is insufficient evidence that the person cited is the person charged and shall immediately notify the Department of Motor Vehicles of its determination. If the Department of Motor Vehicles determines the citation or citations in question formed the basis of a suspension or revocation of the person's driving privilege, the department shall immediately set aside the action.

(4) If the prosecuting attorney or issuing agency fails to respond to a court referral within 45 days, the court shall make a finding of factual innocence pursuant to Section 530.6 of the Penal Code, unless the court finds that a finding of factual innocence is not in the interest of justice.

(5) The citation or notice to appear may be held by the prosecuting attorney or issuing agency for future adjudication should the arrestee who received the citation or notice to appear be found.

(Amended by Stats. 2003, Ch. 467, Sec. 8. Effective January 1, 2004.)

40505. Whenever any traffic or police officer delivers a notice to appear or notice of violation charging an offense under this code to any person, it shall include all information set forth upon the copy of the notice filed with a magistrate and no traffic or police officer shall set forth on any notice filed with a magistrate or attach thereto or accompany the notice with any written statement giving information or containing allegations which have not been delivered to the person receiving the notice to appear or notice of violation.

(Amended by Stats. 1969, Ch. 1056.)

40506. The officer shall, as soon as practicable, file a copy of the notice with the magistrate or before a person authorized by the magistrate or judge to receive a deposit of bail specified therein, and a copy with the commissioner, chief of police, sheriff or other superior officer of the arresting officer.

(Enacted by Stats. 1959, Ch. 3.)

40506.5. Prior to the date upon which the defendant promised to appear and without depositing bail, the defendant may request a continuance of the written promise to appear. A judge of the superior court may authorize the clerk to grant the continuance.

(Amended by Stats. 2002, Ch. 784, Sec. 604. Effective January 1, 2003.)

40507. A written promise to appear in court may be complied with by an appearance by counsel.

(Enacted by Stats. 1959, Ch. 3.)

40508. (a) A person willfully violating their written promise to appear or a lawfully granted continuance of their promise to appear in court or before a person authorized to receive a deposit of bail is guilty of a misdemeanor regardless of the disposition of the charge upon which the person was originally arrested.

(b) A person willfully failing to pay bail in installments as agreed to under Section 40510.5 or a lawfully imposed fine for a violation of a provision of this code or a local ordinance adopted pursuant to this code within the time authorized by the court and without lawful excuse having been presented to the court on or before the date the bail or fine is due is guilty of a misdemeanor regardless of the full payment of the bail or fine after that time.

(c) A person willfully failing to comply with a condition of a court order for a violation of this code, other than for failure to appear or failure to pay a fine, is guilty of a misdemeanor, regardless of their subsequent compliance with the order.

(Amended by Stats. 2023, Ch. 356, Sec. 2. (AB 1125) Effective January 1, 2024.)

40508.6. The superior court in any county may establish administrative assessments, not to exceed ten dollars ($10), for clerical and administrative costs incurred for recording and maintaining a record of the defendant's prior convictions for violations of this code. The assessment shall be payable at the time of payment of a fine or when bail is forfeited for any subsequent violations of this code other than parking, pedestrian, or bicycle violations.

(Amended by Stats. 2022, Ch. 800, Sec. 22. (AB 2746) Effective January 1, 2023.)

40509.1. If any person has willfully failed to comply with a court order, except a failure to appear, to pay a fine, or to attend traffic violator school, which was issued for a violation of this code, the magistrate or clerk of the court may give notice of the fact to the department.

(Amended by Stats. 1998, Ch. 877, Sec. 77. Effective January 1, 1999.)

40510. (a) Prior to the date upon which a defendant promised to appear, or prior to the expiration of any lawful continuance of that date, or upon receipt of information that an action has been filed and prior to the scheduled court date, the defendant may deposit bail with the magistrate or the person authorized to receive a deposit of bail.

(b) For any offense which is not declared to be a felony, a deposit of bail or a penalty may be by a personal check meeting the criteria established in accordance with subdivision (c).

(c) Each court, sheriff, or other agency which regularly accepts deposits of bail or penalties, shall adopt a written policy governing the acceptance of personal checks in payment of bail or penalty deposits. The policy shall permit clerks and other appropriate officers to accept personal checks under conditions which tend to assure the validity of the checks.

(d) The written policy governing the acceptance of personal checks adopted pursuant to subdivision (c) shall provide that the payee of the deposit made by personal check shall be the agency accepting the deposit.

(Amended by Stats. 1992, Ch. 1244, Sec. 34. Effective January 1, 1993. Operative July 1, 1993, by Sec. 39 of Ch. 1244.)

40510.5. (a) The clerk of the court may accept a payment and forfeiture of at least 10 percent of the total bail amount for each infraction violation of this code prior to the date on which the defendant promised to appear, or prior to the expiration of any lawful continuance of that date, or upon receipt of information that an action has been filed and prior to the scheduled court date, if all of the following circumstances exist:

(1) The defendant is charged with an infraction violation of this code or an infraction violation of an ordinance adopted pursuant to this code.

(2) The defendant submits proof of correction, when proof of correction is mandatory for a correctable offense.

(3) The offense does not require an appearance in court.

(4) The defendant signs a written agreement to pay and forfeit the remainder of the required bail according to an installment schedule as agreed upon with the court. The Judicial Council shall prescribe the form of the agreement for payment and forfeiture of bail in installments for infraction violations.

(b) When a clerk accepts an agreement for payment and forfeiture of bail in installments, the clerk shall continue the appearance date of the defendant to the date to complete payment and forfeiture of bail in the agreement.

(c) Except for subdivisions (b) and (c) of Section 1269b and Section 1305.1, the provisions of Chapter 1 (commencing with Section 1268) of Title 10 of Part 2 of the Penal Code do not apply to an agreement to pay and forfeit bail in installments under this section.

(d) For the purposes of reporting violations of this code to the department under Section 1803, the date that the defendant signs an agreement to pay and forfeit bail in installments shall be reported as the date of conviction.

(e) When the defendant fails to make an installment payment according to an agreement under subdivision (a) above, the court may charge a failure to appear or pay under Section 40508 and impose a civil assessment as provided in Section 1214.1 of the Penal Code or issue an arrest warrant for a failure to appear.

(f) Payment of a bail amount under this section is forfeited when collected and shall be distributed by the court in the same manner as other fines, penalties, and forfeitures collected for infractions.

(g) This section shall become operative on January 1, 2022.

(Repealed (in Sec. 43) and added by Stats. 2021, Ch. 257, Sec. 44. (AB 177) Effective September 23, 2021. Operative January 1, 2022, by its own provisions.)

40511. If bail has not been previously fixed and approved by the judges of the court in accordance with a schedule of bail, the magistrate shall fix the amount of bail which in his judgment, in accordance with Section 1275 of the Penal Code, will be reasonable and sufficient for the appearance of the defendant and shall endorse upon the notice a statement signed by him in the form set forth in Section 815a of the Penal Code.

(Enacted by Stats. 1959, Ch. 3.)

40512. (a) (1) Except as specified in paragraph (2) and subdivision (b), if at the time the case is called for arraignment before the magistrate the defendant does not appear, either in person or by counsel, the magistrate may declare the bail forfeited and may, in his or her discretion, order that no further proceedings be had in the case, unless the defendant has been charged with a violation of Section 23111 or 23112, or subdivision (a) of Section 23113, and he or she has been previously convicted of the same offense, except if the magistrate finds that undue hardship will be imposed upon the defendant by requiring him or her to appear, the magistrate may declare the bail forfeited and order that no further proceedings shall be had in the case.

(2) If the defendant has posted surety bail and the magistrate has ordered the bail forfeited and that no further proceedings shall be had in the case, the bail retains the right to obtain relief from the forfeiture as provided in Section 1305 of the Penal Code if the amount of the bond, money, or property deposited exceeds seven hundred dollars ($700).

(b) (1) If, at the time the case is called for a compliance appearance before the magistrate, the defendant has entered into a bail installment agreement pursuant to Section 40510.5 but has not made an installment payment as agreed and does not appear, either in person or by counsel, the court may continue the arraignment to a date beyond the last agreed upon installment payment, issue a warrant of arrest, or impose a civil assessment as provided in Section 1214.1 of the Penal Code for the failure to appear.

(2) If, at the time the case is called for a compliance appearance before the magistrate, the defendant has paid all required bail funds and the defendant does not appear, either in person or by counsel, the court may order that no further proceedings shall be had in the case, unless the defendant has been charged with a violation of Section 23111 or 23112, or subdivision (a) of Section 23113, and he or she has been previously convicted of the same offense, except that if the magistrate finds that undue hardship will be imposed upon the defendant by requiring him or her to appear, the magistrate may order that no further proceedings shall be had in the case.

(c) Upon the making of the order that no further proceedings shall be had, all sums deposited as bail shall be paid into the city or county treasury, as the case may be.

(d) If a guaranteed traffic arrest bail bond certificate has been filed, the clerk of the court shall bill the issuer for the amount of bail fixed by the uniform countywide schedule of bail required under subdivision (c) of Section 1269b of the Penal Code.

(e) Upon presentation by a court of the bill for a fine or bail assessed against an individual covered by a guaranteed traffic arrest bail bond certificate, the issuer shall pay to the court the amount of the fine or forfeited bail that is within the maximum amount guaranteed by the terms of the certificate.

(f) The court shall return the guaranteed traffic arrest bail bond certificate to the issuer upon receipt of payment in accordance with subdivision (d).

(Amended by Stats. 2007, Ch. 738, Sec. 49. Effective January 1, 2008.)

40512.5. (a) Except as specified in subdivision (b), if at the time the case is called for trial the defendant does not appear, either in person or by counsel, and has not requested in writing that the trial proceed in his or her absence, the court may declare the bail forfeited and may, in its discretion, order that no further proceedings be had in the case, or the court may act pursuant to Section 1043 of the Penal Code. However, if the defendant has been charged with a violation of Section 23111 or 23112, or subdivision (a) of Section 23113, and he or she has been previously convicted of a violation of the same section, the court may declare the bail forfeited, but shall issue a bench warrant for the arrest of the person charged, except if the magistrate finds that undue hardship will be imposed upon the defendant by requiring him or her to appear, the magistrate may declare the bail forfeited and order that no further proceedings shall be had in the case.

(b) If the defendant has posted surety bail and the magistrate has ordered the bail forfeited and that no further proceedings shall be had in the case, the bail retains the right to obtain relief from the forfeiture as provided in Section 1305 of the Penal Code if the amount of the bond, money, or property deposited exceeds seven hundred dollars ($700).

(Amended by Stats. 1993, Ch. 524, Sec. 7. Effective January 1, 1994.)

40512.6. (a) If a defendant who elects or is ordered to attend a traffic violator school in accordance with Section 42005 and has paid the full traffic violator school bail amount required under Section 42007 fails to successfully complete the program within the time ordered by the court or any extension thereof, the court may, following notice to the defendant, order that the fee paid by the defendant be converted to bail and declare the bail forfeited. The bail forfeiture under this section shall be distributed as provided by Section 42007. Upon forfeiture of the bail, the court may order that no further proceedings shall be had in the case.

(b) This section shall become operative on July 1, 2011.

(Repealed (in Sec. 11) and added by Stats. 2010, Ch. 599, Sec. 11.5. (AB 2499) Effective January 1, 2011. Section operative July 1, 2011, by its own provisions.)

40513. (a) Whenever written notice to appear has been prepared, delivered, and filed with the court, an exact and legible duplicate copy of the notice when filed with the magistrate, in lieu of a verified complaint, shall constitute a complaint to which the defendant may plead "guilty" or "nolo contendere."

If, however, the defendant violates his or her promise to appear in court or does not deposit lawful bail, or pleads other than "guilty" or "nolo contendere" to the offense charged, a complaint shall be filed that shall conform to Chapter 2 (commencing with Section 948) of Title 5 of Part 2 of the Penal Code, which shall be deemed to be an original complaint, and thereafter proceedings shall be had as provided by law, except that a defendant may, by an agreement in writing, subscribed by him or her and filed with the court, waive the filing of a verified complaint and elect that the prosecution may proceed upon a written notice to appear.

(b) Notwithstanding subdivision (a), whenever the written notice to appear has been prepared on a form approved by the Judicial Council, an exact and legible duplicate copy of the notice when filed with the magistrate shall constitute a complaint to which the defendant may enter a plea and, if the notice to appear is verified, upon which a warrant may be issued. If the notice to appear is not verified, the defendant may, at the time of arraignment, request that a verified complaint be filed. In the case of an infraction violation in which the defendant is a minor, the defendant may enter a plea at the arraignment upon a written notice to appear. Notwithstanding any other provision of law, in the case of an infraction violation, no consent of the minor is required prior to conducting the hearing upon a written notice to appear.

(Amended by Stats. 2001, Ch. 830, Sec. 1. Effective January 1, 2002.)

40514. No warrant shall issue on the charge for the arrest of a person who has given his written promise to appear in court or before a person authorized to receive a deposit of bail, unless he has violated the promise, the lawfully granted continuance of his promise, or has failed to deposit bail, to appear for arraignment, trial or judgment, or to comply with the terms and provisions of the judgment, as required by law.

(Amended by Stats. 1979, Ch. 235.)

40515. (a) When a person signs a written promise to appear or is granted a continuance of his or her promise to appear at the time and place specified in the written promise to appear or the continuance thereof, and has not posted full bail or has failed to pay an installment of bail as agreed to under Section 40510.5, the magistrate may issue and have delivered for execution a warrant for his or her arrest within 20 days after his or her failure to appear before the magistrate or pay an installment of bail as agreed, or if the person promises to appear before an officer authorized to accept bail other than a magistrate and fails to do so on or before the date on which he or she promised to appear, then, within 20 days after the delivery of the written promise to appear by the officer to a magistrate having jurisdiction over the offense.

(b) When the person violates his or her promise to appear before an officer authorized to receive bail other than a magistrate, the officer shall immediately deliver to a magistrate having jurisdiction over the offense charged the written promise to appear and the complaint, if any, filed by the arresting officer.

(Amended by Stats. 2007, Ch. 738, Sec. 51. Effective January 1, 2008.)

40516. (a) The expenses incurred by the Department of the California Highway Patrol and the Department of Motor Vehicles in executing any warrant issued as a result of a notice to appear issued by a member of the California Highway Patrol shall be a legal charge against the city or county in which jurisdiction the warrant was issued except where the commissioner authorizes the acceptance of a warrant for execution within 30 days of the date of its issuance.

(b) The commissioner or director shall certify to the Controller the cost of executing warrants on behalf of each city or county under this section. The departments shall be reimbursed for costs as provided in Section 11004.5 of the Revenue and Taxation Code.

(c) The peace officer to whom a warrant has been delivered for execution, upon demand, shall transfer the warrant, if it has not been executed within 30 days of the date of its issuance, to any member of the California Highway Patrol or to the Department of Motor Vehicles for execution.

(Amended by Stats. 1959, Ch. 1996.)

40518. (a) Whenever a written notice to appear has been issued by a peace officer or by a qualified employee of a law enforcement agency on a form approved by the Judicial Council for an alleged violation of Section 22451, or, based on an alleged violation of Section 21453, 21455, or 22101 recorded by an automated traffic enforcement system pursuant to Section 21455.5 or 22451, and delivered by mail within 15 days of the alleged violation to the current address of the registered owner of the vehicle on file with the department, with a certificate of mailing obtained as evidence of service, an exact and legible duplicate copy of the notice when filed with the magistrate shall constitute a complaint to which the defendant may enter a plea. Preparation and delivery of a notice to appear pursuant to this section is not an arrest.

(b) (1) A notice to appear shall contain the name and address of the person, the license plate number of the person's vehicle, the violation charged, including a description of the offense, and the time and place when, and where, the person may appear in court or before a person authorized to receive a deposit of bail. The time specified shall be at least 10 days after the notice to appear is delivered. If, after the notice to appear has been issued, the citing peace officer or qualified employee of a law enforcement agency determines that, in the interest of justice, the citation or notice should be dismissed, the citing agency may recommend, in writing, to the magistrate or the judge that the case be dismissed. The recommendation shall cite the reasons for the recommendation and be filed with the court. If the magistrate or judge makes a finding that there are grounds for dismissal, the finding shall be entered on the record and the infraction dismissed.

(2) A notice to appear shall also contain all of the following information:

(A) The methods by which the registered owner of the vehicle or the alleged violator may view and discuss with the issuing agency, both by telephone and in person, the evidence used to substantiate the violation.

(B) The contact information of the issuing agency.

(c) (1) This section and Section 40520 do not preclude the issuing agency or the manufacturer or supplier of the automated traffic enforcement system from mailing a notice of nonliability to the registered owner of the vehicle or the alleged violator prior to issuing a notice to appear. The notice of nonliability shall be substantively identical to the following form:

COURTESY NOTICE: THIS IS NOT A TICKET

[insert name of jurisdiction]
PHOTO ENFORCEMENT PROGRAM
Agency Address:

<Name>
<Address>
<City State, Zip>

VIOLATION #						
ADDRESS			CITY		STATE	ZIP
COLOR	YEAR	MAKE	MODEL	STYLE	LICENSE PLATE	STATE
MONTH	DAY	YEAR	TIME			
LOCATION			VEHICLE SPEED		POSTED SPEED	
Statute			Violation Description			
Officer's Name			Badge #			

SCENE A	SCENE B
ZOOM FACE	ZOOM PLATE

Certificate of Mailing

I, (name_of_mailer), of______________________________, do certify that I am over 18 years old and not a party to the above entitled case. On (Print_Date) I placed this Notice in an envelope addressed to the registered owner or lessee as shown above, sealed it and deposited the envelope in a United States Postal Service receptacle located in (city, state). In the ordinary course of business, the envelope is sealed, affixed with proper postage and mailed. I declare under the penalty of perjury under the laws of the State of California that the foregoing is true and correct.

Dated:

Signature of Mailer

(Code of Civil Procedure 1013a [3], 2015.5)

COURTESY NOTICE: THIS IS NOT A TICKET

[Insert agency name]

INSTRUCTION PAGE

The Reason You Received This Notice:
A vehicle registered in your name was photographed failing to stop for an official red light traffic control signal. This is a violation of the State of California Vehicle Code Section 21453(a) or (c) pursuant to Section 21455.5.

You are encouraged to view the video of this violation and to respond to this notice. You may make an appointment to view the evidence by calling the [insert agency name] at (000) 000-0000. During this viewing, an officer or qualified employee will show you a high quality video and still images depicting the violation in greater detail than the printed photos in this notice.

You can also view the video online at www.0000000000.

The video is available online for 60 days from the date of violation. After 60 days an appointment must be made with [insert agency name].

DO NOT CALL THE COURT REGARDING THIS NOTICE. For additional questions contact the Photo Enforcement Program at (000) 000-0000.

Tear Here Tear Here Tear Here

NOTICE OF NON-LIABILITY

IF YOU WERE NOT THE DRIVER/OWNER
Violation #: <<Enter #>>

Last Issued To: <<Enter Name>>

[Insert agency name]

CHECK ONE:
- ☐ The person named below was the driver of the vehicle.
- ☐ I sold the vehicle prior to the violation date to the person named below.
- ☐ I have never owned this vehicle or license plate.

CHECK ONE:
- ☐ I am an individual.
- ☐ I am a car rental or leasing company.

Print Actual Driver/New Owner's Name: ______________________ **Driver's License/ID No.:** ____________

Address: ______________________________________ **Issued in the State of:** ____________

City, State, ZIP Code: ______________________________ **Date of Birth:** ____________

Gender: ________ **Hair Color:** ________ **Eye Color:** ________ **Height:** ________ **Weight:** ________

DECLARATION
I CERTIFY THAT THE FOREGOING IS TRUE AND CORRECT

Signature ______________________________ **Print Name** ______________________________

Your Telephone Number (   ) _____ - ________ **Date** ______________________________

(2) The form specified in paragraph (1) may be translated to other languages.

(d) A manufacturer or supplier of an automated traffic enforcement system or the governmental agency operating the system shall not alter the notice to appear or any other form approved by the Judicial Council. If a form is found to have been materially altered, the citation based on the altered form may be dismissed.

(Amended by Stats. 2012, Ch. 735, Sec. 4. (SB 1303) Effective January 1, 2013. Note: See published chaptered bill for complete section text. Forms relating to the Notice of Nonliability appear on pages 7 to 8 of Ch. 735.)

40519. (a) Any person who has received a written notice to appear for an infraction may, prior to the time at which the person is required to appear, make a deposit and declare the intention to plead not guilty to the clerk of the court named in the notice to appear. The deposit shall be in the amount of bail established pursuant to Section 1269b of the Penal Code, together with any assessment required by Section 42006 of this code or Section 1464 of the Penal Code, for the offense charged, and shall be used for the purpose of guaranteeing the appearance of the defendant at the time and place scheduled by the clerk for arraignment and for trial, and to apply toward the payment of any fine or assessment prescribed by the court in the event of conviction. The case shall thereupon be set for arraignment and trial on the same date, unless the defendant requests separate arraignment. A deposit of bail under this section does not constitute entry of a plea or a court appearance. A plea of not guilty under this section must be made in court at the arraignment.

(b) Any person who has received a written notice to appear may, prior to the time at which the person is required to appear, plead not guilty in writing in lieu of appearing in person. The written plea shall be directed to the court named in the notice to appear and, if mailed, shall be sent by certified or registered mail postmarked not later than five days prior to the day upon which appearance is required. The written plea and request to the court or city agency shall be accompanied by a deposit consisting of the amount of bail established pursuant to Section 1269b of the Penal Code, together with any assessment required by Section 42006 of this code or Section 1464 of the Penal Code, for that offense, which amount shall be used for the purpose of guaranteeing the appearance of the defendant at the time and place set by the court for trial and to apply toward the payment of any fine or assessment prescribed by the court in the event of conviction. Upon receipt of the plea and deposit, the case shall be set for arraignment and trial on the same date, unless the defendant requests separate arraignment. Thereafter, the case shall be conducted in the same manner as if the defendant had appeared in person, had made his or her plea in open court, and had deposited that sum as bail. The court or the clerk of the court shall notify the accused of the time and place of trial by first-class mail postmarked at least 10 days prior to the time set for the trial. Any person using this procedure shall be deemed to have waived the right to be tried within the statutory period.

(c) Any person using the procedure set forth in subdivision (a) or (b) shall be deemed to have given a written promise to appear at the time designated by the court for trial, and failure to appear at the trial shall constitute a misdemeanor.

(Amended by Stats. 2009, Ch. 35, Sec. 30. (SB 174) Effective January 1, 2010.)

40520. (a) A notice to appear issued pursuant to Section 40518 for an alleged violation recorded by an automatic enforcement system shall contain, or be accompanied by, an affidavit of nonliability and information as to what constitutes nonliability, information as to the effect of executing the affidavit, and instructions for returning the affidavit to the issuing agency.

(b) (1) If a notice to appear is sent to a car rental or leasing company, as the registered owner of the vehicle, the company may return the notice of nonliability pursuant to paragraph (2), if the violation occurred when the vehicle was either leased or rented and operated by a person other than an employee of the rental or leasing company.

(2) If the affidavit of nonliability is returned to the issuing agency by the registered owner within 30 days of the mailing of the notice to appear together with the proof of a written rental agreement or lease between a bona fide renting or leasing company and its customer and that agreement identifies the renter or lessee and provides the driver's license number, name, and address of the renter or lessee, the agency shall cancel the notice for the registered owner to appear and shall, instead, issue a notice to appear to the renter or lessee identified in the affidavit of nonliability.

(c) Nothing in this section precludes an issuing agency from establishing a procedure whereby registered owners, other than bona fide renting and leasing companies, may execute an affidavit of nonliability if the registered owner identifies the person who was the driver of the vehicle at the time of the alleged violation and whereby the issuing agency issues a notice to appear to that person.

(Added by Stats. 1998, Ch. 828, Sec. 26. Effective January 1, 1999.)

40521. (a) Except when personal appearance is required by the bail schedule established under Section 1269b of the Penal Code, a person to whom a notice to appear has been issued under Section 40500, who intends to forfeit bail and to pay any assessment may forward by United States mail the full amount fixed as bail, together with the appropriate amount of any assessment, to the person authorized to receive a deposit of bail. The amounts may be paid in the form of a personal check which meets the criteria established pursuant to subdivision (c) of Section 40510, or a bank cashier's check or a money order. Bail and any assessment shall be paid not later than the day of appearance set forth in the notice to appear or prior to the expiration of any lawful continuance of that date.

(b) Bail forwarded by mail is effective only when the funds are actually received.

(c) Paragraph (1) of subdivision (a) of Section 40512 is applicable to bail paid pursuant to this section. Upon the making of the order pursuant to Section 40512 that no further proceedings be had, the amount paid as bail shall be paid into the city or county treasury, as the case may be, and the assessment shall be transmitted to the State Treasury in the manner provided in Section 1464 of the Penal Code.

(Amended by Stats. 2007, Ch. 738, Sec. 52. Effective January 1, 2008.)

40522. Whenever a person is arrested for violations specified in Section 40303.5 and none of the disqualifying conditions set forth in subdivision (b) of Section 40610 exist, and the officer issues a notice to appear, the notice shall specify the offense charged and note in a form approved by the Judicial Council that the charge shall be dismissed on proof of correction. If the arrested person presents, by mail or in person, proof of correction, as prescribed in Section 40616, on or before the date on which the person promised to appear, the court shall dismiss the violation or violations charged pursuant to Section 40303.5.

(Amended by Stats. 1992, Ch. 258, Sec. 5. Effective January 1, 1993.)

Article 3. Notice of Violation

(Article 3 added by Stats. 1969, Ch. 1056.)

40600. (a) Notwithstanding any other provision of law, a peace officer who has successfully completed a course or courses of instruction, approved by the Commission on Peace Officer Standards and Training, in the investigation of traffic accidents may prepare, in triplicate, on a form approved by the Judicial Council, a written notice to appear when the peace officer has reasonable cause to believe that any person involved in a traffic accident has violated a provision of this code not declared to be a felony or a local ordinance and the violation was a factor in the occurrence of the traffic accident.

(b) A notice to appear shall contain the name and address of the person, the license number of the person's vehicle, if any, the name and address, when available, of the registered owner or lessee of the vehicle, the offense charged, and the time and place when and where the person may appear in court or before a person authorized to receive a deposit of bail. The time specified shall be at least 10 days after the notice to appear is delivered.

(c) The preparation and delivery of a notice to appear pursuant to this section is not an arrest.

(d) For purposes of this article, a peace officer has reasonable cause to issue a written notice to appear if, as a result of the officer's investigation, the officer has evidence, either testimonial or real, or a combination of testimonial and real, that would be sufficient to issue a written notice to appear if the officer had personally witnessed the events investigated.

(e) As used in this section, "peace officer" means any person specified under Section 830.1 or 830.2 of the Penal Code, or any reserve police officer or reserve deputy sheriff listed in Section 830.6 of the Penal Code, with the exception of members of the California National Guard.

(f) A written notice to appear prepared on a form approved by the Judicial Council and issued pursuant to this section shall be accepted by any court.

(Amended by Stats. 2003, Ch. 292, Sec. 12. Effective January 1, 2004.)

40604. (a) If the person charged with the offense has not signed a promise to appear, no warrant for arrest may be issued following the filing of the written notice to appear issued pursuant to Section 40600, until 15 days after a notice of the filing has been served upon the person by personal delivery or by mail, addressed to the person at the address shown in the accident report.

(b) The notice shall contain the name and address of the person, the license number of the vehicle involved, the name and address, when available, of the registered owner or lessee of the vehicle, the offense shown on the written notice to appear, and the approximate time of the commission of the offense. The notice shall inform the person that, unless he or she appears in the court designated in the notice within 10 days after the service of the notice and answers the charges, a warrant will be issued for his or her arrest.

(c) Proof of service shall be made by the affidavit of any person over 18 years of age making the service showing the time, place, and manner of service and facts showing that the service was made in accordance with this section. If service is made by mail, no warrant for arrest may be issued until 14 days after the deposit of the notice of filing in the mail.

(Amended by Stats. 1992, Ch. 1243, Sec. 107.7. Effective September 30, 1992. Operative January 1, 1993, by Sec. 118 of Ch. 1243.)

Article 4. Notice to Correct Violation

(Article 4 added by Stats. 1978, Ch. 1350.)

40610. (a) (1) Except as provided in paragraph (2), if, after an arrest, crash investigation, or other law enforcement action, it appears that a violation has occurred involving a registration, license, all-terrain vehicle safety certificate, or mechanical requirement of this code, and none of the disqualifying conditions set forth in subdivision (b) exist and the investigating officer decides to take enforcement action, the officer shall prepare, in triplicate, and the violator shall sign, a written notice containing the violator's promise to correct the alleged violation and to deliver proof of correction of the violation to the issuing agency.

(2) If a person is arrested for a violation of Section 4454, and none of the disqualifying conditions set forth in subdivision (b) exist, the arresting officer shall prepare, in triplicate, and the violator shall sign, a written notice containing the violator's promise to correct the alleged violation and to deliver proof of correction of the violation to the issuing agency. In lieu of issuing a notice to correct violation pursuant to this section, the officer may issue a notice to appear, as specified in Section 40522.

(b) Pursuant to subdivision (a), a notice to correct violation shall be issued as provided in this section or a notice to appear shall be issued as provided in Section 40522, unless the officer finds any of the following:

(1) Evidence of fraud or persistent neglect.

(2) The violation presents an immediate safety hazard.

(3) The violator does not agree to, or cannot, promptly correct the violation.

(4) The violation cited is of subdivision (a) of Section 27151 for a motorcycle.

(c) If any of the conditions set forth in subdivision (b) exist, the procedures specified in this section or Section 40522 are inapplicable, and the officer may take other appropriate enforcement action.

(d) Except as otherwise provided in subdivision (a), the notice to correct violation shall be on a form approved by the Judicial Council and, in addition to the owner's or operator's address and identifying information, shall contain an estimate of the reasonable time required for correction and proof of correction of the particular defect, not to exceed 30 days, or 90 days for the all-terrain vehicle safety certificate.

(e) This section shall remain in effect only until January 1, 2027, and as of that date is repealed.

(Amended by Stats. 2022, Ch. 595, Sec. 4. (AB 2496) Effective January 1, 2023. Repealed as of January 1, 2027, by its own provisions. See later operative version added by Sec. 5 of Stats. 2022, Ch. 595.)

40610. (a) (1) Except as provided in paragraph (2), if, after an arrest, crash investigation, or other law enforcement action, it appears that a violation has occurred involving a registration, license, all-terrain vehicle safety certificate, or mechanical requirement of this code, and none of the disqualifying conditions set forth in subdivision (b) exist and the investigating officer decides to take enforcement action, the officer shall prepare, in triplicate, and the violator shall sign, a written notice containing the violator's promise to correct the alleged violation and to deliver proof of correction of the violation to the issuing agency.

(2) If a person is arrested for a violation of Section 4454, and none of the disqualifying conditions set forth in subdivision (b) exist, the arresting officer shall prepare, in triplicate, and the violator shall sign, a written notice containing the violator's promise to correct the alleged violation and to deliver proof of correction of the violation to the issuing agency. In lieu of issuing a notice to correct violation pursuant to this section, the officer may issue a notice to appear, as specified in Section 40522.

(b) Pursuant to subdivision (a), a notice to correct violation shall be issued as provided in this section or a notice to appear shall be issued as provided in Section 40522, unless the officer finds any of the following:

(1) Evidence of fraud or persistent neglect.

(2) The violation presents an immediate safety hazard.

(3) The violator does not agree to, or cannot, promptly correct the violation.

(c) If any of the conditions set forth in subdivision (b) exist, the procedures specified in this section or Section 40522 are inapplicable, and the officer may take other appropriate enforcement action.

(d) Except as otherwise provided in subdivision (a), the notice to correct violation shall be on a form approved by the Judicial Council and, in addition to the owner's or operator's address and identifying information, shall contain an estimate of the reasonable time required for correction and proof of correction of the particular defect, not to exceed 30 days, or 90 days for the all-terrain vehicle safety certificate.

(e) This section shall become operative on January 1, 2027.

(Repealed (in Sec. 4) and added by Stats. 2022, Ch. 595, Sec. 5. (AB 2496) Effective January 1, 2023. Operative January 1, 2027, by its own provisions.)

40611. (a) Upon proof of correction of an alleged violation of Section 12500 or 12951, or any violation cited pursuant to Section 40610, or upon submission of evidence of financial responsibility pursuant to subdivision (e) of Section 16028, the clerk shall collect a twenty-five-dollar ($25) transaction fee for each violation. The fees shall be deposited by the clerk in accordance with Section 68084 of the Government Code.

(b) (1) For each citation, ten dollars ($10) shall be allocated monthly as follows:

(A) Thirty-three percent shall be transferred to the local governmental entity in whose jurisdiction the citation was issued for deposit in the general fund of the entity.

(B) Thirty-four percent shall be transferred to the State Treasury for deposit in the State Penalty Fund established by Section 1464 of the Penal Code.

(C) Thirty-three percent shall be deposited in the county general fund.

(2) The remainder of the fees collected on each citation shall be

deposited in the State Court Facilities Construction Fund, established in Section 70371 of the Government Code.

(c) No fee shall be imposed pursuant to this section if the violation notice is processed only by the issuing agency and no record of the action is transmitted to the court.

(Amended by Stats. 2021, Ch. 79, Sec. 37. (AB 143) Effective July 16, 2021.)

40612. An exact, legible copy of the notice to correct shall be delivered to the alleged violator at the time he or she signs such notice.

(Added by Stats. 1978, Ch. 1350.)

40614. Any person who signs a notice to correct or a certificate of correction with a false or fictitious name is guilty of a misdemeanor.

(Added by Stats. 1978, Ch. 1350.)

40616. Any person willfully violating a written promise to correct or willfully failing to deliver proof of correction of violation is guilty of a misdemeanor. Proof of correction may consist of a certification by an authorized representative of one of the following agencies that the alleged violation has been corrected:

(a) Brake, lamp, smog device, or muffler violations may be certified as corrected by any station licensed or contracted to inspect and certify for the violation pursuant to Article 6.5 (commencing with Section 9888.5) of Chapter 20.3 of Division 3 of the Business and Professions Code or Section 27150.2.

(b) Driver license and registration violations may be certified as corrected by the Department of Motor Vehicles or by any clerk or deputy clerk of a court.

(c) Any violation may be certified as corrected by a police department, the California Highway Patrol, sheriff, marshal, or other law enforcement agency regularly engaged in enforcement of the Vehicle Code.

(Amended by Stats. 2023, Ch. 681, Sec. 27. (AB 1263) Effective January 1, 2024.)

40618. Whenever proof of correction of violation is not received by the issuing agency in accordance with Section 40610, the issuing agency may deliver the signed promise to the court having jurisdiction of the violation with a certification that no proof of correction has been received. If prepared on a form approved by the Judicial Council, the promise under Section 40610, together with the certification under this section, shall constitute a complaint to which the defendant may enter a plea, and upon which a warrant may be issued if the complaint is verified.

(Added by Stats. 1978, Ch. 1350.)

Chapter 3. Illegal Evidence

(Chapter 3 enacted by Stats. 1959, Ch. 3.)

Article 1. Prosecutions Under Code

(Article 1 enacted by Stats. 1959, Ch. 3.)

40800. (a) A traffic officer on duty for the exclusive or main purpose of enforcing the provisions of Division 10 (commencing with Section 20000) or Division 11 (commencing with Section 21000) shall wear a full distinctive uniform, and if the officer while on duty uses a motor vehicle, it shall be a distinctive color specified by the commissioner.

(b) This section does not apply to an officer assigned exclusively to the duty of investigating and securing evidence in reference to the theft of a vehicle, failure of a person to stop in the event of an accident, violation of Section 23109 or 23109.1, in reference to a felony charge, or to an officer engaged in serving a warrant when the officer is not engaged in patrolling the highways for the purpose of enforcing the traffic laws.

(Amended by Stats. 2016, Ch. 59, Sec. 9. (SB 1474) Effective January 1, 2017.)

40801. No peace officer or other person shall use a speed trap in arresting, or participating or assisting in the arrest of, any person for any alleged violation of this code nor shall any speed trap be used in securing evidence as to the speed of any vehicle for the purpose of an arrest or prosecution under this code.

(Enacted by Stats. 1959, Ch. 3.)

40802. (a) A "speed trap" is either of the following:

(1) A particular section of a highway measured as to distance and with boundaries marked, designated, or otherwise determined in order that the speed of a vehicle may be calculated by securing the time it takes the vehicle to travel the known distance.

(2) A particular section of a highway with a prima facie speed limit that is provided by this code or by local ordinance pursuant to Section 22352, 22354, 22357, 22358, or 22358.3, if that prima facie speed limit is not justified by an engineering and traffic survey conducted within five years prior to the date of the alleged violation, and enforcement of the speed limit involves the use of radar or any other electronic device that measures the speed of moving objects. This paragraph does not apply to a local street, road, school zone, senior zone, business activity district, or speed limit adopted under Section 22358.7 or 22358.8.

(b) (1) For purposes of this section, a local street or road is one that is functionally classified as "local" on the "California Road System Maps," that are approved by the Federal Highway Administration and maintained by the Department of Transportation. It may also be defined as a "local street or road" if it primarily provides access to abutting residential property and meets the following three conditions:

(A) Roadway width of not more than 40 feet.

(B) Not more than one-half of a mile of uninterrupted length. Interruptions shall include official traffic control signals as defined in Section 445.

(C) Not more than one traffic lane in each direction.

(2) For purposes of this section, "school zone" has the same meaning as defined in Section 22352.

(3) For purposes of this section, "senior zone" means that area approaching or passing a senior center building or other facility primarily used by senior citizens, or the grounds thereof that is contiguous to a highway and on which is posted a standard "SENIOR" warning sign, pursuant to Section 22352.

(4) For purposes of this section, "business activity district" means a section of highway described in subdivision (b) of Section 22358.9 in which a standard 25 miles per hour or 20 miles per hour speed limit sign has been posted pursuant to paragraph (1) of subdivision (a) of that section.

(c) (1) When all of the following criteria are met, paragraph (2) of this subdivision shall be applicable and subdivision (a) shall not be applicable:

(A) When radar is used, the arresting officer has successfully completed a radar operator course of not less than 24 hours on the use of police traffic radar, and the course was approved and certified by the Commission on Peace Officer Standards and Training.

(B) When a laser or any other electronic device is used to measure the speed of moving objects, the arresting officer has successfully completed the training required in subparagraph (A) and an additional training course of not less than two hours approved and certified by the Commission on Peace Officer Standards and Training.

(C) (i) The prosecution proved that the arresting officer complied with subparagraphs (A) and (B) and that an engineering and traffic survey has been conducted in accordance with subparagraph (B) of paragraph (2). The prosecution proved that, prior to the officer issuing the notice to appear, the arresting officer established that the radar, laser, or other electronic device conformed to the requirements of subparagraph (D).

(ii) The prosecution proved the speed of the accused was unsafe for the conditions present at the time of alleged violation unless the citation was for a violation of Section 22349, 22356, or 22406.

(D) The radar, laser, or other electronic device used to measure the speed of the accused meets or exceeds the minimal operational standards of the National Highway Traffic Safety Administration, and has been calibrated within the three years prior to the date of the alleged violation by an independent certified laser or radar repair and testing or calibration facility.

(2) A "speed trap" is either of the following:

(A) A particular section of a highway measured as to distance and with boundaries marked, designated, or otherwise determined in order that the speed of a vehicle may be calculated by securing the time it takes the vehicle to travel the known distance.

(B) (i) A particular section of a highway or state highway with a prima facie speed limit that is provided by this code or by local ordinance under paragraph (1) of subdivision (b) of Section 22352, or established under Section 22354, 22357, 22358, or 22358.3, if that prima facie speed limit is not justified by an engineering and traffic survey conducted within one of the following time periods, prior to the date of the alleged violation, and enforcement of the speed limit involves the use of radar or any other electronic device that measures the speed of moving objects:

(I) Except as specified in subclause (II), seven years.

(II) If an engineering and traffic survey was conducted more than seven years prior to the date of the alleged violation, and a registered engineer evaluates the section of the highway and determines that no significant changes in roadway or traffic conditions have occurred, including, but not limited to, changes in adjoining property or land use, roadway width, or traffic volume, 14 years.

(ii) This subparagraph does not apply to a local street, road, or school zone, senior zone, business activity district, or speed limit adopted under Section 22358.4, 22358.7, or 22358.8.

(Amended by Stats. 2025, Ch. 555, Sec. 5. (AB 382) Effective January 1, 2026.)

40803. (a) No evidence as to the speed of a vehicle upon a highway shall be admitted in any court upon the trial of any person in any prosecution under this code upon a charge involving the speed of a vehicle when the evidence is based upon or obtained from or by the maintenance or use of a speedtrap.

(b) In any prosecution under this code of a charge involving the speed of a vehicle, where enforcement involves the use of radar or other electronic devices which measure the speed of moving objects, the prosecution shall establish, as part of its prima facie case, that the evidence or testimony presented is not based upon a speedtrap as defined in paragraph (2) of subdivision (a) of Section 40802.

(c) When a traffic and engineering survey is required pursuant to paragraph (2) of subdivision (a) of Section 40802, evidence that a traffic and engineering survey has been conducted within five years of the date of the alleged violation or evidence that the offense was committed on a local street or road as defined in paragraph (2) of subdivision (a) of Section 40802 shall constitute a prima facie case that the evidence or testimony is not based upon a speedtrap as defined in paragraph (2) of subdivision (a) of Section 40802.

(Amended by Stats. 1996, Ch. 124, Sec. 147. Effective January 1, 1997.)

40804. (a) In any prosecution under this code upon a charge involving the speed of a vehicle, an officer or other person shall be incompetent as a witness if the testimony is based upon or obtained from or by the maintenance or use of a speed trap.

(b) An officer arresting, or participating or assisting in the arrest of, a person so charged while on duty for the exclusive or main purpose of enforcing the provisions of Divisions 10 (commencing with Section 20000) and 11 (commencing with Section 21000) is incompetent as a witness if at the time of that arrest he was not wearing a distinctive uniform, or was using a motor vehicle not painted the distinctive color specified by the commissioner.

(c) This section does not apply to an officer assigned exclusively to the duty of investigating and securing evidence in reference to the theft of a vehicle or failure of a person to stop in the event of an accident or violation of Section 23109 or 23109.1 or in reference to a felony charge or to an officer engaged in serving a warrant when the officer is not engaged in patrolling the highways for the purpose of enforcing the traffic laws.

(Amended by Stats. 2007, Ch. 682, Sec. 19. Effective January 1, 2008.)

40805. Every court shall be without jurisdiction to render a judgment of conviction against any person for a violation of this code involving the speed of a vehicle if the court admits any evidence or testimony secured in violation of, or which is inadmissible under this article.

(Enacted by Stats. 1959, Ch. 3.)

40806. In the event a defendant charged with an offense under this code pleads guilty, the trial court shall not at any time prior to pronouncing sentence receive or consider any report, verbal or written, of any police or traffic officer or witness of the offense without fully informing the defendant of all statements in the report or statement of witnesses, or without giving the defendant an opportunity to make answer thereto or to produce witnesses in rebuttal, and for such purpose the court shall grant a continuance before pronouncing sentence if requested by the defendant.

(Enacted by Stats. 1959, Ch. 3.)

40807. No record of any action taken by the department against a person's privilege to operate a motor vehicle, nor any testimony regarding the proceedings at, or concerning, or produced at, any hearing held in connection with such action, shall be admissible as evidence in any court in any criminal action.

No provision of this section shall in any way limit the admissibility of such records or testimony as is necessary to enforce the provisions of this code relating to operating a motor vehicle without a valid driver's license or when the driving privilege is suspended or revoked, the admissibility of such records or testimony in any prosecution for failure to disclose any matter at such a hearing when required by law to do so, or the admissibility of such records and testimony when introduced solely for the purpose of impeaching the credibility of a witness.

(Added by Stats. 1977, Ch. 804.)

40808. Subdivision (d) of Section 28 of Article I of the California Constitution shall not be construed as abrogating the evidentiary provisions of this article.

(Added by Stats. 1992, Ch. 538, Sec. 2. Effective January 1, 1993.)

Article 2. Civil Actions

(Article 2 enacted by Stats. 1959, Ch. 3.)

40830. In either of the following circumstances a violation of any provision of this code does not establish negligence as a matter of law, but in any civil action under either of the circumstances negligence must be proved as a fact without regard to the violation. The circumstances under which this section applies are either:

(a) Where violation of the provision was required by a law of the federal government or by any rule, regulation, directive or order of any agency of the federal government, the violation of which is subject to penalty under an act of Congress or by any valid order of military authority.

(b) Where violation of the provision was required in order to comply with any regulation, directive, or order of the Governor promulgated under the California Emergency Services Act.

(Amended by Stats. 1971, Ch. 438.)

40831. In any civil action proof of speed in excess of any prima facie limit declared in Section 22352 at a particular time and place does not establish negligence as a matter of law but in all such actions it shall be necessary to establish as a fact that the operation of a vehicle at the excess speed constituted negligence.

(Enacted by Stats. 1959, Ch. 3.)

40832. No record of the suspension or revocation of the privilege to operate a motor vehicle by the department, nor any testimony of or concerning or produced at the hearing terminating in the suspension or revocation, shall be admissible as evidence in any court in any civil action.

(Enacted by Stats. 1959, Ch. 3.)

40833. Neither the report required by Sections 16000, 16001, 16002, or 16003, the action taken by the department pursuant to Chapter 1 of Division 7 (commencing at Section 16000), the findings, if any, of the department upon which action is based, nor the security filed as provided in that chapter shall be referred to in any way, or be any evidence of the negligence or due care of any party, at the trial of any action at law to recover damages.

(Enacted by Stats. 1959, Ch. 3.)

40834. A judgment of conviction for any violation of this code or of any local ordinance relating to the operation of a motor vehicle or a finding reported under Section 1816 shall not be res judicata or constitute a collateral estoppel of any issue determined therein in any subsequent civil action.
(Added by Stats. 1963, Ch. 1530.)

Chapter 3.5. Evidence

(Chapter 3.5 added by Stats. 1973, Ch. 616.)

40900. Notwithstanding any other provision of law, a verification by telegraph, teletype, facsimile transmission, or any other electronic device, from the department, of ownership of a vehicle registered pursuant to this code, is admissible in evidence as proof of ownership of the vehicle in any proceeding involving a parking violation of this code, or any local parking ordinance adopted pursuant to this code.
(Amended by Stats. 1991, Ch. 13, Sec. 65. Effective February 13, 1991.)

40901. (a) A court, pursuant to this section, may by rule provide for the trial of any alleged infraction involving a violation of this code or any local ordinance adopted pursuant to this code.

(b) The rules governing the trials may provide for testimony and other relevant evidence to be introduced in the form of a notice to appear issued pursuant to Section 40500 and, notwithstanding Division 10 (commencing with Section 1200) of the Evidence Code, a business record or receipt.

(c) Prior to the entry of a waiver of constitutional right pursuant to any rules adopted under this section, the court shall inform the defendant in writing of the nature of the proceedings and of his or her right to confront and cross-examine witnesses, to subpoena witnesses on his or her behalf, and to hire counsel at his or her own expense. The court shall ascertain that the defendant knowingly and voluntarily waives his or her right to be confronted by the witnesses against him or her, to subpoena witnesses in his or her behalf, and to hire counsel on his or her behalf before proceeding.

(d) In any jurisdiction with a non-English speaking population exceeding 5 percent of the total population of the jurisdiction in any one language, a written explanation of the procedures and rights under this section shall be available in that language.

(e) Except as set forth above, nothing contained herein shall be interpreted to permit the submission of evidence other than in accordance with the law, nor to prevent courts from adopting other rules to provide for trials in accordance with the law.
(Amended by Stats. 1996, Ch. 124, Sec. 148. Effective January 1, 1997.)

40902. (a) (1) The court , pursuant to this section, shall, by rule, provide that the defendant may elect to have a trial by written declaration upon any alleged infraction, as charged by the citing officer, involving a violation of this code or any local ordinance adopted pursuant to this code, other than an infraction cited pursuant to Article 2 (commencing with Section 23152) of Chapter 12 of Division 11.

(2) The Judicial Council may adopt rules and forms governing trials by declaration in accordance with this section. Any rule or form adopted by the Judicial Council pursuant to this paragraph shall supersede any local rule of a court adopted pursuant to paragraph (1).

(b) If the defendant elects to have a trial by written declaration, the defendant shall, at the time of submitting that declaration, submit bail in the amount established in the uniform traffic penalty schedule pursuant to Section 40310. If the defendant is found not guilty or if the charges are otherwise dismissed, the amount of the bail shall be promptly refunded to the defendant.

(c) Notwithstanding Division 10 (commencing with Section 1200) of the Evidence Code, the rules governing trials by written declaration may provide for testimony and other relevant evidence to be introduced in the form of a notice to appear issued pursuant to Section 40500, a business record or receipt, a sworn declaration of the arresting officer, or a written statement or letter signed by the defendant.

(d) If the defendant is dissatisfied with a decision of the court in a proceeding pursuant to this section, the defendant shall be granted a trial de novo.
(Amended by Stats. 1998, Ch. 265, Sec. 1. Effective January 1, 1999.)

40903. (a) Any person who fails to appear as provided by law may be deemed to have elected to have a trial by written declaration upon any alleged infraction, as charged by the citing officer, involving a violation of this code or any local ordinance adopted pursuant to this code.

(b) Notwithstanding Division 10 (commencing with Section 1200) of the Evidence Code, testimony and other relevant evidence may be introduced in the form of a notice to appear issued pursuant to Section 40500, a notice of parking violation issued pursuant to Section 40202, a notice of delinquent parking violation issued pursuant to Section 40206, a business record or receipt, a sworn declaration of the arresting officer, or a written statement or letter signed by the defendant.
(Added by Stats. 1992, Ch. 696, Sec. 95. Effective September 15, 1992.)

Chapter 4. Presumptions

(Chapter 4 enacted by Stats. 1959, Ch. 3.)

41100. In any action involving the question of unlawful speed of a vehicle upon a highway which has been signposted with speed restriction signs of a type complying with the requirements of this code, it shall be presumed that existing facts authorize the erection of the signs and that the prima facie speed limit on the highway is the limit stated on the signs. This presumption may be rebutted.
(Enacted by Stats. 1959, Ch. 3.)

41101. (a) Whenever a traffic sign or traffic control device is placed in a position approximately conforming to the requirements of this code, it shall be presumed to have been placed by the official act or direction of lawful authority, unless the contrary is established by competent evidence.

(b) Any sign or traffic control device placed pursuant to this code and purporting to conform to the lawful requirements pertaining to it shall be presumed to comply with the requirements of this code unless the contrary is established by competent evidence.
(Enacted by Stats. 1959, Ch. 3.)

41104. In any case, involving an accident or otherwise, where any rear component of a train of vehicles fails to follow substantially in the path of the towing vehicle while moving upon a highway, the vehicle shall be presumed to have been operated in violation of Section 21711.
(Added by Stats. 1959, Ch. 44.)

Chapter 5. Defenses

(Chapter 5 enacted by Stats. 1959, Ch. 3.)

41400. Whenever any person is charged with a violation of this code, it is a sufficient defense to such charge if it appears that in a criminal prosecution in another state or by the Federal Government, founded upon the act or omission in respect to which he is on trial, he has been convicted or acquitted.
(Enacted by Stats. 1959, Ch. 3.)

41401. No person shall be prosecuted for a violation of any provision of this code if the violation was required by a law of the federal government, by any rule, regulation, directive or order of any agency of the federal government, the violation of which is subject to penalty under an act of Congress, or by any valid order of military authority.
(Amended by Stats. 1973, Ch. 78.)

41402. No person shall be prosecuted for a violation of any provision of this code when violation of such provision is required in order to comply with any regulation, directive, or order of the Governor promulgated under the California Emergency Services Act.
(Amended by Stats. 1971, Ch. 438.)

41403. (a) In any proceedings to have a judgment of conviction of a violation of Section 14601, 14601.1, 14601.2, 23152, or 23153, or Section 23103 as specified in Section 23103.5, which was entered in a separate proceeding, declared invalid on constitutional grounds, the defendant shall state in writing and with specificity wherein the defendant was deprived of the defendant's constitutional rights, which statement shall be filed with the clerk of the court and a copy served on the court that rendered that judgment and on the prosecuting attorney in the present proceedings at least five court days prior to the hearing thereon.

(b) Except as provided in subdivision (c), the court shall, prior to the trial of any pending criminal action against the defendant wherein the separate conviction is charged as such, hold a hearing, outside of the presence of the jury, in order to determine the constitutional validity of the charged separate conviction issue. At the hearing the procedure, the burden of proof, and the burden of producing evidence shall be as follows:

(1) The prosecution shall initially have the burden of producing evidence of the separate conviction sufficient to justify a finding that the defendant has suffered that separate conviction.

(2) After the production of evidence required by paragraph (1), the defendant then has the burden of proof by a preponderance of the evidence that the defendant's constitutional rights were infringed in the separate proceeding at issue. If the separate conviction sought to be invalidated is based upon a plea of guilty or nolo contendere, the defendant shall provide the court with evidence of the prior plea, including the court docket, written waivers of constitutional rights executed by the defendant, and transcripts of the relevant court proceedings at the time of the entry of the defendant's plea. These records shall be provided to the defendant without cost to him or her, when the defendant is represented by the public defender or counsel appointed pursuant to Section 987.2 of the Penal Code.

(3) If the defendant bears this burden successfully, the prosecution shall have the right to produce evidence in rebuttal.

(4) The court shall make a finding on the basis of the evidence thus produced and shall strike from the accusatory pleading any separate conviction found to be constitutionally invalid.

(c) If the defendant fails to comply with the notice requirement of subdivision (a) or fails to produce the evidence required by paragraph (2) of subdivision (b), the court shall hear the motion at the time of sentencing in lieu of continuing the trial, unless good cause is shown for failure to provide notice pursuant to subdivision (a) or produce the evidence required by paragraph (2) of subdivision (b), in which case the court shall grant a continuance of the trial for a reasonable period. The procedure, burden of proof, and burden of producing evidence as provided in subdivision (b) shall apply regardless of when the motion is heard.

(Amended by Stats. 1995, Ch. 83, Sec. 1. Effective January 1, 1996.)

Chapter 6. Nonprosecution of Violations

(Chapter 6 added by Stats. 1970, Ch. 1163.)

41500. (a) A person shall not be subject to prosecution for a nonfelony offense arising out of the operation of a motor vehicle or violation of this code as a pedestrian that is pending against them at the time of their commitment to the custody of the Secretary of the Department of Corrections and Rehabilitation, the Division of Juvenile Justice in the Department of Corrections and Rehabilitation, or to a county jail pursuant to subdivision (h) of Section 1170 of the Penal Code.

(b) Notwithstanding any other law, a driver's license shall not be suspended or revoked, and the issuance or renewal of a license shall not be refused as a result of a pending nonfelony offense occurring prior to the time a person was committed to the custody of the Secretary of the Department of Corrections and Rehabilitation, the Division of Juvenile Justice of the Department of Corrections and Rehabilitation, or a county jail pursuant to subdivision (h) of Section 1170 of the Penal Code, or as a result of a notice received by the department pursuant to subdivision (a) of former Section 40509 when the offense that gave rise to the notice occurred prior to the time a person was committed to the custody of the Secretary of the Department of Corrections and Rehabilitation or the Division of Juvenile Justice of the Department of Corrections and Rehabilitation.

(c) The department shall remove from its records notice received by it pursuant to subdivision (a) of former Section 40509 upon receipt of satisfactory evidence that a person was committed to the custody of the Secretary of the Department of Corrections and Rehabilitation, the Division of Juvenile Justice of the Department of Corrections and Rehabilitation, or a county jail pursuant to subdivision (h) of Section 1170 of the Penal Code, after the offense that gave rise to the notice occurred.

(d) The provisions of this section shall not apply to a nonfelony offense if the department is required by this code to immediately revoke or suspend the privilege of a person to drive a motor vehicle upon receipt of a duly certified abstract of the record of a court showing that the person has been convicted of that nonfelony offense.

(e) The provisions of subdivisions (a), (b), and (c) do not apply to an offense committed by a person while that person is temporarily released from custody pursuant to law or while they are on parole or postrelease community supervision.

(f) The provisions of subdivisions (a), (b), and (c) do not apply if the pending offense is a violation of Section 23103, 23152, or 23153.

(Amended by Stats. 2022, Ch. 800, Sec. 25. (AB 2746) Effective January 1, 2023.)

41501. (a) After a deposit of bail and bail forfeiture, a plea of guilty or no contest, or a conviction, the court may order a continuance of a proceeding against a person, who receives a notice to appear in court for a violation of a statute relating to the safe operation of a vehicle, in consideration for successful completion of a course of instruction at a licensed school for traffic violators and pursuant to Section 1803.5 or 42005, the court may order that the conviction be held confidential by the department in accordance with Section 1808.7. The court shall notify a person that only one conviction within 18 months will be held confidential.

(b) Subdivision (a) does not apply to a person who receives a notice to appear as to, or is otherwise charged with, a violation of an offense described in subdivisions (a) to (e), inclusive, of Section 12810.

(c) This section shall become operative on July 1, 2011.

(Amended (as added by Stats. 2010, Ch. 599) by Stats. 2011, Ch. 296, Sec. 311. (AB 1023) Effective January 1, 2012.)

Chapter 7. Arrest Quotas

(Chapter 7 added by Stats. 1976, Ch. 1111.)

41600. For purposes of this chapter, "arrest quota" means any requirement regarding the number of arrests made, or the number of citations issued, by a peace officer, or parking enforcement employee, or the proportion of those arrests made and citations issued by a peace officer or parking enforcement employee, relative to the arrests made and citations issued by another peace officer or parking enforcement employee, or group of officers or employees.

(Amended by Stats. 2002, Ch. 105, Sec. 1. Effective January 1, 2003.)

41601. For purposes of this chapter, "citation" means a notice to appear, notice of violation, or notice of parking violation.

(Added by Stats. 1976, Ch. 1111.)

41601.5. For purposes of this chapter, "agency" includes the Regents of the University of California.

(Added by Stats. 2002, Ch. 105, Sec. 2. Effective January 1, 2003.)

41602. No state or local agency employing peace officers or parking enforcement employees engaged in the enforcement of this code or any local ordinance adopted pursuant to this code, may establish any policy requiring any peace officer or parking enforcement employees to meet an arrest quota.

(Amended by Stats. 2002, Ch. 105, Sec. 3. Effective January 1, 2003.)

41603. No state or local agency employing peace officers or parking enforcement employees engaged in the enforcement of this code shall use the number of arrests or citations issued by a peace officer or parking enforcement employees as the sole criterion for promotion, demotion, dismissal, or the earning of any benefit provided by the agency. Those arrests or citations, and their ultimate dispositions, may only be considered in evaluating the overall performance of a peace officer or parking enforcement employees. An evaluation may include, but shall not be limited to, criteria such as attendance, punctuality, work safety, complaints by civilians, commendations, demeanor, formal training, and professional judgment.

(Amended by Stats. 2016, Ch. 99, Sec. 7. (AB 1953) Effective January 1, 2017.)

Chapter 8. Consolidated Disposition

(Chapter 8 added by Stats. 1983, Ch. 989, Sec. 1.)

41610. (a) Whenever a person who is in custody enters a guilty plea to an infraction or misdemeanor under this code and there is outstanding any warrant of arrest for a violation of this code or a local ordinance adopted pursuant to this code that is filed in any court within the same county, the defendant may elect to enter a guilty plea to any of these charged offenses of which the court has a record, except offenses specified in subdivision (b). The court shall sentence the defendant for each of the offenses for which a guilty plea has been entered pursuant to this section, and shall notify the appropriate court or department in each affected judicial district of the disposition. After receiving that notice of disposition, the court in which each complaint was filed shall prepare and transmit to the department any certification required by applicable provisions of former Section 40509 as if the court had heard the case.

(b) Subdivision (a) does not authorize entry of a guilty plea as specified in that subdivision to an offense for which a notice of parking violation has been issued, nor to any offense specified in Section 14601.2, 14601.3, 20002, 23103, 23104, 23105, 23152, or 23153, subdivision (a) of Section 14601, or subdivision (a) of Section 14601.1.

(Amended by Stats. 2022, Ch. 800, Sec. 26. (AB 2746) Effective January 1, 2023.)

Division 18. Penalties and Disposition of Fees, Fines, and Forfeitures

(Division 18 enacted by Stats. 1959, Ch. 3.)

Chapter 1. Penalties

(Chapter 1 enacted by Stats. 1959, Ch. 3.)

Article 1. Public Offenses

(Article 1 enacted by Stats. 1959, Ch. 3.)

42000. Unless a different penalty is expressly provided by this code, every person convicted of a felony for a violation of any provision of this code shall be punished by a fine of not less than one thousand dollars ($1,000) or more than ten thousand dollars ($10,000), or by imprisonment pursuant to subdivision (h) of Section 1170 of the Penal Code, or by both such fine and imprisonment.

(Amended by Stats. 2011, Ch. 15, Sec. 615. (AB 109) Effective April 4, 2011. Operative October 1, 2011, by Sec. 636 of Ch. 15, as amended by Stats. 2011, Ch. 39, Sec. 68.)

42000.1. Notwithstanding Section 42001, every person convicted of an infraction for a violation described in subdivision (b) of Section 22348 shall be punished by a fine not exceeding five hundred dollars ($500).

(Added by Stats. 1983, Ch. 980, Sec. 4.)

42000.5. Every person convicted of an infraction for a violation of Section 22350, 22406, or 22407 while operating a bus, motor truck, or truck tractor having three or more axles, or any motor truck or truck tractor drawing any other vehicle, shall be punished by a fine not exceeding one hundred dollars ($100) for a first conviction, except that if the person has exceeded the specified speed limit by 10 miles per hour or more, the fine shall not exceed two hundred dollars ($200) for a first conviction, and not exceeding three hundred dollars ($300) for a second or subsequent conviction.

(Amended by Stats. 1989, Ch. 980, Sec. 1.)

42001. (a) Except as provided in this code, a person convicted of an infraction for a violation of this code or of a local ordinance adopted pursuant to this code shall be punished as follows:

(1) By a fine not exceeding one hundred dollars ($100).

(2) For a second infraction occurring within one year of a prior infraction that resulted in a conviction, a fine not exceeding two hundred dollars ($200).

(3) For a third or subsequent infraction occurring within one year of two or more prior infractions that resulted in convictions, a fine not exceeding two hundred fifty dollars ($250).

(b) A pedestrian convicted of an infraction for a violation of this code or any local ordinance adopted pursuant to this code shall be punished by a fine not exceeding fifty dollars ($50).

(c) A person convicted of a violation of subdivision (a) or (b) of Section 27150.3 shall be punished by a fine of two hundred fifty dollars ($250), and a person convicted of a violation of subdivision (c) of Section 27150.3 shall be punished by a fine of one thousand dollars ($1,000).

(d) Notwithstanding any other provision of law, a local public entity that employs peace officers, as designated under Chapter 4.5 (commencing with Section 830) of Title 3 of Part 2 of the Penal Code, the California State University, and the University of California may, by ordinance or resolution, establish a schedule of fines applicable to infractions committed by bicyclists within its jurisdiction. A fine, including all penalty assessments and court costs, established pursuant to this subdivision shall not exceed the maximum fine, including penalty assessment and court costs, otherwise authorized by this code for that violation. If a bicycle fine schedule is adopted, it shall be used by the courts having jurisdiction over the area within which the ordinance or resolution is applicable instead of the fines, including penalty assessments and court costs, otherwise applicable under this code.

(Amended by Stats. 2006, Ch. 900, Sec. 3. Effective January 1, 2007.)

42001.1. (a) Every person convicted of an infraction for a violation of Section 2815 or a violation of subdivision (a) or (b) of Section 22526 at an intersection posted pursuant to subdivision (d) of Section 22526 shall be punished as follows:

(1) For a first conviction, a fine of not less than fifty dollars ($50) nor more than one hundred dollars ($100).

(2) For a second conviction within a period of one year, a fine of not less than one hundred dollars ($100) nor more than two hundred dollars ($200).

(3) For a third or any subsequent conviction within a period of two years, a fine of not less than two hundred fifty dollars ($250) nor more than five hundred dollars ($500).

(b) In addition to the fine specified in subdivision (a), the court may order the department to suspend the driver's license for up to 30 days of any person convicted of a third or any subsequent conviction of Section 2815 within a period of two years, and the department shall suspend the license for the period of time so ordered.

(Amended by Stats. 2005, Ch. 716, Sec. 7. Effective January 1, 2006.)

42001.2. (a) A person convicted of an infraction for a violation of Section 27153.5 with a motor vehicle having a manufacturer's maximum gross vehicle weight rating of 6,001 or more pounds is punishable by a fine for the first offense of not less than two hundred fifty dollars ($250) and not more than two thousand five hundred dollars ($2,500), and for a second or subsequent offense within one year of not less than five hundred dollars ($500) and not more than five thousand dollars ($5,000).

(b) A person convicted of an infraction for a second or subsequent violation of Section 27153, or a second or subsequent violation of 27153.5, with a motor vehicle having a manufacturer's maximum gross vehicle weight rating of less than 6,001 pounds, is punishable by a fine of not less than one hundred thirty-five dollars ($135) nor more than two hundred eighty-five dollars ($285).

(c) Notwithstanding Section 40616, the penalties in subdivision (b) apply when a person is guilty of willfully violating a written promise to correct, or willfully failing to deliver proof of correction, as prescribed in Section 40616, when an offense described in subdivision (b) was the violation for which the notice to correct was issued and the person was previously convicted of the same offense, except that costs of repair shall be limited to those specified in Section 44017 of the Health and Safety Code.

(d) Notwithstanding any other provision of law and subject to Section 1463.15 of the Penal Code, revenues collected from fines and forfeitures imposed under this section shall be allocated as follows: 15 percent to the county in which the prosecution is conducted, 10 percent to the prosecuting agency, 25 percent to the enforcement agency, except the Department of the California Highway Patrol, and 50 percent to the air quality management district or air pollution control district in which the infraction occurred, to be used for programs to regulate or control emissions from vehicular sources of air pollution. If the enforcement agency is the Department of the California Highway Patrol, the revenues shall be allocated 25 percent to the county in which the prosecution is conducted, 25 percent to the prosecuting agency, and 50 percent to the air quality management district or air pollution control district in which the infraction occurred. If no prosecuting agency is involved, the revenues that would otherwise be allocated to the prosecuting agency shall instead be allocated to the air quality management district or air pollution control district in which the infraction occurred.

(e) For the purposes of subdivisions (a), (b), and (c), a second or subsequent offense does not include an offense involving a different motor vehicle.

(Amended by Stats. 2003, Ch. 482, Sec. 4. Effective January 1, 2004.)

42001.3. (a) Violations of Section 34506.3, with respect to any regulation adopted under Section 34501 relative to the maintenance of driving logs, shall be punishable by a fine of not more than five hundred dollars ($500).

(b) Violations of subdivision (a) of Section 34506, with respect to any regulation adopted under Section 34501 relative to drivers' hours of service, shall be punishable by a fine of not less than five hundred dollars ($500) nor more than one thousand dollars ($1,000). In addition, the violations may be punishable by imprisonment in the county jail for not more than six months.

(Amended by Stats. 1988, Ch. 631, Sec. 1.)

42001.4. Every person convicted of an infraction for violation of Section 23117 shall be punished as follows:

(a) By a fine of not less than fifty dollars ($50) nor more than one hundred dollars ($100).

(b) For a second infraction occurring within one year of a prior infraction which resulted in a conviction, a fine of not less than seventy-five dollars ($75) nor more than two hundred dollars ($200).

(c) For a third or any subsequent infraction occurring within one year of two or more prior infractions which resulted in convictions, a fine of not less than one hundred dollars ($100) nor more than two hundred fifty dollars ($250).

(Added by Stats. 1987, Ch. 224, Sec. 2.)

42001.5. (a) A person convicted of an infraction for a violation of subdivision (i) or (l) of Section 22500, or of Section 22522, shall be punished by a fine of not less than two hundred fifty dollars ($250).

(b) No part of any fine imposed under this section may be suspended, except the court may suspend that portion of the fine above one hundred dollars ($100).

(c) A fine imposed under this section may be paid in installments if the court determines that the defendant is unable to pay the entire amount in one payment.

(Amended by Stats. 2003, Ch. 555, Sec. 8. Effective January 1, 2004.)

42001.6. Every person convicted of an infraction for a violation of Section 22511.1 is punishable by a fine of one hundred dollars ($100). No part of any fine imposed shall be suspended, except the court may suspend that portion of the fine above twenty-five dollars ($25) for a violation of Section 22511.1 if the person convicted possessed at the time of the offense, but failed to display, a valid zero-emission vehicle decal identification issued pursuant to subdivision (a) of Section 5205.5. The fine may be paid in installments if the court determines that the defendant is unable to pay the entire amount in one payment.

(Amended by Stats. 2013, Ch. 414, Sec. 4. (SB 286) Effective January 1, 2014.)

42001.7. (a) Every person convicted of a violation of Section 23111 or 23112, or subdivision (a) of Section 23113, shall be punished by a mandatory fine of not less than one hundred dollars ($100) nor more than one thousand dollars ($1,000) upon a first conviction, by a mandatory fine of not less than five hundred dollars ($500) nor more than one thousand dollars ($1,000) upon a second conviction, and by a mandatory fine of not less than seven hundred fifty dollars ($750) nor more than one thousand dollars ($1,000) upon a third or subsequent conviction.

In no case may the court order imprisonment in the county jail for a violation punishable under this subdivision, unless imprisonment is ordered pursuant to Section 166 of the Penal Code.

(b) The court shall, in addition to the fines imposed pursuant to subdivision (a), order the offender to pick up litter or clean up graffiti at a time and place within the jurisdiction of the court as follows:

(1) For a first conviction punished pursuant to subdivision (a), the court shall require the offender to pick up litter or clean up graffiti for not less than eight hours.

(2) For a second conviction punished pursuant to subdivision (a), the court shall require the offender to pick up litter or clean up graffiti for not less than 16 hours.

(3) For a third or subsequent conviction punished pursuant to subdivision (a), the court shall require the offender to pick up litter or clean up graffiti for not less than 24 hours.

(c) It is the intent of the Legislature that persons convicted of highway littering be required to bear the penalty for their actions. Therefore, the court may not suspend the mandatory fines required by subdivision (a) except in unusual cases where the interest of justice would best be served by suspension of the fine. If the court suspends imposition of any fine required by subdivision (a), it shall, as a condition of that suspension, require the offender to pick up litter or clean up graffiti at a time and place within the jurisdiction of the court for not less than eight hours for every one hundred dollars ($100) of fine suspended. The court may not suspend the order to pick up litter or clean up graffiti required by this subdivision or subdivision (b) except in unusual cases where the interest of justice would best be served by suspension of that order.

(Amended by Stats. 1990, Ch. 982, Sec. 1.)

42001.8. Every person convicted of an infraction for a violation of Section 4000 shall be punished by a fine of not less than fifty dollars ($50) and not more than two hundred fifty dollars ($250).

(Added by Stats. 1985, Ch. 1126, Sec. 8. Effective September 28, 1985. Operative April 1, 1986, by Sec. 12 of Ch. 1126.)

42001.9. Every person convicted of an infraction for a violation of Section 23135 shall be punished by a fine of fifty dollars ($50).

(Added by Stats. 1978, Ch. 421.)

42001.10. Every person convicted for a violation of Section 38020 shall be punished by a fine of not less than fifty dollars ($50) for a first offense, and not more than two hundred fifty dollars ($250) for every subsequent offense.

(Added by renumbering Section 42001.9 (as amended by Stats. 1987, Ch. 1027) by Stats. 1988, Ch. 160, Sec. 184.)

42001.11. Every person convicted of an infraction for a violation of Section 21655.5 or 21655.8 shall be punished as follows:

(a) For a first conviction, a fine of not less than one hundred dollars ($100), nor more than one hundred fifty dollars ($150).

(b) For a second conviction within a period of one year, a fine of not less than one hundred fifty dollars ($150), nor more than two hundred dollars ($200).

(c) For a third or any subsequent conviction within a period of two years, a fine of not less than two hundred fifty dollars ($250), nor more than five hundred dollars ($500).

(Added by Stats. 1988, Ch. 1054, Sec. 5.)

42001.12. Every person convicted of an infraction for a violation of Section 21806 shall be punished as follows:

(a) For a first conviction, by a fine of not less than one hundred dollars ($100) nor more than two hundred fifty dollars ($250).

(b) For a second conviction within one year, by a fine of not less than one hundred fifty dollars ($150) nor more than five hundred dollars ($500).

(c) For a third or any subsequent conviction within three years, by a fine of not less than two hundred fifty dollars ($250) nor more than five hundred dollars ($500).

(Added by Stats. 1991, Ch. 13, Sec. 67. Effective February 13, 1991.)

42001.13. (a) A person who commits a violation of Section 22507.8 is subject to either a civil notice of parking violation pursuant to Article 3 (commencing with Section 40200) of Chapter 1 of Division 17 or a criminal notice to appear.

(b) If a notice to appear is issued and upon conviction of an infraction for a violation of Section 22507.8, a person shall be punished as follows:

(1) A fine of not less than two hundred fifty dollars ($250) and not more than five hundred dollars ($500) for the first offense.

(2) A fine of not less than five hundred dollars ($500) and not more than seven hundred fifty dollars ($750) for the second offense.

(3) A fine of not less than seven hundred fifty dollars ($750) and not more than one thousand dollars ($1,000) for three or more offenses.

(c) The court may suspend the imposition of the fine if the person convicted possessed at the time of the offense, but failed to display, a valid special identification license plate issued pursuant to Section 5007 or a distinguishing placard issued pursuant to Section 22511.55 or 22511.59.

(d) A fine imposed under this section may be paid in installments if the court determines that the defendant is unable to pay the entire amount in one payment.

(Amended by Stats. 2010, Ch. 328, Sec. 233. (SB 1330) Effective January 1, 2011.)

42001.14. (a) Every person convicted of an infraction for the offense of disconnecting, modifying, or altering a required pollution control device in violation of Section 27156 shall be punished as follows:

(1) For a first conviction, by a fine of not less than fifty dollars ($50), nor more than one hundred dollars ($100).

(2) For a second or subsequent conviction, by a fine of not less than one hundred dollars ($100), nor more than two hundred fifty dollars ($250).

(b) (1) The fines collected under subdivision (a) shall be allocated pursuant to subdivision (d) of Section 42001.2.

(2) The amounts allocated pursuant to paragraph (1) to the air pollution control district or air quality management district in which the infraction occurred shall first be allocated to the State Air Resources Board and the Bureau of Automotive Repair to pay the costs of the state board and the bureau under Article 8 (commencing with Section 44080) of Chapter 5 of Part 5 of Division 26 of the Health and Safety Code.

(3) The funds collected under subdivision (a) which are not required for purposes of paragraph (2) shall be used for the enforcement of Section 27156 or for the implementation of Article 8 (commencing with Section 44080) of Chapter 5 of Part 5 of Division 26 of the Health and Safety Code.

(Added by Stats. 1992, Ch. 972, Sec. 3. Effective January 1, 1993.)

42001.15. Every person convicted of an infraction for a violation of subdivision (a) or (c) of Section 21453, subdivision (c) of Section 21454, or subdivision (a) of Section 21457 shall be punished by a fine of one hundred dollars ($100).

(Added by Stats. 1997, Ch. 852, Sec. 4. Effective January 1, 1998.)

42001.16. (a) Every person convicted of an infraction for a violation of subdivision (c) of Section 21752, subdivision (c) of Section 22526, or Section 22450, involving railroad grade crossings, or Section 22451 or 22452 shall be punished as follows:

(1) For the first infraction, by a fine of one hundred dollars ($100).

(2) For a second infraction of any of the offenses described in this subdivision occurring within one year of a prior infraction that resulted in a conviction, by a fine not exceeding two hundred dollars ($200).

(3) For a third or any subsequent infraction of any of the offenses described in this subdivision occurring within one year of two or more prior infractions that resulted in convictions, by a fine not exceeding two hundred fifty dollars ($250).

(b) In addition to the fine imposed pursuant to subdivision (a), a court, in a county in which Section 369b of the Penal Code applies, may require the person to attend a traffic school as described in Section 369b of the Penal Code.

(Amended by Stats. 2005, Ch. 716, Sec. 8. Effective January 1, 2006.)

42001.17. Notwithstanding any other provision of law, every person convicted of an infraction for a violation of Section 21951 shall be punished as follows:

(a) For the first infraction, by a fine of one hundred dollars ($100).

(b) For a second infraction for a violation of Section 21951 occurring within one year of a prior infraction of violating of that section that resulted in a conviction, by a fine not exceeding two hundred dollars ($200), as provided in paragraph (2) of subdivision (a) of Section 42001.

(c) For a third or any subsequent infraction for a violation of Section 21951 occurring within one year of two or more prior infractions of violating that section that resulted in convictions, by a fine not exceeding two hundred fifty dollars ($250), as provided in paragraph (3) of subdivision (a) of Section 42001.

(Added by Stats. 2000, Ch. 833, Sec. 14. Effective January 1, 2001.)

42001.18. Notwithstanding any other provision of law, every person convicted of an infraction for a violation of Section 21971 shall be punished as follows:

(a) For the first infraction, by a fine of two hundred twenty dollars ($220).

(b) For a second infraction for a violation of Section 21971 occurring within one year of a prior violation of that section that resulted in a conviction, by a fine of three hundred twenty dollars ($320).

(c) For a third or any subsequent infraction for a violation of Section 21971 occurring within one year of two or more prior infractions of violating that section that resulted in convictions by a fine of three hundred seventy dollars ($370).

(Added by Stats. 2000, Ch. 833, Sec. 15. Effective January 1, 2001.)

42001.19. Notwithstanding any other provision of law, a person convicted of a violation of Section 21070 is punishable, as follows:

(a) For a violation involving bodily injury, by a fine of seventy dollars ($70).

(b) For a violation involving great bodily injury, as defined in Section 12022.7 of the Penal Code, by a fine of ninety-five dollars ($95).

(Added by Stats. 2006, Ch. 898, Sec. 5. Effective January 1, 2007.)

42001.20. Notwithstanding any other provision of law, a person who violates subdivision (b) or (c) of Section 27000 is punishable as follows:

(a) By a fine of one hundred fifty dollars ($150).

(b) For a second infraction occurring within one year of a prior infraction that resulted in a conviction, a fine not exceeding two hundred dollars ($200).

(c) For a third or any subsequent infraction occurring within one year of two or more prior infractions that resulted in convictions, a fine, not exceeding two hundred fifty dollars ($250).

(Added by Stats. 2005, Ch. 166, Sec. 4. Effective January 1, 2006.)

42001.25. Notwithstanding any other provision of law, a person who violates Section 23140 is punishable as follows:

(a) By a fine of one hundred dollars ($100).

(b) For a second infraction occurring within one year of a prior infraction that resulted in a conviction, a fine of two hundred dollars ($200).

(c) For a third or any subsequent infraction occurring within one year of two or more prior infractions that resulted in convictions, a fine of three hundred dollars ($300).

(Added by Stats. 2006, Ch. 899, Sec. 3. Effective January 1, 2007.)

42002. Unless a different penalty is expressly provided by this code, every person convicted of a misdemeanor for a violation of any of the provisions of this code shall be punished by a fine of not exceeding one thousand dollars ($1,000) or by imprisonment in the county jail for not exceeding six months, or by both such fine and imprisonment.

(Amended by Stats. 1983, Ch. 1092, Sec. 404. Effective September 27, 1983. Operative January 1, 1984, by Sec. 427 of Ch. 1092.)

42002.1. A person convicted of a misdemeanor violation of Section 2800, 2801, or 2803, insofar as it affects a failure to stop and submit to inspection of equipment or for an unsafe condition endangering a person, shall be punished as follows:

(a) By a fine not exceeding fifty dollars ($50) or imprisonment in the county jail not exceeding five days.

(b) For a second conviction within a period of one year, a fine not exceeding one hundred dollars ($100) or imprisonment in the county jail not exceeding 10 days, or both that fine and imprisonment.

(c) For a third or a subsequent conviction within a period of one year, a fine not exceeding five hundred dollars ($500) or imprisonment in the county jail not exceeding six months, or both that fine and imprisonment.

(Added by Stats. 2006, Ch. 898, Sec. 6. Effective January 1, 2007.)

42002.4. A violation of Section 10751 shall be punished by imprisonment in the county jail not exceeding six months if the value of the property does not exceed nine hundred fifty dollars ($950), and by imprisonment in the county jail not exceeding one year if the value of the property is more than nine hundred fifty dollars ($950).

(Amended by Stats. 2009, 3rd Ex. Sess., Ch. 28, Sec. 55. (SB 18 3x) Effective January 25, 2010.)

42002.5. Notwithstanding Section 42002, every person convicted of a violation of Section 10852 or 10853 involving a vehicle that has been modified for the use of a disabled veteran or any other disabled person and that displays a special identification license plate issued pursuant to Section 5007 or a distinguishing placard issued pursuant to Section 22511.55 or 22511.59, if those facts are known or should reasonably have been known to the person, shall be punished by a fine of not more than two thousand dollars ($2,000) or by imprisonment in the county jail for not more than one year, or by both the fine and imprisonment.

(Amended by Stats. 1994, Ch. 1149, Sec. 13. Effective January 1, 1995.)

42003. (a) A judgment that a person convicted of an infraction be punished by a fine may also provide for the payment to be made within a specified time or in specified installments. A judgment granting a defendant time to pay the fine shall order that if the defendant fails to pay the fine or any installment thereof on the date that it is due, he or she shall appear in court on that date for further proceedings. Willful violation of the order is punishable as contempt.

(b) A judgment that a person convicted of any other violation of this code be punished by a fine may also order, adjudge, and decree that the person be imprisoned until the fine is satisfied. In all of these cases, the judgment shall specify the extent of the imprisonment which shall not exceed one day for every thirty dollars ($30) of the fine, nor extend in this case beyond the term for which the defendant might be sentenced to imprisonment for the offense of which he or she was convicted.

(c) In any case when a person appears before a traffic referee or judge of the superior court for adjudication of a violation of this code, the court, upon request of the defendant, shall consider the defendant's ability to pay. Consideration of a defendant's ability to pay may include his or her future earning capacity. A defendant shall bear the burden of demonstrating lack of his or her ability to pay. Express findings by the court as to the factors bearing on the amount of the fine shall not be required. The reasonable cost of these services and of probation shall not exceed the amount determined to be the actual average cost thereof. The court shall order the defendant to appear before a county officer designated by the court to make an inquiry into the ability of the defendant to pay all or a portion of those costs or the court or traffic referee may make this determination at a hearing. At that hearing, the defendant shall be entitled to have, but shall not be limited to, the opportunity to be heard in person, to present witnesses and other documentary evidence, to confront and cross-examine adverse witnesses, to disclosure of the evidence against him or her, and to a written statement of the findings of the court or the county officer. If the court determines that the defendant has the ability to pay all or part of the costs, the court shall set the amount to be reimbursed and order the defendant to pay that sum to the county in the manner in which the court believes reasonable and compatible with the defendant's financial ability; or, with the consent of a defendant who is placed on probation, the court shall order the probation officer to set the amount of payment, which shall not exceed the maximum amount set by the court, and the manner in which the payment shall be made to the county. In making a determination of whether a defendant has the ability to pay, the court shall take into account the amount of any fine imposed upon the defendant and any amount the defendant has been ordered to pay in restitution.

The court may hold additional hearings during the probationary period. If practicable, the court or the probation officer shall order payments to be made on a monthly basis. Execution may be issued on the order in the same manner as a judgment in a civil action. The order to pay all or part of the costs shall not be enforced by contempt.

A payment schedule for reimbursement of the costs of presentence investigation based on income shall be developed by the probation department of each county and approved by the presiding judge of the superior court.

(d) The term "ability to pay" means the overall capability of the defendant to reimburse the costs, or a portion of the costs, of conducting the presentence investigation, preparing the presentence report, and probation, and includes, but is not limited to, all of the following regarding the defendant:

(1) Present financial position.

(2) Reasonably discernible future financial position. In no event shall the court consider a period of more than six months from the date of the hearing for purposes of determining reasonably discernible future financial position.

(3) Likelihood that the defendant will be able to obtain employment within the six-month period from the date of the hearing.

(4) Any other factors that may bear upon the defendant's financial capability to reimburse the county for the costs.

(e) At any time during the pendency of the judgment rendered according to the terms of this section, a defendant against whom a judgment has been rendered may petition the rendering court to modify or vacate its previous judgment on the grounds of a change of circumstances with regard to the defendant's ability to pay the judgment. The court shall advise the defendant of this right at the time of rendering of the judgment.

(Amended by Stats. 2002, Ch. 784, Sec. 605. Effective January 1, 2003.)

42004. For the purpose of determining the penalty to be imposed pursuant to this code, the court may consider a written report from the Department of Motor Vehicles containing information from its records showing prior convictions; and the communication is prima facie evidence of such convictions, if the defendant admits them, regardless of whether or not the complaint commencing the proceedings has alleged prior convictions.

For the purpose of this chapter a prior bail forfeiture shall be deemed to be a conviction of the offense charged.

(Repealed and added by Stats. 1968, Ch. 1192.)

42004.5. Upon conviction of any violation of any provision of this code, other than a felony violation and except this section, execution of sentence of imprisonment in the county jail shall be suspended, at the request of the convicted person, for a period of 24 hours, unless the judge determines that the person would not return. If, prior to the end of such period, the person does not deliver himself into custody for commencement of the execution of such sentence, his failure to appear shall constitute a misdemeanor.

(Added by Stats. 1973, Ch. 1184.)

42005. (a) Except as otherwise provided in this section, after a deposit of the fee under Section 42007 or bail, a plea of guilty or no contest, or a conviction, a court may order or permit a person who holds a noncommercial class C, class M1, or class M2 driver's license who pleads guilty or who pleads no contest or who is convicted of a traffic offense to attend a traffic violator school licensed pursuant to Chapter 1.5 (commencing with Section 11200) of Division 5.

(b) To the extent the court is in conformance with Title 49 of the Code of Federal Regulations, and except as otherwise provided in this section, the court may, after deposit of the fee under Section 42007 or bail, order or permit a person who holds a class A, class B, or commercial class C driver's license, who pleads guilty or no contest or is convicted of a traffic offense, to complete a course of instruction at a licensed traffic violator school if the person was operating a vehicle requiring only a class C license, or a class M license. The court may not order that the record of conviction be kept confidential. However, the conviction shall not be added to a violation point count for purposes of determining whether a driver is presumed to be a negligent operator under Section 12810.5.

(c) The court shall not order that a conviction of an offense be kept confidential according to Section 1808.7, order or permit avoidance of consideration of violation point counts under subdivision (b), or permit a person, regardless of the driver's license class, to complete a program at a licensed traffic violator school in lieu of adjudicating an offense if any of the following applies to the offense:

(1) It occurred in a commercial motor vehicle, as defined in subdivision (b) of Section 15210.

(2) Is a violation of Section 20001, 20002, 23103, 23104, 23105, 23140, 23152, or 23153, or of Section 23103, as specified in Section 23103.5.

(3) It is a violation described in subdivision (d) or (e) of Section 12810.

(d) A person ordered to attend a traffic violator school pursuant to subdivision (a) or (b) may choose the traffic violator school the person will attend. The court shall provide to each person subject to that order or referral the department's current list of licensed traffic violator schools.

(e) A person who fails to comply with a court order to attend traffic violator school shall not be assessed any additional penalties for their failure to comply, however the provisions of Section 1808.7 shall not apply to a person who fails to attend traffic violator school.

(Amended by Stats. 2023, Ch. 85, Sec. 2. (AB 466) Effective January 1, 2024.)

42005.1. The court may order a person designated to attend a traffic violator school to instead participate in a study of traffic violator schools licensed pursuant to Chapter 1.5 (commencing with Section 11200) of Division 5. The person's participation in that study constitutes attending a licensed traffic violator school program.

(Amended by Stats. 2010, Ch. 599, Sec. 13.7. (AB 2499) Effective January 1, 2011.)

42005.3. (a) A local authority shall not allow a person who is alleged to have committed a traffic offense in violation of this code, or an ordinance or resolution adopted under this code, to participate in a driver awareness or education program or in any other diversion program as an alternative to the procedure required to be followed under this code for alleged violations of this code.

(b) This section does not apply to a diversion program sanctioned by local law enforcement for a person who committed an infraction not involving a motor vehicle.

(Amended by Stats. 2015, Ch. 306, Sec. 1. (AB 902) Effective January 1, 2016.)

42005.5. Notwithstanding Section 46300 or 84500 of the Education Code or any other provision of law, on and after September 1, 1985, attendance at a school for traffic violators permitted or ordered pursuant to Section 41501 or 42005 shall not be included in computing the average daily attendance of any school district, community college district, or other public educational institution for purposes of allocation of state funds.

(Amended by Stats. 2010, Ch. 599, Sec. 15. (AB 2499) Effective January 1, 2011.)

42006. (a) Except as provided in subdivision (c), there may be levied a special assessment in an amount equal to one dollar ($1) for every fine, forfeiture, and traffic violator school fee imposed and collected by any court that conducts a night or weekend session of the court, on all offenses involving a violation of a section of this code or any local ordinance adopted pursuant to this code, except offenses relating to parking.

(b) When a person makes a deposit of bail for an offense to which this section applies, in a case in which the person is required to appear in a court that conducts a night or weekend session, the person making the deposit shall also deposit a sufficient amount to include the assessment prescribed in this section for forfeited bail. If bail is forfeited, the amount of the assessment shall be transmitted by the clerk of the court to the county treasury for disposition as prescribed by subdivision (d).

(c) If a court conducts night or weekend sessions at two or more locations, the court may do either of the following:

(1) Levy assessments only on those persons who are required to appear at the location where night or weekend sessions are held.

(2) Levy assessments on persons who have the option to appear at a location where night or weekend court sessions are held and that is within 25 miles of the location of the court where the person is otherwise required to appear.

(d) After a determination by the court of the amount of the assessment due, the clerk of the court shall collect the amount and transmit it as provided in subdivision (g).

(e) In any case where a person convicted of any offense to which this section applies is imprisoned until the fine is satisfied, the court shall waive the penalty assessment.

(f) As used in subdivisions (g) and (h), the following terms have the following meanings:

(1) "Court Facilities Trust Fund" means the fund established by Section 70352 of the Government Code.

(2) "Location" means a court facility holding night or weekend sessions under this section.

(3) "Transfer of responsibility" means the transfer of responsibility for court facilities from the counties to the state pursuant to Chapter 5.7 (commencing with Section 70301) of Title 8 of the Government Code.

(g) (1) If transfer of responsibility for a location has occurred, the clerk shall collect any assessment imposed pursuant to subdivision (c) and transmit it to the Court Facilities Trust Fund. Moneys deposited pursuant to this subdivision shall be used for any purpose provided by subdivision (b) of Section 70352 of the Government Code.

(2) If transfer of responsibility for a location has not occurred, the clerk shall collect any assessment imposed pursuant to subdivision (c) and transmit it to the county treasury to be deposited in the night court session fund, and the moneys in the fund shall be expended by the county for maintaining courts for which transfer of responsibility has not occurred and that have night or weekend sessions for traffic offenses.

(h) (1) The county treasurer of each county shall transfer from the night court session fund to the Court Facilities Trust Fund an amount that is the same percentage of the night court session fund as of January 1, 2009, as the square footage of locations for which transfer of responsibility has occurred on or before January 1, 2009, is to the total square footage of locations.

(2) For locations for which transfer of responsibility occurs after January 1, 2009, the county treasurer shall, at the time of transfer of any location, transfer from the night court session fund to the Court Facilities Trust Fund an amount that is the same percentage of the night court session fund as the square footage of the location for which transfer of responsibility is occurring is to the sum of the square footage of locations for which transfer of responsibility has not occurred and the square footage of the location being transferred.

(3) Upon the transfer of responsibility for all locations, the county treasurer shall transfer to the Court Facilities Trust Fund any amount remaining in the night court session fund.

(4) Any expenditures made from the fund for a purpose other than those specified in paragraph (2) of subdivision (g) shall be repaid to the state for deposit in the Court Facilities Trust Fund.

(Amended by Stats. 2008, Ch. 218, Sec. 7. Effective January 1, 2009.)

42007. (a) (1) The clerk of the court shall collect a fee from every person who is ordered or permitted to attend a traffic violator school pursuant to Section 41501 or 42005 in an amount equal to the total bail set forth for the eligible offense on the uniform countywide bail schedule. As used in this subdivision, "total bail" means the amount established pursuant to Section 1269b of the Penal Code in accordance with the Uniform Bail and Penalty Schedule adopted by the Judicial Council, including all assessments, surcharges, and penalty amounts. Where multiple offenses are charged in a single notice to appear, the "total bail" is the amount applicable for the greater of the qualifying offenses. However, the court may determine a lesser fee under this subdivision upon a showing that the defendant is unable to pay the full amount.

The fee shall not include the cost, or any part thereof, of traffic safety instruction offered by a traffic violator school.

(2) The clerk may accept from a defendant who is ordered or permitted to attend traffic violator school a payment of at least 10 percent of the fee required by paragraph (1) upon filing a written agreement by the defendant to pay the remainder of the fee according to an installment payment schedule of no more than 90 days as agreed upon with the court. The Judicial Council shall prescribe the form of the agreement for payment of the fee in installments. When the defendant signs the Judicial Council form for payment of the fee in installments, the court shall continue the case to the date in the agreement to complete payment of the fee and submit the certificate of completion of traffic violator school to the court. The clerk shall collect a fee of up to thirty-five dollars ($35) to cover administrative and clerical costs for processing an installment payment of the traffic violator school fee under this paragraph.

(3) If a defendant fails to make an installment payment of the fee according to an installment agreement, the court may convert the fee to bail, declare it forfeited, and report the forfeiture as a conviction under Section 1803. The court may also charge a failure to pay under Section 40508 and impose a civil assessment as provided in Section 1214.1 of the Penal Code or issue an arrest warrant for a failure to pay. For the purposes of reporting a conviction under this subdivision to the department under Section 1803, the date that the court declares the bail forfeited shall be reported as the date of conviction.

(b) Revenues derived from the fee collected under this section shall be deposited in accordance with Section 68084 of the Government Code in the general fund of the county and, as may be applicable, distributed as follows:

(1) In any county in which a fund is established pursuant to Section 76100 or 76101 of the Government Code, the sum of one dollar ($1) for each fund so established shall be deposited with the county treasurer and placed in that fund.

(2) In any county that has established a Maddy Emergency Medical Services Fund pursuant to Section 1797.98a of the Health and Safety Code, an amount equal to the sum of each two dollars ($2) for every seven dollars ($7) that would have been collected pursuant to Section 76000 of the Government Code and, commencing January 1, 2009, an amount equal to the sum of each two dollars ($2) for every ten dollars ($10) that would have been collected pursuant to Section 76000.5 of the Government Code with respect to those counties to which that section is applicable shall be deposited in that fund. Nothing in the act that added this paragraph shall be interpreted in a manner that would result in either of the following:

(A) The utilization of penalty assessment funds that had been set aside, on or before January 1, 2000, to finance debt service on a capital facility that existed before January 1, 2000.

(B) The reduction of the availability of penalty assessment revenues that had been pledged, on or before January 1, 2000, as a means of financing a facility which was approved by a county board of supervisors, but on January 1, 2000, is not under construction.

(3) The amount of the fee that is attributable to Section 70372 of the Government Code shall be transferred pursuant to subdivision (f) of that section.

(c) For fees resulting from city arrests, an amount equal to the amount of base fines that would have been deposited in the treasury of the appropriate city pursuant to paragraph (3) of subdivision (b) of Section 1463.001 of the Penal Code shall be deposited in the treasury of the appropriate city.

(d) The clerk of the court, in a county that offers traffic school shall include in any courtesy notice mailed to a defendant for an offense that qualifies for traffic school attendance the following statement:

NOTICE: If you are eligible and decide not to attend traffic school your automobile insurance may be adversely affected. For drivers with a noncommercial driver's license, one conviction in any 18-month period will be held confidential and not show on your driving record if you complete a traffic violator school program. For drivers with a commercial driver's license, one conviction in any 18-month period will show on your driving record without a violation point if you complete a traffic violator school program.

(e) Notwithstanding any other provision of law, a county that has established a Maddy Emergency Medical Services Fund pursuant to Section 1797.98a of the Health and Safety Code shall not be held liable for having deposited into the fund, prior to January 1, 2009, an amount equal to two dollars ($2) for every ten dollars ($10) that would have been collected pursuant to Section 76000.5 of the Government

Code from revenues derived from traffic violator school fees collected pursuant to this section.

(Amended by Stats. 2013, Ch. 523, Sec. 31. (SB 788) Effective January 1, 2014.)

42007.1. (a) The amount collected by the clerk pursuant to subdivision (a) of Section 42007 shall be in an amount equal to the total bail set forth for the eligible offense on the uniform countywide bail schedule plus a forty-nine-dollar ($49) fee, and a fee determined by the department to be sufficient to defray the cost of routine monitoring of traffic violator school instruction pursuant to subdivision (c) of Section 11208, and a fee, if any, established by the court pursuant to subdivision (c) of Section 11205.2 to defray the costs incurred by a traffic assistance program.

(b) Notwithstanding subdivision (b) of Section 42007, the revenue from the forty-nine-dollar ($49) fee collected under this section shall be deposited in the county general fund. Fifty-one percent of the amount collected under this section and deposited into the county general fund shall be transmitted therefrom monthly to the Controller for deposit in the State Court Facilities Construction Fund, established in Section 70371 of the Government Code.

(c) The fee assessed pursuant to subdivision (c) of Section 11208 shall be allocated to the department to defray the costs of monitoring traffic violator school instruction.

(Amended by Stats. 2021, Ch. 79, Sec. 38. (AB 143) Effective July 16, 2021.)

42007.3. (a) Notwithstanding Section 42007, revenues derived from fees collected under Section 42007 from each person required or permitted to attend traffic violator school pursuant to Section 41501 or 42005 as a result of a violation of subdivision (a) or (c) of Section 21453, subdivision (c) of Section 21454, or subdivision (a) of Section 21457 shall be allocated as follows:

(1) The first 30 percent of the amount collected shall be allocated to the general fund of the city or county in which the offense occurred.

(2) The balance of the amount collected shall be deposited by the county treasurer under Section 42007.

(b) This section does not apply to the additional forty-nine-dollar ($49) court administrative fee assessed pursuant to subdivision (c) of Section 11208 collected under subdivision (a) of Section 42007.1.

(Amended by Stats. 2010, Ch. 599, Sec. 18. (AB 2499) Effective January 1, 2011.)

42007.4. (a) Notwithstanding Section 42007, revenues derived from fees collected under Section 42007 from each person required or permitted to attend traffic violator school pursuant to Section 369b of the Penal Code as a result of a violation of subdivision (c) of Section 21752, involving railroad grade crossings, or Section 22451 or 22452 shall be allocated as follows:

(1) If the offense occurred in an area where a transit district or transportation commission established under Division 12 (commencing with Section 130000) of the Public Utilities Code provides rail transportation, the first 30 percent of the amount collected shall be allocated to the general fund of that transit district or transportation commission to be used only for public safety and public education purposes relating to railroad grade crossings.

(2) If there is no transit district or transportation commission providing rail transportation in the area where the offense occurred, the first 30 percent of the amount collected shall be allocated to the general fund of the county in which the offense occurred, to be used only for public safety and public education purposes relating to railroad grade crossings.

(3) The balance of the amount collected shall be deposited by the county treasurer under Section 1463 of the Penal Code.

(4) A transit district, transportation commission, or a county that is allocated funds pursuant to paragraph (1) or (2) shall provide public safety and public education relating to railroad grade crossings only to the extent that those purposes are funded by the allocations provided pursuant to paragraph (1) or (2).

(b) This section does not apply to the additional forty-nine-dollar ($49) court administrative fee assessed pursuant to subdivision (c) of Section 11208 collected under subdivision (a) of Section 42007.1.

(Amended by Stats. 2010, Ch. 599, Sec. 19. (AB 2499) Effective January 1, 2011.)

42008. (a) Any county may operate an amnesty program for delinquent fines and bail imposed for an infraction or misdemeanor violation of the Vehicle Code, except parking violations of the Vehicle Code and violations of Section 23103, 23104, 23152, or 23153. The program shall be implemented by the courts in accordance with Judicial Council guidelines, and shall apply to infraction or misdemeanor violations of the Vehicle Code, except parking violations, upon which a fine or bail was delinquent on or before April 1, 1991.

(b) Under the amnesty program, any person owing a fine or bail due on or before April 1, 1991, that was imposed for an infraction or misdemeanor violation of the Vehicle Code, except violations of Section 23103, 23104, 23152, or 23153 or parking violations, may pay to the superior court the amount scheduled by the court, which shall be either (1) 70 percent of the total fine or bail or (2) the amount of one hundred dollars ($100) for an infraction or five hundred dollars ($500) for a misdemeanor. This amount shall be accepted by the court in full satisfaction of the delinquent fine or bail.

(c) No criminal action shall be brought against any person for a delinquent fine or bail paid under this amnesty program and no other additional penalties shall be assessed for the late payment of the fine or bail made under the amnesty program.

(d) Notwithstanding Section 1463 of the Penal Code, the total amount of funds collected by the courts pursuant to the amnesty program created by this section shall be deposited in the county treasury.

(Amended by Stats. 2002, Ch. 784, Sec. 606. Effective January 1, 2003.)

42008.5. (a) A county may establish a one-time amnesty program for fines and bail that have been delinquent for not less than six months as of the date upon which the program commences and were imposed for an infraction or misdemeanor violation of this code, except parking violations of this code and violations of Section 23103, 23104, 23105, 23152, or 23153.

(b) A person owing a fine or bail that is eligible for amnesty under the program may pay to the superior or juvenile court the amount scheduled by the court, that shall be accepted by the court in full satisfaction of the delinquent fine or bail and shall be either of the following:

(1) Seventy percent of the total fine or bail.

(2) The amount of one hundred dollars ($100) for an infraction or five hundred dollars ($500) for a misdemeanor.

(c) The amnesty program shall be implemented by the courts of the county on a one-time basis and conducted in accordance with Judicial Council guidelines for a period of not less than 120 days. The program shall operate not longer than six months from the date the court initiates the program.

(d) No criminal action shall be brought against a person for a delinquent fine or bail paid under the amnesty program and no other additional penalties, except as provided in Section 1214.1 of the Penal Code, shall be assessed for the late payment of the fine or bail made under the amnesty program.

(e) Notwithstanding Section 1463 of the Penal Code, the total amount of funds collected by the courts pursuant to the amnesty program shall be deposited in the county treasury until 150 percent of the cost of operating the program, excluding capital expenditures, have been so deposited. Thereafter, 37 percent of the amount of the delinquent fines and bail deposited in the county treasury shall be distributed by the county pursuant to Section 1464 of the Penal Code, 26 percent of the amount deposited shall be distributed by the county pursuant to Article 2 (commencing with Section 76100) of Chapter 12 of Title 8 of the Government Code, and the remaining 37 percent of the amount deposited shall be retained by the county.

(f) The deposit of fines and bails in the county treasury as described in subdivision (e) is limited to the amnesty program described in this section, and it is the intent of the Legislature that it shall not be considered a precedent with respect to affecting programs that receive funding pursuant to Section 1463 of the Penal Code.

(g) Each county participating in the program shall file, not later than six months after the termination of the program, a written report with the Assembly Committee on Judiciary and the Senate Committee on Judiciary. The report shall summarize the amount of money collected, operating costs of the program, distribution of funds collected, and when possible, how the funds were expended.

(Amended by Stats. 2007, Ch. 682, Sec. 21. Effective January 1, 2008.)

42008.7. (a) The State of California continues to face a fiscal and economic crisis affecting the State Budget and the overall state economy. In light of this crisis, a one-time infraction amnesty program would do the following:

(1) Provide relief to individuals who have found themselves in violation of a court-ordered obligation because they are financially unable to pay traffic bail or fines.

(2) Provide increased revenue at a time when revenue is scarce by encouraging payment of old fines that have remained unpaid.

(3) Allow courts and counties to resolve older delinquent cases and focus limited resources on collecting on more recent cases.

(b) A one-time amnesty program for fines and bail meeting the eligibility requirements set forth in subdivision (e) shall be established in each county. Unless agreed otherwise by the court and the county in writing, the government entities that are responsible for the collection of delinquent court-ordered debt shall be responsible for implementation of the amnesty program as to that debt, maintaining the same division of responsibility in place with respect to the collection of court-ordered debt under subdivision (b) of Section 1463.010 of the Penal Code.

(c) As used in this section, the term "fine" or "bail" refers to the total amounts due in connection with a specific violation, which include, but are not limited to, the following:

(1) Base fine or bail, as established by court order, by statute, or by the court's bail schedule.

(2) Penalty assessments imposed pursuant to Section 1464 of the Penal Code and Sections 70372, 76000, 76000.5, 76104.6, and 76104.7 of the Government Code.

(3) Civil assessment imposed pursuant to Section 1214.1 of the Penal Code.

(4) State surcharge imposed pursuant to Section 1465.7 of the Penal Code.

(5) Court security fee imposed pursuant to Section 1465.8 of the Penal Code.

(d) In addition to and at the same time as the mandatory one-time amnesty program is established pursuant to subdivision (b), the court and the county may jointly agree to extend that amnesty program to fines and bail imposed for a misdemeanor violation of this code and a violation of Section 853.7 of the Penal Code added to the misdemeanor case otherwise subject to the amnesty. The amnesty program authorized pursuant to this subdivision shall not apply to parking violations and violations of Section 23103, 23104, 23105, 23152, or 23153 of this code.

(e) Violations are only eligible for amnesty if paragraph (1), (2), or (3) applies and the requirements of paragraphs (4), (5), and (6) are met:

(1) The violation is an infraction violation filed with the court.

(2) It is a violation of subdivision (a) or (b) of Section 40508, or a violation of Section 853.7 of the Penal Code added to the case subject to paragraph (1).

(3) The violation is a misdemeanor violation filed with the court to which subdivision (d) applies.

(4) The due date for payment of the fine or bail was on or before January 1, 2009.

(5) The defendant does not owe victim restitution on any case within the county.

(6) There are no outstanding misdemeanor or felony warrants for the defendant within the county, except for misdemeanor warrants for misdemeanor violations authorized by the court and the county pursuant to subdivision (d).

(f) Each amnesty program shall accept, in full satisfaction of any eligible fine or bail, 50 percent of the fine or bail amount, as defined in subdivision (c) of this section. Payment of a fine or bail under an amnesty program implemented pursuant to this section shall be accepted beginning January 1, 2012, and ending June 30, 2012. The Judicial Council shall adopt guidelines for the amnesty program no later than November 1, 2011, and each program shall be conducted in accordance with Judicial Council guidelines.

(g) No criminal action shall be brought against a person for a delinquent fine or bail paid under the amnesty program.

(h) The total amount of funds collected under the amnesty program shall as soon as practical after receipt thereof be deposited in the county treasury or the account established under Section 77009 of the Government Code. Any unreimbursed costs of operating the amnesty program, excluding capital expenditures, may be deducted from the revenues collected under the amnesty program by the court or the county that incurred the expense of operating the program. Notwithstanding Section 1203.1d of the Penal Code, the remaining revenues collected under the amnesty program shall be distributed on a pro rata basis in the same manner as a partial payment distributed pursuant to Section 1462.5 of the Penal Code.

(i) Each court or county implementing an amnesty program shall file, not later than September 30, 2012, a written report with the Judicial Council, on a form approved by the Judicial Council. The report shall include information about the number of cases resolved, the amount of money collected, and the operating costs of the amnesty program. Notwithstanding Section 10231.5 of the Government Code, on or before December 31, 2012, the Judicial Council shall submit a report to the Legislature summarizing the information provided by each court or county.

(Amended by Stats. 2011, Ch. 662, Sec. 1. (AB 1358) Effective January 1, 2012.)

42008.8. (a) The Legislature finds and declares that a one-time infraction amnesty program would do all of the following:

(1) Provide relief to individuals who have found themselves in violation of a court-ordered obligation because they have unpaid traffic bail or fines.

(2) Provide relief to individuals who have found themselves in violation of a court-ordered obligation or who have had their driving privileges suspended pursuant to Section 13365.

(3) Provide increased revenue at a time when revenue is scarce by encouraging payment of old fines that have remained unpaid.

(4) Allow courts and counties to resolve older delinquent cases and focus limited resources on collections for more recent cases.

(b) A one-time amnesty program for unpaid fines and bail meeting the eligibility requirements set forth in subdivision (g) shall be established in each county. Unless agreed otherwise by the court and the county in writing, the government entities that are responsible for the collection of delinquent court-ordered debt shall be responsible for implementation of the amnesty program as to that debt, maintaining the same division of responsibility in place with respect to the collection of court-ordered debt under subdivision (b) of Section 1463.010 of the Penal Code.

(c) As used in this section, the term "fine" or "bail" refers to the total amounts due in connection with a specific violation, including, but not limited to, all of the following:

(1) Base fine or bail, as established by court order, by statute, or by the court's bail schedule.

(2) Penalty assessments imposed pursuant to Section 1464 of the Penal Code, and Sections 70372, 76000, 76000.5, 76104.6, and 76104.7 of, and paragraph (1) of subdivision (c) of Section 76000.10 of, the Government Code, and Section 42006 of this code.

(3) State surcharges imposed pursuant to Section 1465.7 of the Penal Code.

(4) Court operations assessments imposed pursuant to Section 1465.8

of the Penal Code.

(5) Criminal conviction assessments pursuant to Section 70373 of the Government Code.

(d) Notwithstanding subdivision (c), any civil assessment imposed pursuant to Section 1214.1 of the Penal Code shall not be collected, nor shall the payment of that assessment be a requirement of participation in the amnesty program.

(e) Concurrent with the amnesty program established pursuant to subdivision (b), between October 1, 2015, to March 31, 2017, inclusive, the following shall apply:

(1) The court shall, within 90 days, issue and file the appropriate certificate pursuant to subdivisions (a) and (b) of Section 40509 for any participant of the one-time amnesty program established pursuant to subdivision (b) demonstrating that the participant has appeared in court, paid the fine, or otherwise satisfied the court, if the driving privilege of that participant was suspended pursuant to Section 13365 in connection with a specific violation described in paragraph (1), (2), or (3) of subdivision (g). For applications submitted prior to January 1, 2017, that remain outstanding as of that date, the court shall issue and file the certificate no later than March 31, 2017. For applications submitted on or before March 31, 2017, all terms and procedures related to the participant's payment plans shall remain in effect after March 31, 2017.

(2) The court shall, within 90 days, issue and file with the department the appropriate certificate pursuant to subdivisions (a) and (b) of Section 40509 for any person in good standing in a comprehensive collection program pursuant to subdivision (c) of Section 1463.007 of the Penal Code demonstrating that the person has appeared in court, paid the fine, or otherwise satisfied the court, if the driving privilege was suspended pursuant to Section 13365 in connection with a specific violation described in paragraph (1), (2), or (3) of subdivision (g). For applications submitted prior to January 1, 2017, that remain outstanding as of that date, the court shall issue and file the certificate no later than March 31, 2017. For applications submitted on or before March 31, 2017, all terms and procedures related to the participant's payment plans shall remain in effect after March 31, 2017.

(3) Any person who is eligible for a driver's license pursuant to Section 12801, 12801.5, or 12801.9 shall be eligible for the amnesty program established pursuant to subdivision (b) for any specific violation described in subdivision (g). The department shall issue a driver's license to any person who is eligible pursuant to Section 12801, 12801.5, or 12801.9 if the person is participating in the amnesty program and is otherwise eligible for the driver's license but for the fines or bail to be collected through the program.

(4) The Department of Motor Vehicles shall not deny reinstating the driving privilege of any person who participates in the amnesty program established pursuant to subdivision (b) for any fines or bail in connection with the specific violation that is the basis for participation in the amnesty program.

(f) In addition to, and at the same time as, the mandatory one-time amnesty program is established pursuant to subdivision (b), the court and the county may jointly agree to extend that amnesty program to fines and bail imposed for a misdemeanor violation of this code and a violation of Section 853.7 of the Penal Code that was added to the misdemeanor case otherwise subject to the amnesty. The amnesty program authorized pursuant to this subdivision shall not apply to parking violations and violations of Sections 23103, 23104, 23105, 23152, and 23153.

(g) A violation is only eligible for amnesty if paragraph (1), (2), or (3) applies, and the requirements of paragraphs (4) to (8), inclusive, are met:

(1) The violation is an infraction violation filed with the court.

(2) It is a violation of subdivision (a) or (b) of Section 40508, or a violation of Section 853.7 of the Penal Code that was added to the case subject to paragraph (1).

(3) The violation is a misdemeanor violation filed with the court to which subdivision (f) applies.

(4) The initial due date for payment of the fine or bail was on or before January 1, 2013.

(5) There are no outstanding misdemeanor or felony warrants for the defendant within the county, except for misdemeanor warrants for misdemeanor violations subject to this section.

(6) The person does not owe victim restitution on any case within the county.

(7) The person has not made any payments for the violation after September 30, 2015, to a comprehensive collection program in the county pursuant to subdivision (c) of Section 1463.007 of the Penal Code.

(8) The person filed a request with the court on or before March 31, 2017.

(h) (1) Except as provided in paragraph (2), each amnesty program shall accept, in full satisfaction of any eligible fine or bail, 50 percent of the fine or bail amount, as defined in subdivision (c).

(2) If the participant certifies under penalty of perjury that he or she receives any of the public benefits listed in subdivision (a) of Section 68632 of the Government Code or is within the conditions described in subdivision (b) of Section 68632 of the Government Code, the amnesty program shall accept, in full satisfaction of any eligible fine or bail, 20 percent of the fine or bail amount, as defined in subdivision (c).

(i) The Judicial Council, in consultation with the California State Association of Counties, shall adopt guidelines for the amnesty program no later than October 1, 2015, and each program shall be conducted in accordance with the Judicial Council's guidelines. As part of its guidelines, the Judicial Council shall include all of the following:

(1) Each court or county responsible for implementation of the amnesty program pursuant to subdivision (b) shall recover costs pursuant to subdivision (a) of Section 1463.007 of the Penal Code and may charge an amnesty program fee of fifty dollars ($50) that may be collected with the receipt of the first payment of a participant.

(2) A payment plan option created pursuant to Judicial Council guidelines in which a monthly payment is equal to the amount that an eligible participant can afford to pay per month consistent with Sections 68633 and 68634 of the Government Code. If a participant chooses the payment plan option, the county or court shall collect all relevant information to allow for collection by the Franchise Tax Board pursuant to existing protocols prescribed by the Franchise Tax Board to collect delinquent debts of any amount in which a participant is delinquent or otherwise in default under his or her amnesty payment plan.

(3) If a participant does not comply with the terms of his or her payment plan under the amnesty program, including failing to make one or more payments, the appropriate agency shall send a notice to the participant that he or she has failed to make one or more payments and that the participant has 30 days to either resume making payments or to request that the agency change the payment amount. If the participant fails to respond to the notice within 30 days, the appropriate agency may refer the participant to the Franchise Tax Board for collection of any remaining balance owed, including an amount equal to the reasonable administrative costs incurred by the Franchise Tax Board to collect the delinquent amount owed. The Franchise Tax Board shall collect any delinquent amounts owed pursuant to existing protocols prescribed by the Franchise Tax Board. The comprehensive collection program may also utilize additional collection efforts pursuant to Section 1463.007 of the Penal Code, except for subparagraph (C) of paragraph (4) of subdivision (c) of that section.

(4) A plan for outreach that will, at a minimum, make available via an Internet Web site relevant information regarding the amnesty program, including how an individual may participate in the amnesty program.

(5) The Judicial Council shall reimburse costs incurred by the Department of Motor Vehicles up to an amount not to exceed two hundred fifty thousand dollars ($250,000), including all of the following:

(A) Providing on a separate insert with each motor vehicle registration renewal notice a summary of the amnesty program established pursuant to this section that is compliant with Section 7292 of the Government Code.

(B) Posting on the department's Internet Web site information regarding the amnesty program.

(C) Personnel costs associated with the amnesty program.

(j) The Judicial Council, in consultation with the department, may, within its existing resources, consider, adopt, or develop recommendations for an appropriate mechanism or mechanisms to allow reinstatement of the driving privilege of any person who otherwise meets the criteria for amnesty but who has violations in more than one county.

(k) A criminal action shall not be brought against a person for a delinquent fine or bail paid under the amnesty program.

(l) (1) The total amount of funds collected under the amnesty program shall, as soon as practical after receipt thereof, be deposited in the county treasury or the account established under Section 77009 of the Government Code. After acceptance of the amount specified in subdivision (h), notwithstanding Section 1203.1d of the Penal Code, the remaining revenues collected under the amnesty program shall be distributed on a pro rata basis in the same manner as a partial payment distributed pursuant to Section 1462.5 of the Penal Code.

(2) Notwithstanding Section 1464 of the Penal Code, the amount of funds collected pursuant to this section that would be available for distribution pursuant to subdivision (f) of Section 1464 of the Penal Code shall instead be distributed as follows:

(A) The first two hundred fifty thousand dollars ($250,000) received shall be transferred to the Judicial Council.

(B) Following the transfer of the funds described in subparagraph (A), once a month, both of the following transfers shall occur:

(i) An amount equal to 82.20 percent of the amount of funds collected pursuant to this section during the preceding month shall be transferred into the Peace Officers' Training Fund.

(ii) An amount equal to 17.80 percent of the amount of funds collected pursuant to this section during the preceding month shall be transferred into the Corrections Training Fund.

(m) Each court or county implementing an amnesty program shall file, not later than May 31, 2017, a written report with the Judicial Council, on a form approved by the Judicial Council. The report shall include information about the number of cases resolved, the amount of money collected, and the operating costs of the amnesty program. Notwithstanding Section 10231.5 of the Government Code, on or before August 31, 2017, the Judicial Council shall submit a report to the Legislature summarizing the information provided by each court or county.

(Amended by Stats. 2016, Ch. 779, Sec. 1. (SB 881) Effective January 1, 2017.)

42009. (a) For an offense specified in subdivision (b), committed by the driver of a vehicle within a highway construction or maintenance area, during any time when traffic is regulated or restricted through or around that area pursuant to Section 21367, or when the highway construction or maintenance is actually being performed in the area by workers acting in their official capacity, the fine, in a misdemeanor case, shall be double the amount otherwise prescribed. In an infraction case, the fine shall be one category higher than the penalty otherwise prescribed by the uniform traffic penalty schedule established pursuant to Section 40310.

(b) A violation of the following is an offense that is subject to subdivision (a):

(1) Section 21367, relating to regulation of traffic at a construction site.

(2) Article 3 (commencing with Section 21450) of Chapter 2 of Division 11, relating to obedience to traffic devices.

(3) Chapter 3 (commencing with Section 21650) of Division 11, relating to driving, overtaking, and passing.

(4) Chapter 4 (commencing with Section 21800) of Division 11, relating to yielding the right-of-way.

(5) Chapter 6 (commencing with Section 22100) of Division 11, relating to turning and stopping and turn signals.

(6) Chapter 7 (commencing with Section 22348) of Division 11, relating to speed limits.

(7) Chapter 8 (commencing with Section 22450) of Division 11, relating to special traffic stops.

(8) Section 23103, relating to reckless driving.

(9) Section 23104 or 23105, relating to reckless driving which results in bodily injury to another.

(10) Section 23109 or 23109.1, relating to speed contests.

(11) Section 23152, relating to driving under the influence of alcohol or a controlled substance, or a violation of Section 23103, as specified in Section 23103.5, relating to alcohol-related reckless driving.

(12) Section 23153, relating to driving under the influence of alcohol or a controlled substance, which results in bodily injury to another.

(13) Section 23154, relating to convicted drunk drivers operating a motor vehicle with a blood-alcohol concentration of 0.01 percent or greater.

(14) Section 23220, relating to drinking while driving.

(15) Section 23221, relating to drinking in a motor vehicle while on the highway.

(16) Section 23222, relating to driving while possessing an open alcoholic beverage container.

(17) Section 23223, relating to being in a vehicle on the highway while possessing an open alcoholic beverage container.

(18) Section 23224, relating to being a driver or passenger under the age of 21 possessing an open alcoholic beverage container.

(19) Section 23225, relating to being the owner or driver of a vehicle in which there is an open alcoholic beverage container.

(20) Section 23226, relating to being a passenger in a vehicle in which there is an open alcoholic beverage container.

(c) This section applies only when construction or maintenance work is actually being performed by workers, and there are work zone traffic control devices, traffic controls or warning signs, or any combination of those, to notify motorists and pedestrians of construction or maintenance workers in the area.

(Amended by Stats. 2007, Ch. 749, Sec. 6.5. Effective January 1, 2008. Operative January 1, 2009, by Sec. 9 of Ch. 749.)

42010. (a) For an offense specified in subdivision (b) that is committed by the driver of a vehicle within an area that has been designated as a Safety Enhancement-Double Fine Zone pursuant to Section 97 and following of the Streets and Highways Code, the fine, in a misdemeanor case, shall be double the amount otherwise prescribed, and, in an infraction case, the fine shall be one category higher than the penalty otherwise prescribed by the uniform traffic penalty schedule established pursuant to Section 40310.

(b) A violation of the following is an offense that is subject to subdivision (a):

(1) Chapter 3 (commencing with Section 21650) of Division 11, relating to driving, overtaking, and passing.

(2) Chapter 7 (commencing with Section 22348) of Division 11, relating to speed limits.

(3) Section 23103, relating to reckless driving.

(4) Section 23104 or 23105, relating to reckless driving that results in bodily injury to another.

(5) Section 23109 or 23109.1, relating to speed contests.

(6) Section 23152, relating to driving under the influence of alcohol or a controlled substance, or a violation of Section 23103, as specified in Section 23103.5, relating to alcohol-related reckless driving.

(7) Section 23153, relating to driving under the influence of alcohol or a controlled substance, which results in bodily injury to another.

(8) Section 23154, relating to convicted drunk drivers operating a motor vehicle with a blood-alcohol concentration of 0.01 percent or greater.

(9) Section 23220, relating to drinking while driving.

(10) Section 23221, relating to drinking in a motor vehicle while on the highway.

(11) Section 23222, relating to driving while possessing an open alcoholic beverage container.

(12) Section 23223, relating to being in a vehicle on the highway while possessing an open alcoholic beverage container.

(13) Section 23224, relating to being a driver or passenger under 21 years of age possessing an open alcoholic beverage container.

(14) Section 23225, relating to being the owner or driver of a vehicle in which there is an open alcoholic beverage container.

(15) Section 23226, relating to being a passenger in a vehicle in which there is an open alcoholic beverage container.

(c) This section applies only when traffic controls or warning signs have been placed pursuant to Section 97 or 97.1 of the Streets and Highways Code.

(d) (1) Notwithstanding any other provision of law, the enhanced fine imposed pursuant to this section shall be based only on the base fine imposed for the underlying offense and shall not include any other enhancements imposed pursuant to law.

(2) Notwithstanding any other provision of law, any additional penalty, forfeiture, or assessment imposed by any other statute shall be based on the amount of the base fine before enhancement or doubling and shall not be based on the amount of the enhanced fine imposed pursuant to this section.

(Amended by Stats. 2007, Ch. 749, Sec. 7.5. Effective January 1, 2008. Operative January 1, 2009, by Sec. 9 of Ch. 749.)

Article 2. Weight Violations

(Article 2 enacted by Stats. 1959, Ch. 3.)

42030. (a) Every person convicted of a violation of any weight limitation provision of Division 15 (commencing with Section 35000), and every person convicted of a violation of Section 21461 with respect to signs provided pursuant to Section 35654 or 35752, and every person convicted of a violation of Section 40001 for requiring the operation of a vehicle upon a highway in violation of any provision referred to in this section shall be punished by a fine which equals the amounts specified in the following table:

Pounds of excess weight	Fine
0 — 1,000	$ 20
1,001 — 1,500	30
1,501 — 2,000	40
2,001 — 2,500	55
2,501 — 3,000	85
3,001 — 3,500	105
3,501 — 4,000	125
4,001 — 4,500	145
4,501 — 5,000	175
5,001 — 6,000	.04 each lb.
6,001 — 7,000	.06 each lb.
7,001 — 8,000	.08 each lb.
8,001 — 10,000	.15 each lb.
10,001 and over	.20 each lb.

(b) No part of the penalties prescribed by this section shall be suspended for a conviction of any of the following:

(1) Section 40001 for requiring operation of a vehicle upon a highway in violation of any provision referred to in this section.

(2) Any provision referred to in this section when the amount of the weight exceeds 4,000 pounds.

(3) Any provision referred to in this section when a second or subsequent conviction of a violation thereof occurs within three years immediately preceding the violation charged.

(c) However, notwithstanding any other provision of this section, the court shall exercise discretion with respect to the imposition of the fine under this section for excess weight not exceeding 1,000 pounds if the load of the vehicle cited consisted entirely of field-loaded, unprocessed bulk agricultural or forest products or livestock being transported from the field to the first point of processing or handling.

(d) Notwithstanding any other provision of this section, the court may exercise discretion with respect to the imposition of the fine under this section if any applicable local permit was obtained prior to the court hearing and, at the time of issuance of the notice to appear, the motor carrier was transporting construction equipment or materials and a valid extra-legal load permit from the Department of Transportation was in effect.

(Amended by Stats. 1996, Ch. 456, Sec. 1. Effective January 1, 1997.)

42030.1. (a) Every person convicted of a violation of any declared gross vehicle weight limitation provision of this code, shall be punished by a fine that equals the amounts specified in the following table:

Pounds in Excess of the Declared Gross Vehicle Weight	Fine
1,001 — 1,500	$ 250
1,501 — 2,000	300
2,001 — 2,500	350
2,501 — 3,000	400
3,001 — 3,500	450
3,501 — 4,000	500
4,001 — 4,500	550
4,501 — 5,000	600
5,001 — 6,000	700
6,001 — 7,000	800
7,001 — 8,000	900
8,001 — 10,000	1,000
10,001 and over	2,000

(b) No part of the penalties prescribed by this section shall be suspended for a conviction of any of the following:

(1) Section 40001 for requiring operation of a vehicle upon a highway in violation of any provision referred to in this section.

(2) Any provision referred to in this section when a second or subsequent conviction of a violation thereof occurs within three years immediately preceding the violation charged.

(Added by Stats. 2000, Ch. 861, Sec. 58. Effective September 29, 2000. Operative December 31, 2001, pursuant to Sec. 67 of Ch. 861.)

42031. Whenever the gross weight and any axle or wheel weight of a vehicle are in excess of the limits prescribed in this code, the excess weights shall be deemed one offense in violation of this code.

(Enacted by Stats. 1959, Ch. 3.)

42032. (a) In addition to any other fines and penalties, any local public agency which owns or operates vehicles used for the collection of garbage, refuse, or rubbish and which has, within any 90-day period, been convicted an excessive number of times for operating those vehicles in violation of any of the weight limitations set forth in Chapter 5 (commencing with Section 35550) of Division 15, taking into consideration the total number of trip routes for those vehicles which are normally scheduled in the same 90-day period, may be assessed a civil penalty not to exceed two thousand five hundred dollars ($2,500) for each violation. Nothing in this section affects the legal standards, proof requirements, or penalty provisions of any other provision of the law.

(b) The penalties imposed by this section shall be assessed and recovered in a civil action brought by the Attorney General or by any district attorney or city attorney. Prior to undertaking a civil action, a reasonable effort for informal resolution of the problem of excessive violations shall be made by the applicable attorney. Penalties recovered shall be paid to the Treasurer for deposit in the State Highway Account in the State Transportation Fund and used, upon appropriation, for purposes of highway maintenance.

(Added by Stats. 1990, Ch. 88, Sec. 1.)

Chapter 2. Disposition of Fees, Fines, and Forfeitures

(Chapter 2 enacted by Stats. 1959, Ch. 3.)

Article 1. Fines and Forfeitures

(Article 1 enacted by Stats. 1959, Ch. 3.)

42200. (a) Of the total amount of fines and forfeitures received by a city under Section 1463 of the Penal Code that proportion which is represented by fines and forfeitures collected from any person charged with a misdemeanor under this code following arrest by an officer employed by a city, shall be paid into the treasury of the city and deposited in a special fund to be known as the "Traffic Safety Fund," and shall be used exclusively for official traffic control devices, the maintenance thereof, equipment and supplies for traffic law enforcement and traffic accident prevention, and for the maintenance, improvement, or construction of public streets, bridges, and culverts within the city, but the fund shall not be used to pay the compensation of traffic or other police officers. The fund may be used to pay the compensation of school crossing guards who are not regular full-time members of the police department of the city.

(b) For purposes of this section, "city" includes any city, city and county, district, including any enterprise special district, community service district, or county service area engaged in police protection activities as reported to the Controller for inclusion in the 1989–90 edition of the Financial Transactions Report Concerning Special Districts under the heading of Police Protection and Public Safety, authority, or other local agency (other than a county) which employs persons authorized to make arrests or to issue notices to appear or notices of violation which may be filed in court.

(Amended by Stats. 1995, Ch. 285, Sec. 2. Effective January 1, 1996.)

42201. (a) Of the total amount of fines and forfeitures received by a county under Section 1463.001 of the Penal Code, fines and forfeitures collected from any person charged with a misdemeanor under this code following arrest by any officer employed by the state or by the county shall be paid into the general fund of the county. However, the board of supervisors of the county may, by resolution, provide that a portion thereof be transferred into the road fund of the county.

(b) The board of supervisors of a county may enter into a contract with the Department of the California Highway Patrol for the purpose of providing adequate protection for school pupils who are required to cross heavily traveled streets, highways, and roadways in the unincorporated areas of the county. When requested, the Department of the California Highway Patrol may provide such service and the county shall reimburse the state for salaries and wages of crossing guards furnished by the Department of the California Highway Patrol pursuant to such contract, including any necessary retirement and general administrative costs and expenses in connection therewith, and may pay the costs thereof from amounts deposited in the road fund pursuant to this section.

(c) Fines and forfeitures received by a county under Section 1463.001 of the Penal Code may be used to pay the compensation of school crossing guards and necessary equipment costs and administrative costs.

(d) When requested by any county which had in effect on June 30, 1979, a contract with the Department of the California Highway Patrol, to provide protection for school pupils at school crossings, the department upon request of a county shall continue to administer such school crossing program until June 30, 1980. The county shall reimburse the Department of the California Highway Patrol for general administrative costs and expenses in connection therewith, except that, effective January 1, 1980, the crossing guards shall be furnished to the California Highway Patrol and such crossing guards shall be employees of the county, the county superintendent of schools, the affected school districts, or both the superintendent and the affected school districts, at the option of the board of supervisors of the county. Any salaries and wages of crossing guards, including necessary retirement and equipment costs and any administrative costs shall be paid or reimbursed by the county from amounts deposited in the road fund pursuant to this section.

(e) The board of supervisors may adopt standards for the provision of school crossing guards. The board has final authority over the total cost of the school crossing guard program of any agency to be paid or reimbursed from amounts deposited in the road fund pursuant to this section. The board of supervisors may specify that a designated county officer, employee, or commissioner is to hire school crossing guards, or, in the alternative, the board may specify that any school district crossing guard program in unincorporated areas shall be maintained by the school districts desiring the program.

(Amended by Stats. 1994, Ch. 308, Sec. 34. Effective July 21, 1994.)

42201.1. Fines and forfeitures received by a county under Section 1463 of the Penal Code may be used to reimburse the state for the construction of platform scales and vehicle inspection facilities in the county.

(Added by Stats. 1985, Ch. 407, Sec. 1. Effective July 30, 1985.)

42201.5. Fines, forfeitures, and deposits of bail collected as a result of a charge or conviction of an infraction shall be deposited and distributed in the same manner as fines, forfeitures, and deposits of bail collected from a person charged with or convicted of a misdemeanor.

(Added by Stats. 1968, Ch. 1192.)

42201.6. (a) A deposit of bail received with respect to an infraction violation of this code, or any local ordinance adopted pursuant to this code, including, but not limited to, a violation involving the standing or parking of a vehicle, shall be refunded by the agency which issued the notice of violation or the court within 30 days of a cancellation, dismissal, or finding of not guilty of the offense charged.

(b) Multiple or duplicate deposits of bail or parking penalty shall be identified by the court or agency and refunded within 30 days of identification.

(c) Any amount to be refunded in accordance with subdivision (a) or (b) shall accrue interest, at the rate specified in Section 3289 of the Civil Code, on and after the 60th day of a cancellation, dismissal, or finding of not guilty or identification of multiple or duplicate deposits, and shall be refunded as soon as possible thereafter along with accrued interest.

(Amended by Stats. 1989, Ch. 290, Sec. 1.)

42202. Failure, refusal, or neglect on the part of any judicial or other officer or employee receiving or having custody of any fine or forfeiture mentioned in this article either before or after deposit in the respective fund to comply with the foregoing provisions of this article is misconduct in office and ground for removal therefrom.

(Enacted by Stats. 1959, Ch. 3.)

42203. Notwithstanding Section 42201 or 42201.5, 50 percent of all fines and forfeitures collected in a superior court upon conviction or upon the forfeiture of bail for violations of any provisions of the Vehicle Code, or of any local ordinance or resolution, relating to stopping, standing, or parking a vehicle, that have occurred upon the premises of facilities physically located in such county, but which are owned by another county, which other county furnishes law enforcement personnel for the premises, shall be transmitted pursuant to this section to the county which owns the facilities upon which the violations occurred. The court receiving such moneys shall, once each month, transmit such moneys received in the preceding month to the county treasurer of the county in which the court is located. Once each month in which the county treasurer receives such moneys, the county treasurer shall transmit to the county which owns such facilities an amount equal to 50 percent thereof. The county owning such facilities shall, upon receipt of such moneys from the superior court of the county in which the facilities are physically located, deposit such moneys in its county treasury for use solely in meeting traffic control and law enforcement expenses on the premises upon which the violations occurred.

This section shall not apply when the county in which such facilities are located performs all law enforcement functions with respect to such facilities.

(Amended by Stats. 2002, Ch. 784, Sec. 608. Effective January 1, 2003.)

42204. Notwithstanding any other provisions of law, all fines and forfeitures collected for violations of Division 16.5 (commencing with Section 38000) shall be deposited in the appropriate fund in the county where the violation occurred and distributed in the same manner as specified in Section 42201.5, and shall be used for enforcing laws related to the operation of off-highway motor vehicles.

(Amended by Stats. 2002, Ch. 563, Sec. 46. Effective January 1, 2003.)

42205. (a) Notwithstanding Chapter 3 (commencing with Section 42270), the department shall file, at least monthly with the Controller, a report of money received by the department pursuant to Section 9400 for the previous month and shall, at the same time, remit all money so reported to the Treasurer. On order of the Controller, the Treasurer shall deposit all money so remitted into the State Highway Account in the State Transportation Fund, or directly into the Transportation Debt Service Fund as provided in paragraph (2) of subdivision (c) of Section 9400.4, as applicable.

(b) The Legislature shall appropriate from the State Highway Account in the State Transportation Fund to the department and the Franchise Tax Board amounts equal to the costs incurred by each in performing their duties pursuant to Article 3 (commencing with Section 9400) of Chapter 6 of Division 3. The applicable amounts shall be determined so that the appropriate costs for registration and weight fee collection activities are appropriated between the recipients of revenues in proportion to the revenues that would have been received individually by those recipients if the total fee imposed under the Vehicle License Fee Law (Part 5 (commencing with Section 10701) of Division 2 of the Revenue and Taxation Code) was 2 percent of the market value of a vehicle. The remainder of the funds collected under Section 9400 and deposited in the account, other than the direct deposits to the Transportation Debt Service Fund referenced in subdivision (a), may be appropriated to the Department of Transportation, the Department of the California Highway Patrol, and the Department of Motor Vehicles for the purposes authorized under Section 3 of Article XIX of the California Constitution.

(Amended by Stats. 2013, Ch. 35, Sec. 15. (SB 85) Effective June 27, 2013.)

Article 2. Refund of Fees and Penalties

(Article 2 enacted by Stats. 1959, Ch. 3.)

42230. Whenever any application made under this code is accompanied by any fee, except an application for an occupational license accompanied by a fee as specified in Section 9262, 9262.5, 11309, or 11820, or an application for a duplicate driver's license, as required by law, and the application is refused or rejected, the fees shall be returned to the applicant, except that, whenever any application is made for the first set of special plates under subdivision (a) of Section 9262 and the application is refused or rejected, the fee for the special plates only shall be returned to the applicant or, when application is made for the first set of special plates under subdivision (1) of Section 9264 and the application is refused or rejected, the fee for the special plates shall be returned to the applicant.

(Amended by Stats. 1996, Ch. 124, Sec. 150. Effective January 1, 1997.)

42231. Whenever any application is made under this code and the application is accompanied by any fee which is excessive or not legally due, or whenever the department in consequence of any error either of fact or of law as to the proper amount of any fee or any penalty thereon or as to the necessity of obtaining any privilege under this code collects any fee or penalty which is excessive, erroneous, or not legally due, the person who has paid the erroneous or excessive fee or penalty, or his agent on his behalf, may apply for and receive a refund of the amount thereof as provided in this article, or the department may refund the same within three years after the date of the payment or collection.

(Amended by Stats. 1961, Ch. 20.)

42232. The application for refund shall be presented to the department in a format prescribed by the department within three years from the date of payment of the erroneous or excessive fee or penalty and shall identify the payment made and state the grounds upon which it is claimed that the payment was excessive or erroneous.

(Amended by Stats. 2000, Ch. 787, Sec. 26. Effective January 1, 2001.)

42233. (a) Whenever any fee or penalty subject to refund under Section 42231 after application therefor has not been paid into the State Treasury, the department shall refund the fee or penalty.

(b) Whenever any fee or penalty subject to refund under Section 42231 after application therefor or Section 10901 of the Revenue and Taxation Code has been paid into the State Treasury to the credit, in whole or in part, of the Motor Vehicle License Fee Account in the Transportation Tax Fund (hereafter referred to in this section as the Motor Vehicle License Fee Account), or to the credit, in whole or in part, of the Motor Vehicle Account in the State Transportation Fund (hereafter referred to in this section as the Motor Vehicle Account), the department shall prepare a claim setting forth the facts pertaining to the fee or penalty sought to be refunded, and the State Controller shall draw his warrant upon the account or accounts to which the fee or penalty was credited. In lieu of filing claims for refund against both the Motor Vehicle Account and the Motor Vehicle License Fee Account when an amount has been determined to be due from both accounts, the director may file a single claim with the State Controller, drawn against the Motor Vehicle Account covering the amount of both refunds, and the State Controller shall thereupon draw his warrant on the Motor Vehicle Account. At least quarterly, the director shall certify to the State Controller the amounts paid from the Motor Vehicle Account which are properly chargeable to the Motor Vehicle License Fee Account supported by such detail as the State Controller may require. Upon order of the State Controller, the amounts so required shall be transferred from the Motor Vehicle License Fee Account to the credit of the Motor Vehicle Account.

(c) This section is an appropriation of any and all amounts necessary to refund and repay any excessive or erroneous fees and penalties collected under this code, and the procedure prescribed in this article for refunds shall be deemed a compliance with the requirements of the Government Code relating to the refund of excessive or erroneous fees or penalties.

(Amended by Stats. 1978, Ch. 669.)

42235. Whenever the department collects any fee which is excessive or not legally due and application for the refund of the fee is not filed within the time prescribed by law because the applicant failed to receive from the department a certificate of registration for the vehicle upon which the refund of fee is sought, the director shall have the power to authorize the payment of a refund in such a case upon a proper showing by the applicant that the delay in applying for the refund was due to the failure to receive the certificate of registration within the statutory period allowed for making application for refund of fees.

(Enacted by Stats. 1959, Ch. 3.)

Article 3. Uncollectible Costs

(Article 3 added by Stats. 2021, Ch. 257, Sec. 45.)

42240. On and after January 1, 2022, the unpaid balance of any court-imposed costs pursuant to Section 40508.5 and subdivision (g) of Section 40510.5, as those sections read on December 31, 2021, shall be unenforceable and uncollectible and any portion of a judgment imposing those costs shall be vacated.

(Added by Stats. 2021, Ch. 257, Sec. 45. (AB 177) Effective September 23, 2021.)

Chapter 3. Motor Vehicle Account

(Heading of Chapter 3 amended by Stats. 1976, Ch. 1079.)

42270. (a) The Department of Motor Vehicles and the Department of the California Highway Patrol each shall file, at least monthly with the Controller, a report of money received by the department covering all fees for applications accepted by the department and all other moneys received by the department under this code and, at the same time, shall remit all money so reported to the Treasurer. On order of the Controller, the Treasurer shall deposit in the Motor Vehicle Account in the State Transportation Fund, into which is merged the Motor Vehicle Account in the Transportation Tax Fund, all moneys so reported and remitted.

Any reference in any law or regulation to the Motor Vehicle Fund, or to the Motor Vehicle Account in the Transportation Tax Fund, shall be deemed to refer to the Motor Vehicle Account in the State Transportation Fund, which is created by subdivision (a) of Section 42271.

(b) The amount of any penalties collected by the department pursuant to Sections 9553 and 9554 of this code and Sections 10770 and 10854 of the Revenue and Taxation Code shall, for purposes of subdivision (a), be deemed to be a percentage of the weight fee, registration fee, and vehicle license fee obtained when applying the total of these fees collected, excluding use tax, against the individual weight fees, registration fees, and vehicle license fees collected on each application. Penalties which cannot be allocated in accordance with this subdivision shall be allocated according to subdivision (c).

(c) The amount of any penalties collected by the department, as provided in Sections 9553 and 9554 of this code and Sections 10770 and 10854 of the Revenue and Taxation Code which cannot be allocated in accordance with subdivision (b), shall, for the purposes of subdivision (a), be deemed to be a percentage of the total fees allocated under this section and under Section 11001 of the Revenue and Taxation Code equal to that percentage of the ratio based on the fees previously allocated under this section and under Section 11001 of the Revenue and Taxation Code in the fiscal year preceding the calendar year for which the penalties are to be allocated. That ratio shall be reevaluated periodically and shall be adjusted to reflect any change in the fee structure that may be provided in this code or in Part 5 (commencing with Section 10701) of Division 2 of the Revenue and Taxation Code.

(d) Whenever any fee paid to the department has not been allocated within one year of the date of collection, the fee shall be allocated to the Motor Vehicle License Fee Account in the Transportation Tax Fund, and the Motor Vehicle Account and the State Highway Account in the State Transportation Fund, in proportion to the revenue allocated to those accounts by the department in the previous fiscal year.

(Amended by Stats. 1986, Ch. 693, Sec. 1.)

42271. (a) The Motor Vehicle Account in the State Transportation Fund is hereby created.

(b) The moneys deposited to the credit of the Motor Vehicle Account in the State Transportation Fund which are appropriated in the Budget Act or any other appropriation act for the support of or expenditure by the Department of Motor Vehicles shall be expended by the department in carrying out the provisions of this code and in enforcing any other laws relating to vehicles or the use of highways.

Regularly employed peace officers of the department may, when authorized by the director, expend such sums as authorized for the purchase of counterfeit, false, forged, or fictitious certificates of ownership, registration card, certificate, license or special plate or permit, or driver's license provided for by this code as evidence, or for expenditures related to the procurement of such evidence, or for expenditures made to investigate other violations of laws administered by the department. When approved by the director, the identity of a peace officer who submits a claim need not be disclosed if the disclosure might materially prejudice the investigation.

The sums so expended shall be repaid to the peace officer making the expenditure upon claims approved by the director. The claims, when approved, shall be paid out of funds appropriated or made available by law for the support of the department.

(c) The moneys deposited to the credit of the Motor Vehicle Account in the State Transportation Fund which are appropriated in the Budget Act or any other appropriation act for the support of or expenditure by the Department of the California Highway Patrol shall be expended by the department in carrying out the provisions of this code and in enforcing any other laws relating to vehicles or the use of highways. The Department of the California Highway Patrol may draw, without at the time furnishing vouchers and itemized statements, sums not to exceed in the aggregate one hundred thousand dollars ($100,000), the sums so drawn to be used as a revolving fund where cash advances are necessary. At the close of each fiscal year, the moneys so drawn shall be accounted for and substantiated by vouchers and itemized statements submitted to and audited by the State Controller.

(Amended by Stats. 1978, Ch. 669.)

42272. For the 2012–13 fiscal year, upon order of the Director of Finance, the Controller shall transfer four hundred thirty-two million two hundred thousand dollars ($432,200,000) from the Motor Vehicle Account to the General Fund as a loan, provided that the loan shall be repaid. The Director of Finance shall order the repayment by the Controller of that four hundred thirty-two million two hundred thousand dollars ($432,200,000) to the Motor Vehicle Account no later than June 30, 2016.

(Added by Stats. 2012, Ch. 22, Sec. 8. (AB 1465) Effective June 27, 2012.)

42273. By the 10th day of each calendar month, the balance remaining to the credit of the Motor Vehicle Account in the State Transportation Fund at the close of business on the last day of the preceding calendar month, after payments of refunds and administration and enforcement, that is not needed for immediate use from the Motor Vehicle Account shall, on order of the State Controller, be transferred to the credit of the State Highway Account in the State Transportation Fund.

(Amended by Stats. 1978, Ch. 669.)

42275. Notwithstanding Section 42273, the State Controller may, after at least 15 days' prior notice, transfer back to the Motor Vehicle Account in the State Transportation Fund amounts transferred to the State Highway Account in the State Transportation Fund pursuant to that section to pay costs incurred against other appropriations from the Motor Vehicle Account.

(Amended by Stats. 1978, Ch. 669.)

42276. Not later than January 10, 1985, and not later than January 10th of each four-year period thereafter, the Secretary of the Business, Transportation and Housing Agency shall submit a report to the Legislature on a study of the fees imposed under this code, including any finding or recommendation on changes in the fees necessary to generate sufficient revenues for the Motor Vehicle Account in the State Transportation Fund to finance those operations of state government to be financed from those revenues.

(Added by Stats. 1981, Ch. 541, Sec. 39. Effective September 17, 1981.)

42277. No money in the Motor Vehicle Account in the State Transportation Fund may be expended for automobile driver training.

(Added by Stats. 1984, Ch. 94, Sec. 1.)

www.ingramcontent.com/pod-product-compliance
Lightning Source LLC
Chambersburg PA
CBHW061351240926
51846CB00007B/1374